ST. JAMES ENCYCLOPEDIA OF POPULARCULTURE

ST. JAMES ENCYCLOPEDIA OF
POPULARCULTURE

VOLUME 4: P-T

EDITORS: Tom Pendergast   Sara Pendergast

with an introduction by Jim Cullen

ST. JAMES PRESS

AN IMPRINT OF THE GALE GROUP

DETROIT • SAN FRANCISCO • LONDON
BOSTON • WOODBRIDGE, CT

Tom Pendergast, Sara Pendergast, *Editors*

Michael J. Tyrkus, *Project Coordinator*

Laura Standley Berger, Joann Cerrito, Dave Collins,
Steve Cusack, Nicolet V. Elert, Miranda Ferrara, Jamie FitzGerald,
Kristin Hart, Laura S. Kryhoski, Margaret Mazurkiewicz
St. James Press Staff

Peter M. Gareffa, *Managing Editor, St. James Press*

Maria Franklin, *Permissions Manager*
Kimberly F. Smilay, *Permissions Specialist*
Kelly A. Quin, *Permissions Associate*
Erin Bealmear, Sandy Gore, *Permissions Assistants*
Mary Grimes, Leitha Etheridge-Sims, *Image Catalogers*

Mary Beth Trimper, *Composition Manager*
Dorothy Maki, *Manufacturing Manager*
Wendy Blurton, *Senior Buyer*

Cynthia Baldwin, *Product Design Manager*
Martha Schiebold, *Graphic Artist*

Randy Bassett, *Image Database Supervisor*
Robert Duncan, Michael Logusz, *Imaging Specialists*
Pamela A. Reed, *Imaging Coordinator*

Library of Congress Cataloging-in-Publication Data
St. James Encyclopedia of Popular Culture / with an introduction by Jim Cullen; editors,
Tom Pendergast and Sara Pendergast.
    p. cm.
    Includes bibliographical references and index.
    ISBN 1-558-62400-7 (set) — ISBN 1-558-62401-5 (v.1) — ISBN 1-558-62402-3 (v.2) —
ISBN 1-558-62403-1 (v.3) — ISBN 1-558-62404-x (v.4) — ISBN 1-558-62405-8 (v. 5)
    1. United States—Civilization—20th century—Encyclopedias. 2. Popular culture—United
States—History—20th century—Encyclopedias. I. Pendergast, Tom. II. Pendergast, Sara.
E169.1.S764 1999
973.9 21—dc21   99-046540

Printed in the United States of America

St. James Press is an imprint of Gale Group
Gale Group and Design is a trademark used herein under license

10 9 8 7 6 5 4 3 2

CONTENTS

EDITOR'S NOTE

Thirty some years ago Ray Browne and several of his colleagues provided a forum for the academic study of popular culture by forming first the *Journal of Popular Culture* and later the Popular Culture Association and the Center for the Study of Popular Culture at Bowling Green State University. Twenty some years ago Thomas Inge thought the field of popular culture studies well enough established to put together the first edition of his *Handbook of Popular Culture*. In the years since, scholars and educators from many disciplines have published enough books, gathered enough conferences, and gained enough institutional clout to make popular culture studies one of the richest fields of academic study at the close of the twentieth century. Thirty, twenty, in some places even ten years ago, to study popular culture was to be something of a pariah; today, the study of popular culture is accepted and even respected in departments of history, literature, communications, sociology, film studies, etc. throughout the United States and throughout the world, and not only in universities, but in increasing numbers of high schools. Thomas Inge wrote in the introduction to the second edition of his *Handbook*: "The serious and systematic study of popular culture may be the most significant and potentially useful of the trends in academic research and teaching in the last half of this century in the United States."[2] It is to this thriving field of study that we hope to contribute with the *St. James Encyclopedia of Popular Culture.*

The *St. James Encyclopedia of Popular Culture* includes over 2,700 essays on all elements of popular culture in the United States in the twentieth century. But what is "popular culture?" Academics have offered a number of answers over the years. Historians Norman F. Cantor and Michael S. Werthman suggested that "popular culture may be seen as all those things man does and all those artifacts he creates for their own sake, all that diverts his mind and body from the sad business of life."[1] Michael Bell argues that:

> At its simplest popular culture is the culture of mass appeal. A creation is popular when it is created to respond to the experiences and values of the majority, when it is produced in such a way that the majority have easy access to it, and when it can be understood and interpreted by that majority without the aid of special knowledge or experience.[3]

While tremendously useful, both of these definitions tend to exclude more than they embrace. Was the hot dog created for its own sake, as a diversion? Probably not, but we've included an essay on it in this collection. Were the works of Sigmund Freud in any way shaped for the majority? No, but Freud's ideas—borrowed, twisted, and reinterpreted—have shaped novels, films, and common speech in ways too diffuse to ignore. Thus we have included an essay on Freud's impact on popular culture. Our desire to bring together the greatest number of cultural phenomena impacting American culture in this century has led us to prefer Ray Browne's rather broader early definition of popular culture as "all the experiences in life shared by people in common, generally though not necessarily disseminated by the mass media."[4]

Coverage

In order to amass a list of those cultural phenomena that were widely disseminated and experienced by people in relatively unmediated form we asked a number of scholars, teachers, librarians, and archivists to serve as advisors. Each of our 20 advisors provided us with a list of over 200 topics from their field of specialty that they considered important enough to merit an essay; several of our advisors provided us with lists much longer than that. Their collective lists numbered nearly 4,000 potential essay topics, and we winnowed this list down to the number that is now gathered in this collection. We sought balance (but not equal coverage) between the major areas of popular culture: film; music; print culture; social life; sports; television and radio; and art and perfomance (which includes theatre, dance, stand-up comedy, and other live performance). For those interested, the breakdown of coverage is as follows: social life, 23 percent (a category which covers everything from foodways to fashion, holidays to hairstyles); music, 16 percent; print culture, 16 percent; film, 15 percent; television and radio, 14 percent; sports, 10 percent; and art and performance, 6 percent. A variety of considerations led us to skew the coverage of the book in favor of the second half of the century. The massive popularity of television and recorded music, the mass-marketing of popular fiction, and the national attention given to professional sports are historical factors contributing to the emphasis on post-World War II culture, but we have also considered the needs of high school and undergraduate users in distributing entries in this way.

The Entries

The entries in this volume vary in length from brief (75 to 150-word) introductions to the topic to in-depth 3,000-word explorations. No matter the length, we have asked our contributors to do two things in each entry: to describe the topic and to analyze its significance in and relevance to American popular culture. While we hope that users will find the basic factual information they need concerning the topic in an entry, it was even more important to us that each user gain some perspective on the cultural context in which the topic has importance. Thus the entry on MTV, for example, chronicles the channel's rise to world popularity, but also analyzes the relationship between MTV, youth culture, and consumerism. The entry on John Ford, while tracing the outlines of the film director's long career, assesses the impact Ford's films have had on the film Western and on Americans' very perceptions of the West. Given the brevity of the entries, we chose to emphasize analysis of a topic's contribution to popular culture over a full presentation of biographical/historical information. The entry on World War I, for example, offers an analysis of how the war was understood in popular film, print culture, and propaganda rather than a blow-by-blow description of the actual military conflict.

Entries are accompanied by a list of further readings. These readings are meant to provide the user with readily accessible sources that provide more information on the specific topic. As befits a multimedia age, these "further readings" come not just from books and magazines, but also from albums, liner notes, films, videos, and web sites. Users of the Internet know well the perils of trusting the information found on the World Wide Web; there are as yet few filters to help browsers sift the useful from the absurd. We cited web sites when they provided information that was unavailable in any other known form and when our reasonable efforts to determine the veracity of the information led us to believe that the information provided was valid and useful. We have occasionally provided links to "official" web sites of performers or organizations, for the same reason that we provide citations to autobiographies. All web links cited were accurate as of the date indicated in the citation.

Organization and Indexing

Entries are arranged alphabetically by the name under which the topic is best known. For topics which might reasonably be sought out under differing names, we have provided in-text cross references. For example, a user seeking an entry on Huddie Ledbetter will be referred to the entry on Leadbelly, and a user seeking an entry on Larry Flynt will be referred to the entry on *Hustler* magazine. Far more powerful than the cross references, however, are the indexes provided in the fifth volume of the collection. The general index is by far the most powerful, for it leads the user searching for information on Humphrey Bogart, for example, to the entries on Lauren Bacall, *Casablanca, The Maltese Falcon, The African Queen,* and several other entries that contain substantive information about Bogie. Equally powerful is the subject index, a list of categories under which we listed all pertinent entries. Consulting the subject index listing for Sex Symbols, for example, will lead the user to entries on Marilyn Monroe, the Varga Girl, *Playboy* magazine, David Cassidy, Mae West, and a long entry on the Sex Symbol, among others. Finally, a time index, organized by decades, provides a list of the entries that concern each decade of the twentieth century. Those entries that concern nineteenth-century topics are indexed by the first decade of the twentieth century.

We encourage readers to use the indexes to discover the fascinating intertwinings that have made the development of popular culture in the twentieth century such a vital field of study. Using the indexes, it is possible to uncover the story of how the American humor that was first made popular on the vaudeville stage evolved into first the radio comedies that entertained so many Americans during the Depression and War years and later the sitcoms that have kept Americans glued to their television screens for the last 50 years. That story is here, in the entries on Vaudeville, the Sitcom, *Amos 'n' Andy,* and the many other programs and comedians that have defined this tradition. A teacher who wishes students to uncover the similarities between sitcoms of the 1950s, 1960s, 1970s, 1980s, and 1990s might well ask the students to use this collection to begin their research into such comedies. Similarly, a teacher who asks students to explore the cross-pollination between musical genres will find that the indexes reveal the mixing of "race music," rhythm and blues, gospel, soul, and rock 'n' roll. It is hoped that this collection will be of particular use to those instructors of high school and undergraduate courses who challenge their students to discover the real cultural complexity of the music, films, magazines, and television shows that they take for granted. This collection should also be of use to those more advanced scholars who are beginning new research into an area of popular culture or who are looking for some context in which to place their existing research.

Acknowledgments

The *St. James Encyclopedia of Popular Culture* represents the work of hundreds of people, and we owe our thanks to all of them. We have had the privilege of working with 20 advisors whose experience, knowledge, and wisdom have truly helped shape the contents of this collection. Each of our advisors helped us to discover hidden corners of popular culture that we would not have considered on our own, and the breadth of coverage in this collection is a tribute to their collective knowledge. Several of our advisors deserve special thanks: Paul Buhle, George Carney, B. Lee Cooper, Jerome Klinkowitz, and Ron Simon all showed an extraordinary level of commitment and helpfulness.

It has been a pleasure to work with the nearly 450 contributors to this collection; we've appreciated their expertise, their professionalism, and their good humor. Several of our contributors deserve special mention for the quality of their contributions to this collection: Jacob Appel, Tim Berg, Pat Broeske, Richard Digby-Junger, Jeffrey Escoffier, Bryan Garman, Tina Gianoulis, Milton Goldin, Ian Gordon, Ron Goulart, Justin Gustainis, Preston Jones, Robyn Karney, Deborah Mix, Leonard Moore, Edward Moran, Victoria Price, Bob Schnakenberg, Steven Schneider, Charles Shindo, Robert Sickels, Wendy Woloson, and Brad Wright. Our team of copyeditors helped us bring a uniformity of presentation to the writings of this mass of contributors, and spotted and corrected innumerable small errors. Heidi Hagen, Robyn Karney, Edward Moran, and Tim Seul deserve special thanks for the quality and quantity of their work; we truly couldn't have done it without them. The contributors and copyeditors provided us with the material to build this collection, but it has been the editors' responsibility to ensure its accuracy and reliability. We welcome any corrections and comments; please write to: The Editors, *St. James Encyclopedia of Popular Culture,* St. James Press, 27500 Drake Road, Farmington Hills, MI 48331-3535.

Gathering the photos for this collection was an enormous task, and we were helped immeasurably by the knowledgeable and efficient staff at several photo agencies. We'd like to thank Marcia Schiff at AP/Wide World Photos; Eric Young at Archive Photos; and Kevin Rettig at Corbis Images. Lisa Hartjens of ImageFinders, Inc. also helped us acquire a number of photos.

We would like to thank Shelly Andrews, Anne Boyd, Melissa Doig, Tina Gianoulis, Heidi Hagen, Robyn Karney, Edward Moran, Victoria Price, Rebecca Saulsbury, Tim Seul, and Mark Swartz for their careful copyediting of the entries.

At the St. James Press, we'd like to thank Mike Tyrkus for his good humor and efficiency in helping us see this project to completion; Peter Gareffa for his usual wise and benevolent leadership; Janice Jorgensen for helping us shape this project at the beginning; the permissions department for smiling as we piled the photos on; and the staff at the St. James Press for their careful proofreading and for all their work in turning so many computer files into the volumes you see today.

Finally, we'd like to thank Lee Van Wormer for his sage management advice and our children, Conrad and Louisa, for their warm morning cuddles and for the delightful artwork that adorns our office walls.

—Tom Pendergast and Sara Pendergast,
Editors

NOTES

1. Cantor, Norman F. and Michael S. Werthman. *The History of Popular Culture to 1815.* New York, Macmillan, 1968, xxiv.
2. Inge, M. Thomas, editor. *Handbook of American Popular Culture.* 2nd edition. Westport, Connecticut, Greenwood Press, 1989, xxiii.
3. Bell, Michael. "The Study of Popular Culture," in *Concise Histories of American Popular Culture,* ed. Inge, M. Thomas. Westport, Connecticut, Greenwood Press, 1982, 443.
4. Browne, Ray B. *Popular Culture and the Expanding Consciousness.* New York, Wiley, 1973, 6.

INTRODUCTION

The Art of Everyday Life

Sometimes, when I'm wandering in an art museum looking at the relics of an ancient civilization, I find myself wondering how a future society would represent a defunct American culture. What objects would be chosen—or would survive—to be placed on display? Would I agree with a curator's choices? Were I to choose the items that some future American Museum of Art should exhibit to represent twentieth-century American culture, here are some I would name: an Elvis Presley record; a Currier & Ives print; a movie still from *Casablanca.* To put it a different way, my priority would *not* be to exhibit fragments of an urban cathedral, a painted landscape, or a formal costume. I wouldn't deny such objects could be important artifacts of American culture, or that they belong in a gallery. But in my avowedly biased opinion, the most vivid documents of American life—the documents that embody its possibilities and limits—are typically found in its popular culture.

Popular culture, of course, is not an American invention, and it has a vibrant life in many contemporary societies. But in few, if any, of those societies has it been as central to a notion of national character at home as well as abroad. For better or worse, it is through icons like McDonald's (the quintessential American cuisine), the Western (a uniquely American narrative genre), and Oprah Winfrey (a classic late-twentieth century embodiment of the American Dream) that this society is known—and is likely to be remembered.

It has sometimes been remarked that unlike nations whose identities are rooted in geography, religion, language, blood, or history, the United States was founded on a democratic ideal—a notion of life, liberty, and the pursuit of happiness elaborated in the Declaration of Independence. That ideal has been notoriously difficult to realize, and one need only take a cursory look at many aspects of American life—its justice system, electoral politics, residential patterns, labor force, et. al.—to see how far short it has fallen.

American popular culture is a special case. To be sure, it evinces plenty of the defects apparent in other areas of our national life, among them blatant racism and crass commercialism. If nothing else, such flaws can be taken as evidence of just how truly representative it is. There is nevertheless an openness and vitality about pop culture—its appeal across demographic lines; its interplay of individual voices and shared communal experience; the relatively low access barriers for people otherwise marginalized in U.S. society—that give it real legitimacy as the art of democracy. Like it or hate it, few dispute its centrality.

This sense of openness and inclusion—as well as the affection and scorn it generated—has been apparent from the very beginning. In the prologue of the 1787 play *The Contrast* (whose title referred to the disparity between sturdy republican ideals and effete monarchical dissipation), American playwright Royall Tyler invoked a cultural sensibility where "proud titles of 'My Lord! Your Grace/To the humble 'Mr.' and plain 'Sir' give place." Tyler, a Harvard graduate, Revolutionary War officer, and Chief Justice of the Vermont Supreme Court, was in some sense an unlikely prophet of popular culture. But the sensibility he voiced—notably in his beloved character Jonathon, a prototype for characters from Davy Crockett to John Wayne—proved durable for centuries to come.

For much of early American history, however, artists and critics continued to define aesthetic success on European terms, typically invoking elite ideals of order, balance, and civilization. It was largely taken for granted that the most talented practitioners of fine arts, such as painters Benjamin West and John Singleton Copley, would have to go abroad to train, produce, and exhibit their most important work. To the extent that newer cultural forms—like the novel, whose very name suggests its place in late eighteenth- and early nineteenth-century western civilization—were noted at all, it was usually in disparaging terms. This was especially true of novels written and read by women, such as Susanna Rowson's widely read *Charlotte Temple* (1791). Sermons against novels were common; Harvard devoted its principal commencement address in 1803 to the dangers of fiction.

The industrialization of the United States has long been considered a watershed development in many realms of American life, and popular culture is no exception. Indeed, its importance is suggested in the very definition of popular culture coined by cultural historian Lawrence Levine: "the folklore of industrial society." Industrialization allowed the mass-reproduction and dissemination of formerly local traditions, stories, and art forms across the continent, greatly intensifying the spread—and development—of culture by, for, and of the people. At a time when North America remained geographically and politically fragmented, magazines, sheet music, dime novels, lithographs, and other print media stitched it together.

This culture had a characteristic pattern. Alexis de Tocqueville devoted 11 chapters of his classic 1835-40 masterpiece *Democracy in America* to the art, literature, and language of the United States, arguing that they reflected a democratic ethos that required new standards of evaluation. "The inhabitants of the United States have, at present, properly speaking, no literature," he wrote. This judgment, he made clear, arose from a definition of literature that came from aristocratic societies like his own. In its stead, he explained, Americans sought books "which may be easily procured, quickly read, and which require no learned researches to be understood. They ask for beauties self-proffered and easily enjoyed; above all they must have what is unexpected and new." As in so many other ways, this description of American literature, which paralleled what Tocqueville saw in other arts, proved not only vivid but prophetic.

The paradox of American democracy, of course, is that the freedom Euro-Americans endlessly celebrated co-existed with—some might say depended on—the enslavement of African Americans. It is therefore one of the great ironies of popular culture that the contributions of black culture (a term here meant to encompass African, American, and amalgamations between the two) proved so decisive. In another sense, however, it seems entirely appropriate that popular culture, which has always skewed its orientation toward the lower end of a demographic spectrum, would draw on the most marginalized groups in American society. It is, in any event, difficult to imagine that U.S. popular culture would have had anywhere near the vitality and influence it has without slave stories, song, and dance. To cite merely one example: every American musical idiom from country music to rap has drawn on, if not actually *rested* upon, African-American cultural foundations, whether in its use of the banjo (originally an African instrument) or its emphasis on the beat (drumming was an important form of slave communication). This heritage has often been overlooked, disparaged, and even satirized. The most notable example of such racism was the minstrel show, a wildly popular nineteenth century form of theater in which white actors blackened their faces with burnt cork and mocked slave life. Yet even the most savage parodies could not help but reveal an engagement with, and even a secret admiration for, the cultural world the African Americans made in conditions of severe adversity, whether on plantations, tenant farms, or in ghettoes.

Meanwhile, the accelerating pace of technological innovation began having a dramatic impact on the form as well as the content of popular culture. The first major landmark was the development of photography in the mid-nineteenth century. At first a mechanically complex and thus inaccessible medium, it quickly captured American imaginations, particularly by capturing the drama and horror of the Civil War. The subsequent proliferation of family portraits, postcards, and pictures in metropolitan newspapers began a process of orienting popular culture around visual imagery that continues unabated to this day.

In the closing decades of the nineteenth century, sound recording, radio transmission, and motion pictures were all developed in rapid succession. But it would not be until well after 1900 that their potential as popular cultural media would be fully exploited and recognizable in a modern sense (radio, for example, was originally developed and valued for its nautical and military applications). Still, even if it was not entirely clear how, many people at the time believed these new media would have a tremendous impact on American life, and they were embraced with unusual ardor by those Americans, particularly immigrants, who were able to appreciate the pleasures and possibilities afforded by movies, records, and radio.

Many of the patterns established during the advent of these media repeated themselves as new ones evolved. The Internet, for example, was also first developed for its military applications, and for all the rapidity of its development in the 1990s, it remains unclear just how its use will be structured. Though the World Wide Web has shown tremendous promise as a commercial enterprise, it still lacks the kind of programming—like *Amos 'n' Andy* in radio, or *I Love Lucy* in television—that transformed both into truly mass media of art and entertainment. Television, for its part, has long been the medium of a rising middle class of immigrants and their children, in terms of the figures who have exploited its possibilities (from RCA executive David Sarnoff to stars like Jackie Gleason); the new genres it created (from the miniseries to the situation-comedy); and the audiences (from urban Jews to suburban Irish Catholics) who adopted them with enthusiasm.

For much of this century, the mass appeal of popular culture has been viewed as a problem. "What is the jass [*sic*] music, and therefore the jass band?" asked an irritated New Orleans writer in 1918. "As well as ask why the dime novel or the grease-dripping doughnut. All are manifestations of a low stream in man's taste that has not come out in civilization's wash." However one may feel about this contemptuous dismissal of jazz, now viewed as one of the great achievements of American civilization, this writer was clearly correct to suggest the demographic, technological, and cultural links between the "lower" sorts of people in American life, the media they used, and forms of expression that were often presumed guilty until proven innocent.

Indeed, because education and research have traditionally been considered the province of the "higher" sorts of people in American life, popular culture was not considered a subject that should even be discussed, much less studied. Nevertheless, there have always been those willing to continue what might be termed the "Tocquevillian" tradition of treating popular culture with intellectual seriousness and respect (if not always approval). In his 1924 book *The Seven Lively Arts* and in much of his journalism, critic Gilbert Seldes found in silent movies, cartoons, and pop music themes and motifs fully worthy of sustained exploration. Amid the worldwide crisis of the 1930s and 1940s, folklorist Constance Rourke limned the origins of an indigenous popular culture in books like *American Humor* (1931) and *The Roots of American Culture* (1942). And with the rise of the Cold War underlining the differences between democratic and totalitarian societies, sociologists David Riesman and Reuel Denny evaluated the social currents animating popular culture in Denny's *The Astonished Muse* (1957), for which Riesman, who showed a particular interest in popular music, wrote the introduction.

European scholars were also pivotal in shaping the field. Johan Huizinga's *Homo Ludens* (1938), Roland Barthes's *Mythologies* (1957), and Antonio Gramsci's prison letters (written in the 1920s and 1930s but not published until the 1970s) have proved among the most influential works in defining the boundaries, strategies, and meanings of popular culture. While none of these works focused on American popular culture specifically, their focus on the jetsam and flotsam of daily life since the medieval period proved enormously suggestive in an American context.

It has only been at the end of the twentieth century, however, that the study of popular culture has come into its own in its own right. To a great extent, this development is a legacy of the 1960s. The end of a formal system of racial segregation; the impact of affirmative action and government-funded financial aid; and the end of single-sex education at many long-established universities dramatically transformed the composition of student bodies and faculties. These developments in turn, began having an impact on the nature and parameters of academic study. While one should not exaggerate the impact of these developments—either in terms of their numbers or their effect on an academy that in some ways has simply replaced older forms of insularity and complacency with new ones—it nevertheless seems fair to say that a bona fide democratization of higher education occurred in the last third of the twentieth century, paving the way for the creation of a formal scholarly infrastructure for popular culture.

Once again, it was foreign scholars who were pivotal in the elaboration of this infrastructure. The work of Raymond Williams, Stuart Hall, and others at Britain's Centre for Contemporary Cultural Studies in the 1950s and 1960s drew on Marxist and psychoanalytic ideas to explain, and in many cases justify, the importance of popular culture. Though not always specifically concerned with popular culture, a panoply of French theorists—particularly Jacques Derrida, Louis Althusser, and Michel Foucault—also proved highly influential. At its best, this scholarship illuminated unexamined assumptions and highly revealing (and in many cases, damning) patterns in the most seemingly ordinary documents. At its worst, it lapsed into an arcane jargon that belied the directness of popular culture and suggested an elitist disdain toward the audiences it presumably sought to understand.

Like their European counterparts, American scholars of popular culture have come from a variety of disciplines. Many were trained in literature, among them Henry Nash Smith, whose *Virgin Land* (1950) pioneered the study of the Western, and Leslie Fiedler, who applied critical talents first developed to study classic American literature to popular fiction like *Gone with the Wind*. But much important work in the field has also been done by historians, particularly social historians who began their careers by focusing on labor history but became increasingly interested in the ways American workers spent their free time. Following the tradition of the great British historian E. P. Thompson, scholars such as Herbert Gutman and Lawrence Levine have uncovered and described the art and leisure practices of African Americans in particular with flair and insight. Feminist scholars of a variety of stripes (and sexual orientations) have supplied a great deal of the intellectual energy in the study of popular culture, among them Ann Douglas, Carroll Smith-Rosenberg, and Jane Tompkins. Indeed, the strongly interdisciplinary flavor of popular culture scholarship—along with the rise of institutions like the Popular Press and the Popular Culture Association, both based at Bowling Green University—suggests the way the field has been at the forefront of an ongoing process of redrawing disciplinary boundaries in the humanities.

By the 1980s, the stream of scholarship on popular culture had become a flood. In the 1990s, the field became less of a quixotic enterprise than a growing presence in the educational curriculum as a whole. Courses devoted to the subject, whether housed in communications programs or in traditional academic departments, have become increasingly common in colleges and universities—and, perhaps more importantly, have become integrated into the fabric of basic surveys of history, literature, and other fields. Political scientists, librarians, and curators have begun to consider it part of their domain.

For most of us, though, popular culture is not something we have to self-consciously seek out or think about. Indeed, its very omnipresence makes it easy to take for granted as transparent (and permanent). That's why trips to museums—or encyclopedias like this one—are so useful and important. In pausing to think about the art of everyday life, we can begin to see just how unusual, and valuable, it really is.

—Jim Cullen

FURTHER READING:

Barthes, Roland. *Mythologies.* Translated by Annette Lavers. 1957. Reprint, New York, The Noonday Press, 1972.

Cullen, Jim. *The Art of Democracy: A Concise History of Popular Culture in the United States.* New York, Monthly Review Press, 1996.

Fiske, John. *Understanding Popular Culture.* Boston, Unwin/Hyman, 1989.

Levine, Lawrence. *The Unpredictable Past: Explorations in American Cultural History.* New York, Oxford University Press, 1993.

Storey, John. *An Introductory Guide to Cultural Theory and Popular Culture.* Athens, University of Georgia Press, 1993.

Susman, Warren. *Culture as History: The Transformation of American Society in the Twentieth Century.* New York, Pantheon, 1984.

ADVISORS

Frances R. Aparicio
University of Michigan

Paul Buhle
Brown University

George O. Carney
Oklahoma State University

B. Lee Cooper
University of Great Falls

Corey K. Creekmur
University of Iowa

Joshua Gamson
Yale University

Jerome Klinkowitz
University of Northern Iowa

Richard Martin
Metropolitan Museum of Art
Columbia University
New York University

Lawrence E. Mintz
University of Maryland
Art Gliner Center for Humor Studies

Troy Paino
Winona State University

Grace Palladino
University of Maryland

Lauren Rabinovitz
University of Iowa

T. V. Reed
Washington State University

William L. Schurk
Bowling Green State University

Alison M. Scott
Bowling Green State University

Randall W. Scott
Michigan State University Libraries

Ron Simon
Museum of Television & Radio
Columbia University

Erin Smith
University of Texas at Dallas

June Sochen
Northeastern Illinois University

Colby Vargas
New Trier High School

CONTRIBUTORS

Nathan Abrams
Frederick Luis Aldama
Roberto Alvarez
Byron Anderson
Carly Andrews
Jacob M. Appel
Tim Arnold
Paul Ashdown
Bernardo Alexander Attias
Frederick J. Augustyn, Jr.

Beatriz Badikian
Michael Baers
Neal Baker
S. K. Bane
Samantha Barbas
Allen Barksdale
Pauline Bartel
Bob Batchelor
Vance Bell
Samuel I. Bellman
James R. Belpedio
Courtney Bennett
Timothy Berg
Lisa Bergeron-Duncan
Daniel Bernardi
R. Thomas Berner
Charlie Bevis
Lara Bickell
Sam Binkley
Brian Black
Liza Black
Bethany Blankenship
Rebecca Blustein
Aniko Bodroghkozy
Gregory Bond
Martyn Bone
Austin Booth
Gerry Bowler
Anne Boyd
Marlena E. Bremseth
Carol Brennan
Tony Brewer
Deborah Broderson
Michael Brody
Pat H. Broeske
Robert J. Brown
Sharon Brown
Craig Bunch
Stephen Burnett
Gary Burns
Margaret Burns

Manuel V. Cabrera, Jr.
Ross B. Care

Gerald Carpenter
Anthony Cast
Rafaela Castro
Jason Chambers
Chris Chandler
Michael K. Chapman
Roger Chapman
Lloyd Chiasson, Jr.
Ann M. Ciasullo
Dylan Clark
Frank Clark
Randy Clark
Craig T. Cobane
Dan Coffey
Adam Max Cohen
Toby I. Cohen
Susann Cokal
Jeffrey W. Coker
Charles A. Coletta, Jr.
Michael R. Collings
Willie Collins
Mia L. Consalvo
Douglas Cooke
ViBrina Coronado
Robert C. Cottrell
Corey K. Creekmur
Richard C. Crepeau
Jim Cullen
Susan Curtis

Glyn Davis
Janet M. Davis
Pamala S. Deane
S. Renee Dechert
John Deitrick
Gordon Neal Diem, D.A.
Richard Digby-Junger
Laurie DiMauro
John J. Doherty
Thurston Domina
Jon Griffin Donlon
Simon Donner
Randy Duncan
Stephen Duncombe
Eugenia Griffith DuPell
Stephanie Dyer

Rob Edelman
Geoff Edgers
Jessie L. Embry
Jeffrey Escoffier
Cindy Peters Evans
Sean Evans
William A. Everett

Alyssa Falwell
Richard Feinberg
G. Allen Finchum
S. Naomi Finkelstein
Dennis Fischer
Bill Freind
Bianca Freire-Medeiros
Shaun Frentner
James Friedman
Adrienne Furness

Paul Gaffney
Milton Gaither
Joan Gajadhar
Catherine C. Galley
Caitlin L. Gannon
Sandra Garcia-Myers
Bryan Garman
Eva Marie Garroutte
Frances Gateward
Jason George
Tina Gianoulis
James R. Giles
Milton Goldin
Ilene Goldman
Matthew Mulligan Goldstein
Dave Goldweber
Ian Gordon
W. Terrence Gordon
Ron Goulart
Paul Grainge
Brian Granger
Anna Hunt Graves
Steve Graves
Jill A. Gregg
Benjamin Griffith
Perry Grossman
Justin Gustainis
Dale Allen Gyure

Kristine J. Ha
Elizabeth Haas
Ray Haberski, Jr.
Jeanne Lynn Hall
Steve Hanson
Jacqueline Anne Hatton
Chris Haven
Ethan Hay
Jeet Heer
Andrew R. Heinze
Mary Hess
Joshua Hirsch
David L. Hixson
Scott W. Hoffman
Briavel Holcomb

Peter C. Holloran
David Holloway
Karen Hovde
Kevin Howley
Nick Humez

Judy L. Isaksen

Jennifer Jankauskas
E. V. Johanningmeier
Patrick Jones
Patrick Jones
Preston Neal Jones
Mark Joseph
Thomas Judd

Peter Kalliney
Nicolás Kanellos
Robyn Karney
Stephen Keane
James D. Keeline
Max Kellerman
Ken Kempcke
Stephen C. Kenny
Stephen Kercher
Matt Kerr
M. Alison Kibler
Kimberley H. Kidd
Matthew A. Killmeier
Jason King
Jon Klinkowitz
Leah Konicki
Steven Kotok
Robert Kuhlken
Andrew J. Kunka
Audrey Kupferberg
Petra Kuppers

Emma Lambert
Christina Lane
Kevin Lause
Nadine-Rae Leavell
Christopher A. Lee
Michele Lellouche
Robin Lent
Joan Leotta
Richard Levine
Drew Limsky
Daniel Lindley
Joyce Linehan
Margaret Litton
James H. Lloyd
David Lonergan
Eric Longley
Rick Lott
Bennett Lovett-Graff
Denise Lowe

Debra M. Lucas
Karen Lurie
Michael A. Lutes
James Lyons
John F. Lyons

Steve Macek
Alison Macor
David Marc
Robin Markowitz
Tilney L. Marsh
Richard Martin
Sara Martin
Linda A. Martindale
Kevin Mattson
Randall McClure
Allison McCracken
Jennifer Davis McDaid
Jason McEntee
Cheryl S. McGrath
Daryna McKeand
Jacquelyn Y. McLendon
Kembrew McLeod
Josephine A. McQuail
Alex Medeiros
Brad Melton
Myra Mendible
Jeff Merron
Thomas J. Mertz
Nathan R. Meyer
Jonathan Middlebrook
Andre Millard
Jeffrey S. Miller
Karen Miller
P. Andrew Miller
Dorothy Jane Mills
Andrew Milner
Deborah M. Mix
Nickianne Moody
Richard L. Moody
Charles F. Moore
Leonard N. Moore
Dan Moos
Robert A. Morace
Edward Moran
Barry Morris
Michael J. Murphy
Jennifer A. Murray
Susan Murray
Pierre-Damien Mvuyekure

Michael Najjar
Ilana Nash
Mary Lou Nemanic
Scott Newman
Joan Nicks
Martin F. Norden
Justin Nordstrom
Anna Notaro

William F. O'Connor
Paul O'Hara
Angela O'Neal
Christopher D. O'Shea
Lolly Ockerstrom
Kerry Owens
Marc Oxoby

D. Byron Painter
Henri-Dominique Paratte
Leslie Paris
Jay Parrent
Felicity Paxton
Sara Pendergast
Tom Pendergast
Jana Pendragon
Geoff Peterson
Kurt W. Peterson
Emily Pettigrew
Daniel J. Philippon
S. J. Philo
Allene Phy-Olsen
Ed Piacentino
Jürgen Pieters
Paul F. P. Pogue
Mark B. Pohlad
Fernando Porta
Michael L. Posner
John A. Price
Victoria Price
Luca Prono
Elizabeth Purdy
Christian L. Pyle

Jessy Randall
Taly Ravid
Belinda S. Ray
Ivan Raykoff
Wendy Wick Reaves
James E. Reibman
Yolanda Retter
Tracy J. Revels
Wylene Rholetter
Tad Richards
Robert B. Ridinger
Jeff Ritter
Thomas Robertson
Arthur Robinson
Todd Anthony Rosa
Ava Rose
Chris Routledge
Abhijit Roy
Adrienne Russell
Dennis Russell

Lisa Jo Sagolla
Frank A. Salamone
Joe Sutliff Sanders

Andrew Sargent
Julie Scelfo
Elizabeth D. Schafer
Louis Scheeder
James Schiff
Robert E. Schnakenberg
Steven Schneider
Kelly Schrum
Christine Scodari
Ann Sears
E. M. I. Sefcovic
Eric J. Segal
Carol A. Senf
Tim Seul
Alexander Shashko
Michele S. Shauf
Taylor Shaw
Anne Sheehan
Steven T. Sheehan
Pamela Shelton
Sandra Sherman
Charles J. Shindo
Mike Shupp
Robert C. Sickels
C. Kenyon Silvey
Ron Simon
Philip Simpson
Rosemarie Skaine
Ryan R. Sloane
Jeannette Sloniowski
Cheryl A. Smith

Kyle Smith
John Smolenski
Irvin D. Solomon
Geri Speace
Andrew Spieldenner
tova stabin
Scott Stabler
Jon Sterngrass
Roger W. Stump
Bob Sullivan
Lauren Ann Supance
Marc R. Sykes

Midori Takagi
Candida Taylor
Scott Thill
Robert Thompson
Stephen L. Thompson
Rosemarie Garland Thomson
Jan Todd
Terry Todd
John Tomasic
Warren Tormey
Grant Tracey
David Trevino
Marcella Bush Trevino
Scott Tribble
Tom Trinchera
Nicholas A. Turse

Anthony Ubelhor
Daryl Umberger

Rob Van Kranenburg
Robert VanWynsberghe
Colby Vargas

Sue Walker
Lori C. Walters
Nancy Lan-Jy Wang
Adam Wathen
Laural Weintraub
Jon Weisberger
David B. Welky
Christopher W. Wells
Celia White
Christopher S. Wilson
David B. Wilson
Kristi M. Wilson
Jeff Wiltse
Wendy Woloson
David E. Woodward
Bradford W. Wright

Sharon Yablon
Daniel Francis Yezbick
Stephen D. Youngkin

Kristal Brent Zook

LIST OF ENTRIES

Ironman Triathlon
Irving, John
It Happened One Night
It's a Wonderful Life
It's Garry Shandling's Show
Ives, Burl
Ivy League

J. Walter Thompson
Jack Armstrong
Jackson Five, The
Jackson, Jesse
Jackson, Mahalia
Jackson, Michael
Jackson, Reggie
Jackson, Shirley
Jackson, "Shoeless" Joe
Jakes, John
James Bond Films
James, Elmore
James, Harry
Japanese American
    Internment Camps
Jaws
Jazz
Jazz Singer, The
Jeans
Jeep
Jefferson Airplane/Starship
Jeffersons, The
Jell-O
Jennings, Peter
Jennings, Waylon
Jeopardy!
Jessel, George
Jesus Christ Superstar
Jet
Jet Skis
Jewish Defense League
JFK (The Movie)
Jogging
John Birch Society
John, Elton
Johns, Jasper
Johnson, Blind Willie
Johnson, Earvin "Magic"
Johnson, Jack
Johnson, James Weldon
Johnson, Michael
Johnson, Robert
Jolson, Al
Jones, Bobby
Jones, George
Jones, Jennifer
Jones, Tom
Jonestown
Jong, Erica
Joplin, Janis
Joplin, Scott
Jordan, Louis

Jordan, Michael
Joy of Cooking
Joy of Sex, The
Joyner, Florence Griffith
Joyner-Kersee, Jackie
Judas Priest
Judge
Judson, Arthur
Judy Bolton
Juke Boxes
Julia
Juliá, Raúl
Jurassic Park
Juvenile Delinquency

Kahn, Roger
Kaltenborn, Hans von
Kansas City Jazz
Kantor, MacKinlay
Karan, Donna
Karloff, Boris
Kasem, Casey
Kate & Allie
Katzenjammer Kids, The
Kaufman, Andy
Kaye, Danny
Keaton, Buster
Keillor, Garrison
Keitel, Harvey
Kelley, David E.
Kelly Bag
Kelly, Gene
Kelly Girls
Kelly, Grace
Kennedy Assassination
Kent State Massacre
Kentucky Derby
Kentucky Fried Chicken
Kern, Jerome
Kerrigan, Nancy
Kershaw, Doug
Kesey, Ken
Kewpie Dolls
Key West
Keystone Kops, The
King, Albert
King, B. B.
King, Billie Jean
King, Carole
King, Freddie
King Kong
King, Larry
King, Martin Luther, Jr.
King, Rodney
King, Stephen
Kingston, Maxine Hong
Kingston Trio, The
Kinison, Sam
Kinsey, Dr. Alfred C.
Kirby, Jack

KISS
Kitsch
Kiwanis
Klein, Calvin
Klein, Robert
Kmart
Knievel, Evel
Knight, Bobby
Knots Landing
Kodak
Kojak
Koontz, Dean R.
Koresh, David, and the Branch
    Davidians
Korman, Harvey
Kosinski, Jerzy
Kotzwinkle, William
Koufax, Sandy
Kovacs, Ernie
Kraft Television Theatre
Krantz, Judith
Krassner, Paul
Krazy Kat
Krupa, Gene
Ku Klux Klan
Kubrick, Stanley
Kudzu
Kuhn, Bowie
Kukla, Fran, and Ollie
Kung Fu
Kwan, Michelle

L. A. Law
L. L. Cool J.
"La Bamba"
Labor Unions
Lacoste Shirts
Ladd, Alan
Laetrile
Lahr, Bert
Lake, Ricki
Lake, Veronica
LaLanne, Jack
Lamarr, Hedy
LaMotta, Jake
Lamour, Dorothy
L'Amour, Louis
Lancaster, Burt
Landon, Michael
Landry, Tom
Lang, Fritz
lang, k.d.
Lansky, Meyer
Lardner, Ring
Larry Sanders Show, The
LaRussa, Tony
Las Vegas
Lasorda, Tommy
Lassie
Late Great Planet Earth, The

Latin Jazz
Laugh-In
Lauper, Cyndi
Laura
Laurel and Hardy
Lauren, Ralph
Laver, Rod
Laverne and Shirley
Lavin, Linda
Lawn Care/Gardening
Lawrence of Arabia
Lawrence, Vicki
La-Z-Boy Loungers
le Carré, John
Le Guin, Ursula K.
Leachman, Cloris
Leadbelly
League of Their Own, A
Lear, Norman
Leary, Timothy
Least Heat Moon, William
Leather Jacket
Leave It to Beaver
Led Zeppelin
Lee, Bruce
Lee, Gypsy Rose
Lee, Peggy
Lee, Spike
Lee, Stan
Legos
Lehrer, Tom
Leisure Suit
Leisure Time
LeMond, Greg
L'Engle, Madeleine
Lennon, John
Leno, Jay
Leonard, Benny
Leonard, Elmore
Leonard, Sugar Ray
Leone, Sergio
Leopold and Loeb
Les Miserables
Lesbianism
*Let Us Now Praise
    Famous Men*
Let's Pretend
Letterman, David
Levin, Meyer
Levi's
Levittown
Lewinsky, Monica
Lewis, C. S.
Lewis, Carl
Lewis, Jerry
Lewis, Jerry Lee
Lewis, Sinclair
Liberace
Liberty
Lichtenstein, Roy

Liebovitz, Annie
Life
Life of Riley, The
Like Water for Chocolate
Li'l Abner
Limbaugh, Rush
Lincoln Center for the
    Performing Arts
Lindbergh, Anne Morrow
Lindbergh, Charles
Linkletter, Art
Lion King, The
Lionel Trains
Lippmann, Walter
Lipstick
Liston, Sonny
Little Black Dress
Little Blue Books
Little League
Little Magazines
Little Orphan Annie
Little Richard
Live Television
L.L. Bean, Inc.
Lloyd Webber, Andrew
Loafers
Locke, Alain
Lolita
Lollapalooza
Lombard, Carole
Lombardi, Vince
Lombardo, Guy
London, Jack
Lone Ranger, The
Long, Huey
Long, Shelley
Long-Playing Record
Loos, Anita
López, Nancy
Lorre, Peter
Los Angeles Lakers, The
Los Lobos
Lost Weekend, The
Lottery
Louis, Joe
Louisiana Purchase Exposition
Louisville Slugger
Love Boat, The
Love, Courtney
Lovecraft, H. P.
Low Riders
Loy, Myrna
LSD
Lubitsch, Ernst
Lucas, George
Luce, Henry
Luciano, Lucky
Ludlum, Robert
Lugosi, Bela
Lunceford, Jimmie

Lupino, Ida
LuPone, Patti
Lynch, David
Lynching
Lynn, Loretta
Lynyrd Skynyrd

Ma Perkins
Mabley, Moms
MacDonald, Jeanette
MacDonald, John D.
Macfadden, Bernarr
MacMurray, Fred
Macon, Uncle Dave
Macy's
MAD Magazine
Madden, John
Made-for-Television Movies
Madonna
Mafia/Organized Crime
Magnificent Seven, The
Magnum, P.I.
Mah-Jongg
Mailer, Norman
Malcolm X
Mall of America
Malls
Maltese Falcon, The
Mamas and the Papas, The
Mamet, David
Man from U.N.C.L.E., The
*Man Who Shot Liberty
    Valance, The*
Manchurian Candidate, The
Mancini, Henry
Manhattan Transfer
Manilow, Barry
Mansfield, Jayne
Manson, Charles
Mantle, Mickey
Manufactured Homes
Mapplethorpe, Robert
March on Washington
Marching Bands
Marciano, Rocky
Marcus Welby, M.D.
Mardi Gras
Mariachi Music
Marichal, Juan
Marie, Rose
Marijuana
Maris, Roger
Marlboro Man
Marley, Bob
Married . . . with Children
Marshall, Garry
Martha and the Vandellas
Martin, Dean
Martin, Freddy
Martin, Quinn

Martin, Steve
Martini
Marvel Comics
Marx Brothers, The
Marx, Groucho
Mary Hartman, Mary Hartman
Mary Kay Cosmetics
Mary Poppins
Mary Tyler Moore Show, The
Mary Worth
*M*A*S*H*
Mason, Jackie
Mass Market Magazine
    Revolution
Masses, The
Masterpiece Theatre
Masters and Johnson
Masters Golf Tournament
Mathis, Johnny
Mattingly, Don
Maude
Maupin, Armistead
Maus
Max, Peter
Mayer, Louis B.
Mayfield, Curtis
Mayfield, Percy
Mays, Willie
McBain, Ed
McCaffrey, Anne
McCall's Magazine
McCarthyism
McCartney, Paul
McCay, Winsor
McClure's
McCoy, Horace
McCrea, Joel
McDaniel, Hattie
McDonald's
McEnroe, John
McEntire, Reba
McGwire, Mark
McHale's Navy
McKay, Claude
McKuen, Rod
McLish, Rachel
McLuhan, Marshall
McMurtry, Larry
McPherson, Aimee Semple
McQueen, Butterfly
McQueen, Steve
Me Decade
Meadows, Audrey
Mean Streets
Media Feeding Frenzies
Medicine Shows
Meet Me in St. Louis
Mellencamp, John
Mencken, H. L.
Mendoza, Lydia

Men's Movement
Merton, Thomas
Metalious, Grace
Metropolis
Metropolitan Museum of Art
MGM (Metro-Goldwyn-Mayer)
Miami Vice
Michener, James
Mickey Mouse Club, The
Microsoft
Middletown
Midler, Bette
Midnight Cowboy
Mildred Pierce
Militias
Milk, Harvey
Millay, Edna St. Vincent
Miller, Arthur
Miller Beer
Miller, Glenn
Miller, Henry
Miller, Roger
Milli Vanilli
Million Man March
Milton Bradley
Minimalism
Minivans
Minnelli, Vincente
Minoso, Minnie
Minstrel Shows
Miranda, Carmen
Miranda Warning
Miss America Pageant
Mission: Impossible
Mister Ed
Mister Rogers' Neighborhood
Mitchell, Joni
Mitchell, Margaret
Mitchum, Robert
Mix, Tom
Mod
Mod Squad, The
Model T
Modern Dance
Modern Maturity
Modern Times
Modernism
Momaday, N. Scott
Monday Night Football
Monkees, The
Monopoly
Monroe, Bill
Monroe, Earl "The Pearl"
Monroe, Marilyn
Montalban, Ricardo
Montana, Joe
Montana, Patsy
Monty Python's Flying Circus
Moonies/Reverend Sun
    Myung Moon

Moonlighting
Moore, Demi
Moore, Michael
Moral Majority
Moreno, Rita
Mork & Mindy
Morris, Mark
Morrissette, Alanis
Morrison, Toni
Morrison, Van
Morse, Carlton E.
Morton, Jelly Roll
Mosley, Walter
Moss, Kate
Mother's Day
Mötley Crüe
Motley, Willard
Motown
Mount Rushmore
Mountain Biking
Mouseketeers, The
Movie Palaces
Movie Stars
Mr. Dooley
Mr. Smith Goes to Washington
Mr. Wizard
Ms.
MTV
Muckraking
Multiculturalism
Mummy, The
Muni, Paul
Munsey's Magazine
Muppets, The
Murder, She Wrote
Murphy Brown
Murphy, Eddie
Murray, Anne
Murray, Arthur
Murray, Bill
Murray, Lenda
Murrow, Edward R.
Muscle Beach
Muscle Cars
Muscular Christianity
Musical, The
Mutiny on the Bounty
Mutt & Jeff
Muzak
My Darling Clementine
My Fair Lady
My Family/Mi familia
My Lai Massacre
My So Called Life
My Three Sons

Nader, Ralph
Nagel, Patrick
Naismith, James
Namath, Joe

Pittsburgh Steelers, The
Pizza
Place in the Sun, A
Planet of the Apes
Plastic
Plastic Surgery
Plath, Sylvia
Platoon
Playboy
Playgirl
Playhouse 90
Pogo
Pointer Sisters, The
Poitier, Sidney
Polio
Political Bosses
Political Correctness
Pollock, Jackson
Polyester
Pop Art
Pop, Iggy
Pop Music
Pope, The
Popeye
Popsicles
Popular Mechanics
Popular Psychology
Pornography
Porter, Cole
Postcards
*Postman Always Rings
    Twice, The*
Postmodernism
Potter, Dennis
Powell, Dick
Powell, William
Prang, Louis
Preminger, Otto
Preppy
Presley, Elvis
Price Is Right, The
Price, Reynolds
Price, Vincent
Pride, Charley
Prince
Prince, Hal
Prinze, Freddie
Prisoner, The
Professional Football
Prohibition
Prom
Promise Keepers
Protest Groups
Prozac
Pryor, Richard
Psychedelia
Psychics
Psycho
PTA/PTO (Parent Teacher
    Association/Organization)

Public Enemy
Public Libraries
Public Television (PBS)
Puente, Tito
Pulp Fiction
Pulp Magazines
Punisher, The
Punk
Pynchon, Thomas

Quayle, Dan
Queen, Ellery
Queen for a Day
Queen Latifah
Queer Nation
Quiz Show Scandals

Race Music
Race Riots
Radio
Radio Drama
Radner, Gilda
Raft, George
Raggedy Ann and Raggedy
    Andy
Raging Bull
Ragni, Gerome, and James
    Rado
Raiders of the Lost Ark
Rainey, Gertrude ''Ma''
Rains, Claude
Raitt, Bonnie
Rambo
Ramones, The
Ranch House
Rand, Sally
Rap/Hip Hop
Rather, Dan
Reader's Digest
Reagan, Ronald
Real World, The
Reality Television
Rear Window
Rebel without a Cause
Recycling
Red Scare
Redbook
Redding, Otis
Redford, Robert
Reed, Donna
Reed, Ishmael
Reed, Lou
Reese, Pee Wee
Reeves, Steve
Reggae
Reiner, Carl
Religious Right
R.E.M.
Remington, Frederic
Reno, Don

Renoir, Jean
Replacements, The
Retro Fashion
Reynolds, Burt
Rhythm and Blues
Rice, Grantland
Rice, Jerry
Rich, Charlie
Rigby, Cathy
Riggs, Bobby
Riley, Pat
Ringling Bros., Barnum &
    Bailey Circus
Ripken, Cal, Jr.
Ripley's Believe It Or Not
Rivera, Chita
Rivera, Diego
Rivera, Geraldo
Rivers, Joan
Rizzuto, Phil
Road Rage
Road Runner and Wile E.
    Coyote
Robbins, Tom
Roberts, Jake "The Snake"
Roberts, Julia
Roberts, Nora
Robertson, Oscar
Robertson, Pat
Robeson, Kenneth
Robeson, Paul
Robinson, Edward G.
Robinson, Frank
Robinson, Jackie
Robinson, Smokey
Robinson, Sugar Ray
Rock and Roll
Rock, Chris
Rock Climbing
Rockefeller Family
Rockettes, The
Rockne, Knute
Rockwell, Norman
Rocky
Rocky and Bullwinkle
*Rocky Horror Picture
    Show, The*
Roddenberry, Gene
Rodeo
Rodgers and Hammerstein
Rodgers and Hart
Rodgers, Jimmie
Rodman, Dennis
Rodriguez, Chi Chi
Roe v. Wade
Rogers, Kenny
Rogers, Roy
Rogers, Will
Rolle, Esther
Roller Coasters

P

Paar, Jack (1918—)

When Jack Paar was chosen to host NBC's faltering *Tonight Show* in July 1957, the program had been reduced to two sponsors and was carried by only 62 network stations. Within eighteen months, the antics of the witty, unpredictable Paar had brought a total of 115 stations on board, and the show, renamed *The Jack Paar Tonight Show,* had full sponsorship. Paar's unique style would both establish the popularity of talk shows and set the standard for all future television hosts.

Born in Canton, Ohio on May 1, 1918, Paar dropped out of high school and began working as a radio announcer for stations in Indianapolis, Youngstown, Cleveland, Pittsburgh, and Buffalo. Working for the army special services during World War II, Paar entertained enlisted men with irreverent gibes at the military brass. He appeared in three movies in the early 1950s: *Walk Softly, Stranger, Love Nest,* and *Down Among the Sheltering Palms.* During the same period, he hosted two television game shows, *Bank on the Stars* and *Up to Paar,* which led to a contract as host of *The Morning Show,* an attempt by CBS to compete with *The Today Show* on NBC. However, none of these programs would ever bring him the amount of success he enjoyed with the *Tonight Show.*

Jack Paar

Temperamental, spontaneous, and at times brilliantly incisive, Paar brought drama to the art of late-night conversation with such semi-regular guests as Washington hostess Elsa Maxwell, Cliff Arquette (who played the character Charlie Weaver), Joey Bishop, Hans Conried, Peggy Cass, Zsa Zsa Gabor, Hermione Gingold, Buddy Hackett, Florence Henderson, Betty White, and Oscar Levant. Levant, a classical pianist with an acid tongue, is remembered for such barbs as "Zsa Zsa has discovered the secret of perpetual middle age" and his nomination of Elizabeth Taylor for the "Other Woman of the Year Award." There were also more serious guests. During the 1960 presidential campaign, John F. Kennedy and Richard Nixon made separate appearances on Paar's show.

In addition to conversing with his guests, Paar featured comic sketches and frequently visited the audience for interviews. On one memorable occasion, Cary Grant was seated in the audience as a surprise to Paar, who pretended not to recognize the international film star while interviewing a little old lady from out of town sitting beside him. Paar's orchestra leader, Jose Melis, liked to play a "telephone game," improvising melodies based on the last four digits of an audience member's telephone number. In another popular routine, Paar showed baby pictures on the screen while supplying humorous captions.

Although he professed to dislike controversy, Paar was continually involved in it, carrying on much-publicized feuds with such celebrities as Steve Allen, Dorothy Kilgallen, Walter Winchell, and Ed Sullivan. Many of the feuds started with a remark made on the show. Paar said, for example, that Winchell's "high, hysterical voice" came from "wearing too tight underwear." The feuds were never easy to quell. Paar's friend and mentor, Jack Benny, finally had to step in to moderate the Paar-Sullivan conflict. But the most famous controversy occurred on February 11, 1960, when an angry Paar walked on stage and began to berate NBC executives for censoring out a joke from the previous night's taped show. Paar then told the audience he was tired of being the center of controversy and bid them an emotional farewell, leaving an astonished Hugh Downs to carry on the show.

Paar returned a month later, but his controversial days had not ended. In September 1961, he took Peggy Cass and a camera crew to Germany to report on the Berlin Wall, which had been erected a month earlier. Paar arranged for a detachment of American troops to be shown in the background of his televised scenes near the Brandenburg Gate. The incident led to a Defense Department inquiry, and the press raked Paar over the coals for the militaristic overtones of his broadcast. Paar maintained that his visit had actually eased East-West tensions. A short time later he announced he would be leaving the show the following spring, and this time he kept his word. His last show aired on March 29, 1962, and dozens of celebrities dropped by or sent tapes to wish him an affectionate farewell.

After his much publicized departure from *The Jack Paar Tonight Show,* he became the owner of Mount Washington TV Inc., broadcasting from WMTW TV and FM, Portland and Poland Springs, Maine. Paar is the author of three humorous books: *I Kid You Not* (1960), *My Saber Is Bent* (1961), and *Three on a Toothbrush* (1965).

—Benjamin Griffith

FURTHER READING:

Brooks, Tim, and Earle Marsh. *The Complete Directory to Prime Time Network TV Shows: 1946 to Present*. New York, Ballantine, 1981.

Galanoy, Terry. *Tonight!* Garden City, Doubleday, 1972.

McNeil, Alex. *Total Television: A Comprehensive Guide to Programming from 1948 to the Present*. New York, Penguin, 1991.

Metz, Robert. *The Tonight Show*. New York, Playboy Press, 1980.

Pachucos

The pachucos were Latino street rebels of the 1940s who innovated a style and attitude that expressed their defiance of mainstream America. Dressed to kill in zoot suits and with pompadour haircuts they hung out on the streets of East Los Angeles, speaking their own language and asserting their difference from everyone around them. They were the first subcultural group to exhibit their rebellion by display—through their clothing and behavior on the street. Their unique brand of defiance opened up an avenue of rebellion which was later followed by youth cultures in genres such as rock and roll.

The pachucos were second generation Mexican-American youths who lived in the barrios of East Los Angeles during the years of World War II. They were branded ''delinquents'' by the Los Angeles Police Department, and held responsible for the wave of juvenile crime that was sweeping the city at the time. The pachucos also incurred the wrath of their Mexican elders by their ''degenerate'' behavior of draft-dodging, marijuana-smoking, and their foppish attention to their clothes.

The style they sported was the zoot suit: a long drape jacket that reached to the knees and high waisted trousers that were baggy on the leg but tapered at the ankle. The suit was worn with a very long key chain and often a crucifix or a medallion over the tie. The hairdo to go with the look was the pompadour, a relatively long hair cut for men, worn greased into a quiff at the front and combed into a duck's tail at the back. In the hair the pachucos kept their fileros (flick knives), the thickness of the hair style providing a secure hiding place for weapons. Distinctive tattoos, such as the Virgin of Guadalupe, where also part of the pachuco look. Their female counterparts, the pachucas, had their own dress code which consisted of short tight skirts, flimsy blouses, dramatic makeup, and longer pompadour hairdos.

The name ''pachuco'' is of uncertain origin but is believed to be derived from the word ''Pachuca,'' a town in east Central Mexico. The pachucos spoke a hybrid slang called ''Calo,'' derived from the gypsy tongue. The word ''Chicano''—a politicized term of self-definition for Mexican Americans—is itself a Calo word. Music was also an important ingredient in the scene, and much of the pachuco lifestyle revolved around the dance halls where they would go to dance and listen to swing bands. A bandleader called Don Tosti had a hit with a song called ''Pachuco Boogie,'' a big band number with lyrics in Calo.

The Sleepy Lagoon Case in 1942 brought the pachucos into the national limelight. This was a murder case in which 13 Mexican-American youths were convicted on varying charges, including that of first degree murder, for the killing of José Díaz. The trial took place at a time when William Randolph Hearst's Los Angeles newspapers had been running incendiary stories about gang violence. The image of the pachuco circulated by these papers was that of a bloodthirsty killer spurred on by the ancestral Aztec desire to let blood. Two years later these convictions were reversed by an appeal court, largely due to the efforts of the Sleepy Lagoon Defense Committee, which featured public figures as illustrious as Orson Welles and Rita Hayworth amongst its number. Luis Valdez's 1981 film *Zoot Suit*, an adaptation of the stage musical, gives a part-fact, part-fiction account of the case from the perspective of Henry Reyna, the leader of the convicted gang of pachucos.

The pachucos' brush with controversy, however, did not end there. In early June 1943, disturbances broke out in East Los Angeles. Mobs of sailors and marines began scouring the streets in taxis looking for zoot-suited pachucos to beat up, supposedly in retaliation for attacks on their number by pachucos. If no candidates could be found the servicemen would storm into movie theaters and drag any young males they perceived as pachucos from the auditorium, take them outside and strip them of their zoot suits, and cut their pompadour hairdos. Eyewitness accounts report the attacks as unprovoked and, furthermore, that they were actively encouraged by crowds of observing civilians.

At a time when national obedience was everything, the pachucos were singled out by servicemen for being bad citizens. Not only were the pachucos dodging the draft, but the zoot suits they wore contravened fabric rationing regulations in the generosity of their cut. ''Pachuquismo''—or the pachuco style—was the total contradiction of military discipline, order, measure, and effort. The pachucos cultivated a manner of languid detachment and were not seen to have a good work ethic. They performed their defiance through their clothes, openly inviting hostile attention. The Mexican poet Octavio Paz described the pachuco as a ''sinister clown'' who courted the hunter by decking himself out as his prey.

The pachuco look was taken up by the mainstream and emerged in the 1950s greaser style. Within marginal groups, the pachucos served as inspirational icons for the Chicano Civil Rights Movement that fomented in the late 1960s. As the first people to forge a position for themselves in opposition both to the American mainstream and their traditional Mexican backgrounds, the pachucos were the first Mexican Americans to self-consciously style and define themselves on exactly their own terms. In the late 1990s renewed interest in swing music by groups such as the Cherry Poppin' Daddies brought ''pachuquismo'' back into vogue. The 1994 film *The Mask*, starring Jim Carrey, characterized the pachuco as the outrageous transformation of the wimpish bankclerk protagonist for the rebellious, maverick, and magical qualities that the style evokes. Quixotic, sinister, and theatrical, the pachuco is continually evoked as one of the mythic figures of American popular culture.

—Candida Taylor

FURTHER READING:

Cosgrove, Stuart. ''The Zoot Suit and Style Warfare.'' *Zoot Suits and Second Hand Dresses*. Basingstoke, United Kingdom, Macmillan, 1989.

Mazón, Mauricio. *The Zoot Suit Riots*. Austin, University of Texas Press, 1984.

Muñoz Jr., Carlos. *Youth, Identity, Power*. New York, Verso, 1989.

Paz, Octavio. *The Labyrinth of Solitude*. London, Penguin, 1985.

Pacino, Al (1940—)

When director Francis Ford Coppola's film masterpiece *The Godfather* was released in 1972, Al Pacino galvanized filmgoers with his brooding, dark good looks and masterfully controlled performance as a Mafia leader. Pacino, already an award-winning stage actor, virtually established a new level of screen intensity, winning an Oscar nomination and launching an international career as a major film star. The film depicts a significant passing of power when the ailing Vito Corleone (Marlon Brando) makes his son Michael (Pacino) the new "godfather." Since both Brando (a film icon) and Pacino (relatively unknown in films) were considered "Method" actors, many critics and filmgoers saw a parallel symbolic passing of influence from one generation of actors to another. For box-office reasons Brando was designated "the star" but Pacino, with his aura of low-key sensuality, compelling screen presence, and underlying explosiveness not only held his ground onscreen with Brando, but mesmerized audiences.

The film completely transcended the traditional gangster picture; Pacino's performance forever changed filmgoers' image of ganglords. The uneducated, raised-in-poverty, loud, brutal Edward G. Robinson/Jimmy Cagney "tough guy" of the past was replaced by Pacino's educated, soft-spoken, unobtrusively wealthy, self-controlled characterization. In this film and his starring role in *The*

Al Pacino

Godfather, Part II (1974 Best Actor Oscar and Golden Globe nominations), Pacino chillingly portrays the metamorphosis of the basically decent Michael—idealistic, patriotic, and gentle—into an austere, steely-eyed, implacably heartless tyrant, deadly to anyone who defies him. His portrayal of Michael's obsessive self-control is so effective that rare displays of temper jar the audience. Pacino shows the gradual erosion of humanity in Michael by infrequent but extreme changes in character intensity, and subtle alterations in manner, speech, posture, facial muscles, and his deep, expressive eyes. Writer Jimmy Breslin said that Pacino "dominates *The Godfather* with a creeping sense of tyranny." Many years later, in *The Godfather, Part III* (1990), Pacino again assumed the role of Michael Corleone, now an aging, ill, demoralized, and ultimately tragic figure. Breslin described Pacino well: "The [*Godfather*] movies unleashed a new force, raw and fearless in his willingness to allow the intrusion of a camera into the soul of a man."

Pacino always seemed determined to become an actor. Although poor, from an early age he regularly saw movies, afterwards reenacting the major roles. He also was excited by and continues to love the stage. Because of family finances he had to quit school early and worked at various jobs; after some acting classes he began to get theater parts. In 1966 the Actors Studio accepted him; two years later he won an Obie Award. His first Tony Award came in 1969 and in that same year he made an effective screen debut in a bit part in *Me, Natalie*. Those performances led to his first leading role in a film at age 31—*The Panic in Needle Park* (1971).

In the 1970s he starred in five film hits, each role garnering him an Oscar nomination: the first two *Godfather* portrayals; an incorruptible, volcanic hippie cop in *Serpico* (1973); a sexually-confused would-be bank robber in *Dog Day Afternoon* (1975); and an idealistic, angry lawyer in *And Justice for All* (1979). In the 1980s he chose far-ranging and unusual scripts, but did not have any major hits. Although included in lists of the top 25 most popular film stars in almost every year, his box-office success was shrinking. Then in 1989 he played a hard-drinking, lonelyhearts police detective having a steamy affair with a possible murderess in *Sea of Love*. The reviews were mostly good and many heralded his "comeback." Most filmgoers do not know that in those two decades, Pacino also was performing onstage in works by playwrights as diverse as Tennessee Williams, Shakespeare, Bertolt Brecht, and David Mamet; he won another Tony Award (1977, for Best Actor) for David Rabe's *The Basic Training of Pavlo Hummel*.

Pacino films made in the 1990s were successful because with few exceptions, such as the comically hammy *Dick Tracy* (1990), Pacino returned to the persona/roles that his fans wanted and expected—the intense, focused, explosive, emotionally-disconnected anti-hero on either side of the law. Successful performances included the haunting and haunted Godfather in *The Godfather, Part III;* the shark-like real estate "closer" in *Glengarry Glen Ross* (1992); the ferociously bitter blind man in *Scent of a Woman* (1992); the charismatic, wheeler-dealer mayor in *City Hall* (1996); and the declining "goodfella" in *Donnie Brasco* (1997). *Looking for Richard,* a 1996 pseudo-documentary Pacino produced, directed, and starred in shows a cast and crew during parts of the rehearsals, discussions, and stage production of Shakespeare's *Richard III*. This unusual and enlightening film makes Shakespeare's gripping drama more accessible to a broader audience.

Pacino is especially effective at changing his facial expressions and altering the volume of his voice, dialect, and speech patterns. But he is best known for using his eyes, which in any one film can be tender and loving, cold and penetrating, full of rage, melancholy, confused, imploring, or cloudy and distant, changing from one look to another in an instant. He is capable of generating an icy heat, of exuding a physical energy while standing perfectly still. Although relatively short, he has a compelling presence and body language that increase his physical stature.

In the sentiments of *Entertainment Weekly* writer Ty Burr, Pacino was ''[the best] fusion of Method acting and charisma since the young Brando.'' He has become an elder statesman of Hollywood; his versatility, integrity, and dedication to his craft are admired and respected by critics, fans, and peers. Eminent film director Sidney Lumet says that ''every star evokes a sense of danger, something unmanageable.'' Pacino is a star; in the best sense, he has become the ''godfather'' of acting.

—Jaye Cohen

FURTHER READING:

Lebo, Harlan. *The Godfather Legacy.* New York, Fireside, 1997.

Maltin, Leonard, editor. *Leonard Maltin's Movie Encyclopedia.* New York, Dutton, 1994.

Schoell, William. *The Films of Al Pacino.* Secaucus New Jersey, Citadel Press/Carol Publishing Group, 1995.

Yule, Andrew. *Life on the Wire: The Life and Art of Al Pacino.* New York, Donald I. Fine, 1991.

Paglia, Camille (1947—)

Following the release of her provocative book *Sexual Personae* in 1990, Camille Paglia, a professor of Liberal Arts at the University of Pennsylvania, established herself as an internationally recognized and highly controversial public intellectual. She is known for being non-conformist in her approach to intellectual life and for her unique methods of communicating her uncommon and sometimes unpopular viewpoints.

Born April 2, 1947 in Endicott, New York, to parents Pasquale John and Lydia Anne (Colapietro) Paglia, she was raised in Syracuse New York where she attended public school. Her academic training continued on a traditional path: she earned a B.A. from SUNY Binghamton in 1968, a M.Phil. from Yale University in 1971, and a Ph.D. in English in 1974, also from Yale. Her teaching career began at Binghamton University in Bennington, Vermont, where she was a faculty member in the Literature and Language department until 1980. Before arriving at Penn's University of the Arts in 1984 she held various fellowships and was a visiting lecturer at both Wesleyan and Yale.

Although Paglia is an accomplished scholar, non-academic influences are instrumental to her work. In her writing, Paglia often identifies herself as a ''daughter of the sixties,'' and its progressive politics are evident in her work. In addition, she was greatly influenced by her Italian-American heritage, using her cultural experience to shape her feminist analyses. She argues that women should view the world as a Darwinian battle for survival. She began to learn such lessons as a child, she writes in *Vamps and Tramps,* when she ''. . . was fed wild black mushrooms, tart dandelion greens, spiny artichokes, and tangy olives flecked with red pepper flakes . . . life lessons in the sour and prickly.''

Sprinkling her prose with such observations, Paglia broke many of the conventions of academic publishing in ways that both thrilled and angered readers. *Sexual Personae* (1990), the scholarly tome that launched her into the public spotlight, is a study of art, social ideas, and sexuality in the Western world. In it, she argues that great art derives from tensions between ''Dionysian lust and Appollonian rationality,'' and makes her argument with salacious discussions of John Keats and Emily Dickinson, and attacks ''sanctimonious P.C. intellectuals'' and the ''weakness of those who cry date rape.'' This best-selling book, which combined standard research with highly abstract philosophies, became controversial for three reasons. First, it espoused a belief in the pagan origins of human sexuality. Second, the book's approach to feminism directly opposed most of the feminist establishment, including institutionalized feminism on American campuses. Third, the format of the book grated on those who rejected her idiosyncratic style of academic argument.

An instant academic celebrity, Paglia was drawn into national controversies over date rape, sexual harassment, censorship, political correctness, poststructuralism, and the role of television, among others. In 1992, she published *Sex, Art, and American Culture,* a collection of essays that chronicled her engagement with these thorny cultural issues; her second book of essays, *Vamps & Tramps* (1994), addressed similar themes. The main essay in *Vamps and Tramps,* entitled ''No Law in the Arena: A Pagan Theory of Sexuality,'' systematically presents Paglia's libertarian views on rape, abortion, battering, sexual harassment, prostitution, stripping, pornography, homosexuality, pedophilia, and transvestitism. ''Vamps and tramps are the seasoned symbols of tough-cookie feminism, my answer to the smug self-satisfaction and crass materialism of yuppie feminism.'' Unlike other feminists—who she claims were focused on victimization—Paglia argues that ''women will never succeed at the level or in the numbers they deserve until they get over their genteel reluctance to take abuse in the attack and counterattack of territorial warfare.''

These and other remarks earned Paglia a reputation as an ''anti-feminist.'' Not surprisingly, this stance contributed to her notoriety and Paglia appeared on a variety of television shows such as CBS's *60 Minutes* (1992) and *Think Tank* on PBS (1995), where she displayed her combative style of discourse. Paglia was featured in or contributed to many of the leading periodicals of the day, including *Playboy, Vanity Fair, New Republic, The New York Times, Time, Rolling Stone, The New York Times Book Review,* and *Harper's Magazine.* In 1991, Paglia even graced the cover of *Village Voice* with the headline ''Counterfeit Feminism, Wanted for Intellectual Fraud.''

Paglia may be one of the most misunderstood thinkers of the century. Not unlike earlier radicals, her innovation was in utilizing unique methods for making her arguments against the status quo. As she explained, ''although I wasn't a follower per se of . . . Allen Ginsberg or Marshall McLuhan . . . those radical thinkers broke through the conventions of tradition and allowed us of the Sixties to find our own voices . . . which is what I wish to do for students of the 1990s.'' Her aggressive conduct befit this goal. In *Vamps and Tramps* she wrote, ''I espouse offensiveness for its own sake as a tool of attack against received opinion and unexamined assumptions.'' Given that she claims her highest ideals are free speech and free thought, this approach corresponds with her philosophy.

Her critics from the feminist establishment notwithstanding, many found her approach liberating. She received a series of stellar reviews for her books, was nominated for a National Book Critics Circle Award in 1991, and has a number of followers in the academic world. In 1997, she became a columnist for the on-line magazine

Salon and in 1998 published a book about Hitchcock's classic film *The Birds* at the behest of the British Film Institute. Only time will tell whether Paglia achieved her goal of helping students of the 1990s find their own voices. There can be no doubt that she found hers.

—Julie Scelfo

FURTHER READING:

Clark, Ve Ve A., et al, editors. *Antifeminism in the Academy*. New York, Routledge, 1996.

Female Misbehavior (film), directed by Monika Treut. Hyena Films, 1992.

hooks, bell, "Camille Paglia: 'Black' Pagan or White Colonizer." In *Outlaw Culture: Resisting Representations*. Boston, South End Press, 1994, 83-90.

Kregloe, K., and J. Caputi. "Supermodels of Lesbian Chic." In *Cross Purposes: Lesbians, Feminists, and the Limits of Alliance*, edited by Dana Heller. Bloomington, Indiana University Press, 1997, 136-154.

Kumar, Mina. "Katha Pollitt on Women and Feminism." *Sojourner*. Vol. 20, No. 9, May 1995.

Paglia, Camille. *Sex, Art, and American Culture: Essays*. New York, Vintage, 1992.

———. *Sexual Personae: Art and Decadence from Nefertiti to Emily Dickinson*. New Haven, Yale University Press, 1990.

———. *Vamps and Tramps: New Essays*. New York, Vintage, 1994.

Satchel Paige

Paige, Satchel (1899?-1982)

In an era when American major league sports were a white man's game, African American Leroy "Satchel" Paige achieved legendary fame as Negro League baseball's undisputed star and standard bearer. In a career spanning three decades, the lanky, limber right-handed pitcher hurled a reputed 2,500 games, won nearly 2,000, and came to symbolize the untapped potential of black professional athletes. He later followed Jackie Robinson and Larry Doby into the Major Leagues as one of baseball's first African-American players and solidified his reputation as one of the game's most talented performers. Joe DiMaggio, facing a Paige well past his prime, praised him as "the best and fastest pitcher I've ever faced."

Controversy has surrounded the issue Paige's age throughout his career, and his date of birth has been placed as early as December 18, 1899 and as late as July 7, 1906. By 1930, the young Alabaman had earned a reputation as one of the brightest young stars in Negro League baseball. He joined Gus Greenlee's Pittsburgh Crawfords in 1931 for an extraordinary $250 a week, and for the next six years teamed up with catcher Josh Gibson to form the dominant battery in black baseball. His performance with the Crawfords quickly demonstrated that he was worth his salary. In 1933, he won 21 games in a row and ended the season with a 31-4 record, racking up a professional record of 62 straight scoreless innings in the process; in 1935, he pitched on 29 consecutive days. Paige later led the Kansas City Monarchs to five pennants, earning both the nickname "the iron man" for his stamina and a reputation as the most respected—as well as one of the most talented—figures in Negro League Baseball. He

also played before sell-out crowds in the Caribbean and Central and South America.

It was Paige's success in exhibition play against white performers, however, which helped earn him nation-wide renown. On barnstorming tours with white pitching aces Dizzy Dean in the 1930s and Bob Feller in the early 1940s, Paige proved that he could stand toe to toe with the best white baseball had to offer. He struck out the game's leading right-handed hitter, Rogers Hornsby, five times in one game and, in a 1930 exhibition match, struck out 22 big leaguers including future Hall-of-Famers Hack Wilson and Babe Herman. His 1934 1-0 victory in 13 innings over Dean is still widely touted as the greatest pitching performance of all time.

When Brooklyn Dodgers' general manager Branch Rickey determined to break Major League Baseball's color barrier during the mid-1940s, Paige's name was circulated widely as a possible candidate. The veteran's age proved to be an obstacle and the pioneer's role fell to Paige's Kansas City Monarchs teammate Jackie Robinson. By the time Robinson entered the National League in 1947, Paige—well into his forties—appeared to be too old for the majors. His high salary demands did little to help his prospects. Although a nationally recognized figure, Paige seemed destined to follow fellow veteran Negro League stars Gibson, "Cool Papa" Bell, and Judy Johnson into obscurity.

Bill Veeck, the owner of the Cleveland Indians, considered purchasing Paige's contract in 1947 but abandoned the plan for fear his efforts would be misinterpreted as a publicity stunt. In 1948, however, Veeck's team was in a tight four-way pennant race and the young executive found himself desperately in need of pitching.

Scouting reports suggested that Paige was the best player available. Confounding his critics, Veeck signed Paige—paying him a full year's salary to pitch the remaining three months of the season—generating one of the most vocal outcries in the history of professional sports. Tom Spink of the *Sporting News* typified Veeck's detractors with the observation that ''to sign a player at Paige's age is to demean the standards of baseball in the big circuits . . . Were Satchel white, he would not have drawn a second thought from Veeck.'' Veeck's reply became legend: ''If Satch were white,'' he said, ''he would have been in the majors twenty-five years earlier and the question would not have been before the house.''

On July 8, 1948, Paige made his Major League debut in Cleveland to a cheering crowd of 34,780 fans—the majority of whom had come to the ballpark to see the Negro League star's debut. In an unprecedented frenzy, press photographers ran onto the field to photograph his warm-up pitches; the forty-something Paige then stunned his audience with two scoreless innings. By the middle of August, he boasted a record of 5-1 and a 1.33 earned run average. Paige became, in historian Jules Tygiel's words, ''the most discussed performer in baseball.'' The Indians went on to win the American League pennant.

Paige later pitched for the St. Louis Browns and the Kansas City Athletics. He ended his Major League stint with a modest 28-31 record and a 3.29 earned run average. Yet throughout his career, Paige continued to be one of baseball's most popular attractions. Author ''Doc'' Young estimated that on one occasion, one in six black residents of Cleveland came out to watch ''Ol' Satch'' perform. After retirement, Paige coached for the Atlanta Braves. He died in 1982 in Kansas City, Missouri.

During a time when many whites disparaged the abilities of black athletes, Paige's perennial feats served as a powerful symbol to the critics of segregated sports. Along with track star Jesse Owens and boxer Joe Louis, he became one of the leading African-American celebrities of the pre-integration era and a unifying, morale-boosting figure in the black community. Sports critic Tom Meany wrote in the *Sporting News* that Paige's Major League debut proved to be an event ''far more interesting than was the news when Branch Rickey broke baseball's color line.'' Paige's celebrity and talent helped pave the way for pioneers Jackie Robinson and Larry Doby. Moreover, he may have been the best pitcher ever to play professional baseball. Quite appropriately, when the Baseball Hall of Fame formed a Committee on Negro Leagues in 1971, Satchel Paige was the first man elected to the shrine in Cooperstown.

—Jacob Appel

FURTHER READING:

Bruce, Janet. *The Kansas City Monarchs: Champions of Black Baseball.* Lawrence, University Press of Kansas, 1985.

Holway, John. *Voices from the Great Negro Baseball Leagues.* New York, Dodd, Mead, 1975.

Paige, Leroy ''Satchel,'' and David Lipman. *Maybe I'll Pitch Forever.* New York, Doubleday, 1962.

Peterson, Robert. *Only the Ball Was White.* Englewood Cliffs, New Jersey, Prentice Hall, 1970.

Ribowsky, Mark. *Don't look back : Satchel Paige and the Shadows of Baseball.* New York, Simon & Schuster, 1994.

Tygiel, Jules. *Baseball's Great Experiment.* New York, Oxford University Press, 1997.

Young, Andrew ''Doc.'' *Great Negro Baseball Stars and How They Made The Major Leagues.* New York, AS Barnes, 1953.

Paley, Grace (1922—)

With the publication in 1959 of the first of three short story collections, *The Little Disturbances of Man: Stories of Women and Men at Love,* Grace Paley, at the age of 37, made an immediate impact on the literary scene. In these stories and the work that followed, readers have been charmed by a voice that is startlingly original yet as familiar as an overheard conversation on a city bus. Paley's work clearly reflects her own experience as a child of the Jewish Bronx, a young wife and mother staked out with the kids in Greenwich Village's Washington Square Park, and an activist involved in many of the important political movements of her time, most notably feminism and various antiwar efforts. Paley's literary output has been relatively small, due in part to time-out for motherhood, but it has been enthusiastically received by a wide audience. A photograph of Paley that accompanies several of her books shows the author bundled up in parka and wool hat, wearing her commentary for the day's political action sandwich-board style over her coat. It reads, from top to bottom: ''Money/Arms/War/Profit,'' and a few other words or phrases that don't fit into the camera's frame. With her characteristic elfin grin, Paley appears to be ready for any weather. The photograph has a caption from the late Donald Barthelme, Paley's fellow fiction writer, neighbor, and friend: ''Grace Paley is a wonderful writer and troublemaker. We are fortunate to have her in our country.''

—Sue Russell

FURTHER READING:

Arcana, Judith. *Grace Paley's Life Stories: A Literary Biography.* Urbana, Illinois, University of Illinois, 1993.

Paley, Grace. *The Collected Stories.* New York, Farrar Straus Giroux, 1994.

———. *Just As I Thought.* New York, Farrar Straus Giroux, 1998.

———. *New and Collected Poems.* Gardiner, Maine, Tilbury House, 1992.

Paley, William S. (1901-1990)

For more than 50 years, CBS and William S. Paley were synonymous. In 1927, Paley was involved with the formation of the Columbia Broadcasting System, and in 1928, his family purchased the company. The network grew quickly under Paley's leadership. Within six years the upstart challenger to the National Broadcasting System had almost 100 affiliate stations, nearly equal to that of NBC. By 1940, CBS was being recognized as the leader in the broadcasting field, in large part because of balanced mass entertainment and highly respected reportage, first in radio, and later in television. Reporter/broadcasters hired by Paley included Edward R. Murrow, Eric

William S. Paley

Sevareid, William L. Shirer, Howard K. Smith, and Walter Cronkite. Paley's leadership kept CBS as the leading network well into the 1980s.

—Lloyd Chiasson, Jr.

FURTHER READING:

Barnouw, Erik. *Tube of Plenty: The Evolution of American Television.* New York, Oxford University Press, 1982.

Bliss, Edward Jr. *Now the News: The Story of Broadcast Journalism.* New York, Columbia University Press, 1991.

Emery, Michael and Edwin. *The Press and America: An Interpretive History of the Mass Media.* 7th ed. Englewood Cliffs, New Jersey, Prentice Hall, 1992.

Weaver, Pat. *The Best Seat in the House: The Golden Years in Radio and Television.* New York, Knopf, 1994.

Palmer, Arnold (1929—)

Modern professional golf began its rise to popularity with the emergence of Arnold Palmer in 1955. The son of a club professional from Latrobe, Pennsylvania, Palmer learned the game as a child. He won the United States Golf Association Amateur Championship in 1954, before entering the professional ranks and dominating in the early 1960s. He won the Masters four times (1958, 1960, 1962, 1964), the British Open back to back in 1961 and 1962, and the U.S. Open in

1960. Palmer won the Seniors Championship, his first event on the Seniors tour, in 1980 and won the U.S. Seniors Open in 1981. Palmer was one of the earliest golfers to use his success on the golf course to create lucrative endorsement and business deals. Legions of fans, known as "Arnie's Army" followed Palmer weekly on the professional tour, and he was responsible for introducing the game to millions.

—Jay Parrent

FURTHER READING:

McCormack, Mark. *Arnie: The Evolution of a Legend.* New York, Simon and Schuster, 1967.

Palmer, Arnold, and William Barry Furlong. *Go for Broke: My Philosophy of Winning Golf.* New York, Simon and Schuster, 1973.

Palmer, Jim (1945—)

From 1965 to 1984, Jim Palmer was among baseball's most successful pitchers, winning three Cy Young Awards for a team that won six pennants. Palmer achieved stardom at the age of 20 when the righthander shut out the Dodgers on the way to a Baltimore Orioles sweep in the 1966 World Series. An injury kept Palmer out of baseball for nearly two years, but in 1969 he was able to come back and establish himself as one of the game's premier pitchers, winning 268 games in a career that spanned 19 years. Despite the team's success, throughout his career Palmer shared a stormy relationship with manager Earl Weaver. When his baseball pitching days ended in 1984, the handsome Palmer embarked on a new career as a pitchman for Jockey shorts. Advertising posters in which he models underwear could be seen in Europe and Asia in addition to the United States.

—Kevin O'Connor

FURTHER READING:

Cohen, Joel H. *Jim Palmer: Great Comeback Competitor.* New York, Putnam, 1978.

Palmer, Jim, and Jim Dale. *Together We Were Eleven Foot Nine: The Twenty-Year Friendship of Hall of Fame Pitcher Jim Palmer and Orioles Manager Earl Weaver.* Kansas City, Andrews and McMeel, 1996.

Pants for Women

As the proverbial question of who "wears the pants" in a relationship suggests, the history of women's pants says as much about the evolution of twentieth century gender roles as it does about the capricious swings of the fashion pendulum. Pants for women emerged from the burgeoning nineteenth century feminist movement, which demanded a change from Victorian dresses to a more practical costume that would permit women to engage in activities beyond those traditionally assigned to the female domestic sphere. Ironically, however, women's pants would achieve widespread social acceptance only when the fashion industry convinced women that pants were a necessary part of a well-dressed woman's wardrobe.

A model wearing Capri pants, c. 1950s.

The first feminine garments approximating pants were "bloomers"—a full skirt reaching just below the knee, with full-cut trousers underneath. Named for their chief advocate, feminist Amelia Jenks Bloomer, the outfit liberated women from heavy skirts, whalebone corsets, petticoats, bustles, and padding. In spite of the unprecedented mobility bloomers permitted, the fashion never spread beyond a small group. The bloomers' association with the suffrage movement stigmatized its wearers and, as an article in the September 1851 issue of *Godey's Lady's Book* hypothesized, bloomers did not take because most women would not wear what did not originate in fashionable Paris.

Though unsuccessful themselves, bloomers influenced the design of the popular feminine bicycling costume of the 1880s and 1890s. The outfit, consisting of a pair of knee-length, very baggy knickerbockers, had a split skirt with stockings worn beneath. These bicycle bloomers marked the first concession made by the fashion industry towards enabling women's participation in skirt-prohibitive activities. Formerly, as with the original bloomers, an activity was deemed immodest and unladylike if it could not be performed in a skirt. While some criticized bicycling for this reason, most women showed no inclination to give up cycling, and the craze for bicycle bloomers raged for the next two decades.

As the somber mood of the World War I replaced the frivolity of the "Gay Nineties," women replaced men in the factories the latter had abandoned for battlefields. At work, when skirts proved too cumbersome, women wore trousers or overalls, although this practice was much criticized. Women worked in the fields too, sometimes wearing overalls, as noted by L.M. Montgomery in her book *Rilla of Ingleside* (1921) which depicts life on Prince Edward Island during World War I. In the novel, some young women wear pants as they work, while the older women working beside them remain in their skirts because pants were still considered indecent or shocking. Clearly, though, those women who wore pants during World War I did so for reasons of practicality and not of fashion.

Following the war, in the 1920s, women exposed their arms and legs, flattened their chests, bobbed their hair to look boyish, and got the vote; but pants remained taboo, except in the realm of sports. Here, ease of movement somewhat dictated fashion. And so the ski-costume, a knitted tunic over knitted trousers which fit into ankle-high ski boots, was created. Riding outfits similar to men's became popular, and women wore the loose trousers of "lounge pajamas" on the beach.

When diva film star Marlene Dietrich appeared in slacks with flared bottoms in her United States debut film *Morocco* in 1930, she signaled the emergence of women's pants from sportswear to high fashion. Wearing them both in films and private life, she popularized the pants look. For summer wear, shorts and beach slacks were stylish, and pants were worn regularly with short-sleeved knit tops. Women's pants had gained such importance by 1939 that in the November issue of *Vogue* the magazine advised, "Your wardrobe is not complete without a pair or two of the superbly tailored slacks of 1939."

During World War II, however, fashion followed the needs of the war. Clothing was simple, sensible, and, in some cases, rationed. In England, the Board of Trade specified the maximum amount of cloth and buttons which could be used in women's slacks. Urged by images like "Rosie the Riveter," shown once on the cover of *The Saturday Evening Post* in 1943 as muscular and wearing coveralls, women returned to factory work; this time they wore their dungarees without looks askance.

In 1947, after the austerity of the war years, Christian Dior introduced his lush New Look, reverting to full skirts and soft femininity. Women's pants, however, were by then an acknowledged fact, and the 1950s brought many innovations to casual wear. Women wore a variety of slacks, ranging from tight-fitting to loose, worn with all types of blouses. Following the post-World War II baby boom, the 1950s ushered in the cult of youth and the creation of a market division specifically for teenage fashions. Girls wore Capri pants, stretch pants with stirrups, and Bermuda shorts.

These innovations set the stage for "unisex" fashions, which were developed in the 1960s. Both men and women wore blue jeans, "hipsters" and close fitting pants with zip fly fronts. The spirit of this latest association of pants with social and sexual liberation can be seen in Alice Walker's novel *The Color Purple* (1982), in which the social victory of the heroine culminates in her opening of a unisex jeans shop. In addition to jeans, pant-suits became popular with women in fabrics ranging from PVC and lurex to velvet and satin.

Since the 1960s, women's pants have run the gamut of trends from the bell-bottoms of the 1970s and the skin-tight jeans of the 1980s, to the return of bell-bottoms and tight jeans in the 1990s. The fashion, however, is not yet entirely divorced from its controversial beginnings. Only in the 1990s has the issue over whether women should wear pants in the workplace cooled, aided by the phenomenon of ''business casual'' days. Perhaps a greater indicator of the merge in the feminist and fashionable aspect of women's pants is reflected in the 1998 Miss America Pageant, where a number of the contestants, having been allowed, for the first time, to choose their outfits for the introductory number, came out wearing jeans.

—Sandra Sherman

FURTHER READING:

Adams, J. Donald. *Naked We Came: A More or Less Lighthearted Look at the Past, Present, and Future of Clothes.* New York, Holt, Rinehart, and Winston, 1967.

de Fircks, Tatiana. *History of Costume and Style.* Melbourne, Pitman Publishing, 1992.

Fifty Years of Fashion: Documented Sketches and Text From the Costume Library of Women's Wear Daily. New York, Fairchild Publications, 1950.

Tyrrell, Anne V. *Changing Trends in Fashion: Patterns of the Twentieth Century 1900-1970.* London, B.T. Batsford Ltd., 1986.

Pantyhose

In 1937 the invention of spinnable nylon made sheer, durable stockings affordable for the average woman, but in the 1960s, pantyhose, a convenient one-piece garment consisting of nylon-spandex stretchable stockings and underpants, made traditional stockings obsolete. Supermodel Twiggy popularized pantyhose when she stepped out on a runway in a miniskirt in 1965. Since then, pantyhose, which come in a wide range of colors, styles, and prices ($3.50-$40.00), have become an indispensable part of virtually every woman's working or fashion wardrobe. Emotionally appealing to women and sexually appealing to men, pantyhose have become a staple product in the global economy, having created a competitive, multi-billion dollar market by the end of the twentieth century that showed no signs of diminishing.

—John R. Deitrick

FURTHER READING:

Bruce, Katherine. ''The Missionary of Pantyhose.'' *Forbes.* December 15, 1997, 116.

Fasel, Penny Proddow. ''Stocking Smarts.'' *In Style.* Vol. 4, September 1998, 131.

Paperbacks

When Pocket Books introduced the paperback to American consumers in 1939, book publishing changed forever. Paperbacks did more than make books affordable to a mass audience; they made books available to readers who did not live near book stores, they helped popularize genre fiction, they turned otherwise obscure writers into best-selling authors, and they ensured a lasting existence for hardback books that went into paperback.

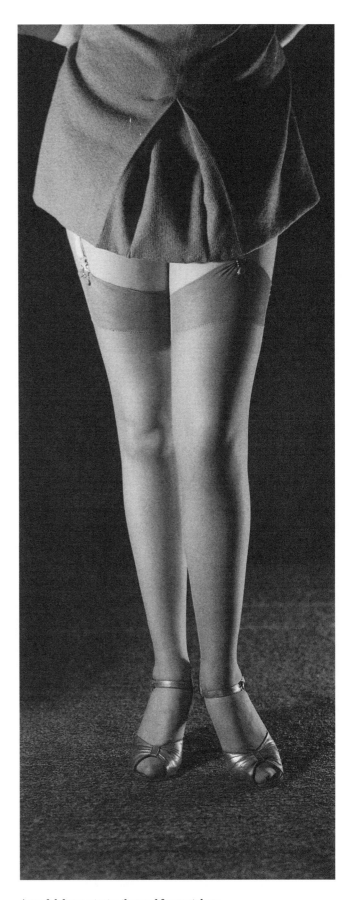

A model demonstrates the need for pantyhose.

Although there had been many earlier attempts to publish books with paper covers, the modern paperback book can be traced to Tauchnitz Books, a German publisher who began issuing paperbound books in 1841. Tauchnitz published English language editions of American and English books, primarily in non-English speaking European countries, assuming that there were enough American and British expatriates as well as Europeans fluent in English to establish a market for inexpensive English language books on the continent. Tauchnitz attempted to publish only the best literature and voluntarily paid royalties to its English and American writers at a time when most European publishers did not, so it was both flattering and financially rewarding to be chosen for publication by Tauchnitz. Perhaps what is most striking about Tauchnitz books is their complete lack of color or decoration; in contrast with American paperbacks, Tauchnitz book covers carried no illustration, only bearing the title and author in black letters against an off-white background.

For 90 years Tauchnitz had the European paperback market to itself. Its primary competitor, Albatross, emerged in 1931. Albatross was founded by German and English publishers; the name Albatross was chosen because that word is the same in nearly every major European language and therefore the company name would need no translation. Albatross brought one major innovation to the paperback market; it color-coded its books, so that one could determine the book's subject matter merely by glancing at the cover: blue books were love stories, red books were crime novels, and so forth. In 1934 Albatross bought out Tauchnitz and the two houses continued to publish until the outbreak of World War II. Meanwhile, an English paperback publisher, Penguin, largely adopted Albatross's book's appearance for its own publications, using a Penguin as its company logo and color-coding its books as well. All Penguin paperbacks were either orange or green in the 1990s.

Robert de Graff brought the paperback to America in 1939. De Graff had worked in book publishing for 14 years and was convinced that there was a market for inexpensive books in the United States. He said he got the idea of selling books for 25 cents when he was driving to work one day, stopped to pay a quarter at a tollbooth and realized that ''Nobody misses a quarter.'' He named his new company Pocket Books because the books were small enough to fit into one's pants pocket; at six and one half inches high and four and one quarter inches wide, the books were one quarter of an inch shorter than paperbacks.

De Graff faced two key obstacles in the development and marketing of the paperback book. He was determined to keep the price to 25 cents, but experts estimated that it would cost a minimum of 27 cents to produce and distribute the books. De Graff dealt with that issue by lowering author's royalty rates and by using cheaper paper, which is why the paperback has always had a reputation of being ''cheaper'' than the hardback book, in terms of quality as well as price. The second problem was a lack of cooperation from book publishers, who were reluctant to sell paperback rights to Pocket Books, fearing that potentials buyers would wait and buy the less expensive version. To prove that paperbacks would not harm the sales of hardback books, De Graff arranged for a test marketing in Texas of Dale Carnegie's *How to Win Friends and Influence People*. When the paperback sold well and sales of the hardback book remained steady, publishers realized that the two formats could co-exist. Eventually it became standard practice to delay the release of a paperback edition for a year or more after the hardback was published.

Pocket Books was launched in June of 1939. Ten titles were published, with a print run of 10,000 copies per title. The selected titles ranged from classics such as *The Way of All Flesh* to popular literature such as Agatha Christie's *The Murder of Roger Ackroyd*. The initial print run sold out in one week, the first indication de Graff had that his new company might be a big success. By the end of the year Pocket Books had sold 1.5 million books. The success of the new paperback format can be attributed to many things. Before the books were printed, De Graff had the edges of the paper dyed red, so that they stood out on a bookrack. He had also insisted that his books be grouped by subject matter, rather than simply divided into fiction and non-fiction, so that a person looking for one specific mystery novel, for example, might see several such novels grouped together and buy two or more. He even insisted that the company's recognizable trademark/mascot, a kangaroo named Gertrude (kangaroos have pockets), had a great deal to do with the company's success. But the most important factor in the success of Pocket Books was distribution. De Graff had managed to have his paperbacks sold in many, many more stores than those who sold hardback books; one estimate was that there were 40 stores carrying paperbacks for every one carrying hardbacks in the United States. Pocket Books were not just available in bookstores; they could be purchased in grocery stores, pharmacies, and candy stores, at bus stations, airports, and train terminals, through Sears, Roebuck and Spiegel catalogs—and at a price of 25 cents. What De Graf had done was make book purchasing an impulse buy, like a candy bar or a pack of gum.

Pocket Books' success did not go unnoticed by the publishing industry and several competitors emerged in 1941. The most successful was Avon Books, which imitated Pocket Books format slavishly. Avon adopted the same dimensions as Pocket Books, also dyed its pages red on the edge, used a bust of Shakespeare as a trademark and originally called its products Avon Pocket-Size Books. Pocket Books sued; eventually Avon dropped the word Pocket-Size from its cover but retained the logo, the red-trimmed pages, and the size.

When America entered World War II it became difficult for either Pocket Books or Avon to obtain as much paper as they needed to meet the demand for paperbacks and the war did substantial damage to the industry—at least in the short term. In the long term, it might have been the best thing that ever happened to paperbacks. During the war Avon, Pocket Books, and Penguin all printed military editions under the auspices of the Council on Books in Wartime, a government organization. These books were given free to servicemen during the war. Military editions were of different size and shape from the regular paperback; wider than they were tall, approximately five and a half inches across but only three and three-quarter inches high, the books could easily be slid into a shirt pocket if a soldier under attack suddenly had to put away his book. The military editions were extremely popular with American G.I.s and helped create a strong market for paperbacks in post-war America; not only did most of the returning soldiers who had read military editions overseas continue to buy and read paperback books, but many recommended them to their family and friends as well.

In 1943 two more publishers entered the paperback market, Dell and Popular Library. Both companies were founded by magazine publishers and therefore were even more attuned to the popular tastes of the American public than was Pocket Books. Dell's noteworthy contribution to the paperback format was the ''map book''—on the back cover of many Dell paperbacks was a map of the setting of the novel to help readers who might otherwise get confused. Bantam Books, like Avon, closely followed the Pocket Books model of red pages, small size, and mascot, a bantam rooster in this case. Bantam was founded in 1945 by Ian Ballantine, a former Penguin editor who went on to found another company, Ballantine, in 1952. New American Library, also founded by former Penguin editors, was established in 1947. NAL, with its Signet and Mentor imprints, soon developed a reputation as the most literary paperback house, publishing William Faulkner and D.H. Lawrence, among others.

The paperback industry changed again in 1950 with the founding of Fawcett Books, certainly the most influential publisher of paperbacks since Pocket Books and arguably the most important publisher in the history of the paperback. Like Dell and Popular Library, Fawcett had published magazines before entering the paperback market and had in fact distributed paperbacks for other companies along with its magazines. Fawcett wanted to enter into paperback publishing, but was contractually bound from producing paperback reprints of hard cover books. So Fawcett by necessity created what was to be the key market innovation of the paperback industry—the paperback original. Fawcett's Gold Medal line published not reprints of earlier works but brand new novels. This was particularly appealing to customers at the time; many publishers changed the titles of books when putting them into paperback so that buyers frequently got home with books they had already read, but Gold Medal novels guaranteed that would not happen. Each Gold Medal book concluded with this phrase: "The End of an Original Gold Medal Novel. The Gold Medal Seal on this book means it has never been published as a book before. To select an original book that you have not already read, look for the Gold Medal seal."

Fawcett attracted better authors than might have been expected from a paperback house; Kurt Vonnegut, John D. MacDonald, Jim Thompson, and Lawrence Block are among the authors who published early works with Gold Medal. The company paid one thousand dollars upon delivery of a manuscript, which meant writers did not have to wait to collect royalties, and a bonus if the book went into reprints. Fawcett also had a genuinely talented editor, Knox Burger, heading up its paperback line. Gold Medal targeted male readers; their books were mostly crime and western novels with titles such as *Second-Hand Nude* or *River Girl,* and their covers were lewd and lurid even by the standards of the paperback industry. They were also very successful and inspired a host of imitators. Dell quickly introduced its line of First Editions and other paperback houses started issuing original novels. New publishers appeared as well, somewhat more disreputable than the older publishers and willing to go even further than Fawcett in using sex and violence to attract a male audience. Paperback houses such as Midwood and Beeline produced hundreds of trashy sex novels, not quite soft-core pornography, in the 1950s. The paperback original boosted sales of softcover books so much that publishers today refer to the "paperback boom" of the 1950s. Ironically, the success of its Gold Medal line led Fawcett eventually to create a reprint line, Crest; the company has published Gold Medal books very infrequently since the early 1980s.

The overt sexual nature of many of the paperbacks published in the early 1950s eventually resulted in the threat of censorship. In 1952 the House of Representatives Select Committee on Current Pornographic Materials began an investigation of the paperback book industry. One representative referred to the three S's of paperbacks: "sex, sadism and the smoking gun." Gold Medal was under particular scrutiny by the Committee, due in part to the lesbian novels the company published. The Committee never made any official move to censor, but the industry did began to restrict the sexual content of paperbacks, with many books actually recalled and reissued with new covers. Furthermore, censorship attempts occurred at state and local levels throughout the 1950s.

Few major paperback publishers emerged after Fawcett. Ace, founded in 1952, added its own market innovation with the double novel—after completing an Ace paperback, readers could turn it over and find another entire (though usually very brief) novel. Harlequin, a Canadian publisher founded in 1949, began publishing its highly successful line of romance books in 1964. In 1969 Pinnacle was founded by former 1950s publishers of "adult" paperbacks. Pinnacle specialized in the "series" novel, books with recurring characters that even included numbers on each new novel so that customers could easily collect an entire series. Pinnacle's most successful characters were the Executioner and the Destroyer; the former was a Vietnam veteran turned vigilante and the latter was a former police officer, who worked for a highly secret government agency. The series novel dominated the 1970s, with westerns, military adventures, and martial arts stories being particularly popular. Finally, DAW books became in the 1970s the first paperback house to specialize in one genre; founded by respected editor and author Donald A. Wollheim, the company published science fiction only.

Other trends developed in the 1970s and 1980s. The relative speed with which a paperback could be published resulted in the "instant" book, a quickly produced volume that discusses a current political or social event. The O.J. Simpson trial, Operation Desert Shield, and the Monica Lewinsky scandal all generated instant books, and there have been instant biographies of stars whose fame seemed destined to be short-lived, such as the Spice Girls and Vanilla Ice. The novelization is a book that is based upon a movie or television program, rather than the other way around. Novelizations of all sorts of TV shows and motion pictures were common in the 1970s and at least one, the novel version of *Jaws 2*, actually achieved bestseller status. By the 1980s, novelizations in the science fiction genre were most common and hundreds of *Dr. Who* and *Star Trek* novels have been written, many featuring original adventures of the characters.

The trade paperback, also called the quality paperback and the oversized paperback, has been in existence at least since 1953, when Doubleday introduced its series of Anchor Books, but has enjoyed its greatest success in the 1980s and 1990s. Trade paperbacks are substantially larger than the regular paperback book, now referred to as the "mass market" book. They are almost as large as a standard hard cover book and cost about one half as much. Trade paperbacks seem to have a cachet of respectability that regular paperback novels were never able to acquire and there is undeniably a certain amount of "snob appeal" involved in the publication of a book in a trade edition.

In the 1990s consolidation of publishers left only a handful of companies producing most of the paperback books in America. Prices have risen considerably from de Graf's 25 cents, and six- and seven-dollar paperbacks have become standard. A great emphasis, especially among mass market publishers, is placed on "category fiction"—novels that can be placed into easily identifiable genres, such as science fiction, westerns, courtroom thrillers, or historical novels. There are fewer original novels published in paper.

The paperback book has played an enormous role in the development of literature in contemporary America. Authors as disparate as J.R.R. Tolkien, Benjamin Spock, Louis L'Amour, and Mickey Spillane all reached mass audiences through the paperback medium. The paperback has been a ubiquitous part of our lives; since the first Pocket Books appeared in 1939, almost anybody in America, living anywhere, has been able to walk into a local store and find a wire rack filled with paperback books.

—Randall Clark

FURTHER READING:

Bonn, Thomas. *Heavy Traffic & High Culture.* Carbondale, Illinois, Southern Illinois Press, 1989.

———. *Under Cover.* New York, Penguin, 1982.

Davis, Kenneth. *Two-Bit Culture.* Boston, Houghton Mifflin, 1984.

O'Brien, Geoffrey. *Hardboiled America.* New York, Van Nostrand Reinhold, 1980.

Petersen, Clarence. *The Bantam Story: Twenty-Five Years of Paperback Publishing.* New York, Bantam, 1970.

Server, Lee. *Over My Dead Body.* San Francisco, Chronicle, 1984.

Parades

Whether to demonstrate military might, to advertise public events and holidays, or simply to entertain, parades traditionally have been part of the community experience, probably since human beings first gathered together in a social order; as far back as 3000 B.C.E., there are records of religious processions and parades. Whether it is a New York ticker tape parade or a ragtag local procession, a parade is a kind of social narrative, as symbols and tableaux approach and pass by, telling cheering spectators a sort of story about their society.

The first public parades were likely military or political in origin, as armies and rulers found that a huge demonstration of power was an effective way both to intimidate opposition and to muster support. Patriotism, that nationalistic pride so important to those who rule nations and those who make war, is still an important product of military and political pageants. Religious institutions also used parades to gain power and solidify connections with the populace. The public welcomed such parades, both as a diversion from workday life and because, for a moment, they put the powerful within reach of the common people. Less enthusiastic were the conquered people forced to watch the victors flaunt their triumph down the main streets of vanquished towns.

Other early parades were connected with fairs and festivals and offered opportunities for people to gather, socialize, and exchange information. In medieval Italy, *carreros,* or carts, were painted with historical scenes and brought out at parade times as a sort of rolling history exhibit. Circus parades were often the most anticipated public events in small towns in earlier centuries. Part flamboyant spectacle and part advertisement for the show, the brightly painted wagons and exotic performers and animals of the circus parade were greeted with enthusiasm by the working people in small, uneventful towns.

More modern parades have tended to fall into the same categories, augmented by modern excesses. The military parade is still a standby, whether to honor veterans of past wars or to celebrate victory in a new one. The end of World War II was cause for hundreds of parades nationwide, but later wars evoked more complicated emotions. Veterans of the undeclared conflicts in Korea and Vietnam complained that their homecomings went unfeted, since most Americans were merely glad to put the controversy and discomfort behind them. In a sort of backlash effect, both public and government seemed almost embarrassingly determined to honor troops. In the next major U.S. conflict, the Persian Gulf War of 1991, the spate of parades celebrating the returning troops lasted longer than the forty-three-day war itself.

Religion has always been a major inspiration for a parade, and many major U.S. parades are at least nominally religious. Mardi Gras parades, major events in many southern cities, the most famous being New Orleans, celebrate the last feast before the beginning of Lent. In practice, Mardi Gras has always been an occasion for revelry and debauchery—and endless parades. In New Orleans, where the first Mardi Gras celebration was held in 1837, social groups called krewes sponsor dozens of balls and parades. The krewes offer a chance of visibility for many who are otherwise marginalized. There are black and Jewish krewes, and, since 1958, several gay krewes. All are welcomed and celebrated in the spirit of Mardi Gras, and all compete for the most artistic and ostentatious parade floats.

The feast of St. Patrick also offers an excuse for a parade in many U.S. cities. In New York City, the nation's largest St. Patrick's Day parade drew one hundred fifty thousand marchers and more than one-and-a-half million spectators in 1998. Though it is on one hand a raucous revel, a St. Patrick's Day parade also often has a subtle political agenda of Irish nationalism. Unlike the Mardi Gras parades, however, St. Patrick's Day parades have often sought to prevent the inclusion of marginalized groups; many have banned contingents of gay Irish marchers, for example.

As in the circus parades, advertising continues to be a motivating factor for parading. Since its beginning in 1924, the famous Macy's Thanksgiving Day parade in New York City is an extravagant advertising gesture, where companies pay hundreds of thousands of dollars to display helium-filled toys and logos before millions of spectators. Many other companies are catching on to parading as a marketing tool, hiring specialized companies to plan and execute their parades to maximum effect.

Gay Pride Day offers an example of the political evolution of a parade. With the beginning of the gay liberation movement in the 1970s, Gay Pride marches were first demonstrations, often angry and challenging, demanding gay rights. As the movement progressed and gays began to feel more strength and solidarity in their communities, the event evolved into a celebratory parade, complete with elaborate floats, commercial advertisements, and glad-handing politicians seeking votes. Though some gays bemoan this change from protest to festivity, others see it as a sign of progress and social acceptance.

—Tina Gianoulis

FURTHER READING:

Davis, Susan G. *Parades and Power: Street Theatre in Nineteenth-Century Philadelphia.* Philadelphia, Temple University Press, 1986.

Ryan, Mary. "The American Parade: Representation of the Nineteenth Century Social Order." *The New Cultural History,* edited by Lynn Hunt. Berkeley, University of California Press, 1989.

Sussman, Mark. "Celebrating the New World Order: Festival and War in New York." *The Drama Review.* Vol. 39, No. 2, Summer 1995, 147.

Paretsky, Sara (1947—)

Creator of Chicago's famous feminist detective V. I. Warshawski, author Sara Paretsky paved the way for a new category of female detectives within the mystery genre. In 1986, angered at the treatment of female mystery writers, who were often ignored, unrewarded, underappreciated, and forced into creating stereotypical protagonists, Paretsky helped to create Sisters in Crime. This group has consistently worked to garner awards for female mystery writers, demand that more reviews of mysteries be written by women, and improve the image of women in mystery novels.

Paretsky, who was born in Iowa and grew up in Lawrence, Kansas, was influenced in her choice of career by her mother, a children's librarian at the Lawrence Public Library. Young Sara began writing at the age of five. As an adult, however, Paretsky worked as a dishwasher, secretary, market manager, and freelance writer before writing her first V. I. Warshawski mystery, *Indemnity Only*, in 1982. In her first novel Paretsky combined her love of writing with her experience in the insurance industry to create a realistic, feminist detective who dealt with real problems on her own terms.

Victoria Warshawski, who prefers to be called V. I. or Vic, is described as being 5'8'' tall, weighing 140 pounds, with dark brown hair and green eyes. She loves Black Label whiskey, red wine, and pasta. V. I. is ferociously loyal to her friends and tenacious when solving crimes. Although she is frequently assisted in her endeavors by her friend Dr. Lotty Herschel and downstairs neighbor Mr. Conteras, V. I. primarily applies her own intelligence and physical abilities to solve cases. Paretsky has succeeded in her goal of creating a female detective who combats the stereotypes of women prevalent in fiction before 1980. In her wake, other mystery writers, such as Dorothy Cannell (Ellie Haskell) and Selma Eichler (Desiree Shapiro), challenged the traditional mode of women in mysteries throughout the 1980s and 1990s. Within the mystery genre, major female characters now include Black, Jewish, lesbian, 60-plus, and divorced protagonists.

In addition to *Indemnity Only*, Sara Paretsky has written eight mysteries featuring V. I. Warshawski: *Deadlock* (1984), *Killing Orders* (1985), *Bitter Medicine* (1985), *Blood Shot* (1988) (entitled *Toxic Shock* in Great Britain), *Burn Marks* (1990), *Guardian Angel* (1991), *Tunnel Vision* (1994), and *Windy City Blues* (1995). She also edited *Women on the Case* (1997), a collection of short stories with female protagonists.

In 1998 Sara Paretsky turned her attention to writing a novel that dealt with the lives of women in a broader context than was possible with the V. I. Warshawski series. *Ghost Country* features a group of women from distinctly different backgrounds who come together in Chicago's underground network of streets. Paretsky's characters become involved with exploring their own identities and their relationship to the world around them.

Sara Paretsky, a mother and grandmother, lives in Chicago with her husband, physicist Courtenay Wright and her golden retriever Cordhu. She was named *Ms.* Magazine's Woman of the Year in 1987, awarded the Mark Twain Award for the Society of the Study for Midwestern Literature, and nominated for a Silver Dagger for *Blood Shot*. In all her novels, Paretsky addresses traditional perceptions regarding the role of women in American society.

—Elizabeth Purdy

FURTHER READING:

Paretsky, Sara. *Blood Shot.* New York, Dell Books, 1989.

———. *Ghost Country.* New York, Delacorte, 1998.

———. *Indemnity Only.* New York. Dell Books, 1991.

Reddy, Maureen T., editor. *Sisters in Crime: Feminism and the Crime Novel.* New York, Continuum, 1988.

Swanson, Jean, and Dean Jones. *By A Woman's Hand: A Guide to Mystery Fiction by Women.* New York, Berkley Books, 1994.

Trosky, Susan M., editor. *Contemporary Authors: A Bio-Bibliographical Guide to Current Writers in Fiction, General Nonfiction, Poetry, Journalism, Drama, Motion Pictures, Television, and Other Fields,* Vol. 129. Detroit, Gale Research, 1990.

Parker Brothers

Parker Brothers is the company most well-known for *Monopoly*, arguably the most famous board game of all. In 1883 a 16-year-old named George S. Parker of Salem, Massachusetts, invented *The Game of Banking*. After two companies rejected the game, he decided to market it himself. With his profits, he established the George S. Parker Company. He later invited his brothers to join and the company officially became Parker Brothers. Long a successful company, alongside its rival Milton Bradley (also located in Massachusetts), Parker Brothers' biggest success came in the 1930s with *Monopoly*, which brought the company revenues of a million dollars by 1936. Over the years, Parker Brothers produced many other popular games, such as *Clue* and *Trivial Pursuit*. In 1968 General Mills bought Parker Brothers—it was spun off as Kenner-Parker two years later—and in 1991 it was acquired by Hasbro, the second leading toy producer after Mattel.

—Robin Lent

FURTHER READING:

Parker Brothers. *Ninety Years of Fun, 1883-1973: The History of Parker Brothers.* Salem, Massachusetts, Parker Brothers, 1973.

Wojahn, Ellen. *Playing by Different Rules.* New York, AMACON, 1998.

Parker, Charlie (1920-1955)

When alto saxophonist Charlie "Bird" Parker died at the age of thirty-four from the effects of drug and alcohol addiction and hard living, graffiti appeared on walls and sidewalks all over New York City proclaiming "Bird Lives!" The grief-stricken graffiti artists were more prescient than they could have imagined. One of the premier jazz artists in history, Parker made a contribution to American music that continues to be strongly felt decades after his own life was cut short. First reckoned as a major influence in jazz when he helped develop the "bebop" style while playing in Harlem clubs in the 1940s, his style is still widely imitated not only by saxophone players, but by jazz musicians on every instrument and even by scat singers. A master improvisationist whose command of theme and counterpoint has been compared by some critics to Bach, Parker was not only a victim of his addictions but also of the contradictions of being a brilliant black musician in the racist United States of the 1940s and 1950s.

Charles Christopher Parker, Jr., was born in Kansas City, Kansas. His father, a singer and dancer who also worked as a Pullman chef for the railroad, left the family when Parker was quite young.

Charlie Parker

Parker was raised by his mother, who doted on her chubby, affectionate, only child. His hearty appetite, especially his love for chicken, may have given rise to his lifelong nickname "Yardbird" or "Bird." When he was eleven, Parker bought his first alto sax, inspired by listening to Rudy Vallee on the radio. By the age of fifteen he had left school to become a professional musician, playing at clubs in the lively Kansas City jazz district. Within a year, through a family friend, he became addicted to morphine.

While developing his music in Kansas City jazz clubs, Parker married a local girl at age sixteen, and by the time he was eighteen he was a father. A year later, in 1939, he asked his wife's permission to leave. He felt that he needed to go to New York to develop his music. Playing with several well-known big bands as well as in the Harlem jam sessions where the direction of jazz evolved, Parker developed a formidable reputation as a saxophone soloist. Modern studies of Parker's recorded music show that he never repeated an improvisation, no matter how often he played the same piece of music.

It was while playing in Harlem with trumpet player Dizzy Gillespie that Parker helped develop the innovative flexible rhythm patterns that became known as bebop or bop. The bebop sound worked better in small combos rather than big bands, and Parker and Gillespie worked together for many years co-leading small jazz groups. From the big bands Parker had learned the delicate art of blending with other instruments while leading them through inventive riffs and motifs. In the five-piece combos and jamming with such greats as Thelonious Monk and Max Roach, he learned to expand on the rhythmic inventions and dynamic phrasing that would revolutionize jazz.

Parker was always a man of contradictions. His warm personality and transcendent horn improvisations made him a revered character in the jazz community, while his ruthless ambition and flamboyant disregard for authority often caused both peers and employers to be wary of him. In the 1920s and 1930s, white America's view of the African-American experience usually came from minstrel shows featuring white (or even black) actors in blackface. With the rise of the jazz age, white audiences thronged to hear black musicians playing the blues and jazz they had developed. Parker was deeply angry and defiant about the contradictions of being famous and black, privileged and oppressed. As a leader in jazz, one of the most American and one of the most truly African-American art forms, Parker constantly rebelled against the power structures in the music business. Unfortunately, his rebellion was often self-destructive, and he became known as a difficult musician. In 1946, after being found naked in his hotel lobby and setting a mattress on fire, he was sent to jail and then to a state mental hospital for six months. Even when he returned to his career, he continued to have problems bowing to authority. In 1949 the famous Birdland Club, named in honor of Parker, opened in Harlem, but in 1954 he was fired, no longer allowed to play there because of his unpredictable behavior.

Parker died in 1955 from complications of pneumonia, but his impact on jazz was immense, affecting not only how jazz is played but also how it is listened to up to the present day. Actor/director Clint Eastwood made a movie about Parker's life called *Bird,* which was released in 1988. Many of Parker's fans complained that it stereotyped the sax player by focusing on his addictions and showing his life through the eyes of his fourth wife, a white woman, and other white characters. Perhaps the only way to really understand Parker is to listen to his music. New mixes of his recordings are continually released, and jazz fans wait for them enthusiastically. It is in these recordings, as well as in the music of thousands of subsequent musicians and singers influenced by Parker's style, that Bird truly lives.

—Tina Gianoulis

FURTHER READING:

Crouch, Stanley. "Birdland: Charlie Parker, Clint Eastwood, and America." *The New Republic.* Vol. 200, No. 8, February 27, 1989, 25.

Giddins, Gary. *Celebrating Bird.* New York, Da Capo Press, 1999.

Woideck, Carl. *Charlie Parker: His Life and Music.* Ann Arbor, University of Michigan Press, 1998.

Parker, Dorothy (1893-1967)

Dorothy Parker was the leading light and most scathing wit of the notorious "Algonquin Round Table"—a collection of literary notables who defined the intellectual tastes of New York City in the 1920s and 1930s. Parker is most often remembered for short verses like "Men seldom make passes at girls who wear glasses." Her wisecracks ("I require only three things in a man. He must be handsome, ruthless and stupid") and acerbic critiques ("This is not a book to be set aside lightly. It should be thrown with great force") filled the gossip columns of the New York press, gained her a national following, and helped to establish the "magazine culture" of the period.

—Barry Morris

FURTHER READING:

The Portable Dorothy Parker. New York, Penguin, 1976.

Meade, Marion. *Dorothy Parker: What Fresh Hell Is This?* New York, Penguin, 1989.

Parks, Rosa (1913—)

One of the most prominent African American women in history, Rosa Parks is regarded as the person who sparked the twentieth century Civil Rights Movement in the United States—although Parks herself downplayed her role. Her refusal to stand up and allow a white man to have her bus seat, however, gave Ms. Parks a permanent place in history. On December 1, 1955, in Montgomery, Alabama, as a city bus filled with passengers, a white bus driver told Parks to stand and give her seat to a white man. She was already seated in the "Negro" section located at the back of the bus and refused to relinquish her seat. The bus driver responded by calling the police who arrested Parks and took her to jail. The act changed the lives of African Americans, especially in the old Confederacy, and changed American history forever.

Rosa Lee McCauley was born on February 4, 1913, in Tuskegee, Alabama, to a farmer father and a schoolteacher mother. Both her grandparents were born slaves. When Rosa was 11, her mother sent her to a private school in Montgomery. Rosa's life changed forever while attending a summer institute at Highlander Folk School in Tennessee. The integrated institution was renowned for producing social activists and Rosa McCauley would become one of them.

In 1932, Rosa married a barber by the name of Raymond Parks and they settled in Montgomery. Ms. Parks gained employment as a seamstress for the Montgomery Ward department store. She also served as the secretary of the local chapter of National Association for the Advancement of Colored People (NAACP), which she joined in 1943. Parks organized the NAACP Youth Council in Montgomery and sat on the National Committee to vindicate the Scottsboro Boys who were wrongfully accused of raping a white woman in Alabama.

Rosa Parks being fingerprinted by a police officer in Montgomery, Alabama.

All over the United States the NAACP was gaining momentum, headed for black civil rights, especially after the 1954 Brown vs. Board of Education decision ended legal segregation. Rosa Parks was well known in Montgomery and maintained a certain respect in the community for her many activities prior to the bus boycott, including failed attempts to try to vote.

Well known were the Montgomery bus system's race discrimination, not just segregation, policies. For example, African American riders were forced to enter busses through the front door to pay their fare, exit, and reenter through the rear door. Sometimes drivers would leave the stop before black passengers could reenter. In an ironic twist, this had happened to Parks. The same driver who had the 43-year-old Parks arrested had driven off on Parks 12 years earlier, an incident she had not forgotten.

Rosa Parks was by no means the first person to be arrested for refusing to give up her seat. In fact, someone had been arrested just the week before for the same offense. What made Rosa Parks unique was that she had standing in the African American community. She was respected for her efforts with the NAACP, and Montgomery leaders knew she would be an exemplary person to support their cause of integration in the court system. On December 5, 1955, the court found her guilty and fined her $14. The stage was set for a long court battle and a battle of wills as the Montgomery Bus Boycott followed the conviction of Parks. The boycott was organized by the new Montgomery Improvement Association (MIA), and brought the young MIA leader Martin Luther King, Jr. to the national forefront. The bus boycott would last 380 days and only end with a United States Supreme Court order in November of 1956 that banned bus segregation.

In 1957, Parks and her husband, fired from employment and victims of harassment, moved to Detroit, Michigan, where Rosa took a job with local United States Congressmen John Conyers. Parks worked for the Congressman in his Detroit office for 25 years. In 1995, she gave a rousing speech at the Million Man March in Washington at the age of 83. Throughout her life, Rosa Parks has continued her social activism. She and Raymond, who died in 1977, founded the Institute for Self-Development to train African American youth to take leadership roles in their community.

Ms. Parks has received numerous honors and accolades throughout her life. In 1987, Parks was venerated with a night in her honor at the John F. Kennedy Center for the Performing Arts in Washington D.C. The Southern Christian Leadership Conference names their award the Rosa Parks Freedom Award in her honor. Rosa Parks represents how one person can make a difference in history.

—Scott Stabler

FURTHER READING:

Abdul-Jabbar, Kareem, and Alan Steinberg. *Black Profiles in Courage: A Legacy of African-American Achievement.* New York, William and Morrow and Co., 1996.

Metcalf, George R. *Black Profiles.* New York, McGraw-Hill, 1968.

Parks, Rosa. *Dear Mrs. Parks: A Dialogue with Today's Youth.* New York, Lee and Low Books, 1996.

———. *My Story.* New York, Dial Books, 1992.

———. *Quiet Strength: The Faith, the Hope, and the Heart of a Woman Who Changed a Nation.* Grand Rapids, Zondervan Publishing House, 1994.

Parrish, Maxfield (1870-1966)

One of the most popular American artists of the twentieth century and one of the most prolific, in his long career Maxfield Parrish produced book and magazine illustrations, landscapes, advertisements, posters, and murals. Although many of his paintings initially give the impression of a meticulous devotion to realism, he actually had a highly individual approach to color and lighting, and many of his most famous illustrations depict giants, dragons, genies, centaurs, mythical kingdoms, and enchanted palaces. Observers of Parrish's work have pointed out that what he really did was rearrange and improve on reality.

Parrish was born in Philadelphia. His father was a landscape painter and etcher. Parrish initially intended to be an architect, but soon shifted to illustration. By the middle 1890s he was starting to get work doing magazine covers. His first was for *Harper's Weekly.* In 1897 Parrish illustrated his first book, *Mother Goose in Prose* by L. Frank Baum, who was still a few years away from discovering Oz. One of Parrish's specialties became the illustrating of children's books, and over the next decade or so he provided imaginative pictures for *The Golden Age* and *Dream Days* by Kenneth Grahame, *Poems of Childhood* by Eugene Field, *A Wonder Book and Tanglewood Tales* by Nathaniel Hawthorne, and *The Arabian Nights.*

He was in large demand as a magazine artist from the 1890s into the 1930s. One checklist of his magazine covers and illustrations includes nearly 400 items. Parrish turned out numerous covers for *Century Magazine, Life, Harper's Bazaar,* and *Collier's.* His work

An illustration of Humpty Dumpty by Maxfield Parrish.

was also to be seen in *Scribner's, McClure's, Ladies' Home Journal,* and *St. Nicholas.* In addition, he did commercial work for a wide range of advertising accounts. These included Jell-O, Wannamaker's, Oneida Silver, H. O. Oats, Columbia Bicycle, Royal Baking Powder, and Swift's Premium Ham. Often he made use of fantasy and fairy tale elements in these pictures, utilizing knights in armor, fantastic palaces, jesters, kings, princesses, dwarfs, goddesses, and nursery rhyme characters.

Probably the most financially rewarding area was the color reproductions of Parrish's paintings that were sold by such distributors as House of Art. *Daybreak,* issued in 1923, has the distinction of being the best-selling art print of all time. During the 1920s and 1930s copies of the work could be seen framed and hanging in many a parlor and living room around the country. The painting shows a colonnade in the foreground with a young woman in vaguely Grecian robes reclining and a nude girl bending over her as dawn tints everything a typically Parrish pink. There are Parrish leafy branches dangling overhead and in the distance Parrish misty mountains. The model for the reclining figure was William Jennings Bryan's granddaughter and the naked little girl was Parrish's daughter. Parrish always worked from photographs that he took himself, except when depicting monsters, elves, and the like. He'd project the photo onto his drawing or painting surface and then trace it in with pencil. Another very successful print was *Stars,* which shows a naked young woman sitting on a rock and gazing contentedly up into the night sky. Painted a few years after *Daybreak,* it was also adapted from a photo Parrish shot of his daughter Jean.

Parrish's favorite model was Susan Lewin. Originally she was the housekeeper for Parrish and his family at their Vermont home, The Oaks. The artist was soon asking the attractive young woman to pose for him, and she can be seen in several of his paintings, including *Sleeping Beauty.* A recent biography of Parrish explained that for many years he lived with Susan and not his wife.

Parrish was responsible for several murals as well. The most famous was *Old King Cole,* painted for the Hotel Knickerbocker. In addition he painted *The Pied Piper* for the men's bar in San Francisco's Palace Hotel and *Sing A Song of Sixpence* for Chicago's Sherman House. His most ambitious undertaking was a series of 18 murals, each over ten feet high, done for the offices of *The Saturday Evening Post* in Philadelphia. Parrish worked form 1911 to 1913 on the project.

An accomplished landscape painter as well, from the middle 1930s onward he concentrated almost exclusively on the genre and did no further illustration of any kind. The landscapes included many paintings of farmhouses, old mills, and small town churches and continued to exhibit the artist's meticulous rendering and his fascination with the effects of light. He stopped painting in 1960, at the age of 90. In 1965 the Metropolitan Museum of Art finally took notice of him and purchased one of his fantasy paintings, *The Errant Pan.* Maxfield Parrish died the following year.

—Ron Goulart

FURTHER READING:

Cutler, Lawrence S., and Judy Goffman Cutler. *Maxfield Parrish: A Retrospective.* San Francisco, Pomegranate Books, 1995.

Ludwig, Coy. *Maxfield Parrish.* New York, Watson-Guptill Publications, 1973.

Partner Swapping
See Swinging

Parton, Dolly (1946—)

Dolly Parton is a country singer, songwriter, movie actress, businesswoman, children's author, and media image, and yet none of these labels, neither singly nor collectively, capture the paradox that is Dolly. Her public image is near caricature, big blonde hair, little-girl voice, and a bust measurement that defies belief. But both her autobiographical lyrics and her multi-million-dollar empire, Dolly Parton Enterprises, testify to the substance beneath the image.

Dolly's life story is the stuff of which American legends are made. Born the third of twelve children in a log cabin in Sevier County, Tennessee, she was delivered by a doctor who was paid with a sack of corn meal milled from corn grown by her then tenant father. The country cliche of humble beginnings where material things were scarce but love and faith were plentiful has been captured in some of her best known songs, including "My Tennessee Mountain Home." But in the skilled hands of this talented songwriter the cliche acquired an unexpected freshness and power. "Coat of Many Colors," the title

Dolly Parton

cut from her 1971 album (RCA Victor), for example, recalls an actual incident from Parton's life. The coat her mother made her from scraps of material becomes an object of ridicule when she wears it to school; her mother assuages her pain by reminding her that the coat was made with love. Parton revealed in interviews that the episode, which she still found hurtful, fired her ambition to become a star. It also gave her a country classic and the material for her first children's book, *Coat of Many Colors.*

Musical ability was not rare in the family of Avie Lee and Lee Parton. Seven of their twelve children would someday work as professional musicians, but Dolly's talent was exceptional even among so talented a group. She began singing before she was two years old and was writing songs on her homemade guitar before she was seven. By the age of twelve, she was singing on a Knoxville radio station, and a year later she recorded "Puppy Love," a song she had written on Gold Band, a small label. A local celebrity by the time she reached high school, Dolly dreamed of Grand Ole Opry stardom. She left for Nashville the day after her high school graduation.

Three years later she had her first charting record, "Dumb Blonde" (Monument); that same year she became Porter Wagoner's "girl singer," appearing regularly on his syndicated television show. Enormously successful as duet partners, Parton and Wagoner during the next thirteen years had fourteen top ten hits and were twice named the Country Music Association's duo of the year. Parton, however, wanted more than being known as Wagoner's duet partner. She signed with RCA in 1968 and became a Grand Ole Opry member in 1969. Successes like "Joshua," number one on country charts in 1970, gave her the courage to strike out on her own, and she left Wagoner in 1974, although she recorded duets with him through 1980.

Recognition as a solo artist was immediate and impressive. The awards began to stack up: the Country Music Association named her Female Vocalist of the Year in 1975 and 1976, and in 1978 she received a Grammy as Best Female Country Vocal Performance and Entertainer of the Year awards from both CMA and the Association of Country Music. As she began appearing on television specials and talk shows, her fan base increased. Dolly's dreams were growing larger.

Parton came under attack within the country music community when it became clear that her plans were not limited to success in a single field. She was not the first country music star to explore different avenues of entertainment, but her independence and ambition were viewed as ingratitude by many in the industry, which was still a man's world. Her switch to Los Angeles management and the firing of her family band made it clear that Parton would ignore critics and chart her own course. Her film debut in *9 to 5* (1980) proved that Dolly could succeed in other media. The million-selling *Trio* album, a 1987 collaboration with Emmylou Harris and Linda Ronstadt, offered further evidence of Parton's range. The irony was that whatever the medium or the message, Dolly remained her inimitable self. Roger Ebert praised her natural acting ability, but Parton perhaps came nearer the truth when she explained that she only played herself. Both Doralee Rhodes (*9 to 5*) and Truvy Jones (*Steel Magnolias*), her two most acclaimed characterizations are essentially Dolly, warm, vulnerable, strong, funny, and as Southern as grits and barbecue.

The best metaphor for Dolly Parton may be found in the history of one of her songs. Parton admitted that she wrote "I Will Always Love You" for Porter Wagoner in an effort to express her reasons for leaving him. She first recorded the song in 1973; a year later it was number one on the country charts. She recorded it again in 1982 and repeated her success. When Whitney Houston recorded it a decade later for the soundtrack of her first film, *The Bodyguard,* it was

number one on the pop charts for fourteen weeks. Dolly recorded it once again, this time as a duet with Vince Gill, and again it was a hit. Like "I Will Always Love You," Dolly Parton continued to appear in new guises even as she remained unmistakably Dolly. "I enjoy making fun of myself and join in when other people are making jokes. I don't *ever* take that personal because I know exactly who I am," Parton provided in a 1998 Country Music Television interview

She became fodder again for clever comics when in 1986 she signed on as a partner in a Smokey Mountain theme park to which she gave her name, but today Dollywood is a flourishing multi-million-dollar business. Dolly's business empire continued to expand, as did her creative efforts during the 1990s. Her 1998 album, self-penned and self-produced, was appropriately entitled *Hungry Again.* Beyond the glitzy image and tabloid headlines and the larger than life public personality lies the mountain child from Sevier County, Dolly Rebecca Parton—always hungry and always pursuing another dream.

—Wylene Rholetter

FURTHER READING:

Bufwack, Mary A., and Robert K. Oermann. *Finding Her Voice: The Saga of Women in Country Music.* New York, Crown, 1993.

James, Otis. *Dolly Parton.* New York, QuickFox, 1978.

Nash, Alanna. *Dolly.* Los Angeles, Reed, 1978.

Parton, Dolly. *Coat of Many Colors.* New York, HarperCollins, 1994.

———. *Dolly: My Life and Other Unfinished Business.* New York, HarperCollins, 1994.

The Partridge Family

From 1970 to 1974, a time when most kids swore by the adage "Don't trust anyone over thirty," ABC aired *The Partridge Family,* an extremely popular sitcom featuring a mom who went on tour with her kids in a band. The hit show was loosely based on the late 1960s folk-music family, the Cowsills.

The Partridge Family (one of two 1970s sitcoms about a big family and a perky blond mom; *The Brady Bunch* was the other) starred Oscar winner and musical theater staple Shirley Jones as Shirley Partridge, the widowed matriarch whose kids started jamming in an impromptu session in the garage of their suburban California home. They asked her to join them, and it sounded groovy. They recorded the song "I Think I Love You," and to everyone's surprise, a record company bought it, it became a smash hit, and a band was born.

And what's a family band without a manager and reluctant father-figure? Enter fast-talking, child-hating, stewardess-dating Reuben Kinkaid (Dave Madden), perpetual foil for ten-year-old con artist, Danny (Danny Bonaduce). The rest of the family included Suzanne Crough as 5-year-old Tracy, Jeremy Gelbwaks (1970-71) and then Brian Forster (1971-74) as 7-year-old Chris, Susan Dey as 15-year-old Laurie, and Jones' stepson, David Cassidy, as 17-year-old Keith.

The Partridge Family toured around the country in a psychedelically-painted school bus (with the astoundingly unhip "Careful, Nervous Mother Driving" on the back) and the show focused on their exploits on the road, and in their California hometown, and their attempt to have normal family lives and be pop stars at the same time. Every show wrapped up in time for a song, during which the

Partridges were usually wearing matching burgundy velvet pantsuits with white ruffled shirts.

Like the Monkees before them, the Partridge Family TV band was heavily cross-promoted in the music business, and "I Think I Love You" sold 4 million copies. Unlike the Monkees, they had no musical pretensions as a band. None of them were professional musicians, and Cassidy and Jones were the only ones providing actual vocals in recordings and on the show. It didn't take a musical genius to figure out that if Cassidy was the lead male vocalist, pre-teen Bonaduce was (impossibly) singing the baritone harmony parts.

The Partridge Family made a huge teen idol out of the androgynous Cassidy, who toured solo to throngs of screaming adolescent girls. His fans were so rabid that one actually asked for one of the gallstones he'd passed as a keepsake. After failing at solo television, he found he was a powerful draw in Las Vegas in the 1990s.

Despite his heartthrob status, Cassidy actually didn't carry the show. That responsibility fell to impish, red-headed, smart-alec Bonaduce. The precocious Bonaduce had the comic timing of an old master. Unfortunately, as he got older and was told he wasn't cute anymore, he went the way of many a child actor—into a drug haze, punctuated with appearances on *The Love Boat* and *Fantasy Island.* His antics included an arrest in 1990 in Daytona Beach, Florida, for attempting to buy cocaine; a year later he was charged with assaulting a transvestite prostitute in Phoenix. He spent the rest of the 1990s as a disc jockey.

The saga of a slightly-hipper-than-Mrs.-Cleaver-mom and family couldn't hold up; ratings of the *Partridge Family* started to sag in 1973, when it was moved from Friday night to Saturday night, up against *All in the Family* and *Emergency.* The 1974-75 season included an ABC Saturday morning cartoon version called the *Partridge Family 2200 AD* which, for some reason, put the family in space. Dey, Bonaduce, Forster, Crough, and Madden provided their voices.

Young viewers in the early 1970s inexplicably felt the need to "choose" between *The Brady Bunch* (which some saw as even more implausible) and *The Partridge Family.* In the end, both shows were representative of the happy, mindless nature of many 1970s sitcoms.

—Karen Lurie

FURTHER READING:

Allis, Tim. "By The Way . . . Whatever Happened to the Other Partridge Kids?" *People Weekly.* 1 November 1993, 73.

Appelo, Tim. "C'mon, Get Happy . . . Fear and Loathing on the Partridge Family Bus." *Entertainment Weekly.* 29 July 1994, 52.

Cunneff, Tom. "Spinning Off His Partridge Past, Danny Bonaduce Rocks Philly as a Raunchy Midnight Deejay." *People Weekly.* 27 February 1989, 97.

Gliatto, Tom. "As Of July 12, Cable's 'Nick At Nite' Is Adding 'The Partridge Family.'" *People Weekly.* 12 July 1993, 11.

Green, Joey; foreword by Shirley Jones. *The Partridge Family Album.* New York, HarperPerennial, 1994.

Patinkin, Mandy (1952—)

Known for his work on Broadway, film, and television, Mandy Patinkin is one of the most versatile performers working in the entertainment industry. The three principal roles he created on Broadway—Che Guevara in Lloyd Webber's *Evita* (1979); George Seurat in Sondheim's *Sunday in the Park with George* (1986); and Archibald Craven in Simon's *The Secret Garden* (1991)—all received critical praise. Film credits include *Ragtime* (1981), *Yentl* (1983), *The Princess Bride* (1987), and *Dick Tracy* (1990).

In the mid-1990s, Patinkin starred in the television series *Chicago Hope,* for which he won an Emmy Award in 1995. His character in *Chicago Hope,* Dr. Jeffrey Geiger, provided the opportunity for Patinkin to showcase his vocal abilities for television audiences. He has recorded a number of solo albums, including *Mandy Patinkin* (1989), *Dress Casual* (1990), *Oscar and Steve* (1995), and the entirely Yiddish *Mamaloshen* (1998).

—William A. Everett

FURTHER READING:

Zadan, Craig. *Sondheim & Company.* New York, Da Capo, 1994.

Patton

Patton, one of the most critically acclaimed films of the 1970s, opened with George C. Scott as United States General George S. Patton, addressing the audience in front of a giant American flag. His speech combined inspiration with profanity: "Now I want you to remember, that no bastard ever won a war by giving his life for his

George C. Scott in a scene from *Patton.*

country. He won it by making the other poor dumb bastard die for his country.''

Based on Omar Bradley's memoirs, *Patton* presented an unflinching look at the volatile general during the European battles of World War II. General Patton was given to poetic, occasionally vulgar evocations of the duty of soldiers in the heat of battle, claiming that he had been a warrior during past lives (''The Carthaginians were proud and brave but they couldn't hold. They were massacred. Arab women stripped them of their swords and their tunics and lances. The soldiers laid naked in the sun. Two thousand years ago. I was here''). To his military colleagues, Patton was a brilliant strategist but emotionally unstable. His instability reached critical mass when, in a fit of rage, he slapped a wounded soldier.

The box-office success of the film surprised many 1970 moviegoers. Hollywood had been inundated with World War II movies since the 1940s, and a movie about the toughest American general seemed a risky commercial proposition during the unpopular Vietnam War; the extensive profanity of the screenplay was also unprecedented for a major studio release in 1970. But director Franklin J. Schaffner, screenwriters Francis Ford Coppola and Edward North, and star Scott crafted a compelling, sophisticated movie that satisfied both conservative and liberal audiences. Critic Pauline Kael observed that Patton's character ''is what people who believe in military values can see as the true military hero—the red-blooded American who loves to fight and whose crude talk is straight talk. He is also what people who despise militarism can see as the worst kind of red-blooded American mystical maniac; for them, Patton can be the symbolic proof of the madness of the whole military complex.''

The outstanding cast included Karl Malden as Omar Bradley and Michael Bates as Field Marshal Montgomery. *Patton* won seven Academy Awards in 1970, including one for Best Picture. Scott won a well deserved Oscar for Best Actor, but he publicly rejected the award (the first such rejection in history), saying he did not wish to compete against fellow actors. Scott had already portrayed a war mongering general (Buck Turgidson) in Stanley Kubrick's landmark 1964 comedy *Dr. Strangelove,* but his performance in *Patton* was more nuanced and sympathetic, and caught the pathos in Patton's gradual loss of control; indeed, it became his signature role. Scott reprised his role in a 1986 made-for-television movie, *The Last Days of Patton.*

One of the most prominent fans of the film was President Richard Nixon, who reportedly watched *Patton* over and over prior to announcing the expansion of the Vietnam War into Cambodia in April 1970. Coppola and North won an Oscar for their screenplay, and on the strength of *Patton*'s success, Coppola was able to green-light his next project—directing *The Godfather* (1972).

—Andrew Milner

FURTHER READING:

Biskind, Peter. *Easy Riders, Raging Bulls: How the Sex, Drugs and Rock'n'Roll Generation Saved Hollywood.* New York, Simon and Schuster, 1998.

Kael, Pauline. *5001 Nights at the Movies.* New York, Holt, 1991.

Paul, Les (1915—)

An influential guitarist and recording artist, Les Paul fundamentally changed the way in which popular music was produced. Among many innovations, he developed the first successful techniques of multi-tracking and the eight-track tape recorder, which led directly to modern recording technology.

Lester Polsfuss was born in Waukesha, Wisconsin, on June 9, 1915. He began playing harmonica at the age of eight, performing at every opportunity. By age 12 he was a sidewalk musician, playing for tips. Over the next few years he taught himself guitar and formed his first band in 1929.

At age 17 Polsfuss dropped out of high school and became a full-time professional musician. During the following six years he performed in a bewildering number of radio and personal appearances, under several different stage names and in a variety of smaller and larger acts. Somewhere along the line he changed his name to the more easily remembered Les Paul. About the same time, he became intrigued by jazz music, especially during a long stay in Chicago in the mid-1930s, and he gradually changed from a hot country picker to a jazz stylist. Soon he gained recognition in the music world as a superior guitarist.

While Les Paul did not invent the electric guitar, he made major improvements in the areas of electronic amplification. He was fascinated by the technical aspects of amplifying and recording sound, often building his own pickups and speaker arrangements, as well as consulting with engineers to produce equipment to his specifications. (The eight-track tape recorder of the late 1950s was developed under this sort of symbiotic relationship with an electronics engineer.) Paul created a major innovation in guitar construction and design with his one-of-a-kind ''Log,'' the world's first solid-body guitar, and he was the first to put two pickups on an electric guitar, now a standard feature.

In 1938 Les Paul and his current sidemen went to New York, quickly landing jobs with Fred Waring and the Pennsylvanians, a prestigious radio and dance orchestra. During three years in Waring's outfit, Paul gained something of a national following, and continued to mature both as a musician and as a technological experimenter. Always a perfectionist and driven by ambition, Paul tired of his relatively small place in Waring's musical empire and once more went out on his own in 1941.

It was a wise move. After a year or two of frequent job changes, Les Paul found his niche in wartime Hollywood. He performed regularly on the NBC radio network, eventually playing on records with Bing Crosby. The added exposure greatly helped his career. During this time in California, Paul continued his experiments in recording technology. Using a homemade lathe, he produced high-quality wax recordings with several generations of overlapped musical tracks. Les Paul succeeded in this where others had failed more from obsessive perfectionism and drive than from any new technological breakthrough. He used this technique to record several separate guitar tracks on one song. His recordings from this point on all used some variation of multi-tracking, giving his work a unique sound.

In 1947 Les Paul became romantically involved with Iris Colleen Summers (1924-1977), a young country singer in southern California. Paul's first marriage was failing, and he would soon marry Summers. Before this, however, she frequently accompanied him on tour. During a road trip in January 1948, with Colleen Summers at the wheel of Paul's Buick, they were in a major automobile accident. She was only slightly injured, while Les Paul suffered numerous broken bones. His right elbow was essentially destroyed, and doctors were seriously considering amputating the arm. Les Paul refused to let the operation be performed; when his elbow had to be fused into an immobile solid mass, Paul directed his surgeons to place it at a roughly 90 degree angle, to facilitate his guitar playing.

Les Paul

After months of recuperation, Les Paul reentered show business. He created a new act with Summers, a gifted singer and guitarist, who he renamed Mary Ford. In 1949 Paul and Ford made numerous records and toured at a frantic pace. Their recordings made use of Paul's multi-tracking to feature many simultaneous guitar and vocal lines, and their work became very popular. Late in the year they were married.

The duo recorded for Capitol Records, for whom they produced almost 40 singles and many best-selling albums over the next decade. Les Paul and Mary Ford became among the most popular and successful musical performers in the world, while Paul masterminded their professional and private lives in a domineering manner. They were sought by radio and television, producing daily programs for the former and a short weekly show for the latter during the early 1950s.

In 1951 Les Paul was approached by the Gibson guitar company, who sought his endorsement for their about-to-be-released solid-body guitar. Although he had almost nothing to do with its design, Les Paul lent his name to what would become one of the most popular electric guitars in existence. This, along with his innovative use of guitar as a solo instrument, helped Paul become the first "guitar hero" of pop music. Partially in response to his popularization of guitar, by the mid-1950s a new wave of music arose: rock 'n' roll, which had roots in R&B and country. Les Paul and Mary Ford were among the many older performers who vanished from the Hit Parade. Their last major hit was "Hummingbird" in 1955.

In 1958 the duo moved to Columbia Records, but had no more success there. A few years later Mary Ford divorced Les Paul, and thereafter both lived in comparative obscurity. By the late 1970s, however, Les Paul began to receive some of the credit he deserved for his innovations in popular music. A documentary film, *The Wizard of Waukesha,* helped promote a comeback. Paul started a long-term weekly performance at a New York night club that soon became highly popular with music business insiders. In 1988 he was inducted into the Rock and Roll Hall of Fame, in the category of "Early Influences."

—David Lonergan

FURTHER READING:

Clarke, Donald, editor. *The Penguin Encyclopedia of Popular Music.* New York, Viking, 1989.

Shaughnessy, Mary Alice. *Les Paul: An American Original.* New York, William Morrow, 1993.

Slonimsky, Nicolas, editor. *Baker's Biographical Dictionary of Musicians.* 8th edition. New York, Macmillan, 1992.

Paulsen, Pat (1928-1997)

Performing perhaps the longest parody skit in history, comic Pat Paulsen ran for president five times between 1968 and 1996. A performer and comedy writer with progressive, rabble-rousing political leanings, Paulsen ran on a satirical platform, which, though relentlessly silly, drew serious attention to the real lack of choices in the American political arena. As Paulsen often said, he represented "the citizen who wants to vote for 'none of the above.'"

Pat Paulsen was born in South Bend, Washington, and raised in Point Bonita, California. He majored in forestry at City College in San Francisco, but his career as a ranger was derailed when he joined the Ric-Y-Tic Players performing troupe. He was performing and working odd jobs as a Fuller Brush salesman and a gypsum miner when he was discovered in the mid-1960s by Tom and Dick Smothers. The Smothers Brothers, quirky comics who did leftist political comedy interspersed with droll dialog and farcical antics, hired Paulsen as a writer for their new weekly television show on CBS.

Paulsen spent three years on *The Smothers Brothers Show,* writing satirical songs and much of the political comedy that kept the show in a constant battle with the CBS censors. He also participated in sketches and performed his own monologues, always with his trademark deadpan expression and loopy, off-the-wall sensibility. In 1968, he won an Emmy for his work on the show.

It was Tom and Dick Smothers too, who first suggested Paulsen run for president in the highly contentious 1968 election. Paulsen reportedly responded, "Why not? I can't dance." Paulsen began his tradition of pointing out the ludicrous contradictions in American politics then, running as a candidate of the Straight Talkin' American Government Party, or STAG Party. He opposed sex education ("Let kids learn it where we did—in the gutter."), and promised to fight poverty (". . . by shooting four hundred beggars a week"). Paulsen's mock campaign was so successful that he went on television to remind people not to really vote for him. Even so, he got 200,000 votes in the 1968 election.

The Smothers Brothers Show was taken off the air in 1970, at least partly because of its continued volatile political content. Paulsen had a short stint on his own network show on ABC in 1970, and when that failed, he moved to Cloverdale, California, where he and his second wife bought a five hundred acre farm and started a winery.

Paulsen's life continued to provide fodder for comedy and for the hang-dog expression he always wore. Even at the winery, he expressed his comedic sensibility—one of his basic wines was called Refrigerator White, and came with Paulsen's mournful face on the label. The winery also featured the satirical Pat Paulsen Museum to entertain visitors. Even thus trading on his fame, the winery was not a successful business, and Paulsen was soon drowning in debt and back-tax penalties. Even his lucky moments were dogged by disaster. His third marriage ended in divorce when he caught his wife embezzling hundreds of thousands of dollars from him, and once while on a comedy tour in Reno, when he won a $300,000 jackpot on a quarter slot machine, the IRS stepped in to claim $285,000 of it. By 1986, Paulsen was forced to sell the winery and go back on the road with his comedy.

Through it all, Paulsen kept his sense of the ridiculous. He continued to perform, both his comedy act and theatrical roles, and he continued to campaign for president every four years. Beginning in 1972, his name was actually on the ballot. For the baby boomers who had nurtured their rebellious politics each week watching the Smothers Brothers, Paulsen was a comforting and irreverent reminder that rebellion still existed even in the complacent 1980s and the cynical 1990s. Paulsen last ran in 1996, under the campaign slogan, "United we sit."

A ubiquitous participant in American political history and popular culture during the latter third of the twentieth century, Pat Paulsen died in 1997 in Tijuana, Mexico, where he was receiving alternative medical treatments for cancer.

—Tina Gianoulis

FURTHER READING:

Paulsen, Pat. *How to Wage a Successful Campaign for the Presidency.* Los Angeles, Nash Publishing, 1972.

Sanz, Cynthia. "Stalked by Tax Woes, Pat Paulsen Tries to Keep his Whine Sparkling." *People.* 19 November 1990, 173.

Payton, Walter (1954—)

Walter Payton is considered one of the greatest running backs in the history of American professional football. Born in Columbia, Mississippi, on July 25, 1954, Payton attended Jackson State University, where he set a college football record for points scored and earned his degree in special education. Although he left his mark on college football, it is in the National Football League that he secured his astonishing reputation.

Drafted by the Chicago Bears in 1975, Payton showed phenomenal talents that had an immediate impact on the team. He led the National Football Conference (NFC) in rushing in 1976, the same year that he made the Pro Bowl team for what would be the first of nine times. In addition to his talents as a running back, Payton was a gifted receiver and team leader, and was chosen the National Football League's Most Valuable Player in 1977 and again in 1985. In 1984 he became football's all-time rushing leader when he broke the record previously held by Jim Brown. After many years of toiling with mediocre teams, Payton finally played in the Super Bowl in 1986, helping to demolish the New England Patriots in the biggest rout in Super Bowl history.

When Payton retired after the 1987 season, he was the NFL's career leader in rushing yards (16,726), rushing touchdowns (100), and total yards gained (21,264). He also held the record for most rushing yards gained in a single game (275), and he had passed for over 300 yards and eight touchdowns. Walter Payton was elected to the Pro Football Hall of Fame in 1993.

While his statistics and on-field accomplishments rank Payton as one of the greatest athletes in the history of professional football, it was his off-field accomplishments that truly set him apart from his contemporaries. His nickname, "Sweetness," not only described his ability as an athlete, but was also an accurate comment on his personality. His charm and understated demeanor made him one of the most endearing of sports personalities and he quickly became a favorite among the fans. Payton never had a negative word to say about his opponents or his city, and his overwhelming love for the game of football was obvious to everybody.

By the end of the 1990s, Walter Payton had been long and constantly dedicated to charity work, particularly causes involving inner-city children and special education. He recognized his position as a role model for youngsters, and made enormous efforts to provide a positive image for them to emulate. In 1988, he helped to start the Halas/Payton Foundation to help the inner-city youth of Chicago. His dedication, integrity, and generosity made him one of the most admired men in the history of professional sports, and his name has become inextricably linked to the city of Chicago.

—Geoff Peterson

FURTHER READING:

Koslow, P. *Walter Payton.* New York, Chelsea House, 1995.

Whittingham, R. *The Bears: A 75-year Tradition.* Dallas, Texas, Taylor Publishing, 1994.

Walter Payton

Peale, Norman Vincent (1898-1993)

A long happy life, national acclaim, professional satisfactions, and accumulating wealth seemed to attest to the success of Norman Vincent Peale's blend of New Thought, psychotherapy, optimism, and Protestant Christianity. The phrase "positive thinking" became part of the national vocabulary, as Peale's books repeatedly topped the bestseller lists. While Pealeism, as his thought came to be known, exactly suited the American post-World War II mood, it also became the object of angry attack from academic theologians for two decades. Along with Billy Graham and Bishop Vincent Sheen (who often found himself introduced as "Norman Vincent Sheen"), Peale became one of the best known American clergymen of his time. His books constituted the greatest commercial success of religion in the middle of the twentieth century. His concepts linger on, though no longer labeled as "Pealeism," in the optimism and mind control techniques of the New Age.

There was much of New England Transcendentalism in Peale's thought. He gratefully acknowledged his debt to Ralph Waldo Emerson, that archbore of American literary classics. There was also much of New Thought in Peale's spirituality. He would have agreed frequently with Mary Baker Eddy, though they did not speak the same theological language. He further learned from both Sigmund Freud and Carl Jung, though he never penetrated the depths of the human psyche or engaged in grandiose speculation about racial archetypes. Most of all, he never discovered the murky underground passages of the human soul; most serious theologians agreed he had a deficient sense of sin.

Norman Vincent Peale

But within modest limits Peale's thought was energizing; his self-applied therapy worked. And people enjoyed reading his books, which made few intellectual demands and abounded in homey anecdotes of folk who became millionaires or successes in their professions. His Bible quotations were invariably sunny.

Peale's best known self-help book was *The Power of Positive Thinking*, published in 1952; it was one of the bestselling books of the decade. Peale became increasingly well known as a public motivational speaker and as regular preacher in the marble Collegiate Church at Fifth Avenue and 29th Street in New York. There he preached to a packed sanctuary and ministered spiritually to Presidents. His message was consistent. The American dream was real; the Protestant work ethic made one virtuous, wise, and prosperous. Material pleasures were not contrary to Christian piety; personal goals were realizable. With the power of positive thought working, a person need not fear any defeat. Good mental and physical health were possible; the goal of life seemed to be contentment, even joy.

Peale described his therapeutic system as "applied Christianity, a simple yet scientific system of practical techniques of successful living that works." His techniques of spiritual healing, derived from his personal experiences and a variety of other sources and ultimately,

he claimed, traceable to the Gospels, involved silent meditation, positive affirmation, creative visualization, and biblical quotations used almost as a mantra. When he talked about getting into "time synchronization" with the Almighty by listening to the sounds of the earth, he sounded suspiciously pantheistic.

Peale was born in Bowersville, Ohio, the son of a Methodist preacher who had given up a medical practice to answer the call. After some hesitation, young Peale accepted ordination in the Methodist ministry, studying theology at Boston University and serving churches in Rhode Island, New York, and New Jersey. Congregations grew and flourished under his care. In 1930 he married Loretta Ruth Stafford, often called "the true positive thinker" of the family, who remained a full partner in his national media ministry. In 1932 Peale was persuaded to accept appointment at the historic Marble Collegiate Church in New York City, founded by the Dutch in 1628 and reputed to be the oldest Protestant church in continuous use in North America. This appointment necessitated Peale's transfer from Methodist to Dutch Reform affiliation. This caused no crisis of conscience, since denominational identity meant little to Peale. Under Peale's direction, Sunday attendance grew from 200 to 4,000.

His calling, however, could never be limited to one congregation, no matter how enormously it expanded. His publications and lectures became central to his national ministry. Early books sold well across the nation, even before the resounding success of *The Power of Positive Thinking*, which stayed at the top of the *New York Times* bestseller list for three years. Other organs of ministry included his monthly pastoral magazine, *Guideposts*, an inspirational book club, the American Foundation of Religion and Psychiatry, emanating from his church's counseling center, and the Foundation for Christian Living, operated by Mrs. Peale with the aim of disseminating her husband's sermons through booklets and recordings. Radio appearances were also frequent and the *Reader's Digest* was the perfect forum for Pealeism.

A Republican and personal friend of Dwight D. Eisenhower and Richard M. Nixon, Peale ventured unsteadily into political controversy during the presidential campaign of John F. Kennedy. Much to his later embarrassment, Peale lent his name to a statement issued by a group of religious leaders opposing Kennedy on the basis of the politics of the Roman Catholic Church and its record of church-state relations. Peale certainly did not harbor personal anti-Catholic prejudice. He maintained cordial relations with Vincent Sheen and other Catholic dignitaries and the Catholic daughter of *Reader's Digest* editor Fulton Oursler called Peale "my Protestant pastor."

To the end of his career, Peale's critics were harsh in their attacks. They found his thinking simplistic, even heretical in its confusion of historic Christianity with American materialism and doctrines of self-reliance and worldly success. Critics found Peale's optimism at variance with reality in a century which had witnessed history's two bloodiest wars, a holocaust, and the advent of nuclear weapons. Peale's own sons attending seminary were forced to listen to their professor's tirades against "Pealeism," and Mrs. Peale especially found the attacks a savagery against a gentle man. It might be supposed that Peale himself, who became a wealthy man from the sale of his books, would have laughed all the way to the bank. On the contrary, he was deeply wounded and even considered dropping out of the ministry. His own brand of positive thinking eventually won over; he forgave his critics, outliving them all, and dying with his optimism unshaken.

—Allene Phy-Olsen

FURTHER READING:

George, Carol V.R. *God's Salesman: Norman Vincent Peale and the Power of Positive Thinking.* New York, Oxford University Press, 1993.

Meyer, Donald. *The Positive Thinkers: Religion as Pop Psychology from Mary Baker Eddy to Oral Roberts.* New York, Pantheon Books, 1980.

Occhiogrosso, Peter. *The Joy of Sects.* New York, Doubleday, 1996.

Peale, Norman Vincent. *The True Joy of Positive Living: An Autobiography.* New York, William Morrow and company, Inc., 1984.

Peanuts

Charles Schulz's famed comic strip, *Peanuts,* had rather modest beginnings. Originally marketed for its flexible size and format (four squares that allowed it to be run horizontally, vertically, or in two rows), it premiered on October 2, 1950, in only seven United States newspapers. United Features Syndicate chose the title; a title, Schulz says in *Charlie Brown, Snoopy and Me,* he has never liked. Sales of the strip climbed slowly at first, worrying United Features Syndicate management. But, by 1960, the strip appeared in over 400 newspapers worldwide. In 1984, *The Guinness Book of Records* listed *Peanuts* as the world's most widely syndicated comic strip, and by its fortieth anniversary in 1990, *Peanuts* was running in over 2,000 newspapers in dozens of countries. Through the years, the *Peanuts* characters

Peanuts creator Charles Schulz.

have appeared in print, animation, and even on stage, making them some of the most popular cartoon characters of the twentieth century.

Charlie Brown, Schulz's main character, first appeared in a panel cartoon called *L'il Folks* that Schulz sold to a St. Paul, Minnesota, newspaper in 1947. Charlie Brown was not named until the first *Peanuts* strip, where he quickly took the lead role. Charlie Brown is insecurity itself. He cannot fly a kite, his baseball team never wins, he receives no valentines on Valentine's Day, and he gets rocks instead of candy on Halloween. The things we fear will happen to us are the types of things that do happen to Charlie Brown. Even so, Charlie Brown displays a plucky spirit. He keeps trying to fly kites, keeps managing the baseball team, keeps sending valentines to his friends, and keeps going out for tricks-or-treats. Faced with continual depression and the torment of his peers, he tends to be friendly and kind. Charlie Brown is a character people identify with because, as Schulz says in *Charlie Brown, Snoopy and Me,* "Who hasn't felt like Charlie Brown after a bad day?" Evidence of the empathy people feel for Charlie Brown came after the first airing of the *Peanuts* animated Halloween and Valentine's Day television specials, when hundreds of people sent Schulz candy and valentines to give to Charlie Brown.

Snoopy, Charlie Brown's exuberant beagle, acts as Charlie Brown's foil. Snoopy is one beagle who does not let being a dog get in the way of his ambitions. He often imagines himself as a writer, a World War I flying ace, an attorney, or the impressive Joe Cool. He plays hockey and baseball. He likes eating and sleeping and picking on the neighbor's cat, his truly dog-like traits, and he particularly likes chocolate chip cookies. He is confident and has an overactive imagination. He is a strange, quirky character who may embody childlike qualities more than the actual children do in this strip. Snoopy is everything Charlie Brown is not, and Snoopy may even exceed his owner's popularity.

The neighborhood children are not quite as depressed as Charlie Brown, but they all have their own insecurities and vulnerabilities. Lucy Van Pelt, Charlie Brown's next door neighbor, is a bossy fussbudget. Generally she is loud and mean-spirited, and is best known for annually coaxing Charlie Brown into kicking the football she has every intention of pulling away at the last minute. Seemingly invulnerable, she has a crush on the musical Schroeder and continually suffers his insults just to be around him. Linus Van Pelt, Lucy's brother, carries a security blanket in spite of the rather loud protests of his sister and grandmother. Sally, Charlie Brown's little sister, worries constantly about her school work. The other neighborhood children are much the same, worrying about school, unrequited crushes, and sports—typical childhood worries. Children and adults see themselves and their own insecurities in these characters.

The *Peanuts* characters, however, are not typical children. They do torment each other (making them some of the first realistic children in comics) and play games, much as other children do, but the *Peanuts* characters are somewhat more serious and intelligent than the average child. Lucy says she would like real estate for Christmas, Linus can philosophize about life's problems while sucking his thumb, and Schroeder's hero is Beethoven. They quote the Bible and have incredible vocabularies. Not only are these children intelligent, they are independent. Adults only appear "off stage," and rarely at that. The *Peanuts* characters seem to go through most of their activities with little adult supervision or interference, and they manage just fine. The characters tend to be a bit less fun-loving than the children we know. They are all somewhat depressed, and when they laugh, they tend to be laughing at each other rather than something innocent that simply strikes them as funny. As Schulz says in *Charlie*

Brown, Snoopy and Me, ''Strangely enough, pleasant things are not really funny. You can't create humor out of happiness.'' Charlie Brown himself is the apex of this philosophy. The *Peanuts* characters have enough childlike qualities to keep children interested, but much of this is adult humor.

The successful transition of *Peanuts* into animation and stage productions has helped maintain and expand the strip's popularity. The first animated television special, *A Charlie Brown Christmas,* premiered on December 9, 1965, and drew 50 percent of the United States viewing audience. It won an Emmy Award and a Peabody Award and has been rerun annually into the 1990s. Other *Peanuts* animated specials have received Emmys, including *A Charlie Brown Thanksgiving* and *You're a Good Sport, Charlie Brown.* On December 11, 1969, the first of several *Peanuts* animated feature films premiered at Radio City Music Hall. The shows and movies continue to be popular, and many have been released on home video. A musical, *You're a Good Man, Charlie Brown,* opened off-Broadway on March 7, 1967, becoming a long-running show especially favored by schools and regional theater groups. Through the animated specials and the musical, the *Peanuts* characters have reached an audience who might never have picked up the funny pages to read the strip.

Through the years, *Peanuts* has stayed in the news and the public eye. In the late 1960s, Snoopy was adopted as the official emblem of NASA (National Aeronautics and Space Administration) for outstanding achievement within the organization. In 1969, the Apollo 10 Lunar Expedition nicknamed their command module ''Charlie Brown'' and the lunar module ''Snoopy.'' Astronaut John Young transmitted a picture of Snoopy back to earth during the mission's fourth telecast. In 1974, when Hank Aaron was approaching Babe Ruth's home run record, Schulz read about people sending Aaron hate mail, angry that a black man was challenging the record. Schulz addressed this in a series of cartoons recounting Snoopy's trials and tribulations as he approaches the home run record. Schulz even commemorated the fiftieth anniversary of D-Day in his strip. *Peanuts* characters have appeared on the covers of *Time, Life, Newsweek, Woman's Day, The Saturday Review,* and *TV Guide.* Additionally, other authors have used *Peanuts* comics to illustrate their books. Therapist Abraham J. Twerski chose *Peanuts* comics to illustrate various psychological concepts in his book, *When Do the Good Things Start.* In *The Gospel According to Peanuts* and *Short Meditations on the Bible and Peanuts,* Robert L. Short uses the cartoons to highlight various lessons in Christian living. The characters have also been spokespeople for Metropolitan Life Insurance, Chex Party Mix, and the United States National Park Foundation. They were some of the first heavily merchandised cartoon characters, starting with calendars and moving on to everything from coffee mugs to tee shirts to shower curtains. Charlie Brown, Snoopy, Lucy, Linus, and the other characters are easily recognized by most Americans and certainly by many people throughout the world.

Charles Schulz himself is highly regarded as a comic artist and has received numerous awards and honors for his work. In 1955, the National Cartoonist's Society awarded Schulz their prestigious Reuben Award; he won it again in 1964. In 1962, Schulz won the National Cartoonist Society's ''Best Humor Strip of the Year'' award. In 1978, he received the ''Cartoonist of the Year'' award from the International Pavilion of Humor of Montreal. In 1990, the Smithsonian's National Museum of American History presented ''This Is Your Childhood Charlie Brown—Children in American Culture, 1945-1970.'' And in 1996, he received a star next to Walt Disney on the

Hollywood Walk of Fame. Clearly, Schulz has been repeatedly recognized for his professionalism, intelligence, and for the quality of his output and has experienced a popularity not enjoyed by many cartoonists.

In his book, *When Do the Good Things Start,* Abraham J. Twerski says, ''The lovable characters created by Charles Schulz do more than amuse; they depict important psychological principles in a manner so deceptively simple that it masks the force of their impact.'' Indeed, *Peanuts* raised a new standard of what could be done in comic art. The intelligence displayed in such comics as Bill Watterson's *Calvin and Hobbes* and Gary Larson's *The Far Side* comes from this tradition—the belief that comics and humor can have more meaning than a simple laugh. The *Peanuts* characters are some of the most popular in the genre. *Peanuts* is intelligent and funny, a combination that has kept it in the public eye for nearly half a century and which should fuel its popularity into the new millennium.

—Adrienne Furness

FURTHER READING:

Johnson, Rheta Grimsley. *Good Grief: The Story of Charles M. Schulz.* New York, Pharos Books, 1989.

Mendelson, Lee, and Charles M. Schulz. *Happy Birthday, Charlie Brown.* New York, Random House, 1979.

Schulz, Charles M. *Around the World in 45 Years: Charlie Brown's Anniversary Celebration.* Kansas City, Andrews and McMeel, 1994.

Schulz, Charles M., and R. Smith Kiliper. *Charlie Brown, Snoopy and Me.* Garden City, Doubleday & Company, Inc., 1980.

Short, Robert L. *The Gospel According to Peanuts.* Louisville, Westminster John Knox Press, 1965.

———. *Short Meditations on the Bible and Peanuts.* Louisville, John Knox Press, 1990.

Twerski, Abraham J. *When Do the Good Things Start.* New York, Topper Books, 1988.

Pearl Jam

When grunge music exploded into the mainstream of popular culture in the early 1990s, it was Pearl Jam, along with fellow Seattle band Nirvana, who filled the column inches and the billboard charts. While Nirvana's September 1991 debut *Nevermind* generated an immediate media frenzy, it was Pearl Jam's more orthodox blues-rock album, *Ten,* released almost simultaneously, that would eventually overtake it in sales—over ten million copies in the United States alone by the end of 1996. The breakthrough single from the album, ''Jeremy,'' won four MTV awards, and recognition for a video that tried to create a coherent story for lead singer Eddie Vedder's typically elusive and obtuse lyrics. What was clear from the video was the sense of pain and anger that characterized Pearl Jam's music: songs that helped recharge rock 'n' roll, a seemingly exhausted genre that had been slipping in both market share and musical relevance since the late 1980s.

Pearl Jam was formed in 1991 by bass guitarist Jeff Ament and rhythm guitarist Stone Gossard. Together with Mike McCready (guitar), drummer Dave Krusen (later replaced by Dave Abruzzese and then Jack Irons), and Eddie Vedder (vocals), the band began

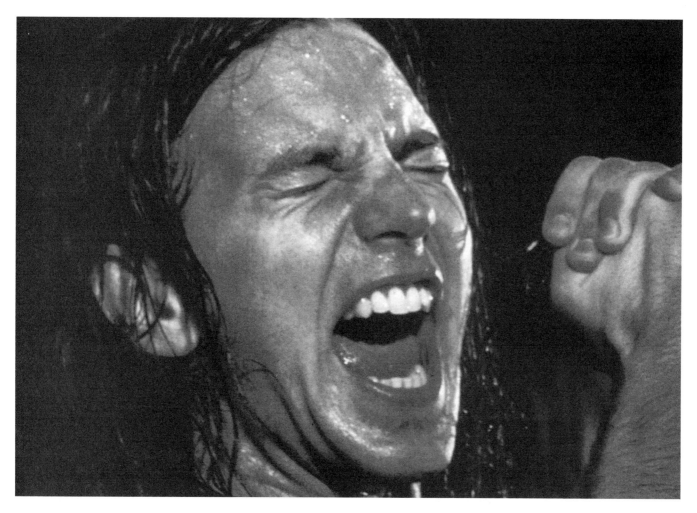

Eddie Vedder, lead singer of Pearl Jam.

recording under the name Mookie Blaylock, after the New Jersey Nets basketball star. After Blaylock objected, they changed to Pearl Jam (allegedly after a jam containing peyote made by Vedder's great-grandmother, Pearl). Their debut album, *Ten,* combined a hard, guitar rock sound with anthemic choruses, slow pop melodies, and Vedder's vocal gyrations that told stories of suicide and childhood neglect. If Nirvana's *Nevermind* was a punk-rock incendiary aimed at classic rock, Pearl Jam's *Ten* provided a more mainstream-sounding attack on the established order. Both albums were instrumental in positioning grunge, or the ''Seattle-sound'' (fellow bands Soundgarden and Alice in Chains also hailed from Seattle), as the dominant MTV aesthetic and confirming Alternative music's arrival overground in the early 1990s.

Pearl Jam's more commercial sound prompted an attack from Nirvana's Kurt Cobain in 1993. The singer called the band a ''corporate, alternative, cock-rock crossover'' and charged Pearl Jam with ''jumping on the alternative bandwagon.'' Their response was to record a much rawer and harder second album, *vs.*, which they refused to support with videos, singles, or a major tour, though the album still managed to sell five million copies and top the billboard charts. In 1994 the band also embarked upon a stand against ticketing agency Ticketmaster, alleging that the company had a monopoly over ticket distribution in U.S. arenas and stadiums. Pearl Jam officially asked

the Department of Justice to investigate Ticketmaster on antitrust charges, and band members Ament and Gossard found themselves testifying before a congressional committee.

The Justice Department dropped its investigation of Ticketmaster in July 1995, but the band gained praise in many quarters for a stand against a stadium system that in some ways mirrored their increasing rejection of stadium rock. The band's third album, *Vitology* (1994), stripped away the grunge sound in favor of a diverse collection of influences, including folk and reggae. One of the standout, Grammy Award winning tracks was ''Spin the Black Circle,'' a homage to vinyl records, and the album was made available on vinyl before its release on other, more polished formats. The move reflected the group's seeming desire to reestablish serious grassroots credibility after tremendous media hype; singer Eddie Vedder had appeared on the front cover of *Time* magazine in October 1993, despite his refusal to be interviewed for the accompanying article. The album also reflected Vedder's musings in light of Kurt Cobain's suicide, an event that increased the attention given the Pearl Jam vocalist. As Andrew Mueller of the British music weekly *Melody Maker* commented at the time, ''Eddie Vedder is out there alone now.''

Vedder and Pearl Jam's response was increasingly to shirk the limelight and to move away from the grunge sound that had helped generate their fame. Their fourth album, *No Code* (1996) employed

Indian drones, psychedelic rock, folk, and punk, only occasionally returning to a high-energy rock sound. Similarly, their 1998 album *Yield* continued with the combination of Vedder's existential musings and more eclectic range of musical instruments. It included a track showing the influence of Pakistani qawwali star Nusrat Fateh Ali Khan, with whom Vedder collaborated for the *Dead Man Walking* soundtrack. Music critics were less receptive to Pearl Jam's attempts to redefine themselves; yet the demise of the grunge phenomenon and a diminished, if still significant, fan base suited the band. Their stated wish was to sustain a lengthy and credible musical career, in line with those they admired, such as Bob Dylan, Pete Townsend, and in particular Neil Young, with whom they collaborated on the *MirrorBall* album.

—James Lyons

FURTHER READING:

Clarke, Malcolm. *Pearl Jam and Eddie Vedder: None Too Fragile.* London, Plexus, 1997.

Humphrey, Clark. *Loser: The Real Seattle Music Story.* Portland, Feral House, 1995.

Morrell, Brad. *Pearl Jam: The Illustrated Biography.* New York, Omnibus, 1993.

Neeley, Kim. *Five Against One.* New York, Penguin, 1998.

Wall, Mick. *Pearl Jam.* London, Sidgwick & Jackson, 1994.

Pearl, Minnie (1912-1996)

Country music's first comedian, Minnie Pearl, entertained Grand Old Opry audiences for more than half a century. Her gingham dress, white stockings, and straw hat complete with $1.98 price tag dangling from it made her a figure recognized wherever country music was heard. Ploughboys and presidents responded to her contagious grin, her homespun humor, and her exuberant greeting. So familiar was her image that upon her death in March of 1996, commentators, columnists, and cartoonists alike pictured her entering the pearly gates and greeting St. Peter with her trademark, "How-dee! I'm just so proud to be here."

Sarah Ophelia Colley Cannon never planned to become a country comic. The sheltered, youngest daughter of conventionally conservative Southern parents and a product of Ward-Belmont, a Tennessee finishing school, she dreamed of becoming a fine dramatic actress. "I planned," she said, "to out-Bernhardt Bernhardt."

The character "Minnie Pearl" evolved from young Ophelia Colley's years working for the Sewell Production Company, an Atlanta-based touring theater company that sent young women directors to stage productions throughout the small-town and rural South. What began as a collection of stories culled from her touring experience gradually developed into a country character that Ophelia used to sell the Sewell productions. She named the character Minnie Pearl because they were common country names, names that were familiar to her audiences. When Ophelia earned her first job, not as a Sewell director but as an entertainer named Minnie Pearl, she was paid the handsome sum of $25 (more than twice her weekly salary). She then added the costume to her act. Minnie Pearl performed for the Pilots Club Convention in Aiken, South Carolina, in 1939, and Ophelia

Minnie Pearl

Cannon acquired an alter ego. That performance, the comedian later revealed, was the first time that she "became the character."

A year after the Aiken appearance, Minnie Pearl debuted on the Grand Ole Opry in a three-minute spot at 11:05 p.m., a time chosen so that if Minnie flopped, the affected audience would be as small as possible. Far from failing, however, Minnie received several hundred fan letters and an offer to become a regular at the Opry. For the next fifty-one years Minnie Pearl, with her tales of Brother, Uncle Nabob, Aunt Ambrosy, and other inhabitants of Grinder's Switch (a name Ophelia Colley borrowed from an abandoned loading switch in Hickman County, Tennessee) captured the affections of Opry audiences and other audiences far from Nashville, including standing-room-only audiences at Carnegie Hall. An early indication that Minnie was on her way to becoming an American icon came in 1948 when Alben Barkley, Harry Truman's vice president, began his first official address to the nation with the words "well, as Minnie Pearl would say, I'm just so *proud* to be here!"

Minnie Pearl with her hillbilly naivete and her inexhaustible search for a "feller" may seem an incongruous figure as a pioneer for women's equality, but Miss Minnie opened doors in the country music business that other women eagerly walked through. She headlined in an era when the only women around were "girl singers" in clearly subordinate roles. Aside from being the first female member of the Grand Ole Opry, Minnie Pearl was also one of the first women to be elected to the Country Music Hall of Fame (1975) as well as the National Comedy Hall of Fame.

The woman who auditioned for WSM knowing nothing about country music became one of the most beloved figures in the country music industry. Initially befriended by Roy Acuff, already an established star when Minnie Pearl came to the Opry, she in turn befriended generations of newcomers, including Chet Atkins and Hank Williams. The esteem in which younger entertainers held her is evident. Dwight Yoakam, who managed to alienate himself from many in the industry, sent fifty dozen roses for Minnie Pearl's fiftieth anniversary celebration on the Grand Ole Opry. And both pop-contemporary Christian music star Amy Grant and country music sensation Garth Brooks named daughters after her.

The same generosity that endeared her to the country music community led her to work for humanitarian causes. Aa a cancer survivor, Minnie Pearl worked tirelessly for the American Cancer Society. Her efforts were recognized in 1987 by President Ronald Reagan, who presented her with the Cancer Society's Courage Award. In 1988 she became the first recipient of the Nashville Network/Music City News humanitarian award, which bears her name. A stroke in 1991 forced her to retire, but her presence continued to be felt in the country music community where good wishes for Miss Minnie were standard fare on award shows. Her husband, Henry Cannon, represented her on tribute shows she could only watch. She died on March 4, 1996.

Minnie Pearl ended her 1980 autobiography by wishing for her readers a Grinder's Switch. ''Grinder's Switch,'' she wrote, ''is a state of mind—a place where there is no illness, no war, no unhappiness, no political unrest, no tears.'' Perhaps it was her ability to evoke such a place that endeared her to fans and peers alike. She allowed her audience to inhabit a space where eccentricities were tolerated, humor was barbless, and laughter was easy.

—Wylene Rholetter

FURTHER READING:

Cannon, Ophelia Colley. *Minnie Pearl: An Autobiography.* New York, Simon and Schuster, 1980.

Tassin, Myron. *Fifty Years of the Grand Ole Opry.* New York, Pelican, 1991.

Peck, Gregory (1916—)

The last of the classic leading men from Hollywood's Golden Age, Gregory Peck became a star during the 1940s when a spinal injury prevented him from joining the armed forces during World War II. With many of its male stars in uniform, Hollywood turned to

Gregory Peck, in the jaws of the great whale, in a scene from the film *Moby Dick.*

the tall, dark, and handsome Peck, who soon made a name for himself playing men of moral fortitude and great dignity. A five-time Academy Award nominee and Oscar winner for Best Actor for his wonderful turn as Atticus Finch in the classic *To Kill a Mockingbird* (1962), Peck was a versatile actor who was able to take on a wide range of roles, including those depicting the darker side of humanity. A tireless supporter of the film industry, Peck has served on almost every major film and arts council. But Hollywood's dedicated elder statesman will undoubtedly always be best remembered as the actor who became a pop culture icon by unflinchingly showing America both the best and the worst about itself.

Eldred Gregory Peck was born in the beach town of La Jolla, California, the son of the town's only pharmacist. Eldred's parents divorced when he was six, but the boy continued to live in the seaside resort community with his mother and grandmother until age ten, when he was sent to St. John's Military Academy in Los Angeles. Upon graduating from the academy after ninth grade, Peck moved in with his father in San Diego, where the teenager attended San Diego High School. The handsome six-foot-two-inch boy was an average student who enjoyed being on the rowing team, but because his father wanted him to become a doctor, Eldred studied at San Diego State University before transferring to study medicine at the University of California, Berkeley. There he quickly realized that he was more interested in literature than in medicine and, as an English major, he fell in with an artistic crowd and was soon persuaded to audition for a production of *Moby Dick*. Cast as Starbuck, Peck so fell in love with the theater that shortly before graduation he dropped out of school and caught the train for New York City.

Arriving in New York in 1939, Gregory Peck, as he now called himself, found work as a barker at the New York World's Fair, before auditioning for Sanford Meisner's famed Neighborhood Playhouse. While studying there with renowned dancer Martha Graham, he received the severe back injury which would eventually keep him out of the war. In the meantime, however, Gregory Peck gradually began to find acting work in stock companies around the East Coast before being "discovered" by distinguished director Guthrie McClintic, who regularly began to use the handsome young leading man in his productions.

Gregory Peck made his Broadway debut in McClintic's 1942 production of an Emlyn Williams wartime drama. The young actor received excellent reviews and soon began to find regular work on Broadway. But not long thereafter, Hollywood, whose ranks of leading men had been depleted by the war, came calling.

With a paucity of available actors, the talented Peck was immediately cast in prime leading roles, working with some of Hollywood's best directors—from John Stahl in *Keys of the Kingdom* (1944) to Alfred Hitchcock in *Spellbound* (1945); and from King Vidor in *Duel in the Sun* (1946) to Elia Kazan in *Gentleman's Agreement* (1947). Overnight the versatile actor became a star, garnering four Academy Award nominations in five years. Despite becoming a famous movie actor, Peck continued to devote himself to the theater, co-founding the prestigious La Jolla Playhouse in his hometown with fellow actors Dorothy McGuire and Mel Ferrer.

Although the gifted Peck could play a wide range of characters, as Baseline's *Encyclopedia of Film* notes, it was "as an authority figure of quiet dignity and uncompromising singlemindedness" that audiences seemed to love Peck best—in such films, for example, as *The Yearling, The Gunfighter*, and *The Man in the Gray Flannel Suit*. Throughout the 1950s, Peck's popularity only seemed to grow. He was a popular leading man opposite such A-list actresses as Audrey

Hepburn, Jean Simmons, and Lauren Bacall, even as he topped the list of Hollywood's favorite action heroes in war films such as *Pork Chop Hill* and *The Guns of Navarone*. But the apex of his career came in 1962, when he was cast in a role that would earn him cinematic immortality. Playing a morally courageous lawyer and single father of two children in a small Southern town who defends a black man accused of rape, Gregory Peck turned in a superb performance as Atticus Finch, epitomizing his appeal as an actor. *To Kill a Mockingbird,* which has become a screen classic, would go on to win three Academy Awards, including Peck's for Best Actor.

Although Peck continued to work in films throughout the 1960s and on into the 1990s, only a few of his later movies, such as *The Omen* and *The Boys from Brazil,* were particularly notable. Peck, however, found an outlet for his creative energies as a founder of the prestigious American Film Institute, three-time president of the Academy of Motion Picture Arts and Sciences, and a member of the National Council for the Arts. Long one of Hollywood's most popular actors, Gregory Peck has managed to meld life and art in creating both an honorable career as well as a career playing some of movies' most honorable men.

—Victoria Price

FURTHER READING:

Everitt, David. "A Bushel of Peck." *Entertainment Weekly.* Issue 423, March 1998, 95-96.

Monaco, James, and the Editors of Baseline. *The Encyclopedia of Film.* New York, Perigee, 1991.

Ross, Bob. "Actor: Gregory Peck." *The Tampa Tribune.* December 7, 1998.

Peep Shows

Contemporary peep shows, featuring video taped or live performances of sexual activity, developed on the heels of several hundred years of interest in optical principles, the construction of novel, very small spaces, and apparent human fascination with the particulars of these settings. The history of today's peep shows might even be much older. Certainly, examples of very small private meal cubicals (often associated with licentious behavior), buskers and tented tableaus, traveling entertainers with all manners of portable containers offering the entrepreneur control and the consumer a sense of security, are mentioned across continents and ages. Today's manifestations exhibit the presence of several particular circumstances: new and cheap materials, changes in public mores and the ability to regulate human behavior, and rapid changes and improvements in technology.

As science became the pastime of leisured gentlemen in the 1700s and through the early quarter of the 1800s (when a transition began to move science into the hands of specialists and Societies), experiments with amusing outcomes were very popular. Thus, the *camera obscura* (a closed device ranging in size from a large box to a reasonable sized room) and the related *camera lucida* both entertained and fostered further work with the phenomena of sight. Literally a "dark chamber," the *camera obscura* allowed the projection of images, often pornographic, onto a wall, through the agency of

An adult entertainment shop on 42nd Street in New York.

the physics of light, a tiny hole, and a willing actor. Meanwhile, the participants inside could act along.

At about the same time, the expanding notion of a hospitality industry allowed commercial eateries and inns to flourish in growing commercial centers. Tiny, secluded chambers away from the restaurant's main hall provided privacy for a range of adult hanky-panky. By the mid-1800s, the commingling of the commercial provision of secure, intimate chambers, and the development of a number of ways to "play" reproductions of titillating forms of entertainment reliably and cheaply offered lucrative opportunities. The early "secure chamber" still exists as the so-called "private room" at contemporary full-service striptease clubs and, indeed, in a slightly changed form at many present day peep shows.

Zoetropes, stereoscopes, crankable flip-card devices, and early movie loops tumbled off the inventor's and manufacturer's conveyor belt from the mid-to late-1800s. Burgeoning city growth and the accompanying cash economy of the factory system virtually guaranteed the lush development of adult entertainment neighborhoods chock-a-block with cafes, dance halls (which also allowed hookers to stroll and display off the street), taverns, theaters, and so on. Well before the assault of Reform Movement "do gooders" in urban

centers after the Civil War, the peep show devices made good sense to entrepreneurs. Images could be loaded to suit the consumer—if the nudes were of brown-skinned women one could deny prurient intent and ride the rage for exotic exploration. Bars would advertise new "shows" and have underemployed day workers hand out tokens. Tokens would work the peep shows and, lured to the tavern, the viewer would buy drinks.

By the time of the Great Depression, movies were commonplace and, through market pressure, cheap. It was hard for a penny peep show to compete with a nickel or dime movie. One result of such competition was a tendency to show increasingly risque content, but what happened more regularly was that peep shows failed at the competition. By the 1960s or so, the peep show machines that still existed were largely curiosities. The sexual revolution stimulated two related but separate updates of the peep show idea.

At first, small booths with a seat, a lock, and a roll of paper towels were made available for individual viewing of 8 or 16 mm stag loops or for access to a usually circular "stage" with living performers. Innovation was rapid and, with the development of cheap video cameras, duplicators, and players—or, in live action settings, willing responses to the consumer's varied tastes—peep shows became an enormously profitable industry. In the privacy of the secure booth, patrons could look on passively to recorded pornography or masturbate, as they preferred. Peep shows featuring live performance booths functioned in several ways, but generally once the patron locked the entry/exit door, feeding tokens or coins to a slot dropped and kept lowered a partition at the front. Depending on the particular business, patrons could "tip" fully or partially nude "models" to act out their directions and requests. In some cases the patron could fondle the performers.

As was the case throughout the history of these secure settings for one or two people, it was commonplace for patrons to hire a loitering sex professional to enter the booth and carry out this or that commercial sexual transaction. Because it was far easier for most regions to regulate prostitution than to regulate the vague, poorly defined activity of viewing live or filmed sexual display, this activity was carefully controlled by the management.

At the end of the twentieth century, wide-spread downtown clean-up campaigns, the explosive growth in availability of inexpensive, technically high-quality pornographic videos and appropriate home viewing units, and a growing awareness of crime combined to make the peep show businesses less profitable. Much investment capital was wooed elsewhere.

—Dr. Jon Griffin Donlon

FURTHER READING:

Balzer, Richard. *Peepshows: A Visual History.* New York, Harry N. Abrams, 1998.

Pee-wee's Playhouse

Despite the taint of scandal, *Pee-wee's Playhouse,* a live-action Saturday morning children's television show, stands as a singularly creative example of successful children's programming. First airing in 1986, *Pee-wee's Playhouse* starred actor and stand-up comedian Paul Reubens as Pee-wee Herman and featured the multicultural Playhouse gang, talking puppets, a robot, and occasional celebrity guests. Despite its time slot, *Pee-wee's Playhouse* appealed to adults as well as their children as Pee-wee led viewers through inventive educational activities that did not condescend to young audiences and held enough double entendres to keep adults laughing. When Reubens was arrested in the summer of 1991 on an indecent exposure charge, CBS pulled the five remaining episodes from its schedule and canceled the series entirely. The scandal and CBS's subsequent action sparked intense public debate and nearly ruined the actor's career.

Reubens conceived of the character at the Groundlings Theater in Los Angeles in 1980 and introduced him to audiences in a sketch that became the basis for the 1981 HBO special *The Pee-wee Herman Show.* The actor claims he took the first name from a toy harmonica with the word "Pee Wee" printed on its side, while the character's last name was borrowed from a disliked childhood acquaintance. Audiences appreciated Pee-wee's obnoxious attitude and silly humor. In 1985, Reubens starred in the summer film *Pee-wee's Big Adventure.* The film cost about six million dollars and earned nearly 50 million, becoming a sleeper summer hit. The film's main character, Pee-wee Herman, was a hyperactive man dressed like a boy in a tight-fitting, grey, glen plaid suit with a perky red bow tie. Although Reubens always maintained in interviews that Pee-wee was male,

Pee Wee Herman appearing at Comic Relief, 1986.

some critics thought that Pee-wee's effeminate body language and mincing manner made the character's gender, not to mention his sexuality, ambivalent at best.

CBS executives liked the character so much that they invited Reubens to develop a children's television show based on Pee-wee Herman. While the network laid down some ground rules (no toilet paper sticking to Pee-wee's shoe as he emerged from the playhouse bathroom, for instance), Reubens basically had carte blanche in developing *Pee-wee's Playhouse.*

Compared to the other Saturday morning television, *Pee-wee's Playhouse* was a breath of fresh, wacky air. While *Sesame Street* was the undisputed leader in children's programming for its seamless blend of education and puppet magic, *Pee-wee's Playhouse* stood out as a smart, creative show among the formulaic animation typically pitched to smaller viewers on weekend mornings. From its carnivalesque score written by former Devo member Mark Mothersbaugh to its visually stimulating set design that mixed vintage decor with plastic toys, *Pee-wee's Playhouse* distinguished itself through sheer difference. This difference was essential to the message that Reubens wanted his character and the show to project to kids. "I'm just trying to illustrate that it's okay to be different—not that it's good, not that it's bad, but that it's all right. I'm trying to tell kids to have a good time and to encourage them to be creative and to question things,'' Reubens told one interviewer in *Rolling Stone* during the program's first season. Ultimately, this message championing difference would come back to haunt the performer in 1991 upon his arrest.

Gary Panter's art direction, the program's title design, and its sound mixing all were recognized with Emmys throughout the program's five-year run. At a time when many children's shows were experimenting with new effects in computer animation, *Pee-wee's Playhouse* was using seemingly outdated techniques such as stop-motion photography to set itself apart. The program also made use of claymation designed by Aardman Animations in Bristol, England, the company that brought to life the beloved Wallace and Gromit characters.

Each episode of *Pee-wee's Playhouse* began with a wild ride through its opening graphics accompanied by a zany theme song. Viewers would learn the day's secret word and were instructed to ''scream real loud'' every time a character on the show said the word, which was given to Pee-wee by his robot friend, Conky. Although the episodes were guided by Pee-wee's childlike stream-of-consciousness, each show revolved around a loosely structured narrative dilemma such as Pee-wee's winning a Hawaiian dinner for two and having to decide which Playhouse friend to invite along. Such plots embodied basic values such as loyalty, honesty, and sharing. Helping Pee-wee to have fun and negotiate personal dilemmas were *Playhouse* regulars such as the glamorous Miss Yvonne (Lynne Stewart), curmudgeonly Kap'n Karl (the late Phil Hartman), sneaky neighbor Mrs. Steve (Shirley Stoler), and amiable Cowboy Curtis (actor Laurence Fishburne).

While many critics faltered in trying to categorize *Pee-wee's Playhouse*, all agreed that its fast pace and frenetic energy made it a natural for children, whose nonlinear thought patterns and short attention spans were matched by Pee-wee's near-manic behavior and the program's quick-moving visuals, which critic Jack Barth described as ''a fast-paced technologically updated Ernie Kovacs in color.''

Given its action-packed innovation, *Pee-wee's Playhouse* was an exhausting show to produce, and by 1989 Reubens decided not to renew his contract with CBS. Instead, he spent the next year working overtime to produce two years' worth of episodes so that he could fulfill his contract to the network and retire the character for good. In the summer of 1991, having completed production on the final episodes, Reubens was visiting family in Sarasota, Florida, when he was arrested in an adult theater for indecent exposure, touching off a media scandal whose hallmark was witty headlines such as ''Today's Secret Word: Suspended.'' CBS abruptly canceled the remaining episodes of *Pee-wee's Playhouse*, and Reubens spent months trying to resuscitate his career while parents tried to explain to their children what had happened to their favorite television character.

Reubens's career did continue, although not with the same pre-scandal promise of success. Episodes of *Pee-wee's Playhouse* were packaged as a set and released for home video rental in the early 1990s. In the fall of 1998, the newly created Fox Family Channel included reruns of *Pee-wee's Playhouse* in its weekday programming blocks.

—Alison Macor

Further Reading:

Barth, Jack. ''Pee-wee TV.'' *Film Comment*. Vol. 22, No. 6, 1986, 78-79.

Doty, Alexander. ''The Sissy Boy, The Fat Ladies, and The Dykes: Queerness and/as Gender in Pee-wee's World.'' *Male Trouble*. Edited by Constance Penley and Sharon Willis. Minneapolis, University of Minnesota Press, 1993, 182-201.

Gertler, T. ''The Pee-wee Perplex.'' *Rolling Stone*. Vol. 493, 1987, 36-40.

Jenkins, Henry. ''Going Bonkers!: Children, Play, and Pee-wee.'' *Male Trouble*. Edited by Constance Penley and Sharon Willis. Minneapolis, University of Minnesota Press, 1993, 157-180.

McNeil, Alex. ''Pee-wee's Playhouse.'' *Total Television: The Comprehensive Guide to Programming from 1948 to the Present*. New York, Penguin Books, 1996, 648.

Wilkinson, Peter. ''Who Killed Pee-wee Herman?'' *Rolling Stone*. Vol. 614, 1991, 36-42.

Pelé (1940—)

Pelé, born Edson Arantes do Nascimento on October 23, 1940 in a small village in the Brazilian state of Minas Gerais, is recognized as the greatest, and most popular, soccer player the world has ever seen. Pelé played professional soccer for Santos Football Club in Brazil from 1956 to 1974. Between 1958 and 1970, he played in four World Cup finals, is the only person to have won three world cups as a player, and scored an astonishing 1,280 goals in 1,362 professional games. In April 1975, the New York Cosmos of the North American Soccer League signed Pelé in an attempt to popularize the sport in the United States. Although thousands came to see him play in New York, only a minority of the American public saw or appreciated his unique skills.

—John F. Lyons

Further Reading:

Arnold, Caroline. *Pele: The King of Soccer*. New York, F. Watts, 1992.

Murray, Bill. *Football: A History of the World Game*. London, Scolar Press, 1994.

Penn, Irving (1917—)

Irving Penn began his photographic career with *Vogue* magazine in 1943. Rejecting the ornate, theatrical style of fashion photography that predominated at the time, he produced simple powerful images that revolutionized the discipline. Penn's subsequent work falls into a variety of categories: fashion, portraits, still lifes, nudes, travel, ethnographic studies, and street photography. In his advertising work, his straightforward manner of focusing on the subject while stripping away superfluous elements is especially apparent, as in the product-centered Clinique advertisements. Penn's photographs—especially his portraits of influential individuals, including actors, artists, politicians, writers, and more—serve as a record of cultural, economic, and political trends in the second half of the twentieth century.

—Jennifer Jankauskas

FURTHER READING:

Penn, Irving. *Passage: A Work Record.* New York, Alfred A. Knopf, 1991.

Westerbeck, Colin, editor. *Irving Penn, A Career in Photography.* Chicago, The Art Institute of Chicago in association with Bulfinch Press/Little Brown and Company, 1997.

Penthouse

Penthouse, "the international magazine for men," became a household name along with its number one competitor, *Playboy,* during the 1960s and 1970s era of "free love" and sexual revolution. Following the 1953 debut of Hugh Hefner's erotic magazine, Bob Guccione rightly sensed that men might prefer to see a bit "more flesh" than was being offered by *Playboy.* In 1965, Guccione launched the London-based *Penthouse,* with slightly racier pictorials as well as investigative stories.

In 1969, the magazine was moved to the United States, where it expanded into a publishing dynasty that included *Forum* (1975), *Penthouse Letters* (1981), and several non-erotic ventures, such as *Omni,* a consumer science magazine (1978), *Compute* (1979), and *Longevity* (1989). Although *Penthouse* (a subsidiary of General Media Publishing) continued to grow and diversify over the next three decades, the company remained privately owned by Guccione and his companion, Kathy Keeton, whose operation was something of a Mom-and-Pop arrangement, staffed by several members of Guccione's family. Working from the nine-story mansion he shared with Keeton on Manhattan's Upper East Side, Guccione became known for his gold chains and lavish lifestyle.

Guccione's enterprise was anything but smooth sailing during the 1980s. Throughout the Reagan era, *Penthouse* was ravaged by attacks from Christian right-wing conservative groups such as the National Federation for Decency. One of the more damaging campaigns came in 1986 when Attorney General Edwin Meese and an 11-member Commission on Pornography sought to intimidate retailers by publishing a blacklist of pornography distributors. Sending its warning on Justice Department stationary, the Commission advised several large booksellers and retail chains that they would be named. Bowing to the pressure, Southland Corporation, parent company of 7-11 convenience stores, announced that it would no longer sell either *Penthouse* or *Playboy* in its 4,500 outlets. By the end of the campaign, some 20,000 retail and convenience stores had been dissuaded from carrying the adult titles.

Penthouse retaliated, along with *Playboy* and the American Booksellers Association, by filing a suit against the Commission, charging it with violating the First Amendment. Although a Federal District Court eventually forced the Commission to retract its letter, it denied the plaintiffs financial relief; in a strange footnote, Edwin Meese was later reported to have said that he did not consider either *Playboy* or *Penthouse* to be obscene.

Penthouse's constant legal battles throughout the 1980s and 1990s cost it millions of dollars in annual litigation fees, but the magazine had another, more threatening problem: videocassette distributors, who now boasted that some ten percent of their sales were in the category of erotica. "People are simply reading less," noted Guccione. "They're into other media."

Overall, *Penthouse* witnessed a steady decline in circulation and never recovered its 1979 high of 4.7 million. By 1987, the numbers had fallen to 3 million; by 1995, circulation was just over the one million mark. That same year, the magazine actually lost money for the first time in its history. *Playboy*'s numbers were also steadily declining, but remained slightly higher than those of *Penthouse.*

To recoup profits, Guccione's team experimented with a range of strategies, including a cover story on celibacy as "the new hot lifestyle." It also launched headlong into three new ventures in the 1980s, including *Spin,* a music magazine to be run by Bob Guccione, Jr., *New Look,* which survived less than six months, and the unexpected *Nuclear, Biological and Chemical Defense Technology,* which targeted defense industry personnel.

Never one to back down from a First Amendment challenge, *Penthouse* found itself under siege yet again in 1990; this time, by the American Family Association, a Christian group which planned to picket 400 Waldenbooks and K-Mart stores for carrying *Penthouse* and *Playboy.* In response to the threat, Ed Morrow, President of the American Booksellers Association, and Harry Hoffman, President and CEO of Walden, took out advertisement space in 28 daily papers, in which readers were asked to respond by "voting" for freedom of expression. The campaign was a success: over 50,000 Americans returned ballots in support of First Amendment rights within the first seven days of the appearance of the advertisements. In contrast, less than 100 picketers showed up for the American Family Association's planned protests.

In 1992, *Penthouse* faced yet another challenge from the United States Navy, which found the distribution and sale of adult magazines on naval bases to be inconsistent with rules and regulations concerning sexual harassment and human dignity. Guccione responded rhetorically, asking, "How do you put a man in uniform, teach him to kill, expose him to images of war and all sorts of inhumanity and in the same breath tell him he is not sanctioned to buy a magazine that shows people making love?" This, however, was a battle that *Penthouse* would lose. In 1996, President Clinton signed The Military Honor and Decency Act, stating that "the Secretary of Defense may not permit the sale or rental of sexually explicit material on property under the jurisdiction of the Defense Department." Although Guccione won an appeal, citing the First, Fifth, and Fourteenth Amendments, the decision was overturned in a 1998 Supreme Court ruling which held that a military base is not a public forum.

So as not to be left behind in the technological race, *Penthouse* went on-line in 1995, and quickly became one of the 25 most frequently-visited web sites. The magazine also found something of a new niche in the early 1990s with unauthorized celebrity sex photos. During this period, it won court battles to publish explicit materials of Tonya Harding (sold to the magazine by ex-husband, Jeff Gillooly), Paula Jones (also obtained from a former boyfriend), and Pamela Lee Anderson and her husband Tommy Lee.

In 1995, *Penthouse* received additional publicity from an unlikely source when the Unabomber named the magazine as his third choice—after *The New York Times* and *The Washington Post*—for publication of a manuscript advocating an anti-technology revolution. Guccione offered the terrorist—who was linked to 16 bombings since 1978—an unedited monthly column in return for his agreement not to strike again; the offer was nullified, of course, by the Unabomber's subsequent capture.

Peter Bloch, *Penthouse* editor since 1983, once claimed that Guccione's publication, unlike *Playboy,* had never been ashamed to portray explicit sexuality in its pages. Indeed, *Penthouse* broke barriers, said Bloch, by being "the first to show full frontal nudity." In 1997, the magazine ventured a step further into carnality, announcing that it would no longer shy away from depicting copulation. It remains to be seen, of course, what the anti-pornography forces will make of this.

—Kristal Brent Zook

FURTHER READING:

Flora, Paul. *Penthouse.* New York, Abrams, 1978.

Reese, Diane. "Penthouse: When Sex Doesn't Sell." *Folio.* January 1987.

The Wonderful World of Penthouse Sex: Radical Sex in the Establishment. New York, Penthouse Press, 1975.

People

When Time, Inc. launched *People* Magazine in 1974, the leading afternoon talk television show, *Donahue,* brought considered debate about important issues into the nation's living rooms and the leading national daily newspaper, the *Wall Street Journal,* brought serious news to the nation's doorsteps. *People* defined the personality-driven style that paved the way for confessional, emotional—often exhibitionistic—television talk shows such as *The Oprah Winfrey Show* in the 1980s, and later, the *Jerry Springer Show,* to lead afternoon ratings. *People*'s reliance on images rather than insightful text anticipated *USA Today*'s visual, less wordy, approach to news in the 1980s and subsequent ascendance to the top position among daily newspapers in the United States. Striving to capture the intimate and everyday lives of celebrities and the occasionally astonishing lives of everyday people, *People* further disintegrated the line between entertainment and news, bringing the personal into the public space.

Time, Inc. conceived *People* as a replacement for its weekly magazine *Life* that had ceased weekly publication in 1972. *Life* covered the grand sweep of world events and the people causing them or caught up in them. It also reported on everyday people, doing everyday things. *Life* lavished many pages and many large or full-page, artful photos on a story. A *Life* story celebrated what made a hero heroic or what made a great event epic—such as coverage of Winston Churchill's funeral or the passing of a U.S. Navy submarine beneath the polar ice cap. It would examine the commonplace with such stories as a detailed account of a day in the life of a small town or what different people in different parts of the country were doing at the exact moment a joke was told on television. This was all reported, sometimes whimsically, but always in a serious journalistic style.

People instead focused on what made public figures seem more like regular people and what made regular people noteworthy. Instead of reporting the great public triumphs of public figures, *People* would report the common personal problems such as divorce or addiction, that they overcame to attain their oft-reported triumphs. This novel formula was described as "extraordinary people doing ordinary things and ordinary people doing extraordinary things." *People*'s

appearance on the media landscape was consistent with changes in the way Americans perceived public figures. Observes Leo Braudy, author of *The Frenzy of Renown: Fame and its History,* "it is not the social order so much as an individual's own emotional problems that are conquered" in the new media spotlight. According to Braudy, the media is now "more likely to stress a victory over alcoholism or personal tragedy than it is to sketch a Lincolnesque rise from poverty."

Years before *People,* fanzines had been trading in gossip and intimate stories about celebrities, relating their favorite recipes, likes and dislikes, or how they relaxed at home. And tabloids such as the *National Enquirer* had long reported on celebrity gossip and the freakish events that could happen to everyday people. But fanzines and tabloids were not published by as respected a journalistic institution as Time, Inc. *People* was designed, graphically and editorially, to look conventional, respectable, and mainstream. While the tabloids and fanzines historically made no pretenses of "respectability," *People* treated the reporting of intimate information about stars and everyday people as a perfectly legitimate undertaking. *People* also expanded the boundaries of celebrity beyond the movie, television, and music stars of the fanzines and the freaks of the tabloids to include religious leaders, business people, fashion designers, models, athletes, and politicians.

People drew on the conventions of television, adopting its visual treatment to news and working within strict constraints of space. By the 1970s, news was beginning to be treated more and more as entertainment, as dramatized in the movie *Network.* This was evidenced by the signing of Barbara Walters as an ABC Nightly News co-anchor for a record setting $1 million, as much for her celebrity status as for her reporting skills. Like television, *People* treated news as another branch of entertainment, but it also reported celebrity gossip and stories as valid news. *Life* had already shown that a magazine could be a collection of pictures, narrated by text. However, where traditional print journalism would allow one, or a few, images to sometimes dramatically stand alone to tell a story, *People* instead adopted television's visual language, displaying a blizzard of many images, none standing dramatically alone.

Financially, *People* found immediate success, selling over 120 million copies in its first two years. The first national weekly magazine to be launched since *Sports Illustrated* 20 years earlier, *People* became profitable within 18 months. The company's flagship weekly publication, *Time,* had taken three years to become profitable. *Sports Illustrated* had taken ten. The news establishment was not as receptive as the average consumer. Said William Safire in the *New York Times,* "*People* fails on its own tawdry terms." Tom Donnelly of *The Washington Post* declared "It will tax none but the shortest attention spans and it is so undemanding that it can be read while the TV commercials are on. It is the reading equivalent of those 'convenience foods.' . . ." *People* was represented no better in popular culture. To indicate that a character in the movie *The Big Chill* had completely sold out his 1960s idealism, he is shown lamenting his life as a writer for *People,* where, he complains, the length of his articles are constrained by the length of time readers spend in the bathroom.

Initially the magazine was not sold by subscription and the cover was crucial in generating copy sales. The staff developed a set of rules for magazine covers based on its experience with sales figures:

Young is better than old.
Pretty is better than ugly.
TV is better than music.
Music is better than movies.

Movies are better than sports.
And anything is better than a politician.
And nothing is better than the celebrity dead.

People's readership was about two-thirds female and experience proved that covers showing women sold more copies than did those with men. In the magazine's first 25 years, Princess Diana, Elizabeth Taylor, (former Duchess) Sarah Ferguson, John Travolta, and Madonna were among the most frequent cover subjects. Best-selling covers included tributes to John Lennon, Princess Grace of Monaco, and Princess Diana, soon after their deaths.

People examined anything and everything through the lens of personalities. Every story was anchored to a person or group of people, and generally concerned the more intimate details of their lives. This approach of covering the personality more than the event began to filter into other media properties. This was reflected not only in the rise of "softer" shows such as *The Oprah Winfrey Show* and *Jerry Springer Show,* or the launch of *USA Today.* It was not even limited to the proliferation of tabloid shows such as *A Current Affair* or the numerous celebrity gossip shows of the 1980s and 1990s such as *Entertainment Tonight* and *Access Hollywood.* Beyond mere imitators such as *Us, People* changed the mainstream, "serious" media. In the 1980s and 1990s, most newspapers developed a "style" or "people" section to report on celebrity news and human interest. These newspapers were more and more likely to report on rumor, stars, and scandal in their news sections. Newsweeklies such as *Time* and *Newsweek* increased their coverage of celebrities and personalities. When, in 1997, sportscaster Marv Albert pled guilty to minor sex crimes committed in private, off the job, the respected paper of record, the *New York Times* reported it on the front page, as news.

The influence of *People* stretches not merely to the dozens of new outlets for celebrity gossip and intimate confession in its wake, but the legitimization of personality journalism in the mainstream press and the introduction of the intimate and personal into the public realm. *People* is the emblem of American celebrity culture and its public intimacy.

—Steven Kotok

FURTHER READING:

Braudy, Leo. *The Frenzy of Renown: Fame and its History.* New York, Oxford University Press, 1986.

Hamblin, Dora Jane. *That was the Life: The Upstairs Downstairs behind-the-Doors Story of America's Favorite Magazine.* New York, W. W. Norton and Company, 1997.

Kessler, Judy. *Inside People: The Stories behind the Stories.* New York, Villard Books, 1994.

Krajicek, David J. *Scooped!: Media Miss Real Story on Crime while Chasing Sex, Sleaze, and Celebrities.* New York, Columbia University Press, 1998.

Schickel, Richard. *Intimate Strangers: The Culture of Celebrity.* Garden City, Doubleday, 1985.

The Peppermint Lounge

The Peppermint Lounge, or The "Pep," a mid-town biker bar on West 45th Street between Sixth and Seventh Avenues in New York,

was the site where rock 'n' roll and youth culture crossed generational and social boundaries. A brief mention by Cholly Knickerbocker (Oleg Cassini) in September of 1961 in the *Journal-American* made the tiny club a mecca for society types and celebrities. Judy Garland, Noel Coward, Elsa Maxwell, Greta Garbo, and the Duke and Duchess of Bedford mingled with a young crowd, many of them New Jerseyites attracted by New York's 18-year-old drinking age. They twisted to the music of the house band, Joey Dee and the Starliters, who shortly thereafter had a number one record with *Peppermint Twist-Part I* and starred in a movie, *Hey, Let's Twist.* Extensive media coverage re-ignited the Twist dance craze and made it an international phenomenon.

—Louis Scheeder

FURTHER READING:

Carpozi, Geroge, Jr. *Let's Twist.* New York, Pyramid Books, 1962.

Dawson, Jim. *The Twist: The Story of the Song and Dance That Changed the World.* Boston and London, Faber & Faber, 1995.

Lucchese, John A. *Joey Dee and The Story of the Twist.* New York, MacFadden, 1962.

Pepsi-Cola

In the early 1890s the beverage that evolved into Pepsi-Cola originated in the North Carolina drugstore of Caleb Bradham. Patterned after other soft drinks and patent medicines of the time, the concoction was initially known as "Brad's Drink." In 1893 the name of the drink was changed to Pepsi-Cola, and a few years later the Pepsi-Cola company was formed. Like industry leader Coca-Cola,

An early six pack of 12-oz. bottles of Pepsi-Cola.

the drink was largely made of sugar and water. Combining the sugar and water with other oils and extracts unique to Pepsi gave it a "citrus" flavor and aroma. Unlike Coca-Cola, however, Pepsi did not find success quickly. Instead Pepsi struggled to challenge Coca-Cola for dominance in the nearly century-long Cola War. Through much of its history Pepsi often found itself playing the role of David to Coca-Cola's Goliath. In the early years of the twentieth century, however, it did not appear as if the beverage would be around long enough to challenge anyone.

Through a combination of poor business decisions, limited distribution, and less than insightful marketing Pepsi spent many of its early years on the fringes of the soft drink industry. By the early 1930s the company manufacturing the beverage had gone bankrupt twice, and rights to manufacture the drink were held by a man who was employed in the candy industry. Charles Guth of Loft Incorporated, attracted to Pepsi only after Coca-Cola refused to grant price concessions on the sale of Coke in his drugstores, resurrected the beverage in 1932. Guth's early fortunes with Pepsi were no better than those of his predecessors, and he was nearly forced into bankruptcy. At one point Guth sent ambassadors to Atlanta to attempt to sell the rights of Pepsi to Coca-Cola. Assuming that the drink would soon disappear of its own accord Coke officials refused to purchase the company. In the decision not to purchase Pepsi, Coke officials, to their lasting regret, allowed Guth to continue to manufacture the drink. A desperate man, Guth soon hit upon a marketing scheme that forever changed the face of the soft drink industry.

Anxious for any means to sell Pepsi, Guth was persuaded to sell the drink in used beer bottles that were 12 ounces in size. Twice the size of the normal six ounce soft drink, he marketed Pepsi at ten cents per bottle, twice the price of the six ounce beverage. Sales of the new larger Pepsi continued to lag, and the drink's future appeared dim. Then, in a move that spoke more of desperation than marketing savvy, Guth decided to sell the 12-ounce Pepsi for five cents per bottle. In Depression era America the "Twice as Much for a Nickel Too" campaign was a success. Within six months of the start of the marketing campaign, sales of Pepsi had grown tremendously and it was soon on its way to prosperity. However, due to the extralegal measures he had used to acquire Pepsi-Cola Charles Guth was forced out of the company and its future.

Despite its growing success, Pepsi manufacturers did not have the advertising capital of industry leader Coca-Cola. Therefore, they were forced to invest in nontraditional sources of advertising. Seizing the new medium of radio, the attributes of Pepsi were soon being hailed in the nation's first musical jingle. The Pepsi jingle not only spurred interest in the drink, but it also revolutionized radio advertisements. Pepsi was also sold through art shows, skywriting, and comic strips. Sales of Pepsi continued to grow until the limitations placed on the drink's ingredients were imposed during World War II.

During World War II, sales of Pepsi, while substantial, paled in comparison to those of Coca-Cola. After the conflict ended Pepsi's identification with youth, labor, and minorities as well as being seen as the "poor man's drink" limited the drink's acceptance. The identification with value that had served Pepsi well during the Depression and war years was less suited for the growing middle class who was looking for prosperity and material comforts. Accordingly Pepsi advertising began to target new American suburban markets and stress its connection to modernity and glamour. Whereas Coke was marketed as a product of nostalgia, Pepsi highlighted its appropriateness for the future. In doing so Pepsi advertising largely identified itself as a youth product.

Slogans such as "Now it's Pepsi for those who think young," and "Come Alive, You're in the Pepsi Generation," made Pepsi appealing among the youth market. Beginning in the 1960s Pepsi began to cement its reputation as the drink for the younger market. Pepsi consistently targeted young people, labeling them the "Pepsi Generation," a slogan that would go beyond advertising into popular jargon. In the 1980s social critics labeled the 18-30 generation as "Generation X" as well as the "Pepsi Generation."

Since the 1960s Pepsi has emphasized itself as the drink of the present and the future. Even though many industry observers argued that it was the taste of Pepsi that caused Coke to change its formula, Pepsi does not challenge the status of Coke. Though Pepsi has had the role of the underdog to Coca-Cola throughout the century, its existence as an alternative to Coke has helped fuel the Cola Wars to the delight of consumers.

—Jason Chambers

FURTHER READING:

Dietz, Lawrence. *Soda Pop: The History, Advertising, Art, and Memorabilia of Soft Drinks in America.* New York, Simon and Schuster, 1973.

Enrico, Roger, and Jesse Kornbluth. *The Other Guy Blinked: How Pepsi Won the Cola Wars.* New York, Bantam, 1986.

Louis, J.C., and Harvey Z. Yazijian. *The Cola Wars.* New York, Everest House, 1980.

Martin, Milward. *Twelve Full Ounces.* New York, Holt, Rinehart, and Winston, 1962.

Stoddard, Bob. *Pepsi: 100 Years.* Los Angeles, General Publishing Group, 1997.

Performance Art

Performance art became known as the distinctive art form of the 1970s, and followed the Happenings and action art of the 1960s. The concept behind performance art has been linked historically to Russian "living newspaper" groups in the 1920s. These groups performed selections of political events and breaking news in the streets, factories, clubs, and colleges. Performance art has been referred to as possessing postmodern qualities and, as such, it tends to be discussed in contrast to modernist art, such as painting and sculpture as well as modernist and avant-garde theater, for its interrogation of language, signs, and visual codes. Unlike most traditional arts and theater, the actual presence, control, and guidance of the artist who conceived the piece was central to performance art. While late-nineteenth- and early-twentieth-century modernist and avant-garde theatrical performers saw their work as part of a new movement in acting, performance artists were generally artists from non-theatrical backgrounds utilizing the act of performance to convey diverse meanings and create a new type of communication.

Though the term "performance" has been vaguely defined, the performance art piece is usually defined as existing in one time and space for the spectators who are there at the time of performance. Unlike other artists, performance artists are in direct contact with their audiences and, unlike a finished painting or sculpture, performance art is not static; it varies from circumstance to circumstance. Commonly, artists draw from a wide range of media to create their art and

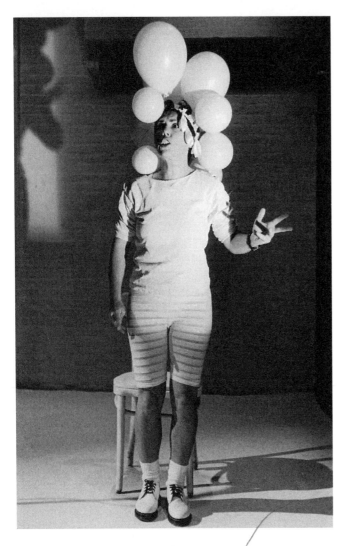

Performance artist Carmelita Tropicana.

choose meaningful durations of time and locations to perform their art. Some have suggested that the migration of artists from traditional art to performance art signaled a shunning of the hierarchical art world for its production of esoteric pieces for a wealthy clientele. But others believe that the move was, for many artists, a matter of professional necessity; a way to enter the art world in a time of diminishing opportunities in painting and sculpture. Performance art offered opportunities to more than traditional artists looking for work. Because performance art did not make creating a masterpiece the artist's ultimate goal and encouraged a blurring between disciplines, it accommodated the work of the non-expert or non-virtuoso.

Performance art has been generally associated with the technology of production and the process of art as opposed to the finished product. In performance art, the idea triumphed over the finished art product and the visual communication of ideas and actions were privileged over pictorial values. Emphasizing the importance of the role of the artist and often times the presence (body) of the artist, performance art highlights the actual production of the work.

A precursor to performance art was the work of music composer John Cage. Cage challenged the disciplinary boundaries between art and performance in the United States and Europe in the 1950s and early 1960s. Cage's work involved the concept of "silence," which he believed the traditional work of art could not convey or embody. Cage's silent pieces were meant to be scored, silent, musical performances which lasted for a specified duration of time, in which no musical instrument was played. Through these pieces, Cage attempted to convey an absence of empty space or time. His music was a compilation of the sounds in any given environment which would have been suppressed by predetermined parameters of other works of music. Cage was opposed to notions of fixity or "real" qualities with respect to art. His work attempted to deflect attention from ideas of the art "object" and focused instead on art's continual state of becoming. The introduction of the concept of silence to the work of art signified, for Cage, the dissolution of the formal integrity and authority traditionally claimed by the art object or piece of music. In addition, Cage's work included the viewer or listener in the art process. By mingling notions of art and non-art, Cage allowed the spectator a hand in the creation of the work.

The poet Vito Acconci became a performance artist when he felt art had reached a stage in which it needed to transcend its standard location on the page or museum wall. Acconci's "body art" of the early 1970s can be said to reveal the ideology behind the historical and cultural construction of the human body. In a 1971 video piece called *Waterways,* Acconci let his mouth fill with saliva until the saliva was forced to spill into his cupped hands. In another performance piece which took place in a restaurant, entitled, "Rubbing Piece" (1976), he rubbed the same spot on his arm until a sore appeared. Both of these pieces emphasized the time in which it takes the body to perform an action. Acconci also produced a short film, *Hand to Mouth* (1970), in which he put his hand in his mouth and pushed it down his throat until he choked.

In 1970, Acconci performed a piece in which he ran in place for two hours, pressed up against a painted wall, and left the wall stained with sweat and parts of his body covered in paint. Acconci explored issues of gender in his 1971 film, *Conversations.* He used a variety of tactics to try to change his body from male to female, including burning the hair off of his breasts and assuming poses in front of the camera in which his penis was strategically hidden. The failure to produce a polished image of a female body for the camera was very much the point of this film as the means in which bodies and genders are constructed and represented was made visible. In his "body art" pieces, Acconci emphasized the degree to which the body's normal functions and productions must be suppressed in order for it to be represented as a natural part of an orderly society. As such, Acconci drew attention to his culture's discomfort and anxiety about notions such as sexuality and uncleanliness.

Performance art tends to intervene in a physical or social reality and to be situational. For example, in 1977, at the Bologna Art Fair, performance artists Ulay and Marina Abramovic stood face to face on either side of the door to the Bologna museum, causing art patrons to pass through the narrow space between the artists' bodies as they entered the museum. The scene was relayed via video camera to a screen in the main gallery of the museum. The performance piece was designed to counter the definition of traditional theater, which creates a set time, place, and space, and attempts to recreate it over and over. This particular performance attempted to expose the hierarchical structure between an art product, the institution surrounding the product, and the consumer of the product.

In another performance art piece, "one year performance: 26 Sept. '81—26 Sept. '82," artist Teh-ching Hsieh lived on the streets of New York city for one entire year without going into a building for shelter. This piece illustrated the ways in which traditional modes of art interpretation are often deconstructed in performance art, as the value of the art does not reside in aesthetic characteristics but in the artist's actions. In this case, interpretation involves considering how and why an action is done. Questions of time and place are also foregrounded in Hsieh's performance piece.

Performance art of the late 1980s and 1990s has been characterized as quieter and perhaps less optimistic than the artform in its earlier stages, with a focus on issues of cultural diversity, spatial politics, and notions of all types of borders and border crossings. For example, in the 1990s in London, as a result of the collapse of a ten-year period of economic prosperity, performance art began to appear in the spatial ruins of the economic boom, taking place in empty factories, warehouses, and office buildings. Along the same lines, adverse conditions with respect to economic, political, gender, and race relations were addressed in the semi-autobiographical performance pieces of such well-known artists as Guillermo Gomez-Peña, Annie Sprinkle, Karen Finley, and Spalding Gray. Radical transformations in city spaces, film, music, video, and television in the last two decades have forced artists to create new contexts for their work: the inclusion of new cultural forms, rather than exclusion, tends to be the rule. In the face of the continued institutionalization of art and culture and prolonged funding crises for independent artists, club-style events have begun to spring up in the United Kingdom and in the United States. These events provide an affordable venue for artists, create a more informal relationship between performance artists and audience members, and incorporate new trends in music and club culture into the performance.

—Kristi M. Wilson

FURTHER READING:

Auslander, Philip. *From Acting to Performance: Essays in Modernism and Postmodernism*. London, New York, Routledge, 1997.

Battcock, Gregory, and Robert Nickas. *The Art of Performance: A Critical Anthology*. New York, E.P. Dutton, 1984.

Bronson, A., and Peggy Gale. *Performance by Artists*. Toronto, Art Metropole, 1979.

Burnham, Linda Frye, and Steve Durland, editors. *The Citizen Artist: 20 Years of Art in the Public Arena*. New York, Critical Press, 1998.

Childs, Nicky, and Jeni Walwin, editors. *A Split Second of Paradise: Live Art, Installation and Performance*. London and New York, Rivers Oram Press, 1998.

Dupuy, Jean, editor. *Collective Consciousness: Art Performances in the Seventies*. New York, Performance Arts Journal Publication, 1980.

Kaye, Nick. *Art into Theatre: Performance, Interviews and Documents*. New York, Harwood Academic, 1996.

Kostelanetz, Richard. *On Innovative Performance(s): Three Decades of Recollections of Alternative Theater*. North Carolina and New York, McFarland, 1994.

Perot, Ross (1930—)

Maverick businessman Ross Perot turned American politics upside down in 1992 when he mounted one of the most effective

Ross Perot

independent campaigns for president in American history. Although he was ultimately unsuccessful, Perot's bid threatened to derail the hopes of Republican incumbent George Bush and Democratic challenger Bill Clinton, who ultimately won the election.

Henry Ross Perot, who normally went by his middle name, Ross, was born June 27, 1930 in Texarkana, Texas. He learned his distinct world-view of self-reliance and ambition as an Eagle scout and later as a Naval officer. He married Margot Birmingham in 1956; they would eventually have five children. After several years as a computer salesman for IBM, Perot founded Electronic Data Systems Corporation (EDS) with $1,000 in 1962. Perot's shrewd dealing and ability to land lucrative government contracts made EDS a major player and Perot a billionaire in a few short years.

Long before he ever ran for elected office, Perot courted controversy several times. He was seen by some as an apologist for the Nixon administration, holding televised ''town hall meetings'' in 1969 that, according to Perot biographer Todd Mason, gave implicit support to Nixon. Nevertheless, Perot's interest in American prisoners of war in Vietnam tended to strain his relationship with Republican administrations. In 1969 he tried to deliver Christmas gifts, food, and medicine to American POWs, and in 1986 and 1987 he strongly criticized the Defense Department and the Reagan administration, accusing them of covering up information that POWs remained in Vietnam.

Perot achieved a reputation as a folk hero and a certain amount of notoriety in 1978, when two of his employees were imprisoned by Iranians who demanded that EDS design a new computer system for Iran. Perot, who made a point of hiring Vietnam veterans, recruited several talented members of his staff to rescue the pair. The tale of the rescue was told in Ken Follett's book *On Wings of Eagles* and adapted as a television movie starring Richard Crenna as Perot.

Perot gained more attention on February 20, 1992, when he announced on the *Larry King Live* talk show that he would run for president if volunteers could get him on the ballot in all 50 states. Within days his Texas offices were swamped with hundreds of thousands of phone calls from volunteers offering to help with the campaign. The following weeks and months were a flurry of activity as word of Perot's intentions spread and volunteers across the country joined the effort to get Perot on the ballot. Eventually the nationwide volunteer effort coalesced into a new political party, known as the Reform Party.

Perot's greatest edge may have been sheer luck. The political scene in 1992 was perfect for a third-party candidate to enter. Voters were fed up with what they perceived as "politics as usual" in Washington: Republicans and Democrats at each other's throats, pointing fingers and spreading blame without really solving any problems. Perot appealed to the large segment of the population who identified with neither Democrats nor Republicans and resented being forced to choose between the two.

Perot energized the segment of the population that was disgusted with politics in general. Cynical voters who had long ago given up any hope of finding a candidate who would stand up for what they believed in suddenly found someone they could believe in. Even those who disagreed with Perot's political stance—and one of the main criticisms leveled at him was that he often appeared to have no real stance—could not deny that he had a powerful personal charisma and rarely allowed himself to be bullied. In addition, many voters were leery of the influence of special-interest money in campaigns. Perot's pledge to pay his own campaign expenses greatly heartened those who feared that politicians were increasingly "for sale."

Despite such grassroots support, Perot had a difficult time being taken seriously by much of the mainstream media. With his short stature, squeaky voice, and large ears, he was rich fodder for late-night comedians and editorial cartoonists. Furthermore, Ross Perot always did and said exactly what Ross Perot thought was best, a trait that tended to both endear and infuriate his followers. In 1990, Perot biographer Todd Mason wrote these oddly prescient words, which perfectly describe the difficulty many had envisioning Perot as president: "(Perot) realizes that his low tolerance for frustration rules out politics. . . . He continues to decline invitations to run for president. He doesn't have the patience to deal with the inanities of public office. He can't compromise. He sees bureaucracy as maddeningly slow and ineffective at its best, and wrongheaded and corrupt at its worst."

As a presidential candidate, Perot had an advantage in the mercurial nature of public opinion, which was unusually difficult to predict in 1992. 1991 had been a historic year, marking the fall of communism and an enormously popular conflict in the Persian Gulf. Bush's approval ratings hovered above 90 percent for months after the war, but an economic recession hurt his approval ratings in 1992. Clinton understood this and ran on a theme summed up by his motto, "It's the economy, stupid." Perot also campaigned on an economic platform and took the bold step of validating the worst fears people had about the economy. Speaking plainly, Perot told America that everything was messed up, that the government had squandered their money, and that if the country continued on the same course things would only get worse. Perot also made a special point of bringing up

the nation's $4 trillion debt, a number so large it almost defied description, and which he insisted must be paid sooner or later.

Perot ran an unorthodox campaign, eschewing large staffs and often ignoring the advice of his experienced campaign strategists, Hamilton Jordan and Ed Rollins. Perot used television as a campaign medium in manners very unlike anything that had been done in major races of the past. He avoided paid advertisements, preferring to appear on the "free media": talk shows, morning news shows, and *Larry King Live*. The differences in his approach to campaigning, his bitter-medicine campaign speeches, and his outsider status struck a chord with many voters early in the summer. At the campaign's peak, Perot ranked ahead of Clinton and Bush in many voter polls, including a June poll which reported that 37 percent of the voting population intended to vote for Perot.

On July 16, Perot made a surprise announcement: He believed that the revitalized Democratic Party was the right choice to lead the nation. Furthermore, the close three-way race would end up throwing the election into the House of Representatives, according to Perot, so he had decided to drop out of the race entirely. The reaction of Perot's followers covered the gamut from complete shock to anger. Most felt betrayed. Supporters and critics alike wondered if Perot's entire campaign had been a rich man's game, a diversion played out with millions of pawns until he had quit when the going got rough. By October, after weeks of speculation, Perot returned to the race, claiming that he was not satisfied that Bush or Clinton were really willing to fix the severe problems with the economy. After quitting once already, Perot had an uphill battle on his hands to regain his credibility.

His biggest advertising effort came late in the campaign, when he purchased half-hour blocks of time on major networks to present his campaign "infomercials." The infomercials were charming, low-budget affairs. For the most part they featured Perot speaking in an office, using his distinctive folksy humor and illustrating economic issues with a pointer. "Let's take a little time to figure out what's happened to the engine (of the American economy)," Perot said in one characteristically homespun analogy. "Let's raise the hood and go to work." Once again Perot flew in the face of conventional political wisdom and managed to come out on top. "The ruling political wisdom was that a single 'talking head' was the most boring thing in television and would drive viewers away rather than attract them," wrote Robert D. Loevy in *The Flawed Path to the Presidency 1992*. Instead, Perot's infomercials attracted large audiences and praise from voters. The first of the presentations attracted 16 million viewers.

Unlike many politicians, Perot ignored negative campaigning almost altogether, even as he painted a drastic picture of the economy. Perot's speeches, advertisements, and infomercials often avoided attacking his opponents by name, which was another popular move. And he also made a strong impression during the presidential debates with Bush and Clinton; many observers felt he was the real winner of the first and third debates and held his own in the second.

Despite the popularity of Perot's approach, Perot was not wholeheartedly embraced. Many of his most devoted followers and volunteers felt betrayed by his quitting; they had put their lives on hold for his campaign and he had failed them by bailing out for reasons that never became quite clear. In addition, negative reports that his management style was dictatorial and autocratic, and that he maintained absolute control over his company and employees repelled some. There were also those that questioned the wisdom of his choice of running mate, retired Rear Admiral James Stockdale. The choice of Stockdale, who had been the highest ranking prisoner of war during the Vietnam conflict, was in character for Perot because of his respect for Vietnam veterans and former POWs. Nevertheless, Stockdale seemed a bit out of touch to some and tended to further turn away those whose support for Perot was wavering.

The week before the elections, Perot harmed his campaign by revealing that he had initially quit the campaign based on information he had that a Republican ''dirty tricks committee'' was planning to sabotage his daughter's wedding. Perot never offered any evidence to support this allegation, and it gave much ammunition to his detractors, who painted him as a conspiracy-theorizing, paranoid eccentric. Ultimately Perot lost the election, garnering 18.9 percent of the popular vote and no electoral votes.

Perot had energized many voters in the 1990s, but he was tapping into a larger zeitgeist that has infused American politics nearly since the country was founded. Reformers in American history such as William Jennings Bryan and ''Battling Bob'' Lafollette have ridden the wave of ''throw the bums out'' public opinion to varying degrees of success. Perot was only the latest reformer to take advantage of his outsider status. Although his campaigns have ultimately been unsuccessful, he left a strong populist legacy and a reminder to both parties that a two-party system was not the unassailable fortress many believed it to be.

His extraordinarily high poll numbers early in 1992 and 18.9 percent of the final vote, one of the highest ever for an independent candidacy, sent a clear message to Washington that voters no longer considered a third party an irrational choice. His presence and influence reminded Republicans and Democrats alike that the two-party system could not be taken for granted, and that may well be his most important political legacy.

—Paul F.P. Pogue

FURTHER READING:

Black, Gordon S., and Benjamin Black. *The Politics of American Discontent: How a New Party Can Make Democracy Work Again.* New York, John Wiley and Sons, 1994.

Follett, Ken. *On Wings of Eagles.* New York, New American Library, 1984.

Loevy, Robert D. *The Flawed Path to the Presidency 1992: Unfairness and Inequality in the Presidential Selection Process.* Albany, State University of New York Press, 1995.

Mason, Todd. *Perot: An Unauthorized Biography.* Homewood, Illinois, Dow Jones-Irwin, 1990.

Pomper, Gerald M., editor. *The Election of 1992: Reports and Interpretations.* Chatham, New Jersey, Chatham House Publishers, 1993.

Perry Mason

America's favorite crime-solving lawyer, Perry Mason, was a character created by lawyer-turned-author Erle Stanley Gardner (1890-1970). Eventually featured in over 80 popular books, Gardner's creation had a modest success in films and radio, but proved a sensation on television. Mason's first appearance came in *The Case of the Velvet Claws,* published in 1933, but it was not until subsequent volumes that Gardner allowed Mason to spend much time in court.

Raymond Burr (left) as Perry Mason in a scene from the television show of the same name.

The mixture of legalistic detail with the time honored whodunit format was a winning combination, but one which Warner Brothers failed to capture in its series of six films (1934-1937); there was also a brief radio series in 1943. Determined not to repeat Hollywood's mistakes, Gardner formed his own production company and oversaw the creation of the *Perry Mason* series, which debuted on CBS-TV in 1957 and ran until 1966.

Cold War viewers who had been exposed to the Army-McCarthy Hearings quickly warmed to this invincible knight who invariably ferreted out the enemy within. With undertones of film-noir, each episode led to a gripping conclusion of almost ritualistic predictability: Mason's courtroom theatrics and cross-examination elicited a sudden confession from the one who had committed the murder for which Mason's client was on trial. This weekly morality play made a television star out of movie villain Raymond Burr, sparked public awareness of America's legal system, and led to countless other courtroom drama series on the tube. The Burr/Mason combo proved so popular that, after starring in the *Ironside* series as the wheelchair-bound detective, the actor reprised his most famous role in *Perry Mason Returns* (1985), the first in a sequence of 90-minute made-for-television movies which ended only with Burr's death in 1993.

—Preston Neal Jones

FURTHER READING:

Collins, Max Allan, and John Javna. *The Critics' Choice: The Best of Crime and Detective TV.* New York, Harmony Books, 1988.

Hughes, Dorothy B. *Erle Stanley Gardner: The Case of the Real Perry Mason.* New York, Morrow, 1978.

Kelleher, Brian, and Diana Merrill. *The Perry Mason TV Book.* New York, St. Martin's Press, 1987.

Perry Mason

See also Burr, Raymond

Personal Watercraft

See Jet Skis

Pet Rocks

Pet Rocks were among the most popular gifts of 1975, and the name has become synonymous with ridiculous fads. Developed by Gary Dahl, a California advertising man who came up with the idea, the Pet Rock—actually rosarita beach stones that Dahl bought for one cent each and sold for two dollars wholesale—was a hit at an August 1975 San Francisco gift show. By Christmas of 1975, Dahl had sold two-and-a-half tons of Pet Rocks, or one million rocks, and had become a millionaire. The Pet Rock was packaged in a cardboard ''pet'' carrying case and came with the *Pet Rock Training Manual.* Dahl rocketed to fame, appearing on *The Tonight Show* twice. Immediately after Christmas 1975, the market for Pet Rocks dried up, and Dahl donated his remaining inventory of one hundred thousand to needy children a year later. Dahl's next attempt to sell nothing for something, the 1976 Official Sand Breeding Kit, was a flop.

—Jeff Merron

Peter, Paul, and Mary

Peter, Paul, & Mary (PP&M) came together in Greenwich Village in 1961. Noel Paul Stookey (1937—) was working as a stand-up comic when he met Mary Travers (1937—). They formed a folksinging duo, but soon they were approached by Albert Grossman, producer for the Kingston Trio. He united them with Peter Yarrow (1938—), who had played at the 1960 Newport Folk Festival. Grossman debuted PP&M at the Bitter End coffeehouse, where the magic of their beautiful harmonies and the skillful, subtle interaction

Gary Dahl, creator of the Pet Rock, rings up $2 million in sales.

Peter, Paul, and Mary

of their two guitars captivated audiences. Soon PP&M were touring across the country, bringing their positive vibes to young, hip audiences.

PP&M embraced many strains of folk music: political songs, love songs, traditional ballads, spirituals, humor, and children's songs. All these elements were featured on their first album, *Peter, Paul and Mary* (1962), which occupied the *Billboard* Top Ten for ten months. Their second album, *Moving* (1963), introduced their hit "Puff, the Magic Dragon" and the Woody Guthrie song, "This Land is Your Land." Their third album, *In the Wind* (1963), included three songs by Bob Dylan, notably "Blowin' in the Wind," and even featured a poem by Dylan on the back cover, thereby introducing their friend and inspiration to a wider audience. Their fourth production, *Peter, Paul and Mary in Concert* (1964) was a double album with plenty of original material, and included Paul's comedy routines. *A Song Will Rise* and *See What Tomorrow Brings* (both 1965) offered more of the PP&M magic, but little in the way of development at a time when the rest of the music world was in state of exciting flux. They acknowledged this on the back cover of *See What Tomorrow Brings,* noting that the "Beatles have gone folk, Bob Dylan has gone pop," but PP&M chose to stick to their roots.

With *Album* (1966) PP&M began to experiment with more instrumentation and a harder sound. Mike Bloomfield, Paul Butterfield, and Al Kooper played on some tracks. "Norman Normal," with its

electric guitar, proved to be their hardest rock song, with supercilious lyrics criticizing the "average" man, in imitation of the Beatles' "Nowhere Man." On *Album 1700* (1967) they continued to experiment with other instruments, but were more at home singing about rock rather than imitating it: "I Dig Rock and Roll Music" is a classic commentary upon the music scene, praising the Mamas and Papas, the Beatles, and other bands who were influenced by folk and in turn enriched folk music.

Their next album, *Late Again* (1968), was another fine performance but again showed little development. Perhaps running out of ideas, PP&M then recorded a collection of children's songs, with the embarrassing title *Peter, Paul and Mommy* (1969). This is easily their worst album of the 1960s. The inclusion of "Puff" and "It's Raining," both of which had appeared on earlier studio albums as well as the live album, made *Mommy* all the more regrettable. The album, however, is valuable for the inclusion of two excellent songs, the folk ballad "Leatherwing Bat" and Gilbert and Sullivan's "I Have a Song to Sing, O!" These two beautiful performances, mercifully appearing back to back, make the album worth having.

In 1970, PP&M split to pursue solo projects. Peter and Mary continued their political activism, while Paul converted to Christianity. Their solo albums tended to fall in with the wishy-washy "singer/ songwriter" trend that emerged in the early 1970s. The many charms that had made the original trio so spellbinding were gone on the solo albums. Special mention, however, should go to Paul's timeless classic "The Wedding Song (There Is Love)."

In 1978 Peter invited Paul and Mary to join him for an anti-nuclear benefit concert, and this was followed by the album *Reunion* (1978). This too lacked the quiet magic of their earlier folk tunes: there seemed to be no going back. Thereafter they produced an album every few years and appeared frequently on PBS to benefit membership drives. Highlights from the reunion period include *A Holiday Celebration* (1988), which found the trio once again drawing on traditional material, and *Lifelines* (1995), which featured an impressive gathering of the "folk family," including Pete Seeger, Judy Collins, and Richie Havens.

PP&M were often objects of ridicule for their smiley, sunshiny image. Their covers usually showed them skipping down a country lane arm-in-arm. This led even the Beatles (who also had a clean cut image in the early days) to call them "Pizza, Pooh and Magpie." Unfortunately, PP&M are often remembered by this G-rated image and dismissed as superficial family entertainment. Some wondered whether PP&M were genuine folk musicians or mere popularizers like the Kingston Trio. Folk purists found them too polished and wholesome, lacking the earthy ruggedness of Dylan or Guthrie. It should be remembered, however, that many of their lyrics dealt frankly and realistically with adult themes such as infidelity, loneliness, death, and the sorrows of growing old. Furthermore, PP&M showed their commitment to folk ideals time and again in many benefit concerts, demonstrations, and marches for civil rights and other causes.

Not least among PP&M's legacy is the recruitment of fans into other kinds of folk music, both contemporary and traditional. Besides introducing Dylan and Gordon Lightfoot, they brought Woody Guthrie, Pete Seeger, and traditional ballads to a new generation, and bridged two eras of folk music when rock was stagnant. Half the fun of spending time with the "folk family" lies in recognizing different versions of songs, sometimes with different lyrics, arrangements, or titles. Anyone well-versed in PP&M and folk-rock will experience a shock of recognition when listening to the *Anthology of American Folk Music* (1952), a collection of recordings from the 1920s and 1930s which often contain the nucleus of songs popularized in the 1960s. For many people, the winding, dusty road back to that winding, dusty anthology begins with Peter, Paul, and Mary.

—Douglas Cooke

FURTHER READING:

Ruhlmann, William. "Peter, Paul, and Mary: A Song To Sing All Over This Land." *Goldmine*. April 12, 1996, 20-50, 62-82, 142-50.

Peters, Bernadette (1948—)

Bernadette Peters is a most distinctive Broadway singer. Her voice encompasses all facets of vocal technique—she can sing with a small, pinched sound, a full-bodied belt sound, or anywhere between the two, depending on the dramatic needs of the song. She made her stage debut at age ten in a revival of *The Most Happy Fella*. Her principal Broadway roles include Dot in *Sunday in the Park with George* (1983), Emma in *Song and Dance* (1985), the Witch in *Into*

the Woods (1987), and Marsha in *The Goodbye Girl* (1993). She won a Tony Award for her performance in *Song and Dance*. Her musical film credits include *Pennies from Heaven* (1981), for which she won a Golden Globe Award, and *Annie* (1982). She provided singing voices for the animated *Beauty and the Beast 2: The Enchanted Christmas* (1997) and *Anastasia* (1997). Her tremendous talent and vocal ability have earned her the well-deserved reputation as one of the finest musical theater performers of the century.

—William A. Everett

FURTHER READING:

Gans, Andrew. "Bernadette's Back." *Playbill*. Vol. 11, No. 10, July 31, 1993, 41-43.

Zadan, Craig. *Sondheim & Company*. New York, Da Capo, 1994.

Pets

For thousands of years people have kept and cared for domesticated animals, often developing strong emotional ties with their pets and regarding them as members of the family. While once important for the services they provided—including rodent control, hunting, and guarding—pets have become even more popular as companions. Noting that relationships between people seem to be less reliable and more complicated, Veterinarian Aaron Katcher described the appeal of pets, explaining that animals offer "a much less difficult relationship." Pets have made an impact on more than just their owners, however. Stories of pets' heroism, hilarious escapades, and loyal companionship abound throughout popular media.

The dramatic heroism and unbreakable devotion of some animals is reflected in literature. In stories like *The Incredible Journey* (1961) loyal pets brave the Canadian wilderness to find their families, Wilbur wins the heart of a small farming community in *Charlotte's Web* (1952), and in *The Odyssey* only Argus, Odysseus' dog, recognizes him upon his return.

Animal stories have proven to be potent material for Hollywood movies. In 1957 *Old Yeller* broke the hearts of American movie audiences with the story of a dog who lost his own life in order to save that of a boy's. The little dog Benji used cunning intelligence to solve crimes in the 1970s. The 1980s and 1990s saw a virtual explosion of live and animated films starring pets. Hooch slobbered his way through a murder mystery with Tom Hanks in *Turner and Hooch* (1989). The true story of Balto the Siberian husky, who carried the diphtheria serum 650 miles from Nenama to Nome in 1925, became a moving animated film in 1995. And hits such as *Beethoven, 101 Dalmatians,* and *Babe* scored at the box office with stories of animal ingenuity.

Since the golden age of television pets have entertained audiences. *Lassie*, television's longest running show, kept people tuned in for seventeen years in the 1950s and 1960s while the loyal dog saved people, solved mysteries, and generally loved his owner. In lesser roles, animals have added insight and comic relief to the tensions in human life. Both Murray, who drinks out of the toilet in *Mad about You*, and Eddie, who won't stay off the furniture in *Frazier*, anger and amuse humans by exposing the triviality of common annoyances. Even Data from *Star Trek: The Next Generation* keeps Spot the cat as a companion in his quarters because the pet makes him feel more human.

In the 1970s, 1980s, and 1990s pets dominated the world of animated cartoons. In 1976, cat and bird duo Sylvester and Tweety began a long-running cartoon showcasing their antics. Comic-born Snoopy entertained audiences with fascinating stories of his imaginary world and *Garfield* comically revealed the intelligence of animals and the foibles of humans.

Even in the comics, stories of pets inspire and excite. In *For Better or Worse,* Farley saved April from drowning and then died from exhaustion; Little Orphan Annie's dog Sandy stays loyally by her side; and Huey, Calvin's real pet hamster, provides amusing comments about the young boy's adventures with his stuffed Tiger in *Calvin and Hobbs.*

Americans have been fascinated by the pets who occupy the White House. Richard Nixon talked about his dog Checkers in a speech which saved his place on the Eisenhower ticket. Barbara Bush helped the cocker spaniel Millie write a best-selling book in 1990 about what it's like to be the President's best friend. The coverage of President Clinton's decision to adopt a dog in 1997 overshadowed major news events. The White House received so many letters concerning the first pets that Hilary Rodham Clinton compiled *Dear Socks, Dear Buddy: Kids' Letters to the First Pets* to share American children's interesting questions about the Clintons' cat and dog. The presence of pets in the White House has become such a part of American life that it would be hard for many Americans to imagine a pet-less president.

The twentieth century was truly a remarkable one for pets, famous or not. Despite the fact that they can be dirty, expensive, and demanding, pets reside in nearly half of all Western European and North American homes. Many people consider their pets to be surrogate children. In 1993 alone Americans spent 17 billion dollars on food, veterinary bills, leashes, apparel, toys, and other accessories and services for their pets. The influence of pets in popular media surely encouraged many people to become pet owners and it is clear that anyone wishing to understand pet-human relationships can understand exactly what pet owners are looking for in an episode or two of *Lassie.*

—Angela O'Neal

FURTHER READING:

Comfort, David. *The First Pet History of the World.* New York, Simon and Schuster, 1994.

Fogle, Bruce. *Pets and Their People.* New York, Viking Press, 1983.

Fogle, Bruce, ed. *Interrelationships Between People and Pets.* Springfield, Illinois, Charles C. Thomas, 1981.

Katcher, Aaron Honori, and Alan M. Beck, eds. *New Perspectives on Our Lives With Companion Animals.* Philadelphia, University of Pennsylvania Press, 1983.

Rice, Berkeley. *The American Way With Pets.* Boston, Little Brown, 1968.

Petting

Though the term "petting" may seem quaintly archaic in the sexually frank latter days of the twentieth century, it reveals a lot about sexual attitudes in the earlier part of the century in which it was coined. Describing pre-intercourse sexual acts, or foreplay, the word petting manages to capture both the innocence and the euphemistic repression that we identify with the 1950s and early 1960s.

This post-World War II period, which is loosely referred to as "the fifties," was characterized by coded and metaphorical references to sex, the baseball metaphor being one of the most common. There are regional differences in the meanings of the bases, but one common definition describes first base as passionate kissing, second base as touching the (girl's) breasts, third base as touching the (girl's) genitals with the (boy's) hands, and home base as intercourse. Likewise, the definitions of necking and petting have been a subject of intense debate, especially among those engaged in the activity, but necking is generally described to be passionate physical contact occurring above the neck, while petting comprises attention to the parts of the body below the neck. Evelyn Duvall, author of a much-used sex education guide of the 1950s, *Facts of Life and Love for Teenagers,* defines petting as, "the caressing of other, more sensitive parts of the body in a crescendo of sexual stimulation." She also warns, "These forces are often very strong and insistent. Once released, they tend to press for completion."

This, then, is the true "fifties" meaning of petting, the unleashing of forces within the body that may then spiral out of control. This idea encapsulates decades of fear of sex, which has its roots, for both sexes, in the church and notions of mortal sin and—for young men—perhaps a latent fear of women as well. Almost all of the sexual metaphors of the era describe heterosexual sex where the male is the aggressor and the woman the defender. The very word petting implies a passive recipient, a "pet" receiving attention from a "petter." If the feelings aroused by petting were to get out of control, they could lead to the most feared result of all—pregnancy out of wedlock, with the attendant stigma that might bring harsh social condemnation, even ostracism, and possibly lead to suicide. That situation, too, was euphemistically couched as "getting in trouble." Sex was viewed as a dangerous force, a threat to young people, to society, to civilization itself. Since boys were largely viewed as slaves to their raging libidos, it was up to girls to control the sexual urge. Most sex education of the time revolved around the general theme expressed in the title of one popular book, *How to Say No.*

Though this was the conventional morality of the 1950s and early 1960s, it had not always been that way. F. Scott Fitzgerald had described ribald "petting parties" in the 1920s, and, in fact, conventional morality often had little to do with people's actual experience even in the 1950s. The Kinsey Report on women's sexuality, released in August of 1953, scandalized the conservative society of the time with its statistics compiled from interviews with women. Kinsey reported that 99 out of 100 of female interviewees born between 1910 and 1929 had petted by the age of 35. In the same age group, one third of the unmarried women were no longer virgins by the age of 25, and a sizable percentage of those had had several sexual partners. There was, and is, so little awareness about women's sexuality at mid-century that these figures remain surprising. Kinsey's statistics challenged the notion that women were by nature less sexual creatures than men. It was not women's nature, but the will of 1950s society that demanded sexual repression. Interestingly, many girls found they preferred the partially permitted petting to the totally forbidden intercourse for purely sexual reasons. Petting was focused on the female body and often led to orgasm for young women, while the self-involved male fumblings of early intercourse seldom did.

The social meaning of petting and other forms of introductory sexuality is explored in Obie Benz's documentary film, *Heavy Petting* (1988), which juxtaposes representations of sex in the media of the 1950s with sex education materials of the time and the reminiscences of celebrities who came of age then.

—Tina Gianoulis

FURTHER READING:

Landers, Ann. *Ann Landers Talks to Teenagers About Sex.* New Jersey, Prentice Hall, 1963.

Peterson, James R. "*Playboy's* History of the Sexual Revolution: Something Cool." (Part IV, 1950-1959). *Playboy.* Vol. 45, No. 2, February, 1998, 72.

Petty, Richard (1937—)

Known throughout the stock car-racing world as "King Richard," Richard Lee Petty compiled an extraordinary record of 200 wins in events sanctioned by the National Association of Stock Car Auto Racing (NASCAR). After 34 years of success in the sport, he retired in 1992 with a record 700 top ten finishes and an astonishing seven Winston Cup championships, based on annual point totals. Finishing in the money nearly every time he raced, Petty earned a career total of $7,757,964. He was widely sought after for commercial endorsements, and his fans voted him the year's most popular Winston Cup Series driver nine times. He also holds the distinction of being the first driver to be inducted into the National Motorsports Press Association's Hall of Fame.

In the 1967 season, Petty won ten consecutive races—another of his records unlikely to be broken—and added to his legend by coming in first in races where all the odds were stacked against him. In a race in Nashville that season, he was leading when a tire blew out, causing him to smash against the fence. He managed to drive his car to the pits, and his crew changed the tires and hammered on the sheet metal to straighten it. While Petty waited, he dropped from first place to ten laps behind, but the crew got him back on the track. "It looked awful," Petty said of the car, "but it ran." No one gave him much of a winning chance, but by the time the race was three-fourths over, he was in fifth place, and with the leaders falling out one by one, "King Richard" won the race by five laps.

Petty also won his 55th race in 1967 and replaced his father, Lee Petty, as the NASCAR driver with the most victories. Lee, a NASCAR pioneer and a three-time winner of the Winston Cup, was the first back-to-back winner of that trophy in the 1958 and 1959 seasons. Lee and Richard Petty were the first of what has become a dynasty of champion stock car race drivers that, by the late 1990s, included

Richard Petty (center)

Richard's son, Kyle, and his grandson, Adam, both young drivers with promising futures.

The period from 1964 through the 1979 season, when Petty won his seven Winston Cup Championships, was to many fans the Golden Age of stock car racing, featuring fierce competition among some of the top drivers in NASCAR history. During those 16 years, both David Pearson and Cale Yarborough were three-time Winston Cup winners. In the three remaining years Ned Jarrett, Bobby Issac, and Benny Parsons each took the trophy once. Petty ranked David Pearson "a better pure driver than I am and probably the best pure driver ever." Pearson, said Petty, "drives smart and hard and he has to be one of the best ever. I respect his record, which is the best ever." Assessing Yarborough, Richard called him a "tremendous competitor, but he runs so close to the ragged edge he'll spin cars more often than most good drivers." Yarborough said, at the mid-point of Petty's career, "The thing that sets Richard apart is his dedication to stock car racing. He's been at it a long time, he knows it as well as anyone, and he works just as hard at it today as he did ten years ago."

The Darlington Speedway, called the "granddaddy" of stock car tracks, was the scene of some bad racing luck for Petty, and it was there in 1970 that he had his most dramatic accident. Coming out of the fourth turn, he lost control of his car, which struck a concrete wall and skidded sideways into the main stretch before becoming airborne, tumbling end over end and then crashing into the pit wall in front of the main stands. Fans were hushed with horror as they saw Richard hanging unconscious, half out of his upturned car. After being rescued by pit crewmen, he was carried off on a stretcher while the crowd watched in stunned silence. When the track announcer spread the good news that he had suffered no more than a dislocated shoulder and a few cuts and bruises, the fans stood and cheered.

Petty has argued that athleticism is required in the sport of stock car racing, stating that the "race driver has to have the reflexes, eyesight, strength, and stamina of any athlete." He pointed out that "driving in tight traffic, speeding up and slowing down at just the right times, passing and being passed, there isn't a time your reflexes aren't important." Eyesight is as important for a race driver as for a baseball hitter, he says, and physical strength is needed to "wrestle a car that weighs three to four thousand pounds for three to five hours." Stamina is vital to compete at a high level for hours in a "roasting hot" car, with no breaks other than the 15 seconds or so during pit stops.

—Benjamin Griffith

FURTHER READING:

Bledsoe, Jerry. *The World's Number One, Flat-Out, All-Time Great, Stock Car Racing Book.* New York, Doubleday, 1975.

Howell, Mark D. *From Moonshine to Madison Avenue: A Cultural History of the NASCAR.* Bowling Green Ohio, Bowling Green State University Popular Press, 1997.

Libby, Bill, with Richard Petty. *"King Richard": The Richard Petty Story.* Garden City, New York, Doubleday, 1977.

Peyton Place

Few imaginary cities are as well known as Peyton Place, and perhaps only Metropolis and Gotham City can rival it for success in a

(Clockwise from left) Ryan O'Neal, Mia Farrow, and Barbara Parkins of *Peyton Place.*

variety of media. The fictitious New England village has been the setting of two novels, two motion pictures, one prime time television series, one daytime drama, and two made-for-television movies—all this from a book written by a New Hampshire homemaker with little formal education.

Grace Metalious published *Peyton Place* in 1956. It was the first novel for Metalious, who was thirty-two at the time, a homemaker with three children and a high school education. Metalious had lived in New Hampshire her entire life, and it is widely assumed that she based her novel on her experiences growing up. *Peyton Place* is set in the late 1930s and early 1940s. The primary character is Allison MacKenzie, a teenager whose mother, Constance, owns a dress store. Constance claims to be widowed but eventually it is revealed that she never married Allison's father. Other major characters in the novel are Betty Anderson, Allison's beautiful and flirtatious classmate; Rodney Harrington, a spoiled rich youth; Selena Cross, Allison's best friend, who comes from an impoverished family; and the new school principal, Michael Rossi. The novel interweaves many stories as it reveals the dirty secrets of many of the townspeople, particularly Allison's illegitimacy and Selena's rape by her stepfather, whom she murders.

Authors had explored the seamy side of small town America before, particularly John O'Hara in his *Gibbsville* stories and Henry Bellamann in *King's Row*, but the fact that Metalious was a woman and a New Englander made Peyton Place more shocking. Critics were not kind to the novel—the *New Yorker* complained that its characters lead "humorless, ungenerous lives" and the *New York Herald*

Tribune commented that "the book reads like a tabloid version of life in a small town." Nevertheless, *Peyton Place* was an enormously popular success, the third best-selling novel in 1956 and the second in 1957. By 1965 it had become the best-selling novel in U.S. history, although it was eventually surpassed by *The Godfather*, *The Exorcist*, and *To Kill a Mockingbird*. Metalious was sued in 1958 by her hometown's high school principal, who claimed she had based one of the novel's character on him; the case was settled out of court. She wrote a sequel, *Return to Peyton Place*, and several other less notable books, but died due to complications from alcoholism in 1964.

Hollywood immediately recognized the potential of Metalious's novel. The six-figure sum she received for the film rights to her book was the highest paid at the time for a first novel. *Peyton Place* the motion picture was released in 1957. Lana Turner starred as Constance MacKenzie, and her casting against type generated a great deal of publicity for the movie, which was the highest grossing film of that year. The film received nine Academy Award nominations, including Best Picture, Best Director, and Best Screenplay. Turner received a Best Actress nomination, and Diane Varsi and Hope Lange, who played Allison MacKenzie and Selena Cross, respectively, each received a nomination for Best Supporting Actress. The sequel, *Return to Peyton Place*, was released in 1961.

Peyton Place reappeared in 1964 as a television series on the American Broadcasting Company (ABC). As it was one of the first prime time soap operas, new episodes of *Peyton Place* were broadcast twice a week, and three times a week from 1965 to 1967, when the series was at the height of its popularity. The television version of *Peyton Place* is best remembered for making stars of Mia Farrow, who portrayed Allison MacKenzie, and Ryan O'Neal, who portrayed Rodney Harrington. The series was canceled in 1969, but it paved the way for subsequent prime time soaps such as *Dallas* and *Knot's Landing*. A daytime drama, *Return to Peyton Place*, ran on the National Broadcasting Network (NBC) from 1972 to 1974. In 1977 the television movie *Murder in Peyton Place* reunited most of the television series cast except Farrow and O'Neal, whose successful film careers kept them from making television appearances. The movie explained the absence of Allison and Rodney by explaining they had been killed, hence the film's title. Another television movie, *Peyton Place: The Next Generation*, also brought back many of the television show's cast members and introduced new characters as well in the hopes of inspiring a television series, but such a program never materialized.

Peyton Place has become a permanent part of American culture. The name itself has become synonymous with deceit and vice. When Jeanine C. Reilly sang in "Harper Valley P.T.A." "Well, this is just a little Peyton Place and you're all Harper Valley hypocrites" all America knew exactly what she meant. And when the Warner Brothers network launched its prime time soap *Savannah*, it seemed almost inevitable that its sluttiest character be named Peyton.

—Randall Clark

FURTHER READING:

Metalious, George and June O'Shea. *The Girl from "Peyton Place": A Biography of Grace Metalious.* New York, Dell, 1965.

Metalious, Grace. *Peyton Place.* New York, Messner, 1956.

Toth, Emily. *Inside Peyton Place: The Life of Grace Metalious.* Garden City, New York, Doubleday, 1981.

Valentino, Lou. *The Films of Lana Turner.* Secaucus, New Jersey, Citadel, 1976.

Pfeiffer, Michelle (1957—)

By 1999, Michelle Pfeiffer had been cited in People magazine as one of the "50 Most Beautiful People in the World" six times. Three-time Oscar nominee Michelle Pfeiffer has proved herself as more than just a pretty face; her physical beauty is accompanied by her dramatic versatility as an actress. Though she began her career playing "dumb blondes," she soon won the chance to captivate audiences with her ability to portray both serious and comedic characters. She has received critical acclaim for such films as *Dangerous Liaisons* (1988) and box office success playing a former Marine turned high school teacher in *Dangerous Minds* (1995), yet rarely have her critical successes also been box office ones.

Born in Santa Ana, California, in 1957 (some sources also list 1958 and 1959), Michelle Pfeiffer was the second of four children by a heating and air conditioning contractor. Never considering herself pretty, Michelle says she was often bigger than all of the other girls. Nevertheless, encouraged by a high school teacher who told her that she had some talent, Michelle studied acting. Upon graduating from

Michelle Pfeiffer

high school, she also studied court reporting at a junior college and simultaneously worked as a supermarket checker. Learning that talent scouts were often judges at beauty pageants, Michelle entered and won the "Miss Orange County" beauty pageant of 1978, and with it, an agent, who got her an episode of *Fantasy Island* and some television work. The next year she landed her first role in a TV series as a character simply known as "the Bombshell" in ABC's short-lived *Delta House* (1979), an *Animal House* derivation.

Pfeiffer won her first starring role in the feature film *Grease II*— the highly-anticipated 1982 sequel to the former box office hit. Though this film failed at the box office, Pfeiffer's performance lead to her first memorable role. As Al Pacino's drug-addicted and doomed wife, Pfeiffer generated considerable critical attention in the box office hit *Scarface* (1983). Though she later played a comedic variation on this role in *Married to the Mob* (1988), critics agree her breakthrough was in playing one of the women romanced by devilish Jack Nicholson in the 1987 hit, *The Witches of Eastwick*. Her dramatic portrayal of Madame De Tourvel, the tortured object of John Malkovich's sexual treachery in *Dangerous Liaisons* (1988), won her her first Oscar nomination as Best Supporting Actress. Her subsequent role as world-weary but sexy lounge singer Suzie Diamond in *The Fabulous Baker Boys* resulted in a second Oscar nomination in 1989, and she was acclaimed for her turn as the tormented Selena Kyle/Catwoman in *Batman Returns* (1992), for which she did her own stunts (except for the back-flips), going through some 60 copies of the Catwoman suit in the process. Pfeiffer won her third Oscar nomination—her second for Best Actress—for the little seen 1992 film, *Love Field,* a character study of a 1960s Dallas housewife who travels by bus to JFK's funeral. Pfeiffer played the part of the mysterious Countess Olenska, the woman who abandoned her philandering husband and fell in love with Daniel Day Lewis' Newland Archer, though they were forced to live a platonic relationship due to the repressive society of the times in Martin Scorsese's prestigious period piece *Age of Innocence* in 1993.

Pfeiffer produced *Dangerous Minds* through her company Via Rosa. A critical disaster, but box office hit, this film was the first on which Pfeiffer had acted as executive producer. Based on the true story of Lou Ann Johnson, an ex-Marine turned inner-city English teacher, the film cost approximately $24 million and grossed over $85 million. This was followed by her *Up Close and Personal* (1996) pairing with Robert Redford in the story of a journalist inspired by Jessica Savitch. Then she tried her hand at romantic comedy opposite George Clooney in *One Fine Day* (1996), and played the ghost of the title character in *To Gillian on Her 37th Birthday* (1996) written by her husband. *A Thousand Acres*—from Jane Smiley's Pulitzer Prize winning novel—followed in 1997, with Pfeiffer playing Rose, the angry sister struggling to expose the debilitating family secrets despite resistance from older sister Jessica Lange, and younger, Jennifer Jason Leigh. While Pfeiffer continued to act in other movies, she had further plans to produce and star in *Faithfull, Privacy, The Ice Queen, Venus to the Hoop,* and *Waltz into Darkness.*

Once married to *thirtysomething*'s Peter Horton, Pfeiffer later married writer-producer David E. Kelley (*Chicago Hope, Picket Fences, Ally McBeal*). The couple has one adopted daughter and one birth son. Since starting her family in the early 1990s, Pfeiffer has limited her roles based on time spent away from her children. She has always considered the level of nudity involved in a role, considering herself "the biggest prude in the industry," and her interest level in a role. Pfeiffer has found that "unless I really had some kind of very strong connection with the character, it wasn't worth it. If you are

playing a character that really energizes you, every day it gives you something. At the end of three or four months, when you might be fighting with the director, they may have completely rewritten the script underneath you, so many things can go wrong. . . . But if you have your character every day, it will get you through the movie. . . .'' Pfeiffer also contends that despite reviews to the contrary, she has not improved as an actress since *Grease II*, but rather the quality of material she's being offered has gotten higher. "And I think I've worked with more and more interesting people and talented people, and I sometimes think that actors are as good as the material that they get to play. I mean, you can see somebody be really shitty in something and then they can turn around and work with a really good director and have a great part and good material and they can just soar.''

—Rick Moody

FURTHER READING:

Corliss, Richard. "California Dream—Michelle Pfeiffer," *Film Comment.* Vol. 21, No. 2, 1985.

Crowther, Bruce. *Michelle Pfeiffer: A Biography.* London, R. Hale, 1994.

The Phantom of the Opera

The Phantom of the Opera (1986) is one of the most popular musicals of the late-twentieth century. Andrew Lloyd Webber's haunting musical score includes such classic musical theater songs as "Think of Me," "The Phantom of the Opera," and "Music of the Night." More than a decade after its premiere, the musical continued to play to sellout audiences in both London and New York. Similarly, numerous other productions also played to packed houses worldwide.

Perhaps Lloyd Webber's most famous work, *The Phantom of the Opera* opened at Her Majesty's Theatre in London (the edifice of which strongly resembles the Paris Opera House) in 1986. Charles Hart was the lyricist, and additional lyrics were provided by Richard Stilgoe. Lloyd Webber and Stilgoe based their libretto on Gaston Leroux's 1911 novel and cast Michael Crawford as the mysterious Phantom, Sarah Brightman as the opera singer Christine Daae, and Steve Barton as Raoul, Christine's suitor. The three singers recreated their roles when the musical opened on Broadway in 1988. Hal Prince's imaginative and impressive staging captivated audiences on both sides of the Atlantic.

The familiar tale of the disfigured, masked Phantom who lives in the lake below the Paris Opera House and is obsessed with the beautiful young soprano Christine Daae and takes her from chorus girl to diva is told in an intensely romantic and operatic style. The Phantom teaches Christine to sing and secures for her the lead role in his opera, *Don Juan Triumphant,* by terrorizing all who would stand in his way, including Raoul, Christine's true love. At the end, the Phantom kidnaps Christine and when she kisses him without being repulsed by his physical appearance, he disappears and leaves her to be with Raoul.

Among the show's most inspired songs are "Think of Me," "The Phantom of the Opera," "Angel of Music," "All I Ask of You," "The Music of the Night," "Masquerade," "Prima Donna," "Wishing You Were Somehow Here Again," and "The Point of No

FURTHER READING:

Everett, William A. "The Mega-Musical as Transcultural Phenomenon." In *The New Europe at the Crossroads,* edited by Ursula E. Beitter. Baltimore, Peter Lang, 1998.

Perry, George C. *The Complete Phantom of the Opera.* New York, H. Holt, 1991.

Richmond, Keith. *The Musicals of Andrew Lloyd Webber.* London, Virgin, 1995.

The Philadelphia Story

In George Cukor's comedy *The Philadelphia Story* (1940), socialite Tracy Lord (Katherine Hepburn) is about to marry George Kittredge (John Howard) when her first husband, C. K. Dexter Haven (Cary Grant), arrives with two reporters from a gossip magazine (James Stewart and Ruth Hussey). Tracy suddenly cannot decide whether she should marry George, Dexter, or Mike Connor (Stewart). Donald Ogden Stewart's witty, Oscar-winning script, derived from a stage play by Philip Barry, satirizes the divisions between classes and argues that people should have sympathy for the flaws of others.

—Christian L. Pyle

FURTHER READING:

Barry, Philip. *The Philadelphia Story: A Comedy in Three Acts.* New York, Coward-McCann, 1939.

Philco Television Playhouse

One of the most distinguished of the live anthology series, NBC's *Philco Television Playhouse* is best remembered for nurturing talent to create original television productions. Producer Fred Coe assembled one of television's most illustrious writing teams, including Paddy Chayefsky, Horton Foote, Tad Mosel, and Gore Vidal. When Philco debuted on October 3, 1948, the series was produced in conjunction with the Actors' Equity Association and specialized in Broadway adaptations, including *Dinner at Eight* with Peggy Wood, *Cyrano de Bergerac* starring Jose Ferrer, and *Counsellor-at-Law,* Paul Muni's TV debut. A year later, *Philco* worked with the Book-of-the-Month Club to present dramatizations of noteworthy novels, including *Sense and Sensibility* with Cloris Leachman. Beginning in the early 1950s, Coe instructed his writers to create intimate dramas for the small screen. What resulted were such acclaimed teleplays as Chayefsky's *Marty* with Rod Steiger (1953); Foote's *A Trip to Bountiful* with Lillian Gish (1955); and Vidal's *The Death of Billy the Kid* with Paul Newman (1955), all of which were later made into films. Goodyear became an alternating sponsor of Coe's *Playhouse* in 1951, and, in all, more than 350 live dramas were produced over eight seasons.

—Ron Simon

FURTHER READING:

Considine, Shaun. *Mad as Hell: The Life and Work of Paddy Chayefsky.* New York, Random House, 1994.

Michael Crawford as "The Phantom" in a scene from Andrew Lloyd Webber's *The Phantom of the Opera.*

Return." The music is decidedly operatic in style, as befits the story. Rock elements permeate much of the score, whether in a hard style as in the title number or in a gentler vein as in "All I Ask of You." Lloyd Webber recreated the atmosphere of nineteenth-century operatic Paris and made it accessible to audiences of the twentieth century.

Spectacular visual effects fill the show, as in the climatic end of the first act when the chandelier rises above the audience during the overture only to be cut down by the Phantom and plummets to the stage. Other lasting images like the grand staircase filled with chorus members and mannequins in the "Masqerade" number at the beginning of the second act and the ghostly candelabra on the Phantom's lake prove that, in *Phantom*, the visual is equal to the aural.

The Phantom of the Opera is representative of two dominant trends in the musical of the 1980s and 1990s: the sung-through musical and the mega-musical. The former type is a musical in which spoken dialogue is minimalized and generally replaced by operatic recitative (speech-singing). The second descriptor refers to a show in which sets, costumes, and special effects are as important to the dramatic narrative as are the traditional coupling of music and words. Every aspect of the work is meant to dazzle the audience.

Lloyd Webber's musical is not the only adaptation of Leroux's novel. No less than five film versions of *Phantom* have been produced. Perhaps the most famous is the first, Lon Chaney's 1925 silent classic. Other musical theater reworkings of the tale include those by Ken Hill (1984) and Mary Yeston (1990).

—William A. Everett

George Cukor (left) directing Cary Grant (right), Katharine Hepburn, and John Howard during the filming of *The Philadelphia Story*.

Krampner, Jon. *The Man in the Shadows: Fred Coe and the Golden Age of Television.* New Brunswick, Rutgers University Press, 1997.

Phillips, Irna (1905-1973)

A pioneering radio writer, Irna Phillips created arguably the first soap opera *(Painted Dreams,* 1930), then spent the next 40 years as the creative force behind everything from *Woman In White, Today's Children,* and *Road of Life* on radio to *As The World Turns* and *Another World* for television. She was among the first soap writers to focus on professional characters—doctors, nurses, and lawyers. Phillips also mentored future soap greats Agnes Nixon and Bill Bell.

—Chris Chandler

FURTHER READING:

Dunning, John. *On The Air: The Encyclopedia Of Old-Time Radio.* New York, Oxford University Press, 1998.

Phone Sex

Computerization and the deregulation of the telephone industry in the United States and Europe in the 1980s made it possible for companies to provide a variety of services, from banking and insurance to mail order shopping, over the telephone. During the 1980s the telephone rapidly became a major source of income for the sex industry. The mostly male callers to premium rate "fantasy lines" pay by credit card to engage in sexually stimulating and anonymous role playing over the telephone. Some commentators suggested that the fear of AIDS contributed to the popularity of phone sex, which in 1995 generated 45 million dollars of income through calls to "900" numbers—so called because they are normally assigned the prefix 900 in lieu of an area code—in California alone.

Opinion has been divided over whether it is the customer or the operator who is being exploited in the phone sex "relationship," but when interviewed, many operators (also known as "call-doers" or "fantasy makers") described what they do as an ordinary job. Many of the companies that provide phone sex services are run by women, and many women in the industry claim that the life is a liberating one.

It allows them to work from home or to look after children; some reported that they are glad to be able to dress the way they want or that the job frees them to work at other things. For others, phone sex is an alternative to prostitution. On the down side, Amy Flowers, who worked for four months as a phone sex operator, pointed to low pay, insecurity, and exposure to abuse as contributors to making employment in the industry a bad experience. For many of the men on the other end of the line, phone sex is an addiction. They spend thousands of dollars on credit cards and run up debts that destroy marriages and break up families.

Phone sex companies provide two basic forms of service: the prerecorded message accessed by the caller making choices through the telephone keypad; and access to live operators, who specialize in performing particular identities and fantasies. These services are advertised in pornographic magazines and sometimes through cards posted in phone booths, placing phone sex somewhere in between the unreality of the magazine and the physical risks of prostitution. Most of the ''fantasy makers'' in the United States are around 30 and describe themselves as white and middle-class. Similarly, most of the callers are middle-class, white, heterosexual males. A small number of lines cater to heterosexual women. In the late 1990s, there emerged a lucrative gay and cross-gender market.

The prerecorded message is the cheaper of the two services, sometimes generating revenue by credit-card subscription, but primarily by keeping the caller on the premium rate line for as long as possible. Although they can be seen as an audio equivalent of pornographic stories, prerecorded adult telephone messages differ significantly from written forms of pornography in that they address the caller directly and involve him in a secret, personal conversation. This illusion of privacy is achieved despite the fact that the brief messages are played continuously and can be accessed by many thousands of callers at the same time.

The illusion of involving the caller in personal contact is created still more effectively on the more expensive live fantasy lines, paid for by the premium rate call, but more importantly from the caller's credit card. Live ''fantasy makers'' can respond to the caller's requirements, adjusting their stated identity, occupation, and the story they tell as they go along. They are trained to begin the call by presenting themselves as the ideal woman, then moving on to various stereotypes, such as lesbian, coed, housewife, or virgin. Operators take pride in being able to take on whatever identity the caller demands, to the extent that African-American roles are often successfully played by European-American women, while the few male operators are able to disguise their voices enough to convince callers that they are talking to a woman. Many regard their work as a form of theater or performance art and describe themselves with titles such as ''telephone fantasy artist.'' One operator, interviewed by Kira Hall, described herself as a storyteller and claimed to have improved her work through studying the techniques of Garrison Keillor.

By adopting stereotyped identities, phone sex operators can protect themselves from much of the racist, sexist, and personal abuse directed at them by callers, but they also help to perpetuate racist, sexist, or antisocial perceptions. Kira Hall acknowledged that while European Americans are often successful in playing the role of African-American women, African-American women themselves are sometimes rejected by clients for not being ''realistic'' enough. The anonymity of the phone sex lines allows the participants on both sides to be whoever they choose to be. As a phenomenon, phone sex can be seen as a metaphor for the way identity and relationships were often defined in the 1990s. In financial terms, phone sex companies are very

successful, but Amy Flowers criticized their role in American society, suggesting that they are not selling sex so much as the fantasy of human intimacy.

—Chris Routledge

FURTHER READING:

Flowers, Amy. *The Fantasy Factory: An Insider's View of the Phone Sex Industry.* Philadelphia, University of Pennsylvania Press, 1998.

Goldstein, Harry. ''The Dial-ectic of Desire: For Women at the Other End of the Line, Some Fantasies Ring Painfully True.'' *Utne Reader.* March/April 1991, 32-33.

Hall, Kira, and Mary Bucholtz, editors. ''Lip Service on the Fantasy Lines.'' *Gender Articulated: Language and the Socially Constructed Self.* London, Routledge, 1995.

Phonograph

Thomas Edison's invention of the phonograph in 1877 opened up a world of recorded sound and created one of the great entertainment industries. The phonograph made it possible to reproduce sounds at will, and the machine eventually emerged as a critical step in the mechanization of leisure time. The first talking machine, the phonograph was an entertainment technology encased in a piece of

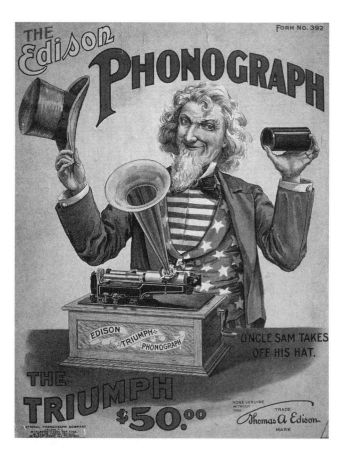

A poster advertising the Edison Triumph phonograph.

furniture; its acceptance into millions of homes made it an important forerunner for the radio and television sets that became the center of home life entertainment in the twentieth century.

The technology of sound recording was conceived as an accessory to the telephone. Alexander Graham Bell's invention was aimed primarily at businessmen, and it followed that once a message was transmitted there should be a device to make a permanent record of it. Thomas Edison was heavily involved in improving all aspects of Bell's telephone and he stumbled upon the principles of acoustic sound recording in the fall of 1877. He found that the sound vibrations of his voice were strong enough to power a stylus to cut a signal into a revolving sheet of tinfoil. Even his own laboratory staff were surprised to hear a faint reproduction of his voice when the tinfoil was rerun under the stylus.

Edison was only one of many inventors and scientists experimenting in telephony and in the years after his famous invention of 1877 several important improvements were made to his phonograph—wax cylinders were used instead of sheets of tinfoil, spring motors replaced hand powered cranks, and a disc format for the recording medium was developed. The latter was the work of the inventor Emile Berliner, who called his machine the Gramophone. Both phonographs and gramophones were based on the same technology; only the format of the record was different. Two large business organizations were founded on each format and the competition between cylinder and disc lasted until the late 1920s when Edison phased out the production of cylinders. Despite the demise of the cylinder-playing phonograph Americans continued to call their talking machines "phonographs" while Europeans called theirs "gramophones," regardless of make or format.

Acoustic sound recording technology was as yet too primitive to be adopted by businessmen; subsequently, the only commercial applications were found in entertainment. First people paid to hear their own voices and then they paid to listen to music. The demand for prerecorded cylinders and discs was so great that the manufacturers of talking machines moved into studio recording and the mass production of records. They recorded all types of popular music—patriotic band music, sentimental Irish and German ballads for immigrants, bawdy songs and the ethnic humor of vaudeville, and selections from opera and classical music.

As mass production techniques were applied to the manufacture of talking machines, more customers had to be found to maintain sales levels, so more types of music were recorded. By 1914 the manufacturers of talking machines had recorded the music of every immigrant group in the United States—including those from Asia—and had delved into the nostalgic antebellum past to recycle the music of the minstrel show, the "coon" songs that made fun of the slaves.

It was not until the 1920s that the manufacturers discovered two groups of customers who would sustain their business for much of the century: African Americans and rural folk. In 1920 the Okeh record company discovered the enormous untapped market of black urban consumers with the phenomenal sales of "Crazy Blues," sung by Mamie Smith. This began the craze for blues and jazz records in the 1920s that prompted the author F. Scott Fitzgerald to label the decade "the jazz age." In 1927 the RCA company sent Ralph Peer to the South to record local music. He recruited (among others) Jimmie Rodgers and the Carter family to sing for the recording machine and enshrined them as the pioneers of country music. During the Great Depression, when sales of records dried up, the demand for "hick discs" sold in general stores or by mail order was an important source of income for the record companies.

The introduction of radio and electronic recording in the 1920s dramatically extended the capabilities of sound recording and reproduction but did little to change the role of the phonograph in popular culture. Nearly every household in the United States had a talking machine and a collection of records in the living room as a source of entertainment. Radio initially cut into sales of phonographs but over time the two learned to coexist; radio depended on recorded sound as a primary source of programming and the phonograph companies found that radio was a good way to introduce new recordings to a national audience. The industry of recorded sound survived the Great Depression and by the 1940s recordings of swing music were selling in the millions of units.

Recorded sound defined popular music in the twentieth century and the record companies determined how it was categorized. Rock 'n' roll bridged the gap between country music for the white audience and rhythm and blues for the black in the late 1950s. The musical tastes of the baby boom generation born after the end of World War II drove the industry of recorded sound in the 1960s and 1970s, as rock 'n' roll on vinyl 45-rpm discs was gradually supplanted by art rock and psychedelic rock recorded on long playing discs.

Although generations of users had learned how to place a needle on a revolving disc and ignore the scratches and pops as it travelled along the groove, the phonograph still suffered from short playing times and lack of a recording capability. Magnetic tape recording proved to be the solution to these problems, and the introduction of the first tape cassettes in the 1960s signalled the beginning of decline for the phonograph. During the 1970s sales of the Philips compact audio cassette equalled those of phonograph records and a tape recorder became an essential part of the home entertainment center. A new form of sound recording based on digital encoding was introduced in the 1980s. The compact disc offered virtually noiseless recordings, ease of operation, and much longer recording times. Slowly, phonograph records disappeared from retail stores and the end was predicted for a technology that was now over a hundred years old. Yet many music lovers refused to throw away their phonographs, and the manufacture of needles and record players continued into the 1990s.

—Andre Millard

FURTHER READING:

Eisenberg, Evan. *Recording Angel: Music, Records and Culture.* London, Picador, 1987.

Frow, George, and Albert Self. *The Edison Cylinder Phonograph.* Sevenoaks, Kent, United Kingdom, Frow, 1978.

Koenigsberg, Allan. *The Patent History of the Phonograph.* Brooklyn, APM Press, 1990.

Millard, Andre. *America on Record: A History of Recorded Sound.* New York, Cambridge University Press, 1995.

Photoplay

The editors of *Photoplay*, Julian Johnson and James Quirk, established one of two most popular fan magazines in the early part of the twentieth century. By 1918, the editors could boast a circulation figure of 204,434. The basic format of *Photoplay* set a precedent for almost all other movie magazines that followed it. It catered largely to the public's craving for information about their favorite stars and reviews of new motion picture releases. A color picture of a movie star, drawn specially for the magazine, appeared on the cover of each issue. Such original art work distinguished *Photoplay* from other fan magazines and made the covers collectors' items.

Inside the magazine, following a few pages of advertisements and the table of contents, there appeared a section of about 10 to 15 pages of photographs of actors and actresses. The key to this layout was a proper balance between pictures and text. And the text could vary between long articles on screen personalities such as D.W. Griffith and the Gish sisters, Lillian and Dorothy, and short opinion pieces written by the editors.

Julian Johnson, the first editor appointed by James Quirk, the vice-president of the magazine from its inception in 1911 until 1917, started a column called "Close-Ups" in which he commented on the state of the moving picture world. He advanced the notion that a better educated public would lead to better films. In order to make this endeavor seem serious, Johnson and Quirk worked to convince their readers that movies were indeed an art-form. For example, when Geraldine Farrar, an opera singer of high repute, crossed over into the movies, Johnson remarked that "the triumph of active photography" was complete. "Let us never hear again the snivel that photodrama is a minor art, or not an art at all." Active photography, he believed, was "destined to raise the art standard of the world by bringing every art, every land and every interpretative genius to every man's door. Broadway will come to Borneo, and Borneo will go right back to Broadway." In fact many contributors to *Photoplay,* such as Terry Ramsaye and Burns Mantle, both respected critics, had frequently published extended pieces on the history of the film industry (Ramsaye) and critiques on movies (Mantle) illustrating that they could be considered serious fun. In a series of editorials that praised the democratic nature of movies, James Quick seemed to exemplify the spirit of a new cultural criticism.

Photoplay performed a double service by catering to the fan's appreciation of movies as entertainment and an escape and by treating the photoplay and its audience with a respect normally reserved for elite patrons of fine arts. As other periodicals appeared devoted solely to expert evaluation of film (even the terms had changed), *Photoplay* settled into a role that accentuated stars over anything else. Photo essays, for example, became the staple of the magazine's success. Fans could browse through pictures of movie stars in and out of their screen roles. Mary Pickford and Douglas Fairbanks—two megastars of the silent era—received considerable coverage on their estate in California known as Pickfair. By the 1940s, *Photoplay* provided the "pin-ups" that teenagers and young adults prized for their collections of Hollywood's stars and starlets.

A second feature that bolstered *Photoplay*'s coverage of stars was the gossip column. James Quirk reportedly hired a young woman named Adela Rogers St. John to begin a regular column that commented (and speculated) on the lives of the famous. This feature grew into an industry—a rumor mill—all its own. Generations of readers were entertained by the gossip of such notable insiders as Hedda Hopper, Sheilah Graham, Dorothy Kigallen, and one of the most powerful voices (and ears) of them all, Louella Parsons. The most valuable currency in the gossip trade was rumors of love—whether illicit, broken, triangular, or innocent. *Photoplay* readers had a chance to hear about Charlie Chaplin's marriages and divorces, Rudolph Valentino's mysterious love-life, and in another generation, the public love affairs of Lana Turner, Clark Gable, Errol Flynn, and many others.

Photoplay merged with another fan magazine—*Movie Mirror*—in 1941 and changed again in 1977 when the name became *Photoplay and TV Mirror.*

—Ray Haberski, Jr.

FURTHER READING:

Gelman, Barbara, editor. *Photoplay Treasury.* New York, Crown Publishers, Inc., 1972.

Jowett, Garth. *Film: The Democratic Art.* Boston, Little, Brown and Company, 1976.

Koszarski, Richard. *An Evening's Entertainment: The Age of the Silent Feature Picture, 1915-1928.* Berkeley, University of California Press, 1990.

Levine, Lawrence. *Highbrow/Lowbrow: The Emergence of Cultural Hierarchy in America.* Cambridge, Harvard University Press, 1988.

Physique Pictorial
See Athletic Model Guild

Picasso, Pablo (1881-1973)

Pablo Picasso's widely reported lifestyle, his wealth and womanizing, and his meticulously documented method of working are legendary; his face has become a mythic symbol of the artist for millions around the world. Likewise, his immediately recognizable paintings, readymades, sculptures, and ceramics virtually stand for modern art. Reproductions of Picasso and his works decorate everything from college dormitory walls to neck ties, coffee cups, flatware, and umbrellas. Protean, bold, a daring experimentalist, and technical master, Picasso stands as the indisputable genius of twentieth-century art.

The process that transforms artworks into commodities reaches its most dizzying heights in the case of Picasso. His paintings, etchings, pottery, sketches, indeed, anything he scribbled upon brought small fortunes even as he produced them. For those who could not afford the real thing, there existed an endless supply of reproductions and imitations long before museum bookshops began covering all variety of consumer items with his images. Art writer and novelist John Berger has written that by the early 1950s Picasso transcended the need for money because "whatever he wished to own, he could acquire by drawing it." The explanation for this incredible reality lay in the technological advances of the era's developing mass media—and the ability of the creative genius Picasso to harness them for an unprecedented experiment in self-promotion. In this, as in so much of his work, Picasso created the model that would generate endless variations. Celebrities of all sorts continue to take cues from his life. He invited expert photographer friends into his studio to capture his eccentric and expansive lifestyle. He constantly reworked stories of his creative influences and accomplishments for sympathetic writers. He painted with specially designed inks before a film crew for the popular 1955 movie *The Mystery of Picasso,* a setting tailor-made to showcase his particular artistic style. The film presents Picasso in all his glory: not meticulous or painterly, but dynamic and mercurial, as if he were a channel through which the Absolute Spirit delivered messages from on high. In fact, his story is one of his masterpieces. His biography has become the archetypal tale of modern genius, inspiring countless fictional and real-life imitations.

Born Pablo Ruiz Picasso in Málaga, Spain, Picasso was accepted into the senior course at the School of Fine Arts in Barcelona when he was 14 years old. He exhibited his works at the Els Quatre Gats gallery five years later. He moved from Barcelona to Paris in 1904 and spent the decade or so thereafter living as an impoverished émigré on the crooked streets of Montmartre, meeting interesting women and enjoying the easy camaraderie of the so-called Picasso Gang of soon-to-be-great men. In 1906 collectors Gertrude and Henri Stein and art dealer Daniel-Henry Kahnweiler began to buy Picasso's paintings. In 1919 Picasso moved forever away from his famously bohemian lodgings to a lavish apartment in one of the most fashionable quarters of Paris. Soon he was a millionaire and one of the first super-star celebrities of the modern era. He was hounded by the press, which he courted and castigated in ritual fashion. He was the subject of tell-all bestsellers written by his beautiful ex-lovers Fernande Olivier and Francoise Gilot. His family and friends made a cottage industry of his life. In the face of all this, he hid behind the curtain of his wealth, retreating to a series of fenced-off villas in the south of France. Estranged from his family and surrounded finally by more sycophants and curiosity-seekers than friends, Picasso nevertheless remained vital and prolific to the end.

It is a testament to the extraordinary power of the modern celebrity-making industry that Picasso's persona came to overshadow his art, for Picasso created unrivalled masterpieces in several of Modernism's widely diverse and rapidly changing styles. The sentimental works of the Blue and Rose periods remain popular favorites, perhaps in part because they seem to conform to reality. Later distorted figures are less immediately appealing, with their characteristic sideways noses, uneven torsos, and twisted limbs. Yet these works, inspired in part by African sculpture, effectively questioned European ways of seeing, freeing Picasso from traditional vanishing-point perspective and naturalistic figuration. After the great masterwork of that era, *Les Demoiselles d'Avignon* (1907), Picasso, together with Georges Braques, turned toward Cubism, where many angles of a figure are portrayed at once, where the constantly varying perspectives of reality constitute the actual subject of the painting. Picasso's anti-war works also represent the standard of the genre. In 1937 Picasso completed *Guernica* (1937), an enormous painting depicting in ferocious allegory the aerial bombing of a Basque town during the Spanish Civil War. *Guernica* contains many of the images that mark Picasso's body of work, including a gored and dying horse, an ominous monster bull, and the upraised arms of a powerless victim.

—John Tomasic

FURTHER READING:

Berger, John. *The Success and Failure of Picasso.* New York, Penguin, 1965.

Gilot, Francoise, and Carlton Lake. *Life with Picasso.* New York, Doubleday, 1989.

Malraux, André. *Picasso's Mask.* New York, Holt, Rinehart, and Winston, 1976.

O'Brian, Patrick. *Picasso: A Biography.* New York, Putnam, 1976.

Richardson, John. *A Life of Picasso.* Vols. 1 and 2. New York, Random House, 1991, 1996.

Rubin, William, editor. *Pablo Picasso: A Retrospective.* New York, MoMA, 1980.

Stassinopoulos, Arianna. *Picasso: Creator and Destroyer.* New York, Simon and Schuster, 1988.

Stein, Gertrude. *Picasso.* New York, Dover, 1959.

Pickford, Mary (1893-1979)

Touted as the first female movie mogul, "America's Sweetheart" Mary Pickford is best remembered for the sticky-sweet Pollyanna image she cultivated in her films of the 1910s and 1920s. The child-like innocence and eternal optimism of her star persona have become somewhat cliche, obscuring the fact that Pickford was one of the most popular international screen icons of her day. Biographer Scott Eyman contends that "she defined her era, roughly 1910-1925, as surely as Marilyn Monroe defined hers."

Born Gladys Smith in Toronto, Ontario, Canada, in 1893, she grew into one of the most powerful figures of early Hollywood. This power was secured in 1919 when she formed the independent studio United Artists with Douglas Fairbanks, Charlie Chaplin, and D. W. Griffith. Her stature was reinforced a year later when she entered into a highly celebrated marriage with Fairbanks. One of the most salient

Mary Pickford

aspects of Pickford's career is the dichotomy between naive, "Little Mary" and the liberated, sophisticated businesswoman which structured her persona. In later life, the star lamented that her public never allowed her to grow up.

Starting her career as a very little girl indeed, Pickford began acting in 1898 in an effort to help support her mother, Charlotte, and two siblings, Jack and Lottie, after her father's death. She made her broadway debut at the age of 14 in David Belasco's *The Warrens of Virginia* and signed a film contract with D. W. Griffith's Biograph Studio two years later. By 1914, Pickford had made 74 films including *In the Bishop's Carriage* (1913), *Cinderella* (1914), and *Rags* (1914). Though her name and off-screen personality were unknown to her audiences, she realized that she was one of the major reasons that her films brought in extraordinary box-office receipts and, on that basis, she continually renegotiated for higher salaries through the 1910s. Adolph Zukor, then head of Famous Players Film Company, grumbled that "it often took longer to make one of Mary's contracts than it did to make one of Mary's pictures." With Zukor, Pickford made a number of high-grossing films, including one of her best-remembered silents, *Tess of the Storm Country* (1914), which the producer later claimed saved Famous Players from bankruptcy.

Pickford's involvement in early Hollywood includes a range of contributions. In addition to being one of the first actors to recognize the economic and social power of film stardom, she achieved many technological "firsts" (albeit some of which are self-proclaimed). For example, Pickford alleged that she conceived of the film "close up" on the set of her picture *Friends* (1912) when she encouraged cameraman Billy Bitzer to move his camera in toward her face—she re-applied her make-up to further facilitate the innovation. She also helped invent the low-level (hazy) lighting which would become a staple of silent, black-and-white films. Hollywood biographer Cari Beauchamp has argued that Pickford's collaborations with screenwriter Frances Marion significantly shaped the story-telling structures which have become classical tradition and that the contribution of these women to early cinema cannot be overestimated.

In 1916, Pickford gained a great deal of creative autonomy by signing a contract with Zukor which afforded her the Pickford Film Corporation, her own production unit, and allowed her films to be distributed separately through Paramount's Artcraft. Pickford had more power to choose her film roles, and she could now contribute to the process of final cut. With her newfound agency, Pickford starred in some of her more memorable roles, including *The Poor Little Rich Girl* (1917), *Rebecca of Sunnybrook Farm* (1917), and *Stella Maris* (1918). In the latter film, she played both the wealthy, sheltered title character and a working-class, homely orphan, impressing critics with her theatrical talents and wowing audiences with her willingness to dress down for the camera.

A distribution contract with First National in 1917 increased Pickford's power even further by allowing her to produce her films. This deal, unprecedented for a female star, meant that she would choose her own scripts, develop them, and be able to exercise final cut. But it was Pickford's organization of United Artists with Fairbanks, Chaplin, and Griffith in 1919 which cemented her position in film history. These four figures considered themselves artists whose creative potential was being squashed by the studio economy. By forming an independent studio, they could engage in a hands-on approach to the development, production, distribution, and, eventually, the exhibition of their films without interference from "above." Their actions provoked the exasperated proclamation (and now infamous quotation) from the president of Metro Pictures that, "The

lunatics have taken charge of the asylum." Despite such skepticism, the founders of United Artists fared quite well for more than a decade with "Little Mary" proving to be one of the company's more capable leaders. Allene Talmey wrote in 1927 that Pickford had a great deal more business sense than her counterpart, Fairbanks, and that she deserved the title "mental arithmetic Mary."

Pollyanna (1920) was one of the star's first United Artists films. The story of an orphan who sees the bright side of every adversity, *Pollyanna* drew on the most charming and endearing qualities of Pickford's persona. Pickford, however, evidenced some disdain for the blind optimism of this character in her autobiography when she wrote, "If reincarnation should prove to be true, and I had to come back as one of my roles, I suppose some avenging fate would return me to earth as Pollyanna—the 'glad girl.'" Her childish naivete seemed particularly well-suited to audiences of her time. As support of this, her films of the 1920s consistently garnered one million dollars at the box office except for those in which she attempted more mature characters (*Rosita* in 1923 and *Dorothy Vernon of Haddon Hall* in 1924). Film critic C. A. LeJeune explained the phenomenon in 1931, remarking that the star's films were "made yesterday for today rather than today for tomorrow." In a historical period of great social upheaval related to industrialization, first-wave feminism, and World War I, Mary reassured audiences with her blend of nostalgic sentimentality and an optimistic eye toward the future. Moviegoers of the early part of the century felt strongly that she was "one of them," a regular person who understood life's difficulties and had summoned the strength to triumph over her hardships.

Pickford's 1920 marriage to Douglas Fairbanks has been celebrated as one of the first Hollywood "fairy tale" marriages. The stars had spent a great deal of time together on the Liberty Bond tour during World War I, so much so that fans were asking studios if they would marry even before they had divorced their respective spouses. At the time, Pickford was married to film star Owen Moore, though the two basically had been separated since the honeymoon. In March 1918, newspaper reports nearly led to scandal after they placed Moore at the scene of New York City's Algonquin Hotel lobby waving a gun around and threatening Fairbanks's life. Scandal was averted again somehow in the spring of 1920 when Nevada district attorneys made it public that Pickford had lied under oath about her residency status in order to obtain a divorce from Moore.

But Pickford and Fairbanks's marriage that spring was received warmly by their fans. It seemed only appropriate that "the Glad Girl" and "the Smile Guy" should come together. While the couple enjoyed an international honeymoon, swamped by massive public attention and mob hysteria, *Photoplay* issued a definitive judgement in a one-page "telegram" that read, "ALL IS FORGIVEN. PLEASE COME HOME." Eventually they did return home to an estate named Pickfair, which boasted fountains, ponds, stables, a swimming pool, a tennis court, a gymnasium, and a home movie theatre. Their estate became a favorite destination for European royalty, and they were often referred to as "American royalty" themselves. Accounts which have emerged since Pickford's death suggest that she suffered from Fairbanks's jealousy and possessiveness, but the precedent they set as Hollywood's premiere star couple is powerful nonetheless.

Pickford won an Academy Award for her performance in *Coquette* (1929), but her popularity had already begun to slip. Her attempts at adult characters found little success, and her 1928 decision to cut off the long curls which had been her signature earned scorn. For her last film, she chose *Secrets* (1933), a remake of a Gloria Swanson movie which she had initiated two years earlier. Her discontent with the project had led her to burn the 1931 print, which was one-third complete. In the version which made it to the screen, Pickford played Mary Carlton from early womanhood to retirement. Her character is forced to confront her husband's adultery and try to rebuild her marriage after the ensuing scandal. (At the time, Pickford's own marriage was headed for divorce because of Fairbanks's strayings.) Predictably, reviewers admired the star in the early part of the picture, when she played a young Mary, but they disliked her as an older woman. Pickford's last film performed decently in theatres, but it signified a disheartening denouement.

Pickford tried her hand at a producing career; however she lacked the cachet and industry intuition which had proven so beneficial for the early films she had starred in. *One Rainy Day Afternoon* (1936), *The Gay Desperado* (1936), and Douglas Sirk's *Sleep, My Love* (1948) failed to launch her as a producer. In the late 1940s, she came very close to starring as the faded silent screen actress Norma Desmond in *Sunset Blvd.* (1950). She and Chaplin sold United Artists in 1953. Sensing that her films would quickly become dated, Pickford made plans to burn all of her original prints, to which she had exclusive rights, but friend and film preservationist Matty Kemp convinced her to create a custodial space for them by forming the Mary Pickford Film Corporation, which eventually led to a retrospective of her work in 1971.

As for her personal life, the "Queen of Hollywood" married *My Best Girl* (1927) costar Charles "Buddy" Rogers in 1937 and remained his wife until her death in 1979. As her career declined, so did her optimistic outlook. In Pickford's later years, she began to be viewed as a rigid relic of the Victorian era. She became increasingly reclusive, withdrawing into Pickfair and, many say, resorting to alcohol as a salve for her poor spirits. According to her niece Gwynne Ruppe Pickford, the star came home from a Paris retrospective of her films in 1965 and announced that "she had worked hard all her life since she was five . . . and she would not get up out of bed or leave the house again, except to go to the hospital."

—Christina Lane

FURTHER READING:

Balio, Tino. *United Artists: The Company Built by the Stars.* Madison, University of Wisconsin Press, 1976.

Beauchamp, Cari. *Without Lying Down: Frances Marion and the Powerful Women of Early Hollywood.* New York, Scribner, 1997.

Carey, Gary. *Doug and Mary: A Biography of Douglas Fairbanks and Mary Pickford.* New York, E.P. Dutton, 1977.

DeCordova, Richard. *Picture Personalities: The Emergence of the Star System in Early America.* Chicago, University of Illinois Press, 1990.

Eyman, Scott. *Mary Pickford: America's Sweetheart.* New York, Donald I. Fine, 1990.

Herndon, Booten. *Mary Pickford and Douglas Fairbanks: The Most Popular Couple the World Has Ever Known.* New York, W.W. Norton & Company, 1977.

Pickford, Mary. *Sunshine and Shadow: An Autobiography.* New York, Doubleday & Company, 1956.

Talmey, Allene. *Doug and Mary and Others.* New York, Macy-Masius, 1927.

Whitfield, Eileen. *Pickford: The Woman Who Made Hollywood.* Lexington, University of Kentucky Press, 1997.

Windeler, Robert. *Sweetheart: The Story of Mary Pickford.* New York, Praeger, 1973.

The Pill

In 1968, a popular writer ranked the Pill's importance with the discovery of fire, among other things. Twenty-five years later, the Pill was still in the news, with *The Economist,* the leading British weekly, listing it as one of the seven wonders of the modern world. In the 1990s, over ten million women in the United States used oral contraceptives, "the Pill," as birth control. During the 1950s, Margaret Sanger, a nurse and feminist who championed birth control education and methods for women, played a pivotal role in finding research funding for the development of the birth control pill.

Shortly after chemist Carl Djerassi first synthesized the Pill, its widespread use helped to catalyze the "sexual revolution" of the 1960s, a time when people were exploring "free love"—sex with multiple partners, without traditional commitment. Because the Pill's accuracy rate in preventing pregnancy is almost 100 percent, it offered an opportunity, before AIDS, for people to be sexually adventurous without the fear of unplanned pregnancies. "The Pill's commercial availability in the early 1960s permitted women far greater reproductive choice, created a new set of ethical and religious questions, encouraged feminism, changed the dynamics of women's health care, and forever altered gender relations," asserted Elizabeth Siegel Watkins in *On The Pill, A Social History of Oral Contraceptives, 1950-1970.* The Pill liberated women's sexual views considerably, making them feel more in control of their bodies, as America was just coming out of the puritanical tyranny of the 1950s, when sex was still confined to the suburban, nuptial bed.

The 1960s was a landmark decade when America questioned conventional ideas about marriage, family, and sex. People continue to look on that period with nostalgia, whether they lived through it or not. The 1960s and 1970s combined student protests/the peace movement with the counterculture and oral contraceptives, to help create a climate where people felt freer about sex. Capitalism was challenged by such "new left" writers as Herbert Marcuse and William Riech, who argued that it demanded self-restraint and compulsive work, which were contrary to any liberated sexual expression. Sexuality was also becoming more political, and with the new freedom and ease that the Pill offered, relations between men and women, among other things, were starting to shift.

Introduced at a time of social reforms, such as the civil rights and gay and lesbian movements, and environmental and peace movements, the impact of the Pill is intertwined with these social changes. The social controversy surrounding the Pill stems from some critics asserting that the Pill encouraged promiscuity. Some analysts think the sexual mentality of the 1960s, which continued well after the decade, has caused devastating consequences for society. "It's woven its way into every single fabric of our society and has literally almost destroyed us," according to Dr. Joe McIlhaney, Jr., president of the National Institute for Sexual Health. In Kristine Vick's CBN report, "The Sexual Revolution Thirty Years Later," Dr. McIlhaney noted the abundance of sexually transmitted diseases (of which the Pill does not safeguard against), non-marital pregnancies, and abortions since the advent of the sexual revolution. Attitudes among the sexes were conflicted because although the Pill took the burden of unwanted pregnancy off women, it put the responsibility of contraception entirely on them. The sudden, widespread acceptance and use of the Pill caused men to often expect and assume that a woman would ''go on the pill'' when a couple began a sexual relationship. The Pill did make preventing pregnancy seem simple and easy, but it is not entirely innocuous, having various side effects ranging in severity, in addition to causing women to gamble with their hormone levels.

The Pill works by stopping ovaries from releasing an egg each month, making the mucus in the cervix thicker so it is harder for sperm to travel into it, and thinning the lining of the uterus, so it is more difficult for a fertilized egg to attach itself. It interferes with a woman's normal cycle of ovulation by creating a hormone imbalance (pills contain estrogen and progestin; progesterone blocks ovulation) that mimics pregnancy. Many women have no problems with it, but there are common, diminishing side effects—nausea, bloating, and changes in skin, are some. Although rare, there are more serious side effects, which include severe headaches, visual changes, blood clots and/or heart attacks. The Pill has been linked to cancer, in that it reduces the risk of ovarian cancer and endometrial cancer, but whether it causes breast cancer remained uncertain in the late 1990s. The Pill has changed the hormonal programming of women's bodies, has revolutionized birth control and sexual attitudes, and has continued to intrigue people at the end of the twentieth century.

—Sharon Yablon

FURTHER READING:

Djerassi, Carl. *The Pill, Pygmy Chimps, and Degas' Horse/The Remarkable Autobiography of the Award-Winning Scientist Who Synthesized the Birth Control Pill.* New York, Basic Books, 1992.

Juhn, Greg. *Understanding the Pill: A Consumer's Guide to Oral Contraceptives.* New York, Pharmaceutical Products Press, 1994.

Sigel, Roberta S. *Ambition and Accommodation: How Women View Gender Relations.* Chicago, University of Chicago Press, 1996.

Vick, Kristine. ''The Sexual Revolution Thirty Years Later.'' February 12, 1998. http://www.cbn.org/news/stories/980212b.asp. April 1998.

Watkins, Elizabeth Siegel. *On The Pill: A Social History of Oral Contraceptives.* Baltimore, Johns Hopkins University Press, 1998.

Watts, Alan. *Summer of Love: The Spirituality and Consciousness of the 1960s.* N.p., Electronic University, 1998.

Pink Floyd

Formed in London in 1965 and named for Georgia bluesmen Pink Anderson and Floyd Council, Pink Floyd performed music that marked the pinnacle of the psychedelic rock scene in the late 1960s. After the departure of drugged-out frontman Syd Barrett in 1968, bassist Roger Waters took charge and penned a string of meditations on madness and the perils of stardom that found great popular favor, including *Dark Side of the Moon* (1973) and *The Wall* (1979). Floyd's expansive, atmospheric sound, combined with over-the-top special effects, packed stadiums across America. The group disbanded in 1983 but was reformed under guitarist David Gilmour's leadership in

1987. Pink Floyd was inducted into the Rock and Roll Hall of Fame in 1996.

—David B. Welky

FURTHER READING:

Dallas, Karl. *Bricks in the Wall.* London, Baton Press, 1987.

Schaffner, Nicholas. *Saucerful of Secrets: The Pink Floyd Odyssey.* New York, Delta, 1991.

The Pin-Up

Although the ''pin-up'' gets its name from the act of display it encourages, which might apply to any mass produced and widely distributed image, the term commonly identifies a more narrow category of pictures, from glossy portraits of Hollywood stars to *Playboy*'s monthly ''centerfolds.'' With an even tighter focus, ''pin-ups'' usually designate pictures of pretty girls wearing skimpy bathing suits, exotic lingerie, or sometimes even less, in ''sexy'' images that only the most puritanical viewer would now condemn as obscene. The term's most evocative use recalls the drawn, painted, or photographed representations of idealized, all-American femininity produced in the decades surrounding World War II. While the pin-up has obvious precursors in naughty French postcards from the turn of

A pin-up of Bettie Page.

the twentieth century, and late variants like the annual *Sports Illustrated* swimsuit issue, the form is exemplified by the odd balance of eroticism, innocence, healthiness, and patriotism found in commercial images of women produced between the 1920s and 1960s.

Viewed within a large frame, the pin-up is a species of the portrait, yanked down off the walls of exclusive galleries and museums and posted in ordinary gas stations and poolhalls. Generated by the development and proliferation of inexpensive processes of photography, lithography, and color printing, the pin-up contributed to more democratic, and perhaps inevitably more vulgar, understandings of celebrity, voyeurism, consumption, and eroticism, closing the gap in taste and appreciation between classical nudes and burlesque showgirls. Early professional photographers like Nadar in France and Napoleon Sarony in New York specialized in the celebrity portrait, redefining the concept of fame through the mass production and distribution of commercial publicity stills. Although pictures of prominent theatrical performers were common by the turn of the twentieth century, the pin-up thrived as a component of the film industry, as talented photographers like Clarence Sinclair Bull, George Hurrell, Eugene Robert Richee, and Ted Allen were exclusively employed by the Hollywood studios to idealize their most precious commodities, the movie stars. Much of the residual glamour of Hollywood's golden age certainly derives from the striking black and white images these photographers produced of screen celebrities like Jean Harlow, Louise Brooks, Greta Garbo, and Joan Crawford.

Preceding the Hollywood dream factory, commercial illustrators and graphic artists such as Charles Dana Gibson and Howard Chandler Christy had already glorified the American girl in the pages of popular illustrated magazines like *Life* and *Collier's*: the cleanly etched "Gibson Girl"—first appearing in 1887—and her younger sisters helped define the modern ideal of femininity that would eventually coalesce as the jazz age's flapper. From the 1920s onward, popular magazine, calendar, and advertising artists like Antonio Vargas, Gil Elvgren, Earl Moran, Zoe Mozert, and George Petty produced hundreds of "cheesecake" images of sleek, flawless, all-American femininity marked by the "tease" of blowing skirts and sheer fabric rather than by explicit nude display. By World War II, the Vargas girl and Hollywood pin-ups like Betty Grable and Rita Hayworth came to represent not only American femininity but the very values American soldiers were defending. The erotic titillation of pin-ups was thus effectively linked to patriotic sentiment and memories of the homefront, especially through the five million prints of Grable's famous bathing-suit pose (photographed by Frank Powolny in 1943) distributed to American soldiers around the globe. As the French film critic Andre Bazin later recognized, "A wartime product created for the benefit of the American soldiers swarming to a long exile at the four corners of the world, the pin-up girl soon became an industrial product, subject to well-fixed norms and as stable in quality as peanut butter or chewing gum."

After the war, the classic, scantily clad pin-up continued to thrive until an underground tradition was brought into the mainstream in 1955 by Hugh Hefner's *Playboy* magazine, which provided an entire "Playboy philosophy" of robust, healthy heterosexuality to justify its monthly inclusion of a nude Playmate at the heart of each issue. *Playboy* redefined the pin-up by shifting the earlier period's emphasis on long legs to an all-but-exclusive fascination with large breasts. Eventually, with the appearance of pubic hair and further investigations of all the classic pin-up had (barely) concealed, *Playboy* and other "men's magazines" left little to the once-necessary erotic imagination. The concept of "tease" which had crucially defined the

voyeur's relation to earlier pin-ups now seemed rather prim. At the very least, the presumably long-standing function of the pin-up as an aid to self-arousal could no longer be denied. Finally, against the widespread competition of explicit pornography in the mainstream market by the 1970s, *Playboy* held its relatively demure ground, maintaining an airbrushed glamour ignored by the more gynecological perspectives provided in subsequent magazines like Bob Guccione's *Penthouse* and Larry Flynt's *Hustler*.

Playboy, by publishing an early nude photograph of Hollywood star Marilyn Monroe, had collapsed the distinction between "innocent" sexiness in mainstream "leg art" and a more surreptitious tradition of straightforward sexual imagery. But for specialized tastes, alternatives to the Vargas girl and Hefner's Playmates were also available. Although fetishistic photographs had been produced in Europe at an early stage in the medium's development, in the United States a mail-order market for "kinky" images only developed much later. In the late 1940s Irving Klaw and his sister Paula, the owners of Movie Star News, a New York shop that sold Hollywood movie stills, began producing their own photographs of women in fetish gear and bondage poses to satisfy the requests of their more discriminating customers. Among Klaw's models, a young woman with jet-black bangs named Betty (or Bettie) Page quickly became a customer favorite, and decades after she disappeared from sight, Page became a cult icon among comic book fans and collectors of 1950s kitsch, perhaps because she so effectively summarized the cultural contradictions of the post-war period: Page, like most pin-ups, was a pretty girl-next-door type, but she also wore stiletto heels and leather bondage gear. In retrospect, Betty Page seemed the ideal pin-up of a period that produced both the McCarthy witchhunts and the Kinsey Reports on human sexuality.

Another specialized market for pin-ups was also first addressed in Europe, where the photographs of nude boys taken by Baron Wilhelm von Gloeden in the Sicilian village of Taormina around the turn of the twentieth century circulated among homosexual collectors. In the United States, a number of studios mirroring Klaw's Movie Star News marketed their images to homosexual consumers. Because the period demanded secrecy and obfuscation, pin-ups of nude or loin-clothed young men were commonly sold to "physique" or "muscle-building" enthusiasts, but the erotic component of images produced by "beefcake" pioneers like Bruce of Los Angeles (Bruce Harry Bellas), Chicago's Kris Studios, and most notably Bob Mizer's Athletic Model Guild, through its regular catalog *Physique Pictorial,* was never very hidden. Although the pin-up has commonly been assumed to be a form depicting women for an audience of heterosexual males, the homosexual tradition of pin-ups has a lengthy history as well: in fact, one of the young artists who regularly contributed his drawings to *Physique Pictorial,* who called himself Tom of Finland, would eventually emerge as the gay Vargas, exaggerating the features of his muscular young men just as the earlier artist idealized his female figures. Recuperated and celebrated in later decades, the "physique" photographs of the post-war period, like Betty Page's bondage pictures, revise simple and nostalgic stereotypes of the era's conservative values and sexual inhibitions.

The legacy of the classic Hollywood pin-up survives in the work of contemporary celebrity photographers like Matthew Rolston, Annie Liebovitz, Bruce Weber, and Herb Ritts, whose subjects are as likely to be rock musicians or "supermodels" as movie stars. Posters of attractive women in bathing suits or underwear, from Farrah Fawcett or Madonna to the Spice Girls, have also never disappeared from adolescent bedroom walls. But the classic pin-up, save for a thriving network of nostalgic collectors, seems to have certainly succumbed to, on the one hand, feminism's largely effective redefinition of women as social subjects rather than simply sexual objects and, on the other hand, the increased availability of hard-core pornography, whose blatant meanings no longer encourage the slightly muted eroticism essential to the classic pin-up.

—Corey K. Creekmur

FURTHER READING:

Bazin, Andre. "Entomology of the Pin-Up Girl." *What is Cinema?* Vol. 2. Translated by Hugh Gray. Berkeley, University of California Press, 1971.

Fahey, David, and Linda Rich. *Masters of Starlight: Photographers in Hollywood.* New York, Ballantine Books, 1987.

Gabor, Mark. *The Pin-Up: A Modest History.* New York, Universe Books, 1972.

Hooven III, F. Valentine. *Beefcake: The Muscle Magazines of America 1950-1970.* Cologne, Taschen, 1995.

Martignette, Charles G., and Louis K. Meisel. *The Great American Pin-Up.* Cologne, Germany, Taschen, 1996.

Smilby, Francis. *Stolen Sweets: The Cover Girls of Yesteryear, Their Elegance, Charm, and Sex Appeal.* New York, Harper & Row, 1981.

Waugh, Thomas. *Hard to Imagine: Gay Male Eroticism in Photography and Film from Their Beginnings to Stonewall.* New York, Columbia University Press, 1996.

Piper, "Rowdy" Roddy (1951—)

One of professional wrestling's hottest renegades and all-time great interviews, "Rowdy" Roddy Piper has been a headliner for over 25 years. Piper, whose real name is Roderick Toombs, was born in Glasgow, Scotland, but spent most of his early years in Canada. He was a gold glove boxer who began his wrestling career at the age of 15. Piper headlined cards in California and the Pacific Northwest throughout the 1970s. While wrestling in Georgia in the early 1980s, he received national attention through exposure on Ted Turner's WTBS Superstation. In a "sport" that receives much criticism for its "authenticity" (or lack thereof), Piper has fashioned himself as one of the twentieth century's more prominent television personas.

Piper's ability to rile a crowd and "draw heat" almost cost him his life in 1982 when a fan stabbed him. His subsequent "turn" into a good guy was a classic wrestling angle. In *Wrestling to Rasslin'*, Gerald W. Morton and George M. O'Brien described the transformation: "the drama finally played itself out on television when one of his [Piper's] hired assassins, Don Muraco, suddenly attacked the commentator Gordon Solie. Seeing Solie hurt, Piper unleashed his Scottish fury on Muraco. In the week that followed, like Achilles avenging Patroklas, he slaughtered villain after villain. . . . In the arenas fans chanted his name throughout his matches." Piper's character went from lunatic villain to a classic hero: standing tall, standing alone, and standing up for right. It is the same character he would play throughout his wrestling career and in most of his film and television work.

Piper was one of the first wrestlers signed in 1984 as part of Vince McMahon's national expansion of the World Wrestling Federation (WWF), although at first Piper was brought in only as a

manager and personality. His manic style shone through in an interview segment called "Piper's Pit," where he would interview other "heel" wrestlers. Famous Piper Pits include Piper interviewing himself on a split screen, attacking Jimmy "SuperFly" Snuka with a coconut, and assailing a wrestler by shouting into the camera "just when they think they have all the answers, I change the questions." Entering the ring to a chorus of bagpipe music, Piper became the most hated wrestler with his penchant for sneak attacks, low blows, and devastating verbal put-downs.

After his feud with Snuka, Piper became new WWF champion Hulk Hogan's greatest foe. It was Piper who started the feud and the "rock 'n' wrestling connection" by smacking Captain Lou Albano over the head during a broadcast on MTV (Music Television) that featured pop singer Cindy Lauper. The feud escalated with Lauper's involvement, leading to "the brawl to settle it all" between Hogan and Piper. Rather than settle anything, this match at Madison Square Garden, broadcast live on MTV and setting a cable ratings record at the time, served as a precursor to *Wrestlemania I*. Teaming with Paul "Mr. Wonderful" Orndorff, Piper squared off in the main event against Hogan and television star Mr. T. The celebrity-laden event put wrestling back on the popular culture landscape. Piper continued the feud with Hogan, as well as with Mr. T, whom he battled in a boxing match at *Wrestlemania II*. Piper's features on NBC's *Saturday Night Main Events* demonstrated a charisma which soon caught the attention of Hollywood.

Piper left wrestling after a "retirement match" at *Wrestlemania III*. He told *TV Guide* that "I'm not just going to go out into the world and wing it, like I always have. I'd like to do some movies and TV. Not as anything in particular—just as a personality. I can always come back and fight." Piper started off strong in movies like *Body Slam* (1987), in which he played himself more or less, and in *Hell Comes to Frogtown* (1987), playing the only virile man left in the world. His biggest role, however, was in John Carpenter's *They Live* (1988). Considered a cult classic, Piper stars as Nana, a homeless man who stumbles upon an alien takeover. In Carpenter's vision yuppies and Reaganites are an alien force as they bombard citizens with subliminal messages to consume and obey. The film's cult following certainly comes from Piper's performance, which was described by *Entertainment Weekly* as "scenery chewing," and from the fight scene that Piper told television personality Joe Bob Briggs had been planned as the "longest fight scene ever." Piper also told Briggs that he ad-libbed the films most famous line: "I have come here to chew bubble gum and kick ass, and I'm all out of bubble gum." Piper continued to make film and television appearances, including shooting a pilot called *Tag Team* with fellow WWF personality Jesse "The Body" Ventura; it was about detectives who moonlight as wrestlers. He also made money in direct-to-video action films like *Terminal Rush* (1995) and *Battleground* (1996).

Like many other WWF wrestlers, Piper found himself in the middle of the steroid scandal when shipments to Piper of illegal steroids from an indicted doctor were entered into court as evidence. Piper weathered that storm and continued to work part-time with the WWF, wrestling, commentating, or playing the role of WWF commissioner while keeping a career in Hollywood. In 1996, Piper unexpectedly left the WWF and showed up in World Championship Wrestling to rekindle his feud with Hulk Hogan. During their interviews, Piper reminded Hogan that fans only "loved you because they hated me." Since coming back from his 1987 retirement Piper has been a fan favorite, but it was his two-year stint as the lead heel in the

WWF that made him a crossover celebrity. He was, true to the cliche, the man the fans loved to hate.

—Patrick Jones

FURTHER READING:

Lentz, Harris M. *Biographical Dictionary of Professional Wrestling.* Jefferson, North Carolina, McFarland & Company, 1997.

Morton, Gerald, and George M. O'Brien. *Wrestling to Rasslin': Ancient Sport to American Spectacle.* Bowling Green, Ohio, Bowling Green State University Press, 1985.

Pippen, Scottie (1965—)

Scottie Pippen has evolved into one of the greatest all-around basketball players in the National Basketball Association. Pippen's road to stardom began at the inauspicious NAIA school, University of Central Arkansas. After joining the Chicago Bulls in a 1987 trade, Pippen quickly became a starter and a major contributor to the team. Along with teammate Michael Jordan, the duo became the cornerstone for six world championship teams in the 1990s. Pippen was named one of the 50 greatest players of all time and has been a mainstay on the All-NBA team and the All-Defensive team. Pippen has had a number of lucrative endorsement deals and has appeared on many television programs, such as the popular NBC series *ER*.

—Jay Parrent

FURTHER READING:

Bjarkman, Peter C. *Sports Great Scottie Pippen.* Springfield, New Jersey, Enslow Publishing, 1996.

Graham, Judith, editor. *Current Biography Yearbook 1994.* New York, H. W. Wilson, 1994.

The Pittsburgh Steelers

The Pittsburgh Steelers are regarded as the most successful professional football franchise of the 1970s, the decade when the sport became a major spectator pastime in the United States thanks to increased live television coverage and the growing momentum of the annual Super Bowl. As millions of American fans were getting hooked on weekly football telecasts in the 1970s, the Steelers won four Super Bowl titles, becoming a sort of touchstone that represented pro football at its best. The team remained a consistent playoff contender in the 1980s and 1990s, though it has not since returned to the league-dominant status of its '70s heyday.

The Steelers were founded in July 1933 by Arthur J. Rooney, who used $2,500 he had won at the racetrack to purchase a football team. The team was known as the Pirates until 1940, when Rooney changed the name to reflect Pittsburgh's steelmaking heritage. Rooney's first obstacle was to circumvent Pennsylvania's blue laws, which did not allow professional sporting events on Sundays; he did so with several clever maneuvers, including inviting high police officials to

be his guests at the team's first game. The Steelers never won any major honors until 1972, when the team captured its first division title. Despite the team's lack of success from the 1930s until the 1970s, Rooney remained dedicated to the team and maintained a constant presence at games and other events with his ever-present cigar.

Despite its poor initial record, the team did have a number of star performers, including the running backs Johnny "Blood" McNally and Bill Dudley, and quarterback Bobby Layne. In the late 1930s, Rooney signed Colorado University star Byron "Whizzer" White for nearly $16,000, making him the highest-paid player in professional football. White played only one season for Pittsburgh. Later, in the 1960s, he was appointed by President Kennedy as a Supreme Court Justice.

The Steelers started to gain a small measure of respectability in the 1950s and 1960s, but the team's turnaround really began in 1969 with the arrival of Chuck Noll as head coach. Noll began his career as a defensive assistant and then coached the Baltimore Colts from 1966 to 1968. At the same time, Dan Rooney, Arthur's eldest son, began to assume greater control over the team. Noll and Rooney proceeded to assemble a group of outstanding players including defensive tackle Joe Greene, quarterback Terry Bradshaw, running back Franco Harris, and wide receivers Lynn Swann and John Stallworth. The hallmark of the Steelers' success in the 1970s was its defense, which earned the nicknamed "Steel Curtain" for its ability to prevent opposing offenses from gaining yardage.

The team's turnaround after Noll's arrival was gradual, as the Steelers won only one game during his first season. However, by 1972, they went 11-3 and won their first divisional title. The team reached its first Super Bowl in 1975, beating the Minnesota Vikings by a score of 16-6. Running back Franco Harris, rushing for a then-Super Bowl record 158 yards on 34 carries, was named Most Valuable Player. The following year, the Steelers returned to the Super Bowl and defeated the Dallas Cowboys 21-17, with wide receiver Lynn Swann earning MVP honors.

In 1978 the Steelers once again beat Dallas in the championship game, 35-31, and returned to defeat Los Angeles 31-19 in the 1979 Super Bowl, becoming the first team ever to win back-to-back Super Bowls on two separate occasions. Quarterback Terry Bradshaw was the MVP in both games, setting records for most career touchdowns (9) and passing yards (932) in the Super Bowl. These honors were a vindication of sorts for Bradshaw, who had initially struggled under high expectations after coming to the team as the first player selected in the 1970 draft. Bradshaw, who came from a rural background and played for an unheralded program at Louisiana State University, suffered from a lack of support and had to endure fans and commentators who habitually questioned his intelligence.

In 1980, however, the Steelers' dominance came to an end when the team suffered a devastating array of injuries and missed the playoffs for the first time since 1972. Gradually, many of the team's stalwarts of the 1970s retired over the next few years. Noll retired as coach after the 1991 season, having served one of the longest head coaching tenures in league history. Bill Cowher succeeded Noll as coach, and the Steelers once again became a perennial playoff team. Under Cowher, the team reached Super Bowl XXX in 1996, only to lose to Dallas 27-17 in its first trip to the championship game since 1979. With its four Super Bowl victories, Pittsburgh ranks second overall only to Dallas and San Francisco, each of which has won five times.

—Jason George

"Mean" Joe Greene (No.75) of the Pittsburgh Steelers takes aim at Dallas Cowboy's running back Walt Garrison (No.32).

FURTHER READING:

Didinger, Ray. *Pittsburgh Steelers.* New York, MacMillan, 1974.

Sahadi, Lou. *Super Steelers: The Making of a Dynasty.* New York, Times Books, 1980.

"Team Histories: Pittsburgh Steelers." http://www.profootballhof.com/ histories/steelers.html. April 1999.

Pizza

Pizza is a popular dish in America that consists of a baked crust, typically between twelve and twenty inches in diameter, topped with a combination of tomato sauce, vegetables, meats, and melted cheese.

Originally an open-face tomato pie, pizza had long been a simple, cheap, and popular "workingman's food" in Italy. Although the dish had been baked since ancient times, the term "pizza" (meaning, "to pluck") started appearing in Italian dictionaries in the 1850s. The quintessential pizza is said to have been created by a baker, Raffaele Esposito of Naples, for the 1889 visit of the reigning king and queen of Italy. Inspired by patriotism, Esposito incorporated Italy's national colors into his creation—tomatoes for red, mozzarella cheese for white, and basil for green—establishing what would become the basic ingredients for the pizza. At the turn of the century Italian immigrants brought pizza to the United States, and Gennaro (or, Giovanni, depending on the account) Lombardi opened the first pizzeria in 1905 in New York City's Little Italy. Very rapidly, other Italians (many trained by Lombardi) opened their own shops, baking their pizzas in coal- or wood-burning brick ovens.

By the 1930s and 1940s, people running small local shops were making and selling pizzas in towns all across the country, enabled in part by new gas-heated ovens that made the baking safer, more efficient, and more reliable. Despite the improvements in technology, the real accelerator in making pizza a national fad came with the return of soldiers after World War II, who had developed a taste for the pizza of Naples. As a food of relative simplicity, pizza allowed for many ethnic and regional variations, making it a foodstuff readily able to please most Americans. Traditional Italian pizzas were round and had thin crusts, while Sicilian versions were square with thick, chewy crusts. Chicago was known for its "deep dish" style, while the midwest in general preferred pizza pies with thin crusts and spicy sauce, and the northeast opted for thick-crusted pizzas with a lot of sauce, extra cheese, and less meat. New Haven was known for its clam pie; California, for its thin crusts, gourmet toppings, and unusual combinations.

While some pizzerias were sit-down restaurants that served other Italian cuisine, the most successful businesses, founded in the later decades of the twentieth century, specialized in take-out and delivery service, making pizza a very mobile food that suited Americans' growing preference for home delivery of convenience meals. Delivery service combined this convenience and the desire for choice: people could call up a nearby pizza shop, place an order selecting as many "pies" with as many different toppings as they liked, and have the food delivered to their door within the hour.

As such, pizza enjoyed a reputation for being a casual food meant for informal occasions, and, indeed, defined these occasions as such. People commonly ate the slices of pizza with their hands, right out of the boxes they were delivered in, foregoing plates and eating utensils. Popular with all age groups and ethnicities, pizzas were commonly associated with children and teenagers, becoming familiar staples at parties and other casual gatherings in college dorm rooms and private homes, around the television and especially during media events like the Super Bowl. Specific occasions, called "pizza parties," were even organized around the food.

The love that Americans shared for pizza gave rise to many successful national chains. Shakey's, the first pizza franchise, began in 1954 in Sacramento. Pizzeria Uno, an Italian restaurant specializing in deep dish Chicago-style pizzas, was first opened in 1943 and had over 110 outlets nationally by the late 1990s. Pizza Hut, a pizza restaurant founded in 1958, grew to more than 10,000 businesses nationally by 1996. Domino's, offering delivery-only service (and promising their pizzas would reach one's doorstep within 30 minutes or the pizza was free), was started in 1960 and enjoyed sales of $2 billion at the end of 1986.

The growth of Americans' taste for pizza also sparked the development of frozen pizzas one could cook oneself. Rose and Jim Totino began one of the most successful of the frozen pizza enterprises in 1962; Totino's was quickly joined by other brands such as Red Baron, Celeste Pizza-For-One, and Stouffer's. In addition, other make-at-home pizza products were successful, including Ragu pizza sauce in a jar, Boboli ready-made pizza crust, and Robin Hood pizza dough mix.

In 1996, Americans ate 100 acres of pizza daily, or 350 slices per second, making it a $30 billion dollar industry. In that same year, 17 percent of all restaurants were pizzerias, many characterized by familiar red and white checkered tablecloths. The overwhelming popularity of pizza in America was mainly due to its convenience, versatility, and its association with pleasure, communal eating, and informality. In cities and suburbs, it was easy to grab a slice for lunch if one's time was limited. It could be made with an almost endless combination of ingredients on which the consumer decided (in the late 1990s pepperoni was the most preferred topping next to cheese), with thick, thin, or stuffed crusts. It could be delivered to one's home and eaten in front of the television set, or, it could be consumed in a restaurant. It could also be the product of a national chain operation or from a local "mom and pop" establishment.

The later decades saw such a proliferation of pizza that anything topped with tomato sauce and cheese was called "pizza," including pizza bagels, pizza English muffins, pizza french fries, and pizza

burgers. Many snack foods, such as tortilla chips and snack crackers, also came in "pizza flavored" varieties.

—Wendy Woloson

FURTHER READING:

Asimov, Eric. "New York Pizza, the Real Thing, Makes a Comeback." *New York Times.* 10 June 1998.

Gabaccia, Donna R. *We Are What We Eat: Ethnic Food and the Making of Americans.* Cambridge, Harvard University Press, 1998.

Gay, Kathlyn, and Martin K. Gay. *Encyclopedia of North American Eating and Drinking Traditions, Customs, and Rituals.* Santa Barbara, ABC-CLIO, 1996.

Hanson, Gayles M.B. "Square, Stuffed, Thin, Frozen, Americans Just Adore Pizza." *Insight on the News.* Vol. 12, No. 25, 42.

A Place in the Sun

George Stevens won an Oscar for directing this 1951 adaptation of Theodore Dreiser's novel *An American Tragedy,* de-emphasizing Dreiser's focus on class and social justice and bringing the romantic angle to the story's center. Montgomery Clift stars as a small-town factory foreman who cannot bring himself to break off a love affair with the equally poor Shelley Winters even after falling in love with the wealthy Elizabeth Taylor. When Winters becomes pregnant, Clift contemplates murder, and she in fact drowns when they go for a canoe ride. The naturalistic Clift delivered a sympathetic performance, and his love scenes with Taylor (in one of her first adult roles) were passionate. Winters proved a formidable opponent, as Clift's passive-aggressive ex-lover. *A Place in the Sun* was both a critical and box-office hit; Charles Chaplin considered it the best movie in Hollywood history. It was the second film based on *An American Tragedy,* a novel Dreiser in turn based upon a 1906 murder case in upstate New York.

—Andrew Milner

FURTHER READING:

Brandon, Craig. *Murder in the Adirondacks: An American Tragedy Revisited.* Utica, New York, North Country Books, 1986.

Laguardia, Robert. *Monty: A Biography of Montgomery Clift.* New York, Arbor House, 1977.

Peary, Danny. *Guide for the Film Fanatic.* New York, Fireside, 1986.

Planet of the Apes

Planet of the Apes, directed by Franklin Schaffner and released in 1968, was almost singlehandedly responsible for elevating cinema's science fiction genre from traditional "B" movie budgets into the lavish and expensive blockbuster art form.

Schaffner's *Planet of the Apes,* based on Pierre Boulle's novel *La Panete des Singes* (1963), portrayed misanthropic George Taylor (Charlton Heston) and his fellow astronauts' deep-space mission to find other forms of life. These voyagers program the ship's computers

Charlton Heston under contol of the Apes in a scene from the film *Planet of the Apes*.

to wake them from their hibernation some 2,000 years in the future, when they expect to be light-years from Earth but in the same physical state due to the effects of travelling at the speed of light. Upon awakening, the crew guides their spaceship to a remote planet, barren and seemingly devoid of life. Soon, though, the astronauts encounter a race of reasoning and talking apes that hold court over a complex aristocratic ape civilization. They also discover a rogue group of primate-like humans, against whom the apes make war. Upon discovering Taylor, the ape leader Dr. Zaius (Maurice Evans) reacts in horror and demands his death. The apes Cornelius (Roddy McDowell) and Zira (Kim Hunter) risk their lives to protect Taylor; in the process, they uncover the damning secret of the planet's history.

Previous science fiction films such as *The Man From Planet X* (1951) and *The Day the Earth Stood Still* (1951) had been big box-office hits despite their shoddy low-budget depictions of futuristic worlds and beings. *Planet of the Apes,* with its expensive makeup and costumes, demonstrated the economic viability of big-budget science fiction fare to Hollywood studios. The following three decades were characterized by a host of similar blockbuster futuristic productions. By the late 1990s, the big-budget science fiction film had become one of the most popular styles of filmmaking and also one of the surest returns on studio investment.

Planet of the Apes became such a cultural phenomenon that it spawned four sequels—*Beneath the Planet of the Apes* (1970), *Escape from the Planet of the Apes* (1971), *Conquest of the Planet of the Apes* (1972), and *Battle for the Planet of the Apes* (1973)—as well as a live action (1974) and an animated (1974-1975) television series.

In addition, the film occasioned its own merchandising line, as children of the 1970s could purchase *Planet of the Apes* action figures and lunch boxes. The film's cultural resonance continued into the 1980s and 1990s. Greenpeace, for instance, seized upon the film's image of Taylor kneeling before the fallen Statue of Liberty as the basis for a series of antinuclear posters. White supremacists have embraced *Planet of the Apes* as well, reading the film's ape dominance as a coded warning against increased racial tolerance.

As of late 1998, Twentieth Century Fox was considering another *Apes*-related production to capitalize on the film's continued cultural appeal and also to honor its contributions to science fiction filmmaking by treating it in the context of elaborate production costs and special effects, both of which the film made possible.

—Scott Tribble

FURTHER READING:

Greene, Eric. *Planet of the Apes as American Myth: Race and Politics in the Films and Television Series.* Jefferson, McFarland & Company, 1996.

Kim, Erwin. *Franklin Schaffner.* Metuchen, Scarecrow Press, 1985.

Pohl, Frederick and Frederick Pohl IV. *Science Fiction: Studies in Film.* New York, Ace Books, 1981.

Plastic

Plastic (from the Greek *plassein,* meaning to mold or shape a soft substance) was originally invented as a substitute for natural resources; by the end of the twentieth century, however, it had become a material in its own right, no longer simulating organic substances, but instead being used to create entirely new products, everything from tableware to car bodies to artificial hearts. More than any other material, plastic changed life in twentieth-century America even as it came to symbolize a particularly artificial and superficial culture concerned more with appearances than substance, more with imitation than reality. In the popular vernacular, ''plastic'' took on a pejorative connotation early on, to mean false or fake or disingenuous. Early Hollywood starlets were called ''celluloid women''; in 1962, Ken Kesey used the phrase ''her fixed plastic smile'' in his writing. In an ironic statement on the condition of the culture, a character in the movie *The Graduate* confided these words of encouragement to Dustin Hoffman's character: ''I just want to say one word to you, Ben. Just one word. Plastics.'' Proof that the material was durable enough to withstand the cybernetic age came when a commencement speaker declared to a 1999 graduating class at a major American university: ''. . . Just one word. Plastics.com.''

The first plastic-like material, celluloid (a derivative of cellulose), was invented in 1869 by John Wesley Hyatt, a man in search of a substitute for the ivory used in billiard balls. While celluloid was never successfully put to this recreational purpose, it did become a viable replacement for coral, marble, bone, and ivory and was used to make things such as piano keys, collars, cuffs, novelties, combs, and brushes. Celluloid democratized a host of consumer goods by making once-expensive goods out of a cheaper but equally functional substitute for those rare materials. In addition, it reflected the growing desire and willingness of people to harness the products of nature and

"Plastics for Living," a display by B.F. Goodrich, at the 9th National Plastics Exposition at the New York Coliseum.

control them for their own interests, expressed most often in the burgeoning industrial ethic.

Celluloid found many applications beyond domestic ones: in the 1920s, it was used as transparent sheeting in automobiles for rear windows and windshields. Cellulose acetate, a nonflammable version of celluloid, could be shaped through injection molding into a variety of objects, from adding machine keys and knife handles to bobbins and eyeglass frames. The use of celluloid that affected American culture the most—and on a grand scale—was its application in the photograph and movie industries. George Eastman revolutionized photography by improving upon a gelatin-coated flexible celluloid film in 1889, which enabled photographers to snap pictures without the encumbrance of a large apparatus and dark room. So popular was this new portable photographic technique that at the turn of the century, about 40,000 tons of the film were sold each year. Thomas Edison ordered film from Eastman to use in his Kinetoscope, and opened up the first "peep" shows in American cities in 1894. Adapted from projection techniques invented in France, Edison's films democratized image-making. Celluloid moving pictures took the power of cultural reproduction away from the academy, and took its products out of museums, exposing them to masses of people. As historian Stephen Fenichell pointed out, "celluloid film succeeded in raising the first plastic's cultural profile from a medium of mere mimicry into a priceless repository of human memory."

Derived from cellulose, celluloid had its roots in nature. Bakelite, in contrast, was the first chemically synthetic plastic; it was invented in 1907 by Leo H. Baekland, later dubbed "the father of plastics."

Known as "the material of a thousand uses," Bakelite was marketed not as a substitute for natural materials, but as an innovative material in its own right. A major advantage of Bakelite over hard rubber and other materials was its ability to conform to the exact details of a mold. It found ready applications in the power industry as electrical insulators, but its formation into pipe stems, billiard balls, buttons, knife handles, radios, telephones, cigarette holders, jewelry, pens, and even airplane propellers indicated the degree to which Americans were willing to accept wholly new materials on their own terms, rather than as nature's substitutes. Indeed, Bakelite was *the* material of the Art Deco 1920s. Industrial designer Henry Dreyfuss used the plastic in his redesign of the Bell telephone, creating its quintessential shape by combining the ear and mouthpiece into a single handset, giving the entire object a streamlined silhouette. Raymond Loewy improved on the design of a mimeograph machine in 1929 by adding a Bakelite shell that concealed its inner workings, coming up with an artful yet utilitarian object for the office. Walter Dorwin Teague used brown Bakelite in 1934 for the body of the "Baby Brownie" camera he designed for Kodak; it was so popular that four million of them were sold in the first year—in the depths of the Depression.

The success of Bakelite and the subsequent popularity of other types of plastic—many of which were much more colorful and versatile than celluloid and Bakelite—moved America from the Machine Age into the Plastic Age. The word "plastic" became a household word between the world wars, and came to be a popularly understood symbol of modernity. As with all new things, however, the increasing intrusion of plastic items into people's lives was met with widespread ambivalence. It at once enabled people to escape the forces and often limited resources of nature and threatened an abrupt disjunction with past materials and manufacturing processes. During the 1920s and 1930s, the world of plastic was a hopeful and stable one, bright and unthreatened by rust and decay. By the late 1930s and 1940s, conservative utopians looked upon plastic as a substance that promised social stability by replacing scarcity with abundance and enabling many more people to own consumer goods. By the 1960s and 1970s, environmentalists were worried about the glut of plastic materials, especially throwaway food containers, disposable diapers, and plastic bags that were clogging landfills and littering the landscape.

Social utopianism, in part, led to the popularity of plastic products like cellophane, a French invention that DuPont purchased the rights to in the 1920s. The first American products wrapped in cellophane, Whitman's chocolates, were soon followed by cigarette packs, which promised to be fresh if wrapped in sheets of this crisp, clear plastic. During the rest of the decade, everything seemed to be wrapped in cellophane—from sheets and towels to tires and pianos. It offered a new sensibility based on ideas of cleanliness and sterility: people wanted to see the products they were buying, but also wanted to be assured of their purity and freshness. Lucite and Plexiglas, more substantial forms of clear plastic which also tapped into this popular ethos, both entered the market in 1937. Cellophane also made things glamorous, immediately conferring a kind of sparkle and sex appeal to the most mundane objects. Cole Porter's 1934 song "You're the Top" exclaimed, "You're the purple light of a summer night in Spain/You're the National Gallery/You're Garbo's salary/ You're cellophane!" The thin plastic film also had practical uses besides heightening the fetishized aspects of consumer goods. In 1930, Richard Drew, an engineer at 3M (then the Minnesota Mining and Manufacturing Company), devised a way to coat cellophane with pressure-sensitive adhesive, coming up with "Scotch" tape, an enduring modern convenience. Cellophane was also used as the lens for gas masks in World War II, and served as an ideal semipermeable membrane for dialysis machines. In a 1940 poll, the most beautiful words in English were identified as "mother," "memory," and "cellophane."

Rayon, or viscose, also a cellulose derivative, was a fabric made out of cellulose fibers, which gave it an attractive sheen and silk-like luster. Elsa Schiaparelli, an avant-garde designer, incorporated this prosaic material into her fashions, immediately democratizing luxury with her drapey, form-fitting outfits. The sales of rayon underwear increased fivefold between 1925 and 1928, and by the mid-1930s, about 85 percent of all American dresses had rayon content, thus moving synthetics into the realm formerly monopolized by such organic materials as cotton, wool, silk, and linen. People were now willing to put plastics intimately close to their bodies ("wrap themselves in plastic," as an acidulous Ralph Nader would sneer in the 1970s).

Polyvinyl chloride (also known as PVC and more commonly called vinyl), was developed into a workable material in 1926 by Waldo Semon. He found that it was water-resistant and fireproof and that it could be molded and extruded into any number of forms. Semon put his new invention toward making things like shower curtains, raincoats, ship's upholstery, and color-coded electrical wires. A related synthetic, polyethylene, was used to coat coaxial cable, an innovation that enabled high-speed telecommunications and revolutionized the methods by which people communicated with one another.

Nylon, which had been primarily used for toothbrush bristles before World War II, was one of plastic's best success stories. Silk was expensive and not durable enough for wartime needs. In addition, most silk imports were coming from Japan, an unreliable supplier by the late 1930s. Invented by DuPont chemist Wallace Carothers, nylon was the first truly artificial fiber that could be woven. Even though nylon stockings (generally called "nylons") were more expensive than their silk precursors, women bought them en masse in the hope that they were more durable (they were, but only slightly); women also loved the sheerness of nylons, a welcome change from the opacity of silk stockings. Like the cellophane sheaths that enhanced and glamorized the products they wrapped, nylons functioned similarly for the women who wore them: they were seen as naughty but sexy. May 15, 1940, known as "N-day," marked the beginning of national sales of nylon stockings. They proved so popular that all five million pairs had been sold by the day's end.

During World War II, plastics reverted to their original purposes as replacements for scarce natural materials, and nylon was no exception. It was made into glider towropes, parachutes, and cords for synthetic rubber tires, among other things. As a result, women had to give up their beloved nylons and often sported the "bare-legged" look to signify their patriotism, often painting a line down the backs of their legs to simulate the otherwise absent stocking seam, so even in its absence, nylon was very much a cultural presence. Other plastics that figured into the war effort included Naugahyde, a form of vinyl, used to upholster military vehicles and furniture; bubbled windshields of Plexiglas that replaced glass in cockpits, allowing pilots to survey their surroundings without visual interference; phenolic resin, a relative of Bakelite, which substituted for steel as a viable helmet liner; and Teflon, whose durability and slipperiness made it ideal for coating the valves and gaskets used in uranium processing and testing at the Manhattan Project. The success of plastic during the war convinced the American public of its worth and value—people could trust it because it had helped the Allied cause win the war. As

Fenichell stated, "If before the war plastic's image had been defined by frivolity, trumpery, and above all, a sleazy pretense at luxury, by the time Teflon was enlisted in the atomic bomb effort, plastic materials had matured under fire."

By the late 1940s, plastic, however artificial, was firmly rooted in the material life of all Americans, especially in the domestic sphere. Tupperware, made from polyethylene, was a brand of housewares developed by Earl S. Tupper in 1942. Even before the war's end, Tupperware and its home sales method of marketing and distribution, which combined entrepreneurialism with domestic duties, enjoyed large success among suburban housewives. Tupperware exploited the very plasticity of plastics—tumblers, bowls, tableware, and resealable containers—were durable yet soft, were strangely organic, and came in many forms and colors, as in pink, blue, orange, yellow, and green pastels. Dacron, another form of polyester, was invented in 1948 by DuPont chemist Hale Charch and woven into fabric to make clothing. Even though it melted, easily pilled, and caused static cling, such fabrics promised drip-dry suits that were machine washable instead of requiring dry cleaning. Magnetic metal particles imbedded in polyester film made audiotapes a viable option for consumers by 1949.

Vinyl experienced similar postwar popularity. Naugahyde, a cheaper and tougher substitute for leather, was now used to upholster recliners such as La-Z-Boys and Barcaloungers and came to symbolize a durable manliness in material form. In 1946, RCA marketed the first vinyl phonograph records, which performed better than earlier versions made from brittle shellac. These were further improved in 1949 as more grooves were pressed into the vinyl, thus producing the first "long-playing" record album. Saran wrap, a vinyl film, could stick to itself, and was therefore used to provide airtight protection; it found use as a kind of disposable Tupperware, covering food either under refrigeration or being transported.

Other plastics that had been around for decades did not experience their heydays until put to especially domestic postwar uses. The durable but slick Teflon, for example, which was invented in 1938 by Roy Plunkett, had unique qualities that made its application to normal life difficult at best: it would neither burn, freeze, nor conduct electricity. As the original space-age material, Teflon was used in space exploration and as an industrial lubricant. But it was not until Teflon was applied to cookware to render it non-stick that it gained a foothold in popular culture. Formica shared a similar history. Invented in 1913 by Westinghouse engineers Daniel J. O'Connor and Harold A. Faber, this cousin to Bakelite was used in institutional settings as an easily wipeable, durable, heat-resistant table surface most apt for hotels, diners, and soda fountains. Since Formica sheets could be manufactured with any number of designs, it frequently was used to simulate natural surfaces like wood grain or marble. After the war it appeared at, or rather on, the dinner table as a popular furniture surface. While utilitarian, it also "provided a blank screen for the unconscious projection of a prime fifties anxiety: the atom bomb. . . . Formica provided protection against internal and external attack, eternally vigilant in its struggle to wipe clean the past," in the words of Fenichell.

The exuberance expressed in postwar America as it reveled in its material abundance was most clearly seen in plastic objects. Children were surrounded by plastic toys, from educational Legos to quirky Silly Putty and faddish Hula-Hoops and Frisbees. Adult versions of these novelties included pink-flamingo or elfin lawn ornaments. Velcro ("velvet hook"), perfected in 1957, was inspired by the sticking power of the cockbur in nature. Pieces of Velcro stuck together could be easily peeled apart from each other, but required considerable shear strength to pull the pieces sideways. The Houston Astrodome, complete with Lucite sky and Astroturf grass, was an almost wholly plasticized environment. The creation of Disneyland and other similar fantasy places during this time symbolized America's willingness to settle for the artificial rather than the real and to prefer the human-made world of plasticized fakery over that of nature. This comfort with the unreal would, by the 1980s and 1990s, emerge in a postmodern culture of simulacra that accepted not only artificial replicas of nature, but also replicas of the replicas.

The 1960s pop aesthetic, influenced by modernity, space flight, and the interrelationships of human and machine, embraced the colors, textures, and forms of plastic, highlighting the materiality of plastic. Inflatable furniture, vinyl go-go boots, and plastic bubble helmets all enjoyed great popularity. Paco Rabanne connected hard plastic pieces to each other with metal rings, creating chain mail-like dresses, vests, and pieces of jewelry. Betsey Johnson designed an entire line of see-through clothing made out of cellophane. Conceptual artist Christo made it his trademark to wrap buildings and landscapes in plastic fabrics, like part of the Australian coast, to celebrate the beauty of synthetic materials as juxtaposed against the natural landscape.

By the 1970s, any clinging romance between people and plastic had disappeared. In this decade, the links between plastics and cancer were becoming clearer, even to the plastics industry, which found that its toxic fumes threatened the health of industrial workers. The wholesale disposability of convenient plastic goods—from contact lenses to cups to diapers—was seen to pose acute environmental hazards. Many forms of plastic would not biodegrade, making them a polluter of seashores and a threat to marine life. In the late 1980s, an anti-Styrofoam campaign launched in a Milford, New Jersey, lunchroom eventually came to pressure McDonald's into finding a more ecologically sound alternative to its Styrofoam sandwich containers and coffee cups. Consumers also debated the relative merits of plastic and paper bags in grocery stores with little consensus; by the end of the twentieth century, both were still offered in most U.S. stores, though the "green" movement seems to have had more of an impact on these matters in Europe. Around this same time, doctors diagnosed a new malady variously called "environmental illness," "twentieth century disease," or "sick building syndrome," which made some people develop an oversensitivity to the toxic environment around them. Concurrently, the first artificial heart made of plastic, the Jarvik-7, was successfully implanted in Barney Clark, underscoring the fact that plastic no longer existed just in people's external world, but that it could also become, literally, a part of them.

Plastic has entered Americans' material lives to such a degree that extricating themselves from their reliance on the simulated stuff would now be impossible without serious impact on the U.S. standard of living. The material has become so "naturalized" that it often seems more real, tangible, and honest than nature itself. It permeates every aspect of daily life, even to the extent that many consumer transactions are carried out via credit cards that are generically referred to as "plastic." As a descriptive term applied to people, "plastic" has come to reflect the larger trends in American culture that have blurred the distinction between animate beings and the inanimate goods that surround them. Ronald Reagan enjoyed notoriety as the "Teflon President" because nothing terrible that happened during his time in office stuck to his reputation. In attempts at self-beautification, large numbers of women and men turned to plastic surgery to alter noses and brows and to dispense with wrinkles and

fat—perhaps in emulation of their idealized plastic counterparts, Barbie and Ken, whose sleek figures remain a sometimes unreachable goal to millions of overweight and aging Americans. In little over a century, the plastic ethos has embraced not only the versatile material but also the lifestyle and mindset that accompanied it, turning America into a prefabricated, simulated environment filled with people hungry for bright surfaces devoid of decay, even including their own.

—Wendy Woloson

FURTHER READING:

Fenichell, Stephen. *Plastic: The Making of a Synthetic Century.* New York, HarperBusiness, 1996.

Friedel, Robert. *Pioneer Plastic: The Making and Selling of Celluloid.* Madison, Wisconsin, The University of Wisconsin Press, 1983.

Katz, Sylvia. *Plastics: Common Objects, Classic Designs.* New York, Harry N. Abrams, Inc., 1984.

Meikle, Jeffrey L. *American Plastic: A Cultural History.* New Brunswick New Jersey, Rutgers University Press, 1995.

Mossman, Susan, editor. *Early Plastics: Perspectives, 1850-1950.* London/Washington, Leicester University Press, 1997.

Plastic Surgery

Plastic surgery is the surgical repair of skin defects and deformities, the removal of skin tumors, and surgical reconstruction. Increasingly, however, this medical specialty includes other procedures such as fatty-tissue removal, wrinkle reduction, breast and penile enlargement or reduction, and even the permanent application of make-up. Technological advances and changing cultural mores have continually broadened the scope of plastic surgery such that it is now primarily equated with cosmetic or aesthetic surgery.

Surgery may well be the oldest branch of medicine, but many centuries passed before modern methods, including plastic surgery, were possible. It was not until precise knowledge of the body was available, anesthesia was understood, and methods of controlling hemorrhage and post-operative infection were devised that complex surgery could be undertaken. There is evidence to suggest, however, that surgery could have been an ancient practice. One Indian text dating from the fourth century B.C.E. includes an extended section on surgery, though it is unknown whether the procedures described were actually practiced. Direct accounts of a plastic surgery performed in Poona in 1793 do exist, and the British physicians who witnessed the procedure described the "Hindu method" as far superior to comparable Western techniques, which suggests that plastic surgery had been performed in India for perhaps centuries. Interestingly, the procedure was a rhinoplasty involving skin grafts and reconstruction for a man whose nose had been amputated as punishment for adultery. Because this method of punishment was common, it may have served as impetus for the development of early plastic surgery. Other records indicate that syphilis, which reached epidemic proportions during European colonial expansion, may have also facilitated advances in surgical techniques that attempted to repair the disease's grotesque manifestations.

Innovations in reconstructive surgery continued through the nineteenth century and, at least in America, interest in cosmetic surgery was already rising. Yet it is World War I which most medical historians designate as the dramatic beginning of modern plastic surgery. The war resulted in unprecedented devastation and death but also in thousands of mutilating facial injuries. The horror inspired one physician, Harold Gillies, to establish a plastic surgery unit in the south of England where he personally attended approximately 2,000 cases of facial trauma with equal sensitivity to the patient's medical needs and appearance. In America, three military hospitals were specifically designated as plastic surgery units to treat soldiers disfigured in battle. In the next 20 years, the American Board of Plastic Surgery was formed, and by 1941 it was certified as a primary specialty board by the American Medical Association.

By the 1960s, evolving attitudes about beauty began to change the course of plastic surgery, and cosmetic, rather than reconstructive, procedures began to dominate the field. In the intervening decades, many new techniques emerged to reduce or reverse the effects of aging, including dermabrasion to remove acne scarring; collagen injection to fill out the lips or sunken skin; and blepharoplasty to eliminate bags under the eye. One procedure on the wane at twentieth century's end is the rhinoplasty or "nose job," which reached its height of popularity in the 1960s and 1970s.

As plastic surgery has become a common cultural phenomenon, its critics have grown increasingly vocal. Some view it as radical conformity to artificial standards of beauty perpetuated by mass media, and its most strident opponents are particularly concerned that women have aesthetic operations more often than men and that even adolescent girls sometimes elect surgery. Nonetheless, each year more cosmetic procedures are performed than ever before, and many plastic surgery patients attest to the psychological benefits of feeling younger, thinner, and more attractive. Perhaps the most notable, if ambiguous, commentary on cosmetic surgery has been offered by the French performance artist Orlan, who explores standards of beauty by undergoing repeated plastic surgery.

—Michele S. Shauf

FURTHER READING:

Camp, John. *Plastic Surgery: The Kindest Cut.* New York, Henry Holt, 1989.

Haiken, Elizabeth. *Venus Envy: A History of Cosmetic Surgery.* Baltimore, Johns Hopkins University Press, 1997.

Porter, Roy. *The Greatest Benefit to Mankind: A Medical History of Humanity.* New York, W.W. Norton & Co., 1997.

Rutknow, Ira M. *American Surgery: An Illustrated History.* Philadelphia, Lippincott-Raven, 1998.

Wangensteen, Owen H., and Sarah D. Wangensteen. *The Rise of Surgery: From Empiric Craft to Scientific Discipline.* Minneapolis, University of Minnesota Press, 1978.

Plath, Sylvia (1932-1963)

Author Sylvia Plath's association with death and madness stemmed from her confessional poetry, her novel *The Bell Jar,* and the facts of her life, but most of all from the cult of readers—many of them teenage girls—that formed after her suicide. Plath's stormy marriage to poet Ted Hughes was a matter for the literary tabloids,

and her work was taken up by scholars as evidence of a troubled soul oppressed by sexist times. Her poems—most particularly those published posthumously in *Ariel*—are an enduring proof of her very real talent.

Plath was born in Boston, Massachusetts, on October 27, 1932. Her father, a college professor and expert on bees, died when she was eight. She was a good student, and published her first short story in the magazine *Seventeen* when she was just a teenager.

In 1950, Plath entered Smith College on a scholarship. She already had an impressive list of publications, and while at Smith she wrote over four hundred poems. She spent some time in New York as a "guest editor" at *Mademoiselle*; when she returned home, she attempted suicide by swallowing sleeping pills. Afterward, she received electroshock and psychotherapy in a mental hospital. (Plath used much of this experience for her autobiographical novel *The Bell Jar,* published pseudonymously in England in 1963 under the name Victoria Lucas. Plath's mother, Aurelia, fought against American publication; the book was not published in the United States until 1970.)

Plath graduated from Smith in 1955 and won a Fulbright scholarship to study at Cambridge, England, where she met poet Ted Hughes. The story of their tempestuous first meeting is now mythic in literary circles: he stole her hair band; she bit his cheek. They were married in 1956.

In June of 1957, Plath attended Robert Lowell's poetry class at Boston University, where she met the poet Anne Sexton; the three of them would later be considered the foci of the intensely personal "confessional school" of poetry. In 1959, Plath and Hughes moved to England. The following year, when she was 28, her first book of poetry, *The Colossus and Other Poems,* was published.

Plath and Hughes separated later that year, when Hughes left Plath for another woman. Plath spent that winter with their two children, Frieda and Nicholas, in a small London flat, waking up at four a.m. in order to write before the children arose. This was a very productive period for her; she wrote almost a poem a day. On February 11, 1963, just days after the publication of *The Bell Jar,* Plath killed herself with kitchen gas.

Ted Hughes became Plath's literary executor. He brought her collection of poetry, *Ariel,* to publication in 1965. Among the "scorching" poems in *Ariel* is Plath's most famous poem, "Daddy," along with "Death and Co." and "Lady Lazarus" ("Dying / Is an art, like everything else. / I do it exceptionally well. // I do it so it feels like hell. / I do it so it feels real. / I guess you could say I've a call"). Other posthumous publications included *Crossing the Water, Winter Trees,* and, in 1981, *The Collected Poems,* edited by Hughes, which won the Pulitzer Prize for poetry.

For feminist scholars, Plath was a talented, brilliant woman done wrong by men and the times. If she had lived in a later era, they ask, would her story have unfolded the same way? Was she a victim of the 1950s ideal of woman as housewife and mother, wedged into a domestic role inappropriate for someone with her skills? Anne Sexton and Sylvia Plath are usually mentioned in the same literary breath—both were women, confessional poets, and suicides; Sexton's poem "Sylvia's Death" discusses their mutual preoccupation with the subjects of death and desire.

After her death, Plath achieved iconic status as a "madwoman" poet. For some cultural critics, she was the epitome of the silenced woman. Hughes had total control over her literary estate, and may have exerted that control to protect his own image; he destroyed at least one journal and censored many other pieces. Many Plath fans had a deep hatred for Hughes, and called him a betrayer, even a murderer. Although her gravestone was inscribed ''Sylvia Plath Hughes,'' it has been repeatedly defaced to read just ''Sylvia Plath.''

Years after her death, Plath remained a literary presence. In 1996, *About Sylvia: Poems* was published, containing works by Diane Ackerman, John Berryman, Rachel Hadas, Robert Lowell, Anne Sexton, and Richard Wilbur. Ted Hughes, British poet laureate, broke his silence on Plath soon before his own death in 1998 with the publication of *Birthday Letters,* a collection of poems about their relationship.

—Jessy Randall

FURTHER READING:

Alexander, Paul. *Rough Magic: A Biography of Sylvia Plath.* New York, Viking, 1991.

Plath, Aurelia Schober, ed. *Letters Home: Correspondence, 1950-1963* (by Sylvia Plath). New York, Harper & Row, 1975.

Rose, Jacqueline. *The Haunting of Sylvia Plath.* Cambridge, Harvard University Press, 1992.

Stevenson, Anne. *Bitter Fame: A Life of Sylvia Plath.* Boston, Houghton Mifflin, 1989.

Platoon

Oliver Stone's *Platoon* (1986), a critically acclaimed Hollywood film about the Vietnam War, was the first in its category to be directed by someone who saw combat in that most divisive of U.S. wars. The film, which cost $6 million to make, grossed $160 million and won four Oscars, including Best Film and Best Director. Like his cinematic alter ego, Chris Taylor (played by Charlie Sheen), Stone abandoned a wealthy family and an Ivy League education for a chance to fight in Vietnam, just as his grandfather had fought in World War I and his father had fought in World War II. In 1967-68, Stone was stationed near the Cambodian border, and it took him about a day to realize that he had made a horrible mistake. More than once, the pressure of battle caused Stone to go over the edge, once shooting at an old man's feet (as Chris does in the film), and once attacking the Viet Cong with such foolish ferocity that he was called a hero and awarded a Bronze Star. He also received a Purple Heart with Oak Leaf Cluster for his two injuries.

Stone's own experiences helped make *Platoon* an especially valuable vehicle for conveying the immediacy and brutality of armed conflict. During Stone's second week in Vietnam, his platoon encountered some Viet Cong and, during the ensuing battle, he was wounded in the back of the neck and the soldier next to him had his

Charlie Sheen (left) and Keith David in a scene from the film *Platoon.*

arm blown off. Suffering only a flesh wound, Stone was soon back in combat. He said most soldiers fell into one of two camps, as shown in the film: the lifers, the juicers, and the unintelligent whites in one camp; and the progressive, hippie, dope-smokers—who wanted only to survive the war with some integrity intact—in the other. Stone fell in with this second group. After being wounded again, he was transferred to the platoon where he met Juan Angel Elias, the inspiration for Sgt. Elias (Willem Dafoe) in *Platoon.* The part-Spanish, part-Apache, compassionate Elias proved to Stone that someone could be both a good soldier and a decent human being. Stone also met a facially scarred officer who would become the inspiration for Sgt. Barnes—the best soldier Stone ever met, but also an angry loner obsessed with killing and getting even.

Platoon is remembered for its authentic and unbiased portrayal of combat. During the war, the only Hollywood movie dealing with the subject had been *The Green Berets* (1968), a laughably bad John Wayne vehicle partially financed by the U.S. government, little more than a World War II-type film with propaganda added, and so inaccurate that the last scene, of the sun setting in the east, seemed appropriate. The *Rambo* and *Missing in Action* films used the war as an excuse for some comic-book macho fantasies, with the U.S. winning some battles for a change. *The Deer Hunter* (1978) and *Apocalypse Now* (1979) were great films, but they seemed to be condemning war in general, not this particular one. *Platoon* immediately dropped the viewer into a jungle so thick that technological superiority became meaningless. Only *Platoon* is so filled with closely observed details—the snakes, the mosquitoes, the ants, the leeches—that it was deemed absolutely authentic in every respect. As Stone says, the film shows kids ''what combat is really like, and what war really means. . . . I hope a lot of kids who see *Platoon* will think twice. Maybe they won't make the same mistake I made.''

—Bob Sullivan

FURTHER READING:

Beaver, Frank. *Oliver Stone: Wakeup Cinema.* New York, Twayne Publishers, 1994.

Kagan, Norman. *The Cinema of Oliver Stone.* New York, Continuum Publishing Co., 1995.

Kunz, Don, editor. *The Films of Oliver Stone.* Lanham, Maryland, The Scarecrow Press, Inc., 1997.

Mackey-Kallis, Susan. *Oliver Stone's America.* Boulder, Colorado, Westview Press, 1996.

Riordan, James. *Stone.* New York, Hyperion, 1995.

Salewicz, Chris. *Oliver Stone.* New York, Thunder's Mouth Press, 1998.

Playboy

The Puritan influence in American culture lasted far longer than did the Puritans themselves. Over the years, the prudishness of the Puritans combined with the rigid moral code of fundamentalist Protestants and the sexually conservative teachings of the Catholic Church to produce a culture in which sex and sexuality were forbidden from virtually all forms of public entertainment and discourse. That culture endured, and dominated, for many years. Beginning in the 1950s, however, the cultural climate in America began to thaw. The heat came from two principal sources. One was Dr. Alfred

Hugh Hefner and Cynthia Maddox (Miss February 1962) enjoying a copy of *Playboy* together, 1962.

Kinsey, who conducted the first scientific research on the sexual practices of Americans, and published the surprising results in a series of *Kinsey Reports.* The other source was Hugh Hefner and his magazine, *Playboy.*

Prior to starting *Playboy* in 1953, Hugh Marsten Hefner, 27, had not achieved much success in life. After college and the Army, he returned to his native Chicago and married his high-school sweetheart. After failing as a freelance cartoonist, Hefner worked in the promotion departments of several magazines, including *Esquire,* the premier ''men's magazine'' of its day. But when *Esquire* moved its headquarters to New York City, it did not invite Hugh Hefner to come along. Frustrated and somewhat desperate, Hefner borrowed a few thousand dollars from relatives and friends and prepared to launch the magazine that had been his dream for years.

The new magazine was very nearly called *Stag Party,* to be symbolized by a drawing of an urbane-looking buck in a smoking jacket. But there was already a magazine devoted to hunting called *Stag,* and its publisher threatened to sue if Hefner used the name. Thus, at the last minute, the magazine was re-christened *Playboy,* with the horny deer transformed into a sophisticated-looking rabbit figure—a name and image that would eventually became known throughout the world.

The first issue appeared in December of 1953. So uncertain of success was Hefner that he left his name off the editorial masthead, and declined to put a date on the magazine's cover. The first decision was designed to allow him to avoid associating his name with a flop if the magazine failed; the second would make the first issue marketable beyond the month of its publication. Hefner need not have worried. Although he would have welcomed the sale of 30,000 copies, the first issue sold over 54,000—helped, no doubt, by a centerfold photo of a nude Marilyn Monroe, one of America's most popular actresses. She had posed for the picture years earlier, while unknown and in need of money. Hefner bought the rights to the photo for $500.

From that point, *Playboy* and its publisher were on their way up. Within a year, the magazine had a circulation of over 100,000, and the figure would eventually reach the millions. The magazine catered to the educated, urban male, who either was affluent and sophisticated or wished to see himself that way. In short, the typical *Playboy* reader was a young man not unlike Hugh Hefner.

As *Playboy* matured, it took on certain features that would eventually help to define it, both within the publishing world and in American culture, as well. These characteristics included profiles of upscale consumer goods, such as sports cars, stereo equipment, and elegant clothing. There would also be articles on fine food, good wine, sophisticated cocktails, and the best places to find them.

Fiction and nonfiction by well-known writers was also incorporated into the magazine. Hefner wanted to compete for *Esquire's* audience, and he also knew that having ''legitimate'' authors writing for him meant he would be able to defend *Playboy* as more than a mere ''skin magazine.'' At first, Hefner's resources were so limited that he was forced to rely on work in the public domain, such as Arthur Conan Doyle's Sherlock Holmes stories. But the magazine's success soon brought in enough money to allow it to purchase original fiction from such notables as Ernest Hemingway, Ray Bradbury, Irwin Shaw, and Gore Vidal. Not surprisingly, one of *Playboy's* favorite writers was Ian Fleming, whose James Bond character embodied many of the fantasies dear to the magazine's readership. The suave secret agent made his first *Playboy* appearance in March 1960, and thereafter the magazine serialized each new James Bond novel until Fleming's death in 1964.

The ''*Playboy* Interview'' was another addition to be greeted with enthusiasm by readers. Beginning with the September 1962 issue, the magazine featured long interviews with prominent figures likely to be of interest to *Playboy* readers. The subjects included no shortages of actors, athletes, and sex symbols, but there were surprising choices, as well, including Malcolm X, Fidel Castro, Albert Schweitzer, Yasir Arafat, and presidential candidate Jimmy Carter (who created a flap by admitting that he sometimes lusted after women in his heart).

Playmates and other naked ladies, of course, were a mainstay of the magazine from the beginning. Each issue of *Playboy* usually offered readers three ''pictorials.'' One of these occupied the center of the magazine and included a folded mini-poster of the young lady designated ''Playmate of the month.'' Hefner's conception of the model who would occupy the centerfold and its surrounding pages has by now become a cultural cliche: he wanted, he said, ''the girl next door.'' She should be beautiful, but not glamorous. The famous Marilyn Monroe picture notwithstanding, the Playmate would not be a celebrity (those would appear elsewhere in the magazine). The photos accompanying the centerfold would show the model in the ''real world''—at home, at school, in a restaurant having lunch. The message sent to the male reader was: ''This girl is real, she is accessible, she really is the 'girl next door''' (always assuming the girl next door had blonde hair, perfect skin, and a 36-22-36 shape).

Other pictorials sometimes featured a montage of young women, grouped around themes that could be educational (''The Girls of the West Coast Conference''), geographical (''The Girls of Australia''),

or occupational (''The Girls of Radio''). Sometimes a pictorial featured a single model who happened to work in an occupation popular in male sexual fantasies. Thus, there were photo layouts devoted to a female police officer, another to a firefighter, and still another to a female stockbroker. And, although Marilyn Monroe's appearance in *Playboy* was not her decision, many well-known women did voluntarily grace the magazine's pages, including Brigitte Bardot, Drew Barrymore, Madonna, Farrah Fawcett, LaToya Jackson, Jayne Mansfield, Kim Novak, Jane Seymour, Nancy Sinatra, Sharon Stone, and Raquel Welch.

The *Playboy* formula was hugely successful, bringing in increasing numbers of readers and advertising dollars throughout the 1950s, 1960s, and 1970s. Hefner spent some of the revenue on a lavish lifestyle (including the Playboy Mansion in Chicago, Playboy Mansion West in Los Angeles, and a luxury, full-sized jet named the Big Bunny), but much of it went into building what would become known as the Playboy Empire. Its components included the chain of Playboy Clubs (best known for their scantily clad waitresses, called Bunnies), followed by resort hotels and then casinos in both Atlantic City and Great Britain. There was a book publishing division, a music division, and a film production company. All of it made money—for a time.

The 1980s, however, were not kind to the Playboy Empire. On the magazine front, it faced competition from rivals like *Penthouse* and *Hustler*. Both were more explicitly erotic than the ''wholesome'' *Playboy,* although they took different approaches—*Penthouse* strove for the same ''sophistication'' as *Playboy,* but with a European accent, while raunchy *Hustler* was blatantly lowbrow.

This competition was not the worst of Hefner's problems. Although he had faced opposition from religious groups in the past, none of them had been sufficiently well organized to be troublesome. But the 1980s saw the rise of arch-conservative televangelists such as Jerry Falwell and Jimmy Swaggart, and the founding of political-religious organizations such as Falwell's Moral Majority and Reverend Pat Robertson's Christian Coalition. Further, many feminists, who otherwise had little in common with the fundamentalists, found common ground with them on the issue of pornography and its supposed danger to women. And, following the 1980 election, the social conservatives had allies in Washington, including the White House. President Ronald Reagan, inclined toward the Christian Right's beliefs in any case, recognized the important role that these groups had played in the last election, and might well play in the next one. Reagan courted them whenever he could, and one of his favors involved the establishment of the Meese Commission on Pornography. Attorney General Edwin Meese assembled a panel that heavily favored the social and religious right, and set out to see whether ''pornography'' had harmful effects on society. To the surprise of no one, he found that it did.

If the political climate of the 1980s was unfavorable to *Playboy,* the economic one was even more so. Playboy Enterprises lost its gaming license in Great Britain for violating gambling regulations. This caused the New Jersey Gaming Commission to reconsider its decision to grant a casino license to the Playboy hotel in Atlantic City. The resulting financial setbacks were enormous, and were soon followed by others. The Playboy Clubs, considered daring in the 1960s, were almost quaint two decades later. Club membership declined greatly, and financial losses followed. Further, advertising in the magazine, the flagship institution of the empire, was down 60 percent from 1970. Clearly, drastic change was in order if *Playboy* were to survive.

Appropriately for an empire founded on the female form, the answer was embodied in a woman: Christie Hefner, adult daughter of founding father Hugh. She agreed to serve as chief executive officer of Playboy Enterprises, while her father enjoyed semi-retirement at Playboy Mansion West (although he retained the majority share of company stock). Working with experienced financial managers, Ms. Hefner sold off the clubs and resorts, as well as other drains on revenue (including her father's jet, The Big Bunny). She recognized the potential of the emerging video market, and Playboy Enterprises was soon profitably producing soft-core adult videos, CD-ROMs, and cable television shows. As the new millennium approached, Playboy Enterprises was again in the black, with *Playboy* magazine (subscribers numbering in the millions) bringing in about half of all revenue.

—Justin Gustainis

FURTHER READING:

Miller, Russell. *Bunny: The Real Story of Playboy.* New York, Holt, Rinehart & Winston, 1985.

The Playboy Book: Forty Years. Santa Monica, General Publishing Group, 1998.

Weyr, Thomas. *Reaching for Paradise: The Playboy Vision of America.* New York, Times Books, 1978.

Playgirl

With its appearance on the stands in May 1973, *Playgirl* magazine became the first magazine for women to focus on men. Although Helen Gurley Brown's *Cosmopolitan* had featured the first nude male centerfold, *Playgirl,* first published by Douglas Lambert and edited by Marin Scott Milam, was more of a female counterpart to *Playboy.* While *Cosmopolitan* may have pushed at the far edges of women's magazines, *Playgirl* went over the line in its effort to bring a newly blossomed feminism to the realm of popular reading material. It desired to offer women "the good life," much as *Playboy* identified a way of life that encompassed the music their male readers listened to, the books they read, the cars they drove—and the women who fed their fantasies.

By the late 1990s, although *Playgirl* could boast a circulation of more than 500,000, this was still nowhere near the much larger circulation figures for *Cosmopolitan* and doesn't enter the sphere of circulation occupied by *Playboy.* Perhaps this is because of the fact that *Playgirl* always had trouble deciding what kind of magazine it wanted to be. Its fiction, although at times featuring such notable authors as Joyce Carol Oates and Margaret Atwood, rarely rose higher than romance novels and confession magazines, while *Playboy*'s fiction often featured the top writers of the day, and it featured interviews with Margaret Thatcher, Henry Kissinger, Warren Beatty, and Jane Fonda, to name a few. While aspiring to emulate *Playboy*, in its early years *Playgirl* periodically featured silly centerfolds, such as actor Rip Torn and Benji the dog. And on the nudity question, it wavered between the extremes of full frontal and none at all.

The magazine's lack of identity reflected the fact that women themselves were struggling to find and assert their identity during the 1970s and 1980s. Could a woman retain her femininity or did she have to ape a man to succeed in a man's world? Her wages were

certainly arguing that she could not compete on equal terms with men. How could she aspire to "the good life" when her wages were often half that of her male counterpart? Women themselves were divided on the issues. Many continued to believe that husbands should work and wives should stay home and care for the family. To these women, working mothers meant bad mothers.

Another reason for the lack of clear focus in *Playgirl* was its publishing history. While the image of *Playboy* boss Hugh Hefner could offer men a vision of what the ultimate playboy was supposed to look like, *Playgirl*'s original publisher was a man. *Cosmopolitan* and *Ms. Magazine* were both headed by strong feminists, able to commit themselves to the message they were proclaiming in the pages of their magazines. In 1986, Drake Publishers bought *Playgirl* and relocated to New York. They believed that women didn't want to see nude men, preferring traditional images of handsome men that they could fantasize about. This romanticized view of women's sexuality didn't go over well with the readers, and the change lasted less than a year before the full frontal nudity was back.

Further, *Playgirl* ignored a vocal part of the women's movement that decried the objectification of women in such magazines as *Playboy* and *Penthouse.* Many men and women argued that sexualizing women led to violent crimes such as rape. It was further argued that men's magazines objectified not only women but men as well, making men nothing more than the sex they were having. While many women's groups called for reform in men's magazines, *Playgirl* was pushing for what many considered equal depravity rather than equal rights. They thought that *Playgirl* actually weakened the arguments for the fair treatment of women.

Despite some of its rocky history, *Playgirl* earned a reputation for listening to what its readers wanted. When the first issue came out, centerfold Lyle Waggoner was featured in a cross-legged pose. Readers complained that *Playgirl* hadn't gone far enough. The next issue featured a fully revealed George Maharis. In 1986, it was the readers' responses to the withdrawal of nudity that convinced Drake Publishers to reintroduce male nudity in the magazine.

In the last years of the twentieth century, *Playgirl*—one voice in a myriad of women's magazines—remained the only women's magazine that regularly featured nude men. Deciding at last to be the only erotic magazine for women, *Playgirl,* in the words of their historical overview, now serves "to legitimize female sexuality and introduce women to the same provocative features and photographs men [have] been enjoying for years." While *Playgirl* may not have presented the fully fleshed-out vision of "the good life" that *Playboy* inspired, it has remained for many women the authority on female sexuality.

—Cheryl A. Smith

FURTHER READING:

Brooks, Gary R., and Lenore Walker. *The Centerfold Syndrome: How Men Can Overcome Objectification and Achieve Intimacy with Women.* San Francisco, Jossey-Bass Pub., 1995.

Chancer, Lynn S. *Reconcilable Differences: Confronting Beauty, Pornography, and the Future of Feminism.* Los Angeles, University of California Press, 1998.

Dines, Gail, Robert Jensen, and Ann Russo. *Pornography: The Production and Consumption of Inequality.* New York, Routledge, 1998.

McElroy, Wendy. *XXX: A Woman's Right to Pornography.* New York, St. Martin's Press, 1997.

Strossen, Nadine. *Defending Pornography: Free Speech, Sex, and the Fight for Women's Rights.* New York, Anchor, 1996.

Playhouse 90

Considered by many to be the most ambitious of the anthology dramas to emerge during the "Golden Age of Television," *Playhouse 90,* according to historian William Boddy, was voted the greatest television series of all time in a 1970 *Variety* poll of television editors. Appearing Thursday evenings on CBS from 1956 to 1959, the program presented new ninety-minute dramas, many of which were telecast live. Like other "anthology dramas" of the era, *Playhouse 90* is often remembered as a fertile ground for quality performances and an opportunity for writers and directors to showcase dramatic talents for a national audience. During its four-year run, *Playhouse 90* launched careers, lured stars back to television, and allowed actors the opportunity to take chances performing roles which they otherwise might not have been offered. The program began on October 4, 1956, with *Forbidden Area,* starring Charlton Heston, Tab Hunter, and Vincent Price. It was followed by Rod Serling's classic *Requiem for a Heavyweight,* which won the Emmy as best single program of the year, and starred Jack Palance, who won an Emmy for best single performance by an actor. Other *Playhouse 90* stars included Johnny Carson (in his first dramatic television role), Errol Flynn, Kim Hunter, Paul Newman (in his last dramatic television role) and Joanne Woodward, Cliff Robertson, Jack Lemmon, Claude Rains, Burt Reynolds, and Robert Redford. Among the memorable programs from this series are *For Whom the Bell Tolls, Judgement at Nuremberg, The Male Animal, The Days of Wine and Roses,* and Joseph Conrad's *The Heart of Darkness. Playhouse 90* was recognized with five Emmys during its first season and won the award for best drama each of the next three years it was on the air. In its final season of production, *Playhouse 90* was limited to sixteen programs or specials as it shared a time slot with *The Big Party.*

—James Friedman

Pocket Books

See Paperbacks

Pogo

Eventually a very political possum, Walt Kelly's Pogo was first seen in 1942 in a comic book. By the time he moved into the funny papers in 1948, he was not only considerably cuter but also much more socially aware. A success, albeit a controversial one, from almost the start of his newspaper days, Pogo soon branched out into a series of popular soft-cover reprint books. As the strip progressed, Kelly took increasing interest, and delight, in poking fun at many of the biggest political targets of the day; these included Senator Joe McCarthy, Lyndon Johnson, Nikita Khrushchev, Spiro Agnew, and J. Edgar Hoover. Needless to say, this was sometimes a risky sort of satire in which to indulge, especially in the social climate of the 1950s.

Born in Philadelphia and raised in Bridgeport, Kelly had always yearned to be a cartoonist. In the mid-1930s he went West to work for the Disney organization. Along with hundreds of other artists, the young Kelly worked on such animated features as *Snow White, Pinocchio,* and *Dumbo.* After leaving Walt Disney in 1941, Kelly came back East and was soon gainfully employed in the comic book business. By then he had become an excellent cartoonist; it was logical that he would find work with *Animal Comics* and *Fairy Tale Parade.*

In 1942 Kelly invented *Pogo* as a backup feature for *Animal Comics,* a magazine wherein the designated star was supposed to be the venerable rabbit gentleman Uncle Wiggily. A very scruffy and too-realistic-looking possum at the start, Pogo soon improved in appearance and eventually came to be the leading character in the feature. Among his swamp companions were the turtle Churchy LaFemme, Porky Pine, Howland Owl, and Albert the Alligator, a likeable ne'er-do-well who smoked cigars and possessed a mind overflowing with sly schemes—a goodly portion of which involved food.

By 1948 Kelly was working as staff artist and chief political cartoonist for the short-lived *New York Star,* which was more or less the successor to the liberal newspaper *PM.* On October 4 of that year, *Pogo* began as a daily comic strip exclusively in the pages of the *New York Star.* When the paper ceased publication three months later, Kelly's swamp denizens were temporarily without a home. The strip, however, was picked up for syndication that May and it immediately began to gather a sizeable client list. Although he had liberal political views, Kelly was at heart a comedian and he also included considerable slapstick, burlesque, puns, and uncontrolled nonsense in his saga of Okefenokee Swamp. In addition to outrageous continuities, mixed frequently with political satire, Kelly was especially fond of having his characters sing somewhat garbled versions of traditional songs. No Christmas, for example, went by without a heartfelt rendering of "Deck Us All with Boston Charlie."

Aware that Kelly's views on such topics as Senator McCarthy, the Ku Klux Klan, and the John Birch Society did not sit especially well with some of their subscribing editors, his syndicate suggested that he prepare a few alternative strips to run in place of an offensive one. Kelly went along with this, creating what he called his "bunny rabbit strips." These featured none of the *Pogo* regulars, but only a bunch of cute little rabbits enacting very tame and quiet gags. Kelly produced at least two dozen of these, and some of them must have been run far more than once.

Because of failing health in his final years, Kelly had to rely on assistants to turn out his strip. After he died in 1973, *Pogo* went on until 1975, written and drawn by others and controlled by his heirs. Early in 1989, the *Los Angeles Times Syndicate* attempted to resurrect Pogo, Albert, and the rest of the gang. A brand new version of the strip, titled *Walt Kelly's Pogo,* was launched with art by Neal Sternecky and scripts by Larry Doyle. This version, which concentrated mostly on whimsy and not social comment, was not particularly successful. By 1992, both members of the creative team had departed and Kelly's daughter Carolyn was drawing it while his son Peter oversaw the writing. *Pogo* closed up shop for the second time soon after.

—Ron Goulart

FURTHER READING:

Goulart, Ron. *The Great Comic Book Artists.* Vol. 1. New York, St. Martin's Press, 1986.

Harvey, Robert C. *The Art of the Funnies.* Jackson, University Press of Mississippi, 1994.

Kelly, Walt. *Pogo.* Vol. 1. Seattle, Fantagraphics Books, 1992.

The Pointer Sisters

Popular music audiences in the late twentieth century had never seen anything like the Pointer Sisters. Throughout their career, they defied categorization like no other female group had ever done, all while maintaining their substantial popularity. They took risks, and in doing so, expanded the boundaries in music for all women. They had a strong, self-aware style that came through whatever type of music they happened to be singing, and this style influenced the changing social mores of the 1970s and 1980s surrounding women.

Born in Oakland, California, sisters Ruth (1946), Anita (1948), Bonnie (1950), and June (1954) had a strict upbringing. Both of their parents were ministers in the West Oakland Church of God, and for many years church singing was their only form of public entertaining. Eventually Bonnie and June began performing in San Francisco clubs as a duo. Their sister Anita joined them later, and in 1971 they officially became the ''Pointer Sisters'' and signed with manager Bill

Graham. For the next few years, they sang backing vocals for a number of popular 1970s recording artists. Eventually, their strong vocal skills brought them to the attention of Atlantic Records, which signed the group. The first few singles, in the rhythm and blues style, were not successful, but the sisters persevered. Ruth quit her job to join the act, and the new quartet of sisters left Atlantic and signed with ABC's Blue Thumb label.

Their self-titled debut album brought them immediate national recognition. The songs moved seamlessly from jazz to rhythm and blues, and showcased the Pointer Sisters' dynamic vocal range, powerful soul-shouting lungs, fierce scat-singing technique, and the effortless beauty of their distinctive vocal blend. The Pointers dressed in 1940s-era clothes, evoking positive comparisons between them and the definitive 1940s vocal group the Andrews Sisters. They performed at Nashville's Grand Ole Opry—the first African-American women to do so. In 1974, they became the first pop act to perform in the San Francisco Opera House, and were the subjects of a PBS documentary.

The group did not restrict themselves to rhythm and blues for long. Bonnie and Anita wrote a country song called ''Fairytale,'' which fared well on the pop charts and won them a Grammy award in 1974 for Best Country Single of the Year. Soon after, however, emotional and financial hardships divided the group for a few years.

The Pointer Sisters

Bonnie decided to be a solo recording artist, so in 1978 she left the group and signed with Motown Records. Although Bonnie found some success with the few songs she released, it was minimal. The remaining trio struggled for a while with an image problem and declining record sales. Because of the 1940s-style image they presented, they were beginning to be thought of, by the late 1970s, as a nostalgia group, albeit a tremendously talented one. The sisters knew they needed to change their image and sound if they were to keep making successful records.

They signed with Planet Records, and with producer Richard Perry's help, they launched a stream of top ten pop records that forever solidified their place in contemporary music history. The new and improved Pointer Sisters seemed, in many ways, like a new group altogether. Their clothes were no longer period pieces, but the latest fashions of their day. Always known for their energetic performances, the Pointers were now dubbed ''high energy'' and seemed to dance faster, jump higher, and sing stronger than they ever had. Seven top ten hits made the Pointers a household name by the mid-1980s. Other groups may have been content to stay with a formula, just as all the girl-groups of the 1960s had done, but the Pointer sisters set out to break every mold they made of themselves in the public eye.

Covering Bruce Springsteen's ''Fire'' got them labeled as a quasi-rock group, but they later recorded the soulful pop ''He's So Shy.'' ''Slow Hand'' seemed to highlight the strong rhythm and blues flavor of their voices, yet they proved again with ''Jump'' that they could deliver pop music with as steady a punch. The nature of the lyrics and the melodies—self-assured, world-wise, sexy, and high-spirited—gave audiences a powerful image of three very independent and energetic women. The advent of MTV (Music Television) and the appearance of the group in a number of music videos (as well as television specials) helped advertise this new image. Audiences all over the country could turn on the television and see these fashionable women—with amazingly seductive voices—laughing, jumping, and having a party on stage because they felt like doing so. Even the title of one of their biggest hits, ''I'm So Excited,'' evokes the kind of party attitude and self-determination the group presented on television, recording, and radio. By revitalizing their career through public image renewal and exploring new styles, the sisters developed a model under which other female artists could emulate and expand upon.

At the end of the 1980s, the group took a break. They occasionally made television appearances, but it was not until the mid-1990s that the group fully stepped out into the spotlight again. This time they turned their attention to Broadway, starring in a revival of *Ain't Misbehavin'*—the hugely successful 1920s musical-revue based on Fats Waller. It seemed, by the end of the twentieth century, that the Pointer Sisters had come full circle—returning, in a sense, to the nostalgic jazz style that first brought them recognition. But for a group that made a career out of sweet musical surprises, there was no way anyone could be certain of anything concerning the Pointer Sisters, except that their powerful voices would not easily be forgotten.

—Brian Granger

FURTHER READING:

O'Brien, Lucy. *She Bop: The Definitive History of Women in Rock, Pop and Soul.* New York, Penguin Books, 1995.

Romanowski, Patricia, and Holly George-Warren, editors. *The New Rolling Stone Encyclopedia of Rock & Roll.* New York, Rolling Stone Press, 1995.

Poitier, Sidney (1927—)

As one of the first African-American actors to consistently appear in serious dramatic roles in American films, Sidney Poitier is acknowledged as a major catalyst for Hollywood offering more substantive roles to black performers. In 1992, the American Film Institute paid tribute to Poitier, with Denzel Washington referring to him as ''a source of pride for many African Americans,'' and James Earl Jones saying that Poitier has ''played a great role in the life of our country.''

Although born in 1927 in Miami, Florida, Poitier grew up on his family's farm in the Bahamas. Despite being a poor man, Poitier has said that his father—a tomato farmer—was never a man of self-pity. As Poitier once said, ''Every time I took a part, from the first part, from the first day, I always said to myself, 'This must reflect well on his name.''' His family moved from the tiny village of Cat Island to Nassau, the Bahamian capitol, when Poitier was eleven years old. It was at that age that he became captivated with the cinema after watching a Western drama unfold on the screen.

After serving in the U.S. Army in the early 1940s, Poitier worked as a dishwasher and janitor until he landed a backstage position with the American Negro Theater. Because his West Indian accent was unintelligible, Poitier developed a more professional voice by listening to radio commercials and imitating the announcers. After perfecting his voice, he was cast in several American Negro Theater productions during the 1940s, including *Days of Our Youth, Lysistrata,*

Sidney Poitier

Anna Lucasta, and *A Raisin in the Sun.* Poitier understudied for actor-singer Harry Belafonte in *Days of Our Youth,* and he impressed critics with his work in *Lysistrata,* despite being so nervous on the play's opening night that he delivered the wrong lines and ran off stage.

Poitier's film career began in 1950 in the feature *No Way Out,* playing a doctor tormented by the racist brother of a man whose life he could not save. Poitier worked steadily throughout the 1950s, most notably in the South African story *Cry, the Beloved Country,* the urban classroom drama *The Blackboard Jungle,* and Stanley Kramer's *The Defiant Ones,* in which Poitier and Tony Curtis played prison escapees whose mutual struggle helped them to gain respect for each other despite their racial divisions.

It was in the 1960s, however, that Poitier produced his most impressive body of work that simultaneously helped to reduce the barriers faced by African-American actors and dispel racial stereotypes on the screen. He appeared in the 1960 film adaptation of the play *A Raisin in the Sun,* in which he played the role he had created on the Broadway stage in 1959. Following that film, Poitier accepted the role of an American serviceman in Germany, in the 1963 production *Lilies of the Field,* which earned him the Academy Award for best actor. He was the first African-American actor to win this award.

Poitier continued throughout the 1960s to break down racial barriers in American film. In 1967, Poitier played a charismatic school teacher in *To Sir, with Love,* and that same year costarred with Rod Steiger in the film *In the Heat of the Night.* In this latter role, Poitier played Virgil Tibbs, an African-American detective from the North who helps solve a murder in a small Southern town with the assistance of a racist police chief. Poitier's role as Virgil Tibbs spawned two sequels and a television series, although Poitier did not appear in the TV project. The actor concluded the watershed year of 1967 by working with Spencer Tracy and Katherine Hepburn in the film *Guess Who's Coming to Dinner*—an important work because it was Hollywood's first interracial love story that did not end in tragedy. Poitier has acknowledged that he suited the needs of filmmakers during this period who wanted to deliver an antiracist message. "I was a pretty good actor," he said. "I believed in brotherhood, in a free society. I hated racism, segregation. And I was a symbol against those things." However, Poitier's involvement in civil rights was more than just symbolic; the actor participated in demonstrations led by Martin Luther King, Jr. in Montgomery, Alabama, and Memphis, Tennessee.

In 1972, Poitier costarred with Harry Belafonte in the revisionist Western *Buck and the Preacher.* It was on this picture that Poitier made his debut as a film director when the original director resigned because of creative differences. Although Poitier and Belafonte wanted Columbia Pictures to hire another director, studio officials liked some of Poitier's own footage so much that they asked him to finish the film himself. His other directorial credits include *A Warm December* (1973), *Uptown Saturday Night* (1974), *Let's Do It Again* (1975), *A Piece of the Action* (1977), *Stir Crazy* (1980), *Hanky-Panky* (1982), *Fast Forward* (1985), and *Ghost Dad* (1990).

In the 1980s, Poitier took only a handful of film roles, primarily *Shoot to Kill* and *Little Nikita,* both action thrillers released in 1988. However, the 1990s produced an upswing in Poitier's film activity, starting with playing Supreme Court Justice Thurgood Marshall in the television film *Separate but Equal.* In 1992, he returned to the big screen costarring with Robert Redford, River Phoenix, and Dan Aykroyd in the espionage comedy-drama *Sneakers.* That same year, the American Film Institute presented Poitier with a Lifetime Achievement Award, with the veteran actor humbly remarking in his acceptance speech: "I enter my golden years with nothing profound to say

and no advice to leave, but I thank you for paying me this great honor while I still have hair, and my stomach still has not obscured my view of my shoe tops." In 1995, Poitier returned to television for a role in the Western drama *Children of the Dust.*

With more than thirty film credits to his name, coupled with his work as a director and civil rights activist, Poitier has emerged from a childhood of poverty to the status of an American icon. Actor Michael Moriarty summed up what Poitier represents both on and off the screen by saying, "You see a face that you've grown up with and admired, someone who was . . . a symbol of strength and persistence and grace. And then you find out that in the everyday . . . work of doing movies, he is everything he symbolizes on screen."

—Dennis Russell

FURTHER READING:

Ceyser, Lester J. *The Cinema of Sidney Poitier.* San Diego, A. S. Barnes, 1980.

Hoffman, William. *Sidney.* New York, Lyle Stuart, 1971.

Marill, Alvin H. *The Films of Sidney Poitier.* Secaucus, New Jersey, Citadel Press, 1978.

Poitier, Sydney. *This Life.* New York, Alfred A. Knopf, 1980.

Polio

Throughout most of human history, polio has caused paralysis and death. Often found in wet areas, the virus is most acute in cities during summer months. The virus inflames nerves in the brain and spinal cord, causing paralysis and can be passed through contact with contaminated feces or oral secretion. Throughout the nineteenth and early twentieth centuries, paralytic poliomyelitis was perhaps the most feared disease in the nation. In 1950 alone, 33,300 people were stricken. In its widespread impact and public awareness, polio bears a striking resemblance to AIDS.

President Franklin Roosevelt, who had been struck by a form of polio in 1921 and left unable to use his legs, declared a War on Polio, and developing a vaccine became a national priority in the 1930s. While he took an active role in getting the leg braces, iron lungs, and other hardware for Polio treatment to all communities in the 1930s, Roosevelt went to great lengths to limit public awareness of his own affliction. Although there are over 35,000 still photographs of FDR at the Presidential Library, only two show him seated in his wheelchair. Through his own experience, Roosevelt seemed to understand that rehabilitation of the polio patient was a social problem with medical aspects, not a medical problem with social aspects. Speaking to a group at the Warm Springs, Georgia, rehabilitation center, FDR said: "The most important point is that people all over the country know about what we are doing and are following our example in their own communities." Iron lungs and rural retreats became well-known possibilities for those suffering from polio, but FDR sought to reduce their stigma.

Roosevelt sought to raise funds for polio victims throughout his presidency. In 1937 he helped to create the National Foundation for Infantile Paralysis, which offered financial assistance to families with polio victims. The Foundation also helped to establish treatment centers in many American communities, whereas previously polio victims had been shunned to remote facilities. Further donations were made to a less medical and more popular organization, "The March of Dimes," also created in 1937. In 1938, the two organizations collected $1.8 million; by 1945 they collected $18.9 million. Treatment was only one use of the funds; these donations combined with government funding to initiate the pursuit of a vaccine. Controlling the virus became one of the first examples of the federal government's involvement in Americans' expectations for a safer standard of living. In essence, the public began to look toward the federal government to ensure a healthy environment. Public awareness campaigns made the virus and its modes of transmission part of the American popular culture through 1950.

With federal funds assisting the search, vaccines became available in the early 1960s. The most well-known was created by Jonas Salk. The Salk vaccine allowed most of the industrialized world to defeat the polio virus, creating a significant economic effect: it is said that the polio vaccine pays for itself every three weeks. By the end of the twentieth century 97 percent of all children have been administered a Polio Vaccine. The scourge of early twentieth century America, polio and its control became indicative of the nation's ability to solve social and medical problems with increasing technology.

—Brian Black

FURTHER READING:

Daniel, Thomas M., editor. *Polio*. Rochester, University of Rochester Press, 1997.

Smith, Jane S. *A Paralyzing Fear: The Triumph over Polio in America*. New York, TV Books, 1998.

Political Bosses

Political bosses are professional politicians who control political machines in cities, counties, or states in ostensibly democratic regimes. Bosses first emerged in the United States in the early 1800s when masses of newly franchised, inexperienced voters provided bosses with opportunities for regimentation, mobilization, and manipulation. Each subsequent expansion of the franchise to new classes of voters, and each new wave of immigrants allowed bosses to strengthen their political power base.

Each individual political boss is a leader within the political machine hierarchy. Little bosses and big bosses are connected in a feudal hierarchy, each with a fiefdom to be exploited, and each bound to the other by mutual self-interest and personal loyalty. The boss is accountable for his actions to no one outside the machine.

The principal methods used by the boss to gain control over voting blocs are patronage, the power to appoint persons to formal positions of power in the government; spoils, the power to distribute tangible rewards, including government contracts for goods and services, tax favoritism, formal and informal exemptions from legal enforcement and prosecution, and the issuance of government permits; the politics of recognition, especially the rapid integration of newly arrived immigrant groups and minority groups into the political system; and the nomination of a balanced electoral ticket in which all supporters of the machine are represented. Bosses secure the public and electoral support of extended families, gangs, business organizations, neighborhoods, ethnic groups, and immigrant groups through patronage, graft, and the granting or withholding of favors,

including government services, government welfare benefits, and social and economic benefits provided by the machine itself. Machine-provided benefits include membership in social clubs, gift baskets for the needy, and make-work employment for unemployed machine supporters.

The political machine is an interdependent community bound together through the boss. Various class, race and ethnic groups are united by the common political objectives of seizing control of government and using government to secure advantages for the constituent groups within the machine. The machine is a vehicle for class, race, and ethnic cooperation and integration, and for the distribution of economic, social, and political benefits across all social groups. Membership in the machine is an achieved status, earned through demonstrated service to the machine. The machine recruits political outsiders into the political system, provides rapid political and social advancement for members of immigrant and minority groups, and helps mainstream and empower groups and individuals previously outside the acting political community.

In jurisdictions where political machines are active, the informal political power of the machine replaces the legal authority of government officials. Bosses typically put their personal self-interest and the machine's self-interest above the interests of political parties, government institutions, and the public. Bosses use their power over politics and government to accumulate personal wealth and social status, and demand deference from leaders of non-political institutions, including businesses, churches, charities, community groups, and criminal organizations. Bosses practice politics for personal profit.

During the course of building the machine, bosses often form mutual-support alliances with corrupt business and criminal elements. These alliances, the conspiracy upon which they are based, and the scintillating lawlessness inherent in reciprocation of power and influence, undermine popular respect for politics and for machine-supported public officials. The resulting scandals and public outrage are the central themes for many novels, films, and television programs, especially police dramatic series. Feelings of helplessness in confronting an overpowering machine also leads to public withdrawal from politics and to political apathy.

Efforts at political reform during the Progressive Era in the late nineteenth and early twentieth centuries, including the civil service system, party primary elections, the multiplication of elected offices, especially in the state and local executive branches, the rotation, staggering, and shortening of elected terms of office, and introduction of the Australian ballot, merely strengthened the power of the boss. First, the reforms further complicated politics, making amateur political leaders less able to compete with the bosses. Second, the diffusion and legal limitations of official authority increased the need and opportunity for unofficial, efficient authority to emerge. Attempts to solve the problem of bossism merely increased the opportunities for bosses to flourish.

Famous bosses include William W. "Boss" Tweed and George Washington Plunkitt, leaders of Tammany Hall, a fraternal aid, charitable, and political organization that controlled the New York City Democratic Party and city politics from 1798 until Tweed's fraud conviction in 1872. Boss Tom Pendergast ran the Kansas City, Missouri, machine throughout the 1930s, paving city streets and rivers and giving Harry Truman his start before being sent to jail on tax evasion charges late in the decade. Mayor Richard Daley controlled the Chicago machine during the mid-twentieth century. Most American cities and states succumbed to the power of similar bosses and political machines at one time or another. There is no distinctive personality type, life history, or other measurable criteria to distinguish a boss from a legitimate political leader. "Bossism" is defined subjectively. E. J. Flynn, author of *You're the Boss,* writes that it is only the leader you do not like who is a boss, and the political organization you do not like that is a machine. Throughout American history, writers, journalists, and political opponents have readily found evidence of bossism in the political leaders they dislike.

—Gordon Neal Diem

FURTHER READING:

Callow, Alexander. *The Tweed Ring.* Westport, Connecticut, Greenwood, 1981.

Croly, Herbert. *Progressive Democracy.* New York, Macmillan, 1914.

Elazar, Daniel J. *American Federalism: A View from the States.* San Luis Obispo, California, Cromwell, 1992.

Erie, Steven. *Rainbow's End: Irish-Americans and the Dilemmas of Urban Machine Politics, 1840-1985.* Berkeley, University of California Press, 1988.

Fadely, James. *Thomas Taggart: Public Servant, Political Boss, 1856-1929.* Indianapolis, Indiana Historical Society, 1997.

Flynn, E. J. *You're the Boss.* New York, Viking Press, 1949.

Menard, Orville. *Political Bossism in Mid-America: Tom Dennison's Omaha, 1900-1933.* Lanham, Maryland, University Press of America, 1989.

Royko, Mike. *Boss: Richard Daley of Chicago.* New York, Dutton, 1971.

Steinberg, Alfred. *The Bosses.* New York, New American Library, 1972.

Van Devander, Charles. *The Big Bosses.* Stratford, New Hampshire, Ayer, 1974.

Zink, Harold. *Bosses in the United States.* Durham, North Carolina, Duke University Press, 1930.

Political Correctness

The social and cultural phenomenon known as political correctness emerged on American college campuses during the 1980s and became a part of the larger cultural scene in the 1990s. Political correctness was neither a social movement nor a coherent political platform, but rather a tendency among governing bodies, especially in academic institutions, to police the spoken, written, or implied beliefs of those with whom they disagreed. Organizations and individuals behaved in a politically correct, or PC, manner when they attempted to restrict the rights of others to espouse opposing beliefs or to use offensive language. To its critics, primarily conservatives, political correctness was censorship, pure and simple; to its proponents, primarily liberals, it was an attempt to create an environment in which no one gave or took offense.

The historical origins of the term political correctness are unclear but telling. Some trace the origins of political correctness to Chinese communist leader Mao Tse-Tung, who debated the origins of correct ideas in his *Little Red Book.* The term was used even earlier, however, when in 1793 a U.S. Supreme Court justice wrote in an opinion, "This is not politically correct." In Russia in the 1930s, Stalinists used the phrase to evoke a "sense of historical certitude." Leninists used the phrase to describe those steadfast to their party affiliations. The phrase was used in the 1960s to describe people who altered their manners and beliefs to fit the prevailing political movements. But political correctness at the end of the twentieth century took on its meaning beginning in the 1980s, when conservative campus advocates began using the phrase to describe the leftist movement to increase multicultural, gay, and feminist studies and to impose codes of conduct that would eliminate behaviors deemed racist, sexist, homophobic, or otherwise unacceptable. Political correctness was thus a pejorative term used by conservatives to describe what they perceived as an attempt to undermine their values.

Whatever its origins, it is clear that political correctness was born of political power, and exerted by socially or politically powerful blocs attempting to establish norms for behavior and speech. When those politically powerful groups first emerged on college campuses in the 1980s, they were largely identified with the generation of academics who had come of age in the 1960s and had recently acquired enough power, through tenure or academic leadership, to enact their agenda. Under the banner of a celebration of American multiculturalism, politically correct academics encouraged the study of feminism, homosexuality, and ethnicity, all in an attempt to give oppressed groups a stronger voice in society. Politically correct theorists proposed that oppressive white males of European descent had dominated American history for long enough, and that it was time to value the contributions of other social and cultural groups.

The concrete impact of political correctness on college campuses came in the creation of codes of conduct and the establishment of courses and departments dedicated to the study of previously marginalized topics. Codes of conduct took many forms across college campuses. Speech and harassment codes punished verbal or physical conduct (epithets, slurs, graphic materials, etc.) that offended an individual or group of individuals. While most such codes were inherently reasonable—how could one favor date rape?—critics claimed that they were used to silence the opinions of conservative white males and that they were enforced, often without regard to due process, by governing bodies eager to serve the needs of the so-called oppressed minorities. As politically correct ideals were mandated, open and honest debate declined. Students and faculty feared being labeled incorrect and faced serious punishment if they violated broadly defined and sometimes subjective speech codes. Although conduct codes were created with good intentions, many students and faculty felt the codes limited academic freedoms and constitutional rights to freedom of speech and assembly.

Multicultural studies were intended to make higher education more demographically and culturally inclusive. Feminist and homosexual studies followed the multicultural movement, and quickly became established in college curricula. Supporters of political correctness claimed that they were attempting to broaden the canons of classical texts and studies by including works by women and minority groups. Conservatives and traditionalists argued that politically correct professors taught the ideas of inferior female or minority authors instead of civilization's greatest authors and philosophers. Stanford University, for one, engaged in a very public and divisive debate over which books to include in its curriculum in the late 1980s.

Political correctness did not descend on campuses overnight, nor did it change college curriculums without a fight. As they began to perceive the ill effects of political correctness, social and political conservatives and liberal proponents of free expression began to articulate their opposition to the changing political atmosphere. Opponents of political correctness decried the inclusion of what they deemed inferior subject matter into the curriculum, charged that politically correct professors were intimidating students into expressing only politically correct beliefs, and hailed the crackdown on anything politically incorrect as a new kind of McCarthyism. These fights between liberals and conservatives were soon carried out in public debates, in articles and books, and on talks shows, thus bringing political correctness to the attention of mainstream culture.

Many governmental organizations soon found themselves facing similar issues to those debated on college campuses in the 1980s as they attempted to define how they would deal with such issues as gays in the workplace and the military, sexual harassment, and hate crimes. On both a state and a national level, legislatures argued over whether to adjust laws to extend special protections to women, homosexuals, or minorities. The passage of the Americans with Disabilities Act in 1990, the backlash against any form of sexual harassment that followed the Clarence Thomas-Anita Hill Senate Hearings in 1991, and the passage of hate crime legislation all seemed to indicate that political correctness had found its way into American law. But the passage of anti-Affirmative Action legislation in California and Washington in the late 1990s indicated that the tide might be turning against legislation intended to protect minority groups.

Perhaps the most pervasive impact of political correctness on American culture came with regard to language. In an effort to show no disrespect for anyone, promoters of political correctness largely succeeded in reducing the number of offensive or inaccurate names used to refer to people. For example, descendants of historically oppressed groups are now called ''Native Americans'' instead of ''Indians'' and ''African Americans'' instead of ''blacks.'' (But descendants of groups that are predominantly of European origin—Italians, Germans, Irish, etc.—did not receive new classifications.) Euphemistic language emerged as a means to prevent offending the sensitivities of others. Examples include using the term ''sanitation engineer'' instead of garbage man, and ''firefighter'' instead of fireman. The mentally retarded or physically handicapped became ''challenged.'' It also became politically correct behavior to recycle, to oppose wearing fur, and to accept homosexuality as an ''alternative lifestyle.'' Though such language became the source of frequent jokes—short people became known as ''vertically challenged,'' for example—its impact was far reaching.

By the late 1990s, open public discussion of political correctness had largely ended, in large part because it had been naturalized into the cultural landscape. To its credit, political correctness helped create a new politeness and sensitivity to differences among American cultural groups. However, by pointing out the differences and mandating codes of behavior, it also heightened hostilities between opposing political sides and contributed to the culture wars of the late twentieth century.

—Debra Lucas Muscoreil

FURTHER READING:

Berman, Paul, editor. *Debating P.C.: The Controversy over Political Correctness on College Campuses.* New York, Dell Publishing, 1992.

CQ Researcher. *Academic Politics.* Washington, D.C., Congressional Quarterly Reports, 1996.

Darnovsky, Marcy, Barbara Epstein, and Richard Flacks. *Cultural Politics and Social Movements.* Philadelphia, Temple University Press, 1995.

Dickman, Howard, editor. *The Imperiled Academy.* New Brunswick, Transaction Publishers, 1993.

D'Sousa, Dinesh. *Illiberal Education: The Politics of Race and Sex on Campus.* New York, Free Press, 1991.

Gitlin, Todd. *The Twilight of Common Dreams.* New York, Holt, 1995.

Henthoff, Nat. *Free Speech for Me but Not for Thee.* New York, HarperCollins, 1992.

Sacks, David O., and Peter A. Thiel. *The Diversity Myth: ''Multiculturalism'' and the Politics of Intolerance at Stanford.* Oakland, Independent Institute, 1995.

Wilson, John. *The Myth of Political Correctness.* North Carolina, Duke University Press, 1995.

Pollock, Jackson (1912-1956)

His aggressive, sometimes violent personality combined with a new painting technique elevated artist Jackson Pollock to legendary status among American painters. His turbulent outbursts and his drip paintings earned him a reputation that would later become the stereotypical idea of the modern artist. Reconciling the unconscious

Jackson Pollock

with the creative act of painting was the impetus behind the paintings of abstract expressionist artist Pollock. His gestural works and technique of flinging and dripping paint over canvas had its inspiration in an exploration of the painting process and stemmed from his association with surrealist artists. Pollock once referenced the act of painting in itself as a source of magic. The art critic Harold Rosenberg picked up on this thought and termed the work ''action painting.'' Pollock's action paintings became the cornerstone of the abstract expressionist art movement. This technique, an all-over approach that redefined pictorial space by doing away with any differentiation between the foreground and the background, stunned the art world when first presented at the Betty Parsons New York Gallery in 1948.

Paul Jackson Pollock, born in Cody, Wyoming, January 28, 1912, spent his early years in the American Southwest, specifically Arizona and California, where he developed an interest in mysticism and mythology. This fascination resurfaced after studying with American Regionalist painter Thomas Hart Benton at the Art Students League in New York from 1930 to 1932. Pollock's imagery began to contrast sharply with the realism of Benton; Pollock had more of an interest in the intangible expressions of emotions as subject matter. Pollock's brush with the work of Mexican muralists Diego Rivera and Clement Orozco during his tenure with the Works Projects Administration Federal Art Project in 1935 reinforced his interest in metaphysical ideas. Pollock also became obsessed with large scale images. In the 1940s some of his canvases grew to sizes over 16 feet long.

Before Pollock began applying the action painting technique, his work in the early 1940s related to the automatic gestural painting practiced by many surrealists and the influence of Wassily Kandinsky and Pablo Picasso. Pollock's earliest images contained loose, gestural figurative forms. The gesture of the painting overtook the subjects beginning in 1947. Soon, recognizable imagery became obliterated by tangles of lines and shapes formed by dripping and poured paint. The movement and layers of the paint intermingled, flattening the plane and often seeming to continue beyond the edges of the canvas. Large scale works such as *Lavender Mist* (1950) and *Full Fathom Five* (1947) were the culmination of this style and became some of Pollock's best known and most successful pieces. Pollock claimed every drip and line was deliberate; he refuted the idea of chance or accident as part of his creative process. Art critic Clement Greenberg, familiar with Pollock's work, encouraged the artist to continue with his unique technique. Greenberg's favorable reviews and his backing of the New York School, with Pollock at the center, led to an exciting period in art history. The abstract expressionists, including Pollock, Mark Rothko, Willem De Kooning, Robert Motherwell, and Franz Kline, in addition to Pollock's wife, artist Lee Krasner, helped make New York the art center of the world. There artists produced exciting new works that defined the idea of avant-garde art.

A return to figurative imagery in Pollock's work after 1950, seen in works such as *#27* (1951) and *Easter and the Totem* (1953), still incorporated the philosophy of applying paint purely for its expressive qualities. Yet, Pollock did not have as much success with these later images as he did with his earlier non-figurative paintings. This lack of success fueled a problem with alcoholism that began to consume Pollock. Moreover, his marriage was disintegrating, and Pollock's life rapidly spiraled downward, culminating in a fatal automobile accident in 1956.

During his short life, Pollock was a prolific and original artist. His works of art had a profound impact on an art community that was ready for reinvention. Pollock and the New York School revitalized the American art scene while filling New York City with a raw, artistic excitement—the discovery of a new way of producing and thinking about art. Pollock and his action paintings were pivotal to the art movement abstract expressionism. Often parodied, Pollock is a legendary figure representing modernity in art in the twentieth century.

—Jennifer Jankauskas

FURTHER READING:

Naifeh, Steven W., and Gregory White Smith. *Jackson Pollock: An American Saga.* New York, C.N. Potter, 1989.

O'Connor, Francis V. *Pollock: A Catalogue Raisonné of Paintings, Drawings, and Other Works.* 4 volumes. New Haven, Yale University Press, 1978.

O'Hara, Frank. *Jackson Pollock.* New York, G. Braziller, 1959.

Potter, Jeffrey. *To a Violent Grave: An Oral History of Jackson Pollock.* New York, G.P. Putnam's Sons, 1985.

Ratcliff, Carter. *The Fate of a Gesture: Jackson Pollock and Post-War American Art.* New York, Farrar, Straus, Giroux, 1996.

Robertson, Bryan. *Jackson Pollock.* New York, Harry N. Abrams, 1960.

Solomon, Deborah. *Jackson Pollock: A Biography.* New York, Simon and Schuster, 1987.

Polyester

The Frankenstein's monster of fabrics, polyester has enjoyed more lives than the evil baron's monstrous creation. The wonder fiber of the post-war West became the fashion rage of the superfueled 1970s. Then, dismissed and disavowed by the cognoscenti, it seemed on the verge of extinction until modern science resurrected its utility in the form of polar fleece in the 1990s. What a long, strange trip it's been.

Other than LSD, perhaps no man-made compound influenced the style of an era quite like polyester. And like LSD, it had its origins in a European laboratory. Polyester, the invention of two chemists working at the Calico Printers Association in England, was not the first man-made fiber. Rayon and Nylon had been in use for years as sportswear and stockings, respectively. But when J.T. Dickson and J.R. Whinfield hit upon a way to spin petrochemical molecules into threads, they created a fiber that was light years ahead in terms of its versatility and utility. The DuPont company sensed the commercial potential of the new invention and purchased the patents for it in 1950. Within three years, polyester was being produced in mass quantities.

Polyester's principal virtue was its plasticity. Natural fibers like cotton or wool cannot be re-engineered, but a man-made fabric like polyester can be custom designed to produce a different aesthetic. With advances in technology, new polyester blends were concocted that simulated the look and feel of ''real'' fabrics. Furthermore, because polyester is naturally permanently pressed, the need for irons and ironing boards was greatly reduced. DuPont even coined a term, ''wash and wear,'' to describe the wondrous properties of its new synthetic.

Throughout the 1960s, polyester was sold to the public as the avatar of a new era of space age convenience in clothing. And for the most part, the people seemed to be buying it. Ads for ''perma-prest,'' ''wash-and-wear,'' and ''double knit'' items began dotting the pages of such barometers of public taste as the *New York Times* and the Sears catalog. In the 1970s, polyester pantsuits, leisure suits, and garishly-colored knit shirts stormed into fashion, as the fabric attained a kind of hipster cachet among suburban moderns. Poly blend sport shirts and flared slacks seemed the perfect attire for weekend barbecues, wife-swapping parties, and trips to the singles bar. Demand for the wonder synthetic became so great by 1974 that manufacturers had difficulty filling their orders.

What killed polyester? Like the fierce debate over "Who lost China?" in the 1950s, the question admits no easy answer. For one thing, there was the problem of ubiquity. By the late 1970s, polyester fashion had become so absorbed into the mainstream that it lost all claim on fashionable taste. Furthermore, with so much polyester on the market—and so much of it cheaply constructed— the fabric's inherent weaknesses began to assert themselves. Simply put, polyester does not breathe the way cotton does. The resultant tendency toward sweatiness gave the clothes a disagreeable downmarket connotation. Finally, the excesses of disco, as personified by John Travolta's egregious white polyester suit in the 1977 film *Saturday Night Fever,* put the final nail in the wonder fabric's coffin.

For almost two decades, polyester languished in popular disrepute. Occasionally used in blends in order to make clothes less expensive, it was all but shunned as an emblem of poor taste by anyone with a shred of fashion sense. Camp film director John Waters even titled his 1981 celebration of tackiness *Polyester.* In the mid-1990s, however, the miracle fiber began to make a comeback in the form of polar fleece. Best known under the trade name Polartec, the fabric was marketed in the form of sweaters, leggings, hats, and mittens by such hip winter wear outfitters as Patagonia and Lands' End. Once again, polyester's utility was the major selling point. Polar fleece is lightweight and does not absorb as much water as other fabrics, making it the perfect lining for outerwear.

And as it had in the 1950s, utility begat fashionability. By 1998, top designers such as Donna Karan and Tommy Hilfiger were integrating polar fleece into their clothing lines. While it was perhaps too early to declare polyester completely rehabilitated, the popularity of winter sports and the rise of casual chic seemed to assure the continued marketability of polar fleece into the new millenium. The wonder fabric's most remarkable attribute, it seemed, was its indestructibility.

—Robert E. Schnakenberg

FURTHER READING:

Stern, Jane, and Michael. *The Encyclopedia of Bad Taste.* New York, HarperCollins, 1990.

Pop Art

Pop art developed in the turbulent cultural milieu of the early 1960s as a response to the brooding intellectual and emotional aspects of abstract expressionism. Originally a British movement of the mid-1950s, in American hands pop art became commentary on the mass production culture and the banality of everyday life. Artists like Andy Warhol, Roy Lichtenstein, and Claes Oldenberg utilized the images and production techniques of daily American life in a consumer society, transforming them into objects that were neither wholly real nor wholly art; in the process, they strove to make viewers aware of the extent to which advertising and the production/consumption cycle had come to dominate their lives.

The phrase "Pop Art" seems to have originated from two sources: from British artist Richard Hamilton's 1956 collage picture *Just What is it that Makes Today's Homes so Different, so Appealing?,* which featured a bodybuilder holding a gigantic "Tootsie Pop" sucker; and as a descriptor of an art which highlighted "popular" everyday objects. The latter definition is more relevant. Pop Art was filled with images of consumer products, rendered in styles derived from advertisements or familiar images. The subject matter, as an early critic described it, was "the twentieth century communications network of which we are all a part." Pop artists borrowed heavily from the slick, flashy, cliché-ridden advertising industry to depict the objects that were a part of American consumerism. Subjects were rendered in a simple, flat manner that emphasized the thinness of the canvas. Strong, bright colors were favored, and the image was centralized within the pictorial space. All of this was in direct contrast to the work of the abstract expressionists, who created formless, nonobjective art that grappled with existential questions of meaning.

The most successful pop artists adopted these techniques in different ways. Roy Lichtenstein used the style of comic strips— bright colors, single scenes, Ben Day dots, and dialogue balloons. He depicted a world of prepackaged emotions (parallel to consumer products) and gender stereotypes. The women in Lichtenstein's paintings were concerned with love and marriage, as in the romance comics; the men inhabited the war comic world of violence and death. In the mid-1960s, Lichtenstein also drew from art history within his comic strip style, integrating such genres as cubism and abstract expressionism. His work thus shifted from a critique of the banal world of everyday America to a commentary on the secularization of high culture.

James Rosenquist's referent was the billboard. A former sign painter, Rosenquist painted on huge canvases a succession of seemingly random fragmented images. For example, his most famous painting, *F-111* (1965), features a military jet, a young girl beneath a missile-shaped hair dryer, and close-ups of spaghetti and an automobile tire. Rosenquist described his work in these words: "I treat the billboard image as it is. I paint it as a reproduction of other things. I try to get as far away from it as possible."

This retreat from the thing itself into the image of the thing was most evident in the work of pop art's most famous practitioner, Andy Warhol. His Campbell's Soup cans, Brillo pad boxes, and Coca Cola bottles epitomized the tension between high art and popular culture. Rather than stacking actual Brillo boxes, he made his own—at a studio appropriately called The Factory—thus demonstrating a preference for the representation over the original. Perhaps this was most cogently demonstrated in Warhol's *The Marilyn Diptych* (1962), which reduced the late actress to a single repeated image that exemplified Hollywood's commodification of the individual. This detachment from the real thing became a desensitization or anesthetization in Warhol's images of automobile crashes and electric chairs. The banality of the every day had spilled over into our emotional lives, numbing us to the real feeling that should naturally arise in the face of violence or tragedy. Warhol, like other pop artists, used the mass production techniques of advertising. His particular favorite was the silkscreen, which he used to repeat identical images across a canvas.

Claes Oldenberg transformed common consumer products into sculptures. In 1961, he turned his New York studio, which occupied a converted shop front that he called The Store. He lined the space with his plaster recreations of food items and consumer goods. Visitors who purchased his work, such as a plaster soda can, were thus recreating the activity of a traditional store. Oldenberg succeeded in treating the gallery as a pseudo marketplace, underscoring the producer/consumer aspect of the artist/patron relationship. Later, he created huge soft sculptures—foam-filled images of everyday items which sagged and drooped, like the human body, under the effects of gravity.

Perhaps the greatest legacy of pop art was the union of art and popular culture. Pop art expressed the idea that the American common stock of shared cultural knowledge no longer came from "high culture" sources like literature or mythology, or from religion, but rather from television, movies, and advertisements. While increasingly fewer Americans in the late twentieth century were familiar with great poetic works, for example, nearly all could recite a good line from a popular movie a cliched phrase from a television advertisement. Pop artists sought to reflect this increasing banality by blurring the distinction between art and consumption. After the heyday of pop art, the public no longer could be sure whether a Coca Cola bottle was an object, a work of art, or both. In pop art and commercial advertising the image became more important than the thing. Pop art begged the question: What is more important, the thing or its image? In the end, pop art may have been, as the poet and critic Frank O'Hara called it, merely a "put on." Nevertheless, it was important in that it facilitated the examination of the effects of consumerism on human thought, emotion, and creativity.

—Dale Allen Gyure

FURTHER READING:

Alloway, Lawrence. *American Pop Art*. New York, Collier Books, 1974.

Lippard, Lucy R. *Pop Art*. New York and London, Oxford University Press, 1970.

Livingstone, Mario, editor. *Pop Art*. London, Royal Academy of Arts, 1991.

Mamiya, Christin J. *Pop Art and Consumer Culture: American Super Market*. Austin, University of Texas Press, 1992.

Mahsun, Carol Anne Runyon, editor. *Pop Art: The Critical Dialogue*. Ann Arbor, Michigan, UMI Research Press, 1989.

Pop, Iggy (1947—)

As the vocalist and leader of the rock band The Stooges, Iggy Pop helped to popularize a new style of music that was loud, raw, and deceptively simple. It dealt with subjects such as boredom, drugs, and violence. Songs such as "Death Trip" and "Your Pretty Face Is Going to Hell" served as a counterblast to flower power idealism of the 1960s, and their stripped down, primal sound worked against the prevailing trends toward longer songs and complex instrumentation. As a result, Iggy and the Stooges were an important influence on the punk and grunge movements.

Pop, born James Osterberg, originally planned to be a blues drummer and moved from his home in Ann Arbor, Michigan, to Chicago, Illinois, to learn the music first hand. Although he sometimes sat in with established musicians, Osterberg came to realize that the best he could do was to parrot their riffs, which he believed was exactly what most prominent white blues bands were doing. Deciding to create a type of simple yet powerful music based on his own experiences, he contacted Ron and Scott Asheton whom he knew from high school, and their neighbor Dave Alexander. They formed a band, first known as the Psychedelic Stooges

Shortly afterward, Osterberg began calling himself Iggy Pop and established an on-stage persona that was designed to shock audiences. Pop would sometimes perform with his head and eyebrows shaved and wearing a maternity dress, but as his reputation emerged and his drug problems worsened, his antics escalated accordingly. Pop lacerated himself on stage, picked fights with members of motorcycle gangs who had come to heckle the band, and routinely dove from the stage to crawl at the feet of audience members. On one infamous occasion, he even vomited into the crowd before a show. Although the Stooges never achieved commercial success, their music and performances set the stage for the punk movement of the late 1970s and 1980s, and a number of groups explicitly acknowledged a debt to Iggy and the Stooges. The Ramones cited the band as one of their favorites, and The Sex Pistols released a version of "No Fun."

While Iggy Pop may have to some cultivated the persona of an idiot, that was far from the truth. He had been class valedictorian in high school, and The Stooges soon collected a number of intelligent and musically savvy supporters. Jazz trumpeter Miles Davis counted himself as a fan, and, although David Bowie was moving toward a heavily produced, complex form of rock that seemed the antithesis of the Stooges, he also praised them. John Cale, then with The Velvet Underground and formerly with La Monte Young's avant garde ensemble The Dream Syndicate, produced their first release in 1969.

That self-titled album drew no shortage of detractors, who claimed that the band was little more than a bunch of amateurs whose popularity rested entirely on Iggy Pop's antics. Although the music seemed basic, its vigor attracted a following. A number of bands attempted to imitate The Stooges' seemingly elementary sound, but few came anywhere near the power and intensity of songs like "I Wanna Be Your Dog." After releasing *Funhouse* in 1970, the band took a four -year hiatus from the studio that was due in part to their increasing drug abuse and, later, to Pop's departure for England to work with David Bowie. Pop would dissolve the band in favor of a solo career, only to reform it when he was unable to find musicians who met his standards. Bowie produced the band's final album, *Raw Power*, in 1974. Songs such as "Gimme Danger" and "Search and Destroy" showed that The Stooges had lost none of their edge, although critics complained that Bowie's production effectively sanitized the band's sound. The Stooges broke up shortly afterward.

Pop's solo work for the rest of the 1970s was more restrained. Still, songs such as "Lust for Life" (later featured in the soundtracks to the films *Trainspotting* and *Basquiat*) and "The Passenger" also garnered some praise, and David Bowie enjoyed a hit single with "China Girl," a song he had co-written with Pop. Turning to acting, Pop appeared in John Waters' *Cry Baby* (1990) and Jim Jarmusch's *Dead Man* (1995).

—Bill Freind

FURTHER READING:

McNeil, Legs, and Gillian McCain. *Please Kill Me: The Uncensored Oral History of Punk*. New York, Grove Press, 1996.

Pop, Iggy. *I Need More*. Los Angeles, 2.13.61, 1992.

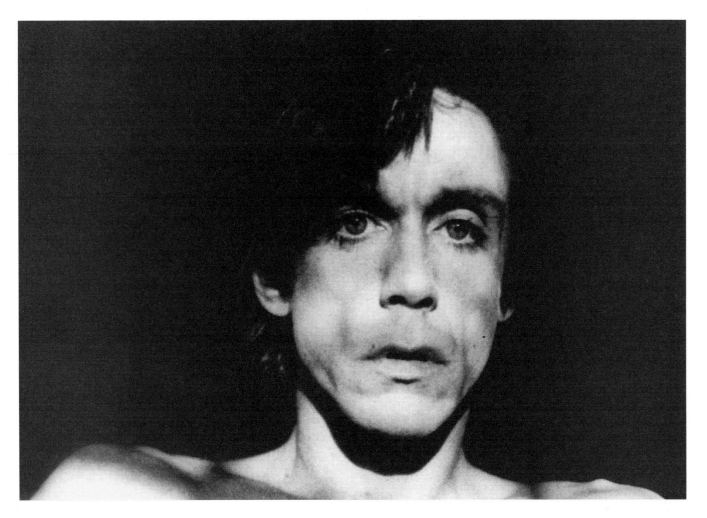

Iggy Pop

Pop Music

While there has always been "popular" music in the United States, and all forms of music are popular with certain audiences, the term "pop music" generally denotes forms of music that are non-classical, very mainstream, intended for very wide audiences, and often controlled by the giants of the music business: sheet music publishers in the early decades of the century, recording companies after 1930. While these companies often produced a great variety of music, their need for profits mandated a constant search for the "next big thing," the next great artist, or style of music whose popularity would generate big record sales. Thus fueled by the profit motive, companies sought to reach the widest markets possible. And while the large companies did produce music targeted at markets considered "marginal," such as the African-American population, they tended to focus on music that was unchallenging, unthreatening, and palatable across the spectrum of listeners.

The focus on palatable, tuneful, and unchallenging music did not necessarily mean music of poor quality. White crooners such as Bing Crosby, Frank Sinatra, Doris Day, Tony Bennett, and other artists, along with black performers such as Ella Fitzgerald and Nat "King" Cole, dominated the popular music charts during the 1940s and early 1950s. They also produced some of the finest pop vocal music ever recorded, often composed by the accepted masters of the popular genre such as the Gershwins, Cole Porter, Jerome Kern, Irving Berlin, Harold Arlen and others, whose best-known songs have become standards of the repertoire—the classics of light, romantic, and/or witty music. Prior to the rise of rock 'n' roll in 1955, this style of music *was* American pop music, and it appealed to white Americans, and listeners in other English-speaking countries, of all ages and classes. The music was easy to produce, and the recording companies knew what material to look for. With the rise of rock 'n' roll, however, things changed. The large companies that defined the pop music field began finding it increasingly difficult to control or predict the course of pop music and the "next big thing" became harder and harder to find with any regularity. Thus, after 1955, the pop music field fragmented and, by the end of the twentieth century, that fragmentation had become so great that the term "pop music" is now very difficult to define.

This fragmentation was the result of numerous of factors. First, while the major record companies such as Columbia, RCA, Decca, and Capitol dominated the pop vocal field during the 1940s and 1950s, they were not the only companies in the music business. Small, independent labels such as Chess, King, Specialty, Sun, and others were busy recording and selling more marginal or specialized music—blues, rhythm and blues, country and western, ethnic music, folk, gospel, and so on. What they were doing was tapping into the diverse musical landscape that existed in the United States. Occasionally, one of these small independents would have a major hit. Chess had huge successes in the mid- and late 1950s with such early rock 'n' roll greats as Chuck Berry and Bo Diddley. Sun was the first to record Elvis Presley, whose amalgamation of country, blues, and rhythm and blues styles hit the charts in the mid-1950s. These successes not only challenged the commercial success of the major labels, but they also shattered the homogeneity of the pop music field. How could Chuck Berry and Tony Bennett both be singing pop music? The answer was that they were not. After the rise of rock 'n' roll, new styles challenged the primacy of pop music dominated by white crooners.

This rupture in the landscape of popular music set off a scramble by the large companies to keep up with the changes. For a brief period, from about 1955 to 1958, they were unable to do so alone. RCA succeeded for a time by buying Elvis Presley's contract from Sun, adopting an "if you can't beat 'em, join 'em" approach, but Presley's experience at RCA was indicative of the entire approach the major labels took to pop music: co-optation. Compared to the raw power of his early Sun recordings, Presley's output on RCA was a rapid devolution into the pop crooner formula. It was the only form the major labels understood. Thus, while Presley scored some early rock 'n' roll hits on RCA ("Jailhouse Rock," "Hound Dog"), by the late 1950s he had been reshaped into the pop crooner mold, recording such songs as "Love Me Tender" and "Treat Me Nice." By the mid-1970s, Presley was recording the same songs as Frank Sinatra, notably "My Way."

By 1958, the major companies had regained much of their position through the process of co-opting many of the more marginal sub-genres of American music. If a record became a hit in one of these more marginal markets, the major labels found someone to record the same song in a way that was palatable to white middle-America. Thus, while black America heard an original like Little Richard singing "Tutti Frutti," white America heard Pat Boone's watered-down version. These major labels also followed the tried-and-true formula that had worked during the crooner era of relying on professional songwriters to write material for young singers. Thus pop music during the 1958 to 1963 period was dominated by teen idols and young vocal groups singing professionally written songs, many written out of New York's Brill Building songwriting center. This was a system the major labels understood, one controlled by professional producers using professional songwriters and studio musicians. While some great music came out of this era, it largely conformed to the major pop requirements, producing unthreatening, easy to listen to music with mass appeal.

Pop music fragmented further after the arrival of the Beatles in 1964. Since the dominance achieved by rock 'n' roll by the late 1950s, the line between rock and pop has never again been clear. The Beatles were simultaneously great rock and great pop artists, and they dominated the pop charts throughout the 1960s. "Yesterday" was undeniably in the pop mold; "Revolution" was clearly rock. Pop music in the 1960s could include both the Rolling Stones "(I Can't Get No) Satisfaction" and Dionne Warwick singing the Burt Bacharach/Hal David song "Walk On By." With this degree of variety, the meaning of the term "pop music" was becoming increasingly hazy, yet the term endures as a loose description of a wide variety of musical styles and trends. And, while earlier periods in pop music can be described as homogeneous (the "crooner" era, the "Brill Building sound," etc.), the pop field after the mid-1960s came to encompass a wide variety of overlapping styles in various stages of waxing or

waning. New styles often emerged from regional, ethnic, racial, gender-specific, or other musical communities, or they arose due to the influence of one particular artist or group. After 1964, no one style could be called "pop music" to the exclusion of all others. This fact reflected the diversity of the record-buying public, now exposed to such a wide variety of music that many were not content listening only to one style.

However, these developments did not mean the extinction of older pop styles. Crooners such as Sinatra and Bennett enjoyed great commercial success in the 1960s and 1970s. The professional songwriting tradition lived on in the work of Burt Bacharach and others and traditional practices in the pop music industry continued. As each new trend emerged, major record companies rushed to take advantage of it. Thus, after the emergence of the Beatles, record companies promoted a host of Beatles knock-offs, and almost any band from Liverpool, England, the Beatles' home town, could get a record contract after 1964. Numerous American groups were also developed and promoted to capitalize on the music and image of the Beatles. Some, such as the Knickerbockers and their song "Lies," were direct rip-offs of the Beatles sound; others, such as the Monkees, aimed to emulate the Beatles in both looks and sound. When the Beatles recorded their psychedelic masterpiece *Sergeant Pepper's Lonely Hearts Club Band* album in 1967, they set off another round of imitators, from the Rolling Stones' *Their Satanic Majesties Request* on down. After 1967, the Beatles moved on from psychedelic music, but their influence meshed with the rising San Francisco psychedelic sound that produced such groups as the Grateful Dead and Jefferson Airplane, both of whom used drug imagery in their music. Both groups might have been too much for the broad range of American pop music listeners, but the pop music field was still able to profit from the sound. Using the old tradition of watering down a musical form, Top 40 radio listeners heard Scott McKenzie singing "San Francisco (Be Sure to Wear Flowers in Your Hair)" or the Mamas and Papas' "California Dreaming."

This trend of co-opting more marginal musical forms and making them palatable to broad audiences remained strong in the late 1960s. The 1960s was a period when several of popular music's most innovative artists were making ground-breaking records, some of which made the pop music charts, but they shared the charts with much lighter fare. Another significant trend during the late 1960s was the rise of manufactured groups. In addition to trying to co-opt other sounds, large corporate record companies tried to manufacture their own groups for the pre-teen and teen market, which, increasingly, had been left behind by psychedelia and other harsher forms of rock music. With such groups as the Monkees, the Partridge Family, and the cartoon group the Archies, companies could make light, pop fare that was extremely palatable to this young market. All of these three groups were promoted with their own television shows. The Monkees and David Cassidy from the Partridge Family became teen idols. This trend was not new to the late 1960s. Earlier teen idols had been similarly "manufactured," and the trend continued in later decades with such singers and groups as Shawn Cassidy, Andy Gibb, Leif Garrett, Menudo, New Edition, Boys to Men, N'Sync, and others.

In the 1970s, the variety of styles that were part of the broad pop music mainstream increased. They included the singer-songwriter tradition, hard rock, southern rock, the California sound, disco, glam rock, stadium rock, heavy metal and others. All entered the pop field at various points. The most important of these trends were the singer-songwriter tradition, the California sound, and disco. The light sound of the singer-songwriter tradition was especially suited to pop music, and brought huge hits for artists such as Carole King, James Taylor, Joni Mitchell, Cat Stevens, Paul Simon, Randy Newman, and John Denver during the decade. All sang introspective songs, often using mostly acoustic instruments that were perfect for the pop sound. Some listeners could find deep meaning in the lyrics of the songs, but these songs were also extremely radio-friendly, soft and often very hummable. Carole King's *Tapestry* album sold over 10 million copies and was on the charts for years; John Denver was all over the airwaves in the later 1970s with such songs as ''Rocky Mountain High'' and ''Sunshine on My Shoulders.'' The singer-songwriter tradition meshed well with the California sound that emerged in the early 1970s. Led by such groups and singers as America, the Eagles, Linda Ronstadt, and Jackson Browne, the California sound was often easygoing, acoustically-oriented music that reflected the laid-back atmosphere of southern California. The Eagles' songs ''Peaceful Easy Feeling'' and ''Take It Easy'' spoke for themselves.

The singer-songwriter tradition and the California sound were largely eclipsed in the late 1970s, as was much of popular music, by disco. Disco, with its thumping, repetitive dance beat and electronic sound was greeted with great enthusiasm by many; for others it was considered the death of pop music. Disco music was dance music, and as such it was part of a much larger club scene rather than simply music for listening. Disco grew, like much of pop music, from the culture of black America, particularly the smooth black urban pop of the early 1970s. Some commentators trace elements of it to dance clubs in Manhattan, in particular to the city's gay culture. Whatever its precise origins, the style reached the pop charts in the mid-1970s with Donna Summer's ''Love to Love You Baby,'' KC & the Sunshine Band's ''Get Down Tonight,'' and others. But the genre exploded in popularity when the film *Saturday Night Fever*, starring John Travolta as a disco-dancing Brooklyn teenager, was released in 1977. Its soundtrack album, featuring the Bee Gees' new disco sound, became one of the most successful records in pop music history. After this success, everyone from the Beach Boys to Rod Stewart to the Rolling Stones jumped on the disco bandwagon for a time. Disco's heyday was short-lived, ending with the 1970s, but its influence continued in the 1980s and beyond.

Pop music's purview widened even further in the 1980s and 1990s, encompassing both old and new trends and styles. The vocal tradition, although far-removed from its crooner days, continued with such major solo vocal divas as Whitney Houston, Mariah Carey, Celine Dion, and Madonna. While most of these singers stayed with predictable and comfortable material, Madonna was unique among them and achieved great success with her meld of disco, pop, r&b, and often outrageous image and controversial material. The teen-idol tradition remained alive and well, but now many of the teen idols were young women such as Debbie Gibson, Tiffany, and the Spice Girls, who offered soft pop to an eager pre-teen market. The 1980s and 1990s, not unlike earlier decades, was also an era of great solo stars such as Billy Joel, Michael Jackson, and Elton John, all of whose songs topped the charts in the 1980s and drew huge crowds for their stadium concerts. Jackson's album *Thriller* was one of the best selling albums of all time, crossing over between pop, disco, and rhythm and blues.

A new trend in the early 1980s was what has been called a ''second British Invasion'' (the first being the Beatles-led invasion of the early 1960s). Coming out of the influential but less widely popular new wave movement of the late 1970s, groups and artists such as Duran Duran, the Eurythmics, Culture Club, U2, Adam Ant, Wham!, and others were significant to the decade. Many relied on synthesizers and drum machines that gave their sound a widely popular electronic feel. There was also a strong fashion consciousness to many of these bands, which—as always in pop and rock—was integral to their image. The visual aspects of this music were heightened by the rise of MTV (Music Television), which began in the early 1980s by playing specially produced music videos of new bands. MTV's increasing influence proved a powerful force in music during the 1980s and 1990s.

Pop music continued to absorb other, more marginal, musical styles. Rap music, a product of black urban youth culture in the 1980s, was one such style. While rap still maintains its authenticity in the hands of many artists, mainstream pop music gradually adopted some of its conventions in diluted form with such performers as MC Hammer and Vanilla Ice, both of whom achieved brief periods of popularity. Another important trend in the late 1980s and into the 1990s was the rise of ''alternative'' music. Originally, alternative music was the harder-edged, guitar-based ''grunge'' sound that emerged out of Seattle with such bands as Nirvana. But the ''alternative'' label could just as easily be applied to somewhat older, influential bands such as Athens, Georgia's R.E.M. and the B-52s. The style was broadened during the 1990s to include a whole host of new bands that challenged the bland pop music that was occupying the official pop charts. Groups such as Nirvana, Pearl Jam, Stone Temple Pilots, and others provided a fresh alternative to such mainstream fare as Phil Collins, Michael Bolton, and Whitney Houston. The alternative genre saw the rise of a new influx of female talent, including the somewhat harder-edged Alanis Morrisette and Joan Osborne as well as more pop-oriented female performers such as Sarah McLachlan and Jewel. As in many of the trends absorbed by pop, the term ''alternative'' widened to such a degree that it had become virtually meaningless by the late 1990s. With the great success achieved by these and other bands, the question ''alternative to what?'' became a hard one to answer by the late 1990s.

As a whole, pop music was much more diverse by the late 1990s than at any other period in its history, and a wide variety of performers and genres could be grouped under its broad umbrella. While that variety certainly proved refreshing to many people, it has raised the problem of defining pop music. However, there are some general characteristics of pop music that have remained fairly constant. First, while pop music is an inclusive genre that draws from a wide variety of styles, it often does so by co-opting them, taking unique musical forms and watering them down for mass consumption. While unique performers and artists continue to find success, the pop charts are often crowded with lesser talents enjoying their ride on the current trends. Second, pop music is primarily commercially driven. All recorded music has its commercial imperatives, but in pop music the drive for commercial success dominates, and this focus often leads to less-than-original music, centered on the lowest common denominator. Third, the style of pop music is fundamentally dictated by trends, and no one in the music industry knows what the next big trend will be. When a trend emerges, often because of a particularly innovative artist or group, a host of imitators follow close on their heels. The originators often move on to new areas, the wave of imitators eventually crashes, and the search for the new begins all over again. Thus, for better or worse, pop music is an ever-changing phenomenon in American popular culture.

—Timothy Berg

FURTHER READING:

Breithaupt, Don, with Jeff Breithaupt. *Precious and Few: Pop Music of the Early '70s.* New York, St. Martin's Press, 1996.

Clarke, Donald, editor. *The Penguin Encyclopedia of Popular Music.* New York, Penguin Books, 1989.

Gregory, Hugh. *A Century of Pop: A Hundred Years of Music That Changed the World.* New York, Acapella Publishers, 1998.

Have a Nice Decade: The '70s Pop Culture Box. CD box set. Rhino Records, 1998.

Miller, Jim, editor. *The Rolling Stone Illustrated History of Rock & Roll.* New York, Rolling Stone Press, 1980.

Whitburn, Joel. *Joel Whitburn's Top Pop Singles 1955-1996: Chart Data Compiled from Billboard's Pop Singles Charts, 1955-1996.* 8th Edition. Record Research, 1997.

The Pope

Within the Roman Catholic Church, the pope serves a dual role as both the Bishop of Rome and the spiritual and symbolic leader of the Church as a whole. According to Catholic doctrine, the pope is the ultimate arbiter of Church tradition and, in specific cases, his teachings are recognized as infallible in matters of faith and morals. As the global personification of Catholicism, the institution of the papacy has exerted a strong influence on American religion, culture, and

Pope John Paul II

politics, shaping not only how Catholics expressed their religious beliefs, but how they were viewed by their Protestant neighbors. Throughout American history, Catholicism in general and the papacy in particular has sparked periodic attacks by ''nativist'' Protestants who saw newly arriving Catholic immigrants as detrimental or dangerous to American society. In the nineteenth century, this resulted in several riots in northern cities and the burning of Catholic churches, schools, and convents. Although tensions between Catholics and Protestants cooled in the twentieth century, attacks against ''popery'' remained a common feature of America's political and cultural institutions. Both evangelical Protestant leaders and the popular press condemned Catholic immigrants as soldiers or spies for Rome who were undermining the Protestant character of the nation.

The crux of the nativist argument was that individuals, particularly newly arrived immigrants, could not be spiritually committed to the pope and remain politically loyal to the American government. One of the most outspoken proponents of this nativist rhetoric was the early twentieth century writer and agrarian Populist Tom Watson. Watson insisted that several Catholic groups in America—parish priests, the Knights of Columbus, and religious orders, particularly the Jesuits—were actually the pope's secret warriors. Their goal, Watson claimed, was to overthrow the American republic and enthrone the pope as supreme ruler over the United States. The same themes were articulated by the prominent anti-Catholic journal *The Menace,* which both warned of a papal coup and blamed Catholic corruption for the failure of progressive political reforms. *The Menace* was founded in 1911 and, within four years, it boasted a circulation in excess of one and a half million and spawned a host of imitators in rural towns throughout the next decade. Tensions with Germany and the rise of World War I brought a halt to *The Menace,* and a lull in anti-Catholicism in general, in the later half of the 1910s as resentment toward the pope was shifted toward the Kaiser. In the 1920s and for the next several decades, however, Catholics were exposed to renewed attacks, largely from the Ku Klux Klan. Catholics were one of many groups singled out as ''un-American'' by the Klan, which became an increasingly powerful and political organization.

American Catholics' own understanding of the papacy have often been ambiguous. On one hand, Catholic prayer, ritual, and iconography had centered on the pope. But, on the other hand, Americans frequently reinterpreted, or even ignored, papal demands that seemed out of place in American life. During the first decade of the twentieth century, Pope Leo XIII and Pius X routinely condemned Catholic leaders for cooperating with Protestants in providing public schooling for Catholic children, involving the laity in parish affairs, and their ecumenical work with other Christian denominations. By labeling these offenses ''Americanism,'' the popes insisted that Americans had broken from longstanding Catholic traditions and needed to bring their behavior in line with the rest of the Catholic world. Yet, on several levels, the breach between America and Rome increased over the next several decades, particularly in the liturgical movement of the 1930s and 1940s, which sought to reform the traditional Latin Mass long before it was altered by the dictates of the Second Vatican Council in the 1960s. Thus, American Catholics were caught in a paradoxical bind, criticized by their religious leaders for being too American and denounced by journalists and politicians as not American enough.

America's uneasiness towards Catholicism often had deep political implications. ''No Popery'' and ''Immigrants Out'' became synonymous slogans in the political battle for immigration restriction in the 1920s. In fact, the immigration quotas adopted in 1924 were designed explicitly to exclude large numbers of immigrants from southern and eastern Europe whose religious beliefs and ethnic stock were deemed inferior to Protestant Americans. In 1928, Al Smith, the Catholic governor of New York, encountered similar resentment when he ran for the presidency. Although he won the Democratic nomination, Smith was denounced and defeated largely over assumptions that he would bring ''Popery'' into public schools and undermine the Protestant character of the nation. Although Smith's criticisms toward prohibition and his Democratic connections also hurt his campaign, his attachment to ''foreign'' Catholicism contributed to Smith's loss to Republican candidate Herbert Hoover.

In 1960, John F. Kennedy faced similar opposition in his presidential campaign against Richard Nixon. Kennedy, a Catholic Senator and Democrat from Massachusetts, was heavily influenced by the anti-Catholic propaganda surrounding his candidacy. Kennedy often downplayed his connections to Rome, insisting that he ''wore his religion lightly'' and that the Constitution, not papal dogma, would dictate his political decisions. In the Senate, Kennedy voted against using federal funds to subsidize parochial schools and opposed the appointment of an American ambassador to the Vatican. While both moves earned him sharp reprisal in the Catholic press, Kennedy's political record also demonstrated to many Protestant voters that Catholicism was not enough to disqualify a candidate from office. Some conservative critics still felt that Kennedy's election was part of a papal plot aimed at subjecting Americans to Roman rule. But Catholics cheered Kennedy's election not simply as a political victory but as a symbol of Catholics' prosperity and success in spite of adversity and bigotry.

According to Catholic doctrine, when a reigning pope dies, a new one is chosen by the college of Cardinals—a group of high-ranking Church officials throughout the world. Although the papacy as an abstract symbol has played a pivotal role in shaping America's politics and culture, the actions of certain individual popes have also attracted American attention among Catholics and non-Catholics alike. One example is Pius X (1835-1914), who reigned as pope from 1903 to 1914 and was the only twentieth century pope to be declared a saint. Pius X seriously offended many Americans by refusing to receive Theodore Roosevelt during his visit to the Vatican because the former president had visited a Methodist congregation earlier on his trip. A more significant example of the papacy's role in American culture is the decision by Pope John XXIII (1881-1963), who reigned from 1958 to 1962, to call the Second Vatican Council. Convened from 1962 to 1965, the rulings of the council transformed Catholic religious services and increased communication and dialogue with other religions. But, more importantly, Vatican II sought to ''shake off the dust'' in Catholicism by signaling a new willingness to participate in and minister to an increasingly complex modern world.

Yet, for many Catholics, John XXIII's successor, Paul VI (1897-1978), did much to undo the enthusiasm and liberalism generated by Vatican II. In 1968, Paul VI issued an encyclical (papal ruling) known as *Humanae Vitae* that denounced all forms of artificial birth control; it was rejected by 90 percent of American Catholics as well as several of his own advisors. While he upheld the rulings of Vatican II, Paul VI represented a conservative shift in Catholic leadership that continued through the late twentieth century. This is particularly apparent in the papacy of John Paul II (1920—), formerly the Archbishop of Krakow and the first non-Italian pope elected in over 400 years. While previous popes had remained in relative isolation within the Vatican, John Paul II has been a tremendous world traveler known for his

charisma and dramatic speaking voice. While he has received criticism in both America and abroad for his condemnation of abortion, birth control, homosexuality, and women's ordination, John Paul II has increasingly brought Catholicism into the public eye. John Paul II has been the twentieth century's longest living pope, as well as one of its most prolific and outspoken. His conservative theology has caused many late-twentieth-century Americans to view the papacy not as an institution bent on national domination, as was feared in earlier decades, but as either a guardian of traditional morality or an outdated model of leadership that has become increasingly out of touch with the modern world.

—Justin Nordstrom

FURTHER READING:

Bentley, James. *God's Representatives: The Eight Twentieth-Century Popes.* London, Constable and Company Ltd., 1997.

Dolan, Jay P. *The American Catholic Experience: A History from Colonial Times to the Present.* Notre Dame, Indiana, University of Notre Dame Press, 1992.

Fuchs, Lawrence H. *John F. Kennedy and American Catholicism.* New York, Meredith Press, 1967.

Hingham, John. *Strangers in the Land: Patterns of American Nativism 1860-1925.* New Brunswick, New Jersey, Rutgers University Press, 1988.

Popeye

A seagoing superhero, Popeye was first seen in 1929 in E.C. Segar's *Thimble Theatre*. The comic strip itself had been running, dispensing fairly cockeyed mock-adventure continuities, since King Features Syndicate introduced it in 1919. Segar, however, did not get around to inventing his tough, spinach-eating sailor until almost ten years later. Already on board when the squint-eyed sailor entered were the quintessentially thin Olive Oyl and her diminutive and entrepreneurial brother Castor Oyl. J. Wellington Wimpy, whose fondness for hamburgers knew no bounds, entered the strip in 1931. By that time the crusty, two-fisted Popeye had long since become the undisputed star and the title had changed to *Thimble Theatre Starring Popeye*.

Never a master cartoonist, Segar compensated for his lack of drawing ability with a gift for audacious comedy. In his long, rambling comic continuities he kidded serious adventure narratives as well as current political and social activities at home and abroad. Segar also frequently made fun of the newspaper business and the cartooning profession. In one early 1930s sequence he showed an artists' bullpen where a group of interchangeable cartoonists spoke nothing but exclamations like ''Zowie,'' ''Zam,'' and ''Bonk,'' and drew strips with such titles as *Zip the Dip* and *Boop the Doop*. A long time science fiction buff, he frequently built stories around strange creatures and odd inventions. Among the eccentrics who frequented *Thimble Theatre* were Alice the Goon, the Sea Hag, the tough café owner Roughhouse, the mystical critter known as Eugene the Jeep, and his foster child Swee'pea. Popeye was a fellow who believed that might made right, and a sock in the snoot was a frequent negotiating tool with him. As the strip progressed his powers continued to increase until he was bulletproof, incredibly strong, and came close—except that he was not nearly as serious—to foreshadowing Superman. Eventually Segar revealed that it was spinach, usually consumed straight from the can, that gave Popeye his incredible abilities.

Popeye also proved to be an impressively successful merchandising figure. In addition to being reprinted in comic books and Big Little Books, he inspired windup toys, toy musical instruments, pull toys, and puppets. According to toy expert Richard O'Brien, "the two most popular comic strip toy characters of the 1930s were Popeye and Buck Rogers." Popeye's image also appeared on every sort of product from canned goods to tooth brushes. In 1933 King Features licensed the Max Fleischer Studios to produce a series of animated cartoon shorts. Though not especially faithful to Segar's strip, the Popeye cartoons were box office hits and continued for over 24 years; later, they became a staple of kids' television. The revenue from all the salty seaman's subsidiary rights eventually reached millions of dollars every year.

Popeye's oft repeated pragmatic statement, "I yam what I yam," was widely quoted during his heyday—as were such Wimpyisms as "I would gladly pay you Tuesday for a hamburger today," "Let's you and him fight," and "Come to my house for a duck dinner—you bring the ducks."

After Segar died of leukemia in 1938 at the age of 44, King replaced him with bullpen artist Doc Winner. They then brought in cartoonist Bela Zaboly and writer Tom Sims. While Zaboly was actually a better cartoonist than either of his predecessors, Sims was never to duplicate the eccentric nonsense and oddly paced adventures that Segar had concocted. During the early 1950s, writer and magazine gag cartoonist Ralph Stein was brought in to work with Zaboly. Finally, Bud Sagendorf took over the writing and drawing in 1958. This was a job Sagendorf had sought for 20 years while working on an assortment of art assignments for King Features; he had been Segar's assistant in the 1930s, starting the job while still in high school. In the mid-1980s, onetime underground cartoonist Bobby London assumed the daily strip. Today *Thimble Theatre* runs in only a handful of papers around the world. Only the Sunday page, drawn by Hy Eisman, offers new material and the daily strip consists of reprints of Sagendorf material.

—Ron Goulart

FURTHER READING:

Marschall, Richard. *America's Great Comic Strip Artists.* New York, Abbeville Press, 1989.

O'Brien, Richard. *The Story of American Toys.* New York, Artabras, 1990.

Segar, E.C. *The Complete E.C. Segar Popeye.* Westlake Village, Ohio, Fantagraphics Books, 1980.

Popsicles

Popsicles are a confection made of fruit juice frozen on a stick. In the 1870s the Ross and Robbins company sold something similar, which they called the Hokey-Pokey. In 1924, Frank Epperson, a powdered lemonade vendor from California, patented a more fully realized version of the product, which he originally named the Epsicle. He sold his patent to the Joe Lowe Corporation, which became Popsicle Industries. The chief Popsicle flavors were grape, orange, and cherry. Later variations of the product included the Creamsicle, the Fudgsicle, the Twin Pop, and the Bomb Pop, and helped keep neighborhood ice cream trucks like Skippy and Good Humor in business during the summer. What made the Popsicle line

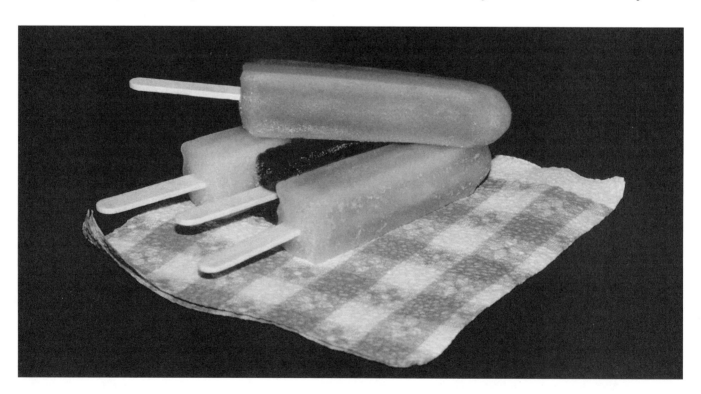

Several popsicles resting on a napkin.

distinctive was the inclusion of the flat wooden stick, allowing the frozen confections to be eaten like lollipops. People saved these sticks and used them for craft projects, making everything from baskets and boxes to lamp bases out of them.

—Wendy Woloson

FURTHER READING:

Dickson, Paul. *The Great American Ice Cream Book.* New York, Atheneum, 1972.

Popular Mechanics

Since 1902, *Popular Mechanics* has been published as a monthly magazine that describes the wonders of twentieth-century technology for the lay reader in a "gee-whiz" style, with do-it-yourself home-workshop projects thrown in for good measure. Debuting just a year before the Wright Brothers' flight at Kitty Hawk, when automobiles and motion pictures were still recent innovations, *Popular Mechanics* has chronicled the breakthroughs of the most productive century in the history of science and mechanics. The periodical made its appearance in Chicago in January 1902 as *Popular Mechanics* and did not become *Popular Mechanics Magazine* until 1910, by which time it had already absorbed another small technical publication by the name of *Technical World.* Its readership grew from only five subscribers in 1902, plus a few readers paying five cents a copy at the newsstand, to a worldwide circulation of 1,428,356 by 1998. In 1947, a Spanish language edition (*Mecanica Popular*) was produced, along with several other foreign language editions in French, Danish, and Swedish.

The story of its founding tells as much about American ingenuity as its content. *Popular Mechanics Magazine* was founded by Henry Haven Windsor, Sr., a former city editor of the Marshalltown, Iowa, newspaper, and the son of an Iowa minister. A strong advocate of science and mechanics, Windsor saw the need for a periodical that could present clearly written technical material to the average man (*Popular Mechanics* continued its focus on a male readership into the 1990s). Prior to his work as founder and editor of *Popular Mechanics,* Windsor had worked for the Chicago City Railway Company in the 1880s. There he started a trade magazine, the *Street Railway Review,* which he edited from 1892-1901. Researching articles for the *Review,* Windsor once spent six months disguised as an operator of an old-fashioned grip car so he could acquire firsthand understanding of the problems of operators.

Windsor brought this same passion for mechanical detail and technical know-how to *Popular Mechanics.* Initially, he wrote every article and sold every advertisement himself for the fledgling eight-page weekly, which by 1904 had grown to 100 pages. Its rapid growth in both size and circulation was testimony to Windsor's vision for the magazine and his ability to tap into a previously unrecognized market. Although Windsor died in 1924, the magazine remained under the control and editorship of the Windsor family through several generations. It became part of the Hearst Corporation in the mid-1950s.

Although developments in science and technology spawned other successful publications, such as the earlier *Popular Science Monthly* (1872), *Mechanics Illustrated* (1928), followed by *Science Digest, Popular Homecraft, Popular Electronics,* and others, none gained the wide appeal of *Popular Mechanics Magazine.* During World War II, the magazine was popular among American G.I.s, who sometimes wrote letters home to request that family members respond to job-training advertisements for them, in anticipation of their return to civilian life. With its practical, down-to-earth, hands-on advice, its focus on "how-to" articles, its clear writing and copious illustrations, the periodical's success lay in its narrow focus, appealing directly to the independent, do-it-yourself reader. With its slogan, "Written So You Can Understand It," *Popular Mechanics* during these years strove to appeal to the general, nonacademic reader who wanted to read about new "modern" advances during the golden years of American science and technology. The publication was also famous during these years for its classified ads section, which offered hundreds of money-making schemes every month, ranging from home locksmithing equipment to furniture building kits to such "untechnical" pursuits as songwriting, stuffing envelopes, and selling patent medicine nostrums.

Especially from the 1930s through the 1950s, *Popular Mechanics* anticipated developments in astronautics by publishing futuristic articles that offered hints about the evolution of rocket science and space exploration, some of which were dismissed as speculative "Buck Rogers" fiction but that were later proven to have been prescient. During the 1970s, when the omnipotence of science and technology began to fade in the minds of some Americans, the magazine and others like it were criticized by environmentalists and others for advancing a worldview based on technological domination of the planet and the exploitation of nonrenewable resources. In the 1980s, *Popular Mechanics* devoted many pages to covering new developments in consumer electronics and personal computers. By the end of the 1990s, the magazine was featuring such articles as "Half Man, Half Machine: New Breakthroughs in Bionics Perfect Battery-Powered Eyes, Ears, Limbs and Muscles," as well as buyers' guides to new cars and trucks, new lawn mowers, and gardening tools. These articles reflected perspectives of the late twentieth century, with awareness of current breakthroughs in medical technology as well as attention to consumer information.

Since its beginnings, a distinctive feature of *Popular Mechanics* has been its emphasis on "descriptive illustration." As Roland E. Wolseley pointed out, Henry Windsor issued a policy statement when he founded the publication: "Most magazines use illustrated articles. We do not. We use described pictures." At the end of the 1990s, articles in *Popular Mechanics* remained profusely illustrated with detailed analyses of machine parts and step-by-step procedures for everything from replacing roof shingles to performing periodic washing machine maintenance.

In the late 1990s, Joe Oldham was editor-in-chief of *Popular Mechanics Magazine,* which by then had its own website, called "PM Zone," and a television version of *Popular Mechanics for Kids.* Offering a detailed chronicle of mechanical and technological innovation throughout the twentieth century, the magazine was as familiar to working- and middle-class Americans as *Harper's Weekly,* with its illustrated coverage of the Civil War, had been to those of the nineteenth century.

—Lolly Ockerstrom

FURTHER READING:

Mott, Frank Luther. *A History of American Magazines 1885-1905,* Cambridge, Massachusetts, Harvard University Press, 1957.

Peterson, Theodore. *Magazines in the Twentieth Century.* Urbana, Illinois, University of Illinois Press, 1956.

"Popular Mechanics Website." http://www.popularmechanics.com. June 1999.

Wolseley, Roland E. *Understanding Magazines.* 2nd edition. Ames, Iowa State University Press, 1969.

Popular Psychology

Popular psychology springs from the desire of people searching for inspiration and self-improvement in a secular form. This desire accounted for some of the success of the eighteenth-century bestseller *Poor Richard's Almanack,* through which Benjamin Franklin conveyed proverbs and aphorisms about human nature along with weather reports and other practical information. By the time psychology emerged as a discipline in the 1880s and 1890s, the United States already had a sizeable reading public that readily consumed literature on self-improvement and the "gospel of success," and there was also a strong market for spiritualism and mental healing. Books and articles of popular psychology merged easily into these two streams, one secular and the other metaphysical, because they aimed to provide an understanding of the mind's workings that could be used for either practical self-improvement or for more mystical psychic explorations.

Although psychology detached itself from religion when it became an academic discipline, popular psychology maintained a fairly close relationship with the religious lives of Americans. This connection was visible from the start. William James, the most influential of all American psychologists, believed in mesmerism, the practice of inducing a trance so as to open the mind of the subject to extrasensory perceptions and healing forces. Mesmerism in America yielded a very popular mind-cure philosophy that predisposed Americans to consider psychology a means for tapping unconscious psychic forces for the general betterment of the person.

The phenomenal 1897 bestseller, *In Tune with the Infinite* by Ralph Waldo Trine, exemplified this "transcendentalist" characteristic of American popular thought. Until the appearance of the not dissimilar *Power of Positive Thinking* (1952) by Norman Vincent Peale, Trine's book was the biggest selling inspirational book of the twentieth century. In it, the author offered his readers peace of mind through a meditative, ecumenical approach for achieving psychic oneness with God. Though not a book of psychology, *In Tune with the Infinite* drew on the concept of the unconscious as a deep spiritual reservoir. Trine urged the reader "to come into the full realization of your own awakened interior powers":

> There is a mystic force that transcends the powers of the intellect and likewise of the body. There are certain faculties that we have that are not a part of the active, thinking mind. . . . Through them we have intuitions, impulses, leadings, that instead of being merely the occasional, *should be the normal and habitual.*

As formally trained psychologists, neurologists, and psychiatrists entered the fray of popular literature, they often seemed to be saying much the same thing, but in a secular form and with titles that were less ethereal, more "scientific" or simply duller. *Directing Mental Energy* by Francis Aveling, for example, a 1927 book whose jacket carried the supertitle "The Business of Thinking," aimed to help readers "economize" their mental and emotional energy so as to lead more productive and satisfying lives. "The successful man or woman of today," the book's promotional copy read, "must know how to organize every ounce of energy to meet the pressure of our complicated existence."

Efficiency in the use of one's inner resources and relaxation of an overtaxed body and mind were common themes of psychological self-help books, all of which were based on the premise that Americans were coping with a complex and nerve-wracking civilization. The words "nervous" or "nerves" frequently appeared in the title of this literature. Some of the most popular books of the 1920s, 1930s, and 1940s were neurologist Abraham Myerson's *The Nervous Housewife (1920),* psychiatrist Josephine Jackson's *Outwitting Our Nerves* (1921), and psychiatrist David Harold Fink's *Release From Nervous Tension* (1943). These authors aimed to help their readers cope with anxiety, insomnia, exhaustion, boredom, and depression, problems that were linked to the peculiar demands of America's fast-paced, competitive, work-oriented, and technologically-driven society.

It is clear that many of the same problems and goals of Americans at the end of the twentieth century were already well articulated in its early decades. Then, as now, the quest for inner reserves of power and tranquility, for methods of maximizing energy and efficiency, and for solutions to vexatious emotional problems has fueled the engine of popular psychology. Yet, across the span of a century, there are discernible phases and eras of popular psychology, which reflected significant changes in American society and culture.

The genesis of popular psychology can be observed partly through the career of Joseph Jastrow, the first person to receive a Ph.D. in psychology in the United States and a pioneer popularizer of the discipline. Born in Warsaw in 1863 and raised in Philadelphia, Jastrow was the son of a prominent rabbi and Talmud scholar. Studying with Charles S. Peirce and G. Stanley Hall, he completed the Ph.D. in psychology at Johns Hopkins in 1886 and went on to the University of Wisconsin, where he set up one of the nation's first and best psychology laboratories. At the Chicago World's Fair of 1893, Jastrow and Hugo Munsterberg, a pioneer of applied psychology, made the first big public demonstration of modern psychology. The two young men set up an apparatus to measure various mental responses and distributed an explanatory pamphlet. For a nominal fee, visitors tried out the testing laboratory and learned something about their mental characteristics.

From the beginning of his career, Jastrow regularly wrote on psychological topics for magazines, but his fame as a popular psychologist was rooted in the 1920s and 1930s, when he wrote syndicated newspaper columns of psychological advice. These became the basis of two popular books, *Keeping Mentally Fit* (1928) and *Piloting Your Life* (1930). Jastrow also hosted a radio program on this subject for NBC from 1935-38. His writing and speaking encompassed all aspects of the field and told something about prevailing attitudes toward psychology at the time. Jastrow authored a book for the general public on the theories of Freud (*The House That Freud Built* (1932)), but he himself was no Freudian. Like many psychologists, as opposed to psychoanalysts, Jastrow preferred to discuss the facts produced by tests of perception and cognition rather than wander into grand theories of childhood sexuality.

One of the purposes he set for himself, and one that typified books of psychology for the layman, was to puncture myths and weigh generalizations with data. "Are bright children weaklings?" "Do school leaders make good?" and "Are city children brighter?"—these were the sort of questions being answered by citing the latest studies of aptitude and achievement. A second goal was simply to explain psychological categories that had come into vogue, such as "complex" and "repression," and to give an explanation of such everyday phenomena as absent-mindedness, fatigue, anxiety over dreams, and sexual self-consciousness. The most obvious defect of these "genres" of popular psychology, even in the hands of an eminent scholar like Jastrow, was their tendency to degenerate into glibness and conviviality. For example, in *Keeping Mentally Fit* Jastrow answered one young woman's appeal for advice about her "sex-consciousness" with the jest that men cannot really understand the way women think about sex: "A man can have only the man's sense of this sex relation, and he sees nothing in other men to get excited about. He isn't blind to the fact that women find men attractive, and he tries to see some compliment in it to himself; he doesn't get much farther than recognizing it as an amiable weakness of women."

By far the overriding theme of Jastrow's psychology, and of many of his contemporaries, was the need for emotional self-control and proper social adjustment to one's work, community, and family. The Mental Hygiene movement of the Progressive Era and 1920s emphasized bodily integrity through exercise and diet, emotional integrity through relaxation, and mental integrity through proper self-assessment and concentration on one's tasks. Americans were dedicated enough to an optimistic philosophy of efficiency and advancement, both personal and social, that they managed to transform even Freudianism in their own image, deleting its atheism and pessimism and making it another program for social betterment. Freud's notion of sublimation, whereby unruly impulses were turned to productive endeavors, was easily compatible with the psychology of usefulness. While child psychology underscored the value of giving children freedom to express themselves, particularly through constructive play, Jastrow's generation nonetheless emphasized the dangers of the self-indulgent personality type. "For efficiency and happiness we must have emotional control," advised the 1929 book *The Healthy Mind: Mental Hygiene for Adults* edited by Henry Elkind:

> The angry man cannot think clearly; the man in fear of losing his job does poor work. . . . The infant, a complete tyrant, absolutely selfish, is a model exhibition of anger, or fear and of most of the undesirable emotions. He has to learn control of his responses through social pressure. That is the object of modern education— the comfortable adjustment of the individual to his surroundings.

Popular psychology entered a second phase of popularity in the 1940s, catalyzed by the Second World War. As had happened in World War I, the reality of war-related mental disorders—"psychoneuroses," as they were then known—stimulated great public interest in the workings of the mind and its effect on the soul. Sympathetic to the plight of GIs who returned home troubled by insomnia, nightmares, nervousness, and malaise, the American public showed not only a heightened interest in psychology but also a greater appreciation of its usefulness for normal people experiencing temporary or occasional problems. Popular magazines ran feature stories candidly conveying the emotional effects of war on fighting men and approving the soldiers' need to express their emotions by crying when necessary. Psychologist Abraham Sperling began his 1946 book *Psychology for the Millions* by discussing this new phenomenon: "The model of courageous behavior is no longer portrayed by a stoic,

tight-lipped, muscle-bound he-man. . . . The supposed hard-bitten soldier bares his soul and is that much better off for it." *Psychology for the Millions,* in its praise of the new emotional openness of Americans, reflected the rising sophistication about psychology and the more exuberant self-expression that characterized American society since the 1920s.

The psychology boom of the 1940s was perhaps most obvious in its penetration of religious inspirational literature. The postwar therapeutic age was heralded in 1946 by an immensely popular book on psychology that was written not by a psychologist but by a clergyman, Rabbi Joshua Loth Liebman. The book, *Peace of Mind,* sold a million and a half copies in a few years, preaching a new creed in which an optimistic neo-Freudian psychology, based on the work of Karen Horney and Alfred Adler, teamed up with religion to help Americans overcome angst and personal problems en route to spiritual fulfillment. Liebman believed in the power of modern psychotherapy to cure ills that had befuddled traditional religion and in this belief he was joined by two of the most influential Protestant ministers of the century, Harry Emerson Fosdick and Norman Vincent Peale.

Both these men had begun to introduce psychology into their pastoral counseling in the 1930s, and along with Liebman, they helped disseminate it to millions of people in the 1940s and 1950s. The special significance of these writers lay in their being clergymen, for their audience included many people who might not otherwise have considered psychology a legitimate resource. Fosdick's *On Being a Real Person* (1943) was based on actual cases of people who came for pastoral counseling. The book, Fosdick hoped, would describe the "familiar mental and emotional maladies" of ordinary people, "their alibis and rationalizations, their ingenious, unconscious tricks of evasion and escape, their handling of fear, anxiety, guilt, and humiliation, their compensations and sublimations also, and the positive faiths and resources from which I have seen help come." Peale, the biggest selling inspirational writer of the century, collaborated with a psychiatrist for the popular 1950 book *The Art of Real Happiness* which, following the lead of Liebman's *Peace of Mind,* showed how psychological insight and religious guidance could solve personal problems. Like Fosdick, Peale discussed real cases, frankly presenting stories of guilt and neurosis induced by repressed sexuality and repressed anger, family harmony ruined by alcoholism, and inundating his readers with uplifting accounts of people overcoming obstacles through prayerful concentration. Peale's 1948 *Guide to Confident Living,* which went through thirty-five printings in seven years, was promoted as a "book of workable spiritual prescriptions [that] used the principles of religion and modern psychiatry to bring practical help and new hope to millions of readers."

In the 1960s and 1970s Peale's blend of Christianity and psychology found a competitor in a "countercultural" melange of Eastern meditation, consciousness-raising, and humanistic and Gestalt psychology. Instead of concentrating on the book of Psalms and the Gospel, some Americans now strove for a "zen mind" and "peak experiences." The venerable American belief in the great hidden capacities of the mind, in a subconsciousness where the mental and the spiritual could be unified, transformed from "the power of positive thinking" to "transcendental meditation." Peale's positive thinking was supposed to produce public success, not just peace of mind. The meditationist trend of the 1960s and 1970s, however, rejected social convention and focused intensely on the state of the mind. At its most extreme, this trend was personified by psychologist Timothy Leary.

Leary's idiosyncratic career started with the prestigious job of directing the Kaiser Foundation Hospital of Oakland, California. Swept up by the current of the times and by experiments with hallucinogenic drugs, Leary quit his practice to preach to American youth about a new drug-based psycho-spiritual creed: "Turn on, tune in, drop out." The college-oriented youth culture produced wide-ranging demands for a new psychology of insight and growth, whether through the fiction of Hermann Hesse's *Journey to the East* (1964) or *Siddhartha* (first published in the United States in 1951), Richard Bach's quirky best-seller *Jonathan Livingston, Seagull* (1970), the lectures and writings of Zen disseminator Alan Watts, or the holistic and growth-oriented theories of Gestalt and humanistic psychology. Gestalt therapists introduced the idea of the "holistic" into American awareness, and the founders of humanistic psychology, especially Abraham Maslow, purveyed the concepts of "self-actualization" and "peak experiences." These ideas gained currency fairly rapidly in the 1960s and 1970s for they conformed to the era's optimistic, almost utopian, expectations of human growth and potential.

In the 1980s and 1990s popular psychology took another turn, this time back toward religion and physiology, both of which were predominant interests at the start of the century. M. Scott Peck, a psychiatrist with a strong Christian orientation, wrote one of the biggest bestsellers of the late twentieth century. *The Road Less Traveled: A New Psychology of Love, Traditional Values and Spiritual Growth* first appeared in 1978 and stayed on the *New York Times* non-fiction bestseller list until the early 1990s. Peck merged psychoanalytic and humanistic insights with a strong commitment to lasting relationships of marriage and family. Turning away from the idealization of the self that was apparent in the popular psychology of the 1960s, he insisted that to love another person required emotional self-discipline, an ability to subordinate one's immediate gratification to the spiritual needs of another. These decades also saw another type of traditionalist return to biology. After several generations dominated by environmentalist approaches, psychologists reasserted the importance of biochemical processes in the brain. Peter D. Kramer's *Listening to Prozac* (1993) was the most popular exposition of the new evidence for physical sources of depression, one that mirrored and stimulated the sudden popularity of this and other antidepressants. Public fascination with the neurology of the brain surfaced in the 1980s with Oliver Sacks' *The Man Who Mistook His Wife for a Hat and Other Clinical Tales* (1985), which detailed case histories of people whose relationships and identity were derailed by discrete forms of brain damage or dysfunction.

The close of the twentieth century also witnessed a flowering of psychology books on interpersonal communication between men and women, such as John Gray's *Men Are from Mars, Women Are from Venus* (1992) and Deborah Tannen's *That's Not What I Meant!* (1986) and *You Just Don't Understand!* (1990). Counterposed to the emphasis on biological roots of behavior, these books emphasized the social and cultural bases of gender differences in language. Interpersonal communication—"getting along with others"—had long been an interest of American popular psychology, although these books showed a new sensitivity to the role of gender differences.

There was, however, one completely new development that defined much of American popular psychology in the final decades of the century. This was the literature of "recovery"—meaning recovery from addictions. Rooted in the Twelve-Step program of Alcoholics Anonymous, a unique American organization founded in the 1930s, the concept of addiction expanded in the 1980s to include not only substance abuse—alcohol and drugs—but also other kinds of

deeply engrained, habitual behavior ranging from temper tantrums to sexual obsessiveness. Although the addiction idea was undoubtedly stretched too far, the A.A. model for coping with seriously troubled people was magnetic. Merging with the newly popular idea of "dysfunctional families," it produced a separate psychotherapeutic literature that counseled individuals on how to maintain their own dignity while involved with "out-of-control" friends and family members. The Twelve-Step idea was grounded in a non-sectarian monotheistic creed and therefore represented a unique fusion of self-help and religion. As addicts came increasingly into the domain of psychiatric rehabilitation centers during and after the 1960s, the grass-roots A.A. approach was adapted by psychiatrists like Abraham Twerski. Founder of a rehabilitation center in Pennsylvania, Twerski, a Hasidic rabbi, wrote a number of popular books on recovery in the 1980s and 1990s. Like M. Scott Peck, he blended traditional religious values with therapeutic insights. For American popular psychology, the twentieth century ended much as it had begun, with intense public interest in both the physiology of the brain and the theology of psychological healing.

—Andrew R. Heinze

FURTHER READING:

Aveling, Francis. *Directing Mental Energy.* New York, George H. Doran, 1927.

Elkind, Henry, ed. *The Healthy Mind: Mental Hygiene for Adults.* New York, Greenberg, 1929.

Fosdick, Harry Emerson. *On Being a Real Person.* New York, Harper & Bros., 1943.

Fuller, Robert C. *Americans and the Unconscious.* New York, Oxford University Press, 1986.

Hale, Nathan G. *The Rise and Crisis of Psychoanalysis in the United States: Freud and the Americans, 1917-1985.* New York, Oxford University Press, 1995.

Holifield, E. Brooks. *A History of Pastoral Care in America: From Salvation to Self-Realization.* Nashville, Abingdon Press, 1983.

Jastrow, Joseph. *Keeping Mentally Fit.* Garden City, Garden City Publishing Co., 1928.

Meyer, Donald B. *The Positive Thinkers: A Study of the American Quest for Health, Wealth and Personal Power from Mary Baker Eddy to Norman Vincent Peale.* New York, Doubleday, 1965.

Peale, Norman Vincent. *Guide to Confident Living.* Englewood Cliffs, Prentice Hall, 1948.

Rieff, Philip. *The Triumph of the Therapeutic: Uses of Faith after Freud.* New York, Harper and Row, 1966.

Sperling, Abraham. *Psychology for the Millions.* New York, Frederick Fell, 1946.

Trine, Ralph Waldo. *In Tune with the Infinite.* New York, Dodd, Mead & Co., 1897.

Pornography

For over a century there has been great debate about the role of pornography in American society. Despite years of social crusades and legal and political wrangling, America remains in the late

The star of *Deep Throat*, actress Linda Lovelace.

twentieth century deeply conflicted about how to handle the "problem" posed by the existence of pornography, which *Webster's International Dictionary* defines as "writing, pictures, etc. intended to arouse sexual desire." To some, any mention or depiction of human sexuality is pornographic and should be censored; to others, no depiction of human sexuality, no matter how "perverse," should be forbidden to adults (with the exception of child pornography, which no one defends). Supreme Court Justice Potter Stewart's enigmatic 1964 statement on pornography perhaps best captured the opinion of most Americans concerning pornography; in his comment regarding *Jacobellis v. Ohio*, Stewart acknowledged that while he couldn't define pornography precisely, "I know it when I see it."

Pornography has always been present in American culture, though the "problem" of pornography has certainly been exacerbated by the ubiquity of media representations of pornography in the late twentieth century. Up until the middle part of the nineteenth century, widely shared social, religious, and cultural prohibitions against pornographic materials kept such materials largely hidden. Because what little existing early pornography was either literary or artistic, and such materials tended to circulate among the literate and well-to-do, who tended not to worry about their corrupting effects. But all that changed with the social and economic convulsions that began in the late nineteenth century. Several factors combined to put pornography into the hands of the growing working and lower classes who, according to their social "betters," were unable to fend off pornography's corrupting influence.

The vastly increased immigration of non-Protestant peoples and the concentration of the working class in urban centers, combined with the expansion of printing operations and the rise in sex trades in cities, all helped to alarm those middle-class Protestant Americans concerned with their lack of control over the direction of American culture. By the turn of the century, a number of forms of pornography became widely available, including French postcards featuring pictures of nude women, flip books (small, multi-paged booklets which revealed an "animated" sex act as the pages flipped by), and, by 1904, the first calendar featuring scantily clad women. As such materials became available to an emerging urban "underclass" no longer willing to subscribe to the moral dictates of a moralizing middle- and upper-class Protestant establishment, pornography emerged as a problem that required the attention of reformers, and the arbitration of lawyers.

The last half of the nineteenth century saw the growth of numerous reform movements in the United States (as in other industrializing nations). Reform groups, typically led by middle-class Protestant women, worked hard to improve the quality of life for urban workers swarming in their crowded warrens. Especially during the Progressive Era, reform-minded activists sought safe work places and humane work hours, especially for children, improved educational opportunity, and the suppression of "dissipating" pastimes such as gaming, festive drinking, and what was called at the time "whoring." The reformers sought to change notions of women's clothing, duties, and rights, and lobbied for womens' suffrage. Through the good agency of these reformers, school attendance was mandated, parks were established, and drinking hours, human sexual interaction, and hunting seasons were routinized.

While social reformers sought to remove or criminalize the forums in which pornography might circulate, prosecutors and lawyers struggled to define what exactly was meant by terms like obscenity and pornography. For years, U.S. obscenity law (which covered pornography) relied on the English case *Regina v. Hicklin* (1868), which overtly supported class, race, and sex divisions. It stated that obscenity be determined by "whether . . . [its] tendency . . . [was] to deprave and corrupt those whose minds [were] open to such immoral influences, and into whose hands a publication of this sort may fall." This benchmark thus assumed that a small group of morally superior people were capable of setting the standards of what was obscene for their social inferiors. Such a standard may have made sense within a rigidly defined social and class structure, but it ran counter to the very freedoms on which the American democracy was based, savaged the First Amendment, and abridged both the letter and spirit of the Constitution as a whole. Technically, it was so unnecessarily broad that even academic or scientific discussion about almost any sexual topic could be suppressed. Supreme Court Justice Felix Frankfurter once opined that the case tended to "reduce the adult population . . . to reading what is fit for children."

The first major case that aimed to clarify the legal standing of pornography was the now famous *Roth v. United States*. The 1957 ruling attempted to establish a uniform and constant standard for determining obscenity. As the result of the case, a three part test was developed to determine whether what was under examination did, in fact, have a realistic tendency to excite lust or lustful thought and thus should be censored. According to *Roth*, the key to dissemination was "whether to the average person, applying contemporary community standards, the dominant theme of the material taken as a whole appeals to prurient interest." Despite the best efforts of the Court, the ambiguity concerning the terms "dominant theme," "community standards," and "prurient interest" meant that the issue was far from being resolved.

Subsequent rulings added to the *Roth* decision. In *Jacobellis v. Ohio* (1964), the Supreme Court added another requirement to the legal definition by declaring that to be pornographic the material must be "utterly without redeeming social importance." Publishers of such magazines as *Playboy* and its many (and often more raunchy) imitators learned that as long as they published articles with some redeeming value, their work as a whole, though it contained images of nudity, would not be deemed pornographic. But the legal resolution of just such a case brought about the most elaborate ruling on obscenity yet issued by the Supreme Court in its 1973 *Miller v. California* ruling. In addition to the *Roth* language, *Miller* offered as a standard that the work in question "depicts or describes in a patently offensive way . . . sexual conduct specifically defined by the applicable law" and "that a reasonable person would find that the work, taken as a whole, lacks serious literary, artistic, political, and scientific value." Chief Justice Warren Burger further clarified the ruling by explaining that the Court meant only to restrict hard-core materials from constitutional protection.

The *Miller* ruling, together with the ongoing sexual revolution that had begun in the 1960s and that generally increased the nation's tolerance for sexual material, meant that most pornographic works (excluding child pornography) were now extended First Amendment protections and that pornographers could safely produce and distribute their works.

The major forums for pornography produced in the twentieth century have been magazines and films. The first pornographic magazines appeared in the United States and England during the Victorian era, and an odd pulp called *Captain Billy's Whiz Bang* published French postcards in its pages in the early 1920s, but it wasn't until the publication of *Esquire* in 1933 that a mass market magazine began to offer pictures of scantily clad women. *Esquire*'s Varga and Petty girls wore only the briefest and flimsiest of night clothes, but they were meant to be respectable. *Playboy* trumped *Esquire* when, beginning in 1953, it began to publish nude photographs of wholesome American "girls-next-door." *Playboy* opened the door for the "girlie" magazine in America, and such imitators as *Penthouse, Oui, Dude, Gent,* and others soon followed. The raunchiest of the girlie magazines, and the only one to truly push the now-loosened definitions of obscenity, was Larry Flynt's *Hustler*.

The presentation of nudity on film also has a long history. Early silent films, including D. W. Griffith's *Intolerance* (1915), sometimes presented brief flickers of nudity, and imported stag films showed much more, but the motion picture Production Code administered by Will Hays successfully barred any mention or depiction of sexuality in major motion pictures for several decades beginning in the 1930s. Truly pornographic films, first imported and then domestically-produced, first caught on in the 1960s, where they were shown in adult theaters and in the homes of those with a movie projector. With the advent of the VCR (videocassette recorder), the pornographic video industry boomed, such that 410 million adult videos were rented in 1991 alone, according to one study. Moreover, images once considered pornographic were by the 1980s and 1990s a regular feature in popular films and even on television.

The widespread availability of pornography beginning in the late 1960s and early 1970s reinvigorated the opponents of pornography. Concerned with whether pornography indeed promoted social problems, the U.S. Congress in 1967 formed the National Commission on Obscenity and Pornography to study the problem. The commission's 1970 findings stated that, according to available data, regulating pornography and obscenity was not a matter of national importance.

Further, it recommended that, "Federal, state, and local legislation prohibiting the sale, exhibition and distribution of sexual materials to consenting adults should be repealed," except in the cases of child pornography. Seventeen of the nineteen commission members concluded that "empirical research designed to clarify the question has found no evidence to date that exposure to explicit sexual material plays a significant role in the causation of delinquent or criminal behavior among youth or adults."

The findings of the commission, which had been appointed by then-President Lyndon Johnson, enraged President Richard Nixon, who denounced the commission as "morally bankrupt." Other conservatives followed suit, and the commission's findings were largely disregarded and led to no new legislation. Fifteen years later, under the even more socially conservative administration of Ronald Reagan, another commission was established to study the "scourge" of pornography. Attorney General Edwin Meese's commission set out to study the effects of pornography on the American people and, according to *Pornography: Debating the Issues* author Ted Gottfried, "to figure out ways to stop it from spreading without stepping on rights guaranteed by the Constitution." The highly-publicized commission findings charged that exposure to pornography led to "anti-social acts of sexual violence" and to other "non-violent forms of discrimination against . . . women," among other evils.

The diametrically opposed findings of these two government commissions made one thing clear: after almost three decades of research, no consistent body of empirical data published in English corroborates the idea that mainstream pornography causes any particular harm or damage to the normal consumer or citizen. Nor, it might be noted, does much data support the contrary theory that pornography acts as a sort of catharsis, that its presence creates a "safety valve" in a stressful society. The absence of any conclusive data on the social effects of pornography meant that the battles over pornography would be based not on reason and science but on emotion and politics. On one side of the debate were those who decried the devastation pornography visited on families and women; on the other side were those who warned of the even greater devastation that censorship caused to civil society. The debate rages on, with no clear winners.

Though they led to only one piece of significant legislation (the Child Protection and Obscenity Enforcement Act of 1988), the Meese Commission's findings energized an array of right-wing forces, pressured the Southland Corporation, owner of the 7-11 convenience store chain, to pull *Playboy* and *Penthouse* magazine from its shelves, and encouraged Senator Jesse Helms of North Carolina, who led an attack on the National Endowment for the Arts for its alleged sponsorship of pornographic art, notably the work of Robert Mapplethorpe and Andres Serrano. Perhaps the most surprising ally of the anti-pornography forces in the 1980s was a vocal group of what came to be known as anti-pornography feminists.

Women Against Pornography founding member Andrea Dworkin announced her group's agenda to audiences in the late 1970s when she declared that: "Pornography exists because men despise women, and men despise women in part because pornography exists." Anti-pornography feminists (including the group Feminists Fighting Pornography) found a potent ally in University of Michigan law professor Catharine MacKinnon, who led the campaign to establish new legislation to suppress pornography (though such laws were largely unsuccessful). Other leading feminists, including Nadine Strossen and Betty Friedan (whose own *The Feminine Mystique* had once been labelled obscene), fought very publicly against what they depicted as the forces of censorship, pure and simple. The issue thus revealed sharp divides within the feminist movement, divides which mirrored those in the public at large.

The rise of the Internet in the 1990s added new fuel to the debate over pornography. With all that the Internet could do, the thing that it seemed to do best in the 1990s was provide ready access to a vast trove of visual pornography. Some studies claimed that as much as 30 percent of the material available via the World Wide Web was pornographic in nature, and industry analysts estimated the revenues from adult web sites could reach $200 million by the end of the century. To be sure, the porn was out there: vast archives of still photography, much of it hard core, were available with the click of a mouse; much of it was available free of charge, and still more for a fee. By the late 1990s technology had made possible the transmission of video clips as well. The most troubling element of Internet pornography was its ease of access. Without special filters to screen out adult content, any child could easily stumble upon material that no parent would deem permissible. Politicians responded to the problem of "cyberporn" in 1996 with the creation of the Communications Decency Act, which prohibited the transmission of material deemed "indecent" over computer networks. The bill attracted the immediate attention of civil liberties groups and was soon found to be unconstitutional. At the end of the century, politicians, parents, and public librarians still struggled to figure out a way to restrict the access of minors to pornography over the Internet without infringing upon the rights of adults.

Throughout the century, Americans have grappled with the problem of pornography. This struggle has illuminated one of the central dramas of the American experience—the struggle between individual freedom and social control—and revealed a prudery that international observers have often found amusing. The agonizing, century-long struggle over pornography has largely supported the rights of adult Americans to have access to sexually explicit materials. But conservative zealots, progressive feminists, and concerned parents alike wonder at the social costs of such freedom of access. As with violence and bigotry, pornography is probably a problem that will remain with us.

—Dr. Jon Griffin Donlon

FURTHER READING:

Arcand, Bernard. *The Jaguar and the Anteater: Pornography and Degree Zero.* London, Verso, 1991.

Christensen, F. M. *Pornography: The Other Side.* New York, Praeger, 1990.

Donlon, J.G. "Strippers: Pandering to Patriarchy or Subverting Bourgeois Authority?" *Popular Culture Review.* Vol. 8, No. 1, 1996, 75-82.

Dworkin, Andrea. *Pornography: Men Possessing Women.* New York, Putnam, 1981.

Gertzman, Jay A. *Bookleggers and Smuthounds: The Trade in Erotica, 1920-1940.* Philadelphia, University of Pennsylvania Press, 1999.

Gottfried, Ted. *Pornography: Debating the Issues.* Springfield, New Jersey, Enslow Publishers, 1997.

Hyde, H. Montgomery. *A History of Pornography.* New York, Farrar, Straus and Giroux, 1964.

Kendrick, Walter. *The Secret Museum: Pornography in Modern Culture.* New York, Viking, 1987.

Kipnis, Laura. *Bound and Gagged: Pornography and the Politics of Fantasy in America.* New York, Grove Press, 1996.

MacKinnon, Catharine A., and Andrea Dworkin. *In Harm's Way: The Pornography Civil Rights Hearings.* Cambridge, Harvard University Press, 1997.

McElroy, Wendy. *XXX: A Woman's Right to Pornography.* New York, St. Martin's Press, 1995.

Nielsen, Alan. *The Great Victorian Sacrilege: Preachers, Politics and the Passion, 1879-1884.* Jefferson, North Carolina, McFarland & Company, 1991.

Stoller, Robert J. *Porn: Myths for the Twentieth Century.* New Haven, Yale University Press, 1991.

Strossen, Nadine. *Defending Pornography: Free Speech, Sex, and the Fight for Women's Rights.* New York, Scribner, 1995.

Porter, Cole (1891-1964)

Cole Porter was one of the most important creators of musicals from the 1920s to the 1950s. He was one of those rare Broadway composers who wrote both lyrics and music. His impressive list of twenty-three Broadway shows included *Anything Goes* (1934), *Kiss Me, Kate* (1948), and *Can-Can* (1953). Porter also wrote songs for

Cole Porter

films such as *Rosalie* (1937) and *High Society* (1956). Porter enjoyed the luxurious lifestyle, and his affluent upbringing is reflected in the wit and sophistication of both his music and his lyrics.

Cole Porter was born on June 9, 1891, in Peru, Indiana, with a proverbial "silver spoon" in his mouth; his grandfather was a multi-millionaire banker. Music was important to the young Cole, and he was already publishing songs at age 11. He continued writing songs and playing piano while a pre-law student at Yale University (B.A., 1913). Law school at Harvard did not fit well with Porter's interests, and he changed his studies to music. This greatly concerned his family, which was fearful that the heir to the family fortune would not have formal training in business acumen.

A devoted francophile, Porter spent a great deal of time in Paris, where he maintained a lavish apartment. He studied in Paris with French composer Vincent d'Indy, and Parisian locales appeared frequently in his shows.

Porter's first show, *See America First* (1916), opened and closed almost immediately. His second show, the revue *Hitchy-Koo* (1920), was as disastrous as its predecessor. Despite these early failures, Porter nevertheless continued to pursue a career as a composer. His first successful song, "Let's Do It," appeared in the musical comedy *Paris* (1928). In this song, Porter's penchant for *double entendre* is readily apparent. Two moderately successful shows, *Fifty Million Frenchmen* and *Wake Up and Dream,* appeared in 1929. During the early 1930s, Porter had hit songs with "Love for Sale" from *The New Yorkery* (1930) and "Night and Day" from *The Gay Divorcee* (1932).

Although he had produced a number of hit songs by the mid-1930s, Porter still had not written a successful show. *Anything Goes* (1934) changed that, playing 420 performances in its initial Broadway run. The plot involved mistaken identity aboard a ship, and the colorful list of characters included Reno Sweeney, an ex-evangelist turned nightclub singer; Billy Crocker, a stowaway; Hope Harcourt, a debutante; and Moon-Face Mooney, Public Enemy No. 13. Songs such as "Anything Goes," "You're the Top," "I Get a Kick out of You," and "Blow, Gabriel, Blow" garnered lavish praise for the show and its creator. Ethel Merman, William Gaxton, and Victor Moore starred in the original production.

Porter's success continued through the 1930s with several important musicals. *Jubilee* (1935), inspired by the Silver Jubilee of Britain's King George V and Queen Mary, concerned a royal family who were able to live *in cognito*. Songs included "Just One of Those Things," "Begin the Beguine," and "Why Shouldn't I?" *Red, Hot and Blue!* (1936), a political satire, starred Jimmy Durante, Ethel Merman, and Bob Hope. "It's De-Lovely," one of Porter's greatest songs, was introduced in this show. Another political spoof, *Leave It to Me!* (1938), is best remembered as the show in which Mary Martin made her Broadway debut. She sang her one solo number, "My Heart Belongs to Daddy," (the lyrics of which are replete with double entendres) while doing a striptease atop a steamer trunk and surrounded by fur-clad chorus boys. *DuBarry Was a Lady* (1939), the fifth longest-running musical of the decade, starred Bert Lahr and Ethel Merman, who introduced the immortal duet "Friendship."

Porter was an avid equestrian. In 1937, he suffered a serious riding accident from which he never would completely recover, despite over two dozen operations and several years in a wheelchair. His right leg, which was crushed in the accident, had to be amputated in 1958. From 1937 to 1958, despite intense, constant pain, Porter continued to write successful musical comedies filled with notable songs.

Porter's shows from the 1940s included *Panama Hattie* (1940), *Let's Face It!* (1941), *Mexican Hayride* (1944), and *Kiss Me, Kate* (1948). *Kiss Me, Kate,* his most successful Broadway show, takes place onstage and backstage during rehearsals for a musical version of Shakespeare's *The Taming of the Shrew.* The book by Samuel and Bella Spewack blurred the distinction between the lives of the characters as actors and as non-actors. The calvacade of hit songs included "Another Op'nin', Another Show," "Why Can't You Behave?" "Wunderbar," "So in Love," "I Hate Men," "Where Is the Life That Late I Led?" and "Brush Up Your Shakespeare." The show starred Alfred Drake and Patricia Morison. Howard Keel and Kathryn Grayson played the lead roles in the 1953 film version.

During the 1950s, Porter continued to compose successful musicals. *Can-Can* (1953) epitomized Porter's love for the French capital. Songs included "C'est Magnifique" and "I Love Paris." While Lido, the French actress who played the lead role, introduced the world to "I Love Paris," it was Gwen Verdon, who danced an Apache dance and the sensuous "Garden of Eden" ballet, who received the greatest accolades. *Silk Stockings* (1955) was Porter's last show, and his sixth to be set in France. The spy plot spawned such songs as "Paris Loves Lovers," "All of You," and "Silk Stockings." The 1957 film version featured Fred Astaire and Cyd Charisse.

Porter also maintained an active career in Hollywood. Twelve of his Broadway shows were made into films, and he wrote songs for numerous other motion pictures. Significant film songs included "I've Got You Under My Skin" from *Born to Dance* (1936), "Rosalie" and "In the Still of the Night" from *Rosalie* (1937), "Be a Clown" from *The Pirate* (1948), and "True Love" from *High Society* (1956).

Cole Porter was one of the most important creators of musicals during the middle part of the century. His sophisticated use of *double entendre* and his love for the city of Paris inspired his greatest work. His ability to create both sophisticated words and chic music made his songs stand out from those of many of his contemporaries.

—William A. Everett

FURTHER READING:

Citron, Stephen. *Noel and Cole: The Sophisticates.* New York, Oxford University Press, 1993.

Eels, George. *The Life that Late He Led.* New York, G. P. Putnam's Sons, 1967.

Howard, Jean. *Travels with Cole Porter.* New York, Abrams, 1991.

Kimball, Robert, editor. *The Complete Lyrics of Cole Porter.* New York, Vintage Books, 1984.

McBrien, William. *Cole Porter: A Biography.* New York, Knopf, 1998.

Morella, Joe. *Genius and Lust: The Creativity and Sexuality of Cole Porter and Noel Coward.* New York, Carroll & Graf, 1995.

Schwartz, Charles. *Cole Porter: A Biography.* New York, Dial Press, 1977.

Postcards

Perhaps no communications medium exemplifies twentieth-century popular culture more accurately than the unpretentious post-card. This simple message-bearer had tremendous public appeal during the final decades of the 1800s, and although it seemed to have reached a peak in popularity during the first 20 years of the twentieth century, now, at the turn of the millennium, the postcard's symbolic power and presence show little sign of giving way to e(lectronic)-mail or other potential electronic replacements. Readily available at any tourist destination along the way, at interstate truck stops, or in the revolving racks at local downtown shops, postcards are an icon of a culture in a hurry. Taped to our refrigerator doors or tacked to the office bulletin board, they have become commonplace signals that someone we know is off traveling. Expressions such as "wish you were here" have become popular parlance ushered into our vocabulary by virtue of being oft-utilized on postcards.

The postcard has a fascinating and well-documented history. Before the idea of a graphic face became popular, plain cards were used for brief correspondence during the mid-nineteenth century. The concept was officially recognized at the 1865 General Postal conference in Karlsruhe, Germany, and four years later the first card published by a government postal agency was issued by the Austrian-Hungary monarchy. It was a plain card with a printed stamp. In the United States, a federal law passed by Congress on May 19, 1898 authorized "Private Mailing Cards" with one side exclusively for the address. This allowed the other side of the card to be used for a picture or drawing. Prior to 1907, one whole side of a picture postcard was reserved for the address, leaving the only place for a written note to be across the picture itself. But in 1907 another law permitted a divided back, one half for the address and the other for the message.

With the sanctioning of a graphical front to the postcard by government postal agencies, picture postcards soon became very popular. This was encouraged by advances in printing and photography allowing mass production. Also, Rural Free Delivery was instituted in 1898, stimulating personal use of the mail system for spontaneous correspondence. People could always find the time to scribble a short note on the back of a postcard, and seemed to enjoy sending these pictures to each other. It has been estimated that more than a billion postcards were produced in this country during the decade preceding World War I. Such volume suggested a significant retail commodity for many commercial establishments, and marketing strategies took advantage of postcard popularity. In *The Book of Postcard Collecting,* Thomas Range reports that "the familiar revolving wire rack for the display of cards has been attributed to one E.I. Dail, who patented this product in 1908." After 1915, the use of postcards declined somewhat, partly due to the war but also because the telephone and the automobile were creating a revolution in communication and transport connectivity.

In the late 1990s, a revival of postcard popularity began in the United States, both for currently published offerings as a means of quick communication, and for the collecting of postcards from the past. Collecting postcards became very popular during the height of their production just after the turn of the twentieth century. Postcards lend themselves to collecting because of their generally uniform size and ease of storage. Postcard collector's clubs first formed during the 1940s, and remain a major storehouse of information and research. There exists a recognized field of study for postcards, which probably began as the popularity of sending postcards declined. As related by Marian Klamkin in the book *Picture Postcards,* "Randall Rhodes of Ashland, Ohio, coined a word in the early 1930s that became the accepted description of the study of picture postcards, 'deltiology,' taken from the Greek word, deltion, meaning a small picture or card." Today there are numerous newsletters and magazines devoted to the hobby. Many postcard collectors concentrate on various themes:

railroad stations, city and town bird's-eye views, steamships, and other symbols of technological progress. These subjects often represent the spirit of the age, what seems or had seemed important to us at the time. Natural disasters commonly became topics for postcards, perhaps going along with what Morgan and Brown, in their book *Prairie Fires and Paper Moons,* have termed an "emphasis on the minor events in out-of-the-way places." Of course, whatever the subject, there was always an imbedded discourse within the image portrayed. And this hidden message continues in the postcards of today, especially for those cards with the "wish you were here" scenery.

Here are the glossy images of lakes, waterfalls, rugged mountains, or bucolic rural scenery. That the picture postcard is produced and designed to be sent through the mail is itself an act of reinforcement for popular perceptions of place, and as such, the lowly postcard can offer insight into both past and present geographies. The record they leave behind is indelible and unmistakable. Postcards represent a sequential snapshot of both the landscape's and society's changes over time. Not only do postcards impart information about trends and cultural shifts, but have themselves been used as vehicles for diffusion of new ideas and styles of artistic expression. Their use in commercial advertising likewise has a long history. The hobby of collecting postcards has resulted in additional value being imparted to them. Ultimately, however, postcards are fun to send and fun to receive, and therefore show little sign of disappearing from popular culture.

—Robert Kuhlken

FURTHER READING:

Carline, Richard. *Pictures in the Post: The Story of the Picture Postcard and its Place in the History of Popular Art.* Philadelphia, Deltiologists of America, 1972.

Fanelli, Giovanni, and Ezio Godoli. *Art Nouveau Postcards.* New York, Rizzoli, 1987.

Klamkin, Marian. *Picture Postcards.* New York, Dodd, Mead & Co, 1974.

Morgan, Hal, and Andreas Brown. *Prairie Fires and Paper Moons: The American Photographic Postcard, 1900-1920.* Boston, David R. Godine, 1981.

Range, Thomas. *The Book of Postcard Collecting.* New York, Dutton, 1980.

Ryan, Dorothy. *Picture Postcards in the United States, 1893-1918.* New York, Clarkson N. Potter, 1982.

Staff, Frank. *The Picture Postcard and its Origins.* New York, F.A. Praeger, 1966.

The Postman Always Rings Twice

James M. Cain's (1892-1977) controversial bestseller *The Postman Always Rings Twice* (1934) is an erotic and violent story about a waitress and a drifter who kill the woman's well-heeled, unattractive older husband. Cain's novel is central to the hard-boiled novel/film noir tradition in American popular culture. As in many novels in this genre, an amoral hero falls victim to his own powerful sexual

Lana Turner and John Garfield in a scene from the film *The Postman Always Rings Twice*.

attraction to a beautiful *femme fatale*. *L'amour fou* (obsessive love) is at the heart of much of Cain's writing, making it eminently adaptable to film noir—a genre where amorality, violence, and a malevolent fate hang over its often psychologically realistic, morally ambiguous characters.

Cain's novel has been adapted four times to film: as *Ossessione* by Luchino Visconti in 1942 (unavailable until very recently because of copyright problems), under its original title in 1946 by Tay Garnett (staring Lana Turner and John Garfield), in 1981 by Bob Rafelson (starring Jessica Lange and Jack Nicholson), and by Marcus DeLeon, in an uncredited version, as *Kiss Me a Killer* in 1991.

—Jeannette Sloniowski

FURTHER READING:

Cain, James M. *The Postman Always Rings Twice.* New York, Vintage Books, 1992.

Dyer, Richard. "Four Films of Lana Turner." *MOVIE.* Vol. 25, Winter 1977-78, 30-52.

Porfirio, Robert G. "Whatever Happened to Film Noir? The Postman Always Rings Twice," *Literature/Film Quarterly.* Vol. 13, No. 2, 1985, 101-11.

Silver, Alain, and Elizabeth Ward, eds. *Film Noir: An Encyclopedic Reference to the American Style.* Woodstock, New York, Overlook Press, 1992.

Postmodernism

The word "postmodernism" means many things to many people. To some it describes a fad or a personal style, to others, a theory of society, a philosophy of human significance (or its lack thereof), a historical epoch, a phase of capitalist development, or a curious feeling of personal weightlessness in a world of synthetic pleasures and meanings. Unlike most "isms," postmodernism has no stock tenets or creeds to fall back on, relying instead on a general attitude of misgiving for all things "modern." The foundational assumptions that undergird modern personal and social beliefs, even the belief in "reality" itself, are, for postmodernists, canon fodder in a relentless "ungrounding" assault waged on modernity. This essay will assess the relevance and achievements of the postmodern critical enterprise (which are significant), while exercising a healthy skepticism about some of postmodernism's more lofty assertions. Postmodernism will be understood for what it is—a product of an academic "idea" industry, meant to describe an awkward period in the history of western society. In this way, postmodernism, the academic fad, will be explained via the use of postmodernism, the critical "ungrounding" of cultural assumptions and beliefs.

To call postmodernism an intellectual fad is neither disparaging nor inaccurate: all cultures are subject to fads, and intellectuals, as any postmodernist would assure you, are no exception. Postmodernism has its origins in the erudite practices of the academic and scholarly world, where new ideas are generated regularly, contested and advanced through the commerce of publishing, hobnobbing at academic conferences, power politicking at faculty meetings and on department budget committees—all processes which are driven by academics' desire to expand personal influence by thinking of something new to say. Beginning in the early 1980s, postmodernism began to emerge as a vanguard movement in the idea market, with all the equipment for a successful intellectual coup—its own fancy vocabulary, a cryptic set of canonical texts, and a seemingly inexhaustible ability to come off cleverer than any of its challengers. Indeed, the ability of the postmodern rhetorician to inflate the significance of familiar issues by describing them with thick jargon has proven a fruitful intellectual stratagem for postmodernists, one whose success rivals that enjoyed by structural functionalist sociologists of the 1950s who, under the leadership of Talcott Parsons, stormed American sociology in a whirlwind of technical sounding lingo.

By the 1990s, the term "postmodern" had crept into the vernacular of American cultural commentary, in much the way that such terms as "existential angst," "mass culture," and "the medium is the message" once held sway over their own distinct periods, promising the key theoretical and rhetorical tools for unlocking the social and cultural mysteries of their time. Of course, fads are never arbitrary: they only catch on because they seem meaningful to people and offer some help in the interpretation of their real lives and the conditions under which they live. For America in the 1980s, many confusing social changes seemed to lend themselves to a postmodern analysis: a new Reagan era emphasis on media theatrics over political realities; a deepening permeation of TV, home videos, and MTV into the most intimate recesses of personal and everyday life; the waning of the promise of left social movements; and the failure in the 1970s of any cultural movements capable of countering the hegemony of consumerism and its seductive culture of images. All suggested a society that had to be fundamentally rethought. In addressing these conditions, postmodernism provided an anti-foundationalist theory for a society struggling with its slipping grasp on any founding reality or system of its own.

To understand postmodernism, we must first understand what postmodernists mean when they speak of "modernity" (a broad term that includes a sweeping host of thinkers and artists from Descartes and Darwin to Jackson Pollock and Mick Jagger). "Modern" thought defines an outlook that grounds human history, social organization, and the human condition in certain essential personal qualities which are, happily, perfecting themselves over time. Modernism proposes that the human capacity for reason, justice, and enlightened knowledge about the world is gradually becoming clearer and more defined, and with those changes, modern society is becoming an increasingly pleasant place to live: modern governments are fairer; technology more capable; capitalist systems, though prone to hard times, are better and more efficient than the older ones they replace; and scientific knowledge is superior to superstition, mysticism, and bunk. Modernists also assume that the greatest share of progress in the development of those personal qualities and the social products they engender has fallen on the shoulders of the Occidental West, and in

particular, its ruling elites. It is thus the duty of those elites to inspire progress elsewhere in the world as best they can. Though this is not an easy task, it is nonetheless a burden modern nations must undertake, even (as critics say) if it means establishing huge colonial empires, stigmatizing and exploiting women, minorities, and other less modern types, and making oneself very rich and influential in the process. In fact, the myth of "progress" provided an immense carpet under which all voices of discontent emanating from the less modern quarter could be quickly and easily swept. In short, modernists maintain that being modern is a fundamentally good and desirable thing for anyone who wants to perfect their innate cognitive and moral potentials (which everyone does, whether they realize it or not).

This is, in short, the modern doctrine of progress: one day, everyone will be perfect, rational, and modern (like us). It is against this doctrine that postmodernists have released their most penetrating, anti-foundationalist critique. Postmodern thought is in many ways quite simple: it repudiates any belief in the foundations that are thought to support various modern institutions and ideologies. The implicit justice and reasonableness of the human character, the moral potential of human social organization, and the bright outlook and optimism supplied by "modernist" apostles of progress is exposed by postmodernists as a fiction of Western civilization. Postmodernists cut away at the foundations of everything, revealing the loftiest of modern principles as silly fetishes, or worse, tools of Western domination. The view of the universality of human reason that led the philosophers of the enlightenment to criticize the teachings of the church as "unscientific" is, for postmodernists, just another quaint European superstition. The vision of universal justice that inspired the democratization of Europe and America is disclosed as another form of social organization, no better or worse than the despotic regimes they opposed. Postmodernists are decidedly relativistic, and their assertion of the ultimate relativity of all values is arrived at by exposing all the great principles of modern thought—science, justice, reason, egalitarianism—as carefully orchestrated shams.

But there is more at stake than the abstract "groundedness" of modern principles: postmodernists use these questions to rethink fundamental questions of contemporary society, from sexuality to racism to social movements to popular culture. Having repudiated the foundational principles that bound modern society, all the fragments of contemporary society have to be somehow collected and pieced back together again. This presents postmodernists with a set of deeply troubling questions: How do you accuse the media of deception without presuming some sort of "truth"? How do you insist that something is unfair without presuming a foundational human morality? How do you separate popular culture from high culture with no objective standard of beauty? And most importantly, how do you think of the historical present and plan for a better future without a modern vision of progress to explain social change? Postmodern relativism has demanded that everything be considered anew, without the help of overarching principles. To understand how postmodernists got to this position, we must consider the connection between modernism's foundational assumptions and its optimistic view of historical development.

From a postmodern perspective, the modernist vision of progress is already in tatters, and has been for years. Perhaps since the Holocaust, perhaps since Dada, or perhaps since the recession of the early 1970s, the rosy modern story or "meta-narrative" of progress has encountered increasing challenges from the many voices it had to silence in order to remain credible. Whether the dream of progress died in the gas chambers at Auschwitz or in the tract homes of Orange

County, this meta-narrative is no longer believable, no longer able to sweep the many unique ''irrational,'' unmodern voices under the carpet of its universal assumptions of rationality and progress.

In light of the unravelling of modern historical consciousness, postmodernism greets a rudderless society, adrift in a sea of fragmented ideas, symbols, and ideologies, where the refuse of history has come unglued. No longer ''obsolete'' (an idea that depends on a belief in ''progress''), figments from the past collide with a contemporary world that no longer thinks of itself as ''new''—as evidenced by the barrage of retro-nostalgic films and fads that have characterized consumer culture since the early 1980s. With hierarchies of taste no longer separating high from low, symphony orchestras play an evening of Warner Brothers' cartoon classics, and prominent art museums feature ''The Art of the Motorcycle.'' With ideologies of ethnic difference no longer holding sway, take-out sushi and Kraft guacamole spread become staples of the American diet. In short, postmodernism announces a world in fragments. Where modernity's narrative of progress used to tell us what belonged where, in a postmodern society everything, past, present, and future intertwines in a pastiche of difference and contrast. A typical feature of postmodernism is its intermixing of reality and representation: Peter Seller's character in *Being There* is often cited in this respect, a man who carries a remote control with him through the streets, trying unsuccessfully to change the channels to remove himself from various situations.

For postmodernists, this fragmenting of society is, in many ways, a good thing: the past presents itself to us like a painter's pallet, offering a range of historical styles for the taking. The blurring of the line between old and new, so troubling to the avant garde 1960s, and the breakdown between real and fake, so troubling in the ''authentic'' culture of the 1970s, is a source of campy joy to the postmodernist, who sees infinite possibilities in the production of new combinations: Why burn a real Christmas log when you can rent a video of a picturesque fireplace burning perfectly for hours? Why buy real flowers when plastic ones are in every way superior? Or even more postmodern: Why try to find your own words to express feelings and sentiments when you can just drop clichés from popular television shows? Indeed postmodernism's assessment of a society without a foundation is always two-sided, sometimes apocalyptic and foreboding, dwelling on the ''death of the subject,'' the ''end of history,'' and the ''disappearance of the social,'' while at other times celebrating the ''multiplicity of meanings'' and the ''carnivalesque'' qualities of a society freed of all foundational obligations.

This perspective has led postmodernists to read culture and society in a unique way, uncovering many subtle dimensions of culture and society that had escaped others. Where modernists saw people as fundamentally reasonable things, postmodernists see people as infinitely shaped by their cultural environments, ''socially constructed'' by the spaces, roles, clothing, and consumer goods they make part of their lives. Gender, for example, is more the product of advertising and fashion than any essential human quality. Revolutionary leaders are not to be found among heroic resistance movements, but rather on TV and in the record store; for instance, volumes have been written by feminist theorists on Madonna for her unapologetic assertion of women's sexuality, and her ability to shift identities by changing her hair color. Though postmodernists were certainly not the first ones to claim to have discovered the social construction of things we usually take to be natural (sociologists have been studying the ''social construction of reality'' since the 1960s), postmodernism launched a new study of everyday life in consumer society, where

language, consumer culture, the body, and the structuring of physical space were understood as the ''sites'' where people acquired identities, shaped ''discourses,'' and formed communities. For this reason, postmodernism's new vocabularies seem justified: naming things that have never been spoken of before (like the effect a TV commercial for lipstick might have on a woman's sense of her body as ''feminine'') required a new critical terminology, and postmodern critics were quick to spin off volumes of innovative terms—''identificatory structures,'' ''liminal sites of resistance,'' ''multiplicity of subject positionalities''—and to pour them thickly in a jargon saturated prose that sent spell-checks reeling, and quickly became the postmodern signature style. The lipstick commercial, rather than ''influencing'' the woman's ''sense'' of her body, ''inscribes'' her body with the ''normative structures'' of ''gender signification.'' To understand why postmodern writing takes on the style it does, how it galvanized such support throughout the 1980s and raised so much ire in the 1990s, we must reach back to the theoretical traditions from which postmodernism developed, and the peculiar understanding of language, writing, and argumentation postmodernists inherited from their intellectual forbearers: the French poststructuralists.

In the 1950s, another intellectual fad, structuralism, swept the French scene. Parisian intellectuals, bored with Jean Paul Sartre's existentialist diatribes that grounded modern angst in the lonely subject of existential philosophy, felt the need for a new, more dispersed ''structural'' take on the individual and its significance. Following Claude Levi-Strauss and Roland Barthes, ''structuralism'' emerged with the model of an individual caught in a fixed network of signs and symbolic relations. Structuralism cut the ground from the under the crucible of the modern subject that had adorned French philosophy textbooks since Descartes, a marvelous and bold gesture that soon drew the admiration of readers across the Atlantic. But structuralism would have to suffer its own ungrounding before it could serve as the theoretical keystone for postmodernism: by the late 1960s, a few French intellectuals (most prominent among them were Jacques Derrida, Jean Francois Lyotard, Jean Baudrillard, and Michel Foucault) undertook a harsh critique of structuralism's own grounds, its assumption that all meanings and social relations could be understood in terms of elements connected in fixed and limited symbolic structures.

The stability of Levi-Strauss's systems of signs was to give way to ''poststructuralism,'' an approach that liquidated assumptions not only about the unique properties of the individual subject, but also the inherent structure of signs and meanings, which included writing and traditional forms of argumentation and explanation. Poststructuralism argued that all structures, which included equally the structures of the human psyche, social institutions, the modern economy, the structures of texts and signs, and the structure of such ideological systems as modernism and its great narrative of progress, always depend on a certain unstated exclusions. Something, some meaning or some voice, had to be pushed to the outside or swept under a carpet if any established meaning or ''foundation'' was to be achieved. Every modern structure, poststructuralists maintained, was premised on a troubling, concealed element, which was never entirely banished, but could be detected lingering at its margins or flickering on its periphery. Reason could never quite escape its nemesis, madness, just as democratic capitalism could never quite come to terms with its history of slavery. From the poststructuralist position, this extra element in every structure never has a ''position'' of any kind—positions are concrete structures in themselves—but is always present as a thing excluded, something ghostlike in its absence. Applying the poststructuralist critique of the destabilizing, outside element to the structure of modern thought, postmodernists pried back the face of modernity to see what outside elements, what ghostlike absences, it had swept under its rug. And of course, modernity's grand narrative of progress was revealed to harbor a whole range of "subordinated" narratives and outside voices: those of women, slaves, gays and lesbians, and other "subalterns" who had haunted the confidence of modern narratives, deemed too irrational to be modern.

In both France and America, poststructuralism couldn't have come at a better time: a Paris student population, disappointed with the results of the uprisings of 1968, met with a splintered American left looking for something to replace the stodgy Marxism and worn-out feminism of their campus years. The new poststructuralism, promising to make criticism sexy again, quickly found space on the bookshelves of American and French academics. Moreover, what made the writings of many poststructuralist authors so enticing was their sense that their own criticism itself should take up that same outside "subordinate," ghostlike relation that poststructuralism had uncovered lurking at the edges of every modern text. To take a position, to speak the language of direct argumentation, or to tell someone in a straightforward manner what postmodernism was all about would be to incorporate oneself into the structure of the argument itself. Poststructuralists like Derrida believed in the importance of elusiveness in their writing, of avoiding taking "positions" in the structure of a text and staying evasive, vague, and irritating. Derrida's philosophy of deconstruction uses indeterminate, multiple meanings in order to keep the poststructuralist's "voice" on the outside of the structure of the debates in which he or she engages, avoiding clarity, producing a style of scholarly writing that insists on remaining open to different readings, with the belief that purposefully unclear and ambiguous writing undermines or "ungrounds" the foundations of writing—and reasoning—itself.

The purposeful ambiguity that postmodernists inherited from poststructuralism and deconstruction and applied to cultural and social commentary has both exasperated its critics while drawing droves of inspired followers to the "critical theory" shelves of university bookstores. Following the poststructuralist lead, the postmodern author stands outside of all structures and systems: permanently defiant, elusive, and clever, remaining faithful to the groundlessness she takes as her only ground, and refusing to explain her evasions for fear she might turn "evasion" into a position, and thus become simply one more element in the structure of its own argument. In reality, of course, postmodern evasiveness has become precisely that: a familiar position, a clearly identifiable style practiced by a group of identifiable postmodern authors. These techniques are by now quite familiar: placing parts of words in (paren)theses so as to suggest double meanings; linking homophones with a backslash, "the body is the cite/site of inscription," or in triplet, "the apparatus of visuality defines the body as the cite/site/sight of inscription"; and the relentless pluralizing of terms, so as to invite, without confirming other meanings—feminism(s), consumerism(s)—and so on. These devices make it appear that one's own position eludes the limitations of language and argumentation that one's opponent remains within. Postmodern argumentation often casts the opposing position as a micro police-state of (modernist) discursive order, converting any effort to sustain a point as an effort to "police the boundaries" of meaning. This move, familiar in discussions between modernists and postmodernists, is a neat trick: it portrays the frustration of the modernist as an anxious response to the destabilization of his own argumentative structure in the face of the subversive instabilities unleashed by the postmodernist's evasive techniques. As the modernist becomes impatient, the postmodernist says "told ya so." By the late 1990s, postmodernism, or "pomo" in academic parlance, had become common fare in college classrooms (thus betraying the spirit of linguistic subversion poststructuralists had in mind.)

No proponent of postmodernism did more to seduce American critical audiences than Jean Baudrillard, whose seemingly bleak pronouncements on the "death of subjectivity" in the postmodern age inspired zealous loyalty and fierce opposition. Baudrillard's expeditions through the dregs of American consumerism took him through Las Vegas, Disneyland, and Los Angeles, where he discovered the European's fantasy of the vulgar (if alluring) American: a nation of crass media addicts whose grip on anything more than the TV's remote was tenuous at best. In America, Baudrillard discovered a new relationship to reality: a simulated "hyper-reality" in which the individual self and all of its experiences were disappearing into a deluge of reproducible copies. Everything, Baudrillard argued, was reproduced in some image or another. In fact, part of what it means to be real, in the postmodern age, is to be copied in one form or anther, either on television or in print. His message was not just critical, it was apocalyptic: it announced an end to reality itself, to criticism, to politics, and to all personal experience, leaving only the mesmeric effects of reproduced images. His dense elliptical terminology and his vague, portentous inflection took American art criticism and downtown bookstores by storm, and soon shaped a new genre of chic cultural commentary. Moreover, Baudrillard's books stung the American left with declarations that politics had "disappeared," been rendered "fictional," lost in a maze of representations. Among his most provocative claims was his assertion in 1992 that "the Gulf War didn't happen," a statement that drew a group of angry anti-war activists to one of his lectures, bearing signs insisting that "the Gulf War DID happen" after all.

No account of postmodernism would be complete without some mention of the events of 1996, and the stunt perpetrated by New York University professor of physics Alan Sokal that did more to draw public attention to the goings on of the scholarly world than any other event in years. Though not a postmodernist himself, Sokal pieced together an essay stuffed with postmodern verbiage, which he titled "Transgressing the Boundaries: Toward a Transformative Hermeneutics of Quantum Gravity," and submitted it to Social Text, a prominent journal of cultural studies with, at times, strong postmodern tendencies. To his surprise, his lark was accepted and published in the spring/summer 1996 issue. When the piece came out, Sokal went public with an article in Lingua Franca, the People Magazine of the academic world. While the editors of Social Text were stunned, Sokal gloated through a firestorm of controversy, touting his essay as the smoking gun that exposed the sham of the entire poststructuralist critical tradition. Though Sokal lacked theoretical savvy, the incident launched his career as a chief critic of the French intellectual oeuvre, and brought Social Text, postmodernism, and the "Sokal scandal" to the front page of the New York Times. It seems a shame that postmodernism, whose chief theoretical asset has been its unique ability to expose the charade of expert narratives, was so lazy about questioning its own emperor's new clothes, leaving the job instead to Sokal. Sokal's lark provided a clear testament to the routinization of postmodern prose and commentary, and if nothing else, the event may have closed or at least tempered what may be remembered as the halcyon days of postmodern rhetorical flourish.

—Sam Binkley

FURTHER READING:

Baudrillard, Jean. *America.* London, Verso, 1988.

Bauman, Zygmunt. *Postmodernity and Its Discontents.* New York, New York University Press, 1997.

Best, Steven, and Douglas Kellner. *Postmodern Theory: Critical Interrogations.* New York, Gilford Press, 1991.

Connor, Steven. *Postmodernist Culture: An Introduction to Theories of the Contemporary.* New York, Blackwell, 1996.

Derrida, Jacques. ''Différance.'' In *Margins of Philosophy,* translated by Allan Bass. Chicago, University of Chicago Press, 1982.

Harvey, David. *The Condition of Postmodernity.* Cambridge, Blackwell, 1989.

Jameson, Frederic. *Postmodernism, or, The Cultural Logic of Late Capitalism.* Durham, Duke University Press, 1991.

Kroker, Arthur, and David Cook. *The Postmodern Scene: Excremental Culture and Hyper-Aesthetics.* New York, St. Martin's Press, 1986.

Lyotard, Jean François. *The Postmodern Condition: A Report on Knowledge,* translated by Geoff Bennington and Brian Massumi. Minneapolis, Minnesota University Press, 1984.

Natoli, Joseph P., and Linda Hutcheon, editors. *A Postmodern Reader.* New York, State University of New York Press, 1996.

Powell, Jim. *Postmodernism for Beginners.* New York, Writers & Readers Publishing, 1998.

Sokal, Alan, and Jean Bricmont. *Fashionable Nonsense: Postmodern Intellectuals' Abuse of Science.* New York, St. Martin's Press, 1998.

Potter, Dennis (1935-1994)

Dennis Potter was one of the most significant and innovative dramatists in the history of British television. From 1965 until his death in 1994, he created an oeuvre of haunting intensity and personal vision that ranks with the greatest achievements in any popular art form. His two best-known works to international audiences, *Pennies from Heaven* (1978) and *The Singing Detective* (1986), are strikingly original miniseries that use the television narrative to journey into an inner, psychological reality. Both series and many of his other dramas, including *Moonlight on the Highway* (1969), *Cream in My Coffee* (1980), and *Karaoke* (produced posthumously in 1996), share a fascination with popular culture and employ songs non-naturalistically to reveal repressed emotions. Although he wrote such films as *Dreamchild* and *Track 29,* Potter considered television ''the most democratic medium,'' and used all his creative powers to open up the artistic possibilities of the medium.

—Ron Simon

FURTHER READING:

Carpenter, Humphrey. *Dennis Potter: The Authorized Biography.* London, Faber and Faber, 1998.

Cook, John R. *Dennis Potter: A Life on Screen.* Manchester, Manchester University Press, 1995.

Fuller, Graham, editor. *Potter on Potter.* London, Faber & Faber, 1993.

Gilbert, W. Stephen. *Fight & Kick & Bite: The Life and Work of Dennis Potter.* London, Hodder & Stroughton, 1995.

The Museum of Television & Radio. *The Television of Dennis Potter* (published in conjunction with an exhibition of the same title). New York, 1991.

Potter, Dennis. *Seeing the Blossoms: Two Interviews and a Lecture.* London, Faber & Faber, 1994.

Powell, Dick (1904-1963)

A pop singer and bandleader, Dick Powell became famous as the perennial youthful star of backstage musical films during the 1930s. He appeared as the juvenile lead opposite dancer Ruby Keeler in a string of films which included *42nd Street, Footlight Parade,* and *Gold Diggers of 1933* (all 1933). Other films included *Gold Diggers of 1935* (1935), *Thanks a Million* (1935), *Gold Diggers of 1937* (1937), *On the Avenue* (1937), *Varsity Show* (1937), and *Star Spangled Rhythm* (1942). Powell later eschewed his clean-cut image and began to aspire to non-singing dramatic roles in films such as *Murder, My Sweet* (1944) and *The Bad and the Beautiful* (1952). He also directed several films, but it is as the energetic, wide-eyed dancer of the 1930s that Powell is best remembered. He married fellow singing actor June Allyson in 1945.

—William A. Everett

FURTHER READING:

Carpozi, George. *The Magnificent Entertainers.* New York, Manor Books, 1978.

Thomas, Tony. *The Dick Powell Story.* Burbank, Riverwood Press, 1993.

Powell, William (1892-1984)

Actor William Powell, who lived to the age of 92, retired from the screen in 1955 having made 94 films, beginning with the role of Moriarty in the 1922 silent version of *Sherlock Holmes* (1922) starring John Barrymore. He was never more than a supporting player, generally a villain of some kind or another during the 1920s, until his accomplished performance in a featured role in Von Sternberg's *The Last Command* (1928) brought him attention. It was, however, the coming of sound, which ruined the career of many a silent star unable to deliver lines, that gradually elevated him to stardom as the quintessential screen sophisticate of the glamorous 1930s—immaculately tailored, impeccably spoken, witty, occasionally attractively caddish, and sometimes cynical. He was as much the perfect embodiment of the type as Gary Cooper was the archetypal emblem of honor, or Clark Gable the prototype of brash and unbridled masculinity. With the later change in styles and trends, Powell was in danger of sharing the obscurity of many of his forgotten films. He escaped such a fate thanks to *The Thin Man* (1934), which has defined his image ever since, despite the fact that the ''thin man'' of the title was not Powell, but some mysterious stranger.

The debonair, urbane, and amusing Powell persona that brightened the lives of moviegoers during the Depression era was famously blended into the perfect screen incarnation of Dashiell Hammett's cocktail-sipping sophisticate-cum-detective, Nick Charles, who, with his wife Nora (Myrna Loy) and their dog Asta, beguiled audiences in *The Thin Man* with such hugely profitable results for MGM, that six more ''Thin Man'' films followed, ending with the inferior *Song of the Thin Man* in 1945. Powell and the glamorous Loy, both needing a bit of a career boost, found it together when director W.S. Van Dyke paired them in *Manhattan Melodrama* (1934), Powell's first for MGM. There followed *The Thin Man,* in which the stars joyously impersonated a couple to whom marriage was clearly an equal and thoroughly enjoyable partnership—a then innovative concept. They were teamed, too, in *Evelyn Prentice* (1934), a melodrama of adultery and blackmail, and in the screwy comedy *Double Wedding* (1937), but it was as Nick and Nora Charles that, after Astaire and Rogers, the Powell-Loy combination was perhaps the most successful star team of the 1930s. As film historian David Thomson puts it, ''The match was perfect: two slender sophisticates, smiling haughtily at each other through a mist of wisecracks.''

William H. Powell was born in Pittsburgh, Pennsylvania, on July 29, 1892, the son of an accountant who intended that he should go into the law. However, he became an avid playgoer, in love with the theater from an early age, and dropped out of the University of Kansas after a week or two to pursue a stage career in New York. He studied at the American Academy of Dramatic Arts (with such talented classmates as Edward G. Robinson and Joseph Schildkraut) and, after a couple of years of struggle, began to find work in vaudeville and stock and on Broadway from 1912. He worked steadily but without particular distinction until 1920 when his performance in a play called *Spanish Love* brought him some notice and led to the beginning of his film career. By then he had honed his craft through performances in some 200 plays.

Powell was under contract to Paramount for seven years from 1924 to 1931, where, as well as *The Last Command,* he made *Dragnet* (1928) for Von Sternberg, and where he made the transition to sound, appearing in *Interference* (1929), a drama whose only distinction lay in being the studio's first all-talkie. In 1929, however, he was cast as S.S. Van Dine's gentleman detective, Philo Vance in *The Canary Murder Case,* establishing the image that was to grow familiar and paving the way for Nick Charles. He played Vance in three more (the last at Warner Bros.), was paired with Kay Francis in three, and made two comedies—*Man of the World* and *Ladies Man*—with Carole Lombard in 1931, the year his first, 15-year marriage to Eileen Wilson ended and his second, two-year marriage to Lombard began.

The actor's professional marriage to Paramount, however, was faltering, and along with Kay Francis, he left the studio for Warner Bros., who revived his pairing with Francis in *One Way Passage* (1932), he a condemned criminal, she the doomed object of his affections. As well as his fourth Philo Vance outing, *The Kennel Murder Case* (1933), directed by Michael Curtiz, he made *The Key* (1934) for the same director, but Warner was proving no more satisfactory than Paramount and he departed the studio. En route to Columbia, he was intercepted by Van Dyke and MGM for *Manhattan Melodrama* (the movie John Dillinger had been viewing just before being gunned down by the FBI), and put under contract to the studio where his talents would be best employed. Powell's next film with Loy was *The Thin Man,* breezily directed by W. S. (''One-Take Woody'') Van Dyke, which earned Powell an Oscar nomination and, more importantly, set the tone for many of his romantic comedies to follow. ''Few images so succinctly convey the essence of thirties comedy,'' asserts critic Tom Shales, ''as a scene from . . . *The Thin*

Man in which Powell's Nick Charles, reclining on the couch, shoots the ornaments off a Christmas tree with the new gun his wife has given him.''

Now one of the brightest lights at MGM, Powell brought his impeccable flair to such comedy-dramas as *Reckless* (1935) with Jean Harlow and *Libeled Lady* (1936) with Harlow, Loy, and Spencer Tracy, and the title role in the biographical extravaganza, *The Great Ziegfeld* (1936), which won the Best Picture Oscar. (He again played impresario Florenz Ziegfeld in *The Ziegfeld Follies* in 1946). On loan to Universal, Powell co-starred with his ex-wife, Carole Lombard, in one of the most exemplary of ''screwball'' comedies, *My Man Godfrey* (1936), and earned his second Oscar nomination. Ever the gentleman in life as well as art, he had insisted that Lombard be cast, explaining, ''Just because we couldn't live together doesn't mean we shouldn't work together.'' As film columnist Robert Osborne has commented, ''For a man with such a perpetual twinkle in his eye, always seemingly in good humor, his personal life was surrounded with a surprising number of tragedies.'' Among these were the sudden death in 1937 of Jean Harlow, with whom Powell was deeply in love and was planning to marry; the bout with cancer that kept the actor off the screen for almost two years and hastened his retirement; and the suicide of his son from his first marriage. In 1940, Diana Lewis became his third and last wife in a union that lasted until his death.

As Powell began to get on in years, he effected a smooth transition to character parts, chiefly by giving an Oscar-nominated and New York Critics' Award-winning performance in the plum role of the elder Clarence Day in *Life with Father* (1947) opposite Irene Dunne. On stage, Day had peppered his pronouncements with profanity; denied these choice words for the film version, Powell put so much persuasive power into his tirades that the epithets were never missed. The way in which Powell bypassed the censors by making ''Gad!'' sound as profane as ''God!'' was a true lesson in the actor's craft. He made *The Senator Was Indiscreet,* a political satire, that same year, and played half the title role in a wistful, rueful fantasy, *Mr. Peabody and the Mermaid.* The actor, who had begun his film career in the days of the silents, continued working into the era of CinemaScope, essaying a key part in *How to Marry a Millionaire* (1953) with Marilyn Monroe and Lauren Bacall. He bowed out as Doc in the film version of *Mister Roberts* (1955) opposite Henry Fonda, giving a performance every bit as expert as his Nick Charles or his Ziegfeld. The three-time Oscar nominee, resting on his laurels as one of the legends of Hollywood's golden era, finally passed away at the age of 92 in his Palm Springs home.

—Preston Neal Jones

FURTHER READING:

Baxt, George. *The William Powell and Myrna Loy Murder Case.* New York, St. Martin's Press, 1996.

Francisco, Charles. *Gentleman: The William Powell Story,* New York, St. Martin's Press, 1985.

Morella, Joe. *Gable & Lombard & Powell & Harlow.* New York, Dell, 1975.

Parish, James Robert. *The Debonairs.* New Rochelle, New York, Arlington House, 1975.

Thomson, David. *A Biographical Dictionary of the Cinema.* New York, Alfred A. Knopf, 1994.

Quirk, Lawrence J. *The Complete Films of William Powell*. Secaucus, New Jersey, Citadel Press, 1986.

Prang, Louis (1823-1909)

Founder of one of America's best-known art education publishers and art supply firms, Louis Prang immigrated to Boston, Massachusetts, from Prussia in 1852. Initially a wood engraver, he became a lithographer, making prints to decorate the homes of New England's growing middle class. He also made labels for manufactured goods, campaign maps for families of Civil War soldiers, and America's first Christmas cards.

In 1870 a Massachusetts law mandated art instruction in the public schools to meet a burgeoning demand for commercial artists. Prang and Company seized on this new market with drawing cards for imitation in the classroom, art textbooks, the Prang Solids (geometric forms to be drawn by the student), paints, crayons, and drawing papers. Although the "art labor" movement receded by the turn of the twentieth century, Prang's firm continued to manufacture art supplies into the 1990s as a subsidiary of the American Crayon Company.

—Nick Humez

FURTHER READING:

Barnhill, Georgia B., et al., editors. *The Cultivation of Artists in Nineteenth-Century America*. Worcester, American Antiquarian Society, 1997.

Freeman, Larry. *Louis Prang: Color Lithographer*. Watkins Glen, New York, Century House, 1971.

Korzenik, Diana. *Drawn to Art: A Nineteenth-Century American Dream*. Hanover, University Press of New England, 1985.

McClinton, Katharine Morrison. *The Chromolithographs of Louis Prang*. New York, Clarkson and Potter, 1973.

Prater, Dave
See Sam and Dave

Preminger, Otto (1905-1986)

During his career, Austrian-born director and actor Otto Preminger worked equally hard at his films and his public persona. With the years he created for himself the identity of the independent producer-director par excellence who refused to submit to the Big Studio system or to restrictive production codes and who could fire a star like Lana Turner, originally cast for Lee Remick's role in *Anatomy of a Murder* (1959), because she refused to wear the pair of trousers he had selected for her. The following statement is as typical of his persona as courtroom scenes are of his movies: "I say what I like because it is completely my picture, an independent picture. I am the producer, the director, the casting director, it's all my decision." This self-consciously iconoclastic and autocratic character endeared him in the 1950s and 1960s to the French critics and directors of *Cahiers du Cinéma*, as well as to auteur-theorists like Andrew Sarris and others writing for magazines such as *Movie* and *The Village Voice*.

Preminger's career can be divided into three periods. After immigrating to the United States in 1936, he signed a contract with Twentieth Century-Fox, where he had several conflicts with producer Darryl F. Zanuck. Together with his first hit *Laura* (1944), Preminger's most interesting films of this period are a series of *noirs* shot during the late 1940s and early 1950s: *Whirlpool* (1949), *Where the Sidewalk Ends* (1950), *The Thirteenth Letter* (1950), and *Angel Face* (1952). Preminger was always quite reluctant to talk about these movies and emphasized instead his contrasts with Zanuck, thus adding to his reputation as a rebel against big studio rules.

The Moon Is Blue (1953) marked the beginning of Preminger's career as an independent producer-director, and was his first movie to be released without Motion Picture Association approval because of Preminger's refusal to cut dialogues containing sexual innuendoes. With his newly gained independence from big studios, Preminger started a successful series of grand-scale movies on, at least superficially, scandalous topics such as drug addiction (*The Man with the Golden Arm,* 1955), rape (*Anatomy of a Murder,* 1959), communism and homosexuality (*Advise and Consent,* 1962), institutions like the United States Army (*The Court Martial of Billy Mitchell,* 1955, and *In Harm's Way,* 1965), and the Catholic Church (*The Cardinal,* 1963). A recurring theme of these rather diverse and eclectic movies is the quest for truth through an apparently objective and scientific "anatomy" whose results, in the end, turn out to be more ambiguous than we would expect. This quest is embodied by the numerous courtroom scenes in Preminger's movies and is usually carried out by solitary male heroes such as U. S. General Billy Mitchell (Gary Cooper) in *The Court Martial of Billy Mitchell* and the lawyer Paul Biegler (James Stewart) in *Anatomy of a Murder*.

His iconoclastic persona notwithstanding, Preminger's use of controversial topics was essentially conservative and embedded in the conformist ideology of the 1950s and early 1960s. Two examples will suffice. As in the case of *The Moon Is Blue, The Man with the Golden Arm* (1956) was released without the seal of approval because of its subject. The film was a great box-office hit and people queued to see the taboo topic of drugs on the big screen for the first time. Yet, what they saw was, in Jackie Byars' words, a movie which is radical only on its surface, having at its base "a very conservative championing of the family, of aspirations to upward mobility, and of traditional gender definitions." Nelson Algren's novel of defeat in the Chicago slums is turned by Preminger into a success story starring Frank Sinatra as the ultimate self-made man: by the end of the movie Sinatra's Frankie Machine gets rid of his addiction and of his hysterical wife Zosh (Eleanor Parker), leaves the slums together with his new supportive girlfriend Molly (Kim Novak), and becomes a musician with the help of American big business. Just as *The Man with the Golden Arm* was perhaps the first mainstream movie to portray drug addiction, *Advise and Consent* (1962) was one of the first to treat explicitly the topic of homosexuality and was to influence the fate of many cinematic gay characters as well as popular perceptions of gay people: tormented by their sexuality, gays have little choice but to die. In this story of political intrigues and scandals, Senator Brig Anderson is appointed chair of the committee investigating the communist past of Senator Robert Leffingwell, who has just been designated Secretary of State. Along his quest for truth, Anderson is blackmailed by Leffingwell's supporters because of a gay affair he had while he was in the army. The movie clearly contrasts the cozy domestic space of Anderson's heterosexual household—filled with a beautiful, supporting wife and a cute daughter—with the squalor of the New York gay neighborhood where Anderson goes to talk to his former lover, Ray. The landlord who first receives Anderson is the very antithesis of his wife. He is ugly and obese; homosexuality is conceived in terms of both moral and physical corruption. In the last instance, as Vito Russo has pointed out, Anderson kills himself "not because he is being blackmailed in Washington, but because he has gone to New York and found people with whom he has something in common and he is so repulsed he sees no alternative to the straight razor."

Preminger's final phase, which includes movies continuing his analysis of contemporary society (race-relations in the South in *Hurry Sundown,* 1967, Palestinian terrorism in *Rosebud,* 1975) and others striving for new directions (the slapstick farce *Skidoo,* 1968), was marked by critical and commercial disappointments. In spite of Preminger's self-appointed role as freedom-fighter, we should wonder, following Dwight MacDonald, if any other director was more skilled than he "at giving the appearance of dealing with large 'controversial' themes in a bold way without making the tactical error of doing so."

—Luca Prono

FURTHER READING:

Byars, Jackie. *All That Hollywood Allows: Re-reading Gender in 1950s Melodrama.* London, Routledge, 1991.

MacDonald, Dwight. *On Movies.* Englewood Cliffs, New Jersey, Prentice Hall, 1969.

Pratley, Gerald. *The Cinema of Otto Preminger.* New York, A. S. Barnes & Co., 1971.

Russo, Vito. *The Celluloid Closet: Homosexuality in the Movies.* New York, Harper & Row, 1981.

Preppy

The word "preppy" (also spelled "preppie") derives from "preparatory" and refers to someone who attends or has attended a college preparatory secondary school. In actual use, preppy implies a wide variety of assumptions about the class, style, and values of such a person. Preppy can be used as a noun ("She dresses like a preppy.") or an adjective ("I'm not interested in your preppy friends.") It can be congratulatory or condescending, though its use is usually humorous and to some degree derisive.

Though preppy was long in use among high school and college students, the word first gained wide national exposure in Erich Segal's 1970 romantic novel *Love Story* and the movie that was made from it. Set on the Harvard University campus, the novel describes the relationship between working-class Radcliffe student Jenny Cavilleri and blueblood Harvard jock Oliver Barrett. Jenny's personality is characterized by salty language, a blue-collar chip on her shoulder, and her hostile references to Oliver as "Preppy." The word preppy entered the national vocabulary at that point in its most common usage—an antagonistic epithet for the elite, used by those who are not in the upper classes.

In 1980, Lisa Birnbaum published *The Official Preppy Handbook,* a tongue-in-cheek look at the very real characteristics, quirks, and foibles of the privileged classes. She focuses her not-altogether-unloving mockery on the "old money" upper crust society of the East Coast, the alumni of such schools as Choate, Groton, Exeter, and Andover. By poking fun at their "Chip and Muffy" nicknames, and their expensive-shoes-without-socks pseudo-casual style, Birnbaum shined a revealing light on the quietly rich. Her book inspired imitators, including some that were more overtly hostile to her subject, such as Ralph Schoenstein's *The I-Hate-Preppies Handbook: A Guide for the Rest of Us.*

Part fashion, part breeding, and part attitude, preppiness denotes wealth, privilege, pomposity, and dissipation. The hostility with which the epithet preppy is hurled casts doubt on the reality behind the U.S. myth of the classless society. Preppy continues to be used regularly in the press, sometimes interchangeably with "yuppie," though yuppie does not carry the East Coast blueblood connotation that preppy does. One of the most memorable outbreaks of preppy in the headlines occurred in the fall of 1996, after Jennifer Levin was strangled in New York's Central Park by Robert Chambers. Levin and Chambers were both members of Manhattan's high-society prep-school elite, and Levin's death was immediately dubbed "The Preppy Murder" in newspapers across the country, giving credibility to the axiom that a particular form of public outrage is reserved for the misdeeds of those who have "all of the advantages."

Though the working classes may have their revenge on preppies in the press and in film, it is the preppies who continue to triumph. With elite boarding schools becoming almost as expensive as private colleges, the prep-school education is more out of reach than ever for working people. A 1997 *Fortune* magazine study showed that corporate executives with upper-class prep-school backgrounds are consistently paid higher salaries than those executives with more middle-class upbringings. Preppies may be targets of fun and ridicule, but grown-up preppies become the power elite who perhaps see themselves safely insulated from the impact of jokes made at their expense.

—Tina Gianoulis

FURTHER READING:

Birnbach, Lisa. *The Official Preppy Handbook.* New York, Workman Publishing, 1980.

Flippin, Royce. *Save an Alligator, Shoot a Preppie: A Terrorist Guide.* New York, A & W Visual Library, 1981.

Schoenstein, Ralph. *The I-Hate-Preppies Handbook: A Guide for the Rest of Us.* New York, Simon & Schuster, 1981.

Presley, Elvis (1935-1977)

It is no accident that Elvis Presley's rise to fame in the 1950s was in tandem with the rise of rock 'n' roll, for the man and the music are indelibly linked. Though not the first rock 'n' roll star, Presley was the most prominent prophet of the pioneering musical form. Moreover, with his daringly unique style, delivery, and sound, he symbolized the cultural shakeup that rumbled throughout the era. As the Pulitzer Prize-winning journalist and social historian David Halberstam proclaimed, "In cultural terms, [Elvis's] coming was nothing less than the start of a revolution."

Presley himself was as complex and as conflicted as the decade he has come to represent. Though shy and beguilingly sweet offstage, his early onstage persona was swaggering, even leering, with performances marked by frenzied bumping and grinding and seemingly gravity-defying bolts, leaps, and slides. To the sexually repressed

Elvis Presley

young people of the day, he was an emblem of rebellious liberation. To the terrified adult establishment, parents especially, he was initially viewed as the devil incarnate. At the time, no one could have predicted that rock 'n' roll would "last," or that Presley's stardom would not only endure, but also grow to mythic proportions following his death in 1977.

Known the world over by his first name, the American legend had decidedly humble beginnings. Elvis Aaron Presley was born on January 8, 1935, in a two-room shack in Tupelo, Mississippi, following the stillborn birth of twin brother, Jesse Garon. The attending country doctor had to collect his fifteen-dollar fee through welfare. Scions of large, sharecropping families, Presley's parents were poor and uneducated. But Vernon and Gladys Presley indulged their precocious, tow-headed son, and Gladys went on to become a pivotal force in his early career. In fact, Presley was so devoted to her that he has often been depicted as a "mama's boy."

Drawn to music from early childhood, Presley was initially exposed to the gospel music that was inherent to the Deep South, and the Pentecostal church he attended in Tupelo. His musical horizons expanded in 1948 when he moved with his family to Memphis, Tennessee. Beale Street, home of the blues, was within walking distance of Lauderdale Courts, the public housing project that became home to the Presleys. Roadhouses were venues for hillbilly bands and cowboy singers. Churches and meeting halls echoed with spirituals. Local airwaves were also diverse. In defiance of the times, Presley avidly listened to so-called "race" stations, which played the music of African-American artists for their primarily African-American audience.

It was during high school that Presley began experimenting with his looks and dress style. At a time when others his age were wearing plaid shirts and blue jeans, he favored flashy "pimp"-type clothing. Colors not ordinarily worn by the era's males, including pink, were a Presley fashion favorite. His hair style was equally distinct. Though crewcuts were the rage, he wore his dark blond hair slicked back with rose oil. That "greaser" look would go on to become a "cool" statement in films and on television. But Presley was far from popular at school. Most students recoiled from the young man with the greasy-looking hair and the acne. His shyness, thick Mississippi accent, and a tendency to stutter, further hampered his status among both classmates and teachers, who were taken aback when he performed in a student show during his senior year. Most were unaware that he sang. But in fact, Presley was consumed by both music and ambition.

It was a July 1953 vanity recording, made just six weeks after high school graduation, that led to his introduction to Sun Records founder Sam Phillips. The blues-loving Phillips was known for recording "colored" artists, such as B.B. King, Bobby Blue Bland, and Big Ma Rainey. But what he was searching for, he used to say, was "a white man who can sing like a Negro." He sensed that Presley, with his wide-ranging voice, might be that person. Presley was working as a truck driver when Phillips teamed him with guitarist Scotty Moore and bass player Bill Black. Their potent chemistry resulted in a sped-up, rhythmically charged version of "That's All Right (Mama)," their first Sun recording. Popular local disc jockey Dewey Phillips, no relation to Sam, played the song multiple times on the night of July 10, 1954. Later that month, as an extra added attraction at a local "hillbilly hoe-down," Presley subconsciously exhibited the gyrating body movements that he would eventually make a trademark.

For the next year and a half, Presley and musicians Moore and Black, who were now Sun Records artists, were on an extended road trip. Traveling throughout east and west Texas, Arkansas, and Louisiana, they played high school auditoriums, Future Farmers of America halls, and backwater honky-tonks. One show found Presley performing atop a flat-bed truck parked at the second base of a baseball diamond. As his regional celebrity grew, disc jockeys and promoters alternately labeled him "the hillbilly cat," the "Memphis flash," a "bebop Western star," and even a "folk music fireball." But if his music was difficult to label, there was unanimity that Presley was one of a kind. Recalling the sensational impact of the early Presley, country music singer Bob Luman once related, "This cat came out in red pants and a green coat and a pink shirt and socks, and he had this sneer on his face and he stood behind the mike for five minutes, I'll bet, before he made a move. Then he hit his guitar a lick, and he broke two strings. . . . So there he was, these two strings dangling, and he hadn't done anything yet, and these high school girls were screaming and fainting and running up to the stage, and then he started to move his hips real slow like he had a thing for his guitar. That was Elvis Presley when he was about 19, playing Kilgore, Texas. He made chills run up my back, man, like when your hair starts grabbing at your collar."

Radio was a pivotal force in Presley's early career. Via the popular *Louisiana Hayride* radio show, his music reached listeners in thirteen states. His sensual, electric performances increasingly drew young women. When he wrapped an act in Jacksonville, Florida, by drawling ''Girls, I'll see y'all backstage,'' hundreds of female attendees took him at his word. The May 1955 incident marked the first riot of his career.

His ascendancy caught the attention of manager-promoter Colonel Tom Parker. The former carnival man had received his honorary ''Colonel'' title in the 1940s, from hillbilly singer-turned-Louisiana governor Jimmy Davis. As shrewd as he was colorful, the Colonel was managing the *Grand Ole Opry*'s Hank Snow when he first heard about the young man from Memphis. He signed Presley to a contract in late summer 1955, and then promptly negotiated the singer's move from the regional Sun Records to the nationally prominent RCA Records.

Even before the move to RCA, Presley proved surprisingly astute about stardom and its demands. From his own office in Memphis, he saw to it that fan mail was answered, and photo requests were filled. Aware that he was becoming the music world's equivalent of James Dean and Marlon Brando, the image-savvy Presley refused to smile for a *Parade* magazine photographer during a late 1955 session, explaining, ''I know that you can't be sexy if you smile. You can't be a rebel if you grin.'' After asking if he could pose himself, Presley casually stripped off his shirt, and stared soulfully at the lens.

A momentous year for Presley, 1956 saw his first RCA single, ''Heartbreak Hotel,'' top the charts and become his first gold record. His first album, *Elvis Presley*, likewise went gold. ''Don't Be Cruel'' and ''Hound Dog'' were top ten hits. TV appearances followed, along with a lucrative film contract, and, in a triumphant homecoming, several now-legendary performances at the Tupelo fairgrounds. Presley's name and likeness also adorned a myriad of products, ranging from charm bracelets to stuffed hound dogs. During their first fifteen months on the shelves, Presley merchandise accounted for $40 million in sales.

There was, after all, a new and burgeoning market: the American teenager. The country's approximately thirteen million teenagers had annual earnings, including allowances, of more than $7 billion. Teen paychecks, the emergence of the 45 rpm record, and the popularity of the jukebox were integral to Presley's meteoric rise.

But not everyone applauded his pervasive presence. Originally, it was ''race'' artists such as Fats Domino, Little Richard, and Chuck Berry who spread the startling sound called ''rock 'n' roll,'' which merged elements of gospel, rockabilly, and rhythm and blues. When white artists performed the music, it became more accessible. As performed by Presley, it became a volatile force. Denounced from pulpits, as well as by educators, the music was targeted for suppression by communities from coast to coast. As moral indignation grew, Presley became a whipping boy. The national boiling point followed his sexually charged performance of ''Hound Dog'' on *The Milton Berle Show*. Critics railed, calling him ''lewd,'' ''obscene,'' and ''suggestive.'' A reprieve came with his third and final appearance on America's premiere variety show, *The Ed Sullivan Show*. Following Presley's performance of January 1957, the respected host assured his audience that Presley was a ''real decent, fine boy.''

Fame brought changes to Presley's personal life. He moved his family into their new home, the Memphis estate named Graceland. He indulged in cosmetic alterations, including capped teeth, a nose-job, and skin treatments. He dyed his hair black, in the belief that black hair made a subject more striking for the cameras.

The inveterate moviegoer had dreamed of becoming a serious actor. But producers did not want Presley to dramatically emote; they wanted him to sing. Thus, anachronistic musical numbers found their way into Presley's 1956 film debut, the bittersweet Civil War romance, *Love Me Tender*, for which he was critically reviled. He fared better in 1957 with the back-to-back, somewhat autobiographical entries *Loving You* and *Jailhouse Rock*. The latter is significant for his surly performance, and the stunning title song musical sequence. His follow-up film, the gritty *King Creole*, boasted his most promising work. Then came his induction into the U.S. Army.

The Memphis Selective Service Commission's 1958 decision to draft Presley prompted congratulatory letters from parents, along with death threats from teenage girls. For many, his haircut by U.S. Army barbers was a powerful and welcome sign that a rebellious era was ending.

The military stint proved significant for Presley. While stationed in Germany he began seriously popping barbiturates in an effort to keep longer hours. In the wake of his mother's death, which left him devastated, he also formed a close relationship with the fourteen-year-old daughter of an Air Force captain. He later had the teenage Priscilla Beaulieu brought to Memphis, to surreptitiously live at Graceland.

Returning from the service in 1960, Presley headed to Hollywood where he and his entourage became renowned for their womanizing and wild parties. Presley's inner circle, which came to be known as the Memphis Mafia, provided a buffer for the star, who increasingly kept his private life private.

His first post-Army film, the formulaic *G.I. Blues*, triggered a series of lightweight romantic musicals set against exotic settings, co-starring myriad pretty girls. Presley cynically referred to them as ''travelogues.'' Still, films such as *Blue Hawaii* and *Fun in Acapulco* were huge moneymakers. And he found his match, in talent and charisma, opposite real life romantic interest Ann-Margret in the 1964 title, *Viva Las Vegas*.

Musically, the post-Army Presley concentrated on ballads. Signifying his shift from rock 'n' roll was ''Are You Lonesome Tonight?,'' as well as ''It's Now or Never,'' which featured Presley in a crooning mode. There were also frothy songs from his movies, and religious entries including ''Crying in the Chapel.'' To young people, it appeared Presley was stagnating. He himself worried that he was being eclipsed by the ''British invasion.'' In desperation, he agreed to star in an NBC-TV special. The resulting *Elvis*, which aired in December 1968, stands as one of the great show business comebacks. Looking slim and sexy, clad in tight-fitting black leather, Presley performed before a live audience in jam session-style. When he returned to TV five years later, Presley was likewise a mesmerizing figure, in white jumpsuit and an American eagle-emblazoned cape. *Elvis: Aloha from Hawaii—Via Satellite*, was beamed to countries around the world, to a record-breaking audience of as many as 1.5 billion.

Enshrined as ''The King,'' the Presley of the early 1970s was the top headliner of Las Vegas, where he was under contract to the Hilton International Hotel. He also played to sold-out crowds in concert arenas across the country. With the revitalization of his career came a tone of playful self-mockery, as evidenced by the inclusion of Richard Strauss's monumental ''Also Sprake Zarathustra'' as the opening music for his concerts.

But Presley's professional triumphs were marred by escalating personal woes. His relationship with Beaulieu, who he had married in May 1967, unraveled shortly after the 1968 birth of daughter Lisa Marie. The couple divorced in 1973. His health also suffered. From late 1973 until his death, Presley was in and out of hospitals, "officially" for treatment of pneumonia, exhaustion, and other ailments. In truth, he was battling a long term dependence on prescription drugs, as well as weight problems. During 1975 and 1976 his performances were increasingly erratic. One Las Vegas engagement was canceled when he collapsed, in tears, on stage.

Despite the warning signs, the world was stunned when Presley died at his Graceland home at age forty-two, on August 16, 1977. President Jimmy Carter observed the passing with a statement saluting the man who symbolized America's "vitality, rebelliousness, and good humor." An estimated 80,000 people lined the streets of Memphis to watch the funeral procession.

Coincidentally, Presley died shortly after the publication of *Elvis: What Happened?*, a lurid exposé penned by former aides. The dark side of his life consequently became fodder for tabloid writers and biographers. Among them was Albert Goldman, whose 1981 book, *Elvis*, is infamous for its cruel tone. Because of the tell-alls, some Presley associates, including the Mafia members and personal physician Dr. George Nichopolous, became familiar names. And there was heightened skepticism over the exact cause of Presley's death. When he died, his system contained traces of ten different drugs, including morphine and codeine. But the medical examiner had determined that "hypertensive heart disease" had caused the death. Autopsy results were reexamined in 1994, and it was concluded that Presley had died of a heart attack. Yet drugs and gluttony certainly contributed to his downward spiral. Presley stands as a preeminent example of the dangers of excess.

But Presley also personifies the American Dream. He ranks as a preeminent musical influence of the twentieth century. At the time of his death, he had sold more than 500 million records. His vast catalog, encompassing blues, rockabilly, country, gospel, rock 'n' roll, and more, is unsurpassed. In revolutionizing popular music, he spawned countless imitators, including the pompadoured rock 'n' rollers who climbed the charts in his aftermath. He also influenced two generations of performers and musicians, professionally and personally.

With his penchant for pink Cadillacs, jewel-encrusted rings, and other audacious trappings, Presley embodied the concept of the superstar as conspicuous consumer. By buying his mother a house, he set a rock-world precedent. By cleverly reinventing himself to suit changing times and tastes, he set a pattern since emulated by rock stars ranging from Elton John to Michael Jackson, from Madonna to Courtney Love. But unlike his successors, his varying images went beyond promotional angles to become cultural benchmarks. When the U.S. Postal Service issued a twenty-nine cent Presley stamp in 1993, the public voted for the image to illustrate the young Fifties-era Elvis. Within the merchandising arena, Elvises of all eras abound, on products ranging from alarm clocks to dolls, from designer ties to doormats. Closely guarding the name, likeness, and image of the entertainer is Elvis Presley Enterprises, Inc., a multimillion dollar business owned by Presley's daughter, Lisa Marie Presley, and overseen by Priscilla Presley. It was Priscilla who salvaged the Presley estate, which was mismanaged during Presley's lifetime due to business dealings balanced in favor of Colonel Parker. The empire's crown jewel is Graceland, which is visited annually by some 750,000 people, making it the second most-toured residence following the White House.

Presley was himself a visitor to the White House, albeit an uninvited one, when he showed up in December 1970 and asked to be part of the country's war on drugs. Unaware of the rock star's own drug dependency, President Richard M. Nixon made Presley an honorary narcotics agent. Their meeting, one of the oddest political

summits, ever, typified the surreal, unsurpassed nature of Presley's stardom. That bizarre quality continued into the 1990s, as personified by Elvis cults, Elvis "sightings," Elvis impersonators, and even Lisa Marie Presley's brief marriage to pop superstar Michael Jackson.

So rife is the Elvis Presley influence that the mere mention of certain foods, such as the fried peanut butter and banana sandwich, a Presley favorite, summon up his memory. Certain clothing attire, including blue suede shoes, immediately suggest Presley. He is the subject of a thriving cottage publishing industry, has been scrutinized in movies and TV shows, and even shows up as a "character" in movies and on TV. His appeal spans all social strata; studied and analyzed in universities, he remains a frequent tabloid subject. The Presley concert closing announcement, that "Elvis has left the building!," has even become part of the lexicon. But Presley hasn't really left. He lives in the collective conscience. In the parlance of Presley fans, Elvis is eternal.

—Pat H. Broeske

FURTHER READING:

Brown, Peter Harry, and Pat H. Broeske. *Down at the End of Lonely Street: The Life and Death of Elvis Presley.* New York, Dutton, 1997.

"Elvis—A Different Kind of Idol." *Life.* August 27, 1956, 101-109.

Goldman, Albert. *Elvis.* New York, Avon, 1981.

Guralnick, Peter. *Last Train to Memphis: The Rise of Elvis Presley.* Boston, Little, Brown, 1994.

Halberstam, David. *The Fifties.* New York, Villard Books, 1993.

Shearer, Lloyd. "I Remember Elvis." *Parade.* January 29, 1978, 4-9.

Torgoff, Martin, editor. *The Complete Elvis.* New York, Delilah Books, 1982.

West, Red, Sonny West, and Dave Hebler, as told to Steve Dunleavy. *Elvis: What Happened?* New York, Ballantine Books, 1977.

The Price Is Right

The longest-running game show in television history is *The Price Is Right,* a proving ground of consumer shrewdness that will serve future historians well as an artifact of capitalist ideology. As it entered its sixth decade on the air during the 1990s, the program continued to beguile millions of shut-ins, homemakers, and truant school children on a daily basis nationwide.

The venerable game show made its debut on NBC in November of 1956, with Bill Cullen as host. In its early days the program had a rigid format centered on contestants guessing the prices of various consumer items. It ran until 1965 in this incarnation, at which point it was canceled and seemed consigned to TV oblivion. But the show came back in 1972 with a new host, genial former *Truth or Consequences* emcee Bob Barker. He would remain with *Price Is Right* throughout the remainder of the twentieth century, logging more man-hours on network television than any other person in history.

Under Barker's stewardship, the show took on a less fixed format. A host of different price-guessing games were introduced,

A typical moment from *The Price Is Right*.

some with complicated rules that bewildered the participants. In "The Clock Game," for example, the contestant was given 30 seconds to guess the prices of two prizes. The price of the items was shown only to the live audience and the viewers watching at home. Barker provided assistance by telling the contestant if the prices he or she guessed were higher or lower than the actual price. The process continued until the contestant guessed the exact price. At the end of every show were "showcase" rounds in which the successful contestants could compete for expensive prizes like trips, cars, and furniture.

A number of staple features gave *Price Is Right* a distinctive look and sound. Announcer Johnny Olson added his unique voice to America's pop cultural consciousness with his booming exhortation to contestants to "Come on down!" Rod Roddy succeeded Olson after his death in 1985. And "Barker's Beauties," an ever changing stock company of leggy models who presented the prizes, were on hand to hook male viewers. Over the years there were a number of notable onstage mishaps as well, including a woman who lost her tube top while "coming on down" and a refrigerator that nearly toppled over onto a contestant.

One of the more unusual aspects of *Price Is Right*'s long television run was the bizarre behavior of its host and star, Barker. A onetime karate student of action hero Chuck Norris, Barker seemed the epitome of blow-dried, hair-dyed emcee cool on stage. Off the set,

however, he often courted controversy. An ardent animal rights activist, Barker enraged the producers of the Miss U.S.A. Pageant in 1988 when he stopped hosting the show to protest the fact that fur coats were being given to contestants. The next year, in response to ads Barker had run in *Variety* accusing them of negligence and incompetence, the American Humane Association, an organization that monitors the treatment of animals in show business, slapped the host with a $10,000,000 suit for libel, slander, and invasion of privacy.

Litigation against Barker was not confined to his political activity, however. It reached into his personal life as well. In 1994, Dian Parkinson, a former *Price Is Right* model, sued Barker for sexually harassing her during their years together on the show. According to the suit, Parkinson claimed Barker frequently called her to his dressing room, told her that "Daddy's bored," and then forced her to perform oral sex on him. The case was eventually dropped.

Such shenanigans might have been the kiss of death for any other game show host, but not for Barker, who kept rolling along even after he stopped dying his hair (with network approval) in 1987. The new, silver-maned Barker gave no indication of slowing down, and *Price Is Right* continued to do well in the ratings. Like its host, this revered television institution has proven that a little snow on the roof does not preclude the existence of a considerable fire in the furnace.

—Robert E. Schnakenberg

FURTHER READING:

Schwartz, David, Steve Ryan, and Fred Wostrbrock. *The Encyclopedia of TV Game Shows*. New York, Facts on File, 1995.

Price, Reynolds (1933—)

Southern novelist and man of letters Reynolds Price has been a distinguished figure in American literature since the 1962 publication of his first novel, *A Long and Happy Life*. With a distinct prose style and rich narrative voice that are firmly rooted in the language and rhythms of his native North Carolina, Price depicts a world of rural familiarity in which characters struggle with personal desires while trying to answer to family duties. Among his many novels, short stories, plays, poems, essays, translations, and memoirs are *Kate Vaiden* (1986), *The Surface of Earth* (1975), and the cancer memoir *A Whole New Life* (1994). Price has also collaborated on songs with singer/songwriter James Taylor, and broadcast personal commentaries on National Public Radio's *All Things Considered*. A graduate of Duke University and a Rhodes scholar, Price has taught in the English Department at Duke since 1958.

—James Schiff

FURTHER READING:

Humphries, Jefferson, editor. *Conversations with Reynolds Price*. Jackson, University Press of Mississippi, 1991.

Kimball, Sue Laslie, and Lynn Veach Sadler, editors. *Reynolds Price: From ''A Long and Happy Life'' to ''Good Hearts.''* Fayetteville, North Carolina, Methodist College Press, 1989.

Rooke, Constance. *Reynolds Price*. Boston, Twayne, 1983.

Schiff, James. *Understanding Reynolds Price*. Columbia, University of South Carolina Press, 1996.

Schiff, James, editor. *Critical Essays on Reynolds Price*. New York, G. K. Hall, 1998.

Price, Vincent (1911-1993)

A veteran of theatre, film, radio, and television, Vincent Price's fifty-five-year acting career ran the gamut from classic film noir to especially bad ''B'' movies, but his lasting legacy is the Gothic horror movies he made with ghoulish glee and good humor. In the era that preceded the cinematic bloodbath of late-twentieth century slasher films, the mellifluous and debonair Price reigned as Hollywood's Master of the Macabre. With his distinctive voice, handsome demeanor, and somewhat tongue-in-cheek approach to Gothic films, as he liked to call them, Price brought style and fun to the horror genre. Generations of film fans reveled in Price's ability to send his audiences on a hilarious horror romp and then scare them to death.

Although his style was decidedly English, Vincent Leonard Price Jr. hailed from Middle America. The youngest child of a successful candy manufacturer, Price was raised in financial comfort among the social elite of St. Louis, Missouri. The son and brother of Yale graduates, Price received an excellent education aimed at prepping him for Yale, which he attended for four years, receiving a degree in English. But Price's passion was art history, which he studied at the prestigious Courtauld Institute in London.

A longtime theatre and movie buff, Price auditioned for a bit part at London's Gate Theatre on a dare and was cast in the role of a Chicago policeman. Bitten by the acting bug, Price next won the coveted role of Prince Albert in *Victoria Regina*. When Broadway producer Gilbert Miller bought the play as a vehicle for Helen Hayes, Price returned to New York, where he made his Broadway debut in 1936. For two years, he appeared nightly in the hottest play on Broadway. Regarded as a matinee idol, the handsome six-foot-four-inch actor eventually struck out on his own and ended up in Orson Welles's Mercury Theatre.

In 1938, Price signed with Universal Pictures, where he was groomed to be a leading man, but after a disappointing screen debut in a light comedy, Price was cast in second and third leads for four years before returning to Broadway in 1941 to star in *Angel Street*. Playing the sadistic villain in a play that would become Broadway's longest-running melodrama (and later a hit movie, *Gaslight*), Price discovered a penchant for playing evil men. A year later, he returned to Hollywood, where he joined the strong stable of actors at Twentieth Century-Fox.

During the 1940s, Price appeared in such screen classics as *Laura* and *The Song of Bernadette* before winning the starring role in *Dragonwyck*. Cast as a despotic, drug-addicted, murdering landowner, Price won rave reviews, but it would be another decade before he fully embraced villainy. It was the 1953 3-D horror classic *The House of Wax* that catapulted Price into horror-movie fame. During the 1950s, when the genre was undergoing a resurgence of public interest, Price appeared in two cult classics, both directed by the master showman of horror, William Castle: *The House on Haunted Hill* and *The Tingler*.

American International Pictures's cycle of films based on the work of Edgar Allan Poe and directed by Roger Corman ultimately transformed Price into the modern King of Horror. Shot on a ridiculously low budget in fifteen days, Corman's *House of Usher* (1960) was a tour de force for Price, who played the tormented Roderick Usher. The film was both critically acclaimed and financially successful. Price and Corman made five more Poe films together, from the lighthearted *Tales of Terror* (1962) to the surreal *The Masque of the Red Death* (1964). *The Raven* (1963), a delectable comedy that united Price with fellow horror stars Boris Karloff and Peter Lorre, became a particular audience favorite and remains a staple of late-night television. Price's tongue-in-cheek approach delighted his fans, as did his willingness to spoof himself in popular TV shows such as *The Brady Bunch* and *Batman,* on which he appeared as the villainous Egghead.

To counteract his horror persona, Price assembled and sold the Vincent Price art collection for Sears, Roebuck & Company; and wrote three best-selling gourmet cookbooks. Cultured and intelligent, Price was often referred to as Hollywood's Renaissance man.

During the early 1970s, Price continued to make horror classics such as *The Abominable Dr. Phibes,* but he grew discouraged as the genre changed from Gothic tales to slasher films and decided to return to his roots in the theatre, spending almost a decade touring the globe with his one-man show about Oscar Wilde. In the mid-1980s, Price was introduced to a whole new generation when Michael Jackson asked the seventy-two-year-old actor to provide the rap for his megahit ''Thriller.'' And in 1987, Price played his first non-horror role in decades in the acclaimed film, *The Whales of August,* starring Bette Davis and Lillian Gish.

In 1982, Price was contacted by a young animator at Disney named Tim Burton who had made a short film about a boy who wanted to grow up to be Vincent Price. When the actor agreed to narrate the film, Price and Burton became friends. Eight years later, it would be Burton who provided the ailing actor with his cinematic swan song as the kind-hearted inventor in *Edward Scissorhands.*

—Victoria Price

FURTHER READING:

Price, Vincent. *I Like What I Know.* New York, Doubleday, 1960.

Williams, Lucy Chase. *The Complete Films of Vincent Price.* Secaucus, New Jersey, Citadel Press, 1995.

Pride, Charley (1938—)

Singer Charley Pride has the distinction of being the only African-American musician to make his career entirely in the field of

Charley Pride

country music, a musical genre dominated by white performers. His string of hits that began in the mid-1960s and continued for more than 18 years broke the color line in country music, even if no other black performers have followed Pride's lead. Pride's smooth voice and country-pop sound carried him to success despite his record company's initial fears that he would not be accepted by the country music establishment, or its fans, because of his race.

Born in 1938 to a sharecropping family on a cotton farm in Sledge, Mississippi, Pride crossed racial lines early in life, preferring to listen to white country music rather than delta blues or other black musical forms. He bought his first guitar from the Sears Roebuck catalog at the age of 14, with money he earned picking cotton, and began to teach himself country songs he heard on the radio. Although he did not want a life as a cotton farmer, Pride did not turn to music at first as a way out. Instead, he left home at age 17 to play baseball with the Negro American League where he played with the Detroit Eagles and later the Memphis Red Sox. He served for two years in the Army and returned to baseball after his discharge, joining the Los Angeles Angels. He tried to break into the major leagues with both the California Angels and the New York Mets, but he missed the cut both times.

His short career in baseball over, Pride returned to his love of country music. While working part-time as a semi-pro baseball player and as a smelter for the Anaconda zinc works in Helena, Montana, Pride also sang in a local nightclub where he was overheard one night by country singer Red Sovine. Sovine, impressed by Pride's voice and singing style, encouraged him to go to Nashville. Unsuccessful at first, Pride was eventually heard by country guitarist and producer Chet Atkins, who was also in charge of RCA Records' Nashville division. Atkins signed Pride to a record deal in 1966. Pride's first single was "The Snakes Crawl at Night." RCA issued the record without any publicity photos, fearing that southern disk jockeys would not play a country record by a black artist. That song, and a follow-up, "Before I Met You," were modest successes. Pride had his first major hit, "Just Between You and Me," at the end of 1966. That success, and the long string of hits that followed, established Pride as a major star in mainstream country music. His acceptance by country music fans soon broke down any initial fears that a black artist could not succeed in country music. In early 1967, Pride became the first black artist to appear on the Grand Ole Opry since Deford Bailey in 1925.

Between 1969 and 1971, Pride released five straight number one singles, including "All I Have to Offer You Is Me," "I'd Rather Love You," "Is Anybody Goin' to San Antone," "Wonder Could I Live There Anymore," and "I'm So Afraid of Losing You Again." His biggest chart successes came in 1971 with "Kiss an Angel Good Mornin'" and "I'm Just Me." These songs topped the country charts and, significantly, also crossed over into the pop charts, providing compelling evidence of Pride's wide appeal among a variety of audiences. Next to Elvis Presley, Charley Pride was RCA's best-selling artist.

Pride maintained his consistent country-pop style throughout the 1970s and 1980s, refusing to follow newer trends in country music. His adherence to his trademark sound encouraged him to break with RCA in 1986 when he felt they were not promoting younger artists at the expense of longtime successes like himself. In the 1990s, Pride continued to record, occasionally forming duets with younger performers such as Travis Tritt, and he maintained an active concert schedule. In 1994, in recognition of his groundbreaking achievements in country music, he was awarded the Academy of Country Music's Pioneer award.

—Timothy Berg

FURTHER READING:

The Country Music Foundation, editors. *Country: The Music and the Musicians.* New York, Abbeville Press, 1994.

Malone, Bill C. *Country Music U.S.A.: A Fifty-Year History.* Revised Edition. Austin, American Folklore Society, University of Texas Press, 1985.

Pride, Charley, and Jim Henderson. *Pride: The Charley Pride Story.* New York, Quill, 1995.

Pride, Charley. *The Essential Charley Pride.* BMG/RCA Records, 1997.

Stambler, Irwin, and Grelun Landon. *Country Music: The Encyclopedia.* New York, St. Martin's Press, 1997.

Prince (1958—)

An exciting live performer and a prolific singer-songwriter, Prince resists easy categorization because of his uncanny ability to transcend genres in music and image. Often a misunderstood and controversial entertainer, Prince emerged on the music scene in 1977 to eventually record a staggering 20 albums in just 20 years. In the 1990s, Prince staged a bitter and highly publicized dispute with his record company, Warner Brothers, over the nature of his contract. Ultimately, the artist changed his name to a symbol in an attempt to regain creative control over his career. While Prince attained the peak of his critical and commercial success in the early 1980s, by the end of the 1990s he had emerged as a musical entrepreneur, continuing to tour regularly while maintaining a legion of fans in the United States and abroad.

Prince Rogers Nelson was born in Minneapolis on June 7, 1958 to Mattie Shaw and John Nelson, a local musician. In his formative years during the 1960s and 1970s, Prince honed his skills on a number of different instruments and immersed himself in the music of artists who would eventually come to influence his sound: Carlos Santana, Joni Mitchell, Curtis Mayfield, Stevie Wonder, Sly and the Family Stone, and Jimi Hendrix. Drawing from this rich legacy, by the late 1970s Prince would help to invent what became known as the Minneapolis Sound: a blend of horns, guitars, and electronic synthesizers supported by a steady, bouncing rhythm.

While Prince has often been classified as a rock musician, his work is much more complex in the way it fuses elements from rhythm and blues, pop, rock, funk, punk, and country. The singer also boasts a wide-ranging vocal ability which includes a growling baritone, a full tenor sound, an elegant falsetto, and a piercing shriek. The multifaceted nature of Prince's music and singing helped earn him a wide and diverse audience throughout his career, allowing him to crossover the racial boundaries that tended to dominate the music scene before his arrival.

In April 1978, Prince released his first album, *For You,* on which he played most of the instruments and overdubbed his voice to heightened effect. While the album was a modest success, his next release, *Prince* (1979), sold over one million copies, producing the hit singles "I Feel for You" and "I Wanna Be Your Lover." The two

albums that followed, *Dirty Mind* (1980) and *Controversy* (1981), were highly influenced by 1980s new wave and punk music. The latter album was aptly named: with each release, Prince become increasingly controversial for his explicit lyrics that would engage sexual themes including oral sex, incest, and sadomasochism.

Prince's outrageous sense of style also proved to be attention-grabbing. Sporting a small, short frame and a full mane of hair, Prince showed an affinity for lacy, frilly, and often suggestive clothing. His rare appearances in media interviews were awkward and self-effacing; yet on stage, he was carnal and exhibitionist in a way audiences had not witnessed before. Along with his musical peers Boy George and Michael Jackson, Prince helped establish a new sense of masculinity in the 1980s that owed a major debt to the images of popular rock stars like David Bowie, Iggy Pop, and Mick Jagger. In Prince's world, men could wear makeup and women's clothes and still maintain a diverse and supportive fan base.

Prince rose to superstar status with the release of his next two groundbreaking albums: *1999* (1982), a double-album set featuring several hit singles, including "Little Red Corvette" and the infectious, prophetic title track; and *Purple Rain* (1984), which became the defining moment of Prince's career. The album functioned as a soundtrack for Prince's first film, also titled *Purple Rain.* Directed on a modest budget by Albert Magnoli (who later became Prince's manager), the semi-autobiographical film presented Prince as the Kid, a struggling rock singer tormented by his dysfunctional relationships with women and his father.

Unexpectedly, *Purple Rain* became the most commercially and critically successful rock film since the Beatles' *Hard Day's Night* (1965). The soundtrack spawned a series of number one and top ten singles on the pop chart, including "Let's Go Crazy" and "When Doves Cry." The album ultimately earned the singer three Grammy Awards, while the title track garnered Prince a 1984 Academy Award for Best Original Song. The unprecedented success of the black-cast film also prepared the way for Spike Lee's groundbreaking independent film, *She's Gotta Have It* (1984), which in turn helped catalyze a new wave of black filmmaking in the 1980s and 1990s.

Although Prince never again attained the commercial visibility of the year in which he released *Purple Rain,* he followed that work with a series of sophisticated and critically praised albums on his own record label, Paisley Park. These albums included *Around the World in a Day* (1985), which sold four million copies and featured the hit single "Raspberry Beret," and *Parade* (1986), which served as the soundtrack for his next film, the disastrous *Under the Cherry Moon.*

After disbanding his backup group the Revolution, Prince released a double-album set, *Sign o' the Times* (1987), which generated a concert film in the same year. The melodic complexity and musical diversity of *Sign o' the Times* helped firmly establish Prince as a "true" artist in many critical circles. His next album, *Lovesexy* (1988), was complemented by a lavish, expensive international tour. The album received attention mostly for its controversial album cover on which Prince appeared fully nude, his loin area strategically covered. Prince also composed the music for two soundtracks, Tim Burton's hugely successful *Batman* (1989) and his own film vehicle, *Graffiti Bridge* (1990), a project that failed miserably at the box office.

During the height of his fame in the 1980s, Prince became linked in the media to a string of glamorous female performers, including Vanity, Appolonia, Sheena Easton, and Kim Basinger. Prince also helped bring a number of artists to visibility, including Morris Day, Tevin Campbell, Sheila E, and Carmen Electra. In the 1990s, he used his formidable talent to produce albums and songs for legendary but

Prince

largely forgotten rhythm and blues and funk artists like Mavis Staples and George Clinton.

In October 1991, Prince released an album titled *Diamonds and Pearls,* featuring his newly formed backup band, the New Power Generation. Although the album was a commercial success, Prince's mix of rap, rhythm and blues, and funk styles no longer seemed fresh or original in the changing scene of popular music in the 1990s. The artist seemed to be ''chasing trends rather than creating them,'' according to his biographer Liz Jones. Moreover, Prince's androgynous

image was no match for the powerfully abrasive images of masculinity that had gained appeal in popular culture in the early 1990s through gangsta rap and black films.

In 1993, Prince's behind-the-scenes battle with Warner Brothers—the record label that had represented him since his debut—came to public attention. In August 1992, Prince had signed a deal with the company which promised him one hundred million dollars for six albums, and a ten million dollar advance. Yet in order to recoup funds spent on Prince in the latter half of the 1980s and into the 1990s, in 1993 Warner Brothers released a double album set of Prince's greatest hits against the singer's wishes. In 1994, the company proceeded to close Prince's struggling Paisley Park label, much to the artist's chagrin. In response, Prince refused to release newly composed music, choosing instead to provide Warner with pre-recorded, and often lesser material from his vault of over 500 unreleased songs.

Yet Prince's attempt to resist Warner Brothers had far reaching effects on his audience and his critics, who longed to hear the quality of music that had defined his early career. Then, in 1993, Prince changed his name to a symbol which combined the generic signs for male and female. Unpronounceable, the new name alienated the singer from many of his fans, who were forced to refer to him as The Artist Formerly Known as Prince or as The Artist. In September 1995, he released a new album, *The Gold Experience,* under the new symbolic name. Eventually, the release went gold, spawning one hit single, "The Most Beautiful Girl in the World." Yet, partly due to poor management, Prince found himself deeply in debt at the end of year. As a result, he was forced to close several of the entrepreneurial ventures he had launched since the 1980s, including his Miami nightclub, Glam Slam, and his merchandise shops in Minneapolis and London.

In 1995, after a commercially and critically disastrous album release, *Chaos and Disorder,* The Artist Formerly Known as Prince met with Warner Brothers and the two entities mutually decided to terminate their contractual agreement. Prince then signed to EMI in 1996 and went on to release a three-CD collection titled *Emancipation.* The album contained new material and covers of songs made famous by artists as diverse Bonnie Raitt and the Stylistics. As a celebration of both his relationship with his new wife Mayte Garcia and his hard-won independence from Warner Brothers, the album rose to number 11 on Billboard's pop album chart and number six on the rhythm and blues charts. The artist's next release, *Crystal Ball,* would not emerge until 1998. In the same year, the Artist continued to develop his independent label by writing, producing, and distributing material for rhythm and blues icons Chaka Khan and Larry Graham of Sly and the Family Stone.

Although Prince continued to be known as an innovator in popular music, he was not able to sustain the commercial success of his early career into the 1990s, partly due to the rise of rap and other changes in popular music. Still, his emphasis on live instrumentation and musical virtuosity served to influence an entire generation of musical artists of the 1990s, including rhythm and blues performers D'Angelo and Maxwell. Prince also helped to establish a crossover scene in popular music, in which black singers were no longer limited to musical styles and became increasingly able to cross racial boundaries. Always ahead of his time, Prince's ambiguous, gender-bending image helped usher in a new, ostentatious style in popular culture and worked to transform the perception of black masculinity in U.S. society. No matter what name he goes by, Prince is truly an American superstar.

—Jason King

FURTHER READING:

Bream, Jon. *Prince: Inside the Purple Reign.* New York, Collier Macmillan, 1984.

Hill, Dave. *Prince: A Pop Life.* London, Faber & Faber, 1989.

Jones, Liz. *Purple Reign: The Artist Formerly Known as Prince.* Secaucus, New Jersey, Carol Pub. Group, 1998.

Prince, Hal (1928—)

Harold S. Prince revolutionized the American musical in the twentieth century. His resistance to the acting and singing conventions of early twentieth-century musical theater, his refusal to construct musicals as star-vehicles, and his use of filmic staging techniques make him one of the world's most original and innovative directors. From his first production, *The Pajama Game,* which cost $170,000, to his 1998 production of *Showboat,* which rang in at $8.5 million, Prince has known his share of artistic and financial successes as well as failures. *New York Times* critic David Richards described Prince as "the undisputed master of the Broadway musical."

Although not from a theatrical family, Prince was constantly exposed to the theater as a young boy. "Mine was a family addicted to theatre, and still there was no effort to encourage me to work in it nor discourage me, and at no time was there any to push me into finance. So I didn't have to resist something I *would* have resisted." Prince was born into what he called a "privileged upper-middle, lower-rich class" German-Jewish family in New York City on January 30, 1928. He was exposed to many of the greatest productions and actors of the time, including Orson Welles's *Julius Caesar* and Burgess Meredith's *Winterset.* In 1944 he graduated from the Franklin School, a private preparatory school, which was also his grandfather's alma mater.

He attended the University of Pennsylvania, where he was a member of the Penn Players. Along with his work in the theater, he also founded and managed the campus radio station and wrote, acted, and directed weekly play adaptations. He enrolled in a liberal arts program with a concentration on English, psychology, philosophy, and history. After graduating in 1948, he wrote plays and sent them to New York producers. After sending one script to ABC-TV, he was referred to the television production office of George Abbott in New York City. There he offered to work "on spec" and, by the end of the month, was earning $25 a week.

Prince worked on all aspects of Abbott's productions, including an original program titled *The Hugh Martin Show.* After Abbott's production company disbanded, Prince was hired by Abbott's production stage manager, Robert E. Griffith. Prince was stage manager for Broadway revues such as *Touch and Go* and *Tickets, Please.* In 1950 Prince was inducted into the army and stationed in Stuttgart, Germany, for two years as an anti-aircraft artillery gunner. There he spent many evenings visiting a nightclub called Maxim's, which would later become the muse for his hit musical *Cabaret.* Prince was discharged in October 1952. He immediately returned to work with Abbott and Griffith on several more hit musicals and began to learn the craft of directing from Abbott. Their production of Leonard Bernstein's *Wonderful Town* ran 500 performances, inspiring Griffith and Prince to become a producing team. Prince directed his first play, *The Pajama Game,* at the age of 26. The following years led to a string of successes for the Griffith-Prince team including *Damn Yankees* (1955), *New Girl in Town* (1957), and *Cabaret* (1966).

Prince's career became much more prominent after 1957 due to two major factors: his collaboration with composer/lyricist Stephen Sondheim and his ability to create his own directorial style free from the influences of George Abbott. His first major success was co-producing the Bernstein-Sondheim musical *West Side Story* (1957). Carol Ilson noted that Prince, "having learned his trade well through his working experiences with Abbott, Robbins, Bernstein, Laurents and Sondheim, would emerge with a unique vision of his own for the American Musical Theatre." Prince would go on to collaborate with

Sondheim on many more breakthrough productions: *Company* (1970), *Follies* (1971), *A Little Night Music* (1973), *Pacific Overtures* (1976), *Sweeney Todd* (1979), and *Merrily We Roll Along* (1981). Prince described their partnership as "creative abrasion," combining Sondheim's shy, introverted nature with Prince's gregariousness.

In the 1980s Prince had a string of box-office and critical failures, including the musicals *A Doll's Life* (1982), *Grind* (1985), and *Roza* (1986). Prince said of those six years, "no matter what I did, it could not please critics or audiences . . . during that period, I thought maybe I'd ceased to be able to create something that people want to see." His career rebounded following a series of successful collaborations with British composer/lyricist Sir Andrew Lloyd Webber. Their productions of *Evita* (1978) and *The Phantom of the Opera* (1986) were international successes. In the following years, Prince directed operas, dramas, and musicals, yet none were as successful as his stagings of *Kiss of the Spider Woman* (1992) and *Showboat* (1997).

Few directors can claim to have revolutionized the theater as much as Prince. His career, spanning the "golden age" of Broadway to the postmodern theater, has been one of incredible success and failure. He set the standard for the musical art form, and his productions are known worldwide for their innovative stagings, astounding effects, and impact on the popular theater. He acknowledged, "I want to leave a mark, to do something of artistic value." Judging from the lasting impact of his work, he has managed to do both.

—Michael Najjar

FURTHER READING:

Bartow, Arthur. "Harold S. Prince." *The Director's Voice: Twenty-One Interviews.* New York, Theatre Communications Group, 1988.

Hirsch, Foster. *Harold Prince and the American Musical Theatre.* Cambridge, Cambridge University Press, 1989.

Ilson, Carol. *Harold Prince: From Pajama Game to Phantom of the Opera.* Ann Arbor, UMI Research Press, 1989.

Prince, Hal. *Contradictions: Notes on Twenty-Six Years in the Theatre.* New York, Dodd, Mead & Company, 1974.

Princess Diana

See Diana, Princess of Wales

Prinze, Freddie (1954-1977)

Comedian Freddie Prinze is one of only a handful of Hispanic Americans to earn national prominence as a popular entertainer. Prinze was born in Washington Heights, New York, a multi-ethnic neighborhood on the Upper West Side. His father was a Hungarian immigrant who worked as a tool-and-die maker; his mother was a Puerto Rican immigrant who worked in a factory. Playing on the name "Neuorican," which is how many Puerto Ricans living in New York identify themselves, Prinze called himself a "Hungarican."

Prinze not only came from a diverse ethnic background, but a diverse religious one as well. His father was part Jewish and his mother was Catholic, but they chose to send him to a Lutheran elementary school. On Sundays he attended Catholic mass. "All was confusing," he told *Rolling Stone* in 1975, "until I found I could

Freddie Prinze

crack up the priest doing Martin Luther." Prinze was also overweight when he was a young boy, which further heightened his anxiety about his "mixed" identity. "I fitted in nowhere," he continued, "I wasn't true spic, true Jew, true anything. I was a miserable fat schmuck kid with glasses and asthma." Like many comedians, Prinze used humor to cope with the traumas of his childhood. "I started doing half-hour routines in the boys room, just winging it. Guys cut class to catch the act. It was, 'What time's Freddie playing the toilet today?'" His comedic talents paid off, as he was selected to attend the prestigious Performing Arts High School in New York.

Prinze did not graduate from the Performing Arts High School, although after his professional successes school administrators awarded him a certificate. The young comedian skipped many of his morning classes, most commonly economics, because he often worked as late as 3:00 A.M. in comedy clubs perfecting his comedy routine. One of his favorite spots was the Improvisation on West 44th Street, a place where aspiring comics could try out their material on receptive audiences.

Prinze called himself an "observation comic," and his routines often included impressions of ethnic minorities and film stars such as Marlon Brando. One of his most famous impressions was of his Puerto Rican apartment building superintendent who, when asked to fix a problem in the building, would say with a thick accent: "Eez not mai yob." The line became a national catch phrase in the early 1970s. His comedy also had a political edge that was poignant and raw. This is perhaps best illustrated by his line about Christopher Columbus: "Queen Isabelle gives him all the money, three boats, and he's wearing a red suit, a big hat, and a feather—that's a pimp." Prinze's comic wit, based in the tradition of street humor pioneered by such comics as Lenny Bruce and Richard Pryor, landed him a number of television appearances, including *The Tonight Show* in 1973.

Prinze's performance on *The Tonight Show* was a major success, and signalled the start of his television career. Indeed, Jimmie Komack, a television producer, liked what he saw in Prinze's routine and cast him to play the part of Chico Rodriquez, a wisecracking Chicano, in a situation comedy called *Chico and the Man* (1974-1978). The series also starred veteran actor Jack Albertson, who played "the Man," a crusty old-timer who owned a run-down garage in a Chicano barrio of East Los Angeles. In the tradition of situation comedies like *All in the Family* and *Sanford and Son,* most of the plots involved ethnic conflicts between Chico, who worked in the garage, and the Man, who was the only Caucasian living in the mostly Latino neighborhood. "Latin music sounds like Montovani getting mugged," the Man says to Chico in one episode. Chico would often respond to the old-timer's bigoted statements with the line, "Looking good," which also became a national catch phrase.

Chico and the Man faced criticism from the Los Angeles Chicano community, who protested the use of Prinze, a New York Puerto Rican, to play a Los Angeles Chicano. Citing dialect and accent differences—and the fact that network television rarely employed Chicano actors—Chicano groups picketed NBC's Burbank studios. Prinze responded with his usual irreverent humor: "If I can't play a Chicano because I'm Puerto Rican, then God's really gonna be mad when he finds out Charlton Heston played Moses." Fearful of the bad publicity, the network and producers of the show changed the character of Chico into a half-Puerto Rican and half-Chicano who was brought up in New York City. The shift in the character's ethnic identity apparently did not bother the audiences, as *Chico and the Man* never slipped below sixth place in the Nielsen ratings when Prinze was its star.

Prinze had a difficult time adjusting to his success. Indeed, friends reported that the comic turned to drugs to cope with the pressures of fame. "Freddie was into a lot of drugs," comedian Jimmy Walker told the *New York Times,* "not heroin, as far as I know, but coke and a lot of Ludes. The drug thing was a big part of Freddie's life. It completely messed him up." During this period, he also experienced many personal problems. His wife of 15 months, Katherine Elaine Cochran, filed for divorce. They had a ten-month-old son, whom Prinze adored. He was also engaged in a lawsuit with one of his business associates. The totality of these events depressed the young comic.

On January 28, 1977, after a night of phone calls to his secretary, psychiatrist, mother, and estranged wife, Prinze shot himself in the head in front of his business manager. He was rushed to the hospital, where he was pronounced dead. He was twenty-two years old. A note found in his apartment read: "I can't take any more. It's all my fault. There is no one to blame but me." According to the *New York Times,* Prinze had previously threatened suicide in front of many of his friends and associates, often by holding a gun to his head and pulling the trigger while the safety was on. It is not known whether the young comedian actually intended to kill himself that night or just allude to killing himself as he had done in the past, but it is clear that he was extremely depressed.

The death of Freddie Prinze is an American success story turned tragedy. His streetwise insight and raw wit are surely missed, perhaps most by the Puerto Rican-American community who have yet to see another politically minded Puerto Rican comedian grab national attention. "I am ee-noyed there is no Puerto Rican astronaut," Prinze

told *Rolling Stone* in an exaggerated Spanish accent, "thee bigots think we will blow thee horn all the way to thee moon, play thee radio, stick our heads out thee window and whistle . . . and then, on thee moon, the white astronaut says, 'Bring in the Rocks now,' and we reply, 'Eez not mai yob, man!'"

—Daniel Bernardi

FURTHER READING:

Burke, Tom. "The Undiluted South Bronx Truth about Freddie Prinze." *Rolling Stone.* 30 January 1975, 38-43.

Edelman, Rosemary. "'Pobrito,' It Ain't Easy Being a Star." *TV Guide.* 15 February 1975, 20-22.

Kasindorf, Jeanie. "'If I Was Bitter, I Wouldn't Have Chosen Comedy.'" *New York Times.* 9 February 1975, D27.

Nordheimer, Jon. "Freddie Prinze, 22, Dies after Shooting." *New York Times.* 30 January 1977, 19.

Pruetzel, Maria, *The Freddie Prinze Story.* Kalamazoo, Michigan, Master's Press, 1978.

Seiler, Michael. "Freddie Prinze: He Didn't Believe in Himself: Friends Reflect on Comedian's Childhood, Sudden Rise to Success and His Death." *New York Times.* 1 March 1977, C1.

The Prisoner

The British television series *The Prisoner* aired in the United States during the summer of 1968, setting a standard for imagination and existential vagary that subsequent shows such as *Twin Peaks* and *The X-Files* aspired, many years later, to match. The brainchild of actor/writer Patrick McGoohan, *The Prisoner* chronicles the travails of Number Six, an unwilling "resident" of what appears to be a sleepy British resort village. Under constant surveillance, and thwarted in his repeated attempts to escape, Number Six may (or may not) be John Drake, the spy hero of McGoohan's previous series, *Secret Agent.* That the events related admitted of no one particular explanation was part of *The Prisoner*'s visionary charm, while the program's recondite plots touched on themes of conformity, rebellion, and free will over the course of 17 increasingly bizarre episodes. In the end, the prisoner managed to turn the tables on his captors and escape to freedom. Or did he?

—Robert E. Schnakenberg

FURTHER READING:

White, Matthew, and Jaffer Ali. *The Official Prisoner Companion.* New York, Warner Books, 1988.

Professional Football

Thanks to television's impact on the viewing public, football threatened to supplant baseball as America's favorite professional sport as the 1950s wound to a close. The December 28, 1958 National Football League championship game, which witnessed the Johnny Unitas-led Baltimore Colts' defeat of the New York Giants 23-17 in overtime, set the stage for professional football's enormous popularity during the years ahead. Some 30 million television viewers watched the stirring contest, which helped the pro game to finally join the same league as both the national pastime and college ball.

First organized at the close of the nineteenth century, professional football remained less highly regarded and considerably less popular than the college game. By 1889, charges were leveled that Ivy League players had been given financial inducements. Then, on November 13, 1892, Yale All-American guard Walter "Pudge" Heffelfinger and Princeton end Ben "Sport" Donnelly received $500 and $250 respectively, plus expenses, to join the Allegheny Athletic Association for a contest against the Pittsburgh Athletic Club. Other players, many from the college ranks, including Bucknell's Christy Mathewson, were soon hired by various teams throughout western Pennsylvania, upstate New York, and Ohio. Football thrived in the Midwest, with teams from Akron, Canton, Columbus, Dayton, and Massillon fiercely competing in the Ohio League. After its 32-game winning streak was broken by Canton in 1906, Massilon won the rematch; more importantly, sportswriter Grantland Rice highlighted the games, allowing pro ball to attain a measure of national attention.

During the 1910s, college athletes like Notre Dame's Knute Rockne, Brown's African American halfback Fritz Pollard, and Rutgers's black All-American end Paul Robeson competed alongside the greatest star of pro football's earliest days, the Canton Bulldog Jim Thorpe, who received $250 a game. An All-American halfback at Carlisle, Thorpe had competed in the 1912 Stockholm Olympics, where he captured both the decathlon and pentathlon. Following revelations that he had been paid for playing baseball in the Carolina League, Thorpe's gold medals were taken away. Led by Thorpe, its stellar performer and gate attraction, Canton dominated the Ohio League, considered the pro game's premier league, from 1916-1919. Thorpe, Robert W. Peterson suggests, "lifted professional football out of the minor sports among the truss ads on the nation's sports pages to a position of some respectability." Yet pro football long proved unable to win the kind of fan allegiance reserved for college football, baseball, or boxing.

On September 17, 1920, representatives from 11 teams, including Thorpe and George Halas, player-coach of the Decatur, Illinois, Staleys, gathered in Canton. They agreed to form the American Professional Football Association and named Thorpe league president. While $100 fees were called for, Halas later acknowledged "that no money changed hands." Sixteen-man rosters were generally employed, thus requiring players to play both offense and defense. Decatur's linesmen averaged 206 pounds, their backs only 174. Players had to provide much of their protective gear, while some teams offered helmets, socks, and jerseys. Stars averaged about $150 a game, with quarterback Paddy Driscoll of the Chicago Racine Cardinals receiving $300. Akron, with an 8-0-3 record, was awarded the Brunswick-Balke Collender loving cup in April 1921 for having captured the "world's professional football championship."

Franchise shuffling abounded, but three teams appeared that provided a foundation for the league's future: Halas's Chicago Bears, Curly Lambeau's Green Bay Packers, and the Chicago Cardinals. In June 1922, team managers renamed their organization the National Football League. Professional football's success remained problematic, however, as the Packers performed on an open field and had to pass a hat among their fans at halftime. Then, in 1925, the pro game received a great boost from Halas's signing of University of Illinois All-American Red Grange. After wrapping up his collegiate career, Grange appeared in a Thanksgiving Day game against the Cardinals,

attended by 36,000 fans. Barnstorming tours followed, enabling Grange, managed by C.C. Pyle, to pull in over $200,000 from gate receipts alone. A knee injury in 1927 ended Grange's broken-field running, but new stars were arriving, including Duluth's Ernie Nevers and Cleveland's tailback Benny Friedman, who immediately established new passing records; on Thanksgiving Day, 1929, Nevers scored all of the Chicago's Cardinals 40 points in a rout of the Bears. As the decade closed, the top teams were Timothy J. Mara's New York Giants, now quarterbacked by Friedman, and the Packers, led by halfback Johnny Blood. The Packer's three-year title streak was ended in 1932, when the Bears, relying on running backs Bronko Nagurski and Grange, defeated Portsmouth 9-0 in the NFL's first playoff game.

As the Great Depression wound on, dooming a number of franchises, seeds were planted for the NFL's eventual ascendancy to the top tier of American sports. Now, passes could be delivered anywhere behind the line of scrimmage, a task soon made easier by the reduction of the ball's size. Goal posts were placed on the goal line, also allowing for increased scoring. Significant too was the establishment of two divisions and the waging of a championship game. Attendance rose, with over 79,000 watching the first annual College All-Star game, in which the finest collegians battled the NFL champ. New owners joined the NFL ranks, including George Preston Marshall, eventual boss of the Washington Redskins, the Philadelphia Eagles's Bert Bell, and the Pittsburgh Steelers' Art Rooney. In 1936, the NFL introduced the player draft, with Heisman trophy winner Jay Berwanger the first player selected. The Packers and the Bears were the decade's top teams, each winning three titles from 1933 onward. The 6'2", 225-pound Nagurski averaged nearly five yards a carry in a run-oriented offense, while halfback Beattie Feathers, in 1934, rushed for a then record 1,004 yards, averaging 9.9 yards a carry. The passing combination of Arnie Herber or Cecil Isbell to Don Hutson accounted for much of Green Bay's success. The lightning fast 6'1", 180-pound Hutson snared 99 touchdown passes in his 11-year career while leading the league in receiving and touchdowns eight times and in scoring on five occasions. Washington also relied on the passing game, thanks to Marshall's signing of TCU's Sammy Baugh, who steered the Redskins to the championship in his initial season in 1937.

The 1940s also ushered in a series of changes, including pro football's first national radio broadcasts, the explosive T-formation, wartime losses, the Cleveland Rams's move to Los Angeles, a competitive struggle with a rival league, and African American ballplayers, who had been excluded from the game for over a decade. The 1940 championship was broadcast nationwide, as the Bears avenged a regular season loss in destroying the Redskins 73-0. The Bears's T-formation attack was guided by quarterback Sid Luckman, who also took Chicago to titles in 1941, 1943, and 1946. Victimized by Chicago in both the 1940 and 1943 championship contests, Washington managed to break the Bears's streak in 1942. The greatest passer of his generation, Baugh, in 1945, established a 70.3-percent completion record (later broken) after setting a season punting mark of 51.3 yards per kick five years earlier.

World War II service depleted the ranks of the NFL, requiring the Chicago Cardinals and Pittsburgh Steelers to merge during the 1944 season. Old-timers like the Bears's Bronko Nagurski temporarily returned to the gridiron, while George Halas served as a naval lieutenant commander in the South Pacific. By 1945, peacetime arrived and attendance rebounded to an average of nearly 29,000 spectators a game. But a new war broke out, a four-year battle with the rival All-American Football Conference. The AAFC was dominated by Paul Brown's Cleveland Browns, starring quarterback Otto Graham and fullback Marion Motley. While taking his team to four consecutive league championships, Brown initiated a series of coaching innovations: employment of full-time, year-round assistant coaches, use of intelligence and psychological tests, reliance on play-books and classroom instruction, timing of players's 40-yard dashes, use of messenger guards, grading of players through film analysis, and placement of spotters in the stadium to help with play selection.

The postwar period ushered in the African Americans' reentry into professional football. In 1946, Motley and guard Bill Willis signed with the Browns, while the Los Angeles Rams' halfback Kenny Washington and end Woody Strode became the first African Americans to play in the NFL since 1933. The Los Angeles county commission pressured the Rams, newly arrived from Cleveland, to give former UCLA All-American running back Washington a tryout, threatening to deny use of the expansive Coliseum. Black ballplayers began to trickle into both major leagues, including Emlen Tunnell, who became a standout defensive back with the New York Giants, and Buddy Young, a 5'5'' scat-back with the New York Yankees.

During the 1950s, professional football began to be perceived as a major sport. The decade opened with the admission of three teams—Cleveland, Baltimore, and San Francisco—from the now dissolved AAFC into the NFL. The Browns immediately proved their mettle, crushing the defending champion Philadelphia Eagles, 35-10, in their opening game. Cleveland went on to take the title that year, captured six straight division crowns, and two more NFL championships through 1955. Other outstanding teams of the era included the Rams, who relied on twin quarterbacks, Bob Waterfield and Norm van Brocklin, throwing to ends Tommie Fears and Elroy ''Crazlegs'' Hirsch; the Detroit Lions, featuring quarterback Bobby Layne and halfback Doak Walker; and the New York Giants, starring halfback Frank Gifford and linebacker Sam Huff, and boasting a brilliant coaching staff that included offensive coordinator Vince Lombardi and defensive coordinator Tom Landry.

By the mid-1950s, televised pro games were drawing in more and more fans. The sudden-death championship game between the Colts and Giants in 1958 proved to be one of those epochal moments in sports history. In the following decade, technological innovations such as instant replays and slow motion shots allowed for a closer examination of the game's key moments. Television even helped to bring about new leagues: the American Football League in 1960, the short-lived World Football League in the mid-1970s, and the United States Football League in the following decade. Managerial acumen helped to ensure the sport's popularity too, ranging from its largely Irish-Catholic early owners to commissioners Bert Bell and Pete Rozelle, who devised a potent economic cartel. Thanks to Rozelle, the NFL signed lucrative television contracts, including one with ABC that resulted in the establishment of the enormously popular *Monday Night Football* game.

Thus, pro football's golden age had arrived, initially illuminating new stars like the Browns's fullback Jim Brown, who won eight rushing titles in nine years and led Cleveland to the 1964 championship, and the Baltimore Colts' Johnny Unitas. Weeb Ewbank's championship teams in 1958 and 1959, quarterbacked by former Steelers castoff Unitas, preceded the Lombardi dynasty in Green Bay. From 1961-67, the Packers, led by quarterback Bart Starr, halfback Paul Hornung, and fullback Jim Taylor, won five NFL championships. In 1960, Hornung, a former Heisman award-winning quarterback at Notre Dame, had scored a record 176 points on 15 touchdowns, 15 field goals, and 41 extra points. Capping a run of three

consecutive NFL titles, Green Bay also won the first two Super Bowls, held after the 1966 and 1967 regular seasons. The Bears, who captured the 1963 championship, remained competitive, with stars like linebacker Dick Butkus, tight end Mike Ditka, and halfback Gale Sayers, who, during his rookie season in 1965, scored a record 22 touchdowns, including six in one game against San Francisco.

The Super Bowl became, along with the World Series and the Olympic Games, the greatest sports extravaganza. It was the by-product of both the television revolution that changed the sporting world and a new territorial skirmish that the NFL now contended with. In 1960, Lamar Hunt had helped to establish the AFL, which was awarded a multi-million dollar television contract from NBC. The AFL's signing of star collegians, particularly Alabama's Joe Willie Namath, who inked a four-year contract with the New York Jets for the then unheard of sum of $427,000 on New Year's Day 1965, eventually brought about a merger of the two leagues. In the first two Super Bowls, pitting winners of the NFL and the AFL, Green Bay displayed the older league's supposedly clear superiority. But in January 1969, the heavily favored Colts fell to the New York Jets, 16-7, a result earlier guaranteed by Namath, who had become a media darling, with his stylish locks, playboy allure, and rifle-like arm. New stars shone brightly, including Buffalo running back O. J. Simpson, who established a rushing record in 1973 with 2003 yards.

The 1972 Miami Dolphins, led by coach Don Shula and quarterbacked by Bob Griese and Earl Morrall, became the first team to complete a season undefeated. The Dolphins repeated their championship run the following year, but Chuck Noll's Pittsburgh Steelers, with quarterback Terry Bradshaw, were the team of the decade, winning four Super Bowls, twice against Tom Landry's Dallas Cowboys. The Cowboys, guided by quarterback Roger Staubach, managed two Super Bowl titles of their own. In the 1980s, Bill Walsh began constructing the latest dynasty in San Francisco, eventually capturing three Super Bowls before turning the team over to George Seifert, who won two more; quarterback Joe Montana led the 49'ers to all but one of those championships. The Cowboys, coached first by Jimmie Johnson and then by Barry Switzer, garnered three additional Super Bowl crowns, relying on the so-called ''Triplets'': quarterback Troy Aikman, halfback Emmitt Smith, and receiver Michael Irvin. By 1994, 135 million fans watched Dallas take a second straight Super Bowl match-up with the Buffalo Bills.

Like other major professional sports, football, by the mid-seventies, was ensnared in a series of legal battles resulting in strikes, cancelled games, and eventually, free agency. Franchise free agency also occurred with one team, the Oakland Raiders, who moved to Los Angeles and then returned to the Bay area. Despite such turmoil, professional football continued to thrive, thanks in part to record-setting performances by the likes of Miami quarterback Dan Marino, 49'er receiver Jerry Rice, and Lion running back Barry Sanders.

—Robert C. Cottrell

FURTHER READING:

Baker, William J. *Sports in the Western World*. Totowa, New Jersey, Rowman & Littlefield, 1982.

Byrne, Jim. *The $1 League: The Rise and Fall of the USFL*. New York, Prentice-Hall, 1986.

Daly, Dan, and Bob O'Donnell. *The Pro Football Chronicle*. New York, Collier Books, 1990.

Golenbock, Peter. *Cowboys Have Always Been My Heroes: The Definitive Oral History of America's Team.* New York, Warner Books, 1997.

Harris, David. *The League: The Rise and Decline of the NFL.* New York, Bantam Books, 1986.

Herskowitz, Mickey. *The Golden Age of Pro Football.* New York, Macmillan, 1974.

Horrigan, Jack. *The Other League: The Story of the AFL.* Chicago, Follett Co., 1970.

Leuthner, Stuart. *Iron Men: Bucko, Crazylegs, and the Boys Recall the Golden Days of Professional Football.* New York, Doubleday, 1988.

McDonough, Will, et al. *Seventy-Five Seasons: The Complete Story of the National Football League, 1920-1995.* Atlanta, Time Publishing, Inc., 1994.

Meggyesy, Dave. *Out of Their League.* Berkeley, Ramparts Press, 1970.

Neft, David, and Richard Cohen. *The Sports Encyclopedia: Pro Football: The Modern Era.* New York, St. Martin's Griffin, 1989.

————, Richard Cohen, et al. *The Sports Encyclopedia: Pro Football: The Early Years.* Ridgefield, Connecticut, Sport Products Inc., 1997.

Oriard, Michael. *Reading Football: Sport, Popular Journalism, and American Culture, 1876-1913.* Chapel Hill, University of North Carolina Press, 1993.

Peterson, Robert W. *Pigskin: The Early Years of Pro Football.* New York, Oxford University Press, 1997.

Rader, Benjamin G. *American Sports: From the Age of Folk Games to the Age of Televised Sports.* Englewood Cliffs, New Jersey, Prentice Hall, 1996.

Roberts, Randy, and James Olson. *Winning Is the Only Thing: Sports in America since 1945.* Baltimore, Johns Hopkins University Press, 1989.

Whittingham, Richard, et al., editors. *The Fireside Book of Pro Football.* New York, Simon & Schuster, 1989.

Prohibition

Prohibition, which lasted from 1919 to 1933, attempted to eliminate the consumption of alcoholic beverages but instead created a legacy of bootleggers, flappers, and speakeasies. Widespread crime in American cities and corruption within the Prohibition enforcement agencies resulted. Profits from illegal alcohol and disrespect for the law grew during the period of legislated moral behavior.

The states ratified the 18th Amendment to the United States Constitution in January of 1919, and nationwide Prohibition began on January 29, 1920. The Amendment made the manufacture, sale, and transport of alcoholic beverages illegal. The widely accepted Volstead Act provided enforcement of Prohibition and was enacted in October of 1919.

Prohibition had its roots in the temperance movements to reduce alcohol consumption in the 1820s. The state of Massachusetts was the first state to enact prohibition laws when it prohibited the sale of spirits in less than 15 gallon containers. This law passed in 1838 and was repealed two years later. In the 1850s, several states enacted

prohibition laws but support for prohibition declined during the Civil War. States maintained jurisdiction over state and local prohibition laws from 1880 to 1914.

The Prohibitionist Party, formed in 1869, began to revitalize the temperance movement to eliminate alcohol consumption. Other reformists such as ministers, physicians, devout middle-class Protestants, and the Woman's Christian Temperance Union drove the prohibition movement. The reformers believed drinking caused numerous social dilemmas: social reformers blamed alcohol for poverty, moral decay, and domestic abuse; physicians argued that alcohol caused health problems; and political reformers saw taverns as corrupt establishments. In addition, employers in the new industrial society believed that employees who drank alcohol were lazy, unproductive, and prone to sickness, absenteeism, and on-the-job accidents. Overall, drinking alcohol was deemed an immoral act by prohibitionists.

Although Prohibition initially reduced the amount of alcohol consumed, it also caused an increase in crime. Where the desire to consume alcohol remained, even increased, a new breed of criminal emerged. Millions of otherwise law-abiding citizens became criminals because they purchased alcohol. Gangsters, enticed by the potentially huge profits related to distributing and manufacturing alcohol, battled for business and settled market disputes with guns. The bootlegger became an American icon. Bootlegged liquor came across Canada waterways, off the Atlantic and Pacific coasts, and from the Caribbean Sea. Bootleggers also manufactured liquor in makeshift distilleries and bathtubs. This liquor was often poor in quality and dangerous to one's health. Drinking patterns also changed; sales of hard liquor rose because it was easier to transport, while beer became less popular to distribute.

Drinking became fashionable during these years. Prohibition created an illegal drinking establishment, the speakeasy, which outnumbered the previous legal drinking establishments. Additionally, only women of ill-repute frequented the saloons of pre-prohibition years, but during Prohibition the number of women who frequented speakeasies rose. It was also during this time that the flapper was born.

Anti-prohibitionists argued that prohibition encouraged crime and widespread disrespect for the law. The dramatic increase in crime overwhelmed the criminal justice system. Citizens lost respect for the system and corruption within enforcement agencies thrived. While some enforcement agents took bribes, others could not be bought. The levels of enforcement varied widely between states, with enforcement agents cracking down harder in areas where the prohibition movement was strongest. Lawmakers thought getting tougher on alcohol crimes would help them achieve success; penalties for the sale of one drink increased to five years and thousands of dollars in fines. Federal prisons operated at over 150 percent of capacity, enforcement budgets increased, and more cops were put on the beat, all to no avail.

Support for Prohibition declined during the Great Depression. People believed that ending Prohibition would create alcohol manufacturing and distribution job opportunities. In 1932, the Democratic Party endorsed a repeal on Prohibition and Democratic presidential candidate Franklin D. Roosevelt won by a large margin. In February 1933, Congress proposed the 21st Amendment to repeal Prohibition. The states ratified the amendment and national Prohibition ended on December 5, 1933. The 18th Amendment is the only repealed Amendment in United States history.

A few states maintained prohibition after the enactment of the 21st Amendment. In 1966, all states abandoned prohibition laws. After Prohibition ended, liquor control laws were created by local

Police inspect equipment at an illegal brewery in Detroit during Prohibition.

government officials. Prohibition ended when public officials and citizens admitted it had failed, but the negative effects of national prohibition continue to echo in American society. Despite the failure of a national prohibition designed to increase moral behavior and eliminate social ills, many Americans in the 1990s still believe prohibition is the answer. When prohibition ended, emphasis was placed on education and treatment. One could argue that today's drug prohibition is history repeating itself. U.S. society is still divided into wets and drys, users and non-users, the moral and the so-called immoral.

—Debra Lucas Muscoreil

FURTHER READING:

Gray, Mike. *Drug Crazy: How We Got into This Mess and How We Can Get Out.* New York, Random House, 1998.

Kyving, David E. *Repealing National Prohibition.* Chicago, University of Chicago Press, 1979.

Rumbarger, John J. *Profits, Power and Prohibition: Alcohol Reform and the Industrializing of America, 1800-1930.* Albany, State University of New York Press, 1989.

Sinclair, Andrew. *Era of Excess: A Social History of the Prohibition Movement.* New York, Harper and Row, 1964.

Prom

Every spring, millions of teenagers across the United States take part in a quintessentially American rite of passage known as the high school prom. Experienced by rich and poor, black and white, Jewish and Catholic, Californians and Virginians, prom night is arguably the most widely shared of all modern American rituals. Certainly, it is one of the most talked about. Though the exact format varies, a traditional prom involves high school students in tuxedos and gowns coming together for a formal dinner dance. Corsages, limousines, favors, photographers, and post-prom festivities are all standard extras. Depending on the location of the school and the age of the participants, proms are held either in school gyms and cafeterias or in hotels, country clubs, and banquet halls. Freshman, Sophomore, and Junior Proms tend to be less extravagant rehearsals for the all-important Senior Prom, the final social gathering of a graduating class.

Though popular historical imagination, influenced by films like *Back to the Future* (1985) and *Grease* (1978), remembers proms as a product of the 1950s, they in fact long pre-date that legendary era of bobby socks and drive-ins. In Philadelphia, home to many of the nation's oldest public, private, and parochial schools, proms first emerged in the 1920s and rapidly replaced ''Senior Play and Dance'' evenings as the high school social events of the year. By the 1930s, proms were commonplace, their rise in popularity linked to several interwoven factors, including ongoing urbanization and industrialization, the expansion of secondary education, the rise of ''youth culture,'' and, stemming from all of these, the mass dissemination of prom stories.

Tales about the glories and mishaps of prom night were first published in the pages of high school magazines which were then exchanged between educational institutions throughout the nation. Early twentieth-century student journalists were extremely zealous about this new event and appear to have regarded prom attendance as an essential marker of good citizenship. ''If You Don't Like This,'' quipped the headline of a 1931 article on the merits of prom night,

''Go Back to the Country Where You Came From.'' There is evidence to suggest that these early proms served an important unifying function, especially in city schools filled with first and second generation immigrants from around the world. Certainly then, as now, prom night was constructed as having been synonymous with ''Americanness.''

Prom night quickly became a hot topic for the writers of popular dramas and romance novels. From 1934 onwards, a whole series of prom plays, short stories, and novels went to press. The 1930s also saw the publication of the first ever prom guidebook, penned by Marietta Abell and Agnes Anderson. Writing in the midst of the Great Depression, the authors hailed the prom as a potential money-saver but admonished readers that ''No one should think of planning and arranging for any one of the proms suggested in less than four weeks.'' To millennial readers, both statements seem laughably ironic. Modern proms cost individual students anywhere from $200 to $2,000, are planned a year in advance, and call on the expertise and services of a vast array of party professionals. Proms, 1990s style, are very big business.

Teenagers jitterbugging at the Anacosta High School Prom in Maryland, 1953.

The exact ritual antecedents of prom night are difficult to trace as proms draw on a number of earlier cultural traditions. To many observers, the prom resembles a democratic version of the elite debutante ball, which is in turn a Republican version of the aristocratic ritual of presenting young ladies at the royal courts of Europe. Proms are also closely related to the cotillions and college dances of the mid to late nineteenth century where formal dress and terpsichorean skill were essential and where the practice of giving out party favors was popularized. Important regional differences existed though: in the Deep South, where religious intolerance of dancing determined the shape and form of early-twentieth-century youthful pleasures, proms were literally "promenades" during which young ladies would take short and keenly supervised walks around the block with male escorts.

Throughout their history, proms have most obviously resembled weddings in both their ritual form and function. Weddings and proms share an emphasis on heterosexual pairing that is reinforced through parallel iconography and corresponding rites of exchange and remembrance. Prom couples often look—from the gown to the tux, flowers, limo, and location—like a young bride and groom. Their night together is subject to many of the same acts of ritual celebration and sanctification. Families gather to send the young couple off, photographs are taken, and flowers and keepsakes are exchanged. Late-twentieth-century prom couples also often share a post-ritual "honeymoon." Indeed, for many teens, these post-prom trips are now more eagerly anticipated than the prom itself.

Prom night's emphasis on heterosexual dating has, since the early 1980s, been a subject of public controversy. Several lawsuits have arisen at schools where students who wanted to attend solo, or who wanted to attend with a same sex partner, were barred. Aaron Fricke's *Reflections of a Rock Lobster* offers an autobiographical account of his legal battle to take his male partner to his senior prom in 1980. As the century draws to a close, many public schools have been forced to relax their boy-girl dating rules and many teenagers now regard prom night less as a night of romance and more as a night to have fun as a group. Meanwhile, since the late 1980s, lesbian, gay, and bisexual teenagers who want to celebrate with a date and who live in major cities in the United States have had the option of attending "gay proms" that provide a safe and friendly environment in which these teens can celebrate. Prom traditions, however, prevail, particularly in parochial schools. In Philadelphia, Catholic schools continue to insist that prom night be a heterosexual affair and they continue to bar both single teens and same-sex couples.

Prom night has also been involved in debates about racial discrimination. In 1994, an Alabama student challenged her school's policy barring interracial prom dating. Meanwhile, at schools around the nation that are de jure desegregated, de facto segregation within the student body often leads to heated disputes over music selection for prom night. Some schools have resolved tensions over musical tastes by holding two proms, one catering to what is seen as "white" musical taste, one to "black."

At all schools, the greatest ongoing prom battle concerns drug use. Prom night is mythically a night for letting go and experimenting, but a series of tragedies, most involving drunk driving, have led teachers, parents, and students across the nation to campaign against prom night's infamous excesses. Some schools have experimented with random breath tests and many lock students inside their prom venues to prevent furtive drinking. Pre-prom safety awareness programs are commonplace and all schools enforce tough penalties for

students involved in prom night drug use. Eager to distance themselves from inappropriate symbolism, most school boards have also now banned the giving of glasses as prom favors. Savvy promware manufacturers have responded quickly; they now fill their ever-popular champagne, wine, and beer glasses with brightly colored wax and market them as "candles."

Perhaps the most famous prom controversy occurred in 1997 when an 18-year-old New Jersey senior gave birth at her prom. According to prosecutors, she then suffocated the infant and returned to the dance floor. She is now serving 15 years for aggravated manslaughter. Her case stands as a vivid reminder that prom night is not always as sweet and innocent an event as popular mythology would have us believe. Students make remarkable sacrifices on prom night, and though these are usually financial they can also be academic, emotional, and physical.

At its best, prom night offers adolescents a unique opportunity to dress up, go out with their peers, and celebrate their high school achievements. Many find the excitement, camaraderie, and grandeur of it all profoundly enjoyable and memorable. At its worst, prom night diverts students' attention away from their academic studies and breeds unhealthy and superficial competition between peers at an age when self-esteem is notoriously fragile. Certainly, this is the angle filmmakers exploit in classic prom movies such as *Carrie* (1976), *Prom Night* (1980) and its sequels, *Pretty in Pink* (1986), and *She's All That* (1999).

Prom night is as much a controversy as it is a national pasttime; few if any rituals are so widely shared, and few are subject to as much hope or hype. Proms are now featured in magazines and movies, talk shows and tabloids, soap operas and songs. They make millions of dollars for the numerous industries that have grown up around them and, for all the talk of declining traditions, proms show no sign of waning in popularity. For better or worse, prom night is a part of American popular culture that is very much here to stay.

—Felicity H. Paxton

FURTHER READING:

Abell, Marietta, and Agnes Andersons. *The Junior Senior Prom: Complete Practical Suggestions for Staging the Junior Senior Prom.* Minneapolis, Northwestern Press, 1936.

Fricke, Aaron. *Reflections of a Rock Lobster: A Story about Growing up Gay.* Boston, Alyson Publications Inc., 1981.

Myrick, Susan. "Whatever Became of the Prom Party?," *Georgia Review.* Vol. 22, No. 3, 1968, 354-59.

Promise Keepers

Public gatherings promoting spiritual revivalism have been a distinctive feature of American religious life since the frontier camp meetings of the early nineteenth century. During the 1990s, a new and controversial expression of this tradition of public revivalism emerged in the activities of the Promise Keepers, a Christian men's organization devoted to restoring conservative family values to American society. Through large outdoor rallies, often held in football stadiums and drawing tens of thousands of participants at a time, the Promise Keepers spread their message of male responsibility and family leadership to millions of American men. The group's name derives

Several thousand men attend a Promise Keeper conference in 1998.

from its members' pledge to maintain an active Christian life, to build strong families and marriages, to seek moral and ethical purity, and to associate with other men who have made the same commitments. The Promise Keepers' insistence on male leadership of the family has produced considerable opposition among feminists, who see the group as a threat to women's equality. Moderates and liberals have also criticized the group for their conservative stance on politically charged social issues like abortion and gay rights. The controversies surrounding the Promise Keepers reflect the ongoing conflict between religious tradition and secular trends within American culture.

The Promise Keepers movement was founded in 1990 by Bill McCartney, a former football coach at the University of Colorado. It began as a local fellowship led by McCartney and other members of the Vineyard Church, a conservative, charismatic group with a strong emphasis on evangelism. By stressing discipline and male bonding, the organization provided support for members trying to lead an exemplary Christian life. The group's leaders also sought to extend its message of religious renewal across denominational boundaries, and so began staging large public rallies to attract new members. Centering on sermons, hymns, prayer, and mutual support, these exclusively

male rallies attracted several million participants during the 1990s, and helped to spread the movement across the United States. The Promise Keepers' largest and most widely publicized rally, held on October 4, 1997, attracted 700,000 men to the Mall in Washington, D.C. Through the success of their public rallies, the Promise Keepers also established a network of thousands of local support groups, led by specially trained leaders or ''key men,'' whose members monitored one another's observance of the organization's principles.

To its supporters, drawn largely from conservative Protestant churches, the Promise Keepers represented a necessary response to moral decay and the decline of the American family. The organization also found many critics, however, among feminists, political moderates and liberals, and mainstream religious leaders. The Promise Keepers' emphasis on the need for male-headed households struck many as an antiquated commitment to patriarchal families and an attack on women's rights. Critics also faulted the group for its ties to the new religious right and that movement's conservative social agenda. The Promise Keepers denied the existence of such ties, but McCartney himself was a featured speaker at meetings of the militant anti-abortion group Operation Rescue, and he publicly supported a

Colorado constitutional amendment limiting the legal recourse available to homosexuals subjected to discrimination in housing or employment. Critics also challenged the Promise Keepers' avowed commitment to racial reconciliation, arguing that the group did little to support concrete efforts to promote political, social, or economic equality for racial minorities.

By the late 1990s, attendance at the Promise Keepers' rallies had begun to decline and financial difficulties led the organization to reduce the size of its paid staff and the scope of its activities. Both critics and supporters questioned the organization's ability to survive in its existing form. During its initial period of growth, however, it had a significant impact on American society by sustaining the resurgence of religious conservatism that had started in the 1970s. In its concern with male responsibility and authority, the Promise Keepers movement also focused attention on the persisting differences of opinion within American society regarding gender roles and family structure, decades after the start of the women's movement.

—Roger W. Stump

FURTHER READING:

Abraham, Ken. *Who Are the Promise Keepers?* New York, Doubleday, 1997.

Kintz, Linda. *Between Jesus and the Market: The Emotions That Matter in Right-Wing America.* Durham, North Carolina, Duke University Press, 1997.

Protest Groups

The United States was created by a revolution and American history is replete with examples of protest groups attempting to alter governmental policies and social and cultural patterns. One of the first things U.S. school children read about is the Boston Tea Party, where a group of colonial protestors, disguised as Native Americans, boarded British ships and destroyed valuable cargoes of tea to demonstrate their opposition to onerous British tax policies. But protest in America only became part of the popular culture during the 1960s, when television brought the strife and turmoil of the Vietnam War and the Civil Rights Movement into the living rooms of the American people. Since that turbulent era, sit-ins, marches, demonstrations, and boycotts have become common protest tactics practiced by various interest groups attempting to gain legitimacy in the eyes of the public.

The nineteenth century witnessed the birth of several important protest groups in the United States. The abolitionists sought the immediate and uncompensated end of slavery. Anti-slavery groups were present as far back as the colonial era, but most had not advocated complete freedom or equality for blacks. For example, the American Colonization Society, which began in 1817, attempted to solve America's race problem by shipping willing blacks back to Africa. In 1831, New England publisher William Lloyd Garrison condemned this gradual approach to ending slavery and called for immediate emancipation. These so-called radical abolitionists included prominent ministers and other activists in the northern states and they flooded the country with anti-slavery literature. At first, they sought to convince slave owners that slavery was a sin and attempted to secure voluntary emancipation. Later, they turned to political action and were potent enough to produce two political parties: the

Liberty Party in the early 1840s and the Free-Soil Party later in that same decade.

Also during the antebellum era, the Women's Suffrage Movement began. Women had always been kept politically and legally subordinate to men; they could not own property, make wills, vote, attend college, or retain wages they had earned. As women became active in various reform activities and social crusades, they began to seek equality. The official beginning of this women's movement dates from an 1848 meeting at Seneca Falls, New York, where a women's right to vote was pronounced as a national goal. Under the leadership of Elizabeth Cady Stanton, Lucy Stone, Julia Ward Howe, and Susan B. Anthony, a variety of women's protest groups championed this cause for the next generation. Some states did pass suffrage laws but it was not until the passage of 19th amendment in 1919 that women gained the right to vote nationally.

The late nineteenth century saw the rise of two different protest groups: farmers and labor activists. Associations of farmers organized in the Midwest after the Civil War. Railroad abuses and high shipping rates compelled U.S. farmers to seek regulatory legislation. In addition, overproduction, resulting from the introduction of sophisticated farm machinery, brought a decline in the price of crops. Farmers and farm protest groups sought to redress these problems with federal regulations. Rural protest groups included the National Grange, the Farmer's Alliances, the National Farmers Union, and various political coalitions like the Greenback Party and the Populist Party.

In that same period, industrial laborers began to protest working conditions. The rapid rise of industrialization after the Civil War stimulated the growth of labor unions at the local, state, and national levels. Unions and labor organizations sought to alleviate dangerous and unhealthy working conditions and resolve problems concerning pensions, disability pay, and child labor. Leading labor protest groups included the Knights of Labor, the National Labor Union, the American Federation of Labor, the Molly Maguires, the Industrial Workers of the World, and the Congress of Industrial Organizations.

The contemporary American view of protests has unquestionably emanated from two mid-twentieth-century issues: Civil Rights and the Vietnam War. During the 1950s, blacks began to challenge the degrading system of segregation in the American South. Leading groups included the National Association for the Advancement of Colored People (NAACP), the Congress of Racial Equality (CORE), and the Southern Christian Leadership Conference (SCLC). Southern blacks used a variety of protest tactics such as boycotts, sit-ins, and marches in attempting to achieve racial equality and end segregation. Perhaps the most famous protest was the Montgomery Bus Boycott in 1955-56. When Rosa Parks was arrested in Montgomery, Alabama, for refusing to move to the back of a segregated city bus, black leaders organized a one-year boycott that inspired black protest groups and eventually ended the segregation of public buses.

In the early 1960s black college students throughout the South passively sat at segregated department store lunch counters in order to force integration. Often, these students were attacked by local whites and carried off to jail for this ''illegal'' practice. In 1961 CORE and the Student Nonviolent Coordinating Committee (SNCC) organized a group of Freedom Riders in an attempt to further integrate bus systems in the South; the Freedom Riders embarked on a long bus ride through the South. In Alabama, they were beaten by white hoodlums and their bus was bombed. The federal government finally dispatched marshals to protect the Freedom Riders although they were ultimately arrested and sent to jail.

The largest demonstration during the Civil Rights era took place in Washington, D.C., in August, 1963. Civil Rights groups organized the March on Washington to pressure the federal government to support the civil rights of African Americans. More than a quarter of a million people gathered and heard Martin Luther King, Jr., give his famous "I Have a Dream" speech. African American protest groups continued to organize throughout the 1960s using sit-ins, boycotts, marches, and voter registration drives in their efforts to gain equality in the South and in the nation as a whole.

The Vietnam War provided a second major protest direction in the 1960s. A peace movement had long existed in the United States, largely based upon Quaker and Unitarian beliefs. While protest groups were active during many of America's wars, they failed to gain popular support until the Cold War era. The escalating nuclear arms race brought about groups like the National Committee for a Sane Nuclear Policy (SANE), Women Strike for Peace (WSP), and the Student Peace Union (SPU). The SPU not only wanted to stop the production of nuclear weapons, but also sought to restructure society on a more equitable basis. But the SPU never became an effective student interest group and faded away by 1964; its banner was taken up by a more active and successful Students for a Democratic Society (SDS).

SDS, centered on college campuses, published the Port Huron Statement in 1962, expressing its disillusionment with the American military-industrial-academic establishment. SDS cited the uncertainty of life in Cold-War America and the degradation of African Americans in the South as examples of social and cultural drift, and called for a revolution of sorts among American youth. Throughout the first years of its existence, SDS focused on domestic concerns. But in 1965, when the United States began bombing North Vietnam, SDS and other student protest groups began focussing on the war. In February and March 1965, SDS organized a series of "Teach-Ins" modeled after earlier Civil Rights seminars. These teach-ins sought to educate large segments of the student population about both the moral and political foundations of America's Vietnam involvement.

As the Vietnam War escalated, the antiwar protests became more raucous. In 1968 protestors occupied the administration building at Columbia University; police used force to evict them. Raids on draft boards in Baltimore, Milwaukee, and Chicago soon followed, as activists smeared blood on records and shredded files. In May 1970, Ohio National Guardsmen fired on a group of antiwar protestors at Kent State University, killing four and wounding 16.

As the Vietnam War became more unpopular in the early 1970s, antiwar sentiment and protest began to gain popular acceptance. During the next three decades, protests became a normal reaction to what were believed to be zealous excesses of power by government and other institutions. After the 1960s, other groups have attempted to continue these protest tactics—although most have met with less success. In the 1970s, environmental activists registered their concerns over the ravaging effects of industrial pollution. The environmental movement was led by older conservation organizations like the Sierra Club and the Wilderness Society, as well as several new protests groups. Greenpeace, founded in 1971, protested nuclear testing and campaigned to save whales, other ocean animals, and rain forests around the world. Earth First!, established in 1981, was a more militant group committed to direct action and the sabotage of projects harmful to the environment.

The Feminist Movement came to fruition during the 1970s, spawning hundreds of new protest groups and advancing radical ideas regarding women's role in society. The National Organization for Women (NOW) advanced three demands: equality for women in employment and education; child care centers throughout the nation; and women's control over their own reproduction, including a woman's right to abortion. Women's protest actions ranged from lobbying Congress to more direct action.

The 1980s and 1990s saw a change in protest and activism. Since the 1950s, protest groups in the United States have come from the left of the political spectrum. But the 1980s saw a political and social counterrevolution—probably in response to the rapid upheaval and perceived permissiveness of the 1960s. Conservatives found voices through the Moral Majority, founded in 1979, while the Christian Coalition advanced its views with more religious fervor. Conservatives also utilized journals and research institutions (think tanks) to advance their message. These included publications like the *National Review* edited by William F. Buckley, and institutions such as the American Enterprise Institute and the Heritage Foundation. A vigorous anti-abortion protest movement has also been a part of the conservative resurgence. Liberal groups remained active in the 1980s and 1990s, but with much less political support than earlier decades. A nuclear freeze movement, gays and lesbians, and AIDS activists have all been active, but the focus of protest continues to change and new issues evolve.

—David E. Woodard

FURTHER READING:

Flexner, Eleanor. *Century of Struggle: The Women's Rights Movement in the United States.* New York, Atheneum, 1973.

Garrow, David. *Bearing the Cross: Martin Luther King, Jr., and the Southern Christian Leadership Conference.* New York, Vintage Books, 1986.

Goldman, Eric. *Rendezvous with Destiny: A History of Modern Reform.* New York, Vintage Books, 1955.

Goodwyn, Lawrence. *The Populist Moment: A Short History of the Agrarian Revolt in America.* New York, Oxford University Press, 1978.

Morris, Aldon. *The Origins of the Civil Rights Movement: Black Communities Organizing for Change.* New York, The Free Press, 1984.

Walters, Ronald. *American Reformers, 1815-1860.* New York, Hill and Wang, 1978.

Wells, Tom. *The War Within: America's Battle over Vietnam.* New York, Henry Holt, 1994.

Prozac

Perhaps more than any prescription medication in history, Prozac has had a profound impact, not only on the patients who have taken it, but on the very practice of psychiatry, and on popular conceptions of mood and personality as well. Within three years of its release in 1987, Prozac (fluoxetine hydrochloride) had become the drug most prescribed by psychiatrists in the United States; by 1994 it was the second-best-selling drug of any kind in the world, with a reported one billion prescriptions written per month. In *A History of Psychiatry: From the Era of the Asylum to the Age of Prozac,* Edward Shorter describes Prozac as the household word of the 1990s; in 1994,

Newsweek proclaimed that Prozac had attained the familiarity of Kleenex and the social status of springwater. The drug has been the subject of numerous television programs, magazine articles, and psychology and self-help books. Much more than a medication, Prozac has come to represent the angst and antidote of a generation, as described in Elizabeth Wurtzel's 1994 best-seller, *Prozac Nation;* and with millions of people taking Prozac each year, and its benefits being touted in the media and discussed at cocktail parties, this new-generation antidepressant arguably has contributed to the destigmatization of mental illness.

Released in December 1987 by the Eli Lilly Company, Prozac was the first in a new class of antidepressant medications: the selective serotonin reuptake inhibitors. The SSRIs are "designer drugs," highly potent chemical compounds that selectively affect a single biological process and, by extension, target a highly specified physiological function. In the case of Prozac (and the other SSRIs, such as Zoloft and Paxil), the target is the brain's reuptake of the neurotransmitter serotonin (5-HT), which is involved in the regulation of mood. By increasing the levels of serotonin available to the brain, Prozac has been found to enhance not only mood, but also energy, assertiveness, and optimism; along with treating anxiety, panic attacks, social discomfort, rejection-sensitivity, and obsessive thoughts. Thus, the effect of Prozac goes beyond the relief of clinical depression: for many people, Prozac ultimately improves one's self-concept.

While earlier antidepressants—such as the tricyclics and monoamine oxidase inhibitors—were effective in controlling depressive symptoms, they were less selective in their action, making them cumbersome to use and difficult to monitor. Tricyclics, which are highly effective in controlling "classical" depression characterized by insomnia, loss of appetite, low mood, and low energy, also interfere with the neurotransmitter acetylcholine, triggering side effects associated with the "flight or fight" response: rapid heart rate, sweating, dry mouth, constipation, and urinary retention. The MAOIs, which effectively alleviate the "nonclassical" depressions that aren't helped by tricyclics, are less "dirty" but more problematic because of their potentially fatal interactions with many foods.

In clinical trials, Prozac has proven to be as effective in treating classical depression as the tricyclics and, for many patients, even more effective in alleviating nonclassical depression than the MAOIs. Because its action is so specific, it is difficult to overdose on Prozac, and doing so does not pose major risk of death. Most significantly, Prozac is "clean": it works without the sedative effects, weight gain, and dangerous interactions associated with the other antidepressant medications. Prozac's tendencies to increase energy and decrease appetite are both highly desirable and supremely marketable traits that have contributed much to its popularity.

Yet, despite the clinical evidence supporting Prozac's marketing as a safe and virtually side-effect-free drug, its initial release was marred by sensational reports of patients "going crazy" on Prozac: some purportedly becoming suicidal for the first time, others claiming to experience episodes of violent behaviors—including murder—triggered by the medication. In 1989, an attorney filed a series of lawsuits against the Eli Lilly Company following an incident in which a man who had taken Prozac (along with several other medications), killed eight people, wounded twelve, and then killed himself. This story was featured on *Donahue* (in a show provocatively titled "Prozac: Medication That Makes You Kill"), and a similar story was featured on *Larry King Live* in 1991, but neither case held up in court. In the end, the claims that Prozac created dangerous behavior in patients who previously had no history of suicide or violence subsided. The sensational headlines soon gave way to a general acceptance of Prozac as a drug safe enough for patients with severe depression and "clean" enough to appeal to a more general public seeking relief from mild dysphoria.

This use of medication to enhance personality in the absence of significant mental illness—a practice that Peter Kramer has called "cosmetic pharmacology"—has been a boon for drug manufacturers and a red flag for naturalists and ethicists. While *Time* hailed the use of Prozac for personality improvement as "a medical breakthrough," others have decried the use of pharmaceuticals to enhance socially desirable traits as a triumph of consumer culture over rational science and an alarming example of social Darwinism. Those concerned about the ethical implications of Prozac argue that, by enabling people who are not clinically depressed to brighten their mood and improve their personalities, Prozac may contribute to a lowering of our cultural tolerance for pessimism, grief, and other manifestations of dysphoria. On the other hand, some have argued that a positive by-product of the widespread popularity of Prozac may be a narrowing of the gap between the so-called "normal" population and the "mentally ill."

—Ava Rose

FURTHER READING:

"The Culture of Prozac." *Newsweek.* February 7, 1994, 41.

Elfenbein, Debra, editor. *Living with Prozac.* San Francisco, Harper, 1995.

Kramer, Peter. *Listening to Prozac.* New York, Viking, 1993.

"The Personality Pill," *Time.* October 1, 1993, 53.

Shorter, Edward. *A History of Psychiatry: From the Era of the Asylum to the Age of Prozac.* New York, John Wiley & Sons, 1997.

Wurtzel, Elizabeth. *Prozac Nation.* Boston, Houghton Mifflin, 1994.

Pryor, Richard (1940—)

In the 1970s and 1980s, Richard Pryor was one of America's top comedians, creating a daring new comedy of character by transforming African-American culture into humorous performance art. Pryor called upon both personal and social tragedy for his comic material, with his irreverent stage appearances laced with salty language and adult humor. His comedy albums during the 1970s and 1980s sold millions, and his work has influenced a new generation of comedians, including Eddie Murphy, Keenen Ivory Wayans, and Arsenio Hall.

Despite his popularity and critical acclaim, tragedy often was just around the corner for Pryor. Throughout much of his career, he battled drug and alcohol abuse. He also survived a heart attack and a suicide attempt, and has incurred the onset of multiple sclerosis. Because of the disease, Pryor now lives a reclusive life in his Bel Air, California, home, almost unable to walk and seeing only a small group of friends. Bill Cosby once summed up the element of tragedy in Pryor's life and work by saying, "For Richard, the line between comedy and tragedy is as fine as you can paint it."

Born in Peoria, Illinois, in 1940 to an unwed mother, Pryor claims to have been raised in his grandmother's brothel, where his mother worked as a prostitute. His parents, LeRoy and Gertrude Pryor, married when he was three years old, but the marriage soon

Richard Pryor

Dick Gregory. Pryor made his television debut in 1964 by appearing on the series *On Broadway Tonight.* Soon thereafter, he appeared on the *Ed Sullivan Show* and the *Merv Griffin Show*. By the mid-1960s, Pryor had moved to Los Angeles, landing small parts in such films as *The Green Berets* and *Wild in the Streets.* During this time, he continued playing live shows, primarily in Las Vegas showrooms, where he dropped the Cosby-influenced act and developed his own raw, raucous stage persona.

By the late 1960s, Pryor's career was in high gear, while his personal life was in chaos with a cocaine habit; clashes with Las Vegas management, landlords, and hotel clerks; a battery lawsuit by one of his wives; and an Internal Revenue Service audit for failure to pay taxes between 1967 and 1970. After laying low in the counterculture community in Berkeley, for several years, Pryor emerged in 1972 with a new stand-up act and a supporting role in the film *The Lady Sings the Blues,* for which he earned an Academy Award nomination. In 1976, he wrote and starred in *The Bingo Long Traveling All-Stars and Motor Kings,* plus co-starred with Gene Wilder in the hit comedy-suspense film *Silver Streak,* which grossed $30 million. Also in the 1970s, two of Pryor's comedy albums went platinum, and the 1979 movie *Richard Pryor Live in Concert* was acclaimed by critics as the comedian's crowning achievement. In the film, the characters portrayed by Pryor include winos, junkies, prostitutes, street fighters, blue-collar drunks, and pool hustlers—all denizens of the underbelly of the American Dream.

During the course of this success, Pryor's life continued on its erratic path, as he suffered a heart attack in 1978 and was divorced after a violent New Year's Eve incident that ended with his riddling his wife's car with bullets. By 1980 Pryor was freebasing cocaine, which apparently precipitated the June 9, 1980, incident in which Pryor caught on fire, suffering severe injuries to half his body. Once again calling upon material from his own life, Pryor in his 1982 concert movie *Live on Sunset Strip* parodied the accident, his drug use, and his stay in the hospital. A year later, he joined a drug rehabilitation program and worked with other addicts to overcome his problems. In 1985, Pryor co-wrote, directed, and starred in the autobiographical movie *Jo Jo Dancer, Your Life Is Calling,* playing a comedian reliving his life following a near fatal accident. Other 1980s films featuring Pryor included *The Toy* (1982), *Brewster's Millions* (1985), *See No Evil, Hear No Evil* (1989), and *Harlem Nights* (1989).

Pryor was diagnosed with multiple sclerosis in 1986, and his later films show him in a weakened condition. In 1990 he appeared in *Another You,* and he also had a small role in David Lynch's 1997 film *Lost Highway.* With more than forty movie credits, more than twenty comedy records, numerous appearances on the *Tonight Show* and other TV programs, and countless live performances, Pryor's legacy is that he turned African American life into a bold one-man theater, and in so doing transformed the face of modern comedy.

—Dennis Russell

FURTHER READING:

Haskins, James. *Richard Pryor: A Man and His Madness.* New York, Beaufort Books, 1984.

Pryor, Richard, and Todd Gold. *Pryor Convictions and Other Life Sentences.* New York, Pantheon, 1995.

Robbins, Fred, and David Ragan. *Richard Pryor: This Cat's Got Nine Lives.* New York, Delilah Books, 1982.

failed. Pryor continued to live with his grandmother, who administered beatings on a regular basis. While in school, the comedian was often in trouble with the law. However, it was at age eleven that Pryor got his first taste of show business when he was cast in a community theater performance by a teacher who also allowed him to entertain fellow students with his comedic antics. Many years later, Pryor gave the teacher an Emmy Award that the comedian had won for writing a Lily Tomlin special.

However, trouble continued to plague Pryor in high school when he was expelled for hitting a teacher. After deciding not to return to school, Pryor worked in a meat-packing house and then joined the Army in 1958. While serving a two-year hitch in West Germany, Pryor clashed with his superiors. In 1960 he returned to Peoria, married the first of five wives, and fathered his second child, Richard Pryor, Jr. Pryor's first child, Renee, had been born three years earlier.

Pryor's first professional break came when a popular African American nightclub in Peoria let him perform stand-up on stage. By the early 1960s Pryor was performing regularly on a comedy circuit that included East St. Louis, Missouri, and Youngstown and Pittsburgh, Pennsylvania. In 1963 he moved to New York City, performing an act highly influenced by his comedic heroes, Bill Cosby and

Williams, John A., and Dennis A. Williams. *If I Stop I'll Die: The Comedy and Tragedy of Richard Pryor.* New York, Thunder's Mouth Press, 1991.

Psychedelia

The word "psychedelic" entered the English language in 1947, courtesy of British psychologist Humphrey Osmond. In a paper he was presenting at a conference of the New York Academy of Sciences, Osmond described his own experiences with mind-altering chemicals such as LSD and mescaline. Dissatisfied with the judgmental terms that his profession typically used to describe such drugs, Osmond came up with "psychedelic" as a more neutral descriptor, and the name stuck.

Psychedelic drugs remained in the cultural background, the sole province of discreet, professional, scientific research, until 1963. That year, it became widely known that two Harvard psychology professors, Timothy Leary and Richard Alpert, were giving controlled doses

A psychedelic promotional poster for a concert with Jefferson Airplane at the Fillmore Auditorium in 1967.

of LSD to graduate student volunteer subjects. Leary and Alpert were engaged in legitimate research, and the LSD (short for lysergic acid diethylamide) had been obtained legally and with government permission. However, Harvard deemed the project irresponsible and fired both men on the grounds of unprofessional conduct.

Freed from the constraints of academia, Leary became a vocal advocate of the use of LSD to expand human consciousness. He was perhaps best known for his pithy admonition to young people: "Tune in, turn on, drop out." By the middle of the decade, many had heard of Leary's advice—and quite a few had taken it. LSD and other psychedelic drugs, such as psilocybin and peyote, came to occupy a prominent place in the youth culture that developed in the 1960s and continued into the 1970s.

One of the focal points for what became known as the "counter-culture" was San Francisco, especially the city's Haight-Ashbury district. An area of traditionally low rent and bohemian lifestyle, "the Haight" attracted many young people who were in search of new experiences, whether chemical, sexual, or social. Although they sometimes referred to themselves as "flower children" or even "freaks," many adults began to use the term "hippie," a word that eventually grew so imprecise that it was often used to refer to anyone who looked, dressed, or acted unconventionally.

An important aspect of the scene was the music, especially the variety that became known as "psychedelic" music or "acid rock"—so named because listening to it could supposedly simulate the experience of a hallucinogenic "trip" without the use of chemicals. Psychedelic music was characterized by extremely high volume, deliberate electronic distortion, the use of synthesizers, extended instrumental improvisations or "jams," and the addition of Eastern instruments, such as the sitar, to the traditional rock instrument repertoire. The accompanying lyrics tended to emphasize mysticism or drug references. Some of the more successful acid rock bands included Jefferson Airplane, Iron Butterfly, Quicksilver Messenger Service, the Grateful Dead, and the British bands Pink Floyd and Led Zeppelin. Other musical groups, while not usually identified as psychedelic, sometimes recorded songs that fit the mold—such as the Beatles' "Lucy in the Sky with Diamonds," Strawberry Alarm Clock's "Incense and Peppermints," and The Jimi Hendrix Experience's "Purple Haze." Scottish folk singer Donovan had a hit record with "Mellow Yellow," which extolled the mind-altering properties of dried banana peels.

Nor was any other aspect of 1960s and 1970s culture left untouched by psychedelia. The publishing world produced books like Aldous Huxley's *The Doors of Perception* and Carlos Casteneda's three-volume *Teachings of Don Juan*—the former a paean to the mind-expanding aspects of hallucinogens, the latter an account of the author's initiation, at the hands of a Yacqui Indian guru, into the mystical dimensions of peyote.

Films were also quick to cash in on the psychedelic scene. Roger Corman, a director best known for his series of horror movies based on the works of Edgar Allen Poe, in 1967 brought *The Trip*, starring Peter Fonda, to audiences. A year later, the Beatles' animated film *Yellow Submarine* was released. Its kaleidoscopic imagery and outrageous use of color hinted, for some, at the surreal experience of an LSD trip.

The world of art was also affected. Psychedelic artists employed glaringly bright colors and unusual shapes to evoke the visual experience that came from the use of mind-altering drugs. The work of Isaac Abrams is notable in this regard, and some of Andy Warhol's paintings also show a psychedelic influence. A number of illustrators also adopted the psychedelic style, especially for display on concert posters and the covers of record albums. Some of the better known work was produced by R. Crumb and Rick Griffin, but the most successful of the psychedelic illustrators was Peter Max. Born in Germany, Max lived for a time in China and Israel before coming to the United States to study art. He had achieved modest success as an illustrator by the mid-1960s, but in 1967 his career really began to take off. Max's bold, colorful designs graced products from posters to shirts to clocks to lamps. In 1968, his posters alone sold over one million copies.

By the mid-1970s, the psychedelic era was over, its LSD and acid rock replaced by cocaine and disco. Although a brief attempt at revival took place in the late 1990s, it was no more than an exercise in nostalgia. The psychedelic era was a product of its time, and, for better or worse, that time is unlikely to come again.

—Justin Gustainis

FURTHER READING:

Henke, James, Parks Puterbaugh, Charles Perry, and Barry Miles. *I Want to Take You Higher: The Psychedelic Era, 1965-1969.* San Francisco, Chronicle Books, 1997.

Stevens, Jay. *Storming Heaven: LSD and the American Dream.* New York, Atlantic Monthly Press, 1987.

Watts, W. David, Jr. *The Psychedelic Experience: A Sociological Study.* Beverly Hills, California, Sage Publications, 1971.

Psychics

Psychics as clairvoyants, fortunetellers, and earth-bound connections to the spirit world can be traced back thousands of years and as far away as ancient Egypt. As an element of American popular culture in the 1990s, the Psychic Friends Network is as close as a 1-900-phone call, though some who claim to be more serious clairvoyants scorn these $3.99-a-minute fortunetellers as charlatans.

The psychic movement in the United States followed closely on the tails of the Mesmeric and Spiritualist movements of the nineteenth century. Austrian doctor Franz Antoine Mesmer (1766-1815) captured followers' attention with his reports of psychic phenomenon such as "thought transference, clairvoyance and 'eyeless vision'" in subjects who came to be referred to as "mesmerized." Mesmer's popularity opened the door for acceptance of the Spiritualist movement by acknowledging the concepts of clairvoyance and communication with the dead. The mesmeric trance, as it had come to be known, led naturally to the idea of the mediumistic trance, the core of the Spiritualist movement. In 1848, Margaret Fox and her two sisters from Hydesville, New York, produced spirit "rappings" in response to questions from the audience. They moved to Rochester, New York, where they grew in popularity until their fame as mediums had spread across the Atlantic. Several imitators followed the Fox sisters, with varying routines: E.S.P. (extrasensory perception), table levitation or "turning," spirit-induced writing, and speaking in a spirit's voice while in trance, later referred to as "channeling." Spiritualism gained such popularity—even First Lady Jane (Mrs. Franklin) Pierce was an

adherent—that many churches and societies were born of the movement. Incidentally, Margaret Fox later confessed to producing the "rapping" noises through her joints.

Connecting the Spiritualist movement with religion did little to shelter the movement from accusations of fraud. In 1882, Sir William Barrett (1844-1925), Henry Sidgwick (1838-1900), and F. W. H. Meyers (1843-1901) founded the Society for Psychical Research (SPR) to scientifically investigate claims of psychic phenomena. The SPR made very few strides toward proving psychic manifestations and instead, uncovered a myriad of fraudulent activities, including those of the famed Russian psychic, Madame Helena Petrovna Blavatsky.

Interest in psychics waxed and waned throughout the twentieth century. In the United States, two psychics in particular had a strong hold on the popular imagination: Edgar Cayce and Jean Dixon. Cayce, known as America's "sleeping prophet," had a remarkable talent for learning clairvoyantly in his sleep, and for diagnosing ailments and describing an appropriate treatment while from a trance-like state. Consistently, doctors confirmed the diagnoses and the treatments were effective. Cayce's individual "health readings" eventually turned into predictions of life events, not only for individual clients, but also for the country and the world at large. Cayce successfully predicted the 1929 Wall Street crash, America's involvement in World War II, the defeat of the Axis powers in 1945, and the collapse of Soviet communism. Cayce also predicted a number of worldwide geological upheavals, many of which simply did not occur. By allegedly predicting the assassination of John F. Kennedy in 1963, Jean Dixon (1918-1997) became something of a media sensation, though she had won the confidence of followers from an early age. Dixon served as a consultant to Presidents Roosevelt and Truman and Britain's Winston Churchill. She successfully predicted the assassination of Gandhi, the suicide of Marilyn Monroe, and the assassinations of Robert Kennedy and Martin Luther King, Jr. Despite her success, however, Dixon began to discredit herself by publicly showcasing her talents and authoring a syndicated horoscope column with worldwide distribution. Her annual "predictions," most of which did not materialize, became a prominent feature in supermarket-tabloid newspapers.

The pop-culture psychic of the 1990s emerged on the crest of New Age metaphysics, Hollywood hype, and a good TV infomercial. For a $3.99-per-minute phone call, the psychics at singer Dionne Warwick's Psychic Friends Network could be consulted about love, money, careers, and even weight loss. In person, a look into the future can cost between $45 and $200. It is estimated that psychic hotlines gross approximately $1 billion per year. Investigative journalists have uncovered evidence that some psychic hotlines do not employ psychics at all, but hire unemployed actors or housewives who offer their consultations from prepared scripts.

Today's psychics are a far cry from the joint-rapping Fox sisters of the early psychic movement. Every large city, and some smaller ones, have their share of storefront "gypsy fortunetellers," and many ethnic groups have their own psychic traditions, such as the "roots" healers in Black and Caribbean communities or the psychics in U.S. Chinatowns that are regularly consulted for advice on business or romantic decisions. Others are more media-savvy, with their 1-900 numbers and Internet websites. Most, it appears, are seasoned entertainers, though they are far shrewder businessmen and women then their early counterparts, with technology clearly on their side. The evolution of the psychic from early charlatan to telephone fortuneteller is proof positive of two basic tenets of human existence: humankind will always have a burning desire to know what the future holds, and nothing, absolutely nothing, can escape commercialization—not even the paranormal.

—Nadine-Rae Leavell

FURTHER READING:

Cavendish, Richard, editor. *Man, Myth, and Magic: The Illustrated Encyclopedia of Mythology, Religion, and the Unknown,* revised edition. Marshall Cavendish Corporation, 1994.

Guiley, Rosemary Ellen. *Harper's Encyclopedia of Mystical and Paranormal Experience.* San Francisco, Harper, 1994.

Melton, J. Gordon, and Leslie A. Shepard, editors. *Encyclopedia of Occultism and Parapsychology.* 4th Edition. Detroit, Gale Research, 1996.

Poinsot, M. C. *The Encyclopedia of Occult Sciences.* Detroit, Gale Research, 1972.

Psycho

Directed by Alfred Hitchcock, this 1960 film thriller based on a novel by Robert Bloch is remembered for its depiction of on-screen violence and for its celebrated ''shower scene.'' Shot on a shoestring budget of $800,000 by the crew of Hitchcock's television show, this black-and-white classic was a carefully crafted work of cinema that also upped the ante on movie mayhem. The staggering box-office success of *Psycho*—it has earned $40 million to date—inspired, and continues to encourage, a host of imitators who are still pushing the envelope on filmic bloodshed, but rarely with the artistry displayed by Hitchcock. *Psycho* is the first classic black-and-white film since Selznick's *The Prisoner of Zenda* that underwent a later, full-color, shot-for-shot remake of its original script.

Mystery/fantasy/science-fiction writer Bloch based his 1959 novel *Psycho* very loosely on the real-life case of murderer Ed Gein. The book tells the story of a lonely, mother-fixated motelkeeper named Norman Bates. Norman and his mom are the sole proprietors of the Bates Motel, a now-seedy establishment patronized by Mary Crane, a young office worker who has impulsively stolen $40,000 of her boss's money. After a chat with Norman in which he discusses his apparently unbalanced mother (''I think perhaps all of us go a little crazy at times'') Mary resolves to return the loot before anyone knows it's missing. But Mary is fated never to leave the Bates Motel alive, cut down in her shower by a butcher knife wielded by someone with ''the face of a crazy old woman.'' Mary's sister initiates an investigation into her disappearance, which, after more murder and mystery, eventually reveals that Norman killed his mother as a youth and has now become a homicidal split personality of Norman/Mother.

It was screenwriter Joseph Stefano who came up with the inspiration to begin the story with the secretary (now Marion) instead of Norman and his mother. By telling the story from Marion's point of view, and engaging audience sympathy for her, the film could shock the audience by disposing of her before the film was barely half over. To add to this impact, Hitchcock cast well-known actress Janet Leigh in the role. To attract sympathy for Norman, the director chose Anthony Perkins, portrayer of sensitive men in such 1950s films as *Friendly Persuasion* and *Fear Strikes Out.* After the release of *Psycho,* public perception of Perkins was irrevocably altered, leading to a career of ''weird'' roles, climaxed by his reprises of Norman Bates in several much-belated sequels.

Shooting on *Psycho* proceeded rapidly, but a week was lavished on one sequence: the shower murder. Working from a storyboard by title designer Saul Bass, Hitchcock shot the death scene from many different angles which, when edited into a rapid montage—and underscored by the piercing strings of Bernard Herrmann's music—had the desired effect of shocking the audience on a primal level. Hitchcock's clever ad campaign, coupled with the stricture against seating anyone after the film had begun, was tongue-in-cheek: ''Don't give away the ending—it's the only one we have!'' The director always claimed that the film was a black-humored joke, not to be taken seriously, but there was no denying its impact on the moviegoers who flocked to the film in great numbers and subsequently swore off taking showers. (Among those claiming still to be afraid of showers: Janet Leigh.) *Psycho* proved to be the capstone of Hitchcock's career, earning him one of his few Oscar nominations.

Compared to the host of horrors which have followed in its wake, from the *Friday the 13th* series to *Scream* and its imitators, *Psycho* was most circumspect in its handling of gore. Hitchcock had been offered the opportunity by his technicians to show a knife actually entering Marion's torso, but had chosen instead to achieve his effects through sheer montage. The monochromatic cinematography he used not only suited the eerie, haunted house mood but also avoided a Technicolor blood bath: The blood seen spattering in the shower sequence was actually chocolate syrup. One proof of *Psycho*'s impact on popular culture came in the 1990s when acquitted murder suspect O. J. Simpson jokingly surprised a TV interviewer by pouncing from behind a door, making stabbing motions, all the while imitating Bernard Herrmann's high-pitched violins.

—Preston Neal Jones

FURTHER READING:

Bloch, Robert. *Psycho.* New York, Simon & Schuster, 1959.

Bogdanovich, Peter. *Who the Devil Made It?* New York, Ballantine, 1998.

Gottlieb, Sidney, editor. *Hitchcock on Hitchcock.* Berkeley, University of California Press, 1997.

Leigh, Janet. *Psycho: Behind the Scenes of the Classic Thriller.* New York, Harmony Books, 1995.

Smith, Steven C. *A Heart at Fire's Center: The Life and Music of Bernard Herrmann.* Berkeley, University of California Press, 1991.

Spoto, Donald. *The Dark Side of Genius: The Life of Alfred Hitchcock.* Boston, Little, Brown, 1983.

Taylor, John Russell. *Hitch: The Life and Times of Alfred Hitchcock.* New York, Pantheon (Random House), 1978.

Truffaut, François *Hitchcock.* New York, Simon & Schuster, 1984.

PTA/PTO (Parent Teacher Association/ Organization)

Parent-Teacher Associations or Organizations are voluntary groups that forge mutually cooperative relationships between parents and public schools. The umbrella organization of these local groups is

Janet Leigh in Alfred Hitchcock's *Psycho*.

the National Parent Teacher Association, which claims affiliation with 27,000 local groups and close to 7 million members. Its mission statement advocates speaking out on behalf of children and youth in schools, assisting parents in their childrearing responsibilities, and encouraging parental involvement in schools. Originally called the National Congress of Mothers, it was formed during the 1890s by Alice McLellan Birney and Phoebe Apperson Hearst, the latter a member by marriage of the prominent newspaper dynasty.

The name of the original national organization—the National Congress of Mothers—reflects its historical context: during the late nineteenth century, women were expected to focus on nurturing and raising children. Most Americans believed these crucial activities took place solely in the domestic sphere and the private home. What women like Birney did was to extend the traditional role of female nurturing to a realm outside the home and into the arena of public advocacy and activity. This new organization both confirmed the special—some would say subordinate—role of women in raising children while extending it to what Settlement House Movement leader, Jane Addams, once called "social housekeeping." This early

group viewed parenting as a specialized activity in need of education and training.

Not surprisingly, the National Congress of Mothers also reflected the spirit of the Progressive Era in American history (roughly 1890-1917), during which time the organization changed its name to the National Congress of Mothers and Parent-Teacher Associations. These years saw an increasing number of middle-class Americans dedicate themselves to reforming the inhumane excesses of industrial capitalism. Perhaps the most famous leader of this movement was President Theodore Roosevelt, who played a major role in the National Congress by serving as a speaker at its conventions. Taking up Roosevelt's call for social and political reform, the National Congress threw itself into numerous Progressive Era causes, including the abolition of child labor, the reform of the juvenile court system, and the passage of the Pure Food Bill in 1906. In addition, the organization helped promote John Dewey's child-centered schooling methods that became known as "progressive education."

During the Progressive Era, the National Congress carved out its particular concern in the midst of other school reform movements.

According to Louise Montgomery, a Chicago educator at the turn of the century, the proliferation of the public school system brought with it new challenges since it divorced the traditional activities of education from the home. She argued, ''The parent has been strangely silent, surrendering his child to the school system with a curious, unquestioning faith.'' Parent-Teacher Associations were meant to challenge this sort of passivity on the part of parents. Members of the organization believed ordinary citizens had a fundamental role to play in America's civic and public life.

Though the original idealism of the groups declined after the Progressive Era, the goals remained the same at century's end, with the National PTA maintaining its role as the nation's biggest child-advocacy organization. The PTA continued to involve parents in decision-making about local schools, and to make child welfare its central focus. Among the contemporary issues important to the PTA in the 1990s were the quality of children's television programming; various attempts to reform the public education system, as by vouchers or charter schools; the threat of violence in many public schools; and the rise of drug and alcohol abuse among many young people.

—Kevin Mattson

FURTHER READING:

Cremin, Lawrence. *The Transformation of the School: Progressivism in American Education, 1876-1957.* New York, Vintage Books, 1961.

Cutright, Melitta. *The National PTA Talks to Parents.* Garden City, Doubleday, 1989.

Swap, Susan McAllister. *Developing Home-School Partnerships.* New York, Teachers College, 1993.

Public Enemy

Public Enemy burst onto the hip-hop scene in 1987 with their debut album *Yo! Bum Rush the Show.* Articulating a militant Black Nationalism over a heavy bass-line and driving rhythms, Public Enemy marked out a new space in the emerging rap genre. They soon attracted attention by their hardline and uncompromising lyrics that sought to bring down the white power system, which had oppressed blacks for so long. Their twin tactics of visibility and militancy soon marked them out as a threat and they were hailed as the ''Black Panthers of rap.''

The members of Public Enemy are more than just rap musicians. Fronted by Chuck D, self-styled prophet of rage, Public Enemy pronounced themselves as the ''Black CNN.'' Originating from Long Island, Chuck D (Carlton Ridenhour), the son of ex-1960s activists, proclaimed his mission as championing the cause of the African-American underclass. He located himself in the tradition of black orators like Jesse Jackson and Martin Luther King, Jr. Chuck D distinguished himself from his rap predecessors by a conspicuous lack of macho clichés and empty boasts. Instead he rapped intelligently and unrelentingly about African-American history while his sidekick, Flavor Flav (William Drayton), incited him on and DJ Terminator X (Norman Rogers) fused the revolutionary teachings of Malcolm X, Kwame Toure, Louis Farrakhan, and Martin Luther King with the beats of LL Cool J and Run-DMC. Public Enemy's emphasis on

education over machismo situated them in a rap tradition begun by the Last Poets and served as a blueprint for other rappers. Paris, KRS-One, Basehead, the Disposable Heroes of Hip-Hoprisy, and Kool Moe Dee soon followed Public Enemy's lead in establishing the new genre of ''hardcore'' rap that fused education with entertainment.

Visibility is a key strand of Public Enemy's hip-hop strategy. On stage, they are backed by Professor Griff (Richard Griffin) and his Security of the First World posse—uniformed, Uzi-toting, paramilitaries—who present a potent image subversive of existing power relations. Their logo—a silhouetted figure between the crosshairs of a gunsight—positions them both as targets of the society at large and society as their target. The figure represents the black man in America, a perceived menace to an establishment bent on excluding him. Many of Public Enemy's fans can be seen wearing this logo on their shirts; and Flavor Flav wears a huge clock as a reminder to ''know what time it is''—it is a stopped alarm clock caricaturing a consumer society that privileges expensive watches while suggesting that time has stopped since social reform is limited.

Their second album, *It Takes a Nation of Millions to Hold Us Back* (1989), extended Public Enemy's campaign to uproot the status quo with tracks like ''Bring the Noise'' and ''Rebel without a Pause.'' ''Black Steel in the Hour of Chaos'' resists the draft as an example of black defiance while ''Louder Than a Bomb'' accuses the Central Intelligence Agency of assassinating Dr. King and Malcolm X. ''Fight the Power,'' on their next album, debunked American icons such as Elvis and John Wayne; this track was Motown Records' biggest-selling twelve-inch. The album has been described as a prototype of what a rap album can achieve. By turning platinum, producing provocative videos, and attracting a vast multiracial audience, Public Enemy set the trend and standards to which rap could aspire.

Accusations of anti-semitism, however, nearly destroyed the group. In May 1989 Professor Griff, Public Enemy's ''minister of information'' and a member of Louis Farrakhan's Nation of Islam, stated that Jews were responsible ''for the majority of wickedness that goes on across the globe.'' Chuck D fired Griff (who later formed his own group) and replied to the media criticism with *Fear of a Black Planet* (1990). By combining news samples with their music and recreating media broadcasts about them, Public Enemy attempted to fight back by depicting themselves as the victims of a white power structure committed to destroying them.

Public Enemy has since made five more albums: *Apocalypse '91* (1991), *Greatest Misses* (1992), *Muse Sick-N-Hour Mess Age* (1994), and *He Got Game* (1998). Chuck D took a break from the group to make a solo album titled *The Autobiography of Mistachuck* (1996). Singles such as ''Shut 'Em Down'' (1991), ''Give It Up'' (1994), and ''I Stand Accused'' (1994) continued their hard-line, myth-breaking militancy.

Not only did Public Enemy raise consciousness among their black following, they also attracted a significant body of white fans. Their ability to sell so many records can be attributed to their influence beyond the confines of inner-city ghettos. Public Enemy proved to be popular among white, middle-class fans and consequently the group drew a sizeable following not only for their music, but also for the rap genre in general. Groups like NWA and other ''gangsta'' rappers have massively benefitted from this new white audience. Undoubtedly it was this consumer bloc that helped rap to crossover into the mainstream music industry such that by the late 1990s, hip-hop singles often reached number one in the charts, selling more than half a million copies.

Pulic Enemy, from left: Terminator X, Flavor Flav, and Chuck D.

Members of Public Enemy were pioneers of the hardcore rap genre. Their rap militancy shifted the genre from the party-style, macho boasting of "electro" toward a more politically conscious music. They set the trend for many others and thus spawned a host of imitators. In doing so, Public Enemy attracted a broad, multiracial following allowing rap to break out of the confines of the inner-city ghettos in which it originated. As a consequence, the group has ensured a wider audience for its vocalization of the problems of blacks in America.

—Nathan Abrams

FURTHER READING:

Abrams, Nathan. "Antonio's B-Boys: Rap, Rappers, and Gramsci's Intellectuals." *Popular Music and Society.* Vol. 19, No. 4, Winter 1995, 1-18.

Fernando, S. H., Jr. *The New Beats: Exploring the Music Culture and Attitudes of Hip-Hop.* Edinburgh, United Kingdom, Payback Press, 1994.

Nelson, Havelock, and Michael A. Gonzales. *Bring the Noise: A Guide to Rap Music and Hip-Hop.* New York, Harmony Books, 1991.

Toop, David. *Rap Attack 2: African Rap to Global Hip Hop.* London, Serpent's Tail, 1991.

Public Libraries

Of all its public institutions, perhaps America's most enduring are its libraries. U.S. libraries arose out of the democratic beliefs in an informed public, enlightened civic discourse, social and intellectual advancement, and participation in the democratic process. Libraries became part of the U.S. commitment to equal educational opportunity and freedom of thought and expression. Though libraries have existed for almost as long as records have been kept, libraries as public institutions are rather recent and the idea to use public funds for library operation had to overcome considerable opposition. In 1854, the Boston Public Library opened, becoming the first American library to be supported by general taxation. Public libraries became products of the nineteenth century due to the influences of the industrial revolution, urban growth, and the accumulation of private and public wealth.

The traditional structure of the public library is based on service, intellectual freedom, education, democracy, and preservation of the record of civilization. For nearly 150 years, the mission of public

The Carnegie Public Library in Snohomish, Washington.

libraries has been to collect, organize, preserve, and provide free and equal access to information, knowledge, and entertainment in different formats. By following this mission, libraries foster community, lifelong learning, recreation, literacy, outreach, and personal advancement. The example of the U.S. public library has been recognized and copied in countries throughout the world.

Though public libraries enjoyed an image of well-organized houses of information at the end of the twentieth century, in the mid-nineteenth century public libraries lacked standards of service, adequate acquisition funds, proper cataloging, and professional librarians. To ameliorate the problems in libraries, library leaders resolved at an 1876 librarian conference to make their occupation professional. Soon an accelerated library movement started; librarians founded the American Library Association and began developing methods and systems for organizing information. Among the methodologies created was the Dewey Decimal Classification created by Melvil Dewey in 1876 for cataloging materials, and William Frederick Poole's authoritative indexing for periodicals, which Poole created while studying at Yale University and later published as *Poole's Index to Periodical Literature* (1887-1908). Dewey went on to establish the first professional school of librarianship at Columbia University in 1887.

While the standardization of organizational methods and professionalization of librarians made public libraries easier to use, private funding provided the boost needed to reach the public they desired to serve. Steel magnate Andrew Carnegie gave over $41 million to erect 1,679 public library buildings in 1,412 communities between 1890 and 1919. His funding helped erect libraries in numbers of underserved communities throughout the country. Many of these libraries are still in use today. Carnegie's level of philanthropy was unmatched until 1997 when once again America's richest man chose the public library as the object of his giving. Bill Gates gave two $200 million grants, one for software and one directed at providing digital

technology and Internet access to underserved libraries. In addition to these two significant philanthropic gifts, federal programs and grants have assisted the local tax base of library budgets. During the 1930s, Roosevelt's Works Progress Administration (WPA) built 350 new libraries and repaired many existing ones. Later, the Library Services Act of 1956 and the Library Services and Construction Act of 1964-65 provided federal dollars for library construction.

The public and private funds used for libraries produced some significant results. In 1876, there were 188 public libraries, a number that had grown to more than 9,000 at the end of the twentieth century. A 1998 Gallup Poll showed that two-thirds of Americans stopped into a public library during the past year, and of these 81 percent checked out one or more books. While public libraries have been criticized as an institution serving the middle class, the library's strength lies in its democracy: equal access to all, free services to people across ethnic, economic, and cultural lines, and a governing board made up of community members.

Libraries and librarianship shifted radically in the latter half of the twentieth century with the development of new information technology. The technology allowed new ways of creating, storing, organizing, and distributing information. Public expectation of the role of libraries also increased, and librarians have responded by taking new initiatives, for example, offering computer access to the library catalog and delivery of full-text items online. While some believe that the virtual world of online information will replace libraries, there is still a need and desire for libraries and librarians. Libraries are the one institution that can fill the gap between the information ''haves'' and ''have nots,'' for example, by providing the public access to computers and teaching them how to navigate for information.

Placing libraries in cyberspace is just one more form of outreach, a role long identified with library service. From the early horse-drawn book wagons to the modern bookmobile, outreach services have extended from telephone and e-mail reference to services for shut-ins and prisoners. Serving the remote online user is just one more extension of service.

Besides adjusting to rapidly changing technology, libraries are faced with challenges in other areas. The rapid rise of book superstores have created competition for libraries. While the information available on the Internet has also generated competition for libraries, librarians have found it necessary to decide whether or not to put filters that block Internet sites unsuitable for children on computers within libraries. In addition, libraries must find ways to contain technology and telecommunications costs, and protect online intellectual property while assuring fair use. Faced with increased competition and costs, libraries continue to struggle with budgetary matters, competing for limited local tax dollars and regularly supplementing their budgets through funds provided from grant writing. With limited funding, public libraries have found it challenging to keep up with changing demographics, especially in serving multi-ethnic and racial populations.

Despite new challenges, it is clear that communities still want libraries. They want them to serve the disadvantaged, provide free access to collections and online technology, promote literacy, provide books and reference service, make a place for community information and programming, and conduct programs for children. Considering that three out of every five library users are children or young adults, public libraries are a vital resource for parents. Libraries cost little, averaging approximately $21 per capita annually. It has been suggested that supporting a public library outranks any other single investment a community can make to help its people.

—Byron Anderson

FURTHER READING:

Garrison, Dee. *Apostles of Culture: The Public Librarian and American Society, 1876-1920.* New York, Free Press, 1979.

Martin, Lowell Arthur. *Enrichment: A History of the Public Library in the United States in the Twentieth Century.* Lanham, Maryland, Scarecrow Press, 1998.

Nunberg, Geoffrey. ''Will Libraries Survive?,'' *American Prospect.* Vol. 41, November 1998, 16-23.

Van Slyck, Abigail Ayres. *Free to All: Carnegie Libraries and American Culture, 1890-1920.* Chicago, University of Chicago Press, 1995.

Public Television (PBS)

With its dedication to the high ideals of presenting the finest in drama, music, children's programs, and political debate, the U.S. public television system has proved a significant cultural force in a nation where broadcasting is largely driven by commercial considerations, often to the detriment of quality. Public television was at least partially born in reaction to Federal Communications Commission (FCC) chairman Newton Minnow's now famous comment that by 1961 American commercial television had become ''a vast wasteland.'' (In 1978 Minnow would become chairman of PBS). From its 1950s roots in educational television, public (or non-commercial)

television has grown, not without problems, internal conflicts, political opposition, and funding setbacks, to enjoy some considerable popular successes as a formidable, if vulnerable, alternative to the increasingly trivial and commercial-sodden programming of late twentieth-century network television.

Public and educational television dates back to the first public radio broadcasts from universities and scientific laboratories. The first radio broadcast of any kind originated from an educational venue, the University of Wisconsin, in 1919, and in the ensuing decade other universities followed suit, forming electronic extension services, though mostly for scattered audiences with crystal sets.

While the first television programs were broadcast in the late 1930s, World War II curtailed the industry's development. By 1945, however, the FCC had set aside 13 channels for commercial television, and by 1949 one million television receivers were in use across the United States. It was during the FCC's four-year freeze on station licenses (1948-1952) that a movement began among educators for channels that would be non-commercial and dedicated to education. In 1952, after its historic Sixth Report and Order, the FCC reserved 242 channels for non-commercial TV, and the Educational Television and Radio Center (ETRC) was established in Ann Arbor, Michigan, on a grant from the Ford Foundation's Fund for Adult Education. The center secured and distributed programs for the emerging system, as well as renting them out to schools and other public institutions.

In 1958 the Center moved to New York where it became National Educational Television (NET), again chiefly supported by the Ford Foundation. NET soon revised the limited classroom approach to educational TV, and shifted to providing a broader range of cultural, public affairs, documentary, and children's programming. It laid the groundwork both for expansion into network status, and for Educational TV's eventual re-designation as Public TV. NET lives on in the spirit and call letters of WNET, New York City's Channel 13 public television station, which is still active in producing original programming for public television.

Public television thus evolved directly out of educational television, a difficult rite of passage due to the fact that ETV originally began as a collection of autonomous stations, each serving in various and sundry ways the cause of education, but with no overriding administrative/creative policy. PBS's non-commercial status was another stumbling block, totally financed as it is by federal and state funding and, increasingly, by voluntary contributions from local viewers and grants from foundations and corporations. The fact that public TV was born after commercial network television had been firmly entrenched in the American mind was another obstacle to its initial development.

When the ETV system was redefined as public television by the Public Broadcasting Act of 1967, some internal confusion remained due to the diversity of the original educational TV system. (This in spite of the ideals for non-commerical TV that had been clarified in the Carnegie Commission Report of that same year). Some stations clung to their original ETV agendas, while others were reluctant to surrender their autonomy to the national system. Regional and political differences further complicated PBS's developmen, and contributed to the factionalism of its first decades. Thus the history of public television is also a history of conflict from within over the definition of the medium's true mission.

Despite internal and organizational conflicts, however, the avowed overall purpose of public television from the start was to make a dedicated attempt to free the television medium from the tyranny of the marketplace and to address the ideal of quality rather mass appeal and commercial profit. In theory, it also marked an attempt to realize the humanistic, social, and intellectual potential of the mass television medium, and to provide a varied menu of cultural, informational, educational, and innovative programming. These ideals were first voiced in the Carnegie Commission Report of 1967, *Public Television: A Program for Action,* the result of a two-year study of educational TV by a prestigious 15-member commission composed of educators, businessmen, producers, and artists. Funded by the Carnegie Corporation, a second Carnegie Commission was formed in 1977 to examine the history of the first decade of public television.

Public television has also been called "a name without a concept," but the system has nonetheless consistently managed to build both an audience and a profile, and to compete positively with, and sometimes even influence, the commercial system. By the 1970s PBS ratings were on the rise due to a flowering of excellent, well-produced original shows displaying variety as well as quality, and ranging from sitcoms and children's programs to documentary series about the arts and classical music. These included *The Adams Chronicles, Great Performances, Nova, Live from Lincoln Center,* and *Sesame Street,* while British imports included the sitcom *Upstairs, Downstairs,* Sir Kenneth Clark's series on the history of art, *Civilization,* Jacob Bronowski's *The Ascent of Man,* and *Monty Python's Flying Circus.* These shows became popular PBS staples, leading to more of the same in later decades. In 1973 the network's detailed coverage of the Senate Watergate hearings was one of its most effective programs ever for fund-raising, and by that year PBS had over a million subscribers, all voluntarily contributing an average annual amount of $15.00 to keep their regional PBS stations on the air. In 1990 *The Civil War,* aired on five consecutive nights, set an all-time ratings record for a series of limited length, and by 1991 the audience had grown to five million, making average yearly contributions up to $56.00. During the 1990s the most popular shows were the *National Geographic Specials,* the *MacNeil/Lehrer News Hour, This Old House, The Frugal Gourmet,* and the British import, *Mystery.*

Two extended mini-series attracted particular attention to public television during the late 1970s and early 1980s. Both were British productions and both pushed the envelope of content and permissiveness for television in general, proving compulsively watchable on a scale that no PBS programming had achieved thus far. *I, Claudius,* a 13-hour BBC drama series, that first aired in 1978, challenged the boundaries of what was acceptable not only on PBS, but for television as a whole. Adapted from two novels by Robert Graves, *I, Claudius,* and *Claudius the God,* the series chronicled in fairly explicit detail the political and sexual intrigues of the reigns of the four decadent Roman emperors who followed Julius Caesar. Told from the viewpoint of Claudius, a presumed idiot who ultimately becomes emperor, the violence and sexuality of the series made many PBS stations uneasy, though none of them failed to air it. *I, Claudius* was one of the most popular entries in PBS's excellent *Masterpiece Theater* series.

In 1982 an elaborate 11-episode adaptation of Evelyn Waugh's novel *Brideshead Revisited* emulated both the critical success and audience ratings of *I, Claudius.* Produced by England's Granada Television International, the twelve-and-a-half-hour production was one of the most expensive British television series to date. The extended story followed an Oxford student who becomes emotionally involved in the life of the semi-decadent upper classes of an England between world wars, and was opulently filmed on location in England, Venice, and Malta. Again, the series created some controversy in its discreet, but unselfconscious depiction of the homosexuality of

one of the leading characters, Sebastian Flyte, and his intense involvement with the story's narrator, Charles Ryder.

Content aside, both *I, Claudius* and *Brideshead Revisited* also pioneered a new genre of high-toned television and literary adaptation. Longer by far than the longest movies ever made, both productions (but *Brideshead* especially) still maintained the production values and prestige of quality filmmaking. While ABC's popular success *Roots* had appeared as a 12-hour, week-long miniseries on ABC in 1977, the PBS broadcasts were the first time that works of classic literature were given their due in a format that finally did justice to both the detail and tempi of the literary originals. Nothing like either *Claudius* or *Brideshead* had ever really been seen anywhere before, and their acceptance and, indeed, overwhelming popularity on American public television laid the groundwork for the global acceptance of a new and somewhat rarefied genre of quality visual entertainment. The genre thrived on PBS, but the style also influenced actual movie making, such as the popular films of James Ivory, who adapted much of E. M. Forster in a similar fashion, and ensuing adaptations of the novels of Jane Austen and others.

Another innovative PBS series also inspired a number of spin-offs, and indeed launched an entire industry: the popular and enduring children's show, *Sesame Street,* with its cast of now globally beloved characters, including Jim Henson's Muppets. The series, which premiered in November of 1969 with an initial budget of only eight million dollars, has been described as "a revolutionary children's program that sought to teach numbers and letters (and, later, social concepts) to preschool children through TV entertainment chiefly by harnessing the techniques used in commercials." *Sesame Street's* original target audience was language-impaired preschool inner-city children, and thus the colorful and ethnically diverse characters (both live and Muppet) were often seen in drab urban settings uncharacteristic of children's shows.

Visual zap animation was the innovative instructional method pioneered on the show, and evaluative tests soon verified that *Sesame's* new formula of teaching letters and numbers though animation, paced at the attention-friendly duration of television commercials and augmented by the use of frequent repetition, was indeed an effective teaching method. The show later expanded from the teaching of educational basics to dealing with more complex issues such as the environment and racial understanding. With the 1984 death of actor Will Lee, who played one of the show's leading characters, Mr. Hooper, the subject of death and dying was raised for what was probably the first time on a children's television program. *Sesame Street* remains *the* most innovative end-product of the venerable educational TV system, and as such changed the face and techniques of children's programming everywhere.

In 1990 the death of Jim Henson, who not only created the show's popular Muppet characters, but lent his distinctive voice characterizations to several of them, left another void in the show. Henson's Muppet characters had made their debut on *Sesame Street,* and quickly became one of its most popular elements. The character of the huge but affable canary-yellow Big Bird became one of the most recognized and exploited characters of the late twentieth century, and PBS's first genuine superstar. Henson's own *Muppet Show* became one of the top-rated prime time CBS shows of the late 1970s, and in 1979 *The Muppet Movie* launched a film series which continues into the 1990s. *Sesame Street's* chief advisor was Dr. Gerald Lesser, a Harvard University psychologist, and the show also launched the songwriting career of Joe Raposo, whose popular *Sesame Street* songs were covered by many adult-geared recording artists of the era.

In spite of its popular successes, PBS has seldom been without its opponents since Lyndon Johnson signed the Public Broadcasting Act that created the Corporation for Public Broadcasting in 1967. That same year Johnson suggested that he would also work out a long-range funding plan for public TV in the coming year, but his withdrawal from the 1968 presidential campaign crushed this hope of extended support. The ensuing Nixon administration is remembered for, among other things, its attacks upon PBS as a "fourth network" and the White House's repeated attempts to decentralize public television. Documents later released under the Freedom of Information Act verify that the Nixon White House's aim was to shift control to individual stations, believing that they would act more conservatively in political terms. In 1972 Nixon vetoed CPB's authorization bill, but after several key members, including the chairman, president, and director of television of CPB resigned, the president signed a bill authorizing public broadcast funding for 1973.

The affair made public television aware of several key issues: that it was vulnerable to presidential political pressure, that it needed to develop a new, decentralized method for distributing production funds, and, especially, that it needed to look for new sources of funding, particularly from the private sector. So it was during this phase that PBS first turned more aggressively toward corporate underwriting, initially from the major oil companies, as a new source of program funding (ergo Exxon's sponsorship of the *Great Performances* series which aired *Brideshead Revisited*).

Congressional Democrats have been traditional supporters of public television, and the Carter administration was relatively hospitable to PBS, which prospered during Carter's term. However, Ronald Reagan's election to the presidency in 1981, just as public TV was becoming a viable alternative to commercial television, occasioned renewed political opposition. During the Reagan years public television's budget was reduced to the extent that some stations came to believe they could only survive by airing commercials. Reagan's drastic budget cuts resulted in FCC approval for experimentation with a form of commercial advertising on public television, though this was termed "enhanced underwriting," and meant that "logos or slogans that identify—but do not promote or compare—trade names, and product and service listings" were now permissible on public television, and have remained so.

In the late 1980s and 1990s PBS continued to produce well-received documentaries such as *The Civil War* and *Vietnam: A Television History*, the latter of which, for conservative viewers, perhaps verified suspicions of PBS's long-standing liberal and even leftist tendencies. In 1992, public television, along with such organizations as the National Endowment for the Arts, came under attack from a coalition of conservative groups led by the Heritage Foundation. The attack was timed to a period when Congress was to consider the reauthorization of public broadcast funding, and the Heritage Foundation simultaneously distributed "Making Public Television Public," a widely quoted report, which, contrary to its title, actually called for the privatization of public television. (One concept espoused was the selling of the Corporation for Public Broadcasting to the private sector, which, the report argued, would "clean up the public television mess.") The outcome, at least as William Hoynes puts it in his book, *Public Television for Sale,* "in the short run," was that a Democratic-controlled Congress passed the reauthorization bill, but with some qualifications. To many the 1992 debate was merely a reprise of ground covered in the Nixon and Reagan years, albeit, as Hoynes also points out, in a "post-cold war climate that celebrated the market in a quasi-religious manner."

On a more mundane level, the frequent periods of air time devoted to lengthy, although necessary, fund-raising campaigns that occur regularly on all public television and radio stations throughout the year sometimes chafe at even the most dedicated supporters of regional PBS. Some of these campaigns, however, also offer audience members the opportunity to appear "on the air" as the vital phone-answering staff for the call-ins from donors, or to see their friends and neighbors become temporary TV personalities on their favorite PBS channel in a kind of throw-back to the older and more audience-friendly days of early local and regional television.

E. B. White once commented on the television medium: "I think television should be the counterpart of the literary essay, should arouse our dreams, satisfy our hunger for beauty, take us on journeys, enable us to participate in events, present great drama and music, explore the sea and the sky and the woods and the hills. It should be our Lyceum, our Chautauqua, our Minsky's, and our Camelot. It should state and clarify the social dilemma and the political pickle." While still far from perfect, and while still both evolving and often in harm's way, public television has come the closest of anything yet in the pervasive and much maligned medium in attempting to fulfill White's ideals.

—Ross Care

FURTHER READING:

Brown, Les. *Les Brown's Encyclopedia of Television.* 3rd Edition. Detroit, Visible Ink, 1992.

Hoynes, William. *Public Television for Sale: Media, the Market, and the Public Sphere.* Boulder, Colorado, Westview Press, 1994.

Macy, John W., Jr. *To Irrigate a Wasteland: The Struggle to Shape a Public Television System in the United States.* Berkeley, University of California Press, 1974.

Miller, Carolyn Handler. *Illustrated T.V. Dictionary.* New York, Harvery House, 1980.

Puente, Tito (1923—)

No individual performer has contributed more to the popularity of Latin music in the United States than the legendary Tito Puente. A musician, arranger, composer, bandleader, and four-time Grammy winner, the internationally acclaimed "King of Latin Music" has moved audiences around the world to the beat of *cha-cha-chas, mambos,* and *pachangas.* Best known as a virtuoso of the timbales, Puente is also an accomplished pianist with a degree from the prestigious Juilliard School of Music. Puente's remarkable career to date has spanned nearly sixty years and produced over one hundred albums. He has been featured in numerous television sitcoms, commercials, music shows, and motion pictures (including *Radio Days* and *The Mambo Kings Play Songs of Love*). The recipient of the Smithsonian Medal and three honorary doctorates, Puente has been nominated eight times for Grammy awards (more than any Latin music artist). His name, which means "bridge" in Spanish, truly captures his achievement—for Puente's music reaches across generational, national, and racial boundaries.

Born April 20, 1923, in New York City to Puerto Rican parents, Ernesto Antonio Puente, Jr., grew up in Spanish Harlem to the sounds of Afro-Cuban and jazz music. By 1949, the successful fusion of these

Tito Puente

influences produced one of his first crossover hit songs, "Abaniquito," and fueled the mambo craze of the 1950s. As one of the famed mambo kings of the era, Puente consistently earned top billing at New York's Palladium Ballroom, a *nuyorican* club that served as the cradle of what is now called "salsa." Jazz greats such as Dizzy Gillespie, Charlie Parker, and Woody Herman often showed up to jam with the mostly Cuban and Puerto Rican musicians appearing nightly at the Palladium. Always in tune with the tempo of his day, Puente contributed to the various Latin music trends of the 1950s and 1960s, first appealing to the early popularity of the cha cha cha, then releasing several hits in the pachanga style that became the rage. In the late 1960s, when an R&B/Latin fusion called *boogaloo* emerged as the latest dance music craze, Puente kept up with the times and obliged his audiences, despite his professed dislike of the form. During those years, Puente recorded and performed with numerous other Latin music stars, including the "Queen of Salsa" Celia Cruz, La Lupe, Santos Colon, Machito, Mongo Santamaria, Mario Bauza, and Xavier Cugat. He also played with Gillespie and would pay tribute to the jazz master in a 1994 concert event at the Apollo Theatre. Puente's "Oye Como Va" and "Para los Rumberos," first recorded in the early 1960s, were later adapted and released by Carlos Santana, introducing audiences in the 1970s to a new synthesis of rock and Latin music. The overwhelming popularity of Santana's remakes led to a joint concert in 1977 and revitalized an interest in Latin music among a new generation of concert-goers. By 1979, when President Jimmy Carter invited him to play at the White House in honor of Hispanic Heritage month, Puente had achieved world-class status.

Puente's musical talent and warm, outgoing personality have made him a favorite among young and old. He has been featured on the popular television sitcom the *Bill Cosby Show,* in a Coca-Cola commercial, and even a 1995 episode of *The Simpsons.* Burger King has used Puente's tune "I Like It like That" in their ads, and he has hosted his own show on Spanish-language television. At the closing ceremony following the 1996 Olympic games in Atlanta, Puente joined B. B. King, Wynton Marsalis, Stevie Wonder, and Gloria Estefan in an extraordinary finale. According to *Time* correspondent Mark Coatney, the group "whipped up an ever-growing conga line that threatened to spill into the streets." Puente's joyous participation in this event helped to rekindle everyone's spirits and proved that Latin music had truly achieved international recognition.

—Myra Mendible

FURTHER READING:

Contemporary Musicians: Profiles of the People in Music. Detroit, Gale Research, 1995.

Loza, Steven Joseph. *Tito Puente and the Making of Latin Music.* Urbana, University of Illinois Press, 1999.

Pulp Fiction

Crime drama is given stylish and original treatment in Quentin Tarantino's 1994 film *Pulp Fiction.* In his take on the genre there is an easy interplay between the mundane and the brutal. Told with visual panache and unconventional dialogue, three stories of the Los Angeles underworld interweave in a complex structure.

The tales were written separately, with two of them written years before the film was conceived. In the first story, two professional hitmen, Jules and Vincent, kill some young men who have stolen a brief case containing something of great beauty and value from gang boss Marcellus Wallace. The routine job becomes a life-changing incident for Jules when one of the young men shoots repeatedly at Jules and Vincent from across the small room, but every shot misses. Jules takes this "miracle" as a sign from God. The job is further complicated when Vincent creates a literal and figurative mess by accidentally blowing their informant's brains out in the back seat of the car. The second story begins when Marcellus Wallace asks Vincent to take his wife Mia out and show her a good time while he is away. After dinner and a dance contest, Vincent and Mia return to the Wallace home where Mia overdoses on Vincent's powerful heroin and almost dies. In the third story, Marcellus Wallace pays an aging fighter, Butch, to take a dive. Instead, Butch wins the fight and attempts to flee the country before Wallace can have him killed. In addition to these three stories, the film begins and ends with a framing incident of a husband and wife team of small-time crooks deciding to hold up the restaurant where Jules and Vincent are having breakfast. The incident takes place chronologically between stories one and two.

The seemingly unrelated stories all tie together in a highly unconventional plot. The structure of the film is not only non-chronological, but there are also repeated actions and parallel actions. A single viewing of the film is a powerful experience, but subsequent viewings are also rewarding, as more of the subtleties and complexities of the film become apparent. It often takes more than one viewing to become comfortable with the film's blending of the horrifying and the oddly funny; not every viewer is prepared to find dark humor in scenes that involve scooping skull fragments off of the upholstery, homosexual rape, or a family heirloom hidden for years in a rectum. The film is an unpredictable mix of the lurid and the absurd, told in dialogue that is alternately hip, mundane, or intriguingly odd.

The dialogue in *Pulp Fiction* does more than simply advance the plot. Tarantino avoids the typical gangster stereotypes by giving his thugs distinctive speech patterns and quirky conversations that bring the characters to life. No two characters in the film speak alike. Mr. Wolf, the professional problem-solver who comes in to take care of Vincent and Jules's mess, speaks in clipped, efficient sentences. Jules freely spices his erudite vocabulary with the harshest profanity, and just before putting a bullet into his target he likes to give a dramatic and frightening recitation of Ezekiel 25:17. Although the dialogue often meanders, just like real conversation, it is still very memorable. On the way to make the hit on the college boys, Vincent explains to Jules that at the Paris McDonalds a Quarter-pounder is called a Royale with cheese. It is just the type of inane conversation that goes on between two co-workers passing the time during the morning commute.

Pulp Fiction's style and originality did not go unnoticed in the film community. At the Cannes Film Festival the film won the Palm d'Or. *Pulp Fiction* revitalized the career of John Travolta, making him the hottest property in Hollywood for the next several years. Travolta garnered Academy Award, Golden Globe, and Screen Actors Guild nominations for Best Actor. The film was nominated for seven Academy Awards, including Best Picture, but only Roger Avary and Quentin Tarantino won for Best Original Screenplay. *Pulp Fiction* established Quentin Tarantino as a major player in Hollywood.

—Randy Duncan

FURTHER READING:

Clarkson, Wensley. *Quentin Tarantino: Shooting from the Hip.* Woodstock, New York, Overlook Press, 1995.

Dawson, Jeff. *Quentin Tarantino: The Cinema of Cool.* New York, Applause, 1997.

Jami, Bernard. *Quentin Tarantino: The Man and His Movies.* New York, HarperPerennial, 1995.

Woods, Paul. *King Pulp: The Wild World of Quentin Tarantino.* Plexus, 1998.

Pulp Magazines

Pulp magazines were a cheap form of popular entertainment that emerged just before the dawn of the twentieth century, grew to immense popularity during the 1930s, and withered away by the early 1950s. Sold for 10 to 25 cents each and chocked full of sensational action, the pulps appealed primarily to the middle class and the educated lower class, but drew avid readers from every strata of society. As pulp publisher Henry Steeger noted in the preface to Tony Goodstone's *The Pulps*, "the names of Harry Truman, President of the United States, and Al Capone, lowest figure of the underworld, graced our subscription lists at the same time." Beneath the garish and lurid covers, the rough-edged pages (made from the cheapest wood-pulp) were often filled with hastily written purple prose. Yet, a few of the pulp magazines contained genuinely fine writing, and many of them contained crude, but powerful storytelling that shaped

American popular culture. The pulps offered a proving ground for some of America's most popular authors, and introduced some of the world's best known fictional heroes.

The pulp magazines grew out of a nineteenth-century tradition of stories for the masses that began with religious chapbooks that warned against "the pernicious effects of dram drinking" and other vices. These small paperbacks were peddled on street corners by hawkers (or chapmen). Although meant to be cautionary tales, some buyers no doubt read these stories of innocent young girls seduced into a life of alcohol and prostitution more for titillation than for moral inspiration. The chapbooks created an appetite for fiction that was satisfied for a time by serialized tales in the weekly story papers that emerged mid-century. In 1860, the publishing house of Beadle & Adams began publishing entire novels in a small paperback format that became known as a dime novel (although many of them actually sold for five cents). Once the format proved successful, Street & Smith, which had been in the weekly fiction business since the 1850s, started their own dime novel line. Street & Smith soon had two very popular dime novel series that would have direct links to the pulps. *Nick Carter Weekly* featured a clean-cut young detective, by the same name, who was a master of disguise. Edward Zane Carroll Judson, writing under the Ned Buntline pen name, elaborated on the exploits of the real-life William Cody in *Buffalo Bill Weekly.* However, the story papers and "nickel weeklies" did not disappear, and at the end of the nineteenth century sensational popular fiction existed in a variety of formats.

Frank A. Munsey is generally considered the father of the pulp magazines. In 1882, he launched *Golden Argosy,* a weekly story magazine for children. Over the next decade, Munsey modified the magazine in a number of ways. He changed the content to all fiction, targeted it for an older audience, switched to cheap wood-pulp paper and shortened the name. By 1896, Munsey had transformed his newly named *Argosy* into the first pulp magazine. Stephen Crane was one of the early contributors to *Argosy.* As the turn of the century approached, *Argosy* was selling half a million copies a month. In 1905, Munsey added *The All-Story Magazine,* followed by *Cavalier Weekly* in 1908. With the publication of the 1912 story "Under the Moons of Mars," *All-Story* introduced Edgar Rice Burroughs, whose work insured the popularity of the pulps and left an indelible mark on popular culture. Later that same year, *All-Story* published Burroughs' "Tarzan of the Apes." The following year Burroughs began his Pellucidar series. After the *All-Story* editor repeatedly quibbled about rate of payment and rejected the sequel to the first Tarzan story, Burroughs began sending his work to other pulp magazines. *All-Story* fell on hard times and was combined first with *Cavalier* and then with *Argosy.* In its 1919 incarnation as *All-Story Weekly,* the magazine published Johnston McCulley's first Zorro story, "The Curse of Capistrano." Munsey's magazines were creating popular culture icons, but they were also facing stiff market competition.

Once again, Street & Smith shifted to a format pioneered by other publishers and soon dominated the field. They began with *Popular Magazine* in 1903 and *Top Notch* in 1910. Street & Smith steadily expanded their offerings until they were one of the largest and most successful pulp magazine publishers. Soon, dozens of other publishers were trying to copy their success. At the end of World War I, only a few dozen pulps were being published. In the midst of the Great Depression there would be several hundred.

By the 1920s, the general interest or family pulp gave way to the specialized pulp. At the height of the pulps in the 1930s, there seemed

A collection of pulp magazines.

to be a magazine for every interest: horror, sports, the exploitative "spicy" pulps, gangsters, romance, cowboys, trains, and even a magazine titled *Zeppelin Stories.* Because profit margins were small, publishers constantly shuffled their offerings and followed new trends. If a title started to lose readers, they dropped it immediately and tried a new genre. The history of the pulps is littered with many esoteric and short-lived magazines.

Street & Smith created the first successful specialized pulp magazine in 1915 when they converted their dime novel *Nick Carter Weekly* into the pulp magazine *Detective Story Magazine* (which was supposedly edited by "Nick Carter"). Police sleuths and private detectives had been a staple in other popular fiction formats and at first the pulps offered nothing new in this genre. Then, in 1920, H. L. Mencken and George Jean Nathan (who published pulps only to subsidize their more literary magazine, *The Smart Set*) began *The Black Mask.* At first, the magazine published general adventure fiction. Within a few years, a distinctive style began to emerge. First, there was Carroll John Daly's brutally tough Race Williams. Next, there was Dashiell Hammett's world-weary and often violent Continental Op. Employing terse dialogue, nuanced characters, and realistic settings, Hammett began to develop the new style of detective story that would become known as hard-boiled fiction. When Joseph T. Shaw took over as editor in 1926, he sought out more writers who

could produce work in the Hammett tradition. In 1933, Shaw made his greatest find, and published "Blackmailers Don't Shoot," the first work of detective fiction by Raymond Chandler. Chandler's tough guys, who followed their own code and dealt their own justice in a harsh world, helped define hard-boiled fiction.

Black Mask was the most significant of the detective pulps, but it was certainly not the only entry in the field. The "Black Mask School" was perpetuated, and even refined, in the pages of *Detective Fiction Weekly, Dime Detective, Thrilling Detective, Ten Detective Aces,* and others. The detective pulps also launched many significant authors in addition to Hammett and Chandler. Erle Stanley Gardner was one of the most prolific and popular of the detective pulp writers. John D. MacDonald and Lawrence Treat had stories published in the waning days of the detective and mystery pulps. As with most genres, the detective pulps had their "spicy" versions that mixed a healthy dose of sex with the detection. Most notable of these was *Spicy Detective Stories,* which often featured the erotic adventures of Hollywood private eye Dan Turner, written by Robert Leslie Bellem. A totally different tradition in detective fiction, the "weird menace," began in *Dime Mystery Magazine.* With covers that often combined the ghoulish and the sadistic, *Dime Mystery* and its spawn offered stories of "impossible" crimes that seemed to be caused by the supernatural, but were eventually revealed by the detective to have a rational solution and a human culprit (oddly enough, the *Scooby Doo* cartoons seem to be a direct descendent of this sub-genre).

The Western, a staple of the dime novels, came to pulp magazines when Street & Smith converted their *Buffalo Bill Weekly* dime novel series into *Western Story Magazine.* With a loyal audience already existing for tales of gunfights, Indian wars, and hairbreadth escapes, the leading Western pulps, such as *Far West, Western Story,* and *Ranch Romances,* easily sold 20 million copies per month. Gradually, the pulp Westerns deviated from the blood-and-thunder style of the dime novels as more pulp writers began to emulate the more restrained and polished style of best-selling Western novelists such as Owen Wister and Zane Grey (who had a number of his novels serialized in the pulps). One of the new breed of Western writers who got their start in the pulps was Louis L'Amour. In creating characters such as Hondo, L'Amour began to crystalize the Western hero. However, the most popular author of pulp Westerns was Frederick Faust, who wrote under numerous pseudonyms, but became best known as Max Brand. While some Western pulp writers strove for gritty realism, Brand elevated the cowboy of the Western pulps to a figure of mythic proportions that could stand shoulder-to-shoulder in the popular culture pantheon with the fantastic heroes of the adventure or single character pulps.

Science fiction, more than any other popular genre, owes a great debt to the pulp magazines. Jules Verne, H. G. Wells, and others had planted the seeds in the previous century, but the true golden age of science fiction flowered in the pulp magazines of the 1920s and 1930s. The "scientific romances" of Edgar Rice Burroughs and his imitators had been appearing in pulp magazines for over a decade, but it was not until an immigrant with a love of science got into publishing that the pulps provided an outlet for true science fiction. Hugo Gernsback immigrated to the United States from Luxembourg in 1904 and immediately became involved with the new science of radio. Gernsback began publishing a magazine, *Modern Electronic,* devoted to his new interest. By 1919 Gernsback had expanded the scope of his magazine and changed the name to *Science and Inventions.* He had also begun including stories of what he called "scientifiction." In 1923, he produced an all-scientifiction issue with six stories, and reader response was enthusiastic.

In 1926, Gernsback published *Amazing Stories,* the first magazine devoted solely to science fiction. While it was not until 1933— and after a change of publishers—that the magazine became standard pulp size, *Amazing Stories* is still considered the first science-fiction pulp. By August of 1928, Gernsback's magazine was publishing landmark science-fiction novels such as E.E. "Doc" Smith's first installment of the Skylark series and Philip Francis Nolan's "Armageddon, 2419 A.D.," the first Anthony "Buck" Rogers story. Gernsback did more than anyone to establish science fiction as a distinct genre, and earned his title as the "father of science fiction." Yet, much of what *Amazing* published tended toward space opera, and Gernsback never quite realized the dream of teaching readers hard science through the stories in his magazine. It was John W. Campbell, editor of *Astounding Stories* (begun in 1930) who truly championed hard science, and issued in the golden age of science fiction. Campbell demanded high-quality fiction based on believable extrapolations of hard science. Campbell also discovered and nurtured many of the authors who would set the standards for science-fiction writing, including Isaac Asimov, Arthur C. Clarke, Lester del Rey, and Robert Heinlein. There were plenty of other science-fiction pulps on the stands over the years, but it was *Amazing Stories* and *Astounding Stories* that defined the future of the genre.

Weird Tales, launched in 1923, was aptly subtitled "The Unique Magazine," and warrants consideration in a category all by itself. The magazine provided an outlet for some of the earliest and most outré work of Clark Ashton Smith, Robert Bloch, Ray Bradbury, Fritz Lieber, and other notable authors. Tennessee Williams' first published work, "The Vengeance of Nitocris," was in *Weird Tales.* However, the writers who did the most to sustain the magazine during its first decade were H. P. Lovecraft and Robert E. Howard. Lovecraft specialized in tales of slithering ancient horrors. Lovecraft's most enduring contributions are his creation of the Cthulhu Mythos, about the indescribably ancient and horrific beings that exist in the dark infinity outside humankind's perception, and the fictional grimoire of forbidden lore, the Necronomicon. In relentlessly vigorous prose, Howard chronicled the adventures of many a brawny and brutal hero, but his best-known creation is Conan of Cimmeria. Although never a consistently profitable magazine, *Weird Tales* was published for 279 issues and was one of the last pulps to grace the newsstands when it finally ceased publication in 1954. Other pulps, such as *Strange Tales, Unknown,* and *Fantastic Adventures,* emerged to compete with *Weird Tales* in the fantasy market, but none managed to match the wonderful strangeness of the original.

The greatest boon to pulp magazine sales was the advent of the single-character pulps, sometimes referred to as the "hero pulps." Recurring heroes such as Tarzan and Zorro had been appearing in various pulp magazines for years, but in 1931 Street & Smith published *The Shadow, A Detective Magazine,* and The Shadow became the first character to appear in a magazine created specifically for his adventures. It did not take long for the Shadow's success to be noticed, and the next wave of characters seemed to hit all at once. *The Phantom Detective, Doc Savage, G-8 and His Battle Aces,* and *The Spider,* the four longest-running hero pulps next to *The Shadow,* all appeared in 1933. These and other hero pulp characters had a direct influence on the superhero comic books that appeared in the late 1930s and early 1940s. Some of the Superman mythos seems to come directly from Doc Savage. To begin with, they are both named Clark. Each hero has a female cousin nearly as remarkable as himself, and each has a secret arctic getaway referred to as a Fortress of Solitude. And while Doc Savage had no true powers, he was often referred to in the stories and in advertisements as a superman. Perhaps no superhero has inherited more from his pulp ancestors than the Batman. His costume and vigilante crusade are reminiscent of Zorro. His *modus operandi* of prowling the night and striking fear in criminals is borrowed from the Shadow. And like Doc Savage, The Batman is a normal human who has, through years of hard work, trained his mind and body to perfection. The immense popularity of progeny, such as Superman and the Batman, is one of the factors that led to the demise of the pulps.

A number of forces converged to bring the pulp magazines to an end. By the early 1940s they faced stiff competition from comic books. Not only were the comic-book heroes flashier, but a number of pulp publishers converted to comic books when the new medium proved profitable. Then, World War II brought about paper shortages. In spite of this, a new format, the paperback book, emerged offering pulp-type content, with authors like Micky Spillane, at the same price and in a more convenient format. After the war, paperback publishing boomed and pulp magazines faded away. By the middle of the following decade, all of the pulps were gone. A few of the science-fiction and mystery titles continued in digest format. The tradition of the hero pulps lives on in comic books and paperback adventure series.

As products, the pulps proved ephemeral. Of the thousands of different magazines and characters that existed, most have been forgotten by everyone except a handful of collectors and historians. More copies of the cheaply made magazines crumble to dust each day, yet they have shaped every genre of popular fiction. Their purple blood runs in the veins of every hero of film, television, and paperbacks. The pulp magazines have proven to be the wellspring of the American mythology.

—Randy Duncan

FURTHER READING:

del Rey, Lester. *The World of Science Fiction: 1926-1976 The History of a Subculture.* New York, Ballantine Books, 1979.

Goodstone, Tony. *The Pulps: Fifty Years of American Popular Culture.* New York, Bonanza Books, 1970.

Goulart, Ron. *An Informal History of the Pulp Magazine.* New York, Ace Books, 1973.

———. *The Dime Detectives.* New York, Mysterious Press, 1988.

Sampson, Robert. *Deadly Excitements: Shadows and Phantoms.* Bowling Green, Ohio, Bowling Green State University Popular Press, 1989.

The Punisher

The Punisher is a superhero character appearing in Marvel comic books. Created in 1974 by Gerry Conway, the Punisher is a costumed vigilante—something of a comic-book answer to *Death Wish.* He is Frank Castle, a Vietnam veteran who embarks on a solemn war against crime after his family is murdered by gangsters. Clad in a black costume emblazoned with a skull-and-crossbones, he punishes the guilty whom the law is either unable or unwilling to convict. After a decade as a recurring character in various Marvel titles, the Punisher won his own series in 1985. The vigilante superhero found a large and receptive audience at the height of the Reagan-Rambo era, and became one of the most popular comic books of the late 1980s and early 1990s.

—Bradford Wright

FURTHER READING:

Daniels, Les. *Marvel: Five Fabulous Decades of the World's Greatest Comics.* New York, Harry N. Abrams, 1991.

Punk

In the mid-to-late 1970s a radical youth culture called punk emerged out of the larger rock 'n' roll scene, and developed its own music, attire, and ideology. The Sex Pistols are the best known of the punk bands; their music, like all punk rock, was aggressive, fast, and loud. Punk attire is characterized by dark clothes, outlandish costumes and ornamentation such as colored hair and earrings and bracelets made from assembled items (the quintessential punk earring was a safety pin). Punk ideology is explicitly at odds with mainstream society and rails against contemporary civilization, which is seen as sterile and banal. Punk is heavily critical of existing political, economic, and cultural institutions, yet is ambivalent about creating alternatives.

The earliest forms of punk rock developed in the United States. The Velvet Underground's minimalist music and commentaries about life outside mainstream society inspired a number of bands, but the first group to be considered a punk rock band was the Ramones. Formed in 1974, the Ramones gained a following around New York City by stripping rock down to its bare essentials and playing with near-anarchic energy. Their first album, *Ramones* (1976) featured a string of songs, most shorter than two minutes, including "Blitzkrieg Bop" and "Now I Wanna Sniff Some Glue." The album became a minor hit in the U.S. and a major hit in England, where a number of bands began to pick up on the energetic rock played by the Ramones and fellow New York-bands the Stooges and the New York Dolls that played at clubs like Max's Kansas City and CBGB's. While punk was a minor sensation in the United States, it gained real popularity in the United Kingdom. The first British punk band was the Sex Pistols, which in the three short years of its existence largely created the ideal of the punk rock band.

The Sex Pistols, led by singer Johnny Rotten (formerly John Lydon) and bassist Sid Vicious and managed by Malcolm McLaren, took the music scene by storm when they began playing in 1976, singing about anarchy, abortion, and fascism in some of the most violent live shows and recordings ever heard. The band alienated several recording labels and frightened the establishment, but they also encouraged the rapid growth of the punk scene in England and sparked the creation of such bands as the Clash, the Damned, the Buzzcocks, and others.

Punk made a very visible, shocking, public display. However, with the drug-related death of Sex Pistols' bass player Sid Vicious in 1979 and the demise of several punk bands, some proclaimed that punk was a short-lived fad that had come to an end. The rumors of punk's death were unfounded, and many bands set about to defend the true meaning of punk and extend its musical influence. The most direct development from early punk is the hardcore punk movement that developed during the 1980s, foremost in the United States, but also in England, France, Italy, and other countries, with bands like the Dead Kennedys, Social Distortion, the Misfits, and Upright Citizens. Since the 1980s there have been any number of bands that have echoed the influence of punk, including Hüsker Dü, the Replacements, Soul Asylum, Green Day, Sonic Youth, and the Minutemen, among others. Though the era of punk rock is generally considered to be the years between 1975 and 1980, the punk ethos lives on.

Musically, rock 'n' roll provided an important foundation for punk, as youths who came of age in the 1970s and 1980s were well acquainted with rock bands like the Beatles, the Rolling Stones, and Led Zeppelin. Many punk bands learned music by playing other people's songs and it was commonplace among young punks, and even well-known bands, to release cover songs. The Dickies, for example, played fast but melodic versions of Led Zeppelin's "Communication Breakdown" and the Moody Blues' "Nights in White Satin." Bands often performed cover versions of older songs that had historical significance or that made a particularly salient political point. Generation X, for example, performed a cover version of John Lennon's "Gimme Some Truth." While cover songs often signaled respect for past music, cover songs could also represent an ironic

Seminal punk rock group, the Sex Pistols

comment on or critique of rock and roll. Although cover songs were common, punk ideology derided cover bands that did not play original songs for a lack of creativity.

Despite the powerful influence of rock, punk music differs significantly from its predecessor. Punk songs are generally short, fast, and loud, and place increased emphasis on distorted guitars. Many punk bands use ''power'' or bar chords, and speed is often emphasized over intricacy. The musical skills of punk musicians are often rudimentary and this lack of virtuosity is connected to an ideology that anyone can write and play songs. Fairly simple songs with basic four-four drum beats are common and many punk bands form with friends picking up instruments and learning as they play. Punk's minimalist three-chord approach and shouted vocals stand in clear opposition to the melodic singing of earlier styles.

Punk music developed ''scenes'' centered on bands, clubs, and fans in a particular area, such as Manchester and London, England. The Damned, Stiff Little Fingers, the Jam, and Sham 69 were particularly influential, as were the Gang of Four, the Mekons, and the Delta 5 from Leeds, England. In the United States, the Los Angeles, California, scene produced such bands as Black Flag, Fear, the Germs, X, and the Circle Jerks. Two documentaries—*The Decline of*

Western Civilization (1981) and *Another State of Mind* (1984)— document the lives of various L.A. punk bands both on stage and off. The Dead Kennedys (San Francisco), the Teen Idols, State of Alert (S.O.A.), and the Bad Brains (all Washington, D.C.), and Hüsker Dü (Minneapolis) were all especially important early punk bands.

Punk was always about more than music, however. For both fans and musicians punk amounted to a kind of lifestyle. From the beginning, punk haircuts and clothing stood in stark contrast to the appearance of rock 'n' rollers. As Dick Hebdige describes, punks rebelled by wearing ripped clothing, black leather, and assembling cultural icons as decoration. Mohawk haircuts, dyed hair, or extreme-ly short cropped haircuts distinguished punks from the typically long-haired rockers. Hardcore attire followed directly from punk, although it tended to be more subdued. Dark clothes, black leather jackets, ripped jeans, sneakers, or boots (especially Doc Martens) were common; however, the outlandish costumes of punk—bright clothes and colored hair—were often toned down. Many hardcore fans simply wear jeans, a tee-shirt (often with a band insignia), and sneakers. In some sense this was a rebellion against the mainstream cooptation of punk dress but it was also an attempt to get beyond an anti-fashion style that was not only a lot of work, but made punks subject to verbal, and occasionally physical, harassment. Less dramatic attire allowed hardcore punks to move more easily between mainstream and alternative cultures. Thus hardcore, while characterized by a louder and more aggressive music, began a tendency back to more mainstream attire.

Punk has offered a radical critique of society and has been noted for its unique ideological characteristics; however, punk has not presented a coherent philosophy but rather a series of related critiques. Punks have been particularly hostile to authority and questioned rules and rulemakers. Rather than focussing simply on politics in the conventional sense, punk challenged the patterns and norms of contemporary social relations. As Dick Hebdige writes, punk has ''signified chaos at every level.'' The politics of everyday life were most central to punk and lyrics question social rules and relationships. Many lyrics are centered on love, relationships, jobs, and so on, but punks put a radical spin on such issues. Punks have aimed to shock and offend and are particularly anti-romantic in their sentiments. Love is frequently referred to only in sexual terms and often quite graphically, as in the Dead Boys' ''Caught with the Meat in Your Mouth.'' Some punks have used Nazi images and ornaments in their outfits, and have made callous reference to such tragedies as the Holocaust in such songs as ''Belsen Was a Gas.'' However, such practices generally reflect an attempt to use images in an ironic sense to question conventional meanings. Furthermore, punks have been by and large anti-Nazi and anti-fascist and have frequently espoused left-wing and humanitarian concerns.

Political issues have been important for many in the hardcore punk scene as well. War, social inequality, and capitalism are common topics of punk lyrics. *Maximum Rock and Roll,* one of the foremost hardcore fanzines, covers these and other topics in its columns, letters, and interviews. Leftist, anarchist, and communist leanings are prevalent as punks express concerns about politics, the military, censorship, corporate crime, and other issues. The band Millions of Dead Cops (MDC) has attacked government and police authority. MDC also railed against corporate capitalism, calling McDonald's hamburgers ''corporate death burgers.'' While a wide range of political views have emerged from the hardcore movement, most of these political statements were rudimentary, as few had worked out the complexities of the many issues they discussed. Typical of a punk political critique was a catch phrase such as ''Reagan sucks.''

Punk has tended to be very cynical regarding political activism, and emphasizes chaos rather than concerted action. While for some punks this has meant an attempt to avoid politics or just to have fun, for others this critique meant an emphasis on social or personal politics rather than large-scale political concerns. Many emphasize personal politics and promote difference as a value; the Big Boys sang: ''I want to be different, I want to make you see, I want to make you wonder is it you or is it me?'' Adherence to the local scene for its own sake is important and punks have tried to establish a core set of values that set punk off from mainstream society. Bands like Reagan Youth, Minor Threat, Youth of Today, and Youth Brigade promote youth power as an ideology opposed to conventional adult married and working life.

Anger is common in punk lyrics. Henry Rollins of Black Flag yelled: ''Everybody just get away/I'm gonna boil over inside today/ they say things are gonna get better/all I know is they fucking better.'' Void growled: ''I'm so fucking filled with hate/ I want to decapitate.'' Boredom is also a common complaint, as Tony of the Adolescents sang: ''We're just the wrecking crew/bored boys with nothing to do.''

Punks launched critiques against hippies and consumerist yuppies alike: the Teen Idles sang ''Deadhead deadhead, take another toke/ deadhead, you're a fucking joke.'' ''Die yuppie scum'' was also a common punk mantra.

While many punks were critical of ''hippie burnouts,'' drug use was and is an element of punk culture and a symbol of punk excess. Punk lore has tended to glorify some of the more outrageous events that transpired under the influence of drugs. Scott Asheton, in *Please Kill Me,* recounts a story about Iggy Pop: ''He was walking down the street and he finally just collapsed. It was from massive amounts of drugs—I mean, you can't take acid and Quaaludes at the same time, it just doesn't work.'' Similarly, in *Please Kill Me,* one person describes the night of the death of Nancy Spungen:

> Nancy was stoned. She was stoned and she was bragging. She's talking in that fucking cockney accent, you know, being Mrs. Sid Vicious. But it wasn't much of a party because Sid was passed out. Sid did not look like he was going to get up. He wasn't moving.
> I said, ''What's wrong with Sid?''
> Someone said, ''Oh, he just ate about thirty Tuinals.''
> I said, ''Oh, he's going to be fun tonight.''

The deaths of Sid Vicious and Nancy Spungen (the subject of the movie *Sid and Nancy,* 1986) were particularly vivid reminders of the presence of drug use and violence in the punk scene. Many other drug-related deaths occurred among punks, particularly in connection with heroin use.

However, in response to frequent cases of addiction and overdose, and in the face of legal restrictions, some punks rejected the use of drugs. The Washington, D.C., straight-edge scene, opposed to drinking, drugs, and casual sex, developed alongside the refusal of clubowners to let underage kids into shows. As a compromise, underage kids were allowed in but were marked with X's on their hands to signify that they couldn't buy alcohol. The kids took this would-be stigma and turned it into a symbol of positive self-identification.

Punk identity has been strengthened by the social networks that developed to organize concerts, start 'zines, and spread ideas. Bands and fans established ties across the country (as well as through much of the world) through which they could share common interests, book shows, or find a needed place to sleep. Many punk musicians, ignored by major record labels, produced their own music on independent labels like Dischord, SST, Touch and Go, and SubPop. Punk was particularly critical of the rock and roll establishment. While rock began as a non-conformist youth culture, punks voiced opposition to the cult of rock stardom and the large stadium concerts that clearly separate the audience from musicians. Punk, by contrast, is premised on the idea that anyone can start a band. Punks have also been critical of major record labels and large–scale industry in general and espoused a ''Do-It-Yourself'' (D.I.Y.) philosophy that emphasizes independent actions and personal creativity.

Centered around punk rock music, the punk movement was an important development in the youth culture of the late 1970s and it remained an identifiable element in youth culture in the late 1990s. Punk was unique for its aggressive and fast musical style, its purposefully shocking visual impact, and its ideological emphasis on chaos, nonconformity, and radical criticism. Punk rock developed as an ideological, musical, and stylistic critique of modern society, and while it is a movement that may be self-limiting in its effectiveness in reaching out to other groups, it has nonetheless had a powerful influence on youth cultures, in particular the emergence of alternative rock and grunge.

—Perry Grossman

FURTHER READING:

Frith, Simon. *Sound Effects: Youth, Leisure, and the Politics of Rock 'n' Roll*. New York, Pantheon Books, 1981.

Hebdige, Dick. *Subculture: The Meaning of Style*. London, Routledge, 1991.

Herman, Andrew. "You're in Suspicion: Punk and the Secret Passion Play of White Noise." *Canadian Journal of Political and Social Theory*. Vol. 14, 1990, 47-67.

Heylin, Clinton. *From the Velvets to the Voidoids: A Pre-Punk History for a Post-Punk World*. New York, Penguin, 1993.

Laing, Dave. *One-Chord Wonders: Power and Meaning in Punk Rock*. Philadelphia, Open University Press, 1985.

Marcus, Greil. *Lipstick Traces: A Secret History of the Twentieth Century*. Cambridge, Cambridge University Press, 1989.

McNeil, Legs, and Gillian McCain. *Please Kill Me: The Uncensored Oral History of Punk*. New York, Grove Press, 1996.

Savage, John. *England's Dreaming: Anarchy, Sex Pistols, Punk Rock, and Beyond*. New York, St. Martin's Press, 1992.

Pynchon, Thomas (1937—)

Though a difficult literary author who has written only five novels in 35 years, Thomas Pynchon has remained a figure who has captured the imagination of a wider public and has avoided the academic and literary communities who revere him. His use of popular culture in his fiction, along with other such "unliterary" subjects as science, have had a highly influential effect on modern fiction. Pynchon, however, is also known to many who have never read his work as an author who has maintained an unheard of level of anonymity in a society that thrives on self-promotion.

Thomas Pynchon was born on May 8, 1937 in Glen Cove, Long Island, New York, into a prosperous family with an American heritage dating back to the early seventeenth century. He studied at Cornell University, served a two-year stint in the Navy, and worked in Seattle for Boeing Aircraft Corporation. From the late 1950s to the early 1960s he published a number of short stories and began work on his first novel, *V.*, published in 1963. *The Crying of Lot 49* was published in 1966 and when *Gravity's Rainbow* came out in 1973, it was selected by the judges for the Pulitzer Prize in literature. They were overruled, however, by the Pulitzer advisory board whose members called the sprawling and bawdy book, with a cast of over 400 characters, "unreadable," "turgid," "overwritten," and "obscene." In 1990 the much awaited *Vineland* came out to mixed reviews but the reception of *Mason & Dixon* (1997) appeared to be more positive.

Pynchon's work has received wide acclaim amongst the literary media and the academic fraternity, but also amongst readers outside these fields drawn towards his use of science and philosophy and his utilization of science fiction and other popular genres. Over his career, his very dense, extensively researched prose has taken him across many periods and many places, studying the motivation and circumstances behind the excesses of empire and the forces of institution and rationalization at the center of Western society. Pynchon uses the "languages" of popular fiction, comics, cinema, and television. *V.* is obviously influenced by the British tradition of spy and adventure fiction, *The Crying of Lot 49* by the detective novel, *Gravity's Rainbow* by spy and war fiction—not to mention a plethora of cinema genres and the comic—and *Vineland* is laced with metaphors surrounding rerun television— from *The Brady Bunch* to *CHiPs*—and the blockbuster movies of the age like the *Star Wars* trilogy. Even *Mason & Dixon* is partly a product of the genre of historical romance. Pynchon utilizes codes, knowledge, and language to both show their worth and to show that anything with a structure can be integrated into rationalized and institutionalized control in order to manipulate and exploit. Ironically, nowhere is this more clear than in the academic reception to his work, where interpreting his wide frames of reference has become an industry in itself.

Although Pynchon may be relatively unread compared to some of the popular writers he adapts in his own writing, he has a broader presence in the popular imagination. Since successfully avoiding a *Time* photographer attempting to take his picture in Mexico in 1963, Pynchon has become famous for maintaining his privacy. In the years following the success of *Gravity's Rainbow*, Pynchon avoided television interviews, lecture tours, and literary prize ceremonies (even when he won prizes); any knowledge of his whereabouts became increasingly valuable and scarce. It was considered something of a scoop in 1974 when *New York* magazine was able to show a 20-year-old photo. *Playboy* magazine printed an article in 1977 by a friend of Pynchon's from Cornell and over the years various magazines and newspapers have run articles by individuals who have run into Pynchon: from reporters attempting to track him down to pundits peddling theories he is anyone from J. D. Salinger to the Unabomber. In the 1980s a series of letters purported to be written by Pynchon in the guise of a local bag-lady appeared in a northern Californian newspaper and were collected in 1996 under the title *The Letters of Wanda Tinasky*. Also in 1996, *New York* magazine finally tracked Pynchon down to a salubrious section of Manhattan and produced a fresh photograph of him for the first time in over 40 years. The magazine chose to print a picture that only showed Pynchon from the back, but, inevitably, the novelist's photo was finally taken by a reporter for the *New York Times* in June 1997. Add to this the number of professional and informative web sites that Pynchon has engendered—carrying both information on all the media says of Pynchon as well as attempting to detail and decipher his work—and the writer appears more a phenomenon than a mere novelist. Clearly, his mixture of intellectual extravagance and biographical frugality has created a fascinated audience larger than his prose alone could muster.

The ability to blend subject matters from so-called "high art" and "low culture," science and literature, and contemporary politics and history, may today almost appear a necessity in the budding "great novelist." Pynchon, however, has been doing this for the last 40 years while maintaining a political agenda that denounces empire and slavery in all its racial, economic, and political manifestations. His maintenance of his privacy is probably both a personal matter and a reflection of his distrust of authority, patently obvious in all his work. Whatever the reasons, Pynchon's wariness of creating a public persona has inadvertently created one for him: a much more intriguing one than most media-friendly writers have achieved.

—Kyle Smith

FURTHER READING:

Factor, T. R. *The Letters of Wanda Tinasky*. Portland, vers libre press, 1996.

Maltby, Paul. *Dissident Postmodernists: Barthelme, Coover, Pynchon.* Philadelphia, University of Pennsylvania Press, 1991.

Weisenburger, Steven. *A Gravity's Rainbow Companion.* Athens, University of Georgia Press, 1988.

Q

Quayle, Dan (1947—)

Fourty-fourth U.S. vice president John Danforth Quayle was a figure of mild controversy from the time he was announced as running mate through his 1989-1993 term with President George Bush. On the summer day in 1988 when Republican presidential nominee Bush declared his choice for a running mate, it was difficult to assess who was more surprised—the journalists covering the convention, Bush's advisors, or the junior senator from Indiana himself.

Quayle was a graduate of DePauw University and Indiana University Law School. He was elected to the House of Representatives in 1976 with a campaign emphasizing conservative issues and was reelected in 1978. He was elected to the Senate in 1980, reelected in 1986, and was identified as a spokesman for the New Right wing of the conservative movement. He had married Marilyn Tucker in 1972 and was the father of three children.

Bush selected Quayle as a running mate for several reasons: it was thought that Quayle, who bore a slight resemblance to actor Robert Redford, might help Bush with the "gender gap" the polls were warning him about—Bush was far more popular among men than women; further, Quayle was politically to the right of the moderate Bush, and his selection might help to reassure conservative Republicans, who had never found Bush a kindred spirit; Quayle also provided the geographic balance that the ticket needed—Bush had roots in both the Northeast and Southwest, and believed that some connection to the Midwest would be helpful in the election; in addition, Quayle was part of the "baby boomer" generation, and Bush advisor Lee Atwater was convinced that this group would prove crucial to the campaign.

Upon being introduced as Bush's choice for a running mate, Quayle was immediately the subject of a media feeding frenzy. As with most modern conventions, the Republican National Convention of 1988 was dull; Bush's nomination had been a foregone conclusion for months, leaving the assembled journalists with little of consequence to cover—until Bush gave them Dan Quayle. The Indiana senator was not well known outside his home state, but the reporters made up for lost time quickly. Quayle's life and record were under the national media microscope within hours, and it did not take long for the blemishes to appear.

There was Quayle's academic record, for example. Professors at DePauw remembered Quayle as an indifferent student, more interested in golf and fraternity life than his political science courses. There was also a story about a golfing trip that Quayle had taken to Florida a few years earlier. He had stayed at a rented house with two other men and Paula Parkinson, a beautiful Washington lobbyist of reputedly easy virtue. But most damaging was the account of Quayle's military service. A strong supporter of U.S. involvement in Vietnam, Quayle had nonetheless joined the Indiana National Guard instead of a unit more likely to see combat. Further, some said that Quayle's influential family had pulled strings to get him into the guard ahead of other applicants.

Unused to the national spotlight, Quayle became flustered easily and tended to be sloppy about details, sometimes contradicting himself from one interview to the next. Bush's staff helped Quayle work out acceptable answers to the questions about his grades, marital fidelity, and patriotism, but considerable damage had already been done to the young senator's credibility. Many people, both in the news media and among the public, had developed the impression that Quayle was an intellectual lightweight who had benefited greatly from his family's money and connections. Privately, there were some in the Bush camp who shared that assessment, but Bush's choice had been made, so damage control became the order of the day. It was decided that Quayle would spend most of the campaign in small towns, away from the major media markets and among audiences who shared his conservative values. This strategy worked well, but it could not protect Quayle from the national exposure of a debate between himself and the Democrats' vice presidential candidate, Senator Lloyd Bentsen of Texas. Quayle worked hard in preparation for the debate, and he committed no major gaffes, but he appeared nervous, and did, at one point, give Bentsen an opening for a devastating retort. In response to a question about his limited experience in the U.S. Senate, Quayle compared his term of service with John F. Kennedy's. Bentsen, in response, shook his head, saying, "I knew Jack Kennedy. I served with him in the Senate. Jack Kennedy was a friend of mine." Then, with a scornful look at Quayle, he concluded, "Senator, you're no Jack Kennedy."

Quayle may be said to have had the last laugh, since he and Bush were elected. But, election results notwithstanding, Quayle had become a national joke. He was a favorite topic in the nightly

Dan Quayle

monologues delivered by Johnny Carson, David Letterman, and others (example: ''Have you heard about the new Dan Quayle savings bond? It has no interest and no maturity''). Unfortunately for Quayle, he was often his own worst enemy. While it must be admitted that a mistake by Quayle received more media attention than a slip by other public figures, Quayle managed to misspeak on a regular basis. It was even possible to buy videotapes containing footage of the vice president's flubs.

During the 1992 campaign, Quayle staked out a position on the ''family values'' issue by publicly criticizing the TV series *Murphy Brown*, in which the lead character, played by Candice Bergen, had a baby out of wedlock. ''Fathers are important,'' Quayle declared, ''and shows like *Murphy Brown* are sending the wrong message.'' But Quayle's ethos was such that few were inclined to take him seriously. A few nights later, David Letterman described the controversy, then sneered to the camera, ''Vice President Quayle, sir, Murphy Brown is a fictional character!'' When the new season of *Murphy Brown* began a few months later, the entire first episode was devoted to making fun of Quayle.

As the 1992 political race became tighter, Bush considered asking Quayle to step down but decided against it for fear of appearing unappreciative of Quayle's loyalty. The Bush-Quayle ticket lost to Clinton-Gore, and Quayle disappeared from the limelight. He continued to act as a spokesman for conservative issues and published his book *Standing Firm* in 1994. In the late 1990s, Quayle indicated a desire to run for president in the 2000 election.

—Justin Gustainis

FURTHER READING:

Goldman, Peter, and Tom Mathews. *The Quest for the Presidency 1988.* New York, Simon & Schuster, 1989.

Quayle, Dan. *Standing Firm: A Vice-Presidential Memoir.* New York, HarperCollins Publishers, 1994.

Queenan, Joe. *Imperial Caddy: The Rise of Dan Quayle in America and the Decline and Fall of Practically Everything Else.* New York, Hyperion, 1992.

Queen, Ellery

The pseudonym of writers Manfred B. Lee (1905-1971) and his cousin Frederic Dannay (1905-1982), and the name of the main character of their popular mystery novel series, Ellery Queen was probably the most popular American mystery novelist of the Golden Era of detective fiction, from the 1920s to the 1940s. The cousins (particularly Dannay) also did much to preserve and promote the mystery short-story form. They produced the long-running *Ellery Queen's Mystery Magazine*, edited short story anthologies that promoted short fiction as a viable mystery vehicle, and avidly collected short-form mystery fiction. As fellow mystery writer Anthony Boucher is often quoted as saying, ''Ellery Queen is the American Detective Novel.''

The cousins grew up together in New York and tried their hands at various careers in adulthood. In the late 1920s, Lee and Dannay (real names Manford Lepofsky and Daniel Nathan) decided to try writing a mystery novel in response to a contest cosponsored by

McClure's magazine and Frederick A. Stokes's Publishing. They chose the name Ellery Queen for their author and, reasoning that mystery readers are better at remembering the names of characters than names of authors, they decided to give their detective the same name. They submitted their story and were told they had won the contest, but the magazine went bankrupt and changed hands, after which the prize was awarded to someone else. Stokes still wanted to publish the book, however, and *The Roman Hat Mystery* (1929) was the first Ellery Queen novel. Queen's career is often divided into three distinct periods: 1929-1935, 1936-1941, and 1942-1970. This first period is notable for titles that all follow the same formula—''The Adjective-of-Nationality Noun Mystery''—such as *The Chinese Orange Mystery.*

After several successful Queen novels, the cousins decided to create another character and pseudonym, and the Barnaby Ross series was born. The detective in this series was a deaf former Shakespearean actor named Drury Lane. This series survived through four books, the first of which was *The Tragedy of X.*

In 1939 they launched the first Ellery Queen radio series. The Queen mystery shows became a popular fixture on the radio and, subsequently, three different television series were produced from 1950-1959, none very successfully. More recently, a critically acclaimed series starring Jim Hutton premiered in 1975. Unfortunately, the ratings were not good and the show was canceled. The show's producers later had more success as the creators of the long-running show, *Murder, She Wrote*, starring Angela Lansbury.

Queen was not any more successful as a motion picture character. There were several Ellery Queen films beginning in 1935 and continuing with a series of films in the 1940s, starring Ralph Bellamy as Ellery. Other motion pictures were made in the 1960s and 1970s, all of them forgettable. None of the films were very good, although the Bellamy series did have a following.

In 1938 Dannay started *Challenge to the Reader*, the first of many anthologies edited as Ellery Queen. In 1941 *Ellery Queen's Mystery Magazine* was launched and it remains the most successful magazine of its type. Also in 1941, Dannay published the anthology, *101 Year's Entertainment*, considered as the definitive anthology of short mystery fiction of its time. Dannay was principally responsible for the magazine and the anthologies while Lee devoted more of his time to the radio show.

The cousins were also among the founding members of the Mystery Writers of America, the organization that annually presents the Edgar Allan Poe awards. They themselves won Edgars in 1945 for Best Radio Play, in 1947 and 1959 for Best Short Story, and in 1960 they were given the Grand Master Award.

Ellery Queen continued to produce novels and short stories throughout the 1950s and 1960s, with the last book, *The Last Woman in His Life,* appearing in 1970. Manfred Lee died in 1971 and Dannay briefly considered continuing with the series with another writing partner, but he later rejected the idea. Dannay did, however continue to produce anthologies and personally edited the magazine until his death in 1982.

Ellery Queen novels are still widely read by fans of older mystery fiction and certainly influenced many mystery writers of today. However, it is probably from the *Ellery Queen Mystery Magazine* that most people recognize the name. The magazine continues to be the most popular and enduring of its kind and is considered a valuable training ground for future mystery novelists.

—Jill A. Gregg

FURTHER READING:

Nevins, Francis M. *Royal Bloodline: Ellery Queen, Author and Detective.* Ohio, Bowling Green University Popular Press, 1974.

Nevins, Francis M., and Ray Stannich. *The Sound of Detection.* Indiana, Brownstone Books, 1983.

Queen for a Day

Queen for a Day, a popular afternoon network television program from 1955 to 1964, originated on radio in 1945. Running five days a week, this program featured five women chosen from a studio audience who competed by presenting their hard-luck stories so as to persuade the audience that each was in the most dire straits. The audience selected the "queen" for each day by applause that was recorded on an applausemeter. The winner was adorned with a sable-collared velvet robe, given a scepter, and crowned by the host, Jack Bailey, who loudly proclaimed "I now pronounce you Queen for a Day!" The queen was then showered with an array of prizes such as appliances, furs, and jewelry—all donated by the show's sponsors in exchange for commercial consideration.

With its obvious Cinderella fantasy, this show added a royal twist to the rags-to-riches myth linked to the American Dream. The show's producers encouraged this comparison by using an opening format in which Bailey pointed at the camera and yelled: "Would *you*

like to be queen for a day?," to which the audience would respond with a resounding "Yes!"

First broadcast on NBC Radio in 1945, with Dud Williamson as the original host, the program moved to NBC Television in 1955. In 1960 it moved to ABC Television where it remained until its demise in 1964. Expanded from 30 to 45 minutes during its peak years of 1955-56, the show reached a daily audience of about 13 million and commanded advertising rates of $4,000 per commercial minute. Its longevity of almost 20 years attests to the show's popularity with the mass audiences of both radio and television. Since *Queen for a Day* was a live show, only a few kinescope recordings remain as historical records of the program.

Queen for a Day was frequently described by critics as a vulgar exploitation of the helpless female contestants' miserable conditions sandwiched in between commercial advertising. They pointed out that the show excluded unattractive or inarticulate women, or contestants who needed more assistance than brand-name merchandise could provide, such as legal or medical counseling. The program was also criticized for rewarding the losers with minor consolation prizes such as hosiery or toasters (also brand-name, of course). "Sure, *Queen* was vulgar and sleazy and filled with bathos and bad taste," former producer Howard Blake wrote in 1966, as quoted in the *New York Times Encyclopedia of Television*. "That was why it was so successful. It was exactly what the general public wanted."

In answering the critics who pointed to the women as victims of a sleazy entertainment production, Blake's retort cynically reflects on the American consumerism of the 1950s, as quoted in *The Ultimate Television Book*:

> Everybody was on the make—we on the show, NBC and later ABC, the sponsors and the suppliers of gifts. And how about all the down-on-their-luck women who we used to further our money-grubbing ends? Weren't they all on the make? Weren't they all after something for anything? Weren't they willing to wash their dirty linen on coast-to-coast TV for a chance at big money, for a chance to ride in our chauffeured Cadillac for the free tour of Disneyland and the Hollywood nightclubs? What about one of the most common wishes they turned in? 'I'd like to pay back my mother for all the wonderful things she's done for me.' The women who made that wish didn't want to pay back their mothers at all. They wanted *us* to.

—Mary Lou Nemanic

The host of *Queen for a Day*, Jack Bailey, receives a manicure from Jeanne Cagney.

FURTHER READING:

Brown, Les. *The New York Times Encyclopedia of Television.* New York, Times Books, 1978.

DeLong, Thomas A. *Quiz Craze: America's Infatuation with Game Shows.* New York, Praeger, 1991.

Fabe, Maxene. *TV Game Shows.* Garden City, New York, Dolphin Books, 1979.

Fireman, Judy, editor. *TV Book: The Ultimate Television Book.* New York, Workman Publishing Company, 1977.

Queen Latifah (1970?—)

Like most realms of mass media, the popular music industry has been historically dominated by men. Rap, the urban music style that developed in the late 1970s, has been characterized as particularly male-defined, with lyrics dedicated to bravado and pleasure derived from the treatment of women as commodities and sexual objects. Though women have always had a presence within the rap and hip-hop culture, it was Queen Latifah who brought women from the sidelines into the limelight.

Queen Latifah, who was born Dana Owens, began her musical career in East Orange, New Jersey, where she performed in high school with a group called Ladies Fresh. Soon after she began her solo career, she rocketed to the top, becoming the first female solo artist to have a gold record. Her musical style is often described as combining elements of hip-hop, jazz, house, and reggae. Queen Latifah's first album, *All Hail the Queen* (1989), showcased her talents as a rap artist with which to be reckoned. Previously, women in rap were considered novelty acts and were not taken very seriously, especially on the East Coast; the style and content of rap articulated issues of oppression, racism, economics, lack of adequate access to the legal and medical systems, inadequate public education, and the need for revolution on all fronts. Queen Latifah added to the mix by noting something not discussed in the lyrics of her male counterparts: sexism.

In some sense Queen Latifah's persona can be described as androgynous, for it combines both masculine and feminine traits. Her

Queen Latifah

chosen moniker, Latifah, which means delicate or sensitive in Arabic, almost contradicts the music she performs as a woman who is strong, independent, ready to challenge any rapper, male or female, while still mainlining her womanhood. On her first album, which was nominated for a Grammy, is a track which critics have called hip-hop's first "womanist anthem." Titled "Ladies First," the song, in a call-and-response pattern performed along with British female rapper Monie Love, clearly challenges sexism in the rap music world: "Some think that we can't flow / Stereotypes they got to go / I'm gonna mess around and flip the scene into reverse / With what? / With a little touch of ladies first."

Queen Latifah has continued her pro-woman stance throughout her career, releasing a single in 1996 that would surpass that first anthem—"U.N.I.T.Y." In this song she tackles issues of sexism that divide the African-American community along gender lines: domestic violence, sexual harassment, and a lack of respect for women.

As the influence of rap and hip-hop culture expanded to other forms of popular culture, Queen Latifah began applying her talents to film and television. As an actress she has appeared in films such as *Jungle Fever* (1991), *House Party II* (1991), and *Juice* (1992). On television she starred on the Fox series *Living Single,* a popular show that countered many African-American stereotypes. She was recognized for her acting talent in the film *Set It Off* (1996) by the Indie Spirit Awards. Her portrayal of Cleo was a daring one, for it was one of the first overt constructions of an African-American lesbian in a big-budget Hollywood production. Queen Latifah has set many precedents in contemporary popular culture, and she continues to influence its changing landscape. In order to make a further impact on that landscape, she formed her own company—Flava Unit—which serves to discover and represent new artists and also functions as a full-fledged record label.

Queer Nation

Formed in March 1990, Queer Nation is an activist organization founded in New York City by four men, all of whom had been victims of anti-gay violence. Its goal was to be a grass-roots, direct-action response to the invisibility of homosexuality in American culture and expressions of homophobic prejudice, using tactics proven effective by the AIDS (Acquired Immune Deficiency Syndrome) Coalition to Unleash Power (ACT UP). It espoused the idea of "outing" persons whose homosexuality was not public knowledge, a concept whose radical nature drew objections from more moderate gay rights organizations. Even its name reflected a defiantly marginal identity, reclaiming a common epithet and reworking it into a newly proud badge, most visible in its trademark slogan of "We're here, we're queer, get used to it."

—Robert Ridinger

FURTHER READING:

Slagle, R. Anthony. "In Defense of Queer Nation: From Identity Politics to a Politics of Difference." *Western Journal of Communication.* Vol. 59, spring 1995, 85-102.

Quiz Show Scandals

In 1958, while television was still in its infancy, Americans were still innocent about the medium's predilection to sacrifice veracity in favor of entertainment. That year, a series of revelations about the fixing of television quiz shows shook the confidence of viewers. The shows had big money, high ratings, and were subject to the whims of sponsors; these aspects combined to corrupt the quiz shows. The more charismatic and telegenic contestants were supplied with answers, while others were told to miss questions intentionally. Shows were so scripted that producers told contestants when to wring their hands, or mop their brow. A series of tie games was often fabricated as a way to build suspense and keep viewers tuning in each week. Contestants, enamored with their newfound fame and prize money, were more than willing to go along with the charade. Finally, a series of revelations in the press from disgruntled former contestants led to a congressional investigation the next year. The rigged contests marred an otherwise innocent era in America, prefiguring the large-scale lies that would surround Vietnam and Watergate.

The most popular of the quiz shows, *$64,000 Question*, was modeled after its radio predecessor, *The $64 Question*. *The $64,000 Question* appeared in 1955, after a 1954 Supreme Court ruling paved the way for high-stakes quiz shows by eliminating jackpot-type quizzes from the category of gambling. However, no specific laws existed to regulate television game shows in the wake of the high court's ruling. The shows were immediately and wildly popular: in August, 1955, approximately 47 million viewers tuned into watch *The $64,000 Question.*

Americans watched these shows because of the big prize money, and their "spontaneous" nature. The prosperity of the 1950s gave rise to the American Dream, as Americans sought to acquire the material goods, homes, and good-paying jobs that were denied to their Depression-era parents. The quiz shows were a reflection of the new materialism. The 1957-58 season featured 22 network quiz shows, broadcast live and mainly during prime time. The most popular shows were those that featured contestants competing for unlimited cash prizes. Some contestants amassed winnings of over $100,000, a large sum for the pre-inflationary dollar. Contestants included future celebrities like television actress Patty Duke, and popular psychologist Dr. Joyce Brothers. Picked by producers to fail, Brothers beat the system by studying so extensively that she won her prize money legitimately.

One former contestant, Antoinette DuBarry Hillman, described a typical screening session which the producers of *Dotto* used to coach contestants. At the time the highest-rated daytime quiz show, *Dotto* required players to answer questions and then identify a puzzle in which drawings of famous people were gradually revealed. In Kent Anderson's *Television Fraud*, Hillman recalled:

> Actually the first day I was on the show (the screener) asked me in the preliminary thing how I would recognize Victor Borge. . . . Then when I got on the show and was answering the questions, I got my first clue (for the emerging dot connections) and it was Danish. I didn't think much about that. Then the second clue was a musician. How many Danish musicians do you know?. . . Finally I had to give in and say Victor Borge. I was right and I won. When I went off stage I popped over to Mr. Green (the screener) and started to thank him, and he said hush, hush, hush.

In his defense, Edward Jurist, the producer of *Dotto,* complained that the world of information was so vast that "you cannot ask random questions of people and have a show. You simply have failure, failure, failure, and that does not make for entertainment."

One major flaw with the quiz shows was that they were created around one sponsor. Companies would act as the show's sole advertiser, and used this to their advantage by exerting its influence on the show's production. The stakes involving the quiz shows were as high for the networks and sponsors as they were presumably for the contestants. For instance, *Twenty-One*'s sponsor, Geritol, advertised as "a relief for tired blood," saw annual sales jump by an average of $3 million a year during the years 1957 and 1958, when the show was being televised. After the scandal erupted, and *Twenty-One* was canceled, Geritol's sales fell back to pre-quiz show levels.

Twenty-One, one of the most popular of the quiz shows, featured two competitors in isolation booths who were required to answer questions on any given topic. Questions were rated by difficulty from 1 to 11. The first contestant to reach a score of 21 without a tie won, and players' scores were concealed from each other until one of them reached 21. The show was not immediately popular after its debut on September 12, 1956, and the show's producers, Jack Berry and Dan Enright, were under pressure to improve its ratings. "*Twenty-One*," writes Walter Karp, "needed talking encyclopedias and human almanacs." The knowledge required was so broad and expert that initial contests ended in 0-0 ties.

Twenty-One recruited Herbert Stempel, a short, awkward New Yorker from Forrest Hills who had a photographic memory, to represent the underdog figure of the "average man." Viewers soon began watching to see if he could continue winning for one more week. Despite his considerable knowledge, Stempel was enlisted to help fix the show. Stempel was told how to dress, how to get his haircut, and was rehearsed with questions that would appear on-air. In his testimony to Congress in 1959, Stempel stated that producer Enright visited him at home to go through questions and answers. "After having done this," Stempel attested, "he very, very bluntly sat back and said with a smile, 'How would you like to win $25,000?' I had been a poor boy all my life, and I was sort of overjoyed."

However, Stempel was not a photogenic man; viewers could see him visibly sweating during the telecast. Geritol felt that Stempel was not the right image, and new contestants were sought in order to attract bigger audiences. Enter Charles Van Doren, an instructor at Columbia University, whose father, Mark Van Doren, was a Pulitzer Prize-winning poet. Charles possessed a cool, WASP-like detachment, and was attractive as well: "He was very American," writes Joseph Epstein, who knew Van Doren. "He looked as if he could have played on our Davis Cup tennis team. . . . Mothers, it was said, saw him as the answer to Elvis Presley." The antipodal contestants played a series of staged ties that delivered big ratings, until Stempel was told by producers to take a dive, giving the wrong response to a question to which he genuinely knew the correct answer. Van Doren continued as reigning champion for 15 weeks.

For his part, Van Doren was told that the riggings were common practice and that the shows were mere entertainment. Karp quotes Van Doren's statement that producer Al Freedman convinced him with "the fact that by appearing on a nationally televised program, I would be doing a great service to the intellectual life, to teachers and to education in general, by increasing public respect for the work of the mind through my performances."

Stempel had grown accustomed to minor celebrity status, and felt betrayed by Enright, who in turn, considered Stempel to be an ingrate. The disgruntled contestant took his ''defeat'' in hard fashion and began seeing a psychiatrist. Stempel tried to tell anybody he could about the fraud, including the newspapers, who were reluctant to print his charges, fearing a libel suit. Enright produced a statement, signed by Stempel, that denied he had been coached in any way while on the program. Stempel was trying to get anyone to listen to his story; meanwhile his nemesis, Van Doren, was being featured on the covers of *Life* and *Time*.

Stempel was not the only former contestant to come forward. One of them, the Reverend Charles E. ''Stoney'' Jackson, Jr., was an unwitting participant in the frauds. After going public with his charges, the Reverend Jackson discovered that the quiz shows were too popular, for he could not even convince his own congregation of the shows' misdeeds. Another contestant on *Dotto,* Edward Hilgemeier, Jr., produced a page from a winner's crib sheet. Hilgemeier refused the initial $500 settlement from the show, which then accused him of trying to blackmail the network. Eventually, a reporter convinced him to accept any form of hush money in order to obtain evidence of the show's corruption. Hilgemeier assented, and left a copy of his affidavit to the Federal Communications Commission at Colgate-Palmolive, *Dotto*'s sponsor. Rumors began appearing in print of the quiz show's misdeeds, and *Dotto* was canceled on August 15, 1958.

Reaction to the revelations was disbelief. As early as April 1957, magazines like *Look* believed the shows were controlled by selecting more or less difficult questions, but ''no TV quiz shows are fixed in the sense of being dishonest.'' Of three polls that appeared shortly after the revelations, the most emphatic response was from the 65 percent who answered in the affirmative to the following statement: ''These practices are very wrong and should be stopped immediately, but you can't condemn all of television because of them.'' Americans liked their new TV sets, and weren't going to let one segment of programming taint the overall ''experience'' of watching television. Some were more alarmed by the public's apathy, or cynicism, than they were by the fixed shows. In the end, the cynicism on the part of Americans may have been justified, since the only people who were legally punished were contestants and not the shows' producers.

The New York District Attorney's office announced its investigation of *Dotto* on August 25, 1958. Three days later, two New York newspapers published Stempel's allegations, which were once considered to be the products of a hysterical, raving maniac. Enright produced a tape of a conversation between himself and Stempel that included revelations of Stempel's receiving psychiatric help, and his gambling debts to a bookmaker. Stempel claimed that part of the tape was altered. Then, after nine months of testimony, the grand jury's report was expunged by the presiding judge ''to protect the dubious reputations of the not-so-innocent.'' Anderson quotes District Attorney Frank Hogan in 1959 as saying that:

> The very essence of the quiz program's appeal lies in its implied representation of honesty. Were it generally understood that these programs do not present honest tests of the contestants' knowledge and intellectual skills, they would be utterly ineffectual in acquiring the public's ''time.''

In July of 1959, Oren Harris (D-Arkansas) announced a House investigation committee, which convened on October 6. Freedman boasted before the committee that not one of the 20 contestants singled out for collaboration had refused. Former *Twenty-One* contestant James Snodgrass produced letters that he sent to himself by registered mail. Snodgrass's letters correctly predicted the outcome of the televised proceedings: ''According to the plan I am to miss the first question, specifically the lines by Emily Dickinson. I've been told to answer Ralph Waldo Emerson. I have decided not to 'take the fall' but to answer the question correctly.'' It was also revealed that, of the 150 witnesses called before the grand jury, 100 of them committed perjury under oath. According to Epstein, when it was suggested to the committee that Van Doren—who by his own testimony was the ''principal symbol'' of the corruption—be spared the exposure of testifying, one member replied, ''It would be like playing Hamlet without Hamlet.''

In response, the networks swiftly canceled the quiz shows during the 1958-59 season. Van Doren lost his job as an assistant professor. President Eisenhower signed a bill in 1960 that declared illegal any contest or game with intent to deceive the audience. People in television began working to get the networks to acquire or produce their programs *before* lining up advertisers. The lasting effects on the quiz shows was a change within their fundamental nature. They returned to television as ''game shows,'' free from any negative associations with the old shows. The overall effect of the scandals, writes Olaf Hoerschelmann, was that they:

> undermined the legitimacy of high cultural values that quiz shows—the term and the genre—embodied. Thus, the new name, ''game shows,'' removed the genre from certain cultural assumptions and instead created associations with the less sensitive concepts of play and leisure.

Thirty years after the scandal, game shows were more likely to present contests with questions requiring everyday knowledge, rather than expert knowledge.

The quiz show scandals have been used to interpret, with varying degrees of plausibility, the downfall of innocence in America. They have been blamed for laying the groundwork for future deceptions involving Vietnam and Watergate. Others saw the scandals as a precursor to the 1960 Nixon/Kennedy presidential debates, in which the telegenic man (Kennedy) wins again. In essence, this is a discussion about Americans' naivete towards a new medium, not the complete shakedown of their innocence; it is dubious as to whether there was an innocence in the first place. Breathless assertions that Van Doren's televised intellectual ability was the American answer to Soviet Russia's Sputnik launch show that people made far too much out of the quiz shows during their broadcast.

The view from the 1990s, as expressed by John Leo, is that the Van Doren/Stempel pairing exploited stereotypes of class and race, by featuring ''the elegant high WASP from a family of famous scholars versus the underachieving and volatile Jewish nerd from Queens.'' *Quiz Show*, the 1994 movie directed by Robert Redford, successfully highlighted this angle. However, the movie's docudrama presentation yielded to making changes of fact in order to enhance dramatic effect. The movie ignored the newspapers, the district attorney, and the grand jury by making bureaucrat Richard Goodwin the singular force behind the exposure of Van Doren. Although widely regarded as a well-made movie, the irony had come full circle: television, represented by *Los Angeles Times*' TV critic Howard Rosenberg, got to stand on the high moral ground for a change. ''How ironic,'' the *U.S. News & World Report* quotes Rosenberg, ''that a movie so judgmental about the TV industry's dishonesty in the 1950s should itself play so fast and loose with the truth for the sake of putting on a good show.''

Television's ''high ground'' is still not solid. One of the reasons the quiz show scandals remain instructive is because television retains the use of deception: it routinely employs the use of dramatic reenactments of crimes, talk-show guests who are rehearsed before tapings, and staged consumer-product safety tests. In the beginning, people believed that television was inherently trustworthy and factual. The quiz shows shattered such beliefs, and showed that television was fictional, engineered, and manipulative, rather than innocent or natural. This is perhaps the longest-lasting effect of the quiz show scandals upon television: they at once uncovered and reinforced the notion that television was solely designed to entertain. Any subsequent successful television show that is inventive, creative, or educational *and* entertaining is regarded as a curious anomaly.

—Daryl Umberger

FURTHER READING:

Anderson, Kent. *Television Fraud: The History and Implications of the Quiz Show Scandals.* Westport, Connecticut, Greenwood Press, 1978.

Diamond, Edwin. *Quiz Show: Television Betrayals Past . . . and Present?* Washington D.C., Annenberg Washington Program in Communications Policy Studies of Northwestern University, 1994.

Epstein, Joseph. ''Redford's Van Doren & Mine.'' *Commentary.* December 1994, 40-46.

Frank, Reuven. '''Quiz Show' Follies.'' *New Leader.* September 12, 1994, 18-19.

Hoerschelmann, Olaf. ''Quiz and Game Shows.'' In *Museum of Broadcast Communications Encyclopedia of Television,* edited by Horace Newcomb. 3 Vols. Chicago, Fitzroy Dearborn Publishers, 1997.

Karp, Walter. ''The Quiz Show Scandal.'' *American Heritage.* May/June 1989, 76-88.

Leo, John. ''Faking It in 'Quiz Show.''' *U.S. News & World Report.* October 17, 1994, 24.

Stone, J., and T. Yohn. *Prime Time Misdemeanors: Investigating the 1950s TV Quiz Scandal—A D.A.'s Account.* New Brunswick, New Jersey, Rutgers University Press, 1992.

R

Race Music

Prior to the emergence of rhythm & blues as a musical genre in the 1940s, "race music" and "race records" were terms used to categorize practically all types of African-American music. Race records were the first examples of popular music recorded by and marketed to black Americans. Reflecting the segregated status of American society and culture, race records were separate catalogs of African-American music. Prior to the 1940s, African Americans were scarcely represented on radio, and live performances were largely limited to segregated venues. Race music and records, therefore, were also the primary medium for African-American musical expression during the 1920s and 1930s; an estimated 15,000 titles were released on race records—approximately 10,000 blues, 3,250 jazz, and 1,750 gospel songs were produced during those years. Race records are significant historical documents of early-twentieth-century African American music and have been and remain influential to artists, audiences, and scholars alike. Most twentieth-century white, popular music—especially rock 'n' roll and country—has roots in race music, in particular jazz, swing, and blues.

The terms "race music" and "race records" had conflicting meanings. In one respect, they were indicative of segregation in the 1920s. Race records were separated from the recordings of white musicians, records solely because of the race of the artists. On the other hand, the terms represented an emerging awareness by the recording industry of African-American audiences. The term "race" was not pejorative; in fact "race was symbolic of black pride, militancy, and solidarity in the 1920s, and it was generally favored over colored or Negro by African-American city dwellers," noted scholar William Barlow in "Cashing In: 1900-1939." The term "race records" first appeared in the *Chicago Defender,* an African-American newspaper, within an OKeh advertisement in 1922.

Race music and records resulted from the concentrated commercialization of American popular music beginning in the early twentieth century. In 1920 Mamie Smith, a female African American singer little known outside of vaudeville, recorded the song "Crazy Blues" for the small OKeh record label. The record unexpectedly sold over 100,000 copies by the end of the year and turned the nascent recording industry's attention to African-American artists and audiences. The early 1920s were a period of declining revenues for the recording industry, and race records emerged in part as a way of expanding the consumer market for recorded music. The two dominant record companies, Victor and Columbia, had seen their status erode dramatically. Victor's sales had fallen from $51 million, and Columbia's sales had declined from $7 million to $4.5 million in the period of 1921 to 1925. The combined impact of radio and competition from new labels were catalysts for the emergence of race records. The onset of commercial radio broadcasts in the early 1920s impacted the recording industry's dominant position as the gatekeeper of recorded music. Prior to a lawsuit in 1919, the two dominant recording companies controlled the patents for phonograph record production. Following this lawsuit, however, the industry was opened to competition. Many of the new record labels that emerged, such as OKeh, Paramount, and Gennett, would be instrumental in the development and production of race records.

The production of race records was a more profitable endeavor than the recording of white artists. As in other endeavors, African-American artists were paid less than their white counterparts for recording sessions and were often exploited. Artists' ignorance of copyright law, and the lack of an independent accounting body to track sales, allowed industry personnel to grossly underpay or waive royalty monies. Bessie Smith, "the queen of the blues," recorded over 160 songs for Columbia and never received royalty payments in the ten years she recorded for the company. Folk blues artists, such as Blind Lemon Jefferson and Son House, were also more profitable to record because their songs could be copyrighted. Unlike their urban peers, folk blues artists' songs generally had not been published, thus record companies could make money off the published songs in addition to sales of records. Once published, songs became commodities and any future recordings would result in royalty payments to the publisher. This practice has remained widespread throughout the twentieth century.

With few exceptions, the labels that produced race records were white-owned and-controlled. One significant exception was Black Swan, formed in 1921 by Harry Pace, W.C. Handy's former partner, as a division of Pace Phonography. Musician and arranger Fletcher Henderson was retained as musical director and recording manager. In 1924, largely due to a lack of sustained financial success, Black Swan sold its catalog to Paramount. Paramount also had a connection to the other major African American-owned label of this time, Black Patti. Black Patti was started in 1927 by J. "Mayo" Williams, an African American who was recording director for the Paramount label. While employed there Williams started the label with money from disgruntled Paramount vice president E.J. Barrett and Richard Gennett, brother of Gennett Records owner Harry Gennett. After releasing approximately 50 records, Black Patti folded in less than a year. Other African American-owned labels include Sunshine and Merritt. Overall, the race labels constituted a small minority in the context of race record production during this period which was dominated by white-owned businesses. Segregation and racism, combined with only fleeting access to capital, technology, and distribution—which were almost exclusively controlled by whites—placed the African-American labels at a disadvantage and ultimately contributed to their quick demise.

Race music and records in the 1920s were characterized by the popularity of two significant genres of music and the dominance of three race record labels. In particular, jazz and blues became part of the American musical idiom in the 1920s, popularized in large part through recordings released on Columbia, Paramount, and OKeh. Jazz, the dominant American indigenous popular music, emerged from the New Orleans area to become national, and eventually international, in popularity and practice. For example, Joe "King" Oliver was a seminal figure in jazz, and his band featured Louis Armstrong. Oliver's Creole Jazz Band came out of New Orleans and was a mainstay in several Chicago clubs; the group recorded some of the earliest and most influential jazz records for the Gennett label. Likewise, Jelly Roll Morton, an influential pianist from New Orleans, recorded groundbreaking songs for the Gennett label.

The blues emerged from diverse regions of the American South and Southwest and had urban and rural progenitors. In the urban North, the vaudeville blues became popular in the early 1920s, especially following the success of Mamie Smith's 1920 recording. Female blues artists in particular were quite successful during the early 1920s. Artists such as Alberta Hunter, who recorded for Paramount, and Sean Martin, who recorded for OKeh, had a large following through their recordings. The folk blues, with origins in the rural South, became popular in the latter half of the 1920s. Artists such as Texan Blind Lemon Jefferson, who recorded 75 songs for Paramount between 1926 and 1930, were popular with audiences and would influence later generations of blues artists. Other folk blues artists of note who recorded during this period were Missippians Charley Patton—a.k.a. "The Masked Marvel"—and Son House; both recorded for Paramount.

During the 1930s, the commercial success and expansion of race music and records were impacted by the Great Depression. While sales of race records had reached $100 million in 1927, they had fallen drastically to $6 million in 1933. In response, the record companies dropped their record prices from an average of 75 cents in the 1920s to 35 cents in the 1930s. Until the mid-1930s, few new songs were released and virtually no new race recordings were made; instead the industry re-released titles and songs that had been previously unreleased. Following the repeal of Prohibition in 1933, the demand for live music increased. And in the late 1930s, the emergence of the jukebox stimulated sales of records. Three race record labels dominated the production of recordings in the 1930s and reflected the impact of the Depression on the music industry: Columbia, RCA-Victor, whose race label was Bluebird, and Decca. Columbia, which had acquired OKeh in 1926, was profitable until 1938 at which time it was sold to CBS. The RCA-Victor label had emerged from RCA's purchase of Victor in 1928. Decca, a new entry into the race market, was a subsidiary of London-based Decca. Despite the economic downturn, the 1930s were a creative period for race music.

In the 1930s race music was expanded by the popularity of swing. Swing grew out of big band jazz ensembles in the 1920s. Unlike the jazz bands of the 1920s, however, swing was more often arranged and scored, instead of improvised, and used reed instruments as well as the brass instruments that dominated earlier jazz. Swing in the 1930s was epitomized by the Fletcher Henderson Band which featured Louis Armstrong on trumpet, Coleman Hawkins on tenor saxophone, and arranger Don Redman. Other notable swing bands during this period included Chick Webb's band, which had vocalist Ella Fitzgerald, Jimmy Lunceford's Band, Duke Ellington's Orchestra, Count Basie's Orchestra, and Cab Calloway's Orchestra.

During the 1940s race records as a distinctly separate catalog of recordings waned due to several factors. The United States' entry into World War II curtailed the production and consumption of recorded music. In 1942 the government rationed shellac, a key component in the manufacture of record discs, which limited the number of releases. Likewise in 1942, the American Federation of Music announced a ban on all recording and as a result the studios were closed for two years. Following the war and the lifting of the recording ban, recording resumed with verve, but the industry concentrated on mass-market sales and neglected their race catalogs. Small labels that emphasized African-American music emerged in the Midwest and South and challenged the status of the major labels. Significantly, these labels—such as Chess, King, and Vee Jay—did not use the nomenclature "race records." Race music during this period was greatly expanded. While blues and jazz titles were still being recorded and released, a diversity of styles, collectively known as "rhythm and blues," began to coalesce. Although race music was still largely produced for and consumed by black audiences, the segregated status of the music and recordings was declining.

—Matthew A. Killmeier

FURTHER READING:

Barlow, William. "Cashing In: 1900-1939." In *Split Image: African Americans in the Mass Media,* edited by Jannette L. Dates and William Barlow. Washington, D.C., Howard University Press, 1990.

Dixon, Robert M.W., and John Godrich. *Recording the Blues.* New York, Stein & Day, 1970.

Dixon, Robert M.W., John Godrich, and Howard Rye. *Blues and Gospel Records 1890-1943.* Oxford, Oxford University Press, 1997.

Foreman, Ronald Clifford, Jr. *Jazz and Race Records, 1920-32: Their Origins and Their Significance for the Record Industry and Society* (dissertation). University of Illinois, 1968.

Kennedy, Rick. *Jelly Roll, Bix, and Hoagy: Gennett Studios and the Birth of Recorded Jazz.* Bloomington, Indiana University Press, 1994.

Oliver, Paul. *Songsters and Saints: Vocal Traditions on Race Records.* Cambridge, Cambridge University Press, 1984.

Russell, Tony. *Blacks, Whites, and Blues.* New York, Stein & Day, 1970.

Southern, Eileen. *The Music of Black Americans: A History.* 5th edition. New York, W.W. Norton Co., 1997.

Race Riots

Although baseball, Mom's apple pie, and the Fourth of July are staples in the cultural fabric of the United States, nothing is more American than race riots. Throughout the nation's history nothing has been more constant than racial warfare. In many ways race riots have taken on a life and a culture of their own.

The 1906 riot in Atlanta, Georgia, would set the stage for the majority of white attacks on African Americans. The conflict erupted on September 22, when approximately 10,000 whites, angry at a report that black men were allegedly assaulting white women, "beat every black person they found on the streets of the city." In all, twelve deaths were registered, at a time when African Americans had begun to assert themselves as men and women, shedding an image of compliancy. Two years later, a similar attack occurred in Springfield, Illinois.

The period of World War I ushered in a new era of racial conflict. As African Americans migrated to urban areas in search of better social and economic conditions, the immediate post-war period was a literal powder keg as white GI's returned home to find a "New Negro" emerging. The first World War I-related riot occurred in East St. Louis, Illinois, in 1917, and left forty African Americans dead, all at the hands of white attackers. This riot foreshadowed the notorious "Red Summer of 1919" when twenty-five cities witnessed racial conflict, leaving 100 dead and another 1,000 wounded. The most dramatic riot of 1919 was in Chicago, where an incident at a Lake Michigan beach touched off thirteen days of rioting, leaving fifteen whites and twenty-three blacks dead. In 1921, Tulsa was the scene of a race "war" after whites destroyed over $1 million worth of black-owned property.

The aftermath of the riots in Watts, Los Angeles.

The World War II period represented a watershed in the history of race riots in the United States. Whereas the previous riots/conflicts were initiated by whites, these new eruptions would be fueled by both black and white frustration. The most notorious World War II riot occurred in Detroit in 1943, leaving twenty-five blacks and nine whites dead. In what was largely a battle over jobs and housing, the all-white Detroit Police Department was responsible for the majority of black deaths.

Following World War II, the second great migration brought over three million African Americans from the South to the urban North and West. But black frustration would set in when black Southerners realized that the ''Promised Land'' was anything but that. Greeted with poor housing, unequal police protection, de-facto school segregation, and employment discrimination, black migrants became increasingly frustrated. As conditions continued to worsen in the mid-1960s, they took their battle to the streets, destroying white property in hopes of drawing attention to their plight. In 1964, Harlem, Chicago, and Philadelphia were the scene of incidents that left more than 100 citizens dead. One year later, the black enclave of Watts in Los Angeles erupted leaving thirty-four dead and approximately $200 million in property damage. In all, the 35,000 active rioters caused 1,000 injuries, but the riot also highlighted the conditions faced by the urban poor.

The year 1967 was by far the worst year of racial disturbances in American history. Serious riots occurred in Newark and Detroit, leaving twenty-six and forty dead, respectively. Most of these deaths were at the hands of white policemen who valued white property over black lives. Thirty-eight other cities experienced outbreaks as well, as black Northerners continued to take out their frustrations upon white property. Similar riots occurred on the night of Martin Luther King, Jr.'s assassination, when over 110 cities erupted.

The decades of the 1970s and 1980s witnessed a decline in rioting; however, in 1992 Americans who were unfamiliar with this aspect of our country's past would be jolted by the Rodney King riots in Los Angeles. In March of 1991 King was brutally beaten by at least four white officers from the Los Angeles Police Department (LAPD). A nearby resident videotaped the incident and within hours the image of a big black man being beaten like a dog was broadcast throughout the world. The officers were indicted but ultimately acquitted of police brutality in the all-white suburb of Simi Valley by a jury composed of eleven whites and one Hispanic. This verdict touched off several days of rioting. At the end of the riot there were thirty-eight fatalities, 4,000 arrests, and over $500 million in property damage. The most infamous image of the riot was the beating of Reginald Denny, a white truck driver who was caught in a black neighborhood. Denny was pulled from his truck and almost beaten to death. Although many Americans expressed shock at the riot, few understood how the Rodney King riots were merely building upon a long-standing tradition in U.S. culture.

—Leonard N. Moore

FURTHER READING:

Hersey, John. *The Algiers Motel Incident.* New York, Alfred A. Knopf, 1968.

Horne, Gerald. *The Fire This Time: The Watts Riot and the 1960s.* Charlottesville, University of Virginia Press, 1997.

Report of the National Advisory Commission on Civil Disorders. New York, Bantam, 1968.

Sugrue, Thomas. *Origins of the Urban Crisis.* Princeton, Princeton University Press, 1997.

Radio

In September of 1895, Guglielmo Marconi, a young Italian inventor, pioneered wireless telegraphy when he transmitted a message to his brother, who was out of sight beyond a hill. By 1906, U.S. inventor Lee De Forest had greatly increased the potential of Marconi's work by developing a three-electrode vacuum-tube amplifier that made modern radio broadcasts possible. From these relatively humble beginnings radio quickly evolved to become the basis of an electronic media revolution that would shape the face of American popular culture during the middle years of the twentieth century. From the early 1920s to the mid-1950s radio both recorded and influenced popular culture in a way that no other media had ever done, forever changing the way information and entertainment would be disseminated and paving the way for television.

An example of an early radio.

The first modern radio station came into being in 1920, when Westinghouse engineer Frank Conrad set up KDKA in East Pittsburgh, Pennsylvania, and began sending out programs "over the ether," in the parlance of the day. On November 2 of that year, KDKA broadcast the results of the Harding-Cox presidential election. However, at that time only about 5,000 Americans had radio receivers, so the broadcast went largely unnoticed. As Susan Smulyan writes in *Selling Radio,* the problem was that "when the first radio station began in 1920, no one knew how to make money from broadcasting." Nevertheless, a number of different groups soon realized that radio could be a powerful and important medium, which resulted in a battle for control of the airwaves.

One faction, spearheaded primarily by educators, believed that radio could be a tool for enriching people's lives. They wanted a government-funded national radio program that would be largely informational and educational. These groups would have to wait nearly fifty years to get their wish; on November 7, 1967, President Lyndon B. Johnson would sign the Public Broadcasting Act into law, resulting in the creation of the noncommercial National Public Radio and the Public Broadcasting (television) networks. But in 1920 the question for broadcasters was, "Who would pay for radio?" The general public was not yet ready to pay for its information and entertainment directly (that would come in the 1970s, with the growth of cable television beyond its humble beginnings as a source for programming in areas beyond the reach of airborne signals). In 1922 New York radio station WEAF—which would later become WNBC—solved the funding dilemma when it aired the first paid radio commercials. Although advertisers were initially unconvinced as to radio's ability to sell products, they eventually realized that it was an incredibly effective way to reach people in their homes. Accordingly, WEAF's commercialization set into motion the private control of U.S. public airwaves. In a now-famous quote, radio pioneer De Forest responded to radio's commercialization by asking, "What have you done with my child? You have sent him out on the street in rags of ragtime to collect money from all and sundry. You have made of him a laughingstock of intelligence, surely a stench in the nostrils of the gods of the ionosphere."

The concept of "selling time" for advertisements had immense ramifications for American popular culture. Since the inception of mass media advertising, the public's conception of life in the United States has become defined not by what people do, but by the products they consume; success or failure in the U.S. is largely defined by material possessions instead of by accomplishments. As Smulyan writes, "broadcasting's programs and structures," which paved the way for later media advertising like television commercials and website banners, were first "developed in radio." However, radio's contribution to popular culture is not exclusively confined to its role in the birth of modern advertising. Just as important are the medium's contributions to the ways in which people are informed and entertained.

Prior to the onset of the Depression, radio had already established its core of music, news, and entertainment programming. Of the three, music and news programming were the most predominant because they were the cheapest to produce; entertainment programming would not enter its golden age until the early 1930s. There were two ways of presenting music on radio: either by playing records or broadcasting musicians as they played live in a studio, concert hall, or hotel ballroom. The widespread integration of musical numbers into more complex variety shows was still a number years off. In addition to musical programming, news broadcasts and issue-based discussion shows also flourished in the 1920s. Never before had the dissemination of news been so immediate. Sports events like the World Series and news events like the infamous Scopes trial, which Chicago station WGN broadcast live, united Americans around their radios. From its earliest days, radio began the move towards instantaneous news.

Radio networks also began appearing in the late 1920s: NBC was established in 1926, and CBS in 1927. Perhaps the most important effect these networks had on radio was their contribution to the establishment of a more national medium. The respective networks began buying up local stations, which became known as "affiliates." Locally produced shows gave way to uniform national shows that the networks broadcast over their affiliates. Concurrently, radio was becoming an item commonly found in every home. As noted by Fred MacDonald in *Don't Touch That Dial,* by the early 1930s approximately 90 percent of Americans had at least one radio in their homes. As a result, American regionalism began to disappear at an accelerated rate as Californians began to hear the same shows as people in Alabama and New Jersey. What in the late 1990s has come to be known as the "homogenization of American culture" can be traced back to the rise of the early radio networks.

Despite the success of radio in the 1920s, something was still missing. Although there were a few popular programs, radio shows had yet to fully come into their own; however, the Great Depression ushered in their "golden age." By the early 1930s, listeners had grown bored with mostly music, news, and talk, and many of them craved escape from the hard reality of their difficult financial circumstances. Radio responded by expanding its programming diversity and broadcasting shows in many genres, including Westerns, detective shows, dramas, soap operas, comedies, romances, and variety shows. Americans danced to the latest rhythms as played by bandleaders who broadcast live from hotel ballrooms, or gathered around their radio sets on Sunday morning to hear prominent preachers and choirs, precursors to the radio and television evangelists of a later era. Many radio shows of the period were serialized so fans could follow the ongoing weekly adventures of their favorite characters. The serialization of radio shows created a continuity in American entertainment that was unique to the medium at that time. *The Lone Ranger,* for example, was on the air for twenty-two years. Likewise, *The Jack Benny Program* enjoyed a twenty-six-year run. Perhaps MacDonald best sums up radio's importance during the Depression when he writes, ''for audiences trapped by the economic depression and social uncertainty of the 1930s, radio became the great wellspring from which came escape, diversion, knowledge, and inspiration.'' As programmers realized that national shows needed national celebrities in order to achieve immediate success, they came to rely heavily on the many popular performers who had been displaced by the rise of electronic media—making radio stars out of ex-vaudevillians like the Marx Brothers, Burns and Allen, Jack Benny, and Fred Allen.

Conversely, in the early 1930s, entertainment's brightest lights— Hollywood movie stars—were reluctant to appear on radio. Most studios, and many stars, believed that appearing on radio would somehow lessen a star's cinematic appeal. Radio loved the movies, on the other hand: most stations ran movie reviews, and syndicated gossip columnists such as Louella Parsons and Walter Winchell often focused on Hollywood figures. Hollywood studios eventually came to the realization that increased exposure for their stars would most likely result in increased revenues for their films. By the early 1940s Hollywood actors, including Humphrey Bogart, Katharine Hepburn, Jimmy Stewart, James Cagney, and Clark Gable, routinely participated in radio reenactments of their films; at the same time a number of actors who got their start in radio, such as Don Ameche, Richard Widmark, Agnes Moorehead, and Art Carney, were beginning to appear in films. As the lines between the two media slowly blurred, America became more and more infatuated with its stars. As a result of the unprecedented media exposure stars received when they began to appear both on radio and in film, the cultural iconolatry of entertainers, which began in earnest with the silent movie stars of the late 1910s and early 1920s, reached new heights in the 1930s and 1940s.

Perhaps the most vivid example of the cultural influence radio had in its heyday is Orson Welles' October 30, 1938, broadcast of an adaptation of H. G. Wells' *The War of the Worlds,* which presented itself as a would-be Martian invasion broadcast in real time. Welles and the other actors meant the broadcast to be dramatic fiction, but millions took it seriously. Although the show did run an opening explanation, many who tuned in late were greeted by an announcer saying, ''Ladies and gentlemen, we interrupt our program of dance music to bring you a special bulletin from the Intercontinental Radio News.'' Listeners mistakenly believed that Martians were invading the United States and that radio was covering it live. All over the country hysteria prevailed for several hours, and the power of radio to influence the American public was confirmed.

Just as radio entertainment became more diversified during the 1930s, so too did the ways in which news was presented. Whereas in the 1920s and early 1930s news had most often been simply read, a new type of reporter was coming into being in the mid-1930s: the broadcast journalist. Reporters began live coverage of developing stories and often offered on-air appraisals of news stories as they

happened. Americans who had previously only heard reporters reading recaps of speeches, conferences, conventions, and military clashes began to hear them live. These live broadcasts of social and political events played a large role in America's national attitude of unity as it entered World War II. The public had been largely uninformed when America entered World War I, but because of radio and its broadcast journalists the American public was keenly aware of the cumulative series of events that had occurred prior to its entering World War II.

As radio grew, politicians realized its importance as a means through which to disseminate their ideology. In an extreme example, European leaders such as Mussolini and Hitler routinely broadcast their fervent speeches live. Although their message was often one of hatred and intolerance, both leaders—but especially Hitler—were brilliant and impassioned speakers who understood just how effective a propaganda tool radio could be. Perhaps the most fervent ideologue on U.S. radio in the late 1930s was Father Charles Coughlin, the ''radio priest'' of Royal Oak, Michigan, who commanded an audience of millions with tirades that became increasingly anti-Semitic and pro-Franco. On the home front, perhaps no U.S. leader used radio as effectively as President Franklin Delano Roosevelt. Beginning in 1933 and lasting until his death in 1945, Roosevelt took his message directly to the people in a series of live radio speeches. Roosevelt called some of these speeches ''fireside chats,'' which were constructed to seem like personal conversations with the public. Opening each chat with the phrase, ''My dear friends,'' Roosevelt carefully explained his policies and programs and used the intimate format to gain popular support from the American people. In addition, Rooseveltian sound bites such as ''the only thing we have to fear is fear itself'' (from his first inauguration) and ''a date which will live infamy'' (from his speech to Congress after Pearl Harbor) were immediately and permanently thrust into the nation'a popular culture, in part because they were broadcast live to an audience of millions.

Throughout U.S. involvement in World War II, radio played a crucial role in the public's perception of the war. Although not televised as the Vietnam War would later be, radio brought World War II into every American living room. From Britain and France's declaring war on Germany in 1939, to Roosevelt's ''day of infamy'' speech after the attack on Pearl Harbor, to the surrender ceremonies aboard the *U.S.S. Missouri* on September 2, 1945, Americans heard the war's major events as they happened. Perhaps the most memorable broadcasts of the war were Edward R. Murrow's reports during the London blitz of 1940, which helped solidify U.S. public opinion on behalf of the Allies. As the war proceeded, and despite strict censorship restrictions, other broadcast journalists reported from military hot spots and the government used radio to communicate with the nation. All through the war Americans turned to their radios for the latest news from the fronts. In addition to the first-hand accounts of those returning from overseas and newsreels, America's memories of World War II have been shaped largely by the immediacy offered by radio.

Although radio continued to enjoy tremendous popularity in the early 1950s, it was never quite the same after World War II. The war had given radio a uniformity of purpose and focus. With the war over, radio was forced to scramble to institute peacetime programming that could match the heady days of broadcasting during the war years. As traditional formats began to lose popularity, it became clear that new formats and ideas were needed; but radio was slow to change. Experimentation was limited by the cold war atmosphere of fear created by the anti-Communist movement of the late 1940s and early

1950s. Producers were afraid that anything different from the norm might be construed as subversive. Concurrently, television was beginning to gain a firm hold in American homes. Many of the shows that had long been broadcast on the radio made the transition to television. By 1960 the golden age of radio was over.

Radio has never fully regained the popularity it enjoyed during its forty-year heyday from 1920 to 1960. The rise of FM radio stations in the 1960s propelled rock 'n' roll to a position of cultural influence unequaled by any other musical genre. FM stations sounded better than AM stations, and came in stereo. The disc jockeys who played records took advantage of their new-found freedom to experiment with the FM dial as "free form" radio. Whereas radio news had chronicled the cultural events of the 1930s, 1940s, and 1950s, rock 'n' roll became the sound track for the cultural revolution ushered in by the Boomer generation in the 1960s and early 1970s. Before World War II, most radio programs, dramas, comedies, musical shows, or quiz shows, were fifteen-minute or half-hour programs; after the war, stations tended to devote round-the-clock programming to specific musical formats, such as rock 'n' roll, Top-40, classical, rhythm & blues, or jazz, for example. In the 1990s, talk radio enjoyed a resurgence, especially on the AM dial, with figures as diverse as Rush Limbaugh, Dr. Laura Schlessinger, and Howard Stern enjoying a cultural influence perhaps never equaled by their radio predecessors—to say nothing of the frank sex therapy dispensed by Dr. Ruth Westheimer and Dr. Judy Kurlansky.

During the height of radio's popularity, as Charles Siepmann writes, "The average man or woman spends more leisure hours in listening to the radio than in anything else—expect sleeping. . . . For radio—cheap, accessible, and generous in its provision for popular tastes—has come to be the poor man's library, his 'legitimate' theater, his vaudeville, his newspaper, his club. Never before has he met so many famous and interesting people, and never have these people been at once so friendly and so attentive to his wishes." On the eve of the year 2000, American audiences had immediate access to more news and entertainment options than any population in the history of the world; radio was the seed from which the structure of contemporary current mass media grew. But America's plethora of options reflects its culture: fractious, scattered, and able to agree on little. Conversely, for a brief forty years in the mid-twentieth century, radio contributed to the creation of at least the semblance of a united country and inspired the national imagination in a way no medium has done before or since.

—Robert C. Sickels

FURTHER READING:

Bray, John. *The Communications Miracle: The Telecommunication Pioneers from Morse to the Information Superhighway.* New York, Plenum Press, 1995.

Hilmes, Michele. *Radio Voices: American Broadcasting, 1922-1952.* Minneapolis, University of Minnesota, 1997.

Ladd, Jim. *Radio Waves: Life and Revolution on the FM Dial.* New York, St. Martin's Press, 1991.

MacDonald, Fred J. *Don't Touch That Dial: Radio Programming in American Life, 1920-1960.* Chicago, Nelson-Hall, 1979.

Maltin, Leonard. *The Great American Broadcast: A Celebration of Radio's Golden Age.* New York, Dutton, 1997.

Nachman, Gerald. *Raised on Radio.* New York, Pantheon Books, 1998.

Ryan, Thomas. *American Hit Radio: A History of Popular Singles from 1955 to the Present.* Rocklin, California, Prima Publishing, 1996.

Smulyan, Susan. *Selling Radio: The Commercialization of American Broadcasting, 1920-1934.* Washington, D.C., Smithsonian Institution Press, 1994.

Urban, George E. *Radio Free Europe and the Pursuit of Democracy: My War within the Cold War.* New Haven, Connecticut, Yale University Press, 1997.

Radio Drama

Before the advent of television in the late 1940s, radio was the most popular mass medium in America. During radio's "Golden Age" from 1929 through the end of World War II, radio's comedy-variety, soap opera, and drama programs were a part of the daily lives of most Americans. Unlike movies, radio brought mass entertainment directly into the home and radio stars like Jack Benny, Gracie Allen, and Orson Welles became familiar presences within the family's private space. For the first time, listeners across the country planned their schedules around the same programs and personalities; for example, movie theaters were forced to pipe in the popular *Amos 'n' Andy* program in 1929 because so many people did not want to leave their homes and miss hearing it. Radio programs functioned as tools of assimilation for many Americans, defining "American" identities through voices. Radio nationalized ethnic, class, and regional accents, creating recognizable standard blueprints for how "Black," "Irish," "rich," and "rural" were supposed to sound. As radio historian Michele Hilmes has written: "In speaking to us as a nation during a crucial period of time [radio] helped to shape our cultural consciousness and define us as a people."

Radio drama emerged in the late 1920s with the formation of national networks and the subsequent commercialization of the industry. In the Radio Act of 1927, the United States government endorsed commercial over government ownership of radio by favoring the networks in allocating wavelengths. Because national networks provided advertisers with the opportunity to sell their products to a mass audience, the government's decision ensured the dominance of mass culture over high culture and educational programming on radio. In order to appeal to this mass audience (especially to women, whom they recognized as the primary consumers within the household), advertisers relied on personalities and programs that seemed to have popular appeal. Throughout the 1920s, music and talk radio had been radio's primary fare, but in 1929 the National Broadcasting Company (NBC) began daily broadcasts of a radio minstrel act that had become quite popular in the Midwest, *Amos 'n' Andy*. It was the network's first attempt at a fictional serial program, and radio was never the same again. The tremendous popularity of *Amos 'n' Andy* convinced advertisers that audiences wanted more narrative programs, and "radio drama," the common inclusive term for radio fiction programs, began to take up more and more network time.

The evolution of radio drama is rooted in the tension between the advertisers and the networks. To make the most money and attract the broadest audience, radio programs had to appeal to the masses without alienating the middle-class family audience. Advertisers thus took a new "lowbrow" approach to advertising, developing programs that emphasized the most pleasurable and stimulating aspects of popular culture like "gag" humor and "shocking" stories. At the time, mass culture was associated primarily with the working classes and the street culture of recent immigrants. Moviemakers and vaudeville entrepreneurs had worked hard to attract a middle-class family audience by toning down their bawdier aspects, but the dominance of mass culture on radio was still a cause for concern among the middle classes. It was the responsibility of the networks to maintain cultural standards before the public in order to keep their licenses; they had to avoid public attacks from the morality-minded who worried about the effects of low-culture programming on society. To avoid public criticism—and hence maintain their monopoly (and their profits),—networks developed two different kinds of radio drama: popular drama, produced by advertisers, and commercial-free "prestige" drama, produced and sustained by the networks to appease their critics. Although these two forms developed separately, by the end of the 1930s they had each begun to take on aspects of the other, blurring the line between popular and high culture.

Popular radio drama drew on a variety of mass culture forms, including pulp fiction, comic strips, and vaudeville. Pulp fiction anthologies of short stories had become immensely popular in the United States from the 1890s to the 1920s with the development of cheap printing techniques and national distribution systems. The "pulps" were usually first printed in magazines, and they offered audiences the predictable satisfactions of standard genres: romance, western, crime, detective mysteries, and horror. Pulp fiction had been the major source of advertising before radio; with the advent of radio drama, advertisers were able to simply shift their sponsorship to a different medium. Pulp fiction genres became well known on radio: programs like *The Shadow, Gangbusters,* and *Gunsmoke* were developed from mystery, crime, and Western pulp fiction, respectively. Romance genres aimed primarily at women were soon segregated into daytime, and became popularly known as soap operas because soap companies sponsored them. Comic strips were also popular sources for radio programs, particularly children's serials like *Little Orphan Annie.* When radio took over these forms, it made them more dramatic. The crime-fighting Shadow, for example, became much more a man of action than he had been in written form, and the constant sound of riot guns in the "real-life" crime show *Gangbusters* produced complaints from parents who charged that the guns frightened their children.

Certainly the most successful of radio's popular programs were comedy-variety shows. In the early 1930s, as the Depression put more and more vaudeville theaters out of business, vaudeville players made increasing use of radio and became the medium's biggest stars. These programs combined vaudeville "gag" humor with nightclub performance, linking the different sections together through one central personality and continuing, familiar stock characters. *The Jack Benny Show* was the most popular of such programs, running from 1932 until 1955; Benny starred as the miserly, childish, vain star of a radio program called *The Jack Benny Show.* Like other popular comedy-variety programs such as *Edgar Bergen and Charlie McCarthy* and *The Bob Hope Show, The Jack Benny Show* relied on ethnic and gender stereotypes widely used in vaudeville. Radio programs differed from vaudeville, however, in that vaudeville shows were much more fragmented and often adapted to local tastes; radio comedy-variety, on the other hand, offered audiences a more predictable narrative structure and consistent characters in order to foster familiarity between players and listeners. Programs that attempted to be more spontaneous or have a more satirical edge either failed to attract a significant audience or, like comedian Fred Allen's show, were streamlined to fit the Benny formula.

While popular drama got much higher ratings with listeners than prestige drama, the latter had a significant impact on the evolution of radio drama because of its technical and artistic innovations. Because prestige drama did not have the constraints of commercial sponsorship, its producers could experiment with sound effects, acting styles, language, and traditional narrative structure. Programs like the *Radio Guild* adapted classical plays for radio audiences, while *The Columbia Workshop* produced original scripts written for radio by some of the country's best known writers, among them Archibald MacLeish, William Saroyan, and Dorothy Parker.

The most famous name associated with radio prestige drama is Orson Welles, whose 1938 adaptation of H.G. Wells' *The War of the Worlds* caused a nationwide panic. Welles' *Mercury Theatre of the Air* program featured radio's first repertory theater, and Welles was the first prestige drama auteur, serving as writer, director, and leading player in most of the program's productions. Welles was also known for his imaginative use of the medium; *War of the Worlds* was so convincing in part because Welles borrowed techniques from radio news programs, giving his program the semblance of a news broadcast. Throughout the 1930s and 1940s, Welles continued to do radio work in both sustaining and sponsored programs, but his name was always linked to "high culture" although he often used material from more popular sources; for every dramatization of *A Tale of Two Cities,* Welles offered a *Dracula* or a *Sherlock Holmes.*

Two other famous names associated with prestige drama were writer-directors Norman Corwin and Arch Oboler. Corwin, who worked for CBS, pushed the boundaries of the radio drama form, developing new radio-specific genres like the "radio opera" (musical-documentary-dramas) and adapting poetic works like Walt Whitman's *Leaves of Grass* and Edgar Lee Master's *Spoon River Anthology* for radio. Oboler, who worked for NBC, focused on realist drama and psychological horror. He is best known for his *Arch Oboler's Plays* series and his original scripts for the horror series *Lights Out.* Oboler's work often explored the supernatural, taking his listeners into settings where they could not ordinarily go; his characters were haunted by ghosts, buried alive, or made bargains with the devil. Where Corwin's work focused on language, Oboler's work exploited radio's potential to unnerve. The war interrupted Oboler and Corwin's experiments, and like other radio writers, they turned their attention to patriotic themes. While prestige dramas were never again given the airtime they enjoyed in the late 1930s, the influence of these dramatists became more obvious in commercial drama during and after the war.

One of the most popular radio genres of the 1940s was the suspense program; programs like *Suspense, Inner Sanctum,* and *Mystery in the Air* were very much products of the radio drama which proceeded them. Unlike most radio genres that originated in pulp fiction, suspense programs shared with prestige dramas a reliance on scripts produced originally for radio. They also utilized several of the techniques of prestige radio programs, including first person narration and interior monologue, psychological complexity, the use of dreams and fantasy, and a preoccupation with the supernatural. Like Oboler's plays, they foregrounded psychological horror, but their context in an uncertain postwar America meant that certain subjects like wartime traumas and sexual tension came to the fore. The most famous and popular original radio play was the *Suspense* play "Sorry, Wrong Number" (1943), written by Lucille Fletcher and starring Agnes Moorehead, which focused on an invalid wife who overhears a murder plot on the phone and does not realize until the last few moments that she is the intended victim. The success of this program influenced radio dramas throughout the 1940s; plots continued to emphasize mistrust between the sexes and feature bizarre, often graphic violence.

As television came to dominate the postwar era in the late 1940s and early 1950s, radio drama faded in significance and popularity; the rise of the disc jockey in the 1950s ensured the resurgence of popular music as the medium's dominant entertainment. Radio drama's lasting influence is most obvious in the content and structure of television programming, which lifted its stars and genres directly from radio fiction, but commercialized radio was distinct from television in its greater acknowledgment of ethnic and class differences. Although both television and radio served to homogenize U.S. culture, much of radio's mass-culture programming remained rooted in the humor and worldview of the nation's underclass, while television's fiction programs moved away from the culture of the urban masses to appeal primarily to middle-class nuclear families.

—Allison McCracken

FURTHER READING:

Fink, Howard. ''The Sponsor's v. the Nation's Choice: North American Radio Drama.'' *Radio Drama,* edited by Peter Lewis. New York, Longman Group Ltd., 1981.

Hilmes, Michele. *Radio Voices: American Broadcasting.* Minneapolis, University of Minnesota Press, 1997.

Lipsitz, George. *Time Passages: Collective Memory and American Popular Culture.* Minneapolis, University of Minnesota Press, 1990.

McDonald, J. Fred. *Don't Touch That Dial: Radio Programming in American Life, 1920–1960.* Chicago, Nelson-Hall, 1979.

Radner, Gilda (1937-1989)

Gilda Radner, with her mass of seemingly untameable curly hair and striking ability to use her voice for comic effect, will be best remembered as one of the original ''Not Ready for Prime Time Players'' who starred in *Saturday Night Live* (1975—), a television series that became a hit with young adults despite its late time slot. She stayed with the series for five years, during which time she parodied many celebrities and created several of her own characters, such as reporters Roseanne Roseannadanna and Baba Wawa (her Barbara Walters parody). Radner married actor Gene Wilder in 1984. She died of ovarian cancer in 1989. After her death, Wilder became active in cancer awareness.

—Denise Lowe

FURTHER READING:

Cader, Michael, editor. *Saturday Night Live: The First Twenty Years.* Boston, Houghton Mifflin, 1994.

Rado, James

See Ragni, Gerome, and James Rado

Gilda Radner as Roseanne Roseannadanna during the ''Weekend Update'' skit on *Saturday Night Live*.

Raft, George (1903-1980)

Screen actor George Raft's greatest lasting contribution to the film industry was in creating the clichéd image of the caring and compassionate gangster who was more victim than victimizer. Raft may be more famous, however, for turning down Humphrey Bogart's four star-making roles than for any of the parts he did play. Raft was offered *Dead End, High Sierra, The Maltese Falcon,* and *Casablanca;* he turned each one down only to be quickly eclipsed by Bogart, who had been struggling to make a name for himself.

Raft's acting career was based on the premise that as a former gangster himself (he was friends with racketeer Owney Maddon and at one time aspired to be a big shot in Maddon's liquor mob), he would excel at playing one. Raft preferred playing tough, brutal men who were revealed to be not as cold and heartless as they pretended. He was very concerned with how crime was portrayed on-screen and would insist on stipulations in his contract about how his character could treat women and children, how knowledgeable about the crime scene his character was, and what his idea of crime was—Raft refused to play an out-and-out rat. Unfortunately, Raft was never a very expressive actor, so he managed to connect with the audience in only a few of his films.

Raft was born in New York City in 1903 and was brought up in the Hell's Kitchen area. As a young man, according to his autobiography, he was a layabout who did some boxing, winning fifteen of his twenty-two matches. He became a dancer and dance hall gigolo, and began to get parts in shows such as *City Chap, Gay Paree, Palm Beach Nights,* and *No Foolin'.* Maddon sent Raft to Texas Quinan's nightclub, where Miss Quinan suggested that he take a part in her movie, *Queen of the Night Clubs* (1929). Heading to Los Angeles, Raft was discovered at the Brown Derby restaurant by director

Rowland Brown, who gave him a bit part in *Quick Millions.* Raft's best parts were in *Taxi!* (1932); *Scarface* (1932), as the coin-flipping best friend of Tony Camonte, the main character; *Each Dawn I Die* (1939), as an idealistic gang leader who learns honesty from James Cagney's con; and *Dancers in the Dark* (1932), as a murderer.

Thinking they had found another Valentino, Paramount signed Raft to a contract and starred him in lackluster features, then suspended him after he refused to appear in *The Story of Temple Drake.* While he had a few tough-guy parts, he did his best work at Paramount as a dancer in *Bolero* (1934) with Carole Lombard and in *Rumba* (1935). Raft also objected to his role in *Souls at Sea* (1937), and went on suspension until his part was more sympathetically written. The gambit paid off and he earned an Oscar nomination for his work as a likeable, romantic tough guy with a sinister slave-trading past who spends most of his time romancing Olympe Bradna. Throughout the story, his character is encouraged to be good by an idealistic Gary Cooper, resulting in Raft's redemption.

By the end of the thirties, Paramount let Raft go, and Warner Brothers made a bid for his services, teaming him with Cagney and Bogart in such pictures as *Each Dawn I Die* and *They Drive by Night* (1940). Raft refused to appear in *South of Suez,* and once Bogart became established, the studio was quite willing to let Raft go. From there, Raft drifted from one minor part to another, appearing mostly in forgettable B films from United Artists or RKO. He finally got a couple of good parts in *Black Widow* (1954) and *Rogue Cop* (1954), but they were not enough to reestablish him in the public eye. He took a cameo role in *Around the World in 80 Days* (1956) and appeared in the television series *I'm the Law* in 1953.

George Raft

Nevertheless, Billy Wilder remembered Raft and cast him as gangster ''Spats'' Baxter in the comedy classic *Some Like It Hot* (1959). He made another cameo appearance in *Ocean's Eleven* (1960), the first Rat Pack film, and was given parts in Jerry Lewis's *Ladies' Man* (1961) and *The Patsy* (1964). In 1965, Raft was indicted for income tax evasion and could have ended his life behind bars, but the court proved merciful and the case did not go to trial. From there Raft traveled Europe and made a few disastrous comedies from a high in *Casino Royale* (1967) to a low in Otto Preminger's *Skidoo* (1968). Unable to get work, he spent his declining years watching television.

—Dennis Fischer

FURTHER READING:

Neibaur, James L. *Tough Guy: The American Movie Macho.* Jefferson, North Carolina, McFarland & Co., 1989.

Shipman, David. *The Great Movie Stars: The Golden Years.* New York, Bonanza Books, 1970.

Thompson, David. *A Biographical Dictionary of Film.* 3rd ed. New York, Alfred A. Knopf, 1994.

Yablonski, Lewis. *George Raft.* New York, McGraw-Hill, 1974.

Raggedy Ann and Raggedy Andy

Raggedy Ann, the central character in a series of children's books about dolls that come alive when their people are away, made her official debut in 1918 with the *Raggedy Ann Stories* by author and illustrator Johnny Gruelle. She was first a real rag doll for a real little girl, then was mass-produced to accompany the nearly 1,000 stories written by Gruelle before his death in 1938. Raggedy Andy, the little rag-brother of Raggedy Ann, was introduced in 1920 with *The Raggedy Andy Stories.* Raggedy Ann's image, with her black shoe-button eyes, red yarn hair, her white pinafore, and scalloped pantaloons over red-and-white striped legs remained surprisingly intact over the years, and was featured on a vast array of children's toys, clothing, furnishings, and other objects. Gruelle produced a series of 40 books, as well as using Raggedy Ann in cartoons, but the dolls themselves remain the most popular collectibles.

John Barton (''Johnny'') Gruelle (1880-1938), the son of a painter, grew up in Indianapolis, Indiana. He first worked as a newspaper cartoonist for several papers, illustrating stories as well as drawing cartoons. He won first prize in 1910 in a comic drawing contest sponsored by the *New York Herald* with the adventures of an elf named Mr. Twee Deedle. His full-color cartoon was syndicated as a full-page feature. Gruelle wrote and illustrated children's stories for popular magazines as well, and in 1914 he produced his first book commission, an illustrated Grimm's fairy tales.

The Gruelles had a daughter, Marcella, who was devoted to an old rag doll that had belonged to Johnny's mother. Resurrected from the attic, and with a new painted face and a new name, this first Raggedy Ann was Marcella's companion through an illness that ended in her death in 1916. Raggedy Ann's initial adventures were stories Johnny told to amuse and divert his bedridden daughter.

Raggedy Ann and Raggedy Andy dolls.

In 1915, Gruelle applied for a patent on Raggedy Ann. The family made a dozen prototype dolls, although accounts differ as to whether the impetus for Raggedy Ann's manufacture came from Gruelle or the P.F. Volland Company of Chicago, with whom he had the book contract. In any event, the dolls and stories were simultaneously produced and were instantly successful. In the time-honored tradition of little brothers, Raggedy Andy came along two years later. Raggedy Andy never acquired the central status of his sister, but remained a secondary character.

Several factors account for Raggedy Ann's great popularity. The dolls, which included an entire cast of other characters—the Scotsman Uncle Clem, Beloved Belindy, Percy the Policeman—were kept at the forefront of consumer consciousness by the large number of books written by their prolific author (a sequel every year and sometimes two). The Raggedy series, while never enjoying great critical acclaim, was very appealing to its young audience. Gruelle's soft line drawings and full-page, color illustrations fill every alternate page of the books. His talents as a cartoonist were well employed in the difficult task of imbuing dolls, whose faces never change, with a full range of expression and attitude. The narratives—romping adventures out of

sight of the "real for sure folks," usually involving peril and a cheerful resolution—are set in an innocent and somewhat dated world, but Gruelle had real insights into the way children think. He uses repetition and naming devices consistent with children's language patterns. He fills his stories with little tiny things, child-sized things, good things to eat, playing games, and (nice) secrets. He creates, in other words, an entire, internally consistent, vicarious world.

Finally, Raggedy Ann and her coterie were easily accessible. Raggedy was not a high-priced porcelain doll with an equally exclusive wardrobe, but a rag doll with a homespun quality that was deliberately preserved despite changes in manufacturers. She could even be made at home, beginning in the 1940s when McCall's Pattern Company marketed an authorized pattern to reproduce Raggedy Ann and Andy.

No discussion of Raggedy Ann would be complete without revealing her secret. She wears stamped over her heart the words "I Love You." And that came about when she fell into a bucket of paint and had to be restuffed by the painter's mother, who sewed into her chest a candy heart with the motto "I Love You" on it. Raggedy Ann was a household presence for the greater part of the twentieth century.

Johnny Gruelle's gifts as an author and illustrator produced a classic American character.

—Karen Hovde

FURTHER READING:

Hall, Patricia. *Johnny Gruelle, Creator of Raggedy Ann and Andy.* Gretna, Louisiana, Pelican, 1993.

Williams, Martin. ''Some Remarks on Raggedy Ann and Johnny Gruelle.'' *Children's Literature,* Vol. 3. Storrs, Connecticut, Children's Literature Association, 1974, 140-146.

Raging Bull

When *Raging Bull,* Martin Scorsese's biopic of 1940s middle-weight boxing champion Jake LaMotta, premiered in November of 1980, critics and audiences alike hailed it as a masterpiece. The film's expressionistic black-and-white photography, its lyrical realism, and Robert De Niro's stunning performance gave it an expressive power of great magnitude. The amazing physical transformation De Niro underwent in the title role—adding an estimated 60 pounds of fat to his slender frame to portray the older, bloated LaMotta without a fat suit—also made it the most extreme example of method acting thus far in filmmaking. De Niro won an Oscar for his work in *Raging Bull,* as did editor Thelma Schoonmaker. But many critics, most notably Pauline Kael, film critic for the *New Yorker* magazine, were uncomfortable with the film, wondering if LaMotta—a violent, troubled wife-abusing lout— was worthy of the spiritual transformation Scorsese attributed to him.

Scorsese undertook the film at a time of crisis in his career. His previous feature, *New York, New York,* had been a critical and commercial bomb. Scorsese was so demoralized by its failure that he embarked on a debauch of epic length, resulting in his 1978 hospitalization. While visiting Scorsese in the hospital, De Niro, who had lobbied to adapt LaMotta's biography for over four years, once again broached the subject of *Raging Bull* with his friend and collaborator.

The picture Scorsese envisioned would be a meditation on the Catholic themes that had inspired his best work of the 1970s: redemption, alienation, morality, and guilt. It would be at once a wholly personal work and a revision of the 1940s movies he had loved as a child. It is the tension generated between the formal aspects of the picture—the stylized black-and-white photography, at times documentary-like in execution—and the subject matter that gives *Raging*

Robert De Niro (left) and Joe Pesci in a scene from the film *Raging Bull.*

Bull its almost hallucinatory ferocity. "What De Niro does in this picture isn't acting, exactly," wrote Pauline Kael, who for the most part took a pejorative view of the film's excesses. "Though it may at some level be awesome, it definitely isn't pleasurable." She was right. In fact, De Niro's portrayal is so harrowing that every moment he is onscreen is excruciatingly tense.

De Niro's LaMotta is a violent, self-centered, egotistical man, a man possessed by uncontrollable paranoia. And like his sobriquet, "The Bronx Bull," LaMotta is bullish. But, as the film begins *in medias res,* the audience never learns the reasons for LaMotta's obstinate behavior, only that it is his fatal flaw, the chink in his armor. Because of his intransigence in dealing with a local mob boss, he remains a contender for years, unable to gain a shot at the title. But only after acquiescing to mob demands—to throw a fight—does he get his chance at the championship. In his final boxing match— against his old nemesis, Sugar Ray Robinson—LaMotta is virtually crucified on the ropes, taking a brutal beating while refusing to go down. With his face reduced to a bleeding pulp, he taunts the victor, repeating, "You never got me down, Ray," in an infantile chant.

Retired in Florida, LaMotta has become an obese parody of himself, presiding over a Miami nightclub where he introduces the acts with a crass version of suave nightclub patter. Indeed, things fall apart: his long-suffering wife leaves him and he is eventually arrested on a morals charge. In a pivotal scene, he retrieves his championship belt, attacking it with a hammer to dislodge the gems he needs for bail money, mindlessly deforming the belt as he has destroyed his life. Finally, locked in solitary confinement, LaMotta reaches a crisis, attacking his confinement, banging his head against the wall, kicking and punching it in anger and frustration, his body half in shadow and half in light. "Why, you're so stupid, an animal," he screams. Finally he collapses, sobbing, "I wasn't that bad." As he cries, a piece of his sleeve catches a beam of light in the darkened cell. It is one of Scorsese's most transcendent moments, perfectly blending religious metaphor with film language.

The film closes as it had begun, with LaMotta, now a nightclub entertainer, practicing Marlon Brando's "I shoulda been a contender" speech—from *On the Waterfront*—in front of his dressing-room mirror. He has achieved a measure of peace. Something is now apparent than was not clear in the first scene, where LaMotta appeared a figure of ridicule, butchering Shakespeare with his ludicrous Bronx accent: looking at his face in the mirror, he says, "Let's face it, it was you, it was you."

Scorsese told an interviewer at the time of *Raging Bull's* release that "those who think it's a boxing picture would be out their minds. Its brutal, sure, but it is a brutality that could take place not only in the boxing ring, but in the bedroom or in an office." Because the film speaks on the level of the specific and the universal notion of man's craving for redemption, its brilliance affects one at a visceral level. As a child, Scorsese had been "taught to hate the sin, but love the sinner." Perhaps no other film so complexly embodies this basic philosophy.

Raging Bull was the culmination of one of several cycles in Scorsese's work, a cycle preoccupied with, in the words of Paul Schrader, "a sense of guilt, redemption by blood, and moral purpose." For Scorsese, filming it seemed to have a salutary effect, resolving the moral conflicts that had permeated *Mean Streets* and *Taxi Driver.*

—Michael J. Baers

FURTHER READING:

Beaver, Frank, editor. *Twayne's Filmmakers Series: Martin Scorsese.* New York, Twayne Publishers, 1992.

Connelly, Marie Katheryn. *Martin Scorsese: An Analysis of His Feature Films.* Jefferson, North Carolina, McFarland, 1991.

Dougan, Andy. *Martin Scorsese Close Up: The Making of His Movies.* London, Orion, 1997.

Ehrenstein, David. *The Scorsese Picture: The Art and Life of Martin Scorsese.* New York, Carol Publishing Group, 1992.

Ferrante, Leonard. *Redemption in the Narrative: Films of Martin Scorsese.* Ann Arbor, UMI Dissertation Services, 1994.

Kael, Pauline. *New Yorker.* 8 December 1980.

Kellman, Steven, editor. *Perspectives on Raging Bull.* New York, Perspectives on Film Series, 1994.

Kelly, Mary Pat. *Martin Scorsese: A Journey.* New York, Thunder's Mouth Press, 1991.

Scorsese, Martin. *Scorsese on Scorsese.* London, Faber, 1989.

Weiss, Marion. *Martin Scorsese: A Guide to References and Resources.* Boston, G.K. Hall, 1987.

Ragni, Gerome (1942-1991), and James Rado (1939—)

The collaborative theatrical team of Gerome Ragni and James Rado created *Hair* (1967), the first rock musical on Broadway. *Hair* was a milestone for musical theater as an art form: experimental in nature, controversial in its subject matter and presentation. It was the first Broadway show to display totally nude performers, and to have a truly racially integrated cast. Supported by composer Galt MacDermot's rock music score, *Hair* celebrated the 1960s hippie lifestyle and examined the concerns of America's youth at that time—anti-war beliefs, sexual freedoms, drug use, and the search for community. Though the show remained Ragni and Rado's only major success, it was a substantial one. *Hair* became wildly popular, even spawning a film version a decade later, and became the only show that fully embodied the youthful energy of the 1960s.

—Brian Granger

FURTHER READING:

Davis, Lorrie, and Rachel Gallagher. *Letting down My Hair: Two Years with the Love Rock Tribe—From Dawning to Downing of Aquarius.* New York, Arthur Fields Books, 1973.

Horn, Barbara Lee. *The Age of Hair: Evolution and Impact of Broadway's First Rock Musical.* New York, Greenwood Press, 1991.

Raiders of the Lost Ark

While on vacation in Hawaii in 1977, filmmakers Steven Spielberg and George Lucas came up with the idea for a movie based on the serials they had loved as children: action movies set in exotic locales

Harrison Ford in a scene from the film *Raiders of the Lost Ark*.

with cliffhangers every second. Recalled Spielberg: ''I wondered why they didn't make movies like that anymore. I still wanted to see them.'' Apparently, so did millions of Americans, as *Raiders of the Lost Ark* (1981), the fruit of the filmmakers' labors, grossed more than $200 million domestically in its first box-office run and re-established the adventure movie genre in U.S. film.

With Spielberg as director and Lucas as executive producer, *Raiders of the Lost Ark* follows the adventures of Indiana Jones (played by burgeoning screen icon Harrison Ford), a mild-mannered, bespectacled archeology professor who leads a double life as a whip-wielding swashbuckler who hunts down ancient treasures and prevents them from falling into the wrong hands, generally those of profit-seekers. Jones's adversaries in this particular episode, set in the 1930s, are Nazis in search of the Ark of the Covenant, allegedly once the storehouse for the Ten Commandments. The Nazis want the Ark because they believe possession of such an ancient treasure would serve as a rallying point for nationalistic pride. Jones and his partner Marion (Karen Allen) venture across the globe in search of the Ark, all the while avoiding the Nazis' best attempts on their lives. The movie climaxes with a fantastic showdown between the two sides over the prized treasure.

With its exotic locations and storyline of ''narrow misses and close calls,'' *Raiders of the Lost Ark* brought adventure back to American cinema. The B-movie adventure story had been out of style since the 1940s, and only in the James Bond films of British cinema could films be found that were remotely adventure-based. In making *Raiders of the Lost Ark,* Spielberg and Lucas attempted to do away with the quintessentially British adventure narrative and restore to the action film the uniquely American flavor of such 1930s serials as *Commando Cody* and *Don Winslow of the Coast Guard.*

Raiders of the Lost Ark was resoundingly popular with both the public and critics. It earned Academy Awards in film editing, visual effects, sound, and art direction. It also ushered in a new era of American action movies, as the 1980s and 1990s gave rise to a host of adventure serials, not the least of which were the two *Raiders of the Lost Ark* sequels: *Indiana Jones and the Temple of Doom* (1985) and *Indiana Jones and the Last Crusade* (1989), also starring Harrison Ford.

An unintended consequence of *Raiders of the Lost Ark* was the way it spawned renewed interest in the profession of archaeology. With series such as *Mysteries of the Pyramids,* the Discovery Channel and the Arts & Entertainment Network maintained the public's fascination with the exotic and fantastic image of archaeology presented by *Raiders of the Lost Ark.* However, much to the chagrin of savants in the field, *Raiders of the Lost Ark* created a less-than-accurate image of professional fieldwork, in which the spoon, not the bullwhip, represents the traditional tool of choice. Professionals have had to disabuse not a few starry-eyed youngsters that the field is not quite as exciting as the movies make it out to be.

—Scott Tribble

FURTHER READING:

McBride, Joseph. *Steven Spielberg: A Biography.* New York, Simon & Schuster, 1997.

Taylor, Philip M. *Steven Spielberg: The Man, His Movies, and Their Meaning.* New York, Continuum Publishing Company, 1992.

Williams, Stephen. *Fantastic Archaeology.* Philadelphia, University of Pennsylvania Press, 1991.

Rainey, Gertrude "Ma" (1886-1939)

Gertrude "Ma" Rainey is known as the "Mother of the Blues." Born Gertrude Pridgett in Columbus, Georgia, on April 26, 1886, Rainey was the first woman known to sing the blues, combining country blues simplicity with more urban styles. Her accompanists included Louis Armstrong and Fletcher Henderson. More commonly, however, her accompaniment consisted of an old-style jug or a washboard band.

Rainey began her entertainment career when she was still a teenager. At fourteen, she started singing in front of audiences, and not long thereafter she began touring with the Rabbit Foot Minstrels.

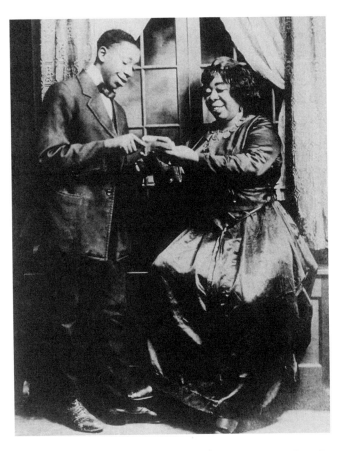

Ma Rainey, sitting, in a promotional photo for the Rabbit Foot Minstrels.

It is commonly held that while touring with the Minstrels she taught Bessie Smith. Rainey is given credit for being the first woman to bring the blues into the popular entertainment of her day—vaudeville, minstrel, and tent shows. In 1904 she married Will "Pa" Rainey, an elderly entrepreneur of the minstrel circuit, and thus got the name by which she became famous. She and her husband had an act billed as "Rainey and Rainey, Assassinators of the Blues."

During the 1910s and 1920s, Ma Rainey became a solo act and the foremost proponent of the blues style. She was the most rural of the classic blues singers, drawing most of her support from a Southern audience. She picked up a number of other nicknames, including the "Paramount Wildcat" (for the Paramount record company) and "Gold Necklace Woman of the Blues" (for the necklace of gold coins which she always wore in performance). She earned for the blues its reputation as a "low down music." Her open bisexuality did a great deal to foster that reputation. Rainey's advertisement for the notorious 1928 record "Prove It on Me," featured her in a man's outfit coming on to two women. The lyrics were similarly challenging: "Wear my clothes just like a fan. / Talk to gals just like any old man; / 'Cause they say I do it, ain't nobody caught me, / Sure got to prove it on me." The song confirmed Rainey's independent image and advocacy of women's issues. Rainey practiced what she preached and controlled her own career; she was famous for her business acumen and always carried a trunk full of money.

In 1923, the thirty-eight-year-old Rainey began recording for Paramount Records. She recorded more than 100 sides in her six years at Paramount, including "C.C. Rider" and "Ma Rainey's Black Bottom." However, male blues singers soon began to surpass female blues singers in popularity while the blues in general went into a decline. Rainey's last recording was in 1928, but she continued to perform until 1935, when she left the circuit and went back home to Columbus, Georgia, where she ran two theaters until she died in 1939 of heart failure.

Rainey had followed the path of other blues singers, returning to the church in her later years. She became active in the Congregation of Friendship Baptist Church, joining her brother who was a deacon there. In 1983 Ma Rainey was posthumously inducted into the Blues Foundation's Hall of Fame. In 1990 the Rock and Roll Hall of Fame followed suit, citing her as an early influence on Rock and Roll. In 1994 the U.S. Postal Service honored her with a stamp.

—Frank A. Salamone

FURTHER READING:

Davis, Angela. *Blues Legacies and Black Feminism: Gertrude "Ma" Rainey, Bessie Smith, and Billie Holiday.* New York, Pantheon Books, 1998.

Lieb, Sandra. *Mother of the Blues: A Study of Ma Rainey.* Amherst, University of Massachusetts Press, 1981.

Stewart-Baxter, Derrick. *Ma Rainey and the Classic Blues Singers.* New York, Stein & Day, 1970.

Rains, Claude (1889-1967)

The words "unique actor" and "consummate professional" are overused in the entertainment industry, but they describe perfectly

Claude Rains, an exceptional character actor of the Golden Age of Hollywood during the 1930s and 1940s. Rains was known for his subtle nuances in style, his perfect diction, and his mellifluous voice as he skillfully created memorable characters on stage, screen, television, and radio for nearly 50 years.

Of the 54 movies Rains made from 1933 to 1965, he is most remembered for his unforgettable performances as the mad chemist in *The Invisible Man* (1933), the smoothly corrupt senator foiled by Jimmy Stewart in Frank Capra's *Mr. Smith Goes to Washington* (1939), the sympathetic and pitiful betrayed husband of Ingrid Bergman in Alfred Hitchcock's *Notorious* (1946), and the charmingly corrupt Vichy police official who joins Humphrey Bogart to fight for freedom at the end of *Casablanca* (1942). But few Americans know that the British-born Rains was an eminent stage actor both in London and with the renowned Theatre Guild in New York for 30 years before he entered motion pictures.

Even though Rains was not particularly good looking, and at 5'6" rather short, he possessed a commanding air, a seemingly inbred impeccable manner, and a sly humor, all of which resulted in a presence more imposing than his slight physical build implied. His acting suggested suaveness with just a hint of wickedness, but it was his elocution and husky-toned velvety voice that became his trademark. Rains could combine words, subtle gestures, and emphatic pauses with perfect timing. His speech and style were all the more remarkable given that he was born into abject poverty in London's slums during the latter part of the Victorian Era, and lived a rather Dickensian childhood on the streets. Until well into his teens, Rains suffered a serious speech defect and also had a strong cockney dialect. As the eminent writer J. B. Priestly stated about the actor's persona in his book *Particular Pleasures,* ''I can imagine an American filmgoer seeing Claude Rains . . . as an autocrat or smooth villain, feeling certain that here was a man who must have left an aristocratic family . . . to amuse himself making films. Rains had that air [of refinement].''

Rains began his career at age ten as a callboy in the British theatre and was encouraged to take voice lessons and overcome his speech problems. His self-discipline and responsible attitude were noticed by theatre owners and, in an unprecedented manner, Rains eventually became stage manager. In this way he learned every aspect of theatrical production, including effective acting.

In 1915 Rains served with the British Army in France, where he suffered the ill-effects of the German's use of mustard gas. Although his vocal cords were damaged, he astonished the doctors when ironically he recovered with a much deeper and unusual voice. In 1919 he returned to the London stage as an actor and performed in diverse plays penned by talents ranging from George Bernard Shaw to Pirandello, and was noticed by critics for his exceptional ability. Prominent writers such as Graham Greene were highly complimentary, describing the actor's interpretations as brilliant: ''Mr. Rains' low husky voice, his power of investing even commonplace dialogue with smoldering conviction, is remarkable. . . . He can catch, as no one else can, the bitter distrust of the world, religious in its intensity'' Rains arrived in the United States in 1925 with a touring company and decided to remain in this country, becoming a naturalized citizen in 1938. By the early 1930s he was one of the leading actors with the Theatre Guild.

Initially Rains avoided films, and he especially refrained from making silent movies. The Great Depression, however, forced him, and many other actors, to leave the theatre for Hollywood. In 1933, he accepted the lead role in Universal's *The Invisible Man*, a film directed by his old theatre friend James Whale, who insisted on Rains

for the part. Whale recognized the power of the actor's extraordinary voice, which was essential since the actor's face was completely covered during the entire film. He made three movies in 1934 and 1935, impressing studio heads, and by 1936 Jack Warner offered the actor a contract, recognizing he had the ability ''to do anything and do it well.'' It was a relationship that lasted ten years.

While most film admirers saw Rains as a reflection of the characters he portrayed—self-assured, cunning, devious, well-educated, polished, and urbane—in reality he was none of these things. He was an extremely honest, entirely self-taught, shy, reserved man who lived quite simply but who always felt very insecure and frightened. Rains' persona of sophistication was self-created and in his acting he never used his own personality, as did so many film stars like Cary Grant and Gary Cooper. Above all, he rarely duplicated his characters and with equal aplomb could be a heavenly messenger (*Here Comes Mr. Jordan,* 1937) or the devil himself (*Angel on My Shoulder,* 1946), a wise and shrewd Caesar (*Caesar and Cleopatra,* 1945), or a naive cuckold to Bette Davis (*Mr. Skeffington,* 1944). Davis considered Claude Rains the greatest actor she ever worked with and they were friends for 20 years. He made two other popular films with her; as the kindly and understanding psychiatrist (in *Now, Voyager,* 1943), and as an egotistical, brilliant, but mean-spirited composer (in *Deception,* 1946). Rains displayed an inherent intelligence in his characterizations, that enabled him to overcome a shallow script or trite dialogue in many films. Producers and directors knew his broad range and his box-office popularity, and they frequently enlarged or built in roles for him. But even when his part was small Rains' presence was commanding, and he made a powerful impression, such as his portrayal of the mysterious Dr. Tower in *Kings Row* (1942).

Rains could suggest thoughts without words, but when he did speak his tone revealed, without affectation, the complexity of his character or set the mood for the scene. He was often labeled a ''villain'' simply because in some parts he implied intrigue and exuded an element of cunning. He used his unique voice to intimidate, suggest, or seduce an audience by controlling the pitch, volume, and innuendo; and his timing was impeccable. Perhaps Rains' uniqueness was that he could ''put on'' a complex personality as easily as other actors use make-up or costumes. This is especially apparent in his suggestive ''effete'' portrayal of Prince John in *The Adventures of Robin Hood* (1938). Often his characters seemed to border between being scrupulous and unscrupulous, and while scheming, not necessarily evil; this is most evident in his performance as the wily police captain in *Casablanca.* Although he was nominated four times for an Academy Award, he never won the honor.

At age 60, and after a 16 year absence, Rains returned to the New York stage in 1951 in Sidney Kingsley's *Darkness at Noon,* playing an old Bolshevik during the Stalinist purge trials. For his remarkable and astonishing portrayal he won every award the theatre world bestows. During the 1950s he attempted a few plays but only found critical success in T.S. Eliot's *The Confidential Clerk* (1954). He also acted in many early prominent television shows such as *Judgement at Nuremburg,* and appeared in a musical version of *The Pied Piper,* along with several Alfred Hitchcock episodes. Sadly, by 1960 his voice began to fail, along with his health, which was very apparent in his portrayal of the devious British official in David Lean's *Lawrence of Arabia* (1962). Rains' last film role was as King Herrod in *The Greatest Story Ever Told* (1965), of which one reviewer wrote: ''After you've seen Rains in the first twenty minutes of the film, you can leave the theatre.''

In the early 1960s, Rains married for the sixth time and moved to New Hampshire, but within a few years his wife died of cancer. Old, quite ill, and alone, he remained isolated in his home until his death in May 1967. His friend Bette Davis best summed up Rains' artistry when she stated during an interview, "an actor of his technique and style was irreplaceable; we shall not see his kind again."

—Toby Irene Cohen

FURTHER READING:

Behlmer, Rudy. *Inside Warner Bros. (1935-1951).* New York, Simon & Schuster, 1985.

Harmetz, Aljean. *Round up the Usual Suspects: The Making of Casablanca.* New York, Hyperion, 1992.

Mank, Greg. *The Hollywood Hissables.* Metuchen, New Jersey. Scarecrow Press, 1989.

Mordden, Ethan. *The Hollywood Studios.* New York, Alfred A. Knopf, 1988.

Raitt, Bonnie (1949—)

Although she is one of rock 'n' roll's biggest names, Bonnie Raitt has always been more concerned with musical integrity and social activism than with easy fame. The daughter of Broadway musical star John Raitt, Bonnie was raised in Los Angeles in a politically active Quaker household. She began playing guitar at age nine, but only began to pursue a musical career while attending Radcliffe, where she played at Cambridge, Massachusetts, blues clubs. Becoming a dedicated student of African-American musical traditions, Raitt dropped out of college to sign with Warner Bros. and released her first album in 1971. A white woman performing classic black blues, Raitt's virtuoso guitar playing and appealing voice made her a critical darling. But she devoted as much time to her political activism as to her music and, struggling with alcoholism, by the late 1970s, her career began to wane. Raitt became sober in the mid-1980s and, in 1989, she released *Nick of Time.* At age 40, after almost 20 years of being overlooked by commercial audiences, Raitt was an overnight success, winning four Grammys. Now one of the music industry's most successful artists, Raitt continues to eschew formulaic pop albums in favor of work that reflects her musical heritage and political beliefs, making her that pop culture rarity—a best-seller with integrity.

—Victoria Price

FURTHER READING:

Bego, Mark. *Bonnie Raitt: Just in the Nick of Time.* New York, Birch Lane Press, 1996.

Rambo

One of the best known and most popular fictional characters of the 1980s, Rambo was introduced in David Morrell's 1972 novel *First Blood* with the words, "His name was Rambo, and he was just some nothing kid for all anybody knew, standing by the pump of a gas

Sylvester Stallone as Rambo.

station at the outskirts of Madison, Kentucky." Rambo's popularity was due especially to the series of films based on the Rambo character, especially the second film, *Rambo: First Blood Part II,* in which the hero, played by Sylvester Stallone, symbolically "wins" the Vietnam War. After the humiliation of Vietnam, the disgust over Watergate, and the four-year presidency of the somber, soul-searching Jimmy Carter, America in the 1980s was ready for a change. Throughout that decade, both President Ronald Reagan and Rambo proclaimed the same message: America is back!

In the novel, the character bears little resemblance to Stallone. Rambo is barely out of his teens. He is only six months home from Vietnam, where he served with the elite Special Forces, was captured by the Viet Cong, escaped, and went a little mad in the process. He has let his hair and beard grow, and now hitchhikes aimlessly around the country. In Madison, Kentucky, Rambo runs afoul of the local sheriff, who arrests him for vagrancy. While being forcibly shaved at the local jail, Rambo has a flashback to the war. In a panic, he kills one deputy, wounds another, and escapes to the nearby wilderness. He is soon the focus of a manhunt by a posse of men who have no idea what kind of tiger they have by the tail. Rambo's hard-won guerrilla skills allow him both to avoid capture and to inflict heavy casualties upon his pursuers. The National Guard is eventually brought in but is no match for the former Green Beret. Many deaths later, Rambo kills his enemy, the sheriff, before being shot dead himself—by his former Special Forces commander, Captain Trautman.

The novel was moderately successful, but the story was not filmed until 1981, and a number of changes were made before Stallone would take on the lead role. The biggest change was in the behavior of Rambo. In the film, he is still a Special Forces veteran of Vietnam, but his use of survival skills is much more restrained. In the novel, Rambo kills his pursuers with no thought of mercy; for him, it is war. Stallone's is a kinder, gentler Rambo. He wounds many people, but kills no one directly, and the one death attributable to him is an accident. Clearly, this rewriting stems from a desire to have Rambo conform more closely to the mold of the "good guy" hero, whereas his literary incarnation is more of an anti-hero. The change in the character may also explain why the savagely realistic Rambo of the novel had to die, while Stallone's character lived to fight another day.

That day was three years in coming, but in May 1985, *Rambo: First Blood Part II* burst upon America's movie screens. Rambo is released from prison to undertake a mission for the CIA. Satellite photos suggest that Americans are still being held prisoner in Vietnam. Rambo is to sneak in through the jungle and find out for certain. The tone of the movie is set early when Trautman, Rambo's former commander, comes to get him out of prison and explain the mission. Rambo asks, "Do we get to win this time?" Trautman's reply: "This time it's up to you." Once in Vietnam, Rambo is betrayed by the CIA, captured by the Vietnamese, and tortured by their Russian "advisors." Refusing to break under torture, Rambo escapes, arms himself, and proceeds to slaughter every Vietnamese and Russian soldier in the vicinity. In an interesting reversal of America's role in the Vietnam War, Rambo is now the wily guerrilla, using stealth, guile, and primitive weapons (a knife and longbow) against a large force of well-armed enemies.

The film was a huge success both in the United States and worldwide, earning more than $150 million in its U.S. theatrical release alone. Even President Ronald Reagan praised it. For some, that was a problem: the character of Rambo seemed to represent the kind of kill-the-Commies machismo that had involved the country in Vietnam in the first place—an attitude that also could be said to typify most U.S. foreign policy in the Reagan years.

Rambo III, one of the most expensive movies made up to that time, was released in 1988. Some estimates put the film's budget at a whopping $63 million, with about a quarter of that going to Stallone. In this incarnation, Rambo is seeking tranquility in a Thai monastery when he is visited by his mentor, Trautman. The Green Beret colonel has been given a dangerous assignment: to help Afghan guerrillas fight the Soviet invaders of their country. Trautman asks Rambo to come to Afghanistan with him, but Rambo is tired of war and declines. Trautman undertakes the mission alone and is captured by the evil Russians. Rambo learns of his friend's plight and vows to rescue him. Reaching Afghanistan, Rambo finds Trautman, frees him, and the two then mow down the Russians in an orgy of grunts, explosions, and automatic weapons fire.

To the surprise of many, *Rambo III* actually lost money, at least in its U.S. release. One reason was its immense budget, but the "Rambo" formula also appeared to be growing stale, and the Soviet invasion of Afghanistan lacked the kind of emotional resonance for Americans that could be found in the second film's refighting of the Vietnam War.

Rambo also saw action as a Saturday-morning cartoon character, battling such enemies as Russian spies, Arab terrorists, and evil American punk rockers. A number of toy companies were licensed to produce action figures of Rambo and his foes, as well as plastic guns and knives modeled after the weapons used by Stallone's character in the films.

—Justin Gustainis

FURTHER READING:

Greenburg, Harvey R. "Dangerous Recuperations: *Red Dawn, Rambo,* and the New Decaturism." *Journal of Popular Film and Television.* Vol. 15, No. 2, 1987, 60-70.

Morrell, David. *First Blood.* New York, M. Evans & Co., 1972.

Walsh, Jeffrey, and James Aulich, editors. *Vietnam Images: War and Representation.* Hampshire, United Kingdom, Macmillan Press, 1989.

The Ramones

Generally regarded as the forefathers of the punk rock movement, the Ramones—Joey, Dee Dee, Johnny, and Tommy—formed in Forest Hills, New York, in 1974. Their influence was felt overseas after several future members of Britain's leading punk acts witnessed the Ramones' 1976 tour of England. Many Americans, though, weren't sure whether the band was a joke or not. Their identical attire of ripped denim and biker jackets, and the use of the same surname ("Ramone" was a pseudonym used by Paul McCartney when he was with the Beatles), poked fun at the pomposity that infected rock during the 1970s. Joey Ramone recalled to Matt Diehl in *Rolling Stone* that "1976 was the height of disco and corporate rock, and we were like nobody else." When other groups were recording songs that lasted the length of an LP's entire side, the Ramones' first album clocked in at 30 minutes, with many songs lasting a mere two minutes. The songs' short length was part of the same minimalist, no-frills technique that characterized the band's career-long discipline and consistency. A Ramones show in 1997 was pretty much the same show as one in 1977, and it was this consistency that helped the band outlast most of its punk peers.

The Ramones were signed in 1975 by Sire Records, an independent American label that had a heavy roster of punk and new wave acts, including the Replacements and the Talking Heads. Their first release in 1976, *Ramones,* contained short, energetic songs that used three chords and shunned existing rock conventions like guitar solos. The combination of surf music and fast rhythm guitar was initially abrasive, something the band undoubtedly knew and capitalized on by recording an actual chain saw to introduce "Chain Saw." Songs like "Beat on the Brat" and "Blitzkrieg Bop" contained elements of aggression and conquest, but this fueled a campaign to overtake the music industry, not one that advocated street violence.

By the time *Rocket to Russia* was released in 1977, the group's cartoonish persona was established; the "joke" band that people thought would fall into obscurity didn't. As many of rock's superstars clung to a leftover 1960s mysticism, the Ramones' records featured cretins, pinheads, lobotomies, and shock treatment. On a more serious level, these elements of fun served to repudiate 1960s hippie culture. The Ramones recaptured the short and simple aesthetic that rock music had abandoned and revived the generation gap, all in the same stroke.

Road to Ruin was released in 1978 and introduced the group's first lineup change. Tommy, the group's drummer and co-producer, gave up performing to produce records; he was replaced by Marky Ramone. *Road to Ruin* included a cover from the British Invasion period and—surprise—a ballad called "Questioningly." The group then starred in the 1979 movie, *Rock 'n' Roll High School*, which fairly represented the group's just-dumb-fun ethos.

The Ramones

The Ramones' last recording was 1995's *Adios Amigos.* They left fans with 11 original recordings and a number of live recordings and retrospectives. Throughout their career the band's style remained largely intact, with the occasional incorporation of metal and psyche-delia. Lyrically, the band expanded into topical subjects, like 1986's ''Bonzo Goes to Bitburg,'' a reference to Ronald Reagan's ill-advised trip to a German war cemetery. The song was subsequently retitled ''My Brain Is Hanging Upside Down'' for its release on *Animal Boy.*

The Ramones characterized the complex nature of punk while exposing the contradictions within rock 'n' roll itself. Their music, lyrics, and image were drawn entirely from popular culture. Some critics, especially those who tried to legitimize rock music to a broader audience, dismissed the Ramones as lowbrow entertainment. These writers missed the point, or forgot, that rock derives a large part of its validity by standing opposite to mainstream culture. Reminding people of this, the Ramones were put in the position of initiating a conservative artistic reaction within the punk movement, a movement that was perceived by many as a radical threat. Even among their songs the group expressed seemingly contradictory ideas: the group that recorded ''Bonzo Goes to Bitburg'' later recorded a pro-NRA song called ''Scattergun.''

The Ramones' cartoonish pose masked their conceptual nature, which Talking Heads bassist Tina Weymouth commented on in 1990: ''What set the Ramones apart from all the hardcore bands that came later was their discipline. They chose to be primitive.'' The Ramones' spontaneous do-it-yourself style made them a mass-scale influence in rock. They launched the development of punk, but they also emboldened musicians outside of punk as well. Once young musicians realized that forming a band did not require anyone else's blessing, local club scenes emerged and independent record labels developed. In the commercially conservative climate of the music business in the late 1970s, the Ramones' appearance showed others that it was possible to work outside an often hostile music industry.

—Daryl Umberger

FURTHER READING:

Bessman, Jim. *Ramones: An American Band.* New York, St. Martin's Press, 1993.

Diehl, Matt. ''The Making of Ramones' Ramones.'' *Rolling Stone.* May 15, 1997, 80.

Eddy, Chuck. ''The Ramones.'' *Rolling Stone.* September 20, 1990, 78-81.

Gaines, Donna. ''My Life with the Ramones.'' *Village Voice.* January 116, 1996, 23-26.

Ramone, Dee Dee. *Poison Heart: Surviving the Ramones.* Wembley, Middlesex, England, Firefly, 1997.

Ranch House

The hiatus in home building enforced by the Great Depression ended in a period when older architectural styles, such as the bungalow, made popular during the housing boom of the turn of the century, was replaced by newer design ideas. After World War II, new designs proliferated due to the largest housing boom in the history of the United States. Unlike designs used at the turn of the century, those used after World War II incorporated a well-thought-out public discourse concerning the design of the modern home. Specifically, many home magazines, such as *Ladies' Home Journal*, linked surveys of home owners with ideas of architects and designers in order to argue that the modern home should pair the latest building technology with the needs of the modern family. In addition, this discourse involved a new attentiveness to domestic life, led by Dr. Benjamin Spock, that suggested that the home design greatly influenced family life. As early as 1940, the ranch house became the form indelibly attached to the new ideal of the American family.

The basic features of the ranch house—its simple, informal, one-story structure, its low-pitched eaves, its large, expansive ''picture'' windows—were fused in the public mind with the easygoing lifestyle identified with the Southwest and West Coast. Although such homes did not necessarily populate the ranches of the Western Prairie—the ranching frontier cared little about architecture—the form of the homes did bear some resemblance to western ranch houses of the

1880s. More directly, the ranch house derived from architect Frank Lloyd Wright's prairie and usonian houses.

Within the overall ranch-house type a pattern of evolution can be traced. Both the size and complexity of the floor plan layouts increase. The modest ranch type evolves into a sprawling, highly articulated ranch rambler, incorporating split and bi-level variants. Three zones of the home are structured around the basic acts of its human occupants: a bedroom zone; family living and entertaining zone; and a garage with adjoining hobby area. The center of the home is the living zone, which incorporates a strikingly open orientation allowing the design to feel free-flowing. While the home appears as a single-story home from the exterior, these zones stretch into a main floor and a lower floor. In this fashion, the ranch form can be deceptively large while placed on a fairly small lot. This, of course, made it a very attractive option for developers.

The ranch house became the most ubiquitous form of American house design after 1950, arguably helping to define family life and structure during this same period through its layout and design. The dominance of the living zone, where it really becomes a multi-purpose area composing the heart of the home, dovetailed beautifully with the life of leisure that awaited many middle-class Americans after 1950. The design was particularly conducive to the television, which could be placed in the main living room and viewed from any number of areas in the living zone. Purchasers associated the form with ''heritage, status, and respectability,'' but functionality was never too far from their minds.

—Brian Black

FURTHER READING:

Clark, Clifford Edward, Jr. *The American Family Home, 1800-1960.* Chapel Hill, University of North Carolina Press, 1986.

Wright, Gwendolyn. *Building the Dream: A Social History of Housing in America.* Cambridge, MIT Press, 1983.

Rand, Ayn
See Objectivism/Ayn Rand

Rand, Sally (1904-1979)

Best known for her sexually provocative dance, using ostrich feather fans, that she introduced at the 1933 Chicago World's Fair (supplemented in 1934 by a bubble dance), Sally Rand eventually made her form of erotic movement more acceptable to mainstream audiences than strip-tease had been. Rand, who came to her calling after stints as a chorine, vaudeville performer, circus acrobat, and Hollywood film star, thought of herself as a ''terpsichorean artiste'' rather than a stripper or exotic dancer. While controversial enough during the 1930s through the mid-1960s to earn arrest for indecency, there was considerable debate about whether she actually wore a body stocking or was naked underneath her feathers. Ultimately, Rand was good at creating the illusion of nudity while she cavorted tastefully under blue or pink lights to the music of Chopin and Debussy, and that was what mattered. She became an American institution, performing into her seventies.

—Frederick J. Augustyn, Jr.

FURTHER READING:

Carskadon, T.R. ''Sally Rand Dances to the Rescue.'' *American Mercury.* Vol. 35, July 1935, 355-358.

Ragan, David. *Who's Who in Hollywood, 1900-1976.* New York, Facts on File, 1991.

Rand, Sally. ''Bubbles Become Big Business.'' *Review of Reviews.* Vol. 91, April 1935, 40-41.

Rap/Hip-Hop

Hip-Hop music, or to use the more popular marketing term, Rap music, was the most popular, influential, and controversial form of black and Latino urban popular music throughout the 1980s and 1990s. It emerged in the early to mid-1970s in the Bronx, though in later years, distinctive East Coast and West Coast styles would emerge and clash, sometimes with fatal results for its performers. Rap and Hip-Hop culture entered mainstream America's collective consciousness as a novelty, resulting from the massive success of the Sugarhill Gang's ''Rapper's Delight.'' ''Rapper's Delight'' contained all the elements that would characterize Hip-Hop's essence: spare instrumentation, rhythmically spoken rhymes, and the borrowing of previously existing musical elements to construct a new song (''Rapper's Delight'' borrowed heavily from Chic's then-current hit, ''Good Times'').

Music is only one part of Hip-Hop culture, which encompasses four major elements: rapping, deejaying, breakdancing, and graffiti-writing. Beyond the rhyming style known as rapping or MC-ing, deejaying uses the turntable as an instrument that the MC raps over while listeners engage in the quasi-acrobatic gyrations of breakdancing. Rapping can take many forms—from the rhythmic vocal delivery of blues artists and the artsy jazz-influenced delivery of the Last Poets to the almost spoken-word delivery of Bob Dylan and Lou Reed. Graffiti ranges from the illegal stylized form of public art often spray-painted on walls to the signature design motifs on clothing, album covers, and posters. As an extension of graffiti, the creative spellings used by many ''aerosol artists'' (''Str8'' for ''straight'' or ''boyz'' for ''boys,'' for example) has constituted a unique vocabulary that has itself become a stylistic signature of the Hip-Hop movement and has spilled over as a shorthand in computer chat rooms.

Hip-Hop's deceivingly simplistic nature and appropriation of other music drew early criticisms about its merits as a musical form, and its graphic and often controversial lyrics delivered mostly from the perspective of African-American urban youth fanned the flames of criticism concerning its social merits. The practice of borrowing fragments from other songs, often with a digital sampler, greatly influenced other forms of music to the point that, by the late 1990s, sampling-based sound collage became recognized as a legitimate musical art form. Throughout the 1980s and 1990s, Hip-Hop music remained one of the only outlets where an inner-city youth's opinion could be heard unfiltered by mass media censors, prompting artist Chuck D to proclaim that form of music ''Black America's CNN.'' By the late-1990s, Hip-Hop has become virtually synonymous with

youth culture (black or white), and its music and associated styles have been appropriated for TV ads, music videos, Pop and R&B songs, fashion magazines, and in malls throughout the United States.

The significance of breakdancing and graffiti should not be downplayed, but it is obvious that the music has become Hip-Hop culture's most noticeable and persistent component. The key figure in the development of Hip-Hop music was the DJ (disc jockey). The role of the DJ during the earliest phases of the style was to spin popular records that kept the party alive and people dancing. In the early 1970s a number of DJs had strong followings in their respective areas. Few of them ever had access to large clubs, so their primary venues were block parties, schools, and parks (where, during the summer, they would plug their sound systems into lampposts and play until the police broke up the gathering).

The most popular of these early DJs was Jamaican immigrant Kool DJ Herc, who is credited with two innovations that, Tricia Rose argues in *Black Noise*, ''separated rap music from other popular musics and set the stage for further innovation.'' The first was Herc's habit of isolating the fragments of songs that were the most popular with dancers and segueing them into one long musical collage. These song fragments were composed of the percussion breaks within the songs and came to be known as ''breakbeats.'' In David Toop's book *Rap Attack 2,* early DJ pioneer Afrika Bambaataa recalls Kool DJ Herc's DJ style: ''Now he took the music of Mandrill like 'Fencewalk,' certain disco records that had funky percussion breaks like the Incredible Bongo Band when they came out with 'Apache' and he just kept that beat *going.*''

Other DJs took this concept and began expanding on the possibilities that two turntables could offer. The endless collages of breakbeats that were an integral part of breakdancing required DJs to draw from massive libraries of obscure records, giving the most popular DJs the title of ''masters of records.'' One of the first DJs to pick up on the breakbeat technique was Grandmaster Flash, who went further than Kool DJ Herc in his turntable wizardry. With two turntables Flash was able to, as told to David Toop, ''take small parts of records and, at first, keep it on time, no tricks, keep it on time. I'm talking about very short beats, maybe 40 seconds, keeping it going for about five minutes, depending on how popular that particular record was.'' Flash continued, ''After that, I mastered punch phasing— taking certain parts of a record where there's a vocal or drum slap or a horn. I would throw it out and bring it back, keeping the other turntable playing. If this record had a horn in it before the break came down I would go—BAM, BAM, BAM-BAM—just to try this on the crowd.'' Another technique that is credited to Grandmaster Flash is ''scratching.'' Scratching consists of moving a record back and forth with one's hand while the needle rests in the groove to produce a rhythmic noise that is completely divorced from the sound the record makes when played at a normal speed. This sound is often used to accent parts of another record playing on the second turntable. These basic Hip-Hop DJ techniques laid the foundation for all Hip-Hop music to come.

Kool DJ Herc is credited with a second important innovation— the development of rapping, or MC-ing. During the parties he began ''dropping rhymes'' or shouting simple phrases that were popular in the streets like ''rock on my mellow,'' ''to the beat y'all,'' or ''you don't stop'' on top of the break beats he played. Herc borrowed this rhythmic form of talking (called ''toasting'') from the microphone personalities who deejayed in his native Jamaica, and he is recognized as the person who brought this style to New York. Early on, when he began concentrating more on mixing break beats, he enlisted the help of his friend Coke La Rock to take over MC duties. The MC was responsible for exciting the dancers and giving the party a live feel; the MC also functioned as a type of crowd control—diffusing tensions that might arise from rival groups in the audience.

Grandmaster Flash, an acrobatic DJ whose showmanship resembled a circus act, saw the importance of having a live MC to keep the crowd dancing and not looking at the DJ. Together with Melle Mel, Scorpio, Kidd Creole, and Raheem & Cowboy, Flash formed Grandmaster Flash & the Furious Five. This trend-setting group inspired numerous rhyme battles throughout the South Bronx, and many "crews" such as Grand Wizard Theodore & the Fantastic Five, the Funky Four Plus One, the Cold Crush Brothers, and the Treacherous Three fought for microphone supremacy.

In the early days of rap, since other venues were unavailable, DJs like Kool DJ Herc, Grandmaster Flash, and Afrika Bambaataa often played for free in outdoor parks, abandoned buildings, and community centers. Soon Grandmaster Flash's popularity surpassed Kool DJ Herc's and Flash began to play for paying customers at numerous high schools and clubs. By 1977 Flash's following had grown to the point where he was playing in clubs to crowds numbering more than 3,000. Until July, 1979, when the Sugarhill Gang released "Rapper's Delight," Hip-Hop was strictly an underground phenomenon that had not been documented beyond the numerous bootleg tapes of live performances that circulated throughout New York City, played on portable radios called "ghetto blasters." The Sugarhill Gang was not a part of the South Bronx Hip-Hop scene that had been developing in the late 1970s; the group was instead put together by Sugarhill Records owners Sylvia and Joe Robinson. They had no street credibility and were not known to anyone involved in the Hip-Hop scene, but this did not stop them from having a huge hit in "Rapper's Delight," which sold more than two million records worldwide.

After the commercial success of "Rapper's Delight" many of the MCs and DJs who were popular on the club circuit began to sign with record labels. By 1982, Afrika Bambaataa was playing for increasingly hip white audiences in downtown Manhattan clubs such as The Ritz, The Mudd Club, and Negril, as well as producing his own hit singles ("Planet Rock" was his biggest). This helped provoke an intense media infatuation with Hip-Hop culture, which singled out and highlighted the elements of Hip-Hop and breakdancing during the early 1980s. Soon after, a deluge of movies began featuring breakdancing and rapping, such as *Wild Style, Beat Street, Breakin',* and *Krush Groove.* Many journalists and music consumers in the mainstream treated Hip-Hop as a passing fad, but Hip-Hop's popularity continued to increase.

Some Hip-Hop artists from its early days—like Grandmaster Flash & the Furious Five, Kurtis Blow, Kool Moe Dee, and Doug E. Fresh—found themselves becoming minor stars while others such as Busy Bee, Spoonie Gee, Debbie Dee, Cold Crush Brothers, and Funky Four Plus One achieved little commercial success. One of the characteristics of what became known as the "old school" of Hip-Hop artists was an avoidance of using DJs and a reliance on live funk bands laying down instrumentals over which the MCs rapped. Also, Hip-Hop artists like Kurtis Blow and Grandmaster Flash & the Furious Five wore flashy outfits that in no way reflected the styles worn by Hip-Hop fans on the street.

By the early 1980s, Hip-Hop music went through its first major stylistic change, ushered in by Run-DMC, which practically invented the "new school." Eschewing the showbizzy outfits and more lightweight backing instrumentals of old school acts, Run-DMC wore the same clothes worn by urban youths on the street. Further, they

stripped the music down to raw basic beats and rhymes, which was more true to Hip-Hop's sound as it was originally heard in Bronx block parties and nightclubs. Run-DMC's influence was enormous, paving the way for the success of more hardcore-sounding Hip-Hop artists like Public Enemy, LL Cool J, the Beastie Boys, and other Def Jam recording acts.

Soon to be a major player in the Hip-Hop music industry, Def Jam Records was co-founded in 1984 by Russell Simmons, the brother of Run from Run-DMC. By 1985, Simmons' label had released a string of seven 12-inch singles that sold over 250,000 each (an unprecedented number at the time), launching the careers of LL Cool J and the Beastie Boys. Simmons' business partner, Rick Rubin, produced their debut albums as well as that of Public Enemy, and also had a hand in producing Run-DMC's *Raising Hell* (the first Hip-Hop album to go platinum). After starting the company with a $5,000 investment, Simmons and Rubin signed a $1 million distribution deal in 1985 with the corporate record label CBS.

While Run-DMC was considered the first Hip-Hop group to attract a predominantly white rock audience (with its cover of Aerosmith's "Walk This Way"), the Beastie Boys, the first white Hip-Hop group, were the first rappers to top the *Billboard* Pop Album charts, a sign that Hip-Hop had finally infiltrated the white suburbs of America. This was another watershed moment in the evolution of Hip-Hop and a wake-up call to major record labels that Hip-Hop was becoming a very profitable genre. These major labels, which had access to large amounts of capital, moved quickly to sign new artists, and began to absorb many of the small independent labels either through distribution deals (such as CBS's relationship with Def Jam Records or RCA's relationship with Jive Records) or by purchasing the independents outright (like Warner Brothers did with the small but profitable Tommy Boy and Sleeping Bag labels).

During the genre's first major commercial explosion (following a number of minor explosions), Hip-Hop entered what is considered to be its golden age during the late 1980s. It was a period of exciting creativity and diversity, with Boogie Down Productions and Public Enemy introducing the Hip-Hop world to overtly political messages with their albums *By All Means Necessary* and *It Takes a Nation of Millions. . . ,* respectively. Rakim radically advanced the art of rhyming on Eric B. & Rakim's *Paid in Full* and *Follow the Leader,* and the likes of Schoolly D, Ice T, and Niggaz with Attitude introduced the harsh, reality-based street rhymes of what would become known as "gangsta rap." Afrocentric groups such as the Jungle Brothers and X-Clan proliferated, and party records by Kid 'n' Play and Rob Base & DJ E-Z Rock were just as popular as Hip-Hop's clown prince Biz Markie and the longest lasting ladies of Hip-Hop, Salt-n-Pepa.

Salt-n-Pepa were not the first female rappers, but they were the first to become extremely popular. Women's participation in Hip-Hop has largely been obscured, primarily because there were few female MCs who were able to release albums during the early 1980s, when Hip-Hop was getting underway. Despite this shortage of female artists, women did participate in the scene. Grandmaster Flash recounted in David Toop's *Rap Attack 2* that there was a greater female presence during the early days, with crews like the Bronx-based Mercedes Ladies playing to large crowds. Other artists like the Funky Four Plus One's Sha-Rock, Dimples D, and the Sequence were among the only recorded female rapper role models that Salt-n-Pepa could look to during the early 1980s.

By the late 1980s, Hip-Hop music was proving itself a big money maker. In 1988, Hip-Hop's annual record sales reached $100 million, which accounted for two percent of the total music industry's sales. The next year *Billboard* added "Rap" charts to its magazine and MTV debuted *Yo! MTV Raps,* which quickly became the network's highest-rated show. By 1992, it was estimated that Hip-Hop was generating $400 million annually, roughly five percent of the music industry's yearly income. These estimates nearly doubled to $700 million in 1993. In 1995 CNN reported that Hip-Hop's annual sales had risen to eight percent of the music industry's annual income. After a brief slump mid-decade, by the late 1990s, Hip-Hop was still going strong, with the majority of gold and platinum albums being awarded not to new pop and rock acts, but to new R&B and Hip-Hop artists. During the first half of 1998, Hip-Hop sales were up twenty-eight percent over 1997.

With the financial success of Hip-Hop came a proliferation of lawsuits involving copyright infringements, owing to the genre's established style of borrowing from previously existing music—a key practice since Hip-Hop's inception, whether by DJs playing fragments of records at Bronx block parties or via the technologically savvy method of collaging found sounds with digital samplers. This method of creation became extremely influential, becoming an accepted and legitimate form of music making by the late 1990s, with many mainstream Pop acts incorporating sampling into their recordings. But for a time during the mid- to-late 1980s, the practice of sampling appeared to be in danger. The deluge of lawsuits began in 1986 when funk artist Jimmy Castor, popular in the 1960s and 1970s, sued Def Jam and the Beastie Boys for their appropriation of the phrase "Yo, Leroy" from Castor's 1977 recording "The Return of Leroy (Part I)." Even though the legal atmosphere surrounding sampling became highly charged, the practice continued. By the early 1990s, businesses called "sample clearing houses" had been established, allowing labels and artists to use them in order to avoid any legal problems that may arise from sampling.

Hip-Hop continued to grow more diverse after its late-1980s golden age, though the mainstream media representations of Hip-Hop were dominated by coverage of gangsta rap during the first half of the 1990s. During this time, artists such as Ice Cube, Dr. Dre, Snoop Doggy Dogg, and Tupac Shakur sold millions of albums, many to white suburban teens. The violent and sometimes misogynist imagery contained in gangsta rap lyrics, and the fact that white teenagers were listening to it, drew protests from many conservative groups, prompting Time-Warner to drop "original gangsta" Ice T from its roster after a much publicized controversy surrounding the lyrics of his song, "Cop Killer." Under pressure, Time-Warner also sold off its investment in Interscope, the distributor of Death Row Records, which was the preeminent gangsta rap label during the first half of the decade. Although gangsta rap sales had been in decline for a year, the violent deaths of Tupac Shakur and Notorious B.I.G. in 1996 and 1997, respectively, marked the symbolic death of that genre.

Even though the West Coast-based gangsta rap genre was in decline by the mid-1990s, many more sub-genres and artists took its place. For instance, the Wu-Tang Clan, a New York City crew of nine talented MCs, bubbled up from the underground in 1993 to become one of the major forces in Hip-Hop by the late 1990s. By 1998, the Wu-Tang Clan had two multi-platinum records. Puff Daddy sold millions of records making popular party raps, and the multicultural Fugees became one of the most successful crossover groups of the 1990s. Female artists like Foxy Brown, Lil' Kim, Lauryn Hill, Lady of Rage, Missy Elliot, Queen Latifah, Bahamadia, Heather B, and others increased women's profiles in the Hip-Hop industry. Also in the late 1990s, the art of deejaying underwent a renaissance, with

turntable crews Invisibl Skratch Piklz, X-ecutioners, and the Beat Junkies, as well as individual turntablists DJ Shadow, DJ Krush, DJ Faust, Kid Koala, and Mixmaster Mike expanding the sonic possibilities of using two turntables.

Despite almost yearly predictions of Hip-Hop's commercial and artistic failure since 1979's "Rapper's Delight," Hip-Hop remained a commercially vital, artistically rich musical tradition well into the 1990s. By the end of the century, Hip-Hop appeared to be more popular and influential than ever.

—Kembrew McLeod

FURTHER READING:

Costello, Mark, and David Foster Wallace. *Signifying Rappers: Rap and Race in the Urban Present.* New York, Ecco Press, 1990.

Fernando, S. H., Jr. *The New Beats: Exploring the Music, Culture, and Attitudes of Hip-Hop.* Garden City, New York, Doubleday, 1994.

George, Nelson, et al. *Fresh: Hip-Hop Don't Stop.* New York, Random House, 1985.

Hager, Steven. *Hip-Hop: The Illustrated History of Break Dancing, Rap Music, and Graffiti.* New York, St. Martin's Press, 1984.

Potter, Russell. *Spectacular Vernaculars: Hip-Hop and the Politics of Postmodernism.* Albany, SUNY Press, 1995.

Ro, Ronin. *Gangsta: Merchandising Rhymes of Violence.* New York, St. Martin's Press, 1996.

Rose, Tricia. *Black Noise: Rap Music and Black Culture in Contemporary America.* Hanover, Wesleyan University Press, 1994.

Toop, David. *Rap Attack 2: African Rap to Global Hip-Hop.* London, Serpent's Tail, 1991.

Rather, Dan (1931—)

Dan Rather succeeded Walter Cronkite as anchor of the *CBS Evening News* on March 9, 1981. After he took over the anchor desk, CBS News dissolved into turmoil due to budget cuts and new owners, and the ratings slipped. Rather had solid credentials, having been with CBS since 1962 (including a stint on *60 Minutes),* but his expertise soon proved less noteworthy than the often bizarre happenings that began to occur around him. His signoff one week was "courage"; he tended to use the vernacular of his Texas upbringing during broadcasts ("that dog won't hunt"); he let CBS "go to black" for six minutes when U.S. Open tennis ran too long, and he tangled on air with then Vice President George Bush. Perhaps oddest was Rather's assault on New York streets by a man asking, "What's the frequency, Kenneth?" (later, during an appearance on *The Late Show with David Letterman,* he joined rock band REM in a performance of their song based on this incident). From 1993 to 1995, Rather co-anchored with Connie Chung, but she was forced out and Rather subsequently trumpeted a "hard news" program. In 1998, he signed a contract to stay with CBS until 2003. Along with Peter Jennings and Tom Brokaw, Rather was one of the leading news broadcasters of the 1980s and 1990s.

—Michele Lellouche

Dan Rather at the Democratic National Convention, 1968.

FURTHER READING:

Goldberg, Robert, and Gerald Jay Goldberg. *Anchors: Brokaw, Jennings, Rather and the Evening News.* Secaucus, New Jersey, Carol Publishing Group, 1990.

Rather, Dan. *Deadlines and Datelines.* New York, Morrow, 1999.

————. *The Camera Never Blinks: Adventures of a TV Journalist.* New York, William Morrow, 1977.

————, and Mickey Hershkowitz. *The Camera Never Blinks Twice: The Further Adventures of a Television Journalist.* New York, William Morrow, 1994.

————, with Peter Wyden. *I Remember.* Boston, Little Brown, 1991.

Reader's Digest

The moral obligation to save time has been a sovereign force in American culture since colonial days. Time saving took on added importance in the late nineteenth and early twentieth centuries when businessmen sought to standardize the performance of the country's growing industrial sector. This movement toward greater efficiency extended into personal lives as well, as people sought to maximize their own working and leisure time. An instant success that went on to become the most powerful vehicle for the printed word in the world, *Reader's Digest* was only one expression of the time-saving vogue when it was introduced in 1922. Printed in a handy booklet form that made it suitable for slipping into a coat pocket or purse, *Reader's Digest* featured 31 articles, one for each day of the month, culled from leading magazines, "each article of enduring value and interest, in condensed and permanent form," as the magazine maintained.

Reader's Digest did not introduce the concept of sampling and condensing other publications. An American magazine called *Littell's Living Age* first reprinted periodical articles in 1844. Almost 50 years later, *Literary Digest,* founded by Isaac Kauffman Funk of Funk & Wagnalls fame, capitalized upon the success of a British periodical, *Review of Reviews,* and presented condensations of articles from American, Canadian, and European publications. The highbrow *Literary Digest* achieved a circulation of over one million by 1927, earning praise from *Time* magazine (another 1920s time-saving publication) as "one of the greatest publishing successes in history." But *Literary Digest* fell out of the reading public's good graces in 1936 when it incorrectly predicted that Franklin D. Roosevelt would lose in a landslide in one of the first national presidential preference polls. The magazine failed the following year, not long after Roosevelt was inaugurated for the second of his record four terms.

The less esoteric *Reader's Digest* was the brainchild of William Roy DeWitt Wallace (1889-1981), a Minnesota-born college dropout who, according to biographer Peter Canning, touted various "schemes and stunts" as a young man. While employed as a traveling salesman, Wallace would condense and memorize important facts from magazine articles on three-by-five slips of paper in an effort to impress customers. He suffered shrapnel injuries fighting in France in World War I, and he read a variety of popular magazines and practiced condensing their articles while he recovered. His college professor father loaned him $300 and in January 1920 Wallace produced a 64-page prototype issue of *Reader's Digest,* complete with 31 articles from publications such as *Ladies' Home Journal, McClure's,* and *Vanity Fair.* Potential publishers—such as William Randolph Hearst—rejected the magazine's concept as interesting but without any commercial promise because of an assumed limited readership and Wallace's determination not to have illustrations or advertisements detract from the reading material in his magazine.

While searching for a publisher, Wallace met feminist reformer Lila Acheson (1887-1984). She was not looking for a husband so much as a business partner in life. She encouraged Wallace to publish *Reader's Digest* himself and helped him advertise and process the first subscription orders. The couple married in Pleasantville, New York, and with $5,000 in advance subscription orders established the Reader's Digest Association in the New York City suburb in 1921. Pleasantville became the headquarters of the *Reader's Digest* empire, as the first issue went out the following January. The magazine was an immediate success, capitalizing on self-education and self-confidence crazes then underway, a growing sense of national pride, and the omnipresent desire of readers to save time.

Except for a signature line drawing of a woman within a circle on the front cover, the drab text-only early *Reader's Digest* was issued without artwork or illustrations until November 1939. That drawing was removed in 1942 to be replaced by the magazine's table of contents. The front-cover table of contents became a trademark for *Reader's Digest* until May 1998, when it was moved inside the magazine, its cover spot replaced by a photograph. A greater number of illustrations began appearing with articles in the 1970s and 1980s, giving the magazine a greater visual appeal. The Wallaces were able to support their publication on circulation revenues until the 1950s, using their financial freedom to espouse populist causes that other magazines were less willing to discuss. Eventually, however, a survey revealed that 80 percent of readers preferred advertising over increased subscription costs and advertisements began appearing in April 1955, generating as much as $91,000 per page by the 1980s. Tobacco advertisements, a mainstay for many periodicals, were never accepted and the first liquor advertisement did not appear in *Reader's Digest* until 1979; no advertisement has ever appeared on the last page of the magazine—an attractive picture or art reprint, suitable for coffee-table display, always graced the magazine's back cover. Many reprints came from the magazine's own collection of original art.

Wallace never surveyed readers about their article preferences. Until he and his wife turned over control of the magazine to senior editors during the 1970s, he selected the articles for condensation based on what interested him, mindful of the need to appeal to a large audience of both sexes and all educational levels. In 1954, *Reader's Digest* business manager Albert Cole called the magazine "the greatest common denominator in communications we have." The topics were almost always universal: science and nature, morals, health, ordeals, education, biography, animals, lifestyle, sex, and humor. The contents remained remarkably similar over the years, including feature departments such as "My Most Unforgettable Character," "Humor in Uniform," "Campus Comedy," "Life in These United States," "Picturesque Speech," "News in Medicine," and "It Pays to Enrich Your Word Power." Occasionally, Wallace's personal tastes intruded. Often, articles were heartwarming and inspirational, involved personal success stories such as his own, or advocated a nondenominational Protestantism that was described as "muscular Christianity."

Carl Sandburg once complained that *Reader's Digest* was "often as solemn as death and now and then funny as a barrel of monkeys." The Wallaces were criticized for their socially and politically conservative agenda, which chided labor, big government, and any form of political radicalism, and their all but open endorsement of the Republican Party. The magazine's staff even wrote articles for other publications, adhering to the Wallaces' conservative leanings, so that they could be reprinted in *Reader's Digest*. The magazine defended such "plants" as a means of providing proper editorial balance. The magazine was also criticized for refusing to publish any letters to the editor, especially corrections or rebuttals. The editors maintained that the mail was usually evenly split, making letters unnecessary. Furthermore, *Reader's Digest* articles were shortened by as much as three-fourths from the manuscripts, leading to complaints that the condensations diluted or lost the entire point of the original. Although conservative, the magazine did not shy away from controversy. Some *Reader's Digest* articles reported on medical or scientific breakthroughs years before details appeared in other publications. The magazine also published crusading articles on venereal disease, cigarette smoking, safe driving, conservation, and other populist-style issues. Competitors such as *Literary Digest, Quick,* and *Esquire's* one-time popular *Coronet* tried but failed to seriously challenge *Reader's Digest*.

From 5,000 first issues, the circulation of *Reader's Digest* soared for most of the twentieth century. The Wallaces kept circulation figures secret until 1936, but the number of copies exceeded 200,000 by 1930, one million in 1935, and nine million by 1950. In 1954, it was estimated that one out of every four families in the United States received the magazine. The domestic circulation peaked at over 17 million copies in 1984, second only to *TV Guide*. The magazine's profits were enhanced by a series of foreign editions, beginning with Great Britain in 1938 and extending to 49 international editions, published in 19 languages, with a total circulation of over 28 million that made *Reader's Digest* the most widely read periodical on the planet.

In 1934, Wallace added a condensed book section as a regular feature to the magazine and it led to a Reader's Digest Condensed Book Club in 1950. In 1965, he purchased Funk and Wagnalls, publishers of the *Literary Digest,* and added their extensive line of encyclopedias, dictionaries, and reference works to his magazine's book publishing division. Records, movies, and video sales were added, along with a direct mail sweepstakes competition that landed the Reader's Digest Association in trouble with the Federal Trade Commission until an agreement was reached in 1983. Their longstanding belief in the Golden Rule induced the Wallaces to fund the Reader's Digest Foundation, one of the greatest philanthropic institutions of its time. The foundation supported a variety of causes, including education, the arts, and major projects such as a new contemporary wing for New York City's Metropolitan Museum of Art and the effort to move Egypt's Abu Simbel temple up the Nile Valley to make way for the Aswan High Dam.

The Wallaces gradually passed on control of their magazine during the 1960s and 1970s. DeWitt died in 1981 and Lila in 1984. As biographer John Heidenry explained, during a management struggle days before her death, Lila sought to return the magazine to "old fashioned American values." The once powerful magazine began to flounder without the Wallaces at the helm. The Reader's Digest Association began buying other magazines in 1986, but the new titles were plagued by mounting losses that hurt the magazine's once-enviable profit margin. Advertising losses, increasing competition, and the aging of its core readership dogged *Reader's Digest* into the 1990s, even in the profitable book and home entertainment groups. The company's stock price dropped from $56 in 1992 to $17 in 1998. An outside chairman and chief executive officer, Thomas Ryder, was hired to revitalize the magazine in 1998. Ryder began a cost-cutting campaign that included employee layoffs, a magazine redesign, the auction of 39 pieces from the magazine's prized art collection, and a self-admitted drop in *Reader's Digest* domestic circulation base from 15 to 12.5 million copies. At the end of the twentieth century, the magazine was discussing such possibilities as *Reader's Digest* made-for-television movies to attract a new and younger audience, along with a merger with another media corporation. Observers, however, could not help but notice that time may have finally caught up with *Reader's Digest*.

—Richard Digby-Junger

FURTHER READING:

Canning, Peter. *American Dreamers: The Wallaces and Reader's Digest, An Insider's Story.* New York, Simon & Schuster, 1996.

Carlson, Peter. "For *Reader's Digest,* a Palatable Makeover." *Washington Post.* May 12, 1998, D1.

Christensen, Reo M. "Report on the *Reader's Digest.*" *Columbia Journalism Review.* Winter 1965, 30-36.

Heidenry, John. *Theirs Was the Kingdom: Lila and DeWitt Wallace and the Story of the Reader's Digest.* New York, W. W. Norton, 1993.

Mott, Frank Luther. *A History of American Magazines, 1885-1905.* Vol. 4. Cambridge, Harvard University Press, 1957.

Peterson, Theodore. *Magazines in the Twentieth Century.* Urbana, University of Illinois Press, 1964.

Russell, Anne M. *''Reader's Digest:* The Condensed Version.'' *Folio.* November 1, 1998, 81-86.

Wood, James Playsted. *Magazines in the United States.* 3rd edition. New York, The Ronald Press, 1971.

———. *Of Lasting Interest: The Story of the Reader's Digest.* Garden City, New York, Doubleday, 1967.

Reagan, Ronald (1911—)

America's fortieth president from 1981-1989, known variously as ''Dutch,'' the ''Teflon President,'' ''The Great Communicator,'' and the father of an economic system named after him (''Reaganomics''), Ronald Wilson Reagan is one of the most controversial political figures of the twentieth century. In fact, an entire system of thought, appropriately titled ''Reaganism,'' was coined to describe the effects of, depending on who you ask, his destructive social legacy or his repositioning of American optimism and strength at the forefront of world politics. In either case, one cannot underestimate the importance of Reagan's influence during the social and political upheavals of the 1980s and beyond.

On February 6, 1911, Ronald Wilson Reagan was born to Nelle and John Reagan in Tampico, Illinois. Although Reagan recalls his younger years as idyllic, his family moved often, living on the fly in five different places in Dixon, four in Tampico, and two in Galesburg, Illinois. His family was involved in the religious revivals hitting Tampico at the time but, though his mother was a leader of church life

Ronald Reagan

in her area, his father displayed a destructive reliance upon alcohol. Ronald's acting skills and religious views were formed together in these early years: he acted in his mother's skits, dated his pastor's daughter for eight years, led the Easter sunrise service, and cleaned and worked at the church.

Ronald attended high school in Dixon and enrolled at Eureka College as a freshman in 1928. He was a fairly good student, studying just enough on the easiest courses to get by, but he displayed a skill for last minute memorization that was, in the words of his brother Neil (who also attended Eureka), ''photographic.'' He performed solidly at the guard position for the football team and was a stellar lifeguard at Lowell Park from 1927 to 1932, rescuing up to 77 swimmers. He performed in seven plays, lettered in two sports and was a cheerleader in others, became president of both the booster club and the senate, and spent time on the school paper and the yearbook, all while majoring in economics.

Upon graduation, he became a radio sports announcer at WHO in Des Moines, Iowa. He was particularly associated with baseball and, curiously enough, was not in attendance at most of the games he called. Though he became wildly popular in Des Moines for his broadcasting, he worked from a telegraph relay, providing his listeners with improvised action and drama. Success as an announcer eventually landed him at Warner Brothers studio in Hollywood. A screen test in 1937 won Reagan a contract and during the next two decades he appeared in 53 films, becoming famous for his cool vocal command and grace under pressure. He became most popular for his role of Notre Dame football coach Knute Rockne in the film *Knute Rockne, All American* (1940) and as the reckless Drake McHugh in *King's Row* (1942), a star vehicle that put Reagan firmly on the Hollywood map. He eventually married actress Jane Wyman, fathering two children, Maureen and Michael. Later divorced, and Reagan married his second wife, Nancy Davis, another Hollywood starlet, in 1952, fathering two more children, Patricia and Ronald.

By this time, Reagan's political career was already underway. As president of the Screen Actors Guild, Reagan became embroiled in disputes over the issue of communism in the film industry and his political views shifted from liberal to conservative. He toured the country as a television host, becoming a spokesman for conservatism and a company man for General Electric. Financially secure by 1962, Reagan then spent a few years delivering speeches to groups across the country, mostly about business and conservative interests and decrying big government. His oratory was dazzling and in 1966 he was elected governor of California by a margin of a million votes. His terms as governor were marked by conflict and controversy. Though he ran as a candidate opposed to taxes (a consideration that carried itself into his presidency), he implemented the highest tax increase in California at the time. He demanded the resignation of University of California, Berkeley, chancellor Clark Kerr during the free speech demonstrations, positioning himself as the voice of moderation exasperated with ''campus radicals,'' yet was lauded by the state for balancing the books. The early stirrings of Reaganism thus became evident during Reagan's stint as governor: a devotion to business interests (General Electric), hard-line stances against liberals seeking to expand social freedoms, the demonization of Communism and the USSR, concern over America's perceived moral disintegration, a delegation of power to the point where the executive's ultimate responsibility lay in his rhetorical influence over party constituents, and finally, the entrenchment of governmental power and influence coupled with the oratorical promise of deregulation.

Reagan won the Republican presidential nomination in 1980 and chose as his running mate former Texas congressman and United Nations ambassador George Bush. The "New Right" program of the minimalist state and the free-market economy adopted by Reagan Republicans hit Washington by force. Primary among these policies was supply-side economics, once called "voodoo economics" by George Bush (before he became Reagan's vice president), a curious theory that relied upon the "trickle-down" of revenue from the wealthy to the poor. This effect would occur when the rich were encouraged to spend money, and to facilitate this, Reagan set about implementing tax breaks and benefits to the wealthy that continued on long past his presidency. He coupled this with cutbacks in domestic spending, especially on the welfare programs AFDC (Aid for Families with Dependent Children) and Medicaid. Welfare recipients were castigated by the Republican Party as loafers who had been coddled by the oversized government that Reagan campaigned against throughout his career. But Reagan's most important political victories came in the arena of foreign policy. He came into power on the heels of a crisis involving Iranian seizure of the U.S. embassy and the taking of hostages, whom former president Jimmy Carter (a Democrat), had been unable to free. Reagan resolved the crisis and freed the hostages shortly after his election to office. He railed against the Soviet Union and Communism as he had done throughout his Hollywood and California years, and set about increasing the budget of the Pentagon and the U.S. defense industries.

At home, he implemented equally aggressive domestic policies against crime, drugs, and pornography; although he championed a United States free from the dictates of oppressive government control, he nevertheless used government to further his conservative social agenda, which included the banning of abortion, reinstatement of school prayer, and promotion of the nuclear, heterosexual family. In hindsight Reagan's programs can be critiqued correctly: American prosperity and position had increased, at least in theory; one can arguably credit the United States' attractive capitalist prosperity for the eventual fall of communism in the Soviet Union that occurred during the Reagan–Bush years. This economic deregulation, however, led to at least one major economic recession, a growth in the unemployment rate, and a stigmatization of those whom Reagan's first domestic policy adviser, Martin Anderson, called the "Dependent American," citizens who relied upon social programs like AFDC and Medicaid for assistance. His punishing stances on social disintegration came back to haunt him during the infamous Iran-Contra Hearings, in which Reagan's cabinet was caught red-handed funneling drug money to the Contras in Central America, a geographical and political zone important to the presidency for its massive drug production. These were the kinds of inconsistencies that coursed throughout the Reagan Revolution, inconsistencies that can be traced all the way back to Reagan's imaginative renderings of baseball games at which he was never present. Some had a hard time sorting out where rhetoric and truth, in the form of policy, met. Yet Reagan, through his incredible oratorical skill and deep-seated beliefs in morality and independence, imparted a sense of relentless optimism and nationalism to a country whose national character and trust in its government had been marred by failures at home (in the form of civil rights dilemmas, the sexual revolution, divisive stances on race and class) and abroad (the Vietnam War, Iran).

A critique of Reaganism would not be complete without a consideration of the major effect Reagan had on the growth and use of media power in the United States. Popular culture can point to

Reagan, much more than John F. Kennedy, as the premier political media presence of the twentieth century. It is obvious that Reagan's history in broadcasting, Hollywood, and advertising played a part in his success as the Great Communicator. Yet Reagan's influence could be felt everywhere in popular culture. In music, down-home heroes like Bruce Springsteen and John Mellencamp climbed the charts on the strengths of their blue-collar, heartland lyrics (Springsteen's biggest album of the period was *Born in the U.S.A.*), yet the birth of rap and its vocal dissatisfaction with unfair treatment of minorities and the poor in the lyrics of groups such as Public Enemy, KRS-One, and Grandmaster Flash & the Furious Five also occurred under Reagan's terms. Films moved toward hard-bodied, masculine heroes such as Sylvester Stallone (whose mythic Rambo was the de facto Reagan icon; in one political speech, Reagan actually compared himself to the character), Chuck Norris, the wildly popular Arnold Schwarzenegger, and, of course, Clint Eastwood (whose character's challenge, "Go ahead, make my day," Reagan appropriated as a motto during a foreign policy speech).

Television became fascinated with the Reagan 1980s, especially the world of glitz and glamour: *Dynasty* was one of the 1980's biggest television hits, while *thirtysomething* provided the Yuppies (Young Urban Professionals, who became the de facto Reaganite model constituents) with a forum for voicing their middle-class concerns. Further, the ultimate conflation of the entertainment industry and political sphere by the end of the Reagan era prefigured the rise in power of so-called tabloid talk shows, news programs (and even 24-hour news channels, such as CNN and CSPAN), "Reality TV" shows such as *Cops,* and an increasing influx of media attention on the personal lives of political figures (Nancy Reagan's alleged affair with Frank Sinatra, the Clarence Thomas-Anita Hill hearings, Gary Hart's indiscretions, the Bill Clinton-Monica Lewinsky affair, among others). Politics and entertainment had finally reached the stage in their evolution where they become linked together; Reagan's persuasive use of the media in his policy implementation strategies, as well as his economic deregulation which allowed media monopolies to grow from film to publishing to sports and further, gave the media heretofor unrealized power. This would be part of the legacy of Reaganism: his presidency while setting the foundations of an economic upswing that would last through the 1990s, had opened the door for all forms of the media, from television to film to publishing to the Internet, to become major players in the American sociopolitical landscape. With the presidency of Bill Clinton, the use of media to manipulate public opinion would perhaps reach its apex in "spin."

—Scott Thill

FURTHER READING:

Feuer, Jane. *Seeing through the Eighties: Television and Reaganism.* Durham, Duke University Press, 1995.

Hill, Dilys, Raymond Moore, and Phil Williams. *The Reagan Presidency: An Incomplete Revolution?* New York, St. Martin's Press, 1990.

Jeffords, Susan. *Hard Bodies: Hollywood Masculinity in the Reagan Era.* New Jersey, Rutgers University Press, 1994.

Schieffer, Bob, and Gary Paul Gates. *The Acting President.* New York, E.P. Dutton, 1989.

Wills, Gary. *Reagan's America: Innocents at Home.* Garden City, New York, Doubleday and Co., 1987.

The Real World

The Real World, MTV's first "reality-based" television series, was launched in the fall of 1991 to immense critical and popular acclaim which has increased over its eight-year run, transforming it from a controversial experiment into a money-making franchise. A pseudo-documentary, its concept—reiterated in the opening credits of each week's half hour episode—is "This is the story of seven strangers, picked to live in a house, and have their lives taped, to see what happens when people stop being polite, and start being real." As columnist Benjamin Svetkey observes, "we get to witness these telegenic urbanites live out their 'real' lives. We watch as they feud with each other (over everything from telephone manners to race relations), flirt with each other, rush off to work or school, chat with their moms on the phone (the ubiquitous microphones eavesdrop on both ends of the conversation), schmooze about sex, get drunk, pass out, and do all the other things twenty-somethings do so well, all of it spliced together as slickly as a Paula Abdul video and set to an in-your-face soundtrack of Guns N' Roses and R.E.M. Voyeurism has never been so cool."

The show's "strangers" are a diverse group of Generation X-ers of various geographic, socioeconomic, religious, and sexual orientations, whom the producers carefully screen and assemble hoping for the most volatile—and therefore sensationally watchable—combination possible. According to producer Jon Murray, "the main point of the series is to tell the story of this group of kids. It's to show them getting involved with each other, learning from each other, sharing fears and dreams."

More often than not, however, this "fishbowl" existence causes the sharing to become ugly, as the cast members must agree to allow themselves to be constantly video- and audio-taped by an arsenal of surveillance and hand-held cameras, as well as microphones hidden in every room, on each character, and in the phone. As the months of recording pass, allegiances and grudges are formed, manifest in direct camera address footage from weekly interviews of the subjects by the filmmakers regarding their feelings about day-to-day incidents, and their changing attitudes toward their roommates. Murray contends that these interviews are held to clear up the narrative, not to create one. The "characters" are also expected to pay a weekly visit to the "confessional" room to air their feelings in private to a camera. Thus, *The Real World* has its antecedents in both cinema verité as well as direct cinema practices of the 1960s.

Once the months of filming are completed, the approximately 180,000 minutes of video are edited down to the 440 minutes that will compose the season; in other words, less than one percent of the actual filmed experience is aired. Footage of everyday activities such as reading, cooking, and cleaning are excised to focus on moments of conflict over philosophies, relationships, and the like. These include controversial moments, such as when abrasive stand-up comic David and the infamous scab-picking bike messenger Puck were booted out of their respective casts due to their inability to get along. Grunge singer Neil sticking his tongue in the mouth of a heckler during a performance only to have it nearly bitten off provided real drama, as did gay cast member Pedro Zamora's marriage to his lover, Sean. While many of the incidents that become the plotlines of an episode are significant, cast members also charge that focusing an episode on what they deem to be insignificant incidents tends to exaggerate their importance way out of proportion—a charge leveled by many subjects of documentary films.

In addition, after each season begins airing and the respective casts are interviewed by the press, the first question often posed to them concerns whether they are being themselves, or playing themselves. Though *Real World*-ers generally contend they quickly grew used to the constant surveillance, paradoxically they also agree that the cameras elevated the intensity of every encounter—so much so that MTV offers each cast free psychological counseling at the end of the taping as a means of recovering from the experience. Producer George Verschoor warns each cast at the outset: "Once you get in this house, you are going to be challenged in ways you never thought of. Every move, every part of your past is going to be questioned. . . . So you'd better be ready to look in that mirror. Because when you do, you're going to see yourself—and not only what you think of yourself, but what others think of you . . . and then what a nation thinks of you."

Consequently, though they are not celebrities in the conventional sense, veterans of the show have found their "15 minutes of fame" through continual public recognition and occasionally harassment; the show's popularity, constant reruns, and updated reports on their respective activities never really allowing them to retire to anonymity. Some cast members have marketed their newfound fame into performing careers—models Jacinda Barrett and Eric Nies and even David "Puck" Rainey turning to acting, with Nies also doing a stint as the host of MTV's dance show, *The Grind,* and creating his own workout video.

The series' popularity also resulted in MTV expanding its slate of reality-based programming, including introducing the equally popular spin-off show, *Road Rules,* in 1995, which is essentially "The Real World-in-a-Winnebego," as five youths take an extensive—often international—road trip involving both thrills (skydiving, swimming with sharks) and chills (staying the night in a haunted house; milking snakes for venom).

—Rick Moody

FURTHER READING:

Johnson, Hillary, and Nancy Rommelmann. *The Real Real World.* New York, Melcher Media, 1995.

The Real World Diaries. New York, Melcher Media, 1996.

Patane, Joe. *Livin' in Joe's World.* New York, Harper-Perennial, 1998.

Reality Television

Reality-based television is an amorphous collection of syndicated thematic shows and one-time episodes that have one unifying basis: they rely, in some fashion, on real or true events. This reality can take numerous forms, and the television industry has defined the genre broadly to include tabloid news, talk shows, comedic style shows, and crime-based shows. Examples include shows such as *Hard Copy, A Current Affair, The Jerry Springer Show, America's Funniest Home Videos, Cops, America's Most Wanted,* and one-time episodes such as "When Good Pets Go Bad," "World's Most Shocking Medical Videos," and "Scariest Chases and Shootouts." These shows rely on film or video footage of actual events, re-enactments of events, and interviews with individuals involved with a specific topic. But the importance of these shows stems from how they shape "reality," emphasizing some aspects over others and limiting some details to create a "news" story. The phenomenon of reality television first gained momentum in the mid-1980s, and due to its popularity and economical production costs, has proliferated into the late 1990s.

Tabloid news shows are a less recognized form of reality television, because shows such as *A Current Affair* and *Hard Copy* have a format that resembles mainstream broadcast news. The tabloids actively try to position themselves as closer to the mainstream news media by using such conventions such as reporters and anchors, a reliance on sources for information, and the occasional presentation of pieces that could be seen as "hard news." Despite complaints from mainstream broadcast journalists who insist that tabloid news shows are very different and very inferior to their own product, in actuality both types of broadcasts have begun to mimic even more of each others' practices. Both investigative broadcast news and tabloid news take a moralizing tone with their stories, and both present a clear villain and victim. Both also rely on real events, and both occasionally turn to re-enactments and amateur home video to tell their stories.

While tabloid news had shaped itself to look like mainstream news programs, the popularity of the tabloid news shows has prompted some mainstream news programs to adopt conventions of tabloid news programs. News magazines such as *Dateline NBC* and *48 Hours* have begun using these techniques, as well as the intermittent use of music and emotion in telling their stories. Although the practice cannot be confirmed, some researchers believe that these more mainstream outlets are employing some form of checkbook journalism, or paying sources for their story, as well. Yet, while news professionals may object to these cross-overs and fight the blurring of these lines, these practices ultimately serve to place tabloid television news more within the broadcast news genre than within the reality television genre.

Television talk shows also have elements of "reality" within them, as they often feature individuals and families presenting their problems to a host and studio audience. Yet, the shows have more in common with radio talk and call-in shows, and tend to identify themselves more as talk shows than reality shows. It should also be pointed out that charges have been leveled against some of the more sensational talk shows, such as *The Jerry Springer Show*, that some of the stories are fabricated, and some of the guests are given scripts directing them how to act and when to become less talkative and more physical.

Comedic style reality includes such shows as *America's Funniest Home Videos* and one-shot specials that rely on audience submitted home videos of their embarrassing moments, funny pets, and precocious children. Often, these shows provide prizes for the best or funniest video clip submitted, which is voted on by a studio audience. Although many of the clips appear to be staged or planned, this does not seem to matter to the shows' producers as long as the results are humorous. Additionally, the continuous advertising for the submission of more clips, often with specific themes, seems to acknowledge and approve of this activity.

Other forms of reality television include shock shows that draw together home video and other amateur video, such as police surveillance footage, on a certain shocking theme. These are often one-shot shows, which occasionally have a sequel. This first one of these specials was *World's Most Dangerous Animals,* which appeared on the Fox network on January 25, 1996. The show collected film clips from nature documentaries, including an elephant stomping on a

trainer and a bear attacking a woman. The show had a moral message—that humanity was to blame for what had happened to these animals. Due to the high ratings it received, this show spawned a series of successors, but without the pro-social message. According to George Gerbner, a communications professor and scholar who studies violence on television, these shows "exploit the worst fears and nightmares of people." NBC executive Don Ohlmeyer called Fox's video of animal attacks "one step short of a snuff film."

The most established reality shows are the crime-oriented shows. Programs such as *Cops, America's Most Wanted,* and *Unsolved Mysteries* appear on a weekly basis and devote themselves to exploring the world of crime and criminals. Because of their established position, they are the form of reality television that has received the most attention from other media and media critics, as well as the television audience. These shows define reality television and provide the best clue as to what reality television reveals about "reality," especially America's beliefs about crime and law and order in the late twentieth century.

The proliferation of reality crime shows can be explained in part, but only in part, by the ratings that they receive. It is true that America's commercial broadcast system relies on profits to continue operating, and that profit comes from advertisers willing to pay money to reach certain audiences or segments of audiences. If reality crime shows did not draw viewers, they would not remain on the air. Yet, this is not the only factor in their continued appearance. According to Mark Fishman, reality crime shows receive below average ratings in the total number of households that watch television. Additionally, they have a mediocre share of the audience that does tune in to television during the time slots that they appear. What high ratings they do get are the result of one or two of these shows— usually *Unsolved Mysteries* and *Cops.* Yet, if these shows do not draw crowds of viewers, how can they stay on the air?

One reason for the continued appearance of reality crime shows, as well as the comedic and shock reality shows, are the low production costs involved in making them. Broadcast television has been in a long-term decline, steadily losing viewers to cable television and other sources of entertainment such as home computers and the Internet. This has led the networks to focus on smaller, more specific audience segments to appeal to advertisers (such as men aged 18-49), and has also led them to invest in low-cost programs. Typically, drama and comedy series are quite expensive. The science-fiction program *Star Trek: Voyager* cost approximately $1.5 million an episode, and the hospital drama *ER* cost NBC $13 million per episode in 1998. In contrast, reality crime shows such as *America's Most Wanted* cost—in its early days—$140,000 to $170,000 to produce one weekly half-hour episode. Thus, although they may not draw the same size audience, these shows are cheaper to produce and so can afford to generate smaller audiences and less advertising revenue.

In addition to their low cost, reality crime shows are valuable to broadcasters for other reasons. For example, many of these shows do not have temporal references in them, and so can be shown again and again in syndication. Once a show has survived at least two seasons, there are enough episodes to sell the show into syndication, where the most profits can be made. Crime reality shows can also fill broadcast station owners' need to provide their viewing audience with "public-service" programming—a requirement for maintaining their FCC license. Because these shows are a somewhat ambiguous mix of news and documentary, station owners can claim that by showing these programs, they are fulfilling their obligation to air public service shows. So, for a host of reasons beyond simply high ratings, these shows remain on the air, and increasing in frequency.

As mentioned above, reality crime shows have likely been watched by the greatest number of viewers, due to their long-running nature and series status. These are also the shows that make the greatest attempt to convey a message to their viewers. Their repetitive messages center on crime and law and order; and through a careful construction of reality, they make their point quite effectively. These shows present crime as rampant, violent, and obvious to spot, criminals as villains, and the police and jails as America's best line of defense against these challenges to decent society. These shows also capture minorities committing a greater percentage of crimes, feature crimes that are readily and easily solved, and are filmed more in less affluent urban areas.

For example, *Cops* features "the men and women of law enforcement" and nightly rides along with police from different parts of the country. *Cops* would appear on the surface to be the most realistic of these shows, as it does not have a narrator or host beyond the police who offer background or context for the situations they encounter. The cameraperson for the show rides along in the squad car, taping hours of footage for what will ultimately become a half-hour show. Although the show is carefully edited to appear "uncut," Debra Seagal reports that shows such as these often rely on stock footage and spend a great deal of time constructing the "stories" that appear on the show. Large portions of tape containing no real action must be edited out, and only the most exciting crimes will be included in the final show. Thus, footage of the police riding around for hours on end or the issuance of a speeding ticket would never appear on *Cops,* unless the receiver of the ticket suddenly engaged the police in a high-speed car chase.

Likewise, shows such as *America's Most Wanted* often use reenactments to explain past criminal activity. The show centers on criminals that are still at large, and urges the audience to become part of the solution, and call the show or police if they see any of these wanted criminals. The show regularly runs updates on wanted criminals that are either still at large or have been captured, thanking viewers if they have called in to provide tips or information. The re-enactments, which attempt to graphically demonstrate the criminal's original lawbreaking, however, often rely on circumstantial evidence or statements, especially if the primary victim does not remember the events or is not around to convey the details. Thus, the show is forced to take some artistic license in creating a reasonable version of events, which viewers are likely to see as the truth of the matter.

Another way these shows construct a version of reality is through the narrative closure they attempt to provide. Resolution of events is preferred over unsolved crimes or escaped or unknown criminals, and these shows attempt to provide viewing audiences with this closure. This leads to a view of law enforcement that is at odds with federal statistics on suspects apprehended and cases closed. For example, Mary Beth Oliver and G. Blake Armstrong report that in a sample of reality-based programs, 61.5 percent of all crimes portrayed were depicted as solved, "as compared to FBI reports of an 18.0 percent arrest rate." Thus, reality shows are far more likely to create the impression that more criminals are being apprehended than is actually the case. Furthermore, the shows perpetuate the idea that minorities are more likely to engage in criminal activities. Oliver and Armstrong also report that "the vast majority of African-American characters are cast in roles of criminal suspects where they are also shown as recipients of police aggression." And while shows such as *Cops* state that "all suspects are innocent until proven guilty in a court

of law," researchers have found that most viewers believe the suspects apprehended are indeed guilty, otherwise the police would not have arrested them in the first place.

Shows such as *Cops* provide a version of society where most criminals are caught and are automatically guilty. These criminals are also more likely to be minorities, and to have come from poorer, more crime-infested areas of cities. In addition to the prevalence of criminal activity, however, reality shows perpetuate the idea that criminals are one-dimensional villains, beyond redemption or reason, and therefore deserving of maximum sentences and harsh justice. Gray Cavender reports that on shows such as *America's Most Wanted* and *Unsolved Mysteries,* "the night teems with drug dealers and satanists, and crazy, cold-blooded killers prowl the mean streets of cities and small towns. . . . Criminals are described in terms that connote physical ugliness. They are depicted as dangerous, depraved, unremorseful people." Because of this portrayal, criminals are caricatures, and are depicted as fundamentally different from the audience and are beyond redemption. This view of criminals as beyond reason, as "rotten to the core," then legitimates strict crime control measures and idealizes justice as something wielded by a community to punish the bad apples that threaten the stability and life of the group.

The view of reality depicted by these crime shows is distorted in many respects. Yet, it provides many people with an interpretation of their society and how crime fits into it. In actuality, during the period in which these shows have become more popular, crime in the United States has decreased and non-violent crimes are now more prevalent than violent crimes. Yet, these are not the sorts of facts presented in reality television. Television has always been criticized for its portrayal of crime and violence. Critics maintain that television presents a world that is more violent, where criminals are one-dimensional and are generally caught. Yet, until reality shows appeared, most of these depictions were either found in fictional series such as crime dramas or in the news. The addition of reality crime shows adds a new dimension to the picture. Although the shows claim to portray reality and therefore real crime, the conventions they rely on and their close association with the police often preclude the possibility that they will accurately portray crime in America.

Reality programs are not strictly an American phenomenon, however. Tabloid television news began in Great Britain, and was brought to America by media magnate Rupert Murdoch. Likewise, according to Justine Boissard, reality programming appears in France and Italy as well, where local versions of crime reality shows are very popular. Thus, viewing reality, or what is attempting to pass for reality on television, appears to be a global pastime. How close television reality comes to actual reality and how distorted views of crime effects people's perceptions of their own surroundings remains a central concern.

—Mia Consalvo

FURTHER READING:

Bauder, David. "90s Turbo-Charged 'Snuff Shows' All the Rage." *Daily Iowan.* February 9, 1999, 5A.

Boissard, Justine. "This Is Their Life." *UNESCO Courier.* October 1992, 14-16.

Cavender, Gray, and Mark Fishman, editors. *Entertaining Crime: Television Reality Programs.* New York, Aldine de Gruyter, 1998.

Seagal, Debra. "Tales from the Cutting-Room Floor." *Harper's Magazine.* November 1993, 50-57.

Rear Window

Alfred Hitchcock's *Rear Window* (1954) belongs indisputably among the director's acknowledged masterpieces of suspense. It sprang from an inspired three-picture collaboration during the 1950s with James Stewart (*The Man Who Knew Too Much,* 1955, and *Vertigo,* 1959) and marked the flowering of the director's Technicolor period (he had ventured into color only twice previously, the first time for *Rope* in 1948, starring Stewart). *Rear Window* continues to be shown regularly on television, at retrospectives of both Hitchcock and Stewart's films, and as an occasional movie theater rerun. It not only endures in popularity but also, despite repeated viewing, never loses its suspense and fascination for the viewer. *Rear Window* is a virtual master class in the concerns, obsessions, and techniques that continue to distinguish Hitchcock's work from that of any filmmaker working in the suspense thriller genre.

Collaborating closely with Hitchcock, John Michael Hayes wrote the skillfully constructed screenplay, in which suspense is tempered by a measure of humor—both salty and sophisticated—sadness, and a rare nod to redemptive compassion. Hayes, who would go on to write Hitchcock's next three films, worked from a novelette called *Window* by Cornell Woolrich (the pseudonym of William Irish), a prolific writer whose fiction had, over the decades, provided

fodder for countless B-thrillers and better *films noirs,* including Robert Siodmak's *Phantom Lady* in 1944. The basic plot is simplicity itself. A news photographer (Stewart), having suffered an accident, has his left leg encased in a heavy plaster cast and is confined to a wheelchair in one room of his small city apartment. Thus immobilized, bored and frustrated, he passes the time in observing the occupants of the apartments across the court through a telephoto camera lens. What begins as a casual way to pass the time turns into compulsion, then voyeuristic obsession, as the details of the lives lived behind the windows opposite begin to emerge, and Stewart grows convinced that one man (Raymond Burr) has murdered his wife and disposed of her body. Stewart's glamorous, society-girl fiancée (Grace Kelly), his down-to-earth nurse-housekeeper (Thelma Ritter), and his police detective buddy (Wendell Corey) are skeptical of his suspicions, but the women are eventually convinced and become dangerously involved in snaring the quarry.

Hitchcock loved to present himself with the challenges of filming in the confinement of a single studio-bound set as, for example, in *Lifeboat* (1943), *Rope,* and *Dial M for Murder,* which immediately preceded *Rear Window.* With *Rear Window,* the director told the entire story through the vantage point of Stewart's character, never straying from the apartment, and showing the audience only what Stewart himself can see. What we have here is a protagonist who

James Stewart in a scene from the film *Rear Window*.

generates the action but is forced into a passive role as observer, a role that is shared by the audience, as is his fascination with the myriad domestic dramas played out in the neighboring apartments. The task of populating the movie posed specific problems. As Hitchcock told Charles Higham and Joel Greenberg: ''The set had to be pre-lit because it was such a tremendous job. We had 31 apartments, 12 of them fully furnished. The people moving around in them had microphones on, which you couldn't see at that distance, through which they received instructions.''

On a purely technical level, what perhaps delighted Hitchcock most about the challenge inherent in filming from so confined a visual set-up was the necessary emphasis this would place on the elementally cinematic device of montage. The building blocks of *Rear Window* are the moments in which the film cross-cuts between Stewart peering through his lens and the various scenes he's watching across the courtyard. It is the constant juxtaposition of the two, back and forth, that tells the story and proves that montage makes a movie more than the sum of its parts. As Hitchcock frequently pointed out, the same shot of Stewart could take on an entirely different meaning for the audience, depending on whether Hitchcock preceded his ''reaction shot'' with that of a mother-with-child or chose to show an attractive blonde disrobing. The director here was self-confessedly working at the height of his considerable powers in dealing with confined settings and exploiting montage.

In discussing *Rear Window* with his great admirer, French filmmaker François Truffaut, for the interview book, *Hitchcock/Truffaut,* Hitchcock explained the importance he had given to the assorted vignettes played out by Stewart's neighbors in their various apartments: ''It shows every kind of human behavior. . . . What you see across the way is a group of little stories that . . . mirror a small universe.'' Truffaut, in turn, points out that ''all of the stories have a common denominator in that they involve some aspect of love. James Stewart's problem is that he doesn't want to marry Grace Kelly. Everything he sees across the way has a bearing on love and marriage.'' In Woolrich's original story, the protagonist had no girlfriend at all. Hitchcock and Hayes supplied this rich secondary theme, which allowed sophisticated verbal sparring between reluctant man and determined woman, for the movie.

In addition to the mini-subplots and the unconventional romantic relationship that add rich and complex dimensions to the film, there is the ambiguity in regard to the Stewart character. As critic Andrew Sarris put it to the director, ''One (argument) says that a good deal of the suspense comes from one's not being sure whether James Stewart is right, whether he's making a fool of himself. The other says that you're meant to be certain that he's right, and the suspense comes from whether he will prove it in time.'' Hitchcock, in reply to Sarris, opted for the latter perspective, but the fact that the film works either way is a testament to its subtextual complexity. On a deeper, more disturbing level, the film explores Hitchcock's recurring theme of the transference of guilt—from the villain to the hero, and, by extension, from the hero to the audience. As Hitchcock admitted to Truffaut, ''(Stewart's character) is a real Peeping Tom. (One critic) complained . . . that *Rear Window* was a horrible film because the hero spent all of his time peeping out of the window. What's so horrible about that? Sure, he's a snooper, but aren't we all?'' And, by implication, aren't we all engaging in an act that is inherently voyeuristic when we sit in a darkened theater and watch the people in a movie?

In both its technique and its story elements, therefore, *Rear Window* exemplifies the duality in Hitchcock's best work, that depth of perspective that so often eludes his imitators and keeps his films

entertaining for contemporary audiences. In his interview with the master, Truffaut confessed that, as a young film critic, ''I (wrote) that the picture was very gloomy, rather pessimistic, and quite evil. But now I don't see it in that light at all; in fact, I feel it has a rather compassionate approach. What Stewart sees from his window is not horrible but simply a display of human weaknesses and people in pursuit of happiness.'' The same movie, the same moviegoer, but in one juxtaposition, he sees darkness, and in the other, he sees light. If that isn't an example of the power of montage, what is?

In a bumper year for the Academy Awards—the year Judy Garland lost out for *A Star Is Born* and *On the Waterfront* was voted Best Picture, *Rear Window* gained only a single nomination, and that for its director. Today, it is regarded as an exemplary piece of filmmaking in every department, from Edith Head's carefully designed clothes and Robert Burk's photography, to Franz Waxman's musical score and an impeccably chosen cast. If the film remains, above all, a masterpiece of screenwriting and direction, it is also a testament to the stature of James Stewart who, in middle age, had matured into an actor of depth and subtlety, able to mine and reflect the darker complexities of character that Hitchcock presented him within this film and, even more tellingly, *Vertigo* five years later.

The potent Woolrich story was remade for television in the 1990s as a vehicle for the paralyzed star Christopher Reeve but, not surprisingly, failed to capture the rich subtexts embodied in Hitchcock's version.

—Preston Neal Jones

FURTHER READING:

Coe, Jonathan. *James Stewart, Leading Man.* London, Bloomsbury, 1994.

Hitchcock, Alfred with François Truffaut. *Hitchcock/Truffaut.* New York, Simon & Schuster, 1985.

Nevins, Francis M. *Cornell Woolrich—First You Dream, Then You Die.* New York, Mysterious Press, 1988.

Sharff, Stefan. *The Art of Looking in Hitchcock's Rear Window.* New York, Limelight Editions, 1997.

Woolrich, Cornell. *Rear Window and Other Stories.* New York, Penguin Books, 1994.

Rebel without a Cause

Rebel without a Cause (1955) is Hollywood's best film about rebellious youth in the 1950s. Promoted as a story about why a kid from a ''good'' family would ''tick . . . like a bomb,'' the film sympathetically presents an adolescent perspective on the rebelliousness of middle-class youth of the time. The film focuses on three frustrated teenagers who seek to form their own identities apart from the world and values of their parents and other adults from which they feel alienated. In his role as James Stark, James Dean presented the American archetype of the troubled and tormented teenager, and in so doing became a spokesman for frustrated youth.

The Jim Stark character is the insecure offspring of a domineering mother (Ann Doran) and henpecked father (James Backus), who

James Dean (right) in a scene from the film *Rebel without a Cause*.

seeks to find a place where his inner gentleness and love can be safely expressed. The other two teenagers include John Crawford (Sal Mineo)—called "Plato"—whose divorced parents have abandoned him, and Judy (Natalie Wood), who cannot understand why her father (William Hopper) seems to have withdrawn his love now that she is a young lady. The three meet at a police station at the beginning of the film, where Plato is brought in for drowning puppies, Judy for being out after curfew, and Jim for being drunk.

The juvenile offenders officer Ray Framek (Edward Platt) is the only sympathetic adult in the film, offering the teenagers a calm and considerate hearing. In contrast, both Judy and Jim's parents seem confused by the needs of their teenagers and misunderstand or avoid their children's desires for comfort and guidance. Plato is cared for by a powerless black nanny (Marietta Canty).

Director Nicholas Ray felt young people and their problems were an important subject matter and regularly made movies that sympathized with outsiders. *Rebel* was adopted from his 17-page "The Blind Run," a series of images of troubled teens that lacked any real story. Taking his idea to Warner Bros., Ray was asked to adapt a nonfiction book by Dr. Robert M. Lindner called *Rebel without a Cause: The Story of a Criminal Psychopath* into a script. Ray refused

because he wanted to dramatize the problems of "normal" delinquents from "ordinary" families. The studio consented, and Ray's movie took Lindner's title but nothing else.

Leon Uris, Irving Shulman—the author of the first novel to deal with modern juvenile delinquency, *The Amboy Dukes*—and Stewart Stern all collaborated with Ray on the script. After Stern spent 10 days in juvenile court passing himself off as a welfare worker and talking to various kids, he created a despairing script which convinced the studio that a film could be made from the project. *Rebel* was a modern-day version of *Peter Pan*, with three kids inventing a world of their own, and expressing teen feelings about the nature of loneliness and love. The story also had a mythic feeling because the action was confined to a single day, recounting the happenings from dawn-to-dawn.

Ray had already selected Dean for the role of Jim Stark, and Dean had helped conceive many of the film's scenes. In playing Stark, Dean portrays the tensions of adolescence, bottling up his feelings to the point of explosion. *Rebel* captures the path Stark takes toward manhood, having him learn that he does not need violence to assert his power, that he can be brave, and that he can go against the pack and risk being unpopular as long as he is true to himself. Dean defined masculinity in a different way for his time, allowing the audience to see the undercurrent of sweetness in a character who longs for a world where people drop their bravado and treat each other gently.

To cast the supporting juvenile roles, Ray held two weeks of mass improvisations at an amphitheater on the Warner's backlot, where 300 boys were asked to run to the top of the bleachers, play King of the Mountain and other games. Ray cast not according to who was the winner, but according to the attitudes he could see expressed by the players as they competed. Ray considered Jeff Silver, Billy Gray, and even Dennis Hopper for the role of Plato, but Mineo expressed such enthusiasm as well as a facility for improvisation for the role that Ray was won over.

For Judy, the studio wanted a star and considered borrowing Debbie Reynolds from MGM, while Ray wanted Carroll Baker, consigning Natalie Wood to playing Judy's scheming friend. Wood badly wanted the part, and after being in a car accident with Dennis Hopper, when the police asked her for her parents' phone number, she supplied them with Ray's instead. She later told the director, "Nick, they called me a goddam juvenile delinquent, now do I get the part?" She did, though Jack Warner initially complained about her delivery, resulting in Ray sending Wood to voice coach Nina Moise.

Censorship demands curtailed some of the violence in the film. There could not be any intention to kill, knives during the chase scene were to be replaced by bicycle chains which could not be whirled about, and there were to be no doubts about the innocent nature of cigarettes furtively palmed or Judy's chastity. Even so, when the movie opened in Great Britain, the British censor was so appalled at the chicken run, where teens watch as Buzz and Jim drive their cars over a cliff (originally over a crowded road, but changed to an empty seacoast at the studio's insistence), that he demanded six minutes of cuts and still gave the film an X rating.

Rebel without a Cause was released four days after Dean's reckless demise in a car accident. The film received three Academy Award nominations, to Ray for Best Original Story, to Mineo for Best Supporting Actor, and to Wood for Best Supporting Actress, but won none of them. It was Ray's only film to be so honored. James Dean, giving the finest performance of his career and one that would cement him forever in the public's imagination, was overlooked entirely, but the film unquestionably belongs to him and his portrayal of an anguished adolescent.

—Dennis Fischer

FURTHER READING:

Archer, Eugene. "Generations without a Cause." *Film Culture.* No. 7, 1956.

Eisenschitz, Bernard. *Nicholas Ray: An American Journey.* London, Faber & Faber, 1990.

Fox, Terry. "Nicholas Ray, with a Cause." *Village Voice.* 1979.

McVay, D. "Rebel without a Cause." *Films and Filming.* August 1977.

Ray, Nicholas. "Rebel—The Life Story of a Film." *Daily Variety.* October 31, 1951.

———. "Story into Script." *Sight and Sound.* Autumn 1956.

Steen, Mike. *Hollywood Speaks.* New York, G.P. Putnam's Son, 1974.

Recycling

Earth Day 1970 suggested to millions of Americans that environmental concern could be expressed locally. Through organized activities, many citizens found that they could actively improve the environment with their own hands. Many communities responded by organizing ongoing efforts to alter wasteful patterns. Recycling would prove to be the most persistent of these grassroots efforts. Though the effort has been trivialized by extremist environmentalists, trash and waste recycling now stands as the ultimate symbol of the American environmental consciousness.

Recycling grew out of a conservative impulse to reduce waste, rather than as an expression of environmentalism. The effort to make worthwhile materials from waste can be traced throughout human society as an application of commonsense rationality. The term "recycling" became part of the American lexicon during wartime rationing, particularly during World War II. Scrap metals and other materials became a resource to be collected and recycled into weaponry and other materials to support the fighting overseas. But the public's enthusiasm for recycling did not last. Historians point to the conclusion of World War II, and the commensurate growth in the U.S. middle class as defining points in the American "culture of consumption"—which reenforced carelessness, waste, and a demand for newness—that became prevalent in the 1950s but extended, in some form, through the end of the twentieth century. The prodigious scale of American consumption quickly made the nation the most advanced and wasteful civilization in the world. It was only a matter of time before a backlash brought U.S. consumption patterns into question. As the 1960s counterculture imposed doubt on much of the American "establishment," many Americans began to consider more carefully the patterns with which they lived everyday life. In the late 1960s and early 1970s, this mindset was met by a litany of examples of American exploitation of resources, ranging from gas shortages to oil spills to toxic leaks. Many Americans began to call for a new ethic to guide everyday life, and, for many, Earth Day 1970 marked the symbolic start of a "greener" perspective.

Belittled by many environmentalists, recycling often seems like busywork for kids with little actual environmental benefit. However, such a minor shift in human behavior suggests the significant alteration made to people's view of their place in nature. Environmental concerns such as overused landfills and excessive litter contributed to a new "ethic" within U.S. culture that began to value restraint, reuse, and living within limits; and gave communities a new mandate in maintaining the waste of their population. Reusing products or creating useful byproducts from waste offered application of this new ethic while also offering new opportunity for economic profit and development. Green, or environmental, industries took form to facilitate and profit from this impulse, creating a significant growth portion of the American economy. Even more impressively, the grassroots desire to express an environmental commitment compelled middle-class Americans to make recycling part of an everyday effort. However, the consumptive momentum of the American economy in the twentieth century made it necessary for citizens to relearn the ethic to decrease waste, and often it was children and schools who fuelled community efforts to recycle. By the end of the twentieth century, many institutions and communities had made recycling a portion of waste disposal service.

Most children born after the 1980s assume the "reduce, reuse, recycle" mantra has been part of the United States since its founding.

In actuality, it serves as a continuing ripple of the cultural and social impact of Earth Day 1970 and the effort of Americans to begin to live within limits.

—Brian Black

FURTHER READING:

Opie, John. *Nature's Nation.* New York, Harcourt Brace, 1998.

Red Scare

The Red Scare of 1919-1920 was the first, but not the last, widespread outbreak of anti-communist sentiment in U.S. history. In a national panic over alleged foreign-inspired subversion, people of varying political beliefs were termed ''Reds'' and became victims of public rage and government suppression. The culmination of these events was the arrest and deportation of hundreds of American citizens—particularly immigrants—in the Palmer Raids of 1920.

The event that initiated the Red Scare was the Bolshevik Revolution of November 1917 in Russia. Inspired by the writings of German philosopher Karl Marx, the Bolsheviks, under the leadership of Vladimir Lenin, believed that the revolution in Russia was the first in a chain of workers' revolutions that would spread throughout the world. In March 1919, the Bolsheviks founded the Communist International to coordinate communist parties worldwide and promote revolution abroad. Many Americans became fearful that, just as a small faction had seized power in Russia, so could a similar group take over the United States. Those under most suspicion were members of the Industrial Workers of the World (IWW), a syndicalist labor union that had espoused revolution for the previous decade, and Bolshevik supporters who formed the Communist Labor Party and Communist Party of the USA in 1919.

The fear of a communist coup in the United States was fueled by a number of events. After World War I, the U.S. economy was in recession, living costs had risen, and many soldiers returned home to a country with high unemployment. In the summer of 1919, as blacks and whites competed for jobs, major race riots broke out in both the North and the South. Also labor unions, which had grown in size and influence during the war years, became involved in a number of major conflicts with employers. In 1919 alone, over four million workers went on strike. There was a general strike in Seattle in January and then a nationwide stoppage of steelworkers in September, both of which, employers alleged, were Bolshevik conspiracies. Worst of all, also in September, the Boston police force walked off the job, and Massachusetts Governor Calvin Coolidge called out the state militia to replace the striking policemen and to stop incidents of looting.

In addition to economic distress and labor unrest, the public was further alarmed by a spate of bomb attacks on prominent figures in commerce and government. Although it was unclear who sent the bombs, newspapers and politicians blamed them on a Communist conspiracy. In April 1919, the maid of U.S. Senator Thomas R. Hardwick of Georgia had her hands blown off when she opened a package delivered to the senator's home. Fifteen other mail bombs were detected that were addressed to other notable figures, including J. P. Morgan, John D. Rockefeller, and Supreme Court Justice Oliver Wendell Holmes, Jr. In June 1919, Attorney General A. Mitchell

Palmer was one of the targets of another series of attempted bombings. Consequently, Palmer organized a new general intelligence division within the Justice Department and placed it under the direction of J. Edgar Hoover, whose job it was to uncover the alleged conspiracy.

The panic over radicalism was chiefly directed at immigrants. Building on a tradition of nativism, many Americans came out of World War I inspired by a militant patriotism and a dislike of foreign influences. Many of the leading radicals were foreign-born, and newspapers and politicians portrayed anarchism, communism, and socialism as foreign ideologies. Moreover, many of the workers who went on strike in 1919 were recent immigrants from Southern and Eastern Europe. Opponents of labor, such as the newly formed American legion, labeled the strikes as un-American and claimed that radical immigrants were fomenting unrest.

Fear and hysteria mounted as the press, politicians, and pressure groups called for action against subversives. All across the nation, police broke up meetings of radical groups, raided their headquarters, and closed down their newspapers. In May 1919, the newly opened offices of the Socialist paper the *New York Call* were ransacked by a mob and its workers hospitalized. On the weekend of November 7 and 8, 1919, federal agents raided the offices of the Union of Russian Workers in New York and arrested over 200 of its members. A few days later in Centralia, Washington, an IWW hall was attacked by American Legionnaires, many of those inside were arrested in the fighting, and one was dragged from jail, castrated, and shot. Also in 1919, socialist leader Victor Berger was elected to Congress from Milwaukee but the House of Representatives refused to allow him to serve his term. In April 1920, the New York State legislature expelled five elected Socialist members. A number of liberal figures and organizations, such as Chicago settlement house worker and pacifist Jane Addams, the League of Women Voters, and the American Civil Liberties Union, also came under attack for their lack of patriotism.

The Red Scare reached a climax with the Palmer Raids of January 2, 1920. On the orders of Attorney General Palmer, around 10,000 people were arrested in 33 cities for their part in alleged subversion. In violation of their constitutional rights, homes were searched, arrested were held without bail, and foreigners were sent to Ellis Island to face deportation hearings without the aid of lawyers. Many of those arrested spent days and weeks in jail with no formal charges filed against them before they were released. Of those arrested, nearly 600 foreigners were ultimately deported.

After the Palmer Raids, the Red Scare quickly subsided. As labor unrest receded, the economy strengthened, bolshevism refused to take root anywhere outside Russia, and the American public became less concerned with subversion. The effects of the Red Scare, however, lingered. Throughout the 1920s reformers were afraid to speak openly, fearing that they would be labeled radical or anti-American. Americanization programs flourished as states sought to stamp out the foreign roots of this radicalism. Twentieth century American radicalism never recovered from the Red Scare. The IWW was virtually destroyed, socialism's electoral strength declined, communism failed to grow, and radicalism was relegated to the margins of U.S. politics.

—John F. Lyons

FURTHER READING:

Murray, Robert K. *Red Scare: A Study in National Hysteria, 1919-1920.* Minneapolis, University of Minneapolis Press, 1955.

Preston, William, Jr. *Aliens and Dissenters, Federal Suppression of Radicals, 1903-1933*. Second edition. Urbana, University of Illinois Press, 1994.

Redbook

Published continuously since 1903, when it was known as *The Red Book* magazine, this mass-circulation American monthly is now targeted toward young wives and mothers, *Redbook* is regarded in the media industry as one of the so-called ''Seven Sisters'' of women's service magazines, a badge shared with *Good Housekeeping, Ladies' Home Journal* and *McCalls*, among others. But it was not until 1951 that its format was revamped to include its now-familiar mix of articles on contemporary living that, in its own words, ''help young working mothers bring balance to a hectic life and focus on what matters most.''

The Red Book was so named because, in the words of founding editor Trumbull White, ''Red is the color of happiness.'' For the first several decades of its existence, many of them under the editorship of Edwin Balmer, the magazine was primarily a vehicle for short fiction. However, even Balmer realized that this format was becoming stale and unattractive to mass audiences, complaining that his publication seemed to appeal only to ''the little old ladies in Kokomo.'' In 1951, following the lead of other periodicals that were redefining their images to appeal to the new post-World War II generation of younger, working women and mothers, the magazine metamorphosed into the *Redbook* that is still recognizable in the 1990s: a lifestyle publication with vivid four-color layouts, departments on childcare, careers, intimacy, fashion, and homemaking, and thoughtful, sometimes controversial features on personal and social issues. With Wade Nichols as editor, *Redbook* became ''The Magazine for Young Adults'' and its circulation soon increased to two million, doubling to 4.5 million by the end of the 1960s. By that decade, *Redbook*'s editorial focus was considered generally more provocative and socially conscious than that of its sister publications, with frank articles that discussed feminism, social and cultural issues, and changing sexual mores. The readership had shifted from ''the little old ladies in Kokomo'' to a new generation of twenty- and thirty-something readers interested in child-care and household tips but also in navigating their way in careers and marriages, the rules of which were being rewritten during a rather turbulent period of American history.

Despite several ownership changes during the 1970s and *Redbook*'s eventual acquisition by Hearst Magazines in 1982, the periodical continued its emphasis on contemporary issues. Editor-in-chief Kate White caused no little controversy when she selected for its December 1997 cover a photograph of actress Keely Shaye Smith and actor Pierre Brosnan looking on as their infant son, Dylan Thomas, is being breastfed by Smith. The graphic cover was ultimately printed on newsstand copies only, about a third of *Redbook*'s circulation; a non-breastfeeding version was supplied to the magazine's regular mail subscribers.

Lesley Jane Seymour took over as *Redbook*'s editor at the end of 1998, with promises to make over the publication. ''My aim is to jazz up the magazine, make it more energetic and a little younger,'' she was quoted as saying. By century's end, *Redbook* had an audited circulation of 2.9 million and was described by the *DrMag* media-watch website as ''an inspiring entertainment magazine'' that ''addresses the needs of young working mothers between the ages of 25

and 45, especially those who work outside the home and have children under 18.'' Hearst's own website touted *Redbook* as ''the must-read magazine for today's young married woman,'' one whose pages offer ''exciting, provocative features that address the fullness of her life—everything from stylish fashion and beauty portfolios and scintillating stories on keeping her marriage fresh, to balancing home and career demands twenty-four hours a day, seven days a week.''

—Edward Moran

FURTHER READING:

''DrMag.'' http://www.drmag.com. April 1999.

''Hearst Magazines.'' http://www.hearstcorp.com. April 1999.

Reed, David. *The Popular Magazine in Britain and the United States*. London, British Library, 1997.

Tebbel, John, *The American Magazine: A Compact History*. New York, Hawthorn Books, 1969.

Tebbel, John and Mary Ellen Zuckerman. *The Magazine in America: 1741-1990*. New York, Oxford University Press, 1991.

Wood, James Playsted. *Magazines in the United States*. New York, Ronald Press, 1978.

Redding, Otis (1941-1967)

Hailing from Georgia, 1960s soul man Otis Redding exemplified the ''Stax sound,'' named after the record company for which he recorded throughout his career as a solo artist. His grainy, emotive vocals backed by the raw but extremely tight house band (Booker T. & the MGs) created a sound that was much copied, and which was responsible for making Memphis-based Stax Records a major player in the 1960s rhythm and blues (R&B) market. Earning a reputation as the penultimate showman and entertainer (rivaling only fellow Georgian James Brown), Redding also became known both as an excellent interpreter (he covered the Rolling Stones' ''Satisfaction'' to great effect) and an exceptional songwriter (he wrote ''Respect,'' which Aretha Franklin later popularized). Though most of his influence was confined to the R&B market, at the time of his death at 26, Redding was on the verge of crossing over to the pop market, which he later did with the posthumously released number-one single, ''Sittin' on the Dock of the Bay.'' It was with this song and earlier crossover hits that Redding helped to merge the gulf between pop and R&B markets during the 1960s.

Redding was born in Dawson, Georgia, and raised in Macon, and was heavily influenced as a young man by the shouting of Little Richard and the more restrained gospel delivery of Sam Cooke. Beginning his career working in small clubs and recording a handful of singles as a Little Richard sound-alike (such as ''Shout Bamalama''), Redding joined Johnny Jenkins' band beginning in the late 1950s, continuing in an off-and-on fashion through the early 1960s. In 1962, when a recording session for Jenkins was going poorly, Redding used the time to step up to the microphone and use the studio band to record ''These Arms of Mine,'' a number 20 R&B hit that established Redding as a solo artist. But his career really did not take off until the mid-1960s when his cover of the Rolling Stones' ''Satisfaction'' and the Redding-penned ''I've Been Loving You Too Long,'' ''Fa-Fa-Fa-Fa-Fa-Fa (Sad Song),'' and ''Respect'' all became top-forty hits.

Otis Redding

His legendary sweat-drenched live shows on the so-called "chitlin' circuit" had already made him one of the most popular black solo artists of the 1960s among African American crowds, and his much-talked-about performance at the Monterey International Pop Festival helped to bring him to the attention of a wider (read "white") audience. By 1967, Redding was not only on the verge of crossing over to the pop market in a big way, but he was expanding his artistic horizons dramatically and redefining what soul music could sound like in the process. "Sittin' on the Dock of the Bay" was the result of his experimentation, and it eventually went to number one on the *Billboard* pop charts, albeit posthumously. On December 10, 1967 Redding's plane went down near Madison, Wisconsin, killing Redding and four members of his back-up band, Stax recording artists the Bar-Kays.

—Kembrew McLeod

Redford, Robert (1937—)

Robert Redford may very well be the last of the classic movie stars. Possessing rugged good looks in the tradition of Clark Gable and Cary Grant, he has been a major leading man since he rocketed to fame in the role of the Sundance Kid in 1969's *Butch Cassidy and the Sundance Kid*, playing opposite another screen legend, Paul Newman. Throughout his 30-year career, which began on Broadway in 1959 in *Tall Story* and continued with his 1962 film debut in *War Hunt,* he has

demonstrated an ability to portray American icons so memorably as to recreate them in his own image. Yet, in most ways, Redford is rather an atypical movie star. Though not necessarily anti-Hollywood, he goes his own way both on the screen and off and is extremely selective about his film roles. Although his blonde, blue-eyed charisma made him the most popular actor in America in 1974, his choice of screen roles were anything but glamorous.

In such films as *Downhill Racer* (1969), *The Candidate* (1972), *Jeremiah Johnson* (1972), and *The Way We Were* (1973), Redford portrayed men who questioned the prevailing political and social systems. In *The Candidate*, for example, he portrayed a man running for the senate on the basis of ethics and idealism, who quickly learns that people care more about appearances than about a candidate's positions on real issues. Winning is what the game was about, he discovers. By the end of the film, the candidate learns how to get himself elected but has no idea of what he will do in office.

This theme is repeated in 1973's *The Way We Were*, in which he plays a popular "most likely to succeed" college athlete paired with Barbra Streisand's idealistic socialist in a marriage of opposites. As in *The Candidate,* Redford's character succeeds in life largely through appearances, connections, and an ability to say the right thing even if it is meaningless. Thus, while he is depicting the American dream, he is troubled by it.

Redford's characters during the early years of his career appeared to be dichotomies: happy on the surface, yet emanating a haunting emptiness. In *Jeremiah Johnson*, he steps out of the system all together by portraying a "frontier trapper" who could not stand the restraints of society and was more at home in the wilderness. This film established the essential Redford character that would dominate the films of his middle and later career. In a string of successful films beginning with *The Great Gatsby* in 1974 and continuing with *Three Days of the Condor* (1975), *All the President's Men* (1976), *Sneakers* (1992), and *Quiz Show* (1994), he took a decidedly mistrusting stance against the government, big business, cultural institutions (such as marriage), and the integrity of the media.

This attitude also typified his behind-the-camera efforts as well. By 1975, he had turned his own production company, Wildwood Productions, into a major player in acquiring film properties, only picking projects that dealt with issues important to Redford. For example, the company acquired film rights to the best-selling book *All the President's Men*, which is about the Watergate investigation and the attempt to impeach President Nixon. The film won an Academy Award. In 1980, Redford won an Academy Award for directing *Ordinary People*, a brilliant dissection of the dark secrets haunting a typical American family. He cast television's most wholesome icon, Mary Tyler Moore, as the overbearingly neurotic mother haunted by the death of her son and blaming it on the youngest sibling. In 1988, he continued his political themes by directing an award-winning documentary *Incident at Ogala*, which investigated the persecution of a Native American by the FBI.

Redford is a passionate environmentalist and political activist for social justice with genuine concerns for the quality of both life and art. He lobbied for the Clean Air Act of 1974, the Energy and the Conservation Act of 1976, and several strip-mining bills. In 1976, he also took three years off from filmmaking to write a book, *The Outlaw Trail,* about the American West.

In 1980, he founded the Sundance Institute in Utah to promote the pure, idealistic side of filmmaking. Eschewing Hollywood, the

Robert Redford

institute aims to nurture young, independent filmmakers by creating an environment in which seasoned professionals can help beginners to find their voice without the pressures of commercialism.

One outgrowth of his creation of the Sundance Institute is an annual film festival dedicated to independent cinema. However, the festival was discovered by Hollywood executives desperate for new ideas in 1990, and a number of films screened there have been subsequently purchased and plunged into the mainstream cinema. While this has been financially beneficial for the artists involved, they rarely go on to experience the creative freedom in Hollywood that they enjoyed at Sundance. By the mid-1990s, the festival became a winter retreat for Hollywood executives. The products screened evolved from truly independent films devoid of big-name stars to Hollywood films utilizing Hollywood talent.

Although he has had some setbacks, Redford has become one of only a few actors who can make his own choices in both his personal life and in his films. He has used his star power to produce and star in films that publicize his beliefs and his causes. Both his lifestyle and his motion pictures have become fully intertwined with their common theme of iconoclastic loners who take on the establishment and live life on their own terms. At the same time, most of his screen roles reflect his political and environmental views to such an extent that one may wonder if he could portray an unsympathetic character. He came

close in 1990's *Havana*, in which he portrayed a Bogart-like professional gambler who only looked out for himself. The film's failure at the box-office may have been because audiences were not used to seeing Redford in such a downbeat role. In 1998, he retreated to his traditional pro-environment, loner character in the successful *The Horse Whisperer*, but broke with his own off-Hollywood stance in his personal life by actually appearing on talk shows around the world to promote the film.

—Sandra Garcia-Myers

FURTHER READING:

De Vries, Hillary. "Robert Redford: Why Does He Still Do It?" *Los Angeles Times Calendar.* December 9, 1990, 8.

Downing, David. *Robert Redford.* New York, St. Martin's Press, 1982.

Hanna, David. *Robert Redford: The Superstar Nobody Knows.* New York, A Leisure Book, 1975.

Redford, Robert. *The Outlaw Trail.* New York, Grossett & Dunlap, 1978.

Weiss, Michael J. "Redford Comes down from His Mountain." *London Times.* September 14, 1984, 9.

Reed, Donna (1921-1986)

With *The Donna Reed Show* (1958-1966), actress Donna Reed was one of the most popular women of early television. While the character she played was a typical television housewife of the 1950s, Reed was also a pioneer as one of the only women at the time who produced her own shows. She began her career playing sweethearts and wives in films of the 1940s—in 1946 she appeared opposite Jimmy Stewart in the film classic *It's a Wonderful Life*. Reed eventually attempted to break out of good-girl roles by portraying a prostitute in *From Here to Eternity* (1953), for which she won an Academy Award. When the film industry did not provide her other parts she wanted, Reed decided turn to the new medium of television, where she became a huge star. After her show went off the air in the 1960s, she continued to act periodically until her death.

—Jill A. Gregg

FURTHER READING:

Fultz, Jay. *In Search of Donna Reed.* Des Moines, University of Iowa Press, 1998.

Reed, Ishmael (1938—)

Ishmael Reed, regarded as one of the greatest satirists in America since Mark Twain, is also one of the best known multi-faceted writers of the twentieth century; his titles include novelist, poet, publisher, playwright, literary critic, songwriter, editor, television producer, founder of the multicultural group Before Columbus Foundation and There City Cinema, and essayist. In 1967, he changed the American literary scene when he published *The Free-Lance Pallbearers,* a novel that set the tone and aesthetic for the eight novels, five collections of poetry, four essay books, and several anthologies that followed. With a writing technique called Neo-HooDoo Aesthetic or Neo-HooDooism, a multicultural style based on Voodoo and African-based religious beliefs which he mixed with elements from other cultural traditions, Reed has consistently supported multiculturalism and argued for a multicultural society in the United States and the world over. Though literary critics have been baffled by his innovative techniques, which include combining several seemingly non-related elements from different time periods into his writings—one novel, *Mumbo Jumbo* (1972), for example, contains photographs, drawings, footnotes, quotes, and a partial bibliography—he has been nationally and internationally recognized as the Charlie Parker of American Fiction. In June 1998, Ishmael Reed received the MacArthur Foundation Award.

—Pierre-Damien Mvuyekure

FURTHER READING:

Bruce, Dick, editor. *Conversations with Ishmael Reed.* Jackson, University Press of Mississippi, 1995.

McGee, Patrick. *Ishmael Reed and the Ends of Race.* New York, St. Martin's Press, 1997.

Reed, Ishmael. *Writin' Is Fightin': Thirty-Seven Years of Boxing on Paper.* New York, Atheneum, 1990.

———. *Mumbo Jumbo.* New York, Atheneum, 1972.

———, editor. *MultiAmerica: Essays on Cultural Wars and Cultural Peace.* New York, Viking, 1997.

Reed, Lou (1942—)

Lou Reed, both as a solo artist and as a member of the Velvet Underground, had an extraordinary influence on the history of rock and roll from the 1960s through the 1990s. Brian Eno once observed that hardly anyone bought the Velvet Underground's albums when they were first released, but the ones who did all formed their own bands.

Born and raised on Long Island, Reed attended Syracuse University, where he met and befriended the poet Delmore Schwartz. After leaving Syracuse, Reed landed a position writing pop songs for Pickwick Records, where he met John Cale, a classically trained cellist who had played with the Dream Syndicate, LaMonte Young's avant-garde ensemble. In 1965, Cale and Reed formed a band, rounding out the lineup with Sterling Morrison, whom Reed had known from college, and Angus MacLise on drums, later replaced by Maureen ''Mo'' Tucker. After going through a variety of names, they finally settled on the Velvet Underground, the title of a pulp pornographic novel. The band's first show was less than auspicious: they were booked as the opening act at a high school dance in Summit, New Jersey. The following year, the Velvets became the house band at The Factory, Andy Warhol's studio and performance space. Warhol convinced them to add Nico, the German actress and model, as a vocalist and signed them on to the Exploding Plastic Inevitable, his touring multimedia show.

Their first album, *The Velvet Underground and Nico*, features topics unheard of in 1960's rock. ''I'm Waiting for the Man'' and ''Heroin'' are frank and even celebratory depictions of drug addiction, while the sadomasochistic themes of ''Venus and Furs'' would provide a model for many gothic bands of the 1980s and 1990s.

Lou Reed

Beyond the lyrics, however, the album was important for a number of reasons. The songs, all of which were written or cowritten by Reed, were deceptively simple (Reed once said he liked the fact that anyone could play them), and the musicianship was deliberately stripped down. Reed's vocals were often laconic, almost spoken, and provided a model for singers such as Ric Ocasek of the Cars, Gordon Gano of the Violent Femmes, and Jonathan Richman. While the band acquired a reputation as both arty and dark, songs such as ''I'll Be Your Mirror,'' ''There She Goes Again'' and ''Femme Fatale'' were straight-up pop songs. That combination of a do-it-yourself attitude, artistic aspirations, and a strong pop sensibility would exert an enormous influence on the punk and independent music scenes of the late 1970s and 1980s.

While the Velvets' first release had used feedback and Cale's dissonant string arrangements as a kind of background noise, *White Light, White Heat*, the band's second album, was a relentless barrage of sound. Experimenting with various effects pedals for his guitar, Reed developed a style in which a squalling wall of feedback was overlaid on every song. It was a wildly different approach from the highly produced and orchestrated sounds which most rock bands of the 1960s had adopted. Even in the 1980s, *White Light, White Heat* remained influential, as bands such as the Gang of Four and the Jesus and Mary Chain incorporated a layer of feedback into their music.

Cale left the band after *White Light, White Heat,* and the Velvets recorded two more albums, *The Velvet Underground* and *Loaded,* as well as unreleased sessions later issued as *VU,* before Reed left the band in 1970. While those efforts at first did not reach the less-than-impressive sales of the first two albums, they indicated the direction Reed's solo career would take. *Loaded* featured ''Sweet Jane'' and ''Rock and Roll,'' two songs which would become among Reed's most famous.

After quitting the band, Reed took a day job as typist at his father's accounting firm, then released two albums in 1972: *Lou Reed* and *Transformer.* The latter was produced by David Bowie, who was an unapologetic Reed admirer. (''Queen Bitch,'' released on Bowie's 1971 album *Hunky Dory,* is an unmistakable tribute to the Velvets.) *Transformer* contains ''Walk on the Wild Side,'' which remains Reed's most popular song.

Reed was exceptionally prolific from the 1970s through the late 1990s, and while his work was often well received, few listeners believed it equaled his work with the Velvet Underground or his early solo efforts. In 1989 he reunited with John Cale on *Songs for Drella,* an album of songs about the Andy Warhol, who had died two years earlier. In 1993, the original Velvet Underground reunited (minus Nico, who had died in 1988) and played a brief reunion tour. Perhaps one of the oddest moments in Reed's career was when he played a twenty-minute set at the White House in 1998 at the request of Czech President Vaclav Havel, who had insisted that Reed and the Velvets were important influences on the Czech underground who had fought against Soviet domination.

—Bill Freind

FURTHER READING:

Bockris, Victor, and Gerard Malanga. *Uptight: The Velvet Underground Story.* New York, Quill, 1985.

McNeil, Legs, and Gillian McCain. *Please Kill Me: The Uncensored Oral History of Punk.* New York, Grove Press, 1996.

Reese, Pee Wee (1918-1999)

Known for his fine defensive play and leadership, shortstop Harold Henry ''Pee Wee'' Reese was the captain of the Brooklyn Dodgers baseball team in the 1940s and 1950s. The ''Little Colonel'' led Brooklyn to seven National League titles and a World Series victory in 1955. The intangibles Reese brought to the game earned him top ten mention in the MVP voting eight times and induction into the Baseball Hall of Fame in 1984. In 1947, Reese gained attention off the field by befriending teammate Jackie Robinson, who was the first black baseball player allowed to play in the major leagues. Reese's friendship with Robinson was instrumental in easing Robinson's acceptance among his Dodger teammates and Major League Baseball. Reese's historic actions remain a symbol of social progress in American civil rights.

—Nathan R. Meyer

FURTHER READING:

Golenbock, Peter. *Teammates.* San Diego, Harcourt Brace Jovanovich, 1990.

Wolpin, Stewart. *Bums No More! The Championship Season of the 1955 Brooklyn Dodgers.* New York, St. Martin's Press, 1995.

Reeves, Martha

See Martha and the Vandellas

Reeves, Steve (1926—)

From 1957 to 1968, Steve Reeves was able to parlay his bodybuilding success and classical good looks into a film career which, for a brief time, made him the highest paid screen performer in the world. Most of his films were ''sword and sandal'' spectaculars, made in Italy, but they provided entertainment for his millions of fans around the world and served as an inspiration for later stars of action films, such as Sylvester Stallone and Arnold Schwarzenegger.

Reeves was born on a ranch outside the small town of Glasgow, Montana, and was not quite two when his father was killed in a farming accident. When Reeves was ten, he and his mother moved to Oakland, California, where the active youngster soon had a paper route and was developing his legendary calves by pedaling the rolling hills of his new hometown. Serendipity brought a teenage Reeves into contact with Ed Yarick, one of the most knowledgeable gym owners

Steve Reeves as Hercules in a scene from the film *Hercules Unchained.*

in the United States. Within two years, Reeves' genetic gifts and Yarick's carefully designed programs had combined to produce a physique equalled by few men in the world at the time.

World War II interrupted Reeves' training for a time, but after fighting in the Philippines he returned to Yarick and began to train for competitive bodybuilding. His first national victory came in 1947, in the biggest contest of all in the United States—the A.A.U. Mr. America. As the holder of this prestigious title, he came to the attention of the media, whose journalists and photographers were drawn to this tall young man, who looked, many said, like a living god.

One of the people who saw photos of Reeves was Hollywood's master of the epic, Cecil B. DeMille, who offered the young body-builder the role of Samson in an upcoming film. The one catch was that Reeves had to reduce his 215-pound weight to 200 pounds, a sacrifice he was unwilling to make, having trained so hard to build himself up, and he passed up the opportunity. However, he went to London in 1950 to compete for the world's most important physique title, Mr. Universe, won the contest, and began getting small roles on the stage and in television. In 1954, the eccentric independent director of poverty row movies, Ed Wood, cast Reeves as a policeman in *Jail Bait*, and later that same year, Reeves was given a much larger role in the musical *Athena*. In 1957, however, the daughter of the Italian director Pietro Francisci saw *Athena*, and suggested to her father that the big, handsome American would make a perfect lead for Francisci's upcoming Franco-Italian production of *Hercules*. Francisci saw Reeves, agreed with his daughter, and a deal was struck that launched Reeves into a series of mythological hero films that made both men wealthy.

A significant factor in the huge success of Reeves' first four European adventure films was the producer/promoter Joseph E. Levine, who took *Hercules* (1957), *Hercules Unchained* (1959), *Morgan the Pirate* (1960), and *The Thief of Baghdad* (1961), dubbed them into English, and premiered them internationally, not only using slick promotion and distribution methods, but also instigating the publication of tie-in paperbacks and comic books. The result was that Reeves rapidly acquired massive marquee value and found himself in demand.

Unfortunately, however, the popularity of these ''neo-classical'' epics resulted in such a rash of Reeves films in a short time that his popularity began a steady decline in the early 1960s. *Hercules* opened in the United States in 1959, but by the summer of 1961 eight of his films had appeared in U.S. theaters. Eight films in 24 months was obviously too much for an American audience to take, and ticket sales fell off. He remained hugely popular in many overseas markets and continued to appear in films throughout the early 1960s. His last, and one of his personal favorites, was the 1969 *A Long Ride from Hell*, a late entry in a genre of violent Italian films dubbed ''spaghetti westerns.'' Ironically, Reeves had turned down the role, which eventually went to Clint Eastwood, in the movie that popularized spaghetti westerns, Sergio Leone's *A Fistful of Dollars* (1964). With the success of the spaghetti westerns, the costume epics in which Reeves had found fame and fortune were eclipsed and faded away as the men who made them turned to the new genre.

Reeves suffered a serious injury to his shoulder in 1959. Over the years the effects of the damage were exacerbated by the often dangerous stunts demanded by his action pictures—stunts that he did himself since, because of his unique build, no suitable stunt man could be found. Reeves prized his health; and as he mourned the early deaths of his friends Errol Flynn and Tyrone Power, he decided to retire while he was young and healthy enough to enjoy it. By 1970 Reeves, who had married Princess Aline Czartjarwitz in 1963, settled on a ranch in southern California to raise Morgan horses.

In 1982, Reeves published a best-selling book, *Powerwalking,* in which he encouraged runners to slow down and save their knees, ankles, and hip joints. Instead, he advocated a form of fast walking using ankle and wrist weights as a safer and equally effective form of aerobic exercise. He was in many ways a pioneer in the field of exercise walking, and in the years since the publication of *Powerwalking* millions of people have switched from running to walking.

For many years, Reeves has been an outspoken opponent of bodybuilding drugs, which were not used during the years in which he competed, and in 1995 he published *Building the Classic Physique—the Natural Way*. Few historians would argue with the premise that no bodybuilder before or since Steve Reeves has ever had such a truly classic physique.

—Jan and Terry Todd

FURTHER READING:

Reeves, Steve, with James A. Peterson. *Powerwalking*. Indianapolis, Indiana, Bobbs-Merrill, 1982.

———. *Building the Classic Physique: The Natural Way*. Calabasas, California, Little-Wolff Group, 1995.

Reggae

Reggae is a broad term encompassing a related variety of musical styles that emerged from the island nation of Jamaica after 1960. These styles include ska, rock steady, reggae, and dancehall, all of which swept Jamaican music in distinct stylistic waves, one after the other, during the 1960s and 1970s. Musically, these styles share a common loping rhythm that accents the subsidiary beat. Reggae, however, is many things to many people. It can be seen as merely another great Caribbean dance rhythm, but at the same time many of its songs have highly political overtones. It is also often associated with the Rastafarian religion, an ascetic, millenarian sect that origi-nated in part in the back-to-Africa teachings of Marcus Garvey in the 1920s and 1930s. Since its arrival on the world scene after 1960, reggae and its associated musical styles have become immensely popular around the world. It is one of the world's first truly interna-tional musical forms, both in its origins and in its worldwide appeal.

Reggae's origins come from a unique blend of Caribbean musical styles and American rhythm and blues from the 1950s. Prior to World War II, the most popular musical style in Jamaica was mento, which drew from Caribbean forms such as calypso, merengue, and rumba, as well as older African-derived folk styles. After World War II, Jamaicans began to hear R&B music being broadcast from the United States, particularly from New Orleans. In comparison to the BBC-style official radio programming coming from within Jamaica, these R&B sounds were a breath of fresh air. Early American R&B pioneers such as Louis Jordan, Roscoe Gordon, and Fats Domino were immensely popular in Jamaica during the 1950s. These records

Reggae artist Jimmy Cliff in concert.

were also promoted in Jamaica by sound-system operators who carried portable speakers and record players in their trucks, playing at parties and selling records. As the classic phase of R&B music dried up in the late 1950s, Jamaicans turned to producing R&B-inspired music themselves. The first result of these efforts was ''ska,'' a hybrid of R&B and mento musical forms that featured shuffling rhythms, accented on the second and fourth beats, a chopped guitar or piano sound, and a loose horn section. Ska became the dominant musical style in Jamaica after 1960, propelled by such groups as the Skatalites, the Ska Kings, the Soul Vendors, the Maytals, and Millie Small, whose song ''My Boy Lollipop'' was an international hit. Much of this music was produced by new Jamaican-run studios, notably those of Coxsone Dodd, Duke Reid, and Prince Buster, all of whom were veterans of the sound-system circuit. Jamaica's political independence from Great Britain in 1962 further strengthened the desire to produce all-Jamaican musical forms, and the dance rhythms of ska provided a soundtrack to the celebrations that accompanied independence. The era of ska's dominance lasted until about 1966, although the style continues to have adherents and practitioners, especially in the United States and Great Britain, where it was revived in the late 1970s.

By 1966, following American R&B's evolution into gospel-inspired soul music, the ska style gave way to slower rhythms called ''rock steady,'' after the Alton Ellis hit ''Get Ready to Rock Steady.'' Other musicians, such as Hopeton Lewis with ''Take It Easy'' and the Heptones with ''Ting a Ling,'' contributed to the new rock-steady style. The music slowed down, and the horns largely disappeared, replaced in dominance by a more melodic bass line. While rock steady was certainly dance music, it was not without its social commentary aspects: Desmond Dekker's ''Shanty Town'' commented on life in the ghetto communities around Kingston; the Ethiopians sang about the wave of strikes afflicting Jamaica in 1968 with their song ''Everything Crash.'' As innovative as rock steady was in Jamaican music, combining sweeter melodies, lyrics worth listening to, and new rhythmic combinations, the rock steady era lasted only until about 1969.

Replacing rock steady was a new sound, reggae, a name that eventually would be applied to all of Jamaican music. The exact meaning of the term is unclear, some claiming it means ragged or street rough. Others defined reggae as a general term referring to poor people who were suffering. For others it was simply a beat. Musically, reggae slowed the rock steady beat down even further with a stronger bass driving the beat, a loping, chopping guitar sound, and more rhythmic freedom for the drummer to play around the beat of the bass. Early reggae records, such as Toots and the Maytals' ''Do the Reggay'' blended elements of rock steady and reggae. Much of this new sound came from new producers such as Lee Perry, Clancy Eccles, and Bunny Lee, who established their own studios in the late 1960s. Unable to hire established studio musicians, they turned to younger talents such as Aston and Carlton Barrett and Leroy Wallace. These producers and musicians established the new reggae beat that soon became the most popular style in Jamaica, eclipsing both ska and rock steady.

Of all the various groups to emerge from the reggae sound, none had a greater impact than Bob Marley & the Wailers. Singer, songwriter, and guitarist Marley became the greatest reggae star ever, with an enduring international appeal. Born in 1945, Marley grew up in Trench Town, a rough slum in Kingston. He formed the Wailers with Peter Tosh and Bunny Livingstone in 1960, and they made their first recordings in 1962. In the later 1960s, Marley became an adherent of Rastafarianism. In 1970, they signed a recording contract with Chris Blackwell's Island Records. Blackwell gave Marley the money and artistic freedom to do largely as he pleased. What followed was a string of some of the most influential reggae recordings in the genre's history. On albums such as *Catch a Fire* and early singles, Marley and the Wailers took on political, religious, and social topics, from ghetto conditions in ''Trench Town Rock'' and ''Concrete Jungle'' to ''Natty Dread'' on Rastafarianism. Tosh and Livingstone left the group in the early 1970s, but Marley continued on, releasing such reggae classics as ''No Woman No Cry,'' ''Get Up Stand Up,'' ''Exodus,'' and ''Them Belly Full (But We Hungry).'' His 1975 album, *Live,* was a bestselling record that encapsulated the live power of Bob Marley & the Wailers' sound. Marley died of cancer in 1981 at 36 years of age.

Along with the success of such reggae ambassadors as Marley and the Wailers during the 1970s, another event that made reggae an international cultural force was the release of the 1973 film *The Harder They Come*. This film, by white Jamaican filmmaker Perry Henzell, starred reggae singer Jimmy Cliff as a young street tough (or ''rude boy'' in Jamaican slang terms) who comes to Kingston, records a hit record, and then gets in trouble with the law. Although fictional, *The Harder They Come* was based on several years of research by Henzell on the culture that surrounded reggae music. The story of success, oppression, and rebellion hit a literal and figurative chord with young people around the world, awakening an interest in Jamaican music and culture that has never completely subsided. The soundtrack album that accompanied it, which included such stars as Jimmy Cliff, the Melodians, the Maytals, and Desmond Dekker, introduced reggae music to millions around the world.

By the early 1980s, reggae was evolving once again. DJs had always been important in Jamaican popular music, bringing music to the masses and sometimes acting as producers of reggae artists. DJs began to dominate Jamaican music in the late 1970s and early 1980s in a style that came to be known as ''dancehall.'' DJs such as Ranking Trevor, U Brown, and Trinity began to revive an earlier style from the 1960s, called ''toasting,'' that had DJs adding vocal effects or talking over instrumental tracks. With toasting, this was an ad-hoc musical form. In the late 1970s, these younger DJs began to record their own songs in the toasting style, which was dubbed ''dancehall.'' The dancehall style became the dominant musical form in reggae with such performers as Yellowman, Sugar Minott, and U Roy, and had direct connections to the emerging rap or hip-hop style among African-American performers in the United States in the early 1980s. The dancehall style continued to be the dominant form of reggae in the late 1990s.

Although the dancehall style now predominates, the earlier Jamaican musical forms continued through the 1980s and 1990s. The reggae style was by no means dead, and groups such as Black Uhuru, Steel Pulse, Peter Tosh, Gregory Isaacs, Third World, and a host of other stars carried the reggae tradition forward. Ska enjoyed a revival in Britain in the late 1970s as young English musicians discovered the music through the many Jamaicans and West Indians living in London. Such groups as the Selector, Madness, the Specials, the Beat, and hundreds of other groups revived the ska sound, using its musical forms while often combining them with socially conscious lyrics that commented on life in Margaret Thatcher's Great Britain. The ska revival also infected the United States, and the style continued to draw a large cult following both in the United States and in Britain during the 1990s.

—Timothy Berg

FURTHER READING:

Chang, Kevin O'Brien, and Wayne Chen. *Reggae Routes: The Story of Jamaican Music.* Philadelphia, Temple University Press, 1998.

Manuel, Peter, et al. *Caribbean Currents: Caribbean Music from Rumba to Reggae.* Philadelphia, Temple University Press, 1995.

Tougher than Tough: The Story of Jamaican Music. Mango Records, 1993.

Ward, Ed. ''Reggae.'' *The Rolling Stone Illustrated History of Rock & Roll.* Edited by Jim Miller. New York, Rolling Stone Press, 1980.

White, Timothy. *Catch a Fire: The Life of Bob Marley.* New York, Owl Books, 1998.

Reiner, Carl (1922—)

Among the most influential comedic actors, writers, directors, and producers of his generation, Carl Reiner has been associated with many of the brightest lights in American comedy during the post-World War II era, including Mel Brooks, Dick Van Dyke, and Steve Martin.

Reiner was born in the Bronx on March 20, 1922. During the Great Depression he got his first taste of show business as a writer and actor in a dramatic workshop sponsored by the Works Projects Administration (WPA). He was drafted into the U.S. Army during World War II, and further developed his performing abilities while acting in a South Pacific service troupe directed by Shakespearean actor Maurice Evans.

After the war, Reiner was part of the first generation of writer-performers on the new medium of television. In 1950 he was signed to write and co-star on NBC's variety series *Your Show of Shows,* starring Sid Caesar and Imogene Coca. Reiner appeared on-screen, serving largely as a straight man to Caesar and Coca's antics. In the writer's room, Reiner worked alongside such greats as Neil Simon, Joe Stein, and a young, maniacal Mel Brooks. Brooks and Reiner developed a rapport for mad improvisation—Reiner would introduce Brooks as a Jewish pirate, for example, and Brooks would begin off-the-cuff dialogue. On one such occasion, Reiner asked Brooks about witnessing the Crucifixion. Brooks's persona became the genesis of the 2,000-Year-Old Man character. The pair developed the routine at

Carl Reiner (left) with Mel Brooks.

show business parties during the 1950s, and on the advice of Steve Allen and George Burns, they recorded an album of the routine in 1960. It became a best-seller and spurred four more records.

Reiner wrote the critically acclaimed autobiographical novel *Enter Laughing* in 1958, which Joe Stein adapted into a hit Broadway play. Reiner realized that the story of his life—a young husband and father who wrote comedy—would also make a good TV situation comedy. The idea eventually became *The Dick Van Dyke Show*, which debuted in 1961 and ran for five seasons. The series was a beautiful combination of physical shtick, verbal jousting, and ensemble acting, and turned Van Dyke and co-star Mary Tyler Moore into TV superstars. Reiner eventually made guest appearances as Alan Brady, the demanding, vainglorious star for whom Van Dyke's character was writing.

During the 1960s and 1970s Reiner branched out as a successful film director. His 1969 movie, *The Comic*, starred Van Dyke as a silent screen comedian. Reiner's next film was the cult classic *Where's Poppa?* (1970), a blissfully off-color farce with something to offend everyone (the film ends with the middle-aged protagonist about to go to bed with his aged mother). He directed the 1977 surprise hit, *Oh, God!*, starring George Burns as the Almighty; the

film was written by fellow Caesar alumnus Larry Gelbart, and its style echoed the 2,000-Year-Old Man routines.

Reiner found his ideal film collaborator in stand-up phenomenon Steve Martin. Reiner directed Martin's first starring role, *The Jerk* (1979), which grossed well over $100 million. Reiner and Martin teamed up three more times, most famously on the 1984 hit, *All of Me* (co-starring Lily Tomlin).

By the 1990s, Reiner was an elder statesman in the comedy field. He reprised his Alan Brady character (and won an Emmy) in a 1995 episode of the popular *Mad about You* sitcom. In 1998 he and Brooks recorded their first 2,000-Year-Old Man album in a quarter century, for which the pair won a long overdue Grammy. "Thirty-nine years ago we were nominated for a Grammy, and lost," Reiner said in his acceptance speech. "We can't wait another 39 years!"

Reiner married singer Estelle Lebost in 1944, and they have three children. The eldest is actor/director Rob Reiner, known for such films as *This Is Spinal Tap* and *A Few Good Men*. Estelle is probably best remembered for her one line—"I'll have what she's having"—in the deli scene in son Rob's 1989 hit, *When Harry Met Sally*.

—Andrew Milner

FURTHER READING:

Reiner, Carl. *Continue Laughing.* New York, Birch Lane Press, 1995.

——. *Enter Laughing.* New York, Simon and Schuster, 1958.

——, and Brooks, Mel. *The 2,000-Year-Old Man in the Year 2000: The Book, Including How to Not Die and Other Good Tips.* New York, Harper Collins, 1997.

Waldron, Vince. *The Official Dick Van Dyke Show Book.* New York, Hyperion, 1994.

Religious Right

Since the 1970s, the Religious Right, often known as the "Christian Right" or the "New Christian Right," has referred to a coalition of organizations and individuals with three major goals in U.S. politics: to get conservative Protestants to participate in the political process, to bring them into the Republican party, and to elect social conservatives to public office. It is not, however, merely an electoral movement. Broadly speaking, the Religious Right is made up of evangelical Christians who are socially, theologically, and economically conservative. Its adherents are primarily, but not exclusively, white middle-class Americans who affirm so-called "family values," promote laissez-faire economics, and believe in a generally literal interpretation of Biblical Christianity. Although the coalition claims support from conservatives among Catholics and other religious groupings, it is generally made up of evangelical Protestants, and it is from this tradition that the movement has emerged. The Religious Right is best known for its positions on contemporary hot-button issues; for example, its adherents oppose abortion on demand, reject homosexuality as an acceptable lifestyle, push for prayer in public schools, and protest high taxes and an expanding welfare state.

The rise of the Religious Right began in 1976, dubbed the "Year of the Evangelical" by *Time* magazine. The *New York Times* claimed that the blossoming evangelical movement was "the major religious force in America, both in numbers and impact,'' and Christian periodicals like *Christianity Today* praised the fact that evangelicals were finally reaching cultural prominence. Americans elected Jimmy Carter, a Southern Baptist, to the White House, a sign to some that the self-indulgence of the 1960s seemed to give way to born-again Christian fervor. Carter himself, however, was a middle-of-the-road Democrat who was far more tolerant of diversity in American culture than many of the outspoken evangelists and politicians who have since come to represent the Religious Right; his election was not so much the fruit of any proactive evangelical movement as it was a result of voters expressing frustration with a decade of Washington-based excesses: unpopular Vietnam policies by the Democrats and the Watergate scandal by the Republicans. Conservative Christians who helped to elect Carter in 1976 turned on him in 1980 as concerns over a variety of social issues caused them to reject Carter's moderate political policies and turn to the socially conservative Republican Party. Since then evangelical Christians largely have been associated with the Republican Party; however, the two are not coterminous and many left-leaning evangelicals decry the evangelical/Republican conflation.

The Religious Right remained an influential political movement through the end of the 1980s until several events caused many to argue that the movement had run its course: a series of televangelist scandals, the failed presidential bid of Pat Robertson in 1988, the disbanding of Jerry Falwell's Moral Majority, and Democratic electoral gains, including the recapture of the White House in 1992. Since the 1980s, however, the Christian Right has established influential new organizations like the Christian Coalition, and has organized many voters on the local level, making conservative Christians an important voting bloc in electoral analysis. For example, the Republican resurgence in 1994 was due in part to the strength of the Religious Right in local politics around the country.

The post-1960s Religious Right draws some of its power from the historical forces that shaped church-state relations in the United States over the past three centuries. The New England Puritans of the seventeenth century believed that they were founding a holy commonwealth and that they were entering into an explicit covenant with God: if they obeyed God's commands they would be blessed, and if they disobeyed they would be punished. Puritans also saw their society as a ''city on a hill,'' an exemplary redeemer nation that the world should revere and imitate. This combination of covenantal thinking and a sense of divine mission has shaped American Protestants' perception of their role in U.S. culture for centuries, as expressed in statements like ''This is God's country and it should be run God's way!'' No matter how many mistakes Americans make, they continue to see themselves as the ''last, best hope of earth.'' Since the Puritan era, evangelical Christians have considered themselves custodians of culture, called not only to serve in churches, but to bring the nation (and the nations) under the rule of God.

During the nineteenth century many of the nation's social reformers were evangelical Christians. Leading revivalists preached the doctrine of perfectionism—the idea that Christians could and should lead sinless lives. Evangelicals tended to be obsessed more with shortcomings in personal piety and opposed such vices as the consumption of alcohol, gambling, fornication, profanity, and dishonesty. While this preoccupation with individual behavior helped to civilize the frontier and encouraged pioneers to lead sober and decent lives, for some it bred social conservatism, causing them to ignore larger cultural issues like political decision-making, economic policies, and social ills such as slavery, exploitation of workers, and

poverty. Many antebellum evangelicals were socially radical in their opposition to slavery, however, and evangelicals founded many of the nation's most prominent institutions of higher learning. Clearly, antebellum evangelicals did not eschew public responsibility, but the dynamic of revivalism did sow the seeds of social conservatism that blossomed in the 1970s with the Religious Right's rigid moralism. For many, God was more concerned about personal moral behavior than problems of social justice and economic equity.

By the mid-nineteenth century, the United States had become, more than at any other point in its history, a Christian republic, though Roman Catholics, as ''foreigners,'' i.e., non-white Anglo-Saxon Protestants, were excluded from this equation because of their supposed allegiance to the Papacy, a foreign power, and because of fears that the poorer Catholic immigrants would upset the social order. Evangelical, revivalistic Protestantism remained the dominant religious expression, church membership had reached record levels, and Americans believed more than ever that through their example they would save the world. Buttressed by the support of wealthy businessmen, evangelists set out to improve the world through personal piety evidenced through public service and reform. Evangelicals pioneered scores of voluntary associations whose attention to single issues made them highly effective instruments of reform. They learned how to raise money and promote their enterprises and how to continually add numbers to their ranks. Most American colleges had evangelical roots, and Protestant clergymen were among the most influential of the country's celebrities. In many ways Victorian America was the heyday of American evangelicalism, as it dominated much of American public life and continued to grow exponentially.

Starting in the second half of the nineteenth century, forces of industrialization, urbanization, and immigration interrupted the evangelical march to cultural preeminence. Multiple subcultures divided by class, ethnicity, language, and religion replaced the relative homogeneity and social cohesion of an earlier era. Expansive immigration from eastern and southern Europe brought Jews, Roman Catholics, and Orthodox Christians to North America, thus weakening Protestant influence over the culture. The growing secularism that came to be found in urban America alarmed many in the country's leading Protestant denominations. The challenges of Darwinism and historical criticism of the Bible made traditional religious belief untenable for many more sophisticated Americans. Many Christian progressives sought to address the social problems accompanying growing industrialism (urban poverty, inadequate public housing, political corruption, for example) with an emphasis on social service, and the Social Gospel movement began to eclipse evangelicalism's traditional emphasis on personal salvation.

Between 1870 and 1925 evangelicals divided into two warring camps: modernists and fundamentalists (with many gradations in between, of course). Modernists adapted the Christian faith to modern science and new Biblical criticism. They espoused ''theistic evolution'' which made room for Darwin's theories and admitted the earth was very old. In addition, conceding that the Bible was often factually untrue and that it was at times supernaturally naive, modernists focused instead on a Social Gospel that emphasized moral instruction and service to fellow humans. Fundamentalists, on the other hand, rejected modernism in all its forms and argued that the Bible could be taken at face value—that it was literally true in all its claims. They also rejected evolution and any findings of modern science that questioned divine creation. Urban revivalists like Dwight L. Moody and Billy Sunday carried the fundamentalist ''old-time religion'' to millions of Americans, and it was from this wing of U.S. Protestantism that the "Old Christian Right" emerged.

After World War I, fundamentalist leaders like Sunday, William Jennings Bryan, and William Bell Riley championed two major causes: prohibiting the sale of intoxicating liquor and banning the teaching of evolution in tax-supported public schools—the two leading causes of the Old Christian Right. By 1920, fundamentalism was well organized and had made some impressive gains. Leaders achieved a stunning moral victory in the passage of Prohibition, the movement had respectable intellectuals who defended the fundamentals of the faith, and a handful of Southern states had passed laws that banned the teaching of evolution in public schools. By the early 1930s, however, the movement had disintegrated and lost its public credibility. Trouble began in 1925 with the trial of John T. Scopes in Dayton, Tennessee, concerning the teaching of evolution. This cultural event, swarming with national media—it was one of the first news events broadcast live on radio—cemented in the minds of Americans the notion that fundamentalists were rural, uneducated, backward simpletons unwilling to embrace advances in science and technology. Within five years all state laws prohibiting the teaching of evolution had been repealed. Prohibition itself was repealed in 1933, ending the fundamentalist dream of an America free from drunkenness and immorality.

By the mid-1930s, modernists had taken control of the largest Protestant denominations as liberals opted for a more flexible faith not imprisoned in fundamentalism's doctrinal rigor. As many Northern denominations embraced modernity, the fundamentalist center of gravity shifted to the rural South where Protestant conservatives stopped short of demanding social transformation. Southern evangelicals had traditionally been socially conservative, seeking to preserve the Southern ideal against Northern capitalistic encroachment. Evangelical Protestantism was now in the hands of social conservatives, and the marriage between the two would grow stronger as each year passed.

Fundamentalists had suddenly become emasculated. No longer capable of redeeming the nation for God, they retreated into culturally conservative communities. Fundamentalists were associated with the Ku Klux Klan in the 1920s and went on to be associated with segregationism and anti-Communism in the 1950s. These links between conservative Christians and retrograde political movements fixed in the minds of Americans the image of fundamentalists as narrow-minded, bigoted, and backward looking—a very different image from that maintained by evangelical progressives a generation earlier. Between 1930 and the 1970s, Americans paid little attention to conservative evangelical Protestants. Having lost key battles in the 1920s, fundamentalists withdrew from public life and nurtured their own institutions. Because they had lost control not only of American culture as a whole but also of the country's major Protestant denominations, fundamentalists set out to create their own organizations that would preserve an unadulterated Christian message. Large independent congregations sprouted up all over the country led by famous preachers such as John Roach Straton, William Bell Riley, J. Frank Norris, Carl McIntire, and "Fighting Bob" Schuler. Individuals and churches formed coalitions that they hoped would increase their strength and effectiveness, the most notable being the World's Christian Fundamentals Association, the National Federation of Fundamentalists, and the Baptist Bible Union. In addition, fundamentalists established Bible colleges all over the country that favored Christian teaching and practical instruction over the liberal arts, the two leading ones being the Moody Bible Institute in Chicago and the

Bible Institute of Los Angeles (BIOLA). Conservative evangelicals also published newspapers and periodicals like the *King's Business,* the *Christian Beacon, Crusader's Champion,* and many others, and also pioneered in radio broadcasting as they attempted to spread the Christian message around the country and the globe.

To the extent that conservative Protestants participated in national political life after 1930, their sympathies generally remained with the Democratic party. In the South, the force of tradition kept conservatives attached to the party that had re-established white political dominance in the wake of Reconstruction. This linkage was further cemented by the popularity of New Deal social-welfare programs that sought to eradicate poverty and assist farmers in financial distress. As evangelicals climbed the social and economic ladders, their affinity for liberal programs faded as they became more conservative. A significant number of conservative evangelicals fled the Democratic party in 1960 when it ran Roman Catholic John F. Kennedy as its presidential candidate. Traditionally anti-Catholic, white, churchgoing Protestants defected to the Republican party and voted for the Republican candidate, Richard Nixon. Southern whites, who fifty years earlier had supported Democrat William Jennings Bryan, responded favorably to the candidacy of Republican Senator Barry Goldwater in 1964, and in 1968 showed significant support for independent presidential candidate George Wallace. Georgian Jimmy Carter won the White House in 1976 and carried most of the Southern states. He did not, however, win the votes of the majority of white Southerners, many of whom were evangelical Christians. By the mid-1970s, most conservative Protestants were Republicans, and they would turn on Carter en masse in 1980 in support of ultraconservative candidate Ronald Reagan.

Scholars refer to the return of conservative Protestants to organized political action as the rise of the "New Christian Right," descendants of the "Old" Christian Right of the 1920s. During the 1950s and 1960s American culture became more liberal. Among many social changes, the Supreme Court under Earl Warren declared segregated schools unconstitutional in 1954 and upheld laws banning organized prayer in public schools in 1963; the Warren Court also progressively lifted prohibitions against books and movies that had been considered obscene. In 1960, the Food and Drug Administration approved use of the birth control pill, removing yet another barrier to nonmarital sex. As the conservative reaction intensified, evangelical Protestants joined in the cultural critique. A number of local movements around the country helped to galvanize conservative Christian political concern and united action. One of particular importance took place in 1974 when a group of fundamentalists led by educators Alice Moore and Mel and Norma Gabler protested proposed public school textbooks in Kanawha County, West Virginia. They argued that the sex education curriculum was too explicit, that the science books pushed evolution at the expense of creation science, and that books with sexually explicit, negative, or morbid language were inappropriate for young people. A culture war of sorts developed in Kanawha County as conservatives and liberals squared off over educational freedom, public school curricula, and issues of public decency. Religious and political conservatives from all over the country offered support to the embattled fundamentalists, among them Paul Weyrich and James McKenna and their Heritage Foundation, a fledgling conservative think tank in Washington, D.C. Journalists observed the "wedding of right-wing politics and right-wing religion" and the Religious Right was back in the limelight of American politics as a major constituency within the Republican party.

As the 1970s advanced, conservative Protestants climbed out of the back seat and were vying for America's cultural steering wheel. *Time* magazine referred to 1976 as the "Year of the Evangelical," noting the prominence of conservative Protestants in American business, political, and social circles. During the 1960s and 1970s evangelist Billy Graham emerged as a celebrity via his well-organized crusades in U.S. cities where he preached a "born again" message. Graham rarely engaged in commentary on specific political issues, nor was he ever tainted by personal scandal, and he is generally regarded as a middle-of-the-road pastor whose political activities were limited to acting as an unofficial chaplain to national political figures. Chuck Colson, one of Nixon's Watergate-era henchmen, found Jesus and fought for an evangelical presence in American politics. Phyllis Schlafly led conservative Christians in their battle against feminism, lesbianism, and the Equal Rights Amendment. Jerry Falwell, pastor of Thomas Road Baptist Church in Lynchburg, Virginia, and host of the *Old Time Gospel Hour* television program, came to the aid of Anita Bryant in her crusade to repeal a gay-rights ordinance in Dade Country, Florida. Robert Billings, James Dobson and scores of evangelical leaders battled the IRS in 1978 when it attempted to remove tax-exempt status from private Christian schools. Fundamentalist ministers who had long warned their constituents to avoid secular politics now encouraged them to reject the division of human affairs into sacred and secular spheres, insisting that there is no area of human activity, including law and politics, that should be outside of Christian influence. The task was "not to avoid this world, but to declare God's kingdom in it."

Political activists with little or no background in the Religious Right attempted to strengthen the Republican party by building bridges between secular and religious conservatives. Howard Phillips of the Conservative Caucus, John "Terry" Dolan of the National Conservative Political Action Committee, Paul Weyrich of the National Committee for the Survival of a Free Congress, and Richard Viguerie, a major fund raiser for conservative causes, all attempted to woo fundamentalist Christians. The basis for this new coalition would be an all-out attack on big government as the major threat to traditional religious and economic values. In addition to their traditional anticommunist, pro-business, and anti-tax stances, conservative activists added the concerns of the Religious Right: feminism, homosexuality, prayer in schools, and sexual laxity, among others. In 1978 Robert Billings, assisted by Paul Weyrich, formed the National Christian Action Coalition, the first national organization of the Christian Right; televangelist Jerry Falwell founded the Moral Majority, a conservative political action group, in 1979. Evangelical leaders embraced conservative political issues, but did so with a religious rationale. Increased defense spending was justified as a way of keeping the world free for ongoing preaching of the gospel; support for the government of Taiwan was key because the U.S. was protecting Christian allies from the godless, communist Chinese; governmental support for Israel was necessary because biblical prophecy demanded a unified and strong Israeli state. Now ideologically and institutionally viable, and savvy about electronic media like television and radio, the Religious Right entered the 1980s stronger than ever before.

Elected president in 1980, Ronald Reagan embraced the views of the Religious Right and pledged to work on its behalf. Among other gestures, he appointed anti-abortion activist and evangelical Christian C. Everett Koop surgeon general, frustrating many conservatives and delighting liberals when Koop took a strong pro-active stance in disseminating nonjudgmental information about the AIDS crisis. In 1980 Republicans regained control of the Senate for the first time in a quarter century, and the Religious Right was credited by many with securing those congressional victories. Throughout the 1980s the Religious Right was constantly on the mind and lips of political commentators and electoral analysts. Falwell became the unofficial spokesperson for conservative Protestants, and Pat Robertson's *700 Club* television show reached record numbers of viewers as it combined revivalistic preaching with analysis of current events in a format similar to the network news. No one could ignore the Religious Right for its profound influence on local and national elections during the Reagan years. Approximately 25 percent of the American public described themselves as "born again" Christians, forcing politicians to contend with conservative Christians as a key voting bloc.

Beginning in 1987, a series of scandals involving prominent televangelists tarnished the image of religious conservatives, and the movement began to lose its cohesion. First, Oral Roberts brought ridicule upon himself by announcing that God would "call him home" if his supporters did not contribute eight million dollars to save his City of Faith Hospital. Then Jim and Tammy Faye Bakker, heroes of the PTL television network and Heritage USA amusement park, found themselves embroiled in controversy. Journalists uncovered Jim's romantic tryst with former secretary Jessica Hahn and discovered that one of Bakker's colleagues had paid her $250,000 in hush money. To make matters worse, IRS investigators charged Jim Bakker with tax evasion and fraud. The Bakkers had mismanaged loyal followers' financial contributions and used them to support their lavish lifestyle. Jim Bakker, though released on parole a few years later, was sentenced to forty-five years in prison, and his wife, Tammy Faye, entered the Betty Ford Clinic to deal with a drug problem brought about by the stress. After this news story broke, televangelist Jimmy Swaggert was caught in a seedy hotel room with a New Orleans prostitute. Taken as a whole, these scandals humiliated the conservative Christian community and sowed seeds of dissention among its constituents.

At the same time journalists and cultural critics were heaping ridicule upon the Religious Right for its leaders' misdeeds, the movement began to disintegrate politically. In 1988, Christian Right religious leaders were politically split during the Republican primary campaign. Falwell endorsed George Bush, while many others supported Jack Kemp and Bob Dole. Television preacher Robertson, head of the multimillion dollar Christian Broadcasting Network, campaigned for president and even made impressive showings in several early primaries. Robertson, however, eventually withdrew from the race after finding himself unable to garner the full support of the Religious Right that he had taken for granted. Falwell disbanded the Moral Majority in 1989, and the hopes of the Religious Right lay in ruins. Many commentators announced the death of the Religious Right in 1992 when Bill Clinton, a liberal Southern, pro-choice, pro-gay rights child of the 1960s, entered the White House.

The Republican congressional resurgence in 1994, revealed these obituaries to be premature. The Religious Right helped to elect political conservatives to office in that year; and Robertson's new organization, the Christian Coalition, was instrumental in that process. In 1989 Robertson, with the counsel of Religious Right leaders Charles Stanley, D. James Kennedy, Beverly LaHaye, Marlene Elwell, James Muffett, and Lori Parker, formed the Coalition as a grassroots conservative political organization independent of the structures of the Republican party. Under the leadership of a young and vibrant Ralph Reed, this new organization would no longer kowtow to Republican presidents but would instead "be a force unto its own.'' The Coalition de-emphasized national politics and followed the principle that the real battles of concern to Christians were in neighborhoods, school boards, city councils, and state legislatures—in other words, they accepted the dictum that all politics is local. During the 1994 election, the Christian Coalition distributed thirty-five million voter guides and seventeen million congressional scorecards, and made telephone calls to three million voters. In 1995 the organization added its support to the Republican ''Contract with America'' and penned its own ''Contract with the American Family'' that called for religious equality, local control of education, school choice, protection of parental rights, family-friendly tax relief, eradication of pornography, privatization of the arts, and victims' rights. By 1995, the Christian Coalition claimed 1.6 million members and a budget of over $25 million. It continues to educate conservative Christians regarding local political issues and candidates in a grassroots campaign to purify the United States.

During the 1990s, a group called the Promise Keepers also garnered national attention. Founded by University of Colorado football coach Bill McCartney and friend Dave Wardell, the Promise Keepers brought together large numbers of Christian men in stadium rallies across the country, asking them to re-commit their lives to Christ and reclaim their traditional role as head of the family. The group's mission statement: ''a Christ-centered ministry dedicated to uniting men through vital relationships to become godly influences in their world'' came under fire by the National Organization for Women and religious-left groups like People of Faith, who claimed Promise Keepers was really advancing a right-wing, homophobic, anti-feminist agenda that wanted to relegate women to traditional, submissive roles. The Promise Keepers organization affirmed, however, that the group has ''no affiliation with the Christian Coalition or any other organization'' and that ''Promise Keepers is not politically motivated in any way.'' It also claimed some success in going beyond the white-Protestant image of the Religious Right by including Catholics and members of racial minorities in its rallies.

Robertson resumed the presidency of the Christian Coalition after the departure of Ralph Reed. In June, 1999, the organization announced it was splitting into two separate organizations after the Internal Revenue Service revoked its tax-exempt status. Under the reorganization, Christian Coalition International would endorse candidates and make political contributions, while the existing tax-exempt body, to be renamed Christian Coalition of America, would continue distributing its controversial voters' guides. The move was seen by critics as yet another example of the decline of the once-powerful organization.

—Kurt W. Peterson

FURTHER READING:

Bruce, Steve. *The Rise and Fall of the New Christian Right.* New York, Oxford University Press, 1988.

Carpenter, Joel. *Revive Us Again: The Reawakening of American Fundamentalism.* New York, Oxford University Press, 1997.

Christian Coalition. *Contract with the American Family.* Nashville, Moorings, 1995.

"Christian Coalition Official Website." http://www.cc.org. June 1999.

Lienesch, Michael. *Redeeming America: Piety and Politics in the New Christian Right.* Chapel Hill, University of North Carolina Press, 1993.

Marsden, George. *Fundamentalism and American Culture.* New York, Oxford University Press, 1982.

Martin, William. *With God on Our Side: The Rise of the Religious Right in America.* New York, Broadway Books, 1996.

Menendez, Albert J. *Evangelicals at the Ballot Box.* New York, Prometheus Books, 1996.

"Promise Keepers Web Site." http://www.promisekeepers.org. June 1999.

Silk, Mark. *Spiritual Politics: Religion and America since World War II.* New York, Simon & Schuster, 1988.

R.E.M.

An alternative rock band of the 1980s and 1990s, R.E.M. served up an eclectic mix of musical styles that included punk, rock, and even country and folk. Comprised of Michael Stipe (vocals), Peter Buck (guitar), Mike Mills (bass), and Bill Berry (drums), R.E.M. had a homegrown feel to its music, with a jangly guitar sound that was reminiscent of the Byrds. R.E.M.'s music also represented a link between the postpunk alternative music of the 1980s and punk forerunners Patti Smith (who appeared on 1996's *New Adventures in Hi-Fi*) and the Velvet Underground. According to *Rolling Stone* magazine, which selected the group as its 1992 Artist of the Year, R.E.M. ascended to ''mainstream popularity without caving in to record-industry dictums or betraying its original college-radio constituency.''

The group began the 1980s in Athens, Georgia, hometown to its members and a small college town with a vibrant and diverse music scene, one that rejected the southern rock establishment's sounds of barroom blues and boogie. Although R.E.M. recalled traditional American songwriting forms, like country and folk, the band was definitely shaped by 1977's punk scene. R.E.M.'s music had very little to do with punk, but the do-it-yourself ethic of punk rock carried tremendous influence within the band. ''You have to remember,'' said Peter Buck, ''growing up at the time I did, there wasn't anyone who made records like us. Rock & roll was full of super-rich guys that had mustaches and were ten years older than me.''

Tiny HibTone Records released R.E.M.'s first single in 1981. Not a hit in conventional terms, ''Radio Free Europe'' still caused considerable excitement. Independent record labels had yet to become a mainstay in the United States, so the single's reach was nothing but astonishing. It almost singlehandedly revitalized the American independent recording scene. If the punk groups of 1977 showed Buck and Stipe that anyone could perform in a band, R.E.M. took things one step further by demonstrating that relative success could be attained without the support of a major record label. A year later, the band signed with I.R.S. Records, a larger independent, and released an extended play single called ''Chronic Town.''

R.E.M.'s first full-length release, 1983's *Murmur*, displayed the group's melodic guitar and harmonies. Stipe's vague lyrics, emphasizing subtlety over abrasiveness, added to the band's idiosyncratic manner. Passionate, atmospheric, and pensive, *Murmur* defined R.E.M.'s sound and set the standard for alternative guitar pop. The follow-up, 1984's *Reckoning*, had a clearer sound and used traditional song forms, like the country sound in ''(Don't Go Back to) Rockville.'' The next two releases—*Fables of the Reconstruction* (1985), and

R.E.M. performing at the 1995 MTV Video Music Awards.

Life's Rich Pageant (1986)—represented a transitional phase. *Fables of the Reconstruction* was depicted in the rock press as either an interesting experiment with dissonance and melody, or an unfocused and meandering mess. Correspondingly, *Life's Rich Pageant* was viewed by some critics as the band's renewal—a return to melodic songs, augmented by powerful guitar riffs—while for others, it was a stop on the way to the big time. All doubts about the band were put to rest in 1987 with *Document*'s succinct pop and its hit single "The One I Love." What sounded at first to be a song of devotion was, on closer inspection, cloaked in spite. For years, people wanted to know what Stipe was singing. When Stipe was once asked if he wouldn't like people to understand him he replied, "I don't see any reason for it. I think music is way beyond rational thinking. It doesn't have to make any sense." Finally, R.E.M. delivered a clear mix with "The One I Love," another song whose meaning bypassed many listeners. By 1988, R.E.M. signed with Warner Brothers Records, becoming a major label artist. The promise of a larger audience made some fans worry that the group would dilute its sound for a new mass audience. They were not disappointed with the release of *Green* in 1988.

Having allayed fans' fears, the group's next series of releases challenged the expectations of their audience. *Out of Time,* released in 1991, featured rapper KRS-One in "Radio Song," and then proceeded to use string arrangements for a large part of the album. *Automatic for the People* (1992) switched moods by being elegiac. In 1994, the group responded to the suicide of Kurt Cobain, and the death of actor River Phoenix, with the furious electric guitar of *Monster.* Its next release, *New Adventures in Hi-Fi* (1996), had been recorded on the band's tour for *Monster,* during sound checks and live performances. That same tour witnessed a series of medical emergencies that affected three of the band's members, with Berry undergoing brain surgery, forcing his departure from the band, which began recording as a trio in 1998.

By helping revitalize the independent recording industry as well as bolstering college radio and local music scenes, R.E.M. contributed to several shifts in American rock. R.E.M.'s success from Athens, Georgia, and the achievements of Prince and the Replacements from Minneapolis, signaled to young musicians that relocating to New York or Los Angeles was no longer a prerequisite to breaking into the music business. R.E.M.'s success with roots-based, traditional forms marked a major shift away from the Anglophilia of album-oriented rock to a more organic, indigenous perspective that reached its full development in grunge rock.

—Daryl Umberger

FURTHER READING:

Bowler, David, and Bryan Dray. *R.E.M.: From "Chronic Town" to "Monster."* New York, Citadel Press, 1995.

Fletcher, Tony. *Remarks: The Story of R.E.M.* London, Omnibus, 1989.

Fricke, David. "Artist of the Year: R.E.M." *Rolling Stone.* 5 March 1992, 45-50.

———. "Michael Stipe." *Rolling Stone.* 15 October 1992, 187-88.

———. "R.E.M." *Rolling Stone.* 15 November 1990, 124-31.

Gray, Marcus. *An R.E.M. Companion: It Crawled from the South.* New York, Da Capo, 1993.

Greer, Jim. *R.E.M.: Behind the Mask.* Boston, Little Brown, 1992.

Sullivan, Denise. *Talk about the Passion: R.E.M., An Oral History.* Lancaster, Pennsylvania, Underwood-Miller, 1994.

Remington, Frederic (1861-1909)

Largely recognized as one of the great artists of the Wild West, Frederic Remington's own life mirrored, in many ways, those of his subjects. Capturing the last days of the exciting, vibrant western frontier, he completed nearly 3,000 works derived from working cowboys whose lifestyles were rapidly vanishing. Although he spent two years at the Yale School of Art and studied at the Art Student's League in New York, in the 1880s he went to the American West, sketching, riding, and prospecting in new territories. His traveling was to be his most practical on-the-job training. Commissioned by *Harper's Weekly* to provide drawings of the West for publication, the artist recorded the Sioux uprisings, Sitting Bull's murder, the capture of Geronimo, and the last great buffalo slaughter in the northern plains. During this time, he continually published, wrote, and illustrated short stories from his experiences with the cavalry and western escapades.

After watching Frederic Ruckstull in 1895, Remington decided to sculpt his cowboy subjects in motion. The clay models he made were then cast in bronze and became immediately successful, with his masterful ability to depict fine details, action, and characterizations. *Bronco Buster*, cast in 1895, depicting a bucking horse and a tenacious rider, became one of Remington's most identifiable works. Multiples were produced for the large audience that had been created through the popularity of his published prints and the art he had produced in *Colliers* and *Scribner's.* Since 1901, these drawings, since 1901, had appeared in full color, double-page spreads, further increasing the demand for his oil paintings.

Remington's work had the ability to connect directly with a vast audience that was often suspicious of "high art," people who were conventionally moral and patriotic. He worked at a time when the proliferation of newspapers and magazines provided a new vehicle for making art available to a mass audience with an insatiable appetite for dramatic content. As the popularity of his work continued to rise, Remington began painting landscapes, broadened his enthusiasm for easel painting, and heightened the exacting demands of his technical standards. Extremely interested in fine detail and a connoisseur of draftsmanship, the artist remarked that he wanted to make his paintings "so you could feel the details instead of seeing them." Two

Tenth United States Cavalry drawings by Frederic Remington, 1891.

of his most famous works, *Downing the Nigh Leader* (1907) and *Dash for the Timber* (1889), realistically show the action and drama of the Wild West.

Sparking even more interest in his work, in 1935, wealthy oilmen, including Amon Carter, Sid Richardson, and the Hogg brothers of Houston, became major collectors of Remington's art. They identified with the dynamics and energy in the trailblazing cowboy and horse images, viewing them as similar to their "wildcat" attitudes in the oil business. Both the artist and the oilmen were enthused by active, physical movement, and the championing of the "little guy."

The value of Remington's work continued to rise into the late 1990s, when a posthumous cast of *Coming through the Rye* was sold in 1998 at Sotheby's in New York for $1,100,000. In his appreciation of U.S. culture one hundred years earlier, Remington had made a significant contribution. His ambition and determination, combined with his position as part of the West's vanishing, romanticized last days, helped to bring his works wide recognition. The printing industry expanded his ability to reach a wide, general audience as well as important men, including Theodore Roosevelt, who believed in Remington's importance and approved his efforts.

—Cheryl McGrath

FURTHER READING:

Ballinger, James. *Frederic Remington.* New York, Harry N. Abrams, 1989.

Foxley, W. C. "Remington, Frederic." *The Dictionary of Art.* Vol. 26. New York, Grove Dictionaries, 1996, 181-2.

Hassrick, P. *Frederic Remington: Paintings, Drawings and Sculpture in the Amon Carter Museum and the Sid W. Richardson Foundation Collections,* exhibition catalog. Ft. Worth, Texas, Amon Carter Museum, 1974.

McCracken, H. *Frederic Remington, Artist of the Old West.* Philadelphia, Lippincott, 1947.

Mehlman, Robert. "Inexplicable Happenings." *Art Newspaper.* Vol. 5, January. 1994, 26.

Samuels, P. and H. Samuels, editors. *The Collected Writings of Frederic Remington.* Garden City, New York, Doubleday, 1979.

Reno, Don (1926-1984)

An early pioneer of bluegrass banjo playing, Don Reno had an instantly identifiable approach to the instrument that was widely admired but seldom imitated. After a brief stint with Bill Monroe in the late 1940s, Reno formed a highly productive partnership with guitarist/singer Red Smiley, and the two made well over 100 influential recordings in the 1950s and early 1960s. When Smiley's health failed, Reno took his tenor vocalizing and banjo style—an innovative blend of country and jazz chording and single-string, guitar-like picking—into a partnership with Bill Harrell, following that with a solo career that lasted until his death. Ironically, it was a casual, short-term studio partnership with Arthur Smith that produced one of Reno's most enduring and influential recordings, the original version of the widely known "Dueling Banjos."

—Jon Weisberger

Renoir, Jean (1894-1979)

A French filmmaker who created some 37 films in the realist tradition during a 40-year career, Jean Renoir is regarded as a mentor to the French New Wave directors of the late 1950s and a mainstay of art films beloved by American cinephiles. The son of Impressionist painter Pierre-Auguste Renoir, he made his first film, *La Fille de l'Eau,* in 1925 and his last, *Le Petit Théâtre de Jean Renoir,* in 1969. Renoir treated complex issues of class and sexuality in his films, in which he created a sense of cinematic space through in-depth staging, location shooting, and camera work noted for its long, complex takes. These processes inflect such seminal works as *La Grande Illusion* (1937), *La Bête Humaine* (1938), and *La Règle du Jeu* (1939). He moved to Hollywood after the outbreak of World War II, making several films in the United States before returning to France after the war. Renoir was given an Academy Award for life achievement in 1975.

—Neal Baker

FURTHER READING:

Bertin, Celia. *Jean Renoir: A Life in Pictures.* Baltimore, Johns Hopkins University Press, 1991.

Faulkner, Christopher. *Jean Renoir: A Guide to References and Resources.* Boston, G. K. Hall, 1979.

Renoir, Jean. *My Life and My Films.* New York, Atheneum, 1974.

The Replacements

A Minneapolis punk quartet that formed in 1979, the Replacements gained quick notoriety for their inebriated, freewheeling live performances. Verging upon success in the mid-1980s, the group mocked rock's conventional marketing tools. Their video for "Bastards of Young," from *Tim* (1985), was a three-minute close-up of a stereo speaker that was not MTV (Music Television)-friendly. Beginning with "Hootenanny" (1983), however, singer Paul Westerberg's songwriting demonstrated a newfound maturity by including styles that veered from punk into country, folk, and jazz. The Replacements pushed aside the purists, who regarded punk as a self-contained musical form closed to any outside influences. Neither musically mainstream nor punk, Westerberg sang in 1987 that the band had "One foot in the door / The other one in the gutter." The group that could not find their niche disbanded in 1991, but became a model for the guitar-pop bands that proliferated in the mid-1990s, when the alternative became the mainstream.

—Daryl Umberger

FURTHER READING:

Mundy, Chris. "Achin' to Be Understood." *Rolling Stone.* June 24, 1993, 51-55.

Ressmer, Jeffrey. "Replacements: A Band on the Verge." *Rolling Stone.* October 18, 1990, 32-33.

Wild, David. "Paul Westerberg." *Rolling Stone.* November 17, 1994, 106-107.

Retro Fashion

The term "retro" applied to stylistic trends in music, film, and fashion in the 1990s, that were characterized by their iconic or kitsch use of the past. Stemming from the late 1960s concept of "retrochic" developed by the Paris avant garde, retro fashion embraced the use of revival or period styles from certain counter-cultural examples of alternative consumerism. Although retrochic began as an impromptu anti-fashion, it soon blossomed into a profitable, commercial style known by fashion critics as "the nostalgia industry." Retro become associated with a playful, postmodern nostalgia where the past is used as a storehouse of fashion. But what distinguished the retro fashion of the 1990s from older forms of revivalism, was the cavalier and eclectic disregard for the past. Designs and styles were used without sentimentality or discrimination; the aura of a previous style inspired revelry more than reverence. Retro was a form of pastiche, less concerned with historical context than with the fashionable and hip qualities of "pastness." Retro can thus be defined as a process of scripting history into nostalgic narratives of the chic and trendy.

The critical and media debate concerning the larger significance of this phenomenon, of various industries marketing the past within new regimes of style, has promoted controversy. In his book *Postmodernism, or, The Cultural Logic of Late Capitalism,* Frederic Jameson suggests that "in a world in which stylistic innovation is no longer possible, all that is left is to imitate dead styles." For critics like Jameson, retro suggests a profound lack of invention; for others, it represents an ironic return to a past given new and creative cachet.

Describing clothing, music, and films as "retro" categorized the style by time period. While certain styles have been described as "retro" because they constitute pop-cultural kitsch of some description, more concrete definitions are available. Within the vintage clothing market, for example, the difference between vintage and retro styles is one of historical era, loosely distinguishing pre-war and post-sixties fashion: retro being commonly associated with kitsch of the 1960s, 1970s, and 1980s. Within the music industry, the term "retro" was used by radio stations, journalists, and marketing managers to categorize music linked to a particular moment or musical zeitgeist, principally Disco and New Wave. While the music cognoscenti in Britain and the United States also used the term to describe the creative character of Britpop (Blur evoked the Kinks, Oasis aped the Beatles), retro is more widely associated with popularized nostalgia for music kitsch of the 1970s and 1980s, from Abba to Duran Duran. Similarly, films described as "retro" have been labeled such because of their music. *Boogie Nights* (1997) and *The Wedding Singer* (1998) both display a self-conscious use of iconic style and sound in their respective evocations of the 1970s and 1980s. Both films illustrate a tendency in postmodern culture, identified by Jameson, to understand the past through stylistic connotation: less 1970s, more 1970s-ness.

The fashion industry embraced retro perhaps more than any other industry. The popularity of stylistic nostalgia and the selling of vintage clothing and retrochic in the 1980s began, in part, as a response to the consolidation of designer fashions like Calvin Klein and Ralph Lauren. Vintage and retro clothing stores (London's American Retro opened in 1986) provided an alternative to the international offerings of the designer labels. The success of these stores influenced mainstream fashion; in the 1990s, both vintage and retro became a distinguishable "look" in Britain and the States. Mathew Rolsten's portraits for *Vanity Fair, Rolling Stone,* and in

Britain *GQ* and *Vogue,* illustrate these looks to some degree. His signature is one of glossy nostalgia, using motifs of 1930s glamour photography and the style of 1940s Hollywood studio stills.

A more particular retro aesthetic was evident in mainstream fashion with the comeback in the 1990s of flares, fly collars, and platform shoes. Witness to the popularity of the trend was the 1998 premier of the Fox Television sitcom, *That '70s Show,* and the McDonald's advertising campaign "Get Back with Big Mac," which featured fashion and dance trends from the 1970s. In each case, the vogue was playful pastness.

—Paul Grainge

FURTHER READING:

Davis, Angela Y. "Afro Images: Politics, Fashion, and Nostalgia." *Critical Inquiry.* Vol. 21, No. 1, 1994, 37-45.

Jameson, Fredric. *Postmodernism, or, The Cultural Logic of Late Capitalism.* London, Verso, 1991.

Kammen, Michael. *Mystic Chords of Memory: The Transformation of Tradition in American Culture.* New York, Vintage, 1993.

Samuel, Raphael. *Theatres of Memory: Past and Present in Contemporary Culture.* London, Verso, 1994.

Reynolds, Burt (1936—)

A motion picture superstar of the late 1970s and early 1980s—thanks largely to his roles in the *Smokey and the Bandit* and *Cannonball Run* movies—the affable and charming Burt Reynolds was voted the Most Popular Box Office Attraction five years in a row during this period and received nine People's Choice Awards for favorite motion picture actor and favorite all-around male entertainer. Reynolds also enjoyed a prosperous television career in series including the western *Gunsmoke,* the detective show *Dan August,* and the sitcom *Evening Shade.* Despite a much-publicized divorce from actress Loni Anderson that left him bankrupt, Reynolds bounced back in the late 1990s with an Oscar-nominated role in *Boogie Nights.*

With his dreams of a career in sports ended by a car accident, Reynolds headed to New York to break into acting and worked on Broadway. He soon landed a role on the TV series *Riverboat* (1959-1960), which led to a popular three-year stint on *Gunsmoke* (1962-1965), where he played the half-breed blacksmith Quint Asper. His husky good looks and muscular physique increased the number of female viewers and, in turn, caused the writers to contrive more opportunities for Quint to take off his shirt. Reynolds' popularity eventually led to his own short-lived detective show, *Dan August* (1970-1971).

Though he had been making a series of forgettable motion pictures since 1961—which Reynolds once explained "were the kind they show in prisons and airplanes, because nobody can leave"—his big movie break came in the widely praised *Deliverance* in 1972. The story of a group of men on a river trip who run afoul of murderous backwoods yokels, Reynolds shined as the macho leader of the group who is seriously wounded early on and must bow to the ministrations of his insecure peers.

1972 was also the year in which Reynolds agreed to appear nude in *Cosmopolitan* magazine, causing sales to soar. Simultaneously his private life also became increasingly public due to his involvement

Burt Reynolds

with a succession of women that included Kim Basinger, Candice Bergen, Catherine Deneuve, Farrah Fawcett, Sally Field, Sarah Miles, Cybill Shepherd, Dinah Shore, and Tammy Wynette. Reynolds' increasing popularity paved the way for his late-1970s fame in a series of films designed to showcase his image as a cocky, carefree, and smooth-talking charmer who wooed women and bucked authority in such films as *Smokey and the Bandit* (1977), *Cannonball Run* (1981), and *Stroker Ace* (1983).

Though Reynolds occasionally attempted to branch out of this mold, the success of these ''lame-brained action comedies directed by and co-starring his pals''—as critic Roger Ebert characterized them—thwarted his efforts. (Intriguingly, Orson Welles once quipped that ''Success is Burt Reynolds' only handicap.'') Reynolds turned to directing with *The End* in 1978, a well-received black comedy about a man who learns he has a short time to live and determines to end his life. This was followed by the highly praised cop thriller *Sharky's Machine* (1981), and the comedy *Paternity* (1981), about a man who hires a woman to have his child.

Reynolds returned to television with the series *B.L. Stryker* in 1989, and on the sitcom *Evening Shade* from 1990 to 1994. His role as a small-town basketball coach won him both a Golden Globe and Emmy Award for Outstanding Lead Actor in a comedy in 1991. Reynolds also created and toured in the one-man stage shows *An Evening with Burt Reynolds* in 1991 and *My Life* in 1992.

Despite the break-up of his second marriage to Loni Anderson (his first was to actress Judy Carne, the ''sock-it-to-me'' girl from TV's *Laugh-In*), and his subsequent declaration of bankruptcy in 1996, Reynolds returned to the big screen with his performance in

Boogie Nights in 1997 as a veteran porn film director serving as a father figure to new discovery Dirk Diggler (Marky Mark). Despite losing the Best Supporting Actor Oscar to Robin Williams, Reynolds won the Golden Globe, the New York Film Critic's Circle Award, the Los Angeles Film Critics Association Award, and the National Society of Film Critics Award for what many critics described as an ''outstanding'' performance. This in turn led to further offers, including a three-picture production deal from Turner Network Television. No longer a muscled hunk, Reynolds survived in the late 1990s thanks to a quality that doesn't fade with age: good acting.

—Rick Moody

FURTHER READING:

Resnick, Sylvia Safran. *Burt Reynolds: An Unauthorized Biography.* New York, St. Martin's Press, 1983.

Reynolds, Burt. *My Life.* New York, Hyperion, 1994.

Smith, Lisa. *Burt Reynolds.* Palm Beach, Florida, Magic Light Productions, 1994.

Streebeck, Nancy. *The Films of Burt Reynolds.* Secaucus, New Jersey, Citadel Press, 1982.

Whitley, Dianna. *Burt Reynolds: Portrait of a Superstar.* New York, Grosset & Dunlap, 1979.

Rhythm and Blues

Rhythm and Blues was the urban popular black music of the 1940s and 1950s. Its antecedents were the jazz and blues of the 1930s, especially Kansas City jazz; in the 1960s, it turned into soul. R&B, as it is often known, was the precursor and the vital center of rock 'n' roll. It used small-group jazz instrumentation, centered on piano and saxophone as often as on guitar, and it moved in the direction of straightforward, danceable rhythms at the time when jazz was moving toward the more complex structures of bebop. Blending the emotional immediacy of the blues, the instrumental intensity of jazz, and the wit of black vaudeville, it became arguably the most irresistible of American musical forms.

Billboard magazine first used the term ''Rhythm and Blues'' as the title for its black music charts in 1949, replacing ''race music.'' But more than the name was new. The postwar era had created an entirely new musical landscape, involving new African American audiences, new black musical styles, and new musical markets that were being serviced by a new music business.

There were social and technological reasons for these changes. The black migration to Los Angeles, New York, Chicago, and Detroit, with their healthy blue collar economy of defense plants that then retooled to service the postwar economy, created a solid urban working class with some disposable income and a changed social dynamic. Black performers, meanwhile, had been hardest hit by the wartime demand for shellac in the defense industry, which had drastically cut back on the production of records, and had made labels trim their rosters dramatically. But a war-created technology was about to open unprecedented possibilities for entrepreneurship in the music industry. The development of recording tape meant that anyone could have a recording studio, and the recording business was no longer in the hands of a few major companies. Thus newly entrepreneurial musicians began producing music for a waiting audience.

The precursors of rhythm and blues came from the jazz and blues worlds, which were starting to come closer together in the 1930s. Singer-pianist Leroy Carr was the first of the Delta blues singers to incorporate jazz influences and smooth urban stylings. Through the early 1930s, until his death in 1935, Carr was one of the most influential figures in blues. Kansas City blues shouter Big Joe Turner created a solo style on a new instrument, the electric guitar. Jazzman Illinois Jacquet, in Lionel Hampton's 1941 recording, "Flying Home," played a honking, emotionally charged tenor sax solo that became the model for rhythm and blues instrumentals.

The most important jazzman to enter rhythm and blues, though, was Louis Jordan, who virtually created "jump blues." Like so much of the music of the 1940s, jump blues came out of the driving dance music of Count Basie's great 1930s bands, in such numbers as "One O'Clock Jump" and "Jumpin' at the Woodside." Jordan adapted Basie's big band swing to small group instrumentation, with an emphatic 2/4 shuffle beat and brilliant comic showmanship derived from Cab Calloway and black vaudevillians. Jordan dominated the charts throughout the early 1940s.

Jordan recorded on Decca. The new rhythm and blues performers of the 1940s, though, were a phenomenon of the new independent labels. Many of these labels were located in the entertainment centers of New York and Los Angeles, but others were regional. They tended to be run by entrepreneurs (more often than not white) who had businesses that serviced the black urban communities and who saw a hugely popular sound ripe for commercial exploitation. Each label contributed some facet of the developing rhythm and blues sound.

The earliest important indie label was Savoy (founded in 1942). Founded by a Newark, New Jersey, record store owner, Herman Lubinsky, Savoy was one of the few labels to specialize in both of the cutting edge black musical styles of the 1940s: bebop and rhythm and blues. Apollo (founded in 1943), a New York label, and King (1944), a Cincinnati label that also recorded country singers, also came along during the war years, but the real explosion of independents began in the postwar era.

Los Angeles, in these years, became a huge center for rhythm and blues recording. T-Bone Walker had settled in Los Angeles. The first breakout rhythm and blues single, "I Wonder," was recorded by Private Cecil Gant in a simple basement studio and released in 1944 on Gilt Edge Records, a short-lived L.A. indie. When "I Wonder" went to the top of *Billboard*'s race charts, a number of labels sprang up to capitalize on the smooth, cool, Leroy Carr-derived L.A. blues style Gant had popularized. The most successful of these was Modern Records, which was to have its biggest success with a T-Bone Walker disciple, B. B. King. Aladdin Records signed Charles Brown, who brought jazz-pop stylings reminiscent of Nat "King" Cole to R&B. Swingtime recorded Lowell Fulson, who combined the smooth L.A. sound with a T-Bone Walker-influenced guitar style and a Charles Brown-influenced singer-pianist who would later develop his own, revolutionary style: Ray Charles.

The two most important postwar independent labels out of L.A. were Imperial and Specialty. Imperial, founded by record producer Lew Chudd in 1945, became a major player—and changed the face of rhythm and blues—when Chudd moved his talent search from Los Angeles to New Orleans and signed Fats Domino. Domino had some of the smooth style of the L.A. singers, but he also had the robust energy of Big Joe Turner, and the rollicking, quirky rhythm that grew up in the Caribbean seaport city of New Orleans. Imperial, which also

recorded other New Orleans R&B performers like Smiley Lewis and Guitar Slim, adopted the finest New Orleans session musicians—producer-arranger Dave Bartholomew, and brilliant instrumentalists like saxophonist Lee Allen and drummer Earl Palmer. Domino was also one of the first successful R&B artists to incorporate the influence of white country music. Generally, when discussing the fusion of rhythm and blues and country that produced rock 'n' roll, music historians point to white singers like Elvis Presley and Carl Perkins, but the real pioneers were Domino and, a few years later, Chuck Berry.

Other L.A. labels started to scout New Orleans for talent. Aladdin signed Shirley and Lee, whose 1950s hits like "Feel So Good" and "Let the Good Times Roll" were a unique amalgam of the mature sexuality of the blues and the teenage sexuality of rock 'n' roll. But the most important Los Angeles beachhead in New Orleans was established by Specialty Records' Art Rupe.

Rupe, who started Specialty in 1946, had developed a successful small label, originally recording jump blues bands like Joe Liggins and the Honeydrippers, then signing former Swingtime artist Percy Mayfield, a fine singer in the L.A. style, and one of the century's greatest songwriters. Mayfield's first recording for Specialty in 1950 was his masterpiece, "Please Send Me Someone to Love."

In 1951, Rupe, excited by Imperial's New Orleans roster, sent producer Bumps Blackwell to scout for talent in New Orleans. Blackwell's first success was Lloyd Price, who hit with "Lawdy, Miss Clawdy," backed by Domino and Bartholomew, in 1952. Specialty had a hit in 1954 with Guitar Slim's "The Things I Used to Do" (with Ray Charles). But the label's most significant performer, also signed and produced by Blackwell, was Little Richard. Richard had made a few marginally successful records for Peacock, a Houston-based indie owned by Don Robey, one of the few black entrepreneurs in the rhythm and blues business (romantic balladeer Johnny Ace recorded for Robey's Duke-Peacock, as did Big Mama Thornton and Bobby "Blue" Bland). With Blackwell, he developed a new, over-the-top style. His first single, "Tutti Frutti," came out in 1955, and was one of the most important developments in the merging of rhythm and blues into rock 'n' roll.

Basically, the big difference between rhythm and blues and rock 'n' roll was that white teenagers, as well as blacks, listened to rock 'n' roll. As a result, rock 'n' roll was generally safer and more conservative. As Robert Palmer pointed out in his book, *Baby, That Was Rock and Roll* (about Jerry Lieber and Mike Stoller), the theme of conflict between blacks and the surrounding white culture turned into the theme of conflict between teens and their parents. Little Richard was an exception to that rule. His songs were full of heavy sexual innuendo, and his performances held nothing back.

Specialty had a strong lineup of gospel singers along with its rhythm and blues line. One of its best gospel groups, the Soul Stirrers, had Sam Cooke as its lead singer. Cooke wanted to go into R&B, but Rupe, afraid of losing his gospel audience, forbade it. Cooke and Blackwell left the label together. Rupe hired Sonny Bono as his new chief talent scout, and Specialty lost its edge.

Chess Records, begun in Chicago in 1947 by Leonard and Phil Chess, drew on a different musical style: the Delta blues singers who had migrated north from Mississippi and electrified their sound. The Chicago audiences, like other postwar urban black audiences, were ready for something newer and livelier than the traditional blues they—or their parents—had left behind in the Mississippi Delta. They wanted the big sound of jump blues, and the loud, electric sound that could be heard in the nightclubs they frequented; but they were also still largely recent Southern immigrants, and they wanted a more down-home sound. The musicians were ready to give the public what it wanted, but they were blues-based guitar and harmonica players, not jazz-based horn players. The most successful performers were the ones who could adapt the country blues style to the group configuration of jump. The best of these was Muddy Waters, who put together bands with such brilliant instrumentalists as Little Walter, Jimmy Rogers, Otis Spann, and Fred Below.

The Chess brothers were nightclub owners who realized that there was a record market for the music that was packing their clubs. Using the talent of a brilliant producer/songwriter Willie Dixon, Chess Records began to sign up the top Chicago rhythm and blues acts. Muddy Waters first recorded for them in 1950, singing traditional blues with only a bass accompaniment. These records were so successful that the Chess brothers were reluctant to change the formula, and it was not until 1950 that they let Waters record with his group. Waters was the prototype of the Chicago blues style; other successful Chess rhythm and blues acts were Howlin' Wolf and Little Walter. These artists did not cross over, at least in the 1950s; their sales were to black audiences. But they were the most profound of influences on the British rockers of the 1960s and the guitar rock bands of the 1970s.

The first Chess rhythm and blues record that made an impact on what was to become the rock 'n' roll market was "Rocket 88," by Jackie Brenston and Ike Turner. Produced in Memphis by Sam Phillips and leased to Chess, it inspired Phillips to go on experimenting with the sound that was to lead to Sun Records and Elvis Presley. The Chess artist who was to change the face of American music most profoundly, though, was Chuck Berry.

Berry, introduced to the Chess brothers by Muddy Waters, was a formidable musician who had absorbed the jump blues of Louis Jordan, the jazz guitar innovations of Charlie Christian, the Chicago rhythm and blues of Waters, and—as with Fats Domino—country. Berry's first recording for Chess was "Maybellene," in 1955, and it was one of the key records to cross black rhythm and blues over to a white audience. Berry's style was so immediately accessible to the new rock 'n' roll market that his hits, unlike Domino's or Little Richard's, were never taken away from him by white artists like Pat Boone. Berry's gifts as a lyricist have led literary critics, as well as pop culture scholars, to hail him as one of the century's most significant writers.

Because of Berry and other rhythm and blues artists who appealed to rock 'n' roll audiences (Bo Diddley, Clarence "Frogman" Henry, and groups like the Flamingoes, the Dells and the Moonglows), Chess became one of the most influential independent R&B labels of the 1950s.

The most important label, though, was unquestionably Atlantic. Founded in 1948 by Ahmet and Nesuhi Ertegun and Herb Abrahamson, Atlantic came to dominate both rhythm and blues and rock 'n' roll.

Atlantic's biggest drawback became its greatest strength. Since there was no blues tradition to speak of in New York, the Erteguns were more or less forced to invent one. Using a brilliant black producer, Jesse Stone, and musicians drawn from the jazz clubs on 52nd street, they created a slick but bluesy sound that redefined American music.

Atlantic's first major star was Ruth Brown, a jazz-pop singer who told Ahmet Ertegun when he signed her, "I don't like blues." But her pop-blues amalgam was perfectly suited to the hip New York audience, and to the white teenagers who were starting to listen to

rhythm and blues. She and Lavern Baker, signed in 1954, became the biggest female stars in R&B.

The vocal harmony group style that came to be known as doo-wop found its most popular manifestation on Atlantic, with the Clovers, the Drifters, and the Coasters as the label's biggest stars. Doo-wop came from one of the oldest traditions of black music: harmony singing. In the early 1940s, the principle harmony purveyors were gospel groups and smooth pop groups, principally the Mills Brothers and the Ink Spots. The doo-wop groups modeled themselves after the smooth groups, but they had something of the rawness and the rocking rhythm of the gospel groups, too.

The first important doo-wop group was the Orioles, on Jubilee Records. Chess developed a significant doo-wop stable with the Flamingoes, the Moonglows, and the Dells. The Los Angeles scene produced the Penguins and the Platters. In New York, record executives George Goldner and Morris Levy, on a succession of labels, recorded a number of classic doo-wop groups, the most famous being Frankie Lymon and the Teenagers.

The Clovers signed with Atlantic in 1951, and from their first recordings—Orioles-influenced harmonies with a stronger, more danceable beat—they were at the top of the charts. The Clovers had a strong career throughout the 1950s. The Drifters were signed by Atlantic in 1953 as a setting for the talents of Clyde McPhatter, whose gospel-tinged voice and erotic passion were the precursors of Sam Cooke, and then the soul singers of the 1960s. McPhatter left the Drifters in 1955, but the group, with a series of other lead singers, continued into the 1960s. The Coasters, originally a West Coast group, were produced by songwriters Jerry Lieber and Mike Stoller, two white men who began by writing blues and who became, along with Chuck Berry, the architects of the rock 'n' roll sensibility. Berry, Lieber, and Stoller had always had a wider range to their writing than sexuality, which was the subject of most blues writing.

Atlantic signed and rejuvenated the careers of R&B pioneers T-Bone Walker and Joe Turner. But artistically, the label's most important solo star was Ray Charles, who had begun on the West Coast as a ballad singer in the Charles Brown/Nat "King" Cole tradition. With Atlantic, Charles moved from the Cole piano trio model to a horn-driven band that was unlike Louis Jordan's Tympany Five, and created a gospel-influenced sound that remains one of the most powerful, original contributions to American music.

In the 1960s, a new group of singers came to Atlantic. The first of these was Solomon Burke, signed to the label to replace the departing Ray Charles. According to Burke, he refused to allow the label to promote him as a rhythm and blues singer, because he had promised his devout mother that he would never sing rhythm and blues. The label had to come up with a new name for this new music, and settled on "soul," a name whose religious overtones would satisfy Burke's mother. Whether or not the story is true, the coming of Burke, Otis Redding, Aretha Franklin and others signaled the beginning of a new musical era.

—Tad Richards

FURTHER READING:

Deffea, Chip. *Blue Rhythms: Six Lives in Rhythm and Blues.* Urbana, University of Illinois Press, 1996.

George, Nelson. *The Death of Rhythm and Blues.* New York, Plume, 1988.

Gillette, Charlie. *Sound of the City.* New York, Pantheon, 1983.

Otis, Johnny. *Upside Your Head! Rhythm and Blues on Central Avenue.* Hanover, New Hampshire, Wesleyan University Press, 1993.

Shaw, Arnold. *Black Popular Music in America.* New York, Schirmer Books, 1986.

————. *Honkers and Shouters.* New York, Collier, 1978.

Ward, Brian. *Just My Soul Responding: Rhythm and Blues, Black Consciousness, and Race Relations.* Berkeley, University of California Press, 1998.

Wexler, Jerry. *Rhythm and the Blues: A Life in American Music.* New York, St. Martin's Press, 1993.

Rice, Grantland (1880-1954)

Grantland Rice, arguably the best-known American sports writer ever, was also one of the most highly regarded personally and professionally. Born in Murfreesboro, Tennessee, Rice attended Vanderbilt University and upon graduation began his journalism career with the *Nashville News,* moving to the *Atlanta Constitution,* then to the *New York Mail* and finally to the *New York Tribune* (later the *Herald-Tribune*). In 1930, his column, "The Sportlight," was nationally syndicated and strengthened Rice's position as the "Voice of Sports." What separated Rice's column from countless others was his writing style and the column's content: a combination of sport news, gossip, and commentary. Since the year of his death, the Football Writers Association of America has awarded the Grantland Rice Trophy to the team it considers the best in college football.

—Lloyd Chiasson, Jr.

FURTHER READING:

Fountain, Charles. *Sportswriter: The Life and Times of Grantland Rice.* New York, Oxford University Press, 1993.

Inabinett, Mark. *Grantland Rice and His Heroes: The Sportswriter as Mythmaker in the 1920s.* Knoxville, University of Tennessee Press, 1994.

Rice, Jerry (1962—)

Maybe the greatest wide-receiver in NFL (National Football League) history, Jerry Rice has been a part of the San Francisco 49ers' success for his entire career, which began in 1986. Coming from small Mississippi Valley State University in Itta Bena, Mississippi, Rice holds numerous NFL regular season and postseason records, including most receptions in a career, most receiving yards in a career, and most touchdowns in a career, to name just three. He was on track for another record, most consecutive games with a reception, before a freak injury in the 1997 season opener stopped that streak. Despite that torn anterior cruciate ligament in his left knee, Rice miraculously returned just three and a half months later in a Monday night game against Denver. Unfortunately, he suffered a shattered kneecap (the same knee), preventing the 49ers' most potent weapon from participating in the postseason. After that injury, Rice returned to his old self

in the 1998 season, racking up over 1,000 yards receiving while leading the 49ers in receptions.

—D. Byron Painter

FURTHER READING:

Bloom, Barry M. "I'm Not Invincible Anymore." *Sport.* September 1998, 76-80.

Rich, Charlie (1932-1995)

A versatile artist whose recording career spanned five decades and seven labels, Charlie Rich is primarily remembered for his 1970s country crossover megahits "Behind Closed Doors" and "The Most Beautiful Girl." Produced by Billy Sherrill, the architect of the crossover country sound, these two songs propelled a reluctant Rich into country music stardom. Despite his identification with country, Rich's music incorporated jazz, pop, rock, gospel, R & B, and soul, making him one eclectic country musician.

Born in Arkansas in 1932, Rich began his musical career as an enlisted man in the early 1950s, playing piano with a jazzy outfit

Charlie Rich

called the Velvetones at the U.S. Air Force base in Oklahoma where he was stationed. After leaving the service in the mid-1950s, Rich farmed by day and worked as a supper-club pianist in Memphis by night. Margaret Ann Rich, Charlie's wife, biggest fan, and sometime collaborator, took his tapes to Sun Records, Sam Phillips's legendary recording label, and the early musical home of Elvis Presley, Jerry Lee Lewis, Johnny Cash, and Carl Perkins. Phillips associate Bill Justis liked the tapes, and Rich was signed to Sun, first as a session man and arranger, and eventually as a recording artist. In 1960, he had his first Top 30 hit with ''Lonely Weekends.'' Unable to score with any of his follow-up singles, Rich's career stalled.

In 1964, Rich left Sun and signed with Groove, an RCA subsidiary, where he recorded several albums that were not commercial successes until they were reissued in the wake of his big 1970s hits. After Groove's demise in 1965, Rich signed with Smash/ Mercury, where he had another Top 30 novelty hit with ''Mohair Sam.'' Once again unable to follow up his hit, Rich switched labels again, signing with Hi Records in 1966, where he was unable to make any impression on the charts.

In 1967, Rich signed with Epic, and with Billy Sherrill he recorded the body of work with which he would become most closely identified. Sherrill's production style, which favored lush string arrangements and vocal choruses over the steel guitar and fiddle found in much recorded country music, was a great fit with Rich's soulful, sultry voice and supple phrasing. In his first five years at Epic, Rich had no commercial successes, but remarkably the label stuck with him. Sherrill had some clout, having scored major hits for Epic with Tammy Wynette and David Houston, and Epic was probably sticking with Rich at Sherrill's insistence. This persistence paid off in 1972 when ''I Take It on Home'' was a hit on the country charts. In 1973, ''Behind Closed Doors'' spent twelve weeks on the Top 40 chart, peaking at number fifteen, and ''The Most Beautiful Girl'' spent seventeen weeks on the same chart, peaking at number one. For those breakthroughs, Rich was named the Country Music Association's Male Vocalist of the Year for 1973, and he won the Grammy for best male country vocal performance. In the wake of these successes, Rich's earlier labels began to re-release the previously unsuccessful material in their vaults, and Rich continued to chart. In 1974, he was the CMA's Entertainer of the Year. After 1974, though the hits kept coming to a degree, Rich never again reached the commercial success of the early 1970s.

While Sun's Phillips called Rich the most talented musician he had ever worked with and the only one who had the potential to rival Elvis Presley, Rich seemed uncomfortable with his status as international sensation. His well-documented drinking problem and occasional erratic behavior (in 1975, while on national television presenting the CMA award to his successor for male vocalist of the year, Rich set fire to the piece of paper that revealed John Denver to be the winner) may be part of what kept him from becoming a superstar. In addition, Rich was always reluctant to do the kind of touring and personal appearances a performer is urged to do to maximize record sales, opting instead to spend time at home with Margaret Ann and their children. Perhaps it had something to do with the fact that commercial tastes dictated that he should temper his tendency for artistic experimentation in blending genres.

Rich left Epic for United Artists in 1978 and had a few country hits there. In 1980, he moved to Elektra and had some successes there through 1981, when he went into semi-retirement for a decade. In 1992, he reemerged to make what would be his final album, a lovely, heart-wrenching, jazzy record called *Pictures and Paintings*. In the

liner notes to Epic's *Feel Like Going Home: The Essential Charlie Rich,* Margaret Ann talks about *Pictures and Paintings:* ''That last album that he did I think was more representative of what he really was all about, because it was all different kinds of music—it was the music he loved, and he was really pleased about that. But I don't think he had any idea of the lives he touched. I'm sure he didn't. Because it was just always about the music. It wasn't about being famous. He never really cared a flip for that. In fact, he kind of ran from it. He just wanted to play music; that's all.'' Charlie Rich died from a blood clot in 1995 while traveling through Louisiana with Margaret Ann.

—Joyce Linehan

FURTHER READING:

Guralnick, Peter. *The Lost Highway: Journeys and Arrivals of American Musicians.* New York, Harper Perennial, 1979.

Richardson, J(iles) P(erry)

See Big Bopper

Rigby, Cathy (1952—)

Though Cathy Rigby never won an Olympic medal, her plucky strength and vulnerability won the hearts of American sports fans in the late 1960s and early 1970s, when she competed as a gymnast. At the 1968 Summer Olympics in Mexico City, ''Little Cathy Rigby'' was the media's darling, finishing 16th in the all-around competition, the best ranking ever for an American female. She continued to compete internationally, becoming the first U.S. female to win a silver medal at the 1970 World Gymnastics Championships. In all, she won 12 medals in international competitions, eight of them gold. She was highly favored, by the U.S. press at least, to take the honors at the 1972 Summer Olympics in Munich until her aspirations were thwarted by the stress of public attention, bringing on eating disorders that jeopardized her health for some years to come. She was 20 when she retired from sports and past 30 before she had healed herself and begun a new and surprisingly successful career on the stage.

Rigby was born in Los Alamitos, California, into a middle-class family. Her father, an aircraft engineer, and her mother, a materials analyst, were protective of their daughter, whose health was poor as a child. At ten years of age, the small and lithe child discovered a talent for the trampoline and tumbling. Her father aggressively encouraged her newfound skills and hired a coach to push along her development. While Rigby was still young, her father lost his job and became an alcoholic, causing tension at home. Though she felt the stress of her father's unhappiness and of his disagreements with her coach, Rigby began to win gymnastic competitions, becoming especially well known for her expertise on the balance beam.

Rigby was just under five feet tall and weighed a slight 92 pounds, but her coach insisted that she needed to reduce even further. Plagued by insecurity and lack of self-confidence, Rigby soon became obsessed with her weight and the need to control it. She tried starvation diets and fasting, but it was difficult to compete without food. By the time of the 1972 Munich games, she had become

Cathy Rigby

bulimic. Having learned the technique from a teammate with similar worries, Rigby ate what she wished, then forced herself to vomit, sometimes as often as six times a day.

Fighting dizziness and exhaustion caused by her bulimia, Rigby placed tenth at the 1972 Olympics, still higher than any American woman ever had. But the press called her performance "disappointing," and flocked to their new darling, Olga Korbut, who had eclipsed Rigby at the games. Feeling like a failure, Rigby retired from the sport and married Tommy Mason, an ex-athlete himself. They had two children and Rigby forged a career doing sports commentary and commercials; still obsessed with being thin, she continued to force herself to vomit several times a day.

It was not until 1981 that Rigby was able to begin dealing with her eating disorder. Offered the role of Dorothy in a revival of *The Wizard of Oz,* Rigby developed a new driving interest—the stage. Buoyed by the enthusiastic critical response to her acting, and supported by a new friend, Tom McCoy, who would become her second husband, she finally defeated her eating disorder. She "came out" in the press as a bulimic and continues to tell her story in the hopes of helping other young women fight their self-destructive obsession with weight.

Soon Rigby found herself cast in other acting roles. She acted in several movies, among them *The Great Wallendas,* a vehicle for her considerable gymnastic skills, and *Perfect Body,* about the problem of eating disorders among young women athletes. Her trademark role, however, is Peter Pan, which she revived on Broadway on the thirty-fifth anniversary of the original production. Once again the American press was charmed by Cathy Rigby, and she got rave reviews for her performance in a role that Mary Martin, a Peter of the 1950s, had once said, "You'd have to be an acrobat," to play.

It was not only her athletic ability that won her a Tony nomination, however, but her spunky, upbeat acting style and her accomplished singing and dancing. When she first joined the cast of *Peter Pan,* the songs were prerecorded by another singer, but Rigby was determined to learn to perform them herself. She studied acting and singing with palpable success. "It's that athlete's obsessiveness," she said of training for her new career, "the need to prove yourself and work harder than anybody else. I think it's what helped me do well in the theater."

Rigby continues to perform regularly. She has done gymnastics exhibitions in Las Vegas, has had lead roles in many other musicals from *Annie Get Your Gun* to *South Pacific,* and continues to play the boy who never grew up with the *Peter Pan* touring company that she and her husband produce. They have also produced a video called *Faces of Recovery* about the dangers of eating disorders. Rigby's resilient career, and the help she has offered those who come after her, continue to make her a role model, not only for young athletes, but for all young women seeking to discover their strengths and use them.

—Tina Gianoulis

FURTHER READING:

Goodman, Mark. "Cathy Rigby: Flying High." *People Weekly.* May 6, 1991, 107.

Hoffman, Greg. "Little Big Woman: Catching Up With Cathy Rigby." *WomanSports.* October, 1980, 12.

Mason, Cathy Rigby. "The Worst Day I Ever Had." *Sports Illustrated for Kids.* August, 1994, 26.

Riggs, Bobby (1918-1995)

In 1939 Bobby Riggs was the number one-ranked tennis player in the world. He is remembered, however, not as much for his skills as for his ill-fated 1973 "Battle of the Sexes" match with Billie Jean King at the Houston Astrodome, in which the 55-year-old Riggs was easily beaten by King in front of a national television audience. Riggs claimed he could beat any woman player despite his age. In fact, Riggs had already beaten the top-ranked women's player, Margaret Court, so King knew she could not avoid playing him. Riggs's loss did wonders for women's sports, not just tennis. King thought that her victory was more symbolic and psychological than athletic, and she hoped it would provide a springboard for women's athletics, which it ultimately did. The timing of her victory was also important; Title IX, which banned gender discrimination in education, had just passed.

—D. Byron Painter

FURTHER READING:

''Robert Lorimore Riggs, American Tennis Champion and Braggart Male Chauvinist Died on October 27, aged 77.'' *The Economist.* November 4, 1995, 113.

King, Billie Jean. ''My Favorite Chauvinist.'' *Sports Illustrated.* November 6, 1995, 118.

———. ''The Battle of the Sexes.'' *Newsweek.* September 21, 1998, 90.

Riley, Pat (1945—)

National Basketball Association (NBA) coach Pat Riley is one of the most successful basketball coaches of all time and his achievements have led him to become one of the country's most respected motivational speakers. After three years starring at Kentucky University, a mediocre nine-year professional playing career, and a two-year stint as a broadcaster, Riley became head coach of the Lakers during the 1981-1982 season. He instituted a fast-breaking style which became known as ''Showtime''—a term that reflected his offense as well as his personal, media-savvy style. Riley coached the team to four NBA championships and, through their battles with the Boston Celtics, helped the NBA become a top spectator sport. After leaving Los Angeles, Riley showed his coaching flexibility by instituting a defensive, slow-down style in taking both the New York Knicks and Miami Heat to the playoffs. During the 1990s, Riley became the career leader for most playoff victories.

—Dr. Robert S. Brown

FURTHER READING:

Riley, Pat. *Showtime: Inside the Lakers' Breakthrough Season.* New York, Warner Books, 1988.

———. *The Winner Within.* Reprint edition. New York, Berkeley Publishing Group, 1994.

Ringling Bros., Barnum & Bailey Circus

Two nineteenth-century American men, Phineas T. Barnum and James A. Bailey, largely defined the image of the circus, with acrobats, animals, band music, clowns, and trapeze artists, that is now deeply embedded in American popular culture. In 1881, they merged their separate circuses into Barnum & Bailey's Circus, which crisscrossed the United States for decades, bringing the excitement of the Big Top to towns and cities from coast to coast. In 1919, the Barnum & Bailey Circus was merged with the Ringling Brothers Circus, which had purchased it in 1907 but ran it as a separate entity for twelve years. In the 1990s, the Ringling Bros., Barnum & Bailey Circus continued to thrill thousands of children and adults nationwide.

The first circuses to be seen in the United States were opened in 1793 in New York and Philadelphia by John Bill Ricketts, who specialized in riding horses through flaming hoops. These shows were performed in semi-permanent structures, but as early as the 1840s, traveling circuses on the Barnum & Bailey model moved slowly overland in their horse-drawn caravans, attracting excited, entertainment-starved crowds to their tents. The idea of presenting the circus in a tent is an American contribution, believed to have begun in 1825 with an itinerant show belonging to J. Purdy Brown. The custom evolved from small tents with a single ring and a few hundred seats to two rings in 1872 and three in 1881, calling for larger and larger canvas coliseums. The distinctive quarter poles that support the canvas roof in large areas between the central ''king poles'' and the side poles, invented by Gilbert Spalding, a former chemist, make it possible to cover much larger areas for spectators. The idea of having a number of acts going on simultaneously in several rings is also an American innovation. In Europe there are many circuses, such as the famous one in Copenhagen, which is staged in a permanent building with a single ring. The nomadic U.S. circuses relied more and more on the railroads, and Ringling Bros., Barnum & Bailey at one time traversed the country in four trains, pulling a total of 107 seventy-foot railroad cars.

Circus impresario Phineas T. Barnum (1810-1891) was a flamboyant showman who bought a five-story marble museum in New York City in 1842 and transformed it into the American Museum, a carnival of live freaks, theatrical tableaux, beauty contests, and other sensational attractions. In the first year he attracted thousands with such exhibits as the Feejee Mermaid, who wore the fake body of a fish; Siamese twins Chang and Eng; and Charles S. Stratton, a 25-inch-tall man whom he renamed General Tom Thumb. In 1850 he risked his entire fortune to bring Jenny Lind, a Swedish soprano he had never heard, to America for 150 concerts, earning Barnum huge returns. With his rare talent for gaining publicity for his enterprises, Barnum became an international celebrity who called himself the ''Prince of Humbugs.'' In 1871, he opened the extravaganza he called the ''Greatest Show on Earth,'' combining traditional circus acts with a menagerie of caged animals and sideshows featuring both human and animal curiosities—alive and dead, real and bogus. There is no evidence he ever spoke or said the words, but Barnum has long been credited with the remark, ''There's a sucker born every minute.'' Although he is not the sole originator of the present-day circus, Barnum made this popular theatrical form into a gigantic spectacle, drawing huge crowds to his famous attractions gathered from all parts of the world. The grand climax of Barnum's circus career was his purchase of Jumbo, an elephant weighing six tons. Barnum's sales pitch was so compelling that the huge pachyderm earned back his purchase price in one season under the Big Top.

James Anthony Bailey (1847-1906) was much more retiring in personality than his partner, but his efficiency and astute sense of business combined well with Barnum's flamboyant salesmanship. Bailey had begun traveling with circuses as a boy and gradually worked up the ladder to responsible managerial positions. In 1872 he became a partner in James E. Cooper's Circus, later called the Great International Circus after a lucrative tour of Australia, New Zealand, Java, and several South American countries. When it was renamed the Cooper, Bailey & Company Circus in 1876, it was seen as a strong competitor to Barnum's Greatest Show on Earth, and in 1881 the two shows merged as Barnum & Bailey Circus. After Barnum's death in 1891, Bailey led the show on several successful tours of Europe and brought his circus to new levels of popularity in America, transporting it coast-to-coast on 85 railroad cars. His version of the greatest show on Earth boasted the largest traveling menagerie and displayed its spectacles in five rings as well as on stages. More than a thousand persons were employed in the enterprise.

Bengal tigers perform with their trainer, Gunther Gebel-Williams, in the center ring of a Ringling Brothers, Barnum & Bailey Circus performance in New York, 1970.

In 1907, after Bailey's death, the Ringling Brothers bought the Barnum & Bailey Circus for $400,000 and ran it as a separate entity until 1919, when their operations were combined into Ringling Brothers, Barnum & Bailey, its present name. The Ringling Brothers of Baraboo, Wisconsin, had begun their tent shows in 1884 with the lengthy name: "Ringling Bros. United Monster Shows, Great Double Circus, Royal European Menagerie, Museum, Caravan, and Congress of Trained Animals." In a short time Alf, Al, Charles, John, and Otto Ringling became known as the Kings of the Circus. Later, two other brothers, Henry and Gus, joined their ranks. By 1889 the show had a seating capacity of 4,000 under its Big Top and was playing cities and towns in the midwest, charging 50 cents for adults and 25 cents for children. That same year they became the twelfth American circus to travel by rail.

American circuses made important contributions to popular spectacle, including the traditional free morning parade down Main Street. Beginning usually at eleven o'clock, a uniformed brass band would step out sharply, their instruments blaring a stirring march. Next would come a long procession of flag bearers, beautiful ladies on horseback, trapeze artists waving from brightly painted circus wagons, and clowns performing their well choreographed highjinks. Cages of wild animals moved by in their horse-drawn cages, followed by cowboys and Indians on horseback, Roman chariots, and a line of elephants, marching trunk to tail in their characteristic shuffling gait. Last in the parade was always the steam calliope, with 32 steam whistles, operated by a keyboard, hissing smoke as well as high-pitched tunes like "The Sidewalks of New York."

Many performers who appeared in the Barnum & Bailey circus became star attractions, notably those who performed daring death-defying feats on the high wire or the flying trapeze. The Wallenda family, who came from Germany to join the circus in 1928, did

acrobatics and rode bicycles on the high wire under the name the Flying Wallendas; they ultimately developed a stunt in which three bikes were balanced on the wire. In 1947 they began performing a seven-man pyramid, and in a tragic fall in 1962, two family members were killed and a third was paralyzed. Another acrobat, Con Colleano, the "Toreador of the Tight Wire," retained his popularity in America for decades, dancing a flamenco on the high wire. Lillian Leitzel, who came from a German circus family, thrilled audiences by performing 150 or more swingovers—pivoting on her shoulder socket like a pinwheel—while suspended by a rope looped around her right wrist. The petite star was fatally injured when her rigging broke during her act. Aerialist Alfredo Codona, her husband, was the first to perform the triple aerial somersault from the high trapeze, and Tito Gaona later began performing the same act blindfolded.

Trained animals, both wild and domestic, were popular in circuses. One of the crowd favorites involved "liberty" horses, who performed intricate routines without rider or reins, guided only by visual or oral commands from the trainer. In 1897 Barnum & Bailey featured an act using a record 70 liberty horses performing simultaneously in one ring. The traditional final in most of the larger circuses was the Great Roman Hippodrome Races, demonstrating the ancient arts of chariot racing and riding horses while the equestrians were standing erect. Clyde Beatty, who appeared with Ringling Bros. Barnum & Bailey in 1934, used a whip and a hand-held wooden chair to subjugate as many as forty lions and tigers in a round cage in the center ring. He also performed with dangerous combinations of other animals, including leopards, pumas, hyenas, and bears. The Knie family of Switzerland also became well known in this country for their gentle training of such exotic animals as giraffes, polar bears, hippopotamuses, and rhinoceroses. Elephants were always popular,

213

and Barnum & Bailey used as many as fifty of the huge animals in three-ring spectacles. By the 1990s, animal-rights activists were boycotting circuses around the world for their practice of using animals for mere spectacle, or for allegedly abusing the beasts. These allegations are denied by circuses, but the boycotts have encouraged the development of new-wave ''non-animal'' circuses, such as Le Cirque du Soleil of Montreal, which uses human performers exclusively.

Clowns, who came in a variety of make-up and costumes, were always immensely popular as they packed themselves in a small vehicle or performed juggling or comic acrobatics. The best known clown of all was Emmett Kelly, who played the sad-faced tramp, ''Weary Willie.'' Kelly joined the Ringling Bros. Barnum & Bailey circus in the late 1930s and was a special favorite until he died in 1979 on the opening day of that year's circus season. Kelly made his motion-picture debut in *The Greatest Show on Earth* (1952).

Through the years the circus has remained one of the most enduring of America's popular entertainments, remaining in much the same format while modes of transportation and venues have changed. Though the canvas Big Top was generally abandoned after 167 people died in a disastrous circus-tent fire in Hartford, Connecticut in 1944, parents and grandparents can still accompany children to Ringling Bros., Barnum & Bailey Circuses with the confidence that the show will still go on, and be much as it was when they were children.

—Benjamin Griffith

FURTHER READING:

Fenner, Mildred Sandison, and Wolcott Fenner. *The Circus, Lore and Legend.* Englewood Cliffs, New Jersey, Prentice-Hall, 1970.

Hammerstrom, David Lewis. *Behind the Big Top.* New York, Barnes & Noble, 1980.

Kirk, Rhina. *Circus Heroes and Heroines.* New York, Hammond, 1974.

Taylor, Robert Lewis. *Center Ring: The People of the Circus.* Garden City, New York, Doubleday, 1956.

Wallace, Irving. *The Fabulous Showman: The Life and Times of P. T. Barnum.* Norwalk, Connecticut, Easton Press, 1990.

Ripken, Cal, Jr. (1960—)

Cal Ripken, Jr., is the person more responsible for the resurgent popularity of baseball in the 1990s than any other individual. His pursuit of Lou Gehrig's consecutive games played record became the focus of national attention in 1995. In addition, his calm, good-natured, ''average guy'' demeanor and clear understanding of his place in history has made him a favorite of millions of baseball fans around the world.

Ripken was born August 24, 1960 in Havre de Grace, Maryland, and grew up in nearby Aberdeen, Maryland. He attended Aberdeen High School, earning All-County and All-State honors. Ripken was selected by the Baltimore Orioles in the second round (48th overall) of the 1978 baseball draft. He rose quickly though the Orioles' minor league system, starting the 1982 the season as the Orioles' third baseman and moving to shortstop in June. That same year he was

Cal Ripken, Jr.

voted the American League Rookie of the Year. The next season, he was selected as the American League's Most Valuable Player (MVP) and he played on the winning team in the 1983 World Series.

Ripken continued to demonstrate his abilities as a player throughout the 1980s and early 1990s. In 1990, he compiled a string of 95 consecutive games without an error that set a major league record for shortstops. In the same year, he set records for fewest errors by a shortstop (3) and highest fielding percentage by a shortstop (.996). In 1991, Ripken became the second player in major league history to be named the league's MVP, Major League Player of the Year (by *Sporting News,* Associated Press, and *Baseball Digest*), All-Star Game MVP, and winner of a Gold Glove in the same season (the other being Maury Wills in 1962). He became the first shortstop ever to hit 20 or more home runs in ten consecutive seasons, and led American League shortstops in fielding percentage for the second straight year.

Although Ripken would have been considered one of the greatest shortstops in the history of baseball without breaking Lou Gehrig's consecutive games played record, it was that honor that ensured his place in baseball history. The excitement surrounding Ripken's ''streak'' was particularly important for baseball because of labor problems during the mid-1990s; baseball players went on strike in late 1994, resulting in the cancellation of the 1994 World Series. The strike continued into the start of the 1995 season, and fans were becoming increasingly disillusioned with both the players and the owners. When baseball finally resumed, attendance for most teams was down a whopping 25 percent or more, and independent estimates put the total lost revenue at nearly $700 million over the two-year span. With predictions of continued fan disenchantment and lost revenue continuing to build, Ripken changed everything.

Ripken had not missed a game since the 1983 season, and on September 6, 1995, he played in his 2,131st consecutive game, breaking the record established by Lou Gehrig in 1939. Baseball fans around the world tuned in on television to watch Ripken play in the historic game, and he capped off the record-breaking event by hitting the game-winning home run. Fans found their interest revitalized, and attendance at the ballparks began to rebound. Ripken was chosen by the Associated Press and United Press International as Male Athlete of the Year, by the *Sporting News* as Major League Player of the Year, and by *Sports Illustrated* as Sportsman of the Year.

Even after breaking Gehrig's record, Ripken continued to play every game of every season. In 1996, The Streak reached 2,216 games, surpassing the world record for consecutive games played set by Sachio Kinusaga of Japan. In 1997 Ripken moved from shortstop to third base, but The Streak continued. On September 20, 1998, The Streak finally ended at 2,632 when Ripken chose to sit out a game. Over the 15-plus years of The Streak, the Baltimore Orioles used 289 other players, had 32 different coaches, and 8 different managers. At the time The Streak ended, Ripken had played in 502 more consecutive games than Gehrig and over twice as many as the player in third place, Everett Scott.

Although The Streak may be what most people remember about Ripken, it is certainly not his only achievement. Ripken has been named to the Associated Press Major League All-Star Team six times, the American League All-Stars 13 times, and the *Sporting News* American League All-Star Team seven times. He has also received nine Silver Slugger Awards for being the most productive offensive shortstop in baseball, and he has won two American League Gold Gloves at shortstop. Ripken owns records for fewest errors in a season by a shortstop, most career home runs as a shortstop, and most consecutive games without an error. He is a lock to be elected to the Baseball Hall of Fame as one of the greatest players ever at his position.

—Geoff Peterson

FURTHER READING:

Gutman, B. *Cal Ripken, Jr.: Baseball's Iron Man.* Brookfield, Connecticut, Millbrook Press, 1998.

Joseph, P. *Cal Ripken, Jr.* Edina, Minnesota, Abdo & Daughters, 1997.

Rosenfeld, H. *Iron Man: The Cal Ripken, Jr., Story.* New York, St. Martin's Press, 1995.

Ripley's Believe It or Not

Truths stranger than fiction have captivated writers ever since there have been books. But for most twentieth-century Americans, the phrase ''Believe it or not!'' is indissolubly wedded to the name of Robert Le Roy Ripley, whose illustrated panel of wonders and curiosities was published in hundreds of newspapers across the

Robert L. Ripley

United States. Although Ripley himself died in 1949, his famous brainchild continued to be produced by his successors throughout the twentieth century.

Ripley's career might have been very different but for several strokes of luck. In 1907, as a boy of 14 in Santa Rosa, California, he sold his first cartoon to the humor magazine *Life*. Later, while he was still a teenager, his talent was recognized by a neighbor, Carol Ennis, who steered him to his first newspaper job with the San Francisco *Bulletin*.

But Ripley's biggest break came after he moved to Manhattan and got hired as a sports cartoonist for the New York *Globe*. Casting about for ideas in a slow week, he hit on the idea of drawing up a panel of surprising sports facts, heading it ''Believe It or Not.'' Reader response was overwhelmingly enthusiastic, and his editors urged him to do more in the same vein.

Ripley soon branched out beyond sports oddities to all of the world's wonders, and ''Believe It or Not'' was in limited syndication, earning him a modest but respectable $10,000 annually by the end of 1927, the year he moved to the New York *Post*. (It was also the year of one of his most famous cartoons, in which he pointed out that ''The Star-Spangled Banner'' was not the national anthem because America had never officially designated one. As a result Congress was flooded with letters, resulting in the statutory adoption of the song in 1931.) In 1929, Ripley was sought out by the head of King Features Syndicate, Joseph V. Connolly, who had been sent a laconic telegram from William Randolph Hearst saying ''SIGN RIPLEY.'' Ripley signed, and his income immediately jumped tenfold; by the mid-1930s he was making $500,000 a year, enabling him to travel worldwide and to buy expensive properties on Long Island and in Florida.

Ripley's staff grew until he had dozens of paid assistants. One of his most loyal researchers was Norbert Pearlroth, who had been hired in the 1920s because he knew 14 languages. Pearlroth became legendary at the New York Public Library reading room, where he could be seen nearly every day for over 50 years, combing foreign journals for the unusual facts that were the feature's stock in trade. (Although Ripley left Pearlroth a surprisingly modest bequest when he died—only $5000—the cartoonist had also put Pearlroth's son through school at his own expense.)

Facts were true to Ripley so long as they were in print somewhere. Hearing of a president of Mexico whose term had set a record for brevity (37 minutes from inauguration to assassination), Ripley set his research team scouring sources, until, in the 9832nd book checked, the desired documentation was found. Some of Ripley's eye-openers were simply matters of deduction: Based on a growth rate extrapolated from two fourteenth-century censuses of China plus the standard day's march for U.S. Army infantry units, Ripley came up with one of his most famous panels, the "Marching Chinese," which purported to demonstrate that if all the inhabitants of China were to begin marching four abreast past a given point, their numbers and birth rate were such that the column would never end.

Ripley's exoticism and ethnocentrism were comfortable bedfellows, and his account of a visit to India in the late 1920s, published in his first book for Simon and Schuster in 1929, is rife with contempt for Hinduism. On the other hand, he had great respect for Chinese civilization and artifacts, collecting the latter avidly, including a motorized junk, the pride of a motley flotilla whose home port was Bion, his Long Island estate. (Like many self-made men of his era, Ripley tended to flout his wealth.)

In addition to his newspaper feature and the books that anthologized it, Ripley went on radio in the 1930s, first as a feature on the *Collier Hour* in 1930 and then with his own show, whose succession of sponsors included Standard Oil, Hudson Motors, General Foods, and Royal Crown Cola. Outmaneuvred for a World's Fair concession in 1939 by a rival, John Hix, who produced the panel "Strange As It Seems," Ripley simply opened up nearby with his "Odditorium;" and though it lost money its first year, he returned in 1940 to turn a healthy profit.

After World War II, Ripley also tried his hand at television, being featured on the show *Truth or Consequences* in the winter of 1948 and in his own show beginning on March 1, 1949. Three months later, he was dead, having blacked out on the set on May 24 and died of heart failure in a hospital bed several days later.

The Ripley organization, however, carried on almost seamlessly. The research team, including Pearlroth, continued to ferret out marvels, which were drawn in the Ripley style by Paul Frehm, who Ripley had hired as an understudy when Frehm was illustrating ads for Borg-Warner. Paul Frehm ran the organization until 1977, when his brother Walter, who had begun his career doing Paul's lettering, took control. In 1989 Walter Frehm retired and was succeeded by Don Wimmer, formerly a freelance artist with United Features Syndicate, which had acquired the rights to *Believe It or Not* and was still distributing it to newspapers nationwide at the end of the 1990s.

Ripley's Believe It or Not continued to be operated under license in a number of U.S. cities, including Chicago, Illinois, and Orlando, Florida. His feature gave rise to numerous parodies as well, from a 1950s *Mad Magazine* spoof titled "Ripup's Believe It or Don't" to the National Lampoon's *True Facts: The Book,* a photo archive of

funny roadside signs, and Kevin Goldstein's *The Leslie Frewin Book of Ridiculous Facts.*

—Nick Humez

FURTHER READING:

Bendel, John. *National Lampoon Presents True Facts: The Book.* Chicago, Contemporary Books, 1991.

Goldstein-Jackson, Kevin. *The Leslie Frewin Book of Ridiculous Facts.* London, Frewin, 1974.

Hansen, William, translator. *Phlegon of Tralles' Book of Marvels.* Exeter, University of Exeter Press, 1996.

Priest, Josiah. *Wonders of Nature and Providence, Displayed.* Albany, J. Priest, 1825.

Ripley, Robert Le Roy. *Ripley's Believe It or Not!* New York, Simon & Schuster, 1929.

———. *Ripley's 35th-Anniversary Believe It or Not!* New York, Simon & Schuster, 1954.

Ripley's Believe It or Not! Book of Chance. New York, Coward, McCann & Geoghehan, 1982.

Sloan, Mark, Roger Manley, and Michelle Van Pargs, editors. *Dear Mr. Ripley: A Compendium of Curiosities from the Believe It or Not Archives.* Boston, Little, Brown & Co., 1993.

Rivera, Chita (1933—)

One of the musical theater's most durable personalities, Chita Rivera is revered as an actress, singer, and dancer. Her first major role was as Anita in *West Side Story* (1957). Other Broadway credits include *Bye Bye Birdie* (1960), *Chicago* (1975), *The Rink* (1983), and *Kiss of the Spider Woman* (1993). She has received numerous accolades for her work, including Tony Awards for *The Rink* and *Kiss of the Spider Woman;* the Drama Desk Award for *The Rink;* and top honors at the 1996 Helen Hayes Awards for contributions to theater. Her film credits include *Sweet Charity* (1969) and *Pippin* (1981). Possessing a voice with a wide dynamic and timbral range, Rivera's talent and charisma both as a singer and a dancer have allowed her to enjoy a successful and diverse stage career for over 40 years.

—William A. Everett

FURTHER READING:

Sandla, Robert. "Chita Rivera: Now Is the Gleam in the Eye." *Dance Magazine.* Vol. 68, No. 2, 1994, 76-81.

Telgen, Diane, and Jim Kamp, eds. *Latinas!: Women of Achievement.* Detroit, Visible Ink Press, 1996.

Rivera, Diego (1886-1957)

Probably more than the work of any other visual artist, Diego Rivera's murals and paintings are representative and emblematic of Mexico's history and culture. A man of his times, Rivera used a language very much his own to express his conception of the world.

Diego Rivera

Through the use of figures representing his socialist ideology and others which went against his beliefs, Rivera created his compositions following simple horizontal and vertical lines. His murals, balanced in terms of colors, forms, and composition, offer us a peaceful world, static and inert yet filled with the energy of the search for a better and just world.

Born in Guanajuato, Mexico, Rivera began his art studies at the age of ten. Three years later, his father insisted that he enroll in a military college, but Diego only lasted two weeks, repelled by the regimented training, and was allowed to enroll in regular classes at the Academy of San Carlos. His first exhibit took place in 1906 at the academy. A year later, he took his first trip abroad, one of many to come, traveling to Spain to study and forming friendships with leading members of the Spanish avant garde. A couple of years later he traveled to Paris and Bruges and studied with several painters, exhibiting his work at the Societé des Artistes Independants. In 1910 he returned to Mexico.

Back and forth between Mexico and Europe, Rivera exhibited at numerous galleries, salons, and studios. In 1913 his work showed a transition to cubism while he was also executing Ingres-style drawings and Cezanne-inspired painting and pencil studies. Several years later he became obsessed with the sensuous quality of paintings by Renoir and traveled to Italy to study Renaissance art. Finally, in 1921, Rivera returned to Mexico and saw his country with new eyes, as a foreigner, the way Gauguin saw Tahiti. With his new outlook, Rivera began his long trajectory of mural painting for public buildings, schools, museums, and chapels. His figures became more and more indigenous, his themes political and social. A reevaluation and dignification of the Indian and the workers of the world would, over the years, turn into a longing for recovery and conquest of a better everyday life for the majorities.

In 1922 Rivera joined the Mexican Communist Party and, in 1927, traveled to the Soviet Union to participate in the celebrations of the tenth anniversary of the October Revolution. The Soviets recognized him as a great Communist artist whose art was dedicated to the public and the masses.

In 1929 Rivera married Frida Kahlo, a union that lasted, on and off, for the rest of her life. Kahlo, a painter in her own right, and

Rivera became a fashionable and much-talked-about couple in Mexico and abroad, their extramarital affairs and frequent separations and divorces the material of gossip columnists and art lovers alike.

The same year, Rivera was expelled from the Communist Party, and a year later he arrived in San Francisco to paint two murals for the California School of Fine Arts. He painted twenty-seven murals depicting auto history for the Detroit Institute of Arts (1932-1933), and in 1933 began working on a mural commissioned by Nelson A. Rockefeller for the RCA building in New York City. Depicting the Soviet May Day celebrations and a portrait of Lenin, *Man at the Crossroads* provoked a series of pro and con demonstrations. When Rivera refused to cover Lenin's face with the portrait of an unknown individual, the mural was destroyed and covered with canvas painted to match the adjoining blank wall. Rivera later reproduced the work at the Palace of Fine Arts in Mexico City.

In 1937, Communist theorist-in-exile Leon Trotsky found asylum in Mexico, and Rivera became his host. However, in 1939, Rivera broke off with Trotsky. Rivera's painting career escalated to the point where he spent most of his time traveling and working. His political trajectory also moved from one end of the spectrum to the other. In 1954 Rivera participated in the demonstrations in support of the fallen Guatemalan president Jacobo Arbenz. That same year Kahlo died, and Rivera was reinstated into the Communist Party. Three years later, on November 24, 1957, Rivera died of heart failure in his San Angel studio and was buried, against his wishes, in the Rotonda de los Hombres Ilustres (Rotunda of Illustrious Men) at the pantheon of Dolores in Mexico City.

—Beatriz Badikian

FURTHER READING:

Bloch, Lucienne. "On Location with Diego Rivera." *Art in America.* February 1986, 102-23.

Herner de Larrea, Irene. *Diego Rivera's Mural at the Rockefeller Center.* Mexico City, Edicupes, S.A. de C.V., 1990.

Kettenman, Andrea. *Diego Rivera (1886-1957): A Revolutionary Spirit in Modern Art.* New York, Taschen, 1997.

Rivera, Geraldo (1943—)

In 1987, Geraldo Rivera became the first Hispanic to host a nationally syndicated talk show, *Geraldo*. In both his personal life and his career in the media, Rivera has experienced roller coaster-like highs and lows. After growing up in the mean streets of New York City, Rivera went on to receive some of the most distinguished awards for broadcast journalism, only to suffer a tarnished reputation for pandering to the masses as an exponent of Trash TV.

Geraldo Miguel Rivera, journalist and television personality, was born to a Puerto Rican father and a Jewish-American mother in New York City. Rivera studied at the University of Arizona and the Brooklyn Law School, but received his a law degree from the prestigious University of Pennsylvania Law School and a degree in journalism from the equally prestigious Columbia University. As such, he was one of the best-prepared and most intellectual of the broadcast and investigative journalists of his generation.

Geraldo Rivera

Rivera began his journalistic career as a reporter for WABC-TV in New York in 1970, and later served as a reporter, producer, and host for various television news and entertainment shows. In 1971 Rivera became the first Hispanic to win the New York State Associated Press Broadcaster Association Award, for his investigative series "Drug Crisis in East Harlem." He also became the first Hispanic to be named Broadcaster of the Year in 1972 and 1974. Rivera went on to become one of the nation's most celebrated and respected investigative television journalists, writing and producing various award-winning documentaries. Over the course of his early career, Rivera also won a Peabody Award and ten Emmys for distinguished broadcast journalism.

In the late 1990s, Rivera was one of the most visible and successful Hispanics in media and entertainment. He hosted a nightly news commentary show for CNBC and produced and starred in NBC broadcast specials. Over the last decade of his career, however, Rivera gained the reputation of being a sensationalist and an exponent of the phenomenon dubbed by critics as "Trash TV." Unfortunately, he is too well remembered for an NBC special in which he was to break into one of Al Capone's long lost treasure vaults on live television, which turned out to be empty. The show will always be remembered as one of TV's greatest fiascoes. He also memorably hosted a sensationalistic Trash TV talk show, one of many that proliferated throughout the 1990s, called *Geraldo*. Since that time, Rivera has exhibited a more serious and sober approach to his coverage and discussions of national topics, such as the O.J. Simpson case and race relations, the Rodney King incident, the Los Angeles riots, and the Clinton-Lewinsky scandal. This work has redeemed him somewhat among critics as a serious journalist.

—Nicolás Kanellos

FURTHER READING:

Kanellos, Nicolás. *Hispanic American Almanac*, 2nd edition. Detroit, Gale, 1997.

Tardiff, Joseph T., and L. Mpho Mabunda, editors. *Dictionary of Hispanic Biography*. Detroit, Gale, 1996.

Rivers, Joan (1933—)

Stand-up comedy has become a pillar of popular culture in the late twentieth century. Among the pioneers of contemporary stand-up was Joan Rivers, whose bold, bitchy, self-deprecating humor broke new ground for women comics. Like Lenny Bruce, whose outrageous

routines set the tone for a wave of new comedy in the 1960s, Rivers' bravura flew in the face of acceptable female behavior and paved the way for future generations of tough-talking, straight-shooting comediennes.

The daughter of a successful doctor and his hardworking wife, Joan Molinsky was born on June 8, 1933, in Brooklyn, New York. A smart girl, Rivers' grades were good enough to get her into competitive Barnard College. After graduating Phi Beta Kappa with a degree in English, Joan ended up working as a publicist at Lord & Taylor. But her dream was to become an actress, and so she auditioned for agents all over Manhattan, trying to find representation. But time after time, she was turned away. As Rivers described it, ''They told me I had everything needed to be a star, except for looks and talent. After hearing such moving responses, I would wander back to the receptionist and makes jokes to cover the hurt I was feeling. And the receptionists began to tell their bosses that I was funny.'' Finally, one of the agents offered her a gig at a small stand-up comedy club.

In the 1950s and early 1960s, comediennes were few and far between. Fannie Brice was no longer alive, and the only other women

Joan Rivers (seated) with Elton John (left), Cher, and Pee Wee Herman.

making a living doing stand-up comedy were Phyllis Diller and Totie Fields. Furthermore, Rivers' humor was edgy, raunchy, and often distinctly unladylike. But she was funny. And she was determined to succeed.

For almost seven years, Joan Molinsky, an overweight Jewish girl from Brooklyn, tried to make it in stand-up. She slogged away at small clubs all over the East Coast, even resorting to using the name Pepper January, before permanently becoming Joan Rivers. In the early 1960s, she started working at Greenwich Village coffee shops, telling jokes that pushed the limits of the acceptable. As Rivers herself later wrote, "I was not unaware of my gender. In a routine about how I got into show business, I used to say: 'How do I get booked? My talent? No, I just go into the agent's office and say, 'Hi, I'm Joan Rivers and I put out.'" In the late 1960s no woman said such things in public. No woman said that when she had her baby, she screamed for 23 hours straight—and that was just during the conception. And certainly no white woman came onstage after a black male singer and said at the end of his applause, "I'm so glad you liked my husband's act." "Critics felt that such jokes entitled me to another line of work, perhaps in a delicatessen," Rivers remarked.

While Rivers' was getting panned, Lenny Bruce was getting praised for his shocking comedy. One day, Bruce came to see her show and sent her a note backstage. He wrote, "Joan, you're right, they're wrong." Encouraged by Bruce, Rivers' stuck with it. In 1965, her big chance finally came—she was booked on the *Tonight Show.* Her routine was a hit, and she continued to be asked back on the program.

Rivers frequently joked that her marriage prospects were so grim that her parents hung out a big sign which said, "Last girl before Thruway." In fact, Rivers' marriage to the erudite, Oxford-educated Edgar Rosenberg was a loving, happy union of 22 years. Rosenberg, who also managed Rivers, was her biggest supporter and, with his encouragement, Rivers became a Vegas headliner, a movie producer, and actress in *Rabbit Test,* and finally, in 1983, the *Tonight Show*'s sole guest host, filling in for Johnny Carson every third week. The now petite blonde was a household name, and her bitchy, self-deprecating humor, which had once been reviled by critics, was now being imitated by young women hoping to follow in Rivers' footsteps. Her signature line "Can we talk?" became ubiquitous.

Although Edgar was sometimes the butt of Rivers's jokes, their marriage was stronger than ever. Despite suffering a heart attack in 1984, Rosenberg orchestrated Rivers' move to a show on the new Fox network, which would be in direct competition with the *Tonight Show.* But the move provoked Carson's wrath, and with low ratings the show floundered. In 1987, after less than a year on the air, *The Late Show Starring Joan Rivers* was canceled. Edgar was distraught and took all the blame on himself. Suffering from a chemical depression brought on by his heart medication, he committed suicide a few months later.

A devastated Rivers' and her daughter Melissa were left nearly broke. A few weeks later, Rivers' agent canceled her contract, saying that no one would book a comedienne whose husband had just died—too unfunny. But Rivers' slowly crawled back into show business, doing gigs at tiny comedy clubs and appearing as the center square on a revival of *Hollywood Squares.* A year later, she was asked to read for a small part in Neil Simon's *Broadway Bound.* She leapt at the chance, and she not only won the part but wowed the critics.

Rivers found her way back in front of a national audience with her syndicated daytime talk show, for which she won the 1990 Emmy for best talk-show host. In the mid-1990s, however, she decided to give up the program to do a Broadway play she had written about Lenny Bruce's mother. *Sally Marr . . . and Her Escorts* was a critical success, but closed after five months due to financial difficulties. When her popular jewelry business fell apart at the same time, Rivers once again found herself in pieces.

Once again, Rivers bounced back. After reconciling a difficult estrangement from daughter Melissa in the wake of Edgar's death, mother and daughter played themselves in a NBC TV movie called *Tears and Laughter: The Joan and Melissa Rivers Story,* and now the mother-daughter duo appear regularly on E! TV, providing commentary on the Oscars and all the major awards shows. A popular author, Rivers has written three top-selling books, *Enter Talking, Still Talking,* and *Bouncing Back,* a humorous self-help memoir.

Like her predecessor in comedy, Fannie Brice, Rivers has survived tragedy through humor. Her petite, ladylike appearance notwithstanding, Rivers is still a tough-talking, funny woman from Brooklyn. Alternately panned and praised, Rivers remains a groundbreaking comic whose unflinching ability to tell it like it is broke longstanding taboos, and whose guts and determination paved the way for other brash women such as Roseanne, Ellen DeGeneres, and Rosie O'Donnell to have their say.

—Victoria Price

FURTHER READING:

Bellafante, Ginia. "Joan in Full Throat." *Time.* May 16, 1994.

Rivers, Joan. *Bouncing Back.* New York, HarperCollins, 1997.

———. "How I Triumphed over Tough Times." *McCall's.* April 1997.

Rizzuto, Phil (1918—)

New York Yankees shortstop and colorful television and radio announcer Phil Rizzuto gave new meaning to the exclamation "Holy Cow!" The wiry New York native debuted with the Yankees in 1940 and, except for a three-year stint in the Navy during World War II, made the baseball team his lifelong living. Keystone of the team's defense in the 1940s and 1950s, he was voted the American League's Most Valuable Player in 1950 and inducted into the Hall of Fame in 1994. "The Scooter" became a Yankees sportscaster after retiring from play in 1956, bringing his tremendous personal warmth to the game. He appealed to fans not only with his enthusiasm and insider's knowledge but with rambling personal anecdotes, amusing commentary, and descriptions of Italian delicacies he consumed with colleagues in the broadcast booth. His *cri de cow*—used to describe everything from bad calls to violent rainstorms and grand slams—was adopted in a rock song by Meat Loaf and served as the title of a book of his on-air musings translated into free verse.

—Daniel Lindley

FURTHER READING:

Halberstam, David. *Summer of '49.* New York, William Morrow and Company, 1989.

Kelley, Brent. *Baseball Stars of the 1950s.* Jefferson, North Carolina, McFarland & Company, 1993.

Peyer, Tom, and Hart Seely, editors. *O Holy Cow! The Selected Verse of Phil Rizzuto*. Hopewell, New Jersey, Ecco Press, 1993.

Road Rage

As American roadways became ever more congested in the 1980s and 1990s, drivers began to experience, either as aggressors or victims, a new phenomenon called "road rage." Reports of violence and shootings provoked by incidental breeches of driving etiquette caused an escalating level of paranoia surrounding driving and heightened its presence in the media and the popular imagination. News headlines announced "Five-Year-Old Victim of Road-Rage Shootout," "Father Charged with 'Road Rage' Killing of Son," "Ugly Increase in Acts of Freeway Fury." While the occurrence of shootings while driving began to epitomize road rage in the 1990s, road rage was characterized by any display of aggression by a driver including verbal abuse, tailgating, hand gestures, intimidating stares, or violence. The American Automobile Association (AAA) reported in 1997 that incidents of "aggressive driving" where an "angry or impatient driver tries to kill or injure another driver after a traffic dispute—has risen by 51 percent since 1990," according to *U.S. News and World Report*.

The term "road rage" was first coined, apparently, in 1988, to describe the increase of aggressive driving behavior. Stemming from the phrase "'roid rage," which refers to sudden, violent outbursts in people taking steroids, the proliferation of the term road rage around the nation led some to call the phenomenon an "epidemic." Although it is difficult to quantify, some researchers believe aggressive driving behavior is a growing trend. A 1996 poll indicated that aggressive driving concerned people more than drunk driving. In 1998, the Department of Transportation listed aggressive driving as one of the top-three highway safety concerns.

Although newspaper headlines announcing incidents of road rage that erupted into shootings or beatings instilled the most fear in drivers, Sandra Ball-Rokeach, co-director of the Media and Injury Prevention Program at the University of Southern California explained, "Aggressive driving is now the most common way of driving. It's not just a few crazies, it's a subculture of driving." In focus groups set up by her organization, two-thirds of drivers said they reacted to frustrating situations aggressively, and almost half admitted to deliberately braking suddenly, pulling close to another car, or driving in some other potentially dangerous way. By 1997 nearly 90 percent of motorists had experienced road rage incidents during the previous 12 months, while 60 percent admitted to losing their temper behind the wheel, according to a survey released by the AAA. The most common examples of road rage include verbal abuse, hand gestures, and driving in an intimidating manner.

Reports of extreme incidences of road rage have made drivers acutely aware of their vulnerability while driving. Knowing that they are susceptible to the unpredictable emotional flare-ups of fellow drivers, many drivers experience anxiety. And when drivers feel provoked, their car is a self-contained place where they can engage in confrontations without the tense proximity of face-to-face interaction. The concern about the ease with which drivers are provoked in the 1990s has generated the research of "road rage experts" who have begun to examine the roots of road rage. John Larson, a psychiatrist at Yale University, linked certain car models to some aggressive driving behavior: "BMWs, pickup trucks, sports cars, or off-road vehicles may be given aggressive motivations; thus aggressive drivers react to the 'personality' they associate with the make and model of the vehicle, not the person inside it." Arnold Nerenberg, a clinical psychologist in Whittier, California, and an expert on road rage, cited evolution as one cause. "This competitiveness on the road is similar to what you see in all social mammals. There is this 'I will not let you get ahead of me.'" Dr. Leon James, professor of psychology at the University of Hawaii, who began researching driving behavior in 1977, defines road rage as a cultural problem, not an individual mental problem, because U.S. culture condones the expression of hostility when people feel wronged. He proposed that drivers should use "emotional intelligence skills" when upset by another driver. Instead of being intent on teaching the other driver a lesson, he advocated that drivers should choose to back out of an escalating conflict. Doing so, he suggested, would help drivers to change their attitude to a more peaceful one.

The righteous indignation often found at the core of many drivers' hostile outbursts may be fostered by other elements of American culture. Talk shows that encouraged emotional venting, such as *The Jerry Springer Show,* as well as the cultural obsession with the self, as indicated by the popularity of confessional and self-help books, promote American's concern for their own problems. And technological advances, such as the fax, e-mail, fast food, and the Internet, have helped nurture American's expectations of convenience. Americans' affection for their automobiles may be the ultimate representation of their cultural obsession with convenience and the self. Sometimes purchased to boost the driver's ego, cars allow people to feel as if they have control over their lives and environments while providing them with the convenience of self-determined travel. But crowded roadways impede their ability to get where they are going.

A study of 50 metropolitan areas by the Federal Highway Administration in the 1990s found each area clogged during rush hour. The study also predicted that congestion would spread to unspoiled locations. Daily commutes have become characterized by long hours of traffic moving at a snail's pace. Radio and television traffic reports during rush hours regularly referred to stretches of highways as parking lots. As the suburban sprawl across America continued, road rage seemed a difficult epidemic to stop, especially when Americans' preferred mode of travel remained the automobile. Advocates of safer roads are lobbying for ways to ease traffic congestion and support mass transportation and better urban planning to make U.S. roadways less lethal.

—Sharon Yablon

FURTHER READING:

Adair, Michael. *Hey! You're Driving Me Crazy! The Definitive Guide to Handling the Stress and Anxiety of Driving.* n.p., A.B. Publishing, 1996.

Altman, Kyoko. "'Road Rage' Runs Rampant in High-Stress U.S. Society." *CNN.* 18 July 1997. http://www.cnn.com/US/9707/18/aggresive.driving/index.html. June 1999.

Fumento, Michael. "'Road Rage' versus Reality." *Atlantic Monthly.* Vol. 282, No. 2, August 1998, 12-17.

Gest, Emily. "Driven Mad." *New York Daily News.* October 23, 1997.

Gorman, Larry, and Tom Gorman, "Inland Empire Leads in Fatal Road Rage." *Los Angeles Times.* March 9, 1999.

James, Leon, "Aggressive Driving and Road Rage: Dealing with Emotionally Impaired Drivers." 1997. http://www.aloha.net/~dyc/testimony.html. June 1999.

Twitchell, James B. *Preposterous Violence: Fables of Aggression in Modern Culture.* New York, Oxford University Press, 1989.

Vest, Jason, Warren Cohen and Mike Thapp. "Road Rage." *U.S. News and World Report.* June 2, 1997.

"Yahoo! News—U.S. Full Coverage: Road Rage." http://headlines.yahoo.com/Full_Coverage/US/Road_Rage. June 1999.

Road Runner and Wile E. Coyote

The Road Runner and Coyote cartoons have endured since 1949, when legendary director Chuck Jones and storyman Michael Maltese created Wile E. Coyote and the Road Runner for the Warner Brothers cartoon short "Fast and Furry-Ous." The cartoon established a formula that has continued to entertain audiences for half a century. The hungry Coyote ("Carnivorous Vulgaris") chases the truly wily Road Runner ("Accelleratii Incredibus") across the desert southwest. In escalating frustration, the Coyote resorts to using a boomerang, a rocket, a boulder, jet-propelled tennis shoes, and the first in a long line of Acme products doomed to failure, the Acme Super Outfit. Each scheme backfires, leaving the Coyote on the wrong end of a boulder, falling off a cliff, or simply exploding.

As Jones recalled in *Chuck Reducks,* studio management, fearful that no one would like the cartoon duo, was reluctant to allow Jones and Maltese to create any more Coyote and Road Runner cartoons. Although it was three years before the release of the second cartoon, "Beep, Beep," Wile E. Coyote and the Road Runner proved so popular that they appeared in 35 cartoons together by 1966, with one, "Beep Prepared," nominated for an Academy Award in 1961. The timeless premise and comedy of these cartoons was common to many successful cartoons produced in the forties and fifties: the bungling predator simply can't outwit his smarter or just plain luckier prey. Such classic pairing as Bugs Bunny and Elmer Fudd (Warner Brothers), Sylvester and Tweety (Warner Brothers), and Tom and Jerry (MGM Studios) thrived on this idea. What set the Coyote and Road Runner cartoons apart was the uniqueness of the characters themselves.

The Road Runner may be one of the most irritating foes any cartoon character has faced. While Bugs, Tweety, and Jerry often display ingenuity, the Road Runner is comparatively oblivious. In the first cartoon, the swift bird displays more aggression, going out of his way to irritate the Coyote. At one point, with the Coyote close on his tail, the Road Runner even looks concerned. In subsequent cartoons, as the Coyote's efforts escalate, the Road Runner generally doesn't seem to even notice his foe. The Road Runner does on occasion take deliberate steps to avoid a trap, but, more commonly, with nothing more than a "beep, beep" and a flick of his tongue, the Road Runner eats the birdseed without setting off traps, runs through rock walls, and stops short at the edges of cliffs while the Coyote goes toppling over.

It is Wile E. Coyote himself who creates the primary appeal of these cartoons. While other predators plow ahead, the Coyote plans, diagrams, and builds. As the cartoons progress and the Coyote's schemes become more and more violent, culminating in a plan involving dynamite or dropping a piano on the Road Runner, the audience realizes that the Coyote's quest is no longer about hunger. With the Coyote, the chase eventually becomes a matter of his wounded pride. Mute, communicating only through the occasional hand-held sign or yelp of pain, his expressive face conveys emotions from cunning to frustration to confusion to fear and back again. He frequently addresses the audience, holding signs that say "Egad" or throwing a sly look toward the camera. Audiences see the effort the Coyote puts into his plans and his doomed hope, making it somehow all the more funny when his plans don't work.

More than anything, the characteristic that truly distinguishes the Coyote is his inability to learn from his mistakes. Despite his diagrams, his schemes fail in often surprising ways. The rocket doesn't take off, it just explodes; the boulder falls backward off the catapult; and the jet-propelled sneakers send him off a cliff. The Coyote often averts one mishap only to find another. When he gets his Acme Bat-Man's Outfit to work only moments before hitting the ground, he smashes into a rock wall. The Coyote faithfully uses Acme products even though, again and again, the explosives, the magnetic birdseed, and the rocket-powered roller skates don't work. The Coyote is surprisingly human in his dogged attempt to attain a goal that doesn't seem to be meant for him. When audiences laugh at the Coyote, it is part slapstick humor and part catharsis, part visual and part mental. People see themselves in the Coyote's continually frustrated attempts to achieve his goal, but no one seems to have it quite as bad as the poor Coyote.

The Road Runner only appeared in cartoons with the Coyote. However, the Coyote proved to be so popular a character, he appeared in other Warner Brothers cartoons. Most notable is a series with Bugs Bunny. In these cartoons, the Coyote is somewhat snooty and introduces himself as "Wile E. Coyote, Genius." Of course, in spite of being a genius, he can't outwit the likes of Bugs Bunny. The Coyote also doubled as a red-nosed wolf, Ralph, in a series of cartoons with Sam the Sheepdog. Again our hero simply cannot seem to catch his dinner. The Coyote is ever the doomed schemer.

Cartoons featuring Wile E. Coyote and the Road Runner first appeared as "curtain-raisers" in theatres, eventually moving to television. In September 1966, *The Road Runner Show,* a repackaged version of the older cartoons, premiered in the CBS Saturday morning lineup. From the sixties through the nineties, the Road Runner and Coyote cartoons have been a staple of children's programming, running on the networks as well as cable stations such as TNT and the Cartoon Network.

—Adrienne Furness

FURTHER READING:

Friedwald, Will, and Jerry Beck. *The Warner Brothers Cartoons.* Metuchen, New Jersey, and London, The Scarecrow Press, 1981.

Jones, Chuck. *Chuck Reducks: Drawing from the Fun Side of Life.* New York, Warner Books, 1996.

Lenburg, Jeff. *The Encyclopedia of Animated Cartoons.* New York and Oxford, Facts on File, 1991.

Woolery, George W. *Children's Television: The First Thirty-Five Years, 1946-1981: Part 1: Animated Cartoon Series.* Metuchen, New Jersy, and London, The Scarecrow Press, 1983.

Robbins, Tom (1936—)

The novelist Tom Robbins was one of the foremost writers of the 1970s and 1980s counterculture, joining Kurt Vonnegut and Robert Pirsig as the gurus of the youth market. His novels wittily debunked the powers that be and challenged conceptions of normalcy, earning him a following of college student groupies. His novels' trademarks are episodic, nonlinear structures that mimic psychedelic LSD trips; casts of eccentric characters with names like Bonanza Jellybean and Marx Marvelous; plots that center on the quest for the Meaning of Life; a flamboyant style characterized by over-the-top metaphors and absurd images; and an optimistic philosophy based on Eastern mysticism, quantum physics, anti-materialism, feminism, and above all, playfulness.

Robbins grew up in Virginia and was raised to be a "southern gentleman," although two years at Washington and Lee University convinced him that he did not fit the mold. In the 1950s, he hitchhiked across the country and was drafted into the military, serving in the air force in Korea. After the war, Robbins earned his degree from the Richmond Professional Institute and started a career as a newspaper arts critic. He fled the conservative South in 1962 and settled in the Seattle area, where he still lives. During the 1960s, Robbins began to experiment with LSD, which he told Steven Dougherty ranks "right up there with the microscope and the telescope as an instrument of exploration." When he began to publish his novels, he was already a prominent figure of countercultural Seattle and New York.

Robbins landed on the national scene in 1973 when his first book, *Another Roadside Attraction* (1971), came out in paperback. Its popularity fueled by word of mouth, the novel became an instant cult favorite on college campuses. In this book, a group of eccentrics discover Christ's mummified body, bring it to a hot dog stand called Capt. Kendrick Memorial Hot Dog Wildlife Preserve, and try to disprove Christianity. The book repudiates the authority of Christianity and offers Eastern religion as a more healthy alternative.

His second book, *Even Cowgirls Get the Blues* (1976), was his most popular. Within four years it sold 1.3 million copies. It tells the story of Sissy Hankshaw, a beautiful woman who learns to live with her socially unacceptable, oversized thumbs, by becoming the best hitchhiker in the country. She ends up at a South Dakota ranch run by cowgirl feminists, where she discovers the path to wisdom with the help of a Japanese hermit. The book struck a chord with readers who had grown disillusioned about America's materialist and patriarchal society. Sissy learns that Americans must reach back to their spiritual roots in Pantheism, which is characterized by feminine receptivity rather than masculine aggression. In 1993, after years of failed deals, the novel was finally made into a film by director Gus Van Sant.

Robbins' next novel, *Still Life with Woodpecker* (1980), a love story about a terrorist and a princess who escape their assailants through the image of the desert on a pack of Camel cigarettes, gained him popularity with a new generation of college students, although critics were growing tired of his style and playfulness, believing him unwilling to grow up and accept the status quo. *Jitterbug Perfume* (1984), an elaborate novel loosely centered around the search for immortality, likewise landed on the best-seller lists. With this novel, his reviews also improved. His last two novels, *Skinny Legs and All* (1990), which features inanimate, everyday objects as characters, and *Half Asleep in Frog Pajamas* (1994), which is told entirely in the second person, employ his trademark style, but their themes are much darker. Robbins has become more serious in his depiction of greed, religious fundamentalism, and destruction of the environment, turning off some readers. Others feel that his style and message have largely lost their appeal for a generation of readers and critics who have outgrown their attraction to absurdity and countercultural ethics. But for Robbins, critiquing the culture he lives in is not a fad but his life's work. His goal as a writer is to help change human consciousness. "We are in this life to enlarge the soul and light up the brain," he has written.

—Anne Boyd

FURTHER READING:

Dougherty, Steven. "Cowgirls May Get the Blues, but Not Tom Robbins, Who Pours It On in Jitterbug Perfume." *People Weekly*. April 1, 1985, 123-124.

Hoyser, Catherine E., and Lorena Laura Stookey. *Tom Robbins: A Critical Companion*. Wesport, Connecticut, Greenwood Press, 1997.

O'Connell, Nicholas. *At the Field's End: Interviews with 20 Pacific Northwest Writers*. Seattle, Madrona Publishers, 1987, 264-284.

Siegel, Mark. *Tom Robbins*. Boise, Idaho, Boise State University Press, 1980.

Roberts, Jake "The Snake" (1955—)

Part of a professional wrestling family, Jake Roberts (who was born Aurlian Smith, Jr.) was known for bringing a pet snake into the ring and for inventing the wrestling finishing hold called "the DDT." Roberts started wrestling in 1975, but achieved his greatest success after entering the World Wrestling Federation (WWF) in 1986. Although never the star of the promotion, Roberts' interview skills, ring psychology, and pet snake gimmick kept him near the top of the card. Roberts, whose career was hampered by substance abuse problems, left the WWF after Wrestlemania VIII in 1992 for a brief stint in World Championship Wrestling (WCW). Retired, he was "born again," and could soon be seen on Christian TV stations talking about his substance abuse. Roberts' short 1996 comeback in the WWF was most notable for his loss to Stone Cold Steve Austin in a match that helped Austin win over WWF fans.

—Patrick Jones

FURTHER READING:

Lentz, Harris M. *Biographical Dictionary of Professional Wrestling*. Jefferson, North Carolina, McFarland & Company, 1997.

Roberts, Julia (1967—)

Julia Roberts became a firm candidate to the title of America's sweetheart with her role as Vivian Ward, a humble hooker retired from the bitterness of street life by a handsome millionaire (Richard Gere) in the romantic comedy *Pretty Woman* (1990). Though Roberts would try serious dramatic roles in the early 1990s, her talents and audiences' attention peaked with her romantic comedies. By the end of the twentieth century she would become the highest paid female actress of her generation, earning $20 million dollars per picture.

Julia Roberts

the course of her career, something which Hollywood seems unable to do. But *Notting Hill* (1999), her film with Hugh Grant, is a comedy in the line of *Pretty Woman* and indicates best the limitations of her career.

Roberts' difficulty breaking away from romantic comedies paralleled the difficulty actor John Travolta had in overcoming his association with *Saturday Night Fever.* Both Travolta and Roberts became connected so closely in the audiences' imagination to their characters that the chance for them to develop a more varied career was limited by public expectations. Travolta managed to overcome his fusion with *Saturday Night Fever* and his years of obscurity thanks to Quentin Tarantino's providential intervention with a role in *Pulp Fiction.* Roberts, however, continues to be in the public eye. She is the champion of the romantic comedy, and no other actress has yet challenged her ability to charm audiences. Unlike Ryan or Bullock, Roberts can portray the all-American sweetheart and the alluring sex symbol. This is what makes her charm unique, but it is also the main dilemma she faces to consolidating her successful career. She might be condemned to be Vivian Ward forever, no matter who she chooses to play.

—Sara Martin

FURTHER READING:

Connelly, C. "Nobody's Fool." *Premiere.* December, 1993, 70-73.

Joyce, Aileen. *Julia: The Untold Story of America's Pretty Woman.* New York, Pinnacle Books, 1993.

McInerney, Jay. "I'm 5'9" with a Famous Smile." *Harper's Bazaar.* September, 1995, 400-405.

Schneller, J. "Barefoot Girl with Cheek." *Gentlemen's Quarterly.* February, 1991, 158-165.

Sessums, K. "The Crown Julia." *Vanity Fair.* October, 1993, 234-241.

Thornton, B. "Right on the Money." *Harper's Bazaar.* June, 1997, 138-141.

The youngest sister of actor Eric Roberts, Julia began her career in 1986 with a minor role in a film starring her brother, soon followed by a leading role in *Mystic Pizza* (1988). A year later, Roberts received her first Oscar nomination at age 22 for her tragic role as a dying bride in *Steel Magnolias* (1989), the film she made just before *Pretty Woman.* The phenomenal success of *Pretty Woman* and her nomination as Best Actress for her role in this film plunged Roberts into the full glare of the public eye, turning her private life into fodder for the predatory sensationalist press. Her string of romantic relationships and one failed marriage to singer Lyle Lovett perpetuated public interest in her.

Roberts, like others including Meg Ryan, has fought hard to dissociate her image from the romantic role that made her famous, but has hardly succeeded. The remarkable box-office performance of the comedy *My Best Friend's Wedding* (1997) indicates that the public prefers to see Roberts in romantic roles. Though her performances in serious roles in suspense films like *Flatliners* (1991), *Sleeping with the Enemy* (1991), and *The Pelican Brief* (1993) were sound, they met only with moderate acclaim. Roberts' dramatic roles in Neil Jordan's *Michael Collins* (1996) and Stephen Frears' *Mary Reilly* (1996) lacked credibility. Like other leading actresses in search of a good role, such as Demi Moore or Sandra Bullock, Roberts has founded her own production company. Her work as producer might well change

Roberts, Nora (1950—)

Nora Roberts is one of the most prolific novelists of all time, with an output approaching 126 novels with 42 million copies in print as of 1999. A popular writer who specializes in "paperback" romances such as *Carnal Innocence* (1992), *Public Secrets* (1990), and *Born in Shame* (1996), she broke into publishing in 1979 as a 29-year-old housewife who turned to writing to avoid being driven stir crazy by a snowstorm that kept her confined to the house for a week. This house-bound experience played a major role in shaping her research and writing style, which does not depend on first-hand knowledge of the world she writes about. In fact, most of her research is performed on the Internet. "I know they say write what you know," Roberts told a *Publishers Weekly* interviewer in 1998, "but I write about what I want to know." Indeed, her "category romances," as she terms them, rely less on reality and fully fleshed out plots than they do on idealized characters and romanticized settings. She views her works as appealing to readers on an emotional level, evoking the feeling of first love, bitter loss, and quiet romance. "That's what people want to learn about."

—Sandra Garcia-Myers

FURTHER READING:

Quinn, Judy. "Nora Roberts: A Celebration of Emotion." *Publishers Weekly*. February 23, 1998, 46.

Tichemer, Louise. "Drive, Discipline, and Desire." *Writer's Digest*. February, 1997, 25.

Robertson, Oscar (1938—)

Although almost unknown to many younger basketball fans in the 1990s, Oscar Robertson ranks among the greatest players in the history of the sport. Red Auerbach, longtime Boston Celtic coach and general manager and one of Robertson's most ardent supporters, called the "Big O" one of the most versatile and complete players he had ever seen. Fellow Hall of Fame member and Celtic player John Havlicek simply stated, "Oscar was the best player I ever played against." Robertson was an unstoppable offensive force, who could also pass, rebound, and play tenacious defense. At 6'5" and 220 pounds, he was the prototype of the modern "big" point guard, paving the way for more recent players who have also excelled at the position, such as Earvin "Magic" Johnson and Anfernee "Penny" Hardaway. Among his many accolades and awards, Robertson is one of only four guards to have ever won the NBA Most Valuable Player (MVP) Award, along with Bob Cousy, Magic Johnson, and Michael Jordan.

While a collegiate player at the University of Cincinnati (1957-1960), Robertson was both a three-time National Player of the Year and three-time national scoring champion, leading the Bearcats to two appearances in the NCAA Final Four (1959 and 1960). He is one of only three players to have scored more than 900 points in three different seasons as a collegiate player, and ranks seventh all time on the NCAA career scoring list with 2,973 points (33.8 points per

Oscar Robertson (No. 12) in mid-air, grabbing a rebound.

game). Prior to his collegiate career, Robertson was a two-time "Mr. Basketball" in Indiana, and led Crispus Attucks High School of Indianapolis to two state championships. The capstone of his amateur career came in 1960, when Robertson was co-captain with Jerry West of the U.S. Olympic Basketball Team, a group that easily won the gold medal at the Games in Rome. This team is considered by many basketball experts to be among the most talented amateur assemblies in the history of the sport.

In 1960 Robertson was drafted by the Cincinnati Royals of the NBA, and began a fourteen-year professional career that ranks among the most prolific and successful of all time. In 1961 Robertson was voted Rookie of the Year and won the first of his three All-Star Game MVP awards. In 1964 Robertson won the league MVP. But his greatest individual accomplishment may have come in his second season (1961-62), when he averaged a triple double for the entire season, (30.8 points, 11.4 assists, and 12.5 rebounds per game). This achievement is undoubtedly his most legendary among basketball players and fans. Many modern players strive to attain this type of production for individual games—not entire seasons—and it has never been duplicated in almost 40 years. Among his many accomplishments in the game, Robertson was a member of the All Star squad 12 of his 14 seasons in the NBA.

Following the 1969-70 season, Robertson was traded by the financially strapped Royals to the Milwaukee Bucks, where he teamed with a young Lew Alcindor (Kareem Abdul-Jabbar) to win the NBA title in 1971. Following a second appearance in the NBA Finals in 1974, Robertson retired from the NBA as the highest scoring guard of all time, with 26,710 points. At the time of his retirement he was also the all-time career assists leader and had made more free throws than any player in NBA history. Additionally, Robertson was an outspoken leader of the NBA Players Association, and is credited with helping bring free agency to the league in the 1970s. Robertson was inducted to the Basketball Hall of Fame in 1979.

Since his retirement as a player, Oscar Robertson has been a community and business leader in Cincinnati, working in both the land development and political arenas to bring economic and civic improvements to lower income neighborhoods throughout the city. In 1996, at the age of 58, he displayed his character and love for his family by donating a kidney to his daughter, who was suffering from severe kidney failure. For his many contributions to the community, his friends, and family, Robertson is among the most beloved citizens that both Cincinnati and the broader basketball community have ever known.

—G. Allen Finchum

FURTHER READING:

Dickey, Glenn. *The History of Professional Basketball*. Briarcliff Manor, New York, Stein & Day, 1982.

Sachare, Alex. *100 Greatest Basketball Players of All Time*. New York, Pocket Books, 1997.

Robertson, Pat (1930—)

The son of a Democratic United States senator from Virginia, Pat Robertson turned from a career in the law to one in religion and made himself one of the most influential and enigmatic leaders of the

Pat Robertson

so-called Christian Right during the Reagan era of the 1980s and beyond. As president of the Christian Coalition, which he founded, from 1989 to 1997, Robertson helped galvanize millions of evangelical Christians toward greater participation in the political process, and has himself considered running for the White House.

Raised in the Southern Baptist tradition, Robertson graduated magna cum laude from Washington and Lee University in 1950. After serving as a Marine Corps officer during the Korean conflict he returned to his education, receiving a J.D. from Yale Law School in 1955. Failures in an early business venture, and his attempts to pass the New York bar exam helped steer him back toward his religious roots. He attended a theological seminary, graduating with a B.Div., and worked for a time with the mostly black inner-city poor in Brooklyn before returning to Virginia where he was ordained a Southern Baptist minister in 1960.

Robertson demonstrated the intensely entrepreneurial side of his character in 1961 when he started operating WYAH, a television station in Virginia that became the first in the nation devoted to primarily religious programming. From this single station Robertson launched what would become a veritable communications empire: the Christian Broadcasting Network (CBN), offshoots of which grew to include a relief agency, cable television holdings, the American Center for Law and Justice, which specializes in First Amendment cases, and Regent University, which came to call itself "America's premier Christian graduate school."

The flagship program of his network was *The 700 Club,* which Robertson hosted from 1966. His success both behind and before the camera led many conservative Christians to promote Robertson's

involvement in U.S. politics. Though he at first thought political organizing was inconsistent with his clerical calling, he had a change of heart by the 1980s, when he began to organize mobilization efforts such as a 1980 "Washington for Jesus" rally and his own Freedom Council (1981-86). In 1984 he changed his party affiliation to Republican. When presented in 1987 with what was purported to be a petition of some 3.3 million names urging him to run for office, he resigned his church offices and launched a campaign for the 1988 Republican presidential nomination. Despite early successes in some primaries, Robertson's candidacy had been decisively rejected by "Super Tuesday" in March of that year, even by many members of conservative Christian churches.

Undaunted by his electoral failure Robertson returned to the idea of grassroots organizing. In 1989 he founded and became the first president of the Christian Coalition, an organization whose mission was to represent evangelical opinion to government bodies, protest anti-Christian bias in public life, train leaders, and develop policies—all while being careful not to lose its tax-exempt status by supporting partisan candidates. The Christian Coalition proved very successful in enunciating the social agenda of the religious right in the United States. With a national membership well in excess of a million, the group raised the political profile of a hitherto-marginalized section of the population. Mirroring the Republican Party's "Contract with America," the Coalition advanced its "Contract with the American Family," which was trumpeted as "A Bold Plan to Strengthen the Family and Restore Common-Sense Values." Many attributed the G.O.P's triumphs in 1996 Congressional races to the efforts of Robertson and his branch of the religious right.

Robertson astonished the media world in 1997 when, on the same day he resigned the presidency of the Christian Coalition, he sold his International Family Entertainment corporation to Rupert Murdoch, a media mogul whose television and newspaper holdings had often been criticized for taking the low moral road. Robertson tried to assuage criticism by promising that the hundreds of millions of dollars the sale had generated would go toward a new global television evangelism campaign as well as to enhance the endowment of Regent University. Part of the deal with Murdoch's Fox Kids Worldwide Inc. was that *The 700 Club* would continue to be aired by the new entity and that CBN itself would remain independent.

At the turn of the century, Robertson remained a figure who defies easy characterization. For many on the politcal left, Robertson is, as described in Robert Boston, "the most dangerous man in America" due to his stances on social issues like homosexuality and the role of women. Those who valued the country's multicultural heritage reacted with horror to Robertson's suggestion that only devout Christians and Jews were fit to hold public office. Other liberals decried his proposals to abolish the Corporation for Public Broadcasting and the National Endowment for the Arts. Robertson's hopes of restoring prayer to public schools and re-establishing teh United States as a "Christian nation" seemed an affront to the constitutional separation of church and state and drew the ire of the Jewish Anti-Defamation League.

Robertson is neither a backwoods fundamentalist nor a one-dimensional Elmer Gantry. He is well educated, well off, and well connected, with two American presidents on his family tree, and his pragmatism has made him an enormously successful businessman. His particular brand of charismatic theology, moreover, is opposed by many right-wing Christians who are uneasy about his claim to receiving divinely inspired "words of knowledge" and his belief that even the faithful will suffer from a pre-millennial period of tribulation before the final coming of Christ. During the 1988 primaries, for example, Robertson's bid for the Republican nomination drew less support from members attending conservative Baptist churches than it did from other white voters. Despite the criticism he has received from some American Jewish groups, he is a leading defender of the state of Israel, which he sees in the context of Biblical end-times prophecies. Robertson resumed the presidency of the Christian Coalition after the departure of Ralph Reed, and presided over the reorganization of the group into two entities—Christian Coalition International and Christian Coalition of America—in the wake of a 1999 IRS ruling that revoked its tax-exempt status.

By criticizing secularism and unbridled personal liberty, Robertson exploited a deep-seated popular discontent and won himself and his organizations a considerable following. Despite his failure to achieve ultimate power, he succeeded in bringing many conservative issues to the public discourse. When he began his career in broadcasting, religious television was in its infancy; forty years later, even after the disasters of the scandal-ridden 1980s, it is a multibillion-dollar industry. From a point on the political fringe, Robertson has helped shape the religious right into a powerful force in U.S. politics.

—Gerry Bowler

FURTHER READING:

Boston, Robert. *The Most Dangerous Man in America?: Pat Robertson and the Rise of the Christian Coalition.* Amherst, New York, Prometheus Books, 1996.

"Christian Coalition Official Website." http://www.cc.org. June 1999.

Foege, Alec. *The Empire That God Built: Inside Pat Robertson's Media Machine.* New York, John Wiley & Sons, 1996.

Robertson, Pat. *America's Dates with Destiny.* Nashville, Thomas Nelson, 1988.

———. *The Secret Kingdom: Your Path to Peace, Love, and Financial Security,* Dallas, Word Publishing, 1993.

Watson, Justin. *The Christian Coalition: Dreams of Restoration, Demands for Recognition.* New York, St. Martin's Press, 1997.

Robeson, Kenneth

Pulp magazine publisher Street & Smith used the house name Kenneth Robeson on two of their publications. Kenneth Robeson was credited as the author of 179 of the original 181 novels that appeared in *Doc Savage Magazine* from 1933 to 1949. The first issue carried the byline Kenneth Roberts and, due to a mistake by an editorial assistant, the March 1944 issue carried the byline Lester Dent, the true author of the novel. Dent wrote the majority of the *Doc Savage* novels, but worked with at least five ghost writers on some 38 of the stories. In 1939, Street & Smith launched *Avenger Magazine* with novels by Kenneth Robeson, "the creator of Doc Savage." All 24 of

the *Avenger* novels were written by Paul Ernst. In the 1960s and 1970s the name Kenneth Robeson appeared on paperback reprints, and in the 1990s it appeared on seven original Doc Savage novels written by Will Murray; they were based on Dent's notes and story fragments.

—Randy Duncan

FURTHER READING:

Cannaday, Marilyn. *Bigger than Life: The Creator of Doc Savage.* Bowling Green, Ohio, Bowling Green State University Press, 1990.

Robeson, Paul (1898-1976)

Paul Robeson must be counted among the most broadly talented men ever born in the United States, but the fact that he was also a "Negro" in a society that could not easily accept exceptional skills in one of his race regularly limited his opportunities to demonstrate his talents. That he accomplished so much in so many public arenas despite the restrictions he faced remains especially remarkable. At times Robeson was probably, often simultaneously, the most famous and controversial black man in America; in retrospect, his long and complex public career marks some of the high and low points in American race relations during the twentieth century.

While Robeson frequently faced racism and, eventually, political intolerance, he nevertheless excelled in whatever field he entered: he was an excellent scholar, an All-American athlete, a riveting stage and screen actor, a spellbinding orator, and one of America's most powerful folk singers. Born and raised in New Jersey, Robeson acted, sang, and delivered speeches in high school before entering Rutgers University, where he then triumphed in several sports, was elected to Phi Beta Kappa in his junior year, and addressed his graduating class as valedictorian. While attending Columbia University Law School, Robeson also played professional football with the Akron Pros, and made his professional stage debut. Recognizing the barriers facing black lawyers, Robeson concentrated on his theatrical career after graduating from Columbia, accepting lead roles in Eugene O'Neill's *All God's Chillun Got Wings* and *The Emperor Jones* in 1924. In the same year Robeson made his screen debut in the independent African-American director Oscar Micheaux's *Body and Soul,* signaling his career-long attempt to address both mainstream and minority audiences.

By 1925, Robeson was frequently recording and singing in concert, as if no single entertainment form could contain his talents; by 1929 he could easily fill both London's Royal Albert Hall and New York's Carnegie Hall. In 1928 he was added to the cast of Jerome Kern and Oscar Hammerstein II's *Show Boat,* beginning his indelible association with the pseudo-spiritual "Ol' Man River," originally a cry of resignation that he eventually reformed in concert as a defiant protest song. By the time the watershed musical was filmed in 1936, Robeson's fame demanded that his small but crucial role be filled out with additional songs provided by the show's composers. Robeson and his wife Eslanda appeared in the experimental film *Borderline* in 1930, and in 1933 *The Emperor Jones* was adapted as Robeson's first

Paul Robeson

talkie. In 1930 Robeson had also opened in London to rave reviews as Shakespeare's Othello, a role that, along with O'Neill's Brutus Jones and *Show Boat*'s Joe, he would often reprise in later years.

As early as 1933 Robeson had become involved with leftist organizations and causes, and his direct involvement with international politics intensified as he continued to act, sing, and make films. Traveling extensively in the late 1930s, Robeson supported the Republicans in Spain fighting Franco's Fascists, sang for dozens of working-class organizations, denounced racial discrimination in every form, and regularly defended the Soviet Union, even after the Nazi-Soviet Pact in 1939. While a number of Robeson's films from this period—including *Song of Freedom* (1936), *Jericho* (1937), *Big Fella* (1937) and *The Proud Valley* (1940)—tacitly supported his political views and growing attachment to Africa, others, such as *Sanders of the River* (1934) and *King Solomon's Mines* (1937), placed him uncomfortably in the role of the exotic native within nostalgic colonialist fantasies. After appearing as an ignorant sharecropper in *Tales of Manhattan* (1942), Robeson announced his rejection of Hollywood films. Almost all of Robeson's films, whether produced in

Hollywood or Europe, betray their uncertainty about how to depict a charismatic black man in entertainment directed at white audiences, so even Robeson's apparent strengths were usually qualified. As Richard Dyer argued, in his films "Robeson was taken to embody a set of specifically black qualities—naturalness, primitiveness, simplicity and others—that were equally valued and similarly evoked, but for different reasons, by whites and blacks."

A high point in Robeson's singing career came in late 1940, when he sang "Ballad for Americans" on the radio. Once recorded, the patriotic piece became one of his best-known numbers, and performing the "Ballad" at the Hollywood Bowl, Robeson set an attendance record by drawing a crowd of 30,000 listeners. Following World War II, Robeson regularly drew attention to the restrictions preventing African-American achievement in the United States, leading the Crusade against Lynching to Washington and meeting with President Truman in 1946. In 1949, two Robeson concerts held in Peekskill, New York, were disrupted by riots, and in the following year the State Department refused to issue Robeson a passport to travel outside of the United States, a restriction that would not be lifted until 1956, resulting in such bizarre circumstances as his singing to 40,000 listeners across the Canadian border in 1952. Declining health and persistent suspicions regarding Robeson's earlier communist and Soviet affiliations prevented him from participating fully in the prominent civil rights struggles of the 1960s, but his last decade was marked by a number of awards and affirmations that would have been unthinkable only a decade earlier, including the renaming of a number of Rutgers University buildings after the school's prominent alumnus. When Robeson died in the first month of the American bicentennial, over 5,000 people attended his funeral.

Although by any measure a remarkable individual, Robeson was fated to represent his race even when his views clashed with those of many other African Americans. Often he was a proud and willing representative of black America, but the persistent demand that he stand for others also exceeded his control, forcing Robeson to carry an impossible symbolic weight. In the long run, the dignity with which he bore the burden of America's racial heritage far outweighs his—or anyone else's—inability to fully contain the varied meanings of blackness in and beyond Robeson's lifetime.

—Corey K. Creekmur

FURTHER READING:

Brown, Lloyd L. *The Young Paul Robeson: "On My Journey Now."* Boulder, Colorado, Westview Press, 1997.

Duberman, Martin Bauml. *Paul Robeson: A Biography.* New York, Alfred A. Knopf, 1988. Reprinted New York, The Dial Press, 1995.

Dyer, Richard. *Heavenly Bodies: Film Stars and Society.* New York, Macmillan, 1986.

Foner, Philip S., editor. *Paul Robeson Speaks: Writings, Speeches, Interviews.* Secaucus, New Jersey, Citadel Press, 1978.

Robeson, Eslanda Goode. *Paul Robeson, Negro.* New York, Harper & Brothers, 1930.

Robeson, Paul. *Here I Stand.* New York, Othello Associates, 1958. Reprinted Boston, Beacon Press, 1988.

Robeson, Susan. *The Whole World in His Hands: A Pictorial Treatment of Paul Robeson.* Secaucus, New Jersey, Citadel Press, 1981.

Stewart, Jeffrey C., editor. *Paul Robeson: Artist and Citizen.* New Brunswick, New Jersey, Rutgers University Press, 1998.

Robinson, Edward G. (1893-1973)

Actor Edward G. Robinson remains inextricably linked with the establishment, in the early 1930s, of a new, popular and influential genre in the cinema: the Warner Bros. gangster movie. The films reflected an era overshadowed by the Depression, Prohibition, and the reign of notorious Chicago mobster Al Capone, expanded into hard-hitting social-conscience dramas, and progressed to film noir in the 1940s with Humphrey Bogart at the center of the Warner contribution. This significant strand in film history dates from *Little Caesar* (1931), which enhanced the reputation of Warner Bros., unleashed a torrent of similar films, established the producer credentials of Darryl F. Zanuck and Hal Wallis and the reputation of director Mervyn LeRoy—and made Edward G. Robinson into a huge star.

Robinson was a man of many contradictions. Despite his world-famous screen image as a crude gangster, in the course of his career he

Edward G. Robinson

demonstrated his artistry and versatility many times over, segueing from mobsters to blue collar workers, business men, and detectives. Off-screen he was a highly cultured man who, over the course of a lifetime, managed to amass two art collections of museum quality. He was a man of the theater who reluctantly turned to movies when the Depression hit, became an instant sensation as *Little Caesar,* and settled into a long and successful career, but claimed never to enjoy the piece-meal process of filming. Despite his stardom, he avoided the trappings of celebrity yet, like many prominent Hollywood citizens of liberal bent, he ran afoul of the House Committee on Un-American Activities—a misfortune that he met by returning triumphantly to the stage. His last years were spent as one of cinema's elder statesmen, gracing films from science fiction to melodrama with his innate dignity and now-vintage craft.

Born in Bucharest in 1893, Emanuel Goldenberg arrived with his Rumanian Jewish family in the United States at the age of nine. The child was fluent in six languages, none of them English, but he quickly picked up the language from his young classmates, and from the Shakespearean actors whose performances thrilled him from his vantage point in the top balcony. The youth turned to political speech making, which in turn led to school plays and the choice of a theatrical career. It was while training at the American Academy of Dramatic Arts that Emanuel became Edward G. Robinson. His short stature and thick features gave him no hope of ever becoming a leading man, but he was determined to make good as an actor and, after a stint in the Navy during World War I that interrupted his progress, he returned to make a career on the New York stage, appearing in some 40 plays.

Robinson appeared in his first film, *The Bright Shawl,* in 1923, and did not make another until *The Hole in the Wall* (1929). He went to Hollywood to play a gangster in *A Lady to Love* (1930), based on Sidney Howard's play *They Knew What They Wanted,* and made four more films that year, including *The Widow from Chicago* in which he played a Prohibition beer racketeer. It was his first film for Warner Bros., who went on to cast him in the title role in the film version of W.R. Burnett's gangster novel, *Little Caesar* (inspired by the career of Al Capone). In Mervyn LeRoy's fast-moving film the stocky, diminutive New York actor electrified audiences, whether sneering, shooting, or uttering one of cinema's most well-remembered curtain lines: ''Mother of mercy, is this the end of Rico?'' For years thereafter, all a comedian had to do was clench an imaginary cigar and sneer, ''Nyah,'' for the audience to recognize his impression of Robinson's iconic mobster. Well into the 1940s and 1950s, comics and animated cartoons were caricaturing Robinson's ''Rico'' face and mannerisms. (Late in his life, Robinson himself jokingly closed off a TV commercial by imitating that famous ''Nyah.'')

Throughout the 1930s, Robinson, along with Cagney and Bogart, made up a triumvirate of Warner Bros.' pre-eminent tough guys. However, not content to become stereotyped, he broke out of the mold as often as he could, going so far as to satirize himself as half of the double role in John Ford's *The Whole Town's Talking* (1935), playing a milquetoast office clerk mistaken for a public enemy. He was a fight manager in Michael Curtiz's *Kid Galahad* (1938), the chief investigating G-man in *Confessions of a Nazi Spy* (1939), and discovered the cure for syphilis in the biopic *Dr. Ehrlich's Magic Bullet* (1940), his personal favorite. During and after the war, Robinson excelled at portraying both the lighter and darker facets of the American businessman, from the insurance investigator in Billy Wilder's classic, *Double Indemnity* (1944), to the war profiteer getting his comeuppance in *All My Sons* (1948), from Arthur Miller's somber play. In two classic Fritz Lang noirs, *The Woman in the Window* (1945) and *Scarlet Street* (1946), Robinson personified to perfection the mild-mannered Everyman caught in a grim web of fate.

The McCarthy era could well have seemed to Robinson a real-life evocation of Lang's dark vision. Never openly accused of disloyalty, yet unable to find work, Robinson made no less than four humiliating appearances at HUAC before his career could resume in full. Ironically, the lack of Hollywood opportunities drove Robinson into a triumphant return to stage acting in Arthur Koestler's anti-Communist drama *Darkness at Noon* (1951). He was forced back into gangster mode in a handful of second-league films, but the year 1956 saw him in the starry line-up of DeMille's remake of *The Ten Commandments* and marked his successful Broadway starring role in Paddy Chayefsky's *Middle of the Night.* But 1956 was unfortunately also the year of Robinson's divorce, after nearly three decades of marriage, from Gladys Lloyd, the terms of which forced the actor (and amateur painter) to sell off his precious art collection.

Eventually, Edward G. Robinson amassed a second art collection equally as distinguished as his first, and enjoyed a second marriage with Jane Adler. In 1973, the 80-year-old veteran filmed his last ever scene, a death scene in *Soylent Green* (1973), in which Sol, an old man, submits himself to euthanasia while bidding farewell to images of a beautiful world. Within a few months, Robinson, the

revered artistic tough guy, was dead of cancer. In his last days, he had been informed that he would be receiving an honorary Academy Award—his first. Jane, his widow, accepted it for him.

—Preston Neal Jones

FURTHER READING:

McDowall, Roddy. *Double Exposure.* New York, Delacorte Press, 1966.

McGilligan, Patrick. *Fritz Lang: The Nature of the Beast,* New York, St. Martin's Press, 1997.

Peary, Danny, ed. *Close-Ups: The Movie Star Book.* New York, Simon & Schuster, 1978.

Robinson, Edward G., with Leonard Spigelgass. *All My Yesterdays.* New York, Hawthorn, 1973.

Shay, Don. *Conversations.* Albuquerque, Kaleidoscope Press, 1969.

Robinson, Frank (1935—)

In the Cleveland Indians' first win of the 1975 season, the new manager Frank Robinson achieved the distinction of entering his own name in the lineup and hitting a home run. A standout ballplayer for over two decades, Robinson was perhaps just as well known for being major league baseball's first black manager. As the only major leaguer to have won the Most Valuable Player Award in each league (1961 and 1966), Robinson was one of those rare players to combine power, an excellent batting average, base-stealing ability, and solid defense. When he retired in 1976 with 586 home runs, only three other men had ever hit more. Although his managerial career was somewhat less successful, his style nevertheless reflected the same kind of intensity he had brought to the game as a player.

Robinson was signed by the Cincinnati Reds out of McClymond's High in Oakland in 1953. Three years later he began his major league baseball career as an unknown 20-year-old outfielder, but by season's end he had established himself as a star, tying the rookie record of 38 home runs. In 1947 another Robinson—Jackie—had paved the way for the first generation of black ballplayers that included Roy Campanella and Larry Doby. Thus, when Frank Robinson began his professional baseball career (the same year Jackie played his final season), black men had been playing major league baseball for less than a decade. Spanning the years 1956 to 1976, his career paralleled that of a remarkable second generation of black players who broke a number of ''unbreakable'' records, including those set by Willie Mays (1951-73), Hank Aaron (1954-76), Ernie Banks (1953-71), and Bob Gibson (1959-75).

In his ten years in Cincinnati, Robinson was an annual All-Star who struck fear into the hearts of opposing pitchers with his bat and played the game aggressively in the field and on the basepaths. In 1961 he led the Reds to their first pennant in 21 years, while winning the National League MVP award with a .323 batting average and 37 home runs. His follow-up season was equally spectacular, as Robinson achieved new career highs in runs (134), hits (208), doubles (51), home runs (39), runs batted in (136), and batting average (.342). By 1965, however, the Reds' front office judged Robinson to be an ''old

Frank Robinson

San Francisco Giants from 1981-1984, but failed to lead his team to a playoff berth. Perhaps his most painful year as a manager was 1988, when he was hired by the Baltimore Orioles after the team had lost its first six games. Unfortunately for Robinson and for Orioles' fans, the team continued its losing streak, setting the league record with 23 losses in a row on their way to a last-place finish. This was followed by a considerably more successful season, in which the Orioles finished only two games behind the division winners, resulting in the American League Manager of the Year award for Robinson in 1989.

Robinson continued to manage the Orioles until 1991, but like many former stars who have tried their hand at managing, with a record of 680 wins against 751 losses, he never achieved anything like the success he enjoyed as a player. During his years as a major league manager and front office employee, Robinson was outspoken about racial issues in baseball, calling attention to the underrepresentation of blacks in baseball's management positions. In 1982, Robinson was elected to the Baseball Hall of Fame on the first ballot.

—Kevin O'Connor

FURTHER READING:

Robinson, Frank. *Extra Innings.* New York, McGraw-Hill, 1988.

————. *My Life in Baseball.* Garden City, New York, Doubleday, 1975.

Robinson, Frank, and Dave Anderson. *Frank: The First Year.* New York, Holt, Rinehart & Winston, 1976.

Thorn, Jim, and Pete Palmer, editors. *Total Baseball.* New York, Warner, 1989.

Robinson, Jackie (1919-1972)

When Jackie Robinson broke Major League Baseball's color barrier in 1947, he was both hailed as a hero and vilified as a traitor. So much attention was paid to the color of his skin that it took the public a little while to realize the scope of his talents. When they did, it only increased the animosity of the men who were determined to keep America's national pastime an all-white bastion. But with his quiet dignity and brilliant athleticism, Robinson tore down the walls of bigotry, forever changing the course of American sports.

Although nineteenth-century baseball had fielded all-black teams and even featured a few black players on white teams, twentieth-century major league baseball had steadfastly been a white-only sport. Black players, however, found an outlet for the sport in various incarnations of the Negro Leagues throughout the first half of the twentieth century. These leagues were widely acclaimed among management, players, and fans of major league baseball both for the depth and scope of their talent as well as for the unique style of quick, tough, and athletic baseball that was played. Stars of the Negro Leagues such as catcher and slugger Josh Gibson, center fielder and brilliant base runner Cool Papa Bell, and the extraordinary pitcher Satchel Paige were known to be as good or better than their white contemporaries such as Babe Ruth and Lou Gehrig. But the only time they could play against these white players was in rare exhibition games.

Although integration was often discussed by fans, owners, and players alike, there was no real thought that it might happen until after the United States entered World War II in 1941. Major League Baseball's ranks were quickly decimated as players joined the armed

thirty'' and after the season traded him to the Baltimore Orioles. This trade proved to be a boon for the Orioles (and a bust for the Reds), as Robinson led the Orioles to their first world championship in 1966. That year Robinson won baseball's triple crown by leading the American League in home runs (49), runs batted in (122) and batting average (.316), while picking up his second MVP award.

The Orioles went on to win another three American League pennants (1969-1971) and a second World Series title (1971) during Robinson's six seasons in Baltimore. Although the team's biggest strength was pitching, he shared the bulk of the offensive load with third baseman Brooks Robinson and first baseman Boog Powell. Back in the National League with the Los Angeles Dodgers in 1972, Robinson appeared to be slowing down. However, when he was traded to the California Angels, his career was extended by the American League's adoption of the designated hitter rule in 1973, which allowed older players like Robinson to hit while not having to play the field.

As his playing career wound down with the Cleveland Indians in the mid-1970s, Robinson was hired as the team's manager, becoming the first black manager to be hired in major league baseball. Midway through the 1977 season, a year after hanging up his spikes as an active player, Robinson became the first black major league manager to be fired as well. He experienced modest success at the helm of the

Jackie Robinson sliding past the tag of Yogi Berra.

services. With black and white soldiers serving together in the newly integrated armed forces, it was inevitable that the prospect of integrating baseball would become a subject of heated discussion. But baseball's commissioner, Judge Kennesaw Mountain Landis, was adamant on the subject of integration: as long as he remained commissioner, Major League Baseball would remain all white. Nonetheless, as the war drew to a close and baseball's ranks remained depleted by the war, the subject continued to surface, and the stars of the Negro Leagues dared to hope that one day they would play in the majors.

In 1945, Commissioner Landis' death brought a new commissioner, Albert Benjamin ''Happy'' Chandler, whose views on integration were diametrically opposed to those of his predecessor. Chandler said, ''I'm for the Four Freedoms. If a black boy can make it in Okinawa and Guadalcanal, hell, he can make it in baseball.'' But a secret vote held among club owners revealed that all but one opposed integration. That one was Branch Rickey of the Brooklyn Dodgers.

A God-fearing, teetotaling Christian and a staunch Republican, Rickey had revolutionized major league baseball when he created the first farm system for the St. Louis Cardinals. Now president, part-owner, and general manager of the Dodgers, Rickey firmly believed that integration would not only be good for both the country and for baseball, but that it would mean big business as well. All he needed

was the right man for the job. That man, he ultimately decided, was Robinson.

Jack Roosevelt Robinson was born on January 31, 1919 in Cairo, Georgia. When his father abandoned the family, Jackie's strongwilled mother, Mallie, moved her five children west to the predominately-white town of Pasadena, California, where her half-brother was living. Although poor, Mallie Robinson found a way to provide her children with a good home and a solid education. She quickly realized that two of her sons were precocious young athletes. Mack excelled in track and field and would eventually earn a spot on the 1936 Olympic team, placing second to Jesse Owens in Berlin in the 200-meter dash. Her youngest son, Jackie, preferred team sports along with the jumping events in track and field. In high school he played baseball, basketball, tennis, and football. Following high school, he enrolled at Pasadena Junior College, where he devoted most of his energy to football, at which he excelled. After two years, he was heavily recruited by many of the West Coast universities. Jackie chose the University of California, Los Angeles, where he would become the first player to letter in four sports—football, basketball, track, and baseball.

In 1941, the United States entered the war and so did Jackie Robinson. But although the armed forces were now integrated, black servicemen faced extreme racial discrimination. Despite being a nationally recognized athlete, Robinson was no exception. Although he was eventually admitted to Officer Candidate School, he continued to be hounded by racism, eventually being subjected to court-martial proceedings based on trumped-up charges. Although he was acquitted in under ten minutes, Second Lieutenant Jackie Robinson resigned from the army in 1944 and took a job playing baseball in the Negro Leagues.

After a year of hitting .387 with the Monarchs, in 1945 Robinson was invited to meet Branch Rickey. In their now-legendary exchange, Rickey told Robinson that he not only needed a great black player to integrate major league baseball, he also needed a great man—someone who would be able to stand up to the abuse he was sure to receive and have the guts not to fight back. After a few minutes of consideration, Robinson accepted Rickey's offer.

On October 23, 1945, Rickey announced that the Montreal Royals, Brooklyn's AAA farm team, had signed Robinson to a contract. Robinson spent the next season in Montreal, playing superb baseball, undergoing daily taunts and abuse from fans and players alike, and ultimately leading the Royals to victory in the minor league World Series.

In 1947, Robinson was called up to the Brooklyn Dodgers, despite the opposition of some of the Southern players on the team, who initially refused to have an African-American teammate. But Rickey and Robinson were ready to make history and, on April 15, 1947, 26,623 fans—over half of whom were African American—turned up to watch Robinson play. Although his first game would prove anti-climactic, the crowd was electrified, as crowds would be all season everywhere the Dodgers played. Robinson endured verbal abuse from fans and players alike, deliberate spikings from opposing teams, and even death threats aimed at his wife, Rachel, and their young son. But Robinson kept his promise to Rickey and never reacted. In the meantime, he brought a brilliant new style of baseball to the major leagues.

As Ken Burns writes, ''It was Robinson's style as much as his statistics or his color that made him a star; the fast, scrambling style of play Negro Leaguers called 'tricky baseball' has largely been absent from the big leagues since Ty Cobb's day. Robinson brought it back, bedeviling pitchers by dancing off base, even stealing home (something he would manage to accomplish 19 times before he was through).'' In just his first year in the majors, Robinson would be voted Rookie of the Year, hitting 12 home runs, stealing 29 bases, and boasting a .297 average. He would also lead the Dodgers to a National League pennant.

With Robinson's success in the majors, the American League soon had their first African-American player when the Cleveland Indians signed Larry Doby and then perhaps the greatest Negro League star of them all, Satchel Paige. More and more great African-American players became baseball stars in the ensuing years, from the Giants' Willie Mays to the Cardinals' Curt Flood to the Braves' Hank Aaron. But it was Robinson who continued to symbolize the integration of America's National Pastime. He was, however, never content to be a mere figurehead. Rather, he became a team leader and a National League Most Valuable Player who, through his brilliant play, helped transform the once hapless Dodgers into a team of perennial contenders.

In 1955, the Dodgers won their eighth pennant. Seven times before they had entered the World Series as National League champions, and seven times they had lost. Although he was 35 years old, Robinson was still a terror on the base paths. His intimidating base running would help lead the Dodgers to their first World Series

championship. A year later, after ten years in the major leagues, Robinson retired.

For the next 17 years, until his death in 1972, Robinson lived an extraordinary yet difficult life. Nominated to the Baseball Hall of Fame in 1962, his legend as a baseball star continued to grow, even as he used his fame to bring the public's attention to the African-American struggle to end racial discrimination, becoming a staunch and outspoken supporter of the civil rights movement. Toward the end of his life, he struggled with illness and suffered the death of his eldest son, before passing at age 53. Eulogized at the time of his death by athletes, politicians, and presidents, Robinson was hailed as a hero—a courageous man, an outstanding athlete, a trailblazer for humanity. He has not been forgotten. In 1997, Major League Baseball honored Robinson by retiring his number—42—forever. More than 25 years after his death, the legacy of Jackie Robinson continues to grow, rendering him one of the true icons of the twentieth century.

—Victoria Price

FURTHER READING:

Kahn, Roger. *The Boys of Summer.* New York, Harper Perennial, 1971.

Rampersand, Arnold. *Jackie Robinson: A Biography.* New York, Alfred A. Knopf, 1997.

Ward, Geoffrey, and Ken Burns. *Baseball: An Illustrated History.* New York, Alfred A. Knopf, 1994.

Robinson, Smokey (1940—)

William "Smokey" Robinson did more to define the Motown sound than anyone except founder Berry Gordy. Involved in all facets of the operation—songwriter, producer, vice president, member of the Quality Control board that approved or rejected every candidate for single release—Robinson somehow found time for a successful singing career, first as leader of the Miracles and then as a solo artist. Along the way, he set a standard for clever wordplay and smooth crooning that has rarely been equaled.

Robinson was born in Detroit, Michigan, on February 19, 1940. He put together his first vocal group, the Matadors, at the age of 14. They were a smooth doo-wop group in the tradition of the Five Satins or the Platters. In 1957, the Matadors became the Miracles, when original member Emerson Rodgers went into the army and was replaced by his sister Claudette, who would later become Mrs. Smokey Robinson and retire from the group. From the start, Robinson had a hand in writing the group's material, as well as handling most of the leads with his pure, expressive tenor. He met Berry Gordy in 1957, and together they wrote the Miracles' first local hit, "Got a Job," an answer to the Coasters' "Get a Job." When Gordy started his own Motown label with his modest songwriting royalties and a loan from his parents, the Miracles were one of the first acts he signed, and Motown's 1960 breakthrough hit was a Miracles tune written by Robinson—"Shop Around." Robinson soon branched out into songwriting and production for other Motown artists. He wrote and produced nearly every hit single for the label's first bona fide star, Mary Wells, including her #1 hit "My Guy." More than his early Miracles numbers, which were often simplistic, this song showed Robinson's genius at creating intelligent, moving music within the

Smokey Robinson

restrictions of the pop single format. He also wrote the first charting Supremes single, "Breathtaking Guy," though their incredible run of success came later with the Holland-Dozier-Holland writing/production team.

From 1963 to 1965, Motown grew at an unprecedented rate, and Robinson grew along with it. His hits with the Miracles included "Mickey's Monkey," "The Tracks of My Tears," "Going to a Go-Go," and "Ooh Baby Baby." He was also chief songwriter for the Temptations, giving them "The Way You Do the Things You Do," "My Girl," and "Get Ready." Robinson was demanding in the studio and often recorded dozens of takes of a track before he was satisfied, but his perfectionism resulted in many of the best-crafted, most memorable recordings of the 1960s. His catchy melodies, painstaking arrangements, and cliché-free love song lyrics influenced such 1960s giants as the Beatles, who covered his "You've Really Got a Hold on Me," and Bob Dylan, who once called Robinson "America's greatest living poet."

Robinson scored more hits in the late 1960s—"I Second That Emotion," "Baby Baby Don't Cry," and "The Tears of a Clown" (his first #1 as a performer)—but musical tastes were changing. The Temptations left Robinson behind, reaching new commercial heights with the psychedelic funk of producer Norman Whitfield. Holland-Dozier-Holland had left Motown, and flagship acts the Supremes and

Four Tops were struggling. The tuneful precision, exemplified by Motown at its peak, had lost popularity to the rawer sounds of hard rock being incorporated by James Brown and Aretha Franklin. After a number of lackluster albums, Robinson left the Miracles, but he was unable to resist the lure of recording, and regained chart success with the 1975 solo album *A Quiet Storm,* which adopted the long song formats and thematic coherency of his former protégés Marvin Gaye and Stevie Wonder. Though he scored a number of hits in his second singing career, including "Cruisin'," "Being with You," and "Just to See Her," Robinson had nothing like his former influence over the pop scene. His key contribution came with the rapid maturity of the pop song in the early and mid-1960s.

—David B. Wilson

FURTHER READING:

Robinson, William "Smokey", and David Ritz. *Smokey: Inside My Life.* 1990.

Robinson, Sugar Ray (1921-1989)

Sugar Ray Robinson's abilities and accomplishments made him the idol not only of a generation of boxing fans, but of a generation of boxers as well. Muhammad Ali idolized Sugar Ray Robinson. During the decades of the 1940s and 1950s, Robinson dominated boxing like no one else, sometimes on the front pages of the newspapers, and always in the ring. Born Walker Smith, the man later nicknamed "Sugar" for his sweet-as-sugar style of fighting, originally borrowed the identity of a friend named Ray Robinson in order to enter an amateur boxing tournament for which he was under the required age. Known in the ring for his raw athletic ability, refined boxing skill, and devastating punching power; Sugar Ray Robinson was identifiable outside the ring by his handsome features and flashy pink Cadillac, both of which he sported all over New York City, and especially Harlem. In an era when most fighters did what they were told when they were told, Robinson remained independent, refusing to do business with organized crime, and negotiating many of the contracts for his own fights by himself. Robinson's reputation as a tough negotiator is legendary and the fact that he in effect managed his own career is part of his legacy as an American original.

Robinson began fighting professionally in 1940 and retired for the final time in 1965. Along the way he defeated a list of champions and near-champions that reads like a roll-call of the boxing Hall of Fame. At his best, as a welterweight (147 pounds), he was nearly invincible. As an older middleweight (160 pounds), he became a five-time champion. Nearly all the fighters who fought him and nearly all the fans who watched him fight insist that Robinson was the best ever. The great Jake LaMotta (of *Raging Bull* fame) managed one single victory against Robinson in six fights, and LaMotta outweighed him in many of their fights by up to 15 pounds. Because the only fighters able to compete with Robinson were fighters larger than him, writers began referring to Robinson as "pound for pound" the best fighter in the world. And indeed, by the time he had completed his career, he had come to be known as the greatest fighter, pound for pound, in the history of boxing. He outboxed all the boxers and out-slugged all the sluggers. "Robinson could knock you out with either hand, while he was going backwards!" was the mantra of those who watched his career unfold.

Sugar Ray Robinson pummeling Carmen Basillo.

The title "pound for pound" is not the only expression developed for the express purpose of describing the career of Sugar Ray Robinson. The term "entourage," widely used in the sporting world of the 1990s, was rather new to the boxing world when it was first used to describe the gang of hangers-on that surrounded Robinson. During the height of his career, after winning the middleweight title against LaMotta in 1951, Robinson and his entourage toured Europe for a year, living the good life. Along the way, however, Robinson lost the title to an Englishman named Randy Turpin. Though Robinson got serious for the rematch and won back the title three months later, it was becoming clear that interests other than boxing were beginning to occupy the time of the greatest fighter the world had ever seen. Sure enough, Sugar Ray Robinson retired in 1952, to become a nightclub entertainer, doing song and dance acts, and not doing them very well. By 1955 he was back in the ring, winning and losing the title three more times before finally hanging his gloves up for good at the age of 45—ancient for a boxer. Sugar Ray Robinson occupies a niche similar to that of Babe Ruth or Michael Jordan, if not in popular culture, then at least in the history of sports. All three were thoroughly dominant during their sport's golden age, and all three represent the standard by which greatness in their sport is measured.

—Max Kellerman

FURTHER READING:

Anderson, Dave. *Sugar Ray.* London, Putnam, 1970.

Schoor, Gene. *Sugar Ray Robinson.* New York, Greenberg, 1951.

Rock and Roll

In the beginning, rock and roll music was a provocation, an affront to parents and proper citizens. As rock critic Jim Miller put it, "It was the music you loved to have them [parents] hate." The name itself was sexual, deriving from black slang for copulation. Dominated by a heavy back-beat and amplified guitars, the music was crude, raucous, easily accessible, and within a few years of its inception, tailored and marketed specifically to the young, now a consumer block of singular importance. And rock was inherently democratic. Any kid could muster up enough money for a guitar, and, gathering together three or four like-minded souls, start a band—many of the best groups were started in precisely this manner. But if the music itself was simple, its origins were not. In fact, rock and roll was the culmination of more than a century of musical cross-pollination between white and black, master and slave; a music born of miscegenation. It was in essence a post-modern medium, one of the first true products of the consumer society. With a whole array of gestures, attitudes, styles, inflections, and narratives, it was endlessly receptive to outside influences and was thus endlessly adaptable—a ground to receive all the narratives of youthful rebellion. Hence, it was far more contingent on history than other musical forms.

When parents first heard rock music in the 1950s, they heard only cacophony. They were unaware of the rich tradition behind rock and roll, that it was playing out a cultural evolution begun in slavery, a blending of musical and cultural forms—African and European, religious and secular—a syncretistic blending of two traditions of music. Prior to the Civil War, white minstrels began to copy the styles of the plantation orchestras, becoming the rage of Europe and America. These slave orchestras had learned a smattering of Europe-an dance tunes, which they combined with traditional African forms played on European instruments (not too dissimilar from the lutes and fiddles used by African *griots*—storytellers—of the Savannah), adapt-ing their traditional music in ways both overt and clandestine, and thereby continuing a cultural heritage that had been in effect outlawed by the slaves' owners. By the time of rock's inception, this musical cross-fertilization had already occurred several times over, creating jazz, blues, gospel, western swing, and rhythm and blues.

These new musical forms—western swing, rhythm and blues, jump blues—proliferated in the years following World War II, the result of migrations out of the rural South and Southwest, as well as greater dissemination through radio and records. Many country musicians introduced blues tunes into their repertoire, while Delta blues musicians adapted to urban nightclubs with electric guitars and small combo arrangements. In the Southwest, small combos and jazz orchestras were combining blues vocals and arrangements with raucous saxophones and a backbeat-heavy rhythm section that spread from its Texas-Oklahoma roots west to Los Angeles and San Francis-co. The birth of rock, however, centers around Memphis and a few farsighted individuals. Sam Phillips moved to Memphis in 1945, lured by the black music that had been his lifelong passion. He set up Sun Studios, recording Beale Street blues musicians, moonlighting and engineering demos to make ends meet. In 1951 he recorded "Rocket 88" by Ike Turner. It became a number-one rhythm and blues hit and is considered by many to be the first rock and roll song. Phillips himself was not concerned with race, but he knew intuitively that all the music he recorded would remain "race" music until a white man recorded it. He boasted to friends that if he could find a white singer who sang like a black man, he would make them both rich.

Memphis was home to a particularly energetic urban blues movement and a magnet for poor blacks and whites seeking to escape the grinding poverty of the countryside. The Presley family was characteristic of this pattern, moving there from rural Mississippi after World War II. They lived in the federal housing (the best housing they had ever had), and the illiterate Vernon Presley got a job driving a truck. Their son majored in shop at Hume High School, where he was regularly beaten for his long hair and effeminate appearance, but despite these eccentricities, it was anticipated that he would follow in his father's marginal footsteps, working some menial job and perhaps playing music on the side.

Elvis Presley's genius lay in his capacity to absorb different influences. He watched *Rebel without a Cause* a dozen times, cultivating a James Dean sneer and memorizing whole pages of dialogue, and visited the late-night gospel revivals, absorbing the religious frenzy. He listened to the radio, to the black gospel stations and groundbreaking DJ Dewey Phillips on WHBQ. At a time when

Memphis itself was thoroughly segregated, Phillips was one of the first DJs in the country with an integrated set-list, playing blues and country alongside each other, and his influence on Elvis was evident by the songs on the singers first legendary Sun single—"I'm All Right, Mama," a blues by well-known Delta transplant Arthur "Big Boy" Crudup, and bluegrasser Bill Monroe's country hit "Blue Moon of Kentucky." The bluesy "I'm All Right, Mama" was countrified, featuring a country-style guitar solo, while Monroe's classic was delivered with a rollicking back beat and a vocal delivery unlike any country singer; Presley sang with the fervor of the gospel musicians he loved to watch. This single 45, the culmination of two hundred years of musical cross-pollination, changed the music forev-er, and because Presley was white (an early radio interviewer made a point of asking what high school Elvis went to simply to prove that this was so), the entire nature of the music industry was stood on its head.

The music had arrived in the night, as it were. Like Dewey Phillips before him, DJ Alan Freed began mixing black and white artists on his late night show, *The Moondog Show,* after a Cleveland record store owner mentioned the droves of white teenagers buying black music at his store. Freed was soon promoting live rock events, drawing crowds well in excess of capacity, and alarming Cleveland's powers-that-be with integrated audiences and performers at a time when the city was largely segregated. "This unprecedented conver-gence of black and white," wrote cultural theorist Dick Hebdige, "so aggressively, so unashamedly proclaimed, attracted the inevitable controversy which centered on the predictable themes of race, sex, rebellion, etc., and which rapidly developed into a moral panic." Freed became a champion of scandal, an unashamed proponent for the young, and one of rock and roll's first martyrs, suffering legal harassment throughout his career and later an indictment in the Payola Scandal (he died sick and penniless in Palm Springs), but he was a crucial figure in its dissemination, especially when his 1954 move to WINS in New York blanketed the East Coast with rock and roll music.

Having seen the commercial potential of rock and roll, the large record companies were eager to profit from the craze but were not altogether enthusiastic about the music itself. Rock and roll was not respectable, nor proper; it was redolent of the kind of culture mainstream America had tried to keep at arm's length for years. Its growing popularity fed into middle-class anxiety that their children were being inextricably corrupted; a study on juvenile delinquency by a Dr. Walter B. Miller asserted among other things that the parental anxiety was not attributable to any increase in delinquency as much as to the adoption by middle-class youth of conduct formerly reserved to the working class; that is, the adoption of a whole array of slangs, styles, and attitudes—proletariat chic—that comprised rock and roll in its essence. Needless to say, the corporate record companies were uncomfortable with Southern and black musicians alike. They were suspicious of rock, could not fathom it, and, as history will attest, did their utmost to tone it down whenever possible. Rock's original journeymen were replaced by sanitized teen idols—Bobby Rydell, Fabian, Frankie Avalon—scrubbed and polished little gems, careful-ly groomed for their role as sex symbols minus the sex. "It [the music] tended to become bowdlerized, drained of surplus eroticism, and any hint of anger or recrimination blown along the 'hot' lines was delicately refined into inoffensive nightclub sound," wrote Hebdige of jazz's mutation into swing. The same could be said of rock and roll in the late fifties. There was pressure to cleanse the music of unwholesome (black or the more obvious poor Southern musician) influences. Jerry Lee Lewis fell victim to this cultural sanitation, convicted by public opinion of incorrigible perversity after he married his teenage second cousin. His music was as heavily influenced by white Pentecostal ecstasy as by black gospel, but Lewis's very personal battle with sin made him an obvious target for the legions of decency. Chuck Berry was dispatched first through violation of the Mann Act, and then by internecine squabbles with the IRS that netted him several jail terms, but it was the infamous Payola Scandal (payola being a term for the bribery to which many small record companies resorted in order to get airplay) that broke the market power of small, independent labels and cleansed the airwaves for the sanitized dreck of the teen idols.

As it was, most of the original rock-and-rollers fell victim to a premature anachronism. Of all the pioneer musicians who carved rock and roll out of the musical wilderness, only Johnny Cash and Elvis survived the early 1960s as anything more than an oldies-but-goodies attraction. A list of these performers reads like a litany of bad luck and willful destruction: Buddy Holly, Ritchie Valens, and the Big Bopper dead in a plane crash, February 3, 1959; Chuck Berry and Jerry Lee Lewis, who found out too late that fame could not insulate them from the law; the flamboyant Little Richard, who traded in rock and roll for the Bible; Carl Perkins, destroyed by alcohol and drugs; rockabilly legend Eddie Cochran, killed in an automobile accident in England just after rock's first decade came to a close. Pioneering always exacts a heavy price on body and soul, and it would appear that bringing rock and roll into fruition turned out to be one of the more lethal endeavors in the creative history of the modern era.

While the pioneering musicians' music and influence was being subsumed in the United States by teen idols, in Great Britain rock and roll was undergoing a parallel evolution that started where stateside rock left off. Vintage rock, blues, rhythm and blues, and country were originally brought over by American servicemen following World War II. For the British youth, it was a revelation, a welcome change from the threadbare music hall tradition of British jazz. The ensuing generation of British rock stars, from ardent blues revivalists to their pop-inflected cousins, all credit the importation of American music as being central to their musical evolution. The British heard rock and roll through a cultural scrim, a sensibility expertly attuned to picking up the subtleties of class differences. With its introduction, the music was formed amid a complex, invisible relationship between its roots in the working-class American South and the chronic dissatisfaction of the British working class, curtailed by the accident of birth from anything more meaningful than menial labor. The British absorbed blues and rock like holy writ, bringing to the music an insouciance born of desperation that had withered in American pop. The British groups that would emerge as vanguards of the new style—the Beatles, the Animals, the Rolling Stones, the Yardbirds, Them, the Dave Clark Five, not to mention a whole host of lesser names—introduced an enthusiasm for American forms that seemed fresh and vital. Incidentally, it caused near riots, panic in the streets, and all sorts of other commotion when it returned to American shores, capturing a new generation grown quite bored by Frankie Avalon, Annette Funicello, Connie Francis, and company.

The expropriation of rock by British artists had a profound effect on rock music and rock fashion, as if, seen through the alien lens of another culture, rock music was revealed as at once more complex and more immediate to American musicians. Many of the British musicians—John Lennon, Pete Townshend, Keith Richards, to name a few—were the products of the English art school system and took influences from the world of art, especially the pop artists and their preoccupation with the language of advertising and their enthusiasm

for obliterating the traditional demarcation between high and low art. In fact, Townshend borrowed the idea of auto-destruction from a lecture by artist Gustave Metzke at Townshend's art school, Ealing. As Chris Charlesworth wrote shortly before that crucial year, 1967, ''Pop music was no longer aimed directly at young fans who screamed at their idols, and neither was it looked upon by its creators as a disposable commodity, good for a quick run on the charts and little else.'' Rock strove to make statements and be considered as serious art. In the Beatles' single ''A Day in the Life'' (on *Sgt. Pepper's Lonely Hearts Club Band*), one can hear echoes of John Cage, Nam June Paik, and the whole current of high art. ''How does the musician compose,'' wrote Dave Marsh, ''when what's being heard is not the noise that the instrument and/or orchestra makes but the noise that the instrument and/or orchestra makes many times removed, on a piece of black plastic with a context of its own? This is what John Russell refers to as the 'element of exorcism' in pop, and it functions as effectively in a Who 45 as in an Oldenberg sculpture. . . . Thus were barriers—between art objects and everyday stuff, between the theory of avant-garde viewers and unaesthetic masses, between high culture and low, between respectability and trash—not simply eradicated but demolished.''

The ecstatic communion of a Fillmore West concert (very similar to the ecstatic communion of the ''holy rollers'' who so influenced Elvis, Jerry Lee Lewis, and others) was a connection to rock's past, but rock music was fundamentally at odds with main-stream culture in a different way than in the 1950s. No longer was it a matter merely of social stigma or cultural chauvinism on the part of the dominant culture. ''For performers like John Lennon, Bob Dylan, and Pete Townshend, Vegas and supper clubs, Hollywood movies and glittering television specials weren't a goal, they were a trap to avoid,'' wrote Marsh. ''Very few of the post-Beatles performers courted the kind of respectability that Col. Tom Parker or Larry Parnes would have understood.'' For generational reasons and in large part because of the Vietnam War, which many rock performers viewed as symptomatic of a larger rot, the options that had satisfied previous generations of performers were no longer open to rock musicians. But as a music, rock was more dependent on the whole armature of consumer capitalism than any previous genre, and in the ensuing decade, these contradictions became glaringly apparent.

Rock is a porous music; this is its value as a social glue and, like other essentially postmodern arts, also its weakness. It is wholly contingent on historical circumstance, not divorced from it, and with the end of the 1960s, rock would once again be in the position it had occupied in the early 1960s—a holding period until the next big thing came along. Early in the 1970s, 1960s rock had become but a vivid memory, with many of its best talents dead or in retirement: Jimi Hendrix, Janis Joplin, and Jim Morrison were dead; the Beatles had broken up. Those bands that remained intact could offer little more than a gesture of resistance (the gesture being an important figuration of the music—think of Pete Townshend's upstretched arm about to rip through his guitar strings, or Mick Jagger's effeminate stage persona, mincing and limp-wristed). Without the cohesion of the Vietnam War behind that rebellious, defiant gesture, it was employed as mere dramatic embellishment. It might be striking, but rock had become essentially hollow.

With nothing left to rebel against, rock devolved into specialized subgenres that bore only a passing resemblance to each other—heavy metal, the singer-songwriter, country rock, disco. The music was reflective of lifestyle choices as much as generational identity, and it no longer spoke to issues of class and youthful rebellion, except in the most base, degraded manner. The gentility of a Joni Mitchell listener bespoke sensitive college-educated professional; Fleetwood Mac and the Eagles, a relaxed middle-class hedonism—nonintellectual, but respectable; while the testosterone bluster of heavy metal—the music of choice for teenage boys and a certain type of blue-collar post-adolescent, hence its status as keeper of rock's rebellious flame—was critically derided. Critics might deride both disco and heavy metal, but appropriately enough, it was these two genres that transcended class distinctions in a similar manner to 1950s rock: as constituting a craze.

In the 1980s, rock, its fire stolen by the punks, appeared even more moribund. Its leading proponents were either aging or one of a variety of manufactured anonymous drones producing vapid, formulaic music not so dissimilar in content from the offerings of the teen idol years. Rock music had been assimilated, contained, and with the advent of MTV, entrenched in an "entertainment" industry to a far greater degree than ever before. Even punk, which had begun its life as a brutal caricature of consumer culture, insisting that rock must be *detourned,* as the French would say, led away from its intended signifier, was finally integrated into the mainstream fifteen years after the fact. One could see the commercial acceptance of bands such as Nirvana, Rancid, and Green Day as evidence of some final co-optation, or the stardom of Marilyn Manson as a final embrace and integration of the *other* (when all is familiar, nothing is strange) or as punk rock's final triumph. More likely, punk's popularity was proof that the gestures of youth rebellion, as they had been since James Dean, were implicitly exciting and thus easily marketed given the proper incentive, which is, if one is a record executive, to swallow one's revulsion all the way to the bank. Was rock finally a dead form, as safe and nonthreatening as swing music?

With such theorizing, it is easy to lose sight of rock's essential nature as being anti-high-art, proletarian, and egalitarian. What was true in the 1950s—that rock in its fundamentals was easy to play, hence easily accessible—remains true in the present, though some rock music is indeed as difficult and as rigorous in composition as any classical music. But there is a possibility inherent in rock, a possibility inherent in all folk forms. The music is not owned by experts or specialists, but by the people; rock celebrates the potential of four kids getting together in a garage and playing. And as a legacy of rock's roots in slave music, where the slave master's strict prohibitions necessitated concealment, rock encodes within it a hidden corrosive message, a secret, a call to arms based on symbols and repetition discernible to anyone with a mind to decipher it, broadcasting its complaint despite the manipulations of record executives. "According to one theory," writes Lester Bangs, "punk rock goes back to Ritchie Valens's 'La Bamba.' Just consider Valens's three-chord mariachi squawkup in the light of 'Louie Louie' by the Kingsmen, then consider 'Louie Louie' in the light of 'You Really Got Me' by the Kinks, then 'You Really Got Me' in the light of 'No Fun' by the Stooges, then 'No Fun' in the light of 'Blitzkrieg Bop' by the Ramones, and finally note that 'Blitzkrieg Bop' sounds a lot like 'La Bamba.' There: twenty years of rock & roll history in three chords, played more primitively each time they are recycled."

—Michael Baers

FURTHER READING:

Arnold, Gina. *Kiss This: Punk in the Present Tense.* New York, St. Martin's Press, 1997.

———. *Route 666: On the Road to Nirvana.* New York, St. Martin's Press, 1993.

Bangs, Lester. "Protopunk: The Garage Bands." *The Rolling Stone Illustrated History of Rock & Roll.* New York, Random House/ Rolling Stone Press, 1980.

———. *Psychotic Reactions and Carburetor Dung.* New York, Alfred A. Knopf, 1987.

Escott, Colin. *Sun Records: The Brief History of the Legendary Recording Label.* New York, Quick Fox, 1980.

Gillett, Charlie. *The Sound of the City: The Rise of Rock and Roll.* New York, Pantheon, 1983.

Gilmore, Mikal. *Night Beat: A Shadow History of Rock & Roll.* New York, Doubleday, 1998.

Herman, Gary. *Rock 'n' Roll Babylon.* New York, Putnam's, 1982.

Loder, Kurt. *Bat Chain Puller: Rock & Roll in the Age of Celebrity.* New York, St. Martin's Press, 1990.

Marcus, Greil. *Mystery Train: Images of Rock 'n' Roll Music.* New York, Dutton, 1975.

———. *Stranded: Rock & Roll for a Desert Island.* New York, Knopf, 1979.

Marsh, Dave. *Before I Get Old: The Story of the Who.* New York, St. Martin's Press, 1983.

Miller, Jim, editor. *The Rolling Stone Illustrated History of Rock & Roll.* New York, Random House/Rolling Stone Press, 1980.

Palmer, Robert. *Rock 'n' Roll: An Unruly History.* New York, Harmony Books, 1995.

Young, Bob, and Mickey Moody. *Language of Rock & Roll.* London, Sidgwick & Jackson, 1989.

Rock, Chris (1966—)

Comedian Chris Rock's blunt, urban honesty quickly gained him a wide following. His stand-up success led to slots on the sketch comedy shows *Saturday Night Live* (1990-1993) and *In Living Color* (1993-1994) and to roles in several movies, including *New Jack City* (1991), *CB4* (1993), and *Lethal Weapon 4* (1998). In 1997 he began his own talk show—*The Chris Rock Show*—on HBO (Home Box Office). His comedy albums include *Born Suspect* (1991) and *Roll with the New* (1997).

—Christian L. Pyle

FURTHER READING:

Rock, Chris. *Rock This!* New York, Hyperion, 1997.

Rock Climbing

Once a chic pursuit for wealthy youth and adventurous others, by the 1990s rock climbing had come to embody a path toward greater self-fulfillment for the average person. Embraced by corporations and schools, rock climbing and the rope skills associated with it became tools to improve corporate teamwork and boost self-esteem in "at risk'' school children. While an international audience could watch extremely skilled athletes scale difficult, dangerous rock faces in televised competitions, rock climbing was available to almost anyone. For the average person, the physical challenges offered by rock climbing were overshadowed by the mental strength participants could gain by learning the sport's skills even if they never stepped foot on an actual mountain top.

Essentially a subset of mountaineering, especially during the early part of the twentieth century, rock climbing involves scaling rock faces ranging in height from tens to thousands of feet and in environments ranging from Southern California seawalls to Alaskan mountain faces. Mountain climbing became a popular sport among the British gentry during the nineteenth century, with most expeditions operating under the guise of scientific study. Yet, not until the 1920s did people begin to climb rock faces simply for the sake of the climbing experience. Over the course of the twentieth century, rock climbing grew into a multifaceted sport that encompassed recreational climbing on crags and cliffs worldwide, extremely difficult mountaineering routes, competitive sport climbing with an international television audience, and afternoons at the gym.

The sport of rock climbing has numerous subsets, all defined by the type of activity in which a climber engages; a rock climber may engage in all or only one of these specific areas of the sport. The simplest form of rock climbing is known as bouldering, in which climbers work out ''problems'' in scaling or traversing boulders or small cliffs without protective ropes. Bouldering is generally considered as training for climbing larger and more committing rock faces, though some climbers, most notably John Gill, have focused solely on this often extremely difficult kind of climbing. Crag climbing consists of climbing rock faces anywhere from seventy-five (considered a half of a standard climbing rope length) to one thousand or more feet. Usually, climbing routes on crags takes no more than a single day to climb. Routes that take longer than a day become considered ''big wall'' climbs. These are climbs in which climbers often spend multiple days on a rock face or may drop to the ground at night before climbing back up fixed ropes to the day's earlier high point. During the 1980s, sport climbing, a type of crag climbing prevalent in France that involved extremely safe pre-placed rope anchors on relatively short climbs, became popular on crags worldwide. This new climbing, with a focus almost exclusively on difficult gymnastic moves to gain the top, led into the sport of competitive climbing that moved off of natural rock walls and into gyms or prefabricated outdoor walls with resin ''holds.'' In this arena, climbers were judged on speed, style, and the highest point reached on any given route (climbing routes here became defined by which resin holds a climber may or may not use.) Climbers who focused on bouldering, crag climbing, or big wall climbing tended to group together, forwarding self-images of adventurers, social outcasts, or heroes, while sport climbers were seen as athletes; sport climbing's competitive nature differed sharply from the recreational enthusiasm of weekend rock-jocks or devoted big wall mountaineers.

Recreational climbing was generally seen as an outdoor activity more akin to hiking, backpacking, or non-technical mountain climbing. Schools devoted to teaching outdoor skills appeared throughout the twentieth century. The two largest and most popular schools were Outward Bound, which started in Wales in 1941 to train young sailors to survive in a lifeboat during World War II, and the National Outdoor Leadership School, which opened in Wyoming in 1965 and focused on leadership training and wilderness skills. During the latter quarter of the century, attending these schools became a rite of passage for

certain groups of generally affluent teenagers (and occasionally their parents during a mid-life search for meaning or adventure). While rock climbing was not the singular focus of these programs, it was a central skill that students learned not only as a wilderness activity, but as a tool toward personal growth and maturity.

By the 1980s, as the popularity of the sport spread and the growth of sport climbing made climbing safer and more accessible to more people, rock climbing became not simply a recreational activity (or a competitive sport), but an avenue toward self-fulfillment. With the increasing development of indoor artificial facilities during the 1990s, a rhetoric of ''facing one's fears'' and increasing one's ''mental fitness'' appeared to make climbing popular for mental well being, rather than for recreational purposes. As an offshoot of rock climbing (mixed with specific kinds of military training), ropes courses in which teams work to get groups or individuals through various climbing oriented tasks (rope climbing, falls, beam walking, etc.) became popular in the 1980s. These courses were not training grounds for future climbing activities, but rather focused on self-improvement and teamwork for its participants. These courses were especially popular among corporations who sent groups of management personnel there to learn skills they could apply to the contemporary corporate culture, particularly the teamwork approach of Total Quality Management. Also, both ropes courses and rock climbing activities became popular as self-empowerment tools for people working with ''at risk'' poor, inner-city youths who had little experience beyond urban centers. By the end of the century, rock climbing had become not only a form of recreation or sport, but a personal empowerment tool.

—Dan Moos

FURTHER READING:

Hattingh, Garth. *The Climber's Handbook*. London, New Holland Publishers, 1998.

Jones, Chris. *Climbing in North America*. Berkeley, University of California Press, 1976.

Randall, Glen. *Vertigo Games*. Sioux City, Iowa, W.R. Publications, 1983.

Roper, Steve, and Allen Steck. *Fifty Classic Climbs of North America*. San Francisco, Sierra Club Books, 1979.

The Rockefeller Family

During the 70 years between oil magnate John D. Rockefeller, Sr.'s emergence as the richest man in the world (c. 1901) and grandson Nelson A. Rockefeller's service as the first U.S. vice president who was appointed, not elected, to that office (1974-77), the Rockefeller family stood as the very epitome of extraordinary wealth and influence, not rivaled in popular imagination until the emergence of Bill Gates in the 1990s. In at least one measure of wealth, John D., Sr. remains the wealthiest American of all time: Bill Gates may have exceeded him in terms of sheer dollars ($40 billion to Sr.'s $1 billion) and he also dominates an industry—computers. But where John D., Sr. at one time received two and a half percent of the national income, Gates has never received more than a half percent. Proof of the pervasiveness and power of the Rockefeller name came in the 1950s, when the Chock Full o' Nuts Coffee jingle that had originally run

John D. Rockefeller, Sr.

"Better coffee Rockefeller's money can't buy" was altered to "Better coffee a millionaire's money can't buy" after the family objected to the allusion. Throughout the twentieth century, several generations of Rockefellers tried to demonstrate how a robber-baron aristocracy could justify its extraordinary wealth by philanthropy and public service.

When John D., Sr. (the founding grandfather) retired from his active business life at Standard Oil in the mid-1890s, he was earning an average of $10 million per year, at a time when the average American earned less than $10 per week. One of the two originators of the modern U.S. corporation—the other was Andrew Carnegie—John D., Sr. was as aloof and secretive as he was before his ascent from utter poverty. Still, Rockefeller remained loyal to the fundamentalist Baptist pieties of his youth. He never bought a yacht, he never sought the treasures of Europe and other continents, and he never exhibited any undue passions for worldly pleasures. Despite glad tidings about his essential humility, the public could not decide what to make of him—just as in years to come, contemporaries and writers could not reach any firm conclusions about his descendants.

On the one hand, John D., Sr. used his money primarily for charitable and educational purposes: to improve health care not only in America but worldwide, to finance great institutions of higher learning such as Spelman College and the University of Chicago, to improve education in the South, and to wipe out hookworm. John D. Rockefeller, Jr. used the family's money to recreate Colonial Williamsburg and to assume quasi-government responsibilities in dealing with the scourge of "white slavery." John D., Sr.'s grandsons (the Brothers) used family funds to help pay for the Museum of Modern

Art and Lincoln Center for the Performing Arts, which not only provided the masses with access to the arts, but raised American standing in the world community. All the Rockefellers, through grants by their foundations, helped catalyze significant advances in knowledge, particularly in medicine and in the sciences.

Its financial benefactions were not the only reasons why the family enjoyed wide respect. John D., Sr. and his descendants symbolized the utter determination and boundless energy that made America a superpower. John D., Sr. had achieved his wealth and position by eliminating competitors so remorselessly that he enjoyed a virtual monopoly in oil production. Americans regarded him as a genius of private enterprise who demonstrated his superiority over his rivals so commendably that he fully deserved all the rewards of his marvelous organizational abilities.

Paradoxically, John D., Sr. was also seen as the great American villain, a living, breathing dollar sign, a corrupter of railroads and legislators, the murderer of free enterprise in the oil industry, someone who declared individualism dead, and the man who made the masses pay double for their kerosene and axle grease. He dealt in millions, saved in pennies, gave away dimes, and savored pettiness. Among examples cited of his miserliness was his directive to use one less drop of solder in the manufacture of each oil can. On the positive side of the ledger, he and John D., Jr. deeply impressed the public with the sincerity of their religious beliefs. John D., Sr. tithed when, as a youth, he did not have the money to buy himself a warm overcoat for cold Ohio winters. Even after he began his climb to fortune, he helped sweep Cleveland's Euclid Avenue Baptist Church. One of the monuments built by Rockefeller money in 1930, the Riverside Church in New York City, remains a contradictory symbol: it is at once a memorial to John D., Sr.'s childhood religion and a bastion of the liberal Social Gospel theology that finds more sin in unbridled capitalism than in personal peccadilloes. John D., Jr., who saw to its building and the appointment of the liberal Harry Emerson Fosdick to its pulpit, was a more sensitive man who suffered from nervous disorders and had few interests in business. His main interest was Christian benevolence. John D., Jr. also collected Renaissance art and Ming Dynasty porcelain. He explained to his father, "I have never squandered money on horses, yachts, automobiles or other foolish extravagances. . . . This hobby [of collecting], while a costly one, is quiet and unostentatious and not sensational."

Yet, even the charities of father and son and their claims of piety struck suspicious observers as nothing but covers for their insatiable need to dominate and to profit from duping the masses. The New York *Herald* commented, "The only thing Standard Oil lacks is a . . . twenty-five-thousand-dollar chaplain who would open their meetings with religious services." At the University of Chicago's first commencement, John D., Sr. said, "The good Lord gave me my money," to which grateful students responded, "John D. Rockefeller, wonderful great man is he/Gives all his spare change to the U. of C."

Few criticisms of Rockefeller's tactics were as withering as muckraker Ida Tarbell's *The History of the Standard Oil Company* (1904). Rockefeller's defenders claimed that the writer's antagonism toward the titan sprang from her background as the fiercely independent daughter of an oil producer broken by Rockefeller. Nonetheless, her analysis of Standard Oil was masterful and would thereafter serve as a model for how to dissect a giant corporation. Readers almost invariably came to believe that Rockefeller (like Carnegie) had to be assigned responsibility for the labor strife that had begun to besiege the country in the early 1900s.

Congress's reaction to such anti-Rockefeller sentiment was not only to pass antitrust legislation, but to refuse to grant the Rockefeller Foundation a federal charter in 1913. A second development, which mightily stoked fires against the family, occurred after Woodrow Wilson appointed Frank Walsh, a prominent Kansas City trial attorney, as head of the United States Commission on Industrial Relations, an agency created to explore causes of industrial violence. Walsh turned commission hearings into lectures at which he declared that the family's huge philanthropic trusts were not only a "menace to the welfare of society" but "attempts to present to the world, as handsome and admirable, an economic and industrial regime that draws its substance from the sweat and blood and tears of exploited and dispossessed humanity."

When the commission met for the first time in the fall of 1913, strikes marked by violence had become commonplace. Possibly the worst took place in Ludlow, Colorado, in April 1914, where about a thousand miners living in tents with their families struck Colorado Fuel and Iron, a Rockefeller-owned subsidiary. The company dug trenches around the tents, bought machine guns, employed a private army to guard its property, and persuaded Colorado's governor to call out National Guard units. Strikers acquired weapons, and guardsmen and workers fought a 12-hour pitched battle, the "Ludlow Massacre," during which several miners, two women, and 11 children were killed.

Walsh moved commission hearings to Denver, Colorado, and then back to Washington, where he called John D., Sr. as a witness. The magnate skillfully deflected Walsh's probing comments and questions. "Let the world wag," he advised John D., Jr., to whom he had already begun to transfer significant assets and authority over family philanthropic and business enterprises. But John D., Jr. had neither his father's studied calm nor his deep conviction of his own saintliness. He wilted under Walsh's ruthless examination, and his weak responses helped convince the public that the family was legally and morally guilty in the Ludlow incident. The manifest rise in public anger toward the family led John D., Sr. to hire a public relations counsel named Ivy Lee (recommended by John D., Jr.) and John D., Sr. began handing out dimes to passersby, a tactic said to increase his popularity. Still, bodyguards had to protect family members. The most surprising development in the aftermath of Ludlow, however, was that John D., Jr. made one of the most abrupt turnabouts of any major capitalist in American history. After first defending Colorado Fuel and Iron, he toured the Ludlow site, ate with miners in their homes, and advised that improvements would be forthcoming. Thereafter, he received an excellent press nationwide. John D., Jr.'s "transformation" distinguished him from his father, who did not relent.

There was no break with fundamentalist outlooks in the family's second generation. Like John D., Sr., John D., Jr. and his six children reserved Sundays for prayer, and the five boys and one girl were taught that careful accounts must be kept of money received and spent. Above all, as befit an imperial family, they received constant reminders that they were Rockefellers, and that their wealth and good name were sacred trusts. The Rockefeller grandsons, John III, Laurance, and David, tended to fall in line uncomplainingly with their father's and grandfather's strict rules. But Abby (Babs) kept sloppy accounts, smoked at 15, drove recklessly, was ticketed repeatedly for speeding, and necked with her future husband in full view of servants. Winthrop's experiences with liquor and women became the stuff of tabloids; he was a cattle rancher who served as Republican governor of Arkansas in the late 1960s.

In the generation of the brothers, it would be Nelson, born on the founding grandfather's birthday in 1908, who not only had the most active and direct contact with the public, but exhibited some of John D., Sr.'s most pronounced characteristics. Everything Nelson did was strategic, and, like his grandfather, he demonstrated the relentless drive of the self-made go-getter and could not be hurried in his decisions. His brother David remarked, "He spent a lot of time in seeing where he wanted to go, and then developing a strategy to get there. In other words, things did not happen by accident in his life."

Nelson was governor of New York four times and unsuccessfully sought nomination as the Republican candidate for president three times. The public had problems deciding what to make of John D., Sr. and had to be persuaded after Ludlow that John D., Jr. truly regretted what had happened. But Nelson's "anything is possible" behavior both confirmed and confused the public's perception of how the very rich behave. Nelson placed no limits on satisfying his demands for personal gratification. Whether in art, real estate, women, or building monuments to himself with public funds, he simply took whatever he wanted. And this was to be a basis for his political undoing. He was perceived as the mainstay of an Eastern Establishment of money and power, which contrasted unfavorably with "cloth coat" Republicans such as Barry Goldwater (in 1964) and Richard Nixon (in 1968 and 1972).

Succeeding generations of Rockefellers (the Cousins followed the Brothers) have not produced personalities who dominated headlines as the earlier ones, except for John D., IV ("Jay"), who went to West Virginia in 1964 as a VISTA volunteer and remained to become its governor and a U.S. senator devoted to progressive causes, and his cousin Abby Aldrich, daughter of David, who came to be seen as the "hippie" of the family for her interest in environmentalism. She formed a company in the 1970s to import a Swedish composting toilet, the Clivus Multrum, and to educate Americans about the value of recycling—showing at least that the Rockefellers still had a knack for nuancing worthy endeavors with their traditional habits of thrift and shrewd business sense.

—Milton Goldin

FURTHER READING:

Chernow, Ron. *Titan: The Life of John D. Rockefeller, Sr.* New York, Random House, 1998.

Collier, Peter, and David Horowitz. *The Rockefellers: An American Dynasty.* New York, Holt, Rinehart and Winston, 1976.

Reich, Cary. *The Life of Nelson A. Rockefeller: Worlds to Conquer, 1908-1958.* New York, Doubleday, 1996.

The Rockettes

The most renowned chorus line in the world, the Rockettes engendered the American form of precision dancing and have remained the paramount practitioners of synchronized tap-dance routines ever since. A quintessential New York tourist attraction, seen by millions of spectators since their debut at Radio City Music Hall in 1932, the Rockettes spawned multitudinous imitations and made precision kick-lines an established element of American entertainment culture—from amateur theatricals and school productions to Broadway musicals, Las Vegas extravaganzas, ice spectaculars, and

The Rockettes on stage.

half-time shows. The Rockettes are often recognized as epitomizing the "all-American girl," perhaps from a bygone era. They are beautiful, but not overtly sexy, they move in unison, but with a natural athleticism, not as automatons.

The Rockettes were the brainchild of Broadway dance director Russell Markert, who was inspired by the Tiller Girls, a precision dance troupe from England that he saw in the Ziegfeld *Follies* during the 1920s. Markert yearned to create an American counterpart of the British troupe, but with taller dancers, longer legs, and higher kicks. In 1925, for stage shows that he was producing in St. Louis, Markert assembled a 16-member precision dance team that he called the Missouri Rockets. The group enjoyed great popularity and soon began touring as the American Rockets. "Hide your daughters—here comes Markert" became a common phrase of the late 1920s as the choreographer scoured the land for suitable girls to join the ever-increasing number of dance troupes he was assembling to meet the growing demand for performances nationwide.

While rehearsing in New York for a Broadway appearance, one of Markert's troupes was observed by Samuel L. "Roxy" Rothafel, who invited them to perform in nightly shows at his Roxy Theatre for the six weeks before their Broadway opening. They were such a hit that Rothafel was reluctant to let them go, so Markert trained yet another group to continue performing at the Roxy. When it came time

for the theatre's big Easter show, Markert combined two groups into a new 32-member troupe called the "Roxyettes." Thus, when when Roxy Rothafel was asked to produce a gigantic stage spectacular for the opening of Rockefeller Center's Radio City Music Hall on December 27, 1932, he cast his Roxyettes as one of the featured attractions, along with the Flying Wallendas, and modern dancer Martha Graham, among others. The production, however, was not a popular success and, by January 1933, the Music Hall decided to abandon full-evening variety shows and adopted what became its signature format—the showing of a first-run family film, accompanied by a live stage show. The only performers retained from the opening night production were the Roxyettes. In 1934 their name was changed to the Rockettes and they became a regular institution at the famous art deco-style music hall.

In 1937 the Rockettes were invited to represent the United States in an international dance festival at the Paris Exposition and won the grand prize. In accepting the award, the director of Rockefeller Center, John D. Rockefeller, Jr., said that the Rockettes remind us that "the only way we can find success in any walk of life is in working for the group and not for personal aggrandizement."

The governing aesthetic principle of the Rockettes is uniformity. Though they range in height from five-foot four inches to five-foot nine (having gotten progressively taller over the years), the illusion that they are all the same height is achieved by placing the tallest dancers in the center of the line and sloping downward. As director of the Rockettes from their inception until his retirement in 1971, Markert was criticized for his ''whites only'' hiring policy, but defended his actions by claiming that visual harmony is the backbone of precision dancing, explaining that he didn't even allow his Rockettes to get suntanned. (In 1988, for the first time, an African American dancer did perform as a Rockette.) When auditioning his dancers Markert looked not only for women who could tap, turn, and kick with proficiency, but who could suppress their individuality to conform to the group dancing style. While many Rockettes have spoken of the ''high'' they get while performing with the troupe on the magnificent Music Hall stage, others have found the experience mechanical, demeaning, and boring for anyone with creative inclinations.

Though the Rockettes have been elaborately costumed over the years as various characters, from cowgirls, poodles, and daffodils, to West Point cadets and astronauts, their routines are choreographically predictable, consisting of a series of tap-danced military drill formations and an obligatory kick-line finale. Unlike the Tiller Girls, who kicked only waist-high, the Rockettes kick to eye-level, straight front, and on the second beat, following a tiny two-footed preparatory jump on the downbeat. The troupe's most distinctive maneuver is the contagious toppling of the annual Christmas show's wooden soldiers: they fall backwards one at a time, neatly collapsing like a row of dominoes.

By the 1970s, as the Music Hall's G-rated films and wholesome variety shows grew out of step with the youth culture of the time, many viewed the Rockettes as kitsch. When, due to sagging box-office receipts, the famous showplace was scheduled to close on April 12, 1978, the Rockettes were instrumental in spearheading the successful efforts to save their home. In order to remain open, however, the Music Hall cut back to producing only three large-scale productions a year and began renting its space to presenters of rock concerts and other entertainment attractions. By the late 1990s the annual ''Christmas Spectacular'' remained the only vestige of the Music Hall's extravagant stage shows.

The Rockettes, however, have continued to perform there, and at entertainment events worldwide. In 1983 their backstage lives were celebrated in the fictionalized ABC-TV movie *Legs*. They franchised in the 1990s, permitting cities such as Las Vegas and Branson, Missouri, to form their own Rockette companies.

Critics have opined that precision dancing, even when considered old-fashioned, continues to attract audiences because it conveys a reassuring sense of stability. In the rapidly changing techno-world of the late twentieth century, the Rockettes and their simulators remained familiar and comforting providers of popular entertainment.

—Lisa Jo Sagolla

FURTHER READING:

Jonas, Gerald. ''From Innovation to High Camp: The Line at Radio City Music Hall.'' *New York Times Magazine*. November 12, 1967, 114-121.

Leavin, Paul. ''Twenty-one Ways of Looking at the Rockettes.'' *Eddy.* No. 8, 1976, 66-79.

Love, Judith Anne. *Thirty Thousand Kicks: What's It Like to Be a Rockette?* Hicksville, New York, Exposition Press, 1980.

Rockne, Knute (1888-1931)

The legend of Knute Rockne goes beyond football. Every school with an active athletic program has its share of sports legends—stories about great athletes and coaches of the past and the games that made them famous. The University of Notre Dame in South Bend, Indiana, is no exception; the school's athletic tradition has produced many legendary figures, especially from its Fighting Irish football team, but the tale of Knute Rockne has transcended Notre Dame to become part of Americana.

Knute K. Rockne was born in Voss, Norway, on March 4, 1888. His family immigrated to the United States in 1893, settling in Chicago. Rockne entered the University of Notre Dame in 1910 and tried out for the football team—unsuccessfully. In that era, football was almost entirely a game of brute force, and Rockne was deemed neither large enough nor muscular enough. The following year, with the Irish under a different coach, Rockne made the team and played for three years, striving to make up in speed and guile what he lacked in size and strength.

Upon graduating in 1914, Rockne was immediately hired as assistant coach of Notre Dame's football team. During his four years in that position, he was credited with introducing two innovations into the game: the forward pass and the shift. In fact, Rockne probably did

Knute Rockne

not invent these tactics (and never claimed that he had), but his teams were the first to integrate these new moves into their regular game plan. The use of the forward pass greatly increased the role of strategy in the game, and the shift (lateral movement on the part of offensive players before the ball is snapped) allowed the offense to adapt to the defense's formation and made the game more exciting.

It was while he was assistant coach in 1916 that Rockne recruited a young man named George Gipp to the team. Gipp turned out to be the best all-round athlete that Rockne ever coached, and when Rockne was appointed Notre Dame's head coach in 1918, George Gipp was his star player. However, in his senior year, Gipp contracted pneumonia following a game. Despite hospitalization, his condition worsened and, tragically, Gipp died on December 13, 1920. But the story of George Gipp did not end with his death. Years later, when a surprisingly mediocre Notre Dame team was trying to salvage a winning season by defeating football powerhouse Army, Rockne gave the locker-room speech that is the centerpiece of the Rockne legend. The team knew who George Gipp had been, but Rockne told them something they didn't know: Gipp's last words to his coach. According to Rockne, the dying Gipp had told him, "I've got to go, Rock. It's all right, I'm not afraid. Some time, Rock, when the team is up against it, when things are wrong and the breaks are beating the boys, tell them to go in there with all they've got and win just one for the Gipper. I don't know where I'll be then, Rock, but I'll know about it, and I'll be happy."

This sentimental story of Gipp's last wish may well be fiction, but it worked for the Fighting Irish, who went on to defeat Army, the heavy favorites. It also became the key scene in the 1940 film about Rockne's life, *Knute Rockne, All American*. Pat O'Brien portrayed the great coach, and the young Ronald Reagan played George Gipp. The role haunted Reagan for the rest of his life, and when he left movies for a career in politics, the name was revived by journalists, who sometimes referred to Reagan in print as "the Gipper." This led to "Win one for the Gipper" being used as a campaign slogan when Reagan ran for President in 1980, and reporters used the term occasionally during his presidency and afterward.

The skill and spirit of Rockne also resides in another enduring aspect of sports mythology that has passed into popular culture, and is arguably the most famous passage in American sports journalism. After another Rockne-coached Notre Dame team defeated Army on October 18, 1924, Grantland Rice wrote in the next day's edition of the *New York Herald Tribune*: "Outlined against a blue-gray October sky, the Four Horsemen rode again. In dramatic lore they are known as Famine, Pestilence, Destruction and Death. These are only aliases. Their real names are: Stuhldreher, Miller, Crowly and Layden. They formed the crest of the South Bend cyclone before which another fighting Army team was swept over the precipice at the Polo Grounds this afternoon as 55,000 spectators peered down upon the bewildering panorama spread out on the green plain below."

Rockne's team was undefeated that season, one of five such triumphant seasons that he enjoyed during his 13 years as Notre Dame's head coach. His overall record during that time was 105 wins, 12 losses and 5 ties. Knute Rockne was killed in a plane crash on March 31, 1931.

—Justin Gustainis

FURTHER READING:

Brondfield, Jerry. *Rockne: The Coach, the Man, the Legend.* New York, Random House, 1976.

Sperber, Murray. *Shake Down the Thunder: The Creation of Notre Dame Football.* New York, Henry Holt, 1993.

Rockwell, Norman (1894-1978)

Despite his distinction as a popular painter of everyday life, Norman Rockwell has, for much of the twentieth century, represented a point of controversy concerning the definition of art and the nature of American culture itself. Although a sizable public embraced the illustrator as America's greatest painter, others have reviled his work as vacuous commercial art depicting a highly restricted spectrum of the national makeup. Rockwell's prominence and the prevailing conception of advocates and critics alike—that his task was to represent America—largely issued from his long association with the popular magazine, the *Saturday Evening Post*. Even when, in the last decades of his life, Rockwell undertook assignments challenging the conservative cultural values of the *Post*—values which were mistakenly ascribed to the illustrator as well—his apparently unselfconscious, realistic style remained out of step with contemporary artistic practices. By the end of the twentieth century, he was widely recognized as a highly successful illustrator though not as an artist, his name serving as a shorthand term for the values of small-town America that he so often depicted.

Rockwell himself enjoyed the pleasant irony that, this reputation notwithstanding, he was born—on February 3, 1894—in the paramount metropolis of New York City. Although his father's family had

Norman Rockwell

once held substantial wealth and his mother took great pride in an English aristocratic ancestry, by the time of Norman Percevel's birth the family's fortune and status had both declined. Rockwell recalled growing up in modest circumstances, and described episodes of acute embarrassment in the face of his own social indiscretions which, he thought, bespoke his lower-middle-class background. Still, his family remained respectably pious, to the extent that Norman and his younger brother Jarvis were conscripted into the church choir by their parents. This religiosity, however, did not stick, and as an adult Rockwell would decline to attend church services.

In his autobiography, Rockwell described a boyhood full of anxieties and punctuated by numerous unpleasant episodes. Amongst his friends he stood out as an awkward and pigeon-toed boy, his face dominated by large, round eyeglasses that earned him the despised nickname "Mooney." He nonetheless participated in all the games and pranks of his neighborhood playmates including, as he later recalled with contrition, incidents of bigoted name-calling. Urban encounters with indigent drunks and rancorous couples enhanced, by contrast, his cherished memories of summer trips away from the city. He would later characterize his early interest in drawing as a compensatory practice that won him admiration from his peers.

As a high school freshman, Rockwell began taking weekly leave in order to attend the Chase School of Art on a part-time basis (c. 1908), and in his sophomore year he left altogether, becoming a full-time student at the National Academy of Design at the age of 15. Finding the academy's program "stiff and scholarly," he enrolled at the Art Students League in New York in 1910. There he devoted himself to the study of the human figure and illustration under instructors George Bridgman and Thomas Fogarty.

Like his fellow students, Rockwell admired and identified with the work of prominent American illustrators such as Howard Pyle and Edward Austin Abbey, particularly their inspiring attention to historically accurate detail and compelling visual narratives. At the same time he esteemed the expressive qualities and technical virtuosity of painters from Rembrandt and Vermeer to Whistler and Picasso. Although modernist practices held little interest for Rockwell in his own art—excepting some brief experiments in the 1920s—neither he nor his peers saw much distinction between the fine arts and illustration. They did, however, disdain other, debased spheres of artistic practice. Rockwell wrote that he and his peers "signed our names in blood, swearing never to prostitute our art, never to do advertising jobs." But the nature of the field of illustration itself was in transition with the proliferation of cheap illustrated magazines (which needed advertisers who in turn needed illustrators), the increasing use of photography, and the demise of handsomely decorated books which had seen their zenith during the so-called Golden Age of Illustration. Rockwell's own practice would soon include the production of successful and highly sought after advertising illustrations.

His first inroads into a professional career included illustrating a didactic children's book called *Tell Me Why Stories*. Landing the position of contributing art director for *Boy's Life* in 1913, Rockwell soon developed a reputation as the "Boy Illustrator," referring both to his young age and his favored subjects rendered for an emerging group of youth magazines. These popular magazines, including *St. Nicholas, American Boy,* and *Youth's Companion,* were intended to entertain white, middle-class adolescents and promote the same ideals of American citizenry embodied in the Boy Scouts and the Young Men's Christian Association movements. But Rockwell sought a more distinguished venue for his art.

Working for the youth magazines, he was soon able to afford a succession of shared studios in New York City and then in New Rochelle where his family took up residence in a boarding house. Despite his steady income, Rockwell aspired to see his work on the cover of what he considered "the greatest show window in America for an illustrator," the *Saturday Evening Post.* Setting his sights on the *Post* he struggled to paint a sample image of a sophisticated society couple in the style of the Charles Dana Gibson, but soon realized that his strength lay in genre scenes, realistically rendered pictures of everyday life. He presented the *Post* editors with two finished canvases depicting scenes of American boyhood and several like sketches. All were approved, and within two months his first illustration for the *Saturday Evening Post* appeared on the cover of the issue for May 20, 1916. In his words, he "had arrived." Having broken into the field of illustration for adult magazines, Rockwell was soon submitting work to *Life, Judge, Leslie's,* and the *Country Gentleman.* By the early 1920s he would gain substantial recognition and could be selective about his assignments, working only for the most prominent magazines.

Throughout Rockwell's 47-year association with the *Post* as its most prominent cover illustrator, he continued to undertake a variety of assignments including calendars, books, and advertisements. Amongst his best known works are the annual Boy Scout calendars painted from 1924 to 1976 (he missed only two years); his illustrations for new editions of Mark Twain's *The Adventures of Tom Sawyer* (1936) and *Huckleberry Finn* (1940); and the long series of pencil-drawn advertisements for Massachusetts Mutual Life Insurance Company done from 1950 to 1963. In 1943, the *Post* published his *Four Freedoms*—illustrating the essential principles declared by President Franklin D. Roosevelt—which soon became successful war bond posters. Each of these has in common the optimism and moral salubrity Rockwell depicted throughout his seven-decade career.

Still, it was his long-standing affiliation with the *Saturday Evening Post* that marked Rockwell's cultural reception. Between the World Wars and under editor George Horace Lorimer, the *Post* advanced illustration as a particularly American art. Illustration was characterized there as speaking a common-sense visual language in opposition to modern art as a rarified and intellectualized foreign import. In short, illustration was wrapped in the magazine's conservative and isolationist positions on culture and politics. This legacy, combined with the *Post*'s pronounced decline and unsteady revival as a discredited voice of nostalgia during the 1960s and 1970s, left Rockwell himself as a representative of obsolescence.

In 1963, Rockwell left the *Post* and soon expanded his repertoire of themes to encompass explicitly controversial social issues. Until this time he had applied his high-detail realism to folksy scenes—usually witty, sometimes poignant—of what appeared to be everyday life in America. As critics would note, this image of the nation's people was generally restricted to white, middle-class, and heterosexual families. Rockwell later explained, in part, that longtime *Post* editor Lorimer had instructed him "never to show colored people except as servants." And so they appeared throughout the *Post* and Rockwell's oeuvre. By contrast, Rockwell's work for *Look* magazine in the mid-1960s explored black-white race relations and the social turmoil which followed the civil rights movement and subsequent legislation. Best known of these is his 1964 image of Ruby Bridges escorted by deputies from the United States Marshall's office as she integrated a white elementary school in New Orleans in 1960 (*Look,* January 14). Thus, it was only in the last decade and a half of his life that Rockwell's own liberal views might have become readily apparent to a broad public.

This late turn towards inclusive subject matter came packaged in Rockwell's brilliant, if familiar, realist style which itself seemed anti-progressive to many art-scene observers. For them, Rockwell's illustrations, though technically accomplished, lacked artistic freedom, intellectual engagement, and creative insight. Still, he remained popular with a substantial portion of the American public. This disparity was played out when art critics dismissed a popular 1968 exhibition of his canvases at a New York City gallery, and again in 1972 on the occasion of a Rockwell retrospective held at the Brooklyn Museum. Any reconsideration of Rockwell's aesthetic and historical significance proposed by these exhibitions was further stymied after 1969 by the apparent crass commercialism of an agreement permitting the Franklin Mint to produce versions of his well-known earlier images as porcelain figurines and silver coins.

Notwithstanding the failure of earlier attempts to present a convincing reassessment of Rockwell in the 1980s and 1990s, he was reasserted as a significant cultural figure. Popular interest in his work hardly abated as witnessed by the proliferation of Rockwell picture books. In the early 1980s a major fund-raising campaign to build a new home for the Norman Rockwell Museum in Stockbridge, Massachusetts, drew substantial support from prominent political figures, including then President Ronald Reagan and Senator Edward Kennedy, indicating that with regard to Rockwell's reception, so-called traditional values might be severed from conservative politics. At the end of the twentieth century, Rockwell remained an iconic figure, his name serving as short-hand for idyllic values promoting family and community. These deeply nostalgic associations recall an America of the past, one imagined as modern, prosperous, homogeneous, and free of the social ills that plagued the late twentieth century.

Rockwell died November 8, 1978 in Stockbridge. His first marriage, which had followed the success of his earliest *Post* cover, ended in divorce in 1930. In that same year he met and married Mary Barstow with whom he was to raise three sons, Jarvis, Thomas, and Peter. After Mary's death he was remarried once more, to Mary (Molly) Punderson. The most comprehensive collection of his works is found at the Norman Rockwell Museum at Stockbridge, to which he left many paintings and papers upon his death.

—Eric J. Segal

FURTHER READING:

Guptill, Arthur L. *Norman Rockwell, Illustrator.* 3rd edition. New York, Watson-Guptil, 1970.

Marling, Karal Ann. *Norman Rockwell.* New York, Abrams, 1997.

Rockwell, Norman. *My Adventures as an Illustrator, by Norman Rockwell, as told to Thomas Rockwell.* Garden City, New York, Doubleday & Company, 1960.

Segal, Eric. "Norman Rockwell and the Fashioning of American Masculinity." *Art Bulletin.* Vol. LXXVII, No. 4, December 1996, 633-646.

Rocky

Rocky (1976) may not be the best sports film ever made, but for many it is the best loved. As much love story as boxing movie, this

Sylvester Stallone and Talia Shire in a scene from the film *Rocky*.

feel-good box-office smash launched Sylvester Stallone's career into the stratosphere, inspired countless imitations (some of which were the *Rocky* sequels), and provided America with a simple blue-collar hero at a time when nonheroes and antiheroes—in movies like *One Flew over the Cuckoo's Nest* and *Dog Day Afternoon*—predominated on American movie screens. As Stallone told the *New York Times* at the time the film came out, "I've really had it with anti-this and anti-that. Where are all the heroes? I want to be remembered as a man of raging optimism, who believes in the American dream."

Much of the film's enjoyment stems from the fact that Rocky Balboa's succeeding-against-all-odds story is neatly paralleled by the succeeding-against-all-odds story of Stallone himself. The actor had been living in a seedy Hollywood apartment with his wife, his savings having dwindled to $106, when he wrote his script about the Italian Stallion. Producers Irwin Winkler and Robert Chartoff showed the script to United Artists, and the studio was sufficiently impressed to offer Stallone $75,000 for the script—then $125,000, then $350,000—so they could make the film starring Ryan O'Neal, Robert Redford, James Caan, or one of the other superstars of the day. But Stallone wanted the role for himself and, realizing that the story was about having faith in yourself and going the distance, he declined the offers, even though he was about to be evicted from his apartment and his wife was pregnant with their first child. When he finally got the chance to star in the film, it launched his career and went on to win the Academy Award for best picture of 1976, beating out such box-office and critical champs as *Network* and *All the President's Men.*

Early in 1975, before Rocky Balboa existed in anyone's imagination, Chuck Wepner was, to many boxing fans, a joke. Living in Bayonne, New Jersey, he sold liquor by day and boxed at night. The 35-year-old Wepner, who was ranked eighth by *Ring* magazine, had been nicknamed ''the Bayonne Bleeder'' because of the 300-plus stitches he had accumulated on his face, mostly around his eyes. He was an unlikely boxer to be facing ''the Greatest,'' Muhammad Ali, in the ring, but Ali was just looking for an easy fight as a warm-up for his next major heavyweight title bout. The fight was such a joke that oddsmakers did not even put out a betting line. The week before the fight, a reporter asked Ali if he thought of Wepner as representing white America in their upcoming bout. Ali rolled his eyes and said, ''White America wouldn't pick *him!*'' Ali called Wepner a ''cinch,'' and someone else suggested that if Wepner was ranked eighth, then a punching bag must have been seventh.

This champ-vs.-chump fight was a joke to everyone—except, of course, to Wepner himself, who spent the two months leading up to the fight in the Catskill Mountains with his trainer and manager, training constantly. On March 15, 1975, the spectators who gathered in the Coliseum outside Cleveland were expecting Wepner to last three rounds at most but, to everyone's amazement, Wepner hung in there round after round after round. At one point Ali's fist broke Wepner's nose. In Round 7, Ali opened a cut over Wepner's left eye, and reopened it in every round thereafter. Wepner's eye swelled shut to the point where he could no longer see Ali's powerful right jabs coming. But in Round 9, Wepner brought the crowd to its feet when he knocked Ali down with a roundabout right—only the fourth time in Ali's long illustrious career that he had been knocked down. When Wepner answered the bell beginning the 15th and final round, he became only the sixth Ali opponent to make it so far. Ali then slammed a powerful right into Wepner's bloody face, the barely conscious Wepner slumped against the ropes and, with 19 seconds remaining in the fight, the referee stopped the bout and awarded Ali a TKO (technical knock-out). Ali later said, ''None of my fights was tougher than this one. There's not another human being in the world that can go 15 rounds like that.'' The spectators had been galvanized, not just in Cleveland but at pay-per-view venues across the country where the fight was carried on closed-circuit television. One of those spectators was Stallone, who had dipped into his $106 in savings to watch the fight at the Wiltern Theater in Los Angeles. Stallone had gone because ''there's something about sweating that inspires me to write,'' and he certainly got his money's worth. According to Stallone, ''That night, Rocky Balboa was born.''

Stallone nurtured the idea for three months before churning out the script in three and a half days. When he first brought up the script to possible investors, he was reluctant to do so because he considered it a rough draft with a number of problems. In this early version, Rocky's trainer, Mickey (played by Burgess Meredith in the film), was a racist, and opponent Apollo Creed (played by Carl Weathers) was much older. At the climax, when Rocky has Apollo on the ropes, Mickey's racism comes out in full force, and he screams at Rocky to kill his opponent. This angers Rocky, who then allows Apollo to land a punch so Rocky can take a dive, and Apollo wins. Rocky retires from fighting and uses his earnings from the fight to buy girlfriend Adrian (played by Talia Shire) a pet shop. During Stallone's next two drafts, he considered having Rocky win, but realized, not only would

this be unbelievable, it would turn Rocky from a common man into a superhero. Cannily, Stallone opted for the ending that was eventually filmed, with Rocky losing the fight but ''going the distance.'' For Stallone, the film was not about winning, it was about courage; the opponent was not Apollo Creed, it was unrealized dreams and fear of failure.

Even though Stallone had refused United Artists' offer of $350,000, Winkler and Chartoff still thought the film might get backing with Stallone as the star if they could come up with a low-enough budget. They finally trimmed the budget to an extremely modest $1,750,000. United Artists executives felt even this was too high, considering the fact they were not sure if Stallone had sufficient charisma to be a leading man, or could be convincing as a boxer. They finally agreed to back the film if the budget were trimmed to an even million, with Chartoff and Winkler paying for any budget overruns. The producers then proceeded to slash salaries in exchange for a percentage of the profits, agreed to take nothing up front, told Stallone he would get only $20,000 for his script and would have to act for union scale, found file footage of crowd scenes from actual fights to save having to hire extras, and scouted real locations to reduce the number of sets that had to be built. Stallone rewrote the scene where Rocky takes Adrian to a crowded skating rink for their first date, substituting a rink that is closed for Thanksgiving in order to save the cost of all those extras on skates. Director John G. Avildsen agreed to direct for half his usual $100,000 fee in exchange for a percentage of the film. For the five months before the cameras rolled, Stallone and Weathers trained together, and Stallone spent every spare moment jogging on the beach, doing pushups, studying fight films, and working out at a gym with a former fight trainer. The film was shot in 28 days, and came in $40,000 under budget.

The movie was a box-office and critical smash, with the public taking to heart this story of a Philadelphia lug who supplements his income as an enforcer for a loan shark but refuses to break thumbs, talks to his pet turtles Cuff and Link, trains at a slaughterhouse by pummeling sides of beef, and makes that triumphant run up the steps of the Philadelphia Art Museum. *Rocky* received ten Academy Award nominations, and Stallone's nominations for both best actor and best screenplay marked only the third time in Oscar history that someone had received both nominations for the same film, previuos nominees being Charlie Chaplin and Orson Welles. The film won for best picture, best director, and best film editing. Following the movie, men flocked to gyms in order to bulk up, drinking raw eggs became a passing fad, and a wave of films flooded out of Hollywood copying the *Rocky* formula, notably *The Karate Kid* films directed by Avildsen, and the *Rocky* sequels. When the first *Rocky* premiered, Stallone said he was planning two sequels: in the first, Rocky would attend night school, enter politics and get elected mayor of Philadelphia; and in the second he would get framed by the political machine because of his honesty, get impeached, and return to the ring. But after the phenomenal success of *Rocky,* Stallone and the producers realized that a fortune could be made by, in effect, remaking the first film, but climaxing it with a Rocky-Apollo Creed championship fight with Rocky winning this time. Stallone directed *Rocky II* (1979) and all involved made fortunes, but the film was a far cry from the original. Stallone then directed *Rocky III* (1982) and *Rocky IV* (1985), and Avildsen returned to direct *Rocky V* (1990), with each generally worse than the one before. This sequel overkill may have tarnished the reputation of the original, though the original still holds up, retaining enough of a reputation to have been selected by the

American Film Institute as one of the 100 greatest films of the last 100 years.

—Bob Sullivan

FURTHER READING:

Daly, Marsha. *Sylvester Stallone*. New York, St. Martin's Press, 1986.

Rovin, Jeff. *Stallone! A Hero's Story*. New York, Pocket Books, 1985.

Stallone, Sylvester. *Official Rocky Scrapbook*. New York, Grosset & Dunlap, 1977.

Wright, Adrian. *Sylvester Stallone: A Life in Film*. London, Robert Hale Limited, 1991.

Rocky and Bullwinkle

The 1990s saw a renaissance in American animation on television, as the phenomenal ratings success of *The Simpsons* prompted network executives to introduce a host of new cartoon series for adult audiences. But the irreverent humor and satirical eye of these postmodern programs owed a great debt to one of the pioneering shows of this genre, *Rocky and Bullwinkle*. The animated series about a moose and a squirrel aired from 1959 to 1964 on various networks, setting the standard for sophisticated cartoon whimsy.

''*Bullwinkle* was a magnificent marriage of concept, writing, performing, and direction,'' observed June Foray in 1991. Foray would know, having served as the voice of Rocket J. Squirrel since the cartoon's inception in 1959. A one-time radio performer, Foray was hired for the long-running gig by Jay Ward, a Harvard Business School graduate who created *Rocky and Bullwinkle* in the late 1950s. Ward, who had no background in writing or animation, relied on a staff of creative types led by writer and vocal stylist Bill Scott, who became the voice of Bullwinkle J. Moose. Others who worked on the show included Allan Burns, a talented comedy writer who would go on to help create *The Mary Tyler Moore Show* in the 1970s.

The program they created, originally titled *Rocky and His Friends*, followed the adventures of Bullwinkle J. Moose, a good-natured, if slightly dim, antlered mammal, and his resourceful cohort Rocky the Flying Squirrel. But this was no ordinary cutesy animal cartoon. *Bullwinkle* episodes were leavened with generous helpings of topical humor, including Cold War satire in the form of Boris and Natasha, dastardly spies from a nebulous Eastern Bloc nation called Pottsylvania. In a typical series plotline, Boris and Natasha attempt to sabotage the U.S. economy by counterfeiting America's most indispensable currency, the cereal box top. ''Serial'' became an operative term for the show itself, as the storylines carried over from week to week in the manner of old-time adventure movies.

There were additional segments of the program as well, including ''The Adventures of Dudley Do-Right,'' about a stolid mountie; ''Fractured Fairy Tales,'' a send-up of the Brothers Grimm and company; and ''Mr. Peabody's Improbable History,'' which followed the exploits of a pedantic pooch who can travel back in time to great moments in the past. All the elements of the show incorporated the same dry humor, reliance on puns, and disdain for the ''fourth wall'' separating the characters from the audience. Thus unlike most cartoons, *Rocky and Bullwinkle* could keep the attention of both children and adults alike.

After concluding its original run of 156 episodes, *Rocky and Bullwinkle* appeared regularly in reruns until 1973. At that point, sophisticated animation sadly went out of style. The moose and squirrel popped up only sporadically in reruns on local stations for the next 18 years. But this long fallow period was only the prelude to a grand *Bullwinkle* renaissance.

In 1991, six video tapes of classic *Rocky and Bullwinkle* episodes were released. With the success of Fox's animated series *The Simpsons* fostering a renewed appreciation for edgy cartoon comedy, sales were brisk. Nostalgic baby boomers and their offspring gobbled up two million copies of the video cassettes in the first year of release. Even an ill-conceived 1992 live-action movie, *Boris and Natasha*, could not slow the moose's long march back to public favor. Cable television's Cartoon Network soon added *Rocky and Bullwinkle* to its lineup of cartoon classics, and it quickly became one of the channel's most watched shows among teenagers, a notoriously hard-to-please demographic. To capitalize further on the cartoon's retro hipness, a handsome commemorative volume, *The Rocky and Bullwinkle Book*, reached bookstore shelves in 1996.

But there was perhaps no greater indication of Rocky and Bullwinkle's return to the pinnacle of the pop culture pantheon than their reinstatement to the front lines of the annual Macy's Thanksgiving Day Parade in New York City. The inflatable moose had disappeared from the parade after 1983, but in 1996 a new Bullwinkle balloon, redesigned with Rocky on his back, once again joined the likes of Bugs Bunny, Mighty Mouse, and Underdog. It seemed a fitting apotheosis for one of cartoondom's most beloved and influential figures.

—Robert E. Schnakenberg

FURTHER READING:

Chunovic, Louis. *The Rocky and Bullwinkle Book*. New York, Bantam Doubleday Dell, 1996.

The Rocky Horror Picture Show

The Rocky Horror Picture Show was not the first midnight movie, but it is arguably the most well known. With its rebellious blend of ''B'' movie science fiction, horror, and a rock 'n' roll soundtrack, *Rocky Horror* celebrates sexual difference. Inspiring viewers with the catch phrase, ''Don't dream it, be it!,'' *Rocky Horror* earned its cult status in part through its transgressive nature. Its fans are legion, and since the film's release in 1975, *Rocky Horror* has developed into a full-fledged cult that has spawned its own cottage industry of merchandise and memorabilia. *Rocky Horror* has become synonymous with participatory cinema, and its history as a midnight feature has helped to define what it meant to be a cult film in the late twentieth century.

The Rocky Horror Picture Show grew out of the fertile imagination of English actor Richard O'Brien, who wrote a rock musical titled *The Rocky Horror Show* over the course of six months in 1972. O'Brien's play combined his appreciation for ''B'' movies and his love of science fiction within a story set in the fictional town of Denton, Ohio. After attending the wedding of two friends, nerdy sweethearts Brad Majors and Janet Weiss are caught up in the moment and decide to get married. En route to the home of Brad's former college professor, Dr. Everett V. Scott, the couple is deterred

From left: Nell Campbell, Patricia Quinn, Tim Curry, and Richard O'Brien in a scene from the film *The Rocky Horror Picture Show*.

by inclement weather. Taking shelter in a roadside mansion, Brad and Janet encounter their host, Dr. Frank-N-Furter, a transvestite overseeing the annual convention of aliens from the planet Transylvania. Although Brad and Janet are less than charmed by the doctor, he insists that they remain in the mansion overnight in order to witness his ultimate scientific creation: the perfect male specimen. In the course of their stay, Brad and Janet both are seduced by Frank, and Janet in turn seduces the doctor's creation, Rocky Horror. Along the way the couple meets Riff Raff, the doctor's sidekick; his sister

Magenta; and a groupie named Columbia. The next morning, Brad's mentor comes to the mansion looking for his nephew Eddie, the former lover of Frank whose brain was used to create Rocky Horror and whose remains become the main dish in an elaborate last supper held at the mansion. In a grand finale, Frank is overthrown as overseer of the Transylvanians and Riff Raff and Magenta take over the group, blasting the mansion back to Transylvania and leaving Brad, Janet, and Dr. Scott to contemplate their experiences.

Premiering at a small theater in the Chelsea neighborhood of London in June 1973, *The Rocky Horror Show* was an instant success.

The popularity of the musical, which starred the charismatic performer Tim Curry as Frank, made it necessary to move the production to successively larger theaters throughout London. After seeing one of these performances in 1974, U.S. movie producer Lou Adler (*Monterey Pop, Brewster McCloud*) struck a deal with O'Brien and fellow *Rocky Horror* producer Michael White that allowed Adler to bring the stage show to Los Angeles and eventually turn the musical into a feature-length film produced by Twentieth Century-Fox.

After O'Brien's musical finished its ten-month run in Los Angeles, Curry returned with some of the other performers to London to shoot the film version at Bray Studios, the former home of the horror films made by Hammer Studios. The film, whose title was changed to *The Rocky Horror Picture Show,* was shot over the course of eight weeks by director Jim Sharman from a script co-written by Sharman and O'Brien. While some of the stage actors, like Curry and O'Brien (Riff Raff), reprised their roles in the film version, actors Susan Sarandon and Barry Bostwick were brought in to play Janet and Brad. Patricia Quinn played Magenta both on stage and in the film, and her wet, red lips provide *Rocky Horror* with its seductive opening sequence as she mouths the words to the song, "Science Fiction/ Double Feature." As J. Hoberman and Jonathan Rosenbaum observe in *Midnight Movies,* this image of Quinn's salacious mouth lip-synching the lyrics sung on the accompanying soundtrack by O'Brien immediately introduces viewers to the tantalizing presence and overwhelming significance of bisexuality within *Rocky Horror.*

After a brief, unsuccessful run of the play on Broadway at the Belasco Theater, *Rocky Horror* the film previewed in California in the summer of 1975. Responses to preview screenings of the film were as negative as those leveled at the Broadway production, but Tim Deegan, the film's publicist, focused on the few viewers who were enthusiastic about the film and kept their responses in mind when promoting it. When it opened in Los Angeles in the early fall of 1975, *Rocky Horror* had little trouble filling the theater. Elsewhere in the country, however, the film did not fare as well. Inspired by the exhibition techniques used to promote George Romero's *Night of the Living Dead,* however, Deegan arranged to release the film in New York only at midnight and to keep it at the same theater for at least one month so the film could find its audience. As it turned out, word-of-mouth drew viewers to the theater, and the movie itself kept audiences coming back for repeat viewings—a defining characteristic of cult films.

Although it is difficult to pinpoint when audiences first began participating in the *Rocky Horror* experience, Hoberman and Rosenbaum suggest one of the earliest instances occurred in New York City in 1976, a few months after the film's release. Dubbed "counterpoint dialogue," this verbal interaction with the film began as a way to fill the awkward pauses between dialogue exchanges and to comment on the poorly written lines uttered by some of the characters. Soon, repeat audiences were staging their own "shows" before the film's midnight screening and during the screening as well. Scripts were written by *Rocky Horror* fans containing counterpoint dialogue for the entire film, and directions for dancing the Time Warp (a dance sequence that occurs in the film) were passed out to audiences—a technique that had its roots in the stage show's early days. Some fans began attending screenings dressed as the film's characters. Props were used as a kind of visual counterpoint to the film as well. During a screening of *Rocky Horror,* for instance, it is customary for audience members to throw rice at the screen during the wedding sequence. When Brad and Janet get caught in a storm, viewers open umbrellas in the theater or hold newspapers over their heads while other members of the audience fire water pistols into the

crowd. Newcomers to the *Rocky Horror* film are called virgins, and their initiation into the experience is gleefully overseen by veterans who have attended the screenings many times over.

The cult surrounding *Rocky Horror* has continued to grow since the film's release in late 1975. Movies like *Fame* (1980), which contains a sequence in which two characters attend a *Rocky Horror* screening, introduced mainstream audiences to a phenomenon that may have otherwise eluded them. During the 1980s in liberal arts classes throughout the country, scholars began to analyze and write about the cult of *Rocky Horror* and to discuss this cultural phenomenon in terms of religion, socialization, sexuality, and ritual. It is customary for the film to screen on college campuses, and this event serves as a kind of initiation into underground culture, sexual difference, and participatory cinema.

For some hard-core *Rocky Horror* fans, the film's acceptance into mainstream society contradicts the very essence of what *Rocky Horror* represents. With its emphasis on unbridled sexuality and transgressive behavior, *Rocky Horror* has been described by Hoberman and Rosenbaum as an "adolescent initiation" that rearticulates the sexual politics of the 1960s. Its release to home video in 1990 struck some as counterproductive since so much of one's enjoyment in the film comes from watching it with an audience. Nonetheless, the video release proved successful enough to spawn a laser disc version in 1992, and in 1996, to celebrate the twentieth anniversary of the film's wide release, FoxVideo unveiled a deluxe, remastered edit of the film. On an alternate audio track, the counterpoint dialogue of two Los Angeles-based audiences of *Rocky Horror* regulars can be heard. The inclusion of this separate audio track, carefully selected from the scores of *Rocky Horror* fan communities in existence, acknowledges the significant role the audience plays in the experience and success of *Rocky Horror.*

In 1981 O'Brien and Sharman re-teamed to direct the sequel to *Rocky Horror,* titled *Shock Treatment.* In the film, Brad (played by Cliff De Young) and Janet (Jessica Harper) are still married but are dissatisfied with their lives and one another. Their hometown has become a large television station, and citizens are either participants or viewers. Although *Shock Treatment* did not fare as well as its predecessor and disappointed many *Rocky Horror* fans, its plot recapitulates *Rocky Horror's* original message, which encouraged viewers to lose their inhibitions and become participants rather than mere viewers of life even decades after its release. *Rocky Horror* continues to screen at midnight in theaters all around the globe and attract new generations of fans on a regular basis. The open text of *Rocky Horror's* narrative allows viewers from a variety of cultural backgrounds to appreciate its campy spectacle. The film's ability to be read by audiences as both transgressive and recuperative, argues Barry K. Grant, has contributed to *Rocky Horror's* longevity.

—Alison Macor

FURTHER READING:

Austin, Bruce A. "Portrait of a Cult Film Audience: *The Rocky Horror Picture Show." Journal of Communications.* Vol. 31, 1981, 450-65.

Grant, Barry K. "Science Fiction Double Feature: Ideology in the Cult Film." *The Cult Film Experience: Beyond All Reason,* edited by J.P. Telotte. Austin, University of Texas Press, 1991, 122-37.

Henkin, Bill. *The Rocky Horror Picture Show Book.* New York, Hawthorn Books, 1979.

Hoberman, J., and Jonathan Rosenbaum. *Midnight Movies.* New York, De Capo Press, Inc., 1991.

Peary, Danny. *Cult Movies.* New York, Delta Books, 1981.

Piro, Sal. *Creatures of the Night: The Rocky Horror Experience.* Redford, Michigan, Stabur Press, 1990.

Roddenberry, Gene (1921-1991)

Gene Roddenberry was the creator of a genuine twentieth-century cultural phenomenon: the *Star Trek* television series. It aired for three seasons between 1966 and 1969 before its cancellation, but went on to thrive in syndication. By the end of the 1990s, the various *Star Trek* manifestations included four live-action television series, one animated television series, nine feature films, and countless novels, short stories, technical manuals, magazines and fanzines, comic books, fan conventions, and Internet sites. There is even a *Star Trek*-inspired ''language'': Klingon. Though Roddenberry died in 1991, the utopian future he envisioned would continue to thrill millions of ''Trekkies,'' as fans are known, via print, television, and cinema.

Growing up in El Paso, Texas, as an isolated and sickly boy who sought temporary refuge from his unhappy circumstances in fantasy, Roddenberry discovered science fiction. Though he grew out of his youthful shell to embark on a varied and adventurous early career, he never lost his appreciation of the genre. After flying for the Army and

Gene Roddenberry and friends.

Pan Am, Roddenberry moved to Los Angeles to become a television writer in the 1950s. While working as a motorcycle policeman for the Los Angeles Police Department, he also wrote episodes for many respected TV series such as *Dr. Kildare, Highway Patrol,* and *Naked City,* and became head writer for *Have Gun Will Travel.* In 1962, he began writing one-hour pilots to sell as potential series, and was the producer of the short-lived show *The Lieutenant.* When it became clear that the series would not last longer than one season, Roddenberry turned to the science-fiction genre for his next project. Tired of the constraints and timidity of American commercial television, he believed that science fiction was a way to covertly address social issues that sponsors, and hence networks, would otherwise shy away from.

Pursuing this idea, Roddenberry wrote up a proposal for a series titled *Star Trek,* which, as every true fan knows, Roddenberry described as a kind of ''*Wagon Train* to the stars.'' He imagined a future in which a united Earth would work together with other alien worlds to create a Federation, which would then dispatch giant starships throughout the galaxy ''to boldly go where no man has gone before.'' The series would focus on the captain and crew of one starship (initially called ''Yorktown'' but later changed to ''Enterprise'') during its five-year mission of exploration. To create limitless story potential, Roddenberry staffed his starship with hundreds of crew members; to save money, he also emphasized that the series would use standing sets and visit only ''Class M'' (Earth-like) planets. He submitted his proposal to MGM on March 11, 1964, and when they failed to respond, he took it to other Hollywood studios. Eventually, it was Desilu, financially strapped and looking for a hit series, that signed Roddenberry to a three-year deal. His next step was to find a network for the show. CBS turned him down, but NBC agreed to give him $20,000 to write three stories, one of which would be chosen for development as a screenplay and pilot episode. Eventually, NBC chose ''The Cage'' (later changed to ''The Menagerie'') as the pilot for *Star Trek.*

Filming on the pilot began on December 12, 1964, and lasted for 12 days. The pilot introduced the characters of Captain Christopher Pike (played by Jeffrey Hunter), the Vulcan officer Mr. Spock (Leonard Nimoy), and the female executive officer Number One (Majel Barrett, also the future Mrs. Roddenberry). The pilot cost $686,000 to make because of post-production special effects and budget overruns, and was eventually rejected by NBC as ''too cerebral'' for the television audience. However, the network took the unprecedented step of requesting another, more action-oriented pilot from Roddenberry. The second pilot, titled ''Where No Man Has Gone Before'' and using a cast much different from the first but for Nimoy, was accepted. The series was scheduled to begin in the fall of 1966, and after personally supervising the show's crucial first half-season, Roddenberry became executive producer. For the next three television seasons, the series regulars included Captain James Kirk (William Shatner), First Officer Mr. Spock (Leonard Nimoy, retained from the first pilot), Chief Medical Officer Leonard McCoy (DeForest Kelley), Chief Engineer Montgomery Scott (James Doohan), Helmsman Hikaru Sulu (George Takei), Communications Officer Uhuru (Nichelle Nichols), and Nurse Christine Chapel (Majel Barrett). Ensign Pavel Chekov (Walter Koenig) was added to the show in the second season. But ratings were low and NBC decided to cancel the next series. Halfway through that second season, Roddenberry capitalized on a tremendous outpouring of fan-mail support for the series' renewal in order to convince network executives to continue the show. However, when the network decided to place *Star Trek* in a late-night Friday time slot, which effectively meant killing the show's ratings once and for all, Roddenberry chose to distance himself from daily production, becoming executive producer again. At the end of the 1969 season, the series was canceled.

Although he began developing other television and movie projects, most of which failed, Roddenberry was very much aware of the extremely enthusiastic following that was growing up around *Star Trek* in syndication. Beginning in 1972, he began working the *Star Trek* convention circuit, asking the ''Trekkers'' to write and/or call Hollywood executives in support of reviving the series. Paramount Studios and Roddenberry worked together over a period of years to bring back *Star Trek* as, alternately, a made-for-TV movie, a series, and a low-budget theatrical movie, but none of the projects panned out. Finally, following the financial success of science fiction feature films such as *Star Wars* and *Close Encounters of the Third Kind* (both 1977), Paramount green-lighted the project that reunited the principals from the television cast and became *Star Trek: The Motion Picture* in 1979. Roddenberry co-wrote the screenplay and served as the film's producer, the first and last time that he would have any direct control over the franchise's films. The finished product proved an expensive, effects-heavy disappointment, although it still earned over one hundred million dollars—enough to justify a sequel.

With the sequels, Roddenberry fought a bitter but futile battle over what he saw as ideas designed to damage the franchise. In particular, he objected to the death of Mr. Spock in the second film, the destruction of the ''Enterprise'' in the third, and the militaristic Federation of the sixth. Nonetheless, he continued as executive producer of the still lucrative films, and in 1987, he created a ''spin-off'' television series titled *Star Trek: The Next Generation.* The second series was set 75 years after the original and featured a fresh new crew, led by Patrick Stewart's cerebral Captain Jean-Luc Picard, and a larger and faster starship, the ''Enterprise D.'' After a shaky start, the *The Next Generation,* with Roddenberry as executive producer, became a bona-fide hit during its third season and ran four more years until the cast graduated to their own feature films in 1994.

Roddenberry died of a heart attack shortly after attending a screening of *Star Trek VI: The Undiscovered Country* in late 1991, but the success of the *Next Generation* films and the syndicated *Star Trek: Deep Space Nine* and *Star Trek: Voyager* series retained its popular appeal and remained a testament to his vision and determination.

—Phil Simpson

FURTHER READING:

Alexander, David. *Star Trek Creator: The Authorized Biography of Gene Roddenberry.* New York, Roc, 1994.

Engel, Joel. *Gene Roddenberry: The Myth and the Man behind Star Trek.* New York, Hyperion, 1994.

Fern, Yvonne. *Inside the Mind of Gene Roddenberry: The Creator of Star Trek.* London, HarperCollins, 1995.

Gross, Edward. *Great Birds of the Galaxy: Gene Roddenberry and the Creators of Star Trek.* New York, Image, 1992.

Roddenberry, Gene. *Star Trek: The First 25 Years.* New York, Pocket Books, 1992.

Shatner, William, with Chris Kreski. *Star Trek Memories.* New York, HarperPaperbacks, 1994.

———. *Star Trek Movie Memories.* New York, HarperPaperbacks, 1995.

Van Hise, James. *The Man Who Created Star Trek: Gene Roddenberry.* Las Vegas, Pioneer, 1992.

Whitfield, Stephen E., and Gene Roddenberry. *The Making of Star Trek.* New York, Ballantine, 1968.

Rodeo

Roping, riding, and bronco busting all form part of one of the oldest American spectator competitions, the rodeo. What began as a way for working cowboys to blow off steam has developed into a lucrative international skills competition replete with glitzy costumes, whooping audiences, and Broadway production values. Less violent than wrestling and even smellier than the circus, rodeo remains an enormously popular family entertainment option across the United States and Canada.

Traditionally, rodeo competition consists of eight events divided into two categories: rough stock and timed. In rough stock events, cowboys (or, in some instances, cowgirls) try to ride bucking horses or bulls for a specified length of time. The traditional rough stock events are bareback bronco riding (or ''busting''), saddled bronco riding, and bull riding.

In timed events, contestants must complete a certain task, such as roping a steer, within a required number of seconds. The five traditional timed rodeo events are calf roping, steer wrestling, team roping, steer roping, and barrel racing. Customarily, female competitors take part only in barrel racing, a precision equestrian event that involves riding a horse in a cloverleaf pattern around an array of barrels. The advent of all-female rodeos, however, has resulted in the easing of this restriction.

The word rodeo derives from the Spanish word *rodear,* meaning to encircle or surround. Spanish settlers in sixteenth-century Mexico used the word rodeo to refer to a cattle round-up. It did not attain its present-day meaning—that of a skills competition devoted to round-up events—until the late nineteenth century. At that time, cowboys looked forward to the Fourth of July holiday (or ''Cowboy Christmas'' as it was also called) as an opportunity, not to grill up some burgers and set off some fireworks, but to ride through town roping steers and corralling them in the public square. Eventually, this activity was systematized into a form resembling today's organized rodeos.

A number of states, including Texas, Colorado, and Wyoming, take credit for being the birthplace of rodeo, though its true place of parentage is unclear. Cheyenne, Wyoming, was the scene of one of the first anarchic exhibitions, on Independence Day in 1872, when a band of cowboys thundered down its main drag on the backs of unruly steers. The next year, bronco busting was added to the mix, and thus began the diversification of activities that led to today's eight standard rodeo events.

Buffalo Bill Cody became one of the first impresarios of the rodeo during the 1880s. In 1883, Cody and others formed *Buffalo Bill's Wild West,* a traveling show that toured the United States and parts of Europe. The show included a mock battle with Indians and a demonstration of Cody's shooting skill. In addition, cowboys competed for prizes in the arenas of roping, riding, and bronco busting, and there was always a show-stopping bull ride finale. Cody used the term ''rodeo'' to sell these extravaganzas to a fascinated public. Sometimes as many as a thousand cowboys participated.

A bull-riding cowboy at a rodeo in Wyoming.

By the 1890s, rodeos had proliferated throughout the cattle-raising regions of the American west. Over time, they spread to other areas of the country as well. Today, rodeos are held in many parts of the United States, Canada, and Australia. The sport's continuing popularity can be credited to its increasing concentration on entertainment value, as a one-time leisure pursuit for drunken cowboys metastasized into a multi-million dollar entertainment extravaganza.

Nowhere were the changes in rodeo more visible than in the contributions of its female participants. Though barred from competing in many of the events, women made significant contributions to the rodeo from its very beginnings. Female equestrian performers carved out a niche with their acrobatic feats, pleasing crowds with their ability to balance themselves on two horses as they traversed the arena. When allowed to take part in the more rough-and-tumble events, they invariably wowed spectators with their steer-roping and bronco-busting prowess.

Women achieved their most noticeable impact on rodeo, however, in the area of costuming. In the early days of motion pictures, many female rodeo performers found that winning rodeo championships was a surefire way to break into silent films, so they began wearing highly decorated outfits to attract the attention of talent scouts. Bright-colored leggings and red velvet skirts with embroidered hems eventually gave way to bold pants, silk blouses, and eye-catching neckerchiefs. Rodeo fans became so enamored with these costumes that they soon demanded the men wear them also—to the chagrin of the blue jeaned and brown-shirted cowboys. Glitzy get-ups like the one worn by Robert Redford in the 1979 film *The Electric Horseman* became de rigueur for the rodeo set, giving the sport a raucous game-show quality that turned off some purists while winning many new adherents nationwide.

Over the decades, rodeo's ''new adherents'' turned up in some strange places. Prison rodeo was, for many years, a popular event in America's Southern penitentiaries, but in recent years it has been deemed cruel and unusual—or at least politically incorrect. The Angola Prison Rodeo, conducted annually at the Louisiana State Penitentiary in Angola, Louisiana, now stands as the only remaining competition of its kind. The official rodeo program promises ''inmate cowboys flying off the backs of those bulls like corn in a popper.''

With its incongruously festive atmosphere, the Angola Prison Rodeo features food booths and a fenced-in bazaar where inmates can sell their handicrafts. Many of the events are unique to Angola and only tangentially derived from rodeo. In fact, the activities of the Roman Coliseum may be a more apt antecedent. In one popular event, ''Convict Poker,'' four inmates sit at a table in the center of the arena and a bull is released. A perverse game of chicken ensues, in which the convict who remains seated longest wins. The showstopper of every prison rodeo is the "Guts and Glory Challenge," in which an especially ferocious bull enters the ring with horns painted bright orange and a $100 chit attached to the front of its head. A group of inmates (whose typical salary for prison work is four cents an hour) are then given three minutes to subdue the beast long enough to retrieve the chit.

Whatever their quarrels with the mainstream culture, the gay and lesbian community has not remained immune from the charm of rodeo either. The idea for a "gay rodeo" originated with Reno, Nevada, gay activist Phil Ragsdale in 1975. It was Ragsdale who decided that a rodeo for homosexuals might be a good way to raise money for the Muscular Dystrophy Association (MDA). At first, Ragsdale was not able to find any ranchers willing to lease livestock for the spectacle, but eventually the animals were procured and the rodeo went on as scheduled. Crowds were sparse the first year, but Ragsdale opted to keep it as an annual event. The extravaganza became known as the National Reno Gay Rodeo and raised thousands of dollars for MDA over the first decade of its existence.

In fact, gay rodeo became so popular that it eventually spread to other localities—and other countries as well. In 1985, the International Gay Rodeo Association (IGRA) was formed with the express intention of "fostering national and international amateur rodeo and other equestrian competition and related arts, crafts and activities which encourage the education on or preservation of Country/Western lifestyle heritage." The group immediately ratified bylaws, approved events, and standardized rodeo rules, largely along the same lines as traditional rodeo. By 1999, the IGRA was comprised of 19 Member Associations representing 22 states, the District of Columbia, and two Canadian Provinces.

—Robert E. Schnakenberg

FURTHER READING:

Coombs, Charles. *Let's Rodeo!* New York, Henry Holt, 1986.

Fredriksson, Kristine. *American Rodeo: From Buffalo Bill to Big Business.* College Station, Texas A&M University Press, 1985.

Jordan, Bob. *Rodeo History and Legends.* Montrose, Colorado, Rodeo Stuff, 1994.

Riske, Milt. *Those Magnificent Cowgirls: A History of the Rodeo Cowgirl.* Cheyenne, Wyoming Publications, 1983.

Westermeier, Clifford P. *Man, Beast, Dust: The Story of Rodeo.* Denver, World Press, 1947; reprinted, Lincoln, University of Nebraska Press, 1987.

Woerner, Gail Hughbanks. *A Belly Full of Bedsprings: The History of Bronc Riding.* Austin, Texas, Eakin Press, 1998.

Wooden, Wayne S., and Gavin Ehringer. *Rodeo in America: Wranglers, Roughstock, and Paydirt.* Lawrence, University Press of Kansas, 1996.

Rodgers and Hammerstein

The collaboration of composer Richard Rodgers (1902-1979) and lyricist/librettist Oscar Hammerstein II (1895-1960) began in 1943 with their landmark musical *Oklahoma!* Each man had already enjoyed a long and impressive career in musical theater. Hammerstein had worked with some of the most famous composers writing for Broadway and Hollywood: Vincent Youmans, Rudolf Friml, Sigmund Romberg, George Gershwin, and, most notably for Hammerstein's own colleague, Jerome Kern, with whom Hammerstein wrote the stunning *Show Boat* in 1927 and whose music Rodgers greatly admired. By 1943, Rodgers had written nearly 30 shows with his previous partner Lorenz Hart (1895-1943), including musicals, film versions of musicals, and original film music. The Rodgers and Hammerstein partnership produced a series of critically and commercially acclaimed musicals, beginning with *Oklahoma!* and ending with *The Sound of Music* in 1959. Rodgers and Hammerstein also excelled in the business aspects of musical theater, establishing a music publishing company and producing the shows of other composers in addition to their own. However, it is their contribution to the evolution of musical theater—the genre's style and form—and the extraordinary number of highly touted shows they wrote together, that determines their unique place in musical theater history.

In the early 1940s Richard Rodgers reluctantly began to contemplate working with a new lyricist. The shows he had written with Lorenz Hart were popular and profitable, and had spawned many durable hit songs, but Hart's drinking problems, poor health, and erratic working habits had become difficult to overcome. Nevertheless, Rodgers wanted to continue the relationship with his close friend and creative partner of 25 years, and asked Hart to join him in a new project, turning Lynn Riggs' play *Green Grow the Lilacs* into a musical. Hart, who could write so compellingly about the darker sides of life, was not persuaded that this play provided good material for a musical and said no. Needful, therefore, of another collaborator for the new show, Rodgers turned to another old friend, Oscar Hammerstein II.

Hammerstein brought a wealth of experience and theatrical wisdom to the endeavor. He was the grandson of opera impresario Oscar Hammerstein I, and both his father, William, and his uncle, Arthur Hammerstein, worked in show business. The well-established lyricist/librettist Otto Harbach had been Hammerstein's mentor, and the two became full-fledged colleagues in 1920. Through the 1920s Hammerstein shared lyricist's responsibilities with Harbach for several important shows: *Wildflower* (music by Vincent Youmans, 1923); *Rose-Marie* (music by Rudolf Friml, 1924); *Sunny* (music by Jerome Kern, 1925); *Song of the Flame* (music by George Gershwin and Herbert Stothart, 1925); and *The Desert Song* (music by Sigmund Romberg, 1926). Then, in 1927, Hammerstein and Kern wrote what many historians consider their masterpiece: *Show Boat*. In this work Kern and Hammerstein took American themes and musical idioms and infused them with a dramatic coherence and intensity that changed the landscape of musical theater. Hammerstein's career seemed secure. He went on to write *The New Moon* with Romberg in 1928 and *Sweet Adeline* with Kern in 1929 but, surprisingly, the 1930s brought little of the recognition he had enjoyed in the 1920s. Although *Music in the Air* with Kern in 1932 was well received, other shows did not prosper—not even *Very Warm for May* with Kern in 1939, which included the much-recorded song "All the Things You Are." Hammerstein had worked steadily through the 1930s writing and directing some productions, but by the 1940s, he needed a new challenge; that challenge appeared in the person of Richard Rodgers.

Rodgers had always been concerned with the integration of words and music, both the careful setting of text to music and the significance of the songs to the plot and character development of the whole work. When working with Lorenz Hart, Rodgers usually wrote the music first, then collaborated with Hart on the lyrics. Even though he and Hart would discuss the libretto and how the musical numbers

Rodgers and Hammerstein

would fit, their songs could often easily and effectively be sung outside the context of the show. Many of these songs have become much-loved standards.

With Hammerstein, however, the creative process worked the opposite way around. Hammerstein often labored over the lyrics for weeks. Rodgers then took the lyricist's carefully polished words and quickly produced the appropriate music to support the text. Working with Hammerstein brought a change to Rodgers' musical style. The typical thirty-two-bar forms of Rodgers' earlier work became less predictable as the musical forms were altered to fit Hammerstein's lyrics, producing many songs which were so fundamental to the thrust of the show that they often carried plot or character development.

Their first show, *Oklahoma!*, already clearly demonstrated Rodgers and Hammerstein's commitment to integrating lyrics, libretto, and music. Its incorporation of dance into the story continued a current in Rodgers' work, which had first appeared in *On Your Toes*, written with Lorenz Hart in 1936 and choreographed by George Balanchine. The dances in *Oklahoma!* were choreographed by Agnes de Mille, whose ballet background imbued her work with a narrative quality. *Oklahoma!* opened during the dreadful years of World War II, on March 31, 1943, and ran for 2,212 performances. Several

elements coalesced to produce a hit like nothing Broadway had ever seen before: the story of frontier life and the Oklahoma land rush at the turn of the century was a perfect vehicle for Hammerstein's gift for fresh, simple poetry, while characters such as Ado Annie were treated with sympathetic humor; the musical was at once folksy (''Oh, What a Beautiful Morning''), romantic and charming (''The Surrey with the Fringe on Top''), yet with hints of dark undercurrents as represented by the character of Judd Fry; the muscular, popular-dance and ballet influenced choreography broke new ground; Rodgers' sensitive score was witty (''I'm Just a Gal Who Cain't Say No''), rambunctious (''Everything's up to Date in Kansas City''), and soaringly romantic (''People Will Say We're in Love'') as the context demanded. *Oklahoma!* held the record as the longest-running musical in Broadway history until 1961. In 1944 the show won a special Pulitzer Prize for drama; touring companies presented it from October, 1943 until May, 1954, and revivals have been frequent. A film version appeared in 1955, and in 1993 the United States Postal Service issued a fiftieth-anniversary commemorative stamp.

Following the phenomenon of *Oklahoma!* Rodgers and Hammerstein continued to astound the musical theater world with a series of extraordinary shows. The first of these, *Carousel* (1945) was hugely successful and proved that *Oklahoma!* had been no mere flash in the pan. Rodgers and Hammerstein dominated the Broadway scene for two further decades. *South Pacific* (1949) brought them a second Pulitzer Prize for Drama (awarded in 1950), and was followed by *The King and I* (1951) and *The Sound of Music* (1959). All enjoyed long runs, critical recognition, and commercial success, and all were made into popular films. The pre-eminent composer/lyricist position that the partnership held was ended with Hammerstein's death from cancer in 1960. Rodgers continued to compose, writing some of his own lyrics, but nothing in his later life equaled the sustained flood of musical and dramatic brilliance that he and Hammerstein had created together.

—Ann Sears

FURTHER READING:

Citron, Stephen. *The Wordsmiths: Oscar Hammerstein and Alan Jay Lerner.* New York, Oxford University Press, 1995.

Ewen, David. *Richard Rodgers.* New York, Henry Holt, 1957.

Fordin, Hugh, with introduction by Stephen Sondheim. *Getting to Know Him: A Biography of Oscar Hammerstein II.* New York, Ungar Publishing Co., 1977. Reprint, New York, Da Capo Press, 1995.

Green, Stanley. *The Rodgers and Hammerstein Story.* New York, John Day, 1963.

Hammerstein, Oscar, II. *Lyrics.* New York, Simon and Schuster, 1949. Reprint, Milwaukee, Hall Leonard, 1985.

Hyland, William G. *Richard Rodgers.* New Haven, Yale University Press, 1998.

Mordden, Ethan. *Rodgers & Hammerstein.* New York, Harry N. Abrams, 1992.

Nolan, Frederick. *The Sound of Their Music.* New York, Walker & Co., 1978.

Rodgers, Richard. *Letters to Dorothy, 1926-1937.* New York, New York Public Library, 1998.

Rodgers, Richard. *Musical Stages: An Autobiography.* New York, Random House, 1975. Reprint, with a new introduction by Mary Rodgers, New York, Da Capo Press, 1995.

Rodgers, Richard, and Oscar Hammerstein. *Six Plays.* New York, Random House, n.d.

Taylor, Deems. *Some Enchanted Evenings: The Story of Rodgers and Hammerstein.* New York, Harper & Brothers, 1953.

Rodgers and Hart

American composer Richard Rodgers (1902-1979) and lyricist/ librettist Lorenz Hart (1895-1943) were one of America's most successful composer/lyricist teams in the golden age of American songwriting. Their works for the musical theater produced a cornucopia of lasting songs. From the beginning of a collaboration that began in 1925 and lasted until Lorenz Hart's death in 1943, Rodgers and Hart shared the goal of writing music for the theater that joined lyrics and music with dramatic and emotional coherence. By the time of their last work together, their experiments in musical theater had prepared the way for Rodgers's later great musicals with Oscar

Hammerstein II—works such as *Oklahoma!* (1943) and *Carousel* (1945), in which the interaction of lyrics, libretto, music, and dance reached a new level. Rodgers and Hart's best known shows are *The Boys from Syracuse* (1938), for which the songs "Falling in Love with Love" and "This Can't Be Love" were written, and *Pal Joey* (1940) which includes "Bewitched (Bothered, and Bewildered)," one of their most popular songs.

Both Rodgers and Hart were born in New York City, and both had evinced an early interest in music and theater. Rodgers studied at Columbia University from 1919 to 1921 and then, from 1921 to 1923, at the Institute of Musical Art, later known as the Juilliard School of Music. He began writing for amateur musical theater productions while still a student, and in 1918 he met Lorenz Hart, a Columbia student majoring in journalism. Rodgers and Hart shared an interest in a style of writing that would integrate words and music in an artistically successful manner. Rodgers's first published song, "Any Old Place with You," interpolated in *A Lonely Romeo* (1919), was a collaboration with Hart. They continued to work together until their 1925 success with *The Garrick Gaieties,* a revue which included the now classic and still immensely popular "Manhattan." By the time of their show *A Connecticut Yankee* in 1927, Rodgers was much in demand as a Broadway composer, and Hart was acknowledged as an accomplished lyricist whose only serious competitor was Ira Gershwin.

From 1926 to 1930 the pair produced 14 shows for both New York and London, along with individual songs for other productions. Following the Wall Street crash in 1929, financing for musical theater in New York became difficult to obtain; thus, like many other Broadway composers and lyricists, Rodgers and Hart turned to Hollywood. From 1930 to 1934 they wrote songs and background music for many films, and were memorably responsible for the score of the smash-hit *Love Me Tonight* (1932) for Maurice Chevalier and Jeanette MacDonald. In 1935 they returned to New York and unleashed a spate of new shows. One of the most notable of their new endeavors was *On Your Toes* in 1936, for which Rodgers wrote his first extensive orchestral music, the ballet score, "Slaughter on Tenth Avenue." This ballet was George Balanchine's first choreography for a book musical, and its importance to the plot presaged the significant "Dream Ballet" which would later be so important in *Oklahoma!* (1943). The string of Rodgers and Hart hits continued with *Babes in Arms* (1937) *and The Boys from Syracuse* (1938).

With *Pal Joey* in 1940, they departed from conventional musical theater practice and built the production around a much darker subject than Broadway was accustomed to contemplating. *Pal Joey* was based on John O'Hara's *New Yorker* stories about Joey Evans, an opportunistic, small-time entertainer. Joey gets a job at a nightclub where he begins a relationship with fellow entertainer Linda English, but when a wealthy older woman, Vera Simpson, notices him, he leaves Linda. Vera builds a glitzy nightclub, Chez Joey, for her lover, but soon tires of him, ultimately leaving Joey to move on to greener pastures. The best known song from *Pal Joey* is "Bewitched," a song whose suggestive lyrics were shocking at the time. The show introduced not only adult themes and provocative lyrics to Broadway, but addressed a segment of American life unfamiliar to musical audiences. Although *Pal Joey* ran for 374 performances following its opening on December 25, 1940, critics were ambivalent about it. However, the revival in 1952 and the 1957 film starring Frank Sinatra were more successful, assuring *Pal Joey* a secure place in the musical theater repertoire.

Rodgers and Hart

In 1942 Rodgers and Hart wrote one final show together, *By Jupiter,* set, as was *The Boys from Syracuse,* in ancient Greece. Starring Ray Bolger, it ran for 427 performances, the longest run of any Rodgers and Hart Broadway collaboration. Rodgers attempted to interest Hart in one more project together, a musical adaptation of Lynn Riggs's play, *Green Grow the Lilacs,* but Hart was unenthusiastic about the suitability of the material and declined to participate. His refusal coincided with the escalation of difficulties—largely the consequence of Hart's futile and self-destructive battle with alcoholism and homosexuality—that had plagued the partnership for years, and the situation was now nearly impossible for Rodgers to cope with. Throughout their 25-year collaboration, Rodgers had usually composed the music first, then asked Hart to write the lyrics. This approach enabled Rodgers to work when Hart was available, while the music Rodgers had already written would stimulate Hart's interest. As Hart's health deteriorated, however, his ability to keep appointments, appear at rehearsals, or revise material also failed. He died only a few months after the show he turned down, *Green Grow the Lilacs,* opened under the new title *Oklahoma!* on March 31, 1943,

beginning an unprecedented run of 2,212 performances and a fruitful new partnership for Rodgers with Oscar Hammerstein II.

Richard Rodgers and Lorenz Hart created some of the most beloved of American songs for their shows, of which "My Funny Valentine," "The Lady Is a Tramp," "Blue Moon," "Mountain Greenery," and "With a Song in My Heart" are just five of many dozens. Written primarily in the 32-measure form popular with Tin Pan Alley's songsmiths, and not generally essential to character or plot development, they were easily excerpted from the shows in which they originally appeared to become standards, recorded time and time again over the years by top vocal artists. Their style combined Hart's witty lyrics, brilliant interior rhymes, and wry twists of meaning with Rodgers's expressive approach to harmony and his highly individual rhythmic choices. Even though Rodgers and Hart's shows are infrequently revived, the individual songs taken from them have become a cornerstone of the musical theater and popular song repertoire.

—Ann Sears

257

FURTHER READING:

Hart, Dorothy, editor. *Thou Swell, Thou Witty: The Life and Lyrics of Larry Hart.* New York, Harper & Row, 1976.

Hart, Dorothy, and Robert Kimball, editors, with an appreciation by Alan Jay Lerner. *The Complete Lyrics of Lorenz Hart.* New York, Alfred A. Knopf, 1986.

Hishchak, Thomas S. *Word Crazy: Broadway Lyricists from Cohan to Sondheim.* New York, Praeger, 1991.

Marx, Samuel, and Jan Clayton. *Rodgers and Hart: Bewitched, Bothered, and Bedeviled.* New York, G. P. Putnam, 1976.

Nolan, Frederick. *Lorenz Hart: A Poet on Broadway.* New York, Oxford University Press, 1994.

Rodgers, Richard. *Musical Stages: An Autobiography.* New York, Random House, 1975. Reprinted with a new introduction by Mary Rodgers. New York, Da Capo Press, 1995.

Rodgers, Jimmie (1897-1933)

Singer and musician Jimmie Rodgers, who rose to national fame through his recordings in the late 1920s and early 1930s, is profoundly connected to a uniquely American form of popular music—country. Since the 1950s, he has been known as the "father of country music" to musicians and fans alike, and his records have continued to sell decades after his death, solidifying a national and international following that was still alive in the 1990s. Rodgers' unique amalgamation of folk blues, popular, and hillbilly music disseminated previously marginal, regional styles to national and international audiences, and he was one of the first nationally recognized musicians to feature and popularize the guitar in his recordings.

Considered a "popular" or "hillbilly" artist in his lifetime, Rodgers was officially canonized as the "father of country music" at a memorial celebration in Meridian, Mississippi, on the twentieth anniversary of his death in 1953. With some 30,000 people in attendance, his songs were played by Hank Snow, Ernest Tubb, Webb Pierce, Bill Monroe, and Roy Acuff. In his lifetime, Rodgers' songs were covered by jazz bands and orchestras, while Gene Autry, the "singing cowboy," recorded 28 Rodgers songs between 1929 and 1937. Tribute songs were recorded after his death by Autry and by Bradley Kincaid and Dwight Butcher. They have also been recorded by the likes of Woody Guthrie, Merle Haggard, the Blasters, and Hank Snow. In 1961 Jimmie Rodgers, Hank Williams, and Fred Rose were the first inductees into the Country Music Association Hall of Fame.

Born James Charles Rodgers in Pine Springs, Mississippi, Rodgers spent his formative years in and around the city of Meridian. Drawn to music at an early age, he won an amateur singing contest when he was 12. At 13 Rodgers went to work on the railroad, where he picked up diverse musical styles, and traded songs with hobos, roustabouts, and rounders throughout the South and Southwest. However, he contracted tuberculosis in 1923, and the resultant health problems, coinciding with a decline in available work, forced Rodgers off the railroad in 1925. Over the next two years he worked a handful of odd jobs to sustain his wife and young daughter while concentrating on music. In 1927 he auditioned and recorded for

Victor in Bristol, Tennessee, in a session that was the first to capture the songs of the Carter Family, another foundational country act.

Although Rodgers was a uniquely radical figure in twentieth-century American popular music, his composition, lyrics, and life epitomize the prototypical country artist. His music featured African-American blues stylings, nasal vocals, and a Southern accent. His lyrics further emphasized his Southern roots, drawing as they did on his difficult life experiences and his travels as a brakeman on the railroad. Many of his songs used the bawdy double-entendres and sexual boasts that characterized African-American blues of the period. Rodgers was deft at rendering the sentimental ("The Mystery of Number Five") as well as the blues ("In the Jailhouse Now"), and he did so with a simplicity and sincerity that touched the working-class audiences who were his biggest fans. His creative works mirrored his life most clearly when he sang about tuberculosis in such songs as "T.B. Blues" and "Whippin' That Old T.B." Although a national star on radio and records, he preferred to play live performances throughout small towns in the South and Southwest. Rodgers rubbed elbows with his fans whenever he had a chance.

While much of his music is an adaptation of the folk blues idiom, Rodgers' work is eclectic and resists simple categorization. He recorded with artists as diverse as the Carter Family, Louis Armstrong, the Louisville Jug Band, and Lani McIntire's Hawaiians during his short, six-year recording career. Traveling with the railroad, Rodgers was likely exposed to African-American folk blues, which he incorporated into his distinct style, and his interpretations of the blues often confused listeners about his race, leading one critic to characterize him as a "White Man Gone Black." Rodgers was an early "crossover" artist who was heard and admired by African-American audiences and working- and middle-class whites alike. Unlike later white blues performers, Rodgers was respectful of the material, interpreting it, rather than imitating black singers; as music scholar Tony Russell noted in *Blacks, Whites, and Blues,* some African-American artists "may have even regarded him as an honorary Negro." Most of Rodgers's songs featured falsetto yodeling, which he termed "blue yodeling," a characteristic that further distinguished him from other musicians during his career, and he was known as "The Singing Brakeman" and "America's Blue Yodeler" during his lifetime.

Rodgers bridged the regional world of the nineteenth century and the modern, mass world of the twentieth. He worked in vaudeville and in blackface minstrel shows, performed on radio, recorded over 100 songs, and appeared in a movie short titled *The Singing Brakeman* in 1929. He played shows in conjunction with movies, headlined at the Earle Theater in Washington, D.C., toured with Will Rogers to raise money for victims of drought and the Depression, and played a plethora of small venues throughout the South. His best known songs include "Blue Yodel (T for Texas)," "T.B. Blues," "Blue Yodel No. 9" (which features Louis Armstrong), and "Blue Yodel No. 8 (Muleskinner Blues)."

Although his health was progressively failing, Rodgers signed autographs, performed in country theaters, and continued to record until his untimely death at the age of 35. He recorded his last songs just two days before his death.

—Matthew A. Killmeier

FURTHER READING:

Malone, Bill C. *Country Music, U.S.A.* Austin, University of Texas Press, 1985.

Paris, Mike, and Chris Comber. *Jimmie the Kid.* London, Eddison Press, 1977.

Porterfield, Nolan. *Jimmie Rodgers: The Life and Times of America's Blue Yodeler.* Urbana, University of Illinois Press, 1992.

Rodgers, Carrie. *My Husband Jimmie Rodgers.* San Antonio, Southern Literary Institute, 1935.

Russell, Tony. *Blacks, Whites, and Blues.* New York, Stein & Day, 1970.

Rodgers, Richard

See Rodgers and Hammerstein; Rodgers and Hart

Rodman, Dennis (1961—)

Dennis "The Worm" Rodman was born in Trenton, New Jersey, but grew up in Dallas's infamous Oak Cliff housing projects. A gangly small child, Rodman lived in the shadows of his two extremely tall older sisters, both of whom were adept with a basketball. In his autobiography *Bad As I Wanna Be,* he describes feeling invisible and clumsy growing up. Everything changed in his late teens, however, when he grew by more than a foot. In his autobiography he announces, "It was like I had a new body that knew how to do

Dennis Rodman

all this shit the old one didn't." At age twenty-one Rodman's new body allowed him to transform himself from a nobody who stole wristwatches and worked the janitorial night shift at the local airport into a somebody who played basketball. After a junior college recruited Rodman to play in the late 1970s, he won a basketball scholarship to Southeastern Oklahoma University in 1983. By his mid-twenties he had made it into the NBA, first drafted by the Detroit Pistons (1986-1992), then later traded into the San Antonio Spurs (1993-1995). Finally, with a reputation as the league's best rebounder (he won Defensive Player of the Year in the 1990-91 season) Rodman realized his ultimate dream: he was acquired by the Chicago Bulls in 1995 and became a World Champion again.

Although Rodman got off to a late start, he has risen to become one of the NBA's top players, earning more than $26 million in NBA salary and corporate endorsements a year. Rodman has also made himself an eccentric celebrity. He makes news headlines with stories of that cover his latest hot-tempered antics on the court (such as head-butting referees), his unlikely romances (including a date with Madonna and his impromptu Las Vegas marriage to actress Carmen Electra), his off-the-court cross-dressing style, and his ever changing hair color. Rodman is willing to try it all. He has penned two autobiographies (*Bad as I Wanna Be* has sold more than 800,000 copies) and has tried his hand at acting, co-starring with Jean-Claude Van Damme in the 1997 film *Double Team.*

—Frederick Luis Aldama

FURTHER READING:

Bickley, Dan. *No Bull: The Unauthorized Biography of Dennis Rodman.* New York, St. Martins Press, 1997.

Rodman, B. Anicka. *Worse than He Says He Is: White Girls Don't Bounce.* New York, Dove Books, 1997.

Rodman, Dennis, and Tim Keown. *Bad as I Wanna Be.* New York, Delacorte Press, 1996.

Rodman, Dennis, and Michael Silver. *Walk on the Wild Side.* New York, Delacorte Press, 1997.

Rodríguez, Chi Chi (1935—)

One of golf's all-time greats, Juan "Chi Chi" Rodríguez was the first Hispanic to become an international champion in golf. Born Juan Rodríguez in Río Piedras, Puerto Rico, on October 23, 1935 into an extremely impoverished family, Rodríguez found his way into golf as a caddy on the links that served Puerto Rico's booming tourism. His is one of the most famous Hispanic "rags to riches through sports" tales, his career earnings having passed the $3 million mark. Included among the important tournaments that he has won are the Denver Open (1963), the Lucky Strike International Open (1964), the Western Open (1964), the Dorado Pro-Am (1965), the Texas Open (1967), and the Tallahassee Open (1979). As a member of the Senior PGA (Professional Golfers' Association) Tour, he won numerous tournaments, including the Silver Pages Classic (1987), the GTE Northwest Classic (1987), and the Sunwest Senior Classic (1990).

—Nicolás Kanellos

Chi Chi Rodriguez

FURTHER READING:

Kanellos, Nicolás. *Hispanic American Almanac.* Detroit, Gale, 1997.

Tardiff, Joseph T., and L. Mpho Mabunda, editors. *Dictionary of Hispanic Biography.* Detroit, Gale, 1996.

Roe v. Wade

In 1973 the Supreme Court of the United States handed down a decision in *Roe v. Wade* that would become arguably the most controversial decision of the twentieth century. Using the concept of privacy and the belief that individuals should be able to make important decisions about their own lives, the Court determined that only a pregnant woman and her medical care provider should be involved in a decision to end a pregnancy within the first three months. States were given the right to limit abortions at any time thereafter. The decision resulted in battle lines being formed, and Pro-Choice and Pro-Life advocates, as they came to be known, engaged in a decades-long struggle to control the reproductive rights of American women.

Before *Roe v. Wade,* only four states and Washington, D.C., provided easy access to abortion. All other states limited access to some degree. Public opinion on abortion shifted, however, when an epidemic of German measles and the exposure of U.S. women to the European tranquilizer Thalidomide resulted in a large number of babies born with serious birth defects. Because abortion access was limited, only those who could afford to travel to one of these states or to a foreign country were allowed the privilege of ending an unwanted or unhealthy pregnancy. Many pregnant women and health care professionals believed that access to safe abortions should be a right and not a privilege and challenged the right of states to restrict access to abortions by trained medical personnel. Desperate women who could not afford to travel often self-aborted or trusted themselves to back-alley abortionists. Both practices frequently led to later health problems, sterility or even death.

Ten years before the decision in *Roe v. Wade* the women's movement had gained momentum with the 1963 publication of Betty Friedan's *The Feminine Mystique.* The birth of this "second wave" of feminism led to a greater awareness of the rights of women. Gaining control of their reproductive rights became a significant way of allowing women to take an equal place in American society. It was argued that women should not be made to become mothers against their will, and the medical community and many churches went on record as supporting the right to choose.

The chief players in this landmark decision were a poor pregnant woman, two young inexperienced lawyers, and a Supreme Court justice with a background in medical law. Norma McCorvey, the pregnant woman who became known as "Jane Roe," claimed that she had been raped by a carnival worker in Augusta, Georgia. She later recanted her story. When McCorvey returned to her home state of Texas and attempted to obtain an abortion, she was told that it was impossible. She was sent to two young lawyers, Sara Weddington and Linda Coffee, who were looking for a pregnant woman willing to serve as a test case to challenge restrictive abortion laws. By the time the case was heard before the Supreme Court, McCorvey had given birth to a baby that was put up for adoption. Weddington presented her first case when she argued before the Supreme Court for the right of "Jane Roe," representing all pregnant women, to determine when and if they gave birth. Coffee continued to consult but took a lesser role as the case progressed through legal channels. Although she was inexperienced, Weddington was a thorough researcher and a quick learner. When it was suggested that she shift her chief argument from equal protection to the right to privacy, she did so. Harry Blackmun, a conservative Republican member of the Supreme Court, was assigned to write the Court's majority opinion in *Roe v. Wade.* Blackmun devised the trimester system based on available medical information tracing the development of the fetus. He became a lifelong proponent of a woman's right to control her reproductive life and remained true to his convictions even when the Supreme Court shifted to the right.

From its inception, *Roe v. Wade* incited strong emotions among both its supporters and detractors. Feminists lauded the control it gave to women, and the religious right began a battle to overturn it that would last for decades. Even though Congress had managed to limit the right of poor women to obtain abortions with its passage of the Hyde Amendment in 1976, the Court stood solidly behind the decision. It was the presidency of Ronald Reagan in 1980 that revived the Pro-Life movement. Throughout the 1980s, political candidates turned their views on abortion into campaign slogans. One's position on this issue became the litmus test for entry onto the federal judiciary, including the Supreme Court of the United States. In 1989, the Court backed away from it position in *Roe* but did not overturn it. *Webster v. Reproductive Health Services* gave control over access to abortion to individual states and resulted in a number of restrictive abortion laws, such as those passed in Louisiana and Guam.

Given the mood of the conservative Reagan/Bush Court, scholars, political activists, and the legal community all predicted that the Supreme Court would overturn *Roe v. Wade* with the 1992 case *Planned Parenthood of Southeastern Pennsylvania v. Casey.* Then Supreme Court justice Thurgood Marshall went so far as to write a dissenting vote that only became public after his death. Contrarily, in that election year the Supreme Court reaffirmed their position in *Roe v. Wade* but upheld restrictions such as informed consent and mandatory waiting periods. They rejected the requirement that married women had to notify their husbands before obtaining an abortion. Once the right to choose was upheld by the conservative court, the focus shifted to the violent attacks on doctors and clinics that performed abortions. After a 1993 decision that, in effect, protected the attackers, the Supreme Court again shifted position and in 1994 allowed severe punishment and fines to serve as a deterrent to the continued attacks on abortion clinics and providers.

The battle between Pro-Choice and Pro-Life supporters is based on core values for both groups. Pro-choice advocates believe that women have the right to control when and if they become mothers and argue that a fetus is not a person in the letter of the law. Pro-Life proponents, on the other hand, insist that a fetus is a person and that its rights should supersede those of the mother. Even though *Roe v. Wade* continues to protect the right to choose, there is little likelihood of ending the controversy that surrounds it.

—Elizabeth Purdy

FURTHER READING:

Craig, Barbara Hinkson, and David M. O'Brien. *Abortion and American Politics.* Chatham, New Jersey, Chatham House Publishers, 1993.

Faux, Marian. *Roe v. Wade: The Untold Story of the Landmark Supreme Court Decision That Made Abortion Legal.* New York, New American Library, 1988.

Reagan, Leslie J. *When Abortion Was Illegal: Women, Medicine, and Law in the United States, 1867-1973.* Berkeley, University of California Press, 1997.

Rogers, Kenny (1938—)

Born in Texas in 1938 and raised in one of the state's poorest Federal Housing projects, the country singer Kenny Rogers grew up to become one of the most recognizable celebrities in the United States. Although variously a television and film actor, photographer, author, and fast food entrepreneur, it is for his music that he has secured a place in popular American culture.

Rogers began his first career, music, in the 1950s when he joined a singing group called the Scholars, who had local hits. He made his first national television appearance in 1958, when a solo hit on a local label, Carlton Records, became popular enough to land him an *American Bandstand* slot. In the late 1950s, he played bass in a jazz combo called the Bobby Doyle Three, and made one record with them before being given a solo contract with Mercury. The arrangement

Kenny Rogers

proved short-lived and commercially fruitless, and when Mercury failed to renew his contract, Rogers joined the folk-pop group the New Christy Minstrels and stayed with them for a year. Together with other members of the group, Rogers left to form the New Edition, with whom he made his first significant national splash. The New Edition performed a mixed bag of styles, but they scored a top ten hit for Reprise in 1968 with the psychedelic "Just Dropped in (To See What Condition My Condition Was In)." They also had success with Mel Tillis's "Ruby Don't Take Your Love to Town," as well as "Reuben James," in which Rogers' country tendencies were becoming apparent. The group parlayed this and a few other minor hits into a prime-time television show in 1972. Rogers left the group in 1974, and the Edition broke up shortly after.

In 1975, Rogers signed with United Artists, and released a number of records, achieving his first major number one smash-hit with "Lucille" in 1977. It was also a big crossover success, peaking at number five on the pop charts. Thus began a run of massive crossover hits, including "The Gambler" in 1978, a song that spawned a series of made-for-television movies starring the singer. In the late 1970s, Rogers teamed up with Dottie West for a series of successful duets, beginning a run of pairings in the early 1980s with such major female stars as Sheena Easton, Kim Carnes, and, memorably, Dolly Parton, with whom he duetted to a number-one smash with the Bee Gees' "Islands in the Stream." He also had a hit with Lionel Richie's "Lady," further blurring the lines between country and pop. Crossover successes like those enjoyed by Rogers and a handful of other artists changed the course of the country music industry. Country artists were no longer satisfied to succeed solely in the country charts, and they began producing music with a sonic quality appropriate for Top 40 radio. The twangy steel guitars and fiddles of the Grand Ole Opry were widely forsaken in favor of the lusher "Nashville" sound as pop success became both desirable and attainable.

In 1983, Rogers signed with RCA records, and though he had several number-one country hits, his crossover appeal was starting to wane. When his contract came up for renewal in 1988, RCA opted out. Though he was no longer as looming a presence on the radio charts, he did appear in several television shows and continued to tour. He invested in the new country music mecca of Branson, Missouri, the Ozark Mountain resort where many older country stars built theaters in which to perform regularly; he also became involved in charity work and published two well-received books of his own photography. He diversified further into the fast food business, lending his name to the Kenny Rogers Roasters franchise, which expanded to hundreds of outlets countrywide.

In 1996, Rogers twice moved into a new spot on the cultural radar. In January that year, his album *Vote For Love* was the first release on "onQ" records, owned by the QVC cable shopping station. It was, of course, marketed exclusively through QVC, and sold over 100,000 copies in its first month of release. Then, in November, the television comedy *Seinfeld* produced a classic episode revolving around Kenny Rogers Roasters. This multi-faceted man has continued to release records almost yearly, but outside of his devoted fan base, they have not made much impact. However, through all of his entertainment and business exploits, he has remained a high-profile figure in the landscape of popular culture.

—Joyce Linehan

FURTHER READING:

Hume, Martha, and Kenny Rogers. *Gambler, Dreamer Lover.* New York, New American Library, 1980.

Rogers, Roy (1912-1998)

Roy Rogers, with his horse, Trigger, came to prominence in the late 1930s and early 1940s, following closely in the footsteps of singing cowboy Gene Autry. Rogers' rise to stardom transformed the "singing cowboy" from an isolated phenomenon to a recognized movie genre, and his popular success, added to Autry's, brought screen stardom in turn to Tex Ritter, Jimmy Wakely, Monte Hale, Johnny Mack Brown, and others. None of them attained the iconic status of Rogers or Autry, but all of them contributed to the mythology of the straight-shooting, clean-living hero who is also sensitive enough, in a folksy, regular-guy sort of way, to pick up a guitar and sing a song or two. The singing cowboy movie was—at least in retrospect—a natural phenomenon for the 1930s. The old West was only a generation or so removed from movie audiences, and the cowboy films or "B" Westerns (as opposed to the weightier Western as conceived by John Ford) spoke to the public's sense of nostalgia. Then, too, the arrival of sound in the cinema created a demand for music and singing, which dovetailed neatly with the Rogers-style

Roy Rogers (right) with Dale Evans.

Westerns, set in an increasingly stylized world not unlike the fanciful Ruritanian villages of light opera, which created a perfect backdrop for good-looking, guitar-playing, singing heroes.

Unlike Gene Autry, Rogers didn't have a western background, but he did come from a rural environment. Born Leonard Slye in Cincinnati, Ohio, he moved to California with his father, a migrant laborer, and worked as a fruit picker and truck driver, as well as singing with a variety of country groups. In the California of the 1930s, country music was influenced by Hollywood pop and by Western Swing, and Rogers (then using the name Dick Weston) was in groups with names like Uncle Tom Murray's Hollywood Hillbillies, the International Cowboys, and the O-Bar-O Cowboys. In 1934, with Bob Nolan and Tim Spencer, he formed a group called the Pioneer Trio which, shortly after, changed its name to the Sons of the Pioneers. The Sons of the Pioneers was a harmony trio, more influenced by barbershop and contemporary jazz-flavored pop groups like the Modernaires than by any country music, but they had a unique sound and, in Nolan, the advantage of a brilliant songwriter ("Tumbling Tumbleweeds," "Cool Water"). They became an important influence on the country and western music that followed them. Rogers, in fact, is the only person to have been inducted into the Country Music Hall of Fame twice—once as a solo performer, and once as a member of the Sons of the Pioneers.

Rogers broke into movies in the mid-1930s, playing bit parts in Westerns, first for Columbia Pictures and then for Republic, Autry's studio and the leading purveyor of "B" Westerns. His first starring role was in *Under Western Stars* (1938), and for the next five years, he and Autry shared stardom at Republic, with Autry still considered the screen's "King of the Cowboys." When Autry went into the Air Force during World War II, Republic threw all the weight of its publicity machine behind Rogers, and his career really took off. From 1943 through 1954, he was listed by a theater owners' poll as the top Western star in Hollywood.

In a genre characterized by stylization, Rogers was perhaps the most stylized of all, as evidenced in his colorful and distinctive outfits, designed by Nudie of Hollywood. Other cowboys had been associated with horses, from Tom Mix (Tony) to Autry (Champion), but no other cowboy had a horse as colorful and identifiable as Rogers's palomino, Trigger, billed as "the smartest horse in movies." Other cowboys had sidekicks, but none quite as colorful as Rogers's Gabby Hayes. Rogers inherited Autry's title of King of the Cowboys, and his wife, Dale Evans, whom he married in 1947, was dubbed the Queen of the West.

Rogers became a symbol of an idealized America in the spirit and style of Norman Rockwell's paintings. He represented the normality that Americans were seeking in the aftermath of the war years but, eventually, his films proved too tame for later postwar audiences. His on-screen romances, generally with Evans, were shy and chaste, and his action sequences had a low violence quotient; he would shoot the gun out of the bad guy's hand, toss away his own, and subdue the baddie in a rousing but fair fist fight. To a generation that had seen the horrors of war, this was at first reassuring, then tame and corny, and Rogers' popularity waned, along with that of the "B" Western.

A shrewd businessman, Rogers took his talents to television, aiming his initial show at younger audiences whose parents, the cowboy's former fans, enthusiastically encouraged their children to enjoy the innocent myths that Rogers perpetrated. *The Roy Rogers Show* debuted in 1951 and continued with first-run episodes until 1957, retaining the familiar style of Rogers' big-screen image. It was all there: Roy and Dale on their ranch, the Double R Bar; sidekick Pat Brady (formerly with the Sons of the Pioneers, replacing Gabby Hayes); wonder horse Trigger and faithful dog Bullet; Dale's horse Buttermilk and Brady's jeep Nellybelle. The show's theme song, "Happy Trails" (by Evans, a skilled songwriter), remains a national catchphrase. Rogers' popularity through the 1950s was international, and of his over 200 fan clubs the one in London, with over 50,000 members, was estimated to be the biggest such club for any performer, anywhere on earth.

In 1962, Rogers and his wife co-hosted a variety program, *The Roy Rogers and Dale Evans Show,* but most of his time since the late 1950s was given over to building a substantial business empire that included ownership of a TV company, interests in thoroughbred horses, real estate, and rodeo, and his well-known Roy Rogers fast food chain. In 1967, he opened the Roy Rogers museum in Apple Valley, California. The most noteworthy display, among other Rogers memorabilia, was Trigger himself, stuffed and mounted in a rearing posture.

During the 1980s and 1990s, Rogers made a singing comeback, recording solo and as a duet performer with Clint Black and others. Some said it was a publicity move to advertise his restaurant chains by reviving his image for a generation that didn't know who he was. Whether or not this was so, his legacy remained strong, with even Bruce Willis's character in *Die Hard* (1988), for example, invoking Roy Rogers as his ideal of courage and decent values.

—Tad Richards

FURTHER READING:

Morris, Georgia, and Mark Pollard, editors. *Roy Rogers: King of the Cowboys.* San Francisco, Collins, 1994.

Phillips, Robert W. *Roy Rogers: A Biography, Radio History, Television Career Chronicle, Discography, Filmography, Comicography, Merchandising and Advertising History.* Jefferson, North Carolina, McFarland & Company, 1995.

Rogers, Roy, and Dale Evans, with Carlton Stowers. *Happy Trails.* New York, Guideposts, 1979.

Rogers, Roy, and Dale Evans, with Jane and Michael Stern. *Happy Trails: Our Life Story.* New York, Simon & Schuster, 1994.

Rogers, Will (1879-1935)

Humorist Will Rogers' impact upon American culture was great and lasting. He made himself into the archetypal American Everyman, apparently baffled and out-smarted by the machinations of politicians and tycoons, but in reality always managing to get the better of them through the shrewd and timely use of common sense and self-effacing humor. Some 35 years before Mort Sahl based his nightclub act on satirical observations of government officials, writer-actor-humorist Rogers told a joint session of Congress, "It's a pleasure to be here in Washington with all these other comedians. The only thing is, when *you* make a joke, it's a law! And when you make a law, it's a joke." But Rogers was not so much a pioneer in the realm of political humor as he was an utterly unique character, whose wry and seemingly naive comments on U.S. politics and society were so integral a part of his public persona that no entertainer could have modeled his act on Rogers' without being dismissed as a mere imitator. When Rogers, a lifelong Democrat ("No, I'm not a member of an organized political party—I'm a Democrat") was introduced to Republican President Calvin Coolidge, he held out his hand and cocked his head to one side. "Pardon," he said, "Didn't catch the name." It was the only occasion during Coolidge's presidency when he was observed to smile.

Born William Penn Adair Rogers on November 4, 1879, on a ranch between Claremore and Oologah, in Oklahoma (then known as the Indian Nation), he became an expert rider and roper at a very early age. Both of Rogers' parents were part Cherokee, and when a reporter asked him if any of his ancestors had come over on the *Mayflower,* he replied, "No, my ancestors met the boat." He received a very light formal education, admitting only to two years at Kemper Military Academy in Booneville, Missouri ("One year in the guardhouse and one in the fourth grade"). He left school for good in 1898 to become a cowboy in the Texas Panhandle, from there drifted to Argentina, and eventually joined Texas Jack's Wild West Circus with a rope-trick act, making his first public appearance in Johannesburg, South Africa, during the Boer War (1899-1902).

When Rogers returned to the United States, he continued with his roping act, playing at county fairs and in vaudeville. Twirling his lariat, making fantastic shapes in the air, he would tell stories and jokes and began to introduce topical humor into his act. As his popularity increased, the humor became more and more important, and by the time his act reached the New York stage in 1905, the rope tricks had become props and punctuation for the jokes. Branching into musical comedy, he had his first taste of real fame: a starring role in the *Ziegfeld Follies* of 1916. His standard lead-in line, "All I know is what I read in the papers," became something of a signature and a ubiquitous watchword in the 1920s. The zenith of his New York stage career came in 1934 when he appeared in Eugene O'Neill's only comedy, *Ah, Wilderness!*, and he made his film debut in 1918. It wasn't until the advent of sound, however, that he became a popular box-office attraction, starring in such memorable John Ford features as *Judge Priest* (1934) and *Steamboat 'round the Bend* (1935). Meanwhile, he had begun a successful parallel career as a writer, at first of humorous books (*The Cowboy Philosopher on Prohibition, The Illiterate Digest*) and, from 1926 onwards, as a syndicated columnist. He also conquered the new medium of radio as a commentator, and had all of America laughing when he announced, "I don't know jokes; I just watch the government and report the facts." All of his brilliant gifts were tragically silenced in 1935 when, flying in Alaska with the noted aviator Wiley Post, the plane crashed and both men were killed.

Will Rogers left other political humorists with very little to do, and the field lay mostly fallow until the late 1950s when Mort Sahl revived political humor. Sahl did so from a very different point of view, commenting that "Will Rogers's act was that he was a country bumpkin up against clever sophisticates, whereas my situation is just the reverse."

—Gerald Carpenter

FURTHER READING:

Alworth, E. Paul. *Will Rogers.* New York, Twayne Publishers, 1974.

Axtell, Margaret S. *Will Rogers Rode the Range.* Phoenix, Allied Printing, 1972.

Brown, William R. *Imagemaker: Will Rogers and the American Dream.* Columbia, University of Missouri Press, 1970.

Carter, Joseph H. *I Never Met a Man I Didn't Like: The Life and Writings of Will Rogers.* New York, Avon Books, 1991.

Robinson, Ray. *American Original: A Life of Will Rogers.* New York, Oxford University Press, 1996.

Rogers, Will. *Autobiography.* Selected and edited by Donald Day. Boston, Houghton Mifflin Co., 1949.

Will Rogers Memorial

Rogers, Will. *The Papers of Will Rogers*. Edited by Arthur Frank Wertheim and Barbara Bair. Norman, University of Oklahoma Press, 1996.

Rolle, Esther (1920-1998)

Emmy award-winning Esther Rolle is best remembered as Florida Evans, the strong matriarch of the hit CBS television series *Good Times* (1974-1979). *Good Times* was a spinoff of Norman Lear's *Maude,* in which Rolle played Florida from 1972-1974. Florida was a feisty sarcastic black maid employed by Bea Arthur's loud, white, middle-aged liberal Maude Findlay. On *Good Times,* Florida was the female head of a lower class family of five in the Chicago projects. At Rolle's insistence, hoping to present positive role models to black Americans, the family was not fatherless. Rolle left the series in 1977 reportedly feeling the storylines involving Jimmie Walker, who played her oldest son, were reinforcing negative stereotypes. Promised changes, she returned in 1978, but ratings had slipped and the show was canceled. Rolle won three NAACP (National Association for the Advancement of Colored People) Image awards throughout her career. She also appeared in numerous feature films. Ironically, she frequently played a maid.

—Joyce Linehan

Roller Coasters

Most everyone can remember the first time they rode a roller coaster, and how it felt. People either love to ride roller coasters or do not, but very few are indifferent to the bone-rattling structures that have become a popular pastime worldwide, ever since the first one— "Flying Mountains," developed in Russia in the fifteenth century— introduced the combination of fear and amusement. The engineering technology of roller coasters defies nature by allowing human beings to be catapulted at varying speeds every which way. There were approximately 475 operating roller coasters in North America as of 1998, all competing in speed, architecture, and inventiveness. The progress of engineering has enabled coasters to travel backward or around inverted loops at alarming speeds (most average in the mid-60-miles-per-hour range), while riders can sometimes stand, be in the dark, or sit in chairlift-style trains with tracks that run along the top, while strapped tightly into their seats. Whether they are steel or wooden, the names bestowed upon roller coasters are always given careful thought, their purpose being to evoke a really good and scary ride (Colossus, Fireball, Cyclone, and the Superman are some examples). As of 1999, there were 13 roller coaster clubs and organizations formed by people who share a similar enthusiasm and spend much of their leisure time engaging in lengthy critiques of coasters all over the world. There are even front- and backseat enthusiasts who argue over which seat will elicit the most surprises and offer the best ride.

The physics are relatively simple: roller coasters are powered by gravity (and operated by computers). As the train is pulled up the hill, "potential energy" is built up and then converted into "kinetic energy" once it begins its descent. Positive gravitational forces ("g-forces") press riders into their seats at the bottom of a dip, whereas

Esther Rolle

"negative g's" create a temporary sense of weightlessness that is pleasurable for some and nauseating for others. During the ride, people experience a communal thrill of traveling at extreme speeds and heights while being in the open air.

Part of the fun of roller coasters is that they are scary, and there is a perverse delight people feel in being afraid, especially when they are (relatively) sure that nothing can go wrong. Some roller coasters have speed to offer (the best usually surpass 70 miles per hour), or the height of dips (225 feet, for example), or the frequency of the dips during a ride (a coaster in Texas boasts 20 additional drops, after the first one, which descends 137 feet). Most trains travel slowly up the track at the ride's beginning to allow the coaster to gain speed during its first plunge that will sustain it for the duration of the ride, but also to build up the anticipation of riders as to what lies ahead (most likely the highest of many drops, loops, or speed). But some blast off instantly, gaining awesome speed in a short amount of time (one popular roller coaster accelerates from 0 to 100 in just 7 seconds). Sometimes the real adventure, though, lies in a roller coaster's stature or age. A creaky, old wooden coaster, without fancy safety mechanisms, can hint at an impending derailment, as well as offer a truly jostling, loud ride.

The Cyclatron roller coaster at Rockaway's Playland in Queens, New York.

The famous, rickety Cyclone in Coney Island, New York, helped to popularize the roller coaster in the United States at the beginning of the twentieth century. Coaster mythology has it that a mute man once rode it and spoke his very first words after riding it: "I feel sick." Even in the 1990s, the coaster still continues to frighten riders who can never be sure if and when it will fall apart. In 1927, a nurse was stationed next to the Cyclone in Crystal Beach, Ontario, just as a precaution, because of its 90-foot drop and hairpin turns. The Zippin Pippin in Libertyland, Memphis, was singer Elvis Presley's favorite amusement park ride. Apparently, the King once rode it nonstop for hours when he rented out the park one night in 1977, just eight days before he died.

There is always an element of uncertainty in riding these man-made machines, and roller coasters have had their share of widely publicized mishaps. Oftentimes the computers that run them fail. Cars have smashed into each other, safety lap bars have suddenly popped open during a ride, and trains have become uncoupled while climbing hills. In turn, riders have been thrown out of trains and suffered other injuries that—combined with the speed, twists, and turns of roller coasters—can be very serious, if not fatal. An extensive study by the Associated Press found that the roller coaster industry was one in which blunders and bad judgment can abound. There is constant competition for companies to design faster, bigger, and more awesome rides, in which riders often serve as guinea pigs, testing the rides' safety when they first open. "It's hard sometimes on paper to anticipate those forces," said Robert Johnson, executive director of the Outdoor Amusement Business Association, a carnival trade group. "People aren't built the same. Some people can withstand

forces differently than others. Any major new ride, it's a trial ride. A prototype. The first year is a trial year." There is a certain degree of misbehaving that goes on in parks with patrons (holding up their hands during a ride, for example), and that coupled with the fact that the industry is one of the least regulated and monitored in the country (there are no federal guidelines for the degree of gravitational forces that people can be subjected to), can produce more risks. But the knowledge that an occasional, injurious accident can occur does not stop enthusiasts from waiting in long lines to ride roller coasters.

—Sharon Yablon

FURTHER READING:

Cartmell, Robert. *The Incredible Scream Machine: A History of the Roller Coaster.* Bowling Green, Ohio, Bowling Green State University Popular Press, 1987.

Costanza, Jared. "Amusement Ride Accident Reports and News." http://members.aol.com/rides911/accidents.htm. June 1999.

Silverstein, Herma. *Scream Machines: Roller Coasters Past, Present, and Future.* New York, Walker, 1986.

Throgmorton, Todd H. *Roller Coasters: An Illustrated Guide to the Rides in the United States and Canada, with a History.* Jefferson, N.C., McFarland and Company, 1993.

Urbanowicz, Steven J. *The Roller Coaster Lover's Companion: A Thrill-Seeker's Guide to the World's Best Coasters.* Secaucas, New Jersey, Carol Publishing Group, 1997.

Van Steenwyk, Elizabeth. *Behind the Scenes at the Amusement Park.* Niles, Illinois, A. Whitman, 1983.

Roller Derby

Roller Derby is a team sport of fast, furious, and often violent action that first appeared in the mid-1930s. The games take place on a banked oval track, where two squads of five men or five women—the sexes do not usually compete against each other—skate around the track, with each team sending out "jammers" in front of the pack. Points are scored when jammers lap an opponent. Like rugby or football, other players act as "blockers" clearing the way for the jammer.

Long-distance bicycle races and marathon dances inspired the original game, invented in 1935 by Leo Seltzer. The objective was to make 57,000 laps around the track, a distance of 4,000 miles. While at that time it was a true athletic contest, it was also quite boring for the spectators because matches would last for hours on end. Similar to the development of professional wrestling, it was when Roller Derby introduced violent contact and shorter matches, and began developing personality players, that its popularity boomed. Legend has it that writer Damon Runyon, after witnessing a fight between two women skaters, suggested that Seltzer turn Roller Derby into something akin to pro wrestling on skates. Like pro wrestling, it is not an authentic competitive sport since the games, fights, and all action are "worked." The participants are heroes and villains, acting out feuds and grudges that pro wrestling fans might find familiar. The most popular skaters were not necessarily the best athletes, but rather the most charismatic characters, dramatic performers, and captivating interview subjects.

The mix of speed and mayhem, coupled with cheap production costs, was perfect for early television, and Roller Derby was the most popular show on ABC during the network's infancy.

The popularity of the sport was such that in 1949 the playoffs of the National Roller Derby League sold out New York's Madison Square Garden for a week. A large part of the Roller Derby audience has always been women, in part because the Roller Derby was almost the only sports activity prior to the 1970s where female athletes could be seen on television. In addition, the Roller Derby integrated very early and many of the skaters were black or Hispanic, among them Ronnie Robinson, son of boxing great Sugar Ray Robinson.

In 1950, Leo Seltzer's son Jerry took over the Roller Derby and moved the base of operations to southern California, then to northern California in 1958. The home team Bay Area Bombers achieved the most success. With stars like Charlie O'Connell, Ann Calvello, and "The Blonde Bomber" Joanie Weston, the Bombers dominated the sport and Weston was the star of the show. She was, according to sports writer Frank Deford, "not only the best skater, but she clearly looks the part as well. With her bleached blonde pigtails flowing out from beneath her shiny black pivot helmet, Joanie appeared like a brave Viking queen in full battle regalia." With huge local shows, which often outdrew those of the expanding Oakland Raiders football team in the early 1960s, the popularity of Roller Derby remained strong. The sport spread to more cities and to other countries, and had ten full-time teams at its peak of popularity. Yet, in 1973, only two years after drawing a record 35,000 people to the Oakland Coliseum, Jerry Seltzer folded the league, selling out to a rival organization based out of Los Angeles called Rollergames. Rollergames was even more outlandish than Roller Derby and featured more professional wrestling gimmicks such as death matches. The Rollergame league's Los Angeles T-Birds, which once featured a huge woman skater with the number 747, was the most dominant team until Rollergames folded in 1975.

Like its cousin, professional wrestling, Roller Derby is considered a trash sport. But fewer people have admitted to watching it than actually do. Eventually, the popularity of Roller Derby found its way into mainstream popular culture. The film *Kansas City Bomber* (1972) featured Raquel Welch as a Roller Derby queen; *Rollerball* (1975) starred James Caan and was a futuristic parable set in a society where an ultra-violent Roller Derby-like sport is used to give anti-social feelings an emotional outlet, thus becoming the most popular mass pastime. In 1978, the TV show *Roller Girls,* centered on the fictional Pittsburgh Pitts Roller Derby team, lasted for less than ten episodes. Numerous attempts at comebacks have been equally unsuccessful. The International Roller Derby League was formed in 1979, but appeared only in the Bay Area and, in 1986, a souped-up version of Rollergames that included "a wall of death" appeared on ESPN. It lasted less than a season.

The most recent revival took place in 1998 and looked to have a chance at success with Jerry Seltzer, as President of the World Skating League, again at the helm. The WSL put together six teams to produce *Roller Jams* for the Nashville Network. While the concept remained the same, the packaging was much different. Rather than roller skates, skaters in the new league donned roller-blades and tight-fitting latex uniforms, and special effects and rock music were introduced to accompany the event. The late 1990s sport was faster and sexier than ever before, and Seltzer expressed the belief that the resurgence of pro wrestling in the 1990s, coupled with the wide attraction of roller-blading, would put Roller Derby back on top for the twenty-first century.

The other inspiration for the new look Roller Derby was Joanie Weston. Even after the Roller Derby folded, Weston kept skating, training new talent, and holding exhibitions in the Bay Area in an attempt to revive the sport. When she died suddenly in 1997, Roller Derby was thrust back into the news. After reading Weston's obituary, TV executive Stephen Land was "inspired to get together with TNN and make Weston's dream come true." Weston has lived on through ESPN's Classic Sports Network show, *Roller Super Stars,* which features old tapes of the golden years of the "blonde bomber" and her teammates.

—Patrick Jones

FURTHER READING:

Deford, Frank. *Five Strides on the Banked Track: The Life and Times of the Roller Derby.* Boston, Little Brown, 1971.

Werts, Diane. "What Goes around Comes Around—Like Roller Derby." *Los Angeles Times.* January 8, 1999.

Rolling Stone

Almost two years before the *Saturday Evening Post*—"America's magazine"—first folded in 1969, a small magazine named *Rolling Stone* began in a San Francisco print shop. With the look of an underground newspaper, *Rolling Stone* targeted a young readership that was attuned to the counterculture. Whereas the *Post* conveyed a consensus within American culture, *Rolling Stone* had more in common with *Playboy*'s approach as the embodiment of a particular lifestyle. At its height, *Rolling Stone*'s cover became an icon in itself—for many, it served as a cultural barometer. At different points in its history, the biweekly had been regarded as a daring anti-establishment voice, or a slick mainstream media product. The magazine's one main constant was its music coverage. *Rolling Stone* deemed rock musicians and their music to be newsworthy, which helped to legitimize one of the key elements of 1960s' oppositional culture. The inception of *Rolling Stone* marked the changes in U.S. culture following the 1960s: one such change held that the personal—one's lifestyle, even the kind of music one listened to—is political.

Jann Wenner, editor and publisher, was a 21-year-old dropout from Berkeley when he began *Rolling Stone* with only $7500 in borrowed capital. "*Rolling Stone* is not just about music," wrote Wenner in the inaugural issue, "but also about the things and attitudes that the music embraces." The magazine's name was taken from a song, by blues legend Muddy Waters, that borrowed its title from an old proverb: "A rolling stone gathers no moss." *Rolling Stone*'s look—newsprint on a quarterfold format—was of an underground newspaper, although that was the furthest thing from Wenner's mind. The intention from the beginning was to make the magazine look as professional as possible, with column rules and Times Roman type. Wenner, who derisively referred to "the hippie press," wanted to be as legitimate as *Time* magazine. Despite Wenner's efforts, outsiders saw *Rolling Stone* as part of the underground press, a perception that lasted into the 1970s.

The magazine took its slogan, "All the News That Fits," from the *New York Times*' "All the News That's Fit to Print"—it was a facetious swipe and a description of the limitless space allotted to *Rolling Stone*'s writers. The magazine's focus on music as a newsworthy topic distinguished it from any other publication before it. Its interviews with musicians (later to include actors, politicians, and other celebrities) went beyond the fan magazine's interest in personal likes and dislikes, and probed the creative processes behind the music instead. One of the magazine's early record critics, Greil Marcus, declared in Robert Anson's *Gone Crazy and Back Again*: "I am no more capable of mulling over Elvis without thinking of Herman Melville, than I am of reading Jonathan Edwards without putting on Robert Johnson's records as background music."

After barely getting off the ground—the first issue had a press run of 40,000 copies where all but 6000 of them were returned—the magazine had a circulation of 325,000 by 1974, a figure that reached 1.25 million in 1998. Along the way, the magazine dropped its quarterfold format for a regular tabloid style and four color. In 1974, 16 percent of its readership was over 25 with a median age of 21. By the end of the 1990s, its original audience was older and more like yuppies. Once a necessity to young Americans, the 1990s *Rolling Stone* faced heavy competition from other music magazines and MTV.

Wenner, dubbed the "hip capitalist" by journalist Robert Draper, once offered the early subscription incentive of a free roach clip (to hold marijuana joints). Hip promotion aside, the magazine's steadily gaining reputation for publishing "some remarkably good reportage," as the *New York Times* was forced to admit in 1973, was what gave *Rolling Stone* its foothold. Wenner's magazine thrived on reporting the cultural events of the late 1960s for which it seemed best suited. While mainstream newspapers condemned the tribal goings-on at the Woodstock festival, *Rolling Stone* reported that the festival crowd temporarily constituted New York State's third-largest city and successfully policed itself. When 1969's Altamont festival self-destructed into violence, *Rolling Stone* weighed in with the headline, "Let It Bleed," and assigned blame to anyone even remotely involved with the festival. Its hard-hitting reporting of Altamont was in sharp contrast to the establishment press that lazily reported facts and figures: how long the traffic jam was, and the estimated crowd, all the while giving no impression of the orgy of violence that ensued there.

Somehow, the optimistic possibilities, ahead of the magazine in the late 1960s, dissipated as it entered the 1970s. The shootings at Kent State in 1970 provoked many on the staff to steer the magazine towards more political coverage. Wenner fought off the revolt and insisted the magazine remain focused on music, which resulted in several resignations. This was problematic because rock music also limped into the 1970s. Many of rock's new legends—like Jimi Hendrix, Jim Morrison, and Janis Joplin—were either dead, or else they were defunct like the Beatles. As rock critic Jon Landau expressed it, as quoted from a 1974 *New York Times* book review: "Bob Dylan has lost much of his impact . . . the end of the Beatles as a group is now irreversible . . . there are no longer any superhumans to focus on."

Enter Hunter Thompson, the iconoclastic writer who became a celebrity through the magazine's pages. Thompson, the "Gonzo Journalist," practiced a bombastic style of writing that pushed aside objectivity, and forced the writer into the stories he covered. Thompson was a cultural outlaw: open about his drug abuse and alcohol consumption, his prose could be gifted in its insights on one page and babbling nonsense on the next. The writer who once wrote that President Richard Nixon had "the integrity of a hyena and the style of a poison toad," managed to find himself, during the 1968 campaign, with the president in Nixon's limousine, where they talked about football. It was the kind of inconceivable situation that endeared Thompson to *Rolling Stone*'s readers. Issues that carried Thompson's installments of his infamous book, *Fear and Loathing in Las Vegas*,

sold out quickly. Soon Thompson was covering the 1972 presidential election for the magazine, which was beginning to display a unique ability to transfer rock-and-roll panache to more sober pursuits, like literature and politics.

Rolling Stone quietly became a literate magazine that happened to cover music. More influential celebrities were granting lengthy interviews, like the ones that had been popularized in *Playboy*. The magazine's literary credentials were further established by the appearance of authors Tom Wolfe and Truman Capote; Richard Goodwin, former speechwriter for John F. Kennedy, helped to give it political cachet. It won the 1970 National Magazine Award for its pieces on Altamont and Charles Manson. Now recognized for challenging its readers' assumptions, *Rolling Stone* had the envious ability to cover stories in ways that major newspapers couldn't, or wouldn't.

Rolling Stone's breakthrough followed in 1975, after being contacted by a San Francisco attorney who claimed he provided refuge for fugitive Patty Hearst, the kidnapped newspaper-chain heiress. "The Inside Story," as the article was titled, scooped the major media outlets on what was an intensely followed story. It was widely recognized that *Rolling Stone*'s Patty Hearst story was the biggest journalistic event since the *New York Times* printed the Pentagon Papers five years before.

Perhaps the magazine's toughest critics were its readers and its staff; every decision, from the changes in format, to the kind of advertising *Rolling Stone* accepted, was subjected to active debate. According to Draper, it was simply that "*Rolling Stone*'s staffers wanted nothing so much as to set a good example for their peers. When they did not, their readers cried 'sellout'—a charge that perhaps no other magazine had ever yet faced." After *Rolling Stone*'s move to New York in 1977, the magazine's culture was altered. Bit by bit, the look and content steered towards more market-driven concerns—Wenner was eager to shake the magazine's hippie image in pursuit of mainstream success. The fragmented music scene and the aging readership helped to underscore the editorial drift that ensued. The magazine, once a haven for writers escaping the establishment press, was put in the unusual position of watching its writers defect to the mainstream press.

"Few things sound less glamorous," proclaimed Louis Menand in a 1991 *New Republic* piece, "than 'the counterculture'—a term many people are likely to associate with Charles Manson." *Rolling Stone*'s constituency had changed. Faced with competition from other music magazines, like *Spin* (alternative music) and *Vibe* (hip-hop/rap), the 1990s presented the challenge of a young audience who could get their music news without having to read *Rolling Stone*. The magazine responded by increasing its content towards fashion and technology. Out of touch with even its core topic, *Rolling Stone* gave covers to major 1980s rock acts like U2 and Talking Heads behind *Time* and *Newsweek*. "Yet this was where the magazine found itself at the close of the eighties," Draper's book concluded: "respected but no longer relied upon, a force among other forces—an institution, surely, and like many such institutions, disregarded."

—Daryl Umberger

FURTHER READING:

Anson, Robert Sam. *The Rise and Fall of the Rolling Stone Generation.* Garden City, New York, Doubleday, 1981.

Arnold, Martin. "Rolling Stone Is Still Gathering Readers, Revenue and Prestige." *New York Times.* October 22, 1973, 32.

Draper, Robert. *Rolling Stone Magazine: The Uncensored History.* Garden City, New York, Doubleday, 1990.

Granatstein, Lisa. "RS Rolls out Fresher Look." *Mediaweek.* August 10, 1998, 6-7.

Menand, Louis. "Life in the Stone Age." *New Republic.* January 7, 1991, 38-44.

Nelson, Alix, review of *The Rolling Stone Reader.* In *New York Times,* April 14, 1974, sec. 7, 19.

Seymour, Corey. "On the Cover of Rolling Stone: A Twenty-Fifth Anniversary Special." *Rolling Stone.* December 10, 1992, 147-154.

Weir, David. "Rolling Stone Gathers No Marx." *Salon.* http://www.salonmagazine.com/media/1998/06/09media.html. 1998.

The Rolling Stones

While the Beatles and other exponents of "the British Invasion" served an updated version of rock 'n' roll to the United States, the Rolling Stones emerged in 1963-1964 as the most prominent of the British acts who brought the Afro-American musical form of blues to a young, white American audience. The group was at the peak of their musical and cultural significance at the end of the 1960s, when their violent lyrics and brooding blues-rock seemed to reflect the potentially cataclysmic clefts in American society. After the early 1970s, the Rolling Stones made very few musically or politically radical records, but their famous 1960s songs continue to resound.

The Rolling Stones

Mick Jagger and Keith Richards attended the same primary school in Dartford, England, during the late 1940s, but lost touch until a legendary reunion at Dartford railway station in 1961, when Richards' interest was piqued by Jagger's selection of Chuck Berry records. Jagger and Richards soon began to play with slide guitar afficiando Brian Jones. The trio recruited jazz drummer Charlie Watts and bassist Bill Wyman, Jones naming the fledgling group the Rollin' Stones after a Muddy Waters song. In April 1962, aspiring pop-group manager Andrew Oldham saw the Stones at the Crawdaddy club in Richmond, London. Oldham later reminisced: "I knew what I was looking at. It was sex."

Oldham negotiated the Stones' contract with Decca Records in early 1963. The group's earliest recorded songs were a compromise between expurgated rhythm and blues (R&B), and pop ballads intended to exploit the popularity of the Beatles. In early 1964, however, Oldham began to promote the Rolling Stones as the antithesis of the "Fab Four," ordering the band to abandon their "Beatle boots" and leather waistcoats and to accentuate the slovenly, surly sexuality which he had seen have such an effect on audiences at their early Crawdaddy gigs. Oldham's propaganda included planting newspaper headlines such as "WOULD YOU LET YOUR DAUGHTER GO WITH A ROLLING STONE?" When the Stones' arrived for their first tour of the United States in June 1964, American newspapers fulminated that the "New Beatles" were a disgrace compared to the adorable, mop-topped originals. Old-school crooner and compeer Dean Martin made sneering references to the Stones' long hair during their appearance on *Hollywood Palace.* But hip American youths embraced the Stones, not least because the Beatles had been coopted by their parents, and, as Lillian Roxon later noted, "No one had ever seen a white man move on stage the way Jagger moved."

The Rolling Stones' commercial appeal to young Americans was confirmed when the single "(I Can't Get No) Satisfaction," a sexually aggressive anthem of disillusion with society, reached number one in June 1965. A run of similarly incendiary hit singles followed, before the 1967 albums *Between the Buttons* and *Their Satanic Majesties Request,* a disastrous foray into fay Anglocentric psychedelia, revealed the extent to which the Stones had neglected their R&B influences during their immersion in the "Swinging London" scene. Nevertheless, the Stones remained notorious during the "Summer of Love." Jagger and Richards were busted for possession of drugs at the latter's English country home, and the June 1967 court case was a very public microcosm of the clash between traditional moral strictures and the liberalized youth culture burgeoning on both sides of the Atlantic.

In May 1968, "Jumpin' Jack Flash" was released, instigating an astonishing period during which the Stones harnessed sinister and salacious lyrics to an intense, rootsy sound. Their finest album, *Beggars Banquet,* released in late 1968, featured "Streetfighting Man," on which Jagger pondered his position as a figurehead for an imminent revolution, and "Sympathy for the Devil," an ironical ode to their own demonic image which incorporated a topical reference to the murder of Bobby Kennedy. In June 1969, Brian Jones was sacked and replaced by young blues virtuoso Mick Taylor. The following month, Jones drowned in his swimming pool. On *Let It Bleed* (1969), the Stones extended their devilish disquisition on violence in contemporary society on such songs as "Midnight Rambler" and "Gimme Shelter" ("Rape, murder, it's just a shot away"). In December 1969, the Stones headlined a free festival, organized in the spirit of Woodstock, at Altamont speedway in California. Hells' Angels, fuelled by liquor and LSD, murdered a young black teenager while the Stones performed. In hindsight, ''Gimme Shelter'' (also the title of the Maysles brothers' brilliant tour film, which concluded with the horror of Altamont), seemed to have anticipated the nihilistic death knell of 1960s idealism.

Sticky Fingers (1971) was a prime piece of Americana featuring ''Brown Sugar,'' a typically scurrilous account of sex and slavery in Dixie. Though criticized at the time, *Exile on Main Street* (1972) has since been recognized as the influential apogee of the Rolling Stones' relationship with the American musical forms of country, blues, and soul. They adapted to the glam era with what Philip Norman called the ''mid-1970s high camp'' of ''It's Only Rock'n'Roll (But I Like It).'' The song's title, however, was telling: creating musically innovative and culturally representative music was no longer the Rolling Stones' top priority. Jagger would later admit that after 1972 the group became ''complacent.'' Instead, the Stones became, along with Led Zeppelin, the archetypal early 1970s rock 'n' roll circus, a touring cavalcade of sexual, chemical, and egotistical excess. On *Some Girls* (1978), the band was somewhat reinvigorated by the influence and challenge of disco and punk, but the ''Glimmer Twins'' were now more media celebrities than musicians: Jagger revelling in his jet-set, high-society lifestyle, Richards' renowned for his decline into heroin addiction.

The group effectively split between 1986 and 1989 due to antagonism between Jagger and Richards. Wyman belatedly emerged as a target of tabloid opprobrium over his relationship with 13-year-old Mandy Smith. During the 1990s, Jagger and Richards made millions from commercials: their seminal mid-1960s attack on consumerism was adapted to promote the ''Satisfaction'' provided by a particular chocolate bar, while the 1981 hit ''Start Me Up'' provided appropriate lyrics for the launch of Microsoft's Windows 95 computer program. The reunited Stones, minus the retired Wyman, continued to undertake extravagant world tours into the late 1990s, during which a bewildering variety of official Stones merchandise was sold. Appropriately, Andy Warhol's lapping-tongue logo had become the massively reproduced signifier of the Rolling Stones' commodifiable cultural endurance.

—Martyn Bone

FURTHER READING:

Booth, Stanley. *The True Adventures of the Rolling Stones.* London, Heinemann, 1985.

Kent, Nick. *The Dark Stuff: Selected Writings on Rock Music 1972-1993.* London, Penguin, 1994.

Norman, Philip. *The Stones.* London, Penguin, 1993.

Wyman, Bill, with Ray Coleman. *Stone Alone.* London, Viking, 1990.

Romance Novels

''Mind candy'' critics declare, adamant about the intellect-eroding properties of romance novels which account for half of all mass-market paperback sales. The phenomenal sales seem only to intensify the attacks of those who object to the simplistic plots and flat characters of the novels. Some see these attacks as a chauvinistic

Romance novelist Danielle Steele.

refusal to take seriously this popular literature, written and edited largely by women for a mostly female audience. But many of the genre's sternest critics are other women who condemn romance novels as dangerously passive texts that encourage readers to find in the fictional world consolation for the fulfillment that a patriarchal culture denies them.

The very term ''romance novel'' is used pejoratively, and the image of romance readers as bored and boring housewives who live vicariously through the fantastic experiences of incredible characters persists even in the face of evidence that refutes the stereotype. Janice Radway's *Reading the Romance* suggests that women's reasons for reading romance are complex. But even a defender like Radway appears ambivalent about the romance genre. Her limited sample reinforces the idea that romance readers are mostly housewives who lead limited lives, and in her introduction to the 1991 edition of her study, Radway makes clear that she sees romance readers as distinctly ''other'' women from whom she and her peers are separated ''by class, occupation, and race.''

Romance novels have always been frowned upon by champions of high culture who value fiction for its originality and see formulaic romance novels as sentimental trash. More than a century ago, Marianne Evans called them ''silly novels by lady novelists,'' distinguishing between this species of sub-literature and her own, more serious fiction, published under the pseudonym George Eliot. Across the Atlantic, Nathaniel Hawthorne complained bitterly of ''that damned lot of scribbling women'' whose novels outsold his own work. Despite the contempt with which denizens of ''real literature'' view the novels, the romance formula can claim roots deep in Western literary tradition. Mikhail Bakhtin's description of classical Greek romances (a male and female of marriageable age experience a mutual, passionate attraction, encounter obstacles that threaten their union, overcome the obstacles and consummate their love within marriage) could as easily describe the latest romance to roll off Harlequin's presses.

Jane Austen's *Pride and Prejudice* has been called the greatest romantic novel of English literature. It, along with Austen's other novels, is entrenched in the literary canon, yet readers of romance novels claim Austen as one of their own. *Pride and Prejudice* was the only pre-twentieth-century work that online fans included in a 1998 list of the top 100 romance novels. While Austen would no doubt be shocked by the frank sexuality of many twentieth-century romantic heroines, she would recognize the sensible, independent women and the arrogant males they humble as descendants of Elizabeth and Darcy. The characters of Emily and Charlotte Brontë also serve as inspiration for romance writers: Heathcliff, the dark and dangerous spirit who serves as hero and villain of the monumental *Wuthering Heights*; Jane Eyre, the plain heroine who wins with courage and integrity; and Rochester, the maimed hero who learns that true love conquers all are stock characters in romance novels.

While the romance novel can claim legitimate kinship with works that have earned established places in the Western literary canon, the most direct precursor of popular romance novels is the "domestic novel" of the nineteenth century. Susan Warner's *The Wide, Wide World* (1851) defined the term "bestseller," and Maria Cummins' *The Lamplighter* (1854) was nearly as popular. These novels focused on the trials of a young heroine, often an orphan, who struggled to survive and cherished her independence, but who ultimately married and surrendered her autonomy. These "scribbling women" recognized that most women could find economic security only within marriage. Yet if marriage offered the young heroine salvation from economic deprivation, her love offered the hero salvation from an emotionally and spiritually barren life. In Augusta Jane Evans' *St. Elmo* (1867), beloved by generations of readers, the beautiful, virtuous Edna Earl capitulates to St. Elmo Murray, the Byronic hero complete with "piercing eyes" and "savage sneer," only after his reformation from hardened cynic to tender lover and Christian minister.

Writers like the prolific Grace Livingston Hill continued this pattern of mutual redemption into the twentieth century. During a career that spanned five decades, Hill produced more than 100 novels, all a retelling of the same story. *White Orchids* is typical: Jeffrey Wainwright, son of a millionaire, falls captive to Camilla Chrystie's beauty and virtue, and discovers in her Christian faith all that is lacking in his own empty life. By the 1920s, however, Hill's strict religious tales were the exception. Women's magazines were enjoying enormous success; periodicals with a circulation of 128,621,000 per issue were flooding U.S. households. Three of the top five consistently brought romance stories with predictable characters and plot and the requisite happy ending. *Ladies' Home Journal, Woman's Home Companion,* and *Pictorial Review* published serialized novels by Kathleen Norris, Faith Baldwin, and other romance novelists. These pre-World War II romances, still formulaic in many ways, had a new heroine, the "New Woman," eager for career success and unwilling to surrender her right to self-expression. These new novels extended the range of romance to reflect the wider experiences available to women in the twentieth century. Meanwhile, Georgette Heyer, only 19 when she wrote her first novel *The Black Moth,* was proving herself a worthy successor to Jane Austen and founding a sub-genre of the romance novel, the regency. Heyer's heroines in *The Grand Sophy* (1950) and *Frederica* (1965) are managing females who put Austen's Emma to shame, and Leonie, the French urchin of *These Old Shades* (1926), prefers masculine clothing and manages her own escape from abductors.

Heyer, Baldwin, and dozens of others continued to write what by the end of the twentieth century would be labeled "gentle romances" to distinguish their novels from the sexually explicit romances of the post-1960s. In Great Britain, Mills and Boon, a name synonymous with the romance novel, was publishing books that were little more than modernizations of the nineteenth-century sentimental novels: an 18-year-old heroine saved from genteel poverty by an older, incredibly wealthy hero who raises her to the heights of luxury as she brings him to his knees in an acknowledgment of love's power. In 1949, Harlequin Enterprises, a Canadian company, began publishing Mills and Boon reprints for a North American audience. The venture was so successful that in 1957 Harlequin suspended publication of other category fiction to focus exclusively on Mills and Boon romances. About the same time, another sub-genre of romance was also experiencing a revival. Phyllis Whitney's *Thunder Heights* and Victoria Holt's *Mistress of Mellyn,* both published in 1960, sold over a million copies, and by the end of the 1970s, gothic romances (35 titles monthly) were outselling every other form of category fiction. But an unsolicited manuscript was about to change the romance scene to an unprecedented degree.

In 1972, Avon published *The Flame and the Flower*, a slush pile find by then unknown Kathleen Woodiwiss. This historical romance, more than twice the length of the average gothic, featured conventional elements of popular romance—mature hero; young, virginal heroine; orphan in peril; forced marriage—but it also introduced explicit sex as part of the formula. Woodiwiss doubtless owed part of her success to timing; greater openness about female sexuality characterized the larger culture of the 1970s. However, Woodiwiss and those who followed her were able to incorporate this new openness within the conventional frame of a monogamous relationship that culminated in marriage. A generation of romance readers and writers date their love affair with the genre from their reading of a Woodiwiss novel.

But the "bodice rippers" had their detractors too. Vehement in their criticism were the feminists who deplored the rape scenes standard in the Woodiwiss-influenced historical romance novels. Some saw such scenes as fodder for those who claimed women wanted to be raped. Others saw the scenes as reflecting a culture in which violence against women was commonplace. But readers, as Radway found, drew a sharp distinction between the hero's passion for the irresistible heroine that led to "forcible persuasion" and "true rape" which brutally dehumanized a woman. More than a decade after Radway's study, Karen Mitchell found that readers glossed over the rape scenes, in effect rewriting the scenes. Romance writers themselves argue that readers are capable of distinguishing between fiction and reality and that these attacks are mere prejudice against romance novels. Jayne Ann Krentz, a Romance Writers of America Lifetime Achievement Award winner and an outspoken defender of the genre, points out that female predators who seduce passive males have long been a feature of male detective fiction with no public outcry. Daphne Clair, an award-winning New Zealand writer, adds that no critic has accused consumers of thrillers and Westerns of being masochists because protagonists in these categories are routinely beaten, tortured, and shot. The controversy was never resolved, but rape scenarios became rarer by the early the 1980s, and the damsel with the ripped bodice, although still around, was replaced by the bare-chested, fantastically muscled hero as the cover model. Eventually, the age of Fabio (the best known of the cover boys) also ended, and the clinches retreated to inside covers.

While detractors and defenders were debating the violence in the new historical romances, readers just kept buying the books, and they were buying not only historical romances. Harlequin Enterprises merged with Mills and Boon in 1971 and began marketing contemporary romances in new outlets. Suddenly romance was everywhere. Women could buy romance novels in supermarkets, variety stores, airports, and drugstores. Harlequin was promoting books like soap powder, and the approach was working. By the end of the decade, Harlequin sales had increased 800 percent, and the company was distributing 168 million copies of its titles in 98 countries. By the end of the century, one in six mass paperbacks sold in North America was published by Harlequin.

Other publishing companies, eager to duplicate Harlequin's success, rushed into romance publishing. Dell, Fawcett, Warner, and Bantam introduced their own romance lines, but Harlequin's stiffest competition came from Simon and Schuster's Silhouette romances. Sexier romances were outselling the traditional, and series with provocative names like Candlelight Ecstasy, Harlequin Temptation, and Silhouette Desire appeared. Harlequin author Anne Mather shattered one barrier in series romance when the heroine of a 1980 novel engaged in premarital sex, but later romance novels were influenced by the explicit sexuality of the historical romances. Promiscuity was unacceptable, and the relationships were love affairs that led to marriage, but graphic descriptions of love scenes became common in the "sensual romances."

By 1984, "the romance wars" were over. A year later Harlequin purchased Silhouette, and only Bantam's Loveswept line, which promoted author over product, challenged Harlequin's absolute rule over series romance fiction. Romance novels had also become subjects of interest for mainstream publications as diverse as *Time, Forbes,* and *Psychology Today.* Scholars too were examining this phenomenally popular category fiction, but most significant were the changes in the novels themselves, changes that accelerated in the next decade. The 18-year-old virgin did not disappear as heroine, but she became a rare species. In her place was an older heroine, often sexually experienced, who had meaningful work, women friends, and a sense of humor. The romantic hero was still handsome, and usually wealthy, but he was now sensitive, expressive, and supportive of a woman's autonomy; and the story line had become socially relevant. While the love story was still primary and the happy ending still sacrosanct, single parents, alcoholism, infertility, divorce, even homelessness were woven into plots.

The romance audience was changing as well. By the 1990s romance readers were largely college-educated women who worked full-time outside the home. These readers saw themselves as mature women who could support themselves, think independently, and contribute to their communities. Though some critics continued to sneer at romance novels, others, including some feminist scholars, had broadened their ideas about women's experience. Those who had predicted the demise of romance novels had been proved wrong. *Dangerous Men and Adventurous Women,* a collection of essays written by romance writers about their craft, became the fastest-selling title in the history of the University of Pennsylvania Press. The idea these essays challenged most firmly was the stereotype of the passive heroine.

Judith Arnold, one of the contributors, described the romance heroines of the 1990s: they "*do*"; they "take steps, hold opinions, and move forward into the world." Any random sampling of romance novels published after 1990 will support Arnold's contention. "Murphy Brown meets June Cleaver" proclaims the cover of a Harlequin Love & Laughter title. Heroines include teachers, lawyers, doctors, corporate executives, small business owners, architects, computer geniuses, builders, psychologists, artists, and country music singers who are also mothers, friends, lovers, soccer coaches, mentors, foster parents, church organists, and volunteers. The romance heroine has not surrendered her place in the domestic world; she has merely added triumph in the public world. She can rescue herself and sometimes the hero as well. It is not a question of the heroine usurping the hero's role, but of her proving the interdependence of their relationship.

The hero may have mixed emotions about this new balance of power but he learns to accept it. Typical is the response of Kenny Traveler, hero of Susan Elizabeth Phillips' humorous *Lady Be Good,* who responds to the news that his genius wife has expunged his bad-boy high school records by thinking of "his own public defender. It was embarrassing . . . but wonderful too." Romantic heroes have always been skillful lovers and conquerors in the public realm, but modern heroes must prove their prowess outside the boardroom and the bedroom. They cook, clean, and change diapers, and this new image seems to hold true across sub-genres. The heroes of historical romances and regencies may do kitchen duty infrequently, but even they regularly show themselves competent caretakers and loving fathers.

Romance novels have always been about relationships, but the relationships in 1990s romances extended beyond the primary relationship of one woman and one man to offer the dream of family. Sheryl Woods's *The Unclaimed Baby* (*Silhouette,* 1999) concludes with the "family gathered to celebrate the day's happy news" of an adoption and a pregnancy. The heroine exults "Cord would have the family he'd always dreamed of." Romance novelists also defined "family" in unconventional ways that reflected new configurations in real life. Barbara Freethy's single-title contemporary *The Sweetest Thing* (Avon, 1999) ends with Alex telling Faith, who has no family, that she will be not only his lover, partner, and best friend but also granddaughter to his idiosyncratic grandfather and mother to Jessie, a teenage girl who may or may not be his daughter.

Nora Roberts, arguably the most successful romance novelist of the late twentieth century, has made a career of novels that place characters within extended families. Roberts has written more than 128 novels since 1981, but her most popular works are the linked tales of the O'Hurleys, the Stanislaskis, the Concannons, the Quinns, and the MacGregors. In her bestselling *The Perfect Stranger,* Roberts describes the heroine Cybil Campbell: "Her mother was a successful, internationally respected artist; her father, the reclusive genius behind the long-running 'Macintosh' comic strip. Together they had given her and her siblings a love of art, a sense of the ridiculous, and a solid foundation." Roberts evokes a world where generations are connected by loving ties. To this she adds the traditional world of the romance novel: a world where a woman can be strong, independent, and articulate without being labeled unfeminine, where problems like glass ceilings, sexual harassment, single motherhood, and uncommunicative males are always happily resolved, where a woman can share passion, intimacy, and blissful monogamy with a powerful and attractive man who fulfills her intellectually, emotionally, and sexually. Small wonder that millions of women are willing to pay their share of the $1 billion romance novels earn annually in order to enjoy the fantasy.

The enduring success of romance novels can be attributed to a paradox. Romance novels remain true to their ancient formula, but they are constantly evolving. More than 20 years ago John Cawelti speculated that the women's movement would render the "moral fantasy" of the popular romance obsolete. But the romance novel has reshaped itself and thrived. At the end of the twentieth century, the lines between popular romance and general women's fiction have blurred. Romance novelists regularly publish in hardcover, are reviewed in mainstream publications, and appear on bestseller lists of the *New York Times, Publishers Weekly,* and *USA Today.* The Romance Writers of America, an organization that includes 8,200 romance writers and other industry professionals, lists on its Honor Roll 47 romance novelists who have made the bestseller lists. Nineteen publishing houses produce romance novels, and the once white-bread industry now publishes lines targeting African-American and Latino-American readers. Romance novels may be historical or contemporary, long or short, inspirational, gentle, or sexy. In cyberspace, publishers, romance writers, and industry-related groups offer author biographies, book summaries, chat rooms, and e-mail newsletters. Fan-generated sites offer independent reviews, reading lists, spirited discussion, and the sense of community that researchers have found central to the experience of romance readers. Forty-five million women in North America alone regularly read romance novels, and experts predict a 22-percent increase in readers by 2010.

—Wylene Rholetter

FURTHER READING:

The Art of Romance: A Century of Romance Art. Toronto, Harlequin, 1999.

Austen, Jane. *Pride and Prejudice* (1813). New York, Knopf, 1991.

Bakhtin, Mikhail. *The Dialogic Imagination.* Austin, University of Texas Press, 1981.

Cawelti, John G. *Adventure, Mystery, and Romance: Formula Stories as Art and Popular Culture.* Chicago, University of Chicago Press, 1976.

Fallon, Eileen. *Words of Love: A Complete Guide to Romance Fiction.* New York, Garland, 1984.

Freethy, Barbara. *The Sweetest Thing.* New York, Avon, 1999.

Frenier, Marian Darce. *Good-Bye Heathcliff: Changing Heroes, Heroines, Roles, and Values in Women's Category Fiction.* New York, Greenwood Press, 1988.

Heyer, Georgette. *Frederica.* London, Bodley Head, 1965.

———. *The Grand Sophy.* London, Heinemann, 1950.

———. *These Old Shades.* London, Heinemann, 1926.

Hill, Grace Livingston. *White Orchids.* New York, Tyndale House, 1995.

Jensen, Margaret Ann. *Love's $weet Revenge: The Harlequin Story.* Bowling Green, Ohio, Bowling Green State University Popular Press, 1984.

Johnson, Victoria M. *All I Need to Know In Life I Learned from Romance Novels.* Santa Monica, California, General Publishing Group, 1998.

Krentz, Jayne Ann, editor. *Dangerous Men and Adventurous Women: Romance Writers on the Appeal of Romance.* Philadelphia, University of Pennsylvania Press, 1992.

Mitchell, Karen S. ''Ever After: Reading the Women Who Read (and Rewrite) Romances.'' *Theater Topics.* Vol. 6, No. 1, 1996, 51-69.

Modleski, Tania. *Loving with a Vengeance: Mass-Produced Fantasies for Women.* Hamden, Connecticut, Archon Books, 1980.

Phillips, Susan Elizabeth. *Lady Be Good.* New York, Avon, 1999.

Porter, Cheryl Ann. *From Here to Maternity. Love & Laughter.* Toronto, Harlequin, 1999.

Rabine, Leslie W. *Reading the Romantic Heroine: Text, History, Ideology.* Ann Arbor, University of Michigan Press, 1985.

Radway, Janice. *Reading the Romance: Women, Patriarchy, and Popular Literature.* Chapel Hill, University of North Carolina Press, 1984.

Roberts, Nora. *The Perfect Stranger.* Silhouette Special Edition. New York, Harlequin, 1999.

Thurston, Carol. *The Romance Revolution: Erotic Novels for Women and the Quest for a New Sexual Identity.* Urbana, University of Illinois Press, 1987.

Wood, Sheryl. *The Unclaimed Baby.* New York, Harlequin, 1999.

Romero, Cesar (1907-1994)

Tall, urbane, and sleekly handsome, Cuban-American actor Cesar Romero helped define the stereotypical ''Latin Lover'' in over 100 film and television appearances beginning in 1933. But he made his biggest impact on American pop culture playing the outlandishly coifed Joker on television's *Batman* from 1966 to 1968. Outfitted in an over-the-top green fright wig and pasty white clown make-up (which took about an hour to apply), Romero mugged and cackled his way through the villainous part with unbridled relish. His campy capering clearly influenced Jack Nicholson's interpretation of the role in the 1989 film adaptation of the comic book adventure. After hanging up his fright wig in 1968, Romero returned to playing elegant rogues on film and television. He died of a blood clot on New Year's Day, 1994, at the age of 86.

—Robert E. Schnakenberg

FURTHER READING:

Eisner, Joel. *The Official Batman Batbook.* Chicago, Contemporary Books, 1986.

Hadleigh, Boze. *Hollywood Gays: Conversations with Cary Grant, Liberace, Tony Perkins, Paul Lynde, Cesar Romero, Brad Davis, Randolph Scott, James Coco, William Haines, David Lewis.* New York, Barricade Books, 1996.

Roots

In 1977, African-American author Alex Haley published *Roots: The Saga of an American Family,* in which he traces the history of his mother's family. *Roots* begins in 1750 with Kunta Kinte, a young man who was captured in Africa by slavers and brought to the United States where he eventually tells the story of Kinte's descendants through seven generations in America. The book immediately captured the imaginations of both whites and blacks in the always racially uneasy United States. By February 1977, it was the number-one-selling book in the nation. *Roots: The Saga of an American Family* spent 20 weeks on the *New York Times* bestseller list, earned its author

LeVar Burton in Alex Haley's *Roots*.

a Pulitzer prize, and, later the same year, was made into a television event: a 12 hour mini-series that was broadcast over eight consecutive nights to more viewers than had watched any program in the history of television. One hundred and thirty million people watched some portion of *Roots,* drawn by its all-star cast and its moving drama. In 1979, the story continued with another hit mini-series, *Roots, the Next Generations.*

Starting with Kunta Kinte's traumatic capture and tracing an African-American family through slavery, the Civil War, and the complex transition into freedom, *Roots* gave blacks something they had been lacking in American popular culture: a history with a human face. Though the days of slavery had been the subject of debate, bitterness, and defensiveness, *Roots* looked at slavery in a different way, as the life experience of real people, bringing the African-American experience vividly to life in an epic tale of family continuity. Black faces were rare on television, and devoting so many prime-time hours to the story of a black family was a fairly radical concept. Though there were some complaints from whites that *Roots* villainized white people, many more whites were themselves captivated by the humanity of the story.

Haley was born in Ithaca, New York, in 1921. His father was an architect, the first of his family to attend college, and Haley's brothers followed his upwardly mobile track, becoming professionals themselves. Alex, however, sought something different, a search that led him to spend 20 years as a cook in the Coast Guard where he honed his writing skills and earned extra money writing love letters for fellow crew members. After his retirement from the Coast Guard, he began his writing career in earnest with adventure stories published in

Reader's Digest, Saturday Evening Post, and *Playboy.* He landed a regular job writing interviews for *Playboy,* and collaborated with civil rights activist Malcolm X to write *The Autobiography of Malcolm X.* Haley remained relatively obscure, however, until his grandmother's stories inspired him to begin to research his family history. The research took him 12 years and led him to the small African nation of Gambia, where he supposedly found the village where his great-great-great-great grandfather had lived before being captured into slavery.

With the publication of *Roots,* Haley became famous and *Roots* would dominate the rest of his career. He outlined another television special, *Roots: The Gift,* which he later wrote in book form as *A Different Kind of Christmas,* and he continued his family research, spending 20 years tracing his father's family. He died in 1992, before he could write up the results of his work, leaving white British writer David Stevens to take over for him. Stevens wrote the epic *Queen,* which was also made into a television mini-series, but critics lambasted both the book and series as boring and derivative. The problems were just as likely the overworked mini-series format and a jaded new audience of readers and viewers. The topic of *Roots,* once innovative, had become "old hat."

Writing the story of Kunta Kinte and his descendants Kizzy, Chicken George, and others, Haley blended history with fictional embellishments to create a writing genre he called "faction." Though *Roots: The Saga of an American Family* was published as nonfiction, its authenticity has always been questioned. Immediately upon publication novelists Harold Courlander (*The African*) and Margaret Walker (*Jubilee*) brought suits against Haley, accusing him of plagiarism. Walker's suit was dismissed, but Haley paid Courlander $650,000 in settlement, admitting that parts of his book "found their way" into *Roots.*

In 1997, as Haley's publisher Doubleday was preparing a twentieth-anniversary celebration for *Roots,* the British Broadcasting Company released a documentary called *The Roots of Alex Haley,* pointing out the many controversies about *Roots.* Along with the accusations of plagiarism, Haley was frequently accused of making up many of the most important facts in the book, even his emotional meeting with the griot, or oral historian, in Gambia, who confirmed for him that Kunta Kinte was Haley's forefather. Haley's critics claim that his family cynically planned to set the beginning of the story in Gambia so that they could use the success of *Roots* to boost the family travel business which arranges tours to Gambia. Haley's supporters call this sort of criticism "literary lynching," and point out that it matters little whether or not the actual facts in the book are true. *Roots,* they say, contains a truth that is deeper than small details of fact, and it continues to resonate with readers and viewers on the basis of that deeper truth. Johns Hopkins historian, Philip Carter, counseled those trying to disprove Haley's story, "You can't win," he advised, "You're fighting TV."

In Gambia, *Roots* has brought a steady stream of African-American tourists, seeking perhaps something of their own roots in the country from which Kunta Kinte was stolen. In June of 1997, the country hosted the Roots Homecoming Festival to celebrate the connection between Africa and the descendants of slaves. Gambia, however, is a poor country, one of the smallest in Africa with a population of 1.2 million, and there are conflicting feelings about the fame that *Roots* has brought. Many Gambians are angry that Haley and his family did not share more of the profits from the books and television shows with their nation of origin, while the Haleys insist that adequate compensation was made.

Both a best-selling book and a record-breaking television production, *Roots* was remarkably influential as literature and entertainment. Though Haley did not invent the expression "tracing one's roots," he did introduce it into everyday parlance, bringing the idea of tracing one's heritage dramatically into the popular imagination. Since the publication of Haley's book, the word "roots" has become a sort of shorthand for the search for a personal history that will give meaning to modern struggles. After Haley's death, many of his possessions were auctioned off to pay debts on his estate. The manuscript of *Roots* sold for $71,000, and the Pulitzer Prize Haley had won for it brought $50,000. Ironically, the man who had impressed upon the nation the importance of gathering one's history together had much of his own history scattered upon his death. He left an enduring legacy, however, an affirmation that each family history is a drama of survival and endurance and an inspiration for people to seek out their own histories. Distinguished African-American writer James Baldwin described the phenomenon this way: *"Roots* is a study of continuities, of consequences, of how a people perpetuate themselves, how each generation helps to doom or helps to liberate, the coming one."

—Tina Gianoulis

FURTHER READING:

Fisher, Murray. "In Memoriam: Alex Haley." *Playboy.* Vol. 39, No. 7, July 1992, 161.

Gonzales, Doreen. *Alex Haley: Author of Roots.* Hillside, New Jersey, Enslow Publishers, 1994.

Reid, Calvin. "Fact or Fiction? Hoax Charges Still Dog *Roots* Twenty Years On." *Publishers Weekly.* October 6, 1997, 16.

Rose Bowl

Long considered college football's premier post-season game, the Rose Bowl was first played on New Year's Day in 1902, when 8,500 fans watched Fielding H. Yost's Michigan "point-a-minute" Wolverines blank Stanford 49-0. The Tournament of Roses committee in Pasadena, California, was the driving force behind the first contest. Disappointed by Stanford's performance, however, the committee arranged chariot races and other events over the next several years. Consequently, 14 years passed before a second Rose Bowl was held, with Washington State shutting out Brown, which was led by the black All-American halfback Fritz Pollard, 14-0. Held continuously since 1916, the East-West classic was played in the Rose Bowl stadium from 1923 onward; ultimately, the capacity crowd surpassed 100,000. Starting in 1947, when Illinois defeated UCLA 45-14, the champions of the Western Conference—later called the Big 10 and eventually joined by Penn State—and the Pacific Coast Conference—superseded first by the Athletic Association of Western Universities, then by the Pacific 10—battled one another. By 1998, the two conferences agreed to join in the Bowl Alliance that sought to bring the top pair of ranked teams in the country to determine an uncontested national champion. Consequently, in the future, such a highly rated Big Ten or Pac-10 championship team could play in the title game, to be waged in the Fiesta, Sugar, Orange, and Rose Bowls on a rotating basis.

Beginning with Michigan's undefeated 1901 team, 19 squads that won Rose Bowls were proclaimed national champions. Two schools, Wallace Wade's Alabama and Pop Warner's Stanford, played to a 7-7 tie and were named co-champions following the 1926 season. Three competitors had already been named the best team in the country prior to their defeat in the Rose Bowl. Other Hall of Famers who guided teams to Pasadena included Notre Dame's Knute Rockne, Southern California's Howard Jones, Ohio State's Woody Hayes, and USC's John McKay. Some of college football's legendary games were played in the Rose Bowl, such as the 27-10 shellacking in 1925 by Rockne's team, featuring its Four Horsemen backfield, of Stanford and fullback Ernie Nevers. In 1948, Fritz Crisler's great Michigan team, boasting a two-platoon system, destroyed USC 49-0, resulting in a second "final" Associated Press poll that placed the Wolverines at its top, not Frank Leahy's unbeaten Notre Dame squad. In one of the most exciting finishes, Wisconsin, in 1963, roared from far behind but still fell to McKay's Trojans, 42-37. In 1968, USC, led by halfback and MVP O.J. Simpson, beat Indiana 14-3. The following year, notwithstanding an 80-yard touchdown scamper by Heisman trophy winner Simpson, USC's bid for a repeat national championship ended with a 27-16 Rose Bowl defeat at the hands of Hayes's Buckeyes.

The stature garnered by the Rose Bowl for both its participants and sponsors, along with the economic doldrums engendered by the Great Depression, led to the formation of additional post-season college games during the 1930s. Hoping for a financial windfall, boosters in the American South helped establish the Orange (1933), Sugar (1935), Sun (1936), and Cotton (1937) Bowls. Initially, monetary rewards were lacing, but a series of additional bowls were created in the following decades. Indeed, by the 1990s, analysts contended that the large number of such bowls enabled mediocre teams to play, while detracting from the quality games. However, the amount of available television revenue ensured that no scarcity of bowl games would likely result. By the end of the decade, universities participating in the Bowl Championship Series received 12 million dollars apiece.

Many bowl games, such as the one generally held on January 1 in Pasadena, are preceded by elaborate parades. Once again, the most famous is the Tournament of Roses carried out in Pasadena, involving scores of elaborately designed floats, richly covered with floral arrangements. Marching bands, festively attired horses and riders, a grand marshal, and the Rose queen are prominently featured for both the gathered throng and large television audiences. The television presence of the Tournament of Roses parade followed by the Rose Bowl every New Year's Day has guaranteed their place in the American popular consciousness.

—Robert C. Cottrell

FURTHER READING:

Hendrickson, Joe, with Maxwell Stiles. *The Tournament of Roses: A Pictorial History.* Los Angeles, Brooke House, 1971.

Hibner, John Charles. *The Rose Bowl, 1902-1929: A Game-by-Game History of Collegiate Football's Foremost Event, from Its Advent through Its Golden Era.* Jefferson, North Carolina, McFarland, 1993.

McCallum, John Dennis. *Big Ten Football since 1895.* Radnor, Pennsylvania, Chilton Books, 1976.

———. *PAC-10 Football, the Rose Bowl Conference.* Seattle, Writing Works, 1982.

Michelson, Herb, and Dave Newhouse. *Rose Bowl Football Since 1902*. New York, Stein and Day, 1977.

Perrin, Tom. *Football: A College History*. Jefferson, North Carolina, McFarland, 1987.

Rose, Pete (1941—)

Although ball player Pete Rose ended a 26-year career with retirement in 1986, at the end of the 1990s he was still actively at the center of controversy in the sport. The holder of several records, including major league records for most career hits, games played, and at bats, he was declared ineligible for the Baseball Hall of Fame because of allegations that he placed bets on games while both a player and a manager in the major leagues. His reputation as a player has also been thrown into question over the years, with some pundits contesting his abilities and arguing that, gambling charges aside, Rose never displayed the talent necessary to be considered for the Hall of Fame.

Rose started playing professional baseball in 1960 with the minor league Geneva (New York) Red Legs. By 1963 he had reached the majors as a rookie second baseman with the National League's

Pete Rose

Cincinnati Reds and was named Rookie of the Year. During his subsequent career as a player he broke one of baseball's seemingly unbreakable records, Ty Cobb's career record of 4,191 hits. Rose ended his career with 4,256 hits, 14,053 at-bats, 3,562 games played, and 3,315 singles—figures that remained unsurpassed 13 years after his retirement.

Although his career numbers are impressive, Rose was arguably more famous for his attitude on the baseball diamond. Known as ''Charlie Hustle'' among fans and fellow players, he was famed for his constant effort, head-first slides, and incredibly competitive demeanor. His presence on the field seemed to energize the players around him, and his willingness to do anything to help his team win was apparent. It was also apparent that Rose was not the most physically gifted player in baseball, but he made up for his lack of physical abilities with an awesome show of determination and persistence that appealed to his fans. Many fans saw Rose as an ''average guy'' who was willing to give everything he had to win, and he actively encouraged this perception.

When Rose retired as a player in 1986, it was unanimously believed that he would be selected for the Baseball Hall of Fame. In 1989, however, everything changed. After months of investigation, Rose was banished from baseball and declared ineligible for the Hall of Fame by Commissioner Bart Giamatti. Giamatti concluded there was substantial and credible evidence that Rose had bet on baseball games, including those involving his own team, the Cincinnati Reds. By 1999, the evidence on which the Commissioner based his decision had not yet been made available to the public. It is a sacrosanct rule of baseball, dating back to the early 1920s, that any player or manager caught gambling on a baseball game is banished for life. After the disaster of the 1919 Black Sox scandal, baseball established a zero-tolerance policy on the gambling issue. Although Rose consistently denied the charges, he signed an agreement with major league baseball and accepted his de facto banishment from the sport.

While there are many who call for Rose's election to the Hall of Fame, others argue that he was never Hall-of-Fame caliber. While it is true that Rose has 65 more hits than Ty Cobb to his credit, it took Rose an extra 2624 at-bats to get those 65 hits. He was never a great home-run hitter, base stealer, or fielder, and did not drive in very many runs, given the number of times he came to the plate; nor did he score very many runs, given the number of times he was on base. In many ways, the argument for Rose's entrance into the Hall is based on his longevity and persistence rather than his abilities. Bill James, baseball's most famous statistician/historian, argued in 1985 that even at his peak Rose was only the 97th greatest player of all time, fanning the continuing debate that surrounds the player's reputation.

Rose was still fighting his banishment from baseball in the 1990s, petitioning the league to lift his banishment and allow him eligibility for the Hall of Fame, a request supported by legions of his fans who continue to call for his punishment to end.

—Geoff Peterson

FURTHER READING:

Reston, James. *Collision at Home Plate: The Lives of Pete Rose and Bart Giamatti*. New York, Edward Burlingame Books, 1991.

Rose, Pete, and Roger Kahn. *Pete Rose: My Story*. New York, Macmillan, 1989.

———, with Hal McCoy. *The Official Pete Rose Scrapbook*. New York, New American Library, 1985.

Sokolove, Michael Y. *Hustle: The Myth, Life, and Lies of Pete Rose.* New York, Simon and Schuster, 1990.

Roseanne

Consistently Nielsen-rated in the top ten programs throughout its 10-year lifespan, the situation comedy *Roseanne* wielded an unprecedented socio-cultural influence on the American television-viewing nation. The series played a key role in revitalizing an ailing television genre by demonstrating that playing for laughs need not preclude intelligent, thought-provoking scripts. As with its contemporary *Cheers* (1982-96), fine ensemble playing and even finer writing ensured this blue-collar sitcom's longevity.

That the show actually reached the nation's television screens is as much a testament to a major shake-up in the world of American television as it is to the creative endeavors of those directly involved in its production. The 1980s witnessed a challenge to the power of the Big Three networks, which saw a substantial drop in their near-monopoly of audience share from 90 percent to 60 percent by decade's end. Shaken by the success of Rupert Murdoch's Fox network, and by the rise of satellite, cable, and VCR ownership, the networks were forced to take a long, hard look at their own output. One positive outcome of this reappraisal was that it led to the commissioning and purchase of innovative programs, often made by independent production companies like Carsey Werner, the makers of *Roseanne.* The challenge to the hegemony of the Big Three, then, undoubtedly helped reinvigorate a tired genre like the situation comedy.

With *Roseanne,* viewers witnessed the return of the blue-collar family to their TV screens. The Conners, led by mother and father Roseanne and Dan Conner (played by Roseanne Barr and John Goodman), were subject to the stresses and strains of contemporary living. The small, midwestern town of Lanford—the sitcom's fictional setting—was recession-hit for much of the series and the family was unable to escape this context. In contrast to so many sitcoms, the domestic arena in *Roseanne* did not provide the Connors with a safe haven in a heartless world; rather, that harsh outside world frequently

Roseanne Barr and John Goodman from the television sitcom *Roseanne.*

threatened to engulf the family as it staggered from one economic crisis to another. As a result of this, *Roseanne*'s literate comedy often took on a clear socio-political dimension, attributable in large measure to the creative influence of the show's star, Roseanne Barr, a successful stand-up comedienne. The sassy humor of Barr's heavily autobiographical ''trailer mom'' monologues supplied the show's writers with a ready-made central character around which to build a variety of relationships. As the show's co-creator, Barr unquestionably stamped both her unique personality and her own agenda on the series that pointedly shared her name. In response to an interviewer's query as to exactly how much of the real her was invested in the screen character, Barr observed ''that's me up there, [although] there's a deliberate choice of what to expose.''

By the early 1990s, on the heels of a successful second season which saw *Roseanne* take over the top slot in the ratings from *The Cosby Show* (1984-1992), Barr had gained complete creative control. It was in these early 1990s shows that an explicit political edge emerged, partly as a result of plots that focused on the workplace as much as the home. In one show Roseanne harasses a vote-canvassing Congressional candidate, first when he calls on her at home, and again when he turns up at her husband's failing motorbike shop. When the politician talks of attracting new businesses to Lanford, Roseanne presses him on how and why these companies would want to set up business in her hometown. Given a familiar clichéd answer which points to the lure of tax incentives and inexpensive production costs, Roseanne pithily notes that the promise of cheap, de-unionized labor and generous corporate-friendly tax breaks simply means that the ordinary working folk in her town will be made to pay twice by making up the shortfall in taxation and then taking jobs at ''scab'' wages. In this same episode, the Connors' son, D.J., ironically wins a regional spelling bee by correctly spelling the word ''foreclosure,'' while an inconsolable eldest daughter, Becky, discovers that there is no college fund for her, despite her having achieved the necessary grades.

While *Roseanne*'s ancestry might appear traceable to early blue-collar sitcoms like *The Honeymooners* (1955-1956), it arguably owed more of a debt to the uncompromising and occasionally uncomfortable humor of a show like *All in the Family* (1971-1979). It certainly did not have much in common with its anodyne immediate predecessors such as *Family Ties* (1982-1989) or *The Cosby Show*. As Judine Mayerle has pointed out, the show simply did not look ''television-ish,'' from the physical appearance, speech, and behavior of the characters themselves through to the variety of cheaply furnished sets that comprise the Connors' household and workplaces (diner, factory, garage, etc). More significantly, the show also consistently denied that familiar sitcom narrative trajectory which offered resolution in the form of the ''warm hug,'' closing moral, or sermon. Instead, *Roseanne* presented the viewer with a ''slice of life'' episodic structure more akin to a drama series, offering ongoing narratives that denied comedic closure since problems such as marital or financial difficulties could not be neatly tied up in under half an hour. The fact that the Conner kids appeared destined to follow in their parents' footsteps was often at the very core of the show's bittersweet humor, and such a recognition rested on a successful narrative carry-over from episode to episode, series to series.

Both plots and characterization prompted a more complex set of audience responses to the adventures of the Connors, simply because on one important level we laughed *with* instead of *at* them. The show avoided lazy stereotypes of ordinary, working Americans, and as a result Roseanne (who, for example, talks to Darlene about Sylvia Plath in one episode) and her family are played as sharp, intelligent, and funny. While life frequently dealt them and their friends a losing hand, they remained defiant in defeat, their one-liners empowering them where few other options were available. *Roseanne* spearheaded a late 1980s revival of the satiric, blue-collar sitcom, in the process bucking the trend for shows in which working-class characters were often represented as loud-mouthed bigots in the Archie Bunker mold. The show arguably paved the way for both *The Simpsons,* begun in 1989 and still running at the end of the century, and *Married .. with Children* (1987-1997). Both of these, while admittedly presenting cognitively disabled characters, nevertheless offered conflict as opposed to resolution, mercilessly lampooned authority figures, and unflinchingly pointed up America's failings.

Despite its early instances of a direct political agenda, David Marc has pointed out that *Roseanne* ''len[t] itself more successfully to the politics of culture than the politics of labor.'' For example, the show stirred up conservative ire because of its perceived failure to back traditional family values. Along with *Murphy Brown* (1988-1998) which the then vice-president Dan Quayle described as ''socially disruptive'' for its depiction of and failure to condemn single-motherhood, *Roseanne* brought complaints from pro-family groups about the prime-time representation of poor parenting displayed by the Connors. In his book *Hollywood versus America,* Michael Medved quoted Ross Perot complaining that ''if you watch Roseanne Barr on television you don't get a very good role model . . . You and I didn't see that kind of stuff growing up.'' Backing Perot, Medved himself drew attention to an episode in which Roseanne takes daughter Becky to her gynecologist for birth control pills. To Medved, this is an act of gross indecency and parental irresponsibility, tantamount to an active endorsement of teenage promiscuity. ''Roseanne's sister Jackie,'' he writes, ''applauds the main character's willingness to facilitate the girl's sex life: 'Isn't it great that Becky has such a progressive, open-minded mom that she can talk to?' When Roseanne moans 'She's all grown up . . . She doesn't need me anymore!' her sister reassures her: 'Of course she needs you! She needs you to pay for her pills.'''

Yet the sheer range of issues aired in the scripts extended the range of subject matter deemed appropriate for future sitcoms. By tackling such subjects as masturbation, lesbianism, same-sex marriage, teenage sex and pregnancy, abortion, drug use, unemployment, and familial abuse in a common-sense way, *Roseanne* surely contributed towards the fostering of a healthy and responsible attitude towards these previously taboo topics. Thus, in the case of the birth control episode, the show pointed up that it was far better that Becky should avoid running the risk of an unwanted pregnancy or disease, particularly if she was going to ''experiment'' anyway.

Sadly, the show limped on a season too long. In its final run, the Connors' multi-million-dollar lottery win deprived the show of its satiric engine, in that so much of the humor had emanated from its portrayal of real people facing real daily struggles with flashes of extraordinary wit. Yet, at its best, *Roseanne* was remembered for its earthy, natural warmth and unabashed display of human imperfection that appealed to millions of viewers, and for fostering a level of audience identification and affection that flew in the face of much critical opprobrium.

—Simon Philo

FURTHER READING:

Aronowitz, Stanley. ''Working-Class Culture in the Electronic Age.'' In *Cultural Politics in Contemporary America,* edited by Ian Angus and Sut Jhally. London, Routledge, 1989.

Barr, Roseanne. *Stand Up! My Life as a Woman.* New York, Harper & Row, 1989.

Dutka, Elaine. ''Slightly to the Left of Normal.'' *Time.* May 8, 1989, 82-83.

Marc, David. *Comic Visions: Television Comedy and American Culture.* Malden, Massachusetts, Blackwell, 1997.

Mayerle, Judine. ''Roseanne—How Did You Get inside My House?: A Case Study of a Hit Blue-Collar Situation Comedy.'' *Journal of Popular Culture.* Vol. 24, No. 4, 1991, 71-88.

Medved, Michael. *Hollywood vs. America: Popular Culture and the War on Traditional Values.* New York, HarperCollins, 1992.

Rowe, Kathleen. ''Roseanne: Unruly Woman as Domestic Goddess.'' *Screen.* Vol. 31, No. 4, 1990, 408-419.

Watson, Mary Ann. *Defining Visions: Television and the American Experience since 1945.* Orlando, Florida, Harcourt Brace, 1998.

Rosemary's Baby

Director Roman Polanski's 1968 film adaptation of Ira Levin's occult novel remains as unsettling at the end of the twentieth century as when it was first released. Mia Farrow and John Cassavetes play the young couple that becomes part of a Manhattan devil cult's plan to impregnate Farrow with Satan's child. Ruth Gordon won an Oscar for her performance as a sinister neighbor whose husband makes Cassavetes a bargain he can't resist. Instead of using graphic violence for shock value as many horror films do, Polanski employs a hallucinatory tone that vacillates between eerie and banal. Set in a creepy, old apartment building, the film questions neighborly friendliness as suspect and posits that home might be the most menacing place of all—ideas that continue to fascinate. Few films since have had the skill to use mood and character, rather than blood and violence, to convey horror.

—Sharon Yablon

FURTHER READING:

Levin, Ira. *Rosemary's Baby.* New York, Random House, 1967.

Ursini, James. *More Things Than Are Dreamt of: Masterpieces of Supernatural Horror—From Mary Shelley to Stephen King in Literature and Film.* New York, Limelight Editions, 1994.

Rosenberg, Julius (1918-1953) and Ethel (1915-1953)

In 1953, Julius and Ethel Rosenberg became the first Americans to be executed for espionage. Their conviction and execution were a crucial factor in the intensification of the Cold War in America, which in turn led to the phenomenon known as McCarthyism. Their guilt and the harshness of their sentence continue to be vigorously debated.

Julius and Ethel Rosenberg

The Rosenbergs have been viewed by leftist intellectuals as martyrs, conveniently sacrificed by an iniquitous United States in the name of anticommunism. They have been remembered for their deaths far more than for their lives and have been the subject of many books, articles, poems, plays, works of art, and documentaries.

Ethel (nee Greenglass) and Julius Rosenberg both hailed from the lower east side of Manhattan. Like many young Americans during the Depression, both became involved in leftist groups. They met at a union-sponsored party in 1936, and they were married in the summer of 1939. In 1943 they curtailed their official affiliation with the Communist party.

The explosion of an atomic bomb by Russia in 1949 led to a search for spies in the American government, and it was discovered that David Greenglass, Ethel's brother, had passed secret information to Soviet agents. Greenglass implicated the Rosenbergs in his confession, and the Rosenbergs were arrested. Their trial lasted from March 6th through March 29th, 1951, and after appeals they were executed on June 20, 1953. A young Richard Nixon made a name for himself as the congressional investigator who originally uncovered the Rosenbergs' crime.

The Rosenberg case divided Americans, many of whom believed the couple were innocent, and had a dramatic impact on U.S. leftists. In particular, it was a watershed for those New York Jewish intellectuals who had become anti-Stalinist, pro-American Cold Warriors. They used the Rosenberg case to dissociate themselves from their previous radicalism at a time when such activity was construed as un-American. U.S. Jewish leaders feared that the case would increase anti-Semitism as the public drew a link between Communism and the Jewishness of the Rosenbergs. Consequently, a great deal of effort was expended by liberal anticommunist organizations and anti-Stalinist intellectuals to dissociate Jews from the actions of the Rosenbergs.

A flurry of literary activity occurred that aimed to discredit the Rosenbergs and to prove the political loyalty of American Jewry. Liberal anticommunist Jewish intellectuals, in particular, Leslie Fiedler and Robert Warshow, wrote vicious critiques of the Rosenbergs. This bloc supported the prosecution's case and argued for the couple's execution. Liberal anticommunists, in contrast, countered these attacks by accusing the prosecution of anti-semitism. They pointed to the flimsiness of the evidence against the Rosenbergs and highlighted the plight of the Rosenbergs' two sons—Robert and Michael—who would be orphaned as a result of the government's actions.

The image of the Rosenbergs as sacrificial lambs, martyred by a complex of Cold War interests, has entered American popular culture. One of the earliest appearances of the Rosenbergs-as-martyrs theme is Arthur Miller's *The Crucible* (1953). The initials of the central protagonists—John and Elizabeth—have been construed as representing Julius and Ethel. In the post-Rosenberg era, further texts have appeared. The Rosenbergs figured in Sylvia Plath's *The Bell Jar* (1966), E.L. Doctorow's *The Book of Daniel* (1971), and Robert Coover's The *Public Burning* (1977). Focusing on the idea of the Rosenbergs, rather than the factual detail of their lives and deaths, the latter two texts interspersed actual historical reality with fictional characterization in postmodern representations of the Rosenberg story. Other popular texts in which the Rosenbergs have appeared include John Updike's *Couples* (1964), Gore Vidal's *Myra Breckinridge* (1968), Howard Fast's *The Outsider,* Joyce Carol Oates' *You Must Remember This* (1988), Don DeLillo's *Libra* (1988), and Tema Nason's *Ethel: A Fictional Autobiography* (1990).

The imagery of the Rosenbergs was further extended in other media. In 1969 Donald Freed's multimedia play, *Inquest,* opened in Cleveland, Ohio. Freed's play highlighted the sensitivity that the Rosenberg case still aroused: the presiding Judge Kaufman contacted the Federal Bureau of Investigation to complain that the play represented politically threatening procommunist propaganda. In 1993, Tony Kushner's two-part drama, *Angels in America,* was produced. Set in the Reagan era, the Rosenberg's prosecutor—Roy Cohn—figured prominently. Rosenberg iconography also animated visual artists. In 1988 an exhibit titled ''Unknown Secrets'' opened under the auspices of the Rosenberg-Era Art Project. Some of the works memorialized the Rosenbergs as Jewish victims of American injustice with titles such as *Roy Judas Cohn, Remembering the Rosenbergs,* and Robert Arneson's *2 Fried Commie Jews.* Other works took a multimedia, postmodern approach that emphasized the Cold War context of the Rosenbergs' death.

—Nathan Abrams

FURTHER READING:

Carmichael, Virginia. *Framing History: The Rosenberg Story and the Cold War.* Minneapolis, University of Minnesota Press, 1993.

Garber, Marjorie, and Rebecca L. Walkowitz, editors. *Secret Agents: The Rosenberg Case, McCarthyism, and Fifties America.* New York, Routledge, 1995.

Radosh, Ronald, and Joyce Milton. *The Rosenberg File.* 2nd edition. New Haven, Connecticut, Yale University Press, 1997.

Ross, Andrew. *No Respect: Intellectuals and Popular Culture.* New York, Routledge, 1989.

Diana Ross and the Supremes

Although their time in the spotlight only lasted six years, Diana Ross and the Supremes quickly became the most successful female group in the history of American popular music. During their years of greatest success from 1964 to 1970, the black female trio brought Berry Gordy's fledgling Motown Records to international visibility through a string of successive number one pop hits. With their flashy gowns, coiffed hairdos, stylized choreography, and polished harmonies, the Supremes helped define the Motown sound. Their crossover

Diana Ross and the Supremes

music reached diverse audiences, acting as a kind of soundtrack for the civil rights movement. Offstage, however, internal conflict often rocked the musical group. In 1970, lead singer Diana Ross left the Supremes to embark on a solo career that would bring her to unprecedented levels of fame in the 1970s, 1980s and into the 1990s.

While the details of their history are somewhat contentious, the development of the Supremes dates back to Detroit in 1958. Originally named the Primettes, the group was created as a female counterpart to the Primes, a male vocal quartet that would eventually rocket to success as the Temptations. The Primettes consisted of sixteen-year-old Ross, then named Diane; Florence Ballard, who was fifteen at the time; sixteen-year-old Mary Wilson; and eighteen-year-old Betty McGlown. Ballard and Ross alternated lead vocals, while Wilson and McGlown mostly sang backup. In the first year of their existence, the Primettes toured around local venues and sock-hops as the opening act for the Primes. In March 1959, the teenage girls had already recorded their first single, which consisted of two songs, "Tears of Sorrow" and "Pretty Baby." Released on a small-time record label called Lu-Pine, the record found little success or circulation outside the Primettes' hometown of Detroit.

Eventually, however, the Primettes' professional demeanor and skill won them a first-place trophy in the 1960 Detroit/Windsor Freedom Festival talent contest. There, the Primettes were spotted by a talent scout from Tamla Records (a division of the Motown Corporation), and the group managed to secure an audition with the founder of Motown, Berry Gordy. Although the audition failed to catch Gordy's interest, the Primettes soon became regulars at the Motown Studios, spending hours after school learning about the music business and singing backup vocals for known acts. When Betty McGlown left the group to get married, she was quickly replaced by Barbara Martin. The Primettes' diligence paid off in January of 1961 when they were contractually signed to Motown. After some debate, the Primettes were renamed the Supremes.

The Supremes' early beginnings were filled with obstacles. Soon after their first two singles in release failed to catch the public attention, Martin left the group to attend to family life. The Supremes decided to continue on as a trio, eventually touring around the country as the opening act for the Motown Revue. Still without a major hit, the Supremes performed strenuous hours for low pay despite their underage status. Touring the American South at the height of the Civil Rights movement, the young trio witnessed first-hand incidents of racial prejudice.

The turning point for the Supremes arrived in early 1963 when Gordy decided to match the female trio with songwriting team, Eddie and Brian Holland and Lamont Dozier, better known as Holland-Dozier-Holland or H-D-H. Gordy also made the contentious decision to have Ross become the group's lead vocalist. Years later, Gordy's decision proved to be a continuing thorn in the side of Ross's co-Supremes, Wilson and Ballard.

The string of hits that followed the pairing of the Supremes and H-D-H proved to be unprecedented and helped introduce the burgeoning Motown Records to wide and diverse audiences across racial lines. The Supremes' first hit, "Where Did Our Love Go?," exemplified the infectious rhythm that was quickly becoming known as the Motown Sound. Sung by Ross in a sultry tone, "Where Did Our Love Go?" reached number one on the pop and R&B charts in July 1964. The Supremes' next two singles, "Baby Love" and "Come See about Me," also reached number one on the pop charts.

The Supremes' first album, *Where Did Our Love Go?* sold over one million copies and remained on the pop charts for more than a year. After record-breaking U.S. and European tours, the Supremes became the first Motown act to appear on the *Ed Sullivan Show,* the most popular variety television show of the era. Surpassed in success only by the Beatles, the Supremes had garnered status as surefire hit-makers. Their new status now meant that black popular music was able to reach audiences across color lines. The group's success also propelled other Motown artists to visibility, boosting the record company's revenue to levels never imagined. While black music had once previously been regarded as "race music" by the entertainment industry, the Supremes' success demanded that styles of black music become integrated into the larger consciousness of American popular music.

As the trio continued to rack up number one hits with songs like "Stop in the Name of Love," internal changes within the group began to threaten their cohesiveness. In January 1966, Ross officially changed her name from Diane to Diana. To enhance their success, the group was subjected to refinement and finishing through Motown's Artist Development Unit. The new clean-cut image of the Supremes would eventually allow them to play sophisticated venues and nightclubs, like New York's Copacabana. As music critic Nelson George claims, these turn of events would "change The Supremes from a diligent, rather juvenile trio into the epitome of upwardly mobile, adult bourgeois charm."

Although each of the Supremes underwent refinement and finishing at Motown, Ross apparently began to show a special knack for audience appeal, charisma, and performing in the spotlight. Around this time, the singer also had begun a romantic affair with Gordy, much to the consternation of Wilson and Ballard. Although their relationship remained a public secret, Gordy would eventually father Diana's first child, Rhonda, in 1971.

When Ballard left the group in 1967, she was replaced by Cindy Birdsong, who had previously been a member of Patti LaBelle and the Bluebelles. As a result of these developments and changes within the group, Gordy decided to change the name of the trio to Diana Ross and the Supremes in order to bring more focus to the attention-grabbing lead singer. By the late 1960s, the group still continued to release chart-topping hits. "Love Child" and "I'm Livin' in Shame" featured lyrics that leaned toward social commentary, reflecting the turbulent changes that marked the era. Moreover, the group began to diversify their interests, starring in Motown's first TV productions and making over twenty-five appearances on popular television shows.

By 1969, however, Ross announced her intentions to leave the Supremes. After having changed the face of popular music over the course of twelve years, the trio played their final historic appearance on the *Ed Sullivan Show* in December of 1969 and made their final live performance in 1970. Their last single, "Someday We'll Be Together," proved to be a fitting tribute to a group ready to disband.

While the Supremes continued on with Jean Terrell as a new lead singer, they never again reached the level of success they had found with Ross. As a Motown solo act, Ross quickly became the most popular black female in pop and R&B, landing chart hits throughout the 1970s that included "Reach out and Touch Somebody's Hand" and "Ain't No Mountain High Enough." After marrying publicist Bob Silberstein in 1971, Ross gained new levels of credibility and acceptance through her much-acclaimed film performance as Billie Holiday in *Lady Sings the Blues* (1972), for which she received an Oscar nomination. She also reunited with her *Lady Sings the Blues* co-star Billy Dee Williams for the romantic film *Mahogany* (1975). In the early 1970s, Ross and Silberstein had two children, Tracee and Chudney, but divorced in 1976. After taking a critical misstep with her performance in the film musical *The Wiz* (1978), Ross left the film business in the 1980s.

In 1980, Ross decided to take greater control of her career by ending her contract with Motown Records. Her last record with the company was the platinum-selling *Diana,* which spawned the hit singles ''Upside Down,'' ''I'm Coming Out,'' and ''It's My Turn.'' As Ross's albums in the 1980s and 1990s became less commercially viable, she married Norwegian shipping magnate Arne Naess in 1986 and the couple had two children. By the late 1990s, Ross continued to exemplify the penchant for glamour and sophistication that she had demonstrated during her tenure with the Supremes, consistently producing work as a singer and an actress.

Diana Ross & the Supremes have proved to be a lasting cultural force. In 1982, *Dreamgirls,* a lavish Broadway musical, opened in New York. Starring Jennifer Holiday and conceived by Michael Bennett of *A Chorus Line* fame, the hit musical was based in large part on the rise and fall of the Supremes. The musical particularly focused on the drama surrounding the group's expulsion of Ballard, who had passed away in 1976. By the late 1990s, the Supremes still held the record for most consecutive number-one hits by a musical group and their legacy formed the basis of hit trios and quartet female musical groups of the 1990s including TLC and En Vogue.

Although they only lasted six years in the limelight, the Supremes managed to leave a lasting impression on U.S. society and culture. The group brought to public attention Diana Ross, the first major international African-American superstar to cross mediums of music, film, and television. The Supremes transformed live performances in R&B music through their emphasis on style, professionalism, and stylized choreography. They also helped to change racial consciousness by being highly visible, successful African-American female performers during a time of civil rights struggles and social upheaval.

—Jason King

FURTHER READING:

Betrock, Alan. *Girl Groups: The Story of a Sound.* New York, Delilah, 1982.

George, Nelson. *Where Did Our Love Go: The Rise and Fall of the Motown Sound.* New York, St. Martin's Press, 1985.

Tarraborelli, J. Randy. *Call Her Miss Ross.* New York, Ballantine, 1989.

Wilson, Mary. *DreamGirl: My Life as a Supreme.* New York, St. Martin's Press, 1986.

Roswell Incident

The Roswell Incident—the alleged government cover-up of the recovery of a crashed flying saucer and the bodies of its crew at a site near Roswell, New Mexico, in 1947—has achieved worldwide notoriety as the strongest ''proof'' of extra-terrestrial visitation.

On June 14, 1947, William ''Mac'' Brazel discovered a sizable amount of debris on the ranch he operated some 75 miles north of the town of Roswell. The material included a tangle of rubber strips, paper, sticks, and tinfoil. Brazel reported his findings to local authorities, which occasioned a minor cause célèbre in the town of Roswell.

The police ultimately referred the matter to the nearby Army Air Field. Base office collected the debris from Brazel and shipped it to Wright-Patterson Air Force Base, where, after much analysis, it was determined to be the wreckage of a weather balloon.

The public accepted the story, and the case was closed for some 40 years. In 1979, Jesse A. Marcel, a former base intelligence officer at Roswell Army Air Field, resurrected the episode in an interview with the *National Enquirer.* Marcel claimed that the wreckage at Roswell had not been of this Earth: it had borne strange alien pictorial markings and it could be neither dented nor burned. A number of civilian witnesses stepped forward to say that they had seen alien bodies among the wreckage. UFOlogists Charles Moore and Stanton Friedman compiled these statements and, in 1980, with the help of well-known occult writer Charles Berlitz, published *The Roswell Incident,* which charged the government with conspiring to withhold the evidence of this alien visitation from the public.

In the 1980s and 1990s, the Roswell Incident came to represent the foundation of faith in the UFO phenomenon for a growing community in the United States; Roswell offered the only known UFO case that involved physical evidence of any sort, and believers considered the incident a validation of their years of belief. A number of books published in the last two decades of the twentieth century explored further the government ''cover-up,'' and thousands of letters poured into Congress, demanding that the ''truth'' be revealed. Filmmakers and television producers capitalized on Roswell mania. The hit film *Independence Day* (1996) re-figured the Roswell tale for its narrative, and the popular television series *The X-Files* routinely dealt with government conspiracies connected with alien visitations.

On July 5, 1997, the fiftieth anniversary of the government's seizure of the wreckage, nearly 40,000 people flocked to Roswell to pay homage to the crash site. They were undeterred by a 231-page government report, published one month earlier, that again asserted there was no crashed flying saucer, no alien bodies, and no cover-up associated with the episode.

—Scott Tribble

FURTHER READING:

Berlitz, Charles, and William L. Moore. *The Roswell Incident.* New York, Grosset and Dunlap, 1980.

Peebles, Curtis. *Watch the Skies! A Chronicle of the Flying Saucer Myth.* Washington, D.C., Smithsonian Institution Press, 1994.

Saler, Benson, Charles A. Ziegler, and Charles B. Moore. *UFO Crash at Roswell: The Genesis of a Modern Myth.* Washington, D.C., Smithsonian Institution Press, 1997.

Roundtree, Richard (1937—)

Born July 9, 1937 in New Rochelle, New York, ex-model Richard Roundtree established himself as one of Hollywood's first black action heroes in only his second feature film, *Shaft* (1971). Expertly directed by Gordon Parks, and with an Oscar-nominated soundtrack by Isaac Hayes, *Shaft* (based on a novel by Ernest

A sign off U.S. 285, north of Roswell, New Mexico, points west to the alleged 1947 crash site of a flying saucer.

Tidyman) is probably the best representative of the genre of low-budget American movies known as "blaxploitation." Roundtree stars as a streetwise private eye who sets out to find the missing daughter of a Harlem ganglord. Two sequels, *Shaft's Big Score* (1972) and *Shaft in Africa* (1973), as well as a short-lived network television show, soon followed. Over the years Roundtree has established himself as a popular character actor. His work numbers over 60 movies and television miniseries, not to mention an album, *The Man Called Shaft.* Films include *Q-The Winged Serpent* (1982), *Seven* (1995), and *Original Gangstas* (1996).

—Steven Schneider

FURTHER READING:

James, Darius. *That's Blaxploitation!: Roots of the Baadasssss 'Tude (Rated X by an All-Whyte Jury).* New York, St. Martin's Griffin, 1995.

Tidyman, Ernest. *Shaft.* New York, Macmillan, 1970.

Rouse Company

During the 1970s and 1980s, the Rouse Company developed and managed a series of "festival marketplaces"—central city shopping malls featuring entertainment and historically themed architecture—that were widely credited with attracting crowds of shoppers and new investment dollars to formerly blighted downtown commercial areas. In the ten years following the 1976 opening of its Fanieul Hall Marketplace in Boston, Rouse built such colorful retail complexes as New York's South Street Sea Port, Baltimore's Harbor Place, Milwaukee's Grand Avenue Mall, and St. Louis's Union Station, a frenzy of development that some observers dubbed the "Rouse-ification" of the American city. Typically such developments depended on extensive subsidies from city government. Critics charged that Rouse projects failed to provide jobs for the urban poor, catered to the nostalgia of yuppie consumers with their use of stylized historical architecture, and squandered scarce public dollars better used elsewhere.

—Steve Macek

FURTHER READING:

Frieden, Bernard, and Lynne Sagalyn. *Downtown Inc.: How America Rebuilds Cities.* Cambridge, Massachusetts, Massachusetts Institute of Technology Press, 1989.

Sorkin, Michael, editor. *Variations on a Theme Park.* New York, Noonday Press, 1992.

Squires, Gregory, editor. *Unequal Partnerships: The Political Economy of Urban Redevelopment in Postwar America.* New Brunswick, New Jersey, Rutgers University Press, 1989.

Route 66

Though it no longer carries travelers across the nation the way it once did, Route 66 remains America's highway. "America's Main Street" spawned popular songs—"Get Your Kicks on Route 66"—and helped to define the culture of the American automobile in its heyday, the 1940s through the 1960s. The escape from reality embodied by the "open road" defined Route 66, and nostalgia continues to imbue the road and road culture with symbolic significance.

From the outset, planners endowed U.S. 66 with a nationalistic goal: to connect the main streets of rural and urban communities along its course. Entrepreneurs Cyrus Avery of Tulsa, Oklahoma, and John Woodruff of Springfield, Missouri, originally conceived of a road to link Chicago to Los Angeles, but more than their efforts were needed to kick off such a massive roadbuilding project. Legislation for public highways first appeared in 1916, but it was not until Congress enacted an even more comprehensive version of the act in 1925 that the government initiated the construction of a national highway. The numerical designation 66 was assigned to the Chicago-to-Los Angeles route in the summer of 1926. America's "main streets" now accessed one common "Main Street," Route 66.

As opposed to existing regional highways, which cut straight to their destination, Route 66 followed a meandering course which linked hundreds of surrounding rural communities to the metropolis of Chicago. Farmers shipping produce and trucking companies soon became some of the greatest users of the road. The more direct route between Chicago and the Pacific coast quickly dropped south toward the flat prairie lands and temperate climates that made Route 66 a favorite of truckers. But the road soon became beloved by more than truckers seeking the fastest route between cities.

In *The Grapes of Wrath* (1939), novelist John Steinbeck proclaimed U.S. Highway 66 the "Mother Road," for it came to stand for personal survival for the thousands of "Okies" who used the road to migrate to California to escape the despair of the Dust Bowl. Such

Wrink's Food Market on old Route 66.

cultural and social significance increased the road's legendary and mythic standing nationwide. With continuous paving completed in 1938, the road was ready to unlock a nation's dreams as well as its hopes.

The increased mobility made possible by the automobile and the expansion of leisure time for America's growing middle-class helped draw ever more drivers to Route 66 after World War II. In such a time of change, relocation was very frequent—particularly to California, where many segments of the defense industry had mobilized during the war. These sensibilities were represented in the song of one such transient professional, former Marine captain Bobby Troup, as he traveled West to begin playing with Tommy Dorsey's well-known band. "Get Your Kicks on Route 66," his song about his move, became a catch phrase for countless motorists. The popular recording was released in 1946 by Nat King Cole, only one week after Troup's arrival in Los Angeles. It became a "musical map" of the traveller's odyssey by listing the stops, the feel, and the aura of the road.

A unique "automobile culture" soon took shape along Route 66. Enterprising entrepreneurs met the needs of even the poorest travelers by building motels, gas stations, diners, and tourist attractions. Most Americans who drove the route preferred motels instead of hotels, because they provided ease of access to their car. Motels evolved from earlier features of the American roadside such as the auto camp and the tourist home. The auto camp had been an entirely informal development as townspeople along Route 66 roped off spaces in which travelers could camp for the night. An outgrowth of the auto camp and tourist home was the cabin camp (sometimes called cottages) that offered minimal comfort at affordable prices.

Gas stations were another new presence on the American landscape. Initially, "filling stations" consisted of a house with one or two gasoline pumps in front. With the addition of service bays the facilities began to grow. Finally, petroleum companies realized that entire structures could serve as advertisements if designed properly. Ordinarily, service stations were developed through regional prototypes and then dispersed across the country. The buildings were distinctive and clearly associated with a particular petroleum company.

Route 66 and the many points of interest along its length had become familiar landmarks by the time a new generation of postwar motorists hit the road in the 1960s. It was during this period that the television series *Route 66* (1960-1964), starring Martin Milner and George Maharis, brought Americans back to the route looking for new adventure. American youth romanticized the image of the road portrayed in the program and in the writings of authors such as Jack Kerouac. The "open road" became a symbol of new opportunities and unfettered living. Driving the route to California became for many a rite of passage into adulthood; for some adults, it became an opportunity to revisit one's youth. The leisure culture of the 1950s and 1960s thus defined itself around sites such as Route 66.

Ironically, such popularity also eroded the future of Route 66. The public cry for easy and rapid automobile travel soon led to improved highways beginning in the 1950s. Under President Dwight D. Eisenhower, massive federal funding went into the construction of a national highway system. When Congress passed the Federal Aid Highway Act of 1956, Route 66 lost its figurative and literal meaning. It became an impractical mode of travel in contrast to the rapidly moving highways. Slowly, Route 66 was taken out of service—the signs removed and the roads taken over by individual states. By the 1970s, the "Mother Road" no longer existed.

Nostalgia, though, can do funny things to practicality. In the 1980s and 1990s, preservationists have reclaimed stretches of the road as a living museum of the evolution of tourist-targeted, roadside architecture. "The Main Street of America" has proven a great attraction, and Historic Route 66 signs now bind the disparate state routes to their common heritage. Route 66 thus binds together the nation's attraction to the automobile and the open road, and the opportunity to control one's own destiny, whether it be for a momentary escape or a lifetime move across the country. Many generations will likely continue to learn about the "kicks" a society got on a seemingly insignificant highway.

—Brian Black

FURTHER READING:

Crump, Spencer. *Route 66: America's First Main Street.* 2nd edition. Corona del Mar, California, Zeta Publishers, 1996.

"Explore Route 66." http://www.national66.com/index.html. June 1999.

Kelly, Susan Croce; photographs by Quinta Scott. *Route 66: The Highway and Its People.* Norman, University of Oklahoma Press, 1988.

Snyder, Tom. *Route 66 Traveler's Guide and Roadside Companion.* New York, St. Martin's Press, 1995.

Rowan and Martin's Laugh-In
See Laugh-In

Royko, Mike (1932-1997)

Pulitzer prize-winning journalist Mike Royko was born on September 19, 1932 in Chicago, the city in which he lived most of his life, and it was as a distinctively Chicagoan journalist that he earned nationwide fame. Royko's journalism awards included the Ernie Pyle Memorial Award, the Heywood Broun Award, the H.L. Mencken Award, the National Headliner award, and the Pulitzer Prize for commentary; however, his readers did not need any award committees to tell them that Royko was a great journalist.

Royko had a sporadic formal education, dropping in and out of school. But he received another form of education by working for his father Michael, a tavern owner, at a young age, and by holding several other jobs. The last degree he earned came when he graduated from Central YMCA High School. Royko then joined the Air Force and was stationed near Seoul, South Korea, during the final months of the Korean War. While in the Air Force, Royko was transferred to O'Hare Field, Chicago. There, he became editor of the base's newspaper. This was his inauguration into newspaper work.

Royko's first job as a civilian journalist was with the *Lincoln-Belmont Booster.* He became a cub reporter for the *Chicago Daily News* in 1959. In January 1964, the paper made him a full-time columnist. The *Daily News* closed down in 1978, but Royko got a columnist position at the *Chicago Sun-Times,* which was owned by the same company as the defunct *News.* In 1984, Royko left the *Sun-Times* for the rival *Tribune;* he despised Australian press baron Rupert Murdoch, who had purchased the *Sun-Times.* At all three papers, Royko wrote a column whose distinctive style set a new standard for journalistic commentary.

Like other opinion journalists, Royko would comment about the news of the day; however, he would approach his topics with a common-sense perspective that often eluded fellow columnists. For instance, in an April 26, 1981 column, Royko dealt with a *Washington Post* reporter who had won the Pulitzer Prize for a story that turned out to be fake. The story claimed that a man was getting his girlfriend's eight-year-old son addicted to heroin. Other columnists were talking about how horrible it was that a journalist had faked a story, but Royko brought up a different issue: What if the fake story had actually been true? Royko argued that the *Post* should have reported the alleged dope-pusher to the authorities, even though the reporter had claimed that she had promised the man confidentiality: "What would the *Post* have done if it had discovered that a congressman knew that an eight-year-old child was being murdered, but had given the killer his word he wouldn't reveal his identity?. . . what does [the publisher of the *Post*] have to say about her editors covering up the murder of an eight-year-old child?"

Royko often used his column to expose injustice. For example, a Royko column of December 10, 1973, described a Vietnam veteran whose face had been mutilated by an enemy rocket. The veteran, who was forced to take his food in liquid form, wanted surgery so that he would be able to eat solid foods. The veteran thought that the Veterans' Administration should pay for the operation, but the VA said that the damage to his face was not a "service-connected disability." Royko discussed the VA's position as follows: "How can this surgery be for anything else but his 'service-connected disability?' Until he was hit by a rocket, [the veteran] had teeth. Now he has none. He had eyes. Now he has none. People could look at him. Now most of them turn away." The day after this column ran, Royko was able to report that the VA would pay the faceless veteran's medical expenses after all. "It shows how efficient a government agency can be—a year late—if its inefficiency is suddenly splashed across a newspaper."

Royko's columns also featured fictional characters who discussed matters of political or cultural importance. One such character, Slats Grobnik, was portrayed as a native of the same area of Chicago as Royko. A column on March 31, 1972, described the young Slats Grobnik's reason for not believing in Santa Claus: "Anybody who can get in and out of that many houses without being seen is going to take stuff, not leave it." Another piece of Slats Grobnik's wisdom (from a column of January 11, 1984): "Everybody says that work is so good for ya. Well, if work is supposed to be so great, how come they got to pay ya to do it?"

Royko published one book (apart from several collections of his columns). That book was the bestseller *Boss,* which was published in 1971 during the reign of Chicago Mayor Richard Daley, whose career the book described. Royko described Daley as the political ruler of Chicago, a man who focused on developing the business district but who neglected the inner city. As portrayed by Royko, Daley was an honest man whose political machine was staffed by less-than-honest men. Royko said that Daley's "moral code" was: "Thou shalt not steal, but thou shalt not blow the whistle on anyone who does." While discussing how members of Daley's machine profited from certain shady deals, Royko reported (but did not claim credit for) a suggested change in Chicago's civic motto. According to the suggestion, the old motto, "Urbs in Horto" ("City in a Garden"), should be replaced with "Ubi Est Mea" ("Where's Mine?").

A 1981 movie, *Continental Divide,* featured a character based on Royko. The Royko character was played by Royko's friend John Belushi, of which Royko noted: "[A]s much as I like Belushi

personally, I think the producers might have made a mistake in casting my part. I think Paul Newman would have been a better choice, although he's older than I am. And in appearance we're different because he has blue eyes and mine are brownish-green." Royko died in his native city on April 29, 1997, in Chicago's Memorial Hospital.

—Eric Longley

FURTHER READING:

Crimmins, Jerry. "Royko's Early Years." *Chicago Tribune.* May 4, 1997.

Crimmins, Jerry, and Rick Kogan. "'Quite Simply the Best': Legendary Columnist, the Voice of Chicago for Decades, Dies." *Chicago Tribune.* 29 April 1997.

Moe, Doug. *The World of Mike Royko.* Madison, University of Wisconsin Press, 1999.

Royko, Mike. *Boss: Richard J. Daley of Chicago.* New York, Signet, 1971.

———. *Dr. Kookie, You're Right!* New York, E. P. Dutton, 1989.

———. *I May Be Wrong, but I Doubt It.* Chicago, Henry Regnery, 1968.

———. *Like I Was Sayin'. . .* New York, E. P. Dutton, 1984.

———, with commentaries by Lois Wille and a foreward by Studs Terkel. *One More Time: The Best of Mike Royko.* Chicago, University of Chicago Press, 1999.

———. *Sez Who? Sez Me.* New York, E. P. Dutton, 1982.

———. *Slats Grobnik and Some Other Friends.* New York, Popular Library, 1976.

———. *Up against It.* Chicago, Henry Regnery, 1967.

Rubik's Cube

Rubik's Cube, the multicolored puzzle with 43,252,003,274, 489,856,000 possible combinations and only one solution, baffled many a partygoer in the early 1980s, when it briefly seized America's attention. The quintessential Reagan-era toy fad was actually a product of the 1970s, when Hungarian professor Erno Rubik came up with the idea as a way to stump his students. He was awarded a patent in 1976 and promptly licensed the product to the Ideal Toy Company. Cube fever soon began spreading across North America in the form of clubs, newsletters, and even a Saturday morning cartoon, *Rubik the Amazing Cube.* Once solved, however, a Rubik's Cube did not have many other uses, and in 1983 the market for the multicolored mind game suddenly disappeared.

—Robert E. Schnakenberg

FURTHER READING:

Rubik, Erno. *Rubik's Cubic Compendium.* New York, Oxford University Press, 1987.

Taylor, Don. *Mastering Rubik's Cube.* New York, Holt, Rinehart and Winston, 1981.

Rudolph the Red-Nosed Reindeer

"The most famous reindeer of all," Rudolph has become a vital ingredient of Christmas lore for generations of children around the world, but few people recall the true genesis of the story. Fewer still would be able to explain how much the original Rudolph fable has been changed by the efforts of songwriters and animators through the decades since its 1939 conception. Yet such is the enduring popularity of this tale in its myriad forms that sociologist James Barnett declared Rudolph the twentieth-century Christmas symbol "most likely to become a lasting addition" to Christmas folklore.

Rudolph the Red-Nosed Reindeer was the brainchild of Robert L. May, a 35-year-old advertising copywriter for the Chicago-based Montgomery Ward department store. In 1939, May was commissioned by his supervisor to create an original Christmas story that the store could give away to shoppers at holiday time. May was tapped in part for his affinity for children's limericks, the form in which the first Rudolph iteration was written.

Drawing on his own childhood experiences (he had experienced ridicule because of his slight frame), May dreamed up a title character who was ostracized by his fellow reindeer because of his glowing red nose. For an alliterative name, he originally suggested Rollo, but this idea was rejected by the Montgomery Ward catalog department. After briefly considering Reginald, May finally settled on Rudolph as the moniker for his creation, a name reputedly arrived at with the help of his four-year-old daughter.

The first Rudolph booklet, with illustrations by Denver Gillen, was distributed to two and a quarter million Montgomery Ward customers during Christmas of 1939. Although quite popular, it was not released again until 1946 due to wartime paper shortages, but by the end of that year, a total of six million copies had been distributed nationwide.

The story of *Rudolph the Red-Nosed Reindeer* that these initial customers enjoyed was quite different from the one that would be immortalized in later versions. In May's original poem, Rudolph is not one of Santa's reindeer—at least, not at first. He is an ordinary reindeer living with his family in an obscure village, and although he *is* ostracized by some of his companions for his glowing red nose, he maintains a positive self-image and has the loving support of his parents. He hooks up with Santa only after the corpulent gift-giver's reindeer team arrives at Rudolph's house one particularly foggy Christmas Eve. Upon noticing his beaming honker, Santa enlists Rudolph to lead his beleaguered team. Rudolph does so with great skill and bravery, prompting Santa to congratulate him upon the team's safe return with the words, "By *you* last night's journey was actually bossed. / Without you, I'm certain we'd all have been lost."

It was in this form that Rudolph first became an icon for wartime Christmas celebrants and a lucrative marketing tool for Montgomery Ward. It made little money for May, however, until 1947, when he persuaded Montgomery Ward president Sewed Avery to transfer the copyright to him. With these rights secured, May set about building the next generation of Rudolphiana. In 1947, a nine-minute *Rudolph the Red-Nosed Reindeer* cartoon, directed by *Popeye* creator Max Fleisher, played in movie theaters nationwide. Two years later, May commissioned his brother-in-law Johnny Marks to write a song based on the Rudolph character. The song, which glossed over many of the key details of May's original story, became an immense hit for vocalist Gene Autry, selling two million copies in 1949 and joining "White Christmas" in the pantheon of Yuletide standards. In 1952, a

now wealthy May quit his job at Montgomery Ward to manage the Rudolph business full-time.

In 1964, the stop-motion animation house of Rankin and Bass produced a new *Rudolph the Red-Nosed Reindeer* TV special that solidified the legend—again in altered form—in the minds of baby-boom viewers. In this new version, narrated by bearded songster Burl Ives, Rudolph is a miserable, self-loathing creature rejected even by his status-conscious parents. The "other reindeer" who taunt him are no longer peers from his village but Santa's actual reindeer, who compete among themselves for the old man's favor. Even Santa himself seems a little ashamed of Rudolph's deformity, and it is only after Rudolph links up with a society of "misfit toys" and proves himself as the head of the sleigh team that he earns the respect of those around him.

This new iteration of the Rudolph legend was to prove almost as popular as the previous ones. In its own way, it was certainly more influential. The innovative stop-motion techniques devised by Rankin-Bass inspired a generation of animators, most prominent among them Tim Burton, who paid homage to Rudolph in his 1993 feature *The Nightmare before Christmas.* The hit movie *Toy Story* and the popular MTV series *Celebrity Death Match* both showed the influence of the Rankin-Bass *Rudolph* as well.

The 1964 *Rudolph the Red-Nosed Reindeer* special continues to generate huge television ratings for its annual holiday broadcast, and the Gene Autry song recording, among many other renditions, is a staple of every radio station's Yuletide music programming. Robert L. May's prototypical creation was commemorated in 1990 with the publication of a handsome facsimile edition—the first time the story had been offered for sale in its original form. Rudolph's fans have thus had many ways in which to appreciate this enduring icon of Americana.

—Robert E. Schnakenberg

FURTHER READING:

Archibald, John J. "Rudolph's Tale Left Him Cold." *St. Louis Post-Dispatch.* December 6, 1989, 3E.

Frankel, Stanley A. "The Story behind Rudolph the Red-Nosed Reindeer." *Good Housekeeping.* December 1989, 126.

Lillard, Margaret. "Rudolph Lit Up Creator's Career." *Los Angeles Times.* December 17, 1989, A7.

Lollar, Kevin. "Reginald the Red-Nosed Reindeer?" *Gannett News Service.* December 21, 1989.

Murphy, Cullen. "Rudolph Redux." *Atlantic Monthly.* August 1990, 18.

Run-DMC

Queens, New York-based hip-hop artists Run–DMC, and Jam Master Jay are responsible for revolutionizing hip-hop in two very important ways. First, during hip-hop's infancy as a recorded form, they changed the direction of recorded hip-hop by stripping it of all its "old school" aural fluff and cutting it down to its barest essentials: hardcore beats and rhymes. Their debut 1983 12" single, "It's like That/Sucker MCs," reflected the way hip-hop sounded as it was performed in local parks and nightclubs, and it laid a blueprint that most 1980s hip-hop artists followed. Second, Run-DMC is credited for almost singlehandedly bringing hip-hop music to a wide scale audience with their Aerosmith collaboration, ''Walk This Way,'' a single that reached number four on the *Billboard* Pop charts in 1986. Among other firsts, they were the first hip-hop artists to earn a gold record, a platinum record, a multi-platinum record, a *Rolling Stone* cover, and have their videos regularly played on MTV.

Run (Joseph Simmons, born November 14, 1964), DMC (Darryl McDaniels, born May 31, 1964), and their DJ, Jam Master Jay (Jason Mizell, born January 21, 1965), were three black middle-class Hollis, Queens, high school kids who grew up listening to hip-hop in New York City parks. Run got his foot in the recording studio door because he was the brother of Russell Simmons, the then manager of hip-hop stars Kurtis Blow and Whodini (and soon-to-be co-founder of one of the most important hip-hop labels, Def Jam). Having rapped professionally since age 12 as ''the son of Kurtis Blow,'' Run often boasted that he could make a record better than the older guys who dominated the early recorded hip-hop scene; Run even went so far as to dismiss those more lightweight records as ''bull——.''

After continually bugging Russell Simmons, the older brother relented and allowed Run and his two friends to cut a 12'' single. Using just their voices and a drum machine (with light touches of synthesizer used to punctuate the rhythm), ''It's Like That'' and

especially ''Sucker MCs'' essentially created hip-hop's first ''new school.'' Rendering previous acts Grandmaster Flash & the Furious Five, the Cold Crush Brothers, Funky Four Plus One, and the Sugarhill Gang ''old school,'' Run-DMC created a new sound that was truer to the way hip-hop sounded in its raw form when it was performed live with a DJ and one or more MCs. This new sound was also extremely popular, earning a gold record (for 1984's self-titled debut), a platinum record (for 1985's *King of Rock*) and a platinum record (for 1986's *Raising Hell*).

Although singles like ''King of Rock'' received significant airplay and were occasionally played on MTV, it was Run-DMC's collaboration with Aerosmith on a cover of that hard rock band's ''Walk This Way'' that put them over the top. Run-DMC was familiar with the song only because they had rapped over the song's beat for years, but they had no idea who Aerosmith was; until they entered the studio with those veterans, they thought the name of the group was Toys in the Attic (the Aerosmith album from which ''Walk This Way'' came). Run-DMC's ''Walk This Way'' smashed down walls between rock and hip-hop audiences, pleasing both crowds and making music history in the process. (It should also be noted that this wasn't Run-DMC's first fusion of rock and rap; they did it before on 1984's ''Rock Box'' and 1985's ''King of Rock.'') The Run-DMC album that contained ''Walk This Way'' also featured a number of

Run-DMC

other popular songs, including ''It's Tricky,'' ''My Addidas,'' and ''You Be Illin'.''

By the late 1980s, Run-DMC found themselves victims of the restless drive for innovation and freshness. After 1988's *Tougher than Leather*, their later albums—*Back from Hell* and *Down with the King*—barely charted, and Run-DMC was seen as ''old school'' has-beens. Before 1993's *Down with the King*, the group embraced Christianity and Run even went so far as to become an ordained minister, founding his own church in Harlem. The group continued to remain active in the late 1990s, touring and performing in a popular 1998 Gap clothing television ad, but they still had not released a record of new material.

—Kembrew McLeod

FURTHER READING:

Fernando, S. H., Jr. *The New Beats: Exploring the Music, Culture, and Attitudes of Hip-Hop.* New York, Doubleday, 1994.

Rose, Tricia. *Black Noise: Rap Music and Black Culture in Contemporary America.* Middleton, Connecticut, Wesleyan University Press, 1994.

Toop, David. *Rap Attack 2: African Rap to Global Hip-Hop.* London, Serpent's Tail, 1991.

Runyon, Damon (1880-1946)

Damon Runyon personified the spirit of Broadway in the Roaring 1920s. A renowned American journalist and sports writer for three and a half decades, he is best remembered for the people he created in his popular short stories of New York during Prohibition—touts, bookies, gamblers, gangsters, and their molls, who frequented the glittering world of speakeasies and nightclubs. ''Runyonesque'' is a commonly used term denoting a rough talking person with a slightly shady purpose, a wisecracking Good Time Charley or grasping Miss Billy Perry. His short story collection, *Guys and Dolls* (1931), became a successful Broadway musical and Hollywood box-office success, starring Frank Sinatra, while his *Little Miss Marker* launched the screen career of Shirley Temple. Together with Walter Winchell and his contemporary, Ring Lardner, Runyon presented a lively, humorous vision of Broadway during this era.

—Joan Gajadhar and Jim Sinclair

FURTHER READING:

Clark, Tom. *The World of Damon Runyon.* New York, Harper and Row, 1978.

Mosedale, John. *The Men Who Invented Broadway.* New York, Richard Marek Publishers, 1981.

RuPaul (1960—)

RuPaul Andre Charles was the first African-American, disco-loving drag queen to secure a contract with a major cosmetics

RuPaul (left) with Joan Rivers.

company (M.A.C., 1995). RuPaul was a stunning beauty at six-feet-seven-inches in heels and propagated an ethic of self-love, acceptance of others, finger-wagging questioning of convention, and self-promotion not seen since Andy Warhol.

A fixture of the fashion and dance club scene in New York City beginning in the late 1980s, RuPaul became a household name when his 1993 debut album, *Supermodel of the World,* earned three #1 Billboard hits and received heavy airplay on cable music video channels and radio stations. In 1994 RuPaul teamed with Elton John to record ''Don't Go Breaking My Heart'' for John's *Duets* album. RuPaul hosted a morning drive-time show on New York City's top-rated WKTU-FM (1996-97), several cable television specials, and a talk show on cable's VH1 music video channel (1997-98). Addressing fashion, music, and current news issues, *The RuPaul Show* was a half hour of glitz, glamour, and infectious self-affirmation.

Between 1994 and 1998 RuPaul appeared in eleven films, sometimes in drag, sometimes not. His roles in *The Brady Bunch Movie* (1995) and *A Very Brady Sequel* (1996) aptly combined his neo-disco style with the retro-chic, tongue-in-cheek revival of the Brady franchise for a bit of cultural nostalgia that was very successful commercially.

RuPaul was forthcoming about his status as a cross-dresser and even used it as a marketing ploy with M.A.C. cosmetics: ''If M.A.C. products can make a big old black man like me look this good,'' he was known to say, ''just think of what they can do for you, girl.'' As co-chair of M.A.C.'s AIDS fund, RuPaul helped raise several million dollars between 1995 and 1997. His fundraising prowess and altruism notwithstanding, RuPaul attracted the criticism of religious leaders worldwide who denounced the use of a drag artist as a spokesperson for an otherwise reputable company and cause.

—Tilney Marsh

FURTHER READING:

M.A.C. Press release. November 6, 1997. http://www.RuPaul.net. February 1999.

Romanowski, Patricia, et al., eds. *The New Rolling Stone Encyclopedia of Rock & Roll*. New York, Rolling Stone Press, 1995.

RuPaul. *Letting it All Hang Out*. New York, Hyperion, 1995.

Rupp, Adolph (1901-1977)

Known as the "Baron of the Bluegrass," Adolph Rupp led the University of Kentucky basketball team to 18 Southeastern Conference championships, a National Invitational Tournament championship, and four NCAA national championships (1948, 1949, 1951, 1958) while compiling a record of 876-190 in his 41 years as head coach. In 1951, three of his star players admitted to taking money to shave points in a 1949 game. The NCAA suspended the team for the 1952-53 season and publicly reprimanded Rupp. Rupp's all-white Wildcats squared off against the all-black Texas Western University in the 1966 National Championship game and lost, prompting Rupp to make some disparaging racist comments after the game. Soon after that season, all southern schools began to lift the unspoken ban on recruiting black athletes.

—Jay Parrent

FURTHER READING:

Laudeman, Tev. *The Rupp Years—The University of Kentucky's Golden Era of Basketball*. Louisville, Kentucky, *The Courier Journal* and *The Louisville Times*, 1972.

Rice, Russell. *Kentucky Basketball's Big Blue Machine*. Huntsville, Alabama, Strode Publishers, 1976.

Russell, Bill (1934—)

In thirteen seasons as a professional basketball player between 1956 and 1969, Bill Russell played on a record eleven National Basketball Association championship teams for the Boston Celtics, serving as both player and coach on the final two. While many believe that Michael Jordan was the best individual player in league history, an accolade that often went to Russell prior to Jordan's ascent in the late 1980s through the 1990s. Russell is still widely recognized for his incredible winning record.

Born in Monroe, Louisiana, in 1934, Russell moved with his family to the San Francisco area and played basketball, without great distinction, at McClymonds High School in Oakland, California. Despite his lack of success at the high school level, Russell was big enough and promising enough to earn a scholarship to the University of San Francisco. There, he developed both physically and skill-wise,

and enjoyed an impressive career, during which he and future Celtic teammate K. C. Jones led the team to two National College Athletic Association championships in 1955 and 1956. Russell averaged more than twenty points and twenty rebounds a game during his college career, one of a very select group of players ever to have done so. He joined the Celtics after helping the United States to win a gold medal at the 1956 Olympic Games in Melbourne, Australia. Russell was initially drafted by the St. Louis Hawks, but Celtics coach Arnold "Red" Auerbach engineered a trade for Russell, as the high-scoring Celtics sorely lacked a player who could rebound and play defense.

Russell's defensive ability, coupled with the team's already high-powered offense, proved the key to an unprecedented string of NBA championships for Boston. In Russell's rookie season, the Celtics defeated the St. Louis Hawks for the league championship in 1956-57, due largely to Russell's nineteen points and thirty-two rebounds in the decisive final game. Although the Celtics lost to the Hawks the following season, with Russell suffering a debilitating ankle injury in the opening moments of the third game of the championship series, the Celtics began a string of eight straight championships from 1958-59 through 1965-66.

The six-foot-nine-inch Russell became the leading rebounder in Celtics' history and the second in NBA history after Wilt Chamberlain. Russell's biggest innovation, however, was related to his ability as a shot-blocker. He would patrol the area near the basket and wait for opposing players to drive for an attempted score. With impeccable timing, Russell would gently swat the ball away to a teammate, who would often take it to the other end of the court for an easy basket. Later, as an outspoken television announcer in the 1970s and 1980s, Russell would criticize players who blocked shots by violently knocking the ball out of bounds. This, according to Russell, was a form of showing off that offended his concept of team play. Unfortunately for Russell, the NBA did not begin keeping track of blocked shots until the 1973-74 season, so his exact number of blocked shots is unknown.

Russell's career-long rivalry with Chamberlain, one of the greatest scorers in NBA history, epitomizes his commitment to team play. While Chamberlain's scoring numbers were much higher (Russell never averaged more than nineteen points a game during the regular season, while Chamberlain averaged at least fifty on several occasions), Russell was famed for his ability to help his teammates, particularly in crucial game situations. Russell won five NBA Most Valuable Player awards, given to the player who contributes the most to helping his team win. As Russell noted in his autobiography, *Second Wind*, "Star players have an enormous responsibility beyond their statistics—the responsibility to pick their team up and carry it. . . . I always thought that the most important measure of how good a game I'd played was how much better I'd made my teammates play."

During the 1966-67 season, Russell became the player-coach of the Celtics, the first African American head coach in league history. Although the Celtics lost to a powerful Philadelphia team in that season, Russell led the aging Celtics to consecutive championships in the 1967-68 and 1968-69 seasons. The 1969 championship was perhaps the team's most dramatic, as the Celtics, who had finished a mere fourth in their own division during the regular season, defeated a heavily favored Los Angeles Lakers team which included future Hall-of-Famers Chamberlain, Jerry West, and Elgin Baylor, winning a decisive game seven in Los Angeles.

Russell retired after the 1968-69 season and was elected to the NBA Hall of Fame in 1974. He undertook stints as the coach and general manager of the Seattle SuperSonics from 1973 to 1977 and as

The Lakers' Wilt Chamberlain tries for a basket over the Celtics' Bill Russell, 1969.

coach of the Sacramento Kings in 1987-88, neither of which approached his success as a player. Part of the problem was that the game had become more and more focused on individual stars since Russell's playing days, and players had a difficult time adjusting to the team style of play that Russell advocated. In addition, even Russell's admirers concede that he had little patience for detail and practice. As a player, notes former coach and close friend Auerbach in *On and off the Court,* Russell would put forth the minimum effort in practice, saving his energy for games. During his stint as player-coach

of the Celtics, Russell would often sit on the bench and drink coffee and read a newspaper while the team practiced. Once the game started, however, Russell was always ready to play.

—Jason George

FURTHER READING:

Auerbach, Arnold ''Red,'' with Joe Fitzgerald. *On and off the Court.* New York, MacMillan, 1985.

"Bill Russell." http://www.nba.com/history/russell,io.html. February 1999.

Fitzgerald, Joe. *That Championship Feeling: The Story of the Boston Celtics.* New York, Charles Scribner's Sons, 1975.

Russell, Bill, and Taylor Branch. *Second Wind: The Memoirs of an Opinionated Man.* New York, Random House, 1979.

Ryan, Bob. *The Boston Celtics: The History, Legends, and Images of America's Most Celebrated Team.* Reading, Massachusetts, Addison-Wesley, 1989.

Russell, Jane (1921—)

It was voluptuous Jane Russell's cleavage that brought her to the attention of eccentric Hollywood producer, Howard Hughes. It was the exposure of too much of said cleavage in the 1941 film, *The Outlaw,* that brought the censors down on Hughes and brought Jane Russell an avalanche of publicity. But it was Russell's ability to both laugh at and rise above her sex symbol status and prove herself a talented actress, a lovely singer, and a gifted comedienne that made her one of Hollywood's top stars during the 1950s.

Ernestine Jane Geraldine Russell was born on June 21, 1921 in Bemidji, Minnesota. The daughter of a former actress and an office manager, Russell moved to Southern California at nine months and it was there she grew up, a tall, fun-loving tomboy. The oldest of five children, and the only girl, she loved the outdoors, and spent much of

Jane Russell in the film *The Outlaw*.

her time riding horses and climbing trees on her family's Van Nuys ranch. Even in high school, Russell's rambunctious spirit was more self-evident than her study habits. But after graduation, her mother insisted that her tall, beautiful, raven-haired daughter go to finishing school. When Russell balked at the idea, they compromised on drama school. After all, when her daughter was born, Russell's mother had named her Jane Russell because she thought the name would look good up in lights.

In September 1939, Russell started taking lessons at the Max Reinhardt School of Drama. But she missed classes more than she attended them and instead hung out at the bowling alley across the street. She dropped out, only to decide a week later to enroll at Maria Ouspenskaya's School of Dramatic Arts. Bitten by the acting bug, Russell stuck with her studies and six months later she was on her to her first screen test at Twentieth Century-Fox. But nothing came of it except that Russell's desire to become an actress grew, as did her disappointment when no one else called for a screen test. At last, she realized that she was going to have to give up her dream and get a real job, which she did, working as a chiropodist's assistant.

One day out of the blue, her mother called to tell her that an agent had been calling every day. But Russell was no longer interested in pipe dreams. The agent persisted and finally got Russell on the phone, telling her that Howard Hughes wanted to test her for a picture. The next day, Russell was at the studio, and met with Howard Hawks, who would direct *The Outlaw* for Hughes. Russell's part in this Western was as a half-Irish, half-Mexican girl whose brother has been killed by Billy the Kid and who tries to kill the Kid with a pitchfork, but is raped by the outlaw in retribution. The nineteen-year-old's knockout figure and devil-may-care attitude may have won her the role, but she didn't care. She was now a working actress.

On the shoot in Arizona, national magazines such as *Look, Life,* and *Photoplay,* photographed the new star in her costume of a low-cut peasant blouse and skirt. As Russell would later write, "My boobs were bulging out over the top of my blouse every time I picked up those pails. But I didn't know it until I saw myself on the covers and centerfolds of practically every magazine on the newsstands . . . Those pictures came out for the next five years."

When Howard Hawks walked off the set of *The Outlaw,* Howard Hughes took over. The result was a film that the Hays office censors took two years to approve, a film which Pauline Kael described as "the definitive burlesque of cowtown dramas . . . Jane Russell swings her bosom around and shows her love for frail, seedy Billy the Kid (Jack Buetel) by hitting him over the head with a coffepot and putting sand in his water flasks when he is setting out across the desert. To reciprocate, he ties her up with wet thongs and leaves her out in the sun. Walter Huston and Thomas Mitchell provide a little relief from the amorous games." But even after the 1943 San Francisco premiere, the film remained hung up in red tape and was not released nationwide until 1947, leaving Russell's dream of becoming a working actress stalled. Hughes owned her contract and refused to lend her out to other studios. She was, however, famous. During World War II, Russell was hailed as the "sexpot of the century," becoming one of the favorite pinup girls for U.S. soldiers overseas.

Finally, after five years of inactivity, during which she married football star Robert Waterfield, Hughes agreed to loan Russell out to make *The Young Widow,* a teary war film. But the weepy widow role didn't suit Russell's strengths and it wasn't until 1948's *Paleface,* in which she starred opposite Bob Hope, playing the strong, sharpshooting straight woman to Hope's timid funny man, that she hit her stride.

When Howard Hughes bought RKO the same year, Russell's career finally took off. She exhibited her singing and acting ability in *His Kind of Woman* and *Macao,* both opposite frequent co-star Robert Mitchum, her appeal as a dark, sexy, leading lady in *The Las Vegas Story,* and her comic talent in two more films with Bob Hope, *Road to Bali* and *Son of Paleface.* But it was 1953's *Gentleman Prefer Blondes,* which best showcased Russell. Starring opposite Marilyn Monroe, Russell gave what Leonard Maltin calls a "sly, knowing, comic performance," more than holding her own against the electric Monroe.

Russell remained an audience favorite in movies through the 1950s and 1960s. But it wasn't until she took over for Elaine Stritch in the Broadway musical, *Company,* in 1970, that Russell found another vehicle suited to her many talents. Playing a blowsy, boozy broad, Russell showed off her ability to sing, dance, act, and have a laugh at her own expense. Though 1970s TV audiences will always associate Russell and her full figure with the many commercials she made touting the virtues of Playtex bras, she has certainly proved herself to be more than the woman Bob Hope once introduced as "the two and only Jane Russell." Beautiful, talented, and funny, Jane Russell is that rare Hollywood sex symbol who can simultaneously laugh at herself and enjoy being the star that she is.

—Victoria Price

FURTHER READING:

Kael, Pauline. *5001 Nights at the Movies.* New York, Henry Holt and Company, 1991.

Microsoft Corporation. *Cinemania 96: The Best-Selling Interactive Guide to Movies and the Moviemakers.* 1995.

Russell, Jane. *Jane Russell: An Autobiography.* New York, Franklin Watts, Inc. 1985.

Russell, Nipsey (1920?—)

With an air of grace and intelligence, and an endless supply of original comic poems, comedian Nipsey Russell was one of the first African Americans to become a national television personality. Russell came to prominence in 1959 after a series of appearances on *The Tonight Show* with Jack Paar. Since then, he has surfaced on a long list of comedy, variety, and talk shows. His forte, however, is as a quiz show panelist. Known as "the poet laureate of television," he entertains with clever conversation and the recitation of his poems, which range in humor from silly to topical. His game show credits include *To Tell the Truth, Match Game 73,* and *Masquerade Party.* During the 1961-62 season, Russell played the character of Officer Anderson on *Car 54, Where Are You?,* a popular situation comedy about police antics in the Bronx. His big-screen credits are sparse, with his most memorable movie performance as the Tin Man in *The Wiz,* a 1978 black-cast musical version of *The Wizard of Oz.*

—Audrey E. Kupferberg

Russell, Rosalind (1911-1976)

Rosalind Russell is best remembered for numerous roles in 1930s and 1940s comedies as high-powered career women (executives, judges, psychiatrists) caught between the problems of ambition and independence, and romantic notions of love and domesticity. Russell was allowed to dominate many of her scenes in these films, playing with power, verve, and perfect comic timing as her roles reversed and questioned gender relationships and exemplified the dilemmas facing women in the war period and beyond. But these roles were played out in the relatively safe haven of comedy and with the promise she would, in the last reel, settle down to domestic bliss with the right man.

—Kyle Smith

FURTHER READING:

Basinger, Jeannine. *A Woman's View: How Hollywood Spoke to Women.* New York, Random House, 1993.

Russell, Rosalind, and Chris Chase. *Life Is a Banquet.* New York, Random House, 1977.

Ruth, Babe (1895-1948)

By most estimates, George Herman (Babe) Ruth was the greatest baseball player in the history of the game, and he is easily the sport's most renowned and enduring symbol. Ruth's legendary power with a baseball bat—many announcers still describe long home runs as "Ruthian" blasts—and his extravagant life off the field contributed to Ruth's extraordinary fame during his lifetime and after his death. Not only did Ruth's prodigious slugging help change the way baseball is played, but his enormous visibility changed the public role and responsibilities of professional athletes. Through team success with the New York Yankees during the 1920s, Ruth helped establish baseball as the "national pastime" and himself as an international celebrity.

Though Ruth was the most famous person in the United States at the time of his death—more people could identify Babe Ruth than film stars or U.S. presidents—his more humble beginnings led Ruth to conclude that he had "gotten a rotten start in life." Born on February 6, 1895, the son of second-generation German saloon proprietors, Ruth grew up in the working-class harbor district of Baltimore. Unsupervised during most of his childhood years, Ruth spent his time "on the street" with the sons of the longshoremen employed at the docks. His refusal to attend school eventually led to his enrollment at St. Mary's Industrial School for Boys, a Roman Catholic protectory for orphans, delinquents, and poor children consigned there by the city. Later in life, Ruth always reminisced fondly on his days at St. Mary's. While Ruth was the most highly paid player in the Major Leagues, he often bragged that he could still make a tailored shirt (the trade he learned as a youth at St. Mary's) in under twenty minutes.

Brother Matthias became Ruth's surrogate father at St. Mary's, and it was the Xaverian priest who became the young man's first instructor in the game of baseball. Baseball was the sport of choice at the school, and Ruth exhibited both passion and talent from the very

Yankee sluggers (l-r) Lou Gehrig, Babe Ruth, and Tony Lazzeri.

beginning. He proved an able understudy, and the lanky left-hander became one of the finest pitching prospects in the city of Baltimore by the age of fourteen. After several unsuccessful attempts, on February 27, 1914, Brother Matthias secured his progeny a tryout with the Baltimore Orioles of the International League, a very competitive minor league franchise. Ruth's first contract as a professional baseball player stipulated a salary of $600 a year.

Ruth got his odd nickname during his first month with the Orioles. While speaking to a reporter about the team's new recruits, one of the coaches suggested that Ruth "is the biggest and most promising babe in the lot." Mistakenly thinking that Ruth's former home of St. Mary's was a refuge for foundlings and "babe" a reference to that past, the reporter used the moniker and it stuck. Ruth's baseball acumen impressed big-league scouts enough that his contract was purchased by the Boston Red Sox in July of 1914. On the eleventh of that same month Ruth began his twenty-two-year major league career as a pitcher, starting and winning his first game.

In order to measure Ruth's importance to the game of baseball, it is necessary to understand his career within the history of the game at

the professional level. At the organizational level, there were at least two significant challenges to the supremacy of the National and American Leagues (the two dominant, and still extant, professional associations in the United States): the creation of a rival organization, the Federal League, in 1914 and the "Black Sox" scandal of 1919. For a brief period, the Federal League posed a serious threat to the two more-established leagues. In fact, a well-supported Federal League team in Baltimore, the Terrapins, forced the owner of the struggling Orioles to sell his top prospects, including Babe Ruth. By competing for players, the Federal League also caused temporary inflation in the market value of athletes, a trend Ruth would continue single-handedly throughout the 1920s. The "Black Sox" scandal of 1919, however, posed a much different threat to the game: widespread corruption. In 1919, just before Ruth began his illustrious tenure with the New York Yankees, a group of players from the Chicago White Sox had accepted bribes in order to "throw" the World Series that year. Details of the incident leaked out during the 1920 season, causing the new commissioner of baseball, Judge Kenesaw Mountain Landis, to ban eight players for life, including Ruth's idol, "Shoeless" Joe Jackson (see the film *Eight Men Out* for more). By that time, however, Ruth's home-run prowess was enough to ensure baseball's growing popularity.

On the field, baseball was played much differently before Ruth changed the game with his powerful batting style. During the era of Ty Cobb, from about 1900-1920, the league's best players specialized in hitting for a high average, bunting well, stealing bases, and cultivating defensive skills. It was also the "dead ball" era, in which pitchers dominated through the use of foreign substances and "lifeless" baseballs. Rule changes and the introduction of a livelier baseball made the 1920s more favorable to hitters. Before 1920, extra-base hits, much less home runs, were an oddity; after Ruth, power-hitters, though rarely as prolific as Ruth, became quite common.

Ruth's transition from pitcher to hitter was gradual, only completed during his final year in Boston. Though he was a fine pitcher (he won 95 games as a hurler and still holds World Series pitching records from his time with the Red Sox), Ruth became a full-time outfielder for the Red Sox in 1919. Though it was still part of the "dead ball" era, Ruth hit twenty-nine home runs in only 130 games, easily shattering the previous single-season record. From 1900-1920 the home run leader in the American League had averaged only ten home runs per year; Ruth's twenty-nine were more than most teams' seasonal output. During the winter of 1919, Ruth was sold to the Yankees for a record $125,000.

Ruth's statistical feats with the Yankees have been well chronicled, but it is worthwhile to note how drastically his performances affected the way baseball is played and watched. Though no player in the American League had topped sixteen home runs during the previous twenty years, Ruth hit twenty-five or more in fifteen consecutive years from 1919-1934, bettering fifty on four separate occasions. At the time, he set modern records for home runs, extra-base hits, runs batted in, runs scored, walks, and strikeouts. The Yankees continually set attendance records both at home and on the road, making the American League club easily the most famous sports franchise in the United States. At its opening in 1923, Yankee Stadium set an attendance mark of 74,000 paying customers, an astounding number in an age before radio broadcasts had widened the sport's fan base. The Stadium later became known as "The House That Ruth Built" (coincidentally, its outfield wall was tailored to Ruth's home run swing). In 1927, he hit sixty home runs, and that Yankee club, after winning 110 games and the World Series, became commonly known as the greatest baseball team of all time.

Ruth's most famous hit came during the 1932 World Series; the story behind it is typical of the mythology surrounding Ruth. During game three of the Series, Ruth allegedly "called" his home run against Charley Root of the Chicago Cubs. With two strikes against him, Ruth pointed in the direction of the centerfield wall, signaling his intent to hit a home run. As the story goes, Ruth hit one over the fence just where he had pointed. Often repeated by reporters but rarely confirmed by Ruth, the tale, widely circulated after his retirement and death, only augments his mythical status. Ruth finished his playing days with more World Series appearances than any other player, and his 714 career home runs were almost three times that of the next highest total. Ruth was honored in retirement by becoming one of the five original inductees to the National Baseball Hall of Fame in Cooperstown, New York.

Ruth's flamboyance off the field of play only added to his enormous fame. Newspapers carried daily reports of his legendary gluttony (it was rumored that he could consume up to eighteen hot dogs and a dozen bottles of soda at one sitting) and nightly debauchery (he rarely returned to the hotel before five in the morning when the team traveled), and towards the end of his career his expanding waistline became a common concern of the press. His stomach problem during the 1925 season was called "The Bellyache Heard 'round the World," while stories about his numerous love affairs caused trouble in both his marriages. Perpetually unsatisfied with his contract, Ruth frequently threatened to quit baseball in favor of boxing (one fight with Jack Dempsey had actually been arranged), Hollywood (he appeared in several films during his baseball days), or professional golf. A great lover of children, Ruth visited hospitals and orphanages with astounding regularity and contributed both time and money to any number of charity organizations during his playing days.

After retirement, Ruth remained a very public figure. He continued to champion a series of philanthropic causes through campaigns all over the country. Acting as an ambassador for baseball, he also traveled the globe, including very successful tours of England, France, and Japan, where Ruth helped establish baseball's popularity. Only thirteen years after his retirement from professional baseball, Ruth developed throat cancer, a result of years of incessant cigar smoking. His number, 3, was "retired" by the Yankees at the Stadium, in front of 70,000 fans, in 1948 before his passing on August 16 of that year. Throngs of supporters crowded New York's Fifth Avenue to catch a glimpse of Ruth's funeral cortege, and thousands later visited Yankee Stadium where his body was displayed before burial. Given the unrivaled popularity of baseball during his playing days and his undisputed dominance of the game, it is unlikely that any single sports figure could captivate the American public in quite the same way.

—Peter Kalliney

FURTHER READING:

Meany, Tom. *Babe Ruth: The Big Moments of the Big Fellow*. New York, A. S. Barnes, 1947.

Smesler, Marshall. *The Life That Ruth Built: A Biography*. New York, Quadrangle, 1975.

Wagenheim, Kal. *Babe Ruth: His Life and Legend*. New York, Praeger, 1974.

Ruth, George Herman

See Ruth, Babe

RV

When technological innovation brought early twentieth-century Americans the liberating effects of the automobile, it also produced ancillary developments in terms of vacation, travel, and shelter. Long-distance auto travel led many Americans to use tents or lean-tos in roadside areas, but trailers and recreational vehicles (RVs) would not begin to appear until the 1920s. What began as haphazard homemade contraptions have evolved into a major industry constructing lavish homes on wheels.

Following the model of the "gypsy kit," which started being marketed in 1909, manufacturers sold trailers and trucks possessing enclosed living areas. The liberation of the American traveler had reached a new level. RVs would become identified with complete autonomy because they represented fully transportable shelter. One of the first applications of the new RVs had little to do with the independence of the open road; instead the military made this form of temporary shelter part of many endeavors. During World War II, trailers replaced tents in the field, and, on the domestic side, trailers became overflow housing outside of military bases.

As leisure time and road quality increased after World War II, many Americans began to purchase RVs for lengthy summer travel, particularly in the American West where motels were rare. Tourist travel fed by the interstate highway system, which had been begun in the late 1950s, made even remote areas of the United States potential tourist destinations. Even infamous commercial sites such as Wall Drug in South Dakota or South of the Border in South Carolina could manufacture a tourist industry through excessive signage along interstates carrying travelers to destinations such as Mt. Rushmore and the southern beaches, respectively. And the popularity of RVs increased as new models—some with the towing vehicle incorporated into the design—appeared after 1950.

Many retirees found such mobility ideal; some even sold their homes in order to own an Airstream trailer or a Winnebago RV. The Airstream culture is one of the nation's most unique. The easily recognizable Airstream trailer campers have a bullet-like, metallic, industrial appearance that makes little claim to aesthetics. This utilitarian design, however, has gathered a huge amount of appreciators, including clubs such as the Vintage Airstream Club. Led by the Wally Byam Foundation, named after Airstream's founder, and with the purpose to "support people to people understanding through trailer travel," Airstreamers have led the way in transforming a form of travel into a culture of its own. With organized trips, called caravans, Airstreamers can be seen throughout the America's highway system.

In the end, RVs have had little to do with outdoor adventure and exploration. By the end of the twentieth century, american families seeking outdoor exploration continued to use tents and hike into areas difficult—if not impossible—for the large-sized RVs to travel. RVs had instead become part of road tourism particularly for retired couples. RVs represent the pinnacle of American mobility, making it possible for Americans to remain "on the road" for as long as they like. This mobility has led Americans of many different ages to explore distant locations along the open road.

—Brian Black

FURTHER READING:

Edwards, Carlton M. *Homes for Travel and Living: The History and Development of the Recreation Vehicle and Mobile Industries.* East Lansing, Michigan, C. Edwards, 1977.

A Winnebago camper.

Meg Ryan

Farlow, Bill, and Sharlene Minshall. *Freedom Unlimited: The Fun and Facts of Fulltime RVing,* edited by Liz McGowen. Lake Forest, Illinois, Woodall Publishing, 1994.

Pollard, Ted. *King of the Road: The Beginner's Guide to RV Travel.* Radnor, Pennsylvania, Remington Press, 1993.

Ryan, Meg (1961—)

Meg Ryan became the queen of romantic comedy by faking a very public orgasm in the memorable restaurant scene of *When Harry Met Sally* (1989). Later, *Sleepless in Seattle* (1993) strengthened her status as America's favorite girl-next-door. Since then Ryan has held her throne against the competition of younger comedy stars Julia Roberts and Sandra Bullock. Her uneven filmography reveals, however, a clear underlying tension between the audience's preference for her romantic roles and her own wish to explore her talent for drama. The revengeful Maggie of *Addicted to Love* (1997) should be seen, thus, as her last unsuccessful attempt to leave her sunny persona behind. The failure of her brave performances as a Gulf War heroine in *Courage under Fire* (1996) and as an alcoholic wife in *When a Man Loves a Woman* (1994) to impress the audience seems to have oriented her career definitively towards romantic comedy.

—Sara Martin

FURTHER READING:

Abramovitz, R. "Private Meg." *Premiere.* May 1996, 52-56.

Collins, A.F. "Faces of Meg." *Harper's Bazaar.* December 1994, 120-123.

Sassums, K. "Maximum Meg." *Vanity Fair.* May 1995, 104-111.

Ryan, Nolan (1947—)

Nolan Ryan was the greatest power pitcher of his era, and certainly the greatest pitcher never to win the Cy Young award. His blazing fastball (consistently measured in excess of 100 miles per hour) and intensity on the mound made him one of the most dominant pitchers in baseball history. His extraordinary work ethic and perseverance became legendary, and his ability to strike out opposing batters made him a role model for thousands of aspiring pitchers. Consigned to playing on mediocre teams for his entire career, Ryan still managed to win 324 games, throw seven no-hitters, and strike out over 5,700 batters in his 27 years in the majors.

Lynn Nolan Ryan, Jr. was born January 31, 1947, in Refugio, Texas, the youngest of six children. He grew up playing Little League baseball under his father's coaching, and later played in high school. It was in high school that a New York Mets scout saw him pitch and signed him to play rookie ball in Virginia.

Early in his career, Ryan's flaming fastball caused many problems. Although he could throw the ball with astonishing velocity, he had little control over where it would actually go. This lack of control translated into a large number of walks and hit batters, and the Mets kept him pitching in middle relief for most of the time he was with the team. In 1969, Ryan made his first appearance in the World Series as a reliever, earning a save in game three.

Nolan Ryan

Although he clearly had the arm to be a major league pitcher, Ryan's poor control became an increasingly big problem for the Mets and in 1971, after four years with the team, he was traded with three other players to the California Angels. It was with the Angels that Ryan began realizing his potential. As a member of the pitching rotation from 1972 to 1979, he threw four no-hitters, compiled a 138-123 won-lost record (far better than the team's overall winning percentage), and set the single-season strikeout record in 1973 with 383. Although Ryan liked pitching for California, he wanted to return to his home state of Texas, and he signed a contract with the Houston Astros for the then record-breaking sum of $1 million per year.

In Houston, Ryan consistently ranked among the league leaders in strikeouts and pitched his record fifth no-hitter in 1981. In 1987, he became the first pitcher to lead the league in earned-run average and strikeouts without winning the Cy Young Award for pitching. This snub was probably due to his record of eight wins and 16 losses, a consequence of the Astros' anemic offense. In 10 of his 16 losses, the Astros scored two or fewer runs. In 1988, at the age of 40, Ryan was asked to take a pay cut by the Astros, but he preferred to leave them rather than accept the cut and signed with the Texas Rangers.

With the Rangers, Ryan earned his 300th win, his 5000th strikeout, and tossed his sixth and seventh no-hitters (no-hitters being previously unthinkable for a pitcher of his age). During his tenure with the Rangers, he finally gained recognition for his astounding achievements, with baseball fans and writers at last recognizing his phenomenal athleticism and perseverance as he approached the end of his career. His amazing conditioning regimen and natural physical gifts allowed Ryan to continue to pitch effectively well past the age of 40, and he reached the status of the ''Grand Old Man'' of the game of baseball.

The 1992 and 1993 seasons were full of injuries, and Nolan Ryan retired from the game he had served on the field for 27 years. He was elected to the Baseball Hall of Fame in 1999, his first year of eligibility. His uniform numbers have been retired by the Angels, the Astros, and the Rangers.

—Geoff Peterson

FURTHER READING:

Rolfe, John. *Nolan Ryan.* Boston, Little, Brown and Co., 1992.

Ryan, Nolan, and Harvey Frommer. *Throwing Heat: The Autobiography of Nolan Ryan.* New York, Doubleday, 1988.

———, and Jerry Jenkins. *Miracle Man: Nolan Ryan, The Autobiography.* Dallas, Word Publishing, 1992.

Trujillo, Nick. *The Meaning of Nolan Ryan.* College Station, Texas A&M University Press, 1994.

Rydell, Bobby (1942—)

Boyishly handsome, with an infectious smile, teen idol Bobby Rydell summoned up the image of the boy next door. Like fellow Philadelphian heartthrobs Frankie Avalon and Fabian, he catered to teenage desires at a time, circa 1959-1960, when the music world wanted safe alternatives to the sexually explosive Elvis Presley.

Still, Rydell stood out as a bonafide talent. A musical prodigy, he began playing drums at six, had a nightclub act at seven, and became a regular on a television amateur show at nine. He was a drummer with the group Rocco and the Saints, which also boasted Avalon on trumpet, when he was approached about a singing career. Resulting hits, including ''Volare'' and ''Wild One,'' were marked by a smooth delivery. In his only major movie, *Bye Bye Birdie* (1963), however, he was eclipsed by volatile Ann-Margret. In the 1990s, Rydell played to former fans in ''oldies'' shows.

—Pat H. Broeske

FURTHER READING:

Miller, Jim, editor. *The Rolling Stone Illustrated History of Rock & Roll.* New York, Random House, 1976.

Rydell, Bobby, as told to Marya Saunders and Bob Gaines. ''Now That I'm of Age.'' *Family Weekly.* April 28, 1963, 4.

Ryder, Winona (1971—)

Actress Winona Ryder's ability to appear both vulnerable and sophisticated won her a devoted following among Generation X viewers. Born Winona Laura Horowitz, she is noted for such diverse roles as a death-obsessed teen (*Beetlejuice,* 1988); Mrs. Jerry Lee Lewis (*Great Balls of Fire!,* 1989); a high school student involved in murder (*Heathers,* 1989); a vampire's love interest (*Bram Stoker's Dracula,* 1992); a struggling Gen Xer (*Reality Bites,* 1994); a vindictive Puritan (*The Crucible,* 1996); and an android (*Alien: Resurrection,* 1997). She received Academy Award nominations for her performances in *The Age of Innocence* (1993) and *Little Women* (1994).

—S.K. Bane

FURTHER READING:

Cawley, Janet. ''Little Woman, Big Career.'' *Biography.* June, 1997, 24-29.

Editors of *US. Winona Ryder.* Boston, Little, Brown and Company, 1997.

Siegel, Scott, and Barbara Siegel. *The Winona Ryder Scrapbook.* Secaucus, New Jersey, Carol Publishing Group, 1997.

Thompson, Dave. *Winona Ryder.* Dallas, Taylor Publishing Company, 1996.

S

Safe Sex

Sex can be considered "safe" if it avoids the risk of one person infecting another with a sexually transmitted disease (STD). Some individuals and groups maintain that the only sex that is 100 percent safe is no sex—that is, abstinence. But since STDs are usually passed on through bodily fluids (genital herpes is an exception, being transmitted by skin-to-skin contact), any form of sexual expression that avoids one partner's exposure to the body fluids of another can be reasonably described as "safe." Although this definition would include such practices as mutual masturbation (once known as "heavy petting"), the most common contemporary definition of the term "safe sex" involves the use of a latex condom to avoid the spread of STDs; such devices have been shown to be 98-100 percent effective.

Safe sex is a vital necessity in the modern age, and has been so ever since the 1980s, when medical science first identified the virus that causes AIDS (Acquired Immune Deficiency Syndrome), a fatal disease with no known vaccine or cure. The Centers for Disease Control and Prevention report that STDs constitute five of the ten most common infectious diseases reported in the United States: AIDS, syphilis, gonorrhea, hepatitis-B, and chlamydia. Further, there

An example of a campaign for condom use among seniors.

are some 12 million new cases of STDs reported in the United States every year.

One of the early efforts to increase public awareness of STDs in the age of AIDS was made by Otis R. Bowen, Secretary for Health and Human Services during the Reagan administration. In a 1987 press conference, he claimed that "When a person has sex, they're not just having it with that partner. They're having it with everybody that partner has had it with in the past 10 years." Bowen's observation made its way into the popular culture quickly. It was picked up by the news magazines, appeared in public service advertisements, and even showed up in television dramas like *L.A. Law.*

When it comes to depictions of sexual activity, however, television entertainment programs are contributors to the STD problem much more frequently then they are part of the solution. A 1999 study by the Henry J. Kaiser Family Foundation showed that 67 percent of prime-time television programs contained verbal or visual references to sex, but only 10 percent made any mention of safe sex or contraception. Within the program sample studied, 88 scenes were identified portraying or implying sexual intercourse, and not one contained any depiction or mention of safe sex. These results were consistent with similar studies performed in 1986, 1993, and 1996: there was considerable sexual activity portrayed on television, but very little mention of STD prevention by any of the sexually involved characters.

There have been a few notable exceptions to this trend. In 1989, an episode of the situation comedy *Head of the Class* caused a stir when one of the characters, a teenage boy, asks his teacher whether he should have intercourse with his girlfriend. The teacher (portrayed by Howard Hesseman) advises the boy not to have sex, but, if he must, to be sure to use a condom. In the late 1990s, several shows on the WB network, including *Dawson's Creek* and *Felicity,* showed characters discussing sex with disease prevention raised as an issue; similar scenes have also been seen on the UPN network's popular show *Moesha.*

If discussion of condoms is rare in network television shows, it is unheard of in the advertising that pays for those programs. Neither the major networks (ABC, CBS, NBC, or Fox) nor the largest independents (WB and UPN) will accept paid advertising for condoms, even during late-night shows. The networks' concern is that such advertisements would cause offense in the more conservative areas of the country, and also that some advertisers of more conventional products would not wish to have their advertisements preceded or followed by a condom commercial.

Local network affiliates, however, are allowed to accept condom advertisements, and several have done so. In August of 1998, CBS affiliate stations in New York and Los Angeles broadcast condom advertisements for the first time, and were followed by Boston a month later. The advertisements were protested by the conservative American Family Association, but the stations continued to run them.

The networks have been more open to the airing of public service announcements (PSAs) for AIDS prevention, which often mention condoms. In 1994, the networks (along with many cable television channels) began broadcasting a series of PSAs sponsored by the Centers for Disease Control. Although Fox and NBC showed the six advertisements without alteration, ABC felt obliged to add this tagline to each: "Abstinence is the safest, but if you do have sex, latex condoms can protect you.'' CBS was willing to air five of the PSAs, but drew the line at one that featured a counselor infected with AIDS and an ''800'' number to call for more information.

Just as concern about safe sex rarely shows up in television programs, it is also generally absent from the movies Americans watch. One exception was *Pretty Woman* (1990), in which prostitute Vivian Ward (Julia Roberts) offers a choice of condoms to her ''date,'' Edward Lewis, played by Richard Gere. More recently, the 1997 sex farce *Booty Call* features two women's insistence on condom use by their men as a central plot element.

Condoms are also becoming more common in the last place where one might expect to find them—XXX adult films. In 1998, porn star Mark Wallice reportedly tested positive for HIV, the virus that causes AIDS. This is not unusual in itself, but it has been alleged that Wallice had tested positive more than a year earlier, and had concealed that fact while continuing to have unprotected sex in films, apparently infecting several of his female co-stars in the process. Consequently, pornography is likely to be showing a lot more latex in the future.

Another unlikely source for safe sex advocacy was Kate Shindle, the 1997-1998 Miss America. Unlike her predecessors, who generally shied away from controversy, Shindle used her many public appearances to discuss AIDS and its prevention through safe sex practices. This caused the cancellation of some of her speaking engagements, but Shindle was undeterred, delivering her message in any venue where she could reach an audience. ''To me,'' she said, ''the most important thing is saving lives.''

—Justin Gustainis

FURTHER READING:

DiClimente, Ralph J., editor. *Adolescents and AIDS: A Generation in Jeopardy.* Newbury Park, California, Sage Publications, 1992.

Edgar, Timothy, Mary Anne Fitzpatrick, and Vicki S. Freimuth, editors. *AIDS: A Communication Perspective.* Hillsdale, New Jersey, Lawrence Erlbaum Associates, 1992.

Lowry, Dennis T., and Jon A. Shidler. ''Prime Time TV Portrayals of Sex, 'Safe Sex' and AIDS: A Longitudinal Analysis.'' *Journalism Quarterly.* Vol. 70, No. 3, Autumn 1993, 628-637.

Nourse, Alan E. *Teen Guide to Safe Sex.* New York, Franklin Watts, 1988.

Patton, Cindy. *Fatal Advice: How Safe-Sex Education Went Wrong.* Durham, Duke University Press, 1996.

Peters, Brooks. *Terrific Sex in Fearful Times.* New York, St. Martin's Press, 1988.

Preston, John, and Glenn Swann. *Safe Sex: The Ultimate Erotic Guide.* New York, New American Library, 1986.

Scotti, Angelo T., and Thomas A. Moore. *Safe Sex: What Everyone Should Know about Sexually Transmitted Diseases.* New York, PaperJacks, 1987.

Sagan, Carl (1934-1996)

Of all the spokespeople for the space sciences active during the last three decades of the twentieth century, astronomer Carl Sagan

Carl Sagan

was the most widely recognized and articulate. Through his accessible and instructive writings on the subject of space and their accompanying television programs, he earned a significant and popular place in American culture, and defined one of the world's most frightening forebodings as ''nuclear winter.''

The explosion of popular interest in astronomy and space travel in the United States following the Soviet Union's launch of Sputnik on October 4, 1957 provided the scientific community with an unparalleled opportunity for public education that continued for several decades. An entirely new genre of writing began to appear from either prominent figures involved in the American space effort, such as Werner von Braun and the members of the newly formed astronaut corps, or science writers knowledgeable in these fields. In addition to the obvious political overtones to the so-called ''space race,'' discussion of humanity's place in the universe and questions regarding the future uses of outer space assumed new importance in both American and worldwide consciousness.

Born in New York City on November 9, 1934, Sagan showed an interest in astronomy early on and pursued it as a career, completing doctoral work at the University of Chicago in 1960 and serving as a faculty member at Berkeley, Harvard, and the Smithsonian Institution before settling at Cornell. While his main research interests lay in planetary studies and the origin of life, many of his writings were designed to educate the general public on these fields, a task he poured heart and mind into throughout his life. His first popular work in this line was the 1973 introduction to the search for extra-terrestrial life and space travel, *The Cosmic Connection.* His interest in the processes through which life might have arisen and developed intelligent awareness was the focus of his next work, *The Dragons of Eden,* awarded the Pulitzer Prize in 1977. But it was with the text of his 1980 volume *COSMOS* (written in conjunction with a series of 13 programs widely broadcast on public television networks) that this unassuming astronomer truly became a recognizable and familiar figure in the public mind of America, if not the planet.

The idea for the *COSMOS* project was born in 1976 while he was part of the imaging team working on the Viking Lander mission to Mars. Journalistic interest in the operation waned swiftly once it became clear that the question of the presence of life on the planet remained unsettled. Sagan and B. Gentry Lee, director of data analysis and mission planning, decided to create a television production company whose goal was the communication of science in an accessible and inviting manner. Several lines in the introduction set forth the essential features of a personal and philosophical view of the space age: these stated that ''the present epoch is a major crossroads for our civilization and perhaps our species . . . our fate is indissolubly bound up with science.'' A lively respect for the intelligence of his audiences, and an unfailing joy and wonder at the infinite diversity of a patterned universe, made Sagan in several ways the ideal teaching voice, able to provide a comprehensible perspective on the flood of new information becoming available from various space missions and orbiting instruments.

His concern for the role of science and its potential to determine the human future was also evident in his involvement with research on the effects of an exchange of nuclear weapons on the Earth's biosphere. Basing their work on models created during analysis of the temperature fluctuations caused by a massive Martian dust storm, encountered in 1971 by the Mariner 9 probe, Sagan and other scientists synthesized available data into the first comprehensive study of the impact of the explosions of numerous megaton atomic weapons on global climate and atmospheric factors. He presented the grim results of these findings as one of the two principal papers at the 1983 Conference on the Long-Term Worldwide Biological Consequences of Nuclear War held in Washington, D.C. It was here that Sagan first publicly coined the phrase ''nuclear winter.''

Arguably, Sagan's most influential contribution made to the popular memory with regard to planet Earth began in 1976. It was then that he was requested to head the team to choose the contents of a message to be sent with the Voyager spacecraft, an unmanned probe that ventured into deep space after its years-long mission through the solar system was completed. Rather than duplicate the aluminum plaques affixed to the earlier Pioneer 10 and 11 probes, Sagan and his team decided to include a long-playing record, containing both audio recordings and visual images gathered from diverse societies, that, collectively, would enable extra-terrestrial beings to gain a sense of human accomplishment. Types of information placed within the final product ranged from 118 pictures representing different aspects of human civilization and its world, through greetings in 54 languages, music ranging from the Navajo Night Chant and Indian ragas to a Mozart aria, and recorded natural sounds, including the cry of a newborn infant. The motivation for sending such a rich record was, in Sagan's view, that ''no one sends such a message on such a journey, to other worlds and beings, without a positive passion for the future.'' Until his death from cancer on December 20, 1996, Sagan continued to promote a clear and well-reasoned perspective on the wonders and complexities of space, and humanity's future within it aboard its ''pale blue dot.''

—Robert Ridinger

FURTHER READING:

The Cosmic Connection: An Extraterrestrial Perspective. New York, Doubleday, 1973.

Poundstone, William. *Carl Sagan: A Life in the Cosmos.* New York, Henry Holt, 1999.

Sagan, Carl. *The Dragons of Eden: Speculations on the Evolution of Human Intelligence.* New York, Random House, 1977.

———, et. al. *Murmurs of Earth: The Voyager Interstellar Record.* New York, Ballantine Books, 1978.

———. *Cosmos.* New York, Random House, 1980.

———, with Paul R. Ehrlich and Walter O. Roberts. *The Cold & The Dark: The World After Nuclear War: The Report of the Conference on the Longterm Worldwide Biological Consequences of Nuclear War.* New York, Norton, 1984.

———. *Pale Blue Dot: A Vision of the Human Future in Space.* New York, Random House, 1994.

Terzian, Yervant, and Elizabeth Bilson, editors. *Carl Sagan's Universe.* New York, Cambridge University Press, 1997.

Sahl, Mort (1927—)

Mort Sahl pioneered the type of biting satirical political humor that inspired so many other comics who came after him, from Lennie Bruce to Jay Leno. Appearing first in nightclubs during the late 1950s, Sahl did not follow earlier comics who told mother-in-law jokes or stuck to ribbing their show business cronies. Instead, he adopted the style of jazz musicians who begin with a theme, are reminded of another idea, and then circle back to the original theme.

Sahl was born May 11, 1927, in Montreal, Canada, but soon moved to Los Angeles, where his father eventually worked as a clerk for the F.B.I. Sahl was a high school member of R.O.T.C. and was stationed, after being drafted, in Alaska. There, he got into trouble as editor of the base paper, ''Poop from the Group,'' and claimed to have served 83 days in a row on KP (kitchen patrol). Nevertheless, Sahl claims that he remained an establishment supporter, the same boy who won an American Legion Americanism award. He served his country with pride, but turned to the comedy of satire as he drifted away from those values.

It took time for Sahl's style of comedy to catch on. Audiences, at first, did not quite know what to make of him. Sahl appeared on stage with a rolled-up newspaper. The paper held a crib sheet of topics and lines he wanted to follow. The owners of San Francisco's Hungry i comedy club believed in him and kept him working until fans came to appreciate the sweater-clad, hip comedian. Here was a man who dared chide President Dwight D. Eisenhower: ''Eisenhower proved we don't need a President,'' Sahl once said. Nothing was sacred to him, and he paraded his ability to expose others' foibles, wondering, ''Is there any group I haven't offended yet?''

Sahl was one of the first comedians to do comedy records. In the late 1950s his recordings—such as 1958's *The Future Lies Ahead*— sold quite well and Sahl's humor became familiar to many that never

Mort Sahl

had the chance to see him in clubs. He set his sights on politicians especially, taking swipes at Eisenhower, Adlai Stevenson, and John F. Kennedy (even though he had once penned one-liners for the Kennedy campaign). Sahl once remarked, ''Whoever the President is, I will attack him.'' But liberals who supported the jibes aimed at Eisenhower failed to appreciate the jokes made at Kennedy's expense and this lack of fan appreciation, coupled with what Sahl complained was a blacklisting by entertainment executives sympathetic to Kennedy, sent his career into a sharp decline in the later 1960s.

Sahl soon became obsessed with Kennedy's assassination, and he felt it was his responsibility to educate the American public that the CIA was responsible for the president's death. His income dropped from about a million dollars a year to $17,000 in 1967. Sahl was reduced to working small clubs and writing movies that never were filmed. He published an autobiography, *Heartland,* in 1976 and in the late 1980s staged a comeback of sorts, appearing in a one-man show on Broadway called simply *Mort Sahl on Broadway,* and acting as host of the radio program *Publishers Weekly's Between the Covers with Mort Sahl* on the ABC Radio Network beginning in 1995. Though he had defined the cutting edge of comedy 40 years earlier, it seemed that Sahl still had something to say to American audiences in the late 1990s.

—Frank A. Salamone

FURTHER READING:

Disch, Thomas. ''Mort Sahl on Broadway.'' *The Nation.* Vol. 245, No. 16, November 14, 1987, 570.

Gross, Ken. ''Not Going Gently into That Good Night, Caustic Comic Mort Sahl Gears Up for a Broadway Comeback.'' *People Weekly.* October 12, 1987, 134-36.

Sahl, Mort. *Heartland.* New York, Harcourt, 1976.

Saks Fifth Avenue

The retail specialty store, Saks Fifth Avenue, has stood as a symbol of American wealth and prestige for most of the twentieth century. The firm was founded in 1902 when Andrew Saks, a street peddler from Philadelphia, opened Saks & Company, a men's clothing shop in Washington, D.C. Saks soon expanded his store operations to Richmond, Virginia; Indianapolis; and New York City. For his New York store, Saks began actively courting the high-end retail market by stocking quality merchandise and offering first-class service. After Horace Saks became firm president upon his father's death in 1912, Saks made a bid to become the premiere specialty store for New York society. Saks buyers scoured the globe for unique and fashionable merchandise in order to build the store's reputation. With the shift of New York retail uptown during the 1910s, it became apparent to Saks that for the firm to continue its fashionable reputation, it needed a more prestigious address than its present location on

Saks Fifth Avenue in New York City.

34th Street near Herald Square. The firm entered negotiations to takeover the site of the New York Democratic Club between 49th and 50th Streets on Fifth Avenue, but lacked sufficient capital to meet Tammany Hall's asking price. Therefore, Horace Saks agreed to merge his retail store chain with Gimbel Brothers department store, which operated stores in Philadelphia; Madison, Wisconsin; and New York. The resultant merger in 1923 created one of the earliest regional department store chains in the United States. Saks' old Herald Square store site was leased to Gimbels and combined with their existing store nearby, making it the largest department store in the world at that time.

The uptown store, christened Saks Fifth Avenue, opened in 1924 with great fanfare. Street windows displayed such luxurious items as raccoon coats and foot muffs for automobile travel. An electric-lighting system signaled chauffeurs when to pick up patrons. In an attempt to capitalize on the growing notoriety of the uptown store, Saks president Adam Long Gimbel decided to rename all the firm's outlets Saks Fifth Avenue, a stroke of marketing genius that conveyed the prestige of the address to every store. Gimbel undertook a branch store building program in 1926 designed to place Saks Fifth Avenues in carefully chosen locations in resort towns and prestigious residential areas in Chicago, Miami Beach, and Beverly Hills. Gimbel establish several trademark services including a gift-buying service for business executives, and they were the first retail store to have their own in-house fashion designer producing collections in the guise of Sophie Gimbel. The store's national reputation grew to the extent that ''very Saks Fifth Avenue'' became a popular euphemism for posh style.

The firm was bought out by Brown & Williamson Tobacco in 1973, and today remains an active retail chain with more than 32 branches, outliving its sister Gimbel Brothers department stores.

—Stephanie Dyer

FURTHER READING:

Harris, Leon. *Merchant Princes: An Intimate History of the Jewish Families Who Built the Great Department Stores.* New York, Harper & Row, 1979.

Hendrickson, Robert. *The Grand Emporiums: The Illustrated History of America's Great Department Stores.* New York, Stein & Day, 1979.

Leach, William. *Land of Desire: Merchants, Power, and the Rise of a New American Culture.* New York, Pantheon, 1993.

Sales, Soupy (1926—)

Comedian Soupy Sales built his reputation on the unlikely skill of pie throwing; he is reputed to have thrown 19,000 pies in a career that stretched from the 1950s into the 1990s. Sales, born Milton Supman, planted pies in the faces of some of America's most noted celebrities, including Frank Sinatra, Sammy Davis, Jr., and Tony Curtis. The comedian appeared on local television variety shows for both children and adults in several major markets before taking the *Soupy Sales Show* national in the mid-1960s. Sales, who delighted fans with his antics, went too far on New Years day in 1965 when he asked the children who watched his show to ''go to Daddy's wallet

Soupy Sales

and get those little green pieces of paper with pictures of George Washington on it and send them to me.'' They did, to the tune of $80,000, but the prank led to the show's brief suspension. Sales made frequent guest appearances on TV and in movies into the 1990s.

—Naomi Finkelstein

FURTHER READING:

Brooks, Tim. *The Complete Directory of Prime Time Network and Cable TV.* New York, Ballentine, 1995.

Salsa Music

Easily the most successful form of music named for a condiment, salsa transcended its humble beginnings as a marketing hook to become a powerful influence on music and culture worldwide. A blend of African rhythms and European harmony born in Cuba and developed in New York City, salsa is a truly international music encapsulating the Latin American experience—and you can dance to it.

Beginning in the sixteenth century, Spanish settlers brought Africans to Cuba to work as slaves, mostly on sugar and tobacco plantations. Afro-Cuban music developed out of traditional West African musical forms, replicated on homemade or Spanish instruments. Some elements stemming from African religious practice, including call-and-response singing and polyrhythms, remain dominant features of Afro-Cuban music to this day, and santería, a typically Cuban blend of African religions and Catholicism, is still a popular musical topic. By the beginning of the twentieth century, Afro-Cuban music had taken three main forms: son, a popular dance music with three contrasting rhythms; rumba, informal street music, enthusiastic and improvised, typically just percussion and vocals; and danzón, derived from European dance forms, spotlighting piano and flute. All three forms are distinguished by their use of the clave, a two-measure, five-beat syncopated rhythm played on small wooden sticks called claves. The music's impact was first felt outside the island beginning in the 1930s, when rhumba (an Americanization of rumba) and mambo (an evolution of danzón) music began to be played by dance bands in the United States, and soon after, jazz pioneer Dizzy Gillespie incorporated Cuban elements into be-bop, a combination Gillespie called "Cubop."

But by the early 1960s, rhumba and mambo had become passé in the United States, at least among those who considered themselves too hip for the likes of Ricky Ricardo. At the same time, many of Cuba's biggest talents moved to New York City, fleeing their country's Communist revolution—most notably Celia Cruz. These artists combined with young, predominantly Puerto Rican, New Yorkers to breathe new life into the city's Latin dance scene, dropping the traditional violins in favor of blaring, often dazzling, horn arrangements. Pianist and bandleader Eddie Palmieri was the first to bring the complex mozambique rhythm—developed in Cuba by Pello el Afrokán—to New York; he was also the foremost of a new generation of jazz-trained pianists, bringing a new harmonic complexity to the music. By the late 1960s, Fania Records, a label owned by Jerry Masucci, had signed most of the rising stars of the new Afro-Cuban music. It is unknown who first applied the word "salsa" to this genre, but Masucci and Fania's musical director Johnny Pacheco relentlessly promoted the use of the term. Many older Latin musicians and fans still bristle at the name, feeling that their cultural heritage is being reduced to tomato sauce. But the name caught on, and is now used—if grudgingly—by nearly all participants.

Almost immediately, sales of salsa records went through the roof, and in the early 1970s there were a wealth of successful bands, making up in energy and swing what they lacked in technical polish and production values: Palmieri, Cruz, Joe Bataan, Ray Barretto, Larry Harlow, Johnny Colón, and most importantly, trombonist Willie Colón (no relation to Johnny). Raised in the Bronx, Willie cut his first record, *Guisando* (1969), in his late teens, and soon established a reputation as salsa's bad boy and biggest hitmaker. His main vocalist in the 1970s was Hector LaVoe, who moved beyond familiar romantic themes to depict the often harsh reality of New York's barrios on such songs as "Piraña," "Barrunto," and "Te Conozco." Colón refused to be limited to Masucci's vision, and he soon expanded his musical palette to include traditional Puerto Rican rhythms—bomba and plena—and Brazilian styles. Of the 1940s and 1950s generation of bandleaders, only the seemingly ageless percussion master Tito Puente remained prominent. Salsa's lyrics have been justly criticized for sexist content, and from the beginning there have been very few female singers—and next to no writers or arrangers—in the form. Central to Masucci's marketing plan was the idea of advertising salsa as a completely new style, and to this end he downplayed the music's Cuban origins, though nearly everything

Fania released—aside from merengue, which came from the Dominican Republic—was Afro-Cuban in character. Partly because of sour United States-Cuba relations, Masucci did not credit Cuban composers on Fania records, even when the majority of an album's tracks were covers of Cuban songs.

In the late 1970s, Panamanian-born Rubén Blades brought a new level of lyrical sophistication to salsa. Both his love songs and his devastating political critiques borrowed the imagery and nuance of Latin American protest music (nueva canción, called nueva trova in Cuba) but brought them to a larger audience by blending them with driving dance rhythms. Blades came to prominence as vocalist and main songwriter for Willie Colón, and their collaboration *Siembra* (1976) is the best selling and probably the most critically praised salsa album of all time; Blades reached his solo peak a few years later with *Buscando América* (1984) and *Escenas* (1985). Thanks in part to his fluency in English, Blades made friends with many rock stars: his 1988 English-language release *Nothing but the Truth* features Sting, Lou Reed, and Elvis Costello, and he also recorded with Joe Jackson and Jackson Browne. In the early 1990s Blades became better known for his character roles in Hollywood films, and in 1994 he put both entertainment careers on hold in favor of an unsuccessful run for president of Panama.

Unlike, say, reggae, salsa was never incorporated into mainstream music in the United States, perhaps because of the language barrier. Even amateur ethnologists Paul Simon and Peter Gabriel ignored the genre: it was at once too close to home, and too far away. Although some New York pop artists, including Janis Ian and Patti LaBelle, recorded salsa tunes, such efforts were few, and no one—traditionalist or imitator—ever hit the Top 40 with a salsa. The best illustration of salsa's failure to cross over to English-speaking markets is that the Puerto Rican act best known to the United States public is not El Gran Combo or Willie Colón, but Menudo: a prefab pretty-boy group with about as much connection to Afro-Cuban rhythms as the Osmonds.

By the late 1980s, Nuyorican youth were buying more high energy dance music than salsa. Many of the old guard had retired or faded into obscurity (Harlow, Barretto) while those who remained had trouble getting their records played (Willie Colón). A film—*Salsa!* (1988)—starring former Menudo vocalist Robby Rosa bombed. The singers who flourished in this environment were those with the least penchant for innovation, the slickest production, and absolutely no political message: for example, Jerry Rivera and Tito Nieves, "the Pavarotti of Salsa." Though salsa was still popular throughout Latin America, as exemplified by Colombia's Grupo Niche and Venezuela's Oscar D'León, the music was stagnating in New York City, where the new hitmakers were lightweight "Latin hip-hop" acts like Exposé, Sweet Sensation, and Brenda K. Starr. These artists relied on static, pre-programmed beats and breathy, high-pitched vocals—the antithesis of salsa.

In a backhanded way, Latin hip-hop provided the impetus for salsa's revival in the mid-1990s. India and Marc Anthony, two artists whose personalities and voices were too strong to be confined by Latin hip-hop's formulas, returned to the music of their childhoods, cutting albums with young producer/arranger Sergio George. George was unafraid to supplement traditional elements with innovative borrowings from funk, soul and hip-hop, but both artists' albums were unmistakably salsa, and they succeeded on those terms, reawakening critical and commercial interest in the genre. At the same time, enormous Latin American immigration into the United States helped bring the music out of its traditional strongholds in New York, Miami,

Salt-n-Pepa

and California. Cuban-born pop singer Gloria Estefan also helped popularize salsa with her tremendously popular *Mi Tierra* (1993), which featured many top salsa artists. Marc Anthony even made it to Broadway, along with Blades, in Paul Simon's ill-fated musical *The Capeman*. Ultimately, salsa outlived Latin hip-hop, and by 1997 Starr was attempting to revive her career with a disc of salsa tunes.

Meanwhile, back in Cuba, the most forward-thinking bands were beginning to incorporate elements of New York salsa into their music. NG La Banda's ''Yo Necesito Una Amiga'' was a perfect New York Sound ballad, and when it became a hit other bands followed suit. By the mid-1990s all the most popular Cuban bands—Los Van Van, Orquesta Revé, Irakere, Dan Den—had cut salsa numbers. Young sensation Manolín even calls himself ''el Médico de la Salsa'' (Dr. Salsa). The music had come full circle—a development Jerry Masucci had probably never imagined.

—David B. Wilson

FURTHER READING:

Gerard, Charley, with Marty Sheller. *Salsa! The Rhythm of Latin Music.* Tempe, Arizona, White Cliffs Media, 1998.

Mauleón, Rebeca. *Salsa Guidebook for Piano and Ensemble.* Petaluma, California, Sher Music, 1993.

Salt-n-Pepa

At a time when hip-hop music was shunned by mainstream radio, Salt-n-Pepa broke through in 1986 with their multi-platinum crossover debut, *Hot, Cool and Vicious*. Along with Run-DMC and the Beastie Boys, Salt-n-Pepa were among the first hip-hop groups to be heard on a wide scale outside American urban centers during the mid-1980s. The Queens, New York-based Salt-n-Pepa also were the first all-female hip-hop group to gain commercial success in a genre dominated by men, opening doors for such female hip-hop artists like MC Lyte, Yo-Yo, Foxy Brown, Lil' Kim, Lauryn Hill, Lady of Rage, Missy Elliot, Queen Latifah, Bahamadia, Heather B, and others. Further, in a genre where the life of a hip-hop career is about one year, Salt-n-Pepa persevered, continued to have hits, and were still active well into the late 1990s.

Formed in 1985 under the name Super Nature, Cheryl ''Salt'' James, Sandy ''Pepa'' Denton, and their Sears department store coworker turned producer Hurby ''Luv Bug'' Azor released a minor hit called ''The Show Stoppa,'' an answer record to the Doug E. Fresh hit, ''The Show.'' Super Nature's song reached number 46 on the *Billboard* R&B singles chart, making enough of a name for the group to perform in local New York clubs. The women changed the group's name to Salt-n-Pepa and added a DJ named Spinderella (Pamela

Greene, who was later replaced by Deidre ''Dee Dee'' Roper). Salt-n-Pepa signed to the independent hip-hop label Next Plateau and released *Hot, Cool and Vicious* in 1986. The album sold successfully with a number of singles doing well on the R&B charts, but it was not until a remix of ''Push It'' was released in 1988 that Salt-n-Pepa were launched into the mainstream of pop music.

In 1988, they followed up their success with a relatively lackluster album, *A Salt with a Deadly Pepa,* which did well enough with the singles ''Twist and Shout'' and the EU collaboration, ''It's Your Thang.'' But after facing the gendered charges of ''selling out'' and ''going pop,'' they put out the Afrocentric-tinged *Black's Magic,* a commercial and artistic success with the number one Rap chart song ''Expression'' and the Top 20 *Billboard* Pop hit, ''Let's Talk About Sex.'' For their fourth album, Salt-n-Pepa signed to the major label, London, and distanced themselves from their longtime producer Hurby ''Luv Bug'' Azor (who the group felt imposed too much control (for instance, he got full songwriting credits on their first album, despite the women's assertions that they also contributed lyrics).

Very Necessary, released in 1993, was a massive hit—the biggest of their career. It spawned the Top Ten Pop hits ''Shoop'' and ''Whatta Man,'' and a lesser hit, ''None of Your Business,'' and won the group a Grammy in 1995 for best Rap performance. Songs like ''Shoop'' and ''None of Your Business'' exemplify the assertive female-centered sexuality that they have cultivated since their earliest recordings like 1986's ''Tramp.'' They have been able to successfully walk the line between engaging in a fun-loving sexual expression and avoiding reducing themselves to purely sexual objects, primarily because of their smart, in-your-face lyrics. For instance, Salt-n-Pepa often engaged in dialogue with their sexist male peers in their songs, challenging traditional notions of femininity and sex-role double standards. In 1995, the group recorded the single ''Ain't Nuthin' But a She Thing,'' the theme song of a documentary about women that aired on MTV in November of 1995.

Having completely split with Azor and taken time off from their careers to raise their children, Salt-n-Pepa entered a new hip-hop era in which many more female hip-hop artists were gaining popularity. For a variety of reasons, including changing audience tastes and poor record company marketing, their 1997 album sold poorly.

—Kembrew McLeod

FURTHER READING:

Fernando, S. H., Jr. *The New Beats: Exploring the Music, Culture, and Attitudes of Hip-Hop.* New York, Doubleday, 1994.

Rose, Tricia. *Black Noise: Rap Music and Black Culture in Contemporary America.* Hanover, Wesleyan University Press, 1994.

Toop, David. *Rap Attack 2: African Rap To Global Hip-Hop.* London, Serpent's Tail, 1991.

Sam and Dave

Sam Moore and Dave Prater were perhaps the most exciting soul duo of the 1960s. Both got their start as gospel singers in Miami, Florida, and after turning to secular music they caught the attention of Atlantic Records co-owner Jerry Wexler, who quickly signed them to a recording contract. Wexler wisely decided to ''loan'' them to Stax Records, the Memphis soul label which was distributed by Atlantic.

At Stax, they secured not only the label's formidable studio musicians but also the songwriting talents of Dave Porter and Isaac Hayes, who penned such hits as ''Hold On! I'm Comin','' and ''Soul Man,'' which was later a hit for the Blues Brothers.

Although Moore and Prater sometimes utilized vocal harmonies, their more distinctive contribution was a call-and-response approach which stemmed from their roots in gospel music. Prater died in 1988.

—Bill Freind

FURTHER READING:

Bowman, Rob. *Soulsville, U.S.A.: The Story of Stax Records.* New York, Schirmer, 1997.

Sandburg, Carl (1878-1967)

A maverick son of Swedish immigrant parents, Carl Sandburg became one of America's best loved poets, as well as one of its most significant. However, he was also a journalist, storyteller, balladeer, and noted biographer of Abraham Lincoln, and his literary works and journalistic writings became ingrained in popular American culture from World War I, through the Roaring Twenties and the Great Depression, to the tumultuous times of World War II and its aftermath.

Part newspaperman, part poet, Sandburg reflected the lives of ordinary people caught up in these events, articulating his concerns through his writings in a career that spanned half a century. He wrote during a time of great industrial and social change. Across America, cities proliferated and grew, while rural populations were displaced from the land and European immigrants flooded the cities. Sandburg wrote in a broad, earthy style, and with honesty and perception, about the burgeoning urban life. Adopting a bold, free verse style reminiscent of Walt Whitman, Sandburg spoke, not in poetically lyrical language, but in the slang and speech patterns of working people, the language of factory and sidewalk. Roger Mitchell, in *A Profile of Twentieth Century American Poetry* explains that ''Sandburg wrote in the language of the people he described and in the belief that their lives mattered.'' Unlike many of his contemporaries, he looked only to America for his inspiration and celebrated the lives of its ordinary citizens.

Born in Galesburg, Illinois, in 1878, the son of hardworking Swedish immigrants, Carl Sandburg grew up on the prairies of Illinois, left school at 13, and, in the wake of a depression, joined the homeless and unemployed in a journey across America. He worked as a laborer and lived as a hobo, sleeping in boxcars and riding the rods of the transcontinental railway for seven years. In 1898 he returned to Galesburg and became a housepainter, but soon after enlisted in the Sixth Illinois Infantry during the Spanish American War. It was during his eight months' service in Cuba and Puerto Rico that Sandburg wrote in his journal of the hypocrisy and injustice of war and its effects on the ordinary soldiers, dying of heat, malaria, and dysentery without firing a shot in battle. After the war he again returned to Galesburg and attended Lombard College, but left without a degree. He pursued journalistic work and become a staunch member of the Socialist Party, through which he met his future wife, Lillian (Paula) Steichen, sister of the great photographer, Edward Steichen. Paula, a university graduate, encouraged Sandburg in his writing, especially his poetry.

In 1916 Sandburg had his first real taste of success as a poet with the publication of his first publicly acclaimed volume, *Chicago Poems* (1916), of which the title poem, "Chicago," attracted popular attention. In the poem, he describes the city as "stormy, husky, brawling . . . a crooked brutal place. . . ." He pictured the people of the city with a harsh reality: prostitutes, gangsters, exploited factory workers and their families starving on low wages. Sandburg's Chicago, however, for all its coarseness and cruelty, was "alive. . . strong. . . cunning. . . ." The poet received negative reviews from critics, but encouraging mail from ordinary Americans proved that his works had their support. This situation prevailed more than once during his long and prolific career, but he had more success with *Cornhuskers* (1918) and *Smoke and Steel* (1920). He was a great storyteller, and his *Rootabaga Stories* (1922) were written for children. When he felt his old wanderlust during this period, he began touring the country as a lecturer and folk singer, accompanying himself on his guitar, and collected folk songs and tales that he published as *American Songbag* (1927). Returning to poetry in "The People Yes" (1936), he expressed his belief in America's people at a time when they needed a champion. His hope for the future lay in the common people. In her biography of Sandburg, Penelope Niven suggests that, in the process, he became "the passionate champion of people who did not have the power to speak for themselves."

The historical writings of Carl Sandburg were the most important twentieth-century factor in Abraham Lincoln's continuing popularity. In 1940 Sandburg received the Pulitzer Prize for his four-volume biography, *Lincoln: The War Years,* published in 1939. For once Sandburg's critics were silenced by the immediate success of the massive work, in which he defines Lincoln as an ordinary person—no idealist, but a beleaguered man struggling to make the right decisions under pressure. Sandburg examines the inside of the government during a time of crisis in American history, and Sandburg reveals his faith in Lincoln as a representative of the American spirit of democracy. Together with his earlier two-volume biography, *Lincoln: the Prairie Years,* (1926), the word-count outstripped that of the collected works of William Shakespeare.

Sandburg's total commitment to World War II led to his greatest undertaking, the novel *Remembrance Rock,* which spans American experience from Plymouth Rock to World War II and beyond. The book was a labor of love for its author, but was never acclaimed as a literary success. He was awarded a second Pulitzer Prize for his *Complete Poems* published in 1951, and in 1953 he wrote an autobiography, *Always the Young Strangers.* Penelope Niven explains Sandburg's life as "an odyssey into the American experience. He helped the American people discover their national identity through songs, poems and that mythical national hero, Abraham Lincoln. "

Together with Robert Frost and William Carlos Williams, Carl Sandburg stands as one of the greatest and best loved poets of the twentieth century. He died on July 22, 1967 and his ashes were buried at his birthplace in Galesburg, beneath a granite boulder called Remembrance Rock.

—Joan Gajadhar

FURTHER READING:

Mitchell, Roger. "Modernism Comes to American Poetry: 1908-1920." in *A Profile of Twentieth Century American Poetry,* edited by Jack Myers and David Wojahn. Carbondale, Southern Illinois University Press, 1991.

Niven, Penelope. *Carl Sandburg: A Biography.* New York, Scribner and Sons, 1991.

Sandburg, Carl. *Chicago Poems.* New York, Henry Holt, 1916, 1944.

Sanders, Barry (1968—)

While many argue whether or not he was the best ever or even the best of his decade, Barry Sanders of the Detroit Lions was the most intriguing running back in the National Football League (NFL) during the 1990s for two reasons: his productivity and personality. Sanders's consistent productivity on the football field was incredible; he averaged more than 100 rushing yards for every game in which he played. Despite never playing for a championship team, Sanders's remarkable on-the-field production—achieved through a combination of power, speed, and tremendous agility—brought him many postseason awards including player-of-the-year honors in 1997. Yet, Sanders may be best known for his humility during an era of professional sports dominated by outspoken and self-absorbed players constantly trying to increase their wealth. According to Paul Attner of the *Sporting News*, Sanders preferred a lifestyle that was "neither flamboyant nor extravagant," which was why he consistently turned down lucrative endorsement opportunities. In the final game of one season, Sanders even took himself out of the game in the closing minutes despite being close to setting the season rushing record. He later explained that the personal achievement meant little to him and he wanted to let his backup have a chance to play. Accentuated by his quiet demeanor, the leadership, modesty, and family values exhibited by Barry Sanders made him not just a great athlete but a uniquely humble superstar. Prior to the 1999 season, in a surprising move, Sanders retired from playing professional football for the Detroit Lions, claiming that he had lost his drive to play.

—Randall McClure

FURTHER READING:

Attner, Paul. "Be Like Barry." *Sporting News.* September 7, 1998, 16-25.

Guss, Greg. "The Father, the Son, and the Holy Numbers." *Sport.* September 1998, 70-75.

Gutman, Bill. *Barry Sanders: Football's Rushing Champ.* Brookfield, Connecticut, Millbrook Press, 1993.

Hinton, Ed, and Paul Zimmerman. "Cut and Run." *Sports Illustrated.* December 5, 1994, 36-46.

Kavanagh, Jack. *Barry Sanders: Rocket Running Back.* Minneapolis, Lerner Publications, 1994.

Sandman

In 1989, a comic book hit the shelves that would change the way fans, critics, and even the indifferent, would view the industry. Its title was *Sandman,* its hero Morpheus. At the height of its popularity, sales of *Sandman* rivaled, and frequently exceeded, those of individual *Superman* or *Batman* titles, the two reliable top-sellers for its parent company, DC Comics. The series and its author, Neil Gaiman, won

Barry Sanders in a game against the San Francisco 49ers.

praise from critics both within and without the comic book industry; even Norman Mailer hailed it as a literary achievement. Among its many awards, the most notable might be the World Fantasy Award, which no comic book had ever won before, and which—as a result of rule changes after *Sandman's* win—no comic book is likely ever to win again. The publication consistently sold over a million copies a year and remained one of the most stable modern titles in the speculators' market. The individual issues became so scarce and valuable that DC released collections of the issues in hardback to meet the demands of new readers. The collections have now sold well over three-quarters of a million copies.

Sandman tells the story of a god-like being who is captured by a group of occultists. He freed himself in the first issue, then spent the next six or seven issues re-establishing his rule after decades in prison. The rest of the series continued to analyze a large diversity of issues, unafraid to tackle concepts that had previously been taboo for comic books.

What is most astounding about *Sandman's* success is that it was achieved in a fraction of the time it has generally taken other champions of the genre to reach high levels of popularity. *Sandman* ran for under a decade—a blink of an eye compared to *Superman's* half-century or the *X-Men's* 30-plus years—and went to a voluntary grave at issue number 75. Within its pages, Gaiman and a host of groundbreaking visual artists floated away from conventional comics with only the thinnest of umbilical cords connecting their work to the mainstream. ''There's definitely a level on which *Sandman* is my creating a superhero I'd be happy writing,'' Gaiman has said. ''One of the things I like best about Sandman is all the wonderful powers he has . . . and they really have nothing to do with anything. They don't get used much, because he doesn't go around doing things heroically.'' In fact, the title character—Morpheus, an enigmatic symbol of the realm of dreams—often appears only at the fringes of the tale. Because of the protagonist's unique perspective on reality and history, the stories can be told from nearly any point of view and at any point in human history.

The themes Gaiman chose likewise push the envelope. He reached an adult audience, a demographic that could not have been depended on before the 1980s, and crafted tales for them that featured homosexuals, alternate histories, unreliable narrators, and an intricately told story that began in the first issue and was explored from a multitude of angles. All this was done within stories structured with careful attention to good storytelling, and readers responded accordingly. "Very few people seem to turn around and say, 'This comic has lesbians in it,'" Gaiman reported. "What they tend to say is, 'This comic has really good people in it.'"

As one critic has pointed out, "Although Gaiman's talent shouldn't be downplayed, it should be noted that his breed of story owes some of its success to the mood of the times, an environment where stories of coincidence and unseen powers fill a nagging cultural need." Gaiman has often stressed that the conclusion of the story in issue 75, is the same story that begins, despite various digressions, in issue one. In the first issue, Morpheus is stripped of his godhood and forced to re-evaluate humanity, precisely at the moment Generation X is questioning the bourgeois values it has been asked to accept from the generations before it.

What is perhaps most important to the field of popular culture is how *Sandman* affected the comic book industry. Stanley Wiater and Stephen R. Bissette, in their *Comic Book Rebels,* say of Gaiman that he is "representative of a new order of creators. Cosmopolitan and nomadic, they successfully maintain their creative autonomy while demanding the respect of their chosen publishers through a clear sense of who they are, what they are worth, and a canny blend of independence and diplomacy." This is revolutionary in that, for most of comic book history, creators who worked for major publishers wrote within the bounds set by their editors and were divested of any right to influence the character created once the individual story was finished. Characters that proved popular would not reap rewards for the creator, but for the publisher who owned the copyright through work-for-hire laws. *Sandman,* under what was almost exclusively Gaiman's guidance, became so popular that, as Wiater and Bissette note, "The first year of its run led to DC's granting an historically unprecedented (and retroactive) creative co-ownership and share of the character and title, including all licensing and foreign sales—rights and revenue DC had always denied creators."

Gaiman's creativity and sheer storytelling power seemed to increase with the continuing monetary rewards, and *Sandman*'s following swelled. Many retailers have credited *Sandman* alone with reaching female fans in a readership that had always been largely male. As the comic's fan base swelled, DC saw that there was a great market for comic books written for adults and, in 1993, only a handful of years after *Sandman*'s debut, the company launched Vertigo, a new imprint which has since produced some of the comic book world's most promising titles. *Doom Patrol* and *Preacher* in particular have enjoyed success through the high-profile creative atmosphere provided only by Vertigo, and, though *Sandman* finished its run in 1999, Vertigo guaranteed that its influence would continue well into the future.

—Joe Sutliff Sanders

FURTHER READING:

O'Neill, Patrick Daniel. "The Master of Dreams, Lost Loves, Old Gods and Unanswered Riddles." *Wizard: The Guide to Comics 9.* May 1992, 32-37.

Wiater, Stanley, and Stephen R. Bissette. *Comic Book Rebels: Conversations with the Creators of the New Comics.* New York, Donald I. Fine, Inc., 1993.

Sandow, Eugen (1867-1925)

Although a native of Koenigsberg, Germany, Eugen Sandow left an indelible mark on American life. Born Friedrich Wilhelm Muller, on April 2, 1867, he became one of the most popular and influential men of his age throughout the world through his activities that gave rise to the modern conceptualization of what we now term bodybuilding. Sandow traveled Europe as an acrobat, artist's model, and wrestler, before achieving prominence in England as a strongman/physique artist in the latter stages of the nineteenth century.

While Eugen Sandow's stage act consisted of the standard weightlifting feats of the era's strongmen, he achieved his greatest recognition for artistic physique posing, in which he displayed hitherto unseen muscular definition and vascularity. In contrast to the barrel-chested and pot-bellied weightlifters of the age, he popularized a new physical ideal that captured the imagination of turn-of-the-century men and women. Appearing on stage in nothing but a pair of briefs or, posing for physique photographs clad only in a fig leaf, Sandow offered an aesthetically appealing, scantily-clad, sexualized physique which challenged the repressive conventions of the late Victorian age.

A leading figure of the late nineteenth and early twentieth century "Physical Culture" movement, Sandow became one of the

Eugen Sandow

most recognized and influential men of his generation. Far from being merely a strongman, or what later generations would term a sex symbol, he branched out into lecturing and publishing, penning five full-length books and innumerable pamphlets and brochures, and editing a physical culture publication, *Sandow's Magazine,* from 1898 to 1907. While not regarded as a leading academic in any sense, his theories were considered scientific and he was respected for his practical knowledge of physiology and medicine.

Sandow's interplay with the scientific and medical authorities extended throughout his professional career. His system of weightlifting and physical fitness was endorsed by a great number of physicians, including blood pressure diagnostics pioneer, Sir Lauder Brunton. In December 1892, Sandow's exhibition before Army cadets was the subject of an article in the medical journal *The Lancet.* He was examined by Harvard professor and medical doctor Dudley Sargent, considered the ''dean of American physical educators,'' and was judged to be ''the most perfectly developed man in the world.'' Sargent then invited Sandow to lecture the students at Harvard, an offer that the strongman took up in 1902. He was also selected by the British Museum to represent the ''Caucasian race'' in the natural history branch's ''Races of the World'' exhibit. His crowning achievement in the field of medico-bodybuilding, however, came when he was named ''Professor of Scientific and Physical Culture'' to King George V in 1911.

While cementing his reputation as a scientistic, if not scientific, entity, Sandow also advanced his career as a popular cultural icon. Having achieved widespread acclaim as a stage star touring the United States with impresario Florenz Ziegfeld, Jr., he was invited by Thomas Edison to star in one of the inventor's Kinetoscope films. On March 10, 1894, Sandow waived his $250 appearance fee to shake the hand of Thomas Edison—who he considered ''the greatest man of the age''—and to become the star of one of the first moving pictures. He later went on to star in ''big screen'' shorts produced by Edison's rival, the American Mutoscope and Biograph studios.

Along with his on-screen exploits, Sandow continued to travel as a stage performer. He incorporated a glass-case posing routine into his act, whereby he would occupy a glass enclosure with a rotating pedestal, which allowed the audience a voyeuristic total view of the bodybuilder's physique. After touring Europe, the British Isles, and the United States, where he was a star attraction at the 1893 Columbian Exposition in Chicago, Sandow set out to take his brand of physical culture and his trademark physique to the rest of the world. In 1902, he toured Australia and New Zealand, preaching his sermon on bodybuilding, and embarked upon a grand tour of South Africa, India, China, Japan, Java, and Burma in 1904. He brought along an entire troupe of performing athletes, and a tent which could comfortably accommodate six thousand people for his exhibitions in areas lacking appropriate theatrical facilities.

While Sandow is noted for his own stage performances, he also organized the first major bodybuilding competition, the so-called ''Great Competition'' of 1901, in Great Britain. Gathering together the foremost British physique artists, he hosted a pageant where, together with sculptor Charles Lawes and Sherlock Holmes creator Sir Arthur Conan Doyle, he set about determining exactly who was the most perfectly developed man in the British Isles. Before a capacity crowd of 15,000 spectators, Sandow put forth an exhibition the likes of which had never been seen. After a parade of athletes, marching to a musical composition written by Sandow, a performance by a boys' choir, wrestling, gymnastics, fencing, exercise displays, and an exhibition by the premier bodybuilder himself,

bronze, silver, and gold statuettes of Sandow were given to those judged to have the three best physiques.

Though age began to take its toll on the athlete's musculature, Eugen Sandow was a very popular figure well into the twentieth century. His likeness was used to sell numerous products from exercisers and dime novels to cocoa and cigars, and he remained active in his adopted homeland of Great Britain through publishing and public speaking. While preparing for a lecture tour of Britain in 1925, he fell ill and was forced to cancel his plans. Hazy details surround his ailment, and when he died at the age of 58 on October 14, 1925, newspaper accounts stated that he suffered a burst blood vessel in his brain after attempting to single-handedly pull an automobile out of a ditch. The story was questioned at the time and is still in question today. Sandow's biographer, David Chapman, speculates that the strongman's death may have been the result of an aortic aneurysm brought about by syphilis.

—Nicholas Turse

FURTHER READING:

Budd, Michael A. *The Sculpture Machine: Physical Culture and Body Politics in the Age of Empire.* New York, New York University Press, 1997.

Chapman, David. *Sandow the Magnificent: Eugen Sandow and the Beginnings of Bodybuilding.* Chicago, University of Illinois, 1994.

Dutton, Kenneth. *The Perfectible Body: The Western Ideal of Male Physical Development.* New York, Continuum, 1995.

Green, Harvey. *Fit for America: Health, Fitness, Sport and American Society.* New York, Pantheon, 1986.

Sanford and Son

The NBC television sitcom, *Sanford and Son,* was created by writer-director and independent producer, Norman Lear, whose lengthy list of successful, long-running, and often controversial television programs revolutionized primetime television during the 1970s. The popular program chronicled the escapades of Mr. Fred G. Sanford, a cantankerous widower living with his thirty-something son, Lamont, played by Demond Wilson, in the Watts section of Los Angeles, California. *Sanford and Son* was the first program with a most Black cast to appear since the cancellation of the *Amos 'n Andy* show nearly twenty years earlier.

Airing from 1972 to 1977, *Sanford and Son* was the American version of a British program called *Steptoe & Son,* which featured the exploits of a Cockney father-and-son junkman team. In the starring role of *Sanford and Son* was veteran actor-comedian John Elroy Sanford, popularly known as Redd Foxx, whose bawdy recordings and racy nightclub routines had influenced generations of Black comics since the 1950s. Foxx was born in St. Louis, Missouri, and began a career in the late 1930s performing street acts. By the 1960s he was headlining in Los Vegas. In 1969, he earned a role as an aging junk dealer in the motion picture *Cotton Comes to Harlem.* This portrayal brought him to the attention of producer Norman Lear, who was casting his newest show, *Sanford and Son.*

In addition to its two stars—Redd Foxx and Demond Wilson—*Sanford and Son* featured a unique, multiracial cast of regular and

Sanford and Son castmembers Desmond Wilson (left) and Redd Foxx.

occasional characters, who served as the butt of Sanford's often bigoted jokes and insults, including Bubba (Don Bexly), Smitty the cop (Hal Williams), Grady (Mayo Williams), Julio (Gregory Sierra), Rollo (Nathaniel Taylor) and Ah Chew (Pat Molina). LaWanda Page played the "evil and ugly" Aunt Esther, Fred's archenemy. Their constant bickering and put-downs of each other provided some of the funniest moments in the show. "I'm convinced that *Sanford and Son* shows middle class America a lot of what they need to know. . . ." Foxx said in a 1973 interview, "The show . . . doesn't drive home a lesson, but it can open up people's minds enough for them to see how stupid every kind of prejudice can be."

The "feigned heart attack routine" became a trademark of the series as Fred, pretending to have a heart attack, clasped his chest in mock pain and threatened to join his deceased wife, saying "I'm coming to join you, Elizabeth!" It was Foxx's enormously funny portrayal that quickly earned *Sanford and Son* a place among the top ten most-watched programs to air on NBC television.

"Certain things should be yours to have when you work your way to the top," declared Redd Foxx in a *Los Angeles Times* article. In 1977 he walked-out on the production of his enormously successful show complaining that the mostly white producers and writers had little regard or understanding of African-American life. He lambasted the total lack of Black writers or directors on the crew. Moreover, he was dissatisfied with his treatment as the star of the program. Believing that his efforts were not appreciated, he left NBC for his own variety show on ABC. The program barely lasted one season. After Foxx left, a pseudo spin-off, called *Sanford Arms* proved unsuccessful and it too, lasted only one season.

Sanford and Son survived five seasons on prime-time television. It earned its place in television history as one of the first successful television sitcoms with a mostly Black cast to appear on American network, primetime television in nearly twenty years. It was an enormously funny program, sans obvious ethnic stereotyping. Redd Foxx died at sixty-eight in October 1994.

—Pamala S. Deane

FURTHER READING:

Adler, Dick. "How Redd Outfoxed the Competition." *Los Angeles Times,* April 12, 1977.

Barnow, Eric. *Tube of Plenty.* Oxford, Oxford University Press, 1982.

Brooks, Tim, and Earle Marsh. *The Complete Directory of Prime Time Network TV Shows, 1946-Present.* New York, Ballantine Books, 1985.

MacDonald, J. Fred. *Blacks and White TV: Afro-Americans in Television Since 1948.* Chicago, Nelson-Hall Publishers, 1983

Marc, David, and Robert J. Thompson. *Prime Time, Prime Movers: From I Love Lucy to L.A. Law, America's Greatest TV Shows and People Who Created Them.* Boston, Little Brown, 1992.

Robinson, Louie. "Sanford and Son: Redd Foxx and Demond Wilson wake up TV's jaded audience." *Ebony*, July, 1972.

Santana

Led by virtuoso guitarist Carlos Santana (1947—), the band Santana has been one of the most successful mainstream ethnic fusion acts in rock history, topping the charts since the 1960s with its signature blend of Latin and African sounds. Carlos Santana grew up to the distinctive mariachi sounds of his native Tijuana, Mexico. As a teenager in the 1950s, he became fascinated by the rhythm and blues and rock and roll sounds he heard on the radio. Upon learning to play guitar, he fused these disparate traditions into an exciting and unique sound that would later become his trademark.

In the mid-1960s, Santana moved to San Francisco, where he and other local musicians formed the Santana Blues Band, later shortened to Santana. The group—featuring Santana (guitar), Gregg Rolie (vocals and keyboards), Dave Brown (bass), Mike Shrieve (drums), Armando Peraza (percussion and vocals), Mike Carabello (percussion), and Jose Areas (percussion)—first gained recognition in the same dance halls that hosted psychedelic rock groups of the era such as the Grateful Dead and Jefferson Airplane. Santana's blend of Latin and African sounds was ill suited to the acid rock scene, but the group's frenetic performances captivated hippie audiences across the Bay Area. Under the direction of concert promoter Bill Graham, Santana landed a spot at the Woodstock Festival in New York, where the band's *tour de force* performance lodged Santana in the mainstream consciousness before the group had even recorded an album.

Santana released its first album, *Evil Ways,* in 1969. The title track from that debut effort reached the Top Ten—an unprecedented feat, given the song's overt Latin sound. The group's 1970 single "Black Magic Woman" enjoyed similar mass appeal and pushed the band's second album, *Abraxas,* to the top of the charts where it remained for six weeks. *Santana III,* released in 1971, likewise topped the charts and established Santana as a major force in the recording industry.

The band underwent frequent personnel changes during the remainder of the decade. Carlos Santana brought drummer Buddy Miles and guitarist John McLaughlin into the fold, while original vocalist Gregg Rolie, along with newer member Neil Schon, departed to form the highly successful band Journey. Despite their internal flux, however, Santana continued to release such stellar albums as *Amigos* (1976) and *Moonflower* (1977), as well as hit singles such as the group's 1977 cover of The Zombies' "She's Not There."

The band continued recording well into the 1980s, but, more often than not, Carlos Santana's supporting cast was a revolving set of hired session musicians. Nevertheless, the group's signature sound remained intact as well as relevant. In 1987, the group took part in "Rock and Roll Summit," the first joint American and Soviet rock concert in history, and, seven years later, Santana made a triumphant return to the Woodstock II anniversary concert in New York. The group also earned a Grammy Award for Best Rock Instrumental Performance in 1988 as well as a *Billboard* Magazine Lifetime Achievement Award in 1996. As of 1998, Santana's albums had sold more than 30 million copies, and the group had performed for more than 13 million people worldwide.

—Scott Tribble

Sarandon, Susan (1946—)

Actress Susan Sarandon is a Hollywood rarity: a strong, sexy, successful, older woman. The five-time Academy Award nominee won her first Oscar just before her fiftieth birthday for *Dead Man Walking* (1995). A former Ford model, her boundary-breaking acting career began with a small role in a 1970 film. In 1975 she appeared in the campy cult film, *The Rocky Horror Picture Show*. A lesbian love scene in *The Hunger* (1983) also attracted attention. First nominated for an Oscar in 1980, she got the nod three more times in the early 1990s for films such as the popular feminist road movie *Thelma and Louise* and true-to-life medical drama *Lorenzo's Oil*. Sarandon's private life is as progressive as her politics. The divorcee has had several high-profile romances with younger co-stars, including common-law husband actor Tim Robbins, father of two of her three children. The two met while filming *Bull Durham* (1988).

—Courtney Bennett

FURTHER READING:

Blau, E. "Susan Sarandon's Roughest Role." *The New York Times.* January 14, 1983.

Neuman, B. "Susan Sarandon: Lover, Lawyer, Marmee." *The New York Times.* July 17, 1994.

Saratoga Springs

Throughout the twentieth century, this upstate New York summer resort—1990 population, 25,001—has jumbled together invalids, nouveaux-riche social climbers, fastidious old-money sportsmen, and both hard-core and petty gamblers. A nineteenth century health resort featuring carbonated waters, the village began promoting summer horse-racing in 1863, and the Saratoga race track is the

oldest still existent in the United States. Saratoga's reputation as a distinctive American congeries was spread in such disparate works as Edith Wharton's unfinished *The Buccaneers,* Edna Ferber's *Saratoga Trunk* (movie version starring Gary Cooper and Ingrid Bergman), and E.L. Doctorow's *Billy Bathgate.* The Kefauver investigation (1951) ended a century of public gaming, but the horse-racing continues unabated and, unlike similar resorts, Saratoga underwent a popular renaissance in the 1970s. It continues to thrive in the 1990s as "the summer place to be," entertaining an appealingly raffish mix attracted to health, history, horses, and the Saratoga Performing Arts Center.

—Jon Sterngass

FURTHER READING:

Spiegel, Ted. *Saratoga: The Place and Its People.* New York, Harry Abrams, 1988.

Waller, George. *Saratoga: Saga of an Impious Era.* Englewood Cliffs, New Jersey, Prentice Hall, 1966.

Sarnoff, David (1891-1971)

A significant innovator in the field of communications, particularly in radio and television, David Sarnoff's influence is indelibly stamped on the cultural development of these media. In creating the National Broadcasting Company (NBC) as the first permanent network, he invented commercial broadcasting as we know it. Sarnoff clearly valued technology and foresaw uses for it beyond the understanding of his contemporaries. In doing so, he helped to propel television from the domain of experimentation to one of global status.

Sarnoff was born in Uzlian, near Minsk, in what is now Belarus. His family emigrated to New York in 1900, and the young Sarnoff was raised in Lower Manhattan's Hell's Kitchen district. In 1906 he was employed as an office worker by the Marconi Wireless Telegraph Company and soon after became a telegrapher. He was first noticed as the lone radioman to relay news from the sinking *Titanic* to the rest of the world. He advanced rapidly, and in 1915 presented his idea for a radio receiving set to the company. In 1919, at the age of 28, Sarnoff became commercial manager of the Radio Corporation of America (RCA) when it absorbed Marconi. He contradicted the current thinking that radio had no application beyond military and corporate use by proposing the "radio music box," a home radio that could receive entertainment programming. Initially, the radio manufacturers financed programming production, but increasing costs led Sarnoff, together with General Electric (GE) and Westinghouse to organize NBC as part of RCA in 1926. Thus, the first advertiser-sponsored national radio network was born, and radio was thereafter established as the medium for home entertainment.

In 1930 Sarnoff became president of RCA and, with radio firmly established, he concentrated his energies on the development of television. He masterminded the independence of RCA from GE and Westinghouse and acquired the Victor Company as a manufacturing base for his assault on the television market. In 1939 he launched television as a new industry at the World's Fair. The onset of World War II, however, caused a temporary hiatus in RCA's advance into television research. Once the war ended, Sarnoff turned back to marketing his new visual technology and spearheaded the development of color television. In 1947 he became chairman of the board of RCA.

Sarnoff was also an enthusiastic partner for governmental initiatives. Prior to World War II he had overseen RCA's total conversion to defense production, and during the war he offered his services to the military and was appointed General Dwight D. Eisenhower's chief of communications. He organized and coordinated all radio communications on the Western front, and in recognition of his services, he was named a brigadier general in the U.S. Army. Sarnoff's involvement with government projects did not, however, end with the war. He was an energetic participant in the Cold War struggle against the Soviet Union; indeed, with the onset of the Cold War, his involvement deepened, as he submitted to the Administration regular proposals for fighting Communism. He also advised Radio Free Europe and Radio Liberation, whose staff members trained at NBC studios. At his suggestion, *Voice of America* adopted the sign-off, "This is the Voice of America, for freedom and peace." RCA also cooperated with the United States Information Agency to produce advertising that would sell its own products as well as promoting America.

David Sarnoff died in 1971, but he will be remembered by many as the "Father of Television." His faith in technology and his support for innovation led to the creation of modern radio and television commercial broadcasting in a manner and on a scale that his contemporaries could not have foreseen, and he has been immortalized by the communications industry.

—Nathan Abrams

FURTHER READING:

Barnouw, Erik. *The Image Empire: A History of Broadcasting in the United States, Volume III—From 1953.* New York, Oxford University Press, 1970.

Bilby, Kenneth W. *The General: David Sarnoff and the Rise of the Communications Industry.* New York, Harper & Row, 1986.

Myers, Elisabeth P. *David Sarnoff: Radio and TV Boy.* Indianapolis, Bobbs Merrill, 1972.

Sarnoff, David. *Looking Ahead: The Papers of David Sarnoff.* New York, McGraw-Hill, 1988.

Sarong

The sarong is a basic form of dress, best known as the fundamental dress form of the Malay Archipelago peoples, men and women alike. A long, straight piece of cloth wraps around the waist. In deference to its primacy in Malay dress, it is generally thought of as being in colorful batik and cognate materials, but metaphorically the sarong can seem to describe the short kilt of ancient Egyptian men. In the 1930s and 1940s, the "exotic South Seas" attire was popularized in Dorothy Lamour films generous in native or para-native skin. Meanwhile, the name lent itself to such imperialist Bob Hope word play as, "what'sarong?" Although never assimilated into mainstream Western dress, the sarong has been used in designer collections and sportswear to connote the beach and/or Orientalism. For America, the sarong symbolizes an exotic, luxurious existence of pleasure.

—Richard Martin

Sasquatch
See Bigfoot

Sassoon, Vidal (1928—)

"Swinging London" of the 1960s, with the Beatles and Carnaby Street, produced no revolution more important perhaps than that of Vidal Sassoon. Sassoon created the bob and easy geometric hairstyles that liberated women from weekly visits to the beauty parlor and the stiff, heavy, fixed hairstyles of prior generations. Sassoon's new ideal of beauty was literally care-free and could, for most women, be cut once a month. Its abiding principle was geometry, letting the hair move naturally, and was typified by the 1960s hairstyles of the Beatles themselves. Freeing women from the beauty parlor and nights of sleeping with curlers and other mechanisms on their heads, Sassoon became emblematic of freedom and sensible good health. His salons became the first chain of worldwide hair styling salons and were complemented by his international sales of hair-treatment products. Sassoon, too, became a television talk-show host and celebrity.

—Richard Martin

FURTHER READING:

Fishman, Diane and Marcia Powell, *Vidal Sassoon: Fifty Years Ahead,* New York, Rizzoli, 1993.

Sassy

Launched in 1988 in the midday heat of conservative Reagan America, *Sassy* was the first magazine aimed at teenage girls and young women to deal frankly with the fact that its readership—despite statutory rape laws, remaining cultural taboos against premarital sex, parental strictures, and limited access to adequate birth control—might indeed be engaging in sexual activity. Instead of addressing the topic of boys and physical attraction in moralistic tones, *Sassy*'s writers tried to provide a realistic viewpoint along with coherent, practical advice, and it forced its competition to do the same. "What *Sassy* did—to its everlasting shame or credit, depending on one's point of view—was to suggest not only that these teenage girls had sexual lives but that it was a proper editorial mission for a magazine to address their urgent informational needs about sex," commented Kathleen T. Endress and Therese L. Lueck in *Women's Periodicals in the United States.* "Perhaps unsurprisingly," the authors continued, *Sassy* became "an immediate success with its teenage readers."

When *Sassy* debuted in early 1988, statistics indicated a population of 14 million young American women aged 14 to 19, with only about 30 percent of that figure purchasing or reading the typical teen fare for females: *YM, Seventeen,* and *Teen,* all holdovers from a more virginal era. *Sassy*'s publishers also recognized the potential force of this captive audience in the realm of advertising dollars: because many teens were being raised in households with two working parents, a combination of guilt and affluence led to a greater "income" level for such young women. With their allowances and access to parental credit cards, it was estimated that they spent an average of $65 a week on clothes and cosmetics. Advertisers were excited at the prospect of reaching such a malleable demographic—buyers with vast leisure time and a desire to conform through consumerism.

Sassy was a knockoff of a successful Australian publication named *Dolly*, but was toned down for its American readership. Key to its success was a young, iconoclastic editor to head it, and Fairfax, Ltd., the American branch of the Australian media company, found one in Jane Pratt, a 24-year-old granddaughter of a onetime executive at Doubleday with a liberal-arts degree and documented wild streak. Pratt had grown up reading teen magazines, and had some experience in the field at a few failed publications. Perhaps more importantly, she had undergone a rough time as a teen after being shipped off to an elite boarding school, and would later say the incident traumatized her so much that she would remain stuck at that age for the rest of her life.

Sassy set itself apart from its major competition in its very first issue in March of 1988. Unlike *Seventeen,* which strove to impart a "good girl" ethos, *Sassy* offered readers the feature, "Losing Your Virginity: Read This Before You Decide." Readers bought *Sassy* in droves. Quickly, *Seventeen* and other magazines got hip to the competition and immediately drew up plans for redesign and refocus. *Sassy* also made media history by allowing ads for condoms. From the start, the magazine was accused of encouraging young women to be boy-crazy and engage in sexual activity, but a more careful reading of its articles showed them to be balanced and frank about the negative physical and emotional consequences of sexual activity.

Most adults seemed to have strong feelings against *Sassy.* Media pundits faulted it for the self-reflexive editorial content—it was not unusual for copy to incorporate penciled rejoinders from dissenting colleagues in the margins—and parents found it threatening, to say the least. In a 1992 *New York* article about Pratt and the success of *Sassy, Seventeen* editor Midge Richardson declared her competition "sometimes vulgar, and the politics are unabashedly liberal. The magazine also pokes fun at traditional values," Richardson said, forgetting that this was usually the perpetual *raison d'être* for teens in general. Yet both *Seventeen* and *YM* immediately jazzed up their features and style to compete and become more "sassy." Its own ad campaign trumpeted the line, "I'm too Sassy to read *Teen.*"

From the start, however, *Sassy*'s critics seemed bent on silencing it. After only a few months on the newsstands, it became the target of a well-organized boycott from the Moral Majority and Christian fundamentalist minister, Jerry Falwell, for what was deemed its promotion of promiscuity and alternative sexuality; a letter-writing campaign managed to scare off a few big advertisers, and Pratt and the staff writers began to tone down the sex features. Unrelated financial difficulties with Fairfax led to Sassy's sale to Lang Communications in 1989, and though it still addressed teen sexuality, it attempted to bring its zingy style to a wider range of issues. In 1991, for instance, it ran articles explaining the Gulf War situation with such titles as "What Saddam Is Irked About."

Under Pratt's guidance, a *Sassy* for boys was launched in 1992 (titled *Dirt*), and Pratt also landed her own television talk show on the Fox Network. Both eventually failed, and Pratt left *Sassy* to create another magazine, a sort of *Sassy* for the 18-to-34 female demographic called *Jane.*

—Carol Brennan

FURTHER READING:

Carmody, Deirdre. "Reaching Teen-Agers, Without Using a Phone." *New York Times.* 18 January 1993.

Daley, Suzanne. "Sassy: Like, You Know, for Kids." *New York Times.* 11 April 1988.

Endress, Kathleen T., and Therese L. Lueck, editors. "Sassy." *Women's Periodicals in the United States: Consumer Magazines.* Westport, Connecticut, Greenwood Press, 311-17.

Smith, Dinitia. "Jane's World! Jane's World!" *New York.* 25 May 1992, 60-71.

Satellites

The launch of the Telstar satellite on July 10, 1962 heralded a new age for communications. Prior to Telstar, live television broadcasts had been confined within continental borders, hindered by the inability of television's high frequencies to bounce off the ionosphere. Although transatlantic telephone cables to Europe existed, as late as 1957 the system could accommodate a mere 36 calls at any one time. Telstar was designed as the first link in a vast network of satellites capable of relaying images and telephone calls around the globe.

While the Soviet Union's Sputnik thrust satellites onto the world stage, its faint chirping beeps served little purpose other than as a tracking signal. However, beyond the immense political ramifications, Sputnik proved that a manmade object could not only be placed into orbit, but it could function in the hostile environment of space. The possibilities for satellites were far reaching—they could be distant sentinels tracking volatile weather formations, spies in the sky for the military, or communication repeater outposts.

The concept of utilizing satellites for communication purposes first appeared in an article penned by space visionary Arthur C. Clarke in October 1945. Entitled "Extra-Terrestrial Relays" the article, published in the trade journal *Wireless World,* predicted three geostationary communication satellites would provide simultaneous worldwide radio broadcasts by the year 1995. Less than 20 years after the publication of this article, science fiction was well on its way to becoming scientific reality, with Telstar blazing the trail.

Realizing the potential of satellites, U.S. telecommunications giant AT&T (American Telephone & Telegraph) initiated funding for a project named Telstar in the fall of 1960. AT&T coined the term "Telstar" by combining "telecommunications" and "star." Their ambitious network of satellites would be an expensive venture, but AT&T's monopoly status at that time allowed the company to simply pass research and operating costs on to the consumer. AT&T even reimbursed NASA $3 million for the use of its Thor-Delta launch vehicle.

From its initial relay, Telstar electrified the world. For the first time an image generated on one side of the Atlantic could be instantly viewed on the other. The telecasting feat answered critics who questioned the practical applications of the Sputnik induced space race. As a propaganda tool, Telstar bolstered America's sagging image as a technological innovator. The Soviets could claim the world's first artificial satellite, but its scientific value paled when compared to the technologically sophisticated instrument designed by American minds.

Reflecting Vice President Lyndon Johnson's statement of Telstar being "another first in the American conquest of space," the first image telecast from three thousand miles above the Earth was an

The Intelsat VI satellite orbits the Earth.

American flag waving in the foreground of AT&T's antenna tracking facility near Andover, Maine. "America the Beautiful" and "The Star Spangled Banner" acted as the musical score for the sequence. Although European tracking stations were unable to receive this broadcast, France was able to establish a link at 7:47 PM EDT. The following evening, July 11, American television viewers were treated to their first live images of Europe courtesy of Telstar; they watched entertainer Yves Montand singing "La Chansonette."

A technological wonder, relaying both television signals and telephone calls, the basic premise of the Telstar network was flawed. Telstar was capable of transatlantic relay for a mere 102 minutes a day. In order to create a stable communications network AT&T estimated 50 to 120 Telstars would need to be placed into orbit. The geostationary concept of Arthur C. Clarke, where a satellite is in synch with the Earth's rotation at a height where it could cover 42 percent of the planet's surface, required only three satellites. On July 26, 1963, Telstar became obsolete as Syncom II became the first satellite to transmit from a synchronous orbit some 22,235 miles in space.

President John Kennedy looked to Telstar as an "outstanding example of the way in which government and business can cooperate in a most important field of human endeavor." Telstar benefitted both the United States and AT&T greatly. The satellite restored America's image as a leader in technology, an image severely battered in the wake of a series of humiliating space firsts achieved by the Soviet Union. An extensive advertising campaign by AT&T featured Telstar linking progress and AT&T firmly in the subconscious of the American public. While geostationary communication satellites quickly eclipsed the Telstar network concept, subsequent satellites failed to achieve the public notoriety of Telstar.

—Dr. Lori C. Walters

FURTHER READING:

Clarke, Arthur C. "Extra-Terrestrial Relays." *Wireless World.* October 1945, 305-308.

Findley, Rowe. "Telephone a Star." *National Geographic.* Vol. 121, No. 5, May 1962, 638-651.

Gavaghan, Helen. *Something New Under the Sun: Satellites and the Beginning of the Space Age.* New York, Copernicus, 1998.

The Saturday Evening Post

Long before *Time* and *Newsweek* recapped the events of the world for millions of Americans, long before *Reader's Digest* and *Life* condensed the world's news in words and pictures, the *Saturday Evening Post* was truly America's magazine. Born at the turn of the century, with roots in colonial America, the *Saturday Evening Post* quickly became required reading for anyone who wished to stay in touch with the issues that mattered in American culture, politics, or the economy. The *Post,* as it is widely known, dominated the American magazine landscape for the first thirty years of the century, both in circulation and in influence. In its heyday, the *Post* was the voice of American common-sense conservatism. When that brand of conservatism declined, so did the magazine, but for a time the *Post* reached its editor's goal of being America's "indispensable magazine."

The modern *Post* was born when magazine magnate Cyrus H. K. Curtis, who published the nation's leading magazine, the *Ladies' Home Journal,* purchased it from Andrew Smythe in 1897 for $1,000. Curtis liked the magazine's pedigree—it claimed to be the oldest magazine in America, and was once printed in Benjamin Franklin's print shop (though historians now doubt that Franklin had anything to

A boy sells the *Saturday Evening Post* in Rochester, New York, 1910.

do with the publication)—but the content of the magazine was without distinction. Curtis soon hired as his editor one George Horace Lorimer, a young preacher's son with a clear idea of how to pitch a magazine to the great middle class. Lorimer believed that the cultural values of the nineteenth-century American middle class—honesty, integrity, hard-work, and self-reliance—would sustain the nation as it entered a new century. By retaining final say on every word that was printed in his magazine, Lorimer made sure that every issue echoed his vision for America. And he soon found readers who agreed with him.

The *Post*'s circulation reached one million per week in 1908, two million in 1913, and three million in 1937. Lorimer had devised what became known as the "*Post* formula," a mix of equal parts business, public affairs, and romance, with sports, humor, illustrations, and cartoons thrown in for spice. The magazine published fiction, much of it in serial form, and much of it romantic, and it published nonfiction articles that celebrated American achievement. The *Post* rarely opposed the status quo and seemed perfectly attuned to the tastes of the "average" American, as long as that American was white, middle-class, middle-aged, and comfortable. Norman Rockwell, who began to illustrate covers for the *Post* in 1916,

perfectly captured the tone of the magazine. While the contents of the magazine remained largely the same for the better part of the 1910s, 1920s, and 1930s, so did the price: until 1942, an issue cost just five cents. The stable price was a measure of the magazine's success, for the magazine attracted so many advertisers eager to peddle their products before the *Post*'s readers that the publisher could cushion his readers from the rising costs of the magazine's production.

Critics complained that the *Post* was sugarcoating the rise of big business in America. They had a point. While other notable American magazines like *McClure's* drew attention to the dangers posed by the rise of large monopolistic corporations, the *Saturday Evening Post* largely applauded the effects that big business was having on the American landscape. As long as pro-business politicians were in office, editor Lorimer was an optimist, for his magazine benefited as much as any large business from the Republican party's dominance over national politics in the first third of the century. But when the political and economic tide turned, Lorimer turned into a scold. It wasn't the stock market crash of 1929 that changed Lorimer's mood—in fact, Lorimer saw the crash and the ensuing economic depression as a healthy correction to an economy that had grown dangerously speculative. Rather, it was the election of President Franklin Delano Roosevelt and the administration of his New Deal programs that turned Lorimer and the *Post* from the spokesman for the common-sense majority into the shrill voice of American conservatism.

Lorimer deplored Roosevelt's New Deal because he felt that what Americans needed to do most was tighten their belts and return to the "old values" he had long promoted in the *Post*. In opposing the New Deal, Lorimer "changed the Post from an organ of entertainment and enlightenment into a weapon of political warfare," writes magazine historian Theodore Peterson. Lorimer's views were popular with many Americans, but fighting these battles took the steam out of the aging editor, who left the *Post* in 1937 with the magazine reaching more Americans than ever before. The magazine experienced a sharp decline during World War II, when the magazine's unpopular isolationist stance and a nasty article on Jews drew bitter criticism, but it soon revived in the post-War boom.

The *Post* reached four million readers in 1949, five million in 1955. While such continually increasing circulation figures would have once convinced both editors and advertisers that the magazine was healthy, major changes in the American magazine market instead revealed the *Post*'s tenuous position in an increasingly competitive market. First, increasingly sophisticated means of tracking magazine readership allowed advertisers and marketers to determine precisely which readerships were likely to bring revenue to potential advertisers. The *Post*, with its aging readership, was no longer the best medium for carrying advertising. Second, the number of magazines on the market had exploded in the 1940s, meaning that the *Post* had more competitors, and the arrival of television in the 1950s meant even more competition for the newly choosy advertising dollar. Hoping to return the *Post* to its former position as the leading medium for advertising in the United States, the Curtis Company experimented with a number of changes to the magazine's format and contents. But the venerable *Saturday Evening Post* was losing so much money that it ceased publication in February of 1969. The *Post* returned from the grave two years later, and was published into the 1990s in one form or another, but it never reclaimed its status as a major magazine.

In its later years the *Saturday Evening Post* was just one among many American magazines struggling to attract enough readers and advertisers to survive, but during its heyday the *Post* was a true phenomenon. According to Jan Cohn, author of *Creating America: George Horace Lorimer and the "Saturday Evening Post,"* "Despite the vast changes in American society between 1899 and 1936, what the *Post* achieved was the fullest expression of a broad American consensual view." Bringing together enthusiasm for the benefits of modern society—economic growth, a wealth of new goods, exciting developments in technology—with a healthy respect for old American truths—reverence for hard work, belief in honesty and sincerity, and love of the home—the *Post* spoke in a language that calmed Americans during a period of dramatic social change. Even during the tumultuous 1920s, a period known for its crazes, enthusiasm, and for its flaming youth, the *Post* managed to contain the burgeoning energy of popular culture within its pages, publishing stories from Jazz Age icon F. Scott Fitzgerald, among others.

Anyone wishing to understand America during the first decades of the century must surely turn to the pages of the *Post*. The story told by the *Post,* week after week, year after year, is not the story of all of America, but of the Americans who wielded power and influence, or at least voted for and revered those who did. It was a consensus magazine for a time when Americans believed that a consensus still existed. The magazine's demise is representative of changes in America as well, for it occurred amid the splintering of American identities that characterized the 1960s. Today, no one magazine could aspire to represent all Americans, but for a brief span of time the *Post* truly was, as it often claimed to be, "America's magazine."

—Tom Pendergast

FURTHER READING:

Bigelow, Frederick S. *A Short History of "The Saturday Evening Post": "An American Institution" in Three Centuries.* Philadelphia, Curtis Publishing Co., 1927, 1936.

Cohn, Jan. *Creating America: George Horace Lorimer and the "Saturday Evening Post."* Pittsburgh, University of Pittsburgh Press, 1989.

Curtis Publishing Company. *A Short History of the "Saturday Evening Post."* Philadelphia, Curtis Publishing Co., 1953.

Friedrich, Otto. *Decline and Fall.* New York, Harper & Row, 1969.

Mott, Frank L. "The Saturday Evening Post." *A History of American Magazines.* Vol. 4. Cambridge, Harvard University Press, 1957, 671-716.

Tebbel, John. *George Horace Lorimer and the Saturday Evening Post.* Garden City, New Jersey, Doubleday, 1948.

Wood, James Playsted. "Magazine Reflection of a Nation: *The Saturday Evening Post.*" *Magazines in the United States: Their Social and Economic Influence.* 3rd ed. New York, Ronald Press, 1971.

Saturday Morning Cartoons

Saturday morning cartoons have been an integral part of the American television scene since the 1960s. Saturday morning is unlike any other time of the programming week in that the viewing audience is more monolithic than any other. At no other time do so many stations broadcast such similar material for such an extended period of time, all aimed at the same audience: children. Several generations of children have planned their weekends around the ritual of pouring huge bowls of sugar-saturated cereal and gathering about the television for the week's dose of animation.

The earliest incarnation of the Saturday morning cartoon came about almost as an accident. In 1949, producer Jerry Fairbanks sold NBC on the idea of a new series of cartoons developed especially for television. His product was a low-budget project titled *Crusader Rabbit,* created by Jay Ward and Alex Anderson. This simply-animated series followed the adventures of an intrepid rabbit and his tiger sidekick. "I don't recall anything special about Saturday morning at that point except that the networks had some vague idea that they wanted programs for kids," Fairbanks said, according to Hal Erickson's *Television Cartoon Shows: An Illustrated Encyclopedia.*

The idea certainly had merit. According to Erickson, statistics going back to the radio years showed that the peak tune-in hours for children were between 10 a.m. and noon on Saturday mornings and 4 p.m. to 6 p.m. weekdays. *Crusader Rabbit* was the very first cartoon created exclusively for television and the first to take advantage of this window of opportunity to market to children. Prior to *Crusader Rabbit,* the only cartoons that had appeared on television were repackaged shorts originally created for the big screen. In order to keep costs down and constantly turn out new material, Ward and Anderson pared *Crusader Rabbit* down to its absolute bare essentials. Characters moved an average of once every four seconds and tended to stay in static poses. The show ran for two years, from 1950-1952.

Crusader Rabbit failed to trigger a deluge of morning cartoons. Television stations preferred to stay with the tried-and-true (and much less expensive) format of a live-action host holding court over a studio audience of children and plugging the sponsors' products. But CBS took a gamble and placed a well-known character, Mighty Mouse, on Saturday mornings in 1955. *Mighty Mouse Playhouse* ran for 12 highly successful seasons and further edged live-action shows out the door in favor of direct-to-television animation.

That same year, another important development was taking place: William Hanna and Joseph Barbera, two talented MGM animators, took over the animation division of MGM, only to be shown the door in 1957. The pair soon set up their own animation studio and started turning out television animation, usually aimed towards prime time or afternoon slots. Such shows as *Ruff and Ready* (the studio's first effort,) *The Jetsons* (1962), and *The Flintstones* (1960-1966) were strong successes for the fledgling studio, but it was in the Saturday morning field that its cost-effective techniques made Hanna-Barbera an industry powerhouse.

In order to feed into the huge time and work demands required to develop a half-hour of animation every week, Hanna-Barbera, Ward, and other early television cartoon pioneers developed a wide array of cost-cutting and corner-cutting techniques. Characters were often drawn with a minimum of motion; if a character was speaking, often the only thing moving on the screen was the mouth. Character design was also geared towards efficiency of action. Many Hanna-Barbera characters, such as those in *The Jetsons* or the seminal *Ruff and Ready,* were designed with wide collars so it would be easier to show them turning their head by simply flopping the drawing of the head on the collar.

In some cases, sharp writing made up for the deficiencies in animation. *The Jetsons* and *The Flintstones* were well known for their occasional double entendres. Jay Ward's adventuresome duo of Rocky and Bullwinkle and their friends appeared in a number of incarnations, including a few Saturday morning runs. They were better known for their sharp gags and jokes that worked on two levels than the rough, sketchy animation that characterized them. The Hanna-Barbera studio was not without its share of critics, many of whom felt that its quickie techniques cheapened all of animation. ''Hanna-Barbera proved to the networks that by cutting corners (actually chunks), it was possible to make cartoons cheaply enough for television's needs,'' Erickson quotes Mark Nardone as writing in 1977.

As the 1960s progressed, animation was increasingly seen as a children's medium. As a result, animation was funneled away from the prime-time slots and into Saturday mornings. 1966 marked an important turning point in the history of Saturday morning cartoons; it was the first year that all three major networks (ABC, CBS, and NBC) broadcast animation blocks on Saturday morning. The ongoing struggle for the support of advertisers, the attention of children, and the money of their parents was waged in earnest. Prime-time animation, though not completely dead, was a flagging form.

Comic books and cartoons are first cousins in the world of entertainment media, and comic books often successfully made the jump to Saturday morning. In the 1960s, *Spider-Man, The Fantastic Four,* and *Iron Man* were among the comic book characters who made their mark on Saturday morning. In the 1970s *Superman, Aquaman,* and *Batman* were individual successes, and the three teamed up with other superheroes to form the *Superfriends.* Spider-Man took the team approach early in the 1980s with *Spider-Man and His Amazing Friends.* Comics were strangely absent from Saturday morning for nearly a decade after that, however. In the early 1990s there was another boom of comic-inspired cartoons, including *Batman, Superman* and *Spider-Man* revivals, *X-Men* and *Silver Surfer.*

A recurring trend in Saturday morning cartoons has been the attempt to break through the animation stranglehold and produce successful live-action programs to compete with the animated stars, often in an updated style of the old 1950s live-action host shows. Not surprisingly, the most successful of the live-action Saturday morning programs have been those that have been most similar to cartoons themselves. *H.R. Pufnstuf,* first produced in 1969, and *Mighty Morphin Power Rangers,* which aired in various incarnations in the 1990s, were live-action shows with liberal doses of garish color, surreal design, outlandish costumes, and fast-paced, cartoon-style plots. The most successful of the live-action Saturday morning shows was *Pee Wee's Playhouse* in the mid-1980s, which deposited comedian Pee Wee Herman into a surreal world of talking chairs, puppets, and wacky neighbors. It was perhaps the most effective of the live-action shows at replicating an animated world in a live environment.

An unusual side development of live-action Saturday morning television was the creation of animated shows based on (and sometimes voiced by) real celebrities. *The Beatles* (1965) was the first Saturday morning show to embrace this concept. In decades to come, Kid 'n' Play, the New Kids on the Block, and the Jackson Five were only a few of the musical groups to follow in the footsteps of the Fab Four. Similarly, animated versions of live-action shows, such as *Mork and Mindy, Laverne and Shirley, Punky Brewster,* and *Alf,* were common Saturday morning fare over the years.

Like most other forms of entertainment media, Saturday morning cartoons exemplify the truism ''Imitation is the sincerest form of flattery.'' When the adventures of *The Smurfs,* a band of friendly blue forest dwellers, debuted on NBC in 1981, the program was one of the most successful animated shows ever. *The Smurfs* is often credited with bringing renewed vigor to an art form that had slipped into a creative slump throughout the 1970s. As a result, studios and broadcasters were encouraged to pay even greater attention to the Saturday morning market. Whatever the subjective effects of the Smurfs' success, one thing is clear: everybody wanted a piece of the action. Hence the endless clones that followed, such as *The Care Bears* and *My Little Pony,* further (much further) expounding on the happy and friendly themes that made *The Smurfs* popular.

Saturday morning cartoons made important and lasting changes to the landscape of American popular culture. One distinct change wrought was a subtle but irrevocable shift in the makeup of the week. Sunday may be a day of rest, but Saturday is a day of entertainment. In a very real sense, Saturday became an unofficial holiday, an event manufactured by advertisers and programmers to take advantage of a captive audience home from school with little to do—except, perhaps, park themselves in front of a television set. By and large, parents didn't mind; it offered them relief from the children in the form of an electronic pacifier.

Parent's groups and government agencies expressed concern about the effect the saturation of Saturday morning cartoons might have on children. Violence was their prime concern; as far back as the 1950s, there were those that had expressed dismay at the alien-blasting antics of Space Ghost or Popeye's tendency to solve problems with a can of spinach and an act of violence. In fact, the majority of scholarly attention paid to television animation focused on the question of whether the violence presented was harmful to children. Additionally, parents and regulators feared the growing phenomenon of ''half hour commercials''—cartoons that were primarily meant as long advertisements for the toys and trinkets relentlessly marketed to children.

Under pressure from many fronts over the course of the 1960s and 1970s, the networks imposed firm standards on themselves to avoid having the FCC or some other regulatory agency do it for them. But standards were nonetheless imposed. One important decision by the National Association of Broadcasters in 1969 dictated that advertisements for toys would not be aired during the same show the toys were based on. In other words, no longer would children watching *The Alvin Show* be regaled with commercials entreating them to run out and purchase doll likenesses of Alvin and the Chipmunks. Violent acts were curtailed by the broadcasters themselves, as was any act that might encourage children at home to imitate their onscreen heroes. Such demands required quite a bit of rewriting and revision; even old cartoon shorts rerun on Saturday mornings were subject to the new slash-and-burn treatment, sometimes rendering them incoherent in the process.

In the late 1970s and early 1980s some the networks attempted to head off accusations of being harmful to children by airing cartoons with social messages. Sometimes these messages were incorporated into the actual storyline of the show; Bill Cosby, producer and creator of *Fat Albert and the Cosby Kids* (1972-1979), was a particular proponent of educating children this way. Quite often, however, the lesson came in the form of a short epilogue to an episode that featured characters breaking ''the fourth wall'' and speaking directly to children, expounding on some educational issue or telling them the moral of the day. Erickson writes critically of this trend: ''While some of these prosocial bites came off with sincerity, most appeared to be hastily inserted with an eye-dropper and wedged in with a shoe-horn—a fleeting conscious-stricken afterthought, a forced apology, for *not* educating the viewers within the body of the program.''

In the 1980s, NBC took this one step further by placing popular live-action stars of the day in *One to Grow On*—short vignettes placed between programs that set up a morally tricky situation (from the 10-year-old standpoint) and resolved it with the help of an all-knowing NBC personality. In a similar vein, from time to time programmers and public agencies have tried to take advantage of the Saturday morning youth monopoly by offering programs that were just enough like standard cartoons to capture children's attention but sent a different message. Educational and religious programming often tried to "draw in" viewers to their message with animation as the hook, but most such efforts fared poorly. As anyone with children knows, kids are very savvy TV viewers.

One of the most successful attempts at educational Saturday morning programming was the *Schoolhouse Rock* project, a series of short educational lessons set to song which aired in the late 1970s and early 1980s. *Schoolhouse Rock* served its purpose well by injecting itself into the long-term language of popular culture, which is to say, its message survived longer than three months. In the 1990s, a generation after *Schoolhouse Rock* first bopped its way onto the scene, it experienced a revival of sorts. *Schoolhouse Rock* T-shirts and albums sold well and many college students could still sing along to "Conjunction Junction, What's Your Function?" and "I'm Just a Bill, Sittin' Here on Capitol Hill."

Possibly the most important economic impact of Saturday morning cartoons was the manner in which their merchandising and influence leaked into the mainstream, beginning in the late 1970s. There seemed to be no end to the variety of media in which the animated characters could be displayed. Characters such as the Smurfs smiled at children from lunchboxes, appeared on their clothes, shoes, party favors, napkins, and school supplies. The potential for toy sales was almost limitless for a successful cartoon.

The increasingly lucrative Saturday morning shows also effected a shift in the business dynamic of other creative forms. Many comic books and animated movies are developed with an eye towards big Saturday morning success a few years down the road. The weekly adventures of *The Little Mermaid, Aladdin,* or *Wild C.A.T.s* can go a long way towards sealing the brand name of a character in the minds of children who had already watched the original movie or read the comic book.

Thanks to the advertising and marketing blitz that accompanies the cartoon takeover of Saturday morning, the characters and memories border on the legendary with those who grew up watching them. Better than ninety percent of all Saturday morning characters slipped into television oblivion—few indeed are those who fondly remember the Snorks or the Orbots—but the ones that succeeded catapulted themselves into the popular imagination in a manner normally reserved for popular music stars or actors. Saturday morning has been a haven for television animation since 1950. Although the Saturday morning cartoon form has suffered through slumps, turmoil, regulation, and change, it still remains a viable and successful form.

—Paul F.P. Pogue

FURTHER READING:

Barbera, Joseph. *My Life in 'Toons: From Flatbush to Bedrock in Under a Century.* Atlanta, Turner Publishing, 1994.

Burke, Timothy, and Kevin Burke. *Saturday Morning Fever.* New York, St. Martin's Griffin, 1999.

Crawford, Ben. "Saturday Morning Fever." In *The Illusion of Life,* edited by Alan Cholodenko. Sydney, Australia, Power Publications, 1994.

Erickson, Hal. *Television Cartoon Shows: An Illustrated Encyclopedia, 1949 through 1993.* Jefferson, North Carolina, McFarland & Company, 1993.

Hanna, Bill, with Tom Ito. *A Cast of Friends.* Dallas, Taylor Publishing, 1996.

Heraldson, Donald. *Creators of Life: A History of Animation.* New York, Drake Publishers, 1985.

Kanfer, Stefan. *Serious Business: The Art and Commerce of Animation in America from Betty Boop to Toy Story.* New York, Scribner, 1997.

Minow, Newton N., and Craig LaMay. *Abandoned in the Wasteland: Children, Television, and the First Amendment.* New York, Hill and Wang, 1995.

Woolery, George W. *Children's Television: The First Thirty-Five Years, 1946-1981.* 2 Vols. Metuchen, New Jersey, Scarecrow Press, 1983-1985.

Saturday Night Fever

A film that captures the essence of the disco craze that flowered in the 1970s, *Saturday Night Fever* (1977) is arguably the quintessential document of an era that came, a decade later, to be one of the most ridiculed periods of the twentieth century. Supported by a best-selling

John Travolta, striking a pose in a scene from the film *Saturday Night Fever.*

movie soundtrack and and instantly iconic leading man in John Travolta, *Saturday Night Fever* survived the demise of 1970s cultural artifacts such as polyester, *Soul Train,* and KC and the Sunshine Band, to become a cult classic. The film enjoyed a resurgence in popularity with the 1990s disco-culture renaissance that was heralded by such films as *Boogie Nights* (1997) and *The Last Days of Disco* (1998). Based on a short story by Nik Cohn and directed by John Badham, *Saturday Night Fever* starred Donna Pescow, Karen Lynn Gorney, and Travolta as Tony Manero, an average, Italian-American working man by day, and a disco demigod by night. The role rocketed Travolta to international stardom, while making him as idolized a figure in America as Farrah Fawcett (a poster of whom Tony Manero has on his bedroom wall in the film).

An over-abundance of foggy, disco-ball dance scenes aside, *Saturday Night Fever* is as much a film about what some consider to be the frivolous, politically neutral disco scene of the 1970s as it is about long-standing class and cultural differences. Set in a lower-middle class, Catholic neighborhood of Brooklyn, New York, *Saturday Night Fever* traces Tony Manero's struggle to attain a sense of self-worth in economically depressed, culturally conservative surroundings. The film opens with an aerial shot of the Manhattan skyline that moves across the Brooklyn Bridge in silence until, as the camera reaches Brooklyn itself, the throbbing sounds of the Bee Gees and the noise of traffic chime in as Tony struts down the streets of his neighborhood. Raised by conservative, Catholic parents, and a revered older brother who is a priest, Tony spends all of his free time and money perfecting his image for weekend appearances at the "2001-Odyssey" discotheque, where he excels as a dancer. Tony's function in his community can be likened to that of shaman, according to critic John Cooke in "Patterns of Shamanic Ritual in Popular Film." Neither a priest nor a medicine man, the shaman's function is to cure the sick in his community. On the dance floor, Tony commands ecstatic admiration from his peers and acts as a new type of spiritual savior in the face of Catholic conservatism. His dancing unites and lifts the spirits of his alienated, economically depressed community of peers. The power of his physical presence and prowess, combined with his confident "attitude" is graphically demonstrated in scenes where the crowd parts when Tony hits the dance floor and his friends cheer as he dances his solos. The bartender of the club even calls him Nureyev.

The opposition between the non-ideological impact of the disco scene and the staunch, ideological power of the Catholic Church in the film is underscored in the relationship between Tony and his brother, Frank. When Frank announces that he has lost his faith in religion and will leave the priesthood, Tony's own faith in his talent as a dancer and his belief in the regenerative space of the discotheque grows. After meeting Stephanie McDonald, an older woman from the neighborhood who is enamored with Manhattan and in the process of refining her image, he begins to drift away from his group of friends. Stephanie, a local girl turned posh, presents the key to escape from his neighborhood and entry into the upscale world of Manhattan, just over the bridge.

John Travolta was a trained actor and dancer by the time he landed the role of Tony Manero. He quit school at he age of 16 to pursue acting, studied dance under Gene Kelly's brother, Fred Kelly, and had appeared in several stage productions, a popular television show (*Welcome Back, Kotter*), and a major motion picture by the time he made *Saturday Night Fever.* He reprised his role as Tony Manero

in *Staying Alive* (1983), but the disco craze had faded and so had Travolta's luster. After a long period out of the limelight, Travolta returned to mainstream Hollywood cinema with a string of 1990s hit films, including *Pulp Fiction* (1994), *Phenomenon* (1996), and *Primary Colors* (1998).

—Kristi M. Wilson

FURTHER READING:

Cohn, Nik. "Another Saturday Night." *Life.* Vol. 8, No. 21, 1998, 48-49.

Cooke, John. "Patterns of Shamanic Ritual in Popular Film." *Literature/Film Quarterly.* No. 12, 1984, 50-57.

Sautman, Francesca Canadé. "Women in the Shadows: Italian American Women, Ethnicity and Racism in American Cinema." *Differentia.* Vol. 6-7, Spring/Autumn 1994, 219-246.

Tamburri, Anthony Julian, Paolo A. Giordano, and Fred L. Gardaphé, editors. *From the Margin: Writings in Italian Americana.* West Lafayette, Purdue University Press, 1991.

Saturday Night Live

A landmark of the 1970s, NBC's *Saturday Night Live* challenged America's comic sensibilities with its outrageous and satirical humor in skits such as "The Samurai Warrior," "Wayne and Garth," "The Coneheads," and "Deep Thoughts by Jack Handey," and launched the careers of many of the brightest comedy performers America has ever known, including Chevy Chase, Eddie Murphy, Bill Murray, Adam Sandler, and David Spade. *Saturday Night Live* made President Gerald Ford into the world's clumsiest man. Mock commercials satirized anything and everything. The show made it a policy to feature musical talent usually not found on network television. Its increasing popularity meant that first-season musical guests such as Harlan Collins and Leon Redbone were replaced by the likes of Aretha Franklin and Billy Joel in the 1994 season. *Saturday Night Live* continues to feature bands that are on the cutting edge of new music: the same 1994 season featured Tony Toni Tone and Crash Test Dummies. For a show that debuted in a dead-end spot on NBC's schedule, *Saturday Night Live* has become an institution that seeks to constantly redefine American comedy.

Producer Lorne Michaels first conceived of *Saturday Night Live* as a reaction to the staid, prime-time comedy of American television. Inspired by Britain's *Monty Python's Flying Circus,* Michaels wanted to produce a comedy show that would break all the rules. He wanted to bring the dangerous energy evident in America's comedy clubs to a television industry that he instinctively distrusted. He was lucky to get the moribund 11:30 p.m. Saturday evening slot, and he began to create a comedy variety show. He was constantly quoted as saying he knew the ingredients of the show, but not the recipe. Michaels scoured the underground comedy scene for his writers and performers, and found many in Chicago's Second City comedy troupe. He established a *Saturday Night Live* repertory of actors, the Not Ready for Prime Time Players, and a core of writers who were raised on TV but were

The original cast of *Saturday Night Live*.

ready to break its rules. They were all aware that few comedians with anything serious to say got to do so on network television, where humor was safe and orderly.

On October 11, 1975, *Saturday Night Live* debuted from the NBC studios in New York City's Rockefeller Center. From the first moment, with its trademark cold opening (no credits or titles), the audience knew something different had arrived on late night television. John Belushi played an immigrant who came for English lessons from writer Michael O'Donoghue's professor. As O'Donoghue was teaching Belushi how to say "Would you like to feed your fingers to the wolverines," he suddenly died of a heart attack. A tremulous Chevy Chase, playing the stage manager, walked into camera shot, looked at the audience with a grin, and bellowed: "Live from New York, it's Saturday Night."

At first, the cast took second place to the guest hosts. The exception in the first few episodes was Chevy Chase, a performer who was originally hired as a lead writer. His suave, sophisticated looks and his recurring role as the anchor of the Weekend Update news parody segment soon set him apart from the rest of the repertory cast. The others, Dan Aykroyd, John Belushi, Jane Curtin, Garrett Morris, Bill Murray, Laraine Newman, and Gilda Radner, got their chance to shine on the third show, hosted by Rob Reiner. The cast felt the host was being dictatorial, and when John Belushi came up to him on stage, as a Bee, their backstage resentment poured out on camera: "[W]e didn't ask to be Bees . . . But this is all they [the writers] came up with for us. DO YOU THINK WE LIKE THIS? No, no, Mr. Reiner, we don't have any choice . . . we're just a bunch of actors

looking for a break, that's all! What do you WANT from us! Mr. Rob Reiner, Mr. Star! What did you expect? THE STING?"

Saturday Night Live was determined to challenge all the standards. Michaels himself stepped from behind the camera in April 1976 to offer the Beatles $3000 to appear on the show and sing three songs. He later came back and upped the offer to $3200. In November, George Harrison showed up and tried to claim all the money himself. Michaels again appeared to say that if it was up to him, George could have the money, but NBC wouldn't agree. When Paul McCartney appeared on the show in 1993, he and Michaels were seen talking about the offer during the monologue.

The cast of *Saturday Night Live* went through numerous changes over the years. At the end of the first season, Chevy Chase departed for Hollywood. Bill Murray joined the repertory, but it was John Belushi who ended up star of the show with his manic weatherman, Samurai Warrior, and Joliet Jake Blues characters. In 1979, Belushi and Aykroyd left to make the *The Blues Brothers* film (1980), followed at the end of the fifth season by Lorne Michaels and virtually the rest of his cast and writers. The season that followed saw the show fall in ratings, but it also saw the debut of the brash young Eddie Murphy. Murphy was hidden for most of his first season on *Saturday Night Live*. His first break came during a commentary he co-wrote for Weekend Update. His "Yo, baby," was belted out with force, and his character of Raheem Abdul Muhammed proceeded to steal the show. Murphy appeared in virtually every other Update segment for the rest of the season, and when new producer Dick Ebersol took over the show in the next season, Murphy was the undeclared star. It was Ebersol who moved away from Michaels's repertory idea, hiring tried and true comics to star as part of the cast (including Billy Crystal and Martin Short), but they did not stay with the show for long.

Michaels returned in 1985 as executive producer. He proceeded to reinvent *Saturday Night Live* as America's one true comedy factory, where new and untried performers and comedians could experiment with their art and in the process reinvent television comedy standards. It was Michaels who brought to the show the likes of Dana Carvey, Chris Farley, Phil Hartman, Mike Meyers, and Dennis Miller. In fact, he continued to add to his repertory even when his actors stayed with the show. It has been suggested that he decided to overstaff this time around to protect himself should more of his stars head for Hollywood. Whatever the reason, the show overcame its legendary past to produce some of its most memorable moments: Carvey presented the viewers with his razor-sharp caricatures of "wouldn't be prudent" George Bush and Ross Perot, while Hartman responded with an uncanny President Bill Clinton. Meyers, with Carvey, brought the world into the basement of "Wayne's World" and was shocked at how big the segments became—Aerosmith came to the show as musical guests in February 1990 and demanded to be included in a "Wayne's World" sketch. Two *Wayne's World* movies followed in 1992 and 1993.

Saturday Night Live was still going strong at the turn of the century, while the early shows were being rerun on cable.

—John J. Doherty

FURTHER READING:

Beatts, Anne, and John Head, editors. *Saturday Night Live.* New York, Avon Books, 1977.

Cader, Michael, editor. *Saturday Night Live: The First Twenty Years.* New York, Houghton Mifflin 1994.

Hill, Doug, and Jeff Weingrad. *Saturday Night: A Backstage History of Saturday Night Live.* New York, Beech Tree, 1986.

Partridge, Marianne, editor. *Rolling Stone Visits Saturday Night Live.* Garden City, New York, Dolphin Books, 1979.

Savage, Randy "Macho Man" (1952—)

Randy Savage (Randy Poffo) entered the World Wrestling Federation (WWF) in 1985. Although other wrestlers had been accompanied to the ring by a female valet, the pairing of Savage and his real-life wife Miss Elizabeth, pushed Savage to the top with this "beauty and the beast" gimmick. With a manic ring style, outlandish wardrobe, and strained voice interviews ending with a shout of "oh yea!" Savage quickly won over WWF fans. He was one of the first "bad guys" to be cheered, a trend which took off in the later half of the 1990s with the success of anti-heroes like Stone Cold Steve Austin. A feud with Hulk Hogan—started on NBC's Main Event— culminated in Hogan defeating Savage for the WWF title at Wrestlemania V in 1989. Like Hogan, Savage made public appearances on television talk shows. He also achieved success as the spokesperson for Slim Jim's beef jerky. Savage left the WWF in 1994 to join Hogan in World Championship Wrestling as they resumed their feud, drawing a record gate for their *Halloween Havoc* Pay-per-view match in 1996.

—Patrick Jones

FURTHER READING:

Lentz, Harris M. *Biographical Dictionary of Professional Wrestling.* Jefferson, North Carolina, McFarland & Company, 1997.

Savoy Ballroom

The Savoy Ballroom was the most popular dance venue in Harlem. Many of the dance crazes of the 1920s and 1930s were perpetuated there. The Savoy was a veritable institution that featured the best of jazz bands, competitions, and dancers. Vocalist Ella Fitzgerald made her famous recording of "A-Tisket, A-Tasket" with the Chick Webb Orchestra, the Savoy's house band, later leading the band after Webb's untimely death. Moe Gale (Moses Galewski), Charles Galewski, and a Harlem real estate investor Charles Buchanan opened the Savoy Ballroom to the public on March 12, 1926. Moe Gale was known as "The Great White Father of Harlem," since he discovered and mentored a number of musicians and groups. Charles Buchanan served as manager. The Savoy Ballroom was connected by landline to a New York radio station and often broadcast the bands that played there. It enjoyed a successful run from its opening in 1926 to 1956, when it closed.

First marketed as "The World's Most Beautiful Ballroom" and later as "The Home of Happy Feet," the Savoy was situated on the second floor of a building that stretched for a whole block on 596 Lenox Avenue between West 140th Street and West 141st Street in New York's Harlem. The interior consisted of a large dance floor of approximately 200 by 50 feet, two bandstands, and a retractable stage. Marble stairs were sandwiched between mirrored walls. The springy dance floor bounced from the dancer's feet and was completely renovated every three years. Street car barns occupied the site prior to the ballroom's opening.

Also known as "The Track" because of its early use for dog racing, the Savoy was a dancer's paradise. Different nights drew different clienteles and emphases. Saturday night saw the largest crowds and was known as "square's night" to the regulars because there was not much room to dance. Wednesday and Friday nights were reserved for social clubs and other voluntary associations. Thursday night was known as the "kitchen mechanics' night" since most of the patrons were domestics off for the evening. Tuesday was the night for serious dancers because there was plenty of floor space. The "Opportunity Contest," where money was given to dancers who won first and second prizes, was held on Sunday nights. Sunday night also attracted a number of celebrities. In addition to its black clientele, the Savoy encouraged and welcomed white dancers and spectators. "The lindy-hoppers at the Savoy even began to practice acrobatic routines, and to do absurd things for the entertainment of the whites. Then Harlem nights became show nights for the Nordics," observed poet Langston Hughes.

The Savoy was a place of intense and creative dance activity— new and old steps were refined and taken to new heights in response to the evolution of swing jazz and be-bop. When the Savoy opened in 1926, it instituted a policy that sprightly dances such as the Charleston were forbidden. Two muscular bouncers enforced the rule; but the dancers evaded the policy by creating "the run," a swift step that allowed them to quickly escape the bouncers. Savoy dancers even adapted to the new and difficult-to-dance-to rhythms of be-bop, and the bands that played there likewise created new rhythms in response to the movement of the dancers. The Savoy dancers were known to add "air steps" to the Lindy that later became known as the Jitterbug. Many dance steps were disseminated after dancers at the Savoy Ballroom were filmed so that others could watch and learn the movements.

In its 30 years of existence, the Savoy featured a veritable who's who of jazz bands of the Swing Era. Some bandleaders were inherently associated with the Savoy because of their long residencies there. The first such band was the Charleston Bearcats, who opened the Savoy and later changed their name to the Savoy Bearcats. Fess Williams and His Royal Flush Orchestra and the Fletcher Henderson band also participated in the opening night's ceremonies. In 1927, the Missourians became the Savoy's house band. By 1935, drummer Chick Webb and vocalist Ella Fitzgerald played frequently at the Savoy, several years later becoming the house band and broadcasting nationally. Trumpeter and bandleader Erskine Hawkins achieved great popularity playing at the Savoy from 1939-1941, and continued playing extended engagements through the 1950s. Another group that enjoyed a long association with the Savoy Ballroom was the Savoy Sultans, a swing band led by Al Cooper, that was extremely popular with dancers and played a powerful swing later known as "jump."

Benny Carter, Coleman Hawkins, Andy Kirk, and Glenn Miller, among many other bandleaders, played single engagements at the ballroom.

Chick Webb's band has been inextricably linked to the Savoy Ballroom. In October 1932, the band was renamed Chick Webb's Savoy Orchestra and began setting record-breaking attendances. More than 4,600 patrons came to one breakfast dance. The Webb band, on most occasions, won out in the battles of the bands. One of the band members, alto saxophonist Edgar Sampson, wrote ''Stompin'

at the Savoy,'' the ballroom's theme song. Sampson's ''Stompin' at the Savoy,'' Eddie Durham's ''Harlem Shout,'' and Sy Oliver's ''Raggin' the Scale'' and ''For Dancers Only'' set the riff instrumental formula for dozens of white swing bands from Tommy Dorsey to Miller to Les Brown. ''Stompin' at the Savoy'' was a hit for the Benny Goodman band and ''Big John's Special,'' his encore for his Carnegie Hall performance, was reportedly named after the Savoy's doorman.

The ballroom usually employed two bands that played alternate sets and became famous for the battles of the bands. One band would

A couple swing dancing at the Savoy Ballroom in Harlem, 1947.

spar with the other for the dancer's favor. The Savoy hosted a number of significant band battles during the Swing Era. One long anticipated battle occurred in 1938 between the Savoy's house band, led by Chick Webb, and the Count Basie Band, with the Basie band receiving the longest applause. The Savoy Ballroom was instrumental in the dissemination of swing dance and played an important role in the coalescence of popular dance and music.

—Willie Collins

FURTHER READING:

Kernfeld, Barry, editor. *The New Grove Dictionary of Jazz.* New York, St. Martin's Press, 1994.

Wood, Ean. *Born to Swing.* London, Sanctuary Publishing, Ltd., 1996.

Schindler's List

The highly anticipated film *Schindler's List,* directed by Steven Spielberg and based on a 1982 historical novel entitled *Schindler's Ark* by Australian writer Thomas Keneally, premiered in December of 1993. In a year that had also seen the opening of the Holocaust Museum in Washington, D.C., the film quickly became a cultural event. The public and many critics praised the harrowing but inspirational tale of individual decency in response to the horrors of genocide. The $23 million film was also a box-office success, eventually earning more than $300 million worldwide, in spite of its black-and-white photography and three-hour-plus running time— normally considered audience deterrents. Given the epic film's high public profile and cross-cultural praise, it was not surprising that *Schindler's List* would go on to garner seven Academy Awards in 1994, winning for best picture and giving Spielberg his first-ever best director honors from the Academy. It should be noted that a great many academic critics are troubled by certain aspects of Spielberg's treatment of such sensitive subject matter, particularly in regard to the film's sentimentalized conclusion, the portrayal of Jews as passive victims, and the perhaps-inevitable trivializing of the Holocaust through traditional Hollywood narrative technique. However, even with the shortcomings, the film was generally acknowledged to be Spielberg's most mature, visually striking, and well-crafted work to date. Not even *Saving Private Ryan,* another Spielberg-directed World War II epic that opened to another round of general praise during the summer of 1998, has come close to capturing the cultural impact of *Schindler's List.*

Ralph Fiennes, walking by a line of women prisoners, in a scene from the film *Schindler's List.*

The film and novel differ in dramatic emphasis and characterization but are both reasonably faithful to the details of the real-life story of a Catholic-German entrepreneur named Oskar Schindler, who saved more than one thousand Polish Jews from the Nazi death camps during World War II. As detailed in the novel, Schindler was born in 1908 in the Sudetenland, in an area that would later become Czechoslovakia. As he grew to manhood, Schindler quickly developed a reputation as a carouser and playboy—a reputation founded in reckless actions that even his early marriage in 1927 to a devoutly religious woman named Emilie did not stop. His parents were prosperous in their hometown of Zwittau until the family business, a farm implement factory, went bankrupt in 1935. At this point, the elder Schindler left his wife, and Oskar was forced to seek his living elsewhere. As a salesman and a member of both the Nazi Party and German military intelligence, Oskar traveled alone to Krakow after the German military occupation of Poland in 1939. (This is the point at which Spielberg's adaptation of the novel begins.) In Krakow, Schindler bought an enamel factory that he then staffed with Jewish workers.

Shortly thereafter, the Germans forced the Jews of Krakow to move to a ghetto within the city and also built a forced labor camp named Plaszow outside the city. The extermination camp of Auschwitz began receiving Plaszow inmates during 1942. Throughout the escalating levels of Nazi persecution and brutality directed against Jews, Schindler was able to keep his well-treated Jewish workforce more or less intact, even after the Krakow ghetto was closed in 1943 and all Jews were forced into Plaszow, commanded by a ruthless man named Amon Goeth. Goeth and Schindler formed an unusual relationship: each exploiting the other for personal advantage but nevertheless reluctantly sharing some similarities of taste and lifestyle. (Spielberg emphasizes their duality of character throughout the middle portion of the film.)

Schindler's employees were able to work in his factory by day until 1944, when orders came to send all of Plaszow's Jews to Auschwitz. Through his close contacts with Goeth and others in the German military hierarchy, Schindler somehow managed to receive permission to relocate one thousand Jewish workers to another camp in the relative safety of Czechoslovakia. In one of the most amazing episodes of the Schindler legend, he even retrieved a group of his female employees from Auschwitz, where their train had been mistakenly diverted. At the Czechoslovakian camp, Schindler provided a haven for another two hundred or so escaped Jewish refugees. With the European war's end in May of 1945, the ''Nazi war profiteer'' Schindler and his wife were forced to flee the camp ahead of its Russian liberators.

After the war, Schindler moved from Austria to Argentina to West Germany, eventually leaving Emilie. He proved consistently unable to make any kind of living and in the end had to rely for daily survival on the financial largesse of the Jews he had so protected during the war. He also visited Israel yearly, all expenses paid by Jewish organizations and individuals. The Holocaust memorial in Jerusalem, Yad Vashem, recognized Schindler as a Righteous Gentile in 1962. He died, perhaps predictably given his lifestyle, of liver failure in 1974 and was buried in a Catholic cemetery in Jerusalem.

The story of Oskar Schindler remained in relative obscurity until the early 1980s, when author Thomas Keneally published *Schindler's Ark*. The historical novel had its origins in a 1980 visit by Keneally to a luggage store in Los Angeles, where Keneally met the storeowner—a Jew who had been rescued by Schindler. Intrigued by the owner's dramatic tale of the long-ago events, Keneally interviewed dozens of the *Schindlerjuden* (Schindler Jews) in several different countries and researched the relevant documents in Israel and Poland. After Keneally's book was published as *Schindler's List* in America, Universal Studios acquired it for development. Director Steven Spielberg, about to achieve yet another spectacular box-office success with *E.T.: The Extraterrestrial,* read the book and was determined that he, too, when he felt he was a mature-enough filmmaker, would someday tell the story of Oskar Schindler.

Ten years passed, during which Spielberg alternated between taking on the project and passing it to others. Finally, in 1992, Spielberg believed the time was personally and historically right to begin active production on the film. He made several important and risky artistic decisions: to use black-and-white film, to shoot on location in Europe, to rely heavily on handheld cameras, to select European extras, and to cast nonstars in the key roles (Liam Neeson as Schindler, Ben Kingsley as Schindler's Jewish accountant Stern, and Ralph Fiennes as Amon Goeth). In spite of Spielberg's determination to use authentic locations, some were unavailable: Spielberg had to painstakingly reconstruct the Plaszow camp; and when his request to film inside Auschwitz was denied by the World Jewish Congress, he and production designer Allan Starski built a chillingly convincing replica directly outside the grounds. After principal photography was finished, Michael Kahn edited the film to its three-and-a-half-hour running length, and longtime Spielberg collaborator John Williams composed the musical score.

The final result, released to theaters at the end of 1993, was generally well received and capped one of Spielberg's most personally and financially successful years ever. (Earlier that summer, his film *Jurassic Park* had earned nearly $360 million domestically.) Many critics reevaluated their previous dismissal of Spielberg as a skilled but trivial filmmaker. But more significantly for history, with the profits from *Schindler's List,* Spielberg established two organizations: The Righteous Persons Foundation, dedicated to memorializing Gentile rescuers of Jews during World War II, and the Shoah Visual History Foundation, set up to record the first-hand accounts of Holocaust survivors before the passage of time silences their voices.

—Philip Simpson

FURTHER READING:

Loshitzky, Yosefa, ed. *Spielberg's Holocaust: Critical Perspectives on Schindler's List.* Bloomington, Indiana University Press, 1997.

Palowski, Franciszek. *The Making of Schindler's List: Behind the Scenes of an Epic Film.* Secaucus, New Jersey, Carol Publishing Group, 1998.

Perry, George. *Steven Spielberg Close Up: The Making of His Movies.* New York, Thunder's Mouth Press, 1998.

Schlatter, George (1932—)

Television producer-writer-director George Schlatter's credits are impressive. He has produced special programming featuring a Hall of Fame of entertainers, from Nat King Cole to Elton John, Frank Sinatra to Michael Jackson, Judy Garland to Bette Midler. He founded the American Comedy Awards, an annual televised event that spotlights the accomplishments of funny-men and women. Over the years he has earned more than two dozen Emmy nominations, and a quartet of Emmy Awards.

Schlatter's greatest contribution to television, however, was as co-executive producer (with Ed Friendly) during the initial—and funniest—seasons of *Rowan & Martin's Laugh-In. Laugh-In,* which aired between 1968 and 1973, was a fast-paced hour crammed with goofy, irreverent sketch comedy. While its often surreal sensibility evolved from Ernie Kovacs's pioneering television humor, *Laugh-In* itself was to alter the future of television comedy from the pacing of sitcom buffoonery to the structure and content of such sketch comedy shows as *Saturday Night Live.* The show also served as the launching pad for the careers of Goldie Hawn and Lily Tomlin.

—Rob Edelman

Schlessinger, Dr. Laura (1947—)

With an estimated weekly listening audience of 18 million, Dr. Laura Schlessinger ranks as the most popular talk radio personality of the late 1990s, surpassing even Rush Limbaugh and Howard Stern. An advocate of high ethical standards and personal accountability, Schlessinger—known to her fans simply as Dr. Laura—takes to the airwaves for three hours each weekday to offer her "never to be humble opinion" on various moral dilemmas. Employing her own brand of tough love, Schlessinger, guided by her Judeo-Christian faith, preaches to her callers, frequently chastising them for their behaviors and nagging them to mend their ways. It is this abrasive manner which causes her to be alternately hailed for her stern morality and criticized for her intolerance of contrary viewpoints. But despite assertions that Schlessinger's message is one of hate, punishment, and vengeance, her audience has continued to grow. Her radio talk show, nationally syndicated in June of 1994, built an audience of 10 million in its first two years; her syndicated column runs in 55 newspapers nationwide, and her self-help books continuously top bestseller lists. Her overwhelming popularity indicates she is doing something right, and many people, including Schlessinger, attribute this success to her tough talk and impeccable timing.

Following nearly three decades of "me generation" ethics—as defined by Fritz Perls' 1960s credo, "I do my thing and you do yours"—Schlessinger offers a radically different message: one of personal responsibility. She challenges her listeners to improve their character by employing a strong moral code when making decisions rather than relying on emotions. In a 1996 interview with Amy Bernstein for *U.S. News and World Report,* Schlessinger stated that between the 1960s and the 1990s Americans, ". . . erected a

Dr. Laura Schlessinger

monument to feelings and made them the vantage point from which to make decisions. That's dangerous.'' Instead, Schlessinger instructs her listeners to take responsibility for their actions by making rational choices and doing the morally correct thing, regardless of emotion. As strident as she sometimes sounds, her message is one Americans want to hear. Indeed, after witnessing numerous high profile personal and political scandals, the American populace has grown tired of excuses. Instead, the public craves integrity, commitment, candor, and conscience—all keystones in Schlessinger's definition of character, and all part of a new counter-culture Americans appear to be embracing. During the presidential elections of 1992 and 1996, ''family values'' were at the foundation of every campaign platform, indicating that Americans were anxious for a return to the simplicity of life symbolized by the 1950s.

In addition to her moral message, Schlessinger offers the idea that individuals have ultimate control of their lives, claiming that even physical addictions such as alcoholism are a matter of personal choice. According to Schlessinger, a person can choose the direction his life will take by practicing self-restraint and religious faith. In a society where many people feel their lives are spinning out of control because violence appears commonplace and marriage is no longer a sacrament, hers is a message which offers stability amidst the chaos.

But for every American who embraces Schlessinger's message, there is another who rejects it. Her critics describe her as narrowminded, self-righteous, and prudish, primarily due to her stances against live-in relationships—which she refers to inimically as ''shacking up''—premarital sex, abortion (in most cases), and gossip. Additionally, Schlessinger regularly badgers listeners who engage in such behaviors, telling them to ''grow up,'' ''stop whining,'' or ''quit cold turkey,''—advice her detractors fault for its harsh, black-and-white nature. Ironically, this is precisely the kind of advice that keeps listeners rushing to their telephones. On average, nearly 50,000 callers vie for a moment on-air with Dr. Laura, seeking her matter of fact opinions, regardless of how severe they may be.

The issue which draws the biggest fire, however, is Schlessinger's position on child care. As evidenced by her assertion following every commercial break that she is, first and foremost, ''her kid's mom,'' children rank high on her agenda. She espouses the belief that once a child is born, a parent should put everything on hold—specifically a career—to stay home and care for that child. In most cases, she believes the at-home parent should be the mother, explaining that women are better and more natural nurturers, especially during a child's first few years. In Schlessinger's view, day-care centers are inadequate methods of child care, and largely to blame for delinquent, immoral, or irresponsible youths who suffer from a lack of one-on-one time with their parents. This view is criticized by many who say Schlessinger abuses her powerful position by placing unnecessary guilt on parents—especially working mothers—and demanding unhealthy amounts of self-sacrifice. Adding more fuel to the fire is Schlessinger's assertion that the feminist movement is responsible for breaking up families by encouraging women to put their own needs before those of their children.

In addition to their disenchantment with her message, detractors have tagged Schlessinger as both a fraud and a hypocrite. The fraud charge stems from her use of the address ''doctor'' on air. While she does have a Ph.D., it is in Physiology, not Psychology, as many listeners may assume. While Schlessinger does have a post-doctoral certificate in Marriage, Family, and Child Counseling, and did practice as a Licensed Marriage, Family, and Child Counselor for 12 years, critics worry that some callers may assume her knowledge of

psychotherapy to be more vast than it is. As for being a hypocrite, detractors cite Schlessinger's assertion that people must accept their faith in whole while simultaneously breaking with her own faith on two important issues. She excuses abortion in cases where the mother's life is in danger, and condones homosexuality, saying it is an issue she and God will work out later. In response, Schlessinger states that the particulars of morality can always be debated; her focus is on the lifelong struggle to be a person of character. Needless to say, Schlessinger's position as ''America's moral compass'' inspires devotion, antipathy, and above all, controversy wherever her message is heard.

—Belinda S. Ray

FURTHER READING:

Bernstein, Amy. ''Dr. Laura Schlessinger's Moral Health Show.'' *U.S. News and World Report.* April 29, 1996, 19.

Perls, Frederick S. *Ego, Hunger & Aggression: A Revision of Freud's Theory & Method.* N.p., Gestalt Journal Press, 1992.

Schlessinger, Laura C. *How Could You Do That? The Abdication Of Character, Courage and Conscience.* New York, HarperCollins, 1997.

———. *Ten Stupid Things Men Do to Mess Up Their Lives.* New York, HarperCollins, 1997.

———. *Ten Stupid Things Women Do to Mess Up Their Lives.* New York, Harperperennial Library, 1995.

Vogel, Stewart, and Laura C. Schlessinger. *The Ten Commandments: The Significance of God's Laws in Everyday Life.* New York, HarperCollins, 1998.

Schnabel, Julian (1951—)

The emergence of artist Julian Schnabel as a mythical figure was a phenomenon of the modern art world in the 1980s. Once considered the bad boy of the New York art scene, Schnabel seemed to rise to prominence from nowhere. After earning a bachelor of fine arts degree from the University of Houston, Schnabel toured Europe before returning to his home of New York City. On his journeys both stateside and abroad, while living a bohemian lifestyle, Schnabel tackled many occupations, including cab driver and cook. Once he began painting as a profession, Schnabel's ability for self-promotion propelled him into the limelight.

Enormous canvases filled with vibrant colors and bold strokes typify Schnabel's paintings. With his first exhibition at Mary Boone Gallery in 1980, which launched him into the New York art scene, he gathered a following for his emotion-filled unusual works. By the time he exhibited his work in a show jointly organized by Boone and Leo Castelli in 1981, he had become firmly established, and a clamoring for his neo-expressionist paintings created on and with remarkable surfaces ensued. Schnabel's signature works, both abstract and figurative, have as a base surface either black velvet or broken crockery. Filled with raw emotion, the paintings contain an underlying edge of brutality while still being suffused with energy. Schnabel claims that he's ''aiming at an emotional state, a state that people can literally walk into and be engulfed by.'' The monstrous canvases have elements of collage, yet his arrival as an artist signified

Julian Schnabel

the return of painting to an art scene that previously revolved around conceptual and minimalist art.

Schnabel's quick rise to popularity became representative of the money-driven 1980s. His notoriety exemplified the commercialization of the art world that related to the economic boom. Considered heroic, with his charismatic and somewhat eccentric personality—the artist worked in pajamas, slippers, and robe—Schnabel became a superstar in art. Controversially, his persona, carefully hyped, often outshone the artwork itself, which inspired debate by critics as to whether it actually held any artistic merit. To the art-buying public, Schnabel's work was the work to own, and his exhibitions often sold out. A proficient artist who worked quickly, Schnabel once claimed to have sold more than sixty canvases in one year. Typifying the era, many critics judged Schnabel's success as an artist based on the incredible demand for his work. With the recession of the late 1980s and the stabilization of the economy in the 1990s, Schnabel's star faded somewhat.

While Schnabel continued to paint successfully through the 1990s, he explored other art forms. In 1996, he wrote and directed the movie *Basquiat*. The $3.3 million independent film related to the life and struggles of his friend and fellow artist Jean-Michael Basquiat. This proved to be a fairly triumphant endeavor, realizing some commercial and critical recognition and success. Schnabel's foray into the cinematic arena again proved his mastery at adapting to the current trends, and this addition of filmmaker to his persona further solidified his reputation as modern artist.

—Jennifer Jankauskas

FURTHER READING:

McEvilley, Thomas, with Lisa Phillips. *Julian Schnabel: Paintings 1975-1987*. London, Whitechapel Art Gallery, 1987.

Schnabel, Julian. *C. V. J.: Nicknames of Maitre D's and Other Excerpts from Life*. New York, Random House, 1987.

Schoolhouse Rock

The *Schoolhouse Rock* series of animated musical shorts that ran on the ABC network on weekend mornings from 1973 to 1985 dazzled a generation of young viewers raised in front of the television. Vibrant, catchy, exuberant, fast-paced, and entertaining: they were also educational and instructive about basic grammar, mathematics, science, and American history.

David McCall, president of New York's McCaffrey and McCall advertising agency, conceived the series. He had observed that his young son had trouble learning his multiplication table but easily and happily recounted the lyrics and music of popular songs. Working with his agency colleagues, McCall commissioned some songs about mathematics and presented them to Michael Eisner, then vice-president of children's programming at ABC (and future chairman of the Walt Disney Corporation), and Chuck Jones, famed for his Bugs Bunny, Daffy Duck, and Road Runner cartoons. ABC bought the series and General Foods sponsored it. The first animated shorts, a series of songs with titles such as "Zero My Hero" and "Three Is the Magic Number," appeared in January 1973. In the early 1970s, Saturday morning cartoons became an institution and the networks were under pressure to run programming that was perceived as having social value. In 1974, the FCC established guidelines for children's programming in an effort to improve their educational content. In this regard, *Schoolhouse Rock*'s timing was perfect.

Over the next 12 years, ABC aired over 41 of these animated musical pieces, running as many as seven different spots in one weekend. The spots were broken into five subject areas: multiplication, grammar, American history, science, and computers. For the "Multiplication Rock" series, the creative team wrote songs concerning the multiplication products from zero to twelve (excluding one), while "Grammar Rock" informed viewers of the parts of speech. "America Rock" was created for the American bicentennial in 1976 and its songs detailed the American Revolution, the Constitution, the westward expansion, racial diversity, and women's suffrage. Later series included "Science Rock" and "Scooter Computer & Mr. Chips."

The series won four Emmy Awards, making McCaffrey and McCall the first advertising agency ever to win the coveted television prize. Advertising art directors working at McCaffrey and McCall, as well as at the Young and Rubicam agency, created most of the designs, and many of the songs were penned by copy and jingle writers. The language of advertising drove the three-minute spots, featuring vivid images supported by a catchy tune and continuous repetition of a key message. As a method for teaching a generation raised on television, *Schoolhouse Rock* was anticipated somewhat by the animated segments interspersed between live action sequences on the Public Broadcasting System's successful *Sesame Street* television program, which debuted a few years earlier. But in style, look, feel, and tone, the series was unique in children's programming.

The creative team that grew out of McCaffrey and McCall created all but a few of the original pieces during the 1970s. The design, colors, and lyrics of the spots were in tune with the aesthetic and the ethic of this era—more so than many of the Saturday morning cartoons and advertisements alongside which they ran. Visually, they were more faithful to the work of underground comic-book artist R. Crumb and the Beatles movie *Yellow Submarine* (1968) than to cartoons by Walt Disney or Hanna-Barbera. The *Schoolhouse Rock* images were bright, colorful, simple, and playfully psychedelic. The colors were earthy, the hip lyrics accessible and vernacular, and the jazzy music had a rock and roll edge. The tone was optimistic and the outlook diverse. The spots presumed that everyone was capable of learning simple mathematics and grammar, and celebrated American history and civic life. The animated spots included refreshingly non-stereotyped people of color, a rarity in the medium.

Among the more renowned *Schoolhouse Rock* pieces was "Conjunction Junction" which asked, "Conjunction junction, what's your function?" while a manic train conductor linked various colored boxcars as an illustration of the conjunction's grammatical role in "Hookin' up words and phrases and clauses." In another well-known spot, a young boy visiting the Capitol spots a "sad little scrap of paper" that turns out to be a bill under consideration by Congress. "Bill" pines to become a law and plaintively sings his predicament to the boy: "I know I'll be a law some day / At least I hope and pray that I will / But today I am still just a bill." Bill then musically explains to the boy the precise legislative process he must endure to become a law.

As the Reagan administration deregulated broadcasters' duties in the area of children's programming in the early 1980s, there was less pressure to include educational pieces during commercial air-time. Production of the program was discontinued in 1985 and ABC took the series off the air. However, in the early and mid-1990s, as the generation that was raised on *Schoolhouse Rock* grew up to become Generation X, the series experienced a resurgence. College students led a national petition drive to bring it back on the air, and in 1993 ABC began re-running the spots and commissioning new ones. That same year, the musical stage show, *Schoolhouse Rock Live*, opened, eventually running on Broadway and across the country. The original songs were re-released on CD and, in 1996, were also re-recorded by popular musicians of the day and released as *Schoolhouse Rock Rocks*. The animated spots themselves were released on video. An "Official Guide" was published by some of the creators in 1996 and *Schoolhouse Rock* T-shirts and other popular paraphernalia began to appear.

Schoolhouse Rock was not only one of the many inventive and original cultural phenomena of the 1970s, but unique as a cultural creation that a generation returned in force to retrieve.

—Steven Kotok

FURTHER READING:

Engstrom, Erika. "Schoolhouse Rock: Cartoons as Education." *The Journal of Popular Film and Television*. Vol. 23, Fall, 1995, 98-104.

Yohe, Tom, and George Newall. *Schoolhouse Rock! The Official Guide*. Hyperion, New York, 1996.

Schwarzenegger, Arnold (1947—)

Born in Austria and naturalized as an American citizen in 1983, Arnold Schwarzenegger is one of the main Hollywood male icons of the 1980s and 1990s. Schwarzenegger—Arnie, as he is known to his fans—has used his spectacular body as a passport to fame, gaining celebrity in bodybuilding contests. Arnie won in 1968 (the first of five times) the title of Mr. Universe, the world's top bodybuilding distinction. He used his initial popularity as a sportsman to start businesses including real estate, gyms, and diet products. The next phase in his rising business career included film stardom, which he reached in the 1980s despite his limited acting skills. Consolidated in the early 1990s as both Hollywood star and businessman, Schwarzenegger is rumored to be planning a political career. This could lead him to run for governor of California.

Schwarzenegger's acting career began with a role as Hercules in a mediocre television film. His first memorable screen appearance was as himself in George Butler and Robert Fiori's documentary on bodybuilding contests, *Pumping Iron* (1977). But Schwarzenegger definitively entered stardom thanks to two roles. One was Robert Howard's sword and sorcery hero Conan in *Conan the Barbarian* (1982) and *Conan the Destroyer* (1984); the other, the ultraviolent cyborg sent from the future to eliminate the mother of mankind's

Arnold Schwarzenegger as "The Terminator."

future leader in James Cameron's *The Terminator* (1984). A number of action films followed, among them the box-office hits *Predator* (1987) and *Total Recall* (1990). In the same period, Arnie started playing leading roles in Ivan Reitman's comedies *Twins* (1988) and *Kindergarten Cop* (1990). Since then, his main hit has been the sequel to *The Terminator, T2* (1991). He has also starred in a rather long list of interesting films, including *True Lies, Eraser,* and the much underrated *Last Action Hero* and *Junior,* in which he played a pregnant daddy. Schwarzenegger became Hollywood's best paid villain with the role of Mr. Freeze in *Batman and Robin* (1997), for which he reaped $25 million.

Several factors contribute to Schwarzenegger's popularity. He is a self-made man in two senses—he has ''made'' his body and has ''made'' himself. He embodies health and heroism, and is, no doubt, perceived as a father figure. Yet each aspect of his success is in itself ambiguous, even contradictory. To begin with, his thick Austrian accent clashes with his roles as all-American hero. Despite his impressive physical appearance, he seems to be more popular with children than with women, who have never seen him as a sex symbol. His harsh facial features—deeply set eyes, prominent cheekbones and jaw—by the 1990s somewhat mellowed by age, and also apparently by cosmetic surgery, have allowed him to play both heroes and villains. Few actors could have successfully transformed, as he did, the murderous first Terminator into the heroic fatherly Terminator of the sequel. Still, this new father has no future and is sacrificed in the end. This capacity to cross the line between good and evil on the screen (and also that between comedy and the action film) seems also closely intertwined with his capacity to quickly overcome the failure of some of his films, such as *Jingle All the Way* and *Last Action Hero.* Schwarzenegger is, in short, a much more malleable, flexible star than he might seem at first glance. This may be, indeed, the secret of his success.

Schwarzenegger's public image is based on his self-presentation as family man and entrepreneuring American citizen, roles that contrast with those he plays in his often violent movies. His long-lasting marriage to journalist Maria Shriver of the Kennedy family has fuelled speculations on his future as a politician. Ironically, although a Catholic like the Kennedys, he is a staunch Republican, having even acted as Counselor for Fitness during the presidency of George Bush. As a public figure Schwarzenegger has also been involved with the Special Olympics, the Inner City Games, diverse charities devoted to caring for sick children, and the Simon Wiesenthal Center. But when he was awarded a Wiesenthal National Leadership award in 1991 for his generous funding of the Center, a museum devoted to the Jewish Holocaust, malicious tongues hinted at young Arnie's alleged involvement with Nazi politics. The open-heart surgery Schwarzenegger underwent shortly before his fiftieth birthday prompted some to insist that this icon of health is in fact a very sick man, placed too early at the gates of death by his (acknowledged) use of steroids in the height of his bodybuilding days. His detractors seemingly find his success as excessive as his body.

Possibly, the key to Schwarzenegger's success is the fierce control he exerts on his career and his innate ability to market himself. Schwarzenegger has confessed his addiction to the public's admiration and his wish to present himself as a role model. He has argued that the lucky combination of the Austrian sense of discipline and the American sense of opportunity are the foundation of his successful career. He is, no doubt, a competitive man gifted with a knack for self-promotion, exuding a positive kind of self-confidence with which people love to identify. But he is also, as David Thomas has noted, a

new phenomenon . . . the star as bully. Schwarzenegger wants, above all, to be in the public eye and for that he has constructed a persona—a mask—that seems impervious to the contradictions that surround him. Nigel Andrews, his unauthorized biographer, insists on the elusiveness of the real man behind the star, speculating that Arnie does believe in the myths he himself has invented. This may be, after all, the fittest definition of Schwarzenegger: he is the star who never doubts himself.

—Sara Martin

FURTHER READING:

Andrews, Nigel. *True Myths: The Life and Times of Arnold Schwarzenegger.* London, Bloomsbury, 1995.

Flynn, John. *The Films of Arnold Schwarzenegger.* New York, Citadel Press, 1996.

Jeffords, Susan. *Hard Bodies: Hollywood Masculinity in the Reagan Era.* New Brunswick, Rutgers University Press, 1994.

Neale, Steve. ''Masculinity as Spectacle: Reflections on Men and Mainstream Cinema.'' *Screen.* Vol. 24, No. 6, 1983, 2-17.

Tasker, Yvonne. *Spectacular Bodies: Gender, Genre and the Action Cinema.* London and New York, Routledge, 1993.

Thomas, David. *Not Guilty: In Defence of the Modern Man.* London, Weidenfeld and Nicolson, 1993.

Science Fiction Publishing

Science fiction is a popular literary genre, abutting such fictional fields as techno-thrillers, fantasy, horror, and the ''lost world'' narratives of the early twentieth century. Less frequently it overlaps spy novels, mysteries, and romantic fiction; it occasionally even surfaces as ''serious'' literature. With varying degrees of success, science fiction narratives and themes have been translated into movies, television, radio dramas, comics, games, and (in one instance) opera. Science fiction has created or popularized such concepts as spaceflight, extraterrestrials, time travel, atomic war, genetic engineering, and ecological disaster. Science fiction mirrors the apprehensions and anticipations of an age; it is increasingly the product of a society that is concerned about the relationship between its continued existence and its dependence upon technological development and scientific knowledge beyond the comprehension of laymen.

Those seeking a worthy pedigree for science fiction have found its ancestors in the works of H.G. Wells and Jules Verne, Mary Shelley's *Frankenstein,* Rostand's *Cyrano de Bergerac,* and *The Golden Ass* of Lucius Apuleius. All were published in their time as ordinary literature without stigma. Modern science fiction is the natural child of those classics, given birth in the ''pulps'' of the 1920s and 1930s, neglected and even despised by its legitimate relatives, and occasionally raised to prominence.

Imaginative stories—notably Edgar Rice Burroughs's tales of Tarzan and John Carter's adventures on Barsoom—had appeared for decades in magazines like Munsey's *All-Story.* In the 1920s fashion changed, however, when general interest fiction magazines lost circulation to more narrowly focused publications, and the remaining

Cover of *Amazing Stories*, August 1927.

readers demanded fiction with ever more conventional settings. Authors without name recognition were thus pushed toward genre magazines, which paid less well but accepted their stories without qualms. Readers with specialized tastes—for interplanetary sagas, plainly told detective yarns, and G-9 and his Battle Aces—defected as well to the newer magazines, which in turn made the general interest publications even more conservative. Ultimately, even Burroughs, Abraham Merritt, and Ray Cummings were banished to the pulps.

By early 1919, Street and Smith's *Thrill Book* already specialized in imaginative literature; it lasted for 16 issues. *Weird Tales*, whose metier was blood-curdling fantasy, fared better, circulating from 1923 to 1953. By general agreement, the first true science fiction magazine was Hugo Gernsback's *Amazing Stories*, which began in April 1926. (The publisher's name is commemorated today in the "Hugos," much-coveted awards presented annually at the official World Science Fiction Convention—a fan-dominated event which Gernsback himself helped institute.) Technically, neither *Amazing Stories* nor the clones later started by Gernsback (*Science Wonder Stories, Air Wonder Stories*) began as pulp magazines, for they were printed on 8.5" x 11" "bedsheet size" paper instead of 7" x 10" sheets.

The distinction of being the first science fiction pulp waited upon January 1930 and the Clayton chain's *Astounding Stories of Super-Science*. From the beginning, *Astounding* outdid its competitors, paying contributors more (with rates of one to two cents per word) and establishing a steady, secure distribution. In addition, *Astounding* was better edited. Both Harry Bates (1930-1933)—who wrote the story which became the movie *The Day the Earth Stood Still*—and F. Orlin Tremaine (1933-1937) were only adequate writers, but excelled as editors who believed in the future of the new genre. Their pursuit of quality and encouragement of new writers secured better authors and better stories for *Astounding,* which helped the magazine build up a higher circulation and to become profitable more quickly than its rivals. These aspects aided *Astounding*'s return from the grave when the Clayton chain fell into bankruptcy in 1933, and the rapid rebuilding of its circulation after the Street and Smith takeover of the Clayton chain in 1933. As of 1998 the magazine was named *Analog Science Fiction and Fact* and published by Dell Magazines.

Tremaine's hand-picked successor, John W. Campbell Jr. (1937-1971), proved to be brilliant. A 27-year-old, well-regarded, but second-string author of superscientific romances (that he was also the author of the moody "Don A. Stuart" stories was generally unknown), Campbell quickly mastered the editorial skills of his mentor and moved on to shape the magazine's—and for a while, the field's—philosophy. Gernsback, mesmerized by turn-of-the-century experimental science, had favored stories whose narrative element was often little more than sugar coating around a core of semi-imaginable technological achievements. Campbell, better educated, and an inveterate tinkerer, controversialist, and promoter of science fiction, placed equal emphasis upon the science and the impact of science and technology upon human beings. Campbell was also a stern advocate of plots with logical consistency, many of which he devised himself and cast wholesale at his contributors in an unending series of letters which doubled as mini-lectures on writing style and technique.

The different emphasis did not make humanists of Campbell and his evolving school of authors—A. E. Van Vogt, Theodore Sturgeon, George O. Smith, C. L. Moore, Henry Kuttner, Robert Heinlein, L. Sprague de Camp, Isaac Asimov, etc. Pulp fiction was fast moving, easily comprehensible, and generally devoid of moral ambiguity; its readers were not disposed to look below the textual surface for deconstructive ironies, and if they had been, they would generally have been disappointed. At a penny a word, writers took no pains to be subtle; they seldom found time to do second drafts.

Fortunately, readers were easily satisfied. Rather than avant-garde literary values, readers of science fiction sought the affirmation of moral or ideological views: that justice was obtainable in a corrupt society in the detective magazines, that courage and gentlemanly virtues coexisted in adventure tales. Science fiction magazines promised an expanding technological and technocratic future and provided ever more grandiose descriptions of action and scenery. Whether the readers sought "transcendence" or a "sense of wonder," this fiction had little to do with the private epiphanies that climaxed much "literary" fiction.

Moreover, pulp fiction was ephemeral. Some pulp authors cracked the book market for detective stories, but most writers' work perished as the yellowing, brittle pages of the magazines crumbled away. A handful of specialist reprint publishers—among them Gnome Books, Shasta, Fantasy Press, Prime Press, and Arkham House—appeared to publish imaginative fiction, but their print runs were small and their material limited. No one expected pulp science fiction to last through the ages, and no one expected to make a living writing it. As the 1930s and 1940s wore on, readers and writers of science fiction were increasingly isolated from the literary values that came to prominence with modernism.

Defenders of science fiction's merits are prone to point at certain masterpieces of the genre, works so carefully told not a comma seems misplaced, so heartbreakingly beautiful that it seems their readers must break into tears. Included among these masterpieces are *More*

Than Human by Theodore Sturgeon, *Childhood's End* by Arthur C. Clarke, *The Year of the Quiet Sun* by Wilson Tucker, *Dying Inside* by Robert Silverberg, and *The Man in the High Castle* by Philip K. Dick. Advocates also list the utilitarianism offered by science fiction as a predictor of inventions used in the modern world—from Verne's Nautilus to Heinlein's waldoes—and the impact of those inventions on modern lives. At the end of 1945, Campbell was predicting in his magazine that men would reach the moon by 1950, and that *Astounding* would be on sale there in 1955. Robert Heinlein's projections, in a 1947 letter to the *Saturday Evening Post,* were only slightly paler, with a moon landing in 1952 and a permanent base there in 1962. But science fiction writers were not alone in contemplating how technology impacted modern lives, as *Collier's* and Walt Disney would demonstrate in the next decade. And science fiction writers had foretold atomic energy, which had become a reality with the devastation of Hiroshima and Nagasaki.

Despite the reality of atomic energy and the promise of space flight, however, there was no great increase in science fiction's prestige in the immediate wake of the war. Much of the internal esprit de corps of Campbell's school had evaporated. The genre was aging; its practitioners were retiring or moving on to other fields. By the early 1950s new authors had come to prominence; this later generation was often better trained in the sciences than their predecessors, more attuned to good prose, more sophisticated politically and more reflective. By large they labored in similar obscurity. Only Arthur C. Clarke would achieve a real reputation among the general public, and that not until 1969, although 1980s film goers might recognize the names of Philip Dick and Frank Herbert.

A few things were different, however. Blessed with a good agent, Robert Heinlein had found it possible in the late 1940s to sell short fiction to the *Saturday Evening Post,* becoming the first pulp science fiction writer to break that market. Later on, Ray Bradbury also made it to the slicks, but for most science fiction authors such high-paying sales remained aspirations rather than reality until *Playboy* proved a receptive audience. Heinlein broke more new ground in 1947, when Scribners published his original *Rocket Ship Galileo,* a novel specifically aimed at teenagers. Throughout the 1950s, he, Andre Norton, Fred Pohl, Jack Williamson, Lester del Rey, Isaac Asimov, and others would write for the juvenile market. Sales were not great, since the hardbound editions usually wound up in public libraries and few were reprinted before the 1960s (Norton proved the exception), but the books were well read, allowing Heinlein to spread his pro-space flight "propaganda" and Asimov to describe the wonders of science to a new crop of readers.

Anthologies of science fiction stories also appeared after the war. Sales were good enough to encourage Simon and Schuster to bring out A. E. Van Vogt's *The World of A* in 1948. In 1950, Doubleday published Max Ehrlich's *The Big Eye,* Asimov's *Pebble in the Sky,* and Heinlein's *Waldo and Magic, Inc.* At last, major publishers were willing to print science fiction between hard covers. Soon thereafter Ace Books and other soft cover publishers were reprinting those editions and original material themselves. For science fiction writers who could break into this market, it was suddenly possible to tell a science fiction story for more than one or two cents a word; it was even possible to tell a story which would pay royalties for years afterward. One could actually make a living as a full time writer.

But not everyone, for the book market was not large enough for all the magazine writers, and the publishers preferred novels to stories. As late as 1959, even Heinlein's story collections *The Menace*

from Earth and *The Unpleasant Profession of Jonathan Hoag* were first printed in hardback by small press publisher Gnome Books, reaching a mass audience only later through paperback. Through the late 1950s, in terms of volume science fiction continued to be a magazine phenomenon. The magazines were smaller than before, the paper of better quality, and the story telling more sophisticated, but circulation figures were small, ranging from 20,000 to no more than 100,000 at *Astounding* (whereas *Playboy* had sales of 2 million by at the end of decade, the *Saturday Evening Post* over 5 million). To make up for this, there were many magazines, twenty to thirty at a time, often no longer lived than mayflies, but all—if briefly—markets for aspiring writers.

The boom in American science fiction magazines peaked in 1953, with 174 issues of 36 magazines. Thereafter the number of magazines fell off first slowly, then abruptly in 1958 when the American News Service folded. Twenty science fiction magazines ceased publication in 1958; sales of those which remained were cut in half. The survivors learned to rely on subscribers rather than newsstand sales. This brought stability, but at a cost; the magazines became increasingly set in molds. Late 1950s issues of *Astounding* and *F&SF* sometimes seemed parodies of themselves in happier times, and of course, without impulse buyers, total circulation figures did not increase. Like other publications, the science fiction magazines also faced competition from television and the increasing volume of paperback books. These juggernauts were not to be defeated; a handful of magazines limp on today with stable (and small) lists of subscribers, but they are peripheral to the film and book markets; most self-professed science fiction "fans" do not read them.

A full account of science fiction in the 1950s would be incomplete without mention of the movies and television, from *Them!* (1954) to *Twilight Zone* (1959-1965). It is enough to note that Hollywood's version of science fiction was a separate art form, with strengths and weaknesses of its own, and that until the 1970s, the influence ran one way: the movies used some themes of genre science fiction, but had virtually no effect on magazine fiction and novels. A similar story could be told of the comics, except that *Superman* and *Flash Gordon* stayed closer to their literary roots.

What noticeably did not happen to science fiction in the late 1950s and 1960s was any improvement in its respectability and sales figures with the advent of the Space Age—a mystery perhaps best explained by the notion that the general public does not want firsthand acquaintanceship with technology and is thoroughly suspicious of science's offerings. Certainly the general repute of scientists deteriorated as the 1960s wore on (as did that of most authority figures). Even that triumphant symbol of science fiction perspicaciousness—the first manned flight to the Moon in July 1969—failed to satisfy; as many Americans (49 percent according to one poll) disapproved of the Apollo program as those who favored it, and space exploration has languished ever since.

Instead, in extraordinary numbers, readers of science fiction (and many authors) turned to the field of heroic fantasy, as exemplified by J. R. R. Tolkein's *Lord of the Rings* trilogy and the Conan tales of Robert E. Howard. The same authors often write both science fiction and fantasy, the same readers buy both genres (more or less, although fantasy is reputed to appeal more to women than does science fiction), and the same publishers print both, so distinguishing between them may be wasted effort. Fantasy's allure continues to increase, and its sales may now rival or even surpass those of traditional science fiction. The material generally runs low on literary merit (with some honorable exceptions, including C. J. Cherryh, Glen Cook, Joel Rosenberg) but brims over with action, villainy, and schmaltz; admirers of Dunsany and Cabell would be disappointed by the generally solemn mood. In tone and style, this material is redolent of the pulps, without the 1930s touch of class consciousness— American fantasy readers turn up their noses at proletarian protagonists but adore heroic lords, ladies, and royalty.

In retrospect, the science fiction of the 1960s looks very like what one might expect of science fiction published during that era. By 1950s standards, it was rebellious. Authors as diverse as Robert Heinlein and Philip Jose Farmer chose sex as their subject matter (Farmer was more successful); others touched upon drugs (Frank Herbert) and mysticism (Philip K. Dick). English authors toyed with surrealism and the multiple-viewpoint characterization of John Dos Passos; these fifty-year-old literary techniques became renowned as a "New Wave." Stylistic experimentation coincided frequently with opposition to the Vietnam War and embrace of "alternative life styles." In the 1970s, Vietnam's fall made political argument pointless; authors perceived that the New Wave was on the ebb, wrote their "unprintable" stories for Harlan Ellison's *Dangerous Visions* series of anthologies, and moved on to cyperpunk and fast paced militaristic sagas.

Meanwhile, the great American public moved on to horror fiction. Horror, one might think, is an offshoot of fantasy, and might be expected to have the same sort of readership and perhaps the same authors. This has not been the case. To generalize, science fiction fans read fantasy and vice versa and the same authors may write in both genres. Science fiction and fantasy readers, however, are not automatically fans of horror. In any event, they form only a small portion of the readership for horror; most horror readers are uninterested in science fiction and fantasy, and most horror writers are not linked to science fiction. This seems rather strange, since science fiction and fantasy elements are often prominent in horror works (consider Stephen King's *The Tommyknockers*), but the visceral appeal of the three genres is evidently quite different.

In the 1980s war novels, in the form of near-future "techno-thrillers" by Tom Clancy, Larry Bond, Steven Coontz, and others made a return to publishing prominence. As with horror, despite the apparent overlap with science fiction, high tech military fiction is a separate market. It has proven impenetrable to science fiction authors, even to those who specialize in military science fiction.

During this period, movie science fiction has passed through several phases, from low-budget "B" movies in the 1950s to studio-breaking spectaculars in the 1970s. In this last period, movies did influence the literary science fiction market: part of making these big-budget films profitable involved extramural marketing of all kinds and the book publishers cooperated to the hilt, with novelizations of the scripts, cocktail table volumes showing off *The Art of Star Wars,* and the like. These in turn have created an audience for novels set in Star Wars settings, semi-facetious non-fiction such as *The Physics of Star Trek,* autobiographies by some principal actors, and even series of novels by those actors (or with those actors' names on the covers). These spinoffs continued to be profitable into the 1990s, producing a slew of science fiction "readers" who seemed familiar with the literature primarily through movies and television. This is good news for publishers; whether the market for science fiction outside the Star Wars-Star Trek "Universes" has increased is another issue.

For all its claims to prescience, science fiction since World War II has been more shaped by popular culture than shaping. The atomic wars and mutants of the 1950s are obvious tokens of the Cold War and ambivalence about atomic energy. The mismanaged battles and angst-torn protagonists depicted in the military science fiction of the 1970s (most memorably, Joe Haldeman's *The Forever War*) were parables of the Viet Nam experience, and the comic book heroics of soldiers in 1980s stories reflected the revival of American morale during the Reagan era. Sagas of pollution, overpopulation, and genetic engineering gone awry also draw more from day-to-day experience and commonplace observation than from esoteric scientific knowledge. Even the omnipresent computer and internet have developed largely without anticipation by science fiction writers; technology evolves today at a faster pace than science fiction authors can accommodate in their stories.

Conservatism has tended to be the norm in recent science fiction's treatment of lifestyles. Despite some claims, science fiction has never been a good medium for presenting feminist ideas, it has not advanced gay rights, and until the 1980s it had problems with multiculturalism. In the 1990s, gay and lesbian characters could be used, but they tended to be in the background; non-Western protagonists were equally unusual. A woman's viewpoint is sometimes used--ironically, male authors seem to do this with more skill. (Deserving of note is C. J. Cherryh's approach of using as protagonist a low-status, insecure male who in the climax must prove himself worthy of a domineering, high-status female love interest.) A similar lack of nerve is present in 1990s-vintage science fiction's treatment of political and economic topics, a rather surprising development given the political consciousness of most authors and the large number of stories dealing with socioeconomic trends in the 1950s and 1960s.

At the end of the 1990s, genre science fiction seemed to be reaching exhaustion. Some magazines continued, notably *Analog, Isaac Asimov's,* and *F&SF.* In technique and literary quality, their material was not much different from the 1940s or 1950s vintages; the "Can Do!" spirit was much rarer.

In book publishing, after a slump in the early 1980s, the flow of both hardbacks and paperbacks continued unabated. Science fiction works tended to be profitable in a small way; they were seldom best-sellers, but since modern technology made print runs of under 5000 copies practical, that had not mattered. With the consolidation of the publishing industry in the 1990s, presumably to be paid for by concentration on best-sellers, and the ever- increasing importance of bookselling chains and "superstores," the situation may change. If so, desktop publishing has already given rise to a new generation of small press operators; methods of distribution need to be improved but science fiction novels and anthologies will likely continue to find a home.

A related trend is the almost universal rejection of over-the-transom manuscripts by major American publishers. It has become very difficult for unagented writers to break into the commercial science fiction field, and difficult even for established authors with mediocre sales to find their manuscripts considered, regardless of merit; this has harmed the careers of European authors who had relied on American sales for the bulk of their income, and probably made science fiction a more insular and parochial field in the 1990s than it was in the 1960s. The book market has effectively adopted the star system; a relative handful of authors can hope to achieve success through being well known and well publicized, while others linger in the shadows. A number of Old Guard authors have died in the last two decades, most notably Robert Heinlein, Isaac Asimov, Clifford Simak, and Theodore Sturgeon. Authors of the later period—Poul

Anderson, Hal Clement, Arthur Clarke, Gordon Dickson, Robert Silverberg, Jack Vance—have reached their 60s or 70s and are declining in productivity. None of their possible successors seems likely to reach the heights attained by Heinlein or Clarke.

Science fiction is ceasing to be a medium in which ordinary authors can make a living simply by writing. Publicity is a necessity for the modern author—frequent convention attendance, a web page, negotiated advertising figures in book contracts, etc.—and ceaseless self-marketing. We need anticipate no shortage of authors who will undergo such rigors; the question an outsider must ponder is whether such a career is as rewarding as the ''school teacher's'' existence L. Sprague de Camp once saw as characteristic of science fiction writers.

Increasingly, the fiction itself, as it attempts to fit itself to the realities of the modern world, seems tired. The excitement of space travel and the expectation that technology may bring wonders to the world are no longer part of the science fiction writers repertoire. Governments are unlikely to underwrite exploration or innovation, modern writers know, and thus books like Michael Flynn's *Fire Ship* and Poul Anderson's *Harvest of Stars* show space flight as the product of gifted, obsessed entrepreneurs stamped from the mold of Ayn Rand's tycoons. Great inventions are now devised by misfits rather than heroic leaders; their impact on the world is often inadvertent, and more often than not, gruesome. In recent science fiction, planetary pioneers are met by bureaucrats and pummelled by paperwork; we learn that it will be hard to colonize new worlds, it will be expensive, it will be tedious, and about as adventurous as sidewalk superintending. In direct contrast to earlier science fiction, which proposed that the future was full of exciting possibility, much recent writing offers the thrilling prospect that the future will be glum and unrewarding. Undoubtedly, this approach brings science fiction closer to ''serious literature.'' But it is not one likely to increase readers or to inspire them with a sense of wonder.

—Mike Shupp

FURTHER READING:

Chapdelaine, Perry A., Sr., Tony Chapdelaine, and George Hay, editors. *The John W. Campbell Letters.* Vol. 1. Franklin, Tennessee, AC Projects, 1985.

Davenport, Basil, editor. *The Science Fiction Novel: Imagination and Social Criticism.* Chicago, Advent, 1959.

De Camp, L. Sprague, and Catherine C. de Camp. *Science Fiction Handbook, Revised.* Philadelphia, Owlswick Press, 1975.

Delaney, Samuel R. *The Jewel-Hinged Jaw: Essays on Science Fiction.* New York, Berkeley Publishing, 1977.

Heinlein, Robert. *Grumbles from the Grave.* New York, Del Rey Books, 1989.

Knight, Damon. *In Search of Wonder: Essays on Modern Science Fiction.* Chicago, Advent, 1956, 1967.

Malzberg, Barry N. *The Engines of the Night: Science Fiction in the Eighties.* Garden City, New York, Doubleday, 1982.

Panshin, Alexi, and Cory Panshin. *The World Beyond the Hill: Science Fiction and the Quest for Transcendence.* Los Angeles, Jeremy P. Tarcher, 1989.

Platt, Charles. *Dream Makers: The Uncommon People Who Write Science Fiction.* New York, Berkley Books, 1980.

Pohl, Frederick. *The Way the Future Was: A Memoir.* New York, Del Rey Books, 1978.

Rogers, Alva. *A Requiem for Astounding.* Chicago, Advent, 1964.

Spinrad, Norman. *Science Fiction in the Real World.* Carbondale, Southern Illinois University Press, 1990.

Warren, Bill. *Keep Watching the Skies! American Science Fiction Movies of the Fifties.* 2 vols. Jefferson, North Carolina, McFarland and Company, 1982, 1986.

Scientific American

The reliable and readable scientific writing published in the *Scientific American* has instructed and entertained readers since its foundation in 1845, and the magazine occupies a unique position in the culture of science. Early readers felt an affinity for the magazine because of its personal contact with inventors. Clarifying patent procedures, the magazine's editors answered readers' questions, stimulated their creativity, and encouraged their ambitions. By being accessible to, and interactive with, its readers, whether nineteenth-century tinkerers or twentieth-century rocket scientists, the magazine had a significant impact on the development, understanding, and acceptance of science in America. Throughout the twentieth century, it remained at the forefront in providing informative articles about current and emerging technology, covering the space age, the development of modern pharmaceuticals, and philosophical debates about science. The *Scientific American,* indeed, has chronicled the inventive spirit of America in the nineteenth and twentieth centuries.

The first issue of *Scientific American* was dated August 28, 1845, and appeared weekly until monthly editions began in November 1921. Inventor Rufus Porter created *Scientific American* in New York City. Experimenting with electrotyping, Porter produced a four-page periodical focusing on new inventions. The early *Scientific American* sold for two dollars per copy and had the subtitle ''The Advocate of Industry and Enterprise, and Journal of Mechanical and Other Improvements.'' At that time, unique technological achievements were forming American industry, and several magazines, such as the monthly *Journal of the Franklin Institute,* addressed the topics of patents and mechanics as applied to mining, transportation, and manufacturing.

Porter served as *Scientific American*'s first editor until Munn & Company purchased the magazine in 1846. Orson Desaix Munn and Alfred Ely Beach, the son of *New York Sun* publisher and inventor Moses Y. Beach, jointly invested money in printing their first edition of *Scientific American* on July 23, 1846. They focused on providing information about patented inventions, including the official list of patents approved by the United States Patent Office. Because so many hopeful inventors asked for help with the patenting process and laws, the partners created a patent agency. *Scientific American* described the models of inventions their clients brought them, among them Thomas Edison's 1877 phonograph. The thriving agency attracted such major inventors as Samuel F.B. Morse, Captain John Ericsson, and Elias Howe. The pages of *Scientific American* published a few lines about every invention the agency promoted, even obscure and unsuccessful ideas, thus revealing insights into the history of invention in the United States.

Expanding to eight pages, the September 26, 1846, *Scientific American* remarked that the editors strived to ''furnish an acceptable family newspaper'' and ''give in brief and condensed form the most useful and interesting intelligence of passing events'' while ''avoiding the disgusting and pernicious details of crime.'' Although inventions dominated the news, information about other aspects of science were included. Circulation reached 10,000 subscribers by 1848, doubling to 20,000 in 1852 and hit 30,000 the next year. While other scientific periodicals struggled for survival, *Scientific American* succeeded, merging with *The People's Journal* in 1854 to boost readership. Readers especially liked such features as Salem Howe Wales's letters from the 1855 Paris Exposition.

In July 1859, *Scientific American* began producing a new series of semi-annual volumes. A Washington D.C. bureau of Munn & Company opened with Judge Charles Mason, a former commissioner of patents, acting as a legal advisor to inventors. During the Civil War, the journal commented primarily on military inventions, and after the war improved its appearance with engraved illustrations and larger pages, increasing the price per issue to three dollars. Also, their editorial and financial support for construction of an underground pneumatic tube 21 feet below Broadway in 1870 increased public curiosity both about inventions and *Scientific American.*

In 1885 Munn & Company founded the monthly *Scientific American: Architects' and Builders' Edition,* later known as *Scientific American Building Monthly.* Demand for specialized periodicals and the incentive to profit from increased advertising resulted in Munn & Company catering to business construction, and they hired architects to provide building plans featured in the magazines. By January 1905, the company was publishing the monthly *American Homes and Gardens* with the subtitle ''New Series of *Scientific American Building Monthly*''; this magazine was absorbed by *House and Gardens* in September 1915. The *Scientific American* house also published export and Spanish editions.

Scientific American featured many inventions and their applications years before the American public was familiar with those ideas—for example, horseless carriages were pictured, with plans for construction, for half a century prior to the popularization of automobiles in America. Such major events as the Chicago World's Fair were also covered and *Scientific American* was the primary source of information for many industries. Promoting aviation, they chronicled the efforts of the Wright Brothers and sponsored monetary prizes for aerospace achievements. The editors were, however, critical of unscientific efforts and designs.

In 1911 the *Scientific American,* for which government, industrial, and university professionals penned articles, began publishing a ''mid-month number'' focusing on a specific topic such as agricultural science or reviews of automobiles. The special issue bore a colored cover, which the main magazine also adopted. The June 5, 1915, issue celebrated the publication's seventieth anniversary, and two years later the price rose to four dollars an issue, with the format by then resembling popular magazines of the era in size and print. The 1919 printers' strike, however, resulted in the suspension of the weekly supplement. Declining circulation due to competitive specialist magazines caused *Scientific American* to become a monthly magazine in 1921 to save costs. Munn & Company changed its name to Scientific American Publishing Company, and the magazine stopped printing lists of patents. No longer primarily an inventor's magazine, it attempted to transmit scientific information to the American public as a popular science magazine. ''It has been the constant aim of this journal to impress the fact that science is not inherently dull, heavy or abstruse,'' an editorial stated, ''but that it is essentially fascinating,

understandable, and full of undeniable charm.'' In the post-World War II era, a revised *Scientific American* reached out to the segment of the community that was already scientifically literate and yearned to learn more. The modern *Scientific American* expanded in size and cost, had glossy covers and illustrations, and increased circulation to hundreds of thousands of readers.

—Elizabeth D. Schafer

FURTHER READING:

Borut, Michael. ''The *Scientific American* in Nineteenth Century America.'' Ph.D. dissertation, New York University, 1977.

Burnham, John C. *How Superstition Won and Science Lost: Popularization of Science and Health in the United States.* New Brunswick, Rutgers University Press, 1987.

Mott, Frank Luther. *A History of American Magazines 1850-1865.* Vol. 2. Cambridge, Harvard University Press, 1938.

''Scientific American.'' http:\www.sciam.com. April 1999.

Scientology
See Hubbard, L. Ron

Scopes Monkey Trial

One of the most sensational court cases in twentieth century America, the Scopes Monkey Trial went infinitely beyond the boundaries of law and the courtroom to question the social, intellectual, and cultural values of America. The explosive and passionate conflicts instigated by the arguments in the case of the State of Tennessee vs. public schoolteacher John T. Scopes in 1925 characterized the decade in which they took place. On one side stood those who emphasized secularism, science, new ideas and theories, and individual self-expression; on the other side stood religious dogma and traditionalism. Thus, there was a bitter division between those Americans who wanted change, and the many others who clung to repressive notions of conformity, moral purity, and order.

The battleground for this conflict between new and old ideas was the public school system within which John Scopes taught Darwin's Theory of Evolution, which contradicted the Bible's interpretation of the origins of man. Although by the 1920s, Darwin's principles were being taught in most American universities and public schools, the middle of the decade brought a concerted drive by religious fundamentalists to stop the teaching of evolution in the schools. School boards, individual schools, and many states in the South prohibited the teachings in public schools of any theory about the origins of human life that conflicted with the teachings of the Bible.

In 1925, the American Civil Liberties Union (ACLU) announced that it was willing to financially support anyone challenging a recently enacted Tennessee law that prohibited the teaching of Darwin in the state's schools. John T. Scopes, a 25-year-old high-school science teacher in Dayton, Tennessee, who taught evolution in his school biology class, accepted the ACLU offer and agreed to stand as the defendant in a test case to challenge the law. On the initiative of

In the courtroom at the Scopes Monkey Trial.

Scopes' friend George Rappelyea, the teacher was reported to the police for breaking the new law, arrested, and sent for trial. A number of prominent legal counselors, led by the famous liberal trial lawyer Clarence Darrow, undertook the defense of Scopes. The prosecuting attorney was William Jennings Bryan, former Secretary of State, three-time Democratic candidate for president, one time Populist, and now a leader of the new fundamentalist movement in Christianity.

During the summer of 1925 the Scopes Monkey Trial grabbed national and international headlines. Almost a thousand people packed the Tennessee courtroom daily, and millions more listened to the proceedings—it was the first trial ever to be broadcast live on the radio. Judge John T. Raulston, a conservative Christian who started each day's court proceedings with a prayer, did not allow the defense to bring any expert scientific testimony about evolution. As a result, Darrow called prosecuting attorney Bryan, an expert on science and religion, as his only witness, and systematically proceeded to humiliate him. With his probing questions, Darrow led Bryan to declare that a big fish had swallowed Jonah, that Eve was literally created from a piece of Adam's rib, and that in 2348 B.C. the world was flooded and fish and animals escaped onto Noah's ark. The press mocked Bryan's literal interpretation of the Bible, thus undermining the fundamentalist cause.

At the conclusion of the hearings, Darrow asked the jury to return a verdict of guilty in order that the case might be appealed to the Tennessee Supreme Court where, he hoped, the anti-Darwin law would be overturned. The jury, complying with Darrow's request, returned a verdict of guilty and Judge Raulston fined Scopes $100. Publicly humiliated and exhausted, Bryan died just a few days after the trial. A year later, however, the decision of the Dayton court was overturned by the Tennessee Supreme Court on a technicality.

Although Scopes was convicted, and the existing anti-evolution law remained on the Tennessee statute books, many Americans

perceived the religious fundamentalist cause as the loser in the trial. The existing statutes banning Darwin's theories were never enforced and evolution continued to be taught in the schools. Moreover, the need for the separation of theology from general education became even more firmly entrenched in the minds of many Americans. Everywhere, prayer and other religious activities were eventually abolished in the public schools.

The Scopes Monkey Trial, wearing only the thinnest of disguises in that the names of the place and the protagonists were changed, became the subject of Jerome Lawrence and Robert E. Lee's successful Broadway play *Inherit the Wind*(1956), which was turned into a film in 1960 with Spencer Tracy and Fredric March as Darrow and Bryan, respectively.

—John F. Lyons

FURTHER READING:

Conkin, Paul K. *When All the Gods Trembled: Darwinism, Scopes, and American Intellectuals.* Lanham, Maryland, Rowman & Littlefield, 1998.

Furnis, Norman F. *The Fundamentalist Controversy.* New Haven, Yale University Press, 1954.

Hansen, Ellen. *Evolution on Trial.* Lowell, Massachusetts, Discover Enterprises, 1994.

Larson, Edward J. *Summer for the Gods: The Scopes Trial and America's Continuing Debate Over Science and Religion.* New York, Basic Books, 1997.

The World's Most Famous Court Trial: Tennessee Evolution Case (complete record of trial). Cincinnati, National Book Co., 1925; Union, New Jersey, Lawbook Exchange, 1997.

Scorsese, Martin (1942—)

By the end of the 1990s, Martin Scorsese was recognized as one of the most significant of American film directors. His uncompromising cinematic examination of New York City's underbelly, beginning with *Mean Streets* (1973), has exerted a profound cultural influence on cinemagoers and filmmakers. Scorsese was initially one of a select group of innovative young filmmakers, famously dubbed the Movie Brats, who began making a mark during the 1960s and went on to secure major reputations. By the 1990s, Francis Ford Coppola, who had led the way for the Movie Brats, had become a venerable but unpredictable artist, veering dizzily between huge successes and dismal failures; George Lucas, the creator of *Star Wars,* was long entrenched in trailblazing technology; Brian De Palma was committed to a controversial, individualistic and uneven course as a skillful specialist in screen violence; and Steven Spielberg reigned as the acknowledged *eminence grise* of the blockbusting commercial cinema. Of them all, it was Scorsese who, with *Taxi Driver* (1976), *Raging Bull* (1980) and *GoodFellas* (1990) as the high watermarks of three decades of filmmaking excellence, had emerged as the most consistently powerful and provocative film director of his generation.

Scorsese's own background provided the fertile soil in which his filmmaking ambitions took root. Born in New York to a first generation Italian-American family, he grew up in Manhattan's Little Italy, the setting of his first full-length features. A sickly child, much confined indoors by asthma, he became addicted to movies at an early age. In the 1960s, he abandoned ambitions to become a Catholic priest

Martin Scorsese

and joined the New York University film school, where he wrote and directed several award-winning shorts, including *The Big Shave* (1968), while the ideas germinated for his first full-length feature, *Who's That Knocking at My Door?* (1969). Starring the young Harvey Keitel, making his film debut, the story concerned an Italian-American trapped by his working-class background and ever present Catholic guilt, which would become characteristic Scorsese themes. Made on a very low budget, the film combined realistic street scenes with *nouvelle vague* techniques that revealed Scorsese's self-confessed enthusiasm for the European cinema of the time, and can be seen as a basic template for work to follow. He then hired himself out as supervising editor on *Woodstock* (1969) and *Elvis on Tour* (1972), and had a directorial breakthrough when Roger Corman gave him *Boxcar Bertha* (1972), a Depression-era tale of Arkansas misfits who turn to robbing trains.

It was, however, with *Mean Streets* that critics and the industry were alerted to the arrival of a major new talent. The film traversed similar territory to that of his first, dealing with the life of streetwise youth and petty crime in Little Italy, and once again starred Harvey Keitel. Pulsating with felt life (and a pounding rock soundtrack) in its depiction of friendship, betrayal, guilt, and casual violence, the film packed a punch and unleashed an electrifying Italian-American New York actor whose future collaboration with Scorsese would result in a handful of major films on which the director's reputation rests: Robert De Niro. After *Mean Streets* came the heavily contrasting *Alice Doesn't Live Here Any More* (1974), a studio picture for Warner Bros. and a tough, contemporary "slice of life" take on the Hollywood "woman's weepie," which won a Best Actress Oscar for Ellen Burstyn.

Then in 1976, came the most completely realized example of Scorsese's particular vision of New York as a hell-on-earth, and the first of his unsurpassed major films with De Niro. Moving away from the bonding of brothers, friends, and hoods that had characterized *Mean Streets, Taxi Driver* focused on an alienated, disturbed loner, the taxi-driving Vietnam veteran, Travis Bickle, whose abhorrence of anti-social behavior he encounters in the city sends him over the edge into psychopathic violence. Self-appointed to cleanse the city of its pimps, prostitutes, and other human detritus, Bickle embarks on a spree of organized savagery, calculated with impeccable logic from his point of view. As Bickle, De Niro gave one of the best screen performances of the later twentieth century, aided by Paul Schrader's penetrating screenplay and Bernard Herrmann's atmospheric and Oscar-nominated score. The film, which introduced a teenage Jodie Foster, Oscar-nominated as a drug-addicted whore, also received nominations for best picture and best actor. Director John G. Avildsen actually won the best picture and director Oscars that year for the highly commercial *Rocky,* but the signal failure of the Academy even to nominate Scorsese as director of *Taxi Driver* displayed a gulf in appreciation for Scorsese's work between the Hollywood powerbrokers who vote at Oscar time and respected critics and serious moviegoers—a gulf which, by the late 1990s, had still not been entirely bridged.

Scorsese and De Niro followed *Taxi Driver* with *New York, New York* (1977), a cynical musical in which De Niro, co-starring with Liza Minnelli, played a saxophonist. This film, much under-rated, was a box-office failure, as were two later excursions into new subject matter—that of ironic comedy—*King of Comedy* (1983, with De Niro) and *After Hours* (1985), both brilliant. After making the "rockumentary" *The Last Waltz* (1978), Scorsese began the 1980s with *Raging Bull* (1980), which many consider to be his masterpiece. Based on the autobiography of heavyweight boxer Jake La Motta, the film—shot in black-and-white—revealed the interior as well as exterior violence of the fight profession and its deleterious effect on the life and relationships of its protagonist. With an astonishing and authentic Oscar-winning performance by De Niro at its center, the film laid bare the brutality of its subject matter, both in the ring (the fights are filmed with uncompromising accuracy, grace, and alternating speed) and out; similarly, the performances are sheer rage, and the documentary style of the domestic scenes resonates with the verbal blows. The whole film, technically flawless, was enhanced by the editing of Thelma Schoonmaker, an integral fixture of Scorsese's team. This time, at least, the Academy nominated both film and director, but the awards went to Robert Redford and his *Ordinary People.*

During the 1980s, continuing his attempts to vary his choice of material, Scorsese successfully entered more reliably commercial territory with *The Color of Money* (1986), a sequel to Robert Rossen's classic, *The Hustler* (1961), starring Tom Cruise and Paul Newman in a reprise of his original role. From there, Scorsese placed himself at the center of an international controversy with *The Last Temptation of Christ* (1988). Adapted by Paul Schrader from the Nikos Kazantzakis novel, the film presents Christ (Willem Dafoe) as a fallible human, a victim of circumstance, who longs to escape his destiny and live the life of a normal man. Overlong and verbose, but rich in ideas and striking photography (by Michael Ballhaus), *The Last Temptation* suffered from the welter of pre-release condemnation it drew, but its director did earn an Oscar nomination, and the film has continued to occupy a respected place in the canon of his work.

In 1989, Scorsese's New York joined that of Woody Allen (and Coppola) in the triptych anthology *New York Stories,* after which came *GoodFellas* (1990) and *Cape Fear* (1991). Adapted by Scorsese and Nicholas Pileggi from the latter's book about real-life Mafia hood Henry Hill, *GoodFellas* joined *Taxi Driver* and *Raging Bull* as a Scorsese masterwork. Starring Ray Liotta and a galaxy of America's finest character actors, including De Niro and Joe Pesci in support, the film graphically depicts the criminal sub-culture in all its shoddy vaingloriousness and misplaced devotions in a masterful blend of uncompromising violence and an exposure of the corruption it renders within the individual. As a piece of filmmaking, *GoodFellas* dazzles with its technique and control, enthrals with its plot, and entertains with its relationships, wisecracks, threats, and performances. It does not, however, neglect to make manifest the complexity of the moral issues that abound within the enclosed world it inhabits. Screenplay and picture were Academy Award-nominated; the director was not.

Opinion remains divided about *Cape Fear.* Once again technically expert, this remake of the 1962 film that had starred Robert Mitchum as a convict released from prison and seeking sadistic vengeance against the lawyer who got him convicted cast De Niro—covered in full-body tattoos—in the Mitchum role. An unqualified success in the delivery of tension and menace, *Cape Fear* bludgeoned its audience with shock tactics and conveyed an unmistakable voyeuristic nastiness that many found hard to swallow. The *New York Times* called it Scorsese's "worst picture—an ugly, incoherent piece of work."

The director—who also makes cameo acting appearances in several of his own films, and in some made by others (Bertrand Tavernier's *Round Midnight,* 1988, and Kurosawa's *Dreams,* 1990, among them)—having commenced both the 1980s and the 1990s with a masterpiece, now turned to a classic literary source to venture into his first period piece. The announcement that this tough chronicler of the sordid, the sleazy, and the violent would film Edith Wharton's

stylish, scathing and poignant Pulitzer Prize-winning novel about a love affair thwarted by the morals and manners of New York high society, was greeted with undisguised scepticism. However, *The Age of Innocence* (1993), set in the 1870s, and starring Daniel Day-Lewis, Michelle Pfeiffer, Winona Ryder, and a starry supporting cast of British actors, marked a complete and impressive change of pace for Scorsese. He rose to the challenge of opulence, elegance, and oblique and disappointed passions with taste, style, and a sumptuous visual display at once seductive and powerful. The film was almost entirely overlooked at Oscar time, but Scorsese did, at least, receive a nomination as co-writer (with Jay Cocks) of the screenplay.

It was unfortunate that after such innovation, perseverance, and restraint, *Casino* (1996) turned out an overblown excursion back into *Goodfellas* territory, set this time amidst the rampant neon-lit greed of Las Vegas, and with De Niro's presence contributing little. *Kundun* (1998), however, signalled a return to higher ambition, as Scorsese made the leap into another culture, philosophy, and place to recount the early years of the Dalai Lama in Tibet. It is a stately film of poetic imagery, and for all the criticism it attracted for its "Western" view of the East, it is an epic—reminiscent of Bernardo Bertolucci's Oscar-winning *The Last Emperor* (1987)—of profound psychological and spiritual impact. Although *Kundun* won Scorsese another nomination for Best Director (he did not win) and the Academy seemed to look on his work with increased favor, it seemed possible that he might someday join the list of great directors, including Orson Welles and Alfred Hitchcock, who never received Hollywood's supreme accolade, the Academy Award, for their incomparable contributions to the art of film.

—Stephen Keane

FURTHER READING:

Dougan, Andy. *Martin Scorsese—Close Up.* London, Orion, 1998.

Pye, Michael, and Linda Myles. *The Movie Brats: How the Film Generation Took Over Hollywood.* London and Boston, Faber, 1979.

Ryan, Michael, and Douglas Kellner. *Camera Politica: The Politics and Ideology of Contemporary Hollywood Film.* Bloomington, Indiana University Press, 1988.

Scorsese, Martin, and Michael Henry Wilson. *A Personal Journey with Martin Scorsese Through American Movies.* London and Boston, Faber, 1997.

Thompson, David, and Ian Christie, editors. *Scorsese on Scorsese.* London and Boston, Faber, 1996.

Scott, George C. (1927-1999)

At once a commanding presence on the screen and a subtly nuanced character actor, George C. Scott was a significant force in American theater, film, and television for almost fifty years. A workmanlike actor, who had always spread his focus among all of the available stages, Scott the man was almost as hard-boiled and sensitive as the characters he played. With little patience for fuss or pandering, he was never a publicity seeker; nonetheless, publicity sought him out, sometimes for his quietly principled stands, but often simply because of his incredibly prolific career.

Born in Wise, Virginia, and raised in Detroit, George Campbell Scott spent World War II in the Marine Corps. When he was

George C. Scott as General George S. Patton.

hack films, such as *Exorcist III,* notable for little else than his august presence. His craggy face, imposing size, and trademark raspy growl might tend to typecast an actor with less skill and versatility, but Scott managed to play everything from tragedy to farce to rugged adventurer. He also succeeded in portraying a widely-diverse range of characters, from sleazy gangsters to tender grandpas, from an antisocial aging Huckleberry Finn (*The Boys of Autumn,* Broadway, 1986) to "Old Blood and Guts," the megalomaniacal General George Patton.

It is perhaps the character of Patton, in the 1970 film of the same name, that will remain as being most identified with George C. Scott. Scott, who once called Patton "a once-in-a-lifetime part," read thirteen biographies of the famous general to prepare for the part. His portrayal of the controversial general is still recognized as a tour de force, and immortalized Patton in a way that the general's checkered military career did not. The other enduring legacy of the film is the famous incident when Scott refused his Best Actor Oscar for the role. Though he had been nominated for Academy Awards before, Scott had made very public his distaste for the Academy's voting methods and for the whole notion of competition among actors. He had announced his intention to refuse the Oscar if it was awarded to him, and, indeed, was home in bed when the award was announced. Nonetheless, Scott's snub to the Academy was felt dramatically and is often still listed among memorable moments of the Oscars.

Scott himself felt a strong attachment to the character of Patton. Though he had, like many actors, agreed to appear in commercials, he adamantly refused to trade on the likeness of himself as Patton. In 1986, Scott bought the rights to the general's memoirs and portrayed him again in a TV movie, *The Last Days of Patton.*

Though he never played the establishment game in Hollywood, Scott remained an admired and highly employable star. Because he always divided his time among television, film, and the Broadway stage, he retained a control and flexibility in his career that few actors have managed. Though he disdained the destructive competition of the awards system, he was nominated for a Tony for his performance in *Inherit the Wind* on Broadway in 1996, and continued in his seventh decade to appear in more television shows, movies, and plays than seems humanly possible.

—Tina Gianoulis

FURTHER READING:

Grobel, Lawrence. "George C. Scott (Interview)." *Playboy.* December 1980, 81.

Harbinson, W.A. *George C. Scott.* New York, Pinnacle Books, 1977.

discharged, he enrolled in journalism school at the University of Missouri on the GI Bill. He soon grew disenchanted with the idea of a writing career; "I discovered I had no talent for it," he said, "so I looked around for something else to do." While looking, he tried out for a college play and discovered where his talents really lay.

In 1951, Scott landed his first professional acting job in the New York Shakespeare Festival, performing in *Richard III, The Merchant of Venice,* and *As You Like It.* At almost the same moment, he began to get job offers on television, an exciting new medium that had just begun to burgeon with programs of serious theatrical merit. Scott starred in productions on such respected shows as *Hallmark Hall of Fame,* the *DuPont Show of the Month, Playhouse 90, Kraft Theater,* and *Omnibus.* By 1959, the movie offers began to roll in. That year, Scott had major roles in *The Hanging Tree* and *Anatomy of a Murder.*

During the 1960s, Scott continued to perform with great vigor and flexibility on the Broadway stage, on television—in TV movies and in his own series (*East Side, West Side,* 1963-64)—and in over forty motion pictures. A few of his best known films from this period are: *The Hustler,* with Paul Newman (1962); *Dr. Strangelove,* with Peter Sellers (1964); and *They Might Be Giants,* with Joanne Woodward (1971). Along with many great films, Scott also made his share of

Scott, Randolph (1903?-1987)

Probably more so than any other Western film star, Randolph Scott symbolized rugged individualism, unwavering honesty, and a gentleman quality seldom matched. As an actor, Scott was noted for his polite, civil manner in an industry filled with out-of-control egos and temper tantrums. A soft-spoken man with a rather passive screen presence, Scott made more than sixty pictures from 1932 to 1962, thus placing him within the ranks of Western film legends Gary Cooper and John Wayne.

Born in Orange, Virginia, in 1903 (some sources say 1898), George Randolph Scott attended Georgia Tech and the University of

Randolph Scott (left) in a scene from the film *Comanche Station.*

North Carolina to prepare for a career in textile engineering. After a brief stint working for his father's textile company in Charlotte, North Carolina, Scott moved to Hollywood to satisfy his growing interest in acting. He found work as an extra in several pictures and landed roles with local theater groups, including the Pasadena Playhouse. This exposure led to Paramount signing him to a seven-year contract. Although many of his early roles were bit parts, Scott received top billing from 1932 to 1935 in a popular series of nine Westerns based on Zane Grey stories. In seven of these films, Scott learned much about the acting process from director Henry Hathaway, a veteran filmmaker best known for directing John Wayne in *True Grit* (1969). Paramount used Scott in several non-Westerns as well, then in 1936 he was cast as James Fenimore Cooper's Leatherstocking hero, Hawkeye, in *The Last of the Mohicans.*

When Scott completed his Paramount contract in 1938, he signed nonexclusive contracts with Twentieth Century-Fox and Universal. In 1938, Fox teamed him with Shirley Temple in *Rebecca of Sunnybrook Farm,* then cast him opposite Tyrone Power and Henry Fonda in the financially successful *Jesse James* in 1939. As he did throughout his career, Scott played the tall, handsome marshal who was bound by his honor in enforcing the law. The box-office success

of Jesse James prompted a Fox sequel, *The Return of Frank James* (1940), and a flurry of other outlaw tales. *When the Daltons Rode* (1940) and *The Desperadoes* (1943) again featured Scott as a law-and-order hero reacting to the colorful exploits of the outlaws.

After paying his dues in numerous Western film supporting roles in the 1930s, Scott finally achieved stardom by the early 1940s and was teamed with some of Hollywood's leading actors. Warner Brothers signed him to play opposite Errol Flynn in *Virginia City* (1940), while Universal teamed him with John Wayne in *The Spoilers* (1942), but those were not as successful as his Westerns. Nor did Scott appear particularly comfortable playing a sword-wielding son of an English nobleman in the pirate movie *Captain Kidd.*

After World War II, Scott returned to the genre that suited him best—the Western. Except for three pictures, Scott's forty-two post-war films were all Westerns. During the next fifteen years, Scott averaged five Westerns every two years. His total of thirty-eight Westerns from 1946 to 1960 made Scott the most prolific Western star of his time. Unlike his acting counterparts Gary Cooper, John Wayne, or Alan Ladd, Scott never made a critical or box-office hit. Instead, he relied on a steady stream of professionally made, action-packed, entertaining movies. In 1951, Scott revealed to a reporter his formula for making movies, saying that he looked for "a strong believable story with seventy-five percent outdoor action and twenty-five percent indoor. If you get any more of your picture indoors, you're in trouble."

Scott did some of his finest work in a series of Westerns he made in the 1950s and early 1960s with director Budd Boetticher. In such pictures as *Seven Men from Now* (1956), *Decision at Sundown* (1957), *Ride Lonesome* (1959), and *Comanche Station* (1960), Scott's presence filled the screen with courageous dignity and laconic stoicism in tales concerning redressing personal tragedy. In each of the films, Boetticher focused on a group of individuals reacting under stress, with Scott and a capable adversary inevitably facing a showdown.

Scott's final film before retiring is considered by critics to be perhaps his finest work—Sam Peckinpah's *Ride the High Country* (1962). In the movie, Joel McCrea was cast as the poor but honest former marshal who is hired to bring in a gold shipment from a mining camp. Scott played McCrea's longtime friend, also an ex-lawman, who hires on to help escort the gold shipment, but who intends to steal it. The theme of the displacement of aging frontier individualists by an encroaching civilization intrigued critics, and Western fans enjoyed watching Scott and McCrea work together. Between them, they had starred in eighty-seven Westerns since the early 1930s.

Following *Ride the High Country,* Scott retired from the movie industry, overseeing his considerable business investments in oil wells, real estate, and securities. By the time of his death in 1987, it was estimated that Scott's holdings were worth anywhere from $50 million to $100 million. But from a popular culture standpoint, Scott left behind more than substantial personal wealth—he left behind a body of work that helped define the rugged individualism theme of American Westerns and provided one of the more convincing portrayals of the frontier hero.

—Dennis Russell

FURTHER READING:

Crow, Jefferson Brim. *Randolph Scott: The Gentleman from Virginia: A Film Biography.* Carrollton, Texas, Wind River Publishing, 1987.

Everson, William K. *A Pictorial History of the Western Film.* Secaucus, New Jersey, Citadel Press, 1969.

Eyles, Allen. *The Western.* South Brunswick, A. S. Barnes, 1975.

Fenin, George N., and William K. Everson. *The Western: From Silents to Cinerama.* New York, Bonanza Books, 1962.

Hitt, Jim. *The American West from Fiction (1823-1976) into Film (1909-1986).* Jefferson, North Carolina, McFarland and Company, 1990.

Scott, C. H., with historical assistance and editing by William C. Cline. *Whatever Happened to Randolph Scott?* Madison, North Carolina, Empire Publishing, 1994.

Scream

Single-handedly resuscitating the horror genre, as well as the sagging career of its director, *Scream,* the 1996 sleeper written by then-Hollywood neophyte Kevin Williamson, brought in a staggering $103 million at the box office and inaugurated a new wave of "teenie kill pics." Self-consciously flagging the hackneyed conventions of post-*Halloween* stalk-and-slash horror movies, *Scream* contrived to grip audiences by mixing genuine scares with affectionate spoofing. Originally titled *Scary Movie,* the name was changed amid concerns that middle America might think this implied it was a comedy. Beyond the startle effects and the self-parody, however, there lies in *Scream* a scathing critique of the way America's mass-media representatives exploit tragedy for profit. In this respect, *Scream* more closely resembles Oliver Stone's serial-killer farce *Natural Born Killers* (1994) than it does Sean Cunningham's stalker classic *Friday the 13th* (1980).

After unsuccessful stints as an actor and as an assistant director of music videos, Williamson had little trouble selling *Scream* (only his second screenplay) to Dimension Films, the newly established "genre division" of Miramax. Wes Craven signed on as director immediately upon reading it. Craven, whose past successes in the horror genre include *The Hills Have Eyes* (1978) and *A Nightmare on Elm Street* (1984), was at the time mired in a decade-long slump, having directed such duds as *A Vampire in Brooklyn* (1995) and *Shocker* (1989). Understandably bored with conventional slasher fare, he saw at once the potential of Williamson's story to bring lapsed horror fans back to their seats while simultaneously initiating a new crop of enthusiasts. In fact, Craven's 1994 contribution to the *Nightmare on Elm Street* franchise, which he wrote as well as directed, can be seen as an ambitious though under-appreciated attempt at generating just the kind of reflexive horror that would come to serve as *Scream's* signature. With a $15 million budget, an experienced director, and an established star (Drew Barrymore) already attached, *Scream* attracted a bevy of gifted Gen-X actors eager to gain recognition in a popular genre.

The intense ten minute opening of *Scream* bears a striking resemblance to the award-winning prologue of *When a Stranger Calls* (1979). An anonymous caller raises the stakes of playing "slasher movie trivia" by threatening the lives of teenage cutie Casey Becker (Barrymore) and her incapacitated boyfriend unless she can answer such questions as "Who was the killer in *Friday the 13th?*" Like everyone else in *Scream,* Casey has some familiarity with the horror film subgenre that began with *Halloween* in 1978. But only copious amounts of insider knowledge are enough to ensure one's survival in this paean to postmodern pastiche. The main storyline centers around the efforts of Sidney Prescott (played with the appropriate mixture of sensibility and sex appeal by Neve Campbell) to avoid the murderous advances of a sadistic slasher film fanatic wielding a very sharp knife and wearing a mask appropriately inspired by Edvard Munch's masterpiece expressionist painting, *The Scream.* With a nod to the traditional whodunit, the identity of Sidney's stalker is kept a secret until the movie's final scene, and not before each of her high school buddies has exhibited just enough dubious behavior to qualify as a suspect. Only the timely intervention of dirt-seeking newshound Gail Weathers (Courtney Cox, of sitcom *Friends* fame) is enough to save Sidney, stunned to discover that her assailant is really a pair of male friends who revel in the motiveless nature of their crimes.

Much has been made of *Scream's* numerous slasher film references and its abundance of in-jokes. Linda Blair (demon-possessed star of *The Exorcist*), Priscilla Pointer (*Carrie*), and Craven himself (playing a Freddy Kreuger lookalike) all make uncredited cameos. One of the killers—Billy Loomis (Skeet Ulrich)—is named after the psychiatrist in *Halloween,* himself named after Janet Leigh's lover in *Psycho* (1960). And at one point, Sidney's friend mentions the director "Wes Carpenter," obviously referring to both Craven and *Halloween* director John Carpenter. At times, however, *Scream* goes

Neve Campbell (left) and Rose McGowan in a scene from the film *Scream*.

beyond mere self-referentiality, approaching something closer to self-reflexivity. Not only do the characters exhibit insider knowledge about slasher films, they occasionally evince awareness of being in one. Thus, an unwitting victim pleads sarcastically, "Oh please don't kill me, Mr. Ghostface, I wanna be in the sequel!" And in response to Sidney's cry that "this is NOT a movie," Billy states, "Yes it is Sidney. It's all one big movie."

As noted by Isabel Pinedo, *Scream* breaks in various ways the "rules" of the traditional slasher. There are two killers, for example, and two heroines, both of whom are sexually active. The victims are bright, articulate, even witty. The nerd survives. And the film ends with the killers' unambiguous deaths. Much of *Scream's* effectiveness, in fact, comes from the setting up and subsequent undermining of audience expectations. It also comes from a blurring of the already hazy line between real-life violence and violent entertainment. Tabloid news reporters in particular are singled out as insensitive instigators of mayhem; one such reporter asks Sydney "how it feels to be almost brutally butchered. How does it feel? People have a right to know!"

Williamson and Craven again teamed up for *Scream 2* (1997), which took the self-reflexivity of its predecessor to new heights; there is a film within the film, for example, supposedly a fictionalized account of the "events" occurring in Part One. And like its predecessor, *Scream 2* grossed over $100 million at the box office (*Scream 3* is in the works.) Williamson's adaptation of a young-adult novel, *I Know What You Did Last Summer* (1997), was another sleeper hit, and his treatment for *Halloween H20* (1998) helped make a success of the "final" installment in that dying series. A $20 million long-term contract with Miramax, a hit television show for teens (*Dawson's Creek*), and permission to direct his own *Killing Mrs. Tingle,* all serve to ensure a steady stream of Williamson-inspired products. Craven too has reaped the benefits of *Scream's* success, his desire for

cinematic respectability finally satiated with a go-ahead to direct Meryl Streep in *50 Violins.*

—Steven Schneider

FURTHER READING:

Pinedo, Isabel. *Recreational Terror: Women and the Pleasures of Horror Film Viewing.* Albany, State University of New York Press, 1997.

Schneider, Steven. "Uncanny Realism and the Decline of the Modern Horror Film." *Paradoxa: Studies in World Literary Genres.* Vol. 3, No. 3-4, 1997, 417-428.

Williamson, Kevin. *Scream: A Screenplay.* New York, Hyperion, 1997.

Screwball Comedies

Born in the early 1930s, during the bleakest years of the Depression, the screwball comedy became a very popular variation of the romantic comedy film. Although the leading characters were usually reconciled to the basic values of polite society by the story's end, most screwball comedies, up until that final reel, were irreverent toward the rich, big business, small town life, government, and assorted other sacred cows, not the least of which was the institution of marriage. Among the unorthodox notions that these movies advocated were the ones that marriage could be fun, that women and men were created equal, and that being bright and articulate was not necessarily a handicap for a woman.

There were, from the early 1930s to the mid-1940s, well over 200 screwball films, almost all of them dedicated to the celebration of eccentric, unconventional behavior and attitudes and the proposition that life could be a lot of fun in spite of war and a fouled-up economy. These movies frequently offered smart, savvy reinterpretations of such classic folk tale plots as *Beauty and the Beast, Sleeping Beauty,* and, most especially, *Cinderella.* Although the plots always dealt with romance, the focal couple might also find themselves involved, while trying to pursue the path of true love, with kidnapping, election campaigns, scandals, runaway leopards, shipwreck, amnesia, divorce, murder, seeming adultery, and all sorts of impersonations.

Of the considerable number of actors and actresses who tried their hands at the screwball category there were several who displayed a true knack for the genre and appeared in quite a few successful titles. Among the women were Rosalind Russell, Carole Lombard, Jean Arthur, Claudette Colbert, Myrna Loy, and Irene Dunne. Top men included Cary Grant, Joel McCrea, Melvyn Douglas, Fred MacMurray, and William Powell. It was not just the madcap heiresses, masquerading shop girls, and disinherited playboys who behaved in wild and eccentric ways. A majority of the films were peopled with a wide variety of odd and outrageous minor characters. Anybody from a rural judge to a Park Avenue cabdriver to a nightclub torch singer might turn out to be a world class screwball. Frequently falling into this category were Alice Brady, Charlie Ruggles, Eugene Pallette, Eve Arden, Mischa Auer, Una Merkel, Robert Benchley, William Demerest, Franklin Pangborn, Billie Burke, and Luis Alberni. Many of these gifted character actors appeared so frequently in this sort of film that they give the impression they must have been permanent residents of a special screwball world. Ralph Bellamy was the ablest portrayer of an essential screwball movie type: the attractive but flawed suitor who is never going to win the leading lady.

Movies with most of the essential screwball ingredients started to show up on the screen in 1932, notably *Trouble in Paradise.* Set in Venice, it dealt with a pair of thieves, played by Miriam Hopkins and Herbert Marshall, who set out to fleece wealthy Kay Francis. Directed by Ernst Lubitsch from a script by Samson Raphaelson, it also made use of several actors who would become part of the screwball stock company throughout the 1930s and into the 1940s—Charles Ruggles, Edward Everett Horton, and Robert Greig (who specialized in grouchy butler parts and worked with everybody from the Marx Brothers to Veronica Lake). The following year saw such films as *Bombshell,* which featured Jean Harlow, aided by the energetic Lee Tracy, in a very funny burlesque version of what looked a lot like her own life as a movie star. Things picked up even more in 1934. Probably the most important screwball comedy was Frank Capra's *It Happened One Night,* scripted by Robert Riskin. Claudette Colbert was the runaway heiress who ends up taking a very strenuous cross country bus trip with salty reporter Clark Gable. Backing them up were portly Walter Connolly, an expert at irascibility, and Roscoe Karns. The film swept the Oscars and put Columbia Pictures firmly in the screwball business for the rest of the decade. Also released in 1934 was *The Thin Man,* adapted from the Dashiell Hammett novel and briskly directed by W.S. Van Dyke. Extremely appealing as the wisecracking husband-and-wife detective team, Myrna Loy and William Powell, went on to make five more movies about Nick and Nora Charles as well as several very good non-mystery comedies, including *I Love You Again* and *Libeled Lady.*

A moderately successful Broadway playwright before going to Hollywood, Preston Sturges started writing comedy screenplays in the mid-1930s. His adaptation of *The Good Fairy* changed the Ferenc

Molnar play completely, turning it into an effective screwball comedy set in Vienna. William Wyler directed, and Margaret Sullavan and Herbert Marshall starred in this variation of the Cinderella story that has orphan Sullavan instrumental in changing the fortunes of struggling attorney Marshall; character actors included Frank Morgan and Reginald Owen. Sturges' *Easy Living* came out in 1937, with Mitchell Leisen directing. Another cockeyed Cinderella story, it has working girl Jean Arthur being mistaken for the mistress of wall street tycoon Edward Arnold. Ray Milland is the young man who falls in love with the transformed Arthur. Demerest and Pangborn are in the cast and Alberni gives a bravura performance as the English-mangling, hyperactive manager of a faltering ritzy hotel who offers Arthur a luxury suite because he thinks it will influence Arnold.

Finally in 1940, Paramount Pictures offered Sturges the opportunity to direct and he proceeded to turn out an impressive string of successful comedies at a rapid rate. They included *The Great McGinty,* with Brian Donlevy, *The Lady Eve,* with Barbara Stanwyck and Henry Fonda, *The Palm Beach Story,* with McCrea and Colbert, *Sullivan's Travels,* with McCrea and Lake, and *The Miracle of Morgan's Creek,* with Eddie Bracken and Betty Hutton. Sturges' comedies had a headlong pace, bright dialogue, social satire, enough eccentrics, curmudgeons, and fatheads to populate a small city, and generous helpings of broad slapstick. He gathered around him a group of gifted comedy actors who appeared in nearly every one of his films. These included Greig, Demerest, Pangborn, Raymond Walburn, Al Bridge, and Eric Blore.

Leisen, working with various writers, provided a string of other screwball comedies. Among them were *Hands across the Table,* with Lombard, MacMurray, and Bellamy—as the fellow who does not get the girl—and *Take a Letter, Darling,* with MacMurray as a very reluctant male secretary to Rosalind Russell. He also directed, with a script by Charles Brackett and Billy Wilder, the quintessential screwball Cinderella movie of the period, *Midnight.* Colbert is a gold digging chorus girl stranded in Paris and she ends up impersonating a countess. Don Ameche is a cab driver who falls in love with her, and John Barrymore and Mary Astor are also on hand.

The performer several critics and historians consider perhaps the best comedienne of these years always thought of herself as a serious actress and a singer. Irene Dunne had to be coerced into taking the starring role in the 1936 comedy *Theodora Goes Wild* at Columbia Pictures. Cast opposite Melvyn Douglas, she plays a quiet small-town young woman who writes a racy bestseller under a pen name. The transformation she undergoes after meeting and falling in love with Douglas, and then realizing that he is even less liberated than she is, forms the basis for the story. Dunne had, in the words of historian James Harvey, "the acutest kind of self-awareness. Where Lombard seems driven and distrait, Dunne seems intoxicated, magical, high-flying. Dunne does not just see the joke—she is radiant with it, possessed by it and glowing with it. Nobody does this so completely or to quite the same degree." The next year Dunne appeared in Leo McCarey's *The Awful Truth,* which has been called "the definitive screwball comedy." It is about infidelity, love, trust, and the inevitability of some relationships. Cary Grant, who did not want to, plays opposite her and establishes the characterization he used for much of his subsequent career. Ralph Bellamy does one of his most memorable turns as the loser of the girl and, for good measure, the dog who played Asta in the *Thin Man* movies appears as the pet over whom the divorcing Dunne and Grant get into a custody battle. As in *Theodora,* Dunne gets to cause considerable embarrassment for the object of her affection by impersonating a different sort of woman, this time

Grant's vulgar, and fictitious, sister. She made a few more comedies, including the equally successful *My Favorite Wife,* again with Grant, in 1940.

On the long list of other screwball comedies many others stand out. They include *Nothing Sacred,* with Lombard, Connolly, and Fredric March; *My Man Godfrey,* with Lombard and William Powell; *Bringing Up Baby,* with Katharine Hepburn and Grant; *Bachelor Mother,* with Ginger Rogers and David Niven; *Ninotchka,* with Melvyn Douglas and, of all people, Greta Garbo; *His Girl Friday,* with Grant and Russell; *The Major and the Minor,* with Ginger Rogers and Ray Milland—the first film directed by Billy Wilder; and *The More the Merrier,* with Arthur, McCrea and Charles Coburn. While attempts have been made in most subsequent decades to revive the genre, for the most part the best screwball comedies remain the ones made more than 60 years ago.

—Ron Goulart

FURTHER READING:

Bassinger, Jeanine. *A Woman's View.* Hanover, Wesleyan University Press, 1993.

Harvey, James. *Romantic Comedy.* New York, Alfred A. Knopf, 1987.

Kendall, Elizabeth. *The Runaway Bride.* New York, Alfred A. Knopf, 1990.

Scribner's

In their heyday *Scribner's* magazine (1870-81) and *Scribner's Monthly* (1887-1942) gave their largely middle-class readership beautiful illustrations and outstanding popular fiction and nonfiction. *Scribner's,* named for a New York publisher Charles Scribner, was founded by Scribner, Roswell C. Smith, a lawyer, and Dr. Josiah Gilbert Holland, a writer of moral tales and poems scorned by critics but popular with young Americans. From the start the men imbued the magazine with their shared Christian outlook, giving it a tone of religious uplift rare among general interest periodicals. As part of their mission they sought to extend art and literature to readers outside the big cities. Promising that *Scribner's* would be "profusely illustrated," Holland proposed it as a "democratic form of literature" for people who lacked time for books. After Scribner died in 1871, Holland became the magazine's guiding light. He emphasized a sort of moderate Christianity, favoring temperance but not prohibition, for instance. "Orthodoxy saves nobody; Christian love and Christian character save everybody," he once wrote.

Spurred by improvements in printing, engraving technology, and other industrial advances, the number of American magazines nearly doubled to 1,200 in the five years after the end of the Civil War. Intended as competition for two older, high-quality rivals, *Harper's Monthly* and the *Atlantic Monthly, Scribner's* published more nonfiction than both. Early on it caught the public's eye with its excellent illustrations and varied articles, many aimed at women. The magazine published much sentimental fiction and poetry and many nonfiction articles on children, gardening, fashion, and the like.

Holland and his assistant editor, Richard Watson Gilder, gradually took a more daring tack later in the 1870s. Walt Whitman's sensual poems offended Holland, and the editor often disparaged the poet in print and even rejected a poem he submitted for publication. Nevertheless, Holland published an article that described Whitman as one of America's leading poets, although "too anatomical and malodorous." *Scribner's* thus became one of the first conventional magazines to recognize Whitman as a great American poet. The magazine also began printing more realistic fiction, including stories by Henry James and Bret Harte. John Muir contributed nature pieces. Illustrators included artists like Winslow Homer. Circulation rose steadily, and by 1878 *Scribner's* was earning a solid profit. It owed part of its financial success to its policy of accepting non-literary advertisements, making it one of the first good quality magazines to do so.

Following a dispute with Charles Scribner's Sons, the editors and part-owners of *Scribner's* separated from the publishing firm and changed the magazine's name to the *Century Illustrated Monthly* in 1881. Holland died after editing just one issue. Gilder took over and led the *Century* to even greater success than its predecessor had enjoyed, nearly doubling its circulation in the 1880s with retrospectives on the Civil War written by leading participants like William T. Sherman and Ulysses Grant. The *Century* continued to flourish until 1900, when it began a long, slow decline brought on partly by competition from cheaper muckraking magazines. By 1930, when it had cut back to quarterly publication with a circulation of just 20,000, it was merged with *Forum* magazine and its name disappeared.

In 1887, meanwhile, Charles Scribner's Sons started *Scribner's Monthly.* Under its first editor, Edward L. Burlingame, the new *Scribner's* continued its namesake's tradition of publishing fine illustrations and articles. Burlingame gained an early advantage over his main competitors, *Harper's,* the *Atlantic,* and the *Century,* by offering the new *Scribner's* at 25 cents an issue, or three dollars a year, compared to the standard 35 cents an issue or four dollars a year. Publishing works by Stephen Crane and Rudyard Kipling, among others, he overtook his rivals in circulation in the 1890s. Important early nonfiction articles like Charles Francis Adams' "The Prevention of Railroad Strikes" and Jacob A. Riis' "How the Other Half Lives" examined labor problems, urban poverty, and other social issues.

The magazine weathered a severe economic depression and challenges from new and cheaper competitors like *McClure's* in the 1890s, and continued to prosper. *Scribner's* largely disdained the muckraking stance most magazines took in the early years of the twentieth century. It continued to concentrate on art, running lavishly illustrated articles with outstanding full-color pictures by N. C. Wyeth, among others. It also printed more outstanding fiction as well as popular travel and adventure features, including a number of articles by Theodore Roosevelt describing his exploits in Africa, South America, and elsewhere. The magazine published fiction by Edith Wharton, Ernest Hemingway, John Galsworthy, and Thomas Wolfe. It reached its peak circulation of more than 200,000 around 1911 and began to decline thereafter.

Dogged by its old-fashioned appearance and the onset of the Great Depression, *Scribner's* suffered a severe slump in the 1930s. Alfred Dashiell, who became editor in 1930, attempted to revive its sagging fortunes by running more left-leaning political articles intended to appeal to young intellectuals. He also continued the magazine's strong literary tradition, publishing stories by Sherwood Anderson, Langston Hughes, Erskine Caldwell, William Saroyan, William Faulkner, and F. Scott Fitzgerald. Nevertheless, he lost many long time readers and did not gain many new ones. By the time he resigned in 1936 to take a job at *Reader's Digest,* circulation had fallen from 70,000 to 43,000.

An English professor and magazine analyst named Harlan Logan became editor in 1936 and redesigned and enlivened the magazine. Although he doubled circulation and cut financial losses, his efforts fell short and *Scribner's* ceased publication in May of 1939. *Esquire* acquired its subscriber list and the title was merged with that of another magazine. The resulting *Scribner's Commentator* met an inglorious death in 1942 after one of its staff pleaded guilty to taking payoffs from the Japanese government in exchange for publishing propaganda favoring United States isolationism.

—Daniel Lindley

FURTHER READING:

John, Arthur. *The Best Years of the Century: Richard Watson Gilder, Scribner's Monthly, and Century Magazine, 1870-1909.* Urbana, University of Illinois Press, 1981.

Mott, Frank Luther. *A History of American Magazines: 1885-1905.* Cambridge, Harvard University Press, 1957.

Peterson, Theodore. *Magazines in the Twentieth Century.* Urbana, University of Illinois Press, 1964.

Tebbel, John. *The American Magazine: A Compact History.* New York, Hawthorn Books, 1969.

Scruggs, Earl (1924—)

An enormously influential musician, North Carolina native Earl Scruggs essentially rescued the five-string banjo from its fate as a country comedian's instrument, moving it into the realm of virtuosity by his work with Bill Monroe's Blue Grass Boys and his own band, the Foggy Mountain Boys, in the 1940s, 1950s, and 1960s. Though he did not invent the three-finger picking style that bears his name, he refined, developed, and popularized it as both a backing and solo approach, winning enthusiastic fans worldwide and earning comparisons to the greatest classical music instrumentalists. In the late 1960s, he left the Foggy Mountain Boys to work with his sons in the Earl Scruggs Revue, bringing a fusion of bluegrass, country, and rock to audiences around the United States, especially on college campuses. Thanks to its use in the soundtrack for the movie *Bonnie and Clyde,* his ''Foggy Mountain Breakdown'' (1949) is one of bluegrass music's best known numbers.

—Jon Weisberger

Scruggs, Earl
See also Foggy Mountain Boys

Scully, Vin (1927—)

One of sports broadcasting's most recognizable voices, Vin Scully is known primarily as the long-time play-by-play announcer for baseball's Dodgers. But his work on national telecasts, including NBC's *Game of the Week* from 1983 to 1989, exposed his mellifluous vocal stylings to viewers from coast to coast. Scully joined the Brooklyn Dodgers' broadcast team in 1950, just a year after graduating from Fordham University. Under the tutelage of Red Barber, he developed a warm, personable on-air style that perfectly suited the national pastime's slow, wheeling pace. His vivid descriptions of such events as Sandy Koufax's perfect game and Kirk Gibson's dramatic home run in the 1988 World Series remain iconic moments in baseball play-by-play. After the 1997 season, Scully retired from national broadcasting to concentrate solely on his local responsibilities with the Dodgers. All told, he called 25 World Series and 12 All-Star Games over the course of his career.

—Robert E. Schnakenberg

FURTHER READING:

Smith, Curt. *The Storytellers: From Mel Allen to Bob Costas: Sixty Years of Baseball Tales from the Broadcast Booth.* New York, Macmillan, 1995.

Sea World

In the highly competitive amusement industry—a $4 billion dollar industry by 1990—Sea World has attempted to provide visitors with a greater understanding of marine life. Unlike Disneyland and other amusement parks, Sea World uses environmental education, spectacle, and science to create an experience that appeals to tourists. The spectacle of Sea World is centered around orca shows; the most famous orca is Shamu. With an environmental experience compared to *Wild Kingdom* and *Jacques Cousteau,* Sea World enables tourists to appreciate nature in a tradition that places humans in control of nature. Sea World performs as a figurehead of green consumerism. "Sea World," Susan Davis notes in her cultural analysis of Sea World, *Spectacular Nature,* "is not so much a substitute for nature as an opinion about it, an attempt to convince a broad public that nature is going to be all right." But Davis contends, "Sea World represents an enormous contradiction. Using living animals, captive seas, and flourishing landscapes, the theme park has organized the subtle and contradictory cultural meanings of nature into a machine for mass consumption." Opened in 1964, Sea World was soon purchased by Anheuser-Busch and by the late 1990s operated four parks in Florida, California, and Ohio.

—Brian Black

FURTHER READING:

Davis, Susan G. *Spectacular Nature: Corporate Culture and the Sea World Experience.* Berkeley, University of California Press, 1997.

Seals, Son (1942—)

One of the strongest live performers to work Chicago's blues circuit, Son Seals brought a new energy to the scene as many of the older musicians were beginning to slow down. Seals was at the forefront of a generation of young guitar players who carried on the traditions of Muddy Waters, Sonny Boy Williamson, and Howlin' Wolf. Seals's father owned the Dipsy Doodle Club in Osceola, Arkansas, exposing young Son to blues at an early age. He took up drums and played with Williamson, Robert Nighthawk, and Earl Hooker while a teenager and toured with Albert King during the mid-1960s. Seals moved to Chicago and formed his own group as a guitarist in 1972, recording *The Son Seals Blues Band* for Alligator Records in 1973; he recorded seven more albums for Alligator through 1996. Seals was shot in the jaw by his wife during a domestic disturbance in January, 1997. He recovered and remained a top draw in Chicago's clubs.

—Jon Klinkowitz

FURTHER READING:

Corbett, John. ''Son Seals.'' *Down Beat.* February, 1995, 52.

Poses, Jonathan. ''Son Seals Blues Band.'' *Down Beat.* March, 1984, 50.

Search for Tomorrow

Producer Roy Winsor developed *Search for Tomorrow* in 1951 and proved that the soap opera could succeed on television. The CBS serial reflected the concerns of postwar America by focussing on a widowed heroine, Joanne Tate (played for all thirty-five years by Mary Stuart), who struggled with issues of marriage and children. Jo was the problem solver for the town of Henderson, counseling friends and neighbors, especially the comic Bergmans (Larry Haines and Melba Rae). Later story lines centered on Jo's children and the exotic adventures of a new family, the Sentells. *Search* moved to NBC in 1982 and, a year later, presented the first live show on daytime in seventeen years (the tape was reportedly stolen). In the mid 1980s the entire community of Henderson was flooded and surviving citizens were forced to live in the same building. The final episode of *Search for Tomorrow* was broadcast on December 26, 1986, and in the last scene Jo was asked for what she was searching. She responded, ''Tomorrow, and I can't wait.''

—Ron Simon

FURTHER READING:

The Museum of Television & Radio. *Worlds without End: The Art and History of the Soap Opera.* New York, Abrams, 1997.

Scherming, Christopher. *The Soap Opera Encyclopedia.* New York, Ballantine Books, 1985.

Stahl, B. ''Mary Stuart's Soap Opera Problems.'' *TV Guide.* November 19, 1960, 17-19.

Stuart, Mary. *Both of Me.* New York, Doubleday, 1980.

The Searchers

Since its release in 1956, John Ford's *The Searchers* has become one of the most controversial films in Hollywood history. At the center of the controversy is Ethan Edwards, played by John Wayne in what many consider his finest performance. Throughout the film Edwards pursues a band of Indians who killed his brother's family and captured the daughters, one of whom, Debbie (Natalie Wood), is still alive. Film scholars, particularly during the late 1980s and early 1990s, have attacked Ford's shabby treatment of Indians, which is perhaps most vividly evidenced in the reactionary persona of Ethan Edwards. Despite its critics, *The Searchers* remains a hugely influential film. It is often cited as a seminal influence by filmmakers as diverse as those of the French New Wave and the American directors who came of age in the late 1960s and early 1970s—most notably Martin Scorsese, Francis Ford Coppola, and Brian DePalma. And in Ethan Edwards filmmakers found a model for the semi-psychopathic antihero so often present in films since the late 1960s.

—Robert C. Sickels

FURTHER READING:

Courtney, Susan. ''Looking For (Race and Gender) Trouble in Monument Valley.'' *Qui Parle.* Vol. 6, No. 2, 1993, 97-130.

Lehman, Peter. ''Texas 1868 / America 1956: *The Searchers.*'' In *Close Viewings: A New Anthology of Film Criticism.* Tallahassee, Florida State University Press, 1990, 387-415.

Nolley, Ken. ''John Ford and the Hollywood Indian.'' *Film & History.* Vol. 23, No. 1-4, 1993, 44-56.

Skerry, Philip J. ''What Makes a Man to Wander? Ethan Edwards of John Ford's *The Searchers.*'' *New Orleans Review.* Vol. 18, No. 4, 1991, 86-91.

Sears Roebuck Catalogue

Known affectionately as ''a department store in a book,'' ''the farmer's wishbook,'' and the ''farmer's Bible,'' the Sears Roebuck mail order catalogue, while not the first of its kind in retail merchandising, was certainly the most famous and the one that inspired the most imitations.

Mail order catalogues—visual and textual descriptions of a store's inventory in print form—were used to select and purchase mass-produced goods. Although the first publication resembling a mail order catalogue was supposedly a mail circular distributed by Ben Franklin in 1744, modern versions became popular in America during the Gilded Age. Montgomery Ward established the modern mail-order industry in 1872, selling his wares, selected primarily for the needs of farming families, through the mail.

Inspired by Ward's success in rural America, Richard W. Sears, a watch salesman who joined forces with Alvah Roebuck, a watch repairman, expanded the line of goods offered to country families, launching his company and publishing his first catalogue in 1886. By 1893 Sears began publishing his catalogue on a regular basis, dubbing it the *Consumer's Guide* in 1894. In the first decade of the twentieth century the Sears catalogue offered over 10,000 different items dealing with every aspect of life from birth to death, including firearms, sewing machines, clothing, bicycles, patent medicines, pianos, and eventually even houses.

The early years of the Sears catalogue were significant in bringing a largely urban and mass-manufactured way of life to rural areas that had until then been relatively isolated from metropolitan goods and culture. In 1897, 318,000 copies of the Sears catalogue were sent to the Midwest; by 1908, 3.6 million copies were sent out. Sears's drawings and verbal descriptions of the items helped sell these otherwise unexaminable goods, through the mail, to customers far

Cover of the Sears Roebuck catalogue, c.1910.

with an additional 250 million tabloid catalogues, per year. The 1897 catalogue has even been successfully reprinted, a testament to its endurance as a cultural icon and as a source of American nostalgia.

The Sears catalogue is perhaps most significant in establishing the viability of mail-order trade, no longer requiring face-to-face interaction between buyer and seller. Thousands of other catalogues sprang up during the twentieth century, including those selling clothing, jewelry, gourmet food, plants, herbs, and art supplies, among other things. Although still a source of revenue for Sears in the 1990s, the mail-order catalogue had paved the way for similarly anonymous sales institutions, such as televised shopping channels like QVC and the Home Shopping Network, and commercial Internet sites.

—Wendy Woloson

FURTHER READING:

Cohn, David L. *The Good Old Days: A History of American Morals and Manners as Seen Through the Sears, Roebuck Catalogues 1905 to the Present.* New York, Simon and Schuster, 1940.

Schlereth, Thomas J. ''Country Stores, County Fairs, and Mail-Order Catalogues: Consumption in Rural America.'' Simon Bronner, ed. *Consuming Visions: Accumulation and Display of Goods in America, 1880-1920.* Winterthur, Delaware, Winterthur Museum, 1989.

Weil, Gordon L. *Sears, Roebuck, U.S.A. The Great American Catalogue Store and How It Grew.* New York, Stein and Day, 1977.

Sears Tower

The Sears Tower looms over downtown Chicago, an unmistakable symbol of the city's pride in its heritage as the birthplace of a uniquely American concept, the modern skyscraper. Built in 1974 to a height of 1,468 feet, the Sears Tower succeeded the Empire State Building as the world's tallest building, and held that title until 1996. The building was designed by the distinguished and world famous firm of architects, Skidmore, Owings and Merrill to serve as the corporate headquarters for Sears Roebuck and Company. Its architectural style, while incorporating significant engineering advances, relates back to the impersonal glass boxes of the 1950s and 1960s rather than looking forward to the more idiosyncratic towers of the 1980s and 1990s. Though large and impressive, the building never quite captured the hearts of Chicago's citizens in the way that the city's John Hancock Center did. Nevertheless, the Sears Tower epitomizes the bustling prairie metropolis that Carl Sandburg called the ''City of Big Shoulders.''

—Dale Allen Gyure

FURTHER READING:

Douglas, George H. *Skyscrapers: A Social History of the Very Tall Building in America.* Jefferson, North Carolina, McFarland & Company, 1996.

away. The success of the mail order business was aided by governmental policies, including the advertiser's penny postcard in 1871, Rural Free Delivery (RFD) in 1898, and parcel post in 1913. Both Sears and Ward took advantage of these policies, remaining mail-order competitors well into the twentieth century. In fact, Sears consistently published a catalogue smaller than Ward's so that it would sit on top of his rival's book in the family home.

As historian Thomas Schlereth pointed out, ''With the spread of mail-order merchandising, people who had lived, to a large extent, on a barter or an extended credit system now became immersed in a money economy.'' Rural merchants, feeling their businesses threatened, decried the use of mail-order catalogues, trying to convince local townspeople that the merchandise offered within was inferior and its delivery unreliable. But Sears allayed people's fears, establishing the familiar ''Satisfaction guaranteed or your money back'' policy. His catalogue impacted rural life in other ways as well. No longer were farmers completely reliant on the food that they grew themselves or procured from local produce merchants. Instead, they could purchase prepackaged food through the mail. The catalogues also presented middle-class styles and tastes and made them accessible to everyone in the country. Further, catalogues were often used as educational tools: children practiced their math by computing the total price of orders, became literate by reading the endless product descriptions, and learned geography by studying the maps inside.

In 1946 the Sears catalogue was selected by the Grolier Society as one of the 100 outstanding American books of all time. By the 1970s Sears was distributing 65 million copies of its main catalogue—by then a familiar adjunct to Sears retail salesrooms—along

Goldberger, Paul. *The Skyscraper.* New York, Alfred A. Knopf Inc., 1992.

Second City

The Second City theater company of Chicago has set the standard for improvisational comedy since the early 1960s, and no single institution has made a greater impact on the development of American comedy since. The comedy troupe has produced a stellar array of improvisational and stand-up comedians, actors, writers, and directors who have had a profound influence on comedy worldwide.

The troupe's roots go back to the progressive campus of the University of Chicago in 1951, where a group of performers and writers began presenting plays. After two years, the group migrated from the university's Southside campus to a Northside converted chop suey house, pooled their resources, and launched the Playwrights Theatre Club, which produced 25 plays over the next two years. When the fire department ordered extensive remodeling, the Club broke apart, forming two new groups: the Compass Players, an improvisational troupe that played nightclubs around Chicago, and the Studebaker Theater Company, which presented repertory theater in a 1200-seat house in the Loop area. Members oscillated back and forth between these two new companies until, a year later, both of them also broke up.

Three former members of the group (or groups)—Mike Nichols, Elaine May, and Shelley Berman—each rapidly achieved individual national recognition. Berman became a successful stand-up comedian and recording star, while Nichols and May played nightclubs across the country, were a hit on Broadway, and produced several smash comedy albums. They parted ways in 1961, with May going on to work variously as an actress, writer, and director, and Nichols forging a major directing career on Broadway and in Hollywood. The comedy background of each was evident in films such as Nichols's *The Graduate* (1967) and May's *A New Leaf* (1971). Meanwhile, the other members of the original group kept in touch, dreaming of reuniting. Their dream came true in 1959 when they obtained use of a defunct Chinese laundry building on the edge of Old Town, which they converted into a coffeehouse. Taking their name from a derisive article about Chicago written by A. J. Liebling for the *New Yorker,* The Second City opened in December 1959 to dazzling reviews, and continued to perform throughout the rest of the century, delighting audiences and training successive generations of comics. Among Second City alumni are several who reached national recognition as cast members of *Saturday Night Live,* including John Belushi, Bill Murray, Dan Aykroyd, Gilda Radner, Martin Short, Mike Myers, Chris Farley, James Belushi, Tim Kazurinsky, Mary Gross, and Robin Duke. Stand-up comics who started at Second City include Robert Klein, David Steinberg, Joan Rivers, and the comedy teams of Stiller and Meara, and Burns and Schriber. Film actors who got their start improvising at this coffeehouse include Alan Arkin (*The In-Laws*), Jane Alexander (*The Great White Hope*), Barbara Harris (*Family Plot*), Ron Liebman (*Slaughterhouse-Five*), and Severn Darden (*The President's Analyst*). Television actors include Ed Asner and Valerie Harper (*The Mary Tyler Moore Show,* then *Lou Grant* and *Rhoda,* respectively), Shelley Long and George Wendt (*Cheers*),

Linda Lavin (*Alice*), Dan Castellaneta (the voice of Homer Simpson), Fred Willard (*Fernwood 2-Night*), Peter Boyle (*Everybody Loves Raymond*), Bob Odenkirk (*Mr. Show*), and David Rasche (*Sledge Hammer*). Directors include Paul Mazursky (*Bob & Carol & Ted & Alice, Moscow on the Hudson*), Betty Thomas (*The Brady Bunch Movie, Private Parts*), indie favorite Henry Jaglom (*Eating, Babyfever*), and actor/director/writer Alan Alda (*Sweet Liberty*).

Apart from its reputation as the most fertile breeding ground for American comics, Second City is best known for the most consistently hilarious sketch comedy show in television history, *SCTV*. In 1976, when the members of the Toronto company of Second City were searching for something to satirize on a proposed television show, they hit upon the perfect topic: television itself. Regulars John Candy, Joe Flaherty, Eugene Levy, Andrea Martin, Rick Moranis, Catherine O'Hara, Harold Ramis, Martin Short, and Dave Thomas week after week acted as various members of the staff of *SCTV*, the call letters for the fictional Second City television station, serving Melonville. The station was owned by wheelchair-bound Guy Caballero (Flaherty), with Moe Green (Ramis) as the station manager—until he was kidnapped by the Leutonian Liberation Front and Edith Prickley (Martin) took over. Other staffers included Monster Chiller Horror Theater host Count Floyd (Flaherty), exercise show host Johnny Larue (Candy), Bob and Doug McKenzie (Thomas and Moranis) with their Great White North, pitchmen Tex and Edna Boil (Thomas and Martin), the polka playing Schmenge Brothers (Candy and Levy) and Ed Grimley (Short)—not to mention cleaning woman Perini Scleroso (Martin) and porn salesman Harry, the Guy with the Snake on His Face (Candy). The show ran for seven years and produced 185 episodes, starting on Canada's Global television and in syndication in the United States, then moving to NBC, and finally to Cinemax. All the show's stars have moved on to success in other projects. John Candy became a film star (*Uncle Buck* and *Planes, Trains & Automobiles*), as did Martin Short (*Innerspace, Three Amigos*) and Rick Moranis (*Little Shop of Horrors, Honey, I Shrunk the Kids*). Catherine O'Hara appeared in films (*Beetlejuice, Home Alone*), and Andrea Martin did both films (*Club Paradise*) and television (*Kate & Allie*). Harold Ramis directed *Caddyshack, National Lampoon's Vacation,* and *Groundhog Day.* Dave Thomas directed and costarred in the McKenzie Brothers movie *Strange Brew* and was a regular on *Grace Under Fire.* And Eugene Levy created the children's show *Maniac Mansion,* starring Joe Flaherty.

The original Second City troupe continues in Chicago, supporting national touring companies and training new generations of improvisational actors. ''In a changing society,'' writes Second City chronicler Donna McCrohan, ''The Second City is a constant, no less committed to quality theater than in 1959.''

—Bob Sullivan

FURTHER READING:

Coleman, Janet. *The Compass: The Improvisational Theatre that Revolutionized American Comedy.* Chicago, University of Chicago Press, 1990.

McCrohan, Donna. *The Second City: A Backstage History of Comedy's Hottest Troupe.* New York, Putnam Publishing Group, 1987.

Sweet, Jeffrey. *Something Wonderful Right Away.* New York, Limelight, 1987.

Thomas, Dave. *SCTV: Behind the Scenes.* Toronto, McClelland & Stewart, 1996.

Sedona, Arizona

The small town of Sedona in Northern Arizona has had a marked influence on late twentieth-century American religious culture. Characterized by its red rocks, and boasting a population of 15,000 people, Sedona is the New Age capital of the world. It is home to UFO enthusiasts, New Religious movements, New Age philosophers, and devotees of paranormal phenomena. Located in the high desert 120 miles north of Phoenix, Arizona, Sedona is on the edge of the Colorado Plateau, surrounded by a landscape of hellfire cliffs, buttes, and spires, and enjoys a climate that is described as near-perfect. Tourism and a thriving community of artists form its economic base. That more people do not live there is a surprise.

Like most Western tourist towns, Sedona is really two places: one where more than four million tourists a year stop to gawk and buy crystals; the other where the real Sedonians live. In popular imagination, however, Sedona is one place, where new churches form—some to die, others to thrive—to worship some alien deity, or follow Native American shamanism, or Eastern mythology. It is the Mecca of the New Age, where people flock to change their lives, and the place of Gabriel of Sedona, who *Dateline NBC* suggested was a fraudulent guru.

Sedona did not always have such a reputation. When the nearby Cline Library of Northern Arizona University began collecting materials relating to Sedona in 1992, little enough could be found to fill one box. Six years later, the collection had overflowed to 18 linear feet of ephemera on the Sedona experience. Things changed for Sedona when psychic Page Bryant announced the discovery of seven vortexes, or natural power spots, of psychic energy. Many today feel that the Sedona area contains the highest concentration of key lines, power centers, and vortexes in the world. These vortexes are said to be wells of natural power emanating from deep within the Earth that, some believe, act as a beacon for intergalactic travelers. People can also heighten their psychic awareness through the vortexes and are able to see beyond this dimension into others. The surrounding hellfire landscape of the place encourages these mystical musings, quests for circles of power, and the communing with spirits or aliens.

Hikers in the wilderness have reported suffering from inexplicable fatigue, and have recounted tales of three-foot-tall "rock people," mysterious rumblings beneath the ground, and floating balls of light. Some have also been confronted by dark-suited secret agents,

Sedona, Arizona

the "Men in Black," who are said to guard the UFO base beneath Secret Mountain.

The area is also the home of many Native American cultures. Scattered throughout the landscape are ruins and wonderfully preserved examples of prehistoric artwork. Until the late 1800s the Yavapai Apache lived in the canyons; before them were the Sinagua and other ancient peoples, or Anasazi. All left their indelible marks on the landscape that spiritualists believe was a result of the magnetic attraction of the vortexes. The descendants of these people, however, believe otherwise, and are concerned that Sedona's popularity is endangering their own sacred sites.

Nearly 400 New Age businesses thrive in the Sedona area, which encompasses the nearby communities of Oak Creek, Cottonwood, and Jerome. These businesses include publishers, retailers, and so forth, but there are also many holistic health practitioners, psychic readers, channelers, Sacred Earth tour guides, and others, who service the demands of the town's ever-growing New Age reputation.

—John J. Doherty

FURTHER READING:

Dannelley, Richard. *Sedona Power Spot, Vortex, and Medicine Wheel Guide.* Sedona, Arizona, R. Dannelley in cooperation with the Vortex Society, 1991.

Johnson, Hoyt. *What's the Name of That Rock?* Sedona, Arizona, Sedona Magazine, 1994.

Mann, Nicholas R. *Sedona—Sacred Earth, Ancient Lore, Modern Myths: A Guide to the Red Rock Country.* Prescott, Arizona, ZIVAH Publishers, 1991.

"Sedona On-Line." http://www.sedona.net. April 1999.

Seduction of the Innocent

In 1948, Dr. Fredric Wertham, a respected New York psychiatrist, began a campaign against comic books. Wertham, the author of two books on the causes of violence, argued in *Collier's* and the *Saturday Review of Literature* that comic books, particularly crime comics, corrupted young minds and contributed to juvenile delinquency. His conclusions were based on his work with juvenile delinquents, who reported that comics showed them how to commit crimes, and on his examination of the violence and sex depicted in comics. Wertham's work on the subject culminated in his 1954 book, *Seduction of the Innocent.* The campaign he spearheaded led to the formation of many committees against comics—mass burnings of comics, Senate hearings, and the formation of the Comics Code Authority (CCA). Wertham and his book would remain for decades after notorious among comic-book fans and professionals, and the word "Werthamite" would come to mean "censor."

In the 1940s, comic books were a popular form of entertainment for both children and adults. The adult readership was particularly important after World War II since many men took up reading comics in the service, largely because the slim magazines could be read quickly and carried easily rolled-up in a pocket. Perhaps to appeal to these older readers, comic-book publishers introduced dozens of crime and horror titles after the war, which often depicted gruesome acts of cruelty.

In *Seduction of the Innocent,* Wertham wrote, "the most subtle and pervading effect of crime comics on children can be summarized in a single phrase: moral disarmament." In crime comics, he argued, the reader is often asked to identify with a criminal on the run from the law. Even though the criminal is usually captured or killed at the story's end, the stories romanticize a violent and immoral life outside the law. The outlaw protagonist "lives like a hero until the very end, and even then he often dies like a hero, in a burst of gun fire and violence."

Wertham did not find the "good guys" of comic books to be any more wholesome. Superman, for example, seemed to embody the fascist idea of a master race that got its way by force: "The superman conceit gives boys and girls the feeling that ruthless go-getting based on physical strength or the power of weapons or machines is the desirable way to behave." Batman and Wonder Woman, Wertham argued, promoted homosexuality because they had child sidekicks of the same gender. He described the home-life of Batman and Robin as "a wish dream of two homosexuals living together." Wonder Woman represented "the cruel, 'phallic' woman," a poor role model for girls because she emphasized power and independence rather than nuturance. Wertham also discovered sadomasochism and other variant sexualities in crime and adventure comics. He titled one of his chapters after a young patient's exclamation, "I want to be a sex maniac!"

Stirred by the outcry against comics that Wertham's charges created, the U. S. Senate put the comics industry on trial. In 1950, a Senate subcommittee chaired by Estes Kefauver found no evidence that linked crime comics to juvenile delinquency. Undaunted, Wertham and others continued to agitate for further government inquiry. In 1954 the Senate Judiciary Subcommittee on Juvenile Delinquency investigated comics again. The committee's verdict was that comics needed to be cleaned up and that the comic-book industry should police itself. Publishers were already moving in that direction. Fearing government censorship, many of the leading comic-book publishers formed the Association of Comics Magazine Publishers in 1948 to establish standards of decency for their publications. Because their efforts at self-censorship were ineffective and failed to convince their critics, these publishers created the Comics Code Authority, an independent board, to evaluate every story before publication. For decades after, most comic books sold in the United States bore a CCA stamp of approval on their covers.

One lasting effect of this era is that by the end of the twentieth century comics were still considered by most Americans to be children's entertainment and to be incapable of conveying substantial artistic content. While countries such as Italy, France, and Japan have developed sophisticated varieties of comics for adult readers, American comics have remained marginalized. The attitude that comics are "bad for you," the intellectual equivalent of junk food, has continued to linger.

—Christian L. Pyle

FURTHER READING:

Barker, Martin. *A Haunt of Fears: The Strange History of the British Horror Comics Campaign.* London, Pluto Press, 1984.

Benton, Mike. *Crime Comics: The Illustrated History.* Dallas, Taylor Publishing, 1993.

Gilbert, James. *A Cycle of Outrage: America's Reaction to the Juvenile Delinquent in the 1950s.* New York, Oxford University Press, 1986.

Wertham, Fredric. *Seduction of the Innocent.* New York, Rinehart, 1954.

West, Mark I. *Children, Culture, and Controversy.* Hamden, Connecticut, Archon Books, 1988.

Seeger, Pete (1919—)

The American singer and composer Pete Seeger was quite simply the foremost popularizer of American folk music of the twentieth century. While others engaged in field work or labored in dusty archives, Seeger recorded over 100 albums in a half a century of performing. An evangelizer with an inborn sensitivity to crowd techniques, Seeger excelled in concert and had few musical peers in working a crowd. An intimate, casual, and charming performer, he often successfully invited his audience to sing along with him. The stringbean performer, bent over his long-necked five-string banjo, dressed in an old work shirt and denims, completely reshaped American musical taste in folk, topical, and protest music. Seeger's banjo read, ''This machine surrounds hate and forces it to surrender,'' and if some segments of America reviled him as a Communist sympathizer, others perceived him as standing for peace, equality,

Pete Seeger

and decency in a troubled world. Seeger formed a bridge from the folk song revival of the 1940s, across the political repression of the 1950s, to the folk/protest scene of the 1960s. A gifted storyteller and musical historian, his influence on American music was incalculable.

Seeger was born in New York City in 1919, the son of a violinist mother and musicologist father, both on the faculty of the Juilliard School of Music. His uncle was the war poet Alan Seeger (who wrote ''Rendezvous With Death,''), his sister Peggy became an accomplished singer and songwriter and married British folk-legend Ewan MacColl, and his brother Mike made a career as one of the foremost proponents of banjo music. Pete Seeger learned banjo, ukelele, and guitar by his teens. He received a scholarship to Harvard in 1936 (same class as John Kennedy) but left in 1938 due to disinterest and poor grades. He then journeyed through the United States, collecting songs, meeting Woody Guthrie and Huddy Ledbetter (Leadbelly), and working with noted folk archivist and field recorder Alan Lomax.

In 1940, Seeger organized the Almanac Singers with Guthrie, Lee Hays, and Mill Lampell, and they recorded an album the next year. Seeger's zeal for labor organizing was nearly religious (''Talking Union''), and the group often performed anti-war songs for left-wing audiences and organizations. After Pearl Harbor, the Almanac Singers emphasized their patriotism (''Reuben James''), and Seeger served in World War II entertaining American troops by singing folk songs. In 1944, he helped create People's Songs Inc. (PSI), which formed a national network of folk music that eventually boasted over 2,000 members. In 1948, he toured with the anti-Cold War presidential candidate Henry Wallace, but PSI drew more interest from the FBI (Federal Bureau of Investigation) than labor unions, and it eventually went bankrupt in 1949.

At the low point of his fortunes in 1948, Seeger joined with Hays, Ronnie Gilbert, and Fred Hellerman to form The Weavers. Despite their unpopular leftward leanings (they were present at the Peekskill ''anti-Communist'' riot of September 1949), The Weavers not only helped to revive national interest in folk music, but also enjoyed astonishing commercial success. Their second single, ''Goodnight Irene'' backed with Leadbelly's ''Tzena, Tzena, Tzena,'' went to the top of the pop charts and sold over two million copies, a phenomenal amount for 1950. They followed with other hits that became (re)established in the American folk tradition, including ''On Top of Old Smokey,'' ''So Long Its Been Good to Know You,'' ''Wimoweh (The Lion Sleeps Tonight),'' ''Rock Island Line,'' and ''Kisses Sweeter Than Wine.'' Concert promoters and the media blacklisted the group in 1952 because of their political views and associations, and The Weavers all but disappeared; Seeger left the group to go solo in 1958 after opposing their participation in a cigarette commercial. Always active in left-wing politics, Seeger refused to answer questions when investigated by the House Un-American Activities Committee (HUAC) in 1955, although he never invoked the Fifth Amendment. He was indicted in 1956, convicted in 1961 on ten counts of contempt of Congress, and sentenced to an astounding ten years in jail. The United States Court of Appeals dismissed all charges against Seeger on a technicality, the very same week in 1962 that the cover version of his song ''Where Have All the Flowers Gone'' hit the Top 40.

In 1958, the success of the Kingston Trio touched off an enormous five-year folk music revival. Seeger's music was ''rediscovered'' and his career once again ascended. In 1962, Peter, Paul, and Mary made a hit out of ''If I Had a Hammer,'' a song Seeger co-wrote in his Weavers' days. The Byrds covered ''The Bells of

Rhymney,'' and eventually had a huge number one hit with "Turn! Turn! Turn!'' (1966), a biblical passage from Ecclesiastes that Seeger had set to music. In 1964, commercial radio listeners heard Seeger's voice for the first time in 12 years when his version of Malvina Reynolds' ''Little Boxes'' became a minor hit. Since the 1940s, Seeger had been one of the guiding lights of folk magazine *Sing Out!* (20,000 subscribers in 1965; bankrupt in 1967); in 1961 he helped Sis and Gordon Friese found *Broadside,* a bulletin of topical songs which helped stimulate the careers of singer/songwriters such as Bob Dylan, Phil Ochs, Tom Paxton, and Eric Anderson.

Paradoxically, Seeger had become a semi-popular success despite being one of the most picketed and blacklisted singers in American history. In 1962, the refusal of the ABC television folk music show, *Hootenanny,* to allow Seeger to perform resulted in a boycott that tore the folk community in half. The incident hurt him commercially, but only served to reinforce his standing as a martyr for freedom of speech. By the mid-1960s, Seeger had become a cultural hero through his outspoken commitment to the anti-war and civil rights struggle. He was involved in several civil rights campaigns in 1962-1965, and helped popularize the anthemic ''We Shall Overcome'' with mainstream audiences. Even supporters had felt that Seeger's belief that music could transform society was hopelessly naive, but for a moment, it all seemed to be coming true. This period of his greatest influence is wonderfully captured on the recording of his concert at Carnegie Hall in June 1963.

Then it all fell apart. The folk-topical song revival came to a crashing halt at the Newport Folk Festival in 1965, when Bob Dylan appeared with electric accompaniment. Seeger, who distrusted electric music as unauthentic, was crestfallen, and literally tried to pull the plug on the amplifiers. He fought on, however, despite Dylan's defection, the crumbling of the civil rights movement, and the escalation of the war in Asia. His anti-Vietnam War ballad, ''Waist Deep in the Big Muddy,'' became a classic of the 1960s, and he dusted off a series of anti-war ballads he had performed with the Almanac Singers a generation before. His disdain for wealth and worldly vanities seemed hopelessly outdated in an indulgent age, but his moral rectitude still inspired, or infuriated, vast numbers of Americans.

In the 1970s, Seeger mirrored the movement away from mass politics to localism and community control. He became particularly interested in ecology, co-founding the organization Clearwater, dedicated to the cleanup and revival of the Hudson river. Through sheer tenacity, he had become a living legend, more frequently parodied than banned. Critics from all over the spectrum praised his life's work, and the grandchildren of his original listeners attended his concerts.

Seeger widely influenced countless performers, and his instructional books and records inspired generations of self-taught musicians and folksingers. He always believed there was something in the best music to inform, stir, rally, direct, or cause social and personal interaction. His moral earnestness often overflowed into self-righteousness, but both friends and foes conceded his indominability. Perhaps his optimism was often naive, but his music helped unionize workers, inspired Americans to revere their own musical traditions, encouraged civil rights and anti-war activists, and helped clean up a river. In his case, at least, one person could make a difference, and the United States was a better place for his having lived in it.

—Jon Sterngass

FURTHER READING:

Cantwell, Robert. *When We Were Good: The Folk Revival.* Cambridge, Harvard University Press, 1996.

Dunaway, David King. *How Can I Keep from Singing: Pete Seeger.* New York, McGraw-Hill, 1981.

Seeger, Pete. *Where Have All The Flowers Gone: A Singer's Stories, Songs, Seeds, Robberies.* Bethlehem, Pennsylvania, Sing Out, 1993.

Seeger, Pete, and Jo Schwartz. *The Incomplete Folksinger.* New York, Simon and Schuster, 1972.

Seinfeld

The weekly situation comedy *Seinfeld,* which aired on NBC from 1990 to 1998, was the most highly-rated show on American television during much of its production run. The show marked the revival of a comic subgenre that had originated on radio and then was adapted for early television by such stars as Jack Benny and the team of George Burns and Gracie Allen. Jerry Seinfeld plays himself, a standup comedian starring in a sitcom about the life of a standup comedian. Like Benny and Burns, Seinfeld retained the privilege of walking back and forth across a metaphoric proscenium, speaking to the audience presentationally (i.e., in the second person) as a standup comic in a nightclub, and representationally (in the actions of a third person). The TV Jerry is a well-to-do New Yorker with a Manhattan

The cast of *Seinfeld*: (from left) Jason Alexander, Michael Richards, Julia Louis-Dreyfuss, and Jerry Seinfeld (center).

apartment, a small group of ''off-beat'' friends, a career, an active sex life, and several other recognizable trappings of a contemporary successful American.

Seinfeld however adds an element that neither Benny nor Burns ever dared venture. As a bridge in his physical movement between the nightclub stage and the apartment, he walks a balancing act of personal identities. He is, to most appearances, Jerry the American, one of TV's ''us,'' a televisually acceptable, conventionally well-dressed single white male. But Jerry is also, by turns of emphasis, one of ''them,'' a New York Jew, a sarcastic wisecracking cynic with an overbite, living on the margin of the American middle class. He can be funny, weird, exotic, lively, obnoxious, or any of the other qualities American ethnic mythology has tagged on to Jewishness.

In this way, *Seinfeld* shares more with the early fiction of Phillip Roth (especially *Good-bye, Columbus,* and *Portnoy's Complaint*) than with the Jewish-American characters that can be found in such sitcoms as *The Goldbergs, Briget Loves Bernie,* and *Rhoda.* Like Alexander Portnoy, Jerry lives out a dilemma that is simultaneously his deepest source of anxiety and the richest resource of his strength. He can easily ''pass'' for an American. Militantly bourgeois in attitude and taste, apparently freed of the burdens of millennial suffering, he is ready and willing to take on the high-end problems of sexual gratification and unchecked consumerism. But somehow, like the early Roth characters (especially the title character ''Eli the Fanatic''), Jerry cannot help but be heir to the legacy of the Diaspora. His sense of humor, the very asset that has allowed him entrée to an advantaged hedonistic secular life among the gentiles, remains rooted in a marginalized point of view that grows out of exclusion—and he is unexcludable without his Jewishness.

Seventy years after Al Jolson opened up the age of talking pictures with *The Jazz Singer,* the theme of Jewish assimilation remains insistent in American popular culture. Like Woody Allen, Jerry Seinfeld is no Yeshiva boy, but he is also under no illusions about transcending his Jewishness. Like Jolson and Allen, he enjoys the money and the small-nosed girls. But no matter how American his show business success makes him, he takes it for granted that he will always carry a second psychological passport. He is neither embarrassed by his Jewishness (like Walter Lippman) nor enamored of it (like Norman Podhoretz). He accepts the cards that were dealt him and makes the most of his hand, moving seamlessly between two spheres of consciousness with as much grace and refinement as he can muster.

His best friend George (Jason Alexander) would like to enjoy the American garden of gentile delights the way that Jerry does, but he cannot. He remains a prisoner of the Bronx. Round, balding, and bespectacled, he is not only physically removed from ideals of gentile televisual masculinity, but he is psychologically mired in a tangle of neuroses that he has inherited wholesale from his parents (played by Jerry Stiller and Estelle Harris). ''Next to George,'' the critic Joshua Ozersky has written, ''Jerry seems like Lee Marvin.'' And this is exactly what Jerry wants. The flexible Jerry is more successful than George at the two most important pursuits in Unmarried-American culture: making money and getting dates.

George embodies all three of the traditional Yiddish comic archetypes. George is a *schlemiel.* He meets a comely WASP woman, and goes away with her for a romantic weekend; however, while trying to build a cozy fire he burns down her father's vacation house. George is a *schlimazel.* When he is accused of racism for telling an African American co-worker that he resembles Sugar Ray Leonard, he finds himself compelled to stop black people on the street to try to

befriend them. George is a *nebbish.* All the principal characters on the show, we learn, masturbate frequently. But only George gets caught by his parents while doing it in their home.

What does a man with successful figures at both the bank and in the mirror see in a friendship with such a broadly defined American failure? Jerry the American needs George around to remind him of his Jewishness, which, despite any problems it might still present, is after all the secret engine of his professional success as a joke-teller. He takes George as his collaborator in creating a new television sitcom. George's surname, Constanza, is not Jewish. To suggest that George is not Jewish, is itself a kind of Jewish joke.

Elaine Benes (Julia Louis-Dreyfus), an outwardly graceful but internally haggard New Yorker, enhances the suggestion of Jerry as a cosmopolitan, enlightened contemporary. A former lover, she is now a member of his small circle of best friends. Elaine's chief identity is that of Unmarried-Gyno-American Worker. Like Mary Richards and Murphy Brown, she has yet to find a man worth slowing down for. Unlike them (or Jerry), however, Elaine lacks a lucrative position in the entertainment-industrial complex. Murphy and Mary both work in TV; when we meet Elaine, she works for a book publisher. Over the course of the series she works at a succession of jobs for neurotic and borderline psychotic men who derive much of their pleasure in life from being her boss. Elaine lacks a traditional ethnic identity, but instead is principally hyphenated by her sex and marital status. This stands in contrast to George's ethnic hyperbole, leaving Jerry just where he likes to be: in perfect balance at the American middle. He has girlfriends and girls as friends. He has money and power enough to play philosopher-king among the working stiffs (a group which includes the other members of the cast as well as the television audience).

Jerry's balance in the order of things is emphasized yet again by his physical positioning between tall, ectomorphic, manic Kramer (Michael Richards) and short, endomorphic, mono-polar George. Kramer functions in the sitcom as a kind of postmodern Ed Norton, entering and leaving Jerry's unlocked apartment at will. (The unlocked door of the inner city apartment somehow endured from *The Honeymooners* to *Seinfeld* as a teledramatic convention in defiance of rational convention.) Kramer's susceptibility to every identity that passes him by—entrepreneur, gambler, chef, playboy, hot-tub owner—puts him in a state of eternal self-image chaos, a sharp contrast to Jerry's elegantly constructed balance of American, Jew and Jewish-American. Jerry, the least marginal of the four characters, is the only one who is specifically and repeatedly identified as a Jew.

Jerry seems to be mocking himself when he refers to the sitcom that he and George pitch to NBC as ''a TV show about nothing'' (the idea is originally George's). But if *Seinfeld* is ''a TV show about nothing,'' as the magazines liked to hail it, then it would have achieved what Samuel Beckett just fell short of in stageplays such as *Waiting for Godot* and *Endgame.* But real life Jerry Seinfeld and his producer, Larry David, learn the lesson of Beckett's struggle: narrative cannot be stamped out. Like God, where it does not exist it will be created.

Jerry is a man committed to only one thing: detachment. He can make fun of fascists when George is mistaken for a neo-Nazi leader. He can make fun of communists when Elaine starts dating one. Jerry makes fun of Elaine when she stops going out with an attractive man ''just because'' he is an opponent of abortion rights. But positing no political beliefs of his own, and glad to take pot shots at anyone who does, he leaves the viewer with the implication that anyone stupid enough to be committed to political causes (or anything, as opposed to nothing) deserves ridicule. The metamorphosis of alienation into detachment is a signal achievement of the sitcom, the most popular of all commercial narrative genres.

—David Marc

FURTHER READING:

Irwin, William. *Seinfeld and Philosophy: A Book about Everything and Nothing.* Chicago, Illinois, Open Court, 1999.

Seinfeld, Jerry, et al. *Sein Off: The Final Days of Seinfeld.* New York, HarperEntertainment, 1998.

Tracy, Kathleen. *Jerry Seinfeld: The Entire Domain.* Secaucus, New Jersey, Carol Publishing, 1998.

Selena (1971-1995)

Singer Selena Quintanilla-Perez's life was short but dynamic. She began her career at the age of five, and was murdered just a month short of her twenty-fourth birthday. Raised in the bicultural world of

Selena

south Texas, she brought a flamboyant new face to Tejano, the Tex-Mex fusion music she performed, and, more significantly, she brought a new kind of pride and ambition to the young Latina women who were her fans. Though her future as an entertainer and businesswoman will forever remain a question mark, her death itself gave Anglo-American society a new perspective on the 28 million of their fellow citizens who comprise the Latino community of the United States.

Selena was born on April 16, 1971, in Corpus Christi, Texas. Her father, Abraham, a musician and restaurateur, put together a family band, playing the traditional Tejano music of the Texas borderland. By the time she was five, Selena was performing regularly with "Los Dinos" ("The Guys"), playing parties, weddings, and bars throughout Texas. Her strong, clear voice and personable interpretations captivated audiences, and by the time she was 15 the band had been renamed "Selena y los Dinos" and she had been chosen as the Tejano Music Awards "Female Entertainer of the Year." She would claim that award for the next eight years.

Once discovered by a major Latin music record label at the Tejano Music Awards, Selena was soon on her way to becoming a star. She was wildly popular with Latino audiences, especially young women, who looked to her as a role model. Raised a strict Jehovah's Witness, she embodied a "clean" moral lifestyle, while at the same time exuding vitality and sexuality on stage, wearing her trademark revealing costumes such as rhinestone-studded brassieres. In fact, the fusion of different cultures is what Selena was all about, and it was her unabashed expression of all of her differing selves that allowed so many Latinos to identify with her.

To understand Selena's contribution to American culture, it is necessary to know a little about the Tejano music tradition. In the early 1900s, Czech and German immigrants brought their accordions and polka beats to the south Texas border towns where they settled. That music blended with traditional Mexican music to form a distinctive music called "conjunto." In the 1930s and 1940s, migrant workers returned from fields in the north bringing with them the big band sounds that were then blended with the conjunto of la frontera (the border). The new music thus created was called Tejano, which is Spanish for Texan, and is the same word used to describe the Mexican-American people of Texas. Like the Latino people, Tejano music has continued to grow and change as it is exposed to new influences. By the time Selena brought her own voice to Tejano, it carried flavors of rap, rhythm and blues, country, and rock, as well as the traditional Mexican songs and the polka beat.

Like Tejano music, Selena herself was that uniquely American product—the fusion of cultures. Raised speaking only English, she learned Spanish songs phonetically and had only begun to learn the Spanish language months before her death. Though in part the obedient and submissive Latina daughter, she had definite plans for herself. In at least two important instances she defied her controlling father, first by marrying fellow band member Chris Perez, then by using her skills at costume design to open a clothing boutique, Selena, Etc. She had ambitions to become a crossover artist, and many critics, comparing her to Madonna and Marilyn Monroe, believe she could have made it.

Before these ambitions could be put to the test, Selena was shot by a trusted friend and employee. Yolanda Saldivar had been president of Selena's fan club when the two met and became friends. When Selena's clothing boutique required more time than she had to spare, she hired Saldivar to manage it for her. In March of 1995, however, Selena began to suspect Saldivar of stealing money and when she confronted her, Saldivar shot and killed her in the parking lot of a motel in Corpus Christi. Though Saldivar always insisted the shooting was an accident, she was convicted of murder and sentenced to life imprisonment. The Latino community across the southwest, reeling with pain and outrage, followed "El Juicio de Selena" ("The Selena Trial") closely, demanding punishment for the woman who had killed the golden girl.

Whether or not Selena would have achieved her crossover goal in life, she certainly achieved it in death. Before her murder, she had won the Grammy Award for Best Mexican-American Performance. Her album *Amor Prohibida* had sold 500,000 copies, and she had performed in Houston's Astrodome to a crowd of 62,000. Just months after her death, her posthumous album, *Dreaming of You,* debuted at number one on the Billboard Top 200 and sold over three million copies. Her songs received play on anglo radio stations, and a feature film and a television movie were made about her life and death. The former, titled *Selena* (1997), was released in two versions—one with Spanish subtitles—and starred Jennifer Lopez; the latter, *True Hollywood Stories: The Selena Murder Trial,* aired in 1996.

Perhaps Selena's greatest achievement, however, was in making Anglo-America take notice of its Latino counterpart. Though there are close to 30 million American Latinos, with over $300 billion in purchasing power, media and corporations often ignore them. After Selena's death, she became something of a folk hero in the United States Latino community, with her face appearing everywhere from street murals to bank checks, and hundreds of babies in Texas and California named after her. Business and the media responded to this surge of grief in unprecedented ways. *People Magazine* not only released a special southwest edition with Selena's death as the cover story, but followed up with a tribute issue, only the third such in the magazine's history, and continued to reach out to Latino readers with *People en Espanol.* During Yolanda Saldivar's trial, *TV Guide* provided bilingual coverage for the first time in its history, with English and Spanish versions of an article about the movie version of "The Selena Trial."

Perhaps in life Selena would not have been able to achieve the crossover she desired. Certainly it would not have come without conflict and controversy. Few Latin music performers have been welcomed into the anglo music scene, and those who have often alienate their Latin audiences by leaving too much of their roots behind them. Though her life was cut tragically short, Selena Quintanilla-Perez remains "una de nosotros" (one of us) to her Latino community, and she unquestionably opened the door for a wider awareness and appreciation of the Latin pop music she loved.

—Tina Gianoulis

FURTHER READING:

Arraras, Maria Celeste. *Selena's Secret: The Revealing Story Behind her Tragic Death.* New York, Simon and Schuster, 1997.

Patuski, Joe Nick. *Selena: Como La Flor.* Boston, Little, Brown, 1996.

Wheeler, Jill C. *Selena: The Queen of Tejano.* Edina, Minnesota, Abdo and Daughters, 1996.

Seles, Monica (1973—)

Yugoslavian-born Monica Seles burst onto the women's professional tennis scene in 1988 at the tender age of fifteen, and made it all the way to number one in the world in just two years. Easily recognizable because of her powerful two-handed groundstrokes and her loud grunting during points, Seles relished in her role as a young female sports celebrity and role model. In April, 1993, well on her way to becoming the most dominant women's tennis player of all time, a deranged Steffi Graf supporter stabbed her in the back during a match in Germany. This life-threatening incident focused public attention on the danger obsessed fans pose to pro athletes. Seles made a comeback in 1995, after an arduous twenty-seven month recuperation period. To the delight of her fans and the astonishment of her peers, she was a winner in her very first tournament back. An eighth Grand Slam victory soon followed.

—Steven Schneider

FURTHER READING:

Layden, Joseph. *Return of a Champion: The Monica Seles Story.* New York, St. Martin's Press, 1996.

Seles, Monica, and Nancy Ann Richardson. *Monica: My Journey from Fear to Victory.* New York, HarperCollins, 1996.

Sellers, Peter (1925-1980)

Born in London to parents who were professional performers in the music halls, Peter Sellers became one of Britain's foremost comic

Peter Sellers

actors of radio, film, and television in the 1950s and 1960s. Famous for his impeccable comic timing, his improvisation skills, and his ability to switch from one character to another, Sellers appeared in films as diverse as *The Ladykillers* (1958), *Lolita* (1962), and *Dr. Strangelove* (1964). But it was the Pink Panther series that both confirmed his versatility as an actor and raised him to an international superstar. Since his death in 1980, four biographies of Sellers have been published, and the actor has gained notoriety for his unpredictable behavior and the excesses of his life as a movie star.

Sellers spent the last couple of years of World War II in the Royal Air Force, where he infuriated high-ranking senior officers by impersonating their voices. After the war he tried to build a career as a drummer, but after an audition at the Windmill theatre in London, he became a comedian. In the late 1940s, Sellers established himself as a comedian and impressionist on BBC radio, working first on *Showtime,* a program that encouraged new talent. Later, he became a regular BBC ''voice man,'' impersonating well-known personalities on a show called *Ray's a Laugh.* In 1951, when he began working with Michael Bentine, Spike Milligan, and Harry Secombe on a radio show called *Crazy People,* later to become known as *The Goon Show,* Sellers's comic talent began to blossom. The anarchic, surrealistic humor of ''The Goons'' marked a significant break with the comedy that had gone before, and paved the way for the comic style of *Monty Python's Flying Circus* and the ''alternative'' comedy of the 1980s and 1990s. It was from working with ''The Goons'' that Sellers was able to move into films, having his first major success with the British-made *The Ladykillers* (1958), in which he worked alongside Alec Guinness and Margaret Rutherford. It was inevitable that he would eventually move to Hollywood, where he made the Pink Panther series of films for which he is, arguably, best known.

Five original Pink Panther movies were made, featuring Sellers as Inspector Clouseau, the endearingly clumsy and incompetent French detective. The first film, *The Pink Panther,* appeared in 1963, followed by *A Shot in the Dark* (1964), *The Return of the Pink Panther* (1975), *The Pink Panther Strikes Again* (1976), and *Revenge of the Pink Panther* in 1978. All the films focus on Clouseau's earnest efforts to solve bizarre, trivial, even non-existent mysteries with a maximum of fuss and melodramatic intrigue. The humor, as with much of Sellers's work, is based on language and voices. Clouseau's comic accent, his inability to understand or pronounce English words, and his attempts to cover up his mistakes with elaborate explanations, satirize our often misplaced respect for authorities of all kinds. A sixth Pink Panther film, *The Trail of the Pink Panther,* appeared in 1982, after Sellers's death. This final, ill-advised outing for Sellers's bumbling detective contains no original material involving him, being constructed from outtakes from the five earlier films. Sellers made over fifty feature films in his relatively short career in Hollywood and in Britain.

After a major heart attack in 1964, his performances, though occasionally brilliant, were no longer as consistent as they had been, and the films to which he contributed in the late 1960s and the 1970s are variable in their quality and their success at the box office. Roger Lewis's 1994 biography of Sellers, *The Life and Death of Peter Sellers,* points to his chaotic private life and dramatic mood swings as part of the reason for the inconsistency of his later work. Throughout the 1960s and 1970s, Sellers's behavior became increasingly unpredictable; he was a drug abuser, became self-destructively obsessed with people, and could be generous and dangerously violent by turns. He married four times, to Ann Hayes, Britt Ekland, Miranda Quarry, and Lynne Frederick, respectively, and was known to be sexually promiscuous. While he was a comic actor of extraordinary abilities, Sellers was also a vain, self-centered man, who enjoyed, and was ultimately let down by, his fame.

Lewis's biography draws loose connections between Sellers's on-screen persona and the private man, suggesting that the megalomania that made his performances so exacting spilled over into his private life. Peter Evans, an earlier, more reserved, biographer, confirms this when he suggests that such was his immersion in whatever role he was playing, Sellers had practically no personality of his own. However difficult or unpleasant he could be as a man, most of those who worked with him agree that as an actor, Sellers has left us a legacy of comic performance and innovation that is among the most rewarding of his generation.

—Chris Routledge

FURTHER READING:

Evans, Peter. *Peter Sellers: The Mask behind the Mask.* London, Severn House, 1981.

Lewis, Roger. *The Life and Death of Peter Sellers.* London, Century, 1994.

Rigelsford, Adrian. *Peter Sellers: A Celebration.* London, Virgin, 1997.

Walker, Alexander. *Peter Sellers: The Authorized Biography.* London, Wiedenfeld and Nicholson, 1981.

Selznick, David O. (1902-1965)

David Selznick's production of *Gone with the Wind* is enough to secure his place in history. While this landmark film was his most successful, his influence on movie production in the 1930s and 1940s also marks his career with greatness. He was a very successful producer and writer with other films to his credit, such as *David Copperfield* (1935), *A Star Is Born* (1937), and *Rebecca* (1940).

Selznick worked for his father's motion picture company, Lewis J. Selznick Productions, until it was forced into bankruptcy in 1923. His first produced feature was *Roulette* in 1924. Selznick joined Metro-Goldwyn-Mayer (MGM) in 1926 as a script reader and assistant story editor. After rapidly rising to supervisor of production he was fired because of disagreements with head of production Irving Thalberg .

Paramount made him their head of production in 1927, but after the depression forced salary cuts he moved to RKO Studios in 1931 as studio boss. While he was there, Selznick personally oversaw such productions as *A Bill of Divorcement* (1932) and *Little Women* (1933), both starring Katharine Hepburn.

When MGM decided that Thalberg's ill health made it sensible to spread some of his production duties around, Louis B. Mayer was able to lure Selznick back to MGM. Since Selznick had married Mayer's daughter Irene in 1929, his return to MGM sparked the saying, ''the son-in-law also rises.'' Intent on bringing more prestigious pictures to the screen, Selznick produced hits such as *Dinner at Eight* (1933) and *Anna Karenina* (1935). In the former picture, Selznick defied conventional wisdom and cast the film with big stars in every role, instead of just one star. By using such performers as Marie Dressler, Jean Harlow, and John Barrymore he produced a blockbuster hit.

David O. Selznick

In 1936 Selznick again left MGM to become an independent producer and founded Selznick International Pictures. His first film was the highly successful *A Star Is Born* (1937). His most memorable is, of course, *Gone with the Wind.* The film was fraught with problems, such as having a total of six directors and having to give up the distribution rights to MGM to get Clark Gable for the male lead. However, Selznick's search for an actress to play Scarlett O'Hara caused a national sensation, as young women everywhere, not just in Hollywood, auditioned for the role. This ultimate triumph won 10 Academy Awards and remains extremely popular. He followed this box office hit with the classic *Rebecca* (1940), directed by Alfred Hitchcock, which won a best picture Oscar.

After a massive tax debt forced his company onto the auction block Selznick formed a new company, David Selznick Productions. In this venue he became more of a talent scout than a producer. One of his biggest personal discoveries was Jennifer Jones, who had won an Oscar for *Song of Bernadette* (1943). While he was not responsible for discovering her, he fell in love with her and did his best to make her a superstar. He produced many films starring her, the most successful of which was 1946's *Duel in the Sun.*

When Selznick and Jones were married in 1949 he virtually gave up his independent producer status and became more of a Svengali to her. Pictures such as *Portrait of Jennie* (1949) and *A Farewell to Arms*

(1957) starring Jones were moderately successful, but Selznick became something of a joke for his obsession with his wife. He continued to work in Hollywood, but his preoccupation with his wife's career relegated him more and more to the background until his death. Nevertheless, David O. Selznick is a name that is firmly planted in motion picture history. He was the biggest of the independent producers at a time when such a thing was rare.

—Jill A. Gregg

FURTHER READING:

Haver, Ronald. *David O. Selznick's Hollywood.* New York, Knopf, 1980.

Selznick, David O. *Memo from David O. Selznick.* New York, Viking Press, 1972.

Thomson, David. *Showman: The Life of David O. Selznick.* New York, Knopf, 1992.

Sennett, Mack (1880-1960)

In February of 1914, Mack Sennett's Keystone company released a comedy called *Kid Auto Races at Venice,* in which a young English vaudevillian who had recently joined Sennett's company of comedians appeared briefly in a battered suit of morning clothes and top hat. His name was Charlie Chaplin and the cameo gave birth to the most famous comedic creation in cinema history, "The Tramp." The very name Mack Sennett resonates with images of early pioneering Hollywood, when rickety, makeshift "studios" sprang up in dusty streets and directors in plus-fours and caps cranked out one and two-reel silent movies with primitive equipment. It was an era both rough and romantic, the earliest days of the Dream Factory when maids and chauffeurs, waitresses, shopgirls, and street sweepers flocked to find fortune, and when fame too often fell victim to scandal in the hothouse atmosphere of the closed film community. It was a time, too, when comedy, brilliantly suited to the technical limitations of the early silent screen, reached a peak of public popularity with stars such as "Madcap" Mabel Normand, Roscoe "Fatty" Arbuckle, Ford Sterling, Chester Conklin, and a host of others. It was to the acumen, imagination, and energy of Mack Sennett, who entered legend and history as the "King of Comedy," that they owed their rise.

Born Michael Sinnott in Danville, Quebec, the son of an Irish Catholic innkeeper, Sennett harbored unfulfilled ambitions to become an opera singer. At age 22 he was working as a laborer in Massachusetts when a chance meeting with actress Marie Dressler led him to New York and an introduction to producer David Belasco. Ignoring Belasco's advice to go home, he embarked on a minor stage career in burlesque and musicals until 1908 when he talked himself into film work at the Biograph studios in Manhattan. He graduated from supporting roles to leads, co-starring with many top leading ladies of the day from Florence Lawrence (the "Biograph Girl") to Mary Pickford and the irrepressible Mabel Normand, who played a profound role in both his professional and personal life for many years. Significantly for his education in the filmmaking process, many of Sennett's films at Biograph were directed by D.W. Griffith, for whom he also wrote some scripts. Driven by curiosity and a desire to learn, by 1910 he was directing shorts at the studio.

In 1912, Mack Sennett, now an experienced director with a pronounced facility for comedy and, with former bookies Charles Bauman and Adam Kessel as his business partners, formed his Keystone company in California. Several of his Biograph colleagues joined him, notably Mabel Normand, the most gifted comedienne of her time. The first ever Keystone program, released in September, 1912, consisted of two split-reel comedies, *Cohen Collects a Debt* and *The Water Nymph*, prototypes for the unrestrained style that became the keystone trademark. Thereafter, Sennett, something of a slave driver, worked at a furious pace, turning out a reel of comedy per week, and rapidly became the foremost purveyor of filmed comedy in America. The earliest Keystone movies were crude, haphazard affairs, largely improvised from the flimsiest of scripts, but they had enormous physical gusto and hilarious sight gags, a stable of major comic acting talents, and Sennett's impeccable sense of timing and skillful editing to control the finished product. Gradually, as the company expanded both its roster of actors, the length of its films and its prodigious output, the frenzied, freewheeling custard-pie-in-the-face-slapstick farce that was its trademark gave way to more carefully considered and controlled material, and the general chaos that prevailed was subjected to better organization.

Within two years, Sennett's Keystone Kops (or ''Cops''), a bunch of inept, accident-prone policemen, were a national American institution in films that poked irreverent fun at the guardians of law and order; a little later they were joined by the famous Mack Sennett Bathing Beauties, a line-up of dizzy ''sexpots'' from whom several successful early female stars emerged in due course. In January 1914, Chaplin arrived, a total newcomer to film, at the invitation of Sennett, who had seen him on stage in Fred Karno's traveling vaudeville company. He stayed almost a year before being lured to Essanay by big money and more artistic freedom, but he made 35 films at Keystone, establishing himself not only as a star actor and creator of the Tramp, but also as a writer and director. He made several with Mabel Normand, and their partnership and his tenure with Sennett concluded with the six-reel *Tillie's Punctured Romance* (1914). Directed by Sennett, the film was unusual in that Chaplin and Normand played second fiddle to a star (Marie Dressler), and historically important in being the first feature-length comedy (90 minutes) to have been made anywhere in the world, exceeding the running time of any previous comic film by two-thirds.

Sennett, dedicated to an ever-increasing production schedule and to the editing process, and retaining final say over each and every film, hired several other directors to come in and make them. To the Kops and the Bathing beauties, he added the Kid Komedies series for children, pre-dating Hal Roach's famous Our Gang series by nearly ten years. In 1915, however, Keystone was absorbed into the new Triangle Film Corporation, which, with Sennett joining directors Griffith and Thomas Ince, could now boast a triumvirate of the American silent screen's most famous filmmaking names. Keystone retained autonomy within Triangle and benefited from larger budgets. Their productions became more polished, and their material more varied, with slapstick no longer the sole product. Humor was broadened to include what would now be called situation comedy, and a series of romantic comedies were made that provided star vehicles for the young Gloria Swanson. For all its seeming advantages, however, Triangle failed to live up to expectation and in 1917—at the cost of relinquishing the Keystone title—Sennett (following the example of Griffith and Ince) broke away and formed Mack Sennett Comedies, his own company releasing first through Paramount, and later Associate Producers and First National.

Living up to its name, the company continued to make two-reel comedies, but also produced several features, some showcasing Mabel Normand and comic Ben Turpin. Then, in 1923, he entered an association with Pathe that saw out the silent era. It was here that, continuing his gift for recognizing and nurturing talent, Sennett launched the career of the great comedian, Harry Langdon in a series of shorts. Throughout his career, Sennett adhered to assembly-line discipline and prodigious working hours (up to 18 a day), but to work for him as a writer or director was tantamount to attending a graduate school in how to make films. He hired Frank Capra to write gags for Langdon, and when the comedian left Sennett he took Capra with him.

The coming of sound toppled Mack Sennett from his throne as the King of Comedy, although he continued producing and directing for some years. He made low-budget shorts for the Educational studio, and produced some comedy shorts with W.C. Fields and a series of musical shorts with Bing Crosby for Paramount in 1932. At Educational in 1935, he directed *The Timid Young Man,* a short starring Buster Keaton (the only time they worked together), before retiring back to Canada, broke and alone. Mabel Normand, dogged by scandal and disillusioned in her long and stormy affair with Sennett that failed to lead to marriage, married actor Lew Cody in 1926 and had died of drug abuse and TB in 1930, aged 35. Their relationship is the subject of Jerry Herman's nostalgic musical, *Mack and Mabel,* first performed on Broadway in 1974 with Robert Preston and Bernadette Peters.

In 1937 Sennett received a special Academy Award ''to the master of fun, discoverer of stars, sympathetic, kindly, understanding comedy genius . . . for his lasting contribution to the comedy technique of the screen, the basic principles of which are as important today as when they were first put into practice.'' Mack Sennett, the self-proclaimed King of Comedy, wrote his autobiography under that title in 1954 and died on November 5, 1960 in Woodland Hills, California.

—Peter C. Holloran

FURTHER READING:

Lahue, Kalton C. *Mack Sennett's Keystone: The Man, the Myth, and the Comedies.* South Brunswick, A.S. Barnes, 1971.

Sennett, Mack. *King of Comedy.* Garden City, New York, Doubleday, 1954.

Sherk, Warren M., editor. *The Films of Mack Sennett.* Lanham, Maryland, Scarecrow Press, 1998.

Serial Killers

During the late 1970s and early 1980s, the threat of serial and mass murder became a topic of great popular and academic interest in America. While there is no murder ''epidemic,'' as hyperbolic writers and law-enforcement officials claimed in the mid-1980s, the apprehension of high-profile serial killers (such as David Berkowitz, Ted Bundy, John Wayne Gacy, and Henry Lee Lucas) and an apparent upswing in mass shootings in schoolyards, post offices, etc., served to bring the problem to public attention. In a capitalistic mass-media age where sensational news stories increase ratings and sell advertising time, the ''random'' killer (especially the serial murderer) provides good source material. He also inspires generations of fiction writers,

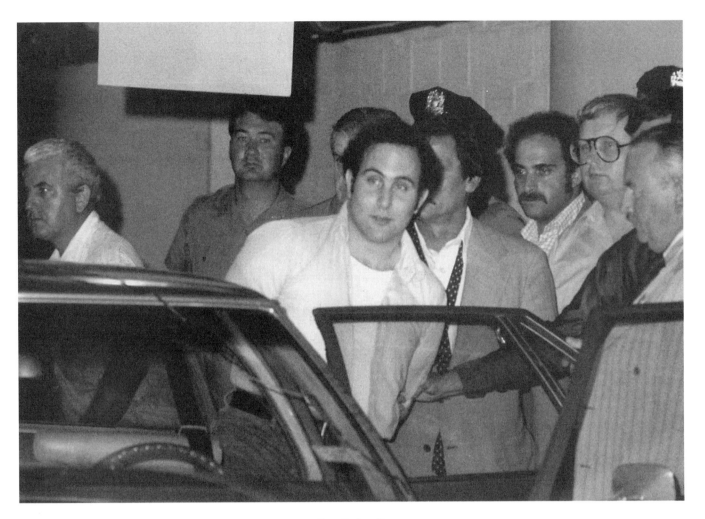

Serial killer David Berkowitz, the ''Son of Sam,'' being arrested by New York police.

who simultaneously view him not only as an artistic metaphor for any number of social ills but a guaranteed moneymaker. Literally thousands of fiction and nonfiction (''true crime'') novels and films centered on multiple killers have grossed hundreds of millions of dollars during the past twenty years in America alone. One of the most recognizable of these is the Oscar-winning film *The Silence of the Lambs*, which is based on a best-selling novel by Thomas Harris. Harris, in turn, was inspired to create his memorable work of fiction by his research into the lives of real-life serial killers and the law-enforcement agents (''profilers'') who pursue them. Most of the well-known fictional stories that feature serial and/or mass murder, then, are contemporary morality plays in which evil, murdering villains threaten the social fabric but are eventually brought to bay by the heroic profilers. The reality of serial and mass murder, however, is much more complicated.

Multiple homicide, whether called serial or mass murder, has always been a part of human history. Gilles de Rais, Countess Elizabeth Bathory, Jack the Ripper, Belle Gunness, Carl Panzram, Albert Fish, Earle Nelson, Peter Kurten, Ed Gein, Albert DeSalvo, Ian Brady and Myra Hindley, Edmund Kemper, Juan Corona, David Berkowitz, Ted Bundy, John Wayne Gacy, Peter Sutcliffe, Angelo Buono, Kenneth Bianchi, Dean Corll, Wayne Henley, Henry Lucas, Ottis Toole, Richard Ramirez, Joel Rifkin, Danny Rolling, Dennis

Nilsen, Jeffrey Dahmer, Andrei Chikatilo, and Aileen Wuornos are only some of the most notorious practitioners of multicide. However, ''serial murder'' has existed only, in the strictest sense, since FBI Agent Robert Ressler coined the term and the American mass media disseminated it throughout the culture during the 1980s. Before ''serial murder'' as a sobriquet came into vogue, the phenomenon in question was usually called ''lust murder'' or ''mass murder'' and included a variety of multiple-homicide crimes. Now, in criminological jargon, serial and mass murder usually refer to two disparate concepts. Complicating matters further, there are many ''subspecies'' of serial and mass murderer. All of them must be distinguished from other varieties of multiple killers, such as paid hit-men or state-sanctioned assassins, executioners, torturers, etc.

Serial murder is most commonly defined as the commission of three or more murders over a period of time, with a ''cooling off'' period or hiatus between each murder. The victims may or may not be known to the killer, but more often than not the social class any one victim represents to the killer is more important than the victim's identity. The fact that victims are often unknown to the killer prior to the murder episode leads many to call serial murder ''irrational'' or ''evil.'' In most cases, no comprehensible motive exists for the crimes, and the murders do not seem to provide the killer with any clearly understood, tangible benefits. According to Elliott Leyton, the serial-killer category most definitely does not encompass those who kill repeatedly for profit or for governments. These killers are performing more of a public "job" than a privately significant act; the motive is basically rational and readily apparent. By contrast, the serial killer, while not without certain "professional" aspirations of his own, works according to a more esoteric agenda which observers often find inscrutable. This leads them to call him insane, psychotic, or schizophrenic: psychiatric terms that all denote a severe and socially crippling disjunction between reality and perception. The terms do not fit most serial killers. The serial killer only appears nonrational because he operates from, as R. M. Holmes and J. De Burger have it, "intrinsic motive systems . . . that originate within the individual; they govern and structure the serial killer's behavior."

The vast majority of known serial killers are males, and the vast majority of their victims females (a fact which understandably leads many to conclude that serial murder is synonymous with sexual murder; however, this is not strictly the case). In August of 1985, the *FBI Law Enforcement Bulletin* published a series of articles (later expanded to a book-length study entitled *Sexual Homicide* in 1988) in which primary offender characteristics were listed. This data was compiled from lengthy interviews with thirty-six incarcerated serial murderers, all of them male. Most writers on the fact and fiction of serial murder, even those critical of law enforcement claims and methods, have been drawing on this specific set of FBI conclusions ever since, so the study is crucial to any analysis of the popular culture's portrayal of the "typical" serial murderer. He is usually a white male between twenty-five and thirty-five years old, though of course there are teen-aged and elderly serial killers as well. Generally, the male serial killer is at the height of his physical powers, a fact which not only serves him in the practical matter of overpowering victims but also empowers him in the public arena: his strength and apparent potency (and of course, choice of innocent victims) render him an effective media monster. He is also likely to be an eldest son or an only child and of average or above-average intelligence. His childhood may have been marked by incidents of sexual or physical abuse, and his parents may be divorced or flagrantly unfaithful to one another. He usually possesses a strong belief that he is more intelligent and privileged than ordinary people (a belief that only grows stronger when confronted by evidence to the contrary) and thus exempted from the social restrictions that govern the masses. No safe predictions can be made about his economic origins, but as Leyton notes, serial murder in our era is more a crime of the middle classes than of the lower or upper ranges of the socioeconomic hierarchy. Also, it should be noted that while males are overwhelmingly responsible for most serial/mass murders, there are more female multicides than commonly believed. A partial list of female American multiple killers alone includes Susan Denise Atkins, Patricia Krenwrinkel, Charlene Gallego, Belle Gunness, Nannie Doss, Martha Beck, Carol Bundy, Dorothea Puente, Priscilla Ford, Amy Archer-Gilligan, Anna Hahn, Mary Elanor Smith, Jane Toppan, Genene Jones, Judy Neeley, and Debra Brown. The most famous female multicide of all is Hungarian Countess Elizabeth Bathory, who with a coterie of female disciples imprisoned and murdered hundreds of women in her castle in the early 1600s.

Not all privately conceived acts of multiple homicide qualify as serial murders. Scholars now generally agree that mass murder forms a separate category. James Alan Fox and Jack Levin point out that mass murderers are generally caught at or near the crime scene, and that the crime is of horrific proportions but relatively short duration.

Unlike serial killers, who typically target strangers and traumatize a community over an extended period of time, the mass murderer plans one ultraviolent assault upon victims who, more often than not, are known to him. The mass murderer category can include depressed people who kill their entire families before committing suicide, but more commonly refers to those who violently retaliate against a specific group or class of people because of a real or imagined grievance; for example, disgruntled employees gunning down supervisors and coworkers. Racism or sexism also often motivates this kind of killer, as was the case with James Huberty, who killed twenty-one people in California because of an obsessive hatred of Hispanics; or Marc Lepine, who killed fourteen women at the University of Montreal because he blamed "feminists" for his romantic and professional difficulties. Massacres in public places (restaurants, schoolyards, classrooms, the work place, the post office, commuter trains, campuses, etc.) typically involve one heavily armed killer who racks up a high death toll. However, the massacre is a one-time-only event that often ends in the death of the killer by the police. Charles Whitman, who opened fire on students from a clock tower on the University of Texas campus in 1966, is probably the best-known example of this kind of mass murderer.

The spree killer occupies an intermediate position between the mass murderer and the serial murderer, although it should be noted that some authorities see no real distinction between spree killing, mass murder, and serial murder. The spree killer does not operate in secret like the serial killer, but neither does he lay siege to one specific locale until a SWAT team cuts him down. Instead, he often drives cross-country, with a companion or two (what R. M. Holmes and S. T. Holmes call "disciple killers"), murdering randomly and noisily as he goes until he is captured or killed. His weapon of choice is the gun, as opposed to the serial killer's more intimate knife. He makes little or no effort to cover his tracks; instead, he exults in the sheer nihilism of destruction and relies on brute mobility to keep him free as long as possible. His crimes are very visible but generally of short duration *because* of their high profile. During the 1950s, for example, embittered garbageman Charles Starkweather and his young girlfriend Caril Fugate rampaged across the Midwest, killing eleven people before they were captured and arousing the nation to new heights of paranoia concerning the dangers of juvenile delinquency. The conspicuousness of the spree killer contrasts significantly with the serial killer, who wishes to remain undetected for a period of time, at least in identity if not in deed.

It is undeniable that during the past half-century the United States has been producing more of these sensational criminals than the other Western industrialized nations. Sociologists point to many possible explanations. One of the most compelling is that the American cult of individuality has always prized violence (particularly for males) as a quick response to frustration. The simple outlaw (Jesse James, Billy the Kid) on the lam from the maddening complexities of communal, multicultural existence remains a heroic American icon. For many (if not most), violence is more attractive as a form of immediate gratification than the intangible results of long-term, peaceful political activism. In spite of the public rhetoric condemning violence, Americans have traditionally accepted even extreme levels of group and individual violence alike as appropriate responses to conditions perceived as intolerable. Marvin Wolfgang and Franco Ferracuti's hugely influential study, *The Subculture of Violence*, analyzes how it is possible for people within a culture to embrace some of its general values while denying, de-emphasizing, or inversing others, and yet remain within that culture. For many segments of the

American public, violence is regarded as a perfectly legitimate form of social expression and problem solving, dependent upon and framed in terms of prevailing local conditions even as it is decried by the supposedly overriding social discourse.

The serial killers and mass murderers of America are no exception or aberration in this sense. Their fantasies of murder and revenge are constructed from accessible cultural symbols recognizable to others. If such killers were truly alien to us, as facile notions of evil and deviance insist, then their motives would not be comprehensible. Indeed, many insist that serial murder *is* incomprehensible. While such exclusionary approaches are undeniably comforting, the unsettling observation must be made that serial murder is clearly rooted in our consensual reality and discourse. Its manifestation and shape obviously relies on the contemporary values, norms, and beliefs it seeks to overturn or, perversely enough, to uphold. In medieval Europe, multiple killers were perceived as, and often believed themselves to be, vampires (Gilles de Rais) or werewolves (Peter Stubb); in modern America, as demonically possessed monsters or formerly abused children, depending on the observer's sociopolitical orientation. The only commonality one can easily discern about multiple murderers from century to century and country to country is their monstrous, outcast status. In ancient legend and contemporary fiction, they lurk on the fringes of civilization, raid us in our vulnerability, then retreat back into the wilderness until a hero (usually an amateur or professional detective) can find them and destroy them. After this ritual expurgation of the murderous exile, the people can reassume their complacency until the next time. In the interval, however, narrative myths keep alive the awareness that somewhere out there, the monsters (be they Grendel or Norman Bates) grow hungry. The names and details may change from one generation's folklore to the next, but the basic plot remains.

—Philip Simpson

FURTHER READING:

Caputi, Jane. *The Age of Sex Crime.* Bowling Green, Ohio, Bowling Green State University Popular Press, 1987.

Douglas, John and Mark Olshaker. *Journey into Darkness.* New York, Pocket, 1997.

———. *Mind Hunter: Inside the FBI's Elite Serial Crime Unit, 1995.* New York, Pocket, 1996.

Fox, James Alan, and Jack Levin. *Overkill: Mass Murder and Serial Killing Exposed, 1994.* New York, Dell, 1996.

Hickey, Eric. *Serial Murderers and Their Victims.* Pacific Grove, California, Brooks/Cole Publishing Company, 1991.

Holmes, R. M. and J. De Burger. *Serial Murder.* Newbury Park, California, Sage, 1988.

Holmes, R. M. and S. T. Holmes. *Murder in America.* Newbury Park, California, Sage, 1994.

Jenkins, Philip. *Using Murder: The Social Construction of Serial Homicide.* New York, Aldine de Gruyter, 1994.

Keppel, Robert and William J. Birnes. *Signature Killers.* New York, Pocket, 1997.

Leyton, Elliott. *Hunting Humans: Inside the Minds of Mass Murderers.* New York, Pocket, 1988.

Norris, Joel. *Serial Killers: The Growing Menace.* New York, Doubleday, 1988.

Ressler, Robert and Tom Shachtman. *Whoever Fights Monsters.* New York, St. Martin's Press, 1992.

Ressler, Robert, Ann W. Burgess, Roger L. Depue, John E. Douglas, Robert R. Hazelwood, Kenneth V. Laming, and Cindy Lent. *FBI Law Enforcement Bulletin.* 54.8, August 1985, 2-31.

Ressler, Robert K., Ann W. Burgess, and John E. Douglas. *Sexual Homicide: Patterns and Motives.* Lexington, Massachusetts, Lexington Books, 1988.

Schechter, Harold and David Everitt. *The A to Z Encyclopedia of Serial Killers.* New York, Pocket, 1996.

Seltzer, Mark. *Serial Killers: Death and Life in America's Wound Culture.* New York, Routledge, 1998.

Tithecott, Richard. *Of Men and Monsters: Jeffrey Dahmer and the Construction of the Serial Killer.* Madison, Wisconsin, University of Wisconsin Press, 1997.

Wilson, Colin and Daman Wilson. *The Killers among Us: Motives behind Their Madness.* New York, Warner, 1996.

Serling, Rod (1924-1975)

Best known as the host of television's *The Twilight Zone*, Rod Serling was a prolific author of live teleplays and television scripts who did much to raise the artistic bar of a fledgling medium in the 1950s and 1960s. With contemporaries such as Paddy Chayefsky and

Rod Serling

Reginald Rose, Serling found television a reprobate cousin to film and theater, and left it a respected forum for expression.

Born Rodman Edward Serling on Christmas Day 1924, he grew up in the sleepy university town of Binghamton in upstate New York. He served in the army during World War II, seeing combat action in the Philippines. Hospitalized with multiple shrapnel wounds, Serling sought an outlet for his pent-up emotions. "I was bitter about everything and at loose ends when I got out of the service," he later recalled. "I think I turned to writing to get it off my chest."

When he returned from the war, Serling began selling radio scripts to programs in New York City. When television's growing popularity created a demand for writers, he moved on to that medium. In four years of freelancing, Serling saw 71 of his teleplays produced, but none of them approached the quality of his 72nd. "Patterns," a powerful drama about internecine warfare within the halls of a major corporation, aired on *Kraft Television Theatre* on January 12, 1955. It earned Serling the first of six Emmy Awards and provided his big break.

The glowing reviews of "Patterns" made Serling one of the hottest commodities in the entertainment industry. "I found I could sell everything I had—and I did," he said later. Some of his scripts were brilliant. The harrowing boxing drama "Requiem for a Heavyweight" became a live television classic, for example. Others should have remained buried in the author's desk drawer. All of them bore the trademark Serling attributes of moral probity and social concern.

Those social concerns occasionally got Serling into trouble with jittery advertisers and network censors, however, and as a defiant defender of free expression, he bristled at every change to his work. In one instance, the word "lucky" was stricken from one of Serling's scripts because the sponsor, a tobacco company, did not want viewers to be reminded of Lucky Strike cigarettes. That was harmless compared to what CBS did to his drama "A Town Has Turned to Dust." An outspoken progressive on civil rights issues, Serling had penned a script based on the case of Emmett Till, a black teenager who was lynched for allegedly whistling at a white woman. The network, afraid that the show would outrage viewers in the South, changed the setting from present-day Mississippi to Mexico in the 1870s. Other racially charged story elements were likewise toned down. Of his original script, the author lamented, "They chopped it up like a roomful of butchers at work on a steer."

In part because of his desire to make an end run around the censors, Serling turned his creative energies in 1959 away from live drama. He envisioned a weekly half-hour fantasy anthology series that could address philosophical and political topics in an oblique way. Intrigued at the prospect of signing up one of television's most respected writers, CBS green-lighted the project, which Serling christened *The Twilight Zone.* He was given total artistic control along with the title of executive producer.

Twilight Zone debuted on October 2, 1959, to generally positive reviews. Literate and highly entertaining, the show raised the science fiction/fantasy genre to a new level of artistic quality. True to Serling's concept, many of the stories used sci-fi trappings to speak to contemporary social issues like racism, cultural conformity, and Cold War paranoia. For actors, the series relied on a dizzying repertory company of seasoned character players and up-and-comers. Serling himself joined their ranks by serving as on-camera host/narrator. His bizarre persona—clenched teeth and gravelly monotone, crisp Kuppenheimer suits and the eternally cupped cigarette—made him seem like some kind of celestial undertaker beamed in to viewers' homes once a week for their edification and enjoyment.

In addition to hosting and serving as executive producer, Serling wrote 92 of *Twilight Zone*'s 156 episodes over the course of five seasons. He contributed some of the show's most memorable teleplays, including "Eye of the Beholder," which explored relative perceptions of beauty through the eyes of a "disfigured" young woman. Unfortunately, the demands on Serling's time and concentration also forced him to write quickly and sloppily. Many of the show's worst installments—and its often preachy and moralizing tone—bore his imprimatur as well.

With the occasional critical brickbat, however, came the fame and recognition due to the unmistakable face and voice of a successful network television series. Serling collected numerous awards for his work on *Twilight Zone,* including another Emmy. After the series was canceled in 1964, he went back to writing dramatic teleplays for anthology shows. In 1968, he wrote the first three drafts of the screenplay for *Planet of the Apes.* His verbose, purple style still can be heard in the finished film, voiced with delicious pomposity by the perfectly cast Charlton Heston.

Lured back to series television in 1970, Serling lent his name and visage to *Night Gallery*, a *Twilight Zone*-esque anthology that ran for two seasons on NBC, but while he penned some exceptional episodes, Serling became frustrated with the network's vision of the show as, in his words, was "Mannix in a cemetery." He even suffered the indignity of having several of his own scripts rejected for insufficiently frightening content. Contractually bound to serve as host, the humiliated fantasist desultorily went through his paces until the show's cancellation. Three years later, he died following complications of heart bypass surgery. To the end, he remained committed to the integrity of his work and the vision of a higher standard of televised entertainment.

—Robert E. Schnakenberg

FURTHER READING:

Sander, George F. *Serling: The Rise and Twilight of Television's Last Angry Man.* New York, Plume, 1994.

Zicree, Marc Scott. *The Twilight Zone Companion.* New York, Bantam, 1989.

Sesame Street

Broadcast on more than 300 Public Broadcasting Service (PBS) stations and in more than 140 countries around the world, this widely acclaimed children's television program celebrated its 30th anniversary in 1998. It has won more than 100 of the top awards in its field, including 71 Emmys, two Peabodys, eight Grammies, four Parent's Choice Awards, and the Action for Children's Television Special Achievement Award. Created by Joan Ganz Cooney for the Children's Television Network to provide educational material to inner-city kids, *Sesame Street* has endured by remaining true to its initial goals while changing with the times. It survived the deaths of Will Lee, who played Mr. Hooper, one of its major characters, and of Jim Henson, its creative force, who made his Muppet characters like Kermit the Frog, Big Bird, and Cookie Monster some of the most familiar faces in American popular culture. Other characters have come and gone, and actors have been replaced over the years, but *Sesame Street* remained an important program by the end of the century.

Joan Ganz Cooney, the creator of Sesame Street, standing with Big Bird and other Sesame Street characters.

The originators of *Sesame Street* spent several years culling the expertise from relevant fields to present a show that would educate and entertain at the same time. It was geared toward a viewing culture in which the typical child will have spent over 5000 hours watching television before entering first grade, and 19,000 hours by high-school graduation. According to Cooney, none of those involved in the beginning realized that *Sesame Street* would become an icon of popular culture and a family to which generations of children would belong. From the beginning *Sesame Street* employed techniques that had been successful in commercials by presenting educational material in the form of fast-paced, highly visual, and oft-repeated commercials. Children who watched the show quickly learned the alphabet, numbers, concepts, and relationships through repetition. The songs sung daily on *Sesame Street* became part of the repertoire of pre-schoolers and parents alike for the same reason. Over the years, the producers of the show developed a specific curriculum for each season aimed at imparting key information and concepts. For example, in Season 29 the show sought to teach social concepts such as acceptance, cooperation, tolerance, conflict resolution, birth, love, and marriage; practical skills such as addition, computers, drawing, geography, and history; and social awareness of such issues as cultural diversity, handicaps, Native Americans, Hispanic, and Chinese Americans.

The adults who appeared on the show at its outset won their roles by auditioning before real kids who chose only those with whom they felt comfortable; many of them have remained with the show for many years. Over the years, the adults have been chosen to represent specific role models for young children. Maria, played by Sonia Manzano, joined *Sesame Street* in 1974 as a young teenager who worked at the lending library. She grew up on the show, married Luis (Emilio Delgado) and had a baby, teaching children about love, marriage, and birth at the same time. Bob McGrath, one of the original cast, has continued to provide stability as children grew up and watched the show with their own children. Gordon, played by Roscoe Orman since 1973, was already married to Susan (Loretta Long) when the show began. Later they adopted a son and taught children about adoption. In response to concerns of the National Organization for Women (NOW) that the character of Susan had become a negative role model for young girls, Susan became a public-health nurse. From the show's inception to his death in 1982, Mr. Hooper (Will Lee) ran the neighborhood store, representing the ideal grandfather as he served up love, comfort, and cookies. *Sesame Street* used his death to help children recognize the importance of memories when someone they love dies and to understand that death is real and final. Other adults have been added to the show, including Buffy St. Marie, a Native American folksinger, comedienne Ruth Buzzi, who uses magical objects in her thrift shop to tell stories to children in the studio and at home, and singer Savion Glover, who entertains and teaches with music.

It was the creative genius of Jim Henson, however, that gave birth to the Muppets, some of the best loved children's characters of all time. Henson had brought the Muppet named Rowlf to national attention on *The Jimmy Dean Show* and was hired to do a series of commercials with his appealing inventions that were a combination of marionettes and puppets. The first Muppets were simple pieces of cloth that came alive under his hand, and the secret of how the Muppets are made is still closely guarded. Originally, the Muppets were not meant to interact with the adults, but tests revealed that young children paid more attention when their favorites were on screen. This allowed the show's producers to use the Muppets as surrogate children. For example, Big Bird, operated by Carol Spinney, is the epitome of a child who with the best of intentions is often confused and who constantly makes mistakes. One of the best loved plots on *Sesame Street* concerned the friendship of Big Bird and Mr. Snuffleupagus, who was thought by the whole neighborhood to be invisible for over a decade. One of the best loved Muppets, Kermit the Frog, appeared on the show only for a short time. In the early days, Kermit served as a roving reporter, attempting to discover the truth behind various tales and usually becoming an unwitting part of the story. Henson chose to remove the frog from *Sesame Street* because he had appeared in commercials before the show aired. Kermit went on to star in *The Muppet Show* and a series of movies.

Bert and Ernie, the Odd Couple of Sesame Street, have demonstrated the give and take of friendship through three decades of manipulation on the part of Ernie and gullibility on the part of Bert. Grover, on the other hand, is bright and patient and always ready to share his wisdom by teaching concepts and relationships. Oscar the Grouch, with his irascible personality, teaches children that some people use gruffness to hide a heart of gold. Cookie Monster allows children to laugh at the selfishness that they sense is part of their own personalities. Perhaps the favorite of the newer Muppets has been Elmo, who represents the sweet, gentle, and trusting child. Elmo frequently visits *The Rosie O'Donnell Show* as a welcomed guest, saying whatever comes to mind and expressing his affection through frequent kisses, just as many small children do. Indeed, with some help from O'Donnell, the Tickle Me Elmo doll became the top-selling toy of 1996. It is impossible to say whether or not *Sesame Street* would have succeeded without the Muppets, but no one would argue that the show has endured in great part because of their charm and originality and because of the hard work of those who manipulate them. In addition to Carol Spinney (Big Bird), Frank Oz continues to operate Bert, Grover, and the Cookie Monster.

Guest stars have been a staple of *Sesame Street* since its inception. Actor Noah Wylie noted that the most exciting thing about being a guest star was being able to meet his idol Big Bird. One of the classic moments in television occurred when a plethora of guest stars, including Willie Nelson, Jane Curtain, and Danny DeVito, implored Ernie to "put down the duckie if you want to play the saxophone." They referred, of course, to Ernie's tendency to clutch his rubber duckie the way that Linus clutches his blanket.

Over 30 years, *Sesame Street* has not escaped criticism, however. Some studies have demonstrated that television stunts imagination, turns out restless and ill-informed students, and that kids who grow up watching *Sesame Street* expect school to be like the show: colorful, fast-paced, and entertaining. In the 1980s, right-wing critics demanded that the show should be removed from the air because the close relationship of Muppets Ernie and Bert suggested that they were gay. Conservatives who deplored the use of tax money to fund public television used this alleged relationship as support for cutting out all funds to public television stations and to the National Endowment for the Arts (NEA). On the other hand, many teachers and parents agreed with a 1988 report that found that watching television may nurture attention-focusing capabilities and self control, while promoting teacher-student responses. Students who watched *Sesame Street* and its sister show for older children, *The Electric Company,* were found to be more proficient in basic skills.

—Elizabeth Purdy

FURTHER READING:

Borgenicht, David. *Sesame Street Unpaved: Scripts, Stories, Secrets, and Songs.* New York, Hyperion, 1998.

Frye, Karen Hill. *Television's Sesame Street: An Experiment in Early Education.* Los Angeles, Center for Afro-American Studies, University of California, 1972.

Lesser, Gerald S. *Children and Television: Lessons from Sesame Street.* New York, Random House, 1974.

Polsky, Richard M. *Getting to Sesame Street: Origins of the Children's Television Workshop.* New York, Praeger, 1974.

Seven Days in May

Released in 1964, director John Frankenheimer's political thriller is based on the 1962 Fletcher Knebel and Charles W. Bailey II novel of the same title. Addressing the issue of nuclear disarmament treaties at the height of the Cold War, *Seven Days in May* tells of a coup by U.S. military leaders in response to American participation in such a disarmament treaty. Fueled by a combination of patriotism and megalomania, Chairman of the Joint Chiefs of Staff General James Mattoon Scott plots to "save" the United States from a President who is willing to trust a nation "who has never honored" a single treaty in their existence. Black and white cinematography adds to the film's tense dialogue provided by screenplay writer Rod Sterling.

—Lori C. Walters

FURTHER READING:

Knebel, Fletcher, and Charles W. Bailey II. *Seven Days in May.* New York, Harper and Row Publishers, n.d.

The Seven Year Itch

Released in 1955, *The Seven Year Itch* represents the epitome of Marilyn Monroe's popular screen persona as the naive and sexually appealing blond. Directed by Billy Wilder and based on the play of the same name by George Axelrod, the film centers around the supposed tendency of men married for seven years to seek extramarital affairs. One hot New York summer, while his wife is vacationing in Maine, a middle-aged publisher (Tom Ewell) considers just such an affair with his pretty, young neighbor (Monroe). In the end, however, he chooses to remain faithful and leaves to join his wife. The film features several humorous sexual fantasy sequences and the famous image of Monroe exposing her shapely legs as she stands over a subway vent in a billowy white dress.

—Scott W. Hoffman

FURTHER READING:

Conway, Michael, and Mark Ricci. *The Complete Films of Marilyn Monroe.* New York, Carol Publishing Group, 1994.

Zolotow, Maurice. *Billy Wilder in Hollywood.* New York, Limelight Editions, 1992.

Seventeen

Seventeen magazine first appeared on newsstands in September, 1944, and it forever changed the media and consumer market for teenage girls. It was not the first publication to notice teenage girls, but it was the first that successfully reached a large teenage audience by devoting an entire magazine to them. Physically larger than today's magazine, *Seventeen* was initially 10 3/8-by-13 1/8 inches, printed on quality, thirty-five pound paper. The reader was first attracted to the colorful cover that promised "Young fashions and beauty, movies and music, ideas and people," as well as the section headings dividing the entire magazine into well-defined categories; "What You Wear," "How You Look and Feel," "Getting Along in the World," "Your Mind," and "Having Fun." Inside its covers, *Seventeen* offered a world of advertising, shopping, responsibility, and advice in the voice of a big sister or aunt, older and experienced, yet friendly and concerned. From the beginning, *Seventeen* was remarkably popular with teenage girls—all 400,000 copies of the first issue sold out in six days. By February, 1947, circulation exceeded one million, and over two-and-a-half million copies sold monthly by July, 1949. This success has continued for over 50 years, and despite stiff competition in the 1980s and 1990s, *Seventeen* is still the most widely read magazine for teenage girls.

In 1944, publisher Walter Annenberg of Triangle Publications decided to overhaul a dying movie screen magazine called *Stardom.* Helen Valentine, promotional director at *Mademoiselle,* agreed to become editor-in-chief of the new magazine if she could design it as a service magazine for teenage girls. She borrowed the name from Booth Tarkington's novel, *Seventeen,* because she thought it fit the thirteen- to eighteen-year-old age group she wanted to reach. While the bulk of the new magazine was designed to focus on fashion and beauty, Valentine insisted that it treat teenage girls seriously and respect what she perceived to be their emotional and intellectual needs. In addition to helping teenage girls choose their first lipstick and survive their first dates, Valentine wanted to teach them about the world and their place in it as responsible citizens.

At a time when advertisers, manufacturers, and media producers were beginning to recognize the economic importance of teenagers, the magazine's editors and publishers invested substantial resources in interpreting and promoting their definition of a prototypical teenage girl, whom they dubbed "Teena." In an effort to help develop the image of the teenage girl as a consumer of the magazine and the products advertised within its covers, *Seventeen's* promotional staff created an advertising advisory board to encourage age-appropriate advertisements and unite advertising and editorial content into a seamless product. Rejecting ads for dark red nail polish or shoes with spiked heels, and discouraging ad copy with heavy slang, *Seventeen* preferred to advertise a "wholesome" teenage girl who dressed neatly and conservatively for high school and dates. Triangle Publications initially invested over $500,000 in a lavish promotional campaign to create and distribute these images, attract advertising, and strengthen the teenage market.

The content balance of *Seventeen* shifted over the years in response to internal institutional changes as well as external social and political changes. During *Seventeen's* early years, articles addressed serious issues such as the political system, preparing to vote, development of the new United Nations, postwar inflation, and atomic energy. Book reviews further encouraged teenagers to read about community forums, the World Youth Conference, and college and career options for young women. These messages were always embedded in a magazine primarily devoted to fashion and beauty that encouraged girls to spend endless hours learning to fix their hair, shape or enhance their body types, pick the right clothes, read up on sports to be interesting for their dates, and learn to cook, decorate, and prepare the perfect party. But reader letters confirm that many of the magazine's consumers read the political articles seriously, could articulate their opinions intelligently, and wanted more coverage of these issues.

As the median age of marriage dropped during the postwar years and more women married in their teens, *Seventeen's* editorial message—not to marry young—was increasingly in conflict with its proliferation of wedding-related advertising for engagement rings, hope chests, silver, linen, china, and carpets. Advertisements pictured dreamy-eyed young women in their new homes with their new, handsome husbands, or sitting in their bedrooms happily collecting china or silver in anticipation of their wedding day. The magazine sought to present a variety of options and to continue to reach its readers who were marrying right out of high school as well as those going on to college and work.

In 1951, Helen Valentine was fired as editor-in-chief due to conflicts within the corporation. The woman who brought the original vision and inspiration to the magazine and her supporters moved on to create other magazines. *Seventeen* retained its basic structure but entered a period of transition toward closer ties with advertisers and away from encouraging responsible citizenship. Categories like "Your Mind" disappeared and "Getting Along in the World" became "You and Others." The sections entitled "What You Wear," "How You Look and Feel," "Home Food and Doings," and "Having Fun" became noticeably longer, encompassing most of the magazine by the mid-1950s.

Seventeen responded to the feminist movement of the 1960s and 1970s with a shift towards self-development and independence. Articles on the Peace Corps, new careers in science, teen democrats and republicans, and prejudice joined the preponderance of articles on clothes, looks, and domestic talents. The thirtieth anniversary edition in September, 1974, heralded the new opportunities that had opened for teenage girls since the 1940s, when their futures were centered around home and family. In the 1970s, the article claimed, discrimination based on sex no longer existed in the workplace. Girls could be anything they wanted to be and could successfully combine their careers with family life. The conservative 1980s, however, marked a return to more domestic and traditionally feminine content, and a decline in articles encouraging self-development. The more serious content, therefore has changed with the years, but the magazine never regained its initial commitment to politics, current events, and civic consumerism.

For over 50 years *Seventeen* has remained a fashion and beauty magazine that addresses teenage girls' interpersonal concerns with boys, family, and friends above all else. Other magazines have tried to copy this formula, but it wasn't until *Sassy* entered the market in the late 1980s that *Seventeen* faced serious competition. *Sassy* was more outrageous and tried harder to imitate the language that readers spoke. Magazines like *Young Miss* also began put more emphasis on boys and sex. While *Seventeen* responded in kind, it tried to remain balanced—to continue to cover fashion, beauty, relationships, school, and entertainment as well as boys.

Seventeen emerged amid economic, social, cultural, and institutional changes that provided the basis for the emerging "teenage girl." The decreasing presence of teenagers in the full-time work force along with growing high school attendance enhanced the separation of teenagers from the adult world and increased the potential for a distinct, age-specific identity. Teenagers began to rely more heavily on their peers and on commercial popular culture, such as movies and music, for guidance and entertainment. With their growing access to disposable income, especially in the years following World War II, they created an opportunity for a magazine that spoke to them directly about issues that were important to them. It is clear that *Seventeen's* messages were significant for the millions of teenage girls who continued to read the magazine and praise its efforts. The magazine played a central role in identifying and constructing teenage girls as a distinct group and in establishing their economic viability as a distinct market.

In the 50th anniversary edition, September 1994, the editorial staff reflected on half a century of *Seventeen,* concluding that it is undoubtedly a different magazine in the 1990s because teens are growing up in a different world. Teenagers today no longer look to adults for information, guidance, and taste. They are more focused on their peers and more likely to reject direct advice. Today's issues, such as gun violence, AIDS, and homelessness, personally affect teenagers who have been exposed to adult topics, violence, and sexuality, whether in their own lives, on talk shows, news, or in movies, far more than their counterparts in the 1940s. Though they may be more knowledgeable and jaded on one level, this veneer of sophistication does not necessarily make teenage girls more mature than they were in the 1940s. Regardless of how much a teenage girl knows about the range of sexual preferences and acts, infidelity, and relationship problems, her first date is still scary and her first kiss still exciting. Although "Teena" in the 1990s is more likely to be Black, Latina, or Asian American, consumer culture for teenage girls is permanently established and continues to thrive. *Seventeen* still interprets teenage girls for advertisers, manufacturers, and society at large, but it is no longer the only voice doing so.

—Kelly Schrum

FURTHER READING:

Budgeon, Shelley, and Dawn H. Currie. "From Feminism to Postfeminism: Women's Liberation in Fashion Magazines." *Women's Studies International Forum.* Vol. 18, No. 2, 1995, 173-86.

McCracken, Ellen. *Decoding Women's Magazines: From Mademoiselle to Ms.* New York, St. Martin's, 1993.

Palladino, Grace. *Teenagers: An American History.* New York, Basic, 1996.

Peirce, Kate. "A Feminist Theoretical Perspective on the Socialization of Teenage Girls through *Seventeen Magazine.*" *Sex Roles.* Vol. 23, No. 9/10, November 1990, 491-500.

Schlenker, Jennifer A., Sandra L. Caron, and William A. Halteman. "A Feminist Analysis of *Seventeen* Magazine: Content Analysis from 1945 to 1995." *Sex Roles.* Vol. 38, No. 1/2, 1998, 135-49.

Schrum, Kelly. "'Teena Means Business': Teenage Girls' Culture and *Seventeen* Magazine, 1944-1950." In *Delinquents and Debutantes: Twentieth-Century American Girls' Cultures,* edited by Sherrie A. Inness. New York, New York University Press, 1998, 134-63.

"Seventeen: A Unique Case Study." *Tide.* April 15, 1945, 19-20.

Sex and the Single Girl

When Helen Gurley Brown's candid primer *Sex and the Single Girl* was published in 1962, both its provocative title and spirited tips on men, money, and morals caused a sensation. It became one of the bestselling books of the year and went on to international success in translation as well. Overnight its author became a media sensation, and Brown just a few years later would be practically handed a magazine of her own—*Cosmopolitan*—to remake according to the *Sex and the Single Girl* principles.

Sex and the Single Girl was published only two years after the oral contraceptive pill appeared on the market in the United States. Though there were tens of millions of unmarried women in the country, conventional attitudes in the media—with the exception of *Playboy*—largely assumed that women did not engage in premarital

Helen Gurley Brown, author of *Sex and the Single Girl*.

sexual relations; if they did, they were usually shown to suffer degradation, unwanted pregnancy, or social ostracism as a result of it. Magazines for young women featured articles that recommended "saying no" as a strategy to avoid a man's pressures for them to have sex while on a date. Brides were then still generally expected to be virgins, and abortion was still illegal in most states.

Belying her glamour-girl persona, Brown was actually of humble origins. A native of the Ozarks, she could not afford college, and so learned how to type and got a job as a secretary. Eventually she became an advertising copywriter, and by 1959 (also the year of her marriage to film producer David Brown) she was the highest-paid woman in advertising on the West Coast. Wishing to write a book, Brown heeded the advice of her husband: "Write what you know." And so Brown began pounding out chapters for a primer on the single life for young women.

Sex and the Single Girl offered tips on decorating, on making one's way through more affluent social circles, and suggestions for looking stylish on a budget. Throughout its pages was the constant message: being single is fun, and there's a whole world of men out there ready to flatter their dates. Never interrupt one when he is telling a story, she cautioned; conveniently "forget" to wear some of your lingerie on a date; or wow guests at your chic little dinner parties with "champagne peach"—a peeled peach in a pilsner glass with bubbly poured over. In the book's recipe for stuffed lobster tails, Brown begins the preliminaries with the helpful hint to "ask that nice gentleman behind the counter to scoop out the lobster meat and then put it back in the tail." She even gave tips for investing in the stock market.

But most significantly, Brown wrote both frankly and coyly about sex. She claimed that single women probably enjoyed far more exciting and satisfying sex lives than married women. Throughout its pages, the text treats married people and their attitudes toward single women rather scathingly. A modern unmarried woman, declared Brown, "is so driven by herself and her well-meaning but addlepated friends to become married that her whole existence seems to be an apology for *not* being married." Elsewhere, Brown theorized that ". . . the single woman, far from being a creature to be pitied and patronized, is emerging as the newest glamour girl of our times." In one of the last chapters, "The Affair: From Beginning to End," Brown wrote of several different reasons a woman might engage in an affair—even with a married man.

The book was an immediate bestseller. Not surprisingly, there was a huge outcry from conservatives against it—it was an era when U.S. courts were still battling over Henry Miller's *Tropic of Cancer,* a novel that had been legally banned for explicit sexual content since the 1930s. Later, Brown would also become an easy target of feminist ire, who accused her of objectifying women and encouraging them to see themselves only as sexual creatures.

But *Sex and the Single Girl* was also a similar hit in translation in numerous other countries, and at one point was selling nearly five thousand copies a week. Brown began to appear often on television and radio, and she did a cross-country lecture tour. She also wrote three other books, including *Sex and the Office,* which actually caused even more of a stir. In it she set forth explicit guidelines for how to make yourself indispensable to a boss. Some newspapers refused to run advertisements for it. Warner Brothers bought the rights to her first book for $200,000, then the highest amount ever paid for a nonfiction title. The film (1964) was less a documentary than a comic tale, starring Natalie Wood as a marriage counselor with a Ph.D. who was the author of a bestselling book for single women.

Brown and her husband came up with the idea for a magazine, *Femme,* which would bring the *Single Girl* attitude to readers on a monthly basis. They were unable to secure funding for a launch, but in early 1965 Brown was hired by the Hearst Corporation to revitalize *Cosmopolitan,* a moribund magazine that was trying to target single, fun-loving women as its readership. By the time of Brown's retirement in 1997, it had become one of the most successful mass-market magazines for women in publishing history.

—Carol Brennan

FURTHER READING:

Alexander, Shana. "Singular Girl's Success." *Life.* March 1, 1963.

Collins, Glenn. "At 60, Helen Gurley Brown Talks about Life and Love." *New York Times.* September 19, 1982, 68.

Ferguson, Marjorie. *Forever Feminine.* London, Heinemann, 1982.

Lippert, Barbara. "Gurley Show." *Mediaweek.* March 4, 1996, MR40.

"Meat Loaf, Anyone?" *Newsweek.* August 31, 1964, 53.

Roberts, Roxanne. "The Oldest Living Cosmo Girl." *Washington Post.* January 31, 1996, D1.

"Sex and the Editor." *Time.* March 26, 1965, 40.

"Sex, the Single Girl and a Magazine." *New York Times.* March 17, 1965.

"What Price the Single Girl?" *Esquire.* October 1964, 108-109.

Sex Scandals

Like the worlds oldest profession, scandals motivated by human sexuality have always been with us. From the Old Testament and those scandalous Greek deities, to modern tabloids which obsessively monitor the erotic misadventures of the modern gods and goddesses of today, the sexual Achilles' heels of the human race has provided hot copy through the ages. Scandal has been defined as "grave loss of or injury to reputation" resulting from actual (or suspected) violation of morality, ethics, propriety, or law. Sex, deceit, bribery, power, excess, and fame are the key elements of most scandals. And of course, it all has to be exposed in some publicized, often lurid fashion, for as George C. Kohn notes: "There has to be some extra element as well—something untoward, shocking, and reprehensible to the public." Kohn might also add, something infinitely fascinating.

Artists and entertainers have always been considered innately scandalous, but at the turn of the twentieth century movies and sex became inextricably linked. In 1921 Roscoe "Fatty" Arbuckle, Hollywood's most popular silent-era comedian, threw a party to celebrate his new $3 million contract. The three day affair resulted in the death of starlet, Virginia Rappe, who suffered a ruptured bladder and died as a result of a questionable sexual encounter with the 266 pound comedian. Arbuckle was charged with Rappe's rape and murder, and became a symbol of all that appeared morally offensive in early Hollywood. Though acquitted, public opinion remained against him. His contract was canceled, his films banned, and he was no longer cast in Hollywood. By 1933 both Hollywood and the public had either forgiven or forgotten, and Arbuckle managed a comeback. But just hours after completing his first film in over a decade, the once beloved comedian died in his sleep of a heart attack in a New York hotel room.

William Randolph Hearst and actress Marion Davies indulged in a long-standing affair which was only partially shielded by the newspaper mogul's wealth and power. The married Hearst became infatuated with Davies in the early 1920s. She became his mistress, and he relentlessly promoted her movie career. Hearst and Davies became the subject of an unresolved scandal when director Thomas Harper Ince died on the Hearst/Davies yacht in 1924. Though the final verdict was death by "heart attack due to acute indigestion," rumors of foul play persisted, including one that Ince had been accidentally shot in a fit of Hearst jealousy aimed at Charlie Chaplin. After the incident the Hearst/Davies relationship continued much as before, and was later fictionalized by Orson Welles in *Citizen Kane,* a 1941 film which enraged Hearst, but which even his vast media empire was unable to suppress.

Sinclair Lewis explored the relationship between sex and evangelism in his famous novel, *Elmer Gantry,* as did Reverend Jim Bakker, mogul of the 1980s "Praise The Lord" Christian TV network. With wife Tammy Faye, Bakker became embroiled in a lurid affair encompassing everything from embezzlement to wife swapping and homosexuality. The scandal was motivated by Bakker's brief extramarital liaison with Jessica Hahn, and his ensuing attempt to bribe her into silence. Bakker was eventually forced to yield control of his lucrative empire to Jerry Falwell, and in 1987 was dismissed from serving as a minister in the Assemblies of God church. But even his ensuing prison term could not quell the controversy, with the tabloids gleefully continuing to report on his alleged affair with another male inmate.

Political sex scandals are among the most venerable, dating back nearly to the creation of the highest office itself: i.e., the recent DNA verification of relations between Thomas Jefferson and his quadroon slave, Sally Hemings. And even well-loved modern presidents, such as Roosevelt and Eisenhower, have not been immune to romantic/ erotic controversy.

John Fitzgerald Kennedy (JFK) was informally known as the "playboy" president, but his extracurricular sex life was carefully suppressed to maintain his well-hyped family image. His erotic exploits commenced while still a Senator, but the first affair to endanger his presidency was with a 26-year-old playgirl, Judy Campbell. Campbell, also known as Judith Exner, was also involved with Chicago Mafia boss, Salvatore "Sam" Giancana. Campbell eventually asserted that Kennedy had encouraged her sexual relationship with Giancana, and used her as a courier to pass intelligence and money to the mob boss, with some of the funds used to buy votes for Kennedy in the 1960 election. In 1962 Federal Bureau of Investigation Chief J. Edgar Hoover, noted for his knowledge of the sexual habits of influential people in all walks of life, lunched with Kennedy, and the affair with Campbell came to an end shortly thereafter.

An explosive relationship that has continued to elicit speculation about both JFK and Bobby Kennedy, was the affair the brothers shared with Marilyn Monroe. The Kennedy/Monroe affairs were blown into history by Monroe's sudden death in 1962, officially a suicide, but still giving rise to persistent rumors that she had been murdered, either by Mafia hit men or by United States intelligence operatives. One investigator claimed that Bobby Kennedy and Monroe shared angry words shortly before her death when Kennedy, fearing public scandal, attempted to end the affair.

John Kennedy's assassination in 1963 threw a sanctified shroud over any scandalous revelations for over a decade. Thus, the American public was considerably jolted when in 1975 word first leaked out concerning Campbell, and Kennedy's other affairs. Kennedy's final involvement was with a Washington socialite, Mrs. Mary Pinchot Meyer. The long term affair may have remained a secret, except for the bizarre fact that Meyer was murdered only 11 months after Kennedy's assassination, and during the investigation their relationship was revealed.

Speculations on Marilyn Monroe's death have continued to the present day, though due to the fact that key data mysteriously vanished shortly afterwards, the truth about the actress' demise may never be known. The ongoing suspicions that she was killed to protect the Kennedy reputation, however, hint at the extremes to which those in high power may have gone to protect themselves from the destructive breath of scandal during the still conservative early 1960s.

Of the later Kennedy controversies, the most publicized was the 1969 incident in which Senator Edward Kennedy's secretary, Mary Jo Kopechne, was killed when the car Kennedy was driving careened off a bridge on Chappaquiddick, a small island near Martha's Vineyard. Kennedy did not report the fatal accident until the following morning, arousing suspicion of an illicit affair between the two. Kennedy pleaded guilty to leaving the scene of an accident, and after suspending his driver's license and a two month suspended jail sentence, local authorities closed the case. It was, however, reopened by the Massachusetts federal district attorney. No one was indicted in the closed inquest in October, 1969, and while Edward Kennedy won re-election to the Senate in 1970, he declined to seek the presidency in 1972.

Not long after Chappaquiddick another senator, Gary Hart, was a leading contender for the 1988 Democratic presidential nomination. But accusations of an extra-marital affair with actress/model, Donna Rice, thwarted his chances, and became an overriding campaign issue. The Hart affair also included reactions against the scandal mongering of the press, particularly the *Miami Herald*, which launched an aggressive investigation that included a secret stakeout of Hart's Washington townhouse. But though no proof of adultery was unearthed, the press rumors persisted, and it was accusations of adultery, rather than any conclusive evidence, that actually cost Hart the candidacy. Before withdrawing Hart made the startling (but prophetic) comment that, if elected he would not "be the first adulterer in the White House."

And certainly not the last. The end of the millennium climaxed with the most graphically documented sex scandal in American history; the 1998/1999 President William Jefferson Clinton/Monica Lewinsky/Paula Jones/Ken Starr/Henry Hyde et al affair. This was state-of-the-art, high-tech scandal, integrating DNA testing, the Internet, new buzzwords such as "censure-plus," and reams of copy from both the legitimate and tabloid media (not to mention a voluminous outpouring of letters to various editors from a passionately divided American public). In contrast to the aggressively guarded Kennedy affairs, the public was spared no detail of the Clinton incident, and articles counseling parents on how to deal with the explicit details of certain highly accessible news stories were a frequent aspect of the scandal.

After the inundation of words, a terse, matter-of-fact item appeared in the "Milestones" column of *Time* magazine's February 22, 1999 issue: "Acquitted, William Jefferson Clinton, 52, of perjury and obstruction-of-justice charges, by the U.S. Senate; in Washington (see cover story)." The cover story: "How the Scandal Was Good For America." After the official verdict, a public consensus seemed to emerge that indicated while many remained disapproving of Clinton's morals, most were satisfied with his performance as president and happy with the state of the American economy.

In a statement on actual character, and a comment on scandal mongering everywhere, Ethan Canin drew a parallel between morality and popular culture in the "Talk of the Town" column of the October 5, 1998 *New Yorker:* "In a novel, I am interested in complex personality, in ranging intelligence, in moral originality - what in fiction is called rounded character. This is also what I want in the President of my country. Ken Starr's zealous and chillingly unambiguous morality suggests to me none of the fullness, none of the complex interplay and recognition of opposing forces that interest the intelligent mind. And this, in fiction, is called flat character. If Bill Clinton and Ken Starr were characters in one of my students' stories, the class could agree that it is Mr. Starr, not Mr. Clinton, who lacks character."

In the wake of the Clinton affair, one might well ask: Is scandal still a decisive issue in modern life, or merely a titillating, rather tiresome diversion? If we define scandal as "a grave loss or injury to reputation resulting from actual or apparent violation of morality, ethics, propriety, or law," we might conclude the latter. In the tabloid age scandal now promotes, rather than ends, careers—the Los Angeles *New Times* comments only half-jokingly that "There is no bad publicity . . . ''—and with the O. J. Simpson case, even children seem to comprehend that certain individuals are now above the law; terms such as "ethics" and "propriety" echoing with a decidedly antiquated ring. As in Bertolt Brecht's mythical American city, *Mahagonny*, when everything is permitted (or accepted), nothing is sacred (or shocking). Where there is no apparent overriding morality left, there can be no scandal, only media buzzwords and cheap, hot copy.

—Ross Care

FURTHER READING:

Brown, Peter Harry, and Patte B. Barham. *Marilyn The Last Take*. New York, A Dutton Book, 1992.

Canin, Ethan, et al. "The Talk of the Town." *The New Yorker*, October 5, 1998, 32-9.

Gibbs, Nancy. "Nightmare's End. Yes, It Was Wretched, and We're Glad to Wake Up. But Even Bad Dreams Can Serve Useful Purposes." *Time*. February 22, 1999, 32-7.

Gordon, William A. *The Ultimate HOLLYWOOD Tour Book: The Incomparable Guide to Movie Stars' Homes, Movie and TV Locations, Scandals, Murders, Suicides, and All the Famous Tourist Sites*. El Toro, California, North Ridge Books, 1998.

Hersh, Seymour M. *The Dark Side of Camelot*. Boston, Little Brown, 1997.

Kohn George C. *Encyclopedia of American Scandal from ABSCAM to the Zenger Case*. New York, Oxford, Facts On File, 1989.

Lord, Lewis. "Jefferson Knew Value of Silence with Press." *U.S. News & World Report*. November 16, 1998, 66.

Miller, Hope Ridings. *Scandals in the Highest Office Facts and Fiction in the Private Lives of Our Presidents*. New York, Random House, 1973.

Wallace, Irving, et al. *The Intimate Sex Lives of Famous People*. New York, Delacorte Press, 1981.

Sex Symbol

The "sex symbol" in twentieth-century American culture is, for the most part, a product of the movies, which over the decades has offered a dizzying variety of male and female images to American audiences: the Vamp, the Red-Hot-Mama, the Golddigger, the Exotic Other, the Girl (and Guy) Next Door, the Femme Fatale, the Strong, Silent Type, the Sex Bomb, the Sex Kitten, the Latin Lover, the Matinee Idol, the Punk, and the Hunk, among many others. Before films became popular entertainment in the 1910s, attractive models having particular standards of "desirability" were only beginning to be seen in the new mass culture, as with the Gibson Girl and Gibson Guy images found in mass-circulation magazines. But once Americans were able to attend films, it was possible for millions to see the same kinds of women and men being held up as models of beauty and sensuality on the silver screen. Over the years, practically the only thread of commonality to be found throughout the various manifestations of the movie sex symbol have been racial and ethnic—the Hollywood sex symbol is almost always white, almost always of northern or western European heritage, and almost always American, though "exotic" examples from Asian, Latino, and African cultures have had their place in film as well as print media. Indeed, two of the earliest sex symbols, Theda Bara and Rudolph Valentino, did not fit

these stereotypes. In general, what defines a person as a "sex symbol" has little or nothing to do with who that person is off the movie or television screen. Instead, sex-symbol status places the emphasis on the "symbol," on the performer's ability to fit into a role that offers, either overtly or covertly, a model for and release of sexual tension. These roles have shaped the development of women's and men's sexual consciousness and confidence during the twentieth century.

One of the earliest sex symbols was Theda Bara (born Theodosia Goodman) who appeared as a vampire woman in the 1915 film *A Fool There Was*. In contrast to the prevailing and desexualized image of wholesome European-American womanhood embodied by Mary Pickford, Bara's Vamp embodied a dark, exotic, and foreign sensuality, a kind of open sexuality not permitted to white American women until much later in the century—though it is precisely this kind of sexuality that was appropriated by some of the black blues divas of the 1920s such as Bessie Smith, Sippie Wallace, and Ma Rainey. In later films, such as *The Vixen* and *The She-Devil*, Bara's Vamp would entrap men with her sexual wiles, only to be punished in the end for transgressing gender roles. Though Bara's career in film was short-lived, the figure of the Vamp as an important sex symbol has marked American film ever since.

As Americans moved into the 1920s, when the androgynous flapper look was in vogue, Mae West, with her unfashionably zaftig figure and unapologetic bawdiness, offered the Red-Hot-Mama as a counterpoint to the more popular ingenue or girl-next-door image of stars like Clara Bow. Known for her humorous quips and innuendo ("Come up and see me some time"; "What're you doin', honey? Makin' love or takin' inventory?"); for styling one of her characters as "Lady Lou, one of the finest women who ever walked the streets"; and even for being jailed in 1926 for obscenity, Mae West both exuded sexuality and contained it through humor, offering a sexual gratification that she never got a chance to deliver, though she played the Red-Hot-Mama role well into her 80s. Sexual transgressiveness has also been a part of Mae West's camp appeal to gay men, especially with her role in the 1970 film adaptation of Gore Vidal's *Myra Breckinridge*, a romp in polymorphous sexuality.

In the 1930s, Hollywood crafted the Golddigger in the person of Jean Harlow. Harlow's platinum-blonde hair and wisecracking persona set her in the tradition of Mae West, but her brassy, open sensuality seemed disconcerting from the mouth of a sweet-looking young woman who was "out to make a killing" in more ways than one. "Would you be shocked if I changed into something more comfortable?" she asked in *Hell's Angels* (1930). The Hays Production Code, which set rules for the depiction of sexuality in the movies in the 1930s, is often seen in part as a response to Harlow's unabashed sensuality.

The other major sex symbol archetype of the 1930s was Swedish actress Greta Garbo, the Exotic Other. Garbo's passions seemed not to stem from erotic desire, but from some unspeakable internal suffering, and the interest in Garbo seemed to stem mainly from the fact that she was foreign, different, and could, therefore, be made to symbolize whatever the viewer desired. Always carefully made up and glamorous, Garbo exuded a melancholy persona that seemed designed to draw viewers in to her personal torment, creating a sense of intimacy between actor and audience. When, in *Grand Hotel* (1932), she uttered her famous line about wanting to be left alone, audiences responded to her faintly mysterious Swedish accent and swooned over her noble, classy, and discreet suffering. Male characters wanted her, but she always wanted the wrong men, almost never achieving on-screen bliss. Her allure for American audiences was so great that, when she left the acting world in 1941, her disappearance excited years of cultish obsession. Don McPherson and Louise Brody fueled this myth in their profile of Garbo, claiming that she "remained an enigmatic and unreachable phenomenon. . . . She seems to wish she were invisible: it is not so much a face as a shadow of one, suggested by isolated glimpses and memories, inscrutable and austere."

World War II ushered in the era of the sex symbol as pinup, the suggestive photos that graced lockers and military barracks in all theaters of war. Actresses that had made their reputations prior to the start of the War—Betty Grable, Rita Hayworth, Jane Russell, Veronica Lake, and Lana Turner—were suddenly in great demand in "pinup" form, usually as images of the sex roles for which they were known. The two most popular wartime versions were the wholesome Girl-Next-Door (personified by Grable) and the Femmes Fatales (Hayworth, Russell, Lake, Turner). The stylized poses taken by these actresses, the most famous being that of Grable, in shorts and high heels, showing off her cleavage and million-dollar gams, offered an image of femininity that seemed to be missing at home, where wives and girlfriends were working and emulating the decidedly unsexy Rosie the Riveter. They offered a reminder of peacetime normality, where women were women, i.e., filled traditional roles. If Grable's look was that of the "good girl," the pinups of Rita Hayworth, Jane Russell, and Lana Turner smoldered openly. These women's provocative poses promised a sexuality just out of reach, and a vision of American womanhood worth fighting for.

World War II had a profound effect on the representation and symbolization of sexuality in general. The term "bombshell" entered American vocabularies as a reference to the openly sexual woman, pointing not only to their power over men but also to their potential for destroying those same men and themselves. Women's sexuality, according to this logic, was dangerous, in need of containment, lest the hapless male end up obliterated by the sex bomb. Coming partly from the portrayals of hardboiled Femmes Fatales in the popular 1940s *film noir* genre, and partly from an anxiety over gender roles destabilized during wartime, the association of women's sexuality with danger continued to linger in American popular culture. (It is this same threatening sexuality that led to the naming of the "bikini" bathing suit after the Bikini Atoll on which nuclear weapons were tested, and the voguish slang word "atomic" to mean splendidly desirable.)

The most popular sex symbol of the 1950s was that great Ingenue-cum-Sex Bomb, Marilyn Monroe. Oozing sexuality but seeming never to recognize it, Monroe offered a soothing sensuality for America's frazzled sensibilities. Monroe's on-screen persona, that of the breathy, innocent girl, provided a welcome return to clear gender roles, to a kind of idyllic sexual past. Monroe was not attired in a sexless coverall like the wartime Rosies, nor did she even want to work: She preferred to marry a millionaire, as in the title of one of her films. But once married, she had no intentions of chewing him up and spitting him out like a Golddigger or a Femme Fatale: Monroe wanted true love, too, in a reassuring return to "lost" femininity. Donald Spoto explained that she represented "the post-war ideal of the American girl, soft, transparently needy, worshipful of men, naïve, offering sex without demands." Though Monroe often sought to transcend her role as symbol (trying to be "taken seriously," marrying the American dramatist Arthur Miller, seeking more challenging film roles), she never managed to separate herself from her Sex Bomb image, eventually becoming almost a parody of herself as in her famous birthday serenade to President John F. Kennedy.

Latching on to Monroe's huge popularity, other studios tried to create their own Sex Bombs, casting American actresses like Mamie Van Doren, Jayne Mansfield, and Kim Novak, or foreigners like Brigitte Bardot, Sophia Loren, and Gina Lollobrigida, in roles that seemed to emphasize a kind of trashy, even sluttish, glamour—women to be played with, not to settle down with. While these women were quite popular in their own right, they never quite reached the stratospheric heights that Monroe did in popular consciousness. Monroe and the other Sex Bombs stood at one end of the continuum of 1950s women's roles, promising a kind of power in sensuality, an ability to control men (though always kindly, always with good intentions); at the other end stood Doris Day, smart, sporty, and perpetual virgin. If Monroe was the archetypal dumb blonde, the kind of girl men wanted to have fun with, the girl they wanted to scratch their *Seven-Year Itch,* Doris Day was the not-so-dumb blonde, the kind of girl men married.

The 1950s ushered in a more "permanent" way to display the sex symbol—as pinup in the form of the *Playboy* magazine centerfold. Created in 1953, Hugh Hefner's risqué magazine catered to the newly developing sex symbol of the Sex Toy, and particularly to the display of the Sex Toy's greatest assets—her breasts. For the unhappy male, caught in what was being portrayed in popular culture as a web of asexual domesticity (June Cleaver and Donna Reed were at the other end of the spectrum), Hefner's magazine offered an escape to a trendy, sophisticated world where men never quite grew up, never had to take on responsibilities, and always had curvaceous women at their sides. If a hapless man couldn't afford to have his own Sex Toy, *Playboy*'s centerfolds offered the next-best thing. Both Jayne Mansfield and Kim Novak appeared in *Playboy*—Mansfield numerous times—and pictures of a younger Monroe eventually did as well, harkening back to Mae West's laughing claim that the only thing she had on during her calendar shoot was "the radio."

With Monroe's death of a drug overdose in 1962, the sex symbol became a symbol of the perils of female sexuality. No longer dangerous to men—magazines like *Playboy* promised that women's eroticism could be tamed and packaged for male consumption—the sexual woman was a danger to herself, a sign that the sexually liberated woman was, after all, desperately unhappy. Thus the 1960s offered up a range of sex symbols that seemed designed to counter the overkill of the 1950s Sex Bomb. These 1960s Icons—Julie Christie, Twiggy, Jean Shrimpton—were sexy, but in attainable ways. Pretty in a healthy kind of way (Christie), or in a waifish way (Twiggy and Shrimpton), these actresses and models were, as Sheila Rowbotham described them: "[d]escendants of Doris Day . . . adapted to an era when virginity was no longer feasible or fashionable." Even stars who seemed closer to the Sex Bomb role—Jane Fonda, Raquel Welch, Faye Dunaway—were, in the end, very much a part of the youthful, no-nonsense image of the Icon.

After the 1960s, it becomes quite difficult to track a specific genealogy of the female sex symbol, and most of the women in subsequent decades seem to be reworkings of aforementioned roles. The 1970s favored sex symbols that combined the Girl-Next-Door qualities of the Icon, the overtness of the Red-Hot-Mama, and the naivete of the Sex Bomb. The walls of many teenaged boys' rooms were decorated with posters of Farrah Fawcett [Majors], Cheryl Tiegs, and other "all-American" women (blond, blue-eyed, fair-skinned) posing semi-provocatively in swimsuits. Television shows like *Charlie's Angels, Three's Company,* and *Wonder Woman* promoted various (re)visions of the sex symbols of decades past. The stars of the former series, Fawcett, Cheryl Ladd, and Jaclyn Smith in particular, seemed to be throwbacks to the Betty Grable-Girl-Next-Door model—women who are smart and resourceful but who also happen to look lovely in the revealing outfits their crime-fighting efforts seemed to require in every episode of *Charlie's Angels.* In *Three's Company* (1977-1984), Suzanne Somers offered a return to the Ingenue-Sex Bomb: blonde, sweet, and not too bright, her antics, comic misunderstandings, tight blouses, and short shorts were one of the show's main attractions. Lynda Carter's Wonder Woman was a street-savvy superhero who just so happened to fight crime wearing a strapless, red, white, and blue bathing suit and go-go boots. The 1960s and 1970s also marked the introduction of non-white sex symbols into American popular culture, such as Pam Grier, the African-American star of the early 1970s "blaxpoitation" films. Perhaps the only "new" sex symbol to come out of this era is the Bimbo, a woman who is all about sex appeal (pneumatic breasts, easy virtue, slow wits) but not about much else.

Changing standards in film, particularly the introduction of more female nudity and explicit sexual content, may have contributed to the shift away from sex symbols as such. The female sex symbol's mystique is, after all, predicated in part on her mystery, on the audience's desire to know more about her. Viewers are captivated by her because they are left to imagine what she would be like; viewers today can find out more or less first-hand. Most of the sex symbols of the 1980s and 1990s seem to have been reinventions of past models. Elvira, Mistress of the Dark, capitalized on the Vamp with her dark clothing, ample cleavage, and promises of gothic intrigue. The Red Hot Mama was reborn in Bette Midler, whose stage performances as "the Divine Miss M" depicted her as the reincarnation of Mae West's brassy, wisecracking dame who knew a thing or two about sex and wasn't afraid to say so. The Femme Fatale was personified by Kathleen Turner and Sharon Stone, among others—women who used their sexual wiles to manipulate and even destroy the men they claimed to love. Cindy Crawford and Claudia Schiffer seemed to combine their roles as exotic fashion models with that of the down-to-earth gal to play the role of the Girl Next Door; no-nonsense talk-show pals one minute, and hot and sultry catwalk models the next, they offered both public and supposedly private visions of what that Girl would be like. Kate Moss, particularly in her Calvin Klein advertisements, has assumed the role of the Waifish Icon, seeming vulnerable and desirable at once. And Madonna, the ever-shifting symbol, has tried on all these roles and more.

Though the female sex symbol has dominated American popular culture, there are male sex symbols as well, and theorists have begun to expand the concept by deconstructing sex symbols outside of traditional heterosexual modes, acknowledging the repressed same-sex eroticism that might have informed sex-symbol interactions in the past. Silent-film actors like Rudolph Valentino offered early visions of the Perfect Lover, effortlessly sweeping his female co-stars off their feet and, presumably, into his bed, and some males have also reported being drawn by his magnetic personality. The Matinee Idol has been the primary manifestation of the male sex symbol during the twentieth century: Actors like Cary Grant, Clark Gable, and Rock Hudson captivated moviegoers during their heydays with their suave masculinity, their classic good looks, and promises of economic security. The 1950s also saw the introduction of the male sex symbol as Bad Boy. Both Elvis Presley and James Dean played this role to the hilt when their shaking hips, brooding looks, and sullen demeanors sent young fans into swoons and parents into paroxysms of worry. Good-looking stars of the 1960s like Paul Newman, Robert Redford, and Warren Beatty combined the Matinee Idol with the Bad Boy,

often manifest in the parts of criminals or outsiders with "hearts of gold" like Butch Cassidy and the Sundance Kid, or Clyde Barrow.

The 1970s saw the introduction of the Sex Machine. Burt Reynolds posed nude in *Cosmopolitan,* a women's magazine. Around this time, *Playgirl* magazine, featuring nude men, was introduced as a "counterpoint" to *Playboy,* attracting a readership of women as well as men with an erotic interest in their own gender. As with female sex symbols, the first non-white male sex symbols appeared during the 1970s, particularly as a result of "blaxploitation" films such as *Shaft,* whose theme song promised that its star, Richard Roundtree, was a "sex machine with all the chicks," and *Dolemite,* starring Rudy Ray Moore. These stars embodied the Sex Machine role, turning women on screen into putty with their sexual prowess and doing the same to fans in the audience. This particular vision also partook of cultural folklore and stereotype about black males' virility. Other male sex symbols of the 1970s assumed the James Bond image of a man as suave, debonaire, and sexually irresistible. In the 1980s and 1990s, male sex symbols included Richard Gere, Harrison Ford, Tom Cruise, Johnny Depp, Leonardo DiCaprio, and Marky Mark. Like their female counterparts, they combined elements of various manifestations of the sex symbols of generations past to create their screen personae.

Despite the introduction of non-white figures into the sex symbol mythos, the majority of sex symbols remain white and European-American, though the growing diversification of the American population may alter that situation in the new century. A double standard for male and female sexuality remains: Despite the fact that men are regularly depicted as sexual objects on television and in film, it is still more likely that the female sex symbol will be punished for her sexuality. In American popular culture, it is more common for a sexually active woman to be regarded as a slut, but a sexually active male as a stud.

—Deborah M. Mix

FURTHER READING:

Da, Lottie and Jan Alexander. *Bad Girls of the Silver Screen.* New York, Carrol and Graf, 1989.

MacPherson, Don and Louise Brody. *Leading Ladies: Photographs from the Kobal Collection.* New York, St. Martin's Press, 1986.

Norman, Barry. *The Story of Hollywood.* New York, New American Library, 1988.

Rowbotham, Sheila. *A Century of Women.* New York, Penguin, 1997.

Shipman, David. *The Story of Cinema.* New York, St. Martin's Press, 1982.

Spoto, Donald. *Marilyn Monroe: The Biography.* London, Arrow Books, 1994.

Sexual Harassment

In the 1990s, sexual harassment became a highly visibile part of American pop culture. In 1991, Anita Hill testified in a televised United States Senate hearing that Supreme Court nominee Clarence Thomas sexually harassed her when she worked for him in the early 1980s at the Equal Employment Opportunity Commission. Thomas was confirmed, but by a very close vote of 52-48. Some of the

Senators who voted for confirmation were defeated for re-election in 1992. In 1994, Paul Corbin Jones accused President William Jefferson Clinton of sexually harassing her when he was Governor of Arkansas and she was an Arkansas state employee. In 1998, Jones' lawsuit was dismissed, but a deposition President Clinton gave about his relationship with Monica Lewinsky, a former White House intern, triggered an investigation by Independent Counsel Kenneth Starr that resulted in Starr recommending to the United States Congress that President Clinton be impeached.

Sexual harassment is defined as unwelcome sexual advances and requests for sexual favors. Other verbal or physical conduct of a sexual nature constitutes sexual harassment when submission or rejection of this conduct explicitly or implicitly affects an individual's employment, unreasonably interferes with an individual's work performance, or creates an intimidating, hostile, or offensive work environment. The two types of harassment are quid pro quo and hostile environment. Quid pro quo, or "this for that," exists when an employee's supervisor or a person of higher employment rank demands sexual favors from a subordinate in exchange for tangible job benefits. Hostile environment, or environmental harassment, is a pattern of intimidating, hostile, or offensive behaviors which affect the person being harassed.

Federal laws on sexual harassment have existed since Congress passed Title VII of the 1964 Civil Rights Act and Title IX of the 1972 Education Amendments. Title VII prohibits sex discrimination in employment; sexual harassment is considered a form of sex discrimination. Title IX prohibits sex discrimination in education. The laws began to have effect when in 1980, and again in 1988, the Equal Employment Opportunity Commission (EEOC) issued guidelines to define sexual harassment.

The courts have defined sexual harassment more precisely, and have been involved in resolving key issues. In 1986, in the *Meritor Savings Bank v. Vinson* case, the Supreme Court ruled that quid pro quo sexual harassment was a form of sex discrimination under Title VII. In the *Meritor* case, the Supreme Court made a very important distinction. It affirmed that a victim may comply voluntarily with sexually harassing behavior, but may not welcome it. If it is unwelcome, it is sexual harassment. The *Meritor* case also set a precedent because it established employer liability for acts of sexual harassment committed by its employees. The Court ruled that quid pro quo and environmental harassment are two distinct claims, but that they can and often do occur at the same time. It is necessary, however, to distinguish between them when employer liability is being determined; the employer is always liable in quid pro quo harassment, but may not always be liable in hostile environment cases.

In education, the United States Supreme Court significantly expanded protection for student victims in *Christine Franklin, Petitioner v. Gwinnett County Public Schools and William Prescott,* on February 26, 1992. For the first time, students had the right to win monetary damages from schools that receive federal funds. This decision provided strong motivation for schools to engage in a proactive strategy to prevent sexual harassment.

On November 9, 1993, the United States Supreme Court ruled, in *Harris v. Forklift Systems,* that harassing conduct need not seriously affect an employee's psychological well-being or cause the plaintiff to suffer injury. On March 4, 1998, the court again ruled, in *Oncale v. Sundancer Offshore Services,* that same-sex harassment in the workplace violates federal law.

The Hill-Thomas hearings led to more legislation. On October 11, 1991, Titles I, II, and III of the 1991 Civil Rights Act were passed.

Title I expands the rights of sexual harassment victims to enable them to collect monetary damages. Title II, commonly referred to as the "Glass Ceiling Act of 1991," encourages corporate practices and policies that promote opportunities for, and eliminate artificial barriers to, the advancement of women and minorities into higher level positions. Title III focuses on fair employment practices and covers employees of the House of Representatives, Senate, and Executive Office of the President.

The military faced the issue of sexual harassment in September 1991, when the "Tailhook" scandal became public. A female Navy helicopter pilot, Lt. Paula Coughlin, complained to Rear Admiral John Snyder, Commander, Naval Air Test Center, that she had been physically and indecently assaulted on September 7, 1991, by a group of naval officers at the 1991 Tailhook Symposium at the Las Vegas Hilton. Commander of the Naval Investigative Service, Rear Admiral Duvall M. "Mac" Williams, was requested to open an investigation. A mammoth investigation was initiated on October 11, 1991. Snyder was relieved of his command for dealing inappropriately with Coughlin's complaint. On February 7, 1994, Coughlin resigned from the Navy and gave as her reason the retaliation she had experienced as a result of her complaint.

Coughlin filed civil law suits against the Tailhook Association and the Las Vegas Hilton. She settled with the Tailhook Association for $400,000 before the trial began. On October 28, 1994, the jury in Las Vegas decided that the Las Vegas Hilton Hotel was negligent because it failed to provide adequate security during the 1991 Tailhook Convention. The jury awarded Coughlin $1.7 million in damages. On October 31, 1994, the jury ordered the Las Vegas Hilton and its parent company to pay Coughlin $5 million in punitive damages for a total award of $6.7 million, an amount later reduced to $5.3 million.

In November 1996, the United States Army brought charges of rape and sexual harassment against military trainers at the Army Ordnance Center at Aberdeen Proving Ground, Maryland. According to the Pentagon, there were more than a dozen victims; all of the victims were female soldiers in their second eight weeks of training. The Army charged 12 staff members of Aberdeen with sex crimes, ranging from inappropriate sexual comments to rape. In September 1997, the Army issued a "scathing report" acknowledging that sexual harassment and discrimination were prevalent.

The Paula Jones case broke legal ground when the Supreme Court ruled that a sitting President can be sued for actions that occurred before he took office and that the case can proceed while the President is still in office. The case went forward and depositions were taken, including a deposition from President Clinton in January 1998 that questioned whether the President had sexual relations with Monica Lewinsky. In March 1998, Judge Susan Webber Wright ruled that Monica Lewinsky "is not essential to the core issues" of Jones' case, and ordered all evidence related to Lewinsky be excluded from the proceedings. Judge Wright dismissed the Jones lawsuit on April 1, 1998.

President Clinton's legal troubles, however, did not end with the dismissal of the Jones' lawsuit. While under oath during his deposition in the Jones case, he denied having sexual relations with Monica Lewinsky. Independent Counsel Kenneth Starr requested and received permission to investigate whether the President had lied under oath. After a seven month investigation, Starr reported to Congress that there were possible grounds for impeachment and the President was impeached by the full House, though the Senate chose not to remove the President from office.

Illustrating the pervasiveness of sexual harassment issues in America, the problem itself has evolved from a behavior without a name, to a social behavior, to a defined legal behavior, and by 1998, to a highly visible social problem for the President of the United States and the nation.

—Rosemarie Skaine

FURTHER READING:

Farley, Lin. *Sexual Shake Down: Sexual Harassment of Women on the Job.* New York, McGraw-Hill, 1978.

MacKinnon, Catherine A. *Sexual Harassment of Working Women: A Case of Sex Discrimination.* New Haven, Yale University Press, 1979.

Skaine, Rosemarie. *Power and Gender: Issues in Sexual Dominance and Harassment.* Jefferson, North Carolina, McFarland & Company, Inc., 1996.

———. *Women at War: Gender Issues of Americans in Combat.* Jefferson, North Carolina, McFarland & Company, Inc., 1998.

The Starr Report: The Independent Counsel's Complete Report to Congress on the Investigation of President Clinton. New York, Pocket Books, 1998.

Vander Schaaf, Derek J. *Tailhook '91, Part 1—Review of the Navy Investigations.* Washington, D.C., DODIG, 1992.

Sexual Revolution

Reports of a "sexual revolution" first appeared in the media in the mid-1960s. The reports identified a number of trends and developments taking place throughout American society. Midway through the decade, the popularity of rock music, the increased use of marijuana, LSD, and other drugs among youth, widespread public displays of nudity, and a new openness about sexuality contributed to the awareness of radical cultural change. Public interest in sex had been growing since the late 1940s and the number of novels, magazine articles, and advice books dealing with sexuality grew to epic proportions. Already in the 1950s, a number of famous novels that had previously been banned because of their sexual explicitness, such as D.H. Lawrence's *Lady Chatterly's Lover* and Henry Miller's *Tropic of Cancer,* began to be published in the United States. Advice books like *Sex and the Single Girl* (1962) by *Cosmopolitan* editor Helen Gurley Brown, and *The Sensuous Woman* (1969) by J. poured from the presses. Betty Friedan's *The Feminine Mystique* (1963) initiated the revival of feminism and stimulated the discussion of sex and gender roles. Popular sociologists like Vance Packard in *The Sexual Wilderness: The Contemporary Upheaval in Male-Female Relationships* (1968) explored the interplay of both feminism and the sexual revolution. In 1966, Drs. William Masters and Virginia Johnson published the first of their scientific studies—*Human Sexual Response* (1966). Sexually explicit pulp novels, like Jacqueline Susann's *Valley of the Dolls* (1966), and sexually explicit movies, like *I am Curious (Yellow)* (1967), attempted to satisfy a public's growing hunger for the vicarious experience of sex. By the 1970s, newspapers with names like *Screw,* offering sexual information, personal ads, and sexually explicit photos and art, were available on street corners in larger American cities. These cultural developments demonstrated an increased public interest in sex and suggested that sexual behavior was undergoing changes as well.

What "sexual revolution" means, when it began (if it did), to whom it applied, and what changes it wrought are highly contested subjects. According to sociologists there is no doubt that patterns of sexual partnering underwent significant change in the 1960s, and it is this shift away from "monogamous" sexuality that is usually signified by the term "sexual revolution." However, the revolution that emerged in the 1960s was as much a change in attitudes about sex as it was a significant shift in sexual conduct. Changes in the way that people thought about sexuality and gender roles stimulated new modes of behavior that were not always measured by increased sexual activity. For example, women entered marriage with greater sexual experience and confidence than women in the past. As a result there was an increased demand for sexual satisfaction in marriage. It contributed to the growth of a market for books and magazine articles about how to improve your sex life, a greater demand for marriage manuals and counselors. It may have also led to an increase in divorces, which reinforced the likelihood of those who were divorced having additional sexual partners in their lifetime. These developments also challenged the double standard—which permitted men to engage in sexual activity outside their marriage, but harshly stigmatized women having extra-marital affairs. In the end, all these experiences probably generated both increased frustrations and greater freedom. Betty Friedan's *The Feminine Mystique* capitalized on precisely these developments—thus the emergence of feminism and women's rights overlapped with and were intertwined with the developments later labeled "the sexual revolution."

The sexual revolution as it emerged in the 1960s was the historical culmination of processes begun during World War II, and it produced significant changes in the decades that followed. The term "revolution" usually implies something that occurs rapidly and dramatically. However, the time frame of the sexual revolution is much longer and it resembles the time frame of the Industrial Revolution—the transition from an agricultural society to one built on new technologies and industrial production. It has been an immense and contradictory process, often not very obvious, stretching out over the life span of two generations. This sexual revolution radically altered the sex/gender system, as anthropologist Gayle Rubin has called the system that translates biological capacities—of sex and gender differences—into the cultural and social patterns that constitute our lives as gendered and sexual human beings. The sexual revolution started as a result of three major cultural forces. First of all, of the explosion of youth culture and the thirst for sexual experience before marriage by young men and women; secondly, the emergence of feminism and the women's movement at the end of the 1960s; and lastly, the gay liberation movement's dramatic Stonewall rebellion in 1969. But the sexual revolution also provoked a profound and powerful counter-revolution—the Religious Fundamentalist Right—which continues to wage a battle against the forces that originally ignited the revolution.

The mobilization of young men for the Armed Services and the recruitment of female factory workers during World War II initiated a profound shift in the social relations of gender and sexuality in the United States. Young men and women left the haven of their families and lived for four years among other people far from parental guidance. These young women and men in their late teens and early twenties were at the threshold of their most sexually active stage of life and usually, they were unmarried. This generation had grown up during the Great Depression and were heavily influenced by the exuberant and free-wheeling culture of swing—a cultural explosion roughly analogous to the rock culture of the 1960s. Throughout the war years young men and women—in constant motion and under the uncertainty and stress of combat—engaged in sexual relations with each other outside of marriage and other constraining contexts.

Recognition of sexual revolution dawned slowly after the war. The publication of Alfred Kinsey's two pathbreaking volumes on human sexuality in 1948 (*Sexual Behavior in the Human Male*) and 1953 (*Sexual Behavior in the Human Female*) probably exerted greater influence on modern conceptions of sexuality than any work since Sigmund Freud's. Moral outrage and a great deal of professional hypocrisy greeted the report, but few Americans remained immune to a new awareness of the gap between public attitudes toward sexual behavior and daily sexual activities. Kinsey was so struck by the extraordinary extent of individual variation in sexual behavior that he argued that any attempt to establish uniform standards of sexual conduct was both impracticable and unjust. He believed that his discovery of the widespread deviation from accepted sexual standards showed that attempts to regulate sexual behavior were doomed to failure and ''the only proper sexual policy was no policy at all.''

Although the research in the Kinsey reports was not based on the generation that experienced the postwar sexual revolution (they had focused on the inter-war generations), the reports did come to symbolize it in the popular consciousness and in the history of American culture. Most of what we mean by sexual revolution refers to non-marital sexual activity. By the early 1960s, shifts had begun to take place along several fronts that consolidated the sexual revolution. One of the most important was that young men and women engaged in their first acts of sexual intercourse at increasingly younger ages. The impact of earlier sexual experimentation was reinforced by the later age of marriage; thus young men and women had more time available to acquire sexual experience with partners before entering into a long-term monogamous relationship. In addition, the growing number of marriages resulting in divorce provided another opportunity for men and women (to a lesser degree) to engage in non-monogamous sexual activity. All three of these developments allowed the generation born between 1935 and 1945 to experience sexual activity with a larger number of sexual partners in their lifetime than most men and women born earlier.

These trends received reinforcement from a number of other developments. Technical improvements and the increased access to birth control methods made it easier for women to engage in sex without the risk of unwanted pregnancy. In 1960, the most popular form of birth control, the oral contraceptive pill, became commercially available. Political developments, such as the emergence of the women's movement, also encouraged women to reject the double standard and to postpone marriage. In the wake of the women's movement, the gay liberation movement emerged in 1969. The gay movement sought to combat the stigma attached to homosexuality. It promoted self-acceptance and a positive evaluation of homosexuality that significantly contributed to the sexual revolution. For example, lesbians and gay men organized dances, coffee houses, and other social activities in order to facilitate sexual and social contacts among men and women with homosexual desires.

If the Kinsey reports represent the first shot fired in the sexual revolution, the research of William Masters and Virginia Johnson represented an ambiguous resolution of some issues raised by the shifts in sexual attitudes and behavior. *Human Sexual Response* (1966) was the first volume published, to be followed four years later by *Human Sexual Inadequacy* (1970); both books were based on

laboratory observations of sexual behavior and became the basis of a therapeutic practice devoted to sexual dysfunction. Nevertheless, their work also exemplified the sexual egalitarianism of the 1960s— not only in their working relationship, but also in the image of sexual relations that they project in their books. Their work stressed the importance of the *quality* of sexual activity—yet they made the couple rather than the unattached individual the preferred unit of analysis and therapy. In the end, Masters and Johnson focused almost exclusively on the quality of sexual experience within committed relationships. They did not discuss improving the quality of sexual experience for those men and women who chose to engage in sex with casual (non-marital) sexual partners, the sex that is essential to the definition of the sexual revolution.

By the late 1960s, social institutions emerged to facilitate non-marital sexual contacts. Singles bars opened so that single men and women could meet and make sexual contacts. Weekly alternative newspapers sprouted in most major cities—all of which carried personal ads of people looking for sexual partners and relationships. Swinging or mate swapping also became the practice among certain social circles where couples swapped partners among themselves. Swingers clubs were started and others took out ads in swinging and alternative publications. Within this context other kinds of sexuality also gained visibility—fetishes, S/M (sado-masochism), and transvestitism. The proportion of the population that participated in the new swinging and singles scene was probably small but the scene was widely publicized in the press and popular culture. The dilemmas of sophisticated sexual experiments like swapping were satirized in movies like *Bob & Carol & Ted & Alice* (1969) and *Shampoo* (1975). Movies like *Looking for Mr. Goodbar* (1977) exploited the vulnerabilities and anxieties of these new trends for young women. The movie *Cruising* (1980) set a police thriller in a gay world of men engaged in an endless and desperate hunt for sex.

Another sign of the sexual revolution was the increased availability of sexually explicit books, magazines, and films. In 1967 the U.S. Congress set up a Commission on Pornography and Obscenity to define pornography and obscenity, provide guidelines for its regulation and to assess its significance in American society. The *Report* of the Commission concluded that its researchers had found no evidence that exposure to explicit sexual materials led to any criminal or delinquent behavior among youth and adults. This report was later criticized by conservatives and some feminists in the 1980s and was countered by a later Commission appointed by the Reagan administration. Nevertheless, the sexual revolution of the 1960s was associated with much greater degrees of sexual explicitness throughout the culture. Mainstream media like Hollywood movies achieved a level of sexual explicitness that receded in the late 1970s and early 1980s.

By the late 1970s, the sexual revolution encountered a number of obstacles. One was the growing opposition of conservative and religious groups to all those new gender roles and forms of sexual conduct that appeared during the peak years (1964—1977) of the sexual revolution: non-marital and youth sexuality, birth control, abortion, and homosexuality. Conservatives established new organizations, elected political representatives, passed legislation, fought to defund sexually progressive programs and to fund sexually conservative programs. These battles continue to take place up until the present. What many call commentators call ''the culture wars'' are, in part, an extension of the sexual revolution.

However, the sexual revolution also encountered obstacles of another sort—sexually transmitted diseases (STD). The diseases spread by sex are numerous and ancient: gonorrhea, syphilis, genital warts, genital herpes, and hepatitis B. AIDS is also transmitted sexually but it was discovered only in 1981; it is the most serious and devastating of sexually transmitted diseases. Starting in the late 1970s, there were a growing number of reports about STD—both *Time* and *Newsweek* produced cover stories on herpes, and the gay male communities were swept by waves of gonorrhea, syphilis, and Hepatitis B. The discovery of an AIDS epidemic among gay men in the early 1980s provoked a major crisis in the sexual politics of the gay community. Medical researchers and gay leaders struggled to find ways of stopping the epidemic without completely excluding all sexual activity. Eventually a number of gay activists invented the idea of "safer sex"—in which gay men could engage in sex, using condoms, without transmitting the virus (HIV) that causes AIDS. Soon after, safer sex was adopted by public health educators and AIDS activists as the basis for HIV prevention. Safer sex and traditional public health treatment programs for the older STD have since reduced the spread of these diseases considerably.

The sexual revolution was not only a revolution in sexual behavior per se—measured by sociologists as an increase in the lifetime number of sexual partners—but also a cultural revolution that was intertwined with many other significant social changes. STD had reached epidemic proportions by the early 1980s, but provided another form of evidence of extensive and casual sexual partnering. Women's sexuality was redefined, and new stress was laid on clitoral orgasm and sexual satisfaction. A culture of sexual experimentation (swinging, S/M clubs, singles bars) emerged that contributed to the evolution of new sexual norms. The women's movement, the counterculture, the development of new lifestyles, lesbian and gay liberation, a greater acceptance of pleasure and all kinds of improvements in the quality of life overlap with the sexual revolution. Religious fundamentalists and the New Right represent the conservative response to the sexual revolution. Many of the social changes and the conflicts engendered by them continue on into the present. Cultural and political changes resulting from the sexual revolution are still in the process of forming. However, the sexual revolution of post-World War II America has changed sexual and gender roles permanently.

—Jeffrey Escoffier

FURTHER READING:

Costello, John. *Love, Sex, War: Changing Values, 1939-1945.* London, Collins, 1985.

D'Emilio, John and Estelle Freedman. *Intimate Matters: A History of Sexuality in America.* 2nd ed. New York, HarperCollins, 1998.

Escoffier, Jeffrey. *American Homo: Community and Perversity.* Berkeley, University of California Press, 1998.

Heidenry, John. *What Wild Ecstasy: The Rise and Fall of the Sexual Revolution.* New York, Simon & Schuster, 1997.

Michael, Robert T., John H. Gagnon, Edward O. Lauman, and Gina Kolata. *Sex in America: A Definitive Survey.* New York, Warner Books, 1994.

Petersen, James R. *The Century of Sex: Playboy's History of the Sexual Revolution, 1900-1999.* New York, Grove Press, 1999.

Seidman, Steven. *Embattled Eros: Sexual Politics and Ethics in Contemporary America.* New York, Routledge, 1992.

Ullman, Sharon R. *Sex Seen: The Emergence of Modern Sexuality in America.* Berkeley, University of California Press, 1997.

Watkins, Elizabeth Siegel. *On the Pill: A Social History of Oral Contraceptives, 1950-1970.* Baltimore, Johns Hopkins University Press, 1998.

The Shadow

For 18 years, from 1931 to 1949, The Shadow, an unrelenting defender of justice, appeared as the title character in 325 novel-length adventures in *The Shadow* magazine, making it the first and most important of the character or hero pulps. A prototypical figure named The Shadow had appeared on radio even earlier, on the *Detective Story Hour,* but the fully-evolved character is best remembered for the radio series that ran from 1937 to 1954, with episodes punctuated by such memorable phrases as "Who knows what evil lurks in the hearts of men? The Shadow knows!" and "The weed of crime bears bitter fruit. Crime does not pay. The Shadow knows!"

The creation of the character named The Shadow is appropriately shrouded in mystery. Although no actual link has been established between the two characters, a seeming prototype of The Shadow appeared in the February 1929 issue of Street and Smith's *Fame and Fortune.* In that story, a character named Compton Moore, with glittering eyes and a mocking laugh, donned a green shroud to fight evil as The Shadow. Whether by imitation or coincidence, when pulp publishers Street and Smith sponsored *Detective Story Hour,* a radio dramatization of stories from their *Detective Story Magazine,* The Shadow was portrayed as the show's narrator, voiced by James La Curto, complete with that familiar haunting laugh.

To get a copyright on their accidental creation and meet what seemed to be a growing demand, Street and Smith quickly created a new pulp magazine, *The Shadow, a Detective Magazine.* John Nanovic, who would a few years later create the Doc Savage character, served as editor for the first twelve years. Journalist and amateur magician Walter Gibson was hired to turn the name and the laugh into a character. In just a few weeks, Gibson produced *The Living Shadow,* the first of the 325 novels that the magazine would publish over the next eighteen years. The stories were all attributed to the house name of Maxwell Grant, and Walter Gibson did not write all of them. However, he did write an astounding 282 of the novels, including the first 112 stories that firmly established the character. When the magazine went from quarterly to twice-monthly publication, Gibson simply picked up his pace and produced two complete novels a month.

In the first story The Shadow is a mysterious presence who works through Harry Vincent and his other operatives. It took a few issues before The Shadow himself was in the center of the action, but the basic look and ambiance was established early on. On the first page of the first story, The Shadow, an ominous figure in a long black coat, seems to materialize out of the thick fog, with only his hawk nose and piercing eyes visible beneath his broad-brimmed felt hat. When The Shadow does go into action, he does so with an automatic pistol spitting death from each hand.

As Walter Gibson fleshed out the mythos, The Shadow acquired scores of agents in addition to right-hand man Harry Vincent. Chief among them were cab driver Moe Shrevitz, gangster Cliff Marsland, reporter Clyde Burke, and the mysterious Burbank, who coordinates communications between The Shadow and his cadre of agents. Another operative, would-be love interest Margo Lane, originated on the radio program but was eventually added to the pulp stories. The Shadow's most interesting relationship is with Lamont Cranston, a wealthy playboy whose guise The Shadow sometimes assumed when Cranston was traveling abroad. The 1937 novel *The Shadow Unmasks* reveals the fact The Shadow is really World War I flying ace and former spy Kent Allard, although some later novels called even this identity into doubt. When The Shadow appeared in other media, his background was simplified—he *was* Lamont Cranston, though he was not so in the original pulps. The final novel in the series, *The Whispering Eyes,* appeared in 1949.

Within a decade after his creation The Shadow had captured the popular imagination. ''As intensely exploited as Tarzan, The Shadow sold wrist watches, coloring books, disguise and fingerprint kits, sheet music, Better Little Books, comic books, and a succession of nearly worthless moving pictures,'' recounts Robert Sampson, author of *Deadly Excitements.* In 1937 The Shadow returned to radio, not just as narrator, but as the lead character, voiced for the first year by Orson Welles. The radio series portrayed The Shadow as less dark and deadly, relying more on his new-found hypnotic powers than on his twin automatics. The show was immensely popular, lasting until 1954. The 1937 feature film *The Shadow Strikes* was based on the radio program, and there was a film serial in 1940 that starred Victor Jory. Some of the later Shadow films were almost domestic comedies, in which the hero is beset with more trouble from his jealous wife than from the villain. The 1994 film starring Alec Baldwin returned to the dark pulp roots for inspiration, pitting The Shadow against his greatest pulp nemesis, Shiwan Khan. The opening scene of the film is even reminiscent of the first chapter of ''The Living Shadow.''

The Shadow had a long and varied life in comic books. Street and Smith published the first of them. Even though Walter Gibson wrote the scripts for the first six years, The Shadow appeared quite differently in the comic book version than in the pulps. Since the radio show had become more popular than the pulp magazine, Gibson was pressured to conform to the radio concept. From 1938 to 1942, Ledger Syndicate distributed a *Shadow* comic strip by Gibson and Vernon Greene. In the 1960s Archie Comics published a series that portrayed The Shadow as a superhero in green and blue tights. One of the most faithful comic-book adaptations was the series published by DC Comics from 1973 to 1975.

—Randy Duncan

FURTHER READING:

Goodstone, Tony. *The Pulps: Fifty Years of American Popular Culture.* New York, Bonanza Books, 1970.

Goulart, Ron. *An Informal History of the Pulp Magazine.* New York, Ace Books, 1973.

Murray, Will. *The Duende History of the Shadow.* Odyssey Press, 1980.

Sampson, Robert. *Deadly Excitements: Shadows and Phantoms.* Bowling Green, Ohio, Bowling Green State University Popular Press, 1989.

''What Evil Lurked?'' *Comics Collector.* Summer, 1984, 33-42.

Shaft

Directed by Gordon Parks and starring Richard Roundtree as the itinerant black detective, John Shaft, Metro-Goldwyn-Mayer's hugely successful 1972 feature, helped initiate Hollywood's Blaxploitation

Richard Roundtree in a scene from *Shaft.*

film craze, a series of cheap and sensational, but lucrative productions featuring provocative ethnic protagonists. Although *Shaft* offers a proud and raw revision of the typical Hollywood African-American hero, the tough spectacle of John Shaft's defiance ultimately contributes little to the cause of racial harmony and understanding.

Provoked by the $10 million in profits of Melvin Van Peeples' independently produced *Sweet Sweetback's Baadasssss Song* in 1971, the aging Hollywood studios observed that Van Peeples had managed to target a widely ignored new box office patronage. Three social factors combined to create a new public taste for successful ethnic ''badasses'' like Sweetback and Shaft. The rise of the civil rights and Black Power movements fostered a popular appreciation for the intelligent, capable, and righteous black individual who triumphed in his attack on the white establishment. The national white flight to the suburbs also contributed to a shifting racial demographic that revised city centers like Chicago, Detroit, and Atlanta where the cinemas of downtown commercial areas now catered to a predominantly middle- and working-class African-American clientele. Lastly, in the late 1960s, Hollywood's long-standing policy of self-censorship gave way to a more liberal rating system that offered mainstream film a new outlet for what had been previously considered uncomfortably blatant expressions of African-American sexuality and anger.

Never as openly revolutionary as the X-rated *Sweet Sweetback,* whose title character escapes white justice after a virulent spree of fornication and murder, *Shaft* tapped into popular feelings of racial tension as it revised the standard Hollywood hard-boiled detective with an R-rated ghetto flavor that tweaked but never attempted to topple the status quo. *Shaft* did much, in Ed Guerrero's words, to "crystallize Hollywood's formula for the 'new' filmic representation of blacks." The film itself revolves around Private Detective John Shaft's rude, but shrewd negotiation of a triple threat. Hired to free the kidnapped daughter of "Bumpy Jonas," a dubious black mob boss, Shaft tangles with the white racist police who attempt to reduce him to a slavish errand boy, navigates the race-complicated grudges between black and white organized crime, and utilizes the revolutionary fervor of militant, but ultimately doomed black urban youth. Throughout the film, Richard Roundtree's performance as the indefatigable private detective subtly revises many of the best hard-boiled moments of Sam Spade and Philip Marlowe. Like Humphrey Bogart in *The Maltese Falcon,* John Shaft overpowers an attacker in his own office, and taunts both his employers and the police, but Shaft also makes deft use of his ethnic appearance when he masquerades as a servile bartending "boy" in order to foil two white assassins. Finally, *Shaft's* dramatic climactic assault on the hired guns in a seedy inner-city hotel references both the war film and the Western in its calculated, paramilitary strike on a fortified outpost of white evil.

Shaft's sexual escapades, boldly aestheticized by Gordon Park's disco-energized cinematography and Isaac Hayes' funky grooves, further exhibit his prowess as a thoroughly masculine black badass. While Shaft shares his most romantic liaisons with a comely African-American woman, he also asserts his manhood by picking up random white women in a local bar. Shaft's post-coital pillow talk with his regular black partner is tender, but his biracial one night stand ends coldly. As Shaft ignores and insults his nameless white lover the following morning, she labels him decidedly "shitty." This brief exchange between the black hero and his white bedfellow powerfully informs the film's finale, when Shaft mimics the angry white woman's insult as a climactic joke on a white establishment cop. Subtly taunting but never openly attacking the racial hierarchy in which he survives, Shaft ends the film disappearing into the city after having effectively "screwed" all his white antagonists.

Aside from two fair sequels, *Shaft's Big Score* and *Shaft in Africa,* Shaft's popularization of the sexy, truculent black male spawned an often bizarre series of Blaxploitation rip-offs and pretenders. A few of these heroes, like *Superfly's* Youngblood Priest and *The Harder They Come's* Ivan Martin, offer some psychological depth. Most Shaft-inspired Blaxploitation heroes, however, are grotesque, ultraviolent perversions of black sexuality. In films like *Welcome Home, Brother Charles* and *Cotton Comes to Harlem,* black male pride and defiance is reduced to crude arrogance, degrading sexual stunts, and brutal vengeance. Hollywood also marketed the feminine side of Blaxploitation through female Shafts, Pam Grier and Tamara Dobson. Films like *Coffy, Foxy Brown,* and *Cleopatra Jones and the Casino of Gold* advertised a shapely, violent black heroine whose arrogant appeal centered around ample doses of ethnic attitude and T&A.

Shaft's new heroic stage in the Hollywood image of the African-American male is clearly limited. Gladstone Yearwood explains, "films such as *Shaft, Superfly,* and *Cooley High* attempt to subvert, or at least question, the dominant tradition in the cinema, but they are effectively harnessed by it in their usage of the Hollywood model as the basis for the development of black heroes." Originally conceived

and scripted for a white actor, MGM quickly darkened its Shaft project for an inner-city African-American audience in order to test drive a new narrative formula where the black won and survived for profitable sequels. Richard Roundtree received a mere $13,000 for his starring role in the first film and the majority of *Shaft's* startling profits were rolled back into MGM's white executive wallets.

Exemplifying the studios' new drive toward customized saturation marketing, *Shaft's* success with the African-American urban audience resulted in a wave of diversified product tie-ins. Aside from more than $10 million in profits from the film's first year of release and the success of Isaac Hayes' Oscar-winning, platinum soundtrack album, MGM capitalized on the popularity of John Shaft's refusal to bow to the man through a merchandising storm that B.J. Mason detailed in *Ebony* as a plague of *Shaft* "suits, watches, belts and sunglasses, leather coats, decals, sweatshirts and night shirts, beach towels, posters, after shave lotion and cologne." Beginning with *Shaft,* Hollywood's cheap and sly appropriation of the racial tensions in America's metropolitan centers became the basis for a parade of crude fantasies and commercial gimmicks revolving around predominantly brutal and misogynistic black heroes who rule the ghetto, but would never garner Sidney Poitier's invitation to dinner.

—Daniel Yezbick

FURTHER READING:

Guerrero, Ed. *Framing Blackness.* Philadelphia, Temple University Press, 1993.

James, Darius. *That's Blaxploitation: Roots of the Baadasssss 'Tude (Rated X by an All-Whyte Jury).* New York, St. Martin's Press, 1995.

Mason, B.J. "The New Films: Culture or Con Game?" *Ebony* December 1972, 68.

Riley, Clayton. "Shaft Can Do Everything—I Can Do Nothing." *New York Times.* 13 August 1972.

Yearwood, Gladstone. "The Hero in Black Film." *Wide Angle.* Vol. 5, No. 2, 32-50.

Shakur, Tupac (1971-1996)

Rapper, film actor, and poet Tupac "Amaru" Shakur, also known as "2Pac," was one of the most influential and greatest rappers of the 1990s, who launched his rap career when he appeared in the Digital Underground's "Same Song" video in 1991. After the video aired, rap fans across America were asking who the young man was in the African outfit with beads beaming down his chest like an "African King." Critic Armond White has noted that it was after his appearance in the Digital Underground video that Tupac Shakur "first realized the thrill of putting a rhyme on tape and getting it to the public." As a solo artist, Tupac Shakur burst on the rap scene with *2Pacalypse Now* (1991), a 13-rap-song album that was destined to change the face of rap music in America and the world over. Through this album, Tupac Shakur vowed to use his poetic power to tell those stories from the streets and the ghetto that the mainstream media refused to talk about, including the plight of black males and other African Americans in America, police brutality, and poverty. In the rap song "Rebel of the Underground," Shakur foreshadowed the conflict between him and the police/media by arguing that they cannot stand the reign of a man like him "who goes against the

Tupac Shakur

grain.'' Furthermore, not only did he characterize himself as ''cold as the devil'' and ''straight out of the underground,'' but he called himself ''the lyrical lunatic, the maniac MC,'' and asserted that ''the most dangerous weapon'' is ''an educated black man.''

Themes of police brutality, black-on-black crimes, the American Dream deferred, black males in America, and the African-American struggle and survival permeate songs like ''Trapped,'' ''Soulja's Story,'' ''I Don't Give a Fuck,'' and ''Words of Wisdom.'' While in ''I Don't Give a Fuck'' and ''Soulja's Story'' Shakur rapped that he does not give ''a fuck'' about the police and other American officials and institutions who oppress African Americans, in ''Words of Wisdom'' he charged America with the ''crime of rape, murder, and assault'' for ''suppressing and punishing'' his people. Additionally, he accused America of falsifying black history and of falsely imprisoning black males by keeping them ''trapped in the projects.'' He concluded the song by warning America that it reaps what it sows and that he is ''2Pacalypse, America's nightmare.'' The rough side and revolutionary stance of *2Pacalypse Now* are what later misled music and popular culture critics to label Tupac Shakur a ''Gangsta Rapper'' and his music ''Gangsta Rap,'' thus blaming the messenger for the message.

Critics who labeled Tupac Shakur a ''gangsta rapper'' and called him controversial and confused failed to see that his music always contained two sides: a tough side bristling with the realities of the ghetto life and a didactic side endowed with positive messages. Such was the case with ''Brenda's Got a Baby'' from *2Pacalypse Now,* one of Shakur's best known rap songs. The song described the carelessness of a cousin who impregnates Brenda, the ignorance of Brenda who tries to throw the baby in the garbage can, and the callousness of the community that fails to realize that Brenda's plight affects the whole community. *Strictly 4 My N.I.G.G.A.Z.* (1993), Tupac Shakur's second album, contained a song called ''Keep Ya Head Up'' in which he both debunks some black men for their misogyny, sexism, and irresponsibility, and advises black women to keep their heads up no

matter what the situation is. Furthermore, Tupac Shakur showed his softer side yet again on *Me Against the World* (1995), with ''Dear Mama,'' a tribute to his mother, Afeni Shakur. Autobiographical in nature, ''Dear Mama'' chronicles the Black Panther days of Afeni Shakur and how she struggled to keep her family together. Also, Shakur reminisced about the stress he caused a mother trying to raise him while struggling with drugs, and how, in the absence of a father, he turned to the streets in search of love and fame.

In 1996, the music scene changed when Tupac Shakur became the first rapper to release a double album, *All Eyez On Me;* it reached number one on rhythm and blues and Pop charts and was certified seven times platinum within ten months. In the late 1990s, *All Eyez On Me* remained the best selling rap album of all time. The most notable and famous song on the album was ''California Love,'' Shakur's single, a song which, according to Armond White, ''certifies a level of achievement, of rap triumph, and American commercial bliss.'' Both Dr. Dre and Tupac Shakur create ''a sense of belonging that neglects rap protest, preferring an affirmation that is vaguely patriotic.'' Other work of Tupac's include two posthumous albums, *Makaveli the Don Killuminati: The 7 Day Theory* (1996) and the double album *R U Still Down? [Remember Me]* (1997).

Shakur influenced the Hollywood film industry by starring in six films in five years: *Juice* (1992), *Poetic Justice* (1993), *Above the Rim* (1994), *Bullet* (1997), *Gridlock'd* (1997), and *Gang Related* (1997). Except for *Poetic Justice,* a film in which he starred beside Janet Jackson and which shows his romantic and soft side, all the other films look like they were written out of Tupac Shakur's tough lyrics; they exploited and contributed to his ''gansta'' and ''thug-life'' image. Though his life was cut short on September 13, 1996, Tupac Shakur has become a legend—some people still think he never died—and his legacy will live forever through his released, and still to be released, records and poems.

—Pierre-Damien Mvuyekure

FURTHER READING:

Alexander, Frank, with Heidi Siegmund Cuda. *Got Your Back: The Life of a Bodyguard in the Hardcore World of Gangsta Rap.* New York, St. Martin's Press, 1998.

Scott, Cathy. *The Killing of Tupac Shakur.* Las Vegas, Huntington Press, 1997.

Vibe magazine editors. *Tupac Amaru Shakur, 1971-1996.* New York, Crown Publishers, 1997.

White, Armond. *Rebel for the Hell of It: The Life of Tupac Shakur.* New York, Thunder's Mouth Press, 1997.

Shane

In 1945 Jack Schaefer, an editor and reporter for the *Norfolk Virginian-Pilot,* wrote and published the story ''Rider from Nowhere'' in *Argosy* magazine. Houghton Mifflin released a revised and expanded version of the story as *Shane* in 1949. Based somewhat on the Johnson Courty War in Wyoming in the early 1890s, it was Schaefer's attempt to reduce the legend of the West to its basic components, and to elevate it to the level of Homeric mythology. It

Alan Ladd (left) in a scene from the film *Shane*.

remains a simple tale of a mysterious stranger who descends into the valley in the midst of a conflict. Choosing sides, he removes his godly raiment to mingle with the common people. He crosses a body of water to challenge the enemy and then, after donning again his godly clothes, recrosses the body of water to vanquish the enemy, before ascending from the valley into the night. The novel has sold over 6 million copies in over 80 editions in more than 30 languages. The resulting movie rendition remains the ultimate statement of the legend of the American West.

Young Bob Starrett watched the lone rider make his way slowly across the valley toward the cluster of small farms. ''Call me Shane,'' he said. He was from Arkansas. At 15 he had left his Arkansas home to wander. He did not say where. The Starretts, Joe Marion, and Little Bob, invited Shane to stay on with them as a farm hand. There was something about him, something mysterious and terrifying, but Joe Starrett sensed they had nothing to fear. ''He's dangerous, all right . . . but not to us.''

The West was changing. The frontier was gone. Homesteaders were fencing off the land in 80 and 160 acre lots. But the old ways die hard. The Fletcher Brothers, owners of the biggest ranch in the valley, had recently contracted with the Army to supply them with beef, and

they needed the range land. This precipitated the conflict between the Fletchers and the farmers that led to several confrontations. Joe Starrett, the strongest willed of the farmers, became their leader, and Shane, sensing the danger of the growing tension, supported Starrett and the farmers.

In two preliminary bouts with the Fletcher cowhands, Shane humiliated them. The first was a fist fight with Chris, a man whom he admired, in which he broke the man's arm. In the second, a barroom brawl at Grafton's Saloon, Shane and Starrett soundly defeated a group of cowhands. In the days following the brawl, young Bob noticed a growing restlessness in Shane, a gradual loss of the serenity that had come over him after he hired on. Fletcher's response to the brawl was to call for a hired gun, Stark Wilson, to come to the valley as their enforcer. When Wilson instigated a face-off with Ernie Wright, and then killed him before Ernie could clear his holster, Shane knew that the conflict had gone far beyond what the farmers could manage. He decided that the time had come to act. ''You seem to know about that kind of dirty business,'' said one of the farmers. ''I do,'' responded Shane.

Fletcher arranged for a meeting with Joe Starrett. But Shane, knowing that it was a trap, knocked Joe unconscious and went to

Grafton's alone, followed by Little Bob. Shane killed Wilson and Fletcher in a gun fight. Then he rode out of town, but not out of memory, as the stories of Shane were told and retold for years after in the valley.

The 1953 film version was produced and directed by George Stevens for Paramount. Alan Ladd played Shane, Van Heflin and Jean Arthur played Joe and Marion, and Brandan DeWilde played Little Joey Starrett. Jack Palance played Wilson and Emile Meyer and John Dierkas played the Ryker Brothers, Rube and Morgan.

In this beautifully filmed movie, the basic elements of Schaefer's story are presented as a mythological tale set in the West. The simple American theme of good winning over evil, and the more complex themes of unstated love, the virtue of economic progress, and the inexorable progress of the order of civilization superseding the chaos of the frontier, are unfolded beneath the dominating peaks of the Grand Tetons.

A lone rider descends into the valley. As a stag bends down to drink from a stream and then raises his head, the rider is framed by the antlers as he comes on slowly toward Little Joey, who is watching him. The audience knows that this is no ordinary drifter. Where is he from? "Here and there." Where is he going? "Someplace I've never been." He learns of the conflict between the homesteaders and the Rykers, who own the largest cattle ranch in the valley. The Rykers want the range opened up and the fences torn down. They are standing in the way of progress. The old ways of open range ranching and cattle drives are inefficient in the face of feed lots and fenced off farming. Shane, in a melancholy surrender to changing times, sees his world coming to an end. The open range is gone. The presence of women and children in abundance requires the banishment of guns and the violent way of life in which he flourished. Reluctantly, he sheds the buckskins of the trail and adopts the drab homespun of the farmer and becomes Starrett's farm hand.

Marion, who watched him ride up, is immediately taken by this handsome Apollo who stands in stark contrast to her dull, dependable husband, Joe. Although she is committed to her family and the farm, she is in love with Shane, as he is with her. Their love, however, is unfulfilled passion, chivalric and pure. This upholds Shane's heroic stature and sets him apart from ordinary men. Little Joey is mesmerized by Shane and his obvious proficiency with guns. He loves his parents, seeks their advice and counsel, and obeys their directives. But he worships Shane. He is a fantasy hero, a little boy's dream.

In the confrontations with Ryker's men, Shane at first backs down. This makes some of the farmers question his dependability. To counter this, Shane picks a fight with Chris Calloway, the ranch hand who first challenged him. The fight turns into a brawl in which Joe and Shane defeat a large group of Ryker's men. Ryker, rebuffed angrily when he offers to hire Shane, responds by sending for Wilson, an evil gunfighter. Played by Palance as a morose, quiet spoken, calculating killer, he personifies evil. As he strolls into the darkened saloon, a dog gets up and walks away, adding an exclamation point to this evil presence. Wilson baits and then kills Torrey, one of the farmers. This prompts an attempt at negotiation between Starrett and Ryker, but Shane is worried that the confab is a set up, that Joe will be killed. Shane then knocks Joe unconscious and rides to meet Wilson at the Saloon. In a beautifully choreographed scene underlined by Gordon Willis' point-of-view photography, Shane kills Wilson and both Ryker brothers in a poetic replay of Wilson's murder of Torrey.

In keeping with the innocent-eye narrative of the novel, the film is presented from little Joey's point of view. Many of the scenes were filmed in low angle camera shots, as if the audience were viewing the action from Joey's level. This technique also solved the problem of photographing the short, 5-foot-5 Ladd in fight scenes with the much taller Heflin and Ben Johnson. The low camera angle makes Ladd look much taller. Joey is presented as an observer in most pivotal scenes, and as such, Ladd is filmed in a manner that depicts Shane as a god-like figure, looming over the action of the story.

Both the novel and the film succeed in transforming the Western legend into a pure and simple tale of the triumph of good over evil. Shane is presented as an incongruous hero, out of his element, in desperate search for a new existence. His world is ending. He tries farming, but he cannot change what is. He appears hopelessly out of place in the family scenes and in the burial scene. He is forced to revert to an existence he realizes cannot exist anymore. He is an ambiguous hero who desires to eliminate violence and killing from the valley, but he must kill to accomplish his objective. Then he must leave the valley. "There is no living with a killing," he tells Joey, "It's like a brand."

Shane's desperate struggle to escape his past thus ends tragically. In order to save the lifestyle he sought to embrace, he was forced to revert to his past life. "I tried it. It didn't work for me," he explains to Joey. As Shane rides off, Joey begs him to come back. "Shane, come back!" he yells into the night. It is a plaintive cry for a return of his lost innocence, of his fantasy hero, and of his hero's way of life. Before civilization came to the West, life was simple and predictable, pure and unambiguous. Personal honor and the law of the gun marked the difference between right and wrong. In the final analysis, *Shane* appeals to that nostalgic longing in urban society for a time long past when life's options remained open, where men were dominant, and where ethical gray areas did not exist. The invocation of a person's moral code was abrupt and final.

This is a towering, landmark Western film. It is the final statement of the legend of the West, reduced to its simplest components and elevated to the status of myth. Yet it is flawed. It is slow and pretentious; it is studied and self-conscious. It lacks spontaneity. At times, the understated dialogue and suggested themes of unfulfilled love, hero worship, male bonding, and the adherence to moral codes seem stagey and lacking in vitality. But these are trivial points. After *Shane,* the Hollywood Western became less and less viable as a genre and, except for *The Searchers* (1957), it remains unmatched in stature or influence by any later Western films.

The Academy of Motion Picture Arts & Sciences nominated *Shane* for Best Picture, Best Director, and Best Writing (screen adaptation by A.B. Guthrie). Brandon DeWilde and Jack Palance were both nominated for the Best Supporting Actor award. Loyal Griggs won an Oscar for his superb color photography. *Shane* was remade by Malpaso Productions in 1985 as *Pale Rider,* starring Clint Eastwood as a lonely preacher riding in to help a group of miners. It is a gritty film and in places almost a frame by frame clone of the original. It marked Eastwood's return to the Western genre after a nine year absence.

—James R. Belpedio

FURTHER READING:

Cawelti, John G. *The Six-Gun Mystique.* Bowling Green, Ohio, Bowling Green University Popular Press, 1971.

Hine, Robert V. *The American West: An Interpretive History.* 2nd edition. Boston, Little Brown, 1984.

Petri, Bruce Humleker. "A Theory of American Film: the Films and Techniques of George Stevens." Ph.D. dissertation. Harvard University, 1974.

Schaefer, Jack. *Shane*. New York, Houghton Mifflin Company, 1949.

Slotkin, Richard. *Gunfighter Nation: The Myth of the Frontier on Twentieth- Century America*. New York, Athenaeum, 1992.

Shaw, Artie (1910—)

One of the three great clarinet-playing band leaders of the twentieth century, along with Benny Goodman and Woody Herman, Artie Shaw was also an experimental leader during the big band era. Born Arthur Arshawsky in New York City, he played in dance bands while in high school and turned professional at age 15, eventually free-lancing in recording studios. In 1935, he played jazz backed by a string quartet and formed a big band that included a string section. Two years later, returning to traditional instrumentation, he recorded his first big hit, Cole Porter's "Begin the Beguine." In 1939, he abandoned his band and went to Mexico. After frequent stops and starts in the music business, Shaw published his autobiography in 1952 and played briefly with a new combo called the Grammercy 5 before a final retirement. He was married eight times to a bevy of beauties that included screen stars Ava Gardner and Lana Turner.

—Benjamin Griffith

FURTHER READING:

Balliett, Whitney. *American Musicians*. New York, Oxford Press, 1986.

Shaw, Artie. *The Trouble with Cinderella*. New York, Farrar, Straus, and Young, 1952.

Simon, George T. *The Big Bands*. New York, MacMillan, 1974.

Shawn, Ted (1891-1972)

Ted Shawn is regarded as the father of American modern dance. Born Edwin Meyers Shawn, he began dancing as a form of physical therapy for his paralysis. He recovered, and became a partner and later husband to dancer Ruth St. Denis, who had become famous for her religious solo dances. The couple formed a pioneering dance company and training school called Denishawn in 1915, which toured across America and the world. Shawn often explored Christian and other world religion themes, and was the first American choreographer to combine nudity with movement. After leaving Denishawn, he created the first all-male dance troupe in America, called simply Men Dancers, and Jacob's Pillow, an international dance festival and training center in Massachusetts. Shawn was responsible for establishing dance as a legitimate career for men in America, inspiring generations of dancers and choreographers.

—Brian Granger

FURTHER READING:

Mumaw, Barton, and Jane Sherman. *Barton Mumaw, Dancer: From Denishawn to Jacob's Pillow and Beyond*. New York, Dance Horizons, 1986.

Shawn, Ted. *One Thousand and One Night Stands*. Garden City, New York, Doubleday, 1960.

Terry, Walter. *Ted Shawn, Father of American dance: A Biography*. New York, Dial Press, 1976.

She Wore a Yellow Ribbon

Director John Ford's *She Wore a Yellow Ribbon* (1949) is the first color feature film shot in Monument Valley, Arizona, and the second of three films Ford made about the 7th Cavalry—the other two are *Fort Apache* (1948) and *Rio Grande* (1950). Collectively these films are known as the "Cavalry Trilogy." Set in the American southwest in 1876, *She Wore a Yellow Ribbon* revolves around Captain Nathan Brittles (played by John Wayne), an aging officer leading a final patrol before retirement. Due to its gung ho glorification of the concept of Manifest Destiny, the film is best known as a reflection of mainstream America's post-World War II optimism.

—Robert C. Sickels

FURTHER READING:

Nolley, Ken. "Printing the Legend in the Age of MX: Reconsidering Ford's Military Trilogy." *Film/Literature Quarterly*. Vol. 14, No. 2, 1986, 82-88.

Place, J. A. *The Western Films of John Ford*. Secaucus, The Citadel Press, 1977.

Stowell, Peter. *John Ford*. Boston, Twayne Publishers, 1986.

Westbrook, Max. "The Night John Wayne Danced with Shirley Temple." *Western American Literature*. Vol. 25, No. 2, 1990, 157-167.

Sheldon, Sidney (1917—)

By the time he wrote his first book at age fifty-three, Sidney Sheldon had already had a substantial impact on popular culture via the creation of successful screenplays and television series, but his subsequent career as a novelist has far eclipsed everything that preceded it. Along with such rivals as Irving Wallace, Jacqueline Susann, Harold Robbins, and Judith Krantz, Sheldon has dominated the bestseller lists by producing fast-moving tales of sex and power among the jet set, such as *Bloodline, The Other Side of Midnight*, and *A Stranger in the Mirror*. And, like these other authors, Sheldon's popularity with the public has been in inverse proportion to his standing with literary critics. Unfazed by the critics' disapproval of his efforts, Sheldon continues to create tales that enthrall readers and-bringing his career full circle—often find a second life dramatized as feature films or television miniseries.

Born in Chicago in 1917, Sheldon entered Northwestern University on a scholarship in 1935, but was soon forced to drop out by the economic hardships of the Depression. He journeyed to Manhattan in hopes of becoming a songwriter, and when that didn't pan out he tried the other coast, where he had better luck. On the strength of the story-sense displayed in his sample précis of Steinbeck's *Of Mice and Men*, Sheldon was hired as a reader by Universal Studios. He had managed to break into screenwriting on a modest basis when World War II broke out, but Sheldon's service proved only a brief interruption, as the Army Air Force quickly discharged him for medical reasons. After some ventures into writing musicals and comedies for the New York stage, Sheldon returned to Hollywood. His acclaim as a scriptwriter was capped by the Oscar he won for the screenplay of *The Bachelor and the Bobbysoxer* (RKO, 1947), a romantic comedy starring Cary Grant, Myrna Loy, and Shirley Temple. The following year, Sheldon collaborated with Frances Goodrich and Albert Hackett on the script for the highly successful MGM musical, Irving Berlin's *Easter Parade*, the only film to unite Judy Garland and Fred Astaire. That script earned the ScreenWriters Guild award for best musical of the year, as did Sheldon's adaptation of Berlin's *Annie Get Your Gun* in 1950.

Other frothy Hollywood vehicles in which Sheldon was involved as writer or producer include *You're Never Too Young* and *Pardners* (1955 and 1956 respectively), both starring Martin and Lewis), Cole Porter's *Anything Goes* (1956, with Bing Crosby), and *Dream Wife* (1953, Sheldon's debut as a director, starring Cary Grant). In the late 1950s, Sheldon made a second assault on Broadway, which proved more successful than his first. He collaborated with Herbert and Dorothy Fields and David Shaw on the 1959 Gwen Verdon vehicle, *Redhead,* which earned four Tony Awards, including best musical.

Following less than stellar work on other shows and movies, Sheldon transferred to the medium of television, where he created and produced two memorable situation comedies for two different networks. ABC premiered Sheldon's *The Patty Duke Show* in 1963. The young actress, most famed for portraying Helen Keller in the serious drama *The Miracle Worker,* played identical cousins, one from America and one from Scotland, who often exchanged identities in Sheldon's frivolous plots. That series ran for three seasons. Even more successful for Sheldon was his NBC series, *I Dream of Jeannie*, starring Barbara Eden as a sweet natured but naive genie and Larry Hagman as the befuddled astronaut for whom she performs her magic. Debuting in 1965, the show ran for five years initially and has been re-running ever since, spawning further *Jeannie* TV movies and commercials. A generation of Americans can probably, if asked, sing the entire lyrics of these two sitcoms' theme songs as readily, if not more so, than they could sing Mr. Berlin's aforementioned "Easter Parade." Sheldon's 1970s ABC series, *Hart to Hart*, was another ratings winner, starring Robert Wagner and Stephanie Powers as wealthy married sleuths in the romantic/comedic tradition of Nick and Nora Charles.

Looking for new worlds to conquer, and anxious to create characterizations with more depth than that afforded by most TV or film scripts, Sheldon tried his hand at writing a novel. His first effort, *The Naked Face* (1970), was a suspense tale about a psychoanalyst who discovers that someone wants him dead. Although it was not a great success in its first printing, *Naked Face* was followed by Sheldon's first blockbuster success, *The Other Side of Midnight* (1974). This rags-to-riches story of a woman's vengeance catapulted Sheldon to the bestseller lists, where he has remained ever since with each successive book. (Thanks to his later volumes, Sheldon's initially moribund *Naked Face* has remained a steady seller in reprints.) *Midnight* brought Sheldon a movie sale, but not, unfortunately, a successful movie. The same pattern was repeated with other Sheldon bestsellers, such as *Bloodline* (1978). Consequently, he elected to write and produce his own adaptation of *Rage of Angels* (1980), among others. Whatever the outcome of these adaptations, however, the hard-working Sheldon takes pride in the success of the

novels themselves. At the age of eighty, on the eve of the publication of his fifteenth novel, *The Best Laid Plans* (1997), the author described his working methods to the *Los Angeles Times*: "I dictate everything to a secretary and she transcribes it. I'll do up to 50 pages a day, but when I get those pages, I'll do a dozen to 15 total rewrites before I ever let my publisher see them." And that, apparently, is when the publisher gets busy: At last count, according to the Guinness Book of World Records, Sheldon is the most translated author in the world, with books in 51 languages in 180 countries.

—Preston Neal Jones

FURTHER READING:

Sheldon, Sidney. *Master of the Game.* New York, Wm. Morrow, 1982.

———. *The Other Side of Midnight.* New York, Wm. Morrow, 1973.

———. *A Stranger in the Mirror.* New York, Wm. Morrow, 1976.

———. *Three Complete Novels (Bloodline; A Stranger in the Mirror; The Naked Face).* New York, Wings Books, 1992.

———. *Windmills of the Gods.* New York, Wm. Morrow, 1987.

Shepard, Sam (1943—)

Playwright, actor, and director Sam Shepard is a serious and distinguished playwright whose work is performed by his peers and admired by critics and theatergoers in many countries. He is, however, most widely and popularly known, particularly in the United States, as a movie actor, notably in *The Right Stuff* (1983), writer-director Philip Kaufman's tribute to the Mercury project astronauts which has become ingrained in American popular culture. Shepard played Chuck Yeager and was Oscar-nominated for his fine performance. His stage and screen persona is in the strong and silent mold—tall, slim, cleft-chinned and good looking—and he has made effective appearances in numerous other films, among them *Crimes of the Heart* (1987), *Steel Magnolias* (1989) and *Thunderheart* (1992) that have varied in both quality and success. He co-starred with Jessica Lange, later his off-screen partner and mother of some of his children, in *Francis* (1982) and *Country* (1984).

It is, however, his work as a playwright that has defined Sam Shepard's cultural contribution. The structure of his dramatic language has received close critical attention as directors and scholars, like Stephen J. Bottoms, have striven to discover "how it is that his strange language and stage imagery so often seem to lodge themselves in the spectator's imagination with such peculiar force." Shepard's "peculiar force" of language earned him Obie awards for three early-career one-act plays in the 1960s, the New York Drama Critics Circle Best Play Award for *Lie of the Mind* (1985), and the Pulitzer Prize for Drama for his play *Buried Child* (1978).

Born Samuel Shepard Rogers in Mount Sheridan, Illinois, he endured an "army brat" childhood until his family eventually settled in California. He became interested in theater early, joined a church dramatic group, and later became a playwright-in-residence at the Magic Theatre in San Francisco. He then moved to New York in the 1960s and began working off-off-Broadway as a writer and actor with such experimental groups as the La Mama company. The origin of Shepard's unique dramatic language can be traced to this early period and his subsequent move to London in 1971. The music scene of

Greenwich Village, the fragmented, improvisational nature of jazz, and the driving, electric sound of rock influenced the tone, structure, and characters of his initial theatrical experiments. Shepard's plays did not conform to the established, traditional dramas of Arthur Miller or Tennessee Williams, a rebellion of approach that became a trademark of his work.

Eschewing both realism and conventional exposition, character conflicts and inner meaning in Shepard's plays are expressed through his use of syntax, imagery, and rhythm. In his preface to *Angel City* (1976), Shepard wrote a "Note to the Actors," revealing how music influences characterization. "Instead of the idea of a 'whole character' with logical motives behind his behavior which the actor submerges himself into, he should consider himself a fractured whole with bits and pieces of characters flying off the central theme. In other words, more in terms of collage construction or jazz improvisation." Although New York had witnessed the staging of almost 20 plays by Shepard between 1964 and 1971, drugs and a troubled affair with rock musician Patti Smith prompted a move to England, where he remained until 1974.

Of his major works, only the rock star/status-struggle drama *Tooth of Crime* (1972) was written and first produced in London; however, this distanced perspective on American culture significantly influenced Shepard's writing. In an interview conducted in England in 1974, he explained this creative dichotomy. "It wasn't until I came to England that I found out what it means to be an American. Nothing really makes sense when you're there, but the more distant you are from it, the more implications of what you grew up with start to emerge." What Shepard "grew up with" was to form what many critics have termed a "family tetralogy," created by the plays *Curse of the Starving Class* (1977), *Buried Child* (1978), *True West* (1980), *Fool for Love* (1983), and *Lie of the Mind* (1985). These works represent his major successes, and while all deal with the psychological dysfunction of the American family, he has remained an artist who resists traditional genre classification, mixing comic absurdism with the faintly sinister.

An actor writing for actors, the power of Shepard's language links him to a renowned tradition of American playwrights; yet, it is precisely this language, which is uniquely his own, that also separates his work from that of his predecessors. Actor Joyce Aaron, who originated many of the female roles in Shepard's early plays, concurs, stating: "Sam is a recorder of the authentic American voice. He starts from a certain perception of daily life, and then transforms that into a specific voice—a voice with its own rhythms and shifting consciousness, its unique, particular curve or leap. . . . That is part of the theatrical challenge and wonder of speaking Sam's language."

Sam Shepard wrote the screenplay for Wim Wenders' *Paris, Texas* (1984), adapted *Fool for Love* to the screen in 1985 (and starred in it), and wrote an original screenplay, *Far North* (1988), in which Jessica Lange starred and which marked his none-too-successful film directing debut. In 1994, he wrote and directed *Silent Tongue,* but it was clear by the late 1990s that his natural metier as a dramatist was the live theater.

—John A. Price

FURTHER READING:

Bottoms, Stephen J. *The Theatre of Sam Shepard: States of Crises.* Cambridge, Cambridge University Press, 1998.

DeRose, David J. *Sam Shepard.* New York, Twayne, 1992.

Marranca, Bonnie, editor. *American Dreams: The Imagination of Sam Shepard.* New York, Performing Arts Journal Publications, 1983.

Wade, Leslie. *Sam Shepard and the American Theatre.* Westport, Connecticut, Greenwood Press, 1997.

Sherman, Cindy (1954—)

To some extent, Cindy Sherman has reached cult figure status in the artworld. With her ability to transform herself into various subjects, Sherman uses her photography as a way to confront and explore the representations of women in society; additionally, she challenges ideas about appearance. With the showing of her first series, the black and white photographs in the *Untitled Film Stills* (1977-80), Sherman burst upon the art scene. Immediately recognized for her new way of approaching photography while promoting a feminist viewpoint, Sherman, in her international exhibitions, has generated a large following and prompted much discussion about many issues. Her images cross the boundaries of several genres, yet, essentially, all of her photographs deal with the ideas of exhibitionism, voyeurism, and in many cases, the portrayal of women. Her theatrical works employ both art theories and critical issues from the 1980s and 1990s, and actively engage critics, collectors, museums, and the general public.

For an artist who so quickly became successful with her images of sometimes surreal, horrific, and always fascinating depictions of invented characters, Sherman had a simple upbringing. She was born, the youngest of five children, on January 19, 1954, in Glen Ridge, New Jersey. Not long after her birth, Sherman's father, an engineer, and her mother, a school teacher, moved the family to Huntington Beach, Long Island, where she grew up. For fun, Sherman would dress up in her mother's and grandmother's clothes, but she was not trying to be "pretty." Even at an early age Sherman was trying to create new characters. As an adult, she continued a form of "dress-up," shopping at second-hand stores to find clothing and props to enhance her characters that she would develop in front of a mirror. This element of her personality would directly feed into later images.

While studying painting at the State University College in Buffalo, New York, Sherman often produced self-portraits. She found difficulty expressing some of her ideas in this medium, however, and turned to photography. Failing her first photography class due to troubles with the technical aspects, Sherman began focusing on ideas rather than technology; this finally produced some success. Sherman's friend, artist Robert Longo, suggested that she incorporate her "dress-up" sessions into her artwork. It was then that Sherman found her niche; it provided her with a way to assert her ideas about the roles and depiction of women. Sherman graduated with a B.A. in 1976 and not long after, received a National Endowment for the Arts grant in 1977. The money gave her the resources to move into New York City and helped finance her first project.

Appropriating ideas and images from "film noir" and movies of the 1950s and 1960s, Sherman's black and white *Untitled Film Stills* carry nostalgic overtones. Sherman has used herself as a model to portray and identify stereotypical roles of women—the femme fatale, the housewife, and the innocent office girl, for example. The photographs are not self portraits, but are studies of characters that Sherman has invented. In each image she dresses up and applies make-up to change or obscure some of her facial features, thus creating new characters. She feels that her face becomes a canvas. The *Untitled Film Stills* are essays influenced by the media. Sherman adapts the messages promoted in the media regarding the universal archetypes of women and holds them up for scrutiny. She questions how the structuring of identity relates to society's visions of womanhood.

Continuing to examine mass media, Sherman began to use her constructed identities exclusively in color images, delving into the emotions and situations of her representations. Her artwork of the early 1980s dealt with portrayals of women in the porn and fashion industries. Commissioned to make fashion images for several designers, boutiques, and magazines, Sherman created unglamorous images that directly contrasted with most fashion photographs. The delineation between commercial photography and fine art becomes blurred with Sherman's work. She has also imbued her works with social commentary, referencing the psychological and emotional toll brought on by conforming to society's ideals. Sherman reveals and highlights internal pathos in her *Fairy Tales* and *Disaster* images (1985-89). These horrific and grotesque images portray the dark side of fairy tales. The subject matter of the photographs becomes less concerned with identities invented by Sherman. She begins to remove herself from the images in a blatant way; yet often found in the photographs are unrecognizable aspects of her body.

In *History Portraits* (1988-1990), Sherman adapted elements from several famous paintings and combined them to create parodies of historical images and icons. She photographed herself with exaggerated make-up, costumes, and props. The characterizations take on specific identities: the Madonna and Bacchus, for example. After this series, Sherman removed her body from the images completely. By manipulating dolls and interchangeable body parts ordered from a medical supply magazine, Sherman created strange still life tableaux in her *Sex Pictures* (1992). This series proved to be controversial; many critics felt this work was pornographic. The work, however, surpasses pornography; the clinical approach that Sherman employed removes any erotic overtones and infuses the images with an artificiality. The images were a reaction to censorship issues caused by the debate in defining obscenity and pornography that the National Endowment for the Arts used in the grant award process in the 1990s. *Horror and Surrealist Pictures* (1994-96) continued to use masks and objects, which become almost undiscernible due to Sherman's use of several photographic processes including double exposures. These color saturated images again refer to the inner psychological and emotional elements that constitute identity.

Sherman's last project, the horror movie *Office Killer* (1997), is a logical extension of her artwork. In all of her images Sherman plays off of existing elements in mass media culture. She finds inspiration in movies, fairy tales, fashion, and books. Using components from these groups in exaggerated forms, Sherman presents her ideas as new representations that attack and transcend universal stereotypes.

—Jennifer Jankauskas

FURTHER READING:

Cruz, Amanda, with contributions by Elizabeth A.T. Smith and Amelia Jones. *Cindy Sherman: Retrospective.* London, Thames and Hudson, 1997.

Fuku, Noriko. "A Woman of Parts." *Art In America.* June 1997, 74-81, 125.

Krauss, Rosalind, with an essay by Norman Bryson. *Cindy Sherman, 1975-1993.* New York, Rizzoli, 1993.

The Shirelles

In 1961, four young African American women known as the Shirelles—original members: Doris Kenner Jackson (1941—), Addie "Micki" Harris (1940-1982), Beverly Lee (1941—), and Shirley Alston Reeves (1941—)—ushered in the girl group era with the Gerry Goffin-Carole King composition "Will You Love Me Tomorrow?" Released on Scepter Records, the song reached number one on *Billboard's* pop charts. The first all-female act to reach the number one position, the Shirelles demonstrated that girl groups could be commercially successful, challenging the music industry's prejudice against female rhythm and blues groups. Subsequent hits included "Baby, It's You" (later recorded by the Beatles) and "Soldier Boy." When their final Top Ten single appeared in 1963, they were competing with other girl groups and their label had turned its attention to new artists, including Dionne Warwick. The Shirelles disbanded in the late 1960s; decades later, original members of the group teamed with new singers to play oldies revival shows. In 1996 the Shirelles were inducted into the Rock and Roll Hall of Fame.

—Anna Hunt Graves

FURTHER READING:

Betrock, Alan. *Girl Groups: The Story of a Sound.* New York, Delilah Books, 1982.

Gaar, Gillian G. *She's a Rebel: The History of Women in Rock and Roll.* Seattle, Seal Press, 1992.

Shirer, William L. (1904-1993)

A globe-trotting newspaperman and author of 15 major works of fiction and history, William L. Shirer is best known for his pioneering work as a radio newscaster during Europe's march toward World War II. From Germany's forcible union with Austria and the Czech Crisis of 1938 to the Nuremberg War Crimes Trials in 1945, Shirer spanned the Atlantic and kept Americans informed of the aggressive intentions of Hitler and the dynamics of Nazism in his memorable *European News Round-Up* broadcasts. By the time he left CBS radio in 1947, he had helped lay the foundation for modern international news broadcasting and achieved, with his "Fall of France" report, one of the biggest on-air scoops in history.

Shirer began his career as a foreign correspondent in 1925 when he joined the Paris office of the *Chicago Tribune*. Before moving to the newspaper's Central European Bureau (Vienna) in 1929, he had the opportunity to cover Charles Lindbergh's famous oceanic flight and the sessions of the League of Nations. Shirer regarded 1930-31 his "most interesting years," when he traveled the breadth of India with Gandhi and reported on the activities of his civil disobedience movement. Shirer returned to Paris in January 1934 after a skiing accident robbed him of part of his eyesight, and he secured a position with the *New York Herald*. He was Universal News Service's Berlin correspondent from August 1934 until the organization was disbanded by William Randolph Hearst in 1937.

Shirer did not remain unemployed for long. Recognizing his vast experience covering European affairs and his facility with German and French, Edward R. Murrow (chief of CBS's European staff) asked him to open the network's office in Vienna and arrange for the

The Shirelles

broadcasts of its correspondents there. At first Shirer was to act only in an administrative capacity, and because his voice was considered inadequate for extensive broadcasts, as an announcer for other speakers. But when the German army moved into Austria on March 12, 1938, in an effort to achieve *Anschluss* (union) between the two states, Shirer was given a rare opportunity. As soldiers swarmed through the streets of Vienna, Shirer managed to locate a microphone, but when he tried to deliver his account, he was forced out of the studio at bayonet-point. Undeterred, Shirer hopped the first flight to London and made his uncensored broadcast there over the network's 117-station hookup. The next day, March 13, CBS news director Paul White charged him with making the arrangements for the first international multiple pickup broadcast, in which a succession of correspondents at various strategic points across the continent would go on the air and provide their own perspective on the crisis. Because this type of direct broadcast had never been done before, Shirer was compelled to improvise. In the few hours before airtime, he located the relevant personnel and ensured their access to short-wave facilities. In order that all scheduled sources could be heard within the

fifteen-minute period allotted for the broadcast, and in the absence of any cueing system or feedback device, Shirer instructed his correspondents to time their words precisely and to go on the air "blind." The success achieved with this first *European News Round-Up* guaranteed it a regular spot in the nightly newscasts of the war period. In many ways, it established the pattern for international coverage later found on television.

As a result of his *Anschluss* performance, CBS made Shirer one of its regular newscasters. In September 1938, he was the man-on-the-scene during the Czech Crisis. As Hitler's conflict with the Czech government over the fate of the Sudetenland threatened to precipitate a major European war, millions of Americans anxiously tuned in to Shirer's nightly five-minute broadcasts from Prague. When the Fuehrer set his sights on Poland in September 1939, Shirer covered the impending crisis from the main vantage point of Berlin itself. On the first day of war, September 1, Shirer captivated listeners with his report of an air raid alarm while it was in progress.

Reporting from the Nazi capital offered distinct opportunities but also had significant drawbacks. Shirer's accounts of German life and strategy during wartime had to pass three rigorous censors prior to airtime, and the approved script could only be read in the presence of official observers from the propaganda office. Shirer used his ingenuity to mitigate the effects of such adulteration. Listeners became sensitive to the way he expressed his true feelings by his ''ironic sense of humor,'' sarcastic tone, and use of peculiarly American phrasing and slang that academically trained German censors could not comprehend. In May 1940 Shirer became one of a handful of correspondents allowed to accompany the German army during its conquest of France and one of the few to beam reports from occupied Paris. The *Wehrmacht*'s (armed forces') advance was so swift that, by the end of the campaign, CBS had lost all contact with Shirer. When he finally reached a transmitter on June 22, he achieved one of the greatest scoops in the history of American broadcasting. Most correspondents had believed the Franco-German armistice would be signed in Berlin, and they took up positions there. Shirer, learning the actual location would be a railroad car in the Compiegne Forest (where the Germans had been forced to capitulate to the French in 1918), was able to arrive there in time to witness the spectacle and relay his account several hours before any other reporter.

In December 1940, the burden of German censorship became intolerable, and Shirer ceased his ''This Is Berlin'' broadcasts. He returned to the United States, embarked upon a vigorous lecture tour, and became technical advisor for the wartime film *Passport to Bordeaux.* While continuing to analyze the news for CBS, he published an uncensored account of the story behind his on-the-spot broadcast from Germany in *Berlin Diary: Journal of a Foreign Correspondent, 1934-41.* In 1941 his book became a best-seller, and the Headliner's Club honored him with an award for ''excellence in radio reporting.'' In 1945, he returned to Germany as CBS's chief European correspondent to cover the Nuremberg War Crimes trials and made it back in time to cover the opening of the United Nations in San Francisco. In 1946, Shirer received the Peabody Award for his ''outstanding interpretation of the news.'' The following year, he resigned from CBS after an ''objectivity'' dispute with Murrow.

Shirer served briefly as a commentator for the Mutual Broadcasting System in 1947-49 but was blacklisted and forced to retire from broadcasting in the early 1950s because of his links with the Hollywood Ten. Thereafter, Shirer sustained himself through his lectures and prolific writings. He wrote substantial articles for *Life, Harper's,* and *Collier's,* and the fictionalized biographies *Traitor* (1950) and *Stranger Go Home* (1954). He produced *End of a Berlin Diary* (1947) as a sequel to his earlier historical work and authored five additional books based on his experience as a correspondent: *Midcentury Journey* (1952), *The Collapse of the Third Republic* (1969), *Twentieth-Century Journey* (1976), *The Nightmare Years* (1984), and *A Native's Return* (1990). His most well-known literary achievement, *The Rise and Fall of the Third Reich,* was published in 1959, after five years of scrutinizing rare Nazi state documents and private memoirs. The work received the National Book Award in 1961. Shirer died in December 1993 in his home state of Massachusetts.

—Robert J. Brown

FURTHER READING:

Brown, Robert J. *Manipulating the Ether: The Power of Broadcast Radio in Thirties America.* Jefferson City, McFarland & Company, 1998.

Cloud, Stanley. *Murrow's Boys: Pioneers on the Front Lines of Broadcast Journalism.* Jefferson City, McFarland & Company, 1996.

Hohenberg, John. *Foreign Correspondence: The Great Reporters and Their Times.* New York, Columbia University Press, 1964.

Shirer, William L. *Berlin Diary: The Journal of a Foreign Correspondent, 1934-41.* New York, Knopf, 1941.

———. *The Rise and Fall of the Third Reich.* New York, Simon and Schuster, 1959.

Shock Radio

The bane of the Federal Communications Commission, shock radio exploded on the American scene in the closing decades of the twentieth century. Some hailed this format as a refreshing example of free speech at work—its very outrageousness proof that any message can be disseminated over America's airwaves if there is an audience willing to receive it. Others decried the success of shock radio as a sign of the coarsening of the nation's popular culture—and pointed to its origins in broadcast hate speech as evidence of its secretly poisonous nature.

Shock radio has a thousand fathers (all of them illegitimate, its detractors might add). From the mid-1920s to the 1940s, Father Charles Coughlin spewed anti-Semitic, pro-Nazi, and crypto-Fascist venom to an audience of millions via his national radio program. The so-called ''father of hate radio'' was one of the first broadcasters to divine the nexus between controversial opinions and a large and avid listenership. Coughlin also established a pattern followed by other successful radio hosts of leaping into other media. He established his own newsletter, *Social Justice,* to disseminate his views. When Franklin Roosevelt dared him to run for president in 1936, Coughlin did so, as the head of the xenophobic Union Party. But America's involvement in World War II dealt a severe blow to the vituperative priest, whose tirades against ''international Jewry'' began to take on a seditious connotation for a nation committed to the struggle against Fascism.

After Coughlin and his imitators departed the airwaves, American radio largely slept through the serene 1950s. The advent of rock and roll presented the only challenge to the heterodoxy of somnambulant top forty fare being offered up on a local and national basis. That all started to change in the 1960s, when big-city markets began to buzz with the controversial opinions of hosts like Joe Pyne. Working out of KABC in Los Angeles, America's first all-talk station, Pyne was one of the first radio hosts to fuse conversation, confrontation, and conservatism in an effort to boost ratings. He once famously directed a caller to ''go gargle with razor blades.'' Pyne's right-wing rants continued in the political tradition of Father Coughlin, a path many subsequent shock jocks followed as well. Others, by contrast, opted to depoliticize their programs in an effort to move beyond an audience of like-minded adherents while still maintaining a high shock value.

In the late 1970s, WNBC in New York became the proving ground for this latest wave of shock radio hosts. Two deejays in particular, Don Imus and Howard Stern, helped perfect the form that each would later take to an even higher level of popularity. Imus, an ex-Marine and one-time rhythm and blues performer, was one of the first to devote the bulk of his show to outrageous, scatological, and offensive humor. Often he would start a conversation with a female guest by asking what she was wearing. Inquiries into breast size and sexual history would invariably follow. There was also an abundance of anti-clerical material, as personified by Imus' popular ''Rev. Billy Sol Hargus'' character, a lapsed minister whose riffs Imus later expanded into a best-selling book and comedy album. All of this chatter was accompanied by a cacophony of quacking noises and sound effects that were to become standard fare for the shock radio genre. A peanut gallery of sidekicks and joke suppliers was on hand to prop up the host when his alcohol and cocaine addictions rendered him unfit to broadcast, which was often.

Playing second fiddle to Imus in those heady days was gangly Long Island native Howard Stern, who at first merely aped the ''I-Man's'' high-volume shtick but would later outstrip him in influence. Stern's daily program took Imus' audacious sex chatter to its logical extreme. Anchored around a running commentary on the news of the day, *The Howard Stern Show* also featured mock game show segments like ''Guess the Jew,'' in which callers try to pick the Semite from a group of three celebrities. Stern's own sexual obsessions, such as lesbianism and the size of his own sex organ, were also given copious attention. ''Conversations'' with guests like Jessica Hahn often devolved into simulated sex acts or on-air stripteases. Despite constant scrutiny by the FCC, Stern managed to remain on the air and export his show to markets across the country. By the early 1990s, he was dubbing himself ''the King of All Media.''

During the 1980s, thanks largely to Stern, ''shock'' became a hot format among radio programmers. Every city, it seemed, had its ''morning zoo'' crew dedicated to keeping alive the art of the prank phone call. Some were fairly tame, never straying far from the standard repertoire of ''big boob'' and dumb politician jokes. Others ventured dangerously far into the minefield of racial and sexual humor. Two St. Louis deejays, Steve Shannon and D.C. Chymes, shocked themselves out of a job in 1993 when they accused a caller to their show of ''acting like a nigger.'' The incident sparked a massive protest by the NAACP and the Urban League and illustrated the perils of on-air confrontation. Most hosts had a better understanding of where their bread was buttered. Even the nascent sports radio format was not immune to the allure of shock. Jim Rome, a host at 690-AM in Los Angeles, was one of the first to bring the arts of insult and confrontation to the task of covering professional athletics. His daily four-hour ''smack-talking'' session proved highly successful and inspired a slew of imitators.

In the 1990s, shock radio reached the apex of its influence. However, in all but taking over the talk radio airwaves, it became a genre increasingly hard to define. Politically oriented hosts like Rush Limbaugh and New York City's conservative firebrand Bob Grant argued that their purpose was not to shock, but to inform and rally support for their viewpoints. Their critics on the other side of the ideological aisle rejected this claim and dismissed their output as ''hate radio.'' Stern and his many imitators treated politics as a mere lark, subservient to their primary mission to titillate and break taboos. Imus, who had blazed the trail in this arena, largely forsook such adolescent shenanigans altogether. His daily forum *Imus in the Morning,* originating out of WFAN in New York beginning in 1988, took on an increasingly topical tone over the years. Gone were the phone calls to semi-nude women, replaced by conversations with U.S. senators and political commentators like Jeff Greenfield and Tim Russert.

Whatever its format, however, there was no denying shock radio's influence on the American pop cultural landscape. The new-and-improved Don Imus became something of a cult figure with the C-SPAN crowd after a well-publicized interview with then-presidential candidate Bill Clinton during the New York Democratic primary in 1992. In 1993, *Imus in the Morning* entered national syndication. Within three years, it aired on over eighty stations across the country. The I-Man's daily audience was estimated at 10 million. Not unexpectedly, Imus later squandered much of his newfound political capital in 1996 during a speech at the annual Radio and Television Correspondents dinner in Washington, calling now-President Clinton a ''pot-smoking weasel'' to his face. Still, his brand of shock continued to sell around the country. A fawning 1999 *Newsweek* cover story on the grizzled shock jock even trumpeted ''The Importance of Being Imus.''

Howard Stern was even more successful. The era of political correctness gave an additional impetus to his transgressive brand of comedy. His listeners were among the most loyal and dedicated in the medium, often prank calling TV phone-in shows to drop the name of their dear leader. Stern briefly stood for election as governor of New York in 1994, but realized his extreme brand of libertarian politics was too idiosyncratic for even a liberal electorate and quickly withdrew. Instead he published a best-selling autobiography, *Private Parts,* and later starred in a movie adaptation well-received by critics. And by adding a weekly national television show in 1998, he seemed perilously close to fulfilling his prophecy to become ''king of all media.'' Stern's meteoric rise in stature, like that of Imus, cemented shock radio's place in the forefront of American popular culture at the turn of the twenty-first century.

—Robert E. Schnakenberg

FURTHER READING:

Reed, Jim. *Everything Imus.* New York, Carol Publishing, 1999.

Stern, Howard. *Private Parts.* New York, St. Martin's, 1997.

Shore, Dinah (1917-1994)

A sultry-voiced pop singer with Southern charm, Dinah Shore recorded 75 hit records between 1940 and 1955. After a modest career in the movies, Dinah found her niche in television, making her debut in 1951 as the cheery host of a fifteen-minute variety show, which aired twice a week. She became even more popular with *The Dinah Shore Chevy Show* (1956-63), singing the jingle ''See the USA in your Chevrolet,'' and smacking a signature sign-off kiss to the audience. Like another of that era's television singers, Kate Smith, Dinah quickly became a national institution.

Born in Winchester, Tennessee, Dinah graduated from Vanderbilt University with a degree in sociology. Moving to New York City after graduation, she sang on radio with Frank Sinatra—who nicknamed her ''Magnolia Blossom''—and tried out unsuccessfully as a vocalist for several top dance bands. Eddie Cantor's daughters heard her singing on WNEW, and she successfully auditioned for Cantor's radio show, which had been a career springboard for singers Deanna Durbin, Margaret Whiting, and Bobby Breen. Within weeks of her debut she had a Columbia recording contract, and Cantor put up $750 of his own money to buy her the rights to the song, ''Yes, My Darling Daughter,'' which became her first hit. By the end of 1940, she was voted Outstanding New Star of the Year by six hundred radio editors.

Shore made her movie debut in the Eddie Cantor musical, *Thank Your Lucky Stars,* perhaps best remembered for a decision made by

Dinah Shore

Warner Brothers' make-up artists to lighten Shore's dark hair to an off-blond color. Samuel Goldwyn chose Dinah to co-star in Danny Kaye's 1944 debut film, a GI comedy, *Up in Arms,* in which she introduced two Harold Arlen songs, "Now I Know" and "Tess's Torch Song." In the few movies that followed (*Belle of the Yukon, Follow the Boys, Till the Clouds Roll By,* and *Aaron Slick from Punkin Crick*), Dinah was featured in guest-singing spots or given minor roles. "I bombed as a movie star," she candidly admitted, but she soon became a superstar on television.

Dinah's warm, friendly manner with her top-name guest stars made her one of the few women to achieve a major success as a variety-series host, and the *Chevy Show* ran for seven seasons as a highlight of NBC's Sunday night schedule. The program allowed Dinah to display a variety of talents in skits and production numbers, in addition to singing such perennial favorites as "Blues in the Night," "I'll Walk Alone," and "Buttons and Bows." In 1961 NBC moved Dinah to Friday nights to give a new Western show, *Bonanza,* the Sunday slot, but her popularity continued.

During her years on television, Dinah received ten Emmy Awards and was regularly named to the list of the nation's most admired women. Making the transition from variety show to talk show host, she continued to win fans with *Dinah's Place* (1970-74), *Dinah and Her Friends* (1979-84), and *A Conversation with Dinah* (1989-91).

In the early 1970s, Dinah's six-year romance with Burt Reynolds, who was 18 years her junior, made big news in the tabloids. A UPI reporter called it "one of the most tastefully handled Hollywood love affairs in recent memory." Both Burt and Dinah openly conversed about it on talk shows and saw no problem with the age difference. They remained good friends after the break-up, and he often appeared on her television shows.

In 1981, at the age of sixty-four, Dinah boldly signed a contract for a series of live stage performances, her first in over thirty years. Although accustomed to television cue cards, she was able, after a few rehearsals, to remember all her new lyrics and arrangements, and the shows went smoothly. During her last years she was an avid tennis player and golfer, also sponsoring a tournament on the Ladies Professional Golf Tour.

—Benjamin Griffith

FURTHER READING:

Brooks, Tim, and Earle Marsh. *The Complete Directory to Prime Time Network TV Shows: 1946 to Present.* New York, Ballantine, 1981.

Hemming, Roy, and David Hajdu. *Discovering Great Singers of Classic Pop.* New York, Newmarket, 1991.

Inman, David. *The TV Encyclopedia.* New York, Perigee, 1991.

Shorter, Frank (1947—)

Often credited with having spurred the running boom of the 1970s, Frank Shorter was one of America's greatest Olympic performers. He is best remembered for his victory in the marathon during the ill-starred games in Munich in 1972, and for his runner-up finish four years later in Montreal. The Munich games were marred by the terrorism meted out against Israeli athletes, but they are also recalled for swimmer Mark Spitz's unprecedented seven gold medals and Shorter's long-distance triumph. On the day of the marathon, September 10, 1972, *Runner's World* later contended, "distance running was changed forever . . . transformed from the cult exercise of an eccentric breed of skinny men into what would become for many a way of life." An international television audience watched as the tousle-haired Shorter, born in Munich in 1947—his father was an American army physician stationed in Germany after the war—and a graduate of Yale University, held the lead from the fifteen-kilometer marker. Days earlier, Shorter had finished fifth in the 10,000 meters race. On entering the stadium near the close of the marathon, he was stunned to encounter jeering and booing, which was intended for a prankster who had landed on the track a short while earlier. Shorter went on to best the Belgian Karel Lismont, who had never lost a marathon previously. "Five seconds beyond the finish line it hit me what I'd done," Shorter, who often ran 140 miles a week, remembered. "I don't have to do it again for a while." The marathon, he reasoned, "is a battle against slowing down."

Four years later in Montreal, Shorter, by then a graduate of the University of Florida School of Law and an associate with French & Stone in Boulder, Colorado, was favored to repeat and thereby

Frank Shorter

duplicate the feat of Ethiopia's Abebe Bikila. Shorter however, was defeated by the little-known East German Waldermar Cierpinski, who established an Olympic record. When he passed the front-running Shorter, Cierpinski later reflected, "I looked right into the eyes of the man who was my idol as a marathon runner. I knew all about him. And yet I could tell by the return glance that he didn't know much, if anything, about me. The psychological advantage was mine."

Shorter's Olympic accomplishments followed earlier victories in the 1969 NCAA six-mile run, the 10,000-meter race in the 1970 U.S.-USSR dual meet in Leningrad, the 1970 AAU outdoor three-mile and six-mile events, the 1971 AAU six-mile run, and the 1971 Pan-American Games 10,000-meter race and the marathon. From 1970-1973, he was also the AAU cross-country champion. Shorter eventually won a record four Fukoka marathons. In 1972, he received the Sullivan Award, given annually to the nation's top amateur athlete. But by 1979, serious foot and back injuries sorely hampered his track performances.

Shorter is a member of the National Track & Field Hall of Fame and the Olympic Hall of Fame. He has served as a television sports commentator for track-and-field performances and founded Frank Shorter Running Gear, headquartered in Colorado. But among his greatest achievements, Shorter helped to challenge the false separation between amateur and professional track-and-field performers, thus ushering in "a new cooperative climate between athletes, sponsors and federations," according to *Runner's World.*

Shorter's Olympic feats, including the first victory in the marathon by an American in 64 years, helped to trigger a running boom in

the United States. (Instrumental, too, were the early successes and later nearly epochal failures in the 1968 and 1972 Olympic games by world record-holding miler Jim Ryun, Dr. Kenneth Cooper's championing of aerobic conditioning, and James F. Fixx's and Joe Henderson's writings extolling running.) By 1970, two million Americans were jogging regularly, according to a Gallup Poll. Following Shorter's triumph, road racing became more popular in the United States, thanks to favorable media coverage and corporate sponsorships. For a time, under-the-table expense payments were often delivered, as the lines between amateur and professional athletes continued to narrow. By 1980, the United States reportedly boasted 30 million runners, while by 1997, *Runner's World* suggested, a second running boom was occurring. This one tended to be less competitive, "more individual- and family-centered, more health- and fitness-oriented, more 'set your own goals and choose your own pace.'" Frank Shorter's contribution to one of late-twentieth-century America's most ubiquitous fitness crazes renders him a significant figure in U.S. popular culture.

—Robert C. Cottrell

FURTHER READING:

Bloom, Marc. "Frankly Speaking." *Runner's World.* Vol. 32, September 1997, 57-58.

———. "Olympic Flashback: Shorter in the Long Run." *Runner's World.* Vol. 27, February 1992, 20.

———. "The Second Boom." *Runner's World.* Vol. 32, November 1997, 66-72.

Cooper, Pamela. *The American Marathon.* Syracuse, Syracuse University Press, 1998.

Espy, Richard. *The Politics of the Olympic Games.* Berkeley, University of California Press, 1979.

Krise, Raymond, and Bill Squires. *Fast Tracks: The History of Distance Running.* Brattleboro, Vermont, The Stephen Greene Press, 1982.

Lovett, Charlie. *Olympic Marathon: A Centennial History of the Games' Most Storied Race.* Westport, Connecticut, Praeger, 1997.

Shainberg, Lawrence. "The Obsessiveness of the Long-Distance Runner." *New York Times Magazine.* February 25, 1973, 28, 30-34.

Shorter, Frank, with Marc Bloom. *Olympic Gold: A Runner's Life and Times.* Boston, Houghton Mifflin Company, 1984.

Wallechinsky, David. *The Complete Book of the Summer Olympics.* Boston, Little, Brown, 1996.

Show Boat

Show Boat (1927), Jerome Kern and Oscar Hammerstein II's immortal tale of life on the Mississippi River from the 1880s to the 1920s, was one of the landmark works of the American musical theater. It not only contained a calvacade of songs that included "Ol' Man River," "Can't Help Lovin' Dat Man," "Make Believe," and "You Are Love," but also helped propel the American musical theater forward with its serious libretto and a musical score that was wedded to the dramatic content.

Howard Keel and Kathryn Grayson in a scene from the film *Show Boat*.

Based on Edna Ferber's 1926 novel of life on the Mississippi River, Hammerstein's libretto focuses on Magnolia (Nola) Hawks, impressionable daughter of Cap'n Andy Hawks—owner of the show boat Cotton Blossom—and his domineering wife, Parthy. Nola falls in love with Gaylord Ravenal, a river gambler, at first sight. They marry and move to Chicago, where their daughter Kim is born. Gaylord loses all his money and deserts his family. The musical ends in 1927, years later, with a reunion of Nola, Gaylord, and Kim on the Cotton Blossom.

Secondary plots and characters are of great importance in the show. Julie, the mulatto actress, is forced to leave the Cotton Blossom when her racial background is exposed. In the second act, Julie sacrifices her career for Nola, who, destitute, auditions to sing at the Trocadero Club. Joe and Queenie, an African-American couple who live on the Cotton Blossom, provide continuity as the personifications of wisdom and the joy of life through numbers such as Joe's "Ol' Man River" and the couple's "Ah Still Suits Me," written for the 1936 film and interpolated into some of the show's subsequent revivals. Frank and Ellie embody the essence of musical comedy with their farcical antics. In Ellie's "Life upon the Wicked Stage," the comic actress describes her profession to her adoring fans.

Show Boat's musical score contained a substantial number of songs that entered the canon of American popular music. Considered the most operatic of Kern's scores, the music in *Show Boat* elevated the standard of popular song. The show's numbers became defining works in the musical theater repertoire. In the music of *Show Boat*, characters were defined through their music. The relationship of Nola

and Gaylord develops from the fantasy world of "Make Believe" to overt expression in "You Are Love" and "Why Do I Love You?" Julie's torch song, "Bill" (written in 1918 for *Oh, Lady, Lady!* but cut from the show), became a classic of the genre, and "Can't Help Lovin' Dat Man," with its opening line "Fish gotta swim, birds gotta fly," emerged as a standard romantic ballad.

Show Boat became an institution in American musical theater because of its skillful integration of operetta, realistic drama, and musical comedy. The fantasy world of the operetta is captured through the show's numerous waltzes. The *credo* of operetta, "Make Believe" (though not a waltz), is the title of one of the musical's early numbers. The fantasy world of the operetta is represented by the show boat and its theatrical escapism. The real world is manifested through the Chicago scenes—the World's Fair, Gaylord's gambling and desertion, and the plights of Julie and Nola. The real world enters the Cotton Blossom in the miscenagation scene, where Julie and her husband Steve are forced to leave the show boat. Musical comedy elements appear in the characters of Ellie and Frank, whose music is decidedly Tin Pan Alley in style. The integration of these diverse musical styles accounts for *Show Boat*'s importance and popularity.

The musical score of *Show Boat* is integrated with the show's dramatic narrative. Music did not exist solely for its own sake—its purpose was to enhance the drama. The standard was set and groundwork was laid for a more serious approach to the Broadway musical. Characters could no longer waltz their way out of difficulty as the tragedy of real life entered the popular musical theater. Kern and Hammerstein did give in to the Broadway tradition of a happy ending, however; Ferber's novel does not include the final scene of reconciliation between Nola and Gaylord.

Show Boat, produced by Florenz Ziegfeld, opened at the Ziegfeld Theatre in New York on December 27, 1927. Howard Marsh and Norma Terris played the lead roles of Nola and Gaylord. Helen Morgan created her legendary role of Julie, and Jules Bledsoe was the first Joe. The show ran for 572 performances, making it the second longest running Broadway musical of the 1920s.

Show Boat has continued to be successful on both stage and screen. Numerous revivals included Ziegfeld's in 1932, Kern and Hammerstein's 1946 production, the Musical Theater of Lincoln Center's 1966 version, and Hal Prince's lavish treatment that opened in Toronto in 1993 and in New York the following year. Three film versions of *Show Boat* were created: a 1929 part-talkie, a 1936 adaptation with Irene Dunne and Allan Jones, and the 1951 classic with Kathryn Grayson and Howard Keel.

In 1988, EMI released what it claimed to be "the first ever complete recording" of *Show Boat*. Under the direction of John McGlinn, it featured opera singers Frederica von Stade, Jerry Hadley, Teresa Stratas, and Bruce Hubbard in the principal roles, thus emphasizing the work's operatic qualities. Music which was cut from the show during its pre-Broadway tryout and songs written for film versions and revivals are included on the recording.

Show Boat is a classic American musical. Its memorable score and its integration of plot and music display a high level of craftsmanship on the part of its creators. The combination of realism and fantasy inherent in the story will ensure that *Show Boat* will continue to delight audiences for generations to come.

—William A. Everett

FURTHER READING:

Block, Geoffrey. "The Broadway Canon from *Show Boat* to *West Side Story* and the European Operatic Ideal." *Journal of Musicology.* Vol. 11, Fall 1993, 525-44.

———. *Some Enchanted Evenings: The Broadway Musical from Show Boat to Sondheim.* New York and Oxford, Oxford University Press, 1997.

Citron, Stephen. *The Wordsmiths: Oscar Hammerstein II and Alan Jay Lerner.* New York and London, Oxford University Press, 1995.

Kreuger, Miles. *Show Boat: The Story of a Classic American Musical.* New York, Oxford University Press, 1977. Reprinted New York, Da Capo Press, 1990.

Mordenn, Ethan. "'Show Boat' Crosses Over." *New Yorker.* July 3, 1989, 79-93.

Shula, Don (1930—)

Don Shula is the winningest coach in National Football League (NFL) history. Born on January 4, 1930, in Grand River, Ohio, Shula started his professional football career as a defensive back with the Cleveland Browns in 1951. He also played for the Baltimore Colts from 1953 to 1956 and the Washington Redskins in 1957. Shula is best known for his thirty-three seasons as a head coach, eight with the Baltimore Colts (1960-1969) and twenty-five with the Miami Dolphins (1970-1995). His teams compiled a record of 347-173-6, and reached the playoffs 20 times. Shula took the Colts to the Super Bowl in 1969, and the Dolphins in 1972, 1973, 1974, 1983, and 1985. He is also the only coach in NFL history to record an undefeated season, capped when his 1972-73 Dolphins beat the Washington Redskins 14-7 in Super Bowl VII. After several disappointing seasons, Shula stepped down as head coach of the Miami Dolphins on January 5, 1996. He was elected in his first year of eligibility to the National Football League Hall of Fame.

—Daniel Bernardi

FURTHER READING:

Brown, Jody. *Don Shula: Countdown to Supremacy.* New York, Leisure Press, 1983.

Shula, Don, with Ken Blanchard. *Everyone's a Coach: You Can Inspire Anyone to Be a Winner.* New York, Harper Business, 1995.

Stein, R. Conrad. *Don Shula: Football's Winningest Coach.* Chicago, Children's Press, 1994.

Shulman, Max (1919-1988)

A popular humorist, Shulman was best known for *The Many Loves of Dobie Gillis,* a CBS television program he created from a volume of short stories of the same name. The television series, for which Shulman was also a writer, ran from 1959 to 1963 and starred Dwayne Hickman and Bob Denver, and was one of the first television shows to focus on the lives of teenagers.

During World War II, Shulman served in the Army Air Corps. He published comic novels concerning college students, civilians during the war, and the difficulties of adjusting to peacetime *(Barefoot Boy with Cheek, The Feather Merchants,* and *The Zebra Derby)* in 1943, 1944, and 1946, a very productive period—during the remainder of his life, he wrote only four more novels. The Dobie Gillis stories were collected in 1951. Shulman adapted his first novel into an unsuccessful musical in 1947, and co-authored the Broadway hit *The Tender Trap* seven years later. In 1957 he published a novel about the establishment of a missile base next to a complacent commuter town in Connecticut, *Rally Round the Flag, Boys!;* Paul Newman, Joanne Woodward, and Joan Collins were the stars of a film adaptation. Shulman himself was an MGM (Metro Goldwyn Mayer) screenwriter for a brief period; three comedies he wrote were released in 1953. In later life Shulman was less productive, writing little after the mid-1960s. He co-authored the film *House Calls* (1978) and was co-creator of the television series of the same name a year later.

—David Lonergan

FURTHER READING:

Contemporary Authors. Vols. 89-92. Detroit, Gale Research, 1980.

Dictionary of Literary Biography. Vol. 11, No. 2. Detroit, Gale Research, 1982.

Shulman, Max. *The Many Loves of Dobie Gillis: Eleven Campus Stories.* Garden City, New York, Doubleday, 1951.

SIDS (Sudden Infant Death Syndrome)

Of all the fears associated with early parenthood, none is greater than the possibility of an infant's unexplainable and sudden death. Sudden Infant Death Syndrome (SIDS) poses such a threat to seemingly healthy babies of all socio-economic and racial backgrounds under one year old. Officially defined and named at a 1969 international conference on causes of sudden death in infants, SIDS has been a political and medical controversy ever since. Although researchers had linked a lower risk of SIDS to babies sleeping on their backs and a higher risk of SIDS to babies exposed to second-hand smoke, by the late 1990s researchers were still uncertain of SIDS' cause(s). SIDS was the leading cause of post-natal mortality from 1980-1994. Heightening the fears surrounding SIDS, controversy rose in late 1997 as an article in *Pediatrics* stated that some SIDS attributed deaths are caused by child abuse and, in 1998, when a large German study associated SIDS with CMV virus, which is common in AIDS patients. As the millennium came to a close, many unanswered questions and innumerable theories surrounded SIDS, which continued to cause grief.

—tova stabin

FURTHER READING:

Bergman, A. B., J. B. Beckwith, and C. G. Ray, editors. *Sudden Infant Death Syndrome: Proceedings of the Second International Conference on Causes of Sudden Death in Infants.* Seattle, University of Washington Press, 1970.

Guntheroth, Warren G. *Crib Death: The Sudden Infant Death Syndrome,* 3rd ed. Armonk, New York, Futura Publishing, 1995.

Bugsy Siegel

Journal of Sudden Infant Death Syndrome and Infant Mortality. New York, Plenum Press, 1996.

Siegel, Bugsy (1906-1947)

Benjamin ''Bugsy'' Siegel is remembered as the visionary mobster who first recognized the enormous money-making potential of the legalized gambling oasis of Las Vegas, Nevada, and who oversaw the construction of the town's first lavish casino and hotel, the Flamingo, in the mid-1940s. Like his close associates Meyer Lansky and Lucky Luciano, Siegel began his underworld career as a street hoodlum on New York's Lower East Side, and with Lansky formed the Bug-Meyer Mob while still in his teens. Specializing in protection rackets, gambling, and auto theft, Siegel also quickly gained a reputation as a brutal hit man and worked alongside Lansky in the formation of Murder Inc., the enforcement arm of the New York syndicate. In the mid-1930s Siegel moved to California, where he worked to expand organized crime operations chiefly in gambling and drug smuggling, and renewed his acquaintance with the movie actor George Raft, a childhood friend. Through Raft, Siegel (who longed for a movie career himself) gained contacts in the film industry and was linked romantically with several actresses, including Wendy Barrie and, most notably, the mob courier Virginia Hill. When the Flamingo failed to bring the promised quick return on their $5 million investment, Luciano and his syndicate associates demanded Siegel settle his debt. Siegel refused and was subsequently shot and killed while he sat in the living room of his Beverly Hills mansion in June 1947.

During the ensuing decades of the twentieth century, Siegel's vision was fully realized as Las Vegas became the chief gambling center of the United States and a favorite location for mob investment. While Siegel himself never found success in Hollywood, several films have traced his career, including *Neon Empire,* a cable television movie that aired in 1989, and the star-studded 1991 biographical feature *Bugsy,* directed by Barry Levinson, in which Siegel and Hill were portrayed by Warren Beatty and Annette Bening. However, perhaps the ultimate ironic tribute was announced in June 1998— more that fifty years after Siegel's murder—when a Las Vegas investment group unveiled plans to construct a $130 million luxury casino named in honor of Siegel. Scheduled to open in early 2000, Bugsy's Resort and Casino will reportedly feature a 1940s Las Vegas decor reminiscent of Siegel's own ill-fated Flamingo.

—Laurie DiMauro

FURTHER READING:

Dorigo, Joe. *Mafia.* Seacaucus, New Jersey, Chartwell Books, 1992.

Jennings, Dean Southern. *We Only Kill Each Other: The Life and Bad Times of Bugsy Siegel.* Englewood Cliffs, New Jersey, Prentice-Hall, 1967.

Nash, Jay Robert. *Encyclopedia of World Crime.* Vol. IV. Wilmette, Ill., CrimeBooks, Inc., 1990.

———. *World Encyclopedia of Organized Crime.* New York, De Capo Press, 1993.

Sifakis, Carl. *The Encyclopedia of American Crime.* New York, Smithmark, 1992.

Wilen, John. *Las Vegas Sun.* June 26, 1998.

The Silence of the Lambs

The film *The Silence of the Lambs,* directed by Jonathan Demme and starring Jodie Foster and Anthony Hopkins, was released in the winter of 1991 to substantial financial and critical success. The film is based on a 1988 novel by Thomas Harris, which in turn is a sequel to Harris's 1981 best-seller on similarly themed material, *Red Dragon.* Both novel and film focus on the strange emotional and intellectual connection between a female FBI Academy student, Clarice Starling, and an imprisoned serial killer, Dr. Hannibal ''The Cannibal'' Lecter. The two work together to apprehend another serial killer, known in the tabloid press as ''Buffalo Bill,'' before he can kill his next female victim. The film version not only introduced Dr. Lecter into the ranks of popular culture villains but garnered the top five Oscars during the 64th annual Academy Awards in 1992. The film won for Best Picture, Best Actor (Hopkins), Best Actress (Foster), and Best Adapted Screenplay (Ted Tally).

—Philip Simpson

FURTHER READING:

Harris, Thomas. *The Silence of the Lambs.* New York, St. Martin's Press, 1988.

Persons, Dan. ''*Silence of the Lambs.*'' *Cinefantastique.* October 1992, 106-11.

———. ''*Silence of the Lambs*: The Making of Director Jonathan Demme's Instant Horror Classic, a Chiller for the '90s.'' *Cinefantastique.* February 1992, 16-38.

Silent Movies

At the advent of the twentieth century, America stood as the most prosperous nation in the world. William S. McKinley was well regarded as President; photographs replaced illustrations in newspapers, and coal was the fuel of choice. There was a strange amalgamation of old and new: horse and buggy and the automobile; covered wagon and locomotive. In Europe, modern art eschewed realism for the abstract, as Sigmund Freud challenged the way people thought about behavior. For those who could indulge in such pleasures, there was the phonograph, the theatre, and vaudeville entertainments. But by 1895, a new curiosity emerged that would slowly but surely inflict profound, controversial, and sometimes curious changes in the moral sensibilities, cultural life, and social order of human society. That new curiosity was the moving picture.

Anthony Hopkins and Jodie Foster in a scene from the film *The Silence of the Lambs.*

393

The moving picture was never intended to be silent but was envisioned by American inventor Thomas Edison as visual accompaniment to his earlier phonograph. It wasn't until late until the late 1920s, however, that "talkies" would be technologically and economically viable. The first three decades of film, therefore, would be the history of the silent movie.

To the average viewer, the silent movie may appear to represent little more than dusty vestiges of a bygone era, featuring storylines with little in common with current issues, and production values that pale in comparison to the slick look of the contemporary cinema. But the silent film can evoke more than nostalgia. The story of the silent film offers a history of the brand new industry of movie-making, as it struggled to overcome the forces of public opinion and censorship, differentiate its products, and create styles of filmmaking that would survive generations. Beyond industry and economics, it is during the period of the silent movie that we see the first glimpses of the film medium as an art form; the surviving collection of silent pictures, produced both in America and abroad, include some of the finest creative achievements in cinematic history. Far from being primitive, a number of silent pictures are today considered marvels, with high levels of technological innovation achieved by their producers (including color and special effects), long before the advent of computers, portable power tools, and motion picture capture and morphing. Moreover, the era of silent moving pictures has left behind a fascinating record of the biases and prejudices, fads and fixations, taboos and preoccupations of human history during the late nineteenth and early twentieth century, and not just in the documentary or fact film, but in the perhaps thousands of shorts, one and two-reelers, and feature films produced between 1896 and 1927.

The history of the early development of the moving picture, from its origins as 1870s series photography to the American studio system, is long, convoluted, and has no single point of origin. Moreover, the history of the invention of the moving picture is associated with a great deal of myth and lore. Americans commonly attribute the invention of the moving picture to the pioneering efforts of Thomas Edison, the flawed genius noted for his patents for electric light, storage batteries, the phonograph, and the telegraph. Contrary to common belief, the birth of the moving picture was not the genius of a single originator but of a kind of competition between inventors in Britain, France, Germany, and the United States. It was in Edison's West Orange, New Jersey, laboratory, however, that the genesis of the American film industry was nurtured through its embryonic stages. In 1894, Edison patented the Kinetoscope, an early movie camera, and in a makeshift studio called the Black Mariah, he and his associates produced the earliest American silent pictures.

Soon after the initial discoveries of Edison and his rivals, the moving picture quickly arose as a phenomenal success. Perhaps thousands of small-time businessmen and women from all backgrounds and ethnic constituencies competed to enjoy the profit-making potential of the newest novelty. Moreover, notes David Cook in his *History of Narrative Film,* the new medium of film moved quickly "toward becoming a mass medium with the then-unimaginable power to communicate without print or speech."

By the turn of the twentieth century, Kinetoscope "shorts" attempted to satisfy a quickly growing audience fascinated with the moving picture. The nickelodeon boom, (a period known as "nickel madness"), saw the growth of film-showing storefronts from a mere handful in 1904 to nearly 10,000 in less than five years. Almost overnight, any available space was converted to a movie theatre. The

moving picture evolved from being a sideshow and filler for vaudeville to an entertainment by itself. Recordings of "entertaining or amusing subjects" as noted in one catalogue, comprised short films such as *The Chinese Laundry, Dancing Bears,* and *The Gaiety Girls Dancing,* featuring comedy, skits, and other brief performances. The storytelling possibilities of film were all but lost on early filmmakers. But whether novelty, filler, or short, as the popularity of this new form of entertainment arose, so did the public concern.

Similar to contemporary debates about film content and effects on society, the emergence of the moving picture as a popular form of entertainment caused an increasing measure of public disapproval. Daniel Czitrom documents early public concern about the movies in *Media and the American Mind,* noting that unlike the near "unanimous praise" afforded the introduction of the telegraph, "the motion picture confronted the accepted standards of culture itself." Film emerged during a time when a glimpse of a woman's bare ankle was considered by some to be obscene. To be sure, there were many early film shorts containing material of an "adult" nature. *The Serpentine Dance* (1895), produced by the Edison Co., was banned because the brief film included titillating glimpses of the female performer's undergarments. But content wasn't the only concern. "Indeed," notes Champlin in an article on the film production code for *American Film,* "it was the instant and immense popularity of the movies that stirred the first fears of their corrupting and inciting power." The culture war had begun.

As all and sundry flocked to the local store theatre to take in the latest short, worried cultural traditionalists and moralists debated the effects of motion pictures on society. "At the turn of the century," notes Janet Staiger in her book on sex and the early cinema, "people argued about what should and should not be said or shown during the first years of the American cinema." The people to whom she refers include the upper classes and the cultural and moral elite who felt themselves to be responsible for the maintenance of public culture and morals and for the governance of the middle and working classes.

To a punctilious Gilded Age society with Victorian moral sensibilities, a knowing glance, a leer, a glimpse of a woman's undergarment, and anything resembling burlesque could be considered inappropriate or outright obscene. In 1908, the seconds-long Edison short *The Kiss* created quite a stir. There, in grainy black and white, were stage actors May Erwin and John Rice bound together in a long and loving caress. Many were shocked at the "brazen" lack of morality in this brief exhibition.

It was not only film content that worried moralists, but also the nature of the audiences that flocked to the theatre and the circumstances of exhibition. The patrons of theatre stores included members of all ethnic constituencies as well as the lower and working classes. Some felt that this opportunity for races and classes of people to comingle could have potentially disastrous effects on the social structure. Moreover, the places where store theaters were located were considered indecorous—including amusement parks, penny arcades, dance halls, and pubs. A woman's reputation could suffer were she seen in such questionable establishments. Sanctioned censorship occurred in Chicago in 1907, where the first ordinances preventing the "exhibition of obscene and immoral pictures" were established. The film industry in America would escape its first decade with only a mild scolding and a bit of self-regulation, including the 1909 National Board of Censorship. But the die was cast, and in subsequent decades, the cries for regulation of the pictures would grow more strident.

The very earliest silent motion pictures were not full-fledged stories, notes Cook, but "unmediated glimpses of real action as it unfolded before the camera." French film entrepreneur Louis Lumière was said to have wandered the streets and set-up his portable camera before any scene that happened to take his fancy, creating what the French called "actualitiés." These brief glimpses of unmanipulated life fascinated viewers because nothing like it had ever been seen before. It is said that during the film screening of a train pulling into a station, panicked audience members rushed from their seats to get out of harm's way (*The Arrival of a Train at the Station*, 1895). In America, surviving "film-as-record" includes glimpses of San Francisco before and after the earthquake and fire; a peek inside a turn-of-the-century factory; footage of the Spanish-American War; and the inauguration and funeral of President William McKinley. Although mostly "staged" for the camera, silent shorts were produced as fillers and teasers for vaudeville, leaving behind a rare peek at Gilded Age theatrical performance and popular entertainment.

Quickly, the moving picture began to evolve into its next phase: story-telling. Film pioneers such as Georges Méliès, Ferdinand Zecca, Emile Cohl, D.W. Griffith, and countless others contributed to the development and refinement of the film narrative. In America, it is Edwin R. Porter whose name is strongly connected with creation of the true film story and who is often afforded much of the credit for the birth of narrative film.

Porter, a protege of Edison, began his filmmaking career in Edison's labs turning out actualities and one-shot film shorts. His 1902 *The Life of an American Fireman* and *The Great Train Robbery* (1903) are seen as the earliest true film narratives produced in the United States. The latter was a popular sensation. Though only 12 minutes in length, the building of suspense and the development of the action captivated an audience used to static shots of a single scene. Porter also produced *The Ex-Convict* (1904) and *The Kleptomaniac* (1905). It is interesting to note that these were more than simply stories for entertainment's sake; they also reflected prevailing "social values." The message movie was born.

Porter's 15-minute long *Uncle Tom's Cabin* (1905?) is considered to be one of the longest and most expensive American movies produced at the time. It would be the first of many adaptations of the 1852 Harriet Beecher Stowe abolitionist classic. Edward Campbell has documented filmdom's romance with various American myths noting, "Significant was the wedding of film to historical myths that were uniquely American . . . storylines which would grow to be the most beloved, the Western and the Old South romance." As the length of the silent movie increased, so did the story possibilities. Filmmakers and the writers of scenarios turned to many sources for material including literature, legend, lore, and stereotypes.

A striking element in film shorts and early narratives is America's painful legacy of racism and bigotry. Early film audiences didn't need to ask why an Indian craved whiskey or a black man was a thief. "Racial stereotyping," note Bohn and Stromberg in *Light and Shadows*, "helped trigger conflict without the need of complex explanations as to motivation." Early filmmakers relied heavily upon rather egregious ethnic typecasting in their depictions of African-American life and culture, of Native Americans and recent immigrants. Contributors to the book *Unspeakable Images: Ethnicity in the Cinema*, document the inclusion of "dumb Irish maids, pilfering, lazy blacks, unscrupulously savvy Jewish storekeepers and naïve Yankee farmers" as the subjects of short subjects and ethnic-based comedies. The racial stereotyping evident in early film didn't suddenly evolve with the medium but emerged from predominant ideas about race and class communicated through literature, sociological studies, vaudeville, and cultural artifacts such as advertisements.

Ruthless and sinister Asian gangsters, whooping savage Indians, and superstitious "coon" characters were common fare in shorts, popular film series, and later, full-length features. "[T]he Mexican bandits were clearly the most vile," notes Allen Woll. "They robbed, murdered, plundered, raped, cheated, gambled, lied and displayed virtually every vice that could be shown on the screen." It took a combination of complaints and the First World War (which provided new villains) to "end the derogatory portrayals." In 1915, Cecil B. DeMille produced the highly successful *The Cheat.* In this story, a white socialite takes out a loan with a rich but lecherous and evil Asian man who viciously brands her with a hot iron when she can't pay him back. Black Americans were viciously lampooned and portrayed as ignorant, ridiculous, and animal-like on the covers of sheet music and advertisements. These same depictions quickly found their way into silent pictures. Early titles (often featuring whites in blackface) included the popular *Rastus* series (1910-1913) about an ignorant black thief and the *Sambo* comedies. "The pages of catalogues were thick with chicken thieves and crapshooters," notes film historian Thomas Cripps, "one catalogue urging its wares because 'these were darkies of the "Old Virginny" type.'"

The year 1900 saw the largest influx of immigrants to the United States ever, and many native-born Americans were distrustful if not outright hostile, toward foreigners. Wars, revolution in Russia, anarchy, and fear of communism led some Americans to view foreigners as war-mongers and to blame them for the sometimes squalid conditions that were the reality in urban centers with high immigrant populations. Early on, foreigners were often used as the butt of jokes in such titles as *How Bridget Served the Salad Undressed* (1900), *A Bucket of Ale*, and *Murphy's Wake*, a film that earned the outrage of Irish movie-patrons because of its stereotypes of the Irish as drunkards.

By the early 1910s, films shorts and one-reelers would expand to multiple reels that later came to be known as "features." The rise of the longer length film was significant in that it helped to make motion pictures respectable for middle-class patrons. Longer films could more resemble legitimate theatre, and classic plays and novels could now be adapted for film.

Silent features expanded to several reels with more defined storylines, creative editing techniques, crosscutting, and innovative use of camera angles (some discovered accidentally). The popularity and success of the feature was in large part caused by the success of Italian-produced spectacles, which transfixed and delighted American audiences. These include Enrico Guazzoni's 1913 *Quo Vadis?* and Giovanni Pastrone's 12-reel masterpiece *Cabiria* (1914). *Cabiria*, more than two hours long, featured elaborated constructed sets, intricately designed costumes, and unique camera-work, dazzling the American movie-going public and influencing American directors like D. W. Griffith and Cecil B. DeMille. Soon, "nickel-madness" gave way to "feature madness."

David Wark Griffith was one of the earliest American filmmakers to realize, perhaps by accident, the dramatic potential of the cinema and its persuasive power over an audience. A failed actor, he turned to directing pictures for Biograph in 1908. As the "master of melodrama," he refined techniques already in use and created new styles of editing, photography, montage, camera movement, and placement—precursors to the emerging classical Hollywood Style. With his "ensemble" of silent film luminaries (including Mary Pickford, Lillian Gish, Lionel Barrymore, and Blanche Sweet) he all but perfected the potboiler and chase scene story and also adapted the serious work of Shakespeare, Tolstoy, and Edgar Allen Poe. He approached his work with an energy, style, and innovation that worried investors while it fascinated and delighted audiences.

Though he enjoyed a respectable career in film, Griffith's name will be forever associated with the notoriety surrounding one particular film. When one and two-reelers could no longer contain Griffith's grand ideas, he turned to the feature. He adapted a civil war novel, *The Clansman*, and to much fanfare, released it in 1915 as *The Birth of a Nation*. It was widely hailed by most, including President Woodrow Wilson, who called it a "remarkable artistic achievement." But the film's scenes of racial violence, including sexually depraved black villains and hooded Ku Klux Klan heroes, were not lost on everyone. In 1916, the Boston Branch of the NAACP led the way in organized protest of the film's patently racist message. In a 47-page pamphlet, supported with endorsements by leading public figures, the group was one of many that sought to have the film banned altogether. Black citizens picketed and protested. In some places where the film was shown, race riots broke out. Wilson was forced to recant his earlier praise. The film was banned in some states. Griffith, a Southerner and the son of a Confederate officer, was surprised, perplexed, and insulted by the criticism of the film. As far as he was concerned, the film was based on a true and accurate portrayal of history. Black citizens knew better, realizing that such pejorative propaganda could only cause more lynchings and distrust, and heighten racial tensions. Griffith responded with a 17-page pamphlet on free speech and counter with his epic production, *Intolerance* (1916). Though one could argue the overall effectiveness of the campaign against this highly successful and groundbreaking silent film, the incident was one of many in a long history of organized protests staged by pressure groups against the images in American cinema.

With so much dissension over Hollywood's depiction of black life and culture, it is not surprising that a number of enterprising film entrepreneurs attempted to fill the void with independently produced, all-black feature films. "Race movies" evolved, in large part, as a response to *The Birth of a Nation*. With the means of financing and distribution often out of reach for the average black filmmaker, all-black, independently produced films were sometimes the products of white producers. Yet, with an all-black cast, black themes, black writers, composers, and sometimes black directors, race-movies provided black audiences a meaningful glimpse of how they saw themselves and their world at the time.

Though there were perhaps hundreds of black film companies, of particular mention is the career of black filmmaker Oscar Micheaux. Like Edison, he was only mildly interested in the cinematic possibilities of the film medium. He was a businessman who wrote, produced, directed, and distributed his own pictures from 1919 to 1948. His subject matter varied widely, but he seemed particularly interested in melodramatic interpretations of personal events in his life. His scenarios included interracial romance, race and color consciousness, lynching, failed marriages, the black bourgeoisie, and issues of class. Most of his work was derived from his own novels, and he was known for his penurious approach to filmmaking. Notes Gehr for *American Film*, "[Micheaux] translated standard Western, gangster and melodramatic fare to a black context, but never without adding something unique, if only in the form of his own rough-hewn, self-taught technique." Not surprisingly, his surviving work has an unfinished look—an odd amalgamation of bad acting, thin storylines, and sometimes nonsensical editing. But the significance of Micheaux and his contemporaries is not aesthetic value. Their films provided work for many black artists and filled the void for a race of people desperately seeking an improved image. Though the scripts may not

have always been perfect, and the production values lacking in contrast to today's standards, in the all-black films, blacks could be doctors, lawyers, police officers, entertainers, and otherwise contributing members of society. Micheaux's surviving works include *The Homesteader* (1919); *Body and Soul* (1925; featuring Paul Robeson in his first film role), *Within Our Gates* (1920), and *The Exile* (1931).

In the 1910s, the American film industry evolved from a scientific oddity to an important big business. Notes Douglas Gomery, a scholar of the economic history of the film industry, "the former system of film sales 'by the foot' was soon replaced with the star system, a finely tuned network of national and international distribution, and the 'run-zone-clearance' system of exhibition." Fights over patents and the eventual monopolistic ownership of the means of production, distribution, and exhibition helped to change the structure of the film industry to one that came to be dominated by a handful of very powerful companies, including the Famous Players-Lasky Co. (later Paramount), the Goldwyn Picture Corporation, Universal, and the Fox Film Corporation. Film production shifted to the West Coast to escape patent litigation and unpredictable weather. Early in film's infancy, the names of the performers and directors of a film were not publicized. It didn't take long however, for the newly organized studios to exploit the profit potential of "star power." By 1915, Little Mary Pickford, nicknamed "America's Sweetheart," would earn a staggering $10,000 weekly and the adoration of millions of fans; Theda Bara became the first screen "vamp," and Clara Bow the "It" Girl. The faces of Lon Chaney, John Barrymore, little Jackie Coogan, Rudolph Valentino, and a young Swedish newcomer named Greta Garbo would grace the covers of fanzines. Striking was the swift development of the new industry. Notes Czitrom, "[o]f all the facets of motion picture history none is so stunning as the extraordinarily rapid growth in the audience during the brief period between 1915 and 1918." As Europeans mobilized for war, the American motion picture industry became an important, legitimate, and powerful facet of American industry.

While film history books have most often chronicled the "great men" of the movies, a number of women managed to carve out respectable filmmaking careers in the new male-dominated industry. Alice Guy Blaché (also known as Alice Guy) was probably the first woman film director, directing nearly 200 films between 1897 and 1920. Born in Paris, by 1912 she used her own money to organize the Solax Film Company. Her mission, notes Alley Acker in *Reel Women,* was to "cater films specific to American tastes and acted in by American artists." Among her American films were *The Vampire* (1915), *The Heart of a Painted Woman* (1917), and *When You and I Were Young* (1917). Former teenage actress Ida May Park was one of several prominent women directors employed at Universal Studios during the late 1910s. Dorothy Arzner began as a script-girl during the silent film era and continued on a respectable career as a director of "women's pictures" well into the 1940s. Similar was the career of Virginia Vann Upp, a former assistant, screenwriter, producer, director, and executive producer and one of few early film women who would later crash the "glass ceiling" of a major film studio. While the current screenwriting industry has endured a reputation as being sexist, most notable are the contributions of women who wrote hundreds of scenarios and screenplays for the early silent pictures. Respected women writers like Grace Cunard, June Mathis, Frances Marion, Julia Crawford Ivers, and Anita Loos created or contributed to the scripts for such films as *Ben Hur* (1907), *The Four Horsemen of Apocalypse* (1914), *The Sheik* (1921), and *Tom Sawyer* (1917).

Although some filmmakers continued the style for years to come, the decade of the 1920s would be the final decade that the silent movie would be a viable, profit-making mode of production. The film industry in United States began to organize itself into what become known as the American Studio System. Though the reasons for this development are many, the evolution of the studio system is often attributed to the success of producer Thomas Ince. Ince's legacy to film history was not the production of a classic film. He was no cinema-auteur, nor did he enjoy a long reign as a mogul of some major studio. His contribution was the institution of "production conventions," including his absolute control over screenplays, shooting script content, and editing. His Inceville Studio served as a model for the efficient and cost-effective running of a motion picture factory. Under his guidance, directors had to adhere to tight budgets and pre-approved schedules. Moreover, he required that scripts not emerge extemporaneously from the muse of a director but be finished products that contained lines of dialogue. The power of the individual would diminish greatly. Variations of Ince's model would soon dominate American film production.

Soon cash would overpower creativity. Film became industry and filmmaking was business. American film studios evolved into factories for the large-scale production of mass entertainment. Filmmakers developed "conventions" and formulas: frequently used devices and techniques that were cheap, economical, easily recognizable, and easy to recreate over and over. Formulas allowed producers to remain within tried and true patterns; they helped keep costs contained since the same sets, props, and costumes could be used more than once. Early mass-produced films quickly began to appear very much alike, with the director's task being to create an "illusion" of variety (keeping well within, of course, the tight economic boundaries that would ensure profit margins). Among other things, producers in the 1920s quickly tried to capitalize on whatever fad, controversy, or preoccupation had caught the imagination of the public: "cycle filmmaking" was born. It is estimated that between 1920 and 1927, nearly 100 films apiece were produced about cars, aviation, and chorus girls, three of the decade's more popular subjects.

Filmmaking strategies in the 1920s also included the development of genres or distinctive categories of films, the continued exploitation of types and stereotypes, the homogenization of cultures, and the creation and propagation of a mythical and filmic view of manners and morals. The process of "standardization" that occurred in silent filmmaking in America had a profound effect on film structure and determined the images and stories audiences would see in the movies for generations to come.

The emerging Hollywood formula film came to include such tried-and-true conventions as: stories with a linear plot (a clearly defined beginning, middle, and "happy" ending); a focus on one or two central characters with clearly defined goals; and in general, a style that didn't call much attention to itself. Moreover, a high premium was placed on the conventions of genre (Western, gangster, women's picture) and the film's entertainment value. It was at this time that many of the more endearing, popular, and successful American film genres would emerge.

With its emphasis on wide open spaces, firearms, exciting action, clear delineation of heroes and villains, and Native American stereotypes, the Western emerged as one of the most popular and endearing genres in American filmmaking. Western formulas included the "myth of the West" stories, Western epics such as *The Iron Horse* (1925), and the Western star vehicle, which included the popular films of William S. Hart including *The Gun Fighter* (1916)

and *The Covered Wagon* (1923), and films featuring Tom Mix, Buck Jones, and Hoot Gibson.

The virile planter bedecked in a white suit; the ever-present mint julep; frail, white womanhood (whose existence never included a day of work!); and happy and contented darkie slaves who profited from the benevolence and care of the overseer—these were some of the conventions of "plantation tales." "The movies of the Antebellum South," notes Campbell, "with their increasingly familiar settings and character types . . . reinforced an image shaped cinematically since 1903."

The suave, dashing, acrobatic, athletic, swashbuckling hero of the action adventure film also found popularity in the silent film, as popularized by screen star Douglas Fairbanks. His films, including *The Three Musketeers* (1921), *Q, Son of Zorro* (1925), *The Black Pirate* (1926), and *Robin Hood* (1922), helped to establish a new kind of filmmaking with a new flow and tempo, dynamic editing, and a building of action scenes still evident in contemporary action adventure films such as the *Indiana Jones* series.

Although film as a visual medium was perfectly suited for physical gags and comic mime, the potential for true comedy went unrecognized by early filmmakers. At first, some directors copied the popular style of trick photography pioneered by Méliès in France, but a true comic style had yet to be identified. By 1913, an amalgamation of foreign and American performers and producers came to create what has been described as American filmmaking's most enduring contribution to the history of film—that of silent screen comedy.

Mack Sennett was a Canadian who became head of the Keystone Co. in 1912. He is the originator of silent slapstick comedy, high-action films signified by their purely visual acrobatic humor including pie-throwing, cliff-hangers, auto-chases, explosions, and last minute rescues. He is notable for his creation of the zany Keystone Cops, and is responsible for "discovering" comedy greats Fatty Arbuckle, Ben Turpin, and Charles Chaplin. Between 1913 and 1935 he produced thousands of one and two-reel films and features, helping to fine-tune a new screen genre in a way that no one ever had done before.

America's favorite comics also included Harry Langdon and Buster Keaton, whose deadpan countenance never changed even as he struggled to hang onto a moving locomotive; Harold Lloyd with his wide-rim glasses, dangling precariously from the hands of a clock suspended over a busy street in a "comedy of thrills"; and Stan Laurel and Oliver Hardy, who continued their successful careers beyond the coming of sound.

By far the most celebrated figure in silent filmmaking was Charles Chaplin, an English vaudevillian who made his first appearance in America in a 1913 film by Keystone Studios producer Mack Sennett. A master of the art of mime, he developed a unique style of humor that exploited the connection between comedy and tragedy—a style that was in sharp contrast to a Sennett picture. He developed his famous persona, the "Little Tramp," while still working for Sennett. In 1919 he formed a partnership with three of the more powerful names in film—Mary Pickford, Douglas Fairbanks, and D.W. Griffith—that they called the United Artists Corporation. There Chaplin produced *A Woman of Paris* (1923) and his signature film, *The Gold Rush* (1925), where in a classic scene he serves up a boiled boot and devours it like a gourmet meal. The success of this film and others caused him to become the most popular, the highest paid, and the most successful figure in film history. "During the silent era," notes Silver for *American Film,* "[Chaplin] was regarded as a indisputable genius by nearly everyone who cared about movies in any remotely serious matter.'' Chaplin continued to produce ''silent'' pictures well after the evolution of sound in film.

The exigencies of World War I and the launching of the industrial age helped to melt away Victorian-age ideals in American society. Women cut their hair and donned short dresses for a night of dancing to the sultry sounds of black jazz artists like Louis Armstrong and Bessie Smith. Formerly secure taboos like divorce were discussed more freely. For some, it was an exhilarating time when the champagne flowed and the party was endless. It is not surprising that this prevailing mood was depicted on Hollywood film screens. Divorce, adultery, sex, drinking, and drugs were now treated openly in the same medium that once gasped at the sight of a woman's bare ankle. Rudolph Valentino resonated a smoldering, on-screen sexuality in films like *Blood and Sand* (1922), while a young Greta Garbo made her U.S. film debut with John Gilbert in the erotic *Flesh and the Devil* (1926).

But dark clouds formed on the Hollywood horizon, as a series of scandals rocked the film world. First, there was Chaplin's highly publicized divorce in 1920. And then Mary Pickford, accused of bigamy for her liaison with Douglas Fairbanks (while still married to Owen Moore). Charles ''Fatty'' Arbuckle, one of the country's more cherished comic figures, was falsely implicated in the brutal rape and death of a young starlet during a party that was described as wild, drunken, and orgiastic. The lurid details of the crime were widely exploited in the press and, even though he was cleared of any charges, Arbuckle's career was over. In 1922, actor Wallace Reid, positioned as an ''all-American boy'' type, was found dead of a drug overdose. Director William Desmond Taylor was found murdered, and the two women film stars he was involved with (Mabel Normand and Mary Miles Minter) were implicated in the crime that was never solved. Notes Champlin in an article on the Taylor murder for *American Film,* ''all were seen as proof that Hollywood, on and off-screen, was an affront to decent men and women everywhere.''

The public outcry was tremendous. *Birth of a Nation,* with its riots and Klan organizing, had shown what damage a film could create. Now this. Some called for government legislation of the film industry. To stave off government regulation, the industry once again turned to self-regulation. They hired a conservative, Presbyterian elder named William Hays to head their trade association, the Motion Picture Producers and Distributors of America (MPPDA). Among other things, a list humorously referred to as *Do's, Don't's and Be Carefuls* was published to serve as a kind of guideline for producers. In truth, the Hays Office was ineffectual, possibly even corrupt. But the die was cast. Censorship of the movies was reality. And as silent pictures evolved into sound, a much more stringent and limiting form of censorship would emerge that would influence filmmaking for decades to come.

Even as American movies were fitted into formulas, shrouded in conventions, and stamped-out in an assembly-line process, the artistic potential of the medium continued to emerge. It was during the era of silent filmmaking that some of greatest artistic achievements in film were produced. And nowhere was the film-as-art movement more evident than in Europe. Emerging from the rubble of World War I, German Expressionists, Soviet Revolutionaries, and French artists and intellectuals sought freedom from the conventions, behaviors, and structures of the former world order. The roots of the phenomenon can be attributed to artistic movements currently in vogue, and the influence of American directors like D.W. Griffith. European filmmakers were particularly interested in the ''visual potential'' of

the medium. They experimented freely with makeshift mobile cameras, bold, new editing techniques, and revolutionary optical effects such as masks, supers, and dissolves. Soon, film production in 1920s Europe would pose the strongest competition ever to the growing Hollywood machine.

In Germany, the art movement known as Expressionism first became important in painting around 1910 and was later adapted to theatre and literature. The motto of filmmakers who adapted the expressionist style was, ''the film image must become graphic art.'' Expressionist artists tended to distort or exaggerate natural appearances in order to create a reflection of an inner world. The stylistic techniques of Schauerfilme (films of fantasy & horror), notes Cook, included extreme stylization—like a ''moving expressionist woodcut.'' The effect was heavily dependent upon *mise-en-scène,* including geometrically stylized sets and nightmarishly distorted decor, actors with heavy make-up moving in jerky or slow motion, chiaroscuro (or Rembrandt) lighting, and unusual camera work. In addition to the prominent expressionist artists hired to design and paint film sets, important German filmmakers include Carl Meyer, with his *Das Kabinett des Dr. Caligari* (1919); F.W. Murnau, with *Nosferatu, A Symphony of Horrors* (1922); and Fritz Lang, with *Dr. Mabuse, der Spiler* (1922) and *Metropolis* (1926-27). So prominent and striking was the work of these men that Hollywood felt compelled to lure many of them away to produce films for American movie screens.

In Denmark, notes Cook, Carl Dreyr concerned himself with ''communicating with the audience's soul'' in his monumental *The Passion of Joan of Arc* (1928), which featured Renee Falconetti, who cropped her hair and wore no make-up for the role. In sharp contrast to America's straightforward approach, Dreyr's directing technique emphasized close-ups that could relay Joan's ''spiritual agony.'' It was the success of French silent filmmaking that perhaps posed the most competition for America. Between 1919-1929, film artists in France developed a style that offered interesting alternatives to the classical Hollywood style. Film, felt the French, should owe nothing to literature or theatre but be an occasion for the artist to express feelings. After surviving near destruction during World War I, the French film industry rose like a phoenix to produce some of the finest silent motion pictures in the history of film. Of particular mention is the work of Abel Gance and his production of the epic *Napoleon* (1926). Notes Cook, ''Cameras were ''carried at arms length, attached to swings, strapped to a horse's back and sent into the air in balloons.'' Gance used 18 cameras during the shooting and introduced the earliest use of wide-screen effects.

''Of all arts, for us cinema is the most important,'' stated Russian revolutionary Vladimir Lenin. Probably the most striking and influential of all the European styles to emerge during the period is the film editing technique that came to be known as Soviet montage. Sergei Eisenstein is possibly the most famous filmmaker to emerge from the silent period. He was a Marxist intellectual and a veteran of the abortive 1905 revolution who saw film as a mass medium designed to appeal to and educate millions of illiterate Russian peasants. His *The Battleship Potemkin* (1925) is considered by some to be one of the most influential films ever made, and is even today the focus of analysis and marvel. Eisenstein's stylistic techniques represented a sharp contrast to the style of American pictures. Eisenstein communicated primarily by means of emotion. He highlighted no individual protagonist (large groups could form a collective hero), used non-actor ''types,'' and promoted a kind of documentary reality in his use of photography. Most significantly, he pioneered a new editing technique, one based on ''psychological stimulation'' rather than narrative logic. As opposed to the seamless or ''invisible'' editing'' that signified American films, Eisenstein used a juxtaposition of shots to create a concept and/or emotion. He felt that in order to create the maximum effect (a jolt for the viewer) shots should not fit together perfectly but create a montage of ''shock stimuli.''

The reality of a second European war would curtail the short-lived triumph of film production in Europe. A host of European actors, performers, designers, and directors made the transition to the sound stages of Hollywood—with varying degrees of success. While no one style would have a profound effect on the American film industry, the influence of montage editing, crosscutting, wide screen, and mosaic narrative would inspire generations of filmmakers on both continents for generations to come.

More than merely a repository of the past, the era of the silent movie represents nearly three decades of sex and scandal, art and angst, sin and censorship, and crime and comedy. From the Gilded Age to the Jazz Age, the silent picture has left behind striking images of American society as it swelled to include the recently manumitted and the thousands of immigrants from many nations who appeared on its shores. From the Black Mariah to motion picture palaces, from seconds-long shorts to feature-length spectacles, from a film-by-the-foot to multinational business, the silent film helped create new and profitable forms of commerce, forms which continued on in the guise of the talking film which has dominated the industry ever since. A combination of myth proffering, image building, and empire construction, the legacy of the silent film still endures, and remains a vital and potent facet of human cultural history.

—Pamala S. Deane

FURTHER READING:

Acker, Ally. *Reel Women: Pioneers of the Cinema 1896 to Present*, New York, Continuum, 1991.

Bogle, Donald. *Blacks in American Films and Television: An Encyclopedia.* New York, Garland Publishers, 1988.

Bohn, Thomas W., and Richard L. Stromgren. *Light and Shadows: A History of Motion Pictures.* Palo Alto, California, Mayfield Publishing Co., 1978.

Campbell, Edward D. C. *The Celluloid South: Hollywood and the Southern Myth.* Knoxville, University of Tennessee Press, 1981.

Champlin, Charles. ''What Will H. Hays Begat (Fifty Years of the Production Code).'' *American Film.* October, 1980.

Cook, David A. *A History of Narrative Film.* New York, W.W. Norton, 1996.

Cripps, Thomas. *Slow Fade to Black: The Negro In American film, 1900-1942.* New York, Oxford University Press, 1977.

Czitrom, Daniel J. *Media and the American Mind: From Morse to McLuhan.* Chapel Hill, University of North Carolina Press, 1982.

Friedman, Lester D., editor. *Unspeakable Images: Ethnicity and the American Cinema.* Urbana, University of Illinois Press, 1991.

Gehr, Richard. ''One Man Show.'' *American Film.* March, 1991.

Gomery, Douglas. *The Hollywood Studio System.* Houndsmills, Macmillan, 1986.

Karney, Robyn, editor. *Chronicle of the Cinema: 100 Years of the Movies.* New York, Dorling Kindersley Publishing, 1995.

Miller, Randall M., editor. *The Kaleidoscopic Lens: How Hollywood Views Ethnic Groups.* Englewood, New Jersey, Ozer, 1980.

Richards, Larry. *African American Films Through 1959: A Comprehensive Illustrated Filmography.* Jefferson, North Carolina, McFarland & Co., .

Silver, Charles. ''Chaplin Redux.'' *American Film.* September, 1984.

Sobchack, Thomas, and Vivian C. Sobchack. *An Introduction to Film.* 2nd ed. Boston, Little, Brown, 1987.

Staiger, Janet. *Bad Women: Regulating Sexuality in Early American Cinema.* Minneapolis, University of Minnesota Press, 1995.

Thomson, David. ''Better Best Westerns.'' *Film Comment.* March-April, 1990.

Turner, Darwin T., editor. *Black Drama in America: An Anthology.* Washington, D.C., Howard University Press, 1994.

The Silver Surfer

The Silver Surfer is a superhero appearing in Marvel comic books. Created by Stan Lee and Jack Kirby in 1965, the Silver Surfer is a noble alien endowed with the ''power cosmic.'' He travels throughout the universe on a surfboard championing good over evil. During the late 1960s the Surfer's comic book became unusually ''adult'' in tone as the character became a vehicle for Lee's existentialist musings and commentary on the failures of human civilization.

The Surfer won a sizable cult following especially among college students. But it was too small to support the series, which was canceled after only a few years. Nevertheless, Lee's ambitious writing influenced young creators seeking to ''make a statement'' even in a medium widely dismissed as ephemeral by the mainstream public. And the Surfer's audience later grew; Marvel revived the character's series in 1986, and it remained a popular title in the 1990s.

—Bradford Wright

FURTHER READING:

Lee, Stan. *Origins of Marvel Comics.* New York, Simon & Schuster, 1974.

Daniels, Les. *Marvel: Five Fabulous Decades of the World's Greatest Comics.* New York, Harry N. Abrams, 1991.

Simon and Garfunkel

Simon and Garfunkel, the extremely popular folk-rock duo of the 1960s, was one of the first groups to emphasize poetry in its lyrics, demonstrating that lyrical complexity and pop music were not mutually exclusive. Simon and Garfunkel were also very influential because, along with the Byrds and a handful of other artists, they were among the first to meld acoustic folk instrumentation with the sounds associated with rock 'n' roll: electric guitar, bass, and drums. Significantly, and symbolically, Simon and Garfunkel's songs were featured prominently in the 1967 Mike Nichols film *The Graduate*, a film starring Dustin Hoffman that is very much about the 1960s generation's coming of age. Taken as a whole, their albums—*Wednesday Morning, 3 A.M., Sounds of Silence, Parsley, Sage, Rosemary and*

Paul Simon (right) and Art Garunkel.

Thyme, Bookends, The Graduate soundtrack, and *Bridge Over Troubled Water*—also provide an eloquent soundtrack to the turbulent second half of the 1960s.

The duo, comprised of Paul Simon (1941—) and Art Garfunkel (1941—), initially met at their elementary school in Forest Hills, New York, and soon realized that they could harmonize to the Doo-Wop songs that were popular on the radio. Soon the two began singing some of the many songs Simon was writing and, when they were both sixteen, the two recorded the song ''Hey Schoolgirl.'' This Everly Brothers-inspired song was released as a single on the independent label, Big Records, under the pseudonym Tom & Jerry, and it sold respectably, reaching the *Billboard* Top 50. The two continued to work with each other intermittently throughout the late-1950s and early-1960s, though they primarily remained solo artists during this time. Garfunkel recorded as Artie Garr and Simon had modest chart success as a member of Tico and the Triumphs (''Motorcycle'' briefly appeared at number 99 in 1962) and as Jerry Landis (''The Lone Teen Ranger'' topped off at 97 in 1963).

The two got back together in 1964, playing in coffee houses in New York's Greenwich Village and recording the album *Wednesday Morning, 3 A.M.,* which sold poorly. The two split up again, with Simon going to England to eke out a living by performing live and recording his first solo album. While Simon was away, folk-rock

producer Tom Wilson added electric bass, guitar, and drums to an obscure track from *Wednesday Morning, 3 A.M.* named ''Sounds of Silence,'' which immediately topped the *Billboard* pop singles chart in 1965. Hearing of his unexpected overnight success, Simon promptly returned to the States for a promotional tour and to record the duo's second album, which was primarily comprised of songs from Simon's U.K. solo album. That second album, *Sounds of Silence,* contained the popular remixed version of the title track and another Top 40 hit, ''I Am a Rock.'' The popularity of their subsequent albums made Simon and Garfunkel among the most popular musical artists of the 1960s, and Paul Simon's complex and occasionally pretentious poetry influenced a number of other imitators.

Because Simon was not a prolific writer (most of the material contained on their first three albums was written between 1962 and 1965), the songs came more slowly near the end of their career together. This, along with the duo's increasing inability to get along, was one of the major reasons Simon and Garfunkel's final album, *Bridge Over Troubled Water,* took two years to record. This album, however, was their most popular and contained their most complex and varied material, from the genre dabbling of ''Cecilia'' and ''El Condor Pasa'' to the symphonic grandiosity of the title track (all of which were Top Forty hits). Since their breakup in 1970, the duo have only played together at two major concerts, a 1972 fund-raiser for presidential candidate George McGovern and a 1981 free concert in New York City's Central Park, which yielded the album, *The Concert in Central Park.*

—Kembrew McLeod

FURTHER READING:

Charlesworth, Chris. *The Complete Guide to the Music of Paul Simon and Simon and Garfunkel.* New York, Omnibus Press, 1997.

Morella, Joseph. *Simon and Garfunkel: Old Friends, a Dual Biography.* London, Robert Hale, 1992.

Simon and Garfunkel: The Definitive Biography. London, Sidgwick & Jackson, 1996.

Simon, Neil (1927—)

Since the early 1960s, Broadway has almost never been without a Neil Simon hit play, which has earned the prolific New Yorker the title of the world's most commercially successful playwright. In his

earlier work, with such hits as *The Odd Couple* and *The Sunshine Boys,* Simon garnered a reputation for churning out charming comedies that were virtually guaranteed long Broadway runs. But in his later work, including the 1980s bittersweet autobiographical trilogy composed of *Brighton Beach Memoirs, Biloxi Blues,* and *Broadway Bound,* Simon conclusively proved that he was capable of more than light comedy. In the early 1990s, when Simon's *Lost in Yonkers* earned four Tony Awards and the prestigious Pulitzer Prize, the transformation of Neil Simon from Broadway wonder to "serious author" was complete. With plays that both bespeak and laugh at the human condition, Neil Simon is one of the world's best-loved playwrights and a fixture of American popular culture.

Born Marvin Neil Simon in the Bronx, New York on July 4, 1927, America's greatest living comedic playwright was raised in a troubled Depression-era household, which would ultimately provide the inspiration for much of his future work. Growing up with a father who frequently abandoned his family, and a mother for whom young Neil felt a great sense of responsibility, the boy looked up to his older brother, Danny, who would become his most important influence. With eight years difference in their ages, Neil idolized his older brother, who had dropped out of high school to become a comedy writer. Danny Simon, about whom Woody Allen would later say, "Everything I know about comedy I learned from Danny Simon,"

Neil Simon

was a comic genius. But so, as it all turned out, was his younger brother, Neil, whom Danny nicknamed Doc, because of Neil's childhood infatuation with a toy medical set. By the time Doc, as he was always called, was sixteen, the two brothers had begun working together.

During World War II, both Simon brothers joined the armed forces, and when they returned to New York City, they soon found work writing for television, which was in its infancy. During the early 1950s, in what would come to be known as the Golden Age of Television, Danny and Doc Simon were staff writers for such classic programs as Sid Caesar's *Your Show of Shows* and Phil Silvers's *The Sergeant Bilko Show*. However, although the Simon brothers almost exclusively wrote for small screen, one of their sketches did make it to Broadway in the 1956 revue *New Faces,* starring Maggie Smith.

After working with his brother for many years, Neil Simon went out on his own. But as the quality of the shows for which he wrote gradually began to dwindle, Simon began dreaming of writing for the theatre. He began his first play when he was thirty years old. Almost two years and twenty-two drafts later, *Come Blow Your Horn*, based on Simon's family and, specifically, the relationship between Neil and Danny, opened on Broadway in 1961. Although the initial revues were lukewarm, audiences loved it. And when Noel Coward and Groucho Marx were quoted in a Broadway column as finding the play hilarious, *Come Blow Your Horn* took off, playing 677 performances.

Neil Simon's career as a playwright was launched. His next effort was the book for a 1962 Cy Coleman-Carolyn Leigh musical called *Little Me,* a vehicle for Sid Caesar, for whom Simon had previously written. A year later, *Barefoot in the Park,* directed by first-timer Mike Nichols and starring Elizabeth Ashley and Robert Redford, opened at the Biltmore. Although the play would go on to become a huge success, running for over 1,500 performances, Simon was greeted with the dual-edged reviews that would forever plague him. Howard Taubman of *The New York Times* wrote that "Mr. Simon evidently has no aspirations except to be diverting, and he achieves those with the dash of a highly skilled writer."

Two years later, Simon followed up with his second unqualified hit, *The Odd Couple*, starring Walter Matthau and Jack Lemmon, for which he won the Tony Award for Best Author. By 1966, with *Barefoot in the Park* still running, Simon, who had also written the book for the 1966 Bob Fosse musical, *Sweet Charity,* was now earning approximately $20,000 a week as a playwright. Not yet forty years old, Simon was already the most commercially successful playwright in the world.

Throughout the 1960s, Simon continued to write hit after hit—*Plaza Suite, Promises, Promises, Star Spangled Girl,* and *The Last of the Red Hot Lovers.* However, despite this string of successes, Simon continued to be attacked by the critics for his glib comedy and commercialism. And so he set out to write his first "serious play." *The Gingerbread Lady* opened in 1971; *The Prisoner of Second Avenue* followed a year later. Both were successful, but still critical recognition continued to elude him. Then tragedy struck in his personal life in 1973 when his wife of twenty years and the mother of his two daughters, Joan Baim Simon, died of cancer. Always a prolific writer, Simon struggled through Joan's illness and death while writing *The Sunshine Boys,* a play about aging vaudevillians, which would open at the end of 1973.

By the early 1970s, Simon had written ten Broadway plays, which had grossed over $30 million and had run almost 7,000

performances. He also had written three books for musicals, which had run over 2,000 performances, and still he continued to work, rarely going a day without writing.

Just a year after his wife's death, Neil Simon married actress Marsha Mason, an Academy-Award nominated actress and the star of Simon's 1974 play, *The Good Doctor.* Not long thereafter, the couple moved to Hollywood, where they soon became popular members of the film community. Although Simon had written a number of screenplays based on his Broadway hits—*Barefoot in the Park, The Odd Couple, Plaza Suite*—he soon began to write exclusively for films, usually creating vehicles in which Marsha Mason starred. *The Goodbye Girl, Chapter Two,* and *Only When I Laugh* earned Mason three Academy Award nominations for Best Actress. Simon himself was nominated for four Oscars for screenwriting. But Simon's heart was still in the theatre, and so he continued to write for Broadway, where his *California Suite* opened in 1976—a play that the *New York Times'* Clive Barnes called "*Plaza Suite* gone West."

Throughout his prolific career, much of Simon's material continued to be inspired by the people in his life. He said, "I've written about my brother over and over, my mother and father, my past wife, good friends. I've tried to write about them truthfully; these are all people I care for. I try to show the good and bad parts." In the early 1980s, Simon embarked on a trilogy that would chronicle his younger years. The first play, *Brighton Beach Memoirs,* opened on Broadway in 1982, with Matthew Broderick playing Simon's alter ego, Eugene. Chronicling the trials and tribulations of a Brooklyn family struggling through the Depression, *Brighton Beach Memoirs* was awarded Best Play by the New York Drama Critics Circle. Running for over 1,500 performances at the Alvin, the theatre was renamed the Neil Simon Theatre during the run of the play.

In 1983, Neil Simon and Marsha Mason were divorced. The next year, Simon returned to Broadway with *Biloxi Blues,* the second play in his autobiographical trilogy. This time, Simon was awarded the Tony for Best Play. Matthew Broderick returned to Broadway as Eugene, undergoing Army Basic Training during World War II. It would be two more years before the third play of the trilogy, *Broadway Bound,* would find it its way to the New York stage.

Simon followed up his award-winning trilogy with a witty piece about an attempted suicide at a dinner party, called *Rumors,* which ran for 531 performances on Broadway during the 1988-89 season. But his next play, *Jake's Women,* would prove one of Simon's first flops in years, initially not even making it to Broadway after a tryout at the Old Globe in San Diego. Thus, it came as a wonderful kind of redemption when Simon's 1991 play, *Lost in Yonkers,* received not only four Tony Awards, including Best Play, but also the coveted Pulitzer Prize. Because Simon had long been decried as a "popular" playwright, he had never expected to win the prestigious Pulitzer. Finally, after years of commercial success, Simon had been accepted into the pantheon of America's great playwrights.

Throughout the 1990s, Simon continued to write at his usual breakneck pace, although his Broadway hits were fewer and farther between. With plays appearing on the London stage and even off-Broadway, Simon focussed his energies on reworking *Jake's Women,* writing *The Goodbye Girl* for the stage, and even penning the first volume of his memoirs, *Rewrites.* Although Simon is not the prolific playwright he once was, he still remains one of the theatre's most recognizable figures. A Pulitzer Prize, New York Drama Critics

Circle, and Tony Award-winning playwright and an Academy-Award nominated screenwriter, Neil Simon is one of the icons of twentieth-century film and theatre—a man whose comic view of American life has helped to shape popular culture.

—Victoria Price

FURTHER READING:

Brown, Gene. *Show Time: A Chronology of Broadway and the Theatre from Its Beginnings to the Present.* New York, Macmillan, 1997.

Costanzo, Peter. ''The Title Page Interviews.'' http://www.titlepage.com/cgi-local/shop.pl/page=simon.htm. January 25, 1999.

Simon, Neil. *Rewrites: A Memoir.* New York, Simon & Schuster, 1996.

Simon, Paul (1941—)

As one half of the 1960s folk-rock team, Simon and Garfunkel, Paul Simon's place in pop music history as a first rate songwriter was

sealed. But after Simon's split with his partner in 1970, this Newark, New Jersey-born musician went on to not only distinguish himself as a veteran songwriter with a substantial body of work, but as a performer who experimented with a variety of musical genres. Throughout his career as a solo artist, Simon has incorporated salsa, jazz, reggae, gospel, doo-wop, Caribbean, South African, and Brazilian music into his finely crafted pop songs. One of his most well-known works, the Grammy-winning album *Graceland*, drew both protest and praise for his use of South African musicians during the height of the Apartheid regime in the 1980s. Paul Simon's music-making method is also interesting for the questions of cultural identity and appropriation that it raises.

Although Simon had experimented with a variety of styles that strayed from Simon and Garfunkel's poetic folk-rock formula when he was part of that duo (''Cecilia'' and ''El Condor Pasa,'' for example), Simon's first post-breakup solo record was more eclectic. The Latino music influence was evident on that self-titled album's cut ''Me and Julio Down by the Schoolyard,'' and the Caribbean-flavored song ''Mother and Child Reunion,'' which was recorded in Jamaica. His even more varied second album, *There Goes Rhymin' Simon,* was recorded at the Muscle Shoals studio, where dozens of classic soul records were made. It contained a Dixieland number, ''Mardi Gras,'' mixed in with songs such as ''Tenderness'' and

Paul Simon

"Loves Me Like a Rock," which featured the gospel-like vocals of the Dixie Hummingbirds. The rest of his albums followed this precedent (excepting the more sober 1975 album, *Still Crazy After All These Years*), with each one charting new musical paths that Simon explored, culminating in 1986's Grammy-winning world music fusion album, *Graceland*.

Graceland is an interesting album because not only is it chock full of Simon's consistently good pop songs, but it has also sparked many debates surrounding the political and cultural implications of a white American working with black South Africans under the Apartheid regime. While the South African vocal group Ladysmith Black Mambazo and other native musicians contributed to the "sound" of the songs, *Graceland*'s songwriting credits were exclusively his. This is significant from an intellectual property vantagepoint, but also from the standpoint of identity politics. Simon could legally "capture" indigenous forms of music and make them his own and, as a famous white American artist, he also had the power to mediate the representation of black South Africans. The critical discourse that surrounds *Graceland* can also apply both to a critique of Simon's frequent use of "exotic" music throughout his career and to the Western music industry's and Western consumers' relationship with World Music.

Throughout his solo career, Simon occasionally rejoined Garfunkel, once for a George McGovern fund-raiser for the 1972 election and later during a free Central Park concert for an estimated half-million fans. Further, Garfunkel intermittently joined Simon on stage as a guest at his concerts and the two worked together on the single "My Little Town," which was featured both on Simon's *Still Crazy After All These Years* and Garfunkel's *Breakaway* albums.

—Kembrew McLeod

FURTHER READING:

Humphries, Patrick. *The Boy in the Bubble: A Biography of Paul Simon*. London, New English Library, 1990.

The Paul Simon Companion: Four Decades of Commentary. New York, London, 1997.

Simpson, O. J. (1947—)

O. J. Simpson was one of America's top college and professional football players in the late 1960s and 1970s, but by century's end he was being remembered not for his gridiron exploits but for his role as the defendant in one of the most celebrated murder trials of the 20th century. Accused of the 1994 slayings of his estranged wife, Nicole Brown Simpson, and of her friend Ron Goldman, Simpson was brought to trial in Los Angeles in a case that attracted enormous media attention both because of his earlier sports celebrity status and because of his race. From his arrest until his eventual acquittal, the Simpson case divided Americans along racial lines, with most blacks believing in his innocence and most whites convinced that he was guilty. Yet prior to these sorry events, Orenthal James Simpson was one of America's most beloved sports heroes. In the late 1960s, he was a college gridiron idol and Heisman Trophy winner. In the 1970s, he starred in the National Football League and earned a reputation as

one of the greatest running backs in the history of college and professional football.

O. J. Simpson, a cousin of Chicago Cubs baseball player Ernie Banks, was born on July 9, 1947 in San Francisco. At age two he suffered from rickets, and wore leg braces for the next three years. In 1960, when he was thirteen, he joined the Persian Warriors, a San Francisco-based street gang. Upon his entry into the Pro Football Hall of Fame in 1985, his mother Eunice observed, "I didn't really think he'd turn out the way he did, but he always said you'd read about him in the papers someday and my oldest daughter would always say, 'In the police report'."

Athletics eventually consumed Simpson's life, and he realized he had a special talent for carrying a football. He earned national attention during two varsity seasons as star rusher at the University of Southern California. In 1967, he scored 13 touchdowns, and added 21 more the following season. In both years he played a total of 18 games, rushing for 3,187 yards. In his senior year, he was handed the ball 40 times in the USC-UCLA contest, allowing him to set an NCAA record of 334 carries in a season. In that game, he ran for 205 yards; his season total of 1,654 yards gained was another NCAA milestone. Simpson earned All-American honors in 1967 and 1968, and topped off his college career by winning the 1968 Heisman Trophy. In 1985, he was elected to the National Football Foundation and College Hall of Fame. John McKay, his USC coach, once observed, "Simpson was not only the greatest player I ever had—he was the greatest player anyone ever had."

Simpson became the number one draft pick of the NFL Buffalo Bills. He played for the Bills from 1969 through 1977, during which time he scored 70 touchdowns and rushed for 10,183 yards on 2,123 carries. In 1972, he gained over 1,000 rushing yards for the first time, and was named AFC Player-of-the-Year. The following season, he set a single-game NFL rushing record with 250 yards ground out against the New England Patriots. In the season finale, in which the Bills faced the New York Jets, Simpson ran for 200 yards, allowing him to finish up with 2,003 yards (in 332 attempts) and become the first player in league history to amass 2,000-plus rushing yards in a season. It was Simpson's greatest year as a pro, and he was named the NFL's Most Valuable Player. He was to enjoy several other solid years with the Bills, along with one more superior campaign: 1975, in which he rushed for 1,817 yards, set an NFL record for touchdowns in a season with 23, and was again named the AFC's Most Valuable Player.

While with the Bills, Simpson played in the NFL Pro Bowl on six occasions, in 1969 and between 1972 and 1976. Two years later, the aging runner, disheartened that the Bills had never reached the Super Bowl, requested a trade to a West Coast team. He soon found himself with the San Francisco 49ers, from which he retired the following year. He eventually was elected to the Pro Football Hall of Fame, and named to the NFL's 75th Anniversary Team.

Simpson's friendly smile, movie-star looks, and extroverted personality also allowed him to become a media fixture who appealed to a cross-section of Americans. While still starring on the gridiron, he established himself as an actor. In 1967, while at USC, he played a student on TV's *Dragnet '67*; the following year, he appeared as himself in "The Big Game," an episode of *Here's Lucy*. In 1974, while playing for the Bills, he debuted on the big screen in *The Klansman* (1974) and *The Towering Inferno* (1974) and went on to appear in *The Cassandra Crossing* (1976), *Capricorn One* (1978),

O. J. Simpson (#32) in a game against the New York Jets.

and three *Naked Gun* comedies as well as additional television series and made-for-TV movies.

In retirement, Simpson remained in the public eye as an actor, a football broadcaster on ABC and NBC and, most famously, a Hertz Rent-a-Car spokesperson who would be seen dashing through airline terminals in TV commercials. Just around the time when Nicole Brown Simpson and Ron Goldman were murdered, Simpson had recently starred in *Frogmen* (1994), a TV series pilot, and the third *Naked Gun* feature had just played in movie theaters.

—Rob Edelman

FURTHER READING:

Baker, Jim. *O. J. Simpson's Most Memorable Games.* New York, Putnam, 1974.

Devaney, John. *O. J. Simpson: Football's Greatest Runner.* New York, Warner Paperback Library, 1974.

Fox, Larry. *The O. J. Simpson Story: Born to Run.* New York, Dodd, Mead, 1974.

Gutman, Bill. *O. J.* New York, Grosset & Dunlap, 1974.

Libby, Bill. *O. J.: The Story of Football's Fabulous O.J. Simpson.* New York, Putnam, 1974.

Simpson Trial

On the night of June 12, 1994, Nicole Brown Simpson and her friend Ronald Lyle Goldman were viciously stabbed to death outside the former's townhouse in Brentwood, California. The murders immediately received an extraordinary amount of media coverage because Nicole Brown was the ex-wife of former football star, minor film star, and celebrity pitchman O. J. Simpson. O. J. Simpson came under immediate suspicion in the murders, was briefly questioned by detectives assigned to the case, and formally notified four days later of his impending arrest on double homicide charges. Rather than surrender, however, Simpson left behind a maudlin note for the media, which some construed to be a suicide note, and took off with his friend A. C. Cowlings in Cowlings's white Bronco. After a few hours of uncertainty and suspense, police cars located the white Bronco on the L.A. freeway and began pursuing it in what the media,

O. J. Simpson's police mug shot.

televising the dramatic event to a spellbound worldwide audience, quickly dubbed a "low-speed chase." In contrast to the public animosity that would soon make Simpson a social outcast, hundreds of people lined the freeway overpasses above the bizarre procession and waved handwritten signs of support for the "Juice." The strangest chase in LAPD history ended at Simpson's estate in Rockingham, where he was quietly placed under arrest, out of camera range of the circling news helicopters, and taken to the L.A. County Jail. Eighteen months later, Simpson, acquitted of all charges, would again be escorted home by the LAPD, but this time to the jeers and contempt of his neighbors and the scorn of much of white America. The reaction to Simpson's acquittal, as well as belief in his ultimate innocence or guilt, was and still is sharply divided along racial lines, with African Americans tending to support Simpson and white Americans ostracizing him. The process by which Simpson became legally vindicated but socially exiled is indicative of the force of the mass media in late twentieth-century America.

The international spectacle of the Bronco chase was only a hint of the media obsession to come regarding the Simpson case. All of the major figures involved in the investigation and trial procedures would become celebrities in their own right, courted by the media and in

many cases given multi-million dollar book deals. The preliminary hearing and the trial were televised in whole or in part by the major networks, and night after night the cable news stations, such as CNN and MSNBC, devoted hours of often-heated analysis from mostly obscure legal pundits to the day's legal developments. (Some of these legal pundits, such as Roger Cossack and Greta Van Susteren, soon gained their own regular cable shows, and much later some of the Simpson trial veterans, such as Johnnie Cochran and Marcia Clark, ironically became pundits themselves.) Millions of viewers across the United States followed the television proceedings throughout the day, and millions more watched the nighttime trial summaries, commentary, and analysis. The wall-to-wall coverage and the high ratings ensured that future extended real-life dramas, such as the 1998 national sex scandal involving President Bill Clinton and a young White House former intern Monica Lewinsky, would receive the same exhaustive treatment from the media.

Simpson was formally arraigned on June 20, 1994, entering a plea of "not guilty." Thus far, public opinion seemed to have more or less reserved judgment on Simpson's guilt, but all of that began to change on June 22. That was the day that the District Attorney's office leaked to the media a tape of a frantic 911 call made by Nicole Simpson back in October of 1993. In that tape, Nicole tearfully pleads for help as an enraged Simpson shouts and swears in the background. The contrast between the chilling tape and Simpson's genial public persona could not have been more striking, and many students of the case point to the release of the tape as the beginning of the public shift of opinion against Simpson. Two other instances of domestic violence in the Simpson household then received widespread media play: a 1985 incident that resulted in no formal charges, and a 1989 incident in which Simpson was charged but eventually pleaded "no contest." On the basis of such abusive incidents, the District Attorney's office, under the leadership of D.A. Gil Garcetti, began formulating its theory of the murders: that O. J. Simpson, already a violent wife-batterer, had killed Nicole and her friend Goldman out of jealousy and rage. Thus began a public debate between various experts as to whether Simpson fit the "profile" of an abuser-turned-murderer.

However, contrary to most expectations, the prosecution's emphasis on domestic violence eventually proved to be a losing strategy. What ultimately carried the day for Simpson was a defense that compellingly argued that a combination of LAPD malfeasance (evidence planting and tampering) and crime lab incompetence (evidence contamination) had conspired to make an innocent man look guilty. Central to this defense strategy was the ambiguous figure of Detective Mark Fuhrman, one of the original investigating detectives at the Bundy crime scene. Fuhrman was in some ways a star witness for the prosecution: movie-star striking in appearance and unwaveringly methodical in crime-scene investigation. However, according to some sources, Fuhrman had a reputation as a racist who allegedly targeted black suspects for brutal treatment. Problematically for Fourth Amendment advocates, Fuhrman also had entered Simpson's Rockingham estate on the night of the murders without a warrant, ostensibly because he and fellow detectives Tom Lange and Philip Vanatter, having just come from one bloody crime scene, feared for Simpson's safety and did not consider him a suspect. (Judge Lance Ito later characterized Vanatter's version of this story as demonstrating "reckless disregard for the truth.") Fuhrman provided a convenient way for defense lawyers to negate one of the most damning bits of evidence against Simpson: a bloody leather glove found by Fuhrman at Simpson's Rockingham home that matched one left behind at the

Bundy crime scene. The defense theory, which was formulated early on and never so much explicitly stated in court as implied, was that racist Fuhrman, alone behind Simpson's house, had motive and opportunity to plant the bloody glove, surreptitiously lifted from the Bundy crime scene, and thus make the case against Simpson ironclad. Such a theory had undeniable resonance in racially troubled Los Angeles, which still remembered all too clearly the deadly riots that followed the 1992 acquittal of four LAPD officers charged with beating African-American motorist Rodney King.

However, it would be some months before the defense could square off against Fuhrman and the LAPD in open court. In July of 1994 at the preliminary hearing, Judge Kathleen Kennedy-Powell found that there was enough evidence for Simpson to stand trial. A few weeks later, Judge Lance Ito became the trial judge. Jury selection began in September and continued into November. The jury was predominantly African American, a fact that would later cause much controversy. The attorneys who represented Simpson, some of them nationally famous, became hyperbolically known in the media as "The Dream Team." Simpson's team of lawyers at various times included F. Lee Bailey, Bob Blazier, Shawn Chapman, Johnnie Cochran, Alan Dershowitz, Carl Douglas, Robert Kardashian, Ralph Lotkin, Peter Neufeld, Barry Scheck, Robert Shapiro, Skip Taft, and Bill Thompson. Robert Shapiro first organized Simpson's defense. Later, the locally famous African-American lawyer Johnnie Cochran joined the defense team and eventually became its lead attorney after public disputes between Shapiro and F. Lee Bailey caused a severe rift in strategy. Against this team were arrayed some forty full-time prosecutors, of which Marcia Clark and Chris Darden (an African American) became the most visible advocates for the People's case.

Clark and Darden delivered opening arguments in the case of *The People vs. O. J. Simpson* on January 24, 1995. The trial lasted for nine months, during which the rapt television audiences witnessed many defining moments, some of high drama and others of low comedy, that have since passed into legal lore. A partial list of those moments includes: Nicole's sister Denise crying on the stand as she described Simpson's contemptuous and abusive behavior toward Nicole; the jury field trip to Simpson's elaborately staged Rockingham estate; the cross-examination of Detective Mark Fuhrman by F. Lee Bailey, in which Fuhrman unwisely denied using the word "nigger" in the previous ten years; the befuddled demeanor and tortured vocabulary of Kato Kaelin, a houseguest of Simpson's who had been with Simpson on the night of the murders; the rigorous cross-examination of LAPD criminalist Dennis Fung by Barry Scheck, in which Fung admitted to numerous errors in processing the crime scene; the horrendous decision by prosecutor Darden for Simpson to try on the killer's leather gloves, which apparently did not fit, in front of the jury; the defense team's first courtroom suggestions that evidence may have been planted by the LAPD in order to frame Simpson; the playing to the jury of tapes which conclusively refuted Fuhrman's contention that he had never said "nigger" in the past ten years; Fuhrman's subsequent pleading of the Fifth Amendment as to whether he had planted evidence in the case; the calling of two sinister-looking mob informants to impeach the testimony of one of the case's detectives; Simpson's in-court assertion to Judge Ito that "I did not, could not, and would not commit this crime;" and Clark's impassioned rebuttal to the defense's closing arguments.

But by far the most dramatic days of the trial were October 2 and 3, when the jury deliberated the case for only four hours before reaching a verdict. Judge Ito decided to delay the announcement of

the verdict until the following day, thus allowing one full night of feverish pundit speculation as to the outcome. On the morning of October 3, 1994, as much of the nation halted work to watch the suspenseful reading of the verdict, Simpson was found "not guilty" of the murders of Nicole Brown Simpson and Ronald Lyle Goldman. Television viewers across the nation saw news video of white audiences stunned by the news and black audiences rejoicing. Official reaction was primarily that of disbelief. A visibly stunned Gil Garcetti and his lead prosecutors held a post-verdict press conference, during which Chris Darden was reduced to tears. Public reaction depended very much on the race of those being asked. Polls taken in the days and weeks after the verdict confirmed that people's views of the verdict tended to break down along racial lines. The voices of the white establishment press, including those of highly visible network news anchors, swiftly grew in protest against the African American jury that, it was implied, freed Simpson for reasons of racial solidarity. Subtly racist criticism was also leveled against Asian American Judge Ito for not having kept tighter control of his courtroom.

The white backlash against the jury and its verdict only grew stronger over the coming months, eventually reaching its crescendo in the wrongful-death civil trial that grew out of a suit earlier filed against Simpson by Fred Goldman, the father of Ron. Fred Goldman had been a highly visible spokesman for his slain son during the criminal trial. The lead lawyer for the plaintiff was Daniel Petrocelli; Simpson's lead lawyer in the civil trial was Robert Baker. The civil trial began on September 16, 1996, in Santa Monica. In contrast to the first trial, the civil trial was not televised, and Simpson himself took the stand to testify. On the evening of February 4, 1997, in another media spectacle that threatened to overshadow President Clinton's annual State of the Union address, a predominantly white jury found Simpson liable for the wrongful deaths of Nicole Brown Simpson and Ron Goldman and assessed combined compensatory and punitive damages of $33 million. Just as the first trial's verdict was roundly condemned by the establishment press, so too was the second verdict hailed as a triumph of justice. O. J. Simpson was forced to sell his Rockingham estate and, as of this writing, stands in jeopardy of losing the custody of his and Nicole's two children, Sydney and Justin. The "Trial of the Century" at which he was acquitted has proved to satisfy no one. Many people remain convinced that Simpson legally, if not financially, got away with murder, while others are equally convinced that institutional racism and police malevolence allowed the real murderer(s) to escape justice.

—Philip Simpson

FURTHER READING:

Bosco, Joseph. *A Problem of Evidence: How the Prosecution Freed O. J. Simpson*. New York, William Morrow and Company, 1996.

Bugliosi, Vincent. *Outrage*. New York, W. W. Norton & Co., 1996.

Clark, Marcia, and Teresa Carpenter. *Without a Doubt*. New York, Viking Press, 1997.

Cochran, Johnnie L., and Tim Rutten. *Journey to Justice*. New York, Ballantine, 1996.

Cooley, Armanda, Carrie Bess, and Marsha Rubin-Jackson. *Madam Foreman*. Beverly Hills, Dove Books, 1995.

Darden, Christopher, with Jess Walter. *In Contempt*. New York, Regan Books, 1996.

Dershowitz, Alan M. *Reasonable Doubts.* New York, Simon & Schuster, 1996.

Elias, Tom, and Dennis Schatzman. *The Simpson Trial in Black and White.* Los Angeles, General Publishing Group, 1996.

Freed, Donald, and Raymond P. Briggs. *Killing Time: The First Full Investigation.* New York, Macmillan, 1996.

Fuhrman, Mark. *Murder in Brentwood.* New York, Regnery Publishing, 1997.

Gibbs, Jewelle Taylor. *Race and Justice: Rodney King and O. J. Simpson in a House Divided.* San Francisco, Jossey-Bass, 1996.

Goldberg, Hank. *The Prosecution Responds.* New York, Birch Lane Press, 1996.

Kennedy, Tracy, Judith Kennedy, and Alan Abrahamson. *Mistrial of the Century.* Beverly Hills, Dove Books, 1995.

Knox, Michael, with Mike Walker. *The Private Diary of an OJ Juror.* Beverly Hills, Dove Books, 1995.

Lange, Tom, and Philip Vanatter, as told to Dan E. Moldea. *Evidence Dismissed.* New York, Pocket Books, 1997.

Morrison, Toni, and Claudia Brodsky Lacour, eds. *Birth of a Nation 'Hood: Gaze, Script, and Spectacle in the O. J. Simpson Case.* New York, Pantheon, 1997.

Petrocelli, Daniel. *Triumph of Justice: Closing the Book on the Simpson Saga.* New York, Crown, 1998.

Resnick, Faye, with Mike Walker. *Nicole Brown Simpson: The Private Diary of a Life Interrupted.* Beverly Hills, California, Dove Books, 1994.

Roberts, Peter. *OJ: 101 Theories, Conspiracies, & Alibis.* Diamond Bar, California, Goldtree Press, 1995.

Schiller, Lawrence, and James Willwerth. *American Tragedy: The Uncensored Story of the Simpson Defense.* New York, Avon, 1997.

Shapiro, Robert, with Larkin Warren. *The Search for Justice.* New York, Warner, 1996.

Simpson, O. J. *I Want to Tell You.* Boston, Little Brown & Co., 1995.

Singular, Stephen. *Legacy of Deception.* Beverly Hills, California, Dove Books, 1995.

Toobin, Jeffrey. *The Run of His Life: The People vs. O. J. Simpson.* New York, Simon & Schuster, 1997.

Uelman, Gerald F. *Lessons from the Trial: The People vs. O. J. Simpson.* Kansas City, Andrews and McMeel, 1996.

The Simpsons

The family situation comedy has long been a staple of American entertainment, and no family brings together more of the foibles and saving graces of the family than *The Simpsons,* which has aired on the FOX network since 1989. Part *Honeymooners,* part *All in the Family,* the animated Simpson family, crudely drawn with bright yellow skin and outlandish stylized hair, have represented the flailing attempts of human beings to keep up with twentieth-century life. Far from being a cartoon show for children only, *The Simpsons* deals with adult and teenage issues as well as world events. At the same time, the show is full of enough visual goofiness to keep the attention of young children.

Living in the Anywhere, USA, town of Springfield, these are the Simpsons:

Homer, the dad, works, between doughnut breaks, as a safety inspector at the Springfield nuclear power plant, where he was once replaced during a strike by a brick placed on a lever. Homer has a taste for just about anything remotely edible, washed down with Duff Beer, which he prefers to drink on the sofa in front of the television or at the local tavern, Moe's. Homer is always on the lookout for a free lunch, or at least a piece of lint-covered candy behind the sofa cushion.

Marge, Homer's better half, sports a towering blue beehive and is, in the main, the sensible anchor of the family. She has what Homer lacks in both common sense and moral fiber, and, though she struggles to stay a step ahead of the damage her family wreaks, she loves them all like—well, like a mother.

Bart is the demon spawn of Homer and Marge. From his first word— ''Cowabunga!''—Bart has faced the world with an irreverent attitude. There is no scheme too depraved for Bart to consider, no mischief too evil to undertake. He is, however, only in the third grade, so, once in a while, even Bart finds himself in over his head.

Lisa, in second grade, is Bart's sister, and must have received her genes solely from Marge's pool. Lisa is a prodigy, and therefore somewhat of a misfit in the Simpson family. She loves school and learning, and plays saxophone like a pro, using its sweet tones to voice her own angst—a sensitive soul trapped in a crude wasteland. However, her Simpson side does show through now and then, and she always gets a laugh out of *Itchy and Scratchy,* the ultra-violent cartoon show Bart loves.

Maggie, the baby, has only uttered one word, ''Daddy.'' For the most part, she only makes suck-suck noises while nursing her ''Neglecto'' brand pacifier. But she shows signs of becoming a true Simpson. When her pacifier is taken away by a brutish day-care worker, Maggie organizes the other babies in a *Great Escape*-style caper to retrieve their contraband ''binkies.'' And, despite her tender age, she has already been responsible for a murder attempt on Homer's boss.

The supporting cast of *The Simpsons* represents a colorful assortment of characters, many of whom play against their stereotype to create a commentary on the wide variation among modern U.S. citizenry: Moe, the hard-boiled bartender, who secretly reads to homeless children at the shelter, weeping over *Little Women*; Waylon Smithers, the closet gay administrative assistant, who harbors a not-so-secret yen for his boss, power plant owner, Mr. Burns; Apu, the Quiki-mart owner, who has a Hindu shrine and a shotgun behind the cash register; Krusty the Klown, who had to leave behind his orthodox Jewish family and his career as a cantor to follow his calling to make little children laugh and make a fortune from licensing his name. Though clearly stereotyped, each character contains surprising quirks and changes, which make the audience laugh but are also surprisingly realistic and reassuring in an ever more complex society.

Each week, *The Simpsons* begins with a long opening sequence. The afternoon whistle blows and Homer packs up to leave work. He doesn't notice that one of the glowing radioactive bars he has been handling falls into his jacket and follows him home. At school, Bart finishes his daily punishment: writing 1000 times on the blackboard ''I will not. . .'' everything from ''waste chalk'' to ''instigate revolution.'' Marge finishes shopping; Lisa blows a blues riff on her saxophone as she leaves band practice. The family reunites in the modern archetypal spot—plopped on the sofa in front of the television.

There is much that speaks to American families in the silliness of *The Simpsons,* and the show appeals to all ages. Adult viewers approaching middle age recognize themselves caricatured in the Simpsons and their friends, from disillusion with dead-end jobs, to children they cannot handle, to fear of nuclear radiation, to the love and warmth they experience in life despite it all. The show functions on several different levels, allowing it to appeal to children as well as adults. The quirky, innovative animation contains visual jokes, some very subtle, that spoof all aspects of American life and culture, from consumerism to baby boomer political values. The light vehicle of animated comedy allows exploration of many normally taboo topics. While network live-action sitcoms still struggle with audience reactions to gay characters, the Simpsons has been a favorite with gay audiences because it has not only had gay storylines, but has a recurring gay character, Smithers, whose crush on the evil Mr. Burns is not always as hopeless as it looks.

Matt Groening is the cartoonist who created the Simpsons, though the television series is produced by an army of writers, animators, and voice actors. Groening, who draws an alternative comic strip called "Life in Hell," first created the Simpsons in 1986, for short spots on *The Tracy Ullman Show,* an innovative variety hour. He named the characters after his own family, except for Bart, who started life as "Matt" but was soon changed to an anagram of "brat." The bright-yellow family soon captured an audience of its own, and, as Groening says, "The phenomenon has gone beyond my wildest dreams—and my wildest nightmares." Their first full-length show was a Christmas special in 1989, called *Simpsons Roasting on a Open Fire,* followed by a half-hour weekly series in January. By the end of 1990, *The Simpsons* was the highest rated show on the FOX network, and was widely syndicated.

"I try not to let anything in our culture be either too high or too low for me," Groening has said, and his work on *The Simpsons* bears this out. With a leftist, alternative point of view, Groening has created a palatable critique of American values, combining sophisticated humor with goofy cartoon slapstick. A husband and father himself, his skewering of the family is incisive, yet loving. Episodes of *The Simpsons* often parody popular movies, movements, and public figures. The perennial mayor of Springfield, for example, speaks with a Kennedy-like Boston accent, and one episode revolves around his attempt to cover up the misdeeds of his spoiled, dissolute nephew. For one vacation, the family goes to a crassly commercial beer theme park, Duff Gardens, which shamelessly promotes alcoholism. Director John Waters guest stars on another episode, as a gay character, Jon, who Homer initially likes until he finds out that Jon is gay. Angriest about being fooled, he sputters, "He should at least have the good taste to mince around and let everyone know he's that way!"

Not to be outdone by Krusty the Klown, Groening is unapologetic about licensing products with the Simpson name. Dozens of products carry pictures of the bright yellow crew. *The Simpsons Comic Extravaganza* put the family in print, along with *Maggie Simpson's Alphabet Book* and *Counting Book,* and there have been Simpsons video games and even a record *The Simpsons Sing the Blues* (1990). In the late 1990s a single cel of Groening's animation sold at Christies' famous art auction house for $24,200.

The Simpsons appeals to its public because it is hilarious entertainment; it is packed with cultural satire and is full of throw-away visual references. The show pulls the audience into its in-jokes, not requiring too much effort, but rewarding a little mental exertion with hidden layers of meaning. Then, just when the viewer seems to find real depth, *The Simpsons* refuses to be predictable, and dissolves into old-fashioned buffoonery. Its cartoon format gives the show that

touch of fantasy which makes it the perfect vehicle for cataloging the stuff of real life.

—Tina Gianoulis

FURTHER READING:

Groening, Matt. *Matt Groening's Cartooning with the Simpsons.* New York, HarperPerennial, 1993.

———; Ray Richmond and Antonia Coffman, editors. *The Simpsons: A Complete Guide to Our Favorite Family.* New York, HarperPerennial, 1997.

Harris, Jessica. "Check Him Out, Man! (Simpson's Creator Matt Groening)." *National Geographic World.* No. 227, July, 1994, 8.

"The Odyssey of Homer." *Entertainment Weekly.* No. 427, March 12, 1993, 84.

Sinatra, Frank (1915-1998)

Frank Sinatra was, by most accounts, the greatest entertainer of his time, known to his legions of fans as "The Voice" of the twentieth century. But his life intersected with worlds beyond show business—with politics, both left and right, with the underworld, and with the celebrity culture of postwar America. An exceedingly complex man, Sinatra articulated in his songs the romantic dreams and existential longings of his generation. His music and life had a Shakespearean "ages of man" arc—from the callow youth of "I Fall in Love Too Easily" to the world-weary maturity of "In the Wee Small Hours" and, ultimately, to the triumphant patriarch of "My Way." But above everything, Sinatra will be remembered, in the words of Pete Hamill, as "a genuine artist, and his work will endure as long as men and women can hear, and ponder, and feel."

During a career that spanned more than 60 years, Sinatra exploited the technology of the century to define and transform his public persona. He received major breaks in his early career when he was heard over the radio by bandleaders seeking a vocalist. During the 1940s his voice seemed to caress the microphone in concert, and Sinatra created a sexual awakening, some say mass hypnotism, among adolescent girls. More than anyone else during the 1950s, he conceived the long-playing record as a vehicle of personal expression for a mature artist. His 60 movies yielded a multitude of Sinatras to contemplate: the joyous song-and-dance man of *Anchors Aweigh* and *On the Town*; the brooding, doomed loner *of From Here to Eternity* and *The Manchurian Candidate*; and the suave hipster of *Pal Joey* and *Ocean's 11.* Sinatra's final project, *Duets,* produced by recording wizard Phil Ramone in the early 1990s, utilized digital fiber optics to create electronic pairings with a new generation of performers and resulted in one of his best-selling albums of all time.

Sinatra's upbringing reflected the immigrant world of urban America. He was born in rough-and-tumble Hoboken, New Jersey, on December 12, 1915. The only child of a hard-working Sicilian household, Sinatra had big dreams to cross the Hudson River and discover his fortune in New York City. He dabbled in sportswriting and engineering before finding his calling at a Bing Crosby concert in the mid-1930s. Determined to become a singer, he polished his act at church suppers and firemen's socials. In September 1935 he and several local musicians made their radio debut as the Hoboken Four

Frank Sinatra

on *Major Bowes' Original Amateur Hour.* Bowes took a liking to the boys, and they began to tour with one of his traveling companies. After immediate success proved elusive, Sinatra went solo.

The ambitious Sinatra did everything he could to nurture his talent. He appeared on local radio with little compensation to attract any type of attention. He undertook voice lessons, which he would continue throughout his career. And, most importantly, he sang publicly, notably at the Rustic Cabin, a small North Jersey roadhouse. His persistence achieved what every singer of his era desired, a featured vocalist spot in a big band. Harry James, a former trumpeter for Benny Goodman, heard Sinatra broadcast from the Cabin and signed him to his first contract in June 1939. James's new orchestra spotlighted the confident Sinatra, especially on ''All or Nothing at All,'' one of the first big band recordings to feature a vocalist from start to finish.

After six months, Sinatra was lured away by a more prominent bandleader, Tommy Dorsey. Inspired by Dorsey's trombone playing, Sinatra crafted a distinctive singing style, gliding from note to note without a semblance of breath. Sinatra's apprenticeship with the band lasted three years, and his recordings of ''I'll Never Smile Again,'' ''I'll Be Seeing You,'' and ''This Love of Mine'' established the boy vocalist as a star in his own right. Sinatra's ascent anticipated the dominance of the singer in postwar popular music.

Beginning in late 1942 Sinatra took control of his destiny, the first of many such moves throughout his mature years. After rancorous negotiations, Sinatra left Dorsey, leading the way for featured vocalists to make it as soloists. His debut performance at the Paramount Theatre on the last day of 1942 created a riotous sensation as thousands of teenage girls, known as the bobbysoxers, swooned (a publicist's description that caught on) at the skinny crooner in a bowtie. Amateur psychologists debated this ardent popularity: did he signify wartime degeneracy or did he bring out the maternal instinct in adolescents? Whatever the reason, Sinatra became a regular on *Your Hit Parade,* network radio's most popular show on Saturday night.

Critics also analyzed the unique communication that Sinatra had with his audience. E. J. Kahn, in one of the first major articles on the Sinatra phenomenon, stated for *The New Yorker* that while singing Sinatra ''stares with shattering intensity into the eyes of one trembling disciple after another.'' His intimacy with the microphone and personalization of the lyrics involved his listeners in a sexual experience. Sinatra learned how to transmit powerful emotions through his songs by studying the haunted textures of Billie Holiday. And in the best jazz tradition, he also liked to come up with innovative ways to treat musical phrases.

Sinatra strove to completely identify with the music in the recording studio. He teamed up with Dorsey arranger Alex Stordahl to produce introspective ballads for Columbia Records throughout the 1940s. Stordahl's lush strings complemented the soulful rapture of Sinatra's baritone. Between 1943 and 1946 he had 17 top singles, including his first Columbia recording, the tender "Close to You" and more upbeat "Saturday Night (Is the Loneliest Night in the Week)," which had special meaning for women whose lovers were away fighting in Europe.

Sinatra made his first movie appearances as a Dorsey vocalist in *Las Vegas Nights* (1941) and *Ships Ahoy* (1942). The hysteria surrounding Sinatra's personal appearances in the early 1940s led to a contract with MGM in 1944. Gene Kelly became his mentor and teacher, and he was groomed for energetic, splashy musicals. He starred as a nerdy, shy sailor in *Anchors Aweigh* (1944); a show business-crazed New Yorker in *It Happened in Brooklyn* (1947); and a baseball playing, tap dancing vaudevillian in *Take Me Out to the Ball Game* (1949) with Kelly. But Sinatra quickly outgrew this manufactured image of cheerfulness and frivolity.

Since his boyhood, Sinatra was immersed in Democratic politics. His mother was a party ward organizer and her only child became a crusader for racial tolerance. Sinatra and his Hoboken sweetheart Nancy named their son Franklin after President Roosevelt for whom the singer had campaigned vigorously. In 1945 Sinatra had received a special Oscar for the short *The House I Live In,* an outspoken attack on religious and ethnic bigotry. But in the late 1940s, when the political mood of cold-war America was shifting rightward, Sinatra was lambasted as a communist sympathizer and fellow traveler as well as criticized for his trip to Havana to meet syndicate boss Lucky Luciano. Questions about his connection to the underworld, especially as the quintessential nightclub and Las Vegas performer, bedeviled the Italian-American entertainer the rest of his career, begetting a nasty feud with the press over personal privacy.

By 1950, Sinatra's public and personal worlds had collapsed. As America began celebrating economic prosperity and organizational conformity, Sinatra's record sales slumped and MGM dropped him from their galaxy of stars. His private indiscretions had become fodder for the gossip columns, and the singer was scandalized for a tumultuous affair with movie goddess Ava Gardner, which disintegrated his marriage. Sinatra also failed to conquer the new medium of the home, television, in the early 1950s as his first series was widely assailed by the critics. The city girls, who had idolized "The Swoon" during the war years, were now busy raising families in the suburbs; Sinatra appeared to be a relic.

Sinatra's comeback, receiving a 1954 Oscar for his portrayal of the downtrodden Maggio in *From Here to Eternity,* has been the stuff of legend. What was more remarkable was the entire transformation of the Sinatra persona. No longer would he be the sensitive balladeer who spoke directly into a woman's heart. Now, he was a man's man, the one who hoped for swinging times, but was often left anguished at the bar alone. His image in the movies was toughened. He played a psychopathic presidential assassin in *Suddenly* (1954), an agonized heroin addict in *The Man With the Golden Arm* (1955), and a disillusioned writer in *Some Came Running* (1958). He also brought a maturity to his musical roles: as the cynical reporter in *High Society* (1956), performing a rousing "Well Did You Evah?" with his inspiration, Bing Crosby, and as the ultimate heel in *Pal Joey* (1957), taking such delight in his crucial number, "The Lady Is a Tramp."

In 1953 Sinatra signed with Capitol Records and, collaborating with arranger/conductor Nelson Riddle, would orchestrate an entirely new sound for his mature self. They pioneered the concept album, which in a suite of songs looked at one aspect of adult love. Riddle, a

former trombonist, brought a pulsating rhythm to the records, helping to define Sinatra's new swinging style. Sinatra adapted a variety of roles to articulate a deeper understanding of romance: the bold sensualist in *Song for Swingin' Lovers* (1956); the tender, intimate companion of *Close to You*; and the gloomy, introspective loner in *Only the Lonely* (1958). Sinatra also hooked up with arrangers Gordon Jenkins and Billy May to explore other masks: the intense and tortured romantic (Jenkins's *Where are You?* And *No One Cares*) and the raucous swinger (May's *Come Fly Me* and *Come Dance with Me!*). In the studio, Sinatra incarnated each role; he was the ultimate "method" singer.

From 1953 to 1962 Sinatra recorded 17 albums for Capitol and exploited the dramatic possibilities of the long-playing twelve- inch disc. Sinatra was at his powers as an interpretative artist and these recordings constitute a treasury of American popular song. Many songs were carefully selected from the golden age of the Broadway musical, and Sinatra's readings plumb the emotional depths of the lyrics. A majority of his meticulously-rehearsed versions are considered definitive, including "I've Got a Crush on You" (George and Ira Gershwin); "I've Got You Under My Skin" (Cole Porter); "One for My Baby" (Harold Arlen and Johnny Mercer); and "I Wish I Were in Love Again (Richard Rodgers and Lorenz Hart). Sinatra always paid tribute to the songwriting art by announcing in concert the name of the composer before each song. During the Capitol years Sinatra also returned to the charts with singles produced for quick recognition and consumption, most notably "Learnin' the Blues," "All the Way," and "Witchcraft." By the end of the 1950s, Sinatra was again America's most prominent performer.

In the early 1960s Sinatra reconfigured his identity once again. He formed his own record company, Reprise, the first major artist-owned label in music history. (He sold the company to Warner Brothers in 1963, retaining a one-third interest.) He became the embodiment of a middle-aged swinging playboy with the release of *Ring-a-Ding Ding!* (1960) and *Swing Along with Me* (1961). He surrounded himself with hard-drinking and high-living friends, called by the press the Rat Pack, whose members included Dean Martin, Sammy Davis Jr., Peter Lawford, and Joey Bishop. The Rats, nicknamed The Summit by the leader, were headquartered in Las Vegas, where Sinatra was established as the premier performer and an owner of the Sands Hotel. Reveling in tuxedo until daybreak, they were, and for some will always be, the epitome of cool.

Sinatra with his pals promulgated a hedonistic philosophy of swagger and style. An outgrowth of Humphrey Bogart's inner circle, they campaigned for the equally fun-loving John F. Kennedy in 1960, with Sinatra supervising the inaugural gala. The Pack made light-hearted slapdash movies, including *Ocean's 11* (1960), *Sergeants 3* (1962), and *Robin and the 7 Hoods* (1964). With the assassination of President Kennedy, who publicly snubbed Sinatra in 1962 because of his mob associations, and the emergence of The Beatles, the Rat Pack seemed tired and out-of-touch by the middle of the decade. And once again, Sinatra reinvented himself.

During his 50th year in 1965, Sinatra contemplated his life and profession. He released *September of My Years,* one of his most personal works, a touching musical reflection on the joys and anguishes of his younger years. Sinatra also compiled and narrated a retrospective album, *A Man and His Music,* which surveyed his career in 31 songs. Both projects received the Grammy Award for album of the year, anointing Sinatra as elder statesman of the industry. Personally, Sinatra was still frisky, marrying actress Mia Farrow, 30 years his junior.

A Man and His Music also inspired a television special, which marked Sinatra's triumphant return to the medium. His two previous weekly series had fizzled, both succumbing to Sinatra's unwillingness to rehearse outside the recording studio. His most noteworthy performances had been one-time only engagements: as the stage manager in a musical adaptation of *Our Town* (which yielded the hit single "Love and Marriage") and as host of a "Welcome Home, Elvis" extravaganza, in which the two former teen idols joined for an incomparable duet. The 1965 special was acclaimed "the television musical of the season," receiving an Emmy Award for outstanding program. Sinatra continued to produce and star in television specials, almost on an annual basis, making sure he remained a force in contemporary music.

During the 1950s Sinatra dismissed rock and roll as music "sung, played, and written for the most part by cretinous goons." By the late 1960s Sinatra had accommodated many diverse sounds in his repertoire. Adapting to changing fashions, he recorded songs composed by Jimmy Webb, Stevie Wonder, Paul Simon, and George Harrison. One of his most advantageous collaborations was with the Brazilian samba stylist, Antonio Carlos Jobim. Sinatra discovered unexpected pleasures in the soft and delicate rhythms of the bossa nova. This embrace of a new beat also provided several popular hits, including "Strangers in the Night," winner of the Grammy Award as record of the year; "That's Life," Sinatra at his bluesiest; and "Something Stupid," a duet with his eldest daughter Nancy. In 1969 he adapted a French ballad, "Mon Habitude," with English lyrics by Paul Anka, and crafted one of his signature songs, "My Way."

Tired of the investigations into his private life, Sinatra announced his retirement from show business in June 1971. He made yet another comeback two years later with the album and TV special, *Ol' Blue Eyes Is Back,* engendering another show business moniker. He was most frequently nicknamed The Chairman of the Board, referring to his pervasive presence in all aspects of the entertainment industry. Although his professional life slowed down, especially after his marriage to Barbara Marx in 1976, Sinatra still made artistic waves. He delivered a classic reading of Stephen Sondheim's innovative "Send in the Clowns," a staple of his concerts during the 1970s. In 1980 he released his most ambitious undertaking, *Trilogy: Past, Present & Future,* three discs that showed off both the swinging and serious facets of his artistry. Sinatra recorded for *Trilogy* yet another defining song, "Theme from New York, New York," which became a showstopper in performance. In movies, he was most comfortable as a hard-boiled, aging sleuth, a role he began in *The Detective* (1968) and further explored in the television movie *Contract on Cherry Street* (1977) and his final starring theatrical role in *The First Deadly Sin* (1980). In 1987 *The Manchurian Candidate,* featuring Sinatra's most complex role as a brainwashed soldier, was re-released, twenty-six years after its premiere. There was a renewed appreciation for Sinatra's acting skills, especially in challenging material.

Like many in his generation, Sinatra's politics drifted rightward as he got older. Becoming an ardent Republican during the Vietnam era (though still a registered Democrat), he campaigned aggressively for Ronald Reagan in 1980. Victorious again, as twenty years before, he produced the presidential inaugural gala. He was appointed to the President's Committee on the Arts and Humanities as well as was awarded the Kennedy Center Honor for Lifetime Achievement (1983) and Presidential Medal of Freedom, America's highest civilian recognition (1985). He still received millions of dollars for concert performances around the world, including a controversial appearance in Sun City, South Africa.

Sinatra's personal life was always riddled with contradictions. His generosity to friends was legendary as was his vicious feuds with targeted members of the press. Back in 1947, he publicly attacked one of his critics, Lee Mortimer, and was ordered to pay a substantial fine. Although his friendship with Chicago mobster Sam Giancana cost him a gambling license in the 1960s, he still associated with the underworld throughout his career, including a 1975 infamous photograph backstage at the Westchester Premier Theater with Mafia boss Carlo Gambino and Jimmy "the Weasel" Frantianno. Many unauthorized biographies focussed on these unsavory aspects of Sinatra's volatile temperament, most significantly the bestselling *His Way* (1986), by Kitty Kelley. Even the 1992 authorized miniseries *Sinatra,* produced by youngest daughter Tina, did not shy away from controversies, portraying Sinatra's relationship with Giancana (played by Rod Steiger).

Sinatra remained a permanent fixture and influence on the American popular culture landscape even in his twilight years. Although his 1988 reunion tour with Sammy Davis Jr. and Dean Martin dissipated when Dino lost interest, the Rat Pack were embraced as the arbiters of hip by the twentysomething generation in the 1990s. At the age of 77, Sinatra made another recording comeback as his *Duets* album unexpectedly sold several million copies. Although his partners were not in the same studio and electronically overdubbed, Sinatra was heard singing with stars from other musical fields, including international personalities Julio Iglesias and Charles Aznavour; from the jazz and soul front, Aretha Franklin, Luther Vandross, and Anita Baker; and from his own genre, Barbra Streisand and Tony Bennett. Rocker Bono of U2, another "duetist," grandiloquently presented Sinatra with the 1994 Grammy Legend Award, enshrining him as "the Big Bang of Pop." Sinatra's 80th-birthday special also featured a wide array of celebrants, including rappers Salt-N-Pepa and rock superstars Bruce Springsteen and Bob Dylan. Sinatra himself toured rigorously well into his 70s, before giving his last concert in February 1995.

Sinatra's death on May 14, 1998 eclipsed one of television's most heavily promoted events, the final episode of *Seinfeld.* Every corner of news, from print to cyberspace, was awash in memorial tributes. As David Hadju of *Entertainment Weekly* pointed out: "No American since JFK (the Sinatra of Presidents) seemed to have received such a grand media memorial, effusive in its praise of his talent and celebratory in its recollection of his life."

The one quality that Sinatra strove for in his nearly 1,300 commercially available recordings and his many different incarnations was honesty. Each song was the personal expression of a deeply felt moment. There was no separating the incomparable singer from the intimate experience of the lyric. Like many other supremely gifted artists, his life did not always live up to the ideals of his art. But, as *New York Times* critic John Rockwell noted, "no singer of our time has better invested the widest range of emotion in his music than Frank Sinatra."

—Ron Simon

FURTHER READING:

Douglas-Home, Robin. *Sinatra.* New York, Grosset & Dunlap, 1962.

Friedwald, Will. *Sinatra! The Song Is You.* New York, DaCapo Press, 1997.

Kelley, Kitty. *His Way.* New York, Bantam, 1986.

Hamill, Pete. *Why Sinatra Matters.* Boston, Little Brown and Company, 1998.

Kahn, E. J. *The Voice: The Story of an American Phenomenon.* New York, Harper & Brothers, 1947.

Lahr, John. *Sinatra: The Artist and the Man.* New York, Random House, 1997.

Levy, Shawn. *Rat Pack Confidential.* New York, Doubleday, 1998.

Lonstein, Albert, and Vito Marino. *The Revised Complete Sinatra.* Privately published, 1981.

O'Brien, Ed, and Scott Sayers. *Sinatra: The Man and His Music.* Austin, TSD Press, 1992.

Petkov, Steven, and Leonard Mustazza, eds. *The Frank Sinatra Reader.* New York, Oxford University Press, 1995.

Rockwell, John. *Sinatra: An American Classic.* New York, Rolling Stone Press, 1984.

Shaw, Arnold. *Sinatra: Twentieth-Century Romantic.* New York, Holt, Rinehart and Winston, 1968.

Sinatra, Nancy. *Frank Sinatra, My Father.* New York, Pocket Books, 1985.

Sinatra, Nancy. *Frank Sinatra: An American Legend.* Santa Monica, General Publishing Group, 1995.

Taraborrelli, J. Randy. *Sinatra: Behind the Legend.* Secaucus, Carol Publishing, 1997.

Wilson, Earl. *Sinatra: An Unauthorized Biography.* New York, Macmillan, 1976.

Vare, Ethlie Ann, ed. *Legend: Frank Sinatra and the American Dream.* New York, Boulevard Books, 1995.

Zehme, Bill. *The Way You Wear Your Hat.* New York, HaperCollins, 1997.

Sinbad (1956—)

A popular African American television comic character of the 1980s and 1990s, Sinbad, whose offstage name is David Adkins, offered wholesome, family-oriented entertainment for children and adults alike. The legitimate heir to Bill Cosby's clean-cut comic style, Adkins, an African American, broke barriers at mainstream studios like Disney by starring in youth-oriented feature films with predominately white casts, such as *Houseguest* (1995) and *First Kid* (1996).

Sinbad first entered mainstream culture as dorm director, Walter Oakes, on the Cosby-produced NBC sitcom *A Different World* (1987-1991), once the nation's number-three rated show. It was this role that catapulted Sinbad into living rooms across the nation. Following the show's run, Sinbad gained further notoriety as host of *It's Showtime at the Apollo,* where his improvisational storytelling on topics such as hair weaves, parenting, and divorce helped to make him one of America's most widely-recognized funny men.

Born in Benton Harbor, Michigan, on November 18, 1956, David Adkins was the child of Baptist minister Reverend Donald Adkins and his wife, Louise. The second of six children, the future comedian was raised in a household in which a high value was placed on morals, personal responsibility, and God. Rejecting both alcohol

Sinbad

and drugs throughout life, Sinbad takes seriously his job as a role model—challenging the need for vulgar language in his performances with the oft-quoted maxim: "If my kids can't watch it, I can't do it."

Tall in stature—he reached 6'5" in adulthood—the comedian grew up feeling "big and goofy," and saw himself as something of an outsider. Luckily his size was of use in pursuing his first love: basketball. He won an athletic scholarship to the University of Denver, but found himself particularly isolated on the largely white campus, where he became increasingly militant during the black-power era of the 1970s. Never one to play by the rules, Adkins surprised his peers by quitting college just short of a diploma. After dropping out, Adkins signed up with the Air Force, where he soon discovered his true calling during a talent contest. Arriving at a steadfast decision to pursue comedy, he got himself discharged from the service—as legend has it—by walking off duty in his underwear. "Kick me out," he told his superiors. "Let's work as a team."

In 1983, embarking on what he has called his "Poverty Tour," the future Sinbad crossed the country by Greyhound bus, performing stand-up routines in small-town clubs and hitching rides with members of his audience. The grueling schedule paid off. By the mid-1980s, the comedian's first big break came through repeated appearances on *Star Search.* With his brightly-colored hair (dyed every shade from gold to red to platinum blond) and feather earrings in both ears, the budding talent had made an impression. He relocated to Los Angeles, and in 1986 was cast as Redd Foxx's foster son on ABC's *The New Red Foxx Show* (1986).

Like his mentor, Bill Cosby, Adkins has consistently challenged stereotypical images in Hollywood film and television productions. On *Houseguest,* for example, he refused to do humor that he termed "very broad and anatomical." During production on his short-lived sitcom, *The Sinbad Show* (1993), which aired on the Fox network during 1993-94, the star's arguments with producers and executives were legend, as he struggled to represent his character, a black single father, in a positive light.

In 1997, Sinbad joined the flurry of black-oriented, late-night talk shows when he was asked to take over hosting duties on *Vibe* (1997-1998). It was a time when competition was stiff for the genre: *The Keenen Ivory Wayans Show* (1997-1998) ran neck-and-neck with *Vibe* before being replaced by Magic Johnson's *The Magic Hour* (1998). But Adkins had also co-hosted, with singer Stephen Bishop, another late-night variety show ten years earlier called *Keep on Cruisin'* (1987).

At the close of the 1990s, Sinbad had expanded his influence beyond the world of entertainment, and had become a pioneer advocate for technology, particularly among inner-city youth. A computer buff who has been known to chat online for hours, he served on an advisory council at Howard University, and as a spokesperson for the National Action Council for Minorities in Engineering, lecturing to some 23 million kids about the importance of math and science in a technologically advanced world. Sinbad also participated in the first annual ThinkQuest Internet competition, along with Ron Howard, Nobel-laureate physicist Kenneth Wilson, and Gene Sperling, advisor to President Clinton, in which more than $1 million in scholarships and cash prizes were awarded to students, teachers, and schools across the country. In 1996, he accompanied first lady Hillary Rodham Clinton to Bosnia to provide comic relief for United States peacekeeping forces stationed there and throughout Europe.

—Kristal Brent Zook

FURTHER READING:

Lovece, Frank. "When Sinbad Says No Offense, He Means It." *Newsday*. City Edition. January 10, 1995, B3.

Sinbad, and Ritz, David. *Sinbad's Guide to Life (Because I Know Everything)*. Bantam Books, 1997.

Watkins, Mel. *On the Real Side: Laughing, Lying, and Signifying*. New York, Touchstone, 1994.

Sinclair, Upton (1878-1968)

American novelist Upton Sinclair is most famous for his 1906 novel *The Jungle* and the reforms to which it gave rise. Sinclair was a muckraker—so dubbed by President Theodore Roosevelt, who regarded them as a nuisance—one of a group of journalists who were relentless in their exposure of corruption in American business and government.

Sinclair intended his book, set in the Chicago meat-packing industry, to arouse support for the plight of immigrant laborers. He exposed the political machinations of the Democratic and Republican parties and put forward the Socialist Party as the only trustworthy organization. Instead, *The Jungle* triggered outrage at the malfeasance of the meat packers, who had little care that much of their processed meat was adulterated with dirt, dung, poisoned rats, and the odd human body part. Roosevelt apparently read the book and dispatched investigators who confirmed the veracity of Sinclair's account. Under threat of releasing the report, Roosevelt forced through the 1906 Meat Packing Act to regulate the industry. Although the act brought the meat packers under the regulatory arm of the government, it had little in the way of enforcement. Moreover, the bigger firms were able to meet the government's requirements, whereas many smaller firms could not, and so the act effectively

increased the strength of big business; certainly not Sinclair's intended outcome. At the time, Sinclair joked, "I aimed at the public's heart and by accident I hit it in the stomach."

The Jungle was Sinclair's sole best-seller, but he went on to publish a series of similarly themed novels. Among them were *Oil!* (1927), about the Teapot Dome Scandal of President Warren Harding's administration, and *Boston* (1928), about the trial and execution of Sacco and Vanzetti, two Italian-American radicals convicted and executed for robbery and murder, a cause celebre of 1927. In 1940 Sinclair began a series of eleven novels with a contemporary setting featuring an antifascist hero, Lanny Budd. Sinclair placed Budd in the action of all major events of his time.

In 1933 Sinclair established and led the End Poverty in California (EPIC) campaign. His solution to Depression-era unemployment was for the state to rent unused land and factories so the unemployed could grow their own food and produce clothing and furniture. In August 1934 he easily won the Democratic primary race for governor. Conservative Democrats then aligned with the anti-New Deal Republican Governor Frank Merriman to defeat Sinclair in the November election. The campaign was marked by the hysterical level of the anti-Sinclair material, which included faked newsreels showing hoboes descending on California and accusations of Communism.

By the end of the twentieth century *The Jungle* was still in print but not included in college anthologies of American literature. EPIC generally is treated as an indication of the sort of political anomalies the Depression produced, and as an aside to Franklin D. Roosevelt's New Deal.

—Ian Gordon

FURTHER READING:

Mitchell, Greg. *The Campaign of the Century: Upton Sinclair's Race for Governor of California and the Birth of Media Politics*. New York, Random House, 1992.

Scott, Ivan. *Upton Sinclair, The Forgotten Socialist*. Lewiston, N.Y., Edwin Mellen Press, 1997.

Singer, Isaac Bashevis (1904-1991)

Singer is considered almost by unanimous consent to be the greatest postwar writer of Yiddish literature. Born on July 14, 1904 in Leoncin, Poland, child of a Chasidic rabbi and pious mother, Singer first made his mark in Yiddish literature in Poland, having published his first novel, *Satan in Goray,* in serialized form in 1934. The next year Singer moved to America where he began writing for the Yiddish-language newspaper the *Jewish Daily Forward*. His creativity blocked by his relocation, Singer produced little fiction until 1943, when an explosion of short stories and novels erupted from his pen that continued until his death on July 24, 1991. In 1966, he published his first of several well-received children's books, *Zlateh the Goat*. In 1978, Singer received the Nobel prize for literature. Several of his works were filmed, including his novels *The Magician of Lublin* and *Enemies, A Love Story,* as well as his short story "Yentl, the Yeshiva Boy," which formed the basis of the musical *Yentl,* which starred Barbra Streisand in the lead role.

—Bennett Lovett-Graff

FURTHER READING:

Farrell, Grace. *Critical Essays on Isaac Bashevis Singer.* Boston, Twayne, 1996.

Farrell, Grace, editor. *Isaac Bashevis Singer: Conversations.* Jackson, University Press of Mississippi, 1992.

Hadda, Janet. *Isaac Bashevis Singer: A Life.* New York, Oxford University Press, 1997.

Lee, Grace Farrell. *From Exile to Redemption: The Fiction of Isaac Bashevis Singer.* Carbondale, Southern Illinois University Press, 1987.

Miller, David Neal. *Fear of Fiction: Narrative Strategies in the Works of Isaac Bashevis Singer.* Albany, SUNY Press, 1985.

Singin' in the Rain

Co-directed by dancer Gene Kelly and Stanley Donen, *Singin' in the Rain* epitomizes how the musical works as Hollywood genre, studio (MGM) product, and instrument of American popular culture. Produced in 1952, the movie's narrative, scripted by Broadway writers Betty Comden and Adolph Green, is set in the 1920s, when viable sound synchronization spawned the "talkie," forcing universal adoption of sound and the invention of the musical. *Singin' in the Rain* is a parody of the backstage musical and the biopic; it playfully mocks the trials of the early studio system and the egos of its silent film stars being tutored to speak and perform in sound pictures.

The movie pays homage to the musical's classical form, tracing its roots from vaudeville to its influence on film. Gene Kelly plays Don Lockwood, who rises from variety shows to the silver screen with dance partner Cosmo Brown (Donald O'Connor). Within the musical's formula of narrative-inspired production numbers and romance, Lockwood guides the object of his desire, Kathy Selden (Debbie Reynolds), into the emotional effects of song-and-dance.

It is the Hollywood kiss, that staple of romantic resolution, which seals the attraction between Lockwood and Selden, then prompts Lockwood to begin "singin' in the rain." Critic Jane Feuer, in *Film Genre Reader II,* dubs such outburst into song-and-dance "the myth of spontaneity" common to the musical genre. Kelly's athletic free spirit in the "singin' in the rain" number celebrates the individual male at play within the American neighborhood. In this liberating, public site, Lockwood moves his feet skillfully through rain with umbrella as ballast, gets soaked and loves it, is chided by a local cop and shrugs it off. His "gotta dance" compulsion not only drives *Rain*'s theme-song number, as if coming from the streets as well as his heart, it also inspires Lockwood to move instinctively into the full-blown artistry and seduction of Cyd Charisse's enigmatic dance/love object in the "Broadway Melody Ballet" fantasy.

Critic Rick Altman, in *The American Film Musical,* calls this device of courtship through dance the male's "loving lesson." In the film's major dance suite, the "Broadway Melody Ballet," the sexual connotations of Lockwood's earlier loving lesson with the neophyte Selden are projected as a fantasy danced with an "other" woman (Cyd Charisse). In the course of the suite, Charisse's vamp transforms into bride, then ethereal "angel", then back to vamp willingly controlled by gangster "hoods." Only dance itself safely permits this eruption of coded sex and this evocation of American culture's darker forces.

These forces, inflected in *Rain* as fantasy, are made central in Charles Vidor's *Love Me or Leave Me* (1955). A biopic of another order, *Love Me or Love Me* is based on singer Ruth Etting's successful career and dark personal life in the 1920s and her marriage to a petty gangster whose possessiveness turns into rape on their wedding night. Domestic melodrama delineates the couple's fraught relationship, with musical numbers playing out of, and off, the drama. In *Rain,* Don's loving protection of the amber-voiced Kathy from the wily, tin-eared silent star Lina Lamont (Jean Hagen) is without social threat, while *Love Me or Leave Me*'s foregrounding of obsessive male control is made tough by it basis in melodrama. In Stanley Kubrick's *A Clockwork Orange* (1971), the darkly parodic "Singin' In the Rain" song-and-dance by Alec (Malcolm McDowell) in the act of torturing a woman makes a cold ritual of violence, a major ideological reach from the original source, *Rain,* but closer to *Love Me or Leave Me.* But in his television special, *You Must Remember This* (1994), Canadian figure skater Kurt Browning's skilled athletic homage restores to family entertainment *Rain*'s 1950s classicism and the nostalgia of Kelly's muscular dancer's persona. Browning's faithful recreation of Kelly's "Singin' In The Rain" number—complete with rain-covered ice surface, look-alike set, and original soundtrack of Kelly's singing and tapping—circulates a memory of the film, specifically a myth of wholesomeness for popular culture of the 1990s. In the 1990s, figure skating's popularity has grown as its imitative performers, tour-shows, and television specials have adopted elements of the production number established and conventionalized by the Hollywood musical, including costuming, lighting, familiar theme songs, dance-step choreography, tributes to screen and pop music stars, and the loving lesson evident in pairs and dance skating.

The impulse to act out in song-and-dance form reveals the gears of social engineering adapted by the Hollywood musical to produce and to promote show-musical culture as a vital ingredient of American popular culture. *Singin' in the Rain* reveals the seams of this process, much as it enfolds audiences into its veiled pleasures.

—Joan Nicks

FURTHER READING:

Altman, Rick. *The American Film Musical.* Bloomington, Indiana University Press, 1987.

Croce, Arlene. "Dance in Film." *Cinema: A Critical Dictionary.* Vol. 1. New York, The Viking Press, 1980.

Feuer, Jane. "The Self-Reflexive Musical and the Myth of Entertainment." *Film Genre Reader II.* Austin, University of Texas Press, 1995.

Maltby, Richard. *Hollywood Cinema.* Oxford, Blackwell Publishers, 1995.

Singles Bars

Singles bars flourished in the 1970s, reflecting the sweeping changes that followed the Sexual Revolution and the attempted passage of the Equal Rights Movement. Commonly referred to as "meat markets," singles bars acted as an open setting in which men and women felt free to engage one another. Statistics cited by sociologist Nancy Netting revealed that by 1980 the rate of premarital sexual intercourse for American college-age women equaled the rate for college-age men. This was a significant change, as the rate for women having premarital intercourse between 1930-1965, studies showed, was 30 percent lower than that of men. One change that resulted from all of these factors was that bar patrons were no longer exclusively male.

Singles bars have a popular image as hotbeds of frenzied, sexual activity, but there is some evidence to suggest that this presumption may be somewhat exaggerated. Despite the promiscuous conduct that many assume occurs, the singles scene operates upon some rather traditional gender roles: men initiate contact, and women flirt as passive objects of desire. By pursuing a female in this environment, the male places his self-assessment at risk, since "rejection may signify that he has miscalculated and is less desirable than he had assumed," concluded a 1991 ethnographic study of singles bars. Another study, published by two psychologists in 1978, found that men avoid the most attractive women because they fear rejection. The study also found that attractive women responded just as positively to researchers as unattractive women. In this respect, the study concluded, "men's anxieties about attractive women may be unfounded."

If a conversation is struck, the talk is likely to be about generalities, wrote Jamie James in *Rolling Stone*:

> They talk about the weather, football (year-round), the latest big murder trial ("Do you think he's guilty?" "Of course he's guilty. But he'll get off"). They talk about everything but what's on their minds. The clincher comes in its own good time: "This place is so noisy I can hardly hear you. Listen, my place is just a few blocks away. . . ."

The 1991 study showed that the micro-order of the singles bar is a fragile one and can fracture when the male "presses forward, failing to accept (the female's) rejection and the chance to save face." The female's rejection can take the form of a polite refusal, a rejection not final ("maybe some other time"), or an excuse: "I'm married," "I have a boyfriend," or "I can't dance in these shoes." Fracturing occurs when the male insults the female to "even the score," or by ignoring her suggestion and continuing his pursuit. When this occurs, the ethnologists noted changes in the female's demeanor through a stiff posture, or sharper tone: "concern with softening the blow is jettisoned for the overriding concern of extricating oneself from the situation."

Faced with excusing oneself, what could possibly serve as refuge in a noisy singles bar? The study noted:

> The most common refuge for escape from unsolicited encounters appeared to be the women's restroom. One of the authors tested this observation by remarking to a queue of women in a restroom that she guessed she wasn't the only one avoiding a man. She was answered by an affirmative nod by a number of women. . . . Women can plan future strategies to avoid male approaches or escape from the necessity of performing these strategies through retreat into an all-female world.

The need to parry male advances is one explanation for findings that show that most women are usually accompanied by at least one other woman at the bars.

An element of danger exists in encountering people who are strangers. This risk was portrayed in the sensational 1975 novel *Looking for Mr. Goodbar*, in which a single woman picks up a stranger in a bar, only to be murdered in her own apartment. "Everybody who hangs out in these places is acutely aware of the intrinsic creepiness of the (singles) scene," explained a woman to James. "It's sort of demeaning, but there has to be some way for us to meet, you know." The one commonly acknowledged taboo among singles is "never go to bed with a stranger."

Although singles bars remained a primary way for singles to meet, other alternatives appeared in the 1980s. Those who desired more control used the screening process of a matchmaking service or did their own screening through newspaper personal ads. More adventurous singles opted for singles cruises, a marketing device that successfully contributed to the boom in cruiseship trips during the 1990s. After AIDS became a serious concern during the 1980s, screening and refraining from risky sexual activity became important for health reasons. In a survey conducted at a college in British Columbia, Canada, the number of students who reported having one-night stands decreased by over 50 percent between the years 1980 and 1990.

—Daryl Umberger

FURTHER READING:

Cory, Christopher T. "The Seven-Second Singles Scene." *Psychology Today*. December 1978, 32.

James, Jamie. "Houston After Dark." *Rolling Stone*. May 31, 1979, 35-40.

Netting, Nancy S. "Sexuality in Youth Culture: Identity and Change." *Adolescence*. Winter 1992, 961-976.

Rossner, Judith. *Looking for Mr. Goodbar*. New York, Simon & Schuster, 1975.

Snow, David A., Cherylon Robinson, and Patricia L. McCall. "'Cooling Out' Men in Singles Bars and Nightclubs: Observations on the Interpersonal Survival Strategies of Women in Public Places." *Journal of Contemporary Ethnography*. January 1991, 423-450.

Spradley, J. P., and J. Mann. *The Cocktail Waitress: Woman's Work in a Man's World*. New York, Wiley, 1975.

Wuethrich, B. "Evolutionists Pick up on One-Night Stands." *Science News*. July 3, 1993, 6.

Sirk, Douglas (1900-1987)

Born Claus Detlev Sierk in Denmark, Douglas Sirk emigrated first to Germany and then, with the rise of Nazism, to the United States where he directed some of the biggest grossing melodramas of the 1950s such as *All I Desire* (1953), *Magnificent Obsession* (1954), *All That Heaven Allows* (1955), *There's Always Tomorrow* (1955), *Written on the Wind* (1956), and *Imitation of Life* (1959). These movies were clearly marketed as "adult films" whose social concerns such as class and race relations justified the graphic, voyeuristic displays of upper-class lifestyle, psychological malaise, sex (ironically Rock Hudson starred in eight of Sirk's movies as the quintessential

Gene Siskel (left) and Roger Ebert

American heterosexual male), and murder. Considered in turn by critics as subversive critiques of family values and of the 1950s sexual repression or as products celebrating the consumeristic and affluent ideologies of the decade, in the 1980s and 1990s, Sirk's melodramas have come to be regarded, in Barbara Klinger's words, ''as 'camp,' as outdated forms that exuded artifice in everything from narrative structure to depiction of romance.''

—Luca Prono

FURTHER READING:

Byars, Jackie. *All That Heaven Allows: Re-reading Gender in 1950s Melodrama.* London, Routledge, 1991.

Halliday, Jon. *Sirk on Sirk.* London, Martin Secker & Warburg, 1972.

Klinger, Barbara. *Melodrama & Meaning: History, Culture and the Films of Douglas Sirk.* Indianapolis, Indiana University Press, 1994.

Mulvey, Laura. *Visual and Other Pleasures.* London, MacMillan, 1989.

Siskel and Ebert

Gene Siskel (1946-1999) and Roger Ebert (1942—) are to film criticism what Arnold Palmer and Julia Child were to golf and cooking respectively. They popularized a formerly stuffy discipline and made it accessible to masses of people. Long after Bosley Crowther, Pauline Kael, and other highbrow critics made reviewing movies an art form, this Mutt and Jeff duo, through their nationally syndicated television program, made it a spectator sport.

Siskel and Ebert established their critical bona fides writing for rival Chicago tabloids. They began their strange odyssey together in 1975, when producers at PBS station WTTW invited them to co-host a weekly film review program. Though initially reluctant, the two men eventually were persuaded that their mutual hostility might make for good television. The series began its run under the name *Opening Soon at a Theater Near You* and was wisely retitled *Sneak Previews*.

The show's low budget allowed the hosts to do little more than air a succession of clips and bicker about the latest theatrical releases, which they then rated with a ''thumbs up'' or ''thumbs down'' in the old gladiatorial tradition. To everyone's surprise, *Sneak Previews* became a huge local hit and was broadcast nationally beginning in 1978. It quickly became the highest rated series in PBS history.

On the surface, the show's appeal lay in the cocktail party simplicity of its premise: two guys sitting around arguing about the merits of the latest crop of movies. But the clash of personalities allowed viewers to feel like they were eavesdropping on a private argument, as the opinionated co-hosts flung invectives at each other. Siskel was arguably the more intellectual of the two. Lean and birdlike, he combed the few thin wisps of hair he had left over the bare crown of his head. Ebert was the people's favorite, a beefy failed screenwriter who amazingly chose not to expunge his name from the credits of the soft-core porn turkey *Beyond the Valley of the Dolls.* Together they were like oil and water, soon referred to nationwide as ''the bald one'' and ''the fat one.''

In 1982, Siskel and Ebert outgrew PBS and moved their show into commercial syndication, retitling it *At the Movies.* Along the way, the show lost some of the ramshackle charm of the original. The ''Dog of the Week,'' a feature honoring the week's worst low-budget film release, was replaced by the ''Stinker of the Week'' and later scrapped entirely. New segments were created to highlight home video releases, a sop to the program's new bourgeois commercial audience. *At the Movies* went through a second, tortuous retitling, to *Siskel & Ebert & the Movies* before settling on the prosaic *Siskel & Ebert.*

With increased popularity came greatly enhanced power. Woody Allen and Eddie Murphy were just two of the stars who railed publicly about the pair's ability to sink a picture with a bad review. On the flipside, the encomium ''two thumbs up from Siskel and Ebert'' soon became prized by publicists all over Hollywood. When they gave their stamp of approval to more outre film fare (both loved 1994's *Pulp Fiction,* for example) it gave mainstream America permission to check it out as well. Their critical criteria—they both put a great emphasis on likability of characters—influenced many mainstream reviewers, as did their show's format (they spawned a host of imitators). Siskel and Ebert became late-night talk show mainstays and frequent targets of parodies like *In Living Color*'s cheeky ''Men on Film.''

The pair continued to host a weekly show and to pop up from time to time on the talk show circuit into the late 1990s. Both men continued to write their weekly reviews in the (Chicago) *Tribune* and *Sun-Times,* respectively. Ebert enjoyed a profitable sideline as the nominal writer of an annual movie reference guide. In 1998, the program even survived a leadership crisis when Siskel underwent an emergency brain operation to remove an unspecified growth. He emerged only slightly worse for wear, his hopeless comb-over an apparent casualty of surgery and his cognitive skills only slightly diminished. Ebert seemed barely to notice the changes, taking Siskel's slowness on the draw as an excuse to lace into his reviews with renewed ferocity. In February of 1999 Siskel died from complications linked to his brain tumor; he was 54.

—Robert E. Schnakenberg

FURTHER READING:

Bernstein, Fred. ''Tough! Tender! Gritty! Evocative! Gene Siskel and Roger Ebert Live to Dissect Films—and Each Other.'' *People Weekly.* August 20, 1984.

Ebert, Roger. *Roger Ebert's Book of Film.* New York, W.W. Norton, 1996.

Sister Souljah (1964—)

Black female rapper Sister Souljah, born Lisa Williamson, made national headlines in 1992 in the wake of the Los Angeles riots when she asked an interviewer, ''If black people kill black people everyday why not have a week and kill white people?'' The interview, in support of her album *360 Degrees of Power,* gained national attention when 1992 Democratic Presidential Candidate Bill Clinton, in order to attract the conservative white vote, condemned her remarks while addressing Jesse Jackson's Rainbow Coalition. Political analysts suggested that this criticism of Sister Souljah in front of an all black gathering was responsible for Clinton attracting a sizable number of white southern voters. Although the media attention increased sales of her disappointing album, it was not enough to energize her rap career. The New York City native resurfaced in 1995 with a quasi-autobiography, *No Disrespect,* which focused on black male/female relationships.

—Leonard Nathaniel Moore

FURTHER READING:

Sister Souljah. *No Disrespect.* New York, Time Warner, 1995.

Sitcom

''Sitcom'' is the abbreviated name for the half-hour television situation comedy. It is a form of television programming, generally 30 minutes in length, and consisting, in writer's jargon, of an opening teaser, two acts, and a closing tag; in all about 22 minutes of program sandwiched between spots (advertisements), PSAs (public service announcements), and station IDs. The situation comedy derives its name from the fact that, at least initially, each episode involved the antics of a regular character who found him/herself in a particular ''situation.''

Like other forms of popular entertainment, commercial television has sometimes suffered from bad press. TV has been derided as a ''boob tube''—a place where delinquents and couch potatoes frittered away the bulk of their sorry lives; in 1961, it was described by the Chairman of the FCC as a ''vast wasteland.'' And what better example of all that was distasteful, moronic, and potentially culturally corrupting than the situation comedy. But the legacy of the television sitcom in popular culture encompasses more than prat falls, canned laughter, and endless reruns in syndication. From the groundbreaking achievements of the *I Love Lucy* show to the phenomenal success of *Seinfeld,* the popularity of the sitcom helped propel American commercial television from its origins as an off-shoot of radio to a multi-billion dollar industry.

Even with images and themes that are often sanitized, circumscribed, and fantasized, the sitcom has provided a compelling portrait of the American landscape throughout periods of plenty, recession, and great societal upheaval. Evolving notions about sex, fashion, urban renewal, child rearing, the government, war, and the changing status of African Americans and women have all been fodder for the producers and writers of the episodic comedy. Other programming formats have also made an impact. Made-for-television movies have sometimes provided thought-provoking portraits of contemporary issues and the historical past, while realistic police-detective dramas offer striking images of the dangers of life on the street. It is the episodic comedy, however, with its humor, weekly format, and regular characters, that has most soundly featured the taboos, preoccupations, prejudices, obsessions, fads and fixations of twentieth century American society—not only by what was shown on the small screen but also by what was sometimes omitted.

Historically, the evolution of the situation comedy on television is firmly anchored to the history of radio programming. Soon after its invention, the new medium of radio emerged from its beginnings in experimental, often amateur-produced "stunts" to organized formats. Early radio programming consisted mostly of music, drama, and public affairs. Early in the Depression years, however, radio began its 20-year reign, known as the Golden Age of Radio, as the primary medium of entertainment in America. Probably the most significant program of early radio, notes Melvin Ely, was *Amos 'n' Andy*. Originating on WMAQ Radio, Chicago, in 1929, the show went on to become the longest-running and most successful radio program in American broadcast history. The show was conceived by Freeman Gosden and Charles Carroll, two white actors who played the part of "Amos" and "Andy" by mimicking so-called Negro dialect. The success of this comedy led to the creation of similar shows, including *Fibber McGee and Molly, The George Burns and Gracie Allen Show,* and *The Jack Benny Show.* All of these, including *Amos n' Andy,* eventually made the transition to the new medium of television.

Very early television programming was largely experimental, consisting of sports (wrestling, baseball, boxing), vaudeville crossovers, and variety shows such as *The Milton Berle Show* (1948-1956) and Ed Sullivan's *Toast of the Town* (1948-1955). But quickly, programming formats that were popular and successful in radio found their way to television, including drama, soap operas, and the situation comedy.

Erik Barnouw has traced the unfolding of two important circumstances that played an important role in the success of the sitcom as a programming format in his book *Tube of Plenty*. During television's infancy in the late 1940s, shows were broadcast live (a throwback from the days of live radio broadcasts). A viable form of videotape recording had not yet been introduced, and film was considered an unnecessary expense. The programs that were preserved for rebroadcast were kinescope reproductions: very bad quality, filmed copies of the video signal. In 1951, Lucille Ball and her husband Desi Arnaz used several thousand dollars of their own money to produce a pilot television program that would be based on their successful radio show, *My Favorite Husband. I Love Lucy* (1951-1957) was wildly successful and quickly dominated the ratings. "The premise of *I Love Lucy*," note Brooks and Marsh in *The Complete Directory to Prime Time TV Shows,* "was not that much different from that of other family situation comedies . . . a wacky wife making life difficult for a loving but perpetually irritated husband. . . ." But beyond the comical antics of the character Lucy Ricardo, the program forged sitcom history.

First, Lucy's show was shot employing a three-camera process and using film, providing high-quality prints that could be broadcast over and over and at previously designated times. In 1953, on the same day that the fictitious Lucy Ricardo character gave birth to her first child (to a captivated 68 percent of the television audience), real person Lucille Ball also gave birth to her son, Desi Arnaz, Jr.

Additionally, Ball shot her show in Hollywood, hastening the migration of television production from the live studios of New York to the motion picture sound stages of Hollywood. The show was filmed before a live audience, an innovation that didn't catch on with other sitcoms until nearly the 1970s. *I Love Lucy,* sponsored by Philip Morris, enjoyed six full seasons as the number one watched program in the nation.

Another important development in the evolution of episodic comedy was the eventual partnership forged between motion pictures and television. At first, the film industry regarded TV as a competitor and refused to allow feature films to be aired on television or for film stars to make television appearances. Eventually, film studios like Paramount and Walt Disney Studios began a dialogue with television. The eventual partnerships that were forged drastically altered the course of prime time television. Motion picture studios began to produce filmed programming for network television, at first mostly Westerns, but soon including the production of sitcoms like *Father Knows Best* (1954-1963), which was produced by Columbia Pictures. By the end of the 1950s, the Golden Age of Television—with its live-broadcast, anthology dramatic series—had begun to fade, to be replaced by more the formulaic fare that is the modern sitcom.

Though the history of television is relatively brief, viewers and critics have already identified distinct periods of television programming. Fifties sitcoms were signified by their vanilla suburbs, their emphasis on hearth and home, and non-threatening humor. Outside of the rare light reference to a social issue like teenage smoking, the characters of *The Aldrich Family* (1949-1953), *Make Room for Daddy* (1953-1965), *Lassie* (1954-1974), and *Father Knows Best* existed in a world that was generally far-removed from the harsh realities of poverty, atomic warfare, and segregated accommodations. In the early 1960s, as America increased its presence in Vietnam, civil rights tensions heightened to the boiling point, and Khrushchev aimed Cuban-based missiles at the U.S., television viewers found solace in the hayseed humor of sitcoms like *The Beverly Hillbillies* (1962-1971), *Petticoat Junction* (1963-1970) and *The Andy Griffith Show* (1960-1968). Moreover, "idiot sitcoms" such as *My Favorite Martian* (1963-1966), *Bewitched* (1964-1972), *The Flying Nun* (1967-1970), and *Gilligan's Island* (1964-1967) occupied spots among the top-ten most watched programs. While news documentaries and variety shows occasionally dotted the program guide, the situation comedy came to dominate the ratings in the 1960s. In less than two decades, television comedy had evolved from transplanted radio shows to fantasy family comedies to scenarios about talking horses. It was the decade of the 1970s, however, that would usher in changes that were at once striking and, at times, controversial.

Leading the changes in the sitcom in the 1970s was Robert D. Wood, who became network president of Columbia Broadcasting System television in 1969. In his chronicle of the CBS network, *This Is . . . CBS,* Robert Slater claims that Wood will be remembered for his "extensive overhaul" of CBS television's programming strategy—a strategy which significantly changed the flavor of prime time American television. Since the 1950s, CBS Television had been the undisputed ratings leader. The network retained its top ranking with a strong line-up of new and old shows, including long-running programs with loyal audiences, such as Western dramas and *The Ed Sullivan Show.* Slater notes, however, that with the great success of programs such as *The Beverly Hillbillies* and *Green Acres* (1965-1971), CBS television was jokingly referred to as "the Hillbilly Network." But by the late 1960s, bigger threats than stereotyping loomed over CBS.

The business side of television had changed a great deal since the days of General Food's sponsorship of *The Aldrich Family*. Programming had slowly evolved from sponsor-owned, sponsor-controlled shows to the selling of "spots" (30 and 60-second commercial messages) to many sponsors. The findings of program research departments took on major significance. Moreover, a new concept was being addressed by television programming executives in the conference rooms of the major networks: demographics. Now it was no longer enough for a program to attract the widest possible audience; it also had to attract the "right" audience, one with disposable income to spend on advertiser's products. CBS's loyal but aging, "fixed-income" audiences for popular shows like *The Beverly Hillbillies* were not representative of the kind of sophisticated spender that advertisers desired. Not surprisingly, during this age of The Beatles and campus anti-war protest, advertisers were eager to orient their products to youth culture. Notes Barnouw: "Older viewers were not big spenders. . . . Programs now tended to survive to the extent that they served the demographic requirements of sponsors." It was clear to Wood and CBS executive William S. Paley that if the network simply rested on its laurels, it would soon lose rating points and advertising dollars.

Not only had the television industry changed, so had life in America. The 1960s was a period of great social and cultural upheaval. Americans had witnessed the assassination of President John Kennedy, his brother Robert, and civil rights activist Rev. Dr. Martin Luther King Jr. The nightly news brought grim footage of the death and destruction of the Vietnam war to American dinner tables. Civil rights protestors were doused with fire hoses and attacked with dogs to the cheers of southern bigots. Student activists created a new American left. College campuses, draft cards, and cities burned. Television programming, it was felt, needed to in some way reflect the needs and feelings of the current culture. Though the situation comedy and the hour-long drama would remain the primary formulas, both genres would experience a shift away from the "consensual mood" of the early years of television to include social issues and themes more appealing and "relevant" to a young, educated audience.

Upon arriving at CBS, Wood initiated a "clean sweep" of the network's programming. Successful shows like *Green Acres, Ed Sullivan,* and *Beverly Hillbillies* were canceled. Banished were old favorites such as *Here's Lucy* (1968-1974), *Gunsmoke* (1955-1975), and *Red Skelton* (1951-1971). Independent producer Norman Lear purchased the rights to a hit British television show called *Till Death Do Us Part*. In the American version, now called *All in the Family* (1971-1979), he cast veteran actor Carroll O'Connor as the "lovable" but bigoted and totally outrageous Archie Bunker. The show included concepts never before approached on television: crude racial epithets, sexual situations, and verbal sparing unheard of around the dinner tables of 1950s sitcom families.

Paley regarded the show as too risky and feared that it might alienate viewers and advertisers alike. But Wood worked hard to allay the fears of censors and advertisers and persuaded Lear to eliminate some of the more risqué language. Notes Barnouw, CBS launched the program "with trepidation" in January 1971. Although *All in the Family* was not an instant hit, within about a year it became the most watched and talked about television sitcom in America.

More importantly, this program's success bred other programs, including more Norman Lear productions. These "spin-offs" of *All in the Family* included *The Jeffersons* (1975-1985), *Maude* (1972-1978), and *Good Times* (1974-1979). In the 1974 comedy *Good Times* (a black-themed show about life in a Chicago tenement),

suburban street crime, muggings, unemployment, evictions, Black Power, and criticism of the government were frequent and resounding themes. Also full of irreverent humor was the show *M*A*S*H* (1972-1983). Set during the Korean War, it was created by veteran writer Larry Gelbart from the successful hit movie. *Sanford and Son* (1972-1977) featured a multi-racial cast and the irreverent and topical humor of black comic Red Foxx as the owner of a junkyard. One of the keys to the success of these sitcoms was that they were "relevant."

The nature of the prime time television sitcom had changed significantly. Now there were interracial marriages, Latino and Asian characters, and scenarios about drag queens and birth control. In one famous and controversial episode of the program *Maude,* the character Maude, a bit past her child-rearing days, agonizes over the idea of having an abortion. At least three sitcoms featured a mostly black cast—the first since the cancellation of *Amos 'n' Andy* nearly 20 years prior. But social realism seemed to end as quickly as it had started. By the 1978-79 season, there was a return to the mythic world of the TV fantasy family. The four tops shows included the safe and congenial humor of *Happy Days* (1974-1984), *Laverne & Shirley* (1976-1983), *Three's Company* (1977-1984), and *Mork and Mindy* (1978-1982).

The evolution of *The Doris Day Show* (1968-73) offers an interesting glimpse of the sitcom's portrayal of the changing status of women. When her show appeared in 1968, Day portrayed a recent widower with two sons who returns to her rural roots to live with her father. By the second season, Doris was a secretary working for the editor of a magazine. In the third season, Doris had moved to San Francisco and was not just a secretary, but did independent writing. By the fourth and final season of the comedy, Doris was a single woman and independent writer with her life as a mother, secretary, and daughter all but forgotten.

To the consternation of traditionalists, the Women's Liberation movement in American unfolded right on the small screens of prime time television. The concerns of the "model moms" of early sitcoms were relegated mostly to issues at home. Although Lucy (*I Love Lucy*), June Cleaver (*Leave It to Beaver*) and Margaret Anderson (*Father Knows Best*) may have occasionally asserted their authority on some issue, it was kept safely within the minor vicissitudes of family life.

Early sitcoms occasionally featured single women with jobs, generally as secretaries, housekeepers, and assistants. In *Comic Visions,* David Marc describes the long-suffering career-women type who "worked for a living in lieu of marriage, which was valorized as the principal or 'real' goal of any woman." Early comedies featuring single, working women include *Our Miss Brooks* (1952-1956), *The Dick Van Dyke Show* (1961-1966) and *Private Secretary* (1953-1957).

Before the end of the 1960s, television featured two interesting precursors to the truly liberated woman. In *That Girl* (1966-1971), Marlo Thomas portrayed a young, independent woman trying to make it as an actress in New York. Some regard the Anne Marie character, with her comical antics and zany behavior, as little more than an extension of Lucy. Moreover, she was often rescued by her understanding boyfriend or doting father. But unlike Marc's long-suffering TV career women of earlier television, Anne Marie actually pursued a viable career—she wasn't simply marking time until her wedding day.

The sitcom *Julia* (1968-1971) is interesting in that it also featured a single, working, and professional woman. Moreover, Julia was black. "Respectably widowed" and a nurse, Julia and her incredibly polite young son Corey lived quiet lives in a safe and accepting world, successfully negotiating the minor challenges of life—far removed it seemed, from the harsh realities that existed in the black community at the time.

The Women's Liberation Movement brought more than bra burning and freedom from Victorian conventions. It shook-up long-held and cherished assumptions about women and sex, gender, marriage, family life, respect, and equal opportunity in jobs and pay. Probably the most celebrated in the vein of liberated women in sitcoms in the highly successful *Mary Tyler Moore Show* (1970-1977). Mary Richards was a career woman employed as an assistant producer at a Minneapolis television station. Her survival did not depend on the support and benevolence of a father figure, steady man, or for that matter, a supportive family. She had a Jewish friend named Rhoda and, in a twist on the typical scenario, together they often joked about—not envied—the life of the married woman on the show. Mary's suitably gruff boss had interpersonal problems and sometimes drank too much, but they developed a unique affection for each other. Moreover, she maintained a close but platonic relationship with a male co-worker. Now, sitcom men and women could be friends without the compulsory romantic relationship. The *Mary Tyler Moore Show* "transcended the model moms" of earlier TV, replaced the widowed career-women role and remade the ambitious, eligible single woman "on-the-make," notes Marc, becoming "a watershed event in American television." Moreover, many of the principle characters of the *Mary Tyler Moore Show* returned in spin-off programs of their own, building the fortunes of the MTM production company.

While Mary Richards, Edith Bunker, and Maude became more liberated and assertive, black women in prime time sitcoms were poorly represented by Florida Evans of *Good Times,* Louise Jefferson of *The Jeffersons,* and occasional characters on shows like *Sanford and Son.* In a 1970s scholarly study of gender and race in television, the authors note that "the black female has become almost invisible."

As a prominent element of American life and culture, race has often been the subject of television programming. But late-century television viewers, raised on a diet of *Family Matters, The Hughleys, Roc, Fresh Prince of Bel Air,* and especially *The Cosby Show* may find it difficult to appreciate the feelings of post-war African Americans about the depictions of black life on network television. For a century or more, African Americans endured vicious lampooning and egregious stereotyping in various forms of popular culture, including sheet music illustrations, advertising, marketing, radio, and motion pictures. Blacks were depicted as ignorant and superstitious, thick-lipped and animal-like; as servants or contented slaves in plantation tales or as dangerous savages in stories rooted in the mythical dark jungles of Africa. For postwar African-Americans, the popularity of television heralded a period of hopeful excitement. The new medium had the potential to forge positive changes in race relations as it nullified decades of pejorative depictions of black life and culture. The frequent appearance on early television of black stars such as Billy Eckstein and Ethel Waters was met with hearty approval. In a 1950 article, *Ebony* magazine endorsed the "liberal exploitation of black talent" as "a sure sign that television is free of racial barriers." However, an untoward amalgamation of economic forces and historical events would soon prove otherwise.

At the same period that television evolved into a viable economic medium, President Harry Truman called for the integration of the U.S. armed services, Jackie Robinson broke the color barrier in professional baseball, and "freedom riders" staged non-violent demonstrations against segregated accommodations. At this time, major sponsors produced much of the network programming that appeared

during prime time. The Southern market was of great concern to advertisers and the agencies that represented them and both were reluctant to have their products too closely associated with the concerns of black people. Media historians Bogel and MacDonald note that the fear of "White economic backlash" and the threat, perceived or real, of "organized consumer resistance" caused advertisers and advertising agencies to steer clear of appearing "pro-Negro rights."

Still, in 1950, film star Ethel Waters became the first black television series "star," capturing the title role in the popular sitcom *Beulah* (1950-1953) The show concerned the life of a black housekeeper working for a white family—a typical role for a black character. After three seasons (and three different dissatisfied actresses in the title role), the *Beulah* show finally succumbed to pressure from the black community regarding its stereotyped images. But the level of black resentment that took *Beulah* off the air hardly approached the clamor of controversy aroused by the appearance of another black-cast, black-themed program.

The sitcom *Amos 'n' Andy* (1951-1953) is probably one of the most protested television programs in broadcast history. After enjoying decades of popularity on radio, television's *Amos 'n' Andy* featured black actors portraying the roles of Amos (a conservative, Uncle Tom-type), the Kingfish (a scheming smoothie), the straight-laced Andy, Lawyer Calhoun (an under-handed crook that no one trusted), Lightnin' (a slow-moving janitor), Sapphire (a nosey, loudmouth shrew), and Mama (a domineering mother-in-law). The Beulah character, although an obvious stereotype, was at least well-mannered and spoke intelligible English. But *Amos 'n' Andy,* with its malapropisms, satire, parody, and ethnic humor, stirred up the level of black indignation almost to the boiling point.

As the series appeared in June of 1951, the NAACP appeared in federal court seeking an injunction against its premiere. To white studio executives, the show was harmless, not much different from *The Goldbergs* (1949-1954), *Life with Luigi* (1952-1953), or any other ethnically-oriented sitcom. It was funny, a testament to a remarkably talented cast and good writing. It was a commercial success and was endorsed by some vehicles of the black press and many in the black entertainment community. "[T]hey are undoubtedly funny," notes an August, 1951 editorial in the *Afro-American.* But, the op-ed continues, "Slapstick comedy of this type does not go well in an age where a great mass of disadvantaged humanity is struggling to lift itself to full citizenship in an often unfriendly atmosphere." This and other articles and editorials underscored the major objection of many postwar blacks. Except for the occasional black entertainer in a guest spot on variety show, the *only* blacks on television were the likes of the Kingfish and Beulah. CBS removed *Amos 'n' Andy* from the air in 1953 after two years. However, the program remained in syndication well into the 1960s, and is available on videocassette today. Moreover, except for the earlier-mentioned, 1968 sitcom *Julia,* another black-cast or black-themed show would not appear on prime time network television for almost 20 years.

In her book *Prime Time Families,* Ella Taylor describes the TV family as "[h]armonious, well-oiled building blocks of a benignly conceived American society founded in affluence and consensus." From the days of the homogenous suburban family life of *Leave It to Beaver* to the "sitcomic social realism" of *Good Times,* many have pondered the supposed effects of TV on the family—the most sacred of American institutions.

In the 1950s, *The Aldrich Family,* the Cleavers (*Leave It to Beaver*), the Andersons (*Father Knows Best*), and the Nelsons (*Ozzie and Harriet*) lived in virtual domestic bliss. By the Kennedy years, single heads of households appeared in the sitcoms *My Three Sons* (1960-1972) and *The Andy Griffith Show.* The 1960s also featured "quirky" families in the form of *The Beverly Hillbillies, The Addams Family* (1964-1966), *Bewitched* (1964-1972), and *The Munsters* (1964-1966). Some consider *The Dick Van Dyke Show* as a standout of the era. It, too, was fashioned amongst the ideals of domestic harmony. But the Petries were different, more sophisticated and hip; Laura Petrie sometimes appeared in pants, while Bob Petrie's co-workers included a Jewish man and a single woman.

In contrast, the 1970s would feature the travails of the Evans, an African-American family eking out an existence in a Chicago slum (*Good Times*), and at the same time present a 1950s fantasy family in the form of the Cunninghams of *Happy Days.* But in the decades since *The Aldrich Family* made the transition from radio to television, the TV family had incurred monumental change. The sitcom would now feature non-traditional families, bi-racial adoption, rebellious teenagers, parent bashing, divorce, twins separated at birth, ghetto families and wealthy ones.

In particular, one unwed mother basked in notoriety that emerged from the most unlikely of places: the American political arena. On the sitcom *Murphy Brown* (1988-1998), the character Murphy was a television journalist and single woman who became pregnant but showed little inclination to marry the father and settle into a life of domesticity. In 1992, former Vice President Dan Quayle led the attack on this highly popular sitcom, condemning the idea of an unmarried woman becoming a mother as being acceptable fare for prime time television. As noted liberally in American newspapers, he regarded the entire affair as "an attack on family values."

The 1980s saw the emergence of the "boomer" audience, the youngish, upscale professionals favored by advertisers who greedily snatched-up commercial time for programs like *Cheers* (1982-1993). For a brief time, nighttime soaps and realistic crime dramas displaced the popularity of the situation comedy. However, the decade is also noteworthy for one particular family-oriented sitcom featuring a predominantly African-American cast which rose to become one of the most watched programs of the period.

The Cosby Show (1984-1992) made its debut on NBC in 1984 and became one of the biggest successes of the decade. If the ratings figures were correct, if you were breathing and watched television, you watched *Cosby.* The popularity and immense success of this sitcom makes clear how programming, once considered mindless entertainment, had attained major stature. Jack Curry, in an article for *American Film,* explains the significance of a hit comedy to the fortunes of television networks. Not only did a popular show like *Cosby* "deliver its own night," but it was used as a "promotional base for other series." It was used to "troubleshoot," assisting with "ratings battles" wherever needed. No sitcom of the decade "had the impact and the acclaim of NBC's *The Cosby Show,*" he notes. Moreover, the show became a cash cow. Notes John Lippman in the *Wall Street Journal,* "The Cosby Show, for example, has generated nearly $900 million in revenue since it was sold into syndication in the late 1980s."

But while *Cosby* may have featured the lives of a professional, educated, upscale black family, another eighties sitcom would forever shatter the image of the TV sitcom family. Like a 1950s Mom, Roseanne Connor cleaned the house, washed the clothes, and made meatloaf for dinner. But that was the end of any similarity to 1950s-style domestic bliss on the quirky, controversial hit sitcom *Roseanne* (1988-1997).

Roseanne was "she who must be obeyed." She sparred (verbally and physically) with her younger, occasionally employed, and sometimes promiscuous younger sister. Roseanne's mother drank too much and at one point thought she was gay. Her boss and later co-worker was indeed gay, as was a female friend who took them for a night of dancing at a gay bar. While Lucy and Desi couldn't share a bed, Dan and Roseanne Connor openly discussed the particulars of their sex life. Over the years, Roseanne's daughter eloped with a mechanic; her college-enrolled daughter was discovered living with her boyfriend; their pubescent son D.J. suffered the embarrassment of getting an erection in math class; and in one show the Connors had their electricity turned off for non-payment. They referred to themselves as "white trash." With so much contention, it is surprising that the show was as funny and successful. It enjoyed top ratings for most of its 10-year run and was probably responsible for the success of other quarrelsome, dysfunctional family scenarios like the Fox Network's, *Married . . . with Children* (1987-1997) and the animated sitcom, *The Simpsons* (1989—).

A 1997 editorial in *The Columbus Dispatch* noted that "something has changed since the days when today's parents sat watching Beaver Cleaver, Andy Griffith, and Gilligan. The three networks have given way to a cornucopia of new channels, and much of the fare is coarser and more irreverent." In the Cleaver household, no one had ever raised their voice, used bad words, or suffered from intestinal gas. There was no sex, ethnic group issues, or alcoholics. Dad was happily, gainfully employed and Mom was always there when you needed her—at home. But sitcom families of the 1990s tended to feature dopey dads, absentee parents, grandparents who had sex, and moms whose behavior sometimes bordered on sadism. The flawless persona of Jim Anderson (*Father Knows Best*) evolved into parents whose flaws are clearly apparent. In an article titled "Father Knows Squat," Megan Rosenfeld of the *Washington Post* notes, "Parents are one of the few remaining groups that are regularly ridiculed, caricatured and marginalized on television. Ask a typical viewer to describe how parents are portrayed on most shows and the answer is: stupid."

Though television changed dramatically in the late 1980s and especially in the 1990s, as widespread cable access brought dozens of channels into American homes, the decade of the 1990s will still be remembered for a sitcom: *Seinfeld* (1990-1998). *Seinfeld* was noteworthy for its unique and quirky cast, its irreverent humor, and the fact that it was described as a show about nothing. Set in New York City, the program followed the life of character Jerry Seinfeld (a comedian), his three friends (Elaine, George, and Kramer), their families, and an odd assortment of occasional characters. In an example of art imitating life, the show even parodied itself as several episodes followed Jerry as he attempted to produce a sitcom about himself on the same network where the real *Seinfeld* program was aired. The group explored former TV taboos and "touchy" subject matter: a chef who neglected to wash his hands after using the toilet, sperm counts, and the size of a man's genitals after a swim. In one episode the group made bets to see who could hold off masturbating the longest. There were ugly babies, cancer scares, bras for men, black-market cable, scary bar mitzvahs, lesbian weddings, and stolen lobsters.

But *Seinfeld* is noteworthy as more than just another success story for NBC. So successful was the program to NBC and its fortunes that the real Jerry Seinfeld was paid one million dollars per episode to continue the show. The cost of advertising during an episode of *Seinfeld* during the 1997-98 season was $700,000 for a 30-second spot. Advertising time for the program's final episode was $1.5 million for 30-seconds, and included big advertisers like Anheuser-Busch, Visa, Mastercard, and the manufacturer of a vegetarian burger. The *Wall Street Journal* noted in 1998 that the one million-per-episode fee that the TBS cable network paid for reruns of *Seinfeld* was "one of the richest rerun deals in cable history." Noted the *Seattle Times,* "The program is poised to become the first television show to generate more than $1 billion in syndication revenues." Moreover, the success of *Seinfeld* was the catalyst for similar shows about well-heeled young professionals with too-much time on their hands, for example, the program *Friends* (1994—).

Unlike the relevant-issues theme sitcoms of the 1970s, 1990s comedies often featured prosperous young professionals sipping expensive coffee and drowning in self-centered angst. Concerns about "real" issues like poverty, nuclear weapons, and the government appeared to be passé. In the Nelson's neighborhood (*Ozzie and Harriet*), the characters couldn't use the word toilet, let alone broach the subject of sex. Nineties sitcom characters talked candidly about orgasms and their choice of sexual partners. On the show *Ellen* (1994-1998), the character Ellen (played by Ellen DeGeneres) even "came out," announcing to the world that she was indeed gay. Beyond the occasional gay supporting character, however, portraits of gay life would remain a scenario much too risky a venture for networks whose fortunes rested on the success of the prime time line-up.

Just decades after the far-fetched scenarios of *My Favorite Martian,* the 1990s also saw the exploitation of "literate humor." Rife with references to Kant and existentialism, shows like *Frasier* (1993—) were created to appeal to upscale audiences with graduate degrees, people who, like the characters Frasier and Niles, had "advanced" cultural tastes. The format itself has evolved, with the "situation" part playing second fiddle. Notes producer Gary Goldberg, now there are sitcom stories with no beginning, middle, and end, or four stories running simultaneously with sometimes no resolution. Moreover, 1990s sitcoms are not always funny, but have often crossed-over (with comic relief) into drama, exploring broken marriages, alcoholism, and teenage sex. Sitcoms of the 1990s featured lovable nerds, soup Nazis, teenage witches, Korean families, dysfunctional families portrayed by cartoon characters, home improvement scenarios, and shows about nothing.

Between the debut of *I Love Lucy* in 1951 and the demise of *Seinfeld* in 1998 spans a period of nearly 50 years. Given the monumental reformation in the television industry, changing concepts of what is considered funny, and the evolution of American society in general, 50 years may seem more like centuries. What is clear, however, is that the situation comedy has come to signify much more than the good old days of black and white television and nostalgic images of Lucy in a hoop skirt. The episodic comedy has ushered America and its people through recession, boom times, war, civil unrest, and conservative and liberal presidencies. It has challenged ideas about sex, morals, reproduction, and fashion. The sitcom

has survived the Family Hour, Prime Time Access Rules, cable TV competition, mergers and takeovers, deregulation, debates, disputes, controversy, scholarly assessment, atomic warfare, and the building and the annihilation of the Berlin Wall to emerge as one of the more enduring forms of commercial television programming in United States.

—Pamela S. Deane

FURTHER READING:

"*Amos 'n' Andy* Protest Rocks Radio, TV Industry." *The Afro-American.* July 21, 1951.

Arney, June. "Ads on last *Seinfeld* outscore Super Bowl." *Baltimore Sun.* May 14, 1998.

Barnouw, Eric. *Tube of Plenty: The Evolution of American Television.* New York, Oxford University Press, 1982.

Blair, Iain. "The Producers of *News Radio, Family Matters . . .* Discuss the Serious Business of Sitcoms." *Film & Video.* April, 1996.

Bogel, Donald. *Blacks in America Films and Television: An Encyclopedia.* New York, Garland Publishers, 1988.

Brooks, Tim, and Earle Marsh. *The Complete Directory to Prime Time Network TV Shows: 1946-Present.* New York, Ballantine, 1985.

Carson, Tom. "The Great Fox Chase." *American Film.* June, 1989.

Curry, Jack. "The Cloning of *Cosby.*" *American Film.* October, 1986.

Ely, Melvin Patrick. *The Adventures of Amos 'n' Andy: A Social History of an American Phenomenon.* New York, The Free Press, 1991.

Gilbert, James. *Another Chance: Postwar America 1945-1985.* Chicago, Illinois, Dorsey Press, 1986.

Gross, Lynne Schaefer. *Telecommunications: An Introduction to Electronic Media.* Brown and Benchmark Publishers, 1997.

Huff, Richard. "What Will Be the Total for *Seinfeld*? Billions and Billions." *Seattle Times.* May 15, 1998.

Lichter, S. Robert, Linda Lichter, and Stanley Rothman. *Prime Time: How TV Portrays American Culture.* Washington, D.C., Regnery Publishing, 1994.

MacDonald, J. Fred. *Blacks and White TV: Afro-Americans in Television Since 1948.* Chicago, Nelson-Hall Publishers, 1983.

Marc, David. *Comic Visions: Television Comedy & American Culture.* Malden, Massachusetts, Blackwell Publishers, 1997.

Marc, David, and Robert J. Thompson. *Prime Time, Prime Movers: From I Love Lucy to L.A. Law, America's Greatest TV Shows and People Who Created Them.* Boston, Little, Brown, 1992.

Mayer, Martin. "Summing Up the Seventies: Television." *American Film.* December, 1979.

Singer, Dorothy, et al. "What Every Parent Should Know About Television." *American Film.* January-February, 1981.

Slater, Robert. *This . . . Is CBS: A Chronicle of 60 Years.* Englewood Cliffs, New Jersey, Prentice Hall, 1992.

Taylor, Ella. *Prime Time Families: Television Culture in Postwar America.* Berkeley, University of California Press, 1989.

''Television Tykes: Series Contemplates Effect on Children.'' *Columbus Dispatch.* July 18, 1997.

Situation Comedy

See Sitcom

The Six Million Dollar Man

First hitting the airwaves as a made-for-TV movie in 1973, *The Six Million Dollar Man* became a weekly hour-long series that aired from 1974 to 1978 on the American Broadcasting Company (ABC) network. The show starred Lee Majors as Colonel Steve Austin, an astronaut who suffered serious injuries from the crash of an experimental craft and was rebuilt into a bionic man by the government. Austin was given bionic legs, a bionic arm, and bionic eye. His new parts gave him super strength, super speed, and super vision. He worked for the OSI, the Office of Strategic Investigation. His superior was Oscar Goldman, played by Richard Anderson, and his doctor/scientist was Rudy Wells, played by Allan Oppenheimer and later by Martin E. Brooks.

During the regular series, Austin faced a variety of foes, including spies, a rogue bionic man, Bigfoot (a robot created by aliens), and the fembots (robots made in the image of women Austin and his fiancée, Jamie Sommers, the Bionic Woman, knew). During most of the episodes, Austin worked as a secret agent. When the character achieved super hero status among young television viewers, the show's producers imitated comic book hero plots with spinoffs and a ''bionic family.'' Sommers ''died'' only to be brought back the next season. Eventually there emerged *The Bionic Women* television

Lee Majors (right) as *The Six Million Dollar Man* with Richard Anderson.

series, involving a bionic boy and Sommers's bionic dog, a German shepherd named Max. The two shows shared a supporting cast and Austin and Sommers crossed over onto each others' shows.

The show lasted longer than several other super spy shows (*The Invisible Man, The Gemini Man*) that appeared around the same time. Both shows were in the top ten rated shows, with *The Six Million Dollar Man* even enjoying the spot as the number one rated show in America. It enjoyed a healthy run in syndication at home and abroad as well, appearing on cable television into the late 1990s. Austin and Sommers also appeared in several movie specials that aired in the late 1980s and early 1990s. (These movies also introduced another bionic man—Austin's son—and a bionic girl.)

Based on the novel *Cyborg* (standing for cybernetic organism), by Martin Caidin, the television series made the terms bionics and cybernetics familiar to the general American population, especially America's youth. Caidin served as technical advisor to the show.

The television shows generated other forms of popular culture. Novels, especially young adult novels, were based on episodes and characters from the series. Steve Austin starred in his own comic book series produced by Charlton Comics. There was a Six Million Dollar Man action figure and lunch box. Dusty Springfield recorded a pop single titled after the show. Parodies also appeared: the Bionic Watermelon debuted on the *Captain and Tenille Show*; a children's joke book was titled *The Bionic Banana*.

The show's opening sequence, showing Austin's crash, gave several phrases to American slang. "He's breaking up! He's breaking up!" and "We can rebuild him; we have the technology. We can make him better than he was before." became expressions among children during play. Pretending to be bionic was easy thanks to the show's low-budget special effects. Every bionic act was usually done in slow motion and was accompanied by a distinctive sound effect, easy to imitate in backyards and school playgrounds.

Besides being a fun thing to say on the playground, the show's opening statement about "making him better than he was before" indicated an American attitude toward technology. After putting a man on the moon, most Americans became extremely proud of technology as a remedy to any problem. The show postulated that technology could even fix a broken person. And of course, scientists involved in the actual field of bionics were attempting to do just that. The show tended to highlight the technology, although *The Bionic Woman* tended to highlight the person. However, although technology solved the problems, it could also be faulted as the source of power for the villains on the show. Killer robots and Venus probes were Austin's biggest challenges. What cannot be overlooked, though, is the significance of Austin's humanness in allowing him to triumph against his machine foes.

The show also expressed a view of government agencies as entities protecting the population. The OSI was concerned with doing good and mostly benign in its practices. This perception of government agencies contrasts radically with the way government is portrayed in the 1990s hit science fiction show *The X-Files*.

—P. Andrew Miller

FURTHER READING:

Cohen, Joel. *The Six Million Dollar Man and the Bionic Woman.* New York, Scholastic Book Services, 1976.

Philips, Mark, and Frank Garcia. *Science Fiction Television Series.* Jefferson, North Carolina, McFarland, 1996.

60 Minutes

Prior to the emergence of prime-time network newsmagazine programs like *20/20, Primetime Live,* and *Dateline,* and before the era of round-the-clock cable news on CNN, MS/NBC, and Fox News Channel, the CBS newsmagazine *60 Minutes* was unchallenged as television's premiere news program. From its initial broadcast on September 24, 1968, *60 Minutes* pioneered the "magazine format" of television journalism, which allowed it to run a mixture of hard news, investigative reports, personality profiles, and light feature pieces. Its prominence enabled it to feature candid stories on the most powerful world leaders, distinguished artists, and crafty villains of the last thirty years. Although it was not a ratings sensation during its first several seasons, by the mid-1970s it grew to become the most prestigious, most watched, and most imitated news program on television.

The creation of *60 Minutes* came about after its producer, Don Hewitt, was fired in 1964 from his position as producer of *The CBS Evening News with Walter Cronkite*. Before his dismissal, he had become a key behind-the-scenes player at CBS News. Hewitt had directed Edward R. Murrow's *See It Now* programs in the 1950s, including the first live coast-to-coast hookup in November 1951 which depicted the simultaneously broadcast images of the Brooklyn and Golden Gate bridges. In 1960, he produced and directed the nation's first televised presidential debate between John F. Kennedy and Richard Nixon. Hewitt was also remembered for such technical achievements as the invention of cue cards, the development of subtitles to identify people and places on screen, the creation of the "double projector" system to enable smoother editing, and coining the term "anchor man." After a dispute with Fred Friendly, president of CBS News, he was relegated to the network's lowly documentary division. He describes his attempts to revive the little-watched, moribund format by stating, "Sometime in 1967 it dawned on me that if we split those public affairs hours into three parts to deal with the viewers' short attention span . . . and come up with personal journalism in which a reporter takes the viewer along with him on the story, I was willing to bet that we could take informational programming out of the ratings cellar."

Hewitt presented his newly fashioned documentary program in the guise of a newsmagazine, such as *Time* or *Newsweek*. Each week his chief correspondents would present several stories on a wide variety of topics. A brief concluding segment in the early years, titled "Point Counterpoint," consisted of debates between liberal and conservative columnists Shana Alexander and James Kilpatrick. In 1978, writer Andy Rooney assumed this segment to present his own brand of short, humorous commentary. Each portion of the program was separated by an image of a ticking stopwatch, which became the show's symbol.

By the late 1970s *60 Minutes* became one of television's most popular shows with its concept of stories presented in a "Hollywood style" that emphasized attractively packaged factual events. In 1979, it was the highest rated television program of the season—a distinction that no other news show had ever attained. Its great popular success made *60 Minutes* one of the most profitable programs in TV history. Costing only about half the price of an hour-long entertainment show while commanding the same commercial rates of such series allowed CBS to earn enormous sums of money from what was once the least-watched network program type. Much of the show's great appeal was based on its increasingly hard-hitting investigative reports. Presented mainly by aggressive correspondents Mike Wallace and Dan Rather, the show exposed a number of frauds and abuses including the sale of phony passports, kickbacks in the Medicaid business, and mislabeling in the meat-packing industry. Reporter Morley Safer commented on the show's ability to get dishonest businessmen and scam artists on camera by saying, "A crook doesn't believe he's made it as a crook until he's been on *60 Minutes.*"

The show's greatest strength derives from its correspondents and their choice of stories. Harry Reasoner, Ed Bradley, Diane Sawyer, Steve Kroft, and Leslie Stahl were correspondents at various times and were able to deliver insightful pieces within the show's potpourri format. One week a reporter would be speaking from a war zone and the next speaking to movie stars or pool hustlers. The large number of correspondents freed each one of them from being studio-bound, thus allowing them to report from the field themselves. Hewitt's focus on "personality journalism" allowed the reporter's own characteristics to shine through. Mike Wallace was seen to embody the image of the tough reporter, while Morley Safer projected a more elegant image. All were considered leaders in their field. The reporter's personal team of six producers, a cameraperson, assistant, soundperson, and electrician supports each on-air personality.

Of all the journalists associated with *60 Minutes,* none is as strongly identified with the program as is Mike Wallace. His intense

reporter's image came only after a long and varied career. He was a radio performer in the 1940s and appeared as an actor on many popular shows like *Sky King, The Lone Ranger, The Green Hornet,* and *Ma Perkins.* After moving to television in 1949, he hosted a variety of talk, interview, and game shows. Following the 1962 death of his son Peter in a climbing accident, Wallace decided to become a straight newsman. He possesses a direct, often abrasive, style that is well suited for the show's confrontational format. He is generally regarded as the most fearless reporter in the business and is unafraid to ask the most provocative questions even of friends. In the 1990s the nearly eighty-year-old Wallace showed no signs of slowing down. His continued tenacity has caused him to be referred to as the "geriatric *enfante terrible* of television."

Although it has long been considered television's most distinguished news program, *60 Minutes* has not been without its critics or controversies. Some claimed it practiced "ambush journalism" by editing its massive amounts of interview footage to distort the positions of some of its subjects. Others have complained the many off-screen producers do the majority of the reporting while the on-air correspondents merely provide each story's narration. In the 1990s, humorist Andy Rooney was temporarily suspended for a supposedly racist remark. Other low moments in the program's long history include its being duped in 1972 by a forged diary of industrialist Howard Hughes and, most seriously, its being forced to delay an exposé on the tobacco industry due to the network's fears of litigation. Despite these problems, *60 Minutes* remains a respected program that is trusted by viewers in Middle America.

An examination of the personalities, issues, lifestyles, and major events covered on *60 Minutes* provides a remarkable window on America from the late 1960s onward. Don Hewitt created a format that has allowed for a varied presentation of ideas that have shaped the

A question is put to a contestant on *The $64,000 Question.*

post-Vietnam era. He and his able correspondents, led by Mike Wallace, revealed to the networks that factual, documentary programming could be highly successful both in terms of journalism and ratings. Their success led to a proliferation of other television newsmagazines in the 1990s. In 1998, it was announced that CBS was planning on expanding the show's franchise by creating *60 Minutes II.*

—Charles Coletta

FURTHER READING:

Coffey, Frank. *60 Minutes: 25 Years of Television's Finest Hour.* Los Angeles, General Publishing Group, 1993.

Hewitt, Don. *Minute by Minute. . . .* New York, Random House, 1985.

The $64,000 Question

During the 1950s, game shows were television's most popular fare, and *The $64,000 Question* (1955-58) was unquestionably America's favorite game show. Every Sunday night, the country came to a stop as millions of households tuned in to watch. The premise behind the show was brilliant—in addition to a profession or vocation, many people have hobbies or avocations about which they are remarkably well informed. The show featured contestants such as a jockey who was an art expert, or a psychologist—the young Dr. Joyce Brothers—who loved prize fighting. Players entered an isolation booth and answered questions, working their way up each week to the final $64,000 Question. Unbeknownst to the viewers and, indeed, to some of the contestants, however, the producers of the show were giving answers to the more charismatic players. A few years later, *The $64,000 Question* came under scrutiny during the investigation by the U.S. Congress known as the Quiz Show Scandal. When the public learned the truth about the "fixed" quiz shows, game shows fell out of favor for years and the American television audience adopted a cynicism that has permeated popular culture ever since.

—Victoria Price

FURTHER READING:

Delong, Thomas. *Quiz Craze: America's Infatuation with Game Shows.* New York, Praeger, 1991.

Holms, John Pynchon, et al. *The TV Game Show Almanac.* New York, Chilton Book Co., 1995.

Skaggs, Ricky (1954—)

A seasoned musical veteran by the time he turned 18, Ricky Skaggs parlayed early bluegrass music prominence and an apprenticeship with Emmylou Harris's country-rock Hot Band into a career

Ricky Skaggs

that put him on top of the country music charts in the early 1980s. While he was capable of brilliance within each genre, it was his creation of a modern sound out of traditional elements from both that earned him widespread acclaim and respect even after the rise of the hot New Country format shut him (and others like him) out of country radio in the early 1990s. Down but not out, he roared back into the limelight in 1997 when the album that signalled a return to his roots, *Bluegrass Rules!*, became the first traditional bluegrass album to break onto the country sales charts.

Born in a small town in the hills of Eastern Kentucky, Skaggs began his career early, playing mandolin and fiddle with his parents' semi-professional band by the time he was five. In 1971, he and partner Keith Whitley were taken under the wing of bluegrass pioneer Ralph Stanley, with whom they toured and recorded for several years. While Whitley continued to work with Stanley through much of the 1970s, Skaggs left to take a short-term job with the Country Gentlemen, and then joined J. D. Crowe and the New South in 1974. Though his tenure with Crowe was brief, it was exceedingly influential; the band toured widely, including a visit to Japan, and made one of the most significant bluegrass albums ever, a self-titled release for Rounder Records in 1975. When Skaggs departed from the New South, he and fellow alumnus Jerry Douglas formed Boone Creek, another influential act that combined traditional bluegrass with a more modern, rock-influenced sound.

Following the breakup of Boone Creek, Skaggs went to work for Emmylou Harris, then an habitual presence at the top of the country music charts. As a member of the Hot Band he both influenced and was influenced by Harris, bringing bluegrass sounds into her material while honing his skills as an electric guitar picker and developing an appreciation for the application of rock beats and accents to traditional country material. A 1979 solo album, *Sweet Temptation,* made while he was still with Harris, showed Skaggs in the process of turning these lessons into a catchy, distinctive sound that melded his influences and experiences into something new; when a single from the album, ''I'll Take the Blame,'' garnered some airplay on country radio, he plunged into a solo country music career, signing with Epic Records and producing *Waiting For The Sun To Shine* in 1981.

Skaggs's first Epic single, ''Don't Get Above Your Raising,'' hit the Top 20, and after his second single reached the Top 10, he had his first number one recording with an updated version of Flatt & Scruggs' ''Crying My Heart Out Over You.'' From then until 1986, he was never absent from the upper end of the country charts, scoring 15 consecutive Top 10 hits, most of which reached the top. The winning formula proved to be a combination of modern-sounding remakes of country and bluegrass classics (''I Don't Care,'' ''I Wouldn't Change You If I Could,'' ''Don't Cheat In Our Hometown,'' ''Uncle Pen'') and well-crafted country-rockers (''Heartbroke,'' ''Highway 40 Blues'') by younger, sophisticated writers, all delivered by a supremely talented band of musicians, many with bluegrass backgrounds. These achievements brought him acclaim—the legendary guitarist/producer Chet Atkins credited him with ''single-handedly'' saving country music—as well as a flood of honors, including membership in the Grand Ole Opry (at the time of his induction he was the youngest person ever to join the cast), eight awards from the Country Music Association, and four Grammies. Though he continued to make occasional guest appearances with bluegrass acts in concert and on record, the 1980s saw Skaggs take up what seemed to be a permanent residence in the world of country music.

By the end of the 1980s, though, Skaggs's releases were no longer topping the charts. Some critics attributed the decline to stagnation and a decline in the quality of his material, while others took note of the changing shape of country music radio, then turning toward a variety of broader rock music influences. Whatever the cause, he had only one number one recording after 1986 (''Lovin' Only Me,'' 1989), and by 1988 most of his singles were failing to reach the Top 20, with his last charting one coming in 1992. Though he continued to maintain a high profile on the Opry and cable television's Nashville Network, hosting a well-received concert series on the latter in the mid-1990s, mutual dissatisfaction between Skaggs and his label found him making a jump to Atlantic Records, for whom he made two strong albums that were favorably received by critics, but not by mainstream country radio.

However, shortly after the release of his second—and, it turned out, final—Atlantic album, Skaggs found a new lease on musical life by returning to his starting point: traditional bluegrass. Turning his country band into a bluegrass one, he recorded an album of standards-*-Bluegrass Rules!* (1997)—that startled virtually everyone by selling well enough to earn a place on Billboard's country album chart. Not by coincidence, the shift came at a time when the death of bluegrass's founder, Bill Monroe, had prompted concern about the longevity of the style; Skaggs was as well-positioned as anyone to contribute to its survival, and the album release was followed by broad-ranging tours and televised appearances, as well as savvy use of the Internet to reach listeners directly, bypassing commercial radio. By the end of the

decade, Skaggs was proclaiming his permanent commitment to bluegrass, and hundreds of thousands of fans appeared to greet the news with equal devotion.

—Jon Weisberger

Skateboarding

Invented in the 1950s by southern California surfers who sought a way to surf without waves, skateboarding has itself experienced several waves of popularity. Almost universally outlawed in the 1960s because it was perceived as dangerous, skateboarding enjoyed a revival in the 1970s and another in the 1980s, helped along by Marty McFly, the skateboarding hero of the *Back to the Future* movies. In the 1990s, skateboarding once again flourished, not only as a popular ''extreme'' sport, but also as a five hundred million dollar a year business. Perhaps because it was spawned by the bohemian surfer culture, skateboarding has always had a rebel image, and it is this that may be responsible for the continuing renewal of its popularity among youth.

In the 1950s bored surfers attached composite roller skate wheels to pivoting axles and put them on the front and back of a wooden plank. The pivoting action helped steer the board, which was maneuvered much like a surfboard on the water, steering by changing the position of the feet and shifting one's weight. In 1973, the old fashioned metal wheels were replaced by newer roller skate wheels made of polyurethane. The new wheels gave the board stability, a smoother ride, and greater traction. Modern boards are made with

Mathias Ringstrom (top) and Max Dufour at the 1997 X-games in San Diego, California.

scientific precision, often at small specialty companies run by skaters, with lighter, more durable decks (the board itself), neoprene wheels, and lightweight tempered trucks (the pivoting axle assembly). Selling at a hundred dollars each or more, skateboards are efficient vehicles both for transportation and for the flamboyant tricks that skaters refer to as "grabbing air."

Unlike surfers, skateboarders need nothing but the streets and concrete structures of the city to hone their skills, and they have nothing but concrete to break their falls. Thus skateboarding has attracted a tough, independent, and rebellious type of urban youth, who have created their own subculture. Skateboarders, who call themselves "thrashers" or "shredders," are largely self-taught. They have their own lingo, their own clothing styles, their own competitions, and their own publications. *Thrasher*, a radical "zine," and *Transworld Skateboarding*, a slightly more clean cut publication, are two of the most successful skateboarding magazines. Each has a circulation of well over 150,000. Skateboarding also spawned its own music genre, with a similarly wild image. Groups with names like Septic Death and Gang Green record their "speed metal" music on small labels devoted to "skate rock." One skate rock disc jockey, Skatemaster Tate, describes the music vividly: "It's punk rock and skating rolled up in a ball of confusion and screaming down the alley in a gutter."

Since skateboarding is often done by groups of teenagers on city streets, parking garages, empty swimming pools and the like, skaters are often subject to hostility from local citizenry and law enforcement officials. Cities have two basic approaches to controlling the thrashers: banning skateboarding or developing special parks devoted to the sport. Banning skating is usually unsuccessful simply because breaking the rules is as much a part of the flashy street sport as wheelies and spins. Skateboard parks offer a compromise that is often at least partially successful. Parks like the Savanna Slamma and Milwaukee's Turf Skateboard Park attract hundreds of skaters to show off their tricks on ramps and half-pipes constructed especially for safe skating. Some skaters however, feel that skating is by right a street sport and that relegating it to special parks robs it of its rebel cachet. This antipathy between thrashers and the law resulted in the most widely known skateboarding slogan, seen on bumper stickers nationwide, "Skateboarding is not a crime."

With an estimated twenty million skaters at the end of the 1990s, skateboarding is well entrenched as a flamboyant mode of transportation and expression for urban youth. Competitions such as ESPN's Extreme Games offer thrashers a chance to win gold, silver, and bronze medals in downhill racing, slalom racing, and freestyle. Though often considered dangerous, skateboarding has far fewer reported injuries than soccer, baseball, or basketball, and many skaters, in addition to the mandatory baggy T-shirt and baggier shorts, now sport kneepads, wrist guards, and helmets. Perhaps those statistics are best kept secret from older generations, however, to avoid ruining a perfectly good rebellious outlet for their offspring.

—Tina Gianoulis

FURTHER READING:

Cocks, Jay. "The Irresistible Lure of Grabbing Air." *Time*. June 6, 1988, 90.

Evans, Jeremy. *Skateboarding*. New York, Crestwood House, 1993.

Fried-Cassorla, Albert. *The Ultimate Skateboard Book*. Philadelphhia, Running Press, 1988.

Greenfeld, Karl Taro. "Killer Profits in Velcro Valley." *Time*. January 25, 1999, 50.

Thatcher, Kevin J. *Thrasher: The Radical Skateboard Book*. New York, Random House, 1992.

Skating

From its ninth-century, Northern European origins as a means for hunting and traveling on ice, skating has been explored for its leisure possibilities. By the time that iron skates—or *schaats* as their sixteenth-century Dutch inventors called them—had replaced their wooden or bone predecessors, their transformation to recreational

Jayne Torvill (right) and Christopher Dean perform their ice dancing routine at the Winter Olympics in Sarajevo, 1984.

usage was well under way. This can be seen in some of Pieter Brueghel's sixteenth-century paintings of peasants skating on the canals of Belgium and the Netherlands, activities that were made famous in Hans Christian Andersen's fairy tales of Denmark. Not so long after iron blades were invented, skates that could snap on to the sole and heel of boots were being manufactured by the Acme Skate Company in Halifax, Nova Scotia. These skates were electroplated in nickel or gold for the wealthy to carry around in expensive carrying cases.

It may be the numerous variations on ice skating that explains its growing popularity today. There is short and long-track speedskating, barrel jumping, pairs, and figure skating. Originally a sport for the Dutch common-folk, speedskating was initially made popular in the Winter Olympics as a sport that involved packs of skaters racing in laps over different distances on a track. The current objective of speedskating is to get around an oval track as quickly as possible (although some of speedskating's most popular races are marathons set on the canals of the Netherlands). Barrel jumping, a common variation of speedskating, was especially popular around the turn of the twentieth century. Skaters, set side-by-side on the ice, would skate as fast as they could, and try to jump over as many barrels as possible. Without a doubt however, it is figure skating, and specifically Sonja Henie's white skates and short skirts in the Olympics of 1928, 1932, and 1936, that commanded the world's attention. Henie's jumps and spins so captured the public imagination that ice skating began to evoke images of talented individuals, alone or in pairs, performing highly technical actions in nearly perfect union with music and all towards the goal of "a clean skate."

Sonya Henie was the most successful figure skater ever, maintaining a public skating career for 46 years. Born in Oslo, Norway, on April 8, 1912, she began skating when she was six years old. At the age of 11 she competed in the Olympics. In 1927 she won the world amateur championship for women, holding that title for 10 consecutive years. She won three gold medals in the Winter Olympics of 1928, 1932, and 1936. Trained in ballet, Henie incorporated some of its maneuvers into female figure skating; she was largely responsible for converting a predictable series of colorless exercises into a spectacular and popular exhibition. After having caught the attention of Americans at the 1930 World Championships in New York, she turned professional after her Olympic triumph in 1936, and toured Europe and the Americas as the star of the *Hollywood Ice Revue,* and for a time (1951-52) she acted as producer of her ice shows. In 1936 she signed with Twentieth Century Fox and starred in 11 popular films including *One in a Million* (1936/37), *Thin Ice* (1937), and *Wintertime* (1943). From 1937 to 1945 she was one of the leading box-office attractions in the motion-picture industry and died in 1969 with a fortune estimated at $47 million dollars.

Since Henie's time, her status as celebrity has been replicated by other female figure skaters. Peggy Fleming, Dorothy Hamill, Katarina Witt, and Kristi Yamaguchi have loomed larger than male figure skaters in the public imagination, paying for this privilege by almost always being cast, as Feuer explains in the anthology *Women on Ice,* as the "wounded bird, a child, or a fairy tale princess." This embodiment of grace has traditionally belied the athleticism necessary to perform the necessary jumps, loops, and spirals that mark elite amateur and professional figure skating careers. The move away from, and reinterpretations of, vestigial images of femaleness and

maleness marked figure skating's skyrocketing popularity in the 1990s. The new figure skating was a media-conscious, entertainment-driven form that thrived in the age of tabloid TV. Although part of the tabloidization of skating is attributable to the death of compulsory figures and endless speculation about who Katarina Witt was dating, the current connection between skating and the tabloids owes much of its origin to the disgraceful but unforgettable Tonya/Nancy scrum.

The rivalry between "trailer trash" Tonya Harding and "ice princess" Nancy Kerrigan, the subsequent scandal in which Harding was found complicit in her husband's assault on Kerrigan at the 1994 US National Championships, and the controversial representation of the two women on the U.S. women's team at the 1994 Lillihammer Winter Olympics is integral in the current popularity of figure skating. Why? Almost 50 percent of U.S. homes with television sets were tuned into the primetime telecasts of the women's figure skating competition, making it the sixth most popular television program ever.

From that point, figure skating increased its allure. Figure skating in the 1990s became a form of public spectacle, the extension of skating beyond competitions like the Olympics to a myriad of touring ice shows and pseudo-competitions that appeared regularly on prime time television. The change was most telling in men's skating, where competitors were acclaimed by fans for their masculine rather than artistic qualities—thus world champion Elvis Stojko performed as a motocross bike-driving, karate-fighting, arm-pumping, quadruple toe loop-jumping super male. More telling were the young members of the audience who hooted and hollered like fraternity brothers at a strip bar as Philippe Candeloro took off his shirt amid squeals of pleasure.

Skating's new popularity was revealed in very full arenas in cities where double axles are more traditionally associated with truckers, not skaters. It was revealed on TV, where the airwaves featured Fox Television's *Rock 'n' Roll Skating Championship,* and six professional championships on 9 Sundays on CBS alone. There were also television specials hosted by individual skaters (Kurt Browning's *You Must Remember This* was considered the best). Finally, rock and roll-like touring such as Campbell Soups' *Tour of World Figure Skating Champions* (televised by CBS as *Artistry on Ice*) ensured complete saturation. Or did it?

In the late 1990s, almost 30 million Americans ice skated. The United States Figure Skating Association membership jumped 25 percent since 1994. It is speculated that 35 percent of the audience for figure skating may be male. According to some marketers, figure skating ranks just behind the NFL in U.S. popularity. In other words, figure skating may have merely completed its compulsory and long programs while its more exciting and even more popular short program awaits.

—Robert VanWynsberghe

FURTHER READING:

Baughman, Cynthia, editor. *Women on Ice: Feminist Essays on the Tonya Harding/Nancy Kerrigan Spectacle.* New York, Routledge, 1995.

Milton, Steve, with photographs by Barbara McCutcheon. *Skate: 100 Years of Figure Skating.* Toronto, Key Porter Books, 1996.

Shivers, Jay S., and Lee J. deLisle. *The Story of Leisure: Context, Concepts, and Current Controversy.* Windsor, Human Kinetics, 1997.

Skelton, Red (1913-1997)

One of television's most popular comedians, Red Skelton is most fondly remembered for *The Red Skelton Show,* which ran on NBC from 1951-1953, and then on CBS from 1953-1970 (with a brief return to NBC for the 1970-1971 season). A very likeable personality and gifted pantomimist, Skelton also starred in a series of comedy films and had a career filled with contradictions. Noted writer Ross Wetzsteon once commented, Skelton was ''a mime whose greatest success was on the radio. A folk humorist in the years when American entertainment was becoming urban. A vulgar knockabout at a time when American comedy was becoming sophisticated and verbal. A naïve ne'er-do-well in the age of the self-conscious schlemiel. Red Skelton's career is a study in how to miss every trend that comes down the pike.''

Skelton was born Richard Bernard Skelton in 1913 (few sources list 1910), and was the son of a circus clown with the Haggenback and Wallace circus. His father died before he was born, and he grew up in punishing poverty. Active in show business from the age of 10, Skelton trained in stock companies, tent shows, burlesque, and vaudeville. In the 1930s, he stumbled upon a formula for finding humor in people's idiosyncracies and displaying his gift for panto-mime, developing his famous routine on the different ways people dunked their doughnuts—he later performed this bit for a two-reel short, *The Broadway Buckaroo.* Skelton developed much of this material with the help of his wife Edna, who served as his manager, writer, and foil for many years.

Red Skelton

Skelton started his film career in 1938 when RKO hired him to perform some of his vaudeville routines for *Having a Wonderful Time.* In the film Skelton plays Itchy Faulkner, the entertainment director of a resort camp in the Catskill Mountains, and performed a routine about the different ways people walk up a flight of stairs. RKO, however, expressed no continued interest in his services. But in 1940, Metro-Goldwyn-Mayer (MGM) assigned Skelton to appear as comedy relief in *Flight Command* and two Dr. Kildare films, but his first starring role and real breakthrough came when he got the lead role of Wally Benton, also known as the radio comic ''The Fox,'' who solves mysteries in a remake of *Whistling in the Dark* (1941). Ace comedy writer Nat Perrin added a bounty of snappy lines for Skelton, and a brief film series of *Whistling* films was launched, which while not wildly funny are unpretentious and diverting, and they represent Skelton's best film work—the other films in the series were *Whistling in Dixie* (1942) and *Whistling in Brooklyn* (1943).

Despite its resources, MGM had difficulty in figuring out how to present their new property, often relegating their new star to more minor comedy relief roles. He was given brief routines in a number of elaborate MGM productions, including *Neptune's Daughter* (1949), *Three Little Words* (1950), *Texas Carnival* (1951), and *Lovely to Look At* (1952), but was most notable in *Bathing Beauty* (1944), where he performed a routine about a woman getting up in the morning, and *Ziegfield Follies* (1946), where his Guzzler's Gin routine was rechristened ''When Television Comes'' and represented the comic highlight of this kitchen sink film.

Skelton had his own radio series from 1941 until 1953, where he developed the characters he was most noted for, including Junior (the Mean Widdle Kid), Freddie the Freeloader, Clem Kadiddlehopper, George Appleby, Sheriff Deadeye, Willy Lump Lump, Cauliflower McPugg, Cookie the Sailor, San Fernando Red, Bolivar Shagnasty, and others.

Skelton served for a time in the army, and his return vehicles at MGM proved unfunny flops (*The Show-off* [1946] and *Merton of the Movies* [1947]). One of Skelton's better efforts, Vincent Minelli's *I Dood It* (1943), was loosely based on Buster Keaton's MGM film *Spite Marriage* (1929). Skelton developed a good relationship with the out-of-work and underutilized Keaton who supplied him with advice about comedy and worked with Skelton on some of his better efforts, notably *A Southern Yankee* (1948) and *The Yellow Cab Man* (1950) both of which credited former Keaton director Edward Sedg-wick as ''comedy consultant'' to keep the resistant front office from getting suspicious. Keaton pinpointed a problem with *A Southern Yankee* right away, noting that when the film began, Skelton, who plays a bumbling northern spy down South, acted like an imbecile and alienated the audience, and so the scenes were re-shot to tone down Skelton's nutty behavior. Keaton also contributed the classic gag where Skelton wears a uniform that is half-Union and half-Confeder-ate, strolling between the two sides to cheers until the charade is discovered.

In *The Yellow Cab Man,* Skelton played a would-be inventor of unbreakable glass and other ''safety'' devices, and featured a classic routine about Skelton's first day at driving a cab. He was also loaned out to Columbia for *The Fuller Brush Man* (1948), where he played a door-to-door salesman who becomes involved in a murder, which was successful enough to spawn a follow-up, *The Fuller Brush Girl* (1950), starring Lucille Ball, in which Skelton made brief appearance.

One of Skelton's most memorable quips occurred on the occasion of Columbia head Harry Cohen's death. When someone remarked on the large number of people who turned out for the hated studio head's funeral, Skelton returned, ''Give the people what they want, and they'll come out for it.''

Skelton's true medium, however, turned out to be television as his remaining film comedies proved rather lackluster. His final film appearance was in a series of comedy sketches at the beginning of *The Daring Young Men and Their Flying Machines* where Skelton mimed various aviation pioneers and their unsuccessful efforts. It was on television where Skelton was most popular and most beloved.

One of Skelton's earliest writers was legendary television host Johnny Carson, who got his first on-camera big break when Skelton knocked himself unconscious one day during rehearsal and Carson was quickly summoned to fill in—CBS liked his appearance enough to offer him his own show in 1955.

Skelton was an inveterate ad libber, much to the consternation of his guest stars who expected him to follow the script (Tim Burton's movie *Ed Wood* (1994) captures the confusion of Bela Lugosi when he appeared on the show). Skelton delighted in getting his guest stars to break up on camera. The rock band the Rolling Stones made one of their earliest television appearances on Skelton's show.

As his professional life was soaring, however, his personal life turned grim. His nine-year-old son Richard Jr. died of leukemia and his second wife tried to commit suicide. Skelton's work became more maudlin and he began losing his audience. He spent his declining years painting a large series of clown faces which were sold in art galleries across the country. These paintings proved enormously lucrative. He died from pneumonia in 1997 at his home in Rancho Mirage, California.

With his television episodes rarely revived, Skelton is in danger of becoming increasingly forgotten, which is a pity because he was a talented comic with a genuinely inspired gift of mimicry. His gifts put him in the same league as Marcel Marceau. One of the most popular comics of the 1940s and 1950s, he was awarded a Golden Globe for Best Television Series in 1959, and received a Cecil B. DeMille Golden Globe years later, as well as a Governor's award from the Emmys in honor of his contributions.

—Dennis Fischer

FURTHER READING:

Maltin, Leonard. *The Great Movie Comedians.* Harmony Books, 1982.

Siegel, Scott, and Barbara Siegel. *American Film Comedy.* Prentice Hall, 1994.

Skyscrapers

The ''skyscraper'' is a uniquely American invention that has come to symbolize the cultural and economic predominance of the United States in the twentieth century. With the invention of the elevator in 1859 and the development of new building materials and

Several skyscrapers across a cityscape.

techniques, tall buildings have been occupying the heart of American cities since the late nineteenth century. They are both soaring examples of technological capability and symbols of deeper concerns. As architectural historian Carol Willis wrote in a 1995 book: ''Skyscrapers are the ultimate architecture of capitalism. The first blueprint for every tall building is a balance sheet of estimated costs and returns.'' The modern city, center of economic activity and capital of culture, is unimaginable without skyscrapers.

While the definition of what qualifies as a skyscraper has changed over the years with increasing technological capabilities, the inherent elements remain the same as a century ago—a tall building of stacked, repetitive office spaces (and sometimes retail and/or residential spaces) located in an urban setting. In 1900, the Park Row Building in New York City was the world's tallest at 382 feet and 32 stories. Today, it would be dwarfed in most large cities. In 1997, the twin 1,476-foot Petronas Towers were completed in Kuala Lumpur, Malaysia, surpassing Chicago's Sears Tower as the tallest occupied building in the world. The fact that they were built in Asia demonstrated the emerging economic power of the region in the late twentieth century and the exportation of American cultural symbols and economic models to all parts of the world.

The century-long evolution of the skyscraper from five-story building to 1,000-foot-plus tower was influenced by many factors. Three of the most important influences were the invention of the passenger elevator by Elisha Graves Otis in the 1850s, the development of steel framing by William LeBaron Jenney of Chicago in the 1880s, and the escalation of real estate prices in downtown areas.

Other factors included stylistic trends, legislation in the form of height restrictions, and civic competition (mainly between New York and Chicago). The first identifiable skyscrapers appeared in Chicago in the 1880s. Masonry buildings, where the stone walls actually carry the weight of the building, were approaching the limits of their capacity. The 16-story Monadnock Building (1891) in Chicago remains the world's tallest masonry building; because of the load created by this height, the Monadnock's walls are six feet thick at the base. By the time of its completion, however, a totally new generation of Chicago-style skyscraper construction was in progress, led by Louis Sullivan, who wrote a famous essay in 1896 entitled ''The Tall Office Building Artistically Considered.'' With the invention of the steel-frame building, in which a lightweight steel skeleton is covered by a masonry skin emphasizing their verticality, buildings could rise higher and provide more interior space while more nearly expressing the spirit of the industrial age. Such tall buildings soon appeared in New York and other cities as downtown real estate became more expensive; the only logical solution was to build upward. The steel-frame building and its derivatives proved indispensable in the development of the twentieth-century American city.

Skyscrapers embody many things, including technical achievement, economic prosperity, urban congestion, and civic and corporate pride. The extent to which the skyscraper has become an American icon demonstrates how corporate capitalism has come to represent America to the rest of the world. Tall buildings have become instantly recognizable urban symbols at home as well. They appear in countless movies and television shows, and have been the subject of paintings, poems, and musical compositions. The Empire State Building in New York, the world's tallest building for four midcentury decades (1931-1972) is one of the most famous silhouettes in the world. Skyscrapers provide an instantaneous means of identification in the modern world; they can be used as shorthand for the anonymous twentieth-century city, like the incomparable forest of tall buildings that occupy the tip of lower Manhattan. Individual buildings like the Empire State Building (1931), Chicago's Sears Tower (1974) and San Francisco's Transamerica Pyramid (1972), stand as prominent civic symbols and tourist attractions, as does the RCA Building (now the GE Building) in the modern Rockefeller Center complex whose original core complex was completed in 1940. One of the most daring and atypical skyscraper designs was never realized: Frank Lloyd Wright's visionary 1930s proposal for a mile-high skyscraper rising not in a congested urban downtown but in the midst of a planned rural complex he called Broadacre City.

More important, however, is the manner in which tall buildings have been used as advertising for America's businesses. In the early 1900s, corporate capitalists discovered that the skyscraper was a more effective advertisement than any billboard, newspaper, or magazine ad. Beginning with Cass Gilbert's Woolworth Building (1913) in New York—the world's tallest building at the time, designed in a striking Neo-Gothic style—skyscrapers have become indelibly linked with America's top companies. Prominent examples of the tall building as corporate symbol include the Gothic-style Chicago Tribune Tower (1922); the American Art Deco Chrysler Building (1930, New York); two International Style skyscrapers: the Seagram Building (1958, New York) and the John Hancock Center (1968, Chicago); and the postmodern AT&T Building (1984, New York). The skyscraper form proved so popular that it was also applied outside the business world. The Nebraska State Capital, designed by Bertram Goodhue and completed in 1932, combined a two-story base with a soaring 400-foot tower that copies the setback style of New York skyscrapers. The United Nations Secretariat (1950) designed by Le Corbusier, and Lakeshore Drive Apartments (1951-52), designed by Mies van der Rohe, are typical examples of a European High Modernist interpretation of an originally American architectural form; these buildings helped pave the way for the International Style ''glass boxes'' typically seen in mid-Manhattan and elsewhere, a style that would become pervasive in the 1950s and 1960s in many other cities of the West. Such incursions of business imagery into the political realm testify to the growing power of business in what has been called ''the American Century.''

Among their other functions, skyscrapers are an index to the economic health of a society. Certain ''boom'' periods have given rise to a proliferation of tall buildings in various cities; Chicago in the 1880s, New York in the 1920s, and Houston in the 1980s are salient examples. By the late 1990s, almost every American city of decent size has at least one tall building—even where real-estate prices do not require them. The skyscraper is a technological and economic solution to an urban problem that has been transformed into a status symbol for cities and developers alike. Because it fulfills so many functions, the skyscraper has proven to be the typical building type for the modern urban world.

—Dale Allen Gyure

FURTHER READING:

Douglas, George H. *Skyscrapers: A Social History of the Very Tall Building in America.* Jefferson, North Carolina and London, McFarland & Company, 1996.

Dupré, Judith. *Skyscrapers.* New York, Black Dog & Leventhal Publishers, 1996.

Goldberger, Paul. *The Skyscraper.* New York, Alfred A. Knopf, 1992.

Huxtable, Ada Louise. *The Tall Building Artistically Reconsidered.* New York, Pantheon, 1984.

Van Leeuwen, Thomas A. P. *The Skyward Trend of Thought.* The Hague, AHA Books, 1986.

Willis, Carol. *Form Follows Finance: Skyscrapers and Skylines in New York and Chicago.* New York, Princeton Architectural Press, 1995.

Slaney, Mary Decker (1958—)

Mary Decker Slaney, the first woman to win the prestigious Jesse Owens track and field award, is considered to be America's greatest mid-distance runner. Slaney won both the 1,500 and 3,000 meters at the 1983 World Championships in Helsinki, has set 36 American and 17 world records, and still holds four American records, all set between 1983 and 1985. In a career that began at age 11, Slaney, who set her first world record at age 14, has established herself as a world-class runner despite a series of painful injuries and remarkable recoveries (19 operations) as well as exercise-induced asthma. After four Olympic tries, Slaney has yet to win a medal. After a successful comeback in 1997 at age 39, however, she made plans to run in the year 2000 Sydney Olympics.

—John R. Deitrick

FURTHER READING:

Kardong, Don. "Bright Speed." *Runner's World.* July, 1997, 86-90.

Slang

Slang is unconventional, hard-hitting, metaphorical language that is colloquial, sometimes vulgar, and always innovative—nothing registers change in cultural thought faster or more dramatically than slang. Lexicologist Stuart Berg Flexner defines slang more precisely as "the body of words and expressions frequently used by or intelligible to a rather large portion of the general American public, but not accepted as good, formal usage by the majority." Linguists Lars Andersson and Peter Trudgill, on the other hand, claim there is no good definition of slang and quote the poet Carl Sandburg: "Slang is a language that rolls up its sleeves, spits on its hands, and goes to work." Although linguists make no value judgments on levels of language, the general public seldom views slang without passion. It is seen as either a harbinger of hope and change (particularly among the young) or as a threat to what is perceived as "proper" language and society.

Informal and spoken rather than formal and written, slang is not the same as dialect, nor is it equal to swearing, although it may take on a vulgar edge, and it almost always evokes negative attitudes. Characterized by its ability to startle, slang falls below the "neutral register" of daily speech: terms such as "whore," "ho," "tart," and "slagheap" for the neutral "prostitute," for example. Perhaps most importantly, slang changes its identity according to who is speaking. What is slang to one, to another is not, depending on one's educational, economic, or social position, and even according to location and generation. Slang is generated from any number of specific language communities or subgroups: jazz musicians, college students, narcotics addicts, immigrants, the military, show business, street gangs, etc. From each of these sometimes overlapping groups come specific terms which identify practices and behaviors particular to its members. Distinct lifestyle choices fuel the need to find a language to name evolving social behaviors and thought, which often challenge more established cultural codes. "Mallie," a term unthinkable prior to the rise of American shopping malls, refers to persons (usually young) who frequent shopping malls for sociability and entertainment. Although most slang is generated by male speakers, the rise of feminism has spawned a female slang or "girl talk," showing the degree to which ideas about gender are changing. Because slang is spoken rather than written, it lacks the status of standard written English. Once slang terms appear in dictionaries, they are seen as having gained currency and, therefore, fuller entrance into the culture. Until then, slang is fully accessible only to insiders of particular subgroups.

Slang also changes over time, and either disappears quickly or becomes fully integrated into the language. Few, if any, would now recognize the word "knucker," which originated from the criminal world of the mid-1880s, but most would understand its current incarnation, "pickpocket," which originated from late eighteenth-century criminal slang. Drug slang changes quickly, in part so that drug dealers can more easily spot undercover agents. "Phone," "bike," and "bus," once slang versions of the more formal "telephone," "bicycle," and "omnibus," have now all but replaced the original terms. Most slang coinages are local in both time and place; much of it, like other cultural phenomena, originates in such large cities as New York or London and fans out to distant towns and cities.

The exact origin of slang is not known, although given the nature of language as a living, changing entity, it is probably as old as language itself. Andersson and Trudgill identify Aristophanes, the fourth-century-B.C. Greek playwright, as the first writer to use slang. The Roman writers Plautus, Horace, Juvenal, and Petronius also employed slang for stylistic purposes. Shakespeare also used slang in his plays. During the nineteenth and twentieth centuries, underworld criminal societies became rich and potent sources of slang, some of which is reflected in early detective fiction by such writers as Wilkie Collins and Agatha Christie.

What differentiates slang from other categories of speech (such as jargon or argot) is one's reasons for using it. In *Slang, Today and Yesterday,* Eric Partridge identifies several reasons for using slang, including the desire to be different, novel, or picturesque; to enrich the language; to engage in playfulness; to identify one's self with a certain school, trade, or social class; to reduce or disperse the pomposity or excessive seriousness of an occasion; to be secret. Slang is always used self-consciously, with a desire to create a particular identity. One might say (but not write) affectionately, "Sweetheart, you da cat's meow," or "Yo—what's happenin'?"

In the twentieth century, the development of slang has paralleled the rise of dominant cultural movements throughout the decades. The 1920s left its mark with jazz and the rise of the machine, creating such terms as "flapper" (a female dancer in a short skirt) and "percolate" (to run smoothly). The 1930s contributed "dehorn," a hobo word for bootleg whiskey or denatured alcohol, and such railroad slang as "groundhog," meaning a train's brake operator. The 1940s was the decade of the military with such coinages as "pea-shooter," from World War II Army Air Force pilots to denote a fighter pilot or plane, and the word "buddy" (meaning "pal"), which, although created in the 1800s, was heavily used by American GIs and took on a particularly sentimental connotation. This term later evolved into several variations such as "ace boon" or "ace buddy" in the black community. The 1950s' beatnik generation revived 1930s jive talk and used such enduring slang phrases as "cool it" to mean relax, and such colorful phrases as "cool as a Christian with aces wired" to signify someone who is tranquilly confident.

By the 1960s, political unrest resulted in the use of such words as "Dove" and "Hawk," which by the 1980s became accepted terms for antiwar advocates and the military. The youth culture (or "NOW generation") coined such phrases as "where it's at" to signify being up-to-date, and also used the term "groady" (with variations of "grotty" and "groddy") to denote anything that was disgusting, nasty, or repellent. Often this was followed by the phrase "to the max" for emphasis. The 1970s' drug scene left numerous terms:

"crack" for cocaine and "narc" for undercover agent (which actually comes from Romany, "nak" or nose). During the 1990s, computers created not only a whole new way of life, but a language to describe it, although this resulted in a computer jargon rather than a computer slang. Nonetheless, such terms as "PC" (personal computer) and "e-mail" (electronic mail) were not even thought of prior to the development and widespread use of personal computers. By the end of the 1990s, the term "Y2K" had gained widespread usage to signify "the year 2000," with particular reference to anticipated problems stemming from the inability of existing programs to recognize dates beyond the year 1999.

While slang itself always reflects contemporary trends of thought, the practice of recording slang in Anglo-American dictionaries goes back more than two hundred years. The British antiquarian Francis Grose published *A Classical Dictionary of the Vulgar Tongue* in 1785, the first known lexicon of slang. Grose's work went through several editions and remained the seminal work in the field until John C. Hotten's *A Dictionary of Modern Slang, Cant, and Vulgar Words* was published in 1859. From the latter nineteenth century through the early twentieth century, several dictionaries of slang were produced, but it was not until 1937 when Eric Partridge published the landmark *A Dictionary of Slang and Unconventional English,* that slang was bestowed with respectability. This text was enlarged and reprinted several times through the 1980s and remains one of the best resources available. Also significant was Harold Wentworth and Stuart Berg Flexner's *Dictionary of American Slang,* published in 1960.

Since then, numerous dictionaries of slang have appeared. The titles of these texts alone trace the degree to which slang has become more accepted by the general public; by the late 1990s, slang was viewed with an increasing degree of amusement, as illustrated in such playful titles as *Juba to Jive: A Dictionary of African-American Slang.* As public sentiment moved toward a greater sense of multiculturalism during the 1990s, slang enjoyed increased acceptance, although with a recognition of its lower than standard status in the language.

—Lolly Ockerstrom

FURTHER READING:

Andersson, Lars, and Peter Trudgill. "Slang." *Bad Language.* Cambridge, Massachusetts, Basil Blackwell, 1990.

Chapman, Robert L., editor. *New Dictionary of American Slang.* New York, Harper and Row, 1986.

Flexner, Stuart Berg. "Preface to the Dictionary of American Slang." *New Dictionary of American Slang.* Edited by Robert L. Chapman. New York, Harper and Row, 1986.

Lewin, Esther, and Albert E. Lewin. *The Thesaurus of Slang.* New York, Facts on File, 1994.

Major, Clarence, editor. *Juba to Jive: A Dictionary of African-American Slang.* New York, Penguin, 1994.

Partridge, Eric. *A Dictionary of American Slang and Unconventional English.* New York, Macmillan, 1953.

———. *Slang, Today and Yesterday.* 2nd Ed. London, George Routledge and Sons, 1935.

Rawson, Hugh. *Wicked Words: A Treasury of Curses, Insults, Put-Downs, and Other Formerly Unprintable Terms from Anglo Saxon Times to the Present.* New York, Crown Trade Paperback, 1989.

Spears, Richard A., editor. *Slang and Euphemism: A Dictionary of Oaths, Curses, Insults, Ethnic Slurs, Sexual Slang and Metaphor, Drug Talk, College Lingo and Related Matters.* New York, Signet, 1991.

Wentworth, Harold, and Stuart Berg Flexner, editors. *Dictionary of American Slang.* New York, Thomas Y. Crowell, 1960.

Slasher Movies

With the possible exception of the hardcore porn flick, no modern film genre has managed to achieve quite the level of commercial success in spite (or because) of its inherent controversiality as has the slasher movie. Otherwise known as the "stalker," "dead babysitter," or "teenie-kill" pic, the "slasher" label has been adopted by most fans and critics to designate the entries in a voluminous collection of remarkably similar post-1960 horror films. In these movies, isolated psychotic males, often masked or at least hidden from view, are pitted against one or more young men and women (especially the latter) whose looks, personalities, or promiscuities serve to trigger recollections of some past trauma in the killer's mind, thereby unleashing his seemingly boundless psychosexual fury.

Although the precise formula of the slasher movie varies depending on one's initial characterization, the genre's exploration (at times its exploitation) of some or all of the following themes has remained strikingly consistent through the years: male-upon-female voyeurism, gender confusion and sexual perversion, the spectacle of murder, the efficacy of female self-defense, the substitution of violent killing for sexual gratification, and the utter inability of traditional authority figures to eliminate a communal threat. Vilified by feminists for supposedly promoting misogynistic messages and targeted for censorship by outraged parents and lawmakers, the slasher movie has nevertheless been treated as unworthy of critical discussion by most mainstream academics, presumably because of its "low-culture" status. In recent years, however, the progressive potential of a genre once dismissed as "violent pornography" has been examined by film theorists as well as cultural historians.

The slasher has its roots in two 1960 films, Alfred Hitchcock's *Psycho* and Michael Powell's *Peeping Tom.* Although the former movie has since received immeasurably more critical and commercial attention than the latter, together they are responsible for establishing many of the slasher's primary generic elements. These elements include an "explanation" of the killer's motive in quasi-psychoanalytic terms, a figuring of the main victim as a sexually transgressive female, and a focus on intimate assault with sharp, phallic, penetrating implements. It is tempting to read the subsequent history of the slasher as little more than elaborations on the themes introduced in these two films.

Like *Psycho* before it, Tobe Hooper's *The Texas Chainsaw Massacre* (1974) took for inspiration the monstrous crimes of necrophilic serial killer Ed Gein. Unlike *Psycho,* however, Hooper's film emphasized gore and bodily carnage, thereby situating itself within the tradition of Herschell Gordon Lewis's notorious ''splatter'' films, *Blood Feast* (1963) and *The Wizard of Gore* (1968). *The Texas Chainsaw Massacre* also contributed two important elements of its own to the slasher movie formula: a group of adolescent victims who are picked off one by one, and a ''final girl'' who undergoes a lengthy, terrifying ordeal in the film's second half, only to come out alive at the end. Although John Carpenter's *Halloween* (1978) eschewed the gore of *Texas Chainsaw Massacre* in favor of impressively subtle startle effects, it kept the latter film's youthful victims, and made its final girl (Jamie Lee Curtis, daughter of *Psycho* star Janet Leigh) even more aggressive and self-reliant. The unprecedented commercial success of this movie ensured its place at the head of the ''Stalker Cycle'' class; between 1978 and 1981, no fewer than 11 *Halloween*-inspired slashers were made (including *Friday the 13th, Prom Night, Terror Train,* and *Graduation Day*), all structural, if not quite stylistic, copies of the original. In these movies, the predator-prey theme takes on unprecedented importance, as does the emphasis on ''creative'' murders, and a reliance on camera shots taken from the killer's point of view. To what extent this camerawork forces viewer identification with the killer, however, remains an open question.

Despite the final girl's ever-increasing strength and ferocity—as exemplified by ''Ripley'' (Sigourney Weaver) in the *Alien* series of outer-space slashers—public debate over the genre's antisocial consequences only intensified in the 1980s. Representatives from numerous states, citing hastily acquired and somewhat dubious ''empirical evidence'' for support, complained of a direct cause-and-effect relationship between the depiction of graphic violence in films such as *Friday the 13th* and the increase in violent crimes perpetrated by youths. In 1984, the ''Video Recordings Bill'' passed through Britain's Parliament on the heels of an effort to restrict the consumption of arbitrarily designated ''video nasties'' (the vast majority of which were slashers). By 1989, bills were passed in Colorado, Missouri, Ohio, and Texas granting local prosecutors the power to decide which videos cross the line of ''excessive violence'' and so cannot be rented to persons under 18 without parental permission.

It is arguable that at least some of this negative attention was unnecessary, even self-defeating. By 1986 the slasher movie was in a state of decline, primarily because of an over-reliance on convention and a glut of predictable entries. But just like its best known psychopaths, Michael Myers and Jason Voorhees, the slasher would rise from the dead. *Fatal Attraction* (1987), *Pacific Heights* (1991), and especially the Oscar Award-winning *Silence of the Lambs* (1996)— the so-called ''yuppie slashers''—brought a heretofore unimagined respectability to the genre. And with the appearance of self-consciously reflexive slashers such as *Scream* (1996), *Scream 2* (1997), and *Halloween H20* (1998) came a whole new range of convention-bending possibilities.

One thing is clear: no easy answer to the question why slasher movies have proven so popular exists. Whether they enforce conservative values by demonstrating ''the inefficacy of sexual freedom'' (Vera Dika), promote tolerance by ''constituting a visible adjustment in the terms of gender representations'' (Carol Clover), or further a feminist agenda by ''articulating the legitimacy of female rage in the face of male aggression'' (Isabel Pinedo), it can hardly be denied that these films appeal to different audiences at different times and for different reasons or that they will continue to engender heated debate in homes, classrooms, and courtrooms.

—Steven Schneider

FURTHER READING:

Barker, Martin, editor. *The Video Nasties: Freedom and Censorship in the Media.* London, Pluto, 1984.

Clover, Carol J. *Men, Women, and Chain Saws: Gender in the Modern Horror Film.* Princeton, Princeton University Press, 1992.

Dika, Vera. ''The Stalker Film, 1978-81.'' In *American Horrors: Essays on the Modern American Horror Film,* edited by Gregory Waller. Urbana, University of Illinois Press, 1987, 86-101.

Pinedo, Isabel. ''. . . And Then She Killed Him: Women and Violence in the Slasher Film.'' In *Recreational Terror: Women and the Pleasures of Horror Film Viewing.* Albany, State University of New York Press, 1997, 69-95.

Schneider, Steven. ''Uncanny Realism and the Decline of the Modern Horror Film.'' *Paradoxa: Studies in World Literary Genres.* Vol. 3, No. 3-4, 1997, 417-428.

Slinky

Since its introduction to the public at Gimbels Department Store in Philadelphia in 1945, the Slinky has been one of the best-selling toys in America. This simple, steel spring developed by Richard James, a naval engineer who was trying to produce an anti-vibration device for ship instruments, has become one of the most widely recognized toys, with over 250 million Slinkys sold by the time of its fiftieth anniversary. When James and his wife, Betty, first demonstrated the Slinky's rhythmical step-by-step movement at Gimbels, they sold their entire lot of 400 Slinkys in ninety minutes.

In addition to playing with Slinkys, innovative Americans have used them as pecan-picking devices, envelope holders, light fixtures, and during the Vietnam War as makeshift radio antennae. Since 1962, children watching television have heard the Slinky jingle with its famous lines, ''It's Slinky, it's Slinky, for fun it's a wonderful toy/It's Slinky, it's Slinky, it's fun for a girl and a boy.'' In addition to being featured in television commercials, the Slinky has appeared in the films *Hairspray, Ace Ventura: When Nature Calls,* and as a leading, animated character, the Slinky Dog, in *Toy Story.* Slinkys have been manufactured in large-size, brightly colored plastic models for younger children, and the elite retailer Neiman Marcus sells an $80 gold Slinky. The original steel model sold in 1945 for one dollar. Fifty years later, in 1995, the same model (changed only by having its ends crimped for safety) sold for a mere one dollar and ninety-nine cents. Its low price has allowed for its presence, at one time or another, in nearly every American home.

—Sharon Brown

FURTHER READING:

Panati, Charles. *Extraordinary Origins of Everyday Things.* New York, Harper and Row, 1987.

The Slinky

Sly and the Family Stone

At their apogee, Sly and the Family Stone made music that broke racial and commercial barriers, combining soul, R & B, doo-wop, white rock, and British Invasion influences into an ineluctably delicious package that slithered and grooved and, at times, shouted from radios and turntables across America. For its time, the group's personnel was no less remarkable: an integrated, multi-gender line-up where the musicians switched instruments and roles with a fluidity as snaky as the band's trademark syncopated backbeat. Emerging in 1968, Sly and the Family Stone filled a vacuum in the musical landscape, presaging a whole new form of music-funk with their musical cross-pollination and incandescent live shows.

Sylvester Stewart, the guiding force behind this musical pot-pourri, was born in Texas and grew up in Vallejo, a tough oil-town across the Bay from San Francisco. As a child, Stewart sang in church choirs, playing music with his siblings and learning guitar, piano, and organ, among other instruments. From all accounts, Stewart was

Sly Stone

already something of a wunderkind by the time he met up with radio personality Tom Donahue and was hired as resident producer for Donahue's Autumn Records label. Sly produced much of the mid-1960s San Francisco rock music, crafting albums for groups like the Beau Brummels, the Mojo Men, and the Vejtables. But Sly was an imperious presence in the studio, a notorious perfectionist, and by the time the acid-rock groups began to beat a path to Autumn Records's doorstep, he decided he had more important things to do besides marshal stoned musicians (he allegedly forced Grace Slick and the Great Society through two hundred takes, resulting in exactly one completed song). Sly took a DJ job at a local black radio station where, always iconoclastic, he interspersed Beatles and Bob Dylan tracks among the regular Stax-Volt and Motown singles fare.

"The pop scene was then at a turning point," writes Dave Marsh, "Both Soul and Rock were trapped—the former by its own conventions, the latter by its increasing solemnity as it pursued High Art. Sensing a gap, Sly moved to fill it with his characteristic mixture of calculation, conviction, and dumb luck." He had formed a bar band and was regularly plying his trade with what would become the nucleus of Sly and the Family Stone while hunting for a record label. His first effort for Columbia, *A Whole New Thing,* being perhaps too

ahead of its time, was an unmitigated failure, but Columbia was interested enough to give him a second chance. Through the rest of the decade, Sly and the Family Stone registered an impressive list of hit singles, music as mold-breaking as it was danceable, with an ideological twist: part populist, part utopian hippie. In songs like "Dance to the Music," "Everyday People," "Everybody Is a Star," and "You Can Make It If You Try," Sly preached a message of total reconciliation, expressing, in the words of Marsh, "the sentiments of the Haight and hopes of the ghetto."

On stage, the band dressed like psychedelic peacocks, sporting fringes, satin shirts, leathers, and bangles. Musically, there were role reversals, epiphanies, unexpected surprises. The woman played instruments, the men sang, the whites grooved, the blacks freaked out. The result was a revelation and a call to arms; when Sly sang "I Want to Take You Higher"—as he did for two million at Woodstock—you believed him.

But being spokesperson for inner-racial unity is a tough act, and like Jimi Hendrix before him, Sly was resistant to becoming swept up in the internecine squabbles between the New Left and the black power groups. And there were other problems. As one of the highest paid performers in the business, excess was not simply a danger, it was almost de rigueur. Sly began missing shows, his behavior became more eccentric, and no new music was forthcoming, although his progeny were filling the charts with their versions of Sly's Whole New Thing. When he broke his silence late in 1971, the resultant album, *There's a Riot Goin' On,* took his formula and stood it on its head. It was an abstract, introspective album that shied away from declamations, acknowledging instead the bitter realities of racial inequity—utopia turned dystopic. It was the perfect soundtrack for the end of the 1960s, a brilliant synthesis of despair, and if the album's success was any measure—it rose to number one on the charts and generated three hit singles—Sly had once again hit the mark.

There's a Riot Goin' On was a tour de force, but it was also a blind alley. Apparently Sly was unable to extricate himself from this self-created musical cul-de-sac. As the seventies progressed, albums from Sly grew fewer, with longer gaps in between. A 1976 *Jet* magazine article reported Sly had gone broke. Rumors abounded that he had spiraled into addiction-fueled seclusion, living alone in his mansion without a telephone or much to eat. 1979 saw the release of a new album, *Back on the Right Track,* but apparently it was an aberration. The silence has continued.

In the dialectic of creativity, Sly's career followed a predictable arc from synthesis to innovation to decline, but if he could only go so far, he left in his wake a legion of imitators that kept his vision very much in evidence. Established soul groups let their hair down and started turning out records with a pointed political subtext. The slinky drum beats, slapped bass lines (a technique Stone bassist Larry Graham is credited with inventing), and minimalist keyboard arrangements were responsible for the evolution of funk and disco. And the sartorial splendor—rhinestones, leathers, gold lame—that was the band's trademark was embellished by everyone from George Clinton to Earth, Wind, and Fire. In their music and flamboyance, artists like Rick James and Prince would pay homage, but Sly and the Family Stone remained the template from which these disparate artists sprang. As Dave Marsh wrote, "No one has gone past them."

—Michael Baers

FURTHER READING:

Henderson, David. *19 Necromancers from Now.* Edited by Ishmael Reed. New York, Doubleday, 1970.

Marsh, Dave. *The Rolling Stone Illustrated History of Rock and Roll.* Edited by Jim Miller. New York, Random House/Rolling Stone Press, 1980.

Smith, Bessie (1894-1937)

Elizabeth ''Bessie'' Smith was born in Chattanooga, Tennessee, and became known as the ''empress of the blues.'' She began her career with Chappelle's Rabbit Foot Minstrels, starring Ma Rainey, who taught Smith the art of blues singing. Smith developed her own style of powerful and theatrical blues with a jazz orientation, which became the accepted classic blues style. Her first recording, ''Down Home Blues'' (1923), sold 800,000 copies. She recorded until 1933, toured extensively with her troupe, the Liberty Belles, and appeared in the film *St. Louis Blues* (1929). Smith died while touring when her car was hit by a truck and run off the road in Mississippi.

—Charles J. Shindo

FURTHER READING:

Albertson, Chris. *Bessie.* New York, Stein and Day, 1972.

Smith, Dean (1931—)

North Carolina's Dean Smith retired after the 1997 season as the all-time winningest head coach in college basketball. Smith's 879 wins over 36 years surpassed legendary Kentucky coach Adolph Rupp by three games. For twenty-seven consecutive years, Smith's squads won 20 or more games, and they captured two national titles along the way.

Smith coached some of the games best players during years at North Carolina, including Billy Cunningham, James Worthy, Mitch Kupchak, and Michael Jordan. Smith also saw many of his assistant coaches go on to become head coaches, including Roy Williams and Larry Brown. But the achievement of which Smith is most proud is that fact that 97 percent of his players graduated with a degree. In the 1980s and 1990s, as college hoops came to seem ever more glamourous under the bright lights of increasing television coverage, Smith represented the finest values of amateur athleticism.

—D. Byron Painter

FURTHER READING:

Chansky, Art, with Michael Jordan. *The Dean's List: A Celebration of Tar Heel Basketball and Dean Smith.* New York, Warner Books, 1997.

Wolff, Alexander. ''Fanfare for an Uncommon Man.'' *Sports Illustrated.* December 22, 1997, 32-43.

———. ''Dean Smith Unplugged.'' *Sports Illustrated.* December 22, 1997, 50-55.

Wulf, Steve. ''Tears for the Tar Heels: North Carolina Coach Dean Smith Takes Himself Out of the Game for Which He Has Done So Much.'' *Time.* October 20, 1997, 93.

Smith, Kate (1907-1986)

Long known as the ''first lady of radio,'' Kate Smith starred on CBS radio from 1931-1947, always opening with her theme song, ''When the Moon Comes Over the Mountain.'' The lyrics of this song were adapted from a poem Kate had written as a teenager to celebrate her native Shenandoah Mountain area. She was also associated in the public mind with Irving Berlin's ''God Bless America,'' which she introduced on Armistice Day in 1938. Berlin was so pleased with her treatment of the song that he granted her exclusive rights to sing it on radio in the late 1930s. Moving to television in later years, Smith's popularity continued, leading a pop music critic to write: ''For at least five decades, Kate Smith ranked close to apple pie, baseball, and the Statue of Liberty among America's best loved and most instantly recognized symbols.''

Smith became a household name from coast to coast within a month of her radio show's debut on her 22nd birthday, May 1, 1931. The long-running show, originally called ''The A&P Bandwagon,'' gave the first radio appearance to such show-business luminaries as Greta Garbo, John Barrymore, Bert Lahr, and Mary Boland. Comedians on their way to the top, including Abbott and Costello and Henny Youngman, were also first brought to national attention on her show.

Kate Smith

The great success of the new show caused NBC to move its popular *Amos 'n' Andy* comedy program to another time slot.

Smith's homey, small-town image flowed naturally out of her upbringing. Her birthplace was the small town of Greenville, Virginia, and she was originally billed on radio as "The Songbird of the South." As a child her singing talents were evident as she began early to sing in church services. During World War I, eight-year old Kate sang at Liberty Loan rallies, where she was introduced to President Woodrow Wilson.

After the war Smith entered amateur contests in the Washington, DC, area and aspired to a career behind the footlights. Her family, fearing that her increasing girth would make her the target of taunts in a theatrical career, insisted that she study nursing. She found that she was unhappy as a nursing student, however, and 16-year-old Kate tried out some song routines in Washington vaudeville houses and then headed for New York City. While waiting her turn in an amateur contest, she saw a young dancer bring down the house doing the Charleston and became convinced that despite her bulk she could do the vigorous, hip-wiggling dance herself. She worked it into her closing number and won a standing ovation. The show's headliner, Broadway star Eddie Dowling, hired her for a small part in a new musical, *Honeymoon Lane*, singing "Half a Moon" and dancing the Charleston. The *New York Times* review read: "*Honeymoon Lane* is Colorful & Lavish; Kate Smith, 250-pound Blues Singer, a Hit."

Several Broadway shows followed. Made up in blackface, she sang "Hallelujah" in Vincent Youman's *Hit the Deck* (1927). In George White's *Flying High* (1930) she played star Bert Lahr's mail-order bride and suffered his relentless jibes about her size. Every performance she heard him say, "When she sits down, it's like a dirigible coming in for a landing." After the show closed, she made her radio debut on the Rudy Vallee variety show, where she attracted the attention of Columbia Records executive Ted Collins, who offered her a recording contract and became her personal manager. Collins got Kate 11 weeks at the vaudeville pinnacle, New York's Palace, as well as a contract with CBS for a 15-minute network radio show four nights a week, and the show became an instant success that was to grow in popularity for the next 16 years. By 1933, during the Great Depression, Kate was making $3,000 a week, the highest salary of any woman in radio.

During the years of World War II, Kate traveled over a half-million miles to entertain service men and women, and she sold more than $600 million in war bonds. Her recording of "God Bless America" sold thousands of copies and, following the lead of Irving Berlin, she gave all her royalties to the Boy Scouts and Girl Scouts of America.

Smith moved to television in 1950, hosting a daytime variety show mainly for housewives. When her popularity lessened in the 1960s, Ted Collins, noting that Judy Garland's career had been rekindled with a famous concert, arranged for Kate to appear at Carnegie Hall in 1963. From this came a new RCA recording contract and numerous guest appearances on television. When Ted Collins died the following year, Kate stopped performing. Her career had another rebirth several years later when the Philadelphia Flyers hockey team discovered that they always won when Kate's record of "God Bless America" preceded the game. The team made her the official team sweetheart, and she was invited for guest appearances on shows hosted by Ed Sullivan, Jackie Gleason, Dean Martin, and the Smothers Brothers.

In the mid-1970s Kate began a major national tour, only to have it interrupted in Lincoln, Nebraska, by an illness that caused the remainder of the tour to be canceled. Severe diabetes made her a virtual recluse for the next ten years. In 1982 she was awarded the U.S. Medal of Freedom by president Ronald Reagan. George T. Simon, former *Metronome* editor, observed, "From 1931 onward, Kate Smith did indeed seem to personify the country—idealistic, generous, home-spun, sentimental, emotional, and proud."

—Benjamin Griffith

FURTHER READING:

Hayes, Richard K. *Kate Smith: A Biography.* Jefferson, North Carolina, McFarland, 1995.

Hemming, Roy, and David Hajdu. *Discovering Great Singers of Classic Pop.* New York, Newmarket, 1991.

Lackmann, Ron. *Same Time . . . Same Station: An A-Z Guide to Radio from Jack Benny to Howard Stern.* New York, Facts on File, 1996.

Pitts, Michael R. *Kate Smith: A Bio-bibliography.* New York, Greenwood Press, 1988.

Smith, Patti (1946—)

Poet, performer, and "queen of punk" Patti Smith made her mark in the disparate worlds of punk, rock and roll, and poetry, with seven albums, six books of poetry, and a world-renowned performing

Patti Smith

style. "Three chord rock merged with the power of the word," Patti Smith's first album *Horses* described itself in 1975.

Smith was born in Chicago but raised in Woodbury, in rural southern New Jersey, the eldest of Grant and Beverly Smith's four children. Isolated and sickly as a child, Patti was encouraged to be creative by her mother and lived an intense, imaginary life in games with her siblings and, as she grew older, in her writing, fed by the work of Arthur Rimbaud, Bob Dylan, James Brown, and the Rolling Stones. A literate punk icon in the 1970s, Smith achieved her greatest success with the single "Because the Night," off her album *Easter* (1978). In 1979, Smith left performing for marriage and children in suburban Detroit with Fred Smith, ex-MC5 guitarist and leader of Detroit's Sonic Rendevous Band. In 1994 Patti lost her husband, Fred Smith, her brother, Todd Smith, and her longtime friend and former lover, Robert Mapplethorpe, to various early deaths. She slowly returned to performing and publishing with a book of poems, *Early Work* (1994), and an album, *Gone Again* (1996).

—Celia White

FURTHER READING:

Johnstone, Nick. *Patti Smith: A Biography.* United Kingdom, Omnibus Press, 1997.

Roach, Dusty. *Patti Smith: Rock and Roll Madonna.* South Bend, Indiana, And Books, 1979.

Smith, Patti. *Early Work, 1970-1979.* New York, W. W. Norton, 1994.

———. *Patti Smith Complete: Lyrics, Reflections and Notes for the Future.* New York, Doubleday, 1998.

Smith, Rosamond

See Oates, Joyce Carol

Smithsonian Institution

Established by an Act of Congress in 1846 with the bequest of English scientist James Smithson, the Smithsonian Institution is a research center that holds some one hundred million artifacts and specimens in sixteen museums and galleries. The mission of the Institution includes public education, national service, and scholarship in the arts, sciences, and history. Artifacts held by the Smithsonian include the Wright Brothers' 1903 Flyer, the Hope Diamond (the world's largest deep blue diamond), the Star Spangled Banner, Judy Garland's Red Slippers from *The Wizard of Oz,* Harrison Ford's fedora and leather jacket from *Raiders of the Lost Ark*, and Archie Bunker's chair and Fonzie's leather jacket from the television shows *All in the Family* and *Happy Days*, respectively. Duke Ellington's papers are housed in the Smithsonian and the Institution also owns the Folkways Records back catalog.

Museums and galleries of the Smithsonian include the National Air and Space Museum, the National Museum of American History, the National Museum of African Art, the National Museum of Natural History, the National Museum of American Art, and the National Portrait Gallery, all of which are in Washington, D.C. The Smithsonian-run Cooper-Hewitt National Design Museum and the National

Museum of the American Indian are in New York City. The Smithsonian is also responsible for the National Zoo and a number of scientific research institutes.

Many of the museums are located on the Mall in Washington and a visit to the Capitol seems to require an obligatory visit to at least one of these buildings. From April through October the various Washington locales of the Smithsonian are packed with visitors. One summer highlight is the Festival of Folklife, which explores the diversity of American and world cultures, that takes place on the Mall in late June and early July.

In 1970 the Institution launched its own magazine, *Smithsonian,* which carries general readership articles on the arts, the environment, sciences, and popular culture. The magazine has a readership approaching eight million. Another magazine, *Air & Space/Smithsonian,* was created as an extension of the Smithsonian Institution's National Air and Space Museum. It examines the culture of aviation and space.

In 1995 the Smithsonian launched its home page (www.si.edu) on the World Wide Web and has since averaged over four million "hits" per month. The site has grown to contain a wealth of information on the various activities and collections of the Smithsonian.

In the 1990s the Smithsonian engendered considerable controversy with its exhibition, *The West as America,* at the National Museum of American Art and its proposed *Enola Gay* exhibition at the National Air and Space Museum to mark the fiftieth anniversary of the atomic bombing of Hiroshima and Nagasaki. These exhibitions questioned received versions of history and the outrage generated broad public debates about history, culture, and the role of academics and museums.

The Smithsonian Institution is a repository of American cultural artifacts. The diversity of its collections and activities place it at the center of public understanding of American history and culture.

—Ian Gordon

FURTHER READING:

America's Smithsonian: Celebrating 150 Years. Washington, D.C., Smithsonian Institution Press, 1996.

Conaway, John. *The Smithsonian: 150 Years of Adventure, Discovery, and Wonder.* Washington, D.C., Smithsonian Institution Press, 1995.

"History and the Public: What Can We Handle? A Roundtable about History after the *Enola Gay* Controversy." *Journal of American History.* Vol. 82, No. 3, 1995, 1029-1144.

Smits, Jimmy (1945—)

Emmy Award-winning television, film, and stage actor Jimmy Smits is one of a very small handful of highly visible Hispanic actors. A co-founder of the National Hispanic Foundation for the Arts, an organization whose mission is to establish opportunities for Hispanic Americans in entertainment, Smits has used his immense popularity and fame—both of which derive in part from his stunning good looks—to publicize the cause of Hispanics and other minority groups in the entertainment industry. An elegant and truthful actor with a persona that combines charm, sex appeal, and vulnerability with a tough and steely inner core, Smits carved a place for himself as an

Jimmy Smits

smoldering Mexican soldier in *Old Gringo* (1989), and a role in the 1997 Chicano family drama *Mi Familia* (*My Family*)—both of them critically respected but commercially unspectacular features—he made only a handful of forgettable films.

Bochco and ABC came to the rescue in 1994, when he joined *NYPD Blue* in its second season. For the next five years, he delivered an elegant, understated portrayal of a quietly complex character, in perfect counterpoint to the explosive acting of Dennis Franz as Simone's troubled, sometimes bigoted partner, Andy Sipowicz. The gritty cop drama was controversial from the outset because of its coarse language and explicit sexual content and, during its first season, many network affiliates refused to carry it. Despite (or maybe because of) this, it was an almost immediate ratings success, as were its sometimes ambiguous lead characters, multi-dimensional and complex, following a trend already set in other cop series such as *Homicide: Life on the Streets* and *Law and Order*. Smits was thoroughly convincing as an introspective widower who joins the 15th precinct after months of tending to his dying wife, and who raises homing pigeons as a hobby. However, the fact that Bobby Simone was conceived as being of French-Portuguese rather than Hispanic descent drew some criticism, emphasized by the fact that the only Hispanic officer was played by an actor of Italian heritage (Nicholas Turturro).

In 1998, with his contract up and due for renewal, Jimmy Smits decided to leave *NYPD Blue* in search of fresh challenges. The challenge to the program in finding a way to write him out resulted in a sequence of tense and tearjerking episodes in which Bobby Simone succumbs to previously undetected heart disease. This turn of events in the plot all but dominated the 1998 series and tested Smits' acting abilities to the limit. He passed with flying colors.

—Joyce Linehan

FURTHER READING:

Cole, Melanie. *Jimmy Smits*. Childs, Maryland, Mitchell Lane, 1998.

American cultural icon when he was cast in Steven Bochco's landmark television ensemble drama series, *L. A. Law* (1986-1991) and went on to an even higher profile as detective Bobby Simone in Bochco's hard-hitting cop series, *NYPD Blue* (1994-1998).

Born in Brooklyn, New York, on July 9, 1955 to a Puerto Rican mother and a South American (Suriname) father, Smits was raised mostly in Brooklyn, though he did live in Puerto Rico for a short time between the ages of nine and 11. While attending school at Thomas Jefferson High, he made the championship football team, but quit playing to become the star of the school's drama club. He went to Brooklyn College where he got his B.A. in Education, and worked for a while as a teacher before becoming a student again, earning his Master's degree in Theater Arts from Cornell in 1982. After graduating, he traveled around the country working in repertory theater until 1984, when he made his television debut in the pilot episode of *Miami Vice*. The experience was short-lived: cast as Don Johnson's partner, he was killed in the course of the episode.

Then, in 1986, Smits landed the ongoing part of Victor Sifuentes, Hispanic public defender turned corporate litigator, in Bochco's critically acclaimed and wildly successful *L. A. Law* for NBC. (The number of law school applications in the United States increased dramatically at the height of the show's popularity). The role of Sifuentes catapulted Smits into stardom, and he became a heartthrob and sex symbol much as George Clooney would in *E.R.* a few years later. He was nominated for a Best Supporting Actor Emmy every year, finally winning it in 1990, but left the show in 1991 to pursue opportunities on the big screen. However, with the exception of his co-starring appearance, alongside Jane Fonda and Gregory Peck, as a

The Smothers Brothers

Comedy/singing team the Smothers Brothers has been entertaining audiences on stage, record album, and, most famously, on television for more than 40 years. "Mom always liked you best!" stuttering, slow-witted comic dunce Tom Smothers on guitar would complain to his supercilious, smooth-talking, straight-man brother Dick on bass as they both crooned folk songs and engaged in comic banter, often with pointed political overtones. The Smothers Brothers' penchant for political satire resulted, in the late 1960s, in one of the most celebrated and infamous cases of television censorship as the brothers battled their network, CBS, over the antiwar and countercultural content of their top-rated variety series, *The Smothers Brothers Comedy Hour*—a precursor of later shows such as *Saturday Night Live*. Attempting to bring some of the political and social turmoil of the era into prime time, the Smothers Brothers discovered the limits set by American commercial television in the 1960s for controversial material in entertainment. Their variety show, with its ongoing battles against network censorship, become a flash point of debate about the role of popular entertainment in the process of social change.

Tom (left) and Dick Smothers

Nothing much in the Smothers' background would indicate that they would become rebels against the system. Tom and Dick, born, respectively, in 1937 and 1938, were sons of West Pointer Thomas Bowen Smothers, who died in a POW camp during the Second World War. The boys were raised by their mother and a stepfather in Redondo Beach, California. Their comic career began while students at San Jose State College where they found themselves working the burgeoning folk circuit of college clubs, blending accomplished folksinging with eminently clean-cut comedy. Their first big break into television came in 1961 when Jack Paar introduced them to a national audience on his show. A few years later, CBS gave the Smothers their first television series. Running for only one season, 1965-66, *The Smothers Brothers Show* featured Tom and Dick in a situation comedy. Similar to other contemporary "magical" shows like *My Mother the Car, My Favorite Martian,* and *Bewitched,* the Smothers' series had Tom as an apprentice angel who made life difficult for his mortal brother Dick. The series failed, but CBS remained committed to finding a more appropriate vehicle for the Smothers Brothers' talents.

Debuting on Sunday night in February 1967, *The Smothers Brothers Comedy Hour,* a variety show, found itself in an unenviable position scheduled next to the long-standing, top-rated NBC stalwart *Bonanza.* CBS's strategy for the *Comedy Hour* was to attract a younger, more urbane audience than was traditionally drawn to the rival network's horse opera. The gambit worked. *The Smothers Brothers Comedy Hour* cracked the top 20 Nielsen ratings in its first two years on the air, and in its second helped to dislodge *Bonanza* from its three-year run as the number-one-ranked series in the country.

In its first season, the series played things fairly safe. The brothers attempted to appeal both to the burgeoning generation of disaffected and politicized baby boomers as well as to the parents. According to *Time* magazine, the Smothers were "hippies with haircuts." The show featured countercultural bands like Buffalo Springfield singing its anthem of youthful paranoia and alienation, "For What It's Worth," and also middle-of-the-road Jim Nabors singing "The Impossible Dream." Like Ed Sullivan, the Smothers' show balanced the tastes and sensibilities of the increasingly polarized generations.

Controversy and censorship began to plague the series beginning most notably following the *Comedy Hour*'s second season premier, aired on September 10, 1967. The Smothers had invited folk singer Pete Seeger as a special guest. While the network expressed no qualms about having the previously blacklisted performer appear on the airways, CBS balked at a song Seeger proposed to sing: "Waist Deep in the Big Muddy." The song was an allegory about Vietnam and contained the following lyrics that CBS found unacceptable: "Now every time I read the papers / That old feelin' comes on / We're waist deep in the Big Muddy / And the big fool says to push on." The network disapproved of the disrespectful reference to the president as a fool and, further, felt political material such as this had no place on an entertainment show. The performance was summarily censored. The network's action led to an avalanche of public criticism of the network's high-handed action. Eventually, CBS relented and allowed Seeger to pay another visit to the Smothers' show later in the season where he was permitted to sing the song in its entirety.

Emboldened by the show's popularity, Tom Smothers began pushing for more confrontational and cutting-edge material. Despite his slow-witted persona, Tom was both highly intelligent and increasingly aligned with anti-establishment youth politics. He was also the major creative force behind the series. Pushing the envelope of political satire, sexual innuendo, and matters of taste, Tom dared CBS to censor his show. The network responded, and the battle was on. Some of the flaps between the show and the censors involved material that now seems benign. CBS objected to a sketch about sex education: the words "sex" and "sex education" were unacceptable. The network also objected to a sketch about censorship in which Tom and guest star Elaine May played motion picture censors at work objecting to the word "breast" in sequence. Says censor Elaine: "I think the word 'breast' should be cut out of the dinner scene. I think that 'breast' is a relatively tasteless thing to say while you're eating." CBS censors were not amused and blue penciled the entire sketch. The network was also uneasy with a recurring character on the show, Goldie O'Keefe, a kooky hippie whose comedy revolved around celebratory references to hallucinogenics. In a recurring sketch, a parody of advice shows for housewives titled "Share a Little Tea with Goldie," the character proclaimed, "A lot of you ladies have written in asking when I'm on. . . . Ladies, I'm on as often as possible and I highly recommend it." Some of the marijuana and LSD references evaded censorship as the elderly guardians of taste didn't understand that "Goldie," "tea" and "Keefe" were drug code words. Comedian David Steinberg created consternation for the network as well with a series of "sacrilegious" sermonettes. The network began demanding that the Smothers make preview copies of their episodes available for affiliated stations to review—a completely unprecedented move by any network.

The most infamous run-ins with the network involved the Smothers' increasingly unapologetic anti-establishment political material. In their third season premier in September 1968, CBS balked at letting guest star Harry Belafonte do a song criticizing the police and institutional violence meted out to youthful demonstrators at the Chicago Democratic Convention the previous month. The number included lyrics such as "Tell all the population / We're havin' a confrontation / Let it be known freedom's gone / And the country's not our own" to images of police rioting against unarmed demonstrators. The network axed the entire number and, to add insult to injury, sold the five minutes worth of air time to the Republican Party for a Nixon/Agnew campaign ad.

The escalating confrontations between Tom Smothers and the network eventually came to a head. On April 3, 1969, with a few weeks yet to go in the television season, Robert D. Wood, president of CBS television, informed Tom Smothers by wire that the brothers were fired. The ostensible reason was that the Smothers had not delivered an acceptable broadcast tape in time for preview by network censors and affiliated stations. The unprecedented forced removal of a television series from a network schedule led to public uproar. Tom Smothers attempted to launch a free speech campaign in Washington, D.C., to force the network to relent, but to no avail. Eventually, the Smothers filed a lawsuit against the network for wrongful dismissal. They won, but it was a Pyrrhic victory as *The Smothers Brothers Comedy Hour* would not be revived for 20 years.

The brothers continued to turn up on the broadcast dial however. A year after being kicked off of CBS, ABC gave the brothers a summer variety series. However, the wind was out of Tom Smothers's sails, and the series was not picked up in the fall. In January 1975, NBC gave the brothers a try with yet another variety series, but that one also did not last the full season. The brothers continued touring in their highly successful stage concerts and were frequent guests on various television shows. Then, 20 years after being booted off CBS's airwaves, the network invited the brothers back to do a twentieth-anniversary special of *The Smothers Brothers Comedy Hour* in 1989. The special brought back the familiar stage set and many of the show's supporting players, such as Leigh French as Goldie O'Keefe, Pat Paulsen, and Bob Einstein as Officer Judy. The special was a big enough hit that CBS agreed to bring *The Smothers Brothers Comedy Hour* back in the regular season. Goldie O'Keefe was now a yuppie, and political commentary tended to focus on American intervention in Central America. Tom also introduced his alter ego, the Zen-like, silent "master of Yo," the "Yo-Yo Man." The revived *Comedy Hour* was moderately successful but did not result in a second season.

After more than forty years in show business, the Smothers Brothers continued to tour extensively and very successfully throughout North America in the 1990s. *The Smothers Brothers Comedy Hour* remained their most important popular cultural achievement. The show was enormously influential on future comics and television shows which attempted to bring political satire to the television, *Saturday Night Live* being the most noteworthy legacy of the Smothers' groundbreaking work. Bill Maher of the late night *Politically Incorrect* talk/comedy series also credited the *Comedy Hour* with inspiring his approach to political satire. *Saturday Night Live* alum Dennis Miller's show on HBO also owes much to the Smothers' example. However, all of these shows are either aired outside prime time or on cable and specialty channels: thirty years after *The Smothers Brothers Comedy Hour,* it would appear that sophisticated political satire and comedy is still not ready for prime time.

—Aniko Bodroghkozy

FURTHER READING:

Bodroghkozy, Aniko. "*The Smothers Brothers Comedy Hour* and Youth Rebellion." *The Revolution Wasn't Televised: Sixties Television and Social Conflict.* Lynn Spigel and Michael Curtin, eds. New York, Routledge, 1997, 201-219.

Carr, Steven Allen. "On the Edge of Tastelessness: CBS, the Smothers Brothers, and the Struggle for Control." *Cinema Journal.* Vol. 31, No.4, Summer 1992, 3-24.

Hendra, Tony. "Death by Committee." *Going Too Far.* New York, Doubleday, 1987, 202-226.

Mertz, Robert. "The Smothered Brothers." *CBS: Reflections in a Bloodshot Eye.* Chicago, Playboy Press, 1975, 293-305.

Spector, Bert. "A Clash of Cultures: The Smothers Brothers vs. CBS Television." *American History/American Television.* John E. O'Connor, ed. New York, Frederick Ungar, 1983, 159-183.

Sneakers
See Tennis Shoes/Sneakers

Snoop Doggy Dogg (1971—)

Perhaps the most recognized performer of the gangsta rap tradition, Snoop Doggy Dogg emerged in 1993 with two commercially successful albums on controversial Death Row/Interscope Records. Notorious for his violent and explicit lyrics, Snoop Doggy Dogg became a central target of political censorship and attack soon after his appearance on the rap scene. Despite his initial commercial success, the rapper's career began to flounder after gangsta rap fell out of favor in the latter half of the 1990s. By 1998, Snoop Doggy Dogg had changed his name to Snoop Dogg, switched music labels, and toned down his graphic and controversial act in an effort to maintain his status in the industry.

Born Calvin Broadus in 1971, he was nicknamed Snoop as a child and raised in an urban ghetto in California, suffering through a childhood of harsh social realities. One month after his high school graduation, the soon-to-be rap star was arrested on drug charges and spent the next three years in and out of jail on three separate charges related to drug possession.

Following his release from jail, Snoop began to hone his skills as a rapper and shopped a demo tape of his work around his hometown. Soon, he was introduced to Dr. Dre, a key member of the controversial rap group N.W.A. Dre invited the young rapper to make a cameo appearance on his song "Deep Cover," which soon reached number one on the rap charts. In 1991, Snoop was invited to appear on Dre's critically acclaimed solo album *The Chronic,* and the young rapper's performances became legendary in the hip-hop community. Their rapping duet on the song "Nothin' but a 'G' Thang" launched the single into the top five on the pop charts, establishing for the first time hardcore rap as crossover music. Snoop's unique rap style—aggressive but melodic, nasal and "cool"—created an instant buzz on the streets. After appearing on three major magazine covers, the widespread anticipation for Snoop's solo project seemed to be unprecedented in the history of rap music.

Nothing could prepare the young rapper for the attention he would receive with his debut 1993 album, *Doggystyle.* The album

Snoop Doggy Dogg

sold eight hundred thousand copies in its first week and debuted at number one on the Billboard charts. With his lanky, six-foot-four-inch frame and his long, braided hair, Snoop presented an image of black masculinity that hadn't been seen before. To his fans, the rapper appeared slightly effeminate but also menacing and hardcore. Through his realistic, graphic lyrics about living in the ghetto, Snoop helped bring to public attention the form of hip-hop known as gangsta rap. In this musical form, rappers portrayed themselves as instruments of menace and terror in order to shed light on the problems of youth living in the harsh social realities of urban ghettos. The success of *Doggystyle* also helped establish the West Coast as a viable center for the production of rap music.

Nonetheless, Snoop's success was a double-edged sword. Along with the Death Row record label and the label's head, Suge Knight, Snoop came under the critical scrutiny of a number of politicians and advocates for his glorification of violence and criminality, his explicit language, and his promotion of hustler and pimp lifestyles. Moreover, Snoop's legal troubles and his portrayal of criminality also seemed to spill into his offstage life. In the month before *Doggystyle* was released, Snoop was charged as an accomplice to the shooting death of a young black man. After receiving the legal services of O. J. Simpson trial lawyer Johnnie Cochran, Snoop was acquitted in 1996. Yet Snoop's brush with the law only boosted his credibility among his

fans, as they witnessed his offstage life blend into his art. As a result, his second album, *Murder Was the Case,* sold more than two million copies. By the mid-1990s, Snoop had also became one of the leading proponents of an escalating and highly publicized war of words between East Coast and West Coast rappers.

Eventually, however, Snoop's career suffered as gangsta rap began to weaken in its cultural power. In 1996, Death Row Records buckled under massive censorship from political conservatives, and as the year wore on, the hip-hop community became revolutionized by the untimely shooting deaths of hip-hop's two biggest stars, Tupac Shakur and the Notorious B.I.G., and by the incarceration of Death Row's Suge Knight. Unprepared to respond to the changing culture, Snoop's third album, *Tha Doggfather* (1997) suffered poor critical reviews and limited commercial attention. To increase his bad fortune, the rapper was then sued by Suge Knight's wife, who also acted as Snoop's manager, for millions of dollars in unpaid management fees. As Time/Warner sold its share of Interscope Records to MCA, Snoop found his musical home of Death Row Records in serious disrepair and public disrepute. Yet the record company continued to claim that the rapper contractually owed them another six albums.

In 1998, Snoop returned to visibility. Louisiana's No Limit Records label, run by emerging hip-hop entrepreneur and rapper Master P, entered into a deal with Death Row Records to release Snoop from future responsibilities. After having sold seven million albums in six years, the rapper released his fourth album, *Da Story Is to Be Sold Not to Be Told* on the No Limit Records label. In the same year, he appeared in bit parts in the straight-to-video movie *The Game of Life* and in the feature film release *Half-Baked,* and he decided to drop the word ''Doggy'' from his name to distance himself from his association with the gangsta rap idiom which he had helped popularize. In media interviews, Snoop Dogg began to publicize his offstage role as a father to two children. The rapper described his newfound image in 1998 as ''more educated, wise, and more of a thinker—more for life.''

—Jason King

FURTHER READING:

Powell, Kevin. ''Hot Dogg.'' *Vibe.* Vol. 1, No. 1, September 1993, 51-55.

Ro, Ronin. *Have Gun Will Travel: The Spectacular Rise and Violent Fall of Death Row Records.* 1st ed. New York, Doubleday, 1998.

Snow White and the Seven Dwarfs

Though criticized for the implied message that every girl needs a ''prince'' to rescue her, Walt Disney's first animated feature remains a classic. Debuting in 1937, the movie had a simple story line. Snow White escapes the murderous Queen and finds refuge with the Seven Dwarfs (Doc, Bashful, Sleepy, Sneezy, Happy, Grumpy, and Dopey). Learning she is alive, the Queen disguises herself and tricks Snow White into eating a poisoned apple. She apparently dies. A handsome prince, however, wakes her with a kiss. Reviewers criticized the human characters for being wooden, but the film broke ground in animation. The illusion of depth in the forrest scenes and such details as rain splashing on the ground had never been seen before. The movie proved animated features could be done and paved the way for later Disney films.

—P. Andrew Miller

FURTHER READING:

Holliss, Richard, and Brian Sibley. *Walt Disney's Snow White and the Seven Dwarfs and the Making of the Classic Film.* New York, Simon & Schuster, 1987.

Krause, Martin F., and Linda Witkowski. *Walt Disney's Snow White and the Seven Dwarfs.* New York, Hyperion, 1994.

Maltin, Leonard. *The Disney Films.* New York, Crown Publishers, Inc. 1973.

Soap Operas

In the 1930s, advertisers such as Procter & Gamble sought sponsorship of daily radio programming targeted to homemakers, who controlled the household purse strings for cleaning and other household product purchases. Daytime serial dramas soon answered this call, focusing melodramatically on women, multi-generational families, and romantic intrigue in live, 15-minute shows. Although derogatory at first, the term ''soap opera'' was eventually embraced and is now the genre's customary designation.

The first soap opera, *Painted Dreams*, was developed in 1931 for WGN radio in Chicago by Irna Phillips, who would go on to become the most prolific creator of soap operas for both radio and television. The program aired without specific product association until content changes were made to accommodate Montgomery Ward & Co., the show's first sponsor. Phillips employed the same enticements to secure advertisers for her other serial inventions, and the genre's characteristic sponsor ties were established. Phillips' *Today's Children*, sponsored by Pillsbury, evolved into the first network soap opera when NBC began airing it nationwide in 1933.

Understanding that women often performed their domestic chores while listening to radio and were, consequently, all the more inclined to buy and use merchandise that could be casually promoted within a program, Procter & Gamble (P&G) initiated its first soap opera, *Ma Perkins*, in 1933. Other P&G ventures, including *The O'Neills* (1935), *The Guiding Light* (1937), and *Kitty Keene* (1937), soon followed.

Once television became a feature of the domestic landscape after World War II, soap operas gradually faded from the radio airwaves and took up residence on the small screen. *The Guiding Light,* a Phillips creation, ran simultaneously on both media for several years and remained in CBS's lineup at the end of the twentieth century. While radio soaps shifted to tape before they faded, television soaps were, until the late 1950s, presented live. The decade saw myriad TV soaps begin and end abruptly, but several in addition to *Guiding Light,* including Roy Winsor's *Search for Tomorrow* and *Love of Life* and Phillips' *As the World Turns*, exhibited staying power. By the 1960s, soap operas were the only television genre whose production was still owned and managed by sponsors, with P&G dominating the field (other shows had shifted to running ''spots'' by a variety of advertisers). As a by-product of the shift to television, an extra measure of redundancy and ''backstory'' exposition was added to the

soap opera formula in order to accommodate viewers' tendency to turn or step away from the screen momentarily in attending to their household tasks. When added to the genre's open, serial form, this element further ingrained feminine domesticity into the very fabric of the soap opera.

The tried-and-true ability of soaps to target the preferred audience of women, aged 18-49, was unmatched by any other type of programming. Younger viewers became ''hooked'' on their shows by watching with their mothers after school, during the summer, and on holidays, and were then counted upon to become loyal viewers for the next three decades. With the lucrative, Baby Boom generation of women coming of age in the late 1950s, 1960s, and 1970s, soap producers geared up to capture a new crop of female consumers.

When *As the World Turns* (CBS) featured the teenaged elopement of Penny Hughes and Jeff Baker in the late 1950s, the strategy of the ''summer storyline'' was inaugurated. Since that time, soaps have made special efforts to highlight and write for younger characters during the summer months in order to attract high school and college students at home during their breaks. New soaps with new angles also attempted to snare these viewers. ABC's Gothic soap opera, *Dark Shadows*, emerged in the mid-1960s to beguile a largely cult audience with vampires, witches, and werewolves for half a decade, creating a fandom which has lingered far longer than the program. Additionally, by the end of the decade, most soaps had expanded to a half-hour format.

The summer storyline became more of a year-round prospect in the 1970s, as Agnes Nixon's *All My Children* (ABC) and William Bell's *The Young and the Restless* (CBS) were devised with Baby Boomers in mind. Meanwhile, NBC's *Another World*, a 1964 co-creation of Phillips and Bell, emerged in 1975 as the first soap to make 60 minutes the industry standard.

In the late 1970s, *General Hospital* evolved into a winner for ABC when ratings increased dramatically due to executive producer Gloria Monty's decision to pair teenaged ''soap babe'' Laura Baldwin (Genie Francis) with bad boy ''soap hunk'' Luke Spencer (Anthony Geary)—a courtship that clicked into full gear after the writers realized the enormous popularity of the couple and recontextualized Luke's previous rape of Laura as a ''seduction.'' Luke and Laura became soap opera's first ''super couple,'' and were promoted in a newfangled fantasy and adventure-oriented ''ice princess'' story. NBC's *Days of Our Lives*, a 1960s creation of Irna Phillips, Ted Corday, and Alan Chase, followed suit with super couples such as Bo and Hope and fantasy scenarios of its own. When Luke and Laura finally wed during the November ratings sweeps of 1981, in excess of 30 million viewers tuned in, the largest audience ever to view an episode of any daytime soap opera.

Although Luke's ''rape redemption'' fueled controversy, taboo topics were addressed on soaps in the 1970s and 1980s as an integral part of the campaign to lure Baby Boomers. Roger Thorpe's rape of wife Holly was the groundbreaking issue on *Guiding Light*. The writers who penned it, Jerome and Bridget Dobson, followed with a similar story on *As the World Turns,* where *General Hospital*'s former scribe, Douglas Marland, eventually took the reigns and conceived socially conscious tales about bulimia, incest, and homosexuality. *Another World,* which tackled addiction, abortion, and alcoholism under the leadership of Irna Phillips, William Bell and, later, Harding Lemay, went on to offer the first AIDS story in the late 1980s.

As much as they tried, soaps that were caught behind the curve during the youth boom soon experienced downturns in popularity and have never completely recovered. Procter & Gamble, the only sponsor to still produce its own soaps in the late 1980s, was especially hard hit, and one of its properties, *Search For Tomorrow,* switched from CBS to NBC before going under in 1986. P&G's *Guiding Light, Another World,* and *As the World Turns* also struggled with their aging viewerships. The 1980s saw efforts to reach other specific demographics with NBC's *Generations,* targeted primarily to African-Americans, and Christian Broadcasting Network's *Another Life,* geared to Christian viewers. Neither achieved long-term success.

Another feature of the 1970s and 1980s was the rise of the prime time soap opera. Although *Peyton Place* (ABC) had attempted such a temporal shift in the 1960s, launching the film careers of Ryan O'Neill and Mia Farrow but little else, it was not until the late 1970s and Lorimar's saga of an oil dynasty in *Dallas,* headed by the infamous J.R. Ewing (Larry Hagman), that the idea finally caught on. Unlike *Peyton Place,* which offered two episodes per week, *Dallas's* once-a-week format proved more palatable to prime time viewers, and the CBS series became immensely popular, enduring for a decade. It's worldwide appeal was even more staggering, and when a 1980 season-ending cliffhanger posed the question, "Who shot J.R.?," massive, global speculation ensued. Elihu Katz and Tamar Liebes' scholarly study of this international phenomenon, published in *The Export of Meaning,* demonstrates how popular texts can be interpreted in numerous ways according to culture, nationality, and other aspects of identity. CBS later added other serial sagas to its lineup, including *Falcon Crest* and *Knot's Landing*—a *Dallas* spin-off. But it was Aaron Spelling's *Dynasty* that answered the challenge for ABC, resonating 1980s' narcissism and opulence and dishing up "soap vixen" Alexis Carrington who, owing to Joan Collins' brazenly camp portrayal, emerged as a cult favorite. Moreover, other nighttime formats began exhibiting seriality and other soap opera conventions as the genre's influence was seen in domestic dramas such as *thirtysomething,* law enforcement, legal, and medical shows such as *Hill Street Blues, L. A. Law,* and *St. Elsewhere,* and "dramedies" such as *Moonlighting.*

By the 1980s, academic study of daytime soap operas had evolved from statistical audience surveys and content analyses such as those contained in Mary Cassata and Thomas Skill's *Life on Daytime Television,* to critical analyses of soap opera texts and the potential identifications of viewing subjects such as those found in Tania Modleski's *Loving with a Vengeance* and Robert Allen's *Speaking of Soap Opera.* Despite their denigration in the larger culture, a feature attendant to most any "feminine" genre from romance novels to film melodrama, soaps were found to provide central female characters through whom women in the audience might seek affirmation and empowerment. Although some scholars found many aspects of these representations lacking, the genre's serial form, its emphasis on and elevation of the domestic sphere, and its focus on feminine subjects, were considered by most to be positive and noteworthy traits.

As the 1990s loomed, soaps began to undergo a period of transition, seeking to retain their audience of Baby Boomers while attracting the younger, MTV generation of viewers. Jerome and Bridget Dobson's 1984 creation for NBC, *Santa Barbara,* took its lesson from *Dynasty* and delivered a spirit of camp postmodernism to daytime. While proving a huge success overseas, the soap failed to capture the domestic demographics the network was hoping for and suffered cancellation nine years later. *All My Children's* devilish "soap diva" Erica Kane and the actress playing her, Susan Lucci,

became household names, as multiple onscreen marriages for Erica and offscreen Emmy losses for Lucci were grist for the publicity mill.

In the late 1980s, another Agnes Nixon soap, *One Life to Live* (ABC), had endeavored to replicate *General Hospital's* winning fantasy adventures by depicting unconventional journeys to the Old West and to a lost city called "Eterna." Under the management of former movie producer Linda Gottlieb and mystery novelist Michael Malone, the program shifted to hard-hitting realism in the 1990s. Stories involving the town of Llanview's homophobic response to a gay teen, Billy Douglas, and the brutal gang rape of a college student by three fraternity brothers led by Todd Manning (Roger Howarth), emerged from the collaboration. Controversy ensued when Howarth's charisma with fans led creators to orchestrate Todd's redemption, much to the chagrin of Howarth, who found himself braving screams of "rape me, Todd," from overly ardent admirers. *All My Children* followed *One Life to Live's* homophobia story with its own tale of a popular teacher who nearly loses his job after revealing his homosexuality during a classroom lecture.

General Hospital adopted a similar tone of verisimilitude during this decade, largely as a result of headwriter Claire Labine's heart-wrenching tales of a child's tragic death, her gift of a healthy heart to an ailing cousin, and a middle-aged woman's battle with breast cancer. The most risky and significant decision during Labine's tenure was to have teenager Robin Scorpio (Kimberly McCullough), who had literally grown up on the program, contract the AIDS virus by engaging in unprotected sex with her boyfriend, Stone. Stone subsequently suffered and died of the dread disease before the eyes of both Robin and viewers. These dark stories garnered *General Hospital* critical acclaim but endangered the program's healthy ratings, as the incoming generation of fans seemed more stimulated by fantasy and escape than by tragedy and catharsis.

Meanwhile, it was NBC's long-running *Days of Our Lives,* under the creative leadership of executive producer Ken Corday and innovative writer James Reilly, which appeared to discover the key unlocking the devotion of this new generation. Taking a lead from *Dark Shadows,* Reilly conjured up Gothic fantasy scenarios, camp "supervillains," never-ending "super triangles," and bizarre sagas involving premature burial and demon possession. This latter escapade required the soap's most beloved diva, Marlena Evans (Diedre Hall), to levitate and morph into wild animals. While many longtime fans could not tolerate the program's drastic change in tone and jumped ship, teens gravitated to its postmodern panache and rushed aboard. While *Young and the Restless* gained and retained the number one spot in ratings during the late 1980s and 1990s, warranting the addition of a second Bell soap, *The Bold and the Beautiful,* to CBS's lineup, *Days of Our Lives* mounted a serious challenge to this ratings leader and at one point surpassed it in terms of demographics—the advertisers' target group of younger women. After a few years, ratings and demographics for *Days of Our Lives* dipped a bit, but its producers seemed not to question whether the "formula" they had concocted might prove to be a short term fix rather than a long term remedy.

Days of Our Lives was very influential in the 1990s, with many programs endeavoring to emulate it and refusing to relinquish their future audience to any other soap or network. Even more than during the Baby Boom influx, "youthification" became the order of the day. Multi-generational or Baby Boom-centered soap operas had become scarce in prime time, with only NBC's *Sisters* breaking out as an instance of both. Most remarkable had been Aaron Spelling's groundbreaking creations for FOX, *Beverly Hills 90210* and *Melrose Place,* which demonstrated that it was possible for soaps to focus almost exclusively on teens and/or twenty-somethings and be successful in prime time. Late in the decade, *Party of Five* (FOX) and *Dawson's Creek* (WB) extended this trend. Despite differences in potential audience and format, some daytime powers hoped they could corner the youth market in similar fashion. With the children of the Baby Boom generation, the Baby Boomlets, lying in wait and nearly as numerous as their parents, there appeared to be no turning back. Although some had predicted that Boomers would dominate the culture well into and even beyond their middle age, the trajectory of soap operas responding to the advertisers' increasing concern with demographics, as opposed to household ratings, portended otherwise.

Most deliberate in its campaign was NBC, making *Days of Our Lives* its standard bearer and pressuring its only other soap, *Another World,* to "backburner" and eventually fire much of its over-forty cast while adopting a decidedly more outrageous tone. The network then picked up Aaron Spelling's first daytime offering, the virtually uni-generational *Sunset Beach,* to complete its menu. After writer James Reilly departed *Days of Our Lives,* the network hired him to develop a new daytime venture. *Another World,* whose ratings continued to spiral downward after the loss of its veteran performers, was the likely candidate for replacement by the new Reilly soap. The fact that Procter & Gamble was a "middle man" for *Another World* did not help its chances, and NBC's contract disputes with *Days of Our Lives,* which was threatening a move to another network, offered the ailing *World* its only glimmer of salvation as the millenium approached. Sadly though, *Another World* was cancelled during the summer of 1999.

Meanwhile, the traditional Procter & Gamble soaps on CBS, *As the World Turns* and *Guiding Light,* were not surviving this period unscathed. The former escorted many of its veterans to the chopping block and was inundated with young, inexperienced performers. The latter bore its own spates of downsizing and had taken to featuring otherworldly stories, including an especially controversial one in which popular diva Reva Shayne (Kim Zimmer) was cloned.

Despite the tenuous success of *Days of Our Lives,* daytime soap operas realized an overall decline in viewership during the 1990s. Competition with the O.J. Simpson trial, more abundant offerings on cable, and the fact that more and more women were in the work force, all had an impact. Although many working women videotaped or "time-shifted" their soaps, advertisers refused to pay for viewers who were apt to fast-forward through ads. Still, avid fans had become more active and, indeed, interactive, establishing communities on the Internet in which they could discuss the latest storylines, root for their favorite "core" characters, families, and/or super couples, or lament some of the genre's more flagrant lapses in logic, including resurrections from the dead, multiple recasts, and the "rapid aging syndrome" in which children are ushered off to boarding school only to return six months later, ten years older, and ripe for romance in a summer teen storyline. Online soap operas such as *The Spot* also sprang up.

Accordingly, during this decade, scholars engaged in cultural studies and other approaches to media analysis turned their attention to soap opera viewers, exploring their interpretations and activities in fan groups, clubs, and Internet forums. In *Soap Opera and Women's Talk,* Mary E. Brown argues that female audiences recognize their subordination through negotiating and celebrating the genre's feminine emphasis, while in a study entitled "'No Politics Here,'" Christine Scodari examines soap opera "cyberfandom" and bemoans

ruptures in the audience attendant to creators' "youthification" efforts and the genre's postmodern turn.

Despite their attempts to enthrall succeeding generations of viewers with controversial and/or outlandish subject matter, some research, such as Mumford's *Love and Ideology in the Afternoon,* maintains that daytime soaps have persisted in their essential conservatism. While many programs welcome African-American and Hispanic characters and viewers, race is still a thorny issue. Soapland's black women and white men have occasionally fallen in love across racial lines, but when *Another World* tried to reverse that equation by developing a flirtation between Caucasian diva Felicia Gallant (Linda Dano) and a handsome black suitor, a backlash apparently prevented the story from moving beyond the initial stages. Similarly, *Soap Opera Digest* received disagreeable letters from fans of *Young and the Restless* in response to a blossoming romance between African-American Neil and Caucasian Victoria. *Another World*'s plan to make race an explicit component of a trial in which an African-American cop accused a popular—and white—"hunk" of raping her, was buried under the negative fallout of fans whose sensibilities it violated. And, although soap opera's focus on female viewers would seem to warrant the overturning of double standards, serious romances between older women and younger men remain taboo. Only one— Vanessa and Matt of *Guiding Light*—was evident in the late 1990s. As soaps became more devoted to younger segments of the audience, such stories were apt to be seen as inimical to commercial goals and, therefore, inadvisable. Moreover, while soaps may depict women in career roles, the workplace continues to serve as a stage upon which women are seen "catfighting" with one another for the love of a man rather than seeking professional accomplishment for its own sake.

Still, soap opera's ongoing focus on human relationships and the "feminine" is exceptional and laudable. Adapted to a plethora of international cultures, featured in numerous fan magazines, celebrated at the *Daytime Emmys* and *Soap Opera Digest Awards,* and lampooned in movies (*Soapdish, Tootsie*) and television (*Mary Hartman, Mary Hartman, Soap, The Carol Burnett Show*), the genre endures as a highly accommodating and exportable staple of American popular culture.

—Christine Scodari

FURTHER READING:

Allen, Robert. *Speaking of Soap Operas.* Chapel Hill, University of North Carolina Press, 1985.

Blumenthal, Danielle. *Women and Soap Opera: A Cultural Feminist Perspective.* Westport, Connecticut, Praeger, 1997.

Brown, Mary E. *Soap Operas and Women's Talk: The Pleasure of Resistance.* Newbury Park, California, Sage, 1994.

Cassata, Mary, and Thomas Skill, editors. *Life on Daytime Television.* Norwood, New Jersey, Ablex, 1983.

Liebes, Tamar, and Elihu Katz. *The Export of Meaning: Cross-cultural Readings of "Dallas."* New York, Oxford University Press, 1990.

Modleski, Tania. *Loving with a Vengeance: Mass-Produced Fantasies for Women.* Hamden, Connecticut, Archon, 1982.

Mumford, Laura. *Love and Ideology in the Afternoon: Soap Opera, Women, and Television Genre.* Bloomington, Indiana University Press, 1995.

Museum of Television and Radio, editors. *Worlds without End: The Art and History of the Soap Opera.* New York, Harry N. Abrams, 1997.

Scodari, Christine. "'No Politics Here': Age and Gender in Soap Opera 'Cyberfandom.'" *Women's Studies in Communication.* Fall 1998, 168-187.

Waggett, Gerard. *Soap Opera Encyclopedia.* New York, Harper Paperbacks, 1997.

Soccer

Soccer in America is in a strangely paradoxical position. It is the world's most popular sport, yet it has never managed to gain much of a spectator footing in the United States. It may be virtually ignored on television as a spectator sport, but it has become one of the biggest participatory forms of leisure activity in America by the late 1990s. Nonetheless, many Americans are still ignorant not only of the rules of the world's biggest game, but also of their country's own soccer history.

The origins of soccer in America are obscure. Folklore suggests that the Pilgrim Fathers discovered the American Indians playing a form of the game along the Massachusetts coastline. British immigrants, however, imported the game that developed into association football (soccer) around the world in the nineteenth century, into America in the seventeenth century; there is documentation of the game as early as 1609. The game was an early folk pastime played mainly in the streets and open squares, and it remained so until the nineteenth century. By the 1820s, soccer was a violent, unorganized, and casual game almost exclusively played on college campuses. The first intercollegiate soccer match took place in 1869 between Princeton and Rutgers. Schoolboys established the first organized soccer club, the Oneidas of Boston, in 1862. They played on Boston common and were undefeated for several years.

At this point it looked as if soccer would develop in the United States. British expatriates had exported soccer around the world and many immigrants from the British Isles arrived in America bringing the game with them. Harvard, however, had other ideas. In an attempt to distinguish itself from the other Ivy League colleges, Harvard adopted rules similar to those developed by rugby football. Since Harvard was the leader in physical education during the nineteenth century and other colleges did not want to lose such prestigious competition, they adopted rugby rules. This set of rules subsequently became the basis for the innovation of American football. Football was then highlighted as a uniquely American sport while soccer was relegated in significance as the game of immigrants, particularly as it was played by the new arrivals from Southern Europe.

Nonetheless, soccer did not die out in America. In 1884 the American Football Association was organized in Newark, New Jersey. And in 1885 the United States played its first "international" against Canada, one of the first soccer games to be played outside the British Isles. The United States soccer team participated in the 1904 Olympic games in St. Louis and in 1914 the United States Football Association (USFA) was granted full membership in FIFA, the governing body of world soccer. In 1916 the USFA team traveled to Sweden and Norway. It played its first international match on foreign soil on August 20, defeating Sweden 3-0. When the first World Cup competition was organized in 1930, America was one of 13 nations to compete and its Bert Patenaude was the first player to score three goals in a single World Cup game. The highlight of the USFA's international games, however, was in the 1950 World Cup when it defeated England 1-0. This has been considered the biggest upset ever in international soccer.

Soccer in America has since undergone many incarnations during the twentieth century. In 1923, the world's first indoor soccer league was organized in Boston. In 1958, the International Soccer League was set up. It was composed of top teams from Europe, South America, and the United States, holding its first championship tournament in 1959. The league survived for a decade as a testing ground for soccer as a spectator sport in America. In 1967 two more soccer leagues were established: the United Soccer Association (USA) and the National Professional Soccer League. At the end of the year, these leagues were merged at the request of FIFA, forming the North American Soccer League (NASL). This newly established professional league had 18 teams by 1974 and it achieved a major success by signing the world's greatest footballer, Pelé, in 1975. Professional soccer as a spectator sport finally appeared to have taken root in America when a seven game contract was signed with national television in 1977. The NASL eventually collapsed, however, due to a combination of highly paid foreign stars, a failure to develop the game at grassroots level, the withdrawal of its sponsors, and falling gate receipts.

Soccer was revitalized once again during the early 1990s. In 1994 the United States hosted the World Cup for the first time. Three and a half million fans filled the stadia and broke all previous attendance records. For the first time in 64 years the USA progressed beyond the first round, eventually losing a creditable 1-0 to the team from Brazil. On the back of the World Cup the United States Soccer Federation set up Major League Soccer, promising a blend of home-grown talent, imported foreign stars, and audiences of 14,000 per game. The World Cup had proven that Americans could both play and watch soccer. Major investment in the sport, from companies such as Nike, has also boosted the popularity of soccer amongst Americans. In America, soccer is now played by both sexes and is a major participatory activity. Indeed, the USA's women's team is currently an Olympic champion. The men's team, however, has not fared so well. At the 1998 World Cup in France, they went out during the first round. The lowest point came when they were defeated 3-1 by Iran, a team who had never previously appeared in the World Cup Finals.

Despite the formation of domestic soccer leagues and international successes, soccer is somehow still not recognized as an American sport. Unlike football and baseball, it is not considered an American invention, but rather as the sport of immigrants. Undoubtedly, soccer has suffered from its lack of prime-time television coverage. Television sport schedules are virtually monopolized by the "big three": football, baseball, and basketball. This lack of exposure has continued to hinder soccer's development at the professional level, while overshadowing its thriving grassroots existence at a participatory level. Until soccer's television and earning power match that of the big three it will continue to remain in their shadows.

—Nathan Abrams

FURTHER READING:

Abrams, Nathan D. "Inhibited but not 'Crowded Out': The Strange Fate of Soccer in the United States." *The International Journal of the History of Sport.* Vol. 12, No. 3, December 1995, 1-17.

Foulds, Sam, and Paul Harris. *America's Soccer Heritage: A History of the Game.* California, Manhattan Beach, 1979.

Manzo, J. "A Ball in the Grass: An Explanatory Look at Soccer in the United States." *Sport Place.* Vol. 1, Winter 1987, 30-38.

Markovits, A. S. "The Other 'American Exceptionalism': Why Is There No Soccer in the United States?" *The International Journal of the History of Sport.* Vol. 7, September 1990, 230-64.

Sugden, John. "USA and the World Cup: American Nativism and the Rejection of the People's Game." *Hosts and Champions: Soccer Cultures, National Identities and the USA World Cup,* edited by John Sugden and Alan Tomlinson. Aldershot, United Kingdom, Arena, 1994.

Waldstein, David, and Stephen Wagg. "UnAmerican Activity? Football in U.S. and Canadian Society." *Giving the Game Away: Football, Politics and Culture on Five Continents,* edited by Stephen Wagg. London and New York, Leicester University Press, 1995, 72-87.

Social Dancing

Social dancing refers to all those forms of dance that are recreational and public. It is not a professional form of dance, except for exhibition dancing or teaching, nor a form of theatrical dancing, like ballet, modern dance, tap dancing, or flamenco, although such forms of art and entertainment incorporate steps and gestures from social dance. In American society almost everyone has some sort of relationship to social dancing. Many people participate with great intensity in social dance activities for a period of their lives. In pre-industrial societies and working-class communities, social dancing has often been a group activity, but by the end of the twentieth century in many parts of the world, social dancing was primarily a form of couples dancing.

Folk dancing is the earliest form of social dancing. Most folk dancing is a group activity, and often includes only a single sex. A common folk dance form is the European round dance that is for both men and women in which the dancers are linked in a circle by holding hands, or holding the arms and shoulders or the waist belts of the other dancers. The couple dance where a man and woman hold each in their arms is a late development in folk dancing. Couple dances probably originated as courtship or wedding dances. Folk dances have often existed in a dialectical relationship with court dancing. Folk dances were usually codified by "dancing masters" when they were introduced to the aristocratic courts so that the dances could be taught more easily.

English country-dances were exported to France, where they were codified and introduced into French aristocratic circles. Known as the *contredanse,* they were group dances that formed circles and lines of dancing to make an elaborate shape through which members of the court could thread. In the minuet, a related dance form, couples danced as part of the group. These early ballroom dances were grouped together under the title of cotillion and quadrille. Elite ballroom dancing of this sort was destroyed by the French Revolution.

After the French Revolution, the waltz swept across Europe; it was considered a "popular" democratic dance—the dance of the rising middle classes. Social dance moved out of the ballroom of the aristocratic court into public dance halls and "assembly rooms." Paris had, in the period after the revolution, over 700 dance halls. It was also the first dance of urban life. The waltz was the first example of the "closed couple" dance—the dance partners faced one another and were in intimate physical contact with one another. Because of that and its whirling and the intoxicating effect of its 3/4 time, it was thought to be vulgar and lascivious. The waltz was introduced to the United States in the early nineteenth-century. The waltz remained the dominant form of social dance in Europe—where it culminated in the Viennese waltzes of Johann Strauss—and North America. Other dances that emerged rivaled it for short periods of time, but did not displace it until late in the nineteenth century.

At the end of the twentieth century in the United States, most forms of social dance were hybrid dance forms descended from European and African musical and dance traditions. During the eighteenth and nineteenth centuries, most of the social dances that Americans participated in were imported from Europe, but since the beginning of the twentieth century American popular forms of social dance have originated in or were primarily influenced by African-American music and dance styles. Even the many forms of Latin dancing that have also been popular—from the tango, to the samba, to salsa—are cross acculturations of African and Hispanic musical traditions.

The emergence of ragtime, in the 1890s, revolutionized social dancing in the United States. Composed by Black musicians as piano music to be played in saloons, bars, brothels, and cafes, ragtime was rarely written down or recorded. The first identifiable style of jazz, ragtime comes from *ragged music,* also known as syncopation, where the musical stress is on an unaccented beat and then held over until the next beat. The most famous ragtime composer in the early twentieth century was Scott Joplin. His pieces, "Maple Leaf Rag" and "The Entertainer" were among the most popular compositions of the day. Ragtime radically changed American dance styles. Before ragtime, there was an emphasis on learning complicated steps and the pleasure in movement. After ragtime, the main impetus of social dancing was the music's rhythm and the impulse that it gave to dancing.

The one-step—called so because one step was taken to each beat of the music with a constant tempo—was the first kind of dancing done to ragtime. The one-step spawned a series of other one-step dances accompanied by different arm and body gestures: the turkey-trot involved flapping one's arms like a turkey, the grizzly bear included lurching like a bear, and so on with the bunny hug, the shiver, and the Boston dip. Vernon and Irene Castle, a world famous, husband and wife team, adapted the one-step as the Castle Walk and popularized it across the country, commanding huge fees for performing ballroom dances in exhibitions, cafes, and theaters. The one-step and the other new dances were much simpler—they undercut the social distinction to be gained by ballroom dancing lessons. Anyone could learn them by observation in an evening of dancing. One English observer noted, that "[A]ll you have to do is grab hold of the nearest lady, grasp her very tightly, push her shoulders down a bit, and then wiggle about as much like a slippery slush as you possibly can." Many new dances also allowed much closer physical contact between the couple, in part because they were somewhat slower than the waltz or the polka.

One offshoot from these early one-steps was the two-step—which is basically a marching step with interpolated skips. Neither the one-step nor the two-step had the major impact of later dance styles on American recreational dancing. The two-step was originally danced to the popular marches of John Philip Sousa. Ragtime, Dixieland jazz, and later swing, offered rhythmically complex musical frameworks for more sophisticated dance forms. With the revival in popularity of country and western music in the late twentieth century, the two-step survived as country and western dancing primarily as a line dance incorporating open couples.

The next dance to sweep the country was the foxtrot; its invention the most significant development in social dancing until the 1960s. Incorporating some aspects of the one-step and other new dances, the foxtrot was more enjoyable to dance because its combination of quick and slow steps allowed greater variety and flexibility than the monotonous one-step. Most ballroom dances that followed—the *shimmy,* Black Bottom, and Charleston—were variations on the foxtrot.

After ragtime, jazz became the dominant idiom of urban dance music and popular song up until the 1950s. The popularity of the foxtrot and its centrality to ballroom dancing was instrumental to the infusion of jazz into mainstream American popular music. The big dance bands of the 1920s and 1930s were the vehicle for the most popular and exciting dance vogue in the era before rock 'n' roll—*swing* and all the dances that grew out of it such as jitterbug, Lindy Hop, and Jive.

Rock 'n' roll, a new style of music that emerged in the late 1950s, and a synthesis of blues, rhythm, and country music—was a popular form of dance music. Songs like ''Shake, Rattle and Roll'' and ''Rock Around the Clock'' typified both this new music as well as a dance style. Couples continued to dance the jitterbug to early rock 'n' roll, but in the early 1960s, Chubby Checker recorded a dance song called ''The Twist''—a dance in which partners shook their shoulders, swiveled their hips, but did not touch. As a dance it swept across the United States. And although the enthusiasm for it faded within a year or two, popular social dance was decisively changed. Coordinated couple dancing was a thing of the past. After the twist, social dancing was characterized by standing in one place, small foot movements (somewhat resembling the motion of putting out a cigarette), dance partners hardly touching one another, or dancing alone on a crowded dance floor. Partners usually maintained eye contact, but dance fashions no longer focused on footwork so much as the motion of the arms and upper body.

Less influential than the dance forms that emerged from jazz, rock 'n' roll, soul, and hip hop, although still highly visible at times, were Afro-Latin dances, such as the tango, rhumba, samba, mambo, cha-cha, and salsa. The tango was the first to arrive—creating a huge dance craze in 1913 and 1914. The tango traveled back and forth throughout the nineteenth century between Europe and Latin America as well as passing through Japan in the 1940s. In the course of these movements the tango was modified by black and Creole influences being transformed once more in the brothels and cafes of Buenos Aires in the 1930s and 1940s. Popular at the end of the twentieth century, the tango had enjoyed several revivals throughout the century.

Rhumba music is popular throughout the Caribbean islands of Jamaica, Haiti, and Cuba. The rhumba as a dance migrated to the United States from Cuba—where it was a sex pantomime danced extremely fast with exaggerated hip movements and very aggressively led by the male partner. The music is played with a staccato beat. The samba, a Brazilian dance form first performed by blacks at carnival time and other holidays, is a difficult dance because of its speed and because its steps are taken on a quarter of a beat with a rocking motion. It was introduced to the United States by Fred Astaire

and Dolores Del Rio in the 1933 movie *Flying Down to Rio,* where they danced the ballroom version of the samba, the carioca. The ''Brazilian Bombshell,'' as movie star Carmen Miranda was known, popularized the samba's rhythms in her movies. Mambo is a voodoo term in Haiti, although as a dance it was created among upper-class Cubans for the ballroom. To some extent it evolved from the rhumba, although it is more difficult and danced fairly fast with jitterbug-like acrobatics and jerky staccato rhythm. The difficulties of the mambo led to the creation of the cha-cha, a simpler and easier dance, which resembled a much slower version of the mambo. In the United States the cha-cha has been the most popular Latin dance since the 1950s, although in the 1990s the mambo, tango, and salsa have eclipsed the cha-cha. Salsa, a Puerto Rican dance, has steadily gained in popularity in the last decade of the twentieth century.

In the 1970s new forms emerged that revived close couple dancing as well as a greater stress on footwork and coordination than did the post-Twist dances. The hustle and its close cousin, disco, grew up among the black and Puerto Rican bars and dance clubs in New York City. *Saturday Night Fever* (1977), starring John Travolta, had an immense impact on the popularity of disco dancing. Disco spurred an exhibition-style dancing, emphasizing improvisation and individual expression—the dancer becoming almost a soloist or choreographer. The hustle (and disco) closely resembles the Lindy except that disco music does not have the rhythmic swing of big band music. Instead, the hustle consists of dancing three beats against the music's four beats. One variation of the hustle was the ''Good Foot'' popularized by soul singer James Brown in his 1969 hit song, ''Get on the Good Foot'' which he performed in an acrobatic style. The ''Good Foot'' pointed towards breakdancing.

Hip hop as a musical style emerged in opposition to the increasing commercialization of disco, funk, and soul. It came out of New York, Los Angeles, and Chicago. This new style was created by DJs (disk jockeys) in dance clubs who blended, scratched, and inter-cut music from different tracks thus creating a new musical form. Break dancing or breaking emerged as dance form in response to a number of new developments. The DJs melding of percussion breaks from two identical records and playing the breaks over and over again generated opportunities for dancers to perform their gymnastic dance routines. Some break dancing routines were derived from the miming of robot-like actions, inspired by the character of Robot on the popular 1970s TV program, *Soul Train.* It also resulted from the incorporation of moves from martial arts—especially Kung Fu and Capoeira, the Brazilian dance-like martial art. In some cases, this also transformed violent conflict between gangs into dance competitions. Break dancing requires great skill and acrobatic abilities and was popularized by the 1983 movie, *Flashdance.* Hip hop musical culture continued to generate variations on break dancing such as popping, uprock, house, and bebop (a swing-like revival) that continued to influence social dancing at the end of the twentieth century.

—Jeffrey Escoffier

FURTHER READING:

Hager, Steven. *Hip Hop: The Illustrated History of Break Dancing, Rap Music, and Graffiti.* New York, St. Martin's Press, 1984.

Hazzard-Gordon, Katrina. *Jookin': The Rise of Social Dance Formations in African-American Culture.* Philadelphia, Temple University Press, 1990.

Stephenson, Richard M., and Joseph Iaccarino. *The Complete Book of Ballroom Dancing.* New York, Doubleday, 1980.

Soda Fountains

The classic American soda fountain was defined as much by its atmosphere as by what it served. Light, cool, and airy places furnished with marble-topped counters and tables, shining mirrors, and sparkling glass and chrome serving dishes, soda fountains began springing up in the early nineteenth century, and kept essentially the same formula until the 1950s. The bill of fare was simple: carbonated beverages and, later, ice cream and combinations thereof. In the heyday of the soda fountain (roughly 1890-1940) one could order a tempting variety of dishes, from an ice-cream soda (soda water and ice cream) to an ice-cream sundae (ice cream topped with nuts and a chocolate or fruit sauce) to a plain soda (carbonated water with fruit syrup mixed in).

For millennia, people have partaken of bubbly mineral water that came from natural springs, which was thought to have therapeutic qualities. After chemists figured out how to make artificially carbonated water, apothecaries and later drug stores featured it as one of their many curatives. In 1770 a Swede named Bergman produced the first artificially carbonated water, and by 1806 Professor Benjamin Silliman of Yale was manufacturing bottled water in Hartford, Connecticut. Early in the nineteenth century druggists began carbonating water in their basements, installing a readily accessible spigot on the first floor to serve customers. Before long the local literati were gathering at the drug store, making it a common meeting place and establishing the soda as a social beverage.

In 1832, John Matthews of New York City invented the first compact soda-water machine and dispenser unit, which popularized the drink and gave tavern owners their first stiff competition. Six years later, Eugene Roussel, a Philadelphia perfume maker, combined fruit syrups with this carbonated water, making the first flavored sodas, including orange, cherry, lemon, teaberry, ginger, peach, and root beer.

The ice-cream soda was not invented until about 1874, at the Franklin Institute Exposition in Philadelphia, when Robert M. Green, a soft drinks vendor, ran out of cream and substituted ice cream in his drinks. This new libation quickly became a national institution. By 1876, helped along by the Centennial Exposition's 30-foot-high fountain, soda fountains replaced ice-cream saloons as the fashionable place for the elite to patronize and see the wonders of technology at work. By 1900 common brand names sold at soda fountains

A soda jerk displaying his skills.

included Hires Rootbeer, Moxie, Dr. Pepper's, and Coca-Cola, the "great national temperance drink."

Prohibition greatly increased the popularity of the soda fountain. By the 1920s the improvement of refrigeration allowed these places to serve meals as well, and soda fountains were incorporated into department stores, luncheonettes, grocery stores, tobacco shops, and five-and-dime stores. While they were popular with all Americans, teenagers frequented soda fountains the most. Soda jerks, named for the way they jerked the handles used to extract fruit syrups from the pumps, worked behind the counter making the sometimes complicated concoctions for the patrons—anything from a Brown Cow to a Bonnie Belle Cream to a Catawba Frappe. Usually good-looking men, soda jerks were a popular attraction to their customers, and even had their own lingo. For example, "shoot (or hang) an honest" meant a cherry coke, "one sweet" or "pull one" referred to milk, "Adam and Eve on a raft" translated as two eggs on toast, a "ninety-five" described someone trying to get away without paying, and "thirteen!" warned that the boss was around.

Such a familiar icon in popular culture, the soda fountain appeared in plays and movies: people drank strawberry sodas at the fountain in *Our Town,* it appears as the place of courtship in the 1919 movie *True Heart Susie,* and Mickey Rooney and Judy Garland flirted over sodas in the 1938 film *Love Finds Andy Hardy.* The legendary soda fountain at Schwab's drugstore in Hollywood was supposedly the place where young hopefuls went to get noticed by the film industry; legend has it that Lana Turner was "discovered" there in 1937.

The "golden days" of the soda fountain were from the end of the nineteenth century to the early 1940s. During the World War II years, soda jerks got drafted, sugar was rationed, manufacturers of soda equipment had to retool for the war effort, and fountain operators saw larger profits in goods like cosmetics and nylon stockings. After the war there was a brief resurgence in soda fountains, but the business was never again as popular as it had been earlier in the century. Americans turned to ready-made food, and began motoring to the new fast-food restaurants sprouting up along the nation's highways, spelling the demise of the time-consuming ice-cream soda and its attendant institution, the soda fountain.

—Wendy Woloson

FURTHER READING:

Dickson, Paul. *The Great American Ice Cream Book.* New York, Atheneum, 1972.

Jonas, Susan, and Marilyn Nissenson. *Going, Going, Gone: Vanishing Americana.* San Francisco, Chronicle Books, 1994.

Morrison, Joseph L. "The Soda Fountain." *American Heritage.* August 1962, 10-19.

Riordan, John Lancaster. "Soda Fountain Lingo." *California Folklore Quarterly.* Volume 4, 1945, 50-57.

Schwartz, David M. "Life Was Sweeter, and More Innocent in Our Soda Days." *Smithsonian.* Vol. 17, July 1986, 114-24.

Soldier Field

Dedicated as a memorial to World War I soldiers, the colonnaded stadium known as Soldier Field has served as a cultural mecca for Chicago residents, hosting professional sports, presidential visits, religious events, and concerts. The architectural firm of Holabird & Roche was awarded the commission for the stadium in 1919. Construction on the $6,000,000 stadium (which was originally known as Grant Park Stadium) began in 1922 and was dedicated in November 1925. Though a centerpiece of Chicago's waterfront, the stadium fell victim to disuse and poor maintenance. Talks were initiated in the 1950s to bring a professional baseball team to the stadium, but it was not until 1971 that the stadium found a permanent resident in the National Football League's Chicago Bears. Plans for demolishing, revamping, or possibly doming the stadium continued until 1983, when the structure was placed on the National Register of Historic Places. The building—with its classic columns and pre-cast concrete resembling slabs of stone—remains a magnificent sight along the shore of Lake Michigan and an anomaly among professional football stadiums.

—Michael A. Lutes

FURTHER READING:

Bruegmann, Robert. *Holabird Roche Holabird Root: A Catalog of Works.* New York, Garland, 1991.

Some Like It Hot

Some Like It Hot, a critically acclaimed farcical romp produced by United Artists and directed by Billy Wilder, premiered at Loew's Capitol Theatre on Broadway in 1959. Set in Chicago in the 1920s, the film stars Tony Curtis and Jack Lemmon as hapless musicians who are pursued by gangsters when they witness the Saint Valentine's Day Massacre. Joe and Jerry decide to disguise themselves as "Josephine" and "Geraldine," and join a female band headed for Florida. (Actually, Jerry takes to his new role quickly, spontaneously introducing himself as "Daphne.") On the southbound train, the pair befriend Sugar Kane, played by Marilyn Monroe, and begin competing for her affections. It turns out that Sugar is on the run as well, fleeing the string of saxophone players who have loved her and left her. In Florida, Joe woos Sugar by masquerading as a millionaire, and "Daphne" is courted by Osgood, who is indeed a millionaire.

Wilder was by this time an established auteur. Reviews of *Some Like It Hot* compare his sophisticated comedy to that of Ernst Lubitsch and refer to "the Wilder touch." Wilder enjoyed a great deal of control over the production of the film. For example, although few films were shot in black and white by the end of the 1950s—especially since Hollywood was competing with television for viewers—Wilder felt that Lemmon and Curtis would look too garish in color and got his way.

Some Like It Hot marked Monroe's emergence from semi-retirement. She had made 21 films between 1950 and 1956, only one in 1957, and none in 1958. She was married to Arthur Miller and pregnant with his child during filming, but suffered a miscarriage shortly after. She had long since earned the reputation of being extremely difficult to work with: showing up late, drinking on the set, stumbling over lines, and consulting with her drama coach constantly. Wilder is the only director ever to work with her more than once, and he was extremely critical of her unprofessionalism afterward. According to Carl Rollyson in his *Marilyn Monroe: A Life of the Actress,* "He had been cautious with the press during filming, but shortly

Haskell, Molly. *From Reverence to Rape: The Treatment of Women in the Movies.* New York, Penguin Books, 1974.

Rollyson, Carl E. *Marilyn Monroe: A Life of the Actress.* Ann Arbor, UMI Research Press, 1986.

Straayer, Chris. "Redressing the 'Natural': The Temporary Transvestite Film." *Wide Angle.* Vol. 14, No. 1, 1992, 36-55.

Sondheim, Stephen (1930—)

Stephen Sondheim is one of the most important creative personalities in the American musical theater of the late twentieth century. Like George M. Cohan and Cole Porter before him, Sondheim is one of those rare songsters who creates both words and music. Sondheim and his shows have almost a cult following because of their sophistication of topic, music, and approach. Sondheim is a composer who creates something unique and different for each show, yet each work bears his unmistakable imprint. His most popular number, "Send in the Clowns," has been recorded by numerous singers worldwide.

Sondheim was born on March 22, 1930, into an affluent New York family and began his musical studies at very young age. He grew up as a neighbor of Oscar Hammerstein II, who took the young Stephen under his wing. He graduated from Williams College with a music degree and continued his composition studies with Milton Babbitt, a pioneer in computer-generated music. He began his career as a composer of musicals in the 1950s with *Saturday Night* (1955), a show which was not staged until 1997. He also wrote incidental music for the play *Girls of Summer* (1956).

Sondheim's first commercial success was as librettist for *West Side Story* (1957). With music by Leonard Bernstein, Sondheim penned the words to such immortal songs as "Maria," "Tonight," "America," "One Hand, One Heart," "I Feel Pretty," and "Somewhere."

Sondheim's next major project was *Gypsy* (1959). He was to write both words and music before the star of the show, Ethel Merman, demanded a more experienced composer. Jule Styne wrote the music, and Sondheim once again created the lyrics for his second hit show of the late 1950s. Songs in *Gypsy* included "Let Me Entertain You," "Everything's Coming Up Roses," "Wherever We Go," and "Rose's Turn."

The first show to appear on Broadway for which Sondheim penned both words and music was *A Funny Thing Happened on the Way to the Forum* (1962). Based on the plays of Plautus, the fast-moving musical farce included such songs as "Comedy Tonight," and "Everybody Ought to Have a Maid." The plot concerned Pseudolus, a slave who must go through a series of hilarious adventures in order to gain his freedom. Zero Mostel received rave reviews for his performance as Pseudolus in the original production. The show won Tony Awards for Best Musical and Best Producer (Harold Prince). It was revived on Broadway in 1972 with Phil Silvers and again in 1996 with Nathan Lane. A number of original songs were dropped for the 1966 film version with Zero Mostel and Phil Silvers.

Two works followed in the succeeding years: *Anyone Can Whistle* (1964) and *Do I Hear a Waltz?* (1965). *Anyone Can Whistle,* a musical about corrupt city officials, played only one week on Broadway. Its cast album, made after the show closed, gained cult status. Sondheim returned to his single role as lyricist for *Do I Hear a Waltz?* (1965), a show for which Richard Rodgers wrote the music. The plot

Tony Curtis (left) and Jack Lemmon in a scene from the film *Some Like It Hot.*

afterwards he allowed his disgust with her to show. She had seldom worked a full day on the set, and because of her the production had gone several weeks past its scheduled end and had exceeded its budget by about half a million dollars. He took his revenge in a series of sarcastic statements''; for example, suggesting that the Screen Directors Guild should give him a Purple Heart for casting her in two of his films, and he was too old and too rich to ever go through such an ordeal again. Curtis also spoke of her contemptuously, describing their love scene as "like kissing Hitler." In the final film, however, the ensemble acting of the cast was considered superb.

According to Bernard F. Dick, "It would not be hyperbole to call *Some Like It Hot* a comic masterpiece. It has the classic comic plot of disguise, deception, and intrigue where a single complication generates a series of subplots the way a single pebble creates concentric ripples in a pool. *Some Like It Hot* also possesses a quality found in the best comedies—a sense of humanity and an attitude of compassion for the lunatics and lovers who play the fool for our sake."

—Jeanne Hall

FURTHER READING:

Dick, Bernard F. *Billy Wilder.* New York, DeCapo Press, 1996.

Dyer, Richard. *Heavenly Bodies.* New York, St. Martin's Press, 1987.

French, Brandon. *On the Verge of Revolt: Women in American Films of the Fifties.* New York, Frederick Ungar Publishing Company, 1978.

Stephen Sondheim (standing) with Richard Rodgers.

centered around the experiences of an American tourist in Venice and, like its immediate predecessor, was a commercial failure.

Sondheim's work during the 1970s began with two concept musicals, *Company* (1970) and *Follies* (1971). A dramatic plot in the traditional narrative sense does not exist in either of these works. Rather, each show revolves around a central theme or concept. *Company* concerned five New York couples and their mutual bachelor friend, while *Follies* centered around four people in their early fifties who attend a reunion and reflect on earlier times. *Company* included the numbers "Being Alive," "You Could Drive a Person Crazy," "Another Hundred People," and "Barcelona." The show won the New York Drama Critics' Circle Award for Best Music and six Tony Awards, including Best Musical, Best Score, and Best Lyrics. *Follies,* with a fifty-member cast and a twenty-two number score, included "Who's That Woman?" "I'm Still Here," and a myriad of pastiche songs in the styles of earlier Broadway composers. Although *Follies* won the Drama Critics' Circle Award for Best Musical and seven Tony Awards, it closed after 522 performances with a loss of its $800,000 investment. A revival of *Follies* appeared in 1987.

A Little Night Music (1973) was based on the 1955 Ingmar Bergman film *Sommarnattens Leende* (*Smiles of a Summer Night*). Set in Sweden at the turn of the century, the book by Hugh Wheeler dealt with the complicated romantic world of the aging actress Desiree Arnfeldt, her former lover—the lawyer Fredrik Egerman, his child-bride Anne, and their circle of acquaintances. Glynis Jones and Len Cariou starred in the original Broadway production, while Elizabeth Taylor and Cariou appeared in the 1978 film. *A Little Night*

Music is entirely in 3/4 time (or multiples thereof), the meter of a waltz, a musical symbol of nostalgia. The show contained a number of memorable songs, including "A Weekend in the Country," "Night Waltz," and "Remember." But the show's most unforgettable number was "Send in the Clowns," Desiree's nostalgic soliloquy.

The Frogs (1974) was one of Sondheim's most curious experiments. Created as incidental music for a Yale Repertory Theatre production of Burt Shevelove's English adaptation of the Greek play of the same name, Sondheim's score received its first performance in the Yale University swimming pool. The score avoided traditional musical theater idioms and contained fiendishly difficult choral writing. Without the experience of writing *The Frogs,* the innovation which Sondheim demonstrated in *Pacific Overtures* may not have been possible.

Pacific Overtures (1976) is one of the most unique shows in the repertory of the American musical theater. The saga of 120 years of Japanese history, from the arrival of Commodore Perry in 1856 to the late twentieth century, is told in the style of traditional Japanese Kabuki theater. The all-male, all-Asian cast performed numbers such as "Chrysanthemum Tea," "Please Hello," and "The Advantages of Floating in the Middle of the Sea." Despite its striking originality (or perhaps because of it), *Pacific Overtures* closed after 193 performances, losing all of its half million dollar budget.

Always wanting to expand the boundaries of the musical theater, Sondheim chose the macabre tale of a murderous barber as the basis for *Sweeney Todd, The Demon Barber of Fleet Street* (1979). The title character, swearing revenge on a judge for the demise of his family and murdering everyone who sits in his barber chair, enters into a business partnership with Mrs. Lovett, owner of a pie shop who has difficulties finding meat for her pies. The pair find a practical, but macabre, solution to both of their problems. The score contains a very high percentage of music—so many, in fact, that the work has sometimes been called an opera. Among the most memorable numbers are "Not While I'm Around," "Epiphany," "A Little Priest," "God, That's Good," "Pretty Women," and "Johanna." The show, described as "one giant step forward for vegetarianism," garnered eight Tony Awards, including Best Musical, Score, and Book. Angela Lansbury and Len Cariou starred in the original Broadway production.

Merrily We Roll Along (1981) was a pastiche score which, like *Follies*, emulated earlier musical comedies. The show ran for only 16 performances on Broadway. Like *Anyone Can Whistle, Merrily We Roll Along* lived beyond its Broadway run through the success of its cast album.

Sunday in the Park with George (1984) revealed yet another approach to Sondheim's efforts to expand the musical theater. Based on characters in Georges Seurat's painting *Sunday Afternoon on the Island of La Grande Jatte,* the book by James Lapine dealt with issues of creativity and the power of art. Mandy Patinkin and Bernadette Peters starred in the original production. The show ran for over a year and a half and won the 1985 Pulitzer Prize for Drama. Among the numbers in its intriguingly intricate score were "Finishing the Hat" and "Move On."

Sondheim, again in collaboration with Lapine, ventured into the world of fairy tales for his next show, *Into the Woods* (1987). The stories of Cinderella, Jack and the Beanstalk, Little Red Riding Hood, Snow White, and Rapunzel were fused around a central tale about a baker and his wife who live under the curse of a witch. In order to break the curse, the baker and his wife must secure an item from each of the other fables. All ends well at the end of the first act. In the second act, the widow of the giant in Jack and the Beanstalk demands revenge, and the characters must join together in order to defeat her. Songs such as "Into the Woods," "Agony," and "Giants in the Sky" appeared in the score, as did the instructive ballads "No One Is Alone" and "Children Will Listen." Bernadette Peters, Joanna Gleason, and Chip Zien starred in the original Broadway production.

With *Assassins* (1991), Sondheim returned to the darker side of the human experience. All of the major characters are people who tried, either successfully or unsuccessfully, to assassinate American presidents. From the opening chorus, "Everybody's Got the Right to Be Happy," to the final scene at the Texas Book Depository, these "anti-heroes" of American society each present the motives behind their actions.

Passion (1994), based on the French film *Passione d'Amore*, concerned the love triangle between a military officer, his beautiful young lover, and an invalid who captures his soul. The story is presented in a rhapsodic manner with a seamless blend of music and dialogue. Songs included "Happiness," "I Wish I Could Forget You," and "No One Has Ever Loved Me."

In addition to original shows, several stage compilations of Sondheim songs have appeared in London and New York: *Side by Side by Sondheim* (1976), *A Stephen Sondheim Evening* (also known as *You're Gonna Love Tomorrow*, 1983), and *Putting It Together* (1992).

Sondheim has also written for the motion pictures. Among his film credits are *The Seven Per-Cent Solution* (1976), *Reds* (1981), and *Dick Tracy* (1990). The song "Sooner or Later" from *Dick Tracy*, performed by Madonna in the film, earned Sondheim an Oscar for Best Original Song. Sondheim's only television musical, *Evening Primrose* (1966), was featured on ABC's "Stage 67" series and starred Anthony Perkins.

Stephen Sondheim is one of the most original creators for the musical theater at the end of the twentieth century. Each of his shows is unique. Sondheim has expanded the boundaries of the musical theater not only through his choice of subject matter (in which he often challenges the audience to extremes) but also in his handling of musical form and structure. Songs are intrinsically joined together in his shows, and are likewise bound to particular characters. Through live performances, video releases, and recordings, Sondheim's music enjoys world-wide dissemination. For Sondheim's avid fans, his work represents a level of accomplishment and innovation which is difficult to match.

—William A. Everett

FURTHER READING:

Banfield, Stephen. *Sondheim's Broadway Musicals.* Ann Arbor, University of Michigan Press, 1993.

Bristow, Eugene K, and J. Kevin Butler. "Company, About Face! The Show that Revolutionized the American Musical." *American Music.* Vol. 5, No. 3, 1987, 241-54.

Fraser, Barbara Meares. "The Dream Shattered: America's Seventies Musicals." *Journal of American Culture.* Vol. 12, No. 3, 1989, 31-37.

Gordon, Joanne. *Art Isn't Easy: The Theater of Stephen Sondheim,* revised edition. New York, Da Capo, 1992.

Gottfried, Martin. *Sondheim.* New York, Abrams, 1993.

Herbert, Trevor. "Sondheim's Technique." *Contemporary Music Review.* Vol. 5, 1989, 199-214.

Martin, George Whitney. "On the Verge of Opera: Stephen Sondheim." *Opera Quarterly.* Vol. 6, No. 3, 1989, 76-85.

Mollin, Alfred. "Mayhem and Morality in *Sweeney Todd.*" *American Music.* Vol 9, No. 4, 1991, 405-17.

Secrest, Meryle. *Stephen Sondheim: A Life.* New York, Alfred A. Knopf, 1998.

Zadan, Craig. *Sondheim & Company.* New York, Da Capo, 1994.

Sonny and Cher

When struggling songwriter and publicist Salvatore Bono met 16-year-old runaway Cher Sarkisian in a Los Angeles Club in 1962, he saw the possibility that he could make her into a performer. What neither of them could have seen was how phenomenal the musical act "Sonny and Cher" would become over the next decade. Sonny and Cher materialized on the pop scene in 1965. Their second radio hit, "I Got You Babe," sold 3 million copies and became their signature song, while their first album, *All I Really Want to Do* (1965), shot to second place on the charts. To a generation of teenagers looking for a more serious message than that found in the pop of the early 1960s, Sonny and Cher represented an exciting new rebellious style. Often pictured with sullen expressions, both had long dark hair and wore clothes that were outlandish even by hippie standards: wide bell-bottomed jeans with fur vests and boots and large peace medallions. The words to their songs were often filled with the resentful pain of

Sonny and Cher

the outsider, and their voices complimented the words perfectly: Cher's, deep and soulful, and Sonny's, nasal and sneering. Adding to the mystique was their relationship; they might be alienated from society, but they had each other, a very appealing concept to their young audience. Though their career as rebel icons lasted only a few years, they were a pivotal part of an important transition in white rock music from 1950s pop to the folk rock of the late 1960s.

Salvatore Bono was born in 1935 in Detroit to working-class Italian immigrant parents. His family eventually moved to Los Angeles where, after dropping out of high school in 1952, "Sonny" drove a delivery van for a butcher shop. Though he had no formal musical training and admitted "I only knew five chords," Bono wanted to become a songwriter. Between meat deliveries, he tried to sell his songs at the music stores on Sunset Boulevard. By 1962, when he met Cher, he was working as a songwriter and publicist.

Cher Sarkisian grew up in Los Angeles. Her Armenian father deserted the family, and though Cher renewed contact with him for short periods during her childhood, she was raised by her mother, whose background was Irish, English, German, and Cherokee. Her mother, Georgia Holt, was an aspiring actress with a transient lifestyle and a long line of boyfriends and ex-husbands, giving Cher's childhood an unstable quality. As the only dark child in a family of blondes, Cher later said she keenly felt the lack of ethnic role models. By age sixteen, she left home for good.

When Bono met Cher, he thought she was a lesbian, since many of her friends were gay. They became friends, but even after they became lovers, neither was compelled by any physical relationship. Eleven years older, and with clear ambitions, Sonny took the role of mentor and promoter in the relationship. Cher was the talent. Sonny wrote songs for Cher and intended that she should sing them alone. When she pleaded shyness, he agreed to sing with her, and Sonny and Cher was created. The immediate success of their first album and several top-ten hits overwhelmed the couple. Luxuriating in their new-found fame, they bought a mansion and treated themselves to nose jobs. However, their second album was a failure, and they began the struggle to stay on top. Though they played themselves in the Beatles-like film entitled *Good Times* (1967), the public had turned away. The new psychedelic music was in vogue, and Sonny and Cher did not fit in.

Sonny's next direction was moviemaking. He wrote the screenplay for *Chastity* (1969), a coming-of-age film about Cher's life. When *Chastity* lost money at the box office, the couple was desperate, since he had invested all their money in making the film. Ever resourceful, Sonny developed a nightclub act for the duo, and they were booked at the Flamingo Hilton in Las Vegas, opening for Pat Boone. The act revolved around Cher's singing and some comedy dialogue, mostly involving put-downs of the gawky Sonny by his glamorous wife. (They had finally been legally married in 1969, shortly after the birth of their daughter, Chastity.) Though the put-down humor was Sonny's idea, and he wrote the jokes, the various strains with his relationship with Cher were beginning to become obvious.

When success finally arrived in the form of a variety show on network television, their relationship was essentially over. From the fall of 1972 until the spring of 1974, Sonny and Cher hosted a weekly show—*The Sonny and Cher Comedy Hour*—that was essentially a recreation of their Vegas act, complete with supposedly good-natured marital carping. The show was widely liked, but by quite a different audience than the one that had loved them in the 1960s. An older, more settled generation watched the show, which was built around

Sonny and Cher as a family. In an era when the Vietnam War and economic problems made society feel insecure, it was reassuring to see that the hippie couple was still together. Though their marriage was famous, it was more a creation of public relations than a reality. They still lived together, but each had a lover living in the household as well. Cher finally divorced Sonny in 1975, citing "involuntary servitude" as the grounds. Though Sonny claimed to be stunned by the charges—he wrote in his diary, "I though I was teaching; she thought I was intimidating"—Cher insisted that he had been controlling and stifling. "I left Sonny for another woman," she has said, "Myself." Their relationship was to remain discordant for years.

Sonny and Cher, who chose to use their one-word names after the divorce, each went on to extraordinary careers separately. Immediately after the cancellation of their television show and the divorce, Cher's career seemed to soar. While continuing to sing, she also starred in several movies, receiving kudos for acting in *Silkwood* (1983) and an Academy award for best actress for *Moonstruck* (1987). Frequently showing up on "worst dressed" lists because of her continued penchant for outrageous and revealing clothes, Cher was a constant figure in the tabloids, which loved to follow her romantic exploits and marriages, often with younger men. With the help of personal trainers, plastic surgery, and cosmetics, she has made her beauty itself a career, creating fitness books and videos and selling a cosmetics line. She was ridiculed by critics when she made a series of infomercials for beauty products, but, always resilient, has continued to make music and movies.

In the meantime, Sonny was reduced to infrequent guest appearances on shows like *Love Boat,* which made a specialty of showcasing forgotten stars. He finally gave up entertainment and opened a restaurant, first in Los Angeles, then in Palm Springs, where he remarried. When he became frustrated with the red tape involved in moving the sign for his restaurant, Sonny decided to run for mayor of Palm Springs, even though he had registered to vote for the first time only in 1987. While some voters thought his candidacy a joke, enough of them agreed with his "less government" message to put him in office in 1988. Discovering a taste for politics, he ran for the U.S. Senate in 1992, suffering a humiliating defeat. Two years later, he made a bid for the U.S. House of Representatives, and won. Many still thought him a joke and called him "Sonny Bonehead" behind his back, but Bono managed to command respect in his new career. Having left his rebellious hippie roots far behind him, Sonny reinvented himself as an uncomplicated conservative with an outsider's fresh viewpoint and a self-deprecating humor that appealed to many constituents. By the time he died, in January, 1998, in a skiing accident, he was a far cry from the sullen hippie in the Eskimo boots and bobcat vest who peered out from under shaggy bangs on his album covers. His colleagues, his ex-wife Cher, and the public who had watched him change along with their own changes, came to eulogize him.

Sonny and Cher's daughter Chastity Bono has made news on her own account. At the age of thirteen, watching a movie kiss between two women, Chastity realized that she was a lesbian. She intended to keep her sexuality a secret, but media scrutiny of her famous parents made it impossible. The tabloids "outed" her in their headlines, and in 1987, Chastity told her parents she was a lesbian and began to work actively on gay-rights issues. Initially horrified, Cher threw her daughter out of their apartment, but they soon reconciled. Her relationship with her father was more problematic. Sonny's conservative politics did not mix well with Chastity's lesbian activism, and at the time of his death they remained estranged.

In retrospect, Sonny and Cher burst on the American scene in an impressionable era. Because they so seemed to capture the spirit of youth—angry, vulnerable, intensely loyal to each other—the young fans who admired them could not forget them. Their resilience continued to give hope to their aging audience, likewise battered by life. Though their musical contributions may not have been exactly classic, they have been enduring, and their signature song, ''I Got You Babe,'' contains a hope for connection that spans generations.

—Tina Gianoulis

FURTHER READING:

Bono, Chastity, and Billie Fitzpatrick. *Family Outing.* New York, Little, Brown and Company, 1998.

Bono, Sonny. *And the Beat Goes On.* New York, Pocket Books, 1991.

Cher, as told to Jeff Coplon. *The First Time.* New York, Simon and Schuster, 1998.

Sosa, Sammy (1968—)

Born in the Dominican Republic, Chicago Cubs outfielder Sammy Sosa became a baseball sensation almost overnight in 1998, when he was named the National League's Most Valuable Player after battling St. Louis Cardinals hitter Mark McGwire neck-and-neck for baseball's home-run championship. In that year, Roger Maris's 37-year-old record was broken twice, by McGwire who hit 70 homers, and by Sosa, with 66. In June, Sosa had hit 20 home runs, the most ever by one player in a single month. Sosa's 158 runs batted in (RBIs) in 1998 ranked him fourth in National League history. His impressive statistics helped the Cubs to make the post-season playoffs for only the third time since 1945. Despite being constantly followed by the media during his home-run chase with McGwire, Sosa maintained his good charm and easy-going manner and helped contribute to a renewal of America's faith in its national pastime, beset by strikes and player scandals in recent years.

—Matt Kerr

FURTHER READING:

Preller, James. *McGwire & Sosa: A Season to Remember.* New York, Aladdin Paperbacks, 1998

Sammy's Season. Introduction by Skip Bayless. Lincolnwood, Illinois, Contemporary Books, 1998.

Smith, Gary.''The Race Is On.'' *Sports Illustrated.* September 21, 1998, pages 48-51.

Soul Music

Soul music emerged in the late 1950s and early 1960s as one of the most distinctive forms in the history of American popular music. For black Americans especially, soul music defined the 1960s, offering a cultural soundtrack to the civil rights movement and the larger awakening of black consciousness and pride. Soul hits dominated the charts during that decade, but defining exactly what soul was proved no easy task, even for some of its greatest artists. Wilson

Soul singer Sam Cooke.

Pickett defined soul as ''nothin' but a feelin'.'' Don Covay said, ''For a singer, soul is total vocal freedom.'' Aretha Franklin explained, ''Soul to me is a feeling, a lot of depth and being able to bring to the surface that which is happening inside. . . . It's just the emotion, the way it affects other people.'' Elements of the genre live on, but the classic period of soul music, from about 1960 to 1975, remains one of the most important contributions to American popular culture for its style, its raw, emotive power, and its depth of feeling. Alongside jazz, it is one of America's most original contributions to world culture.

If defining soul music proved elusive, its origins were not. Soul music emerged during the 1950s as a cross between rhythm and blues and gospel music. Soul music combined the Saturday-night sinner and the Sunday-morning repentant into one person or one song, just as they existed in real life. In combining the R&B themes with gospel elements (call-and-response singing, close harmonies, and themes of celebration, loss, and longing), early soul artists often secularized gospel tunes by changing key words: the gospel song ''Talkin' 'Bout Jesus'' became ''Talkin' 'Bout You''; ''This Little Light of Mine'' became ''This Little Girl of Mine''; ''I've Got a Savior'' became ''I Got a Woman.'' This transition reflected changes occurring in the black community after World War II as more and more black Americans moved from the rural South to the urban North. Early arrivals in the North had created R&B music in the mid-1940s as an expression of the new realities of life in these urban neighborhoods. Later, as more Southern blacks poured into these communities, they brought with them elements of Southern gospel music. Both musical forms coexisted as separate expressions of black life. They soon crossed, however, producing what became soul music.

The acknowledged father of this cross was Ray Charles. All of the secularized gospel songs mentioned above were hits for Charles in the mid-1950s. Born in 1930 in Albany, Georgia, Charles moved to Seattle as a teenager and emerged in the late 1940s as a Nat ''King'' Cole-style crooner playing local clubs such as the Rocking Chair and the Black and Tan. There he caught the attention of Swingtime

Records, one of the early black-owned R&B recording companies, and he released a number of blues and Cole-inspired tunes, among them "Kissa Me Baby" and "Confession Blues." Moving to Atlantic Records in 1952, Charles began developing an earthier style that he picked up working with blues musicians Guitar Slim and Lowell Fulsom. At Atlantic, he began to combine blues elements with gospel stylings he had picked up as a child in Georgia. That style became the basis for soul music and provided Charles with a string of hits during the 1950s, including "Lonely Avenue," "I Got a Woman," "Hallelujah I Love Her So," and perhaps his biggest hit, "What'd I Say," which combined a gospel call-and-response segment between Charles and his backup singers, the Raelettes, moans that could easily have come from either the bedroom or the pulpit, and a driving R&B band.

Following close on Charles's heels was Sam Cooke, who had come to prominence as the lead singer of the gospel group the Soul Stirrers before developing a more pop-oriented soul style which brought him such hits as "You Send Me," "Twistin' the Night Away," and "Bring It on Home to Me." Jackie Wilson similarly had started out in a vocal group, the Dominoes, before forging a driving pop-soul style with such songs as "Reet Petite," "Lonely Teardrops," and "Baby Workout." While Charles's music maintained a close connection with the raw elements of R&B music, Wilson and Cooke moved the R&B and gospel marriage closer to the realm of pop.

It took three record companies to bring soul into the mainstream. They were Atlantic Records in New York City, Motown Records in Detroit, and Stax/Volt Records in Memphis. While numerous smaller labels made invaluable contributions to soul music, these three labels were responsible for some of the most explosive soul music of the 1950s and 1960s. Most of the major talents in soul music, with some very notable exceptions, were on these three record labels. And, while there were major individual talents on each label roster, each company managed to build a unique sound that identified each artist with his or her particular label.

Herb Abramson and Ahmet Ertegun formed Atlantic Records in 1947. Their initial releases were in the jazz vein, but they moved into R&B in 1949 and became one of the dominant independent record labels in that field in the 1950s due to their successes with such R&B artists as Ruth Brown, Ray Charles, Joe Turner, LaVern Baker, the Clovers, and others. With the success of Charles's records in the emerging soul style, Atlantic moved even further into soul music. In the early to mid-1960s, Atlantic had soul hits with The Drifters' "Up on the Roof," "This Magic Moment," and "Save the Last Dance for Me"; Ben E. King's "Stand by Me" and "Spanish Harlem"; Percy Sledge's "When a Man Loves a Woman"; Wilson Pickett's "Land of 1000 Dances," "Mustang Sally," and "Funky Broadway"; Don Covay's "Seesaw"; and Solomon Burke's "Just out of Reach." Atlantic's major sound innovation was to bring soul "uptown" with a more polished, professional sound accomplished by adding string arrangements and by using professional Brill Building songwriters.

Atlantic's biggest success, however, came in 1967 with the discovery of singer Aretha Franklin. Franklin was the perfect embodiment of soul music, combining a strong background in church music (her father, the Reverend C. L. Franklin, was the well-known minister of the New Bethel Baptist Church in Detroit) with the depth of feeling and style required to take her gospel training to the secular music world. She had first signed with Columbia Records in the early 1960s, where she attempted to become a pop/soul singer in the Sam Cooke style. Her records in this vein fared poorly, and when her contract with Columbia expired in 1967, producer Jerry Wexler signed her to

Atlantic. There, Wexler took Franklin to Rick Hall's Fame Studios in Muscle Shoals, Alabama, where he had had success remolding Wilson Pickett's sound. Hall's Muscle Shoals, with its combination of black and white Southern musicians, was developing a reputation as a hotbed of soul music, a place where the all-important *feeling* necessary in soul music seemed to come out more readily. There, Franklin remade her sound, letting her gospel roots come out. She debuted on Atlantic in 1967 with the album *I Never Loved a Man the Way I Love You,* which went to number two on the album charts that year. Both the title song and Franklin's cover of Otis Redding's "Respect" went to number one on the R&B charts that year. The album also contained "Do Right Woman—Do Right Man," "Baby, Baby, Baby," and "Save Me," all of which have become soul classics. Franklin released two more records in the space of a year, unleashing such hits as "Baby I Love You," "Chain of Fools," and the smash "(You Make Me Feel Like) A Natural Woman," a top ten hit on both the pop and R&B charts. These releases earned Franklin the undisputed title of "The Queen of Soul" and cemented Atlantic as the home of some of the most powerful soul music ever produced.

Songwriter, producer, and one-time record shop owner Berry Gordy, Jr. founded Motown Records in 1960 in a simple white bungalow at 2648 West Grand Boulevard in Detroit, Michigan. Gordy had successfully written and produced songs for Jackie Wilson ("Lonely Teardrops") and Barrett Strong ("Money") during the late 1950s that drew upon Ray Charles's innovations in fusing R&B and gospel styles. In 1960, Gordy moved from independent producing (where he would lease songs to other labels) and began his own label, Tamla, which later became part of Motown. In Motown, Gordy put together a songwriting/producing/recording formula that would sell more singles by the end of the 1960s than any other company. He did this with what resembled assembly line production, and Gordy referred to his role as "quality control." First, he assembled a team of crack songwriters and producers, including Smokey Robinson and the team of Brian Holland, Lamont Dozier, and Eddie Holland, who wrote one hit after another for Gordy. Next, he put together a house band that included Benny Benjamin on drums, Joe Messina on guitar, James Jamerson on bass, Earl Van Dyke on keyboards, and other regulars. Together, the songwriting, production teams, and house band established a signature style that was unmistakable. Then, drawing from the rich local talent of Detroit, Gordy assembled or signed vocal groups or individual singers to record the songs.

Part of Gordy's gift lay in transforming raw street talent into a polished musical product, which he did using this assembly line process and his eye for promising young talent, calling Motown the "Sound of Young America." Motown's roster of stars included the Supremes ("Baby Love," "You Can't Hurry Love," "Love Child"), Marvin Gaye ("I Heard It through the Grapevine," "Pride and Joy"), the Four Tops ("Standing in the Shadows of Love," "Bernadette," "Reach out I'll Be There"), the Temptations ("My Girl," "Ain't Too Proud to Beg"), Mary Wells ("My Guy"), Martha and the Vandellas, Smokey Robinson and the Miracles ("I Second That Emotion," "The Tracks of My Tears"), the Marvelettes, Jr. Walker and the All-Stars, Stevie Wonder ("Uptight," "Signed, Sealed, Delivered, I'm Yours," "For Once in My Life"), and Gladys Knight and the Pips, among many others. Motown's nationwide success with this formula lay in the ability of its music to resonate in both the black and white communities, and many of the above hits topped both the R&B and Pop charts throughout the 1960s. From the very beginning, for commercial reasons or otherwise, Gordy followed an integrationist approach, and his success pushed the soul music created at Motown closer and closer to the larger pop realm.

Although Gordy's formula was responsible for most of Motown's success, in the later 1960s and early 1970s, a few of his early artists began to break out of the Motown formula, maturing musically to create very personal, signature styles all their own. The two most prominent and unique were Marvin Gaye and Stevie Wonder. Gaye broke out of the Motown mold in a decisive way with the topical album *What's Going On* in 1971: both its title track and "What's Happening Brother" addressed the war in Vietnam, "Mercy Mercy Me" the environment, and "Inner City Blues" the urban crisis in America's ghetto communities. Wonder became a musical force unto himself with a string of important albums in the early 1970s on which he wrote and sang all of the songs and played most of the instruments. Included in albums such as *Innervisions, Talking Book, Fulfillingness First Finale, Music of My Mind,* and his double-album opus *Songs in the Key of Life,* Wonder scored huge hits with such songs as "You Are the Sunshine of My Life," "Isn't She Lovely," "I Wish," and "Superstition." His songs also often took a topical turn, with such songs as "Living for the City" and "Village Ghetto Land" on urban problems, and "Too High" on drug addiction. "Higher Ground" was an exhortation for black self-empowerment, and "You Haven't Done Nothin'" a larger critique of the white power structure. The classic Motown era ended after 1971 when Gordy moved the company to Los Angeles and gave up direct hands-on control over studio production. With those changes, the trademark sound disintegrated.

If Atlantic and Motown defined soul in the urban North, Memphis's Stax/Volt Records, during its classic period from 1960-1968, virtually defined Southern soul, a sound at once relaxed and easy yet filled with musical tension that left listeners begging for more, which became as easily recognizable as the Motown sound. Jim Stewart and his sister Estelle Axton founded Satellite Records in 1959, changing the name to Stax by 1961 (Volt Records was a later subsidiary), and began to record local black musicians, eventually establishing a studio in an old Memphis movie theater at 926 E. McLemore Avenue. Among their first recording artists were local DJ Rufus Thomas and his daughter Carla. Carla Thomas scored an early hit in 1960 with "Gee Whiz," which reached the top ten on both the R&B and Pop charts. Stax's next hit was "Last Night," an instrumental number by the Mar-Keys that featured a unique combination of organ, guitar, and horns that would become the hallmark of Stax/Volt's sound. Although not quite as tightly run as Motown, Stax/Volt did employ some of the same techniques. The instrumental band Booker T. and the MGs became in essence Stax's house band in addition to scoring numerous hits on its own such as "Green Onions" and "Time Is Tight." Stax also benefited from a core group of songwriters and producers, most prominent among them David Porter and Isaac Hayes, who wrote many of Stax's great hits, including "Hold On! I'm Comin'" and "Soul Man" by Sam and Dave and "B-A-B-Y" by Carla Thomas. A number of Stax/Volt's stars were also writers, including Eddie Floyd, who cowrote his own hits "Knock on Wood" and "Raise Your Hand," among others. Even more prolific was MG guitarist Steve Cropper, who, in addition to playing guitar on many Stax/Volt records, also cowrote many songs with other Stax/Volt artists, including the best selling Stax/Volt single of all time, "(Sittin' on) The Dock of the Bay," with Otis Redding. Like Aretha Franklin at Atlantic, Redding was far and away Stax/Volt's greatest star, and one of the most distinctive soul singers ever, with a powerful, raw, emotional style that seemed to wring every bit of feeling from every note of a song. A prolific songwriter as well, Redding had some of Stax/Volt's biggest hits, including "Respect," "Try a Little Tenderness," "These Arms of Mine," "Mr. Pitiful," "The Happy Song (Dum-Dum)," and literally dozens of others before his untimely death in a plane crash in December 1967.

Stax/Volt continued after the death of Redding, but things were never quite the same. Despite a number of hits in the 1968-1972 period, Stax declined with the dissolution of Booker T. and the MGs and the loss of its deal with Atlantic Records, which had given Atlantic distribution rights to Stax's recording, since the early 1960s. With the breakup of that deal, Atlantic took Stax's biggest sellers, the Otis Redding and Sam and Dave catalogs, which were in many ways the heart of the Stax/Volt empire. These problems slowly eroded Stax's signature style, and the company folded in bankruptcy in 1975.

While the artists on Atlantic, Motown, and Stax/Volt did much to define soul music in the 1960s, the genre's most distinctive, and perhaps most influential, innovator came not from these three labels but in the person of Augusta, Georgia's James Brown. Born in 1933, Brown emerged as an early R&B/soul singer in the mid-1950s with such hits as "Please, Please, Please," and "Try Me." He scored more hits in the early 1960s, but his heyday came later in the decade when he diverged from more standard soul forms to fashion his own brand of soul/funk, a harder-driving, more intense and powerful sound that came through on such songs as "Cold Sweat," "Papa's Got a Brand New Bag," "Get Up (I Feel Like Being a) Sex Machine," and "I Got You (I Feel Good)." Brown also made powerful statement songs during the heyday of black power, including "Say It Loud—I'm Black and I'm Proud," "I Don't Want Nobody to Give Me Nothing (Open Up the Door I'll Get It Myself)," "Get Up, Get into It, and Get Involved," and "Soul Power." Brown's stylistic innovations in soul music influenced the development of both funk music in the 1970s and rap music in the 1980s.

Although great soul artists such as Al Green, the Staple Singers, Curtis Mayfield, the aforementioned Marvin Gaye and Stevie Wonder, and many others continued to record soul music, the classic soul era ended in the mid-1970s as black music fragmented into such styles as disco and funk, which emphasized dance rhythms over well-crafted singing and songwriting. The great record labels that had acted as important conduits for soul music had moved in other directions as well. Atlantic moved more toward rock acts, Motown left for Los Angeles, and Stax/Volt fell apart in financial trouble. In terms of style, the connection to gospel music that was such a hallmark of soul became less influential in black music generally, and soul evolved into a more homogenous sound known as "urban contemporary" music.

—Timothy Berg

FURTHER READING:

George, Nelson. *The Death of Rhythm and Blues.* New York, Plume, 1988.

Guralnick, Peter. *Sweet Soul Music: Rhythm and Blues and the Southern Dream of Freedom.* New York, Harper & Row, 1986.

Haralambos, Michael. *Right On: From Blues to Soul in Black America.* New York, Drake Publishers, 1975.

Hirshey, Gerri. *Nowhere to Run: The Story of Soul Music.* New York, Times Books, 1984.

Miller, Jim, editor. *The Rolling Stone Illustrated History of Rock & Roll.* New York, Random House/Rolling Stone Press, 1980.

Shaw, Arnold. *The World of Soul: Black America's Contribution to the Pop Music Scene.* New York, Cowles Book Company, 1970.

Szatmary, David P. *Rockin' in Time: A Social History of Rock-and-Roll.* Englewood Cliffs, N.J., Prentice Hall, 1991.

Various Artists. *Atlantic Rhythm and Blues: 1947-1974.* Atlantic Recording Corporation, 1985.

Various Artists. *Beg, Scream, and Shout!: The Big Ol' Box of '60s Soul.* Rhino Records, 1997.

Various Artists. *The Complete Stax/Volt Singles, 1959-1968.* Atlantic Recording Corporation, 1991.

Various Artists. *Hitsville U.S.A.: The Motown Singles Collection, 1959-1971.* Motown Records, 1992.

Soul Train

Since 1970, fans have been grooving every week to America's top soul and R&B hits on a televised boogie down called *Soul Train.* Known as "the black *American Bandstand,*" the syndicated dance party proved to be more than just a musical showcase: It established an African American presence on television at a time when such representation was almost nonexistent.

Created and hosted for 23 years by Don Cornelius, a former Chicago disc jockey with a silky, measured baritone, *Soul Train* was conceived around the notion of "soul music going from city to city as a train would." The program relied on a sequence of stock elements that gave it an air of familiarity. The show's distinctive squealing "Soooulll Traaain" opening, devised by a deejay friend of the host, has remained unchanged since 1970. Each week, Cornelius opened the show by promising viewers they could "bet your last money it's gonna be a stone gas, honey." A series of musical performances followed, with the camera alternating between the lip-synching band and the gyrating denizens on the dance floor. Occasionally stopping to banter with his musical guests, Cornelius closed each program by wishing his viewers "love, peace, and soul!"

The show was a first of its kind on mainstream American television, a weekly forum for the best in African-American rhythm and blues. "It was trailblazing," observed J. R. Reynolds, R&B editor of *Billboard Magazine,* "not in terms of being a dance music show, but in terms of R&B being offered a platform on a consistent basis." In its heyday during the 1970s, *Soul Train* was able to attract some of the top names in the entertainment industry. Guests on the first national telecast were Gladys Knight and the Pips; the performers

Chaka Khan performs with the group Rufus on the *Soul Train* television show.

who made regular appearances included Barry White, Marvin Gaye, Aretha Franklin, and James Brown. Several of the dancers went on to show business careers of their own, including Jody Watley, Rosie Perez, and Fred ''Rerun'' Berry. *Soul Train* shows from the 1970s even became popular staples of Japanese TV in the 1990s.

In the 1980s, with the advent of rap, *Soul Train* began taking on a hip-hop orientation. The appearance of the politically charged rap group Public Enemy was a sure sign that the torch had been passed to a new generation of African-American musicians. Through it all, Cornelius continued to beam beatifically and tout his program as ''the hippest trip on television.''

The transition from trailblazing series to revered television institution did not diminish the show's impact. Young people of all races continued to watch *Soul Train* for tips on dress and personal style. ''*Soul Train* showed a generation what it meant to be cool,'' declared Todd Boyd, assistant professor of critical studies at the University of Southern California's School of Cinema-Television. In the 1990s, the show became a cultural touchstone for the African-American artistic community, cropping up in movies like Spike Lee's *Crooklyn* and the Hughes Brothers' *Dead Presidents*. But *Soul Train* had a wider pop cultural impact as well, as witnessed by *Soul Trek,* a 1992 comic book parody that placed the affable Cornelius in command of the *U.S.S. Enterprise.*

Cornelius served as host of *Soul Train* until 1993, when he assumed the role of ''host emeritus,'' introducing a new guest emcee every week. He graduated from independent producer to partner with the Tribune Entertainment Co., the show's distributor. In 1995, he was inducted into the Broadcasting & Cable Hall of Fame. Despite the show's success, however, Cornelius continued to have difficulty getting exposure from TV stations. Even in cities with large black populations like Cleveland and St. Louis, *Soul Train* continued to air at irregular times well into the 1990s.

Soul Train is the longest running program in television history originally produced for first-run syndication. While originally created by African Americans for young African American viewers, it has grown to attract a much larger and more diverse audience. ''I've been a fan for a long time!'' gushed President Bill Clinton on the *Soul Train* 25th Anniversary Special in 1995.

—Robert E. Schnakenberg

FURTHER READING:

Dean, Chuck. '''Soul Train' Rolls into Its 25th Year; Get Down with Your Bad Self.'' *Entertainment Weekly*. March 17, 1995.

Elber, Lynn. ''Don Cornelius Reflects on 'Soul Train,' His 'Little Dance Show.''' *Star Tribune*. August 11, 1995, 18E.

Moody, Lori. ''Durable 'Soul Train' Is Pop History in the Making.'' *Star Tribune*. November 22, 1995, 1E.

''Soul Train Still Chugging Down the Track.'' *Michigan Chronicle*. June 17, 1997.

The Sound of Music

The longest running Broadway musical of the early 1960s, *The Sound of Music* marked the last collaboration between composer

Richard Rodgers (1902-1979) and lyricist/librettist Oscar Hammerstein II (1895-1960), just before Hammerstein's death from cancer. Based partially on Maria Von Trapp's autobiography, *The Trapp Family Singers*, and partially on a German film, *Die Trapp Familie*, the show was written for Mary Martin, who had already appeared as Nellie in Rodgers and Hammerstein's musical *South Pacific*. Like many other Rodgers and Hammerstein productions, *The Sound of Music* included a remarkable number of popular songs: ''The Sound of Music,'' ''My Favorite Things,'' ''Climb Ev'ry Mountain,'' ''Do-Re-Mi,'' and ''Edelweiss.''

The setting for *The Sound of Music* is Salzburg, Austria, where Maria, a postulant at Nonnberg Abbey, is too free-spirited to accept the discipline of the order easily and frequently escapes to the mountains. Thus, the Mother Abbess arranges for Maria to work as a governess for the wealthy, aristocratic Captain George Von Trapp—a widower with seven children. By adding music and outdoor expeditions to the children's normally rigorous schedule, Maria wins the children's hearts. Although Captain Von Trapp is engaged to the elegant socialite, Elsa Schraeder, through the course of the play he falls in love with Maria and eventually marries her. But it is 1938, and the Von Trapp's married life is quickly disrupted by Nazi Germany's annexation of Austria. The family has become well known as an amateur singing group, and after a final appearance at a local contest, they manage to escape and cross the mountains on foot to Switzerland. The first romance of Von Trapp's oldest daughter Liesl, unfortunately with a young Nazi, provides a bittersweet subplot.

The Sound of Music was originally the idea of director Vincent J. Donehue with Mary Martin's husband, Richard Halliday, and Leland Hayward producing. Howard Lindsay and Russel Crouse adapted Maria Von Trapp's book. Rodgers and Hammerstein were approached to write only one song, but ended up doing the entire score and lyrics as well as co-producing the show. *The Sound of Music* opened at the Lunt-Fontanne Theatre on November 16, 1959, and ran for 1,443 performances. In 1965 Twentieth Century-Fox released a film version starring Julie Andrews as Maria and Christopher Plummer as Captain Von Trapp. Featuring a young, exuberant Julie Andrews, one of Rodgers and Hammerstein's most accessible scores, and spectacular views of the Alps and Salzburg, *The Sound of Music* garnered ten Oscar nominations and won five: Best Picture, Best Director (Robert Wise), Best Adapted Score, Best Film Editing, and Best Sound. The film also won awards from the Directors Guild of America, the Golden Globes (Best Actress in a Musical Comedy), and the National Board of Review. It was the top box office draw from 1966 thorough 1969, and it has remained one of the most popular films ever made.

—Ann Sears

FURTHER READING:

Fordin, Hugh. *Getting to Know Him: A Biography of Oscar Hammerstein II*. New York, Da Capo Press, 1995.

Green, Stanley. *Broadway Musicals Show by Show*. 3d ed. Milwaukee, Wisconsin, Hal Leonard Publishing Corporation, 1990.

———. *Encyclopaedia of the Musical Film*. New York, Oxford University Press, 1981.

Rodgers, Richard. *Musical Stages: An Autobiography*. New York, Da Capo Press, 1995.

Julie Andrews (right) in a scene from the film *The Sound of Music*.

Trapp, Maria Augusta. *The Trapp Family Singers*. New York, J. B. Lippincott Company, 1949.

Sousa, John Philip (1854-1932)

Known as the "March King," John Philip Sousa created more than 100 marches which reflected the optimism, patriotism, and military prowess of late nineteenth and early twentieth century America. Sousa was called the "Dickens of Music" and "Knight of the Baton." He described himself as a "Salesman of Americanism, globetrotter, and musician."

Sousa was born on November 6, 1854, in Washington, D.C., to John Antonio and Maria Elisabeth (Trinkhaus) Sousa. His father played a trombone for the United States Marine Band. Musically gifted at a young age, John Philip Sousa studied at a local conservatory and was inspired by Civil War marches he heard during his boyhood. At age 13, Sousa considered joining a circus band, and his father enlisted him in the United States Marine Band.

By the summer of 1872, Sousa conducted and played in orchestras in Washington, D.C., and began composing music. His first published composition was "Moonlight on the Potomac Waltzes." Sousa's early work revealed his unique style that would gain him international distinction. Touring as orchestra conductor for various companies, Sousa performed as a violinist during the Philadelphia Centennial Exhibition in 1876. He composed his first comic opera, "The Smugglers," for a Philadelphia choir.

On September 30, 1880, Sousa became conductor of the United States Marine Band. During his leadership, the band improved in quality from a mediocre ensemble into a superb group. Sousa's exacting standards enabled the band to achieve fame internationally for its spirited style. The Marine Band became the model for other bands to emulate. Sousa led the band on national and international tours while composing music such as "Semper Fidelis" (1888).

In the spring of 1892, Sousa resigned from the Marines Corps to create a concert band of civilians. Sousa assembled talented musicians and staged his band's first concert on September 26, 1892, at Plainfield, New Jersey. The band's programming was a unique blending of instrumentalists, a soprano vocalist, and violinist. "In

John Philip Sousa

dynamics, I have never heard any orchestra that could touch us,'' Sousa told *Music* magazine in 1899. Sousa's band appeared throughout the United States and traveled to Europe, including an around-the-world trip from 1910 to 1912. Sousa and his band enhanced the image of American culture in Europe, proving that American musicians were not inferior to European performers.

Sousa constantly composed new music for his band, such as ''The Stars and Stripes Forever,'' which later was designated the United States's official march. Some critics argue that this composition alone secured Sousa's acclaimed status as a composer. A patriotic and emotional musician, Sousa sought to create music that was assertive and energetic like the United States was militarily at the turn of the twentieth century. He wanted his music to make people proud to be Americans. During the Spanish-American War, Sousa was musical director of the VI Army Corps and prepared a pageant, *The Trooping of the Colors*.

Nicknamed the ''Pied Piper of Patriotism,'' Sousa thought a march should ''make goose pimples chase each other up and down your spine.'' He stressed that marches should be characterized by simplicity with a steady, stimulating rhythm. Sousa's marches reflected the country's spirit of optimism, and his driving, pulsating tunes emphasized the strength of the country. Sousa's martial music standardized the march form and became popular classics. In addition to

his music, Sousa developed a new instrument, the Sousaphone, which resembled a tuba. He also devoted time to protecting composers' rights. He coined the term ''canned music'' in 1906 when he protested the phonograph industry recording music without compensating composers.

During World War I, Sousa joined the United States Naval Reserve as a lieutenant, directing the Great Lakes Naval Training Station Band which toured the country to raise millions of dollars in Liberty Loan drives. Sousa was a familiar figure, wearing his uniform and carrying his sword at the head of parades. After the war, he toured with his band, promoted music education, and testified to Congress about composers' rights. Sousa's dramatic performances reinforced his reputation as a showman. Choosing entertainment over education, he vowed to present audiences the music that they wanted. His band played in remote parts of the United States where people had never heard a symphony orchestra. Town dignitaries declared ''Sousa Day'' when the band arrived, and performances were often standing-room-only. Sousa strived to present music that people appreciated while making unfamiliar music, such as early jazz, accessible to them thus influencing Americans' musical taste. Sousa often invited the audiences to sing along with the band.

Americans' interest in bands peaked between 1890 and 1910, and Sousa helped to disseminate band music. Before televisions, radios, and movies, instruments provided entertainment in homes, and people played Sousa pieces, especially popular dance songs. The July 4, 1898, *Musical Courier* commented, ''go where you may, you hear Sousa, always Sousa. . . . It is Sousa in the band, Sousa in the orchestra, Sousa in the phonograph, Sousa in the hand organ, Sousa in the music box, Sousa everywhere.'' The name Sousa became a household term, and at one time he was the best known musician in America. Vaudeville comedians imitated him, and towns hosted public celebrations for his birthday. Sousa also received many honors and medals.

Although he refused to perform on the radio because he preferred interacting with live audiences, Sousa was convinced to broadcast concert series in 1929 and 1931 because of overwhelming public demand. Sousa especially focused on encouraging young musicians. He accepted invitations to help amateur bands and supported the school music movement and the National Music Camp at Interlochen, Michigan. Every year John Philip Sousa awards are given by high school band directors to talented band members. The John Philip Sousa foundation recognizes excellent high school, college, and community bands.

Sousa died on March 6, 1932, after a rehearsal at Reading, Pennsylvania. The last piece he conducted was ''The Stars and Stripes Forever.'' The Marine Band played ''Semper Fidelis'' during his funeral procession. Buried at Congressional Cemetery in Washington, D.C., Sousa's gravestone was carved with a bar from ''The Stars and Stripes Forever.'' His music library was donated to the University of Illinois. The movie *Stars and Stripes Forever* (also called *Marching Along*) premiered in 1952 with Clifton Webb playing Sousa, and Sousa's family and band members criticized the movie's inaccuracies. In 1957, George Balanchine choreographed the ballet *Stars and Stripes*. The Public Broadcasting Corporation televised the documentary *If You Knew Sousa*. The Sousa Stage was dedicated at the John F. Kennedy Center for the Performing Arts in Washington, D.C., and other Sousa memorials include schools and band shells. Sousa's former band members belonged to chapters of the Sousa Band Fraternal Society. In 1997, the United States Postal Service issued a 32 cent stamp, "The Stars and Stripes Forever!," to celebrate the centennial of Sousa's most famous march.

—Elizabeth D. Schafer

FURTHER READING:

Berger, Kenneth. *The March King and His Band*. New York, Exposition Press, 1957.

Bierley, Paul E. *John Philip Sousa: American Phenomenon*. 2nd edition. New York, Appleton-Century-Crofts, 1973.

———. *The Works of John Philip Sousa*. Columbus, Integrity Press, 1984.

Heslip, Malcolm. *Nostalgic Happenings in the Three Bands of John Philip Sousa*. Revised edition. Westerville, Ohio, Integrity Press, 1992.

Newsom, Jon, editor. *Perspectives on John Philip Sousa*. Washington, Music Division, Research Services, Library of Congress, 1983.

Sousa, John Philip. *Marching Along: Recollections of Men, Women and Music*. Westerville, Integrity Press, 1994.

———. *Book of Instruction for the Field-Trumpet and Drum: Together With the Trumpet and Drum Signals Now in Use in the Army, Navy and Marine Corps of the United States*. Westerville, Integrity Press, 1985.

South Pacific

With Mary Martin and Ezio Pinza in the lead roles, the musical *South Pacific* opened at the Majestic Theatre in New York on April 7, 1949, and ran for 1,925 performances. It was the fifth collaboration between composer Richard Rodgers (1902-1979) and lyricist/librettist Oscar Hammerstein II (1895-1960), following *Oklahoma!* (1943), *Carousel* and *State Fair* (1945), and *Allegro* (1947). The phenomenal success of *Oklahoma!* and *Carousel* had made Rodgers and Hammerstein the dominant figures in American musical theater; *South Pacific* only added to their stature and reputation. Director Josh Logan suggested that Rodgers and Hammerstein base a musical theater production on one of the short stories from James Michener's *Tales of the South Pacific*, winner of a 1948 Pulitzer Prize. They decided to combine two stories, "Fo' Dolla'" and "Our Heroine," and the resulting musical went on to win Rodgers and Hammerstein their second Pulitzer Prize in a decade (the first was for *Oklahoma!* in 1943). *South Pacific* starred Mary Martin, in her first Rodgers and Hammerstein show, and Metropolitan basso Ezio Pinza in his Broadway debut, and was co-produced and directed by Logan. Like *Oklahoma!*, *South Pacific* yielded a remarkable number of songs that became popular apart from the show: "Some Enchanted Evening," "There Is Nothin' Like a Dame," "Bali Ha'i," "I'm Gonna Wash That Man Right Outa My Hair," "A Wonderful Guy," and "Younger Than Springtime." A film version, also directed by Logan, was released by Twentieth Century-Fox in 1958 starring Mitzi Gaynor, Rossano Brazzi, Ray Walston, Juanita Hall, and France Nuyen.

The story takes place in the islands of the South Pacific during World War II, as two very different romantic couples face similar obstacles to their happiness together. First, French plantation owner Emile deBecque and young Navy nurse Nellie Forbush from Arkansas fall in love. When Nellie encounters his children with a deceased Polynesian wife, she reconsiders married life with him. Meanwhile, Lt. Joe Cable from Philadelphia has a brief romance with Liat, a native girl, but like Nellie wonders how he can explain the racial issues to his family back home. DeBecque and Cable go on a secret mission behind the Japanese lines. Cable is killed, but deBecque returns to find Nellie transformed. She has faced her racism and realized that the children are fellow human beings whom she has already begun to love.

Commenting on social issues through music was a pattern in Rodgers and Hammerstein's work from the beginning of their partnership. The issue of racism has rarely been addressed directly on stage in musical theater, with the exception of the revolutionary musical *Show Boat* (1927), which not so coincidentally also had book and lyrics written by Oscar Hammerstein II. However, *South Pacific* meets Caucasian versus Asian racial prejudice head on through the stories of its main characters and through the song "You've Got to Be Carefully Taught to Hate." This approach to social justice continues in later Rodgers and Hammerstein shows; for example, there are gender and racial issues in *The King and I* (1951), conflict between generations and cultures in *Flower Drum Song* (1958), and issues of freedom and patriotism in *The Sound of Music* (1959).

The initial touring company of *South Pacific* traveled for five years. The musical was revived at Lincoln Center in 1967 and staged by the New York City Opera in 1987. The popular film version of 1958 was shot in the Fiji and Hawaiian Islands, but the colored filters that changed lighting effects from scene to scene hinder appreciation of the scenic beauty and the glorious music. Nonetheless, the film has kept the musical before the public, and *South Pacific* remains a perennial favorite with amateur theater groups around the world.

—Ann Sears

FURTHER READING:

Fordin, Hugh, with introduction by Stephen Sondheim. *Getting to Know Him: A Biography of Oscar Hammerstein II*. New York, Ungar Publishing Co., 1977. Reprint, New York, Da Capo Press, 1995.

Green, Stanley. *Broadway Musicals Show by Show*. 3d ed. Milwaukee, Hal Leonard Publishing Corporation, 1990.

———. *Encyclopaedia of the Musical Film*. New York, Oxford University Press, 1981.

Hyland, William G. *Richard Rodgers*. New Haven, Yale University Press, 1998.

Michener, James. *Tales from the South Pacific*. New York, The Macmillan Company, 1947.

Mordden, Ethan. *Rodgers & Hammerstein*. New York, Harry N. Abrams, 1992.

Rodgers, Richard. *Musical Stages: An Autobiography*. New York, Random House, 1975. Reprint, with a new introduction by Mary Rodgers, New York, Da Capo Press, 1995.

Mitzi Gaynor (center) belts out a song in a scene from the film *South Pacific*.

Taylor, Deems. *Some Enchanted Evenings: The Story of Rodgers and Hammerstein.* New York, Harper and Brothers, 1953.

South Park

The animated comedy *South Park,* created by animators Trey Parker and Matt Stone, premiered on Comedy Central in August 1997 to rave reviews and loud criticism. The main characters, four round-headed third graders, have been involved in unlikely adventures with zombies, aliens, and Mr. Hanky the Christmas Poo. Stan, Kyle, Cartman, and Kenny respond to most situations by belching, vomiting, or swearing. Kenny is killed in nearly every episode to the refrain: "They killed Kenny! You bastards!" The show is wildly popular among children, teens, and twenty-somethings. Its unflinching look at how sweet and innocent most children *really* are when left to themselves takes the portrait of childhood offered by such popular comics as *Peanuts* and *Calvin and Hobbes* several steps further. In a town where Jesus has his own cable access show, Parker and Stone

have created an environment where nothing is sacred and everything is fodder for their satire.

—Adrienne Furness

FURTHER READING:

Gegax, T. Trent, et al. "South Park: The Rude Tube." *Newsweek.* March 23, 1998, 56-62.

Southern, Terry (1924-1995)

Texas-born writer Terry Southern is best remembered for the wildly written satires—usually featuring a Candide-esque heroine—that earned him acclaim in the early 1960s. Southern also cut a wide swathe through the 1960s film world. His writing on *Dr. Strangelove* (1964) and *Easy Rider* (1969) earned him two Academy Award nominations and helped define the rebelliousness and paranoia of that era. But by all accounts, Southern's exposure to Hollywood had an unwholesome effect. By 1970, his fictional output had slowed to a trickle. What he did publish belied the promise of his early work. Silent for the next two decades, in 1992 he published *Texas Summer,* a poorly received autobiographical novel. At his death he left behind more than 40 unproduced screenplays and an unpublished spoof of Virgin Records, titled *Virgin.* While many found his writing sophomoric, Southern had a special gift for unmasking hypocrisy, and while he used it, he was among the funniest writers working.

—Michael Baers

FURTHER READING:

McAninch, Jerry. "Terry Southern." In *Dictionary of Literary Biography.* Volume 2. *American Novelists Since World War II,* edited by Jeffrey Helterman and Richard Layman. Detroit, Gale Research Company, 1978.

Murray, D. M. "Candy Christian as a Pop-Art Daisy Miller." *Journal of Popular Culture.* Vol. 5, 1971, 340-48.

Silva, Edward T. "From *Candide* to *Candy:* Love's Labor Lost." *Journal of Popular Culture.* Vol. 8, 1974, 783-91.

Spacek, Sissy (1949—)

Sissy Spacek is a fine actress who has made an indelible impression, both through her unique quality as an eternal waif, and because of four particular films whose overall quality was matched by her performances. Texas-born Elizabeth Mary Spacek won a singer-songwriter contest, went to New York to pursue a music career, but studied with Lee Strasberg instead. A little modeling and TV, and an extra's job in Warhol's *Trash* (1970) preceded her debut in *Prime Cut* (1972). Then, at twenty-four, she played the first of her dangerously disturbed yet sympathetic teenagers, on a killing spree in *Badlands* (1973); at twenty-seven she was *Carrie* (1976), the tormented teenager with telekinetic powers, which brought her first Oscar nomination; at thirty she essayed thirteen-year-old country singer Loretta Lynn in *Coal Miner's Daughter* (1979) and won the best actress Oscar and, in 1982, playing grown-up but barely looking it, she was Oscar-nominated for Costa-Gavras' *Missing* (also for *The River,* 1985, and *Crimes of the Heart,* 1990). She took a four-year break between 1986 and 1990, and by the late 1990s, although working consistently, was no longer a major box-office draw.

—Robyn Karney

FURTHER READING:

Emerson, Mark, and Eugene E. Pfaff. *Country Girl: The Life of Sissy Spacek.* New York, St. Martin's Press, 1988.

Willsmer, Trevor. *Who's Who in Hollywood.* Edited by Robyn Karney. New York, Continuum, 1994.

Spaghetti Westerns

Spaghetti westerns were hyper-violent, low-budget genre films made in Europe by European (usually Italian) studios between 1961

and 1977. The more than five hundred of these films, many forgettable, used European crews, writers, directors, and, for the most part, actors. Location shooting often took place in Spain, parts of which resemble the geography of the American Southwest.

The spaghetti western shot its way into mainstream American culture in 1964 with the release of *A Fistful of Dollars,* directed by Sergio Leone and starring a little-known American actor named Clint Eastwood as The Man with No Name, an amoral bounty hunter with a lightning-fast draw. The film was immensely popular in the United States and around the world, and led to the production of two sequels: *For a Few Dollars More* (1965) and *The Good, the Bad, and the Ugly* (1966). Two other Leone films were also successful in the United States: the lavish, sprawling 1969 epic *Once upon a Time in the West,* starring Charles Bronson, Jason Robards, Claudia Cardinale, and a cast-against-type Henry Fonda playing a ruthless killer; and *Duck, You Sucker,* also known as *A Fistful of Dynamite* (1971), which paired James Coburn with Rod Steiger.

Spaghetti westerns had several stylistic elements in common. They were often very violent (for their time) and did not flinch from portraying brutal beatings, rape, and the murder of women and children. The films were usually made cheaply, and their production values showed it (exceptions were *The Good, the Bad, and the Ugly* and *Once upon a Time in the West,* both of which had large budgets for production). Further, since the supporting actors (and sometimes the stars) of spaghetti westerns were usually Italian, most of the speaking parts had to be dubbed for release outside Italy (in some cases, limited budgets made for sloppy dubbing and unintentionally hilarious results). Finally, the films often made use of tight close-up shots, which meant that the actors, even bit players, tended to have interesting (if not always handsome) faces. This photographic technique was especially common in scenes leading to a showdown: the camera would alternate between the two (or more) characters who were preparing to duel, with the close-ups growing increasingly tight until only the eyes could be seen. Then the tension would be broken as the gunmen drew and fired. This trademark motif was labeled by some critics the "squint and shoot" style of cinematography.

The musical scores for spaghetti westerns tended to be moody and atmospheric. The best-known composer to work in the genre was Ennio Morricone, who went on to write music for a variety of other films. Morricone's scores for Leone constitute some of the best-known movie music of the 1960s and early 1970s. In addition to traditional instruments, Morricone made use of bells, jangling spurs, whistling, and a Jew's-harp to create a distinctive, and much-imitated, sound.

An attempt was made to revive the genre in 1998, when Turner Network Television produced and broadcast a made-for-cable homage called *A Dollar for the Dead,* starring Emilio Estevez as yet another Man with No Name.

—Justin Gustainis

FURTHER READING:

Frayling, Christopher. *Spaghetti Westerns: Cowboys and Europeans from Karl May to Sergio Leone.* London and Boston, Routledge & Kegan Paul, 1981.

Weisser, Thomas. *Spaghetti Westerns—The Good, The Bad and the Violent.* Jefferson, N.C., McFarland Publishing, 1992.

Spalding, Albert G. (1850-1915)

After fully dedicating his career to baseball in 1871, Albert Goodwill Spalding went on to become pro baseball's first recorded 200 game winner, dividing his time between the Boston Red Stockings and the Chicago White Stockings. As first captain/manager and later as president/owner of the White Stockings, Spalding helped mold Chicago into the baseball dynasty of the 1880s. Yet, it was as an owner that Spalding had his greatest cultural impact. In 1876, he helped found the National League and became its president in 1901. Through such actions, he was key in establishing baseball as a viable and acceptable commercial enterprise. Spalding helped to solidify professional baseball as a business. In addition to his baseball duties, in 1876 he and his brother opened their first sporting goods store in Chicago, the beginning of the Spalding sporting goods chain.

—S. Paul O'Hara

FURTHER READING:

Bartlett, Arthur Charles. *Baseball and Mr. Spalding: The History and Romance of Baseball.* New York, Farrar, Straus and Young, 1951.

Levine, Peter. *A.G. Spalding and the Rise of Baseball: The Promise of American Sport.* New York, Oxford University Press, 1985.

Spartacus

Spartacus represents the pinnacle of the epic film trend which included spectaculars such as *Cleopatra, Ben Hur,* and *Fall of the Roman Empire.* It was acclaimed as the first truly intelligent epic, but its director, the highly acclaimed Stanley Kubrick, has largely disowned it. Kubrick took the assignment, partially as a way of escaping the ill-fated *One-Eyed Jacks* project he was working on with Marlon Brando (Brando himself took over direction and went heavily overbudget with the film).

Kubrick was belatedly brought aboard by producer/star Kirk Douglas, who was impressed with their classic collaboration on *Paths of Glory.* Initial director Anthony Mann resigned after only a week's shooting, only completing the opening scenes at the rock quarry. Kubrick picked up the project from the gladiator school on.

Kubrick objected to the script for *Spartacus* on the grounds that it was dumb and rarely faithful to what is known about the actual Spartacus. The former slave in reality twice led his victorious slave army to the northern borders of Italy and could have easily gotten out of the country, but instead he led his army back to pillage Roman cities. Instead of exploring the question of why he chose to do this or whether the intentions of the rebellion changed, whether Spartacus lost the control of his followers who became more interested in the spoils of war rather than in freedom, Trumbo's script simply has Spartacus prevented from escaping by a silly contrivance in which a pirate leader (played by Herbert Lom) reneges on a deal to take the slave army away in his ships.

Nor did Spartacus die by crucifixion as the film depicts. He was actually killed in battle and hacked into pieces on the battlefield. However, six thousand of his followers were later crucified along the Appian Way. As a director-for-hire, Kubrick discovered he had to bow to the wishes of his producer.

Spartacus happened because producer Eddie Lewis brought the Howard Fast novel to Douglas's attention, and he optioned the book, seeing its potential to become a popular epic. He hoped to interest United Artists in the film, but they were planning their own version of the tale called *The Gladiators* which was to be directed by Martin Ritt

Battle scene from the film *Spartacus*, with Kirk Douglas leading the charge (center).

and star Yul Brynner and Anthony Quinn with a script by Abe Polonsky. Howard Fast was given first crack at adapting the material into a screenplay, but his work had a political axe to grind and was quickly rejected. Douglas needed somebody who could write both well and fast, and so pitched the project to blacklisted writer Dalton Trumbo, who hated Fast but agreed to write the script under the name Sam Jackson.

Douglas needed some high-powered talent to convince a studio to back the film, and so he approached Laurence Olivier, Charles Laughton, and Peter Ustinov. Olivier expressed interest in both starring and directing the film as well, but then committed to appearing in *Coriolanus* in Stratford-on-Avon, and consented to appear as Crassus, provided the part was improved. Laughton did not care for the material but needed the money and so agreed to appear as Gracchus, the rotund Republican senator who opposes Crassus, while Ustinov was eager to play the role of an ingratiating middleman for once (he usually had played kings or peasants) and had suggestions for improving his part. Universal agreed to undertake the film.

Douglas wanted Ingrid Bergman to play his love interest Varinia, but she turned it down as being ''too bloody.'' Jean Simmons wanted the role, but Douglas preferred a foreigner who was not British. Jeanne Moreau refused to leave a play she was in to take the part. Douglas thought German actress Sabina Bethmann had the right look and hired her for the part, despite her thick accent. She was sent to be coached by blacklist victim Jeff Corey.

Spartacus began with Anthony Mann as director on January 27, 1959, when Mann filmed the mine sequence in Death Valley, but when the production started filming the sequences at the gladiator school, it started to fall apart and Universal pushed for Mann's replacement, and Douglas paid him off $75,000 and asked for Kubrick to come in. Universal was against hiring the 30-year-old maverick director, but with the clock already running up large expenses, they capitulated and filming resumed under Kubrick on February 16.

Kubrick immediately realized that the inexpressive Bethmann was not going to work out, and decided to test her powers of improvisation by telling her that she had just lost the part in the movie. Rather than reacting emotionally, the actress froze and thereby ensured her departure from the production. Simmons was quickly summoned to take her place. However, shortly afterwards she had emergency surgery and could not work for over a month, so the production had to shoot around her.

One of Kubrick's innovations was to film the scene where Varinia serves food to the gladiator trainees without dialogue, using only Alex North's music to make his point, and thereby improving the scene. Indeed, the scenes in the gladiatorial school are some of the best in the film, especially those where Marcellus Charles McGraw) uses Spartacus to demonstrate where to maim or kill one's opponent and the famous scene where because of an idle whim by two Roman ladies, Draba (Woody Strode) is forced to fight Spartacus in the ring, but the Ethiopian chooses to attack Crassus at the cost of his own life rather than kill a fellow slave.

Tony Curtis begged to be put in the film, and so the part of Antoninus was written for him as a sensitive young man who becomes like a son to Spartacus and is forced to fight him to the death at the end of the film. Curtis severed his Achilles tendon and had to spend some time in a wheelchair. Even Douglas became sick, the film went months over schedule, and 250 percent over budget.

Douglas, Lewis, and Kubrick got into a discussion over who should get the writing credit on the film. Lewis did not feel right

taking credit for Trumbo's work, and Douglas was uneasy about crediting the film to a Sam Jackson who did not really exist. Kubrick put forth the suggestion that he be given credit for the script. Revolted, Douglas decide to break the blacklist by crediting Trumbo and summoning him to the studio. (Soon afterward, Otto Preminger announced that Trumbo would be credited on *Exodus* as well, and soon other blacklisted artists were finding employment again). One of *Spartacus*'s most significant accomplishments was this breaking of the blacklist, considered a risky move at the time.

Kubrick's rough assemblage of the film was not well-received. Trumbo wrote a critique running over 80 pages, detailing the changes made and what he felt was wrong with them. Douglas agreed and declared that the film would have to be restructured and a battle scene added (originally, the battle was just to have been suggested, much like Kurosawa did in *Kagemusha*). Visual design consultant Saul Bass was hired to design the battle sequence and noted that scenes of preparation for the battle helped build up more excitement than the actual battle itself. The Spanish government loaned their army to play the Roman army, and the scenes were shot in Spain. The budget became $12 million, or $750,000 less than MCA paid for Universal Pictures in its contemporaneous takeover.

Finally, *Spartacus* was ready for release. The American Legion sent a letter demanding a boycott of the film because of Trumbo's involvement to 17,000 local posts. Hedda Hopper joined the fray, attacking the film's use of ''Communist'' writers. Still, despite its shortcomings, the film stands up as one of the best of the Roman screen epics, and won Peter Ustinov an Academy Award for best supporting actor for his role as Batiatus, the conniving purveyor of slaves.

In 1988, *Spartacus* was restored and re-released to theaters in all its glory. Kubrick, although he had never expressed a fondness for the film, was involved in carefully re-editing the film, adding numerous small snippets that had been trimmed previously. One of the most significant additions was the scene where the bisexual Crassus attempts to seduce Antoninus while Antoninus is bathing him by asking Antoninus if he eats oysters and snails, explaining that it is a matter of appetites rather than morals. (Crassus then proceeds to compare himself to Rome, expounding, ''No nation can withstand Rome. No man can withstand her. And how much less—a boy. There's only one way to deal with Rome, Antoninus. You must serve her. You must abase yourself before her. You must grovel at her feet. You must love her.''

The footage for the scene was located, but not the original soundtrack. Tony Curtis agreed to revoice his part, but Olivier was dead, and so Anthony Hopkins imitated Olivier's vocal inflections in order to restore this scene that had so outraged the censors of the 1960s. The scene does add to the film's portrait of Crassus as a self-serving manipulator obsessed with demonstrating his power and authority.

—Dennis Fischer

FURTHER READING:

Baxter, John. *Stanley Kubrick.* New York, Carroll & Graf Publishers, Inc., 1997.

Ciment, Michel. *Kubrick.* Paris, Calmann-Levy, 1980.

Douglas, Kirk (with Linda Civitello). *The Ragman's Son: An Autobiography.* London, Simon & Schuster, 1988.

Harris, W. V. "Spartacus," *Past Imperfect: History According to the Movies,* edited by Mark C. Carnes. New York, Henry Holt, 1995.

Kagan, Norman. *The Cinema of Stanley Kubrick.* New York, Continuum, 1994.

Monaco, James. *The Films of Stanley Kubrick.* New York, New School Department of Film, 1974.

Nelson, Thomas Alan. *Kubrick: Inside a Film Artist's Maze.* Bloomington, Indiana, Indiana University Press, 1982.

Walker, Alexander. *Stanley Kubrick Directs.* New York, Harcourt, Brace Jovanovich Books, 1971.

Spawn

Todd McFarlane's *Spawn* comic book changed the dynamics of the comic book industry in the 1990s. *Spawn* set sales records, helped an upstart new company become a major publisher, and enticed the top talents in the industry to leave Marvel and DC to make their fortunes with creator-owned properties.

In the late 1980s, Todd McFarlane gained some notoriety as a comic-book artist for his work on Marvel Comics' *Incredible Hulk* title. At the time, "hot" artists drove comic-book sales, and when McFarlane moved to penciling *Amazing Spider-Man,* it quickly became Marvel's best-selling book. In 1990, Marvel created a new *Spider-Man* title for McFarlane to write, pencil, and ink. It immediately became their top selling monthly, and the first issue sold an incredible two and a half million copies. McFarlane began to wonder why, if he was so popular, he needed to do work-for-hire on a character that someone else owned.

Born of this thinking, McFarlane formed a partnership with a few of Marvel's other popular young artists in 1992. Together they founded Image Comics in order to publish creator-owned comic books and reap the full rewards of their popularity. For the first few years, Image Comics, true to its name, proved to be more flash than substance. However, when McFarlane came up with *Spawn,* it proved to be the backbone of the company. Unlike the majority of Image books, *Spawn* was consistently published on time and, thus, enjoyed consistently high sales. The first issue sold 1,700,000 copies, far outstripping the circulation of any other independent comic book. For decades, Marvel and DChad so dominated the industry that any comic not published by one of the "big two" was considered "independent." By its second year, Image Comics had such volume of sales that the industry press began to suggest the possibility of "the big three," and by 1996 Image, albeit briefly, surpassed DC to become number two in market share.

McFarlane proved to have the best head for business of the young Image artists, and was aggressive in marketing his characters. *Spawn* became a multi-million dollar industry. By 1993, there was a "Spawnmobile" super-competition funny car touring with car shows, and Mattel was selling a "Spawnmobile" Hot Wheel. A comics industry trade magazine, *Hero Illustrated,* named Todd McFarlane the "Most Important Person in Comics," and in 1995, with New Line Cinema's McFarlane-scripted live-action *Spawn* movie in pre-production (it was released in 1997), he signed contracts for a *Spawn* animated series on HBO. Also in 1995, Sony began developing a *Spawn* video game, a *Spawn* board game was in stores, Halloween costumes were licensed, and McFarlane Toys brought out a new line of action figures. Somehow, McFarlane found time to keep producing

a new *Spawn* comic book each month, remaining number one in industry-wide sales for a fourth year in a row. Both the sales and the marketing frenzy then began waning somewhat, but in the space of four years Todd McFarlane had become one of the wealthiest people in the comic book industry.

The name and face of McFarlane's main character were borrowed from his real-life friend Al Simmons, who became somewhat of a minor celebrity on the comic convention circuit. The fictional Al Simmons is a principled but efficient killer for a mysterious branch of the government. When he begins to question the orders of his commander, Jason Wynn, he is burned to death with laser weapons by two of his fellow agents. Sent to Hell for the bloody deeds he has committed, Simmons becomes a pawn of the Dark Lord Malebolgia, who needs just such a soldier to lead Hell's army in the final battle against Heaven. For a chance to return to Earth to see his family again and take revenge on Wynn, Simmons forfeits his soul and agrees to become Malebolgia's general. Simmons's horribly burned body is reanimated, and he returns to Earth as a grotesque but incredibly powerful Hellspawn. Spawn is clothed in a symbiotic uniform and wields hell-born energy that is seemingly capable of anything that he can imagine. Yet, once this energy is fully expended, Simmons will have to return to Hell to fulfill the rest of his bargain. As Spawn regains memories of his former life, he begins following his own agenda and using his powers against the forces of evil. He lives with homeless people in a Bowery alley and becomes their defender. He watches over his family and his love for his wife begins healing him spiritually. However, he is constantly plagued by his "guardian demon," The Clown, whose task is to keep Spawn from straying too far from Hell's path.

Spawn provides savage, gory adolescent fantasy with sexy images; McFarlane has admitted that much of the success of his book is probably due to his ability to draw a "really cool looking cape." As other "hot" artists migrated to Image, or copied the Image style, there was an ascendancy of what comics pioneer Will Eisner refers to as "wallpaper comics," filled with splash pages, double-page spreads, and bravura artwork but not much story. In a medium that already stressed the visual over the verbal, the success of *Spawn* and other "wallpaper" comic books further diminished the role of the writer.

—Randy Duncan

FURTHER READING:

Malloy, Alex G., editor. *Comic Book Artists.* Radnor, Pennsylvania, Wallace-Homestead Book Company, 1993.

Jones, Gerard, and Will Jacobs. *The Comic Book Heroes.* Rocklin, California, Prima Publishing, 1997.

Special Olympics

The first International Special Olympics was held in Chicago's Soldier Park in July of 1968. Before this event, there was no opportunity for mentally disabled children and adults to compete in sporting events. With the help of the Kennedy Foundation, mentally disabled citizens have been given the chance to take part in the kinds of sporting events unavailable to them before the advent of the competition. Under the leadership of Eunice Kennedy Shriver and with the efforts of thousands of volunteers, mentally disabled children and adults now compete locally, regionally, and internationally in games based on the Greek Olympics.

Traditionally, mentally disabled children did not receive many opportunities to take part in physical activities because popular theory held that they did not need physical activity. As a result, these children were never given the chance to excel in sports or physical activity, and many mentally disabled children were doomed to accept a lifestyle without exercise. As early as 1963, however, a movement was underfoot to change these perceptions. The Joseph P. Kennedy, Jr. Foundation, in conjunction with the American Alliance for Health, Physical Education, and Recreation, began work in providing a physical fitness program for the mentally disabled. In addition, President John Kennedy established the President's Council for Physical Fitness and Sports, and by 1967, after considerable study by different organizations, research indicated that lack of opportunity, not lack of ability, was the major reason for the low physical ability of mentally disabled children.

In 1967, members of the Chicago Park District decided to organize a track and field meet for mentally disabled children based on the Greek Olympics. When letters were sent to the individual states inviting them to join, they received mixed responses. Reasons for not participating included a lack of support or a lack of interest based on the premise that promoting physical activity among the mentally disabled would be a waste of time and effort. These and other reasons kept nearly half the states from participating in the first Special Olympics. Unwilling to give in to negative feedback, several states and Canada pressed on to hold the event. The Kennedy Foundation donated $20,000, and the games were to be held at Soldier Field as planned.

At a press conference shortly after the success of the first International Special Olympics, Eunice Kennedy Shriver reiterated the mission of the Special Olympics—to provide all mentally disabled children a chance to participate in athletic events—and pledged $75,000 in monetary support on behalf of the Kennedy Foundation to build the Special Olympics program. This support allowed communities across the United States to take part in the Special Olympics originally planned to be held every two years. Because the response to the first Special Olympics was so positive, Senator Edward Kennedy announced the formation of Special Olympics, Inc., and named Eunice Kennedy Shriver its president. The new foundation's purpose was to provide the means for all mentally disabled citizens to have access to a physical fitness program like the Special Olympics.

The games are modelled after modern-day Olympic competition. They are divided into winter and summer games with both team and individual competitions. Held every two years, they alternate summer and winter games with the same schedule as the modern Olympics. Anyone eight and above, with an IQ of 75 and below, is eligible to compete free of charge. Ranging in age from eight to seventeen years-old, 1,000 children from 26 states and Canada competed in the first International Special Olympics in 1968. By 1970, all 50 states, the District of Columbia, and Canada had Special Olympics organizations and state directors. In 1975, the event had grown to 3,200 participants. In planning for the 1999 Special Olympics, organizers estimated that 7,000 athletes from 150 countries will participate, generating a need for 35,000 volunteers to organize 19 sports.

In the 1980s and 1990s, the Special Olympics came under intense scrutiny by mental health professionals who questioned the games and their benefit. Critics cite such reservations as the value of segregating the mentally retarded from mainstream athletic events and the theory that the games are becoming overly competitive. In response to criticism, Special Olympics organizers emphasize the positive physical, mental, and emotional achievements of the athletes. The debate remained a controversial one at the end of the 1990s, with professionals on both sides of the question presenting strong arguments to back up their opinions.

Though still controversial, the International Special Olympics continues to grow and over one million athletes take part in local, area, and chapter competitions each year. The motto of the Special Olympics states, "Let me win, but if I cannot win, let me be brave in the attempt." The motto sums up the attitude and accomplishments of both organizers and participants throughout the more than 30 years of the Special Olympics.

—Kimberley H. Kidd

FURTHER READING:

Haskins, James. *A New Kind of Joy: The Story of the Special Olympics.* New York, Doubleday, 1976.

Klein, Tovah, et al. "Special Olympics: An Evaluation by Professionals and Parents." *Mental Retardation.* Vol. 3, No. 1, 1993, 15-23.

Spector, Phil (1940—)

As the developer of a style of production so lush it was dubbed "the wall of sound," Phil Spector was arguably the most influential record producer in the history of popular music. From the late 1950s through the early 1960s, Spector, along with his arranger, Jack Nitzsche, produced a sound characterized by complex arrangements of strings, horns, and percussion. Although that sound is most evident in pop songs by the Ronettes, Crystals, and Righteous Brothers, all of whom recorded for Spector's label, he also produced a variety of other performers. The Beatles enlisted his skills in the studio, and Spector also produced solo efforts by John Lennon and George Harrison. Acts as diverse as the Ramones and Leonard Cohen worked with him, and Bruce Springsteen cited him as a major influence on his own music.

When he was seventeen, Spector wrote "To Know Him Is to Love Him," which became a number one single for his band the Teddy Bears. It was the beginning of an impressive songwriting career, but Spector's real achievements were in the studio. He learned the craft of production under Lee Hazlewood, who had given Duane Eddy his trademark guitar sound by a variety of techniques, including manipulating tape speeds and recording in an empty grain elevator. Spector left California for New York, ostensibly in hopes of securing a position at the United Nations, but within a few months he had cowritten "Spanish Harlem" with Jerry Leiber, half of the songwriting team of Leiber and Stoller. The song would become a hit for Ben E. King.

Spector also began producing prominent performers such as LaVern Baker, Ruth Brown, and Gene Pitney, but his most original and influential work came after he established Philles Records. Although he originally had three partners, Spector was sole owner when he was only twenty-one; he was also a millionaire. The Crystals's "He's a Rebel" was the label's first hit and is generally regarded as the first "wall of sound" song. It's worth noting that the phrase is something of a misnomer: although Spector employed an extraordinary number of musicians, and although the primitive technology of the time required an extensive use of overdubbing, the instruments remain surprisingly distinct. That is certainly a result of Spector's obsessiveness in the studio. According to one story, Spector once listened to the same note for twelve hours, trying to determine whether it needed to be rerecorded. Although probably apocryphal, it is undeniable that he worked with a vastly higher degree of attention than most other producers of the time. Labels usually worked on a variety of singles simultaneously in an attempt to get a hit single. Spector, on the other hand, focused his energies on one single at a time, and that approach proved extraordinarily successful. Songs such as the Ronettes's "Be My Baby" and the Righteous Brothers's "You've Lost that Lovin' Feeling" are some of the most recognizable hits of the 1960s, and Spector's collection of Christmas songs, *A Christmas Gift for You,* remains an exceptionally popular holiday album.

Spector shut down Philles Records in 1966. Some have claimed that he did so because Ike and Tina Turner's "River Deep, Mountain High" failed to achieve the success he had expected. A more likely explanation is that he recognized the music industry had changed fundamentally. The increasingly corporate nature of record distribution pushed independent labels to the margins; additionally, listeners began to favor full-length albums instead of singles. Spector no doubt understood that those shifts worked against his emphasis on the hit song. Ironically, however, other changes showed just how deeply Spector had influenced contemporary music. Although the Beach Boys had been known for their hit singles, in 1966 they released *Pet Sounds,* an album of complex and highly orchestrated pop songs which showed a clear debt to the wall of sound. The following year, the Beatles issued *Sergeant Pepper's Lonely Hearts Club Band;* in part a response to *Pet Sounds,* it also bore the hallmarks of Spector's work.

Despite his undeniable genius, Spector's megalomania and eccentricities became so infamous that fewer artists sought his talents in the 1980s and 1990s. At the same time, however, Spector became almost reclusive and certainly showed little interest in searching out new acts to produce. In 1998, a short-lived collaboration with Celine Dion ended amid rumors that Spector had been impossible to work with in the studio.

—Bill Freind

FURTHER READING:

Puterbaugh, Parke. "The Wall of Sound." *Rolling Stone.* August 23, 1990, 113-14.

Wolfe, Tom. *The Kandy-Kolored Tangerine-Flake Streamline Baby,* New York, Farrar, Strauss, Giroux, 1965.

Spelling, Aaron (1928—)

The most successful producer in the history of television, Aaron Spelling began his career with writer/producer credits on such classic early television fare as *Zane Grey Theater* and *Playhouse 90* in the 1950s, and 40 years later has more than 3,000 productions to his credit, including such audience favorites as *The Mod Squad* (1960s); *Charlie's Angels, Love Boat,* and *Fantasy Island* (1970s); *Dynasty* and *Family* (1980s); *Beverly Hills 90210, Melrose Place, Dawson's Creek, 7th Heaven,* and *Charmed* (1990s). Interspersed with these

series were critically acclaimed television series such as *Day One* and *And the Band Played On.*

Despite his success, Spelling has never been a favorite of the critics. "There is good and there is bad Spelling," a *Washington Post* TV critic stated in a 1996 *Los Angeles Times Magazine* article, "but there is never great Spelling, only degrees of terribleness." Yet, even his severest detractors agree that the producer has an uncanny knack for knowing what the public wants to see. During the 1980s, it was his *Dynasty,* a clone of the popular CBS hit *Dallas,* that propelled ABC to the top of the ratings charts; and during the 1990s his *Beverly Hills 90210* and *Melrose Place* helped transform the FOX network from an also-ran in the ratings into a major player. With *Felicity,* in the late 1990s, he is performing the same feat with the fledgling Warner Brothers network.

Spelling's background is remarkably similar to those of many of the legendary pioneers of both television and motion pictures. He began life as the youngest of five children born to struggling immigrant parents in Dallas during the 1930s. Two decades later, after an acting stint in *Gunsmoke,* he approached the producers of the Western anthology *Zane Grey Theater* with an idea of how to write the host's segments on the show and was given an assignment to write it on a continuing basis for $100 per week. The spots were so successful that he was approached by producer Martin Manulus who wanted to do a Western story on his *Playhouse 90* and offered Spelling the task of writing it. The resulting program, *The Last Man,* proved so popular that Twentieth Century-Fox optioned it as a feature film project within 48 hours of its airing.

The experience of writing the film version convinced Spelling that his rightful place was on television. Chided by his superiors for writing too fast, he completed the screenplay, which was finally released as *One Foot in Hell,* starring Alan Ladd, and returned to television where he went to work with Four Star productions where his creative speed paid dividends. At one point during the late 1950s, he was producing eight shows at once including *Johnny Ringo, Alcoa Presents, The June Allyson Show, Kaiser Presents Lloyd Bridges, The Dick Powell Theater,* and *Honey West.*

As Spelling's TV career began to take off during the 1960s, his forte became his ability to capture the mood of the American public at just the right time: his 1960s series *Burke's Law* coincided with the detective and spy craze incited by the emergence of the James Bond films on the big screen; *Mod Squad,* which premiered at the end of the decade, combined the always popular police genre with a teenage-rebels-seeking-social-justice motif that captured the unrest of a turbulent decade and managed to be entertaining at the same time. Although some shows, particularly *Amos Burke Secret Agent,* the spy-spoof sequel to *Burke's Law,* and, later, *Dynasty* were open to accusations of being less on the cutting edge of public taste and more derivative of existing films and shows such as the James Bond series and *Dallas,* Spelling always managed to imbue his shows with qualities that differentiated them from their predecessors through unpredictable plot devices and eccentric characters (notably Joan Collins's Alexis in *Dynasty*).

It was during the 1960s that Spelling produced his defining vision—one that would be evident in every one of his subsequent shows in one form or another. It was his role, he decided, to present the audience with the vision of itself it most wanted to see. In most cases, this meant putting together a glossy, idealized version of Southern California. The public was fascinated, he reasoned, with the trials and tribulations of the wealthy, particularly problems that could not be solved by money (unrequited love, legal entanglements, and incurable diseases). During the next three decades, he packaged and exported the Southern California lifestyle.

During the 1970s, he caught the viewers' interest in sex and titillation with *Charlie's Angels,* which combined crime fighting action with glamorous women and lots of skin. Although it was based in Los Angeles, the show's action routinely roamed to Palm Springs and Las Vegas—anywhere sex could be combined with wealth and glamour. During the 1980s, Spelling took it even farther with *Dynasty* and its spin-off, *The Colbys,* which presented life among the wealthy in less "black-and-white" terms. Unlike *Charlie's Angels,* there were no clear-cut heroes; it all depended on where individual viewer's sympathies lay. For those who hated the rich and famous, it was simply fun to watch all of the characters strive to do the others in.

By the end of the 1980s, Spelling's star began to dim. The emergence of the sitcom (*Cosby* and *Cheers*) and the public's growing fascination with the gritty realism of Steven Bochco's *Hill Street Blues* signaled trends that Spelling was slow to pick up on. In 1989, to headlines announcing "Spelling Dynasty Over," ABC canceled the show that had led them to the top of the ratings charts. Two of Spelling's medical dramas, ABC's *HeartBeat* and NBC's *Nightengales,* were also canceled. Suddenly, Spelling was unable to sell any of his one-hour programs, prompting him to admit to the *Los Angeles Times,* "I can honestly say that I don't know what the networks want anymore."

Within a year, however, he was back on top with *Beverly Hills 90210* suddenly putting the fledgling Fox network on the map. He followed it with the successful spin-off *Melrose Place,* which proved once and for all that if there was one thing that Spelling knew, it was how to combine money, glamour, and the Southern California lifestyle into an unforgettable package. His knowledge of the youth market paid big dividends in the mid-1990s with such successful shows as *7th Heaven, Dawson's Creek,* and *Felicity* reworking his traditional formula to incorporate more real-to-life people and their problems in other areas of the country besides California.

—Sandra Garcia-Myers

FURTHER READING:

"Aaron Spelling." *Daily Variety Special Issue.* Nov. 17, 1995.

Archambault, Dennis. "Aaron Spelling." *Producers Interviews.* Los Angeles, USC School of Cinema-Television, 1989.

De Vries, Hillary. "He's Made TV What It Is Today." *Los Angeles Times Magazine.* Sept. 8, 1996, 17.

Finke, Nikki. "Can Spelling Cast His Spell Again?" *Los Angeles Times Calendar.* March 26, 1989, 3.

Spelling, Aaron. *Aaron Spelling: A Prime-time Life.* New York, St. Martin's Press, 1996.

Wild, David. *The Official Melrose Place Companion.* Introduction by Aaron Spelling. New York, Harper Perennial, 1995.

The Spice Girls

After half a decade of alternative rock authenticity ruling the popular culture landscape, Britain's Spice Girls burst upon the scene in 1996 and—seemingly within five minutes after the release of their debut single, "Wannabe,"—helped change the direction of mainstream pop music for the latter half of the 1990s. While their explosion happened on a smaller scale than Madonna, Prince, or the nuclear bomb that was Michael Jackson, the Spice Girls nevertheless left a noticeable crater in the pop culture landscape that was still evident by the turn of the century. Just as alternative angst-ridden demigods Nirvana and Pearl Jam wiped away the superficial spectacle that was pop music in the late 1980s, the Spice Girls made being shallow and fun cool again, paving the way for a number of other commercially successful soul/dance-influenced, good-looking boy and girl bands.

The Spice Girls comprised five young women chosen to be in the group after auditioning in 1993, making them similar to many of the "manufactured" girl groups of the early 1960s. But that is where the comparison ends. Writing or cowriting many of their songs, publicly acting fiercely independent, and, importantly, firing their manager before the release of their second album, these women were no mere puppets. Nor were they revolutionaries but, instead, existed very much as sexily dressed commodities who nonetheless brought the fire and brimstone rhetoric of the pro-woman punk rock riot girl movement to pubescent and prepubescent girls—which was either a calculated marketing strategy or a positive, empowering move, depending on one's perspective.

Early on, the girls carved out very specific identities for themselves: Geri Estelle Halliwell (Ginger Spice), Melanine Janine Brown (Scary Spice), Victoria Addams (Posh Spice), Melanie Jayne Chisholm (Sporty Spice) and Emma Lee Bunton (Baby Spice). This made the group more distinctive and, with the help of a number of catchy singles ("Wannabe," "Say You'll Be There" and "2 Become 1"), by the end of 1997 they were one of the top selling acts in the world. Many dismissed them as a passing fad that couldn't last a year and—after a series of Pepsi commercials, Top 40 singles and a feature film—several media watchers believed they would become overexposed and fade from the public's consciousness. Their second album, *Spiceworld,* was considered a flop (even though it went multiplatinum), and in late 1997 it seemed that those predictions might have been true. But the critical and commercial success of their movie, *Spiceworld,* and their subsequent sold-out world tour proved those prophecies to be incorrect. The departure of Geri Halliwell at the beginning of the American leg of their world tour similarly did not keep the group down and certainly did not discourage Spice Girl fans from attending their concerts.

On the surface, the Spice Girls seemed as plastic as Barbie dolls, just as artificial as the numerous dance-pop groups that preceded them before the alternative rock explosion (and those groups that followed in the Spice Girls's wake, such as the popular "boy bands" N-Sync and the Backstreet Boys). While the Spice Girls may be the farthest thing from being "real," debates over their authenticity become moot upon seeing thousands of energized young girls chanting "girl power," the group's slogan. The Spice Girls are certainly not as complex as female-centered artists like Ani DiFranco and Bikini Kill, but at their best they provided a self-esteem boost for thousands of young girls and, at their worst, may have only been "mere" entertainment.

—Kembrew McLeod

FURTHER READING:

Aplin, Rebecca. *Spice Girls: Giving You Everything.* London, UFO Music, 1997.

Shore, Nancy. *The Spice Girls.* Philadelphia, Chelsea House, 1998.

The Spice Girls

Spider-Man

Spider-Man, a character appearing in Marvel comic books from 1962, ranks not only as Marvel's most popular superhero, but as one of the most instantly recognizable comic-book characters of all. Of the many superheroes to appear over the years, only Superman and perhaps Batman have had a greater impact on the history and fortunes of the comic-book industry. And no other comic-book character has more perfectly realized the adolescent angst and male fantasies at the heart of the modern superhero genre.

With innovative characters like the Fantastic Four and the Incredible Hulk, Marvel, in the 1960s, pioneered the formula for superheroes who evinced such human failings as jealousy, insecurity, and alienation. This stood them in sharp contrast to the impossibly noble and stiff superheroes offered by competitors like DC Comics. Marvel's formula would attract an expanding fan base throughout the 1960s and beyond, ultimately making it the preeminent comic-book company. Although he was not the first of the new Marvel superheroes, Spider-Man was the true archetype of the Marvel formula. In a calculated stab at the teenage market, which had dwindled since the institution of the Comics Code in 1954, writer-editor Stan Lee set out to create a superhero who was himself an adolescent—one who had to wrestle with his own insecurities and personal difficulties as often as

he had to fight the bad guys. This superhero, in Lee's words, "would lose out as often as he'd win—in fact, more often." Lee bypassed his chief artist Jack Kirby and chose Steve Ditko to illustrate the concept, feeling that Ditko's own offbeat style was more appropriate for such an odd character as Spider-Man. The premise was so unusual, in fact, that Lee chose to debut Spider-Man in the fifteenth and final issue of *Amazing Fantasy,* a series slated for cancellation.

The August 1962 issue of that title introduced readers to Peter Parker, a shy bespectacled teenager ridiculed by his classmates for his social awkwardness and his love of science. One day when he attends an exhibit on radioactivity, Peter is bitten by a spider that unbeknownst to him has just been irradiated. Later, Peter discovers that somehow the radioactive spider's bite has transferred its power to him. Now possessing superhuman speed and agility, the ability to cling to walls, and the proportionate strength of a spider, Peter designs himself a pair of web-shooters attached to his wrists, tailors a costume to conceal his identity, and becomes Spider-Man.

What came next in the originating story set the character apart from his costumed predecessors. Instead of swearing an altruistic oath to aid humanity, Peter sets out to cash in on his new powers. Why, after all, should he do anything for a society that has done nothing but ostracize him? He cares only for his Aunt May and Uncle Ben, who have raised him since the death of his parents. So selfish is his pursuit of fortune and glory that Spider-Man refuses to come to the aid of a policeman who fails to apprehend an escaping burglar. Then one night, Peter comes home to discover that his beloved Uncle Ben has been murdered. As Spider-Man, he pursues the killer only to discover that it is the very same criminal whom he had earlier neglected to stop. The shocking revelation that his self-interest has indirectly led to the death of his uncle forces Spider-Man to accept the role that fate has forced upon him. He learns that ''with great power must come great responsibility.'' It is this painful lesson that would form the guiding principle and tragic quality of his life as a superhero.

It is difficult to conceive of a more perfect origin story for a comic-book superhero. Lee and Ditko created a hero instantly relevant to the many shy, lonely, and disoriented adolescents who read comic books at a time when anxieties over the perils of atomic energy prevailed in the culture. Young people had a new superhero whom they could truly claim as their own. But Spider-Man's story imparted an important moral message as well. Although inclined to be a loner, Spider-Man was compelled by tragedy to enlist in a cause. This call to commitment proved to be a watchword not only for Spider-Man, but for the discontented baby boomers who mobilized their numbers in the service of political, social, and cultural change. In this important respect, Spider-Man meshed effortlessly with the currents then shaping 1960s youth culture.

Spider-Man immediately became Marvel's most popular superhero—a distinction that he has held ever since. Responding to overwhelmingly positive reader mail, Stan Lee in 1963 launched the character in his own series, *The Amazing Spider-Man,* which remained in circulation in the late 1990s. Spider-Man's commercial

A *Spider–Man* novel cover.

success fueled Marvel's mid-1960s superhero revival and set the company on the course toward becoming the industry leader.

Stan Lee quite ingeniously billed Spider-Man as ''the superhero who could be you.'' Peter Parker lived at home with his Aunt May, whose motherly doting was a constant source of inconvenience, as Peter had to fabricate explanations for the late nights and extended absences that Spider-Man's lifestyle demanded. His high school and college life figured prominently into the stories, as did his job as a photographer for the cranky publisher J. Jonah Jameson's *Daily Bugle.* His perennial money problems and romantic travails with high school sweetheart Liz Allen, co-worker Betty Brant, and college flames Gwen Stacy and Mary-Jane Watson became an integral part of what was arguably the first comic-book soap opera. Spider-Man's good-natured wise-cracking, irreverence for authority, and self-deprecating humor made him an especially endearing antihero to the young. Although he battled a colorful array of middle-aged villains like Dr. Octopus, the Green Goblin, and the Vulture, Spider-Man was himself branded an outlaw by the press, the police, and other sources of adult authority who always seemed to suspect and misunderstand the hero's motives and actions.

Spider-Man's popularity only grew over the following decades with a proliferation of licensed products, several Saturday-morning television cartoon series, and a long-running syndicated newspaper strip. In keeping with industry trends, Spider-Man's stories became increasingly sophisticated during the 1970s and 1980s. Three notable issues in 1971 defied the Comics Code Authority by dealing explicitly with the subject of drug abuse. The controversy over the anti-drug stories led immediately to the liberalization of the Comics Code. Mindful of the fact that Spider-Man was especially popular among the youngest comic-book readers, Marvel has tended to keep the series rather squarely within the boundaries of mainstream cultural acceptability.

Several new comic-book titles featuring the hero increased his presence in the market to near-saturation point during the late 1980s and 1990s. In 1990 the first issue of *Spider-Man* sold a record two million copies in multiple printings. The proliferation of the *Spider-Man* series and crossover stories prompted a number of fans to charge that Marvel was over-marketing their favorite hero at the expense of coherent stories, but this controversy has done little to diminish his standing among general comic-book readers. The lack of a major movie deal and accompanying hype on par with that of DC's Superman and Batman has limited Spider-Man's exposure in American mass culture. But that fact may also help account for his continuing popularity among comic-book fans, a subculture generally resistant to mainstream media trends.

It is Spider-Man who most completely epitomizes the ideal of the comic-book superhero for people raised since the 1960s. As a personification of adolescent anxieties and fantasies, Spider-Man truly deserves his status as the quintessential modern comic-book superhero.

—Bradford W. Wright

FURTHER READING:

Daniels, Les. *Marvel Comics: Five Fabulous Decades of the World's Greatest Comics.* New York, Harry N. Abrams, 1991.

The Essential Spider-Man, Vol. 1. New York, Marvel Comics, 1996.

Jacobs, Will, and Gerard Jones. *The Comic Book Heroes.* Rocklin, California, Prima Publishing, 1998.

Lee, Stan. *Origins of Marvel Comics.* New York, Simon and Schuster, 1974.

Spiegelman, Art

See Maus

Spielberg, Steven (1946—)

Reviewing Steven Spielberg's first theatrical film, *Sugarland Express,* in 1974, critic Pauline Kael wrote, "The director, Steven Spielberg, is twenty-six; I can't tell if he has any mind, or even a strong personality . . . but he has a sense of composition and movement that almost any director might envy . . . He could be that rarity among directors—a born entertainer." The next year, Spielberg came out with *Jaws,* the blockbuster that helped launch a new era in Hollywood, and put Spielberg on the road to becoming the most successful filmmaker of his time. By the 1990s, not only was he considered by many critics to be one of the most talented filmmakers in history, but he had broken three modern box office records (with *Jaws, E.T.,* and *Jurassic Park*), owned his own studio, and was reportedly worth almost $2 billion.

Steven Allan Spielberg was born on December 18, 1946 (not 1947, as traditionally reported) in Cincinnati, Ohio. His youth—displaced from Ohio to New Jersey to Arizona to California, obsessed

Steven Spielberg

with movies, television, and comic books, bullied by anti-Semites, and culminating in his parents' divorce—seems to form the subtext of many of his films. Crucial to his success has been his ability to invest the horror, science fiction, and other Hollywood genres he has continually recycled with the emotional force of his childhood obsessions. His early family difficulties, for example, seem to have provided raw material for a filmography crammed with broken homes, abandoned children, and wayward, would-be, or substitute fathers.

Spielberg started making amateur films at age ten. He made the amateur 8mm sci-fi feature *Firelight* in 1964, at age 17. Rejected from the prestigious film schools at the University of Southern California and the University of California Los Angeles, he attended California State College at Long Beach. While contemporaries such as George Lucas, Francis Ford Coppola, and Martin Scorsese became the first "Film School Generation," Spielberg was essentially self-taught, spending three days a week during college hanging around the Universal lot, observing and hobnobbing. His last amateur film, the short *Amblin'* (1968), won him a directing contract at Universal, prompting *The Hollywood Reporter* to call him the youngest filmmaker ever contracted to a major studio. For the next two years, he directed television programs like *Night Gallery, Marcus Welby, M.D.,* and *Columbo.*

Spielberg's professional feature debut, the made-for-television road thriller *Duel* (1972), made an international splash, prompting *LA Times* television critic Cecil Smith to remark, "Steve Spielberg is really the *wunderkind* of the film business." Spielberg quickly established himself as a leading figure in American mass culture. In nine years, he made five of the highest grossing films of his era, a feat certainly unsurpassed in film history. *Jaws,* essentially a horror film starring a huge mechanical shark, was so successful that it helped transform the whole American film industry from the post-studio dispersion of the 1960s to "the blockbuster mentality" of the 1980s. It also marked Spielberg's debut as an impresario of cutting-edge special effects. In *Close Encounters of the Third Kind* (1977), Spielberg transformed the 1950s movie alien from a monster into a saint. Ray Bradbury called it a religious film; Jean Renoir called it poetry. The more nakedly commercial *Raiders of the Lost Ark* (1981) and its two sequels (1984 and 1989) re-popularized the adventure serial genre with tongue planted firmly in cheek. With *E.T. The Extra-Terrestrial* (1982), a fairy tale about a boy's friendship with an alien stranded on Earth, Spielberg made what is probably the most cherished film of modern times. It made him a celebrity in his own right, and even garnered him a United Nations Peace Medal. Spielberg's influence on American culture in this period cannot be overestimated. Indiana Jones, E.T., and the shark became durable American icons, helping to transform the national Zeitgeist from the turbulence of the 1960s to the high-tech nostalgia of the 1980s.

In 1985, Spielberg began a series of attempts to break away from the kind of genre-dominated filmmaking that had previously defined his career. *The Color Purple* (1985) was his first feature entirely about people (no car chases, sharks, or aliens). He took a huge risk in tackling Alice Walker's historical novel of black female liberation, and the results were ambiguous. While successful with the mainstream of American viewers and critics, *The Color Purple* was the first in a series of "serious" Spielberg films accused by a vocal minority of substituting sentimentality for an honest engagement with historical and political realities. The apparently perfect marriage between art and commerce that Spielberg had attained in his earlier genre films began to founder. *Empire of the Sun* (1987), *Always* (1989), and *Hook* (1991) met with mixed reviews.

In 1993, Spielberg regained commercial and critical success, though not in the same film. First came another box office smash, *Jurassic Park,* a return to the horror genre, with computer-generated dinosaurs instead of a mechanical shark. Then came *Schindler's List,* a self-consciously European-style Holocaust film in black and white, and winner of seven Academy awards, including Best Picture and Spielberg's first for Best Director. This alternating pattern repeated with two films in 1997: a *Jurassic Park* sequel, and *Amistad,* the true story of a maritime slave revolt. It remains to be seen whether *Saving Private Ryan* (1998) signifies a reunion of Spielberg's commercial and artistic ambitions.

Considering their authorship by a variety of screenwriters and their mass appeal, Spielberg's films display a striking degree of thematic and stylistic unity. In Spielberg's world, the highest ideal is childlike innocence—embodied by children themselves, endangered by monsters and villains, defended by heroes, reclaimed by grown men, and symbolized by flying. Human relationships in the films are based on the model of the family broken and mended. Emotions tend to the extremes of terror and wonder. Stylistically, Spielberg's talent for visual composition is unsurpassed. With his embrace of high technology, his blending of genre and art cinema traditions, his prodigious quotation of other films, and his increasing concern with themes of vision and artifice, Spielberg is a consummate postmodernist. During the 1990s, his thematics and stylistics have tended to become unified under the banner of excessive, if sometimes historically justified, violence.

While Spielberg's directorial career alone would guarantee him a place in the history of mass culture, he has also made his mark as a film producer, studio mogul, and civic personality. He formed the highly successful production company, Amblin Entertainment, in 1984, producing or executive producing such films as *Gremlins* (1984), *Back to the Future* (1985), *An American Tail* (1986), and *Who Framed Roger Rabbit?* (1988), and such television series as *Tiny Toon Adventures* and *ER.*

In 1994, Spielberg launched both DreamWorks and the Survivors of the Shoah Visual History Foundation. DreamWorks SKG, co-founded with film executive Jeffrey Katzenberg and music mogul David Geffen as the first new major Hollywood studio since the 1930s, produces film, television, music, and computer-based entertainment. With *Schindler's List,* Spielberg publicly reclaimed his Jewish heritage and proclaimed his civic ideals. Seeded with $6 million from his *Schindler's List* earnings, the Shoah Foundation set out to videotape 50,000 testimonies by Holocaust survivors around the world, to catalogue them, and to make them available for research and education via a sophisticated interactive computer system.

Thematically, economically, and ideologically, Spielberg's truest predecessor was Walt Disney. For many, he represents Hollywood at its best. For some, he represents it at its worst. His films have been criticized as both infantile and manipulative—essentially as theme park thrill rides. His adherence to a liberal political agenda has been accused of masking a retrograde paternalism in both his films and his business dealings. The new Hollywood he helped create has been viewed as the embodiment of the most greedy and destructive tendencies of capitalism. Even his Shoah Foundation has been criticized for Hollywood-izing history. A genius without, as Kael put it, "a mind," Spielberg embodies the contradictions of late twentieth-century American mass culture.

—Joshua Hirsch

FURTHER READING:

Brode, Douglas. *The Films of Steven Spielberg.* New York, Citadel, 1995.

Kael, Pauline. *For Keeps.* New York, Dutton, 1994.

Loshitzky, Yosefa, editor. *Spielberg's Holocaust: Critical Perspectives on Schindler's List.* Bloomington, Indiana University Press, 1997.

McBride, Joseph. *Steven Spielberg: A Biography.* New York, Simon and Schuster, 1997.

Spillane, Mickey (1918—)

In terms of sales, Mickey Spillane is one of the most popular writers of the twentieth century, and of all time. In terms of the content of the books themselves and the two fictional heroes for which he is best known, he has been widely reviled for his portrayal of extreme violence, sexual excess, and right-wing bigotry. Whatever the opinions of his critics, since the 1940s Spillane has proved himself to be a talented comic book writer, an author of prize-winning books for

Mickey Spillane

children and young adults, and, through his *Mike Hammer* series, a key player in the history of the hard-boiled detective novel.

Frank Michael Morrison Spillane was born in Brooklyn, New York, and brought up by working-class parents during the Great Depression. He began publishing stories in the pulp magazines soon after graduating from High School and, dropping out of college and frustrated with his sales job, eventually ended up working on comic books. In *One Lonely Knight* Max Allan Collins and James L. Traylor suggested that he was particularly successful at this, producing three times the output of other writers and devising a new, more efficient method of composition. When the war intervened, Spillane became a fighter pilot instructor, and afterwards found that comic books were no longer popular enough to provide a reliable source of income. This led him to write his first novel and to create the New York-based detective, Mike Hammer.

The first Mike Hammer novel, *I, the Jury*, was published in 1947 and is a landmark in the development of private-eye fiction. Famously, in *I, The Jury,* Mike Hammer discovers his lover, Charlotte, to be the killer he has been pursuing. When she tries to save herself by seducing him, Hammer shoots her and leaves her to die. The underlying moral logic of this (that the villain must be punished at whatever cost to the hero) is no different from Sam Spade's turning Brigid O'Shaunnessy over to the police in Dashiell Hammett's *The Maltese Falcon* (1930). However, Spillane's novel represents a significant shift from public to private justice. Sam Spade investigates but does not punish crime. Mike Hammer is investigator, judge, jury, and executioner. Spillane's other series hero, the spy Tiger Mann, is also successful in his use of violence to solve problems. *Tiger Mann* differs in very little other than name from Mike Hammer and appears to have been written in response to successful spy stories, including Ian Fleming's *James Bond* novels in the 1950s and 1960s.

After publishing seven novels between 1947 and 1952, Spillane seemed to respond to criticism of his portrayal of sex and violence by producing no more for the next nine years, although he continued to write and publish short stories during this period. When he began publishing novels again in 1961, the violence in them, and particularly the link between sex and violence, was hardly diminished, but over the years since, Spillane's reputation with critics gradually improved. He became respected as one of the most influential mystery writers of the late twentieth century. After producing over 30 adult novels, including 13 Mike Hammer adventures and four in the Tiger Mann spy series, Spillane surprised critics by publishing a novel for children and young adults, *The Day the Sea Rolled Back*, in 1979, which won a Junior Guild Literary Award.

Spillane has always been heavily involved in promoting his work. He has appeared as Mike Hammer on film and on the covers of some of the later novels, as well as reading his work on audio recordings. He made numerous chat show and game show appearances during the 1970s and even appeared as a parody of Mike Hammer in TV commercials for Miller beer. Somewhat notoriously, his second wife, Sherri, posed nude for the dustjackets of *The Erection Set* (1972), and *The Last Cop Out* (1973). Despite this, Spillane remains a rather private man, and his desire for publicity is perhaps summed up in a comment he made, quoted in *One Lonely Knight*: "Hell, I'm not an author, I'm a writer. I've got to make a living, somehow."

—Chris Routledge

FURTHER READING:

Cawelti, John G. *Adventure, Mystery, and Romance.* University of Chicago Press, 1976.

Collins, Max Allan, and James L. Traylor. *One Lonely Knight: Mickey Spillane's Mike Hammer.* Bowling Green University Popular Press, 1984.

Palmer, Jerry. *Thrillers: Genesis and Structure of a Popular Genre.* London, Edward Arnold, 1978.

Symons, Julian. *Bloody Murder: From the Detective Story to the Crime Novel.* New York, Viking Penguin, 1985.

Van Dover, J. Kenneth. *Murder in the Millions: Erle Stanley Gardner, Mickey Spillane, Ian Fleming.* New York, Frederick Ungar, 1984.

Spin

Just as a tennis player puts spin on the ball in order to influence the direction of its bounce, so too do public figures (especially politicians) try to "spin" events so as to favorably influence coverage by the news media. The first uses of the term "spin" in this context date to the U.S. elections of 1984, and the term "spin doctor," meaning a press secretary, publicist, campaign manager, or other surrogate adept at dealing with the press, came into use about 1990. Given the growing plethora of news outlets and the undeniable power of the news media to influence public opinion, the concept of spin control has only become more prevalent by the end of the century.

Political campaigns are prime occasions for the exercise of spin control, because everything that occurs in a campaign, short of the final vote count, is open to interpretation. The candidate who placed second in a primary, for example, may spin the result as a moral victory or as a sign of growing momentum. The candidate in third place may claim that the result is acceptable, considering the very limited time and money that he or she spent in the state. The candidate coming in fourth may claim to have gained valuable experience and name recognition that might bode well for future primary contests.

One aspect of campaigns that is especially amenable to spin is the political debate, which lacks clear criteria for victory, and the television audience is not, in any case, made up of trained debate judges. As a result, the opinions of media pundits can have a great influence on public perceptions of a political debate's outcome. This is well illustrated by Gerald Ford's remark, during a 1976 televised debate with Jimmy Carter, about the status of Poland. In response to an earlier statement by Carter, Ford claimed that Poland was not under the domination of the Soviet Union. Opinion polls conducted immediately after the debate showed that a significant portion of the audience thought Ford had done well. But by the next day, after the news media had made much of Ford's gaffe about Poland, many viewers apparently decided that Carter was the debate's clear winner. Occasions like this, demonstrating the media's power to sway public perceptions, have convinced political professionals of the necessity of effective spin control.

Wartime provides another instance of the usefulness of spin, especially in the post-Vietnam War era. It is virtually doctrine at the highest levels of the U.S. armed forces that the news media "lost" the Vietnam War for America by writing and broadcasting stories that undermined the public's will to win. News stories about human rights abuses by the South Vietnamese government, mistreatment of prisoners and other atrocities allegedly committed by U.S. troops, and the effects upon civilians of indiscriminate bombing of North Vietnam—along with vivid images of dead, dying, and horribly disfigured American troops—are believed by the Pentagon to have convinced many citizens that the war was unwinnable.

That does not mean that spin control was absent during the Vietnam War. It was, in fact, widely attempted by politicians at home and by the Military Assistance Command in Vietnam. But the official spin on the war lost effectiveness as the conflict dragged on. President Lyndon Johnson, whose Vietnam policies had enjoyed wide support in 1964, was alleged to have developed a "credibility gap" concerning the war by 1967—a euphemism for the belief that Johnson had been caught lying. In Vietnam, military Public Information Officers held daily press briefings in Saigon at 5 p.m. In time, many journalists grew so cynical about the official spin on the war that they began to refer to the briefings as the "Five O'Clock Follies." Fed up with the official line, many reporters went off on their own, and in the process sometimes uncovered stories embarrassing to both the U.S. military and its commander in chief.

Having learned what it saw as the public relations lesson of Vietnam, the Pentagon has since taken careful and comprehensive steps to ensure that media coverage of military conflict receives the proper spin. The new policy involves the close supervision of reporters in combat zones, restriction of journalists from "sensitive" areas, and frequent official briefings so as to ensure that journalists receive the military's version of events. This approach was followed successfully by the military in Grenada (1984) and Panama (1990). However, the crowning achievement in military spin control probably came in the Persian Gulf War. In the Saudi Arabia staging area for Coalition forces, correspondents were forbidden to travel on their own; instead, battlefield newsgathering was only permitted by a closely supervised "pool" of reporters, while the others were left behind. Then, the journalists were brought back to the press area to brief their colleagues. Military briefings during the Gulf War were much more effective as spin than the "Five O'Clock Follies": the carefully scripted briefings created the desired impression of the Coalition Forces' invincibility.

A more recent spin control campaign began in the spring of 1998, when stories began to surface in Washington alleging that President Bill Clinton had engaged in a sexual relationship with a young White House intern named Monica Lewinsky. The Clinton White House, especially Press Secretary Mike McCurry, tried hard to spin the story into something innocuous. Observing McCurry at work over a long period, writer Howard Kurtz derived some of the press secretary's "spin strategies," including: 1) Don't let television break a scandal. If it's inevitable, leak it to the print media, which tend to provide more nuance and are seen by considerably fewer people; 2) Do not let Senate committees break scandals, either. Beat them to the punch by informing the media yourself, providing your own "spin" in the process; and 3) Leak favorable but boring stories to one media outlet as an "exclusive"—chances are, they'll be grateful enough to give the story a positive spin.

—Justin Gustainis

FURTHER READING:

Kurtz, Howard. *Spin Cycle: Inside the Clinton Propaganda Machine.* New York, The Free Press, 1998.

Maltese, John Anthony. *Spin Control: The White House Office of Communications and the Management of Presidential News.* 2nd ed. Chapel Hill, University of North Carolina Press, 1994.

Spiritualists
See Psychics

Spitz, Mark (1950—)

The first Olympian ever to win seven gold medals in a single Olympics, U.S. swimmer Mark Spitz became part hero and part controversial athlete during his Olympic career. With his black mustache and movie star looks, Spitz dominated his sport in 1972 and retired to find even greater fame as the first athlete to become a commercial success in corporate America. Even the specter of terrorism at the 1972 Munich games did not lessen his extraordinary appeal. With 11 Olympic medals under his belt and a reported $5 million in endorsements, Spitz enjoyed enormous popularity and success in the 1970s.

Spitz began training at an early age, and by the age of eight he was already swimming in competitions. With his family firmly behind him, the Spitzes relocated to California in search of a better training environment. Spitz received encouragement and training from both his father, Arnold, and three coaches during the course of his career. Coaches Sherm Chavoon, Doc Counsilman, and George Hains, all Hall of Fame members, guided Spitz to success in competition.

Known for his self-confidence, Spitz was not always popular with his teammates but continued to train for both team and individual competitions. By the 1968 Summer Olympics in Mexico City, the outspoken Spitz had already made a name for himself as a cocky, self-assured young man. In the days before the games, he boasted that he would take home six gold medals. Unfortunately, his prediction fell far short; he won only two gold medals, one silver medal, and one bronze medal. Disappointed, but not daunted, Spitz returned home to train with the Indiana University swim team in preparation for the 1972 Summer Olympics in Munich, West Germany.

By the beginning of the 1972 Olympics, Spitz had matured as both an athlete and as a person. His personal appearances lacked the boasting predictions of 1968, and he appeared more focused on his goal of winning as many medals as possible. His determination paid off. By the end of his second Olympiad, Spitz had won seven gold medals and set seven world records in only eight days, a record that remained unbroken throughout the century. Even amid the terrorism during the Munich games, in which nine members of the Israeli team, a West German police officer, and all five Arab terrorists were killed, Spitz's victories remained a high point for both himself and the U.S. Olympic swim team.

Spitz's popular appeal did not wane following the 1972 Olympics, and he returned home a hero with seven gold medals, endorsement contracts, and even a popular poster underscoring his achievements as the winner of seven gold medals. With a contract from the William Morris Agency, Spitz promoted a range of items from swimwear and pool accessories to milk, razors, and even hair dryers. In addition to his endorsements, Spitz also made numerous television appearances with such stars as Sonny and Cher and Bob Hope.

However, Spitz never really found success in the advertising world. Lacking the agents and the public relations experts employed by athletes in the 1990s, Spitz did not receive the guidance he needed to succeed in product endorsement. He was considered "too quiet" by some and was criticized for his often stiff appearance on camera.

Mark Spitz

But by the standards of the 1990s, the most surprising criticism Spitz received was that he endorsed too many products. After clearing the way for future athletes to carve out lucrative niches in advertising, Spitz left both his swimming career and his endorsements behind for a life out of the spotlight.

By the time he retired from swimming shortly after his 1972 Olympic victories, Spitz, at age 23, had won 11 Olympic medals and had set 26 individual world records and 24 national records. In 1972, he was named World Swimmer of the Year and was inducted into the International Swimming Hall of Fame as an Honor Swimmer in 1977. In the years following Munich, Spitz led a busy life pursuing a wide variety of interests including real estate investments, sailing, speaking engagements, and appearances at swimming events.

In the 1990s Spitz attempted a comeback at the age of 40. His attempt to qualify in the 100-meter butterfly for the 1992 games fell short, and he retired again. But this setback did not alter his love of the sport or his active participation in it. At the 1998 World Championships in Perth, Australia, Spitz proposed the creation of a position dealing with the problem of performance-enhancing drugs used by swimmers. Though no longer a competitor, Spitz retains his love for and interest in the sport through personal appearances at competitions and the enjoyment he still finds in swimming. Though his outstanding career has been punctuated with disappointments in 1968, tragedy in

1972, and a failed comeback in 1992, Mark Spitz remains a national hero and a shining star in the Olympic firmament.

—Kimberley H. Kidd

FURTHER READING:

Noden, Merrell. ''Catching Up with . . . Swimming Champion Mark Spitz.'' *Sports Illustrated.* August 4, 1997, 11.

Reed, Susan. ''Mark Spitz.'' *People.* January 15, 1990, 86.

Spitz, Mark, and Lemond Alan. *The Mark Spitz Complete Book of Swimming.* New York, Thomas Y. Crowell, 1976.

Spock, Dr. Benjamin (1903-1998)

By introducing new child-rearing techniques that contradicted those practiced for hundreds of years, pediatrician Dr. Benjamin McLane Spock changed the way several generations of parents raised their children. Through his practice, his books, and his articles in numerous child-rearing magazines, he taught parents that their own common sense, their own instincts, their unique bond with their children, were to be trusted more than any theories. He told them to listen to their children and to respect their unique individual abilities. Dr. Spock gave parents flexible tools to use for child rearing, which he called "a long, hard job." Without being an idealogue or professing to be a guru, Dr. Spock and his liberal views on child rearing also opened or reinforced new directions in education. From the 1950s education moved away from the force-fed teaching of pre-digested materials toward a nurturing of children's natural desires for knowledge.

As North America's foremost pediatrician and parenting authority for over fifty years, Dr. Spock had the privilege of witnessing firsthand the results of his earlier recommendations to parents. His best-known book, *Common Sense Book of Baby and Child Care* (later re-titled *Baby and Child Care*), was published in June 1946 and became the predominant how-to guide for parents in the post-World War II baby boom. In it, Dr. Spock urged parents to trust their instincts and their own parenting abilities. The book became a virtual bible of child rearing, guiding many parents from the 1950s to the 1990s. By the end of the century, virtually all parents with young children in the United States had grown up within the child-rearing and educational framework advised by Dr. Spock. Though parts of the book have been criticized as fostering over-permissiveness, the book remained one of the most influential books on parenting at the end of

Dr. Benjamin Spock

the twentieth century. Dr. Spock embraced the flexibility he asked of parents by adapting his basic volume to changes in society, expanding and revising it several times during his lifetime.

The United States was ripe for change when Dr Spock first introduced his radical ideas. The end of World War II in 1945 meant the end of many social values inherited from the nineteenth century, and, with the disappearance of those—along with so many millions of human beings the world over—there was a need for new beginnings and different ways of tackling the world. If the atomic bomb created a constant nuclear death threat, the joys of reunion with the homecoming veterans spurred a celebration of life.

Dr. Spock's optimistic vision of parents was welcomed in this climate. His confidence in parental instincts probably found its source, deep down, in Jean-Jacques Rousseau's romantic vision of mankind as fundamentally good. Nevertheless, Spock's optimism found willing readers from veterans who had experienced cruelty, savagery, and crimes against humanity during the war. Parents of children during the 1950s clearly wanted to turn their backs on misery and despair and to believe that the world was good, that life could only get better, that progress was now unlimited, and that the future was wide open. Gone was the rigid discipline and sacrifice used to contribute to the war effort; gone was the rationing of sugar, bananas, meat, cigarettes, butter, chocolate, and gasoline. Americans could rejoice in their lives and their new prosperity. Such optimistic views and indulgence luxuries would last until the "difficult times" of the 1970s and beyond—times that Dr. Spock would address in his further writings.

The generation most influenced by Dr. Spock was the baby-boom generation, which would give the second half of the twentieth century many of it characteristics. The significant increase in the number of babies born in 1946 over those born in 1945 is attributable to the return of veterans of the war to their current or future wives. In 1945 2,873,000 babies were born compared to 3,500,000 in 1946, a 20 percent increase. In 1954 the number increased to 4,000,000 and remained high through 1964, the last year of the baby-boom generation. The sheer number of babies born at the same time gave tremendous importance to Dr. Spock's writings and teachings. Dr. Spock's opinions would shape the first generation of children born into a United States that was a dominant world power.

From the Middle Ages, children raised within Western traditions had been considered trainees, who should be taught early on to obey specific rules. Feeding was restricted to specific hours and toilet training had to be done according to specific principles and at precise ages. The rules applied to all children regardless of their individual differences. This approach, still widely practiced in some European contexts and in highly socialized countries in Asia, for instance, runs counter to the advice given to the parents of baby boomers by Dr. Spock. "I wanted to be supportive of parents rather than to scold them," Dr. Spock said. "My book set out very deliberately to counteract some of the rigidities of pediatric tradition, particularly in infant feeding." He emphasized what may have been obvious to parents with some degree of common sense (especially parents of multiple children), but may not have been obvious to authors of books on parenting: there were enormous differences between individual babies. These differences were important, and had to be taken into account. Parents needed to be flexible and did not need to worry constantly about "spoiling" as a danger. Aside from giving parents permission to make their own decisions, Dr. Spock also needed to dispel many myths about what was good or bad for children. When he began practicing pediatrics, bananas were considered hazardous to a young child's health and castor oil was praised as a cure-all. Obviously, that first book was needed. In the 52 years since its publication, 50 million copies of *Baby and Child Care* have been sold, and the book has been translated into 39 languages.

This extremely influential man did not live his life in the ivory tower of some academic community. Born on May 2, 1903, in the New England community of New Haven, Connecticut, he had gone to Yale University, and been a member of the crew team that won a gold medal for the United States in the 1924 Olympics. He then went on to receive his medical degree from Columbia University and went to the New York Psychoanalytic Institute for further studies. He was not an advisor who did not practice what he preached either: from his marriage in 1927 with Jane Cheney (that would end in divorce after 48 years) two sons were born, Michael and John.

While maintaining a private practice in New York City, he taught pediatrics at Cornell University from 1933 to 1943. He participated in World War II as a psychiatrist in the U.S. Naval Reserve Medical Corps, and was discharged as a Lieutenant Commander in 1946. He then went on to teach psychiatry at the University of Minnesota, which he left in 1951 to join the University of Pittsburgh as professor of child development. In 1955, he joined the faculty at Case Western Reserve University.

The enormous influence Spock had through his books exemplified the changes in society. The traditional way of handling child-rearing practices had been through confidential, direct information from doctor or nurse to the parent, or from parents to children of parenting age. Such practices continued, of course, but they did not correspond to the needs of a new age, with growing mass media where everything had to be made available to the largest possible number, through paperbacks or newspaper articles, radio broadcasts or cassette tapes. To reach these audiences, he wrote or collaborated on 15 books over the years. With his wife, Mary Morgan, he wrote an autobiography, *Spock on Spock,* published in 1989. He also wrote columns for more than 30 years in mass-market publications such as *Ladies Home Journal* or *Redbook*. He was a contributing editor to *Parenting* magazine (including the Web version for the last year of his life) from 1992 until his death. The editors of *Parenting* magazine mourned his death by saying, "We will miss his common sense approach to parenting and his dedication to raising healthy, happy children. The work he did at *ParentTime* will continue to be available as *Dr. Spock's Perspective* and soon we will publish a number of columns he did for us that have never been seen before. It is our hope that future generations of parents and children will benefit from his beliefs." From his perspective, the Internet was certainly new, but did not modify the basic realities of parenting: "Despite the newness of this setting," Spock said, "parents and children really haven't changed, and I anticipate addressing many of the same concerns and issues I have for the past six decades."

As the baby boomers have aged, Dr. Spock has been criticized for preaching permissiveness and was held responsible for a "Spock-marked" generation of hippies. Such criticism should certainly be put in perspective. There is no doubt that Spock did endorse beliefs held by the younger generation. He certainly was neither a fundamentalist of any kind, nor an arch-conservative. He joined protests against nuclear technology and the Vietnam war. While Vice President Spiro Agnew accused him of corrupting the youth of America, Dr. Spock only took credit, though, for having a "mild influence." His message had not been to substitute the preaching of a "doctor" for sound parental judgment. This included a measure of discipline and parental authority. Respecting and understanding children was not letting

them do anything they wanted. Contrary to the claims of his critics, Dr. Spock was always a firm believer in sound, responsible parental authority. He said: "Respect children because they deserve respect, and they'll grow up to be better people. But I've always said, ask for respect from you children, ask for cooperation, ask for politeness. Give your children firm leadership." He went beyond this statement, though, by saying: "strictness or permissiveness is not the real issue. Good-hearted parents who aren't afraid to be firm when it is necessary can get good results with either moderate strictness or moderate permissiveness. On the other hand, a strictness that comes from harsh feelings or a permissiveness that is timid or vacillating can each lead to poor results."

The basic message Dr. Spock sent to parents remains: "Don't take too seriously all that the neighbors say. Don't be overawed by what the experts say. Trust yourself, you know more than you think you know." It is a message of respect in all possible ways: respect for parents by a health professional, respect for children by parents, respect for parents by children. It is a deeply humanist message, stating that the real values are always individual values, that the only valid judgment is the judgment made by responsible individuals. It is the very opposite of cults and of every theory or system that would diminish, reduce, or even annihilate the fundamental duty that we have to our individual decision-making process, in child rearing or in any other matters. Dr. Spock left a deep impression of wisdom. He died at the age of 94 at his home in San Diego, with his family by his side.

—Henri Parette

FURTHER READING:

Bloom, Lynn Z. *Doctor Spock: Biography of a Conservative Radical.* Indianapolis, Bobbs-Merrill, 1972.

Kaye, Judith. *The Life of Benjamin Spock.* New York, Twenty-first Century Books, 1993.

Maier, Thomas. *Dr. Spock: An American Life.* New York, Harcourt Brace, 1998.

Spock, Benjamin. *Common Sense Book of Baby and Child Care.* 1946. Revised and updated, with Michael B. Rothenberg, *Baby and Child Care.* New York, Dutton, 1985.

Spock, Benjamin and Mary Morgan. *Spock on Spock: A Memoir of Growing up with the Century.* New York, Pantheon Books, 1989.

Sport Utility Vehicles (SUVs)

Short for sport utility vehicle, the SUV earned its name by its ability to transport people and their gear to outdoor recreation areas. While the SUV has been available to drivers in the United States since the end of World War II, its immense popularity arose only in the 1980s and 1990s, when baby boomers discovered that the more luxurious models were a sporty and practical alternative to the family sedan, minivan, or station wagon. Even though the majority of SUVs rarely go off road, many owners appreciate the rugged potential of SUV, while safety-conscious drivers value its handling on snow and ice.

The first SUVs in the United States were much more spartan than the Mercedes, Lexus, and Cadillac versions of the 1990s. Surplus military Jeeps converted to meet the needs of the civilian market at the end of World War II, the first SUVs met the recreational demands of consumers who sought escape from the deprivation of the Great Depression and war-time rationing.

The supply of surplus military Jeeps did not last long, however, and the Willys-Overland Company began to produce models specifically for the civilian market. Ranchers, farmers, hunters, and campers appreciated their affordability and the fact that they were four-wheel drive. These early models did not compete with passenger automobiles because they lacked space for both people and luggage and because they handled like the trucks on which they were based. Although International Harvester manufactured the Travelall and the Scout, and Jeep brought out the Jeep Wagoneer, the first dedicated sport utility from a major manufacturer was the Ford Bronco, introduced in 1966 and followed in 1969 by the Chevy Blazer and GMC Jimmy. These relatively compact SUVs were joined in 1973 by the Suburban, which was marketed by both Chevrolet and GMC and came in a choice of two- or four-wheel drive versions. (An earlier version of the Suburban, which appeared in the 1930s, was a delivery truck, not a true SUV.) Still the largest SUV in the 1990s, the Suburban offered interior spaciousness and towing capacity unknown to earlier models.

The gas shortage of the 1970s created numerous changes in U.S. driving habits. Gasoline shortages, long lines at the pumps, and the encouragement of public figures, including President Jimmy Carter, caused many Americans to abandon their gas-guzzling muscle cars for a more socially responsible alternative. Although many drivers chose either small European or Japanese cars, others discovered the versatility of imported trucks. Still others found that they needed a vehicle that could tow a boat or trailer. In 1983, both General Motors and Ford offered alternatives to the imports, a smaller version of the Blazer and the Jimmy and the Bronco II. Although SUVs in the early 1980s counted for only two percent of all vehicle sales in the United States, drivers were very different from those who had purchased converted military jeeps. Instead of wanting a vehicle for off-road use, the new generation of SUV owners included a high percentage of women who wanted an alternative to the station wagon and later to the minivan.

Attempting to appeal to these diverse drivers, manufacturers offered more amenities, including more horsepower, sophisticated sound systems, better handling, and the ability to "shift on the fly" from two-wheel drive to four-wheel drive. In addition, manufacturers began offering a variety of sizes from the tiny sub-compact Suzuki Sidekick (which weighed under 3,000 pounds and towed a modest 1,500 pounds) to the behemoths of the SUV set, the Chevrolet and GMC Suburbans, weighing over two tons and able to tow 10,000 pounds. In 1998, about one in every eight vehicles sold in the United States was a SUV, and that trend shows no signs of diminishing as the children of baby boomers leave the nest while their still-youthful parents have time and energy for recreational activities.

Enthusiasm for SUVs was dampened briefly in 1997 when Consumers Union, publishers of *Consumer Reports,* petitioned the National Highway Traffic Administration to investigate the Isuzu Trooper (1995/96) and the Acura SLX (1996) for placing occupants at a higher risk for rollovers. Other studies, including those by NHTSA, reported different conclusions, including the fact that the additional size and weight of SUVs made them safer than passenger automobiles. Nonetheless, many manufacturers aggressively addressed the perceived threat by warning consumers to drive SUVs a bit differently.

While SUVs have gained popularity with consumers, they are not popular with everyone. In fact, groups like the Sierra Club and

Friends of the Earth criticize SUVs for their impact on the environment. Classified as light trucks under federal rules, SUVs must meet less stringent fuel and emission standards than are required of passenger automobiles; and because they can also go off road, they can inflict greater damage on the environment. In addition, their higher ground clearance means that they can inflict costly damage on smaller cars. As a result, some insurance companies have raised their liability rates on SUVs.

Sales of SUVs continue to be strong at the end of the 1990s because they provide both a sporty feel and the ability to transport everything from boats and trailers to Labrador Retrievers to a gaggle of school children and their gear. More fun than the sedans and station wagons that baby boomers remember from their childhoods and more versatile than their chief competitor, the minivan, SUVs (many with designer labels, such as the Orvis Edition Jeep Grand Cherokee and the Eddie Bauer Ford Explorer) offer American drivers both more practicality and panache than their ancestors, the Jeep and Land Rover of the post World War II years.

—Carol A. Senf

FURTHER READING:

Delong, Brad. *4-Wheel Freedom: The Art of Off-Road Driving.* Boulder, Colorado, Paladin Press, 1996.

Jacobs, David H. *Sport Utility Vehicles: The Off-Road Revolution.* New York, Todtri Productions Ltd., 1998.

Ramsey, James L. "Birth of a Phenomenon." http://www.best4x4. landrover.com. June 1999.

The Sporting News

Known as the "Bible of Baseball," *The Sporting News* helped to expand the popularity of baseball among Americans in the first half of the twentieth century, before coverage of the sport was saturated by daily newspapers, radio, and television. A weekly newspaper, *The Sporting News* provided in-depth coverage of baseball that reflected its close connections to the game's inner circles and thoroughly informed its readers, helping to elevate baseball to its status as the national pastime. For many years, the tagline "The Base Ball Paper of the World" ran on the paper's front-page masthead.

"*The Sporting News*' coverage of baseball issues, ranging from the reserve clause and the farm system to night baseball, radio, and the major leagues' color barrier, represents more than an incidental source of information about baseball," G. Edward White wrote in his book *Creating the National Pastime: Baseball Transforms Itself 1903-1953.* "*The Sporting News* was consistently traditionalist to the point of being reactionary about most innovations in the game, although it made an effort to give a fair-minded presentation of most issues."

The Sporting News was owned and operated by the Spink family from 1886 to 1977. Its founder was Al Spink, a Canadian emigre who became a St. Louis promoter interested not only in baseball but also horse racing and the theater. When Al Spink suffered a financial setback, he enticed his brother Charlie to leave his homestead in the Dakotas and take over the fledgling newspaper. In its early years, the newspaper covered horse racing and the theater, as well as baseball, boxing, hunting, track, and cycling. In the early 1900s, Charlie Spink set the editorial direction that would distinguish the publication for decades to come—the paper would cover only baseball.

With a circulation of a meager 3,000 readers at the turn of the century, Charlie Spink hoped to capture more readers by establishing editorial positions that stood for the good of the game, not necessarily the position of the baseball team owners. Perhaps the paper's most controversial position was to support Ban Johnson in his 1901 quest to establish the American League as a second major league to the National League. ''The success of these crusades, combined with the changing nature of baseball, helped to consolidate the paper's editorial position,'' Stanley Frank wrote in his 1942 *Saturday Evening Post* article entitled ''Bible of Baseball.''

Sparse advertising revenue in the early years led Charlie Spink to contract with correspondents rather than hire permanent writers for much of the paper's content. Born out of frugality, the correspondent system became one of the paper's great strengths, giving readers the insight of a local scribe who witnessed the action and conversed with the participants as opposed to the basic details of wire reports. The correspondent system was especially important to the paper's extensive coverage of the minor leagues, a hallmark of its Bible of Baseball reputation. While most readers could get at least an overview of results of major league competition in their local daily newspapers, *The Sporting News* was the only publication that consolidated coverage of the minor leagues, covering the up-and-coming players as well as the big league stars and players. Another hallmark of *The Sporting News* was its printing of box scores from both major and minor league games.

When Charlie Spink died in 1914, his son J. G. Taylor Spink took over as publisher of the newspaper. During his 48-year tenure, he cemented the publication's place in baseball journalism. In his *Saturday Evening Post* article, Frank described Taylor Spink as ''the game's unofficial conscience, historian, watchdog and worshipper; and happily, he has made a nice piece of change in these public-spirited roles.'' Taylor Spink piloted *The Sporting News* as baseball emerged as the nation's favorite spectator sport in the 1920s and 1930s, campaigning for progressive policies to improve baseball and keep it an honest game following the 1919 Black Sox scandal. Two of his innovations had lasting impacts on the game of baseball. In 1925 he introduced *The Sporting News* annual major league all-star team, selecting the best players at each position and best left- and right-handed pitchers. This was the precursor to an actual game among all-stars that began in 1933. In the late 1920s, *The Sporting News* also picked the most valuable players in each major league, filling a void in the abandoned haphazard approaches previously used to select players for this honor. This led to the establishment of today's MVP selection system by vote of the Baseball Writers of America Association.

While Spink was said to have his finger on the pulse of baseball, critics of *The Sporting News* contended that the paper was overly one-sided to the baseball powers, as the paper initially resisted integration (it virtually ignored the Negro Leagues), night baseball, and radio broadcasts. ''Despite its traditional bias,'' White noted in *Creating the National Pastime,* ''*The Sporting News* had a sense of when changes were on the verge of taking place in baseball.''

In 1942, *The Sporting News* took over from Spaulding the publication of baseball's annual *Official Record Book and Guide.* This furthered its baseball influence and spurred the newspaper into even greater publication pursuits, for which it was best known for in the 1990s. Restricted advertising revenues during World War II also forced Taylor Spink to abandon the newspaper's baseball exclusivity, as it expanded into coverage of football, basketball, and hockey.

When Taylor Spink died in 1962, his son C. C. Johnson Spink assumed the helm of *The Sporting News.* In the 1960s, Johnson Spink further expanded coverage into golf, tennis, and auto racing. With no children to transfer the business to, Johnson Spink sold the newspaper in 1977 for $18 million to the Times-Mirror Company.

The paper remained an influential force in baseball through the 1950s, but it dissipated thereafter. Daily newspapers had significantly improved the quality and volume of baseball-related material following World War II. Television also offered faster transmission of information. While the paper no longer exerts the influence it once had in baseball, the J. G. Taylor Spink Award established in 1962 honors outstanding writers with a place of high acclaim at the Baseball Hall of Fame.

—Charlie Bevis

FURTHER READING:

Frank, Stanley. ''Bible of Baseball.'' *Saturday Evening Post.* June 20, 1942, 9-10.

Reidenbaugh, Lowell. *The Sporting News: First Hundred Years 1886-1986.* St. Louis, The Sporting News Publishing Company, 1985.

White, G. Edward. *Creating the National Pastime: Baseball Transforms Itself 1903-1953.* Princeton, Princeton University Press, 1996.

Sports Heroes

Americans look to their sporting heroes to be models of courage, discipline, strong character, and success; those perceived to be breaking the rules of the game are stereotyped as villains. In the last third of the century, the media has demanded that the hero's off-field conduct matters nearly as much as the onfield performance. In addition to winning the physical contest, the hero must negotiate other conflicts: the technicalities of the game's rules; overcoming physical pain; and negotiating the pitfalls of private self-doubt. This accounts for the American notion that sports, in addition to building physical skills, also builds moral character. Therefore, the sports hero often transcends the athletic arena: ''Because their lives helped, in part, to shape our values, habits, and, arguably, the content of our character, no full understanding of America is possible without an understanding of its sports idols,'' argue Robert Lipsyte and Peter Levine in *Idols of the Game.*

Developments in communications technologies throughout the twentieth century changed the sports they broadcast. The rise of radio transformed local hero athletes into national icons. As television began reaching a wider audience, the expanded broadcasting of events created an insatiable need to find and promote heroes. Televised sports created a shared experience, in which national audiences participated in their heroes' victory or defeat, or bore witness to an athlete's sportsmanship or misconduct. ''The most outstanding [athletes],'' writes John Izod in ''Television Sport and the Sacrificial Hero,'' ''become media personalities, and as such they reveal their hopes and fears as well as their thoughts about the game to the viewer.'' The proliferation of statistics in modern-day sport has helped create an overabundance of sports heroes. Figures such as ''most career home runs'' or ''career average rushing yards per carry'' help the transfixed fan distinguish a pantheon of great athletes emanating from the television factory.

According to sociologist Orrin Klapp, author of the 1949 study ''Hero Worship in America,'' the emotional behavior of hero worship encompasses ''popular homage, familiarity, possessiveness, curiosity, identification, and imitation.'' Fans identify with their heroes by adopting their uniforms, mannerisms, and even their style. As an ad from the 1920s proclaimed: ''A Spalding Swimming Suit won't teach you to swim. But it will make you *feel* like an Olympic champion.'' Following his 1969 Super Bowl triumph with the New York Jets, fans began wearing sideburns in emulation of pro quarterback Joe Namath. The veneration bestowed upon the sports hero often creates demigods, as this piece on Namath from *Esquire* demonstrates:

> Once in a generation, more or less, a chosen figure detaches himself from the social matrix and swims into mythology, hovering somewhere near the center of the universe, organizing in himself our attention, monopolizing our hopes and fears, intruding on our dreams, compelling our hearts to beat as his.

The sports hero is at once distant, placed in high-esteem, and simultaneously the subject of intense personal interest. This intense curiosity sometimes turns into a possessive need need to learn more about the hero. Klapp quotes boxer Jack Dempsey's description of the fans who forced themselves into his dressing room:

> They want to look at your eyes and your ears to see how badly you may have been injured. They want to pick up a word here or a gesture there which, later on, they can relay, magnified, to their own little public. I have always regarded these curious fans in a tolerant, even friendly way.

By the 1990s, superstars such as Michael Jordan could scarcely venture forth in public for fear they would be crushed by the onslaught of fan interest.

The genesis for the American sports hero can be traced back to the the 1920s—often referred to as ''The Golden Age of American Sports.'' The then-largest paying crowd to witness a sports event was for the 1926 Dempsey-Tunney bout in Philadelphia, which was watched by 120,757. Figures like Babe Ruth, Lou Gehrig, Knute Rockne, Helen Wills, Bobby Jones, and Jack Dempsey enabled each sport to claim its own titan.

The most towering object of hero worship during the 1920s was aviator Charles Lindbergh. Like sports heroes, Lindbergh performed a colorful feat that received tremendous admiration. ''Lindbergh,'' writes Klapp about the aviator's overnight recognition following his transatlantic flight, ''was literally jerked upward in status and in his vertical ascent became almost a demigod.'' Americans' hero worship of Lindbergh literally set the tone for later fan behavior. A story about Lindbergh in Klapp's study could be in reference to any celebrity of the twentieth century: ''A respectable-looking woman of middle age came up to Lindbergh, at dinner in a New York hotel, and tried to look into his mouth to see whether he was eating 'green beans or green peas.'''

In a similar fashion, Ruth's home run-hitting feats captured the popular imagination. Prior to Ruth, the game of baseball was played in a methodical fashion, by stringing together a series of singles in order to achieve runs. Ruth's powerful swats ignored the assembly line of singles-hitting by producing runs instantly. ''Ruth was like the

movie stars of the time who were discovered overnight,'' noted sports historian Benjamin Rader. ''Their seemingly effortless rise to fame and fortune was so unlike the arduous work of a bureaucrat or an assembly line worker.''

By the 1920s, the subjects of popular biographies shifted from worshiping ''idols of production''—politicians, or captains of industry—to the ''idols of consumption,'' or sporting and entertainment heroes. These new heroic tales, writes Mark Dyreson, were ''every bit as didactic as a tale about Horatio Alger,'' that describe the triumphs of heroes ''who succeeded against the odds, not simply because they got the breaks, but because of their adherence to the traditional values of perseverance, hard work and clean living.''

For decades following the rise of the sports hero, those enshrined in the public spotlight basked in the uncritical admiration of the media and fans alike. It wasn't that the private exploits of such heroes as baseball's Mickey Mantle and Ted Williams, basketball's Bill Russell, and football's Jim Brown were exempt from scrutiny; rather, it was that they were judged first and foremost on their public acts, and their private lives remained private. As the century wore on, however, a serious debate about what constitutes a true hero emerged among fans, the media, and athletes. Whereas the heroes of the 1920s were lionized for committing a specific feat that captured the public's imagination, by the 1990s the sports hero was asked to behave as a ''role model'' whose personal conduct was as important as his or her athletic feats.

Perhaps the figure that best marks this change was New York Yankees great Mickey Mantle. The Oklahoman who broke Ruth's record for home runs in a World Series in 1964 joined the Yankees during the 1950s. This was a decade of conflicting demands for those who were coming of age, writes Michael Anderson: ''their best was never good enough. Only by overachieving could they live up to their parents, those grimly stoic survivors of war and want.'' Mantle—as the old athletic cliche goes—lived hard and played hard, and few faulted him for it. Once he left the game of baseball, Mantle was no longer able to outplay others on the field so he seemed to try to outdrink them. In 1994, Mantle publicly admitted his alcoholism and promptly assumed the role of the socially-responsible role model by imploring others to avoid his mistakes. He also underwent a failed liver transplant and urged others to sign organ donor cards. ''I have thought about trying to define what a hero is,'' wrote Mantle's son David, shortly after his father's death. ''Dad was one throughout his baseball career, and a different kind at the end of his life.''

In the 1980s and 1990s, as the private lives of all celebrities (even political celebrities) came under increasing scrutiny, it was no longer enough for sports figures to swat a baseball the farthest, or catch a game-winning touchdown pass: they were increasingly sought after to set examples for the young. After sports fans witnessed several player strikes, and watched well-paid athletes land in drug abuse clinics, many yearned for an edenic time when athletes were clean-cut role models. This was a mythic notion: Ruth attained his legendary status alongside his womanizing, and a rather unathletic regimen of beer and hot dogs that showed in his overweight condition. Sociologist Charles Payne in *Newsweek* sums up this mistaken notion of innocence before the advent of big-money sports: ''If you were to go through baseball's or football's Hall of Fame, you're not going to come up with a bunch of choirboys.''

Atheletes themselves disagree over their obligation to lead exemplary privates lives. In a 1993 *Newsweek* article basketball star Charles Barkley, in his typically forthcoming manner, declared ''I'm not paid to be a role model. I'm paid to wreak havoc on the basketball court.'' Karl Malone, another basketball great, openly disagreed with Barkley, stating that ''We don't choose to be role models, we are chosen.'' Fans, devoted as they may be, had become hardened to the complaints of multimillionaire pro athletes. ''Funny,'' objects sports columnist Phil Mushnick, speaking for many fans, ''how big shots accept all the trappings of role modeldom—especially the residual commercial cash—before they renounce their broader responsibilities to society.''

Although it is true that not every athlete deserves a role model status, critics inflate the debate somewhat by failing to recognize that children have the capacity to distinguish between real-life heroes and daydream ones. As one 12-year-old told Sports Illustrated for Kids, if his sports hero were to ''mess up'' then ''he wouldn't be my favorite player anymore. I would sell all his cards. I have about 65 of them, and I'd give them away.'' It is possible that the adults are the ones who have changed, and not the kids. An enduring piece of baseball lore describes Shoeless Joe Jackson, a participant in the 1919 Black Sox Scandal, passing a young boy in public, who plaintively cries to the fallen hero: ''Say it ain't so, Joe!''

Americans learned to look for their heroes' faults, even while they were in the process of exalting them. In 1993 Michael Jordan, who is generally acknowledged as the greatest basketball player ever, was reported to have lost a substantial amount of money from gambling and was subjected to months of media attention and a brief diminishment of his reputation for his strictly legal activities. A few years later, in the midst of 1998's home run record chase, record-setter Mark McGwire was spotted with a legal performance enhancement drug sitting in his locker, prompting one editorial from St. Louis to proclaim: ''There probably aren't going to be any heroes anymore. The media won't let us have them.'' Yet it is the media that has helped create the impossible dilemma that confronts the sports hero. On the one hand they feed athletes on a steady diet of adulation beginning in college and increasing exponentially once they reach a professional level. Told for years that he (and, rarely, she) can do no wrong, the hero is then subjected to equally intense scrutiny aimed at uncovering faults and weaknesses. Wrote a St. Louis paper after McGwire's legal steroid was reported, ''In an oftentimes desperate attempt to get the story no one else has, the media look behind closed doors . . . to come up with something that might taint the reputation of an otherwise unblemished character.''

Other instances have caused Americans to examine themselves. In 1994, crowds gathered along a California freeway to witness ex-football star O.J. Simpson engage police in a surreal, televised car chase as a suicidal fugitive. Like fans urging on a self-destructive rock star, the crowd implored O.J. Simpson to run—as if he still carried the football—or made pronouncements like ''I can't believe he did it.'' Tom Verducci of Sports Illustrated commented that ''it sounded as if half of America lived next door to Simpson.''

Not all athletes have a choice about whether to act as a role model or not. Some, by virtue of their gender, race, or ethnicity, have no choice but to perform to higher expectations. Early on, female athletes—like Babe Didrikson, the winner of three track and field medals at the 1932 Los Angeles Olympics—found that their exploits were not viewed with the same legitimacy reserved for their male counterparts. ''America has lionized the male athlete to the female athlete's disadvantage,'' write Lipsyte and Levine; ''there is a definite misogynist streak in the sensibility of the big-time locker room and its boys-will-be-boys rationale.'' By the 1990s, women were still fighting against media images that trivialized female athletic accomplishments. This despite the fact that, in 1991, women outspent men

in the purchase of athletic shoes and apparel, and more women participated in sports and fitness than did men. In 1994, athletic shoemaker Nike used an ad depicting a female volleyball player lying on satin sheets in her underwear. CBS Sports, in 1996, suspended a golf commentator for characterizing professional female golfers as lesbians and opined that women with ''big boobs'' were less able to play the sport. In the absence of serious, authentic portrayals of female athletes, the focus for young girls upon female athletes is more than just upon skill; the female sports hero is also a model who counteracts a broad social stereotype.

Sports heroes have often been used as an avenue for disenfranchised groups to participate in an American life that was otherwise closed to them—politically, economically, or socially. It is hard for late twentieth-century Americans, who take the achievements of African-American athletes for granted, to appreciate Boxer Joe Louis's significance. As Lipsyte and Levine reconstruct it: ''Louis was out there representing all black people in those bitter days when most colleges admitted few if any blacks, when college-educated blacks were lucky to get jobs as railroad waiters, when even the Army was segregated.'' Ethnic athletic heroes bear the similar weight of carrying the hopes of millions. Unlike their parents, second-generation ethnics had the time to devote to leisure and recreation, and sports heroes began serving as important role models.

The best example of a single athlete representing the aspirations of an entire people was Jackie Robinson, the first African-American major league baseball player. On the field, and off, Robinson was subject to racial slurs, hate mail, and death threats; once in Philadelphia, Robinson's Brooklyn Dodger teammates were refused admittance into a hotel because of his presence on the team. Robinson was an integral symbol of the African-American struggle against discrimination in the pre-civil rights era. Robinson's enormous burden is palpable in this 1947 passage by sportswriter Jimmy Cannon, as quoted by Sports Illustrated in 1997:

> In the clubhouse Robinson is a stranger. The Dodgers are polite and courteous with him, but it is obvious he is isolated by those with whom he plays. . . Robinson never is part of the jovial and aimless banter of the locker room. He is the loneliest man I have ever seen in sports.

Sports heroes often say as much about the larger social milieu as they do about themselves: ''Independent of their own intentions and beliefs—sometimes even counter to those intentions and beliefs—idols can be coopted to represent both the dominant culture and the concerns and interests of outsiders,'' write Lypsite and Levine. Every so often, though, a dominant figure emerges in sport to renew the fan's emotional involvement with sports that, according to historian Benjamin Rader, ''encourages a kind of primitive solidarity among the population despite our diverse backgrounds. Our society has many forces that pull it apart . . . (Sports) is a tie that binds.''

—Daryl Umberger

FURTHER READING:

Anderson, Michael. ''Like a Colossus.'' New York Times. April 7, 1996, sec. 7, 12.

''Batting Down a Hero.'' St. Louis Business Journal. August 31, 1998, 58.

''Demi-God.'' Esquire. October 1969, 103-13.

Dyreson, Mark. "The Emergence of Consumer Culture and the Transformation of Physical Culture: American Sport in the 1920s." In *Sport in America: From Wicked Amusement to National Obsession,* edited by David K. Wiggins. Champaign, Illinois, Human Kinetics, 1995.

Fimrite, Ron. "A Sad Tale of Self-Loathing: Mickey Mantle Was Striving to Exorcise His Personal Demons When Death Intervened." *Sports Illustrated.* November 11, 1996, 10.

Gelman, David, and Sudarsan Raghavan. "I'm Not a Role Model." *Newsweek.* June 28, 1993, 56-57.

Izod, John. "Television Sport and the Sacrificial Hero." *Journal of Sport and Social Issues.* May 1996, 173-93.

Klapp, Orrin E. "Hero Worship in America." *American Sociological Review.* February 1949, 53-62.

Lipsyte, Robert, and Peter Levine. *Idols of the Game: A Sporting History of the American Century.* Atlanta, Turner Publishing, 1995.

Lopiano, Donna. "Women Athletes Deserve Respect from the Media." *USA Today Magazine.* March 1996, 74-76.

Nack, William. "The Breakthrough." *Sports Illustrated.* May 5, 1997, 56-65.

Rader, Benjamin. "The Home Run Mystique Involves the Power of One Dramatic Blast to Pull a People Together." *Christian Science Monitor.* October 1, 1998, 11.

"Role Models: What Kids and Athletes Say." *Sports Illustrated for Kids.* September 1995, 26-27.

Verducci, Tom. "The Hero Trap." *Sports Illustrated.* July 11, 1994, 88.

William, Peter. *Sports Immortals: Deifying the American Athlete.* Bowling Green, Ohio, Bowling Green State University Popular Press, 1994.

Sports Illustrated

Using a blend of groundbreaking photography and revolutionary writing, *Sports Illustrated* changed the way spectator sports fit into American culture during the 1960s and 1970s. As the first weekly magazine devoted solely to sports, *Sports Illustrated* was a media leader that contributed, along with television, to sports moving from a pleasant diversion into big business, spewing out multi-million-dollar player salaries. The magazine's influence also cast beyond sports, as its annual mid-winter swimsuit issue became a popular phenomenon and created lasting changes in the modeling industry. "*Sports Illustrated* served as a counterbalance to the persistent hype of television, offering a way for new and educated fans to put the endless rounds of games and matches into a meaningful context," Michael MacCambridge observed in his book *The Franchise.* "It made an art out of in-depth reporting on those games, and thereby made the games themselves more important to more Americans."

Henry Luce, founder of Time Inc., the publisher of *Time* and *Life,* conceived the idea for *Sports Illustrated.* Though not much of a sports fan, Luce saw the potential for a weekly sports magazine based on the increased leisure time of the burgeoning post-war middle class, a large percentage of whom were migrating to the suburbs. Against the advice of his aides, who thought the idea folly, Luce launched

Sports Illustrated on August 16, 1954. Initially, the magazine covered an eclectic assortment of sports—big game hunting, yachting, horse racing, dog shows, and fishing, along with cooking, fashion, and travel—in addition to more traditional sports such as baseball, football, and boxing.

The magazine was positioned as a "class" magazine, much like the *New Yorker,* with sophisticated, intelligent, critical writing with no pandering. But it attracted neither readers nor advertisers in large numbers early on. The magazine began to fulfill its promise with the installation of Andre Laguerre as managing editor in 1960. Laguerre, a cosmopolitan and urbane native of France, had a keen appreciation for good writing. He focused the magazine on the four major team sports (baseball, football, basketball, and hockey) plus boxing, golf, and tennis. Fishing, which had ranked fourth among all sports in articles per year in the magazine's third year, ranked number 13 by 1963.

Laguerre hired two writers who would forever change the face of sports journalism: Dan Jenkins and Frank Deford. These two writers gave readers insight and analysis unavailable elsewhere and helped *SI,* as the magazine was often called, to create a new approach to sportswriting. MacCambridge described the *SI* style as "not just reporting or covering an event, but distilling it, capturing its essence and presenting it in a compressed, lyrical image of deadline literature and photojournalism."

SI became a part of the weekly routine as much as the daily sports page. Millions watched the games on the weekend, then waited for *SI* to arrive in their mailboxes on Thursday or Friday to tell them what had really happened behind the scenes. To many sports fans, *SI* was "the final word" and "an event wasn't real until ratified in the pages of *SI.*" From its initial 350,000 subscriber base in 1954, circulation grew to 1 million readers in 1960, 2 million in the mid-1970s, 3 million in the mid-1980s, and topped out at nearly 3.5 million in the late 1980s.

As James Michener explained in his book *Sports in America,* "*Sports Illustrated* has become the bible of the industry, and it has done so because it appreciated from the start the facts that faced printed journalism in the age of television: don't give the scores, give the inside stories behind the scenes. And deal openly with those topics which men in saloons talk about in whispers." Besides the ongoing sports seasons, the magazine also took on hard subjects as exemplified by Jack Olsen's 1968 series on the exploitation of the black athlete, "The Black Athlete - A Shameful Story." In the late 1960s, *SI* also published series about the growing threat of drugs in sports, women's rights in athletics, and the electronic revolution in sports.

In addition to great writers, Laguerre also hired two photographers named Neil Leifer and Walter Iooss, who would transform the nature and art of sports photography. Leifer and Iooss shot many of the *SI* cover photos in the 1960s. As *SI* continually pushed the technological limits in color photography printing, Leifer and Iooss captured on film the very essence of a weekend sports event and had it appear within a few days in *SI.* Laguerre thus merged the best color with the latest analysis to expand the *SI* influence. In 1965, Leifer also shot what is considered one of the most famous sports photos of all-time, Muhammad Ali standing over a prostrate Sonny Liston with Ali's fist angrily imploring Liston off the canvas, with three faces—mouths agape—seen between Ali's legs. The image, oddly, was not chosen for the cover shot that week.

An athlete's appearance on the cover of *Sports Illustrated* became a cultural icon, proof of an athlete's legitimacy. People framed *SI* covers for keepsakes, beginning with the cover of its first issue in 1954, Milwaukee Braves' third baseman Eddie Mathews. The top cover subject in the magazine's first 40 years was Ali, who appeared on 32 covers, followed closely by Michael Jordan with 30. Being on the *SI* cover also became identified as a jinx, a double-edged sword of being on top of the sports world but at risk for malfunctioning in the big game. The first incident occurred shortly after the release of the January 31, 1955 issue, with skier Jill Kinmont on the cover, when Kinmont fell in a ski meet that left her paralyzed below the neck.

Laguerre also pioneered the swimsuit issue in 1964. The original concept was as a "sunshine issue" in the bleak winter days of late January. It was designed to bridge the gap between the New Year's Day college bowl games to the start of baseball spring training in early March, in the years when basketball, either pro or college, had little national following. What might have been just a single issue article blossomed into an annual event, with the commotion about the issue. It brightened some people's winter, but outraged others. The issue went "from moral outrage to hallowed tradition in only one generation," Deford wrote in his 1989 retrospective on the swimsuit issue, "How It All Began."

To take charge of the swimsuit issue, Laguerre tapped Jule Campbell. After fashion model Babette March graced the 1964 initial cover, Campbell used unknown women with "natural" or "healthy" looks instead of the gaunt high fashion look. As the issue gained popularity, Campbell blended known faces with her "healthy" look. She even used the models' names in photo captions, providing a degree of identity that fashion magazines did not at the time. This helped to accelerate the career of Cheryl Tiegs, who appeared on the cover of the 1970 swimsuit issue, and some say, helped to usher in the supermodel era. Other famous models that appeared early in their careers on the cover of the swimsuit issue were Christie Brinkley (1979), Elle MacPherson (1986), and Kathy Ireland (1989).

As the issue's swimsuits became skimpier, the battlefield changed from moral corruption of youth to sexism. "Women should stop screaming about that one issue and start screaming that *SI* doesn't carry enough women's sports. That's sexism," tennis star Billie Jean King said. The debate came to a head with the 1978 issue, when Iooss photographed Tiegs wearing a fishnet swimsuit. When dry, the suit was sensual but not revealing in the upper body area. Tiegs, however, had dipped into the water and the wetness created an exceptionally provocative pose, leaving nothing to the viewer's imagination. The picture caused a furor, eliciting more letters and canceled subscriptions in the history of the swimsuit issue. But it was a defining moment for both the swimsuit issue and the supermodel industry. "If there was any doubt before that modeling was, like everything else, about to lose its virginity (or illusion of virginity) in the 70s, the January 1978 *Sports Illustrated* swimsuit issue put an end to it," Stephen Fried wrote in *Thing of Beauty.* "The uproar caused by one picture of Cheryl Tiegs reinforced the new truth that the way straight men perceived fashion models would determine the future of the business." "It's a sweet little picture, that's it," Tiegs told Michael Gross, author of *Model: The Ugly Business of Beautiful Women.* Gross went on to write, "But in fact, it was a major coup, adding the powerful appeal of the pinup picture to modeling's arsenal of promotional gimmicks."

As the swimsuit issue gained popularity, *SI* stepped up its marketing of the issue in the mid-1980s by introducing the swimsuit calendar and touting the models on the talk show circuit before the issue hit the newsstand. The 1986 issue with MacPherson on the cover sold 1.2 million copies at the newsstand, up from just 300,000 in 1983. The 25th anniversary issue in 1989 sold 2.7 million single

copies. Newsstand sales by 1996 had slumped back to 1986 levels, a reflection of the changing dynamics in sports journalism.

The creation of ESPN and other round-the-clock media in the 1980s made the magazine's original mission less compelling. Its influence began to wane as sports fans no longer depended on the magazine to explain what had happened a few days before, as a plethora of television highlight shows and the Internet had already done so. In the 1989 merger of Time with Warner, *SI* moved away from writing and began to pursue a strategy to "extend the brand." Videos and calendars were hawked in crass television advertisements, as were magazine subscriptions (example: this awesome [item] is free with your one-year subscription to *Sports Illustrated,* which includes the swimsuit issue!). A spin-off magazine was also introduced, *Sports Illustrated for Kids.*

In the 1990s, *Sports Illustrated* was as well known, if perhaps not more so, for its swimsuit issue, free videos, and clothing line as it was for the writing and photography that had made it famous in the first place. And thousands of loyal readers still treasured its arrival every week.

—Charlie Bevis

FURTHER READING:

Deford, Frank. "How It All Began." *Sports Illustrated.* Special Issue. February 1989, 38-46.

Fried, Stephen. *Thing of Beauty: The Tragedy of Supermodel Gina Carangi.* New York, Pocket Books, 1993.

Gross, Michael. *Model: The Ugly Business of Beautiful Women.* New York, W. Morrow, 1995.

MacCambridge, Michael. *The Franchise: A History of "Sports Illustrated" Magazine.* New York, Hyperion, 1997.

Michener, James A. *Sports in America.* New York, Random House, 1976.

Spring Break

Each year, as the cold and gray of winter gives way to the bright new green of spring, human beings also experience an influx of energy: hopeful, youthful, and, at least partly, sexual. Psychologists explain this phenomenon with a variety of theories, but all agree that "spring fever" is normal and fairly universal. For the past six decades, American college students have celebrated this vernal "rising of the sap" with a unique ritual called "spring break," which involves travel to a sunny beachside resort to participate in drunken revelry and sexual debauchery. Though people of all ages, races, and classes may feel the urge to head somewhere sunny and warm as spring approaches, it is the fairly well-off, mostly white full-time students at four year colleges and universities that have created the famous phenomenon of spring break, celebrated in movies, television, and police blotters.

Traditionally, college spring vacations are scheduled sometime between the first Saturday in March and Easter Sunday in April. Students converge on the most fashionable spot they can afford to go to, often cramming 15 to 20 people in a motel room to limit expenses. Local bars cater to partying students, offering drink specials and rowdy entertainment such as Belly Flop, Hot Bod, and Wet T-shirt contests, designed to appeal to the young and inebriated. Vacationers

Young adults doing "The Twist" during a typical spring break.

sport T-shirts with such spirited slogans as, "I'm too drunk to fuck," "Party Naked," and "University of Heineken." Crowds of tourists become a nightmare for local police, snarling traffic, littering and vandalizing the streets of resort towns. Many spring breaks have turned literally riotous, resulting in destruction of property and arrests. Cleaning up after spring break becomes a major expense for cities that draw large numbers of students, though the money the students pour into a community during those first weeks of spring tends to offset the disadvantages.

In 1936, the swim coach at Colgate University in Hamilton, New York, unwittingly began a tradition when he brought a few members of his swim team to train at the Casino Pool by the beach in Fort Lauderdale, Florida. The experiment was so successful that the entire team returned for Christmas vacation. In 1938, Fort Lauderdale continued to attract students as the Casino Pool hosted the first College Coaches' Swim Forum, and the famous Elbo Room opened in the Seabreeze Hotel. By 1946, in spite of wartime travel restrictions, Fort Lauderdale had become a regular destination for college students on spring vacation. Fifteen thousand student revelers came in 1953, and in 1954, 20,000 arrived and started another spring break tradition: trouble with the police. That year, eight students were arrested for disorderly conduct and two for public indecency. Two were killed in drunk-driving incidents.

Time magazine reported on the phenomenon in 1959, and in 1960 a new film solidified Fort Lauderdale as spring break capitol of the United States. *Where the Boys Are,* starring Connie Francis, Paula Prentiss, and Yvette Mimieux, was the film version of a 1958 novel by Glendon Swarthout. It describes the adventures of three young college women on spring vacation in Fort Lauderdale, seeking independence, fun, and romance. The film, with its clean-cut adventure and obligatory cautionary tale of the tragic end of the girl who went too far, became an icon of the spring break experience. Along with the "Beach Party" movies of Frankie Avalon and Annette Funicello, *Where the Boys Are* advertised a beach vacation culture

that many students were eager to emulate. By 1961, 50,000 of them flocked to Fort Lauderdale to find it.

In 1963, *Palm Springs Weekend,* starring Connie Stevens and Troy Donahue, advertised Palm Springs, California, as another mecca for students and by the late 1960s Florida's Daytona Beach was actively promoting itself as a spring break destination, trying to lure students and their dollars away from Fort Lauderdale. One hundred thousand students responded and converged on Daytona Beach.

The self-indulgent 1980s were peak years for the hedonistic spring revels. In 1983, the film *Spring Break* was released, with Tom Cruise and Shelly Long, and *Where the Boys Are* was remade in 1984. In 1985, spring break in Fort Lauderdale reached its height as 350,000 students crammed into the city. Fort Lauderdale had had enough. By erecting barricades between the beach and the streets and enforcing room occupancy rules and alcohol laws, the city managed to reduce its spring break tourism numbers back to 20,000 by 1989. Of those, 2,400 were arrested. Fort Lauderdale, while still a popular destination on a much smaller scale, relinquished its title of "spring break capitol" to Daytona Beach. By the mid-1990s, Daytona too was trying to find ways to manage the rowdy crowds without alienating the tourist dollars.

By the end of the 1990s, spring break vacation spots were much more varied, though there were still "hot spots" that attract hundreds of thousands of visitors. Panama City, Florida, hosted 550,000 student tourists in 1997, and little South Padre Island, Texas, which has a resident population of just over 1,000, welcomed 130,000 visitors in the spring of 1997. California also welcomed its share of visitors, especially in San Diego and Palm Springs. Ski vacations have become more and more popular and destinations like Colorado's Vail and Steamboat Springs and California's Lake Tahoe are flooded with students looking for both ski and apres-ski adventures. Foreign travel has an appeal as well, not the least of which is a drinking age of 18 in Mexico, the Bahamas, and Canada. Even in the United States, many resort towns resisted enforcing laws like the drinking age that might drive tourists away.

Many businesses not specifically related to the tourist trade also take advantage of the huge audiences drawn to spring break meccas. Daytona Beach hosts ExpoAmerica, a giant trade show with high-tech exhibits designed to appeal to modern students. Both CBS and MTV offer extensive spring break special telecasts from spots like Daytona and San Diego, to bring the festivities to those who had to stay at home. Some businesses even try to recruit employees among the crowds of student vacationers, though some report difficulties finding sober prospects.

Each generation has added its own personality to the celebration of spring break. Crazy Gregg, manager of venerable Fort Lauderdale institution the Button, explained in 1986, "Basically, we've had three different generations here. In the '50s, the kids were more mellow and conservative, not blatant. In the late '60s and early '70s, they weren't gung ho or rah-rah. They didn't seem to want to have fun. When we played 'God Bless America,' they booed us. But now the pendulum has swung completely around. They enjoy themselves to the hilt. The morality is looser. Golly, I saw a guy walk through the hotel stark naked. They wouldn't have done that 15 or 20 years ago." The 1990s has brought its own influences to the spring break phenomenon. A sharpened awareness of the problems of alcoholism has resulted in a marked decrease in the glorification of drink at resort destinations. While there is still a high level of consumption, liquor and beer company advertisements are more likely to advise caution and adherence to drinking age laws, where a decade earlier they might have focused only on the fun and excitement of drinking. Also evidence of a more serious generation is the "Breakaway" program at Vanderbilt University in Nashville, Tennessee. Started in 1991, Breakaway is a national network that arranges what it terms "alternative spring break" for students who would rather volunteer in soup kitchen, homeless shelters, and other community programs than spend a week getting drunk and having casual sex. In its first year, the Breakaway network served 2,500 students in 40 colleges nationwide. By the late 1990s, it arranged volunteer work for close to 15,000 students in 350 colleges.

Spring break came of age in the 1950s and 1960s when students needed a hedonistic outlet from a repressive society. Perhaps in the pleasure-seeking culture of the 1990s, what young people really seek is an escape from self-indulgence.

—Tina Gianoulis

FURTHER READING:

Flanagan, William P., and Diane Merelman. "Spring Break Alert." *Forbes*. Vol. 159, No. 4, February 24, 1997, 188l.

Kalogerakis, George. "How to Win Friends . . . And Throw Up on People." *Esquire*. Vol. 117, No. 4, April, 1992, 82.

Waldrop, Judith. "Spring Break." *American Demographics*. Vol. 15, No. 3, March, 1993, 52.

Springer, Jerry (1944—)

Jerry Springer has taken the talk show genre to a new level, and placed himself at the helm of a growing public controversy. Banned by placard-carrying ministers who protest outside its Chicago studios, *The Jerry Springer Show* combines drama and sensationalism that borders on the hilarious. Since its debut in 1991, the show's outrageous style and often perverse topics have either strongly enticed or offended individuals. The show not only allows but encourages brawls between its guests, egged on by Springer's audience of adoring fans, who repeatedly chant, "Jerry, Jerry, Jerry!" Guests are permitted to vent antagonistic emotions that often result in physical fights, quelled at the last minute by clean-cut, beefy bouncers. In addition to his public defense of his show, Springer has also been in the news as the subject of an alleged sex scandal with a porn star and her stepmother (the romping was supposedly caught on tape), both of whom were guests on his show. Springer has also starred in the 1998 film *Ringmaster* (also the title of his autobiography).

Before becoming a talk show host, Springer, who has a law degree from Northwestern University, had a brief political career as the mayor of Cincinnati in the 1970s and worked as a news anchorman and commentator in Cincinnati in the 1980s, during which time he won seven Emmys. But when a Chicago station in the 1990s hired him, an anchorwoman promptly resigned in disgust, calling him "the poster child for the worst television has to offer."

Talk shows have served different purposes. They can act as an informal, supportive forum for topics and guests varying in controversy. But with a growing interest people have in hearing titillating, personal, and sometimes shocking details concerning others' lives, formats have swiftly veered towards the sensational. The trend was first started on the *Rikki Lake Show* (1993), when producers began encouraging confrontations among guests. A success, it spawned

Jerry Springer

imitators, as well as a growing group of those opposed to what has been labeled "trash TV." *The Jerry Springer Show* took the sensationalism one step further and became the first talk show to include physical confrontation on a regular basis. The show's swift rise in ratings and the popularity of its host have confirmed for many that people find the show entertaining. Critics say people watch the show for the same reasons they would drive slowly by a traffic accident. Because *The Jerry Springer Show* tends to deal with such outrageous and often hopeless problems, some contend that people viewing it tend to feel better about their own lives.

Guests on the show are often marginalized people who solve their problems through physical conflict. The regularity of the fights on the show have prompted speculation into whether the fights are staged with out-of-work actors. If the fights are genuine, one can imagine the pre-show akin to a cockfight, in which guests are purposely baited against each other. Because of the nature of the show's topics and the often consistent personality traits of its guests, it has come to be known as a humorous "white trash" sensation. Springer says that he encourages guests to be as outrageous as possible, but defends his show against charges of exploitation, stating that his critics are "elitists" who only want to see beautiful or rich people discussing their problems on television. But poverty should not be an excuse for extreme, inappropriate behavior, like mothers sleeping with their 13-year-old daughter's ex-boyfriends (a past show topic). Other topics include a family of strippers, and possibly the most perverse in all of talk show history—bestiality.

Not every topic on the show has shock value, however, the appearance of brawling guests has been consistent. Springer has featured interracial couples facing disapproval from their families, for example. And, at the end of every show, Jerry offers a brief but eloquent epitaph, his ''Final Thought,'' that functions as the show's ''moral'' thermometer. After an episode on cheating lovers, for example, he counseled viewers that it is unhealthy to pursue someone who does not want you, and to work on raising their self-esteem. Delivered with an authentic smile, he manages to convey that although he will quietly observe the antics onstage, he may really want people to be happy.

Jerry Springer is most certainly an enigma, and a man of contradictions. As the ''ringmaster'' of his exhibitionist show, he maintains a relatively private life. He often takes pride in his work, stating that it gives a platform to people media ''snobs'' would rather ignore, but he is often surprised at his own success, dismissing his program as a ''circus'' and saying, ''I don't have any talent.'' He has been an active voice and fundraiser for various charities. He also has country music aspirations. ''It struck me that the subjects of country songs and talk shows are very similar,'' he said. Springer now has a music CD out, and will tour as his schedule permits. He has even impersonated Elvis.

—Sharon Yablon

FURTHER READING:

Collins, James. ''Talking Trash.'' *Time*. 30 March 1998, 62-66.

Gamson, Joshua. *Freaks Talk Back: Tabloid Talk Shows and Sexual Nonconformity*. Chicago, University of Chicago Press, 1998.

Scott, Gini Graham. *Can We Talk? The Power and Influence of Talk Shows*. New York, Insight Books, 1996.

Seitz, Matt Zoller. ''Springer's Circus Comes to Town.'' http://www.nj.com/entertainment/stories/1124ringmaster.html. January 1999.

Springer, Jerry, and Laura Morton. *Ringmaster!* New York, St. Martin's Press, 1998.

Springsteen, Bruce (1949—)

Bruce Springsteen has placed himself in a lineage of folk and popular musicians, including Woody Guthrie and Bob Dylan, who have sought to effect social change. An acclaimed songwriter and energetic performer, Springsteen spent his early years singing in New Jersey bars, garnered a sizable commercial audience by 1975, and achieved superstar status with the release of *Born in the USA* (1984). His tremendous popularity, combined with his own ambition for success, opened his music to interpretations that seemed to conflict with his populist lyrics. Anxious to ride the bandwagon of his success, politicians and pundits appropriated his image to support their own perspectives. In much of the work that followed *Born in the USA*, however, Springsteen made a self-conscious effort to elucidate a liberal cultural politics.

Born in Freehold, New Jersey, Springsteen grew up in an austere working-class household. Uninterested in school, he was fascinated by Elvis Presley's 1957 performance on the *Ed Sullivan Show* and began to imagine that rock and roll might provide a ticket out of his socioeconomic situation. After leading several bands in the late 1960s, Springsteen was performing acoustic shows in Greenwich Village when he auditioned for the legendary Columbia Records

Bruce Springsteen

talent scout, John Hammond, in 1972. ''The kid absolutely knocked me out,'' recalled Hammond, who billed the guitarist as the successor to another of his ''discoveries,'' Bob Dylan.

Springsteen's first two albums, *Greetings from Asbury Park, N.J.* (1973) and *The Wild, the Innocent, and the E Street Shuffle* (1973), chronicled the culture of the New York streets and Jersey boardwalks in a familiar Dylanesque style. Despite lackluster sales figures, Springsteen enjoyed a warm critical reception and began to establish a loyal following along the eastern seaboard. Backed by the E Street Band, he was renowned for electrifying performances that often exceeded three hours. His tremendous energy caught the eye of former *Rolling Stone* critic Jon Landau, whose enthusiastic review of a 1974 concert transformed Springsteen's career. ''I saw the rock and roll future,'' wrote Landau in *The Real Paper*, ''and its name is Bruce Springsteen.'' Columbia enlisted this hyperbole to launch a marketing blitz for *Born to Run* (1975), which landed Springsteen on the covers of the October 27, 1975 issues of *Time* and *Newsweek*. The album was both a critical and commercial triumph, attaining platinum status within four months.

Springsteen's career stalled, however, when he became entangled in a legal battle with manager Mike Appel. In 1976, Springsteen and Appel filed countersuits involving copyrights and royalty payments. Appel won a court injunction that prohibited Springsteen from recording a new album with Landau, who became the musician's manager when the dispute ended a year later.

The hiatus was intellectually productive for Springsteen. At Landau's urging, he read the works of Flannery O'Connor and John Steinbeck, and watched the films of John Ford and Sergio Leone. Inspired in part by Steinbeck's *Grapes of Wrath* (1939) and Ford's 1940 adaptation of it, *Darkness on the Edge of Town* (1978) marked a turning point in his career. While *Born to Run* expressed a longing to escape the rigors of working-class life, *Darkness* explored the human costs of social and economic injustices.

This change in perspective compelled Springsteen to develop a political consciousness. Following the 1979 Three Mile Island crisis, he headlined several shows for Musicians United for Safe Energy, an anti-nuclear power consortium that included Bonnie Raitt and Jackson Browne. Two years later, he staged a benefit for the Vietnam Veterans' Association, asking the audience to help heal the physical and psychological wounds inflicted on the soldiers who fought the nation's most unpopular war.

Meanwhile, Springsteen's double album, *The River* (1980), soared to number one on the *Billboard* chart and produced "Hungry Heart," his first top ten hit. *The River* treated familiar topics of cars and girls, but also revealed Springsteen's burgeoning interest in both traditional music and social issues. In the late 1970s, he had begun to listen to classic country recordings as well as the Folkways Records *Anthology of American Folk Music* (1952). Based on Hank Williams's "Long Gone Lonesome Blues," the album's title track was a particularly moving ballad about two teenagers who have a child, marry, and watch their dreams evaporate in the face of economic uncertainty. Springsteen later identified this song as a breakthrough in his writing.

In November 1980, Springsteen acquired a copy of Joe Klein's *Woody Guthrie: A Life* (1980). Impressed with Guthrie's artistry and political commitments, he began to cover the folksinger's "This Land Is Your Land" (1940) in his concerts. Guthrie's influence was palpable on *Nebraska* (1982), a largely acoustic and remarkably uncommercial album that Springsteen recorded in his home. Sparse guitars, wailing harmonicas, and somber vocals guided listeners through a desolate, deprived landscape where individuals committed acts of desperation, ranging from petty crimes to mass murders. Greil Marcus described *Nebraska* as "the most convincing statement of resistance and refusal that Ronald Reagan's U.S.A. has yet elicited"; *Rolling Stone,* one of Springsteen's staunchest supporters, called it his "bravest" album, a work that solidified his reputation as a performer who cared more about artistic integrity than commercial success.

The validity of such observations was complicated when Springsteen attained unimagined fame and fortune in 1984. *Born in the USA* sold 20 million copies, generated seven top ten singles, fueled a world-wide stadium tour (1984-1985), and, with the aid of music video, introduced Springsteen to a younger generation. This success, which Springsteen actively cultivated and obviously enjoyed, clouded his politics. Unlike most of the album's songs, which eschewed the bleak realities of *Nebraska*, "Born in the USA" told the story of an unemployed Vietnam veteran who lost his brother in the war. The lyrics clearly questioned the morality of war as well as the country's treatment of its veterans, yet much of Springsteen's audience misconstrued his intentions. The ringing melody and the exuberant chorus of "Born in the USA" led listeners to interpret it as a

jingoistic celebration of American militarism. Moreover, the working-class woes that Springsteen expressed were lost in the celebration of his own success story.

Politicians scrambled to claim Springsteen as their own. Syndicated columnist George Will lauded him for both his optimism and the work ethic he demonstrated in his four-hour shows. Will's enthusiasm convinced Reagan to invoke the musician during a campaign stop in New Jersey. "America's future rests in the message of hope in songs of a man so many young Americans admire: New Jersey's own Bruce Springsteen," remarked the president. "And helping you make those dreams come true is what this job of mine is all about." Springsteen's anti-war song conflicted with Reagan's aggressive military policies, but the president's appropriation confused the musician's intentions. The song was further obscured by Sylvester Stallone's *Rambo: First Blood Part 2* (1985), a film that sought to redeem America's performance in Vietnam. Soon after its release, major newspapers dubbed Springsteen, whose muscle-bound body resembled Stallone's, "The Rambo of Rock."

Springsteen was not an innocent bystander in this process. The Los Angeles Summer Olympic Games and the presidential election made 1984 a year for stars and stripes, a fact he exploited by placing the flag on the album cover and using it as a backdrop to his concert stage. Moreover, as his detested sobriquet "The Boss" suggested, he projected a commanding masculine presence that made it difficult to separate him from the hard-nosed aggression and conservatism that both Reagan and Rambo represented. But if Springsteen capitalized on the resurgence in American patriotism, he made an effort to clarify his politics. At a Pittsburgh concert, he dedicated "Johnny 99," a song about an unemployed autoworker, to the president. Three days after Reagan's remarks, he initiated a $2 million personal charity campaign by donating $10,000 to a union-sponsored food bank.

In 1986, Springsteen documented his concert legend with the release *Live/ 1975-1985*, a 40-song compendium that used long introductory speeches to "The River" and a rendition of Edwin Starr's "War" to express his disapproval of American military policy. He continued to articulate liberal viewpoints following the release of *Tunnel of Love* (1987), a collection inspired by his failing marriage to actress Julianne Phillips. In 1988, he underscored his connection to Guthrie by recording ballads about homelessness for the tribute album, *A Vision Shared.* More importantly, he headlined Amnesty International's Human Rights Now! Tour, where he criticized the "economic apartheid" that existed in the United States.

After divorcing Phillips and breaking up the E Street Band in 1989, Springsteen entered a period of depression and took a sojourn from cultural politics. Like *Tunnel, Human Touch* and *Lucky Town* (1992) explored the dynamics of gender relationships, celebrating his subsequent marriage to former band member Patti Scialfa and the birth of their children. Disappointing sales prompted many critics to question Springsteen's viability in a changing market, but success returned when he reembraced social issues in "Streets of Philadelphia." Written for Jonathan Demme's motion picture about an AIDS (Acquired Immune Deficiency Syndrome) patient, the composition won an Academy Award in 1994. A year later, Springsteen earned his second Oscar nomination with "Dead Man Walkin."

Springsteen reconvened the E Street Band to record four new songs for *Greatest Hits* (1995), but promptly returned to solo work. *The Ghost of Tom Joad* (1995) reasserted his connection to Steinbeck,

Ford, and Guthrie: Joad was the protagonist of *Grapes of Wrath* and the subject of a lengthy Guthrie ballad. Following in the footsteps of its cultural predecessors, the folk-styled album explored the plight of the underclass and identified injustices endured by Mexican immigrants. To ensure that his political intentions were understood, Springsteen embarked on an acoustic tour during which he performed his most socially engaged songs and explained the meaning of and inspiration for his lyrics. He reiterated his politics on a 1996 edition of *60 Minutes,* where he criticized the policies of the Reagan-Bush years and urged his audience to promote values of human welfare rather than individualism.

In the late 1990s, Springsteen remains one of the most influential and politically engaged performers in popular music. His historical awareness has led him to become involved in the promotion of the Rock and Roll Hall of Fame, into which he was inducted in 1999.

—Bryan Garman

FURTHER READING:

Appel, Marc. *Down Thunder Road: The Making of Bruce Springsteen.* New York, Simon and Schuster, 1992.

Cullen, Jim. *Born in the U.S.A.: Bruce Springsteen and the American Tradition.* New York, Harper Collins, 1997.

Garman, Bryan. "The Ghost of History: Woody Guthrie, Bruce Springsteen, and the Hurt Song." *Popular Music and Society.* Vol. 20, No. 2, 1996, 69-120.

Marsh, Dave. *Glory Days: Bruce Springsteen in the 1980s.* New York, Pantheon, 1987.

Sprinkle, Annie (1955—)

American performance artist Annie Sprinkle (born Ellen Steinberg) made her mark as one of the pre-eminent practitioners of the art form in the 1980s with her one-woman show "Post-Porn Modernist." Described in a British broadsheet newspaper in 1999 as "porn-queen-turned-new-age-sex-goddess," Sprinkle's onstage antics invoked the wrath of conservatives, who used her work, along with that of certain others, as a weapon for the argument to cut funding to the National Endowment for the Arts. Although allying her work to the feminist cause, she has also offended mainstream feminists. Her controversial exhibition, which aimed to demystify the female body and encourage sex as a spiritual act, included simulating oral sex, performing masturbation, and inviting audience members to inspect her cervix. Sprinkle began her career as a prostitute in a massage parlor and went on to act in over 200 adult films and videos throughout the 1970s and 1980s, in addition to serving as the editor of a pornographic magazine and contributing to many others.

—Geri Speace

FURTHER READING:

June, Andrea, and V. Vale. *Angry Women.* San Francisco, RE/ SEARCH Publications, 1991.

Sprinkle, Annie. "Some of My Performances in Retrospect." *Art Journal.* December 22, 1997, 68.

Sputnik

A thin plume of orange rising into the Soviet sky on October 4, 1957, carried aloft humankind's first artificial satellite. A 22-inch, 184-pound, beeping sphere, Sputnik ("Fellow Traveler") marked the beginning of a new chapter in the Cold War, where national prestige would be measured by a race in space. An incredible technological achievement in which all of humanity should have taken pride, the flight of Sputnik 1 and its successors (launched through 1961), was transformed into propaganda by the intense political posturing of the Cold War. For the Soviets, a supposedly technically backward nation, Sputnik instilled national pride; for the United States, watching their own puny Vanguard rockets fizzle and blow up on the launch pad, it enhanced fears of the growing Red Menace. While the satellite fell from orbit in January 1958, the word Sputnik became embedded in the American lexicon—symbolizing a period in time in which the United States first realized space exploration would not be a wholly American enterprise.

The International Geophysical Year, a period of worldwide scientific study spanning from July 1957 to December 1958, prompted efforts toward the development of satellites. President Dwight

The Soviet satellite Sputnik I.

Eisenhower announced that the United States would orbit a scientific package—Project Vanguard—during the IGY with an anticipated launch date in March 1958. Unlike Soviet Premier Nikita Khrushchev, the administration failed to foresee the propaganda coup of placing the first manmade object into space. Sputnik captured headlines around the world. The Soviet News agency TASS boasted how the people of a Socialist society turned dreams into reality.

Noted atomic weapons pioneer Edward Teller professed, "America has lost a battle more important and greater than Pearl Harbor." Following the revelations of the Rosenberg trial, McCarthy hearings, the fall of mainland China to a Red Mao, conflict in Korea and the Revolt in Hungary, Sputnik only added to a sense of fear toward the Red Menace by Americans. Eisenhower sought to alleviate anxiety by reminding the nation that U.S. satellite efforts had not been conducted as a race with other nations. Not only was Vanguard on schedule, it would make serious contributions to science, while Sputnik did little more than transmit its location. Such reassurances did little to calm the citizenry as a blanket of paranoia and insecurity unfurled across the nation.

The role of the United States as the leader in science and technology was being directly challenged. Before Sputnik, there was a widespread belief by Americans that the Soviets were far behind the United States in such areas, relying on espionage rather than originality. Had such smugness bred mental stagnation among Americans? Senator Styles Bridges made this case declaring, "The time has clearly come to be less concerned with the depth on the new broadloom rug or the height of the tail fin of the car and to be more prepared to shed blood, sweat and tears if this country and the free world are to survive."

A second Sputnik launched in less than a month, on November 3, only served to increase the nation's anxiety. Sputnik II weighed an incredible 1,100 pounds and contained a living passenger, a dog named Laika. Clearly, any booster capable of such feats had to possess a massive thrust capacity. This brought to light fears the Soviets were on the verge of perfecting the first Intercontinental Ballistic Missile and with it nuclear warheads that could rain down upon the United States at any given moment.

Attempting to bolster national pride domestically and the United States image abroad, the White House ordered an acceleration of Vanguard's timetable by four months to attempt a December 1957 launch. With the nation's eyes transfixed on Cape Canaveral, the pencil-like Vanguard rose four feet, dropped, and burst into a pyrotechnic display of brilliant orange and white flames. The Soviet United Nations delegation promptly inquired if the United States desired to enlist rocketry aid under their nation's program of technical assistance to backward nations.

The United States did successfully launch the 31-pound Explorer 1 on January 31, 1958. In May, the Soviets launched Sputnik 3, which carried the first space laboratory and used solar energy to power its instruments and transmitters. Sputniks 5 through 10 (four of which carried dogs) were launched 1960-61; these were working models of the spacecraft that carried Yury Alekseyevich Gagarin, the first human passenger, into space in 1961.

Politically, the impact of Sputnik within the United States would be far-reaching. In Washington, critics charged that the president's policy of fiscal responsibility hindered the military's ability to develop ICBMs. Senate Majority Leader Lyndon Baines Johnson opened a subcommittee of the Senate Armed Services Committee to review the nation's missile and space programs. Eisenhower succumbed to such pressures, increasing defense dollars allocated for

missiles. To ensure the peaceful exploration of space, the president called for the creation of a civilian space agency. The National Aeronautics and Space Act of 1958 formally established the National Aeronautics and Space Administration. Through NASA the nation set forth to combat the Soviets in this new arena of the Cold War called the space race. Because some critics charged the U.S. educational system with not stressing the same fundamentals in science and mathematics as the Soviet system, the National Defense Education Act allocated nearly $1 billion to increase science, mathematics, and foreign languages in elementary, secondary, and collegiate education. American school children needed to be as versed in algebra formulas as they were in baseball batting averages if the United States hoped to surpass Sputnik.

While average Americans found themselves terrified by Sputnik, it became a phenomenon filtering into their everyday lives. Sputnik-watching became a popular evening event. Broadcast in a frequency range that amateur short-wave radio operators could receive, the beeps of Sputnik were as familiar to many families as the "Ballad of Davy Crockett." Toy stores found their shelves lined with Sputnik-inspired toys. David Glover wrote and published the song "Go! Sputnik Boogie." Bartenders concocted Sputnik cocktails—with vodka as a primary component, naturally.

—Dr. Lori C. Walters

FURTHER READING:

Clowse, Barbara Barksdale. *Brainpower for the Cold War: The Sputnik Crisis and National Defense Education Act of 1958.* Westport, Connecticut, Greenwood Press, 1981.

Divine, Robert A. *The Sputnik Challenge.* New York, Oxford University Press, 1993.

Harford, James. *Korolev.* New York, John Wiley and Sons, 1997.

Killian, James A. *Sputnik, Scientists and Eisenhower: A Memoir of the First Special Assistant to the President for Science and Technology.* Cambridge, Massachusetts, MIT Press, 1977.

McDougall, Walter A. *The Heavens and the Earth: A Political History of the Space Age.* New York, Basic Books, 1985.

St. Denis, Ruth (1879?-1968)

Early-twentieth-century American dancer and choreographer Ruth St. Denis is often considered to be the mother of modern dance. Born Ruth Dennis in Newark, New Jersey, she began her dance career as a teenager and took the stage name Ruth St. Denis. St. Denis traveled extensively, performing on the vaudeville circuit in the United States and using her visits abroad to learn about the dances of other countries. She was the first to present Eastern dance forms and themes to American audiences, developing a nationwide acceptance of Eastern art. She performed her first dance work, *Radha,* in New York in 1906 after studying Hindu art and philosophy. With her husband and dance partner, Ted Shawn, she created a dance school and popular performing company known as Denishawn in 1915 in Los Angeles, California. The two profoundly influenced modern dance through their company, the first organized center for dance experiment in the United States; they separated, both professionally and personally, in 1931. St. Denis will be remembered for her teachings and often religious choreographic works that helped to establish modern dance as a serious artistic genre for later generations. A dancer of considerable power and beauty, St. Denis was a great inspiration to her three most accomplished students: Martha Graham, Doris Humphrey, and Charles Weidman, who each became legendary modern dance figures in their own right. Called the ''First Lady of American Dance,'' St. Denis performed into the 1960s.

—Brian Granger

FURTHER READING:

Shelton, Suzanne. *Divine Dancer: A Biography of Ruth St. Denis.* Garden City, New York, Doubleday, 1981.

Sherman, Jane. *The Drama of Denishawn Dance.* Middletown, Connecticut, Wesleyan University Press, 1979.

St. Denis, Ruth. *Ruth St. Denis, An Unfinished Life: An Autobiography.* New York and London, Harper & Bros., 1939.

St. Elsewhere

Medical dramas like *Dr. Kildare, Medical Center, Chicago Hope,* and *ER* have long been one of the most popular television show formats. Of the many programs that presented the issues surrounding major medical institutions, none was more unique, ambitious, and unpredictable than *St. Elsewhere.* The series, which ran on NBC from 1982 to 1988, focused on the lives of the doctors, nurses, and patients at St. Eligius, an inner city Boston teaching hospital. Each episode offered a realistic look at the fallibility of doctors, the stresses of being hospitalized, and the ethical dilemmas inherent in the practice of medicine. Mixed in with the often tragic storylines were oblique in-jokes, subtle bawdy humor, and countless intertextual references to other works of popular culture. Although the series often struggled with mediocre ratings, its strong appeal to the demographically important baby-boomer and upscale urban professional audiences allowed the idiosyncratic show to remain on the air. After its surreal final episode, *St. Elsewhere* was widely hailed as one of television's most literate and original programs.

The term ''St. Elsewhere'' is derived from medical school jargon for a hospital that serves as a dumping ground for patients not wanted by more prestigious medical facilities. Unlike its namesake, however, the series had a distinguished pedigree. Joshua Brand and John Falsey, staff writers on the basketball series *The White Shadow,* were encouraged to create the series after hearing of a friend's experiences as an intern at the Cleveland Clinic. They assembled a core group of young producers and writers, including Bruce Paltrow, Mark Tinker, John Masius, and Tom Fontana, who crafted a program distinctly different than previous medical dramas featuring noble and perfect physicians. Their stories presented flawed doctors trying, and often failing, to provide the best medical care in less than ideal circumstances. The show's narrative center was held by three veteran physicians: Daniel Auschlander (Norman Lloyd), a liver specialist faced with liver cancer; Donald Westphall (Ed Flanders), a widowed chief of staff raising an autistic son; and Mark Craig (William Daniels), a brilliant and heartless heart surgeon. Many young residents, who confronted their own problems, surrounded them. That the

series was set in a large, decaying urban institution, featured a large and diverse cast, and continued plots over a number of episodes caused many to initially consider the series as little more than *''Hill Street Blues''* in a hospital.''

In 1986, executive producer Bruce Paltrow said of the series: ''The original concept was to try to do an ensemble medical drama in a real way, with a kind of spontaneity and snap—and comedy.'' The intense realism of the series was evident in its willingness to frankly address such issues as breast cancer, rape, infertility, impotence, and addiction. A 1983 episode contained one of network television's first dramatic presentations of the AIDS (Acquired Immune Deficiency Syndrome) crisis. To heighten the sense of reality, the writers routinely placed their main characters in life-threatening situations from which they did not always survive. Over the years main characters left the show through such means as committing suicide, being murdered, going to prison, and contracting fatal diseases. Howie Mandel, who played a resident, reflected that the characters were as vulnerable as real people when he said: ''I could get hit by a car and killed on my way to work and so could Fiscus (Mandel's character). You always felt they could've killed anybody off. It wasn't past what they would do on *St. Elsewhere.''*

The harshly realistic tone of the series was tempered by the writers' willingness to experiment with the show's form and their frequent use of black humor and pop culture references. The obnoxious patient Mrs. Hufnagel entered St. Eligius for an entire season only to die in a freak accident when her bed folded up on her. Another recurring patient, the amnesiac John Doe number six, became convinced he was ''Mary Richards'' from the *Mary Tyler Moore Show.* For that episode the writers included dozens of references to the classic series and other MTM productions. A highlight was a scene in a psych ward featuring actor Jack Riley as ''Mr. Carlin,'' his neurotic character from *The Bob Newhart Show.* Episodes that departed from the show's usual format included one doctor's journey to heaven where he met God and another structured like the play *Our Town.* Robert Thompson, director of the Center for the Study of Popular Television at Syracuse University, stated ''More than any other series in the history of American television, *St. Elsewhere* rewarded the attentive viewer.''

Careful viewers were aware of the writers' affinity for placing dirty, but subtle, jokes in many episodes. The most infamous was one of the first references to oral sex on network television. While dictating a novel Dr. Craig stated: ''She came in from the garden, cheeks flushed, arms filled with flowers. I sat playing the Wurlitzer. She said 'Where would you like these?' I smiled. 'Put the roses on the piano and the tulips on the organ.''' Such hidden gags were a bonus for active viewers. The series' final episode itself contained dozens of references to other programs throughout television history. In its final moments the writers offered devoted viewers a great surprise as it was revealed that the hospital was only a model within a snowglobe. The entire series had sprung from the imagination of Westphall's autistic son.

Few television programs can claim to be as thoroughly dramatic, humorous, and inventive as *St. Elsewhere.* The writers demonstrated respect for their audience's intelligence on a weekly basis and revealed that network television can provide a level of sophistication beyond mere mindless entertainment. Furthermore, the constant intertextual references demonstrated that television possesses a rich heritage that can be drawn from by capable artists. Although it may not have been high in the ratings, the series stands as a high point in television history that has rarely been matched by other series.

—Charles Coletta

FURTHER READING:

Bianculli, David. *The Dictionary of Teleliteracy.* New York, Continuum, 1996.

Okie, Susan. ''Too Close to Real?'' *The Plain Dealer.* February 17, 1986, C1.

Thompson, Robert. *Television's Second Golden Age.* Syracuse, Syracuse University Press, 1996.

Stadium Concerts

In the 1970s, stadiums became the main venue for staging concert performances of popular music. From country and rock music stars to more traditional singers like Frank Sinatra and Barbra Streisand, popular performers attracted audience sizes anywhere from 20,000 to 100,000 people at a time. Rock music—with its mass participation and the sheer volume that was necessary to reach so many people at once—was particularly suited to playing concerts at football stadiums and in sports arenas. Rock musicians looked to the stadium as a way to play in front of the most people, for the most money, as audiences broadened during the seventies. Rock's dominance on the concert circuit continued into the 1990s. Of the 20 top-grossing North American concert tours between 1985 and 1994, the average tour grossed $55 million and visited 42 cities; nearly all of them were rock artists.

Rock's first stadium concert was in 1965, when the Beatles performed in New York's Shea Stadium to 55,000 screaming fans. Newspaper reports treated the concert as a curious aberration. The *New York Times* referred to the screaming fans' ''immature lungs,'' which produced a ''magnificent and terrifying voice,'' and quoted a policewoman who called the fans ''psychos.'' The Shea Stadium concert, at which the Beatles earned more than $160,000 for 28 minutes' work, prefigured rock's commercial power. By 1967, outdoor rock festivals began attracting audiences on an even larger scale. The Monterey Pop Festival in 1967 drew more than 50,000 people, while the 1969 Woodstock festival attracted more than 400,000. The festivals accustomed rock fans to attend concerts in large numbers, but they were plagued by major problems. Festival promoters were

Queen guitarist Brian May (left) performing with Slash at the Freddie Mercury Tribute Concert at Wembley Stadium, 1992.

often corrupt or inept, and violence was a looming threat that was realized at Altamont. In ensuing years, concert promoters—by having to coordinate 40-city tours—had no other choice but to improve; violence, as always, remained a threat.

Rock's development toward big business can be partly tracked by the growing professionalism among rock acts. At the beginning of the seventies, rock acts like the Rolling Stones and Led Zeppelin would routinely arrive at concerts an hour or more late; in addition, the Stones would not do encores. Jefferson Airplane's Paul Kantner, in *Bill Graham Presents,* expressed the attitude toward performing in rock's pre-stadium era: "A show was not just a performance. . . . A show was a whole social something-or-other. Bonfire ceremony or something. After we played, we wanted to go out and hustle girls. Get drunk and party, come back and play another set, go out and party again, and pretty soon dawn was there. To break that up was business." The move toward the stadiums was inevitable, however, as rock artists commanded greater receipts. Madison Square Garden and places like it, "could not have had an artist play there unless the artist said they wanted to," said Graham, who added that, at the time, he thought stadiums "should just be for . . . Roller Derby and boxing."

In the 1970s, declared *Rolling Stone* magazine, "there was no unifying presence in rock . . . and no artist whose latest record had to be heard by every fan and musician. By the time the decade began, rock was entertainment; in fact, it was well on its way to being the entertainment industry." Soon, performers were accompanied by special effects, like pyrotechnics or laser light shows. Professionalism had become the norm, as the stadium concert gave birth to one of rock's biggest cliches: the audience ritual of requesting encores by holding lit cigarette lighters into the darkness of the arena. If the outdoor festivals were characterized by their free-form nature, then the stadium concert was defined by its ritualistic showmanship.

Holding the attention of 20,000 (or more) people at a time was a serious challenge to those performing, and the rock star was well-armed. Any given tour might include several buses, a couple of trailer rigs, and a road crew ("roadies") to set up and dissemble increasingly elaborate stages; stacks of speakers became impossibly high towers that could allow performers to reach 120 decibels. The amplifiers were as much an assault on the poor acoustics as they were upon the audiences.

The dark side to such mass gatherings, when part of the audience was drinking, drugging, or both, was security concerns. The "stage rush," where people in front rows pushed forward toward the stage, sometimes threatened performers. At other times, the concert frenzy could produce tragedy, like the December 1979 Who concert at Cincinnati's Riverfront Stadium. A stampede of 7,000 people, through two open banks of doors, resulted in the trampling deaths of 11 people. A later-abandoned practice known as "festival seating," in which concertgoers entered the stadium by dashing to secure the best seat possible, was held to blame.

By the late 1980s, rock and country artists used stadium concerts as a way to voice their social concerns. Stadium-sized benefits of the late 1980s included Farm Aid—relief for America's farmers—and the Conspiracy of Hope Tour for Amnesty International. The biggest benefit concerts were the simultaneous Live Aid shows in Philadelphia and London. On July 13, 1985, between one-and-a-half and two billion people worldwide watched the televised concert. In the process, the event raised more than $100 million for African famine relief. Tours for individual groups grew to comparable proportions. The top two touring acts of 1994, the Stones and Pink Floyd, grossed

$121 million and $103 million, respectively. Stadiums with a 20,000-seat capacity, which were considered to be the big prizes in the 1970s, had became second-tier venues when superstar groups were on the road.

—Daryl Umberger

FURTHER READING:

Coleman, Mark. "The Revival of Conscience." *Rolling Stone.* November 15, 1990, 69-73.

Coleman, Ray. *The Man Who Made the Beatles: An Intimate Biography of Brian Epstein.* New York, McGraw-Hill, 1989, 211-14.

Funk & Wagnalls Corporation. *The World Almanac and Book of Facts 1996.* Funk & Wagnalls Corporation, 1995.

Graham, Bill, and Robert Greenfield. *Bill Graham Presents: My Life inside Rock and Out.* New York, Doubleday, 1992.

Mayer, Allan J., and Jon Lowell. "Cincinnati Stampede." *Newsweek.* December 17, 1979, 52-53.

Microsoft Corporation. *Microsoft Bookshelf '97* (CD-ROM). Microsoft Corporation, 1996.

Neely, Kim. "Music Versus Muscle: Is Concert Security a Necessary Evil? And How Much Is Too Much?" *Rolling Stone.* April 15, 1993, 15-17.

Schumach, Murray. "Shrieks of 55,000 Accompany Beatles." *New York Times.* August 16, 1965, 1.

"70s." *Rolling Stone.* September 20, 1990, 51-55.

Stagecoach

The critically-acclaimed classic film, *Stagecoach* (1939), not only helped to revive the A-movie Western, which had been out of favor since the advent of the sound era, but it cemented director John Ford's reputation as one of America's greatest filmmakers. And, as if that weren't enough, *Stagecoach* was the movie that catapulted John Wayne into stardom. Based on Ernest Haycox's short story, "Stage to Lordsburg," *Stagecoach* follows eight travelers on a trip through Indian country and explores the tensions and relationships that emerge during times of crisis.

Despite its big-movie pretensions, *Stagecoach* shares many similarities with B-movie Westerns. Its main characters are standard clichés from any number of low-grade cowboy flicks: Ringo (John Wayne), the young outlaw bent on revenge; Dallas (Clare Trevor), the prostitute with a heart of gold; Boone (Thomas Mitchell), the drunken doctor; Gatewood (Benton Churchill), the pompous businessman; Hatfield (John Carradine), the chivalrous gambler; Lucy (Louise Platt), the snobbish rich lady; and Peacock (Donald Meek), the timid whiskey drummer, are hardly unique to this film. Nor is the plot particularly original, with chases and shootouts that are typical Western fare.

What makes the film special is its character development and, more importantly, the clear social vision it presented to movie audiences mired in the Great Depression. Primary to this vision was the idea of community. The coach itself, set adrift in the savage wilderness of Indian country, represents a microcosm of civilized society. The passengers in the stagecoach-society are clearly from

Claire Trevor and John Wayne in a scene from the film *Stagecoach*.

diverse backgrounds. In the course of the film, however, these outlaws, out-of-towners, and snobs work through their differences to form a cohesive unit (with one notable exception). The driving force behind their union is crisis. The premature birth of Lucy's baby forces Dr. Boone to sober up, brings Dallas and Lucy together, and draws sympathy from the others. Similarly, the climactic (if not slightly stereotypical) Indian-coach chase requires these disparate elements to join forces to repel the common foe. The message was clear for contemporary audiences, who themselves faced a different sort of crisis: The best way to persevere through hard times is to band together and fight. Ford was no utopian idealist, however. Once the danger had passed and the stage reached Lordsburg (an ironic name, considering the amount of gambling, prostitution, and gunplay that took place there), the group went their separate ways. Clearly, such a community could only exist in extraordinary times.

But Ford's community is not all-inclusive. Significantly, the banker Gatewood is left out, as if he had no role in society. Depression-era audiences, who largely blamed bankers for the decade's ills, found in Gatewood a figure richly deserving of their scorn. While others try to help Lucy after she gives birth, Gatewood impatiently demands that the coach continue its trip. He is notably absent in the chase scene, remaining invisible inside the moving coach while the others desperately fire at the marauding Indians from its windows.

Gatewood presents an alternative social vision, which is roundly rejected. The other passengers are noticeably bored when he demands that bankers be free from government inspection and proclaims that America needs a "businessman for president." Their disinterest is a swipe at the conservative Republican administrations of the 1920s and is an implicit nod of support for the more liberal Franklin Roosevelt and his New Deal. At the film's end, Gatewood is revealed as a thief and dragged off in handcuffs.

Ford extended his vision beyond this call for community and used *Stagecoach* to present a largely traditionalist idea of the perfect man and woman. *Stagecoach*'s heroic men are tough and rugged problem-solvers who are not afraid to use weapons to defend themselves and their civilization from outside threats. Fainthearted men like Peacock are lampooned and exposed as effeminate. "I've had five children," Peacock notes when Lucy is in labor. "I mean," he notes, "my dear wife has." Throughout the movie, Peacock, doing his best impression of a disapproving nurse, tries to dissuade the alcoholic Dr. Boone from imbibing. Women, conversely, are most sympathetic when acting as mothers. The cold and aloof Lucy becomes a much more likable character once she has her baby, and Ringo first expresses his feelings for Stella after he admires her as she holds Lucy's baby. These ideal types are as important to *Stagecoach*'s message as its presentation of a society in crisis; to weather times of trouble, a community needed to be made up of the right kind of people.

Stagecoach struck a chord with both critics and audiences. The *New York Times* hailed the film as "a noble horse opera," and declared the film "a beautiful sight to see." *Variety* called *Stagecoach* a "sweeping and powerful drama" and enthusiastically lauded its "photographic grandeur." The film packed movie houses and won Academy Awards for Best Supporting Actor (Thomas Mitchell) and Best Score.

Stagecoach was John Ford's first Western since 1926's *3 Bad Men,* and was his first "talkie" Western (he had made forty-three silent Westerns). He would go on to make many more, including *Fort Apache* (1948), *She Wore a Yellow Ribbon* (1949), and *The Man Who Shot Liberty Valance* (1962), all of which starred John Wayne. Many, however, still consider *Stagecoach* to be Ford's best.

—David B. Welky

FURTHER READING:

Bergman, Andrew. *We're in the Money: Depression America and Its Films.* New York, New York University Press, 1971.

Davis, Ronald L. *John Ford: Hollywood's Old Master.* Norman and London, University of Oklahoma Press, 1995.

Ford, Dan. *Pappy: The Life of John Ford.* Englewood Cliffs, New Jersey, Prentice-Hall, 1979.

Gallagher, Tag. *John Ford: The Man and His Films.* Berkeley, University of California Press, 1986.

Roberts, Randy, and James S. Olson. *John Wayne: American.* New York, The Free Press, 1995.

Stagg, Amos Alonzo (1862-1965)

Amos Alonzo Stagg, the charismatic "Grand Old Man" of college football, was one of the sport's immortal leaders and innovative strategists. Stagg coached on the college level for an astounding 57 seasons. He started out at Springfield College in Massachusetts and, in 1892, became head football coach and associate professor of physical culture at the University of Chicago, where he enjoyed his lengthiest coaching tenure of 40 years. After retiring from the Big Ten school in 1932, he went on to the College of the Pacific in Stockton, California, where he headed up the football program through 1946.

Stagg was born in West Orange, New Jersey, and attended Yale University, where he participated in several sports. In 1886, he pitched Yale to a victory over Harvard to win the college championship. He also played end on the football team, coached by Walter Camp and made the 1889 All-America squad. It was under Camp's peerless guidance that he became a student of the game. Stagg, who originally wished to become a minister, also developed the conviction that within football there existed the positive force with which to mold men's characters. This concept, which he adhered to with evangelical zeal, was to become one of the cornerstones of his football philosophy.

At the University of Chicago, Stagg became the nation's initial tenured football coach, as well as his era's most imaginative, enterprising, and dominant athletic mentor. His on-field innovations ranged from the "ends back" flying wedge formation to end-around plays and hidden-ball plays (in which he had his runners hide the pigskin under their jerseys). He instituted the modern T-formation and the flea-flicker pass and was the first coach to spotlight the forward pass in his team's offense. He also was fabled for devising forceful defenses. The one he employed against the powerful Harold "Red" Grange of Illinois resulted in a 21-21 tie in 1924 and a moral victory for his underdog Maroons.

Stagg was the first to organize scrimmage games. In order to decrease injuries during practice, he devised the tackling dummy. He also was the first to add numbers to the jerseys worn by his players. As a coach, Stagg was noted for his intensity. Occasionally, he would even suit up and illustrate for his players the way he wished them to block and tackle. "No coach ever won a game by what he knows," he observed. "It's what his players have learned."

Stagg coached in the era in which professional football first emerged and was in its infancy. As his University of Chicago football program became renowned nationwide, he seized on the idea to commercialize the sport. In this regard, he and the university's president, William Rainey Harper, served to transform football from an intercollegiate pastime to a high-profile, moneymaking industry. In their wake, for better or worse, universities came to be defined by the success or failure of their football programs. Stagg also was a crafty recruiter of athletic talent. In 1902, he established the University of Chicago interscholastic, a national track-and-field tournament for high school students—an event which served to acquaint him with the country's top scholastic athletes, whom he then could entice to enter his athletic program.

At the University of Chicago, Stagg amassed a 268-141 record and earned six Big Ten conference titles, along with a tie for a seventh crown. Upon his retirement in 1932 at age 70—when his football program was in the process of deteriorating—he moved on to coach at the College of the Pacific. At the end of the decade, the University of Chicago decided to close down its varsity football program. However, its unofficial demise came in 1938, when it was blanked 32-0 by a rising football power from California: Stagg's College of the Pacific team.

Stagg was 84 years old when he retired from the College of the Pacific in 1946. Incredibly, the following year, he became an assistant coach at Susquehanna College in Selinsgrove, Pennsylvania, working under his son, Amos Alonzo Stagg, Jr. The younger Stagg coached at Susquehanna between 1935 and 1954; his father remained at the school for six seasons. Stagg, Sr. did not officially retire until 1960, when he was 98-years old. During his career, he guided his teams to 314 victories, which ranks third among major college coaches (behind Glenn "Pop" Warner's 319 wins and Paul "Bear" Bryant's 323; division I-AA Grambling's Eddie Robinson is the all-time NCAA leader, with 408).

Stagg was the initial individual inducted into the College Football Hall of Fame as both a player and coach and was cited as coach of the all-time Big Ten team. Across the land, high schools and athletic facilities are named for him, including those at the schools in which he coached. Each year, the American Football Coaches Association hands out the Amos Alonzo Stagg Award, honoring "the individual, group or institution whose services have been outstanding in the advancement of the best interests of football."

—Rob Edelman

Amos Alonzo Stagg (center) amidst prospective University of Chicago football players.

FURTHER READING:

Considine, Bob. *The Unreconstructed Amateur: A Pictorial Biography of Amos Alonzo Stagg.* San Francisco, Amos Alonzo Stagg Foundation, 1962.

Lester, Robin. *Stagg's University: The Rise, Decline, and Fall of Big-Time Football at Chicago.* Urbana, University of Illinois Press, 1995.

Lucia, Ellis. *Mr. Football: Amos Alonzo Stagg.* South Brunswick, New Jersey, A. S. Barnes, 1970.

Stallone, Sylvester (1946—)

The most pervasive action star of the 1970s and the 1980s, Sylvester Stallone became renowned for his depictions of inarticulate, larger-than-life heroes, most notably the lovable pugilist Rocky Balboa, and the alienated Vietnam War veteran John Rambo. As a creative force, who wrote/directed/produced many of his movies, he also became a favorite target of critics, who took aim at the overt

sentimentality of the formulaic *Rocky* sequels, and at the revisionist politics of the *Rambo* series. Yet Stallone triumphed with audiences, to become one of the biggest movie stars in the world.

Not coincidentally, the Hollywood anomaly rose to fame in the shadow of the Watergate scandal. Amid the cynicism of the 1970s, moviegoers flocked to *Rocky,* the uplifting 1976 saga of the Philadelphia southpaw, also known as the Italian Stallion, who inadvertently gets a shot at the title. The year's sleeper hit made its screenwriter-star the year's most talked-about talent.

As with the character of Rocky Balboa, whose saga was underscored by the line, ''his whole life was a million to one shot,'' Michael Sylvester Stallone was an unlikely contender for success. A native of Hell's Kitchen, New York, he was born with droopy eyes and slurred speech, the result of a forceps injury. His childhood and adolescence were troubled; growing up in a broken home, he had behavioral problems that resulted in frequent expulsion. By age 15 he had attended a dozen schools. After graduating from a high school for troubled youth, his athletic prowess led to a scholarship to the American College in Switzerland. He went on to study dramatics at the University of Miami. He was just a few credits shy of graduating when he headed to New York.

He once described his earliest efforts in show business as "off the wall." Indeed, he co-starred in the 1970 soft-core adult movie, *A Party at Kitty and Studs,* which was later rereleased and retitled *The Italian Stallion,* and he appeared nude in several off-off Broadway plays. He made his mainstream movie debut in 1974, with the 1950s-era look at Brooklyn buddies, *The Lords of Flatbush*, and was followed by roles in *Capone, Bananas,* and *Death Race 2000*. But his career remained in stasis.

Stallone was 30 years old, with a pregnant wife and $106 in the bank, when he chanced to see a closed-circuit prize fight between Muhammad Ali and Chuck Wepner, a longshot who thrilled the crowd by going the distance. Over the next three days, Stallone wrote his screenplay about Rocky Balboa, who squares off against the champion, Apollo Creed. By fight's end, Rocky has not only won respect, but also the love of the shy, bespectacled Adrian, who works in a pet shop. Initially, the producers Irwin Winkler and Robert Chartoff envisioned a vehicle for a leading actor such as Robert Redford or Al Pacino. But Stallone refused to sell the script unless he could also star.

Filmed over 28 days for $960,000, *Rocky* became the year's top-grossing movie, and won the year's Best Picture Oscar. Its ten nominations included those for best actor and best screenplay, putting Stallone in prestigious company. At that time, the dual honor had previously been bestowed only on Charles Chaplin for *The Great Dictator* and Orson Welles for *Citizen Kane*. Of his watershed movie, Stallone once said, "It was never a script about boxing. It was always about a man simply fighting for his dignity. People require symbols of humanity and heroism."

With its prolonged training sequences, and publicity about Stallone's own body building regimen, *Rocky* also evoked the benefits of health and fitness, foreshadowing the fitness movement of the 1980s. Much of the Stallone oeuvre has celebrated physicality. The five *Rocky* movies have all included a rigorous workout sequence. With their loving close-ups of the title character's rippling pectorals

and abs, the three *Rambo* movies are as much a paean to the body beautiful as they are about the adventures of a modern-day warrior. Moreover, it was under Stallone's supervision that actor John Travolta resculpted his body, to sinewy perfection, for the 1983 movie, *Staying Alive,* which Stallone directed, co-wrote, and co-produced. Stallone has said that as a teenager he was inspired to body build after watching the gladiator movies of Steve Reeves; doubtless, teenagers of the 1970s and 1980s were similarly inspired by Stallone.

His own movies certainly impacted the action-adventure arena—particularly *Rambo: First Blood Part II,* the 1985 sequel to *First Blood.* In fact, *Rambo* redefined the genre, with elements that became genre staples. Among them, the visceral style, minimal dialogue, the ticking time clock that gives Rambo limited time to carry out his covert mission, and scenes of the hero readying for war. Because the plot took the disenchanted veteran back to Vietnam, to rescue forgotten American POWs (Prisoners of War), and because Rambo asked, "Sir, do we get to win this time?," critics and commentators assailed the movie for rewriting history. They also took personal aim at the star-co-writer, noting that, like John Wayne, another star famed for his patriotic alter egos, Stallone had managed to elude real life military service. But *Rambo* proved critic-proof, touching a responsive chord that transcended language and cultural barriers.

Stallone, or "Sly" as he is called, shrewdly parlayed his 1980s-era power into deals that included creative control, and the highest salaries of the day. His celebrity was further amplified by his colorful personal life, which has included a string of public romances and marital woes. In the 1990s, however, as the action arena sought new direction, his career waned. He tried playing against type in several comedies that failed. More successful was his turn as a paunchy, lonely, sheriff in the 1997 crime drama, *Copland.* At the time it was widely publicized that Stallone had gained 30 pounds for the role. Today, it is the career, not the man, that needs redefinition. But if Stallone is a star in transition, there is no denying his charisma and star quality, or the crowd-pleasing appeal of his most famous creations, Rocky and Rambo.

—Pat H. Broeske

FURTHER READING:

Broeske, Pat H. "The Curious Evolution of John Rambo." *Los Angeles Times.* October 27, 1985, 32-38.

———. "Sly Stallone's Rocky Road." *The Washington Post.* May 22, 1985, F1, F4.

Rovin, Jeff. *Stallone! A Hero's Story.* New York, Pocket Books, 1985.

Sackett, Susan. *The Hollywood Reporter Book of Box Office Hits.* New York, Billboard Books, 1990.

Sylvester Stallone

Stand and Deliver

Stand and Deliver (1987) is a movie about mathematics—yes, mathematics. It also features a most unusual movie hero: an educator. Yet this independently produced 1987 drama is as riveting and satisfying as the most cleverly plotted, edge-of-your-seat thriller. It is the fact-based story of Jaime Escalante, a math teacher in an East Los Angeles barrio high school, brought brilliantly to life by Hispanic actor Edward James Olmos in an Oscar-nominated performance.

Engaging, affecting, and inspirational, the film gave Escalante's philosophy and methods wide popular exposure, exercising a positive influence on American attitudes to education culture among those who saw it.

Jaime Escalante transformed a classroom of potential dropouts into calculus wizards, and *Stand and Deliver* shows how he did it. In so doing, the film's title takes on extra resonance. The phrase "stand and deliver" (originally a military term) has come to define how a person—any person—is capable of succeeding if he or she works hard, stands tall, and presents him or herself positively and intelligently, and thus the film's title takes on a specific resonance. The bespectacled educator's nondescript, slightly paunchy appearance in no way obscures his extreme intensity and his dedication to his job, and he wins the attention of his charges by the sheer force of his enthusiasm for his subject, and his ability to communicate it.

Several of Escalante's students start off as underachievers. A few are nice enough youngsters but destined never to progress beyond serving fast food or stocking shelves in a supermarket. Others are Hispanic Dead End Kids, macho punks with boulder-sized chips on their shoulders. Under Escalante's patient and gifted tutelage, 18 students learn the intricacies of calculus, and take an extremely difficult advanced placement exam. Each and every one passes the test. However, the story of *Stand and Deliver* only begins when this success is tainted by a charge of cheating, leading to an invalidation of the test results.

Stand and Deliver (the pre-release title was *Walking on Water*) is a multi-themed film, at once a tale of institutional racism and false accusation and an allegory of how an individual can accomplish a task through sheer will-power. In its most incisive scenes, director Ramon Menendez, who co-scripted with Tom Muscia, tellingly conveys how youthful minds and spirits can be dulled by parents who quash their children's natural eagerness for knowledge. Ultimately, it is Escalante, always aware of the pressures in their lives, who pushes, manipulates, cajoles, and hustles the kids, and gets results.

At the heart of *Stand and Deliver* is the wonderfully lively and expressive acting of Olmos. His performance is crammed with keenly observed inflections and mannerisms. Without ever having met the real Jaime Escalante, one can be certain that Olmos does not so much act the role as become the man. "When we see a film like *Rocky*," Olmos explained while promoting the film prior to its release, "we see an Anglo in a boxing ring. I'd say about 98 per cent of us, black, white or Hispanic, will never step in a boxing ring. But imagine how people must feel when they see a film set in a classroom—a place where everybody has been. Everyone has at one point or another sat behind a desk, and everyone knows that calculus is hard. But in this movie, you realize that calculus really isn't that hard—if you have an exceptional teacher."

Most of the real-life Escalante's calculus prodigies went on to complete college. When the film was released, several were in graduate school, and one had even joined Escalante as a colleague. "You can get anything you want in this country, as long as you are willing to pay the price and the price is right," Escalante declared, nine years after his story was told on screen. "You don't get anything unless you work for it." He also stressed that schools alone cannot be responsible for educating children, noting that he prescribes the "Three Ts" to parents: Tell your kid, 'I love you'; touch your kid; and time. "It is important to devote time to your kid. The best investment you can make in your kid is time."

—Rob Edelman

FURTHER READING:

Byers, Ann. *Jaime Escalante: Sensational Teacher*. Springfield, New Jersey, Enslow Publishers, 1996.

Mathews, Jay. *Escalante: The Best Teacher in America*. New York, Holt, 1988.

Standardized Testing

Standardized testing is so much a part of American culture that almost everyone can recognize its multiple choice format, even young children. It is no wonder; for most Americans, the testing starts in kindergarten. This testing culture seems to be uniquely American. In fact, Europeans refer to these tests as "American tests." A standardized test is called such because everyone takes the same test with the same questions, so one's performance can be compared to everyone else's, in order for a relative score to be obtained. Schools across the country vary greatly, so an A at one school might not be equal to an A from another; standardized tests thus serve to offer an equitable measure of aptitude. Because they are designed to screen applicants and are nearly impossible to finish, many people freeze when taking them. Perhaps their fear would change to anger if they knew the checkered history of these tests.

In 1912, Henry Goddard, who coined the word "moron," ran his version of an intelligence test at Ellis Island, and "proved scientifically" that the majority of Jews, Hungarians, Italians, and Russians were what he considered "feebleminded." A few years later, the president of Columbia College, disappointed by all the recent Jewish immigrants enrolling after World War I, made Columbia the first school to use an "intelligence" test for admissions; he hoped these tests would limit the number of Jewish students without instituting an overt policy to do so.

World War I provided a perfect opportunity to test large numbers of people. The Army Mental Tests were created in 1917, with the help of Goddard and Carl Campbell Brigham. Results of these tests were to be used in assigning recruits to jobs in the army. Questions had the familiar multiple choice format, but pretty odd subject matter. For example, "Crisco is a (A) patent medicine (B) disinfectant (C) toothpaste (D) food product" and "The forward pass is used in (A) tennis (B) hockey (C) football (D) golf." Few would agree that these questions test not intelligence, but rather an awareness of consumer and leisure culture, things to which impoverished immigrants without American hobbies and with little or no English skills probably would not know the answers to.

Brigham used questions like these to prove his thesis. In analyzing the "data" from the Army tests, Brigham concluded that there are four racial strains in America. In order of their supposed "intelligence," and using his terminology, they are: Nordic; Alpine; Mediterranean; and last, American Negroes. The data gathered from Brigham's army tests was continually invoked in Congress and was instrumental in fostering congressional debates that led to the Immigration Restriction Act of 1924. The act imposed quotas on immigrants entering the United States.

In 1925, the College Board, which had been established in 1900 to standardize the entrance exams that Harvard, Yale, Princeton, and a few other elite colleges had all been administering separately— and today includes more than 2,500 colleges, schools, school systems, and educational associations—hired Brigham to develop an intelligence test for use in college admissions. That test was called the Scholastic Aptitude Test (SAT). The first SAT, published in 1926 and administered to 8,040 people, included questions about brand names, chicken breeds, and cuts of beef, and had a section on artificial language that included made-up vocabulary and grammar rules, and asked testers to make sentences. There was also an analogy section that gave testers only six minutes to answer 40 questions. The test was—and still is, albeit in dramatically modified form—used to "predict" one's success in college.

Because so many people were going to college after World War II, there was a huge demand for the SAT. In 1947 the College Board created the non-profit Educational Testing Service (ETS) to take care of the testing demand. The next year, 75,000 students took the SAT. In 1954 the College Board instituted a "test use" requirement, which forced all members of the Board to use at least one of its exams; a monopoly was thus established. Until 1957 neither the testers nor their high schools were even told their scores. Annual administrations of the SAT passed over one million in 1963, and were at 1.8 million by 1994.

Henry Chauncey, ETS' first president, thought of the SAT as an IQ test. He admired such tests and believed that testing could help define vocational goals of students, especially those whose "talents" lend themselves to stopping education after high school. He suggested that students get tested at the end of the eighth or ninth grade, and then every one or two years thereafter. One does have to pay a fee each time one takes a standardized test. Some estimates of the amount Americans spend on testing in general are as high as $500 million annually.

Standardized tests are being used more than ever to aid overworked and understaffed admissions departments. The tests come by their nickname "the Gatekeepers" honestly; the score is the first, and often the only thing, an admissions officer looks at on an application. If the prospective student has too low a number, they do not get in, no matter how impressive the rest of the application. And schools sometimes jack up the "average" incoming test scores of students in their admissions material so the school will seem more "selective." Yet these gatekeepers are not crafted by academicians; writing test questions requires no special academic training. College professors do not write the SAT; lawyers do not write the LSAT, much less the Bar exam.

Most of ETS' tests contain some combination of math and verbal questions (analogies, sentence completions, and critical reading passages); some throw in "analytic" questions such as logic games. The MCAT (Medical College Admissions Test) contains curriculum based questions on biology, chemistry, and physics; this is more like the non-ETS (and less expensive) ACT (American College Testing) Assessment Test, a curriculum-based test that is also used for college admissions. The GRE (Graduate Record Examination) and GMAT (Graduate Management Admissions Test) were by the 1990s given only on computer, as opposed to pencil and paper, in a format called "computer adaptive" or CAT. The CAT format redefines "standardized," since each tester gets questions from a pool and the computer "adapts" each time she gets a question right or wrong by giving her a harder one if her last answer was correct and an easier one if her last answer was incorrect. It is therefore possible that no two test takers will take the exact same test.

ETS does seem to be distancing itself from the idea of "aptitude" testing. Until 1982, the GRE General Test was called the GRE

Aptitude Test. And in 1994, the A in SAT began to stand for "Assessment." ETS now says that native intelligence is not what their tests are designed to detect; the SAT measures "developed ability, not innate intelligence; a test of abilities that are developed slowly over time both through in-school and out-of-school experience."

The world of standardized testing starts long before high school. Estimates report that 127 million tests a year are being given at the K-12 level alone (including the Iowa Test of Basic Skills, a widely-used achievement test for grade schools). Also at that level, teachers have complained that because their peers are "teaching to the test," the resulting scores are meaningless. ETS has always maintained that coaching is not effective on its tests; it did not even publish its own practice questions until 1978. But the million-dollar cottage industry of coaching businesses, whose existence depends on these tests, disagrees. Some such coaching programs claim that a student can raise his or her SAT score by up to 300 points after taking a coaching course.

Not only do testing opponents insist that high scores reveal little more than a talent for taking tests and understanding the testing "mentality," but they also seem to correlate with the income and education of the tester's parents. College Board data shows that someone taking the SAT can expect to score about 30 points higher for every $10,000 in her parents' yearly income. Unfortunately, these tests still seem to do what Brigham meant for them to do. For many years now, the median score for African Americans on the SAT has been 200 points below that for whites; females have been scoring 35 points lower on the math sections than males. ETS has made some changes to answer these charges. The 1996 "recentering" of SAT scores, done technically to create a better distribution of scores around the test's numerical midpoint, boosted the average scores for groups like African Americans and Hispanics. Additionally, the Preliminary Scholastic Assessment Test (PSAT), a test used to determine who gets the National Merit Scholarship, replaced its old scoring formula, which assigned equal weight to the math and verbal sections, with a formula that doubles the verbal score, usually the higher one for female testers, in the hope that more women might get the scholarship.

School entry might be the most common way people are introduced to the entrenched testing culture, but it is not the only way. A partial list of organizations that buy tests from ETS includes, but is not limited to: the CIA (Central Intelligence Agency), the government of Trinidad and Tobago, The American Society of Plumbing Engineers, and The Institute for Nuclear Power Operations. One might also be required to take an ETS exam to become a golf pro, and in some states, a travel agent, a real estate salesman, and a beautician.

—Karen Lurie

FURTHER READING:

Brigham, Carl C. *A Study of American Intelligence.* Princeton, Princeton University Press, 1923.

Gould, Stephen Jay. *The Mismeasure of Man.* New York, Norton, 1981.

Kellaghan, Thomas, George F. Madaus, and Peter W. Airasian. *The Effects of Standardized Testing.* Boston, Kluwer-Nijhoff Publications, 1982.

Lemann, Nicholas. *The Big Test: The Secret History of the American Meritocracy.* New York, Farrar, Straus, and Giroux, 1999.

Murray, David W. ''The War Against Testing.'' *Commentary*. September 1998, 34.

Owen, David. *None of the Above: Behind the Myth of Scholastic Aptitude*. Boston, Houghton Mifflin, 1985.

Sacks, Peter. ''Standardized Testing: Meritocracy's Crooked Yardstick.'' *Change*. March-April 1997, 24.

Zenderland, Leila. *Measuring Minds: Henry Herbert Goddard and the Origins of American Intelligence Testing*. Cambridge and New York, Cambridge University Press, 1998.

Stand-up Comedy

Born in the smoky halls of turn-of-the-century vaudeville and thrust into mainstream American culture by the advent of radio and television, stand-up comedy is the entertainment industry's most accurate social thermometer. From Milton Berle to Roseanne Barr, comics have used the power of laughter to challenge Americans to face the controversial issues of the day, whether sex, government or

Stand-up comedian Jerry Seinfeld

religion. A good routine can turn the most tragic headlines into a gut-wrenching guffaw. Sometimes comics go too far for a laugh; sometimes they're the only ones brave enough to point out hypocrisy and social injustice.

The profession developed long before the discovery of electricity. Court jesters performed the first stand-up routines in medieval times. Elements of stand-up also pervaded William Shakespeare's work in the form of a fool providing the audience with a dose of comic relief. If the nineteenth-century American humorist did his work on paper, like Mark Twain, the twentieth century ushered in the age of performance. Vaudeville, a pre-cursor to the television variety show, provided a stage for the first generation of stand-up comedians such as Bob Hope, Jack Benny, George Burns and Gracie Allen, Bud Abbott and Lou Costello.

In Oscar Hammerstein's Victoria theatre, opened in Times Square in 1899, or the Palace Theatre, opened on Broadway and 47th Street in 1913, you could find singing women (Sophie Tucker, Nora Bayes, Elsie Janis), monologists (Milton Berle, Julius Tannen), the earliest comedy teams (Burns and Allen) and an assortment of freak acts. This was nothing like the high profile comedy showcases that would come later in the century, filled with Hollywood agents and television scouts. These variety shows were for the masses, which is why the young Berle, the brilliant monologist, might find himself on the same stage as the Armless Lutz Brothers, who could assemble a car with only their feet.

The foundations of stand-up were laid in the age of vaudeville, with terms like the ''one-liner'' and ''straight man'' entering the lexicon. Comics also developed different styles, deciding whether to space out laughs, build elaborate routines or just deliver the punch lines. Legendary society columnist Walter Winchell dubbed Henny Youngman, the ''King of the One Liner.'' Youngman relied on vivid imagery in his jokes. ''If a joke is too hard to visualize, then what the hell good is it?'' he asked in his autobiography, *Take My Life, Please!* ''I tell easy jokes where people don't have to think.''

His clear and concise one-liners continue to amuse. ''I'm so old, that when I order a three-minute egg here, they make me pay up front,'' went one of those jokes, and another, ''A guy came up to me and said he'd bet me fifty dollars that I was dead. I was afraid to take the bet.''

George Burns and Gracie Allen became the first great comedy team. Performing for the first time in Newark, New Jersey, Burns cast himself as the joke man, with Allen delivering the straight lines. A funny thing happened: Allen got all the laughs. Burns rewrote the show to refine what he called her ''illegal logic.'' With the new formula, the couple continued to get laughs for years. One example of how Burns' highlighted Allen's humorous logic follows:

GRACIE: Where do you keep your money?
GEORGE: In the bank.
GRACIE: What interest do you get?
GEORGE: Four percent.
GRACIE: Ha! I get eight.
GEORGE: You get eight?
GRACIE: I keep it in two banks.

The vaudeville generation made a natural transition to the next stage of stand-up: radio and television. Burns and Allen debuted on radio in 1932 with *The Adventures of Gracie* show (later renamed *Burns and Allen* (1932-1950)) and then moved to television with *The Burns and Allen Show* in 1950 for another eight years. On the small screen, Burns would often talk to the viewing audience, dropping all pretenses that the show they were watching was in fact reality. Called "breaking the fourth wall," this method would be practiced years later by another former stand-up, Garry Shandling, in the 1980s. Berle became known as "Mr. Television" because of his popular variety show, *The Texaco Star Theater,* which ran from 1948 to 1953. Bud Abbott and Lou Costello, before trying television and the big screen, debuted their famous "Who's On First?" routine on radio in 1938. As the people of vaudeville moved to radio, film, and television, these new media soon eclipsed vaudeville, which disappeared by the 1940s.

Without the vaudeville stage to help hone their acts, stand-up comedians turned to strip clubs and the growing nightclub circuit. The new clubs proved fertile ground for comedians like Bob Newhart, Woody Allen, Bill Cosby, and Lenny Bruce. No longer forced to shout over a rowdy audience riled by dancing girls or fish swallowing Swedes, comics could develop stories for their acts in the more controlled atmosphere of these new venues. While one-liners still ruled many acts, younger comics worked to draw the audience into a "bit" which might run for 20 minutes—about the time it took Henny Youngman to blast through a few dozen punch lines.

At the forefront of the movement stood Lenny Bruce, the comic philosopher. One of the first truly controversial stand-ups, he used vivid, sometimes obscene, language and sexually charged subject matter. Unlike comics who used profanity and went "blue" for cheap laughs, Bruce's monologues spoke to the simmering social war, the contrast between the emerging hipster cool and the prosperous, conservative, postwar America. At the time, Communists—both in Asia and in Hollywood—were under attack, and Pat Boone, the five-cent hamburger, and nondescript but affordable subdivisions were embraced. Into this cultural milieu came Bruce—a barely concealed heroin addict—with his thirst for controversial talk about race, censorship, and sex. "Show me the average sex maniac, the one who takes your eight-year-old, schtupps her in the parking lot, and then kills her, and I'll show you a guy who's had a good religious upbringing," went one of his routines. "You see, he saw his father or mother always telling his sister to cover up her body when she was only six years old, and so he figured, one day I'm going to find out what it is she's covering, and if it's as dirty as my father says I'll kill it."

Woody Allen benefited from the nightclub scene as much as Bruce. Though he went on to become one of stand-up's greatest success stories, Allen would never have made it in the vaudeville era. His quiet, intentional half-stutter delivery would have been drowned out after the first few rows of a burlesque hall. In a nightclub world, he was a headliner, known for his satiric stories and willingness to always poke fun at himself, using his noodly, bookish physique to his advantage. On stage, Allen carved out a niche as the loveable schlemiel, an intellectual comic who referenced philosophers, shrinks, and college. He would tell long stories, presented as autobiographical. But somewhere before the punch line, an absurd twist would let the audience into the tall tale; their comedic confessor was in fact a master yarn spinner.

Not interested in radio, and frustrated by the constraints of television, many among Allen's generation tapped into the growing comedy album industry. The 1960s and 1970s were a golden age for the comedy record, starting with Bob Newhart's million-selling 1960 release, *The Button-Down Mind Of.* For racier comics, George Carlin, Richard Pryor, and Eddie Murphy in particular, comedy records would prove invaluable, enabling them to use hot material that would

either not be allowed on television or have to be softened for the viewing audience.

Sparked by the general loosening of social rules brought on by the sexual revolution and youth-oriented civil rights and antiwar movements, stand-up comedy continued to push boundaries in the 1970s. Stuffy network executives were often tested or outright mocked, as in George Carlin's famous "Seven Words You Can Never Say On Television." Female comics also began to get more stage time, in particular Lily Tomlin, Gilda Radner and Joan Rivers. It wasn't until the 1980s, when Roseanne Barr (later Arnold) developed a successful sitcom out of her stage act, that female comics made a true mark in the male-dominated industry. *Saturday Night Live,* a sketch comedy show based largely on stand-up principles, was created in 1975. In addition to a cast that included Dan Aykroyd, John Belushi, Jane Curtin, Chevy Chase, and Bill Murray, *SNL* guest hosts like Carlin, Pryor, and Steve Martin gained exposure.

The 1970s generation included two of the more important comedians in Richard Pryor and Andy Kaufman. Pryor grew up in a poor, black neighborhood; Kaufman was white and from Long Island. But they shared a thirst for original and unpredictable behavior, both on and off stage, leaving audiences and critics wondering where the act ended and reality began.

Kaufman didn't just tell jokes; he wrestled with women on stage, slipped into a bad toupee to play the lounge lizard, Tony Clifton, and according to legend, read *The Great Gatsby* in its entirety to an audience in Iowa. (On another occasion, after being asked to stop reading, Kaufman agreed and put on a record instead—of him reading *The Great Gatsby.*) He had the talent to succeed with more conventional fare; his "Foreign Man" character was adapted as Latka Gravas for the popular television series, *Taxi;* his Elvis impersonation was so hilarious the pop band, R.E.M., centered its 1992 Kaufman tribute, "Man on the Moon" around it. But Kaufman preferred to push his act into performance art territory. On *Late Night with David Letterman,* he and professional wrestler Jerry Lawler appeared to get into a genuine argument, ending with Lawler slapping the comedian off his chair. The Clifton routine could run for a half-hour, with Kaufman—as Clifton—growing angry at the suggestion that he was simply doing an impression. "Listen, folks, what I'm doing up here—that's how I make my living," Clifton would yell. "I don't have to take this kind of crap!" For several years, he became so consumed by professional wrestling that his friend, comedian Robin Williams, noticed during lunch that Kaufman was wearing trunks under his clothing. When Kaufman died of cancer in 1984, many wondered whether it was the ultimate put-on.

Pryor was equally unpredictable. The most important black comics who preceded him, Bill Cosby and Flip Wilson, tended to be non-confrontational and television-ready. And Dick Gregory's biting routines were political instead of personal and less effective in the post-activist climate of the 1970s. Pryor was unique in that he based his act on common black experience in America. He grew up poor, in a world of pimps, wife beaters, and poolroom hustlers. Even as he became one of Hollywood's most bankable comic stars, Pryor remained erratic, cursing, yelling, and storming off the stage when he didn't feel right. On *The Tonight Show,* Pryor suggested to the studio audience: "If you want to do anything—if you're black and still here in America—get a gun and go to South Africa and kill some white people." He also bared his soul. In 1980, after setting himself on fire while free-basing cocaine, Pryor worked it into his routine. Pryor's red-hot stage show paved the way for the generation of black comics that would include Eddie Murphy, Martin Lawrence, and Chris Rock.

His sexually-oriented material also led to the one-dimensional, smut routine of Andrew Dice Clay.

The success of the late 1970s and early 1980s comics led to a boom in the stand-up business. Clubs opened, comedy specials were produced for cable television, John Belushi and Dan Aykroyd's Blues Brothers toured the country playing rhythm and blues, Sam Kinison's manic re-recording of ''Wild Thing'' climbed the *Billboard* charts. But the inevitable crash which came in the 1990s, when headliners moved onto television or films, and left behind a glut of second and third-rate comedians. Nearly 5,000 were listed by *Comedy USA,* the bible of stand-up comedy, in the mid-1990s. There were fewer stages, as well: The 450 clubs registered in 1991 had dwindled to 350 by the middle of the decade.

The scene was unforgiving, as described by *The New York Times'* Neil Strauss in 1999: ''The bottom rung of the comedy ladder can be uglier, crueler and more demeaning than in any other line of entertainment—be it actor, model, musician, writer or clown. Sexism and racism run rampant, club-owners ask struggling comedians to scrape gum off the bottom of tables to get a booking, competition between comics is fierce, and newcomers have to pay to perform.'' In a way, stand-up comedy had returned to the days of vaudeville, when Burns and Allen were competing against acrobats or dancing dwarfs. And the sheer volume of comics led to an important development: the rise of the alternative stand-up scene. At places like the Luna Lounge in New York City, the Velveeta Room in Austin, Texas, and the Subterranean Cabaret in Chicago, comics didn't dare trot out stand-up's war horses—jokes about mother-in-laws, terrible airplane flights or the single life. With an audience packed mainly with other comics, the performers retired well-worn bits for fresher, more experimental material. That could be, as Strauss notes, a struggling comic delivering her monologue with her pants at her ankles or a male comic acting out how a cat feels.

If the late 1990s marked the decline of the comedy club, stand-up grew even more pervasive. Bill Maher's *Politically Incorrect,* which featured four different roundtable guests each night, was hailed as one of the freshest talk shows. Books by Dennis Miller, Paul Reiser, and Martin—among others—climbed *The New York Times* bestseller list. And even the veritable CBS news, launching the *60 Minutes II* newsmagazine, chose a Boston stand-up, Jimmy Tingle, to offer a commentary at the end of each program. Jerry Seinfeld, after deciding to retire his groundbreaking television sitcom, took his stand-up routine back on the road.

Not much had changed on the front lines. In comedy clubs all across America, managers continued to strain to make money on unknowns. Drink minimums kept crowds unruly and joke-hungry. Entertainers exposed themselves, under the glare of the klieg light, defended by only a microphone and every rage, fear, and insecurity that might be cashed in for a laugh. It had been this way since Milton Berle's day, and there was never a shortage of young comics vying for that chance to deliver the perfect punch line. Because, as Steve Allen wrote in his book, *Funny People*: ''Without laughter, life on our planet would be intolerable.''

—Geoff Edgers

FURTHER READING:

Allen, Steve. *Funny People.* New York, Stein and Day, 1981.

Bruce, Lenny, with introduction by Eric Bogosian. *How to Talk Dirty and Influence People.* New York, Simon and Schuster, 1992.

Gottfried, Martin. *George Burns and The Hundred-Year Dash.* New York, Simon and Schuster, 1996.

Leno, Jay, with Bill Zehme. *Leading With My Chin.* New York, HarperCollins, 1996.

Pryor, Richard, with Todd Gold. *Pryor Convictions and Other Life Sentences.* New York, Random House, 1995.

Slide, Anthony. *The Encyclopedia of Vaudeville.* Westport, Connecticut, Greenwood Press, 1994.

Youngman, Henny, with Neal Karlen. *Take My Life, Please!* New York, William Morrow, 1991.

The Stanley Brothers

During the late 1940s, the Stanley Brothers (Carter, 1925-1966, and Ralph, 1927—) and their band the Clinch Mountain Boys helped to establish bluegrass— as Bill Monroe's new style came to be known--as a musical genre. According to folklorist Neil Rosenberg, their 1948 recording of ''Molly and Tenbrooks''—featuring Darrell ''Pee Wee'' Lambert, a tenor singer and mandolin player like Monroe—offers the first proof that Monroe's sound was being copied by other groups. Merging the old-time sound of traditional mountain music, haunting vocal harmonies, and bluegrass instrumentation, the early recordings of the Stanley Brothers have become bluegrass classics. When lead singer Carter Stanley died in 1966, Ralph took control of the group. He revitalized the band with new members (including Keith Whitley and Ricky Skaggs during the 1970s), and over the next two decades they developed and maintained a following among bluegrass and traditional folk fans that continued into the late 1990s.

—Anna Hunt Graves

FURTHER READING:

Artis, Bob. *Bluegrass.* New York, Hawthorn Books, 1975.

Rosenberg, Neil V. *Bluegrass: A History.* Urbana, University of Illinois Press, 1985.

Stanwyck, Barbara (1907-1990)

From her modest beginnings as a Broadway chorus girl named Ruby Stevens, Barbara Stanwyck forged a long and versatile career as one of Hollywood's strongest female stars. Her breakthrough performance occurred in 1930's *Ladies of Leisure,* directed by Frank Capra, who said her emotionally charged acting could ''grab your heart and tear it to pieces.'' In her earliest roles she epitomized the self-sacrificing woman, culminating in her title part in the 1937 woman's picture, *Stella Dallas.* The 1940s transformed her into a sexy, ruthless femme fatale. She played the movies' first woman to murder for no reason nobler than avarice in the 1944 seminal film noir, *Double Indemnity.* Unlike Bette Davis and Joan Crawford, her peers in melodrama, Stanwyck also made an impression as a comedienne in canonical romantic comedies like 1941's *Ball of Fire* and *The*

Lady Eve. Her image, onscreen and off, as a tough, independent woman overcoming a hardscrabble childhood is her legacy.

—Elizabeth Haas

FURTHER READING:

DiOrio, Al. *Barbara Stanwyck: A Biography.* New York, Coward-McCann, 1983.

Madsen, Axel. *Stanwyck: A Biography.* New York, HarperCollins, 1995.

Star System

With the rise of the Hollywood film industry in the 1920s and thereafter, the world came to recognize that fame, like American automobiles or hot dogs, could also be manufactured and successfully marketed. In a democratic, officially classless culture, where "personality" provided a vehicle for upward mobility, it came to be increasingly understood that personality required manufacturing and regular maintenance. As a mass movie audience, the anonymous public also began to recognize that many of the most notable people in the world were manufactured, like the movies featuring their close-up faces, in a semi-mythic place called Hollywood. Carefully crafted to complement the technical components of the entertainment industry, the "star system" focused attention of the public onto idealized "picture personalities" that simultaneously embodied familiar social types and represented privileged individuality for their fans.

While American show business, exemplified by early impresarios like P. T. Barnum, Florenz Ziegfeld, and "Buffalo Bill" Cody, had relied upon the promotion of featured "players" throughout the nineteenth century, the construction of a regulated system for the production and promotion of Hollywood stars was designed along the industrial model pioneered by Henry Ford and his Detroit assembly lines. Commercial cinema did not have stars in its early years, not until film producers, perhaps goaded by audiences, came to understand the commercial appeal of specific actors. Among the first "stars" so identified were such as Charlie Chaplin, Lillian Gish, Mary Pickford, Douglas Fairbanks, Rudolph Valentino, and Clara Bow. As Hollywood's financial and cultural power grew, it came to heavily depend upon the distinctive charisma of specific actors to promote its product to an adoring audience. Working behind the scenes from the mid-1920s through the 1950s, the Hollywood star system relied on a coordination of working parts that both imitated and rivaled Ford's efficient factories: dance and singing lessons; careful decisions about names, makeup, hair, and clothing; the posing of glamour photographs; carefully chosen publicity appearances and constructed gossip. Using these tools, the major film studios groomed and marketed their most visible products, the stars whose weekly secular worship sold millions of tickets, fan magazines, and tie-in consumer goods. Beginning with *Motion Picture* in 1911 and dominated by the long-running *Photoplay*, the fan magazine provided the public's key link to the "real lives" of their favorite actors; the construction of an offscreen image for its contract players thus became just as important for the studios as the tailoring of a specific star's screen persona. Fans were hungry for information on the "real" Clark Gable or the "actual" Joan Crawford that supplemented their film roles, and so the star system negotiated a careful balance

of identification and adoration. Stars like Judy Garland and Mickey Rooney were kids "just like us" who we knew we would never really be.

The underlying tension between studio-controlled information about stars and less-regulated gossip occasionally surfaced when major stars were caught in scandals that threatened to create wide gaps between their onscreen and offscreen images. Shocking trials in the 1920s featuring beloved comedians like Charlie Chaplin and Roscoe "Fatty" Arbuckle, and widespread rumors about the sex lives of Clara Bow or Rudolph Valentino, redefined the star system's promotional work as crisis management until the industry adoption of the Production Code allowed the studios to fully enforce "morality" clauses in actors' contracts. As far as the film studios were concerned, there was a direct relationship between a star's public behavior and his or her box-office receipt, so controlling the image of contract players was an economic imperative, even if it appeared under the guise of moral guardianship. Only in later decades would serious ethical questions be raised about, for instance, a film studio's arranging dates and even a sham marriage for Rock Hudson so that his legions of female fans might not suspect that he was in fact a homosexual.

Of course, as a capitalist structure well aware of the quick gratifications of mass culture, the star system also demanded a regular selection of fresh products, so new names and new faces were constantly put before the public even as the careers of older stars were retooled as long as the public showed interest in them. While some stars, like Mae West, Boris Karloff, or John Wayne, were narrowly defined by their iconic star personas, other stars were transformed in attempts to attract changing audiences and reflect shifting fashions. Popular child stars like Elizabeth Taylor or Shirley Temple were or were not successfully redefined for adult roles as they grew up, and performers once closely associated with one genre were reconceptualized for others: the 1930s boy singer Dick Powell reemerged as a screen tough-guy in the 1940s, and Barbara Stanwyck moved with relative ease from women's melodramas and screwball comedies in the 1930s into 1950s Westerns.

The Hollywood star system began to weaken as the studio system itself lost prestige and power in the 1950s, especially after a number of major stars, including Burt Lancaster and Kirk Douglas, declared themselves "independent" by forming their own production companies. In other cases, a star's contracts with studios, once long-term and binding, were redrawn as short-term, profit-sharing deals that linked an actor's salary directly to the success of a specific film. In 1950, James Stewart received half of the profits of his hit western *Winchester '73,* dramatically revising the industry's understanding of a star's earning potential. With stars, along with their personal agents and talent agencies, increasingly responsible for their own public images and career choices, the control over performers once secured within the studio hierarchy had clearly shifted. By the 1980s, the old Hollywood concept of the "star vehicle," a film specifically tailored to the image and talents of its leading player, was again fully active, but only a handful of stars called the shots that determined which major films were produced and promoted. The self-styled moguls of the studio era had been displaced by their former puppets, the "talent" whose survival skills now included, most significantly, a keen business sense.

Certainly a contemporary "celebrity system" remains visible in the small army surrounding any major celebrity: agents, publicists, managers, and personal assistants all work to secure film projects, recording deals, promotional endorsements, talk-show appearances, and cameo roles for their employers. The earlier star system, however, has merged into a much larger "culture of celebrity" that extends massive fame not only to film stars and professional athletes or pop musicians, but also to the legions of "minor celebrities" necessary to regularly replenish television talk shows, fashion catwalks, award presentations, and "special guest" appearances on weekly sitcoms. The pop artist Andy Warhol's notorious designation of previously unknown figures as "superstars" and his famous allotment of 15 minutes of fame to everyone in a media-saturated world perhaps signaled the real end of any remaining purpose for a coherent "system" that was once constructed to transform mere mortals into minor gods and goddesses.

—Corey K. Creekmur

FURTHER READING:

de Cordova, Richard. *Picture Personalities: The Emergence of the Star System in America.* Urbana, University of Illinois Press, 1990.

Dyer, Richard. *Heavenly Bodies: Film Stars and Society.* London, Macmillan, 1986.

———. *Stars.* London, British Film Institute, 1979, 1998.

Fowles, Jib. *Starstruck: Celebrity Performers and the American Public.* Washington, D.C., Smithsonian Institution, 1992.

Gamson, Joshua. *Claims to Fame: Celebrity in Contemporary America.* Berkeley, University of California Press, 1994.

Marshall, P. David. *Celebrity and Power: Fame in Contemporary Culture.* Minneapolis, University of Minnesota Press, 1997.

Morin, Edgar. *The Stars.* New York, Grove Press, 1960.

Schickel, Richard. *Intimate Strangers: The Culture of Celebrity.* New York, Doubleday, 1985.

Walker, Alexander. *Stardom: The Hollywood Phenomenon.* New York, Stein & Day, 1970.

Star Trek

A worldwide science-fiction pop culture triumph, Star Trek has become a veritable empire of movies, television shows, novels, comic books, fanzines, clubs, conventions, board games, video games, and memorabilia. Star Trek began as a television series originally conceived by writer-producer Gene Roddenberry (1921-1991) in the early 1960s. Airing on NBC from Fall 1966 through Spring 1969, *Star Trek* episodes chronicled the adventures of the twenty-third century starship Enterprise, serving the interplanetary Federation on a five-year mission to "explore strange new worlds" and "boldly go where no man has gone before."

Initially assembled at Desilu Studios, the series took shape with significant help from the actors, all of whom had the sense that they were involved with something quite new and important. Captain James T. Kirk (played by William Shatner) was the young, handsome leader of the mission, the youngest captain in the history of Starfleet. Though occasionally headstrong and impetuous, and with a weakness for beautiful women of all races (and all species), Kirk was an inspiring and resourceful leader, often the most popular character of the show. Rivaling and sometimes surpassing Kirk in popularity was Mr. Spock (Leonard Nimoy), a native of the planet Vulcan, where emotions are suppressed in an attempt to achieve complete objective

William Shatner (right) and Leonard Nimoy as they appeared in *Star Trek: The Motion Picture.*

logic. Spock's tapered eyebrows and pointed ears were at once sinister and fascinating, like a hybrid between a devil and an elf. Spock was particularly interesting because he was half human; though raised as a Vulcan, he was torn between the rigors of logic and the "irrational" pull of friendship and love. The third major character was Dr. "Bones" McCoy (DeForest Kelley), a curmudgeonly and quick-tempered older man. McCoy had little patience for the impossible idealism that often accompanied Kirk's confidence, and even less patience for the self-importance that often accompanied Spock's self-restraint.

The other prominent members of the original Enterprise crew were a deliberate mixture of races and nationalities, as Roddenberry felt an accurate vision of the future must depict humanity as having transcended ethnic and political strife. Montgomery Scott—"Scottie"—(played by James Doohan) was the ship's Scottish engineer; he could push the ship beyond its limits and work miracle repairs. The Japanese Lieutenant Sulu (George Takei) and the Russian Ensign Chekov (Walter Koenig) were the ship's helmsmen. The African Lieutenant Uhura (Nichelle Nichols) was the communications officer.

Star Trek was originally conceived as a rather dark and serious show, but it quickly became much more than this. There is a great variety in the original *Star Trek* episodes: tragedy, comedy, mystery, romance, action, adventure. Among the most popular humorous episodes is "The Trouble with Tribbles," during which some members of the Enterprise crew purchase some cute, round, fur-covered creatures known as tribbles from an intergalactic merchant, only to discover that the creatures multiply at a rate fast enough to threaten engulfing the entire ship. Often voted the best all-time episode is "The City on the Edge of Forever," a time-travel drama written by Harlan Ellison and co-starring Joan Collins. In this heart-wrenching episode, Kirk is forced to choose between saving the life of the woman he loves or forever altering the natural course of history.

Other popular episodes feature the Enterprise in conflict with the Federation's redoubtable alien enemies, the warlike Klingons and the scheming Romulans.

The 1960s *Star Trek* is justly famous for its social commentary. A few episodes, including "A Private Little War," offer thinly veiled criticism of Vietnam by showing the problems of getting involved in other nations' internal struggles. Indeed, Starfleet's "Prime Directive" is that no technologically advanced society may interfere with the normal development of a more primitive society. Other episodes promote racial harmony and equality; the exciting "Last Battlefield" episode shows a planet of racists engaged in a futile and self-destructive war. A few episodes, including "A Way to Eden," critique the communal counterculture: intergalactic hippie types are seen spoiled by drugs or foolishly deluded into thinking they will find a perfect paradise. Overall the show is upbeat, suggesting that many of the problems of twentieth-century Earth will ultimately be solved. The tradition of social commentary in the episodes of the original *Star Trek* series carried into the later *Star Trek* series, which have examined issues such as overpopulation, environmentalism, homelessness, drug abuse, bisexuality, and religious fanaticism.

The original *Star Trek* is also remarkable for its breaking of television taboos. Apparently, the show's being set in the future allowed it to get away with content that would have been unacceptable in a "real life" show. Many episodes feature scantily clad men and women, often in thin and flimsy outfits that seem about to fall off entirely; but as many of these men and women were "robots" or "aliens" the network censors allowed them on the show. *Star Trek* was also historic in condoning interracial (or even inter-species) love. The fine "Plato's Stepchildren" episode (aired 1969) features television's first interracial kiss, between Shatner and Nichols.

Over the years, the original *Star Trek* series has furnished its fans with a multitude of inside jokes. Drinking games have developed during which fans take one drink every time the show's most famous motifs are repeated: the ship's teleporting "Transporter" always breaks down; red-shirted security officers always die at the hands of evil aliens; Kirk always finds a way to talk attractive female aliens into bed; Uhuru always taps the microphone in her ear to get better reception across the light years; Spock and his fellow Vulcans greet each other with mystic hand-signals and with the words, "Live long and prosper"; after McCoy examines a dead body, he always turns sadly to the captain and says, "He's dead, Jim"; after a mission accomplished (and after the ship's Transporter has been conveniently repaired), Kirk radios his engineer and chimes, "Beam me up, Scotty." Yet all these jokes, along with the occasional silly-looking sets and ham-acting, have become a source of endearment rather than derision.

Despite the tremendous efforts of everyone involved with the show, and despite the high cost of close to $200,000 per episode, media critics considered the show a failure. Worse still, after some initially high Nielsen ratings, the show's popularity began to decline. Although fan mail increased week after week, the number of viewers appeared to be dwindling. NBC came close to canceling the show after the first season but relented after being deluged by letters written during a "save *Star Trek*" campaign organized by prominent science-fiction writers. But the show's second season still failed to capture high ratings. Again the show was nearly canceled, but again a "save *Star Trek*" campaign (this time organized by fans) saved it. The third season was the show's last, but the total of 79 episodes were enough to allow syndication.

In syndication, *Star Trek* became an immediate hit. Fanzines and fan clubs proliferated, enough to inspire the first Star Trek convention in January 1972 in New York City. In response to this burgeoning popularity, NBC revived the show as an animated series, featuring the original actors as the voices of their original characters. Unfortunately, though the animated show featured stories as complex as the live action series, it was aired for young viewers on Saturday mornings and thereby was misplaced. It was canceled after a brief 22-episode run from Fall 1973 into Winter 1974. Plans for a second television series were in the works, but after the spectacular success of *Star Wars* in 1977, Star Trek's new owner Paramount decided to make the show into a movie. *Star Trek: The Motion Picture* (directed by Robert Wise) hit theaters in 1979, and while it was not well-liked by critics or hardcore fans (mostly because of its extravagant special effects and emphasis on concept over character), the picture drew tremendous crowds and was a financial success.

Star Trek movies have since hit theaters regularly every few years. *Star Trek II: The Wrath of Khan* (1982, directed by Nicholas Meyer) was an action-packed adventure co-starring Ricardo Montalban and Kirstie Alley; it became both a critical and popular success despite the death of Mr. Spock in the film's final scenes. *Star Trek III: The Search for Spock* (1984, directed by Leonard Nimoy) was another all-around success; the Enterprise is lost, but Spock is resurrected. *Star Trek IV: The Voyage Home* (1986, directed by Nimoy) time-warped the crew back to 1980s San Francisco in search of a pair of humpback whales; possessing a playful sense of delight, it has become the most successful Star Trek film of all. *Star Trek V: The Final Frontier* (1989, directed by William Shatner) gave the crew a rebuilt Enterprise and sent them in search of an evil alien whom they mistake as God; the movie also purposefully suggested that the characters were perhaps getting too old to be adventuring in outer space. *Star Trek VI: The Undiscovered Country* (1992, directed by Meyer), in which the Klingons and the Federation make peace, was the last film to feature the original cast.

Star Trek: Generations (1994, directed by David Carson) portrayed the death of James T. Kirk, and was also the first film to feature the second generation of Star Trek characters from the already-successful *Next Generation* television show. *Star Trek: First Contact* (1996, directed by Jonathan Frakes) was a multi-layered time-travel film showing Earth's first contact with an alien race. And *Star Trek: Insurrection* (1998, directed by Frakes) portrayed a power-struggle over a beautiful pleasure-planet.

The success of the first Star Trek movies inspired Paramount to produce a second television series, *Star Trek: The Next Generation*, that took place 78 years after the first series. The new show (aired 1987-94) took a more contemplative and peaceful approach to its episodes; there was less action but more science and more diplomacy. Beautiful computer-generated special effects added further breadth. But as with the original series, a prime appeal of the second series was the emphasis on character. With families and couples on board a much larger starship, the show had a balanced "group" feel. Captain Jean-Luc Picard (played by Patrick Stewart) was mature and dignified, while First Officer Riker (Jonathan Frakes) was suave and sturdy. Klingon security officer Worf (Michael Dorn) was often torn between his hereditary codes of honor and his duties serving the Federation, while android Lieutenant Data (Brent Spiner) struggled to compare his thoughts and his "emotions" with those of human beings. Major characters also included the empathetic Counselor Troi (Marina Sirtis), the young engineer Geordi La Forge (LeVar Burton), and the doctor Beverly Crusher (Gates McFadden). Some episodes featured Dr. Crusher's son Wesley (Wil Wheaton), the Ukrainian security officer Tasha Yar (Denise Crosby), and the 500-year-old Guinan (Whoopi Goldberg). Like the original series, *The Next Generation* offered fans a great variety of shows ranging from the very lighthearted to the very serious. Popular episodes feature the Romulans (now a major enemy of the Federation), the Borg (frightening and hostile aliens who resemble a cross between insects and robots), and the nearly-omnipotent alien ''Q'' (John DeLancie), who enjoys teasing the earnest but helpless humans.

After seven seasons, it was decided that *The Next Generation* be replaced by a new show, *Star Trek: Deep Space Nine* (created largely by Rick Berman and debuting in 1993), whose characters inhabit a space station rather than ship. The station is precariously situated at the edge of the Federation near an intergalactic ''wormhole'' through which all manner of alien spaceships frequently pass. Besides accommodating their alien visitors, the Deep Space Nine crew faces the challenge of a conflict raging in their sector between the empire of the Cardassians (reptilian Federation adversaries) and the inhabitants of the planet Bajor. In later shows the crew faces the threat of the hostile Jem'Hadar alien troops and their masters in the ''Dominion.'' The look and mood of the show is darker than in the earlier shows, but the optimistic vision remains. The characters include widower Captain Benjamin Sisko (Avery Brooks) and son Jake (Cirroc Lofton), the Bajoran first officer Kira (Nana Visitor), the unscrupulous merchant Quark (Armin Shimerman), the symbiont-hosting alien Dax (Terry Farrell), and the shapeshifting officer Odo (Rene Auberjonois). As in the earlier shows, the *Deep Space Nine* crew is a harmonious mixture of peoples: Sisco is black, the ship's doctor (Siddig El Fadil) is an Arab, the operations officer (Colm Meany) is Irish, the botanist (Rosalind Chao) is Japanese.

With *Deep Space Nine* still intended to run a full six or seven seasons, in 1994 yet another Star Trek TV series debuted, entitled *Star Trek: Voyager* (also created largely by Rick Berman). As in the first two series, the characters serve on board a space ship, but this ship is lost light years from the Federation and must find its way home. The Voyager crew must also deal with internal Federation rebels known as The Maquis, some of whom serve on the Voyager bridge. Crew members include the scientist-captain Kathryn Janeway (Kate Mulgrew), Native American officer Chakotay (Robert Beltran), ex-convict Lieutenant Paris (Robert Duncan McNeill), youthful Ensign Kim (Garrett Wang), Vulcan Lieutenant Tuvok (Tim Russ), half-Klingon engineer Torres (Roxann Biggs-Dawson), holographic-projection ''Doctor'' (Robert Picardo), chef Neelix (Ethan Phillips), telekinetic Kes (Jennifer Lien), and part-Borg Seven of Nine (Jeri Ryan). As with the preceding series, there is an underlying sense of optimism about the future, but also a broad variety of episodes that deal with serious subjects such as personal versus professional loyalties, legitimate versus illegitimate forms of authority, foreign (or alien) codes of ethics, and the loss of families and loved ones.

In all its manifestations, Star Trek has made an incalculable impact on American culture. Social critics have viewed Star Trek as something of a modern mythology basing itself on the future rather than the past. Few Americans exist who have not seen at least one Star Trek movie or television show. The stars of the original *Star Trek* series have virtually become national legends, regularly featured on talk shows or as the subjects of biographical articles, books, and documentaries. NASA named one of its space shuttles ''Enterprise''

in tribute to the show. World-renowned physicist Stephen Hawking appeared on a *Next Generation* episode, as did Mae Jemison, the first African-American woman in space. In the late 1990s, Star Trek television shows are seen in more than 100 countries worldwide and viewed by an audience of 30 million each week. There are more than 63 million copies of Star Trek books in print, and every newly-released Star Trek novel has been a best-seller—making this the most successful series in publishing history. There have been more than a dozen different Star Trek comic book series since the early 1970s, and there are thousands of Star Trek websites. There have been Star Trek museum exhibits, and there is a permanent ''Star Trek: The Experience'' museum/spaceship-simulator at the Hilton Hotel in Las Vegas.

There are many reasons for Star Trek's successes—the deep and compelling characters, the charismatic actors, the intelligent themes and plots of individual shows, the consistency of the future technologies and devices, the believability of the future universe. Perhaps one of the most important reasons is Star Trek's positive vision of the future. Star Trek shows and movies are an inspiration and hope for a twentieth-century world dealing with crime, homelessness, ethnic strife, and AIDS. In the twenty-third century, Earth has solved all its biggest problems. Political and racial harmony is so strong that warfare no longer exists. Understanding and altruism are so universal that money is no longer necessary. Sickness and hunger have all but vanished; humans live to age 130 and beyond.

For hardcore fans, Star Trek has truly become a way of life. Costumes from each of the television series are available, as are the tools of the trade—''phaser'' weapons, ''communicator'' radios, and scientific or medical ''tricorders.'' Nearly every science fiction shop in the country carries tribble dolls and Klingon dictionaries. The biggest Star Trek fans—''Trekkies'' or ''Trekkers''—have become something of a culture of their own, the subject of serious sociological studies as well as condescending satires. Trekkies are occasionally stereotyped as overweight nerds, but are in fact a very diverse bunch, as ethnically mixed as Star Trek characters themselves. Trekkies are the only fans listed in the OED, and they have become so numerous that, by the late 1990s, during every weekend of every year there is a Star Trek convention held somewhere in the world.

—Dave Goldweber

FURTHER READING:

Asherman, Allan, and Kevin Ryan, editors. *The Star Trek Compendium.* New York, Pocket, 1993.

Bjorklund, Edi. ''Women and *Star Trek* Fandom.'' *Minerva.* Vol. 24, No. 2, 1986, 16-65.

Blair, Karin. ''Sex and *Star Trek.''* *Science-Fiction Studies.* Vol. 10, No. 2, 1983, 292-97.

Dillard, J.M. *Star Trek: Where No One Has Gone Before.* New York, Pocket, 1996.

Harrison, Taylor, et al, editors. *Enterprise Zones: Critical Positions on Star Trek.* Boulder, Colorado, Westview, 1996.

Jindra, Michael. ''*Star Trek* Fandom as a Religious Phenomenon.'' *Sociology of Religion.* Vol. 55, No. 1, 1994, 27-51.

Okuda, Michael, et al, editors. *The Star Trek Encyclopedia.* New York, Pocket, 1997.

Reeves-Stevens. *The Art of Star Trek: Thirty Years of Creating the Future.* New York, Pocket, 1997.

Richards, Thomas. *The Meaning of Star Trek.* New York, Doubleday, 1997.

Shatner, William. *Star Trek Memories.* New York, HarperCollins, 1994.

Solow, Herbert F., and Robert H. Justman. *Inside Star Trek: The Real Story.* New York, Pocket, 1997.

Worland, Rick. ''Captain Kirk: Cold Warrior.'' *Journal of Popular Film and Television.* Vol. 16, No. 3, 1988, 109-17.

Star Wars

In 1977, George Lucas released a space opera titled *Star Wars: A New Hope* that has become not only one of the most important movies ever made, but one of the largest merchandising enterprises ever. The *Star Wars* phenomenon has led to two sequels (*The Empire Strikes Back* [1980], and *Return of the Jedi* [1983]), a set of prequels set for release at century's end, a score of books, numerous awards, and more toys than was once thought imaginable. *Star Wars* the movie was a

remarkable piece of filmmaking, but *Stars Wars* the industry permeated popular culture in an unprecedented fashion—and looks to do so for years to come.

The *Star Wars* trilogy (as it was known before the release of the first Star Wars prequel, *Star Wars Episode I: The Phantom Menace*, in May of 1999) was one of the most successful movie endeavors of all time. All three of the movies rank in the top ten of box office revenue and by 1999 it was estimated that the trilogy had earned $1.5 billion, plus three times that amount in merchandising. Beyond ticket sales the importance of the movies can be seen in the numerous Oscars, Golden Globes, and many other awards it has received. The movies were so popular that on the twentieth anniversary of the original, Lucas re-released the *Star Wars* trilogy with additional new footage (made with special effects that were not technologically possible in the late 1970s and early 1980s) and again drew viewers to theaters by the millions. Lucas stated that *Star Wars* was only 70 percent of what he had imagined and he described the release of the Special Edition not as the director's cut, but as the ''director's wish.''

The *Star Wars* movies are often described by critics as ''corny'' or ''hokey'' and as having a childishly simplistic plot, but these corny plots have taken hold of popular culture in an astounding fashion. The overall story has the simplicty of myth: rebel forces do battle with an evil empire, led by a cruel Emperor and his dark enforcer, Darth

(From left) Mark Hamill, Harrison Ford, Peter Mayhew as Chewbacca, and Carrie Fisher in a scene from *Star Wars***.**

Vader. The movies depict the struggle between good (Luke Skywalker, Princess Leia, Han Solo, Obi-Wan Kenobi, etc.) and evil (Darth Vader, Emperor Palpatine, and the Storm Troopers); they are populated with heroes, villains, warrior-wizards, wise mentors, ogres, and princesses. The story tells of the transmission of good and evil from father to son; it is also a story, according to Lucas, about "redemption." There is little that is new in the movies, much that is familiar. As scholar Andrew Gordon put it, "*Star Wars* is a masterpiece of synthesis, a triumph of American ingenuity and resourcefulness, demonstrating how the old may be made new again: Lucas has raided the junkyard of our popular culture and rigged a working myth out of scrap."

Prior to *Star Wars,* merchandising was only used to help promote a movie and rarely lasted after the movie had finished its run. But *Star Wars* merchandising became a business unto itself and and produced the most important licensing properties in history. The commercialization of *Star Wars* can be seen everywhere, from action figures to comic books to bank checks; there are even *Star Wars*-themed versions of Monopoly, Trivial Pursuit, and Battleship. Kenner toys once estimated that for most of the 1980s they sold in excess of $1 billion a year in *Star Wars* related toys. In 1996, *Star Wars* actions figures were the best selling toy for boys and the second over-all best-seller, after Barbie; in 1999 Legos introduced new models based on space ships from the early movies. Even in the late 1990s, *Star Wars* toys remained incredibly popular.

As time wore on the amazing popularity of *Star Wars* items did not falter. In 1991, Timothy Zahn's *Heir to the Empire* became the first in a series of books based upon the *Star Wars* universe. It surprised the publishing world by going to No. 1 on the *New York Times* hardcover-fiction list. Marketers quickly discovered a new generation of fans who had never seen the movies in theaters but were nevertheless obsessed with *Star Wars*. This popularity can be easily seen, as a majority of the books published in the 1990s have reached the *New York Times* best seller list. The books have in one respect mirrored the real world; as the first generation of fans, now parents, take their children to see the re-release of *Star Wars* several of the books have focussed on the adventures of the children of Han Solo and Princess Leia.

Other books and movies spun off characters found in the trilogy. One set of books focused on the adventures of Lando Calrissian; two made-for-television movies featured the Ewoks (characters introduced in *Return of the Jedi*). The movies, *The Ewok Adventure: Caravan of Courage* (1984) and *Ewoks: The Battle for Endor* (1985) benefited greatly from the splendid special effects provided by Lucas's Industrial Light and Magic, providing a rare treat for television movies. Both were considered superior fare for television, and were released theatrically abroad. The popularity of the two Ewok movies among children led to two half-hour animated adventure series. One featuring the Ewoks (1985-86) and the other the Droids R2D2 and C3PO (1985). Not only did the spin-offs demonstrate the appeal of the plethora of characters created by Lucas, but they further ingrained the *Star Wars* story into the cultural consciousness of fans old and new.

Star Wars merchandising kept pace with technology as LucasArts (the division of Lucas Industries tasked with developing computer games) created several games designed for the Nintendo system and for personal computers. Among the most popular of these games are

X-Wing (1993), which was the best-selling personal computer game of the year; Rebel Assault (1993), which sold 1.5 million copies, and the sequel Rebel Assault II: The Hidden Empire (1995); and Dark Forces (1995). In the late 1990s LucasArts became one of the top 5 producers of video games in the United States. As Lucas did in the film industry, LucasArts has pushed the outer limits of what was possible in computer games.

The popularity and long-term interest in *Star Wars* merchandise has given rise to a substantial collectors industry. With the high-level demand for original run *Star Wars* toys the value of many has skyrocketed. A vinyl-caped Jawa, which sold in 1978 for approximately $3, brought as much as $1,400 in the late 1990s. This has led to a number of conventions, books, and websites dedicated to collectibles. The demand and hoped for return on investment has led many toy stores to limit the number of any one item that can be purchased by customers.

Star Wars has had other far-reaching influences on Ameriocan popular culture. The theme music by John Williams, which won both the Oscar and the Golden Globe in 1978, is one of the most identifiable pieces of film music ever created. The sound of Darth Vader's artificially enhanced breathing is universally connected to dark foreboding danger, in much the same way that the theme music to films like *Psycho* and *Friday the 13th* connote coming horror. "May the force be with you" is just one of the most widely known of the many phrases from the movies that have worked their way into popular terminology. Nearly as well known is Obi-wan Kenobi's admonition to Luke Skywalker, uttered during the hurtling chase scene in the high-walled metallic canyon of the Death Star, to "trust the force, Luke."

Perhaps the most obvious influence *Star Wars* had in the political arena was its use as a linguistic device in the debate over the Strategic Defense Initiative (SDI). In an unrehearsed speech that took many foreign policy analysts by surprise, on March 23, 1983 President Ronald Reagan announced a goal of rendering nuclear weapons "impotent and obsolete" by constructing a space-based defensive system. For 30 years, the American defense against nuclear attack had rested on the policy of MAD (Mutual Assured Destruction). MAD assumed that the threat of massive retaliation would deter Soviet attack. SDI would provide an actual defense against the weapons themselves. Opponents of Reagan's plan bitterly argued that not only would SDI prod the Soviet into developing new nuclear weapons that could penetrate SDI but that it wouldn't work anyway. Shortly after President Reagan's March 1983 speech, Senator Ted Kennedy derided SDI as "Star Wars" fantasy that was reckless, costly, and technologically unfeasible.

Senator Kennedy's term of derision stuck. Years after President Reagan's proposal was made, SDI is still known as "Star Wars." Indeed, the Federation of American Scientists, an interest group opposed to SDI, has on its web site page for SDI issues a moving picture of Darth Vader menacingly waving his lightsaber. And in an academic conference sponsored by Northwestern University, one group of scholars claimed that "Star Wars" was worse than simply defensive weapons in space: SDI was in reality a "Death Star," a potential offensive device in orbit that could destroy Earth just as Princess Leia's homeworld of Alderaan was destroyed.

Not surprisingly, the *Star Wars* series has directly influenced many subsequent science fiction films, first, in its upbeat and individualist theme and characterizations, and second, (and perhaps contradictorily) in its "mindless" special effects-induced action and weak plotline. In the first half of the 1970s science fiction films were either themed around gloom and doom messages of imminent environmental catastrophe—as in *The Andromeda Strain* (1971), *The Omega Man* (1971), and *Soylent Green* (1973)—or depicted an oppressive, corporate-controlled future in films such as *Rollerball* (1975) and George Lucas's own *THX-1138* (1970). These films reflected the public backlash against government corruption in the Watergate-era and government dishonesty during the Vietnam conflict.

Star Wars abruptly changed the previously dispiriting and grim view of the future taken by science fiction films, offering a pro-freedom, anti-tyranny theme where the good guys actually won. (In *The Omega Man* and in *Soylent Green,* the lead characters are killed at the film's conclusion.) *Star Wars,* with its backdrop of a totalitarian universe, promoted the values of the individual against the state and the "freedom fighter," foreshadowing and congruent with the decade of the 1980s. The Empire is seen as a synthesis of Nazi Germany and the Soviet Union, a faceless bureaucratic tyranny that disturbs the agrarian, peaceful, trading peoples of the galaxy. Indeed, two of the primary heroes of the *Star Wars* saga, Han Solo and Lando Calrissian, are depicted as entrepreneurial privateers struggling against the oppressive state and avoiding its regulators.

The revival of religious values in the 1980s was also indicated in the *Star Wars* series. The individual-against-state theme of *Star Wars* is qualified by its solemnly spiritual individualism. With the mysticism of The Force, a plot device that Lucas had not originally intended to be a centerpiece of the series, *Star Wars* conveys the values of faith over reason and simplicity over complexity. *Star Wars* may be libertarian, but it is definitely not libertine and as such served as a precursor to the revival of small-town traditional values in the 1980s.

In keeping with its upbeat theme, *Star Wars* also resurrects the role of the unambiguous hero. In the 1960s and 1970s the heroes of many films were dubious heroes at best, and at worst anti-heroes. Among the films in this category are Francis Ford Coppola's *Godfather* series; Martin Scorcese's *Taxi Driver* (1976); Sam Peckinpah's *The Wild Bunch* (1969); and the "Man with No Name" westerns and Dirty Harry cop films of Clint Eastwood. On the other hand, *Star Wars* offers the likes of Luke Skywalker, Han Solo, and Lando Calrissian as genuinely good-hearted, if not faultless, characters. The faults they do possess—Luke leaving his Jedi training too soon to rescue Han and Leia—are faults of judgment that arise out of a love and concern for friends and not of character. In short, *Star Wars* reverses the bleakness, grimness, and unsettling tragedy inherent in many early 1970s films by, in part, offering characters to cheer for. Other science fiction films—indeed Hollywood in general—would come to mimic the heroic characterizations of *Star Wars*. The Indiana Jones series, Chuck Norris's *Delta Force* series, the *Superman* series, the *Conan* series, and of course the *Rocky* series all revive the heroic archtype central character. Nearly gone were the no-name, angst-ridden, amoral "heroes" of the late 1960s and 1970s.

A second influence of the *Star Wars* series was the way in which it heightened the use of special effects in film, especially science fiction film, to the detriment of plot. *Battlestar Galactica* (1978), for example, was an obvious and cheap *Star Wars* reproduction that was wholly devoid of plot. While other science fiction films succeeding *Star Wars* such as the *Alien* series, *Superman* (1978), *Close Encounters of the Third Kind* (1977), *E.T.* (1982), the *Jurassic Park* series all

possessed passable plots, the emphasis on the effects is clear. One film, *Independence Day* (1996), went so far as to mimic Luke's attack run through the Death Star's trench, replacing TIE fighters and X-Wings with F-18s and alien fighters.

Lucas has stated that the next *Star Wars* films are prequels to the released films, taking place approximately 35 years prior to the events of the original *Star Wars* (which is the fourth episode in the saga). The first of the prequels, *Star Wars—Episode 1: The Phantom Menace,* takes place in the last years of the Jedi Republic and deals with the early Jedi training of Luke's father, Anakin Skywalker, under Obi-Wan Kenobi, his love for a young Queen, and the maneuverings of Senator Palpatine to the throne. The film stars Liam Neeson, Ewan McGregor, Natalie Portman, and Frank Oz as the voice of Yoda. According to David Ansen in *Newsweek,* while the first film took audiences by surprise, the prequel came out "amid a cacophony of media hype, carrying on its shoulders the wildest hopes of several generations of worshipful moviegoers. . . . It's not hype to say that *Phantom Menace* [was] the most eagerly awaited movie ever made." The prequel was directed by George Lucas himself (the first film Lucas will have directed since the original *Star Wars*), and was reported to have cost $115 million to produce, with a 20-minute finalé alone costing a reported $22 million. The first prequel contains over 1,500 special effects, five times the number in effects-laden *Independence Day*. If one can judge by the hype that preceded the release of the movie on May 19, 1999, the force remains with the *Star Wars* franchise.

—Craig T. Cobane and Nicholas A. Damask

FURTHER READING:

Ansen, David. "Star Wars: The Phantom Movie." *Newsweek*. May 17, 1999, 56-60.

Cavelos, Jeanne. *The Science of Star Wars: An Astrophysicist's Independent Examination of Space Travel, Aliens, Planets, and Robots as Portrayed in the Star Wars Films and Books.* New York, St. Martin's Press, 1999.

Champlin, Charles. *George Lucas: The Creative Impulse.* New York, Harry N. Abrams, 1997.

Edwards, Ted. *The Unauthorized Star Wars Compendium: The Complete Guide to the Movies, Comic Books, Novels, and More.* Boston, Little Brown, 1999.

Gordon, Andrew. "Star Wars: A Myth for Our Time." *Literature/Film Quarterly.* Vol. 6, No. 4, 1978, 314-26.

Jenkins, Garry. *Empire Building: The Remarkable Real-Life Story of Star Wars.* Secaucus, New Jersey, Carol Publishing Group, 1999.

Kelly, Kevin and Paula Parisi. "Beyond Star Wars: What's Next for George Lucas." *Wired.* February, 1997, 160-67, 210-12, 216-17.

Sansweet, Stephen J. *Star Wars Encyclopedia.* New York, Ballantine Publishing Group, 1998.

Sansweet, Stephen J. with Josh Ling. *Star Wars: The Action Figure Archive.* San Francisco, California, Chronicle Books, 1999.

Seabrook, John. "Why Is the Force Still with Us?" *The New Yorker.* January 6, 1997, 40-53.

Snyder, Jeffrey B. *Collecting Star Wars Toys, 1977-1997: An Unauthorized Practical Guide.* Atglen, Pennsylvania, Schiffer Publishing, 1998.

"Star Wars." http://www.starwars.com. May 1999.

Weinberg, Larry. *Star Wars: The Making of the Movie.* New York, Random House, 1980.

Starbucks

The brand recognition of Starbucks coffee, and its elevation to a catchword denoting the ultimate corporate commodification of the anti-corporate, ''slacker'' lifestyle, is all the more phenomenal for the company's marked refusal to achieve that status through the medium of advertising. A chain of retail coffee outlets that offer fresh specialty drinks and beans to go, the Seattle-based company expanded across North America at a quick pace during the 1990s, and by early 1998 Starbucks stores could boast a combined foot-traffic count of five million visitors weekly. Because of Starbucks, Americans can now pronounce the foreign terms ''latte'' and ''barista'' when discussing complex coffee beverages and the food-service professionals who make them.

Starbucks' corporate origins date back to 1971, but the company did not really begin its march to massive success until 1986, when a Starbucks executive, Howard Schultz, created a coffeehouse in Seattle to serve upscale espresso drinks. He called it Il Giornale, and modeled it on the coffee-imbibing locales ubiquitous to Italian cities. The following year, Schultz put financing together and bought out Starbucks' two original founders, who had little faith in his attempt to introduce European-style coffee and coffee culture.

Starbucks was a hit in Seattle, however, and soon began expanding down the Pacific Coast. Exporting the concept to Chicago in the early 1990s was equally successful, and forays into the Northeast and Canada were also lucrative. The trade journal *Restaurants & Institutions,* naming Starbucks as its ''Changemaker'' for 1995, explained

Starbucks president, Howard Behar, poses in front of the first Starbucks in China.

that ''with ethnic influences shaping the American palate, consumers demand more from everything they consume.... Along comes Starbucks with a flavor profile stronger than many Americans had ever experienced.'' With a featured ''coffee of the day'' and a variety of espresso, cappuccino, and latte drinks priced from $1.15 to $3.15, Starbucks became a morning stop for urban commuters in major American cities, and a hangout for the home-office-bound and stroller-mom brigade of the more affluent suburbs. In some urban spots, Starbucks outlets were so successful that the company simply opened up a second Starbucks across the street.

By 1998, Starbucks was the number-one roaster and retailer of specialty coffee in the United States, closing in on its goal of 2,000 stores by the year 2000, expanding into Asian markets, and introducing bottled beverages and packaged beans in supermarkets. Yet it was the actual Starbucks space that attracted both devotees and disparagers. The stores are carefully designed to look just slightly cutting-edge and modern in their fixtures and fabrics; the lighting is subdued and ambient. Sociologists term it a ''third place''—neither work nor home, but a neighborhood spot where it's okay to sit alone, offering the chance of running into old friends or making new ones. ''I don't think Starbucks' success has that much to do with coffee,'' urban sociologist Peter Katz told *Seattle Weekly*'s Bruce Barcott. ''Starbucks is selling community.''

Katz and other academics have contemplated Starbucks' success and increasing ubiquity, and cite certain elements in North American culture and demographics as key factors. First is the importance of the ''private sphere'' in American life, and because of it a near-planned lack of designed community spaces, as in Europe. The predominance of suburban living spaces has led, in turn, to too much isolation. Economic considerations have also contributed to Starbucks' empire: By the 1990s, the workplace no longer offered the security and stabilized socialization of the past and more Americans had opted to work at home. Coupled with the extreme transientness of North America culture in general, these factors engendered this longing for just such a ''third place.''

Furthermore, coffeehouse culture allows, to a certain extent, people from different social and belief strata to mix, and fulfills a post-Yuppie era desire to appear sophisticated and European. It also allows more straitlaced personality types to participate in what had been the coffeehouse culture pre-Starbucks, when such places were frequented by artists, college students, and the underemployed. ''Square America needs a hangout too,'' observed the *Seattle Weekly*'s Barcott. ''Starbucks joins the concept of the coffeehouse with mainstream America's demand for brand-name assurance.'' Locating the stores near or even inside mega-bookstores such as Barnes & Noble or Borders creates what Barcott calls the ''upscale leisure ghetto.''

Yet anti-Starbucks sentiment is strong, especially among the original slacker coffeehouse crowd. Stores under construction are sometimes vandalized, there are Internet web sites that rail against ''McLatte,'' and National Public Radio host Ira Glass speaks of the common bond uniting his audience as ''a fear of Starbucks.''

—Carol Brennan

FURTHER READING:

Barcott, Bruce. ''Starbucks Nation.'' *Seattle Weekly.* February 19, 1997.

Kugiya, Hugo. ''Seattle's Coffee King.'' *Seattle Times Pacific Magazine.* December 15, 1996.

McDowell, Bill. ''The Bean Counters.'' *Restaurants & Institutions.* December 15, 1995.

———. ''Starbucks Is Ground Zero in Today's Coffee Culture.'' *Advertising Age.* December 9, 1996, 1, 49.

Starr, Bart (1934—)

Bart Starr retired from the Green Bay Packers as the winningest quarterback in the history of professional football. From 1956 to 1971 he directed the Packers to six Western Division titles, five World Championships, and two Super Bowl victories. He won the National Football League's (NFL) Most Valuable Player award in 1966, made four Pro Bowl teams, and won the league passing title three times. Even as the talented starting quarterback of the NFL's best team during the decade that saw football became America's number one sport, Starr's humble personality was initially overshadowed by more outspoken Packers like Ray Nitschke, Paul Hornung, and coach Vince Lombardi. But his stature rose among both football fans and the general public as the Packers evolved from a running to a passing team during their championship run. Teammates and outsiders recognized the balance his cool personality offered the intense Packers. Like other American celebrities from Gary Cooper to Dwight Eisenhower, Starr's public persona sprang from a dependable, appealing toughness and self-effacing gentility.

Bart Starr

Born in Montgomery, Alabama on January 9, 1934, Bryan Bartlett Starr struggled through his playing days in high school and college. Although he was not a high school star and was considered too shy to be an effective starting quarterback, his career at the University of Alabama began well. As a freshman he was all-SEC (South Eastern Conference) and started in the 1953 Orange Bowl, which Alabama won 61-6. Due to injuries and a coaching change, however, Starr rode the bench his final two years.

At the urging of his former coach at Alabama, the Green Bay Packers selected Starr in the seventeenth round of the 1956 NFL draft. For his first four seasons, Starr alternated at quarterback and observers echoed concerns at Alabama: Starr's arm was weak and he was too passive and nice to develop the presence necessary for a championship quarterback. When Vince Lombardi became head coach of the Packers in 1959 he too shared in that assessment, and like Starr's previous coaches, badgered the quarterback to assert himself. In time, Lombardi recognized that Starr's future depended upon quiet encouragement instead of public humiliation. Starr responded, embracing Lombardi's single-minded will to succeed and dogged preparation for games. Starr's liabilities—his quiet focus and selflessness—became advantages for the team, which needed a firm but unassuming presence amidst Lombardi's tumultuous personality. By mid-1961, Starr was the starter for good. ''Everything I am as a man and a football player I owe to Vince Lombardi,'' Starr later told *Sport* magazine. ''He is the man who taught me everything I know about football, about leadership, about life. He took a kid and made a man out of him, with his example, with his faith.''

Starr developed into an inspiring leader and one of the most efficient passers in the history of football. A clever quarterback who expertly read defenses and studied game films year-round, he set NFL records for the lowest percentage of passes intercepted in a season (1.2 percent), fewest interceptions in a full season (3), and lifetime passing completion percentage (57.4 percent). In 1964 and 1965 he threw a record 294 passes without throwing an interception.

Starr came to symbolize the clutch player, creating a model for later NFL quarterbacks like Terry Bradshaw and Joe Montana. His post-season quarterback rating set records as the highest in NFL history. In six NFL championship games he threw 11 touchdowns but only one interception. Starr made big plays, too. Most famously, he engineered ''The Drive'' in the final moments of the 1967 NFL Championship game against the Dallas Cowboys. One of the most famous series in the history of professional football, The Drive culminated in Starr's quarterback sneak behind Jerry Kramer to give the Packers the victory in the game later known as the ''Ice Bowl.''

Throughout all his successes and his failures, like his disappointing nine years as head coach of the Packers from 1974 to 1983, Starr retained his likeable, modest, hard-working personality. After coaching, he remained in Green Bay, setting up businesses in Wisconsin and his home state of Alabama, and working for charitable causes. To many, he will always be the sturdy conscience behind the Packer dynasty.

—Alexander Shashko

FURTHER READING:

Devaney, John. *Bart Starr.* New York, Scholastic Book Services, 1967.

Gruver, Ed. *The Ice Bowl: The Cold Truth About Football's Most Unforgettable Game.* Ithaca, New York, McBooks Press, 1998.

Starr, Bart, with Muray Olderman. *Starr.* New York, William Morrow, 1987.

Starr, Kenneth (1946—)

Kenneth Starr will be remembered in the popular imagination as the soft-spoken but tenacious Republican special prosecutor locked in mortal combat with Democratic President William Jefferson Clinton and his White House—a battle which culminated in impeachment proceedings for only the second time in U.S. history. Starr, a former Federal Appeals Court judge and solicitor general under President George Bush, was appointed as Independent Counsel by U.S. Attorney General Janet Reno in 1994 to investigate allegations of wrongdoing by the former Arkansas governor William Jefferson Clinton, his wife Hillary Rodham Clinton, and their various business and personal associates. Starr's investigation, which began as an attempt to ascertain if the President and First Lady had illegally benefited from a land deal in Arkansas, culminated in the referral of a controversial report to the U.S. House of Representatives regarding President Clinton's affair with a 21-year-old White House intern named Monica Lewinsky. The story of the affair, and the legal clash between Starr and Clinton, dominated the media during 1998 and well into 1999.

Kenneth Starr

From the beginning of his investigation, Starr was accused of partisan bias and conflict of interest, particularly in representing tobacco companies for his law firm of Kirkland & Ellis and nearly filing a Supreme Court brief in support of Paula Jones's sexual harassment suit against Bill Clinton. The charges against Starr intensified when the Lewinsky story broke in January of 1998. Though Starr had received permission from a three-judge panel and the Attorney General to expand his Whitewater investigation to include the Lewinsky matter, critics took issue with some of the Office of the Independent Counsel's legal tactics, such as its wiring of a Pentagon employee named Linda Tripp to record Lewinsky, its justification for expanding the investigation, and its subpoenaing of sympathetic witnesses such as Betty Currie (the President's personal secretary) and Monica Lewinsky's mother. Seemingly unheedful of his public relations problems even as the President's approval ratings climbed, Starr pressed forward with his grand jury investigation throughout the first half of 1998. For months, the President stood by his initial denial of having had "sexual relations" with Lewinsky, but before Starr's grand jury on August 17, the President reluctantly admitted to at least some details of what he called an "inappropriate relationship."

The Starr Report, submitted to Congress on September 9, 1998, and quickly released to the American public both on the Internet and through various publishers, was widely criticized not only for its omission of most matters relating to the original Whitewater investigation, but for its explicitness in detailing specific sexual encounters between President Clinton and Ms. Lewinsky. Starr's office and its defenders argued that the detail was unfortunate but necessary in order to prove that the President had obstructed justice and committed perjury first in a deposition in the Paula Jones sexual harassment case against him and later before the grand jury investigating the matter. The referral went to the House Judiciary Committee, charged with the task of debating and drawing up articles of impeachment against the President. Starr himself appeared before the committee in order to defend his office's investigation and the report that resulted. Following often acrimonious debate between Republicans and Democrats in the Judiciary Committee, President Clinton was formally impeached on December 19, 1998, on a mostly party-line vote by the full House on two charges of obstructing justice and committing perjury before a federal grand jury—only the second such presidential impeachment in American history. The Senate declined to remove the President from office. The man singly most responsible for the President's impeachment, Kenneth Starr, remained as Independent Counsel into 1999, though analysts predicted that the case against Clinton would go no further.

—Philip L. Simpson

FURTHER READING:

Bugliosi, Vincent. *No Island of Sanity: Paula Jones v. Bill Clinton: The Supreme Court on Trial.* New York, Ballantine, 1998.

Carville, James. *—And the Horse He Rode in on: The People v. Kenneth Starr.* New York, Simon & Schuster, 1998.

Coulter, Ann. *High Crimes and Misdemeanors: The Case against Bill Clinton.* Lanham, Maryland, Regnery, 1998.

Dershowitz, Alan. *Sexual McCarthyism: Clinton, Starr, and the Emerging Constitutional Crisis.* New York, Basic Books, 1998.

Drew, Elizabeth. *On the Edge: The Clinton Presidency.* New York, Simon & Schuster, 1994.

Kurtz, Howard. *Spin Cycle: How the White House and the Media Manipulate the News.* New York, Simon & Schuster, 1998.

The Starr Report. New York, Pocket, 1998.

The Starr Report: The Evidence. New York, Pocket, 1998.

Stewart, James B. *Bloodsport: The President and His Adversaries.* New York, Touchstone, 1997.

Starsky and Hutch

A popular detective show during the 1970s, *Starsky and Hutch* (1975-1979) brought violence on television to the forefront of national debate in that decade. Shot in Los Angeles, but set in a city that was never named, *Starsky and Hutch*—unlike previous detective shows—featured a shootout and a car chase in each episode. The show starred dark haired Paul Michael Glaser as the wisecracking, street smart David Starsky and blue-eyed blonde David Soul as the educated, soft-spoken Ken ''Hutch'' Hutchinson. Every week, the two undercover

police officers came in contact with big city criminals, drug dealers, prostitutes, mobsters, cultists, and murderers, and managed to catch the bad guys in less than 60 minutes while wearing skin tight bell bottom pants. Drawing inspiration from hit movies like *The French Connection,* the capture of the criminal always required a car chase, which featured Starsky's prize possession, the ''red tomato,'' a 1974 Ford Torino with a white racing stripe.

When the show debuted on ABC in 1975, much was written about the chemistry between the two lead actors. *Starsky and Hutch* was one of the first shows where men could be friends and openly care about each other. These two young, hip, bachelor plain clothes detectives were as vulnerable as they were tough. Not afraid to hug each other, they were a far cry from the cardboard Joe Fridays and Mike Stones that preceded them, and the relationship between the two men had sensitive qualities rarely—if ever—seen before on television.

The show also featured blaxploitation film star Antonio Vargas as the flamboyant Huggy Bear, a con man who moonlighted as a police informant, and had the fashion sense of a pimp. *Starsky and Hutch*'s boss was Captain Harold Dobey, played by Bernie Hamilton. Captain Dobey, a member of the old guard, often butted heads with his two new-breed detectives about the manner in which police work should be done. The gruff-but-lovable Dobey was a glimpse of what would later become a staple in many television cop dramas—the

David Soul (left) and Paul Michael Glaser as *Starsky and Hutch*.

almost one dimensional African-American police boss. The use of the African-American actor as a supervisor in these kinds of dramas became very popular in the 1990s, with the likes of *Homicide*'s Lieutenant Al Giardello, *NYPD Blue*'s Lieutenant Arthur Fancy and *Law and Order*'s Lieutenant Anita Van Buren.

William Blinn created the show. Aaron Spelling and Leonard Goldberg acted as executive producers and produced 92 episodes of *Starsky and Hutch,* which ended its television run in 1979. Glaser and Soul directed several episodes of the show themselves, which was unusual for actors at the time. In subsequent decades, the practice of stars performing directing and producing duties would become more common.

Starsky and Hutch's influence can be seen in TV cop shows in which the partners have a very close relationship. But the good looking hipster cops were descendants of television's *The Mod Squad* (1968-1973), and they were part of a post-*Serpico* spate of cop narratives, including *Baretta* and *Toma,* which depicted law enforcement's battle with the dark side of America's crime-ridden urban landscape. The contentious relationship they had with their superior has become a staple in cop dramas. The violence in the show, shocking in 1975, seems tame by later standards.

In the late 1990s, though it had been off the air for a couple of decades and had not been a terribly popular network choice for reruns, *Starsky and Hutch* surfaced in a rather odd way. An August 18, 1997 *New York Times* article by Amy Harmon about fan fiction, an Internet phenomenon in which fans write and post new episodes of their favorite shows, mentions *Starsky and Hutch* as a favorite of the ''slash'' genre writers and readers. In ''slash'' fan fiction, the sexual orientation of the main characters has been changed, and in 1999, there were about a dozen web pages devoted to the homoerotic exploits of the two detectives.

—Joyce Linehan

State Fairs

A reflection of American life and its diverse people and interests, state fairs featuring exhibits, rides, shows, and food have been popular since the mid-nineteenth century and became an American tradition in the twentieth. The pride, nostalgia, and entertainment that make up a state fair experience have transcended political, social, and economic changes that America has faced during the twentieth century. By the 1990s state fairs have come to represent a nostalgic, ''old-fashioned'' form of family entertainment that emphasizes state and national pride, agricultural roots, and good times.

Fairs have existed for centuries and can even be dated back to ancient Mesopotamia in 3000 B.C. Modern American fairs grew out of an 1807 idea by Elkanah Watson, a banker and farmer in Pittsfield, Massachusetts. He decided that the best way to convince other farmers to raise sheep was to show them his own animals. The townspeople were so impressed with Watson's idea that they gathered together to form the first Berkshire Cattle Show in 1810. Although many people were concerned about attending a nonreligious celebration, Watson convinced the people of New England that the show was an acceptable event for upstanding citizens because of its importance

to the business of farming and its educational value. Throughout the next decade the show expanded to include men's and women's manufacturing exhibits, a parade, and a dance. The fair quickly spread throughout the United States, and by the time of the Civil War, agricultural societies in 25 states were holding annual fairs.

With the success of county and local agricultural fairs, state governments quickly realized that fairs could be used to highlight the growth and achievements of their states. New York held the first state fair in September 1841, and several states in the Midwest quickly followed its example. State fairs were among the first places in the nation where people could see electric lights, automobiles, solar homes, and dozens of other modern inventions. Railroads contributed to the popularity of state fairs by allowing people to travel quickly and cheaply. Some railroads even provided discounts for exhibitors and families going to the fair. People attended the early state fairs in overwhelming numbers and still do: more than 900,000 people attended the 1997 Ohio State Fair, the second largest state fair next to Texas.

State fairs attempt to feature the most appealing aspects of their respective state. Each year people who have made a difference, such as sports heroes, celebrities, teachers, and activists are chosen to be recognized at the state fair. In cooperation with the state wildlife bureau, many state fairs offer an area showcasing native birds and animals. Prominent businesses, churches, and social organizations highlight their own achievements. Each organization is given a booth in which it can introduce people to its work. Visitors shopping for certain items are offered a large selection, while those who are just browsing are introduced to many new and exciting people and goods that they may not have known existed. Agriculture continues to be a vital component of state fairs in the twentieth century. Exhibits of farm machinery and tools are common. Competitions for crops and farm animals remain much the same as in the nineteenth century, except that advances in technology have allowed for stronger and healthier crops and livestock.

Young people are an important part of the state fair experience. Their presence allows older people to recall their own experiences at fairs past, and their participation helps to forge a new bond between the young and the old that often does not exist the rest of the year. High school marching bands come from around the state to play at the fair. Youth groups such as the 4-H, Future Farmers of America, and Girl and Boy Scouts hold competitions for raising animals, cooking, sewing, woodworking, citizenship, art, and gardening. In the 1970s, 1980s, and 1990s many young people who participated in state fairs were far removed from the rural farm setting of the traditional fairgoers. Encouraged by their parents' fond memories, young people living in urban areas often will concentrate on home manufacturing areas or raise small animals.

Mechanical rides became common at state fairs in the years following their introduction at the 1893 world's fair in Chicago. The Ferris wheel, first introduced there, became a hit at state fairs around the nation and remained popular throughout the twentieth century. In the 1990s, a state fair would not be complete without a diverse and abundant selection of rides for people of all ages. The Bumper Cars, the Himalaya, and the Scrambler are just a few of the rides that have kept Americans returning to the state fair since the 1950s. State fair rides are popular with teenagers and have been romanticized as the starting place for many first dates.

A State Fair in Louisville.

Sideshows featuring multiheaded people or animals, bearded women, and extra-human contortionists are expected at state fairs and were once part of the novelty of discovery that made up the fair. Since the 1970s, however, sideshows have declined in popularity and presence at state fairs, either because of an effort to provide ''wholesome'' entertainment for families or simply due to lack of interest. Nonetheless, sideshows remain part of the nostalgic image of state fairs.

Food is an essential part of the state fair experience. French fries, coney dogs, Polish sausage, cotton candy, and apple pie fill the air with a smell that only a state fair can create. State fairs often offer specialty foods that are made of locally grown ingredients, but many foods highlight the ethnic diversity of the state. It is common for a single state fair to have food from dozens of countries around the world—Mexican, Greek, Chinese, Polish, and German are especially popular—creating a common ground where ethnic and racial tensions present in everyday life may be muted.

Since the 1950s, state fairs have offered shows featuring popular musical groups of many different styles—rock, Christian, blues, folk, gospel, and even some classical. Country music is usually the most popular, however. In the 1980s and 1990s, country musicians Alabama, Willie Nelson, and Garth Brooks sold out shows at state fairs around the country. While big names such as these do attract crowds, other sorts of shows such as rodeos, exhibition sporting events, and magic shows are also popular and can sometimes attract crowds as large as those for concerts.

—Angela O'Neal

FURTHER READING:

Alter, Judy. *Meet Me at the Fair.* New York, Franklin Watts, 1997.

Auger, Helen. *The Book of Fairs.* New York, Harcourt, Brace and Company, 1939.

Braden, Donna. *Leisure and Entertainment in America.* Detroit, Wayne State University Press, 1998.

Dellinger, H. Paul. *Fairs Are for Everybody.* N.p., 1965.

Perl, Lila. *America Goes to the Fair: All about State and County Fairs in the USA.* New York, William Morrow and Company, 1974.

Rydell, Robert W. *All the World's a Fair.* Chicago, The University of Chicago Press, 1984.

Staubach, Roger (1942-)

In his eleven-year career with the Dallas Cowboys from 1969 to 1979, quarterback Roger Staubach frequently engaged in last-second heroics to help his team to two Super Bowl victories and four National Football Conference titles.

A native of Cincinnati, Ohio, Staubach played quarterback for the United States Naval Academy, where he won the 1963 Heisman Trophy, awarded to the top player in college football each season. Staubach was drafted by the Cowboys in the tenth round of the 1964 NFL draft, but first served in the navy for four years before beginning his professional career.

After Staubach began his career with the Cowboys in 1969, he played sparingly during his first several seasons, when Dallas Coach Tom Landry was using Craig Morton as the team's starting quarterback. In 1971, Dallas had suffered a disappointing 16-13 loss to the Baltimore Colts in Super Bowl V, and the following season, Landry decided that he would give Staubach the opportunity to compete for the job of starting quarterback. At the end of preseason, Landry decided to alternate Staubach and Morton at the position during 1971-72, a situation which did not seem to work out particularly well, as the

Roger Staubach

team lacked cohesion in the early part of the regular season. However, in mid-season, Landry made Staubach the starting quarterback, and he responded by leading the Cowboys to the Super Bowl. Staubach earned the Most Valuable Player Award in Super Bowl VI in 1972, as his Dallas Cowboys defeated the Miami Dolphins by a score of 24-3. Staubach completed 12 out of the 19 passes that he attempted, for 119 yards and two touchdowns.

Staubach had little chance to savor his success, however, for he badly separated his right shoulder in a game the following preseason, which required surgery and caused him to miss much of the 1972 regular season. Staubach's injury came while he tried to fight through several defenders in an attempt to score, a style unlike that of most other quarterbacks, who generally try as hard as possible to avoid physical contact on the playing field.

Staubach was able to return later that season, however, and in the 1972 playoffs, he delivered a performance that defined much of the rest of his career and earned him the title "Captain Comeback." He entered a first-round game against the San Francisco 49ers with his team trailing at the end of the third quarter and the 49ers already beginning their celebration. Staubach, however, led the Cowboys to two dramatic touchdowns in the last two minutes and an improbable come-from-behind 30-28 victory. Despite Staubach's heroics, the Cowboys lost that season's NFC title game 26-3 against the Washington Redskins.

The Cowboys reached the Super Bowl three times in the late 1970s with Staubach at quarterback. Twice, in Super Bowls X and XIII, they lost to Pittsburgh teams that were considered by many to be among the greatest of all time. However, the Cowboys defeated the Denver Broncos in Super Bowl XII in 1978 by a 27-10 score, giving Staubach his second Super Bowl victory. In that game, Staubach threw a 45-yard touchdown pass in the third quarter to give the Cowboys an insurmountable 20-3 lead. During this period, the Cowboys came to be known as "America's Team."

Staubach retired following the 1979 season, despite the fact that at 37, he was still playing at a very high level. The quarterback, however, cited a desire to spend more time with his family, a declining enthusiasm for football, and concern over the possibility of permanent injuries, as he had already suffered numerous concussions and a variety of other physical problems as a result of his tenacious style of play.

Staubach was enshrined in the Professional Football Hall of Fame in Canton, Ohio in 1985. He was the leading passer in the NFL during four of his 11 seasons, and was an All-NFC selection four times during his career. "Captain Comeback" also managed to lead the Cowboys to 21 come-from-behind victories in the fourth period, living up to his nickname.

—Jason George

FURTHER READING:

"Roster of Enshrinees: Roger Staubach." http://www.profootball-hof.com/enshrinees/staubach.html. April 1999.

St. John, Bob. *The Landry Legend: Grace Under Pressure.* Dallas, Word Publishing, 1989.

Staubach, Roger, with Frank Luksa. *Time Enough to Win.* Waco, Texas, Word Books, 1980.

Steamboat Willie

Premiering in 1928, *Steamboat Willie* was the first of Disney's Mickey Mouse cartoons to feature sound, which helped to launch the character's phenomenal career. Unlike other cartoons of the time where sound served simply as a background to the action, both music and sound effects were essential to the film's structure and visual rhythm. The clever animal concert (in which Mickey plays a cow's teeth like a xylophone and transforms a nursing sow into a bagpipe) illustrates Disney's ability to successfully blend sight and sound, so that neither element dominates the other. It also anticipates the complex musical sequences, featured in later films like *Fantasia,* which transformed the art of animation and became key to Disney's financial success.

—Scott W. Hoffman

FURTHER READING:

Maltin, Leonard. *Of Mice and Magic: A History of American Animated Cartoons.* New York, McGraw-Hill Company, 1980.

Schickel, Richard. *The Disney Version: The Life, Times, Art and Commerce of Walt Disney.* New York, Simon and Schuster: 1968.

Watts, Steven. *The Magic Kingdom: Walt Disney and the American Way of Life.* New York, Houghton Mifflin Company, 1997.

The Steel Curtain

The Steel Curtain was the name given to the defensive line of the Pittsburgh Steelers football team during their glory days in the 1970s. Composed of L. C. Greenwood, Ernie Holmes, "Mean" Joe Greene, and Dwight White, the four members of the Steel Curtain routinely dominated the opposition, crushing opposing running backs and sacking quarterbacks. Although the Steelers defensive unit as a whole was one of the greatest of all time, it was the Steel Curtain that was the focus of public attention. Joe Greene, the leader of the Steel Curtain and two-time Defensive Player of the Year, was also a media celebrity in his own right. Greene appeared in one of the most famous soft-drink advertisements in television history. The advertisement featured Greene trading his football jersey to a small child in exchange for a bottle of Coca-Cola.

—Geoff Peterson

FURTHER READING:

Bouchette, E. *The Pittsburgh Steelers.* New York, St. Martin's Press, 1994.

Livingston, P. *The Pittsburgh Steelers: A Pictorial History.* Virginia Beach, Virginia, Jordan & Co. Publishers, 1980.

Steffens, Lincoln (1866-1936)

At the beginning of the twentieth century, when corruption in city government ran rampant in large American cities, one of the original muckrakers—so named by Theodore Roosevelt for their aggressive journalistic tactics in investigating controversial stories—was Lincoln Steffens. Steffens hounded corrupt city officials all across the United States. He faced numerous death threats and stood up to local political machines in many cities, including Pittsburgh, New York City, and Minneapolis. His first effort at a story came in Philadelphia, where he compared the local extortionists' control of the city voting to that of the disenfranchisement of African-Americans in the South. He wrote in *McClure's* magazine, "The honest citizens of Philadelphia have no more rights at the polls than the Negroes in the South." Over the course of his career, Steffen's muckraking led to the indictment of eighteen municipal legislators in St. Louis and the ouster of twenty corrupt city councilman in Chicago. Through the journalistic ideology of muckraking, Steffens challenged the way in which city business was done and set a standard many others would follow.

Lincoln Steffens was born in 1866 in San Francisco. He failed his first attempt at the entrance exam to the University of California-Berkley. On his second try he succeeded and graduated in 1889 with a degree in philosophy. In 1891, Steffens moved to Paris and married Josephine Bontecou. He returned to New York City in 1892 after landing a job with the *New York Evening Post.* He later became managing editor of *McClure's,* joining other muckrakers like Ida Tarbell and Ray Stannard Baker. In a nationwide publication, Steffens exposed corrupt city officials, who often received and gave bribes, and bought and sold privilege at all levels. Steffens published six articles on corruption in local city governments and these articles formed the hallmark on city reform for the next half-century. The six articles were published together in a book in 1904. *Shame of the Cities* quickly became a bestseller and stood out for its prose and style.

Lincoln Steffens' public call for the end of democracy led to a permanent split with *McClure's.* In 1906, he became co-owner of *American* magazine, but sold his shares in 1907, after a little more than a year. By 1910, Steffens had become disillusioned with muckraking and concerned himself with the radical revolutionaries in Mexico. This involvement led him to become even more skeptical of capitalism. In 1917, he traveled to Soviet Union, proclaimed himself a Marxist, and joined the Communist Party. At the conclusion of the Great War, Steffens attended the 1919 Paris Peace Conference at Versailles. After leaving Paris, Steffens returned to the United States and embarked on a cross-country tour promoting the Bolshevik Revolution. By late 1921, Steffens was pressured out of America with the onset of the first Red Scare. He first returned to Paris then later moved to Italy, where he wrote his autobiography in 1931. *The Autobiography of Lincoln Steffens,* and its theme of an intellectual reformer turned revolutionary, appealed to many during the Great Depression. The book, with its witty, charming, and compassionate narrative, sold well in the United States and laid the groundwork for autobiographical style for years to come. Steffens moved back to the United States in 1927 and died in 1936 in Carmel, California. He is buried in San Francisco. Lincoln Steffens' life will be remembered for many achievements in journalism. He helped end city corruption, published two popular books nearly thirty years apart, and became the first truly revolutionary writer. Steffens has left his mark on journalistic history.

—Scott Stabler

FURTHER READING:

Connery, Thomas, ed. *A Sourcebook of American Literary Journalism: Representative Writers in an Emerging Genre.* New York, Greenwood Press, 1992.

Palermo, Patrick. *Lincoln Steffens.* Boston, Twayne Publishers, 1978.

Steffens, Lincoln. *The Autobiography of Lincoln Steffens.* New York, Harcourt, Brace, and Co., 1931.

———. *Shame of the Cities.* New York, P. Smith, 1904.

Stinson, Robert. *Lincoln Steffens.* New York, F. Ungar Publishing Co., 1979.

Steinbeck, John (1902-1968)

A native Californian, writer John Steinbeck built his career on stories based primarily in Northern and Central California, around his hometown of Salinas, near Monterey. Best known for the novels *Of Mice and Men* (1937), *The Grapes of Wrath* (1939), and *East of Eden* (1952), along with numerous short stories, Steinbeck also published non-fiction, plays, and screenplays. He was awarded the Pulitzer Prize for *The Grapes of Wrath,* and, in 1962, he received the Nobel Prize for Literature. Steinbeck's works have been widely read and have been the subject of many motion pictures.

Born John Ernest Steinbeck in the fertile valley of Salinas, California, inland from Monterey Bay, Steinbeck grew up in an

John Steinbeck

environment caught between the transition from farming and ranching to the "respectable culture" of universities and businessmen. Steinbeck's parents were middle-class citizens of Salinas (his father served as Monterey County Treasurer and his mother was a schoolteacher), but John himself often worked as a laborer on nearby farms. Attending Stanford University as a marine biology major, Steinbeck left without completing his degree, having made the decision to try making his living at writing, first in New York and then back in California. His early works, *Cup of Gold* (1929), *Pastures of Heaven* (1932), and *To A God Unknown* (1933), went largely unnoticed until the publication of *Tortilla Flats* (1935), which described the exploits of a group of *Paisanos* (Mexican-Americans) living in Monterey. Steinbeck's reputation as an advocate for farm labor organization began with the publication of *In Dubious Battle* (1936), which recounts the efforts of farm labor organizers during a fruit pickers strike. His next work, *Of Mice and Men* (1937), was first conceived as a stage play and was produced simultaneously as a play and a novel. The play received the Drama Critics' Circle Award, and the novel, the compelling story of two itinerant farm hands, firmly established Steinbeck as a major California writer.

Steinbeck's most acclaimed work, *The Grapes of Wrath* (1939), has become a classic work of the Depression era. The book was awarded the Pulitzer Prize in 1940 in addition to being made into a classic motion picture by John Ford that same year. Following the success of *The Grapes of Wrath*, Steinbeck concentrated on non-fiction works such as *Sea of Cortez* (with Edward F. Ricketts, 1941) and *Bombs Away: The Story of a Bomber Team* (1942). During World War II, he worked as a war correspondent—his articles were published collectively as *Once There was a War* in 1958. He returned to fiction with *Cannery Row* (1945), *Sweet Thursday* (1954), *The Red Pony* (1945), *The Pearl* (1947), and his most ambitious novel, *East Of Eden* (1952), which tells the stories of three generations of the Trask family, focusing on the conflict between two brothers. In the 1960s Steinbeck once again returned to non-fiction with *Travels with Charly in Search of America* (1962) and *America and Americans* (1966). In addition to having many of his works adapted for the screen, including *Of Mice and Men* (1939 and 1992), *The Grapes of Wrath* (1940), *Tortilla Flat* (1942), *The Moon is Down* (1943), *The Pearl* (1947), *The Red Pony* (1949), *East of Eden* (1955), and *Cannery Row* (1982), Steinbeck himself wrote several original screenplays, including Alfred Hitchcock's *Lifeboat* (1944) and Elia Kazan's *Viva Zapata* (1952).

In his acceptance speech for the Nobel Prize, Steinbeck described his belief in the power of literature to improve the condition of humankind: "I hold that a writer who does not passionately believe in the perfectibility of man has no dedication nor any membership in literature." The realism of his writing, along with the intensity of his belief in the transformative power of literature, has helped develop an American literary style, which influenced the protest writings, both literary and musical, of the late 1950s and 1960s.

—Charles J. Shindo

FURTHER READING:

Benson, Jackson J. *The True Adventures of John Steinbeck, Writer.* New York, Viking, 1984.

Davis, Robert. *Steinbeck: A Collection of Critical Essays.* Englewood Cliffs, New Jersey, Prentice-Hall, 1972.

Fensch, Thomas. *Conversations with John Steinbeck.* Jackson, University of Mississippi Press, 1988.

Lisca, Peter. *John Steinbeck: Nature and Myth.* New York, Thomas Y. Crowell, 1978.

Steinbeck, Elaine, and Robert Wallsten, editors. *Steinbeck: A Life in Letters.* New York, Viking Penguin, 1975.

Steinbeck, John. *The Portable Steinbeck.* New York, Viking, 1946.

Steinberg, Saul (1914-1999)

Best known for the hundreds of enigmatic, captionless drawings and frequent covers he has contributed to the highbrow *New Yorker* magazine since 1941, the Romanian-born, world-traveled Saul Steinberg has employed in his long career an eclectic range of media and styles that are rarely straightforward and frequently attest to his literary and philosophical musings. Steinberg has often incorporated the likes of unintelligible calligraphy, watercolor, rubber stamps, tracings, thumbprints, graph paper, and collage into his pen-and-ink drawings for books and magazines. Recurring themes have included the relationships among abstract concepts, as in "Ship of State" (1959), and places he has known, such as "Bleecker Street" (1971), in which a parade of street characters are rendered in dozens of cartoon styles. Few have so successfully blurred the line between popular and high art as Steinberg.

—Craig Bunch

FURTHER READING:

Rosenberg, Harold. *Saul Steinberg.* New York, Alfred A. Knopf and the Whitney Museum of American Art, 1978.

Steinbrenner, George (1930—)

The word "controversial" has preceded the name George Steinbrenner ever since the multimillionaire shipbuilder from Cleveland became the principal owner of the New York Yankees in 1973. Considered to have been the driving force behind baseball's escalating salary structure in the late 1970s and 1980s, Steinbrenner was loathed for his frequent criticism of his players and managers while being credited with bringing winning baseball back to New York City. Never one to shy away from the media limelight, Steinbrenner's brash personality and penchant for grabbing newspaper headlines often overshadowed his team's play on the field.

With his father's retirement from the family shipping business in 1963, George M. Steinbrenner III, a former football player for Ohio State University, was called upon to take over the company. With the millions he made in business, Steinbrenner returned to the sports world, attempting in the early 1970s to acquire the Cleveland Indians. When that deal fell through, Steinbrenner's attention turned to the floundering New York Yankees, then owned by the Columbia Broadcast System. In 1973, CBS sold the team to a syndicate headed by Steinbrenner for $10 million. Although he had vowed not to take a prominent role in running the club, the new Yankees president soon became one of the most controversial owners in the game.

After a decade of disappointing seasons, under the new ownership the Yankees quickly became competitive again, finishing a close second in 1974, followed by a pennant in 1976, and world championships in 1977 and 1978. Through a series of shrewd trades and large free-agent contracts, "Boss" Steinbrenner had brought winning baseball back to New York. On New Year's Eve 1974 he signed American League Cy Young Award winner Jim "Catfish" Hunter to a five-year contract worth an estimated (and unprecedented) $3.75 million, following this up in later years with huge contracts to sluggers Reggie Jackson, Dave Winfield, and many other players.

Although successful on the baseball diamond during his first decade with the Yankees, Steinbrenner's tenure was marred by legal battles and feuds with managers and players. In 1974, baseball's commissioner Bowie Kuhn barred Steinbrenner from serving as Yankees president for one season for having made illegal contributions to President Richard Nixon's campaign two years earlier. Steinbrenner's tempestuous relationship with his managers began with the resignation of longtime manager Ralph Houk after the 1973 season. Over the next 20 years Steinbrenner made 18 more managerial moves involving 12 different managers. His most turbulent relationship was with former Yankees second baseman Billy Martin, who was first hired as the Yankees' manager in 1975 and first fired in 1978—a sequence that was repeated four more times before Martin's last firing in 1988. After being dismissed 16 games into the 1985 season, Yankees manager (and former star catcher and fan favorite) Yogi Berra vowed never to set foot in Yankee stadium again as long as Steinbrenner continued to run the Yankees.

Despite the team's success on the field, in the late 1970s and early 1980s the Yankee clubhouse was awhirl in controversy. As Yankee third baseman Graig Nettles recalled, "When I was a little boy, I wanted to be a baseball player and join the circus. With the Yankees, I've accomplished both." Egos clashed in the Yankee clubhouse with the arrival of highly paid free agents. Outfielder Reggie Jackson, signed to a record-setting, free-agent contract in 1977, made himself unwelcome to his Yankee teammates even before his arrival when he announced, "I'm the straw that stirs the drink." Though dubbed "Mr. October" for his World Series heroics, Jackson's five years with the Yankees were marked by a love-hate relationship with Steinbrenner and an even more acrimonious relationship with manager Billy Martin, who once said of Jackson and Steinbrenner that "One is a born liar, the other convicted." The animosity shared by many players toward the team's owner—despite all the big contracts—was partly fueled by Steinbrenner's frequent public criticisms of his players, including an apology to the city of New York after the team's poor performance in the 1981 World Series.

Steinbrenner's years with the Yankees reached an all-time low in 1990, when after a decade of steady decline the team finished in last place for the first time since 1966. That year Steinbrenner once again found himself embroiled in controversy when Commissioner Fay Vincent learned that the Yankees owner had paid a professional gambler named Howard Spira $40,000 to dig up damaging information on Dave Winfield, a player with whom Steinbrenner had feuded for nine years (Steinbrenner unfavorably compared the millionaire outfielder to Reggie Jackson by sticking Winfield with the demeaning moniker "Mr. May"). On July 30, 1990, Steinbrenner agreed to resign permanently as general managing partner of the Yankees for his violation of "the best interests of baseball" rule.

Steinbrenner's campaign to have himself reinstated brought success in July 1992, when the outgoing Vincent lifted the ban,

George Steinbrenner

effective March 1, 1993. The seasons that followed proved to be among the most placid—and successful—in the history of the Steinbrenner era. Steinbrenner now seemed to defer more often to the expertise of his front office staff, and Yankee field managers breathed easier. In the strike-plagued year of 1994 the Yankees finished in first place for the first time since 1981. Under the calm leadership of manager Joe Torre, in 1996 the Yankees staged an unlikely come-from-behind World Series victory over the defending champs (Atlanta Braves). However, Steinbrenner's greatest baseball success came two years later, when the Yankees astounded the baseball world by winning 114 games en route to their second world championship in three years. What made this team different from the rowdy 1970s crew was that these Yankees seemed to actually like each other, and their visibly mellowed owner appeared content to avoid controversy. For once, Steinbrenner remained silent while the accomplishments of the team itself received most of the attention.

—Kevin O'Connor

FURTHER READING:

Jacobson, Steve. *The Best Team Money Could Buy: The Turmoil and Triumph of the 1977 Yankees.* New York, Atheneum, 1978.

Lyle, Sparky and Peter Golenbock. *The Bronx Zoo.* New York, Crown, 1979.

Madden, Bill and Moss Klein. *Damned Yankees: A No-Holds-Barred Account of Life With ''Boss'' Steinbrenner.* New York, Warner, 1991.

Schaap, Dick. *Steinbrenner!* New York, Putnam, 1982.

Steinem, Gloria (1934—)

American feminist and journalist Gloria Steinem is perhaps the most visible representative of the women's rights movement, an effort that has resulted in immeasurable effects in contemporary society. She is best known for founding the groundbreaking women's magazine *Ms.* in the early 1970s and for being heavily involved in spearheading the drive to ratify the Equal Rights Amendment, which, although it was never adopted, generated a maelstrom of dialogue on the topic and contributed to a new consciousness for women in America. Though more radical feminists have criticized Steinem for having too much of a middle-class approach to the struggle, some have noted that her mainstream persona helped make women's rights accessible to a greater number of women.

Steinem was born March 25, 1934, in Toledo, Ohio, to Leo and Ruth (Nunevillar) Steinem. When she was a youth, her parents divorced, leaving her mother—who had already been prone to nervous breakdown—extremely depressed. Steinem spent much of her youth caring for her incapacitated mother, who enriched her daughter by exposing her to literature and instilling in her a deep respect for others. In high school, Steinem moved to Washington, D.C., to live with her older sister, Suzanne, then went on to attend Smith College. After graduating *magna cum laude* in 1956, Steinem earned a fellowship to study in India, where she learned of the nonviolent philosophy of Mahatma Gandhi.

Steinem returned to the United States and aspired to a career in journalism. In 1960 she began writing for periodicals, and in 1963 went undercover as a Playboy ''bunny,'' a cocktail waitress in the famous men's club, in order to write a wry expose detailing the degradation women faced there. By the late 1960s, Steinem began emerging as a serious journalist when she was tapped to produce a weekly political column for the newly launched *New York* magazine. Brimming with advocacy and pleas for activism, her pieces tackled

subjects ranging from the fight to free Angela Davis, to support of Cesar Chavez and the United Farm Workers, to backing author Norman Mailer in his bid for mayor of New York City. She was not considered a leader in the women's movement until she produced the article ''After Black Power, Women's Liberation'' in 1968, following a meeting by a group called the Redstockings that addressed the issue of abortion.

From 1969 to 1972, Steinem rose to acclaim as a figure head of the women's rights movement. Appearing regularly in the media, she was articulate and humorous, thus endearing many to the cause. She was in stark contrast to the far-left feminists of the day, who quickly earned derision and ridicule by much of the press for their Marxist views and lesbian orientation. In July of 1971, Steinem joined Betty Friedan, Bella Abzug, and Shirley Chisholm to found the National Women's Political Caucus, which supported women running for public office. Also that year, Steinem founded *Ms.,* a magazine by, for, and about women. The first full issue was published in January of 1972 and sold out its print run of 300,000 in just over a week. By summer of 1972, it had become a monthly magazine, financed by

Gloria Steinem

Warner Communications. Beginning in 1979, it operated as a nonprofit organization.

As she gained prominence, Steinem faced opposition from various radical feminist camps because her views did not always agree with theirs. In addition, men from both the conservative and liberal camps were threatened by her attacks on male power as well as issues like pornography, which she opposes. In addition, the Redstockings began accusing Steinem in the mid-1970s of working for the CIA in the 1950s. She had indeed briefly been employed with a liberal student group after college that was funded by the agency, but maintained that she was not aware of the ties. Meanwhile, the Equal Rights Amendment was introduced and passed Congress in 1972. It was a proposed amendment to the Constitution that guaranteed equal rights to women under the law. Though it was never approved, Steinem was one of its leading advocates, helping to stir up debate that went far in changing the role of women in society. Due to this cultural shift, more and more women began entering the work force, thus empowering themselves economically. It became illegal to discriminate against and harass women, and it is no longer legal for a man to rape or beat his wife. As recently as the 1960s, classified ads for jobs were segregated by sex; that practice is no longer acceptable. Though women still may not have achieved the full status of men in American business and politics, the effects of the women's movement on society has been enormous.

Into the 1980s, Steinem continued to urge for more fairness in the treatment of women. She championed the concept of equal pay for equal work and wanted to see it come to fruition, though studies show that it has not yet happened. She also began shifting her focus from mainly financial and job-related issues to a more humanistic approach, hoping to encourage a world where gender lines will not be so strictly defined. Pushing for men to accept more of the responsibility of child-rearing and domestic duties, she espoused that men and women should be less bound by traditional roles in order to make their lives more well-rounded. In 1983 Steinem published a well-received collection of essays titled *Outrageous Acts and Everyday Rebellions.* She also stayed involved with *Ms.,* but in 1987 Australian company John Fairfax, Ltd. bought the magazine and readership fell drastically. The legendary publication was in dire straits. In 1990, it returned without paid advertising. For the first of the new issues, Steinem wrote a scathing commentary on the control that advertisers have in editorial operations of women's magazines. In 1994 she released a new set of essays, *Moving Beyond Words,* and continued to stand as the leading spokesperson for feminist activism in America.

—Geri Speace

FURTHER READING:

Glickman, Simon. "Gloria Steinem." *Newsmakers 1996 Cumulation.* Edited by Louise Mooney Collins and Frank V. Castronova. Detroit, Gale Research, 1996.

Gorney, Cynthia. "Gloria: At 61, Steinem Wants Straight Talk, More Fun, and a New Congress." *Mother Jones.* November-December 1995, 22.

Steinem, Gloria. *Outrageous Acts and Everyday Rebellions.* New York, Penguin, 1983.

Winokur, L.A. "Gloria Steinem." *The Progressive.* June 1995, 34.

Stengel, Casey (1890-1975)

Baseball legend Casey Stengel spent fifty-five years in baseball as both player and manager. He is best remembered for managing the highly successful New York Yankees and the highly unsuccessful New York Mets. While his management skills sustained his career, his outrageous use of the English language gained him equal fame.

He was born Charles Dillon Stengel in Kansas City, Kansas, and began playing semiprofessional baseball while in high school, where he was known as "Dutch" because of his German ancestry. An outfielder, he played with different minor league teams before joining the Brooklyn Dodgers in 1912. It was there he acquired the nickname "K.C." because he was from Kansas City, a nickname that soon eased into "Casey," after the poem *Casey at the Bat.* After Brooklyn, he played major league ball for the Pittsburgh Pirates (1918-19, with time out for the U.S. Navy), Philadelphia Phillies (1920-21), New York Giants (1921-23, where in 1923 he batted .339 and won two World Series games with two home runs), and the Boston Braves (1924-25). He ended his playing career as a player-manager for the minor league Toledo (Ohio) Mud Hens.

Stengel was a jokester and a fighter, and was thrown out of many games both as a player and a manager. For one of his early pranks, he stepped back from the plate, doffed his hat, and out flew a sparrow. The fans loved his antics. Stengel was also famous for his "Stengelese," with statements such as "I've always heard it couldn't be done, but sometimes it don't always work." Yet, he could be succinct and telling: when he married his wife in 1924 he said of himself in the third person, "It is the best catch he ever made in his career." He said of Willie Mays, who played in a notoriously windy Candlestick Park in San Francisco: "If a typhoon is blowing, he catches the ball." Sometimes he could describe someone in a phrase: a nervous batter had "jelly leg," bad players were "road apples," rookies were "green peas," and a player who didn't carouse was a "milkshake drinker."

From 1934 to 1948, Stengel managed the Dodgers, Boston Braves, Milwaukee Brewers, Kansas City Blues, and Oakland Oaks. In October of 1948, the Stengel legend began when he was named manager of the Yankees. In Stengel's first year as manager the Yankees beat the Dodgers in the World Series and went on to win six more out of ten appearances under Stengel, thus being the team to beat in the 1950s. Stengel managed such outstanding players as Joe DiMaggio, Billy Martin, Yogi Berra, and Mickey Mantle. Stengel's critics said that anyone with that kind of talent playing for him could win, and many wouldn't give him credit for his knowledge of baseball and players. "Ability," Stengel once said, "is the art of getting credit for all the home runs someone else hits." His ability ran out when the Yankees lost the World Series to the Pirates in 1960 and he was fired, although the public story was that he was stepping aside as part of a youth movement at the Yankees. A bitter seventy-year-old Stengel quipped: "I'll never make the mistake of being seventy again."

He was down, but not out. A year later he was the manager of the expansion National League New York Mets, a team he was to call the "Amazin' Mets." What was amazing was that they ever took the field. In his four seasons as manager, the team never played better than .327. "The only thing worse than a Mets game was a Mets doubleheader," Stengel once said, and "Without losers, where would the winners be?" But because they were bad, they were endearing and they drew a better crowd than their cross-town rivals, the Yankees, viewed by many as an elitist team.

Casey Stengel (right)

A broken hip finished Stengel's managing career. He retired one month after turning seventy-five. He was inducted into the Hall of Fame on a fast-track vote. The honor was obviously important to him, for afterward he signed his letters ''Casey Stengel, N.Y. Mets & Hall of Famer.'' Stengel died the day after the 1975 season ended.

—R. Thomas Berner

FURTHER READING:

Bak, Richard. *Casey Stengel: A Splendid Baseball Life.* Dallas, Taylor Publishing, 1997.

Berkow, Ira, and Jim Kaplan. *The Gospel According to Casey.* New York, St. Martin's Press, 1992.

Creamer, Robert W. *Stengel: His Life and Times.* New York, Simon and Schuster, 1984.

Durso, Joseph. *Casey: The Life and Legend of Charles Dillon Stengel.* Englewood Cliffs, New Jersey, Prentice-Hall, 1967.

Steppenwolf

With landmark power-chord anthems like ''Born to Be Wild,'' the popular late-1960s band Steppenwolf coined the phrase for the bombastic, fast-paced genre it created: heavy metal, one of the most popular musical styles of the late twentieth century. The group came to prominence in 1969, when ''Born to Be Wild'' was featured in the opening sequence of the landmark film *Easy Rider* (1969). The song became a call-to-arms for a generation of rebellious youth, and its reference to ''heavy metal thunder'' became the tagline for the musical style it adopted. ''Born to Be Wild'' ultimately reached number two on the *Billboard* singles chart that year. By 1999, the song had appeared in more than sixty films and television programs.

Steppenwolf's founder and lead vocalist John Kay was born as Joachim Krauledat in the former East Germany in 1944, where he grew up listening to an Armed Forces Radio playlist that featured American blues-rock artists such as Chuck Berry and Little Richard. Emigrating to Toronto in the early 1960s, Kay joined a local blues

Steppenwolf

band known as The Sparrows. After attempts to record with The Sparrows for Columbia Records, Kay left the group, relocating to New York and later to San Francisco. In 1967, he formed Steppenwolf, named after the novel by Herman Hesse. The band featured guitarist Michael Monarch, keyboard player Goldy McJohn, drummer Jerry Edmonton, and bass player Rushton Moreve, later replaced by John Morgan.

Steppenwolf's eponymous debut album, released in 1968, belied some of Kay's blues influences as well as the group's ties to the Bay Area psychedelia scene. However, it was the fierce power-chord stomp "Born to Be Wild" that captured the counterculture's imagination. Steppenwolf largely forsook its blues influences to hone this tough hard-rock sound on its next two albums, *The Second* (1968) and *At Your Birthday Party* (1969). The albums spawned two Top Ten hits, "Magic Carpet Ride" and "Rock Me," as well as a host of heavy metal classics such as "Move Over" and "Hey Lawdy Mama." The band reached its creative peak in 1970 with the release of *Monster,* a concept album based on Kay's jaundiced view of contemporary America. *Monster* featured newcomers Larry Byrom on guitar and Nick St. Nicholas on bass, both former members of the band called Time.

Constrained by the pressure of making music for bikers and frustrated by continued personnel turnover, Kay disbanded Steppenwolf in 1972. After a less-than-successful solo career, Kay reconstituted the band in 1980 with Ron Hurst on drums and longtime writing partner Michael Wilk on keyboards and bass. This most recent incarnation of Steppenwolf had produced five albums as of 1999, but none had enjoyed the commercial success of the group's 1960s hits.

The success of the heavy metal genre that the group spawned as well as the continued popularity of "Born to Be Wild," has ensured Steppenwolf's legacy in rock history. The band toured well into the 1990s, headlining numerous "oldies" shows and selling out concerts throughout the country. In 1996, John Kay was inducted into the Canadian Academy of Recording Arts and Sciences (CARAS) Hall of Fame.

—Scott Tribble

FURTHER READING:

The Billboard Encyclopedia of Music. Cincinnati, 1998.

Kay, John, and John Einarson. *Magic Carpet Ride: The Autobiography of John Kay and Steppenwolf.* Kingston, Ontario, Quarry Press, 1994.

Stereographs
See Stereoscopes

Stereoscopes

Stereoscopy—creating three-dimensional visual experiences from two-dimensional materials—informed most every visual medium of the Modern age: art, photography, cinema, television, and newspapers. In the nineteenth century the marriage of stereoscopy, photography, and industrial production resulted in the first photographic mass media: the Victorian stereoscope. Popular from 1850-1920, the stereoscope answered desires for greater realism in visual representation while its popular, yet intimate, visual experience prefigured visual media like cinema and television. Eventually overshadowed by cinema and later electronic visual technologies, the optical principles of the stereoscope grounded many popular visual entertainments of the twentieth century: View-Master viewers, 3-D cinema and comic books, and Magic Eye stereograms.

The Victorian stereoscope was part of a general trend in the nineteenth century towards more realistic visual representations, mass-produced for an emergent commodity culture. It has been long known that two-dimensional representations, like drawing and painting, are a poor imitation of human visual experiences. Paintings present but a single image, while in normal binocular vision the two different images received by each eye are synthesized by the brain into a single image, allowing us to perceive depth and spatial relationships. In 1832 British physicist Charles Wheatstone invented a device—the reflecting stereoscope—which induced normal binocular vision using prepared imagery. Wheatstone created two drawings of an object which mimicked the slightly different perspective our two eyes have of a single scene. By using mirrors the reflecting stereoscope channelled vision so that only one of the drawings could be seen by each eye. The viewer's brain combined the two images into a single stereoscopic image with qualities similar to that of unaided vision. It was soon discovered that stereo-photographs could be prepared for Wheatstone's device by simultaneously taking two photographs with a double-lensed camera. If the imagery was properly prepared, the visual effects of solidity, depth, and realism were unparalleled.

Wheatstone's awkward device was merely a scientific curiosity until modified by William Brewster in 1849. Brewster's lenticular stereoscope, a small box outfitted with lenses and a slot to hold stereographic imagery, debuted in 1851 at London's Great International Exhibition. Although the interest of Queen Victoria ensured immediate popularity, early photographic technologies hampered broad circulation. In the 1840s Wheatstone's device used daguerreotypes and calotypes, but only after the 1851 introduction of glass-plate negatives could stereo-photographs be mass-produced. With cheap viewers and abundant imagery, stereoscopic viewing came within reach of a broad middle-class audience, fulfilling the London Stereoscopic Company's motto ''A Stereoscope In Every Home.''

Popularity depended on a plentiful supply of imagery in the form of stereographs, also called stereocards or stereoviews. Generally, stereographs are four-by-seven inch rectangular cards having two stereo-photographs pasted side-by-side. The photographer's, or more commonly publisher's, imprint and a short caption might be shown on the front, with a longer text on the reverse. Later thematic boxed sets were accompanied by maps and an explanatory guidebook. Since the overall size and shape of the stereograph was dictated by the stereoscope (similar to later standardized mass media like cassette tapes or CDs) stereographic publishers anticipated consumer desire and sought market niches through aesthetic innovation. Collectors attest to the bewildering diversity of stereographs: examples are known with tintype, daguerreotype, ambrotype, and lithographic images; pasted on paper, cardstock, glass, and porcelain mounts. Usually a stereograph can be dated to within a few years based solely on physical details.

Initially, stereographs were produced by lone figures who often took the photograph, processed the film, assembled the stereograph and sold it to tourists. Stereo-photographers included the obscure and the famous; William Henry Jackson, Carleton Watkins, Timothy O'Sullivan, Eadweard Muybridge, and Matthew Brady are better known producers. Historian William Culp Darrah estimated that between 1860 and 1890 as many as 12,000 stereo-photographers took between 3.5 and 4.5 million individual images, which were printed on upwards of 400 million stereographs. In the later nineteenth century large factories churned out thousands of stereographs a day using assembly-line methods. Stereographs were sold at tourist spots, from storefronts, through mail order catalogues, and door to door. Production gradually consolidated until, in 1921, the Keystone View Company was the sole purveyor of stereographs in America.

If the invention and early developments of stereoscopy belong to Europeans, the phenomenon attained its greatest success in America. Stereoscopes were known in America from the early 1850s. In 1854 the Langenheim Brothers of Philadelphia became the first large-scale retailers of stereoscopic equipment. Between 1859-63 noted essayist Oliver Wendell Holmes promoted the stereoscope in three enthusiastic articles in *The Atlantic Monthly*. Holmes also designed a simple hand-held wooden stereoscope, improved and marketed by Boston photographer J.L. Bates. Stereo-photography was central to convincing skeptical Eastern audiences of the wonders of the American West, as well as conveying in realistic detail the horrors of the Civil and Spanish-American Wars.

By delivering news of the world in visual form, stereographs were roughly analogous to cinematic newsreels and television. Stereographs were a way to travel the world and experience its events from the security of one's armchair. Subjects included cities, famous places, tourist destinations, and resorts, portraits of famous people, fine art works, modes of transportation, international expositions,

wars, natural disasters, aftermaths of fires and earthquakes, erotica and pornography, educational and scientific matter. One card showed the full moon, which when viewed through a stereoscope showed every crater and mountain with a degree of detailed relief unattainable even using a telescope. Similar to early narrative silent film, a short series of stereographs could present a comedy or morality play. Subject matter accommodated and anticipated the taste of the white Euro-American middle class, its primary consumer. Racial and social stereotyping was prevalent especially in images of Native and African Americans, urban immigrants, and colonized peoples in Africa and Asia. Collecting, trading, organizing, viewing, and sharing stereocards was a prominent family pastime. Home filing cabinets for stereographs allowed collectors to construct a personal visual cartography of the world, infinite in its variety, endlessly malleable in form.

With the emergence of cinema, and especially after the 1920s, the stereoscope became largely an educational tool and later a children's toy. Tru-Vue stereoscopic filmstrips (1920s-1950s) and the better-known View-Master system introduced at the 1939 New York World's Fair employed a similar optical apparatus. View-Master reels held ten translucent celluloid stereoscopic images on a thin plastic disk which was inserted into a lightweight View-Master viewer. Translucent celluloid imitated the luminescence of cinematic projections, injecting new life into an old gadget. View-Master contracted with Walt Disney studios to publish its popular animated films as View-Master reels suggesting a growing audience among children. In the 1980s View-Master viewers appeared in the shape of popular children's animated characters like Mickey Mouse, Casper the Ghost, Big Bird, Batman and Tweety Bird.

Three-dimensional cinema of the early 1950s briefly revived adult interest in three-dimensional viewing. Broadcast television reduced theater attendance and to attract viewers Hollywood introduced Natural Vision, or 3-D movies. Between 1952-54 Hollywood produced over 70 3-D movies beginning with *Bwana Devil* (Arch Oboler, 1952), the most famous being Alfred Hitchcock's *Dial M For Murder* (1954). To see a movie in 3-D, moviegoers wore special throwaway glasses with one red and one blue lens which permitted each eye to perceive only certain parts of a color-polarized film. The process had been known since the mid-nineteenth century, and a few monochromatic 3-D films were made in the 1920s and 1930s. Due to technical limitations and the uncomfortable glasses the novelty was short-lived. It was briefly reintroduced in early 1980s horror flicks and television broadcasts, and in panoramic IMAX 3-D movies of the 1990s.

Hollywood's flirtation with 3-D heralded the first comic book in 3-D by Norman Maurer and Joe Kubert: *Three Dimension Comics* featuring Mighty Mouse (1953). Over 50 3-D comics were produced from 1953 to 1954. Three-dimensional comics are viewed with the same glasses as in 3-D cinema. The necessity of hand-drawing limited early 3-D comics to bi-color images but after the 1970s limited polychromy was possible using computer drafting technologies. Three-dimensional comics appeared sporadically into the 1990s engaging some venerable talents of comic arts: Ray Zone, Jack Kirby, and Wally Wood.

In the 1990s, computer-generated Magic Eye stereograms put a new twist on traditional stereoscopic viewing. Based on the theories of Bela Julesz and Christopher Tyler, Magic Eye artists employed a sophisticated computer algorithm which manipulated images at the pixel level, disguising simple stereoscopic images within another unrelated pattern. By free viewing (seeing a stereoscopic image without a stereoscope) the hidden image emerges from the generic background. Between 1992 and 1995 Magic Eye sold 25 million books in 26 languages worldwide and in 1994 Magic Eye syndicated a weekly image to over 200 newspapers.

By the late 1990s, computerized flight simulators, high-altitude surveillance photography, and weapon targeting systems employed stereoscopic science. Using stereo-photography NASA's Pathfinder Mission (1997) produced interactive topographical maps of Mars. For its report on the Mars mission, *National Geographic* featured some of the 3-D images from the Pathfinder Mission and included a pair of 3-D glasses to view them. Gradually, this technology became available to a broader consumer culture through holographic and virtual reality devices. Amateur and professional interest in stereoscopy was accompanied by intense collecting of antique stereo-viewers and stereoscopic imagery. There were regional, national, and international associations; a magazine devoted to the topic, *Stereo World*; and numerous internet sites. Although Victorian stereographs have become the province of antiquarians and museums, the desire to see in 3-D remains of unfailing interest to a popular audience.

—Michael J. Murphy

FURTHER READING:

Darrah, William C. *The World of Stereographs.* Nashville, Land Yacht, 1997.

Earle, W. E., editor. *Points of View: The Stereograph in America-A History.* Rochester, Visual Studies Workshop, 1979.

Higham, Charles. *Hollywood at Sunset.* New York, Saturday Evening, 1972.

Jones, John. *Wonders of the Stereoscope.* New York, Knopf. 1976.

N. E. Thing Enterprises, et al. *Magic Eye: the 3D Guide.* Kansas City, Andrews, McMeel, 1995.

Nelson, M. A. "Dots of Science." *Popular Science.* Vol. 245, September 1994, 56-9.

Newcott, William. "Return to Mars." *National Geographic.* Vol. 194, No. 2, August 1998.

Sell, Wolfgang, and Maryann Sell. *View Master Viewers-An Illustrated History.*

Terrell, Maria and Robert Terrell. "Behind the Scenes of a Random Dot Stereogram." *The American Mathematical Monthly.* Vol. 101, October 1994, 715-24.

Waldsmith, John. *Stereoviews: An Illustrated History and Price Guide.* Iola, Wisconsin, Krause, 1995.

Wing, Paul. *Stereoscopes: The First One Hundred Years.* Nashua, Transition, 1996.

Zone, Ray. *The 3-D Zone.* http://www.ray3dzone.com. April 1999.

Stern, Howard (1954—)

Howard Stern evokes the kind of controversy that you wouldn't expect from a typical celebrity. Stern, however, is not a typical celebrity. The audience for his nationally broadcast morning show numbers in the millions, and it is comprised mostly of men, aged 25 to 54, who listen religiously. A typical morning on the Howard Stern Show might include discussions on sex, lesbianism, race relations, lawyers, the latest tabloid stories, or flatulence. His radio show

Howard Stern

transcends the bounds of good taste and has tested the limits of radio broadcasting codes and regulations for over 20 years.

Howard Allen Stern was born on January 12, 1954, in the Queens borough of New York City. His father, Ben, was an engineer at a Manhattan radio station and was hard on his only son, frequently calling him a "moron." Stern describes his mother, Ray, as an overprotective woman who thought that her son would grow up sensitive if he played with puppets. The idea backfired, however, when little Howard put on X-rated puppet shows for his friends in his parent's basement.

Stern graduated from high school in 1972 and enrolled at Boston University, where he pursued a degree in broadcasting. Graduating in 1976, he started working for WRNW-AM in Briarcliff, New York, as an afternoon disc jockey (DJ) and eventually took over several other duties, including both program and production directors. It was at WRNW that Stern realized that he would have to be funnier than normal DJs if he wanted to be a success. His first antics on the air included bizarre commercial spots complete with weird sound effects and off-color calls to the business owners. Stern lasted about two years at WRNW before moving to Hartford, Connecticut, to work for WCCC. Further honing his comedic technique, he experimented with on-air gags such as the "Cadaverathon," a fundraiser for the Yale University Medical School, which was purported to lack corpses for its students. Another event was his "To Hell With Shell" campaign aimed at gas companies and the long lines at the pumps during the late 1970s fuel shortage. Routines like these got him noticed by WWWW-FM in Detroit, a rock station that took him on in 1979. More irreverent gags and sketches followed, including a bra-burning demonstration in support of the Equal Rights Amendment, and a raunchy daily piece in which a dominatrix would call in and give the weather forecast. Then, literally overnight, WWWW changed its format to country and Stern left.

In 1978 Stern married his college sweetheart, Alison Berns, a social worker. Stern tested the strength of his marriage by making it the subject of frequent on-air conversations. When his wife miscarried their first child Stern did a sketch on it, a call from God himself who denigrated him for not being able to reproduce. The consequences were disastrous, for the gag hurt his wife severely. Reaching a point where nothing was sacred on his show, Stern would even make fun of his wife's clients and their odd behavioral habits. Stern apologized for such antics in his first book, *Private Parts* (1993), but still jokingly attacks his marriage to Alison on his show. The two have three children, all girls, and Stern does insist that he is a family-oriented man.

In 1981 Stern began working for WWDC-FM in Washington, D.C. Building a base for his morning show, he persuaded his supervisors to hire Fred Norris, a comedy writer with whom he worked in Hartford. Though Stern jokes that Norris does nothing for the show, Norris's part is a large one, doing voices, sound effects, and bogus recordings of celebrity voices. It was at WWDC that Stern first met Robin Quivers, who has been Stern's news anchor ever since. Quivers, a Baltimore native, had her reservations about working with Stern at first, but was clearly impressed with his spontaneous, unrehearsed style. In February 1982, Stern pulled what may have been his most outrageous stunt when, in the wake of the crash of Air Florida Flight 90 into the 14th Street Bridge, he called the airline and asked how much a one-way ticket to the bridge would cost. The call offended many listeners, though Stern claimed that he was expressing his own outrage against the flight crew that allowed the plane to take off without the wings being de-iced. Shortly thereafter Stern was fired from DC-101 (though not for the prank call—he was fired for referring to station management as "scumbags").

Stern was quickly hired to work for WNBC-FM, fulfilling his dream of working in New York City. But Stern found himself in frequent disagreements with his superiors at NBC. In order to control Stern's antics, his superiors would often write new rules and regulations for him to follow. Stern usually refused and was suspended several times before he was fired in September of 1985. It wasn't long before a competing New York station, WXRK-FM (K-Rock), picked him up. The station promised Stern no restrictions in running his show. Stern brought along Quivers, Norris, Gary Dell'Abate, a former producer for NBC and the show's punching bag, and his chief comedy artist, Jackie "The Jokeman" Martling, who did a large part of the show's writing. One addition to his crew of regulars was "Stuttering" John Melendez, whose own speech impediment was put to use by Stern. Stern believed that no one would turn down an interview with a stutterer, even one that asked rude questions. Only months after starting at K-Rock, Stern was given the chance to move his show to the coveted morning slot, in direct competition with fellow "shock jock" Don Imus. Stern prized the rivalry with Imus, who remained the whipping boy for Stern and his crew into the 1990s.

In 1986 Stern completed his objective, surpassing Imus in the ratings. To celebrate the event, Stern organized a mock funeral at Rockefeller Center.

In 1990 Stern launched the TV version of the *Howard Stern Show* on WWOR-TV in New York. The program was a visual rendition of his radio show but was ultimately canceled because of budget setbacks. *The Howard Stern Interview* followed but also didn't last. In 1994 the E! network began broadcasting a 30-minute simulcast of his radio show, using several stationary cameras placed in the radio studio. In August 1998, Stern launched yet another talkshow, called *The Howard Stern Radio Show,* which aired directly opposite *Saturday Night Live.*

Private Parts is mostly a memoir of events in Stern's broadcasting career as well as his childhood, and became the fastest selling item in the history of its publisher, Harper Collins. The book saw a resurgence in sales in 1995 when Stern released his second book, *Miss America,* which featured Stern himself on the cover in drag. *Private Parts* was made into a full-length film in 1997. Stern supposedly rejected 13 scripts before settling on what he thought was the best representation of his book. The film received positive reviews and is mostly a tribute to his relationship with his wife. A very funny and surprisingly touching film, it reenacts many of the sketches that marked his early career. It also gives more insight into his partnership with Robin Quivers and their undying friendship.

Though his radio show has brought him millions of fans, he has had one consistent enemy throughout his career: the Federal Communications Commission (FCC). Stern's radio station owner, Infinity Broadcasting, was fined $600,000 in 1992 after Stern boasted about masturbating to pictures of Aunt Jemima and having rough sex with Michelle Pfeiffer. It was not the first but only the most dramatic in a series of inquiries, reprimands, and fines aimed at Stern since 1986. Stern alleged that the FCC had a personal vendetta against him, and told *Rolling Stone* that he'll never win against the powerful government organization "because they're bureaucrats . . . they've got all the time in the world and they're going to sit there and just wear me down."

Howard Stern has been called the "poet laureate of urban American white trash" and the funniest man on radio. He cites as his major influence Lenny Bruce, another comedian with the same disregard for moral standards. In total contrast to the neurotic personality he portrays on the radio, Stern and his wife practice transcendental meditation and lead a very normal life.

—Tom Trinchera

FURTHER READING:

Cegielski, Jim. *The Howard Stern Book: An Unauthorized, Unabashed, Uncensored Fan's Guide.* Secaucus, New Jersey, Carol Publishing, 1994.

Colford, Paul D. *Howard Stern, King of All Media: The Unauthorized Biography.* New York, St. Martin's, 1996.

Kunen, James S. "Howard Stern: New York's Mad-Dog Deejay May Be the Mouth of the '80s." *People Weekly.* October 22, 1984.

Lucaire, Luigi. *Howard Stern, A to Z: The Stern Fanatic's Guide to the King of All Media.* New York, St. Martin's, 1997.

Marin, Rick. "Man or Mouth: The Rolling Stone Interview with Howard Stern." *Rolling Stone.* February 10, 1994.

Menell, Jeff. *Howard Stern: Big Mouth.* New York, Windsor, 1993.

Remnick, David. "The Accidental Anarchist." *The New Yorker.* April 10, 1997, 56-67.

Stern, Howard. *Miss America.* New York, Regan Books, 1995.

———. *Private Parts.* New York, Simon & Schuster, 1993.

Stetson Hat

When Philadelphia hat maker John B. Stetson went west in 1859 to cure his tuberculosis, he worked the Gold Rush at Pike's Peak, Colorado, where he designed a hat for working in the hot sun. Stetson returned to Philadelphia to mass-produce the "Boss of the Plains" hat, made of tan felt with a wide brim and high crown. Worn by Presidents, Buffalo Bill, and the Texas Rangers, the hat became a symbol of the West. Stetson felt hats continued to be popular into the 1990s.

—S. Naomi Finkelstein

FURTHER READING:

Stetson Hat Company, *The Stetson Century 1865-1965.* St. Louis, Stetson Hat Company, 1965.

Stevens, Ray (1939—)

Before Ray Stevens, a country humorist was a guy in overalls, chewing on a stalk of straw and telling homespun stories about cow pies and two-seater privies. Stevens changed all that in 1962, when he released "Ahab the Arab," an off-the-wall saga of a Mideastern camel driver, complete with sound effects. Stevens went on to score

Ray Stevens

hit records with a wide range of approaches. He spoofed Tarzan and rock 'n' roll at the same time in "Gitarzan," a 1970s public nakedness fad in "The Streak," and 1980s televangelism with "Would Jesus Wear a Rolex?" He also displayed a talent for sophisticated musical humor when he transformed the jazz standard "Misty" into a bluegrass romp, and had a way with sentimental country in his 1970 chart-topper, "Everything Is Beautiful." But through all that, he maintained his identification as a country artist. Stevens became one of the leaders in music marketing in the 1990s, with his aggressive and successful television mail order promotions of his music videos.

—Tad Richards

Stewart, Jimmy (1908-1997)

One of the most universally recognized and loved movie stars of the twentieth century, the prolific and popular career of iconic actor Jimmy Stewart spanned six decades, from the 1930s to the 1980s, as well as many filmmaking genres, from comedy to serious drama, from the dark Westerns of the 1950s to the brilliant suspense of Alfred Hitchcock. No matter what part Jimmy Stewart played, audiences responded to the gangly, good-looking actor, believing that underneath it all, he was always a good man, as his "aw shucks" personality endeared him to fans around the world.

Born in the small town of Indiana, Pennsylvania, to Elizabeth and Alexander Stewart, James Maitland Stewart was raised in a loving middle class home. His father was the proprietor of the local J.M. Stewart Hardware Store (which would become famous as the home of Stewart's Academy Award, which stayed in the store window for many years), and by all accounts Jimmy had a happy and normal childhood. Upon graduation from high school, he decided, with encouragement from his very practical father, to study civil engineering and architecture at Princeton University, from which he graduated in 1932 with honors. While at college, however, he became involved in the theater group, the Triangle Club, where he met fellow student (and future director), Joshua Logan. After graduation Logan invited Stewart to join the University Players, his summer stock theater company in Massachusetts.

After making his professional debut with the Players, Stewart abandoned architecture forever, much to his parents' displeasure. He eventually moved to Broadway to appear in the production, *Carry Nation*, which was not successful. His next role, however, was in *Goodbye Again,* in which he had appeared in Massachusetts. This production was a hit, earning Stewart excellent notices, and by 1934 he was working steadily, when he was hired by producer/director Guthrie McClintic, husband of stage actress Katharine Cornell, to appear in the play *Yellow Jack.* Stewart received rave reviews. It was during this production that Stewart also appeared in his first motion picture, a small uncredited role in *Art Trouble.*

In 1935, while Stewart was visiting his family, he received an offer from Metro-Goldwyn-Mayer to appear in a small role in *Murder Man* starring Spencer Tracy. MGM signed him to a standard seven-year contract and put him in several productions, but his first real break came when an old friend from his University Player days, actress Margaret Sullavan, insisted on him as her co-star in *Next Time We Love* (1935). A second break came when Stewart played opposite Eleanor Powell in *Born to Dance,* where he introduced the Cole

A young boy wearing a Stetson hat.

Porter song, "Easy to Love." While his singing was unremarkable, *Born to Dance* was one of the biggest hits of 1936. Stewart continued to appear in films such as *After the Thin Man* and *Seventh Heaven.*

It was a film released in 1939 that finally made Stewart a major star. He had worked with director Frank Capra previously on the classic comedy, *You Can't Take it With You.* When Capra needed a leading man for his new picture, *Mr. Smith Goes to Washington,* he wanted no one else for the role of the idealistic young man who is thrust into the corrupt world of Washington politics. The film and

Stewart were a sensation, although many political figures denounced the inference that the government of the United States might contain corrupt elements. For his performance, Stewart won the New York Film Critic's Best Actor Award. He was also nominated for an Academy Award, but was a surprising loser to Robert Donat in *Goodbye, Mr. Chips.* The following year he costarred with Katharine Hepburn and Cary Grant in *The Philadelphia Story* and took home an Oscar for that performance, though many felt it was a consolation prize for *Mr. Smith.*

Jimmy Stewart

In 1941 America entered World War II, which put a temporary hold on Stewart's career. He was one of the very first movie stars to enlist in the military, earning a distinguished record as an Air Force pilot and commander and becoming one of the highest ranking officers in the U.S. Auxiliary Air Force, rising to the rank of colonel.

For his first film project after the war, Stewart chose to work with Frank Capra again. *It's a Wonderful Life* is now considered a classic and a Christmas staple, but when it was originally released the audience and critics alike did not particularly care for it. Capra and Stewart were disappointed with the reception the picture received and both maintained in later years that it was their favorite film.

The late 1940s saw many changes in the life of Jimmy Stewart. First, at the age of 41, Stewart married Gloria McLean and became an instant father to Gloria's children from a previous marriage. He also decided that his career needed to take a different direction. This led to two successful collaborations each with directors Anthony Mann and Alfred Hitchcock. The results were some of Stewart's darkest and most critically acclaimed works—*Winchester 73* and *Broken Arrow* with Mann, and *Rear Window* and *Vertigo* with Hitchcock. The latter is considered by many to be Stewart's finest performance and Hitchcock's masterpiece.

After the 1950s Stewart continued to do film work, although good roles became more infrequent. By the 1970s, he had turned to television, appearing in two shorted-lived television series, *The Jimmy Stewart Show* (1971-1972) and *Hawkins* (1973-1974). He also did several made-for-television movies, such as *Mr. Krueger's Christmas* in 1980 and *Right of Way* with Bette Davis in 1983. In 1980 he received the American Film Institutes Lifetime Achievement Award.

His last film performance was as the voice of the gunfighting dog, Wylie Burp in *An American Tail: Fievel Goes West.* Stewart continued to be active until the death of his wife, Gloria, in 1994. His health began failing soon after and he died in 1997.

Jimmy Stewart will long be remembered as exemplifying the best of America. His heroic roles and his devotion to his family made Americans feel he was a part of their own family, making him one of the best-loved figures of twentieth-century American popular culture.

—Jill A. Gregg

FURTHER READING:

Coe, Jonathan. *Jimmy Stewart: A Wonderful Life.* New York, Arcade, 1994.

Dewey, Donald. *James Stewart: A Biography.* Georgia, Turner Publications, 1996

Fishgall, Gary. *Pieces of Time: The Life of James Stewart.* New York, Scribner, 1997.

Pickard, Roy. *James Stewart: The Hollywood Years.* England, F.A. Thorpe, 1992.

Quirk, Lawrence J. *James Stewart: Behind the Scenes of a Wonderful Life.* New York, Applause Books, 1997.

Robbins, Jhan. *Everybody's Man: A Biography of Jimmy Stewart.* New York, Putnam, 1985.

Stickball

Stickball refers to a form of baseball developed to accommodate play on streets and sidewalks. A janitor's mop handle is the preferred bat, and a pink rubber ball—known as a "Spaulding" or "Spauldeen"—is considered to be the best ball. The ball is pitched or bounced towards the hitter; sewers and chalk markings are used for bases, and a hit may be played off of fire escapes, cars, stoops, or any other urban obstacle.

Stickball traces its origins eighteenth-century English games such as old cat, rounders, and town ball, although some sources trace it back to games played by Plains Indians. As of the 1990s, stickball is still played in its purest form in summer leagues in New York City, and exists in some form in most American cities. Other versions are known as Strikeout, Fast Pitch, Corkball, Bottle Caps, and Fuzzball, and are played with a wide range of bats and balls, sometimes against walls with painted strike zones. Stickball and its variations offer players the chance to use basic baseball skills without requiring full teams of players, expensive gloves or bats, or the rarest of all urban commodities, an open stretch of grass.

—Colby Vargas

FURTHER READING:

Ravielli, Anthony. *What Are Street Games?* New York, Atheneum, 1981.

Schindler, Steven. *Sewer Balls.* Los Angeles, Elevated Press, 1996.

Wirth, Cliff. *Stickball, Streetcars, and Saturday Matiness: Illustrated Memories.* Greendale, Wisconsin, Reiman Publications, 1995.

Stiller and Meara

For 35 years the comedy team of Stiller and Meara—five-foot-six Jewish actor Jerry Stiller and his five-foot-eight Irish-Catholic wife Anne Meara—have been best known for wringing laughter out of improvisational situations, appearing 36 times on *The Ed Sullivan Show* in the 1950s and 1960s. They have also acted on Broadway—separately and as a team—and have each starred in a number of television sitcoms and motion pictures. Jerry's role as George Costanza's short-fused father on *Seinfeld* in the late 1990s sent his revitalized career to a higher level, leading to further work on Broadway and in network television commercials. In recent years Stiller and Meara have also been known as the parents of talented writer-director-actor Ben Stiller and actress Amy Stiller.

Both born in New York City, Jerry Stiller and Anne Meara were stage-struck in their teens. When they met in the early 1950s at an agent's office in Manhattan, Jerry had already acted in a number of plays, including *Peter Pan* with Veronica Lake. The pair signed with a comedy improv group, the Compass Players in St. Louis, and set out on their own as a "boy-girl" act in comedy clubs. They appeared first in a small Greenwich Village club, then moved to the popular Blue Angel, followed shortly by bookings into other major nightclubs and guest spots on television. The first comedy sketch they wrote was called "Jonah," with Anne playing a TV news reporter and Jerry an older Miami Beach man who had been swallowed by a whale.

They were married in 1954 at a time when Jewish-Catholic marriages raised eyebrows. Stiller explains: "But when I met Anne, nobody of my own background wanted to marry me. I was an actor, and an actor had no credentials. Anne was an actress, and she had no credentials either. What brought us together was unconditional love." They were also attracted to each other's comic talent and offbeat humor. Besides performing on stage, the couple wrote and performed radio commercials. The best known of these—a commercial for an obscure wine called Blue Nun—increased the product's sales 500 percent overnight.

Honing her talents by writing comedy routines and commercials, Anne Meara has become a successful playwright. Her comedy, *After-Play*, had a long run on Broadway as well in major cities coast-to-coast. She and Jerry starred in this comedy about two New York couples, the Shredmans and the Gutemans, having dinner, many drinks, and tossing around hundreds of witty one-liners, after seeing a Broadway play they reviewed in total disagreement.

The couple has also enjoyed a varied career in films. Anne has appeared in nine movies, including the recent *Jetters* (1997), *The Search for One-Eye Jimmy* (1996) and *The Daytrippers* (1996). Jerry has appeared in eighteen, ranging from *The Taking of Pelham One Two Three* (1974) and *Airport 75* to the more recent *A Rat's Tale* (1998), as well as three films in 1997: *Camp Stories, The Deli,* and *Stag.*

The comedy team has appeared in a variety of television sitcoms, both together and separately. They were regulars on *The Paul Lynde Show* in the 1970s, and made numerous guest appearances as a couple on *Love, American Style, The Courtship of Eddie's Father,* and *The Love Boat.* Jerry was a regular on two sitcoms in the late 1980s,

Tattinger's and *Nick and Hillary,* and in the 1990s, on *The King of Queens* in addition to *Seinfeld.* Anne was a regular on such popular sitcoms as *Rhoda,* (1976-1977), *Archie Bunker's Place,* (1979-1982), and *ALF* (1987-1990).

—Benjamin Griffith

FURTHER READING:

Inman, David. *The TV Encyclopedia.* New York, Perigee, 1991.

Marc, David. *Comic Visions: Television Comedy in American Culture.* New York, Blackwell, 1997.

Schleier, Curt. "Jerry Stiller's Youth in Brooklyn Set Stage for Lifetime of Laughs." *Jewish Bulletin of Northern California.* March 20, 1998.

Waldron, Vince. *Classic Sitcoms: A Celebration of the Best in Prime-Time Comedy.* New York, Silman Jam, 1998.

Stine, R. L. (1943—)

In just over a decade, R. L. Stine went from being an obscure humor magazine editor to the biggest name in books for youth. Though his achievement is sometimes discounted as a fluke, Stine found a formula and tapped an audience that brought him unprecedented success. Many attribute his success to the great entertainment

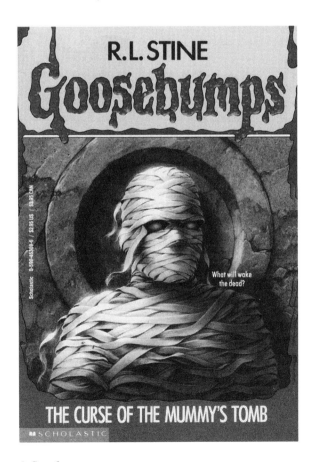

A *Goosebumps* cover.

his books provide kids. Like Stephen King, to whom Stine is often compared, Stine knows how to tell a story. He knows how to keep readers interested and involved and, most importantly, how to satisfy them. Stine is not creating well-rounded characters; he is not using symbolism, metaphor, or any of the tricks of the trade in his writing. Instead, he practices the tricks of his own trade: that of entertaining people with "cheap thrills." He uses humor, roller-coaster plots, suspenseful chapter endings, gross-outs, credible kids' dialogue, recognizable if stereotypical characters, cliffhangers and red herrings, and a bare-bones style that gets to the point: to scare his readers. He is not interested in educating, enlightening, or informing; he is only interested in entertaining kids by terrifying them with gruesome, plot twisting, scary thrillers.

Robert Lawrence Stine had been telling and writing scary stories since he was a kid growing up in Columbus, Ohio. He wrote and illustrated his own magazines throughout his school years, then was the editor of the Ohio State humor magazine, *The Sundial,* during his college years. After a brief stint as a social studies teacher, Stine moved from Ohio to New York to break into the writing business. After a series of short-lived jobs writing for fan magazines and trade industry publications, he landed a job at Scholastic. Within a few years he had moved from a staff writer to editor of the youth humor magazine *Bananas.* While he was editing *Bananas,* he was writing joke books like *How to Be Funny* and *The Beast Handbook.* Soon after *Bananas* folded, Stine was downsized at Scholastic and began freelancing fulltime, turning out more joke books, penning numerous *Choose Your Own Adventure* style multiple storyline books, writing a television show, and even writing bubble gum cards and coloring books. All his work eventually paid off with the success of *Fear Street* and *Goosebumps.*

Stine had learned in childhood that he could entertain by telling stories, like those he shared with his brother as they tried to go to sleep at night. He also learned that he could entertain his peers by writing the stories as well. He so enjoyed entertaining his peers that he decided to make a career of it. Stine told *People* magazine that "I started writing when I was nine. I think I knew then that I wanted to write. I don't really know why. I just always loved it more than anything else." As an adult, Stine described himself as a "writing machine" in *USA Today* and continues to effectively use what he learned at age nine about how to entertain nine-year-olds.

Stine's first financial success came in 1992 with the debut of his *Goosebumps* book series for upper elementary/middle school kids. Edited by his wife Jane and packaged through her company Parachute Press, *Goosebumps* quickly became the most popular children's book series of all time; by the late 1990s there were 180 *Goosebumps* books in print in over 30 languages. The numbers for *Goosebumps* products were just as impressive. Additionally, since its debut in 1995, the *Goosebumps* television show has been a top-rated show and remains a centerpiece in the Saturday morning schedule of the Fox network in 1999; *Goosebumps* prime-time and after-school specials are rating winners as well. Videos based on the shows have sold over one million copies, while the first CD-ROM based on the books, *Escape from Horrorland,* was a big seller. The World Wide Web overflows with kids' personal *Goosebumps* pages, not to mention Scholastic's official site. By 1999, a movie was also in the works with Fox Family Films, while Disney has cashed in with a *Goosebumps* Horror Land at its Metro Goldwyn Mayer Studios site in Florida. It should be of no surprise that the roller coaster plot twister is tied in with an amusement park with an attraction featuring a live *Goosebumps* show

performed five times a day and a *Goosebumps* Fun House with a scary hall of mirrors. Disney also sponsored a *Goosebumps* parade and signed Stine for a *Goosebumps* cruise on the Disney Cruise ships.

Parachute Press had watched Stine's *Fear Street* series become popular among teens and pre-teens. Parachute and Stine then developed an idea for another scary series, this one to be aimed at younger kids. There still needed to be scares and dangers, but no blood, no guts, no bullets, and no guns. In these books for younger readers Stine played up the humor—another of his strengths—while playing down the violence. In order for the books to be scary, there would still need to be a threat to the character, but the threats would be different— most *Fear Street* stories are not monster stories and therefore contain an edge of realism.

In his autobiography *It Came From Ohio,* Stine writes that he saw an advertisement in *TV Guide* to promote horror films which read, "It's *GOOSEBUMPS* week." With that, he was off and running, turning out the first title, *Welcome to Dead House,* in ten days. It was not, however, an instant success. *Welcome to Dead House* sold less than a million copies. Nor did the next book—*Stay Out of the Basement*—set the publishing world afire. Like *Fear Street* before it, *Goosebumps* was a series without a central set of characters, and in this case, not even a central location. *Fear Street* also came out after some seeds had been sown by Stine and other authors in books like *Twisted.* In contrast, there was nothing even remotely like *Goosebumps* on the market: it was a brand new field. It was not until the third book, *Monster Blood,* that the series caught on, mostly due to word of mouth. With their easy availability through Scholastic book clubs, the growing number of mega-bookstores, and discount stores like Wal-Mart, *Goosebumps* soon began selling well. By the sixth title, *Let's Get Invisible, Goosebumps* cracked *Publishers Weekly's* children's bestseller chart. The books received a boost in visibility when *USA Today* began its own bestseller list in 1994. Unlike other rankings that do not include paperbacks or children's books—or if they do include them, they do not compare their sales to adult bestsellers—*USA Today*'s premise was, a book is a book is a book. On *USA Today*'s list, it became obvious that *Goosebumps* was outselling adult authors like Michael Crichton.

But the bubble burst on February 21, 1997, when Scholastic Inc., publishers of Stine's *Goosebumps* series, saw its stock drop 40 percent after an announcement that its earnings would not meet expectations. Blame for this dramatic drop fell on the decline in sales figures of the *Goosebumps* franchise, in particular their older titles. Five years into the life of the series, it had "simply peaked." The wide coverage given to this news—which ended up on the front page of most newspaper business sections—demonstrates the impact and importance of R.L. Stine. One writer, it seems, can influence the fate of an entire company. Stine, however, is not just any writer; he is, without a doubt, the most famous of all writers for children. Perhaps only Judy Blume in her heyday rivals Stine in this regard. He has appeared on countless television shows, helped create two successful television series (*Goosebumps* and *Eureka's Castle*), and has been widely written about in the media. His first adult novel—*Superstitious* (1996)—earned a big advance and a movie deal. Needless to say, in spite of the series' declining sales, the *Goosebumps* brand name still appears on fast-food drink cups, snack foods, calendars, clothing, and everywhere else in the retail world.

Goosebumps are more than books; they are popular culture products. From the movie tie-ins to the Cheetos bags, *Goosebumps* stopped being just books very soon into the series and Stine went from hack writer to celebrity in just a few months. Stine told *People* that "No one over 14 has ever heard of me." By 1998, however, there were few people with any significant contact with kids who had not heard of R.L. Stine.

—Patrick Jones

FURTHER READING:

Donahue, Deirdre. "R.L. Stine Has a Frightful Way with Pre-Teen Readers." *USA Today*. December 3, 1993, D6.

Jones, Patrick. *What's So Scary About R.L. Stine?* Lanham, Maryland, Scarecrow Press, 1998.

."R.L. Stine." *People Weekly*. December 25, 1995/January 1, 1996, 102-3.

Santow, Dan, and Toby Kahn. "The Scarier the Better." *People Weekly*. November 14, 1994, 115.

Silver, Marc. "Horrors, It's R.L. Stine." *U.S. News and World Report*. October 23, 1995, 95.

Stine, R.L., as told to Joe Arthur. *It Came from Ohio: My Life as a Writer*. New York, Scholastic, 1997.

———. "Why Kids Love to Get *Goosebumps*." *TV Guide*. October 28, 1995, 24.

West, Diana. "The Horror of R.L. Stine." *The Weekly Standard*. September 25, 1995, 42-5.

Stock-Car Racing

From February through November there is a stock-car race somewhere in America, with tracks drawing up to 150,000 racing fans, eager to watch their favorite drivers zoom around the oval tracks in cars much like their own automobiles. From humble beginnings in a farmer's field in the mid-1930s, the sport has become so popular nationwide that its television ratings are second only to the National Football League, and top drivers make millions of dollars a year from racing and advertising endorsements. When Jeff Gordon won the opening race of the 1999 season at Daytona Beach, Florida, he collected more than $2.1 million.

The earliest stock-car racers got their training by transporting moonshine whiskey over the dusty roads of Appalachia in the dead of night, outrunning the revenuers by driving flat-out in dangerous conditions. These moonshine runners were a part of a legend, later to be etched in the public mind by a movie, *Thunder Road* (1958), starring Robert Mitchum. In the mid-1930s, the drivers began arguing about who was fastest, and a race was set up in a quarter-mile dirt track carved out of a farmer's field near Stockbridge, Georgia. Unpublicized, the first race drew about 50 people, but after that thousands began showing up for the race, and the moonshiners began to collect cash prizes that surpassed their pay for nocturnal whiskey runs.

Among these early drivers were the Flock brothers—Tim, Bob, and Fonty—whose uncle owned one of the biggest stills in Georgia, and Junior Johnson, whose father had the largest moonshine operation in Wilkes County, North Carolina. Johnson, a legend in his own time, was featured in 1965 in a famous *Esquire* article by Tom Wolfe—"The Last American Hero is Junior Johnson-Yes!"—that

was made into a movie. Unbeatable on the dirt tracks, Junior had his own special style of accelerating through the turns by cocking his steering wheel hard left and fishtailing the rear end of the car. Other drivers, who slowed their cars on turns and tried catching up on the straightaways, had little chance.

At about the time the Georgia farmer was carving a race track out of a cornfield, an auto mechanic and weekend dirt-track race driver named William Henry "Bill" France was beginning a journey that would eventually make him the pioneer and prime mover of organized stock-car racing. He moved to Daytona Beach, where 25 miles of hard-packed sand, 500 yards wide, had attracted Sir Malcolm Campbell, who made annual visits to attempt new land-speed records with his racing car "Bluebird." In 1935 France watched as Campbell made his last runs at Daytona before moving his operation to the less windy conditions of the Bonneville Salt Flats in Utah. To continue attracting speed-minded tourists to Daytona Beach, the city fathers organized beach races, with little success.

In 1938 they recruited the personable France, whose gasoline station was a hangout for drivers and mechanics, to organize the races. A natural promoter, France signed up drivers, gathered prizes from local merchants, and set his race for July 4. Over 4,500 spectators showed up, each paying 50 cents a ticket. France and his financial backers split $200 in profits, and the young promoter started planning a beach race for Labor Day. By the following year, attendance was sharply up and ticket prices had doubled to a dollar. His races were a roaring success, but World War II brought a temporary end to his operation.

When he returned to the Daytona track after the war, France started the National Championship Stock-Car Circuit (NCSCC) to sponsor monthly races, with a winner's fund and a cumulative point system to reward the circuit's champion driver. NCSCC's inaugural year in 1947 was a great success, with Fonty Flock declared national champion. France's next bold step came in December of that year when he invited the most influential members of the stock car clan to a meeting in Daytona. He addressed 35 of his colleagues, urging them to "unite all stock car racing under one set of rules, with national point standings whereby only one driver could be crowned national champion." He urged consistent, enforceable rules concerning the modification of cars, insisting that the races admit only standard cars that could be bought at automobile dealerships. After a brief debate, the group supported such an organization and named France president. The National Association for Stock Car Racing (NASCAR) was incorporated on February 15, 1948, and a technical committee wrote rules to promote fair competition and provide for the safety of drivers and spectators.

Another important figure in stock car racing history is Harold Brasington, who brought to reality his dream of building a 1.25 mile paved speedway in his hometown of Darlington, South Carolina, and hosting the first 500 mile race for stock cars, the South's version of the Indianapolis 500. Bill France, in his second year of sanctioning races with his newly formed NASCAR, was called in to recruit drivers for the inaugural Southern 500 on Labor Day, 1950. Expecting to attract perhaps 5,000 paying customers to his 9,000 seat stadium, Brasington and France were astounded when 25,000 people showed up along with the first traffic jam in Darlington history. Tickets were sold for the infield, and the fans saw Johnny Mantz win the first Southern 500 driving a 1950 Plymouth with an average speed of 76 miles per hour, going the distance without a change of tires. By 1955 the Darlington track, known to racing fans as "the Granddaddy of them all," was

The Pepsi 400, Daytona International Speedway, October 17, 1998.

attracting a maximum of 75,000 fans to the annual race, and the crowds remain that size every year. Harold Brasington's dream succeeded beyond all expectation.

Another event that boosted NASCAR to national prominence came in 1951 when the Detroit Chamber of Commerce called on Bill France to organize an automobile race as part of the Motor City's 250th anniversary celebration. France chose a one mile dirt racetrack in the Michigan State Fairgrounds and planned a race for stock cars that would run 250 miles, one for each year of the city's age. He also asked all the automobile manufacturers to enter at least one car in the race, and 15 agreed. On August 12, a crowd of 16,500 racing fans filled the track for the Motor City 250, and they saw 59 cars in a close, exciting race, with the lead changing 14 times. The winner was undecided until the last lap, when Tommy Thompson, in a 1951 Chrysler, out-foxed Joe Eubanks in a 1950 Oldsmobile 88.

The Motor City 250 enabled France to make two important breakthroughs: stock car racing, a sport bred in the South, became accepted in the North, and Detroit's auto makers became convinced that this popular sport could be good for a corporation's bottom line. Corporate sponsorships immediately began to bolster NASCAR's profits and winners' purses, and companies like Chevrolet, Ford, Goodyear, and Unocal began partnerships that have enhanced more than 50 years of NASCAR's history. Before these sponsorships, race

drivers could hardly earn enough in prizes to keep their cars in tires; in the Motor City race, the first three cars won $5,000, $2,000, and $1,000, with the next seven making a few hundred dollars, and the other 52 cars only $25 or $50. In 1999, winners' purses have escalated so much that the top drivers employ racing teams to build as many as 12 cars a season at a cost of $70,000 each, all meeting NASCAR's exact specifications and assembled with the hope that the driver will gain 2/10 of a second advantage.

To move NASCAR into the modern era, Bill France risked his entire fortune to build the plush Daytona International Speedway, a 2.5 mile oval designed for high speeds with sweeping turns banked at 31 degrees. Fireball Roberts, a popular 1960s driver, said you could "flat-foot it all the way." Lee Petty, father of Richard and winner of the first Daytona 500, said there was not a driver there who was not "scared" of the steeply banked track. "We never had raced on a track like that before." It all added to the mystique of the race, and the fans came in droves. In 1959, there were 42,000, and today the grandstands at Daytona for the annual opening event of the NASCAR season hold over 140,000. This success led to other major tracks, and construction on super speedways in Atlanta, Charlotte, and Hanford, California, started in 1960. In 1969 France lapped the field again with the building of the spectacular Talladega, Alabama, track—2.66 miles long and a lane wider than Daytona—which took the sport to a new level, with cars racing three abreast at higher speeds than ever before. It was at Talladega that Bill Elliott drove the fastest lap in the NASCAR books: 212 miles per hour.

One of the reasons for NASCAR's continued success has been the "consistent, enforceable rules" that France had envisioned for governing the sport. He always believed that it was close, side-by-side racing that drew the fans, and to preserve fair competition NASCAR showed no favoritism. Whether the rule violator was a champion or a rising star, the penalty was consistent. Seven-time Winston Cup champion Richard Petty was caught with an illegal engine in 1983 and fined $35,000. Jeff Gordon was the series leader and eventual Winston Cup champ in 1995 when his team was fined $65,000 for using an unapproved wheel hub. Such strict inspection had begun in the very first "Strictly Stock Car" race in 1949, when Glenn Dunnaway crossed the finish line first but was disqualified when a post-race inspector discovered a wedge had been placed in the rear suspension to stiffen the springs and improve handling, a trick long known by moonshine runners.

In 1999, NASCAR is sanctioning approximately 2,000 events a year in 12 separate divisions at over 100 race tracks across the United States. More than 16 million people attend these events, which are watched by another 150 million on television. The premier series is the Winston Cup, featuring the top drivers and cars that are factory-supported by Chevrolet, Ford, and Pontiac. Second is the Busch Series, Grand National Division, a training ground for Winston Cup drivers of the future. Also popular is the Winston Racing Series of weekly races at more than 100 short tracks, a grassroots level of racing that produces its own national champion.

On February 7, 1999, a stock-car race driver came in second in the ARCA 200 at Daytona after having taken three years off to give birth to two children and start an interior design business. The driver was Shawna Robinson, who walked away from racing in 1995 after five seasons in the Busch Grand National Series, in which she became the first woman to win a NASCAR national series race. From its beginning, stock car racing has changed with the times while continuing to give its fans thrills and surprises.

—Benjamin Griffith

FURTHER READING:

Bledsoe, Jerry. *The World's Number One, Flat-Out, All-Time Great, Stock Car Racing Book.* Garden City, New York, Doubleday, 1975.

Hagstrom, Robert G. *The NASCAR Way: The Business That Drives the Sport.* New York, Wiley, 1998.

Howell, Mark D. *From Moonshine to Madison Avenue: A Cultural History of the NASCAR Winston Cup Series.* Bowling Green, Ohio, Bowling Green State University Popular Press, 1997.

Stock Market Crashes

Information concerning the stock market fills American daily newspapers and television reports. With so many Americans belonging to pension plans and other long-term investment programs, stock market shifts touch more people now than ever before. When the stock market is on the rise, everyone views it is a positive signal; investments are increasing in value and a bullish market must mean the economy is good. But what are the repercussions when the stock market goes sour? What happens to American society and culture when the stock market falters or even crashes? In order to evaluate the full social and cultural implications of market crashes, an understanding of the 1929 crash and subsequent Great Depression is necessary. For it was the 1929 crash that has left a permanent mark on American society. That crash led to important policy changes and basically defined the terminology and standards by which the United States would judge future market shifts.

The 1920s had been very good economic times for most Americans. By 1929, production and employment were high, wages were increasing, and prices were stable; there were more middle-class Americans than ever before. American capitalism was in a lively phase and business was good. But while most of the American public did not understand the nuances of the stock market, they did understand there was a lot of speculation and many "get-rich-quick" schemes. In fact, rich and well-connected investors were buying stocks with little or no money down. And there was a feeling throughout the nation that these speculative designs were immoral and might soon lead to severe economic problems.

Still, by the summer of 1929, the stock market boom was a dominant topic of conversation. The bull market not only dominated the news, it also dominated the culture. At any posh party was an investment broker willing to tell his rich friends what to do. Everybody seemed to be a stock market expert and many regular investors were looking to make a quick fortune. Economist John Kenneth Galbraith wrote of the diversity of people playing the stocks: "The rich man's chauffeur drove with his ears laid back to catch the news of an impending move in Bethlehem Steel; he held fifty shares himself . . . The window cleaner at the broker's office paused to watch the ticker . . . [I was told of] a broker's valet who made nearly a quarter of a million in the market, of a trained nurse who cleaned up thirty-thousand following the tips given her by grateful patients; and of a Wyoming cattleman, thirty miles from the nearest railroad, who bought or sold a thousand shares a day."

Then came the famous Stock Market Crash. At first, it seemed like this might be just another downturn. Most assumed the market would just right itself as it had done on earlier occasions. On October 24, 1929, the day now called "Black Thursday," however, thirteen million shares were traded and many of America's key businesses, including RCA and Westinghouse, lost nearly half of their value. It is a day in which millions lost all of their money, savings, and hope. By 11:00 a.m. there was a wild scramble to sell, but few buyers. Prices continued to drop as crowds began to form around brokerage houses throughout cities all over the nation. That day, suicides had already begun as 11 well-known speculators killed themselves. There was a last-ditch effort by some key bankers to prop up the market but that only worked for several days. Then came October 29, a day in which over 16 million shares were dumped. The holes which the bankers had closed opened wide. One precocious messenger boy at the Stock Exchange decided to bid a dollar for a block of stocks and he actually got them! No bankers were around to bale the market out, for they were all broke too.

The stock market never righted itself and for a variety of reasons, a severe depression ensued. By 1932 unemployment had reached 25 percent—it had been 3 percent in 1929. The Gross National Product (GNP) fell to 67 percent of its 1929 level. Farm prices fell 60 percent from 1929 to 1932, and between 1930 and 1933 more than 5,500 banks closed. In addition, the suicide rate climbed 30 percent between 1929 and 1932. This Great Depression lasted from 1929 to 1941, and ended only when the United States began to prepare for World War II.

The Great Depression had a lasting effect on several generations of Americans. Even when World War II ended, many assumed the depression would resume. The conservative culture of the 1950s, marked by its lack of dissent and need for social acceptance, can be traced back to that 1929 depression. By 1950, many American families feared another economic crash and remained uncomfortable with economic expansion, credit, and cheap loans. It is accurate to say that the generation of Americans who lived through the 1929 crash and the subsequent depression never forgot it. And it has been those Americans who have continued to make the crash and Great Depression part of American culture and lore.

Evidence shows that the American people and its government, from 1945 to about 1973, were indeed influenced by the depression in several ways. First was the belief that both the federal budget and family budgets should be balanced. On the federal level, the budget deficit did not begin in earnest until 1980. On the personal level, families only purchased major household items when they could pay cash. There was little or no credit for most Americans, as debt was considered a poor judgement at best, and even immoral to some. Second, people also saved more money in the post-depression years. Savings reached a peak during the 1950s as the American public still worried about economic downturns. The belief in society was that if families stayed out of debt and saved their money, they could survive another serious economic downturn.

Personal economic paradigms, however, began to change in the United States—along with everything else—during the 1960s. First, the federal government began to spend more than it took in. This started during the Vietnam War and although the deficit never reached 1980 levels, the mere fact deficits existed provided a startling change in economic policy. Second, as the economy boomed during the 1960s, more and more consumer spending was needed to keep the economy vigorous. Because of this, more credit cards and cheap loans were issued and people were actually encouraged to spend more than they earned. Business leaders argued that spending was good for the economy while too much savings were counterproductive—saving too much money would slow economic growth and cost American jobs. Third, going in debt did not seem immoral to the new generation of Americans who did not remember the depression. The youth of the 1960s and 1970s only heard stories about the Great Depression but had not faced the economic challenges of their parents and grandparents. These new consumers wanted to purchase goods and did not want to wait until they had the cash. Consumer credit and personal debt began to soar.

Clearly, since 1929 the effects of stock market dips have changed with generational perceptions. Market downturns in the late 1940s and early 1950s were met by citizens who lived through the depression. Their survival tactics during these periods included increased savings, earning extra income, and in rural areas, growing and selling their own food and produce. Those were all lessons learned from earlier times; the key during an economic downturn was not to borrow or increase your debt.

The new generation of consumers that came of age in the early 1970s, however, viewed the economy in a much different way. When the market dipped in the 1970s, people actually spent more, went into debt, did not save, and assumed they would make up the difference when the economy rebounded. To these Baby Boomers coming of age, the market would always right itself and debt was not an immoral thing.

There have been crashes since 1929, and each time the stock market falls, the 1929 terminology permeates newspapers and other media outlets. But the crashes that have occurred since 1929 have not had the same economic, social, or cultural effects because the salience of the Great Crash has disappeared. In 1987 there was a stock market crash reminiscent to the 1929 fall. Several brokerage houses collapsed and thousands of investors lost money. The Dow Jones industrial stocks fell 22.6 percent. This time, however, things did right themselves relatively quickly. Fearing the economic repercussions of the 1987 crash, the Federal Reserve Board, the White House, and Congress acted swiftly. Passing legislation to right the economy was not considered in 1929 because politicians believed it more prudent not to tinker with the free market system. A major result of the 1929 crash was that the government began to take an active role in times of economic downturn by enacting fiscal and monetary policy changes.

In 1998, the stock market again fell precipitously. Investment portfolios declined but it seemed to cause little panic and few economic worries. Again, the federal government and Federal Reserve Board offered policy alterations and the market recovered in a short period of time. Those most adversely effected by the 1998 crash were small nations with strong economic ties to the United States. The American economy, with fiscal and monetary policy changes, is able to weather market fluctuations. But many smaller nations are hurt when the American economy goes into a tailspin, even if for a short period of time.

With fewer and fewer people who remember the 1929 crash still living on the eve of the twenty first century, fears about stock market crashes have been blunted. In 1929, many American economic and business structures were still weak and could not handle the crash. But because of the 1929 crash, American banks, businesses, and policy makers are prepared for problems and make the necessary adjustments. In every crash since 1929, the market has rebounded and subsequent recessions or depressions have been avoided. But because the 1929 crash had such dire economic consequences, it remains an important social and cultural event—even if its economic significance has lost salience. Drops in the current market are always compared with 1929 declines. Unemployment rates, productivity figures, and other economic data is generally contrasted with 1929 figures. And post-crash depression stories are still part of American popular culture. There are many tales about those who lived through the depression and in later years refused to put their money in banks, opting instead to place all their savings in mattresses or freezers. While more enlightened economic policies have made it possible to easily survive a stock market crash, the 1929 calamity and its aftermath will forever be the standard against which Americans measure economic and social problems.

—David E. Woodard

FURTHER READING:

Brinkley, Alan. *The End of Reform: New Deal Liberalism in Recession and War.* New York, Vintage Books, 1995.

Galbraith, John Kenneth. *The Great Crash.* Boston, Houghton Mifflin, 1954.

Leuchtenburg, William. *The Perils of Prosperity, 1914-1932.* 2nd edition. Chicago, The University of Chicago Press, 1993.

Nash, Gerald. *The Crucial Era: The Great Depression and World War II, 1929-1945.* 2nd edition. New York, St. Martin's Press, 1992.

Stockton, "Pudgy" (1917—)

The unofficial queen of Muscle Beach, Santa Monica's Abbye "Pudgy" Eville Stockton inspired thousands of women to join gyms and take up weight training in the 1940s and early 1950s in much the same way that John Grimek ushered in the modern era of men's bodybuilding. Before Stockton, there were a few professional strongwomen who trained with weights, but they were generally massively proportioned women who unintentionally helped perpetuate the myth that weight training would make women large, unattractive, and perhaps a trifle coarse. Stockton, with her glowing skin, shining hair, miraculous curves, and amazing strength, changed all that. At the end of the Depression, Stockton became emblematic of the new type of woman needed to win the war. Competent, feminine, strong, yet still traditionally sexy, Stockton became the media darling of Muscle Beach and famous around the world.

Abbye Eville was born August 11, 1917, and moved to Santa Monica in 1924. Called Pudgy as a small child by her father, the name stuck, even though at five feet two inches she normally weighed about 115 pounds. Pudgy began seeing UCLA student Les Stockton during her senior year in high school. Their favorite date was to go to the beach and practice gymnastics. In the early days of Muscle Beach, Pudgy and Les, whom she married in 1941, primarily worked on acrobatic and gymnastic feats. With their friend Bruce Conner, they performed at football game half-time shows and other venues in an acrobatic act known as the Three Aces. Their practice sessions attracted other gymnasts, adagio dancers, and handbalancers, and began drawing audiences to the beach. On weekends following World War II, it was not uncommon for several thousand people to see their performances. To capitalize on the interest, the City of Santa Monica erected an outdoor platform to slightly elevate them above the crowd, and Muscle Beach was born.

The media also gathered at Muscle Beach on the weekends and quickly capitalized on Pudgy's rare combination of strength, physical beauty, and charisma. The main photo pictorials of the era—*Life, Pic,* and *Laff*—included her in photo essays, and two newsreels, *Whatta Build* and *Muscle Town USA,* also featured her. She appeared in ads for the Ritamine Vitamin Company and the Universal Camera Company in the late 1930s and, by her own count, was on the cover of forty-two magazines from around the world by the end of the 1940s.

In 1944, Stockton began writing a regular women's training column in *Strength & Health* magazine, a task she did for most of the next decade. Writing in what was then the most influential fitness magazine in the world, Stockton featured the women who trained with her at Muscle Beach as she argued for the benefits of weight training for women. In article after article in her "Barbelles" column, Stockton demonstrated that weights would enhance a woman's figure and make any woman a better athlete; and as proof, she showed her readers photographs of herself and other women who trained with weights. Stockton also helped to organize the first sanctioned weightlifting contests for women and publicized them in *Strength & Health.* The first such meet to carry an Amateur Athletic Union sanction was held February 28, 1947, at the Southwest Arena in Los Angeles. In that contest Stockton pressed 100 pounds, snatched 105 pounds, and clean and jerked 135 pounds. In 1948, Les and Pudgy opened a women's gym in Los Angeles, and for the next several decades she continued to instruct in her own and others' gyms in the Los Angeles area, preaching her message of the benefits of weight training for women.

Although Pudgy held only one "bodybuilding title" during her career (she was selected by Bernarr Macfadden as Miss Physical Culture Venus for 1948 at the age of thirty-one), her influence on women's bodybuilding and weight training has been enormous. Every woman bodybuilder who puts on a swimsuit and steps up on the posing dais, every woman weight lifter who strains under a clean and jerk, and every woman power lifter who fights through the pull of a heavy deadlift owes a debt of gratitude to Stockton, whose personal example helped make these modern sports possible. Stockton's great and enduring gift to the world of bodybuilding was the living proof that muscles could be feminine, womanly strength could be an asset, and that working out was fun.

—Jan Todd, Ph.D.

FURTHER READING:

Chowder, Ken. "Muscle Beach." *Smithsonian.* November 29, 1998, 124-37.

Matzer, Marla. "The Venus of Muscle Beach." *Los Angeles Times Magazine.* February 22, 1998, 20-22.

Todd, Jan. "The Legacy of Pudgy Stockton." *Iron Game History.* Vol. 2. January 1992, 5-7.

Stokowski, Leopold (1882-1977)

A brilliant symphony orchestra conductor and arranger of classical music, Leopold Antoni Stanislaw Stokowski achieved his greatest fame as conductor of the Philadelphia Orchestra, beginning in 1912. His statuesque physique, flowing hair, and theatrical temperament came to symbolize for generations of Americans—and for other conductors—how the musical directors of symphony orchestras should look and behave. Stokowski was especially admired and respected for creating an ensemble with so unique a sound that the Philadelphia Orchestra was considered by many musicians to be the greatest in the world. Eventually, celebrity entered his personal life when he married heiress Gloria Vanderbilt.

In the 1930s, Hollywood beckoned and Stokowski appeared with singer Deanna Durbin in films that were merely vehicles for their talents. The exception was Walt Disney's *Fantasia,* in which animation was blended with Stokowski conducting superb renditions of works by classical composers. The films reinforced Stokowski's image, allowing millions to see him in action.

—Milton Goldin

FURTHER READING:

Daniel, Oliver. *Stokowski: A Counterpoint of View.* New York, Dodd, Mead, 1982.

Leopold Stokowski

Stone, Irving (1903-1989)

A prolific, best-selling author whose entertaining biographical novels and "biohistories" have proved far more popular with readers than with scholars or critics, Irving Stone is best known for works that, in the words of one critic, are pleasing to people who like their history "a little embellished with fiction." By far his two most memorable works are a pair of books that offer monumental, sweeping accounts of the lives of two world-class artists: *Lust for Life: A Novel of Vincent van Gogh* (1934) and *The Agony and the Ecstasy: A Novel of Michelangelo* (1961). Stone also wrote a series of popular fictionalized histories of the nation's First Families: *The President's Lady* (1951), about Andrew and Rachel Robards Jackson; *Love Is Eternal* (1954), about Abraham and Mary Todd Lincoln; and *Those Who Love* (1965), about John and Abigail Smith Adams. American political radicals figured in some of Stone's other works, such as *Sailor on Horseback: The Biography of Jack London* (1938), a book that, in translation, was immensely popular in the former Soviet Union; *Clarence Darrow for the Defense* (1941), and *Adversary in the House* (1947), an account of Socialist leader Eugene V. Debs.

Irving Stone, who took his family name from his stepfather after his mother's remarriage, was born Irving Tennenbaum in San Francisco, California, on July 14, 1903 to Charles and Pauline Rosenberg Tennenbaum. As a child, Stone was a self-described "hopeless bookworm," who was inspired to be a writer after devouring the work of Jack London, Frank Norris, Sherwood Anderson, and Gertrude Atherton. In order to continue his education after graduating from high school, Stone took a variety of odd jobs to work his way through the University of California, including saxophone player, fruit picker, meat packer, and hotel clerk. He majored in political science, graduating with honors in 1923, and taught economics at the University of Southern California while working toward his Masters degree there. But he soon abandoned his academic career to indulge his passion for writing. With ambitions to be a dramatist, he moved to New York, but few of his scripts made it to the stage. Like many American intellectuals of the period, he spent some time in Paris, where he chanced to see an exhibit of van Gogh's paintings that forever changed his direction. "It was the single most compelling emotional experience of my life," he later said, and immediately embarked on extensive research into the life of the nineteenth-century Impressionist painter. After rejection by more than a dozen publishers, during which time Stone supported himself by writing pulp-detective stories, his Van Gogh biography was finally published in 1934, as *Lust for Life,* and quickly became a best-selling book. (It would later be made into a popular film starring Kirk Douglas.)

Stone made one more foray into playwriting, however; but when his Broadway drama, *Truly Valiant,* closed after one performance in 1935, he realized he had no talent for the medium and, from then on, he devoted himself exclusively to biographical subjects with the help of his new bride, Jean Factor, who collaborated with him as an editor or co-writer. Among the works they jointly edited was *Dear Theo* (1937), based on the correspondence between Vincent Van Gogh and his brother. Several of the biographies Stone wrote over the next ten years were favorable portraits of progressive political figures admired by their author, including Jack London, Clarence Darrow, and Eugene V. Debs. Another book, *Earl Warren* (1948), featured the then-California governor and future Chief Justice of the United States. In the 1950s, Stone began using the term "biohistory" to describe his works, such as *Men to Match My Mountains* (1956), written for Doubleday's Mainstream of America series, a fictionalized narrative of the settling of the American West.

Next turning his attention to the life of Michelangelo Buonarroti, Stone commissioned the first complete translation of the Renaissance artist's letters into English and spent more than two years living in Italy, near sites significant to his subject. The result, *The Agony and the Ecstasy* (1961), sold several million copies, was made into a motion picture starring Charlton Heston, and earned Stone decorations from the Italian government. Stone and his wife subsequently edited 600 of the letters into *I, Michelangelo, Sculptor* (1962), a first-person portrait. That year also saw the publication of *Lincoln: A Contemporary Portrait,* which Stone edited with historian Allen Nevins. Other subjects for Stone's works have included Charles Darwin (*The Origin,* 1980); and Sigmund Freud (*The Passions of the Mind,* 1971). In a century in which popular culture appropriated politics, art, literature, and history, Stone was a preeminent purveyor of the accessible mainstream biography. Stone died on August 26, 1989.

—Edward Moran

FURTHER READING:

Stone, Irving. *The Agony and the Ecstasy: A Novel of Michelangelo.* New York, Doubleday, 1961.

———. *An Irving Stone Reader.* New York, Doubleday, 1963.

———. *Love Is Eternal.* New York, Doubleday, 1954.

———. *Lust for Life: A Novel of Vincent Van Gogh.* New York, Longmans Green & Company, 1934.

———. *Men to Match My Mountains.* New York, Doubleday, 1956.

———. *The Origin.* New York, Doubleday, 1980.

———. *The Passions of the Mind: A Novel of Sigmund Freud.* New York, Doubleday, 1971.

Stone, Irving and Jean Stone, editors. *Dear Theo.* New York, Houghton Mifflin, 1937.

———. *I, Michelangelo, Sculptor.* New York, Doubleday, 1962.

Stone, Oliver (1946—)

Since the mid-1970s, Oliver Stone has been involved in writing, directing, and producing over 30 films in a wide range of styles and genres. Most of his work has been critically and commercially successful, but, since the 1980s, it has also been controversial. Films like *Salvador* and *Platoon,* both released in 1986, criticized United States government policy over El Salvador and Vietnam, sidestepping the prevailing confident patriotic mood to deal with the effects of war in a realistic and thoughtful way. In the 1990s, films like *Natural Born Killers* (1994), in which two young lovers travel around New Mexico, killing as they go, have led to further accusations of exploitation and gratuitous violence. Since *Salvador,* the subject matter of Stone's films has ranged from political conspiracy in *JFK* (1991) and *Nixon* (1995), to war and its cultural effects in *Platoon* (1986) and *Born on*

Oliver Stone

the Fourth of July (1989), to rock biopic in *The Doors* (1991). With their roots in the "New Cinema" of Hollywood at the end of the 1960s, Stone's films contain a blend of realism, social documentary, and political enquiry that has made him a difficult but important commentator on American culture in the late twentieth century.

After spells teaching English, and later fighting in Vietnam in the 1960s, Stone returned from the war in 1968 to study film at New York University. Like many other directors of his generation, Stone benefitted from the new graduate programs in film history, theory, and production that appeared in the 1960s. Film schools at the University of California Los Angeles and New York University, among others, produced directors and writers such as Francis Ford Coppola, Brian de Palma, and Martin Scorsese, many of whose films, like Stone's, have been among the most influential of the 1970s, 1980s, and 1990s.

Stone began his filmmaking career as the writer, director, and editor of a horror film, *Seizure* (1974), and won his first academy award, for Best Adapted Screenplay, in 1978, for *Midnight Express.* In the early 1980s, Stone had his most success as a screenwriter, taking writing credits for *Conan the Barbarian* (1981) and *Scarface* (1983). He has also been influential as a producer of many of his own films, as well as the television series, *Wild Palms* (1993), and films such as *The Joy Luck Club* (1993) and *Reversal of Fortune* (1990), among others. Additionally, he has acted, making appearances as a reporter in *Born on the Fourth of July,* as a professor in *The Doors,* and as a financial trader in his 1987 film, *Wall Street.*

Graduates of the film schools have often become known for their technical skill and mastery of visual effects, and Stone is no exception. His best known visual technique is the use of a variety of different types of film stock to present different viewpoints. In films like *JFK* and *Natural Born Killers,* Stone also used news and amateur film, mixed in with "made" footage, to reconstruct events and give them an "authentic" appearance. Since the late 1980s, the mixing of images using digital techniques has become much cheaper and easier, and other directors, such as Stone's contemporary, Steven Speilberg, also a film school graduate, have used the technique to good effect, for example in *Schindler's List* (1993). But while Spielberg tends to blend "real" and "made" footage to create a continuous visual quality, Stone plays on the different textures of formats like Super 8, 35mm, and video to disrupt the flow of the narrative, and make the viewer's position less secure.

Salvador (1986) was Stone's first major success as a film director. Based on the experiences of Richard Boyle, a journalist in El Salvador in 1980-1981, the film portrays the Salvadoran government's violent suppression of opposition, and is deeply critical of American support for the right-wing regime. In the same year, *Platoon* took a similarly realistic approach to representing the war in Vietnam. The film won four Academy awards, including for Best Picture and Best Director, and marks the beginning of Stone's rise as an influential director and producer. Following *Platoon,* several films dealing in a new way with the issue of Vietnam found success for other directors; these included *Full Metal Jacket* (Stanley Kubrick, 1987) and *Good Morning, Vietnam* (Barry Levinson, 1988). As David Cook points out, however, the fashion for films about Vietnam did not only include sensitive treatments of modern warfare; *Platoon* came along at around the same time as more exploitative films, like *Born American* (Renny Harlin, 1986) and *Rambo: First Blood, Part II* (George Pan Cosmatos, 1985).

Stone's second Vietnam film, *Born on the Fourth of July* (1989), contains some combat footage, but concentrates on the cultural issues of the treatment of war veterans, and in particular those, like Ron Kovac, whose injuries made them an embarrassment to the military authorities and the general public. Having dealt with Vietnam from the point of view of soldiers in combat in *Platoon* and of veterans in *Born on the Fourth of July,* in 1993 Stone considered the experience of war from the other side. *Heaven and Earth* describes the war from the point of view of a Vietnamese peasant woman who experiences the fighting as a child and later marries an American soldier. Besides his efforts to represent war in more realistic ways, and from the point of view of its victims, Stone is also known as a shrewd social and cultural commentator. In the late 1980s, for example, films like *Wall Street* (1987) and *Talk Radio* (1988) dealt with current concerns about the financial markets, greed, and the media's manipulation of celebrities and its audience. In 1991, *The Doors* appeared as a film portrait of the rock band and its charismatic singer, Jim Morrison. While the portrait of Morrison is a fan's account, the film is ruthless in its treatment of drug and rock culture.

Since the early 1990s, Stone's trademark technique of switching between film stocks, as well as using hand-held cameras and natural lighting, has made watching his films a more directly engaging experience. The disorienting effect of the unstable camera involves the viewer in the unfolding scene in ways that are not possible with more formal styles of filmmaking. Perhaps his most important film, *JFK* (1991), relies on such techniques to make telling comments on the creation of myths by the media and government. Dealing with the assassination of President Kennedy in November 1963, the film revives the 1967 theory of New Orleans District Attorney Jim Garrison that Kennedy could not have been shot by Oswald as the Warren Commission had found. Following the release of the film, Stone was attacked for having rewritten the facts about the assassination. Critics pointed to the way in which the famous amateur film of the killing had been enhanced and manipulated to prove Garrison's theory, but Stone also came in for criticism for his speculation about plots against Kennedy in the security forces and government. Despite the opinions of critics, the film was a success with audiences, prompting a run on books about the Kennedy assassination, and eventually putting pressure on Congress to release records of the Warren Commission through a special act in 1992. Perhaps because of the controversy, *JFK* received no Oscars, but Stone did receive a Golden Globe Award for Best Director.

JFK was significant for its technical effects as well as the public response it triggered, and *Natural Born Killers,* perhaps Stone's most vilified film, takes the techniques learned in making *JFK* still further. The movie includes animation and other electronic imaging methods, as well as live action shots on several different film stocks, with the effect that the images themselves, as well as the subject matter, bombard the viewer in a quite relentless way. David Cook speculates that the film is Stone's response to the media's treatment of *JFK*. *Natural Born Killers* exposes the hypocrisy of a media that criticized him for twisting the truth, yet makes fortunes out of goading the public to ever greater voyeuristic excesses. Certainly the murderous couple in Stone's film are presented in such a way as to make their acts of violence fascinating rather than repellent. Manipulating the viewer, even though it admits to doing so, *Natural Born Killers* speculates about how much more manipulative the supposedly objective media might be.

Many of Stone's films look at the way individuals are controlled and used by bigger organizations. As a result, he has often found himself in opposition to current thinking, and has been described as a dissident by his supporters. Like those of many directors who came

through the film schools in the 1960s, Stone's films have a reputation for provoking strong emotional responses in audiences. Perhaps for this reason, films like *JFK* and *Natural Born Killers* have sometimes received harsh treatment at the hands of their critics. Oliver Stone's main achievement as a film director, however, has been his contribution to the valuable tradition of socially challenging independent filmmaking that began in the 1960s with directors such as Arthur Penn, Sam Peckinpah, and Stanley Kubrick.

—Chris Routledge

FURTHER READING:

Cook, David A. *A History of Narrative Film.* New York, W.W. Norton, 1996.

Kagan, Norman. *The Cinema of Oliver Stone.* New York, Continuum, 1995.

Kunz, Don. *The Films of Oliver Stone.* Lanham, Maryland, Scarecrow Press, 1997.

Riordan, James. *Stone: The Controversies, Excesses, and Exploits of a Radical Filmmaker.* New York, Hyperion, 1995.

Stonewall Rebellion

In the early hours of June 28, 1969 patrons of a gay men's bar in Greenwich Village, and their allies in the street, vigorously resisted a routine police raid. The event, which has been described as "the hairpin drop heard around the world," and as one of those "specific sparks that ignites protest," was both timely and inevitable. It came about during an era of cultural and social ferment, and after years of efforts on the part of homosexuals to gain a public voice and legitimate place in U.S. society. The Stonewall Rebellion became a "metaphor for emergence, visibility and pride," one that publicly affirmed the identity of a people burdened with a tradition of invisibility and abuse.

A variety of factors including modernity, changes in cultural and sexual mores, and a politicized environment have been identified as supporting the development of urban homosexual subcultures and subsequently a homosexual movement. In New York City, the geographic and cultural setting for these radical changes was established in the bohemian, avant-garde atmosphere that began developing in Greenwich Village during the 1940s. Significant influences included the Beat Culture, pop art, psychedelics, the New American Cinema, off-Broadway theatre, and the activist folk music scene. In short, the area was an incubator for oppositional attitudes toward convention and traditional authority and these attitudes spread across the country.

Cultural critic Daniel Harris, has also proposed that "diva worship," among male homosexuals, was another factor that unwittingly contributed to gay militancy. Since homosexual males had no other gay positive images, many projected themselves either into the tragic and resilient Judy Garland ("the ultimate bellwether of the docile gay masses"), or the "invincible personas" portrayed by the likes of Joan Crawford and Bette Davis. In short, homosexuals "recycled the refuse of popular culture and reconstituted it into an energizing force."

Homosexual militancy was also nurtured by the politicized atmosphere of the time. Since the 1950s, Mattachine, ONE, and Daughters of Bilitis had publicly advocated for respect and civil rights for homosexuals. In the 1960s, the activities and gains of the Civil Rights Movement and other social movements also promoted a new sense of hope and assertiveness among politicized homosexuals.

For some gay men, the death of Judy Garland a few days before the Stonewall uprising, symbolically transformed the stereotype of the quiet, suffering homosexual. Activist Alkarim Jivani observed that "Garland had been the archetypal gay icon because she represented bravery through adversity, but that bravery was characterized by a passive stoicism. With the death of Judy Garland, that image of the gay man died."

Meanwhile, for those who identified with the battling, invincible divas, the moment of truth was fast approaching. According to one report, the day of Judy's funeral was "sweltering and humid, and that night there was a full moon." Vito Russo, who later wrote a book on homosexual themes in U.S. films (*The Celluloid Closet*), recalled that "I was in a foul mood that night because of the funeral." Ira Kushner, who was 15 at the time, remembers standing outside the Stonewall as part of a crowd that had gathered to honor Garland. Then the police arrived.

At first the police arrested some of the younger men standing outside and then they went into the bar. As the patrons were roughly hustled out of the bar, it was those most used to confrontations with the police (drag queens, street people, students, and a few butches), who were in the vanguard of the resistance. Drag queen Rey "Sylvia Lee" Rivera recalled that "that night, everything clicked." Rivera and some of the people he knew were already involved in other social movements. He told himself, "Great, now it's my time. I'm out there being a revolutionary for everybody else, now it's time to do my own thing for my own people," according to E. Marcus' book, *Making History*. In the midst of the Vietnam War, the civil rights movement, counterculture, student and women's movements, patrons of the Stonewall bar refused to go quietly into the police van.

There are also reports that, as the tension increased, a well-placed spark was contributed by a butch in drag. She had been visiting a male friend in the bar. When the police pulled her out of the bar and into a police car, she struggled. When she was hit, the audience exploded. Coins (symbolizing the bribes paid to the police by the bars), an uprooted parking meter, bottles, fists, and insults flew. Queens engaged in campy street theatre that included sexual repartee aimed at the police and a chorus line singing "We are the Stonewall girls. . ." The bar was set on fire, the police called for reinforcements, and the melee escalated into a riot. Although this was not the first time that homosexuals had resisted police abuse, this time, there were significant political consequences.

While moderate homosexuals condemned the violence, more radical activists used the event as an organizing opportunity. In New York, the event galvanized those sympathetic to confrontation politics. By July, these activists had coalesced into the co-gender Gay Liberation Front (GLF), a name that suggested solidarity with Third World resistance movements, such as the National Liberation Front in Vietnam. Across the United States, scores of groups with the same name sprang up. GLF was the first of many homosexual activist groups of that era, most of whom were politically at odds with one another. What these groups did have in common was a radical

commitment to the civil rights of homosexuals. The groups were loosely connected into a network known as the Gay Liberation Movement. By 1973 there were over 800 gay and lesbian groups and organizations in the United States.

Main Street U.S.A. took little notice of the Stonewall event. News of the riot was buried in the back pages of the *New York Times.* Other mass market publications such as *Life, Newsweek, Time,* and *Harper's,* which had previously published sympathetic articles about homosexuals, also failed to recognize the importance of the event. While the mainstream press missed the significance of Stonewall, the homosexual press which was politically moderate, treated the riot with ambivalence. *The Advocate,* a national gay male publication, published several reports, and one writer wondered if "the spark" set off by Stonewall, would endure. *The Ladder,* a national lesbian publication gave the event two pages of coverage, but the article did not appear until October of 1969.

After Stonewall, coverage of homosexual issues in the mainstream media increased significantly. In October of 1969, *Time* magazine featured the "Homosexual Movement" as a main story. *The Reader's Guide to Periodical Literature,* an index to popular magazines, listed nine entries on "sex perversion" in 1950, the year in which the first Homophile Organization (Mattachine) was founded. By 1970, *The Reader's Guide* listed thirty items under "homosexuality" and one under "lesbianism."

Gradually, the story of Stonewall came to occupy a central position in the folklore and chronology of U.S. gay and lesbian history. It remains so even in the face of claims that it was but one significant event in a long history of individual and collective resistance that spans 400 years of U.S. history. According to Martin Duberman, the event simply "gave meaning and coherence to a struggle that was already underway." However, to many, the special appeal of the Stonewall Rebellion is based on it being a defiant and defining moment that took place during an era filled with similar moments. As in the Boston Tea Party, the use of confrontation radicalized a movement that had, up to that time, relied on documents and discourse.

Since 1970, lesbians and gays in cities across the United States have held annual Gay Pride parades and rallies to commemorate the event. There have been significant turnouts in San Francisco, New York, Los Angeles, and Chicago. San Francisco's event attracts between 350,000 and 500,000 participants and onlookers. Unlike the celebrations of other marginalized groups, Gay Pride memorializes the public emergence of a people and a movement that are still outside the equal protection of the law and are widely unwelcome at the diverse cultural table of this nation.

Stonewall signifies a dividing line between the brave but understandably more conservative efforts of homophile groups founded during the McCarthy Era; those of liminal 1960s groups like the Society for Individual Rights in San Francisco and the Homosexual Action League in Philadelphia; and radical homosexual activists, many of whom had gained organizing skills and new political perspectives in other civil rights movements. The title of a well-known documentary film on gay and lesbian history, *Before Stonewall* (1979), suggests that the event was a radical departure from the homophile era. For those who subscribed to the new liberation ethos, assimilation and dissimulation were out. Instead, they were inspired by slogans like "gay is good" and "out of the closets and into the streets.'' For these lesbians, gay men, and other ''sexual outlaws,'' Stonewall was a watershed event, one that galvanized them into radical activism on behalf of an historically despised group. For a specific generation of activists, the event ''became the symbol of an oppressed and invisible minority at last demanding its place in the sun,'' according to Wayne Dynes in the *Encyclopedia of Homosexuality*.

—Yolanda Retter

FURTHER READING:

Duberman, Martin. *Stonewall*. New York, Penguin, 1994.

Dynes, Wayne, ed. *Encyclopedia of Homosexuality*. New York, Garland, 1990.

Harris, Daniel. ''The Death of Camp: Gay Men and Hollywood Diva Worship, From Reverence to Ridicule.'' *Salmagundi*. Fall 1996, 166-91.

Marcus, E. *Making History: The Struggle for Gay and Lesbian Rights*. New York, Harper, 1992.

Stout, Rex (1886-1975)

U.S. detective-story writer Rex Stout is best remembered for having created the characters of eccentric crime-solver Nero Wolfe and his assistant Archie Goodwin, a memorable duo who appeared in more than 50 books over four decades beginning in the mid-1930s. Wolfe and Goodwin quickly endeared themselves to readers not only for their adeptness at solving crimes but for their trenchant comments on American life, war, big business, and politics. Nero Wolfe, the puffing, grunting, Montenegrin-born heavyweight gumshoe with a

Rex Stout

fondness for food and orchid-growing, made his appearance in 1934 with the publication of *Fer de Lance*. A steady stream of Nero Wolfe books followed, to the point where the character became more well-known than its creator. Often compared by literary critics to Sherlock Holmes and Dr. Watson, Wolfe and Archie played complementary roles in Stout's fiction. Detective work for Wolfe was a business, and his clients were charged handsomely for his services, allowing the investigator to indulge his penchant for orchids and food. Goodwin, like Watson, is the legman, the hardboiled detective who satirically narrates the events in the story. He is dispatched to do all the detecting that Wolfe, the consummate detective, refuses to do. Wolfe is portrayed by his partner as partly human, partly godlike, with an arrogant intelligence, a gourmand's appetite, and an orchid grower extraordinaire. Goodwin treats clients, cops, women, and murderers with the same degree of wit and reality he applies to Wolfe. Singly they would be engaging but together they form a brilliant partnership that brought a new, humorous touch to detective fiction. Another character in the Nero Wolfe series, Inspector L. T. Cramer, NYPD, has been described by George Dove in his book, *The Police Procedural* (1992) as probably the most familiar policeman in classic detective fiction. Cramer's feelings toward Wolfe move from skepticism to open hostility to open admiration within the space of a single novel.

Rex Todhunter Stout was born in Noblesville, Indiana, in 1886, the sixth of nine children of John and Lucetta Todhunter Stout, who were Quakers. The family later moved to Kansas, where by the age of nine, Stout was a child prodigy, especially in mathematics. He attended the University of Kansas but did not complete a degree, leaving to enlist in the United States Navy, where he served as a yeoman on President Theodore Roosevelt's yacht. When he returned to civilian life in 1908 he began working as a bookkeeper, and devised a system of school banking that netted him a considerable fortune, making possible a trip to Paris and an opportunity to write. Among his early freelance articles was one in which he purported to analyze the palm prints he personally obtained from President William Howard Taft. Stout turned out three critically acclaimed novels before *Fer de Lance* that never attained the popularity he later achieved with his Nero Wolfe novels. In his private life Stout was outspoken, first against Nazism and then later against the use of nuclear weapons. In 1941, he served as emcee of the radio program ''Speaking of Liberty'' and, during World War II, he wrote propaganda and volunteered for the Fight for Freedom organization.

In Stout's Nero Wolfe series, the detective is portrayed as solving crimes from his brownstone on New York's 35th Street, adhering to a schedule regardless of murderers with guns, bombs in guest rooms, or clients with problems. In *The League of Frightened Men* (1935), Goodwin suggests that Wolfe step out into the street in front of the house to bring his powers to bear on a cabdriver there, an important witness. ''Out?'' Wolfe exclaims, looking at Goodwin in horror. When Goodwin explains that his employer would not even have to step off the curb, the unflappably cool Wolfe replies, ''I don't know, Archie, why you persist in trying to badger me into frantic sorties.'' Wolfe did, however, leave the house upon occasion to attend orchid shows as in *Some Buried Caesar* (1938) or to be incarcerated in the local jail in *A Family Affair* (1973).

In Stout's novels, character and dialogue are more important than plot. Goodwin is portrayed as dashing around—even falling in love—while Wolfe is defined as a slightly comic but always impressive figure, even if only for his sheer bulk. Weighing a full seventh of a ton, the enormous Wolfe can cross his legs only with great difficulty whenever he finds a strong enough chair in which to seat himself. Goodwin takes great delight in his observation and recording of Wolfe's movements and habits, his glasses of beer, his tending of a collection of 10,000 orchids, or his method of entering a room. Stout himself summed up his career in this quotation: ''You know goddam well why, of all kinds of stories, the detective story is the most popular. It supports, more than any other kind of story, man's favorite myth, that he's *Homo sapien,* the rational animal. And of course the poor son-of-a-bitch isn't a rational animal at all—I think the most important function of the brain is thinking up reasons for the decisions his emotions have made. Detective stories support that myth.''

—Joan Gajadhar

FURTHER READING:

Dove, George. *The Police Procedural.* Bowling Green, Ohio, Bowling Green University Press, 1982.

Keating, H. R. F. *Crime and Mystery, the 100 Best Books.* New York, Carroll and Graf, 1987.

Stout, Rex. *Fer de Lance.* New York, Farrar and Rinehart, 1934.

———. *The League of Frightened Men.* New York, Farrar and Rinehart, 1935.

''Stout, Rex.'' In *World Authors 1900-1950.* New York, H. W. Wilson, 1996.

Symons, Julian. *Bloody Murder: From the Detective Story to the Crime Novel, a History.* London, Faber and Faber, 1972.

Strait, George (1952—)

When George Strait burst on to the national scene in 1981, he was identified with a movement in country music known as New Traditionalism, a return by young country artists to old country styles. Pop music had come to dominate the country charts during the 1970s, and Strait, along with Ricky Skaggs, Randy Travis, and others, were among the dissenters. Before long, Strait went on to become one of music's most commercially successful recording and touring artists.

Born in Poteet and raised in Pearsall, Texas, Strait and his brother lived with their father, a junior high school math teacher and part-time rancher. A true Texas cowboy, Strait helped out on the family ranch. Growing up, he ignored country music in favor of the pop music of the British Invasion of the 1960s, as did many of his peers. In high school, Strait played in a number of garage bands. After graduation, he eloped with Norma, his high-school sweetheart, and after a short flirtation with college, joined the Army in 1971. It was while he was stationed in Hawaii that he began performing country music, as a singer in a band on the base.

Strait finished his military service in 1975, and returned to Texas to study agriculture at Southwest Texas State University. It was there that Strait formed the Ace in the Hole Band, which became a big

George Strait

regional draw. The group released a couple of records on the Dallas-based D Records label and made several trips to Nashville, though they failed to draw the attention of anyone in the music industry there. Erv Woolsey, a Texas club owner and former record-promotions executive, saw the band one night and took an interest. In 1980, Woolsey convinced MCA to sign Strait, and eventually became and remained his manager.

Strait's first single was released in the spring of 1981, and reached the top ten. His 1982 offering ''Fool Hearted Memory'' was his first number-one single, and since then he has had an amazing string of chart successes, including more than 30 number-one country singles. Every album he has released since 1981's *Strait Country* (more than 20 in all) has been certified gold or platinum. He holds many concert box-office records, having mounted some of the most successful United States concert tours in the 1980s and 1990s. In 1992, he made his silver screen debut with a starring role in a film called *Pure Country.* In 1995, MCA released a four-disc career retrospective called *Strait out of the Box,* which became one of the best-selling box sets in country-music history.

Though country music has become increasingly more pop since the 1980s, Strait seldom strays too far from Texas honky-tonk and the shuffle beat of western swing. He has successfully negotiated the line between commercial and traditional for quite some time. He is a song stylist, greatly influenced by Merle Haggard, known for his subtle phrasing and supple vocals. His style is evocative of such classic country singers as Lefty Frizzell and Ray Price. Though he is not a songwriter, he has proven his skills in song selection. His glitter-free cowboy-hat-and-denim fashion style has helped to spawn a legion of faceless ''hat acts'' in country music over the years, but Strait has an understated and elegant presence, existing in stark contrast to the bombastic style of Garth Brooks, country music's other giant male country superstar.

—Joyce Linehan

FURTHER READING:

Bego, Mark. *George Strait: The Story of Country's Living Legends.* New York, Kensington Books, 1997.

Cantwell, David. *George Strait.* New York, Boulevard Books, 1996.

Sgammato, Jo. *Keepin' It Country: The George Strait Story.* New York, Ballantine Books, 1998.

Stratemeyer, Edward (1862-1930)

It seems ironic that America's most prolific creator of juvenile popular fiction is a man whose name is hardly known. Edward Stratemeyer revolutionized the world of children's writing by adapting it to the methods of mass production. His Stratemeyer Syndicate,

Edward L. Stratemeyer

founded at the turn of the twentieth century, hired ghostwriters to develop hundreds of stories based on Stratemeyer's outlines. From this ''fiction factory,'' as some have called it, came such durable American heroes as the Bobbsey Twins, Tom Swift, the Hardy Boys, and Nancy Drew.

Born in New Jersey in 1862, the son of German immigrants, Stratemeyer grew up admiring the rags-to-riches stories of Horatio Alger and aspired to write similar books. The progress of Edward Stratemeyer's career is reminiscent of an Alger plot as well. Although he did not quite start in rags, Stratemeyer eventually obtained riches by steadily climbing the ranks of the professional fiction-writer's business. As a child, he had a small printing press which he used to print and distribute copies of his own stories. As a young adult he sold several small pieces, for small sums, to various papers. But his first important sale came in 1889 when the popular *Golden Days* story paper bought ''Victor Horton's Idea'' for the substantial sum of $75.

Encouraged by this success, Stratemeyer spent the following years publishing widely, using both his own name and several pseudonyms. In addition to selling serials to story papers, he branched out to writing dime novels, and became a regular contributor to the various publications owned by Street and Smith, the premier publisher of popular fiction in its day. In 1893 Stratemeyer became an editor at *Good News,* a Street and Smith publication, while also supplying it with original material. During his years as a writer and editor of dime novels and story papers, Stratemeyer learned principles he would later apply to his own syndicate. He saw, for example, the value of establishing ''house names'' as pseudonyms, for this allowed several authors to work interchangeably on a series without disrupting the public's relationship with the ''author.'' He also saw that copyright holders earned the greatest financial rewards: an author could be hired at a flat rate to produce a story, but the copyright holder could print and reprint that story at will and reap the benefits indefinitely.

Stratemeyer steadily steered his career toward the more respectable world of hardcover fiction. In 1894 he began recycling some of his former story-paper serials as complete books, shaping the volumes into series. The thrifty system of recycling, renaming, and reworking would become a hallmark of the Stratemeyer's operations, influencing his own work and that of the Syndicate for years after his death. In 1898 Stratemeyer enjoyed his first great success with hardcover fiction. He had been circulating a war-themed manuscript just as the Spanish-American war broke out. The publishers reviewing the manuscript asked Stratemeyer to revise it, incorporating the news of Dewey's naval victory in the Philippines. *Under Dewey at Manila* became an immediate bestseller, initiating one of Stratemeyer's many series on historical and military themes.

In 1899 Stratemeyer launched his watershed series, The Rover Boys, under the name Arthur M. Winfield. Stratemeyer later claimed to have chosen this pseudonym for its cryptic symbolism: Arthur stood for ''author,'' and Winfield represented his desire to win in his field. The initial ''M'' stood for the number of books he hoped to sell--first ''a thousand '' (as the Roman numeral for one thousand), and then ''a million,'' depending on when he was asked. The Rover Boys series was an enormous success and was the first series to exemplify what later became the Stratemeyer Syndicate formula: average teenage heroes having extraordinary adventures, with lots of action and excitement driving the plot. Despite his early training in the blood-and-thunder milieu of dime novels, Stratemeyer kept his hardcover fiction for youngsters clean and wholesome. After 1900 Stratemeyer's work for story papers and dime novel houses diminished, as he focused more attention on his own series books. Within a few years he had several series going at once, and decided that an assembly-line approach would be a more efficient method for producing the quantity of material he had in mind.

The Stratemeyer Syndicate, begun in 1905, employed the methods Stratemeyer had learned earlier in his career. He devised plots and titles for stories, then hired ghostwriters to flesh out the skeletons, making them sign agreements not to reveal their identities. His hired hands were other dime novel authors like himself, some of whom he had known at Street and Smith, as well as journalists and other professionals skilled in turning out high quantity on tight deadlines. His most important employee was his friend Howard Garis, who would later become famous in his own right as the author of the Uncle Wiggily stories. For Stratemeyer he wrote several series, most famously Tom Swift. Howard's wife, Lilian Garis, also a children's writer, contributed volumes to the Syndicate's Bobbsey Twins series and others.

Not all of Stratemeyer's properties were for children. He repackaged dime novels from his early career as fare for young adult readers. Moreover, he also functioned as a literary agent who purchased manuscripts from other writers and had them published under various house pseudonyms. A handful of his properties were written for the adult fiction market, such as a series of mysteries written by "Chester K. Steele." But children's series were the backbone of the Stratemeyer Syndicate, and their themes were wide-ranging, covering school stories, westerns, mysteries, sports, career stories, and other genres. The popularity of these books was enormous. The catalogs of Cupples & Leon and Grosset & Dunlap, two of his main publishers, were laden with Syndicate fare—although, thanks to the pseudonyms, young readers were unaware that all of the books they were devouring came from the same source.

Stratemeyer's near-monopoly of the children's series market brought him some unwelcome scrutiny. Franklin K. Mathiews, librarian for the Boy Scouts of America, published a scathing article in *Outlook* magazine in 1914, "Blowing Out the Boys' Brains." In it, Mathiews asserted that sensationalist series books, marked by rapid-fire plots, absurd coincidences, multiple cliff-hangers, and a total lack of character-development, damaged boys' imaginations by over-stimulation, thus ruining them for the subtleties of better literature. There was a degree of sense in Mathiews' complaints, and educators and librarians around the country took up the cry. Stratemeyer's success, however, was never seriously compromised because children loved his books and could afford to buy them themselves. But down through the decades there always remained a strain of protest against the vapidity and sensationalism of series books. The books, however, were not working in a vacuum; they were part of a general trend, catering to the same appetite for speed and superficiality that would later be exemplified by television. Despite disapproval from the more educated segments of the population, children craved this style of entertainment and the great demand called for an equally great supply.

Accordingly, the 1910s and 1920s were prolific decades for the Stratemeyer Syndicate. In the five year span between 1912 and 1917, the syndicate was producing nearly 50 distinct series, and a similar amount ten years later, from 1922-27. But in the spring of 1930 Edward Stratemeyer succumbed to pneumonia, and died at age 68. After attempting unsuccessfully to find a buyer for the syndicate, Stratemeyer's daughters, Harriet Adams and Edna Stratemeyer, assumed operation of the family business.

Stratemeyer left behind enough material to allow the syndicate to continue normally for another two years; after 1932, however, the material was gone and the Great Depression had damaged the book market. The sisters trimmed the business down considerably, killing off nearly their whole line of series. They kept only the proven cash-cows, including Nancy Drew and the Hardy Boys, among a few others. A few new series were begun during the depression, but the syndicate remained a much more conservative and narrowly-focused business than it had been during Stratemeyer's tenure. The body of series was cut down even further when the advent of World War II required conservation of paper and the metal plates used for printing books. By the late 1940s, the syndicate was producing only half a dozen series.

In 1942 Edna Stratemeyer married and moved away, leaving Harriet Adams as the active partner. Adams' strategy for success involved maximizing the value of the syndicate's back-catalog. She resurrected old series in reprint editions with new publishers and signed deals to have her characters translated into foreign languages and other media. Former bestseller Bomba the Jungle Boy benefitted from this treatment, as he became the hero of a string of "B" movies, from 1949-52, and a reprint series of books, both of which were released in other countries as well as the United States. In 1954 Adams revitalized the Tom Swift legacy by launching the Tom Swift, Jr. series, based on the original hero's son. Guided by talented ghostwriter James Lawrence, this series became a major latter-day success for the syndicate. Other new series were attempted during the following years, but the only other substantial hit was The Happy Hollisters (1953-1970), written by syndicate partner Andrew Svenson.

Adams' most controversial decision came in 1959, when she launched a project to revise and rewrite all the volumes in the Hardy Boys and Nancy Drew series, as well as many of the Bobbsey Twins. Her decision was caused primarily by concerns that modern children were impatient with the now old-fashioned texts of the original books. A further motivation came from complaints the syndicate received about the insulting portrayals of ethnic characters. Not only had the syndicate historically tended to cast minorities as villains, but early ghostwriters often used ethnic stereotypes as sources of humor. Adams responded to both concerns with one remedy, gradually replacing original books with new versions that were shorter, thoroughly modern, and (relatively) stereotype-free. The revisions were mere shadows of their former glory, however, as much of the books' charm and style had been erased.

Another controversy erupted in 1979 when Adams changed publishers. Dissatisfied with the practices of Grosset and Dunlap, her primary publishers for nearly 50 years, Adams signed a contract with Simon and Schuster. Grosset sued, and the litigation put the famous syndicate series at the center of a well-publicized custody battle. The case was decided in favor of the syndicate, and Simon and Schuster brought out new versions of Nancy Drew, Tom Swift, the Hardy Boys, and the Bobbsey Twins. Harriet Adams died in 1982, and her partners sold the business to Simon and Schuster two years later. Throughout the 1980s and 1990s the publishers continued to work with their properties in much the same way the syndicate had, hiring ghostwriters and swearing them to secrecy. Despite efforts to revitalize Tom Swift and the Bobbsey Twins, both series were discontinued in the early 1990s, but Nancy Drew and the Hardy Boys continued and even expanded into a variety of spin-off series.

Simon and Schuster's greatest service to the Stratemeyer Syndicate, however, came with its donation of nearly all of the syndicate's paperwork to the New York Public Library. This collection of records, which opened to the public in September 1998, dates from the earliest years of Edward Stratemeyer's career and forms the largest single location for research into the syndicate's history. During the 1990s an increasing number of scholars noted the massive influence of the Stratemeyer Syndicate, not only as the single largest contributor to children's popular fiction in the twentieth century, but also as a model of a publishing phenomenon. Reaching several generations of American readers, the products of the Stratemeyer Syndicate have had an incalculable effect on America's consciousness.

—Ilana Nash

FURTHER READING:

Billman, Carol. *The Secret of the Stratemeyer Syndicate: Nancy Drew, the Hardy Boys and the Million Dollar Fiction Factory.* New York, The Ungar Publishing Company, 1986.

Dizer, John T. *Tom Swift & Company.* Jefferson, North Carolina, McFarland & Co., Inc., 1982.

Garis, Roger. *My Father was Uncle Wiggily.* New York, McGraw-Hill, 1966.

Johnson, Deidre. *Stratemeyer Pseudonyms and Series Books.* Westport, Connecticut, Greenwood Press, 1982.

———. *Edward Stratemeyer and the Stratemeyer Syndicate.* New York, Twayne Publishers, 1993.

Stratemeyer Syndicate
See Stratemeyer, Edward

Stratton-Porter, Gene (1863-1924)

Gene Stratton-Porter was a popular author, photographer, and illustrator whose prolific output of romance-spiced nature writings found an enthusiastic audience with middle-class Americans in the early 1900s. Her 26 books have been through multiple editions (many of the titles still in print at the close of the century), and the most popular of these sold millions of copies in the years leading up to and encompassing World War I.

Stratton-Porter's novels have not endured on the basis of their literary merit. Even at the height of her popularity, critics were not fond of her work, which they considered to be formulaic and unrealistic. The broad appeal of Stratton-Porter's fiction lay in her unique and seemingly effortless ability to portray and foster the vicarious involvement of the reader in the vivid and detailed goings-on of natural dramas: the hatching of great moths, the breeding and nesting of birds, the gurglings and whisperings and unfoldings of swamp and woodland. Nature writing was already an established and successful genre, with authors such as John Burroughs, Ernest Thompson Seton, and John Muir. Stratton-Porter added her own twist, tempering the nature message with enough romantic fiction to engage the reader's interest.

Stratton-Porter wrote what she knew best. Born Geneva Stratton, the youngest of 12 children, in Wabash County, Indiana, she spent long unsupervised hours in fascinated contemplation of the plant and wildlife that abounded in what was as yet largely untamed wilderness. When her family moved into town in her 11th year, she took with her a collection of pet birds. Marriage, in 1886, to Charles Darwin Porter, and the birth of her only daughter, Jeannette, two years later, kept

Stratton-Porter occupied with homely concerns, but the family's move to Geneva, Indiana, in 1890 placed her adjacent to a unique natural setting—Limberlost Swamp. Here, in the kind of personal metamorphosis characteristic of her future plots, Stratton-Porter became the Bird Woman. Bored and discontented with the social boundaries of small-town housewifery, and spurred by the chance pairing of a gift camera with the need to illustrate some writing projects on bird life, Stratton-Porter took to the swamp.

The long and arduous field hours and her bird studies, at which she became increasingly proficient, provided not only the raw material for her nonfiction, but also the experiences, observations, and many of the characterizations (modeled after interactions with farmers, loggers, and other people she found in the swamp) for her fiction. Her first book, *The Song of the Cardinal* (1903), illustrated with her own photographs and detailing the life of a cardinal and its mate, was well-received, albeit by a small audience.

Stratton-Porter decided to try her hand at a second book—natural history with, this time, a human love story running through it—and *Freckles* (1904) set the stage for the rest of her career. While publishers were initially concerned about the predominating natural world in her work, Stratton-Porter's adamance that it remain, and her subsequent sales records, won the day. Those of her novels to achieve bestseller status were *Freckles, A Girl of the Limberlost* (1909), *Laddie* (1913), and *Michael O'Halloran* (1915). Recognizing that her fiction found better sales than her natural history works, Stratton-Porter arranged with her publishers to alternate nonfiction with the novels. *What I Have Done with Birds* (1907) and *Moths of the Limberlost* (1912) are representative of the best of her nonfiction. They tended to be lavishly produced volumes with her own photographic illustrations accompanied by text in a descriptive, informal style. This presentation, while accurate in great detail, appealed more to nature lovers than naturalists, and contributed to her recognition as a novelist rather than for the substantial contributions she made to photography and bird behavior studies.

Stratton-Porter's interests and abilities coalesced with a literary output for which an American readership lay ready and waiting. She wrote about nature when nature-writing was in vogue. She wrote overwhelmingly positive and uplifting stories—her primary theme being the overcoming of personal obstacles through faith, trust, and hard work in the atmosphere of peace bestowed by interaction with nature—at a time when Americans were not only avid consumers of fiction but were attracted to themes that would, however temporarily, divert them from the urban grind and the grim reality of World War I.

Stratton-Porter's exposure benefited from yet another popular medium with the proliferation of women's magazines. She had regularly contributed articles to publications such as *Outing* and *Recreation,* but in 1921 she was approached by *McCall's* and offered an editorial page. "Gene Stratton-Porter's Page" gave her a powerful forum for disseminating her message of positive thinking and right living. Novel serializations and poems appeared in *Good Housekeeping* as well.

Not surprisingly, Stratton-Porter's success drew the attention of Hollywood. She had moved from Indiana to California in 1920 and had initially contracted with filmmaker Thomas Inca, billing "Clean Pictures for Clean People." Dissatisfied with the results of the first project to produce *Michael O'Halloran,* and by now a very wealthy and determined woman, Stratton-Porter established her own production company. Ultimately seven of her novels were made into films.

In 1924 Stratton-Porter died in an automobile accident. At the close of the twentieth century her novels no longer are sought by mainstream readers, but they are still on the shelves of public and academic libraries; especially *Freckles,* which remains after others have been relegated to storage. Stratton-Porter and her audience were made for each other, her work providing a gentle reflection of American mores and desires that saw drastic change in the years between the two world wars.

—Karen Hovde

FURTHER READING:

Long, Judith Reick. *Gene Stratton-Porter, Novelist and Naturalist.* Indianapolis, Indiana Historical Society, 1990.

Richards, Bertrand F. *Gene Stratton-Porter.* Boston, Twayne Publishers, 1980.

Trosky, Susan M., and Donna Olendorf, editors. *Contemporary Authors.* Vol. 137. Detroit, Gale Research, 1992.

Strawberry, Darryl (1962—)

Darryl Strawberry's life reads like a soap opera. This major league ballplayer was the first pick overall in the 1980 free-agent draft, selected by the New York Mets. Without a doubt, he possessed the raw talent that could have earned him a spot in the Hall of Fame, but his erratic career has been a textbook case of overindulgence resulting in underachievement.

Professionally speaking, Strawberry's best years were the late 1980s. Yet while he was entrenched as a slugger-hero for the Mets, he never blossomed into superstardom. Furthermore, he was to earn as much publicity for drinking, drugs, and marital and tax problems. By the 1990s he had evolved into an injury-prone underachiever. A low point came in 1993, when he hit a measly .140 in 32 games for the Los Angeles Dodgers. In the mid-1990s, however, an older, humbled Strawberry was resurrected by the New York Yankees. Although he did not complain that he was relegated to part-time status, he spent most of 1997 on the disabled list; near the end of the 1998 season, as the Yanks were on their way to a record-breaking 125-win campaign, he faced the biggest challenge of his life when he was diagnosed with colon cancer.

—Rob Edelman

FURTHER READING:

Klapish, Bob. *High and Tight: The Rise and Fall of Dwight Gooden and Darryl Strawberry.* New York, Villard Books, 1996.

Saxon, Walt. *Darryl Strawberry.* New York, Dell, 1985.

Strawberry, Darryl, with Art Rust, Jr. *Darryl.* New York, Bantam Books, 1992.

Streaking

Streaking, the practice of running naked through a public gathering, has been around for many years, but it attained full-fledged craze status only in the 1970s when, it seemed, all manner of strange behavior was soaring into public consciousness. Some historians

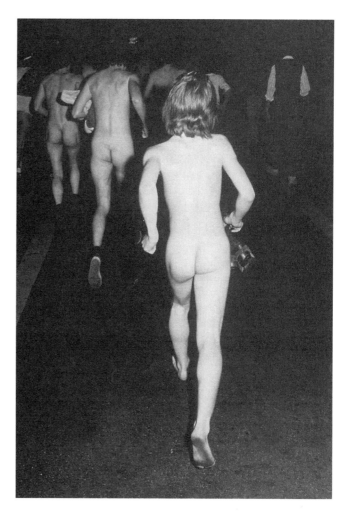

A group of men streaking through the streets of New York City.

have tagged Lady Godiva as the world's first streaker, but she rode— not ran—while deliberately concealing her nudity under her long, flowing hair. Not to be confused with simple nudism, streaking is an inherently exhibitionist act and thus the perfect public gesture for an exhibitionist age.

The spring of 1974 represented the high moment of modern streaking. In March of that year, the University of Missouri endured a mass streaking by more than 600 students. The nude collegians paraded past the campus's Ionic columns as a crowd estimated at 1,500 watched and cheered. In April, hayseed comedian Ray Stevens's single "The Streak" rocketed to number one on the pop charts. "He ain't rude. He ain't rude. He's just in the mood to run in the nude," crooned Stevens of the eponymous nudist. Full national exposure came that same month. During the broadcast of the Academy Awards ceremony, streaker Robert Opal shocked the crowd of Hollywood swells by letting it fly during David Niven's introduction of Elizabeth Taylor. "The only way he could get a laugh was by showing his shortcomings," quipped an unruffled Niven. Undeterred, the 33-year-old streaker managed to extract his full fifteen minutes of fame from the situation. As a result of the Oscar publicity, he pursued a brief career as a stand-up comic and was hired as a "guest streaker" for Hollywood parties. When the streaking craze died down, Opal moved to San Francisco, where he was found murdered in 1979.

Not surprisingly, academics and opinion writers tried to explain the streaking craze. In 1974, a psychology professor at the University of South Carolina did one of the first studies on the phenomenon. After much research, he concluded that the average male streaker was "a tall Protestant male weighing 170 pounds with a B grade average [who] dated regularly, came from a town with a population less than 50,000 and a family where the father is a business or professional man and the mother is a housewife." Female streakers, the study found, "tended to be small, 5 feet 3 inches and 117 pounds."

Others tried a more sociological approach. At the low end, streaking was dismissed as little more than an outrageous fad on the order of swallowing goldfish or packing phone booths. At the high end, it was touted as a lifestyle choice, a non-violent form of protest, and even a type of therapy. E. Paul Bindrim, the so-called "father of nude psychotherapy," coached more than 3000 people through their first experience of public nudity. Explaining his philosophy to the *Los Angeles Times,* Bindrim declared: "Clothing is kind of a mask. So there are reasons to think if you remove clothing, you get a freer atmosphere where people would talk more openly."

When streaking became a national craze, Bindrim wrote an op-ed piece for the *Los Angeles Times* in which he commented more specifically on the trend: "Streaking is healthy, and I predict that it is here to stay," he wrote. "It may change form, but its essential ingredient, the tacit sanctioning of public nudity, will remain. . . . Running is the only aspect of streaking that will die out." Belying Bindrim's prediction, scampering in the nude enjoyed something of a revival in the 1990's. It even briefly gained front-page status again when it invaded the pristine world of lawn tennis. In 1996, Melissa Johnson, a 23-year-old London student, streaked across Centre Court moments before the men's Wimbledon final. The topless woman, wearing only a tiny maid's apron, pranced momentarily in front of finalists Richard Krajicek and MaliVai Washington as they posed near the net for photographs. She was quickly escorted off the court by two policemen as both players and most of the 14,000 fans broke into laughter.

—Robert E. Schnakenberg

FURTHER READING:

Pleasant, George. *The Joy of Streaking.* New York, Ballantine, 1974.

Streep, Meryl (1948—)

Considered by many to be "the" actress of her generation, Meryl Streep remains in a class by herself in terms of critical acclaim and career longevity. A two-time Oscar winner, she has been nominated for ten Academy Awards throughout a career which has spanned more than twenty-five films. Known primarily for her heavy dramatic roles as neurotic or obsessed characters—many of which have required her to assume an accent—Streep has also proven versatile in playing both comedy and action roles.

Ironically, Mary Louise Streep was not driven to be an actress during her affluent New Jersey childhood. More drawn to athletics, she was a swimmer who later became a cheerleader in high school. It was upon enrolling at the exclusive Vassar College that Streep became obsessed with both literature and acting—in addition to singing with a musical group and acting as vice president of her sophomore class. Besides extensive work behind the scenes in

Meryl Streep

designing lighting and costumes, one of her many leading roles was in Strindberg's *Miss Julie,* in which she asserts she was not "any good" but did have her first moment of epiphany as an actress "where you leave everything behind" and achieve "transcendence or something." Subsequent graduate work at Yale allowed her to play approximately forty roles, which were most often not reality-based, which she considered ironic in view of the heavy reality of the vast majority of her film work. After graduation in 1975, Streep won major roles at Joseph Papp's Public Theater in New York and the New York Shakespeare Festival. She made her Broadway debut in *Trelawny of the Wells* and won rave reviews and a Tony nomination for her performance in Tennessee Williams's *Twenty-Seven Wagons Full of Cotton.*

Her first film role—most of which ended up on the cutting-room floor—was with Jane Fonda and Vanessa Redgrave in *Julia* in 1977. It was followed by an Emmy-winning performance in the highly praised TV miniseries *Holocaust* and a performance opposite Robert De Niro (in the first of three films with him) in her first Oscar-nominated role in *The Deer Hunter.* Of the latter film, Streep contends that since the role was basically unwritten she was required to improvise her own lines of dialogue and interaction.

Streep made a series of high-profile films throughout the 1980s, beginning with her role in *Kramer vs. Kramer,* for which she won her first Academy Award for best supporting actress for her portrayal of Joanna, Dustin Hoffman's neglected wife who abandons her family. She subsequently received Oscar nominations for *The French Lieutenant's Woman, Silkwood, Out of Africa,* and *A Cry in the Dark.* Her second Oscar—this time for best actress—as well as many other prestigious awards resulted from her role as a tortured Polish concentration camp survivor in 1983's *Sophie's Choice.* Streep also returned to the theater, winning an Obie award for acting, singing, and dancing the lead in a musical adaptation of *Alice in Wonderland.*

Seeking a break from a succession of heavy, character-driven roles, Streep then made a succession of comedies such as *She-Devil,* costarring reigning TV sitcom queen Roseanne; then, in a surprise move, performing her own stunts in a demanding role as a whitewater rafting guide in the action thriller *The River Wild.* Her tenth Oscar-nominated performance was as a bored Italian war bride who finds love with costar and director Clint Eastwood in the highly acclaimed *The Bridges of Madison County* in 1995.

Streep has worked with nearly every important director and every leading man of note, all of whom praise her talents. Sydney Pollack, who directed her in *Out of Africa,* claimed that not only is Streep capable of becoming "a totally new human being," but, further, is able to effectively communicate the character's struggles to the audience. Alan J. Pakula, who directed Streep in *Sophie's Choice,* once commented, "If there's a heaven for directors, it would be to direct Meryl Streep your whole life."

Throughout her career Streep has been nominated for and received many other prestigious awards. In 1997 she received the first Bette Davis Lifetime Achievement Award to "honor an actor or actress whose career distinctly parallels the high professional standards set by the late movie legend"; the Women in Film's Crystal Award, reserved for women whose work has helped enhance the role of women within the entertainment industry; the prestigious Silver Medallion at Telluride Film Festival's 25th Anniversary Celebration; and in 1998 received her star on the Hollywood Walk of Fame to coincide with the release of her twenty-fifth feature film, *One True Thing.*

A political activist, Streep has also hosted and narrated television specials championing the rights of women and children, literacy, and ecological issues. She not only testified in congress against the use of pesticides but organized "Mothers and Others," an antipesticide organization, which has grown from thirty-five members to thirty-eight thousand.

Known for avoiding Hollywood glitz, Streep is fiercely defensive of her private life in the hills of northwest Connecticut, on a secluded eighty-nine-acre estate with a forty-seven-acre private lake. Married since 1978 to sculptor Don Gummer, Streep is the mother of four children and claims "Even my decisions about what films I make are predicated on the fact that I think about how my children will view them . . . and how it will either enhance it or strafe the soul of their future." Considering herself a mother first and a movie star second, she often takes her family with her on location, and she was once named one of the outstanding mothers of the year by the National Mother's Day Committee.

—Rick Moody

FURTHER READING:

Maychick, Diana. *Meryl Streep: The Reluctant Superstar.* New York, St. Martin's Press, 1985.

Street and Smith

One of America's oldest publishing houses, Street and Smith helped to ensure the spread of mass literacy in the United States. Producing inexpensive books and periodicals, Street and Smith was long known for its dime novels, pulp fiction, popular magazines, and comic books. Featured prominently were the tales of Jesse James, Buffalo Bill, Nick Carter, Frank Merriwell, and the Shadow. Noteworthy authors included Edward Z. C. Judson, Horatio Alger Jr., Gilbert M. Patten, and Eugene T. Sawyer, while reprints of Rudyard Kipling, Sir Arthur Conan Doyle, Robert Louis Stevenson, and Victor Hugo abounded. In the 1850s, Street and Smith began producing dime novels, soon becoming the most successful publisher in the field, surpassing even Beadle and Adams, Munro, and Tousey. As one commentator quipped, "Munros to the left of them, Tousey to right of them, Street and Smith behind them, Onward they blood-and-thundered." Beginning in 1859, many of Street and Smith's serialized novels appeared in the *New York Weekly,* recently purchased by Francis S. Street and Francis S. Smith.

From the mid nineteenth century onward, Street and Smith helped to shape the image of the American hero, while moving from dime novels—which frequently sold for a nickel—to pulp fiction. Real-life individuals with anti-heroic qualities, such as the outlaw Jesse James and the Western adventurer Buffalo Bill, were presented in a glorified light. Alger's *Ragged Dick,* whose protagonist was a former bootblack turned bank clerk, helped to reinforce a belief in self-reliance and individualism as America entered an era of rapid modernization. Detective Nick Carter, who first appeared in the *New York Weekly* in 1886, was a more cerebral figure: "He was a master of disguise, and could so transform himself that even old Sim (his father) could not recognize him. And his intellect, naturally keen as a razor blade, had been incredibly sharpened by the judicious cultivation of the astute old man." In 1896, Patten offered Frank Merriwell, a genius of an athletic stripe who invariably bested his competitors—but always did so honorably—in the pages of *Tip-Top Weekly.* Thus, the Street and Smith heroes included men of the Wild West, city lads and slickers, and athletes, in a period when urbanization and industrialization were transforming the national landscape.

Street and Smith was known for its pulp fiction, which was initiated by Frank Munsey's *Argosy* at the close of the nineteenth century, supplanting dime novels and story papers. Street and Smith contributed gaudy, three-colored covers. Russell Nye contends that Street and Smith's *New Buffalo Bill Weekly,* published in 1912, was "the last genuine dime novel." Pulp magazines, most of the general adventure variety, thrived, while Street and Smith contributed *Detective Story* (1915), *Western Story* (1919), and *Love Story* (1921). Created by a young woman, Amita Fairgrieve, *Love Story* began as a quarterly but ended up as a weekly. By 1938, *Love Story* produced a score of imitators, including *True Love Stories, Pocket Love, Romantic Range,* and *Real Love.* Selling as many as 10 million copies by the 1930s, the pulps suffered from heightened production charges during the following decade. The death-knell of pulp magazines was ushered in by radio, television, and 25 cent paperback books. Along with other publishers, Street and Smith began emphasizing publications that garnered large advertising budgets.

Street and Smith was known for far more than its pulp, producing periodicals like *Popular Magazine,* which began in 1903 as a quarterly intended "for boys and 'Old Boys'," but soon became an action, adventure, and outdoors semimonthly. With a circulation of nearly a quarter of a million, *Popular Magazine* was published until 1928. Upton Sinclair contributed to the publication, as did top pulp authors suck as B. M. Bower, H. H. Knibbs, and Rex Beach. Appearing in 1937, *Pic* began printing risque photographs of young women, while posing questions such as, "Do White Men Go Berserk in the Tropics?" With World War II coming to a close, *Pic* became a more respectable men's magazine, with its circulation surpassing the 600,000 mark; mounting costs, however, doomed it.

By the late 1940s, Street and Smith closed its last pulp and a series of comic books, opting to highlight slick periodicals like *Charm, Mademoiselle,* and *Living for Young Homemakers. Mademoiselle,* which targeted women from 17-30, had been introduced in 1935. Quentin Reynolds referred to Street and Smith as "a fiction factory," while contending that the company had long thrived because of its diversity and readiness to discard increasingly unpopular publications. Family control of Street and Smith terminated in 1959, when the company was purchased by Condé Nast Publications, reportedly for $4 million and stock options. Among the magazines acquired were *Charm, Living for Young Homemakers, Astounding Science Fiction, Air Progress,* and *Hobbies for Young Men.*

—Robert C. Cottrell

FURTHER READING:

Mott, Frank Luther. *A History of American Magazines 1865-1885.* Cambridge, Harvard University Press, 1967.

————. *A History of American Magazines 1885-1905.* Cambridge, Harvard University Press, 1957.

Noel, Mary. *Villains Galore - The Heyday of the Popular Story Weekly.* New York, MacMillan Company, 1954.

Nye, Russell. *The Unembarrassed Muse: The Popular Arts in America.* New York, Dial Press, 1973.

Peterson, Theodore. *Magazines in the Twentieth Century.* Urbana, University of Illinois Press, 1964.

Reynolds, Quentin. *The Fiction Factory, or from Pulp Row to Quality Street.* New York, Random House, 1995.

Smith, Henry Nash. *Virgin Land: The American West as Symbol and Myth.* Cambridge, Harvard University Press, 1970.

Tebbel, John, and Mary Ellen Zuckerman. *The Magazine in America 1741-1990.* New York, Oxford University Press, 1991.

A Streetcar Named Desire

According to Brooks Atkinson, the major theater critic of the mid-century, Tennessee Williams' urban tragedy, *A Streetcar Named Desire,* was "a modern masterpiece" that "took Broadway by storm." Considered by many to be the finest drama of America's finest post-war playwright, *A Streetcar Named Desire* made an indelible impression on American culture. Under the muscular direction of Elia Kazan, the incendiary play, which won both the Pulitzer Prize and the Critics' Circle Award in 1947, was the follow-up to Williams' 1944 debut, *The Glass Menagerie*; but whereas the earlier play was primarily a meditative memory piece, *Streetcar* is rife with activity. Its melodramatic structure, however, is never allowed to eclipse the emotional and atmospheric authenticity of the play. It is particularly revered for its multi-faceted characterizations; its rich

dialogue, which is masterful in its lyricism as well as its use of working-class vernacular; and the role it played in popularizing a new, naturalistic style of American acting, known colloquially as the "The Method."

Streetcar depicts domestic strife. At the start of the play, an unmarried, thirtyish, out-of-work schoolteacher, Blanche DuBois, arrives at the home of her younger sister, Stella. Since both young women were reared in the lap of luxury on a lush Mississippi homeplace called Belle Reeve, the cultivated Blanche is somewhat shocked to find Stella living in rather squalid conditions in the French Quarter of New Orleans. More troubling to Blanche is her sister's marriage to a loutish, "common" ex-serviceman named Stanley Kowalski. For her part, Stella is dismayed to learn that Belle Reeve was forfeited to creditors under Blanche's watch. Clearly, both sisters have lost their social and economic footing, but while Stella is perfectly content in her rough-hewn but passionate marriage, Blanche is dispossessed, one step away from poverty.

The play recounts Blanche's efforts to adapt to her new circumstances with her dignity and sanity intact, and documents her poignant attempts to conceal her advancing age, her professional failure and her highly sexual nature from those who might judge her harshly. "A woman's charm is fifty-percent illusion," Blanche confides to Stella, and Stella indulges her fragile sister, encouraging Blanche's blossoming courtship with Stanley's gentle co-worker, Mitch. But Stanley ultimately becomes Blanche's destroyer, tearing away her tissue of lies and insulting her fine sensibilities. "I've been on to you from the start," he bellows to her at *Streetcar*'s climax. His subsequent rape of Blanche causes what scholar Harold Bloom calls "a psychic rending" that is enough to nudge Blanche into madness. In the end, bound for a state asylum, Blanche leaves the home of her merciless brother-in-law and disbelieving sister, a lovely but broken spirit in an inhumane world. Her destruction is so complete that some critics, Kenneth Tynan for one, have read the play as a comment on the decline of civilization, the trampling of man's finer instincts by the implacable brutality of the modern world.

Several of the play's lines have found an affectionate place in the American vocabulary. Stanley's anguished, full-throated cry, "Stella, STELLAAAA!" has become something of a cultural touchstone, and Blanche's lilting final line, "I have always depended on the kindness of strangers," has endured as Blanche's perfect motto, as it utilizes a genteel euphemism for sexual promiscuity to reconcile Blanche's poetic frailty with her more desperate animal behavior.

Though Blanche is the role of greater complexity and sympathy, both major characters continue to live in the cultural imagination. Blanche's mix of cultivation, hysteria, and tragedy makes her an unforgettable creation, while Stanley, "the exuberantly macho American Pole," in Ronald Hayman's felicitous description, has been accorded iconic status. Much of this stature is no doubt due to the role's close identification with Marlon Brando, for rarely has an actor taken possession of a role so effectively and completely. Many actresses have triumphed as Blanche ("a relatively imperishable creature of the stage," according to Williams), not only Jessica Tandy in the original production, but Vivien Leigh in the 1951 film version, and in the 1990s, Jessica Lange on stage and television. But as for Stanley, Brando's remains the definitive interpretation. His Stanley is cunning, explosive, overtly sexual, and the ways in which the actor communicated character through his body language was startlingly modern to 1947 audiences, a living advertisement for the Method and

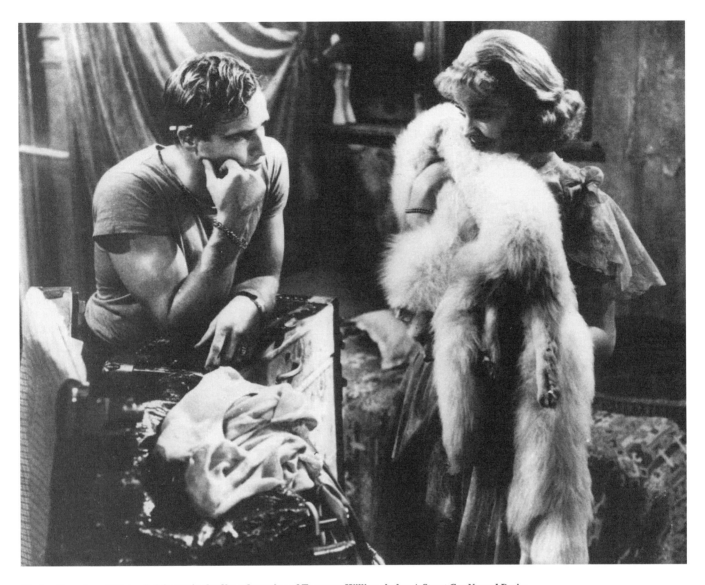

Marlon Brando and Vivian Leigh star in the film adaptation of Tennesee Williams' play *A Street Car Named Desire*.

the acting school that advanced it, Lee Strasberg's Actor's Studio. It is ironic that in early drafts of the play this emblem of machismo appeared as a considerably more androgynous figure. According to *New Republic* writer Geoffrey O'Brien, the final product in the form of Brando—grunting and sweating with exhibitionistic virility—''proposed a different way for men to be. Talking was small part of it.''

After originating the role on Broadway, Brando revived his performance for the acclaimed 1951 film, which was also directed by Kazan. Original Broadway cast members Kim Hunter (Stella) and Karl Malden (Mitch) recreated their supporting roles, carrying off Academy Awards for their efforts. Oscars were also awarded to the film for Best Picture, and to Leigh as Best Actress; oddly, only Brando was passed over (he won three years later for the Kazan-directed *On the Waterfront*).

The great success of the Kazan movie adaptation has deterred any subsequent attempts to film the play as a feature. However, television producers have proven more intrepid; prior to the 1995 version that starred Jessica Lange and Alec Baldwin, Ann-Margret and Treat Williams filled the shoes of Blanche and Stanley for the

1984 TV movie, and the play continues to be performed at both the amateur and professional levels all over the world. Composer Andre Previn based an opera on the play, and debuted it at the San Francisco Opera House in 1998 (Previn's *Streetcar* was also broadcast on public television that year), further attesting to the enduring legacy of Williams' masterpiece.

—Drew Limsky

FURTHER READING:

Bloom, Harold. *Tennessee Williams's A Streetcar Named Desire: Modern Critical Interpretations*. New York, Chelsea House Publishers, 1988.

Hayman, Ronald. *Tennessee Williams: Everyone Else is an Audience*. New Haven, Yale University Press, 1993.

Leverich, Lyle. *Tom: The Unknown Tennessee Williams*. New York, Crown, 1995.

Manso, Peter. *Brando: The Biography*. New York, Hyperion, 1994.

O'Brien, Geoffrey. Review of *Brando: Songs My Mother Taught Me,* by Marlon Brando, and *Brando: The Biography,* by Peter Manso. In *The New Republic.* December 5, 1994, 35.

Williams, Tennessee. *Memoirs.* New York, Bantam, 1976.

———. *A Streetcar Named Desire.* New York, Signet, 1947.

Streisand, Barbra (1942—)

Since she first got her break on the Broadway stage in 1962, Barbra Streisand has elicited extreme reactions from her public and from critics. Either adored or detested, the Streisand persona has, almost from the beginning, been larger than life. Indeed, it has almost overshadowed her considerable talents as singer, actress, director, producer, and writer. Though she has often been confused, frightened, and angered by both the homage and the vitriol heaped upon her, she has remained a strong personality, a productive artist, and a phenomenon in the entertainment field.

Born Barbara Joan Streisand in 1942, in Brooklyn, New York, to Jewish working-class parents, Streisand's father died when she was 15 months old. Within a few years her mother had remarried. Streisand's stepfather was an emotionally abusive man, who her mother described as "allergic to children." Her mother was undemonstrative, calling her daughter "ugly" and ridiculing the young Barbara's aspirations to be an actress. Streisand, however, was not to be deterred and as a young girl she sang in the halls of her

Barbra Streisand

Flatbush apartment building, learning to appreciate the sound of her own voice as it echoed off the walls. As a teenager she began taking acting lessons and haunting the theaters and clubs of Manhattan's Greenwich Village, seeking an entrance to the stage.

She moved to the Village in 1960. Although she wanted to become an actress, friends who heard her sing encouraged her to enter talent night at a local club, and soon she embarked on a career as a cabaret singer, dropping the middle "a" from her name so that it would stand out. Her vibrant soprano soon won Streisand a loyal local audience, mostly of gay men. Working in the Village she also met the drag queens who worked the clubs and learned from them the campy flamboyance of the diva, which she used to cover her insecurity on-stage.

Her big break came in the 1962 show *I Can Get It for You Wholesale,* when she was cast as the frumpy Miss Marmelstein. Making the most of a small part, Streisand impressed critics and audience, and, when she sang her one song, she stopped the show. The following year, *The Barbra Streisand Album* was released and won the Grammy Award for Album of the Year.

In 1964, she was cast in the leading role of the new play *Funny Girl,* playing comic and singer Fanny Brice. The role could have been made for her, as Brice too was a Jewish girl, not conventionally pretty, but with a powerful talent and an intense will to succeed. The play was a success—23 curtain calls on opening night—and overnight Streisand became a star. The girl whose mother had recommended she give up the stage and seek a secure secretarial job was on the cover of *Time* and *Life* magazines, and on television. *My Name is Barbra,* the first of many Streisand television specials, won an Emmy in 1965.

Streisand's voice has always been her most dependable asset. Most comfortable singing show tunes and popular classics, she has sung everything from Christmas carols to rock 'n' roll. Since 1964, she has sold more than 60 million records. Thirty-eight of her albums have made the top 40, and at least 24 have sold one million copies, more than anyone except Elvis Presley and the Beatles. She has won eight Grammy Awards, was named a Grammy Legend in 1992, and won a Grammy Lifetime Achievement Award in 1995. But she never lost her insecurity about performing on stage, and after she received death threats before a concert in New York's Central Park in 1967, she stopped giving public concerts. It was almost 30 years later, in 1993, that she performed for an audience again, doing what she called her last concert tour.

As an actress, Streisand's work has been less universally acclaimed. After starring in the movie of *Funny Girl,* for which she won the Academy Award for best actress, Streisand went on to make many films; some successes like *The Way We Were* in 1973; and some failures, like *The Main Event* in 1977. Many, like *A Star Is Born* (1976) were critical flops, but did well at the box office, proving the loyalty of Streisand's fans.

Often accused of trying to control production in the films she appeared in, Streisand wanted to direct films herself. In 1983, she realized her dream by becoming the first woman to co-write, direct, produce, and star in a feature film. *Yentl* was the story of a Jewish girl in eighteenth-century Russia who disguised herself as a boy so that she could go to school and gain the education that was forbidden to girls. The project was close to Streisand's heart and she was hurt and angered by the mixed critical reception and the almost total snubbing of the film by the Academy of Motion Picture Arts and Sciences. She went on to direct and produce other films, but continued to be ignored by the Academy. Even when her film *Prince of Tides* was nominated for Best Picture, she did not receive the Best Director nomination traditionally given to Best Picture nominees.

The motion picture establishment and many critics have been hard on Barbra Streisand. Even audiences have been polarized, some loving her ethnic looks and Brooklyn accent, others finding her abrasive and ugly. Her reputation in Hollywood ranges from hard-working perfectionist to neurotic narcissist. She has defended herself against accusations of egotism by citing the sexism of the Hollywood system. "A man is forceful," she has said, "a woman is pushy . . . He's assertive—she's aggressive. He strategizes—she manipulates."

As a young singer, Streisand's raw emotion, ineffectively masked by awkward brashness and affected diva mannerisms, touched a chord with audiences. They identified with her endearing insecurity, respected her refusal to change her nose or her accent, and admired her drive to succeed and be respected. Streisand's response to the adoration of her fans has been complex. Stunned and overwhelmed by her sudden popularity after *Funny Girl,* she called the crowds that mobbed the stage door "the crazies," and slipped out alternate exits to avoid them. As she has achieved the success she sought, Streisand has become more polished. Her speech has softened, and, while she has still not changed her nose, in part fearful of affecting her voice, her face and body show the effects of expensive care. She treats her fans with respect but still keeps aloof. Her fans, who have seen her progress flamboyantly through three decades of fashion and ideology, seem to welcome each transformation.

Unlike many performers who got their start before gay audiences, Streisand has never tried to distance herself from her gay fans. She has remained an icon among gay men and cheerfully acknowledges the connection, joking on-stage about being outdone by a group of Barbra drag queens, and even hiring a Barbra impersonator to fool her friends at a party. In a serious vein, she has raised money for AIDS (Acquired Immune Deficiency Syndrome) research, made a television movie about the career of lesbian coast guard officer Margarethe Cammermeyer, and spearheaded a celebrity boycott of Colorado after anti-gay legislation passed there.

Politically liberal and wealthy (in 1997, her worth was estimated at $100 million), she created the Streisand Foundation, which donates money to such causes as civil rights, AIDS, and the environment. With the election of Bill Clinton as president, she became a frequent visitor to Washington and an active fund-raiser for the Democratic party. Though she sometimes drew ridicule for speaking about politics, she insisted on the rights of artists to free expression, and on respect for liberal traditions.

Though her career, like her persona, has often been controversial, and though she has not always lived up to the expectations of critics or fans, Barbra Streisand accomplished what she intended from the beginning—she became a star. "I always knew I would be famous. . . I was never contented. . . I wanted to prove to the world that they shouldn't make fun of me."

—Tina Gianoulis

FURTHER READING:

Edwards, Anne. *Streisand: A Biography.* Boston, Little Brown, 1997.

Kimbrell, James. *Barbra—An Actress who Sings.* Boston, Branden Publishing Company, 1992.

Riese, Randall. *Her Name is Barbra.* Secaucus, New Jersey, Carol Publishing Group, 1993.

Streisand, Barbra. "The Artist as Citizen." *New Perspective Quarterly.* Vol. 12, No. 2, Spring 1995, 36.

Strip Joints/Striptease

Strip joints feature females engaging in provocative dance and titillating disrobing for a predominantly male clientele. Some strip joints do cater to females with male strippers like the Chippendales. Antecedents of the modern striptease include the auletrides of ancient Greece, geishas of Japan, belly dancers of Arabia, and a variety of singing and dancing "strumpets" found throughout history.

Dance is a self-conscious display of personal charms for excitation. Virtually all species of animals, birds, and fishes engage in conscious display to stimulate sexual excitement and attraction. Striptease adds simultaneous disrobing to the dance. Striptease costumes often use clothing associated with the mores and taboos of society, including religious taboos (the nun's habit and crucifix), sexual taboos (the school girl uniform and anklet socks), hunting fetishes (feathers and animal skins), and socio-economic symbols

Burlesque queen Blaze Starr.

(jewels and furs). Removing clothes both flaunts mores and taboos associated with the clothes and leads to sexual arousal. The gradual revelation of nudity as the stripper's clothes are slowly removed evoke fantasies that lead to sexual arousal. The female breast has been the primary historic focus of striptease. According to Desmond Morris, *The Naked Ape,* the appeal of the breast is probably associated with the imprinting of the female breast on the male during early childhood resulting in a permanent sexual reflex behavior, in addition to the human erect posture and face-to-face copulation in which the female breast substitutes for the buttocks, which is the primary sexual stimulus of all other primates.

Modern titillation and tease was perfected in the 1860 music halls of Paris and London. After World War I, risqué nudity became commonplace in the cabarets of Berlin, reviews of Paris, and the nightclubs of the New York Bowery, where the term ''striptease'' was first used. With the sexual revolution, and the civil rights, woman's rights, and free speech movements of the 1960s, striptease became more mainstream and moved into the discotheques, theater districts, cinemas, and adult entertainment districts in most cities worldwide. As striptease became more widespread, it influenced popular dance by introducing sensual and erotic body movements.

In the late twentieth century, striptease evolved from titillating dance into more radical ''show routines,'' ''lap dances,'' ''performance art exhibitions,'' and ''sex shows.'' In the show routine, the striptease is continued to full nudity and to a full gynecological exhibition of the vagina, often with simulated or actual masturbation by the dancer. In the lap dance (and table dance) simulated sex acts are performed on the male observer as the dancer gyrates in extremely close proximity to the observer's body. Some criticize performance art exhibitions for seeking to exploit state and federal grants for arts funding and to avoid zoning restrictions by claiming to exhibit a more artistic and aesthetic rendition of many of the same acts performed in show routines and lap dances. In the sex show, found throughout Europe and the developing world but rarely in the United States, two or more performers engage in simulated or actual sex acts and copulation for the voyeuristic enjoyment of observers.

The strip joint, and its historic antecedents, have served a variety of social functions. The venue has maintained gender separation, providing a males-only retreat where affairs of business, politics, and sport could be conducted. This function was highly criticized by feminists who demanded access to those affairs. The strip joint also has provided an outlet for the male libido. Lewis Berg and Robert Street offer a typical warning in their 1953 marriage manual, *Sex: Methods and Manners*: ''A woman should realize that all normal men are sexually responsive to the exposure of the female body. This is particularly true where strange women are concerned, since the male perpetually seeks variety. It accounts for the popularity of burlesque and girl shows in general, and for exhibitions of the strip-tease, bubble-dance, and fan-dance character. Few husbands, if any, are totally indifferent to these attractions.'' Thirdly, striptease has offered lucrative wages for female performers, some of whom lack the education, skills, or enthusiasm for other employment. Research has reported that many skilled and educated women abandon traditional careers for higher-paying and less demanding careers in striptease. Some strippers remain active into age 50 or 60.

Offering unconditional sexual stimulation, the striptease artist has functioned as a surrogate lover for noncompetitive men who fear rejection in the post-feminist social world. The striptease offers genuine entertainment and a ration of female companionship for males in military camps, gold fields, industrial centers, and other isolated locations away from opportunities for social interaction with females. Despite the contributions of strip joints and strippers, they are relegated to low social status. Indeed, the strip joint is occasionally a front for prostitution, substance abuse, gambling, and other illegal activities. To limit their impact on the larger society, many communities try to restrict strip joints to certain locations safely away from schools and churches.

Striptease has been used as a symbol of both feminism and antifeminism. While striptease represents the female right to self-expression and control of her body, it also represents the male chauvinistic exploitation of women as purely sexual objects for entertainment.

—Gordon Neal Diem

FURTHER READING:

Allison, Anne. *Nightwork: Sexuality, Pleasure, and Corporate Masculinity in a Tokyo Hostess Club.* Chicago, University of Chicago Press, 1994.

Berg, Lewis and Robert Street. *Sex: Methods and Manners.* New York, McBride, 1953.

Jarrett, Lucinda. *Stripping in Time: A History of Erotic Dancing.* San Francisco, HarperCollins, 1997.

Langner, Laurence. *The Importance of Wearing Clothes.* New York, Hastings House, 1957.

Morris, Desmond. *The Naked Ape: A Zoologist's Study of the Human Animal.* New York, McGraw-Hill, 1967.

Scott, David Alexander. *Behind the G-String: An Exploration of the Stripper's Image, Her Person, and Her Meaning.* Jefferson, North Carolina, McFarland, 1996.

Wilson, Robert Anton. *The Book of the Breast.* Chicago, Playboy Press, 1994.

Zeidman, Irving. *The American Burlesque Show.* New York, Hawthron Books, 1967.

Stuart, Marty (1958-)

Beneath a rock 'n' roll hairdo that makes donning a cowboy hat impossible, and with a collection of flamboyant jackets that would have made Liberace jealous, Marty Stuart emerged in the 1980s as a talented country instrumentalist—he plays both guitar and mandolin—songwriter, and performer. Born in Philadelphia, Mississippi, in 1958, Stuart first picked up a mandolin at the age of five. By 1972, the 13-year-old was playing the instrument with legendary bluegrass guitarist Lester Flatt. After Flatt's death in 1979, Stuart signed on as a guitarist with one of his all-time heroes, country-music great Johnny Cash and remained with Cash's band for six years before leaving in 1986 to begin a solo career. Stuart has also performed with such stars as Bill Monroe, Bob Dylan, the Everly Brothers, Willie Nelson, guitarist Doc Watson, Billy Joel, Neil Young, fiddler Vassar Clements, and Emmylou Harris. Songs penned by Stuart have been recorded by Harris as well as Wynonna Judd, George Strait, and Buck Owens.

Stuart produced his first solo album, *Busy Bee Cafe,* in 1982, while still a member of Cash's band. For this album, he enlisted the

Marty Stuart

help of fellow pickers like guitarists Doc Watson and Cash, Dobroist Jerry Douglas, and banjo-great Carl Jackson, catching the eye of CBS Records, which signed him on and produced *Marty Stuart* four years later. In 1990, with his first MCA effort, *Hillbilly Rock,* Stuart caught fire with country-music listeners in a big way. His ''hillbilly music— with a thump!,'' as he called it, had fans clamoring for more, and he served it up on the 1991 release, *Tempted.* The album allowed Stuart to focus on his own distinct style, especially in its best-known single, ''Burn Me Down,'' which had a long run on country radio.

This One's Gonna Hurt You, Stuart's first gold record, was driven up the charts by the momentum of *Tempted* and the celebrated ''No Hats'' tour he made with fellow country artist Travis Tritt. Released in 1993, *This One's Gonna Hurt You* blends the best of bluegrass, delta blues, and 1950s rockabilly with honky-tonk swing, ringing gospel harmonies and some gutsy guitar work. One of the album's most popular cuts, ''The Whiskey Ain't Workin' Any-more''—sung with fellow ''No-Hatter'' Tritt—earned Stuart a Grammy award, his first Country Music Association Award, and three BMI songwriter awards. But Stuart's proudest moment had already come:

in 1992 he became the 72nd performer to be honored by membership in Nashville's Grand Ole Opry, the ''high church'' of country music.

The kudos heaped on *This One's Gonna Hurt You* made it a tough act for Stuart to follow, and he postponed release of his seventh album, *Love and Luck* (1994), until he could get the mix of songs just right. Other recordings made in the 1990s, including *The Marty Party Hit Pack,* continue to provide a musical panorama of country influences that all come together under the musicianship of Stuart and his ever-changing, four-star lineup of collaborators, among them bluegrass fiddler Stuart Duncan, country vocalists Vince Gill, guitarist Ricky Skaggs, and banjoist Bela Fleck.

Throughout his career in country music, Stuart has consistently striven to keep alive the musical traditions of old-time country, traditions that continue to influence him greatly. On stage he plays country-rock pioneer Clarence White's 1954 Fender Telecaster, and he owns several Martins that belonged to Hank Williams, Sr. and Lester Flatt. His tour bus is modeled on the one used by honky-tonker Ernest Tubb. He still likens his career to the tours he used to make with the Sullivans, a family of bluegrass gospel singers, during the

1980s. ''You know, sometimes I feel like it's a crusade, or a mission, a crusade for hillbilly music,'' he once told an interviewer.

—Pamela L. Shelton

FURTHER READING:

Barnard, Russell, D., and others, editors. *Comprehensive Country Music Encyclopedia.* New York, Times Books, 1994.

Country: The Music and the Musicians: From the Beginnings to the '90s. New York, Abbeville Press, 1994.

Stambler, Irwin, and Grelun Landon. *Country Music: The Encyclopedia,* third edition. New York, St. Martin's Press, 1997.

Stuckey's

If you grew up in the 1950s or 1960s, chances are you might have gone on a cross-country car trip with your family. And your journey probably included a stop at Stuckey's, a turquoise-roofed building along one of America's highways. At Stuckey's you bought gas, food, and souvenirs. You also used the clean restrooms and basked in the atmosphere of air conditioning. Finally, before you left Stuckey's, you purchased some candy, probably one of their famous Pecan Log Rolls. You were ready to continue your trip.

The 1950s marked the first time in American history when families were able to travel throughout the United States. These benefits came about due to the post-World War II economic boom and the availability of leisure time afforded workers in the new American corporate structure. This freedom was also greatly enhanced by the introduction of the Interstate Highway system in 1956. Highways had a tremendous impact on American life. Average annual driving increased by 400 percent while shopping centers, suburbs, drive-in movies, gas stations, and fast food establishments entered the popular culture.

And as people began traveled cross-country on these new 41,000 miles of roads, they needed gas, restrooms, and a places to eat—that is where Stuckey's came in. Vacationing by car became the American way after the war and Stuckey's was an important part of that experience. Stuckey's were especially prevalent in the South and Western United States. In the 1950s and 1960s, they seemed to be everywhere. Stuckey's billboards lined the interstate, ''Slow Down, Stuckey's 1000 feet'' or ''Pecan Log Rolls, 4 for $1 with gas Fill-up.''

Stuckey's opened its first store in 1934 when Bill and Ethyl Stuckey began selling their family pecan candy to motorists in Georgia. After some success, they opened other stores along busy highways in Georgia and Florida and began including gasoline pumps, restaurants, and souvenirs along with their famous Pecan Log Roll candy.

While the Pecan Log Rolls might have been Stuckey's most significant contribution to America's sweet tooth, Stuckey's also distinguished itself with other items. Souvenirs like rubber snakes, T-shirts, novelty cigarette lighters, state salt-and-pepper shakers, and more recently, anything with Elvis on it, gave Stuckey's a lasting place in the hearts and minds of traveling American's during the 1950s and 1960s.

By the mid-1960s, Stuckey's enjoyed a virtual monopoly on American highways. During the early 1970s, at its peak, there were 360 Stuckey's stores in 31 states. But monopolies do not last forever and things began to change for Stuckey's. Fast food chains like McDonald's and Dairy Queen saw a golden opportunity to increase their business with highway travelers. Soon, even those fast food giants were joined in the competition by gas station-convenience store chains like Super America. And by the late 1970s, cheap air fares made long distance traveling by car less common. New highways were also replacing some of the older routes and many Stuckey's were left on less traveled roads. Furthermore, says one business analyst, ''Stuckey's image became a little tired and often synonymous with our parents and grandparents. And the need for those personal touches traditionally associated with Stuckey's and those plastic souvenirs were replaced by fast food, fast service, and extended hours.'' Consequently, the number of Stuckey's began to fall in the late 1970s.

In 1985, Bill Stuckey, Jr., tried to reinvigorate the store by mixing some well-known brand names with traditional Stuckey's merchandise. More recently, Stuckey's has entered into partnerships with other fast food chains like Dairy Queen and Citgo, to sell Stuckey's candies and souvenirs at those businesses. The idea is to develop a number of Stuckey's Express locations within the more successful fast food chains. Finally, Stuckey's has replaced the turquoise roof and old pecan shop look with a more contemporary facade and logo. From its peak of 361 stores, Stuckey's operated just over 50 establishments in the late 1990s.

Stuckey's no longer rules the roadsides of America. However, the chain still sells thousands of its Pecan Log Rolls and souvenir salt-and-pepper shakers. But for anyone who traveled during the 1950s and 1960s along America's roadways, Stuckey's will always be a fond memory of that experience.

—David E. Woodard

FURTHER READING:

Andrews, Greg. ''Stuckey's Staples and Souvenirs Still Draw Travelling Customers.'' *Indianapolis Star/News,* 24 January 1998.

Brooks, Hugh. ''Road Trip.'' *http://www.retroactive.com/mar97/roadtrip.html* February 1999.

Caruso, Dale. ''Stuckey's: Pecan Log Roll and Coffee Make a Comeback.'' *American Reporter,* Raleigh, North Carolina, 17 February 1998.

Student Demonstrations

Colleges and universities have historically been centers of political dissent. Perhaps because university students are in a rarefied state of independence, suspended between parental control and the mundane responsibilities of adult life, perhaps because the very nature of university education inspires students to form opinions and to take those opinions seriously, students have frequently been leaders in movements for social change. As early as the fourth century, Common Era, throughout the middle ages, and continuing into the modern era, university students have protested against politics and policies they find distasteful. The 1960s, shorthand for an era that began in the 1950s and continued into the 1970s, marked a time of massive social upheaval. African Americans began to organize to fight the state supported racism that oppressed them. Women

Student protest in the 1960s.

and gays began to question the social order that kept them subservient and invisible. There was open dissent about government policies, particularly regarding the undeclared war in Vietnam. Citizens began to mistrust the government officials they had always been told knew best. And at the core of each of these growing movements were the energetic, angry challenges of the student movements, both in the United States and around the world.

Though media representations of the student protest movements of the 1960s may be content with showing long-haired demonstrators waving flowers at police, the fact is that many complex political movements evolved in the 1960s. Some students were deeply involved in these movements, while others were simply swept up in their wake. The 1960s really began with the formation of two radical student organizations that would exemplify major waves of student activity of the era, the Student Non-Violent Coordinating Committee (SNCC, pronounced ''snick'') and Students for a Democratic Society (SDS).

SNCC was formed in 1960 with the support of a major civil rights organization, the Southern Christian Leadership Conference, to give a voice to young black civil rights activists who were impatient with the careful tactics of their elders. Almost immediately, SNCC

took a more radical approach to the fight for civil rights, though it maintained a commitment to non-violence. SNCC organized demonstrations, became involved in the ''Freedom Rides'' campaign to desegregate Southern buses, and worked to reform voting laws. In one of its most successful demonstrations, SNCC was instrumental in organizing the Freedom Summer of 1964, when busloads of mostly white students from the north came south where they lived with black families and did extensive organizing, from teaching in the Freedom Schools to registering black voters. Besides the extraordinary accomplishment of public education and outreach, the Freedom Summer played a large part in the passage of the United States Voting Rights Act.

By 1966, impatient with continued prejudice and discrimination, the membership of SNCC grew increasingly radical. Members like Stokely Carmichael and H. Rap Brown embodied this change of attitude. New catch phrases became, ''Black Power!'' and ''Violence is as American as cherry pie.'' SNCC joined with another new organization for young black militants, the Black Panther Party, and demonstrations were no longer peaceful sit-ins, but angry, threatening near-riots. The Black Panther Party also began to look outside the

United States for support, to countries like Cuba for whom revolution was more than a symbol.

Also formed in 1960, the Students for a Democratic Society put out its famous statement of purpose, the Port Huron Statement, in 1962. Drafted at a national meeting of SDS in Port Huron, Michigan, the statement began, "We are people of this generation, bred in at least modest comfort, housed now in universities, looking uncomfortably to the world we inherit." The statement was an indictment of modern American values and called for students to demand a truly "participatory democracy," and to fight against social injustice and materialistic capitalism. In 1963, in an effort to act on this statement, SDS formed the Economic Research and Action Project to put participatory democracy into practice. In the summer of 1964, 125 SDS organizers attempted political organizing among the urban poor in various cities across the country. But it was its mobilization against the Vietnam War for which the SDS is best remembered.

By the mid-1960s, television broadcasts of wartime violence and American casualties were causing doubt among many Americans as to the rationale behind the war, and the greatest doubters of all were college students of draft age and their friends. Demonstrations against the war sprang up on college and university campuses everywhere, some at military recruiting offices, some at ROTC buildings, anywhere that held some connection to the war. On April 17, 1965, SDS organized the first of several mass demonstrations against the Vietnam War in Washington, D.C. Fifteen thousand demonstrators joined them. In November, SDS cosponsored another demonstration that drew 30,000 antiwar protesters.

Like SNCC, SDS members grew impatient with the slowness of governmental response to their impassioned protests, and the group became more militant. By the time over 700 demonstrators were arrested at an SDS protest at Columbia University in 1968, the organization was already beginning to metamorphose into the fiercely militant Weathermen. In 1969, the Weathermen organized the "Days of Rage" of violent protest and rioting at the Democratic convention in Chicago. Eventually, radical members formed the Weather Underground, which considered itself a guerrilla warfare group, and continued to be active until 1977, taking responsibility for 12 bombings, and releasing 22 political communiques and a book, *Prairie Fire*. While many radicals later disavowed their militant stands, many others, like SDS' Bernadette Dohrn, stand behind their youthful politics and continue to work on the left for social change.

Most students were not members of any group, but a large number felt strongly about the social and political issues that motivated the organizations. Raised by a generation that had been largely unquestioningly patriotic, the students of the 1960s questioned everything their parents and their government told them. They began to feel they had been lied to, that the privilege they enjoyed was tainted because it came at the expense of people of color both at home and in Vietnam. Most of all, they did not want themselves or their friends to kill or be killed in Vietnam defending the lie. Following the pattern of groups like SNCC and SDS, student demonstrations of the early 1960s were largely peaceful rallies and marches, with the occasional teach-in about the war or sit-in in a controversial building on campus.

Unfortunately, university administrations and campus police did not understand how to deal with such challenges to their authority and often responded by attempting to clamp down with tighter control, which usually resulted in greater and more violent rebellion. Along with antiwar protests, "student power" movements developed as students insisted on having a voice in the way their schools were run. The Free Speech Movement (FSM) at the University of California at

Berkeley began when the university attempted to ban student political organization on campus. When campus police tried to arrest a student distributing civil rights literature, 3,000 students sat down, immobilizing the police car, until beaten back by police with clubs. The FSM continued to protest the university policy, resulting in the occupation of Sproul Hall on campus on December 2, 1964 and the arrest of almost 800 students. Though large universities like Berkeley and Columbia are famous for dramatic student demonstrations, the wave of protest was nationwide and effected a broad spectrum of colleges. Buildings were occupied and even bombed in institutions from Washington University in Saint Louis to the College of William and Mary in Virginia. Student organizers reasoned that since they were fighting to save lives, both American and Vietnamese, damage to mere property was imminently justified.

Perhaps the most famous example of overreaction to student protest occurred at Ohio's Kent State University in May, 1970. Following an announcement by President Richard Nixon of a new escalation in the war, students across the United States rose up in a series of angry protests. The national guard was called out to control crowds of demonstrators at Kent State, not an unusual practice for frustrated administrators. With little training in handling crowds, overwrought guardsmen fired into the crowd, killing four students and setting off a fresh wave of outraged protests. Fourteen days later, a similar incident at Jackson State University in Mississippi caused the deaths of two students and wounding of nine others. Though these incidents provoked public horror, little investigation was done, and the guardsmen involved were never punished.

While American students were organizing demonstrations across the United States, around the world students in France, Japan, England, Spain, Czechoslovakia, and other countries were also rising up in protest against university or government policies. May and June of 1968, a turbulent year in the United States, saw a nationwide strike of students and workers in France. One of the differences between demonstrations in the United States and those in many other countries, especially in France, was that the European students often allied themselves with labor, protesting in conjunction with working people. In the United States, many working class people viewed protesting students with angry suspicion, as privileged brats who despised their achievements and denigrated their flag. Though some American students sought alliances with working people, others referred to them derisively as "hard-hats" and saw them as the enemy, the arms and voices of unthinking patriotism that supported the state lie and the materialistic American dream. These stereotypes—the wealthy, downwardly-mobile, foul-mouthed hippie and the "America, love it or leave it" narrow-minded hard-hat—often prevented communication between students and laborers that might have revealed their common interests.

There was some truth to the rebel stereotype. Counterculture young men did wear their hair long, both because it was fashionable and to challenge the authority that insisted they cut it. Young women wore their hair long and straight too, and eschewed makeup and bras and often did not shave their legs. Both sexes wore clothes that were casual to the point of raggedness. These styles were adopted by the youth of the 1960s, along with a direct mode of speech liberally peppered with profanity, partially as a reaction against the careful facades of propriety so important to their parents' generation, and partially to conform with the careful facade of impropriety so necessary to the rebel generation. There was a culture of protest and, along with its mandated style of dress and speech, it had its own literature and music. Radicals read Richard Wright's *Native Son*, Eldridge

Cleaver's *Fire and Ice,* and Angela Davis' speeches in the *Guardian.* They listened to rock music that was specifically political, like Buffalo Springfield's ''For What It's Worth'' and Country Joe and the Fish's ''I'm-Fixin'-to-Die Rag,'' or to music filled with a raw and painful passion, like Janis Joplin and the Doors.

Student protests continue around the world, with each generation defining its style and its issues. SDS activist Tom Hayden described the achievements of his generation grandly, ''We ended a war, toppled two presidents, desegregated the South, and broke other barriers of discrimination.'' While some former protesters of the 1960s might be more jaded as to the long-lasting effects of their efforts, there is no doubt that the idealistic energy of the youth of that period did change history. Richard Nixon later admitted that fears of heightened protest limited his escalation of the war in Vietnam. While racial discrimination clearly still exists in the United States, state-sanctioned segregation no longer does. Shortly after the dramatic demonstrations of 1968, both France and the United States lowered their voting age to 18. The Green Party in Germany continues to fight for the causes that German youth demonstrated for in the 1960s. For a period of a few years, the hippies and activists of the New Left felt sure they could change the world, and that passion is perhaps their greatest legacy.

—Tina Gianoulis

FURTHER READING:

deGroot, Gerard. ''Reagan's Rise.'' *History Today.* Vol. 45, No. 9, September 1995, 31.

Koning, Hans. *Nineteen Sixty Eight: A Personal Memoir.* New York, W.W. Norton, 1987.

Longman, Wesley. *Student Protest: The 1960's and After.* New York, Addison, 1998.

Miller, Jim. *Democracy is in the Streets: From Port Huron to the Siege of Chicago.* Cambridge, Harvard University Press, 1994.

Students for a Democratic Society (SDS)

SDS was one of the largest and most militant organizations to oppose the Vietnam War. It grew from a small group of young socialists to an organization of over 100,000 members, with chapters on over 350 college campuses. The small Student League for Industrial Democracy became Students for a Democratic Society in 1960, and 1962 saw the publication of its Port Huron Statement, a manifesto critiquing American society and proposing student activism as a solution to the problems identified. The document was circulated widely, causing student interest in SDS to grow significantly.

In 1964, some SDS chapters organized demonstrations against the growing American involvement in Vietnam. As the war intensified, so did SDS opposition, including attacks on ROTC programs, the occupying of campus buildings, and student strikes. Media coverage of these protest activities tended to focus not only on the most disruptive and violent acts, but also on the most radical SDS spokesmen. The coverage was to the group's disadvantage—it tended to attract the most politically extreme young people (thus radicalizing SDS even further), and it gave the impression to middle-class Americans that SDS consisted entirely of violent would-be revolutionaries.

In 1968, SDS participated in the demonstrations at the Democratic National Convention in Chicago. SDS president Tom Hayden was one of the ''Chicago Seven'' who were later tried on federal charges of conspiracy to riot. In 1969, internal dissension caused SDS to self-destruct, leaving only a core of its most radicalized members, who soon began to call themselves the Weathermen.

—Justin Gustainis

FURTHER READING:

Gitlin, Todd. *The Whole World Is Watching: Mass Media in the Making & Unmaking of the New Left.* Berkeley, University of California Press, 1980.

Miller, James. *Democracy Is in the Streets: From Port Huron to the Siege of Chicago.* New York, Simon & Schuster, 1987.

Sale, Kirkpatrick. *SDS.* New York, Random House, 1973.

Studio 54

A legendary New York nightclub, Studio 54 was infamous for its sexual licentiousness (nudity on the dance floor, topless busboys, a unique gay/straight clientele mix) and an eclectic/elitist door policy that integrated the beautiful, the eccentric, and a vast array of celebrities (the Jaggers, Andy Warhol, Liza Minelli, Michael Jackson, etc.). Studio 54 was opened in April 1977 by Steve Rubell and Ian Schrager; early in 1980, they were both sent to prison for tax evasion. The nightclub ownership then changed hands twice before it finally closed in March 1986. Immortalized, in a fictional form, in the films *54* (1998) and *The Last Days of Disco* (1998), Studio 54 has come to symbolize a historical transition point: from the freedom and hedonism of the 1970s into the yuppie elitism and self-destructiveness of the 1980s.

—Glyn Davis

FURTHER READING:

Haden-Guest, Anthony. *The Last Party: Studio 54, Disco, and the Culture of the Night.* New York, William Morrow, 1998.

Studio One

Although it had its genesis as a radio program, *Studio One* became the longest running anthology drama series of the ''Golden Age of Television,'' with more than 500 live teleplays on CBS from 1948 through 1958, and earned a reputation as a visual innovator in broadcast storytelling. A product of television's infancy, the series disseminated drama of a high order, bringing classical works and serious ''one-off'' plays to a wide popular audience, and sowing the seeds for a generation of Hollywood writers and directors to learn their craft on the small screen. While other series were known for psychological realism, *Studio One,* under its first producer, Worthington Miner, explored the technical and stylistic potentials of the medium.

Worthington Miner thought with his eyes, and focused on a highly inventive, visual mode of storytelling. For him, *Studio One* existed somewhere between live drama and film. It was a ''live

Inside Studio 54.

performance staged for multiple cameras.'' Whereas most dramatic series efficiently relayed a live performance using a static three-camera set-up, the camera movement was an integral part of the *Studio One* performance. The actors were positioned and choreographed so they could be shot through apertures in the scenery, and flying walls were employed. Elaborate physical productions filled the studio above Grand Central Terminal, and in the first two years of the show, Miner himself created 39 of the 44 live productions, employing techniques that kept audiences constantly attentive.

In a modern dress production of William Shakespeare's *Julius Caesar* during the first season, for example, Miner moved the camera in extremely tight for a close-up of the eyes of one of the conspirators, while the pre-recorded voice of the actor played over the live close-up. In this attempt to reveal thought, Miner jumped inside the character's mind, using methods that both unnerved and excited the viewers. For *Battleship Bismarck* the producer featured inventive camera angles, tight groupings, and quick, live-camera cuts in place of post-production editing—he often used long, shallow sets that allowed him to shoot from sharp angles. He also employed arresting lighting techniques for outdoor scenes, as in *Macbeth* starring Charlton Heston, one of the show's regular performers. This array of technical and stylistic devices created a specific form of visual storytelling appropriate for the infant medium.

These innovations were vital to the success of the program. Most outstanding dramatic material was already under option to Hollywood, which was not about to share it with an upstart medium that was perceived as a threat to the livelihood of the film industry. In addition, the film studios argued that kinescopes (a film of the image from the picture tube), which were broadcast later in markets other than New York, violated their rights to certain properties. Also, there were not yet seasoned television writers and television could not afford to hire established stage or screen dramatists. Consequently, Miner not only adapted plays from the great classical canon and other work in the public domain, but also drew on lesser Broadway vehicles and short stories.

In 1953 Felix Jackson became producer of *Studio One* and began his stewardship with a critically acclaimed production of George Orwell's *1984*. He established the emphasis on original drama, most notably with Reginald Rose's *Twelve Angry Men,* but despite these and other successes (*The Defender*) many of the works from the mid-1950s were ''kitchen sink'' dramas, stories of ordinary people dealing with a range of ordinary domestic and emotional problems. Larger social and political themes were largely left untouched. In spite of high ratings, sponsors and advertising agencies were generally unhappy with the quotidian locales and stories, feeling that they were sabotaging the implicit fantasies and dreams of consumerism presented in their commercials. CBS and Westinghouse demanded that Rose's *Thunder on Sycamore Street,* based on an actual incident involving a black family moving into a white neighborhood, be altered. Fearing for the sensibilities of Southern affiliates and their white viewers, the black protagonist was changed to an ex-convict. Rose partially managed to subvert this revision by withholding this information until the very end of the show. As Erik Barnouw notes, viewers responded with their own predilections, and the sponsors and network discovered that they had unwittingly presented the type of controversy they had hoped to avoid.

Actress Betty Furness did the commercials during the first year's telecasts and continued to do so for the remainder of the program's life on the air. Her live demonstrations of Westinghouse's household appliances made her the most famous and recognized spokesperson in American television.

The shift to Hollywood and film allowed the networks and sponsors to create something more akin to the production values of feature films. Intimate, minimalist settings and the "marvelous world of the ordinary" were on their way out. Filmed productions for television had the potential for an economic after-life in syndication, while action-oriented genres, especially Westerns, could be churned out quickly on film. Sponsors were relieved of the worry of approving a new set of characters and a potentially problematic script each week—they, and their audiences, could happily identify with a few ongoing characters and personalities instead. In 1957, the amount of prime time programming originating on the West Coast jumped from 40 per cent to 71 per cent. *Studio One in Hollywood* premiered in January of 1958. It still broadcast live but was off the air by September.

—Louis Scheeder

FURTHER READING:

Barnouw, Erick. *Tube of Plenty: The Evolution of American Television.* New York and Oxford, Oxford University Press, 1975.

Studio System

As Herbert Hoover's oft-quoted aphorism states, the business of America is business. But what this truism fails to take into account is the powerful urge for respect, for status, that accompanies the simple aim of making a buck. Though there is no aristocracy in America, not so far as recognized by law, no one who has ever thirsted after power and influence with only money as a weapon, and then come face to face with the invisible blue-bloods arrayed before the gate, can have any faith in this homily to America's virtuous democracy. So it was with the founders of the major Hollywood studios. Immigrants or the sons of immigrants, Eastern Europeans, and Jews, of slight education and deprived backgrounds, they knew from bitter experience to what extent they would be allowed within the provinces of power: not at all. So they created an empire of their own and called it Hollywood, a domain where they could play as philosopher kings or petty tyrants while they remade America in their own image; the better to be accommodated.

It all started in New York City, where several perspicacious young Jews—independently of each other—recognized in the nascent film business the possibility of future wealth. Unlike their competition, they saw that film, far from being a passing novelty, would ultimately have a nearly universal appeal. This fact was not lost on men like Adolph Zukor, a young Hungarian immigrant who made a small fortune in the fur business, and whose story is fairly representative. "[T]here was something in Zukor that went unsatisfied," writes Neal Gabler in *An Empire of Their Own.* "It could have been that he felt his social mobility was blocked by the fur business; no matter how much wealth he accumulated, he would still be associated with something unmistakably Jewish, as the fur trade was, and slightly declasse, as all the garment trades were." In 1903, when a cousin of Zukor came to him for a loan to open an arcade of electric novelties and "peep" machines, the usually cautious Zukor thought to himself: "A Jew could make a lot of money at this." Zukor had an advantage that the purveyors of these machines lacked: from his years in the fur business, Zukor had become adept at judging the market. At the time, films were only beginning to be shown on large screens. Their more common form was the "peep" machine, where a brief film, like *The Great Train Robbery* (1903), could be viewed for a nickel. Zukor saw the commercial potential of movie theaters, and his experience in opening one bore him out. Zukor also perceived the potential market for longer films—"canned" theater as it were, a revolutionary idea for its time—and he believed that movies could both entertain and edify. He obtained the rights for an hour and a half French film starring Sarah Bernhardt, which became an instant success.

Across America, a similar narrative was being played out among ambitious first generation Jews, in touch with the desires of their audience and willing to go out on a limb to satisfy their only half formulated desires. Nickelodeons were popular in the immigrant community, and subsequently were viewed as somewhat disreputable by established businessmen, precisely because of that popularity. The Jews, who had no such qualms, made a killing and then, in their efforts to satisfy the viewing public, began making films of their own. At the time, Thomas Edison had put together a trust of older, more established film producers and distributors, with the intent of enforcing the patent payments he held on film equipment. Incensed, the upstart film producers waged a covert war on the Edison Trust, many of them fleeing to Los Angeles, outside of the long arm of Edison. Coincidentally, the sunny, clement weather in Los Angeles was also conducive to film-making.

In the 1910s a period of consolidation occurred, resulting in several large conglomerates that both produced, distributed, and owned theaters; thus were born the major Hollywood studios. By the mid-1920s, a distinct pecking order existed in Hollywood between the smaller, poverty row studios and the powerful conglomerates such as Paramount (Zukor's company), Universal, RKO, Twentieth Century-Fox, and Metro-Goldwyn-Mayer (MGM) . With the coming of sound film in the late 1920s, filmmakers had realized Zukor's ambition of "canned" theater. Paramount, MGM, Universal, Twentieth Century-Fox, and to a lesser extent, Warner Brothers and Columbia vied for supremacy in this period, each establishing a distinctive style and stable of stars that in many ways reflected the personalities and conceits of their respective heads.

With the coming of sound and with the popularity of films during the Depression, the studios found themselves shaping the entertainment of an entire nation. Many studio heads took their role as cultural arbiters seriously, and shaped their studio's pictures to fit a certain image. Zukor had a penchant for "quality" entertainment, scouring the European continent for artists and presenting his finds in lavish period pieces wholly devoid of any concern for realpolitick. Louis B. Mayer, who as a result of luck and business cunning had finessed himself into heading the conglomeration of three rival companies, was preoccupied with family values. He perceived himself as a patriarch at the head of an enormous extended family (the studio), and by extension the viewing public. A man who had refused to allow his two daughters to go to college for fear they might acquire subversive ideas, he evinced the same concern for the viewing public as a whole. As can be expected from such a man, the pictures MGM made were wholesome things, and in the 1930s, Mickey Rooney and his Andy Hardy movies and wholesome sporting epics were examples of the good, clean fun that predominated at MGM. Universal and Twentieth Century-Fox had both made early successes in silent pictures, but were unable to adapt as readily. Universal, outside of their classic 1930s horror movies and a few lavish production pieces, merely weathered the storm. It was Columbia and Warner Brothers, both marginal upstarts, that adapted best to the changing current of American life, Warner with their fast-paced, starkly lit gangster films, and Columbia with breezy, wise-cracking screwball comedies.

Film succeeded so far beyond the studio presidents' dreams that they were soon involved in a continental search to expand the talent-pool. Agents and scouts were sent scurrying across Europe to lure directors, technicians, and actors to Hollywood. Ernst Lubitsch and Erich von Stroheim came early, impressed by the technical innovations in American films. Fritz Lang came later, a refugee from Hitler's Germany, as were an increasing number of novelists, playwrights, musicians, artists, and composers who, while playing only a marginal role, enlivened the atmosphere considerably. New York was not immune to studio agent's incursions. Throughout the 1930s, novelists and playwrights lit out west after the brass ring. Some, like F. Scott Fitzgerald and Dorothy Parker, were feted and cajoled into writing for pictures, and in turn, reacted with derision. Others, like William Faulkner and Raymond Chandler, were failed authors who relied on Hollywood to sustain them. Nathaniel West, whose books had sold as poorly as Faulkners, turned his bile into artistry, penning the caustic *Day of the Locust,* which would reign as the most venal, acerbic take on Hollywood until the much less distinguished *What Makes Sammy Run* supplanted it in 1941.

In 1939, the year *Gone with the Wind* and *The Wizard of Oz* were released, film was the nation's eleventh-largest industry, with studios turning out some five hundred new movies each year. A decade later, the major studios were losing money, and films' influence was slipping, superseded by its lilliputian rival, television. The HUAC(House Un-American Activities Committee) hearings investigating communist influences in Hollywood further reduced any lingering sensations of omnipotence among the studio heads, who were forced to blacklist some of their most notable talent. What damaged the studios most, however, was the success of an anti-trust suit in the Supreme Court in 1948. Investigations of the studios' monopolistic practices dated back to 1920, when the consolidation of production and distribution had effectively squeezed out all but a few independents, with the studios building enormous temples to themselves with their ornate theaters. Practices such as block-booking and blind selling enabled studios to cram a slew of mediocre films down the throats of theater owners to get the one film they wanted to show. By 1948, the Justice Department had finally drawn a line in the dirt. RKO was the first to cave in, followed in short order by Loew's and then the other majors. Hollywood would never recover.

The system these men created to sustain their vision, the studio system, lasted a little over a quarter century, from the mid-1910s to the early 1950s. By the mid-1950s, control of many majors had reverted to Wall Street and the pioneers were retiring or succumbing

to the stress of running a studio. Harry Cohn died of a heart attack in the mid-1950s, Louis Mayer succumbed to Leukemia, and Jack Warner lived until 1967 before dying of a stroke. Only Adolph Zukor, the grand old man of the studios, would live past his seventies, dying peacefully in his sleep at the age of one hundred and two.

For the common man—and the movies made the common man a recognizable demographic—the movies became, like the flickering images in Plato's cave, a simulacrum of reality. "A picture, all it is is an expensive dream," Harry Warner once said, and there is ample evidence to suggest that the studio heads themselves thought it so, and made their own version of America out of believing it. By recreating the world in dream form, they could supersede the accident of birth that delivered the studio heads to such a lowly station, and overcome the chance of birth that appeared to have precluded them from tasting the fruits of the high and mighty.

—Michael Baers

FURTHER READING:

Davis, Ronald L. *The Glamour Factory.* Dallas, Southern Methodist University Press, 1993.

Friedrich, Otto. *City of Nets.* New York, Harper & Row, Publishers, 1986.

Gabler, Neal. *An Empire of Their Own.* New York, Crown Publishers, 1988.

Mordden, Ethan. *The Hollywood Studios: House Style in the Golden Age of Movies.* New York, Knopf, 1988.

Schatz, Thomas. *The Genius of the System: Hollywood Filmmaking in the Studio Era.* New York, Pantheon, 1988.

Sturges, Preston (1898-1959)

After a childhood abroad, a stint in the army, and a turn as an inventor creating kiss-proof lipstick, in 1929 Chicago native Preston Sturges staged his first Broadway play. From that nearly accidental debut, he fashioned a career in Hollywood's "Golden Age" that film critic Andrew Sarris calls "one of the most brilliant and bizarre bursts of creation in the history of the American cinema." Hired as a writer in 1932, by 1940 Sturges became the first screenplay author to direct his own script when he penned and directed *Christmas in July, Remember the Night,* and Academy Award winner, *The Great McGinty.* By 1944 he had secured his lasting legacy with signature romantic comedies: *The Lady Eve* and *Sullivan's Travels* (both 1941), *The Palm Beach Story* (1942), and *The Miracle of Morgan's Creek* (1944). Sturges was hailed for his brilliance in studio publicity and for his movies' eccentric, visionary critiques of American society.

—Elizabeth Haas

FURTHER READING:

Harvey, James. *Romantic Comedy in Hollywood from Lubitsch to Sturges.* New York, A.A. Knopf, 1987.

Jacobs, Diane. *Christmas in July: The Life and Art of Preston Sturges.* Berkeley, University of California Press, 1992.

Rozgonyi, Jay. *Preston Sturges's Vision of America: Critical Analyses of Fourteen Films.* Jefferson, North Carolina, McFarland, 1995.

Sturges, Preston. *Preston Sturges.* New York, Simon & Schuster, 1990.

Styron, William (1925—)

The novels of William Styron have won major literary awards, received tremendous popular attention, and been the subject of controversy. Styron's two best known novels, *The Confessions of Nat Turner* (1967) and *Sophie's Choice* (1979), deal respectively with an American slave rebellion and the holocaust. *The Confessions of Nat Turner,* based on a documented revolt by slaves in Virginia's Tidewater area in 1831, won the Pulitzer Prize, yet sparked much hostile criticism from black writers and critics. Many charged Styron with historical falsification while others believed it was unconscionable for a white novelist to presume to enter the mind of a black slave. *Sophie's Choice,* set in post-World War II Brooklyn, is the story of an Auschwitz survivor who is plagued by horrible memories and caught in a turbulent love relationship. Styron has also chronicled his battle with depression in a memoir, *Darkness Visible* (1992).

—James Schiff

FURTHER READING:

Casciato, Arthur D., and James L. W. West III, editors. *Critical Essays on William Styron.* Boston, G. K. Hall, 1982.

Clarke, John Henrik, editor. *William Styron's Nat Turner: Ten Black Writers Respond.* Boston, Beacon Press, 1968.

Coale, Samuel Chase. *William Styron Revisited.* Boston, Twayne, 1991.

West, James L. W. III, editor. *Conversations with William Styron.* Jackson, University Press of Mississippi, 1985.

———. *William Styron: A Life.* New York, Random House, 1998.

Suburbia

The development of suburbs—residential communities on the outskirts of cities—was one of the most dominant features of American life in the twentieth century. Far from being merely a way Americans organized their housing and ordered their landscape, the suburbs created an entirely new way of ordering American social life and culture. The result was a phenomenon known as "suburbia," a term denoting not only a physical place but often a cultural and social mind-set as well. The rise of suburbia in the nineteenth and twentieth centuries had a major role in the development of American culture, extending long-cherished American beliefs in individuality and an agrarian ideal in new ways while simultaneously working to reshape both the American physical and social landscape.

While suburbia had its major impact during the twentieth century, it originated and developed in the nineteenth century. "I view large cities," Thomas Jefferson once wrote, "as pestilential to the morals, the health, and the liberties of man." Jefferson's anti-urban view was shared by a growing number of people in the nineteenth century. As cities became crowded with people, bringing

A suburb in south Phoenix, 1998.

increased sanitation, transportation, and crime problems, those Americans who could afford to, namely the growing middle class, began moving to larger, single-family homes on the outskirts of major American cities. This was in direct opposition to European cities, where the middle and upper classes preferred to remain in the central city, and poorer people were pushed to the outskirts. Prior to the mid-nineteenth century, work and home were closely intertwined, and cities reflected this mixture as well with residential buildings coexisting with commercial ones. As industrialization advanced, home and work became increasingly separated as men went off to work and women stayed at home. New innovations in transportation, from ferries and omnibuses to steam railroads and horse-drawn streetcars, helped make this transition possible.

These new 1840s and 1850s suburbs contributed to the monumental shift in middle-class culture in key ways. New suburban homes became a measure of success for these middle classes, a way of telling the world they had arrived. Having money and success meant that the man of the house was able to move his family out of the increasingly grimy and dangerous city to a more pastoral, Edenic place separated from the world of work and commerce. It also allowed these families to reestablish at least a symbolic connection to Jefferson's agrarian ideal, where every family owned its own piece of land and thus remained independent—a key necessity for the success of liberty, and thus the republic. With fewer people making their living in farming as the century progressed, suburban homes with their often ornate gardens offered the closest approximation possible to this agrarian ideal. The suburbs also contributed to the development of the cult of domesticity. Separated from the world of work in their suburban enclaves, women were placed at the center of the domestic world, caring for hearth and home, husband and children, a role exalted as one of supreme importance. Women were viewed as the centers of morality and the important transmitters of this morality to their children and thus to future generations.

These ideals were not unique to the nineteenth century. The exaltation of the domestic sphere for women, the intense desire of Americans to own their own homes, the need to keep some kind of connection to the rural past in an increasingly urbanized present, the desire for social status, and the need for physical and economic security continued to find resonance within American culture throughout the twentieth century. Transportation factors again played an important role, from the development of streetcars in the late nineteenth century to the increasing dominance of the automobile after the 1920s and particularly after the development of the national highway system that began in the 1950s. Suburbs throughout the twentieth century continued to act as an increasingly attractive alternative to inner-city living for those who could afford it. Suburbs grew tremendously throughout the 1920s and 1930s, as bungalow houses and other styles sprang up one after the other on the more affluent sides of major cities around the United States. Throughout this period, suburbs remained closely tied to their urban cores, and their growth accompanied the larger process of urbanization occurring in the United States. In 1920, the number of people living in urban centers became a majority of the population (51.7 percent) for the first time.

With this increase in urban growth, developers across the country took advantage of the continuing desire for suburban living, buying up huge parcels of suburban land and developing it into neighborhoods and subdivisions. One of the most successful was J. C. Nichols of Kansas City, Missouri, whose Country Club District development played upon the deep cultural imperatives behind suburbanization. Nichols combined the lure of the new with the pastoral beauty of the past. His homes built during the 1920s had the most modern of conveniences: gas and electric service, the latest household appliances, and access to transportation connections. He set the homes amid a park-like setting, with generous set-back lines from the street, and ensured his development's success by enacting permanent deed restrictions that limited the extent to which residents could change their houses and yards. He also enacted racially restrictive covenants, ensuring that no resident sold his or her house to African Americans, Jews, or members of other minority groups. In doing so, Nichols ensured that his development remained exclusive. His homes were expensive, and both he and his buyers made sure their investments did not decline in value. More importantly, these restrictions preserved the reason many people were moving to the suburbs in the first place: to avoid the problems (and peoples) of the cities and to provide an environment in which they would not only be surrounded by the bounty of nature, but also by their own kind of people. Nichols's formula, and success, proved a powerful example to developers across the country who mimicked the restrictive covenants, design, and prestige of Nichols's Country Club District. Many similar developments sprang up across the United States during the 1920s.

The depression of the 1930s, and the collapse of the housing market, brought a temporary end to the great wave of exclusive suburban developments, but suburbia, and the needs it served, was hardly finished. After World War II, the United States experienced its greatest wave of suburban development, one that showed little sign of abating at the end of the 1990s. The same cultural factors that had influenced suburban development in the period in the nineteenth and early twentieth centuries remained in the postwar period. One crucial difference was that as suburbia grew, it became available to a wider spectrum of Americans, reflecting the growth of the middle class during the postwar economic boom; however, it still remained largely closed to minorities. No longer were suburbs the exclusive domain of the well-to-do. Indeed, it is the 1950s that many associate with the suburbs, even though they existed long before, and continued long after, that decade. That association is the result of the vast cultural and social impact suburbia had on the United States in the postwar years.

The widening access to suburbia largely can be attributed to one man, developer William Levitt. Like his predecessor Nichols, Levitt's approach proved immensely successful and thus very popular, spawning an untold number of imitators. Levitt's idea was rather simple: he brought mass-production techniques and low prices to suburban housing just as Henry Ford had done in the automobile industry. Taking advantage of the great demand for housing, and benefiting from federal government housing policies which provided mortgage guarantees for both developers and homeowners, Levitt purchased a large parcel of rural land in suburban Long Island. There, he used mass-production techniques to construct more than ten thousand small, inexpensive homes. All were virtually identical, and all sold almost immediately. They proved immensely popular with young couples eager to raise their new families in a comfortable and safe environment. The result was an almost instant community, called Levittown. With low initial and monthly payments for houses in such communities, many families could afford to leave the cities in greater and greater numbers for the relative space, comfort, and security of the suburbs. The result was "white flight," as urban whites moved out of the inner cities to escape the growing influx of black, Hispanic, and other minority groups. This population movement eventually took jobs, tax money, and a diverse population away from America's inner cities, contributing to the decline of cities across the country.

But for those who could enjoy these new suburban developments, suburbia had a strong impact on American social life, so much so that the suburban lifestyle dominated American culture from the 1950s on. Television shows such as *Leave It to Beaver* and *Ozzie and Harriet* centered around white middle-class families in the suburbs. Their lives were idyllic ones, representing peace and harmony. The suburbs and their images on television also worked to promote a reworking of gender roles. Fathers were usually dressed in business suits and were often shown coming home from work to discover the mishaps or other plot twists that had occurred during the day. Women were portrayed as homemakers content with baking cookies, making dinner, and caring for their children and husbands. This idyllic view of suburbia was not entirely incorrect, however, as the suburbs reinforced traditional notions of family and gender that had been challenged by working women during the World War II years. With the strict division of the home from the world of work, suburbia in the 1950s and after continued trends that had begun in the mid-nineteenth century. The suburbs also contributed to what many soon labeled the "culture of conformity." New suburban developments such as Levittown were homogenous places. Not only were the houses virtually identical, but their inhabitants were as well. These new communities were quickly filled by new families, many of them headed by young veterans eager to return to a normal life after the traumas of World War II, with similar backgrounds, experiences, needs, and ages. Group socialization and the adherence to established social norms was encouraged; individuality and isolation were not. Many found this new environment appealing, but critics soon began to criticize the social conformity demanded by the suburbs. John Keats, in his book *The Crack in the Picture Window* (1956), attacked the conformity of suburbs as a "postwar, homogenous hell" of rigid social roles that produced an environment of mediocrity. Folksinger Pete Seeger sang in "Little Boxes": "Little boxes, on the hillside, little boxes made of ticky-tacky . . . little boxes all the same." And not only were the houses all the same, but the people were as well, going through exactly the same experiences, living in identical social boxes that, as Seeger sang it, might well have been coffins.

In addition to its cultural impact, suburbs also had a great impact on the American landscape and environment, encouraging the development of an automobile culture and suburban sprawl. Spread out away from cities, without access to older public transportation systems such as subways and rail lines, suburbanites depended on their cars for access to jobs in the city. This development was encouraged by the 1956 Federal Highway Act which provided more than $25 billion to construct more than forty thousand miles of highways. It was the largest public works project in the history of the United States. In a culture that was already in love with the automobile, the suburbs encouraged even greater reliance on them. The result was suburban sprawl. Instead of tightly compacted centers where most services, entertainment, and employment were easily accessible on foot, suburbs encouraged all of these functions to spread out. Thus restaurants, stores, and other facilities each occupied their own buildings with parking surrounding them. Some were clustered in strip malls or enclosed shopping malls, but like the suburbs as a whole, all were geared to the need of the automobile.

Suburbia also encouraged the unique American social phenomenon of obsession with lawns and lawn care. Among the deeper ideological bases for suburbia was the need to recreate an Edenic natural setting that was believed to be superior to the concrete jungles of city life. Preserving the image of life in a garden, however, was difficult with so many houses so close together. As a substitute, Americans began to view their lawns as each contributing to a seamless expanse of grass that created as much of a park-like setting as possible. Maintaining this lawn became an important cultural imperative, as homeowners were responsible for keeping up their portion of the "park." Encouraged by magazines, advertising, seed companies, and often by homeowners associations' restrictive clauses that mandated proper upkeep of lawns, lawn care became a major suburban activity. In suburban developments during the warmer months, weekends were filled with the drone of lawn mowers. Competitions were held in neighborhoods to establish the "yard of the month," and people who refused to do their part were often shunned and occasionally sued for their noncompliance. The lawn obsession was also part of a larger cultural interest in outdoor life, and suburbs promoted such things as outdoor barbecues, swimming pools, and gardening.

While the classic 1950s image of suburbia still exists at the turn of the century, suburbs in the 1980s and 1990s were in the midst of change. The biggest shift came in the relationship between suburbs and the cities they surrounded. By the 1980s, many suburbs were beginning to evolve into self-contained communities where people not only lived, but worked. In Orange County, California (outside Los Angeles); Cobb County, Georgia (north of Atlanta); Tyson's Corner, Virginia (outside Washington, D.C.); and in similar communities across the country, suburbs became the locations for major office complexes that were home to thousands of workers. With their living and working needs now available in the suburbs, there was less and less need for suburbanites to travel to the downtowns of central cities. They developed into their own small cities that writer Joel Garreau labeled "edge cities." That trend, which historian Jon Teaford called "postsuburbia," was indicative of a new age in the history of suburbs. While still a relatively new phenomenon, this shift may also portend a change in the ability of suburbia to fill certain cultural needs. With work and home sites now close together, the role of suburbs as an idyllic retreat from the world of commerce was changing by the late 1990s, reversing a trend that began in the early nineteenth century. These developments, and the increasing concern over suburban sprawl with its often negative effects on the environment and on what many were calling a loss of community in American life, were still in their infancy by the late 1990s. The long-term effects of these changes on the historic roles suburbia has played in American social and cultural life remain to be seen.

—Timothy Berg

FURTHER READING:

Gans, Herbert. *The Levittowners.* New York, Pantheon, 1967.

Garreau, Joel. *Edge City: Life on the New Frontier.* New York, Doubleday, 1991.

Hayden, Delores. *Redesigning the American Dream: The Future of Housing, Work, and Family Life.* New York, W.W. Norton, 1986.

Jackson, Kenneth T. *Crabgrass Frontier: The Suburbanization of the United States.* New York, Oxford University Press, 1985.

Jenkins, Virginia Scott. *The Lawn: A History of an American Obsession.* Washington, D.C., Smithsonian Institution Press, 1994.

Palen, J. John. *The Suburbs.* New York, McGraw-Hill, 1995.

Teaford, Jon C. *City and Suburb: The Political Fragmentation of Metropolitan America, 1850-1970.* Baltimore, The Johns Hopkins University Press, 1979.

———. *Post-Suburbia: Government and Politics in the Edge Cities.* Baltimore, The Johns Hopkins University Press, 1997.

Suicide

While actual reasons for suicide stem from complicated and often indeterminate causes, the public is left to sort out the implications of what Primo Levi calls this "noninstinctive, unnatural choice." In the early part of the twentieth century, suicide was a taboo subject. Popular opinion held that madness was the most plausible explanation for a person taking his or her own life. When suicides were mentioned in the 1910s and 1920s, they were characterized in terms of trends: *Literary Digest* once reported of "rashes" of childhood suicides, and again of college campus suicides. Suicide was seen as virtually a contagious disease.

The stock market crash of 1929 brought the first widespread acknowledgement of suicide in the twentieth century, with instantly legendary images of despondent former millionaires leaping to their deaths. As some news accounts of the time would have it, a person walking through New York City would have had difficulty navigating the bodies littered on Wall Street. Without question, the crash did eventually cause a number of suicides, but as John Kenneth Galbraith reported, statistics suggest that the "suicide wave" of 1929 was largely a myth: "For several years before 1929, the suicide rate had been gradually rising. It continued to increase in that year, with a further and much sharper increase in 1930, 1931, and 1932—years when there were many things besides the stock market to cause people to conclude that life was no longer worth living." This notwithstanding, the widely-reported millionaire suicides expanded America's understanding of the causes of suicide to include not only madness but also great financial loss. Capitalism itself became a credible contributing factor in suicides.

For decades, suicide receded into the shadows, until the 1962 death of movie star and legendary sex symbol Marilyn Monroe. Events surrounding Monroe's death became fodder for gossip columns and investigative reports throughout the rest of the twentieth century. Instead of repudiating her for committing suicide, the nation shared her tragedy. Her death helped spawn the growth of suicide hotlines, where people who felt suicidal were encouraged to discuss their feelings with counselors. Monroe's later well-publicized dependence on prescription drugs fueled the opinion that the pressures of celebrity became too much for her. With the acceptance that the public might have contributed to Monroe's final act, suicide moved from private blame into the arena of shared responsibility. Unfortunately, statistics subsequent to her suicide also lend credence to the theory that suicides can be "contagious"; according to Herbert Hendin, "Just after Marilyn Monroe's death, the notes of a number of suicides linked their own deaths to her presumed suicide . . . A sense of sharing the tragic death or suicide of someone famous . . . enables some people to feel that their death has a meaning it would otherwise lack."

Throughout the 1960s and into the 1990s the pressures celebrities experience were also linked to drug abuse and overdose, nowhere more than in the music industry. The deaths of rock stars Janis Joplin, Jimi Hendrix, and Elvis Presley, all of whom accidentally overdosed, were received with a sense of tragedy similar to Monroe's death. Though these deaths were officially "accidental," fame had surely influenced self-destructive behavior. Other high-profile victims of the deadly combination of fame and drug abuse included comedian Freddie Prinze, who shot himself in 1977 at the age of 22, comedian John Belushi, who died of a drug overdose in 1982, and "grunge" music pioneer Kurt Cobain, with a history of treatment for a heroin addiction, who shot himself in 1994.

The connection between a creative personality and suicide has seemed particularly close among writers. The most prominent instances of the twentieth century were the deaths of Ernest Hemingway in 1961, Sylvia Plath in 1963, and Anne Sexton in 1974. While Hemingway's suicide was attributed to poor physical and mental health, it seemed in keeping with his gonzo personality. The deaths of Plath and Sexton, however, seemed more tragic because they were comparatively young and healthy. Their deaths were especially indicative of the troubled female artist. As A. Alvarez writes of Sylvia Plath, public perception perverted her death into "a myth of the poet as a sacrificial victim, offering herself up for the sake of her art." Her suicide intimated to the public that art had the power to destroy.

Religious fervor, long attributed as a cause for insanity and suicide, also showed its powers of destruction. When 914 followers of the Reverend Jim Jones committed mass suicide in Jonestown, Guyana in 1978, suicide became inextricably linked to religious cults. Jones was seen as a charismatic brainwasher who convinced his members that their deaths were, according to him, "an act of

revolutionary suicide protesting the conditions of an inhuman world." Subsequent cases confirmed the apocalyptic and suicidal nature of cults, most notably the Branch Davidians in Texas in 1993, and the 39 suicides of members of the Heaven's Gate cult in California in 1997.

The early 1990s saw rock musicians Judas Priest and Ozzy Osbourne of the group Black Sabbath defend their music in separate court cases which accused that their songs influenced teens to commit suicide. In both cases, the first amendment rights of the musicians were upheld. Still, Osbourne's song "Suicide Solution," as well as other songs such as "Goodbye Cruel World" by Pink Floyd, books such as *Illusions* by Richard Bach, and films such as *Dead Poet's Society* continued to draw criticism for what some saw as glorifying the act of suicide.

At the close of the twentieth century, physician-assisted suicide dominated the headlines, with purported "suicide doctor" Jack Kevorkian challenging laws across the country that made assisted suicide illegal. In 1998 he appeared on the news program *60 Minutes* which aired a tape of him assisting a suicide. Kevorkian orchestrated the publicity stunt in an effort to force a Supreme Court ruling on the constitutionality of a person's "right to die."

While suicide remained complex for most Americans, by the end of the twentieth century the topic had emerged from the shadows to be discussed in the light of the shared public arena.

—Chris Haven

FURTHER READING:

Alvarez, A. *The Savage God: A Study of Suicide.* New York, Norton, 1990.

Durkheim, Emile. *Suicide: A Study in Sociology.* New York, Free Press, 1997.

Galbraith, John Kenneth. *The Great Crash 1929.* Boston, Houghton Mifflin, 1955.

Hendin, Herbert. *Suicide in America.* New York, Norton, 1982.

Kushner, Howard I. *Self-Destruction in the Promised Land: a Psychocultural Biology of American Suicide.* New Brunswick, Rutgers University Press, 1989.

Lester, David. *Encyclopedia of Famous Suicides.* Commack, New York, Nova Science Publishers, 1997.

———. *Making Sense of Suicide: An In-Depth Look at Why People Kill Themselves.* Philadelphia, Charles Press, 1997.

———. *Patterns of Suicide and Homicide in the World.* Commack, New York, Nova Science Publishers, 1994.

Sullivan, Ed (1902-1974)

Ed Sullivan, who could not sing, dance, or act, was television's greatest showman in its early years. For twenty-three years, from 1948 to 1971, he hosted America's premiere variety show every Sunday night on CBS, on which he introduced an eclectic array of talent that included everything from opera singers to dancing bears to Elvis Presley and the Beatles. Sullivan, a former newspaper columnist, appeared on the nation's television screens as a most untelegenic presence. He was everything that a professional television host is not supposed to be—awkward, stiff, and prone to frequent malapropisms.

Ed Sullivan with Lucille Ball on the *Ed Sullivan Show*.

His real talent was behind the scenes, as a man who had his finger on the pulse of America's cultural tastes. He understood instinctively that a variety show should present acts that would appeal to the various demographic segments of its audience. Only on *The Ed Sullivan Show* could you see such diverse talents as Van Cliburn, Rudolf Nureyev, Robert Goulet, Richard Pryor, a plate spinner, and The Rolling Stones. With his distinctive nasal voice, Sullivan regularly promised audiences "a really big shew" and delivered by offering up virtually every form of twentieth-century entertainment.

Edward Vincent Sullivan was born on September 28, 1902, in the Harlem section of Manhattan, New York City, the son of a customs inspector. He was one of seven children (his twin brother, Daniel, died in his first year) and was raised in Port Chester, New York. Young Edward was a poor student, but a strong athlete who won ten letters in sports. Upon graduating from high school he became a newspaper sports reporter. In 1932, he joined the *New York Daily News* as a Broadway columnist and soon came into contact with many figures in the entertainment industry. While serving as emcee of the newspaper-sponsored Harvest Moon Ball dance contest in 1947, he was "discovered" by Worthington Miner, a general manager at CBS-TV, who asked Sullivan to host a planned variety series called *Toast of the Town*. The series debuted on June 20, 1948, reflecting from the beginning Sullivan's keen sense of diversity in programming. That initial episode featured Broadway's Richard Rodgers and Oscar Hammerstein, the rising comedy team of Dean Martin and Jerry Lewis in their first TV appearance, classical pianist Eugene List, ballerina Kathryn Lee, a group of singing New York City firemen, and six June Taylor dancers (called the "Toastettes"). Within that

single hour was something for everyone, from the highbrow to the most common man.

During his 23-year run on CBS, Ed Sullivan served as the cultural arbiter for much of middle America. He worked constantly to insure that his audience witnessed the very best entertainment available, as he was deeply involved in all aspects of the show. He booked all the acts himself, helped edit each performer's material, and frequently juggled the show's running order. Some claimed he was a dictatorial taskmaster, but Sullivan took full responsibility for the success or failure of each week's episode. In 1967 he revealed his show-business philosophy when he stated, "An audience will forgive a bad act but never bad taste." For a man who sought perfection in even his silliest performers, Sullivan always presented himself as a rather bumbling persona. An article in *TV Guide* once described him by writing: "Not since radio's Major Bowes have the airways been subjected to such a bumbling Barnum. Cod-eyed, cement-faced and so scaredy-cat stiff that he's been suspected of having a silver plate in his head, Sullivan has yet to complete gracefully the smallest gesture, unravel his vowels, or conquer a simple introduction." Sullivan's distinctive voice and mannerisms made him the target of many comics and impressionists, including John Byner and Will Jordan. While he may have been awkward, Sullivan knew his job was to introduce the talent and leave the stage so they could shine.

The format of Sullivan's show, which was re-titled *The Ed Sullivan Show* in 1955, changed little over its many years. It was basically a filmed vaudeville show with acts chosen to appeal to the broadest possible audience. Guests from the world of the classical arts included violinist Itzhak Perlman, dancer Margot Fonteyn, and opera star Roberta Peters. For a rare TV appearance by diva Maria Callas, Sullivan staged a full scene from *Tosca*. Guests designed to attract more middle-class audiences included Broadway and movie stars, such as Richard Burton and Julie Andrews performing a scene from *Camelot*, songs by Barbra Steisand, Dinah Shore, and Eddie Fisher, and Henry Fonda reading Lincoln's Gettysburg Address. Sullivan was very fond of comics and often invited Borscht Belt veterans like Alan King and Henny Youngman to perform. His most frequently returning comedy guests, however, were the Canadian team of Wayne and Shuster. For the youngsters in the audience, Sullivan was always sure to include a novelty act. These included acrobats, mimes, animal acts, and much more. The specialty act most associated with Sullivan was the lovable Italian mouse puppet, Topo Gigio, who frequently exclaimed, "Hey, Eddie, kees-a-me goodnight!" Occasionally, Sullivan would devote an entire show to one subject, such as honoring the works of Irving Berlin, Cole Porter, and Walt Disney.

By the mid-1950s Sullivan became aware that American popular culture was changing drastically. He helped to promote racial diversity by showcasing black performers, such as Pearl Bailey, Nat "King" Cole, George Kirby, and Leontyne Price. Other television shows refused to present African-American guests due to sponsor complaints. Furthermore, Sullivan began inviting rock and roll stars onto the show to raise its appeal to the demographically important teen audience. Elvis Presley made three memorable visits in 1956. Although cameras showed him from only the waist up on his last appearance to calm adult fears of the singer's swiveling pelvis, the fact that Presley was on the show seemed to legitimize rock to the adult audience. On February 9, 1964, an appearance by the Beatles earned Sullivan his highest rating ever. That broadcast is considered a milestone event in television history. Throughout the 1960s, more members of the counterculture appeared with Sullivan, such as Janis Joplin, Marvin Gaye, and The Rolling Stones. While he liked the ratings they brought, he was often uncomfortable with their attitudes and material. He had heated confrontations with The Doors and Bob Dylan over his attempts to censor their songs. Younger comedians like George Carlin, Woody Allen, and Bill Cosby were also more visible in the 1960s. After 1087 episodes that presented over 10,000 performers, *The Ed Sullivan Show* left the air on June 6, 1971. Ed Sullivan died in October, 1974.

Ed Sullivan and his variety program are monuments to a form of entertainment that no longer exists. Today, the mass television audience has nearly disappeared and has been dispersed with the advent of cable and more specialized programming. *The Ed Sullivan Show* provided one of the last opportunities for the entire family to gather round the tube and be entertained by a single program. The show was immortalized by the hit Broadway musical *Bye, Bye Birdie* as the emblem of all that was good with television. For contemporary viewers it offered a rare opportunity to witness the performances of many of the twentieth century's greatest artists. As authors Harry Castleman and Walter Podrazik wrote of Sullivan in 1989, "He was good because he was a good packager of entertainment. . . He could spot talent, knew how to balance an hour program, and didn't waste time calling attention to himself. We could use more hosts like him now." Sullivan's legacy is enshrined in the many "really big shews" that entertained a generation.

—Charles Coletta

FURTHER READING:

Bowles, Jerry. *A Thousand Sundays: The Story of the Ed Sullivan Show.* New York, Putnam's, 1980.

Brooks, Tim. *The Complete Directory to Prime Time TV Stars.* New York, Ballantine Books, 1987.

Castleman, Harry, and Walter Podrazik. *Harry and Wally's Favorite TV Shows.* New York, Prentice Hall Press, 1989.

Harris, Jay. *TV Guide: The First 25 Years.* New York, New American Library, 1980.

Marschall, Rick. *The History of Television.* New York, Gallery Books, 1986.

Sullivan, John L. (1858-1918)

Bare-knuckle prizefighter John L. Sullivan became a symbol of ethnic pride and working-class masculinity to the nineteenth-century, Irish-American community from which he emerged. Because of his boisterous claims to "lick any son of a bitch in the house" and his ability to back up his claim, many Irish Americans saw in Sullivan a way to take revenge upon the unwelcoming American society. The working-class Irish took pride as Sullivan knocked out his Anglo-Protestant opponents, yet Sullivan's popularity went beyond mere ethnic and class identity; the rest of American society slowly began to accept Sullivan as well. Because of his mass appeal, Sullivan became one of the first cultural heroes and sporting celebrities of the nineteenth century. Along with his rise in popularity, boxing earned a measure of respectability as a sporting endeavor. When Sullivan began boxing, prizefights were against the law. By the time he quit, boxing matches were a cultural event attended by all segments of society.

John L. Sullivan

John Lawrence Sullivan was born into the Irish working-class community of Roxbury, Massachusetts, in 1858. Like many Irish immigrants, Sullivan's father worked as a hod carrier in the lowest-paying of the new industrial jobs. As was the norm for the youth of his community, Sullivan moved into the industrial work force quickly. He worked a variety of odd jobs but was unable to hold down steady work because of a tendency to get into fights with his fellow workers. To support himself, Sullivan began to play baseball and box semiprofessionally. He complemented his boxing with neighborhood fights in theatres and movie halls. Sullivan and his friends soon earned reputations through such street fights. It was in these theatres, the Sullivan legend later suggested, that he first stood up and made his famous boast, "I'm John L. Sullivan and I can lick any son of a bitch in the house." These claims, along with strongman demonstrations of lifting beer kegs above his head, soon earned Sullivan the nickname "Boston Strong Boy" and the reputation of an up-and-coming pugilist. On the strength of his reputation, Sullivan issued a challenge to Paddy Ryan, the reigning champion.

Prizefighting in nineteenth-century America was a working-class amusement, and fights often took place inside the ethnic saloons that dotted the working-class community. Middle-class society frowned upon the practice of boxing, so much so that bare-knuckle prizefighting was outlawed. Champions often held a questionable position within the community. They often split their time between boxing, breaking up barroom scuffles, and brawling at the ballot box for the local political machine. Paddy Ryan was just such a champion. By 1882, however, he could ignore the young challenger from Boston no longer and agreed to a bout. In February, Ryan and Sullivan met for the first time in Mississippi City, Mississippi. Sullivan dominated the champion from the start, winning not only first fall and first blood, but knocking out Ryan after nine rounds.

Now recognized as the heavyweight champion, Sullivan did not become, like Ryan, political muscle. Instead, Sullivan issued his most famous and broad sweeping challenge. He dared anyone in the United States to last four rounds with him in a gloved match and offered a $1,000 prize to those who could. With the offers lining up, Sullivan began a whirlwind tour of the states. His travels took on a carnivalesque atmosphere with juggling acts and vaudeville shows preceding his defeat of whoever challenged him. From 1878 to 1905, Sullivan won 31 of 35 bouts, 16 by knockout. Because of his tour and the fact that he rarely lost his bet, Sullivan's popularity soared. Irish Americans across the country flocked to see the man who fought with both the colors of the United States and Ireland in his corner. Because Sullivan fought gloved matches, his bouts were legal and could be seen by people who had not watched prizefighting before. Sullivan quickly became a cultural icon whose name and image appeared in advertisements and vaudeville shows.

Sullivan was still considered the champion of boxing and, as such, was required to defend his title in a bare-knuckle fight. He had managed to stave off most challengers with gloved matches, but by 1889, Jake Kilrain demanded a bare-knuckle bout. Kilrain had taken a path similar to Sullivan's, rising out of the Irish working class by his fists. His impressive record combined with the accumulated effect of years of Sullivan's legendary drinking made the odds even at the time of the fight. On July 8, 1889, the two men squared off in what would be the last bare-knuckle championship bout. Despite years of hard drinking and weak fights, Sullivan had trained himself back into shape. Fighting under the scorching Mississippi sun, Sullivan and Kilrain faced each other for more than two hours and 75 rounds until Kilrain was unable to start the 76th.

Although Sullivan did enjoy a great deal of popularity outside his working-class community, not every one accepted his display of masculine aggression and violence. Parts of the American middle class, especially the emergent Irish-American middle class, distanced themselves from the bruiser from Roxbury. Many cheered when "Gentleman" Jim Corbett, a man of breeding who had learned to box in a club instead of the street, knocked out Sullivan in 21 rounds in New Orleans in September 1892 to earn the U.S. world heavyweight boxing champion title.

During his career, Sullivan earned more than $1 million, but spent it all. He became an advocate of prohibition and delivered lectures on the topic.

—S. Paul O'Hara

FURTHER READING:

Gorn, Elliot J. *The Manly Art: Bare-knuckle Prizefighting in America.* Ithaca, Cornell University Press, 1986.

Isenberg, Michael T. *John L. Sullivan and his America.* Urbana, University of Illinois Press, 1986.

Summer Camp

For over a century, summer camps have provided millions of American children with their first taste of the world outside their family and neighborhood. The first commercial camp began in 1881; at the end of the nineteenth century, a handful of camps served elite Protestant boys almost exclusively. In the early twentieth century, the industry extended and diversified its reach. At its peak in the prosperous years after World War II, about one in six children attended camp. Camp is still an important part of many children's summers: while the traditional eight week private camp is no longer as popular as once it was, in the late 1990s over eight million children and adolescents between the ages of five and seventeen attend a wide variety of camps—5500 overnight and 3000 day camps—each summer. While day camps, short-term overnight camps and specialty camps serve increasing numbers of children, many camps feature traditional activities that have varied little for generations: living in cabins with children of similar backgrounds; taking daily swims and engaging in other water and land sports, hikes and overnight trips; doing arts and crafts; singing camp songs and roasting marshmallows around campfires. The industry has reflected disparate and changing goals, but the basic premise remains the same: that camps foster community life, personal development, and skill-building, while providing retreats from the problems and dangers of the outside world.

Summer camp is a distinctly American invention, whose origins reflect the aspirations and anxieties of late nineteenth century middle and upper class life. First, as cities grew, particularly in the Northeast, industrialization and urbanization inspired some well-to-do men (and a few women) to travel to wilderness areas to experience the reinvigorating romance of nature, and its fortification for urban life. Second, concepts of child-rearing among the upper and middle class were in transition; as the birthrate among urban well-to-do families declined, parents devoted increasing resources toward providing a sheltered and longer childhood for their smaller families. Acknowledging that children had their own peer cultures, adults expressed anxiety about how best to supervise and guide them. Rural children had traditionally helped their parents on farms during the summer, but increasing numbers of urban children and upper class children had no set tasks over the long vacation. In addition, the first summer camps reflected the particular anxieties of their founders, a group of white middle- and upper-class Protestant men who worried about the effects of modernity upon elite boys' manliness. Youth leaders feared the enfeeblement of those who, they believed, ought by virtue of their class to lead the nation. Camp was to be an antidote to the "softness" of the modern work regime and vacations at resort hotels: a place where privileged boys would experience the toughening effects of outdoor life, albeit amidst the safety of select peers and adult supervision.

Given that camps claimed to be an antidote to modern urban life, it is unsurprising that they achieved their greatest popularity near the largest urban centers, particularly at lakes and mountains within a day's travel of the densely settled Northeast. While smaller camping districts—such as the Upper Midwest and the mountains of North Carolina—emerged in the early twentieth century, summer camps have always been most popular in the Northeast, where they first started. The Gunnery Camp near Milford, Connecticut (1861-1879) has long been cited as the earliest camp model. It was not a separate camp but part of the summer term of a boarding school; for two weeks each summer, the boys lived in tents by the sea and simulated the life of soldiers. Other early efforts included the North Mountain School of

Physical Culture, northeast of Wilkes-Barre, Pennsylvania, run in the late 1870s for "weakly boys," and the first church-sponsored camp, run by the Reverend George Hinckley of Hartford, Connecticut during the summers of 1880 and 1881 near Wakefield, Rhode Island. Ernest Balch's Camp Chocorua, which ran from 1881 to 1889 on Asquam Lake, New Hampshire, was the first commercial organized camp. Chocorua provided a model that camps of all kinds would cite for years to come, in which children with similar family backgrounds lived together away from home, sharing leisure activities, chores, camp rituals and inside jokes.

Chocorua, like later camps, lauded the wilderness but took advantage of modern innovations. The boys made their own boats and did extensive chores around the grounds, but within a few years they were living in cabins instead of tents, and the camp had inaugurated a complex financial system to teach the boys about modern commerce. In general, while many camps started small, with a few tents and a rowboat, if they were successful they sheltered children from the wilderness that they extolled, and provided comforts and improved recreational facilities as quickly as they could afford them. From the 1880s onward, innovations have run the gamut from electricity to miniature golf courses, leading to countless discussions among camping professionals about what exactly makes a camp "campy."

At the turn of the twentieth century, the field of camping expanded to benefit the poor as well as the rich. Progressive Era reformers worried particularly about the plight of new immigrant children growing up in city tenements, where poverty and overcrowding bred malnutrition and disease. Hoping both to assert a moral control over potentially unruly new Americans, and to provide healthful and pleasurable activities in rural settings for needy youth, a variety of nonprofit and charitable organizations started their own camps. Settlement Houses, church groups, and charitable organizations all sponsored short trips to the country for poor urban children. At the same time, camping opportunities for middle class children grew as YMCAs, YMHAs and their female counterparts began to work more intensively with children and adolescents. By the 1910s, reflecting new models of athletic girlhood, increasing numbers of girls' camps opened. New youth organizations such as the Boy Scouts, Girl Scouts, and Camp Fire Girls specifically exhorted children to camp outdoors. By the early twentieth century, boys and girls of many ethnicities and social classes were camping at their own facilities (as in other forms of commercial recreation, children of color experienced more limited camping opportunities).

As ideas about child-rearing and recreation shifted over the course of the century, so did camps' daily routines. Most of the very early camps had a decidedly religious character. Protestants, and later Jews and Catholics, saw in camp a means to reinforce their religious communities. By the 1920s, camping had expanded to serve a variety of interest groups, all of whom saw in camping communal possibilities that transcended their individual political, religious, and social differences. Zionists, Progressive educators, hiking enthusiasts, socialists, and military types all created camps in their own image. But they also were responsive to larger trends in children's recreation. During the First World War, many camps adopted military drill and army-style discipline. In the 1930s, influenced by the pedagogical theories of John Dewey, a countering discourse stressed creativity, social adjustment, and personality development. One enduring legacy is the place of Indian-style ritual. In the first years of the twentieth century, Ernest Thompson Seton's youth organization, the Woodcraft League, inspired many camps to "play Indian" by making teepees and totem poles, telling Indian stories by the campfire, and wearing

moccasins and headdresses. Driven by nostalgia and desire for premodern "authenticity," many camps have continued to invoke Indian pasts.

Across the country, overnight camps flourished in the postwar years, as a generation of baby boomers grew to camping age. In 1948 the national umbrella organization, the American Camping Association, finally instituted national standards for camp accreditation, after decades of debate. But the years since have been rocky ones. Since the mid 1970s, more than 2500 camps, or about one in five, have gone out of business. In the late 1960s and 1970s, camp owners found themselves competing against not only trips to Europe but also the anti-authoritarian youth culture of that era. Camps near major cities and tourist centers have fallen victim to high expenses and the temptation of high real estate prices. In response, many traditional eight-week camps have inaugurated shorter sessions to accommodate parents who are scheduling their children's summers more tightly around competing interests, including joint custody issues and alternate family vacation plans. In addition, traditional camps now compete against newer specialty camps which focus on particular skills or provide specific experiences: computer skills, weight loss, gymnastics or soccer, and bike tours across the country. At the end of the 1990s, 75 percent of all camps were run by nonprofit groups and social service agencies, serving children of all economic classes. In other words, the popular image of the extended vacation at a private eight-week camp does not fully reflect the experience of most contemporary campers, for whom the average stay is one week at a non-profit camp. But in the popular imagination, camps represent sites for children's adventurous "coming of age," rather than quick trips. In films such as *Meatballs* (1979), *Little Darlings* (1980), and *Addams Family Values* (1993), camps are a place where children and adolescents embark upon voyages of self-discovery, friendship, and loneliness, pranks of all kinds, and, if they are teenagers, sexual and romantic exploration. For adults who once attended them, camps often represent a nostalgic reminder of childhood.

For over a century, disparate groups have held in common the belief that rural spaces are healthier and safer for children, and that camps in particular can be spaces of social transformation, in which adults can teach children the arts of acculturation and good (class, racial, ethnic, religious, political and gender-appropriate) citizenship before returning them to their homes. Collectively, summer camps have shown an ability to change with the times and to accommodate different and sometimes diametrically opposed groups. They provide a window into the expansion of children's recreation in the twentieth century, and to the changes in American social order that have enabled a widening range of communities to create children's leisure in their own image.

—Leslie Paris

FURTHER READING:

Buckler, Helen, Mary F. Fiedler and Martha F. Allen. *Wo-he-lo: The Story of the Campfire Girls 1910-1960.* New York, Holt, Rinehart, and Winston, 1961.

Deloria, Philip J. *Playing Indian.* New Haven, Yale University Press, 1998.

Eells, Eleanor. *Eleanor Eells' History of Organized Camping: The First 100 Years.* Martinsville, Indiana, American Camping Association, 1986.

Gibson, H. W. "The History of Organized Camping." *Camping.* Jan.-Dec. 1936.

Gutman, Richard J. S. and Kellie O. Gutman. *The Summer Camp Memory Book: a pictorial treasury of everything, from campfires to color wars, you loved about camp.* New York, Crown Publishers, 1983.

MacLeod, David. *Building Character in the American Boy: The Boy Scouts, YMCA, and Their Forerunners, 1870-1920.* Madison, University of Wisconsin Press, 1983.

A Worthy Use of Summer: Jewish Summer Camping in America. Edited by Jenna Weissman Joselit with Karen S. Mittelman. Philadelphia, Museum of American Jewish History, 1993.

Summer, Donna (1948—)

Singer Donna Summer was the first and perhaps only true luminary of the disco era. Beginning with a breakthrough 1975 hit that pigeonholed her as a libidinous electrified diva, Summer recorded several albums over the next few years that brought her international fame; for a brief time her style even seemed to be breaking down racial barriers in American pop music. She was often referred to as the "queen of disco" and by 1979 had topped the charts with *Bad Girls,* the best-selling album by a female performer that year.

Summer was born La Donna Gaines in 1948 and grew up in Boston. As a youth, she sang gospel in her church and moved to

Donna Summer

Europe before finishing high school when offered a role in the stage version of the popular hippie musical *Hair.* She spent the next several years in Germany, married an Austrian named Helmut Sommer (and kept his name after their 1974 divorce), and appeared in theater productions before beginning to work with two successful Munich producers, Giorgio Moroder and Pete Bellote, at their Musicland Studios. The duo made minor disco hits for the European dance-club scene that were quietly making their way to the underground nightclubs frequented by gays, blacks, and Latinos in New York City. Such discos grew in popularity when a downturn in the economy made such clubs—with their five-dollar cover for an evening of entertainment—a preferable alternative to concerts.

Billboard magazine had introduced a disco chart in early 1975 after savvy record companies realized the huge potential of the emerging dance-club scene: certain records were selling in the thousands without any radio airplay at all. Summer had two minor hits in Europe, then suggested to her producers that they record something similar to a breathy French hit from 1959, "*Je t'aime . . . moi non plus*" by Jane Birkin and Serge Gainsbourg. What they came up with was three minutes of Summer singing the words "love to love you, baby," a few other phrases, and a lot of moaning. When the track found its way to a party at the Los Angeles home of Neil Bogart, who had made a fortune in the sixties with a label that put out bubble-gum pop, his guests clamored to hear it over and over. He contacted Moroder and Bellote, asked them to make a longer version, and signed Summer to his new label, Casablanca.

Summer had a huge hit in the United States with "Love to Love You, Baby," and a debut album of the same name went gold. "It was a disc that spun day and night throughout the summer of 1975," wrote Albert Goldman in *Esquire* just two years later. "To the layman, it was just another catchy tune; to the initiate, it was the first unambiguous sign that we were in for another epidemic of the dancing sickness--that recurrent mania that sweeps over this country and Europe on an average of once every ten years. . . ." *Time* journalist Jay Cocks wrote, three years after its debut, that the song seemed to signify "disco's coming-out party," the emergence of homosexual subculture into mainstream America. Goldman termed it "the first frankly erotic album ever to achieve wide currency and airplay. Broadcasting the cries and moans of a woman enjoying intercourse may not sound like much of a breakthrough in this age of explicit sex and rampant pornography," Goldman wrote in 1977, "but it must be borne in mind that phono-recording is the most oppressively censored medium in America."

Summer became a household name. For a time she had a constant bodyguard, since fans were known to trap her in elevators. She released a number of albums over the next few years, including two in 1976, *A Love Trilogy* and *Four Seasons of Love.* A less-discofied album, *I Remember Yesterday,* had a great hit the following year with "I Feel Love." The song was notable for what came to be known as the "galloping bass line," a thumping, 140-beat-per-minute backbone of drum-machine rhythm structure that became the staple of many a disco hit. "Donna Summer snapped her choruses over booming rhythm tracks that moved the artfully tied construction boots of gay men and the teetery hetero platforms of the Saturday Night Fever disco hordes," wrote Gerri Hirshey in *Rolling Stone.* Summer's 1978 double-live album, *Live and More,* sold millions.

In 1978 Summer made her film debut in *Thank God It's Friday,* and a song she wrote and sang for it, "Last Dance" won her one of several Grammy Awards that year. The album *Bad Girls,* released in 1979, featured a blend of rock and disco—much of which she actually wrote herself—and garnered both good reviews and, again, huge sales. Yet it would also be her last for Casablanca, and in 1980 she became the first act signed by record industry executive David Geffen on his new label. She made *The Wanderer* in 1980 but had only a few minor chart successes over the next decade.

Despite her low profile for so many years after the death of disco, Summer has long enjoyed a cult following. The resurgence of disco kitsch in the mid-1990s—which helped breathe a bit of life into the careers of the Village People and the Bee Gees—was also beneficial to her. In March of 1998 she gave a benefit concert for New York City's Gay Men's Health Crisis at Carnegie Hall. "After nearly two hours of mature ovations and controlled excitement . . . the remarkably well-behaved audience could no longer be contained," wrote Larry Flick in *Billboard*. "As she began a salacious, guitar-drenched rendition of 'Hot Stuff,' fans rushed down the red carpeted aisles toward the stage." Summer lives in Nashville and hopes to see a musical she wrote, *Ordinary Girl,* debut on Broadway in 1999.

—Carol Brennan

FURTHER READING:

Cocks, Jay. "Early Reign of the Disco Queen." *Time.* December 4, 1978, 93.

Flick, Larry. *Billboard.* March 16, 1998.

Goldman, Albert. "Disco Fever." *Esquire.* December 1977, 60-66.

———. "Studio 54, Driver!" *Sound Bites.* New York, Random House, 1992.

Jacobson, Mark. "Disco Dreams." *Very Seventies: A Cultural History of the 1970s from the Pages of Crawdaddy.* New York, Fireside/Simon & Schuster, 1995.

Porter, Evette. "Awaiting the Diva." *Village Voice.* December 17, 1996, 61-62.

Rockwell, John. "The Disco Drum-Beating in Perspective." *New York Times.* February 25, 1979.

———. "Donna Summer Has Begun to Win Respect." *New York Times.* July 26, 1979.

Sun Records

Established in Memphis by visionary Sam Phillips in 1952, Sun Records revolutionized pop music. At his Memphis Recording Service, Phillips recorded blues artists and then started Sun as a home for some of them. In 1954 Phillips recorded Elvis Presley, whose blending of musical genres had a major impact on the course of popular music. In his book on Sun, Colin Escott quotes Phillips on Elvis: "He sings Negro songs with a white voice which borrows in mood and emphasis from the country style, modified by popular music. It's a blend of all of them." After selling Elvis' contract to RCA for $35,000, Phillips had the capital to continue work with influential artists like Carl Perkins, Johnny Cash, Jerry Lee Lewis, and Charlie Rich. In 1969, Sun was sold to recording executive Shelby Singleton who went about reissuing many of Sun's important early recordings.

—Joyce Linehan

FURTHER READING:

Escott, Colin, and Martin Hawkins. *Sun Records: The Brief History of the Legendary Record Label.* New York, Quick Fox, 1975, 1980.

Sundance Film Festival

The Sundance Film Festival helped to revolutionize the world of American independent cinema by cultivating an audience for daring and innovative films, and often catalyzing theatrical distribution deals for such films that otherwise would not have a chance for release. In 1981, actor Robert Redford, interested and concerned about the state of film in the United States, founded the Sundance Institute, an organization devoted to the support and development of emerging screenwriters and directors. Quickly turning into a fertile ground for new artists (over 300 filmmakers benefit annually from its various film, screenwriting, and cultural programs), the Institute ballooned into the high-profile Sundance Film Festival, an annual, winter event held in the quaint village of Park City, Utah, that is attended by over 10,000 people. The festival runs over a period of ten days, and screens international films, documentaries, short films, and American independent premieres—making the festival the pre-eminent showcase for American independent films in the world. Understanding the importance of encouraging the spectrum of visions that film artists have, Redford and his Institute have helped to enhance the quality of American films, along with giving an array of talented people the opportunity to develop and refine new work. The Sundance Film Festival has also helped to launch the careers of talented, eccentric actors and actresses that mirror its hip, young aesthetic, such as Lily Taylor and Parker Posey. Because of Sundance's widely publicized success stories of past participants (Quentin Tarantino/*Reservoir Dogs,* Neil Labute/*In the Company of Men,* and Allison Anders/*Gas, Food, Lodging,* for example), and the diverse and bold style of the films it supports, the festival has attracted a great deal of attention in and out of Hollywood, making it one of the most talked about events related to the film industry.

Studios tend to pursue more commercial scripts; stories that offer the guarantee of drawing in large audiences and funds. Scripts bought by large studios are often reworked without the original writer to match the studio's market-driven vision, and not the artist's. But with Sundance and its persistent focus on risky choices that were pleasing audiences, sleek studio executives armed with cellphones and celebrities began to flood the Sundance Film Festival, giving it sudden prestige. As American audiences began to lust after such stories, studio executives became more sycophantic towards their writers and directors. Wining and dining cutting-edge filmmakers, during the course of the festival they often foster careers that prove to be long-lasting.

Films screened at Sundance started a new trend towards dramatizing stories of a darker nature. Whether it be physical violence with an edge of black humor (Quentin Tarantino), or emotional violence (Neil Labute), people were becoming more drawn to films that explored different terrain and did not necessarily have happy endings. Large studio films tend to offer easy entertainment. Even when they are sad, there can be excessive sentimentality that allows for an audience to have an emotional release and leave the theater satisfied after having had a good cry. But the new wave of films and

Carl Perkins, one of the original Sun Records recording artists.

filmmakers that Sundance was producing did not do that. Instead, they offered worlds with little solace or answers where characters were cruel to each other, as in Labute's film *In the Company of Men* (which premiered at Sundance in 1997, launching his independent film career), which told the story of disillusioned and bored corporate men who seduce a mute woman in their office just so they can have the satisfaction of dumping her. It is important to tell these kinds of stories, because they explore the intricate ways people relate to one another, which are often unhealthy. These films leave audiences feeling uncomfortable, and that is a new and confusing feeling, but not necessarily a bad one. There is nothing wrong with ''feel-good'' entertainment, but it is refreshing to have a film take chances with character, storyline, and behavior.

Sundance has even produced an ''illegitimate offspring'' in the form of ''Slam Dance.'' Also in Park City, it supposedly includes films that were rejected by Sundance, as well as others, and holds its festival concurrently with Sundance's. Slam Dance, too, has caught on and now Hollywood executives have to divide their time between both festivals, always on the lookout for fresh, undiscovered talent.

Independent film's involvement with larger studios has not always been a smooth relationship. Writer/director Todd Solondz, for example, whose film debut *Welcome to the Dollhouse* hit big after premiering at Sundance in 1996 (it was the winner of the Grand Jury

Prize), was courted by a studio that wanted to back his next film, *Happiness.* But when executives balked at Solondz' delicate, dark story about a tortured suburban pedophile, Solondz would not tone it down, and was promptly dropped by that studio (another studio picked up the film, and it was released and received good reviews).

For two weeks in winter, throngs of entertainment people flock to the little town of Park City, Utah, as the world watches via entertainment programs and the news, to network and buy independent films. There is no restaurant, bar, or street corner in town that is without somebody affiliated with the film industry and ready to deal.

—Sharon Yablon

FURTHER READING:

Anders, Allison, editor. *Four Rooms: Four Friends Telling Four Stories Making One Film.* New York, Miramax Books/Hyperion, 1995.

Gilroy, Frank D. *I Wake Up Screaming!: Everything You Need to Know About Making Independent Films Including a Thousand Reasons Not To.* Carbondale, Southern Illinois University Press, 1993.

McKee, Robert. *Story: Substance, Structure, Style, and the Principles of Screenwriting.* New York, Regan Books, 1997.

Sunday, Billy (1862-1935)

A former professional baseball player with an entertainer's flair and a mastery of idiomatic language, Billy Sunday set the pace for modern evangelism. His tabernacle crusades of the early 1900s combined showmanship with Fundamentalism and produced thousands of converts. His influence on the cultural dynamics of the country is incalculable for, while many doubted the sincerity of Sunday's believers, his ''Elmer Gantry'' style would be copied by American evangelists throughout the twentieth century, serving to increase and cement the religious right as a significant force in society.

Born William Ashley Sunday on November 19, 1862 in a farmhouse near Ames, Iowa, Billy Sunday seemed an unlikely candidate for the ministry. While a stint in an orphanage instilled habits of honesty, Sunday was also known to fight, drink, and chase women. He held a series of odd jobs until a baseball scout noticed his athletic abilities, and in 1883 he joined the Chicago White Stockings and enjoyed the boisterous life of a professional athlete. One afternoon in 1886, while out with friends at a Chicago saloon, Sunday encountered an evangelistic group from the Pacific Garden Mission. Intrigued by their singing, he accepted an invitation to services and was soon converted, joining the Jefferson Park Presbyterian Church a short time later. He continued to play baseball, but gave up his habits of drinking and swearing, and began giving inspirational talks to young fans. Sunday left baseball in 1891 to work for the Chicago YMCA. In 1893, he joined J. Wilburn Chapman's evangelistic services as an advance man, handling technical details for the revival

Billy Sunday

services. When Chapman retired in 1895, Sunday assumed his place and began a touring ministry.

Sunday's tabernacle crusades were conducted in temporary wooden structures with sawdust covered floors. While the revival meeting was not new to America—the tradition stretched back to the Second Great Awakening of the early 1800s and the camp meetings on the frontier—Sunday added new elements to make his events successful. Careful planning went into the crusades, and teamwork was essential. A Sunday campaign resembled a vaudeville show as much as a mission; advance men promoted the coming attraction, secretaries made local arrangements, and bands and choirs were hired to provide entertainment. In 1909, Homer A. Rodeheaver, a song leader and trombone player, joined Sunday's troupe, and the tabernacle rang with music and excitement in the build-up to Sunday's explosive sermons.

Combining athletic gestures with colorful language, Sunday harangued his audiences about the need to get right with God. He defended the brevity of his visits by saying, ''They tell me a revival is only temporary: so is a bath, but it does you good.'' He linked religion to patriotism and upright living, urging people to accept Christ as their savior and to signify their intention to convert by walking down the aisle and shaking Sunday's hand. Thousands did so. A New York campaign alone drew a million and a half people with 100,000 conversions. The weakness in his work was that he did not encourage people to join any specific church, and thus many of his converts never became committed to a particular faith.

Sunday did not avoid controversial issues or tone down his Fundamentalist message in order to court popularity. He advocated Prohibition and wholeheartedly embraced the war effort, using religion to promote the sale of war bonds during World War I. He denounced Modernism in religion, advocated the enactment of laws to ban the teaching of evolution in schools, and was a friend and advisor to conservative politicians. Unlike most evangelists, who settled down to become pastors or teachers in religious colleges, Sunday remained a fixture on the ''sawdust trail.'' By his death on November 6, 1935, he had led over 300 campaigns and claimed to have brought 300,000 souls to Christ.

By using the modern techniques of show business and linking religion not to intricate theology, but to common language and experiences, Billy Sunday established a unique American form of evangelism. Later leaders, most notably Billy Graham, would continue his practice of large-scale campaigns aimed at emotional conversions.

—Tracy J. Revels

FURTHER READING:

Bruns, Roger. *Preacher: Billy Sunday and Big Time American Evangelism.* New York, W. W. Norton, 1992.

Dorsett, Lyle W. *Billy Sunday and the Redemption of Urban America.* Grand Rapids, W. W. Eerdmans Publishing Co., 1991.

McLoughlin, William G. Jr. *Billy Sunday was His Real Name.* Chicago, University of Chicago Press, 1955.

Sunday Driving

A catchphrase that made specific reference to people who broke the Sabbath by driving their automobiles, especially during church services, Sunday driving stood as a metaphor for what many believed was a nationwide decline in morality. For many Americans, the twentieth century marked an irreversible decline in everything they held dear. Uncontrollable "outside forces" seemed to be tearing apart families, destroying tight-knit communities, and eroding the foundations of morality on which previous generations had built their lives. Ministers around the country railed against these changes and identified the accoutrements of modernity as prime culprits: telephones, radios, movies, and professional sports all received a measure of blame for corrupting the American spirit. To many people, however, nothing symbolized the degeneration of the modern era quite as well as the automobile. And to ministers facing declining church attendance, a particular cause for alarm was the increase in Sunday driving.

Ministers were not the only ones who believed that Sunday driving was cause for public concern. In a 1922 article in *Scribner's* magazine, Allen Albert claimed that "in good motoring weather I have attended Sunday-morning services from Waycross, Ga., to Manistee, Mich., and it would be hard to find any pews emptier anywhere." Ruth Suckow also illustrated the concern that the growing popularity of Sunday driving caused in her novel, *Country People* (1924): "It was a wonder to Emma to sit on the porch on Sunday afternoons and count how many vehicles went by. But grandpa wouldn't even try to count. '*Ach*, no! no! no!' was all that he would say. This was all so wicked on Sunday!" In Nashville, a 1923 ordinance forbade any business to sell gasoline, oil, or automobiles on Sundays, and prohibited automobile service facilities from operating as well. "Everyone wanted to enjoy a Sunday outing in the automobile," editorialized the *Tattler* in 1929, "but realized he was taking a big chance. He might run out of gas, have a puncture or break down miles away from home. Then the whole family would have to walk back."

Despite protests against Sunday driving, however, the practice always had many more advocates than opponents. Some people pointed out that automobiles could just as easily carry people to church as away from it. As *Motor Age* commented in 1919: "Even the farmer in the remotest rural district may wait until the last minute, jump into his car and go to church, attend services and be home in less than the time it used to take him to get there alone." Others, such as a writer for the *Christian Advocate* in 1920, rationalized that automobiles might encourage "many immoral practices," including "desecration of the Sabbath," but that "all good things are liable to abuse." Some believed the freedom and mobility of automobiles would encourage religious celebration. "He . . . would take his religion out of doors, where God smiled and spoke to burdened business men," wrote a writer for *Christian Century* in 1928. "In serene solitude he would drive his car over smoky and smelly roads, oblivious of all but the deeper invisible realities. To the care-free accompaniment of the motor he would raise hymns of joy to the God of breeze and field." And of course there were all of the Americans who took to the roads on Sundays, disregarding protests from those who held onto older notions of morality. For better or for worse, Sunday driving became a standard feature of American culture—more notable for its unremarkable regularity than for the emotionally charged controversy it once provoked.

—Christopher W. Wells

FURTHER READING:

Berger, Michael. *The Devil Wagon in God's Country: The Automobile and Social Change in Rural America, 1893-1929.* Hamden, Connecticut, Archon Books, 1979.

Sunset Boulevard

Axel Madsen writes of *Sunset Boulevard* (1950) that it is "a gnawing, haunting, and ruthless film with a dank smell of corrosive delusion hanging over it." A classic film noir, *Sunset Boulevard* is a cynical and decadent tragi-comedy narrated, in true noir fashion, by a dead man. Populated by faded silent movie stars like Gloria Swanson, Erich von Stroheim, and Buster Keaton, it is the story of a weak-willed writer (William Holden) who, in trying to escape his creditors, happens upon the mansion of a wealthy, but slightly mad, silent movie star who perpetually waits for a phone call from a studio which has long since forgotten about her. The handsome writer becomes a kept man who struggles to make it in the movie business, only to fall prey to his keeper as he tries to make his escape from her obsessive love for him.

Typical of Billy Wilder's sophisticated and cynical style, *Sunset Boulevard* is a black comedy about the casualties of the Hollywood dream machine, and those obsessed by fame and success in the cruel world of the movie studios. The film is filled with stylish settings and wonderfully biting dialogue, and it has attained the status of a cult classic with quotable lines like the famous, "I'm ready for my close up now, Mr. De Mille." There is also a Broadway musical version of the film created by Andrew Lloyd Webber.

—Jeannette Sloniowski

FURTHER READING:

Corless, Richard. "The Authors-Auteurs." *Talking Pictures: Screenwriters in the American Cinema.* New York, Penguin Books, 1975, 141-161.

Madsen, Axel. *Billy Wilder.* London, Secker and Warburg, 1968.

Mundy, Robert. "Wilder Reappraised." *Cinema.* No. 4, October, 14-19.

Super Bowl

More than any other sporting event in America, the Super Bowl has truly become a cultural phenomenon. According to 1999 National Football League figures, more than 138 million people in the United States alone watched the Super Bowl, with over 750 million total Super Bowl viewers in 187 countries. The Super Bowl has become, according to writer Michael Real (as quoted in Dona Schwartz's *Contesting the Super Bowl*), a "mythic spectacle," that "in the classical manner of mythical beliefs and ritual activities. . . is a communal celebration of and indoctrination into specific socially dominant emotions, life-styles, and values." The Super Bowl brings together several institutions: sports, television, advertising, and the American corporate culture. The Super Bowl serves as an end-of-the-season celebration, glorifying revenues accumulated by team owners, advertisers, media outlets, and many other businesses that share in the tremendous profits generated by professional football.

The Super Bowl itself stems from a fierce rivalry between two football leagues. In 1960, the upstart American Football League (AFL) challenged the popular and well-established National Football League (NFL). The AFL was well funded and soon began to contest the NFL in a bidding war for college players. In 1965, the AFL scored its first major coup when the New York Jets signed University of Alabama star quarterback Joe Namath. Namath's personality, media appeal, and on-field success gave the AFL an early degree of legitimacy. The AFL was also helped by a television contract. Under an exclusive deal with the American Broadcasting Company (ABC), each AFL team was paid $150,000, money that kept the league afloat during the difficult, early years of its existence.

In 1966, the AFL decided to further assert itself by attempting to sign established, veteran NFL players. When several of its stars signed lucrative contracts, the NFL found it had little choice but to accept the situation and started working on a merger of the two leagues. In June 1966, an NFL-AFL merger was announced. The merger called for a common draft of college players and a championship game—the Super Bowl—to start in 1967. The new league would be called the National Football League with the previous rivals split into two divisions: the National Football Conference (NFC) and the American Football Conference (AFC). The full merger would take place in 1970. The Super Bowl pitted the winners of the two conferences in one game in late January, following the regular season and a series of playoff games.

During the first few years of the new National Football League, the two conferences maintained separate identities and schedules. Initially then, the Super Bowl became a contest where the upstart AFL would try to prove its meddle against more established teams. As might be expected, in the first two Super Bowls (Super Bowls I and II), the NFL Green Bay Packers easily defeated their AFL opponents. Most believed it would take years before an AFL team would actually win a Super Bowl. Then in Super Bowl III, the AFL champion New York Jets were matched against the powerful Baltimore Colts. Jets quarterback ''Broadway Joe'' Namath, on the eve of the contest in which the Colts were heavily favored, ''guaranteed'' a Jets victory. On January 12, 1969, the Jets stunned the sports world by defeating the Colts 16-7. The Jets victory finally gave the AFL its due and helped bring the two leagues together when the merger officially began the next year.

Enhancing the merger of the two leagues in 1970 was a television package from ABC. For just over $8 million each season, ABC agreed to televise thirteen prime-time games on Monday nights. Television revenues for the NFL totaled nearly $150 million. Overall, it meant that each of the twenty-six NFL teams in 1970 would receive about $1.7 million. The popularity of football stemmed primarily from its television exposure. During the 1970s, television transformed football into America's premier spectator sport. Before the 1973 season, Congress lifted TV blackouts on home games that were not sold out. While some predicted that this legislation would make it hard for some small market teams to fill the stands, that did not prove to be the case. Not only did TV viewing increase, but teams actually sold more tickets. And it was TV contracts that became the meal ticket for the NFL—not single game sales. In 1978, the NFL signed the most lucrative sports TV contract ever. In January of that year, a Lou Harris poll found that 70 percent of the nation's sports fans followed football, compared to 54 percent who followed baseball.

With the help of television, over the past three decades the game on the field has become just an ancillary part of the entire Super Bowl experience. More than anything else however, the Super Bowl is about money and corporate advertising. This January spectacle is the most lucrative sporting event in the United States and has become as much an advertising contest as a sports production. The NFL sold the broadcast rights for the 1999 Super Bowl for over $60 million and NFL properties, the licensing arm of the league, sells approximately $200 million in merchandise for the game. At the Super Bowl itself, logo placement, advertising angles, and television commercials have taken on more importance than the outcome of the game. In fact, television commercials slated for the Super Bowl are often shown as news items on local broadcasts days before the game. There are even postgame telecasts that examine and evaluate the quality of Super Bowl commercials.

To demonstrate the serious connection between advertising and the Super Bowl, one need look no further than Anheuser-Busch's ''Bud Bowl,'' which has been a part of Super Bowl television broadcasts since 1989. The Bud Bowl is a fictitious football game, played out in expensive commercial spots, between animated beer bottles of Budweiser and Budweiser Light. The Bud Bowl employs real announcers and millions of dollars are spent to show these beer bottles running up and down the field attempting to score touchdowns. But the key to the Bud Bowl is Anheuser-Busch's promotions, which begin months before the game itself at hundreds of retail outlets. The beer company offers thousands of prizes that are tied into these advertising spots at the Super Bowl. Because of the advertising and prize giveaways, the final score of the Bud Bowl has become more important to the American television viewer than the results of the Super Bowl. Anheuser-Busch even set up a toll free number so potential prize winners could call and find out the final score of the Bud Bowl.

By 1999, 30-second Super Bowl advertising spots were selling for well over $1 million. Yet the evidence indicates that those sums are well worth the price for American corporate advertisers. In 1991, the Gillette Company used the Super Bowl to introduce its new Sensor razor. Gillette spent over $3 million on Super Bowl advertising to reach their male audience. By focusing its ads on Super Bowl Sunday, Gillette sold out its Sensor inventory through February and March following the broadcast, and the company was able to increase its market share by 35 percent in 1991. Evidence gathered by writer Phil Schaaf for his book *Sports Marketing* indicated that 66 percent of people tested recall Super Bowl commercials.

Money and corporate infiltration of the Super Bowl has also influenced the type of fans that attend the January event. In a sport that caters to the ''average'' fan during the regular season, few of those ordinary team boosters will ever have the opportunity to see a Super Bowl. Tickets are not sold to the general public—most go to corporate sponsors, celebrities, National Football League owners and officials, other players, and news organizations. In fact, during Super Bowl XXIX, 646 news organizations and 407 international media representatives were given Super Bowl credentials. The number of journalists working at the Super Bowl for these newsgroups totaled 2846. An actual statistical breakdown of fans who attends a Super Bowl shows the following: 35 percent attend on corporate expense accounts; 33 percent earn more than $100,000 annually; 27 percent own their own company; 25 percent are corporate officers; and 22 percent sit on corporate boards of directors. So the look of a Super Bowl is far different from the look of a football game on a regular Sunday in October or November.

But a Super Bowl does brings in a great deal of money to a host city. It is estimated that the Phoenix metropolitan area brought in

$187 million when it hosted the Super Bowl. In Minneapolis, Minnesota, during the 1991 Super Bowl, 2,000 jobs were created for that event. All but the first Super Bowl has been a sellout, even though the cheapest tickets at the 1999 game sold for just over $250. Scalpers, or illegal ticket brokers, generally get four times that much for a Super Bowl ticket. Tim Green, a former professional football player, wrote in his book *The Dark Side of the Game* that, "January is when the big money really starts to drop." Green is referring to the legal and illegal betting that accompanies the Super Bowl. The game is the most gambled on sporting event in the United States. A person can lay a wager on just about any facet of the game: the first quarter score, which team will score first, which running back will get the most yards, the total score, or how many yards a particular quarterback will throw for. Between $35 and $60 million in legal gambling goes on for each Super Bowl game—illegal estimates are much higher.

Since television and media coverage dominates the Super Bowl, it is inevitable that politics has entered the formula. The Super Bowl is the most watched one-day event in the world. There is no worry about a rain-out and viewers represent a wide demographic range (41 percent of all American television viewers are female). The Super Bowl is also the third biggest eating day in America—behind only Christmas and Thanksgiving. In 1993, several national women's groups announced that Super Bowl Sunday was the worst day of the year for violence against women. Women's shelters claimed that hot lines were "flooded with more calls from victims [on Super Bowl Sunday] than any other day of the year." And a study was released by Old Dominion University in Norfolk, Virginia, which showed that hospital admissions of women rose after games won by the Washington Redskins. While many subsequently questioned the links between domestic violence and the Super Bowl, the women's groups had scored a public relations coup by releasing their finding just before the Super Bowl, when national and world media attention was so focused upon that event. But additional evidence showed that the Super Bowl brings out the worst in American sports fans. After Denver won its second consecutive Super Bowl in 1999, rowdy fans rioted in that city, overturning cars, breaking windows, and starting fires. One sports psychologist determined that testosterone levels of young males rose by 20 percent when their team won a big game. During the 1992 game between the Buffalo Bills and the Washington Redskins, American Indian groups used the Super Bowl media glare to call attention to what they believed were racist and demeaning use of nicknames and mascots on professional sports teams. The Redskin team nickname was considered especially egregious to the American Indian Movement (AIM) and protestors ringed the stadium on Super Bowl Sunday chanting slogans to voice their cause. Because of the media saturation in town for the Super Bowl, the American Indian Movement appeared on television and were interviewed for national and international media outlets. While nothing came of the protests, AIM was able to get their message out and even forced the National Football League to issue a statement about the team nicknames.

The Super Bowl has offered the American sports fan a plethora of heroic players and exciting teams: Joe Namath, Terry Bradshaw, Joe Montana, John Elway, the Miami Dolphins, Pittsburgh Steelers, Dallas Cowboys, and San Francisco 49ers. But player statistics and heroics have become overshadowed by economic, social, and cultural issues: Who will sing the national anthem? Who will perform at the half-time festivities? What television commercials will catch the attention of the American public? What political issues might arise this year? And, what is the betting line on the game? These issues have turned the Super Bowl into more of a media event than a sporting contest.

—David E. Woodard

FURTHER READING:

Duden, Jane. *The Super Bowl.* Parsippany, New Jersey, Crestwood House, 1992.

Green, Jerry. *Super Bowl Chronicles: A Sportswriter Reflects on the First 30 Years of America's Game.* 2nd edition. New York, Masters Press, 1995.

Green, Tim. *The Dark Side of the Game.* New York, Warner Books, 1996.

Hanks, Steven. *The Game That Changed Pro Football.* New York, Birch Lane Press, 1989.

Neft, David, Richard Cohen, and Rich Korch. *The Sports Encyclopedia: Pro Football, The Modern Era, 1960-1995.* 14th edition. New York, St. Martin's Griffin, 1996.

Rosentraub, Mark S. *Major League Losers: The Real Cost of Sports and Who's Paying For It.* New York, Basic Books, 1997.

Schaaf, Phil. *Sports Marketing: It's Not Just a Game Anymore.* Amherst, New York, Prometheus Books, 1995.

Schwartz, Dona. *Contesting the Super Bowl.* New York, Routledge, 1998.

Weiss, Ann. *Money Games: The Business of Sports.* Boston, Houghton Mifflin, 1993.

Superman

The first and most important comic book superhero, Superman looms large not only in comic books but in all of twentieth-century American popular culture. Among the few American characters instantly recognizable in virtually every corner of the globe, Superman is truly a pop culture icon. Certainly there is no purer representative of the fantastic possibilities inherent in the comic book medium.

Superman sprang from the imagination of two Jewish teenagers growing up in Cleveland during the Great Depression. Jerry Siegel and Joe Shuster were both lower-middle-class sons of immigrants who believed in the American dream. Avid readers of science fiction and pulp magazines, the two youths aspired to write and draw their own adventure comic strip. In 1934, after several try-outs in their school newspaper, Siegel and Shuster hit upon the idea that they suspected would be a salable comic strip. In his striking red-and-blue costume with flowing red cape and red "S" emblazoned on his chest, Superman was the ultimate strongman, capable of achieving almost any physical feat. He was a fantastic being from a doomed alien planet (later revealed to be Krypton), come to apply the superhuman blessings of his native home in the service of his adopted world. And perhaps most importantly, he assumed the persona of an undistinguished mild-mannered newspaper reporter named Clark Kent. Unpretentious and seeking no glory, he was a superhero who would retreat into the anonymity of American society when his spectacular deeds were accomplished. Here was the crucial point of reference for a Depression-era culture that extolled the virtues of the "common man."

Superman was a brilliant creation—ingenious in its very simplicity and instantly accessible to a mass audience. It was, of course,

Superman

not an entirely original concept. Superheroes of various sorts had a long history in popular myth and folklore. But the Superman/Clark Kent dichotomy was original as a contemporary expression of adolescent wish-fulfillment. Siegel and Shuster, both of whom wore glasses and admitted to being shy, insecure, and unsuccessful with girls in high school, put much of themselves and their fantasies into the character. In truth, the essence of Superman's appeal was almost universal—especially to young males. Any boy or man who has felt in any way inadequate in a society of formidable male gender expectations has at times wished that he could transcend his human frailty as easily as Clark Kent removed his glasses.

Such a concept was destined to be a popular one with young people. But the middle-aged men who ran the newspaper syndicates failed to recognize Superman's appeal. After several years of failing to sell their idea to the newspapers, Siegel and Shuster reluctantly sold it to a fledgling comic book company called Detective Comics (DC), for whom they had done some freelance work. As part of the contract, the two young men would write and draw the series as long as DC allowed them to, but they also forsook all rights to the character in exchange for $130 ($10 per page for the 13-page story). It proved to be one of the most infamous contracts ever signed in the history of the American entertainment industry.

Superman debuted in the first issue of DC's *Action Comics*, dated June 1938. The cover of the classic issue, which now fetches prices of over $50,000 from collectors, showed the costumed hero

lifting an automobile over his head as stupefied criminals flee in terror before him. It was an impossible image that DC's publishers feared would only confuse readers. But the audience responded positively and quickly. Only a few issues into publication, *Action Comics* became the best-selling comic book on the market, and the reason—confirmed by informal newsstand surveys—was obvious: Superman was a winning concept.

In later years Superman evolved into a character who was stoic, morally beyond reproach, and frankly rather humorless and dull. But Siegel and Shuster initially portrayed him as a feisty character who most closely resembled a super-powered ''hard-boiled'' detective. He was a wise guy, who took to crime fighting with an adolescent glee, routinely took time to mock and humiliate his adversaries as he thrashed them, and did not shrink from breaking the law when it stood in the way of true justice. It was a macho world into which only the glamorous Lois Lane intruded. Although she had no time for the plain Clark Kent, she was, of course, infatuated with Superman, who rarely had time for her. Siegel and Shuster cast their superhero as a populist ''champion of the oppressed,'' who defended common Americans from the evils of big money, political corruption, and greed in all its forms. As the United States drifted into war, Superman turned his attention to foiling spies and saboteurs on the American home front, although his creators deliberately kept him away from the front so as not to upstage America's real-life heroes in uniform.

At a time when most successful comic book titles sold between 200,000 and 400,000 copies per issue, each issue of *Action Comics*—featuring only one Superman story—consistently sold around 900,000 copies. Mindful of these figures, DC featured the character in a second title, *Superman*, which established industry records by selling a staggering average of 1,300,000 copies per bimonthly issue. The Superman phenomenon was not limited to comic books either. By 1941 Superman was featured in a syndicated newspaper strip, a series of short animated films produced by Paramount, and a highly popular radio show that opened with the immortal lines: ''Faster than a speeding bullet! More powerful than a locomotive! Able to leap tall buildings in a single bound! Look! Up in the sky! It's a bird! It's a plane! It's . . . Superman!'' Within a few short years of his comic book debut, Superman had become a cartoon figure almost as widely recognized as Disney's Mickey Mouse.

It is difficult to overestimate the influence that Superman has had on the comic book industry. Before his appearance, comic books hardly constituted a medium distinct from newspaper comic strips. Most featured either reprinted newspaper strips or derivative variations thereof. Superman was the first original character to exploit the fantastic creative possibilities of the comic book medium—possibilities limited only by the imagination and skill of writers and artists. Images that would have been technically onerous or impossible to represent in motion pictures or radio could be easily adapted to the comic book format. Superman's improbable adventures demonstrated this, and he single-handedly gave the comic book industry a reason for being. Superman became the most widely imitated character in comic books, spawning a host of costumed superheroes from DC and its competitors. These superheroes established the comic-book industry as a viable commercial entertainment industry, and they have been the mainstay of comic books ever since.

Superman also established DC Comics as the industry's leading publisher. For a time, even his creators benefited financially from Superman's profits. But Siegel and Shuster saw diminishing returns for themselves even as their creation continued to generate massive revenue for the publisher. In 1947 they sued DC, trying to secure the profits that they claimed Superman should have earned them over the years. The court ruled against them, claiming that under the original 1938 contract, they had no rights to the character. For the next several decades they saw no royalties from the comic book industry's most lucrative property. In the late 1970s, after the news media reported that Superman's creators were living in poverty, DC relented and paid them a yearly stipend for the remainder of their lives. A notorious tale well known to comic-book creators, the plight of Siegel and Shuster helped to rally writers and artists to push for new royalties and financial incentives, which the major publishers subsequently introduced in the 1980s.

Superman remained the most popular and best-selling comic-book character well into the 1960s. Under the close editorial direction of Mort Weisinger, Superman evolved into a character befitting his status as the elder statesman among superheroes. Abandoning all semblance of his rambunctious younger days, Superman became a staid, predictable, and paternalistic figure, always adhering to the strict letter of the law. He also gradually acquired an array of powers that made him almost invincible: flight, X-ray vision, telescopic vision, super-hearing, super-breath, the ability to move through time, the strength to move planets, and invulnerability to virtually everything except Kryptonite, the meteoric remnants of his native world Krypton. Weisinger created a fairy-tale Superman mythos that incorporated Superman's youth (as Superboy in the Midwestern town of Smallville), his friends (Lois Lane and Jimmy Olson were featured in their own comic books), villains like Lex Luthor and Braniac, and spin-off characters like Supergirl and Krypto the Superdog. To overcome the creative limitations of the virtually omnipotent superhero, Weisinger also conceived a variety of "imaginary" stories that explored such questions as, "What if Superman had gone to another planet besides Earth?" and even "What if Superman had died?" These simple and entertaining stories were clearly aimed at children, and they sold well. Airing from 1953 to 1957, the highly successful *Adventures of Superman* television series, to which Weisinger was a consultant, kept Superman in the public consciousness and served to promote his comic books to the new generation of baby boomers. In the mid 1990s, an ABC television series called *Lois and Clark: The New Adventures of Superman* introduced the characters—played by Teri Hatcher and Dean Cain, respectively—to a new generation of viewers.

Superman's popularity among comic-book readers waned in the late 1960s. Faced by intense competition from Marvel's wave of more "human" superheroes like Spider-Man, the Hulk, and the Fantastic Four, Superman's irreproachable Boy Scout image had become a commercial liability for new generations of young people grown expectant of anti-establishment trends in youth culture. By the mid 1970s, the character's comic book sales were at an all-time low, although his image remained the most lucrative comic book licensed property for toys and other products. The pinnacle of the character's earning power came in the late 1970s and early 1980s in a series of major Warner Brothers *Superman* movies starring Christopher Reeve in the title role. Success in other media, however, did not translate into impressive comic book sales, which continued to lag well behind those of trendy morally ambivalent superheroes like the X-Men, the Punisher, and even DC's Batman, who began as a follow-up to Superman and proved to be far more adaptable to changing times.

The history of Superman in the comic books over the past several decades has largely been shaped by DC's periodic attempts to revitalize the character by making him less "super." In 1971 Superman's powers were halved. In 1988, DC contracted popular writer/artist John Byrne to rewrite Superman's origin, hoping to spark fan interest. Surely the most blatant of these efforts came in 1992 with the much-hyped "Death of Superman." To no one's surprise, the event produced a short-term boom in Superman's sales and concluded in the "Rebirth of Superman." In 1997 Superman got a radical new costume change. While nostalgic fans disapproved, DC responded that it had little choice but to try new things to reverse Superman's steady commercial decline.

Superman will probably never be as popular as he once was. But that in no way diminishes his significance. As the archetype for the superhero genre so intrinsic to American comic books, he deserves his stature as the industry's de facto world ambassador. His presence is firmly etched into a global popular culture, encompassing motion pictures, television, advertising, music, and common language. And for the generations weaned on his adventures, Superman will forever remain the quintessential champion of truth, justice, and the American way.

—Bradford Wright

FURTHER READING:

Daniels, Les. *DC Comics: Sixty Years of the World's Favorite Comic Book Heroes.* Boston, Little, Brown, and Company, 1995.

Dooley, Dennis, and Gary Engle. *Superman at Fifty: The Persistence of a Legend.* Cleveland, Octavia Press, 1987.

Feiffer, Jules. *The Great Comic Book Heroes.* New York, Dial Press, 1965.

The Greatest Superman Stories Ever Told. New York, DC Comics, 1987.

Jacobs, Will, and Gerard Jones. *The Comic Book Heroes.* Rocklin, California, Prima Publishing, 1997.

Supermodels

The word "supermodel" was first used in the 1940s, but the supermodel phenomenon belongs to the 1980s and 1990s, when a few women epitomizing glamour and opulence captured the American popular consumer's imagination. For most of the supermodel era, the pantheon included Cindy Crawford, Naomi Campbell, Kate Moss, Claudia Schiffer, Linda Evangelista, and Christy Turlington—all of them tall, architectural, and distinctive in appearance—who represented both the triumph of unadulterated image and the mass marketing of fashion.

Models had been famous before—Suzy Parker in the 1950s, Twiggy in the 1960s, Christie Brinkley in the 1970s—but the supermodels were touted for taking charge of their own careers, marketing themselves assiduously, and commanding huge fees for themselves and their agents. They cast themselves in discrete roles: Crawford was the confident sexual one, Moss the waif, Schiffer the one who looked like Brigitte Bardot. Like most models, they tended to launch their careers in Europe, where the pay was relatively low but a girl (often as young as fourteen or fifteen) could accumulate photographs and develop a distinctive "look." Once in New York, the U.S. modeling capital, a girl hoped to sign or continue a relationship with a powerful agency such as Elite and Ford, where clients in search of an

Naomi Campbell leads a group of models on the catwalk for the Versace collection in Milan, 1997.

seventy-two hours at a cost of sixty thousand dollars was a good way for a company to display its success, confidence, and solvency. Models and supermodels alike made most of their money in advertising: Turlington's 1991 contract with Maybelline, for example, netted her eight hundred thousand dollars for twelve days' work a year. The more prestigious work, including magazine covers, was comparatively unremunerative—in 1995 *Vogue, Glamour,* or *Mademoiselle* might pay as little as one hundred dollars a day—though the exposure did help establish a model as a commodity. But a woman who had achieved supermodel status never had to worry: in 1995 Claudia Schiffer, modeling's biggest wage earner, made twelve million dollars from various assignments. In the eras of Reaganomics and, later, recession, such well-publicized paydays were part of a supermodel's allure.

The wild and bratty behavior that often accompanied the models' sudden wealth was another element of their mystique; unleashed on New York, a number of them danced and drugged the nights away, and they were known for prima donna behavior such as sulkily kicking their limo drivers in the neck. Off the runway and out of the magazine, they lived larger than life, and the careers of many would-be supermodels ended in financial ruin and despair. Psychologists Vivian Diller and Jill Muir-Sukenick, both former models, explained in *Psychology Today* that many in the business suffer from a "fragile personality that makes them potentially self-destructive . . . what we call 'extreme narcissistic vulnerability.'" Without a secure sense of and liking for herself, argued Diller and Muir-Sukenick, such a young woman might easily fall prey to exploitative agents, clients, drug dealers, and others who prey on the young and attractive. Models' dissolution became a popular subject for articles, books, and movies, as audiences craved to see the girls consumed like the products they represented.

As it turned out, despite the supermodels' status, the public was interested in them as images, not as women. Though Campbell wrote a novel, and Crawford (who once referred to herself as "Cindy, Inc.") made TV specials and a movie, these attempts at establishing themselves as personalities largely failed. While some photographers and designers achieved respect and enduring fame as artists, their models, including the celestial six, were often considered merely a medium for expression. In the late 1990s, magazines started heralding "The Fall of the Supermodel," noting that reglamorized actresses were claiming many of the most prestigious modeling jobs and that consumers (in the words of superagent Katie Ford) had grown tired of "just seeing six people at the center of most magazines." Image was not enough to guarantee an enduring place in the popular imagination.

—Susann Cokal

FURTHER READING:

Bellafante, Ginia. "The Runway Girls Take Off." *Time.* Vol. 125, No. 16, April 17, 1995, 66-68.

Gross, Michael. *Model: The Ugly Business of Beautiful Women.* New York, William Morrow and Company, 1995.

Lieberman, Rhonda. "Supermodels." *Artforum.* Vol. 31, No. 4, 1992, 8-9.

Marano, Hara Estroff. "Model Existence: Women Psychologists Look at Fashion Modeling." *Psychology Today.* Vol. 27, No. 3, 1994, 50-58.

Stein, Joel. "The Fall of the Supermodel." *Time.* Vol. 128, No. 19, November 8, 1998, 102-03.

image looked first. The supermodels were lucky to enter the American scene at the moment in which fashion designers were changing their target market from the wealthy elite to the masses. When Calvin Klein began to advertise on television, billboards, and bus shelters, the subliminal message seemed to be that even common people and their clothes could attract attention; paradoxically, perhaps, his model Brooke Shields shot to celebrity (as, later, did his muse Moss). At the same time, Hollywood actresses had de-glamorized themselves; now that they were more inclined to appear in jeans and unwashed hair rather than in evening gowns and jewels, models stepped in to feed America's hunger for opulence, harking back to the glamour of stars such as Myrna Loy and Grace Kelly. Yet, perhaps because they had no real careers beyond posing, and didn't even select the clothes or products they would wear, the supermodels were able to represent a product, an image, completely—in this regard they were forums for display, not fleshed-out characters.

The individual supermodels themselves achieved name-brand recognition. Advertisers focused on the same six (and a few slightly less enduring lights, such as Elle MacPherson, Paulina Porizkova, and Tyra Banks) in part to show they could afford to: hiring Turlington for

Surf Music

Surf music, while not always about surfing, emerged out of the subculture created by surfers in Hawaii and California in the late 1940s and 1950s. Two distinct streams of surf music developed, one primarily instrumental, the other predominately vocal, each expressing a distinctive aspect of the surfer subculture. The sound was most prominent in the early and mid-1960s, when instrumental surf music was heard accompanying television shows such as *Hawaii Five-O,* and vocal surf music by The Beach Boys was topping the sales charts.

While surfing as a form of recreation and sport developed in the nineteenth century as a Polynesian pastime, it was not until the early twentieth century that surfing caught on outside of Hawaii. Olympic swimming champion Duke Kahanamoku (1912 and 1920 Olympics) toured the mainland U.S. in the wake of his Olympic triumphs and created interest in surfing through exhibitions on both the East and West coasts. Early in the twentieth century, surfboards were made usually of solid wood, but big-wave riders increasingly preferred hollow boards after Tom Blake introduced one in 1928. Still, the lightest boards made of plywood weighed around 50 pounds, with big-wave boards weighing more than twice that. Blake introduced other design modifications, such as the addition of a tail fin, which aided in maneuvering.

World War II stalled surfing's development for the duration, then it transformed the sport as technological developments in plastic foams and resin revolutionized surfboard construction. Bob Simmons, a hydrodynamics student from Santa Monica, California, sandwiched polystyrene between two pieces of wood, wrapped the entire board in fiberglass, and sealed it with resin. The result was a lightweight, durable board that was shaped easily and could be maneuvered well with minimum experience. Postwar prosperity led to the development of local surfing communities in southern California, Hawaii, and eastern Australia. For many of these surfers, dedication to the sport required them to maintain "open" work schedules that allowed them to hit the surf whenever it was good. This often meant many of them were unemployed or worked only during low periods in the surf. This preference for surf over employment, reinforced by the traditional Hawaiian ideas of leisure, community, and nature, went against the grain of mainstream American postwar thinking, in which conformity and economic success were paramount.

Creating a counterculture of sorts, surfers not only promoted their sport but a way of life as well. This surfer lifestyle included Hawaiian "palapas," or palm-frond huts appearing on California beaches, with after-surf barbeques and campouts serving to bind this community together. *Surfer* magazine appeared in 1960 to inform the surfing community of events, products, developments, and achievements. Surfing films portrayed spectacular rides from Hawaii and Australia to California and vice versa, but these documentaries, shot on 16mm film, received little attention outside of the surfing community. Bud Browne, the pioneer of the surf documentary, presented *The Big Surf, Hawaiian Surfing Memories,* and *Trip to Makaha,* all in the 1950s. This subculture was too small to have an impact on mainstream culture until writer Frederick Kohner penned a 1956 novel based on some of the exploits of his daughter Kathy on a Malibu beach where she "hung out" with several prominent surfers including Mickey Dora (one of the sport's first superstars), Billy Al Bengston (aka "Moondoggie"), and Terry "Tubesteak" Tracey. Tubesteak began calling Kathy a "girl-midget" since she was around five feet tall, and the name quickly transformed into "Gidget." The

film *Gidget,* based on these stories, appeared in 1959, starring Sandra Dee and James Darren. Numerous sequels and knockoffs followed, such as *Gidget Goes Hawaiian* (1961), *Beach Party* and *Gidget Goes to Rome* (1963), *Muscle Beach Party* (1964), *Beach Blanket Bingo* and *How to Stuff a Wild Bikini* (1965).

The sound tracks for these movies were composed primarily of pop music with lyrics pertaining to the beach, but a new sounding music also made an appearance in these films, surf music. Created by Dick Dale, "King of the Surf Guitar," surf music began as a musical attempt to recreate the sensation of riding a wave. Dale's combination of cascading licks, rapid playing, and a powerful bass line served as a perfect soundtrack for surf documentaries, and occasionally turned up in Hollywood beach movies, but like films based on surfing, the music also developed along two different lines. Surf music by instrumental groups like Dick Dale and the Deltones, The Ventures, The Chantays, and the Surfaris, found a devoted audience among surfers themselves, as did classic documentaries such as Bruce Brown's *Endless Summer* (1964). Meanwhile, beach music by vocal groups like Jan and Dean and The Beach Boys flooded the mainstream airwaves and, along with beach movies, represented the surfing subculture to most other Americans.

Instrumental surf music reached its widest audience with the Ventures' theme for the television series *Hawaii Five-O.* The group also had hits with "Walk, Don't Run" and "Perfida" (both 1960). The Surfaris (from inland Glendora, California) are best known for their 1962 song "Wipe Out," characterized by the hysterical laugh and high-pitched "wipe out" that opens the song. The Chantays reached number four on the sales charts with its classic "Pipeline," while Dick Dale and the Deltones continued their reign as the official cult band of the surf crowd with songs like "The Victor" (1964) and "Let's Go Trippin'" (1961). These instrumentals took elements of popular music and transformed them by emphasizing the bass line and using the guitar as a melodic instead of rhythmic instrument. A good example of this is found in The Ventures' "Walk, Don't Run." Written and originally recorded by jazz guitarist Johnny Smith, who was inspired by a "walk, don't run" sign in a New York subway, the song was recorded by country guitarist Chet Atkins in 1957 as a lilting ballad. By adding a driving beat and bass line, The Ventures created a version that recalled elements of Atkins' guitar work plus jazz elements such as "bending" notes and a blue tonality, all with a rock and roll beat. The song peaked at number two on the sales chart in 1960, right behind another beach-inspired song, Brian Hyland's "Itsy Bitsy Teenie Weenie Yellow Polka Dot Bikini."

Despite the popularity of instrumental surf music, or perhaps because of it, vocal surf music became the more widely disseminated form of the genre. While the music had little to do with the blazing guitars and heavy bass of Dick Dale and The Ventures, the lyrics of vocal surf music sought to capture the feel of the surfer subculture. "Surfin'" (1962), the first hit by a teen group from Hawthorne, California, called The Beach Boys, describes the dedication of surfers to their sport: "Surfin' is the only life, the only way for me." Written by non-surfer Brian Wilson and based mainly on stories from Beach Boy members and surfers Mike Love and Dennis Wilson, the songs of the Beach Boys presented an American youth market with an image of sunshine, beautiful girls, and surfing that was wholesome and superficial. In songs like "Surfin Safari" (1962), "Surfin' USA" and "Surfer Girl" (1963), "Fun, Fun, Fun" and "I Get Around" (1964), "Help Me, Rhonda" and "California Girls" (1965), "Wouldn't it Be Nice" and "Good Vibrations" (1966), the leisure pursuits of young southern Californians became a national industry. Reinforced by other performers, such as Jan and Dean (''Surf City'' 1963) and the beach movies of Frankie Avalon and Annette Funicello, the surfer subculture became a marketing tool used to sell not only entertainment, but a whole range of products as well, such as clothing. Hang Ten, founded in 1961, produced clothing with its trademark symbol of two bare feet representing the act of hanging ones toes off the front end of a surfboard. Offshoot sports also developed, like skateboarding, originally called ''sidewalk surfing,'' and, in the 1980s, sailboarding.

Instrumental surf music witnessed a resurgence in the 1990s with the release of compact disc compilations of surf music and its use in new films like Quentin Tarrantino's *Pulp Fiction* (1994) and Bruce Brown's *The Endless Summer II* (1994), a sequel to the 1964 original .

—Charles J. Shindo

FURTHER READING:

Carroll, Nick, editor. *The Next Wave: The World of Surfing.* New York, Abbeville Press, 1991.

White, Timothy. *The Nearest Faraway Place: Brian Wilson, The Beach Boys, and the Southern California Experience.* New York, Henry Holt and Co., 1994.

Susann, Jacqueline (1921-1974)

Jacqueline Susann, sometimes called the Joan Crawford of novelists, wrote only three works of fiction between 1966 and 1973, but her first novel, *Valley of the Dolls,* was one of the 10 most widely distributed books of all time. While her often maligned books eventually went out of print, Susann was still remembered as the first writer to become a media celebrity through her aggressive promotional appearances on television talk shows. A mid-1990s revival saw *Dolls* back in print again, some relatively serious re-evaluations of her campy, but charismatic work, and Susann's perhaps inevitable ascension into the pantheon of gay male pop culture icons.

Born in Philadelphia, Pennsylvania, in 1921, Susann moved to New York in 1936, a beauty contest winner anxious to crash show business. In 1939 she married Irving Mansfield, and worked as both model and actress, appearing in Broadway and road company productions, including *The Women* in 1937. Lacking the talent, luck, and angles to really hit performing big time, Susann was still addictively drawn to celebrities and their world, and her 15 years on the fringes of show business paid off in a shrewdly exploited literary career. This commenced in 1963 with the nonfiction success, *Every Night, Josephine,* about Susann's beloved pet poodle. But Susann's next book, the novel *Valley of the Dolls* in 1966, channeled her inside show business savvy into a best-selling combination of romance, lurid sex, and sensationalism which, as the publishing blurb used to say, ripped the lid off the entertainment industry. Susann and her press agent husband also launched the kind of hard-sell promotional campaign that had previously been exploited only by Hollywood. The first author to effectively exploit the television talk show circuit, Susann became as famous as her controversial books. In a legendary media incident she and Truman Capote traded insults during separate talk show appearances, Capote delivering his now infamous jibe that Susann reminded him of ''a truck driver in drag.''

While commercially successful, Susann's work was savaged by critics, instilling in her a longing for approval and prestige that was never to be truly gratified. While prestigious Random House distributed Susann's first two books, they often denied being her publisher because the titles were actually published by Bernard Geis, an outsider in the New York publishing world. James B. Twitchell observes: ''. . . the modern phenomenon of celebrity-as-author was rediscovered by publishers like Bernard Geis after the collected wisdom of Art Linkletter became a best-seller. Geis realized that just as out-and-out hacks can be made into celebrities, celebrities can be made into authors''—and thus, Susann instinctively realized, authors could be made into celebrities. After Simon and Schuster published her second book of fiction, *The Love Machine* in 1969, an editor reputedly sent Susann a rose and a note saying simply ''For us, once was enough,'' as her third and final novel, *Once Is Not Enough,* was being published by William Morrow in 1973.

Ironically, Susann's private life became more dramatic than any of her fiction. In 1962 she was diagnosed with breast cancer, which a mastectomy failed to alleviate, and, until her death in 1974, spent the rest of her life on painkillers. Her condition was never announced publicly. In addition, Susann and Mansfield's only son, Guy, was autistic, a fact also concealed from the world at large. Thus while Susann pushed the envelopes of content in her fiction, in real life she adhered to what she perceived as the expectations of her era, believing the public demanded celebrities who conformed to a positive, if manufactured image, no matter what the actuality of their private lives.

Valley of the Dolls, a lurid, sudsy saga of three young women coping none too well with the challenges of show business, remains Susann's key work. Aside from its delirious camp excesses, the cult status of the 1967 film version (in which Susann briefly appears) was instantly certified when Judy Garland was replaced by Susan Hayward shortly after production commenced, and retrospectively by co-star Sharon Tate's brutal death in the Charles Manson clan multiple murder case. Leonard Maltin calls the film a ''terribly written, acted, and directed BOMB''—he also cites an updated and expanded four-hour 1981 television remake as ''superior to the 1967 theatrical version.'' A 1971 in-name-only sequel, Russ Meyer's equally cultish *Beyond the Valley of the Dolls* took Susann's hyperbole into the realm of deliberate (and violent) camp.

In late 1997 Grove Press reissued the long-out-of-print *Valley of the Dolls,* peaking a mainstream Susann renaissance which had been percolating within gay culture for over a decade—the cult status of Susann among American gay men was the subject of a detailed feature article, ''Pink Trash,'' in no less than the usually staid *New York Times,* in July of 1997. The revival also included a New York City drag stage production of *Dolls,* the trendy popularity of gay smart-set *VOD* parties featuring jelly beans in the form of Susann's famous Valium pills (or ''dolls''), a 1998 television movie bio, *Scandalous Me,* and the announcement of a theatrical film of Susann's life to star Bette Midler. But perhaps the most bizarre manifestation of 1990s Susann-mania was an ''interview'' with the deceased author published in *Interview* magazine in October 1997, and based on a seance involving drag performer Lypsinka and a medium named Miss Eek.

Nora Ephron comments on Susann's work: ''With the possible exception of *Cosmopolitan* magazine, no one writes about sadism in modern man and masochism in modern woman quite so horribly and accurately as Jacqueline Susann. *Valley of the Dolls* had a message that had a magnetic appeal for women readers: it describes the standard female fantasy—of going to the big city, striking it rich, meeting fabulous men—and went on to show every reader that she was far better off than the heroines in the book. It was, essentially, a morality tale.'' *Art Forum* editor Sydney Pokorny gushes: ''She's camp, she's glam, she's frivolous, she understood the appeal of modern celebrity better than anyone else (except maybe Andy Warhol), and on top of it all her heroines were always powerful, independent women. Jackie is a prophet of pop culture.''

Jackie herself put it this way: ''People who read me can get off the subway and go home feeling better about their own crappy lives, and luckier than the people they've been reading about.''

—Ross Care

FURTHER READING:

Carvajal, Doreen. ''Pink Trash—Camp and Glam and Still Badly Dressed, Jacqueline Susann Stages a Comeback.'' *New York Times.* July 27, 1997, Sec. 1, 23-24.

Korda, Michael. ''Wasn't She Great?'' *The New Yorker.* August 14, 1995, 66-72.

Mansfield, Irving, with Jean Libman Block. *Life With Jackie.* New York, Bantam Books, 1983.

Twitchell, James B. *Carnival Culture: The Trashing of Taste in America.* New York, Columbia University Press, 1992.

Susskind, David (1923-1987)

David Susskind was one of the few successful television producers to also star in front of the camera. He began his career in the late forties as an agent, eventually representing such stars as Jerry Lewis and Dinah Shore. After forming Talent Associates with Alfred Levy, he started to package live dramas, before becoming a full-time producer in the mid 1950s. Over the course of more than thirty years, he produced hundreds of television dramas for such series as *The DuPont Show of the Week* and *Armstrong Circle Theater;* over a dozen movies, including *Raisin in the Sun* (1961) and *Alice Doesn't Live Here Anymore* (1974); and numerous stage plays. Aspiring to be the Cecil B. DeMille of television, Susskind especially cherished prestige specials and among his award-winners were *The Ages of Man* (1966), with John Gielgud; *Death of a Salesman* (1967), starring Lee J. Cobb; and *Eleanor and Franklin* (1976), with Edward Hermann. In 1958 he became a celebrity as host of his own talk series, *Open End,* which had unlimited time to examine an issue. The brash Susskind liked to confront his guests, exemplified by his heated exchange with Soviet Premier Nikita Khrushchev. His often-controversial series, which was trimmed to two hours in the early sixties, covered a wide range of topics, from such weighty issues as racism and organized crime to tabloid fare, including astrology and sex change operations. Retitled *The David Susskind Show* in 1967, the program continued for nineteen years until the host's untimely death in February 1987.

—Ron Simon

FURTHER READING:

Asinof, Eliot. *Bleeding between the Lines.* New York, Holt, Rinehart, and Winston, 1979.

Gehman, Richard. ''David Susskind Wants to Be Goliath.'' *TV Guide.* November 23, 1963, 15-19.

Swaggart, Jimmy (1935—)

A leading televangelist of the 1980s, Jimmy Swaggart became an American celebrity whose rise and fall were both comedy and tragedy. A self-trained piano virtuoso, whose hot Gospel stylings were barely distinguishable from the rock 'n' roll standards performed by his cousin, Jerry Lee Lewis, Swaggart might have become a major popular music artist. But he chose preaching, evolving a pulpit manner characterized by physical gyrations, abundant tears, and impassioned Biblical declamations. Scorning as bland sentimentality the positive thinking of other religious opinion makers, he further rejected the ecumenical spirit of Billy Graham. Swaggart chose instead to deliver fire-and-brimstone sermons, always tough on sin, especially that of a sensual nature. Though he first imitated the preaching of the tent evangelists of his Southern youth, he quickly learned the masterful use of media, first radio and later television. Often regarded as the most effective of the televangelists of the 1970s and 1980s, his blend of show-business hucksterism and old-fashioned Holy Ghost revivalism perpetuated a long tradition of American folk evangelism.

Born in 1935 near Ferriday, Louisiana, Jimmy Lee Swaggart was the son of a lay preacher in the charismatic Assemblies of God. Derisively called ''holy rollers'' in the early years of the century, members of this denomination moved into the middle class after World War II. Their spirit-filled devotional style began to influence the older, mainline churches, both Protestant and Catholic. Young Swaggart started preaching at age six, though he was not ''born again'' until two years later. Religion remained the major preoccupation of his entire youth. Offered a recording contract, about the time

Jimmy Swaggart

his cousin and best friend Jerry Lee was becoming famous, Swaggart vowed to use his own musical talents only in the service of the Lord. He even advised God to strike him with paralysis should he ever perform "the devil's music."

By the time he was 23, Swaggart was regularly traveling the gospel preaching circuit, along with his wife, Francis, who would remain a full partner throughout his ministry, and their two-year-old son, who would grow up to become his father's lieutenant. Backcountry evangelism, always as much entertainment as religion, put Swaggart's temperament and talent to good use. By 1964, despite success as a traveling preacher, he yearned for more respectability and was properly ordained by the Assemblies of God. He then took his "crusades" into cities. He also inaugurated a Gospel recording career and eventually sold more than 15 million recordings. In 1973 he added a weekly television program.

By the end of the 1980s Swaggart's telecasts and publications were addressing a regular national audience of almost two million. His outreach extended to 53 countries. Like other media preachers, Swaggart sought to anchor his operations; he chose Baton Rouge, Louisiana, as home base, where he built a Family Worship Center to seat 7,500. Perhaps in compensation for his own meager schooling, he readily followed the precedent of other celebrity preachers such as Aimee Semple McPherson and Oral Roberts by founding his own Bible college to train Christian workers for domestic and foreign service.

Politically conservative and openly judgmental, Swaggart made enemies. He could be fierce and even personal in his attacks. Among his targets were Roman Catholics, lukewarm Protestants, social "liberals," and fellow preachers with moral failings. He seemed oblivious to his own vulnerability when in early 1987 he launched the national scandal that came to be known as "Gospelgate." He accused rival televangelist Jim Bakker of adultery. Though the charges were easily substantiated, it did not take long for Swaggart's enemies to publicly expose his own predilections. They revealed that he had engaged in a series of voyeuristic acts with a prostitute in a Louisiana motel.

Owning up to his wrongdoing, labeling it "sin" rather than merely inappropriate behavior, Swaggart gave the premier performance of his life on February 21, 1988, to a capacity audience gathered at his Family Worship Center. His lips quivered as he weepingly apologized to his wife, his son, his daughter-in-law, and the Assemblies of God "which helped bring the gospel to my little beleaguered town, when my family was lost without Jesus." Finally, Swaggart apologized to Jesus Himself and asked to be renewed by His cleansing blood. So powerful was this confession that subsequent public acknowledgements of moral lapses by national figures have come to be known as "doing a Swaggart."

The Assemblies of God eventually defrocked Swaggart as later transgressions surfaced. Even without their blessing, his ministry continued throughout the 1990s, but his force was largely spent, and the impressive evangelistic compound he had built in Louisiana fell into some disrepair. With admissions of wrongdoing and investigations of financial irregularities of several televangelists, the influence of "the electronic church" went into general decline. Religious journals stopped lamenting that the seat in front of the television set was replacing the church pew. But Swaggart's career had become part of his century's unique body of religious lore, and he would be remembered in all his passion and moral ambiguity as a genuine American type.

—Allene Phy-Olsen

FURTHER READING:

Balmer, Randall. "Still Wrestling with the Devil: A Visit with Jimmy Swaggart Ten Years after His Fall." *Christianity Today.* Vol. 42, No. 3, March 2, 1998.

Nauer, Barbara. *Jimmy Swaggart: Dead Man Rising.* Baton Rouge, Glory Arts, 1998.

Packard, William. *Evangelism in America: From Tents to TV.* New York, Paragon House, 1988.

Reid, D., et. al. *Dictionary of Christianity in America.* Downers Grove, Illinois, Intervarsity Press, 1990.

Swaggart, Jimmy, with R. P. Lamb. *To Cross a River.* Baton Rouge, Jimmy Swaggart Ministries, 1987.

Wright, Lawrence. *Saints and Sinners.* New York, Vintage Books, 1995.

Swann, Lynn (1952-)

During the late 1970s, a period when professional football players were joining the ranks of U.S. pop-culture icons, wide

Lynn Swann at the University of Southern California.

receiver Lynn Swann was at the peak of his highly successful nine-year career in the National Football League. Swann played on four Super Bowl championship-winning teams for the Pittsburgh Steelers when that team was dominating NFL play. Swann's trademark was his ability to make acrobatic catches, especially at key junctures of important ballgames.

The Pittsburgh Steelers drafted Swann, a Tennessee native, in the first round of the 1974 NFL Draft following his graduation from the University of Southern California (USC), where he had been a unanimous choice for All-American honors during his senior year. While at USC he also earned a letter as a long jumper at track.

Swann was named the Most Valuable Player in Super Bowl X in 1976, as Pittsburgh defeated the Dallas Cowboys by a 21-17 score to become only the third team to win back-to-back Super Bowls. Swann caught four passes for a total of 161 receiving yards. The highlight was Swann's catch of a 64-yard touchdown pass from quarterback Terry Bradshaw for a game-deciding score. Swann also made a diving 53-yard catch during the second quarter, a feat that is considered by many to be one of the greatest in Super Bowl history.

In Super Bowl XIII, Swann caught an 18-yard touchdown pass from Bradshaw that was the decisive play in the Steelers' 35-31 victory over the Cowboys. Swann caught seven passes for 124 yards in that victory, an accomplishment made even more impressive because of doubts he would even play in that game due to a concussion he incurred in the American Football Conference (AFC) Finals against the Oakland Raiders. He had even been confined to his bed for several days prior to the Super Bowl, with doctors warning him that another hard hit could cause more extensive, and even career-threatening, damage. Despite the risks, Swann decided to play, with spectacular results.

Swann's performance in Super Bowl XIII was the culmination of his best professional season. In that year, 1979, he caught 61 passes for a total of 880 yards, and scored 11 touchdowns. During the 1979 season, Swann caught a decisive 47-yard touchdown pass from Bradshaw in the third quarter of Pittsburgh's 31-19 victory over the Los Angeles Rams, a play in which Swann leapt between two defenders to catch the ball before reaching the end zone.

Part of Swann's great success came from his being teamed with another wide receiver drafted in 1974, John Stallworth, who formed another threat at the wide-receiver position and prevented other teams from focusing all of their attention on Swann. The two men gave quarterback Terry Bradshaw an inviting choice of targets. As Swann noted in Lou Sahadi's *Super Steelers: The Making of a Dynasty,* "John [Stallworth] and I are both moving targets. It's just up to Terry to hit us. What's happened is that we developed a remarkable, almost undefinable rapport among the three of us."

Swann ranks second in receiving yards in the Super Bowl (364) and touchdowns (3) to San Francisco great Jerry Rice. During his playing career, he was named to the NFL Pro Bowl on three occasions. He has been a finalist for induction into the Professional Football Hall of Fame in Canton, Ohio, every year that he has been eligible. Regarding Swann's failure to be inducted into the Hall of Fame, his teammate Joe Greene noted "Lynn Swann didn't have the stats, but he sure as heck had an impact. . . . He didn't play a long time, but he made an impact. . . . He played a lot of big games. I'm a great Lynn Swann fan. He deserves a lot more consideration."

Following his retirement from professional football in 1982, Swann worked as a sports broadcaster for the ABC network, covering football as well as a diverse array of other sports, ranging from rugby to dog-sled racing. Swann has also been active in a wide variety of

charitable and other causes. He has served as the national spokesperson for the Big Brothers and Big Sisters of America since 1980, and on the Board of Trustees of the Pittsburgh Ballet Theater, for which he created a youth scholarship. He was named the NFL Man of the Year in 1981, and has also competed in several marathons. Swann had a cameo as a television announcer in the 1991 movie *The Last Boy Scout.*

—Jason George

FURTHER READING:

Sahadi, Lou. *Super Steelers: The Making of a Dynasty.* New York Times Books, 1980.

"MVP Profiles." http://www.nfl.com/history/mvp/sbx.html. April 1999.

"Where Are They Now?: Lynn Swann." http://www.steelref.com. April 1999.

Swatch Watches

The Swatch watch was released in 1983 as a response by the Swiss watch industry to the encroaching Japanese influence on the market for inexpensive high tech timepieces. The first Swatch was made of slim plastic with only 51 components, allowing it to be sold cheaply. By the 1990s the Swatch had become the most successful wristwatch brand of all time. The key to the popularity of Swatch was its collectibility. By rotating designs and discontinuing popular lines at key moments, the Swatch company was able to give their watches a cult status, especially among young people.

—Deborah Broderson

FURTHER READING:

Hall, John. *Bringing New Products to Market: The Art and Science of Creating Winners.* New York, AMACOM, 1991.

Komar, Daniel. *Swatch Watches I.* Switzerland, Chrono Time, 1992.

Swatch AG. *Pop Swatch.* Switzerland, Swatch AG, 1994.

The Sweatshirt

The humble gray cotton sweatshirt with fleece lining was one of the last garments to come out of the gym locker into high-style fashion. The wonderfully practical sports coverup was determinedly unglamorous: it was affiliated with no one sport in particular; its heavy cotton tended to lose shape over time and, unlike jeans, move away from sexual outline to a gray blob. Technology, which around the early 1980s introduced just enough synthetic stretch (generally less than 5 percent) to maintain shape, collar, and cuffs without losing the integrity and feel of cotton, catapulted the sweatshirt out of the bottom of the locker. In 1981, Norma Kamali made a woman's jumpsuit ensemble for day or evening in gray sweatshirt material; by 1986, Emporio Armani styling showed hooded sweatshirts with sports jackets; in 1987, Quincy Jones appeared in an American Express advertisement in a short-sleeved sweatshirt. Perhaps a more influential popularizer of sweatshirts as fashionable garb was actress

Jennifer Beals, who wore cut up sweatshirts in the 1983 movie *Flashdance*. Since the 1980s, sweatshirt gray has become a popular color for diverse clothing.

—Richard Martin

FURTHER READING:

Martin, Richard, and Harold Koda. *Jocks and Nerds: Men's Style in the Twentieth Century.* New York, Rizzoli, 1989.

Swimming Pools

In 1988, a local dispute in East Hampton, Long Island, received national attention. An affluent couple was threatening to sue their town for refusing them a permit to build a second swimming pool at their ocean-front home. While the dispute hinged on issues of zoning restrictions and environmental protection, the story was widely reported due to its almost comical justification of Thorstein Veblen's 1899 critique of the "leisure class." If one backyard pool is an emblem of comfort and leisure, two pools at an ocean-front home exemplify conspicuous consumption run amok.

At the same time, a different sort of swimming pool controversy was raging in Greenspoint, New York. Residents of this Brooklyn neighborhood bitterly disagreed about what should be done with the crumbling remains of the McCarren Park municipal pool. Some in the community, especially the Latino and African American residents, wanted the pool restored to its former splendor. Built in 1936, this enormous pool, which could accommodate 6,800 swimmers at a time, had served as a recreation resort for locals unable to afford memberships at private pools and, according to a *New York Times* writer, had been "the hub of the working-class neighborhood's summertime social life." Other area residents, most of whom were white, wanted the pool closed permanently or rebuilt on a much smaller scale. They feared that such a large public pool would become a locus for urban crime.

These two episodes reveal the diverse and often discordant cultural meanings Americans attach to swimming pools. Private pools symbolize, sometimes in an extreme way, the "good life"—a life of material comfort and leisure. Public pools, however, evoke

A swimming pool.

very different images. Some of the residents of Greenspoint associated public pools with urban decay and social disorder, while others saw the possibility of a rejuvenated and vibrant community life. These contradictory cultural meanings date back to the first swimming pools built in America and highlight some of the successes and failures of twentieth-century American society.

Athletic clubs, colleges, and wealthy homeowners built the first private swimming pools in America during the Gilded Age. These pools were used for both sport and leisure, which at the time were the almost exclusive domain of the well-to-do. Early public swimming pools, built in and around large northern cities, served a different purpose for a different segment of society. Brookline, Massachusetts, opened the first municipal pool in 1897. Like most early public pools, it was located within a bathhouse. Progressive reformers and municipal leaders viewed these swimming pools as public health institutions and intended them to promote cleanliness among the nation's growing population of urban poor. Gradually, public pools evolved from baths to fitness institutions to, by the second decade of the twentieth century, recreation and leisure facilities.

Social and cultural conflict dominated the history of swimming pools in America during the first half of the twentieth century. The vast majority of pools during this period were public. They were intensely contested civic spaces—controversies over where pools should be built, who should be allowed to use them, and how they should be used reflected the dominant tensions in American society. These racial and class tensions, often obscured in other areas of life, appeared with striking clarity and definition at public pools because Americans perceived them to be intimate and potentially hazardous spaces. Swimming in a pool necessitated exposing one's body; it brought swimmers visually and, in a way, physically into intimate contact with one another. Swimming also exposed people to the dirt and disease of other swimmers. Consequently, the class, ethnic, and racial phobias that circumscribed and limited social interaction in general at this time became heightened at swimming pools.

In the early twentieth century, the social and cultural contests over swimming pools divided along class lines. A controversial proposal to build a swimming pool in New York's Central Park illustrates this class dynamic. John Mitchel, president of the Board of Aldermen, proposed the pool so that the city's poor, especially the children, would have a clean and cool place to bathe and play during the summer. Without such a pool, these children had no place to swim except among the rats, garbage, and sewage in the East and Hudson Rivers. The mostly middle-class New Yorkers who opposed Mitchel's proposal were determined to maintain the park in its original form. A pool would "desecrate" the park, they feared, by transforming their oasis of genteel recreation into a popular amusement center. "No Coney Island, if you please, in the park," one opponent pleaded. These critics were also determined to protect the park's social landscape. "I have never been in favor of putting a swimming pool in Central Park," affirmed Park Commissioner Charles Stover, "I should consider it disastrous if the only swimming pool belonging to the city was put there. It would attract all sorts of undesirable people." Stover suggested instead that this swimming pool for the masses be built in a more appropriate location: "under the approaches to the Manhattan bridge." By keeping the swimming pool out of Central Park, New York's middle class defended their Victorian pastimes and reinforced the physical distance between themselves and their working-class neighbors.

The late 1920s and early 1930s marked an important transition in the history of swimming pools. The number and popularity of public pools increased dramatically. Large northern cities doubled and even tripled the number of pools they provided for their residents, while southern cities and smaller communities built municipal pools for the first time. The social contest over these pools changed as well: race replaced class as the most important distinction in determining patterns of discrimination. This racial contest, however, still occurred within a larger class context. Middle- and working-class blacks competed with working- and lower middle-class whites for the use of public pools, while wealthy whites swam at private pools.

The pattern of the racial struggle at public swimming pools was closely tied to the size of the community and the region in which the pool was located. In the South, black Americans were excluded from using public pools entirely. In large northern cities, racial discrimination took the form of segregation. Cities like New York, Chicago, and Boston largely avoided direct racial conflict and violence by providing separate pools for black residents. However, in smaller communities, black and white residents often competed over the use of a single pool. The dynamic of this struggle varied from town to town, but generally involved exclusion, protest, and violence.

Elizabeth, New Jersey, for example, opened its municipal pool in June, 1930. By August of that year, a group of black residents had filed a complaint with the city protesting their exclusion from the pool. The city's Board of Recreation Commissioners ruled that blacks should have equal access to the facility. The pool remained tenuously integrated for two summers, but in 1933, black residents stopped using it because white swimmers continually harassed and assaulted them. In 1938, black residents tried to integrate the pool again, but were once again subjected to the same abuse. Finally, the Board closed the pool. It could no longer condone the discrimination and violence, but apparently would not arrest the perpetrators.

The history of swimming pools fundamentally changed after World War II. America's rising economic tide, the increased rate of suburbanization, and racial desegregation combined to cause a dramatic increase in the number of private and residential pools. The economic prosperity of the postwar era coupled with advances in pool construction made backyard pools affordable to America's expanding middle class. In 1950, Americans owned only 2,500 private residential swimming pools; by 1970 they owned 713,000. During the same period, proliferating suburban communities often chose to build private swim clubs instead of public pools.

This general trend towards privatization was, at least partially, in response to the forced desegregation of municipal pools. During the 1940s, black Americans won several important legal victories against communities with segregated swimming pools. One such community was Montgomery, West Virginia, which built a public pool in 1940 but did not open it. The city's elected officials faced a conundrum: they did not want Montgomery's black residents swimming in the pool, but they were reluctant to defy West Virginia's anti-discrimination statutes by openly turning them away. The city eventually leased the pool to a private non-profit community association in 1946 for one dollar. The pool finally opened that summer and the now "private" administrators denied blacks admittance. The African American residents of Montgomery quickly sued the city, arguing that leasing the pool to private interests did not relieve the city of its obligation to afford black citizens equal rights. The federal courts agreed: "Justice would be blind indeed if she failed to detect the real purpose in this effort of the City of Montgomery to clothe public function with the mantle of private responsibility. 'The voice is Jacob's voice,' even though 'the hands are the hands of Esau.'" The court-ordered desegregation of Montgomery's pool, however, was a hollow victory for the city's black residents. In response to the court's decision, Montgomery closed the pool until 1961. White residents were apparently more willing to go without a community pool than swim with their black neighbors.

Pool use continued to divide along racial lines in the 1970s and 1980s. Just as many white Americans chose to avoid living next to black Americans during this period by moving to restricted neighborhoods, they chose to avoid swimming with them by joining private swim clubs or building backyard pools. African and Latino Americans, many of whom continued to live in large cities, were left to swim at deteriorating public pools. Even most whites who remained in urban areas did not swim at public pools. As the Greenspoint controversy shows, some did not want municipal pools in their neighborhoods at all. America's history of segregated swimming pools thus became its legacy.

The shift from public to private pools has, in some ways, transformed the quality of community life in America. Throughout much of the twentieth century, the public swimming pool served as a stage for public discourse. Community life was fostered, monitored, and disputed at these municipal institutions. The recent privatization of swimming, however, constitutes a retreat from public life. Private pools, especially residential ones, have stifled the public discourse that used to occur at community pools. Instead of swimming, chatting, and fighting with their neighbors at municipal pools, private pool owners have fenced themselves into their own backyards. The Greenspoint controversy shows that public debate at and about municipal pools has not been silenced completely; however, too many controversies in contemporary America resemble the East Hampton dispute: people fighting to get away from their community rather than fighting to be a part of it.

—Jeffrey Wiltse

FURTHER READING:

Jackson, Kenneth T. *Crabgrass Frontier: The Suburbanization of the United States.* New York, Oxford University Press, 1985.

Leeuwen, Thomas, A. *The Springboard in the Pond: An Intimate History of the Swimming Pool.* Cambridge, MIT Press, 1998.

Nasaw, David. *Going Out: The Rise and Fall of Public Amusements.* New York, HarperCollins Publishers, 1993.

Riess, Steven A. *City Games: The Evolution of American Urban Society and the Rise of Sports.* Urbana, University of Illinois Press, 1989.

Sugrue, Thomas J. *The Origins of the Urban Crisis: Race and Inequality in Postwar Detroit.* Princeton, Princeton University Press, 1996.

Williams, Marilyn Thornton. *Washing ''The Great Unwashed'': Public Baths in Urban America, 1840-1920.* Columbus, Ohio State University Press, 1991.

Swing Dancing

In the 1930s swing bands emerged at the forefront of American popular music, evolving from the jazz genre, which was primarily produced and listened to by blacks, into one patronized also by urban whites. Long before baseball was integrated, the big swing bands—led by Duke Ellington, Benny Goodman, and Count Basie—brought together black and white musicians in a new social amalgam that decisively changed American culture. Musically, swing offered rhythmic flexibility. Swing music is marked by a subtle swaying, living pulse, which came from musicians playing just ahead of the beat enough to be syncopated, or dragging behind it enough to be bluesy. Swing, notes historian Lewis Erensberg, caused ''a general revolution in the popular dance in the United States'' as white youth took up the black dance innovations in order to banish whatever ballroom gentility remained in the Depression. After World War II, swing grew increasingly fragmented, and became less of a dance music and more of a concert music. Although bebop succeeded it as the new wave of jazz innovation, it did not stimulate a new form of social dancing.

Harlem became the cultural capital of black America in the late 1920s and it is here that swing dancing began, first appearing as the Lindy Hop. Originated among secret gangs in Harlem—which was quickly being populated by African-Americans as whites departed—the steps were refined and made famous by dancers at Harlem's Savoy Ballroom. Lindy Hop refers to Charles Lindbergh's ''hop''—his historic solo flight—across the Atlantic Ocean in 1927. Observing the acrobatics of some dancers at the Savoy Ballroom, ''Shorty George'' Snowdon, a dance enthusiast, said ''Look at them kids hoppin' over there. I guess they're doin' the Lindy Hop.'' The swing combined steps from the shag, the Texas tommy, and vaudeville into a ballroom dance—a syncopated two-step or box step that accented the offbeat; the fundamental innovation of the dance was the ''breakaway,'' when the partners spun away from each other and improvised a break. The acrobatic or ''air steps'' were judo-like variations in which partners would roll and flip each other over the back. The Lindy Hop evolved into the jitterbug—a more acrobatic and an almost ''choreographed'' version of the Lindy Hop. ''The white jitterbug is oftener than not uncouth to look at,'' reported the *New York Times* according to swing historian David Stowe, ''but his Negro original is quite another matter. His movements are never so exaggerated that they lack control, and there is an unmistakable dignity about his most violent figures.''

Jitterbug enjoyed enormous popularity from 1936 until the end of the war. Every soda shop had a jukebox where teenagers were able to jitterbug after school. Eventually, in the late 1940s, the Lindy and jitterbug evolved into what has come to be called ''East Coast swing''—which had a rotating character, the couple has no fixed relation to the room. An almost separate version of swing dancing developed on the West Coast, in which the two partners remain in a narrow slot on the dance floor. Even after swing was musically moribund, jitterbug remained the basic framework for couples dancing in the early days of rock 'n' roll. It passed from the scene only after the Twist had introduced the stand alone form of dancing in the early 1960s.

In the late 1990s, partnered social dancing began to make a comeback, with swing dancing an integral part of the revival. There has also been a renaissance of swing and big band music—typified by groups like the Royal Crown Revue and Big Bad Voodoo Daddy. Ballroom dance classes became extremely popular, particularly on college campuses. In the larger cities, ballrooms, dance clubs, and the larger dance teaching studios offer special nights of swing dancing. Contemporary social dancing reflected an extensive process of blending: for instance, hip hop dance styles have incorporated elements of the Lindy and jitterbug and new swing styles showed a strong Latin influence.

—Jeffrey Escoffier

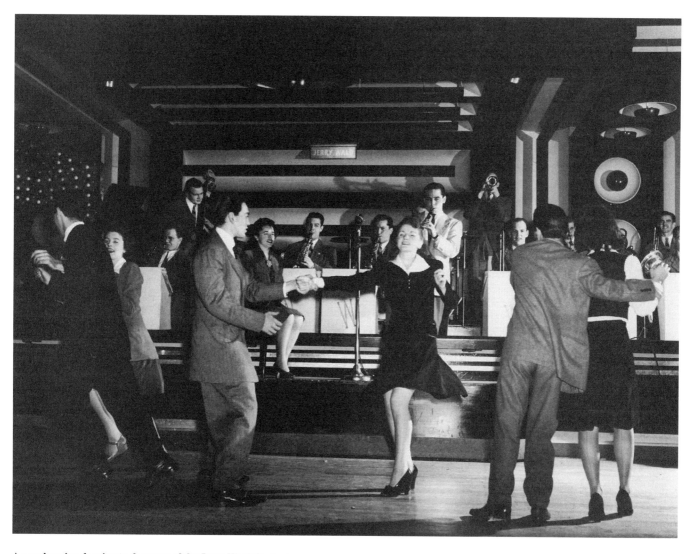

A couple swing dancing to the tunes of the Jerry Wald Orchestra.

FURTHER READING:

Erenberg, Lewis A. *Swingin' the Dream: Big Band Jazz and the Rebirth of American Culture.* Chicago, University of Chicago Press, 1998.

Stearns, Marshall, and Jean Stearns. *Jazz Dance: The Story of American Vernacular Dance.* New York, Macmillan, 1968.

Stowe, David. *Swing Changes.* Cambridge, Harvard University Press, 1994.

Swinging

Of all the social phenomena of the 1970s, one of the least practiced but most discussed was swinging, sometimes called partner swapping or wife swapping. Though few couples actually indulged in this practice, there were enough who did, or who knew about someone who did, to give the phenomenon widespread awareness. When the trend lost its popular buzz, however, swinging returned to what it had always been—the casual avocation of a group of hardcore enthusiasts.

There have always been swingers throughout history. The Bible records enough incidents of men lying down with other men's handmaidens to fill the *Penthouse* letters page many times over. And informal "clubs" devoted to extramarital experimentation have been around from the early days of the Republic. But the emergence of "swinging" as a loosely organized lifestyle coincided with America's "sexual revolution" in the 1960s.

Generally conducted at poolside parties and potluck dinners, partner swapping claimed about one million adherents during its heyday in the 1970s. Sometimes swinging involved couples placing ads in adult publications or choosing other couples they might like to pair up with. At other times, the encounters were purposely made random. One popular forum for selecting partners was the "key party," in which the men tossed their car keys into a bowl and the women fished them out to determine with whom they would spend the night. The climate of sexual freedom espoused in such magazines as *Playboy* and *Penthouse* accelerated acceptance of the practice and eventually led to coverage in more mainstream publications as well.

Partner swapping even made it onto prime-time television. A 1971 episode of *All in the Family* traced the comic consequences of Edith Bunker's inadvertent reply to an ad from a pair of swingers.

Vincent Gardenia and Rue McClanahan played the bewildered couple, who met up with the old morality in the form of Archie Bunker, America's avatar of sexual counterrevolution. But such downbeat portrayals of the lifestyle were the exception rather than the rule, as more people briefly flirted with the idea that maybe this open-marriage thing had some advantages to it after all.

An even surer sign that partner swapping had hit the mainstream came in 1973, when two members of the New York Yankees pitching staff swapped wives for the long haul. Lefties Mike Kekich and Fritz Peterson announced the spouse exchange in a bizarre press conference during spring training. The unique trade was completed with the addition, not of the customary "player to be named later," but of the rest of their families: children, pets, and, residences. For the record, Kekich broke up with Marilyn Peterson soon after the switch, while Fritz Peterson remained married to the former Susan Kekich more than 25 years later. The high-profile swap briefly captured national headlines, but the fact that it did not scandalize baseball indicated just how much American sexual mores were changing.

The novelty of swinging eventually wore off, however. During the 1980s, AIDS and sexually transmitted diseases made all but its diehard believers reconsider the advantages of monogamy. With a conservative administration in Washington, promiscuity regained some of its negative stigma. Swinging once again became the private preserve of a little-publicized subculture. Still, during the 1990s, three million Americans were estimated to be swinging on a recreational basis. Facilitated by the Internet, and fueled by a reaction against the sexual moderation invoked during the AIDS era, sexual adventurousness was once again on the rise. House parties still provided a prominent medium for partner swapping, although a new wave of institutions, including affinity groups, travel agencies, and even bed and breakfasts, were catering to the burgeoning swinging lifestyle. In August of 1997, more than 4,000 people attended a convention of the North American Swing Club Association in Palm Springs, California, where seminars were offered on such topics as "Recipes for a Successful Orgy" and "Growing Up with Kinky Parents."

The prevailing ethos at swinging encounters continued to be freewheeling sexual experimentation. But there were some changes from the wild and lawless 1970s. The spread of AIDS sensitized many partner-swapping enthusiasts to the primacy of good hygiene and a more judicious choice of partners. And society's growing acceptance of homosexuality allowed more swingers to experiment with same-sex partners. There was even a mini-wave of nostalgia for the old ways subsumed in the larger national wistfulness about the 1970s, as evidenced in such films as Ang Lee's *The Ice Storm* (1998), based on Rick Moody's novel of the same name. The film, whose harrowing climax occurs during a "key party" attended by its suburban Connecticut protagonists, captured the emotional sterility that allowed swinging to spread beyond a small hedonistic cult to briefly capture the fancy of middle-class America.

—Robert E. Schnakenberg

FURTHER READING:

D'Emilio, John, and Estelle B. Freedman. *Intimate Matters: A History of Sexuality in America.* 2d edition. Chicago, University of Chicago Press, 1997.

Michael, Robert T., John H. Gagnon, Edward O. Laumann, and Gina Kolata. *Sex in America: A Definitive Survey.* New York, Warner Books, 1995.

Thomas, Patti. *Recreational Sex: An Insider's Guide to the Swinging Lifestyle.* Cleveland, Ohio, Peppermint Publishing Company, 1997.

Sylvia

Since its inception in a suburban Chicago newspaper in 1978, Nicole Hollander's comic strip, *Sylvia,* has evolved to become a leading expression of postmodern feminism in satiric form. Appearing daily in newspapers coast-to-coast, Hollander's popular strip has also been reprinted in many books, including such titles as *I'm in Training to be Tall and Blonde,* and *Ma, Can I Be a Feminist and Still Like Men?*

If the title character in Cathy Guisewite's *Cathy* strip represents the relationship struggles—romantic, parental, and inter-office—of a neurotic, thirtysomething working woman, *Sylvia* portrays a somewhat older, stouter, work-at-home woman comfortable with herself but at war with the foibles of contemporary society. Actually, Sylvia herself does not always appear in the strip that bears her name, a sly, surrealistic stream-of-consciousness in which Hollander applies her own witty touch to subjects both slight and substantial, from such comedy staples as pets and airlines to such fresher ground as gender inequality and goddess spirituality. Sylvia is a plump, fiftyish advice columnist who is as likely to be found conversing with her cats or a space alien as her nubile daughter, Rita, or her friend, Beth-Ann. Like many of us, Sylvia also talks back to the media: When a commercial on the radio announces, "Spray N' Wash gets out what America gets into," bubble-bathing Sylvia responds: "Send some to El Salvador!"

Nicole Hollander, the strip's creator, had also worked as an art instructor and book illustrator, but she found fame as a comic strip writer/artist when *Sylvia,* initially created for a suburban Chicago newspaper in 1978, was picked up for syndication by the Universal Press Syndicate in 1979. The increased visibility led inevitably to *Sylvia* books and a line of greeting cards; in 1981, another syndicate, Field Enterprises, bought the *Sylvia* rights and added a Sunday strip, since discontinued. For a time, Nicole Hollander incorporated herself as The Sylvia Syndicate and took over her own distribution. By the end of the 1990s, *Sylvia* was being distributed by the Los Angeles Times Syndicate, although Hollander retained the copyright on her daily creations. Hollander was featured prominently in a PBS documentary about contemporary female comic strip artists.

Although there are recurring themes in *Sylvia,* there are no storylines; each day's strip is self-contained. Her visual style is purposefully slapdash, in keeping with *Sylvia*'s cutting-edge humor. What distinguishes the *Sylvia* strip is its celebration of the life of the mind of its heroine. As often as not, there is nothing happening in the strip *per se* except what Sylvia is imagining, in the fashion of a latter-day Little Nemo in Slumberland, except that she is wide awake both physically and ideologically. The strip's innovative fancies and conceits include "Menacing Supercops of the Future" such as the "fashion cop," policing errors of taste and style, or the "love cop," seeking to break up incompatible couples or prevent them from forming; the eternally annoying "Woman Who Does Everything More Beautifully Than You"; "Alien Lovers"; "Special Goddesses"; "The Woman Who Worries About Everything"; "The Cat Who Hypnotizes His Mistress"; "From the Diary of a Woman Who Never Forgets a Slight"; "Gender-Based Differences—How to Tell if You're a Gal or a Guy"; and "The Lonely Detective," in which

Sylvia imagines herself a noirish Phillipa Marlowe-type private eye tackling contemporary societal issues.

Popular culture has always been a rich source for *Sylvia*'s satire. At times, her advice column was featured in the strip—she once addressed one of her troubled readers as "Dear disgusting wimp"—although in recent years the column is seldom referred to directly. Other gambits have included Sylvia's proposals for TV game shows, such as the one in which recently divorced couples would have tried to guess each other's most annoying habits, or her extreme take-offs from *The Three Faces of Eve,* imagined dramas about women with three-way personality splits, one of which is always a housewife, as in: "housewife, snake-handler, and educator," or "housewife, hair stylist, and brain surgeon." Considering that Hollander's *Sylvia* strip has always been frankly feminist, multiethnic, multispecies, and unabashedly liberal in outlook, it is not surprising that it will sometimes refer to current events, although the "ripped from the headlines" approach has never been *Sylvia*'s prime focus as it has been for strips such as *Doonesbury.* In any given year, however, *Sylvia* will manage to reflect—and have fun with—the mood of a small but hearty band of free-thinkers as they warily eye the shenanigans of the world at large.

—Preston Neal Jones

FURTHER READING:

Hollander, Nicole. *Female Problems.* New York, Dell, 1995.

————. *Hi, This Is Sylvia: I Can't Come to the Phone Right Now, So When You Hear the Beep, Please Hang Up.* New York, St. Martin's Press, 1983.

————. *Mercy, It's the Revolution, and I'm in My Bathrobe.* New York, St. Martin's Press, 1982.

————. *Never Take Your Cat to a Salad Bar.* New York, Vintage Books, 1987.

————. *Sylvia on Sundays.* New York, St. Martin's Press, 1983.

————. *That Woman Must Be On Drugs: A Collection of Sylvia.* New York, St. Martin's Press, 1981.

————. *The Whole Enchilada: A Spicy Collection of Sylvia's Best.* New York, St. Martin's Press, 1986.

Horn, Maurice. *100 Years of American Newspaper Comics: An Illustrated Encyclopedia.* New York, Gramercy Books, 1996.

"This Is Sylvia's Home Page." http://www.suba.com/~sylvia. May 1999.

Syndication

Syndication refers to the sale or distribution of television programs that are offered to multiple markets for non-network exhibition. As a practice, syndication stands opposed to network broadcasting where content and schedule are determined nationally for all affiliated stations. Syndication includes a variety of program types including movies, first-run series, re-runs of network programming, talk shows, game shows, foreign programs, and children's series. While syndication may resemble network distribution in that the same programs air over many separate outlets, the timing (day of the week as well as time of day) may vary from location to location. Serving as a counterbalance to network control, syndication has developed from

the simple sale of off-network programming in the early 1950s, into a number of complex and varied business practices including off-net, first run, re-run, and barter syndication. More than just the distribution of programs, syndication regulations and practices have played a major role in the development of contemporary television. From the Federal Communication Commission's (FCC) "Prime-Time Access Rules" (PTAR) and "Financial Interests and Syndication" (Fin/ Syn) rulings, to the programming of UHF, cable, and even entirely new networks, syndication has been one of the most debated—and most important—business and programmatic practices within the television industry.

During the 1950s the television networks owned and controlled most of the programming they aired. The networks were able to present re-runs of programs, or sell the rights, even if they had minimal or no investment in the actual production. Networks defended this practice by arguing that they were equally responsible for the success of a series, since they promoted, placed, and provided the exposure for the program. This left them in the enviable position of taking minimal financial risk in a show's production, while at the same time enjoying long term profit from its being broadcast (and re-broadcast). Unable to risk the capital necessary to produce a series on their own, many independent production companies disappeared during these early years, and by the 1960s, almost all programming was produced by the networks or movie studios. In an attempt to limit the networks' monopolization of television production, exhibition, and distribution, the FCC examined syndication and made sweeping changes to network practices in 1970-1971. The FCC's motivation was to re-invigorate local and independent production, and to accomplish this goal they adopted the Fin/Syn and PTAR rulings.

The Fin/Syn rulings effectively ended network monopolies on syndication. Following these rulings networks could not syndicate domestically and could only sell a program internationally if they had completely financed the production. Furthermore, networks were limited in the number of programs they could produce, thus creating greater dependence on outside production companies. The PTAR, on the other hand, limited prime-time network broadcasts to the 8:00 to 11:00 pm slot in the top 50 television markets. In adopting these rules the FCC hoped that they would open access to programming, and encourage affiliates to air shows that were independently or locally produced. Rather than generating a resurgence of local programming, however, the PTAR led to the development of inexpensive shows which attracted a significant audience—often in the form of game shows like *Wheel of Fortune* or *Jeopardy.* Ironically the FCC's decisions had tremendous economic ramifications which affected the television and movie industry alike. Given one year to divest themselves of their syndication services, networks sold these divisions. Such sales led to the formation of new companies like Viacom which, once a division of CBS, now owns Paramount Pictures and its own television network (UPN).

Syndication became increasingly important as television expanded and the new and independent Ultra High Frequency (UHF) television stations looked for programming. With the expansion of non-network stations syndicators found themselves in the enviable position of supplying content for a significant portion of the daily television schedule. Separated from the networks, the syndication industry became more profitable, powerful, and competitive, leading to new practices intended to make programs more economically attractive to affiliates. One such example is "barter syndication," which was designed to meet the needs of advertisers and affiliates alike. In this form of syndication, the distributor would give the program to affiliates free of charge in exchange for ad time on the program. By placing a program in enough markets around the country, the syndicator could then sell commercials to national advertisers and keep the revenue as their payment. During the early days of UHF, stations needing to fill their schedules were cash-poor, and barter syndication offered them a way to gain programming without expending their limited capital. Eventually, as stations became more established, syndicators would move towards a combination of cash payments and ad time for their programs.

The most common form of syndication is "off-network syndication," which refers to programs that have already aired on network television. The cost of these programs was generally recouped during their network runs, which meant that most of the syndication revenue became profit. Anyone who grew up watching television after the 1960s is familiar with a host of programs, from *Gilligan's Island, F-Troop,* or *Rockford Files,* to name a few, which were (and still are) aired in this manner. With the growth of cable, entire networks, such as TV Land, were built on the strength and popularity of off-network programming. A more recent trend has been "first run syndication," which refers to programs that are syndicated when they are new. While there is more financial risk in this type of syndication—since the costs are not absorbed through network exhibition—these programs offered tremendous control and profit potential to the producers. Perhaps the most famous shows distributed in this fashion include *Baywatch, Star Trek: The Next Generation*, and a number of game shows. By the 1980s, the emergence and success of "first-run syndication" led to a new type of inexpensive programming know as "reality programming," "trash," or "tabloid TV."

With the success of cable television in the 1980s, syndicators once again experienced an increased demand for programs. Following the growth of independent stations, the expanded cable market made syndication one of the most profitable businesses in television. This all began to change by the late 1980s, however, as production companies recognized the greater value of their programs, and new networks emerged, reducing the number of independent stations. The first blow came with the formation of the Fox network, which combined a number of previously independent stations and supplied them with regular network programming. By the end of the 1980s syndicators experienced additional setbacks when the FCC eased syndication rules and polices, thus allowing networks more freedom to produce and distribute programming. This situation was then further exacerbated by the development of two new networks (WB and UPN) which committed many of the remaining independents to network programming. Nevertheless, syndication remains a viable, powerful, and profitable method of television distribution.

In addition to the economic ramifications, syndication has also created a unique cultural phenomenon: cross-generational exposure to television programming. Because of syndication, the favorite programs of one generation of television viewers may remain popular decades after they have aired. This practice appeals to a sense of nostalgia for some, and demonstrates the timelessness of television's generic programmatic qualities to others. In either case television is somewhat unique in that series and children's programs continue to be enjoyed for generation after generation.

—James Friedman

FURTHER READING:

The Economics of TV Programming and Syndication. Carmel, California, Paul Kagan Associates, 1994.

Erickson, Hal. *Syndicated Television: The First Forty Years, 1947-1987.* Jefferson, North Carolina, McFarland, 1989.

MacDonald, J. Fred. *One Nation Under Television.* New York, Pantheon Books, 1990.

Head, Sydney W., et al. *Broadcasting in America: A Survey of Electronic Media.* 8th edition. Boston, Houghton Mifflin, 1998.

T

Tabloid Television

During the 1980s, the proliferation of popular television shows focusing on sex, crime, and gossip, such as *A Current Affair, Hard Copy,* and *Inside Edition,* led some media critics to fear that the lines between responsible journalism and sensationalism were being blurred. These "tabloid television" shows, so designated because of their resemblance to supermarket tabloid newspapers, relied for their content on gossip, barely credible sources, an appeal to emotion, and the use of checkbook journalism, staged reenactments of events, and home video footage. These practices have had an impact on mainstream broadcast journalism, which has been charged with downplaying more serious news in order to compete for viewers and advertising revenue.

Tabloid television began in earnest in 1986 when media magnate Rupert Murdoch created *A Current Affair* and put it into syndication. The half-hour show featured anchorman Maury Povich and stories focusing on sex, crime, and sleaze. At the height of its popularity, it claimed ninety million viewers in the United States. This show spawned a series of copies, such as *Hard Copy* and *Inside Edition,* which for many uninformed people blur the distinction between responsible journalism and gossip. In the 1990s, such events as the O. J. Simpson murder trial and the death of Princess Diana offered much fodder for the purveyors of tabloid television.

The methods used by the producers of tabloid television are at odds with acceptable journalistic practice as defined by mainstream television news. Checkbook journalism is one of the most hotly contested practices. The tabloids commonly pay their sources for interviews, especially exclusive ones. Mainstream journalists argue that this encourages sources to embellish their stories in order to make more money. Likewise, the use of re-enactments of crimes or other activities blurs the line between what actually happened and a fictionalized account of what may have happened. Yet, even as mainstream journalists condemn these practices, they are increasingly using them in their own shows.

The O. J. Simpson trial offered an important case study in tabloid television. Coverage of the trial became continuous, and mainstream journalists began to compete with the tabloids, often by employing many of their methods. NBC News, for example, using computer modeling, "re-created" the murder for viewers. In another example, *Dateline NBC* rigged the gas tanks on some Ford trucks to explode as a way of dramatizing their alleged danger. Some mainstream broadcasters have also begun citing tabloid reports as "news" in their own reports, justifying it with the disclaimer that they are reporting information, though its truth or falsity could not be verified. This sort of "peeping tom" journalism—reporting on what the tabloids are saying and even criticizing it—offers to the mainstream journalists a way of carrying the same information, but with reduced risk. Yet, the continued use of this activity means that ultimately, there is little differentiation between the tabloids and the mainstream.

Author Matthew Ehrlich argues that this separation between mainstream and tabloid news has never been that concrete. In *The Journalism of Outrageousness: Tabloid Television News vs. Investigative News,* he points out that the principle characteristics of the tabloids have always been similar to the characteristics of investigative news. For example, both take a stand on the guilt or innocence of the particular parties involved, both take a moralizing tone, and both examine crime and sex. The only difference, Ehrlich argues, is that investigative news uses this material to inform and possibly rectify the world, while the tabloids use the material merely for entertainment.

The zenith of tabloid journalism may have come with the death of Princess Diana in August 1997. In a statement made after her death, her brother, Lord Spencer, expressed his belief that the "press would kill her in the end," a reference to the high-speed car chase involving *paparazzi* photographers in Paris. Although print tabloids were most implicated in the event, the criticism implicated tabloid television as well.

—Mia Consalvo

FURTHER READING:

Bishop, Ronald. "From Behind the Walls: Boundary Work by News Organizations in Their Coverage of Princess Diana's Death." *Journal of Communication Inquiry.* Vol. 23, No. 1, 1999, 90-112.

Ehrlich, Matthew J. "The Journalism of Outrageousness: Tabloid Television News vs. Investigative News." *Journalism & Mass Communication Monographs.* No. 155, 1996, 1-24.

Krajicek, David J. *Scooped! Media Miss Real Story on Crime While Chasing Sex, Sleaze, and Celebrities.* New York, Columbia University Press, 1998.

Tabloids

Tabloids were originally pint-sized newspapers specializing in the sensational. Once confined to so-called "scandal sheets," or magazine-style newspapers that many people saw only in grocery store checkout lines, during the last years of the twentieth century their subject matters of sex and scandal seeped into the mainstream press and virtually all other media, including magazines, radio, television, and the Internet. Nearly all of American journalism seemed affected by the spread of tabloid news, as coverage of the personal foibles and problems of celebrities and presidents became commonplace. The line between the splashy press and the serious journal became blurred.

Once a proprietary name for a pill or tablet, the word "tabloid" came to be almost exclusively associated with sensational journalism. Later, "tabloid" described a newspaper about half the size of most broadsheets. Tabloids popularized the news by featuring bold pictorial coverage of sex escapades, murder and gore, sports, and scandals of all sorts, but especially those relating to the lives of the rich and famous. The word tabloid also sprouted offshoot words, such as "tabloidese" for the breezy writing style of many tabloids, "tabloidesque" to connote tabloid-type publications, and "tabloidization" to mean compression of stories or literature, according to *The New Shorter Oxford English Dictionary.*

To understand the incursion of tabloids and the tabloid style into the mainstream media, it is helpful to consider three eras of journalism: the early days of the media barons, the era of young, free-spirited reporters in the anything-goes years around the "Roaring Twenties," and the electronic age when new forms of media mushroomed. Although *Vanity Fair* in its late twentieth century incarnation dubbed the 1990s the "Tabloid Decade," the last several decades of the century could be called a tabloid age when stories of murders, sex, scandal, and the once-private lives of public officials spread into every home through newspapers or the electronic media.

In the early years of U.S. journalism, power belonged to those who owned a printing press. There was no competition from radio, television, or other media in news coverage, advertising, or audience appeal. In the 1800s and early 1900s, the pulse of American journalism ticked away in New York City, where publishers found gold in what was called the "penny press," a new form of American papers that produced eye-opening stories that were long on scandal and mayhem but short on analysis or depth. Publisher Benjamin Day launched the early penny press trend with his *New York Sun* in 1833. Another New York publisher, James Gordon Bennett, followed with *The Herald* in 1835. Six years later the famed Horace Greeley edited the *Tribune* as a penny press.

But the best known promoters of mass-appeal newspapers were mogul William Randolph Hearst and his rival, Joseph Pulitzer. Hearst created an empire in New York and a dozen other cities of big-circulation newspapers, successful magazines, and a wire service (International News Service). His power extended to American foreign policy. When his headline-shouting newspapers published reports about Cuba's demands for independence from Spain, the articles helped bring on the 1898 Spanish-American War.

Hearst was in fierce combat for newspaper circulation dominance with Pulitzer, a Hungarian-born newspaperman who bought and created newspapers, including the *St. Louis Dispatch* and the *St. Louis Post,* which he formed into the *Post-Dispatch.* Later, Pulitzer entered the New York journalism wars, buying the *World* in 1883 and four years later the *Evening World.* Pulitzer and Hearst battled furiously for readers through hyped-up news accounts that gave rise to the derogatory "yellow journalism" brand. After his death, however, Pulitzer's name became associated with high journalistic standards. Through his will, he endowed Columbia University's School of Journalism and started the distinguished Pulitzer prize for news excellence. Hearst too left a legacy of newspapers, magazines, and broadcast outlets.

If Pulitzer and Hearst drove the popular press wagons, the workhorses and talent pulling them were the reporters. In the early days, they were often a rough-and-tumble bunch who had little education but shared a knack for digging up stories and dirt and spinning a good yarn. Although they were poorly paid for their efforts, some of the nation's biggest literary figures of the twentieth century, such as Ernest Hemingway, got their start in newspapering.

What they lacked in college education, many of these young reporters of the 1920s made up on the streets and in the police stations of the nation. H. L. Mencken, the great Baltimore newspaperman, writer, and all-around curmudgeon, belonged to this breed. He wrote in 1942 of his early newspaper days:

> At a time when the respectable bourgeois youngsters of my generation were college freshmen, oppressed by simian sophomores and affronted with balderdash daily and hourly by chalky pedagogues, I was at large in a

wicked seaport of half a million people with a front seat at every public show, as free of the night as of the day, and getting earfuls and eyefuls of instruction in a hundred giddy arcana, none of them taught in schools. I was laying in all the worldly wisdom of a police lieutenant, a bartender, a shyster lawyer, or a midwife. And it certainly would be idiotic to say that I was not happy. . . . Life was arduous but it was gay and carefree. The days chased one another like kittens chasing their tails.

If there was one work of literature that encapsulated this wild and woolly journalism, it was the highly celebrated play *The Front Page* about newspapering in Chicago written by two former Chicago newsmen, Ben Hecht and Charles MacArthur. Hecht, who later gained fame as a screenwriter and author, recalled his early days as a newspaperman fondly, much as Mencken did, in his 1963 book about reporting days, *Gaily Gaily.* Hecht wrote: "I came to Chicago at the age of sixteen and a half and went to work immediately as a newspaper reporter on the *Chicago Journal.* I write of the five merry years that followed. As sang Bliss Carman: Oh, but life went gaily, gaily . . . ."

The essential trait among the memorable early newsmen, whether it was Damon Runyon, who wrote humorously of the guys and dolls of the underside of life, or sports writer and columnist Ring Lardner, it was the ability to spin a good yarn. Gene Fowler, called "the last of the troubadours," was one of the best on Park Row (the Fleet Street of New York, where many newspaper offices were located) during the early era of the 1920s. A talented writer and gifted reporter, Fowler portrayed the news scene in his 1961 book of reminiscences of the 1920s:

> I still can see the incredibly fast flutter of bandit Gerald Chapman's small feet as he dies on the hangman's rope. I again can hear Queen Marie of Romania tell her lady-in-waiting 'get rid of that damned thing!' after the Dakota Indians have given Her Majesty a war bonnet. Once again I am present at Carnegie Hall as the addled Mayor Hylan makes his ghostwritten address of welcome to President Woodrow Wilson; but unthinkingly keeps his back turned to Mr. Wilson during the ceremony. I remember also the lean Irish statesman Eamon de Valera, clad in his long underwear and huge boxing gloves on his hands, as he spars with his bull-necked secretary in a sitting room at the old Waldorf.
>
> Even as I write, there unaccountably springs to mind an occasion when I asked Henry Ford about the sleep habits of his good friend [Thomas] Edison. Was it true, as legend had it, that Mr. Edison, like Napoleon, slept but four hours? Yes, said Mr. Ford, but Mr. Edison slept twice and sometimes three times a day. . . ! Little things about big men. Or, if you will, big things about little men. . . . The stories of my day are no longer big in the public attention, or else have been chewed upon until the taste is gone.

There were scores of sensational and landmark stories in those days that were covered by the serious papers as well as tabloids, although more colorfully in the latter. There was the manslaughter trial of top comic film actor Fatty Arbuckle, who was acquitted of brutally assaulting a young actress while he was at the peak of his career, his fame second only to that of Charlie Chaplin. There was Charles Lindbergh's historic transatlantic flight and the later trial of Bruno Hauptmann for the kidnap-murder of the Lindbergh baby. There were riveting accounts of murders and prohibition, the constitutional amendment giving women the right to vote, elections, the Depression, and World Wars I and II.

After World War II, journalism started maturing and opening up its pages to previously untouched stories as competition grew from radio and the new medium of television. In the prewar days, for example, few Americans knew that President Franklin Delano Roosevelt was crippled from infantile paralysis, or polio. An unwritten rule in the press was to protect Roosevelt from being shown, described, or referred to as confined to a wheelchair or wearing braces to stand briefly, assisted by crutches. It was not until after Roosevelt's death in 1945 that his true condition became universally known.

During the postwar era, most of the misdeeds of celebrities were still confined to gossipmongers and a magazine called *Confidential,* which exploited the private lives of movie stars. Few newspapers followed up with front-page stories on material *Confidential* dug up. Major exceptions included the sensational trial and subsequent acquittal of dashing Hollywood actor Errol Flynn on a charge of rape on a yacht.

Stories of large public scope, rather than scandal, dominated traditional newspapers and television news. There were the assassinations of President John Kennedy, Martin Luther King, and Senator Robert Kennedy; space travel; the Civil Rights Movement; the Vietnam War; the Watergate scandal; the resignation of President Richard Nixon. But then came scandals that forced themselves onto front pages by their very dramatic nature and the public stature of those involved, such as the accidental drowning of Mary Jo Kopechne, a young aide of Senator Edward Kennedy, after a car driven by Kennedy went off a small wooden bridge following a party on Chappaquiddick Island, Massachusetts in 1969.

The Chappaquiddick story was the first of a series of news reports about the exploits of Washington figures. The most powerful congressman at the time, House Ways and Means Committee Chairman Wilbur Mills, splashed his way onto front pages after his girlfriend, a striptease artist nicknamed "The Argentine Firecracker," jumped unexplainably into the Tidal Basin in the wee hours after the married and very private Mills and the woman had spent an argumentative evening together. Another powerful congressman, Wayne Hays, made news when it became known he had hired a woman with whom he had an intimate relationship to work in his office as a secretary, although she later admitted she couldn't take shorthand or type. The presidential ambitions of Senator Gary Hart ended after reporters learned the married candidate was socializing with a young woman. Especially damaging to Hart was a widely circulated photograph of him and the woman together on a Miami boat called "Monkey Business."

The scope of news coverage was revolutionized again when cable television began filling 24 hours a day with nonstop news, talk, and gossip. "Television tabloid" programs such as *Hard Copy* and *Inside Edition* delivered exposés and inside scoops on celebrities. The mainstream press started paying attention. *The Washington Post*, for example, promoted a new gossip column. The mainstay *New York Times* even started running short pieces on celebrities.

In the 1990s, scandals reported in mainstream media included Washington Mayor Marion Barry's conviction and sentencing on a drug possession charge after being caught on videotape smoking crack cocaine in a hotel room with a woman who was not his wife during a police raid. Tales of sex and other titillating topics started cascading. The Senate confirmed Clarence Thomas, a black jurist, as an associate justice of the Supreme Court, but not before a former aide, Anita Hill, testified she was sexually harassed by him. There was John Wayne Bobbitt, whose penis was cut off by his wife, Lorena Bobbitt, and who later became a pornographic film curiosity after his organ was surgically replaced. There was the rape trial and acquittal of Senator Edward Kennedy's nephew William Kennedy Smith. But no story to date had captured the public interest as did the nationally televised "trial of the century" in 1995 of O.J. Simpson, who was accused of stabbing his wife, Nicole, and a young man, Ron Goldman, to death. The acquittal of the former professional football hero produced emotions across the nation ranging from outrage to joy. For worldwide coverage, few stories could match the 1997 death of Britain's Princess Diana, who, along with her boyfriend and driver, was killed in an automobile crash after a high-speed chase by photographers through the streets of Paris.

The proportions of the news coverage of the O.J. Simpson case and the death of "Princess Di" were surpassed in the United States when a young woman named Monica Lewinsky arrived in Washington, D.C., and nearly brought down the President of the United States. Her story of sexual intimacy with President William Jefferson Clinton in the Oval Office while she was a White House intern and President Clinton's persistent denials resulted in the House of Representatives' impeachment of Clinton on charges of perjury and obstruction of justice. After much agonizing, the Senate, in only the second impeachment trial of a president in U.S. history, acquitted Clinton of the charges, thus keeping him in office.

The story of the Clinton presidency involved scandal even before he was elected. Voters elected him despite stories he had had an affair while Arkansas governor with a night club singer named Gennifer Flowers. That story, picked up by the mainstream media, was broken by a grocery store tabloid, the *Star,* with the bold headline "My 12-Year Affair with Bill Clinton." By coincidence, it was the same publication that brought down Dick Morris, one of Clinton's top political advisers, during the 1996 Democratic convention by breaking the story that Morris had been conducting an extramarital affair with a Washington prostitute at a hotel near the White House.

Media revelations about President Clinton's extramarital affair brought out defenders who pointed out that other presidents, going back to Thomas Jefferson and including Franklin Roosevelt and John Kennedy, had also had affairs. Pundits said future presidential candidates would routinely be queried on their sexual pasts. Where journalists once left the private lives of politicians alone, it appeared the personal problems of politicians would no longer be off the record. There appeared to be no limits to the public's appetite—already stimulated by stories of sex on daytime TV soap operas and in movies and now fed by newspapers, cable TV, and the Internet—for salaciousness and sensation. The last years of the twentieth century saw the way paved for universal coverage of the foibles of the famous, profoundly changing the tone of American politics, largely because of the irresistible dynamics of tabloid journalism.

—Michael L. Posner

FURTHER READING:

Fowler, Gene. *A Reporter's Reminiscence of the '20s.* New York, Viking Press, 1961.

Greenberg, Gerald S. *Tabloid Journalism: An Annotated Bibliography of English-Language Sources.* Westport, Connecticut, Greenwood, 1996.

Kamp, David. "The Tabloid Decade." *Vanity Fair.* Number 462. February 1999, 62-82.

Mencken H. L. *The Vintage Mencken.* Gathered by Alistair Cooke. New York, Vintage Books, 1955.

Tales from the Crypt

Tales from the Crypt was one of the most popular and notorious horror comic books of the early 1950s. Like other titles published by EC Comics, *Crypt* featured stories that explored the depravity of human nature and the hypocrisy of middle-class society. Brutality, bloodshed, and sadism were the norm in these stories, and—much to the horror of American parents—the kids loved it.

When the series became widely imitated by competing publishers, the proliferation of horror comics provoked a public backlash that led ultimately to a 1954 U.S. Senate investigation into the comic-book industry. Chastised publishers adopted a stringent Comics Code that year which prohibited the publication of horror comic books like *Crypt.*

—Bradford Wright

FURTHER READING:

Barker, Martin. *A Haunt of Fears: The Strange History of the British Horror Comics Campaign.* London, Pluto Press, 1984.

Benton, Mike. *Horror Comics.* Dallas, Taylor Publishing, 1991.

Talk Radio

Credited with shaping presidential elections and blamed for creating a climate of intolerance, talk radio rose to prominence in the 1990s by offering Americans a free, unfiltered, and often national forum. Whether the issue was a pushy boss, a hapless sports team, or a downtown-parking crunch, talk radio became a sort of water-cooler for the masses. The rise also reflected the increasingly combative nature of American discourse, with on-air arguments, taunts, and racy, satiric routines often the key to a talk show's success. As ratings increased, so did the critics who believed that the radio hosts were, in part, to blame for the increasingly hostile environment that led to a series of high-profile incidents, including the terrorist bombing in Oklahoma City. Leading talk show hosts Howard Stern, G. Gordon Liddy, and Don Imus were branded "shock jocks" for their brash, obnoxious, and often controversial points of view. As Howard Kurtz notes in *Hot Air,* "When White House chief of staff Leon Panetta wanted to attack Newt Gingrich, the strongest insult he could muster was to accuse the House speaker of acting like 'an out-of-control radio talk show host.'" But whether agitator or great equalizer, talk radio offers anyone with a telephone a chance to become part of the national debate. And its influence can be felt off the dial as well, as radio jocks write best-selling books, star in films, and are spoofed on the television sketch comedy show, *Saturday Night Live.*

The emergence of talk radio came about because of technological advances as much as the need for an open forum. Commercial

Don Imus

radio had existed since the 1920s, but the toll free telephone lines and satellite hook-ups that encouraged the spread of the format were not in place for another 60 years.

In the early days of radio, before television, the best known voices were comedians making the jump from the vaudeville stage, old-style newsmen, and sportscasters. The first true talk radio host may have been celebrity interviewer Barry Gray, who began broadcasting out of New York City in the mid-1940s. But Gray's show was without one key element: the caller. Jerry Williams, who went on the air in Boston in 1957, became the first to take calls. He used two tape recorders to comply with the federal regulations requiring delays.

In addition to technical limitations, talk radio was held back by a 1949 law, the Fairness Doctrine, which required equal time for opposing views. The change began in the late 1950s when machinery made the seven second delay possible, enabling hosts to put callers on the air without fear. Talk radio received a similar boost in the 1980s with the spread of satellite and digital phone technologies, which made toll free numbers more affordable for station managers. Emboldened by the fact that these calls were being made not only to a radio station, but also in many cases a radio station in another time zone, callers embraced this new forum. They could yell at another human and risk nothing more than being cut off by the host. In addition, Ronald Reagan abolished the Fairness Doctrine in 1987.

Talk radio spread from 75 stations nationwide in 1980, to 125 by 1987, and 1,350 by 1998.

From the start, talk radio proved a strong voice for political protest. Jerry Williams brought consumer advocate Ralph Nader onto the air to criticize automobile makers in the 1960s. Twenty years later, Williams led a repeal of a law requiring the mandatory use of seat belts in Massachusetts. In 1988, Congress wanted to vote itself a 51 percent pay raise. A nationwide network of talk show hosts, led by Detroit's Roy Fox, suggested listeners send tea bags to Washington, D.C., to show their displeasure. More than 150,000 tea bags were dumped in front of the White House; Congress withdrew the pay raise. A decade later, lawmakers had not forgotten. A survey of members of Congress revealed that 46 percent of them found talk radio the most influential media source during the health care debate; 15 percent cited the *New York Times.*

As talk radio gained stature, so did the voices behind it. In many cases, these were failed disc jockeys who had tried, in vain, to fit into the more conventional music format. Larry King was a broadcasting veteran who first went on the air in 1960 in Miami, Florida, struggled later with a gambling problem and three bad marriages, and was eventually arrested for misusing $5,000 from a business associate. In 1978, King got what just about everyone in radio gets: a second chance. From the 12th Floor Studio in Crystal City, Virginia, he launched the first nationally broadcast radio show, talking from midnight to 5:30 a.m. The success of his show proved that national talk shows could make it. King eventually left radio for his nightly interview television talk show on the Cable News Network and launched a regular column in the *USA Today,* laying the foundation for the rise of the talk star.

Rush Limbaugh, a college dropout who had failed repeatedly as a rock 'n' roll disc jockey, launched his talk show in the mid-1980s, immediately establishing himself as a conservative voice; his show went national in 1988. No matter that Limbaugh had not registered to vote for several presidential elections; he was courted by then-President George Bush as the 1992 elections approached. Seeking his on-air support, Bush invited Limbaugh to the White House and even carried the talk show host's bags. Limbaugh's influence was considered so widespread that an effort by Congress to bring back the Fairness Doctrine in the 1990s was quickly dubbed the "hush-Rush" bill by the *Wall Street Journal.*

Limbaugh's success provided ample fodder to talk radio's critics. A Times Mirror poll showed Limbaugh's audience to be 92 percent white and 56 percent male. And his on-air mistakes created a strong anti-Rush backlash. The *Flush Rush Quarterly* spurred much of it, reporting Limbaugh's errors. On the Reagan-era Iran Contra scandal, for example, Limbaugh stated: "There is not one indictment. There is not one charge." In reality, there had been 14 people indicted and 11 who had either pleaded guilty or been convicted.

Limbaugh's histrionics were mild compared to those of the freewheeling Howard Stern, the self-proclaimed "moron" of talk radio. Stern made no secret of his distaste for his profession. "Radio is a scuzzy, bastard industry that's filled with deviants, circus clown rejects, the lowest of the low," he said.

Off the air, Stern was the dedicated family man who did not go to parties and spent most of his time with his college sweetheart turned wife, Alison. On the air, he discussed his sexual fantasies, argued with his staff, belched, and complained about the size of his penis. Unlike many other talk shows, Stern attacked celebrity culture instead of celebrating it. He called Oprah Winfrey "a big dolt with an empty, oversized head" and Roseanne "a fat slob." He also promoted a

series of B-level figures, from Jessica Hahn, known for her affair with television preacher Jim Bakker, to Frank Stallone Jr., the less-famous brother of Sylvester. Stern's reporter, Stuttering John, carried out further attacks on celebrity culture. Disarmed by the stutter, expecting another *Entertainment Tonight*-styled softball interview, celebrities were shocked when confronted by John's questions. When Gennifer Flowers held a press conference to address her affair with then-Presidential candidate Bill Clinton, Stuttering John stole the show from the pack of mainstream reporters. "Gennifer," he asked, "did Governor Clinton use a condom?"

Stern also drew the wrath of the Federal Communications Commission (FCC), receiving 21 of 44 fines levied. When Alfred Sikes, chairman of the FCC, fined Stern's employer, Infinity, $1.7 million for allegedly broadcasting obscenities, the radio host responded, on the air, by hoping that Sikes would develop cancer.

If Stern and Limbaugh were considered too controversial by many, Don Imus found a proper balance between shock radio and serious discourse. A radio star whose first career collapsed in the 1970s due to his addiction to cocaine and alcohol, Imus returned to the national airwaves in 1988. His morning show was a mix of news, racy skits, and spoof songs. Imus found himself in line with the media elite, interviewing President Clinton at one point and regularly hosting serious news veterans like Cokie Roberts, Dan Rather, and Tim Russert. He also appeared on the David Brinkley show.

It is this range—from the serious to the frivolous—that talk radio proponents say makes the medium more powerful than the generally entertainment focussed programming on television talk shows. *Talkers* magazine reports that the top five issues on talk radio between 1990 to 1995 were the O.J. Simpson case, the 1992 elections, the Persian Gulf War, the Oklahoma City Bombing, and the Los Angeles riots. But lest it be taken too seriously, *Talkers* also rated discussion of John Wayne Bobbitt, the man whose penis was surgically reattached after it had been cut off by his wife, higher than debates on Bosnia and gays in the military.

For those more interested in serious-minded talk, National Public Radio (NPR) emerged a decade before Limbaugh, Stern, and Imus. Known for lengthy reports and the breathy but understated delivery of its hosts, NPR's style is so distinctive it has also been spoofed on *Saturday Night Live.* NPR made its debut on May 3, 1971 with its first broadcast of *All Things Considered.* That first broadcast reached a few hundred thousand listeners through only 104 public radio stations. Twenty five years later, *All Things Considered* would reach 16 million Americans through NPR's 520 member stations, all the while holding faithful to the wishes of its first director, Bill Siemering, who wanted "calm conversation, analysis and explication."

By the late 1990s, NPR had long established itself as a dependable voice, but the influence of hot talkers like Limbaugh and Stern was still being debated. Limbaugh took credit for the Republican victories during the 1994 Congressional elections and made the cover of *Time* magazine, the headline posed: "Is Rush Limbaugh Good For America?" But by the end of 1996, Clinton had won a second term and the conservative movement was floundering.

Nobody debated whether talk radio would survive. It had made stars of big mouths (Stern, Imus), political impresarios (Limbaugh, G. Gordon Liddy), shrinks and sex therapists (Dr. Laura Schlesinger, Dr. Judy Kuriansky), and even discarded politicians (former New York Governor Mario Cuomo, former New York City mayor Ed Koch).

Whether we liked it or not, we had become, as Howard Kurtz wrote, ''a talk show nation.''

—Geoff Edgers

FURTHER READING:

Colford, Paul D. *The Rush Limbaugh Story: Talent On Loan From God.* New York, St. Martin's Press, 1993.

Fowler, Gene, and Bill Crawford, with a foreword by Wolfman Jack. *Border Radio: Quacks, Yodelers, Pitchmen, Psychics and Other Amazing Broadcasters of the American Airwaves.* Austin, Texas Monthly Press, 1987.

Kurtz, Howard. *Hot Air: All Talk All the Time.* New York, Random House, 1996.

Stern, Howard. *Private Parts.* New York, Simon & Schuster, 1993.

Werthheimer, Linda. *Listening to America: Twenty-five Years in the Life of a Nation as Heard on National Public Radio.* New York, Houghton Mifflin Company, 1995.

Talking Heads

From their earliest days, Talking Heads were a band that defied categorization. Playing in New York during the height of the mid-1970s punk scene, Talking Heads were a preppy-looking trio that became a punk band by association. Despite being musically different, Talking Heads' minimalist sound, their musical combination of energy and intelligence, and their self-conscious and unpretentious demeanor connected them to punk. Some critics tried using the term ''Art Rock'' to describe the band's intellectual approach to their music, but the term fell short: Talking Heads were cerebral, but they were also eminently danceable, too. Like the characters in their songs, Talking Heads' music dramatized the human predicament of the duel between head and heart.

David Byrne (vocals and guitar), Tina Weymouth (bass), and Chris Frantz (drums) began as a trio in 1975, after dropping out of the Rhode Island School of Design and relocating to New York. Their first single, ''Love Goes to a Building on Fire,'' was released in early 1977 and displayed the band's spare technique. That same year, the band signed to Sire Records, an independent label whose roster included the Ramones, and released *Talking Heads '77.* The album added keyboardist Jerry Harrison, a former graduate student at Harvard. Their debut appeared to often ecstatic reviews. The lyrics to ''Don't Worry About the Government'' celebrated civil servants and life's more mundane qualities: ''My building has every convenience/ It's going to make life easy for me.'' The song's simplicity was almost shocking in its honesty. Hardly a tentative songwriter, Byrne was also capable of writing tense music in ''No Compassion'' and ''Psycho Killer.'' The latter song, although not a hit single, brought the group widespread attention for the song's psychodrama: ''I can't sleep 'cos my bed's on fire/Don't touch me I'm a real live wire.'' The notoriety of ''Psycho Killer'' was fueled even further by Byrne's physical resemblance to actor Anthony Perkins, who played Norman Bates in Alfred Hitchcock's *Psycho.*

The group's 1978 release, *More Songs About Buildings and Food,* began a long collaboration with producer Brian Eno, who essentially became a fifth member of the group. The album produced a Top-40 hit, a cover of soul singer Al Green's ''Take Me to the

River.'' The modest hit provided a glimpse into the band's future commercial successes, as well as their developing forays into dance, funk, and international rhythms. ''Take Me to the River'' also vindicated the band's commercial philosophy: ''It wouldn't please us to make music that's impossible to listen to,'' said Byrne in *Rolling Stone,* ''but we don't want to compromise for the sake of popularity. It's possible to make exciting, respectable stuff that can succeed in the marketplace.''

The opening track on 1979's Fear of Music, ''I Zimbra,'' had polyrhythmic arrangements that announced the group's new musical direction. Not everyone was paying attention. ''Life During Wartime,'' one of the group's best-known songs, contained the line, ''This ain't no disco,'' and some mistakenly thought that Talking Heads were the new standard-bearers for the anti-disco movement. The irony around ''Life During Wartime'' was all too real. Around the time that Talking Heads began incorporating international rhythms, rock critic Ken Tucker wrote that ''seldom in pop music history has there been a larger gap between what black and white audiences are listening to than there is right now.'' *Remain in Light,* which was released in 1980, was the realization of the polyrhythmic experiment in ''I Zimbra.'' Augmented by a host of outside musicians, *Remain in Light* had the feeling of a free-flowing jam session at first, but it was tightly structured and disciplined. The album displayed funk and African influences when many whites took the phrase ''Black music'' to describe several distinct musical forms, like disco, funk, soul, and rhythm and blues.

The next year found the band pursuing solo projects that continued the group's musical blends. Weymouth and Frantz's side project, *The Tom Tom Club,* contained a merger of new wave with dance music, and also rap. The self-titled album included ''Genius of Love,'' a song whose rhythm was used by several R & B and rap artists of the 1990s. Byrne completed a score for *The Catherine Wheel,* a dance performance by Twyla Tharp that proceeded with *Remain in Light*'s sound. In 1985, Byrne's next project was for an experimental theater piece called *Music for the Knee Plays,* which employed traditional New Orleans brass band struts and funeral marches. Byrne's skill in working with other musical forms was hitting its stride.

The band's first album in three years was 1983's *Speaking in Tongues.* Eno was no longer sharing production chores, and the band shed many of its guest musicians. Talking Heads had a hit with ''Burning Down the House'' and reached the peak of their popularity with the 1984 film, *Stop Making Sense.* Directed by Jonathan Demme, the film documented the Talking Heads' 1983 tour, and won the National Society of Film Critics Award for Best Documentary. The group recorded three more albums before they unofficially broke up in 1988. In 1996, at the peak of alternative music's popularity, the group decided to reform without Byrne, as the Heads, and recorded *No Talking Just Head.* Byrne sued his former bandmates and asked for an injunction against the album's release. Then, shortly before the album's release date, a settlement was reached and the album was released to generally abysmal reviews.

Talking Heads expanded the musical borders of American popular music. By the late 1980s, international musical styles were being adopted by mainstream artists, like Peter Gabriel and Paul Simon. What the mainstream considered to be acceptable was broadening. In another sense, Talking Heads extended personal musical borders as much as they were intent on stretching national ones. Ken Tucker, in his review of *Remain in Light,* summed up the climate in which the group was attempting to bridge musical gaps: ''By 1978, punk and disco had divided the pop audience. What did Talking Heads do? They recorded Al Green's 'Take Me to the River.' The gesture was a heroic one.''

—Daryl Umberger

FURTHER READING:

Davis, Jerome. *Talking Heads.* New York, Vintage/Musician, 1986.

Gans, David. *Talking Heads.* New York, Avon, 1985.

Reese, Krista. *The Name of This Book Is Talking Heads.* London, Proteus Books, 1982.

Tucker, Ken. "Africa Calling." *Rolling Stone.* December 11, 1980, 55.

Tang

Tang instant beverage entered American popular culture in the 1960s with a remarkable journey to outer space. The vitamin-fortified drink was first marketed in the late 1950s as a healthy alternative to soda pop. After being chosen by the National Aeronautic and Space Administration (NASA) to be the drink of the astronauts, Tang flew on several flights in the 1960s and soon became a drink of choice for children hoping to emulate the feats of the astronauts. Despite the introduction of new flavors in addition to the classic orange, Tang's popularity diminished in the 1980s and 1990s along with America's excitement over the space program.

—Angela O'Neal

FURTHER READING:

Holland, Gini. *The 1960's.* New York, Lucent Books, 1999.

Varnum, Allan H., and Jane P. Setherland. *Beverages: Technology, Chemistry and Biology.* London, Chapman Hall, 1994.

Tanning

In the late nineteenth century, high fashion dictated the maintenance of alabaster skin. Creamy white skin signified a person of privileged status, not an unfortunate sun-darkened field laborer. But as the industrial age dawned and laborers increasingly spent long hours in factories and the coal haze above city streets blocked the sun from reaching their tenement windows, the professional-managerial class, with its increased leisure time, embraced a culture of outdoor living. Furthermore, the consumer culture that emerged along with the products of the industrial age prompted a cultural shift toward an emphasis on appearance. Advertising, motion pictures, and the popular press inundated people with images of the body: images that emphasized the display of hedonism, leisure, and sexuality. A tan soon became a status symbol.

Fashion proved the greatest influence on the popularity of the suntan. Many learned about fashion through film; in the early 1920s Bela Balàzs had noticed that film was a major influence in the cultural shift away from "words" and toward "visual images" that "drew attention to the appearance of the body, the clothing, demeanour, and

A sunbather gets a tan in the Florida sun.

gesture," according to Mike Featherstone in *Theory Culture and Society.* Douglas Fairbanks Sr. was among the first to popularize the suntan. In his films and publicity shots in the popular press his bronzed skin became an emblem of his vigorous pursuit of outdoor activities. While other male celebrities quickly followed his lead, women, even Douglas' wife Mary Pickford, preserved their light skin. Europe continued to dictate fashion at this time, so when fashion designer Coco Chanel returned from vacation with a deep bronze tan and began using tanned mannequins for her designs in the 1920s, tanning transformed into a cultural obsession in and of itself. Consequently, the deep cut backs of women's dresses in the 1920s and 1930s required tanned skin for the wearer to be appropriately fashionable. The more revealing fashions became adornments for bronzed skin, and by 1946, women could tan their skin publicly in as little as a bikini.

The new sun worship prompted by fashion had support from science, which had begun to report the healthful benefits of sunshine at the turn of the century. Previous warnings about the sun's harmful effects on the skin gave way to new research that had proven the sun's healing qualities on diseases like rickets and tuberculosis in the late 1800s. Articles announcing the healing benefits of heliotherapy and tanned skin proliferated. An antebellum health advisor, William A. Alcott, promoted the idea that "Not a few individuals would be gainers in point of health, especially children and females, by being slightly tanned over their surface." Dr. Edwin E. Slosson reported in *Daily Science News Bulletin* in 1923 that, instead of being harmful, "It seems that ultra-violet and violet rays may be positively beneficial," according to *Literary Digest,* which featured a photo of babies at the beach with the caption: "Nothing is better for babies—or grown people either—than a good coat of tan, we have it on high scientific authority." And by 1929, an American article proclaimed that "the skin of a healthy man is brown, smooth, and sleek," according to Featherstone.

During the warm months, interest in sunbathing on beaches began in the interwar years and continued unabated into the early 1980s. But while many could sunbathe during the summer, only the well-off could afford the cost of air travel, which allowed them to spend winters in sunny locations. There were few status symbols as obvious as tanned skin during the winter. *Newsweek* reported in 1966 that in the "jet age" the tan had become a status symbol that could "be worn like Brooks Brothers clothes as a sure sign of affluence." Tanned skin became synonymous with health, wealth, leisure, and style.

"Nothing is as transient, useless, or completely desirable as a suntan," a pre-feminist Gloria Steinem wrote in *The Beach Book* in 1963, adding "What a tan will do is make you look good, and that justifies anything." Steinem perfectly captured the kind of zeal that fueled many hours of sunbathing. The desire for tanned skin prompted formulas for obtaining the perfect tan to abound. People coated themselves in baby oil and red iodine believing this mixture would turn their skins a fashionable caramel brown color. Some smoothed on a purple peroxide foam which promised to speed the tanning time and bleach the body hair to enhance the depth of the tan's color by contrast. Others restricted their diets before tanning, eating vitamins and avoiding wine and spicy foods, to increase their chances of getting a coppery glow. Some even rubbed their skin with salt to tan faster. The truly fanatical sun worshipers lay inside aluminum coffins or ringed their necks with sun reflectors to ensure themselves an even tan. The proliferation of tanning salons and tanning booths promised people of every class access to a year-round tan by the late 1970s. (Indoor tanning became one of the fastest growing industries in North America, increasing 54 percent between 1986 and 1988, according to *U.S. News and World Report.*) People willingly sought out these seemingly ridiculous activities because, according to *Newsweek,* "only the result counts." An episode of the sitcom *Seinfeld* highlighted the folly of these tanning strategies when the character Kramer coats himself in butter as he basks in the sun, only to appear and smell like a well-roasted turkey to his hungry friend, Newman.

Any number of brands sought to capitalize on the craze for suntanned skin. The first branded suntan cream available in America was a Coppertone brand cream made mostly of cocoa butter that was introduced in 1944. By 1945 Coppertone Suntan Oil was advertised with an "Indian Head seal" and the slogan "Don't Be a Paleface." But Coppertone's most enduring image—"Little Miss Coppertone"—debuted on Miami-areas billboards in 1953. The illustration of the tanned young girl whose dog is pulling down her panties to display her white-skinned bare bottom soon graced billboards, advertisements, and product labels across the country. The little girl came to represent the youthfulness associated with tanned skin. If Little Miss Coppertone represented the youthfulness of tanned skin, Ban de Soliel Orange Gelée advertisements captured the sexual appeal of the suntan. The 1970s and 1980s advertisements for the Bain de Soliel brand using the sultry and darkly tanned model, Kriss Ziemer, epitomized the glamour many hoped a tan would confer.

While the hazardous effects of a sunburn and the detrimental effects of sun bathing on fair-skinned people had long been known, worries about tanning began to reach a wider audience by the 1970s as the incidence of skin cancer had begun to rise noticeably. Between 1930 and 1986 the Skin Cancer Foundation of the American Cancer

Society figured that the incidence of melanoma had risen tenfold, from one in every 1,500 people to one in every 150. Research into the ill effects of sun bathing resulted in the proliferation of products to protect the skin from burning. The Coppertone Solar Research Center created and initiated the use of SPF factors—a standardized measurement of a sunscreen's ability to protect the skin and prevent sunburn—in sun lotions in 1972, but SPF numbers (2, 4, 6, 8) did not appear on product labels until 1977. And not until 1980 did the Skin Care Foundation grant Coppertone Supershade 15 an acceptance seal as an "effective aid in the prevention of sun-induced skin cancer." When research in the 1980s revealed that most exposure to the sun occurs during childhood, Little Miss Coppertone began to promote sun protection over tanned skin for children. The first offering of SPF 30 formulas appeared in 1993, and by 1998, Coppertone had joined with the American Academy of Dermatology to promote the use of sun-blocks in the "Stop the Sun, Not the Fun" campaign, the first in-school sun safety program. By 1994, Little Miss Coppertone could be seen with a hat, sunglasses, and T-shirt, when she was used to help promote the new UV Index.

The scientific authority of the 1990s condemned tanning. Doctor Darrel Rigel, professor of dermatology at New York University, Manhattan, told *FDA Consumer Magazine* contributor Alexandra Greeley that "There is no such thing as a safe tan. Why does the body tan? Because the body is being injured by ultraviolet radiation that hits it. This causes the body to make melanin, a natural sun screen. So to get tan, you must get injured first." The American Cancer Society reported that by the late 1990s the incidence of malignant melanoma had risen to one in 75 and predicted that 44,200 people would be diagnosed with the disease in 1999, of which 9,200 would die, according to Gandee. The scientific community has linked the rise in the number of affluent young people afflicted with melanoma to air travel. Dermatologist Patricia Wexler told Gandee that the melanoma rate is higher in younger generations "because our parents didn't go to the Delano or the Hamptons or St. Bart's."

Despite the overwhelming evidence of the negative effects of the suntan, tanning products companies continued to promote the benefits of a tan. The Bain de Soliel brand began to use lightly tanned women in its ads, but continued to promote products to help obtain deeply bronzed skin into the 1990s, as did many other brands. One significant change in the promotion of tanning products was the residual rhetoric about how "healthy" tanned skin looks. A 1999 radio ad for the Go Bronze sunless tanning lotion sold at the Bon Marché department store, for example, featured a woman saying that she wanted tan, healthy looking skin too.

Sunless tanning products could offer the "look" without the damage. Sunless tanning products that turned the skin a realistic tan color made the sunless tanning market more viable in the 1990s than it had been when the first sunless tanning products were introduced in 1960. These first products, including Schering-Plough Healthcare Products' Quick Tanning lotion, the first sunless tanning lotion, offered an orange-ish tan color that was easily identified as fake. Some fashion magazines, like *Vogue,* furthered the interest in sunless tanning lotions by presenting articles about the harmful effects of the sun in the same issue that featured photos of bathing suit clad models covered in sunless tanning lotions frolicking on a sun-drenched beach.

Though by the late 1990s some continued to mimic the looks of actor George Hamilton, who *Newsweek* dubbed the "Sultan of Suntan" for the year-round tan he has maintained for three decades, there had been a steady increase in the numbers of people who Coppertone identified as "sun concerned"—a category based on sales of products with an SPF number of 8 and over—since the early 1980s. A 1994 survey by the American Academy of Dermatology reported that one third of the respondents never sunbathe and always use a sun screen, according to Greeley. And dermatologist Dennis Gross indicated that in assessing his patients from the mid- to late 1990s, ''the number of women who consider a tan desirable has gone from the majority to the minority,'' according to Gandee. Aside from the medical reasons to curb suntanning, the sexual appeal of pale skin was beginning to gain followers with the admirers of public figures, including Gwyneth Paltrow, Nicole Kidman, and Uma Thurman. In addition, fashion magazines like *Elle* began to feature paler models for spring and summer issues. Future historians may well look back on the fashionable suntan as an oddity of the twentieth century.

—Sara Pendergast

FURTHER READING:

Adler, Jerry, with Mariana Gosnell, Karen Springen, and Nikki Finke Greenberg.

''The Advantage of Tan.'' *Literary Digest.* September 22, 1923, 27-8.

Alcott, William A. *The Home-Book of Life and Health; or, the Laws and Means of Physical Culture Adapted to Practical Use.* Boston, 1858, 229-30.

''Brown as a . . . '' *Newsweek.* August 1, 1966, 58-9.

''The Dark Side of the Sun.'' *Newsweek.* June 9, 1986, 60-4.

Featherstone, Mike. ''The Body in Consumer Culture.'' *Theory Culture and Society.* 1.2, 1982, 18-33.

Gandee, Charles. ''Safety in Numbers.'' *Vogue.* May 1999, 310-13, 339.

Greeley, Alexandra. ''Dodging the Rays.'' Rockville, Maryland, Department of Health and Human Services, Public Health Service, Food and Drug Administration, 1994; reprint from *FDA Consumer,* 1993.

Harris, Marvin. ''The Rites of Summer: History of the Sun Tan.'' *Natural History.* August 1973, 20-2.

Levine, Art. ''A New Bronze Age for the Tanning Industry: Indoor Tanning Salons Take on Their Critics.'' *U.S. News and World Report.* September 8, 1997, 48.

Steinem, Gloria. *The Beach Book.* New York, Viking, 1963.

Sweet, Cheryl A. '''Healthy Tan'—A Fast-Fading Myth.'' Rockville, Maryland, Department of Health and Human Services, Public Health Service, Food and Drug Administration, 1990.

Tap Dancing

An indigenous American dance form that evolved as African and British dance traditions merged during the eighteenth and nineteenth centuries, tap dancing involves the production of syncopated sounds by the dancer's feet. Tap dancing has been a mainstay of virtually every type of popular performing-arts entertainment in the United States, from minstrel shows to vaudeville, revues, extravaganzas, Broadway and Hollywood musicals, nightclubs, precision dance teams, and television variety programs. A remarkably adaptive dance form, tap has fused with and reflected the changing entertainment sensibilities of American audiences for almost 200 years. Tap routines figure prominently in children's dance recitals, as dance instruction is a popular enrichment activity for youngsters and many are too young for, or uninterested in, the serious discipline of ballet. Adult amateurs also find tap dancing a fun form of recreation and exercise.

Though some trace the roots of tap back to the ships that transported enslaved Africans to America (as the Africans' dancing was observed by the Europeans, and vice versa) the significant merging of the two dance traditions began on southern plantations. When a mid-eighteenth century law forbade slaves from playing drums, they increased the use of their feet to embody rhythms in their dancing. Their observations of the articulated foot actions of Irish step dancing and other European dances practiced by their masters engendered a new hybrid dance form in which the Africans combined fancy footwork with their sophisticated rhythmic sensibilities. Oftentimes they were put into contests by their masters and won prizes for the most daring or complex dancing. This inspired individual creativity and competition, characteristics that continued to drive the development of tap dancing well into the twentieth century.

In the minstrel shows, the most popular form of American entertainment during the mid-nineteenth century, tap dancing became a codified stage dance form. Its most esteemed practitioner was William Henry Lane, known as Master Juba, a free African American who was one of the only blacks to be allowed to perform onstage with whites. The new social dances that sprang up around the turn of the twentieth century were incorporated into the developing tap dance vocabulary. By 1910 the use of metal plates attached to the bottoms of the shoes' heels and toes became commonplace; previously, the dancers wore wooden-soled shoes or pounded nails or pennies into leather soles.

Vaudeville became the next important breeding ground for the advancement of tap dancing. Striving to earn a living in a business that depended on continuously pleasing and surprising audiences, tap dancers were constantly inventing more impressive maneuvers. Different categories of tap dancers evolved: eccentric dancers, such as Ray Bolger, sported a loose, rubbery movement style; comedy dancers, such as Bert Williams and George Walker, were duos who danced as foils to one another; flash acts, such as the Nicholas Brothers, added spectacular acrobatic tricks to their tapping; class acts, such as Charles ''Honi'' Coles, were elegant in their costuming and movements; and the rhythm- or jazz-tappers, such as John W. Bubbles, explored the complicated rhythms of jazz music.

By the 1930s tap dancing chorus lines had become a prominent feature of Broadway and Hollywood musicals. While such stars as Fred Astaire, Gene Kelly, Ann Miller, Eleanor Powell, Shirley Temple, and Bill ''Bojangles'' Robinson advanced the popularity and artistry of tap dancing, the ensembles stunted tap's artistic growth. The art of tap dancing lies in the subtle nuances and complex rhythmic interchanges between the beat, the music, and the tapping sounds. When executed by large groups, the sounds must be simple, otherwise multiplication breeds muddiness. Precision teams, such as the Rockettes, have solidified tap dancing's place in American popular entertainment, but have frozen it, artistically. It was at the Hoofers Club in Harlem that the art of tap flourished as the great jazz-tappers held improvisational ''challenge'' contests and pushed each other to further develop their skills.

During the 1950s and 1960s tap ''hibernated'' as its performance outlets vanished. The Hoofers Club had closed and jazz-tappers found that the crowded rhythms of be-bop, the new form of jazz music, left no space for tap sounds. Rock 'n' roll was too loud for tapping. The age of movie musicals was ending, nightclubs turned to comedy and music acts, ballet had overtaken Broadway, and vaudeville had long since died.

The tap revival began when a group of old-time hoofers appeared at the Newport Jazz Festival in the early 1960s and intrigued the public with their artistry. In 1968 a series of ''Tap Happenings,'' held in Manhattan, provided opportunities for audiences to witness the legendary jazz-tappers. By the 1970s the rhythmic explorations of these early hoofers were recognized as an integral part of the development of jazz music. Their work, and tap dancing in general, began to be viewed with serious eyes.

The 1970s was a nostalgic decade on Broadway and re-introduced tap dancing in new musicals, such as *No, No, Nanette* (1971) and *Bubbling Brown Sugar* (1976). The release, in 1974, of Metro Goldwyn Mayer's *That's Entertainment!* re-acquainted audiences with the tap dance stars of old Hollywood musicals. New tap dance stars soon emerged and put a contemporary urban face on tapping. Gregory Hines appeared in the Broadway musicals *Sophisticated Ladies* (1983) and *Jelly's Last Jam* (1991), and in the film *Tap* he pioneered an electronic form of tapping, originally engineered by Al Desio, whereby the dancer makes music through electronic transmitters built into the tap shoes. Savion Glover fused tap with hip-hop sensibilities and wowed audiences with his fierce, heavy-footed style in the Broadway revue *Bring in 'da Noise, Bring in 'da Funk* (1996). In 1989 Congress declared National Tap Dance Day to be celebrated annually on May 25, Robinson's birthday.

Though many dancers of the 1990s approach tap as art, it is not commonly perceived as serious dance. Tap dancing has been called America's folk dance and, as such, will probably always be most appreciated for the joy it gives to its participants—both professional and amateur—and to spectators of popular entertainment.

—Lisa Jo Sagolla

FURTHER READING:

Ames, Jerry, and Jim Siegelman. *The Book of Tap: Recovering America's Long Lost Dance.* New York, David McKay Company, Inc., 1977.

Frank, Rusty E. *Tap! The Greatest Tap Dance Stars and Their Stories, 1900-1955.* New York, Da Capo Press, 1990.

Stearns, Marshall, and Jean Stearns. *Jazz Dance: The Story of American Vernacular Dance.* New York, Schirmer Books, 1968.

Tarantino, Quentin (1963—)

Best known for writing and directing the Oscar winning film *Pulp Fiction* (1994), Quentin Tarantino is one of the most critically lauded film directors of the 1990s. In *Reservoir Dogs* (1992) he redefined the primary elements of the pulp genre—murder, drugs, sex, violence, and betrayal—by introducing self-consciously witty dialogue, formal inventiveness, and slick yet casual violence. As a result he raised what had been traditionally judged as a B movie genre to an avant-garde art form. His style has become like a brand name in the film industry. Celebrating popular culture and capitalizing on the political correctness backlash of the 1990s, Tarantino's audiences are served a hearty dose of shallowness, ease, and familiarity combined

with as much violence and sex as an R rating can indulge. In addition to writing and directing he also acts, produces, and distributes films.

—Adrienne Russell

Tarbell, Ida (1957-1944)

One of *McClure's* muckrakers, Ida Tarbell changed the oil business in America. A female journalist was not common at the turn of the twentieth century, especially not one who muckraked or scandalized industry. From *McClure's* excerpts, Tarbell published the two volume *History of Standard Oil* in 1904. In it she revealed the many unfair business practices of Standard Oil and owner John Rockefeller. Tarbell became a whistleblower on the most powerful trust in America. She earned the name the Joan of Arc of the oil region. The government broke up the Standard Oil Company in 1911.

Ida Tarbell was born in Titusville, Pennsylvania, to an oil baron father, Franklin Tarbell. Ida, the only female freshmen, attended Allegheny College and gained a degree in biology in 1880, and joined the staff at *McClure's* magazine with muckrakers Ray Stannard Baker and Lincoln Steffens. Her inquiry into Rockefeller was not all from professional interest; her father invented wooden barrels to hold oil and attained great wealth, but nearly went bankrupt when he failed to sell his business to John Rockefeller. His ultimate victory, however, would come when *The History of Standard Oil* and its revelations led to the break up of the largest corporation in America.

Ida Tarbell was also a historian. Her first major publication in 1895 was on Napoleon and Josephine Bonaparte. She wrote eight books on Abraham Lincoln, his relatives, and his family. In fact, until the release of Abraham Lincoln's Papers in 1947 she was considered the measure of Lincoln history. Ida Tarbell made her mark in an era when women journalists were often not taken seriously.

—Scott Stabler

FURTHER READING:

Brady, Kathleen. *Ida Tarbell: Portrait of a Muckraker.* New York, Seaview/Putnam, 1984.

Tarbell, Ida. *The History of the Standard Oil Company.* New York, McClure, Phillips and Co., 1904.

Tarkanian, Jerry (1930—)

Jerry Tarkanian—ever so appropriately nicknamed ''Tark the Shark''—is both one of the most talented and controversial college basketball coaches in the history of the sport. His nineteen-year tenure at the University of Nevada-Las Vegas began in 1973, and was highlighted by a quartet of appearances in the Final Four, a national championship in 1990, and an overall record of 509-105. Nonetheless, throughout his UNLV career, Tarkanian constantly was in conflict with the National Collegiate Athletic Association, the governing body of college sports. In the late 1970s, the NCAA placed the Runnin' Rebels' hoops program on two years' probation for recruiting violations. The school was directed to suspend its coach—an action that Tarkanian blocked with a court order. He also sued the NCAA, albeit unsuccessfully—although the case went all the way to the Supreme Court. And yet another clash between Tark and the NCAA ended up in the Supreme Court, in which the justices rejected the coach's attempt to resurrect a Nevada state law that had shielded Tarkanian and his UNLV associates, who had been charged with breaching NCAA regulations.

Two years after UNLV won the national championship in 1990, the NCAA commenced another major investigation of Tarkanian. This time, the coach resigned under pressure—and yet again sued the NCAA, accusing the organization of trying to run him out of college basketball. The suit was settled in 1998, just before it was set to go to trial. While admitting no liability, the NCAA paid Tarkanian $2.5 million. ''They can never, ever, make up for all the pain and agony they caused me,'' Tarkanian observed. ''All I can say is that for 25 years they beat the hell out of me.'' Tarkanian eventually signed on as the basketball coach of Fresno State, from which he had graduated in 1955. However, the conflict surrounding him did not subside. In 1997, controversy again swirled on campus when it was revealed that the Bulldogs had recruited a convicted wife abuser, and two of his players were accused of assaulting their girlfriends. The following year, two players were jailed on charges of grand theft and assault with a deadly weapon. Nonetheless, Jerry Tarkanian remains a seminal figure in the sport of college basketball, where his unconventional style combined with his phenomenal success, have left a deep and lasting impact on the game.

—Rob Edelman

FURTHER READING:

Harp, Richard, and Joseph McCullough. *Tarkanian: Countdown of a Rebel.* New York, Leisure Press, 1984.

Valenti, John, with Ron Naclerio. *Swee'pea and Other Playground Legends: Tales of Drugs, Violence, and Basketball.* New York, M. Kesend, 1990.

Yaeger, Don. *Shark Attack: Jerry Tarkanian and His Battle With the NCAA and UNLV.* New York, HarperCollins, 1992.

Tarkington, Booth (1869-1946)

A prolific and versatile writer of mainstream fiction, (Newton) Booth Tarkington is remembered for his portrayals of middle-class life in late nineteenth- and early twentieth-century Indiana. His best known works, *The Magnificent Ambersons* (1918) and *Alice Adams* (1921), were awarded the first and the fourth Pulitzer Prizes for literature. The former was adapted for the screen by Orson Welles in 1942, and the latter is considered by critics to be Tarkington's finest accomplishment. A novelist, playwright, essayist, and briefly a politician, Tarkington produced a total of 171 short stories, 21 novels, 9 novellas, and 19 plays along with a number of movie scripts, radio dramas, and even illustrations over the course of a career that lasted from 1899 until his death in 1946. Having achieved a wide audience but not the lasting respect of critics, most agree that his finest work was done around the time of World War I.

Born in Indianapolis, Indiana, to the sort of comfortably well-established family that he later popularized in his fiction, Tarkington dictated his first short story to his sister at the age of six, and by the age of 16 had written a 14-act work on Jesse James. After graduation from Princeton, Tarkington moved to New York and labored futilely for

Booth Tarkington

five years to get his work published before turning to his own background for inspiration. Said Tarkington, ''I had no real success until I struck Indiana subjects.'' He later described his first book, *The Gentleman from Indiana*, as ''an emotional tribute to the land of my birth.'' A commercial success, it received only lukewarm comment from critics, many of whom labeled it an unrealistic romance. Thus was a general pattern set for Tarkington's career. A 1991 *Dictionary of Literary Biography* entry on Tarkington suggested that ''Although he had more talent than most of his contemporaries, his work never quite achieved major significance, and he had to be content with a large rather than a discriminating audience.''

In 1902, Tarkington married Laurel Louisa Fletcher and was elected to the Indiana House of Representatives as a Republican, though he was forced to vacate his seat a year later due to an illness. The couple spent most of the next decade traveling through Europe, but Booth's happiness, as well as his writing, were disrupted by bouts of excessive drinking and finally by divorce in 1911. One year later he married Susanah Keifer and took up his literary career again full-time. In 1914 he began work on his ''Penrod'' stories, which recaptured boyhood life in the late nineteenth century. In the postwar years, Tarkington's career reached its zenith with two Pulitzer Prizes. His prolific output during this time was not accidental; by all accounts he was a literary workhorse sometimes putting in 18-hour days of solid writing with little or no diversion until the task of the moment was complete. The popularity of this work made him financially comfortable, and beginning in the 1920s Tarkington settled in to what he called ''the milk run''—summers at Kennebunkport, Maine, and winters in Indianapolis. Cataracts gradually diminished his sight, and in 1930 he went completely blind. Surgeries successfully returned a part of his vision a year later, but his vitality was diminished. He turned primarily to children's stories in the final phase of his career, while also becoming a significant collector of art. He died in 1946 after an illness.

The volumes that Tarkington completed over the course of the first half of the twentieth century form a documentary testament of industrialization, urbanization, and social flux in urban middle America. Biographer James Woodress characterized his body of work as ''a paradigm of growth in the Midwest.'' In his fiction, Tarkington clearly expressed his distaste for the bustle and grime of urban life. *The Magnificent Ambersons* documented the incursion of the dirty streets, unkempt masses, and smoke-filled air of the industrializing metropolis into an idyllic nineteenth-century world. Part of the tragedy of the book is aesthetic as the beautiful estate of the great family is vanquished by bland, utilitarian architecture and uncultured people. Yet, ironically, Tarkington chose to spend much of his adult life in the city whose fall he lamented in his fiction. Addressing this paradox, Tarkington said, ''I belong here, I am part of it, and it is part of me. I understand it and it understands me. I would be out of touch with what I know best if I did not spend at least part of each year in Indianapolis.''

In describing his style, an anonymous reviewer in the *North American Review* commented, ''Mr. Tarkington is neither a realist, nor a romanticist, nor a localist, nor an impressionist, nor any special kind of literary artist, but simply a complete novelist.'' Tarkington himself fought the impetus to pigeonhole his work, vehemently rejecting the label of ''romanticist'' that some reviewers tried to force upon him. His literary heroes were Mark Twain and especially William Dean Howells. Dickinson quoted Tarkington on his wholesome, all-American tastes: ''[He] admires all those things which every decent, ordinary, simple-hearted person admires,'' and ''hates precisely those things hated by all honest, healthy, 'American,' people.'' Yet, Tarkington was nonetheless criticized by some conservative contemporaries for his critique of the American fascination with wealth, superficiality, and what he often referred to as ''bigness'' as ends in themselves, an overriding selfishness that he saw leading society toward mental and spiritual degeneration.

Tarkington lives on through his two Pulitzer-winning novels, the ''Penrod'' stories, and Orson Welles' 1942 film adaptation of *The Magnificent Ambersons*. These are remembered for their sentimental and socially conscious renderings of boyhood and middle-class life in the American Midwest around the turn of the century. Tarkington is not considered a literary genius, despite the Pulitzers. Instead, his legacy is as one of the most popular writers of the first half of the twentieth century—a period in which he sold more than five million volumes.

—Steve Burnett

FURTHER READING:

Dickinson, Asa Don. *Booth Tarkington: A Sketch.* New York, Doubleday, 1928.

Dictionary of Literary Biography. Vol. 9. *American Novelists, 1910-1945.* Detroit, Gale Research, 1981.

Fennimore, Keith J. *Booth Tarkington.* Boston, Twayne, 1974.

Mayberry, Susanah. *My Amicable Uncle: Recollections about Booth Tarkington.* West Lafayette, Purdue University Press, 1983.

Tarkington, Booth. *The World Does Move.* New York, Doubleday, 1928.

Twentieth-Century Children's Writers. 3rd ed. Detroit, St. James Press, 1989, 947-949.

Woodress, James. *Booth Tarkington: Gentleman from Indiana.* Philadelphia, Lippincott, 1955.

Tarzan

Edgar Rice Burroughs' Tarzan, the world's best-known apeman, first swung into view in the pages of a pulp fiction magazine in 1912. The Lord of the Jungle went on to conquer the media, including books, movies, comic strips, radio, comic books, and television. Burroughs was in his middle thirties and had failed in several professions—including being an instructor at a military academy, running a stationery store, and working as a salesman of pencil sharpeners—when he turned to the writing of pulp fiction in the second decade of the twentieth century. His first published work was a serial titled *Under the Moons of Mars.* It introduced his science fiction hero John Carter and started in the February 1912 issue of *All-Story* magazine. Later that same year, borrowing from the works of such writers as H. Rider Haggard and Rudyard Kipling, Burroughs invented his major character. His novel *Tarzan of the Apes,* subtitled ''A Romance of the Jungle,'' appeared in its entirety in the October issue of *All-Story.*

Tarzan, like Kipling's Mowgli, was a feral child. In the case of young John Clayton, the future Lord Greystoke, the little boy was raised by apes in the wilds of Africa. His parents, Lord and Lady Greystoke, were marooned on the African coast by the mutinous crew of the ship they'd been traveling on. Tarzan's father built a hut for himself and his pregnant wife, and it was there that the boy was born. His mother died soon after and his father was later killed by an attacking band of great apes. But a female ape named Kala, who'd just lost her own offspring, adopted and raised the child. ''The apes called him Tarzan, meaning white-skin,'' as the comic strip version explained. ''He grew up among them. He learned to speak their language and he lived as they did, in the trees.'' Somewhere along the way the wild child learned modesty and took to wearing a sort of sarong fashioned from a leopard skin. He later, after stumbling upon his family's hut, discovered books and taught himself to read. As his knowledge increased, the boy began to suspect that he was no ordinary ape.

Burroughs was basically a fantasist and well aware that in a real life situation, his little white-skinned hero wouldn't have made it to his first birthday. But it was more fun ignoring reality. The novice author also didn't have much of an idea of what Africa was really like. In the pulpwood version of *Tarzan of the Apes,* Burroughs included a tiger named Sabor among his animal cast. His editor didn't catch this, and it took a reader to write in and point out that ''the tiger is not and never has been included in the fauna of the African continent.''

Eventually Tarzan encountered other humans. Initially they were natives, and the earliest interactions were far from cordial. Then

The cast of the *Tarzan* films (from left): Jane (Maureen O'Sullivan), Tarzan (Johnny Weismuller), Boy (Johnny Sheffield), and Cheetah.

another group of mutineers arrived in his stretch of wilderness. This bunch had captured a group of treasure seekers headed up by Professor Porter and included his daughter Jane and Tarzan's cousin William Cecil Clayton, the present Lord Greystoke and suitor of Jane Porter. Once Tarzan, now a full grown young man, encountered Jane, he was smitten. He proceeded to rescue her and her friends and to arrange a jungle interlude, perfectly innocent, with her. Eventually, however, she sailed back to America, leaving her Jungle Lord behind. Tarzan, with the help of a new friend, was able to establish that he was the true Lord Greystoke. But when he followed Jane to her home, he became convinced that she actually loved the other Clayton. So rather than tell her or William Clayton the truth, he delivered one of the great curtain lines in fiction—"My mother was an Ape. I don't know who my father was."

In addition to Kipling and Haggard, Burroughs was very much influenced by Victorian fiction in general. Tarzan is very much a typical Victorian hero, a fellow who is a gentleman to the core. And just as true gentlemen like Oliver Twist and David Copperfield survived in the urban jungle of nineteenth century London, Tarzan survived in the jungles of Africa and proved that he, too, was a gentleman. A gentleman, if he's honest and right-thinking, can't be kept from rising to his true rank in society. And in the next several books John Clayton did just that, eventually winning back his title and marrying Jane. Burroughs, knowing his audience well, always made certain that there was an abundance of jungle action, lost cities, cruel villains, lovely maidens, wild savages, white goddesses, and untamed beasts in each subsequent Tarzan book.

Tarzan's conquest of the media began almost at once. In 1914, *Tarzan of the Apes* appeared as a hardcover novel. Eventually there would be two dozen novels about the apeman, the majority of them serialized in pulp magazines, such as *Argosy* and *Blue Book,* prior to publication. *Tarzan of the Apes* became a silent movie in 1918. Barrel-chested Elmo Lincoln, who'd portrayed a blacksmith in *The Birth of a Nation,* was the first screen Tarzan. He was followed in the role by such actors as Frank Merrill, James Pierce (who married Burroughs' daughter Joan) and P. Dempsey Tabler. In the talkies of the 1930s, Buster Crabbe, Bruce Bennett (under his real name of Herman Brix) and Glenn Morris all took turns at wearing the leopard skin. But the definitive Tarzan of that decade, as well as of the 1940s, was Johnny Weissmuller. Not an actor but a record-breaking swimmer, he was in his late twenties when he first took to the trees for MGM's *Tarzan the Ape Man*. It's said that he beat out such contenders as Joel McCrea, Johnny Mack Brown, and Clark Gable for the part. W. S. Van Dyke directed the film, and Maureen O'Sullivan played Jane.

MGM's Tarzan was not the articulate gentleman of the novels. He was a rather primitive fellow not much more versed in human speech than one of his apes. ''My lines read like a backward two-year-old talking to his nurse,'' Weissmuller once complained. The major reasons for making his screen apeman less than fluent were probably Weissmuller's slightly flutey voice and his evident inability to get conviction into any line of dialogue containing more than a half dozen words. For swimming, grappling with man and beast, rescuing Jane, and swinging from tree to tree on a vine, though, he had no equal. An assortment of others, usually athletes rather than actors, succeeded him in the role in the more than 50 films created around the Tarzan character. Of all the Tarzan films, however, the 1984 *Greystoke: The Legend of Tarzan, Lord of the Apes,* best captures Burroughs' original vision of the character.

Tarzan came to the comic pages as a daily strip in 1929, with a Sunday page added in 1931. The dailies, for several years, were anonymous adaptations of the Burroughs' novels. There were no dialogue balloons or sound effects, and the copy, set in type, ran below the pictures. Hal Foster, a seasoned advertising illustrator by then, drew the first sequences. Having little faith in comics and even less love for Tarzan, he soon dropped the project, and a less gifted artist named Rex Maxon took over drawing the daily and the Sunday. Burroughs, who had originally wanted pulp illustrator J. Allen St. John for the job, never thought much of Maxon's rendering of his hero, nor of the jungle denizens. Since United Feature Syndicate had the final say, all the author could do was write disgruntled letters to the editors there. These apparently had some effect, because Foster was eventually persuaded to come back and draw the Sunday *Tarzan* page.

Foster's pages were impressively and ambitiously drawn, and he could render ancient Egyptian civilizations surviving in contemporary Africa, Viking pirates, prehistoric monsters on the rampage, and even a foxhunt in rural England with equal ease. When he left the feature in the middle 1930s, he was replaced by Burne Hogarth. Among the subsequent artists were Bob Lubbers, Russ Manning, Gil Kane and Gray Morrow.

United Feature included reprints of *Tarzan* in the lineup of *Tip Top Comics,* launched in 1936, and subsequently also in *Comics On Parade* and *Sparkler Comics.* Dell introduced original adventures of the jungleman in 1947 with artwork by former Disney artist Jesse Marsh. In later years, both Marvel and DC Comics tried, unsuccessfully, to make a go of a comic book devoted to the character. The chief artist at DC was Joe Kubert. Tarzan's influence in the comics did not die with his strip; other comic strips used the character for comic effect, including Sam Watterson's *Calvin and Hobbes* (in 1986), Gary Larson's *The Far Side* (1991), Dan Piraro's *Bizarro* (1997), Gary Blehm's *Penmen* (1997), Wiley Miller's *Non-Sequitur* (1997), and Mike Peters' *Mother Goose and Grimm* (1998), among others. Burroughs' hero also appeared in Big Little Books, on the radio, and on television. Disney also produced a full-length animated feature.

—Ron Goulart

FURTHER READING:

Foster, Hal. *Tarzan.* Vol. 1. New York, Flying Buttress, 1992.

Goulart, Ron, editor . *The Encyclopedia of American Comics.* New York, Facts-On-File, 1990.

Porges, Irwin. *Edgar Rice Burroughs: The Man Who Created Tarzan.* Provo, Brigham Young University Press, 1975.

Sampson, Robert. *Yesterday's Faces.* Vol. 2. Bowling Green, Popular Press, 1984.

Taxi

At the Sunshine Cab Company on the television series *Taxi* (1978-1983), everyone comes off a little angry for putting in long hours at an unrewarding job while yearning for something better. Everyone that is except for Alex Reiger (Judd Hirsch), the only practical thinker in the entire garage who declares in the initial episode, ''Me? I'm a cab driver. I'm the only cab driver in this place.'' Like Ralph Kramden in *The Honeymooners*, each week the characters of *Taxi* would take a new chance at success only to return to the garage defeated but still hopeful about the future.

Taxi was not only one of the best situation comedies of the latter 1970s, it was also one of the most awarded and critically acclaimed. It won 18 Emmys in its five year run (winning the Outstanding Comedy Series Emmy the first three of those years), and helped to launch the careers of Danny DeVito and Christopher Lloyd.

The cast of *Taxi*.

The series came into existence solely on the track record of its writer-producers, James L. Brooks, Stan Daniels, David Davis, and Ed Weinberger, who had been behind the highly successful *Mary Tyler Moore Show* and its spin-offs. The four men decided to leave MTM and form their own production unit at Paramount Studios, which they named John Charles Walters Productions after a sign Weinberger had seen in an English pub. There was no such person at the company, but the name sounded dignified.

Wanting to get away from shows about white collar women workers, James Brooks decided to revive an idea he had with David Davis about doing a show concerned with taxi drivers, an idea once considered in conjunction with Jerry Belson (co-creator of *The Odd Couple* TV series) before it was abandoned. The producers had persuaded MTM to purchase the rights to an article on cabbies by Mark Jacobson that ran in the June 21, 1976 issue of *New York* magazine. Grant Tinker of MTM agreed to sell the rights for the article to the new production company for the same amount that he had purchased them for—$1,500.

The part of Alex Reiger was written with Judd Hirsch in mind, but after the failure of his series *Delvecchio*, Hirsch was reluctant to return to television until he read the show's first script. While Reiger would sometimes be troubled by philosophical questions when not dispensing advice to the others, Louie DePalma (DeVito), the firm's disagreeable, dishonest dispatcher never seemed to suffer from hurt feelings or a troubled conscience.

The DePalma character was originally a minor part until casting director Joel Thurm brought in Danny DeVito who walked into the office in character and quickly came to dominate the show just as he did the garage. By and large, the show resisted using gratuitous insults and wisecracks, with the exception of DePalma, who was given to saying thinks like, ''Banta, sometimes I wish you were smarter just so you could see how dumb you are'' or ''Fill out this form, and I hope you fill it out better than you fill out your pants.'' DePalma provides the conflict and is the enemy that the other cabbies band against.

Other characters went through changes as well. Tony Danza's Tony Banta character was originally supposed to be a punch-drunk Irish heavyweight rather than an unsuccessful young boxer, while Marilu Henner's Elaine Nardo character was supposed to be a tough-minded Italian woman in her thirties rather than a young, divorced woman looking to make ends meet, but the producers altered the characters to fit the performers they selected.

The characters on the show were realistic, except for Latka Gravas (Andy Kaufman), the cheerful mechanic from a mythic foreign country, who was included because the producers had enjoyed Kaufman's stand-up act and wanted to incorporate the kind of material he did into the show. Other characters included an aspiring actor Bobby Wheeler (Jeff Conway) unable to land a part, and Reverend Jim Ignatowski (Christopher Lloyd), a former hippie burnout and minister of the ''Church of the Peaceful'' who seemed off in his own world and had an infinite number of peculiarities. Rev. Jim had been written as a one-shot, and was recruited to become a regular the second season when the shy John Burns' character—played by Randall Carver—was written out of the show.

What makes the show a classic is the enormously high quality of the writing and the acting that went into the series. *Taxi,* like *M*A*S*H*, found a way to bring humor to what would often be potentially tragic situations. The characters are often estranged from other family and by being co-workers become friends, forming an unlikely family of their own. Hirsch was particularly adept at picking out subtle, perceptive nuances in his performances, while Kaufman,

Carol Kane (who played Latka's wife Simka), and Christopher Lloyd were simply off-the-wall wacky and amusing. The entire cast was nominated for a Golden Globe Award in 1979.

Left alone by the network and given a good time slot, *Taxi* started off as a resounding success, finishing its first two seasons in the top twenty. However, in the third season, ABC moved the series to Wednesday night and saw the ratings fall off. When it was moved to Thursdays the following season, it did even worse, falling to 53rd place, and it was soon canceled despite its Best Comedy Series Emmy wins.

Strangely enough, Grant Tinker left MTM in 1981 to become the head of the NBC Network, where he promoted the idea of quality programming. He beat out a bid from HBO for giving the series a second chance, and *Taxi* was picked up by NBC for its fifth and final season. (DeVito recorded a promo as DePalma snarling, ''Same time, better network!'').

Unfortunately for the show's followers, the numbers remained low. The following September when the Academy of Television Arts and Sciences presented the series with three Emmys, Outstanding Lead Actor in a Comedy Series winner Hirsch quipped, ''Don't they know we've been canceled?'' In accepting his award, Hirsch declared, ''If you can't get it out of your mind, if you have to keep giving laurels to us, then you should put it back on the air.'' However, there was to be no second reprieve, though the series proved very successful in syndication.

—Dennis Fischer

FURTHER READING:

Lovece, Frank, with Jules Franco. *Hailing Taxi.* New York, Prentice-Hall, 1988.

Sorensen, Jeff. *The Taxi Book: The Complete Guide to Television's Most Lovable Cabbies.* New York, St. Martin's Press, 1987.

Waldron, Vince. *Classic Sitcoms: A Celebration of the Best in Prime-Time Comedy.* New York, Collier Books, 1987.

Taxi Driver

Taxi Driver captured the angst felt throughout America in the post-Vietnam era. Directed by Martin Scorsese, *Taxi Driver* (1976) is a psychological drama and a tale of alienation, displaced sexuality, and life in the big city. The film stars Robert De Niro, Harvey Keitel, Cybill Sheperd, Jodie Foster, Peter Boyle, and Albert Brooks. Scorsese's male protagonists tend to be energetic, violent, and driven toward public recognition; Travis Bickle, played by De Niro, is no exception. Travis is a Vietnam-era vet who yearns to ''be somebody'' but only succeeds in becoming increasingly deranged and lonely as the film progresses. Scorsese's cinematography and the cast's skillful acting made *Taxi Driver* an enduring portrait of one of America's most disconcerting periods.

Set in New York City, *Taxi Driver* traces the daily habits of Travis as he drives his cab through the city, working long hours to avoid the monotony of his life. The film opens with shots of De Niro's eyes looking at the world from behind the glass windshield of his cab, calling to mind his isolation from society, which becomes magnified with time. Travis' life changes when he falls for a political campaign manager named Betsy, played by Cybill Sheperd. Betsy's rejection of

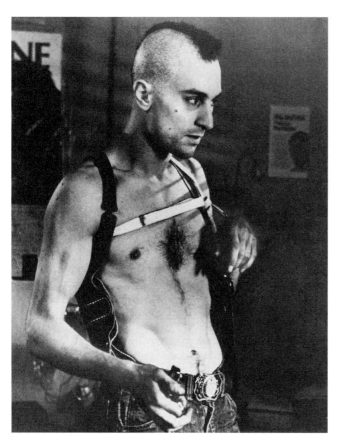

Robert De Niro as Travis Bickle in *Taxi Driver*.

Travis instigates his obsession with guns and fixation with the idea of rescuing a teen-age prostitute he meets in his cab, played by Jodie Foster.

Travis simultaneously destroys his body with drugs, alcohol, and junk food, and yearns to get himself into shape and to get his life organized. These two poles of his personality are best illustrated by an infamous scene in which Travis has a standoff with his mirror image. Travis looks at himself in the mirror and utters the most frequently quoted lines in the film: "You talking to me? You talking to me? You talking to me? . . . Well I'm the only one here." This scene enacts the construction, rehearsal, and performance of masculinity. In the privacy of his own room, Travis practices the role of the type of man he would like to be and calls to mind the anxiety embedded in the process of striving for this masculine ideal in the American post-Vietnam era.

The score for *Taxi Driver* was written by Alfred Hitchcock's composer, Bernard Herman, and completed the day before he died. While he collaborated with Hitchcock on many films, Herman is most famous for composing the soundtracks for *Psycho* and *Vertigo*. Like many of Hitchcock's films, *Taxi Driver* is a film about making movies. In a direct reference to Hitchcock, Scorsese appears in a shot at the beginning of the film. He later acts in a scene in which he and De Niro gaze at the silhouette of a woman through an apartment window (calling to mind Hitchcock's *Rear Window*). The cinematic spectator is continually addressed by shots of De Niro watching movies, films, projectors, the gazes of secret service men through photographic lenses, Travis' mirror, and the car window through which Travis experiences much of the world.

Director Martin Scorsese grew up in an Italian-American community in Little Italy. He entered a seminary after grammar school

only to be asked to leave at the age of fourteen after falling in love with a girl. Scorsese attributes much of his cinematic fascination with issues of family loyalty, hierarchy, and spirituality to his early years in Catholic school. He made his first short film in high school and went on to study film at New York University. While most of Scorsese's earlier body of work deals with issues pertaining to Italian-American identity, later in life, he began to turn his camera away from Little Italy with films such as *Alice Doesn't Live Here Anymore, The King of Comedy, After Hours, The Last Temptation of Christ,* and *Kundun.* This is certainly not to say that Italian-American themes have not played a continual role in Scorsese's work. His 1990s films such as *Goodfellas* and *Casino,* and standards such as *Raging Bull* and *Mean Streets* point to his continuing interest in exploring stereotypes of Italian-Americans through mafia narratives.

—Kristi M. Wilson

FURTHER READING:

Lourdeaux, Lee. *Italian and Irish Filmmakers in America: Ford, Capra, Coppola and Scorsese.* Philadelphia, Temple University Press, 1990.

Odabashian, Barbara. "Double Vision: Scorsese and Hitchcock." *Social and Political Change in Film and Literature.* Edited by Richard Chapple. Gainesville, UP of Florida, 1994, 21-36.

Page, Ken. "Going Solo: Performance and Identity in *New York, New York* and *Taxi Driver.*" *You Tarzan: Masculinity, Movies and Men.* Edited by Pat Kirkham and Janet Thumin. New York, St. Martin's Press, 1993, 137-43.

Tamburri, Anthony Julian, Paolo A. Giordano and Fred L. Gardaphé, editors. *From the Margin: Writings in Italian Americana.* West Lafayette, Purdue University Press, 1991.

Taylor, Elizabeth (1932—)

Fame and notoriety attached themselves to Elizabeth Taylor very early in her life and never left her. It is more than likely that she will forever occupy a place in both cultural and social history as twentieth-century America's most celebrated woman—as well as one of its most beautiful—and certainly Hollywood's last genuine star in the great tradition. Whether in good films or bad, the pull of her magnetic presence continually drew hordes of fans, mesmerized by her screen persona and her off-screen life, which took on the aura of myth.

A national institution and a living legend, Taylor became the paradigmatic exemplar of media-driven notions of celebrity, and an emblem of outrageous excess—conditions that defined her adult image. Her extraordinary, colorful and, indeed, remarkable life, made her an object of constant fascination to the public, among whom she variously evoked admiration, even worship, as well as periodically inviting derision or attracting moral outrage. However, the notoriety that has attached to her fabled marriages (seven husbands, eight weddings), her abundant wealth, her disappointments and tragedies, her many illnesses, weight problems, and battles with substance abuse, served seriously to overshadow her acting achievements to the detriment of her professional reputation.

By the time she voluntarily retired from filmmaking after a character role as Pearl Slaghoople in *The Flintstones*(1994), her 51st

Elizabeth Taylor

and last film, Elizabeth Taylor had the longest postwar career of any actress in Hollywood. It was largely as undistinguished as it was lengthy, her abundance of talent and intelligence too often buried, as she herself observed with her customary candor, in a welter of mediocrity. Nevertheless, among her credits, the handful of good roles in worthwhile films rightfully earned her five Academy Award nominations and two Oscars, the French Legion d'Honneur, and the American Film Institute Lifetime Achievement award; while her eloquent campaigning for causes, notably in the field of AIDS research, brought her the Academy's Jean Hersholt Humanitarian Award.

Elizabeth Rosemond Taylor was born in Hampstead, London, on February 27, 1932, the daughter of American parents. Francis Taylor was an art dealer and his wife Sara was a socially ambitious former stage actress. Thanks to their influential connections, Elizabeth and her elder brother Howard enjoyed a privileged early childhood. To escape World War II, the Taylors returned to the United States in 1939, finally settling in Beverly Hills, where Francis opened a fashionable gallery in the Beverly Hills Hotel. With child and teen stars a popular fixture of Hollywood movies at that time, Sara Taylor was determined that her pretty, violet-eyed daughter would be one of them.

A shy child who loved animals, Elizabeth had no desire to become an actress but, in the grip of an iron-willed mother, found herself at age nine auditioning for MGM, who turned her down, and Universal who took her on. She made her debut playing an objectionable brat with little to say in a poor comedy programmer called *There's One Born Every Minute* (1941), after which the studio dropped her. She lived the natural life of a child again until late the

following year when she made *Lassie Come Home* for MGM, beginning a contractual association with MGM that lasted until the early 1960s. The studio immediately lent her to Fox for a tiny role as the child who dies in *Jane Eyre* (1943), after which she was enrolled in the MGM schoolroom, and appeared (mostly in small featured roles) in a string of films that were largely forgettable. It was the death of normality. Owned by the studio and controlled by her mother, Elizabeth did as she was told, her self-image gradually shaped by her movies, her adolescence a fantasy lived through the roles she played.

In 1943, while training for her first major role—in *National Velvet*—Elizabeth fell from her horse and sustained a spinal injury, the first of several such over the course of her life. When the film was released in 1944, her performance as Velvet Brown who, disguised as a boy jockey, wins the Grand National, enchanted critics and audiences alike. Fresh, natural, and vivacious, the 12-year-old also revealed the beginnings of her great beauty that even the braces on Velvet's teeth failed to mar. Over the next few years Elizabeth was transformed from sparkling teenager to ripening, sensuous woman, with no intermediate stage. As the eponymous *Cynthia* (1947), her role sounded a perilous echo of her own life—an over-protected, over-controlled teenager battling with her mother (Mary Astor) to gain adolescent freedoms; in *A Date with Judy* (1948) she was the sophisticated, sexy, and knowing teenager who sets out successfully to catch the man (Robert Stack, aged 29) earmarked for Judy (Jane Powell).

In a radio interview with Louella Parsons just before the release of *Cynthia,* the 15-year-old rising star, who had not yet been allowed a boyfriend, said that she wanted to be a great actress, but added, with ironic prescience, "most of all, I want to snare a husband." Meanwhile, MGM sent her to England in late 1948 to play a wife—married to Robert Taylor—in *Conspirator,* a film whose only merit was to reveal the actress's burgeoning beauty, talent, and physical maturity. She was 17.

All eyes were on the young Elizabeth Taylor by 1949, a year in which she made the cover of *Time* magazine, became engaged to the wealthy and eligible William Pawley Jr. in a blaze of publicity, broke the engagement when he demanded she give up the career to which she was now totally committed, and, on loan to Paramount, began work on *A Place in the Sun*. Under the guidance of director George Stevens, her performance marked a new seriousness in what was the most significant film of her career to that date and one of the best she had ever made. Elizabeth, at her most incandescent as the young heiress ensnared in a doomed love affair, starred opposite Montgomery Clift. Offscreen, they adored one another, but it was a hopeless situation for the deeply infatuated Elizabeth, who learned to settle for a close and enduring friendship with the homosexual Clift, and fell in love with Nicky Hilton instead.

She met Hilton, heir to the hotel fortune, while filming *A Place in the Sun* and married him in May 1950. The extravagant "fairytale" wedding was glitteringly stage-managed by MGM, as was the release of her new film, rushed out to coincide with her nuptials. The resulting publicity made *Father of the Bride*, in which Elizabeth starred as the about-to-be wed daughter of Spencer Tracy and Joan Bennett, one of the studio's most profitable hits. The real-life, 18-year-old bride left on an extended European honeymoon during which she discovered that her husband was a neglectful, abusive, womanizing drunk. By December the marriage was over. Bruised and bewildered, Elizabeth went back to work, moved to her own apartment for the first time, and was squired by choreographer and director Stanley Donen. MGM disapproved, and sent her to England in June of 1951 to play a secondary role in *Ivanhoe.*

By the time she returned, *A Place in the Sun* had placed her firmly in the upper echelon of stardom, and she was in love with Michael Wilding, the British actor who, at 38, was twice her age. Demonstrating the willful determination that became one of the hallmarks of her character, she virtually proposed to him, and they married in 1952. The couple had two sons, but their floundering marriage, doomed from the start by the inequity of age and status, was over by 1956, the release year of *Giant* in which Elizabeth gave a fine dramatic performance opposite Rock Hudson and James Dean, and the year she began making *Raintree County.*

A lavish period drama which cast Elizabeth as a Southern belle tormented in love, *Raintree County* (1957) brought the actress her first Oscar nomination but, during filming, Montgomery Clift had the car crash which famously left its mark on his beauty. Elizabeth, who had been devastated by the death of her friend James Dean in similar circumstances, was first at the scene, cradling his bloody head in her lap. She remained his closest friend, and it was reportedly at her insistence that the by then seriously drug- and alcohol-addicted actor was cast in *Suddenly Last Summer* (1959)—the film which brought her an Oscar nomination for her performance as Katharine Hepburn's traumatized niece.

In 1957, Elizabeth was swept off her feet by the flamboyant producer and impresario Mike Todd (born Avrom Goldbogen), 24 years her senior. She converted to Judaism and married him in Acapulco in February 1957. The best man was Todd's great friend, crooner Eddie Fisher. August brought the premature and difficult birth of Liza Todd, and Elizabeth was warned that she could have no more children. (Three years later she adopted a German-born daughter, to be known as Maria Burton). In March 1958, Elizabeth had begun filming *Cat on a Hot Tin Roof* with Paul Newman when Todd's plane, *Lucky Liz,* crashed in a storm. A hysterical and grief-stricken Taylor emerged from sedated seclusion to complete the film, giving a performance of powerful depth as Tennessee Williams's unhappy Maggie the Cat and earning a well-deserved Oscar nomination.

Eddie Fisher provided solace in her grief. When he divorced his wife, Debbie Reynolds, to become Taylor's fourth husband, the star's sympathetic public, fueled by the tabloids, turned hostile, branding her a home-breaker. (In truth, the Fisher-Reynolds marriage had been in crisis for some time.) Eddie and Elizabeth married in a Las Vegas synagogue in May 1959, the year she was approached by Walter Wanger to play the title role in *Cleopatra.* Facetiously agreeing to consider the offer for a fee of one million dollars, Taylor was astounded when Twentieth Century-Fox agreed to this unprecedented and astonishing sum. But first she had a contractual obligation to fulfill at MGM.

The vehicle chosen for her was *Butterfield 8,* in which she played Gloria Wandrous, high-class hooker and nymphomaniac who pays for her sins by dying in the wreckage of her sports car. The moral climate and censorship rules of the time caused endless headaches in the search for compromise, resulting in a sub-standard and tacky film that, from the outset, Elizabeth was opposed to making. Despite the roller-coaster ride of her private life and her volatile temperament, she was no scarlet woman, and her eventual forced acquiescence represented a tough battle that the studio won. She co-starred with Laurence Harvey and, at her insistence, her husband Eddie Fisher. Despite the odds, Elizabeth, the throat scar from her recent surgery largely concealed, gave a convincing performance which, ironically, brought her first Oscar win, thought to have been awarded on the

sympathy vote. (Co-nominee Shirley MacLaine famously remarked, "I lost to a tracheotomy.")

In September 1960, Elizabeth Taylor arrived in London to begin work on *Cleopatra* for director Rouben Mamoulian. Her co-stars were Stephen Boyd (Antony) and Peter Finch (Caesar). By October 10, Elizabeth was ill, and by November 18, her recurring infections led to the temporary shutdown of filming. She flew to Palm Springs to recuperate and returned in January 1961 to resume work. Mamoulian had resigned and was replaced by Joseph L. Manckiewicz who set to work on script changes. At this time, the *Motion Picture Herald* top ten box-office poll was announced, with Elizabeth Taylor at number one. While work on the script dragged on, the Taylor-Fisher retinue, installed at the Dorchester Hotel, lived like royalty, with "Queen" Elizabeth exhibiting the extravagance for which she became renowned. She had her favorite foods specially flown in from several corners of America, as well as from France and Italy and, while Manckiewicz rewrote the script, she shopped. The marriage to Fisher was not turning out to be a success.

On March 4, 1961, Elizabeth became dangerously ill and was rushed to the London Clinic where emergency surgery was performed. For some days she hovered between life and death while the world (and Twentieth Century-Fox) held its anxious breath, but emerged from the clinic on March 11 having made, according to the surgeons, a miraculous recovery. Restored to favor by her adoring public, the world's most famous glamour icon departed to California for necessary rest and recuperation, and collected her *Butterfield 8* Oscar while *Cleopatra* was once again shut down and rescheduled to shoot in Rome.

The Taylor-Fisher entourage—three children, several dogs and cats, and a large staff—arrived in Rome on September 1, and took up residence at the Villa Papa, a seven-bedroom mansion set in eight acres of gardens a few minutes from the Cinecittà studios. Delays in filming had brought cast changes, and the new Mark Antony, Richard Burton, was occupying a nearby villa with his family. Filming began on September 25, fraught with the problems of a half-finished script and uncompleted sets. Amid the chaos, Elizabeth remained calm and professional—and fell head-over-heels in love with Richard Burton.

Their affair was most protracted and public adultery that the modern world had yet beheld; and the world remained at once scandalized and transfixed by the affair for the best part of 14 years in the face of the Taylor-Burton antics. The complexities of double divorce prevented the couple from marrying until March 1964, during Burton's Canadian season of *Hamlet,* by which time they had made *The VIPs* (1963) together. It was a feeble British film that cashed in shamelessly on the couple's notoriety, but worse was to follow with the risibly awful *The Sandpiper* (1964). Professionally, the liaison marked a period of decline for both of them. Their fees (never less than a million plus for Taylor) were grossly disproportionate to the quality of their joint ventures, with the shining exception of *Who's Afraid of Virginia Woolf?*; this screen adaptation of Edward Albee's play revealed a hitherto unthinkable Taylor: blowzy, loud, passionate, and vitriolic as the embittered Martha, locked in a poisonous game with her husband George. It was a *tour de force,* the finest work of her career, and her second Oscar was a fitting tribute to her committed and lacerating performance.

The Burtons, inescapably, were famous for being famous. They were also famous for their drinking binges, their rows, and their astonishing extravagances. They became a kind of traveling circus, buying an ocean-going yacht, several homes, priceless paintings and, for Elizabeth, jewelry. Burton bought his wife the Krupp diamond

($305,000), the historic "La Peregrina" pearl ($37, 000), the Cartier diamond ($1.1 million), and the Shah Jahan yellow diamond ($900,000). By 1972, the marriage was in trouble and 1973 saw the announcement of a separation and a failed attempt to reconcile. They were divorced in 1974, remarried on the banks of an African river in Botswana in 1975, and parted finally in 1976.

Between their endless travels and upheavals, Elizabeth had made numerous films, of which only *The Taming of the Shrew* with Burton and *Reflections in a Golden Eye* with Brando (both 1967) merited any real attention. At the end of 1976 she married ex-Secretary to the Navy John Warner, and settled in Virginia to play the role of the loyal politician's wife. Her high profile campaigning helped her husband to the U.S. Senate, but she grew bored and put on weight; the couple separated in 1981. With her film career gradually petering out, Elizabeth took to the stage for the first time, playing Regina in *The Little Foxes* on Broadway and in London's West End (1981-82). It was a brave stab at a medium for which she was totally untrained, but the public flocked to the show, and in 1983 she joined forces with Richard Burton, playing Amanda to his Elyot in Noel Coward's *Private Lives* on Broadway. It was a risible exercise, really, but the public willingly paid inflated ticket prices to see the legendary pair.

In August 1984 Richard Burton died of a cerebral hemorrhage. Elizabeth collapsed at the news, but stayed away from the funeral for fear of causing a media stampede. She subsequently made a pilgrimage to Burton's family in Wales and attended a memorial service in London before returning to make a TV movie (one of several during the 1980s, among them *North and South* and *Sweet Bird of Youth*). The following year brought more grief with the news that her friend Rock Hudson was ill with AIDS. Her publicized visit to Hudson's bedside marked the beginning of her high profile campaigning for AIDS awareness and research funds, and it became her primary occupation as her acting career wound down.

Throughout the late 1980s, Elizabeth Taylor's name was romantically linked with numerous men, among them actor George Hamilton and the multi-millionaire Malcolm Forbes. She made *Young Toscanini* (1987) in Italy for Franco Zeffirelli, which was shown at the Venice Film Festival, but was barely released. It was her last major screen appearance. Alongside her AIDS work, she launched the first of her perfumes (the aptly named "Passion"), and gave attention to her children and grandchildren. She continued, however, to be dogged with illnesses of various kinds and, increasingly, relied on pain-killing drugs. (According to biographer Donald Spoto, she suffered 73 illnesses, accidents and injuries requiring hospitalization between 1947 and 1994). Suffering the effects of drug dependency, she checked herself into the Betty Ford Clinic in 1988, where she met construction worker Larry Fortensky.

In October 1991, in a ceremony held at singer Michael Jackson's ranch, thirty-nine-year-old Fortensky became fifty-nine-year-old Elizabeth Taylor's seventh husband. It was a last act of personal folly, and the marriage was over by 1997, the year that she had an operation to remove a brain tumor. Once again, people the world over waited anxiously for the outcome but Elizabeth Taylor emerged, shaven-headed, to continue crusading on behalf of the less fortunate, demonstrating the truth of her own words, spoken in a 1987 interview: "I have no plans to succumb. I am a survivor."

—Robyn Karney

FURTHER READING:

Bragg, Melvyn. *Richard Burton: A Life*. Boston, Little Brown, 1988.

Spoto, Donald. *Elizabeth Taylor*. New York, Little Brown, 1995.

Taylor, Elizabeth. *Elizabeth Taylor*. New York, Harper and Row, 1965.

Vermilye, Jerry, and Mark Ricci. *The Films of Elizabeth Taylor*. Secaucus, Citadel, 1976.

Walker, Alexander. *Elizabeth: The Life of Elizabeth Taylor*. New York, Grove Weidenfeld, 1990.

Taylor, James (1948—)

Blending folk, country, and blues to create his own distinctive musical sound, James Taylor spearheaded the singer-songwriter movement in the 1970s. Born in Boston in 1948, Taylor began playing guitar at twelve and soon was performing at small folk gigs. But having struggled with depression at boarding school, at sixteen, Taylor checked himself into a mental hospital, where he graduated from high school. After moving to London in 1968, Taylor was the first outside artist signed to the Beatles' Apple Records. Following the release of his first album, he returned to the United States in 1969, where his first single, "Carolina In My Mind" climbed the charts. In 1971, Taylor was featured on the cover of *Time* magazine as the "originator of the singer-songwriter era." Described in *Time* as "a blend of Heathcliffian inner fire with a melancholy sorrows-of-young-Werther look," Taylor was romantically linked to Joni Mitchell, but married singer Carly Simon in 1972, the same year he won his first Grammy. Throughout the 1970s and 1980s, Taylor continued to release critically and commercially successful albums, refining his style while maintaining his superb musical craftsmanship. Still touring to packed houses in the 1990s, Taylor's 1997 album, *Hourglass*, rose to Number 9 on the Billboard chart and went platinum. Now in his fifties, James Taylor may be the granddaddy of singer-songwriters, but he remains a thoroughly contemporary musician and an ever-popular star.

—Victoria Price

FURTHER READING:

Herbst, Peter. "James Taylor: The *Rolling Stone* Interview." *Rolling Stone*. September 6, 1979.

"James Taylor: One Man's Family of Rock." *Time*. March 1, 1971. http://www.james-taylor.com/ September 1998.

"James Taylor Unofficial Home." http://www.james-taylor.com/ September 1998.

Taylor, Robert (1911-1969)

Typecast for most of his career as a handsome ladies man, Robert Taylor became a top box office attraction after his first major film in 1936 and continued to star in big budget movies for the next twenty years. The list of leading ladies who played opposite Taylor include some of the biggest stars of Hollywood's Golden Age: Irene Dunne, Loretta Young, Barbara Stanwyck, Joan Crawford, Greta Garbo, Jean Harlow, Hedy Lamarr, Ava Gardner, Greer Garson,

Robert Taylor

Vivien Leigh, Norma Shearer, Katharine Hepburn, Elizabeth Taylor, and Deborah Kerr. Of his long association with MGM, Taylor said: "I stayed with one studio for twenty years, took what they gave me to do, did my work." Summarizing his treatment at the hands of movie critics, he said, "I never got raves, but neither did I get pans."

Born Spangler Arlington Brough (a name dear to trivia buffs), the son of a physician in Filley, Nebraska, Taylor initially decided on a medical career, but acting in amateur productions in college soon led him in another direction. He enrolled in a Los Angeles drama school, where a talent scout saw him in a production of *Journey's End*. After a screen test, he was signed by MGM to a seven-year contract, starting at $35 a week. In his first film he played a supporting role to Will Rogers in *Handy Andy* (1934). A succession of low-budget pictures followed, but in 1936 he moved to number four in the box office ratings with the teary film, *Magnificent Obsession*, opposite Irene Dunne. Taylor starred in the role of a playboy who becomes a respected surgeon in order to restore the sight of a woman he had blinded in an automobile accident. After the film was released, all of the most glamorous Hollywood leading ladies wanted to play opposite the handsome young actor.

Two other important films followed in 1936—Taylor starred with Barbara Stanwyck in *His Brother's Wife* and with Joan Crawford in an historical drama, *The Gorgeous Hussy*. His sudden appeal at the box office led MGM to star him opposite Greta Garbo in *Camille*. Comparing him with the uniquely talented Garbo, critics were almost unanimous in calling the pairing one of the great mismatches of cinema history. Studio executives pointed out, however, that in the important area of ticket sales, Taylor ranked number three in 1937,

while Garbo was only number six. In 1937 Taylor played the more macho role of a secret service agent, who is ordered by President McKinley to join a gang of robbers to expose a powerful mob, in *This is My Affair*, opposite Barbara Stanwyck as a saloon-girl. Taylor and Stanwyck were married in 1939, a much-publicized Hollywood romance that lasted until 1952.

In the late 1930s, studios gave Taylor parts designed to draw more men to his pictures. He was the cocky, athletic young American in *Yank at Oxford* (1938), a boxer in *The Crowd Roars* (1938), and he even starred in a Western, *Stand Up and Fight* (1939). Taylor's own favorite film was the romantic *Waterloo Bridge* (1940), in which he played a soldier who meets a ballet dancer (Vivien Leigh) during a London air raid.

His most expensive film was *Quo Vadis* (1951), in which he essayed the role of a Roman centurion, which Gregory Peck had turned down. In the lavishly made movie, shot in Italy, Taylor falls in love with a Christian beauty (Deborah Kerr), in a plot that threatens to throw both of them to the lions. The movie grossed $11 million, at that time the fourth biggest moneymaker in history. Other big budget spectacles followed: *Ivanhoe* (1952), *Knights of the Round Table* (1953), and *Valley of the Kings*, filmed in Egypt in 1954. In the next few years Taylor's popularity dwindled, and his contract with MGM ended, but he continued to work in minor films and in a television series called *The Detectives*. In his last movie in 1969, he and Charles Boyer played secret agents in *The Day the Hot Line Got Hot*. He died that same year after a long struggle with cancer. Fellow actor Ronald Reagan, then governor of California, said at his funeral: "He was more than a pretty boy, an image that embarrassed him because he was a man who respected his profession and was a master of it."

—Benjamin Griffith

FURTHER READING:

Jarvis, Everett G. *Final Curtain: Deaths of Noted Movie and Television Personalities.* New York, Carol, 1995.

Shipman, David. *Cinema: The First Hundred Years.* New York, St. Martin's, 1993.

——. *The Great Movie Stars: The Golden Years.* New York, Hill and Wang, 1973.

Teddy Bears

Most adults carry fond, even significant memories of their own teddy bear, a possession integral to the childhood of all but the severely deprived in America and beyond. Although these days one can find stuffed toys representing every animal from an aardvark to a zebra, the figure of the bear remains the most popular choice, among children and adults alike. By the latter part of the twentieth century, teddy bears had become something of an industry in the United States and Europe.

Both the United States and Germany lay claim to the invention of the teddy bear, each for good reasons. In fact, however, the teddy bear seems to be the product of a remarkable historical coincidence occurring in 1902. One part of the story starts in Mississippi, where President Theodore Roosevelt was on a hunting trip. One of his companions captured a black bear cub, tied a rope around its neck, and brought it to Roosevelt to shoot, but the President, seeing no sport in

A young girl hugs a giant teddy bear.

killing an exhausted, bound, and defenseless animal, declined. A reporter traveling with the hunting party telegraphed the story to *The Washington Post,* which ran a front-page cartoon by Clifford Berryman the following day, showing Roosevelt refusing to shoot the bear cub with the caption "Drawing the line in Mississippi." In Brooklyn, New York, the cartoon was seen by one Morris Michtom, the owner of a small novelty store, who had been trying unsuccessfully to sell a few stuffed toy bears made by his wife, Rose. Inspired by Berryman's cartoon, Michtom wrote to the White House, received permission to use the presidential name, and put the toys in his shop window with a sign reading, "Teddy's bears." The bears sold quickly, and the demand for more was so great that Michtom soon founded the Ideal Novelty and Toy Corporation and put "Teddy's bears" into mass production.

Meanwhile, thousands of miles away in Germany, Richard Steiff was also in the grip of a big idea. While watching some trained bears performing in a circus, Steiff had the thought that a toy bear standing upright with jointed arms and legs might be a marketable commodity. He made some drawings of his conception and took them to his aunt, Margarete Steiff, a well-known toy and doll maker. She designed a stuffed bear based on her nephew's ideas, and exhibited them at the 1903 Leipzig Toy Fair. European stores initially expressed no interest in the new toys, but an American buyer was enthusiastic and ordered several thousand for export to the United States. Consequently, the teddy bear may be said to have two birthdays, although the name is clearly owed to its American maker and the president who inspired it.

Today, teddy bears are big business; there are an estimated 2.5 million collectors in the United States alone. So significant has this

"bear market" become, the industry now distinguishes between two kinds of teddy bears: toys and collectibles. Toy bears are distinguished by their soft stuffing, designed to make them "huggable," while collectible teddys are characterized by jointed arms and legs, firm stuffing, and a relatively unyielding exterior. Many experts regard Gund, Inc. as the premier maker of cuddly toy bears, but to collectors, Steiff still reigns supreme, with antique Steiff bears sometimes fetching in excess of $10,000 at auctions.

The popularity of the teddy bear soon spread beyond the United States to Britain and elsewhere, and some teddys are based on characters in universally loved children's stories by English writers. Winnie the Pooh, the honey-loving bear created by A. A. Milne in 1926, has been a perennial favorite, as has Paddington Bear, who first appeared in the 1950s storybook *A Bear Called Paddington* by Michael Bond and Peggy Fortnum. A stuffed Smokey the Bear has been around for decades to remind bear lovers that "Only *you* can prevent forest fires." Teddy bears have also been based on human characters, both real and fictional, several with movie connotations. Thus, we have had such creations as "Humphrey Beargart," "Theda Beara," and the macho "Rambear."

Any popular collectible tends to spawn enterprises designed to feed it, and teddy bear collecting is no exception. There are mail-order catalogs devoted to bears and other bear products (such as T-shirts and posters), magazines for the teddy bear collector, bear calendars, teddy bear conventions, and innumerable internet sites devoted to commerce in stuffed bears.

—Justin Gustainis

FURTHER READING:

Bull, Peter. *The Teddy Bear Book.* New York, Random House, 1970.

Severin, Gustav. *Teddy Bear: A Loving History of the Classic Childhood Companion.* Philadelphia, Courage Books, 1995.

Waring, Philippa. *In Praise of Teddy Bears.* London, Souvenir Press, 1997.

Teen Idols

As long as there are teenagers, there will be teen idols. From the vintage "Frankie" Sinatra to Elvis Presley, from the Beatles to David Cassidy, from the New Kids on the Block to 'N Sync, the names and faces may change with the decades, but the emotions that drive the phenomenon do not. Teen idols are a rite of passage for pre-teens and early teens. They are dream mates who fuel romantic daydreams, and provide a safe release for hormonally-charged emotions. After all, unlike flesh-and-blood boyfriends or girlfriends, the teen idols make no demands.

Collectively, teen idols have long been dismissed as lightweight and flashes-in-the-pan. But, in fact, many notable performers have passed through the teen idol ranks. Before becoming one of Hollywood's most prolific and acclaimed leading men, John Travolta was a popular pin-up, the result of his co-starring role in the 1975 TV series, *Welcome Back, Kotter.* The 1997 box office blockbuster, *Titanic,* derived much of its drawing power from the casting of teen idol, Leonardo DiCaprio. Pop-soul maestro Michael Jackson was a teen idol in the 1980s, as well as the previous decade, when he was one of the Jackson Five. The Beatles were huge teen idols in the 1960s, as

Bobby Darin in concert.

was Elvis Presley in the 1950s. In the 1940s, females screamed for Sinatra.

Even those teen idols who did not successfully make a transition as their fans matured continue to be regarded with affection. To their fans, they represent a special time in their lives. To the credit of these teen idols, they also left imprints on popular culture. For example, many of the icons of the 1950s—the decade in which the modern teen idol is rooted—became fixtures on the record charts. From late 1957 through 1963, the young performers were responsible for at least thirteen number one hits. They included Tab Hunter's ''Young Love'' and Frankie Avalon's ''Venus.'' Another twenty tunes by teen idols climbed to the top five.

Just as Presley had gone from recording studio to Hollywood, the idols made the leap to the big screen. Theirs were major names during the final years of the so-called Hollywood ''star system.'' Sandra Dee, who became a teen favorite with her depiction of the surfing-obsessed Gidget, went on to become a top-ten box office draw for the years 1960, 1961, 1962, and 1963—an astonishing feat, considering the list also included Doris Day, Cary Grant, Elizabeth Taylor, and Frank Sinatra. Between 1959 and 1964, Fabian appeared in no less than ten films, ranging from comedies to teen genre flicks to

a John Wayne action adventure. Tab Hunter clocked in seventeen films between 1950 and 1964.

Of course, teen idols did not originate in the 1950s. Back in the 1930s, singer-actor Rudy Vallee induced swoons from schoolgirls when he performed while clutching a megaphone. But it is Frank Sinatra who is credited as the official pioneer of the teen idol movement. At age 27, Sinatra had a skinny, vulnerable look. That look, combined with his lush romantic ballads, elicited mass hysterics and stampeding among teenage ''bobby soxers'' at his December 1942 performances at New York's Paramount Theater. When Sinatra later appeared at the Boston Armory, the seats were bolted down as a security measure.

In the 1950s, the emergence of American teenage culture prompted another kind of hero worship. Before he cinched his eternal stardom with his car crash death of 1955, James Dean had come to symbolize the teenager in pain, with his angst-ridden performance in *Rebel Without a Cause.* The early Elvis Presley had his own angst-ridden performances in song, including the bravado *Heartbreak Hotel.* But Dean and Presley also summoned up a sense of looming danger. In Presley's case, his sexy stage antics and the fact that he was a white singer who sounded ''black'' made him anathema to authority figures.

A much safer alternative was found in Charles Eugene Boone. Better known as Pat Boone, the young performer from Nashville, Tennessee, emerged as the flip side of the coin that bore the imprints of Dean and Presley. Considering the era's controversy over rock 'n' roll, it is significant that Boone rose to fame by singing cover versions of songs originally recorded by African-Americans. His easy-going delivery and boyish charm helped to defuse the volatility of rock 'n' roll. Furthermore, Boone did not emote sexual magnetism. It was Boone who set the stage for what transpired, following a Richter-scale shift in the world of rock 'n' roll.

Denoting that upheaval was the U.S. Army's 1958 decision to draft Elvis Presley. Other significant careers also came to a standstill. Chuck Berry faced a prison term for having transported a minor over a state line for sexual purposes. Jerry Lee Lewis was blackballed because of his marriage to his thirteen-year-old cousin. Plane and car crashes took the lives of Buddy Holly, Ritchie Valens, and Eddie Cochran.

With the music world in transition, promoters moved in to provide an antidote—a new commodity to entice the growing teenage spending power. The idea was to cater to teenage desires, but without the erratic undercurrent or explosive passion that had made Presley an infamous household name. So the new teenage idol was created. It was no coincidence that, along with the lure of their talent—some of it legitimate, some wholly manufactured—the teen idols were exceedingly clean cut and attractive. Or that the male teen idols appeared vulnerable as opposed to predatory. After all, strong masculine qualities can be off-putting to young females. Thus, over the years, many teen idols have had an androgynous look.

More than any of the others, Fabian and Frankie Avalon set the standards against which the 1950s teen idols were measured. Both young men had the engaging affability of the boy-next-door. And not coincidentally, both were managed by Philadelphia producer-promoter Bob Marcucci, who was teamed with Peter DeAngelis in Chancellor Records. The label was based in Philadelphia, a city that specialized in turning out teen idols.

Phil Spector—the legendary producer known for his work with girl groups, the Righteous Brothers, and the Beatles, and the "wall of sound" that backed their tunes—has called Philadelphia of the 1950s "the most insane, most dynamite, the most beautiful city in the history of rock 'n' roll and the world." The city's thriving music industry included competing record labels and their respective producers, and promoters. Their collective goal was to get their performers booked on the Dick Clark-hosted *American Bandstand*. As the premiere showcase for rock 'n' roll performers, the show was essential to the careers of would-be teen idols.

When the pioneering rock 'n' roll artists had made their ascent, there were no national television shows devoted to rock 'n' roll. The performers made their reputations after months or even years of touring. Prior to his famed appearances on the *Ed Sullivan Show*, Presley was a regional star, the result of having played the hinterlands. Only after becoming known regionally did he enjoy exposure on national TV variety shows. By contrast, the teen idols could become "overnight" successes as a result of a single, carefully-promoted TV appearance. Ricky Nelson's rise as a teen idol began when he sang a single song on his family's long-running series, *The Adventures of Ozzie and Harriet*. Tommy Sands was an unknown seventeen-year-old when he appeared in the NBC telecast of *The Singing Idol*, which generated eight thousand pieces of fan mail. Avalon, Bobby Rydell, and Fabian all owed their fame to *American Bandstand*.

The rise and fall of Fabian stands as a cautionary chapter in the teen idol annals. Fabiano Forte was a 14-year-old boy literally sitting on his front porch when he was spotted by Marcucci, who was already managing Avalon. Though Fabian's father had just been taken away by ambulance after having suffered a heart attack, Marcucci was brazen enough to ask, "Say, kid, can you sing?" Fabian was not interested. After continuing to see the teenager in the neighborhood, including at the corner drug store where he worked, Marcucci returned to the family home. This time Fabian agreed to become a Marcucci protégé.

At the time, Avalon was finally enjoying success as a singer—after having bombed with a trio of singles. But unlike Avalon, who could carry a tune and was an accomplished musician, Fabian had no natural musical prowess, in fact, he had failed his high school chorus class. But Marcucci persisted, taking the youth to a series of vocal coaches and introducing him to local audiences via sock hops. He also launched a major promotional campaign touting Fabian as "The Fabulous One." Still, despite several *American Bandstand* appearances, the teenager's initial records failed. "You gotta find this kid a hit record!" Clark told Marcucci. That hit turned out to be "I'm a Man," which Fabian lip-synched on a December 1958 show. The single climbed the charts, and paved the way for additional hits, tours, and movie roles. But Fabian's fame and largely off-key singing also led to cruel barbs from the press, which left the teenager both hurt and bewildered.

Ironically, Fabian garnered some of his best notices when he played a psychopathic killer in a 1961 episode of the TV anthology series, *Bus Stop*. But the casting of the teen idol also generated controversy, for teen idols of the day were not expected to have dimension as artists. For that reason, they were not taken seriously by the very industry that created them. Thus, when times and tastes changed, and his teenage fan base grew older, Fabian had to grapple to survive as a performer. Of his reign as an icon, Fabian once said, "I was just a street-punk kid who got into all this because my father had a heart attack and the family needed money. I didn't know nothing. Sure I had girls—I was a healthy young man. But what all this teen idol stuff comes down to is business. Big business."

In the 1960s, that big business was typified by the staggering success of the Beatles, and the fellow and female Britons and Americans who followed in their wake. Foremost among the latter was the fabricated-for-TV group, the Monkees. Selected from a casting call that drew more than 400 applicants, the group starred in their own series and a major movie, and had eight Top 40 hits, two of which went to number one.

Integral to the success of Monkeemania, Beatlemania, and myriad other teen idol-manias was the teen fan magazine industry, which thrived during this era. A hybrid of the "girl's" magazines which debuted in the 1940s and early rock 'n' roll magazines, some of these publications had monthly sales of more than 900,000 copies.

Reflecting the relationship between the idols and publishing, teen fan magazine pioneer Charles Laufer once related how he honed in on the appeal of 1970s teen icon, David Cassidy. It happened as he was watching an episode of TV's *Marcus Welby, M.D.* "A kid comes on, and he's got diabetes. I didn't know who he was, but he was raw-boned and vulnerable, and I thought, this kid's terrific. So I waited for the credits. The next day I came into the office and said, 'Who the hell is David Cassidy?'" Laufer tracked down Cassidy, who was about to begin work on the 1970 TV show, *The Partridge Family*, about a family singing group. Laufer went on to publish the *Partridge Family* teen magazine, and to oversee the group's fan club. Though it was a fictional group, in which only two of the show's cast members, Cassidy and stepmother Shirley Jones, actually sang, the Partridge Family went on to have a number one hit, with "I Think I Love You." The shag-haired Cassidy would later call the group "the last gasp of innocence in America."

In truth, there have been many more gasps of innocence within the teen idol roll call. During the 1970s the roster included Cassidy's half-brother, Shaun Cassidy, as well as Donnie and Marie Osmond, Robbie Benson, and Andy Gibb. Among 1980s names were Scott Baio, John Stamos, Menudo, and Debbie Gibson. The safe, sweet side of teen idoldom continued in the 1990s, with the actor Jonathan Taylor Thomas and singing groups such as Hanson.

But another kind of teen idol, who is less than wholesome, also managed to exist in a parallel universe. The metamorphosis began in the late 1970s, and is exemplified by Kiss, which became a potent teen idol force despite the group's shock-value tactics. According to fan magazine publishers, kids rallied to the group's larger-than-life stage theatrics, as well as to the members' comic book-like appearances. Those appearances made them seem more like fictional characters, as opposed to "real" and therefore threatening heavy metal artists. Madonna, meanwhile, was embraced as the enticing embodiment of the disobedient girl and a proud boy toy, something about which young females fantasize. In the 1990s, that naughty but cool mantle shifted to the Spice Girls and their mantra espousing "girl power!"

Of course, the Spice Girls could not have succeeded in a more modest era; by the same token, a Connie Francis would today be considered an anachronism. For teen idols are both a product and a reflection of their times. As with all product, their success/failure is indelibly linked to marketing, as well as timing. The stakes are tantalizing. According to the Recording Industry Association of America, of the 532 million albums purchased in the United States in 1996, twenty-five percent were bought by 10 to 19-year-olds. That same group comprised a significant percentage, fifty-eight and thirty, respectively, of the rap and rock markets.

Just as the teen idols of the 1950s were able to become overnight successes as a result of television, the current teen idols are able to become multi-millionaires on the basis of synergy and mass-marketing. Consider: At their height in the late 1980s, the New Kids on the Block, comprised of five rapping Boston "boys," sold eighty million albums and $500 million worth of merchandising. Their 1990 earnings were $1 billion.

But the power of teen idoldom is not summed up merely by dollars and cents. "When you're talking about teen idols, you're talking about being godlike," said Bobby Sherman, a leading 1970s teen idol. But there are distinctions between the teen idol types. As explained by Sherman: "See, there's an A group and a B group. The A group is like the Beatles. They create a lifestyle which changes people. Then there's the B's, like I was. I was like a number in a system that was created in a succession of molds that perform well for their time and place."

Yet when the Beatles first arrived on the scene, they were perceived by the media to be no more than a fad. To young females, they were cause to celebrate, en masse, and to release sexual energy. The group's musical evolution and staying power could not have been foreseen. The same can be said of the young performers who carry on the teen idol tradition. Some may go on to achieve greatness. If not, they will doubtless live on in the scrapbooks and the memories of the fans whose hearts and lives they touched.

—Pat H. Broeske

FURTHER READING:

Broeske, Pat H., and Cheryl A. Latuner. "Teenzine: A Loss of Innocence." *Los Angeles Times Sunday Calendar.* August 25, 1985, 42-46.

Brown, Peter Harry, and Pat H. Broeske. *Down at the End of Lonely Street: The Life and Death of Elvis Presley.* New York, Dutton, 1997.

Cartnal, Alan. "Teen Idols. The Truth! . . . About Shaun and Scott and Jimmy and Leif and Willie! . . . What They Think About Everything!" *New West.* January 1, 1979, 38-43.

Farley, Ellen. "The Story of Frank and Fabe and Bob." *Los Angeles Times.* November 23, 1980, 30-31.

"50 Years of Teen Idols." *People Weekly.* July 27, 1982, 42-128.

Finn, Timothy. "Teen Idols Are the Profits of Today for Record Companies and Marketers." *Kansas City Star.* February 12, 1998, 21.

Miller, Jim, editor. *The Rolling Stone Illustrated History of Rock & Roll.* New York, Random House, 1980.

Morgan, Thomas B. "Teen-Age Heroes: Mirrors of Muddled Youth." *Esquire.* March 1960, 65-68.

Teenage Mutant Ninja Turtles

The Teenage Mutant Ninja Turtles cartoon characters—Leonardo, Raphael, Donatello, and Michaelangelo—were one of the greatest cross-media phenomena of the 1980s and early 1990s. The Turtles, ordinary pets mutated into superheroes, began as an underground comic book created by cartoonists Peter Laird and Kevin Eastman in the mid-1980s as a spoof of such comics as the mutant X-Men and the grim, urban Daredevil. An instant smash, the Turtles soon branched out into other media, including films, an animated television series, multiple toy and merchandise tie-ins, even a live-action television program. The success came at the cost of their identity, however, as the original, funky nature of the Turtles comics became more cartoonish and child-friendly to better facilitate their mass acceptance.

—Jay Parrent

FURTHER READING:

"Eastman & Laird & Their Pet Turtles." *Comics Sense.* July 1987, 50-52.

"Lights! Camera! Turtles!" *Comics Sense.* August 1989, 17-19, 50.

Teenagers

Initially invented as a marketing target, "teenagers" only came into existence after World War II. Possibly our most important years, our teenage years are a time of transition, a period in which we develop from children into adults. We may remember them as either the best or the worst days of our lives, but the life experiences encountered between the ages of 12 and 20 leave a lasting impression: burgeoning emotional and sexual feelings; physiological development of secondary sexual characteristics; entry into the order of

Teenagers in 1956.

society through individual and group affiliations. Since the instantiation of teenagers as a category, they subsequently may have been exploited ruthlessly as such by commercial interests, but this also has allowed (and continues to allow) the identification and interrogation of issues affecting one of the most important groups within society.

Following World War II, a sudden boom in affluence in the West produced new market forces: a growth in original consumer goods (nylon, televisions, fridge freezers) and the appearance of new groups at whom those goods could be marketed. Teenagers were one; they were initially invented as a target marketing group, a new demographic to be tapped, whose wealth came from their parents' increased financial freedom. The number of products created for and aimed at teenagers since World War II has been phenomenal, and shopping remains popular. In the 1990s, teens made 40 percent more trips to the mall than other shoppers. What is particularly interesting is what those products tell us about teenagers: what they're (supposedly) interested in and what their concerns are, plus how we think about them and how that thinking has changed over the decades. The realms of pop music, television, and cinema provide especially illuminating examples.

Pop music is seen as music for children. Passion for the predictable and disposable three-minute song is perceived as an immaturity of taste; we supposedly "grow out of" listening to pop music and

start listening to classical music, jazz, the blues, and so on. In addition, the short shelf-life of pop bands and the general transience and ephemerality of pop music is representative of the fickle tastes of changeable teenagers; it reflects the "passing phase" nature of teenage life. Elvis Presley was (and remains, even after his death in 1977) one of the most successful pop stars; unlike most pop musicians, Elvis's career spanned two decades. His meteoric rise to fame as a singer and guitarist was cashed in on with a raft of low-budget movies, often named after his song titles, including *Love Me Tender* (1956), *Jailhouse Rock* (1957), and *Blue Hawaii* (1961). At the beginning of his musical career, Elvis drew attention by dancing in a way branded as sexually lewd; he gyrated his hips while crooning, earning him the nickname "Elvis the Pelvis." Teenage girls screamed and swooned at his concerts, behavior that has become a common female reaction to male pop stars, especially boy bands.

The sexual aspect of Elvis's music was a cause for concern. A supposedly trivial form of music suddenly seemed subversive. Could the lyrics of pop music, or the antics of pop stars, pass on unwanted messages to a susceptible teenage audience? This has been a persistent worry for moral guardians and would-be censors. Teenagers are still seen as children and thus vulnerable and worthy of protection, yet in their journey toward adulthood, they are interested in adult issues such as sex and drugs. Girls also screamed, notably, at the Beatles, the

British four-piece whose enormous popularity and lengthy career challenged the status of pop music as trivial and ephemeral. Like Elvis, the Beatles also appeared in films specifically made for their teenage audience, including *A Hard Day's Night* (1964) and *Help!* (1965). In addition, as with Elvis, no marketing opportunity was too silly. It was possible, for instance, to buy Beatle "moptop" wigs. Teenagers, it seemed, would spend their money on anything, so long as it had a faint connection to their pop idols. Similarly, they would buy anything targeted directly at them; thus, in pop music, songs could be found targeted directly at teenagers and their concerns, such as "Teenage Idol," "Teenager in Love," and "Sweet Sixteen."

If longevity and/or success is achieved (which can be assisted by the possibility of cross-media synergy), the potential financial rewards for pop stars are large. This has led to the artificial manufacture of a great number of pop musicians and bands, from the Monkees in the 1960s (who also had their own television show) to the Backstreet Boys in the 1990s. The formula remains an occasionally successful one. If there has been one change in the form of pop music, it is that lyrics have become raunchier as restrictive moral codes have relaxed; the songs of teenage soul/R & B star Usher are exemplary of this fact. Generally, however, pop music remains anodyne, all sexuality being expressed in a suggestive yet naive way. Pop stars themselves may be styled to be attractive to the teenage audience, but it is an ambiguous, soft-edged, safe kind of attractiveness. It is unclear whether this is really what teenagers want, or merely what the producers and manufacturers of pop music will allow.

The invention of the teenager category coincided with the widespread introduction of the television set into American society, but, initially, television had problems programming material for teenagers; in contrast, children's programs and those for adults were clearly identifiable. Teenagers had to make do with shows with a broader appeal, such as popular family-oriented dramatic series, variety shows, and comedy programs, some of which featured teenage characters: *Little House on the Prairie, I Love Lucy, Bewitched, The Brady Bunch, The Johnny Carson Show.* This is not to say that programs for teenagers were not made; pop music shows, though usually lifeless and presented by adults, were popular, as were examples such as *The Monkees* television show. Teenagers were conceptualized by television during this period as "older children"; if they had their own interests, they were those dictated to them.

The gradual expansion of television over the decades, including the introduction of satellite and cable arenas, has produced a plethora of channels, all of which need filling with material. The 1980s and 1990s saw the production of an enormous number of programs aimed directly at teenagers, mostly comedies and drama series set in and around schools: *The Wonder Years, Beverly Hills 90210, Party of Five, My So-Called Life, Saved by the Bell,* and so on. In the 1990s, there were entire channels devoted to teenage programming. These programs projected a very different conception of teenagers than those of the 1960s. The adolescents of the 1990s were now "young adults," confronted with a raft of difficult social issues such as drug use, pregnancy, bullying, sexual identity, and homelessness. In addition, the stars of teenage television programs often appeared much like pop stars—physically attractive, yet sexually ambiguous and, therefore, safe.

Unlike television, cinema speedily capitalized on the existence of a solvent teenage audience. The 1950s was a decade in which drive-in movies became popular with high school students, and so a range of quickly produced films, in identifiable genres, were made specifically for this audience. These included a lengthy series of beach/surf movies, a wealth of teenage gang movies, and such cheaply made horror films as *I Was a Teenage Werewolf* (1957) and *I Was a Teenage Frankenstein* (1957). Also released during this decade were films about teenagers with a broader audience appeal, such as *The Wild One* (1954) and *Rebel without a Cause* (1955). Because of the film rating system, these movies about teenagers were able to offer a corrective to television's sanitized conception; the adolescents in *Rebel without a Cause*, for instance, deal with alcohol, suicide dares, gang bullying, knife fights, and homelessness, among other factors. Films about teenagers are numerous. This may be because the tribulations of adolescence are effective (melodramatic) narrative devices; it may be because Western culture tends to associate youth with beauty. The 1980s were notable for the number of films produced about teenagers; with the recurrent presence of certain actors, a series of these became known as the Brat Pack films: *Sixteen Candles* (1984), *Pretty in Pink* (1986), *The Breakfast Club* (1985), and *Ferris Bueller's Day Off* (1986). Issues affecting the teens in these narratives included truancy, detention, dating, and drug use— issues similar to those impinging on 1950s movie teenagers.

Cinematic representations of adolescence tend to depict it as either a difficult time of angst, alienation, and loneliness, or as an idyllic period of innocence, unlimited fun, and growth through misadventure. The first set produces iconic images of rebel teens— James Dean, River Phoenix, Drew Barrymore, Natalie Wood. The second—including such films as *American Graffiti* (1973) and *Stand by Me* (1986)—serves a similar mythologizing purpose, reinforcing the cultural conception of adolescence as "the best years of your life." In the 1990s, there have been two minor developmental trends in the filmic depiction of teenagers. First, teenagers actually may be portrayed as sexually active, rather than this simply being suggested; for example, the audience sees two of the teenage characters having sex in *Inventing the Abbotts* (1997). Second, it has become possible to represent teenagers as vicious, unpleasant individuals; in *Kids* (1995), the two lead characters commit acts of racial and sexual violence without remorse.

—Glyn Davis

FURTHER READING:

Austin, Joe, and Michael Willard, editors. *Generations of Youth: Youth Cultures and History in Twentieth-Century America.* New York, New York University Press, 1998.

Barson, Michael, and Steven Heller. *Teenage Confidential: An Illustrated History of the American Teen.* San Francisco, Chronicle Books, 1998.

Bernstein, Jonathan. *Pretty in Pink: The Golden Age of Teenage Movies.* New York, St. Martin's Press, 1997.

Jaffe, Michael L. *Adolescence.* New York, John Wiley and Sons, 1998.

Munk, Nina. "Girl Power!" *Fortune.* Vol. 136, No. 11, December 8, 1997.

Owen, Robert. *Gen X TV: The Brady Bunch to Melrose Place (Television Series).* New York, Syracuse University Press, 1997.

Tejano Music

During the 1930s and 1940s a music developed which mirrored the evolution of Hispanics in southwestern cities into Mexican Americans, a bicultural community emerging from Mexican roots within the United States. This was the first generation of Americans of Mexican descent to aspire for inclusion in Anglo-American life. Popular dance band ensembles catered to this generation's biculturalism by playing genres chosen from both the Latin and the American traditions: *bolero, danzón, guaracha,* and *rumba* alternating with boogie, swing, and fox-trot, among others. After World War II, a type of fusion of the traditions took place that developed into a distinctive sound, especially among the *orquestas* and *conjuntos* in Texas, where the largest Hispanic recording companies existed at that time. The result was a music that came to be known as Tejano.

As orchestras became more professional and ballroom dance circuits extended throughout the Southwest, the Texas recording artists became the greatest in demand and spread their new music throughout the Southwest and northern Mexico. Among the first prominent big bands were Beto Villa's from Falfurrias, Texas, whose leader is sometimes called the father of the Mexican American *orquesta*. Villa popularized a folksy, ''country''-style polka; this polka, in particular, came to be known as ''Tex-Mex,'' especially when compared with the more sophisticated urban sounds of *danzones, guarachas,* fox-trots, and swings. Villa's influence was so strong that many followers appeared throughout the Southwest, most noteworthy of them being singer-saxophonist Isidro López, also from Texas, who is known for adding the working-class *canción ranchera* to the Tex-Mex repertoire. Balde González of Victoria, Texas, and Pedro Bugarín of Phoenix, Arizona, smoothed out the musical deliveries and broadened the repertoire of genres included in Tex-Mex.

The peak years for the Mexican-American orquesta were the 1960s and 1970s, during which emerged Little Joe Hernández, one of the greatest all-time performers and popularizers of Tex-Mex. Little Joe led a band made up of family members and friends under a series of names and struggled to get studios to record his music and radio stations to play it in Texas. Finally, he had to form his own recording and distribution companies. Little Joe, in addition, fused the Tex-Mex *ranchero* sound with American jazz and rock within the same musical number to achieve a unique bi-musical sound which came to be called ''La Onda Chicana'' (The Chicano Wave). Little Joe's first experiment in this Chicano Wave occurred on his hugely successful 1972 LP *Para La Gente* (*For the People*). Backing Joe and his brother Johnny's harmonic duet were the usual instruments of a well-organized Mexican American band of those years: two trumpets, two saxophones, a trombone, and a rhythm section of bass, electric guitar, drums, and keyboards. On the album, many of the arrangements were augmented with strings from the Dallas symphony—a novelty for Tex-Mex music—and with the interlacing of jazz riffs. Even at the turn of the century, many of the numbers included on this historic LP are standard fare among dance bands in Mexican American communities.

Texas continues to be the center for Tejano music, from whence dance bands and recording artists tour to as far north as Chicago and New York City and as far south as Mexico City. The advent of the three Spanish-language television networks further popularized the music into the Caribbean and South America. Younger generations of Mexican Americans further infused the music with rock influences in the 1990s and took it far afield from its country roots, mirroring the overwhelming concentration of Hispanics in big cities today.

—Nicolás Kanellos

FURTHER READING:

Peña, Manuel. *The Texas Mexican-Conjunto: History of a Working-Class Music.* Austin, University of Texas Press, 1985.

———. ''From *Ranchera* to *Jaitón:* Ethnicity and Class in Texas-Mexican Music.'' *Ethnomusicology.* Vol. 29, No. 1, 1985, 29-55.

Telephone

The telephone is a device for conducting spoken conversations across any distance beyond the range of the unaided human ear or the unamplified human voice. It works by transferring the atmospheric vibrations of human speech into a solid body, and by converting those vibrations into electrical impulses sent through a conducting medium—originally metal wires, but now optical fibers and electromagnetic microwaves as well. The word is a compound of two Greek words, ''*tele*'' (''far'') and ''*phone*'' (''sound''), and the instrument is the most widely-used of all telecommunications appliances, with hundreds of millions of telephones in use all over the world. On any given

Alexander Graham Bell with his invention, the telephone.

business day, approximately two billion calls are placed, just in the United States. The telephone is also the archetypal electronic "medium," in the sense of the word intended by Marshall McLuhan—an "extension of man"—but its social impact is grossly understudied in favor of the more readily observable "bully blow" of the television. Telephones are small and unobtrusive and their impact on our visible environment (except for the poles and wires) has not transformed our relationship to it.

Notwithstanding a host of rival claimants, the traditional account of the telephone's invention by the Scottish-born Alexander Graham Bell (1847-1922) remains substantially the correct one. While the word "telephone" itself had been used to describe a device similar to a children's string telephone as long ago as the seventeenth century, and although the general concepts on which the invention was based had been known for several decades, it was certainly Bell who experienced the sudden flash of insight which he immediately translated into a working model.

Bell and his assistant Thomas Watson had been trying to develop not a telephone, but something Bell called a "harmonic telegraph," by which he hoped to expand the bottleneck throttling communications traffic and permit the transmission of more than one telegraph message over a single wire at the same time. Bell's ideas involved a series of vibrating metal reeds (like those used in wind instruments). Of course, once he had developed that technology, his goal was, in fact, to discover a way to transmit all the sounds of the human voice via his "harmonic telegraph." On June 2, 1875, Bell and Watson were working at opposite ends of a line and Bell heard the distinct sound of a plucked reed coming through the line. He ran to the next room and shouted to his assistant, "Watson! What did you do then? Don't change anything!" From that moment, it took only an hour or so more of plucking the reeds and listening to the sounds they made before Bell was able to give Watson instructions on making the first "Bell telephone," which was capable of transmitting only the sounds of the human voice, not words. Bell and Watson worked through the summer of 1875, and in September, Bell began to write the specifications for his basic patent, which was issued on March 7, 1876 (#174,465). It is, to date, the most valuable patent ever issued. (The famous "Mr. Watson, come here! I want you!" was spoken after the first patent was issued, when Bell and Watson were working on perfecting their transmitter.) Ultimately victorious, Bell had to defend his patent in over 600 separate lawsuits.

The Bell Telephone Company, first of its kind, was founded on July 9, 1877. That same July, Bell married Mabel Hubbard and sailed to England to introduce his telephone there. Well before 1900, Thomas Watson, Thomas Edison, Emil Berliner, and others had worked with Bell's patented technology to produce what would be recognized as a telephone in the late 1990s. The telephone has consisted of the same basic components: a power source, switch hook, dialer, ringer, transmitter, and receiver.

The social impact of the telephone has been literally incalculable. Although the telegraph, patented by the painter Samuel B. Morse in 1840, enjoys pride of place as the first electric instrument to extend and greatly speed human communication, it never became a ubiquitous home appliance like the telephone—it was too complicated to use, and required too much special knowledge (codes, key technique). All a person needs to know in order to use a telephone is how to talk and to listen; it is not necessary to be literate or to have more than a

minimal mechanical aptitude. It is, moreover, next to impossible to gossip using a telegraph. Like a religion, telegraphy has its privileged class, the operators, and gossip passes most freely between equals, without going through an intermediary. Because the telephone enables two people to exchange gossip directly, though they may be on opposite sides of the Earth, the telephone has, more than any other invention, produced what Marshall McLuhan called "the global village."

The telephone has changed war and business and the whole gamut of public activities, as well, but it has not transformed them out of recognition, the way it has altered the fundamental relationship of one individual to another and of one individual to society. Warfare is altered by the invention of a new weapon, from the metal sword to the atomic bomb; business is altered by intellectual inventions like double entry book-keeping or speculation or advertising or market capitalism. Public life has changed with the emergence of new institutions—the law, the "Republic," democracy, dictatorship— and is now being replaced by the television camera.

But the telephone began the seismic shift in sensibility described by Martin Pawley in his book *The Private Future*: "Western societies are collapsing not from an assault on their most cherished values, but from a voluntary, almost enthusiastic abandonment of them by people who are learning to lead private lives of an unprecedented completeness with the aid of the momentum of a technology which is evolving more and more into a pattern of socially atomizing appliances." The telephone, which has been traditionally promoted as a means of bringing people together, of connecting them, is in fact the archetype of Pawley's "socially atomizing appliance." The filmmaker Bill Forsyth gives a perfect example of this in his film, *Local Hero*. The character played by Peter Riegert wants to invite to dinner a girl standing less than 20 feet away from him on the other side of a glass partition—so he dials her extension. That is "the Private Future" in action.

Cordless phones, answering machines, cellular phones, "call waiting," phones in automobiles, headset phones which free up both hands—all these seem likely to increase our dissociation from the here and now, and to hasten our withdrawal from the public sphere into "private lives of an unprecedented completeness." The dangers inherent in the disappearance of any meaningful public life should be obvious. On the most primitive level, consider the person driving a big shiny suburban wagon, about to negotiate a tricky left turn through a busy intersection while they chat on the telephone with a friend. This person has the illusion of being in two places at once— with the friend and in traffic—but is in fact nowhere at all. The friendship, however, is not in physical danger—the other vehicles approaching that intersection, along with their passengers, are in the gravest peril. By the end of the 1990s legislation restricting the use of telephones in automobiles in the United States began to pass in several states. The whole concept of interdependence, of civic responsibility, is losing its force. The huge juggernaut of communications technology which was launched when Alexander Graham Bell burst in on Thomas Watson and shouted "Don't change anything!" has changed everything. Whether for the better or the worse depends on the relative importance you ascribe to the social contract.

—Gerald Carpenter

FURTHER READING:

Casson, Herbert Newton. *The History of the Telephone*. Chicago, A.C. McClurg, 1910.

Televangelist Jimmy Swaggart

Coe, Lewis. *The Telephone and Its Several Inventors: A History.* Jefferson, North Carolina, McFarland, 1995.

Fischer, Claude S. *America Calling: A Social History of the Telephone to 1940.* Berkeley and Los Angeles, University of California Press, 1992.

Harlow, Alvin F. *Old Wires and New Waves: The History of the Telegraph, Telephone, and Wireless.* New York, D. Appleton-Century, 1936.

McLuhan, Marshall. *Understanding Media: The Extensions of Man.* New York, McGraw-Hill, 1964.

Pawley, Martin. *The Private Future: Causes and Consequences of Community Collapse in the West.* London, Thames and Hudson, 1973.

Prescott, George B. *Bell's Electric Speaking Telephone: Its Invention, Construction, Application, Modification, and History.* 1884. Reprint, New York, Arno Press, 1972.

Stehman, Jonas Warren. *The Financial History of the American Telephone and Telegraph Company.* Boston, Houghton Mifflin, 1925.

Stern, Ellen, and Emily Gwathmey. *Once Upon a Telephone: an Illustrated Social History.* New York, Harcourt Brace, 1994.

Televangelism

Since the beginnings of commercial radio, evangelical Christians have recognized the effectiveness of the broadcast media as a vehicle for disseminating their faith. By enabling them to reach new audiences as well as committed believers, broadcasting has provided evangelists with a means of building large and widespread followings. As a result, religious broadcasters have continually taken advantage of new broadcast technologies, from local radio programs in the early 1920s to 24-hour cable television networks by the late 1970s. The use of television by evangelists as a medium for expressing their views proved to be an especially influential development during the last quarter of the twentieth century, as conflicts between religious conservatives and mainstream popular culture grew. In this context, the term ''televangelism'' became widely adopted to describe the use of broadcasting to promote not only evangelical Christian beliefs, but also a wide range of social and political views espoused by Christian fundamentalists.

The roots of contemporary televangelism can be traced to the 1950s, when evangelists such as Billy Graham, Rex Humbard, and Oral Roberts started to use television programs to spread their conservative Protestant beliefs. Most early examples of televangelism adopted a traditional format, concentrating on sermons, church services, and revival meetings, and operated on fairly small budgets. Early televangelist programming was also generally restricted to Sunday mornings, and was usually broadcast over a small number of stations covering a limited geographical area. Over time, however, technological changes and increasing resources allowed televangelists to reach much larger audiences. The advent of videotape, for example, provided an inexpensive and flexible means of distributing programs, so that they did not have to be broadcast live or recorded on expensive motion picture film. And the proliferation of television stations during the 1950s and 1960s provided a broader variety of outlets for televangelism, as did the subsequent expansion of cable television.

As a result of these innovations, televangelism underwent a major period of growth during the 1970s. Organizations like Pat Robertson's Christian Broadcasting Network and Jim Bakker's Praise The Lord (PTL) Satellite Network were able to use local cable television systems, linked by satellite transmissions, to bring their programming to virtually all parts of the country, and throughout the week, not just on Sundays. To take advantage of this increase in exposure, televangelists also adopted new programming formats, such the talk show and the news magazine, which had become staples of commercial television. The rapid growth in their operations also brought greater political influence to televangelists during the late 1970s and 1980s. With the conservative turn in American politics at this time, and the rise of the Christian right as a political force, prominent televangelists like Jerry Falwell and Pat Robertson found that broadcasting provided them with a powerful tool for publicizing their views and shaping the nation's political agenda.

Towards the end of the 1980s, however, televangelism went into a period of decline, primarily as a result of separate financial and sexual scandals involving Jim Bakker and Jimmy Swaggart, two leading religious broadcasters. Their sexual misconduct and Bakker's misappropriation of funds donated to the PTL Network exposed televangelism to increasing public criticism and suspicion. The core audience of the television evangelists did not turn away from them, but their broader influence within American society dropped, as did their television ratings. The failure of Pat Robertson to win the Republican presidential nomination in 1988 also marked a downturn in the political influence of the conservative televangelists. Christian broadcasters responded to these trends by trying to broaden the appeal of their programming, experimenting with new formats and offering an increasing number of family-oriented programs without an explicit religious or political message.

Through their successful use of broadcasting technology, televangelists have established a notable presence in American popular culture over the past several decades. Considerable disagreement exists over the size of their audiences, even before the scandals of the 1980s, and a number of studies have suggested that televangelists have had more success in reinforcing the faith of existing believers than in reaching new converts. Nonetheless, televangelism has become a persistent feature of the American broadcast media, and as such has contributed substantially to the diversity of views that constitute American popular culture.

—Roger W. Stump

FURTHER READING:

Armstrong, Ben. *The Electric Church.* Nashville, Thomas Nelson Publishers, 1979.

Bruce, Steve. *Pray TV: Televanglism in America.* London, Routledge, 1990.

Hadden, Jeffrey K., and Anson Shupe. *Televangelism: Power and Politics on God's Frontier.* New York, Henry Holt, 1988.

Hadden, Jeffrey K., and Charles E. Swann. *Primetime Preachers: The Rising Power of Televangelism.* Reading, Massachusetts, Addison-Wesley, 1981.

Schultze, Quentin J. *Televangelism and American Culture: The Business of Popular Religion.* Grand Rapids, Michigan, Baker Book House, 1991.

Television

At the same time radio began to achieve commercial viability in the 1920s, the United States and Britain began experimenting with "television," the wireless transmission of moving pictures. Although Britain was initially somewhat more successful, both countries experienced a lot of difficulty in the early stages. There were a variety of reason for this. In America, many people whose livelihoods were tied to radio were also responsible for developing television. Accordingly, they were in no hurry to see radio, a sure money maker, usurped by the new medium. In addition, the Depression greatly slowed the development of television in the 1930s. There was also a tremendous amount of infighting between potential television manufacturers and the Federal Communications Commission (FCC) in trying to establish uniform technical standards. And finally, just as it seemed as though television was poised to enter American homes, the onset of World War II delayed its ascendancy until the war's end. However, in the late 1940s and early 1950s commercial television exploded on the American market, forever changing the way products are sold, people

A couple ponders the purchase of their first television.

are entertained, and news events are reported. In the years immediately following World War II television quickly became America's dominant medium, influencing, shaping, and recording popular culture in a way no other media has ever equaled.

Although televisions first appeared on the market in 1939, because there were virtually no stations and no established programming, it wasn't until just after World War II that TV began its meteoric rise to media dominance. As John Findling and Frank Thackeray note in *Events That Changed America in the Twentieth Century,* in 1946 only 7,000 TV sets were sold. However, as television stations began appearing in an increasing number of cities, the number of sets sold rose dramatically. In 1948 172,000 sets were sold; in 1950 there were more than 5,000,000 sets sold. By 1960 more than 90 percent of American homes had TV sets, a percentage which has only climbed since. Before television, Americans had spent their leisure time in a variety of ways. But as each new station appeared in a particular city, corresponding drops would occur in restaurant business, movie gates, book and magazine sales, and radio audiences. By the early 1960s Americans were watching over 40 hours of TV a week, a number that has remained remarkably stable ever since.

Television originally only had 12 Very High Frequency (VHF) channels—2 through 13. In the late 1940s over 100 stations were competing for transmission on VHF channels. Frequency overcrowding resulted in stations interfering with one another, which led to the FCC banning the issuance of new licenses for VHF channels for nearly four years, at the conclusion of which time stations receiving new licenses were given recently developed Ultra High Frequency (UHF) channels (14 through 88). However, most TV sets needed a special attachment to receive UHF channels, which also had a worse picture and poorer sound than VHF channels. Unfortunately, it was mostly educational, public access, and community channels that were relegated to UHF. Because of the FCC's ban, the three major networks, ABC, CBS, and NBC, were able to corner the VHF channels and dominate the television market until well into the 1980s.

From its introduction in American society, television has proven itself capable of holding its audience riveted to the screen for countless hours. As a result, people who saw television as a means through which to provide culturally uplifting programming to the American public were gravely disappointed. Instead, TV almost immediately became an unprecedentedly effective means of selling products. Most Americans weren't interested in "educational" programming, and if people don't watch advertisers don't pay for air time in which to sell their products. TV shows in the late 1940s followed the model established by the success of radio; single advertisers paid for whole shows, the most common of which were half hour genre and variety shows. But in 1950 a small lipstick company named Hazel Bishop changed forever the way companies sold their products.

When Hazel Bishop first began advertising on TV in 1950 they had only $50,000 a year in sales. In two short years of television advertising, and at a time when only 10 percent of American homes had TV sets, that number rose to a stunning $4.5 million. As advertisers flocked to hawk their products on TV, TV executives scrambled to find a way to accommodate as many companies as possible, which would result in astronomical profits for both the advertisers and the networks. TV executives realized that single product sponsorship was no longer effective. Instead, they devised a system of longer breaks during a show, which could be split up into 30

second "spots" and sold to a much larger number of advertisers. Although this advertising innovation led to television's greatest period of profitability, it also led to advertising dictating television programming.

In the early 1950s television advertisers realized they had a monopoly on the American public; they were competing with each other, not with other mediums, such as books or magazines. Americans watched regardless what was on. Advertisers discovered that what most people would watch was what was the least objectionable (and often the most innocuous) show in a given time slot; hence the birth of the concept of "Least Objectionable Programming." A TV show didn't have to be good, it only had to be less objectionable than the other shows in the same time slot. Although more "serious" dramatic television didn't entirely disappear, the majority of shows were tailored to create the mood advertisers thought would result in their consumers being the most amenable to their products. By the mid-1950s lightweight sitcoms dominated the American television market. The relative success and happiness of television characters became easily measurable by the products they consumed.

Prior to the twentieth century, "leisure time" was a concept realized by generally only the very wealthy. But as the American middle class grew astoundingly fast in the post World War II boom, a much larger population than ever before enjoyed leisure time, which helped contribute to television's remarkable popularity. Perhaps even more important was the rise of the concept of "disposable income," money that people could spend on their wants rather than needs. Advertisers paying for the right to influence how people might spend their disposable income largely funded television. As a result, television was ostensibly "free" prior to the late 1970s. Nevertheless, television's cost has always been high; it has played perhaps the single largest role in contributing to America's becoming a consumer culture unparalleled in world history. Countless television shows have achieved an iconic stature in American popular culture, but none have had as powerful an effect on the way American's live their day to day lives as have commercials.

By the mid-1950s it became clear that television's influence would not be confined to the screen. Other forms of media simply could not compete directly with television. As result, they had to change their markets and formats in order to secure a consistent, although generally much smaller than pre-television, audience. Perhaps the most far reaching consequence of the rise of television is that America went from being a country of readers to a country of watchers. Previously hugely popular national magazines such as *Colliers, Life,* and *The Saturday Evening Post* went out of business in the late 1950s. Likewise, as television, an ostensibly more exciting visual medium than radio, adapted programming previously confined to the radio, radio shows quickly lost their audience. Magazines and radio stations responded similarly. Rather than trying to compete with TV they became specialized, targeting a singular demographic audience. Simultaneously, advertisers grew more savvy in their research and development and realized that highly specific consumer markets could be reached via radio and magazine advertising. Strangely, television's rise to prominence secured the long term success of radio and magazines; their response to the threat of television eventually resulted in a much larger number of magazines and radio stations than had been available before television. In the late 1990s audiences can find a radio station or magazine that focuses on just about any subject they might want.

Perhaps the industry struck hardest by the advent of television was the American film industry. Hollywood initially considered TV an inferior market, not worthy of its consideration. And why not, for in the late 1940s as many as 90 million people a week went to the movies. But television's convenience and easy accessibility proved much competition for Hollywood. By the mid-1950s the industry's audience had been reduced to half its former number. Hollywood never recovered as far as actual theater audiences are concerned. In fact, by the late 1990s only 15 million people a week attended the cinema, and this in a country with twice the population it had in the late 1940s. However, Hollywood, as it seemingly always does, found a way to adapt. Rather than relying exclusively on box-office receipts, Hollywood learned to use television to its advantage. Now after market profits, including the money generated from pay-per-view, cable channels, premium movie channels, and, most of all, video sales and rentals, are just as important to a film's success, if not more so, than a film's box-office take.

In addition, television's media domination has contributed greatly to blurring the lines between TV and Hollywood. Most Hollywood studios also produce TV shows on their premises. Furthermore, just as radio stars once made the jump from the airwaves to the silver screen, TV stars routinely make the jump from the small screen to the movies. As a result, many American celebrities can't be simply categorized in the way they once were. Too many stars have their feet in too many different mediums to validate singular labels. Take, for example, Oprah Winfrey, a television talk show maven who has also been involved in several successful books, promoted the literary careers of others, frequently appeared on other talk shows and news magazines as a guest, and has acted in and produced a number of both television and Hollywood films. Although hers is an extreme example, television's unequaled cultural influence has resulted in turning any number of stars who would have formerly been confined to one or two mediums into omnipresent multimedia moguls.

If radio ushered in the era of "broadcast journalism," TV helped to further define and legitimize it. In addition, television newscasts have changed the way Americans receive and perceive news. By the late 1950s TV reporters had learned to take advantage of emerging technologies and use them to cover breaking news stories live. Television broadcasts and broadcasters grew to hold sway over public opinion. For, example, public sentiment against the Vietnam War was fueled by nightly broadcasts of its seemingly senseless death and destruction. Walter Cronkite added further fuel to the growing fire of anger and resentment in 1968 when he declared on-air that he thought the war in Vietnam was a "terrible mistake." When most Americans think of the events surrounding JFK, Martin Luther King, and Bobby Kennedy's assassinations, the civil rights movement, the first moon walk, the Challenger space shuttle disaster, the Gulf War, and the 1992 riots in Los Angeles after the Rodney King trial verdict, it is the televised images that first come to mind.

Unfortunately, by the late 1990s many Americans had come to rely on television news as their main source of information. In addition to nightly news and news oriented cable networks, cheap-to-make and highly profitable "news magazines" such as *Dateline NBC, 20/20,* and *48 Hours* have become TV's most common form of programming. Rarely do these shows feature news of much importance; instead, they rely on lurid and titillating reports that do nothing to enrich our knowledge of world events but nevertheless receive consistently high ratings, thus ensuring the continuing flow of advertising dollars. That most Americans rely on television for their information means that most Americans are underinformed; for full accounts of a particular story it is still necessary to seek out supporting written records in newspapers, magazines, and books. The problem with relying on television for information is, as Neil Postman writes, "not that television presents us with entertaining subject matter but that all subject matter is presented as entertaining." Accordingly, it is Postman's contention that America's reliance on TV for information is dangerous, for when people "become distracted by trivia, when cultural life is redefined as a perpetual round of entertainments, when serious conversation becomes a form of baby-talk, when, in short, a people become an audience and their public business a vaudeville act, then a nation finds itself at risk."

Because of news broadcasting and the fact that television is the best way to reach the largest number of Americans, television has helped shape American politics in the second half of the twentieth century. Effective television advertising has become crucial to the success or failure of nearly any national election. Unfortunately, such advertising is rarely completely factual or issue oriented. Instead, most such advertisements are used to smear the reputation of a particular candidate's opponent. Perhaps the most famous example of such advertisements occurred in the 1988 Presidential campaign, during which Republican George Bush ran a series of slanted and inflammatory spots about his Democratic opponent, Michael Dukakis. Furthermore, the careers of several presidents have become inextricably intertwined with TV. For example, President Ronald Reagan, a former minor movie star and television product pitchman, used his television savvy so effectively that he came to be known as "the Great Communicator." Conversely, President Bill Clinton, whose initial effective use of television has reminded some of JFK's, became victim to his own marketability when in August of 1998 he admitted in a televised speech to the nation that he had lied about his affair with a young intern named Monica Lewinsky. His admission, which was meant to put the incident behind him, instead spawned a virtual television cottage industry, with literally dozens of shows devoting themselves to continual discussion about his fate, which was ultimately decided in a televised impeachment trial.

Strangely, considering the man was wary of the medium, perhaps no politician's career has been more tied to television than Richard Nixon's. As a vice presidential candidate on Dwight Eisenhower's 1952 Republican Presidential bid, Nixon came under fire for allegedly receiving illegal funding. A clamor arose to have Nixon removed from the ticket. On September 23, 1952, Nixon went on TV and delivered a denial to the accusations, which has since become known as "the Checkers speech." More than 1 million favorable letters and telegrams were sent supporting Nixon; he remained on the ticket and he and Eisenhower won in a landslide. Conversely only eight years later TV would play a role in Nixon's losing his own bid for the White House. Nixon agreed to a series of televised debates with his much more telegenic opponent, John Fitzgerald Kennedy. Nixon's pasty face and sweaty brow may have cost him the election. Many historian's believe that Kennedy "won" the debates as much by his more polished appearance and manner than by anything he said. Nixon learned from his error. While again running for the Presidency in 1968, Nixon hired a public relations firm to run his campaign. The result was a much more polished, image conscious, and TV friendly Nixon; he won the election easily. In the last chapter of Nixon's political career, broadcast and print media helped spur investigations into his involvement with the Watergate affair. The hearings were broadcast live on TV, which helped to turn public opinion against the President, who resigned from office as a result. One of the most famous images in TV history of television is that of Nixon turning and waving to the crowd as he boarded the helicopter that removed him from power forever.

Prior to World War II, baseball was widely recognized as America's national pastime. Games were often broadcast live, and the country blissfully spent its summers pursuing the on-the-field exploits of larger than life figures such as Babe Ruth. However, after the war other sports grew to prominence, largely because of television, beer, and, until 1970, cigarette advertisers, who saw in sports audiences a target market for their products. Individual sports such as golf and tennis, grew in popularity, but team sports such as hockey, basketball, and most of all, football had the greatest increases. By the late 1960s and with the advent of the Super Bowl, annually America's most viewed broadcast, football surpassed baseball as America's favorite pastime. Because of their nature, team sports have a built in drama that escalates in intensity over the duration of a season. Americans are drawn to the players in this drama, which has resulted in athletes hawking products perhaps more than any other cultural icons. In fact, as advertising revenues increasingly fund sports, athletes have become perhaps the highest paid workers in America. Michael Jordan earned a reported $30 million to play for the Chicago Bulls in the 1997-98 season. In the Fall of 1998 pitcher Kevin Brown signed with the Los Angeles Dodgers for a seven year deal worth $105 million. Accompanying their paychecks is a rise in media scrutiny. Elite athletes are hounded by paparazzi in a way once reserved for movie stars and royalty. Such is the price of television fame in America.

Despite the ridiculous salaries and the accompanying out-of-control egos of many athletes and owners, it could be argued that television has made sports better for most people. Seeing a game live at a venue remains thrilling, but TV, with its multiple camera angles and slow motion instant replays, is by far a better way to actually see a game. In addition to better vision, one has all the comforts of home without the hassle of inclement weather, expensive tickets, heavy traffic, and nearly impossible parking. And because of TV and its live transmission of sports, certain moments have become a part of America's collective cultural fabric in a way that never would have been possible without television. Heroes and goats achieve legendary status nearly immediately. Just as important to our culture as the televising of events of political and social importance is the broadcast of sporting events. Although not particularly significant in their contribution to human progress, because of television the images of San Francisco 49er Joe Montana's pass to Dwight Clark in the back of the endzone in the 1981 NFC championship game to beat the Dallas Cowboys or of a ground ball dribbling between Boston Red Sox first baseman Bill Buckner's legs in the sixth game of the 1986 World Series are just as much a part of American culture's visual memory as the image of Neil Armstrong walking on the moon.

As the twentieth century careens to a close and America prepares to embark on a new century, debates over television's inarguable influence continue to rage. Is TV too violent? Is television's content too sexually oriented? Has television news coverage become vacuous and reliant on the superfluous and tawdry? Is TV damaging our children and contributing to the fraying of America's social fabric? Regardless of the answers to these and countless other questions about television's influence, the inarguable fact is that television is

the most important popular culture innovation in history. Our heroes and our villains are coronated and vanquished on television. Sound bites as diverse in intent and inception as "where's the beef," "read my lips," and "just do it," have become permanently and equally ensconced in the national lexicon. Television is not without its flaws, but its accessibility and prevalence has created what never before existed: shared visual cultural touchstones. As one America mourned the death of JFK, argued about the veracity of the Clarence Thomas/Anita Hill hearings, recoiled in horror as Reginald Denny was pulled from his truck and beaten, and cheered triumphantly as Mark McGwire hoisted his son in the air after hitting his 62nd home run. For better or for worse, in the second half of the twentieth century television dominated and influenced the American cultural landscape in an unprecedented fashion.

—Robert C. Sickels

FURTHER READING:

Baker, William F., and George Dessart. *Down the Tube: An Inside Account of the Failure of American Television.* New York, BasicBooks, 1998.

Barnouw, Erik. *Tube of Plenty: The Evolution of American Television.* New York, Oxford University Press, 1990.

Caldwell, John Thornton. *Televisuality: Style, Crisis, and Authority in American Television.* New Brunswick, Rutgers University Press, 1995.

Comstock, George. *The Evolution of American Television.* Newbury Park, Sage Publications, 1989.

Findling, John E., and Frank W. Thackeray. *Events that Changed America in the Twentieth Century.* Westport, Connecticut, Greenwood Press, 1996.

Himmelstein, Hal. *Television Myth and the American Mind.* Westport, Praeger Publishers, 1994.

Postman, Neil. *Amusing Ourselves to Death.* New York, Penguin Books, 1985.

Stark, Steven D. *Glued to the Set: The 60 Television Shows and Events that Made Us Who We Are Today.* New York, Free Press, 1997.

Sturcken, Frank. *Live Television: The Golden Age of 1946-1958 in New York.* Jefferson, North Carolina, McFarland & Co., 1990.

Udelson, Joseph H. *The Great Television Race: A History of the American Television Industry 1925-1941.* The University of Alabama Press, 1982.

Television Anchors

According to television news legend Walter Cronkite, the term "anchorman" was invented by Sig Mickelson, the first head of the television and radio news department at CBS. It was expressly coined for use at the political conventions of 1952, the first ever covered by modern television. These conventions were made coherent by one

Walter Cronkite

broadcaster who provided perspective on events and introduced reporters bringing news from various parts of the convention; in short, a man who anchored the broadcast. In the United States and other developed countries around the world, television news anchors have become the de facto source of news for much of the public. With fewer people reading newspapers, and more and more getting their information from television, television news anchors on national and local newscasts have become the people the public turns to with the question, "What happened today?" Television news anchors, with their individual quirks and inflections, help to put a human face on the news. The power of the anchor to slant or comment on the news has been a source of concern for conservative and liberal critics alike. In totalitarian systems, they are often seen as nothing more than the face of the government, reporting news which is patently false or propagandistic.

Walter Cronkite set the standard for anchors in the United States during the period when he was known as the "most trusted man in America." Cronkite was even urged to run for president at various times in his career. His sign off, "And that's the way it is," rivaled Edward R. Murrow's "Good night and good luck" as the most popular signature piece of any news person. Other significant news

anchors of the 1960s included Chet Huntley and David Brinkley, who brought a partnership sensibility to the job that became a template for other newscasts. Their familiar signature—"Goodnight Chet. Goodnight David"—was often invoked in both comedy and drama.

The first television news anchors were used on weather reports and national and local television newscasts. Many of the first news anchors had worked originally in radio where the news format consisted of a news "reader" announcing the news in sonorous and serious tones. This immediately translated to television, where a clock or sheet of paper were used as props to make the set design appear serious. Early local television news instituted the "anchor" as the centerpiece of the show, delivering news, sports, and weather. It was only late in the 1960s that news programs began to have separate segments for different types of news, each presented by its own reporter. During this period, the news anchor began to rise in prominence, since he (early anchors were almost exclusively male) was the person that attracted viewers to the channel. The most popular anchors were those who appeared trustworthy and serious.

In the 1970s, feminism began to lead to the installation of female co-anchors on many newscasts. Soon the serious reading of the news was supplemented with repartee and chat among co-anchors. News consultants, such as Frank Magid and Associates, helped to bring about a more "scientific" method of choosing news anchors based on demographic sensibilities and entertainment style. Men and women with telegenic looks and breezy ad libbing skills are used to attract viewers, while older news people with significant experience are usually retired or given reporting assignments in the field. Audiences seem to want reporters they can trust, but anchorpeople who entertain them.

The conflict caused by the changing role of the news anchor was probably best highlighted in *Network* (1976), Paddy Chayefsky's vivid send-up of the news industry, which presaged the merging of news and entertainment. In the film, the news anchor, after suffering a mental breakdown, returns to the news desk only to entreat his audience to "get out of their chairs, go to the window and scream, I am as mad as hell and I'm not going to take it anymore!" The anchor's complaint became a popular catch phrase for the universal frustration of modern life. Ted Baxter, the fictional news anchor on the *Mary Tyler Moore Show* (1970-77), perhaps best exemplified the stereotype of the modern anchorman: the vacuous, handsome man, puffed up with self-importance and barely aware of the meaning of anything he is reading on the air.

—Jeff Ritter

FURTHER READING:

Cunningham, Liz. *Talking Politics: Choosing the President in the Television Age.* Westport, Connecticut, Praeger, 1995.

Fensch, Thomas, editor. *Television News Anchors: An Anthology of Profiles of the Major Figures and Issues in United States Network Reporting.* Jefferson, North Carolina, McFarland, 1993.

Goldberg, Robert, and Gerald Jay Goldberg. *Anchors: Brokaw, Jennings, Rather and the Evening News.* Secaucus, New Jersey, Carol Publishing Group, 1990.

Marlane, Judith. *Women in Television News Revisited: Into the Twenty-First Century.* Austin, University of Texas Press, 1999.

Temple, Shirley (1928—)

Shirley Temple, Hollywood's quintessential child star during the 1930s and 1940s, became a diplomat in later years, serving as Ambassador to Ghana and Czechoslovakia and as the U.S. Ambassador to the United Nations under her married name, Shirley Temple Black. But it is the diminutive smiling moppet with golden ringlets that most older Americans remember from the Saturday afternoon matinees of their own childhoods. Her unique appeal and immense popularity were without precedent and have never been equaled by the junior members of the Hollywood acting fraternity. The child star who acted, danced, and sang her way into the hearts of millions was the sun that shone through the clouds of the depression years. In a series of box-office smashes, Little Shirley Temple dispensed sweetness and light, beguiling her adult audiences and upstaging her adult co-stars in a series of films specially concocted to capitalize on her qualities. Decades before the rise of film-product merchandising, Temple's popularity gave rise to a profitable industry in Shirley Temple products such as dolls, cut-outs, and clothes, and her name has passed into the language as a synonym for cute, smiling, curly-haired, doll-like little girls—and even as the eponym for a non-alcoholic cocktail served to children and teetotaling adults.

Shirley Temple

Shirley made her first feature film appearance in 1932. She was awarded a special Academy award "in grateful recognition of her outstanding contribution to screen entertainment during the year 1934," and was the number-one box-office attraction in the United States and Britain from 1935 to 1938. During this time her salary had risen to $100,000 per picture, but by the end of 1939, unable to keep advancing age at bay, her career began its downward slide. She was 11 years old.

Born in Santa Monica, California, on April 23, 1928, Shirley was taken to dancing classes at age three by an ambitious stage mother who later hawked around her daughter to various film studios. The child was first chosen for a series of one-reel movies called "Baby Burlesks," a quick stepping stone to her first small roles in features. In 1934, Fox Studios, needing a tot to perform a song and dance number in *Stand Up and Cheer,* engaged her at $150 per week. She made an immediate impact with the number, "Baby Take a Bow" and emerged with a Fox contract. Meanwhile, *Little Miss Marker,* the first film under a two-picture deal that Mrs. Temple had previously made with Paramount, was released several weeks after *Stand Up and Cheer,* and became a huge hit. Based on a story by Damon Runyon, it was this film—something of a classic and frequently remade—that catapulted the six-year-old Temple to stardom.

As little Miss Marker, little Miss Temple was paired with Adolphe Menjou, the smooth veteran of many a more sophisticated screen liaison. She played the daughter of a gambler who, in debt to his bookie, dumps his small daughter on the man as "security" and disappears. Menjou played the seemingly flint-hearted bookie who softens under the influence of the charming, loving child, reforms his ways, and embraces the role of surrogate father. With minor variations on its basic idea, *Little Miss Marker* established the formula for the subsequent string of mediocre films whose success rested on their star's tiny shoulders. Most of the stories were formulaic: a child, generally an orphan or, at the very least, motherless, is packed off by some inept or mildly villainous guardian to live with a reluctant relative. In double-quick time she melts the stony heart of whichever aunt or grandfather she has been inflicted upon, never wants to leave, is reclaimed for purposes of exploitation by the original caregiver and, after much phony but effectively plotted tension, is blissfully reunited with her loved ones.

Exploiting the success of her number in *Stand Up and Cheer,* Fox rushed her into *Baby Take a Bow* (Shirley as the daughter of an ex-con who straightens out under her sunny influence); then it was back to Paramount for *Now and Forever* with Gary Cooper and Carole Lombard (he a jewel thief, she his mistress and Shirley his motherless daughter); the year ended with *Bright Eyes,* in which an orphaned Shirley sang the hit song "On the Good Ship Lollipop." In 1935 she danced with Bill "Bojangles" Robinson in *The Little Colonel* and *The Littlest Rebel;* in *Our Little Girl* she succeeded in reuniting her two estranged parents; in *Curly Top,* a loose retelling of *Daddy Longlegs,* she sang another hit song, "Animal Crackers in My Soup" as she took control of her adoptive playboy-father's affairs, both professional and romantic.

And so it continued. Temple, remaining cute as a button, proved herself a real trouper, delivering her lines and dispensing wisdom to adults with unnerving authority and breaking effortlessly into song and dance with breathtaking ease. In *Stowaway* (1936), the eight-year-old impersonated Eddie Cantor, Al Jolson, and Ginger Rogers dancing with a Fred Astaire doll; the film version of *Heidi* (1937) suited her to perfection and won critical plaudits; *Wee Willie Winkie* the same year shamelessly changed the original Rudyard Kipling character from a small boy to a small girl. Directed by John Ford, the tale of a child who becomes the mascot of a British army regiment in colonial India was the most expensively produced of the Temple vehicles, with sentimentality taking second place to action. *Rebecca of Sunnybrook Farm* (1938), about an orphan who becomes a radio star, reprised Shirley's career and remains an excellent introductory film for those who have never seen her.

Neither her novelty nor her popularity faded until 1939 when her ratings began to slip after *The Little Princess* and *Susannah of the Mounties*. In 1940, with her asking price now $300,000, she starred in Maurice Maeterlinck's *The Blue Bird,* adapted by the author and filmed in color; it was the first Shirley Temple vehicle to lose money. At the end of the year, Mrs. Temple and the studio (now Twentieth Century-Fox), who had long had an uneasy relationship, agreed to terminate Shirley's contract. She returned to the screen via MGM, who did not know what to do with her and, after a feeble performance in *Kathleen* (1941), she went to United Artists and appeared in *Miss Annie Rooney* (1942). She disappeared for two years and came back in *Since You Went Away* (1944), a popular wartime family drama in which she played third fiddle to Claudette Colbert and Jennifer Jones.

The world had changed, and so had Shirley Temple, now 16. She was rejected by a disappointed public unable to accept her transformation from dream child to attractive but ordinary teenager, and ten more films between 1945 and 1949 (including *The Bachelor and the Bobby-Soxer* with Cary Grant), and marriage, at 17, to John Agar, only continued the downward slide. Two comeback attempts with television series in 1958 and 1960 failed to generate any enthusiasm and finally marked the end of her career. Divorced from Agar, she married TV executive Charles Black in 1950 and, as Shirley Temple Black, entered Republican politics during the 1960s. Her congressional bid was unsuccessful, but she was appointed a U.S. representative to the United Nations, became the American ambassador to Ghana (1974-76), then the U.S. Chief of Protocol and, finally, in 1989, ambassador to Czechoslovakia.

Described by David Thomson as not ''just a child leading her life under adult shadows, but a Lilliputian moralist in ringlets, tap-dancing into your heart and then delivering the sententious message that sorts out confusion,'' Shirley Temple certainly had her detractors. There were those who found her unbearable, and those who noted the shortcomings in her singing and dancing. Novelist and one-time film critic Graham Greene was famously sued for a review in which he asserted that she was an adult masquerading as a child. But to most, she was the perfect antidote to reality in a difficult era, who later said of her career, ''I class myself with Rin-Tin-Tin. At the end of the Depression people were perhaps looking for something to cheer themselves up. They fell in love with a dog and a little girl. It won't happen again.''

—Robyn Karney

FURTHER READING:

Black, Shirley Temple. *Child Star, USA.* New York, Warner Books, 1989.

Hammontree, Patsy Guy. *Shirley Temple Black: A Bio-Bibliography.* Westport, Connecticut, Greenwood Publishing, 1998.

Thomson, David. *A Biographical Dictionary of Film.* New York, Alfred A. Knopf, 1994.

Windeler, Robert. *The Films of Shirley Temple.* New York, Citadel Press, 1995.

The Temptations

While many believe the Temptations to be the favorite soul singing group of all time, this assessment of the band's accomplishments is limited considering their substantial impact upon both the look and sound of popular music. Formed in Detroit, Michigan, in 1960 at a time when AM radio was a multi-layered media format that gave access and success to a large quantity of artists from rock, pop, country, soul, blues, and rockabilly music, the Temptations set a standard for vocal performers and created a sound and style that remains distinctly their own. Built around the remnants of two previous bands, the Distants and the Primes, the Temptations were a major force in the success of Berry Gordy's Motown Records and have been referred to as the originators of the ''Motown Sound.'' Rising to popularity with other precedent-setting Motown performers such as Marvin Gaye, Martha and the Vandellas, and the Supremes, the Temptations were at the center of a huge music explosion. Over the course of nearly 40 years the Temptations would have 19 members and earn 3 Grammy Awards. The group would place 43

The Temptations

singles in the rhythm and blues (R&B) Top 10 as well as earn 14 R&B number one hits. As pop artists, the Temptations would hit number one four times and place 15 sides in the pop Top 10.

Known for their lush harmonies, smooth on-stage choreography, and a bold sense of fashion which made them immediately recognizable, the Temptations conquered pop, rock, R&B, and the soul music market during the course of a career that remains strong. From the start, the membership of the Temptations was ever changing. The Distants, a local Detroit outfit, who recorded for the Northern label and released a single in 1959, "Come On," included Elbridge Bryant, bass singer Melvin Franklin, and baritone Otis Williams. The Primes were a trio of transplants from Alabama comprised of tenor Eddie Kendricks, Kell Osborne, and Paul Williams. It was Otis Williams who brought Kendricks and Paul Williams into the fold when the Primes broke up. Impressed by the Primes' use of choreography, Otis Williams wanted to incorporate that into the Distants' live performances. The Distants changed their name to the Temptations and by 1961 they were signed to a Motown subsidiary, Miracle. While at Miracle the Temptations released several sides with only one achieving any commercial success, "Dream Come True," in 1962. By 1963 Bryant was out of the band and was replaced in 1964 by the notable tenor voice of David Ruffin.

At this point the Temptations began working with William "Smokey" Robinson. A songwriter of immeasurable talent and a producer who would go on to achieve his own success with the Miracles, Robinson gave the Temptations their first hit, "The Way You Do the Things You Do." It would be the first of many Top 10 hits for the group. Their debut album, *Meet the Temptations,* was released in 1964. In 1965 the Temptations scored big and gave the world what would become their signature song, "My Girl." Another Robinson composition, "My Girl" was number one on both the pop and R&B charts. Crossing over as they were, in an era of racial strife and turmoil, made their accomplishments even more meaningful and paved the way for others to follow. They continued this pattern and in 1965 they release another hit from the pen of Smokey Robinson, "Get Ready." Harder and more edgy, "Get Ready" was of tremendous appeal to rock audiences. Two albums resulted from their early association with Robinson, *Sing Smokey,* in 1965 and *Gettin' Ready,* which also contained the stunning, "Ain't Too Proud to Beg," another signature tune for the Temptations.

Moving on, the Temptations began working with producers Norman Whitfield and Brian Holland and also moved Ruffin into the lead vocal position, a spot Kendricks had filled admirably for some time. Ruffin's voice soared on well known hits "Beauty's Only Skin Deep" and "(I Know) I'm Losing You." Together, Kendricks and Ruffin shared lead vocal duties on the classic romantic hit, "You're My Everything," from the 1967 album *With a Lot o' Soul.* Ruffin pushed to have his name placed in front of the band's name, a request that resulted in his firing from the Temptations. He was replaced by Dennis Edwards, a former member of another band, the Contours. Edwards' voice was a perfect fit as the Temptations took their sound into a more psychedelic direction. Edwards' arrival ushered in a time of change for the Temptations and their sound when he recorded the stinging lead vocal for "I Can't Get Next to You," the most significant cut from the Puzzle People project in 1969.

With Whitfield in full control of production, the Temptations were moving away from the smooth, soulful love songs that had made

them so successful. Tunes like "Cloud Nine," "Psychedelic Shack," and "Ball of Confusion (That's What the World is Today)" were commentary on America's drug culture and politics. Changing their sound and style to fit into the world around them, the Temptations remained current, timely, and part of the mainstream. Furthermore, their influence carried over as rock and pop acts sought to emulate not only their moves, but their material.

By 1971 Kendricks was leaving the band. His swan song with the Temptations was "Just My Imagination," a mellow, flowing tune that showed off the group's skillful harmonies. Paul Williams, who suffered from alcoholism, also left around this time. Damon Harris and Richard Street joined the Temptations. Rumors of the band's demise circulated. But, the Grammy-winning single, "Papa Was a Rolling Stone," displaying vast expanses of instrumental work and Edwards' strong vocals, was a huge crossover hit that only seemed to underscore the versatility and tenacity of the group. Their album, *All Directions,* released in 1972, put an end to the idea that the Temptations were about to disband as did a Grammy Award for their album *Masterpiece* the following year.

After more lineup changes, the Temptations recorded their final project for Motown Records in 1976. *The Temptations Do the Temptations* signaled the end of an era as the act moved to Atlantic Records. Atlantic had designs on turning the Temptations into a disco act. Unsuccessful and dissatisfied, the Temptations returned to Motown and hit the charts once again in 1979 with the single, "Power." A reunion tour and album followed in 1982. Ruffin and Kendricks joined the five current Temptations in what was a brief, but glorious moment in time that included an impressive SRO performance at Radio City Music Hall in New York City. Problems, both personal and professional, made it impossible for Ruffin and Kendricks to remain. In 1984 Ali-Ollie Woodson was on board as lead singer.

Inducted into the Rock 'n' Roll Hall of Fame in 1989 by blue-eyed soul duo Daryl Hall and John Oates, the Temptations were formally acknowledged for their contribution to popular culture and to America's music. Yet, their success was marked by tragedy all along the way. Original member Paul Williams died in 1973 of a self-inflicted gunshot wound. Later, Ruffin passed away in 1991 of a drug overdose while Kendricks succumbed to lung cancer in 1992. Another founding member, Melvin Franklin, lost his life in 1995 after a brain seizure. By the 1990s Otis Williams was the only original member left performing with the group and had spent years in court defending his right to use the Temptations' name after Edwards left and formed a rival group. Publishing his autobiography in 1988, he carried on while Motown released a number of anthologies and greatest hits packages, including *Emperors of Soul* in 1994, and the critically acclaimed *Ultimate Collection* in 1996.

A 1990s renaissance of sorts, however, caused renewed interest in the band. Romantic R&B singing acts of all racial persuasions looked to the work of the Temptations for inspiration. The Temptations' sound was found in the work of chart topping 1990s acts such as BoyzIIMen, Babyface, and the Backstreet Boys. Further interest in the group was fueled by an NBC television movie, *The Temptations,* shown in two parts in November, 1998. Based upon Williams' book, the miniseries focused upon the classic Temptations lineup, the drama of their collective rise to fame and fortune, and the individual trials and tragedies of each member. The 1998 release of a brand new CD, *Phoenix Rising,* also on Motown, refuted the idea that the Temptations were merely an oldies act resting upon their laurels. Williams, along with tenor Ron Tyson, Barrington Henderson, Terry Weeks, and Harry McGilberry, Jr., give credence to the original member's expression, ''Temps forever.''

—Jana Pendragon

FURTHER READING:

Gordy, Berry. *To Be Loved.* New York City, Warner Books, 1994.

Williams, Otis, and Patricia Romanowski. *Temptations.* New York, Putnam Publishing, 1988.

The Ten Commandments

The annual network presentation of Cecil B. De Mille's 1956 epic film *The Ten Commandments* has been an American television standard every Easter for decades. Highlighted by Oscar-winning special effects, such as the spectacular parting of the Red Sea, *The Ten Commandments* vividly tells the Biblical story of the life of Moses, with 1950s superstar Charlton Heston in the lead role. Featuring a cast of thousands, the three-plus hour saga remains a perennial audience

favorite, proving that larger-than-life spectacle continues to be among Hollywood's principal contributions to popular culture.

One of the most important early motion picture directors, Cecil B. De Mille helped define Hollywood's early cinematic style in silent films such as the classic 1915 melodrama *The Cheat.* Primarily a comedy director in his early career, De Mille made his first epic film, *The Ten Commandments,* in 1923. In this earlier version, De Mille interwove the Biblical story with a modern-day parable of two brothers, one a saint, the other a sinner. Even though the shooting budget exceeded a million dollars, the film was a huge moneymaker for Paramount Pictures and made De Mille the top director of his day.

In the mid-1920s, the director started his own studio and his reputation reached legendary proportions. As noted in Baseline's *Encyclopedia of Film,* ''By the middle of the decade De Mille, with his Germanic swagger, boots and riding crop, had come to represent the archetypal director to the moviegoing public.'' After movies switched to sound, De Mille remained one of Hollywood's most bankable directors throughout the 1930s and 1940s, known for his sweeping historical epics.

In 1950, the sixty-nine-year-old director reunited with his great silent star, Gloria Swanson, to make the classic *Sunset Blvd.* Two years later, he directed *The Greatest Show on Earth,* which won the Oscar for Best Picture—DeMille's first. In 1955, rumors began

Charlton Heston (right) and Yul Brynner in a scene from the film *The Ten Commandments*.

circulating Hollywood that the legendary director was planning to remake his 1923 classic, *The Ten Commandments.* Everyone wanted to audition. As actor Vincent Price, who would be cast as Baka, the Master Builder of the Pyramids, recalled, "I think all of us, Eddie Robinson, myself, Judith Anderson, we all really wanted to be in a De Mille picture. We really felt that you couldn't call yourself a star unless you had been in a De Mille picture! So we all took these sort of small, but rather arresting parts." Indeed, the cast was star-studded, with Charlton Heston as Moses, Yul Brynner as Ramses, and Anne Baxter as Nefretiti, and featuring Edward G. Robinson, Yvonne De Carlo, Debra Paget, Nina Foch, Judith Anderson, Vincent Price, and John Carradine. Bit players included future television stars Mike Connors and Robert Vaughn and musician Herb Alpert.

In *The Ten Commandments,* Golden Age Hollywood filmmaking meets the 1950s. As described by film critic Pauline Kael, "Charlton Heston is the highly athletic Moses; Anne Baxter is the kittenish princess who loves him; Judith Anderson is the sinister slave who knows the secret of his Jewish birth; Cedric Hardwicke is the likable old Pharoah; Yul Brynner is the prince who beats Moses to the Egyptian throne; Edward G. Robinson is the traitor to the Jews; Debra Paget is the young slave old Robinson has got his eyes on. Stir them all together, throw in stone tablets, a whopping big Golden Calf, part the Red Sea, and you've got Cecil B. De Mille's epic—3 hours and 38 minutes of it. As old-fashioned hokum, it's palatable and rather tasty." Filmed in VistaVision, *The Ten Commandments* was nominated for seven Academy Awards, winning for Special Effects.

Both Hollywood and Cecil B. De Mille made better films than *The Ten Commandments,* but few have remained as popular for as long. A family favorite, a good old-fashioned epic, a television tradition, *The Ten Commandments* has become a staple of American popular culture.

—Victoria Price

FURTHER READING:

Barson, Michael. *The Illustrated Who's Who of Hollywood Directors: The Studio System in the Sound Era.* New York, The Noonday Press, 1995.

Monaco, James. *Encyclopedia of Film.* New York, Perigee, 1991.

Shipman, David. *The Story of Cinema: A Complete Narrative History from the Beginnings to the Present.* New York, St. Martin's Press, 1982.

Tennis

A ball, a racket, and a net. The simplicity of tennis is one reason that its origins are difficult to pinpoint. At any one point in time, variations of the game were probably played in almost every country in the world. Some historians believe the game was first invented in the Middle Ages—it is mentioned in twelfth-century manuscripts—but exactly when and where is probably lost to antiquity. The word tennis is derived from the French word "tenez," meaning "to hold." Certainly the French greatly enjoyed the game, and by the sixteenth

century up to 2,000 Jeu-de-Paume (the name for the ball) courts had been built in France, and it is thought that every western European country had courts at the time.

Perhaps until the nineteenth century, tennis courts were walled, and the exact rules of the game may have differed from country to country, perhaps even court to court. In 1858, however, a lawn court was constructed in England, and by 1873 an Englishman, Major Walter Clopton Wingfield, modernized and standardized the game. Calling his game Sphairistike (Greek for ball and stick), the net was set at four feet eight inches, while the court was shaped like an hourglass, narrow at the net and wider at the baseline. The game was played to 15 points. This standardization probably was the reason for an increased interest in the game. At about the same time, the game spread to the United States, and soon after, worldwide.

The early establishment of national championships in major tennis-playing countries demonstrates the fast-growing popularity of tennis during this period. In 1877, Wimbledon, the British championship, was first played. In 1881, the United States National Championship (now the U.S. Open) was held. Ten years later the French National championship (now the French Open) began, and by 1905 the national championship of Australia (now the Australian Open) was played. In addition, in 1900 the Davis Cup, a team competition between the United States and England, was first held, and the tournament has since become an annual international championship.

Over the years, various surfaces have been used to play the game, ranging from grass to clay to concrete to composition. Each is generally better suited to different aspects of the game, and rather than undermining the standardization of the game, it has added a diversity to both amateur and tournament play. For example, the French Open is played on clay while Wimbledon is on grass.

Unlike most sports, tennis had a remarkably difficult time meshing amateur and professional status into its organizational format. Although a professional tournament had been held in the United States as early as 1927, not until the 1960s did the "Open Era" of professional tennis begin.

Tennis in the twentieth century is highlighted by a litany of great players from different eras. In the 1920s, American Bill Tilden enjoyed great popularity. In the 1930s, 1940s, and 1950s, Ellsworth Vines, Fred Perry, Don Budge, Jack Kramer, Pancho Gonzales, and Lew Hoad, were, at various times, either ranked number one or regarded as such. In the 1950s and early 1960s, a host of Australian players reached the top echelon, most notably Rod Laver. Others included Hoad, Ken Rosewall, Frank Sedgman, and Neal Fraser. By the late 1960s and 1970s, players like Arthur Ashe, Stan Smith, and John Newcombe came to the forefront. By the 1980s, Bjorn Borg, Ivan Lendl, and John McEnroe were marquee names while Pete Sampras, Boris Becker, and Andre Agassi have been dominate players in the 1990s.

Women's tennis has also had an illustrious list of notable players such as Frenchwoman Suzanne Lenglen in the 1920s, Americans Helen Wills and Helen Hull Jacobs in the 1920s and 1930s, Americans Maureen "Little Mo" Connolly and Althea Gibson, the first to break the color line in tennis, in the 1950s, Australian Margaret Court, Brazilian Maria Bueno, and American Billie Jean King in the 1960s, Australian Evonne Goolagong, American Chris Evert, and Czech Martina Navratilova in the 1970s and 1980s, and German Steffi Graf, American Monica Seles, and Swiss Martina Hingis in the 1990s.

Pete Sampras

In part, professional tennis has been somewhat of a battle of the sexes. The battle was perhaps best exemplified by the much ballyhooed "match of the century" held in the Houston Astrodome in 1973. The match pitted women's star Billie Jean King against former Wimbledon champion Bobby Riggs. Months earlier Riggs, a self-appointed "king of the chauvinist pigs," challenged all women athletes in general, but specifically the top ranked woman's player in the world, to a tennis match. The number two ranked women's tennis player Margaret Court accepted, and Riggs promptly beat her 6-2, 6-1 in what was called the Mother's Day Massacre. This led to the King-Riggs Astrodome match in front of 30,000 fans and a worldwide television audience of 50 million. Although Riggs claimed to be a chauvinist, he probably did more for women's tennis than any male player in history. In front of the large audience, King beat Riggs in three straight sets and took home the $100,000 winner-take-all prize. The resultant publicity drew attention to the growing complaint from women professionals that their prize money should be equal to men's, particularly since many women players felt their blend of finesse and power made women's matches more enjoyable for spectators. The

Women's Tennis Association, coincidentally founded the year of the King-Riggs match, has consistently worked toward greater equity in prize money and purses for women have become substantially larger, but generally remain smaller than those awarded to men.

—Lloyd Chiasson Jr.

FURTHER READING:

Cummings, Parke. *American Tennis: The Story of a Game and Its People.* Boston, Little Brown, 1957.

Grimsley, Will. *Tennis: Its History, People and Events.* Englewood Cliffs, New Jersey, Prentice-Hall, 1971.

Lorimer, Larry. *The Tennis Book: A Complete A-to-Z Encyclopedia of Tennis.* New York, Random House, 1980.

Schickel, Richard. *The World of Tennis.* New York, Random House, 1975.

Schwabacher, Martin. *Superstars of Women's Tennis.* Broomall, Pennsylvania, Chelsea House, 1997.

Tennis Shoes/Sneakers

Although a nineteenth century American lexicographer described sneakers as ''shoes with canvas tops and rubber soles,'' the vernacular meaning has come to include any shoe with natural or synthetic rubber soles. Uppers can be of leather, nylon, canvas, plastic, or combinations of these. Alternative names for sneakers include tennis shoes, gym shoes, plimsolls, felony shoes, cross trainers, boat shoes, and running shoes. The most popular type of shoe, sneakers accounted for just over a third of all shoes sold in 1996 according to Sporting Goods Marketing Association.

Modern sneakers have beginnings in various sports shoes. One ancestor is the expensive British upper-class footwear of the late 1800s, used for lawn tennis, cricket, croquet, and at the beach. Worn by both sexes, these canvas or leather lace-up oxfords—or high tops—had rubber soles. By the end of the nineteenth century they were priced for the average consumer. Field and track shoes are also forerunners in the industry. At the turn of the twentieth century, football and baseball players wore essentially the same shoe: leather high-topped lace-ups with leather soles and cleats. Sears sold leather shoes made specifically for runners as early as 1897.

From 1900 through the 1920s not much changed, but in the 1930s through the 1960s technical improvements that ultimately made sneakers trendy were implemented. The quintessential sneaker—the Converse All Star—premiered in 1917. In 1922, Montgomery Ward offered high and low top sneakers—for ''work, play or everyday wear''—for children and adults. Paul Sperry introduced his wavy sole for boating shoes in 1935 and other shoemakers produced non-skid soles in patterns including diamonds, feathers, and chainlinks. Keds offered a variety of colored uppers, and sponge rubber, plastic foam, cushioned heels, and soles adding comfort were later introduced. In addition, it was in the 1940s and 1950s that Dassler Brothers (later split into Puma and Adidas), Converse, Spalding, and other companies were gaining reputations as sports shoemakers. Also during this time, sneakers, coupled with blue jeans, became symbols of youth. Adidas eventually made shoes with nylon uppers and velcro began to be used as a fastener in the 1960s. The 1970s pushed sneakers into the spotlight with the optimum shoe pursued by both consumers and manufacturers. Geoffery Beene, Calvin Klein, and other designers transformed sneakers into fashion.

When jogging became a popular pastime *Runner's World* printed surveys comparing the qualities of shoes. The running fad of the late 1970s propelled shoe manufacturers such as Saucony, Brooks, and Etonic to develop anti-pronation devices on their shoes so athletes would land flatfooted. Flared and elevated heels, in addition to soft molded and cantilevered soles, were some of the improvements

A pair of tennis shoes.

designers offered. One of a number of athletes turned sneaker designers, Bill Bowerman, a University of Oregon coach, created the waffle sole for added traction. With their popularity well established, by 1978 sneakers amounted to 50 percent of all shoes sold.

By the 1980s many shoe brands had become household words. The aerobic exercise trend of this time called for a new kind of shoe that Reebok pioneered. Nike joined in with a gas-filled midsole in the late 1970s, and by the 1980s added windows in the sole to display this air. Hip-hop musicians soon adopted sneakers as part of their style and referenced them in their songs. In 1986 rappers Run-DMC issued "My Adidas," an anthem to the Super Star model they wore without laces. The same year, Reebok came out with a pump shoe for the excessive price of $175: the strong desire to be in vogue, coupled with an inability to afford expensive sneakers, even pushed a few young people to rob, and sometimes kill, others for their costly sneakers.

From the 1980s into the 1990s, the technologically-crafted sneaker looked ready for space trekking—take, for example, L. A. Gear's flashing lights, straps, and intricate lacing systems, along with the sculptured, multicolored soles of Puma, New Balance, and other brands. With lighter materials, shoes could afford to be bulky, resembling moon boots more than sports shoes. Still, despite the style and technology, the questionable labor practices of Southeast Asian manufacturers contracted to make shoes for brands like Nike and Reebok eventually caused consumer boycotts.

While athletic styles were similar for males and females, non-sport sneakers were distinctively for women. Keds advertised low-heeled pumps with toe bows in 1917 for "Milady." Sequin sneakers, stitch-it-yourself needlepoint sneakers, and wedge heeled satin sneakers were all 1970s products. About this time fashion designer Betsy Johnson created high-heeled sneakers, a style that would gain popularity in the 1990s, along with sneaker clogs. Another 1990s style, homemade platform sneakers, was copied by Converse and fashion designer Donna Karan, among others.

Meanwhile, new retail venues were created to meet the demand for sneakers. Into the 1960s, sporting goods stores sold athletic shoes with their low-tech siblings available in regular shoe shops. By the early 1960s specialty stores such as The Sneaker Shop of Bridgeport, Connecticut opened. Department stores had designated athletic footwear and accessories sections. In shopping malls, the Athlete's Foot, Foot Locker, and, exclusively for women, Lady Foot Locker, among others, sold only sneakers. By the late 1990s, super stores such as Sneaker Stadium and The Sports Authority dotted the landscape. Nike owners Phil Knight and Bill Bowman, who had retail outlets as importers for Tiger (now Asics), opened Nike Towns, selling Nike shoes, apparel, and accessories.

Athletes' endorsements for sneakers were common after 1920. Chuck Taylor, whose signature was added to the Converse All Star in 1923, had directed basketball clinics for Converse and had been on the Akron Firestones basketball team. Northwestern University coach "Dutch" Lonborg lent his name to the 1932 Montgomery Ward basketball shoe. Jim Thorpe endorsed B. F. Goodrich's "Chief Long Lance" brand sneakers. Female endorsers in the 1970s included Chris Evert for Converse and Virginia Wade for ProKeds. Endorsements, however, created mixed loyalties in the 1970s and 1980s. Some athletes wore favorite shoes with the logo of their endorser hiding the brand they wore. Others changed shoes during the course of a game, giving multiple endorsers equal time. But in the commodified

culture of the 1990s, endorsements by athletes like Michael Jordan for Nike propelled manufacturers into hero-selling machines.

—ViBrina Coronado

FURTHER READING:

Cheskin, Melvyn P. *The Complete Handbook of Athletic Footwear.* New York, Fairchild, 1987.

Vanderbilt, Tom. *The Sneaker Book.* New York, New York Press, 1998.

Walker, Samuel Americus. *Sneakers.* New York, Workingman Publishing, 1978.

Wolkomir, Richard, with illustrations by Lane Yerkes. "The Race to Make a 'Perfect' Shoe Starts in the Laboratory." *Smithsonian.* September 1989, 94-104.

10,000 Maniacs

Formed under the name Still Life in rural Jamestown, New York in February 1981, 10,000 Maniacs became noted for its melodic folk music and the wistful lyricism and distinct vocal patterns of its lead singer, Natalie Merchant. After releasing one EP and three albums, the group blossomed into prominence in the late 1980s on the strength of its single "What's the Matter Here." The hit put them in the Top 40 along with friends R.E.M. Following the success of its fifth album, *Blind Man's Zoo* (1989), the band's participation in the MTV (Music Television) Inaugural Ball for President Clinton in 1992, and its swan song performance on MTV Unplugged (1994), Merchant left to pursue a successful solo career. The remaining members of the band, guitarist Robert Buck, keyboardist Dennis Drew, and bassist Steve Gustafson, recruited an old collaborator, singer-violinist Mary Ramsey, releasing *Love Among the Ruins* (1997) to critical praise, marking a new chapter in the band's eventful career.

—Scott Thill

Tenuta, Judy (1951—)

Stand-up comedienne Judy Tenuta is the goddess of her own religion, Judyism, and she encourages the "pigs" in her audience to worship her. Her performances may include accordion music, sadomasochistic play with audience members, and stories of dating the Pope punctuated by her catch-phrase, "It could happen!" In 1997, she hosted an Internet talk show, *The Princess of Pop Culture.* Her comedy albums include *Buy This, Pigs!* (1987) and *In Goddess We Trust* (1995).

—Christian L. Pyle

FURTHER READING:

Tenuta, Judy. *The Power of Judyism.* New York, Harper Perennial, 1991.

Terkel, Studs (1912—)

Studs Terkel was born Louis Terkel in New York City. When he was eight, his family moved to Chicago, a city of raw midwestern muscularity and deep jazz rhythms that sharply influenced his life and career. His love of acting and jazz combined with his urban working-class environment spawned his dual role as local radio personality and oral historian.

Though he graduated from college and law school at the University of Chicago, Terkel never practiced law. Instead, taking his nickname from a famous literary character of the day, Studs Lonigan, he succumbed to the lure of the stage, acting in radio and community theater productions and even in the exciting new medium of television. From 1949 until 1951, he had his own weekly show on NBC, *Studs' Place*, an innovative, improvisational situation comedy about "regular folks." Terkel took the show's loose, unscripted format from the jazz he loved.

In 1951, anticommunist fever was rising, and Terkel's television career was cut short when NBC discovered he had signed leftist petitions seeking reform on such controversial issues as rent control and segregation. With his typical stubborn conviction, Terkel refused to renounce the petitions, and his show was canceled. His next step was to approach radio station WFMT with a proposal for an hour-long interview show. The station hired him and became Terkel's home for the next 45 years, until his retirement in 1997.

During those years, Terkel interviewed hundreds of politicians, writers, artists, and "regular folks," becoming in the process the quintessential "regular folk" himself. Dressed in his trademark uniform, a red and white checked shirt, and red socks, Terkel developed an interviewing style that was homey yet incisive, respectful yet downright curious, which made many people comfortable in revealing their insights and experiences to him.

His interviews with celebrities and politicians were sensitive and probing, often undressing sides of figures in popular culture that were previously concealed. Terkel often ventured out across the United States with his show, interviewing ordinary people. Many of his fans would agree that he made his biggest contributions to society in these treks as a chronicler of the impact of historical events on everyday life.

Terkel often quoted a poem by Bertold Brecht:

When the Chinese wall was built, where'd the masons
    go for lunch?
When Caesar conquered Gaul was there not even a cook
    in the army?
When the Armada sank, King Philip wept.
Were there no other tears?

It is these individuals whom history leaves out of its story who most deeply interested Terkel, and he strove to become their scribe. Beginning with *Giants of Jazz* in 1957, which extolled previously little known black musicians, Terkel produced a series of books that gave voice to the experience of the "regular folks." In 1967 he wrote *Division Street America,* the first of his oral histories, quickly followed by *Hard Times: An Oral History of the Great Depression* (1970), *Working: People Talk About What They Do All Day and How They Feel About What They Do* (1974), *American Dreams, Lost and Found* (1980), *The Good War: An Oral History of World War II* (1985), *The Great Divide: Second Thoughts on the American Dream* (1988), *Race: How Blacks and Whites Think and Feel About the American Obsession* (1992), *Coming of Age: The Story of Our Century By Those Who Have Lived in It* (1995), and *My American Century* (1997).

Each book depicts a multifaceted picture of the historical period it covers and the society that lived through it. Not interested in pat answers or definitive statements, Terkel took delight in the astonishing variety of human experience, and it is that delight he passes on to his readers, like a jovial host at a huge gathering.

"Oral journalism is associated with me," Terkel has said, "and I like that, and it's true. Because it's the sound of the voice that I'd like to capture." Terkel indeed captured the sound of hundreds of voices, previously unheard, but his own voice is apparent in his books as well, often merely in what he chose to write about. He jokingly related that his red checked shirt represents his politics. Terkel's ideological beliefs as a long-time socialist and his interest in working people went hand in hand. A resister of technology, he never used an electric typewriter or drove a car, preferring to take the bus to work. His down-to-earth style perhaps contributed to his success in radio, a much less superficial and glamour-oriented medium than television. He expressed his concern over how high-tech media has affected interpersonal relations when he complained, "We are more and more into communications and less into communication."

—Tina Gianoulis

FURTHER READING:

Baker, James Thomas. *Studs Terkel.* New York, Twane Publishers, Toronto, Maxwell Macmillan, 1992.

Parker, Tony. *Studs Terkel: A Life in Words.* New York, H. Holt, 1996.

Terkel, Studs. *Talking to Myself: A Memoir of My Times.* New York, Pantheon Books. 1977.

The Terminator

The Terminator is one of the most popular robots of film. There are actually two models of Terminator: the metal skeleton covered by human flesh (technically a cyborg) first seen in *The Terminator* (James Cameron, 1984); and the liquid metal, shape-shifting new T-1000 introduced in the sequel, *The Terminator 2: Judgment Day* (Cameron, 1991). Both were created by Stan Winston, following Cameron's designs. The older Terminator (Arnold Schwarzenegger) comes from the near future to kill Sarah, the mother of the still unborn John Connor, who will become the guerrilla leader that fights the rebellious machines in a future war. In the sequel, this evil Terminator becomes the fatherly protector of mother and son, saving them from the murderous T-1000. The *Terminator* films have appealed to the popular imagination thanks to their special effects (especially the infographics of the sequel) and the magnetic presence of Schwarzenegger in the title role.

—Sara Martin

FURTHER READING:

Jeffords, Susan. "Can Masculinity be Terminated?" *Screening the Male: Masculinities in Hollywood Cinema.* Ed. Stephen Cohan and Ina Rae Hark. London and New York, Routledge, 1993, 245-261.

Arnold Schwarzenegger as the Terminator in a scene from the film
Terminator 2: Judgement Day.

Mann, Karen. "Narrative Entanglements: *The Terminator.*" *Film Quarterly.* Vol. 43, Winter 1989-1990, 17-27.

Rushing, Janice Hocker, et al, editors. *Projecting the Shadow: The Cyborg Hero in American Film.* Chicago, University of Chicago Press, 1995.

Telotte, J.P. "Chapter 8: The Exposed Modern Body: *The Terminator* and *Terminator 2.*" *Replications: A Robotic History of Science Fiction.* University of Illinois Press, 1995.

Terry and the Pirates

A popular and highly influential adventure strip, *Terry and the Pirates* was set in China and began in the autumn of 1934. It was written and drawn during its heyday by Milton Caniff. The cinematic layouts and the impressionistic inking style that Caniff perfected influenced a whole generation of comic strip and comic book artists.

Terry Lee was a kid of 12 when he arrived in the Orient, accompanied by an avuncular adventurer named Pat Ryan. Almost immediately the pair was tangling with an assortment of pirates on land and sea. Among them was the quintessential femme fatale, the Dragon Lady. During World War II, Caniff, who had been dealing with the Japanese invaders since the late 1930s, turned *Terry and the Pirates* into a fairly authentic chronicle of combat activities in the China-Burma-India theater. He left his strip at the end of 1946 to do

Steve Canyon. Terry and the Pirates, taken over by George Wunder, continued until early in 1973.

—Ron Goulart

FURTHER READING:

Harvey, Robert C. *The Art of the Funnies.* Jackson, University Press of Mississippi, 1994.

Marschall, Richard. *America's Great Comic Strip Artists.* New York, Abbeville Press, 1989.

Tex-Mex Music
See Tejano Music

Thalberg, Irving G. (1899-1936)

Irving Grant Thalberg may have been the most influential motion picture executive of his time. "The Boy Wonder," as he was called, was an expert in knowing what the public wanted and how to get it to them under budget. As head of production for Metro Golwyn Mayer (MGM) he oversaw countless productions during his tenure, including *The Big Parade* (1925) and *Mutiny on the Bounty* (1935) although *The Good Earth* (1937) was the only picture for which he ever received on-screen credit as producer.

Despite suffering from a weak heart his entire life, Thalberg was a classic workaholic. After their marriage in 1927, he personally oversaw the career of his wife, actress Norma Shearer. Thalberg was often quoted as saying, "Credit you give yourself is not worth having." The Thalberg Award, given by the Academy of Motion Picture Arts and Sciences, is named for him.

—Jill A. Gregg

FURTHER READING:

Flamini, Roland. *Thalberg: The Last Tycoon and the World of MGM.* New York, Crown Publishing, 1994.

Marx, Samuel. *Mayer and Thalberg: the Make-Believe Saints.* New York, Random House, 1975.

Thomas, Bob. *Thalberg: Life and Legend.* New York, Doubleday, 1969.

Thanksgiving

A national holiday in the United States since 1863, Thanksgiving has come to play a number of important roles in popular culture. It was customary in Europe to hold days of thanksgiving both for successful harvests and for events such as military victories, deliverance from plagues, and royal births. The date and site of the first Thanksgiving in what is now the United States are still debated, but the most famous in pre-independence times was that held in October, 1621 in the Plymouth Colony. There, European immigrants, "the Pilgrims," and indigenous Wampanoag Indians celebrated the harvest season with feasting that included the dish that would become a traditional part of the day: turkey. Throughout the colonial era, days of thanksgiving were common, especially in New England, but not universal or regular. Although national days of thanksgiving were proclaimed by the Continental Congress in 1777 and by President Washington in 1789, there was no great clamor for an annual festival until the nineteenth century.

Credit for the establishment of Thanksgiving Day as a nation-wide holiday must go to Sarah Josepha Buell Hale, the editor of an influential women's magazine (and author of "Mary Had a Little Lamb") who lobbied legislatures and presidents from 1827 on. In 1863 Abraham Lincoln proclaimed the last Thursday of November as a day of "thanksgiving and praise to our beneficent Father who dwelleth in the Heavens," and since then it has been an annual celebration, though the date has varied. From 1939-1941 President Franklin Delano Roosevelt, in response to the complaints of business-men that there was insufficient shopping time between Thanksgiving and Christmas, proclaimed Thanksgiving to be the third Thursday in November. This, however, created conflicts with the dating of the holiday in many states which had their own Thanksgiving legislation, so Congress in 1941 passed a joint resolution decreeing that the observance should fall on the fourth Thursday of November.

Thanksgiving, as a non-denominational harvest festival, is part of the American civic religion, able to be celebrated by people of any faith or none at all. It is marked by Pilgrim pageants, the decoration of schools, churches, and shopping malls with harvest themes, procla-mations by politicians voicing gratitude for the country's prosperity, and the televising of college and professional football games. Above all, it is the day the extended family gathers for a dinner with a menu that has become stereotypical, almost invariably including turkey, stuffing, mashed potatoes, sweet potatoes, cranberries, and pumpkin pie. Americans abroad observe the day (in a way they would not trouble themselves for Memorial Day or Presidents' Day, for exam-ple) and attempt to duplicate this traditional meal as best they can in a foreign setting. The illustrator Norman Rockwell's depictions of this family feast have become American icons.

Thanksgiving, in the shorthand of popular culture, stands for family togetherness for good or ill. Motion pictures such as *Planes, Trains & Automobiles* (1987) and *Dutch* (1991) have been built around the utter necessity of returning home, whatever the obstacles, for this holiday. The final scene of *Raising Arizona* (1987) is a dream sequence in which a dysfunctional and childless couple are blessed in the future by the arrival of children and grandchildren for a Rockwell-style Thanksgiving. On the other hand, films like *The Ice Storm* (1997) and *Home for the Holidays* (1995) use the Thanksgiving setting in a claustrophobic way to emphasize the troubles of a family gone wrong.

Thanksgiving also marks the semi-official launch of another holiday: Christmas. As early as 1889 a New York newspaper claimed that "as soon as the Thanksgiving turkey is eaten the great question of buying Christmas presents begins to take the terrifying shape it has come to assume." Thanksgiving Parades, especially Macy's in New York and that on Los Angeles' Santa Claus Lane, usher in the shopping season.

—Gerry Bowler

FURTHER READING:

Cohen, Hennig, and Tristam Potter Coffin, editors. *The Folklore of American Holidays.* Detroit, Gale Research, 1987.

Hatch, Jane M. *The American Book of Days.* New York, H.W. Wilson, 1978.

Tharp, Twyla (1941—)

A leading choreographer of modern dance and ballet, Twyla Tharp rose to prominence during "the dance boom" of the 1960s and 1970s. Tharp's choreography incorporates dance elements from roll 'n' roll, blues, and jazz, and has been set to the music of Jelly Roll Morton, Bix Biederbecke, and Fats Waller, as well as Chuck Berry, the Beach Boys, and David Byrne. In the mid-1970s, Tharp began to cross-over into ballet choreography. *Push Comes to Shove* and *Nine Sinatra Songs* were the two finest works that grew from her collabora-tion with Mikhail Baryshnikov and the American Ballet Theater. Other important works are *The Catherine Wheel* and *In the Upper Room.* Although her work continues to draw on modern dance, she is arguably the most important ballet choreographer since George Balanchine. Tharp's choreography can be seen in the movies, *Hair, Ragtime, Amadeus,* and *White Nights* and a Broadway version of *Singin' in the Rain.* She continues to choreograph for and tour with her own company.

—Jeffrey Escoffier

FURTHER READING:

Baryshnikov Dances Sinatra and More: A Dance Creation by Twyla Tharp: The Little Ballet, The Sinatra Suite, Push Comes to Shove, with American Ballet Theater, Kultur International Films, 1984.

Tharp, Twyla, *Push Comes to Shove: An Autobiography,* New York, Bantam Books, 1992.

Them!

First and best of the giant insect/arachnid subgenre of horror films, *Them!* was directed by Gordon Douglas and released by Warner Brothers in 1954. Atomic bomb testing in the American Southwest causes ants to mutate, growing to great size. A scientist (Edmund Gwenn), his daughter (Joan Weldon), an FBI agent (James Arness), and a police officer (James Whitmore) lead the effort to find and destroy the migrating horde of ants before it is too late.

The film is characterized by a matter-of-fact approach. Early witnesses to the ants' existence are either semi-catatonic, like the young girl who can say only "Them!" or the pilot (Fess Parker) who is placed in a psychiatric ward after claiming to have seen giant bugs. The climax, an all-out assault on the ant colony living in the Los Angeles sewers, is moody and frightening, especially by the standards of 1950s' special effects.

Later, lesser films in this genre included *Tarantula* (1955) and the 1957 films *The Deadly Mantis, Beginning of the End,* and *The Black Scorpion.*

—David Lonergan

FURTHER READING:

Parish, James, and Michael Pitts. *The Great Science Fiction Pictures.* Metuchen, N.J., Scarecrow Press, 1977.

Walker, John. *Halliwell's Film Guide*. New York, HarperPerennial, 1994.

The Thing

John Carpenter's *The Thing* (1982) is one of the peaks of sci-fi horror cinema, comparable only to *Alien* (1979). Its premise is simple and effective. A group of American scientists working in Antarctica are stalked by a shape-shifting alien, which kills them one by one and then assumes the victim's physical and mental identity. This extraterrestrial creature has lain dormant for centuries, buried in the Arctic ice, until a team of Norwegian scientists defrosts it. The originality of Carpenter's film, otherwise quite conventional as regards character development and plot structure, stems from the shape-shifting abilities of the alien. Suspense is consistently maintained throughout the film because the creature's nature makes it impossible for the audience to predict the shape it will take next. Intense horror is achieved by each new manifestation of the Thing, based on the truly scary designs of special effects wizard Rob Bottin.

The Thing is actually a double adaptation. Its main inspiration is Christian Nyby's 1951 film *The Thing (from another world)*, an adaptation of "Who Goes There?," a short story by John W. Campbell Jr. which was also the basis of Carpenter's version. Nyby's *Thing* is one of the many monster films produced in the 1950s, a vogue fueled by terrors related to the Cold War and its feared alien—that is to say, communist—invasion of America. The first *Thing* failed to truly frighten the audience because the horrific potential of Campbell's original shape-shifting alien could not be adequately realized on the screen. Producer Howard Hawks wanted to achieve what would be achieved thirty years later by special effects artist Rick Baker and director John Landis in *An American Werewolf in London* (1982): a complete on-screen transformation of human into horrific non-human creature. The rudimentary special effects available to Nyby and his crew made this utterly impossible and they had to rely on the traditional man in a rubber suit, shaped in this case—its detractors claim—as a rather unimpressive giant carrot.

After the success of Ridley Scott's *Alien* (1979)—a story loosely based on another sci-fi pulp tale about a hostile alien fond of invading human bodies—the time seemed ripe to face the challenge Hawks had failed to meet. By 1981 special effects had progressed far from the poor 1950s standards under the guidance of make-up pioneer Dick Smith. Two of his disciples, Rick Baker and Rob Bottin, had discovered the wonders of latex foam, a new, supple material invented by George Bau, which enabled them to turn their wild flights of

From left: T. K. Carter, Kurt Russell, and Donald Moffat in a scene from the film *The Thing*.

fancy into actual sculptures and models. Baker and Bottin commenced a fierce competition for the position of king of special effects, beginning with a werewolf film on which they worked together, Joe Dante's *The Howling* (1981). Baker won the first round by reaping the first Oscar for Best Make-Up thanks to his work in *An American Werewolf in London*, but the quality of Bottin's work for Carpenter's *The Thing* certainly did not lag behind Baker's.

The Thing is now a cult film. Its original release, however, was badly timed, for it coincided with that of Steven Spielberg's *E.T.* Audiences charmed by Spielberg's cute, homesick alien found little to enjoy in Carpenter's grim tale, which, in addition to horrific scenes of mutation, offers one of the most pessimistic endings on record. By the late 1990s, *The Thing* had been fully vindicated by devoted fans who carved a niche for Carpenter's film in the roll call of top horror films. Its new-found popularity could be accounted for by two main factors: one, no doubt, the quality of Bottin's extraordinary work, which aged well and is hailed by many contemporary monster-makers as seminal inspiration. The scene of the post-mortem that reveals the bizarre, nightmarish shapes the alien can assume is one of the most terrifying metamorphoses ever filmed.

The other factor that contributes to the cult status of *The Thing* is the atmosphere of despair that surrounds Carpenter's doomed heroes. Unlike countless monster films which conclude with the victory of humankind and the destruction of the alien monster, the end of *The Thing* suggests that the monster is alive as one of the only two survivors—either the sensible black scientist Nauls (T. K. Carter) or McReady, the rugged white hero played by Kurt Russell. Suggesting that the monster might find its last refuge in an African American man may have come to seem provocative enough with the onset of political correctness; but even more provocative is the suggestion that it is perhaps the hero, with whom our sympathy has lain throughout the film, who is the monster. Very little hope is left for trust among human beings or for the survival of humankind. This bleak prospect awoke an echo of sympathy in the more pessimistic late 1980s and 1990s, when fears of nuclear annihilation or alien conquest were superseded by fears of more subtle invasions, such as that by the AIDS virus. Fortunately for the admirers of Carpenter's masterpiece, no trivializing sequel followed—doubtless because of its downbeat conclusion and poor box-office returns.

—Sara Martin

FURTHER READING:

Cumbow, Robert C. *Order in the Universe: The Films of John Carpenter*. Metuchen, New Jersey, Scarecrow Press, 1990.

Salisbury, Mark, and Alan Hedgcock. *Behind the Mask: The Secret of Hollywood's Monster Makers*. London, Titan Books, 1994.

Timpone, Anthony. *Men, Make-up and Monsters: Hollywood Masters of Illusion and FX*. New York, St. Martin's Griffin Press, 1996.

The Third Man

Holly Martins (Joseph Cotton) arrives in postwar Vienna to visit his friend Harry Lime (Orson Welles) only to find that Harry is dead. When Major Calloway (Trevor Howard) claims that Harry was a black marketeer, Holly begins to investigate Harry's mysterious death. He discovers that Harry is still alive and is as

corrupt as Calloway claimed. Holly's conscience is torn between Calloway and the beautiful Anna Schmidt (Alida Valli), Harry's lover who urges Holly to remain loyal to his friend. *The Third Man* (1949) is remembered for its compelling tale of mystery, Anton Karas' haunting zither score, and the blend of expressionism's jagged angles and *film noir*'s shadows in Robert Krasker's Oscar-winning cinematography.

—Christian L. Pyle

FURTHER READING:

Greene, Graham, and Carol Reed. *The Third Man*. New York, Simon & Schuster, 1968.

This Is Your Life

A human-interest show that presented documentary-style biographies of celebrities through the recollections and testimonials of colleagues, friends, and relatives, *This Is Your Life* was one of the most popular shows on radio and television during its lengthy run. Although occasionally lesser-known but accomplished guests appeared on the program, the show is best remembered for its surprise tributes to Marilyn Monroe, Jack Benny, Bette Davis, and other Hollywood stars.

Created by perennial host Ralph Edwards for radio in the 1940s, *This Is Your Life* came to television on October 1, 1952 as a half-hour series lasting for nine seasons on NBC. On both radio and television, the show's format was the same. Edwards would appear to encounter the evening's guest by happenstance in or near the television studio. After a brief exchange of pleasantries, Edwards would announce ''This is your life!'' and the startled guest would be taken to the

A scene from the television show *This Is Your Life*.

show's set where his or her life story would unfold before a live studio audience. Reading from the *This Is Your Life* book, Edwards would recount the celebrity's childhood, school years, and rise to fame with a sentimental flare certain to elicit an emotional outpouring from both guest and audience. Edwards was so effective, in fact, that one show celebrating the life of educator Laurence C. Jones inspired his television audience to send $700,000 in contributions to a Mississippi college. The show's specialty, however, seemed to be orchestrating parades of long-lost teachers and friends whose appearance was sure to trigger tears from the honored guest.

From time to time a planned show would have to be scrapped because the celebrity learned of the project in advance, but for the most part Edwards was remarkably successful in his *Candid Camera* style ruses, especially since the show was broadcast live until the 1959-1960 season. *This Is Your Life* did, however, tip off two guests: Lillian Roth, so that producers could obtain permission to discuss her successful struggle with alcoholism, and Eddie Cantor, who producers feared might experience a heart attack at too dramatic a surprise.

The show generated two spin-offs, a British version of *This Is Your Life* and, in 1953, *The Comeback Story,* which each week presented the inspiring tale of a faded star who was regaining fame and fortune. It also spun off several incarnations of itself. Edwards revived *This Is Your Life* in 1971, this time featuring the Nelson Riddle Orchestra, but the syndicated show lasted only one season. It re-emerged for another try in 1983, and over the years several *This Is Your Life* specials have appeared on NBC, with Ralph Edwards hosting until 1993. Despite its reputation for sentimentality and sensationalism, *This Is Your Life* has proven to be a resilient formula for the surprise party, whether televised or not. Not only have television producers fit it into every decade's programming, if only for an evening, but the words "This is your life!" have entered the popular imagination as a theme appropriate to almost any kind of party or celebration.

—Michele S. Shauf

FURTHER READING:

Brooks, Tim, and Earle Marsh. *The Complete Directory to Prime Time Network and Cable TV Shows 1946-Present.* New York, Ballantine Books, 1995.

McNeil, Alex. *Total Television.* New York, Penguin Books, 1996.

Thomas, Clarence

See Anita Hill-Clarence Thomas Senate Hearings

Thomas, Danny (1912-1991)

Although he later starred in the longest running situation comedy in television history and became one of TV's top producers, Danny Thomas once denounced the new medium as a "workplace for idiots." He made this comment after spending two years hosting NBC's *All-Star Revue,* rotating with comedians Jack Carson, Jimmy Durante, and Ed Wynn. He quit the show in 1952 to return to the

Danny Thomas

nightclub circuit. A year later, he was back on the small screen, well on his way to becoming one of the icons of television's Golden Age.

Born Muzyad Yakhoob in Deerfield, Michigan, the fifth of nine children of Catholic immigrants from Lebanon, Danny's first experience in show business was selling candy at a burlesque theater. At age twenty he began singing on a Detroit radio station, and six years later he started a career in nightclubs, as a standup comic and master of ceremonies. His popularity steadily increased during the 1940s, leading to a brief career in films. In his two best remembered films, he played pop composer Gus Kahn in *I'll See You in My Dreams* (1951), and the Al Jolson role in the remake of *The Jazz Singer* (1953).

In 1953, Thomas began developing a situation comedy for ABC. Discussing the project with writer Mel Shavelson, Danny explained that he wanted to stay home with his family in Los Angeles. As he wrote in his autobiography in 1990, "I was away on the road so much that they hardly knew me. They called me 'Uncle Daddy.'" Shavelson realized at once that they had a concept for a comedy show, featuring a nightclub entertainer trying to have a normal family life along with a career in show business. Danny's wife Rose Marie suggested the title, *Make Room for Daddy.* While Danny was on the road, the children took over his space in the home, and when he returned, they had to shift bedrooms and move their belongings to "make room for Daddy."

The show made its debut on ABC in September 1953, running for four seasons with its ratings near the bottom, ranking 107th of the 118 shows in that period. The low ratings came despite the fact that the show won an Emmy as Best Situation Comedy Series in 1954, the same year Danny won his Emmy for Best Actor Starring in a Regular Series. After the third season, Jean Hagen, Danny's on-screen wife, quit the show and became the first leading character in a sitcom to die in the off-season. When the next season started, little Terry and Rusty were told, ''Mommy's gone to Heaven.''

In 1957 the renamed *Danny Thomas Show* was moved to CBS and aired on Monday night in the 9 p.m. time slot. In the first episode Danny had just married his new bride (Marjorie Lord), who arrived with a cute, precocious five-year-old stepdaughter, played by Angela Cartwright. Another popular character on the show was Danny's Lebanese Uncle Tonoose, played by Hans Conried. Ratings immediately soared to the top ten, and the newfound audience remained loyal throughout the run of the series, which ended in 1964.

In 1967, a special, *Make More Room for Daddy,* aired on NBC. Two years later, another special entitled *Make Room for Granddaddy,* reuniting Thomas, Marjorie Lord, Angela Cartwright, Rusty Hamer, and Hans Conried, proved so popular that it became a pilot for the 1970-71 series on ABC. Danny's ''grandson,'' played by Michael Hughes, was introduced on that show. Danny's real-life children also became important in show business; son, Tony, produced such hit shows as *Golden Girls* and *Empty Nest,* and daughter, Marlo, starred in the hit series *That Girl.*

In the 1950s, Thomas had branched out into production, forming partnerships first with Sheldon Leonard and later with Aaron Spelling. He became one of the most successful television producers of the 1950s and 1960s, whose blockbuster programs included *The Andy Griffith Show*, *The Dick Van Dyke Show*, *Gomer Pyle*, and *The Mod Squad*.

In 1991 Danny Thomas made a rare guest appearance on his son Tony's series, *Empty Nest.* A week later, his fans were stunned to learn that he had died of a heart attack. His later years were marked by his generosity in giving and raising money for his favorite charity, St. Jude's Hospital.

—Benjamin Griffith

FURTHER READING:

Books, Tim, and Earle Marsh. *The Complete Directory to Prime Time Network TV Shows: 1946 to Present.* New York, Ballantine, 1981.

McNeil, Alex. *Total Television: A Comprehensive Guide to Programming from 1948 to the Present.* New York, Penguin, 1991.

Sackett, Susan. *Prime-Time Hits: Television's Most Popular Network Programs.* New York, Billboard, 1993.

Thomas, Isiah (1961—)

National Basketball Association (NBA) legend Isiah Thomas starred for two seasons at the University of Indiana, where he won All-American honors in 1981, led the Hoosiers to a national title, and was cited as the NCAA (National Collegiate Athletics Association) tournament's Most Valuable Player. Following that season, Thomas chose to leave school and turn pro. He was drafted in the first round by the Detroit Pistons, and went on to play 13 seasons in the NBA. The six-foot-one, 185-pound point guard became the Pistons' captain and star, leading the team to three successive appearances in the NBA finals (from 1988 through 1990). In the latter two years, the Pistons emerged as champs. In 1990, Thomas was cited as the MVP (Most Valuable Player) of the finals. Between 1982 and 1993 he started in

12 successive NBA All-Star games, and was the contest's MVP in 1984 and 1986.

In his time in the NBA, Thomas teamed with Joe Dumars to make up one of pro basketball's top backcourts. Upon his retirement after the 1993-1994 season, he was the Pistons' all-time scoring leader, with 18,822 points. He also was tops in assists with 9,061, steals with 1,861, and games played with 979. One of the keys to his success has been his mental approach to the game. ''I've always believed no matter how many shots I miss,'' Thomas once said, ''I'm going to make the next one.''

Although he left college before graduation, Thomas continued his studies and in 1988 earned a degree in criminal justice. Since his retirement, he has transferred his intelligence and ambition to off-court endeavors. ''If all I'm remembered for is being a good basketball player,'' he declared, ''then I've done a bad job with the rest of my life.'' Thomas first became a part-owner and vice president of the NBA expansion Toronto Raptors. He hoped to take over the team, but the deal, involving majority owner Allan Slaight, fell apart, resulting in Thomas leaving the Raptors and joining NBC as a basketball analyst. He has also been involved in banking, land development, sports and amusement activities, and other business ventures in the Detroit area. Nonetheless, Isiah Thomas's greatest glory came on the basketball court. In 1996, he was named one of the 50 Greatest Players in NBA history.

—Rob Edelman

FURTHER READING:

Challen, Paul C. *The Book of Isiah: The Rise of a Basketball Legend.* Chicago, Login Publishers Consortium, 1996.

Thomas, Lowell (1892-1981)

A best-selling author, globe-trotting adventurer, and legendary broadcaster, Lowell Thomas travelled from the arctic to the outback, covering stories ranging from World War I to Lawrence of Arabia. He came to radio in 1930 and stayed—for a variety of sponsors and two different networks—until 1976. His 15-minute nightly broadcast was rarely far from the top of the news ratings chart, and his sign-off line is well remembered: ''And so long until tomorrow.''

—Chris Chandler

FURTHER READING:

Dunning, John. *On The Air: The Encyclopedia Of Old-Time Radio.* New York, Oxford University Press, 1998.

Thomas, Marlo (1943—)

Marlo Thomas will always be best remembered as the naively innocent and exhaustingly enthusiastic Ann Marie of the television show *That Girl* (1966-1971). One of the first series to present an unmarried female pursuing anything other than a husband, it was more traditional than it claimed. Although the show made a great deal of the fact that she was an aspiring actress living on her own in New York City, both Ann's father and her ever-present boyfriend were just a phone call away when she found herself in one of her never-ending predicaments. Moreover, she was seldom seen auditioning and worked at only low-paying temporary jobs suitable for women of the period. Despite her inability to find a reliable source of income, she somehow managed to live in a three-room apartment in a good neighborhood in New York City and dress in the height of fashion.

After the series ended Thomas became a producer and in that capacity won Emmy Awards for her work on *Marlo and Friends in Free to Be . . . You and Me* and *The Body Human: Facts for Girls.* She won a third Emmy for her role in *Nobody's Child* (1986). She has also been a strong advocate for a variety of women's causes. In 1980, Thomas married talk-show host Phil Donahue.

FURTHER READING:

Atholl, Desmond and Michael Cherkinian. *That Girl and Phil.* New York, St. Martin's Press, 1990.

O'Donnell, Monica M., editor. *Contemporary Theatre, Film, & Television.* New York, Gale Research, 1986.

Thompson, Hunter S. (1939—)

Hunter S. Thompson represents life on the edge, the counter to culture, the man who has listed his religion as none, his politics as

Hunter S. Thompson

anarchist, and his hobby as collecting guns. He claimed membership in the American Civil Liberties Union, the National Rifle Association, and the National Organization for the Reform of Marijuana Laws, and once ran for sheriff of Aspen, Colorado. Strange as it may seem, the drug- and alcohol-abusing Thompson at one time worked for *Time* magazine, the *New York Herald Tribune,* and the *National Observer* before he went straight and started writing for the voice of the counterculture, *Rolling Stone,* and invented "gonzo journalism," or at least that's the storyline. He was even turned into a character in the comic strip *Doonesbury.*

Thompson made his first major visit to the edge in 1965, when he wrote an article for *The Nation* about the Hell's Angels entitled "The Motorcycle Gangs: Losers and Outsiders." The article led to a book contract. Thompson spent a year with the Angels as a field study for the book. He was charged with separating fact from fancy and in doing so he condemned the press for coverage that he felt misrepresented the Angels. Generally, the press merely repeated what law enforcement officials chose to say rather than learning the truth by riding with the members.

Thompson's book portrayed the Angels as drug-using and alcohol-abusing gang members who believed that women were put on earth to service them. Perhaps the lowest point of the book was Thompson's description of gang sex with one woman. And at the end, some Angels nearly stomped him to death and Thompson suddenly seemed not so fond of the motorcyclists.

The titles of Thompson's books say something about Thompson and his subject matter: *The Great Shark Hunt: Strange Tales from a Strange Time; Gonzo Papers, Volume One, The Curse of Lono, Generation of Swine: Tales of Shame and Degradation in the '80s; Gonzo Papers, Volume Two, Songs of the Doomed: More Notes on the Death of the American Dream; Gonzo Papers, Volume Three, The Proud Highway: The Saga of a Desperate Northern Gentlemen; Fear and Loathing in Las Vegas: A Savage Journey to the Heart of the American Dream,* and *Fear and Loathing on the Campaign Trail '72.* "Fear and Loathing in . . . " became a trademark Thompson headline on many of his *Rolling Stone* articles.

The two *Fear* books followed *Hell's Angels* and helped establish Thompson as a writer with an attitude. The Las Vegas book was purported to be an autobiographical account of Thompson's failure to cover two events for a magazine because he spent more time on drug trips than reporting. The book includes a character named Raoul Duke, who was really Thompson, and who in Garry Trudeau's *Doonesbury* became "Uncle Duke." More than 25 years after the book was published, it was made into a movie that received some good reviews, but wasn't in the theaters very long.

Fear and Loathing on the Campaign Trail '72, a collection of articles Thompson wrote for *Rolling Stone,* to some extent continued to reflect Thompson's loathing of the mainstream press, while at the same time making Thompson the center of the reportage rather than the candidates. Another *Rolling Stone* writer, Timothy Crouse, wrote a book about how the press covered the 1972 presidential campaign, and he provided many of the stories about Thompson's non-journalistic antics. Crouse even claimed that, when *Rolling Stone* dispatched him and Thompson to Washington to open a bureau, Crouse was "to write the serious backup pieces, keep Thompson out of trouble, and carry the bail bond money." Thompson showed up on the campaign trail in sneakers, sunglasses, a Miami sports shirt, and a hunting jacket; everyone else in the press corps wore coats and ties. Thompson was downright irreverent, Crouse reported, offering to share his beer, Wild Turkey, and drugs and wondering outloud if at the next campaign stop he'd have time to drop some acid. Eventually, however, many members of the press came to respect Thompson because he was able to write what they couldn't. While his colleagues were committed to objective reporting, Thompson's talent was in his ability to fill his pieces with his own opinions expressed in descriptive language.

Thompson invented "gonzo journalism" while covering the Kentucky Derby (Thompson was born in Louisville) for *Scanlan's Magazine* in 1970. He claimed later that the article did not come about through any careful plotting of storyline and subsequent revision the way most writing is born, but had been created out of necessity when Thompson, unable to write, merely ripped pages out of his notebook, numbered them and sent them on to his editor. The result was "The Kentucky Derby Is Decadent and Depraved," a hilarious account of Thompson in Louisville. Thompson's claim aside, the article worked too well to have been assembled randomly, but no one noticed, and Thompson later proclaimed himself the inventor of gonzo journalism.

Thompson continued to be published, if not in *Rolling Stone* or other magazines and newspapers, then in book collections of his journalistic pieces—namely, the "gonzo papers." Meanwhile, he continued to behave outrageously. "I'm afraid I've become addicted to my own adrenaline," he told a *Washington Post* writer in 1991. His writing style has been badly imitated but hardly duplicated. Generally, those who continued to follow him enjoyed his irreverent and rich writing, and he remained a larger-than-life example of the counterculture of the 1960s.

—R. Thomas Berner

FURTHER READING:

Berner, R. Thomas. *The Literature of Journalism: Text and Context.* State College, Pennsylvania, Strata Publishing, 1999.

Carroll, E. Jean. *Hunter: The Strange and Savage Life of Hunter S. Thompson.* Dutton, 1993.

Crouse, Timothy. *The Boys on the Bus.* New York, Random House, 1973.

Mckeen, William. *Hunter S. Thompson.* Boston, Twayne Publishers, 1991

Perry, Paul. *Fear and Loathing: The Strange and Terrible Saga of Hunter S. Thompson.* Thunder's Mouth Press. 1993.

Vetter, Craig. "Playboy Interview: Hunter Thompson." *Playboy.* November 1974.

Whitmer, Peter O. *When the Going Gets Weird: The Twisted Life and Times of Hunter S. Thompson.* Hyperion, 1993.

Thompson, John (1941—)

Olympic and college basketball coach John Thompson, Jr. became the first African American to guide an NCAA championship basketball team in 1984. Thompson led the Georgetown University Hoyas team from 1972-1999. Thompson turned around Georgetown's abysmal record, making it a national powerhouse in the Big East Conference that he helped to charter in 1979. Under his leadership, the team compiled 24 consecutive victorious seasons (excluding his first year there), beating its opponents in more than 70 percent of its games. Thompson's college athletes were known for their aggressive playing styles as well as for their commitment to academic achievement at their elite Catholic institution. The coach supervised both his players' scholarly progress as well as their outside friendships, rescuing some stars from the bad influence of drug dealers. Thompson's shoulder-resting trademark towel that he used on court to wipe away his perspiration symbolized his hard-driven temperament. But he also kept a deflated basketball on his desk as a symbol to Georgetown players that there should be more to their lives than the game.

—Frederick J. Augustyn, Jr.

FURTHER READING:

Porter, David L., editor. *African-American Sports Greats: A Biographical Dictionary.* Westport, Connecticut, Greenwood Press, 1995.

———. *Biographical Dictionary of American Sports: Basketball and Other Indoor Sports.* Westport, Connecticut, Greenwood Press, 1989.

Shapiro, Leonard. *Big Man on Campus: John Thompson and the Georgetown Hoyas.* New York, Henry Holt, 1991.

Thomson, Bobby (1923—)

Robert Brown "Bobby" Thomson played major league baseball from 1946 through 1960. On October 3, 1951, as a New York Giant, he belted a home run to win the National League Pennant in his team's final at-bat. That "shot heard round the world" became what many consider the most dramatic event in the history of American sports. The home run capped a thrilling pennant race between the New York Giants and their bitter rivals, the Brooklyn Dodgers. In front of a national television audience, Thomson and the Giants reveled in their victory just as New York delighted in its place at the cultural center of a thriving postwar America. But Thomson's home run retained significance well beyond the 1950s. Beginning in the 1970s, as Major League Baseball increasingly cloaked itself in the garb of nostalgia, the shot heard round the world symbolized a simpler America, where an average guy who lived with his mother on Staten Island could drive to Manhattan one autumn afternoon and return home a hero.

Bobby Thomson was born in Glasgow, Scotland, on October 23, 1923. At the age of two, he moved with his mother and five siblings to join his father James in New York. James Thomson was a cabinetmaker who had moved to America to seek a better living. The Thomsons would struggle financially throughout Bobby's youth on Staten Island.

Thomson first played professionally, without much success, in the Giants' minor league organization in 1942. He then postponed his

Bobby Thomson

baseball career to join the U.S. Army Air Corps. After spending three years stationed in Victorville, California, he went to a Giants training camp for returning serviceman. The Giants assigned him to their Triple-A affiliate in Jersey City where he played for one year. After an outstanding rookie season with the Giants in 1947, Thomson showed only occasional flashes of brilliance. Critics accused him of harboring a nonchalant attitude that adversely affected his play. By 1951, Thomson seemed destined for an average career on a mediocre New York Giants team.

In the early part of the 1951 season, neither Thomson nor the Giants had improved. The Giants lost 12 of their first 14 games. Over that period Thomson hit a dismal .193. Although the Giants recovered from their disheartening start, in early August they found themselves a distant second, 13 1/2 games behind the Brooklyn Dodgers. The press and most fans predicted that the championship would go to Brooklyn. But on August 11, the Giants started a 16-game winning streak fueled by Thomson's hot hitting and climbed within reach of the Dodgers. The Giants caught the Dodgers with one day left in the season, and after the season's final game, the two teams remained tied for first place. New York and Brooklyn split the first two games of a three-game playoff series. The winner of the third game would take the National League pennant.

The deciding game started inauspiciously for the Giants, as they fell behind 4 to 1, thanks in part to Thomson's poor base running. The Dodger pitcher Don Newcombe appeared indestructible until the bottom of the ninth inning. After three base hits the Giants closed the gap to 4 to 2 and had base runners on second and third. With the

winning run coming to the plate, and his pitcher clearly tiring, Brooklyn manager Charlie Dressen made a call to the bullpen for Ralph Branca. With one out, Bobby Thomson stepped into the batter's box. Thomson watched Branca's first pitch blow past him for a strike. Branca's second pitch came in hard, high, and inside. Thomson lashed out at the ball, and it shot off his bat toward the left field wall. Russ Hodges, the Giants announcer, called the action on WMCA radio: "There's a long drive . . . it's gonna be . . . I believe . . . The Giants win the pennant! The Giants win the pennant! The Giants win the pennant! The Giants win the pennant! I don't believe it! The Giants win the pennant!" Thomson claimed his feet never touched the ground as he circled the bases.

The shot heard round the world immediately gained legendary status, epitomizing New York's and America's postwar optimism. The series was the first sporting event to be telecast live from coast to coast, and its dramatic finish affirmed New York's place as the de facto capital of a thriving American culture. New York sportswriter Red Smith captured the euphoric sense of disbelief. "Now it is done," he wrote, "Now the story ends. And there is no way to tell it. The art of fiction is dead. Reality has strangled invention. Only the utterly impossible, the inexpressibly fantastic can ever be plausible again." Bobby Thomson's home run spoke for a city and a nation where the impossible had become the attainable.

Bobby Thomson played solid baseball for eight more years, but never recaptured the glory of 1951. Following the 1953 season, the Giants traded him to Milwaukee. He played briefly for several other teams before retiring in 1960. Thomson settled in New Jersey with his wife Elaine and their three children, where he worked as a paper products salesman.

In the 1970s, amid salary disputes and escalating ticket prices, Major League Baseball began to market itself through nostalgia, attempting to connect the contemporary game to a mythical past. Thomson's homer became the crowning moment of that myth. The shot heard round the world symbolized a time of innocence and purity, when players played for the love of the game, and the fans loved their players—a time when the tall, plodding, immigrant son of a cabinetmaker could swing a bat and become a hero.

—Steven T. Sheehan

FURTHER READING:

Robinson, Ray. *The Home Run Heard Round the World.* New York, HarperCollins, 1991.

Rosenfeld, Harvey. *The Great Chase: The Dodgers-Giants Pennant Race of 1951.* Jefferson, North Carolina, McFarland and Company, 1992.

Thomson, Bobby, with Lee Heiman and Bill Gutman. *The Giants Win the Pennant! The Giants Win the Pennant!.* New York, Zebra Books, 1991.

Thorogood, George (1952—)

George Thorogood's gritty blues-rock music earned him the title of "today's master of yesterday's rock 'n' roll" and brought a working-class consciousness to the 1980s pop scene. Beginning as a blues guitarist in the vein of Elmore James and Hound Dog Taylor, Thorogood and his group the Destroyers crossed over to a pop/rock audience in 1978 with his cover of Hank Williams's "Move It On Over." In 1982 he released his major-label debut, *Bad to the Bone,* and its title track remains his best-known single, due in large part to its repeated exposure on MTV.

Though three subsequent albums all went gold, Thorogood's audience began to shrink. His only major success in the 1990s was the single "Haircut," a rebellion against authority figures who urged the song's protagonist to "get a haircut, and get a real job." Thorogood nevertheless continued to tour and record, releasing a "comeback" album, *Rockin' My Life Away,* in 1997.

—Marc R. Sykes

FURTHER READING:

Stambler, Irwin. *Encyclopedia of Pop, Rock & Soul.* New York, St. Martin's Press, 1989.

Thorpe, Jim (1888-1953)

Few would argue that Jim Thorpe is one of the most accomplished American athletes of the entire twentieth century. His time in the National Football League (NFL) and Football Hall of Fame enshrinement data attests to this fact. Here, it is noted that he was an "All-America halfback at Carlisle [and] 1912 Olympic decathlon champion . . . First big-name athlete to play pro football, signing with the pre-NFL Canton Bulldogs in 1915 . . . Named 'The Legend' on the all-time NFL team . . . Voted top American athlete of first half of 20th century. . . ." Additionally, Thorpe won Olympic gold in both the decathlon and pentathlon. That his medals were ingloriously stripped away because he had briefly played professional baseball is one of the less-than-honorable deeds of the International Olympic Committee.

James Francis Thorpe, a Sac and Fox Indian, was born in the Oklahoma Territory. His indian name was Wa-tho-biuck (or "Bright Path"), and he, his twin brother Charles, mother, and rancher father resided in a one-room cabin near the small town of Bellemont. Young Jim was a natural athlete who loved and excelled in all sports. His early life, however, was laden with disappointment and tragedy. When he was eight, his brother was stricken with fever and subsequently passed away. Five years later, his mother died of blood poisoning. In 1904, at age 16, he headed east to Pennsylvania's Carlisle Indian School. His small size—he was 5 feet 5 inches tall and weighed 115 pounds—prevented him from finding a spot on the Carlisle varsity football team. This frustration, coupled with the death of his father, resulted in declining grades, alienation, and eventual sequestering in the Carlisle guardhouse.

By his late teens, Thorpe had grown five inches, adding bulk and muscle. Pop Warner, Carlisle's legendary coach, first took note of his track-and-field skills, and eventually recruited him for the football team. He started out as a kicker, became the starting halfback during the 1908 season, and his athletic career began to blossom. During that

Jim Thorpe

season, his running, punting, place-kicking, and occasional passing guided Carlisle to a 10-2-1 record; Walter Camp, America's reigning football expert, cited him as a third-team All-American.

After playing professional baseball in the Carolina League, Thorpe returned to Carlisle and solidified his legend as an all-time-great college gridiron star. In 1911, he was involved in two out of every three of Carlisle's offensive plays. His 50 and 60 yard punts soared through the sky. In the year's penultimate contest, an 18-15 victory over Harvard, he carried the ball on 40 percent of all plays and kicked four field goals. Carlisle ended the campaign with an 11-1 record; the following season, Thorpe added to his luster by leading Carlisle to a 12-1 mark. In both years, Camp cited him as a first-team All-American.

Perhaps Thorpe's greatest triumph came in the 1912 Olympics, held in Stockholm. He was set to compete in two punishing events: the pentathlon, made up of five track-and-field competitions (javelin throw, discus throw, running broad jump, 200-meter dash, and 1,500-meter race); and the decathlon, consisting of 10 events (javelin throw, discus throw, long jump, high jump, pole vault, shot-put, 400-meter run, 1,500-meter run, 100-meter dash, and 100-meter hurdles). He won gold medals in each, and King Gustav of Sweden proclaimed that Thorpe was the "greatest athlete in the world."

Thorpe returned to the United States a bona fide hero. But the cheering was to be short-lived. A journalist soon discovered that Thorpe had played professional baseball. Therefore, he could not be classified an amateur athlete; only amateurs could compete in the Olympics. In a letter to the Amateur Athletic Union, Thorpe wrote, "I did not play for the money . . . but because I like to play ball. I was not wise to the ways of the world and I did not realize this was wrong and that it would make me a professional in track sports."

Back when Thorpe was in his athletic prime, it was a common practice for college athletes to pass their summers playing pro ball to pick up a few extra bucks. They played under assumed names—so no one was the wiser—and they could retain their amateur status. Had Thorpe done so, his indiscretion would have remained a secret. When confronted with the accusation that he had played ball for money, he was honest enough to admit the truth. Nevertheless, he was divested of his medals by the International Olympic Committee. This dishonor is particularly ironic considering that, today, professionals with million-dollar salaries are allowed to compete for Olympic gold. For the "crime" of playing pro baseball, Thorpe pulled down a salary of $25 to $30 a week.

Thorpe was to be the Bo Jackson and Deion Sanders of his day, as he went on to play major league baseball and pro football. His debut in the majors came in 1913, when he patrolled the outfield for the New York Giants. From then through 1919 he played in 289 games, mostly for the Giants, but with brief stints in Cincinnati and Boston. In 1915, Thorpe made his pro football debut with the Canton Bulldogs. Between 1915 and 1928, he played halfback for the Bulldogs (where he spent the bulk of his career), Cleveland Indians, Oorang Indians, Rock Island Independents, New York Giants, and Chicago Cardinals. In 1916, he was the Bulldogs' starting halfback and head coach, guiding his team to an undefeated season. In 1920, he became the first president of the American Professional Football Association, the precursor of the NFL. Thorpe also was an innovator; during his pro career, he conceived the style of tackling in which the tackler attempts to halt the runner with his shoulder, rather than arm.

Jim Thorpe was 40 when he retired from football. For the next two decades he held various menial jobs—often, ironically, working under an assumed name because of the humiliation. He toiled as a B-movie actor in Hollywood. He accepted public speaking engagements in which he would be garbed in Indian gear as he discussed athletics and the plight of the American Indian. During these hard times, he also became an alcoholic.

In January 1950, the Associated Press surveyed 391 sportswriters and broadcasters to determine the greatest athletes of the first half of the twentieth century. Thorpe was cited as the top football player, and bested Babe Ruth as the finest all-around athlete. A year later, his life story was told in the Hollywood movie *Jim Thorpe—All American,* with Burt Lancaster in the title role. Thorpe died in 1953, after suffering his third heart attack. The following year, his remains were placed in a mausoleum in Mauch Chunk, a Pennsylvania town of 5,000 located at the foot of the Pocono mountains, which was summarily renamed for Thorpe.

Since his death, his honors have multiplied. In 1955, the NFL's Most Valuable Player trophy was named for Thorpe; the trophy awarded to college football's top defensive player also was named for him. In 1958, he was admitted into the National Indian Hall of Fame, and in 1961, he was chosen for the Pennsylvania Hall of Fame. By 1963, he had become a charter inductee in the Football Hall of Fame—and, when arriving at the Hall, located in Canton, one is greeted by a statue of Thorpe. Most importantly, in 1982—29 years after his death—Juan Antonio Samaranch, the new president of the International Olympic Committee, reestablished Thorpe's amateur status. The following year, his children were presented with facsimiles of his Olympic medals.

—Rob Edelman

FURTHER READING:

Nardo, Don. *Jim Thorpe (The Importance Of).* San Diego, Lucent Books, 1994.

Newcombe, Jack. *The Best of the Athletic Boys: The White Man's Impact on Jim Thorpe.* Garden City, New York, Doubleday, 1975.

Schoor, Gene, with Henry Gilfond. *The Jim Thorpe Story: America's Greatest Athlete.* New York, Messner, 1951.

Wheeler, Robert W. *Jim Thorpe: World's Greatest Athlete.* Norman, University of Oklahoma Press, 1985.

The Three Caballeros

Produced with the newly formed Office of Inter-American Affairs, Walt Disney Studio's animated film *The Three Cabelleros* (1945) presented stellar technical achievements, blending live action and animation in color on a scale never achieved before, and putting the film years ahead of its time. Rooted in the World War II era, the film was one of a series of features, beginning with *Saludos Amigos* (1943), attempting to celebrate diplomatic relations between the United States and Latin America by erasing the stereotyped images of Latin American culture and people common in Hollywood cinema:

the untrustworthy Mexican womanizing Latin lover "guerillero"; his female counterpart, the lascivious Latin woman; and the stupid, lazy "poncho."

These films are also noted for being the first concerted effort to use animation as an instructional medium for popular audiences and as an effort to atone for what Eric Smoodin in *Animating Culture* describes as "the previous sins of Yankee cultural chauvinism." Yet what started out as a lesson in geography with more balanced depictions of place and people evolved into fantastical depictions of what Smoodin notes as "geographies animated by imagination and desire." *The Three Cabelleros* actually reveals more about the culture and ideologies of the United States than it does about the nations of Mexico and Brazil, the featured countries. Latin America is presented to the star of the film, Donald Duck, as a series of birthday presents. It constructs a tourist representation of Latin America, its peoples and culture, exotic with pleasures and fun offered for the delight of North America. This is well-illustrated by Donald Duck's reaction to Latin American women as constructed in the text. The film renders the people of Latin America, and particularly the women, as homogeneous. The diversity of racial types on the continent is not presented, rather the women are "recognizably" Latin American. Their portrayal is linked directly to the images of Latin American women popularized by Carmen Miranda, and they are linked to hyper-sexuality, both in the male's reaction to them and visually, as in the Carmen Molina dance sequence with phallic cacti. Though the effort to present a truer vision of Latin America is made obvious, *The Three Cabelleros* reveals an underlying set of messages of American imperialism and racism.

—Frances Gateward

FURTHER READING:

Maltin, Leonard. *The Disney Films.* New York, Crown Publishers, 1984.

———. *Of Mice and Magic: A History of American Animated Cartoons.* New York, Plume, 1987.

Smoodin, Eric. *Animating Culture.* New Brunswick, New Jersey, Rutgers University Press, 1993.

3-D Imagery
See Stereoscopes

Three Investigators Series

The Three Investigators series, a 43-volume set of mysteries for juvenile readers published by Random House between 1964 and 1987, featured three 13-year-old male amateur sleuths, Jupiter Jones, Pete Crenshaw, and Bob Andrews. Jupiter, a former child actor, was the group's leader, Pete the impulsive athlete, and Bob the reserved, studious type. Although the sleuths were amateurs, they were portrayed handling themselves in a thoroughly professional manner,

including offering business cards and maintaining scrupulous files in their office, a trailer hidden in a junkyard owned by Jupiter's aunt and uncle. The office had several secret entrances, including a tunnel which could be accessed through a loose board on the junkyard fence. The Three Investigators also used modern equipment in their investigations, including the telephone and portable tape recorders.

Film director Alfred Hitchcock served as a consultant to the Three Investigators at the beginning and end of each story. After Hitchcock's death in 1980, the series stopped using his name as a character, replacing him with a fictitious film director, Hector Sebastian, for new titles and paperback reprints of the first thirty volumes. The early volumes (1-8, 10) were written by Robert Arthur Feder (1909-1969), who served as an editor for the *Alfred Hitchcock Magazine,* the author of many screenplays for *Alfred Hitchcock Presents,* and the compiler of several short-story collections bearing the director's name. The title pages of the Three Investigators books identified the authors of each volume. Some of them wrote under pen names, such as "Robert Arthur" for Robert Arthur Feder, "William Arden" for Dennis Lynds, and "Marc Brandel" for Marcus Beresford; others, such as Nick West and Mary Virginia Carey, used their real names.

The Three Investigators were too young to drive, and in the early books were chauffeured around their native Rocky Beach (near Hollywood, California) in a gold-plated limousine whose services they had won in the first volume. In later books, their chauffeur returned to help the boys during his time off. This transportation complication made the Three Investigators series more believable to readers who were just a few years younger and facing the same problems. Because of the more realistic adventures experienced by the trio, librarians preferred them over the mass-market—and old-fashioned—Hardy Boys books.

After the publication of the earlier volumes, Random House issued a new series of Three Investigators Crimebusters stories, but they were discontinued after a little more than a dozen paperback volumes were published. In these stories, written by some of the same writers as the original series, Jupe, Pete, and Bob were old enough to drive and hold down part-time jobs. The Crimebusters series had a modern theme with more action and violence, erasing the innocence of the original series. The Three Investigators have proven popular in Germany and several new stories were written specifically for that market in a series known in translation as the "Three Question Marks."

—James D. Keeline

The Three Stooges

Although they spent more than three decades making films, it was television that turned the Three Stooges into one of the most recognizable and beloved comedy teams in the world. Specializing in unsophisticated, violent slapstick, the Three Stooges slapped, poked, and generally abused each other in more than two hundred short films between 1934 and 1958, when their shorts were released to television, to the delight of a whole new generation of Three Stooges fans.

Formed in vaudeville in 1923, the team's original members were Moe Howard (born June 19, 1897, as Moses Horowitz; died May 4, 1975) and his brother Shemp (born March 17, 1895, as Samuel

The Three Stooges

Horowitz; died November 23, 1955), who acted as sidekicks to their boyhood friend, comedian Ted Healy. In its early years, the act was billed "Ted Healy and His Stooges" and sometimes "The Racketeers." While various "stooges" moved in and out of the act, each virtually interchangeable with another, the addition of Larry Fine (born October 5, 1902, as Louis Feinberg; died January 24, 1975) in 1925 rounded out the troupe. For the next several years Healy's Racketeers were Moe, Larry, Shemp, and Fred Sanborn. Although there was very little that was innovative about the team's act—the physical comedy they performed was borrowed from old vaudeville slapstick—their success in vaudeville led them to Broadway in the late 1920s and to film in 1930, where this lineup supported Healy in the feature film *Soup to Nuts.* Although the film was not a hit, the Stooges found a warm audience.

In the meantime, a rift had grown between Healy and his players, as the trio resented the pay inequity by which they were paid only one-tenth of the more than one thousand dollars Healy earned weekly. Such financial disagreements were exacerbated by Healy's problems with alcohol, which were worsening. The Stooges left Healy when he nixed a contract offered to them by Fox (to perform without Healy),

striking out on their own as "Howard, Fine and Howard" while Healy hired new stooges to do the old act. Although Healy managed to convince them to return, Shemp left the act to pursue a career in feature films and was replaced by Curly (born October 1903 as Jerome Lester Horowitz; died January 18, 1952), who soon emerged as the most popular stooge. Signed to a one-year contract with Metro-Goldwyn Mayer studios in 1933, the Stooges appeared in six feature films, including *Meet the Baron, Dancing Lady* (with Joan Crawford), *Fugitive Lovers,* and *Hollywood Party.* But it was short films such as *Plane Nuts* that allowed them to reproduce their vaudeville act. When their contract was up, Healy stayed with MGM, while the Three Stooges went on as a trio, signing a deal with Columbia for a series of two-real comedies—a commitment that would end up lasting twenty-five years.

It was during the early Columbia years that Moe, Larry, and Curly developed into recognizable characters, with hairstyles that scarcely changed over the decades: Moe's thick black mop with its evenly cut bangs was as much a fixture of the act as the two large tufts of curly hair that protruded from Larry's balding head. Moe assumed Healy's role as the leader (off camera as well), slapping, poking, or punching the childlike Curly or the hapless Larry. However, it was the bald and portly Curly who usually stole the show, delighting audiences with his masterful body language, which he exercised with his feet as much as his hands, sometimes dancing or spinning on the floor. Curly's high-pitched voice was also used to great effect by singing, barking, and most of all, wise-cracking—while his occasional defiance of the bossy Moe almost always resulted in more abuse.

The films generally followed a standard plot, which of course was merely a vehicle for their slapstick set pieces and verbal gags. In most films, the group would take on occupations such as plumbers, waiters, doctors, salesmen, soldiers, or businessmen, where they would proceed to make a mess of the situation. Although the tiniest disagreements would usually result in an exchange of slaps, pokes, and insults—a formula that was usually repeated several times in each film—in the end Moe, Larry, and Curly always stuck together in their efforts to resolve whatever problem they faced.

Working under directors such as Edward Bernds, Charlie Chase, Del Lord, and Jules White, the Stooges didn't write their own scripts, but their ad-libbing frequently survived the films' final cut. Highlights of their early years with Columbia include their World War II parodies of Hitler in *You Nazty Spy* (1940) and *I'll Never Say Heil Again* (1941). Such performances had personal resonance because of the Stooges' Jewish background but were nevertheless enhanced by Moe's striking transformation into the German fuehrer. Although the trio appeared in occasional feature films, including *Start Cheering* (1938), *Time Out for Rhythm* (1941), and *Swing Parade* (1946), short subjects remained the principal format for their films.

With his health steadily deteriorating, Curly suffered a stroke while on the set of *Halfwit's Holiday* in May 1946 and was forced to retire from the act. His brother Shemp returned from a solo career as a character comedian and rejoined the group. Although it was difficult to fill the shoes of the trio's most popular member, Shemp helped to sustain the group's success for the next decade, until his unexpected death in November 1955. Despite the loss of another brother, Moe chose to continue the act with one-time burlesque star Joe Besser replacing Shemp. While the Three Stooges had starred in Columbia's top-grossing short-subject series for many years, the era of short-subject films was nevertheless coming to a close by the early 1950s. With most major studios having phased out two-reelers, the Stooges' career with Columbia ended in 1958 when the studio closed its short-subjects department.

Just as the act seemed on the verge of retiring, a new generation discovered a quarter century of face-slapping, nose-tweaking, eye-poking comedy with the release of seventy-eight Columbia shorts (featuring Curly) to television. Capitalizing on their renewed popularity, the group carried on by making numerous personal appearances (which had always been their most lucrative source of income) and launching a line of merchandise and comic books. Meanwhile, by 1959 Joe Besser had been replaced by Joe De Rita, who became known as "Curly Joe," and the trio ventured into a series of feature films aimed primarily at children, including *Have Rocket, Will Travel* (1959), *Snow White and the Three Stooges* (1961), *The Three Stooges Meet Hercules, The Three Stooges in Orbit* (both 1962), and *The Outlaws Is Coming* (1965). In 1965 the group produced live-action wraparounds for a series of five-minute animated cartoons.

The impact of the Three Stooges' comeback in the late 1950s and 1960s was part of a general renewal of interest in slapstick comedy. During this period many of the works of the Marx Brothers, Laurel and Hardy, and the silent films of Charlie Chaplin were revived and found new television audiences. On the big screen, the success of high-budget feature films such as *It's a Mad, Mad, Mad, Mad World* (1963), *Those Magnificent Men in Their Flying Machines* (1965), and *The Great Race* (1965) was probably due in no small part to the Three Stooges' role in the renaissance of physical comedy. Long after the Three Stooges' demise, homage continued to be paid to Curly's antics in cartoons such as "Jabberjaw" in the 1970s.

Although they had retired by the end of the 1960s, the Three Stooges' popularity continued to grow in succeeding decades, weathering criticism from parents concerned with the group's excessive violence and from some women offended by the Stooges' objectification of women. In the 1990s the images of the "classic" Three Stooges—Moe, Larry, and Curly—endured not only in their short films, but also in television commercials and merchandise such as calendars, books, and computer screen savers.

—Kevin O'Connor

FURTHER READING:

Besser, Joe, with Jeff and Greg Lenburg. *Not Just a Stooge*. Orange, Calif., Excelsior Books, 1984.

Feinberg, Morris. *My Brother Larry: The Stooge in the Middle*. San Francisco, Last Gasp of San Francisco, 1984.

Hansen, Tom, with Jeffrey Forrester. *Stoogemania*. Chicago, Contemporary Books, 1984.

Howard, Moe. *Moe Howard and the Three Stooges*. Secaucus, N.J., Citadel Press, 1977.

Kurson, Robert, and Martin Short. *The Official Three Stooges Encyclopedia: The Ultimate Knucklehead's Guide to Stoogedom*. Lincolnwood, Ill., Contemporary Books, 1998.

Maurer, Joan Howard. *Curly: An Illustrated Biography of the Superstooges*. Secaucus, N.J., Citadel Press, 1985.

Scordato, Mark. *The Three Stooges*. New York, Chelsea House, 1995.

Three's Company

Three's Company was the definitive mindless television sex comedy, speaking to a generation ripe for the numbing. Running on ABC from 1977 to 1984, it reflected the swinging needs of the viewers, and was the vehicle through which a major Hollywood blackballing took place.

Three's Company starred John Ritter as the prat-falling chef Jack Tripper, Joyce DeWitt as the sensible florist Janet Wood, and Suzanne Somers as the prototypical dumb blond secretary (and minister's daughter), Chrissy (full name: Christmas) Snow. As the series opened, Janet and Chrissy needed a third roommate for their Santa Monica apartment. The morning after the going-away party for their last roommate, they found a man sleeping in their bathtub, and, upon learning that he could cook, they let him move in. Nothing sexual ever went on between the roommates, but not for Jack's lack of

The cast of *Three's Company*.

leering. While he was hitting on anything in a skirt, he had to pretend to be gay so the landlord would allow the living arrangement, which was still a new idea in the 1970s.

Usually joining the trio at the local hangout, the Regal Beagle, was Jack's sleazy best friend Larry Dallas (Richard Kline). The landlords were impotent Stanley and sex-starved Helen Roper, played by Norman Fell (who also played an uptight landlord in *The Graduate*) and Audra Lindley. Jack often had to distract Mr. Roper by coming on to him and disgusting him into leaving; though it was never given a name, Jack's faux homosexuality manifested itself in limp wrists, simpering, and hissing. The Ropers were spun off in 1979, and Jack, Janet and Chrissy's new landlord was Ralph Furley, a leisure-suited nebbish played by Don Knotts.

Three's Company was chock-full of pratfalls (Ritter's forte), double entendres, and misunderstandings ("I overheard Janet say she's late . . . oh my God, she must be pregnant!"). In a typical episode Jack gives someone cooking lessons, but a roommate thinks he's giving "love lessons."

The show became hugely popular, and was featured on the cover of *Newsweek* in February 1978, with a staged shot of Somers with her underwear falling off and Ritter leering over her shoulder, something that never happened on the show. Even the theme song (". . . where the kisses are hers and hers and his. . . ") implied sex where there was none.

Three's Company made a celebrity out of the buxom Somers, who got her big break with a few seconds of screen time in George Lucas' *American Graffiti*, along with half a dozen other actors. In the

summer of 1980, Somers asked her *Three's Company* producers for the same amount of money the male stars of the era were bringing home—a share of the profits and a fivefold salary increase, from $30,000 to $150,000 per episode. The producers didn't go for it, and, making an example of her, held her to her contract for a final year. During the 1980-1981 season, Somers appeared only in one-minute inserts at the end of each show, featuring Chrissy talking on the phone to one of the characters; it was explained that Chrissy was tending to her sick mother in Fresno. The inserts were taped separately on a closed set. Soon Chrissy was written out of the show, and Hollywood closed its doors on Somers.

Somers' first replacement, in the fall of 1980, was Chrissy's cousin, the blond and clumsy Cindy Snow (Jennilee Harrison). After a year, Cindy moved out to go to UCLA Vet school, but still stopped by. In the fall of 1981, lanky nurse Terri Alden (Priscilla Barnes) moved in. In 1984, Janet got married, Terri moved to Hawaii, and Jack met his true love Vicky Bradford. Jack and Vicky spun off into *Three's a Crowd* (1985-86), where they lived together (Vicky didn't believe in marriage) above Jack's restaurant. Jack's foil this time was Vicky's disapproving father, who also owned the building.

Most of the show's stars became indelibly associated with their roles (with the exception of Knotts, who will always be remembered as Barney Fife in *The Andy Griffith Show*). Somers did make a comeback, mostly by continuing to look good as she aged, which she owed to a product she will be forever associated with, the Thighmaster (and later, the Buttmaster). Besides exercise books and videos, she also wrote and spoke out about surviving abuse.

—Karen Lurie

FURTHER READING:

Brooks, Tim, and Earle Marsh. *The Complete Directory to Prime Time Network and Cable TV Shows 1946-present.* New York, Ballantine Books, 1995.

McNeil, Alex. *Total Television.* New York, Penguin, 1996.

Somers, Suzanne. *After the Fall: How I Picked Myself Up, Dusted Myself Off, and Started All Over Again.* New York, Crown Publishing, 1998.

Thurber, James (1894-1961)

Ohio-born satirical writer James Thurber was most noted for his ability to illustrate, through the use of humor, the frailties of human beings in a world seemingly dominated by forces of their own making. His primary media, the short story and his famous pen-and-ink cartoon sketches, have served as models for later critics and observers of the social scene who write in a casual style reminiscent of the *New Yorker,* which began publication in the 1920s and for which Thurber was a regular contributor. Much of his work, including his writings and drawings of animals, especially dogs, and the unforgettable Walter Mitty have become permanent fixtures in American literary folklore.

Thurber was born in Columbus in 1894, during a time when the United States was experiencing great change due to the forces of industrial development: explosive urban growth, immigration, labor upheavals, and the dizzying pace of technological advancement. All of these influenced Thurber's work. Thurber's poor eyesight—as a child his brother William accidentally shot him in the eye with a bow and arrow—prevented him from enjoying an active childhood and later in life rendered him legally blind. After a difficult start at Ohio State University, Thurber found his stride as editor of the school newspaper and literary magazine. While in college, he befriended future playwright and film director Elliott Nugent, with whom he would collaborate in New York in later years.

Thurber's writing career foundered from the start. He accepted a job as a reporter for the Columbus *Dispatch* after World War I, moved to Europe in the 1920s to write for overseas newspapers, then returned to the United States and wrote for the New York *Post*. While living in New York, Thurber met author E. B. White, who introduced him to the editors of the *New Yorker,* a new magazine that hoped to capitalize on the "Roaring Twenties" image of the city by developing a smart, lighthearted, and slightly irreverent literary style. Thurber was hired as an associate editor, and then later managed to get himself "demoted" to a contributing author. The marriage of the *New Yorker* and Thurber was fortuitous: his articles and sketches graced the pages of the magazine for years to come and helped set the overall tone for the publication. Thurber and White collaborated on the 1929 bestselling book *Is Sex Necessary?,* a spoof on the sex-psychology books popular during the 1920s.

Thurber's use of humor to point out human shortcomings took several forms. His cartoons often depicted people struggling with the trials and tribulations of everyday life, especially in the face of modern technology that often made things more, rather than less, troublesome. Thurber believed that humans often unnecessarily complicated their lives through an excess of "abstract reasoning" instead of being practical. Thus, he always portrayed animals in a sympathetic light, commending their reliance on instinctive wisdom instead of the fuzzy reasoning of humans. Males were especially targeted for ridicule by Thurber; his cartoons often included spineless husbands being berated by their domineering and opinionated wives. In "The Secret Life of Walter Mitty," (1939) Thurber's most famous *New Yorker* story, he created a title character who escaped his meager, workaday world by becoming a larger-than-life hero in his daydreams, a gentle symbol of humanity's loss of direction and purpose in modern times. Thurber's work also found its way to the stage, as in *The Male Animal* (1940), a Broadway collaboration with Elliott Nugent, and *A Thurber Carnival* (1960), an off-Broadway revue in which Thurber himself performed.

Beset with alcoholism, rage, and blindness, Thurber's last years were not happy ones for him or his friends, and his personal problems were reflected in his creative output. In a piece for the *New York Times Book Review,* John Updike commented that "The writer who had produced *Fables for Our Time* and *The Last Flower* out of the thirties had become, by the end of the fifties, one more indignant senior citizen penning complaints about the universal decay of virtue." Still, Thurber is considered one of the century's most prominent humorous writers, with works that took many forms over the span of his career, including novels, short stories, articles, and sketches—almost all of them containing a strain of melancholia that is distinctly modern in style. A quotation from one of his many fables perhaps best describes Thurber's attitude: A dinosaur, talking to a

human, remarked "There are worse things than being extinct, and one of them is being you." Thurber was not a hater of mankind; he was a modernist who saw the limitations of man in a conspicuously optimistic age.

—Jeffrey W. Coker

FURTHER READING:

Holmes, Charles S. *The Clocks of Columbus: The Literary Career of James Thurber.* New York, Atheneum Books, 1972.

Thurber, James. *Thurber's Dogs.* New York, Simon & Schuster, 1955.

———. *A Thurber Carnival.* New York, Samuel French, 1962.

———. *Vintage Thurber.* 2 Volumes. London, Hamish Hamilton, 1963.

Tierney, Gene (1920-1991)

Debuting as a teenage model and budding stage actress, Gene Tierney soon metamorphosed into one of Hollywood's most recognizable movie stars of the 1940s and 1950s. Her reputation relied on promotion of her distinctive looks and physical elegance. Twentieth Century Fox founder Darryl Zanuck famously proclaimed her, "unquestionably the most beautiful woman in movie history." With high cheekbones and unusually shaped eyes, Tierney, a New Yorker, was considered "exotic." Studios cast her in films that highlighted her mystique like *The Shanghai Gesture* (1941) and *The Egyptian* (1954). In seeming contradiction with her inscrutable features, Tierney's image also reflected her Swiss finishing school poise and sophistication, garnering her the cosmopolitan title role in the film noir classic *Laura* (1944) and that of the love-obsessed femme fatale of *Leave Her to Heaven* (1945). Offscreen, Tierney's life embraced another incongruity. The popular star suffered well publicized misfortunes and subsequent breakdowns, and her aura of graceful beauty came to signify tragedy.

—Elizabeth Haas

FURTHER READING:

Ellrod, J.G. *The Stars of Hollywood Remembered: Career Biographies of 82 Actors and Actresses of the Golden Era, 1920s-1950s.* Jefferson, North Carolina, McFarland, 1997.

Lambert, Gavin. "Gene Tierney: Beverly Hills Backdrop for the Enigmatic Star of *Laura.*" *Architectural Digest,* 1992.

Tierney, Gene, with Mickey Herskowitz. *Self Portrait.* New York, Berkley Books, 1980.

Tiffany & Company

Tiffany, a name long synonymous with elegance and style, owes its lustre to the New York firm founded by Charles Lewis Tiffany which, since becoming Tiffany & Company in 1853, has provided the well-to-do with exquisitely crafted jewelry and home furnishings. Louis Comfort Tiffany, a brilliant and famous glass designer, founded Tiffany Studios in 1900 and succeeded his father as head of Tiffany & Company. Tiffany's place in America's popular imagination was given a boost by Truman Capote's 1958 novel *Breakfast at Tiffany's* and the 1961 film of the same title, in which Audrey Hepburn as Holly Golightly accepts from her admirer a Tiffany-engraved toy Crackerjack ring. No doubt the popularity of the girls' name Tiffany in the last decades of the twentieth century owes much to its associations with the beautiful creations of Tiffany & Company.

—Craig Bunch

FURTHER READING:

Loring, John. *Tiffany's 150 Years.* Garden City, New York, Doubleday & Company, 1987.

———. *Tiffany's 20th Century: A Portrait of American Style.* New York, H.N. Abrams, 1997.

Tijuana Bibles

It is surely no accident that illicit pornographic comic books, popularly known as Tijuana Bibles, thrived during the heyday of media censorship in modern America, roughly the mid-1920s to the mid-1950s. In the early decades of the century, movies, comic strips, and pulp magazines all had ample room for the naughty and risque, but by the 1920s the pressures of social respectability were increasingly hemming in popular culture. The acceptance of the stringent Hays Code by Hollywood in 1934 was a significant turning point in this larger trend. Like girlie magazines and stag movies, Tijuana Bibles represented an escape from the puritanism of mainstream culture. As the cartoonist Harvey Kurtzman, creator of *Mad* magazine, once noted, "The obvious repression of sexual fantasy in [mainstream comic strips] brought its release in the little dirty books, or Tijuana Bibles."

Almost as ephemeral as washroom graffiti, Tijuana Bibles were anonymous in every sense imaginable. For the most part, no one knows who wrote them, who drew them, or who published them. The name "Tijuana Bible" plays off the fictitious foreign addresses that were given as the place of publication. In addition to erotic and exotic Mexico, Tijuana Bibles were said to be produced in Cuba, England, and even Canada. Some suggested that organized crime was behind these tawdry sex books. Cartoonist Will Eisner, best known for creating the masked crime fighter the Spirit, frequently has recounted the story of how as a struggling artist in the 1930s he was approached by a gangster who wanted him to draw Tijuana Bibles.

Yet, despite their obscure origin, almost one thousand separate Tijuana Bibles were published and managed to circulate throughout North America. "The distribution system was mysterious, but it worked," commented Kurtzman. Comic book historian Donald Gilmore, in the first scholarly study of the genre, noted that Tijuana Bibles were "conceived in dark attics, published in dingy garages on unnamed alleys, and distributed from the hip pockets of vendors across the nation. . . . [but] accounted for a multi-million-dollar business in the tight economy of the Great Depression."

The earliest Tijuana Bibles of the 1920s and 1930s were comic strip parodies. Often deftly done imitations, these books featured such stars of the funny pages as Betty Boop, Popeye, Olive Oyl, Mickey Mouse, and Dick Tracy all engaging in activities forbidden in family newspapers. In positing a secret sex life for popular cultural icons, Tijuana Bibles both influenced and anticipated the work of such later cartoonists as Kurtzman, whose *Little Annie Fanny* started running in *Playboy* in the 1960s. The work of countercultural cartoonists of the late 1960s like Robert Crumb and S. Clay Wilson—who drew Disney-esque animals with earthy human appetites—also shows the influence of Tijuana Bibles.

By the early 1930s, Tijuana Bibles had expanded from their origins as cartoon parodies and started featuring Hollywood celebrities such as Laurel and Hardy, Mae West, the Marx Brothers, and Clark Gable. These Tijuana Bibles played off the rumors of "Hollywood Babylon" that flourished in the tabloid press. Hollywood was shown as a happy playground of orgies and bisexuality. Noting the large number of strips featuring celebrities, cartoonist Art Spiegelman observes that Tijuana Bibles "were not overtly political but were by their nature anti-authoritarian, a protest against what Freud called Civilization and Its Discontents. Here was a populist way to rebel against the mass media and advertising designed to titillate and manipulate, but never satisfy."

Some Tijuana Bibles that were more explicitly political in one way: they featured such world figures as Hitler, Mussolini, Stalin, Chiang Kai-shek, and even Whittaker Chambers (a Cold War spy who, a recent biography confirms, was a bisexual, just as he was portrayed in a Tijuana Bible from the late 1940s). As with the Hollywood strips, the politics of these Tijuana Bibles was implicitly anti-authoritarian, ridiculing the powerful by showing that they had base needs. Of course, there was a limit to how subversive Tijuana Bibles could be. In all these strips, the main goal was to titillate, and they replicated the racial and ethnic stereotypes found in mainstream culture.

Artistically, the quality of Tijuana Bibles varied greatly. Two talented cartoonists, "Doc" Rankin and Wesley Morse, have been identified and singled out by aficionados of the genre. Bob Adelman praised Rankin's "graceful, articulate, Deco style" and Morse's "wonderful graphic flair." (Morse went on to do *Bazooka Joe* comics in the 1950s.) Only a few other Tijuana Bible cartoonists, all of them anonymous, were as good as Rankin and Morse. The worst Tijuana Bibles were also among the worst comic books ever done: crudely drawn, illiterate, and mean-spirited.

With the decline of censorship in the mid-1950s, signaled by the emergence of *Playboy* in 1955, Tijuana Bibles lost their reason to exist. However, as with other trashy and throw-away bits of the past, Tijuana Bibles continue to have a nostalgic appeal. In the mid-1970s, the novelist John Updike wrote that the type of pornography he "most missed" was "Popeye, Olive Oyl, and Wimpy fellating and gamahuching one another, in comic books circulating in southern Pennsylvania in the late 1940s." Not surprisingly, books reprinting Tijuana Bibles continue to roll off the press.

—Jeet Heer

FURTHER READING:

Adelman, Bob, with additional commentary by Art Spiegelman, Richard Merkin, and Madeline Kripke. *Tijuana Bibles: Art and*

Wit in America's Forbidden Funnies, 1930s-1950s. New York, Simon & Schuster, 1997.

Gilmore, Donald H. *Sex in Comics: A History of the Eight Pagers.* 4 vols. San Diego, Greenleaf Classics, 1971.

Time

Published weekly without interruption since March 3, 1923, *Time: The Weekly News-Magazine* (the final word is no longer hyphenated) pioneered a new genre of publication that was invented in the United States after the First World War and spawned many imitators at home and abroad. *Time* was the first mass-circulation magazine to offer a weekly digest of current events and commentary organized into departments, written in an oft-parodied breezy, idiosyncratic style. As the inaugural publication in Henry Luce's publishing empire that within little more than a decade included *Fortune, Life,* and *Architectural Forum,* the periodical quickly established itself as a "lengthened shadow" of its founder, who maintained close control over its content and used it to shape public opinion toward accepting his views about the role of the United States in "the American Century." As such, it frequently was thought to be a Republican-oriented publication: it published highly favorable coverage of the presidential aspirations of Herbert Hoover, Wendell Willkie, and Dwight Eisenhower—though, surprisingly, Luce voted for Alfred E. Smith, Hoover's Democratic opponent in 1928. Not surprisingly, *Time*'s opinions were frequently at odds with that of Franklin D. Roosevelt, though Luce gave his wholehearted support to the administration in the interest of national unity during World War II. *Time* was one of the earliest and most vocal critics of the right-wing tactics of Senator Joseph McCarthy in the 1950s. Even though the Time-Life empire had evolved into Time-Warner by the 1990s, with Time, Inc. New Media establishing a brand-conscious presence on the World Wide Web, *Time* "the weekly newsmagazine" still maintains an important role as one of the three leading American newsweeklies along with *Newsweek* and *U.S. News and World Report.*

The genesis of *Time* magazine had its roots in the deep but often contentious friendship between two old schoolmates from Hotchkiss and Yale: Henry R. Luce and Briton Hadden. Luce was born and raised in China, the son of a Presbyterian missionary and the grandson of a Scranton, Pennsylvania grocer. Hadden was a native of Brooklyn, New York, the son of a stockbroker and the grandson of a bank president. The two had worked together on publication boards at their alma maters and served in a military-reserve unit during World War I, an experience that convinced them that the typical American was poorly informed of current events. They graduated with Yale's class of 1920, Luce winning the DeForest award for oratory with a speech that foreshadowed his later "American Century" editorial stance at *Time* and *Life* with its idealism in advocating American benevolent hegemony as "the great friend of the lame, the halt and the blind among nations, the comrade of all nations that struggle to rise to higher planes of social and political organization. . . ."

It was while working together as reporters on the *Baltimore News* in 1922 that Luce and Hadden hatched plans for their weekly magazine, which they originally wanted to call *Facts.* Earlier, while

working briefly as a reporter for the *New York World,* Luce had proposed to Hadden an idea "for a magazine that comes out every Friday with all the news condensed so you and all the other rich millionaires commuting home for the weekend can catch up on the news that they have missed. How's that?" The two men quit the *News* after three months, drew up a prospectus, convinced some wealthy friends to invest in their enterprise, and spent most of 1922 setting up editorial offices in New York and hiring a staff. Among the part-timers listed on *Time*'s first masthead were two men who later became somewhat prominent poets: Stephen Vincent Benét, a book reviewer, and Archibald MacLeish, who wrote the Education section for ten dollars a week. For National Affairs editor, Luce hired Alan Rinehart, the son of novelist Mary Roberts Rinehart. In days when gender roles were somewhat stratified, men were hired as editors and reporters while women researchers were hired as "secretarial assistants."

Luce projected a first-year income of $155,000, most of it from twenty-five thousand subscriptions at $5 each, and the remaining $30,000 from advertising. The fledgling publishers were disappointed when a mailing of half a million promotional pieces yielded only six thousand subscribers. Another five thousand were earmarked for newsstand distribution. The folksy tone affected in a stockholders' report just before Christmas 1922 hardly suggests that the fledgling venture would within a generation grow into one of the world's most powerful media conglomerates: "*Time* knows well that the people that will help it most are those who are best satisfied with it. For that reason it does not desire to antagonize any of its stockholders by asking to do anything that is distasteful. From time to time summary requests will be made. . . : 'Give me a letter to this potential advertiser.' 'Get me 13 subscriptions.'"

A sketch of retiring House Speaker Joseph G. Cannon graced the cover of *Time*'s Volume I, No. 1 when it was published on March 3, 1923. The thirty-two-page magazine (including covers) carried a relatively steep newsstand price of fifteen cents. Half of the newsstand's allotment of five thousand copies came back unsold, for a total of about nine thousand copies circulated, far less than optimistic projections of twenty-five thousand. For the first year or so, both circulation and advertising revenue remained sluggish. When Volume I was completed, the publishers sent bound copies to charter subscribers. Among those who sent back endorsements was Franklin D. Roosevelt, the unsuccessful vice-presidential candidate in 1920, who wrote in part "I do not think the articles are too brief—they are just about right in length and they are unbiased as far as it is possible for red-blooded Americans to make them so."

There was little original reporting in *Time*'s early issues, which were cobbled together from newspapers, wire-service reports, speeches, and other sources, rewritten in the inimitable *Time* style that was largely the brainchild of Briton Hadden. The first issue defined what would remain *Time*'s approach over the years, with only minor variations: items organized into departments such as national news, foreign news, the arts (and their subdivisions), books, religion, education, finance, and so forth. The first issue also featured three light-humor departments: Imaginary Interviews, Point with Pride, and View with Alarm. Stories were created by teams of writers and researchers, supplemented in later years by reporters and correspondents from bureaus around the world. A brief *New York Times* notice heralding the launch of the publication was headlined "Time a New Weekly—First Issue of Magazine Devoted to Summarizing Progress." True to its mission as articulated by Luce to Hadden, the magazine was designed to be read by busy millionaires and others in less than an hour; columns were at first restricted to seven inches. An unusual feature of the new magazine was its regular coverage of the number of lynchings in the Southern states. Robert T. Elson, in his semiofficial two-volume history *The World of Time Inc.,* quoted Luce: "We were what would be called pro civil rights for Negroes from the beginning. One of the things in which we may have been useful is the fact that we tried to report every single lynching. We tried to print the exact story, without moralizing." *Time* was also the first publication to apply the honorific "Mr." to both black and white subjects.

Time, especially in its earlier decades, is perhaps best known for the idiosyncratic style favored by Hadden, which has been variously termed "breezy," "arch," or "cute." It was notable for the liberal use of word coinages, especially portmanteaus or puns, as in describing a young would-be newspaper publisher as a "Hearstling"; for its resuscitation of words and allusions from classical Greek such as "kudos" or "katabasis"; for its syntax-bending, especially through the use of inverted word order, as in "Forth from the White House followed by innumerable attendants, Mr. and Mrs. Warren G. Harding set out. . . ." (their return, not surprisingly, was termed a "katabasis"); for its historical and literary allusions; and for its pomposity-deflating identification of subjects with their middle names, as in "Walter Percy Chrysler," or with nicknames in parentheses, as in "Bernarr ('Body Love') Macfadden." *Time's* stylists also pioneered in the stringing together of frequently alliterative adjectives, as when describing George Bernard Shaw as "mocking, mordant, misanthropic"; and in the uncanonical use of nouns as attributives, as in "Teacher Scopes." Clearly, *Time* was being written for an educated and well-read audience: Elson suggested that Hadden's admiration for Homeric Greek prompted him to pepper his copy with a plethora of hyphenated modifiers: "At all times Hadden had by him a carefully annotated translation of the *Iliad.* In the back cover he had listed hundreds of words, especially verbs and the compound adjectives, which had seemed to him fresh and forceful. The classic ring of this vocabulary, which he frequently reviewed, served him as a tuning fork for the language that he wanted in *Time.*" Luce is credited for the popularization of several words, such as "tycoon," a term previously used to describe a Japanese shogun which he applied to American business moguls, and "pundit," after the name of a Yale literary club he had joined.

As a cost-saving measure, *Time's* editorial offices moved to Cleveland, Ohio, in 1925 but returned to New York City within three years. By the end of the 1920s, the publication had published several sixty-page-plus issues and was reporting net profits of $125,000 on total revenues of $1.3 million, with a circulation guarantee approaching three hundred thousand. Newsstand sales doubled in a year, to twenty-three thousand copies. In 1928, with the selection of Charles Lindbergh, *Time* initiated its notable custom of selecting a "Man of the Year"—hero or villain—which over the years has been expanded to included women, anonymous groups (such as the under-thirty generation), and even the personal computer. The Man of the Year philosophy echoed Luce's secular-evangelical belief that history was mightily shaped by individual will, a phenomenon he saw himself embodying as the most influential publisher of his era at the time of his death in 1967.

In February of 1929, Hadden, then thirty-one, died of a streptococcal infection exacerbated by overwork, and Luce assumed even greater day-by-day oversight of the publication, confirming his reputation as a shrewd businessman as well as a savvy journalist. In the months before the stock-market crash ushered in the Great Depression, *Time's* tilt toward business had become quite evident. Within a month after Hadden's death, Luce said in a speech, with characteristic flourish: "Business is, essentially, our civilization; for it is the essential characteristic of our times. . . . Business is our life. It is the life of the artist, the clergyman, the philosopher, the doctor, because it determines the conditions and problems of life with which either artist or philosopher, let alone ordinary mortals, have to deal." It thus struck some observers as strange that Luce should have packed the editorial staff of his new publication, *Fortune* (which debuted February 1930), with such imaginative writers as Archibald MacLeish, Dwight Macdonald, and Russell Davenport. "There are men who can write poetry, and there are men who can read balance sheets," said Luce. "The men who can read balance sheets cannot write. . . . Of necessity, we made the discovery that it is easier to turn poets into business journalists than to turn bookkeepers into writers."

During the early 1930s, Luce enlisted the new medium of radio to expand *Time's* reach while simultaneously shaping the way radio would present news and documentary material. Luce hired Fred Smith of a Cincinnati radio station to develop a radio program based on *Time's* weekly content. Originally titled *Newscasting,* the project quickly evolved into the *NewsActing,* in which short news items were dramatized with sound effects, and then into the full-blown radio program *The March of Time*, which employed leading radio performers and announcers to reenact the week's events in a Friday night, half-hour, CBS-network program, introduced by a fanfare and the words "On a thousand fronts the history of the world moves swiftly forward. . . ." Agnes Moorehead and Orson Welles were among the graduates of the early broadcasts of *The March of Time*. Within a few years, a moving-picture-newsreel version was created, and the legend "Time Marches On" soon became a familiar sight on movie screens from coast to coast. Although, as Elson wrote, "the method of *The March of Time* is no longer acceptable as journalism . . . TV, the modern film documentary, the new school of *cinéma vérité* owe much to its pioneering methods."

Despite the success of this and other ventures, *Time* and its sister publications suffered through the Depression years, especially when factoring in the huge start-up costs of *Life* in 1936. In the period before the United States entered World War II—*Time* coined that designation in a September 1939 issue when it confidently reported "World War II began last week at 5:20 a.m. (Polish time) Friday, September 1"—Luce had come to believe that Americans had a fateful role to play in world affairs and urged military aid to the beleaguered European allies. After Pearl Harbor, Luce committed *Time* to the cause of "absolute victory." He also threw his support to the Nationalist Chinese forces of Chiang Kai-shek, much to the consternation of *Time's* correspondent in China, Theodore H. White (later of *Making of the President* fame), who broke with Luce when ordered to write flattering pieces about the man White called "China's somber tyrant." John Heidenry complained in his *New York Times* review of a 1995 book about Luce and White that the publisher "believed that ideological distortion of the news was often preferable to objectivity, particularly where China and the Republican Party were concerned." In the years that followed, *Time* maintained a firm anti-Communist tack, but it also was among the first publications to challenge the demagoguery of Wisconsin Senator Joseph McCarthy. Still, *Time* during the 1950s and 1960s was perceived as having a Republican bias—at least an "Eastern establishment" Republican bias, for *Time* endorsed, for the first time, the Democratic presidential candidate in 1964, favoring Lyndon B. Johnson over Barry Goldwater. Luce had retired as editor-in-chief earlier that year, handing over the reins to Hedley Donovan. Andrew Heiskell had already taken over as chairman of the parent company. At Luce's retirement, the firm that had started forty-some years earlier with an investment of $86,000 had grown to a conglomerate with revenues of more than $400 million.

In January of 1990, Time, Inc. and Warner Communication combined to form an even larger conglomerate, the largest in the United States, bringing together Luce's company "with its rich journalistic history and its aristocratic, traditional leadership" and Warner, "with its lucrative stable of movie, entertainment and cable television properties," in the words of the *New York Times*. During the 1980s, the management of Time, Inc. decided that it was time to deemphasize the role of its magazines as future sources of revenue and corporate viability, leading some observers, like Richard M. Clurman, to worry about the future of its journalistic integrity, as described in his 1992 book *To the End of Time: The Seduction and Conquest of a Media Empire*. Clurman's fear of "people in Time Warner who believe and act as if the purpose of business is only business" stands ironically against Henry Luce's declaration in 1929 that "Business is, essentially, our civilization."

In 1998, *Time* celebrated its seventy-fifth anniversary with a gala at New York's Radio City Music Hall to which were invited all living men and women who had appeared on the magazine's cover, a star-studded affair with guests ranging from President Bill Clinton to Russian ex-premier Mikhail Gorbachev to Billy Graham to Sharon Stone to Toni Morrison. By century's end, managing editor Walter Isaacson has been credited with restoring some of the old luster of *Time*'s authority and credibility in a "post-magazine" era by leading the publication into the new-media era via its Pathfinder Internet service, by increasing science and technology coverage, and by planning *The Time 100* series on CBS Television. Revenues at the publication increased 21 percent in 1997 to about $94 million, and circulation rose slightly to 4.2 million, earning *Time* the designation "Hottest Magazine of '97" by *Adweek*.

—Edward Moran

FURTHER READING:

Clurman, Richard. *To the End of Time: The Seduction and Conquest of a Media Empire*. New York, Simon & Schuster, 1992.

Elson, Robert T. *Time, Inc.: The Intimate History of a Publishing Enterprise 1923-1941*. New York, Atheneum, 1968.

———. *Time, Inc.: The Intimate History of a Publishing Enterprise 1941-1960*. New York, Atheneum, 1973.

Griffith, Thomas. *Harry and Teddy: The Turbulent Friendship of Press Lord Henry R. Luce and His Favorite Reporter, Theodore H. White*. New York, Random House, 1995.

Hamblin, Dora Jane. *That Was the Life*. New York, W. W. Norton & Co, 1977.

Reed, David. *The Popular Magazine in Britain and the United States*. London, The British Library, 1997.

Tebbel, John. *The American Magazine: A Compact History*. New York, Hawthorn Books, 1969.

Tebbel, John and Mary Ellen Zuckerman. *The Magazine in America: 1741-1990*. New York, Oxford University Press, 1991.

Wainwright, Loudon. *The Great American Magazine: An Inside History of Life*. New York, Alfred A. Knopf, 1986.

Wood, James Playsted. *Magazines in the United States*. New York, Ronald Press, 1978.

Times Square

Less of a square and more like two triangles located at the intersection of Broadway and Seventh Avenue in New York City, Times Square has been associated over the years with a series of seemingly opposite combinations: both high and low culture, glitz and grime, and exciting bright lights and seedy dark corners. The history of Times Square is a direct reflection of the history of Americans' relationship with their cities.

The origin of Times Square can be traced to the 1811 New York Commissioner of Streets and Roads' plan, which laid out the Manhattan grid above Fourteenth Street. The significance of this plan, and many others like it across the United States prior to and after 1811, is that the future growth of the American city was partitioned off and predetermined as easy-to-develop slices of land. This not only assured efficient exploitation, but also brought about a sort of "democratization" of the city, which the older cities of Europe with their main squares, large cathedrals, and prominent town halls did not possess. By virtue of this new grid, every building was just as important as the next, at least in terms of location on the grid. And so, the nineteenth-century American city gradually filled up its preplanned grid, creating uniform streets between often not-so-uniform buildings. American city-dwellers of this time lived in cities because they wanted to; that is, because they preferred the orderly and paved conditions of the city over the often irregular and muddy conditions of the rural areas, the only other option at this time (just before the suburbanization of America).

As New York expanded north from 14th Street, the diagonal path of the former Indian trail known as "the Bloomingdale Road" (later Broadway) was so strong that it ignored the 1811 grid plan and cut right through it. As a result, at every intersection of Broadway with a north-south avenue, a "square" came into being: Union Square at Fourth (Park) Avenue, Madison Square at Fifth Avenue, Herald Square at Sixth Avenue, and Long Acre (Times) Square at Seventh Avenue.

In the 1890s, live-performance theatres (or "legitimate theatres") began to locate themselves in and around Long Acre Square: Oscar Hammerstein's 1895 Olympia Theatre on Broadway between 44th and 45th streets was one of the first and most famous. Others soon followed from their former locations below 23rd Street, and the area soon became known as a "theatre district." At its peak in 1925, there were approximately 80 legitimate theatres within the vicinity of Times Square.

The story goes that because the City of New York had not yet installed street-lighting as far north as Long Acre Square, theatre owners took it upon themselves. Exploiting the new technology of electric lighting, the fronts of the new theatres became giant advertisements, spelling out the play on offer and sometimes also the main players. Later, multiple-story-high advertisements for chewing gum, soft drinks, and other products appeared. The result was that by about 1910, Broadway was dazzlingly lit up at night and became known as "The Great White Way."

In 1904, Long Acre Square changed its name to Times Square after the completion of the *New York Times* tower at 42nd Street and Broadway. The newspaper decided to celebrate the opening of its new building by counting down the last minutes of 1904 from the top of it. Two years later, the festivities grew to include the lowering of a ball at midnight. This event soon grew into the enormous annual party held every year in Times Square.

Also in 1904, a subway shuttle was opened which linked Times Square with Grand Central Station at 42nd and Park Avenue. This was followed by an IRT line (1918) and a BMT line (1923), both with stops at 42nd Street—and thus another aspect of Times Square was born: a transportation hub, an interchange, a "Crossroads of the World." This nickname later was strengthened by an IND line stop (1932) and the New York City Port Authority Bus Terminal (1950) at 42nd Street and Eighth Avenue, and the first Lincoln Tunnel entrance/exit (1937) at 42nd and Tenth Avenue.

The theatres (and their accompanying restaurants, bars, and hotels), the fantastic lights, and the busy transportation interchanges were all direct reflections of how the concept of "city" was portrayed in the mind of an American at the turn of the twentieth century. The city at that time was a place of energy, excitement, and culture. It was the place to be, the place where anything could happen and where most things did. The theatre represented high culture, and those who attended the performances were the elite. The lights, however, could be enjoyed by anyone, and Broadway, Times Square, and 42nd Street (it is difficult to separate them) at the turn of the twentieth century was a place to see and be seen.

With the arrival of talking movies in the late 1920s and the Depression of the 1930s, the character of the Times Square area began to change. It still remained a center for entertainment, but at that time both high and low culture were represented: live performance and musical comedy theatres on one side, and burlesque houses and "movie palaces" on the other. In addition, in that time before plane travel became commonplace, New York City was a port of call for anyone traveling between Europe and America, especially during World War II when most every American soldier passed through and spent some time at Times Square. It was a crowded and popular place, as exemplified by the estimated two million people who thronged Times Square on August 14, 1945, to read the official announcement of Japanese surrender on the *Times* building's "zipper" (news bulletin board).

In the years following World War II, the rise of television (which brought entertainment into the home, no need to go out) and city suburbs (which were clean, spacious, and safe) further strengthened the decline of Times Square and also the American city. The area began to take on vulgar associations, and its large-scale advertisements reflected this with block-long flashing neon gin bottles and 30-foot-high heads which puffed cigarettes boasting real smoke. The

42nd Street corridor became known not only for pornographic movies, but also its easy access to prostitution, and by extension, it also became a place for illegal drug trading and street gambling.

To many city-dwellers, the new burlesque houses, movie palaces, and general gawking crowds were an insult to the city but were part of a growing trend; it was changing from being a special place where special things happened to being an ordinary, common place associated with dirt and grime, overcrowded conditions, degeneracy, and crime, and, as a result, neglect and dereliction. After World War II, the American city was not seen as a place to live. Instead, it was seen as a place to get away from—hence the growth of suburban communities which, however, paradoxically still depended upon the city as the "place to work."

During the late 1970s and early 1980s, as foreshadowed by the 1967 replacement of the 1904 *Times* building's original facade with blank marble panels, the Times Square area again dramatically changed. This time it was a physical, not social change: from a mixture of different-sized theatres and commercial buildings into a wasteland of overscaled and faceless skyscrapers. Many famous turn-of-the-century theatres were demolished to make way for new developments, which were carried out with the promise that they would "revitalize" Times Square, but all they really did was add to its density.

One of the reactions to this change of Times Square was the 1987 city ordinance that required new buildings to include "super" signage several stories high and with varying degrees of animation. In addition, a 1988 ruling gave "landmark" status to most remaining theatres in the area, following the general trend in New York and other American cities of building preservation by government intervention. At the same time, large-scale musical productions with hummable tunes and easy lyrics catering to a simpler audience than live theatre became successful at Times Square theatres.

Various urban planning development studies and inquiries were undertaken to ascertain if anything could be done for the area, but no consensus was reached. In 1992, the private Times Square Business Improvement District, composed of area property owners and residents, was established. This organization, similar to others set up across the United States at this time, was privately funded to undertake those duties normally associated with the city government: public safety, sanitation, community services, economic strategy, and tourism promotion.

The city ordinances concerning the aesthetics of future development, the listing of "historic" buildings, and the creation of private entities to do the city's job all had the goal of retaining a sort of street-life status quo, but at the expense of turning Times Square into a regulated and controlled public amusement park. This last stage reflects the state of the American city at the turn of the twenty-first century: the city as a place to visit, as one might visit an amusement park. As Americans began to not only live and work in the suburbs, they also began to realize that while the suburbs might be cleaner, more spacious, and safer than the city, they were also more boring. The city, at this point, became that preserved exciting piece of the past whose purpose was to be used when one wanted that "urban experience."

In 1996, the next logical step along this road was taken as The Disney Corporation renovated the Amsterdam Theatre (1903), once home to the Ziegfeld Follies, for its own use in staging offerings such as *Beauty and the Beast* and *The Lion King*. Dick Clark's Rock 'n Roll New Year's Eve celebration of 1998 (his twenty-seventh), complete with its ever youthful and tanned host, was reportedly attended by half a million people and watched on television by an estimated 300 million. At that point, the only things missing were crying kids and the long lines for the rides.

—Christopher S. Wilson

FURTHER READING:

Dunlap, David W. *On Broadway: A Journey Uptown over Time*. New York, Rizzoli International, 1990.

Ellis, Edward Robb. *The Epic of New York City: A Narrative History*. New York, Kondansha International, 1966.

Jackson, Kenneth T. *Crabgrass Frontier: The Suburbanization of America*. New York, Oxford University Press, 1985.

Rencoret, Francisco Javier. *New York City: The Edge of Enigma*. Princeton Architectural Press, 1991.

Stern, Robert A. M., Gregory Gilmartin, and John Massengale. *New York 1900: Metropolitan Architecture and Urbanism 1890-1915*. New York, Rizzoli International, 1983.

Stern, Robert A. M., Gregory Gilmartin, and Thomas Mellins. *New York 1930: Architecture and Urbanism between the Two World Wars*. New York, Rizzoli International, 1987.

Stern, Robert A. M., Thomas Mellins, and David Fishman. *New York 1960: Architecture and Urbanism between the Second World War and the Bicentennial*. New York, The Monacelli Press, 1995.

Timex Watches

The introduction of the Timex watch in 1956 revolutionized the time-keeping industry. The relatively simple design, with fewer parts than other watches, made the Timex more durable, a feature which led to one of the world's most important advertising campaigns. Capitalizing on the country's growing fascination with television, Timex hired veteran newsman John Cameron Swayze to run an elaborate series of torture tests—live on Steve Allen's popular Sunday night program. Timex watches were smashed by jackhammers, sloshed through dishwashers, and strapped to world class divers taking flops off the cliffs of Acapulco. By 1956, sales of the watch that "takes a lickin' and keeps on tickin'" surpassed the five million mark. One of the more famous commercials occurred in 1958, when Swayze strapped a Timex to an outboard motor. When the watch slipped off the propeller and disappeared into the tub of water, Swayze had to promise to try again the following week. Timex decided to end the torture tests campaign in 1977 with a staged failure: an elephant stomped and crushed a watch. "It worked," Swayze quipped to the television audience, "in rehearsal."

—Geoff Edgers

FURTHER READING:

McDermott, Kathleen. *Timex: A Company and its Community, 1854-1998*. Timex Corporation, 1998.

Tiny Tim (1927?-1996)

"Tiny Tim" was the last and most successful of many stage names adopted by singer and ukulele player Herbert Khaury. Born in New York, Khaury was a struggling performer as Derry Dover, Larry Love, Julian Foxglove, and Sir Timothy Thames, before being given a small part in the counterculture movie *You Are What You Eat* in 1968. He became modestly well-known as Tiny Tim, the pseudonym he was currently employing, and received his first national exposure shortly afterwards on NBC's *Rowan and Martin's Laugh-In*. His odd garb, odder stage presence, and falsetto renditions of old songs quickly made Tiny Tim a celebrity. His signature song (and 1968 hit) was "Tip-Toe Thru' the Tulips with Me"; it was first recorded in 1929.

A frequent guest on *The Tonight Show*, Tiny Tim made history when he married "Miss Vicki" during the episode of December 18, 1969; the ceremony was witnessed by over 20 million viewers in America—a daughter, Tulip, was born in 1971, and the couple divorced six years later.

Both in falsetto and a quavery baritone, Tiny Tim recorded hundreds of popular songs from the nineteenth and twentieth centuries, and knew thousands more. He had probably performed a more varied repertoire of songs, in more venues, than any other singer of his generation. He died in Minneapolis, where he had moved with his third wife, "Miss Sue," on November 30, 1996.

—David Lonergan

FURTHER READING:

"Deaths: Tiny Tim." *Billboard*. Vol. 108, No. 50, December 14, 1996, 69.

Grimes, William. "Tiny Tim, Singer, Dies at 64; Flirted (Chastely) with Fame." *New York Times*. December 2, 1996, B12.

"Unconventional Pop Figure Tiny Tim Dies." *Washington Post*. December 2, 1996, B4.

The *Titanic*

In the realm of popular culture, the *Titanic* has turned out to be more than just a ship that sank; it has become an icon of an era long past, as well as a contemporary phenomenon. It seems that each generation since the sinking has rediscovered the shipwreck in new books, movies, and even music.

When the luxury ocean liner *Titanic* left Queenstown, Ireland, on April 11, 1912, the ship's fame was far different than it would become in just a few short days. The voyage of the *Titanic* was a tremendous news event all around the world. The *Titanic* was the largest and most luxurious liner of its time. The world was thrilled with the improvements the industrial age had brought to their lives and *Titanic* seemed to be the ultimate realization of their dreams; many began to speak of conquering Mother Nature. When *Titanic* was called "unsinkable," some saw the description as proof of man's supremacy, while others saw it as a direct challenge to God.

When the *Titanic* struck an iceberg on April 14, 1912 and sank two hours later, with over 1,500 souls losing their lives, the world also

The *Titanic*

lost much of its innocence and faith in man as a superior being. If this ship, so carefully planned and built to withstand anything, could sink on its maiden voyage, on what could society depend? Was the sinking a warning from God, as some religious leaders claimed? Was it meant to warn the public against the materialism of ''the Gilded Age,'' as some proposed? Would it reverse the progress the age of industry was bringing? As is often the case with tragedies, many used the event to argue an ideological perspective. Religious leaders, for example, used the example of Ida Strauss, who chose to remain with her husband on the ship, as an example to argue against divorce. Among some groups, women who survived were scolded for not following Mrs. Strauss' example and remaining with their husbands to perish. Both sides of the suffrage issue also used the *Titanic* tragedy to argue their case.

Ironically, the sinking of the *Titanic* also came to illuminate growing disparities in class around the world. In 1912, the world was marked by very distinct social classes, and it was a time when those with money were perceived as rarefied beings, somehow superior to others. Sailing on the *Titanic* were many who were of immense wealth, such as John Jacob Astor and Benjamin Guggenheim. While neither man survived, many other first class passengers did. When those numbers were compared to the number of steerage passengers rescued, an outcry was heard against the privileged. Why did they seemingly have more right to be rescued than the others? While the

industrial revolution continued, there was a backlash against progress and the wealthy. Change was in the air.

The tragedy also spawned increased efforts to launch rescue operations for those involved in water accidents. In the hope of averting a repeat of the event, the International Ice Patrol was founded by the nations of the North Atlantic. The official inquiries in America and Britain also produced changes in the laws regarding lifeboats and other safety issues. After its use on the *Titanic*, the Marconi wireless apparatus was popularized to send distress signals so that rescuers on land could receive messages regarding survivors.

In a media-saturated society, it is only appropriate that it would not take long before the *Titanic* tragedy became a popular commodity. Between 1912-1913, there were at least 100 songs about the *Titanic* published, including Leadbelly's recording of ''Down with the Old Canoe.'' The first motion picture, starring survivor Dorothy Gibson and titled *Saved from the Titanic*, appeared just one month after the disaster and was filmed on the Titanic's sister ship, the *Olympic*. Survivor Lawrence Beesley published his account, *The Loss of the S.S. Titanic*, six weeks after the tragedy. Additionally, articles appeared in *Scientific American* and other popular magazines of the time, and countless books were written surrounding the sinking. One such book, a 1898 novel by Morgan Robertson, was also rediscovered. *Futility* was the story of a ship so similar to the *Titanic* in every way, including its name, Titan, that many felt it had predicted the sinking of the *Titanic*.

After 1913, most of the interest in the *Titanic* died down rapidly. The great ship occasionally showed up again, mainly in motion pictures, including the British film *Atlantic* (1929) and the German film *Titanic* (1943). The German film, made during World War II, was a propaganda exercise with the only heroic person on the ship a fictional German crew member. In 1953, the United States finally produced their version of the story in true Hollywood style. Starring Barbara Stanwyck and Clifton Webb, *Titanic* was a melodrama with the shipwreck used largely as a background for the fictional story of an estranged couple who reconcile as the ship sinks.

By November 1955, the *Titanic* myth experienced its first resurgence. Walter Lord, a longtime student of *Titanic* lore, published his classic—*A Night to Remember*—retelling the story of *Titanic*'s short life. By January 1956, it had sold 60,000 copies, and has never been out of print since. Another book appeared two months after Lord's, but *Down to Eternity* by Richard O'Connor was received poorly.

Not to be left out of the ''picture,'' so to speak, in March 1956, a teleplay about the *Titanic*, directed by George Roy Hill and narrated by Claude Rains, was shown on network television. By May, an episode of the popular *You Are There* series dealt with the *Titanic*. In addition, motion pictures began appearing, including *Abandon Ship* (1957) and *A Night to Remember* (1958). The latter film, produced in documentary style, is regarded as the most faithful and accurate telling to that time. Now a permanent part of popular culture, the story of the woman who was the most famous survivor of the *Titanic*, Margaret Tobin Brown, was chronicled in *The Unsinkable Molly Brown*. The story was first reproduced as a musical on Broadway with Tammy Grimes (1960) as the title character, and then in a motion picture with Debbie Reynolds (1964). Both were huge successes and proved there was continued interest in the shipwreck.

The *Titanic* again slipped to semi-obscurity in the mid-1960s. It did, however, remain a popular subject for the occasional television show. In 1966, the premier episode of the television adventure show, *The Time Tunnel,* dealt with the disaster. A television miniseries, *S.O.S. Titanic,* starring David Janssen as John Jacob Astor, was also produced in 1979. The ship also played an important role in fictional books such as Clive Cussler's *Raise the Titanic* (1976) and *The Memory of Eva Ryker* (1978), written by Norman Hall.

On September 11, 1985, Dr. Robert Ballard of the Woods Hole Oceanographic Institute and Jean-Louis Michel of the French IFREMER Institute returned the *Titanic* to the front pages when they located the wreck of the ship. It had long been a Holy Grail of sorts to those fascinated by it, and previous expeditions had tried unsuccessfully to locate the wreckage. Dr. Ballard became an instant celebrity and a vocal critic of those who wanted to salvage items from the ship. There were even those who wanted to try to raise the *Titanic.* Articles in *National Geographic* and other magazines appeared, along with more books on the subject, including reprints of Walter Lord's book. Documentaries such as *Secrets of the Titanic* (1986) soon began to appear, and it seemed that the event was taking on a mystical quality. There was even a video game, *Search for the Titanic,* appearing in 1989, that allowed players to finance and plan an expedition to locate the wreckage.

Interest remained high over the next few years as periodic new books and television specials kept the *Titanic* visible to the public. Much debate went on about whether or not to salvage any of the ship. Those who argued to salvage the ship were concerned that time was of the essence, and felt that artifacts would soon be all that was left of the event. Those against salvaging it, championed by Ballard, felt the wreck was a memorial and should be left alone. Eventually, the pro-salvage group won, and artifacts from the ship were eventually brought to the surface.

On April 23, 1997, a new interpretation of the disaster appeared when *Titanic: A New Musical*—a big budget theater production—debuted on Broadway. In a theater season with few successes and even fewer legitimate hits, this musical was the smash of the season; it won 5 Tony awards, including one for Best Musical.

Nothing, however, could prepare the world for the coming of the James Cameron film, *Titanic,* in 1997. Amid rumor and innuendo regarding "the most expensive film ever made," the public waited for its release and a chance to it judge for themselves. When the release date was delayed and the film went over budget, many predicted another disaster, this one of a business nature. Would it be a hit or the most expensive miss in motion picture history? It became obvious after the film's initial release that Cameron did not need to worry. *Titanic* became the largest grossing movie ever and tied previous Academy Award winner *Ben Hur* (1959) for most trophies won, with 11. The soundtrack from the movie became the best selling movie soundtrack in history; the love theme from the movie, "My Heart Will Go On" performed by Celine Dion, quickly became a number one song. And the stars of the motion picture, Leonardo DiCaprio and Kate Winslet, both relatively unknown before the film, became superstars.

The public could not get enough of the film or the ship. Using life-size models and computer generated images, the film was generally considered the most historically accurate, although some historians disagreed with liberties taken with some of the characters in the film. The Edwardian hairstyles and wardrobe depicted sparked a fashion craze, and the blue diamond necklace that was a centerpiece of the plot became a bestselling piece of costume jewelry.

In the late twentieth century, the *Titanic* continues to fascinate the public. There are faithful *Titanic* buffs who have read about and pondered the fate of the vessel for many years. Many of them are members of the Titanic Historical Society, whose headquarters are in a jewelry store in Indian Orchard, Massachusetts. Membership increases every time the *Titanic* returns to the front page of the news, but it took a blockbuster film to make the *Titanic* a true cultural phenomenon among the general public. The *Titanic* remains a commodity to be bought and sold. The sinking of the *Titanic* is a historic tragedy which will forever be a part of history and of poplar culture.

—Jill A. Gregg

FURTHER READING:

Ballard, Robert D., and Rick Archbold. *The Discovery of the Titanic.* New York, Warner Books, 1988.

Biel, Steven. *Down with the Old Canoe: A Cultural History of the Titanic Disaster.* New York, W. W. Norton, 1996.

Lord, Walter. *A Night to Remember.* New York, Holt, Rinehart, and Winston, 1955.

Lynch, Don. *Titanic: An Illustrated History.* New York, Hyperion, 1992.

Spignesi, Stephen J. *The Complete Titanic: From the Ships Blueprints to the Epic Film.* New Jersey, Carol Publishing Group, 1998.

Wade, Wyn Craig. *The Titanic: End of a Dream.* New York, Viking Penguin, 1986.

To Kill a Mockingbird

Harper Lee's novel *To Kill a Mockingbird* gives an accurate reflection of race relations in the Southern United States during the 1930s. The novel, set around a single-father family in small-town Alabama, contains a vast array of symbolism to intertwine the main plot with several subplots. Through her novel, Lee debunked the quaint antebellum Southern society for the realism of Southern culture. The timing of this publication, which denounced prejudicial attitudes, coordinated with the early Civil Rights Movement in the United States. This best selling novel became a classic and required reading for many American high school students.

Author Harper Lee was born in Monroeville, Alabama, in 1926. She spent four years at the University of Alabama and one year at Oxford University in England. She also attended law school, leaving six months short of finishing her coursework to pursue a writing career in New York City. There she helped author Truman Capote research *In Cold Blood.* To earn money she took a job as an airline reservation clerk. In 1960, Lee published *To Kill a Mockingbird,* and in 1961 the novel won the Pulitzer Prize. By 1962, an Academy Award-winning motion picture was produced from the novel, and, in the same year, Lee won the Paperback of the Year award given by *Bestsellers* magazine to the best selling paperback of the year.

Harper Lee, a direct descendant of General Robert E. Lee, recommended to potential authors, "Write what you know and do so thoughtfully." She emphatically denied the her prize-winning work

Gregory Peck (standing) in a scene from the film *To Kill a Mockingbird*.

was autobiographical. The similarities it contains to her own life are striking, however. Her father, Amasa Coleman Lee, for instance, was a lawyer.

The novel's symbolism and clarity made it a literary classic. It is narrated in the voice of a white six-year-old tomboy named Jean Louise "Scout" Finch. She lives with her ten-year-old brother, Jem, and her father, Atticus Finch, in the small town of Maycomb, Alabama. The story centers on the alleged rape of the white Mayella Ewell, daughter of the wicked Bob Ewell, by the black Tom Robinson. Atticus serves as Robinson's attorney. The all-white jury finds Robinson guilty even after Atticus proves reasonable doubt of Robinson's guilt.

The novel portrays common, real-life stereotypical racist events of the time. Atticus faces taunts of "nigger lover" and "lawing for niggers." There also is the attempted lynching of Mr. Robinson. The perceived threat of blacks to white women and the salvation embodied in white males are mocked.

Throughout the novel, Lee pursues various themes like ignorance versus knowledge, cowardice versus heroism, and children versus adults. Courage versus cowardice is portrayed in Atticus's demeanor in a confrontation with Bob Ewell over Atticus's open disbelief of Mayella's accusation. The dispute also represents an old stereotype of race cohesion that Ewell believes Atticus is breaking. Lee draws parallels of ignorance in her handling of characters Boo Radley and Tom Robinson; they are both presumed guilty with no one having taken the time to get to know them. Radley is the Finch's neighbor who has an evil reputation, especially among the children, who fear him without ever having met him. Radley turns out to be a hero when he saves Scout and Jem from murder at the hands of Bob Ewell. Tom Robinson dies while trying to escape prison, representing how the racist South has endured and egalitarian measures have floundered.

Explicitly symbolic is Jem's attempt to make a snowman during a rare Alabama snowfall. As he makes the snow into a ball he roles it to accrue more snow. While rolling the snowball it picks up dirt giving the snowman a dirty surface. The snowman signifies the superficiality of skin color.

To Kill a Mockingbird underscores many themes and represents a universal story from a regional perspective. The overall argument involves the obvious plea for justice while mocking the mores of Southern society. It is Lee's only major published work. Though she faded back into the obscurity of Monroeville, Alabama, her mark in literary persuasion endures.

—Scott Stabler

FURTHER READING:

Johnson, Claudia D. *To Kill a Mockingbird: Threatening Boundaries.* New York, Twayne Publishers, 1994.

Lee, Harper. *To Kill a Mockingbird.* Philadelphia, Lippincott, 1960.

To Tell the Truth

To Tell the Truth was one of the most durable and popular panel quiz shows ever to appear on television, having a run of more than twenty years in both network and syndicated form. Along with *What's My Line?* and *I've Got a Secret, To Tell the Truth* was one of three similar shows introduced by Mark Goodson-Bill Todman Productions in the 1950s. These shows were designed to appeal to a relatively upscale television audience and to counter the effects of widely publicized quiz show payola scams. In the original version of *To Tell the Truth,* which ran from 1956 to 1968 on CBS, Bud Collyer was host (he also hosted *Beat the Clock*), moderating a group of celebrity panelists that included Orson Bean, Polly Bergen, Kitty Carlisle, Peggy Cass, and Tom Poston. The show ran on prime time from 1956 to 1967 and in the daytime from 1962 to 1968.

The panelists' goal was to determine which one of three players was telling the truth about an unusual event or circumstance in which they were involved. All three claimed by affidavit to be the authentic truth-teller, and each panelist was given an opportunity to question the contestants individually for a designated amount of time. After the panelists completed their questioning, the host asked, ''Will the real John Doe please stand up?'' The contestants were then awarded money based on their success in fooling the panel. Because the genuine contestant was not identified until the end of the question sessions, those in the home and studio audience were able to play along. After the ''real John Doe'' introduced himself or herself, the impostors identified themselves to the panelists. The information disclosed in these introductions was almost as entertaining as the game itself, as the impostors were often struggling actors or individuals employed in careers that could not have been more dissimilar from that of the ''real'' truth-teller.

To Tell the Truth had a second run in syndication from 1969 to 1978 with hosts Garry Moore (1969-1977) and Joe Garagiola (1977-1978). Orson Bean, Peggy Cass, and Kitty Carlisle returned as panelists and were joined by Bill Cullen. Another short-lived version ran in syndication from 1980 to 1981 with host Robin Ward and regular panelists Peggy Cass and Soupy Sales. The longevity of this show and others like it probably had much to do with its extremely low production costs. The consistent appearance of familiar panelists also added to the show's popularity, as the personal style of each of the celebrities was part of the entertainment. Kitty Carlisle could be expected to make her appearance in floor-length gown and feather boa, Peggy Cass would look erudite but down-to-earth in her horn-rimmed glasses, and Orson Bean could be counted on to ask questions that revealed a font of obscure knowledge. After the demise of the show, these personalities would continue to be remembered by the public primarily in their roles as panelists on *To Tell the Truth,* although each went on to other unrelated ventures: Peggy Cass, for example, joined the company of the popular musical *Nunsense,* and Kitty Carlisle Hart established herself as a prime mover in the arts world through her role as head of the New York State Council on the Arts.

—Sue Russell

To Tell The Truth Master of Ceremonies, Bud Collyer (rear) presides over a panel including (from left): Polly Bergen, Ralph Bellamy, Kitty Carlisle, and Hy Gardner.

FURTHER READING:

Brooks, Tim, and Earle Marsh. *The Complete Directory to Prime Time Network TV Shows, 1946-Present.* New York, Ballantine, 1979.

DeLong, Thomas A. *Quiz Craze: America's Infatuation with Game Shows.* New York, Praeger, 1991.

Harris, Jay S., editor. *TV Guide: The First 25 Years.* New York, Simon and Schuster, 1978.

Schwartz, David, Steve Ryan, and Fred Wostbrock. *The Encyclopedia of TV Game Shows.* New York, Zoetrope, 1987.

Today

The longest-running early-morning network television program, the *Today* show premiered on NBC on January 14, 1952, just months after the first live coast-to-coast television broadcast in the United States. Aired live from New York at 7 a.m. Mondays through Fridays, the two-hour show—the prototype of the news-magazine format—added a live Saturday program in the 1990s. By the late 1990s, nearly half a century after its origin, the *Today* show was still relying on its original format: a combination of news, interviews with leading newsmakers, features on topics such as health, personal finance, and food, and entertainment segments.

Sylvester "Pat" Weaver, who developed *Your Show of Shows* and the *Tonight* show, created the *Today* show as a type of broadcast news magazine that could be watched in segments while viewers ate breakfast or prepared to go to work or school. It premiered when television sets were a rarity and early-morning broadcasting was unknown. In 1952, daytime television was still a rarity in many parts of the United States.

After a considerable search, the man Weaver chose to host the show was Dave Garroway, a relaxed, witty conversationalist who wore professorial horn-rimmed spectacles. His early experience as a radio newscaster, plus his wide audience gained on the variety show *Garroway at Large* over WMAQ-TV in Chicago, convinced Weaver he was the performer needed to attract and hold a nationwide audience that was just out of bed. Jack Lescoulie was picked to report sports as well as the amusing stories from the day's news, and Jim Fleming read a news summary every half hour. *Today* opened in its own studio in the RCA Exhibition Hall on West 49th Street in Manhattan, outfitted with a large plate-glass window that allowed passers-by to see the show and be seen on camera. President Harry Truman, known for his morning walks, happened to lead his entourage by the *Today* window one morning when he was in New York and was stopped for a brief interview. During the show's first year, television critics complained of the show's slow pace and obsession with technological gadgets.

The show began making money in its second year, attracting larger audiences and luring thousands of children and their parents by adding J. Fred Muggs to the cast. Muggs was a strong-minded ten-month-old chimpanzee, owned by trainers Buddy Menella and Roy Waldron, and his unpredictable antics sometimes intimidated the staff but delighted the audience. Within the year J. Fred was making

personal appearance tours and meeting his adoring fans. He became more difficult to handle each year, and after five years gave way to a new chimp named Mr. Kokomo. The press release announcing his retirement said that Muggs was leaving to "extend his personal horizons."

In 1953 Frank Blair became the show's newscaster and remained on *Today* for 23 years, longer than anyone else connected with the show. That same year the show began to feature shapely young women as "*Today* girls," who read the temperature and a one-word description of the weather in major U.S. cities. The first of these was actress Estelle Parsons, followed by Lee Ann Meriwether (Miss America of 1955), singer Helen O'Connell, and actresses Betsy Palmer, Florence Henderson, and Maureen O'Sullivan. The only one of them to gain long-running status on the show was Barbara Walters, whose role was gradually expanded to that of co-anchor. Walters, who had appeared on the rival CBS *The Morning Show* was originally hired by *Today* as a writer. Pressed into on-camera service during the events surrounding the assassination of President John F. Kennedy, she became a regular in 1963.

In July of 1961 Dave Garroway closed the show for the last time, giving his audience a smile, a raised open palm, and his trademark "peace" signoff. He was replaced by John Chancellor, a veteran newscaster who was never comfortable in the show's format and left after 14 months. Hugh Downs replaced Chancellor in October, 1962, becoming the only television personality to have a regular position on all three of Pat Weaver's program creations, *Today, Tonight,* and *Home.* Downs had been Jack Paar's announcer and sidekick during the entire run of the Paar show from 1957-62. He continued to appear regularly on *ABC's 20/20,* co-anchoring the show with Barbara Walters, in the late 1990s.

Frank McGee replaced Downs in October, 1971, and Walters's growing stature on the show strained their relationship. Jim Hartz, hired with Walters's approval, replaced McGee—who died of bone cancer in 1974—and after a short stay was himself replaced by Tom Brokaw. When Walters left the show for a lucrative ABC contract in 1976, an extensive search was begun to replace her, and six candidates were tested on air: Cassie Mackin, Betty Rollin, Linda Ellerbee, Kelly Lange, Betty Furness, and Jane Pauley. Pauley, born in 1950, was only two years older than the show itself, but she won over all the contenders, and the new team of Brokaw, Pauley, and Willard Scott was able, in 1977, to bolster the show's declining ratings and maintain the show's number-one rank among morning shows. Bryant Gumbel joined the show as a sportscaster in 1980 and became a co-host in 1982. By that time, *Today* no longer was the dominant force in the early morning. ABC's *Good Morning America,* which had previously beaten *Today* in the ratings for a few weeks in 1979, now won the ratings race consistently in 1982 and 1983, and in one week in 1983, the *CBS Morning News* nudged *Today* into third place.

During the 1980s the Gumbel-Pauley-Scott team increased the show's ratings and won the race against *Good Morning America* frequently until 1989, when a well-publicized incident sent the series into another decline. In February, 1989, an intra-office memo in which Gumbel was harshly critical of Scott and Gene Shalit was leaked to the press, causing fans to express their loyalty by changing channels. The second move that proved unpopular with the viewers was the reduced role played by Jane Pauley when Deborah Norville was added to the show as newscaster. Pauley announced her departure on December 28, 1989, but continued on other NBC shows, filling in for Tom Brokaw on the *NBC Nightly News* and hosting her own prime-time series, *Real Life with Jane Pauley.*

Bryant Gumbel interviewing Richard Nixon on the *Today* show, 1990.

Today's ratings plunged 15 percent in the spring of 1990, and *Good Morning America* was atop the charts again, but in April, 1991, the popular Katie Couric was named co-host with Bryant Gumbel, and *Today* soon became dominant again. She had joined the show in June, 1990, as its first national correspondent and had served as substitute anchor since February, 1991. A native of Washington, D.C., and an honor graduate of the University of Virginia, Couric showed an intelligent, probing, but polite and friendly style in memorable segments of the show, including Hillary Rodham Clinton's first television interview as First Lady, General Colin Powell's

farewell to his position on the joints chiefs of staff, Anita Hill's first interview after the crisis with Clarence Thomas, and General Norman Schwarzkopf's first interview after the Persian Gulf War. She has also co-hosted, with Dick Enberg, NBC's morning coverage of the Summer Olympics in Barcelona (1992) and Atlanta (1996).

Matt Lauer, a native of New York City, replaced Bryant Gumbel as co-anchor of *Today* in January, 1997, and the show has continued to gain viewers. A graduate of Ohio University with a degree in communications, Lauer worked as co-anchor of *Today in New York* for the city's NBC affiliate before joining the network *Today* show's news desk in 1994. His frequent filling in for golfing buddy Gumbel led to an outpouring of cards and letters from fans throughout the nation, and Lauer was promoted to co-anchor. Another factor in the show's continued high ratings was the moving of the show into a glass-walled, ground-floor production center in June, 1994. Just as in the early days of the show, the crowd outside the window has become a vital part of the *Today* show, and the stars frequently conduct on-the-spot interviews with visitors. In January, 1999, *Today* had national ratings nearly twice those of the next highest competitor.

The *Today* show remains a window on the world for its viewers, with live shows originating from the Orient Express streaking across Europe, as well as from China, the Soviet Union, the French Riviera, Italy, the United Kingdom and Ireland, Australia, South America, and Cuba. Other familiar faces on the 1999 *Today* show include Ann Curry, news anchor; Al Roker, weather; Gene Shalit, film critic; and Willard Scott, known for his comic remarks and his daily list of America's latest centenarians.

—Benjamin Griffith

FURTHER READING:

Castleman, Harry, and Walter J. Podrazik. *Watching TV: Four Decades of Watching Television.* New York, McGraw-Hill, 1982.

Kessler, Judy. *Inside Today: The Battle for the Morning.* New York, Villard, 1992.

McNeil, Alex. *Total Television: A Comprehensive Guide to Programming from 1948 to the Present.* New York, Penguin Books, 1991.

Toffler, Alvin (1928—)

Alvin Toffler, the most popular futurist in America, became a celebrity in the 1960s and 1970s for his predictions and suggestions for ways people could cope with the unprecedented rate of change initiated by new technologies. With the publication of his bestseller *Future Shock* in 1970, Toffler became a household name and won many admirers in government and business. *The Third Wave* (1980) made him internationally known, and with *Powershift: Knowledge, Wealth, and Violence at the Edge of the Twenty-First Century* (1991) and *Creating a New Civilization: The Politics of the Third Wave* (1994), Toffler became a prominent political advisor. Since 1993, Toffler's wife, Heidi, has begun to share authorial credit with him, although he claims that she co-authored all of his previous books as well. Together they are known as the couple "who brought futurism to the masses," as Michael Krantz has written in *Time* magazine.

In *Future Shock,* Toffler argued that Americans were experiencing confusion and denial about the changes they were witnessing in society. He called this "future shock," a concept he derived from the anthropological concept of "culture shock," which means the inability of members of primitive cultures to adapt to a more advanced culture. Very similarly, Toffler argued, Americans were growing unable to cope with the new culture that was coming into being as technology changed the way people worked and lived. Witnessing the social upheaval of the 1960s, Toffler believed that the mass hysteria of the protests and growing divorce and crime rates were signs that

Americans were reaching a limit beyond which they could accept no more change. As remedies to future shock, Toffler argued that children should read more science fiction and that the study of the future should become a standard part of American education.

The main problem, according to Toffler, was that America was undergoing a fundamental shift from a Second Wave to a Third Wave society. The First Wave was the adoption of the agrarian way of life 10,000 years ago, the Second Wave was the urbanization and industrial revolution of the nineteenth century, and the Third Wave that began after the Second World War he called a "super-industrial revolution." This last phase of human development was fueled by the rise of technologies that were driven by knowledge rather than raw material power. In 1980 he predicted in *The Third Wave* that the personal computer would become a household item, three years before IBM (International Business Machines) introduced computers for home use. Toffler also believed that an information superhighway would become an important part of our everyday lives and that changes in our economy would effect a fundamental restructuring of our society; a "demassification" that would turn back some of the effects of centralization and standardization of the industrial era. Workers would return to the home, establishing living patterns similar in some ways to the First Wave of human development. The difference, however, is that people would be linked by new technologies that enabled them to communicate with others all over the world. And instead of having to purchase identical, mass-produced products, consumers would be presented with a growing number of choices as smaller industries became more feasible. Finally, in what became the focus of his last two books, the federal government would become less centralized as power shifted to smaller interest groups and local governments.

Toffler looked forward to the changes that would take place, arguing optimistically that a more direct democracy, more varieties of family structure and home life, greater utilization of renewable energy resources, a decentralized government, and a more accessible media would result from the Third Wave, effectively eliminating social hierarchies. He attempted to ease the fears of Americans about the rapid rate of change. In *The Third Wave* he argued that "we are the final generation of an old civilization and the first generation of a new one . . . much of our personal confusion, anguish, and disorientation can be traced directly to the conflict within us, and within our political institutions, between the dying Second Wave civilization and the emergent Third Wave civilization that is thundering to take its place." His optimism about the positive effects this shift would have on the quality of life and his urgent message that we must prepare for these changes rather than impede their progress drew many disciples, most notably Ronald Reagan and Newt Gingrich. Ted Turner even claimed to have gotten the idea for *CNN (Cable News Network)* from *The Third Wave.*

Alvin and Heidi Tofflers' main goal has been to prepare people for the changes ahead and to make them more comfortable with the concept of change. They want Americans to abandon their nostalgia for small-town life, the nuclear family, and employment stability of the past, and to embrace a future in which knowledge and flexibility will be the greatest assets. As Alvin Toffler told Charles Platt in *Dream Makers,* he wants to "open up the reader's mind to other ways of conceptualizing our political and social structures. I think that helps people adapt."

—Anne Boyd

FURTHER READING:

Judis, John B. "Newt's Not-So-Weird Gurus: In Defense of the Tofflers." *The New Republic*. October 9, 1995, 16-23.

Krantz, Michael. "Cashing in on Tomorrow: A Generation After the Tofflers' *'Future Shock,'* Professional Prognosticators See Nothing But Blue Skies." *Time*. July 15, 1996, 52-54.

Platt, Charles. *Dream Makers: The Uncommon Men and Women Who Write Science Fiction,* Vol. 2. Berkeley, Berkeley Publishing, 1983.

Toffler, Alvin. *Future Shock*. New York, Random House, 1970.

———. *The Third Wave*. New York, Morrow, 1980.

Toga Parties

At the turn of the twentieth century, when the poet Ezra Pound advised writers to "make it new," he was referring to the need for a new vision that would propel artists through a new century. But as artists, intellectuals, writers, and other makers of culture turned to their crafts in order to create a new world, they found themselves looking to the past as much as they looked to the future. They looked not to the recent past, from which they wanted to free themselves, but to the ancient past of Greece and Rome. Homage to the Classical world sometimes manifested itself in the form of the toga party, which took place throughout the century and became particularly popular during the 1970s. Revising Classical culture to modern sensibilities, toga parties represented not only youthful exuberance, but an underlying desire to maintain a link to the past. (The name derives from the "toga," a simple cloth wrap worn loosely around the body in imitation of the national garment of the early Romans). Such parties played out the legendary excess of the Roman god, Bacchus, the god of wine, and his Greek precursor, Dionysus.

It is not hard to see why the figure of Dionysus had such appeal to those in the twentieth century, when more open attitudes toward sexuality began to take hold. At the beginning of the century, "modern women" announced their modernity by cropping their hair short and wearing Greek bangs, and during the 1920s, Classical style tunics became popular. One motto of the 1930s—"wine, women, and song"—was a direct call from the ancient rite of the Bacchanal, or Dionysian rites of spring. The call of the ancient Greeks and Romans was even heard at the Roosevelt White House in the early 1930s, when Eleanor Roosevelt hosted a great toga party in an attempt to poke fun at the politicians and newswriters who viewed F.D.R. as a second Caesar.

The toga was revived when the 1978 film *Animal House* featured a fraternity house toga party, prompting a new fad on college campuses. Across the United States, students wrapped themselves in bedsheets draped like togas in an attempt to imitate Greek and Roman figures and the Bacchanal. At times, John Belushi and other actors from *Animal House* would show up at such parties. Perhaps the most widely publicized, if not the largest, toga party was held at the University of Wisconsin, where 10,000 persons attended, all wearing sheets draped like togas, many of them sporting garlands of flowers in their hair. Much as rock concerts of the 1960s defined the 1960s generation, toga parties became an identifying rite of passage for the generation of the 1970s. During the 1990s, toga parties were still known to take place, although largely as a nostalgic gesture.

—Lolly Ockerstrom

FURTHER READING:

Hope, Thomas. *Costumes of the Greeks and Romans*. New York: Dover, 1962.

Marum, Andrew, and Frank Parise. *Follies and Foibles: A View of 20th Century Fads*. New York, Facts on File, Inc., 1984.

Tokyo Rose

During the fight with Japan in World War II, Allied (mostly American) fighting men in the Pacific were assailed with Japanese radio propaganda broadcast from radio stations throughout the Japanese empire. Many of the broadcasters were women, and they began to be known by the term "Tokyo Rose." The American Office of War Information (OWI), based on a study of the Japanese propaganda broadcasts, concluded that none of these women referred to herself as Tokyo Rose; the OWI considered the name "Tokyo Rose" to be "strictly a GI invention."

The various "Tokyo Rose" broadcasters spread different types of propaganda. Some of the woman broadcasters taunted the Allied soldiers by implying that their wives and sweethearts back home were being unfaithful to them. Although the United States Foreign Broadcast Information Service (FBIS) did not pick up any Japanese broadcasts which predicted specific military movements, some soldiers later claimed that "Tokyo Rose" announcers would identify Allied units, predict Japanese bombing raids, warn soldiers who were about to go into battle that they would be cut to pieces, and make otherwise demoralizing remarks.

Some of the Japanese broadcasts were less blatant than this. There was one Tokyo-based program, known as *Zero Hour,* which consisted of musical numbers, readings of letters from Allied POWs, and some news. A woman DJed the musical portions of the program; the woman interspersed the music with brief, and generally innocuous, commentary. The woman DJ on "Zero Hour" was an American named Iva Toguri (later d'Aquino). Though she never referred to herself as "Tokyo Rose" in her broadcasts—her moniker was "Orphan Ann"—she ended up being assigned the role of Tokyo Rose.

Iva Toguri was born in the United States to Japanese parents. In 1941 she was in graduate school, studying to be a doctor, but she left the country for Japan to take care of a sick aunt. Although she was a native of the United States, she had problems getting a passport and had to travel without one. After Pearl Harbor, the war stranded her in Japan. While seeking work to support herself in Japan, Toguri got a part-time clerical job at NHK, the government radio service. She was noticed by Charles Cousens, a POW who had served with the Australian army and who had been ordered by his Japanese captors to make radio propaganda aimed at the Allies. Cousens—who was later cleared of treason charges by Australian authorities—claimed that he was trying to sabotage the "Zero Hour" program by making it useless as propaganda. As part of that plan, Cousens claimed, he hired Iva Toguri because she was anti-Japanese and had a bad radio voice.

While she was working for Japanese radio, Toguri helped out many Allied POWs who were interned in the Tokyo area, giving them food and expressing pro-American sentiments. At the end of the war in 1945, the newly-married Iva Toguri d'Aquino did not seem to regard herself as a traitor, and she was willing to talk to the American press about her activities.

Tokyo Rose

Following the war, two Hearst reporters looking for the famous "Tokyo Rose" were led to d'Aquino, who signed a contract with one of the reporters giving various Hearst enterprises the exclusive rights to her story. In return, d'Aquino was promised $2,000 (which for various reasons she never got). In the contract, d'Aquino identified herself as "the one and original 'Tokyo Rose'" and gave numerous autographs identifying herself as "Tokyo Rose." D'Aquino was stretching the truth, and it soon lead her into serious trouble.

American authorities held d'Aquino in a Japanese prison for nearly a year while investigators tried to determine whether her broadcasts on behalf of Japan amounted to treason. Released in 1946 for lack of evidence, she faced a renewed campaign to block her return to the United States in 1947. The American Legion and broadcaster Walter Winchell did not want the traitress Tokyo Rose to be a free woman in the United States, and they campaigned for a reopening of the case. In 1948, Attorney General Tom Clark directed that d'Aquino be tried for treason.

D'Aquino was brought from Japan to San Francisco, where she was tried in 1949. Of the eight charges against her, the jury found her guilty of only one charge. According to the jury, she claimed in one broadcast that the Japanese had won the battle of Leyte Gulf (which they had not) and she allegedly taunted Allied soldiers about this imagined defeat. D'Aquino received a ten-year sentence and, as a convicted traitor, she was stripped of her American citizenship. After spending eight years in prison, d'Aquino was released in 1956. The United States commenced deportation proceedings, but dropped them in 1958. D'Aquino went to work in her family's store in Chicago, which she was still running in 1998.

Beginning around 1974, the Japanese American Citizens League (JACL) took an interest in d'Aquino's case. The JACL believed that d'Aquino had been a loyal American who had done what she could to assist American POWs, who had taken a job as a disc jockey and made innocuous broadcasts, and who had been targeted by unscrupulous journalists and prosecutors who were trying to transform her into the mythical "Tokyo Rose." Media reports sympathetic to d'Aquino appeared in 1976. The jury foreman at her trial told *60 Minutes* that he thought d'Aquino was innocent of all charges. Articles in the Chicago *Tribune* indicated that two of the witnesses against her had lied. (Later, documents acquired through the Freedom of Information Act indicated that the two witnesses had made statements to the FBI in identical language, raising the inference that they had been coached.)

The JACL received support from other important quarters. The California legislature, several municipal governing bodies, conductor Seiji Ozawa, and the American Veterans Committee all endorsed a pardon. Influential Japanese-American politicians joined the campaign, particularly S. I. Hayakawa, who was soon to become a republican senator from California and who had access to President Gerald Ford. In January 1977, just before his term of office came to an end, President Ford pardoned d'Aquino. The pardon restored d'Aquino's civil rights, including her American citizenship.

—Eric Longley

FURTHER READING:

Chapman, Ivan. *Tokyo Calling: The Charles Cousens Case.* Sydney, Hale, 1990.

Duus, Masayo, translated from the Japanese by Peter Duus. *Tokyo Rose: Orphan of the Pacific.* New York, Kodansha International, 1979.

Harper, Dale P. "Personality: American-born, UCLA-educated Tokyo Rose Was Convicted of Treason Against the United States." *World War II.* September 1994, 8, 67-69.

Howe, Russell Warren. *The Hunt For "Tokyo Rose."* New York, Madison Books, 1990.

Uyeda, Clifford I. "The Pardoning of 'Tokyo Rose': A Report on the Restoration of American Citizenship to Iva Ikuko Toguri." *Amerasia.* Vol. 5, 1978, 69-93.

Tolkien, J. R. R. (1892-1973)

Born in South Africa in 1892 to English parents and resident of the United Kingdom from 1895 until his death in 1973, J. R. R. Tolkien is the most prominent fantasy writer of the twentieth century. He is beloved for his epic fantasy trilogy, *The Lord of the Rings* (1954-1955), and its prequel, *The Hobbit* (1937). Although exactitude is impossible, Patrick Curry estimates worldwide sales of *The Lord of the Rings* at approximately 50 million copies—"probably the biggest-selling single work of fiction this century." *The Hobbit* has sold an estimated 35 to 40 million copies, and Tolkien's books have been translated into more than 30 languages. A 1997 survey of some 25,000 readers in England found *The Lord of the Rings* to be the runaway winner as the most important book of the past 100 years.

Tolkien was also a prominent philologist. His academic career encompassed 39 years, dating from his appointment in 1920 as Reader in English Language at Leeds University. He became the Rawlinson and Bosworth Professor of Anglo-Saxon at Oxford University in 1925, and held the prestigious Merton Professor of English position at Oxford from 1945 until his retirement in 1959. His essay, "*Beowulf*: The Monsters and the Critics" (1936), is regarded as a landmark scholarly work, as is his examination of regional dialect in the *Canterbury Tales,* "Chaucer as a Philologist" (1949). His critical edition of *Sir Gawain and the Green Knight* (1925), developed in collaboration with E. V. Gordon, is still taught today.

"There were not two Tolkiens, one an academic and the other a writer," asserts T. A. Shippey, "They were the same man, and the two sides of him overlapped so that they were indistinguishable—or rather they were not two sides at all, but different expressions of the same mind, the same imagination." Tolkien's academic research delved deeply into ancient Northern literatures, and led him to learn such languages as Finnish, Gothic, Middle English, Old English, Old Norse, and Welsh. This research in turn shaped his fiction. In the United States foreword to the Ballantine edition of *The Lord of the Rings* (1966), Tolkien avers that his trilogy is "primarily linguistic in inspiration."

The blurring of Tolkien as an academic and a fantasy writer is no more apparent than in his essay "On Fairy-Stories," first presented as the 1938 Andrew Lang Lecture at the University of St. Andrews and later expanded for the collection, *Tree and Leaf,* in 1964. Here, Tolkien demarcates a territory for fantasy that is distinct from stories that are framed—that is, normalized—as travellers' tales, dreams, or beast fables. Fantasy entails an act of sub-creation, namely, a "Secondary World" that is separate from the "Primary World" of everyday life. Secondary worlds must be internally consistent, thereby structuring a sense of "credible, commanding Secondary Belief." Central to fantasy are the elements of Recovery, Escape, and Consolation. Tolkien coined the term "Eucatastrophe," which denotes the "sudden joyous 'turn'" that is the hallmark of fairy-tale happy endings.

J. R. R. Tolkien

Tolkien applied the precepts of ''On Fairy-Stories'' to the secondary world that occupied much of his life: Middle-earth. The genesis of Middle-earth was a poem written by Tolkien during his student days, based on a line from the Old English Advent poem ''Crist,'' by Cynewulf. ''Hail, Earendel, brightest of angels, over middle-earth sent to men,'' sparked the imagination of Tolkien and established the basis for a cosmology that began to emerge during World War I. As a lieutenant with the Lancashire Fusiliers, Tolkien was posted to France and fought in the battle of the Somme. He later explained in a letter to his son, Christopher, that many of the early

writings about Middle-earth were composed ''in grimy canteens, at lectures in cold fogs, in huts full of blasphemy and smut, or by candle lights in bell-tents, even some down in dugouts under shell fire.'' These writings bore the title *The Book of Lost Tales.*

Tolkien returned to Oxford after a bout with trench fever and found sustenance in the English countryside. He was seized with the desire to create a mythology for England. Humphrey Carpenter quotes Tolkien on this point in his definitive biography, where the Oxford professor recollects how he ''had a mind to make a body of more or less connected legend, ranging from the large and cosmogonic to the level of romantic fairy-story—the larger founded on the lesser in contact with the earth, the lesser drawing splendor from the vast backcloths—which I could dedicate simply: to England; to my country.''

A small literary circle of Christian academics—The Inklings—acted as midwife for Tolkien's mythology. At Oxford, Tolkien regularly met with Owen Barfield, Charles Williams, and C. S. Lewis, whose *Chronicles of Narnia* would later adorn the lists of fantasy literature. The Inklings read aloud passages of their work, including a ''children's'' novel that Tolkien had been writing since one fateful day in the late 1920s, when he scribbled on the page of a blank exam book, ''In a hole in the ground there lived a hobbit.''

The Hobbit was published in 1937 to popular and critical acclaim. Set in Middle-earth, it narrates the adventures of Bilbo Baggins, a staid halfling who embarks on a quest with the wizard Gandalf and a party of dwarves to reclaim treasure stolen by the dragon, Smaug. Along the way, Bilbo finagles a magic ring away from a twisted hobbit named Gollum. ''Prediction is dangerous,'' ventured the *Times Literary Supplement,* ''but *The Hobbit* may well prove a classic.''

Bilbo's inheritance is at the heart of *The Lord of the Rings,* which approached completion in 1950. Frodo Baggins undertakes a perilous journey to Mount Doom in the land of Mordor, ruled by the dark lord, Sauron. There he must cast away Bilbo's ring, revealed by Gandalf to be the One Ring of Power lost by Sauron in the distant past. Humans, dwarves, and elves aid Frodo in his quest, while the War of the Ring ignites across Middle-earth. Tolkien unsuccessfully negotiated with Collins publishing house for the joint issuing of his epic with *The Silmarillion,* a revised version of *The Book of Lost Tales.* Allen and Unwin, publishers of *The Hobbit,* eventually agreed to publish *The Lord of the Rings* in three volumes—*The Fellowship of the Ring* (1954), *The Two Towers* (1954), and *The Return of the King* (1955).

Reaction to *The Lord of the Rings* varied. If some critics waxed rhapsodic, others derided Tolkien's work as medievalist pablum. The trilogy was received as an independent work, since *The Silmarillion* languished unpublished for over 20 years. The trilogy did not achieve widespread attention until 1966, following its publication in the United States by Ballantine Books in the wake of an unauthorized Ace Books paperback edition in 1965. It quickly vaulted to the top of the bestseller ranks and mushroomed into a full-blown cult phenomenon on college campuses during the 1960s and early 1970s.

The Silmarillion was finally published posthumously in 1977. Fans were perplexed by the lofty creation myth, biblical language, detailed genealogies, and the almost complete lack of characterization. Critics were equally baffled until the scope of Tolkien's mythology was communicated via the editorship of his son, Christopher. *Unfinished Tales of Númenor and Middle-earth* appeared in 1980, followed by the 12-volume opus of textual criticism, *The History of Middle-earth* (1983-1996). Christopher Tolkien combed his father's papers for seemingly every story fragment and draft pertaining to Middle-earth; the scale of his findings will likely occupy scholars for years.

Tolkien's influence on fantasy and science fiction has been profound. His example of a consistent, detailed secondary world is now the norm for imaginative writing. He is furthermore credited with the rekindling of fantasy as a narrative art. Among his descendants one might include such contemporary novelists as Peter S. Beagle, Stephen R. Donaldson, Robert Jordan, and Tad Williams. Tolkien has inspired a legion of lesser imitators as well, with the result being derivative, multi-volume series boasting faux medieval Europe

settings and fit to bursting with cookie-cutter elves, inns, wizards, and megalomanic dark lords. If Tolkienesque fantasy seems hackneyed today, few of his successors come close to rivaling the width and depth of the Middle-earth cosmos.

—Neal Baker

FURTHER READING:

Carpenter, Humphrey. *Tolkien: A Biography.* Boston, Houghton Mifflin, 1977.

Carpenter, Humphrey and Christopher Tolkien, editors. *The Letters of J. R. R. Tolkien.* Boston, Houghton Mifflin, 1981.

Curry, Patrick. *Defending Middle-Earth: Tolkien, Myth, and Modernity.* New York, St. Martin's, 1997.

''Review of *The Hobbit.''* *Times Literary Supplement.* October 2, 1937, 714.

Shippey, T. A. *The Road to Middle-Earth.* Boston, Houghton Mifflin, 1983.

Tolkien, J. R. R. ''On Fairy-Stories.'' *Tree and Leaf.* Boston, Houghton Mifflin, 1965.

Tom of Finland (1920-1991)

After 30 years of limited circulation in gay magazines and exhibitions in gay clubs, Tom of Finland's frankly pornographic drawings have enjoyed a vast popularity since the 1970s: They have been exhibited worldwide and even mainstream publishers have produced collections of his work. Tom of Finland is now considered, in the words of his biographer, ''the foremost name in gay erotic art'' and the critic Nayland Blake has defined him ''one of the gay world's few authentic icons,'' noting Tom's influence on artists as different as Robert Mapplethorpe, Bruce Weber, and Rainer Werner Fassbinder. A foundation was established a few years before Tom's death to preserve and perpetuate his work and, in the 1990s, Tom of Finland's influence has even extended to fashion, as the name of the pornographer has become a trademark for a line of male clothes.

Tom of Finland was born Touko Laaksonen in 1920 in Kaarina, then a rural area in the southwestern part of Finland. In 1939, after graduating from high school, Laaksonen went to art school in Helsinki to study advertising, but he soon had to suspend his studies because of World War II. After the war he completed his degree and also learned to play the piano at the renowned Sibelius Institute. In these early post-war years, Laaksonen kept his ''dirty drawings'' (as he liked to call them) to himself and earned his living by working as a freelance advertiser during the day and playing the piano at parties and cafés in Helsinki's bohemian districts in the evenings. It was not until 1957 that Laaksonen decided to submit some of his less graphic drawings (which he signed as Tom of Finland) for publication in *Physique Pictorial,* an American muscle magazine. The editor was so enthusiastic about them that the cover of the Spring 1957 issue of the magazine featured a drawing by Tom of Finland.

During the late 1950s and the 1960s, Tom of Finland's drawings were published regularly in American and European magazines and sold to private publications all over the world; but homosexual art did not sell very well at the time and Tom of Finland could not give up his advertising job any earlier than 1973, the same year of his first

European exhibition. Five years later Tom of Finland went to the United States for the first American exhibition of his drawings in Los Angeles. During this trip he met Durk Dehner who was to become Tom of Finland's successful manager and co-founder of the Tom of Finland Foundation. After the death of his companion of 28 years, Veli, in 1981, Tom of Finland divided his life equally between Finland and the United States until his own death ten years later. In 1987 the anthological volume, *Tom of Finland Retrospective,* was published to such a great success that a companion volume, *Retrospective II,* was also produced. Both volumes document Tom of Finland's career from the naturalist drawings of the late 1940s to the 1987 "safe-sex" poster urging the use of condoms, passing through his mature work featuring perfect physiques, exaggerated poses, and improbable sizes.

The characters in Tom of Finland's drawings are mostly men in uniform (soldiers, policemen, sailors, lumberjacks, and bikers in leather) involved in homosexual sex of all kinds and in every (im)possible position. Their huge pectorals and muscles, their perfectly-rounded bottoms and their enormous penises point to the exaggerated maleness of Tom of Finland's men, an iconography that goes against the dominant representation of gay men as effeminate and is thus an important point of reference for the leather gay subculture. Tom of Finland's drawings counteract also the enduring stereotype of "the sad and unhappy homosexual": the men in them are clearly having a lot of fun and are proud of their sexual orientation. Tom of Finland once declared that when he started to draw, "a gay man was made to feel nothing but shame about his feelings and his sexuality. I wanted my drawings to counteract that, to show gay men being happy and positive about who they were." Even if some of Tom of Finland's drawings take place in prisons or police-stations or depict sadomasochistic situations, there is always a strong sense of play underlying them and drama never intervenes.

A complex network of looks takes place in most of Tom of Finland's drawings. As Nayland Blake has pointed out, Tom of Finland has challenged the framework of the single gaze of traditional pornography where the object presents itself passively to the eyes of the viewer. In Tom of Finland's drawings there is an interaction of looks between the different characters, which complements the gaze of the viewer. Often the two men having sex in the foreground are observed by a third man in the background. Sometimes the characters even respond to the gaze of the viewer, as in the case of Tom of Finland's re-elaboration of Michelangelo's David (commissioned by the conservative Italian film-director Franco Zeffirelli). Tom of Finland's David, much better endowed than Michelangelo's, wears a defiant look on his face and seems to be telling the viewer: "I know what you're looking at."

Tom of Finland's *oeuvre* is a lot more than just a series of "dirty drawings." As Dennis Forbes and Fred Bisonnes have pointed out, when the cultural history of the late twentieth century's Gay Liberation Movement will be written, Tom of Finland will have to be acknowledged as having created an effective iconography for part of the gay world.

—Luca Prono

FURTHER READING:

Blake, Nayland. "Tom of Finland: An Appreciation." In *Out in Culture: Gay, Lesbian, and Queer Essays on Popular Culture,* edited by Corey K. Creekmur and Alexander Doty. Durham, Duke University Press, 1995.

Forbes, Dennis, and Fred Bisonnes. "Tom of Finland—An Appreciation." In *Tom of Finland Retrospective.* Los Angeles, London Press, 1988.

Hooven, Velentine F., III. *Tom of Finland: His Life and Times.* New York, St. Martin's Press, 1993.

Tom Swift Series

A popular series of forty boys' novels published by Grosset & Dunlap between 1910 and 1941, the Tom Swift books were mostly published under the pen name "Victor Appleton," though they were produced by the Stratemeyer Syndicate, a book packager that created other popular juvenile literature. Attempts were made to revive the series three times over the years, once in the 1950s with the Tom Swift, Jr. books, and again in the 1980s and 1990s, but they were never as successful as the originals. The hero of the first series was Tom Swift, a young inventor, portrayed as a plucky, ingenious figure who used modern technology and American know-how to create new devices and foil his rivals. An excerpt from an advertisement written by Edward Stratemeyer (1862-1930) for the first Tom Swift books characterizes the scope of this series: "It is the purpose of these spirited tales to convey in a realistic way the wonderful advances in land and sea locomotion and to interest the boy of the present in the hope that he may be a factor in aiding the marvelous development that is coming in the future."

The Stratemeyer Syndicate, which created more than 1400 books between 1904 and 1984, devised the series concepts and hired writers to complete book-length stories from a limited outline in exchange for a flat-fee compensation ($75.00 for the first Tom Swift book in 1910). The writer hired to become "Victor Appleton" for the majority of the Tom Swift volumes was Stratemeyer's close friend, Howard Roger Garis (1873-1962), who created the Uncle Wiggily stories and ghostwrote nearly 300 books for the Syndicate. Stratemeyer and Garis worked closely to craft a series of adventure stories with inventions inspired by the real-world work of inventors who were mentioned in magazines like *Scientific American.* Other writers involved on a limited basis for this series included W. Bert Foster and John W. Duffield.

The early Tom Swift volumes featured existing vehicles, like a motorcycle and a motorboat that Tom acquired and improved with suggestions from his father, "the aged inventor," Barton Swift. Next, Tom helped others with their inventions, the *Red Cloud,* an airship designed by John Sharp, and a submarine built by his father. By the fifth volume (all five were published in 1910), Tom built his first invention, an alkaline battery for an electric car. Later inventions of note included his sky racer (1911), a revolutionary photo telephone (1914), a coast-to-coast airline express (1926), a motor home called a "house on wheels" (1929), and a device to allow radio listeners to see the performers on a silvery screen with his "talking pictures" (1928).

In most cases, Tom Swift's vehicles were bigger and faster than their real-world counterparts, which often did not become practical until much later. A typical story involved a discussion of an exotic locale or strange event by the main characters, Tom, Barton, Tom's chum Ned Newton, and their eccentric friend, Mr. Wakefield Damon, who "blessed" more than 1,200 items and parts of his body throughout the series. Tom and friends were usually dogged by rivals, including Andy Foger, the squint-eyed redheaded bully who seemed to be on the scene no matter how remote the locale.

The Tom Swift series generated a combined sales of more than six million volumes so it is no surprise that in the early 1950s, the Stratemeyer Syndicate created a spin-off series, Tom Swift Jr., to try to reclaim part of the market share lost to the *Rick Brant* series (1948-1967), published under the "John Blaine" pseudonym. Work on the Tom Swift, Jr. series was begun in 1951 and by January 1952, a manuscript of the first volume was far enough along to receive comments by one of the Syndicate's science consultants, Robert H. Snyder. Despite this early start, the first five books in the series would not be published until 1954 after rewrites. Between 1954 and 1971, Grosset & Dunlap published thirty-three books about Tom Swift, Jr., his sister Sandra, pal Bud Barclay, and potential girlfriend, Phyllis Newton, daughter of Ned Newton from the original series. Tom Swift, Sr. makes appearances as a middle-aged man who remains active in science and invention. While the original series had titles like *Tom Swift and His Electric Rifle* (1911), the Tom Swift, Jr. series used atomic, electronic, and outer-space themes, like *Tom Swift and His Atomic Earth Blaster* (1954). For the Tom Swift, Jr. series, plot took a back seat to title in the early development of a volume. Long lists of proposed titles were considered. Once a title was selected, a story idea would be devised to match it.

"Victor Appleton II" was said to have "inherited his wonderful storytelling ability from the original Victor Appleton" in dust jacket ads for the early books. It is hard to say whether the Syndicate was referring to the ghostwriters or itself. While several writers wrote a volume or two, most of the newer series (volumes 5-7, 9-29) were written by James Duncan Lawrence (1918-1994), a Syndicate ghostwriter who also wrote for a number of different media, including screenplays for television and radio, books, and comic strips.

The Tom Swift, Jr. series was discontinued in 1971 due to declining sales, which had more to do with the aging Baby Boomers than it did with the perceived problem of Tom's achievements being surpassed by a real-world NASA. At the close of the Tom Swift, Jr. series, an anonymous memo laid the groundwork for yet another new Tom Swift series set in the far future where Tom Swift's inventions have become a reality. This new series was, indeed, set in the far future and contained science-fiction stories of interplanetary space travel with titles like *Terror on the Moons of Jupiter* (1981). Very little in the way of invention was included in the stories, and little or no reference was made to the previous two series. Part of the reason for this was that the new group of ghostwriters had published science fiction books under their own names, and because this series was published by Wanderer, a division of Simon & Schuster, which had purchased the Stratemeyer Syndicate in 1984. The third Tom Swift series was discontinued at this time.

In 1991, Simon & Schuster decided to try the venerable name of Tom Swift again in a new series published under its Archway imprint. Thirteen volumes were published of Tom Swift in a contemporary setting with inventions again being the focus, as in *Cyborg Kickboxer* (1991) and *Death Quake* (1993). This new series did not sell well and it was soon discontinued. All in all, Tom Swift appeared in ninety-nine stories in four series since the first volume was published in 1910.

—James D. Keeline

FURTHER READING:

Dizer, John T., Jr. *Tom Swift and Company: "Boy's Books" by Stratemeyer and Others.* Jefferson, North Carolina, McFarland and Company, 1982.

———. *Tom Swift, the Bobbsey Twins, and Other Heroes of American Juvenile Literature.* Lewiston, New York, Edwin Mellen Press, 1997.

Johnson, Deidre. *Edward Stratemeyer and the Stratemeyer Syndicate.* New York, Twayne, 1993.

———, compiler and editor. *Stratemeyer Pseudonyms and Series Books: An Annotated Checklist of Stratemeyer and Stratemeyer Syndicate Publications.* Westport, Connecticut, Greenwood Press, 1982.

Tomlin, Lily (1939—)

Lily Tomlin, a gifted comedienne, writer, and actress, emerged on American television in the early 1970s as a featured performer on the highly innovative and successful comedy variety series *Rowan & Martin's Laugh-In.* She became noted for her gallery of memorable characters, such as Ernestine the telephone operator and the sassy, five-year-old Edith Ann, and for her ability to transform herself into many vivid personas without costume changes or make-up. Throughout the 1970s and 1980s she established herself as "America's reigning female comic genius" by appearing in a series of praised television specials, releasing a bestselling comedy album, and making a successful transition onto the movie screen. Known for her versatility, Tomlin occasionally appeared in more dramatic roles for some of Hollywood's most respected directors. In 1985, she scored her

Lily Tomlin

greatest artistic triumph by appearing in her one-woman Broadway smash *The Search for Signs of Intelligent Life in the Universe,* which presented Tomlin's attempt to summarize a generation of social history through a series of character sketches. By the 1990s, Tomlin was displaying her talents on series television, film, animation, and commercials.

Mary Jean Tomlin, born on September 1, 1939, in Detroit, Michigan, had a great interest in observing people from childhood. Raised by a factory worker and housewife who had moved north from Paducah, Kentucky, in search of jobs during the Depression, Tomlin expressed an interest in theatre while attending Wayne State University. She combined her desire to perform comedy with talents for observation and mimicry in order to find her own style as a performer. Author Jeff Sorensen comments on Tomlin's comedic evolution when he writes: "Unlike other comics who stick with one successful persona, she was determined to play as many parts as she could dream up. Characters impressions were what interested Tomlin; she had no intention of standing up and telling topical jokes on subjects." Of her comic style she has said, "My comedy is actual life with the slightest twist of exaggeration. I construct compressed accuracy, a character essence that is as true as I can get it. I don't go for laughter. I never play for a joke *per se.* If the joke gets in the character's way, I take it out."

Tomlin began her career playing in Detroit coffeehouses while still in college, eventually making her way to New York. While honing her routines at a Manhattan nightclub and in several off-Broadway productions, Tomlin's career took off after she landed a part on *Laugh-In* in 1969. Tomlin became an instant celebrity during her tenure on *Laugh-In,* which lasted from 1969 to 1973. She endeared herself to audiences by inventing characters embodying both humor and intelligence. The most recognizable of her zany characters was Ernestine the telephone operator, a nasal and over-bearing woman who began her sketches with the catchphrase: "One ringy-dingy, two ringy-dingy, is this the party to whom I am speaking?" The wise-cracking Ernestine became so popular that AT&T offered Tomlin $500,000 to do a commercial, but the comedienne refused noting it would compromise the character's comedic integrity. One of Ernestine's most famous lines was "We don't care. We don't have to. We're the Phone Company." Tomlin's next most popular character of the early 1970s was Edith Ann, an uninhibited, lisping, five-year-old who sat in an oversized rocking chair as she discussed her life. Edith Ann would conclude her observations with her trademark expression "And that's the truth." Tomlin continued to create memorable characters after she left *Laugh-In* to star in a series of comedy specials. Her most famous creations include Trudy the bag lady, Sister Boogie-Woman, and Mrs. Beasley. The great popularity of these and other characters transformed Tomlin into a national comedic phenomenon.

The comedienne's versatility continued to expand as she moved beyond television. Her film debut came in 1975 when she was cast in Robert Altman's music industry epic *Nashville.* Tomlin, in a noncomedic role, played Linnea, a devoted mother and gospel singer who had an affair with a rock star. For this performance she received an Academy Award nomination. She followed this early screen success with such acclaimed films as *The Late Show* (1977), *9 to 5* (1980), *All of Me* (1984), and *Big Business* (1988). Her career suffered its greatest setback in 1978 with the release of *Moment by Moment,* which paired her with John Travolta in a romance. Critics lambasted the film, and audiences ignored it. Tomlin bounced back in 1985 with her Broadway triumph *The Search for Signs of Intelligent Life in the Universe.* She and writer Jane Wagner produced the acclaimed feminist look at the human condition that appealed to all audiences. Tomlin continued to express her versatility into the 1990s by appearing in such diverse roles as a TV executive on the sitcom *Murphy Brown,* the teacher/bus driver on the animated educational show *The Magic School Bus,* and through many film and TV guest appearances. Two of her best characterizations of this period were as an aging hippie in the film *Flirting with Disaster* and as a murderous Christmas spirit in a 1998 episode of *The X-Files.*

—Charles Coletta

FURTHER READING:

Anderson, Christopher. *The New Book of People.* New York, G. P. Putnam's Sons, 1986.

Brooks, Tim. *The Complete Directory to Prime Time TV Stars.* New York, Ballantine Books, 1987.

Grace, Arthur. *Comedians.* New York, Thomasson-Grant, 1991.

Sorensen, Jeff. *Lily Tomlin: Woman of a Thousand Faces.* New York, St. Martin's Press, 1989.

Tone, Franchot (1905-1968)

In the succinct words of David Thomson, "Tone was perhaps all that Franchot had—that and Joan Crawford," the first of his four wives. Born the son of a wealthy industrialist in Niagara, New York, and educated at Cornell, Franchot Tone had a distinguished stage career, working with the Group Theater among others. His film career, however, although long and prolific (1933 to 1965), consigned him to roles as wealthy café-society sophisticates, weak cads, or the losing end of love triangles in archetypal romances of the 1930s and 1940s. In 1935 he was Oscar-nominated for a supporting role in *Mutiny on the Bounty,* and married Crawford "after one of the most denied, affirmed, and re-denied romances Hollywood had ever witnessed," as one columnist commented. Unhappy with his film roles, he returned to Broadway, starring in Ernest Hemingway's *The Fifth Column* in 1940, but was soon back in Hollywood. Although he lacked the necessary screen charisma for leading-man stardom, he worked with many of the top directors, including John Ford, Von Sternberg, and Billy Wilder. He made several films with Crawford, and was with Jean Harlow in *Bombshell* (1933) and Bette Davis in *Dangerous* (1935), but gave his most memorable performances towards the end of his career and his life: the dying president in Otto Preminger's *Advise and Consent* (1962) and the grim Ruby Lapp in Arthur Penn's *Mickey One* (1965).

—Benjamin Griffith

FURTHER READING:

Jarvis, Everett G. *Final Curtain: Deaths of Noted Movie and TV Personalities.* New York, Carol Publishing Co., 1995.

Shipman, David. *The Great Movie Stars: The Golden Years.* New York, Crown, 1970.

The Tonight Show

NBC's venerable late-night talk show *The Tonight Show* has provided a unique window into the changing times and mores of contemporary American culture. Beginning in 1954, its four principal hosts have used the program as a pulpit for nightly commentary on events both profound and piddling. Over the decades, the show has fluctuated wildly in terms of its influence and quality. At various times it offered groundbreaking comedy, scintillating conversation, and instructions for stylish living. Even Jay Leno's tepid, non-threatening *Tonight Show* of the 1990s seemed somehow to reflect the tenor of its self-satisfied times.

The first host of *The Tonight Show* was Steve Allen, a former disc jockey who had presided over a succession of Golden Age TV offerings. During his innovative three-year run as host, Allen established the program's basic format: a monologue followed by a comedy set piece and a series of conversations with celebrity guests. Allen also inaugurated the show's long-running practice of breaking in new stand-up comics. Lenny Bruce and Mort Sahl were just two of the comedians who got their start slinging jokes at Allen's audience. In later years, such prominent entertainers as George Carlin, Richard Pryor, and Roseanne Barr would gain their initial national exposure on the program.

In 1956, NBC moved Allen onto another show and briefly retooled *The Tonight Show*. That experiment failed and the network eventually brought in Jack Paar, a garrulous game show host, as Allen's replacement. Beginning in July of 1957, Paar brought a more erudite presence to *The Tonight Show*. He eschewed comedy skits for genteel conversation, often booking guests from the political arena. Robert F. Kennedy, Richard Nixon, and labor leader George Meaney were a few of the luminaries who chatted with Paar over the years.

Behind the veneer of a highbrow gabber, there was a darker side to Paar as well. He picked fights with notable figures in broadcasting, Walter Winchell and Ed Sullivan among them. On numerous occasions he threatened to quit the program, citing network interference and his own ennui with the late-night grind Paar was the first of *The Tonight Show* hosts to cut his work week down from five days to three. On February 11, 1960, Paar finally walked out on the program—literally, in the middle of a broadcast. He did return to his desk a few weeks later, but after a series of additional controversial incidents, Paar took his leave of *The Tonight Show* in March of 1962.

After a half-year interregnum, during which guest hosts filled the command chair, Johnny Carson became Paar's successor. A glib boy magician from Nebraska, Carson brought a midwestern geniality, along with a sharp wit, to the hosting chores. He also introduced America to Ed McMahon, his second banana from the game show

Frank Sinatra (left) and Johnny Carson on *The Tonight Show* in 1976.

Who Do You Trust, to serve as announcer and sounding board. The pair would remain together on the program for the next 30 years, with McMahon's famous introduction, ''Heeeeere's Johnny!'' becoming a globally recognized refrain.

For a time, Carson retained Paar's reliance on learned guests, though over the decades Hollywood glitz began to trump intelligent conversation. In a reflection of this shift, the show moved from New York to Los Angeles in 1972. Out west, *The Tonight Show* took on more of an adult urban contemporary feel. Hipsters like Burt Reynolds and Hugh Hefner replaced the stodgy Hubert Humphreys of the Paar years. *The Tonight Show* became more popular than ever, as ''Johnny'' reveled in his shaman of late-night status.

The show's veneer of cool began to melt away in the 1980s, as *The Tonight Show* grew old along with its audience. Once the icon of hipness, Carson now seemed a mainstream fuddy-duddy, as edgier comics like David Letterman and, later, Arsenio Hall began to steal some of his limelight. The nadir of *The Tonight Show* came with the 1983 installation of Borscht Belt fossil Joan Rivers as Carson's permanent guest host. The whining, shrewish Rivers alienated many of the show's loyal viewers—and eventually enraged her patron by jumping ship for her own, competitive late-night program. Carson replaced her with comedian Jay Leno, who took over when Carson abruptly announced his retirement as of May 1992.

Leno, who beat out the more talented Letterman for the job after a well-publicized internecine struggle, took over the day after Carson signed off. He made almost no changes to the format, apart from dropping the unnecessary second banana. A workaholic stand-up, Leno relied on his strong monologues to distract attention from his sub-par interviewing skills. He seemed on the verge of losing control of the show when Letterman fielded a competitive program on CBS, but rode back to the top of the ratings on the strength of his jokes about the O.J. Simpson murder trial. Though Leno's tame take on late-night chat offered little to differentiate it from its competitors, the equity in *The Tonight Show* franchise and the host's skill with a one-liner ensured it would remain a subject of office water cooler conversation for years to come.

—Robert E. Schnakenberg

FURTHER READING:

Carter, Bill. *The Late Shift.* New York, Hyperion, 1995.

Tootsie

Named one of the top 100 American Films by the American Film Institute, *Tootsie* was released in 1982, and became the year's blockbuster romantic comedy. The 1980s saw the opening of several films featuring cross-dressing, including *Yentl, Victor/Victoria,* and *Torch Song Trilogy*; and yet it was *Tootsie* that garnered the most critical attention and popular acclaim. The American cultural obsession with cross-dressing surfaces in newspaper stories, television talk shows, children's tales, and movies. Anthropologists, literary critics, and historians all have paid a great deal of attention to cross-dressing, producing studies of hermaphrodites, boy actors, and the politics of camp. Cross-dressing and the treatment of cross-dressing raises, in a relatively concise if somewhat confusing fashion, questions of the

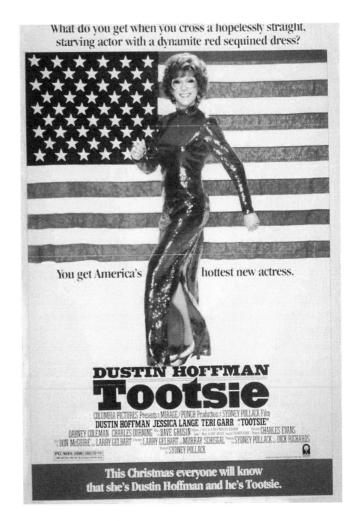

Film poster for *Tootsie.*

construction of gender and sexuality. If a man can dress up successfully as a woman, does that mean that gender itself is merely a performance, albeit a culturally dictated one? What does it mean to ''become a woman?'' That is, what are our culture's definitions of femininity, and, by implication, masculinity? Upon its release, *Tootsie* quickly became a focus for popular and critical debate of these questions. Both critics and popular audiences responded to the film's investigation of gender roles as well as its interrogation of what it means to be a woman and what it *could* mean to be a man.

In *Tootsie,* Dustin Hoffman plays Michael Dorsey, an out-of-work New York actor who dresses as a woman, Dorothy Michaels, in order to land a role in a very successful soap opera, *Southwest General.* His character, named Emily Kimberley, becomes a fan favorite because of his/her improvised feminist protests on the set. Off stage, Hoffman falls in love with Jessica Lange, another actress in the series, who, thinking Hoffman is a woman, becomes his/her confidante. Finally, Dorothy unmasks, and the movie concludes with a stereotypically happy romantic ending and with Michael's understanding of the difficulties of being a woman. Becoming a woman for Michael means more, the movie implies, than simply shaving more often, wearing makeup, and donning pantyhose. In other words, while pretending to be Dorothy in order to make a living, Michael realizes that it's no easy game to live as a woman in our culture.

Michael Dorsey and Dorothy Michaels are both familiar figures in Hollywood's long history of representations of male-female impersonators in movies such as *Pat and Mike, Easy Living, Bringing up Baby,* and *Some Like It Hot.* In fact, Hoffman modeled Dorothy Michaels's mannerisms on Jack Lemmon's Daphne in *Some Like it Hot. Tootsie*'s appeal, however, lies in the way that it moves beyond the farcical transvestitism of its predecessors. *Tootsie* attempts to be social commentary, not just comedy. Dustin Hoffman's performance in the film does not resemble drag or camp, but rather presents itself as a serious comment about playing a woman in contemporary American culture (just as it is serious business for Michael Dorsey within the context of the movie).

Tootsie quickly became the ground from which to spring feminist critiques of women in mainstream film, including analyses of positive and negative images of women and feminism in film, as well as of the potential co-optation of feminism for enormous commercial profit. Many critics asserted that *Tootsie*'s lesson is that women are simply better than men—Dorothy Michaels, they argue, is not only more successful than Michael Dorsey, but she is more sympathetic, feeling, and observant as well. (Indeed, Hoffman's oft-repeated claims in interviews that playing Dorothy made him a better man, less prone to anger and more sensitive to others' needs, seems to attest to this interpretation.) Since Dorothy Michaels is really a man, however, others have argued that the hidden message of the film is that men are actually better than women. After all, no matter whether one thinks that *Tootsie* destabilizes gender roles or reaffirms them, a man disguised as a woman seems to be better at being a woman than a real woman (as Teri Garr's character learns, when she discovers that Dustin Hoffman has won the role of Emily over her). Many critics read the film as arguing that only a man can be tough and honest enough to express women's rights. In fact, "Tootsie" has become slang among some literary and film critics for a man who claims his identity as a feminist even while maintaining a sexist understanding of women. The image of Dustin Hoffman in a long red sequined dress operates simultaneously, it seems, as both a feminist icon and a parody of feminism.

Although *Tootsie* is all about acting, in the end it is unclear whether or not the film implies that all gender roles are performances. Do the daily rituals of becoming a woman which *Tootsie* obsessively documents—tweezing eyebrows, applying mascara, shaving legs, applying nail polish, and fixing one's hair—mean the same thing for a man dressing as a woman as they do for a woman dressing up? There does not seem to be any question, for example, that Dorothy Michaels is "really" Michael Dorsey (that is, that his masculinity is a performance). In addition, the film does not investigate the ways in which femininity is a performance that the *women* in the movie perform as well (or not as well) as the men. "Genuine" gender roles are reasserted at the end of the movie, suggesting that cross-dressing or the understanding of gender as performance should take place only on stage, or for limited periods. In other words, one could read *Tootsie* as a slick (some would argue exploitative) poke at gender roles, whose conclusion leaves those roles finally intact (as a film that is, in the end, not good for women). And yet, such a reading might be too simplistic, for it denies what makes the film so popular in the first place—the basic ambiguity of cross-dressing itself.

—Austin Booth

FURTHER READING:

Garber, Marjorie. *Vested Interests: Cross-Dressing and Cultural Anxiety.* New York, Routledge, 1992.

Showalter, Elaine. "Critical Cross-Dressing: Male Feminists and the Woman of the Year." *Raritan.* Vol. 3, No. 2, Fall 1983, 138-52.

Top 40

Top 40 is a listing of the 40 most popular single records in the nation for a given week, and is derived from radio station playlists and retail sales. The listing is based on trade magazines including *Gavin Report, Cashbox,* and *Billboard.* Top 40 also is an AM radio format that consists of music, trivial talk, news, and promotions including services, money, and goods given to listeners. Though Top 40 radio has undergone many changes in its 45-year history, it remains a viable format. From 1956 to the present, Top 40 has provided Americans, especially those born in the 1940s, a musical smorgasbord served up through their favorite disc jockey. Disc jockeys were chosen on the basis of their voice, excitement, and sex appeal. The Top 40 format did not leave much room for personalities, and for that reason did not appeal to some disc jockeys. At first, Top 40 was not aimed at a teenage market; instead disc jockeys, adhering to a playlist, entertained and did what was called "formula radio." But Top 40 soon became a bridge from adult-oriented music to rock 'n' roll and rhythm and blues to other styles. The youth market gravitated to Top 40, and with the evolution of rock 'n' roll contributed to its early success. By 1958, Top 40 stations had spread from the Midwest to the rest of the country.

While the Top 40 format originated in 1956, there were earlier developments in radio that helped in its formation. In 1935, *Your Hit Parade,* a program on NBC, featured live performances of the most-liked songs based on sheet music, records, and airplay. In 1941, *Lucky Lager Dance Time,* a Los Angeles radio program on KFAC, first aired playing hit records and a "Lucky Ten" countdown. By 1949, KOWH, an Omaha, Nebraska, radio station, featured a playlist of popular records. Popular disc jockey Alan Freed produced the *Moondog Rock and Roll Party* in 1951 that introduced black music to a mostly white audience. In 1953, radio still held its own against television, with 96 percent of homes and 76 percent of cars having radios. Americans listened to radio on a daily basis or at least once per week. In 1953, New Orleans radio station WDSU played the top 20. Top 40 became an expanded version of previous programs, including *Your Hit Parade* and *Lucky Lager Dance Time,* and was programmed over a full broadcast day with disc jockeys and local advertisements.

The exact origin of the Top 40 is disputed and there are several explanations of its beginning. In one instance, Top 40 began in the context of several bars in several cities, including Omaha, New Orleans, Dallas, San Antonio, and Houston. Another story credits radio programmer Bill Gavin with having invented the Top 40 chart. Most scholars of radio and disc jockey Dick Clark, however, give credence to Top 40 beginning at a bar in Omaha where in an interval of two years from 1953 to 1955, Todd Storz, operator of KOWH devised the format. The story goes that Storz and his program director, Bill Stewart, were sitting in a bar in Omaha, when they became aware that patrons played the same jukebox selections repeatedly over the course of four hours. When one of the patrons was asked why, she plainly responded, "I like 'em." Inspired by her response, Stewart, based on the most-played records on the jukebox, developed a playlist of thirty songs. Storz implemented this playlist at KOWH and the ratings improved drastically. Yet, another etymology of Top 40 has Storz developing a radio program at his New Orleans station WTIX called *Top 40 at 1450* immediately after acquiring it in 1953. The program was in response to rival station WDSU's *The Top 20 at 1280* show. Disc jockey Bob Howard, reasoned that if a list of 20 hits was satisfactory, then 40 would be outstanding, and consequently developed a show of 40 selections called *Top 40 at 1450*. In 1955, influenced by Howard, Storz at WTIX radio in New Orleans continued the concept at an Omaha radio station. KLIF owner Gordon McLendon also initiated the Top 40 format, including goofy promotions and jingles. By 1956, Top 40 had developed into a popular format.

Several key individuals were considered pioneers of Top 40, with each bringing an innovation that became part and parcel to the format. Gordon McLendon, called "the Orson Welles of radio," was a creative talent with programming and promotional ideas that gave early Top 40 its form, vitality, and innovative jingles. In radio, jingles are the most reliable indicators for listeners remembering a station. Jingles existed before Top 40, but it was McLendon who hired a music director, who in turn employed a vocal group to record jingles designed for Top 40.

Mike Joseph and Chuck Blore were also two important programmers in early Top 40 radio. It was McLendon who employed Blore as a disc jockey and program director. Blore is credited with the concept of "Color Radio," a term inspired by color television and a format developed in 1958 at KFWB in Los Angeles. "Color Radio" had nothing to do with ethnic diversity, but rather diversity in promotions, news, music, and a strong amusement and entertainment element. Joseph, a radio consultant, kept the industry focused on playing the hits and giving listeners what they wanted—always a central mission of Top 40 radio. Bill Gavin, programmer for the *Lucky Lager Dance Time* programs heard on 48 western stations, monitored sales and combined these data with other statistics, creating the *Bill Gavin's Record Report* in 1958. This information base became the foundation on which the Top 40 playlist was created. *The Gavin Report* was an innovation in the radio business that gave statistics on various markets and was essential to the development of Top 40.

In its early years, from 1956 to around 1962, Top 40 was democracy in radio. Musical categories including pop, rock 'n' roll, country, rhythm and blues, novelty tunes, jazz, and movie soundtracks made the format and were played to a mass audience. For example, from a list of Top 40 singles, the following songs and artists were represented in the following categories in 1960: pop ("Save the Last Dance for Me," the Drifters), rock 'n' roll ("It's Now or Never," Elvis Presley), country ("He'll Have to Go," Jim Reeves), rhythm and blues ("Finger Poppin' Time," Hank Ballard & the Midnighters), novelty tune ("Itsy Bitsy Teenie Weenie Yellow Polka Dot Bikini," Brian Hyland), jazz ("Georgia on My Mind," Ray Charles), and movie soundtrack ("Theme from 'A Summer Place,'" Percy Faith). A clock, sometimes called a "hot clock" in the early days and now a computer readout with a written scenario, drives Top 40. Disc jockeys have to religiously follow the clock. Relying on its popularity, a song, could be repeated every hour or every six hours. Top 40 has not been without criticism, and while the format purported to play what people wanted to hear and espouse democratic ideals, critics, including Columbia Records, accused disc jockeys of relinquishing air time and kowtowing to teenage tastes. Obviously, during the course of its maturity, Top 40 changed in that each of the various subgenres of pop

and rhythm and blues either now has its own radio format and niche market or no radio home at all.

The disc jockey, a term coined by record executive Jack Kapp in 1940, was the heart and soul of Top 40. A good disc jockey could imbue the staid format with a personality and identity. Entertainers in their own right, disc jockeys of Top 40 radio, would introduce and build up a song by talking while playing the instrumental introduction, finishing just before the vocal would start. This practice was called "hitting the post" or the art of the talk-up. While it is questionable whether disc jockeys could accurately predict what records would become hits, Top 40 radio disc jockeys always took credit for selecting certain hits. Disc jockey Wolfman Jack takes a more conservative stance on the role of disc jockeys making hits. "As long as I can remember there've been lists," he said. "Top 40 lists in the trade magazines, and in my life since 1960 I've been going by the goddamned charts. You didn't vary too far. There's no disc jockey alive who can make a record happen. All you can do is give it exposure." Many stations featured a pick hit based on a disc jockey's recommendation that actually turned out to be a hit.

The exposure of diverse musical styles, including African American popular music, owes much to the Top 40 format. By 1957, led by Chuck Berry and Fats Domino, a number of African American styles, from calypso to rhythm and blues, made the format, including records by Harry Belafonte, the Del Vikings (the first successful interracial group in rock 'n' roll), the Drifters, Della Reese, Little Richard, the Coasters, Little Anthony and the Imperials, the Platters, Larry Williams, Roy Brown, Jimmy Reed, and Ruth Brown. The first Motown entry in the format was Barrett Strong's "Money," followed in succeeding years with records by the Supremes, and the Four Tops, among others. Some of the most enduring rock 'n' roll also debuted on the Top 40. In 1957, Jerry Lee Lewis, Buddy Holly and the Crickets, and the Everly Brothers all appeared on the Top 40.

While black popular music could be heard on Top 40 by the original performers of the music, the Top 40 format often played emasculated and watered-down versions of black popular music. "Cover" records had made their debut many years before Top 40. A narrow definition of "cover" referred to a song that was successful by a black artists and then recorded by a white artist on a major label. Black bluesman Joe Turner's "Shake, Rattle and Roll" was recorded by Bill Haley and His Comets. "Sincerely" by the Moonglows, a black vocal group, was recorded by the McGuire Sisters. The covers in many instances climbed to the top of the charts while the "authentic" originals were shut out. Eventually, the black originals began to outshine the covers, as Sam Cooke's "You Send Me" did over the Teresa Brewer's version.

Top 40, according to radio consultant Guy Zapoleon, can be a format envisioned in four cycles, each lasting from seven to nine years. Each cycle has three stages: birth, extremes, and doldrums. Cycle 1 (1956-1963) encompasses pop, rock, R&B, dance, and country. Cycle 2 (1964-1973) embodies pop, rock, R&B, acid rock and soft rock, and country. Cycle 3 (1974-1983) embraces pop, rock, R&B, the disco, adult/contemporary, and country. Cycle 4 (1984-1993) includes pop, rock, R&B, rap/funk, adult/contemporary, and country. By the end of the twentieth century, rap or hip-hop, country, and hard rock have yet to penetrate the Top 40. When rap first broke into the pop charts, Casey Kasem, the originator of the countdown and *Casey's Top 40,* is credited with playing the hits, but other Top 40 stations have taken a harder line irrespective of how rap songs charted, most Top 40 stations have consistently avoided rap. Perhaps mainstream rap artists such as Mase and Will Smith will eventually be palatable to the format.

Payola, the act of paying for air play, long suspected in the radio industry, was investigated by Congress in 1960. Representative Oren Harris and his subcommittee targeted Alan Freed, an extremely popular disc jockey who was found guilty of two counts of commercial bribery by the New York District Attorney's Office. His fine was small, but as a result he lost his job and was subsequently indicted for back income taxes. Payola scandals gained notoriety and resurfaced in 1984 and again in 1986. Despite these scandals, Zapoleon believed that Top 40 remained robust and continued to mirror the best of all types of music.

While Top 40 may have been democratic in its selection of playlists where each song was evaluated on its on merit, it was less so in terms of the diversity in race and gender of Top 40 disc jockeys. The majority of Top 40 disc jockeys were white males. No satisfactory explanation exists as to why more disc jockeys of color were not employed in Top 40 radio. In 1964, after Top 40 had been in existence for more than nine years, several black disc jockeys were hired, including Larry McCormick, reportedly the first African American disc jockey to work at KFWB in Los Angeles. In 1965, Chuck Leonard was hired for New York's WABC radio, and in 1968, Frankie Crocker was a Top 40 DJ on WMCA. Also in 1968, Walt Love was hired as a Top 40 disc jockey at Houston's KILT. In 1973, Yvonne Daniels, daughter of singer-dancer Billy Daniels, broke gender and race by becoming the first woman and first African American to be hired as a Top 40 disc jockey at WLS in Chicago.

By 1965, disc jockey and program director Bill Drake experimented with programming ideas to transform KHJ in Los Angeles to a Top 40 station, devising the concept of "Boss Radio." This Top 40 format was copied by numerous stations across the country. By 1968, the listening audience for Top 40 began to erode from competition by FM "free form" (later called "progressive" rock) radio. During most of the 1970s, Top 40 did maintain a smaller audience, even as the popularity of disco peaked in 1978. Though Top 40 regained some of its listening audience in 1983, by 1993, mainstream Top 40 disappeared as new appellations, including rock and alternative, were added to Top 40 formats. The number of radio stations identifying themselves as Top 40 also dwindled from 578 to 441. Gavin noted that the strong competition experienced by Top 40 stations brought the ratings down. In addition to competition from other radio stations, MTV (Music Television) launched in 1981, was an immediate success with young viewers. MTV essentially did what Top 40 had purported to do all along, and that was play the hits and give listeners what they wanted to hear.

In 1997, Top 40, fueled by popular artists such as the Spice Girls, made a comeback, and in its more than 45 years of existence continued to be the best format for variety in music. The Top 40 radio format was a general standard that achieved intermittent success and impacted the music industry. It was a format and system that monopolized playlists, not only dictating songs radio listeners heard, but the number of times, the order, time of day, and even to some extent the professional lives of the artists printed alongside the titles on the list. Top 40 inherently became its own worst enemy, since as listeners tended to mature, they developed preferences for certain types of music instead of the melange of popular songs on the playlists. Radio stations began emphasizing light rock, classic soul and R&B, classical, and jazz in efforts to capture a particular segment of the market. In spite of its vacillations, Top 40 has presented a diverse repertoire of songs that reflects the world of popular music.

Top 40 has remained resilient in spite of its many changes. "Through forty years, it (Top 40) had weathered one payola scandal after another, one competing format after another, one new technology after another, and all the shifts in fortune that society, culture, politics, and the economy can bring," observed noted writer and editor, Ben Fong-Torres. By the end of the twentieth century, Top 40 continued to be a viable format.

—Willie Collins

FURTHER READING:

Fong-Torres, Ben. *The Hits Just Keep on Coming: The History of Top 40 Radio.* San Francisco, Miller Freeman Books, 1998.

Pollock, Bruce. *When Rock Was Young: A Nostalgic Review of the Top 40 Era.* New York, Holt Rinehart and Winston, 1981.

Zapoleon, Guy. "What Goes Around Comes Around." *Gavin Report.* June 20, 1997.

Tora! Tora! Tora!

A 1970 motion picture recounting the attack on Pearl Harbor by the Japanese during World War II, *Tora! Tora! Tora!* was at the time of its release the second most expensive movie ever made, just behind *Cleopatra* in actual cost. Based on the historic novels *Tora! Tora! Tora!* by Gordon W. Prange and *The Broken Seal* by Ladislas Farago, the film recounts what happened on both the American and Japanese sides. The title refers to the Japanese code word which signaled the launch of the attack.

The idea for making the film came from Elmo Williams, who was hoping for another financial triumph along the lines of *The Longest Day.* From the beginning it was planned as a film of monumental scale that would examine the events of Pearl Harbor in precise detail. A tremendous amount of research had been done by Dr. Gordon Prang and his staff at the University of Maryland. (Prang had been appointed by General Douglas MacArthur as the official historian of the Pacific war, and had the advantage of being fluent in Japanese). In order to further enhance the authenticity of the film, Akira Kurosawa, Japan's most famous and possibly greatest director, was hired to direct the Japanese scenes.

The production faced numerous problems. For example, apart from one destroyer, nothing was left of the original Japanese fleet, requiring the filmmakers to construct a Japanese aircraft carrier and a plywood battleship and have them sent to Japan for filming. With no Japanese Zeroes available, 28 Vultee AT-6's were "stretched" six feet so that they would appear to be the same size and were then fitted with appropriate cowlings, windshields, and wheel skirts (with the result that parts were always falling off during flight).

Nor was there much left of the American fleet either, now that it had been mothballed. One floating battleship set alone cost $1 million to construct. The Fox miniature department built models of 19 Japanese ships and ten American ships at a scale of three-quarters of an inch to the foot, thereby creating forty-foot "miniatures." They also had to build to scale the Battleship Row docks and surrounding land areas.

Tora! Tora! Tora! took two years to prepare under the supervision of Williams. American director Richard Fleischer was called in

A scene from the film *Tora! Tora! Tora!*

during the last six months of preparation before shooting was to begin. He met with Kurosawa and Williams in Hawaii. Williams wanted Kurosawa to cut several scenes from the script that he felt were extraneous. Kurosawa was reluctant but agreed. Kurosawa also felt it was important to depict the Japanese military as all spit and polish, formal, correct, obsessed with protocol and ceremony, while Fleischer would depict the American military as relaxed, laid-back, a bit sloppy, and casual.

Ultimately, the producers of the film spent $25 million to reenact the attack on Pearl Harbor, more than the Japanese had spent to launch it. The attack itself was a complex sequence requiring smoke, flames, explosions, planes diving or bombing or crashing, torpedoes running; hangers, planes, and ships blowing up; anti-aircraft and machine guns firing, as well as actors in almost every shot.

The American sequences were scripted by Larry Forrester and starred Martin Balsam as Admiral Kimmel, Joseph Cotten as Secretary of War Stimson, E.G. Marshall as Lt. Colonel Bratton, James Whitmore as Admiral Halsey, and Jason Robards as General Walter C. Short. The Japanese sections were scripted by Hideo Oguni and Ryuzo Kikushima and starred Soh Yamamura as Admiral Yamamoto, Tatsuya Mihashi as Commander Genda, Takahiro Tamura as Lt. Commander Fuchida, Eijiro Tono as Admiral Nagumo, and Koreya Senda as Prince Konoye.

In Japan, Kurosawa began to resent the intrusion of five American production people sent to oversee things. He insisted on shooting interior scenes from 4:00 p.m. to midnight. He did not like the American design of the prefabricated structure sent to Toeiga Studios to serve as his administration building. He cast the heads of several large corporations in bit parts (in hopes that they might finance his next film), and insisted that everyone on the crew wear special *Tora! Tora! Tora!* jackets and regulation Navy caps and salute the actors whenever one passed by.

When the first day of shooting came, set inside a shrineroom on board a battleship, Kurosawa decided it was the wrong shade of white and insisted that every member of the crew work to repaint it. He became obsessed with endless minor details while overlooking a major one, despite warnings from the Americans. The plywood battleship sent over from America was being constructed facing the wrong direction.

Soon the Japanese portions were falling far behind schedule. The studio became intolerant of the delays, and Kurosawa was receiving threats from politically important people who did not want the film to be made at all. (On his way to the set, Kurosawa would lie down on the floor of the limousine to avoid assassination). As he became more abusive, his own crew started to turn against him. The story was released that illness forced him off the picture, but the truth was the studio had finally had enough and fired him. Two commercial Japanese directors, Toshio Masuda and Kinji Fukasaku took over.

Perhaps it was because of the Japanese involvement, but the final film downplays the real reasons for the United States contemplating war with Japan before the attack. There is no mention of Japanese aggression in China or the much-publicized atrocities committed by the Japanese during their occupation. The film also fails to portray opposition to the war from within the ranks of the Japanese military.

Six servicemen were injured during the filming of the attack, and after rumors circulated of Naval carriers transporting props for the shoot, Representative John M. Murphy of New York proposed legislation to forbid the military to participate in commercial motion picture production.

The film is notable for how accurately it depicts the actual events, and it won an Academy Award for A.D. Flowers and L.B. Abbott for its spectacular battle effects. However, it did not prove to be the major league blockbuster its producers had hoped it would be, easily being eclipsed by the year's other great war epic, Franklin Schaffer's *Patton*. Many Americans did not like having to read Japanese subtitles during the Japanese portions of the film, and others feared that the Zero pilots would be made to seem heroic at the expense of American servicemen who struggled vainly to defend the base.

—Dennis Fischer

FURTHER READING:

Fleischer, Richard. *Just Tell Me When to Cry.* New York, Carroll & Graf Publishers, 1993.

Iriye, Akira. *"Tora! Tora! Tora!" Past Imperfect: History According to the Movies.* Edited by Mark Carnes. New York, Henry Holt, 1995.

Prange, Gordon W. *At Dawn We Slept: The Untold Story of Pearl Harbor.* New York, McGray-Hill, 1981.

Wohlstetter, Roberta. *Pearl Harbor: Warning and Decision.* Stanford, California, Stanford University Press, 1962.

Tormé, Mel (1925-1999)

One of the most versatile entertainers of all time, Mel Tormé, known as the "Velvet Fog," was one of America's most acclaimed vocalists as well as a composer-arranger, drummer, actor in films and television, and star performer on records and the live concert stage. In 1996, his 67th year in show business, he broke all records by performing for the twentieth consecutive year at both Carnegie Hall and the Hollywood Bowl. The popular holiday classic "The Christmas Song" ("Chestnuts roasting on an open fire") is his best-known composition.

Born in Chicago, Tormé began his career at age four, singing on weekly radio broadcasts with the Coon-Sanders Nighthawk Band in 1929 and with Buddy Rogers and his Band in the early 1930s. When he was six, he worked regularly with vaudeville units around Chicago, and at nine he was cast as Jimmy the newsboy on the popular NBC radio soap opera *Song of the City.* Remaining as a regular in the show

Mel Tormé

from 1934-40, Mel used his spare time to study drums and songwriting. At age fifteen he wrote his first hit song, "Lament to Love," which was recorded by Harry James in 1941. The following year he joined the Chico Marx Band in California as a drummer, singer, and arranger.

When the band broke up in July, 1943, the young singer's career began to soar. He made his debut in a feature film with Frank Sinatra in RKO's *Higher and Higher,* followed shortly by *Pardon My Rhythm* and *Let's Go Steady,* minor musicals with a high school setting. These two films featured the Mel-Tones, a singing group formed by students from Los Angeles City College, featuring Tormé as lead singer and arranger.

After serving in the army during World War II, Mel signed a contract with MGM studios. There he played in *Good News* (1947), a popular college film starring June Allison and Peter Lawford and featuring the "Varsity Drag." Mel also appeared in *Words and Music* (1948) with Mickey Rooney and Judy Garland. During the 1950s he recorded a string of hit records and toured widely on the concert stage as the leading jazz singer of the new "Cool School."

Making the transition to television in 1951, he starred with Peggy Lee on *TV's Top Tunes,* a summer replacement for *The Perry Como Show.* For the next two years he hosted a daily talk show on CBS. In 1957 he earned an Emmy nomination for best supporting actor in a *Playhouse 90* production entitled "The Comedian." During this time he was frequently featured on television variety shows.

His career as an author began in 1963 when producer George Schlatter hired Mel to write scripts for *The Judy Garland Show* on CBS. His experiences in coping with the unpredictable star of the show led him to write *The Other Side of the Rainbow,* which was published by William Morrow and became a best seller. His later books include his autobiography, *It Wasn't All Velvet, Drummin' Men: The Heartbeat of Jazz, the Swing Years,* and *The World of Gene Krupa: That Legendary Drummin' Man.*

His long career includes appearances with most of America's best-known symphony orchestras. In 1983 Mel won the Grammy Award as Best Male Jazz Vocalist for the album *An Evening with George Shearing and Mel Tormé.* While performing at the White House for President and Mrs. Reagan the following year, he was told he had received a second Grammy for the album *Top Drawer.* As the aging superstar of pop music, Tormé won an even wider audience with frequent appearances as himself on the popular television comedy, *Night Court.* Tormé passed away in June of 1999.

—Benjamin Griffith

FURTHER READING:

Balliett, Whitney. *American Singers: 23 Portraits in Song.* New York, Oxford, 1988.

Friedwell, Will. *Jazz Singing: America's Great Voices from Bessie Smith to Bebop and Beyond.* New York, Da Capo, 1996.

Tormé, Mel. *It Wasn't All Velvet: An Autobiography.* New York, Viking, 1988.

———. *My Singing Teachers: Reflections on Singing Popular Music.* New York, Oxford, 1994.

Touched by an Angel

Premiering in 1994, the television series *Touched by an Angel* chose a unique formula to achieve success. The series relied on spiritual faith, love, and redemption to send positive messages in an age of dramatic television filled with tremendous violence and negativity. The three main characters, all angels, include: Tess (Della Reese), the supervisor and mentor; Monica (Roma Downey), the new angel; and Andrew (John Dye), the angel of death. The angels assist a wide range of different characters with their personal relationships and tackle many serious issues along the way, including AIDS (Acquired Immune Deficiency Syndrome), capital punishment, and teenage pregnancy. While the series focused on spiritual thoughts and does use the word ''god,'' it does not assert any specific religion or religious agenda. With little fanfare at first, *Touched by An Angel* consistently gained in popularity over the late 1990s to become a top ranked and unique drama series.

—Randall McClure

FURTHER READING:

Reese, Della, with Franklin Lett and Mim Eichler. *Angels Along the Way: My Life with Help from Above.* New York, G.P. Putnam's Sons, 1997.

Sheets, Robin, and Martha Williamson. *Touched by an Angel.* Grand Rapids, Michigan, Zondervan Publishing House, 1997.

Williamson, Martha. *When Angels Speak: Inspiration from Touched by an Angel.* Columbus, Fireside, 1997.

Tour de France

The Tour de France bicycle race is the world's largest annual sporting event, having been run every year since 1903 except for periods during the two World Wars. With a live television audience of 900 million viewers in 163 countries in 1998, its popularity is surpassed only by the World Cup and the Olympics. Unfolding during a three-week period every July, it covers approximately 2,500 miles and is divided into daily segments that traverse France by various routes. The race pits some 21 teams of riders against mountainous segments in the Alps and Pyrenees and flat segments in Brittany and Normandy, culminating with a spectacular symbolic finish on the Champs-Elysées in Paris. Individual riders also compete against each other in time trials. The overall leader earns the right to wear an illustrious yellow jersey. Victories by American Greg Lemond in 1986, 1989, and 1990 enhanced the event's popularity profile in the United States.

—Neal Baker

FURTHER READING:

Abt, Samuel. *Tour de France: Three Weeks to Glory.* San Francisco, Bicycle Books, 1991.

Brunel, Philippe. *An Intimate Portrait of the Tour De France: Masters and Slaves of the Road,* second edition. Denver, Bounpane Publications, 1996.

Town Meetings

Typically held once a year, town meetings bring citizens together to vote on decisions about local affairs, including ordinances, taxes, town officers, and local improvements. Most historians associate town meetings with the region and culture of New England, especially Massachusetts and Vermont. Town meetings symbolize a strong belief in political equality and direct democracy (versus the representative democracy of America's constitution), which explains why town meetings continue today. Some historians and political scientists argue that town meetings are not truly democratic because citizens simply defer to an unspoken leadership when attending them. The meetings were re-popularized by Bill Clinton's presidential campaign in 1992.

—Kevin Mattson

FURTHER READING:

Bryan, Frank, and John McClaughry. *The Vermont Papers: Recreating Democracy on a Human Scale.* Chelsea, Vermont, Chelsea Green, 1989.

Lockridge, Kenneth. *A New England Town: The First Hundred Years: Dedham, Massachusetts, 1636-1736.* New York, Norton, 1985.

Mansbridge, Jane. *Beyond Adversary Democracy*. New York, Basic Books, 1980.

Toy Story

This joint venture between Pixar Animation Studios and Walt Disney Productions was the first fully computer-animated feature-length film. Pixar's John Lasseter, who won an Academy Award for Special Achievement in honor of his leadership, directed and co-wrote the film. Disney released the film on November 22, 1995, with what has become its characteristic media blitz, spawning products as diverse as toys in Burger King Kids Meals, T-shirts, shoes, hats, and *The Toy Story Animated StoryBook*. Celebrity voices abound in the film with Tom Hanks as Woody, Tim Allen as Buzz Lightyear, and Don Rickles as Mr. Potato Head. The combination of 3D computer animation, the Disney label, and star power made for a sure-fire hit that was one of the highest-grossing films of 1995. *Toy Story* has made Woody and Buzz familiar household names, and the profits led to further collaborative projects between Disney and Pixar, including a sequel, *Toy Story II*.

—Adrienne Furness

FURTHER READING:

Kaplan, David A. "High Tech in Toon Town." *Newsweek*. December 4, 1995, pp. 54-56.

Toys

Pushed out by a celebrity-driven popular culture, beloved toys of the past, including blocks, erector sets, doll houses, trains, tops, and tea sets, have almost disappeared because of media advertising that targets children not as imaginative players but as pop culture consumer imitators. Material objects, such as *Citizen Kane*'s Rosebud, Mattel's Barbie, and Hasbro's GI Joe, are reflections of society's attitudes towards children. Toys mirror cultural notions about family and childrearing values, while concomitantly resonating with a child's inner-world of play. Thus contemporary toys mimic ideas found on television rather than creative possibilities found in a child's imagination. Children today may be able to dress Barbie in a vast array of wardrobe options, but gone are the days of popular toys that allowed a previous generation of children to build, imagine, and interact with unique forms from a more diverse range of choices, choices that were not prescribed by celebrity icons on places like television, computer, and movie screens.

Although toys have been around for thousands of years, the relationship between toys, children, and culture has shifted with the passing of time. Gary Cross, in *Kid's Stuff*, notes the discovery of 5,000-year-old dolls, balls, rattles, and ancient artifacts resembling smaller versions of adult tools and weapons. Many of these early toys and miniatures were made for religious rites or for the exclusive use of adults. Wooden Noah's Arks and fashion dolls, for example, were favorite gifts of aristocratic women in the Middle Ages, while clay soldiers and knights were a source of entertainment for adult men. Eventually these "adult toys" were given to children. Brian Sutton-Smith, in his book *Toys as Culture*, explains that play and toys

became a part of children's culture in the 1600s as a result of a decreased need for child labor combined and a new and related concern with controlling children's behavior. Play and toys began to be considered by such serious thinkers as John Locke and Jean Jacques Rousseau, who held that children were different than adults and needed protection and special activities, like play, to progress.

Changes in American domestic life facilitated the introduction of toys into the home. Over the course of the nineteenth century, work was done with greater frequency away from the house and not by children, furthering the notion that children needed to be treated differently. Toys and children's books began to claim more importance in this new children's culture of the nineteenth century, for it was thought that they could provide for the moral and intellectual development of the child.

Developing industrial and technological capacities brought innovations to the making of toys; rubber, plaster, and sheet metal made toys easier to manufacture. Germany was the largest exporter of toys in the early nineteenth century, and more than any other country was responsible for the modern world of toys. Just another dry good in the United States, toys offered gender-typed play tools for boys and dolls for girls. After the Civil War, however, chain stores like Woolworth's (1879) and Sears (1887) emerged and began to sell toys as gifts. Other stores, such as Macy's, designated specific sections of their consumer spaces for the sale of toys. FAO Schwartz opened in 1870 as a specialty retailer of toys.

Notions about the amount of toys required in children's lives changed when Christmas became a legal holiday in the mid-nineteenth century, helped along by the popularization of Santa in Clement Moore's 1823 poem, "A Visit from St. Nicholas." The promise of Santa's arrival promoted an even larger children's market. Santa added a sense of mystery and a morality theme as "His List" told him who was "naughty or nice"; at the same time, this happy image of St. Nick served to disguise the crass commercialism of the Christmas spirit. Ultimately, indulging children became part of a family's status reinforced by new advertising and commercial interests.

Toys bought for boys in the early twentieth century reflected a fascination with industrialization and technology; early "industrial" toys include Lionel trains (1906), Moline Buddy trucks (1910), Gilbert Erector sets (1913), Tinker toys, and Lincoln Logs (1916). These construction toys were the antecedent of Legos (1954), the very successful Danish Toy that allows children to follow a design or build their own creations. "Theodore Roosevelt and the Spanish American War set the stage for the development of numerous male-identified toys" explains David Brody in his dissertation, *Fantasy Realized*. The famous and durable Teddy Bear (based on Teddy Roosevelt's popularity) became a favorite as well as the Daisy Air Rifle (1898), Admiral Dewey Dolls, and the very successful, yet racist, Billikens (1912) with their Orientalized physical traits. In contrast toys for girls reflected domestic life, featuring dolls and miniature kitchen appliances. Doll companies like E. I. Horsman and Effanbee and manufacturers like Schoenhut and Steiff produced the Patsy Doll (1924), Raggedy Ann, and other companion dolls.

In 1901 John Dewey wrote about the importance of toys promoting the psychological needs of the child. Dewey ushered in a whole group of child experts in the twentieth century including the psychologist Stanley G. Hall and later the author of *Baby and Child Care*, Benjamin Spock, who promoted toys that fostered imagination and creativity. Educators, psychologists, and politicians soon had a great deal to say about childrearing and family values. Beginning in 1912, Maria Montessori began making parents aware of the importance of the objects children played with in terms of their ability to learn. Educational toys started to be promoted by a very aggressive *Parent's Magazine* (1926), whose subscribers were mainly mothers with expendable income. Urged on by such experts, parents grew interested in creating children who could navigate the more industrialized twentieth century with a greater sense of ease.

Noel Barrett, toy expert and star of PBS's *Antique Road Show,* is particularly impressed with how toys changed from what he calls "Sunday Toys with religious significance" to toys like mechanical banks, which adults could justify buying for their children since they taught thrift. Children were now considered as a special and vulnerable group in society. Toys were meant to help prepare the young for success as Playskool (1928) and Fisher-Price (1930) sold more blocks, desks, and doll houses. What was not considered by the child experts was how new developments within the realm of popular culture were impacting children's lives. As the celebrity glow of Teddy Roosevelt and Charles Lindbergh sold dolls and toy airplanes, toy makers began to look ahead to other venues for child-marketing connections.

In 1904, the Brown Shoe Company bought the exclusive rights to the popular comic strip character Buster Brown in an effort to sell more children's shoes at the World's Fair in St. Louis. It worked, and Buster also sold dolls and toys with both his and his dog's image on them. Later radio characters, like Little Orphan Annie, Tom Mix, and Jack Armstrong sold cereal and advertising premium toys. In the 1940s Captain Midnight asked children to use their Ovaltine decoder to decipher secret messages. The Dionne Quintuplets sold dolls and cutouts, as did Shirley Temple and Charlie McCarthy.

But it took a strange character, related to the rodent family, with the ears of Bing Crosby, a mouth like Martha Ray, and a high pitched squeaky voice, to really launch children's popular culture. Walt Disney understood the value of successful children's characters. Beginning in 1928, he parlayed Mickey Mouse and others like him into dolls, toys, theme parks, movies, and billions of dollars. Even before the advent of television, Disney marketed Pinocchio dolls and Snow White coloring books. When he discovered the power of TV, he produced the incredibly commercial *Mickey Mouse Club* (1955). *The Wonderful World of Disney* became the first kid's infomercial highlighting upcoming Disney toys and theme park attractions. Later films of the 1980s and 1990s such as *The Little Mermaid, Tarzan, Pocahontas, Mulan,* and *Lion King* all have their own dolls, puzzles, and tapes. The stories told are not just Disneyfied for dramatic reasons, but very often modified to sell more toys and are intensely self-referential, with each medium encouraging the involvement in the other. Each character becomes a brand that begs children to buy more. Indeed, the movies *Pocahontas* and *The Little Mermaid* featured irrelevant hair brushing scenes designed to make their heroines more appetizing for little girl doll play.

In the late 1940s, television replaced radio as children's predominant form of entertainment. Beginning in 1947 under the title *Puppet Playhouse, Howdy Doody* was the first successful children's TV show. The selling of products related to the show began in 1949 when, according to Stephen Davis author of *Say Kids What Time Is It?,* Western Printing offered a surprising royalty for a Howdy Doody Comic book. The producer thought this would be great publicity. But after 10 million comic books were sold, property rights and merchandising became the focus of the program. Howdy soon began selling cards, dolls, and toys related to the characters on the show. Scripts were modified, as children reacted in an almost Pavlovian manner to anything promoted. Princess Summer Fall Winter Spring, who was

pushed onto the stage to provide a female character, helped sell little girls untold Indian dolls and costumes. Television thus not only entertained children but shaped their consumer decisions. Sensing the power of this new media, both Hasbro, starting with Mr. Potato Head in 1951, and Mattel, with the Burp-Gun in 1955, made the decision to market on TV. As Stephen Kline points out in *Out of the Garden,* these marketing decisions revolutionized the toy industry. Up until the 1950s, yo-yos, toy tanks, Slinkys, Frisbees, play dishes, Silly putty, and cap guns held their own as companies like Marx and Ideal made their profits with efficient production techniques and little Christmas advertising. Mattel's and Hasbro's decision now tied toys to electronic images, not Santa. Toy making became a year round business, and the most highly promoted toys soon began to drive the others from the market.

Perhaps the most prominent member of this new genre of toys was Barbie, who was created by Ruth Handler, the wife and business partner of Mattel executive Elliot Handler. Ruth Handler created Barbie to fill a void in the girl's fashion doll industry. Originally discovered as a sex novelty toy in Europe, Barbie has the shape of a young woman, with long legs, large bust, and narrow waist. She reflects a teenage fantasy world, for she is beautiful and sexy, well dressed, and autonomous; Barbie has no parental ties. With her accessories and play environments she stresses the virtue of consumerism. In Barbie's world, consumerism means happiness. While not really a TV series tie-in toy, she was among the first toys to be heavily marketed by television. In the 1990s, Barbie is everywhere. Barbie's marketers use what Mattel calls a "segmentation strategy" of not one Barbie doll, but many, for different types of play. With every young girl in the country having an average of eight Barbies, she is America's most successful commercial toy.

Puppeteer Jim Henson and Joan Ganz Cooney met in 1969 and formed The Children's Television Workshop; their creations included Big Bird, Cookie Monster, Rubber Ducky, and, of course, Bert and Ernie. These amusing characters began selling letters of the alphabet, words, and pro-social values on *Sesame Street* but soon moved into dolls, toys, pajamas, and almost any other consumer good imaginable. There was even more merchandising as Henson's *Muppets* and their movies became blockbusters and Tickle Me Elmo became the most sought after Christmas toy in 1997. At a ceremony following Henson's untimely death, his daughter told a Vasser College audience that "the bond between the Muppet's characters and their ever renewing audience was the Henson's Company biggest asset."

The 1970s was the height of old time TV merchandising, as *Scooby Doo* and Hanna Barbera, with their *Jetsons* and *Flintstones,* continued the media success of children's television and licensed products. Still, the show came first and the merchandising followed. This was all to change with the 1976 release of George Lucas's *Star Wars.* From the beginning, Lucas sought to promote the interrelation between the licensed products and the movies, using the movies as a long commercial for the products and vice-versa. Using the myth-creating principles of Joseph Campbell, Lucas formed a magical universe populated by phenomenal characters like Luke Sky Walker, Hans Solo, and Princess Leia. These movies and their related products remained top sellers twenty years after their introduction and promised to surge in sales with the release of the new Star Wars movie, *The Phantom Menace* in 1999.

By 1980 Strawberry Shortcake's creators got this licensing message and acted quickly, according to Tom Engelhardt in "The Strawberry Shortcake Strategy." American Greeting Card's surveyed young girls about the qualities they would find most appealing in a doll and toy maker Kenner introduced her at the Toy Fair in New York City. Strawberry Shortcake was pink, soft, and spoke of her "berry" nice friends. One billion dollars in products sold quickly after she was given her own TV special. *My Little Pony* and *The Care Bears* (both 1983) followed with more programming and merchandising. The toys and lunch boxes now came first. Children's groups were outraged by this type of activity and a sympathetic FCC spoke out about television's obligation to children. But the deregulation of the airwaves that proceeded under the administration of President Ronald Reagan (1980-1988) brought no guidelines concerning appropriate marketing to children. As a result, the after school air waves became filled with product-driven programs like *Masters of the Universe, He-Man,* and other such shows. The new Fox Children's Network and Nickelodeon began to not only impact on a child's Saturday mornings but their after school time as well, with shows like *The Teenage Mutant Ninja Turtles* (1980s), *The Mighty Morphin Power Rangers* (1993), and *The Rugrats* (1991). Programming now became a series of infomercials where movies and live shows related to the program were promoted and every character or hideout was for sale. While networks worried about audience share during prime time, children's television advertising revenues continued to soar as new toys needed both program time-slots and commercials to be successful.

Toy production in the 1990s was dominated by two major manufacturers: Mattel, which owned Barbie, Tyco, Hot Wheels, and Fisher-Price; and Hasbro, parent to Kenner, Milton Bradley (who created the Game of Life in 1860), Playskool, Tonka (maker of trucks and Play-Doh), Coleco (Cabbage Patch Kids), and Parker Brothers. As described in G. Wayne Miller's book about the Hassenfeld family's progression from pencil manufacturer to world-wide toy maker Hasbro, *Toy Wars,* Mattel and Hasbro are huge global conglomerates locked in a bitter struggle for world toy dominance; they continuously swallow up lesser manufacturers and mass produce toys that have brand and media recognition. Their on-going battle involves stock prices and options rather than children and play, as toy executives answer only to Wall Street. Controlling the brand names in toys like Mr. Potato Head, G.I. Joe, Batman, Star Wars, Etch-a-Sketch, and Monopoly is not enough. Even the huge distributors like Toys "R" Us and Target are small time compared to a omnipresent media promoting what children should buy, as program content and advertising commingle.

At the millennium a whole new set of toy manufacturing options are becoming available. The very nature of what constitutes our previous conceptions of media-based possibilities is being radically reconfigured by cyberspace and DTV. New "Toy Stories" are emerging with the advent of on-line web sites where a child's favorite licensed characters sell toys. Children want more than a functioning toy, they want a share of the media's emphasis on celebrity, a piece of purchasable personality. This personality represents power, glamour, money, beauty, respect, and invulnerability. Information and media mega-companies fill this need with the syndication and synergy of electronic characters. Ever-growing media corporations are now our most important children's story tellers and the new toy makers.

—Michael Brody

FURTHER READING:

Brody, David. *Fantasy Realized: The Philippines, Orientalism and Imperialism in Turn-of-the-century American Visual Culture* (Ph.D. dissertation). Boston, Boston University, 1997.

Brody, Michael. "The Wonderful World of Disney: It's Psychological Appeal." *American Imago.* Vol. 33, No. 4, Winter 1976.

Cross, Gary. *Kid's Stuff.* Cambridge, Harvard University Press, 1997.

Davis, Stephen. *Say Kids! What Time Is It?* Boston, Little Brown, 1987.

Engelhardt, Tom. "The Strawberry Shortcake Strategy." In *Watching Television.* New York, Pantheon Books, 1986, 68-110.

Fleming, Dan. *Powerplay.* Manchester, Manchester University Press, 1996.

Kline, Stephen. *Out of the Garden.* London, Verso, 1993.

Miller, G. Wayne. *Toy Wars.* New York, Times Books, 1998.

Seiter, Ellen. *Sold Separately.* New Brunswick, New Jersey, Rutgers University Press, 1993.

Sutton-Smith, Brian. *Toys as Culture.* New York, Gardner Press Inc., 1986.

Winnicott, D.W. *Playing and Reality.* New York, Basic Books, 1971.

Tracy, Spencer (1900-1967)

Spencer Tracy, frequently defined by his peers as "an actor's actor," was the prime exemplar of understated acting in both comedy and drama. The unrufflable simplicity was deceptive, for beneath the surface of that craggy face and chunky frame simmered anger, passion, compassion, or grief, as the role required. It is for his famous

Spencer Tracy

on-screen partnership with his legendary off-screen love, the redoubtable Katharine Hepburn, that Tracy remains best remembered, but his other achievements in a film career that spanned thirty-seven years and some seventy-three films were substantial.

Tracy was cast in a unique mold. He achieved leading man status of the first rank without a vestige of glamour or movie-star good looks. His strikingly natural persona, combined with many of the characters he played, became a benchmark for solid values and dependability as he worked his way through a succession of priests, fathers, judges, and down-to-earth avenging angels. Avuncular, often gruff, and sometimes irascible (a reflection of his own temper), there generally lurked an understanding heart beneath the rough exterior. Stern but kindly, often with a twinkle in his eye, Tracy was a rock of integrity who, but for graying hair and the lines of age that barely disturbed his familiar face, never essentially changed in either appearance or manner.

Born in Milwaukee, Tracy was the son of a truck salesman. He was educated at a Jesuit school and initially intended to enter the ministry, but he later found he preferred dramatics and decided to become an actor. In 1922, he enrolled in the American Academy of Dramatic Arts in New York. After graduation, he embarked on a succession of menial jobs until he eventually found work in a stock company. Gradually he made it to Broadway where, in 1930, his lead performance in a successful prison drama, *The Last Mile,* caught the attention of Hollywood director John Ford, who cast him as the lead in *Up the River,* a gangster film, that same year.

The next five years were spent under contract to Fox, where Tracy made a couple of interesting films, including *The Power and the Glory* (1933), but his best roles came among the frequent loan-outs to other studios, notably in the hard-hitting *20,000 Years in Sing Sing* (1933), made for Michael Curtiz at Warner Brothers. In this film, Tracy starred as a criminal who confesses to a murder of which he is innocent, and the actor was given ample opportunity to display toughness and humanity in equal measure. Indeed, during these early years, Tracy frequently was cast as a rough-hewn character, either made good or gone to the bad. Having married in 1923 and always a devout Catholic, a guilt-ridden Tracy courted unwelcome publicity in the early 1930s when his affair with Loretta Young was revealed in the scandal sheets. When, in 1935, he was arrested for drunkenness, Fox fired him. MGM hired him and, in time, provided fertile ground for a rich crop of roles that established Tracy as a star.

His first major success at MGM was as the man who survives an unjust lynching and seeks vengeance in Fritz Lang's powerful drama *Fury* in 1936, the same year he played the priest in *San Francisco* and earned his first Oscar nomination. He won the Oscar the following year for his role as the Portuguese sailor protecting Freddie Bartholomew in *Captains Courageous* and in 1938 became the first actor to win two in a row when he was again voted best actor as Father Flanagan in *Boys Town*—the first of his biopics.

In 1942 the Tracy-Hepburn collaboration began with *Woman of the Year,* in which his sports reporter and her politician, wonderfully ill-matched, fall in love. The film set the tone for the most successful and popular of their films together as sparring partners in the battle of the sexes, competitive, witty, sometimes acidic, but always affectionate. In Frank Capra's political comedy *State of the Union* (1948) Tracy is a presidential candidate, Hepburn his estranged wife; in George Cukor's *Adam's Rib* (1949) they are married lawyers on opposite sides of an attempted murder case; in Cukor's *Pat and Mike* (1952), she is a sporting phenomenon, he a sports promoter of dubious connections who sets out to exploit her money-making

potential. *Without Love* (1945), an uncertain romance from a failed Broadway play, sank without a trace (the only one to do so), while there were more serious but less popular excursions with Cukor's *Keeper of the Flame* (1942), Tracy impressive as a reporter destroying the reputation of a dead politician, and *Sea of Grass* (1947), a brooding drama with Tracy cast as a work-obsessed cattle tycoon.

In 1950, directed by Vincente Minnelli, Tracy played the gruff, bumbling, and put-upon *Father of the Bride* to daughter Elizabeth Taylor, a huge hit which won him an Oscar nomination and was followed by a hit sequel, *Father's Little Dividend* (1951), but quality vehicles were growing thinner and, correspondingly, so were the memorable performances. The only truly noteworthy contributions to the 1950s were his political campaigner in John Ford's *The Last Hurrah* and his one-armed, dark-suited avenger in John Sturges's *Bad Day at Black Rock* (1955). Descending on a crumbling one-horse outpost to unearth a terrible secret and seek justice, Tracy was never better than in this superb Western morality tale, unconquerable, implacable, ironic, compassionate, and heroic. It earned him a third Academy nomination, and there was a fourth for *The Old Man and The Sea* (1958).

The 1960s brought the onset of illness. During his last years, Tracy grew increasingly moody and difficult to work with, and producers shied away from using him. An exception was Stanley Kramer, and it was for him that the actor gave his impressive last three performances: a thinly disguised Clarence Darrow defending in an equally thinly disguised Scopes Trial in *Inherit the Wind* (1960), the presiding judge wrestling with the Nazi legacy in *Judgment at Nuremberg* (1961), and, in a last glorious reunion with Hepburn, another irascible, bewildered, and tender-hearted father in *Guess Who's Coming to Dinner?* Already very ill, Tracy died a few weeks after filming was completed.

—Robyn Karney

FURTHER READING:

Davidson, Bill. *Spencer Tracy, Tragic Idol.* New York, Dutton, 1987.

Fisher, James. *Spencer Tracy: A Bio-Bibliography.* Connecticut, Greenwood Publishing, 1994.

Kanin, Garson. *Tracy and Hepburn: An Intimate Memoir.* New York, Bantam, 1972.

Tozzi, Romano. *Spencer Tracy: 1900-1967.* New York, Galahad Books, 1973.

Trading Stamps

Trading stamps are small pieces of glue-backed colored paper, given in proportion to purchases made and redeemable for merchandise. They were first used in the United States in Schuster's Department Store in Milwaukee, Wisconsin, in 1890. Schuster's gave the stamps to customers paying in cash in an effort to limit credit use. The S&H Green Stamp Co. attributes their invention to their founders (the Sperry and Hutchinson of S&H) in 1896 as a way to "say thank-you" to customers and calls the trading stamps "America's first frequent shopper program and grandfather of marketing promotions such as frequent flyer miles." The first S&H redemption center opened in 1897 as a kiosk. One of the earliest items in the catalog was a Bissell carpet sweeper; its modern counterpart was still in the catalog 100 years later.

The heyday of the trading stamp came during the 1950s and 1960s when large numbers of Americans got the stamps with their groceries and exchanged filled books (usually 1500-3000 stamps) for a variety of household goods. At the height of stamp fever, S&H distributed its catalogs free in supermarkets and operated multiple redemption centers, the size of small shops, in towns all over the United States. They claim that in 1964 its catalog was the largest single publication in the United States.

S&H Green Stamps, Top Value, King Korn, Triple S, Gold Bell, and Plaid were among the most popular nationally circulated brands of stamps. Attesting to the pop chic of trading stamps, artist Andy Warhol painted a series of S&H green stamps posters along the lines of his famous Campbell Soup works.

As consumers opted for lower prices in lieu of stamps in the 1970s and 1980s the movement waned but never disappeared. One of the last major grocery chains to carry the stamps was the Publix chain in Florida, which dropped them in favor of coupons and other promotions that were less costly to the store. A 1988 study in the *Academy of Marketing Science Journal* notes that a survey of retail stores showed that stores that gave trading stamps had significantly lower gross profit margins and net profit returns than did stores that did not.

At the end of the twentieth century, the consumer's persistent desire to be tangibly rewarded for patronage continued in other forms—frequent flier miles, the return of percentages of credit card purchases—but only a few retail establishments offered actual trading stamps. The stamp movement tried to keep pace with changes in technology. Although S&H continued to distribute stamps and offer merchandise catalogs, they began to offer "paperless green stamps" saved on an ID card and added automatically at the register. In addition to redemption for gifts in the catalog, the stamps could be used to save in the store, as coupons for entertainment, frequent flyer miles, and donations toward a charity or community project.

—Joan Leotta

FURTHER READING:

Lynn, Judy, and Bobby Vaught. "Three Different Variables and Their Relation to Retail Strategy." *Academy of Marketing Science Journal.* Vol. 16, Fall 1998.

Trailer Parks

Any film or television program refers to certain "stock" devices to create a chosen visual and emotional environment. A frequent image in modern culture is a tightly-packed row of homes, similar in style and each with a tiny fragment of land, which serves for parking, storage, recreation, gardening, and decoration. The homes follow the model of the tight suburb, but they are not American ranch houses. This image is dominated by rectangular trailers, most of which have removed wheels or at least concealed them with a trelice covering. During its history, the trailer, or mobile home, has been viewed as progressive, adventurous, and, finally, as the opposite of these American ideals. Today, when a director or producer incorporates the trailer park into a visual narrative, she seeks most often to depict Americans locked in—spiritually and physically—to a lower economic class by

social strictures. Some call the trailer park America's modern tenement; yet, the trailer park's existence also suggests one of the nation's most democratic achievements—home ownership available to all classes.

The enlightened thought of Thomas Jefferson helped to make personal home ownership an American ideal. As they configured capitalist thought, economic philosophers/visionaries Adam Smith and Thomas Hobbes incorporated property value into the scheme by making personal land ownership possible within enlightened societies at the end of the 1700s. The owner could then increase the value by "improving" the property so that it would be sold for a higher price. This philosophy made up the foundation for Jefferson's dream of an agrarian republic, full of small property owners who each tended (and improved) his own land. The American housing ideal has not ventured too far from these foundations over 200 years of development. Urban growth has provided alternative models—such as apartments and condos—but the ideal of the vast majority of Americans is to own their own home. Rising home prices after 1950 forced developers to construct a new version of this ideal that would involve classes previously unable to own their own property. The effort to appeal to lower and lower-middle class American urges for home ownership bred the trailer park.

The trailer grew out of Americans' early-twentieth-century impulse to travel the nation by automobile. The trailer-camper allowed complete freedom to pull over at any time and enjoy the comforts of home. This travel filled an important void when services were few, and allowed many Americans to reject the rapidity and regiment of train travel for the slow, wandering travel of the open road. Prior to the spread of hotels and following the proliferation of automobile ownership, roadside camping offered the most reliable form of comfort during travel. An autocamper's outfit was an instant hotel to which one had to add only water. "Just back off the main road," instructs one guide, "in a little grove of white birches on the bank of a noisy brook, which will furnish water and perchance fish enough to fill the breakfast frying pan!" While tents remained the most popular implement for car camping, the trailer grew in popularity from 1920 to 1950. By tent or trailer, car camping spread from fad to institution during this era, giving form to the autocamp: an open site in which campers pooled together. A unique culture rapidly grew out of such sites, particularly the male effort to assess and rate others' camping equipment and technology. Not dissimilar from the shared space of the modern trailer park, campers interacted with others whenever they left the cover of their tent or trailer. In the autocamps, the travelers discussed other sites, the road, and equipment. Out of such ingenuity, the "gypsy-trailer form" began standardized manufacture after 1920.

Cabin camping also grew in popularity during the inter-war years; by 1935, however, the nation was most enthused with the evolving trailer technology. Between 1935 and 1937, popular articles included "Back to the Covered Wagon," "Nation of Nomads," "Tin-Canners," "Nomads of the Road," "Home of the Free," and many other related topics. Futurists even began to predict that every American would soon live permanently in a cheap trailer. Their thinking revolved around the common sense of such mobility as well as the Depression-era thoughts of limiting waste. The trailer, after all, offered Americans the fulfillment of their most basic needs of shelter and safety, with few unnecessary frills. Modernist thinkers rallied around this model as the wave for the standardized future—the geodesic dome with wheels. Such thinkers, however, overlooked Americans' unique cultural preferences. Americans who could still afford

A mobile home/trailer park in Wyoming.

nicer homes would want them. But the trailer offered possibilities for those of lesser means. As developers created standardized suburbs for the middle and upper-middle class from 1950 to 1980, the same drive for conformity and ownership fueled the construction of the first trailer parks. Now, of course, the sites were not for transients who would take their trailer and leave in the morning; they were not, however, intended as end homes. The mobility behind the trailer park was economic: developers assumed young families would use them as a temporary home while saving for their suburban dream home.

Used originally as temporary housing, trailer parks became noticeable to most Americans after World War II, when they were clustered around Army posts and construction sites. Today, mobile home parks are not temporary aberrations on the landscape. More than 13 million Americans, most of them from young blue-collar families, call trailers their temporary homes. Few Americans or architectural historians are willing to consider such mobile homes dwellings. Critics stress that the trailer is not architecture; instead, it is an industrial product, mass-produced, low-cost, and disposable. By-passing craftsmen, the trailer comes out of a midwestern factory by truck almost ready for occupancy. The attraction, of course, is the low cost of the trailer, compared even to the smallest house. Standardized suburban homes, such as the bungalow, have achieved dwelling status; but the mobile home remains without a place in our architectural lexicon. Quite literally, most communities also exclude trailer

parks from the mainstream, relegating them to the least desirable tracts of land, such as along rail lines, highways, or flood areas. Additionally, the odd transience of the trailer place it outside of taxation and even standard land ownership. The trailer park is not dissimilar from the autocamps of the early twentieth century: ordinarily, residents own their trailer but only lease or rent the plot on which it rests. The home, though, will normally remain at the site long after residents move.

At once, the trailer park represents the proliferation of American ideals of ownership to all economic classes and also a culture of exclusion and transience. The trailer park, then, clearly becomes ironic as it begins young families on the track to owning their own home while also divorcing them from enduring community connections. As the media reported the housing crisis of the 1970s, it also helped to create the enduring stereotypes of trailer parks. Townhouses and trailers were consistently presented as inadequate, makeshift substitutes for detached suburban dwellings. The new alternatives were posed as a threat to the postwar suburban ideal. Currently, between 50 and 70 percent of American communities ban mobile homes from privately owned lots in residential neighborhoods. This restricts Americans who may only be able to afford a mobile home to reside within the lowly trailer park. Over half of the nation's mobile homes are sited in parks, surrounded by high walls required by local codes. It is likely that the trailer park, a construction of modern, industrial sensibilities, will remain ''lower-class'' squatter settlements into the future.

—Brian Black

FURTHER READING:

Belasco, Warren James. *Americans on the Road.* Cambridge, MIT Press, 1981.

Jackson, John Brinckerhoff. *A Sense of Place, a Sense of Time.* New Haven, Yale University Press, 1994.

Wright, Gwendolyn. *Building the Dream.* Cambridge, MIT Press, 1981.

Tramps

The tramp or hobo (the tramp's name for himself) refers to a wandering foot traveler, often a vagrant, thief, or beggar with no fixed abode or destination. The term hobo, originally a migratory American worker hitching rides on freight trains, has disappeared as modern society increasingly controlled the outcast individuals who chose the itinerant or homeless life.

In the 1870s, American Civil War veterans and immigrants swelled the ranks of unemployed boys and men traveling from job to job, and the ''tramp menace'' alarmed newspaper editorialists and civic leaders concerned about the growing number of homeless vagrants descending on towns and cities. Tramps were often driven from town or sentenced to the jail or the workhouse for vagrancy; even skilled craftsmen, such as itinerant or tramp printers, were unwelcome in small towns. Allan Pinkerton, the legendary American detective, warned of the danger tramps posed in his 1878 book *Strikers, Communists and Tramps.* But tramps found in the new railroad system mobility to seek work in harvests, lumberjacking, mining, or construction projects.

Hostility to the independent tramp may be found as early as St. Benedict's rule in 535 A.D. against the *girovagi* or wandering monks for whom religious life was but a pretense, and who led their lives

A homeless man.

without restraint or obedience to church authority. The Elizabethan Poor law of 1603 also condemned England's wandering, sturdy beggars, as did early American courts. By 1700 Boston selectmen, for example, warned migrant strangers or vagabonds to leave town and refused them public charity.

By the Victorian era the hobo had become a fixture in the American circus; perhaps the most famous hobo clown was Emmett Kelly (1898-1979), who portrayed Weary Willie the Hobo on television and in films such as The Greatest Show on Earth (1952). In silent movies, Charlie Chaplin's Little Tramp was his signature character in seventy films such as *The Kid* (1921) and *The Gold Rush* (1925). Another famous tramp clown was Red Skelton's television character Freddie the Freeloader in the 1950s and 1960s. In the theater of the absurd, Samuel Beckett's *Waiting for Godot* (1954) portrayed two pensive tramps on a country road musing about the nature of human existence. American literature celebrated the romantic hobo or tramp life, from Mark Twain's *Huckleberry Finn* (1884) to Beat Generation writer Jack Kerouac's *On The Road* (1957) and *Dharma Bums* (1958), as well as in folk music by the Industrial Workers of the World (the IWW or Wobblies) and troubadours like Woody Guthrie and Pete Seeger. Harry Kemp (1883-1960), the hobo poet, wrote autobiographical poems and narratives about his tramp adventures. But other works documented the grim reality of the hobo life, as in Jack London's *The Tramp* (1911) and George Orwell's *Down and Out in Paris and London* (1933).

During the Depression of the 1930s, the number of tramps increased dramatically as more than a million homeless men, women, girls, and boys rode the rails and lived in hobo jungles in search of work or adventure. By that era, reformers such as Father Edward Flanagan, who opened the Workingmen's Hotel and Boys' Town in Omaha, and Dorothy Day, who established the Catholic Worker Movement in New York, addressed serious social problems associated with tramping. By the 1980s homelessness was recognized as a major social issue in the United States when a rapid increase in people without adequate housing reached one million. Many of these contemporary tramps are young or mentally ill, unlike the older white alcoholic men found earlier in skid-row flophouse hotels.

The movies *Boxcar Bertha* (1972) and *Ironweed* (1987) celebrate female hoboes. Hollywood featured hoboes in socially conscious movies, *Wild Boys of the Road* (1933) and *Sullivan's Travels* (1941), and later in *Joe Hill* (1971), *Emperor of the North* (1973), and *Bound for Glory* (1976). Most tramp songs glorify the freedom of the open road and the autonomy of the hobo life while overlooking its chronic poverty, hunger, violence, and insecurity.

The bum, a sedentary beggar who avoids work, is a variant of the tramp or hobo. This derogatory name originated in the German word *bummler*, or loafer. In the 1860s it meant a foraging soldier, and later to loaf, beg, or wander like a vagabond or tramp. By the 1890s it referred to a hobo hitching a ride on a freight train. In the 1920s it came to mean ejection from a saloon via the bum's rush, or inferior quality as in a bum job. By the 1960s it referred to resort habitués such as the beach bum or ski bum. Today, however, the tramp tradition survives in the annual National Hobo Convention at Britt, Iowa, and in the memory of men and women who last rode the rails in the Great Depression of the 1930s.

—Peter C. Holloran

FURTHER READING:

Brevada, William. *Harry Kemp, the Last Bohemian.* Lewisburg, Pennsylvania, Bucknell University Press, 1986.

Flynt, Josiah. *Tramping with Tramps.* Montclair, New Jersey, Patterson Smith, 1972.

Gray, Frank. *The Tramp, His Meaning and Being.* London, J. M. Dent, 1931.

Orwell, George. *Down and Out in Paris and London.* New York, Harcourt Brace Jovanovich, 1933.

Traveling Carnivals

In American culture, the traveling carnival evokes all things seamy, dubious, and lurid. In their heyday, some three hundred different traveling carnivals roamed the United States offering a glimpse of mystery and excitement, and sometimes danger. It was the rare child who did not think of joining a traveling carnival or circus to escape a stultifying small-town environment. The carnival was the poor man's entertainment. An egalitarian institution, carnivals practiced equal-opportunity speculation, and thus acquired a reputation for trickery and deceit, if not outright fraud, and as a consequence of America's developing network of train lines and highways, these carnivals were able to penetrate the most remote backwaters of the country. The carnival remains one of America's most enduring cultural institutions.

The United States, being a young country, has long had fairly primitive tastes in entertainment. For the better part of the nineteenth century, entertainment in rural America consisted of traveling circuses and burlesque troops, vaudeville and magic-lantern shows, all traversing the country by train or horse-and-buggy, offering temporary relief from the boredom of country life. The showmen were both exalted and disdained; occupants of an insular class, they were much maligned but envied for their carefree lifestyle. Cities contained a richer palette of diversions, but actors and showmen were no less scorned there. Going to dime museums exhibiting freaks of nature, magic acts, or flea circuses was a popular pastime with the people, and in the latter half of the century, resort towns located near urban centers sprang up to accommodate a growing middle class. Resort entertainment choices mirrored those of the city, with freak shows, burlesque, and primitive amusement parks relocating for the summer season. From these disparate entertainments, the traveling carnival emerged. It was an ad-hoc gathering of shows and concessions that traveled under the casual imprimatur of a manager or showman who handled the business end of things, and was responsible for hiring and firing acts.

Most histories credit the 1893 Chicago World's Fair—which brought together the largest agglomeration of showmen ever assembled up to that point—with the traveling carnival's origination. Along the Midway Plaisance, an avenue at the fair's periphery, the freak shows, games of chance, burlesque, wild west shows, and other more unsavory diversions assembled, and their close proximity led many of the showmen to compare notes on their business. "The showmen working the Midway Plaisance," writes Robert Bogdan, "not only shared the same grounds and experiences but even met to discuss common problems . . . it was in the area around Buffalo Bill's Wild West Show, that the idea for a collective amusement company was first discussed."

Otto Schmidt, a participant in these meetings, organized the Chicago Midway Plaisance Amusement Company, and he and his acts set out on a tour of the Northeast. The show featured thirteen attractions, some direct form the Midway Plaisance, but failed to make its final booking in New Orleans, folding due to poor organization and business practices. Nevertheless, it provided the model for a new type of traveling amusement—part circus, part amusement park—and several showmen from Schmidt's troupe revamped the idea with success, going on to operate some of the first traveling carnivals.

From spring to fall of 1902, seventeen carnivals toured the United States. They pitched their tents in empty fields or vacant lots, or were booked in conjunction with state and county fairs, these having become a welcome diversion for the small towns that served as the center of isolated farm communities. By 1905, there were forty-six traveling carnivals plying their trade. By 1937, an estimated three hundred different shows traversed the country.

The average carnival consisted of a circular avenue, the midway (the name derived from that of the avenue leading to the big top in a circus), ringed by the different attractions and circumscribing the rides and food vendors within a circular enclosure of colorful tents. Among the different attractions, a pre-World War II carnival would invariably include a model show, where naked (if the police could be sufficiently bribed) or scantily clad young women were exhibited behind a see-through fabric; a sex exhibit in which grift was especially common (anything even loosely associated with sex— fetuses preserved in formaldehyde, anatomical aids, or caged guinea pigs— could suffice); a palm reader; a dance pavilion; games of chance; food concessions; and, of course, the rides.

The rides were usually owned and operated by the carnivals manager, and they provided a constant draw, an insurance against the vagaries of local jurisprudence, which often prohibited many acts from performing, or made grift a difficult and hazardous endeavor. Most carnivals would also include a free act, usually some spectacular dare-devil stunt, for instance, plunging off a tower into a small pool of water. This act was performed at the peak hour of carnival business, providing a climax and focal point to the day's events. If the rides were the bread-and-butter of a carnival, games of chance were the jam. Extremely lucrative for the concessionaire, when the police would allow them, games of chance were in great part to blame for the carnival's dubious reputation, and a frequent source of animosity between the townies and the carnies. The games were almost always rigged, and the "marks" duped out of a considerable amount of cash. Where the police were vigilant, vendors laid off the "grift." Where gambling was illegal or heavily frowned upon, the games paid off in "slum," or trinkets.

Every carnival featured a freak show, often called a "ten-in-one" or "string show," consisting of a number of different acts appearing in a single tent. The freak show provided the mystery to a carnival and, although now moribund as an institution, it remains of abiding interest, with freak show paraphernalia commanding high prices by collectors. Most shows had at least one genuine *lusus naturae*—a fat woman, a living skeleton, Siamese twins—and a number of "made" acts. These ranged from outright frauds—a wild man of Borneo (or geek) who might have grown up in Brooklyn, or a mind-reader who worked his dazzling clairvoyance by means of an elaborate code—to acts that were semi-legitimate. Tattooed men, torture acts, sword-swallowers, and snake charmers were the most common sort of act, constituting a sort of middle class of the carnival

world; they ranked slightly lower than nature's aristocrat, the freak, but far above the lowly geek.

To attract an audience, a "talker," a quick-talking announcer, would gather a crowd, attracted by the talker's "pitch" as well as by the exhibitions, several of whom would appear with him on the "bally platform" giving short demonstrations. This was called "turning the tip." Once the tip had been turned, that is, lured into paying the entrance fee, they would be further induced to buy cheap merchandise—photos, pamphlets, and the like—and then to pay an additional fee to see the "blow-off," a genuine freak—a fat man or woman, a bearded lady, pin-heads, or victims of other birth defects. A good "blow-off" could underwrite the operating expenses of a ten-in-one, therefore, freaks were a highly valued commodity.

Carnival life fostered an us-and-them attitude. You were either "with it" (in the know), or a mark. There was no middle ground, and sometimes pitched battles, deemed "clems" by the carnies, would erupt. Often small-town carnival-goers were simply suspicious, and often the fights started after the games of chance had bled them dry. In small town America of 1930s, it was simply second-nature to distrust the carnies. And yet, the lurid quality of the carnival, the danger of being swindled, appears to have been part of the attraction. Carnival and carny alike were exotic, simultaneously feared and envied. The carnies rejection of the "normal" world, of proper society, was an affront, but it was also an invitation. In the midst of the Great Depression, when the traveling carnivals were at their most popular, customers could still be counted on to spend their hard-earned pennies. Perhaps it was because escape from the hardship of everyday life had assumed a monumental importance for the hard-pressed citizenry.

After World War II, the number of carnivals in operation dropped substantially. No one single reason can account for their precipitous decline. Perhaps it was that small-town audiences had become more sophisticated; perhaps changing social mores diminished the popularity of the freak show; or perhaps it was simply that society had become more regimented, and the escape carnivals represented had become anomalous. In addition, corporatism had invaded the carnival world. The result is today's pallid excuse for a carnival: no freak shows, games of chance that pay off in worthless trinkets, and not even a faint hint of danger or sex. The forbidden, as much a part of the carnival mystique as cotton candy or the smell of sawdust, had been excised from the carnival, and without the danger, the fun and excitement was simply less alluring.

But the image of the carnival remains powerfully alluring. Carnival paraphernalia—banners and promotional materials—are now much sought-after by collectors. In literature, as well, the carnival works its distinctive magic. By cleverly inverting the carnival-goer's presumption of fraud, Charles G. Finney's novel, *The Circus of Dr. Lao* (1935), wrote of a traveling circus in which all the attractions are fantastically real, yet the townies fail to see past their suspicions. Katherine Dunn's best-selling novel, *Geek Love* about a family of carnival freaks, purposefully deformed *in utero*, captured the public imagination in the late 1980s, becoming a best-seller. Since Todd Browning's 1932 masterpiece, *Freaks*, the carnival has routinely appeared in motion pictures, and its appearance is usually metaphor for subterfuge and betrayal. More recent films such as *Carny* (1980) treat the wayward carny with more affection, but one need only read David Foster Wallace's essay, "Getting Away from Being Pretty Much Away from It All," to comprehend the slightly sinister quality of the carnival and its workers.

Carnivals conjure up a host of associations in American culture. Heirs to both the showmanship of a Wild Bill Hickock and the entertaining mendacity of the snake-oil salesman, carnivals tap deeply into the American psyche: its restlessness, its love/hate relationship with conformity, its romance with all things criminal. The carnival was a non-judgmental environment where the deformed, the drifter, the loser could find a place that would accept him unconditionally; it was a metaphor for freedom from troubles, from the mundane, and into a magical world where the rule is that things aren't always what they seem.

—Michael Baers

FURTHER READING:

Bogdan, Robert. *Freak Show: Presenting the Human Oddities for Amusement and Profit.* Chicago, University of Chicago Press, 1988.

Dunn, Katherine. *Geek Love.* New York, Knopf, 1989.

Finney, Charles G. *The Circus of Dr. Lao.* New York, Viking, 1935.

Gorham, Maurice. *Showmen and Suckers.* London, Percival Marshall, 1951.

Hall, Ward. *Struggles and Triumphs of a Modern Day Showman.* Sarasota, Carnival, 1981.

Mannix, Daniel P. *Memoirs of a Sword Swallower.* San Francisco, V/Search, 1996.

McKennon, Joe. *A Pictorial History of the American Carnival.* Sarasota, Carnival, 1972.

Wallace, David Foster. *A Supposedly Fun Thing I'll Never Do Again: Essays and Arguments.* Boston, Little Brown, 1997.

Travolta, John (1954—)

There are two John Travoltas. One is the late 1970s star who rose to the dizzy heights of worldwide fame thanks to his roles in *Saturday Night Fever* (1977) and *Grease* (1978). The other is the actor who was reborn from the embers of his cooling popularity thanks to Quentin Tarantino's cult mega-hit *Pulp Fiction* (1994). Other facets of John Travolta include his membership of the much-questioned Church of Scientology—seemingly the secret of his perseverance against all odds in his road towards permanent fame—and his early image as a dancing and singing idol.

Travolta's first taste of stardom came with his role as Tony Manero in John Badham's *Saturday Night Fever*. This film followed Travolta's noted appearances in the TV series *Welcome Back Kotter*, as high-school troublemaker Vinnie Barbarino (1975-6); the TV tearjerker, *The Boy in the Plastic Bubble* (1976); and in the first adaptation of a Stephen King novel, director Brian de Palma's *Carrie* (1976), in which Travolta played a sadistic classmate of the victimized heroine. *Saturday Night Fever,* the film that came to epitomize the booming disco culture of the 1970s, created a sweeping worldwide craze around Travolta—complete with countless dancing imitators vying for fame in Manero's famous cheap, white, three-piece suit. It also gave Travolta his first nomination for an Oscar as Best Actor. The second would come years later for his supporting role as Vincent Vega in *Pulp Fiction.*

Among his many admirers, actress Bette Davis remarked that although Travolta was talented, he would not last. Davis' prophetic

John Travolta in a scene from the film *Saturday Night Fever.*

words proved, if not true, at least remarkably accurate. The role of Tony Manero was followed by the very popular Danny Zuko of *Grease,* a musical Travolta knew well from his early theater days—in which he became a teenage cult icon with Olivia Newton-John—and *Urban Cowboy*'s Bud (1980). But the 1980s proved much less congenial to Travolta's supple talent and he was relegated to a string of mediocre films that did badly at the box office. The first signs of his renewed popularity came with the popular but insubstantial *Look Who's Talking* trilogy (1989, 1990, 1993), which was punctuated by Travolta's ineffectual resurrection of Tony Manero in Sylvester Stallone's *Staying Alive* (1993).

Just when Travolta seemed definitively condemned to playing uninspired roles like the James Ubriacco of *Look Who's Talking* for the rest of his acting life, Quentin Tarantino stepped in, convincing his much adored idol to play heroine fiend hit man Vincent Vega. Travolta's return was but one of the ingredients that turned *Pulp Fiction* into a massive hit, and the film placed the tarnished star back into the top list of Hollywood icons. Since 1994 Travolta has hardly had time to savor the sweet taste of his success, as he has been busy working non-stop in films of a varied range. His performances include an action villain in *Broken Arrow* (1996), a gangster-cum-producer in *Get Shorty* (1996), a mechanic turned supernatural hero in *Phenomenon* (1996), a devoted de-faced FBI agent in *Face Off* (1997), and even the contradictory roles of angel in *Michael* (1996) and the Bill Clinton-inspired character Governor Jack Stanton in *Primary Colors* (1998).

Travolta has amply displayed both his abilities as an actor and his understanding of the vagaries of show business, securing a sheltered financial position for himself that has allowed him to weather the difficult years in comfort. As a cultural phenomena, Travolta's career further begs the question: To what degree are actors shaped by the roles they play? As with Julia Roberts and *Pretty Woman,* it is unclear whether Travolta made the roles he played in films such as *Saturday Night Live* and *Grease* unique, or whether these unique roles made him. Like all other contemporary Hollywood big names, Travolta is subjected to a system in which the individual talent of each performer is very hard to assess, as acting is but one ingredient in the complex process of filmmaking. His popularity, like that of many other major stars, results from a capricious combination of talent, adroit choosing of roles, availability, luck and the mysterious ''x'' factor, best defined as being in the right place at the right time. And finally, Tarantino's idolization of Travolta, which perhaps had a touch of irony, appears to be a crucial factor, without which Travolta would not be the star he is at the end of the twentieth century.

—Sara Martin

FURTHER READING:

Amis, Martin. ''Travolta's Second Act.'' *The New Yorker*. February 20-27, 1995, 212-16.

Andrews, Nigel. *Travolta: The Life*. London, Bloomsbury, 1998.

Clarkson, Wendy. *John Travolta: Back in Character*. New York, Overlook Press, 1997.

Cohn, N. ''Rebound for Glory.'' *Vogue*. October, 1994, 191-92.

Millea, H. ''Stayin' Alive.'' *Premiere*. August, 1996, 54-60.

Schruers, F. ''Travolta: The *Rolling Stone* Interview.'' *Rolling Stone*. February 22, 1996, 40-43.

The Treasure of the Sierra Madre

Long acknowledged as a classic of Hollywood cinema, director John Huston's 1948 film *The Treasure of the Sierra Madre* was among the first to make extensive use of on-location shooting and anticipated the themes that would come to characterize film noir: paranoia, greed, and duplicity. The virtue of the film is that it can be understood on a variety of levels—as an adventure story, as an etiology of one man's mental disease, as a subtle critique of capitalism, or as an anthropologic study of the clash of cultures. Laced with disturbing psychological truths, it is precisely the fable-like quality of the film—the timeless and acute observation of human nature—that makes the film so remarkable. Huston won Oscars for best direction and screenplay, and his father, Walter, for best supporting actor.

In the Mexican town of Tampico, booming oil fields have attracted adventurers from every continent, lured by the scent of easy money. Fred C. Dobbs (Humphrey Bogart) is a drifter of dubious temperament who has bottomed out in Tampico but stills dreams of the big score—he covets luxury but has not the patience or perseverance to work for it. As the first scene shows, Dobbs is unscrupulous; he repeatedly panhandles from a wealthy American (played by John Huston) and then uses the money for such unnecessary luxuries as a haircut, buying lottery cards, and coffee. After teaming up with another young American, Bob Curtin (Tim Holt), and an aging prospector, Howard (Walter Huston), who has dazzled the younger men with stories of rich gold deposits in the surrounding mountains, he sets out on a quest for riches that will ultimately prove his undoing.

A book cover of *The Treasure of the Sierra Madre*.

Dobbs is the weak link in the chain. Curtin and Howard, although not paragons of virtue, are basically decent, realistic individuals. In one scene, the three discuss what they will do with their newfound wealth; Howard plans to open a business to sustain him in his old age: Curtin dreams of buying a farm. Dobbs, on the other hand, thinks only of the luxuries and women he will buy, and the people he will impress. The more gold they find, the further Dobbs descends into a delusional world—gold fever, as prospectors call it—in which his compatriots are mortal enemies. Every incident becomes proof of his partners' duplicity. For example, Dobbs becomes convinced Curtin is hunting for his stash, when in fact, he has unwittingly stumbled upon a gila monster and is trying to drive it off. Curtin dares Dobbs to put his hand under the rock. Dobbs hesitates, and Curtin kills the reptile.

Further evidence of Dobbs's evaporating morality is evidenced when an American, Cody, who has followed Curtin back from a trip to restock supplies wishes to join in their venture. Curtin, though unhappy, is amenable to the proposal, but Dobbs is adamantly opposed—he wants to kill the newcomer. It remains for Howard to cast his vote, and he has reluctantly sided with Dobbs when Mexican bandits—who had earlier waylaid the prospectors' train—stumble on the encampment, claiming to be *Federales*. In the ensuing melee (the source of the famous quote ''Badges? We ain't got no badges. We don't need no badges. I don't have to show you any stinking badges.''), Cody is killed, and the prospectors find a letter to his wife in his pocket. Curtin and Howard resolve to give a share of their gold to Cody's widow, but Dobbs abstains, saying, "You two must've been born in a revival meeting."

The Treasure of the Sierra Madre is a morality play, and Dobbs is its Richard III, undone by his own instability. After Howard is temporarily separated from the two younger men, the last restraint on Dobbs's behavior is removed. Dobbs attacks Curtin, who manages to disarm his attacker, but then finds himself captive to Dobbs's psychosis, keeping watch over him until he can no longer stay awake. Dobbs seizes his chance and guns Curtin down. As he sits before the fire, his face enveloped in the flames, he is consumed by his madness as the flames dance about him: "Conscience—what a thing—if you believe you got a conscience, it'll pester you to death . . . but if you don't believe ya got one . . . what can it do to ya?'' Appropriately, Dobbs meets his fate at the hands of his brother in bestiality, Jefe the bandit leader, who kills him, seizing the burros and provisions, and discarding the gold, which the bandits take for sand. The gold dust scatters in the wind. "O laugh, Curtin, old boy," cries Howard, when the two men (Curtin having escaped death) find the empty bags. "It's a great joke played on us by the Lord or fate or nature or whoever you prefer . . . but whoever or whatever played it certainly had a sense of humor!''

Psychiatrist Harvey R. Greenberg has written that *The Treasure of the Sierra Madre* "is much more than a clinical vignette of a diseased personality driven mad by gold. It is, by turns, the story of a young man's coming of age, of an aging man's search for his last resting place. It is a rousing adventure tale, a subtle commentary on the capitalist mentality . . . But I am always drawn back to Dobbs himself, to this mean-spirited, vicious, yet strangely sympathetic figure." Paranoids litter the literature of western man—Richard III, Lady Macbeth, Rebekka West in Ibsen's *Rosmersholm*. It is a testament to Huston's ability as a storyteller and the breadth of his psychological insight that 50 years after its making, *The Treasure of the Sierra Madre* is still a powerful, convincing film. Dobbs has become one of the most memorable anti-heroes in film history, not because he is a villain, but because in his madness there lurks something all audience members can recognize. Dobbs is a reminder that the real villain is most often within.

—Michael Baers

FURTHER READING:

Cooper, Stephen, editor. *Perspectives on John Huston.* Boston, G.K. Hall, 1994.

Greenberg, Harvey R., M.D. *The Movies on Your Mind: Film Classics on the Couch, From Fellini to Frankenstein.* New York, E.P. Dutton, 1975.

Madsen, Axel. *John Huston.* New York, Doubleday, 1978.

Miller, Gabriel. *Screening the Novel: Rediscovering American Fiction in Film.* New York, Frederick Ungar Publishing, 1980.

Pratley, Gerald. *The Cinema of John Huston.* South Brunswick, A.S. Barnes, 1977.

Thomas, Sam, editor. *Best American Screenplays.* New York, Crown, 1990.

Traven, B. *The Treasure of the Sierra Madre.* New York, Knopf, 1935.

Treviño, Lee (1939—)

In 1968, Lee Treviño became the first Mexican American to win a major professional golf championship at the U.S. Open, and he became the first player in history to shoot all four rounds of the event under par. Born in Dallas, Texas, and raised by his mother, who worked as a housekeeper, and his maternal grandfather, a grave digger, Treviño got involved in golf because their four-room farmhouse overlooked the back of the Glen Lakes Country Club fairways. As a boy, Treviño studied the form of golfers on the course from his own backyard. He dropped out of school in the seventh grade and made his way into what was then an exclusively Anglo rich man's sport by working as a caddie and greenskeeper.

Treviño became a professional golfer in 1966, and by 1970 he was the leading money winner on the Professional Golfers' Association tour. In 1971, Treviño became the first player to win the U.S., British, and Canadian opens in a single year, and was the first Hispanic ever named PGA Player of the Year, Associated Press Athlete of the Year, and *Sports Illustrated* Sportsman of the Year. He won the British Open again in 1972 and the PGA again in 1974 among many other tournaments. He was awarded the Vardon Trophy for the fewest strokes per round (69.73 for 82 rounds), the lowest since Sam Snead in 1958. Treviño was struck by lightning in 1974, and the

Lee Treviño

resulting back problems and surgeries restricted his play in the early 1980s. He served as a TV sports commentator, but came back to win the PGA in 1984 and the British Masters in 1985. Treviño retired from the PGA tour in 1985, with his thirty victories and a total career earnings of more than $3 million (third highest). Treviño has been elected to the Texas Sports, American Golf, and World Golf Halls of Fame.

—Nicolás Kanellos

FURTHER READING:

Kanellos, Nicolás. *The Hispanic American Almanac.* 2nd ed. Detroit, Gale Research, 1997.

Trevor, Claire (1909—)

Born in New York City, trained at the American Academy of Dramatic Arts and Columbia University, Claire Trevor has sustained a long and prolific acting career that includes over 150 movies, 200 radio shows, 20 stage plays, and scores of television dramas. Trevor began her film career in 1933 in *Jimmy and Sally.* Playing a boozy moll in *Key Largo* (1948), she won an Oscar as best supporting actress. In 1956 she won an Emmy for best single performance by an actress for her role in the Producer's Showcase television drama, *Dodsworth,* with Frederic March. As late as 1987 she appeared in a motion picture *Breaking Home Ties,* based on Norman Rockwell images.

—Benjamin Griffith

FURTHER READING:

Shipman, David. *Cinema: The First Hundred Years.* New York, St. Martin's, 1993.

Shipman, David. *The Great Movie Stars: The Golden Years.* New York, Crown, 1970.

Trillin, Calvin (1935—)

Calvin Trillin, journalist and storyteller of the American scene, has introduced his readers to friends in unlikely places like Horse Cave, Kentucky, exposed several small-town scandals, and revealed a great many of his own idiosyncrasies along the way. Readers know a little bit about the way he thinks and a lot about the way he eats from the pages of his self-titled "tummy trilogy," *American Fried* (1974), *Alice, Let's Eat* (1978), and *Third Helpings* (1983). We've also met his family: his wife Alice, who "has a weird predilection for limiting our family to three meals a day," and his two daughters, Abigail and Sarah, the latter of whom "refused to enter a Chinese restaurant unless she was carrying a bagel in reserve. . . 'just in case.'" (*Alice, Let's Eat*). Since many of these pieces originated as columns in the *New Yorker* and other magazines, Trillin's cast of characters has become a memorable and anxiously awaited feature for regular readers. Trillin enthusiasts have also developed an appetite for the best barbecue in the world, available only in his hometown, Kansas City, Missouri. Trillin writes about food not as an expert nor, indeed, as a cook—we learn that Alice does the cooking at home—but as the owner of a prodigious appetite for foods that the doctor generally does not recommend.

Calvin Trillin's journalistic career began after his graduation from Yale in 1957 and a subsequent stint in the U.S. Army. From 1960 to 1963 he worked as an Atlanta correspondent for *Time,* as well as in various other departments of the magazine, until he was invited by editor William Shawn to join the *New Yorker* staff. His initial assignment for the *New Yorker* led to his first book, *An Education in Georgia* (1964), about the forced integration of the University of Georgia at Athens. Trillin continued to demonstrate his reportorial ability in his regular *New Yorker* feature, "U.S. Journal," in which he recorded the experiences of ordinary American people in times of stress. Many of these articles later appeared in book collections such as *Killings* (1984), a compilation of short pieces on wrongful deaths and suicides, and *American Stories* (1991), which includes a few more tales of crime mixed in with profiles of favorite Trillin characters like Fats Goldberg, the formerly fat pizza baron who shuttles between New York and Kansas City, Missouri, where he always stops for a chili dog at Kresge's.

Trillin is equally at home in many genres. His short satirical commentaries from *The Nation* are collected in *Uncivil Liberties* (1982) and *With All Disrespect: More Civil Liberties* (1985). He has also written fiction, including three compilations of short stories "written for Alice" and a novel entitled *Runestruck* (1977), the story of a pre-Columbian artifact discovered in a small town in Maine. Trillin has tried his hand at light verse as well in *Deadline Poet* (1995). His more ruminative side is shown in memoirs like *Remembering Denny* (1993), about a Yale friend who never lived up to his initial promise as a "golden boy" and eventually killed himself.

As a journalist, Trillin knows the value of a good lead, in both senses of the word: as story idea and as reader enticement. A few examples of the latter:

> Not long ago, I ran across a man who pulls his own teeth. ("Ouch," *With All Disrespect*, 55)

> Not long ago, I became preoccupied with the cost of the wristwatches worn by the New Jersey State Legislature. ("The Dark Side," *Uncivil Liberties*, 75).

> In my version of a melancholy walk on the waterfront, I find myself walking through a cold Atlantic mist along the docks of some East Coast city, wearing a turned up trenchcoat, making the best approximation of footsteps echoing on the cobblestones that can be expected from a man wearing crepe-soled shoes, and ducking into a passage that turns out to be the entrance to a gourmet kitchen-supply shop called something like the Wondrous Whisk—where I soberly inspect imported French cherry pitters and antique butter molds and Swedish meat slicers.
> ("Weekends for Two," *Alice, Let's Eat*, 155)

Like Kansas City barbecue, Calvin Trillin's writing can be addictive.

—Sue Russell

FURTHER READING:

Trillin, Calvin. *Alice, Let's Eat: Further Adventures of a Happy Eater.* New York, Random House, 1978.

———. *American Stories.* New York, Ticknor & Fields, 1991.

———. *Uncivil Liberties.* New Haven, CT, Ticknor & Fields, 1982.

———. *With All Disrespect: More Uncivil Liberties.* New York, Ticknor & Fields, 1985.

Trivial Pursuit

Trivial Pursuit can be credited with creating a whole new category of board games for adults as well as an entire industry of trivia games. On December 15, 1979, Canadian photographer Chris Haney and sportswriter Scott Abbott were inspired to create the game after competing against each other in a Scrabble game. They had originally planned to call their game Trivia Pursuit until Haney's wife jokingly referred to it as Trivial Pursuit, and the name stuck. The first 1,100 sets cost $75 each to manufacture. But after selling them to retailers for $15 a game, by early 1982 Haney and Abbott were in debt. Then the U.S. game company, Selchow and Righter, became interested after hiring a PR consultant who saw Trivial Pursuit's potential as a popular leisure-time diversion. After Selchow and Righter bought the rights to the board game, 3.5 million games had been sold by late 1983. A year later, the figure had jumped to 20 million. By the 1990s, retail sales had exceeded $1 billion, and the game was available in 19 different languages and 33 countries. There has been a Trivial Pursuit television show, and the game is available on computer and on the Internet. Since its debut in 1982, there have been 40 variations of the game, and Trivial Pursuit has become an essential part of the universal language of popular culture.

—Frank Clark

FURTHER READING:

Butters, Patrick. "What Biggest Selling Adult Game Still Cranks Out Vexing Questions." *Insight on the News.* January, 26, 1998, 39.

Krane, Magda. "'Trivial Pursuit' Come to the U.S. to Take the Bored out of Games and the Profit Away from Pacman." *People Weekly.* September 19, 1983, 84-85.

"Let's Get Trivial." *Time.* October 24, 1983, 88.

Silver, Marc. "Endless Pursuit of All Things Trivial." *U.S. News & World Report.* November 6, 1989, 102.

Trixie Belden

"Schoolgirl shamus" Trixie Belden was featured in mysteries beginning with #1 *The Secret Mansion,* published by the Whitman Company in 1948, and concluding with #39 *The Mystery of the Galloping Ghost,* issued in 1986. Julie Campbell wrote the first six volumes. Then the new publisher, Golden Press, hired ghostwriters who used the pseudonym Kathryn Kenny. Thirteen-year-old Trixie lived in rural New York. She, her brothers, and friends, all members of the club Bob Whites of the Glen, participated in American and international adventures, usually solving thefts. Trixie appealed to teenage readers because her lifestyle and dreams were more familiar to them than those of Nancy Drew. The Trixie Belden mysteries enabled readers to explore and solve problems vicariously. Set in a wholesome country environment, the stories were often didactic, criticizing wealthy socialites while praising the virtue of domesticity and self-sacrifice and reinforcing middle- and lower-class values. In each book, Trixie heroically rescued people or property from danger. Often impulsive and impatient, Trixie was always capable and honest, and worked to earn money for such charity projects as UNICEF. Adult fans continue to collect the out-of-print books and sponsored internet sites about Trixie.

—Elizabeth D. Schafer

FURTHER READING:

Mason, Bobbie Ann. *The Girl Sleuth: A Feminist Guide.* Old Westbury, The Feminist Press, 1975.

Trout, Robert (1908—)

Robert Trout was radio broadcasting's first true anchorman. The concept was purely a practical innovation: the networks' foreign correspondents and highly paid analysts were the stars, yet someone had to introduce their reports, kill time during technical problems, or read late-breaking bulletins as they poured into the studio. Trout was hand-picked for this role as war clouds gathered over Europe in 1938, and gradually—broadcast after broadcast, day after day, crisis after crisis—he turned what had been a simple announcer's chore into a star role, creating the "broadcast news" institution that continues to this day.

Trout came out of local radio in Washington. Assigned to introduce President Roosevelt's "fireside chats," FDR was said to be so impressed with the young announcer's ad-libbing skill, he sometimes delayed the start of his talk a few seconds just to see how Trout would fill the time. The CBS network soon beckoned, even as the European situation worsened. The networks were beefing up their news operations, assigning correspondents to every major world capital; when the March 1938 German-Austrian crisis exploded, CBS brass picked Trout to sit in the studio, reading the late bulletins and introducing reports from the network's far-flung correspondents. And while the job could (and, on NBC, *was*) handled by any number of nameless staff announcers, Trout took the role at CBS and made it his own.

Broadcasting legend, of course, holds that the great innovation of that Austrian crisis was the invention of the "news roundup," the blending of several European correspondents' reports into a single live broadcast. Indeed, even the notion of CBS letting its own European staff speak on the air was an innovation in these pioneering days, but the idea of Trout holding the coverage together from New York, broadcast after broadcast—one steady, instantly identifiable voice speaking for the network over the long days or weeks of crisis— was equally revolutionary, and Trout seemed instinctively to understand the potential of his new role. His delivery was fast and facile, his manner urbane but not arrogant, his voice authoritative yet not pompous. By the time Germany invaded Poland in September 1939, it was impossible to imagine coverage of a major event without Trout at the CBS microphone, smoothly steering listeners from one event to the next, juggling shortwave reports and incoming bulletins while masterfully hitting every cue and station break.

Strangely, NBC never imitated this single "Voice of Authority" idea; even Trout's own bosses seemed not to realize what they had created. When CBS European chief Edward Murrow returned from his London posting in late 1941, the network brass sent Trout overseas—as a reporter. It was an obvious sign that they understood Trout's star status, yet the admittedly prestigious London assignment was ill-advised at best. Trout acquitted himself adequately, but his absence from the New York studio deprived CBS of the central force that had spearheaded its crisis coverage for so long. Without him, CBS's coverage of the attack on Pearl Harbor seemed particularly disjointed and rudderless.

Trout was back in New York by midwar, turning the London job back over to Murrow, and picking up right where he'd left off. It was Trout whose voice sounded across the nation just after 3:30 on the morning of June 6, 1944: "This means invasion!" he intoned, and America knew the D-Day landings were officially under way. It was Trout whose leaden, disbelieving tones addressed the nation upon the unexpected death of President Roosevelt in April 1945, and it was Trout (after sleeping on a cot just outside the studio for several days, so as not to miss the big moment) who told the world at 7 p.m. on August 14, 1945, "The Japanese have accepted our terms fully . . . this, ladies and gentlemen is the end of the Second World War!"

Tougher times followed. Murrow again returned to New York, this time taking a job as chief of CBS's news operation. In 1946, Trout was given a real plum: his own nightly broadcast, a five-evening-a-week extravaganza sponsored by Campbell's Soup. It didn't last long. By 1948, Murrow realized he hated the executive suite, and Campbell's jumped at the chance to return the legendary broadcaster to the air . . . alone. Trout was off the show, a pill so bitter he resigned and defected to NBC for a time before patching things up and returning to CBS in the early 1950s.

And there he stayed, reporting everything from political conventions to the 1961 Alan Shepard spaceflight to a series of war-years retrospectives in the mid-1960s. His one big television break came in 1964, when low ratings and behind-the-scenes turmoil led CBS bigwigs to oust Walter Cronkite from the anchor chair, replacing him with Trout and Roger Mudd—a combination which was a blatant effort to copy the wild success of NBC's Huntley-Brinkley team. Trout and Mudd did no better against NBC, however, and viewer protests quickly guaranteed Cronkite's return to center stage.

Trout continued to work on radio, reporting on the political conventions into the late 1980s (more recently for ABC). He could always be counted on to reminisce about the war years or the glory days of network radio.

—Chris Chandler

FURTHER READING:

Dunning, John. *On the Air*. New York, Oxford University Press, 1998.

Slater, Robert. *This . . . Is CBS*. Englewood Cliffs, New Jersey, Prentice Hall, 1988.

Sperber, A. M. *Murrow: His Life and Times*. New York, Bantam Books, 1986.

Trudeau, Gary

See Doonesbury

True Detective

One of the first "pulp" magazines—so named because it was printed on cheap, grainy wood-pulp paper—*True Detective* helped pioneer the American crime story genre in the 1920s. The monthly periodical, which started life as *True Detective Mysteries* in 1924, was retitled *True Detective* with the October 1939 issue. As the name suggests, the magazine devoted itself to true crime stories, making full use of the manners and language of the United States. The "hardboiled" investigators featured in its pages represented a break with the European "Great Detective" tradition. Dashiell Hammett, creator of Sam Spade, was among the crime writers whose work appeared in the pages of *True Detective*.

—Robert E. Schnakenberg

FURTHER READING:

Goodstone, Tony. *The Pulps*. New York, Chelsea House, 1970.

Winn, Dilys. *Murder Ink*. New York, Workman, 1984.

True Story Magazine

In 1919 the eccentric publisher Bernarr Macfadden began publication of *True Story Magazine*. According to Macfadden the magazine was inspired by personal letters of "confession" sent to him in his capacity as the editor/founder of *Physical Culture*. Sensing a widespread interest in the changing social/sexual codes of modern America, Macfadden put out a new magazine filled with first-hand accounts of social problems such as pre-marital sex, illegitimacy, adultery, unemployment, social relations, and crime (alongside ever-so slightly risque movie-stills of each story's most dramatic moments—the kiss, the temptation, the horrible realization). The magazine personalized issues that were hotly debated in Jazz Age America (dancing, drinking, partying, petting) and offered a unique working-class perspective on issues that were not necessarily unique to the working class. Sensational, emotional, and controversial, *True Story* disseminated tales of sex, sin, and redemption that seemingly revealed the ubiquity of modern sexual and social "irregularity." Most educated observers hated the magazine, figuring that it depicted the worst aspect of the "revolution in manners and morals" that occurred in the 1920s.

But workaday America loved the new confessional magazine. *True Story* became the publishing smash hit of the 1920s. In 1934 one critic offered Macfadden a back-handed complement when he noted that millions of Americans "wallow in the filth of his politely dressed confessions." Achieving circulation figures close to the two million mark by 1929, *True Story* easily matched the sales of traditional big-sellers such as *Ladies Home Journal* and the *Saturday Evening Post*. *True Story* (along with siblings *True Romance* and *True Experience*, and competitors like *True Confessions*) would maintain a large and devoted readership right into the 1990s. However the *True Story* which can be found on back shelves in supermarkets today bears only a slight resemblance to the popular original. Macfadden lost control of his publication during the 1940s, but even by that time the magazine had come to represent a much more muted version of the original "confessional" genre. Over time *True Story* evolved into a magazine that told mild tales of women's sexual misadventure, tempered by strong doses of normative moral sermonizing. In the 1920s, the period in which *True Story* shocked middle-class Americans into a series of renewed (and somewhat successful) efforts at censorship, the magazine was an innovative, raunchy, working-class pulp that purveyed an eclectic range of stories designed to appeal to both a male and female audience.

The popularity of *True Story* has too often been ascribed solely to its "sex sells" credo. In fact, in the 1920s *True Story* offered the reader much more than titillating sex tales; it offered working-class Americans stories told in their own voice (the magazine offered money for reader's personal stories). Although scholars have, and not without reason, scoffed at Macfadden's claims that his stories were both true and written by authentic working-class Americans, there is little question that his idea that stories of everyday working-class life were important was an original one. *True Story* argued, both explicitly and implicitly, that the story of modern working-class America was drama of epic proportions. In its original guise, *True Story* told tales of how working-class men and women struggled to negotiate the changes wrought by modernity. The central premise of the magazine in those early days was the notion that "it is a new world . . . and it might be well to get ready for it." *True Story* claimed to help its readers make sense of the "maelstrom of chaotic inconsistency" that was modern life and taught them how to safely embrace "the enthusiastic, buoyant spirit" of the Jazz Age. In short *True Story* told tales of seemingly particular modern moral downfall (drugs, crime, sex)—even if it did then offer up some patently old-fashioned and universal remedies for redemption (confess, make amends, walk a straighter path).

The importance of *True Story* lies in the ways in which it challenged the hegemony of middle-class publishing norms. Failing to apologize for the cheapness of his endeavor, Macfadden outraged middle America (even as it tempted its youth) by daring to elevate rowdy, raunchy, working-class youth into modern heroes and heroines. *True Story* not only revealed and popularized the ways in which working-class youth flouted convention; it argued that its working-class antihero/ines were the success stories of modern America. *True Story* valorized the lifestyles of the new American working class, with their extra dollars in their pockets, their love of material goods, and their desire for things previously denied. The magazine did not deny the realities of modern temptation; rather, *True Story* explicitly argued that it could teach working-class youth how to safely negotiate their path through modern life—through the vicarious (albeit entertaining) experience of stumbling, falling, and getting up again.

As the 1920s progressed *True Story* lost its radical edge. Bernarr Macfadden, influenced by new marketing credos, sought to expand his advertising and his audience base. In order to achieve greater circulation figures and larger advertising revenues, Macfadden successfully transformed his confessional magazine into a women's magazine. He achieved this transformation by erasing most of the "men's stories," including advertising that targeted women, and—as a pander to conservative advertisers—toning down the content of the confessional stories. By the 1930s *True Story* was a tamer version of the original confessional concept, and a decidedly less exciting one. Although *True Story* lost its male readership along with its male confessions, the magazine did continue to offer one of the few working-class voices in the marketplace. However that voice was less raw, more conservative, and increasingly mediated by the concerns of advertisers and editors. *True Story* would barely change its format in the following seven decades. Although the transformation of the magazine into a women's romance magazine proved an effective survival strategy, the moment at which *True Story* was most vital, most alive, was undoubtedly during that time in the 1920s when Macfadden's confessional stories seemed to herald (terrifyingly and excitingly) the dawn of a raunchy modern American moment.

—Jackie Hatton

FURTHER READING:

Ernst, Robert. *Weakness is a Crime: The Life of Bernarr Macfadden.* New York, Syracuse University, 1991.

Hatton, Jacqueline Anne. *True Stories: Working-Class Mythology, American Confessional Culture, and True Story Magazine, 1919-1929.* Unpublished Ph.D. Thesis, Cornell University, 1997.

Hersey, Harold. *Pulpwood Editor: The Fabulous World of Thriller Magazines Revealed By a Veteran Editor and Publisher.* New York, Frederick A. Stokes, 1937.

Oursler, Fulton. *The True Story of Bernarr Macfadden.* New York, Lewis Copeland, 1929.

T-Shirts

Sex, work, and democracy together advanced the T-shirt as a clothing icon of the late twentieth century. Until the 1940s, the T-shirt was exclusively an undershirt. Sailors, however, in shipboard fraternity, worked in T-shirts. These World War II, T-shirted heroes appeared in *Life* Magazine (cover, *Life,* July 13, 1942) and cavorted in the musical *South Pacific.* The private world was now public, and the undershirt entered society, sometimes with the renegade image of Marlon Brando, other times with the innocent white shirt of James Dean. The T-shirt would not have the authority of the cut-and-sewn shirt with collar until the 1980s when Bruce Springsteen reinforced the T-shirt's proletarian roots but also identified the T-shirt with the new 1980s masculinity of sex-object, gym-built male bodies.

—Richard Martin

FURTHER READING:

Harris, Alice. *The White T.* New York, Harper Collins, 1996.

Tupperware

Perhaps no product line epitomizes post-World War II American suburbia as much as Tupperware plastic kitchen containers. Earl Tupper (1907-1983), inveterate experimenter from Harvard, Massachusetts, used his experience in 1937 working for Dupont to develop his own kind of plastic, which he used to make all types of products.

A Tupperware party.

He founded the Earl S. Tupper Company in 1938, which had some success selling gas masks and signal lamp parts to the Navy during World War II. But when he applied his flexible and durable material to civilian needs, Tupper achieved his greatest success.

In 1945 Tupper trademarked his perfected plastic, Polyethylene-Tupper, or "Poly-T," the "material of the future." Forever interested in women's daily lives (he experimented with designs for garter belt hooks and brassieres, for example), Tupper used this innovative material to create an entirely new line of housewares which revolutionized the way women dealt with food and other things in their kitchens. Up until this time, plastics like Bakelite and celluloid were common materials but had limited uses—products made from them were either brittle or heavy and were not suitable for use with foods. In contrast, Tupperware was perfect in the kitchen. It came in many forms, including tumblers, bowls, pitchers, ice cube trays, butter dishes, and even cocktail shakers. Tupper's most famous and effective innovation, in 1947, was a set of storage canisters with resealable lids that could be "burped" to let out and keep out excess air. They were light-weight, air-tight, indestructible, and waxy-textured for a good grip. These canisters proved to be great improvements over the more common glass and metal containers women had been using in the kitchen, which were heavy, not air-tight, were prone to sweating from refrigerator condensation, and broke easily.

Tupper's plastic products were not only utilitarian, but also materially seductive. The drinking tumblers came in many colors, including lime, raspberry, lemon, plum, and orange. The bowls were attractively shaped and could even be used to display fresh-fruit centerpieces. Tupperware was such an embodiment of post-war materialism that some of its pieces became part of the Museum of Modern Art's permanent collection in 1955, and were described as "carefully considered shapes . . . marvelously free of that vulgarity which characterizes so much household equipment." It is ironic that Tupper, such a pioneer bringing the modernity of his translucent

plastic designs into the home, was an antiquarian at heart. He believed, nostalgically, in the traditional values of hand-craftsmanship and manual labor, and his home was filled with antiques. In contrast, the products he engineered and manufactured were truly "tomorrow's designs with tomorrow's materials."

While Tupper brought new materials and new forms into the domestic sphere, his products also introduced a new kind of sociability among women through private home sales. From 1950 on, Tupperware was marketed and distributed only by direct selling, through Tupperware Parties, overseen by Tupperware Home Parties Incorporated, established in 1951 and also known as the Cinderella Company. These parties were actually commercial opportunities orchestrated as social events. A hostess would throw a party in her home, inviting friends and neighbors in order to provide first-hand demonstrations of the products (like how to "burp" the storage canisters), and to give her guests a chance to purchase Tupperware items. Here, women also played games and could win Tupperware prizes, and the hostess would try to recruit potential hostesses to give their own parties—all in exchange for Tupperware items for herself.

This method of product distribution paradoxically offered women the freedom to be entrepreneurs while it emphasized their domestic duties as wives and mothers, giving them the chance to socialize on their own, yet in a way that channeled them into their traditional gender roles. However ambiguous, Tupper's marketing strategy—overseen by homemaker Brownie Wise until 1958—was clearly successful. In 1954 over 200,000 women were dealers, distributors, and managers. In that same year sales topped $25 million and allowed Tupper to double the size of his Blackstone, Massachusetts, manufacturing facility. In 1958 he sold his interest in the company to Justin Dart of the Rexall Drug Company.

Tupperware and the party system both successfully entered Britain in 1961. By 1979 there were over 50,000 people selling over $700 million worth of Tupperware. In the 1980s Tupperware was sold in over 42 countries and carried product lines fitting specific cultural needs, like the sushi saver in Japan. To bring it up to date, Morris Cousins redesigned Tupperware in the 1990s, giving it "Euro styling" with brighter colors and sleeker shapes. The company introduced "Tupperkids," a line of children's toys, in 1994. What is more, Tupperware is so familiar to Americans that it has become a generic word applied to all such plastic storage containers with resealable lids, and has come to symbolize the unique blend of domesticity, materialism, and superficiality that is seen to characterize life in the American suburb.

—Wendy Woloson

FURTHER READING:

Clarke, Alison J. "Tupperware: Product as Social Relation." *American Material Culture: The Shape of the Field,* edited by Ann Smart Martin and J. Ritchie Garrison. Winterthur, Delaware, Henry Francis du Pont Winterthur Museum and Knoxville, Tennessee, University of Tennessee Press, 1997.

Fenichell, Stephen. *Plastic: The Making of a Synthetic Century.* New York, HarperBusiness, 1996.

Meikle, Jeffrey L. *American Plastic: A Cultural History.* New Brunswick, New Jersey, Rutgers University Press, 1995.

Turner, Ike (1931—) and Tina (1938—)

Formed in 1959 in St. Louis, Missouri, the partnership of Mississippi rhythm-and-blues musician Ike Turner and a young singer from Nutbush, Tennessee, named Annie Mae Bullock would result in one of popular music's most combustible sounds. Known for their impressive live performances, Ike and Tina Turner were an immediate crossover sensation who eventually released some 29 albums on various labels. As significant as their contribution was to American black music, their 16-year union as the Ike and Tina Turner Revue also left an indelible impression upon rock and pop music the world over. Supported by a full R&B orchestra and choreographed backup singers, Ike was bandleader, arranger, and producer for the duo. With a distinctive on-stage style, the Ike and Tina Turner Revue created a whirlwind of sensation and emotion that inspired audiences and performers alike. Compatible with R&B, straight blues, Motown soul, and hard-core rock and roll, Ike and Tina Turner shared bills with many top performers including the Rolling Stones. While Ike was the competent instrumentalist and songwriter, it was Tina who created for herself an enduring place within popular culture. As both a woman and a performer of strength, grace, and spirit, Tina overcame poverty, self-doubt, and abuse in order to succeed personally and professionally.

Starting out as a piano player, Ike Turner made history early on in 1951 when he played on the Sun Studios session that produced one of the first rock and roll records ever recorded, Jackie Brenston's

Ike and Tina Turner

"Rocket 88." Picking up the guitar shortly thereafter, Turner became a busy session player who worked with blues greats Howlin' Wolf, Elmore James, and Otis Rush. It was at this time that he developed his distinctive stinging guitar style.

His own band, Ike Turner's Rhythm Kings, was the toast of East St. Louis when Annie Mae Bullock (Tina), the daughter of sharecroppers, met Ike Turner for the first time. Tina joined Turner's touring band as a backup vocalist in 1956, when she was 18. By 1958 she was the star of the show. It was her lovely growl and wild, gospel accents that set her apart from other singers at the time. The high-energy performer filled the stage with her powerful presence and made every lyric of a song come to life. As sexual as she was talented, Tina was not simply a soul singer or an R&B singer: she was something new and different, and this captured the attention of both white and black audiences.

As Ike and Tina Turner, they recorded their first single in 1959 for Sue Records, "A Fool in Love." By 1960 this side was a No. 2 hit on the R&B charts. Following up with "I Idolize You," "It's Gonna Work Out Fine," and "Poor Fool," the Ike & Tina Turner Revue had five Top 10 hits on the R&B charts in less than 3 years. Their first album, *The Soul of Ike and Tina Turner* was released in 1964 on Sue. Working for top labels such as Warner Brothers, Liberty Records, London, Hallmark, Valiant, Sunset and United Artists, Ike and Tina released at least one project every year until their final album, *Nutbush City Limits,* was recorded in 1973. Their most successful project, in 1970, was *Workin' Together.* Released on Liberty, this recording included Tina's version of "Proud Mary." Another highlight of their years together was working with producer Phil Spector, whose "Wall of Sound" production style dominated American pop music during the 1960s. This big sound complimented Tina's vocal prowess dramatically as is evidenced on *River Deep and Mountain High,* released in 1966.

While Ike and Tina's stage union produced spectacular results and Tina had carved a name for herself as one of the premier women of rock and pop, their personal life together was hardly satisfactory. Ike Turner was a taskmaster who insisted upon total control in everything, including his marriage. Using fear and her own youthful inexperience against her, Ike finally married Tina in Mexico. After years of mistreatment and abuse, Tina left Ike in 1975, eventually divorcing him and rebuilding her career as a solo artist. In 1984, at the age of 45, she was once more an international sensation, making the charts again with her album *Private Dancer.* In 1985 she had a starring role in the popular Mel Gibson film *Mad Max Beyond Thunderdome,* for which she also recorded the hit single "We Don't Need Another Hero." The 1993 film *What's Love Got to Do With It?* chronicled Tina's rocky career and starred Angela Bassett along with Laurence Fishburne as Ike Turner. Ike spent the 1980s battling drugs and legal problems. In 1991 Ike and Tina Turner were inducted into the Rock and Roll Hall of Fame and EMI America released *Proud Mary: The Best of Ike and Tina Turner,* a 23-track collection detailing their career from the early 1960s through the mid-1970s.

—Jana Pendragon

FURTHER READING:

Ivory, Steven. *Tina.* New York, Putnam, 1985.

Mills, Bart. *Tina.* New York, Warner Books, 1985.

Turner, Tina, with Kurt Loder. *I, Tina: My Life Story.* New York, Avon, 1986.

Wynn, Ron. *Tina: The Tina Turner Story.* New York, Macmillan, 1985.

Turner, Lana (1920-1995)

Nicknamed the ''Sweater Girl,'' actress Lana Turner defined feminine sexuality for a generation during the World War II era. She portrayed an archetypal character in *The Postman Always Rings Twice,* the first American film version of a James Cain novel and a seminal film noir, and helped reestablish the melodrama genre in the 1950s with her appearances in *Peyton Place* and *Imitation of Life.* But Turner's importance is not rooted in her acting. Turner was a movie star in the old style, a product of the studio system, a glamour girl, a femme fatale.

Jean Mildred Frances Turner's film career began when she was fifteen years old and was hired to be an extra in *A Star Is Born.* MGM gave her the name Lana, and studio publicity claimed she had been discovered by the editor of the *Hollywood Reporter* while having a strawberry soda at Schwab's drugstore; Turner later said she was drinking a Coke at the Top Hat Café. Her first significant role came in what was only her second film, Mervyn LeRoy's *They Won't Forget* (1937), in which she played Mary Clay, a teenage girl who is raped and murdered twelve minutes into the film. In her most famous scene,

Lana Turner

Turner has no dialogue and simply walks across the screen wearing the tight sweater that earned her her nickname. The scene launched Turner's career; critics wrote about ''the girl in the sweater,'' and filmgoers sent fan letters to MGM.

Turner went on to make fifty-three films in thirty-nine years. In most of them she played a variation on one characterization: sexy but not quite slutty, strong but vulnerable. In 1945 Turner was one of the most highly paid actresses in Hollywood, and by the time she appeared in *The Postman Always Rings Twice* in 1946, she had already been a top box office draw for several years. Still, the film provided her with her definitive role; writing in *The Films of Lana Turner,* Lou Valentino observed, ''if Turner fans had to make a choice, *Postman* is the movie they would most elect to have time-capsuled.'' In it, Turner plays the unhappy wife of a much older man who plots with a handsome young drifter to murder her husband. Because the Hays Code would not allow MGM to film a faithful adaptation of Cain's overtly sexual novel, director Tay Garnett dressed Turner in white for most of the film, which, according to Garnett, ''made everything she did seem less sensuous. It was also attractive as hell. And it somehow took a little of the stigma off.''

At the height of her popularity, Turner was a pervasive presence in American society. Children could buy Lana Turner paper dolls and coloring books. Her likeness was painted on airplane noses. There was a song titled ''The Lana Turner Blues.'' Perhaps most significantly, Turner played a major role in defining the manner in which women would be portrayed in American popular culture. In the 1940s she appeared on magazine covers almost monthly. She endorsed beauty products and made the buxom look popular—in 1948 4.5 million breast pads were sold to American women, who wanted to look like the Sweater Girl.

In the late 1950s Turner moved into melodramas. She received her only Academy Award nomination for *Peyton Place,* in which she plays a widowed woman who becomes the subject of scandal when she is forced to reveal that her teenaged daughter is illegitimate. In 1957, the signing of a sex symbol like Turner to the role of the mother made headlines. In *Imitation of Life,* Turner's most financially successful film, she plays an actress and mother who arranges for an unemployed African American woman, Annie, and her daughter to live with her and act as her servants. As the two women's daughters grow older, Annie's daughter ''passes'' for white and grows ashamed of her mother.

Turner was married seven times, most notably to bandleader Artie Shaw and actor Lex Barker. In 1958, Turner's daughter, Cheryl Crane, stabbed and killed Turner's boyfriend, mobster Johnny Stompanato. Turner survived the bad publicity surrounding Stompanato's murder and her daughter's trial with no visible damage to her career. She made nine more motion pictures after *Imitation,* and she appeared on television and on stage in the 1970s and 1980s. Turner died of throat cancer in 1995.

—Randall Clark

FURTHER READING:

Basinger, Jeanine. *Lana Turner.* New York, Pyramid, 1976.

Crane, Cheryl. *Detour.* New York, Arbor House, 1988.

Morella, Joe, and Edward Epstein. *Lana: The Public and Private Lives of Miss Turner.* New York, Citadel, 1971.

Root, Eric. *The Private Diary of My Life with Lana.* Beverly Hills, Dove Books, 1996.

Turner, Lana. *Lana: The Lady, the Legend, the Truth.* New York, Dutton, 1982.

Valentino, Lou. *The Films of Lana Turner.* Secaucus, New Jersey, Citadel, 1976.

White, Jane Ellen. *Lana: The Life and Loves of Lana Turner.* New York, St. Martin's Press, 1975.

Turner, Ted (1938—)

Ted Turner, a flamboyant Southern entrepreneur and sportsman, first came to prominence in 1977 when, as the skipper of the winning yacht in the America's Cup race, he shocked the rather staid community of Newport Rhode Island with his wild celebrations and partying. Yet, this notoriety masked the fact that he was also in the process of creating television's first "superstation," a local television station that, through the power of satellite communications, could broadcast its signal to cable-equipped households across the United States and ultimately around the world. In the process, he reinvented television viewing patterns for most Americans and forced the networks to rethink their traditional broadcasting options.

His career, in fact, began very quietly in 1970 when his Turner Communications, a small family-owned and billboard-oriented advertising agency, merged with Atlanta's Rice Broadcasting and took over a controlling interest in local television station WTCG. During the first year of the Turner regime, the station's most popular show

Ted Turner

became *Georgia Championship Wrestling.* Ironically, news programming, for which Turner would later become famous, received scant attention, being broadcast only at three or four a.m. when there were few viewers. Even at that hour, serious news stories were, for the most part, treated "tongue in cheek" and more as entertainment than as a public service. To Turner, there seemed to be no such thing as good news and viewers were regarded as being much better off watching reruns of old television series instead of dreary recounts of what went on in the world.

His purchase of the television station, however, led him to a development that would turn television on its head. Turner eventually discovered the existence of a communications satellite in a geosynchronous orbit over the earth that could be used on a 24-hour basis by anyone willing to pay the rent. The technology which was then in its infancy and which relied on the National Aeronautics and Space Administration for its positioning was not highly publicized and had been, as a consequence, under-utilized by broadcasting entities, few of which saw the possibilities for global programming. Yet, to the flamboyant Turner, the idea of a small local station being able to send its signal all over the world made perfect sense.

Beginning with a tall television tower and a lone earth station microwave dish maintained by one technician, Turner proudly proclaimed his operation to be the world's first "superstation." Utilizing an eclectic blend of movies, sports, reruns of discontinued television series, and his own original programming produced by a subsidiary company, the station achieved the status of a basic cable selection on most systems around the country and, in fact, probably helped spread the growth of cable during the next decade. Under Turner's direction, the station went from a money losing operation to generating a profit of almost $2 million within its first 18 months. It was renamed WTBS in 1979 to reflect its corporate affiliation and became the primary revenue source financing the next components of the Turner empire.

Doing a flip-flop on his anti-news stance, Turner expanded his broadcasting base the following year by creating the innovative Cable News Network (CNN), a 24-hour news service carried by satellite to cable systems around the world. He correctly noted that the proliferation of cable programming had placed its emphasis on entertainment programming, ignoring the fact that continuous newscasting would be an ideal melding with cable since public interest was high and because the traditional networks dismissed 24-hour news service as too costly. To Turner, however, the financial risk was a gamble worth taking. He put the service on the air in June 1980 by leveraging most of his holdings and routing all of the profits from WTBS and his other interests into the fledgling enterprise.

At first, the station was regarded as something of a novelty by the critics and the networks alike, who dismissed the ambitious programming as "light weight journalism" at best. Yet, the new network with news bureaus around the world began to get its reporters to breaking stories well before the established news organizations. By 1990, it surpassed the networks with its on-the-spot coverage of the Persian Gulf War and established itself as the premier television news service in the United States. As a result, by the mid-1990s, it had expanded its viewership to 140 countries around the world and had created such off-shoots as CNN Headline News and CNN International.

In 1986, Turner took another risk by purchasing the Metro Goldwyn Mayer (MGM)/United Artists motion picture studio in a complicated cash/stock transaction valued at approximately $1.5 billion. In order to finance his portion, Turner had to break up the studio and divest himself of a number of subdivisions to keep the money coming in. He immediately sold the United Artists portion of the studio back to financier Kirk Kerkorian, who had sold him the entire studio to begin with; he also included MGM's film and television production and distribution in the Kerkorian package. Additionally, he sold the lot itself to television production entity Lorimar-Telepictures and wound up only with MGM's large library of motion pictures, which included the pre-1948 Warner Bros. and RKO films. Turner was now the owner of perhaps the largest library of filmed entertainment in the world—sufficient programming to keep WTBS going forever, in addition to being able to market the films on video and lease them to other networks.

Turner's next move, the controversial "colorizing" of many of the black-and-white films in his new library, raised the ire of film purists aghast at the thought of seeing such classics as *Casablanca* (1941) and *Citizen Kane* (1941) broadcast with computer-enhanced artificial color. Congress even got into the act by holding hearings to determine authorship and copyright issues relating to film to see if the Southern mogul actually had the right to contradict the original artistic intent by introducing color. The issue was never resolved but it did sensitize Turner to the issues involved, and his company has subsequently played a leading role in film preservation efforts in the United States. He also established the Turner Classic Movie channel in the early 1990s to show motion pictures in their original manifestations, with a knowledgeable host to introduce each one and talk about its production history.

Turner has also played a leading role in a number of other altruistic endeavors as well. For most of his life, he has been an ardent environmentalist, but in the mid-1980s, he began to take an equally strong stand against warfare by exploring viable methods of bringing people together. In 1985, he founded the Better World Society to produce film and television documentaries to educate people about such issues as pollution, hunger, and the perils of the arms race. He followed this a year later with The Goodwill Games, a scaled down version of the Olympic Games in an effort to promote brotherhood and world peace. He lost $26 million on the first games staged in Moscow in 1986, and followed that with another $44 million shortfall in the 1991 games held in Seattle. In 1992, he created the "Turner Tomorrow Awards" to provide an incentive for writers around the world to come up with positive solutions to problems effecting the world.

With his 1991 marriage to actress and political activist Jane Fonda, he expanded his concerns to share and support his longtime interest in Native American issues. He produced a number of documentaries and fact-based feature films on his TNT channel to show the development of American history from the Native American point of view and to spotlight the contributions of indigenous Americans to the United States. In recent years, he has expanded his commitment to his social concerns by creating a list of volunteer initiatives that individuals can do to make the world a better place. The tenets include initiatives on family size, pollution, and conservation of the environment.

In 1997, with his typical flamboyance, Turner pledged a gift of $1 billion to the United Nations to be distributed over the following decade. He emphasized, however, that the money could not be used for administrative or "housekeeping expenses." It had to be used for programs such as disease control, cleaning up landmines, UNICEF (United Nations International Children's Emergency Fund) children's programs, refugee relief, and peacekeeping.

The proposed gift to the United Nations was based on money that he received in stock shares for merging his company with Time Warner in 1997 to form the world's largest media company. Under the terms of the deal, Time Warner gained access to Turner's interests in cable and satellite television and, importantly, the rights to the library of pre-1948 Warner Bros. films, RKO films, and the MGM collection. In effect, Time Warner reclaimed its heritage and then some. The possibilities of commercial exploitation of the Turner materials in the Warner Bros. stores, and fledgling theme parks with videos, new character licensing, and reissues of restored films is seemingly unlimited. In return, Turner became Time Warner's largest stockholder, with "clout" only surpassed by Chief Executive Officer Gerald Levin. He immediately began pressing the company to initiate an austerity program to reduce what he considered to be an untenable corporate debt approaching $17 billion. This included selling the corporate jets and consolidating redundant departments created by the merger.

While many find the combination of unbridled ambition in the business world juxtaposed with a genuine concern for environmental and social causes in his personal life to be an odd mix, his closest associates view it as an inevitable consequence of Turner's unsettled childhood. As the son of an equally ambitious businessman, Robert Edward Turner II, who had seen his own parents lose their South Carolina home during the Great Depression, he was conscious of the value of a dollar. This was amplified, at the age of 24, by his father's suicide after losing the family billboard advertising business due to debts. Turner also suffered through his younger sister's extended illness and death from lupus erythematosus only four years earlier. The combined experiences turned him away from organized religions but left him with an equally religious fervor to cure some of the ills of the world. "One should not set goals that he cannot reach," he told *Time* magazine in 1992. "I'm not going to rest until all the world's problems have been solved. Homelessness, AIDS [Acquired Immune Deficiency Syndrome]. I'm in great shape. I mean the problems will survive me—no question about it."

Still, Ted Turner will seemingly continue to manage the contradictory feats of creating a corporate empire and also to continue to give much of it away for worthy causes as long as he is able to "wheel and deal" his way through American finance and industry.

—Steve Hanson

FURTHER READING:

Andrews, Suzanna. "Ted Turner Among the Suits." *New York.* December 9, 1996, 32.

Bart, Peter. "Ted's Trail of Tears." *Variety.* August 31, 1998, 4.

Bethell, Tom. "The Hazards of Charity." *The American Spectator.* July 1998, 18.

Dempsey, John. "Ted, Time: New Tower of Cable." *Variety.* July 22, 1996, 1.

Goldberg, Robert. "Citizen Turner." *Playboy.* June 1995, 100.

Goldberg, Robert and Gerald Jay Goldberg. *Citizen Turner.* New York, Harcourt Brace, 1995.

Meyer, Michael. "I Want to See What it's Like to Be Big." *Newsweek.* October 2, 1995, 62.

Miller, Judith. "What Makes Ted Turner Give?" *The New York Times.* September 20, 1997, 7.

Painton, Priscilla. "Man of the Year." *Time.* January 6, 1992, 35-39.

Range, Peter Ross. "Ted Turner." *Playboy.* August 1983, 59.

Sharpe, Anita. "Not so Retiring." *The Wall Street Journal.* November 27, 1995, A1.

TV Dinners

Introduced in the 1930s, General Foods offered the first proto-TV dinner, which was a frozen Irish stew. Successfully reaching a larger market, Swanson manufactured pot pies in 1951, and followed four years later with their mass-marketed "TV Dinners." The first TV Dinner was turkey with cornbread dressing, peas, and sweet potatoes; other varieties like Salisbury steak, ham, and chicken quickly followed.

These frozen dinners reflected changes in cultural patterns. Americans bought 70 million TV Dinners in 1955, 214 million in 1960, and 2 billion in 1994. The first meals were indeed meant to be eaten in front of the television, a relatively new technology in American homes at mid-twentieth century. To satiate larger appetites, Swanson introduced the "Hungry Man's Dinner" in 1972, and changed the generic name from "TV Dinner" to "Frozen Dinner." Producers of frozen dinners in the 1980s and 1990s reflected shifting preoccupations with foods, emphasizing low-calorie yet upscale meals—calling their products Lean Cuisine, Budget Gourmet, and Le Menu—and making cooking times even shorter by utilizing the microwave oven.

—Wendy Woloson

A TV Dinner

FURTHER READING:

"Better Than TV Dinners?" *Consumer Reports.* March 1984, 126-27, 170.

I'll Buy That! 50 Small Wonders and Big Deals that Revolutionized the Lives of Consumers. Mount Vernon, New York, Consumers Union, 1986.

Stern, Jane, and Michael Stern. *The Encyclopedia of Bad Taste.* New York, HarperCollins, 1990.

Volti, Rudi. "How We Got Frozen Food." *Invention and Technology.* Spring 1994, 47-56.

TV Guide

In 1953, when television was still a brand-new and growing phenomenon on the American scene, the president of Philadelphia's Triangle Publishing—Walter H. Annenberg—conceived the idea of a national television magazine. Inspired by the wide circulation of a local magazine called *TV Digest,* Annenberg envisioned one central nationwide magazine with separate editions containing the different local television listings. Annenberg moved quickly, keeping the convenient digest size and adding glossy color photographs and articles. On April 3, 1953, *TV Guide* was born and remains the premier listing for television fanatics in the late twentieth century.

Beginning what was to be a tradition of exclusive reportage on television and its surrounding issues, the cover of the first issue showed one of the first photos of comedy queen Lucille Ball's new baby. The magazine was issued in 10 editions, each geared to a different locality, and it sold more than one and a half million copies. The idea had proved to be a good one, and *TV Guide* went on to become the best-selling weekly in the United States, with a circulation of more than 13 million readers. The 10 editions grew to 119 regional editions, and *TV Guide* became the name most often associated with not only television program listings but also with television journalism. Though perhaps not the most glamorous aspect of the television industry, *TV Guide* is certainly one of the most familiar.

The main office of *TV Guide* is still in Radnor, Pennsylvania, but the staff of over 1,300 is scattered in more than 20 bureaus around the country. Because *TV Guide*'s competition includes the free television sections of local newspapers, the weekly had to offer viewers something special, not available in the local listings. Because of this, the editorial staff of *TV Guide* has always employed a two-pronged approach—the listings and the articles.

To maximize the value of its program listings, *TV Guide* writers are assigned to cover individual television shows. Rather than using studio press releases, these writers screen programs and even read scripts themselves to ensure that their descriptions of the shows are accurate. The National Features Department of the journal moved to New York City in 1991, to be even closer to the television industry there.

TV Guide's other approach to creating public demand for its product has been its articles. The pages not filled with program listings contain photographs of stars, reviews of weekly programs and television movies, and articles. Some articles are the predicable fluffy pieces highlighting the off-camera antics of sitcom casts, or lightweight interviews with current popular stars. Light though they may be, these articles are often exactly what the television viewer wants to see—alternate views of favorite shows and stars, and the critics' opinion of the shows they watch. But *TV Guide* takes itself seriously as a television magazine as well. In the sentiments of the editorial staff, "*TV Guide*'s remarkable success stems from its ability to present not only broad, objective reporting about what is on television but also in-depth, provocative coverage about the TV industry itself and the effect television has on society."

To accomplish this purpose, the journal employs its own staff of distinguished reviewers and commentators, and has also sought outside contributors who would draw readers. Politicians such as John F. Kennedy and Gerald Ford, and eminent writers like Joyce Carol Oates and John Cheever have been found in its pages along with names more commonly associated with the entertainment industry but no less distinguished, such as David Brinkley and Katherine Hepburn; even political activists like Gloria Steinem and Coretta Scott King have found their way into *TV Guide*. While printing the writing of such famous personalities is clever editorial policy on the part of a magazine eager to boost sales, appearing in such a popular magazine is also a smart move for a writer who wants to be widely read.

In 1988, *TV Guide* was sold to Rupert Murdoch—a flamboyant Australian entrepreneur associated with sensational journalism—who was accumulating a vast entertainment empire. *TV Guide* joined the London *Times,* the Fox television network, Twentieth Century Fox movie studio, Harper and Row publishers, and dozens of other publications and companies as part of Murdoch News Corporation. Murdoch continued and expanded the *TV Guide* tradition of entertainment coverage that is both entertaining and thoughtful. Senator Paul Simon gave the *TV Guide* report on television violence much credit for encouraging Congressional hearings about television violence, and the Public Relations Service Council also acknowledged the magazine's role in prompting them to set ethical standards for video news releases. Along with the serious side of television reportage, Murdoch brought some of the flashy side of television to *TV Guide*. In 1998, the first annual *TV Guide Awards Show* was broadcast, with winners selected by reader vote, and the USA Network has signed a deal to produce several *TV Guide* specials.

In 1998, News Corp. sold *TV Guide* to Tele-Communication Incorporated (TCI), one of the major cable companies in the United States. Competing not only with the Sunday newspaper pull-outs but also with new print competitors like Time, Inc.'s *Entertainment Weekly* and the cable on-screen guides, the circulation of *TV Guide* began to slip. Acquisition by TCI, however, marries the venerable and highly recognized *TV Guide* name with cable. A "TV Guide Channel" runs continuously to inform viewers of programming, and an on-line *TV Guide* magazine offers readers instant links to a variety of entertainment sites. Even the familiar pocket-sized digest format will change when *TV Guide* puts out its first full-sized edition in the late 1990s, offering reviews and commentaries for the first time on theatrical release movies as well as television.

As *TV Guide* changes with the times, it also offers a link to a simpler time—the early days of television when viewers, not yet inundated with entertainment, eagerly awaited news of the week's programs supplemented with pictures and stories about the stars. Viewers appreciated a journal that took the new medium as seriously as they did, and they devoured the magazine that was all about television—right down to the crossword puzzle. In the 1960s, Marshal McLuhan envisioned a global community with television at its center. Television has no doubt been a huge force in modern culture, but not perhaps in the way he foresaw. By the late 1990s, there are more television stations and more different kinds of programming than could have been imagined at the birth of the medium. Though

there are hundreds of channel and program guides, *TV Guide* was the first and, to many American viewers, the only "real" guide to the exciting world promised by television. A glance back through the past issues of *TV Guide* provides a good chronicle of what television has been and what it has to say for itself.

—Tina Gianoulis

FURTHER READING:

Kerwin, Ann Marie. *"TV Guide Turns Gaze to Big Screen." Advertising Age.* Vol. 69, No. 17, April 27, 1998, 62.

TV Guide Online. http://www.tvgen.com/tv/magazine/index.sml. June 1999.

Tweety Pie and Sylvester

When Friz Freleng directed 1947's "Tweetie Pie," he may not have known he was making history. This, the first pairing of Sylvester the sputtering cat and Tweetie (later Tweety) the wide-eyed canary, won an Academy Award and united a duo that would appear in more than 40 Warner Brothers cartoon shorts by 1962. Sylvester and Tweety earned their studio another Academy Award for 1957's "Birds Anonymous" and several other Oscar nominations through the years. Generations of Americans have grown up watching Sylvester's classic, ever-thwarted attempts to catch Tweety. With two of the most famous voices in cartoons, both supplied by Mel Blanc, Sylvester's sloppy "sufferin succotash" and Tweety's baby-voiced "I tawt I taw a puddy tat," Sylvester and Tweety are two of the most quickly identified characters in cartoons.

A number of Warner Brothers cartoons featuring a predator unable to catch his prey appeared and gained popularity in the 1940s, including such classic pairings as Elmer Fudd and Bugs Bunny and the Road Runner and Wile E. Coyote. Other studios created similar cartoons, one of the earliest examples being MGM's Tom and Jerry. Many of these cartoons, like Sylvester and Tweety, survived into the 1990s. Few characters, however, have attained the status Sylvester and Tweety enjoy.

Primarily responsible for uttering his tag lines ("I tawt I taw a puddy tat! I did! I did taw a puddy tat!" and "You bad old puddy tat!") and looking cute, Tweety isn't known for his superior wit or intelligence. Then again, that little canary is consistently able to get away from Sylvester, an animal who is both larger and faster than he is. Tweety is a popular character, both liked and disliked by audiences. Some like him because he does always get away from Sylvester, and also because he is so cute—bright yellow with big blue eyes and a baby voice. On the other hand, many people find him irritating for the same reasons. Either way, Tweety is one of the most recognized and imitated characters in cartoons.

If Tweety is not known for his superior wit and intelligence, Sylvester is known for his decided lack thereof. He generally goes barreling into situations, never considering the possibilities or consequences. When, in an effort to catch the delectable Tweety, Sylvester dresses up in a dog suit and is caught by the dog catcher, the moment he's thrown in the back of the truck with a group of mangy mutts, he takes off his costume and shouts, "But I'm a cat!" Sylvester's son, Junior, is so ashamed of his father, he generally walks around with a paper bag over his head. Sylvester's only virtue may be his dogged persistence. In the face of constant failure, he continues to try. A combination of stupidity, audacity, and sputtering temper, Sylvester defies the image of the cat as smart, cool, and collected. He continues to be, along with the likes of Bugs Bunny and Daffy Duck, one of the Warner Brothers's most popular and liked characters.

Both Sylvester and Tweety appeared in other cartoons before being paired for "Tweetie Pie." Since this first pairing, Tweety has appeared almost exclusively with Sylvester. Other regular characters added spice to the Sylvester and Tweety cartoons, including Granny, Tweety's owner and protector, and a bulldog, who, in his general dislike for cats, often saves Tweety from Sylvester's schemes. Sylvester was also given a son, Junior, for 1950's "Pop 'Im Pop." Sylvester has had other adventures, appearing in cartoons with Speedy Gonzales, the world's fastest mouse, and Hippety Hopper, the baby kangaroo. Sylvester even made a cameo appearance as the Grand Duke in "The Scarlet Pumpernickel."

The Sylvester and Tweety cartoons, like their counterparts, began as "curtain-raisers" in theatres. A 1949 U.S. Supreme Court ruling that declared it illegal for studios to demand that theaters book a cartoon, newsreel, or live-action short in addition to hit films marked the beginning of the end of curtain-raisers. The advent of television and less public interest in movies made it difficult for studios to recover the costs of creating a cartoon short. Some less expensive cartooning methods came out of this time, but, ultimately, cartoon shorts had to make the move to television or perish. Sylvester and Tweety made this transition, culminating in a self-titled repackaging of their older cartoons as well as other Warner Brothers shorts which premiered on September 11, 1976 on CBS. Sylvester and Tweety shorts appear into the 1990s on various programs on network and cable stations.

Perhaps one of the most important factors in the continuing popularity of Tweety and Sylvester is Warner Brothers Studio's ability to keep the characters' faces in front of viewers. Sylvester and Tweety have been reincarnated in a new cartoon series, *Sylvester and Tweety Mysteries,* which premiered on September 9, 1995 on the WB Television Network. The duo appeared in 1996's *Space Jam* with legendary basketball player Michael Jordan. The cat and canary have been seen endorsing products such as Miracle Whip dressing and MCI long distance. On April 27, 1998, the United States Post Office honored Tweety and Sylvester with a 32 cent postage stamp. Sylvester and Tweety are on tee shirts, shorts, socks, underwear, and other articles of clothing. They appear prominently in products from clothing to cups to clocks sold at the Warner Brothers Studio Stores in malls across the United States.

Sylvester and Tweety are just two of numerous Warner Brothers cartoon characters who appeared in the first half of the 20th century and have enjoyed continuing popularity. Warner Brothers's marketing of the characters is no small part of their fame, but Sylvester and Tweety have an appeal that goes beyond marketing. Sylvester is not the cat we might expect, and Tweety certainly isn't as innocent as he appears. Their interactions are what makes great comedy. With Sylvester and Tweety, it is always the unexpected that makes audiences laugh. When people have seen the cartoons repeatedly and are still laughing, Sylvester and Tweety Pie's continuing popularity seems to be assured.

—Adrienne Furness

FURTHER READING:

Friedwald, Will, and Jerry Beck. *The Warner Brothers Cartoons.* Metuchen, New Jersey, and London, The Scarecrow Press, 1981.

Lenburg, Jeff. *The Encyclopedia of Animated Cartoons.* New York and Oxford, Facts on File, 1991.

Woolery, George W. *Children's Television: The First Thirty-Five Years, 1946-1981: Part 1: Animated Cartoon Series.* Metuchen, New Jersey, and London, The Scarecrow Press, 1983.

Twelve-Step Programs

Addiction-recovery treatments modeled on the techniques of Alcoholics Anonymous (AA), Twelve-Step programs are manifestations of the nineteenth-century self-help and social collectivist movements. AA and similar organizations also represent a form of secularized religion, involving both Christian and Eastern philosophical principles, that became popular in the twentieth century. The Twelve Steps are a series of behavior-modification principles that appeal to a higher power, take action through personal inventories, make amends to others, and spread the message. Beginning with alcoholism, the treatment philosophy has been applied to gambling, eating disorders, drug addictions, sexual disorders, physical health problems, and a variety of other damaging compulsive behaviors, with varying degrees of success and not without some controversy.

The industrialization and resulting prosperity of mid-nineteenth-century Victorian Britain encouraged a renewed belief in restraining moral attributes such as hard work, respectable behavior, and personal responsibility. These values were not only embraced by the new, growing middle class in England, but appealed to other classes as well. Author Samuel Smiles enshrined what he called his "gospel of work" in a series of best-selling books including the 1859 *Self-Help.* This book, which was based on a series of self-improvement lectures that Smiles gave to young men, taught that financial success and personal happiness were based entirely on individual initiative and faith in God. Smiles' self-help movement spread across the Atlantic to the rapidly industrializing United States and influenced a generation of American self-help activists including physician John Harvey Kellogg. Kellogg was hired to supervise the Seventh Day Adventists' Health Reform Institute, located in Battle Creek, Michigan, in 1876. Beyond the breakfast cereal he helped invent as a health food, Kellogg became the most prominent self-help health advocate in the world until his death in 1943. He spread, popularized, and helped make nearly universal the Adventist notion that individuals are responsible for and can do something about their physical and spiritual health.

During the early twentieth century, a Protestant evangelist named Frank N. D. Buchman established the Oxford Group, a religious movement that encouraged conversion experiences through confession, restitution, and self-survey. Before the group became involved with Fascism in the late 1930s, it attracted two converts with severe drinking-related problems, New York City stockbroker William Griffith Wilson, or "Bill W." as he was known to his AA friends, and Akron, Ohio physician Robert Holbrook Smith, or "Dr. Bob." The pair adapted the principles and practices of the Oxford Group in tandem with the well-known self-help health dogma of Kellogg to the problem of controlling drinking. Previously, alcoholism had been treated as a matter for moral persuasion, institutionalization, or law enforcement. Bill W. and Dr. Bob's new program consisted of helping, talking to, or otherwise maintaining contact with other drunkards to engage in spiritual activity. On June 10, 1935, Dr. Bob had his last drink, marking the official start of Alcoholics Anonymous.

The circles of recovering alcoholics in AA grew slowly at first. The noble experiment of Prohibition, which ended in 1933, had changed the culture of alcoholism in American society. All-male saloons died with the introduction of Prohibition in 1920, replaced by mixed-sex drinking that continued after 1933. Gone was the fraternity of men supporting each other in and out of alcoholism. Prohibition forced drinking undercover, into homes, hotel rooms, and other places where it had not been common previously. Bootleg beverages, especially beer, were often weak or reduced with other substances so that they could be consumed in greater quantities.

The end of Prohibition meant the return of alcoholic beverages to their traditional strengths, a reality to which many drinkers could not adjust. Coupled with enticing stories in the press, advertisements promoting drinking as sophisticated and glamorous, and the abundant use of alcohol in Hollywood movies, alcoholism gradually increased in the years during and after the Great Depression. There were over 100 members of AA by 1939, the same year the basic Twelve-Step program, *Alcoholics Anonymous,* or the "Big Book" as it was known in the movement, was published. A national AA service office was established in New York City in 1940 and the *Saturday Evening Post* gave the AA and the Twelve-Step program its first extensive national publicity in 1941.

Bill W. wrote The Twelve Steps in a burst of inspiration during 1938 and 1939, but they were based on debate among members and reflected the collective nature of the organization and its religious underpinnings. Though the original version was written in the stilted language of the day, subsequent editions of the "Big Book" have kept the original wording. The founders described themselves as "average Americans," but most were male, Protestant, white, and middle class. Their perspective reflected their environment, although the group had made efforts to distance itself from the earlier temperance movement that had flourished among the same social-economic class by stressing that alcohol was not in itself bad, only that some individuals were unable to drink in moderation. The first tenet of the Twelve-Step program was that members had to admit their powerlessness in their addiction. AA maintained that a person had to "hit bottom" and find him or herself in a totally powerless situation before redemption was possible. After members were introduced on the anonymous, first-name basis pioneered by AA (every member is greeted with "Hi" and their AA name), Twelve-Step meetings were built around the near-destruction testimonials of new and old members.

Next, the member had to express the crucial element of belief: adherence to a power greater than him or herself. Only with faith could the member move on to Step Three, turn his or her life over to God, Step Six, be ready to have God remove defects of character, and Step Seven, ask Him to remove shortcomings. Steps Four to Nine, including the making of a moral inventory, the admission of past wrong-doings to another person, and the listing and making of amends to people who had been wronged, were called the action Steps. The action Steps said nothing about drinking, for in AA parlance, "liquor was but a symptom." Steps Ten to Twelve continued inventory taking and wrong-doing admission, the improvement of one's knowledge of God through prayer and meditation, and the undergoing of a conversion experience. A "spiritual awakening" as the result of these Steps, which permitted the member to spread the Twelve-Step method to other addicts and practice the principles in

everyday life, was considered to represent the continuance or maintenance of the Steps. In AA's conception, helping other alcoholics was considered the best means by which to maintain an individual's own continued sobriety. It also perpetuated the AA organization and spread the Twelve-Step concept.

From its modest beginnings, AA has grown into a worldwide organization with hundreds of thousands of members. Fellowship continues to be organized on a local level with no dues payable. Contributions for expenses are accepted from those attending meetings only. Affiliation of the AA or its local groups with churches, political organizations, or other official institutions is barred by the AA Twelve Traditions, another seminal document. More than 200 other organizations have developed their own versions of the Twelve-Step program, including Al-Anon, the organization for members of the families of alcoholics founded in 1951, Narcotics Anonymous, Gamblers Anonymous, Overeaters Anonymous, Debtors Anonymous, Augustine Fellowship Sex & Love Addicts Anonymous, Survivors of Incest Anonymous, and more recently, Cocaine, Nicotine, and Co-Dependents Anonymous.

The Twelve-Step program continues to be a focus of debate. Experts argue that it is difficult to evaluate recidivism rates of Twelve-Step program participants because of their anonymity. AA's insistence that alcoholism is a disease counters more recent research that alcoholism is a behavior without physical cause. The first continuing female member of AA, Marty Mann, joined in 1937, but feminists and minorities argue that AA is oppressive through language in the Twelve Steps, which they perceive as constraining, repressive, and fostering co-dependence. They hold also that AA literature does not allow for discussion of social issues, such as discrimination and poverty, which often affect individual drinking patterns. The Twelve-Step's insistence in God or a "Higher Power" has run afoul of the doctrine of the separation of church and state, especially when the AA cooperates with law enforcement officials in mandating AA treatment for convicted offenders. And AA's Protestant Christian roots has led to criticism that it is in itself a form of religion, or at least a quasi-religious organization like Transcendental Meditation or Scientology, an allegation AA denies.

The Twelve-Step program has been borrowed by numerous, less serious behaviors such as shop and fish-o-holics. The AA meeting format, with members' accounts of desperate experiences and the "Hi, I'm so-and-so" introduction, have been the object of lampoons and parodies. In an episode of the popular 1990s television sitcom *Seinfeld,* the character George harassed a new AA member friend for failing to properly complete Step Eight, making amends to persons harmed, to the extent that the friend was driven to binge on liquor-flavored ice cream. Still, most experienced therapists agreed that any form of treatment for addictive behavior is most likely to show a higher rate of success if the patient joins Alcoholics Anonymous or another Twelve-Step Organization. In the face of the omnipresent social problem of alcoholism and its detrimental effects on children and families, the growing social acceptance of gambling and tolerance of compulsive gamblers, and an ever-increasing variety of other addictive behaviors, Twelve-Step programs provide adequate substitutes for a dependent way of life.

—Richard Digby-Junger

FURTHER READING:

Carr, Neil J. "Liberation Spirituality: Sixty Years of A. A." *America.* June 17-24, 1995, 20-22.

Conlon, Leon S. "*Griffin v. Coughlin*: Mandated AA Meetings and the Establishment Clause." *Journal of Church and State*. Vol. 39, Summer 1997, 427-54.

Kurtz, Ernest. *A.A. The Story: A Revised Edition of Not-God: A History of Alcoholics Anonymous*. San Francisco, Harper and Row, 1988.

Makela, Klaus, et. al. *Alcoholics Anonymous as a Mutual-Help Movement: A Study in Eight Societies*. Madison, University of Wisconsin Press, 1996.

Rudy, David R., and Arthur L. Greil. "Is Alcoholics Anonymous a Religious Organization? Meditations on Marginality." *Sociological Analysis*. Vol. 50, No. 1, 1988, 41-51.

Thomsen, Robert. *Bill W*. New York, Harper and Row, 1975.

Wuthnow, Robert. "How Small Groups Are Transforming Our Lives." *Christianity Today*. February 7, 1994, 2-24.

The Twenties

The 1920s were a period of rapid industrial growth, economic prosperity, and cultural change. Due mainly to the automobile industry, building and road construction, the development of the radio and advertising industries, and the emergence of "the new woman," the 1920s are often seen as the first "modern" decade in which the major characteristics of the twentieth century first emerged. Tensions between ideas of modernity and accepted traditional values characterize the popular culture of the twenties.

Following American involvement in the First World War, the 1920s witnessed an emphasis on domestic concerns such as the economy and the cultural values of American society. The economic boom of the 1920s, best illustrated by Henry Ford's dominance of the automobile industry through the use of interchangeable parts in automobile production, led to a high standard of living for many Americans as wages increased while working hours decreased. This was possible mainly through the increased mechanization of industry and production on a massive scale. Ford's River Rouge plant in Michigan, in which raw materials were processed, parts fabricated and assembled all under Ford's control, illustrates the strengths of the 1920s economy. Ford produced an automobile which required little in highly paid skilled labor and could be sold at a relatively cheap price. The automobile industry, in turn, fueled growth in related industries such as construction, glass, rubber, oil, and tourism. This boom created an American economy in which industrial production, for the first time, outpaced consumer demand. In order to accommodate this increase in production, corporations turned to advertising as a way to increase demand. It was during the 1920s that businesses began advertising directly to consumers and not retailers. The purpose of the advertisements became less about the presentation of information about a product and more about creating a positive image for a corporation or product by implying various benefits resulting from the product's purchase. Employing popularized ideas about the expression of desires taken from Sigmund Freud's theories of sexual repression leading to neurosis, advertisers sought to exploit the desires of the consuming public by emphasizing the benefits of consumption.

The emphasis on expression over repression went beyond the realm of advertising and can be seen in the popular culture of the 1920s. From novels such as F. Scott Fitzgerald's *The Great Gatsby* (1925) and Sinclair Lewis' *Babbitt* (1922) to the increasingly frenetic sound of jazz music and new dances such as the Lindy Hop (named after famous flyer Charles Lindbergh), American popular culture reflected a modern sense of ethics and values focused on individual pleasure and expression. Even all-American celebrities, such as Douglas Fairbanks and Mary Pickford, were challenged by more sexually expressive personalities such as Rudolph Valentino and Greta Garbo. This more modern approach to popular culture was reinforced by modern media, such as the radio, phonographs, and sound film. Both the form and content of 1920s popular culture demonstrated a sense of modernity.

In literature, the 1920s were characterized by the writings of what Gertrude Stein called "the lost generation." Writers such as Fitzgerald, Lewis, Ernest Hemingway, John Dos Passos, T. S. Eliot, Ezra Pound, e. e. cummings, and Sherwood Anderson critiqued American society, especially the traditions and values of rural life, or in their words, "the village." These writers were disillusioned by their involvement in the First World War and this disillusionment is reflected in their writings. It was a lost generation, according to Malcolm Cowley in *Exile's Return: A Literary Odyssey of the 1920s* "because it was uprooted, schooled away, and almost wrenched away from its attachment to any region or tradition." But the "lost generation" writers were not the only significant writers during the 1920s. Women like Edna St. Vincent Millay attempted to capitalize on the less repressive atmosphere of the 1920s by flaunting sexual expression in their poetry and life, and African American writers such as poets Langston Hughes and Countee Cullen, novelists Claude McKay, Jean Toomer, Jessie Faust, and Zora Neale Hurston joined artists such as Aaron Douglas and Augusta Savage in leading the "Harlem Renaissance."

This greater mainstream acceptance of African-American culture is also reflected in the growing influence of jazz music on American popular music. The First World War was instrumental in the spread of jazz music. The military's forced closure of New Orleans' red light district, Storyville, forced many jazz musicians employed there out of Louisiana northward in search of other opportunities, and war mobilization provided greater contact between races at military installations and wartime manufacturing plants. These two factors led black musicians to adapt black blues and jazz to the expectations of a white audience. Jazz spread first among younger audiences, mainly due to its spontaneous nature and its association with chaotic dancing, and critics denounced it as unmusical, intoxicating, and immoral. Despite these objections, jazz became the most popular form of music during the 1920s, dominating the radio airwaves, record sales, and even influencing movies such as *The Jazz Singer* (1927). As jazz music became more popular, it also became more standardized, organized, and arranged. What had once been music that emphasized improvisation throughout a piece became a highly structured, formulaic genre in which improvisation was limited to specific breaks in the arrangement of jazz "riffs." What had been "hot" jazz, by musicians such as Louis Armstrong and his Hot Five, became "sweet" jazz at the hands of band leaders like Guy Lombardo and his Royal Canadians, or "symphonic" jazz in the words of Paul Whiteman. Whiteman's orchestra debuted George Gershwin's "Rhapsody in Blue," in 1924, subtitled "for jazz band and piano." The work was primarily symphonic with jazz motifs. These orchestras and large bands developed what would become Big Band swing music in the 1930s and 1940s.

Like jazz music, motion pictures also gained greater acceptance during the 1920s as they moved out of working-class storefront nickelodeons into grand movie palaces attracting a middle-class and middle-brow audience. In the various conflicts between traditional values and modernity, movies challenged accepted middle-class values. According to Robert Sklar, in his book *Movie-Made America: A Cultural History of American Movies,* ''movies came to be seen as offering values distinctly different from those of middle-class culture, and providing greater opportunities for ethnic minorities than other economic sectors.'' Not only was the movie industry dominated by recent immigrants, the films themselves (being silent in the early 1920s) were easily adapted to a variety of immigrant cultures and easily understood by immigrant audiences, and as the audience for movies grew, so did the respectability of movies as an art form and acceptable leisure activity. The movie industry portrayed a changing America not only through the opportunities it created for a more heterogeneous population, or the attractions it held for a mass audience, but the movies themselves presented the values of modern America at the same time as it reinforced traditional middle-class values. Two of the most popular male stars illustrate this point. Rudolph Valentino, in his short career before his sudden death in 1926, embodied the modern, passionate, and sexually expressive male of the 1920s in such films as *The Sheik* (1921) and *Blood and Sand* (1922), while Douglas Fairbanks, in *The Mark of Zorro* (1920), *Robin Hood* (1922), and *The Thief of Bagdad* (1925), embodied the traditional, robust, athletic, all-American male. Both men became celebrities and helped to cultivate the studio star system in which performers became the major commodity used in selling a movie to the public.

The 1920s witnessed the consolidation of the power of the studios, especially Paramount Studios under Adolph Zukor, which was the largest of the silent film producers. Metro-Goldwyn-Mayer was created by theater owner Marcus Loew, who bought and combined Metro Picture Company with Samuel Goldwyn's Picture Company under the direction of Louis B. Mayer. Chafing under the influence of powerful producers and studio executives, director D. W. Griffith, and actors Charlie Chaplin, Douglas Fairbanks, and Mary Pickford formed the United Artists Corporation in 1919 to distribute individually produced films, and thereby avoid the formal structure of a studio. Each of these companies controlled several aspects of film production, distribution, and exhibition, yet the greatest change in Hollywood film occurred at the fledgling Warner Brothers Studio when they purchased and began producing films with the Vitaphone (sound-on-disc) technology in 1926. Within a few years, sound film production outpaced silent film. With the premiere of *The Jazz Singer* in 1927, the silent era ended.

In many ways, the silent era in popular culture ended earlier with the spread of radio technology in the 1920s. From amateurs broadcasting in basements and garages to fully formed and regulated networks after the Radio Act of 1927, the radio industry developed into Americans' most utilized and trusted source of news, information, and entertainment. The 1920s were a decade of growth for the radio industry, not only in its technical aspects, but in regards to programming as well. Radio stations learned what worked well on radio and what did not. The most attractive aspect of radio for the audience was its immediacy. Broadcasts of sporting events, from boxing matches and baseball games, political conventions and election returns, live remote broadcasts from big-city ballrooms, and news reporting all became mainstays of the radio industry. Radio also

found itself the new home of variety entertainment after the decline of vaudeville. The most popular radio comedy, *Amos and Andy,* featured white vaudevillians Freeman Gosden and Charles Correll portraying two black southerners whose simple ways and common misunderstandings provided the humor for the show. The pervasive nature of radio reinforced, to a national audience, many regionally held stereotypes, especially of minorities. Many people believed what they heard on the radio, not only because it was capable of presenting news upon its occurrence, but because the radio produced a certain form of intimacy in which the listener identified with the broadcast in ways unlike other forms of media. The presence of a radio set within one's home and the necessity of the listener to create images from the sounds presented resulted in each listener creating a very personal program, unique and individual. This transformation in communications and entertainment, through its immediacy and national appeal, reinforced the feeling that the 1920s were the start of the ''modern'' era.

This modern shift in social and cultural values did not take place unopposed. Several social movements can be explained as a revolt against the changes occurring in American society; as a revolt against modernity. Nativism, prohibition, and counter-evolution were all attempts to save traditional values in the face of change. Nativism came in three basic forms. All, however, expressed a deep discomfort with the changes occurring in American society and mainly with the changes occurring as a result of immigration. Anti-radicalism was a form of nativism in which people who disagreed with the government were seen as undesirable. The attacks on foreigners during and after WWI, in such notable instances as the Palmer raids and the unfair trial of anarchists Sacco and Vanzetti were all part of this fear of radicals, especially in the wake of the Bolshevik Revolution in Russia in 1917. This fear of radicals spilled over into a fear of non-Protestants, especially against Jews, but even against Catholics. Michigan and Nebraska both passed laws prohibiting parochial schools, and critics of President Woodrow Wilson called him ''the puppet of the Pope.'' This fear of others naturally translated into fierce support of white Anglo-Saxon Protestants. In 1921, Madison Grant wrote *The Passing of the Great Race* in which he described not only the hierarchy of races, with whites being at the top, but he also distinguished between whites by dividing Europeans into three main groups, Mediterraneans, Alpines, and Nordics, with Nordics being the superior group. This belief in the inferiority of Asians, Africans, and southern and eastern Europeans led to the passage of the National Origins Act of 1924 in which immigration quotas were designed to increase the number of nordic immigrants while decreasing all others; this also meant the complete exclusion of Asian immigrants and small quotas for southern and eastern European immigrants. The most dramatic example of nativism during the 1920s can be seen in the revival of the Ku Klux Klan (KKK). Unlike the post-Civil War era, when the purpose of the Klan was to intimidate African Americans, the 1920s Klan advocated white supremacy over not only Blacks, but also Jews, Catholics, and any immigrants who were not white Anglo-Saxon Protestants. The Klan also became modern by using expert advertisers to promote themselves and recruit new members. By 1923 over 3 million Americans were members of the Klan, with the strongest Klan organizations in the Midwest and the West.

In January of 1919 the 18th Amendment was passed, prohibiting the manufacturing, selling, or transporting of intoxicating beverages in the United States. The Volstead Act of 1919 defined intoxicating beverages as anything with more than 0.5 percent alcohol. This move towards prohibition of alcohol was yet another attempt to return

America to what many perceived as its past. The proliferation of saloons in the late nineteenth and early twentieth centuries was seen by many people as an expression of change, of encroaching foreign influence. Halting this process of change meant reinforcing and retaining traditional values.

Part of the attack on things foreign and things new was the attack on science, and especially in those areas where scientific theory and practice conflicted with deeply held religious beliefs, such as in the case of the theory of evolution and the belief in creationism. In 1925, the state of Tennessee passed a law prohibiting the teaching of evolution in public schools and colleges. In a test case in July of 1925, schoolteacher John T. Scopes was tried under this law in Dayton, Tennessee. The case became a national sensation, with two of the most prominent attorneys representing each side. The American Civil Liberties Union hired the famous trial lawyer Clarence Darrow to argue against the law, while the state got William Jennings Bryan (the populist and Democratic presidential hopeful) to argue its side. The "monkey trial," as it was known, argued over the issue of evolution versus creationism, but in the end the judge ruled that the only thing that mattered was the fact that Scopes did teach evolution and therefore was guilty. He was fined $100, which was suspended by the state supreme court. It was a victory for the anti-modernists, but it would be their last one. A few days after the trial ended, William Jennings Bryan died, and with him died much of the 1920s fundamentalist movement.

Each of these social movements (nativism, prohibition, and anti-evolutionism), seen in conjunction with the rapid spread of automobiles, economic prosperity, and the radio and film industries, illustrates the conflicted state of American culture during the 1920s.

—Charles J. Shindo

FURTHER READING:

Cowley, Malcolm. *Exile's Return: A Literary Odyssey of the 1920s.* New York, Penguin, 1976.

Dumenil, Lynn. *The Modern Temper: America Culture and Society in the 1920s.* New York, Hill and Wang, 1995.

Hentoff, Nat, and Albert J. McCarthy, editors. *Jazz: New Perspectives on the History of Jazz.* New York, DeCapo, 1959.

Nash, Roderick. *The Nervous Generation: American Thought, 1917-1930.* New York, Ivan R. Dee, 1990.

Sklar, Robert. *Movie-Made America: A Cultural History of American Movies.* New York, Vintage, 1975.

23 Skidoo

Though commonly associated with the "roaring twenties," the popular catch phrase, "23 Skidoo," actually originated around the turn of the twentieth century. Its origin has been accredited to two contemporaneous sources: *The Only Way*, a Broadway adaptation of Charles Dickens' *Tale of Two Cities,* and telegraphic code. In the last act of the aforementioned play, an old woman solemnly intones the number of victims on their way to the gallows, with special emphasis on number 23, the play's protagonist. The cry, "23!," was soon taken up by Broadway habitués. In telegraphic code, 23 is an abbreviation

for "Away with you!" Skidoo, a derivation of skedaddle, was soon added to "23" for the edification of those who had not seen the play or were unfamiliar with telegraphic code. For the next 20 years, the expression, or one of its variants, was commonly heard amongst students and young sophisticates, where it ordinarily meant "Get lost!," but was frequently used without any precise meaning. By the end of the 1920s, "23 Skidoo" had fallen out of common usage, but has since proved more enduring than other catch phrases of the period.

—Michael Baers

FURTHER READING:

Mathews, Mitford W. *A Dictionary of Americanisms on Historical Principles.* Chicago, University of Chicago Press, 1951.

Partridge, Eric. *A Dictionary of Catch Phrases, American and British, from the Sixteenth Century to the Present Day.* New York, Stein and Day, 1987.

20/20

With the premiere on June 6, 1978 of its program *20/20,* ABC Television launched its first ever news magazine. The youngest and the most troubled television network in the late 1970s, ABC was engaging in a major initiative to revise its news programming under the tutelage of its newly appointed president, Roone Arledge. Arledge targeted a number of ways in which ABC could improve its news division with the goal being to attract the average American viewer rather than news junkies. One result of this push was *20/20,* which was based on the success of the CBS program *60 Minutes,* which, since its premiere in 1968, had enjoyed significant popularity as a different means to present news through the use of longer segments and non-traditional news time slots.

The very first *20/20* program was hosted by *Time* magazine critic Robert Hughes and former *Esquire* editor Harold Hayes. The kick-off story featured a report on rabbit abuse at greyhound tracks, and signally failed to attract critical enthusiasm. The initial reviews ranged from "dizzyingly absurd" from *The New York Times* to "the trashiest stab at candycane journalism yet" from *The Washington Post.* Arledge immediately realized that the program's concept had to be reworked if it was to succeed. He rearranged the show's focus and introduced a new anchor, the longtime *Today* show personality Hugh Downs. Under the beloved Downs, *20/20* thrived and took on more of a consumer focus. In 1984, Arledge decided to bring on Barbara Walters, also a *Today* show alumnus but more recently a rising star within ABC. The combination of the two anchors was a hit with the viewers and, through *20/20,* Walters and Downs earned a place among the most respected journalists in television history.

20/20 has featured countless groundbreaking and exclusive interviews with world-famous figures drawn from many different arenas of public life. Often controversial, they have ranged from politics and show business to sportsmen, and even criminals. Among the most memorable interviewees have been Cuba's president, Fidel Castro; Bill and Hillary Clinton, appearing at the height of the Whitewater controversy; Olympic diving champion Greg Louganis, who revealed for the first time that he was stricken with AIDS and had been HIV-positive when he competed in the 1988 Olympics; and former White House intern and presidential paramour, Monica Lewinsky. Also contributing to *20/20*'s success with viewers has been its numerous health-related stories, one of the most personal involving Downs being shadowed by a crew who filmed him during his knee procedure and subsequent recovery.

Encouraged by the strong showing of *20/20* and the continued popularity of the rival *60 Minutes,* and spurred on by NBC's competitive bid into the news magazine forum with *Dateline,* ABC has created other news magazines over the years. With NBC's *Dateline* airing up to five times per week, in 1997 ABC decided to increase *20/20* showings to several nights a week. While this proved mildly successful, the network made a more radical move for the 1998-1999 season, combining all ABC news magazines (notably *PrimeTimeLive*) under the *20/20* brand. Airing at least three times weekly, *20/20* expanded its original consumer focus to embrace the more investigative pieces and hard journalism that had marked *PrimeTimeLive,* as well as to include more features on the day's top news. Additionally, Downs and Walters were no longer the sole anchors of the expanded program, but shared responsibilities with several other top ABC journalists, notably Sam Donaldson, Diane Sawyer, Charles Gibson, and Connie Chung.

—Alyssa L. Falwell

FURTHER READING:

Gunther, Marc. *The House that Roone Built: The Inside Story of ABC News.* Boston, Little, Brown, 1994.

Twiggy (1949—)

Arguably the very first "supermodel," England's Twiggy became an international star in the mid-1960s, bringing the world an idealized image of a youthful "Swinging London" and, for better or worse, heavily influencing popular conceptions of femininity. On the one hand, the ninety-one-pound, saucer-eyed Twiggy (born Lesley Hornby) was a positive celebration of androgyny and a radical break from the 1950s' insistence that female sex symbols possess curvaceous figures. Conversely, some critics have argued that Twiggy's slight physique helped push standards of thinness too far, leading many young women toward personal dissatisfaction with their bodies and, in some cases, anorexia. After saturating the pages of fashion magazines at the end of the 1960s and appearing in a handful of films in the early 1970s, notably Ken Russell's *The Boyfriend,* Twiggy adopted the last name Lawson and largely remained out of the limelight. However, Twiggy's influence upon the fashion industry never truly waned, as svelte boyishness recurred as a theme in female models for decades.

—Shaun Frentner

FURTHER READING:

DeLibero, Linda Benn. "This Year's Girl: A Personal/Critical History of Twiggy." *On Fashion,* edited by Shari Benstock and Suzanne Ferriss. New Jersey, Rutgers University Press, 1994, pp. 41-58.

Twiggy

Twiggy. *Twiggy: How I Probably Just Came Along on a White Rabbit at the Right Time, and Met the Smile on the Face of the Tiger.* New York, Hawthorne Books, 1968.

The Twilight Zone

Created by the visionary writer Rod Serling, *The Twilight Zone* proved both a landmark of televised science fiction and a powerful touchstone in America's pop cultural consciousness. The black-and-white anthology series, which ran on CBS from 1959 to 1964, generated lukewarm ratings at the time but has grown in public estimation over time. Over the course of its five-year network run, *The Twilight Zone* explored themes never before examined on television. It exposed the talents of a generation of talented character players, like Jack Klugman, William Shatner, and Robert Duvall, who would go on to become household names for subsequent portrayals. It also cemented the legacy of its creator, at the time known principally as the author of socially concerned live dramas.

Serling created *The Twilight Zone* to serve as a forum for his commentary about technology, conformity, discrimination, and a whole host of other issues. Frustrated by his inability to explore these

A scene from *The Twilight Zone* episode "Time Enough at Last."

topics in mainstream dramas in the face of censorship by network executives and skittish advertisers, he hoped that the show's science fiction anthology format might allow him to introduce a little liberal orthodoxy to viewers without alarming the suits. But if Serling was in it for the advocacy, the show's other creative collaborators consistently pulled it back into the realm of traditional fantasy. This dialectic proved good for all parties concerned.

The Twilight Zone premiered on October 2, 1959. Its introductory episode, "Where Is Everybody," established the tone and creative parameters of the series. In it, a young man in Air Force garb finds himself in a seemingly deserted town. After increasingly frantic attempts to locate its inhabitants, he breaks down in despair. Only at the end is it revealed that the man is an astronaut being subjected to an experiment in an isolation booth, and that the proceedings have been an hallucination. In countless subsequent installments, *The Twilight Zone* would rely on this same formula of an ordinary human being suddenly beset by extraordinary circumstances. Quite frequently, there was an unexpected twist at the denouement that cast the strange events in a new or supernatural light. To provide context and codify the cosmic significance of the events, Serling himself provided opening and closing narration, usually on camera in an immaculate Kuppenheimer suit.

To supply these dark melodramas from week to week, *The Twilight Zone* relied upon a stable of writers seasoned in the macabre arts of science fiction and fantasy. Along with Serling, short story veterans Richard Matheson and Charles Beaumont formed a creative troika that was responsible for much of the series' high-quality

teleplays. Matheson's scripts tended toward more hard-science content, like the classic "Little Girl Lost," about a child who vanishes through her bedroom wall into another dimension. Beaumont crafted some of the show's more horrific installments, like the gothic gem "The Howling Man," in which a traveler in Europe happens upon the devil being kept locked up in a cell in a monastery. Other important contributors to the series included George Clayton Johnson; Montgomery Pittman; Earl Hamner, Jr.; Reginald Rose; and Ray Bradbury, who eventually wrote for the show as well.

But it was the workaholic Serling who took on the bulk of the creative burden. All told, Serling would write 92 of the 156 broadcast episodes, more than one-third of the total. His influence over the show was especially keen during the first three seasons, when he personally penned some of the program's signature installments. "Eye of the Beholder" addressed people's perceptions of beauty, through the eyes of a bandaged and "disfigured" young woman whom viewers see revealed in a shocking climax. "Mirror Image" explored the nature of identity when a woman waiting in a bus station is suddenly confronted by her exact double. And the chilling "The Obsolete Man" touched on Cold War themes in relating the last days of a librarian of the future condemned to death for defending the utility of books.

Episodes like these allowed Serling to fulfill his vision of commenting on existential and political themes without incurring the wrath of advertisers and network executives. But the show's social concern also emboldened Serling to write all too pontifically at times, a problem that was exacerbated by his heavy workload. Too many of his episodes seem written in a rush of sanctimony, with long, windy speechifying from the central characters on the major issues of the day. Even the many gems could not spare the program from lukewarm public interest. *The Twilight Zone* was never a hit in the ratings and was in danger of cancellation by CBS almost from the start. At the end of the third season, the network elected to expand the show to an hour in hopes that that might change its fortunes. But the quality of the scripts suffered, with many seeming interminably padded at the new running time. After a desultory fifth season, during which most of the series best creative talent left, the axe finally fell.

The Twilight Zone may have ended in 1964, but its influence continued to grow. Many of the show's writers, like Richard Matheson, took their talents to the big screen. Others continued to work in television. Earl Hamner, Jr., who wrote several episodes for *The Twilight Zone* set in the rural backwoods, went on to create *The Waltons,* the long-running cornpone drama on CBS. Fittingly, Serling remained the busiest of all. He co-wrote the screenplay for *Planet of the Apes* in 1968, among other theatrical ventures. He also released a series of short story adaptations of his classic *Twilight Zone* teleplays. But Serling's talents remained best suited for the small screen. He hosted a very *Twilight Zone*-like anthology series, *Night Gallery,* from 1970 to 1972, but network interference eventually drove him out of the medium altogether. He died following complications from open heart surgery on June 28, 1975.

Long after its network run had ended, *The Twilight Zone* remained a staple of syndicated reruns nationwide. Often aired late at night, it gave the creeps to a whole new generation of insomniacs who had not been around for the initial airings. The show's appeal was so broad that in 1977, *Saturday Night Live* could do a parody of it (with Dan Aykroyd doing a dead-on Serling) that had the audience howling with recognition. Serling's widow even launched a *Twilight Zone* magazine featuring new fiction in the series tradition. The time seemed ripe for a major revival of the franchise.

But all did not work out as planned. In 1982, a *Twilight Zone* movie was released to much anticipation. In keeping with the spirit of the series, producer Steven Spielberg had opted for an anthology format, comprised of three remakes of classic *Twilight Zone* installments and a fourth, all-new story. Up and coming directors Joe Dante (*The Howling*), John Landis (*An American Werewolf in London*), and George Miller (*The Road Warrior*) were brought in to helm three of the segments, with Spielberg handling the fourth. Despite all that talent, however, and the best efforts of screenwriter Richard Matheson, the result was a tepid mishmash that bombed at the box office. Each of the three remakes was markedly inferior to the original, while Landis' segment, the lone original story, was a sanctimonious misfire, dismissed by the show's aficionados as an unintentional parody of Serling. The fact that actor Vic Morrow was beheaded during filming did little to enhance the picture's public relations cachet, and embroiled Landis in a career-threatening lawsuit.

Somewhat more successful—artistically, if not commercially—was a new *Twilight Zone* television series, launched in 1985 on CBS. The new show boasted a stellar lineup of creative talent, from Ray Bradbury, Stephen King, and Harlan Ellison on the writers' side to directors like William Friedkin, Joe Dante, and John Milius. Actor Charles Aidman, who had appeared in two original *Twilight Zone* episodes, assumed Serling's post as narrator/moral contextualizer. A number of top-flight episodes were produced, like Ellison's brilliant "Paladin of the Lost Hour," that recaptured the spirit of the old series. But budget cuts, network interference, and low ratings eventually took their toll, and the series was mothballed for good in 1989.

Four decades after its network debut, *The Twilight Zone* continued to intrigue both the general public and fans of the science fiction/ fantasy genre. The phrase "Twilight Zone kind of feeling" has entered the popular lexicon as a term for the series' quintessentially eerie sensation of otherworldly alienation. Marathon airings of the nearly 40-year-old episodes generated powerhouse ratings for local syndicated stations well into the 1990s, making the syndication package a prized possession within the broadcast industry. In 1996, cable's Sci-Fi Channel secured exclusive rights to air reruns of the original series—albeit in a truncated form allowing for additional commercial time, something of which Serling would most assuredly not approve. Nevertheless, its viability into a second millennium ensured that Serling and his unique vision would remain a permanent marker on America's pop cultural landscape.

—Robert E. Schnakenberg

FURTHER READING:

Presnell, Don, and Marty McGee. *A Critical History of Television's The Twilight Zone, 1959-1964*. New York, McFarland & Company, 1998.

Zicree, Marc Scott. *The Twilight Zone Companion*. New York, Bantam, 1989.

Twin Peaks

With a quirky mixture of murder mystery, soap opera, film noir, and the avant-garde, *Twin Peaks* rewrote the formula for prime-time television drama in the early 1990s. Created by American filmmaker David Lynch (*The Elephant Man, Blue Velvet, Lost Highway*), *Twin Peaks* was a character-driven show, sporting a cast of more than one

hundred, and used intricately interwoven subplots to keep viewers tuned in. This unconventional epic revolves around the murder of Laura Palmer, small-town beauty queen, and the investigating FBI agent whose dreams and quasi-Buddhist methods reveal the Black Lodge, a surreal waiting room inhabited by the personification of pure evil known only as BOB. *Twin Peaks* was canceled in 1991 after only twenty-nine episodes.

—Tony Brewer

FURTHER READING:

Chion, Michel. *David Lynch*. London, British Film Institute, 1995.

Lynch, Jennifer. *The Secret Diary of Laura Palmer*. New York, Simon and Schuster, 1990.

Twister

Invented by Reyn Guyer, this game asks several players to reach over, under, and across each other to place their hands and feet on colored circles on a large vinyl game board. Named "Twister" by Milton Bradley, the game was demonstrated on the *Tonight Show* in 1966. While Eva Gabor was on her hands and knees, show host Johnny Carson stood over her and reached for another circle; the sexual innuendo and close physical contact made for controversial television and helped attract American youths to the game. Twister sold 13 million games in its first year. In 1987, at the University of Massachusetts campus in Amherst, 4150 contestants set a record for the number of simultaneous Twister players.

—S. Naomi Finkelstein

FURTHER READING:

Hoffman, David. *Kid Stuff: Great Toys*. New York, Chronicle Books, 1978.

2 Live Crew

2 Live Crew, the primary progenitors of a hip-hop sub-genre called Miami Bass, will probably be better remembered for their important legal battles than their music. Their sexually explicit songs that often objectified women and which featured relatively simple bass-driven beats drew the attention of many conservative law enforcement officials from their hometown of Miami, as well as elsewhere. 2 Live Crew's legal perils during the late 1980s and early 1990s opened up debates about censorship and made them unwitting proponents of free speech.

Foreshadowing the legal battles over intellectual property that dogged the group a few years down the line, the group's first legal confrontation involved the appropriation of the name Luke Skywalker as a stage name by the group's leader (born Luther Campbell, Dec. 22, 1960). Lucasfilm, the owner of the *Star Wars* trilogy trademark,

2 Live Crew

promptly sued the group when they began to find aboveground exposure when 2 Live Crew's second album, *Move Somethin'* (1987), reached number 68 on the *Billboard* pop chart. As a result, Luther Campbell's stage and record company names were shortened to ''Luke'' and ''Luke Records,'' respectively. The album that gained the most attention, though, was *As Nasty As They Wanna Be* (1989) which reached the pop album charts' Top Forty and spawned a hit single, ''Me So Horny.'' Despite its many detractors, from conservative law enforcement officials, right-wing Christian groups, and music critics, *As Nasty As They Wanna Be* sold over two million copies, many of which were likely sold because of publicity drawn from criticism of the group.

Enraged by the explicit content of 2 Live Crew, a Coral Gables attorney named Jack Thompson launched an all-out war against the group, culminating in a Broward County, Florida judge deeming the album obscene under state law in March of 1990. Soon after, a record store owner in Ft. Lauderdale, Florida and another in Huntsville, Alabama were arrested by local sheriffs departments for violating obscenity laws. Around the same time, 2 Live Crew was arrested for

performing songs from *As Nasty As They Wanna Be* in a Florida nightclub and, when visiting the same town, alternative band Too Much Joy was arrested for performing songs from that album in an act of protest. These events escalated into a full scale debate within the media over free speech and first amendment protection, with radio and television talk show pundits arguing over 2 Live Crew's social and musical merits.

The two record store retailers were eventually acquitted, as were 2 Live Crew and Too Much Joy—all by juries that either criticized local authorities for wasting their time or, in one case, wanted to deliver the not guilty verdict in the form of a rap. In May 1992 the obscenity ruling was reversed by the eleventh United States Circuit Court of Appeals and an appeal was refused to be heard by the United States Supreme Court. But 2 Live Crew's legal woes were not over, as they faced another suit filed against them for the unauthorized sampling of Roy Orbison's ''Oh, Pretty Woman.'' The owners of the song's copyright, Acuff-Rose, argued that 2 Live Crew's use of the song devalued the original's worth. After a protracted legal battle that eventually went to the United States Supreme Court, that court ruled in 1994 that the 2 Live Crew version constituted fair use under copyright law and was therefore legal. In a time dominated by easy access to digital recording and transferring technology, this was seen as a significant ruling by legal scholars.

Riding the wave of publicity after the *As Nasty As They Wanna Be* scandal, 2 Live Crew milked another couple of minor hit albums in 1990 and 1991 (*Banned in the USA* and *Sports Weekend,* respectively). Soon after, however, the group's mainstream success fizzled and the original lineup disbanded, with Luke going on as a solo artist, periodically releasing solo albums on his own label.

—Kembrew McLeod

FURTHER READING:

Campbell, Luther. *As Nasty as They Wanna Be: The Uncensored Story of Luther Campbell of the 2 Life Crew.* Kingston, Kingston Publishers, 1992.

Shabazz, Julian L. D. *The United States of America vs. Hip-Hop.* Hampton, United Brothers, 1992.

2001: A Space Odyssey

In 1964 film director Stanley Kubrick approached science fiction writer Arthur C. Clarke seeking a plot for "the proverbial good

A scene from the film *2001: A Space Odyssey*.

science fiction movie." They worked together to craft a story inspired by Clarke's short story "The Sentinel," in which an astronaut discovers a mysterious pyramid on the moon. As Clarke wrote a novel derived from their script, Kubrick created a unique movie which continues to amaze and frustrate viewers, the 1968 MGM film *2001: A Space Odyssey*.

The film presents an abbreviated and speculative version of human evolution. The story opens at "The Dawn of Man" as pre-human man-apes discover a large, upright black slab. The apes are drawn to the monolith as it sings to them. After this, one ape, Moon-Watcher (Daniel Richter), discovers that a bone can be used as a club and learns how to use the club's power to acquire food and to dominate the emerging ape society. The setting shifts in one of the most famous cuts in film history: Moon-Watcher tosses his club into the air; as it falls, the club suddenly transforms into a spaceship sliding through space. The plot now focuses on Heywood Floyd (William Sylvester), an official with the National Astronautics Council, who is traveling to the moon to investigate a mysterious black monolith discovered there. The monolith had obviously been created by intelligent extraterrestrial beings and deliberately buried in a lunar crater. When Floyd arrives at the monolith, it emits a piercing shriek.

The setting shifts again to the Discovery, a spaceship en route to Jupiter. The ship carrying three scientists in suspended animation is staffed by astronauts Dave Bowman (Keir Dullea) and Frank Poole (Gary Lockwood) and the HAL 9000 computer (voice of Douglas Rain). After a mysterious equipment failure, Dave and Frank become suspicious of the supposedly infallible HAL. The astronauts conspire to disconnect HAL but the all-seeing computer learns of their plot. HAL murders the sleeping scientists, sets Frank adrift in space, and traps Dave outside the ship. After he manages to reboard the Discovery via an airlock, Dave dismantles HAL's memory, reducing the computer to infancy and, finally, death. As HAL's red eye goes black, a video begins to play in which Floyd explains the Discovery's secret mission. The moon monolith's shriek had been a transmission aimed at Jupiter, and the Discovery had been sent in search of the signal's destination. In the film's final segment ("Jupiter and Beyond the Infinite"), Dave flies a pod toward a monolith floating in space near Jupiter and is transported through a stargate (depicted as a psychedelic lightshow) into a surreal, symbolic world where he ages and dies in ornate but sterile white rooms. His death seems to produce a celestial fetus, the next stage in human evolution.

The film polarized the critics; their responses tended to be either strongly positive or strongly negative. The film was daringly different from other major studios' big-budget releases. It did not have a clear storyline or a central protagonist. There was little dialogue, and what dialogue there was was deliberately innocuous. Overall, *2001* presented a cold universe in which humans behave like passionless automatons and in which the most sympathetic character is the homicidal computer HAL. Some critics responded to *2001*'s uniqueness as a step forward in the art of filmmaking. For example, Mike Steele, reporting in *The Minneapolis Tribune,* saw *2001* as a step "closer to the purity of the film" and away from a sequential storyline imposed by literary aesthetics. Other critics found the movie to be a confusing muddle. In *The Village Voice,* Andrew Sarris called the movie a "thoroughly uninteresting failure" and the ending "an exercise in mystifying abstract fantasy in the open temple of High Art." As *2001* found its audience, several critics who had panned it wrote second reviews to reassess the movie's merits under a different set of criteria. Although Sarris, for his part, wrote a second review only to say that his opinion had not changed.

Despite the confusion and disfavor of many viewers, *2001* quickly gained the status of a "cult film," a movie which inspires fanatical devotion in a relatively small audience. The film continues to be a film for several cults. For science fiction fans, it is a realistic depiction of space travel. No other movie in the genre before or since has remained so true to the laws of physics. For film buffs, it presents a dazzling experiment with the elements of filmmaking. While viewers accustomed to conventional American movies may bemoan the long sequences of play with sight and sound which do not advance a linear plot, lovers of the filmmaker's art delight as a spaceship and a space station waltz to Johann Strauss' "On the Beautiful Blue Danube." For devotees of the hallucinogenic drug culture, the surreal imagery, particularly in the final segment, was "The Ultimate Trip" promised by the tagline of a 1974 re-release. *2001* remains an active part of the popular imagination and is often imitated, referenced, and parodied in various media. In the 1996 film, *Independence Day,* for example, David Levinson (played by Jeff Goldblum) opens his laptop, and HAL's red eye appears on its screen.

Kubrick succeeded in offering the "proverbial good science fiction movie" because *2001* addresses universal, eternal questions: What is the meaning of life? What is the nature of God? What is the destiny of humanity? Are we alone in the universe? What is the relationship between humans and their machines? One of the aspects of the movie that frustrates viewers is that Kubrick provides no clear answers to these questions, but the nature of the questions is that they are unanswerable. As Clarke put it, "If you understood *2001* completely, we failed. We wanted to raise more questions than we answered." The film poses ancient questions in a relatively new language, science, and in a new medium, film. The extraterrestrial monoliths seem to be guiding human evolution; thus, they serve as a metaphor for the hand of God or destiny. However, *2001* explores theological issues outside of the framework of any religion or established mythology. It forces its audience to rethink the assumptions such a framework might provide.

Perhaps the most memorable ingredient of *2001* is HAL, the fullest development of a sequence of human tools which began with the bone club. One of the major issues of science fiction has been whether a machine capable of independent thought would be "human." In *2001,* HAL is a terrifying monster, but he also seems to be more human than the humans. The audience cannot help but find the computer sympathetic as he begs for his life; we see that HAL only killed out of fear. As interaction with computers becomes increasingly a part of everyday life, HAL remains a powerful symbol of both the peril and the promise of artificial intelligence. Fans have noticed that if each letter of HAL is replaced by the next letter in the alphabet, HAL becomes IBM (Clarke denies that this was intentional). In 1997 (the year HAL was supposedly created), David Stork published a collection of essays, *Hal's Legacy: 2001's Computer as Dream and Reality,* in which scientists explore how close current technology comes to creating a HAL 9000.

—Christian L. Pyle

FURTHER READING:

Agel, Jerome, editor. *The Making of Kubrick's "2001."* New York, New American Library, 1970.

Bizony, Piers. *"2001": Filming the Future.* London, Aurum, 1994.

Clarke, Arthur C. *The Lost Worlds of "2001."* New York, New American Library, 1972.

Clarke, Arthur C. *2001: A Space Odyssey.* New York, New American Library, 1968.

Coyle, Wallace. *Stanley Kubrick: A Guide to References and Resources.* Boston, G. K. Hall, 1980.

Geduld, Carolyn. *Filmguide to "2001: A Space Odyssey."* Bloomington, Indiana University Press, 1973.

Stork, David, editor. *Hal's Legacy: 2001's Computer as Dream and Reality.* Cambridge, MIT Press, 1997.

Tyler, Anne (1941—)

Anne Tyler, a novelist who has received much critical and popular acclaim, is known for her insightful, often comic depictions of family relationships and ordinary life. Her novels, the best of which include *Dinner at the Homesick Restaurant* (1982), *The Accidental Tourist* (1985), and *Breathing Lessons* (1988), have won such prestigious awards as the Pulitzer Prize and the National Book Critics Circle Award. A longtime resident of Baltimore, where she often sets her novels, Tyler is viewed by many as a Southern novelist, largely because of her concern with family, home, and place.

—James Schiff

FURTHER READING:

Evans, Elizabeth. *Anne Tyler.* New York, Twayne, 1993.

Petry, Alice Hall. *Understanding Anne Tyler.* Columbia, University of South Carolina Press, 1990.

Petry, Alice Hall, editor. *Critical Essays on Anne Tyler.* New York, G. K. Hall, 1992.

Salwak, Dale, editor. *Anne Tyler as Novelist.* Iowa City, University of Iowa Press, 1994.

Stephens, C. Ralph, editor. *The Fiction of Anne Tyler.* Jackson, University Press of Mississippi, 1990.

Tyson, Mike (1966—)

Born in Brooklyn and educated in the pugilistic arts on the New York streets, Mike Tyson went on to become history's youngest world boxing champion at age nineteen. From the start of his professional career in 1985, Tyson displayed contradictions of character that dogged him in controversy. An efficient powerhouse of a fighter, his inability to control his anger in his personal life sidelined his career more than once. When this anger finally caused him to lose control in the ring and bite an opponent's ear, many thought the incident signaled the end of his boxing career. However, Tyson proved himself as skilled at comebacks as at knockouts. By the end of the twentieth century, 15 years after his debut in the ring, it was

Mike Tyson

evident that so long as promoters were able to make millions of dollars on every round he fought, ''Iron Mike'' Tyson would continue to be welcomed whenever he might choose to enter the ring.

Boxing has often been a controversial and paradoxical sport. Many see it as simple brutality, a gladiator-like contest where bloodthirsty audiences cheer as opponents batter each other senseless. Others claim boxing as one of the earliest refined athletic skills, a noble art requiring balletic precision, muscular power, and that indefinable yet essential quality—''heart.'' Perhaps it is because of that engaging quality of heart that boxing has given rise to so many heroes who have captured the public imagination. And yet, like boxing itself, boxing heroes are often contradictory figures with whom the public has a love-hate relationship. Boxing requires many of the same fighting skills that are necessary to the survival of young men growing up in poverty on urban streets. Thus many champs have come from underprivileged backgrounds, using their skills and toughness to pursue the wealth and fame that championship boxing promises those that succeed. The rise of the ghetto-bred fighter, particularly among African Americans and other minority groups, symbolizes the American dream of rising from poverty and obscurity to wealth and fame. From Jack Dempsey to Muhammad Ali, boxing champions have become national icons, glorifying the attributes of brashness, guts and furious strength.

Mike Tyson is a paradigm example of the phenomenon. Born into a poor African-American family and raised by a single mother on welfare, he has said of his own origins, ''I was born in guck, mud. Humiliation.'' On his own from around age ten, Tyson was not tall, but he was powerfully built and filled with rage, and he learned early how to earn his way by mugging and purse-snatching. By the time he was 13, he had been arrested 38 eight times, finally ending up at the ''bad cottage'' at Tryon School for Boys in Catskill, New York. Tyson has described the reformatory with a poignant simplicity that a sociologist might envy: ''Just a bunch of bad kids no one cared about

in a square box.'' It was at Tryon School that ex-boxer Bobby Stewart recognized the tough youngster's fighting talent, and introduced him to Cus D'Amato, a visionary trainer who had been behind boxing champions Floyd Patterson and Jose Torres.

D'Amato recognized Tyson's potential and undertook his training. Tyson's amateur career was only mildly distinguished—he competed in trials for the 1984 Olympics, and earned a place on the team as an alternate—but in 1985 he entered the professional arena like a steamroller. From 1985 until 1990, he won every fight, most with knockouts and most in the first round. By 1986, he was world heavyweight champion. Then, in 1990, displaying the inconsistency fans would later come to expect, he suffered his first professional defeat at the hands of Buster Douglas, a virtual unknown with 50-1 odds against him. In 1988, at the height of his glory days, Tyson married actress Robin Givens. The petite Givens and her ''gentle giant'' husband were a pair made for the media, and they received an onslaught of attention from tabloids and television. The fairy tale union did not last however, and, though it was shocking, it surprised few when Givens confessed in a television interview with Barbara Walters that Tyson abused her and that life with him was ''pure hell.'' The couple was divorced in 1989.

In 1992, the fighter made world headlines when he was convicted of rape and given a six-year prison sentence. Although persistently denying the charge, he served three years in a minimum-security prison where he converted to Islam, and came out declaring he was a changed man. He immediately resumed his boxing career, and by 1996 again held both the WBC and WBA heavyweight titles. Working with flamboyant boxing promoter Don King, Tyson negotiated one of the most lucrative boxing contracts in history, a $158 million deal with the Las Vegas MGM Grand Hotel and Showtime Entertainment Television for six fights or two and a half years, whichever came first.

Tyson's comeback success did not last. In 1997, in a rematch fight with Evander Holyfield, who had previously beaten him, ''Iron Mike'' lost control and bit pieces off both of Holyfield's ears. The boxing world, as well as the larger public, reeled in shock and disgust. Ear-biting jokes became a television staple, and Tyson's boxing license was suspended for life. However, after some 18 months of therapy and anger counseling, Tyson approached the boxing commissions in New Jersey and Nevada with assurances that he had once again mended his ways. Both commissions voted him mentally fit to box, and he made another comeback.

Tyson has continued to win matches, often within an embarrassingly short time. After his release from prison in 1995, fans who paid up to $1500 a seat to watch him fight the hopelessly outclassed Peter McNeeley were disgruntled when the fight lasted only a few minutes. However, the fighter has continued to be plagued by the consequences of his uncontrolled rage. In 1999, he was sentenced to another year in jail for violating parole by assaulting two motorists after an automobile accident, and was facing assault charges by two women.

In over a decade of intense and dramatic career boxing, Mike Tyson has only fought 200 rounds in all, and only three of his fights have gone the distance. Out of 48 fights, he has won 45, knocking out his opponent in 39 of them. The press and the public have tended either to glorify him as the poor kid who made good, or to demonize him as a thug and a felon. In reality, Tyson is the uncomfortable sum of many contradictory parts, and often expresses these with the simple, incisive perception of a self-educated man. Pummeling other men to the mat was the only way for a painfully poor black street kid to rise to the top of the heap, and Tyson channeled his deep anger at life into boxing. He achieved unprecedented success, but has remained isolated, distrustful and angry even during his best times. Five foot eleven and weighing in at 220 pounds, Tyson is a massive man who looks like a fighter. His voice is incongruously soft and high, hinting at a gentle core overlaid by years of depression, defensiveness, and pure rage. Perhaps it is this ambiguous combination of qualities, the suggestion of the hurt child beneath the brutal physical powerhouse, which keeps the public from giving up completely on ''Iron Mike.'' After all, this juxtaposition is what gives boxing its appeal—the glory through the pain. Robin Givens added perhaps the most telling dimension to the picture, ''I think he's probably going to turn out to be the all-American tragedy. There's something about Michael that's dangerous.''

—Tina Gianoulis

FURTHER READING:

Hoffer, Richard. *A Savage Business: The Comeback and Comedown of Mike Tyson.* New York, Simon and Schuster, 1998.

Jordan, June. ''Requiem for the Champ.'' *The Progressive.* Vol. 56, No. 4, April, 1992, 15.

Samuels, Allison, and Mark Starr. ''Will He Get Up?'' *Newsweek.* Vol. 129, No. 26, June 30, 1997, 80.